Chronology of
Western Classical Music

Chronology of
Western Classical Music

Charles J. Hall

Routledge
Taylor & Francis Group

NEW YORK AND LONDON

Published in 2002 by
Routledge
29 West 35th Street
New York, NY 10001
www.routledge-ny.com

Published in Great Britain by
Routledge
11 New Fetter Lane
London EC4P 4EE
www.routledge.co.uk

Routledge is an imprint of the Taylor & Francis Group.
Printed in the United States of America on acid-free paper.

10 9 8 7 6 5 4 3 2 1

Cataloging-in-Publication Data is available from the Library of Congress.

ISBN 0-415-94216-0 (vol. 1)—0-415-94217-9 (vol. 2)
      0-415-93878-3 (set)

Contents

❄

Preface   vii

Acknowledgments   x

Chronology, 1751–1900   1

Composition Index   I1

Historical Index   I159

Preface

❄

This two-volume chronology of music in what the author calls cultivated/art music (the term *classical music* applies to music of the eighteenth century) is the further outgrowth of the author's continual research into music chronology, which originally resulted in a program on a local FM station titled *Hall's Musical Years*. Those early notes eventually evolved into three volumes of musical chronicles published in the eighties. Further interest in and research into American music resulted in *A Chronicle of American Music* in 1996. These volumes on world music contain much more information than the earlier chronicles and hopefully present the material in a more usable form.

As in the earlier works, the volumes are arranged chronologically, with volume one covering the years 1751 to 1900 and volume two concerned with the twentieth century. In an attempt to make the volumes more meaningful in all the arts, each year is introduced with a brief synopsis of history and highlights from the related fields of art and literature.

The musical highlights are divided into nine major categories, many of which are subdivided and arranged as follows:

A. **Births**—births are divided into five categories: composers, conductors, singers, performers, and others.

B. **Deaths**—deaths are divided into the same categories as above.

C. **Debuts**—in these volumes, only one debut date for singers and performers is given. Care has been taken to provide the real debut date, but it is patently impossible to ensure the veracity of all debut information, particularly in the years of the baroque and classical periods.

D. **New Positions**—divided into two parts, the conductors section being much larger. The second category contains mainly positions in education (only directors or other important positions are noted), organ or opera administration, and so on. In the opera and symphony field, there are many categories: artistic director, principal director, and so on. Here the author has chosen to use the year when the individual first becomes associated with the organization.

E. **Prizes/Honors**—divided into the two obvious parts. In deference to space, many of the titles, particularly in the honors class, will be abreviated (for example, American Academy for the American Academy of Arts and Sciences, or CBE for Commander of the British Empire).

F. **Biographical Highlights**—short items of a more personal nature concerning important musical personalities.

G. **Cultural Beginnings**—consisting of beginning dates for musical organizations and anything related to music, this section is divided into eight subcategories as follows:

Performing Groups—Choral
Performing Groups—Instrumental
Festivals—primarily a twentieth-century phenomenon
Educational—schools, conservatories, and anything related thereto
Music Publishers
Music Publications—primarily music magazines and periodicals
Performing Centers
Others—the miscellaneous file of anything else in music
H. Musical Literature—individual biographies are not included except for a few recognized landmarks.
I. Musical Compositions—divided as follows:
Chamber Music:
  String Quartets—all works included use the classical string quartet
  Sonata/Solos—anything for solo instrument, with or without piano
  Ensembles—anything left after the categories directly above
  Piano—works for the solo instrument alone
  Organ—same as above
Choral/Vocal Music:
  Choral—in some of the earlier years, this category will list such things as oratorios and Bach Cantatas as a separate section
  Vocal—works for solo voice and various accompaniments
  Musical Stage—primarily operas and operettas
Orchestra/Band Music:
  Concerted Music—music of solo instruments or small groups with orchestral accompaniment
    Piano
    Violin
    Orchestra—the orchestra concerto seems to concentrate more on displaying the abilities of the various orchestral sections and thus is included here
    Other
  Ballet/Incidental Music
  Program Music—any work by any name that has an extra-musical background
  Standard Works—basically all orchestra or band works outside of the above or the symphonies (below)
  Symphonies
  Electronic—twentieth century only

The dates given for the above are, as far as can be ascertained, the date of composition, but it is very hard, particularly in the baroque and early classical periods, to separate the premiere date from the date of composition. Considering the multitude of sources from which this work has been compiled, it would seem inevitable that differences and contradiction should arise on birth dates, debuts, and so on, and such is the case. At one time, the author had five different birth dates for Maria Callas, all of them being only a year apart. To alleviate the situation, a question mark appears in parentheses next to each item that is in doubt. In most cases of differing opinions of this sort, the compiler has taken the *New Grove Dictionary of Music* and the eighth edition of *Baker's Biographical Dictionary of Music* as the final word.

As can be expected, the material will thin out as we approach the present—how can one tell which of the works among the myriads that are being written will endure or predict which composers will be heard ten or twenty years from now. The author truthfully admits to a great degree of subjectivity in choosing material available. The author would also like to acknowledge the publishers of the magazines *Fanfare* and *American Record Guide* for the excellent material they present, which aids the author in making a publication such as this relevant to those who love the higher things in musical life.

Acknowledgments

�֎

To my loving wife, Mary, for her many hours of input and for being my best critic and proofreader

To Lorena Bidwell, for computer help and that wonderful macro program that shortened my task considerably

1751

❄

Historical Highlights: The British Parliament finally changes to the Gregorian calendar; Chinese forces invade Tibet; in the New World, tension between England and France increases with the colonizing of the Ohio Valley by English settlers; the Currency Act forbids any issuance of paper money in the New England colonies.

Art and Literature Highlights: Births—artists James Sharples, Johann Friedrich Tischbein, Ralph Earl, writers Richard Sheridan, Nikolai Lvov; Deaths—artists Charles A. Coypel, John Smibert. Art—Falconet's *Allegory of Music*, William Hogarth's *Cheap Gin and Beer Street*, Longhi's *The Painter in His Studio*; Literature—Fielding's *Amelia*, Klopstock's *Messias I*, Smollett's *The Adventures of Peregrine Pickle*.

Musical Highlights

A. Births

Composers: Supply Belcher (U.S.A.) April 19; Carl Joseph Birnbach (Germany); Dimitri Bortniansky (Russia); Ferdinand Kauer (Austria) January 18; Blas de Laserna (Spain) February 4; Jean-Baptiste Lemoyne (France) April 3.

Singers: Mary Ann Pownall (British-born singer/composer) February; Corona (Elisabeth) Schröter (German soprano/composer) January 14; Carl David Stegmann (German tenor/harpsichordist).

Performers: Benjamin Blake (British violinist) February 27; Bartolomeo Campagnoli (Italian violinist/composer) September 10; Josephus Andreas Fodor (Dutch violinist/composer) January 21; Karl Haack (German violinist) February 18; Johann Baptist Kucharz (Bohemian organist) March 5; William Mahon (Brazilian cellist); David Moritz Michael (German-born violinist/composer) October 21; Maria Anna Mozart (Austrian pianist) July 30.

Others: Louis-François Beffara (French music author) August 23; Emanuel Schikaneder (Austrian librettist) September 1; Nikolaus Simrock (German publisher) August 23.

B. Deaths

Composers: Tomaso Albinoni (Italy) January 17; John F. Lampe (Germany) July 25; Georg Caspar Schürmann (Germany) February 25; Domingo Terradellas (Spain) May 20.

Singers: Henry Theodore Reinhold (German-born bass) May 14.

Performers: Giuseppe Matteo Alberti (Italian violinist/composer) February 18; Pierre Dumage (French organist) October 2; Anton Englert (German organist) November.

Others: Heinrich Bokemeyer (German music theorist/composer) December 7; Jacobus Franciscus Moreau (Dutch organ builder) October 9; Christopher Schrider (German-born organ builder) May.

C. Debuts

Singers: Joseph Vernon (British tenor—London); Isabella Young (British contralto—London).

Performers: Carlo Francesco Chiabrano (Italian violinist—London).

D. New Positions

Conductors: Manuel Gaytan y Arteaga (maestro de capilla, Cordoba Cathedral); Ignaz Holzbauer (oberkapellmeister, Stuttgart); Antonio Mazzoni (maestro di cappella, S. Giovanni, Monte).

Others: Charles Burney (organ, St. Margaret's, King's Lynn, Norfolk); Francois Francoeur (co-director, Paris Opera); Johann Christian Kittel (organ, Langensalza); Jose Nebra (director, Royal Choir School and deputy director, Royal Chapel, Madrid); François Rebel (co-director, Paris Opera); John Worgen (organ, Vauxhall Gardens, London).

E. Prizes/Honors

Honors: Johann Friedrich Agricola (court composer, Frederick the Great); Francois Colin de Blamont (Order of St. Michel); Quirino Gasparini (Accademia Filarmonica, Bologna).

F. Biographical Highlights

Faustina Bordoni retires from the stage but continues singing in the court; Charles Burney moves his family to King's Lynn for a nine-year stay; Carl Ditters von Dittersdorf enters the service of the Prince of Sachsen-Hilburghausen; Elizabeth Duparc returns to the concert stage; Francois Joseph Gossec arrives in Paris with a letter of introduction to Rameau; George Frederic Handel is stricken with blindness; Johann Adam Hiller enters the law school of the University of Leipzig.

G. Cultural Beginnings

Performing Groups—Instrumental: Maresch Hunting Horn Ensemble (St. Petersburg).

Educational: James Logan Library (bequeathed to the city of Philadelphia).

Music Publishers: Peter Thompson Music Publishing House (London).

Performing Centers: King Street Theatre (Birmingham); Teatro Nuovo (Padua).

Other: Johann A. Stein, organ builder (Augsburg).

H. Musical Literature

Thomas A. Arne, *Vocal Melody III*; Charles-Henri de Blainville, *Essai sur un troisième mode*; Pierre Esteve, *Nouvelle découverte du principe de l'harmonie*; Francesco Geminiani, *The Art of Playing the Violin*; Georg J. Hahn, *Wohl unterwiesene General-Bass Schuler*; William Hayes, *The Art of Composing Music by a Method Entirely New*; Johann Mattheson, *Sieben Gespräche der Weisheit und Musik samt zwo Beylagen: Als die dritte Dosis der Panacea*; Johann X. Nauss, *Grundlicher Unterricht der General-Bass recht zu erlernen*; Georg C. Wagenseil, *Geig-Fundamenta, oder Rudimenta panduristae*.

I. Musical Compositions

Chamber Music:

Sonata/Solos: Felice de' Giardini, *Six Violin Sonatas, Opus 1*.
Piano: Johan J. Agrell, *Three Harpsichord Sonatas (A, B♭, G)*; C. P. E. Bach, *Sonata in e, H.66*.

Choral/Vocal Music:

Choral: George Frederick Handel, *Jephtha* (oratorio); Johann A. Hasse, *Mass in d–Te Deum in D*.

Musical Stage: Girolamo Abos, *Tito Manlio*; Andrea Adolfati, *Adriano in Siria–La gloria e il piacere*; Johann F. Agricola, *La ricamatrice divenuta dama*; Francesco Araja, *Eudossa incoronata*; Ferdinando Bertoni, *Le Pescatrici*; Giuseppe Bonno, *Il re pastore*; William Boyce, *The Shepherd's Lottery*; Pasquale Cafaro, *Ipermestra*; Egidio Duni, *La semplice curiosa*; Baldassare Galuppi, *Dario–Antigona–Lucio Papirio–Artaserse*; Carl H. Graun, *Britannico–L'Armida*; Johann A. Hasse, *Ciro riconosciuto*; Niccolò Jommelli, *Talestri–Ifigenia in Aulide–Cesare in Egitto–Ipermestra–L'uccellatrice*; Nicola Logroscino, *Amore figlio del piacere–La finta frascatana*; Antonio Palella, *Il Geloso*; Domenico Paradies, *La forza d'amore*; David Perez, *Ezio–La Didone–La Zenobia*; Giovanni Pescetti, *Artaserse*; Jean-Philippe Rameau, *Linus–Acante et Céphise*; Georg Reutter, *La virtuosa emulazione*; Rinaldo di Capua, *Gli impostori–Il ripiego in amore di Flaminia*; Domingo Terradellas, *Sesostri*; Tommaso Traetta, *Il Farnace*.

Orchestra/Band Music:

Concerted Music:
Piano: Johan J. Agrell, *Three Harpsichord Concertos (F, D, A), Opus 3*; C. P. E. Bach, *Harpsichord Concerto in B♭, H.434*.
Other: Charles Avison, *Six Concertos in Seven Parts, Opus 3*.

Ballet/Incidental Music: Thomas A. Arne, *The Country Lasses* (IM); Jean-Philippe Rameau, *La guirlande* (B).

Standard Works: Thomas A. Arne, *Eight Overtures*; Niccolò Pasquali, *Twelve Overtures*.

Symphonies: Charles de Blainville, *Six Symphonies, Opus 2*; François Martin, *Six Symphonies (D, F, c, g, A, E♭), Opus 4*; Papavoine, *Six Symphonies, Opus 1*.

1752

❋

Historical Highlights: The Treaty of Aranjuez is signed between Spain and the Holy Roman Empire; the British break the French siege of Trichinopoly in India; The Liberty Bell is installed in Philadelphia but cracks on its first trial; the Treaty of Logstown settles the Allegheny Mountain problems and opens the territory for colonial expansion.
Art and Literature Highlights: Madrid Academy of Fine Arts opens. Births—artists John R. Cozens, Ann Eliza Bleecker, writers Fanny Burney, Thomas Chatterton, Timothy Dwight, Friedrich von Klinger; Deaths—artist Charles A. Coypel. Art—Giaquinto's *Birth of the Virgin*, Longhi's *The Family Concert*, Tiepolo's *Beatrix Arrival to the Emperor*; Literature—Sedaine's *Poèsies Fugitives*, Charlotte Lennox's *The Female Quixote*.

Musical Highlights

A. Births
Composers: Francesco Bianchi (Italy)(?); André de Silva Gomes (Brazil) December; Ambrogio Minoja (Italy) October 22; Johann Friedrich Reichardt (Germany) November 25; Nicola Antonio Zingarelli (Italy) April 4.
Conductors: Johann Friedrich Krantz (Germany) April 6.
Singers: Charles Knyvett, Sr. (British tenor) February 22; Johann Georg Spangler (Austrian tenor) March 22; Carl Stenborg (Swedish tenor/impresario) September 25; Elisabeth Augusta Wendling (German soprano) October 4.
Performers: Friedrich Ludwig Benda (German violinist/composer) September 4; Isidore Bertheaume (French violinist/composer)(?); Charles Broche (French organist) February 20; Muzio Clementi (Italian pianist/composer) January 23; Georg-Friedrich Fuchs (French clarinetist/composer) December; Edward Jones (British harpist) May 29; Justin Heinrich Knecht (German organist/music theorist) September 30; Ludwig August Lebrun (German oboist/composer) May; José Mauricio (Portugese organist/music theorist) March 19; Josef Reicha (Czech cellist/composer) March 13.
Others: Giuseppe Carpani (Italian music author) January 28; Carl Friedrich Cramer (German publisher) March 7; Sébastien Érard

(French piano/harp maker) April 5; Count Andreas Razumovsky (Russian patron of the arts) November 2.

B. Deaths

Composers: Agostino Bonaventura Coletti (Italy); Girolamo Donnini (Italy); John Christopher Pepusch (Germany-England) July 20.
Performers: Johann Ludwig Benda (Bohemian violinist/composer); Pietro Castrucci (Italian violinist) February 29; Michael Festing (British violinist/composer) July 24; Henri-Guillaume Hamal (Belgian organist) December 3; Conrad Michael Schneider (German organist) November 23; John Shore (British trumpeter) November 20; Nicolas Vibert (French violinist/composer) August 16.
Others: Louis Fuzelier (French librettist) September 19.

C. Debuts

Singers: Jean-Louis Laruette (French tenor—Paris).

D. New Positions

Conductors: Benjamin Cooke (Academy of Ancient Music, London); Adolph Carl Kunzen (kapellmeister, Mecklenburg-Schwerin); David Perez (maestro di capella, Royal Chapel, Lisbon); Giuseppe Sarti (Faenza Theater); Joseph Umstatt (kapellmeister/composer, Bamburg).
Others: Ferdinando Gioseffo Bertoni (first organist, St. Mark's, Venice); Chapel Bond (organ, Holy Trinity, Coventry).

F. Biographical Highlights

The family of Tommaso Giordani, comprising a traveling opera group of their own, make their Amsterdam debut; Christoph Willibald Gluck goes to Naples to oversee the performance of his commissioned opera, *La clemenza di Tito*; Nicola Antonio Porpora is pensioned from the Dresden Court and moves to Vienna, where he begins private teaching, Franz Joseph Haydn becoming one of his students; Antonio Soler takes the Holy Orders at El Escorial and remains there for the rest of his life.

G. Cultural Beginnings

Educational: Académie de Musique de Reims.
Music Publishers: Samuel Lee, Music Store (Dublin).
Music Publications: *Covent Garden Journal; Gray's Inn Journal.*
Performing Centers: Rococo Theater (Schwetzingen).

H. Musical Literature

Jean d'Alembert, *Treatise on Rameau's Theories–The Elements of Music*; Thomas A. Arne, *Vocal Melody IV*; Charles Avison, *Essay on Musical*

Expression; Christian G. Krause, *Von der musikalischen Poesie*; Francesco Provedi, *Paragone della musica antica e della moderna*; Johann J. Quantz, *Versuch einer Anweisung, die Flote traversiere zu spielen*; Joseph Riepel, *Anfangsgrunde zur musikalischen Setzkunst*; Caspar Ruetz, *Widerlegte vorurtheile von der Beshaffenheit der heutigen Kirchenmusik und von der Lebens-Art einiger Musicorum.*

I. Musical Compositions

Chamber Music:

Sonata/Solos: Louis de Caix d'Hervelois, *Pièces di viole, Book 5*; Georg Philipp Telemann, *Seven Duets for Flutes*.

Piano: Johan J. Agrell, *Three Harpsichord Sonatas (G, E, —)*; C. P. E. Bach, *Sonata in D, H.67–Sonata in g, H.68–Variations in F on "Ich schlief, da träumte mir," H.69*; Domenico Scarlatti, *Thirty Keyboard Sonatas I–Thirty Keyboard Sonatas II* (publication).

Choral/Vocal Music:

Choral: Baldassare Galuppi, *Gerusalemme convertita* (oratorio); George Frederick Handel, *Jephtha* (oratorio); Niccolò Jommelli, *La nativita della beatissima Vergine* (oratorio); Niccolò Piccinni, *Gioas, re di Giuda* (oratorio); Giovanni Alberto Ristori, *Mass in C*; Johann H. Roman, *Swedish Mass*.

Musical Stage: Girolamo Abos, *Erifile–Lucio Vero*; Andrea Adolfati, *Vologeso–Ipermestra*; Francisco de Almeida, *L'Ippolito*; Thomas A. Arne, *Harlequin Sorcerer*; Giuseppe Bonno, *L'eroe cinese–Didone abbandonata*; Gioacchino Cocchi, *Il Tutore*; Baldassare Galuppi, *Didone abbandonato–Le virtuose ridicole–La calamita de' cuori*; Christoph Willibald Gluck, *La clemenza di Tito–Issipile*; Carl H. Graun, *L'Orfeo–Il giudicio di Paride*; Johann A. Hasse, *Adriano in Siria*; Franz Joseph Haydn, *Der krumme teufel*; Niccolò Jommelli, *I rivali delusi*; Nicola Logroscino, *La Griselda–Lo finto Perziano*; Jean-Joseph de Mondonville, *Venus et Adonis*; Antonio Pampani, *Venceslao*; David Perez, *Adriano in Siria–Demofoonte*; Rinaldo di Capua, *La donna superba–La forza della pace*; Jean-Jacques Rousseau, *Le devin du village*; Joseph N. Royer, *Pandore*; Giuseppe Sarti, *Pompeo in Armenia*; Giuseppe Scarlatti, *Adriano in Siria–Demetrio–L'impostore–I portentosi effetti della Madre Natura–L'amor della Patia*; Jean-Joseph Vadé, *La Fileuse–Le Poirier.*

Orchestra/Band Music:

Concerted Music:

Piano: William Felton, *Six Organ/Harpsichord Concertos, Opus 4*.

Other: Christoph Willibald Gluck, *Flute Concerto in G*.

Ballet/Incidental Music: Thomas A. Arne, *The Oracle* (IM); Michel Blavet, *Floriane, ou La Grotte des spectacles* (B); Antoine Dauvergne, *Les amours de Tempe* (B).

1753

Historical Highlights: The British Parliament finally provides for the naturalization of Jews; Austria, Russia, and France unite against Frederick II of Prussia; Fort Presque Isle (Erie, Pennsylvania) and other forts are built by the French in the Ohio Territory, and George Washington is sent by the Virginia governor to demand French withdrawal.

Art and Literature Highlights: The British Museum Library is built. Births—writers Phillis Wheatley, Elizabeth Inchbald, August G. Meissner, artist William Beechey; Deaths—artist Georg W. Knobelsdorff, philosopher George Berkeley. Art—Boucher's *Setting of the Sun*, Chardin's *The Blind Man*; Literature—Destouche's *Le Dissipateur*, Richardson's *History of Sir Charles Grandison*, Smollett's *Ferdinand Count Fathom*.

Musical Highlights

A. **Births**

Composers: Angelo Baldan (Italy); Stanislas Champein (France) November 19; Nicolas Dalayrac (France) June 8; Friedrich Christoph Gestewitz (Germany) November 3; Otto Carl Kospoth (Germany) November 25; Johann Baptist Schenk (Germany) November 30; Johann Gottfried Schicht (Germany) September 29; Pedro Etienne Solère (Spain).

Conductors: Friedrich August Baumbach (Germany) September 12.

Singers: Jean-Joseph Imbault (French violinist/publisher) March 9; Giovanni Rubinelli (Italian castrato alto); Luiza Rosa Todi (Portuguese mezzo-soprano) January 9.

Performers: Johann Braun (German violinist) August 29; Jean-Baptiste Sébastien Bréval (French cellist/composer) November 6; Franz Anton Dimmler (German horn virtuoso/composer) October 14; Peter Fuchs (Austrian violinist/composer) January 22; Anton Stadler (Austrian clarinetist) June 28; Carl Türrschmidt (German horn virtuoso) February 24; Johan Wikmanson (Swedish organist/composer) December 28.

Others: Franz Ambros Alexander (German instrument maker) July 22; Franciscus Geissenhof (Austrian violin maker) September 15; Antoine-Marcel Lemoine (French publisher) November 3; Christian Friedrich Ruppe (German music theorist/composer) February 18.

B. **Deaths**

Composers: Joseph Christoph Deichel (Germany) August 2; Giacomo Facco (Italy) February 16; Nicolas Recot de Grandval (France) November 16; François-Lupien Grenet (France) February 25; Louis-

Maurice de La Pierre (France) January 1; Giovanni Alberto Ristori (Italy) February 7.

Performers: Jacques Aubert (French violinist) May 17; Johann Nicolaus Bach (German organist/composer) November 4; Carl Joseph Einwald (Austrian organist) November; Barnabas Gunn (British organist/composer) February 6; James Worgan (British organist) April.

Others: Gerhardus Havingha (Dutch organist/music theorist) March 6; Gottfried Silbermann (German organ builder) August 4.

C. Debuts
Singers: Giuseppe Aprile (Italian castrato soprano—Naples).

D. New Positions
Conductors: Gioacchino Cocchi (maestro di cappella, Conservatorio degli Incurabili, Venice); Ignaz Holzbauer (kapellmeister, Mannheim); Giuseppe Sarti (Mingotti's Opera Co., Copenhagen).

Others: Christlieb Siegmund Binder (organ, Dresden Court); Richard Langdon (organ, Exeter Cathedral).

F. Biographical Highlights
The operatic family of Tommaso Giordani moves on to England and makes their debut at Covent Garden; André Gretry, age twelve, is dismissed from the choir of the St. Denis church and begins taking violin and singing lessons; music historian John Hawkins marries into a wealthy family leaving him free to devote his time to music and literature study; Franz Joseph Haydn meets and receives encouragement from Carl Ditters von Dittersdorf.

G. Cultural Beginnings
Music Publishers: Hummel Music Publishing Co. (Amsterdam).
Performing Centers: Residenztheater (Cuvilliestheater, Munich).

H. Musical Literature
Thomas Arne, *Agreeable Musical Choice I*; Charles Avison, *A Reply to the Author of Remarks on the Essay on Musical Expression*; C. P. E. Bach, *The Proper Method of Playing Keyboard Instruments I*; Michel Corrette, *Le maître de clavecin*; Pierre Esteve, *L'esprit des beaux-arts*; Friedrich Grimm, *Le petit prophète de Boemisch-broda*; William Hayes, *Remarks on Avison's Essay on Musical Expression*; Friedrich Marpurg, *Abhandlung von der Fuge I*; Friedrich Riedt, *Versuch uber die musikalischen Intervalle*; Jean-Jacques Rousseau, *Lettre sur la musique francaise*; Louis Travenol, *Histoire du théâtre de l'opéra en France*.

I. Musical Compositions
Chamber Music:
Ensembles: Jean-Marie Leclair, *l'aine*, *Three Ouvertures et sonates en trio, Opus 13*; Carlo Tessarini, *Six Trio Sonatas, Opus 16*.

Piano: C. P. E. Bach, *Six Sonatas (C, d, A, b, E♭, f)*, *H.70–75*; Domenico Scarlati, *Thirty Keyboard Sonatas III–Thirty Keyboard Sonatas IV*.

Choral/Vocal Music:

Choral: Francesco Durante, *Mass in A*; José Nebra, *Mass in B♭*; Antonio Pampani, *Magnificat III*; Giovanni Sammartini, *La reggia de' fati–La pastorale offerta* (cantatas).

Vocal: Willem De Fesch, *Mr. De Fesch's Songs Sung at Marybone Gardens*.

Musical Stage: Andrea Adolfati, *La clemenza di Tito*; Maria Teresa Agnesi, *Ciro in Armenia*; Ferdinando Bertoni, *Ginevra–I bagni d'Abano*; Michel Blavet, *La fête de Cythère*; Gioacchino Cocchi, *Il Pazzo glorioso*; Antoine Dauvergne, *Les troqueurs–La coquette trompée*; Giovanni Ferrandini, *Catone in Utica*; Baldassare Galuppi, *I bagni d'Abano* (with F. G. Bertoni)–*Sofonisba–L'eroe cinese*; Carl H. Graun, *Silla–Il trionfo della fedelta*; Johann A. Hasse, *Solimano–L'eroe cinese*; Ignaz Holzbauer, *Il figlio delle selve*; Niccolò Jommelli, *La clemenza di Tito–Fetonte–Bajazette–Demofoonte II*; Giovanni Lampugnani, *Vologeso*; Nicola Logroscino, *Olimpiade–Elmira generosa–La Pastorella scaltra*; Jean-Joseph de Mondonville, *Titon et l'Aurore*; Antonio Pampani, *Madama Dulcinea*; David Perez, *L'eroe cinese–Olimpiade*; Jean-Philippe Rameau, *Daphnis et Egle–Lysis e Délie*; Rinaldo di Capua, *La Zingara–La serva sposa–L'amante deluso*; Giovanni M. Rutini, *Semiramide*; Giuseppe Sarti, *Il re pastore*; Giuseppe Scarlatti, *Alessandro nell'Indie–De gustibus non est disputandum*; Tommaso Traetta, *I pastori felici*; Jean-Joseph Vadé, *Le Rien–Le Suffisant*.

Orchestra/Band Music:

Concerted Music:

Piano: Johan J. Agrell, *Three Harpsichord Concertos, Opus 4 (A, b, G)*; C. P. E. Bach, *Harpsichord Concerto in A, H.437*.

Ballet/Incidental Music: Thomas Arne, *Lethe* (IM); Michel Blavet, *Le jeux olympiques* (B); Antoine Dauvergne, *La sibylle* (B); François Giraud, *Les hommes* (B); Jean-Philippe Rameau, *Les Sybarites* (B).

Symphonies: Pierre Talon, *Six Symphonies (F, D, E♭, C, B♭, A), Opus 1*.

1754

❊

Historical Highlights: England and France begin their battles in the Old World (Seven Years War) and the New (French and Indian War); at the Battle of Great Meadows, George Washington, in charge of the Virginia militia, is forced to surrender Fort Necessity; King's College (Columbia University) is founded in New York City.

Art/Literature Highlights: Births—artists Andrea Appiani, Asmus Jakob Carstens, Amos Doolittle, writers Joel Barlow, George Crabbe, Vincenzo Monti; Deaths—writers Philippe Destouches, Ludvig Holberg, Henry Fielding. Art—Boucher's *The Captive Cupid*, Copley's *Mars, Venus and Vulcan*, Fragonard's *Psyche with Cupid's Presents*; Literature—Gessner's *Daphnis*, Rousseau's *On the Inequality of Man*.

Musical Highlights

A. Births

Composers: David August von Apell (Germany) February 23; Luigi Caruso (Italy) September 25; Vincenzo Federici (Italy) October 6; Gaetano Marinelli (Italy) June 3; Vicente Martin y Soler (Spain) May 2; Silvestre (De) Palma (Italy) March 15; Joseph Schubert (Bohemia) December 20; Peter (von) Winter (Germany) August 28.

Singers: Maddalena Allegranti (Italian-born soprano); Matteo Babbini (Italian tenor) February 19; Josefa Dušek (Czech soprano) March 6; Elizabeth Ann Linley (British soprano) September 5; Luigi Marchesi ("Marchesini") (Italian castrato soprano) August 8.

Performers: Anton Felix Bečvařovský (Bohemian organist) April 9; Ignaz Böck (German horn virtuoso)(?); Étienne Ozi (French bassoonist/composer) December 9; Anton Teyber (Austrian pianist/organist/composer) September 8.

Others: François Callinet (French organ builder) October 1; Franz Anton Hoffmeister (German publisher/composer) May 12.

B. Deaths

Composers: Giovanni Carlo Maria Clari (Italy) May 16; Louis de Lacoste (France); Gaetano Maria Schiassi (Italy).

Performers: Jacques de Bournonville (French harpsichordist/composer)(?); Johann Christian Hertel (German violist/composer) October; Ferdinando Antonio Lazzari (Italian organist/composer) April 19.

Others: Camillus Camilli (Italian violin maker) October 21.

C. Debuts

Singers: Anna Lucia de Amicis (Italian soprano—Florence); Rosa Curioni (Italian mezzo-soprano—London).

D. New Positions

Conductors: Pierre-Montan Berton (Paris Opera); Giovan Brunetti (maestro di cappella, Pisa); Ignazio Fiorillo (hofkapellmeister, Braunschweig).

Others: John Christopher Smith (organ, Foundling Hospital, London).

E. Prizes/Honors

Honors: Gregorio Ballabene (Accademia Filarmonica, Bologna).

F. **Biographical Highlights**
Johann Christian Bach travels to Bologna to study with Padre Martini; Franz Joseph Haydn becomes a valet-pupil of Porpora who gives him composition lessons in exchange for menial tasks; Francis Hopkinson's *Ode to Music* is the first known work by a native American; Pierre-Alexandre Monsigny, his imagination fired by a performance of Pergolesi's *La Serva padrona*, decides to begin writing operas; Giovanni Paisiello, on recommendation of his choir director, is sent to the Conservatorio de S. Onofrio in Naples; Gaetano Pugnani begins concertizing throughout Europe; Jean-Jacques Rousseau returns to Geneva and reenters the Calvinist faith.

G. **Cultural Beginnings**
Music Publishers: Robert Bremner (Edinburgh).
Music Publications: *Historisch-Kritische Beytrage zur Aufnahme der Musik.*
Performing Centers: Drottningholm Palace Theater I (Stockholm); Teatro Filarmonico II (Verona).
Other: Inventionshorn (by Anton Hampel).

H. **Musical Literature**
Jean-le-Rond d'Alembert, *Réflexions sur la musique en général et sur la musique françaises en particulier;* Thomas Arne, *Agreeable Musical Choice II;* Jean de Bethizy, *Exposition de la theorie et de la pratique de la musique;* Charles-Henri de Blainville, *L'Esprit de l'art musical;* François Collin de Blamont, *Essai sur les goûts anciens et moderne de la musique française, relativement aux paroles d'opéra;* Francesco Geminiani, *Guida Armonica*(?); Johann A. Hiller, *Abhandlung uber die Nachahmung der Natur in der Musik;* Friedrich Marpurg, *Abhandlung von der Fuge nach dem Grundsätzen den besten deutschen und ausländischen Meister;* Jean-Philippe Rameau, *Observations sur notre instinct pour la musique;* Johann A. Scheibe, *Abhandlung vom Ursprung und Alter der Musik;* Johann M. Schmidt, *Musico-Theologia;* Giuseppe Tartini, *Trattata di musica secondo la vera sienza dell'armonia.*

I. **Musical Compositions**
Chamber Music:
Sonata/Solos: François Granier, *Six Solos for Cello;* Nicola Porpora, *Twelve Violin Sonatas.*
Ensemble: C. P. E. Bach, *Trio Sonata in G, H.583–in E♭, H.584.*
Piano: C. P. E. Bach, *Sonata in G, H.77–Sonata in E♭, H.78;* Pietro D. Paradies, *Twelve Harpsichord Sonatas, Vol. 2;* Ferdinando Pellegrini, *Six Harpsichord Sonatas, Opus 1;* Domenico Scarlatti, *Thirty Keyboard Sonatas VII–Thirty Keyboard Sonatas VIII–Thirty Keyboard Sonatas IX.*

Choral/Vocal Music:
Choral:
Oratorios: Anton Adlgasser, *Christ on the Mount of Olives*; Ignaz Holzbauer, *La Passione de Gesu Christo*; Niccolò Jommelli, *La reconciliazione della Virtu e della Gloria*; Antonio Pampani, *Messiae praeconium–Carmine complexum.*
Others: Francis Hopkinson, *Ode to Music*; François Philidor, *Mote, Lauda Jerusalem.*
Vocal: Vincenzo Ciampi, *Six Arias*(?)–*Six Arias with Recitative accompaniment*(?).
Musical Stage: Johann Agricola, *Cleofide–La nobilità delusa*; Thomas Arne, *Eliza*; Andrea Bernasconi, *L'huomo*; Ferdinando Bertoni, *La moda*; Giuseppe Bonno, *L'isola disabitata*; Vincenzo Ciampi, *Didone*; Francesco Durante, *S. Antonio di Padua*; Baldassare Galuppi, *Siroe– Il filosofo di campagna–Alessandro nelle Indie*; Manuel García, *Le finta schiava*; Christoph Willibald Gluck, *Le cinesi*; Carl H. Graun, *Semiramide*; Johann A. Hasse, *Artemisia*; Ignaz Holzbauer, *L'isola disabitata–L'issipile*; Niccolò Jommelli, *Lucio Vero–Catone in Utica–Don Falcone*; Jean-Joseph de Mondonville, *Daphnis et Alcimadure*; Antonio Pampani, *Eurione*; Giovanni Pescetti, *Tamerlano*; David Perez, *L'Ipermestra–Lucio Vero*; Niccolò Piccinni, *Le donne dispettose*; Georg Reutter, *Il tributo di Rispetto e d'Amore–La Corona*; Rinaldo di Capua, *Attalo–La Chiavarina*; Giuseppe Sarti, *Antigono–Vologeso–Ciro riconosciuto*; Giuseppe Scarlatti, *Caio Mario–Antigono–La madamigella*; Tommaso Traetta, *Le nozze contrastate*; Jean-Joseph Vadé, *Le Trompeur trompé–Il était temps.*
Orchestra/Band Music:
Concerted Music:
Other: Franz X. Richter, *Six Concertos for Horn and Orchestra.*
Ballet/Incidental Music: Jean-Philippe Rameau, *Anacreon I* (B)–*La naissance d'Osiris* (B).

1755

Historical Highlights: Great Lisbon Earthquake kills more than 60,000 people and causes extensive damage; the British sign a Treaty of Alliance with Russia; General Braddock is mortally wounded at the Battle of the Wilderness, and George Washington takes over command.
Art and Literature Highlights: Births—artists Thomas Stothard, John Flaxman, Gilbert Stuart, writers Jean F. Collin d'Harleville, Marie Anne Elisabeth Vigee-Lebrun; Deaths—artists Gustavus Hesselius, Jean Baptiste Oudry. Art—Boucher's *Shepherd and Shepherdess*, Falconet's *The*

Punishment of Cupid, Oudry's *The White Duck;* Literature—Fielding's *Journal of a Voyage to Lisbon,* Johnson's *Dictionary of the English Language.*

Musical Highlights

A. **Births**
Composers: Mateo Pérez de Albéniz (?Spain); Gaetano Andreozzi (Italy) May 22; Luigi Braccini (Italy)(?); Thomas Hamly Butler (England); Franz Götz (Bohemia) July 29(?); Antoine-Frédéric Gresnick (Belgium) March 2; Peter Albrecht van Hagen (Holland); Christian Kalkbrenner (Germany) September 22; Angelo Tarchi (Italy).
Singers: Brigida Giorgi Banti (Italian soprano); Sarah Bates (British soprano)(?); Louis Chardiny (French baritone); Louise Dugazon (French mezzo-soprano) June 18; Adrian Ferraresi del Bene (Francesca Gabrielli) (Italian soprano); Sabina Hitzelberger (German soprano) November 12; Marie-Josephine Laguerre (French soprano).
Performers: Giuseppe Antonio Capuzzi (Italian violinist/composer) August 1; Pierre-Louis Couperin (French organist/composer) March 14; Federigo Fiorillo (Italian violinist/composer) June 1; François-Joseph Garnier (French oboist/composer) January 18; François-Joseph Hérold (French pianist/composer) March 18; Philipp Christoph Kayser (German pianist/composer) March 10; Pierre Leduc (French violinist) October 17; Vincenz Mašek (Bohemian pianist/organist) April 5; John Christopher Moller (German-born organist/publisher); Gaspard-Claire Prony (French harpist/music theorist) July 12; Franz Ries (German violinist) November 10; Giovanni Battista Viotti (Italian violinist/composer) May 12.
Others: John Betts (British violin maker); Thomas Busby (British music author) December; Albert Christoph Dies (German artist music author) February 11; Pierre Leduc (French violinist/publisher).

B. **Deaths**
Composers: Francisco António de Almeida (Portugal); Johann Caspar Bachofen (Switzerland) June 23; Pietro Paolo Bencini (Italy) July 6; Joseph Bodin de Boismortier (France) October 28; John Clark (Scotland); Francesco Durante (Italy) September 30; François Estienne (France) March 5; Gottlob Harrer (Germany) July 9; Giovanni Battista Porta (Italy) June 21; Joseph-Nicolas Royer (France) January 11.
Singers: Alexander Gordon (Scottish tenor)(?); Anastasia Robinson (British contralto) April.
Performers: Jean-Jacques-Baptiste Anet (French violinist) August 14; Georg Gebel, Jr. (German organist) September 24; Maurice Greene (British organist/composer) December 1; Johann Georg Pisendel (German violinist/composer) November 25; Theodor Christlieb Reinhold (German organist) March 24; Jean-Baptiste Stuck (Italian-born cellist) December 8.

Others: Azzolino Bernardino Della Ciaia (Italian organist/builder/ composer) January 15.

C. **Debuts**

Singers: Charlotte Brent (British soprano—Dublin); Henri Larrivée (French bass-baritone—Paris); Frederick Charles Reinhold (British bass—London).

D. **New Positions**

Conductors: Andrea Bernasconi (kapellmeister, Munich Court); Giovanni Battista Costanzi (maestro di cappella, St. Peter's, Rome); José Duran (maestro de capilla, Palau, Barcelona); Francisco Javier García Fajer (maestro di cappella, Terni Cathedral); Johann Andreas Giulini (kapellmeister, Augsburg Cathedral); Gottfried August Homilius (music director, Dresden's three main churches); Jean Joseph de Mondonville (Concerts Spirituel, Paris); Giuseppe Sarti (kapellmeister, Copenhagen Court).

Others: Felice de' Giardini (impresario, Italian Opera, London); Johann Gottfried Müthel (organ, Lutheran Church, Riga).

E. **Prizes/Honors**

Honors: Antoine Dauvergne (Composer to the King, Paris).

F. **Biographical Highlights**

Francesco Araia writes the first known opera to be based on a Russian libretto, *Cephal i Prokris*; Thomas Arne and his wife separate over his affair with the soprano Charlotte Brent; Gioacchino Conti survives the Great Lisbon Earthquake but is so impressed by his escape that he decides to enter a monastery; Christoph Willibald Gluck, traveling in Italy, meets Franz Joseph Haydn; Michael Haydn is dropped from the St. Stephen's choir when his voice changes; Francesco Antonio Uttini goes to Stockholm as conductor of an Italian opera group and stays there permanently.

G. **Cultural Beginnings**

Music Publishers: Thomas Cahusec (England).

Performing Centers: Municipal Theater on the Place Stanislas (Nancy); Teatro des Pacos de Ribeira (Lisbon).

Other: W. Hill and Son, organ builders (London).

H. **Musical Literature**

Francesco Algarotti, *Saggio sopra l'opera in musica*; Jean-Antoine Berard, *L'art du chant*; Philippe Caffiaux, *Histoire de la musique*; Ranieri Calzabigi, *Dissertazione su le poesie drammatiche del Sig. Abate Pietro Metastasio*; Francesco Geminiani, *The Art of Accompaniment*; Friedrich Marpurg, *Anleitung zum Clavierspielen der schönen Ausübung der heutigen Zeit gemäss–Handbuch bey dem Generalbasse und der Composi-*

tion; Christoph Nichelmann, *Die melodie nach ihren Wesen*; Pierre Roussier, *Observations sur differents points d'harmonie*; William Tans'ur, *The Royal Melody Compleat*; Antonio Tonelli, *Trattado di Musica*.

I. Musical Compositions

Chamber Music:

Ensembles: C. P. E. Bach, *Four Concertos (b, c, g, F)–Trio Sonata in B♭*, H.587; François Philidor, *Six Quartets for Oboe and Strings*; Giuseppe Tartini, *Six Trio Sonatas II*.

Piano: C. P. E. Bach, *Sonata in E, H.83–Fantasia and Fugue a 4 in c, H.103*; Felice de' Giardini, *Six Cembalo Sonatas, Opus 3 (with violin obbligato)*; Friedrich Marpurg, *Six Harpsichord Sonatas*; Domenico Scarlatti, *Thirty Keyboard Sonatas X–Thirty Keyboard Sonatas XI*.

Organ: C. P. E. Bach, *Four Sonatas (F, a, D, g), H.84–87*.

Choral/Vocal Music:

Choral: Carl H. Graun, *Der tod Jesu* (cantata); Niccolò Jommelli, *Gerusalemme convertita* (oratorio); Antonio Pampani, *Sofonea id est Joseph pro Rex Aegypti*; Georg Wagenseil, *Gioas, re di Giuda–La redenzione* (oratorios).

Vocal: William Boyce, *Lyra britannica* (cycle); William Jackson, *Twelve Songs, Opus 1*(?).

Musical Stage: Andrea Adolfati, *Sesostri, re d'Egitto*; Johann F. Agricola, *Il tempio d'amore*; Francesco Araja, *Alessandro nell'Indie*; Thomas Arne, *Britannia*; Andrea Bernasconi, *Adriano in Siria*; Egidio Duni, *Olimpiade*; Giovanni Battista Ferrandini, *Diana placata*; Baldassare Galuppi, *Attalo–Le nozze–La diavolessa–Il poverto superbo*; Manuel García, *La pupilla–Pompeo Magno in Armenia*; Christoph Willibald Gluck, *La danza–L'innocenza giustificata*; Carl H. Graun, *Ezio–Montezuma*; Johann A. Hasse, *Ezio II–Il re pastore–Il Calandrano*; Ignaz Holzbauer, *Don Chisciotte*; Niccolò Jommelli, *Pelope–Enea nel Lazio–Il giardino incanto*; Giovanni Lampugnani, *Siroe*; Antonio Pampani, *Astianatte*; David Perez, *Alessandro nell'Indie*; Niccolò Piccinni, *Le Gelosie*; Georg Reutter, *La Gara*; John C. Smith, *The Fairies*; Tommaso Traetta, *L'incredulo*; Francesco Uttini, *Il re pastore*; Georg Wagenseil, *Le cacciatrici amanti*.

Orchestra/Band Music:

Concerted Music:

Piano: C. P. E. Bach, *Organ/Harpsichord Concerto in G, H.464*; William Felton, *Six Organ/Harpsichord Concertos, Opus 5*.

Other: Charles Avison, *Eight Concertos in Seven Parts, Opus 4*.

Ballet/Incidental Music: François Giraud, *Deucalion et Pyrrha* (B).

Symphonies: Louis Aubert, *Six Symphonies (F, G, B♭, d, A, D), Opus 2*; C. P. E. Bach, *Three Symphonies (C, F, D), H.648–650*; Papavoine, *Six Symphonies, Opus 3*; Georg Wagenseil, *Three Symphonies, Opus 1*.

1756

❊

Historical Highlights: The Seven Years War continues with Great Britain against most of the European nations; the Treaty of Westminster is signed between England and Prussia; stagecoach service begins between New York City and Philadelphia; the *New Hampshire Gazette*, one of the United States' longest running newspapers, is founded.

Art and Literature Highlights: Births—artists Peter Francis Bourgeois, Henry Raeburn, John Trumbull, William Rush, writer Willem Bilderdijk; Deaths—artists George Vertue, Jean-Louis Lemoyne, writer Thomas Cooke. Art—Hagenauer's *Christ Tied to the Column*, Longhi's *The Fortune Teller*, Natoire's *San Sebastian and the Angel*; Literature—Amory's *The Life of John Buncle I*, Swedenborg's *The Heavenly Arcana*.

Musical Highlights

A. **Births**
Composers: Nicolas-Joseph Hüllmandel (France) May 23; Henrik Klein (Moravia) June 13; Joseph Martin Kraus (Germany-Sweden) June 20; Wolfgang Amadeus Mozart (Germany) January 27; Vincenzo Righini (Italy) January 22; Johann Christoph Vogel (Germany) March 18.
Singers: Cecilia Davies (British soprano)(?); Mme. (Antoinette) Cêcile Saint-Huberty (French soprano) December 15.
Performers: Olof Åhlström (Swedish organist) August 14; Laurent-François Boutmy (British organist/pianist) June 19; Jean Gehot (Belgian violinist/composer) April 8; Józef Jaruwek (Czech-born pianist/conductor) October 2; Antoine Lacroix (French violinist/publisher); Thomas Linley, Jr. (British violinist/composer) May 5; Alexander Reinagle (British-born pianist/impresario/composer) April 23; Franz Teyber (Austrian organist/conductor/composer) November 15; Paul Wranitzky (Bohemian violinist/conductor/composer) December 30.
Others: Ernest Chladni (German acoustician) November 30; Carl Augustin Grenser (German instrument maker) May 2; Augustus Frederic Kollmann (German-born music theorist/organist) March 21; Christian Gottfried Körner (German music theorist) July 2; Bernard Germain Lacépède (French music theorist) December 26; Josef Preindl (Austrian music theorist/organist) January 30.

B. **Deaths**
Composers: Riccardo Broschi (Italy); Giacomo Antonio Perti (Italy) April 10.

Singers: Antonio Maria Bernacchi (Italian castrato alto) March 13; Catherine Tofts (British soprano).
Performers: Charles-Placide Caraffe, *le cadet* (French violinist) October 24; Jean Odo Demars (French organist) November 7; Johann Gottlieb Goldberg (German pianist) April 13; William McGibbon (Scottish violinist/composer) October 3; Johann Theodor Römhild (German organist) October 26; Georg Gottfried Wagner (German violinist/composer) March 23.
Others: John Byfield, Sr. (British organ builder); Johann C. Donati (German organ builder) September.

C. Debuts
Singers: Angiola Calori (Italian soprano—Venice); Rosalia Guerrero (Spanish soprano—Madrid); Elizabeth Young (British soprano—Dublin).
Performers: Luigi Boccherini (Italian cellist—Italy); Pierre Vachon (French violinist—Paris).

D. New Positions
Conductors: Antonio Aurisicchio (maestro di cappella, S. Giacomo degli Spagnuoli, Rome); Johann Ernst Bach (kapellmeister, Weimar); Giuseppe Maria Carretti (maestro di cappella, S. Petronio, Bologna); Johann Friedrich Doles (cantor, St. Thomas School, Leipzig); Francisco Javier García Fajer (maestro di cappella, Saragossa Cathedral); Francois Giroust (maître de musique, Orleans Cathedral); Johann Valentin Görner (kapellmeister, Hamburg Cathedral); Luis Misón (Royal Opera, Madrid); Giuseppe Paolucci (maestro di cappella, S. Maria Gloriosa dei Frari, Venice); Johann Michael Schmid (kapellmeister, Mainz).
Others: Franz Xaver Brixi (organ, Prague Cathedral); Johann Ludwig Krebs (organ, Castle Church, Altenburg).

E. Prizes/Honors
Honors: Giovan G. Brunetti (Accademia Filarmonica, Bologna); Pierre de La Garde (Chamber Composer to the King, Paris); Christoph Willibald Gluck (Order of the Golden Spur); Pietro Longhi (Venice Academy).

F. Biographical Highlights
Caffarelli retires from the opera stage and, with his considerable fortune, buys the dukedom of Santo-Durato in Naples; Christoph Willibald Gluck goes to Rome to oversee the production of his *Antigono*, then returns to Vienna to oversee the production of his *Il re pastore*; Franz Joseph Haydn begins the limited teaching of music; Jean Jacques Rousseau is set up at the Hermitage by Mme. d'Epinay.

G. Cultural Beginnings
Music Publishers: Breitkopf und Hartel (Breitkopf since 1719, Leipzig).
Music Publications: *Samenspraaken over Musikaale Beginselen.*
Performing Centers: Princes Street Rooms (Bristol); Russian Royal Court Theater (first known permanent Russian theater).
Other: Thomas Haxby, instrument maker (York).

H. Musical Literature
Ernst Baron, *Abriss einer Abhandlung von der melodie*; Joseph Blanchet, *L'art ou les principes philosophiques du chant*; Robert Bremner, *The Rudiments of Music*; Philippe Caffiaux, *Nouvelle méthode de solfier la musique*; Giacomo Durazzo, *Lettre sur le Méchanisme de l'opéra Italien*; Pierre Esteve, *Dialogue sur les Arts*; Pierre Fournier, *Essai d'un nouveau caracteres de fonte pour l'impression de la musique*; Barthold Fritz, *Tuning of Keyboard Instruments*; Friedrich Marpurg, *Principes de clavecin*; Giovanni Martini, *Regole agli organiste per accompagnare il canto fermo*; Leopold Mozart, *Fundamentals of Violin Playing.*

I. Musical Compositions
Chamber Music:
Ensembles: Charles Avison, *Six Trio Sonatas, Opus 5*; C. P. E. Bach, *Trio Sonata in F, H.590*; Giuseppe Tartini, *Twelve Trio Sonatas, Opus "3."*
Piano: C. P. E. Bach, *Sonata in d, H.105–in e, H.106*; Domenico Scarlatti, *Thirty Keyboard Sonatas XII.*
Organ: C. P. E. Bach, *Preludio in D, H.108*; Michel Corrette, *IIIe livre d'orgue.*
Choral/Vocal Music:
Choral:
Oratorios: Anton C. Adlgasser, *Die wirkende Gnade Gottes (David in der Busse)*; Georg Philipp Telemann, *Der Tod Jesu*; Georg C. Wagenseil, *Il roveto di Mose.*
Others: C. P. E. Bach, *Oster-Musik, H.803*; Carl H. Graun, *Te Deum*; Franz Joseph Haydn, *Salve Regina in E*; Niccolò Jommelli, *Missa pro defunctis in E♭*; José Nebra, *Mass, "Jubilate in conspectu Regis"*; Antonio Pampini, *Magnificat IV*; Nicola Porpora, *Te Deum I.*
Vocal: Domenico Scarlatti, *Salve Regina* (soprano, strings).
Musical Stage: Thomas Arne, *The Pincushion*; Andrea Bernasconi, *Didone abbandonata*; Pasquale Cafaro, *Ladisfatta di Dario*; Vincenzo Ciampi, *Catone in Utica*; Egidio Duni, *La buona figliuola*; Giovanni Battista Ferrandini, *Demetrio*; Baldassare Galuppi, *Idomeneo–Le nozze di Paride–La cantarina–Le pescatrici*; Francisco García Fajer, *Lo Scultore deluso*; Quirino Gasparini, *Artaserse*; Felice de' Giardini, *Olimpiade*; Tommaso Giordani, *La Comediante*

fatta cantatrice; François Giraud, *La gageure de village*; Christoph Willibald Gluck, *Antigono–Il re pastore*; Carl H. Graun, *La Merope–I fratelli nemici*; Johann A. Hasse, *L'Olimpiade*; Ignaz Holzbauer, *Le nozze d'Arianna–Il filosofo di campagna*; Giacomo Insanguine, *Lo funnaco revotato*; Niccolò Jommelli, *Artaserse II*; Nicola Logroscino, *I disturbi–Le finte magie*; Antonio Pampini, *Antigono— Artaserse*; François Philidor, *Le retour du printemps*; Niccolò Piccinni, *Zenobia–Il curioso del suo proprio danno*; Rinaldo di Capua, *Il capitano napolitano*; Antonio Sacchini, *Fra Donato*; Giuseppe Sarti, *Arianna e Teseo*; John C. Smith, *The Tempest*; Tommaso Traetta, *La fante furba–Buovo d'Antona*; Jean-Joseph Vadé, *Les Raccoleurs*.

Orchestra/Band Music:
Concerted Music:
  Piano: Vincenzo Ciampi, *Six Harpsichord Concertos, Opus 7*.
  Other: Franz Joseph Haydn, *Organ Concerto No. 1 in C, H.SVIII/I*.
Ballet/Incidental Music: Thomas Arne, *Injured Honor* (IM).
Symphonies: C. P. E. Bach, *Symphony in e, H.652–Symphony in e, H.653*; François Gossec, *Six Symphonies (D, E, C, G, F, D), Opus 3*; Papavoine, *Six Grande Symphonies, Opus 4*; Georg C. Wagenseil, *Six Symphonies, Opus 2*.

1757

Historical Highlights: Robert Clive defeats the French in India and consolidates the British influence in that country; Chinese emperor curtails foreign trade and limits it to the city of Canton; French forces capture Fort William Henry in upper New York; Benjamin Franklin is sent to London as a special agent for the colonies.

Art and Literature Highlights: Births—artists Antonio Canova, William Blake, writers Harriet Lee, Wojciech Boguslawski; Deaths—artists Antoine Pesne, Rosalba Carriera, writers Colley Cibber, James Davenport. Art—Falconet's *The Bather*, Greuze's *La Paresseuse Italienne*, Longhi's *The Masked Reception*; Literature—Bodmer's *Das Niebelungenlied*, Klopstock's *Geistliche Lieder I*, Smollett's *The Reprisal*.

Musical Highlights

A. Births
Composers: Louis-Abel Belfroy de Reigny (France) November 6; George K. Jackson (England-U.S.A.) April 15; Józef Kozlowski (Poland); Daniel Read (U.S.A.) November 16; Klaus Scholl (Denmark) April 28.

Performers: Antonio Bartolomeo Bruni (Italian violinist/composer) January 28; Henry Condell (British violinist/composer); Christian Danner (German violinist) July 12; Christian Ludwig Dieter (German violinist/composer) June 13; Jacob Eckhard (German-born organist/composer) November 24; Willem de Fesch (Dutch violinist/composer); Giovanni Battista Gaiani (Italian organist/composer) November 20; William Reeve (British organist/composer); Alessandro Rolla (Italian violinist/composer) April 6; Johann Abraham Sixt (German organist/composer) January 3; Richard Wainwright (British organist) July 8; Charles Wesley (British organist/composer) December 11.

Others: Antonio Calegari (Italian music theorist/composer) February 17; François-Louis Pique (French violin maker); Ignace Joseph Pleyel (Austrian publisher/composer) June 18; George Thomson (Scottish folksong collector) March 4.

B. **Deaths**

Composers: Paolo Benedetto Bellinzani (Italy) February 25; Fortunato Chelleri (Italy) December 11; Bartolomeo Cordans (Italy) May 14; Domenico Scarlatti (Italy) July 23; Jean-Joseph Vadé (France) July 4; Andrea Zani (Italy) September 28.

Conductors: Johann Stamitz (Bohemia) March 27.

Performers: Willem De Fesch (Dutch violinist/composer)(?); Michel Forqueray (French organist) May 30; Johann Paul Kunzen (German organist) March 20; François Martin (French cellist/composer); Niccolò Pasquali (Italian violinist/composer) October 13.

Others: Johann Konrad Brandenstein (German organ builder) November 21; Louis Bertrand Castel (French acoustician) January 11; Zacharias Hildebrandt (German organ builder) October 11.

C. **Debuts**

Singers: (Madeleine) Sophie Arnould (French soprano—Paris).

D. **New Positions**

Conductors: Gioacchino Cocchi (Haymarket Theater, London); Pascual Fuentes (choirmaster, Valencia Cathedral); Michael Haydn (kapellmeister, Bishop of Grosswardein); Antonio Soler (maestro de capilla, El Escorial); Matheo Tollis de la Roca (assistant maestro de capilla, Mexico City Cathedral).

Others: Jean-Joseph Boutmy (organ, St. Baaf Cathedral, Ghent); François Francoeur (director, Paris Opera and co-director, Royal Academy, Paris); Adolph Carl Kunzen (organ, Marienkirche, Lubeck); Samuel Porter (organ, Canterbury Cathedral); François Rebel (co-director, Royal Academy, Paris); Wilhelm August Roth (music editor, *Der Freund*).

F. **Biographical Highlights**
Johann Gottlob Clemm moves his organ-building business to Bethelem, Pennsylvania; Friedrich William Herschel settles in England and begins teaching music; Johann Gottlieb Naumann goes to Italy and receives instruction from Tartini, Martini, and Hasse; David Tannenberg moves to Bethlehem, Pennsylvania, in order to work with Clemm.

G. **Cultural Beginnings**
Educational: Lord Mornington's Musical Academy (Dublin).
Performing Centers: Bolshoy Kamenniy Theater (Moscow); Large Stone Theater (St. Petersburg); Teatro Comunale (Bologna); Teatro de Operas y Comedias (Buenos Aires); Theater Royal (Norwich); University Theater (Moscow).
Other: Philadelphia Public Concerts.

H. **Musical Literature**
Johann F. Agricola, *Anleitung zur Singekunst*; Johann P. Kirnberger, *Der allzeit fertige Polonaisen- und Menuetten-componist*; Friedrich W. Marpurg, *Systematische Einleitung in die musikalische Setzkunst, nach den Lehrsätzen des Herrn Rameau–Anfangs-gründe der theoretischen Musik*; Giovanni Martini, *Storia della musica I*; Niccolò Pasquali, *Thorough-Bass Made Easy*; Antonio Rodriguez de Hita, *Diapason instructivo*; Johann G. Sulzer, *Pensees sur l'origine des sciences et des Beaux-Arts*.

I. **Musical Compositions**
Chamber Music:
    Ensembles: Johann J. Agrell, *Six Trio Sonatas (G, G, C, G, G, G), Opus 3*.
    Piano: C. P. E. Bach, *Six Sonatas (B♭, E, g, G, C, c), H.16–21*; Georg Benda, *Six Harpsichord Sonatas (B♭, G, d, F, g, D)*; William Jackson, *Six Harpsichord Sonatas, Opus 2*; Domenico Scarlatti, *Thirty Keyboard Sonatas XIII*.
Choral/Vocal Music:
    Choral:
        Oratorios: Agostino Accorimboni, *Giuseppe riconosciuto*; Johann F. Agricola, *Trauerkantate*; Johann Albrechtsberger, *Christo Kreutz-Erfindung*; Georg Benda, *Der Sterbende Jesus*; George Frederick Handel, *The Triumph of Time and Truth*; Ignaz Holzbauer, *Isacco*; Jan Oehlenschlägel, *Captiva filia Sion*; Antonio Pampani, *Triumphus Judith*; Johann Seyfert, *Der sterbentag Jesu*; Georg Philipp Telemann, *Passion According to John V*.
        Others: Johann F. Agricola, *Psalm 21–Trauerkantate*; Johann Albrechtsberger, *Christo Kreutz-Erfindung*; Johann Christian Bach, *Requiem in F*; Wilhelm Friedemann Bach, *Ja, Ja, es hat mein*

Gott–Halleluja, wohl diesen volk (cantatas); William Boyce, *Ode in Commemoration of Shakespeare*; Carl H. Graun, *Te Deum Laudemus*; José Nebra, *Mass in D*; Antonio Pampani, *Magnificat V*; Nicola Porpora, *Te Deum II–Salve Regina No. 5*; Georg Philipp Telemann, *Cantata for the Birthday of King Friedrich V*.
Vocal: C. P. E. Bach, *Geistliche Oden und lieder, H.686*; Hinrich P. Johnsen, *Church Music for Easter Sunday*.
Musical Stage: Ferdinando Bertoni, *Lucio Vero*; Giuseppe Bonno, *Colloquio amoroso fra Piramo e Tisbe*; Pasquale Cafaro, *L'incendio di Troia*; Vincenzo Ciampi, *Il clemenza di Tito–Il chimico*; Gioacchino Cocchi, *Semiramide I–Demetrios*; Egidio Duni, *Le peintre amoureux de son modèle*; Baldassare Galuppi, *Ezio–Sesostri*; Florian Gassmann, *Merope*; Felice de' Giardini, *Rosmira*; Pietro Guglielmi, *Lo solachianello 'mbroglione*; Ignaz Holzbauer, *La clemenza de Tito*; Giacomo Insanguine, *La Matilde generosa*; Niccolò Jommelli, *Temistocle–Creso*; Antonio Pampani, *Demofoonte*; David Perez, *Solimano*; François Philidor, *Blaise le savetier*; Niccolò Piccinni, *Caio Mario– L'amante ridicolo deluso–La schiava seria*; Georg Reutter, *Il sogno*; Antonio Sacchini, *Il giocatore*; Giuseppe Scarlatti, *L'isola disabitata–Il mercato di Malmantile*; Tommaso Traetta, *La Didone abbandonata–La Nitteti–Ezio*; Jean-Joseph Vadé, *L'Impromptu du coeur–Le Mauvais plaisant*.
Orchestra/Band Music:
Concerted Music: Giovanni Sammartini, *Six Concerti grossi, Opus 6*.
Ballet/Incidental Music: Thomas Arne, *Isabella* (IM); Jean-Philippe Rameau, *Zéphyre* (B)–*Anacréon* (B).
Symphonies: Ignaz Holzbauer, *Six Symphonies in Four Parts, Opus 2*; Johann Stamitz, *Six Symphonies, Opus 2*.

1758
❃

Historical Highlights: Burma becomes an independent state with the capitol at Rangoon; the British take over the Bengal state in India; French forces suffer the loss of Fort Duquesne, rebuilt and renamed Fort Pitt by the English; the first Indian reservation is opened in Burlington County, New Jersey.
Art and Literature Highlights: Births—artists Pierre-Paul Prud'hon, Alexander Nasmyth, Antoine Charles (Carle) Vernet, writers Peter Andreas Heiberg; Deaths—writers John Dyer, Francoise Grafigny. Art— Boucher's *The Mill at Charenton*, Pigalle's *Love and Friendship*, Greenwood's *American Sea Captains Carousing in Surinam*; Literature— Lennox's *History of Henrietta*, Prime's *The Unfortunate Hero*, Voltaire's *Candide*.

Musical Highlights

A. **Births**
   Composers: Domingo Arquimbau (Spain)(?); Frédéric Blasius (France) April 24; Johann Chrysostomus Drexel (Germany) January 24; Christian Ignatius Latrobe (England) February 12; António Leal Moreira (Portugal) June 30; Bernardo Porta (Italy); Carl Friedrich Zelter (Germany) December 11.
   Singers: Antonio Bianchi (Italian baritone); François Lays (French tenor) February 14; Benedikt Schack (Bohemian tenor) February 7; Josepha Weber (German soprano).
   Performers: José Manuel Aldana (Mexican violinist/composer); Josepha Barbara Auernhammer (Austrian pianist) September 25; Henri-Joseph de Croes (Belgian violinist) August 16; Francisco Galeazzi (Italian violinist); Joseph Gelinek (Bohemian pianist/composer) December 3; Thomas Greatorex (British organist/conductor) October 5.
   Others: Johann Simeon Buchholz (German organ builder) September 27; Bohumir Jan Dlabač (Bohemian music scholar) July 17; Nicolas Lupot (French violin maker) December 4; Timothy Swan (American compiler/composer) July 23.

B. **Deaths**
   Composers: Johann Friedrich Fasch (Germany) December 5; Joseph Meck (Germany) December 2; Matteo Palotta (Italy) March 28; Johan Helmich Roman (Sweden) November 20.
   Singers: Domenica Casarini (Italian soprano)(?); Domenico Gizzi (Italian castrato soprano) October 14; Richard Leveridge (British bass) March 22; Angelo Maria Monticelli (Italian castrato soprano).
   Performers: Giuseppe Antonio Brescianello (Italian violinist) October 4; François Dagincour (French organist/composer) April 30; Alessandro Toeschi (Italian violinist) October; John Travers (British organist/composer) June; Bernard Christian Weber (German organist) February 5.
   Others: Richard Bridge (British organ/piano maker) June 7; Johann Balthasar König (German music scholar) March 31; Johann Tobias (German organ builder) November 24.

C. **Debuts**
   Singers: Marie-Therese Laruette (French soprano—Paris).

D. **New Positions**
   Conductors: Charles Gauzargues (sous maître, Royal Chapel, Paris); Johann Philipp Kirnberger (kapellmeister, Princess Amalie, Berlin); Pierre van Maldere (Brussels Opera); Hermann Friedrich Raupach

(kapellmeister, St. Petersburg); Tommaso Traetta (maestro di cappella, Duke of Parma).
Others: Laurent Desmazures (organ, Notre Dame, Rouen); Charles-Simon Favart (director, Opéra-Comique, Paris); Pierre-Claude Foucquet (organ, Chapel Royal, Paris); Jean-Pierre Legrand (organ, St. Germain-des-Près).

E. Prizes/Honors
Honors: Giovanni Battista Consoni (Accademia Filarmonica, Bologna); Giuseppe Antonio Consoni (Accademia Filarmonica, Bologna); Thomas Dupuis (Royal Society of Musicians); Giovanni Battista "Padre" Martini (Accademia Filarmonica, Bologna); Giovanni Plantanida (Accademia Filarmonica, Bologna).

F. Biographical Highlights
Carl Friedrich Abel leaves Dresden and moves to London, where he settles permanently; Caterina Gabrieli is forced to leave Padua early due to one of her many scandals; Johann Adam Hiller, while tutoring the nephew of Count Bruhl, travels to Leipzig and decides to settle there, reviving the Liebhaberkonzerte subscription series some time later; Antonio Lolli becomes solo violinist in the court orchestra of the duke of Wurttemberg in Stuttgart; Vincenzo Manfredini goes to Russia for an eleven-year stay in the St. Petersburg Court; Italian castrato Giusto Ferdinando Tenducci is enthusiastically received in London.

G. Cultural Beginnings
Music Publishers: Louis Balthazard La Chevardiere (Paris); Johann Haffner (Nuremburg).
Music Publications: *Journal de Musique Française, Italienne (Echo).*
Performing Centers: Crow Street Theater (Dublin).
Other: Aberdeen Musical Society (Scotland); Accademia Filarmonica (Milan).

H. Musical Literature
Jacob Adlung, *Anleitung zu der musikalischen Gelehrtheit*; Alexander Baumgarten, *Aesthetica*; Robert Bremner, *Instructions for the Guitar*; Charles F. Clément, *L'Accompagnement du Clavecin*; Michel Corrette, *Le parfait Maître à chanter*; Francesco Geminiani, *The Harmonical Miscellany*; Friedrich W. Marpurg, *Anleitung zur Singe-composition*; Niccolo Pasquali, *The Art of Fingering the Harpsichord*; Louis Travenol, *Mémoire sur le sieur Travenol, ex-musicien du roi de Pologne.*

I. Musical Compositions
Chamber Music:
    Sonata/Solos: John Collett, *Six Violin Solos, Opus 1.*

Piano: C. P. E. Bach, *Ten Sonatas (B♭, c, d, e, F, a, b, A, B♭, A), H.126–135.*
Choral/Vocal Music:
  Choral—Oratorios: Johann F. Agricola, *Die auferstehung des Erlösers*; Jean-Joseph de Mondonville, *Les Israelites au Mont Oreb*; Jan Oehlenschlägel, *Fortis in bello amor et maeror*; Niccolò Piccinni, *La morte di Abele*; John C. Smith, *Judith–Paradise Lost*; Georg Philipp Telemann, *Passion According to Matthew IV.*
  Choral: Johann Christian Bach, *Dixit Dominus, T.202–Magnificat in C, T.207–Beatus vir in F, T.209*; William Boyce, *Ode to the New Year*; Vincenzo Ciampi, *Missa Solemnis–Te Deum*; Baldassare Galuppi, *L'oracolo del Vaticano* (cantata); José Nebra, *Missa, "Domino exaudi vocem meam"–Missa Pro de functis.*
  Vocal: August B. Herbing, *Musikalische Belustigungen I.*
  Musical Stage: Thomas Arne, *The Sultan*; Vincenzo Ciampi, *Arsinoe*; Antoine Dauvergne, *Enée et Lavinie*; Egidio Duni, *Le docteur Sangrado–La fille mal gardée–Nina et Lindor*; Giovanni Battista Ferrandini, *Demetrio*; Baldassare Galuppi, *Adriano in Siria–Ipermestra–Demofoonte*; Florian Gassmann, *Issipile*; Christoph Willibald Gluck, *L'ile de Merlin–La fausse esclave*; Pietro Guglielmi, *Il filosofo burlato*; Johann A. Hasse, *Demofoonte II–Nitteti–Il sogno di Scipione*; Franz Joseph Haydn, *Der neue krumme Teufel*; Ignaz Holzbauer, *Nitteti*; Niccolò Jommelli, *L'asilo d'amore* (serenade)–*Ezio III–Tito Manlio*; Giovanni Lampugnani, *Ezio III–Le cantatrici*; Giovan di Majo, *Ricimero re dei Goti*; Niccolò Piccinni, *Alessandro nelle Indie–La Scaltra letterata–Gli uccellatori–Madame Arrighetta*; Georg Reutter, *Le Grazie vendicate*; Rinaldo di Capua, *Adriano in Siria*; Antonio Sacchini, *Olimpia tradita*; Giuseppe Sarti, *Anagilda*; Tommaso Traetta, *Olimpiade–Demofoonte.*
Orchestra/Band Music:
  Concerted Music:
    Piano: Charles Avison, *Six Harpsichord Concertos, Opus 6.*
    Other: Jean-François Tapray, *Six Organ Concertos.*
  Ballet/Incidental Music: Thomas Arne, *The Prophetess* (IM); Antoine Dauvergne, *Les fêtes d'Euterpe* (B).
  Symphonies: Franz Beck, *Six Overtures, Opus 1*; François Gossec, *Six Symphonies (D, E, F, E, d, F), Opus 4*; André Gretry, *Six Small Symphonies*; Franz X. Richter, *Three Symphonies, Opus 10*; Johann Stamitz, *Four Symphonies, Opus 4.*

1759

Historical Highlights: The Jesuit Order is expelled from Spain and Portugal, and the Jesuit University in Portugal is closed; British forces take over Fort Niagara, Crown Point, and Fort Ticonderoga; British General James Wolfe and French General Louis Joseph de Montcalm are both killed in the Battle of the Plains of Abraham.

Art and Literature Highlights: Births—artist Julius Caesar Ibbetson, writers Johann Friedrich von Schiller, Bobby Burns; Deaths—artists Charles Brooking, Philip Mercier, Lambert S. Adam. Art—Longhi's *The Tooth-Drawer*, Tiepolo's *St. Thecla Praying for the Plague-Stricken*, Wilson's *Portrait of Benjamin Franklin*; Literature—Thomas Godfrey's *Prince of Parthia*, Samuel Johnson's *History of Rasselas*.

Musical Highlights

A. **Births**

Composers: Maria Rosa Coccia (Italy) January 4.

Singers: Joseph Carl Ambrosch (German tenor) May 6; Brigida Banti (Italian soprano); Salomea Deszner (Polish soprano); Charles Duquesnoy (Belgian tenor/composer) May 18.

Performers: Andrew Ashe (Irish flutist)(?); Wilhelm Friedrich Ernst Bach (German harpsichordist/pianist) May 23; Gervais-François Couperin (French organist/composer) May 22; François Devienne (French bassoonist/composer) January 31; Carolus Emanuel Fodor (Dutch-born harpsichordist) October 31; Johann Christian Haeffner (German-born organist) March 2; Franz Vincez Krommer (Czech violinist/composer) November 27; Jean Lebrun (French horn virtuoso) April 6; Antonio da Silva Leite (Portugese guitarist/composer) May 23; Marie Theresia von Paradies (Austrian pianist/composer) May 15; Jacob Scheller (Bohemian violinist) May 16; Jacques Tours (Dutch organist); Sophia Maria Westenholz (German pianist) July 10.

Others: Giuseppe Bertini (Italian musicographer) January 20; Franz Gleissner (German lithographer); Johann Carl Friedrich Rellstab (German publisher) February 27; Guillaume-André Villoteau (French music scholar) September 6.

B. **Deaths**

Composers: Paolo Benedetto Bellinzani (Italy) February 25; Ignazio Maria Conti (Italy) March 28; Carl Heinrich Graun (Germany) August 8; George Frederick Handel (Germany) April 14; François de La Croix (France) April 8.

Singers: Francisco Senesino (Francesco Bernardi) (Italian castrato alto) January 27; Gustavus Waltz (German bass)(?).

Performers: Johann Christoph Altnikol (German organist) July 25; Francisco Manalt (Spanish violinist) January 16; Charles-Joseph Sohier (French violinist/composer) June 29.

Others: Pietro Mingotti (Italian impresario) April 28; Heinrich Titz (German organ builder) May 4; Tobias Heinrich Trost (German organ builder) August 15.

C. Debuts

Singers: Antonia Maria Girelli (Italian soprano—Venice); Thomas Norris (British tenor—Oxford).
Performers: Carl Friedrich Abel (German viola da gamba virtuoso—London).

D. New Positions

Conductors: Johann Friedrich Agricola (music director, Potsdam Opera); Johann Georg Albrechtsberger (organ, Melk Abbey); Giovanni Battista Borghi (maestro di cappella, Macerata Cathedral, Naples); Pascal Boyer (maître de chapelle, Nimes Cathedral); Franz Xaver Brixi (kapellmeister, St. Vitus' Cathedral, Prague); Giacomo Carcani (maestro di cappella, Ravenna Cathedral); Giovanni Battista Casali (maestro di cappela, St. John Lateran, Rome); Johann Ridinger (director, Stuttgart Academy).

E. Prizes/Honors

Honors: Thomas Arne (D.Mus., Oxford); John Beard (doctorate, Oxford); Francois Bedos de Celles (Bordeaux Academie des Sciences); William Boyce (Master of the King's Music); Giovanni B. Cirri (Accademia Filarmonica, Bologna).

F. Biographical Highlights

André Grétry is sent to Rome on a scholarship to study music; Francis Hopkinson writes *My Days Have Been So Wondrous Free*, the first known song written in the New World; Pietro Locatelli, traveling to Russia with his opera company, introduces comic opera to Moscow audiences for the first time; James Lyon graduates from the College of New Jersey (Princeton) with a degree in theology; Giovanni Paisiello graduates from the Conservatorio di S. Onofrio in Naples and is given a teaching position there for the next four years.

G. Cultural Beginnings

Music Publications: *Kritische Briefe uber die Tonkunst.*
Performing Centers: Moscow Opera House.
Other: Michael Hillegas Music Shop, first known in the New World (Philadelphia).

H. Musical Literature

Jean d'Alembert, *De la liberté de la musique*; Pietro Gianotti, *Le guide du compositeur I*; Henri Hardouin, *Bréviaire du Diocese de Reims*; Johann A. Ludwig, *Versuch von den Eigenschaften einer rechtschaffenen*

Orgelbauers; Friedrich W. Marpurg, *Kritische einleitung in die Geschichte und Lehrsätze der alten und neuen Musik–Historisch-kritische beyträge IV;* Jean-Philippe Rameau, *Nouvelles réflexions sur le principe sonore.*

I. Musical Compositions
Chamber Music:
String Quartets: Franz Joseph Haydn, *Six Divertimentos (B♭, E♭, D, G, E♭, C), Opus 1.*
Ensembles: Johann J. Quantz, *Six Flute Duets, Opus 2.*
Piano: Johan J. Agrell, *Twenty Harpsichord Sonatas, Opus 2;* C. P. E. Bach, *Eight Sonatas (F, G, a, d, c, F, d, a), H.136–143;* Ferdinando Pellegrini, *Six Harpsichord Sonatas, Opus 4*(?).
Choral/Vocal Music:
Choral:
Oratorios: Giuseppe Bonno, *Isacco figura del redentore;* Vincenzo Ciampi, *Vexillum fidei;* Jean-Joseph de Mondonville, *Les fureurs de Saul;* Jan Oehlenschlägel, *Justitia et clementia;* Nicola Porpora, *Israel ad Aegyptiis liberatu;* Georg Philipp Telemann, *Miriam und deine Wehmut–Das befreite Israel–Die Hirten bei der Krippe zu Bethlehem–Passion According to Mark I.*
Other: André Grétry, *Messe Solennelle;* José Nebra, *Missa, Sie benedicam Domino.*
Vocal: August B. Herbino, *Musikalischer Vesuch;* Francis Hopkinson, *My Days Have Been So Wondrous Free.*
Musical Stage: Pietro Aulette, *Didone;* Ferdinando Bertoni, *Il Vologeso;* William Boyce, *Harlequin's Invasion;* Vincenzo Ciampi, *Gianguir;* Egidio Duni, *La veuve indécise;* Baldassare Galuppi, *Melite riconosciuto–La ritornata di Londra;* Florian Gassmann, *Gli uccellatori;* Christoph Willibald Gluck, *L'arbre enchanté–La Cythere assiégée–Le diable à quatre;* Pietro Guglielmi, *La ricca locandiera–I capricci di una vedova–La moglie imperiosa;* Johann A. Hasse, *Achille in Sciro;* Ignaz Holzbauer, *Alessandro nell'Indie–Ippolito ed Aricia;* Niccolò Jommelli, *Nitteti–Endimione;* Pierre Monsigny, *Les aveux indiscrets;* Vincenzo Orgitano, *Il finto pastorello;* David Perez, *Enea in Italie;* François Philidor, *Blaise le savetier– L'huître et les plaideurs;* Niccolò Piccinni, *Siroe, rè di Persia–Ciro riconosciuto–La Cecchina;* Jean-Philippe Rameau, *Le procureur dupé sans le savoir;* Rinaldo di Capua, *Le Donne ridicole;* Antonio Sacchini, *Il copista burlato;* Giuseppe Sarti, *Armida abbandonata– Achille in Sciro;* Giuseppe Scarlatti, *La serva scaltra;* Tommaso Traetta, *Solimano–Ippolito ed Aricia–Ifigenia in Aulide.*
Orchestra/Band Music:
Concerted Music:
Piano: C. P. E. Bach, *Harpsichord/Organ Concerto in E♭, H.446.*

Ballet/Incidental Music: Christian Cannabich, *Ippolito e Aricia* (B). **Symphonies:** Carl F. Abel, *Six Symphonies in Four Parts, Opus 1*; François Gossec, *Six Symphonies, Opus 4*; Franz Joseph Haydn, *Symphony No. 1 in D*.

1760
❄

Historical Highlights: Berlin is burned by the Russians; Prussia is defeated at Landshut and the Austrians at Liegnitz and Torgau; the French give up both Montreal and Detroit; Baron Amherst is appointed governor-general of British North America; New York passes the first law requiring the licensing of physicians and surgeons.

Art and Literature Highlights: Royal Society of Arts founded in London. Births—writers Johann Peter Hebel, Leandro Fernandez de Moratin, George Richards; Deaths—writer Isaac Hawkins Browne. Art—Canaletto's *San Marcus Plaza*, Stubb's *Mares and Foals in Landscape*; Literature—Musaus' *Grandison der Zweite I*, Macpherson's *Fragments of Ancient Poetry Collected in the Highlands of Scotland*, Sterne's *Tristram Shandy I, II*.

Musical Highlights

A. Births

   Composers: Inácio António de Almeida (Portugal) February 18; Johann Evangelist Brandl (Germany) November 14; Luigi Cherubini (Italy-France) September 14; Johann Ladislaus Dussek (Bohemia) February 12; Henri-Philippe Gerard (France) November 9; Jean-François Le Sueur (France) February 15; Cándido José Ruano (Spain) June 14; Angelo Tarchi (Italy)(?) April; Johann Rudolf Zumsteeg (Germany) January 10.

   Singers: Catharina Cavalieri (Austrian soprano) February 19; Celeste Coltellini (Italian mezzo-soprano) November 26; Pierre Gaveaux (French tenor/composer) October 9; Samuel Harrison (British tenor) September 8; John Page (British tenor)(?); Therese Teyber (Austrian soprano) October 15; Aloysia Weber (German soprano).

   Performers: Johann Dalberg (German pianist/author) May 17; Johann Georg Distler (Austrian violinist/composer); Joseph Graetz (German pianist/composer) December 2; John Moorhead (Irish violinist/composer); Maria Hester Park (British pianist) September 2; William Shrubsole (British organist) January; Gaetano Valeri (Italian organist/composer) September 21.

Others: Charles Albrecht (American piano maker); Jacques-Georges Cousineau (French harp maker) January 13; Louis Alexandre Frichot (French instrument inventor) April; Claude-Joseph Rouget de Lisle (French poet/composer) May 10.

B. Deaths

Composers: Girolamo Abos (Malta) October; Andrea Adolfati (Italy) October 28; François Colin de Blamont (France) February 14; François Bouvard (France) March 2; Roque Ceruti (Italy-Peru) December 6; Anton Filtz (Germany) March 14; (Johann) Christoph Graupner (Germany) May 10; Michele Masciti (Italy) April 24; Giuseppe Maria Orlandini (Italy) October 24; Giacomo Rampini (Italy) May 27.

Singers: Giovanni Carestini (Italian castrato contralto)(?); Annibale Pio Fabri (Italian tenor) August 12; Maria Rosa Negri (Italian mezzo-soprano) August 4; Tommaso Scarlatti (Italian tenor) August; Aloysia Weber (German soprano)(?).

Performers: Ernst Gottlieb Baron (German lutenist) April 12; Louis de Caix d'Hervelois (French viola da gamba virtuoso); Jean-Baptiste Chrétien (French cellist) December 1; César François Clérambault (French organist/composer) October 26; René Drouard de Bousset (French organist) May 19; Vicente Rodriguez (Spanish organist/composer) December 16.

Others: Louis-Alexandre Clicquot (French organ builder) January 25; Wolf Wilhelm Haas (German instrument maker) February 21; Philip Hollister (Italian organ builder) May; Abbé Jean Lebeuf (French music scholar) August 10; Giuseppe Serassi (Italian organ builder) August 1.

C. Debuts

Singers: Cecilia Grassi (Italian soprano—Venice).
Performers: James Cervetto (British cellist—London).

D. New Positions

Conductors: Paolo Tommaso Alberghi (maestro di cappella, Faenza Cathedral); Johann Samuel Endler (kapellmeister, Darmstadt); Quirini Gasparini (maestro di cappella, Turin Cathedral); José de Orejon y Aparicio (maestro de capilla, Lima Cathedral, Peru), Francesco Zanetti (maestro di cappella, Perugia Cathedral).

Others: Theodore Aylward (organ, Oxford Chapel, London); Johann Christian Bach (organ, Milan Cathedral); William Selby (organ, Holy Sepulchre, London); John Worgen (organ, St. John's Chapel, London).

E. Prizes/Honors

Honors: François Francoeur (Director of the King's Music, Paris); François Rebel (ennobled); Garret Wellesley (Earl of Mornington).

F. **Biographical Highlights**
Carl Friedrich Abel is given royal publication privileges in London; Andrea Adolfati is appointed maestro di cappella at Padua just six months before his death; Johann Christian Bach joins the Catholic faith in order to be able to find a position in Italy; William Billings becomes a tanner's apprentice; Johann Adolf Hasse loses his property and his manuscripts in the siege of Dresden; John Mainwaring's *Memoirs of the Life of the Late G. F. Handel* is the first musical biography of any composer; Wolfgang Amadeus Mozart begins piano lessons with his father Leopold.

G. **Cultural Beginnings**
Festivals: Hampshire Musical Festival (Winchester).
Other: English Horn (by Ferlandis of Bergamo); Gelehrte Clubb (Magdeburg); Musikalische Gesellschaft (Riga).

H. **Musical Literature**
Giorgio Antoniotto, *Treatise on the Composition of Music*; Jean-Joseph Boutmy, *Traité abrégé de la basse continue*; William Boyce, *Cathedral Music I*; Francesco Geminiani, *The Art of Playing the Guitar*; Johann P. Kirnberger, *Construction der gleichschwebenden Temperatur*; Martin Madan, *Collection of Psalm and Hymn Tunes*; James Nares, *A Regular Introduction to Playing on the Harpsichord or Organ*; Johann J. Quantz, *New Church Melodies*; Jean-Philippe Rameau, *Code de musique pratique*; William Tans'ur, *The Psalmsinger's Jewel*; Benjamin West, *Sacra Concerto; or the Voice of Melody*.

I. **Musical Compositions**
Chamber Music:
Sonata/Solos: Gaetano Pugnani, *Six Violin Sonatas, Opus 3*(?); Pierre Vachon, *Six Violin Sonatas, Opus 1*.
Ensembles: Charles Avison, *Six Trio Sonatas, Opus 7*; Luigi Boccherini, *Six String Trios (F, B♭, A, D, G, C), Opus 1*; Felice de' Giardini, *Six Trios for Guitar and Strings, Opus 2b*.
Piano: C. P. E. Bach, *Three Sonatas (C, B♭, B♭), H.150–152–Allegro in C, H.153–Two Sonatas (C, c), H.156,7*; Ferdinando Pellegrini, *Six Harpsichord Sonatas, Opus 5*.
Organ: Johann Gottlieb Janitsch, *Organ Sonata*.
Choral/Vocal Music:
Choral:
Oratorios: Vincenzo Ciampi, *Virgines prudentes et fatuae*; Ignaz Holzbauer, *La Betulia Liberata*; Johann Mattheson, *Das fröhliche Sterbelied*; Jan Oehlenschlägel, *Innocentia de pietas*; Antonio Pampani, *Prophetiae evangelicae ac mors Isaiae*; Georg Philipp Telemann, *The Resurrection and Ascension of Jesus–Passion According to Luke IV*.

Others: François Gossec, *Messe de morts*; Nicola Logroscino, *Stabat Mater in E♭*; José Nebra, *Missa, In viam pacis*; Georg Philipp Telemann, *Aus Zion! Und lass in geheilinten Hallen, TWVl:l09* (cantata).
Vocal: William Jackson, *Six Elegies, Opus 3*; Ferdinando Pellegrini, *Eight Italian Songs*.
Musical Stage: Thomas Arne, *Thomas and Sally*; Johann C. Bach, *Artaserse*; Antoine Dauvergne, *Canente*; Egidio Duni, *La boutique du poète–L'isle des foux*; Baldassare Galuppi, *Solimano–La clemenza di Tito–L'amante di tutte*; Florian Gassmann, *Filosofia ed amore*; Christoph Willibald Gluck, *Tetide–L'ivrogne corrigé*; Pietro Guglielmi, *L'Ottavio*; Johann A. Hasse, *Artaserse II–Alcide al bivio*; Niccolò Jommelli, *Alessandro nell'Indie–Caio Fabrizio*; Giovanni Lampugnani, *Amor contadina–Giulia*; Nicola Logroscino, *Il vecchio marito–Il natale di Achille*; Vincenzo Manfredini, *Semiramide*; Pierre Monsigny, *Le maître en droit*; François Philidor, *Le soldat magicien–Le volage fixé*; Niccolò Piccinni, *La furba burlata–Il ré pastore–L'Origille*; Nicola Porpora, *Il trionfo di Camilla II*; Jean-Philippe Rameau, *Les paladins*; Antonio Sacchini, *Il testaccio–La vendemmia–I due fratelli beffati*; Giuseppe Sarti, *Andromaca–Il testaccio–Astrea splacata*; Giuseppe Scarlatti, *L'Issipile–La clemenza di Tito*; Tommaso Traetta, *Enea nel Lazio–I Lindaridi*; Georg C. Wagenseil, *Demetrio*.
Orchestra/Band Music:
Concerted Music:
    Piano: William Felton, *Eight Organ/Harpsichord Concertos, Opus 7*.
    Violin: Michael Haydn, *Violin Concerto No. 2 in B♭*.
    Other: Johann A. Hasse, *Twelve Concertos in Six Parts, Opus 3* (flute, strings).
Symphonies: Christian Cannabich, *Symphony (No. 5) in G*; Franz Joseph Haydn, *Symphony No. 2 in C*; William Herschel, *Six Symphonies (G, D, C, d, f, B♭)*; Franz X. Richter, *Six Symphonies, Opus 2–Six Symphonies, Opus 3*; Georg C. Wagenseil, *Six Symphonies, Opus 3*.

1761

Historical Highlights: The Russians capture Kolberg while the Austrians take Schweidnitz; Mikhail Lomonosov discovers the existence of an atmosphere on Venus; the A. W. Faber and Co., pencil makers, is founded; the unpopular Writs of Assistance giving soldiers freedom to search any house at their will is abolished; a treaty with the Cherokees eases the Indian troubles in the Carolinas.

Art and Literature Highlights: Births—artists John Opie, Louis-Leopold Boilly, Edward Savage, writers Friedrich von Matthisson, August F. von Kotzebue; Deaths—writers William Law, Samuel Richardson, sculptor Francois Balthasar Adam. Art—Reynold's *Garrick between Comedy and Tragedy*, J. Hesselius' *Charles Calvert and His Slave*; Literature—Gozzi's *Love of Three Oranges*, Gray's *The Fatal Sisters*, Rousseau's *Julie*.

Musical Highlights

A. **Births**

Composers: Giovanni Battista Cimadoro (Italy); Evstigney Ipatovich Fomin (Russia) August 16; Jacob Kimball, Jr. (U.S.A.) February 22; Friedrich Ludwig Kunzen (Germany) September 24; Joseph Lefèbvre (France) July 20; Giovanni Domenico Perotti (Italy) January 20; Vittorio Trento (Italy); Georg Friedrich Wolf (Germany) September 12.

Performers: Johann Christian Ludwig Abeille (German organist/ composer) February 20; François Alday (French violinist/organist); Willem De Fesch (Dutch violinist); Joseph Augustin Gürrlich (German doublebass virtuoso); Ernst Häusler (German cellist); William T. Parke (British oboist) February 15; Peter Nikolaus Petersen (German flutist) September 2; Anton Wranitzky (Czech violinist/composer) June 13.

Others: Frederick Hollister (Irish piano maker) September; James Leach (British psalmist) December 25; Prince Carl Lichnowsky (Polish patron of the arts) June 21.

B. **Deaths**

Composers: Carlo Cecere (Italy) February 15; Francesco Feo (Italy) January 18; Antonio Palella (Italy) March 7; Meinrad Spiess (Germany) July 12.

Singers: Gioacchino Conti ("Gizziello") (Italian castrato soprano) October 25.

Performers: Adam Falckenhagen (German lutenist); Nicolas-Gilles Forqueray (French organist) October 22; Frédéric-Hubert Paulin (French organist/composer) January 25; Angelo Maria Scaccia (Italian violinist/composer) September 29.

Others: Pierre François de Beauchamp (French music/literature historican) March 22; François Etienne Blanchet, *pére* (French harpsichord maker); Louis Hotteterre (French flute maker) August.

C. **Debuts**

Performers: Nicolas Capron (French violinist—Paris); Jean Pierre Duport (French cellist—Paris).

D. New Positions
Conductors: Esprit Joseph Blanchard (maître de chapelle, Versailles); Michel Richard Delalande (maitre de musique, Chartres Cathedral); Egidio Duni (Comédie-Italienne, Paris); Jakob Friedrich Kleinknecht (kapellmeister, Bayreuth).
Others: John Beard (manager, Covent Garden); Filippo Maria Gherardeschi (organ, Livorno Cathedral); Feodor Volkov (director, Russian Imperial Theater, St. Petersburg).

E. Prizes/Honors
Honors: Matthew Dubourq (Master of Her Majesty's Band of Music); Filippo Gherardeschi (Accademia Filarmonica, Bologna); James Oswald (Chamber Composer to the King); Antonio Tozzi (Accademia Filarmonica, Bologna).

F. Biographical Highlights
Luigi Boccherini begins a two-year stay in Lucca playing cello in the local orchestra; João de Sousa Carvalho enters the Naples Conservatory on a royal grant from the Portuguese government; Domenico Cimarosa is given a free scholarship to enter the Conservatorio di Santa Maria di Loreto; Farinelli leaves Spain and retires to a grand villa he had built near Bologna; Franz Joseph Haydn becomes the second kapellmeister at Esterhazy estate in Eisenstadt; Josef Mysliveček becomes a master miller but still continues his study of music.

G. Cultural Beginnings
Performing Groups—Choral: Noblemen and Gentlemen's Catch Club (London); St. Cecilia Society of Charleston, South Carolina (first known in the New World).
Performing Groups—Instrumental: Riga Symphony Orchestra (Estonia).
Music Publishers: Giovanni Pirenesi Publishing House.
Performing Centers: Konzertsaal auf dem Kamp (Hamburg).
Other: Glassychord (Glass Harmonica, invented by Benjamin Franklin); Johannes Zumpe, piano and harpsichord maker (London).

H. Musical Literature
Johann Albrecht, *Grundliche Einleitung in die Anfangslehren der Tonkunst*; James Lyon, *Urania*; Friedrich W. Marpurg, *Die Kunst das clavier zu spielen II*; Johann Mattheson, *George Frederick Handel*; John Parry, *Collection of Welsh, English and Scotch Airs*; Manuel Romero de Avila, *Arte de canto, llano y organo*; Joseph (L'Abbé) Saint-Sevin, *Les principes du violon*; John Wesley, *Select Hymns with Tunes Annext*.

I. Musical Compositions

Chamber Music:

String Quartets: Luigi Boccherini, *Six Quartets (c, B♭, D, E♭, E, C), Opus 2.*

Ensembles: Luigi Boccherini, *Six Duets for Two Violins, Opus 3*; Giuseppe Tartini, *Six Trio Sonatas, Opus 9, for Violin, Cello and Cembalo.*

Piano: C. P. E. Bach, *Sonata in g, H.158.*

Choral/Vocal Music:

Choral:

Oratorios: Anton C. Adlgasser, *Esther*(?); Thomas Arne, *Judith*; John Abraham Fisher, *Judith*; Nicola Logroscino, *Ester*; Jean-Joseph de Mondonville, *Les titans*; Jan Oehlenschlägel, *Patientia et humilitas*; Antonio Sacchini, *Gesù presentato al tempio*; Johann M. Schmid, *Tod und Begrabnis Jesu*; Georg Philipp Telemann, *Passion According to John VI–Resurrection.*

Others: C. P. E. Bach, *Psalm 2, H.773–Psalm 4, H.774*; Baldassare Galuppi, *Gloria*; Antonio Pampini, *Magnificat VI*; Georg Philipp Telemann, *Siehe, ich verhündige Euch* (cantata).

Musical Stage: Charles G. Alexandre, *Georget et Georgette*; Michael Arne, *Edgar and Emmeline*; Thomas Arne, *Florizel and Perdita*; Johann Christian Bach, *Catone in Utica*; Ferdinando Bertoni, *La bella Cirometta*; Antonio Boroni, *Le Moda*; Vincenzo Ciampi, *Amore in caricatura*; Antoine Dauvergne, *Hercule mourant*; Egidio Duni, *La bonne fille–Mazet*; Baldassare Galuppi, *Li tre amanti ridicoli–Il caffe di campagna–Demetrio*; Florian Gassman, *Catone in Utica*; Christoph Willibald Gluck, *Le cadi dupé*; François Gossec, *Le périgourdin*; Johann A. Hasse, *Zenobia*; Niccolò Jommelli, *L'Olimpiade–L'isola disabitata*; Giovan di Majo, *L'Almeria*; Pierre Monsigny, *Le cadi dupé–On ne s'avise jamais de tout*; Vincenzo Orgitano, *Le pazzie per amore*; Giovanni Pescetti, *Zenobia*; François Philidor, *Le maréchal ferrant–Le jardinier et son seigneur*; Niccolò Piccinni, *Demofoonte–Lo stravaganti–La schiavitù per more*; Antonio Sacchini, *Andromaca–La finta contessa*; Giuseppe Sarti, *Nitteti–Issipile*; Georg Philipp Telemann, *Don Quichotte der Lowenritter*; Tommaso Traetta, *Enea e Lavinia–Armida.*

Orchestra/Band Music:

Concerted Music:

Violin: Michael Haydn, *Concerto No. 1.*

Ballet/Incidental Music: Christoph Willibald Gluck, *Don Juan* (B).

Symphonies: Thomas A. Erskine, *Six Overtures in Eight Parts (D, C, D, E♭, G, F), Opus 1*; Ignaz Fränzel, *Symphony in B♭*(?); François Gossec, *Symphony in D* (*"Périodique No. 38"*); Franz Joseph Haydn,

*No. 6 in D, "Le matin"–No. 7 in C, "Le midi"–No. 8 in G, "Le soir"–No.
10 in D*; William Herschel, *Six Symphonies (d, c, F, g, f, d)*; Pierre Talon,
Six Symphonies, Opus 2; Pierre Vachon, *Six Symphonies, Opus 2*.

1762
❋

Historical Highlights: Czar Peter III is assassinated and is succeeded
by wife, Catherine the Great; Russia concludes an alliance with Prussia
and drops out of the war; the Louisiana Territory is secretly ceded to
Spain by the French via the Treaty of Fontainebleau in order to prevent
the British from taking over the territory during the fighting; the Ethan
Allen ironworks are founded in Salisbury.

Art and Literature Highlights: Sorbonne Library opens in Paris.
Births—artist Paul Troger, writers Joanna Baillie, George Colman, Jr.,
André Marie de Chenier; Deaths—artists Edme Bouchardon, Louis-
François Roubiliac, poet Crebillon. Art—Falconet's *Christ in Gethsemane*,
Pannini's *Trevi Fountain* (Rome), Roubiliac's *Handel Monument*; Litera-
ture—Godfrey's *The Court of Fancy*, Macpherson's *Fingal*, Rousseau's
Social Contract.

Musical Highlights

A. Births

Composers: Santiago Ferrer (Spain) August 10; Samuel Holyoke
(U.S.A.) October 15; Georg Godfrey Müller (Germany-U.S.A.) May
22; Giuseppe Nicolini (Italy) January 29; Marcos António Portugal
(Portugal) March 24; Marco Santucci (Italy) July 4; Stephen Storace
(England) April 4.

Singers: Girolamo Crescentini (Italian castrato mezzo-soprano) February 2; Adelheid Eichner (German soprano)(?); Pierre Garat (French
tenor/baritone) April 5; Friedrich Franz Hůrka (Czech tenor/com-
poser) February 23; Michael Kelly (Irish tenor/composer) December
25.

Performers: Andrew Adgate (American organist/composer) March
22; Carl Christian Agthe (German organist/composer) June 16; Karl
Friedrich Horn (German organist) April 13; Feliks Janiewicz (Polish
violinist/composer); Theobald Monzani (Italian flutist/publisher);
Georg Gottfrey Müller (Moravian-born violinist/composer) May 22;
Francesco Pollini (Italian pianist/composer) March 25; Franz Tausch
(German clarinetist/composer) December 26; Johann Christian Till
(Moravian-born organist/composer) May 18.

Others: Carlo Gervasoni (Italian music theorist/historian) November 4; Jérôme-Joseph de Momigny (Belgian-born music theorist/composer) January 20; Carlantonio de Rosa (Marquis de Villarosa) (Italian music author) January 1; (Count) Ferdinand Ernst Waldstein (Bohemian patron of the arts) March 24.

B. **Deaths**

Composers: Jean Audiffren (France) August 8; Laurent Belissen (France) February 12; Vincenzo Ciampi (Italy) March 30; Johann Ernst Eberlin (Germany) June 19; Johann Samuel Endler (Germany) April 23; Francesco Geminiani (Italy) September 17; Giovanni Giorgi (Italy) June; Johann Valentin Görner (Germany) July; Jacques Martin Hotteterre, "le Romain" (France) July 16; Francesco Onofrio Manfredini (Italy) October 6; Christoph Nichelmann (Germany) July 20; Johann Christian Schickhardt (Germany-Holland) March 26; Joseph Umstatt (Austria) May 24.

Performers: Ernst Christian Hesse (German viola da gamba virtuoso) May 16; Johann Tobias Krebs (German organist) February 11; Jacques-Christophe Naudot (French flutist) November 26.

Others: Jakob Adlung (German music scholar/organist) July 5; Johann Clemm (German organ builder) May 5; Pietro Guaneri (Italian violin maker) April 7; Alexandre Jean de La Pouplinière (French patron of the arts) December 5.

C. **Debuts**

Singers: Josef Valentin Adamberger ("Adamonti" in Italy) (German tenor—Italy); Antonia Bernasconi (Italian soprano—Munich); Anne Catley (British soprano—London); Polly Young (British soprano—London).

D. **New Positions**

Conductors: Antoine Dauvergne (Concerts Spirituels, Paris); Ignazio Fiorillo (Kassel Court Theater); Baldassare Galuppi (maestro di cappella, Venice); Pietro Gnocchi (at age 85, maestro di cappella, Brescia Cathedral); Michael Haydn (kapellmeister, Salzburg); Pierre van Maldere (Grand Theater, Brussels); Johann Gottfried Schwanenberg (kapellmeister, Brunswick).

Others: Rafael Anglés (organ, Valencia Cathedral); Benjamin Cooke (organ, Westminster Abbey); Henry Delamain (organ, Christ Church, Oxford); William Herschel (director, Leeds Concerts); Johann Christian Kittel (organ, Predigerkirche, Erfurt); Giovanni Battista Pescetti (organ, St. Mark's, Venice).

E. **Prizes/Honors**

Honors: Giovanni Rutini (Accademia Filarmonica, Bologna).

F. Biographical Highlights
    Johann Christian Bach leaves Italy and moves permanently to Lon-
    don; Wilhelm Friedemann Bach is offered a post at Darmstadt but
    loses it by his inaction; Robert Bremner moves his publishing head-
    quarters to London; Franz Joseph Haydn is kept on as kapellmeister
    at Eisenstadt by the new prince, Nikolaus Esterhazy; Wolfgang
    Amadeus Mozart and his sister are taken on their first performance
    tour by their father, Leopold; Pietro Nardini becomes solo violinist
    with the Stuttgart Court Orchestra; Jean-Jacques Rousseau flees
    Paris after the government condemns his *Social Contract*.

G. Cultural Beginnings
    Performing Groups—Instrumental: Band of the Royal Regiment of
    Artillery (oldest permanent musical organization in England).
    Music Publishers: Bremner Publishers, London Branch; Welcker
    Music Publishers (London).
    Music Publications: *Journal de Clavecin.*
    Performing Centers: St. Cecilia Hall (Edinburgh).
    Other: Harp Pedal System (by Michael K. Ogiński).

H. Musical Literature
    C. P. E. Bach, *The Proper Method of Playing Keyboard Instruments II*;
    James Beattie, *On Poetry and Music*; Charles Clement, *Essai sur la
    basse fondamentale*; Henri Hardouin, *Méthode nouvelle pour apprendre
    le plainchant*; Johann A. Ludwig, *Gedanken über die grossen Orgeln*;
    John Potter, *Observations on the Present State of Music and Musicians*;
    Antonio Soler, *Llave de la modulación y antigüedades de la música en que
    se trata del fundamento necessario para saber modular.*

I. Musical Compositions
    Chamber Music:
        String Quartets: Franz Joseph Haydn, *Six Quartets (A, E, F, B♭)*,
        Opus 2.
        Sonata/Solos: C. P. E. Bach, *Harpsichord Sonata in G, H.563*; Luigi
        Boccherini, *Sonata in C for Two Cellos–Four Cello Sonatas (F, D, E♭, B♭).*
        Ensembles: Charles G. Alexandre, *Six Trios, Opus 4*; Franz Joseph
        Haydn, *Four Divertimentos, Opus 2.*
        Piano: C. P. E. Bach, *Harpsichord Sonata in b*; Giuseppe Sarti, *Six
        Clavier Sonatas.*
    Choral/Vocal Music:
        Choral:
            Oratorios: Johann G. Albrechtsberger, *Oratorium de Passione Do-
            mini*; Jan Oehlenschlägel, *Vox filiae Sion*; Georg Philipp Tele-
            mann, *The Day of Judgment–Passion According to Matthew V.*

Choral: Johann Christian Bach, *Te Deum in D, T.210*; Wilhelm Friedemann Bach, *Lobe den Herrn in seinem Heiligtum* (cantata); Vincenzo Manfredini, *Requiem for Empress Elizabeth–La pace degli eroi* (cantata); Georg Philipp Telemann, *Der Herr hat offenbart* (cantata).

Musical Stage: Thomas Arne, *Artaxerxes–Love in a Village–Beauty and Virtue*; Johann Christian Bach, *Alessandro nell'Indie*; Giuseppe Bonno, *Latenaide*; Antonio Boroni, *Demofoonte*; Vincenzo Ciampi, *Antigona*; Baldassare Galuppi, *Viriate–Il marchese villano–L'orfana onorata*; Florian Gassmann, *Un pazzo ne fa Cento*; Christoph Willibald Gluck, *Orfeo ed Euridice*; Johann A. Hasse, *Il trionfo di Clelia*; Franz Joseph Haydn, *La vedova–Il dottore–Il scanarello–La Marchesa Nespola–Acide*; Nicola Logroscino, *La viaggiatrice de bell'umore*; Vincenzo Manfredini, *Olimpiade*; Jean-Joseph de Mondonville, *Psyche–Les Fêtes de Paphos*; Pierre Monsigny, *Le roi et le fermier*; Johann G. Naumann, *Il tesoro insidiato*; David Perez, *La Berenice–Giulio Cesare*; François Philidor, *Sancho Pança dans son isle*; Niccolò Piccinni, *Artaserse–Antigono–Amor senza malizia*; Antonio Sacchini, *I due bari–L'amore in campo*; Giuseppe Sarti, *Semiramide–Didone abbandonata*; Johann Schwanenberg, *Solimano–Adriano in Siria*; Tommaso Traetta, *Sofonisba–Zenobia–Alessandro nelle Indie*; Georg C. Wagenseil, *Prometeo Assoluto*.

Orchestra/Band Music:
Concerted Music:
   Piano: C. P. E. Bach, *Harpsichord Concerto in B♭, H.447*.
   Other: Johann George Albrechtsberger, *Organ Concerto*.
Ballet/Incidental Music: Antoine Dauvergne, *Alphée et Arethuse* (B); Vincenzo Manfredini, *Amour et Psyche* (B); Carlo G. Toeschi, *Telemaque* (B).
Symphonies: Carl F. Abel, *Six Overtures in Eight Parts (Symphonies No. 7–12), Opus 4*; C. P. E. Bach, *Three Symphonies (E♭, G, F), H.654–656*; Christian Cannabich, *Symphony No. 25 in C*; François Gossec, *Six Symphonies (F, E♭, D, E, E♭, D), Opus 5–Six Symphonies (D, A, c, A, g, B♭), Opus 6*; William Herschel, *Seven Symphonies (D, D, E♭, E♭, C, E♭, c)*; Franz Joseph Haydn, *No. 3 in G–No. 4 in D–No. 5 in A–No. 9 in C*; Carlo G. Toeschi, *Six Symphonies, Opus 1*.

1763
❄

Historical Highlights: The Peace of Paris ends the Seven Years War—the British receive Canada, Florida, and control of India—France loses all of her New World holdings east of the Mississippi River; excavations begin at Pompeii and Herculaneum in Italy; the Proclamation Line limits settlements west of the Appalachians.

Art and Literature Highlights: Births—artists George Morland, Jean Germain Drouais, writers Jean Paul Richter, Janos Bacsanyi; Deaths—artist Franz Bustelli, writers Thomas Godfrey, Pierre Carlet de Marivaux, Hedvig Charlotta Nordenflycht, Antoine Prévost d'Exiles. Art—Lorenzoni's *Mozart Portrait*, Van Loo's *Venus and Cupid*; Literature—Churchill's *The Duellist*, Lessing's *Minna von Barnhelm*, Sheridan's *The Discovery*.

Musical Highlights

A. Births

Composers: Joseph Arquier (France); Franz Ignaz Danzi (Germany) June 15; John Davy (England) December 23; Matthäus Fischer (Germany) November 28; Giacomo Gotifredo Ferrari (Italy) April 2; Adalbert Gyrowetz (Bohemia) February 19; (Johannes) Simon Mayr (Germany) June 14; Étienne-Nicolas Méhul (France) June 22; Giovanni Benedetto Platti (Italy) January 11; Karl Gottlieb Umbreit (Germany) January 9.

Conductors: Johannes Andreas Amon (Germany).

Singers: Dorothea Bussani (Austrian soprano); Anna Marie Crouch (British soprano) April 20; Charles Incledon (British tenor) February 5.

Performers: Paul Alday (French violinist/composer)(?); Johann Sébastian Demar (German organist/composer) June 29; Domenico Dragonetti (Italian contrabass virtuoso) April 7; Jean Xavier Lefevre (Swiss clarinetist/composer) March 6; Peter Ritter (German cellist/composer) July 2; Thomas Wright (British organist/inventor) September 18.

Others: Gottfried Christoph Härtel (German publisher) January 27; John Relfe (British music theorist/composer).

B. Deaths

Composers: Maximilian Joseph Hellmann (Austria) March 20; Johann Gottlieb Janitsch (Germany)(?); Richard Mudge (England) April 3; Giuseppe Paganelli (Italy)(?); Claude Mathieu Pellegrin (France) October 10; Giovanni Benedetto Platti (Italy) January 11; Johann Caspar Vogler (Germany) June 1.

Performers: James Heseltine (British organist) June 20; Louis Antoine Lefebvre (French organist/composer) July 20; Christoph Schaffrath (German harpsichordist/composer) February 17; Giovanni Battista Somis (Italian violinist) August 14.

Others: Anton Dulcken (Belgian harpsichord maker); Christian Müller (German organ builder) March 8.

C. Debuts

Singers: Francesco Bussani (Italian bass—Rome).
Performers: Simon Leduc (French violinist—Paris); Thomas Linley, Jr. (British violinist—Bristol).

D. New Positions

Conductors: Carlo Antonio Campioni (maestro di cappella, Cathedral of S. Maria del Fiore, Florence); Filippo Maria Gherardeschi (maestro di cappella, Volterra); Orazio Mei (maestro di cappella, Livorno Cathedral).
Others: François Bainville (organ, Cathedral of St. Maurice, Angers); Thomas Ebdon (organ, Durham Cathedral); Christian Friedrich Schale (organ, Berlin Cathedral); Jean-François Tapray (organ, Besançon Cathedral); Ernst Wilhelm Wolf (organ, Weimar Court).

E. Prizes/Honors

Honors: Paolo Morellati (Accademia Filarmonica, Bologna).

F. Biographical Highlights

Pasquale Anfossi has his first opera production, *La serva spiritosa*, in Rome; Carl Ditters von Dittersdorf accompanies Christoph Willibald Gluck on his trip to Italy; Johann Adolf Hasse and his wife, Faustina Bordoni, are dismissed from Dresden and move to Vienna; Wolfgang Amadeus Mozart has his first works published; Johann Gottlieb Naumann becomes composer of sacred music at the Dresden Court; Joseph Boulogne Saint-Georges begins music study with Leclair and Gossec; Georg "Abbe" Vogler enrolls in the University of Würzburg to study theology and law.

G. Cultural Beginnings

Educational: Bremner School of Music (Philadelphia).
Music Publishers: Johann Hartknoch (Mitau).
Music Publications: *Frusta Litteraria*.
Other: Leipzig Subscription (Leibhaber) Concerts (revived by Johann Hiller).

H. Musical Literature

John Brown, *The Rise, Union and Power, the Progressions, Separations and Corruptions of Poetry and Music*; Francis Hopkinson, *A Collection of Psalm Tunes with a Few Anthems*; Johann H. Lambert, *Sur quelques instruments acoustiques*; Friedrich W. Marpurg, *Anleitung zur Musik überhaupt und zur Singkunst besonders mit Übungsexampeln erläutert*; Philippe J. Meyer, *La vraie maniere de jouer de la Harpe*; Jean-Adam Serre, *Observations sur les principes de l'harmonie*; Georg A. Sorge, *Kurze erklärung des Canonis Harmonici*; Aaron Williams, *The Universal Psalmist*.

I. **Musical Compositions**
   Chamber Music:
   Sonata/Solos: Franz Benda, *Six Violin Sonatas, Opus 1*; Luigi Boccherini, *Three Cello Sonatas (G, g, G)*(?); Ferdinando Pellegrini, *Six Harpsichord Sonatas, Opus 6*.
   Ensembles: Johann Christian Bach, *Six Trios, Opus 2* (violin, cello, harpsichord).
   Piano: C. P. E. Bach, *Three Sonatas (E, C, C), H.163–165–Seven Sonatas (f, A, B♭, e, D, C, d), H.173–179*; Johann G. Eckard, *Six Sonatas, Opus 1*; Franz X. Richter, *Six Sonatas for Harpsichord, Set II*.
   Choral/Vocal Music:
   Choral:
      Oratorios: Anton C. Adlgasser, *Ochus regnans (Samuel und Heli)–Bela Hungariae Princeps (David und Jonathas)*; Bonaventura Furlanetto, *La sposa de' sacri cantici*; Baldassare Galuppi, *Maria Magdalena*; Nicola Logroscino, *La spedizione di Giosue contro gli Amalechiti*; Jan Oehlenschlägel, *Patientiea victrix*.
      Others: Johann F. Agricola, *Triumphlied bei der Rückkehr Friedrichs II* (cantata); Paolo T. Alberghi, *Mass*; Johann A. Hasse, *Requiem in C*; José Nebra, *Missa, per singules dies*.
   Musical Stage: Pasquale Anfossi, *La serva spiritosa–Lo sposo di tre e marito di nessuna*; Thomas Arne, *The Birth of Hercules*; Johann Christian Bach, *Zanaida–Orione*; Andrea Bernasconi, *Artaserse*; Giuseppe Bonno, *Il sogno di Scipione*; Antonio Boroni, *L'amore in musica–La pupilla rapito*; Antoine Dauvergne, *Polyxene*; Egidio Duni, *Le rendez-vous–Les Deux Chasseurs et la laitière*; Baldassare Galuppi, *Arianna e Teseo–Il re alla caccia–La donna di governo*; Felice de' Giardini, *Siroe*; Christoph Willibald Gluck, *Il trionfo di Clelia*; Pietro Guglielmi, *Tito Manlio–La francese brillante–L'Olimpiade*; Niccolò Jommelli, *La pastorella illustre–Il trionfo d'amore–Didone abbandonata*; Giovanni Lampugnani, *Enea in Italia*; Vincenzo Manfredini, *Carlo Magno–La pupilla–La finta ammalata*; Pierre Monsigny, *Le nouveau monde*; François Philidor, *Le bûcheron–Les fêtes de la paix*; Niccolò Piccinni, *Il cavaliere per amore–Le contadine bizzarre–Le donne vendicate*; Antonio Sacchini, *Alessandro Severo–Olimpiade–Alessandro nell'Indie*; Giuseppe Sarti, *Cesare in Egitto–Il Narciso*; Giuseppe Scarlatti, *Pelopida*; Tommaso Traetta, *Ifigenia in Tauride*.
   Orchestra/Band Music:
   Concerted Music:
      Piano: C. P. E. Bach, *Harpsichord Concerto in F, H.454*; Johann Christian Bach, *Six Clavecin Concertos, Opus 1*.
      Other: Luigi Boccherini, *Two Cello Concertos (E♭, A)*; Carl Ditters von Dittersdorf, *Flute Concerto in e*; Carlo G. Toeschi, *Four Flute Concertos*.

Ballet/Incidental Music: Christian Cannabich, *Ceyx et Alcyone* (B); Vincenzo Manfredini, *Pygmalion* (B); Carlo G. Toeschi, *Feste del seraglio* (B).
Standard Works: Nicola Porpora, *Ouverture Royale in D.*
Symphonies: Johann Christian Bach, *Symphony in B♭, Opus 9, No. 3–Symphony in E♭, Opus 18, No. 1*; Christian Cannabich, *Symphony No. 26 in F*; François-Joseph Gossec, *Symphony in D (Périodique No. 48)*; Franz Joseph Haydn, *No. 12 in E–No. 13 in D–No. 40 in F*; William Herschel, *Three Symphonies (C, D, a)*; Josef Mysliveček, *Sinfonie a quatre, Opus 1*; Franz X. Richter, *Simphonie Periodique No. 49–Sinfonias (No. 12–14) a piu stromenti obbligati.*

1764
❄

Historical Highlights: The Russian government confiscates all lands of the Russian Orthodox Church; France expels the Jesuit order; the British begin the system of numbering houses along each street; the Currency Act and the Sugar Act brings on protests from the colonists; St. Louis is founded on the Mississippi River by French fur traders.

Art and Literature Highlights: Births—writers Ann Radcliffe, Jens Immanuel Baggesen, André Marie de Chenier, Gabriel Marie Legouvé; Deaths—artist William Hogarth, writers Charles Churchill, Joseph Brown Ladd. Art—Trumbull's *Oath of Brutus*, Hogarth's *The Bathos*, Van Loo's *The Magic Lantern*; Literature—Goldsmith's *The Traveler*, Hutchinson's *History of the Colony of Massachusett's Bay*, Voltaire's *Dictionnaire Philosophique*.

Musical Highlights

A. Births
Composers: Alexander Campbell (Scotland) February 22; Valentino Fioravanti (Italy) September 11; Georg Christoph Grosheim (Germany) July 1; Jeremiah Ingalls (U.S.A.) March 1; Richard Mount-Edgcumbe (England) September 13; Luigi Piccinni (Italy).
Singers: Franz Xaver Gerl (French bass/composer) November 30; Louis-Sébastien Lebrun (French tenor/composer) December 10; Jeanne Charlotte Saint-Aubin (French soprano) December 9.
Performers: János Bihari (Hungarian violinist) October 21; Matthew Camidge (British organist) May 25; Franz Lauska (Moravian pianist) January 13; János Lavotta (Hungarian violinist/composer) July 5; Heinrich Gerhard Lentz (German pianist)(?); Jean Henri Levasseur (French cellist) May 29; Charles-Henri Plantade (French cellist/com-

poser) October 14; Bernhard Anselm Weber (German pianist/conductor) April 18.

Others: William Forster, Jr. (British violin maker) January 7; Franz Xaver Glöggl (Austrian music author/conductor) February 21; Johann Heinrich Grenser (German woodwind instrument maker) March 5; Felix Joseph Lipowsky (German music historian/lexicographer) January 25; Richard Mount-Edgcumbe (British music author) September 13.

B. **Deaths**

Composers: Jaime de Casellas (Spain) April 27; Giovanni Antonio Giai (Italy) September 10; Jean-Marie Leclair, *l'aîné* (France) October 22; Pietro Antonio Locatelli (Italy) March 30; Wilhelm Hieronymus Pachelbel (Germany); Jean-Philippe Rameau (France) September 12.

Singers: Daniel Sullivan (Irish counter-tenor) October 13; Robert Wass (British bass) May 3.

Performers: Nicola Fiorenza (Italian violinist) April 13; Musgrave Heighington (British organist) June; Johann Xaver Nauss (German organist) November 15; John Reading (British organist) September 2; Lorenzo Gaetano Zavateri (Italian violinist) December.

Others: Francesco Algarotti (Italian poet/music scholar) May 3; Johann Mattheson (German music theorist/composer) April 17.

C. **Debuts**

Singers: Lucrezia Aguiari ("La Bastardina") (Italian soprano—Florence); Joseph Legros (French tenor—Paris); Corona Elisabeth Schröter (German soprano—Leipzig); Antoine Trial (French tenor—Paris); Frederica Weichsell (British soprano—London).

D. **New Positions**

Conductors: Johann Gottlieb Görner (Leipzig Gelehrtenkonzert); Esteban Salas y Castro (maestro de capilla, Santiago de Cuba).

Other: Edmund Broderip (organ, Mayor's Chapel, Bristol); Cornelius Heinrich Dretzel (organ, St. Sebald, Nuremberg); August Bernhard Herbing (principal organ, Magdeburg Cathedral); David Traugott Nicolai (organ, Hauptkirche, Leipzig); Johann Siebenkäs (organ, St. Lorenz, Nuremberg).

E. **Prizes/Honors**

Honors: Carl Friedrich Abel (Chamber Musician to the Queen); Johann Christian Bach (Chamber Musician to the Queen); Charles Burney (Royal Society of Arts).

F. **Biographical Highlights**

Carl Friedrich Abel, with Johann Christian Bach, begins a twenty-year concert series in London; Anton Cajetan Adlgasser is sent by the

archbishop of Salzburg for a year's study in Italy; Wilhelm Friedemann Bach leaves Halle and begins teaching privately; Charles Burney and his family move to Paris in order to provide the type of
education they wish for their daughters; Jean-Marie Leclair, *l'aîné*, is
murdered in his own home; Wolfgang Amadeus Mozart plays for
Louis XV and meets Johann Christian Bach while in London.

G. Cultural Beginnings
Performing Groups—Choral: Giuseppe Bustelli Opera Co. (Prague).
Educational: University of Dublin Chair of Music.
Music Publications: *Journal de Musique Francaise et Italienne.*
Performing Centers: Bratislava Theater; Dublin Rotunda.
Other: Philadelphia Subscription Concerts (by Frances Hopkinson
and Robert Bremner).

H. Musical Literature
Johann Albrecht, *Abhandlung über die Frage: Ob die Musik beim Gottesdienst zu dulden sei oder nicht*; John Camidge, *Six Easy Lessons for the
Harpsichord*; Leonhard Euler, *Conjecture sur la raison de quelques disso-
nances . . .* ; Josiah Flagg, *Collection of the Best Psalm Tunes*; Pietro
Gianotti, *Méthode abrégée d'accompagnement à la harpe e au clavecin*; Johann A. Hiller, *Anekdoten zur lebensgeschichte französischer, teutscher,
italienischer, holländischer und anderer Gelehrten*; Johann A. Ludwig,
Den unverschamten Entehrern der Orgeln; Friedrich Marpurg, *Kritische
Briefe über die Tonkunst . . . von einer musikalisch Gesellschaft in Berlin*;
Antonio Roel del Rio, *Reparos musicos*; Pierre-Joseph Roussier, *Traité
des accords, et de leur succession*; Francisco Solano, *Nova instrucção musical, ou Theorica pratica.*

I. Musical Compositions
Chamber Music:
   String Quartets: CarloTessarini, *Six Grand Overtures for String
   Quartet, Opus 18.*
   Sonata/Solos: Johann Christian Bach, *Six Violin Sonatas (F, G, D, C,
   D, E♭), Opus 2*; Luigi Boccherini, *Three Cello Sonatas (F, E♭, E♭)*; Wolf-
   gang Amadeus Mozart, *Violin Sonata in C, K. 6–in D, K. 7–in B♭, K.
   8–in G, K. 9–in B♭, K. 10–in G, K. 11–in A, K. 12–in F, K. 13–in C, K.
   14–in B♭, K. 15.*
   Ensembles: Giuseppe Agus, *Six String Trios, Opus 3*; Charles Avi-
   son, *Six Trio Sonatas, Opus 8* (two violins, cello, harpsichord);
   Franz X. Richter, *Six Trio Sonatas, Opus 3–Six Sonatas da Camera*
   (cembalo, flute, violin, cello).
   Piano: C. P. E. Bach, *Four Sonatas (B♭, a, b, F), H.180–183*; Johann G.
   Eckard, *Two Sonatas, Opus 2–Menuet d'Exaudet with Variations.*

Choral/Vocal Music:
Choral:
Oratorios: Baldassare Galuppi, *Sacrificium Abraham*; Antonio Pampini, *Pro solemni die BMV*; Georg Philipp Telemann, *Passion According to Luke V*.
Others: Ignacio de Jerusalem, *Matins for the Virgin of Guadalupe*; José Nebra, *Missa, benedicamus Domino*; Antonio Pampini, *Messa a più voci–Magnificat VII*; François Philidor, *Requiem in Memory of Rameau*.
Vocal: C. P. E. Bach, *Twelve Geistliche oden und lieder, H.696*.
Musical Stage: Pasquale Anfossi, *Il finto medico*; Michael Arne, *Hymen*; Thomas Arne, *The Guardian Outwitted–The Arcadian Nuptials*; Andrea Bernasconi, *Olimpiade*; Antonio Boroni, *Sofonisba–Siroe*; Christian Cannabich, *Le jugement de Paris*; Charles Dibdin, *The Shepherd's Artifice*; Baldassare Galuppi, *Cajo Mario–La partenza il ritorno de' marinari*; Florian Gassmann, *L'Olimpiade*; Felice de' Giardini, *Enea e Lavinia*; François Giraud, *Acanthe et Cydippe*; Christoph Willibald Gluck, *La rencontre imprévue*; Pietro Guglielmi, *Siroe re de Persia–Li rivali placati*; Johann A. Hasse, *Egeria*; Johann A. Hiller, *Die verwandelten weiber*; Niccolò Jommelli, *Demofoonte–Il re pastore*; Pierre Monsigny, *Rose et Colas*; Josef Mysliveček, *Medea*; Johann Naumann, *Li creduti spiriti*; Giovanni Paisiello, *Il ciarlone–I Francesi brillanti*; François Philidor, *Le sorcier*; Niccolò Piccinni, *Berenice(?)– L'equivoco–Il nuovo Orlando–Gli stravaganti*; Jean-Philippe Rameau, *Abaris*; Rinaldo di Capua, *Il caffè di campagna*; Antonio Sacchini, *Semiramide riconosciuta–Lucio Vero–Eumene*; Giuseppe Sarti, *Il gran Tamerlano–Il naufragio di Cipro*; Tommaso Traetta, *Antigono*.
Orchestra/Band Music:
Concerted Music:
Other: Michael Haydn, *Trumpet Concerto*.
Ballet/Incidental Music: Christoph Willibald Gluck, *Alessandro* (B).
Symphonies: Ignaz Fränzel, *Symphony in C(?)*; Franz Joseph Haydn, *No. 14 in A–No. 15 in D–No. 21 in A–No. 22 in E♭, "Philosopher"–No. 23 in G–No. 24 in D*; William Herschel, *Three Symphonies (D, C, e)*; Wolfgang Amadeus Mozart, *No. 1 in E♭, K. 16*; Papavoine, *No. 1*; Franz X. Richter, *Sinfonia Periodique No. 61*.

1765

Historical Highlights: Joseph II, as Holy Roman Emperor, becomes coruler of Austria with Maria Theresa; James Watt perfects his steam engine; more discontent caused by the Stamp Act and Quartering Act; the

Declaration of Rights and Grievances, issued by the Stamp Act Congress, is sent to the British Parliament.

Art and Literature Highlights: Births—artist/inventor Robert Fulton, writers Manuel Maria du Bocage, William Hill Brown; Deaths—artists Charles André (Carle) Van Loo, George Lambert, writer Edward Young. Art—Chardin's *Attributes of Music*, Copley's *Boy with a Squirrel*, Pratt's *The American School*; Literature—Brooke's *The Fool of Quality*, Jonathan Edward's *Personal Narrative*, Walpole's *The Castle of Otranto*.

Musical Highlights

A. Births

Composers: Charles-Louis André (Belgium) February 23; Joseph Leopold Eybler (Austria) February 8; Friedrich Heinrich Himmel (Germany) November 20; Oliver Holden (U.S.A.) September 18; Joseph Mazzinghi (England) December 25; Prince Michal Cleofas Ogiński (Poland) September 25; Jakub Jan Ryba (Czechoslovakia) October 26; Pietro Terziani (Italy).

Conductors: Bernard Sarrette (France) November 27.

Singers: Elizabeth Billington (British soprano) December 27; Nancy Storace (British soprano) October 27.

Performers: Thomas Attwood (British organist/composer) November 23; Jean-Baptiste Cartier (French violinist/composer) May 28; Charles Dignum (British violinist)(?); Frédéric Nicolas Duvernoy (French horn viruoso) October 16; Anton Eberl (Austrian pianist/composer) June 13; Alexander Juhan (American violinist/conductor); Joseph Mazzinghi (Italian pianist/composer) December 25; Friedrich Ludwig Seidel (German organist) July 14; Daniel Steibelt (German pianist/composer) October 22.

Others: Karl Gottlieb Hering (German music theorist) October 25; Bernard Sarrette (French music administrator) November 27.

B. Deaths

Composers: Francesco Ciampi (Italy)(?); Giuseppe Antonio Consoni (Italy) March 7; Nicola Bonifacio Logroscino (Italy)(?); Johann Melchior Molter (Germany) January 12.

Singers: Elisabetta de Gambarini (British soprano/composer) February 9.

Performers: Johan Joachim Agrell (Swedish violinist/composer) January 1; Gabriel Besson (French violinist/composer) August 23; Louis Antoine Dornel (French organist/composer)(?); Pietro Gianotti (Italian countrabassist/composer) June 19; Carlmann Kolb (German organist) January 15; José de Orejón y Aparicio (Portugese organist/composer) May; Wilhelm August Roth (German organist) April 20; Antonio Tonelli (Italian cellist/composer) December 25. **Others:** Christophe Ballard (French music publisher) September 5; Anne Claude Philippe Caylus (French music author) September 5.

C. Debuts
Singers: Venanzio Rauzzini (Italian male soprano—Rome).

D. New Positions
Conductors: Carl Ditters von Dittersdorf (kapellmeister, Bishop of Grosswardein); Baldassare Galuppi (Italian Opera, St. Petersburg); Georg Wilhelm Gruber (kapellmeister, Nuremberg); Julien-Amable Mathieu (maître de chapelle, Versailles); Raynor Taylor (Sadler's Wells and Marylebone Gardens).
Others: Pieter Joseph van den Bosch (organ, Antwerp Cathedral); Tommaso Traetta (director, Conservatorio dell'Ospedaletto S. Giovanni, Venice); Richard Woodward (organ, Christ Church Cathedral, Dublin).

E. Prizes/Honors
Honors: Giovanni Fioroni (Accademia Filarmonica, Bologna); Bernardo Ottani (Accademia Filarmonica, Bologna).

F. Biographical Highlights
Johann Georg Albrechtsberger leaves the Melk Abbey and goes to Silesia; Baldassare Galuppi introduces Italian contrapuntal style of writing into Russian liturgical music; Wolfgang Amadeus Mozart and his father spend time in England and Holland on a concert tour; Johann Gottlieb Naumann begins a three-years stay in Italy conducting several of his operas; Giuseppe Sarti is sent by the king of Denmark to Italy to recruit singers for the reopening of the Italian Opera in Copenhagen; David Tannenberg continues his organ-building career in Lititz, Pennsylvania.

G. Cultural Beginnings
Performing Groups—Instrumental: Bergen Harmonic Society; Societa Filarmonica Pisana (Pisa).
Educational: Allgemeine Deutsche Bibliothek.
Music Publishers: Giovanni Artaria and Co. (Mainz-Vienna).
Performing Centers: Ackermann Theater (Hamburg); Sadler's Wells Music House II (London); Theater of the Estates (Ljuljana).
Other: Bach-Abel Subscription Concerts (London).

H. Musical Literature
Johann L. Albrecht, *Vom Hasse der Musik: Versuch einer Abhandlung von der Ursachen des Hasses, welche einige Menschen gegen die Musik von sich blicken*; John Arnold, *Church Music Reformed*; Georg S. Löh-

lein, *Clavier-Schule I*; Johann A. Scheibe, *Abhandlung über das recitativ*; Carlo Tessarini, *Grammatica di musica* (English translation published); John Wesley, *Sacred Melody*.

I. Musical Compositions
Chamber Music:
String Quartets: Carlo Tessarini, *Six Grande Overtures, Opus 20*.
Sonata/Solos: Pietro Nardini, *Six Sonatas for Two Flutes/Violins*(?).
Ensembles: Gaetano Pugnani, *Six Trio Sonatas, Opus 2*(?).
Piano: C. P. E. Bach, *Six Sonatas (d, D, A, G, e, E♭), H.184–189*; Franz Joseph Haydn, *Sonatas (Divertimenti) 3, 4 (C,D)*; Vincenzo Manfredini, *Six Harpsichord Sonatas*; Ferdinando Pellegrini, *Six Harpsichord Sonatas, Opus 7* (with violin).

Choral/Vocal Music:
Choral:
Oratorio: Anton C. Adlgasser, *Amysis (Jechonias und Evilmerodach)–Iphigenia mactata (Chalcis expugnata)*; Luigi Boccherini, *Gioas, re di Giudea–Il Giuseppe riconosciuto*; Baldassare Galuppi, *Triumphus divini amoris*; Felice de' Giardini, *Ruth*; Antonio Sacchini, *S. Filippo Neri*.

Other: Luigi Boccherini, *La Confederazioni dei Sabini con Roma* (cantata)–*Dixit Dominus*; Domenico Cimarosa, *Mass in F* (male voices); Baldassare Galuppi, *La virtu liberata* (cantata); Franz Joseph Haydn, *Te Deum in C*; Vincenzo Manfredini, *Le rivali* (cantata); Wolfgang Amadeus Mozart, *Motet, "God Is Our Refuge"*; José Nebra, *Missa de difuntos*; Giovanni Paisiello, *Le nozze di Bacco ed Arianna*; Niccolò Piccinni, *La pace fra Giunone ed Alcide* (cantata).

Vocal: C. P. E. Bach, *Phillis un Thirsis, H.697* (cantata); Johann Christian Bach, *Six Canzonettes, Opus 4*; William Jackson, *Twelve Songs, Opus 4*(?).

Musical Stage: Maria Teresa Agnesi, *Sofonisba*; Johann F. Agricola, *Achille in Sciro*; Charles G. Alexandre, *Le Tonnelier*; Thomas Arne, *Bacchus and Ariadne*; Johann Christian Bach, *Adriano in Siria–The Maid of the Mill*; George A. Benda, *Xindo riconnoscíuto*; Antonio Boroni, *Le Villeggiatrici ridicolo*; Egidio Duni, *L'École de la jeunesse*; Florian Gassmann, *Il trionfo d'amore*; Felice de' Giardini, *Il re pastore*; Tommaso Giordani, *The Enchanter–Love in Disguise–Don Fulminone*; Christoph Willibald Gluck, *La corona– Telemaco*; François Gossec, *Le faux lord*; André Grétry, *La vendemmiatrice*; Johann A. Hasse, *Romolo ed Ersilia*; Giacomo Insanguine, *La vedova capricciosa–Il nuovo Belisario*; Niccolò Jommelli, *Imeneo in Atene*; Nicola Logroscino, *La gelosia–Il tempo dell' onore*; Jean-Joseph de Mondonville, *Thesée*; Giovanni Paisiello, *Madama l'umorista– Demetrio– L'amore in ballo–I bagni d'Abano*; François Philidor, *Tom Jones*; Niccolò Piccinni, *Il barone di Torreforte*; Antonio Sacchini, *Il Creso–La contadina in corte–Il finto pazzo per amore*; Giuseppe Sarti, *Mithridate*; Johann Schobert, *Le Garde-chasse et le braconnier*; Tommaso Traetta, *Semiramide*.

Orchestra/Band Music:
Concerted Music:
Piano: C. P. E. Bach, *Harpsichord Concerto in B♭, H.465.*
Violin: Franz Joseph Haydn, *Concerto No. 1 in C–Concerto No. 2 in D*; Pietro Nardini, *Six Violin Concertos, Opus 1*(?).
Ballet/Incidental Music: Christian Cannabich, *Ulisse et Circée* (B)–*Les amours de Télémaque* (B); Christoph Willibald Gluck, *Semiramis* (B).
Symphonies: Johann Christian Bach, *Six Symphonies (C, D, E♭, B♭, F, G), Opus 3*; François Gossec, *Three Grand Symphonies (E♭, F, E♭), Opus 8*; Franz Joseph Haydn, *No. 28 in A–No. 29 in E–No. 30 in C, "Alleluia"–No. 31 in D, "Hornsignal"*; Wolfgang Amadeus Mozart, *Symphony in F, K. a223–Symphony in C, K. a222–No. 4 in D, K. 19–No. 5 in B♭, K. 22*; Papavoine, *No. 2*; Franz X. Richter, *Six Symphonies, Opus 4*; Johann G. Schetky, *Symphony in C–Symphony in D*(?); Carlo G. Toeschi, *Six Symphonies, Opus 3*.

1766
❄

Historical Highlights: The British Parliament repeals the Stamp Act but passes the Declaratory Act; Benjamin Franklin becomes the American representative to Parliament; Catherine the Great grants freedom of worship to all Russians; the Mason-Dixon Line is established; Queens College (Rutgers University) is founded in New Jersey.

Art and Literature Highlights: Dresden Academy of Art founded. Births—artists Wilhelm von Kobell, John Brewster, Jr., writers Isaac d'Israeli, Mme. de Stael; Deaths—artists Jean Marc Nattier, Johann Christoph Gottsched. Art—Fragonard's *The Swing*, Olivier's *Mozart Playing for Afternoon Tea*, Wright's *The Orrery*; Literature—Goldsmith's *Vicar of Wakefield*, Lessing's *Laocoön*, Roger's *Ponteach; or, The Savages in America*.

Musical Highlights

A. Births
Composers: Stepan A. Degtiarev (Russia); Franz Xaver Süssmayr (Austria); Friedrich Dionys Weber (Bohemia) October 9; Joseph Weigl (Austria) March 28.
Conductors: Feodor Petrovich Lvov (Russia).

Singers: Luigi Bassi (Italian baritone) September 4; Johann Friedrich Döring (German bass) July 16.

Performers: John Addison (British contrabassist/composer)(?); Jacques-Marie Beauvarlet-Charpentier (French organist) July 3; Johann August Burgmüller (German organist/conductor) April 28; John Wall Callcott (British organist) November 20; Joseph-Denis Doche (French organist/conductor) August 22; Charles Duvernoy (French clarinetist); Rodolphe Kreutzer (French violinist/composer) November 16; Ignaz Antoine Ladurner (French pianist) August 1; Louis Massonneau (German violinist) January 10; Samuel Wesley (British organist) February 24.

Others: James Power (Irish publisher).

B. Deaths

Composers: Giovanni Battista Pescetti (Italy) March 20; Gregor Joseph Werner (Austria) March 3.

Singers: Susanna Maria Cibber (British mezzo-soprano/actress) January 31.

Performers: André Chéron (French organist/composer) October 7; August Bernhard Herbing (German organist) February 26; Luis Misón (Spanish flutist/composer) February 13; Ferdinando Pellegrini (Italian harpsichorist/composer); Johannes Ritschel (German violinist) March 25; Thomas Roseingrave (British organist) June 23; Carlo Tessarini (Italian violinist/composer) December 15.

Others: John Brown (British music author) September 23; Barthold Fritz (German clavichord/organ builder) July 17; Johann Hencke (Austrian organ builder) September 24; Friedrich Dionys Weber (Bohemian music author) October 9.

C. Debuts

Singers: Tommaso Guarducci (Italian male soprano—London); Rosalie Levasseur (French soprano—Paris); Marie Jeanne Trial (French soprano—Paris).

D. New Positions

Conductors: Giuseppe Colla (maestro di cappella, Duke Ferdinand of Parma); Domenico Fischietti (kapellmeister, Dresden); Filippo Gherardeschi (maestro di cappella, Chiesa Conventuale di S. Stefano, Pisa); Benedik Istvanffy (choir master, Gyor Cathedral); Feodor Lvov (Imperial Chapel Choir, St. Petersburg); Anton Schweitzer (kapellmeister, Hildburghausen).

E. Prizes/Honors

Honors: Joseph dall'Abaco (baronet).

F. Biographical Highlights
Luigi Boccherini goes on a concert tour of France with Vincenzo Manfredini; André Grétry, in Geneva as a teacher, meets Voltaire who encourages him to seek his musical fortune in Paris; Franz Joseph Haydn is promoted to full kapellmeister at the Esterhazy estate; Wolfgang Amadeus Mozart visits Paris and returns to Salzburg by way of Switzerland and Munich; Giovanni Battista Viotti is taken into the house of Prince Alfonso of Turin and given music lessons.

G. Cultural Beginnings
Performing Groups—Choral: Anacreontic Society of London.
Performing Groups—Instrumental: Musikalische Gesellschaft (Kassel); Beauvais Société de Musique.
Music Publications: *Wochentliche Nachrichten und Anmerkungen.*
Performing Centers: Drottningholm Palace Theater II (Stockholm); Leipziger Schauspielhaus (Stadttheater); Southwark Theater (Philadelphia).

H. Musical Literature
François Bedos de Celles, *L'Art du facteur d'orgues I*; Charles H. Blainville, *Harmonie theoretico-pratique*; Jean Dubreuil, *Dictionnaire lyrique portatif*; Josiah Flagg, *Sixteen Anthems to Which Is Added a Few Psalm Tunes*; John Heck, *The Art of Fingering*; Joseph Lacassagne, *Traité général des elemens du chant*; Georg F. Lincke, *Die Sitze der musikalischen Haupt-Satze in einer harten un weichen Tonart*; John Trydell, *Two Essays on the Theory and Practice of Music.*

I. Musical Compositions
Chamber Music:
    String Quartets: Charles Avison, *Twelve Concertos in Four Parts, Opus 9.*
    Sonata/Solos: Luigi Boccherini, *Four Cello Sonatas (c, E♭, B♭, A)*; Ferdinando Pellegrini, *Six Harp Sonatas* (with violin), *Opus 16.*
    Ensembles: Johann C. Bach, *Six Trio Sonatas (G, D, E, F, B♭, E♭), T.317*; Luigi Boccherini, *Six String Trios (E♭, B♭, E, f, D, F), Opus 4*; Christian Cannabich, *Six Trio Sonatas, Opus 3*; Florian Gassmann, *Six String Quintets*; François Gossec, *Six String Trios, Opus 9*; Wolfgang Amadeus Mozart, *Six Violin Sonatas (E♭, G, C, D, F, B♭), K. 26–31.*
    Piano: C. P. E. Bach, *Sonata in A, H.192–Eleven Pieces, H.193–203– Ten Sonatas (F, C, B♭, A, d, c, g, g, B♭, E), H.204–213–Six Pieces, H.214–219–Three Fantasias (G, d, g), H.223–225–Romance with Twelve Variations H.236*; Johann C. Bach, *Six Sonatas (B♭, D, G, E♭, E, c), Opus 5*; Franz Joseph Haydn, *Keyboard Sonatas No. 5–11 (d, A, B, B♭, e, C, A).*

Choral/Vocal Music:
Choral: Carl Ditters von Dittersdorf, *Isaac, figura del redentore* (oratorio); Baldassare Galuppi, *La pace tra la Virtu e la Bellezza* (cantata); Franz Joseph Haydn, *Cacilienmesse in C*; Ignaz Holzbauer, *Il Guidizio di Salomone* (oratorio); Niccolò Jommelli, *Missa solemnis in D*; Wolfgang Amadeus Mozart, *Stabat Mater, K. 33c–Kyrie in F, K. 33*; José Nebra, *Missa, De profundis clamavi*; Tommaso Traetta, *Rex Salomone* (oratorio).
Vocal: C. P. E. Bach, *Bachus und Venus, H.698–Der wirth und die gäste, H.699*.
Musical Stage: Anton C. Adlgasser, *La Nitteti*; Maria Teresa Agnesi, *Insubria consolata*; Pasquale Anfossi, *Fiammetta generosa*; Samuel Arnold, *Harlequin Dr. Faustus*; François Barthélémon, *Pelopida*; George A. Benda, *Il buon marito*; Antonio Boroni, *La notte critica*; João de Sousa Carvalho, *La Nitteti*; Egidio Duni, *La clochette*; Baldassare Galuppi, *La Cameriera spiritosa*; Florian Gassmann, *Achille in Sciro–Il viaggiatori ridicolo*; Tommaso Giordani, *L'eroe cinese*; François Gossec, *Les pecheurs*; André Ernest Grétry, *Isabelle et Gertrude*; Franz Joseph Haydn, *La Canterina*; Michael Haydn, *Rebekka als Braut*; Johann A. Hiller, *Der Teufel ist los*; Giacomo Insanguine, *Le quattro mal maritate*; Niccolò Jommelli, *Vologeso–La critica–Il matrimonio per concorso*; Pierre Monsigny, *Philémon et Baucis*; Giovanni Paisiello, *Le finte contesse–La vedova di bel genio*; Antonio Pampini, *Olimpiade*; David Perez, *Demetrio*; François Philidor, *Le nozze disturbate*; Niccolò Piccinni, *La pescatrice–Il gran Cid–La Molinarella*; Antonio Sacchini, *L'isola d'amore– La contadine Byarre*; Giuseppe Sarti, *Ipermestra*; Giuseppe Scarlatti, *Armida*; Tommaso Traetta, *Le serve rivali*; Jean-Claude Trial, *Esope a Cythere*.
Orchestra/Band Music:
Concerted Music:
Violin: Carl Ditters von Dittersdorf, *Four Violin Concertos*.
Other: Luigi Boccherini, *Cello Concerto in C(?)*; Franz Joseph Haydn, *Organ Concerto in C, H.XVII/8*; Michael Haydn, *Flute Concerto No. 1*; Franz X. Richter, *Cello Concerto in G*.
Ballet/Incidental Music: Christian Cannabich, *L'amour espagnol* (B)–*L'amour jardinier* (B); Vincenzo Manfredini, *Les amants réchappés du naufrage* (B)–*Le sculpteur de Carthage* (B); Pierre Monsigny, *Aline, reine de Golconde* (B).
Symphonies: Charles G. Alexandre, *Six Symphonies "à 8," Opus 6*; Christian Cannabich, *Six Symphonies, Opus 4–Six Symphonies for Large Orchestra*; John Collett, *Six Symphonies (E, E♭, G, C, E♭, G), Opus 2*; Carl Ditters von Dittersdorf, *Six Symphonies, Opus 1— Symphony in E♭, Opus 8, No. 1*; Franz Joseph Haydn, *No. 16 in*

B♭–No. 17 in F–No. 18 in G–No. 19 in D–No. 20 in C–No. 25 in C–No. 27 in G–No. 32 in C.

1767

Historical Highlights: The first Mysore War breaks out in India; the Jesuits and their Inquisition are expelled from Sicily; the Austrian government begins large-scale educational reforms, especially for the young; the New York Assembly is disbanded for refusing to honor the Quartering Act—Parliament passes the Townshend Acts.

Art and Literature Highlights: Births—artists Anne-Louis Girodet-Trioson, Charles Peale Polk, writers Maria Edgeworth, August Wilhelm von Schlegel; Deaths—poet Michael Bruce, artist François-Hubert Drouais. Art—Copley's *Girl with Bird and Dog,* Vien's *Greek Girl at the Bath,* Williams' *Woman with Hour Glass and Skull;* Literature—Marmontel's *Belisaire,* Mercier's *L'Homme Sauvage;* Sterne's *Letters of Yorick to Eliza.*

Musical Highlights

A. Births

Composers: Francesco Basili (Italy) January 31; Henri-Montan Berton (France) September 17; José Mauricio Nunes García (Brazil) September 22; Francesco Ruggi (Italy) October 21; (Johann) Franz Volkert (Bohemia) February 4.

Conductors: Wenzel Müller (Austria) September 26.

Singers: Martin Joseph Adrien (Belgian bass) May 26; Luigi Asioli (Italian tenor)(?); Georgina Oldmixon (British-born soprano); Dorothea Wendling (German soprano) January 27; Luigi Zamboni (Italian bass).

Performers: Julie Candeille (French pianist/composer) July 31; Heinrich Domnich (German horn virutoso) March 13; Friedrich Johann Eck (German violinist/composer) May 25; Ferdinand Fränzl (German violinist/composer) May 25; Gottlieb Graupner (German-born instrumentalist/composer) October 6; Friedrich Hiller (German violinist)(?); August Eberhard Müller (German organist) December 13; Andreas Jakob Romberg (German violinist) April 27; Bernhard Heinrich Romberg (German cellist/composer) November 11; Christian Friedrich Schwencke (German pianist/composer) August 30.

Others: Karl August Lichtenstein (German impresario) September 8.

B. Deaths

Composers: Thaddäus Ferdinand Lipowsky (Germany) March 18; Juan F. de Iribarren (Spain) September 2; Luca Antonio Predieri (Italy) January 3; George Philipp Telemann (Germany) June 25.

Singers: Francesca Bertolli (Italian contralto) January 9.
Performers: Per Brant (Swedish violinist/composer) August 9; Matthew Dubourg (British violinist/conductor) July 3; Johan Henrik Freithoff (Norwegian violinist) June 24; Johann Christoph Ritter (German organist) February 18; Johann Schobert (German harpsichordist) April 19.
Others: James Grassineau (British music compiler) April 5; Johann Haffner (German publisher) October 22; Thomas Johnston (American organ maker) May 8.

C. Debuts
Singers: Elizabeth Ann Linley (British soprano—London); Gertrud Mara (German soprano—Dresden).
Performers: Etienne-Joseph Barrière (French violinist—Paris).

D. New Positions
Conductors: Antonio Gaetano Pampani (maestro di cappella, Urbino Cathedral); Gaetano Pugnani (King's Theater, London); Luigi Antonio Sabbatini (maestro di cappella, Basilica of S. Barnaba, Marino); Francesco Uttini (Stockholm Opera).
Others: Jean-Claude Trial (co-director, Paris Opera); Christian Ehregott Weinlig (organ, Evangelist Church, Leipzig).

E. Prizes/Honors
Honors: Francesco A. Uttini (Master of the King's Music, Sweden).

F. Biographical Highlights
Thomas Arne begins work with the Noblemen and Gentlemen's Catch Club in London; John Beard retires from active music life because of increasing deafness; João de Sousa Carvalho joins the Brotherhood of St. Cecilia; André Grétry arrives in Paris to seek his musical fortune; Pietro Alessandro Guglielmi goes to England for a five-year stay of writing and conducting operas; Wolfgang Amadeus Mozart visits Vienna, where he and his sister contract smallpox; Johann Schobert and his family all die from eating poisonous mushrooms.

G. Cultural Beginnings
Performing Groups—Choral: Old American Co. (New York); Opera Velha (Rio de Janeiro); St. Cecilia Society of Ratisbon; Venice Opera Co.
Music Publishers: Longman and Broderip, Music Publishers (London).
Other: Joshua Shudi, harpsichord maker (London).

H. Musical Literature
John Arnold, *The Essex Harmony*; Charles-Henri de Blainville, *Histoire générale, critique et philologique de la musique*; Ernst Dressler, *Fragmente einiger Gedanken des musikalischen Zuschauers*; Jean Dubreuil,

Manuel harmonique; Francis Hopkinson, *The Psalms of David;* Johann
S. Petri, *Anleitung zur praktischen Musik;* Jean-Jacques Rousseau,
Dictionnaire de Musique; Georg A. Sorge, *Anleitung zur Fantasie;* Giuseppe Tartini, *De' principi dell'armonia musicale contenuta nel diatonico
genere;* Carlo G. Testori, *La musica raggionata;* Giuseppe Viale, *L'arbre
genealogique de l'harmonie.*

I. Musical Compositions
Chamber Music:
Sonata/Solos: Luigi Boccherini, *Four Cello Sonatas (C, B♭, E♭, c)*(?);
Jean-Baptiste Canavas, *Six Cello Sonatas I.*
Ensembles: Johann C. Bach, *Six Trio Sonatas (B♭, A, E♭, G, D, C),
Opus 6;* Franz Joseph Haydn, *Divertimento in E♭ for Horn, Violin and
Cello;* Gaetano Pugnani, *Six Trio Sonatas, Opus 6*(?).
Piano: C. P. E. Bach, *Eleven Pieces, H.228–238;* Franz Joseph Haydn,
Sonata No. 2 (Partita in D).
Organ: François Bainville, *Nouvelles pièces d'orgue composées sur dif-
férens tons;* Wolfgang Amadeus Mozart, *Organ Sonatas No. 1–3.*
Choral/Vocal Music:
Choral:
Oratorios: Anton Adlgasser, *Hannibal, Capuanae urbis hospes;* Fe-
lice Alessandri, *Il Tobia;* Samuel Arnold, *The Cure of Saul;* Tom-
maso Giordani, *Isaac;* Johann G. Naumann, *La Passione di Gesù
Christo;* Antonio Sacchini, *Gioas;* Georg Philipp Telemann, *Pas-
sion According to St. Mark II.*
Others: Georg Benda, *Ode auf des sterbemorgan der . . . Herzogin
zu Sachsen-Gotha und Altenburg;* Franz Joseph Haydn, *Stabat
Mater in g;* Wolfgang Amadeus Mozart, *Grabmusik, K. 42* (can-
tata); George "Abbe" Vogler, *Missa Pastorella in A.*
Vocal: Johann A. Hasse, *Salve Regina in E♭;* August B. Herbing,
Musikalische Belustigungen II.
Musical Stage: Johann F. Agricola, *Amor e Psiche;* Felice Alessan-
dri, *Ezio–Il matrimonio per concorso;* Charles G. Alexandre, *L'esprit
du jour;* Pasquale Anfossi, *I matrimonio per dispetto;* Michael Arne,
Cymon; Johann C. Bach, *Carattaco;* Georg Benda, *Il mestro di capella;*
Antonio Boroni, *Artaserse;* Carl Ditters von Dittersdorf, *Das Reich
der toten;* Florian Gassmann, *L'amore artigiano–Amore e Psyche;*
Tommaso Giordani, *Phyllis at Court;* Christoph Willibald Gluck,
Alceste–Il prologo; François Gossec, *Toinon et Toinette–Le double
deguisement;* André Grétry, *Isabelle et Gertrude;* Johann A. Hasse,
Partenope; Johann A. Hiller, *Die Muse–Lottchen am Hofe;* William
Jackson, *Lycidas;* Niccolò Jommelli, *La Semiramide in Bernesco;*
Pierre Monsigny, *L'isle sonnante;* Wolfgang Amadeus Mozart, *Die
Schuldigkeit des ersten Gebots–Apollo et Hyacinthus;* Josef Mys-

liveček, *Farnace–Il Bellerofonte–Il trionfo di Clelia*; Johann G. Naumann, *L'Achille in Sciro*; Giovanni Paisiello, *L'idolo cinese–Lucio Papirio dittatore–Il furbo malaccorto*; David Perez, *L'Isola disabitata*; François Philidor, *Ernelinde princesse de Norvège*; Niccolò Piccinni, *La notte critica–La finta baronessa*; Antonio Tozzi, *Il re pastore*; Tommaso Traetta, *Siroe re di Persia*; Pierre Vachon, *Les femmes et le secret.*

Orchestra/Band Music:
Concerted Music:
    Piano: Franz Joseph Haydn, *Keyboard Concerto No. 5 in G.*
    Violin: Luigi Boccherini, *Violin Concerto in F*(?).
    Other: Luigi Boccherini, *Two Cello Concertos (D, A)*(?); Franz Joseph Haydn, *Organ Concerto No. 2 in D.*

Ballet/Incidental Music: Christian Cannabich, *Mirtil et Amarilis* (B)–*L'enlèvement de Prosperine* (B); Vincenzo Manfredini, *La constance récompensée* (B).

Standard Works: Franz X. Richter, *Periodic Overture No. 18.*

Symphonies: Carl F. Abel, *Six Symphonies (Nos. 13–18), Opus 7*; Christian Cannabich, *Six Symphonies, Opus 4*; Carl Ditters von Dittersdorf, *Six Symphonies, Opus 4–Symphony in B♭, Opus 8, No. 2*; John A. Fisher, *Four Symphonies (C, F, E♭, c)*; Ignaz Fränzel, *Symphony in F*; Wolfgang Amadeus Mozart, *No. 6 in F, K. 43–(No. 43) in F, K. 76*; Franz X. Richter, *Six Symphonies, Opus 7*; Pierre Talon, *Six Symphonies (E♭, F, D, g, d, E♭), Opus 5.*

1768

❖

Historical Highlights: Turkey declares war on Russia to begin a century of on-and-off warfare between the two powers; Russia crushes a Polish bid for independence; Captain James Cook begins the first of his world voyages; unrest mounts against the Townshend Acts; the Regulator Movement is founded in North Carolina.

Art and Literature Highlights: Royal Academy of Art is founded in London. Births—artists John Crome, Joseph Koch, writer François René de Chateaubriand; Deaths—artists Canaletto, Johann Wincklemann, writers Sarah Fielding, Laurence Sterne. Art—West's *Agrippina Landing at Brindisium*, Zuccarelli's *The Finding of Moses*; Literature—Goldsmith's *Good-Natured Man*, Sterne's *Sentimental Journey*, Sumarokov's *The Usurer.*

Musical Highlights

A. Births
    Composers: Benjamin Carr (England-U.S.A.) September 12; José Pons (Spain)(?).

Singers: Gaetano Crivelli (Italian tenor) October 20; Margarethe Danzi (German soprano/composer); Jean-Blaise Martin (French baritone) February 24; Marianne de Tribolet (Austrian soprano) February 17; Johann Michael Vogl (Austrian baritone/composer) August 10.
Performers: Johann Georg Backofen (German harpist/clarinetist) July 6; Carlos Baguer (Spanish organist/composer) March 13(?); Francisco Javier Cabo (Spanish organist/composer) May 24; Robert Cooke (British organist); Xavier Désargus (French harpist)(?); Carolus Antonius Fodor (Dutch pianist/conductor) April 12; Sebastian Ludwig Friedl (German cellist) February 15; Johann Baptist Henneberg (Austrian organist/conductor) December 6; Louis Emmanuel Jadin (French pianist/composer) September 21; Antoine de Lhoyer (French guitarist/composer); Jean-Englebert Pauwels (Belgian violinist/conductor) November 26; Franz Anton Schubert (German double-bass virtuoso/composer) July 20; Samuel Webbe, Jr. (British organist) October 15.
Others: Johann Friedrich Kind (German librettist) March 4.

B. **Deaths**
Composers: Conrad Beissel (Germany-U.S.A.) July 6; Nicolas-Antoine Bergiron (France) April 27; Vigilio Blasio Faitello (Italy) March 14; Pascual Fuentes (Spain) April 26; José Nebra (Spain) July 11; Nicola Porpora (Italy) March 3; Gregor Schreyer (Germany) June 6.
Singers: Gregorio Babbi (Italian tenor) January 2.
Performers: Michel Blavet (French flutist/composer) October 28; Pierre-Gabriel Boufferdin (French flutist) January 13; Georg Donberger (Austrian organist/composer) April 2; Pierre-Simon Fournier (French organist) October 8; Joseph Friedrich Majer (German organist/author) May 22; Pierre van Maldere (Belgian violinist) November 1; Michel Mathieu (French violinist/composer) April 7(?); Francesco Maria Veracini (Italian violinist/composer) October 31.
Others: John Wainwright (British hymnist) January 28.

C. **Debuts**
Performers: Jean-Louis Duport (French cellist—Paris).

D. **New Positions**
Conductors: Carl Philipp Emanuel Bach (cantor, Johanneum and music director, Hamburg churches); Filippo Gherardeschi (kapellmeister, Duke of Tuscany); Johann Ernst Hartmann (Copenhagen Royal Orchestra); Antonio Ripa (maestro de capilla, Seville Cathedral).
Others: Carlo Monza (organ, Milan Court); Paolo Morellati (organ, Vicenza Cathedral); Antonio Sacchini (director, Conservatorio dell' Ospedaletto, Venice); Christian Friedrich Schubart (court or-

ganist, Ludwigsburg); Robert Wainwright (organ, Collegiate Church, Manchester).

E. Prizes/Honors
Honors: Lucrezia Aguiari (Court Virtuoso, Parma); Carlo Monza (Accademia dei Pugni).

F. Biographical Highlights
Johann Georg Albrechtsberger settles in Vienna; William Boyce resigns due to his increasing deafness and retires to Kensington; Baldassare Galuppi leaves Russia and returns to Venice to resume his position at St. Mark's; Franz Joseph Haydn loses much of his music in a fire at the Esterházy estate; Wolfgang Amadeus Mozart again visits Vienna and receives from Joseph II a commission for *La Finta Semplice*; Giuseppe Sarti returns to Copenhagen and resumes his duties as kapellmeister at the court; Giuseppe Tartini suffers a mild stroke.

G. Cultural Beginnings
Festivals: Birmingham Music Festival (England).
Music Publishers: Johann Michael Götz (Mannheim).
Performing Centers: Esterhazy Opera House (Eisenstadt, Hungary).

H. Musical Literature
Jakob Adlung/J. F. Agricola, *Musica mechanica organoedi*; Jakob Adlung, *Musikalisches siebengestirn*; Charles Davy, *Essay upon the Principles and Powers of Vocal and Instrumental Music*; William Hayes, *Anecdotes of the Five Music Meetings*; John Heck, *A Complete System of Harmony*; Johann H. Lambert, *Sur la vitesse du son*.

I. Musical Compositions
Chamber Music:
   String Quartets: Franz X. Richter, *Six Quartets, Opus 5*.
   Sonata/Solos: Luigi Boccherini, *Six Violin Sonatas (B♭, C, B♭, D, g, E♭), Opus 5—Four Cello Sonatas (F, c, C, G-?)*; Nicolas Capron, *Violin Sonatas, Book I, Opus 1*.
   Ensembles: Alessandro Guglielmi, *Six Concerti da Camera, Opus 1*; Franz Joseph Haydn, *Piano Trio (No. 14) in F*; Josef Mysliveček, *Six Trio Sonatas, Opus 1*; Francesco Uttini, *Violin Trios, Opus 1*.
   Piano: Johann Christian Bach, *Six Keyboard Sonatas, Opus 5*.
Choral/Vocal Music:
   Choral:
      Oratorios: Anton C. Adlgasser, *Abraham und Isaak–Kampf der Busse und Bekehrung–Philemon und Baucis (Der Besuch Jupiters)*; Michael Haydn, *Der Kampf der Busse und Bekehrung*; Antonio Sacchini, *Il popolo di Giuda, liberto della morte per intercessione della Regina Ester*.

Others: Domenico Cimarosa, *Mass in F*; Wolfgang Amadeus Mozart, *Missa Brevis, K. 49*; Josef Mysliveček, *Narciso al fonte* (cantata); Giovanni Paisiello, *Ebone* (cantata); George "Abbe" Vogler, *Missa Pasatorita in D.*

Vocal: Antonio Pampini, *Amor divino e urbana* (cantata).

Musical Stage: Agostino Accorimboni, *Le scaltre contedine di Montegelato*; Felice Alessandri, *L'Argentino–La moglie fedele*; Samuel Arnold, *The Royal Garland*; François Barthélémon, *The Judgment of Paris*; Antonio Boroni, *Didone*; Egidio Duni, *Les Moissonneurs–Les sabots*; Baldassare Galuppi, *Ifigenia in Tauride*; Florian Gassmann, *La notte critica*; Tommaso Giordani, *The Elopement*; François Gossec, *Les agréments d'Hylas et Silvie*; André Grétry, *Le huron–Les Mariages samnites*; Johann A. Hasse, *Piramo e Tisbe*; Franz Joseph Haydn, *Lo speziale*; Michael Haydn, *Die hochzeit auf der Alm*; Johann A. Hiller, *Die liebe auf dem lande*; Ignaz Holzbauer, *Adriano in Siria*; Niccolò Jommelli, *La schiava liberata–L'unione coronata*; Wolfgang Amadeus Mozart, *Bastien und Bastienne, K. 50–La finta semplice, K. 51*; Johann G. Naumann, *Alessandro nelle Indie*; Giovanni Paisiello, *Olimpia–La luna abitata–La finta maga per vendetta*; François Philidor, *Le jardinier de Sidon*; Niccolò Piccinni, *Lo sposo burlato–La locandiera di spirito–Il napoletani in America*; Antonio Rodriguez de Hita, *Briseida–Las Segadoras de Vallecas*; Antonio Sacchini, *Artaserse*; Giuseppe Sarti, *La giardiniera brillante–La calzolaia di Strasburg*; Johann Schwanenberg, *Antigono*; Tommaso Traetta, *L'isola disabitata–Amor in trappola*; Nicolo Zingarelli, *I quattro pazzi.*

Orchestra/Band Music:

Concerted Music:

Piano: Luigi Boccherini, *Concerto for Harpsichord in E♭*.

Violin: Josef Mysliveček, *Six Sinfonia concertante, Opus 2*.

Ballet/Incidental Music: Christian Cannabich, *Acis et Galathée* (B)–*Roland furieux–Les filets de Vulcain* (B).

Symphonies: Johann Albrechtsberger, *No. 1 in F–No. 2 in C*; Johann Christoph Friedrich Bach, *Symphonies No. 1–3*; Franz Joseph Haydn, *No. 49 in f, "La passione"*; Wolfgang Amadeus Mozart, *No. 7 in D, K. 45–No. 8 in D, K. 48–(No. 55) in B♭, K. a214*.

1769

❈

Historical Highlights: Poland is partitioned off by Prussia and Austria; George Washington introduces the Virginia Resolves to the Virginia Assembly; San Francisco Bay is discovered by the Spanish—Padre Crespi names their new colony in lower California Nuestra Senora la Rena de Los Angeles; Dartmouth College is founded.

Art and Literature Highlights: Births—artists Thomas Barker, Thomas Lawrence, writers Charles Julien de Chenedolle, Joseph Doddridge; Deaths—writers William Falconer, Christian Furchtegott Gellert, Joseph Sewall. Art—Fragonard's *The Love Letter*, Stubbs' *Lion Attacking a Horse*, West's *Self-Portrait*; Literature—Fonvizin's *The Brigadier*, Klopstock's *Hermanns Schlacht*, Smollett's *Adventures of an Atom*.

Musical Highlights

A. **Births**

Composers: Bonifacio Asioli (Italy) August 30; Pietro Casella (Italy)(?); Dominique Della-Maria (France) June 14; Joseph Antoni Elsner (Poland) June 1; Giuseppe Farinelli (Italy) May 7; Francesco Gneccho (Italy)(?); Thomas Haigh (England) January; Daniil Nikitich Kashin (Russia); Josef Alois Ladurner (Austria) March 7; Giovanni Agostino Perotti (Italy) April 12; Alexei Nikolaivich Titov (Russia) June 23.

Conductors: Johann Georg Lickl (Austria) April 11.

Singers: Maria Theresa Bland (British soprano)(?); (Pierre) Jean Elleviou (French tenor) June 14.

Performers: Paolo Bonfichi (Italian organist) October 6; Friedrich Ludwig Dülon (German flutist/composer) August 14; Jean-Jacques Grasset (French violinist/conductor)(?); Benedikt Hacker (German violinist/composer) May 30; Charles Hague (British violinist) May 4; Hyacinthe Jadin (French pianist/composer) April 23; Louis-Luc Loiseau de Persuis (French violinist/composer) July 4; Johann Georg Voigt (German organist) May 14.

Others: Adolph Martin Schlesinger (German publisher) October 4; Christian Friedrich Wilke (German organ builder) March 13.

B. **Deaths**

Composers: Chevalier d'Herbain (France).

Performers: William Felton (British organist/composer) December 6; Marianus Königsperger (German organist) October 9.

Others: Charles-Henri de Blainville (French music theorist/cellist); Pietro Nachini (Italian organ builder) April 16; James Oswald (Scottish publisher/composer) January 2.

C. **Debuts**

Singers: Francesco Benucci (Italian bass—Pistoia); Magdelena Heroux (German soprano—Mannheim).

D. **New Positions**

Conductors: Pedro Aranaz y Vides (maestro de capilla, Cuenca Cathedral); François Giroust (maître de musique, Saint Innocents,

Paris); François-Joseph Krafft (maitre de chapelle, St. Baaf Cathedral, Ghent); Bernardo Ottani (maestro di cappella, S. Giovanni, Monte); Franz Xaver Richter (kapellmeister, Strasbourg Cathedral); Giovanni Marco Rutini (maestro di cappella, Modena).
Others: Antoine Dauvergne (co-director, Paris Opera); Ignaz Vitzthumb (director, Grand Theatre, Brussels).

E. **Prizes/Honors**
Honors: Jean Baptiste Huet (French Academy).

F. **Biographical Highlights**
Luigi Boccherini moves to Madrid and becomes virtuoso to the Infante Luis; Dmitri Bortniansky receives a scholarship for study in Italy, where he begins studying with Galuppi; Charles Burney receives his doctoral degree from Oxford; Franz Joseph Haydn has his first music published; Niccolò Jommelli returns to Italy when the Stuttgart Court orchestra disbands; Wolfgang Amadeus Mozart leaves on a two-year Italian journey with his father; Christian Gottlob Neefe studies law at the University of Leipzig while continuing with his music writing and study.

G. **Cultural Beginnings**
Educational: Regia Scuola de Canto (Parma).
Performing Centers: Hôtel de Musique (Berne); Teatro Accademico (Mantua).
Other: Composers Concerts (by Giovanni Gualdo in Philadelphia— first known series in the New World); Concerts de la Loge Olympique (Paris); Concerts des Amateurs (Paris); Polytonal Clavichord (by J. A. Stein).

H. **Musical Literature**
Johann Altenburg, *Lebens-Umstande des Organisten Altenburg*; Paul-Cesar Gibert, *Solfèges ou leçons de musique*; Christoph Willibald Gluck, *Preface to Alceste*; Giovanni Martini, *Compendio della teoria de' numeri per uso del musico*; John Trydell, *Analogy of Harmony*; Daniel Webb, *Observations on the Correspondance between Poetry and Music*.

I. **Musical Compositions**
Chamber Music:
  String Quartets: Luigi Boccherini, *Six Quartets (D, c, E♭, g, F, A), Opus 8*; François Gossec, *Six Quartets, Opus 14*; Franz Joseph Haydn, *Six Divertimentos, Opus 9*.
  Sonata/Solos: Isidore Bertheaume, *Six Violin Sonatas, Opus 1*; Pietro Nardini, *Six Violin Sonatas, Opus 5*; Francesco Petrini, *Six Harp Sonatas, Opus 1*; Pierre Vachon, *Six Violin Sonatas, Opus 3*.

Ensembles: John Antes, *Three String Trios (E♭, d, C)*; Luigi Boccherini, *Six String Trios (B♭, E♭, A, F, g, C), Opus 6*; Thomas A. Erskine, *Six Trio Sonatas*; Florian Gassmann, *Six Quartets, Opus 1* (flute, strings).

Choral/Vocal Music:

Choral:

Oratorios: C. P. E. Bach, *Die Israeliten in der Wüste, H.775–St. Mattthew Passion I, H.782*(?); Johann Christoph Friedrich Bach, *Der Tod Jesu*; Baldassare Galuppi, *Tres Mariae ad sepulchrum Christi*; Josef Mysliveček, *La famiglia di Tobia*; Niccolò Piccinni, *Sara*(?); Johann H. Rolle, *Christmas Oratorio*.

Others: Domenico Cimarosa, *Magnificat–Gloria patri*; Baldassare Galuppi, *Flora, Apollo, Medoaco* (cantata); Luigi Gatti, *Virgilio e Manto* (cantata); Felice de' Giardini, *Italian Hymn* ("Come, Thou Almighty King"); Tommaso Giordani, *The Castle Ode*; Franz Joseph Haydn, *Missa honorem Beata Maria virgine in B♭ (Missa Sancti Joseph)*; Wolfgang Amadeus Mozart, *Missa Brevis in D, K. 65–Mass in C, K. 66, "Dominicus"–Te Deum in C, K. 141*.

Musical Stage: Felice Alessandri, *Il re alla caccia*; Antonio Boroni, *Il carnevale*; Pasquale Cafaro, *L'Olimpiade*; João de Sousa Carvalho, *L'amore industrica*; Baldassare Galuppi, *Il villano geloso*; Florian Gassmann, *L'opera seria*; Christoph Willibald Gluck, *Le feste d'Apollo*; André Grétry, *Lucile–Le tableau parlant*; Pietro Guglielmi, *Ruggiero–L'impresa d'opera*; Franz Joseph Haydn, *Le Pescatrici*; Michael Haydn, *Die Wahrheit der Natur*; Giacomo Insanguine, *La finta semplice*; Pierre Monsigny, *Le déserteur*; Josef Mysliveček, *L'Ipermestra–Il Demofoonte*; Johann Naumann, *La clemenza di Tito*; Giovanni Paisiello, *L'arabe cortese–Don Chisciotte della Mancia*; David Perez, *Il cinese*; François Philidor, *L'amant déguisé–La rosière de Salency*; Niccolò Piccinni, *Demetrio–La finta ciarlatana–l'innocenza riconosciuta*; Gaetano Pugnani, *Nanetta e Lubino*; Venanzio Rauzzini, *Piramo e Tisbe*; Giovanni M. Rutini, *La Nitteti*; Antonio Sacchini, *Nicoraste–Il Cidde*; Giuseppe Sarti, *L'asile de l'amour*; Ernst W. Wolf, *Das Gärtnermädchen*.

Orchestra/Band Music:

Concerted Music:

Piano: C. P. E. Bach, *Harpsichord Concerto in E♭, H.469*; Vincenzo Manfredini, *Harpsichord Concerto in B♭*.

Violin: Luigi Boccherini, *Concerto for Two Violins, Opus 7*; Franz Joseph Haydn, *Concerto No. 4 in G*; Carlo Toeschi, *Concerto in B♭*.

Other: Johann G. Albrechtsberger, *Trombone Concerto*; Charles Avison, *Six Concertos in Seven Parts, Opus 10*.

Ballet/Incidental Music: Christian Cannabich, *Cephales et Procrid* (B)–*Renaud et Armide* (B); Pierre Monsigny, *La Rosière de Salency*; Pierre Vachon, *Hippoméne et Atalante* (B).

Standard Works: Christian Cannabich, *Six Symphonia Concertantes, Opus 7*; Wolfgang Amadeus Mozart, *March in D, K. 62*.
Symphonies: Johann Christoph Friedrich Bach, *No. 4 in E*; François Barthélémon, *Six Symphonies (D, F, g, G, D, E♭), Opus 3*; Carl Ditters von Dittersdorf, *Three Symphonies, Opus 5*; François Gossec, *Six Symphonies for Large Orchestra (D, G, C, B♭, E♭, F), Opus 12*; Christian Graf, *Six Symphonies, Opus 9*; Franz Joseph Haydn, *No. 36 in E♭–No. 38 in C–No. 59 in A, "Fire"*; Ignaz Holzbauer, *Six Symphonies in 8 Parts, Opus 3e*; Wolfgang Amadeus Mozart, *Three unnumbered symphonies—D, D. a215–B♭, K. a217, B♭, K. a218*; Carlo Toeschi, *Six Symphonies, Opus 6–Three Grandes Symphonies, Opus 8*.

1770
❊

Historical Highlights: The Townshend Acts are repealed—Lord North becomes British prime minister; Captain Cook explores New Zealand and Australia; the estimated population of the colonies is about 2,000,000; the so-called Boston Massacre takes place March 5—the British, under provocation, kill several colonists.

Art and Literature Highlights: Births—writers Thomas Chatterton, Étienne de Sénancour, Georg W. F. Hegel, Johann F. Hölderlein, William Wordsworth; Deaths—writer Thomas Craddock, artists François Boucher, Giovanni Battista Tiepolo, Joseph Feuchtmayer. Art—Gainsborough's *Blue Boy*, Tiepolo's *St. Francis Receiving the Stigmata*; Literature—Chatterton's *The Revenge*, Goldsmith's *Deserted Village*, Mumford's *The Candidates*.

Musical Highlights

A. **Births**
Composers: João José Baldi (Portugal); Ludwig van Beethoven (Germany) December 16; Carl Friedrich Ebers (Germany) March 25; James Hewitt (England-U.S.A.) June 4; Anton Reicha (Czechoslovakia-France) February 26; Jan August Vitásek (Bohemia) March 22.
Singers: Thomas L. Bellamy (British bass); Marie Dickons (British soprano)(?); Giuseppe Naldi (Italian bass) February 2.
Performers: Josef Bähr (Austrian clarinetist) February 19; Ferdinando Carulli (Italian guitarist) February 10; John Clarke (British organist/composer) December 13; Jean-Baptist-Edouard Dupuy (French violinist/composer)(?); August Duranowski (Polish violinist)(?); Antoine-Charles Glachant (French violinist) May 19; Peter Hänsel (German violinist) November 29; Johann Christian Rinck (German organist) February 18; Georg Abraham Schneider (German horn virtuoso) April 19; Friedrich Witt (German violinist/composer)

November 8; Johann Nepomuk Wittassek (Bohemian pianist/composer) March 23.
Others: William Gardiner (British music author/editor) March 15; Aloys Mooser (Swedish organ builder) June 27; José Virués (Spanish music theorist) June 27.

B. **Deaths**
Composers: Francesco Araja (Araia) (Italy); Charles Avison (England) May 10; Esprit Joseph Blanchard (France) April 19; Gian Francesco Majo (Italy) November 17; Gottlieb Muffat (Austria) December 9.
Performers: Pasquale Bini (Italian violinist) April; John Broderip (British organ) December; Louis-Gabriel Guillemain (French violinist/composer) October 1; Giuseppe Tartini (Italian violinist/composer) February 26.
Others: Charles Dallery (French organ builder) January 10; Jean Dumas (French music theorist); Christian Gottfried Krause (German aesthetician/composer) May 4.

C. **Debuts**
Singers: Maddalena Allegranti (Italian soprano—Venice); Mary Ann Pownall (British soprano—London); Luiza Rosa Todi (Portugese mezzo-soprano—Lisbon).
Performers: Jean-Jerome Imbault (French violinist—Paris); Pierre Leduc (French violinist—Paris); Francesco Petrini (German-born harpist—Paris).

D. **New Positions**
Conductors: Daniel Dal Barba (maestro di cappella, Verona Cathedral); Antonio Boroni (kapellmeister, Stuttgart); Carl Ditters von Dittersdorf (kapellmeister, Count von Schaffgotsch, Johannesburg); Stanislao Mattei (maestro di cappella, S. Francesco, Bologna); Pietro Nardini (maestro di cappella, Florence); Giuseppe Paolucci (maestro di cappella, S. Martino, Senigallia); Giuseppe Sarti (Danish Court Theater).
Others: Nicolas Framery (editor, *Journal de Musique*).

E. **Prizes/Honors**
Honors: Armand-Louis Couperin (Organist to the King, Paris); Carl Ditters von Dittersdorf (Knight of the Golden Spur); Wolfgang Amadeus Mozart (Knight of the Golden Spur).

F. **Biographical Highlights**
Charles Burney begins his continental travels gathering material for his books; Wolfgang Amadeus Mozart writes out Allegri's *Misere* from memory after hearing it performed at the Vatican and also gets to study with Padre Martini; Gaetano Pugnani returns to Turin to take

up the concertmaster's position in the local orchestra; Jean-Jacques Rousseau, back in Paris, takes up music copy work; William Tuckey conducts the first performance of Handel's *Messiah* in the New World; Giovanni Battista Viotti begins studying violin with Pugnani in Turin.

G. **Cultural Beginnings**
Performing Groups: Liebhaber Konzerte (Berlin).
Festivals: Norwich Festival (England).
Music Publishers: Alessandri and Scattaglia (Venice); Luigi Marescalchi (Venice); B. Schotts Sohne (Mainz); Jean Georges Sieber, Publisher (Paris); George Smart, Publisher (London).

H. **Musical Literature**
William Billings, *New England Psalmsinger*; John Binns, *Dictionary of Musical Terms*; Johann F. Daube, *Der musikalische dillettant I*; John Hawkins, *An Account of the Institution and Progress of the Academy of Ancient Music*; John C. Heck, *The Art of Playing the Harpsichord*; John Holden, *An Essay towards a Rational System of Music*; Giovanni Martini, *Storia della Musica II*; Pierre Roussier, *Mémoire sur la musique des anciens*; Giovenale Sacchi, *Della divisione del tempo nella musica nel ballo e nella poesia*; Aaron Williams, *The Psalmody*.

I. **Musical Compositions**
Chamber Music:
String Quartets: Luigi Boccherini, *Six Quartets (c, d, F, E♭, D, E), Opus 9*; Wolfgang Amadeus Mozart, *No. 1 in G, K. 80.*
Sonata/Solos: Pietro Nardini, *Six Violin Sonatas, Opus 2*; Gaetano Pugnani, *Six Violin Sonatas, Opus 7(?)–Six Sonatas for Two Violins, Opus 4.*
Ensembles: Johann Christian Bach, *String Quintet in B♭, T.305*; Luigi Boccherini, *Six String Trios (c, D, E♭, A, B♭, F), no opus no.*; Felice de' Giardini, *Six Quintets, Opus 11* (cembalo, strings); Justin A. Just, *Six Piano Trios (C, F, B♭, D, a, G), Opus 2.*
Piano: Muzio Clementi, *Six Keyboard Sonatas, Opus 1–Three Keyboard Sonatas, Opus 2d*; Franz Joseph Haydn, *Keyboard Sonata No. 18 in B♭.*
Choral/Vocal Music:
Choral:
Oratorio: Anton C. Adlgasser, *Die gereinigte Magdalena*; C. P. E. Bach, *St. Mark Passion I, H.783(?)*; Johann Christian Bach, *Gioas, re di Guida*; Julije Bajamonti, *La translazione d. San Domino*; Carl Ditters von Dittersdorf, *Davidde penitente*; Michael Haydn, *Der reumütige Petrus*; Antonio Sacchini, *Machabaeorum mater.*
Other: Johann F. Agricola, *Les voeux de Berlin* (cantata); C. P. E. Bach, *Die Letzten Leiden des Erlösers, H.776* (cantata); Johann A.

Hiller, *Cantata Profana*; Wolfgang Amadeus Mozart, *Miserere in a, K. 85.*

Vocal: William Jackson, *Twelve Songs, Opus 7*(?)–*Twelve Canzonets, Opus 9.*

Musical Stage: Agostino Accorimboni, *Le contadine astute*; Johann F. Agricola, *Il re pastore*; Pasquale Anfossi, *Armida–Cajo Mario*; Thomas Arne, *The Ladies' Frolick*; Antonio Boroni, *Le orfane svizzeri*; Pasquale Cafano, *Antigono*; Egidio Duni, *Themire*; Baldassare Galuppi, *Amor lunatico*; Florian Gassmann, *Ezio–La contessina*; Tommaso Giordani, *Il Padre e il figlio rivali*; Christoph Willibald Gluck, *Paride ed Elena*; André Grétry, *Les deux avares–Silvain–L'amitie a l'epreuve*; Johann A. Hiller, *La Didone abbandonata*; Giacomo Insanguine, *Die Jagd–Der dorfbarbier*; Niccolò Jommelli, *Armida abbandonata*; Vincenzo Manfredini, *Armida*; Pierre Monsigny, *Pagamin de Monèque*; Wolfgang Amadeus Mozart, *Mitridate*; Josef Mysliveček, *La Nitteti*; Johann G. Naumann, *Il villano geloso*; Giovanni Paisiello, *Le trame per amore*; François Philidor, *La nouvelle école des femmes*; Niccolò Piccinni, *Catone in Utica–Cesare e Cleopatra–Didone abbandonata*; Rinaldo di Capua, *I finti pazzi per amore*; Antonio Sacchini, *Calliroe–L'eroe cinese–Scipione in Cartagena*; Antonio Salieri, *Le donne letterate–L'amore innocente*; Giuseppe Sarti, *Soliman II.*

Orchestra/Band Music:
Concerted Music:
> **Piano:** C. P. E. Bach, *Harpsichord Concerto in F, H.470*; Franz Joseph Haydn, *Keyboard Concerto No. 8 in G.*
> **Violin:** Franz Joseph Haydn, *Concerto No. 3 in A*; Maddalena Laura Lombardini-Sirmen, *Six Concertos*; Carlo Toeschi, *Concerto in D.*
> **Other:** Luigi Boccherini, *Cello Concerto in C*; Antonio Salieri, *Triple Concerto in C* (violin, oboe, cello); Carlo Toeschi, *Six Concertos for German Flute and Orchestra.*

Ballet/Incidental Music: Christian Cannabich, *Bacchus et Ariadne* (B)–*Angélique et Médor* (B); Antoine Dauvergne, *La tour enchantée* (B).

Standard Works: Giuseppe Agus, *Six Notturnos for Strings, Opus 4.*

Symphonies: Johann Albrechtsberger, *No. 3 in D*; Johann Christian Bach, *Six Symphonies (G, D, E♭mB♭, E♭, g), Opus 6–Six Symphonies périodiques (E♭, G, D, F, B♭, E♭), Opus 8*(?); Johann Christoph Friedrich Bach, *No. 6 in C*; Carl Ditters von Dittersdorf, *Three Symphonies, Opus 6*; John A. Fisher, *Six Symphonies in Eight Parts (E, D, E♭, B♭, D, c)*; Franz Joseph Haydn, *No. 26 in d, "Lamentatione"–No. 39 in g–No. 41 in C*; Wolfgang Amadeus Mozart, *No. 10 in G, K. 74–No. 11, K. 84–(No. 44) in D, K. 81–(No. 45) in D, K. 95–(No. 47) in D, K. 97.*

1771

Historical Highlights: James Cook completes his first round-the-world voyage; Russia conquers the Crimea to the alarm of Prussia and Austria; the *Encyclopedia Britannica* is first published; North Carolina "Regulators" enter into a losing battle with the British troops over what they consider to be repressive taxes and laws.

Art and Literature Highlights: Births—writers Sir Walter Scott, Louis Jean Lemercier, artist Antoine Jean Gros; Deaths—artist Louis Michel Van Loo, writers Christopher Smart, Tobias George Smollett. Art— David's *Combat of Mars and Minerva*, Fragonard's *The Progress of Love*, West's *Penn's Treaty with the Indians*; Literature—Klopstock's *Oden*, Mackenzie's *Man of Feeling*, Smollett's *Expedition of Humphrey Clinker*.

Musical Highlights

A. **Births**

    Composers: Daniel Belknap (U.S.A.) February 9; C. G. August Bergt (Germany) June 17; Carl Cannabich (Germany) October; Gioseffo Catrufo (Italy) April 19; William Linley (England) February; Ferdinando Paër (Italy) June 1; Friedrich Christian Ruppe (Germany) February 18.

    Singers: Antonio Pellegrino Benelli (Italian tenor/composer) September 5; Matthäus Stegmayer (Austrian singer/librettist/composer) April 29.

    Performers: Pierre Baillot (French violinist) October 1; Johann Baptist Cramer (German pianist/pedagogue) February 24; Giuseppe Maria Festa (Italian violinist/conductor); Giuseppe Naldi (Italian bass) February 2; Johann Joseph Rösler (Bohemian pianist/composer) August 22; Armand-Emmanuel Trial (French pianist) March 1.

    Others: Johann August Apel (German music author) September 17; Alexandre Choron (French editor/music theorist) October 21.

B. **Deaths**

    Composers: Pietro Auletta (Italy) September; Franz Xaver Brixi (Bohemia) October 14; Pietro Gnocchi (Italy) September 4; Johann Gottlieb Graun (Germany-U.S.A.) October 27; Giovanni Gualdo (Italy) December 20; Isfrid Kayser (Germany) March 1; Jean-Claude Trial (France) June 23.

    Singers: Antoine Fel (French bass) June 27.

    Performers: Philip Barth (German oboist) October 21; Martin Berteau (French cellist) January 23; Benjamin Blake (British vioinist) February 22; Giuseppe Maria Festa (Italian violinist); Anton Joseph

Hampel (German horn virtuoso) March 30; Giuseppe de Majo (Italian organist/composer) November 18; Giovanni Battista Mastini (Italian organist) February 20.
Others: Joseph Gabler (German organ builder) November 8; Blasius Ugolinus (Italian music theorist).

C. Debuts
Singers: Giovanni Battista Rubinelli (Italian castrato alto—Stuttgart).

D. New Positions
Conductors: Anton Laube (choirmaster, St. Vitus Cathedral, Prague).
Others: Joseph-Lazare Audiffren (organ, St. Victor, Marseilles); Jean-Jacques Beauvarlet-Charpentier (organ, St. Victor, Paris); Pasquale Cafaro (director, Conservatorio della Pieta, Naples); Francesco Corbisieri (first organist, Naples Royal Chapel); Justin Heinrich Knecht (organ and music director, Biberach).

E. Prizes/Honors
Honors: Maxim Berezovsky (Accademia Filarmonica, Bologna); Carlo Monza (Accademia Filarmonica, Bologna); Josef Mysliveček (Accademia Filarmonica, Bologna); John Hawkins (knighted); Richard Woodward (Mus.D., Dublin University).

F. Biographical Highlights
Domenico Cimarosa leaves the Conservatory and studies privately with Piccinni; Johann Gottfried von Herder joins the Buckeburg Court and works with Johann Christoph Friedrich Bach on several of his operas; Gertrud Mara leaves the Dresden Opera and joins the Berlin Court Opera of Frederick the Great; Marcos Antônio da Portugal enters the Seminario Patriarchal in Lisbon and studies music with Carvalho; William Selby moves to the United States and settles in Boston, where he becomes organist at various churches including the King's Chapel.

G. Cultural Beginnings
Performing Groups—Instrumental: Accademia Filarmonica Modenese.
Educational: Johann A. Hiller Singing School (Leipzig); Swedish Royal Academy of Music.
Performing Centers: Bath Assembly Rooms ("The Upper Room").

H. Musical Literature
Anselm Bayly, *The Sacred Singer*; James Beattie, *The Minstrel I*; Anton Bemetzrieder, *Leçons de Clavecin et principes d'harmonie*; Charles Burney, *The Present State of Music in France and Italy*; Johann F. Daube, *Der musikalische Dillettant II*; Fernando Ferandiere, *Prontuario Musico para el instrumentista de Violin y Cantar*; Johann P. Kirnberger, *Die*

Kunst des reinen Satzes in der Musik, aus sicheren Grundsätzen hergeleitet und mit deutlichen Beyspielen erläutert I; William Tans'ur, *Melodia Sacra*.

I. **Musical Compositions**
   Chamber Music:
   String Quartets: Franz Joseph Haydn, *Six Quartets (C, E♭, G, D, B♭, A), Opus 9–Six Quartets (E, F, E♭, c, G, D), Opus 17.*
   Ensembles: Luigi Boccherini, *Six String Quintets (A, E♭, c, C, E♭, D), Opus 10–Six String Quintets (B♭, A, C, f, E, D), Opus 11*; Gaetano Brunetti, *Six String Quintets, Opus 1*; Tommaso Giordani, *Six Quintets, Opus 1* (harpsichord, strings); Gaetano Pugnani, *Six Trio Sonatas, Opus 9.*
   Choral/Vocal Music:
   Choral:
   Oratorios: C. P. E. Bach, *St. Luke Passion II, H.784–St. John Passion I, H.785*(?); Bonaventura Furlanetto, *Moyses in Nilo*; Baldassare Galuppi, *Nuptiae Rachelis–Dialogus sacer–Adam*; Michael Haydn, *Der büssende sünder*; Wolfgang Amadeus Mozart, *La Betulia liberata, K. 118*; Josef Mysliveček, *Adamo ed Eva–Giuseppe riconosciuto*; Antonio Sacchini, *Jephtes Sacrificium.*
   Others: Franz Joseph Haydn, *Salve Regina in g*; Michael Haydn, *Requiem in c*; Wolfgang Amadeus Mozart, *Regina Coeli in C, K. 108–Litany in B♭, K. 109*; Niccolò Piccinni, *Giove piacevole nella regia di Partenope* (cantata).
   Musical Stage: Maria Teresa Agnesi, *Nitocri*; Pasquale Anfossi, *Quinto Fabio–Il barone di Rocca Antica*; Thomas Arne, *The Fairy Prince*; Samuel Arnold, *The Magnet*; Venanzio Buzzini, *L'eroe cinese*; Carl Ditters von Dittersdorf, *L'amore disprezzato–Il viaggiatore americano in Joannesberg*; Baldassare Galuppi, *L'inimico delle donne*; Florian Gassmann, *Il filosofo inamorato–Le pescatrici*; Giuseppe Gazzaniga, *Il Calandrino–La locanda*; Giuseppe Giordani, *L'astuto in imbroglio*; André Grétry, *L'ami de la maison*; Pietro Guglielmi, *Le pazzie di Orlando*; Johann A. Hasse, *Il Ruggiero*; Niccolò Jommelli, *Ifigenia in Tauride–Achille in Sciro*; Jean-Joseph de Mondonville, *Les projets de l'Amour*; Pierre Monsigny, *Le faucon*; Wolfgang Amadeus Mozart, *Ascanio in Alba*; Josef Mysliveček, *Montezuma–Il gran Tamerlano*; Christian Neefe, *Die Apotheke–Der Dorfbarbier*; Giovanni Paisiello, *Artaserse–I scherzi d'amore e di fortuna–Annibale in Torino*; Niccolò Piccinni, *Antigono II–La Corsala–Le finte gemelle–La donna di bell'umore*; Gaetano Pugnani, *Issea*; Rinaldo di Capua, *La donna vendicativa*; Antonio Sacchini, *Ezio–Adriano in Siria*; Antonio Salieri, *Armida–La moda–Don Chisciotte alle nozze di Gamace*; Giuseppe Sarti, *La clemenza di Tito–La contadina fedele.*

Orchestra/Band Music:
Concerted Music:
Piano: C. P. E. Bach, *Six Concertos (F, D, E♭, c, G, C), H.471–6*.
Other: Luigi Boccherini, *Four Cello Concertos (C, D, G, C)*; Michael Haydn, *Flute Concerto No. 2*.
Ballet/Incidental Music: Antoine Dauvergne, *Le prix de la valeur* (B); André Grétry, *Zémire et Azor* (B).
Symphonies: Luigi Boccherini, *Six Symphonies (D, E♭, C, d, B♭, A), Opus 12*; Franz Joseph Haydn, *No. 42 in D*; Wolfgang Amadeus Mozart, *No. 12 in G, K. 110–No. 13 in F, K. 112–No. 14 in A, K. 114–(No. 42) in B♭, K. 75–(No. 46) in C, K. 96*.

1772

Historical Highlights: Another partitioning of Poland takes place between Russia, Prussia, and Austria; James Cook begins his second round-the-world voyage; Samuel Adams forms the Committees of Correspondance with the sole intent of fomenting revolution; the British revenue cutter *Gaspee* is burned by the colonists after it runs aground.

Art and Literature Highlights: Births—writers Samuel Taylor Coleridge, Friedrich von Schlegel, Sándor Kisfaludy; Deaths—sculptor Johann Feuchtmayr, philosopher Samuel Johnson. Art—David's *Apollo, Diana and the Children of Niobe*, Peale's *George Washington*, Zoffany's *Academicians of the Royal Academy*; Literature—Graves' *The Spiritual Quixote*, Trumbull's *The Progress of Dulness, Volume I*, Wieland's *Der goldene spiegel*.

Musical Highlights

A. Births
Composers: Pietro Carlo Guglielmi (Italy) July 11; Stephen Jenks (U.S.A.) March 17; Giuseppe Mosca (Italy).
Conductors: Gottlob Benedikt Bierey (Germany) July 25; Franz von Destouches (Germany) January 21; Ignaz Franz von Mosel (Austria) April 1.
Singers: Domenico Ronconi (Italian tenor) July 11; Giovanni Liverati (Italian tenor/conductor) March 27; Nicola Tacchinardi (Italian tenor) September 3.
Performers: Maurice Montagney Artôt (French horn virtuoso/conductor) February 3; Charles Jane Ashley (British cellist) December 30; Carl Gottlieb Bellman (German organist) September 6; William Carnaby (British organist); Franz Cramer (German violinist) June 12; Pierre Dalvimare (French harpist) September 18; Casper Fürstenau

(German flutist) February 26; John Pratt (British organist); Henri-Jean Rigel (French pianist/composer) May 11; Josef Triebensee (Bohemian oboist/composer) November 21; Karl Jakob Wagner (German oboist/conductor) February 22; Johann Wilhelm Wilms (German-born pianist/composer) March 30.

Others: James Shudi Broadwood (British piano maker) December 20; Joseph Franz Lobkowitz (Bohemian patron of the arts) December 7; Johannes Nepomuk Maelzel (German inventor) August 15; François Louis Perne (French music historian) October 4.

B. Deaths

Composers: Francesco Barsanti (Italy-England); Giulia Frasi (Italian soprano) October; Johann Giulini (Germany) August 21.

Singers: Jean Antoine Bérard (French counter-tenor) December 1; Giovanni Dreyer (Italian castrato soprano) April 13; Marie Favart (French soprano) April 21; Julia Frasi (Italian soprano).

Performers: Louis-Claude Daquin (French organist/composer) June 15; Alessandro Felici (Italian harpsichordist) August 21; Pierre-Claude Fouquet (French organist) February 13; Johann Peter Kellner (German organist) April 19; Jean-Joseph de Mondonville (French violinist/composer) October 8; Georg von Reutter (Austrian organist/composer) March 11.

Others: Johann Patroklus Möller (German organ builder) July 24.

C. Debuts

Singers: Franz Christian Hartig (German tenor—Mannheim); Franziska Dorothea Lebrun (German soprano—Schwetzingen); Carl David Stegmann (German tenor—Breslau).

Performers: John Mahon (British clarinetist—London); Joseph Boulogne de Saint-Georges (West Indian-born violinist—Paris).

D. New Positions

Conductors: Domenico Fischietti (kapellmeister, Salzburg); Friedrich Hartmann Graf (kapellmeister, Augsburg Protestant Church and St. Anne's Gymnasium); Ernst Wilhelm Wolf (kapellmeister, Weimar).

Others: Johann Georg Albrechtsberger (organ/choir, St. Joseph's, Vienna); Pietro Maria Crispi (organ, S. Luigi dei Francesi, Rome).

E. Prizes/Honors

Honors: Antonio Bianchi (Accademia Filarmonica, Bologna); Michael Esser (Knight of the Golden Spur).

F. Biographical Highlights

Johann Christian Bach visits the Mannheim court; Charles Burney, traveling in the Low Countries, meets Christoph Willibald Gluck; Hieronymus Colloredo becomes the archbishop of Salzburg; Johann

Adolf Hasse retires to Vienna; Étienne Méhul, at age ten, becomes the organist at the convent in Givet; Wolfgang Amadeus Mozart, after a brief Salzburg visit, returns to Italy; Nicola Antonio Zingarelli graduates from Naples Conservatory.

G. Cultural Beginnings
Educational: Kerzelli Music College (Moscow).
Music Publishers: C. G. Ghera (Lyons); Lemoine Music Publishers (France); William Napier (London).
Performing Centers: Lyceum Theater (London); Teatro dei Nobili Fratelli Prini (Pisa).
Other: Barrel Organ (by Flight and Kelly); Celestina (patented by A. Walker); Melodika (by Johann Andeas Stein); St. Petersburg Music Club; Wiener Tonkünstler-Sozietät (Haydn Sozietät in 1826).

H. Musical Literature
Michel Corrette, *Method for Mandolins*; Louis J. Francoeur, *Diapason général de tous les instruments à vent*; Johann A. Hiller, *Anekdoten zur lebensgeschichte grosser Regenten und berühmter Staatsmänner*; Giuseppe Paolucci, *Arte pratica di contrappunto*; Christoph G. Schröter, *Deutliche answeisung zum generalbass*; William Tans'ur, *The Elements of Music Displayed*; Girolamo Tiraboschi, *Storia della letteratura italiana*.

I. Musical Compositions
Chamber Music:
String Quartets: Luigi Boccherini, *Six Quartets (D, F, E, F, E♭, c), Opus 15*; Florian Gassmann, *Six Quartets, Opus 1*; François Gossec, *Six Quartets, Opus 15*; Franz Joseph Haydn, *Six Quartets (E♭, C, g, D, "Sun Quartet," f, A), Opus 20*; Wolfgang Amadeus Mozart, *Quartet in D, K. 155*; Antonio Salieri, *Six String Quartets, Opus 20*.
Ensembles: Giuseppe Agus, *Twelve Duets* (two violins, harpsichord); Johann C. Bach, *Six Quintets (C, D, E♭, F, G, B♭), Opus 8* (flute, strings); Luigi Boccherini, *Six String Quintets (E♭, C, F, d, A, E), Opus 13–Six String Trios (F, c, A, D, E♭, F), Opus 14*; Nicolas Capron, *Six Quartets, Opus 1–Six Quartets, Opus 2*; Pierre Vachon, *Six String Trios, Opus 5–Six String Trios, Opus 6*(?).
Piano: Wolfgang Amadeus Mozart, *Piano Sonata in D, K. 381* (four hands)–*Three Church Sonatas, K. 67–69*.
Choral/Vocal Music:
Choral:
Oratorios: Anton C. Adlgasser, *Pietas in hospitem–Mercurius (Pietas in Deum)*; Johann Albrechtsberger, *Oratorium de nativitate Jesu*; C. P. E. Bach, *St. Matthew Passion II, H.786*(?); Baldassare Galuppi, *Debbora prophetissa*; Johann Naumann, *Isacco, Figura del Redentore*; Antonio Sacchini, *Nuptiae Ruth*.

Others: Johann Christian Bach, *Endimione* (cantata); Domenico Cimarosa, *Mass in C*; Franz Joseph Haydn, *Missa St. Nicolai in G*; Wolfgang Amadeus Mozart, *Litany in B♭, K. 125–Regina Coeli in B♭, K. 127*; Antonio Rodriguez de Hita, *Missa del Pange Lingua.*

Vocal: Georg Benda, *Amynte Klagen über die Flucht der Llage–Die Zurückkunst der Llage.*

Musical Stage: Agostino Accorimboni, *L'amante nel sacco*; Johann F. Agricola, *Oreste e Pilade*; Pasquale Anfossi, *Alessandro nell'Indie–L'amante confuso*; Thomas Arne, *The Cooper*; Johann Christian Bach, *Themistocle*; Josef Bárta, *La Diavolessa*; Domenico Cimarosa, *Le stravaganze del conte*; Nicolas Dezède, *Julie*; Baldassare Galuppi, *Montezuma–Gl'intrighi amorosi*; Carl Ditters von Dittersdorf, *Il finto opazzo per amore*; Florian Gassmann, *I Rovinati*; Tommaso Giordani, *Artaserse*; Johann A. Hiller, *Der Krieg*; Giacomo Insanguine, *Didone abbandonata*; Niccolò Jommelli, *Cerere placata–Le avventure di Cleomede*; Vincenzo Manfredini, *Artaserse*; Wolfgang Amadeus Mozart, *Il sogno di Scipione–Lucio Silla, K. 135*; Christian G. Neefe, *Amors guckkasten–Der Einsprüche*; Giovanni Paisiello, *Montezuma–La Dardané–L'innocente fortunata*; Niccolò Piccinni, *Ipermestra–Scipione in Cartagena–L'americano–L'astratto*; Gaetano Pugnani, *Tamas Kouli-Kan nell'India*; Johann F. Reichardt, *Hänchen und Gretchen–Amors Gückkasten*; Antonio Sacchini, *Armida–Vologeso*; Antonio Salieri, *La fiera de Venezia–La secchia rapita–Il barone di Rocca antica*; Giuseppe Sarti, *Deucalion og Pyrrha*; Tommaso Traetta, *Antigona*; Ernst W. Wolf, *Die Dorfdeputierten–Die treuen Köhler.*

Orchestra/Band Music:

Concerted Music:

    Piano: Johann F. Reichardt, *Concerto No. 8 in G.*

    Violin: Jean-Baptiste Davaux, *Two Symphonies concertantes (F, D), Opus 5(?).*

Ballet/Incidental Music: Franz Asplmayr, *Ifigenia* (B); Christian Cannabich, *Les mariages de Samnites* (B)–*Médée et Jason* (B); George "Abbe" Vogler, *Le rendez-vous de chasse* (B).

Standard Works: Josef Mysliveček, *Four Orchestral Trios for Strings.*

Symphonies: Johann Albrechtsberger, *No. 4 in D*; Johann Christoph Friedrich Bach, *No. 10 in E♭*; Antonio Boroni, *Symphony*; Gaetano Brunetti, *Six Overtures (Symphonies 1–6)*; Franz Joseph Haydn, *No. 43 in E♭, "Mercury"–No. 44 in e, "Trauersinfonie"–No. 45 in f♯, "Farewell"–No. 46 in B–No. 47 in G*; Wolfgang Amadeus Mozart, *No. 9 in C, K. 73–No. 15 in G, K. 124–No. 16 in C, K. 128–No. 17 in G, K. 129–No. 18 in F, K. 130–No. 19 in E♭, K. 132–No. 20 in D, K. 133–No. 21 in A, K. 134.*

1773

Historical Highlights: British Parliament passes the Regulating Act seeking to reform the British East India Company; the Jesuit order along with its Inquisition is banned from the Holy Roman Empire and is temporarily dissolved by Clement XIV; British Parliament passes the so-called Coercive Acts resulting in the Boston Tea Party.

Art and Literature Highlights: Births—artist François Frédéric Lemot, writers Robert Treat Paine, Johann Ludwig Tieck, Heinrich W. Wackenroder; Deaths—writers John Hawkesworth, George Lyttelton, artist Hubert François Gravelot. Art—Reynold's *The Graces Decorating Hyman*, Tiepolo's *Abraham and the Angels*, Trumbull's *Rebecca at the Well*; Literature—Burger's *Lenore*, Goethe's *Urfaust*, Goldsmith's *She Stoops to Conquer*.

Musical Highlights

A. Births

Composers: Charles-Simon Catel (France) June 10; François René Gebauer (France) March 15; Pietro Generali (Italy) October 23.

Conductors: Johann Philipp Schulz (Germany) February 1.

Singers: Josephina Grassini (Italian contralto) April 8; Margarete Luise Schick (German soprano) April 26.

Performers: Johann Gottfried Arnold (German cellist) February 1; George Baker (British organist/composer); Charles-Nicolas Baudiot (French cellist) March 29; Arthur Thomas Corfe (British organist) April 9; Michael Gottard Fischer (German organist/composer) June 3; Karl Ludwig Hellwig (German organist/composer) July 23; Pierre-Louis Hus-Desforges (French cellist/conductor) March 14; Charles Knyvett, Jr. (British organist); Wenzel Thomas Matiegka (Austrian guitarist/composer) July 6; Joseph Wölfl (Austrian pianist/composer) December 24.

Others: August Friedrich Donati (German organ builder) May 21; Raphael Georg Kiesewetter (Austrian music author) August 29; Matthew Peter King (British music theorist/composer); Hans Georg Nägeli (Swiss publisher/author) May 26.

B. Deaths

Composers: Carlo Pietro Grua (Italy) April 11; Jan Zach (Czechoslovakia) May 24.

Singers: Elisabeth Duparc (French soprano).

Performers: Florian Johann Deller (Austrian violinist) April 19; Carl Höckh (German violinist) November 25; Louis-Alexandre Legrand

(French organist) November 30; Johann Joachim Quantz (German flutist/composer) July 12.
Others: Matthew Peter King (British music theorist)(?); Burkhard Tschudi (Shudi) (Swiss harpsichord maker) August 19.

C. Debuts

Singers: Giacomo Davide (Italian tenor—Milan); Manuela Guerrero (Spanish soprano—Madrid); Luigi Marchesi (Italian castrato soprano—Rome); Carl Stenborg (Swedish tenor—Stockholm).
Performers: Giovanni Mane Giornovichi (Italian violinist—Paris); Marie-Alexandre Guénin (French violinist—Paris).

D. New Positions

Conductors: João de Sousa Carvalho (mestre de capela, Seminário Patriarchal, Lisbon); Pierre Gaviniés (Concerts Spirituel, Paris); François Joseph Gossec (co-director, Concerts Spirituels, Paris); Joseph Boulogne St. Georges (Concerts de Amateurs, Paris).
Others: Nicolas Séjan (organ, Notre Dame, Paris); Johann Gottfried Vierling (organ, Stadtkirche, Schmalkalden); Christoph Martin Wieland (editor, *Der Teutsche Merkur*).

E. Prizes/Honors

Honors: Ferdinando Bertoni (Accademia Filarmonica, Bologna); Jean-Baptiste Cupis (baronet); Carl Ditters von Dittersdorf (ennobled, Empress Maria Theresa).

F. Biographical Highlights

Christoph Willibald Gluck moves with his family to Paris; Johann Adolf Hasse and his wife, mezzo-soprano Faustina Bordoni, leave Vienna and settle in Venice; Franz Joseph Haydn writes and performs his *Symphony No. 48* for the Empress Maria Theresa during her visit to the Esterhazy estate; Antonio Lolli goes to the Court of Catherine the Great in St. Petersburg, where he soon becomes a favorite of the empress; Wolfgang Amadeus Mozart tries for a position at the Viennese Court but fails to obtain it; George Joseph "Abbe" Vogler, sent by the elector of Mannheim to study music in Italy, takes Holy Orders while in Rome.

G. Cultural Beginnings

Performing Groups—Choral: Swedish National Opera (Stockholm).
Performing Groups—Instrumental: New York Harmonic Society.
Music Publishers: Christian Ludwig Weber (St. Petersburg).
Music Publications: *Der Teutsche Merkur*.
Performing Centers: Innsbruck Redoutengebäude; Swedish National Theater (Stockholm); Teatro della Nobile Academia del Casino (Perugia).

H. Musical Literature

Daniel Bayley, *New Universal Harmony*; Charles Burney, *The Present State of Music in Germany, the Netherlands and the United Provinces*; Michel Corrette, *Method for the Doublebass*; Johann F. Daube, *Der musikalische Dillettant III*; Johann A. Hiller, *Anweisung zur Singekunst in der deutschen und italienischen Sprache*; Johann P. Kirnberger, *Die wahren Grundsätze zum Gebrauch der Harmonie*; Johann A. Scheibe, *Über die musikalische Composition I*; Georg M. Telemann, *Unterricht in Generalbass-Spielen*; John Watts, *Psalms of David Imitated*.

I. Musical Compositions

Chamber Music:

String Quartets: Florian Gassmann, *Six Quartets, Opus 2*; Wolfgang Amadeus Mozart, *Quartet in C, K. 157–in F, K. 158–in B♭, K. 159–in E♭, K. 160–in F, K. 168–in A, K. 169–in C, K. 170–E♭, K. 171–in B♭, K. 172–in d, K. 173*; Joseph Boulogne de Saint-Georges, *Six Quartets, Opus 1*; Pierre Vachon, *Six Quartets, Opus 6–Six Quartets, Opus 7(?)*.

Sonata/Solos: Johann C. Bach, *Six Violin Sonatas (B♭, C, G, E, F, D), Opus 10*; Luigi Boccherini, *Cello Sonata in B♭(?)*; Jean-Baptiste Canavas, *Six Cello Sonatas II*.

Ensembles: Luigi Boccherini, *Six Flute Sextets (D, F, A, E♭, A, C), Opus 16–Six Flute Quintets (D, C, d, B♭, G, E♭), Opus 17*; Jean Baptiste Davaux, *Six Quartets for Strings, Opus 6*; Florian Gassmann, *Five Trios for Flute, Violin and Bass*; Wolfgang Amadeus Mozart, *String Quintet in B♭, K. 174*; Johann G. Schetky, *Six String Trios, Opus 1*.

Piano: Muzio Clementi, *Six Keyboard Sonatas, Opus 2*; Franz Joseph Haydn, *Piano Sonatas No. 19–24*; Christian G. Neefe, *Twelve Piano Sonatas I*.

Choral/Vocal Music:

Choral: Johann Christoph Friedrich Bach, *Die Kindheit Jesu–Die Auferstehung und Himmelfahrt Jesu* (oratorios); Luigi Cherubini, *Mass in d*; Carl Ditters von Dittersdorf, *L'Esther* (oratorio); Thomas Lindley, *Let God Arise*; Wolfgang Amadeus Mozart, *Missa Brevis in G, K. 140–Mass in C, K. 167, "Trinitatis"*; Josef Mysliveček, *La Passione di Gesù Cristo*.

Vocal: Wolfgang Amadeus Mozart, *Motet in F, K. 165, "Exultate, Jubilate"*; Johann F. Reichardt, *Vermischte Musicalien*.

Musical Stage: Felice Alessandri, *Argea*; Johann André, *Der Töpfer*; Pasquale Anfossi, *L'incognita perseguitata–Demofoonte–Antigono*; Maximus Berezovsky, *Demofoonte*; Francesco Bianchi, *Il Grand Cidde*; João de Sousa Carvalho, *L'Eumene*; Domenico Cimarosa, *La finta parigina*; Nicolas Dezède, *L'erreur d'un moment–Le Stratagème découvert*; Carl Ditters von Dittersdorf, *Il tutore e la pupilla*; Baldassare Galuppi, *La serva per amore*; André Grétry, *Le magnifique–*

Cephale et Procris–La Rosière de Salency; Franz Joseph Haydn, *L'in-fedelta delusa* (burletta)–*Philemon und Baucis–Acide II*; Johann A. Hiller, *Die Jubelhochzeit*; Giacomo Insanguine, *Arianna e Teseo–Merope–Adriano in Siria*; Pierre Monsigny, *La belle Arsène*; Josef Mysliveček, *Il Demetrio–Romolo ed Ersilia–La clemenza di Tito*; Johann G. Naumann, *Armida–Solimano–L'isola disabitato*; Giovanni Paisiello, *Alessandro nell' Indie*; François Philidor, *Le bon fils–Zémire et Mélide*; Niccolò Piccinni, *Le quattro nazioni; l vagabondo fortunato*; Antonio Sacchini, *Il cidde–Tamerlano*; Antonio Salieri, *La locandiera*; Tommaso Traetta, *Amore e Psyche*; Francesco Uttini, *Thetis och Pelée*; Pierre Vachon, *Sara*; Ernst W. Wolf, *Der Abend im Walde*.

Orchestra/Band Music:

Concerted Music:

> **Piano:** Carl Ditters von Dittersdorf, *Harpsichord Concerto in B♭*; Maddalena Laura Lombardini-Sirmen, *Six Harpsichord Concertos*; Wolfgang Amadeus Mozart, *Concerto No. 5 in D, K. 175*; Johann F. Reichardt, *Concerto for Two Pianos*; Antonio Salieri, *Concerto No. 1 in C–No. 2 in B♭*.
>
> **Violin:** Jean-Baptiste Davaux, *Two Symphonies concertantes (C,A), Opus 7*; Johann F. Reichardt, *Concerto No. 7 in B♭*; Joseph Boulogne de Saint George, *Two Violin Concertos (G, D), Opus 2*.
>
> **Other:** Johann G. Albrechtsberger, *Harp Concerto*; Johann Christian Bach, *Symphonie Concertante in A, T.284*; Antonio Salieri, *Organ Concerto*.

Ballet/Incidental Music: Franz Asplmayr, *Acis et Galathée* (B)–*Alexandre et Campaspe de Larisse* (B); Luigi Boccherini, *Ballet espagnolo* (B).

Symphonies: Carl F. Abel, *Six Symphonies, Opus 10*; C. P. E. Bach, *Six Simphonies (G, B♭, C, A, b, E), H.657–662*; Johann Christian Bach, *Three Symphonies (B♭, E♭, B♭), Opus 9*; Carl Ditters von Dittersdorf, *Four Symphonies, Opus 7–Symphony in E♭, Opus 8, No. 3*; François Gossec, *Three Symphonies for Large Orchestra*; Franz Joseph Haydn, *No. 50 in C*; Wolfgang Amadeus Mozart, *No. 22 in C, K. 162–No. 23 in D, K. 181–No. 24 in B♭, K. 183–No. 25 in g, K. 183–No. 26 in E♭, K. 184–No. 27 in G, K. 199*; Johann F. Reichardt, *No. 1–No. 2*; Carlo Toeschi, *Six Symphonies, Opus 7–Three Symphonies, Opus 10*.

1774

Historical Highlights: In their treaty, Turkey gives Russia free use of the Black Sea and the Dardanelles; Louis XV of France dies—succeeded by Louis XVI; the First American Continental Congress presents a Petition of Grievances to Parliament who passes the Intolerable Acts; the Quebec Act pushes the Canadian border down to the Ohio River.

Art and Literature Highlights: Births—writers Robert Southey, Isaac Story, artists Pierre Guérin, Raphaelle Peale, Casper David Friedrich; Deaths—poet Oliver Goldsmith, artists Jean-Baptiste Lemoyne, Jeremiah Theüs. Art—Clodion's *St. Cecilia*, David's *Antiochus and Stratonice*; Literature—Goethe's *The Sorrows of Young Werther*, Jefferson's *Summary View of the Rights of British America*, Wieland's *Story of the Abderites*.

Musical Highlights

A. Births
Composers: Gaspare Luigi Spontini (Italy) November 14; Václav Jan Tomášek (Bohemia) April 17.
Singers: John Braham (British tenor) March 20.
Performers: Philip Barth (German oboist/composer) October 21; Franz Eck (German violinist); Guillaume-Pierre Gatayes (French guitarist) December 20; William Horsley (British organist/composer) November 15; Karl Möser (German violinist/conductor) January 24; Pierre Rode (French violinist/composer) February 16; Christoph Ernst Weyse (Danish organist/composer) March 5.
Others: Archibald Constable (Scottish publisher) February 24; François Joseph Fayolle (French music author) August 15.

B. Deaths
Composers: Johann Friedrich Agricola (Germany) December 2; Joseph Baildon (England) May; Florian Leopold Gassmann (Bohemia) January 20; Niccolò Jommelli (Italy) August 25; František Ignác Tůma (Czechoslovakia) January 30.
Performers: Jean-Pierre Guignon (Italian-born violinist) January 30; Charles-Nicolas LeClerc (French violinist/publisher) October 20; Francis Linley (British organist/composer).
Others: John Byfield, Jr. (British organ builder).

C. Debuts
Singers: Louise Dugazon (French mezzo-soprano—Paris).
Performers: William Mahon (British oboist—London); Andreas Jakob Romberg (German violinist—Münster, age seven).

D. New Positions
Conductors: Giuseppe Bonno (hofkapellmeister, Vienna); Christian Cannabich (Mannheim Orchestra); Carl Friedrich Christian Fasch (Berlin Royal Opera); André da Silva Gomes (mestre de capela, São Paulo Cathedral); Andrea Lucchesi (kapellmeister, Bonn); Antonio Salieri (Italian Opera, Vienna Court); Antonio Tozzi (hofkapellmeis-

ter, Munich); Daniel Gottlob Türk (kantor, Ulrichskirche, Halle);
Giovanni Zanotti (maestro di cappella, S. Petronio, Bologna).
Others: Johann Michael Demmler (organ, Augsburg Cathedral);
James Hook (organ, Vauxhall Gardens).

E. **Prizes/Honors**
Honors: Christoforo Bartolomeo Babbi (Accademia Filarmonica,
Bologna); Christoph Willibald Gluck (Court Composer, Vienna);
Georg Joseph "Abbe" Vogler (Knight of the Golden Spur).

F. **Biographical Highlights**
Wilhelm Friedemann Bach leaves Halle and decides to try his luck in
Berlin; Franz Chrismann installs the new organ at St. Florian;
Nicholas Marie Dalayrac is appointed a member of the elite Guard
of Honor at Versailles but continues taking music lessons from Honoré François Langlé and André Grétry; Wolfgang Amadeus Mozart
travels to Munich for the premiere of his *La finta giardiniera* and becomes acquainted with the music of Haydn.

G. **Cultural Beginnings**
Music Publishers: Johann André Publishing Co. (Offenbach); John
Preston and Son, violin maker and publishers (London).
Music Publications: *Deutsche Chronik* (Augsburg); *Gentleman
and Lady's Musical Companion; The New Musical and Universal Mag-
azine.*
Performing Centers: New Street Theater (Birmingham, England).
Other: Christopher Ganer, piano maker (London); Gray and Davi-
son, organ builders (London); Pantheon Concerts (London); Spath
und Schmahl, piano and organ builders (Regensburg); Tannenberg
Organ (Holy Trinity Church, Lancaster, Pennsylvania).

H. **Musical Literature**
Leonhard Euler, *Lettres a une princess d'Allemagne*; Antonio Eximeno,
*Dell'origine e delle regole della musica colla storia del suo progresso, deca-
denza e rinnovazione*; Martin Gerbert, *De cantu et musica sacra*; Johann
A. Hiller, *Anweisung zum musikalisch-richtigen Gesange*; Johann H.
Lambert, *Remarques sur le tempérament*; Richard Langdon, *Divine
Harmony*; Georg S. Löhlein, *Violinschule*; Giambattista Mancini, *Pen-
sieri e riflessioni pratiche sopra il canto figurato*; Giovanni Martini, *Es-
emplare ossia Saggio fondamentale pratico de contrappunto I*; Johann F.
Reichardt, *Über die deutsche comische oper–Briefe eines aufmarksamen
Reisenden die Musik betreffend*; Théodore-Jean Tarade, *Nouveaux
principes de musique & de violon beaucoup plus instructifs que ceux qui
ont paru jusqu'à présent.*

I. Musical Compositions

Chamber Music:

String Quartets: Gaetano Brunetti, *Six Quartets, Opus 2–Six Quartets, Opus 3*; Johann F. Reichardt, *Quartet*(?); Pierre Vachon, *Six Quartets, Opus 9*.

Ensembles: Johann Christian Bach, *Six Quintets (C, G, F, E♭, A, D), Opus 11*; Luigi Boccherini, *Six String Quintets (c, D, E♭, C, d, E), Opus 18–Six Flute Quintets (E♭, g, C, D, B♭, D), Opus 19*; Samuel Wesley, *Trio Sonata in G*.

Piano: C. P. E. Bach, *Five Sonatas (F, C, b, G, a), H.243–247*; Johann Christian Bach, *Six Sonatas (G, e, E♭, G, A, B♭), Opus 17*; Franz Joseph Haydn, *Piano Sonatas No. 25–30*; Christian G. Neefe, *Six Piano Sonatas II*.

Choral/Vocal Music:

Choral:

Oratorios: C. P. E. Bach, *St. Mark Passion II, H.787*(?); Giuseppe Bonno, *Il Giuseppe riconosciuto*; Baldassare Galuppi, *Tres pueri hebraei in captivitate Babylonis*; François Gossec, *La nativité*; Franz Joseph Haydn, *The Return of Tobias*; Antonio Salieri, *La sconfitta di Borea–Il triofa della gloria e della virtù*.

Others: Johann Christian Bach, *Amor vincitore* (cantata); Luigi Cherubini, *Mass No. 1 in C–La pubblica felicità* (cantata); André da Silva Gomes, *Christmas Matins*; Franz Joseph Haydn, *Missa Sancti Josephi in E♭*; Benedek Istvánffy, *Missa sanctificabis annum quinquagesium vel sanctae Dorotheae*; Niccolò Jommelli, *Miserere*; Wolfgang Amadeus Mozart, *Dixit Dominus-Magnificat in C, K. 193–Missa Brevis in F, K. 192–Missa Brevis in D, K. 194–Litany in D, K. 195*; Johann Naumann, *Mass in A*.

Vocal: Johann A. André, *Scherzhafte lieder–Auserlesene Scherzhafte und zärtliche lieder*; Christian G. Neefe, *Freimaurerlieder*.

Musical Stage: Agostino Accorimboni, *Le finte zingarelle*; Felice Alessandri, *Il Medonte re d'Epiro–Creso–*; Pasquale Anfossi, *Lucio Silla–La finta giardiniera–Olimpiade*; Johann Christian Bach, *Lucio Silla*; Johann Christoph Friedrich Bach, *Brutus*; François Barthélémon, *The Maid of the Oaks*; Carl Ditters von Dittersdorf, *Il tribunale di Giove*; Tommaso Giordani, *Antigono* (adapted from Hasse); Christoph Willibald Gluck, *Iphigenie en Aulide*; François Gossec, *Sabinus*; Michael Haydn, *Titus*; Niccolò Jommelli, *Il trionfo di Clelia*; Pierre Monsigny, *Le rendezvous bien employe*; Josef Mysliveček, *Antigona–Artaserse–Atide*; Johann Naumann, *Ipermestra–La villanella incostante*; Giovanni Paisiello, *La frascatana–Il credulo deluso–Andromeda–Il duello*; David Perez, *Creusa in Delfo–Il ritorno di Ulisse in Itaca*; Niccolò Piccinni, *Alessandro nelle Indie–Gli amanti* *mascherati*; Vincenzo Righini, *La vedova scaltra*; Antonio Sacchini, *Nitetti–Perseo*; Antonio Salieri, *La Calamita de' Cuori*; Tommaso Traetta, *Lucio Vero*.

Orchestra/Band Music:

Concerted Music:

Piano: Johann F. Reichardt, *Six Keyboard Concertos, Opus 1*; Samuel Wesley, *Two Harpsichord Concertos (G, D)*.

Violin: Joseph Boulogne de Saint-Georges, *Two Concertos (D, C), Opus 3–Concerto in D, Opus 4*.

Other: Wolfgang Amadeus Mozart, *Bassoon Concerto in B♭, K. 191*; Antonio Salieri, *Concerto for Oboe and Strings*.

Ballet/Incidental Music: Christian Cannabich, *Achille reconnu* (B)–*La fête marine* (B); Felice de' Giardini, *Elfrida* (IM); Franz Joseph Haydn, *Der Zerstreute* (IM).

Standard Works: Wolfgang Amadeus Mozart, *Serenade in D, K. 203*.

Symphonies: François Gossec, *Symphony in F, "Tobias"*; Franz Joseph Haydn, *No. 51 in B♭–No. 52 in c–No. 54 in G–No. 55 in E♭, "Schoolmaster"–No. 56 in C–No. 57 in D–No. 60 in C, "Il Distratto"*; Wolfgang Amadeus Mozart, *No. 28 in C, K. 200–No. 29 in A, K. 201–No. 30 in D, K. 202–(No. 50) in D, K. 161,3*; Johann F. Reichardt, *No. 3 in e–No. 4*.

1775

❄

Historical Highlights: Peasant's Revolt takes place in Bohemia; Second Continental Congress meets in Philadelphia; American Revolution begins with the Battles of Lexington, Concord, and Breed's Hill; George Washington appointed commander of the colonial forces; Daniel Boone leads the first settlers into the Kentucky territory.

Art and Literature Highlights: Births—artists Raphaelle Peale, Joseph Turner, John Vanderlyn, writers Charles Lamb, Jane Austen, Friedrich Wilhelm von Schelling; Deaths—artists François-Hubert Drouais, Ignaz Günter, writer Pierre Dormont de Belloy. Art—Clodion's *Satyn and Bacchante*, Houdon's *Portrait, Christoph Willibald Gluck*; Literature—Beaumarchais' *The Barber of Seville*, Sheridan's *The Rivals*.

Musical Highlights

A. Births

Composers: François-Adrien Boieldieu (France) December 16; Catterino Cavos (Italy-Russia) October 30; Moritz Dietrichstein (Austria) February 19; Nicolò Isouard (Malta, France) December 6; Luigi Mosca (Italy).

Singers: Edmée Sophie Gail (French vocalist/composer) August 28; Manuel García (Spanish tenor) January 21; Andrea Nozzari (Italian tenor).

Performers: Richard G. Ashley (British violist); João Domingos Bomtempo (Portugese pianist) December 28; Sophia Giustina Corri (Italian pianist) May 1; William Crotch (British organist/composer) July 5; Bernhard Henrik Crusell (Finnish clarinetist/composer) October 15; Traugott Maximilian Eberwein (Germany violinist/composer) October 27; Philippe Libon (French violinist/composer) August 17; Felice Alessandro Radicati (Italian violinist).

Others: Johann Anton André (German publisher) October 6; Giuseppe Baini (Italian music author) October 21; Prince Anton Heinrich Radziwill (Polish patron of the arts) June 13.

B. Deaths

Composers: John Collett (England); Egidio Romualdo Duni (Italy) June 11; Giovanni Battista Sammartini (Italy) January 15.

Singers: Vittoria Tesi-Tramontini (La Moretta) (Italian contralto) May 9.

Performers: Cornelius Dretzel (German organist) May 7; Jean Dubreuil (French pianist); Heinrich Nikolaus Gerber (German organist) August 6; Johann Georg Holzbogen (German violinist) September 7; François Rebel (French violinist/conductor) November 7; Lorenzo Giovanni Somis (Italian violinist/composer) November 29.

Others: Johann Hildebrandt (German organ builder) November 7; Samuel Powell (Irish publisher) November 27; Karl Joseph Rieppe (German organ builder) May 5.

C. Debuts

Singers: Harriett Adams (British soprano—London); Catarina Cavalieri (Austrian soprano—Vienna); Louis-Joseph Guichard (French vocalist—Paris); Vincenzo Righini (Italian tenor—Parma).

Performers: Maria Theresia von Paradis (Austrian pianist—Vienna).

D. New Positions

Conductors: Christoforo Bartolomeo Babbi (Teatro Comunale, Bologna); Giuseppe Gazzaniga (maestro di cappella, Urbino Cathedral); Carlo Monza (maestro di cappella, Milan); Johann Friedrich Reichardt (Royal Opera, Berlin); Friedrich Wilhelm Rust (kapellmeister, Dessau); Paolo Scalabrini (kapellmeister, Copenhagen—second term).

Others: Pierre-Montan Berton (general director, Paris Opera); Ernst Ludwig Gerber (court organ, Sondershausen); Giuseppe Sarti (director, Conservatorio dell'Ospedaletto, Venice); Johann Siebenkäs (organ, St. Sebald, Nuremburg); Richard Wainwright (organ, Collegiate Church, Manchester); Robert Wainwright (organ, St. Peter's, Liverpool).

F. Biographical Highlights
Thomas Attwood at age nine joins the Chapel Royal as a chorister; Ludwig van Beethoven receives his first music lessons from his father; John Behrent builds the first known piano in the New World; Benjamin Cooke receives his doctorate from Cambridge; Alessio Prati leaves Italy and takes up a composing career in Paris; Tommaso Traetta, in ill health, leaves Russia and goes to London; Georg Joseph "Abbe" Vogler returns to Mannheim and becomes vice-kapellmeister as well as spiritual advisor to the elector.

G. Cultural Beginnings
Performing Groups: Musikübende Gesellschaft (Leipzig).
Music Publishers: Simon et Pierre Leduc (Paris).
Performing Centers: Gotha Court Theater; Hanover Square Concert Hall (London).
Other: Keith Prowse and Co. (London); John Snetzler, organ builder (London Branch); Robert Stodart Piano Co. (London).

H. Musical Literature
Marie Engramelle, *La Tonotechnie*; Antonio Eximeno, *Dubbio de Antonio Eximeno sopra il saggio fondamentale, pratico di contrappunto del reverendissimo Padre Maestro Giambattista Martini*; Fedele Fenaroli, *Regole musicali per i principianti di cembalo*; Pietro Gianotti, *Le guide du compositeur II*; Paul-Cesar Gibert, *Mélange musical: premier recueil*; Johann H. Lambert, *Observations sur les sons des flutes*; Joseph de Laporte, *Anecdotes Dramatiques*; Vincenzo Manfredini, *Regolo armoniche*; Giovanni Martini, *Saggio fondamentale pratico di contrappunto II*; Johann F. Reichardt, *Schreiben über die berlinische musik*; Pierre Roussier, *L'harmonie pratique*; Johann G. Sulzer, *Allgemeine theorie der schönen kunste*.

I. Musical Compositions
Chamber Music:
String Quartets: Luigi Boccherini, *Six Quartets (C, D, E♭, B♭, a, C), Opus 22*; Pierre Vachon, *Six Quartets, Opus 5*.
Sonata/Solos: Johann Christian Bach, *Six Violin Sonatas, Opus 10*; Jean-Frédéric Edelmann, *Six Sonatas for Violin and Cembalo, Opus 1*.
Ensembles: Charles G. Alexandre, *Six Duets for Two Violins, Opus 8*; Luigi Boccherini, *Six String Quintets (E♭, B♭, F, G, d, a), Opus 20*; Jean Baptiste Breval, *Six Quatuors concertante, Opus 1*; Felice de'

Giardini, *Six String Trios, Opus 17*; Tommaso Giordani, *Three Quartets for Flute, Violin and Cello with Cembalo–Six Chamber Concertos for German Flutes*; Antonio Sacchini, *Six Trio Sonatas, Opus 1*; Johann G. Schetky, *Six Duos, Opus 2, for Violin and Cello–Six Piano Trios, Opus 3.*

Piano: Giuseppe Agus, *Six Sonatas, Opus 6*; C. P. E. Bach, *Six Easy Clavier Pieces, H.248*; Johann Christian Bach, *Six Keyboard Sonatas, Opus 7*; Wolfgang Amadeus Mozart, *Sonata in D, K. 284*; Josef Mysliveček, *Six Sonatas* (with violin); John Stanley, *Six Concertos for Keyboard, Opus 10.*

Organ: Wolfgang Amadeus Mozart, *Sonata No. 6, K. 212.*

Choral/Vocal Music:

Choral:

Oratorios: C. P. E. Bach, *The Israelites in the Wilderness–St. Luke Passion II, H.788*(?); Bonaventura Furlanetto, *Jerico*; Baldassare Galuppi, *Exitus Israelis de Aegypto*; Giuseppe Giordani, *La fuga in Egitto*; Franz Joseph Haydn, *Il ritorno di Tobia*; Michael Haydn, *Oratorium de Passione Domini nostra Jesu Christi*; Josef Mysliveček, *La liberazione d'Israele*; Johann G. Naumann, *S. Elena al calvario.*

Others: C. P. E. Bach, *Weihnachts-Musik, H.815*; Johann Christoph Friedrich Bach, *Michaels Sieg* (cantata); Luigi Cherubini, *Mass No. 2 in C–Magnificat*; Domenico Cimarosa, *Il giorno felice* (cantata); Bonaventura Furlanetto, *Melior fiducia vos ergo* (cantata); Baldassare Galuppi, *Venere al tempio* (cantata); Franz Joseph Haydn, *Missa brevis Sancti Joannis de Deo in B♭ (Kleine Orgelmesse)*; Joseph M. Kraus, *Requiem*; Wolfgang Amadeus Mozart, *Missa Brevis in G, K. 220–Missa Longa in C, K. 262*; George "Abbe" Vogler, *Missa pastoritia in E–Te Deum in D.*

Vocal: Johann F. Reichardt, *Gesänge für Schöne Geschlecht.*

Musical Stage: Felice Alessandri, *La novità–Alcina e Ruggero–La sposa persiana–Sandrina*; Johann André, *Erwin und Elmire*; Pasquale Anfossi, *L'avaro–Didone abbandonata*; Thomas Arne, *Caractacus*; George A. Benda, *Medea–Ariadne auf Naxos–Der Dorfjahrmarkt*; Francesco Bianchi, *La Réduction de Paris*; Antonio Boroni, *Le Déserteur–Zémire et Azor–L'isola disabitata*; Carl Ditters von Dittersdorf, *Lo sposo burlato–Il maniscalco*; François Gossec, *Alexis et Daphne–Philemon et Baucis*; André Grétry, *La fausse magie*; Franz Joseph Haydn, *L'incontro improvviso*; Gaetano Monti, *L'Adriano in Siria*; Wolfgang Amadeus Mozart, *Il re pastore–La finta giardiniera*; Josef Mysliveček, *Ezio–Merope*; Giovanni Paisiello, *Demofoonte–Il grand Cid–Le astuzie amoroso*; David Perez, *L'eroe coronato*; François Philidor, *Berthe–Les femmes vengées*; Niccolò Piccinni, *I viaggiatori–La* *contessina–L'ignorante astuto*; Johann Reichardt, *Der Holzbauer–Le feste galanti*; Vincenzo Righini, *La bottegha del caffe*; Jean-Jacques Rousseau, *Pygmalion*; Antonio Sacchini, *Montezuma*; Antonio Salieri, *La finta scema*.

Orchestra/Band Music:
Concerted Music:
  Piano: Johann F. Reichardt, *Concerto No. 8 in g*.
  Violin: Felice de' Giardini, *Six Concertos, Opus 15*; Wolfgang Amadeus Mozart, *Concerto No. 2 in D, K. 211–No. 3 in G, K. 216–No. 4 in D, K. 218–No. 5 in A, K. 219*; Joseph Boulogne de Saint-Georges, *Two Concertos (C, A), Opus 5–Two Symphonie concertante (C, B), Opus 6* (two violins).
  Other: François Barthélémon, *Six Concerti grossi (g, D, d, A, F, E), Opus 3*; Jean-Baptiste Davaux, *Two Symphonie concertante (B♭, D), Opus 8* (two violins, flute); Antonio Salieri, *Organ Concerto*; John Stanley, *Six Concertos for Organ and Strings, Opus 10*.
Ballet/Incidental Music: Christian Cannabich, *L'embarquement pour Cythère* (B).
Standard Works: Wolfgang Amadeus Mozart, *Serenade in D, K. 204*; Josef Mysliveček, *Six Overtures*.
Symphonies: Johann Christian Bach, *Three Symphonies, Opus 9*; Luigi Boccherini, *Six Symphonies (B♭, E♭, C, D, B♭, F), Opus 21*; Ignaz Fränzl, *Symphony in D(?)–in C*; Franz Joseph Haydn, *No 58 in F*; Guillaume Navoigille, *Six Symphonies (G, D, c, a, E♭, F), Opus 5(?)*; Antonio Salieri, *Symphony in D, "Il giorno onomastico"*; Peter von Winter, *Symphony in D(?)*.

1776
❊

Historical Highlights: Russia and Denmark sign the Treaty of Copenhagen; Russia begins building a large-size Black Sea navy; the American Declaration of Independence is signed in August; New Jersey becomes the first colony to grant women suffrage; Thomas Paine publishes his *Common Sense* and *The American Crisis*.

Art and Literature Highlights: Births—artists John Constable, Jaob Eichholtz, Gottlieb Schick, novelist Jane Porter; Deaths—artists Francis Hayman, Alexei Egorov, writers Cadwallader Colden, David Hume. Art—Cozens' *Hannibal Crossing the Alps*, Pigalle's *Nude Voltaire*, West's *Helen Brought to Paris*; Literature–Gibbon's *Decline and Fall of the Roman Empire I*, Klinger's *Sturm und Drang*, Smith's *The Wealth of Nations*.

Musical Highlights

A. Births
Composers: Juan Bros (y Bertomeu) (Spain) May 5; E. T. A. Hoffmann (Germany) January 24; Vincenzo Lavigna (Italy) February 21.
Conductors: Philipp Jakob Riotte (Germany) August 16; Ignaz Xaver Seyfried (Austria) August 15.
Singers: Teresa Bertinotti (Italian soprano) November 29; Bianchi Jackson (Lacy) (British soprano).
Performers: Joseph Valentin Dont (Bohemian cellist) April 15; Charles Duvernoy (French clarinetist/composer); Robert Lindley (British cellist) March 4; George Schetky (Scottish-born cellist/ publisher) June 1; Ignaz Schuppanzigh (Austrian violinist) November 20; George Thomas Smart (British organist/conductor) May 10.
Others: Richard Mackenzie Bacon (British music author/editor) May 1; Charles Édouard Delezenne (French acoustician) October 4; Rodrigo Ferreira da Costa (Portugese music author/composer) May 13; John Parry (British music author/composer) February 18; Thaddäus Weigl (Austrian publisher/conductor) April 8.

B. Deaths
Composers: Giuseppe Paolucci (Italy) April 24; Matthias Venta (Italy) November 22.
Singers: Filippo Finazzi (Italian castrato soprano/composer) April 21; Barbara Lucietta Westenholz (Italian soprano) September 20.
Performers: Joseph Canavas (Italian violinist) September 26; Bartolomeo Felici (Italian organist) June 12; Antonio Guerrero (Spanish guitarist) November 23; James Kent (British organist) May 6.
Others: Giorgio Antoniotto (Italian music theorist) November 22; Johann Adolf Scheibe (German music theorist/composer) April 22; Johann Philipp Stumm (German organ builder) June 27; Leopold Widhalm (German violin maker) June 10.

C. Debuts
Singers: Brigida Giorgi-Banti (Italian soprano—Paris); Marie Joséphine Laguerre (French soprano—Paris).

D. New Positions
Conductors: Joah Bates (Concerts of Ancient Music, London); Henri-Joseph de Croes (maître de chapelle, Regensburg); Johann Gottlieb Naumann (kapellmeister, Dresden); Gaetano Pugnani (general director, instrumental music, Turin).
Others: Franz Vollrath Buttstett (organ, St. Jakob's, Rothenburg); Philip Hayes (organ, New College, Oxford); Thomas Norris (organ, Christ Church, Oxford); William Selby (organ, Trinity Church, Boston); Jean-François Tapray (organ, École Royale Militaire, Paris).

E. Prizes/Honors

Honors: Johann Baptist Baumgartner (Swedish Academy); Francesco Bianchi (Accademia Filarmonia, Bologna); Georg "Padre" Martini (Roman Academy); Jean-Baptiste Rey (Court Musician to Louis XVI).

F. Biographical Highlights

Domenico Dragonetti, at age thirteen, becomes the principal bass player at the Venice Opera Bouffe; Franz Joseph Haydn loses more music in a second fire at the Esterhazy estates; Wolfgang Amadeus Mozart meets the Haffners and writes the *Serenade* for their daughter's wedding; Giovanni Paisiello goes to St. Petersburg for an eight-year stay at the court of Catherine the Great; Niccolò Piccinni arrives in Paris and the controversy known as the "War of the Buffoons" begins with the followers of Gluck's operatic reforms.

G. Cultural Beginnings

Performing Groups—Choral: Bolshoi Opera Co. (Moscow); Concerts of Ancient Music (London); Opera Nova (Rio de Janeiro); Polish Opera Co. (Lvov).

Performing Centers: Belfast Assembly Rooms; Bratislava Opera House; Societäts-Theater (Dresden); Teatro Coliseo (Havana); Théâtre de Rouen.

Other: Concerts Spirituels (Leipzig).

H. Musical Literature

Hyacinthe Azaïs, *Méthode de musique sur un nouveau plan*; Anton Bemetzrieder, *Traité de musique concernant les tons, les harmonies, les accords et les discours musical*; Charles Burney, *General History of Music I*; John Hawkins, *A General History of the Science and Practice of Music*; Johann H. Hesse, *Kurze doch hinlängliche anweisung zum General-Basse*; Joseph de Laporte/S. Chamfort, *Dictionnaire Dramatique contenant l'histoire des théâtres et les règles du genre dramatique*; Antonio Lolli, *École du violon en quatuor*; Friedrich Wilhelm Marpurg, *Versuch über die musikalische Temperatur . . .* ; Jean-Baptiste Mercadier, *Nouveau système de musique théorique et pratique*; Johann Reichardt, *Über des Pflichten des Ripien-violinistens*; Georg Vogler, *Tonwissenschaft und Tonsetzkunst–Stimmbildungskunst*.

I. Musical Compositions

Chamber Music:

String Quartets: Etienne Barrière, *Six Quartets, Opus 1* (two violins, viola, bass); Pierre Vachon, *Six Quartets, Opus 6*; Johann Vanhal, *Quartets, Opus 3*.

Sonata/Solos: Jean-Frédéric Edelmann, *Six Violin Sonatas, Opus 2–Two Divertissements for Clavecin and Violin, Opus 3*; Johann G. Schetky, *Six Cello Sonatas, Opus 4*.

Ensembles: Johann A. André, *Three Trio Sonatas, Opus 1*; Johann Christian Bach, *Three Quartets (D, C, A)*, T.309; Luigi Boccherini, *Six String Sextets (E♭, B♭, E, f, D, F), Opus 23*; Gaetano Brunetti, *Six String Sextets–Six Sextets for Oboe and Strings–Six String Trios, Opus 1–Six String Trios, Opus 2*; Jean-Frédéric Edelmann, *Sinfonie pour le clavecin, Opus 4*; Simon Le Duc, *Six Trio divertimenti (F, B♭, g, D, A, f), Opus 5*; George "Abbe" Vogler, *Six Piano Trios, Opus 1*.

Piano: Christian G. Neefe, *Six Piano Sonatas III*.

Choral/Vocal Music:

Choral:

Oratorios: C. P. E. Bach, *St. John Passion II*, H.789(?); Johann Christoph Friedrich Bach, *Der Fremdling auf Golgotha*; Bonaventura Furlanetto, *David in Siceleg*; Baldassare Galuppi, *Mundi salus–Moyses de Synai revertens*; Giuseppe Giordani, *Good Friday Passion*; Josef Mysliveček, *Isaaco Figura del Redentore*; Antonio Salieri, *La Passione di Gésu Cristo*.

Others: Domenico Cimarosa, *Mass in D*; Thomas Linley, Jr., *A Shakespeare Ode*; Wolfgang Amadeus Mozart, *Mass in C, K. 257, "Credo"–Missa Brevis in C, "Spaur," K. 258–Missa Brevis in C, "Organ Solo," K. 259–Litany in E♭, K. 243*; George "Abbe" Vogler, *Requiem in g*.

Vocal: Johann A. André, *Musikalischer Blumenstrauss*; Christian G. Neefe, *Klopstock Odes*.

Musical Stage: Johann André, *Der Barbier von Sevilien–Der alte Freyer*; Pasquale Anfossi, *Montezuma–La vera costanza*; Thomas Arne, *May Day*; Friedrich L. Benda, *Der Barbier von Sevilla*; George A. Benda, *Romeo und Julie–Walden*; Fernando Bertoni, *Orfeo*; Dmitri Bortniansky, *Creonte*; Domenico Cimarosa, *I matrimoni in ballo–La Frascatana nobile*; Carl Ditters von Dittersdorf, *La contadina fedele–Il barone di rocca antica–L'Arcifanfano*; Giuseppe Gazzaniga, *La fedeltà d'amore alla pruova*; Ignaz Holzbauer, *Günther von Schwarzburg*; Vicente Martín y Soler, *La Madrileña*(?); Josef Mysliveček, *Adriano in Siria*; Johann Naumann, *L'Ipocondriaco*; Christian G. Neefe, *Zemire und Azor–Heinrich und Lyda*; Giovanni Paisiello, *La disfatta di Dario–Le due contesse*; Niccolò Piccinni, *Radamisto*; Venanzio Rauzzini, *Le'ali d'amore*; Vincenzo Righini, *Il Convitato di pietra*; Giovanni Rutini, *Il finta amante*; Antonio Salieri, *Daliso e Delmita*; Giuseppe Sarti, *Farnace–Le gelosie villane*; Tommaso Traetta, *La Merope–Germondo*; Francesco Uttini, *Aline Queen of Golconda*.

Orchestra/Band Music:
Concerted Music:
Piano: Wolfgang Amadeus Mozart, *Concerto No. 6 in B♭, K. 238–No. 7 in F for Three Pianos, K. 242–No. 8 in C, K. 246.*
Violin: Jean-Baptiste Davaux, *Two Symphonies concertantes (B♭, D), Opus 8* (two violins); Michael Haydn, *Concerto No. 3;* Joseph Boulogne de St. George, *Concerto No. 9, Opus 8.*
Other: Etienne-Joseph Barrière, *Two Symphonies concertante (F, A), Opus 2;* Michael Haydn, *Horn Concerto.*
Ballet/Incidental Music: Giuseppe M. Cambini, *Les Romains* (B).
Standard Works: Luigi Boccherini, *Serenade in D*(?); Wolfgang Amadeus Mozart, *Serenade in D, "Notturna," K. 239–Serenade in D, "Haeffner," K. 250.*
Symphonies: C. P. E. Bach, *Four Symphonies in Twelve Voices, H.663–6;* François Barthélemon, *Six Overtures (G, B♭, A, c, D, E♭), Opus 6;* Giuseppe M.Cambini, *Three Symphonies (D, G, B♭), Opus 5;* François Gossec, *Symphonie de Chasse (in D);* Marie-Alexandre Guénin, *Three Symphonies (D, C, d), Opus 4*(?); Franz Joseph Haydn, *No. 61 in D;* Honoré Langlé, *Six Military Symphonies, Opus 1* (winds); Vincenzo Manfredini, *Six Symphonies;* Guillaume Navoigille, *Three Symphonies (D, C, A), Opus 87;* Johann F. Reichardt, *No. 6;* Tommaso Traetta, *Symphony in D.*

1777

❄

Historical Highlights: Spain and Portugal come to terms on their respective holdings in South America; a colonial victory at Saratoga encourages the French to enter the American conflict against the British; the Articles of Confederation are adopted by the Congress; Vermont, by their State Constitution, becomes the first state to outlaw slavery.

Art and Literature Highlights: Births—artist Philipp Otto Runge, writers Thomas Campbell, Heinrich von Kleist; Deaths—artist Charles J. Natoire, writers Claude Crébillon, Jean-Baptiste Gresset. Art—Gainsborough's *The Watering Place*, Goya's *The Parasol*, West's *Saul and the Witch of Endor*; Literature—Bessenyei's *The Philosopher*, Brackenridge's *The Death of General Montgomery*, Sheridan's *A School for Scandal.*

Musical Highlights

A. Births
Composers: Ludwig Berger (Germany) April 18; Stepan Ivanovich Davïdov (Russia) December 16; János Fusz (Hungary) December 16;

Joseph-Henri Mees (Belgium) May 28; Filippo Traetta (Italy-U.S.A.) January 8.

Conductors: Charles Frédéric Kreubé (France) November 5.

Singers: Elizaveta Semyonova Sandunova (Russian mezzo-soprano) September 10.

Performers: William Ayrton (British organist/critic/editor) February 24; Ramón Félix Cuéllar y Altariba (Spanish organist/composer) September 20; Charles William Hempel (British organist) August 28; Johann Bernhard Logier (German pianist/composer) February 9; Nicolas-Joseph Platel (French cellist); William Russell (British organist) October 6; Johann Gottlob Werner (German organist).

Others: George Catlin (American instrument maker) December 16; William Marcellus Goodrich (American organ builder) July 21; Johannes Franciscus Pressenda (Italian violin maker) January 6; Johann Heinrich Scheibler (German music theorist) November 11.

B. Deaths

Composers: Ernst Eichner (Germany) December 22; Pietro Antonio Gallo (Italy) August 15; Giuseppe Scarlatti (Italy) August 17; Georg Christoph Wagenseil (Austria) March 1; Richard Woodward (Ireland) November 22.

Singers: Maximus Berezovsky (Russian tenor/composer) April 2.

Performers: Johann Cajetan Adlgasser (German organist/composer) December 22; Johann Ernst Bach (German organist/composer) September 1; Emanuele Barbella (Italian violinist) January 1; William Hayes (British organist) July 27; Jean-Marie Leclair, *le cadet* (French violinist/composer) November 30; Simon Le Duc (French violinist/composer) January 20.

Others: Andrea Basili (Italian music theorist/composer) August 29; Bernhardt Christoph Breitkopf (German publisher) March 23; Johann Lambert (German music theorist) September 25.

C. Debuts

Singers: Sarah Bates (British soprano—London); Paolo Mandini (Italian tenor—Brescia); Antoinette Cécile Saint-Huberty (French soprano—Paris).

D. New Positions

Conductors: Friedrich August Baumbach (Hamburg Opera); Fedele Fenaroli (maestro di cappella, Conservatorio S. Maria di Loreto, Naples); Franz Ignaz Kaa (kapellmeister, Cologne Cathedral); Pierre La Houssaye (Concerts Spirituel, Paris); Giacomo Rust (kapellmeister, Salzburg).

Others: Olof Åhlström (organ, Marian Church, Stockholm); Charles Broche (organ, Rouen Cathedral); Laurent Desmazures (organ, St.

Férréol, Marseilles); William Jackson (organ, Exeter Cathedral); Joseph Legros (manager, Concerts Spirituel, Paris); John Randall (organ, Trinity College).

E. **Prizes/Honors**
Honors: Thomas Linley (Royal Society of Musicians).

F. **Biographical Highlights**
Felice Alessandri, at the invitation of Joseph Legros, moves to a conducting job in Paris; Sébastien Erard manufactures the first known French-made piano; Christoph Willibald Gluck goes to Paris for the production of his opera *Armide*; Wolfgang Amadeus Mozart, fired by the archbishop of Salzburg, begins a tour with his mother and meets the Weber family in Mannheim; Johann Gottlieb Naumann, at the request of Gustavus II, reorganizes the Swedish Court music; Christian Friedrich Daniel Schubart, due to his political writings, is imprisoned by the duke of Wurttemberg for ten years.

G. **Cultural Beginnings**
Festivals: Manchester Festivals (England).
Educational: Nobile Accademia di Musica.
Performing Centers: Norwich Pantheon.
Other: Gesellschaft zur Beförderung des Guten un Gemeinnützen (Basel); Felix Meritis Society (Amsterdam).

H. **Musical Literature**
Jean d'Alembert, *Réflexions sur la théorie de la musique*; Ernst Dressler, *Theater-Schule für die Deutschen, das . . . Singe-Schauspiel betreffend*; Johann N. Forkel, *Über die Theorie der musik, sofern sie Liebhabern und Kennern derselben nothwendig und nützlich ist*; Martin Gerbert, *Monumenta veteris liturgiae alemannicae*; John C. Heck, *The Art of Playing Thorough Bass*; William Jones, *Observations in a Journey to Paris*; Carl L. Junker, *Tonkunst*; Joseph M. Kraus, *Etwas von und über Musik für Jahr 1777*; Jean F. Marmontel, *Essai sur les révolutions de la musique en France*; Samuel Wesley, *Eight Lessons for Harpsichordists*.

I. **Musical Compositions**
Chamber Music:
String Quartets: Luigi Boccherini, *Six String Quartets (D, A, E♭, C, e, g), Opus 24*; Johann G. Schetky, *Six Quartets*.
Sonata/Solos: Johann G. Schetky, *Six Flute Duets, Opus 5*.
Ensembles: Johann Christian Bach, *Six Instrumental Quintets, Opus 11*; Jean-Baptiste Bréval, *Six String Trios, Opus 3*; Wolfgang Amadeus Mozart, *Quartet for Flute and Strings, K. 285*.
Piano: Jean-Frédéric Edelmann, *Four Clavecin Sonatas, Opus 5* (violin ad. lib.); Ludwig Lachnith, *Six Sonatas, Opus 2* (violin obbli-

gato); Wolfgang Amadeus Mozart, *Sonata in C, K. 309–Sonata in D, K. 311–Church Sonata in C, K. 274–Church Sonata in G, K. 278*; Josef Mysliveček, *Six Easy Divertimentos.*

Choral/Vocal Music:

Choral:

Oratorios: C. P. E. Bach, *St. Matthew Passion III, H.790*(?); John Abraham Fisher, *Providence*; Bonaventura Furlanetto, *Israelis liberatio–Mors Adam*; Gottfried Homilius, *Die Freude der Hirten über die Geburt Jesu*; Thomas Lindley, *The Song of Moses*; Johann G. Naumann, *Giuseppe riconosciuto*; Antonio Sacchini, *Esther*; George "Abbe" Vogler, *Die auferstehen Jesu.*

Others: Luigi Cherubini, *Te Deum*; Tommaso Giordani, *Aci e Galatea* (cantata); Michael Haydn, *Missa Sancte Hieronyni*; Wolfgang Amadeus Mozart, *Missa Brevis in B♭, K. 275*; Josef Mysliveček, *Il tempio d'eternita* (cantata); Venanzio Rauzzini, *La partenza* (cantata); George "Abbe" Vogler, *Deutsche Kirchenmusik in a.*

Musical Stage: Agostino Accorimboni, *Nitteti–Il finto cavaliere–l'amor artigiano*; Johann André, *Die Bezauberten*; Pasquale Anfossi, *Gengis-Kan–Il curioso indiscreto*; Thomas Arne, *Phoebe at Court*; Giuseppe M. Cambini, *Rose d'amour*; Domenico Cimarosa, *I tre Amanti–Il fanatico per gli antichi romani–L'Armida immaginaria*; Nicolas Dezède, *Fatmé–Les Trois Fermiers*; Christoph Willibald Gluck, *Armide*; André Grétry, *Matroco*; Franz Joseph Haydn, *Il mondo della luna*; Giacomo Insanguine, *Pulcinella–Le astuzie per amore*; Pierre Monsigny, *Félix, ou L'enfant trouve*; Christian G. Neefe, *Die Zigeuner*; Giovanni Paisiello, *Nitteti–Lucinda e Armidore*; David Perez, *La pace fra la virtùe la Bellezza*; Niccolò Piccinni, *Vittorina*; Joseph Saint-Georges, *Ernestine*; Antonio Salieri, *La partenza inaspettata*; Giuseppe Sarti, *Medonte–Ifigenia–Il militare bizarro*; Tommaso Traetta, *Telemacco– Il cavaliere errante.*

Orchestra/Band Music:

Concerted Music:

Piano: Johann Christian Bach, *Six Keyboard Concertos, Opus 13*; Wolfgang Amadeus Mozart, *Concerto No. 9 in E♭, K. 271*; Johann F. Reichardt, *Six Harpsichord Sonatas, Opus 2* (violin ad. lib.).

Violin: Carl Ditters von Dittersdorf, *Violin Concerto in D*; Joseph Boulogne de Saint-Georges, *Two Symphonies concertante (C, A), Opus 9–Two Symphonies concertante (E♭, G), Opus 12.*

Other: Jean-Baptiste Bréval, *Two Symphonies concertante (D, A), Opus 4*; Carl Ditters von Dittersdorf, *Three Viola Concertos*; Antonio Salieri, *Concertino for Flute and Strings.*

Ballet/Incidental Music: Michael Haydn, *Zaire* (IM).

Standard Works: Luigi Boccherini, *Serenade in D.*
Symphonies: Ignazio Raimondi, *Symphony: Les Aventures de Télémaque*; Carlo G. Toeschi, *Six Symphonies, Opus 12.*

1778
❄

Historical Highlights: France declares war on England to help the American colonies; the Continental Congress signs a Treaty of Alliance with France, the first country to recognize the new government; Savannah, Georgia, falls to the British; the War of the Bavarian Succession is fought between Prussia and Austria.

Art and Literature Highlights: Births—artist Rembrandt Peale, writers Clemens Brentano, Ugo Foscolo, James K. Paulding; Deaths—philosopher Voltaire, artists John Hesselius, Jean-Baptiste Lemoyne, Pieter Vanderlyn. Art—Copley's *Watson and the Shark*, Fuseli's *Oath on the Rütli*, Nollekens' *Venus Chiding Cupid*; Literature—Fanny Burney's *Evalina*, Herder's *Stimmen der Völker in Lieder I*, Francis Hopkinson's *The Battle of the Kegs.*

Musical Highlights

A. Births
Composers: Charlotte-Antoinette-Pauline Duchambge (France) December 29; Joseph Funk (U.S.A.) April 6; Johann Baptist Gänsbacher (Austria) May 8; Antonio Francesco Pacini (Italy) July 7; Carl Friedrich Rungenhagen (Germany) September 27.

Singers: Anton Fischer (German tenor/composer) January 13.

Performers: Alexandre-Jean Boucher (French violinist) April 11; George Bridgetower (Polish-born violinist) October 11; Simon Hermstedt (German clarinetist) December 29; Johann Nepomuk Hummel (Austrian pianist/composer) November 14; Benjamin Jacob (British organist/composer) May 15; Joseph Kemp (British organist) December 29; Nicolaus Kraft (Hungarian cellist) December 14; Jean Nicolas Auguste Kreutzer (French violinist) September 3; Sigismund von Neukomm (Austrian pianist/conductor) July 10; Carl Borromaus Neuner (German violinist/composer) July 29; Fernando Sor (Spanish guitarist/composer) February 13.

Other: Domenico Barbaja (Italian impresario) December 29; Francesco Caffi (Italian music scholar) June 14; Fortunato Santini (Italian music scholar) January 5.

B. Deaths
Composers: Thomas Augustine Arne (England) March 5; Francesco Corselli (Italy) April 3; Giovanni Fioroni (Italy) December 14;

Quirino Gasparini (Italy) October 30; Jean-Noël Hamal (Belgium) November 26; Benedek Istvánffy (Hungary) October 25; Johann Balthasar Kehl (Germany) April 7; David Perez (Italy) October 30.

Singers: Francesca Cuzzoni (Italian soprano) June 19; Elisabeth Duparc (French soprano); Pasquale Pisari (Italian bass/composer) March 27.

Performers: Angelo Antonio Caroli (Italian organist) June 26; Giovanni Battista Costanzi (Italian cellist) March 5; Laurent Desmazures (French organist) April 29; Johann Gottlieb Görner (German organist) February 15; Albertus Groneman (German violinist) June 1; Johann Heinrich Hesse (German organist) June; Thomas Linley, Jr. (British violinist/composer) August 5; Georg Tzarth (Czech violinist/composer).

Others: Lorenz Christoph Mizler (German music scholar) March; Georg Andreas Sorge (German music theorist/organist) April 4.

C. Debuts

Singers: Salomea Deszner (Polish soprano—Warsaw); Elizabeth Mahon (British soprano—London), Therese Teyber (Austrian soprano—Vienna).

Performers: Ludwig van Beethoven (German pianist—Bonn, age eight); Jean-Baptiste Breval (French cellist—Paris).

D. New Positions

Conductors: Giovanni Battista Borghi (maestro di cappella, Santa Casa, Loreto); Antonio Boroni (maestro di cappella, St. Peter's, Rome); Pietro Maria Crispi (maestro di cappella, Oratorio di S. Girolamo della Caritá, Rome); Ignaz Fränzl (Nationaltheater, Mannheim); Karl Hanke (kapellmeister, Brünn); Anton Schweitzer (kapellmeister, Gotha).

Others: Johann Nikolaus Forkel (music director, University of Göttingen); Richard Langdon (organ, Bristol Cathedral); William Selby (organ, Stone Chapel, Boston); Ignaz Umlauf (director, German Opera, Vienna).

E. Prizes/Honors

Honors: Pehr Frigel (Swedish Royal Academy).

F. Biographical Highlights

Ludwig van Beethoven's father, with the Mozart "wunderkind" in mind, lies about his son's age at his first recital appearance; Luigi Cherubini is given a grant by Duke Leopold II of Tuscany to study music with Sarti in Milan; Charles Dibdin, forced with all foreigners to leave France, returns to England; Christoph Willibald Gluck makes his last visit to Paris; Leopold Kozeluch gives up on law study and goes to Vienna, where he becomes an important teacher and pianist; Wolfgang Amadeus Mozart loses his mother in Paris, but meets Johann Christian Bach in London.

G. Cultural Beginnings

Performing Groups—Choral: German National Singspiel Co.
Music Publications: *Betrachtungen der Mannheimer Tonschule.*
Performing Centers: Bonn Nationaltheater; La Scala Opera House (Milan).
Other: Akademie-Konzerte (Mannheim); Astor and Co., flute manufacturers (London).

H. Musical Literature

François Bedos de Celles, *L'Art du facteur d'orgues III*; Anton Bemetzrieder, *Réflexions sur les leçons de musique*; William Billings, *The Singing Master's Assistant*; Johann N. Forkel, *Musikalisch-kritischen Bibliothek I*; William Hales, *Sonorum doctrina rationalis et experimentalis*; Carl L. Junker, *Betrachtungen über mahlerey, ton' und bildhauer kunsts*; Christian G. Thomas, *Praktische beiträge zur geschichte der Musik*; Vasili Trutovsky, *Russian Folksongs II*; Georg Vogler, *Kuhrpfälzische Tonschule.*

I. Musical Compositions

Chamber Music:

String Quartets: Charles G. Alexandre, *Six String Quartets*; Luigi Boccherini, *Six Quartets (B♭, g, E♭, A, F, f), Opus 26*; Antonio Sacchini, *Six Quartets, Opus 2*.

Sonatas/Solos: Johann F. Reichardt, *Six Violin Sonatas*.

Ensembles: Etienne Barrière, *Six Quartets, Opus 3* (two violins, viola, bass); Friedrich (W. H.) Benda, *Six Trio Sonatas, Opus 1*; Luigi Boccherini, *Six String Quintets (d, E♭, A, C, D, a), Opus 25*; Jean-Baptiste Bréval, *Six Quatuors concertants, Opus 5*; Wolfgang Amadeus Mozart, *Quartet in G for Flute and Strings, K. 285b–Quartet in A for Flute and Strings, K. 298*; Johann F. Reichardt, *Six Trio Sonatas, Opus 1*; George "Abbe" Vogler, *Piano Quartet in E*.

Piano: C. P. E. Bach, *Three Rondos (C, D, a), H.260–2–Twelve Variations in a on "Folie d'Espagna," H.263*; Jean-Frédéric Edelmann, *Three Clavecin Sonatas, Opus 6*; Tommaso Giordani, *Six Keyboard Sonatas, Opus 15*; Wolfgang Amadeus Mozart, *Sonata in a, K. 310*; Maria Theresia von Paradis, *Four Sonatas*; Samuel Wesley, *Eight Keyboard Sonatas (B♭, D, E, C, A, E, G, B♭), Opus 1*.

Choral/Vocal Music:

Choral: C. P. E. Bach, *Heilig, H.778–St. Mark Passion III, H.791(?)–Oster-Musik, H.804–Oster-Musik, H.805(?)*; Franz Joseph Haydn, *Missa St. Johannis de Deo in B♭*; Johann Naumann, *Mass in d, "Pastoalmesse"*; Johann F. Reichardt, *Gott ist unser Gesang* (cantata).

Vocal: Venanzio Rauzzini, *Twelve Italian Duettinos, Opus 5*; John S. Smith, *To Anacreon in Heaven* (tune, "Star-Spangled Banner").

Musical Stage: Agostino Accorimboni, *Le virtuose bizzarre*; Felice Alessandri, *Calliroe*; Johann André, *Der Alchymist*; Pasquale Anfossi, *Ezio–La forza della donne*; Johann Christian Bach, *La clemenza di Scipione, Opus 14*; Georg A. Benda, *Der Holzhauer*; Dmitri Bortniansky, *Quinto Fabio–Alcide*; Christian Cannabich, *Azakia*; João de Sousa Carvalho, *L'Angelica*; Domenico Cimarosa, *La stravaganze d'amore–Il retorno di Don Caladrino–Gli amanti comici*(?); Nicolas Dezède, *Zulima–Le Porteur de chaise*; Tommaso Giordani, *Il re pastore*; Christoph Willibald Gluck, *Iphigenie en Tauride*; François Gossec, *La fête de village*; André Grétry, *Le jugement de Midas–Les trois âges de l'opéra–L'amant jaloux*; Michael Haydn, *Abels Tod*; Johann A. Hiller, *Der Greis, Mann und Jungling*; Giacomo Insanguine, *Eumene*; Josef Mysliveček, *L'Olimpiade– Las Calliroe*; Johann G. Naumann, *Amphion*; Christian G. Neefe, *Sophonisbe*; Giovanni Paisiello, *Achille in Sciro–Lo sposa burlato*; Niccolò Piccinni, *Roland–Phaon*; Antonio Sacchini, *L'avaro deluso–L'amore soldato–Erifile*; Joseph Saint-Georges, *Europa riconosciuta*; Antonio Salieri, *L'Europa riconosciuta–La scuola de' gelosi*; Giuseppe Sarti, *Olimpiade–Scipione–I Contrattempi*; Joseph Schuster, *Der Alchymist*; William Shield, *The Flitch of Bacon*; Tommaso Traetta, *Artenice–La disfatta di Dario*; Peter Winter, *Armida*.

Orchestra/Band Music:

Concerted Music:

Piano: C. P. E. Bach, *Two Concertos (G, D), H.477,8–Double Concerto in E♭, H.479* (harpsichord, piano); George "Abbe" Vogler, *Six Easy Concertos, Opus 2*.

Violin: Etienne Barrière, *Concerto in A, Opus 5*.

Other: François Gossec, *Symphonie Concertante No. 2 in F Major*; Wolfgang Amadeus Mozart, *Flute Concerto in G, K. 313–Flute Concerto in D, K. 314–Concerto for Flute and Harp in C, K. 299*.

Ballet/Incidental Music: Luigi Boccherini, *Cefalo e Procri* (B); Christian Cannabich, *Das liebe des Cortes* (B); Felice de' Giardini, *Sappho* (IM); François Gossec, *Annette et Lubin* (B); George "Abbe" Vogler, *Hamlet* (IM).

Standard Works: Samuel Wesley, *Overture No. 2 in D*.

Symphonies: Christian Cannabich, *Six Symphonies, Opus 10*; Marie-Alexandre Guénin, *Three Symphonies (D, A, C), Opus 6*(?); Franz Joseph Haydn, *No. 53 in D–No. 64 in A, "Tempora mutantur"–No. 65 in A*; Wolfgang Amadeus Mozart, *Symphony No. 31, "Paris," K. 297*; Ignaz Pleyel, *Symphony in c, B.121–Symphony in A, B.122*.

1779

❅

Historical Highlights: The Treaty of Teschen ends the War of the Bavarian Succession; Spain joins France in the war against England; the British fight the Mahrattas in India; the first known iron bridge is built over the River Severn in England; the British are defeated at Stony Point, New York, by General Anthony Wayne—George Rogers Clark succeeds in taking over the Old Northwest Territory.

Art and Literature Highlights: Births—artists Washington Allston, Augustus Callcott, dramatist Adam Gottlob Oehlenschläger; Deaths—artists Thomas Chippendale, Jean-Baptiste Chardin, Anton Raphael Mengs. Art—Canova's *Daedalus and Icarus*, Chandler's *River View with Figures and Trees*; Longhi's *The Alchemist*; Literature—Lessing's *Nathan, the Wise*, Sheridan's *The Critic*, Warren's *The Motley Assembly, a Farce*.

Musical Highlights

A. Births

Composers: Angelo Maria Benincori (Italy) March 28; Ignacy Dobrzyński, Sr. (Poland) February 2; August Ferdinand Häser (Germany) October 15; Mariano Rodríques de Ledesma (Spain) December 14; Franz de Paula Rosa (Austria) August 17; Stefano Pavasi (Italy) January 22; Louis Alexandre Piccinni (France) September 10; Johann Baptist Schiedermayer (Germany) June 23; Johann Philipp Schmidt (Germany) September 8; Peter Ivanovich Turtchaninov (Russia) December 1.

Conductors: Johann Kaspar Aiblinger (Germany) February 23.

Singers: Josef Blahack (Hungarian tenor); Alexis de Garaudé (French vocalist) March 21; William Knyvett (British countertenor/composer) April 21; Thomas Moore (Irish singer/composer) May 28; Luise Reichardt (German soprano) April 11.

Performers: François Aimon (French cellist/conductor) October 4; Jean Ancot, *père* (Belgian violinist) October 22; Angelo Maria Benincori (Italian violinist) March 28; Ernst Köhler (German organist/composer) May 28; Friedrich Wilhelm Riem (German organist/composer) February 17; Oliver Shaw (American organist) March 13; Gottlob Wiedebein (German organist) July 27.

Others: Asa Hopkins (American woodwind maker) February 2; Auguste Leduc (French publisher) December 19; Carl Friedrich Peters (German publisher) March 30; (Jacob) Gottfried Weber (German music theorist/composer) March 1.

B. Deaths

Composers: Johann Adam (Germany) November 13; M. Romero de Avila (Spain) December 15; William Boyce (England) February 7; Tommaso Traetta (Italy) April 6.

Singers: Domenico Annibali (Italian castrato alto) December 19; Ernst Christoph Dressler (German tenor) April 6.

Performers: Josse Boutmy (Belgian organist/composer) November 27; Edmund Broderip (British organist) September 9; François Granier (French cellist/composr) April 18; Georg Philipp Kress (Germany violinist) February 2.

Others: Dom François Bedos de Celles (French organ scholar) November 25; Hinrich Philipp Johnson (German organ builder) February 12; Joseph de Laporte (French music author) December 19; Johann Georg Sulzer (Swiss aesthetician/lexicographer) February 25.

C. Debuts

Singers: Luigi Bassi (Italian bass—Pesaro, age thirteen); François Lays (French tenor—Paris); Aloysia Weber (German soprano—Vienna).

Performers: Friedrich Ludwig Dulon (German flutist—Berlin); Johann Ladislav Dussek (Bohemian pianist—Malines); Anne-Marie Krumpholtz (German harpist—Paris); Etienne Oxi (French bassoonist—Paris).

D. New Positions

Conductors: Bernardo Bittoni (maestro di cappella, Rieti Cathedral); Dmitri Bortniansky (Russian Imperial Church Choir, St. Petersburg); Luigi Braccini (maestro di cappella, ss Annunziata Monastery, Florence); Christian Gottlob Neefe (Grossmann-Hellmuth Co., Bonn); Giuseppe Sarti (maestro di cappella, Milan Cathedral); Jan Stefani (Warsaw Court Opera).

Others: Thomas Dupuis (organ, Chapel Royal, London); Giacomo Rampini (organ, Udine Cathedral); Johann Baptist Rauch (organ, Strasbourg Cathedral); Daniel Gottlob Türk (music director, University of Halle).

E. Prizes/Honors

Honors: Friedrich H. Graf (Swedish Royal Academy); John Stanley (Master of the King's Music, London).

F. Biographical Highlights

Ludwig van Beethoven begins futher piano lessons with Tobias Pfeiffer in Bonn; Dmitri Bortniansky leaves Italy after ten years to return to Russia and begin his career in choral conducting at the Imperial Court; William Crotch, age four, plays at Buckingham Palace for the king and queen; Christoph Willibald Gluck, suffering a severe stroke that leaves him partially paralyzed, retires from the music scene and returns to Vienna; Antonio Lolli leaves Russia for a wasteful life of gambling in which he loses the fortune he gained in Russia; Wolfgang Amadeus Mozart leaves Paris and returns to Salzburg.

G. Cultural Beginnings

Performing Groups—Choral: Mannheim National Opera Co.; Russian Imperial Chapel Choir (St. Petersburg).
Music Publishers: James Harrison (London).
Performing Centers: Mannheim National Theater; Teatro del Fondo (Naples); Teatro della Cannobiana (Milan).
Other: Erard Piano and Harp Manufacturers (Paris).

H. Musical Literature

John Alcock, *An Instructive and Entertaining Companion*; Jean-Joseph Amiot, *Mémoire sur la musique des Chinois*; Anton Bemetzreider, *Le Tolérantisme musical*; William Billings, *Music in Miniature*; Michel de Chabanon, *Observations sur la musique . . .* ; Johann Kirnberger, *Die Kunst der reinen Satzes in der Musik, aus sicheren Grundsätzen hergeleitet und mit deutlichen Beyspielen erläutert II*; Andrew Law, *Select Harmony*; John Smith, *Collection of English Songs, c. 1500*; Francisco Solano, *Novo tratado de musica metrica e rythmica*; Francesco Vallotti, *Della scienza teorica e pratica della moderne musica*; John Wesley, *The Power of Music*.

I. Musical Compositions

Chamber Music:

String Quartets: Jean-Baptiste Davaux, *Six Quartets, Opus 9*; Václav Pichl, *Six Quartets, Opus 2*; Samuel Wesley, *No. 1 in G.*
Sonata/Solos: Johann Christian Bach, *Six Violin Sonatas (D, G, C, A, D, F), Opus 16*; Antonio Sacchini, *Six Violin Sonatas, Opus 3.*
Ensembles: Johann Christian Bach, *Four Sonatas (Trio Sonatas–C, A, D, B♭), Opus 15*; Luigi Boccherini, *Six String Quintets (A, G, e, E♭, g, b), Opus 27–Six String Quintets (F, A, E♭, C, d, B♭), Opus 28–Six String Quintets (D, c, F, A, E♭, g), Opus 29*; Felice de' Giardini, *Six String Trios, Opus 20.*
Piano: C. P. E. Bach, *Four Rondos (E, F, B♭, G), H.265–8*; Johann Christian Bach, *Six Keyboard Sonatas (G, c, E♭, G, A, B♭), Opus 17*; Jean-Frédéric Edelmann, *Two Sonatas for Clavecin and Violin, ad. lib., Opus 7–Three Sonatas for Clavecin and Violin, ad. lib., Opus 8*; Wolfgang Amadeus Mozart, *Two Church Sonatas, K. 328 and 329.*

Choral/Vocal Music:

Choral: C. P. E. Bach, *St. Luke Passion III, H.791(?)*; Luigi Cherubini, *Mass "Te laudamus Domine"*; Johann A. Hasse, *Mass in E♭*; Michael Haydn, *Missa S. Aloysli*; Wolfgang Amadeus Mozart, *"Coronation" Mass in C, K. 317–Vesper Service in C, K. 321–Regina*

Coeli in C, K. 276; François Philidor, *Carmen saeculare*; Johann H. Rolle, *Thirza und ihre söhne*; Tommaso Traetta, *The Passion According to St. John.*

Vocal: Johann F. Reichardt, *Oden und Lieder I–Frohe lieder für deutsche männer.*

Musical Stage: Agostino Accorimboni, *Il marchese di Castelverde*; Felice Alessandri, *Adriano in Siria*; Pasquale Anfossi, *Cleopatra–Il matrimonio per inganno*; Johann Christian Bach, *Amadis de Gaule*; George A. Benda, *Philon und Theone–Pygmalion*; Giuseppe M. Cambini, *Rose et Carloman*; João de Sousa Carvalho, *Perseo*; Domenico Cimarosa, *L'infedeltà fedele–L'Italiana in Londra*; Evstigney Fomin, *Melnik*; Giuseppe Giordani, *Epponina*; Christoph Willibald Gluck, *Echo et Narcisse*; André Grétry, *Aucassin et Nicolette–Les evénements imprévus*; Franz Joseph Haydn, *L'isola disabitata–La vera costanza*; Michael Haydn, *Der englishche Patriot*; Johann A. Hiller, *Das Grab des Mufti*; Ignaz Holzbauer, *La morte di Didone*; Giacomo Insanguine, *Medonte*; Vicente Martín y Soler, *Ifigenia in Aulide*; Gaetano Monti, *Il gelosa sincerato*; Wolfgang Amadeus Mozart, *Zaide, K. 344*; Josef Mysliveček, *Armida–Il Demetrio–La Circe*; Christian G. Neefe, *Macbeth*; Giovanni Paisiello, *Gli astrologi immaginari–Il matrimonio inaspettato*; Niccolò Piccinni, *Il vago disprezzato*; Johann Reichardt, *Ino*; Antonio Sacchini, *Enea e Lavinia*; Giuseppe Sarti, *Siroe–Adrianno in Sciro*; William Shield, *The Cobbler of Casterbury.*

Orchestra/Band Music:

Concerted Music:

Piano: Wolfgang Amadeus Mozart, *Concerto No. 10 in E♭, K. 365, for Two Pianos.*

Violin: Václav Pichl, *Three Concertos, Opus 3*; Joseph Boulogne de Saint-Georges, *Two Symphonie concertantes (F, A), Opus 10–Two Concertos (A, B♭), Opus 7*; Samuel Wesley, *Concerto No. 1 in C.*

Other: Friedrich (W. H.) Benda, *Two Flute Concertos, Opus 2*; Wolfgang Amadeus Mozart, *Symphonie concertante in E♭, K. 364.*

Ballet/Incidental Music: Felice Alessandri, *Venere in Cipro* (B)–*L'enlèvement des Sabines* (B); Friedrich L. Benda, *Narren ballett* (B); François Gossec, *Mirza* (B)–*Les scythes enchainés* (B).

Standard Works: Wolfgang Amadeus Mozart, *Serenade in D, K. 320, "Posthorn"–Sinfonia Concertante in E♭, K. 364*; Joseph Saint-Georges, *Two Symphonies Concertantes, Opus 10.*

Symphonies: Franz Joseph Haydn, *No. 66 in B♭–No. 67 in F–No. 68 in B♭–No.69 in C, "Laudon"–No. 70 in D*; Ludwig W. Lachnith, *Six Symphonies, Opus 1(?)*; Wolfgang Amadeus Mozart, *Symphonies No. 32 in G, K. 318–No. 33 in B♭, K. 319*; Joseph Boulogne de Saint-Georges, *Two Symphonies (G, D), Opus 11*; George "Abbe" Vogler, *Symphony in G.*

1780

Historical Highlights: Second Mysore War takes place in India; Bo-hemia and Hungary both abolish serfdom in their territories; Maria Theresa dies—Joseph II becomes sole ruler of the Austrian Empire; the estimated colonial population is 2,781,000; colonial forces are defeated at the Battle of Camden but win a victory at King's Mountain.
Art and Literature Highlights: Births—artists Alfred E. Chalon, Jean-Auguste Ingres, Ferdinand Jagemann, writers William E. Channing, Anna Maria Porter; Deaths—philosopher Étienne Bonnot de Condillac, artists Canaletto, Nicolás Fernández de Moratín. Art—Copley's *Death of the Earl of Chatham in the House of Lords*, Morland's *The Angler's Repast*; Literature—Cowley's *Belle's Stratagems*, Crabbe's *The Candidate*, Wieland's *Oberon*.

Musical Highlights

A. Births
   Composers: Victor-Charles Dourlen (France) November 3; Uri Keeler Hill (U.S.A.) December 10; Conradin Kreutzer (Germany) November 22; Franz Lessel (Poland)(?).
   Singers: François van Campenhout (Belgian tenor/composer) February 5; Angelica Catalani (Italian soprano) May 10; Henri Etienne Dérivis (French bass) August 2; Louis Nourrit (French tenor) August 4; Giuseppe Vincenzo Siboni (Italian tenor) January 27.
   Performers: Friedrich Wilhelm Berner (German organist) May 16; Auguste Bertini (French pianist/composer) June 5; Franz Clement (Austrian violinist/conductor) November 17; François-Joseph Dizi (Belgian harpist) January 14; Michael Henkel (German organist/composer) June 18; (Christian) Theodor Weinlig (German organist/composer) July 25.
   Others: Friedrich von Drieberg (German music historian) December 10; Joseph Fröhlich (German music theorist) May 28; Friedrich Heinrich von der Hagen (German scholar/music author) February 19; Johann August Heinroth (German music author/composer) June 19; Peter Lichtenthal (Austrian music author/composer) May 10; Charles-Simon Richault (French publisher) May 10.

B. Deaths
   Composers: Pierre-Montan Berton (France) May 14; Francesco Antonio Vallotti (Italy) January 10.
   Singers: Benedetta Emilia Agricola (Italian soprano) September.

Performers: Domenico Ferrari (Italian violinist/composer) September; Johann Ludwig Krebs (German organist/composer) January 1.

C. Debuts
Singers: Matteo Babbini (Italian tenor—Italy); Louis Chardiny (French baritone—Paris); Celeste Coltellini (Italian mezzo-soprano—Milan); Nancy Storace (British soprano—Florence).
Performers: Antonio Bartolomeo Bruni (Italian violinist—Paris); Rodolphe Kreutzer (French violinist—Paris).

D. New Positions
Conductors: Eleutério Leal (mestre de capela, Lisbon Cathedral)(?); Antonio Lolli (kapellmeister, St. Petersburg); Johann Abraham Schulz (kapellmeister, Rheinsberg).
Others: Robert Broderip (organ, Mayor's Chapel, Bristol); Philip Cogan (organ, St. Patrick's Cathedral, Dublin); Antoine Dauvergne (director, Paris Opera—third term).

E. Prizes/Honors
Honors: Franz Joseph Haydn (Modena Philharmonic Society); Joseph Martin Kraus (Swedish Royal Academy).

F. Biographical Highlights
Muzio Clementi begins a concert tour of the main cities of Europe and engages in a friendly keyboard "duel" with Mozart in Vienna; Sébastien Erard builds what is believed to be the first "modern" piano; François-Joseph Gossec becomes second conductor at the Paris Opera; William Herschel joins the Bath Literary and Philosophical Society; Antonio Lolli, broke from gambling, returns to Russia and regains his position as kapellmeister and soloist in the court of Catherine the Great; Wolfgang Amadeus Mozart moves to Munich for the production of his *Idomeneo*; Johann Peter Salomon, on the disbandment of the orchestra in Rheinsburg, leaves Germany, visits Paris, and finally settles in London; Giovanni Battista Viotti joins Gaetano Pugnani in a concert tour of Germany, Poland, and Russia.

G. Cultural Beginnings
Performing Groups—Choral: Dramatiske Selskab (Oslo).
Performing Centers: Bordeaux Grand Theater; Leipzig Gewandhaus; Petrovsky Theater (Moscow).
Other: John Betts, violin maker (London); Dilettanti Musical Society (Birmingham); Johannes Kohler, wind instrument maker (London).

H. Musical Literature
Johann J. Engel, *Über die musikalische Malerei*; Johann N. Forkel, *Genauere Bestimmung einiger musikalischer Begriffe*; Philipp J. Frick,

The Art of Musical Modulation; Johann A. Hiller, *Anweisung zum musikalisch-zierlichen Gesang*; Jean de La Borde, *Essai sur la musique ancienne et moderne*; Louis F. Lefébure, *Nouveau Solfège*; James Nares, *Treatise on Singing*; Giovenale Sacchi, *Delle quinte successive nel contrappunto e delle regolo degli accompagnamenti*; Francisco Solano, *Dissertaçâo sobre o caracter do musica*; Georg Vogler, *Entwurf einer neuen Wörtersbuch für die Tonschule*.

I. **Musical Compositions**
   Chamber Music:
   String Quartets: Johann G. Albrechtsberger, *Six "quators en fugues"*; Luigi Boccherini, *Six Quartets (E♭, e, D, C, g, A), Opus 32*; Giuseppe A. Capuzzi, *Six Quartets, Opus 1–Six Quartets, Opus 2*; Jean-Baptiste Davaux, *Six Quartets, Opus 10*; Ludwig Lachnith, *Six Quartets, Opus 7*; Josef Mysliveček, *Six Quartets, Opus 1*; Giovanni Paisiello, *Six Quartets (A, C, E♭, D, A, C)(?)*; Johann B. Vanhal, *Six Quartets, Opus 4*; Samuel Wesley, *Quartet No. 2 in c.*
   Sonata/Solos: Christian G. Neefe, *Violin Sonata*; Francesco Petrini, *Six Harp Sonatas, Opus 3–Two Harp Sonatas, Opus 4.*
   Ensembles: Luigi Boccherini, *Six String Quintets (B♭, a, C, E♭, e, C), Opus 30–Six String Quintets (E♭, G, B♭, c, A, F), Opus 31*; Felice de' Giardini, *Six Trios, Opus 18* (guitar, violin, piano)*–Six Harpsichord Quartettos, Opus 21.*
   Piano: Johann E. Altenburg, *Six Sonatas* (publication); C. P. E. Bach, *Two Sonatas (F, A), H.269,70–Rondo in G, H.271*; Luigi Cherubini, *Six Sonatas (F, C, B♭, G, D, E♭)*; Muzio Clementi, *Five Piano Sonatas, Opus 1–Three Four-Hand Duets (C, E♭, G), Opus 3–Three Keyboard Sonatas (B♭, F, E♭), Opus 5–Six Piano Sonatas (D, E♭, C, G, B♭, F), Opus 4* (violin ad. lib); Franz Joseph Haydn, *Piano Sonatas No. 31–36*; Johann Baptiste Krumpholz, *Harpsichord Sonata No. 1(?)*; Wolfgang Amadeus Mozart, *Church Sonata in C, K. 336*; Alexander Reinagle, *Twenty-Four Short and Easy Pieces, Opus 1–Twenty-Four Short and Easy Pieces, Opus 2.*
   Organ: Luigi Cherubini, *Sonata for Two Organs.*
   Choral/Vocal Music:
   Choral: Paolo T. Alberghi, *Magnificat*; C. P. E. Bach, *Auferstehung und Himmelfahrt Jesu, H.777–St. John Passion III, H.791(?)–Oster-Musik, H.806*; Prosper-Didier Deshayes, *Les Macchabées*; Carl Ditters von Dittersdorf, *Job*; Baldassare Galuppi, *L'Anfione* (cantata); Wolfgang Amadeus Mozart, *Solemn Mass in C, K. 337–Vespers in C, K. 339*; Johann F. Reichardt, *Ariadne auf Naxos–Der May* (cantatas); Vincenzo Righini, *La sorpresa amorosa.*
   Vocal: C. P. E. Bach, *Geistliche gesänge I, H.749*; Johann Reichardt, *Oden und lieder II.*

Musical Stage: Agostino Accorimboni, *Il podestà di Tufo antico;* Felice Alessandri, *Erifile–Attalo re di Bitinia;* Pasquale Anfossi, *Tito nelle Gallie–La finta cingara per amore;* Michael Arne, *The Artifice;* Georg Benda, *Das tartarische Gesetz;* João de Sousa Carvalho, *Testoride argonauta;* Luigi Cherubini, *Il Quinto Fabio;* Domenico Cimarosa, *Cajo Mario–I finti nobili–Le donne rivali–Il Falegname;* Franz Danzi, *Azakia–Cleopatra;* Antoine Dauvergne, *Le sicilien;* Nicolas Dezède, *Cécile–A trompeur, trompeur et demi;* André Grétry, *Andromaque;* Franz Joseph Haydn, *La fedelta premiata;* Giacomo Insanguine, *Montezuma;* William Jackson, *Lord of the Manor;* Vicente Martín y Soler, *Ipermestra–Andromaca;* Josef Mysliveček, *Antigono–Medonte;* Christian G. Neefe, *Adelheit von Veltheim;* Giovanni Paisiello, *La finta amante–Alcide al bivio;* François Philidor, *Persée;* Niccolò Piccinni, *Atys;* Johann Reichardt, *Liebe nur beglückt;* Joseph Saint-Georges, *L'amant anonyme;* Anton Schweitzer, *Rosamunde;* William Shield, *The Deaf Lover–The Siege of Gibraltar;* Ernst W. Wolf, *Alceste;* Johann Zumsteeg, *Das tartarische Gesetz.*

Orchestra/Band Music:

Concerted Music:

    Violin: Etienne Barrière, *Concerto in D, Opus 7*(?).

    Other: Tommaso Giordani, *Six Flute Concertos, Opus 19;* Joseph Boulogne de Saint-George, *Two Symphonies concertante, Opus 10.*

Ballet/Incidental Music: Christian Cannabich, *La descente d'Hercule* (B); Vicente Martín y Soler, *La bella Arsene* (B)–*I ratti Sabini* (B); Joseph Boulogne de Saint-Georges, *L'amant anonyme* (B).

Standard Works: Samuel Wesley, *Overture No. 3 in C.*

Symphonies: Carl Philipp Emanuel Bach, *Four Hamburg Symphonies, Wg.183;* Gaetano Brunetti, *Nos. 14, 15 (C, B♭)–Nos. 18–20 (D, b, E♭);* Franz Joseph Haydn, *No. 71 in B♭;* Wolfgang Amadeus Mozart, *No. 34 in C, K. 338;* Peter von Winter, *Symphony in D–Symphony in F*(?).

1781

❊

Historical Highlights: Emperor Joseph II abolishes serfdom, grants religious tolerance and freedom of the press in the Austrian territories; in America, the British forces under General Cornwallis surrender at Yorktown after the French Navy blockades Chesapeake Bay; the Articles of Confederation are ratified by Maryland, the last colony to do so.

Art and Literature Highlights: Births—sculptor Francis Chantrey, writers Achim von Arnim, Adelbert von Chamisso; Deaths—writers Johannes Ewald, Gotthold Lessing, Josiah Smith. Art—Mansfield's *Por-*

trait of Franz Joseph Haydn, Nepomuk's *The Mozart Family*, C. W. Peale's *George Washington at the Battle of Princeton*; Literature—Freneau's *The British Prison-Ship*, Kant's *Critique of Pure Reason*, John Witherspoon's *The Druid*.

Musical Highlights

A. **Births**

Composers: Albert Auguste Androt (France); Felice Blangini (Italy-France) November 18; Anthony Philip Heinrich (Bohemia-U.S.A.) March 11; Friedrich Wollanck (Germany) November 3.

Conductors: John Charles Clifton (England) November 7; François-Antoine Habeneck (France) January 22; Martin-Joseph Mengal (Belgium) January 27.

Singers: Giovanni Battista Velluti (Italian castrato soprano) January 28.

Performers: Louis-François Dauprat (French horn virtuoso/composer) May 23; Dorothea von Ertmann (German pianist) May 3; Mauro Giuliani (Italian guitarist/composer) July 27; Charles-Philippe Lafont (French violinist) December 1; François-Joseph Nadermann (French harpist) December 18; Giovanni Battista Polledro (Italian violinist/composer) June 10; Louis Barthélemy Pradher (French pianist) December 18; Christian Friedrich Uber (German violinist/ conductor) April 22; Michael Umlauf (Austran violinist/conductor) August 9; Gustave Vogt (French oboist/composer) March 18.

Others: Anton Diabelli (Austrian publisher/composer) September 6; Karl C. F. Krause (German music author) May 6; Vincent Novello (British publisher) September 6; Guillaume-Louis Wilhelm (French music educator) December 18.

B. **Deaths**

Composers: Antonio Aurisicchio (Italy) September 4; Thomas Alexander Erskine (Scotland) October 9; Garret Wesley Mornington (Ireland) May 22; Josef Mysliveček (Bohemia) February 4; Giacomo Puccini (Italy) May 16; Anton Zimmermann (Austria) October 16.

Singers: Faustina Bordoni (Italian mezzo-soprano) November 4; Anna Franziska Hatašová (Benda) (Bohemian soprano) December 15.

Performers: John Barker (British organist) April 3; Adolph Carl Kunzen (German organist/composer) July 11; Giacomo Puccini (Italian organist/composer) May 16; Johann Siebenkäs (German organist) January 22.

Others: Jean Laurent de Béthizy (French music theorist) November 17; Giuseppe Bustelli (Italian impresario) April; Jean-Esprit Isnard

(French organ builder) March 16; Georg Simon Löhlein (German music theorist/composer) December 16.

C. Debuts

Singers: Martin Joseph Adrien (Belgian bass—Paris); Samuel Harrison (British tenor—Gloucester).

Performers: Johann Baptiste Cramer (French pianist—London); Heinrich Domnich (German horn virtuoso—Paris); Jean Lebrun (French horn virtuoso—Paris).

D. New Positions

Conductors: Domenico Corri (Edinburgh Opera); Karl Hanke (music director, Warsaw); Giacomo Antonio Insanguine (maestro di cappella, Cappella del Tesoro di San Gennaro); Pierre La Houssaye (Comédie-Italienne, Paris); Jean François Lesueur (maître de chapelle, Dijon Cathedral); Jean-Baptiste Rey (Concert Spirituel, Paris).

Others: Thomas Greatorex (organ, Carlisle Cathedral).

E. Prizes/Honors

Honors: Giovanni Gaiani (Accademia Filarmonica, Bologna).

F. Biographical Highlights

Ludwig van Beethoven quits school and begins studying music privately with Neefe, Koch, and Rovantini; Christoph Willibald Gluck suffers a second stroke; Johannes Simon Mayr begins the study of theology at the University of Ingolstadt; Wolfgang Amadeus Mozart cuts his ties with Salzburg and moves permanently to Vienna, where he meets Franz Joseph Haydn with whom he becomes fast friends; Georg Joseph "Abbe" Vogler goes to Paris for the production of his *La Kermesse*.

G. Cultural Beginnings

Performing Groups—Instrumental: Leipzig Gewandhaus Orchestra.

Educational: Collège Dramatique et Lyrique (Amsterdam); Università de' Filarmonici (Piacenza).

Music Publishers: Heinrich Bossler Co. (Speyer—to Darmstadt in 1792); William Forster Publishing Co. (London); Friedrich Meyer (St. Petersburg).

Performing Centers: Esterházy Opera House II; Nuovo Teatro Civico del Verzaro (Perugia); Ständetheater (Prague).

Other: Broadwood Grand Piano (first known).

H. Musical Literature

Salvatore Bertezen, *Principi della musica teorico-prattica*; William Billings, *Psalm Singer's Amusement*; Johann A. Hiller, *Über die Musik und deren werkungen*; Johann P. Kirnberger, *Grundsätze des General-*

basses, als erste Linien zur Composition; Georg S. Löhlein, *Clavier-Schule II*; Giovanni Martini, *Storia della Musica III*; John Maxwell, *An Essay upon Tune*; John Parry, *Cambrian Harmony: A Collection of Ancient Welsh Airs*; Girolamo Tiraboschi, *Biblioteca Modenese I*; Georg F. Wolf, *Kurzer aber deutlicher Unterricht in Klavierspielen*.

I. Musical Compositions
Chamber Music:

String Quartets: Luigi Boccherini, *Six String Quartets (E, C, G, B♭, e, E♭), Opus 33*; Nicolas Dalayrac, *Six String Quartets*; Franz Joseph Haydn, *"Russian" Quartets, Opus 33: No. 1 in e–No. 2 in E♭, "The Joke"–No. 3 in C, "The Bird"–No. 4 in B♭–No. 5 in G, "How Do You Do?" No. 6 in D*; Vincenzo Manfredini, *Six String Quartets*(?); Josef Mysliveček, *Six String Quartets, Opus 2*.

Sonata/Solos: Johann Christian Bach, *Four Violin Sonatas (G, D, E♭, G), Opus 18*; Friedrich (W. H.) Benda, *Three Violin Sonatas, Opus 3*; Benjamin Blake, *Six Duets for Violin and Viola*; Wolfgang Amadeus Mozart, *Variations in G, K. 359–Variations in g, K. 360* (violin, piano)–*Violin Sonatas in F, K. 376–in F, K. 377–in G, K. 379–in E♭, K. 380*; Jan Vaňhal, *Four Viola Sonatas, Opus 51*.

Ensembles: Johann Albrechtsberger, *Twelve Preludes and Two Fugues, Opus 3*(?); Luigi Boccherini, *Six String Trios (f, G, E♭, D, C, E), Opus 34*; Jean-Baptiste Bréval, *Six Quartuors concertants, Opus 7*; Jean-Frédéric Edelmann, *Four Quartets, Opus 9* (clavecin, strings); Wolfgang Amadeus Mozart, *Quartet in F Major, K. 370* (oboe, strings); Joseph Boulogne de Saint-Georges, *Three harpsichord/piano Sonatas* (with violin).

Piano: Marianna von Auenbrugger, *Sonata*; C. P. E. Bach, *Sonata in G, H.273–Rondo in E, H.274*; Muzio Clementi, *Keyboard Duet, Opus 6, No. 1–Two Keyboard Sonatas, Opus 6, No. 2,3*; Wolfgang Amadeus Mozart, *Sonata in D, K. 448, for 2 Pianos*.

Choral/Vocal Music:
Choral:

Oratorios: Johann G. Albrechtsberger, *Die Pilgrime auf Golgotha*; Felice Alessandri, *Bethulia liberata*; C. P. E. Bach, *St. Matthew Passion IV, H.794*(?); Jean-Frédéric Edelmann, *Esther*; Bonaventura Furlanetto, *Dies extrema mundi–David Goliath triumphator*; Giuseppe Gazzaniga, *I profeti al Calvario*; Johann Vogel, *Jephte*.

Others: Francis Hopkinson, *The Temple of Minerva* (dramatic cantata); Wolfgang Amadeus Mozart, *Kyrie in d, K. 341*.

Vocal: C. P. E. Bach, *Geistliche gesänge II, H.752*; Luigi Boccherini, *Stabat Mater*; Franz Joseph Haydn, *Six Songs, Set I–Six Songs, Set II*; Johann Reichardt, *Oden und Lieder III–Gedichte von R. C. I. Rudolphi*.

Musical Stage: Felice Alessandri, *Arbace–Il vecchio geloso*; Johann André, *Die Entführung aus dem Serail*; Pasquale Anfossi, *Il trionfo d'Arianna–Lo sposo per equivoco*; Michael Arne, *The Choice of Harlequin*; Ferdinando Bertoni, *Ezio*; Christian Cannabich, *Electra*; João de Sousa Carvalho, *Leleuco, rè di Siria*; Domenico Cimarosa, *Alessandro nell'Indie–Giannina e Bernardone*; Nicolas Dalayrac, *Le petit Souper–Le Chevalier à la mode*; Luigi Gatti, *Antigono*; Giuseppe Gazzaniga, *La stravagante*; Giuseppe Giordani, *Elpinice*; François Giroust, *Rosemonde*; André Grétry, *Emilie*; Vicente Martín y Soler, *Astartea*; Gaetano Monti, *Le donne vendicate–La contadina accorta*; Wolfgang Amadeus Mozart, *Idomeneo, K. 366*; Johann G. Naumann, *Elisa–Osiride*; Giovanni Paisiello, *La serva padrona*; Niccolò Piccinni, *Iphigénie en Tauride–Adéle de Ponthieu*; Venanzio Rauzzini, *L'omaggio de paesani al signore del contado*; Antonio Sacchini, *Mitridate*; Antonio Salieri, *Der Rauchfangkehrer*; Giuseppe Sarti, *Giulio Sabino*; William Shield, *Robinson Crusoe*; George "Abbe" Vogler, *Erwin und Elmire–Albert III von Baiern*; Nicola Zingarelli, *Montezuma*.

Orchestra/Band Music:
Concerted Music:
   Violin: Wolfgang Amadeus Mozart, *Rondo in C, K. 373*; Samuel Wesley, *Concerto No. 2 in D*.
   Other: Wolfgang Amadeus Mozart, *Concerto Rondo, K. 371, for Horn and Orchestra*; Georg "Abbe" Vogler, *Symphonie concertante in E♭*.
Ballet/Incidental Music: Franz Danzi, *Laura Rosetti* (IM); François Gossec, *La fête de Mirza* (B); Vicente Martín y Soler, *La regina di Golconda* (B).
Standard Works: Wolfgang Amadeus Mozart, *Serenades, K. 361 and 375, for Winds*; Christian G. Neefe, *Lessings Totenfeier-Overture*.
Symphonies: Johann Christian Bach, *Six Grand Overtures (E♭, B♭, D, b, E, D), Opus 18*; Jean-Baptiste Cardonne, *Symphony in G*(?); Carl Ditters von Dittersdorf, *Six Symphonies, Opus 13*; Franz Joseph Haydn, *No. 72 in D–No. 74 in E♭–No. 75 in D*; Ludwig W. Lachnith, *Three Symphonies, Opus 6*(?); Samuel Wesley, *Sinfonia obligato in D–Symphony in A*.

1782
❄

Historical Highlights: The British sign a peace treaty with the Mahrattas in India; the Spanish fail in an attempt to take Gibraltar away from the British; James Watt builds the first working rotary steam engine; the

American Revolution ends; the Great Seal of the United States is adopted by the Continental Congress; the bald eagle is chosen as the official national bird.

Art and Literature Highlights: Births—artists John Cotman, Charles Fraser, Johannes de Troostwijck, writers Steen Blicher, Félicité de Lamennais, Giovanni Niccolini. Deaths—artists Charles Fraser, Richard Wilson, writer José de Cadalso y Vázquez. Art—Fuseli's *The Nightmare*, Stuart's *Gentleman Skater*, Wright's *Benjamin Franklin*; Literature—Fanny Burney's *Cecilia*, Fonvizin's *The Minor*, Trumbull's *M'Fingal, A Modern Epic*.

Musical Highlights

A. Births

Composers: Daniel-François Auber (France) January 29; Jonathan Blewitt (England) July 19; Carlo Coccia (Italy) April 14; Joseph Drechsler (Bohemia-Austria) May 26.

Singers: Thomas (Simpson) Cooke (Irish tenor/instrumentalist) December 21; François Foignet (French tenor/composer) February 17; Jacques Émile Lavigne (French tenor).

Performers: Thaddäus Amadé (Hungarian pianist/composer) January 11; Antoine Tranquile Berbiguier (French flutist) December 21; Joseph von Blumenthal (Belgian violinist) November 1; John Field (Irish pianist/composer) July 26; Jacques-Féréol Mazas (French violinist/composer) September 23; Niccolò Paganini (Italian violinist/composer) October 27.

Others: Conrad Graf (Austrian piano maker) November 17; Friedrich Griepenkerl (German music editor) December 10; Friedrich Hofmeister (German publisher) January 24.

B. Deaths

Composers: Pedro Antonio Avondano (Portugal) October 23; Johann Christian Bach (Germany-England) January 1; Placidus Camerloher (Germany) July 21; Giuseppe Farinelli (Italy) July 15.

Singers: Cecilia Grassi (Italian soprano) May.

Performers: Johann Baptist Baumgartner (German cellist) May 18; John Burton (British harpsichordist/pianist) September 3; Jean-Baptiste Forqueray (French viola-da-gambist/composer) August 15; Catherine Hamilton (British harpsichordist) August 27; Samuel Howard (British organist/composer) July 13; Johann Christoph Monn (Austrian pianist/composer) June 24; Louis-Henri Paisible (French violinist) March 19; John Parry (British harpist) October 7; Joseph Riepel (Austrian violinist/music theorist) October 23; Christoph Gottlieb Schröter (German organist/music theorist) May

20; Josef Ferdinand Seger (Bohemian organist/composer) April 22; Robert Wainwright (British organist) July 15.
Others: Daniel Bernoulli (Swiss mathematician/acoustician) March 17; Pietro Metastasio (Italian poet/librettist) April 12; Kane O'Hara (Irish librettist) June 17; Johann N. Ritter (German organ builder) February 28; Carlo Giovanni Testori (Italian music theorist) May 20.

C. **Debuts**
Singers: Girolamo Crescentini (Italian castrato mezzo-soprano—Padua).
Performers: (Amélie) Julie Candeille (French pianist—Paris); Francois Devienne (French flutist—Paris); Charles H. Florio (British flutist—London); Giovanni Battista Viotti (Italian violinist—Paris).

D. **New Positions**
Conductors: Joachim Albertini (hofkapellmeister, Warsaw); Cándido José Ruano (maestro de capilla, Avila Cathedral).
Others: Carl Christian Agthe (organ, Ballenstedt Court); Benjamin Cooke (organ, St. Martin-in-the-Fields); Giovanni Battista Grazioli (organ, St. Mark's, Venice); Richard Langdon (organ, Armagh Cathedral); Christian Gottlob Neefe (organ, Bonn Court); William Shrubsole (organ, Bangor Cathedral); Richard Wainwright (organ, St. Peter's, Liverpool).

F. **Biographical Highlights**
Carl Friedrich Abel visits Germany and begins performing and composing for the Russian Court at St. Petersburg; Ludwig van Beethoven begins substituting for Neefe at the organ in the Bonn court chapel; Domenico Cimarosa becomes the music master at a girl's school in Venice; William Herschel makes his last public appearance as a musician before turning permanently to astronomy; Wolfgang Amadeus Mozart marries Constanze Weber and moves to Vienna; Joseph Weigl begins the study of music with Johann Georg Albrechtsberger.

G. **Cultural Beginnings**
Educational: Royal Irish Academy of Music (Dublin).
Music Publishers: F. Ernst Leuckart Publishing Co. (Breslau).
Music Publications: *Musikalisches Kunstmagazin*.
Performing Centers: Riga City Theater (Latvia); Stockholm Opera House; Teatro degli Armeni (Livorno).
Other: Alexander Brothers, instrument makers (Mainz); William Southwell, piano maker (Dublin).

H. **Musical Literature**
Johann F. Christmann, *Elementarbuch der Tonkunst*; Christian E. Graf, *Thoroughbass Method*; William Jackson, *Thirty Letters on Various Sub-*

jects; Carl L. Junker, *Einige der vornehmsten pflichten eines Kapellmeister oder Musikdirector;* Johann P. Kirnberger, *Gedanken über die verschiedenen Lehrarten in der Komposition, als Vorbereitung zur Fugenkenntniss;* Heinrich Koch, *Versuch einer Anleitung zur Composition;* Andrew Law, *Collection of Hymns for Social Worship;* Pierre-Joseph Roussier, *Mémoire sur la nouvelle Harpe de M. Cousineau;* Christoph G. Schröter, *Letzte beschäftigung mit musikalischen dingen;* Georg Vogler, *Essai de diriger le goût des amateurs de musique;* Ernst W. Wolf, *Kleine musikalische Reise.*

I. Musical Compositions
Chamber Music:
String Quartets: Johann G. Albrechtsberger, *Six quatuors en fugues, Opus 2;* Ludwig W. Lachnith, *6 Quartets, Opus 7;* Wolfgang Amadeus Mozart, *Quartet in G, K. 387;* Pietro Nardini, *Six Quartets;* Pierre Vachon, *Six Quartets Concertant, Opus 11.*

Sonata/Solos: Friedrich L. Benda, *Violin Sonata;* Jan L. Dussek, *Three Violin Sonatas (B♭,G,C), Opus 1;* Wolfgang Amadeus Mozart, *Violin Sonata in A, K. 402* (unfinished)–*Violin Sonata in C, K. 404* (unfinished).

Ensembles: Johann Christian Bach, *Six Sinfonia for Woodwind Quintet, T.285;* Etienne Barrière, *Six Quartets, Opus 8* (two violins, viola, bass); Benjamin Blake, *Six Duets, Opus 2* (violin, viola); Jean-Baptiste Bréval, *Six Trios, Opus 8* (flute, violin, cello); Gaetano Brunetti, *Six String Trios, Opus 3;* François Devienne, *Six Trios, Opus 17* (bassoon, violin, cello); Carl Ditters von Dittersdorf, *Six String Quintets;* Ludwig W. Lachnith, *Six Trio Sonatas, Opus 5*(?); Wolfgang Amadeus Mozart, *Quintet in E♭, K. 407* (horn, strings); George "Abbe" Vogler, *Six Trio Sonatas, Opus 6.*

Piano: Muzio Clementi, *Three Keyboard Sonatas (E♭, C, g), Opus 7*–*Three Keyboard Sonatas (g, E♭, B♭), Opus 8;* Jean-François Edelmann, *Four Clavecin Sonatas, Opus 10* (violin ad. lib.); Ludwig W. Lachnith, *Five Harpsichord Sonatas, Opus 8*(?); Wolfgang Amadeus Mozart, *Variations on "Ah vous dirai-je, maman," K. 265;* Johann F. Reichardt, *Six Sonatas, Opus 3*–*Three Sonatas, Opus 4.*

Organ: François Barthélémon, *Six Organ Voluntaries, Opus 2.*
Choral/Vocal Music:
Choral: Joachim Albertini, *Missa solemnis;* Felice Alessandri, *Il tempio della fama* (cantata); Francesco Azzopardi, *La [Passione di Cristo;* C. P. E. Bach, *St. Mark Passion IV, H.795*(?); Domenico Cimarosa, *Mass in G–Giuditta–Absolamo* (oratorios); Baldassare Galuppi, *Il ritorno di Tobia* (oratorio); Christoph Willibald Gluck, *De Profundis;* Franz Joseph Haydn, *Missa Cellensis in C (Mariazeller-Messe);* Michael Haydn, *Missa Sancte Ruperti–Sanctificatio Julilaei* (cantata); Étienne Méhul, *Ode Sacrée.*

Vocal: Carl Christian Agthe, *Lieder eines leichten und fliessenden Gesangs*; Georg C. Grosheim, *Hessische kadettenlieder*; William Jackson, *Twelve Canzonets, Opus 13*(?); Johann G. Naumann, *Forty Freymäuerlieder zum Gebrauch der teutschen auch französischen Tafellogen*; Johann F. Reichardt, *Oden und lieder von Kleist und Hagedorn*.

Musical Stage: Felice Alessandri, *La finta principessa*; Johann André, *Elmine–Die Werbung aus Liebe*; Pasquale Anfossi, *Zemira–Il trionfo della costanza*; Michael Arne, *Vertumus and Pomona*; João de Sousa Carvalho, *Penelope nella partenza da Sparta–Everado II rè di Lituania*; Luigi Cherubini, *Il Messenzio–Adriano in Siria–Armida abbandonata*; Domenico Cimarosa, *L'eroe cinese–L'amor constante–La ballerina amante*; Philip Cogan, *The Contract*; Nicolas Dalayrac, *L'éclipse totale*; Giuseppe Gazzaniga, *Amor per oro*; Giuseppe Giordani, *Ritorno d'Ulisse*; Tommaso Giordani, *Il bacio*; François Gossec, *Thésée*; André Grétry, *La double épreuve–L'embarras des richesses*; Franz Joseph Haydn, *Orlando paladino*; Giacomo Insanguine, *Calipso*; Vicente Martín y Soler, *Partenope–L'amore geloso*; Wolfgang Amadeus Mozart, *The Abduction from the Seraglio*; Johann G. Naumann, *Cora och Alonzo*; Giovanni Paisiello, *Il barbiere di Siviglia–Il mondo della luna*; Vincenzo Righini, *Armida*; Antonio Salieri, *Semiramide*; Giuseppe Sarti, *Fra i due litiganti il terzo gode–Attalo, Re di Bitinia–Alessandro e Timoteo*; Johann Schwanenberg, *L'Olimpiade*; William Shield, *Lord Mayor's Day–Friar Bacon*; Peter Winter, *Bellerophon*.

Orchestra/Band Music:

Concerted Music:

Piano: Wolfgang Amadeus Mozart, *Rondo in A, K. 386–Concerto in A, K. 414*; Jean-Frédéric Edelmann, *Clavecin Concerto, Opus 12*; Christian G. Neefe, *Piano (Harpsichord) Concerto*; George "Abbe" Vogler, *Concerto in C, Opus 8*.

Violin: Joseph Saint-Georges, *Two Concertos, Opus 7–Two Symphonies concertante, Opus 13* (two violins); Giovanni Viotti, *Concertos Nos. 1–6*; Johann Vogel, *Concerto*; Samuel Wesley, *Concerto No. 3 in A–No. 4 in B♭–No. 5 in C*(?).

Other: Friedrich (W. H.) Benda, *Three Flute Concertos, Opus 4*(?); Luigi Boccherini, *Cello Concerto in D*(?); François Devienne, *Flute Concerto No. 1 in D*; Wolfgang Amadeus Mozart, *Horn Concerto No. 1 in D, K. 412*; Francesco Petrini, *Two Harp Concertos, Opus 18*.

Ballet/Incidental Music: David August von Apell, *Euthyme und Lysis* (B); François Gossec, *Electre* (IM); Vicente Martín y Soler, *Cristiano II, rè di Danimarca* (B).

Standard Works: Wolfgang Amadeus Mozart, *Serenade in c, K. 388* (winds).

Symphonies: Hyacinthe Azaïs, *Six Symphonies*; Johann Christian Bach, *Six Sinfonias, Opus 18*; Luigi Boccherini, *Six Symphonies (D, E♭, A, F, E♭, B♭), Opus 35*; Gaetano Brunetti, *No. 26 in B♭*; Franz Joseph Haydn, *No. 73 in D, "La Chasse"–No. 76 in E♭–No. 77 in B♭–No. 78 in c*; Wolfgang Amadeus Mozart, *No. 35 in D, "Haffner," K. 385*; Georg "Abbe" Vogler, *Symphony in d, "Pariser."*

1783

Historical Highlights: William Pitt becomes prime minister of Great Britain; Russia proceeds to annex the Crimea region, provoking further warfare with Turkey; the Montgolfier brothers make the first balloon ascent; the Treaty of Paris formally ends the American Revolution; slavery is abolished in both Massachusetts and Maryland.

Art and Literature Highlights: Births—writers Victor Henri Ducange, Washington Irving, Stendhal, artist Samuel Lovett Waldo; Deaths—artist Jean-Baptiste Perroneau, poet Ann Eliza Bleecker. Art—Copley's *Death of Major Pierson*, David's *The Grief of Andromache*, Lange's *Portrait of Wolfgang Amadeus Mozart*; Literature—Cowley's *A Bold Stroke for a Husband*, Crabbe's *The Village*, Day's *History of Sandford and Merton*.

Musical Highlights

A. Births

Composers: Nicola Benvenuti (Italy) May 10; Johann Nepomuk Poissl (Germany) February 15.

Singers: Filippo Galli (Italian bass) December 28; Joseph August Röckel (German tenor) August 28.

Performers: Anton Dimmler (German clarinetist) April 24; Friedrich Dotzauer (German cellist) January 20; August Alexander Klengel (German pianist/organist/composer) June 29; Joseph Lincke (German cellist) June 8; Heinrich Aloys Praeger (Dutch violinist/conductor) December 23.

Others: Nathan Adams (American brass instrument maker) August 21; Gottfried Wilhelm Fink (German music critic/editor) March 8; Reginald Heber (British hymnist) April 21; George Hogarth (Scottish music author) December 28.

B. Deaths

Composers: Franz Habermann (Bohemia) April 8; Johann Adolf Hasse (Germany) December 16; Ondřej František Holý (Bohemia) May 4; Ignaz Holzbauer (Austria) April 7; Antonio Soler (Spain) December 20.

Singers: Lucrezia Agujari ("La Bastardina") (Italian soprano) May 18; Caffarelli (Italian castrato soprano) November 30; Marie-Joséphine Laguerre (French soprano) February 14; Thomas Lowe (British tenor) March 1; Antonio Uberti ("Il Porporino") (Italian castrato soprano) January 20.

Performers: Giacomo Basevidetto Cervetto (Italian-born cellist/composer) January 14; Daniel Dow (Scottish guitarist) January 20; Gaspard Fritz (Swiss violinist/composer) March 23; James Nares (British organist/composer) February 10; Thomas Pinto (British violinist) December 20; William Tans'ur (British organist/music author) October 7.

Others: Jean-le-Rond d'Alembert (French encyclopedist) October 29; Leonhardt Euler (Swiss mathematician/music theorist) September 3; Johann Philipp Kirnberger (German music theorist) July 26 (27?); Johann Andreas Silbermann (German organ builder) February 11.

C. **Debuts**
   Singers: Maria Mandini (Italian soprano—Vienna); Georgina Oldmixon (British soprano—London).
   Performers: William Brown (American flutist—New York); Jean Xavier Lefévre (Swiss clarinetist—Paris).

D. **New Positions**
   Conductors: Federigo Fiorillo (kapellmeister, Riga); Luigi Gatti (kapellmeister, Salzburg Cathedral); Ignace Joseph Pleyel (assistant kapellmeister, Strasbourg Cathedral); Giacomo Rust (maestro di cappella, Barcelona Cathedral).
   Others: Jean-Jacques Beauvarlet-Charpentier (organ, Notre Dame, Paris); John Ross (organ, St. Paul's Episcopal Chapel, Aberdeen); Nicolas Séjan (organ, St. Sulpice, Paris).

E. **Prizes/Honors**
   Honors: William Jones (knighted); Marcos de Portugal (Lisbon St. Cecilia Society); Jean-Baptiste Regnault (French Academy).

F. **Biographical Highlights**
   Thomas Attwood, on a royal grant, begins two years of music study in Italy; Ludwig van Beethoven is made court cembalist in Bonn with no salary; Christoph Willibald Gluck suffers a third stroke; Antonio Lolli is finally relieved of his duties in St. Petersburg and is replaced by Paisiello; Giovanni Battista Viotti gives up public performances but continues to perform privately for small occasions; Georg Joseph "Abbe" Vogler travels to England seeking approval of his new musical system; Elizabeth Weichsel marries musician James Billington and begins her Dublin career.

G. Cultural Beginnings

Performing Groups: Casino- und Musikgesellschaft (Worms).
Educational: Caracas Academy of Music (Venezuela); Pio Istituto Filarmonico (Milan).
Music Publishers: Joseph Dale (London); Franz Anton Hoffmeister (Vienna); Jean Imbault (Paris); Soren Sonnichsen (Denmark).
Music Publications: *Magazin der Musik* (Hamburg); *The New Musical Magazine* (London).
Performing Centers: Hermitage Theater (St. Petersburg); Teatro de la Ranchería (Buenos Aires); Tyl Theater (Prague).
Other: Concerts Spirituels (Berlin); Rellstab Music Lending Library (Berlin).

H. Musical Literature

Esteban de Arteaga, *Le rivoluzioni del teatro musicale italiano dalla sua origine fino al presente I*; Johann A. Eberhard, *Théorie der schönen Wissenschaften*; Johann S. Gruber, *Literatur der Musik*; Carl L. Junker, *Musikalischer Almanach, 1783*; Johann C. Kellner, *Grundriss des Generalbasses*; Andrew Law, *The Rudiments of Music*; Edward Miller, *Institutes of Music*; Henri Moreau, *L'harmonie mise en pratique*; Franz Christoph Neubahr, *Eine Erleichterung zu der musikalische composition*.

I. Musical Compositions

Chamber Music:

String Quartets: Wolfgang Amadeus Mozart, *String Quartet in d, K. 421–String Quartet in E♭, K. 428*; Ignace Pleyel, *Six Quartets (C, E♭, A, B♭, G, D), Ben. 301–6 (Opus 1)*; Giovanni Viotti, *Six Quartets (A, C, E♭, B♭, E♭, E), Opus 1–Six Quartets (A, C, F, B♭, E♭, E), Opus 3*.
Sonata/Solos: Luigi Boccherini, *Cello Sonata in C(?)*; Jean-Baptiste Bréval, *Six Cello Sonatas, Opus 12*; Johann Baptiste Krumpholz, *Variations on an Air by Mozart, Opus 10* (harp).
Ensembles: Carl F. Abel, *Four Flute Trios, Opus 16–Six String Trios, Opus 16*; Johann Christian Bach, *Sextet in C, T.302*; François Devienne, *Six Quartets for Flute and Strings, Book I*; Wolfgang Amadeus Mozart, *Piano Trio in d, K. 442*; Václav Pichl, *Six String Trios, Opus 7*; George "Abbe" Vogler, *Six Trio Sonatas, Opus 7*.
Piano: Ludwig van Beethoven, *Rondo in C–Rondo in A*; Muzio Clementi, *Three Keyboard Sonatas (B♭, C, E♭), Opus 9–Three Keyboard Sonatas (A, D, B♭), Opus 10*; Étienne Méhul, *Three Sonatas, Set I*; Wolfgang Amadeus Mozart, *Sonata in C, K. 330–Sonata in A, K. 331–Sonata in F, K. 332*; Alexander Reinagle, *Six Sonatas with Violin Accompaniment*.
Organ: Johann G. Albrechtsberger, *Twelve Fugues, Opus 1* (organ/harpsichord); Michel Corrette, *Noëls with Variations*.

Choral/Vocal Music:
Choral: Felice Alessandri, *La virtu rivali* (cantata); C. P. E. Bach, *Morgengesang am Schöpfungsfaste*, *H.779–St. Luke Passion IV*, *H.796*(?); Domenico Cimarosa, *Angelica et Medoro* (cantata); Christoph Willibald Gluck, *Ode an der Tod*; Johann Naumann, *Zeit und Ewigkeit* (cantata); Giovanni Paisiello, *La passione di Gesù Cristo* (oratorio); Johann Reichardt, *La Passione di Gesu Cristo* (oratorio); Joseph Weigl, *Mass in E♭*.
Vocal: Luigi Boccherini, *Four Villancios for Voices and Orchestra*; Gaetano Brunetti, *Concert Aria, "E ver' por troppo."*
Musical Stage: Agostino Accorimboni, *Lo schiavo fortunato–Il regno delle Amazzoni*; Joachim Albertini, *Don Juan*; Felice Alessandri, *I puntigli gelosi*; Johann André, *Der Barbier von Bagdad*; Pasquale Anfossi, *I vecchi burlati–Le gelosie fortunate*; Lugi Boccherini, *La Clementina*; João de Sousa Carvalho, *L'Endimione*; Luigi Cherubini, *Lo sposo di tre e marita di nessuna*; Domenico Cimarosa, *Nina e Martuffo–La villana riconosciuta*; Nicolas Dalayrac, *Le Corsaire–Les deux soupers*; Nicolas Dezède, *Balise et Babet–Péronne sauvée*; Giuseppe Giordani, *Erifile*; André Grétry, *La caravane du Caire*; Franz Joseph Haydn, *Armida*; Ignaz Holzbauer, *Tancredi*; William Jackson, *The Metamorphosis*; Vicente Martín y Soler, *Vologeso*; Gaetano Monti, *Lo studente*; Wolfgang Amadeus Mozart, *Lo sposo deluso–L'oca del Cairo*; Niccolò Piccinni, *Didon–Le faux lord–Le dormeur éveillé*; Venanzio Rauzzini, *Creusa in Delfo*; Antonio Sacchini, *Renaud–Chimène*; Giuseppe Sarti, *Olimpiade–Il trionfo della pace–Idalide*; William Shield, *Rosina*; Angelo Tarchi, *Ademira*; Georg "Abbe" Vogler, *La kermesse–Le patriotisme*.
Orchestra/Band Music:
Concerted Music:
   Piano: Wolfgang Amadeus Mozart, *Concerto No. 11 in F, K. 413–Concerto No. 13 in C, K. 415*.
   Violin: Franz Joseph Haydn, *Concerto No. 2 in D*; Rodolphe Kreutzer, *Concerto No. 1 in G, Opus 1*; Samuel Wesley, *Concerto No. 6 in G*; Giovanni Viotti, *Concerto No. 7 in B♭–No. 8 in D–No. 9 in A–No. 10 in B♭*.
   Other: Jean-Baptiste Bréval, *Two Symphonie concertante, Opus 11*; François Devienne, *Flute Concerto No. 2 in D*; Franz Joseph Haydn, *Cello Concerto No. 2 in D*; Wolfgang Amadeus Mozart, *Horn Concerto No. 1 in E♭, K. 417*.
Symphonies: Carl F. Abel, *Six Overtures, Opus 17* (Nos. 31–36); Gaetano Brunetti, *No. 22 in g–No. 23 9n F–No. 24 in C–No. 25 in D–No. 29 in C–No. 30 in E♭–No. 31 in d*; Michael Haydn, *Symphony in G* (formerly known as Mozart's No. 37); Ludwig Lachnith, *Three*

Symphonies, Opus 4(?); Wolfgang Amadeus Mozart, *No. 36 in C, K. 425, "Linz."*

1784

❋

Historical Highlights: The British India Act strengthens the British hold on India; the Hungarian Constitution is abrogated by Joseph II; Denmark abolishes all serfdom in its borders; trade with China is opened by the voyage of the *Empress of China* to the port of Canton; the Mason-Dixon Line is extended westward into the new territories; Connecticut and Rhode Island abolish slavery in their states.

Art and Literature Highlights: Births—artists Bass Otis, Allan Ramsay, François Rude, writers James Nelson Barker, Allan Cunningham, Denis Diderot; Deaths—poets Robert Munford, Phillis Wheatley. Art—David's *Oath of the Horatii*, C. W. Peale's *George Washington at Yorktown*, West's *Call of the Prophet Isaiah*; Literature—Beaumarchais' *The Marriage of Figaro*, Peter Markoe's *The Patriot Chief*, Schiller's *Kabale und Liebe*.

Musical Highlights

A. Births

Composers: Henri-Montan Berton (France) May 3; Pierre-Auguste-Louis Blondeau (France) August 15; Francesco Morlacchi (Italy) June 14; Georges Onslow (France) July 27; Giuseppe Pilotti (Italy) December 1; Louis Spohr (Germany) April 5.

Conductors: Carl Wilhelm Henning (Germany) January 31.

Singers: Teresa Belloc-Giorgi (Italian mezzo-soprano) July 2.

Performers: Dionisio Aguado (y García) (Spanish guitarist) April 8; Heinrich Bäermann (German clarinetist) February 14; William Beale (British organist) January 1; Franz Xaver Gebauer (German organist) December 1; Karl Leibl (German organist/conductor) December 1; Martin-Joseph Mengal (Belgian horn virtuoso/conductor) January 27; Charles Neate (British pianist) March 28; Ferdinand Ries (German pianist/composer) November 28.

Others: François-Henri-Joseph Blaze (Castil-Blaze—French music author) December 1; François-Joseph Fétis (Belgian music theorist/historian) March 25; Thomas Hastings (American hymnist) October 15; Edward Taylor (British musician/author) January 22; Carl von Winterfeld (German music author) January 28.

B. Deaths

Composers: Wilhelm Friedemann Bach (Germany) July 1; Andrea Bernasconi (Italy) January 24; Anton Laube (Bohemia) February 24; Benedetto Micheli (Italy) September 15.

Performers: Giuseppe Arena (Italian organist) November 6; John Bennett (British organist) September; Manuel Blasco de Nebra (Spanish pianist) September 12; Jean-Baptiste Canavas (Italian cellist/composer) June 7; Nicolas Capron (French violinist/composer) September 14; Antonin Kammel (Bohemian violinist) October 5; Giovanni Battista Martini (Italian organist/composer) August 3; Friedrich Wilhelm Riedt (German flutist/music author) May 2.

Others: Denis Diderot (French man of letters) July 30; Jean-Baptiste Nicolas Lefèvre (French organ builder) December; Ferdinand Philipp Joseph Lobkowitz (Bohemian patron of the arts/composer) January 11; Giovanni Battista "Padre" Martini (Italian pedagogue/music author/composer) August 3; Girolamo Tiraboschi (Italian musicologist) June 3.

C. Debuts

Singers: Joseph Carl Ambrosch (German tenor—Bayreuth); Luigi Bassi (Italian baritone—Prague, adult debut); Elizabeth Billington (British soprano—Dublin); Charles Dignum (British tenor— London); Friedrich Franz Hŭrka (Czech tenor—Leipzig); Charles Incledon (British tenor—Southampton); Luisa Laschi (Italian soprano— Vienna); Halifax Lowe (British tenor—London); Dorothea Wendling (German soprano—Munich).

Performers: Anton Eberl (Austrian pianist—Vienna).

D. New Positions

Conductors: Franz Paul Grua (hofkapellmeister, Munich); Johann Antonin Kozeluch (kapellmeister, St. Vitus Metropolitan Cathedral, Prague); Jean François Lesueur (maître de chapelle, Tours); Melchor López Jiménez (maestro de capilla, Santiago Cathedral); Giovanni Paisiello (maestro di cappella, Naples); Brizio Petrucci (maestro di cappella, Ferrara Cathedral); Giuseppe Sarti (kapellmeister, St. Petersburg); Georg "Abbe" Vogler (kapellmeister, Munich).

Others: François Joseph Gossec (director, École Royal du Chant).

E. Prizes/Honors

Honors: Edmund Ayrton (D.Mus., Cambridge); Franz Joseph Haydn (Gold Medal of Prince Henry of Prussia); Pietro Terziani (Accademia Filarmonica, Bologna).

F. Biographical Highlights

Ludwig van Beethoven is appointed second court organist at Bonn, this time with a salary; Luigi Cherubini is invited to London for the production of his operas; Johann L. Dussek enjoys a very successful German concert tour; Wolfgang Amadeus Mozart, settled in Vienna, meets Sarti and Paisiello and joins the Masonic Order; Giuseppe Sarti leaves for St. Petersburg and the Court of Catherine the Great; Daniel Steibelt deserts the Prussian Army and flees the country; Franz X. Süssmayr begins the study of law and philosophy.

G. Cultural Beginnings
Performing Groups—Choral: Brotherhood of St. Cecilia (Brazil).
Educational: Armonici Uniti (Bologna); École Royale du Chant et de Déclamation (Paris, founded by François Gossec).
Music Publishers: Bland and Weller, publishers and instrument makers (London); Kozeluch Music Publishing Co. (Vienna).
Music Publications: *Review of New Music Publications.*
Performing Centers: Italian Opera House (Prague); New Swedish Theater (Stockholm); Teatro della Società (Casale Monferrato); Teatro Eretenio (Vicenza).
Other: Institution for the Encouragement of Church Music (Uranian Society in 1787, Philadelphia); Royal Bohemian Academy of Sciences.

H. Musical Literature
Joseph Gehot, *A Treatise on the Theory and Practice of Music*; Martin Gerbert, *Scriptores ecclesiastici de musica sacra potissimum*; Christian F. Gregor, *Choralbuch* (Moravian); Johann A. Hiller, *Lebensbeschreibungen berühmter Musikgelehrten und Tonkunstler*; Edward Jones, *Musical and Poetical Relicks of the Welsh Bards*; William Jones, *Treatise on the Art of Music*; John Keeble, *The Theory of Harmonics*; Daniel Schubart, *Ideen zu einer aesthetik der Tonkunst*; Frédéric Thiéme, *Éléments de musique pratique.*

I. Musical Compositions
Chamber Music:
String Quartets: Wolfgang Amadeus Mozart, *Quartet in B♭, K. 458, "The Hunt"*; Ignace Pleyel, *Six Quartets (A, C, g, E♭, B♭, D), Ben. 307–12.*
Sonata/Solos: Johann Baptist Krumpholz, *Symphony No. 2 for Harp, Opus 11*; Wolfgang Amadeus Mozart, *Violin Sonata in B♭, K. 454.*
Ensembles: Johann Christian Bach, *Four Quartets (C, D, G, c), Opus 19* (flute, strings); Luigi Boccherini, *Six String Quintets (E♭, D, G, a, g, F), Opus 36*; Jean-Frédéric Edelmann, *Four Sonatas, Opus 13* (clavecin, strings); Felice de' Giardini, *Six String Trios, Opus 26*; Franz Joseph Haydn, *Piano Trios No. 1 and 2*; Wolfgang Amadeus Mozart, *Quintet in E♭ for Piano and Winds, K. 452*; Ignace Pleyel, *Three Keyboard Trios (C, F, G), Ben. 428–30.*

Piano: C. P. E. Bach, *Sonata in e, H.281–Sonata in B♭, H.181–Rondo in c, H.283–Fantasie in C, H.284*; Muzio Clementi, *Sonata in E♭, Opus 11–Four Sonatas (B♭, E♭, F, E♭), Opus 12*; Franz Joseph Haydn, *Sonatas No. 39–42*; Wolfgang Amadeus Mozart, *Sonata in c, K. 457–Sonata in F, K. 533–Ten Variations on a Theme of Gluck, K. 455–Eight Variations on a Theme of Sarti, K. 460.*

Choral/Vocal Music:

Choral: C. P. E. Bach, *St. John Passion IV, H.797(?)–Oster-Musik, H.807(?)*; Friedrich (W. H.) Benda, *Pygmalion* (cantata); Joseph L. Eybler, *Christmas Oratorio*; Johann G. Naumann, *Psalm 96, "Singet dem Herrn ein Neues Lied*; George "Abbe" Vogler, *Missa solennis in d–Missa de quadragesima in F*; Joseph Weigl, *Mass in F.*

Vocal: Carl C. Agthe, *Der Morgan, Mittag, Abend und Nacht*; Johann A. André, *Neue Sammlung von Liedern*; Michel Corrette, *Tenebrae Lessons*; Johann G. Naumann, *Sammlung von (36) Liedern*; Johann F. Reichardt, *Lieder von Gleim und Jacobi.*

Musical Stage: Felice Alessandri, *L'imbroglio delle tre spose–Al villanella rapita*; Antonio Calegari, *Le Sorelle rivali*; Giuseppe M. Cambini, *La statue*; Christian Cannabich, *Corésus et Callihoé*; João de Sousa Carvalho, *Adrasto rè degli Argivi*; Luigi Cherubini, *L'Idalide–Alessandro nell'Indie*; Domenico Cimarosa, *L'Olimpiade–Artaserse–La vanità delusa–La bella greca*; Nicolas Dalayrac, *Les deux tuteurs*; Valentino Fioravanti, *Le avventure di Bertoldino*; Giuseppe Giordani, *Tito Manlio–Pizarro nell'Indie*; Tommaso Giordani, *Gibraltar–The Haunted Castle*; André Grétry, *Théodore et Paulin–Richard Coeur-de-Lion–L'épreuve villageoise*; Vicente Martin y Soler, *Le burle per amore*; Gaetano Monti, *La donna fedele*; Giovanni Paisiello, *Antigono–Il re Teodoro in Venezia*; Niccolò Piccinni, *Lucette–Diane et Endymion*; Gaetano Pugnani, *Adone e Venere*; Venanzio Rauzzini, *Alina*; Antonio Sacchini, *Dardanus*; Antonio Salieri, *Les Danaïdes–Il ricco d'un giorno*; Giuseppe Sarti, *Didone abbandonata–Gli amanti consolati*; William Shield, *Robin Hood–The Noble Peasant*; Georg Vogler, *Castor e Polluce*; Peter Winter, *Scherz, List und Rache.*

Orchestra/Band Music:

Concerted Music:

Piano: Leopold Kozeluch, *Concerto No. 7*; Wolfgang Amadeus Mozart, *Concerto No. 14 in E♭, K. 449–No. 15 in B♭, K. 450–No. 16 in D, K. 451–No. 17 in G, K. 453–No. 18 in B♭, K. 456–No. 19 in F, K. 459.*

Violin: Rodolphe Kreutzer, *Concerto No. 2 in A, Opus 2*; Ignace Pleyel, *Concerto in C, B.101–Concerto in D, B.102.*

Other: Jean-Baptiste Bréval, *Cello Concerto No. l in A, Opus 14–No. 2 in G, Opus 17*; Jean-Baptiste Davaux, *Two Symphonies concertante*

(G, D), *Opus 12* (two violins, flute); François Devienne, *Flute Concerto No. 3 in G*; Ignace Pleyel, *Two Cello Concertos (C, D)*, Ben. 101,2.
Ballet/Incidental Music: Christian Cannabich, *Persée et Andromède* (B); Vicente Martín y Soler, *Aci e Galatea* (B); Carlo Toeschi, *Florine* (B)–*Die Amerikaner* (B).
Symphonies: Gaetano Brunetti, *No. 21 in E♭*; Jean-Baptiste Davaux, *Three Symphonies (E♭, F, D), Opus 11*; Franz Joseph Haydn, *No. 79 in F–No. 80 in d–No. 81 in G*; Franz A. Hoffmeister, *Grand Symphonie, Opus 14, "La Chasse"*; Ludwig W. Lachnith, *Three Symphonies, Opus 3*; Ignace Pleyel, *Three Symphonies (F, D, B♭)*, Ben. 123–25; Samuel Wesley, *Symphony No. 1 in D–No. 2 in A–No. 3 in E♭*.

1785
❄

Historical Highlights: The Russians end the ongoing peasant reforms and give the nobility full right to property and ownership of serfs; Russia begins the settlement of the Aleutian Islands of Alaska; the United States and Spain begin arguments over navigation rights on the Mississippi River; stagecoach service begins between the major east-coast cities; New York outlaws slavery; Thomas Jefferson appointed minister to France and John Adams to England.

Art and Literature Highlights: Births—artist David Wilkie, writers Bettina Brentano von Arnim, Caroline Lamb, Alessandro Manzoni, Pierre A. Lebrun; Deaths—artists Giovanni Cipriani, Pietro Longhi, Jean-Baptiste Pigalle. Art—Fragonard's *The Fountain of Love*, Gainsborough's *Morning Walk*, Reynolds' *The Infant Hercules*; Literature—Bürger's *Der wilde Jäger*, Raspe's *Baron Munchausen's Narrative of His Marvelous Travels*.

Musical Highlights

A. **Births**
Composers: Karol Kurpiński (Poland) March 6.
Conductors: William Hawes (England) June 21; Henri-Justin-Armand Valentino (France) October 14.
Singers: Violante Camporese (Italian soprano) December 26; Isabella Colbran (Spanish soprano) February 2; Alberico Curioni (Italian tenor); Adelaide Malanotte (Italian contralto); (Pauline) Anna Milder-Hauptmann (Austrian soprano) December 13.
Performers: Thomas Adams (British organist) September 5; Alexandre Pierre Boëly (French organist/composer) April 19; Johann Leopold Fuchs (German pianist/music theorist) November 2; Frédéric Kalkbrenner (French pianist/composer) November 8; Friedrich

Wieck (German pianist/pedagogue) August 18; Pierre-Joseph Zimmerman (French pianist/composer) March 19.

Others: John Abbey (British organ builder) December 22; Thomas Appleton (American organ builder) December 26; Alpheus Babcock (American piano maker) September 11; James Alexander Hamilton (British music theorist); John Meacham, Jr. (American instrument maker) May 2; Giovanni Ricordi (Italian publisher) December 26.

B. Deaths

Composers: Bernard de Bury (France) November 19; Étienne Joseph Floquet (France) May 10; Baldassare Galuppi (Italy) January 3; Antonio Mazzoni (Italy) December 8; Karl Siegmund Seckendorff (Germany) April 26.

Singers: Catherine "Kitty" Clive (British soprano) December 6.

Performers: Paolo Tommaso Alberghi (Irish violinist/composer) October 11; Gabriel-Louis Besson (French violinist) August 24; Carlo Cotumacci (Italian organist) July 29; Johann Michael Demmler (German organist/composer) June 6; Gottfried August Homilius (German organist/composer) June 2; Johann Heinrich Rolle (German organist/composer) December 29; Pierre Talon (French cellist/composer) June 25; Matthias Van den Gheyn (Belgian organist/carillonneur) June 22.

Others: Johann Snetzler (Swiss organ builder) September 28.

C. Debuts

Singers: Vincenzo Calvesi (Italian tenor—Venice); Franz Xaver Gerl (Austrian bass—Erlangen); Sarah Mahon Second (British soprano—London).

D. New Positions

Conductors: Ferdinando Gioseffo Bertoni (maestro di cappella, St. Mark's, Venice); Antonio Rosetti (kapellmeister to Prince Öttingen-Wallenstein); Johann Gottfried Schicht (Leipzig Gewandhaus Concerts); Joseph Mazzinghi (King's Theatre, London); Christian Ehregott Weinlig (cantor, Kreuzschule, Dresden); Georg Friedrich Wolf (kapellmeister, Stolberg).

Others: Giovanni Battista Grazioli (primo organ, St. Mark's, Venice); Giacomo Insanguine (director, Conservatorio di San Onofrio, Naples); Gaetano Valeri (organ, Padua Cathedral).

E. Prizes/Honors

Honors: Bernard de Bury (ennobled, Louis XVI); Joseph Farington (Royal Academy, London); Evstigney Fomin (Accademia Filarmonica, Bologna).

F. **Biographical Highlights**
Ludwig van Beethoven studies violin with Ries; Domenico Cimarosa becomes the second organist at the Neapolitan Chapel; Friedrich Heinrich Himmel begins the study of theology at Halle University; Rodolphe Kreutzer becomes first violinist in the Chapelle du Roi, Paris; Antonio Lolli, leaving Russia, visits in London, Paris, and Naples before settling in Palermo; Johann Gottlieb Naumann is given the task of reforming the Danish Hofkapelle in Copenhagen; Johann Reichardt's London performances meet with great success.

G. **Cultural Beginnings**
Performing Groups—Choral: London Caecilian Society.
Educational: Adgate Free School (Uranian Academy, Philadelphia).
Music Publishers: Krämer and Bossler, Darmstadt Branch; Pascal Boyle Publishing Co. (Paris); William Rolfe and Co., piano maker and publisher (London).
Music Publications: *Les Lunes.*
Performing Centers: Redoutensale Theater (Brno); Teatro do Salitre (Lisbon).
Other: Robert Woffington, organ and piano maker (Dublin).

H. **Musical Literature**
Andrew Adgate, *Lessons for the Uranian Society*; Charles Burney, *Account of the Musical Performances in Westminster Abbey and the Pantheon . . . in Commemoration of Handel*; Michel de Chabanon, *De la musique considérée en elle-même et dans ses rapports avec la parole, les langues, la poèsie et le théâtre*; Louis F. Despréaux, *Cours d'éducation de Clavecin ou Pianoforte*; Johann S. Gruber, *Beyträge zur literature der musik I*; James Hook, *Guida de Musica I*; Justin H. Knecht, *Erklärung einiger missverstandenen Grundsätze aus der Vogler'schen Theorie*; Bernard Lacépède, *Poétique de la Musique*; Jean F. Lirou, *Explication du système de l'harmonie*; Daniel Read, *The American Singing Book*; Armand Vanderhagen, *Méthode nouvelle et raisonnée pour la clarinette*; Ernst W. Wolf, *Vorbericht als eine Anleitung zum guten Vortrag beim Klavier-Spielen*.

I. **Musical Compositions**
Chamber Music:
   String Quartets: François H. Barthélémon, *Six Violin Sonatas, Opus 9*(?); Tommaso Giordani, *Six Quartets, Opus 18*; Franz Joseph Haydn, *Quartet in d, Opus 42*; Wolfgang Amadeus Mozart, *Quartet in A, K. 464–Quartet in C , "Dissonance", K. 465*; Franz C. Neubauer, *Three Early Quartets*; Ignace Pleyel, *Six Quartets (B♭, A, e, C, E♭, D), Ben. 313–18*; Joseph Boulogne de Saint-Georges, *Six Quartets, Opus 14*; Johann B. Vanhal, *Six Quartets, Opus 33*.

Sonata/Solos: François H. Barthélémon, *Six Violin Sonatas, Opus 10(?)*; Benjamin Blake, *Six Duets for Violin and Viola, Opus 3*; Wolfgang Amadeus Mozart, *Violin Sonata in E♭, K. 481*.

Ensembles: Johann Christian Bach, *Two Quintets (D, F), Opus 22*; Jean-Baptiste Bréval, *Six Quators concertants, Opus 18*; Jean-Frédéric Edelmann, *Three Concerts, Opus 15* (clavecin, strings); Franz Joseph Haydn, *Piano Trios No. 3–7*; Wolfgang Amadeus Mozart, *Piano Quartet in g, K. 478*; Václav Pichl, *Six String Trios, Opus 4*; Ignace Pleyel, *Two String Quintets (E♭, g), Ben. 271,2*.

Piano: Muzio Clementi, *Six Sonatas (G, C, E♭, B♭, F, F), Opus 13–Three Four Hand Duets (C, F, E♭), Opus 14*; Tommaso Giordani, *Six Harpsichord Sonatas, Opus 25–Six Harpsichord Sonatas, Opus 28*; Ludwig Lachnith, *Three Harpsichord Sonatas, Opus 8* (opt. violin); Wolfgang Amadeus Mozart, *Fantasy in c, K. 475*.

Choral/Vocal Music:
Choral: C. P. E. Bach, *St. Matthew Passion V, H.798(?)*; Johann Christoph Friedrich Bach, *Singet dem Herrn ein neues Lied* (cantata)–*Die Hirten bei der Krippe Jesu* (oratorio); Friedrich L. Benda, *Trauercantate*; Wolfgang Amadeus Mozart, *Die Mauerfreude, K. 471* (cantata); Johann Naumann, *Il ritorno del figliolo prodigo* (oratorio)–*Unserer Brüder* (cantata); Giovanni Paisiello, *Il ritorno di Perseo* (cantata); Johann Reichardt, *Auferstehungs-oratorium*.

Musical Stage: Agostino Accorimboni, *Il governatore delle Isole Canarie*; Joachim Albertini, *Circe und Ulisses*; Friedrich (W. H.) Benda, *Orpheus*; João de Sousa Carvalho, *Nettuno ed Eglé*; Luigi Cherubini, *La finta principessa*; Domenico Cimarosa, *Il marito disperato*; Nicolas Dalayrac, *La Dot–L'amant-statue*; Jean-Baptiste Davaux, *Théodore*; Nicolas Dezède, *Alexis et Justine*; Giuseppe Giordani, *Osmano*; Tommaso Giordani, *Calypso–Gretna Green–The Hypochondriac*; André Grétry, *Panurge dans l'île des lanternes*; Ludwig Lachnith, *L'heureuse réconciliation*; Vicente Martín y Soler, *La vedova spiritosa*; Étienne Méhul, *Alonzo et Cora*; Johann Naumann, *Tutto per amore*; Giovanni Paisiello, *La grotta di Trofonio*; François Philidor, *Thémistocles–L'amitié au village*; Niccolò Piccinni, *Pénélope*; Ignace Pleyel, *Ifigenia in Aulide*; Gaetano Pugnani, *Achille in Sciro*; Antonio Salieri, *La grotta di Trofonio*; Giuseppe Sarti, *I finti eredi*; William Shield, *The Choleric Fathers–Frederick in Prussia*; Franz X. Süssmayr, *Karl Stuart*; Peter Winter, *Der Bettelstudent*; Nicola Zingarelli, *Alsinda–Ricimero*; Johann R. Zumsteeg, *Armide*.

Orchestra/Band Music:
Concerted Music:
Piano: Ludwig Lachnith, *Three Harpsichord/Piano Concertos, Opus 9–Three Harpsichord/Piano Concertos, Opus 10*; Wolfgang

Amadeus Mozart, *Concerto No. 20 in d, K. 466–No. 21 in C, K. 467–No. 22 in E♭, K. 482*.

Violin: Christian Danner, *Concerto*; Rodolphe Kreutzer, *Concerto No. 3 in E, Opus 3*; Samuel Wesley, *Concerto No. 7 in B♭*.

Other: Jean-Baptiste Breval, *Cello Concerto No. 3 in F, Opus 28*; François Devienne, *Symphonie concertante No. 1 in F* (horn, bassoon)*–No. 2 in C* (oboe, bassoon)*–Bassoon Concerto No. 1 in C–Horn Concerto No. 1 in C*; Étienne Ozi, *Symphonie concertante No. 1 in B♭, Opus 5*.

Ballet/Incidental Music: François Gossec, *Athalie* (IM).

Standard Works: Wolfgang Amadeus Mozart, *Masonic Funeral Music in c, K. 477*.

Symphonies: Johann Christian Bach, *Two Symphonies (D, D), Opus 18*; Étienne-Joseph Barrière, *Three Symphonies (D, F, G), Opus 10*; Franz Joseph Haydn, *No. 83 in g, "La Poule"–No. 85 in B♭–No. 87 in A*; Ludwig Lachnith, *Three Symphonies, Opus 11–Three Symphonies, Opus 12*; Ignace Pleyel, *Symphony in D, Ben. 126*; Ignazio Raimondi, *Symphony, The Battle*.

1786

❄

Historical Highlights: Lord Cornwallis becomes the governor-general of India and seeks to bring about reforms in the governing of that country; Shays' Rebellion in Massachusetts is put down by state militia; the Annapolis Convention sets the stage for the first Constitutional Congress; John Fitch sails the first steamboat in the New World.

Art and Literature Highlights: The Shakespeare Gallery opens in London. Births—poet Marceline Desbordes-Valmore, artist Franz Riepenhausen; Deaths—artist Alexander Cozens, poets Jacobus Bellamy, Joseph Brown Ladd. Art—David's *Death of Ugolino*, Stuart's *Portrait of Chief Joseph Brant*, Trumbull's *Death of Montgomery at Quebec*; Literature—Burns' *Poems, Chiefly in the Scottish Dialect*, Rowson's *Victoria*.

Musical Highlights

A. Births

Composers: Francisco Andrevi y Castellar (Spain) November 7; Tommaso Gasparo Barsotti (Italy) September 4; Henry Rowley Bishop (England) November 18; Giacomo Cordella (Italy) July 25; José Mariano Elízaga (Mexico) September 27; Conrad Kocher (Germany) December 16; Pietro Raimondi (Italy) December 20; Carl Maria von Weber (Germany) November 18.

Singers: Charles Edward Horn (British-born singer/composer/conductor) June 21; Johanna Sophia Kollmann (British soprano) July 20.
Performers: Marie Bigot (de Morogues) (French pianist) March 3; Carl Eberwein (German violinist/composer) November 10; Friedrich Kuhlau (German-born pianist/composer) September 11; Friedrich Müller (German clarinetist/conductor) December 10; Iwan Müller (German clarinetist/inventor) December 14; Karel F. Pitsch (Bohemian organist) February 2; Friedrich Schneider (German organist/composer) January 3; Jean-Louis Tulou (French flutist/composer) September 12.
Others: Louis Callinet (French organ builder) April 19; John Crosse (British musicologist) July 7; John Feltham Danneley (British music theorist) March 9; Marie-Pierre Hamel (French jurist/organ builder) February 24; Henri Lemoine (French publisher) October 21.

B. **Deaths**
Composers: Michael Arne (England) January 14; Franz Asplmayr (Austria) July 29; Frederick the Great (Germany) August 17; Carlos d'Ordonez (Austria) September 6; Antonio Sacchini (Italy) October 6; Johann Georg Schürer (Germany) February 16.
Singers: Johanna Elisabeth Döbricht (German soprano) February 23; Frederica Weichsell (Brazilian soprano) January 6; Elisabeth Augusta Wendling (German soprano) February 20.
Performers: Franz Benda (Bohemian violinist/composer) March 7; Henri-Jacques de Croes (Belgian violinist/composer) August 16; John Keeble (British organist) December 24; Johann Wolfgang Kleinknecht (German violinist) February 20; Johann Michael Quallenberg (German clarinetist) April 16; Friedrich Schwindl (German violinist/composer) August 7; John Stanley (British organist/composer) May 19; Franz Wendling (German violinist) May 16.
Others: Giovanni Guadagnini (Italian violin maker) September 18.

C. **Debuts**
Singers: Maria Theresa Bland (British soprano—London); Dorothea Bussani (Austrian soprano—Vienna); Adriana Ferraresi del Bene (Francesca Gabrielli) (Italian soprano—London); Jeanne Charlotte Saint-Aubin (French soprano—Paris); Anna de Santi (Italian soprano—Venice); Benedikt Schack (Austrian tenor—Salzburg).
Performers: Alexandre-Jean Boucher (French violinist—Paris); Nicola Mestrino (Italian violinist—Paris).

D. **New Positions**
Conductors: Jean François Lesueur (maître de chapel, Notre Dame, Paris), Raimondo Lorenzini (maestro di cappella, S. Maria Maggiore, Rome), Juan José Morata (maestro de capilla, Segorbe Cathedral), Wenzel Muller (Leopoldstadt-Theater, Vienna), Ignaz

Vitzthumb (maître de musique, Brussels Royal Chapel), Georg Joseph "Abbe" Vogler (kapellmeister, Stockholm).
Others: Olaf Åhlström (organ, Jacobskyrka, Stockholm); Jacob Eckhard (organ, St. John's Lutheran, Charleston, South Carolina).

E. **Prizes/Honors**
Honors: Andrew Law (M.A., Yale); William Parsons (Master of the King's Music, London).

F. **Biographical Highlights**
Luigi Cherubini leaves London and his position as composer to the king and begins a year's stay in Paris; Jan L. Dussek begins three years of concertizing and teaching in Paris; Franz Joseph Haydn writes his "Paris Symphonies" for the Concerts de la Loge Olympique in Paris; Alexander Reinagle travels to New York, but finally settles in Philadelphia; Johann Peter Salomon introduces the symphonies of Haydn and Mozart in London.

G. **Cultural Beginnings**
Performing Groups—Choral: Stoughton Musical Society (Massachusetts).
Music Publishers: George Goulding and Co. (London); Pierre-Jean Porro (Paris).
Music Publications: *American Musical Magazine; Columbian Magazine.*
Performing Centers: Besançon Opera House (France); Liverpool Concert Hall; Nationaltheater (Old French Theater, Berlin).
Other: J. J. Astor Music Shop (New York); Salomon Concert Series (London).

H. **Musical Literature**
William Billings, *The Suffolk Harmony*; Philipp S. Frick, *Treatise on Thorough-Bass*; Johann S. Gruber, *Biographien einiger Tonkünstler*; Johann A. Hiller, *Über Metastasio und seine Werke*; Carl L. Junker, *Über den werth der Tonkunst*; James Nares, *A Concise and Easy Treatise on Singing with a Set of English Duets for Beginners*; Daniel Schubart, *Musikalisches Rhapsodien*; Johann G. Tromlitz, *Kurze abhandlung vom flötenspiel*; Joseph C. Walker, *Historical Memoirs of the Irish Bards*.

I. **Musical Compositions**
Chamber Music:
String Quartets: Wolfgang Amadeus Mozart, *String Quartet in D, "Hoffmeister," K. 499*; Ignace Pleyel, *Six Quartets (C, G, F, A, B♭, D), Ben. 319–24*.
Sonata/Solos: C. P. E. Bach, *Flute Sonata in G, H.564*; Isadore Bertheaume, *Two Violin Sonatas "dans le style de Lolly," Opus 2*; Jo-

hann L. Dussek, *Six Violin Sonatas (C, F, B♭, C, D, G), Opus 2–Three Sonatas for Flute/Violin (G, D, C), Opus 4*.

Ensembles: Jean-Baptiste Bréval, *Six String Trios, Opus 27*; François Devienne, *Six Quartets for Flute and Strings, Book 2, Opus 16*; Johann L. Dussek, *Three Trio Sonatas (C, B♭, e)*; Wolfgang Amadeus Mozart, *Piano Quartet in E♭, K. 493–Piano Trio in G, K. 496–Piano Trio in E♭, K. 498–Piano Trio in B♭, K. 502*; Johann Naumann, *Six Quartets, Opus 1* (flute, violin, bass, piano); Ignace Pleyel, *Three String Quintets (C, a, f), Ben. 273,76,77*.

Piano: C. P. E. Bach, *Two Sonatas (D, G) H.286,7–Two Rondos (E♭, d), H.288, 290–Two Fantasias (B♭, C), H.289, 291–Six New Sonatinas (G, E, D, B♭, F, d), H.292-7–Two Sonatas (E♭, G), H.298,9*; Friedrich (W. H.) Benda, *Three Sonatas, Opus 5* (with flute); Muzio Clementi, *Three Sonatas (E, C, B♭), Opus 15* (with violin)–*Capriccio in B♭, Opus 17*; Jean-Frédéric Edelmann, *Airs pour clavecin ou le forte piano, Opus 16*.

Organ: Johann Albrechtsberger, *Fugue in C, Opus 4*(?).

Choral/Vocal Music:

Choral: C. P. E. Bach, *St. Mark Passion V*; Johann Christoph Friedrich Bach, *Pygmalion* (secular cantata); Friedrich L. Benda, *Psalm 97*; Domenico Cimarosa, *Il sacrificio d'Abramo* (oratorio); Prosper-Didier Deshayes, *Jephthé* (oratorio); Carl Ditters von Dittersdorf, *Giobbe*; Giuseppe Giordani, *La morte di Abelle*; Michael Haydn, *Missa hispanica in C*; Giovanni Paisiello, *Amore vendicato*; François Philidor, *Te Deum*; Johann F. Reichardt, *Weihnachts-Cantilene–Te Deum laudamus*; Antonio Sacchini, *Esther* (oratorio).

Vocal: William Jackson, *Twelve Pastorals, Opus 15*; Maria Theresia von Paradis, *Twelve Lieder auf ihrer Reise in musik qesetz*.

Musical Stage: Joachim Albertini, *Virginia–Scipione africano*; Pasquale Anfossi, *L'inglese in Italia*; Friedrich (W. H.) Benda, *Alceste*; Luigi Boccherini, *La Clementina*; Dmitri Bortniansky, *Le faucon–La fête du Seigneur*; Antonio Calegari, *L'amor soldato*; Luigi Cherubini, *Il Giulio Sabino*; Domenico Cimarosa, *Il credulo–L'impresario en angustie*; Nicolas Dalayrac, *Nina–Azémia*; Carl Ditters von Dittersdorf, *Doktor und Apotheker–Betrug durch Aberglauben*; Evstigney Fomin, *Novgorod Hero Vassily Boyeslavich*; Giuseppe Giordani, *La vestale–Ifigenia in Aulide*; François Gossec, *Rosine*; André Grétry, *Amphitryon–Le comte d'Albert*; Pietro Guglielmi, *Enea e Lavinia–L'inganno amoroso*; Honoré Langlé, *Antiochus et Stratonice*; Vicente Martín y Soler, *Una cosa rara–Il burbero di buon cuore*; Wolfgang Amadeus Mozart, *Die Schauspieldirektor, K. 486–The Marriage of Figaro, K. 492*; Johann Naumann, *Gustaf Wasa–Orpheus og Eurydike*; Giovanni Paisiello, *Olimpiade–Le gare generose*; Johann Reichardt, *Panthée–Tamerlan*; Antonio Sacchini, *Oedipe à Colone*; Antonio Salieri, *Les Horaces*; Giuseppe Sarti, *Armida e Rinaldo*;

William Shield, *Richard Coeur de Lion–The Enchanted Castle* (operettas); Franz X. Süssmayr, *Die Drillinge*; Johann Vogel, *La Toison d'or*; Nicola Zingarelli, *Armida–Antigono*.

Orchestra/Band Music:
Concerted Music:
   Piano: Ludwig W. Lachnith, *Six Harpsichord Concertos, Opus 18*; Wolfgang Amadeus Mozart, *Concerto No. 23 in A, K. 488–No. 24 in c, K. 491–No. 25 in C, K. 503.*
   Violin: Rodolphe Kreutzer, *Concerto No. 4 in C, Opus 4*; Ignace Pleyel, *Symphonie Concertante in E♭, Opus 111.*
   Other: Jean-Baptiste Bréval, *Cello Concerto No. 4 in C, Opus 22–No. 5, Opus 24–No. 6 in C, Opus 26*; Wolfgang Amadeus Mozart, *Horn Concerto in E♭, K. 495*; Francesco Petrini, *Harp Concerto No. 1, Opus 25.*

Ballet/Incidental Music: Domenico Mazzochi, *Le premier navigateur* (B)–*L'amour jardinier* (B)–*La fête Marine* (B)–*Les deux solitaires* (B).

Symphonies: Luigi Boccherini, *Four Symphonies (C, D, d, A), Opus 37*; Franz Joseph Haydn, *No. 82 in C , "The Bear" (Paris No. 1)–No. 84 in E♭, "La reine" (Paris No. 3)–No. 86 in D (Paris No. 5)*; Ludwig W. Lachnith, *Three Symphonies, Opus 11–Three Symphonies, Opus 12*; Wolfgang Amadeus Mozart, *No. 38 in D, K. 504, "Prague"*; Ignace Pleyel, *Six Symphonies (B♭, G, C, G, C, B♭), Ben. 127–32–Six Symphonies (D, E♭, B♭, F, A, f), B.133–138.*

1787

❄

Historical Highlights: The Hapsburgs claim the Austrian Netherlands; Turkey once again goes to war with Russia; the Edict of Versailles gives French Protestants religious freedom; in the United States, the Constitutional Convention sends the new Constitution to the states for ratification—Delaware, Pennsylvania, and New Jersey become the first to do so; the Northwest Ordinance provides for the territory north of the Ohio River and east of the Mississippi River.

Art and Literature Highlights: Births—writers Matthew Jouett, Johann L. Uhland, Konstantin Batyushkov; Deaths—artists Arthur W. Devis, Pompeo G. Batoni, writers Johann K. A. Musäus, Charles Chauncey. Art—David's *Death of Socrates*, Tischbein's *Goethe in the Roman Campagna*, Trumbull's *Declaration of Independence*; Literature— Barlow's *The Vision of Columbus*, Goethe's *Iphigenie auf Tauris*, Schiller's *Don Carlos.*

Musical Highlights

A. **Births**

Composers: Alexander Alexandrovich Aliabiev (Russia) August 15; Michele Carafa (Italy) November 17; Franz Xaver Gebel (Germany).

Conductors: Karl Guhr (Germany) October 30; Edward Lannoy (Belgium-Austria) December 3; Christian Rummel (Germany) November 27.

Singers: Pierre Ignace Begrez (French tenor) December 23; Eliza Salmon (British soprano).

Performers: Christian Frederik Barth (Danish oboist) February 24; Johann Fredrik Berwald (Swedish violinist) December 4; Ludwig Böhner (German pianist/composer) January 8; John Burrowes (British organist) April 23; Hieronymus Payer (Austrian organist/conductor) February 15; Joseph Sellner (German oboist/composer) March 13.

Others: Charles François Gand, *père* (French violin maker) August 5; Franz Gruber (Germany hymnist) November 25; Tobias Haslinger (Austrian music publisher) March 1.

B. **Deaths**

Composers: Carl Friedrich Abel (Germany) June 20; Charles-Guillaume Alexandre (France); Anna Amalia (Germany) September 30; Joseph Bárta (Bohemia) June 13; Giovan Gualberto Brunetti (Italy) May 20; Pasquale Cafaro (Italy) October 25; Ignazio Fiorillo (Italy) June; Paul-César Gibert (France); Christoph Willibald Gluck (Germany) November 15; Johann Friedrich Gräfe (Germany) February 8; Antonio Rodriguez de Hita (Spain) February 21; Leopold Mozart (Germany-Austria) May 28; Joseph Starzer (Austria) April 22; Anton Schweitzer (Germany) November 23.

Singers: Adelheid Eichner (German soprano) April 5.

Performers: Gottfried Joseph Beck (Bohemian organist) April 8; Johan Daniel Berlin (German-born organist/composer) November 4; François Francœur (French violinist/composer) August 5; Carlo Graziani (Italian cellist); Matthias Hawdon (British organist) March.

C. **Debuts**

Singers: John Braham (British tenor—London, as boy soprano); Margarethe Danzi (German soprano—Munich); Louis-Sébastien Lebrun (French tenor—Paris).

Performers: Johann Nepomuk Hummel (Austrian pianist—Vienna); Feliks Janiewicz (Polish violinist—Paris).

D. **New Positions**

Conductors: Ignazio Alberghi (kapellmeister, Faenza Cathedral); Domenico Cimarosa (maestro di cappella, St. Petersburg); Johann

Adam Hiller (civic music director, Breslau); António Leal Moreira (mestre de capela, Royal Chapel, Lisbon); Vincenzo Orgitano (primo maestro di cappella, Naples); Vincenzo Righini (kapellmeister, Mainz); Johann Abraham Peter Schulz (hofkapellmeister, Copenhagen).
Others: José Lidón (first organist, Chapel Royal, Madrid); Josef Preindl (organ, St. Michael's, Vienna); Franz Seydelmann (director, Royal Danish Theater); Joseph Supries (organ, St. Sauveur Cathedral); Daniel Gottlob Türk (organ, Liebfrauenkirche, Halle).

F. **Biographical Highlights**
Ludwig van Beethoven meets Mozart while in Vienna but returns to Bonn when he hears of his mother's death; Domenico Cimarosa is invited to the Russian Court in St. Petersburg by Catherine the Great, and is given a hero's welcome at Vienna, Warsaw, and St. Petersburg as he travels northward; Wolfgang Amadeus Mozart visits Prague, where he learns of the death of his father; Giuseppe Sarti loses his Russian position due to the intrigues of soprano Luiza Todi and is hired by Prince Potemkin; Samuel Wesley suffers severe skull damage in a fall causing him considerable difficulty in future concert work.

G. **Cultural Beginnings**
Performing Groups—Choral: London Glee Club; Opéra de Marseilles.
Music Publications: *Harrison's New German Flute Magazine* (London).
Performing Centers: Casino dei Nobili (Bologna); Lille Opera House.
Other: Irish Music Fund (Dublin); Konzerte fur Kenner und Liebhaber.

H. **Musical Literature**
John Aitken, *Compilation of Litanies and Vespers, Hymns and Anthems*; Daniel Bernoulli, *Essai théorique sur les vibrations des plaques vibrantes*; Ernst Chladni, *Entdeckungen über der Theorie des Klanges*; Domenico Corri, *A Complete Musical Grammar*; Johann F. Dalberg, *Blicke eines Tonkünstlers in die Musik der Geister*; Johann A. Hiller, *Über alt und neu in der Musik*; James Johnson, *The Scot's Musical Museum*; William Jones, *The Nature and Excellence of Music*; Jean F. Lesueur, *Exposé d'un musique une, imitative et particulière à chaque solemnité*; Edward Miller, *Elements of Thorough Bass and Composition*; Daniel Read, *American Singing Book Supplement*; Daniel G. Türk, *Von den wichtigsten Pflichten eines Organisten: ein Beytrag zur verbesserung der musikalischen Liturgie*; Georg F. Wolf, *Kurzegefasstes musikalisches Lexikon*.

I. **Musical Compositions**
Chamber Music:
String Quartets: Luigi Boccherini, *Three Quartets (A, e, C), Opus 39*; Giuseppe A. Capuzzi, *Six String Quartets, Opus 6*; Franz Joseph

Haydn, *"Prussian" Quartets, Opus 50: No. 1 in B♭–No. 2 in C–No. 3 in E♭–No. 4 in f♯–No. 5 in F, "Ein Traum"–No. 6 in D, "The Frog"*; Ignace Pleyel, *Six Quartets (B♭, E♭, A, C, G, F), Ben. 325–30–Twelve "King of Prussia" Quartets (B♭, G, d, C, A, E♭, D, F, g, G, c, D), Ben. 331–42.*

Sonata/Solos: Isidore Bertheaume, *Two Violin Sonatas, Opus 4*; Jean-Baptiste Bréval, *Six Cello Sonatas, Opus 28*; Johann L. Dussek, *Three Violin Sonatas (F, E♭, f), Opus 4*; Wolfgang Amadeus Mozart, *Violin Sonata in A, K. 526*; Václav Pichl, *One Hundred Variations for Solo Violin, Opus 11*; Johann F. Reichardt, *Flute Sonata No. 1 in D–No. 2 in C(?)*; Johan Vanhal, *Viola Sonata No. 5 in E♭(?).*

Ensembles: Thomas Attwood, *Three Piano Trios, Opus 1*; Luigi Boccherini, *Five Sextets (E♭, B♭, E♭, E♭, E♭) and Octet in G, Opus 38–Three String Quintets (B♭, F, D), Opus 39*; Dmitri Bortniansky, *Quintet in C*; François Devienne, *Six Trios for Two Flutes and Cello, Opus 19*; Wolfgang Amadeus Mozart, *String Quintet in C, K. 515–String Quintet in g, K. 516–A Musical Joke, K. 522*; Václav Pichl, *Three Quartets for Flute and String, Opus 12*; Ignace Pleyel, *Nocturne-Serenade in C, Ben. 215–String Septet in E♭, Ben. 251–Two String Quintets (D, B♭), Ben. 274,5–Three String Trios (E♭, D, F), Ben. 401–3.*

Piano: C. P. E. Bach, *Freie Fantasie in f♯, H.300*; Isidore Bertheaume, *Three Sonatas, Opus 7* (with violin)–*Three Sonatas, Opus 8* (with violin); Muzio Clementi, *Sonata in C, Opus 20–Three Sonatas (D, G, C), Opus 21–Three Sonatas, Opus 22*; Wolfgang Amadeus Mozart, *Sonata in C, Piano, Four Hands, K. 521.*

Organ: Johann Albrechtsberger, *Six Fugues and Two Preludes, Opus 6(?)*; Michel Corrette, *Pièces pour l'orgue dans un genre nouveau.*

Choral/Vocal Music:

Choral: Carl Philipp Emanuel Bach, *St. Luke Passion V, H.800*; Johann Christoph Friedrich Bach, *Gott wird deinen Fuss nicht gleiten lassen* (cantata); Luigi Cherubini, *Amphion* (Freemason cantata); Domenico Cimarosa, *Requiem pro defunctis in g*; Bonaventura Furlanetto, *Judith triumphans* (oratorio); Michael Haydn, *Jubelfeier* (cantata); Johann Naumann, *La passione Gesù Christo II*; Franz C. Neubauer, *Hymne auf die Natur*; Giovanni Paisiello, *Baldassare* (oratorio); Antonio Salieri, *Le jugement dernier* (cantata).

Vocal: Johann Heinrich Egli, *Schweizerlieder*; Friedrich F. Hůrka, *Schez und Ernst in zwölf Liedern*; Johann Naumann, *Zwölf von Elisens geistlichen liedern*; Johann F. Reichardt, *Deutsche gesänge.*

Musical Stage: Pasquale Anfossi, *Creso–L'orfanella americana*; Dmitri Bortniansky, *Le fils rival*; Giuseppe M. Cambini, *Le Tuteur avare–La croisée*; Domenico Cimarosa, *Domenico, Il fanatico burlato–Vôlodimirö*; Nicolas Dezède, *Alcindor*; Carl Ditters von Dittersdorf, *Die Liebe im Narrenhause*; Anton Eberl, *La marchande des modes*; Evstigney Fomin, *The Coachmen*; Luigi Gatti, *Demofoonte*;

Giuseppe Gazzaniga, *Don Giovanni Tenorio–La Didone–L'amor costante*; Giuseppe Giordani, *Alciade e Telesia*; André Grétry, *Le prisonnier anglais*; Michael Haydn, *Andromeda e Perseo*; Vicente Martín y Soler, *L'arbore di Diana*; Étienne Méhul, *Hypsipile*; Wolfgang Amadeus Mozart, *Don Giovanni*; Johann Naumann, *La reggia d'Imeneo*; François Philidor, *La belle esclave*; Niccolò Piccinni, *Clytemnestre*; Venanzio Rauzzini, *La Vestale*; Johann Reichardt, *Andromeda*; Joseph Saint-Georges, *La Fille Garçon*; Antonio Salieri, *Tarare*; Giuseppe Sarti, *Alessandro nell'Indie*; William Shield, *Marian–The Farmer*; Nicola Zingarelli, *Ifigenia in Aulide*; Johann Zumsteeg, *Zalaor*.

Orchestra/Band Music:
Concerted Music:
> **Piano:** Thomas Arne, *Six Favorite Concertos for Keyboard*; Jan L. Dussek, *Concerto in E♭, Opus 3*.
>
> **Violin:** Isidore Berteaume, *Two Concertos, Opus 5–Symphonie-concertant, Opus 6/1* (two violins)*–Symphonie-concertant, Opus 6/2* (two violins, viola/horn); Jean-Baptiste Davaux, *Two Symphonies concertante (D, A), Opus 13* (two violins); Rodolphe Kreutzer, *Concerto No. 5 in A, Opus 5*; Giovanni Viotti, *Concerto No. 11 in A*.
>
> **Other:** François Devienne, *Flute Concerto No. 7 in e*; Wolfgang Amadeus Mozart, *Horn Concerto in E♭, K. 447*; Samuel Wesley, *Organ Concerto No. 1 in A*.

Ballet/Incidental Music: François Gossec, *Le pied de boeuf (B)*; Domenico Mazzochi, *L'heureux événement (B)–Zémire et Azor (B)–Les offrandes à l'amour (B)*; Johann Reichardt, *Macbeth* (IM).

Standard Works: Wolfgang Amadeus Mozart, *Serenade in G, K. 525, "Eine kleine Nachtmusik."*

Symphonies: Luigi Boccherini, *Two Symphonies, Opus 37/3, 4*; Gaetano Brunetti, *No. 27 in B♭*; Giuseppe M. Cambini, *Symphony in F–in e–in D*; Muzio Clementi, *Symphony in B♭–in D, Opus 18*; Franz Joseph Haydn, *No. 88 in G–No. 89 in F*; Ignace Pleyel, *Six Symphonies (D, E♭, B♭, F, A, f), Ben. 133–8*.

1788

Historical Highlights: A list of grievances from the common people causes Louis XVI to call for a meeting of the French Estates-General; the first British convicts are settled in Sydney, Australia; the Russo-Swedish War begins; in the United States, all of the states ratify the new Constitution except for Rhode Island and North Carolina, who eventually are coerced into joining the Union; Virginia and Maryland donate territory for the proposed District of Columbia.

Art and Literature Highlights: Births—writers Lord Byron, Friedrich Rückert, Arthur Schopenhauer; Deaths—artists Thomas Gainsborough, Robert Edge Pine, Francesco Zuccarelli. Art—Barry's *King Lear Weeping over Cordelia*, David's *Paris and Helen*, Dunlap's *Artist Showing Picture from Hamlet to His Parents*; Literature—Alsop's *The Charme of Fancy*, Goethe's *Egmont*, Rowson's *The Inquisitor*, Smith's *Emmeline*.

Musical Highlights

A. Births

Composers: José Bernardo Alcedo (Peru) August 20; Erik Drake (Sweden) January 8.

Conductors: Giuseppe Donizetti (Italy) November 9.

Performers: Caspar Ett (German organist/composer) January 5; Mateo Ferrer (Spanish organist/composer) February 25; Johann Peter Pixis (German pianist/composer) February 10; Camille Pleyel (French pianist/piano maker) December 18; Aloys Schmitt (German pianist/composer) August 26; Simon Sechter (Austrian organist/composer) October 11; Prosper-Charles Simon (French organist) December 27.

Others: Christian Frederick Albrecht (German-born piano maker) January 6; François Chanot (French violin maker) March 25; Johann Theodor Mosewius (German musicologist/conductor) September 25; Felice Romani (Italian librettist) January 31; Count Mikhail Wielhorsky (Russian patron of the arts) November 11.

B. Deaths

Composers: Carl Philipp Emanuel Bach (Germany) December 14; Giuseppe Bonno (Italy-Austria) April 15; Carlo Antonio Campioni (France-Italy) April 12; Gaetano Latilla (Italy) January 15; Alessio Prati (Italy) January 17; Carl Joseph Toeschi (Germany) April 12; Johann Christoph Vogel (Germany) June 27; Francesco Zannetti (Italy) January 31.

Performers: François Bainville (French organist) September 26; Jean-Baptiste Cardon (French violinist/composer) October 18; Jean-Baptiste Cupis (French violinist/composer) April 30; Joseph Gibbs (British organist/composer) December 12; Orazio Mei (Italian organist/composer) March 1; Johann Gottfried Müthel (German organist/composer) January 17; Théodore Tarade (French violinist/composer) September 14.

Others: Johann Heinrich Stumm (German organ builder) August 23; Charles Wesley (British clergyman/hymnist) March 29.

C. Debuts
Singers: Francesco Albertarelli (Italian bass—Vienna).

D. New Positions
Conductors: Gaetano Brunetti (Royal Chamber Orchestra, Madrid);
Franz Götz (kapellmeister, Archbishop of Olomouc); Joseph Martin
Kraus (hofkapellmeister, Stockholm); Johann Christoph Kühnau
(music director, Trinity Church, Berlin); Vicente Martín y Soler
(kapellmeister, St. Petersburg); Antonio Salieri (kapellmeister, Vi-
enna); Carl Bernhard Wessely (Berlin State Theater).
Others: Theodore Aylward (organ, St. George's Chapel, Windsor).

E. Prizes/Honors
Honors: Jean Baptiste Cordonne (Master of the King's Music, Paris).

F. Biographical Highlights
Olof Åhlström is given a monopoly on all music printing done in
Sweden; Gottlieb Graupner, discharged from the army band, goes to
London, where he begins playing in local orchestras; Thomas
Greatorex returns to London and soon becomes a popular singing
teacher; Johann Nepomuk Hummel begins a four-year concert tour
throughout Europe; Jean-François Lesueur retires from active con-
ducting and moves to the country in order to be able to compose in
peace; Franz Xaver Süssmayr moves to Vienna; Francesco Antonio
Uttini retires from the active musical life of the Swedish Court.

G. Cultural Beginnings
Performing Groups—Choral: New York Musical Society.
Music Publishers: Nathaniel Gow Music Shop and Publisher (Edin-
burgh).
Music Publications: *The Gentleman's Musical Magazine* (London);
Journal de Guitare (by P. J. Porro); *The Lady's Musical Magazine* (Lon-
don); *Musikalische Realzeitung*.
Performing Centers: Mainz Nationaltheater; Teatro Communale
(Faenza).
Other: Chromatic (sic) Trumpet and French Horn (by C. Clogget);
Gentlemen's Private Concerts (Glasgow); Valentine Metzler Music
Shop (London—publishing by 1814).

H. Musical Literature
Andrew Adgate, *The Rudiments of Music*; Esteban de Arteaga, *Rivoluzioni del teatro musicale italiano IV*; Johann F. Bellermann, *Bemerkungen über Russland*; Thomas Busby, *The Divine Harmonist*; Charles
Dibdin, *The Musical Tour of Mr. Dibdin*; Johann N. Forkel, *Allgemeine
geschichte der musik I*; Vincenzo Manfredini, *Difesa della musica moderna*; Etienne Ozi, *Méthode de basson*; Johann J. Walder, *Anleitung zur*

Singkunst; Ernst W. Wolf, *Musikalischer unterricht für Liebhaber und diejenigen, welche die Musik treiben und lehren wollen.*

I. Musical Compositions
Chamber Music:
String Quartets: Luigi Boccherini, *Two String Quartets, Opus 41;* Carl Ditters von Dittersdorf, *Six String Quartets;* Adalbert Gyrowetz, *Six Quartets, Opus 1;* Franz Joseph Haydn, *"Tost" Quartets, Opus 54: No. 1 in G–No. 2 in C–No. 3 in E–"Tost" Quartets, Opus 55: No. 1 in A–No. 2 in f, "The Razor"–No. 3 in B♭;* Wolfgang Amadeus Mozart, *Adagio and Fugue in c, K. 546;* Václav Pichl, *Three Quartets, Opus 13;* Ignace Pleyel, *Nine Quartets (F, A, F, C, F, E♭, G, B♭, A), Ben. 343–352; Quartet in E♭, Opus 352* (violin, two violas, cello).

Sonata/Solos: Jan L. Dussek, *Two Violin Sonatas (G, B♭), Opus 5;* Tommaso Giordani, *Three Violin Sonatas, Opus 34;* Ludwig W. Lachnith, *Six Sonates concertantes, Opus 14* (violin, harpsichord); Wolfgang Amadeus Mozart, *Violin Sonata in F, K. 547;* Giovanni B. Viotti, *Six Violin Sonatas, Opus 4.*

Ensembles: Luigi Boccherini, *Six String Quintets (A, D, D, C, e, B♭), Opus 40;* Jan L. Dussek, *Sonata in A♭, Opus 5/3;* Wolfgang Amadeus Mozart, *Piano Trio No. 8 in E♭, K. 542–No. 9 in C, K. 548–No. 10 in G, K. 564–String Trio in E♭, K. 563;* Franz C. Neubauer, *Six Quartets for Flute and Strings;* Ignace Pleyel, *Five String Quintets, (G, C, E♭, F, D), Ben. 280–84–Six Keyboard Trios (C, G, B♭, A, e, D), Ben. 431–6;* Georg "Abbe" Vogler, *Variations in G* (piano, string quartet).

Piano: Muzio Clementi, *Sonata in F, Opus 21–Three Keyboard Sonatas (D, G, C, "La Chasse), Opus 22;* Franz Joseph Haydn, *Piano Sonata No. 47 in D;* Franz Kotzwara, *The Battle of Prague;* Étienne Méhul, *Three Sonatas II;* Wolfgang Amadeus Mozart, *Sonata No. 15 in C, K. 545;* Samuel Wesley, *Two Keyboard Sonatas (D,E♭), Opus 5/3,4.*

Choral/Vocal Music:
Choral: Giuseppe Amendola, *Orfeo* (cantata); C. P. E. Bach, *St. John Passion V, H.801–St. Matthew Passion VI, H.802*(?); Friedrich L. Benda, *Unser Vater–Der Tod–Dio Religion* (cantatas); Domenico Cimarosa, *Atene edificata* (cantata); Bonaventura Furlanetto, *De solemni nuptiae in domum Lebani* (oratorio); Michael Haydn, *Missa in Honorum Sancte Gotthardi;* Vincenzo Righini, *Il natal d'Apollo* (cantata); Antonio Salieri, *Grand Mass in D, "Kaisermesse."*

Vocal: C. P. E. Bach, *Twelve Masonic Songs, H.704;* Friedrich L. Kunzen, *Weisen und lyrische Gesänge.*

Musical Stage: Pasquale Anfossi, *Artaserse–La maga Circe;* Samuel Arnold, *The Gnome;* Jean-Baptiste Bréval, *Ines et Leonore;* Giuseppe M. Cambini, *Colas et Colette–Le Bon Père;* Christian Cannabich, *Le Croisée;* Luigi Cherubini, *Demophon–Ifigenia in Aulide;* Domenico

Cimarosa, *La vergine del sole–La felicità inaspettata*; Nicolas Dalayrac, *Sargines–Fanchette–Les deux sérénades*; Franz Danzi, *Die Mitternachtsstunde–Der Sylphe*; Carl Ditters von Dittersdorf, *Das rote Käppchen*; Giuseppe Giordani, *Scipione–Il Corrivo–Caio Ostilio*; André Grétry, *Le Rival confident*; Michael Haydn, *Die Ährenleserin*; Johann Naumann, *Medea in Colchide*; Franz Neubauer, *Fernando und Yariko*; Giovanni Paisiello, *Fedra–L'amor contrastato*; Gaetano Pugnani, *Demofoönte*; Johann Reichardt, *Andromeda*; Joseph Boulogne de Saint-Georges, *Le Marchand de Marrons*; Antonio Salieri, *Il talismano*; Giuseppe Sarti, *Cleomene*; William Shield, *Alladin*; Johann C. Vogel, *Démophon*; Georg "Abbe" Vogler, *Gustaf Adolph*; Johann Zumsteeg, *Tamira*.

Orchestra/Band Music:
Concerted Music:
    Piano: Wolfgang Amadeus Mozart, *Concerto No. 26 in D, K. 537, "Coronation."*
    Violin: Rodolphe Kreutzer, *Concerto No. 6 in e, Opus 6*(?); Ignace Pleyel, *Concerto in D, Ben. 103–Concerto in C, Ben. 104*; Giovanni Viotti, *Conerto No. 13 in A–No 14 in a.*
    Other: François Devienne, *Symphonie concertante No. 3 in F, Opus 22* (flute, clarinet, bassoon)–*No. 4 in B♭, Opus 25* (two clarinets); Johann Zumsteeg, *Cello Concerto No. 1.*
Ballet/Incidental Music: Domenico Mazzochi, *L'Amour et Psisché* (B)–*Les fêtes de Tempe* (B).
Symphonies: Luigi Boccherini, *Symphony in c, Opus 41*; Giuseppe M. Cambini, *Three Symphonies (D, B♭, E♭)*; Carl Ditters von Dittersdorf, *Five Symphonies*; Alexandre Guénin, *Three Symphonies (D, A, C), Opus 6*; Franz Joseph Haydn, *No. 90 in C–No. 91 in E♭*; Wolfgang Amadeus Mozart, *No. 39 in E♭, K. 543–No. 40 in g, K. 550–No. 41 in C, "Jupiter," K. 551*; Franz Anton Schubert, *Symphony da camera in D.*

1789
❄

Historical Highlights: The French Estates-General declares itself a National Assembly and passes the Declaration of the Rights of Man—the Parisian Bastille is stormed on July 14; the Brabant Revolution takes place in the Low Countries; *H. M. S. Bounty* mutineers settle on the remote island of Pitcairn; in the United States, the new Constitution goes into effect—George Washington chosen as first president; the Federalist Party is formally founded.

Art and Literature Highlights: Births—artists John "Mad" Martin, Johannes Riepenhausen, Horace Vernet, writers James Fenimore Cooper, Friedrich von Heyden; Deaths—artists Claude-Joseph Vernet, Johann Heinrich Tischbein. Art—David's *Brutus Receiving His Son's Body*, Regnault's *Descent from the Cross*, Trumbull's *Battle of Bunker Hill*; Literature—Alfieri's *Brutus the Second*, Blake's *Songs of Innocence*, Goethe's *Torquato Tasso*.

Musical Highlights

A. Births

Composers: György Adler (Hungary) April 20; József Danse (Poland) December 15; John Fawcett (England-U.S.A.) December 8; Friedrich Fesca (Germany) February 15; Friedrich Silcher (Germany) June 27; Joseph Maria Wolfram (Bohemia) July 21.

Conductors: Ramón Carnicer (Spain) October 24.

Singers: Davidde Banderali (Italian tenor) January 12; Giulio Marco Bordogni (Italian tenor) January 23; Christian Wilhelm Fischer (German bass) September 17; Joséphine Fodor-Mainvielle (French soprano) October 13; Johann Nepomuk Schelble (German tenor/pedagogue) May 16.

Performers: Nicolas-Charles Bochsa (French harpist) August 9; Hippolyte-André Chélard (French violinist/composer) February 1; Joachim Kaczkowski (Polish pianist); George Augustus Kollmann (British pianist/inventor) January 30; Ludwig Maurer (German violinist) February 8; Joseph Mayseder (Austrian violinist/composer) October 26; Johann Schneider (German organist/pedagogue) October 28; Maria Agate Szymanowska (Polish pianist/composer) December 14.

Others: August Heinrich Cranz (German publisher); Horace Meacham (American piano maker) July 19.

B. Deaths

Composers: Franz Xaver Richter (Bohemia) September 12; Lukas Sorkočević (Croatia) September 11.

Singers: Pasquale Bondini (Italian bass/impresario) October 31; Anne Catley (British soprano) October 14; Cecilia Young (British soprano) October 6; Carl Westenholz (German tenor/composer) January 24.

Performers: Christlieb Siegmund Binder (German organist/composer) January 1; Armand-Louis Couperin (French organist/composer) February 2; Pierre-Louis Couperin (French organist) October 10; Jacques Duphly (French harpsichordist/composer) July 15; Johann Wilhelm Hertel (German violinist/composer) June 14; Nicola Mestrino (Italian violinist) July; Joaquín de Oxinaga (Spanish organist/composer) October 24.

Others: Robert Bremner (Scottish publisher) May 12; Johann Friedrich Hartknoch (German publisher) April 1; Sir John Hawkins (British music historian) May 21; Don Giovenale Sacchi (Italian music scholar) September 27; Johann G. Wagner (German piano maker) July 21.

C. Debuts

Singers: Josephina Grassini (Italian contralto—Parma); Jean-Blaise Martin (French baritone—Paris); Giuseppe Naldi (Italian bass—Milan).

Performers: George Bridgetower (Polish-born violinist—Paris, age nine).

D. New Positions

Conductors: João José Baldi (mestre de capela, Guarda Cathedral); Johann Adam Hiller (cantor, Leipzig Thomaskirche); Johann Friedrich Krantz (Weimar Opera); Stanislao Mattei (maestro di cappella, S. Petronio, Bologna); Ignace Joseph Pleyel (first kapellmeister, Strasbourg Cathedral); Antonio Rosetti (kapellmeister, Duke of Mecklenburg-Schwerin).

Others: Carlos Baguer (organ, Barcelona Cathedral); Cayetano Carreño (organ, Caracas Cathedral); Gervais-François Couperin (organ, St. Gervais, Paris); Pierre-Louis Couperin (organ, St. Gervais).

E. Prizes/Honors

Honors: Pierre-Louis Couperin (Organist to the King, Paris).

F. Biographical Highlights

Charles Dibdin begins his extremely popular "Table Entertainments" in London; Jan L. Dussek flees from the French Revolution to London, where he settles for an eleven-year stay; Nicolò Isouard, forced to leave France during the Revolution, goes to Italy; Wolfgang Amadeus Mozart visits Berlin, Leipzig, and Dresden with Prince Lichnowsky; Johann Friedrich Peter writes what is believed to be the oldest preserved chamber music written in the New World.

G. Cultural Beginnings

Performing Groups—Instrumental: Hamburger Harmonic Gesellschaft.

Educational: French Conservatory of Music (Paris).

Performing Centers: Théâtre de Monsieur (Paris); Théâtre de Société (Montreal).

Other: Charles Albrecht, piano maker (Philadelphia); Bacon Piano Co. (New York); Saitenharmonika (by Johann Andreas Stein).

H. Musical Literature

Andrew Adgate, *Philadelphia Harmony*; Olof Åhlström, *Musikaliskt tidsfördrif*; Esteban de Arteaga, *Investigaciones filósoficas sobre la belleza*

ideal, considerata como objeto de todas las artes da imitacion; Anselm
Bayly, *The Alliance of Musick, Poetry and Oratory*; François-Henri Clic-
quot, *Théorie pratique de la facture de l'orgue*; Johann N. Forkel,
*Geschichte der italienischen Oper von ihrem ersten Ursprung an bis auf
gegenwärtige Zeiten*; Jacob French, *New American Melody*; Bonaventura
Furlanetto, *Lezioni de contrappunto*; André Grétry, *Mémoires*; John
Gunn, *Theory and Practice of Fingering the Violoncello*; Johann A. Hiller,
Wer ist wahre Kirchenmusik?; Christian Kalkbrenner, *Theorie der
Tonkunst*; Luigi Sabbatini, *Elementi teorici della musica colla pratica dei
medesimi, in duetti e terzetti a canone accompagnate dal basso*; Daniel G.
Türk, *Clavierschule*.

I. **Musical Compositions**
   Chamber Music:
   String Quartets: Luigi Boccherini, *Two Quartets (A, C), Opus 42*;
   Adalbert Gyrowetz, *Six Quartets, Opus 2*; Wolfgang Amadeus
   Mozart, *"Prussian" Quartets: No. 1 (No. 21) in D, K. 575*; Ignace
   Pleyel, *Six Quartets (D, F, A, G, B♭, C), Ben. 381–6*.
   Sonata/Solos: Johann G. Albrechtsberger, *Six Sonatas for Two Violins,
   Opus 8*; Gaetano Brunetti, *Viola Sonata in b*; Jan L. Dussek, *Three Flute
   Sonatas (C, G, E♭), Opus 7–Three Violin Sonatas (C, F, A), Opus 8–Three
   Violin Sonatas (B♭, C, D), Opus 9–Three Violin Sonatas (A, g, E), Opus 10*.
   Ensembles: Luigi Boccherini, *Octet in E♭–Four String Quintets (f, C,
   b, g), Opus 42*; Carl Ditters von Dittersdorf, *Six String Quintets*;
   Domenico Mazzochi, *Three Quartets, Opus 3*; Wolfgang Amadeus
   Mozart, *Clarinet Quintet in A, K. 581*; Johann E. Peter, *Six String
   Quintets (D, A, G, c, B♭, E♭)*; Ignace Pleyel, *Two String Quintets (B♭,
   G), Ben. 278,9–String Quintet in F, Ben. 285–Six String Trios (C, E♭, D,
   e, B♭, G), Ben. 404–9*.
   Piano: Johann Christian Bach, *Sonata in C*; Ludwig van Beethoven,
   Two Preludes, Opus 39 (piano/organ); Muzio Clementi, *Two
   Sonatas, Opus 24*; Franz Joseph Haydn, *Sonata No. 43–Sonata No.
   44–Fantasie in C*; Wolfgang Amadeus Mozart, *Sonata No. 17 in D, K.
   576*; Samuel Wesley, *Three Sonatas (C, F, D) Opus 3*.
   Organ: Johann Albrechtsberger, *Fuga sopra do, re, mi, fa, sol, la,
   Opus 5*; David T. Nicolai, *Fantasy and Fugue*.
   Choral/Vocal Music:
   Choral: Franz Ignaz Beck, *Stabat Mater*; Friedrich (W. H.) Benda,
   Die Grazien (cantata); Luigi Cherubini, *Circé* (cantata); Bonaventura
   Furlanetto, *Triumphus Jephte* (oratorio); Giovanni Paisiello, *Requiem
   in c for Double Choir*; Giuseppe Sarti, *Te Deum*; Georg "Abbe" Vogler,
   Miserere in E♭; Christian T. Weinlig, *Die Feier des Todes Jesu* (oratorio).
   Vocal: George Benda, *Cephalus und Aurore* (solo cantata); Franz
   Joseph Haydn, *Arianna a Naxos* (solo cantata).

Musical Stage: Ferdinando Bertoni, *Nitteti*; Giuseppe M. Cambini, *Aleméon–Alcidas–Cora*; João de Sousa Carvalho, *Numa Pompilio II rè dei romane*; Stanislas Champein, *Le Nouvelle Don Quichotte*; Domenico Cimarosa, *La Cleopatra*; Nicolas Dalayrac, *Raoul, sire de Crequi–Les deux petits Savoyards*; Franz Danzi, *Der Triumph der Treue–Der Quasi-Mann*; Nicolas Dezède, *Auguste et Théodora*; Carl Ditters von Dittersdorf, *Hieronymus Knicker–Der Schiffspatron*; Tommaso Giordani, *Perseverance*; André Grétry, *Aspasie–Raoul Barbe-bleue*; Friedrich L. Kunze, *Holger Danske*; Vicente Martín y Soler, *The Unfortunate Hero Kosometovich*; Johann G. Naumann, *Protesilao*; Giovanni Paisiello, *Nina–Catone in Utica–I zingari in fiera*; Gaetano Pugnani, *Demetrio a Rodi*; Johann Reichardt, *Brenno–Jery und Bätely–Claudine von Villa Bella*; Francesco Rosetti, *Das Winterfest der Hirten*; Antonio Salieri, *La cifra–Il pastor fido*; Josef Schuster, *Rübezahl*; Stephen Storace, *The Haunted Tower*; Franz X. Süssmayr, *Die väterliche Rache–Die liebe auf dem Lande*; Paul Wranitzky, *Oberon, Konig der Elfen*; Nicola Zingarelli, *Antigone–Artaserse*.

Orchestra/Band Music:

Concerted Music:

Violin: Giovanni B. Viotti, *Concerto No. 15 in B♭–No. 16 in e*.

Other: Jean-Baptiste Bréval, *Symphonie concertante, Opus 30* (oboe, horn)(?).

Ballet/Incidental Music: Domenico Mazzochi, *Admète* (B)–*Les caprices de Galatée* (B).

Symphonies: Luigi Boccherini, *Symphony in D, Opus 42*; Gaetano Brunetti, *No. 16 in D–No. 17 in B♭–No. 28 in A*; Franz Joseph Haydn, *No. 92 in G, "Oxford"*; Ignace Pleyel, *Three Symphonies (E♭, F, G), Ben. 139–41*.

1790
❖

Historical Highlights: The French National Assembly draws up a constitution forming a limited monarchy; Austria crushes the Brabant Revolution in Belgium; the Third Mysore War is fought in India; in the United States, the census shows a population of 3,929,214 within thirteen states; Philadelphia, the largest colonial city, becomes the temporary new capital; the Treaty of Greenville made with the Indians settles the Ohio problem.

Art and Literature Highlights: Births—sculptor John Gibson, writers Per Daniel Atterbom, Fitz-Greene Halleck, Alphonse de Lamartine; Deaths—artists John Bacon, Winthrop Chandler, writer Antoine de Bertin, philosopher Adam Smith. Art—Fuseli's *Titania and Bottom*,

Houdon's *Apollo*, Stubbs' *Two Hunters by a Lake*; Literature—Burns's *Tam O'Shanter*, Radcliffe's *A Sicilian Romance*, Warren's *Poems Dramatic and Miscellaneous*.

Musical Highlights

A. Births

Composers: Ignaz Assmayer (Austria) February 11; Louis-Joseph Daussoigne-Méhul (France) June 10; Isaac Nathan (England-Australia).

Conductors: Christian August Pohlenz (Germany) July 3.

Singers: Giovanni David (Italian tenor) September 15; Domenico Donzelli (Italian tenor) February 2; Anton Forti (Austrian tenor/baritone) June 8; Nicola Vaccai (Italian singing teacher/composer) March 15.

Performers: Wilhelm Johann Agthe (German pianist) July 13; Luigi Legnani (Italian guitarist) November 7; Carl Lipínsky (Polish violinist/composer) October 30; Wilhelm Speyer (German violinist/composer) June 21; Waldemar Thrane (Norwegian violinist/conductor/composer) October 8; Chrétien Urhan (French violinist/violist) February 16; Wenzel Wilhelm Würfel (Bohemian pianist/conductor) May 6.

Others: Franz Joseph Antony (German music author) February 1; Luigi Lambertini (Italian piano maker) March 17; William Letton Viner (British hymnist) May 14.

B. Deaths

Composers: Charles-Joseph van Helmont (Belgium) June 8; Johann Küchler (Germany) January 16.

Conductors: Johann Friedrich Klöffler (Germany) February 21.

Singers: Angiola Calori (?Italian soprano); Halifax Lowe (British tenor) October; Thomas Morris (British tenor/organist) September 3; Giusto Ferdinando Tenducci (Italian castrato soprano) January 25.

Performers: Chapel Bond (British organist) February 14; Wilhelm Gottfried Enderle (German violinist/composer) February 12; Carlo Ferrari (Italian cellist) April 2; Johann Baptist Krumpholtz (Bohemian harpist/composer) February 19; Ludwig August Lebrun (German oboist/composer) December 16; John Worgan (British organist/composer) August 24.

Others: François-Henri Clicquot (French organ builder) May 24; C. H. Eisenbrandt (German instrument maker) April 13; Nicholas Esterházy (Hungarian patron of the arts) September 28.

C. Debuts
Singers: Antonio Peregrino Benelli (Italian tenor—Naples); Jean Elleviou (French tenor—Paris); Elizaveta Semyonova Sandunova (Russian mezzo-soprano—St. Petersburg).
Performers: Jacques-Pierre Rode (French violinist—Paris).

D. New Positions
Conductors: Inácio António de Almeida (mestre de capela, Nossa Senhora de Oliviera, Guimaraes—official in 1793); Antonio Brunetti (maestro di cappella, Chieti Cathedral); Luigi Caruso (maestro di cappella, Cingoli); Franz Xaver Glöggl (kapellmeister, Linz Cathedral); Johann Baptist Henneberg (Theater an der Wien); Pierre La Houssaye (Théâtre de Monsieur, Paris); António Leal Moreira (Italian Opera Theater, Lisbon); Philippe Jacques Pfeffinger (maître de musique, Strasbourg); Christian Ruppe (kapelmeester, University of Leiden).
Others: Frédéric Blasius (director, Comédie-Italienne, Paris); William Crotch (organ, Christ Church, Oxford); Philip Hayes (organ, St. John's College); Johann Christian Rinck (municipal organ, Giessen); Nicolas Séjan (organ, Royal Chapel, Paris).

E. Prizes/Honors
Honors: Anton Walter (Royal Court Chamber Organ and Instrument Maker).

F. Biographical Highlights
Ludwig van Beethoven meets Haydn; Muzio Clementi makes his last public appearance; Johann L. Dussek, settled in London, quickly becomes a favorite of the public; Franz Joseph Haydn is retired with a pension; Johann Nepomuk Hummel begins a two-year stay in London; Johann Reichardt is given a three-year leave of absence with pay; Daniel Steibelt takes up permanent residence in Paris; Joseph Weigl becomes assistant to Salieri at the Vienna Court; Joseph Wölfl goes to Vienna to study with Mozart; Paul Wranitzky becomes concertmaster of the Vienna Opera.

G. Cultural Beginnings
Performing Groups: Åbo Musical Society (Finland).
Educational: Perugia Musical Institute; Society of Musical Graduates (London).
Music Publishers: Maurice Hime, music publisher (Liverpool); George Walker, music publisher (London).
Music Publications: *Journal de Modinhas*.
Performing Centers: Théâtre Royal (Nice).
Other: J. A. Baader and Co., zither makers (Mittenwald); Oliver Holden Music Store (Charleston, South Carolina); James Johnson

Music Shop (Lawnmarket); Theobald Monzani Flute Co. (London); Tannenberg Organ, Zion Lutheran Church (Philadelphia).

H. Musical Literature

Olof Åhlström, *Skaldestycken satte i musik*; Johann G. Albrechtsberger, *Gründliche Anweisung zur Composition*; Franz F. Böcklin, *Beyträge zur Geschichte der Musik besonders in Deutschland*; Guillaume Gatayes, *Guitar Method*; Joseph Gehot, *The Art of Bowing the Violin–Complete Instructions for Every Musical Instrument*; Ernest L. Gerber, *Historisch-biographisches Lexikon der Tonkünstler I*; Ferdinand Kauer, *Singschule nach dem neuesten System der Tonkunst*; Friedrich Marpurg, *Neue Methode, allerley Arten von Temperaturen dem Claviere aufs bequemste mitzutheilen*; Johann A. Schulz, *Gedanken über den Einfluss der Musik auf die Bildung eines Volks*; Francisco Solano, *Exame instructivo sobre a Musica multiforme, metrica e rythmica*.

I. Musical Compositions
Chamber Music:

String Quartets: François Barthélémon, *Six Quartets (D, A, E♭, c, B♭, E), Opus 12*; Luigi Boccherini, *Two Quartets, Opus 43*; Jean-Baptiste Davaux, *Four Quartets, Opus 14*; Felice de' Giardini, *Six Quartets, Opus 29*; Adalbert Gyrowetz, *Six Quartets, Opus 3*; Franz Joseph Haydn, *"Tost" Quartets, Opus 64: No. 1 in C–No. 2 in b–No. 3 in B♭–No. 4 in G–No. 5 in D, "The Lark"–No. 6 in E♭*; Wolfgang Amadeus Mozart, *"Prussian" Quartets: No. 2 (No. 22) in B♭, K. 589–No. 3 (No. 23) in F, K. 590*.

Sonata/Solos: Jan L. Dussek, *Three Violin Sonatas (F, B♭, C), Opus 12–Three Violin Sonatas (B♭, D, G), Opus 13*.

Ensembles: Luigi Boccherini, *Three String Quintets (E♭, D, F), Opus 43*; François Devienne, *Six Trios for Two Clarinets and Bassoon, Opus 27*; Felice de' Giardini, *Six String Trios, Opus 28–Six Piano Trios, Opus 30*; Adalbert Gyrowetz, *Six Piano Trios, Opus 4*; Franz Joseph Haydn, *Piano Trios No. 11–14*; Michael Haydn, *Quintet in E♭*; Wolfgang Amadeus Mozart, *String Quintet in D, K. 593*; Václav Pichl, *Three Quartets for Clarinet and Strings, Opus 16*; Ignace Pleyel, *Serenade in F, Ben. 216–Three Keyboard Trios (F, G, E♭), Ben. 437–9*.

Piano: Carl C. Agthe, *Three Easy Sonatas*; Muzio Clementi, *Three Sonatas (E♭, F, E♭), Opus 23–Two Sonatas (F, B♭), Opus 24–Six Sonatas (c, G, B♭, A, f♯, D), Opus 25*; Felice de' Giardini, *Two Keyboard Sonatas, Opus 31*; Tommaso Giordani, *Six Keyboard Sonatas, Opus 34–Six Keyboard Sonatas, Opus 35*.

Organ: Wolfgang Amadeus Mozart, *Adagio and Allegro, K. 594, for Mechanical Organ*.

Choral/Vocal Music:
Choral: Ludwig van Beethoven, *Cantata on the Death of Joseph II*; François Gossec, *Te Deum* (male voices); Johann Naumann, *La morte d'Abel* (oratorio)–*Psalm 103, "Lobe den Herrn, Meine Seele"*; Giovanni Paisiello, *Cantata per la sollennità del S. Corpo dei Cristo*; Niccolò Piccinni, *Giove revotato* (cantata); Vincenzo Righini, *Mass in D, "Krönungsmesse"*; Antonio Salieri, *Te Deum de incoronazione.*
Vocal: Johann Heinrich Egli, *Lieder des Weisheit un Tugend*; Samuel Holyoke, *Washington*; William Jackson, *Twelve Songs, Opus 16*(?); Maria Theresia von Paradis, *Leonore*; Johann F. Reichardt, *Geistliche Gesänge von Lavater.*
Musical Stage: Felice Alessandri, *L'ouverture du grand opéra italien à Nankin*; Samuel Arnold, *New Spain*; Friedrich L. Benda, *Der verlobung*; Francesco Bianchi, *La vendetta de Nino*; Luigi Cherubini, *Marguerite d'Anjou*; Giovanni Battista Cimadoro, *Pimmaglione*; Nicolas Dalayrac, *La Soirée orageuse–Le Chêne patriotique–Vert-Vert*; François Devienne, *Le mariage clandestin*; Nicolas Dezède, *Les trois noces–Ferdinand–Adéle et Didie*; Carl Ditters von Dittersdorf, *Hokus-Pokus–Der Teufel ein Hydraulikus*; Giuseppe Giordani, *Caio Mario*; André Grétry, *Pierre le Grand*; Pietro Guglielmi, *La serva innamorata*; Leopold Kozeluch, *Didone abbandonata*; Rodolphe Kreutzer, *Jeanne d'Arc*; Louis S. Lebrun, *L'art d'aimer, ou L'amour au village*; Vicente Martín y Soler, *La melomania*; Étienne Méhul, *Euphrosine*; Wolfgang Amadeus Mozart, *Cosi fan tutti, K. 588*; Wenzel Müller, *Der Sonnenfest der Braminen*; Giovanni Paisiello, *Zenobia in Palmira–Le vane gelosie*; Johann Reichardt, *L'Olimpiade*; Vincenzo Righini, *Alcide al Bivio*; Antonio Salieri, *Catilina–Sappho*; William Shield, *The Czar Peter*; Nicola Zingarelli, *La morte de Cesare.*
Orchestra/Band Music:
Concerted Music:
  Piano: Daniil Kashin, *Concerto.*
  Violin: Rodolphe Kreutzer, *Concerto No. 7 in A, Opus 7*(?), Giovanni Viotti, *Concerto No. 17 in d–No. 18 in e.*
  Other: François Devienne, *Bassoon Concerto No. 3 in F*; Ignace Pleyel, *Viola/Cello Concerto in D, Ben. 105.*
Ballet/Incidental Music: Johann Reichardt, *Faust I* (IM).
Symphonies: Luigi Boccherini, *Symphony in D, Opus 43*; Gaetano Brunetti, *No. 34 in F*; Franz I. Danzi, *No. 1 in D*(?); José M. García, *Sinfonia funebre*; Franz Neubauer, *No. 1, Opus 1*; Ignace Pleyel, *Five Symphonies (c, C, E♭, D, G), Ben. 142–46.*

1791

Historical Highlights: Louis XVI and his family are put under house arrest in Paris; the Canada Act divides the country into the provinces of Ontario and Quebec, the English and French sectors; the International Copyright Agreement is passed by several European countries; in the United States, the Bill of Rights is ratified; Vermont becomes state number fourteen, the first to enter following the original thirteen states.

Art and Literature Highlights: Births—artists Jean-Louis Géricault, Samuel F. B. Morse, writers Franz Grillparzer, Benjamin Young Prime, Augustin Eugène Scribe; Deaths—sculptor Étienne Maurice Falconet, poet Benjamin Young Prime. Art—Copley's *Siege of Gibraltar*, Langhan's *Brandenburg Gate* (Berlin); Literature—Bellman's *Fredmans Sänger*, Klinger's *Fausts Leben, Toten und Höllenfahrt*, Rowson's *Charlotte*.

Musical Highlights

A. Births

Composers: Marie-Désiré Beaulieu (France) April 11; Joseph Bengraff (Germany) June 4; José Melchor Gomis y Colomor (Spain) January 6; Ferdinand Hérold (France) January 28; Giacomo Meyerbeer (Germany) September 5; Jan Václav Voříšek (Bohemia) May 11.

Conductors: Friedrich Wilhelm Grund (Germany) October 7; Peter Joseph von Lindpaintner (Germany) December 9; Pietro Romani (Italy) May 29.

Singers: Nicolas Levasseur (French bass) March 9; John Sinclair (Scottish tenor) December 9.

Performers: Henri-Louis Blanchard (French violinist/critic) April(?); Carl Czerny (Austrian pianist/pedagogue/composer) February 20; Johann Wilhelm Gabrielski (German flutist) May 27; Johann Gottlob Töpfer (German organist/author) December 4.

Others: Félix Savart (French acoustician) June 30.

B. Deaths

Composers: Joseph Bengraf (Germany); Luigi Braccini (Italy); Giovanni Battista Ferrandini (Italy) September 25; Francis Hopkinson (U.S.A.) May 9; Johann August Just (Austria) December; Wolfgang Amadeus Mozart (Austria) December 5; Domenico Paradies (Italy) August 25.

Singers: John Beard (British tenor) February 5; Franziska (Dorothea) Lebrun (German soprano) May 14; Marie-Anne-Catherine Quinault (French soprano).

Performers: John Alcock, Jr. (British organist) March; Carlo Besozzi (Italian oboist) March 22; Guillaume Boutmy (Belgian organist/harpsichordist) January 22; Franz Kotzwara (Czech violinist) September 2; Carl Türrschmidt (German horn virtuoso) November 1.
Others: Christian Friedrich Schubart (German music author/poet/composer) October 10; John Wesley (British hymnist) March 2.

C. **Debuts**
Singers: Margarete Luise Schick (German soprano—Righini); Luigi Zamboni (Italian bass—Ravenna).
Performers: Sophia Giustina Corri (Dussek-Italian pianist—London).

D. **New Positions**
Conductors: Johann G. Albrechtsberger (kapellmeister, Vienna); Pasquale Anfossi (maestro di cappella, St. John Lateran, Rome); Domenico Cimarosa (kapellmeister, Vienna); Giuseppe Gazzaniga (maestro di cappella, Crema Cathedral); Giuseppe Giordani (maestro di cappella, Fermo Cathedral); Johann Baptist Kucharz (Italian Opera, Prague); Friedrich L. A. Kunzen (kapellmeister, Copenhagen); José Mauricio (mestre de capela, Coimbra Cathedral); José Pons (choirmaster, Gerona Cathedral); Johann Rudolf Zumsteeg (German Opera, Stuttgart).
Others: George Thomas Smart (organ, St. James Chapel, London).

E. **Prizes/Honors**
Honors: Antonio Calegari (Accademico Filarmonica, Bologna); Franz Joseph Haydn (Mus.D., Oxford).

F. **Biographical Highlights**
Domenico Cimarosa leaves Russia and returns to Vienna; Franz Joseph Haydn visits London for the first time when his symphonies are performed at Salomon's concerts; Wolfgang Amadeus Mozart receives a visit from the "mysterious stranger" who commissions him to write a *Requiem*; Ignace Joseph Pleyel begins a year's stay in London conducting the Professional Concerts.

G. **Cultural Beginnings**
Performing Groups—Choral: Berliner Singakademie; St. Cecilia Society of New York.
Performing Groups—Instrumental: Boston Philo-Harmonic Society.
Music Publishers: Hug and Co., music house and publishers (Zürich).
Music Publications: *Musikalisches Magazin auf der Höhe* (Brunswick); *Musikalisches Wochenblatt*.
Performing Centers: Her Majesty's Theater II (London); Teatro Riccardi (Bergamo); Théâtre de St. Pierre (New Orleans); Théâtre Français de la Rue Richelieu (Paris).

Other: Noblemen's Subscription Concerts (London); Orchestrion (by Thomas Anton Kunz).

H. Musical Literature

Giuseppe Aprile, *The Modern Italian Method of Singing;* Bartolomeo Campagnoli, *Nouvelle méthode de la mécanique progressive du jeu de violon;* Johann F. Dalberg, *Vom Erfinden und Bilden;* Francesco Galeazzi, *Elementi teorico-pratici di Musica I;* Samuel Holyoke, *Harmonia Americana;* William Jackson, *Observations on the Present State of Music in London;* Giuseppe Sarti, *Trattato del basso generale;* Daniel Schubart, *Leben und gesinnungen von ihm selbst im Kerker aufgesetz;* Johann G. Tromlitz, *Ausführlicher und gründlicher unterricht die Flöte zu spielen;* Daniel G. Türk, *Kurze anweisung zum generalbassspielen;* Hardenack Zinck, *Kompositionen für den Gesang und das Clavier I.*

I. Musical Compositions

Chamber Music:

String Quartets: Johann G. Distler, *Three Quartets, Opus 1;* Ignace Pleyel, *Six Quartets (C, B♭, e, G, A, f), Ben. 353–8;* Anton Wranitzky, *Six Quartets, Opus 1–Three Quartets, Opus 2, Book 1.*

Sonata/Solos: Thomas Attwood, *Three Cello Sonatas, Opus 2;* Jan L. Dussek, *Three Violin Sonatas (C, G, F), Opus 14–Three Violin Sonatas (C, F, G), Opus 16;* Franz C. Neubauer, *Violin Sonata.*

Ensembles: Muzio Clementi, *Three Piano Trios, Opus 27;* François Devienne, *Three Quartets for Flute and Strings, Book III, Opus 62;* Wolfgang Amadeus Mozart, *String Quintet in E♭, K. 614–Adagio and Rondo in c, K. 617;* Ignace Pleyel, *String Sextet in F, Ben. 261–Three Keyboard Trios (B♭, C, f), Ben. 440–2.*

Piano: Muzio Clementi, *Sonata in F, Opus 26–Three Sonatas (F, D, G), Opus 27;* Johann N. Hummel, *Variations, Opus 1–Variations, Opus 2.*

Choral/Vocal Music:

Choral: Domenico Cimarosa, *La serenata non preveduta* (cantata); François Gossec, *Le chant du 14 juillet;* Michael Haydn, *Der fröhliche wiederschein* (cantata); Wolfgang Amadeus Mozart, *Motet, "Ave verum corpus," K. 618–Eine Kleine Freimauer–Cantata, K. 623–Requiem Mass in d, K. 626* (finished by Franz X. Süssmayr); Johann Naumann, *Mass in A;* Giovanni Paisiello, *Te Deum–Cantata epitalamica.*

Musical Stage: François Alday, *Geneviève de Brabant;* Felice Alessandri, *Dario;* Samuel Arnold, *The Surrender of Calais;* Friedrich L. Benda, *Louise;* Giuseppe Cambini, *Nantilda and Dagobert;* Luigi Cherubini, *Lodoïska;* Nicolas Dalayrac, *Camille–Philippe et Georgette–Agnès et Olivier;* Evstigney Fomin, *Magician, Fortune-Teller and Matchmaker;* Giuseppe Gazzaniga, *La disfatta dei Mori;* Giuseppe Giordani, *Don Mitrillo contrastato–Medonte;* Tommaso

Giordani, *The Distressed Knight*; André Grétry, *Guillaume Tell*; Franz Joseph Haydn, *L'anima del filosofo*; Rodolphe Kreutzer, *Paul et Virginie–Lodoiska–Le franc breton*; Honoré Langlé, *Corisandre*; Louis S. Lebrun, *Montansier*; Vicente Martín y Soler, *Il castello d'Atlante*; Étienne Méhul, *Cora*; Wolfgang Amadeus Mozart, *The Magic Flute, K. 620–La clemenza di Tito, K. 621*; Wenzel Müller, *Der Fagottist*; Johann Naumann, *L'Olimpiade*; Ferdinando Paër, *Circe*; Giovanni Paisiello, *Ipermestra*; Johann Reichardt, *Erwin und Elmire*; Giuseppe Sarti, *Il trionfo d'Atalanta*; Johann Schenk, *Der Erntekranz*; William Shield, *The Woodman*; Franz X. Süssmayr, *Der rauschige Hans*; Nicola Zingarelli, *Pirro, Ré d'Epiro*.

Orchestra/Band Music:
Concerted Music:
> **Piano:** Jan L. Dussek, *Concerto in F, Opus 14*; Wolfgang Amadeus Mozart, *Piano Concerto No. 27 in B♭, K. 595*; Georg "Abbe" Vogler, *Variations on Air de Marlborough*.
> **Violin:** Johann G. Distler, *Concerto*; Ignace Pleyel, *Symphonie concertante in B♭* (violin, viola); Giovanni Viotti, *No. 19 in g*.
> **Other:** François Devienne, *Symphonie concertante in F* (flute, oboe, bassoon); Wolfgang Amadeus Mozart, *Clarinet Concerto in A, K. 622*; Ignace Pleyel, *Symphonie concertante in B♭, Ben. 112* (violin, viola); Giovanni B. Viotti, *Concerto No. 17 in d–No. 19 in g*.

Ballet/Incidental Music: Johann Reichardt, *Egmont* (IM).
Symphonies: Franz Joseph Haydn, *"London Symphonies": No. 1 (No. 93) in D–No. 2 (No. 94) in G, "Surprise"–No. 3 (No. 95) in c–No. 4 (No. 96) in D, "Miracle"*; Franz C. Neubauer, *Symphony, Opus 1*; Ignace Pleyel, *Symphony in d, Ben. 147*.

1792
❄

Historical Highlights: Poland suffers invasion by both Russia and Prussia; the Russo-Turkish War ends; the War of the First Coalition begins—France declares war on Austria and Prussia; Denmark abolishes the slave trade by her ships; in the United States, George Washington is re-elected as president; Congress passes a Coinage Act establishing the first mint at Philadelphia and providing for a decimal system of money; Kentucky becomes state number fifteen.

Art and Literature Highlights: Births—artists George Cruikshank, George Hayter, poet John Keble; Deaths—artists John Greenwood, Joshua Reynolds, dramatist Denis Fonvizin. Art—Fuseli's *Falstaff in the Buck Basket*, Hardy's *Portrait of Franz Joseph Haydn*, Jennings' *Liberty Dis-*

playing the Arts and Sciences; Literature—Belknap's *The Foresters, an American Tale*, Legouvé's *La Mort d'Abel*, More's *Village Politics*.

Musical Highlights

A. Births

Composers: Gioacchino Rossini (Italy) February 29.

Conductors: Philippe Musard (France) November 8.

Performers: Louis François-Philippe Drouet (French flutist/composer) April 14; Marie Leopoldine Pachler-Koschak (Austrian pianist) October 2; (Philip) Cipriani Potter (British pianist/composer) October 2; Giovanni Puzzi (Italian horn virtuoso); Johann Friedrich Schwencke (German organist/composer) April 30; Charles Thibault (French-born pianist/composer) September 5.

Others: Anton Bernhard Fürstenau (German music author/flutist) October 20; Guillaume Charles Gand (French violin maker) July 22; Moritz Hauptmann (German music theorist/composer) October 13; Emanuel Langbecker (German musicologist) August 31; Lowell Mason (American music educator) January 8; John Osborne (American piano maker); Sylvanus Billings Pond (American publisher/composer) April 5; Peter Joseph Simrock (German publisher) August 18.

B. Deaths

Composers: Antonio Boroni (Italy) December 21; Giovanni Battista Casali (Italy) July 6; Nicolas Dezède (France) September 11; Nathanael Gottfried Gruner (Germany) August 2; Joseph M. Kranz (Germany) December 15; Antonio Rosetti (Bohemia) June 30; Johann M. Schmid (Bohemia) December 19; Ernst Wilhelm Wolf (Germany) December 1.

Singers: Gaetano Guadagni (Italian castrato contralto/soprano) November; Pierre de La Garde (French baritone)(?); Jean-Louis Laruette (French tenor/composer) January 10; Elizabeth Ann Linley (British soprano) June 28.

Performers: Bernardo Aliprandi (Italian cellist/composer); Johann Friedrich Beckmann (German organist/composer) April 25; Friedrich Ludwig Benda (German violinist/composer) March 20.

Others: Charles-Simon Favart (French librettist/impresario) May 12; Ernst Johann Haas (German instrument maker) February 29; Jacob Kirckman (German-born harpsichord maker) June 9; Abbé Pierre-Joseph Roussier (French music author) August 18.

C. Debuts

Performers: Andrew Ashe (Irish flutist—London); John Field (Irish pianist—Dublin, age nine); Jozef Jawurek (Polish pianist—Warsaw).

D. New Positions

Conductors: Joseph A. Elsner (kapellmeister, Lemberg); Leopold Anton Kozeluch (kapellmeister, Vienna); Cándido José Ruano (maestro de capilla, Toledo Cathedral); Franz Xaver Süssmayr (Vienna National Theater); Bernhard Anselm Weber (Berlin Nationaltheater). **Others:** Joseph Corfe (organ, Salisbury Cathedral); Johann Christian Friedrich Haeffner (director, Swedish Royal Opera); Friedrich Ludwig Seidel (organ, Marienkirche, Berlin).

E. Prizes/Honors

Honors: Olof Åhlström (Swedish Academy).

F. Biographical Highlights

Ludwig van Beethoven goes to Vienna, where he studies a short time with Haydn; Charles Dibdin opens his own theater in London in which to produce his "entertainments"; Franz Joseph Haydn, following a highly successful London adventure, returns in triumph to Vienna; James Hewitt moves to the United States and settles in New York; Johann Nepomuk Maelzel settles in Vienna as a music teacher; Joseph Boulogne de Saint-Georges becomes a colonel in the French Negro Regiment; organist Raynor Taylor leaves London and emigrates to the United States; Isaiah Thomas moves his publishing firm to Boston.

G. Cultural Beginnings

Performing Groups—Choral: Royal Opera Co. of Berlin.
Festivals: Belfast Harp Festival.
Music Publishers: Johann Gerstenberg Music Store and Publishing House (Leipzig); Hans Nägeli (Wetzikon).
Music Publications: *The Music Magazine* (U.S.A.).
Performing Centers: Sans Souci Theater (London); Spectacle de la Rue St. Pierre (New Orleans); Teatro La Fenice (Venice).

H. Musical Literature

Johann G. Albrechtsberger, *Kurzegefasste methode, den Generalbass zu erlernen*; Johann N. Forkel, *Allgemeine literature der Musik*; Ernst L. Gerber, *Historisch-biographisches Lexicon II*; Johann A. Hiller, *Anweisung zum Violinspiel*; Oliver Holden, *American Harmony*; Christian Kalkbrenner, *Kurzer Abriss der Geschichte der Tonkunst*; Justin H. Knecht, *Gemeinnützliches elementarwerk der harmonie und des generalbasses I*; Jean P. Martini, *Mélopée moderne*; Johann Reichardt, ed., *Studien für Tonkünstler und Musikfreunde*; Daniel Türk, *Kurze Anweisung zum Klavierspielen*; Amand Vanderhagen, *Méthode nouvelle et raisonnée pour le Hautbois*; Hardenack Zinck, *Kompositionen für den Gesang und das Clavier II, III*.

I. Musical Compositions
Chamber Music:

String Quartets: Luigi Boccherini, *Six Quartets (B♭, e, F, G, D, E♭)*, *Opus 44*; Franz C. Neubauer, *Six Quartets (no opus number)–Three Quartets, Opus 3–Three Quartets, Opus 4*; Ignace Pleyel, *Six Quartets (F, B♭, D, E♭, G, E)*, Ben. 359–364; Anton Wranitzky, *Three Quartets, Opus 2, Book 2–Three Quartets, Opus 4*.

Sonata/Solos: Jan L. Dussek, *Three Violin Sonatas (B♭, a, E♭)*, *Opus 18*; Giovanni B. Viotti, *Six Violin Sonatas, Book II*.

Ensembles: Luigi Boccherini, *Four Quintets (c, A, B♭, C), Opus 45*; Jean-Baptiste Davaux, *Six Trios, Opus 15* (two violins, viola).

Piano: Ludwig van Beethoven, *Sonata in F*; Muzio Clementi, *Three Sonatas (c, E♭, G), Opus 28*; Jan L. Dussek, *Sonata in a, Opus 18/2*; Johann N. Hummel, *Sonata in C, Opus2a/3*; August E. Müller, *Three Sonatas, Opus 3*; Maria Thesesia von Paradis, *Six Sonatas, Opus 1–Six Sonatas, Opus 2*; Ignace Pleyel, *Twelve German Dances*, Ben. 601–12.

Choral/Vocal Music:
Choral:

Oratorio: Friedrich (W. H.) Benda, *Die Jungen am Grabe des Auferstandenen*; Bonaventura Furlanetto, *Gideon*; Friedrich H. Himmel, *Isacco figura del redentore*; Niccolò Piccinni, *Gionata*.

Other: François Gossec, *Hymne à la Liberté*; Michael Haydn, *Missa Sancte Crucis*; Friedrich H. Himmel, *La danza* (secular cantata); Joseph M. Kraus, *Funeral Cantata*; Maria Theresia von Paradies, *Trauerkantate*.

Vocal: Georg Benda, *Bendas Klagen*; Luigi Boccherini, *Twelve Concert Arias*; Dmitri Borniansky, *Eight Alexseyevna Songs*; Franz Joseph Haydn, *Twelve English Ballads*; Oliver Holden, *Coronation* (hymn tune, "All Hail the Power"); Claude Rouget de l'Isle, *La Marseillaise* (French National Anthem).

Musical Stage: Samuel Arnold, *The Enchanted Wood*; Thomas Attwood, *The Prisoner*; Friedrich L. Benda, *Mariechen*; Benjamin Carr, *Philander and Silvia*; Domenico Cimarosa, *Il matrimonio segreto*; Dominique Della Maria, *Il maestro di cappella*; Franz von Destouches, *Die Thomasnacht*; Nicolas Dezède, *Paulin et Clairette–Mélita*; Giuseppe Farinelli, *Il Dottorato di Pulcinella*; Evstigney Fomin, *Orpheus and Eurydice*; Pierre Gabeaux, *Les deux Suisses–Le Paria*; Giuseppe Giordani, *Atalanta*; André Grétry, *Les deux couvents–Basile*; Georg C. Grosheim, *Titania*; Rodolphe Kreutzer, *Charlotte et Werther–La Siège de Lille*; Johann Naumann, *Amore Giustificato*; Giovanni Paisiello, *Elfrida–Il ritorno d'Idomeneo in Creta– Didone abbandonata*; Niccolò Piccinni, *La serva onorata*; Giovanni Rossi, *Piramo e Tisbe*; Giuseppe Sarti, *Lo stravagante inglese*; William Shield, *Hartford Bridge*; Stephen Storace, *The Pirates*;

Franz X. Süssmayr, *Moses*; Angelo Tarchi, *Le Danaidi*; Georg Vogler, *Gustav Adolph*; Joseph Weigl, *Der strassensammler*; Paul Wranitzky, *Rudolf von Felseck*; Nicola Zingarelli, *Atalanta–Annibale in Torino–Il mercato di Monfregoso*.

Orchestra/Band Music:

Concerted Music:

Piano: Jan L. Dussek, *Concerto in F, Opus 17*; Johann H. Hummel, *Variations in F on a Theme from Vogler, Opus 6*; August E. Müller, *Concerto No. 1, Opus 1*; Johann G. Naumann, *Concerto for Harpsichord/Piano*.

Violin: Ignace Pleyel, *Symphonie concertante in F, Ben. 113–Symphonie concertante in F, Ben. 115* (two violins); Giovanni Viotti, *Concerto No. 20 in D–No. 21 in E*.

Other: Jean-Baptiste Bréval, *Symphonie concertante, Opus 33* (violin, viola)(?).

Ballet/Incidental Music: Rodolphe Kreutzer, *La journée de Marathon* (IM); Vicente Martín y Soler, *Didon abandonée* (IM); Domenico Mazzochi, *Le volage fixé* (B)–*La foire de Smirne* (B); Étienne Méhul, *Stratonice* (B); Gaetano Pugnani, *Correso e Calliroe* (B).

Program Music: James Hewitt, *Overture, Expressive of a Battle (Battle of Trenton)*.

Symphonies: Luigi Boccherini, *Symphony in d, Opus 45*; Franz Joseph Haydn, *"London Symphonies:" No. 5 (No. 97) in C–No. 6 (No. 98) in B♭–Sinfonia Concertante in B♭, Opus 84*; Louis Massoneau, *No. 1, 2 (E♭, D), Opus 3*; Franz C. Neubauer, *Three Symphonies, Opus 4*.

1793

Historical Highlights: The Reign of Terror under the control of Robespierre begins in France—Louis XVI and Marie Antoinette are both sent to the guillotine—Catholicism is banned in the Revolutionary Republic; the Second Partition of Poland takes place; in the United States, Congress passes the Proclamation of Neutrality in regards to the Anglo-French warfare; a Fugitive Slave Law is passed by Congress.

Art and Literature Highlights: The Louvre opens in Paris. Births—artists Francis Danby, Charles Eastlake, Ferdinand Waldmüller; Deaths—artists Francesco Guardi, Pierre Verschaffelt, Joseph Wright, writers William H. Brown, Carlo Goldoni. Art—David's *The Death of Marat*, Rush's *The River God*, Tiepolo's *Pulcinellos on Holiday*; Literature—Chénier's *Fénelon*, Smith's *The Old Manor House*, Alsop's *American Poems*.

Musical Highlights

A. **Births**

Composers: Carl Jonas Almquist (Sweden) November 28; Pietro Antonio Coppola (Italy) December 11; William Henry Havergal (England) January 18; Bernhard Klein (Germany) March 6; George Frederick Perry (England).

Conductors: August Neithardts (Germany) August 10; Joseph Hartmann Stuntz (Switzerland) July 23.

Singers: Giuseppe de Begnis (Italian bass); Julius Cornet (Austrian tenor/author) June 15; Anna Fröhlich (Austrian soprano/pianist) November 19; Benedetta Rosmunda Pisaroni (Italian soprano/contralto) May 16; Geltrude Righetti-Giorgi (Italian contralto).

Performers: František Tadeáš Blatt (Bohemian clarinetist); Céleste Couperin (French organist/pianist).

B. **Deaths**

Composers: Marc-Antoine Désaugiers (France) September 10.

Singers: Louis Armand Chardiny (French baritone/composer) October 1; Joseph Legros (French tenor) December 20.

Performers: Andrew Adgate (American organist/conductor) September 30; Alexandro Besozzi (Italian oboist/composer) July 26; Johann Joachim Bode (German instrumentalist/composer) December 13; Benjamin Cooke (British organist/composer) September 14; Johann Ernst Hartmann (Danish violinist/composer) October 21; Leopold Hofmann (Austrian organist/violinist) March 17; Pietro Nardini (Italian violinist/composer) May 7; Papavoine (French violinist/composer).

Others: Jean-Joseph Amiot (French music scholar) October 8; Alselmo Bellosio (Italian violin maker) August 21; Martin Gerbert (German music scholar) May 13; Christian Gottlob Hubert (Polish-born piano maker) February 16; Pascal Taskin (Belgian instrument maker) February 9.

C. **Debuts**

Performers: Auguste Bertini (French pianist—London); Johan Fredrik Berwald (Swedish violinist—Stockholm).

D. **New Positions**

Conductors: Johann Georg Albrechtsberger (kapellmeister, St. Stephen's, Vienna); Domenico Cimarosa (maestro di cappella, Naples); Pietro Alessandro Guglielmi (maestro di cappella, St. Peter's, Rome); António Leal Moreira (Teatro San Carlo, Lisbon); José Pons (choir, Cordoba Cathedral); Joseph Preindl (kapellmeister, St. Peter's, Vienna); Vincenzo Righini (hofkapellmeister, Berlin—director, Italian Opera); (Abbé) Johann Franz Sterkel (kapellmeister,

Mainz); Johann Baptist Toeschi (kapellmeister, Munich); Nicola Antonio Zingarelli (maestro di cappella, Milan Cathedral).
Others: Samuel Arnold (organ, Westminster Abbey); Robert Broderip (organ, St. Michael's, Bristol); Robert Cooke (organ, St. Martin-in-the-Fields).

F. **Biographical Highlights**
Ludwig van Beethoven meets the Baron von Swieten and Prince Lichnovsky who become his friends and patrons; Benjamin Carr leaves London, moves to the United States, and settles in Philadelphia; Domenico Cimarosa leaves Vienna and returns to Naples; Franz Joseph Haydn, following his return from London, buys a home in Vienna; Friedrich Heinrich Himmel travels and studies music in Italy on a royal grant; Johann Nepomuk Hummel, back in Vienna, studies with Haydn and Salieri; Alexander Reinagle helps to set up a stock company in New York for the presentation of comic operas; Georg "Abbe" Vogler returns to his position in the Stockholm court.

G. **Cultural Beginnings**
Performing Groups—Choral: Newport St. Cecilia Society; New York Uranian Society.
Educational: Groton Academy (New Hampshire—founded by Samuel Holyoke).
Music Publishers: Gaveaux Music Publishing Co. (Paris); Moller and Capron (New York); Simrock Music Publishers (Bonn).
Music Publications: *Carr's Musical Repository* (Philadelphia); *Musikalische Zeitung* (Berlin).
Performing Centers: Boston Theater; Casa de Comedias (Montevideo); New Theater Opera House (Philadelphia); Teatro S. Carlos (Lisbon).
Other: Haydn Monument (Rohrau); Institute National de Musique (Paris); New York "City Concerts."

H. **Musical Literature**
Jacob French, *The Psalmodist's Companion*; Hans Gram, *Sacred Lines*; John Gunn, *The Art of Playing the German Flute*; Johann A. Hiller, *Allgemeines Choral-Melodienbuch für Kirchen und Schulen*; Oliver Holden, *Union Harmony*; Jacob Kimball, *The Rural Harmony*; Heinrich Koch, *Versuch einer anleitung zur composition III*; Honoré Langlé, *Traité d'harmonie et de modulation*; Francesco Petrini, *Nouveau système de l'harmonie en 60 accords*; Daniel Read, *Columbian Harmonist I*; Johann Reichardt, *Briefe über Frankreich*; George Thomson, *Original Scottish Airs I*.

I. Musical Compositions

Chamber Music:

String Quartets: Adalbert Gyrowetz, *Three Quartets, Opus 5*; Franz Joseph Haydn, *"Apponyi" Quartets, Opus 71: No. 1 in B♭–No. 2 in D–No. 3 in C–"Apponyi" Quartets, Opus 74: No. 1 in C–No. 2 in F–No. 3 in g, "The Rider"*; František Krommer, *Three Quartets, Opus 1–Three Quartets, Opus 3*; Franz C. Neubauer, *Three Quartets, Opus 7*.

Sonata/Solos: Ludwig van Beethoven, *Variations on Mozart's "Se vuol ballare," Opus 156* (violin, piano); Jan L. Dussek, *Flute and Cello Sonata in C, Opus 21*.

Ensembles: Luigi Boccherini, *Six String Quintets (B♭, d, C, g, F, E♭), Opus 46–Six String Trios (A, G, B♭, E♭, D, F), Opus 47*; François Devienne, *Six Quartets for Flute and Strings, Book IV, Opus 66–Six Quartets, Book V, Opus 67*; Adalbert Gyrowetz, *Three Piano Trios, Opus 8–Three Piano Trios, Opus 9*; Franz Neubauer, *Three Trios for Flute, Violin and Viola, Opus 14*; Ignace Pleyel, *Three Keyboard Trios (C, F, D), Ben. 443–5*; Jan Václav Stich, *Twelve Small Trios for Three Horns*.

Piano: Muzio Clementi, *Three Sonatas (C, G, D), Opus 29–Three Sonatas (F, D, C), Opus 32* (both with violin); Jan L. Dussek, *Sonata in B♭, Opus 24*; Carolus A. Fodor, *Two Sonatas (F, f♯), Opus 2*; Georg C. Grosheim, *Theme with Twelve Variations*; Franz Joseph Haydn, *Variations in f*; Ignace A. Ladurner, *Three Sonatas, Opus 2* (piano, four hands); August E. Müller, *Three Sonatas, Opus 5*; Samuel Wesley, *Keyboard Sonata in B♭, Opus 5/2*.

Choral/Vocal Music:

Choral: François Boieldieu, *Chant populaire pour la fête de la raison*; François Gossec, *Hymne à la nature–Hymne à l'égalité–Hymne à la statue de la liberté*; Étienne Méhul, *Hymne à la raison*; Giuseppe Sarti, *Requiem for Ludwig XVI*; Christian Weinlig, *Der Christ am Kreuze Jesu* (oratorio).

Vocal: Adalbert Gyrowetz, *Six Italian Ariettas, Opus 6*; Friedrich F. Hůrka, *Twelve Deutsche Lieder I*.

Musical Stage: Felice Alessandri, *Virginia*; Bonifazio Asioli, *Cinna*; Thomas Attwood, *The Mariners*; François Boieldieu, *La fille coupable*; Giuseppe M. Cambini, *Les trois gascons*; Luigi Cherubini, *Koukourgi*; Domenico Cimarosa, *I traci amanti–Amor rende sagace*; Nicolas Dalayrac, *Ambroise–Urgande et Merlin*; Anton Eberl, *Die Zigeuner*; Pierre Gaveaux, *Les deux ermites–Le famille indigente*; Johann B. Henneberg, *Die Waldmänner*; Rodolphe Kreutzer, *Le déserteur*; Friedrich L. Kunzen, *Das Fest der Winzer, oder Die Weinlese*; Ignace Ladurner, *Wenzel*; Jean F. Lesueur, *La caverne*; Étienne Méhul, *Le jeune sage et le vieux fou*; Ferdinando Paër, *I molinari*;

Niccolò Piccinni, *La Griselda*; Vincenzo Righini, *Enea nel Lazio*; Giovanni Rossi, *Pietro il grande–L'impresario delle Smirne*; William Shield, *The Midnight Wanderers–The Relief of Williamsburg*; Daniel Steibelt, *Roméo et Juliette*; Franz X. Süssmayr, *L'Incanto superato–Piramo e Tisbe*; Vittorio Trento, *La finta ammalata*; Armand E. Trial, *Le Siège de Lille–La cause et les effets*; Peter Winter, *Psyche*; Paul Wranitzky, *Merkur, der Heurat-Stifter*; Nicola Zingarelli, *La Rossana–La secchia rapita*.

Orchestra/Band Music:
Concerted Music:
   Piano: Ludwig van Beethoven, *Rondo in B♭*; Johann L. Dussek, *Concerto in B♭, Opus 22.*
   Violin: Rodolphe Kreutzer, *Symphonia concertante No. 1 in F for Two Violins*; Giovanni Viotti, *Violin Concerto No. 22 in a–No. 23 in g–No. 24 in b–No. 26 in B♭.*
   Others: Domenico Cimarosa, *Concerto in G for Two Flutes*; François Devienne, *Bassoon Concerto No. 4 in C–Flute Concerto No. 9 in e*; Francesco Petrini, *Harp Concerto No. 3, Opus 27–No. 4 in B♭, Opus 29*; Jan Václav Stich, *Horn Concerto No. 3–No. 4.*
Ballet/Incidental Music: Vicente Martín y Soler, *Amour et Psyche* (B)–*L'oracle* (B); Étienne Méhul, *Le jugement de Paris* (B).
Standard Works: Georg "Abbe" Vogler, *Trauermusik auf Ludwig XVI (Begrafnings musik).*
Symphonies: Franz Joseph Haydn, *"London Symphonies"*: *No. 7 (No. 99) in E♭*; Franz C. Neubauer, *Three Symphonies, Opus 8*; Ignace Pleyel, *Symphony in E♭, Ben. 148.*

1794
❋

Historical Highlights: Robespierre himself is taken to the guillotine, bringing to an end the Reign of Terror in France; a revolt of Polish patriots led by Thaddeus Kosciusko is crushed by Russian troops; in the United States, the Battle of Fallen Timbers permanently ends the Indian problem in the Ohio Territory; the Whiskey Rebellion by the farmers of western Pennsylvania is put down by government troops; the U.S. Navy is officially formed by an act of Congress.

Art and Literature Highlights: Births—artists Julius Schnorr von Carolsfeld, Karl Begas, poets William Cullen Bryant, Wilhelm Müller; Deaths—writers Gottfried August Bürger, André Chénier, John Witherspoon. Art—Blake's *Ancient of Days*, David's *Luxembourg Gardens*, Goya's *Procession of the Flagellants*; Literature—Lemercier's *Agamemnon*, Radcliffe's *The Mysteries of Udolpho*, Paine's *The Age of Reason*.

Musical Highlights

A. Births

Composers: Carl Arnold (Germany-Norway) May 6; François Benoist (France) September 10; Anselm Hüttenbrenner (Austria) October 13; George Jackson Lambert (England) November 16.

Singers: Franz Hauser (Bohemian baritone) January 12; Luigi Lablache (Italian bass) December 6; Giovanni Battista Rubini (Italian tenor) April 7; Catherine Stephens (British soprano) September 18.

Performers: Friedrich Berr (German clarinetist/bassoonist) April 17; Theobald Böhm (German flutist/inventor) April 9; Aristide Farrenc (French flutist/editor) April 9; Joseph Binns Hart (British organist/composer) June 5; Ignaz Moscheles (Polish-born pianist/composer) May 23; Antoine Prumier (French harpist) July 2.

Others: Ignaz Bösendorfer (Austrian piano maker) July 27; Samuel Graves (American instrument maker) July 2; Thomas Hall (American organ builder) February; Carl August Hüttenrauch (German organ builder) March 21; Alexander Dmitrievich Oulibicheff (Russian music author) April 13; Josef Proksch (Bohemian pianist) August 4; Carl Proske (German music scholar/editor) February 11; Eberhard Friedrich Walcker (German organ builder) July 3.

B. Deaths

Composers: Salvatore Bertini (Italy) December 16; Pascal Boyer (France) July 7; Johann Georg Clement (Germany) May 23; Pablo Esteve y Grimau (Spain) June 4; James Lyons (U.S.A.) October 12; Franz Xaver Pokorný (Bohemia) July 2.

Conductors: Josiah Flagg (U.S.A.) December 30.

Singers: Marie Fel (French soprano) February 2; Elisabeth Augusta Wendling (German soprano) February 18.

Performers: Leopold Auguste Abel (German violinist) August 25; Gaetano Besozzi (Italian oboist); Jean-Jacques Beauvarlet-Charpentier (French organist) May 6; Jean-Frédéric Edelmann (French pianist/harpsichordist) May 5; Jakob Friedrich Kleinknecht (German flutist/composer) August 14; Jean-Benjamin de La Borde (French violinist/music author) July 22; Johann Anton Maresch (Bohemian horn virtuoso) June 10; Henry Mountain (Irish violinist/publisher) November 15.

Others: Johann Gottlob Breitkopf (German publisher) January 28; Abraham Kirckmann (German harpsichord/piano maker) April.

C. Debuts

Singers: Gaetano Crivelli (Italian tenor—Brescia); Pierre Jean Garat (French tenor/baritone—Paris); Andrea Nozzari (Italian tenor—Bergamo); Luise Reichardt (German singer—Berlin).

Performers: Niccolò Paganini (Italian violinist—Genoa).

D. New Positions
Conductors: João José Baldi (mestre de capela, Faro Cathedral); Francesco Bianchi (King's Theater, London); Friedrich Ludwig Kunzen (Prague Theater); Franz Xaver Süssmayr (Vienna Court Opera); Nicola Antonio Zingarelli (maestro di cappella, Santa Casa, Loreto). **Others:** Louis-Joseph Francoeur (administrative director, Paris Opera); Benjamin Jacob (organ, Surrey Chapel); August Eberhard Müller (organ, Nikolaikirche, Leipzig).

F. Biographical Highlights
Ludwig van Beethoven, settling in Vienna, enters into a fashionable keyboard competition with Joseph Wölfl; Benjamin Carr opens a branch of his Musical Repository in New York and concertizes as both singer and pianist; Franz Joseph Haydn makes his second visit to London for Salomon's second series of concerts; Étienne Méhul is given a yearly pension from the Comédie-Italienne; Niccolò Piccinni, on returning from his Vienna trip, is unjustly put in house arrest for four years.

G. Cultural Beginnings
Performing Groups—Instrumental: Philharmonische Gesellschaft (Ljubljana).
Music Publishers: Joseph Carr Publishing House (Baltimore); Johann D. Gerstenberg (St. Petersburg); Johann Traeg (Vienna); George Willig (Philadelphia).
Performing Centers: Chestnut Street Theater (Philadelphia); Drury Lane Theater II (London); Federal Street Theater (Boston); Leeds Music Hall II.
Other: Bevington and Sons Organ Co. (London); Ibach and Sons, piano makers (Beyenburg); Motta and Ball, piano makers (London).

H. Musical Literature
Friedrich A. Baumbach, *Kurzgefasstes Handwörterbuch über die schönen Künste*; Supply Belcher, *The Harmony of Maine*; William Billings, *The Continental Harmony*; James Hook, *Guida de Musica II*; Andrew Law, *The Art of Singing*; Daniel Read, *Columbian Harmonist II*; Nicola Sala, *Regole del contrappunto prattico*; William Tattersall, *Improved Psalmody*; Johann G. Vierling, *Versuch einer Anleitung zum Präludieren*.

I. Musical Compositions
Chamber Music:
String Quartets: Luigi Boccherini, *Six Quartets (F, A, b, E♭, G, C), Opus 48*; Adalbert Gyrowetz, *Three Quartets (A, F, C), Opus 9*; František Krommer, *Three Quartets, Opus 4*.

Sonata/Solos: Benjamin Blake, *Six Violin Sonatas, Opus 4.*
Ensembles: Johann Christoph Friedrich Bach, *Septet in E♭ for Winds*; Ludwig van Beethoven, *Trio, Opus 87* (two oboes, English horn); Luigi Boccherini, *Five String Quintets (D, B♭, E♭, d, E♭), Opus 49*; Franz Joseph Haydn, *Four Trios for Two Flutes and Cello–Piano Trios No. 15–18*; Ignace Pleyel, *Six Keyboard Trios (C, B♭, A, C, G, B♭), Ben. 446–51.*
Piano: Muzio Clementi, *Sonata in C, Opus 30–Sonata in A, Opus 31–Three Sonatas (A, F, C), Opus 33*; Johann H. Hummel, *Variations, Opus 3*; Alexander Reinagle, *Preludes for Piano*; Samuel Wesley, *Keyboard Sonata, Opus 5, No. 1.*
Choral/Vocal Music:
   Choral: Gaetano Brunetti, *Miserere–Lamentations*; Domenico Cimarosa, *Il trionfo della fede* (cantata); Joseph L. Eybler, *Der Hirten bei der Krippe* (oratorio); Michael Haydn, *Missa tempore quadragesimae–Missa proquadragesimae sec cantum choralem*; Johann G. Naumann, *Davide in Terebinto, figura del Salvatore* (oratorio); Giovanni Paisiello, *Christus* (oratorio); Nicola Zingarelli, *Gerusalemme distrutta* (oratorio).
   Vocal: Luigi Cherubini, *Clytemnestre*; Adalbert Gyrowetz, *Eight German Songs, Opus 22*; Friedrich F. Hŭrka, *Twelve deutsche Lieder II*; Johann Reichardt, *Goethes' lyrische Gedichte–Deutsche gesänge von Matthisson*; Daniel Steibelt, *Mélanges d'airs et chansons en forme de scène, Opus 10.*
   Musical Stage: Felice Alessandri, *Zemira–Armida*; Thomas Attwood, *The Packet Boat*; Christian Cannabich, *Cortez et Thélaire*; Luigi Cherubini, *Eliza*; Domenico Cimarosa, *Le astuzie femminili*; Nicolas Dalayrac, *La prise de Toulon*; Carl Ditters von Dittersdorf, *Das Gespenst mit der Trommel*; André Grétry, *Joseph Barra–Denys le tyran–La rosière républicaine*; James Hewitt, *Tammany–The Patriots* (ballad operas); Friedrich Himmel, *Il primo navigatore*; Nicolò Isouard, *Artaserse*; Rodolphe Kreutzer, *Le congrès des rois*; Jean F. Lesueur, *Tyrté–Paul et Virginie*; Simon Mayr, *Saffo*; Étienne Méhul, *Horatius Coclès–Mélidore et Phrosine*; Wenzel Müller, *Die Schwestern von Prag*; Ferdinando Paër, *Una in bene e una in male*; Giovanni Paisiello, *Elvira*; Niccolò Piccinni, *Il servo padrone*; Andreas Romberg, *Der Rabe*; Giuseppe Sarti, *Der ruhm des Nordens*; William Shield, *Netley Abbey–The Travellers in Switzerland* (operettas); Franz X. Süssmayr, *Der Spiegel von Arkadien–Il turco in Italia*; Joseph Weigl, *Das Petermännchen*; Paul Wranitzky, *Das Fest der Lazzaronen.*
Orchestra/Band Music:
   Concerted Music:
      Piano: Jan L. Dussek, *Concerto in F, Opus 27*; Johann G. Naumann, *Concerto*; Alexander Reinagle, *Concerto.*

Violin: Jean-Baptiste Breval, *Symphonie concertante in F, Opus 38;* François Devienne, *Symphonie concertante in G;* Rodolphe Kreutzer, *Symphonie concertante No. 2 in F* (two violins, cello); Giovanni B. Viotti, *Concerto No. 27 in C(?);* Ignace Pleyel, *Symphonie concertante in F, Ben. 115.*

Other: Jean-Baptiste Bréval, *Cello Concerto No. 7 in A, Opus 35;* François Devienne, *Bassoon Concerto No. 2–Flute Concerto No. 6 in D–No. 8 in G.*

Ballet/Incidental Music: Étienne Méhul, *Timolén* (IM); Alexander Reinagle, *Slaves in Algiers* (IM).

Standard Works: François Devienne, *Ouverture* (wind band); Rodolphe Kreutzer, *Overture, La journée de Marathon.*

Symphonies: Johann Christoph Friedrich Bach, *No. 20 in B♭;* François Devienne, *Grand Symphony in D, "La Bataille de Gemmapp";* François Gossec, *Symphony in C–Military Symphony in F;* Franz Joseph Haydn, *"London" Symphonies: No 8 (No. 100) in G, "Military"–No. 9 (No. 101) in D, "The Clock"–No. 10 (No. 102) in B♭;* Louis E. Jadin, *Symphony* (band); Louis Massonneau, *No. 3 in c, "La tempête et la calme," Opus 5;* Ignace Pleyel, *Symphony in B♭, Ben. 149.*

1795

❉

Historical Highlights: The French Directory is formed—Napoleon Bonaparte becomes head of the French Army in Italy—the French invade and occupy the Lowlands; the Third Partition of Poland takes place; Prussia and Spain both sue for peace with France; the Treaty of San Lorenzo gives the United States navigation rights on the Mississippi River—the Pinckney Treaty gives the United States the right of deposits at the mouth of the Mississippi at New Orleans.

Art and Literature Highlights: Births—artists William Jewett, Ary Schaffer, writers Thomas Carlyle, John Keats; Deaths—writers James Boswell, Raniero di Calzabigi, Johan Henrik Kellgren. Art—Carsten's *Night with Her Children,* C. W. Peale's *The Staircase Group,* Stuart's *George Washington, The Vaughan Portrait;* Literature—Dunlap's *Fountainville Abbey,* Gifford's *The Maeviad,* Goethe's *Wilhelm Meisters Lehrjahre.*

Musical Highlights

A. Births

Composers: Heinrich Marschner (Germany) August 16; (Giuseppe) Saverio Mercadante (Italy) September 17; Robert Lucas Pearsall (England) March 14.

Conductors: Francisco Manuel da Silva (Brazil) February 21.

Performers: Pedro Albéniz y Basanta (Spanish organist/composer) April 14; Friedrich August Belcke (German trombone virtuoso) May 27; Henri Bertini (British-born pianist) October 28; Joseph Böhm (Hungarian violinist) March 4; Jacques François Gallay (French horn virtuoso) December 8; Joseph Merk (Austrian cellist) March 18; Charles Nicholson (British flutist) August 12; Anton Felix Schindler (Moravian violinist/conductor) June 13; Charles Zeuner (German-born organist) September 20.

Others: Johann Friedrich Bellermann (German music scholar) March 8; Adolf Bernhard Marx (German music theorist) May 15; George Peabody (American patron of the arts) February 18.

B. Deaths

Composers: Hyacinthe Azaïs (France); Johann Christoph Friedrich Bach (Germany) January 26; Georg Anton Benda (Bohemia) November 6; Giacomo Insanguine (Italy) February 1; François-André Philidor (France) August 31; Francesco Antonio Uttini (Italy) October 25.

Conductors: François-Joseph Krafft (Belgium) January 13.

Singers: Antoine Trial (French tenor) February 5; Isabella Young (British contralto) January 5.

Performers: Maria Teresa Agnesi (Italian harpsichordist/composer) January 19; Michel Corrette (French organist/composer) January 22; Jeremiah Dencke (Moravian-born organist/composer) May 28; Pietro Grassi Florio (Italian flutist) June 20; Friedrich Graf (German flutist/composer) August 19; Thomas Linley, Sr. (British harpsichordist/concert manager) November 19; Franz Christoph Neubauer (Czech violinist/composer) October 11; Josef Reicha (Czech cellist) March 5; John Christopher Smith (German-born organist/composer) October 3.

Others: Benjamin Banks (British violin makers) February 18; Carl Michael Bellman (Swedish poet/composer) February 11; Ranieri Calzabigi (Italian poet/composer) July; Franz Xavier Chrismann (Austrian organ builder) May 20; Christian Gottlob Donati (German organ builder) November 13; Friedrich Wilhelm Marpurg (German music theorist) May 22.

C. Debuts

Singers: Angelica Catalani (Italian soprano—Venice); Marianne de Tribolet (Austrian soprano—Vienna); Johann Michael Vogl (Austrian baritone—Vienna).

Performers: Anton Dimmler (German clarinetist—Munich).

D. **New Positions**
Conductors: Domingo Arquimbau (maestro de capilla, Seville Cathedral); Friedrich Heinrich Himmel (kapellmeister, Berlin); Friedrich Ludwig Kunzen (kapellmeister, Copenhagen).
Others: Nicolò Isouard (organ, St. John of Jerusalem, Malta); Raynor Taylor (organ, St. Peter's, Philadelphia).

E. **Prizes/Honors**
Honors: Joachim Albertini (life pension by Prince Poniatowski of Poland); François Gossec (French Institute); André Grétry (French Institute); Étienne Méhul (French Institute).

F. **Biographical Highlights**
Ludwig van Beethoven has his first work published, his *Piano Trios, Opus 1*; Carl Czerny's family moves to Vienna in order to escape the unrest in Poland; Carl Ditters von Dittersdorf, on the death of his patron, the Prince-Bishop of Breslau, is invited by Baron von Stillfried to his estate, where he spends the rest of his life; Gottlieb Graupner leaves London and, emigrating to the United States, settles in Charleston, South Carolina; E. T. A. Hoffmann graduates from his law studies; Vicente Martín y Soler leaves Russia for a year in London; Joseph Wölfl gives up his post in Warsaw and returns to Vienna as pianist and teacher.

G. **Cultural Beginnings**
Performing Groups—Choral: Columbian Anacreontic Society of New York; Norwich Anacreontic Society.
Educational: Paris Conservatory of Music (merger of the Institute of Music and the École Royal de Chant).
Music Publishers: Rudolph Becker Publishing House; Cramer Publishing House (Paris); Maison Pleyel (Paris); Peter Urbani (Edinburgh).
Music Publications: *Glaneur lyrique; Die Hören.*
Other: Thomas Boosey Book Store (London); Duncan Phyfe Shop (New York); Schlesinger'sche Buch- und Musikalienhandlung (Berlin).

H. **Musical Literature**
Johann Altenburg, *Versuch einer Anleitung zur heroisch-musikalischen Trompeter- und Pauker-Kunst*; Jonathan Blewitt, *Complete Treatise on the Organ*; Carlo F. Chiabrano, *Compleat Instructions for the Spanish Guitar*; François Devienne, *Méthode de Flûte*; Charles Dibdin, *History of the Stage*; Guillaume Gatayes, *Harp Method*; Oliver Holden, *Massachusetts Compiler*; Nicolas J. Hüllmandel, *Principles of Music, Chiefly Calculated for the Pianoforte*; George K. Jackson, *First Principles, or a Treatise on Practical Thorough Bass*; Justin H. Knecht, *Kleines . . . Worterbuch . . . aus der musikalischen Theorie*; Honoré Langlé, *Traité*

d'harmonie et de modulation; Cesare Mussolini, *A New and Complete Treatise on the Theory and Practice of Music*; George Vogler, *Introduction to the Theory of Harmony*.

I. Musical Compositions
Chamber Music:
String Quartets: Luigi Boccherini, *Four Quartets (C, D, G, f), Opus 52*; Johann G. Distler, *Three String Quartets, Opus 2*; Adalbert Gyrowetz, *Three Quartets for the Prince of Wales*(?); Friedrich Hiller, *Three String Quartets, Opus 1*; Rodolphe Kreutzer, *Three Quartets, Opus 2*(?).

Sonata/Solos: Benjamin Blake, *Nine Divertimentos, Opus 5* (violin, piano); Jean-Baptiste Bréval, *Six Cello Sonatas, Opus 40*(?); Jan L. Dussek, *Six Violin Sonatas (C, F, B♭, D, g, E♭), Opus 28–Two Sonatas, Opus 25/1,3–Two Sonatas Opus 31/1,3*.

Ensembles: Georg G. Albrechtsberger, *Six Trio Sonatas, Opus 11b*; Ludwig van Beethoven, *Three Piano Trios (E♭, G, c), Opus 1–String Quintet in E♭, Opus 4*; Luigi Boccherini, *Six String Quintets (A, E♭, B♭, E, C, B♭), Opus 50–Two String Quintets (E♭, c), Opus 51*; François Devienne, *Six Woodwind Trios, Opus 6*; Adalbert Gyrowetz, *Three Piano Trios, Opus 10–Three Quartets for Flutes and Strings, Opus 11–Three Piano Trios, Opus 12*; Jan L. Dussek, *Sonata in D, Opus 25/2–Sontata in D, Opus 31/2*; Franz Joseph Haydn, *Piano Trios No. 19–24*; Josef Mysliveček, *Six Trios* (flute, violin, cello); Ignace Pleyel, *Three Keyboard Trios (D, B♭, A), Ben. 452–4*.

Piano: Ludwig van Beethoven, *Three Sonatas (f, A, C), Opus 2*; François Boieldieu, *Three Sonatas, Opus 1–Three Sonatas, Opus 2*(?); Jean-Baptiste Bréval, *Petite airs variées, Opus 36*; Muzio Clementi, *Two Sonatas, Opus 34 (G, g)–Two Capriccios (A, F), Opus 34*; Ignace Ladurner, *Three Sonatas, Opus 5* (with violin); August E. Müller, *Three Sonatas, Opus 7*(?)–*Variations, Opus 8*.

Organ: Johann Albrechtsberger, *Six Preludes and Fugues, Opus 15*.

Choral/Vocal Music:
Choral: Samuel Arnold, *Elisha* (oratorio); Domenico Cimarosa, *Il Matirio* (oratorio); Johann G. Naumann, *Gottes Wege* (cantata).

Vocal: Ludwig van Beethoven, *Adelaide, Opus 46*; Benjamin Cooke, *Nine Glees and Two Duets*; Friedrich F. Hŭrka, *Die Farben–Die Geburtstagfeier*; Honoré Langlé, *Hymne à la Liberté*; Johann G. Naumann, *Sechs neue lieder*.

Musical Stage: Carle Agthe, *Der Spiegelritter*; François Boieldieu, *Rosalie et Myrza*; Domenico Cimarosa, *Penelope–Le nozze in garbuglio–L'impegno superato*; Nicolas Dalayrac, *Adèle et Dorsan–La pauvre femme*; Franz Danzi, *Deucalion et Pirrha*(?); Prosper-Didier Deshayes, *Bella*; Carl Ditters von Dittersdorf, *Don Quixotte der Zweite–Gott Mars und der Hauptmann von Bärenzahn*; Pierre Gaveaux, *La Gasconade–Sophronime*; Friedrich H. Himmel, *La morte di Semiramide*; Nicolò Isouard, *L'avviso ai maritati*; Rodolphe Kreutzer, *La journée du 10 août 1792*; Louis S. Lebrun, *Emilie et Melcour–Le bon fils*; Vicente Martín y Soler, *L'isola del piacere–La scuola dei maritati*; Étienne Méhul, *Doria–La caverne*; François Philidor, *Bélisaire*; Johann F. Reichardt, *Macbeth*; Francesco Ruggi, *L'ombra di Nino*; Antonio Salieri, *Il mondo alla rovescia–Eraclito et Democrito–Palmira Regina di Pergia*; Johann Schenk, *Achmet und Almanzine*; William Shield, *The Irish Mimic–The Mysteries of the Castle*; Franz X. Süssmayr, *Die edle Rache–Idris und Zenide*; Joseph Wölfl, *Der Höllenberg*; Paul Wranitzky, *Die gute Mutter*; Nicola Zingarelli, *Gli orazi e curiazi*.

Orchestra/Band Music:
Concerted Music:
   Piano: Ludwig van Beethoven, *Concerto No. 1 in C, Opus 15–Concerto No. 2 in B♭, Opus 19*; Jan L. Dussek, *Concerto in C, Opus 29–Concerto in G, Opus 30*.
   Violin: Rodolphe Kreutzer, *Concerto No. 8 in d, Opus 8*(?); Niccolò Paganini, *Variations on "La carmagnola"*; Giovanni Viotti, *Concerto No. 25 in a*(?).
   Other: J. A. André, *Flute Concerto in c, Opus 13*; François Boieldieu, *Clarinet Concerto No. 1*; Jean-Baptiste Bréval, *Symphonie concertante in e, Opus 38* (clarinet, horn, bassoon); Franz C. Neubauer, *Flute Concerto, Opus 13*; Ignace Pleyel, *Cello Concerto in C, Ben. 106*.
Ballet/Incidental Music: Joseph Weigl, *Der Raub der Helena*.
Standard Works: Ludwig van Beethoven, *Twelve German Dances, Opus 140*; Benjamin Carr, *Federal Overture*.
Symphonies: Anton André, *Symphony No. 4 in C, Opus 4–No. 5 in F, Opus 5–No. 6 in C, Opus 6*; Franz Joseph Haydn, *"London" Symphonies: No. 11 (No. 103) in E♭, "Drum Roll"–No. 12 (No. 104) in F, "London"*; Franz C. Neubauer, *Three Symphonies, Opus 12*.

1796

❄

Historical Highlights: Spain joins France in the war against Great Britain; Napoleon conquers all of Northern Italy—the Austrians push the French back to the Rhine River; in the United States, George Washington refuses to run for a third term as president—John Adams is elected as second president; Tennessee becomes state number sixteen; Congress passes the Land Act, which makes it possible to sell public lands by auction.

Art and Literature Highlights: Births—artists George Catlin, Jean-Baptiste Corot, Asher Durand, writers Theodore Dwight, Jr., Karl L. Immermann; Deaths—artist Franz Anton Maulbertsch, poets Robert "Bobby" Burns, James Macpherson. Art—Canova's *The Penitent Magdalen*, Robertson's *New York from Long Island*, Turner's *Fishermen at Sea*; Literature—Barlow's *Hasty Pudding*, Dunlap's *The Archers*, Lewis' *The Monk*.

Musical Highlights

A. Births

Composers: Franz Berwald (Sweden) July 23; Carlo Conti (Italy) November 14; Carl Loewe (Germany) November 30; Giovanni Pacini (Italy) February 17.

Singers: Anton Haizinger (Austrian tenor) March 14.

Performers: Edward Hodges (British organist/composer) July 20; Nicholas Mori (British violinist/publisher) January 24.

Others: Melchiore Balbi (Italian music theorist/composer) June 4; Louis Lambillotte (French author/organist) March 27.

B. Deaths

Composers: Giuseppe d'Avossa (Italy) January 9; Giovanni Battista Borghi (Italy) February 25; Joseph Lederer (Germany) September 22; Jean-Baptiste Lemoyne (France) December 30; Nicola Sabatino (Italy) April 4; Stephen (John Seymour) Storace (England) March 19.

Singers: Caterina Gabrielli (Italian soprano) February 16.

Performers: Henry Delamain (Irish organist) December 19; Georg Wilhelm Gruber (German violinist/composer) September 22.

Others: Samuel Green (British organ builder) September 14; Thomas Haxby (British instrument maker) October 31; Friedrich Wilhelm Rust (German violinist/composer) February 28.

D. New Positions

Conductors: Dmitri Bortniansky (Russian Imperial Court Orchestra); Anton Franz Eberl (kapellmeister, St. Petersburg); Christian Gottlob Neefe (Dessau Theater); Luigi Piccinni (kapellmeister, Stockholm); Carl Bernhard Wessely (kapellmeister, Rheinsberg).

Others: John L. Birkenhead (organ, Trinity Church, Newport); Domenico Cimarosa (first organist, Naples Court); Charles Knyvett, Sr., (organ, Chapel Royal, London); John Christopher Moller (manager, New York City Concerts).

E. Prizes/Honors

Honors: Karl Friberth (Knight of the Golden Spur); François Giroust (French Institute).

F. Biographical Highlights

Muzio Clementi decides to give up conducting and concentrates on performance and composition; Gottlieb Graupner gets married while in Charleston, South Carolina, and soon moves to Boston; Rodolphe Kreutzer makes a triumphal concert tour of Italy, Germany, and the Netherlands; Vicente Martín y Soler leaves London and returns to St. Petersburg, where he remains until his death; Daniel Steibelt, in financial stress, leaves Paris for a concert tour of the Netherlands and England, where he settles temporarily in London; Carl Maria von Weber receives his first formal music training.

G. Cultural Beginnings
Performing Groups—Choral: Apollo Glee Club (Liverpool); New York Harmonical Society.
Music Publishers: Euroditio Musica (Amsterdam); Falter und Sohn (Munich); Lewis Lavenu (Lavenu and Mitchell in 1802—London); A. Senefelder, Fr. Gleissner and Co., lithographers (Munich).
Performing Centers: Boston Haymarket Theater.
Other: Liceo Filarmonico (Bologna); Musical Box (patented by Antoine Favre).

H. Musical Literature
Esteban de Arteaga, *Del ritmo sonoro e del ritmo muto nella musica degli antichi*; Mathieu-Frédéric Blasius, *Clarinet Method*; Giuseppe M. Cambini, *Nouvelle Méthode théorique et pratique pour le violon*; Jan L. Dussek, *Instructions on the Art of Playing the Pianoforte or Harpsichord*; Nicolas E. Framery, *De la nécessité du rythme et de la césure dans la hymnes ou odes destinées à la musique*; Francesco Galeazzi, *Elementi teorico-pratici di Musica II*; John Gunn, *School of the German Flute*; Karl G. Hering, *Praktisches handbuch zur leichten Erlernung des Klavier-Spielens*; James Hook, *New Guida de Musica*; Augustus Kollmann, *An Essay on Practical Harmony*; António Leite, *Estudo de Guitarra*; August E. Müller, *Anweisung zum genauen vortrage*.

I. Musical Compositions
Chamber Music:
   String Quartets: Luigi Boccherini, *Six Quartets (E♭, D, C, A, C, E♭)*, *Opus 53*; Adalbert Gyrowetz, *Three Quartets, Opus 13–Three Quartets, Opus 16*; František Krommer, *Three Quartets, Opus 5*.
   Sonata/Solos: Rodolphe Kreutzer, *Forty-two études ou caprices for Solo Violin*; Václav Pichl, *Twelve Capriccios for Solo Violin, Opus 19*.
   Ensembles: Luigi Boccherini, *Six String Trios (D, G, E♭, C, d, A)*, *Opus 54*; Adalbert Gyrowetz, *Two Piano Trios, Opus 14–Two Piano Trios, Opus 15*; Ignace Pleyel, *Thirteen Keyboard Trios (G, C, B♭, G, D, C, D, F, D, B♭, F, C, E♭)*, Ben. 455–67; Jan Václav Stich, *Three Quartets for Horn and Strings, Opus 18*.
   Piano: Ludwig van Beethoven, *Two Sonatinas: Sonata No. 19 in g, Opus 43a–Sonata No. 20 in G, Opus 44a–Six Variations on Paisiello's*

"Nel cour piu," Opus 180–Twelve Variations on a Russian Dance by Wranitzky, Opus 182; Muzio Clementi, *Three Sonatas (C, G, D)*, Opus 35; Jan L. Dussek, *Sonata in C* (four hands); Ignace Pleyel, *Swiss Air with Variation in B♭*, Ben. 614; August E. Wenzel, *Variations, Opus 9–Variations, Opus 12*; Joseph Wölfl, *Three Sonatas*, Opus 2 (with violin). **Organ:** Johann G. Albrechtsberger, *Six Fugues, Opus 7* (organ/harpsichord).

Choral/Vocal Music:

Choral: Domenico Cimarosa, *Mass in E♭*; François Gossec, *Chant martial pour la fête de la victoire*; Franz Joseph Haydn, *Missa Sancti Bernardi, "Heiligmesse"–The Seven Last Words*; Michael Haydn, *Missa hispanica*; Friedrich A. Kunzen, *Die Auferstehung* (oratorio); Venanzio Rauzzini, *Old Oliver, or The Dying Shepherd* (cantata); Franz X. Süssmayr, *Der Retter in Gefahr* (oratorio).

Vocal: Ludwig van Beethoven, *"Ah, perfido," Opus 65*; Adalbert Gyrowetz, *Eight Italian Ariettas, Opus 17*; Friedrich F. Hürka, *Ehelicher guter Morgen und gute Nacht*; August E. Müller, *Twelve German Songs, Volume 1*.

Musical Stage: Johann André, *Der Bräutigam in der Klemme*; Thomas Attwood, *The Smugglers*; Francesco Bianchi, *Antigona*; François Boieldieu, *Les deux lettres*; Benjamin Carr, *The Mountaineers of Switzerland*; Domenico Cimarosa, *Gli Orazi ed i Curiazi–I nemici generosi*; Nicolas Dalayrac, *Marianne–La famille américaine*; Carl Ditters von Dittersdorf, *Ugolino–Der schöne Herbsttag*; Valentino Fioravanti, *Il furbo contro al furbo*; Pierre Gaveaux, *Le petit matelot–Céliane–Lise et Colin*; Tommaso Giordani, *The Cottage Festival*; François Gossec, *La reprise de Toulon*; Antoine Gresnick, *Le baiser donné et rendu–Les faux mendians*; Nicolò Isouard, *Rinaldo d'Asti–Il barbiere di Siviglia*; Rodolphe Kreutzer, *Imogène*; Friedrich A. Kunzen, *Festen i Valhal–Hemmeligheden*; Ignace A. Ladurner, *Les Vieux foux*; Jean F. Lesueur, *Télémaque*; Simon Mayr, *La Lodoiska*; Étienne Méhul, *Tancrède et Chlorinde*; Victor Pelissier, *Edwin and Angelina*; Marcos Portugal, *Zulima–La Donna di genio volubile*; Gaetano Pugnani, *Werther*; Alexander Reinagle, *The Witches of the Rock*; Antonio Salieri, *Il Moro*; Johann Schenk, *Der Dorfbarbier*; William Shield, *Lock and Key*; Gaspare Spontini, *Li Puntigli delle donne*; Stephen Storace, *The Iron Chest*; Franz X. Süssmayr, *Die freiwilligen*; Alexei Titov, *The Brewer*; Joseph Weigl, *L'amor marinaro*; Nicola Zingarelli, *Andromeda–Giulietta e Romeo*.

Orchestra/Band Music:

Concerted Music:

Piano: Muzio Clementi, *Concerto in C*; Adalbert Gyrowetz, *Concerto No. 1, Opus 26*; Daniel Steibelt, *Concerto No. 1 in C–No. 2 in e*.

Other: Johann A. André, *Flute Concerto, Opus 10*; Franz Joseph Haydn, *Trumpet Concerto in E♭*.
Ballet/Incidental Music: Franz Joseph Haydn, *Alfred, König der Angelsachsen* (IM); Domenico Mazzochi, *Les trois sultanes, Opus 20* (B)–*Le bouquet, Opus 22* (B); Joseph Weigl, *Alonzo e Cora* (B).
Symphonies: Franz Danzi, *No. 2 in d, Opus 19*(?).

1797
❊

Historical Highlights: The Treaty of Campo Formio forces Austria out of the War of the First Coalition; Talleyrand becomes the French foreign minister—the XYZ Affair strains relations with the United States; the British Navy defeats the Spanish fleet; in the United States, the Lancaster Pike in Pennsylvania opens to traffic; the frigate *United States* is launched, the first in the new country; Fort Adams (Memphis) is built on the banks of the Mississippi River.

Art and Literature Highlights: Births—writers Michel Jean Sedaine, Mary Wollstonecraft Shelley, Heinrich Heine, Alfred Victor de Vigny; Deaths—artist Christian Bernhard Rode, writers Edmund Burke, Horace Walpole. Art—Berczy's *Joseph Brant, Mohawk Chief*, Blake's *Night Thoughts*, Goya's *The Clothed Duchess—The Nude Duchess*; Literature— Goethe's *Hermann und Dorothea*, Lewis' *The Castle Spectre*, Tyler's *The Algerine Captive*.

Musical Highlights

A. Births
Composers: Gaetano Donizetti (Italy) November 29; Aimé-Ambroise-Simon Leborne (France) December 29; Franz Schubert (Austria) January 31.
Singers: Luigia Boccabadati (Italian soprano); Barbara Fröhlich (Austrian contralto) August 30; Edward Franz Genast (German baritone) July 15; Giuditta (Maria Costanza) Pasta (Italian soprano) October 28; Domenico Reina (Italian tenor); Lucia Elizabeth Vestris (British contralto) January 3(?).
Performers: Lucy Anderson (British pianist) December 12; Charles François Angelet (Belgian pianist) November 18; Charles Hart (British organist) May 14; Johann Hermann Kufferath (German violinist/conductor) May 12; Friedrich August Kummer (German cellist) August 5; Charles Franz Schoberlechner (Austrian pianist/composer) July 21; Ernst Johann Wiedemann (German organist/conductor/composer) March 28; Heinrich Wohlfahrt (German pianist) December 16.

Others: Auguste Bottée de Toulmon (French music author/librarian) May 15; Ludovicus Coenen (Dutch organ builder) April 29; Johann Christian Lobe (German music author) May 30; Heinrich Engelhard Steinweg (Steinway) (German piano maker) February 15; Alexandre-Joseph Vincent (French music theorist) November 20.

B. **Deaths**
Composers: Pasquale Anfossi (Italy) February; Antoine Dauvergne (France) February 11; Johann Friedrich Doles (Germany) February 8; John Hill (England) January 19; Giovanni Marco Rutini (Italy) December 22; Pietro Pompeo Sales (de Sala) (Italy) November 21; Joseph Anton Steffan (Bohemia) April 12.
Singers: Giovanni Battista Andreoni (Italian castrato mezzo-soprano) April 23; Elisabeth Böhm (German soprano); Pierre de Jélyotte (French counter-tenor/composer) October 12; Mary Ann Pownall (British singer/composer) August 11; Anton Raaff (German tenor) May 28.
Performers: Carl Christian Agthe (German organist/composer) November 27; Anton Bachschmidt (German violinist/composer) December 29; Stephen Clarke (Scottish organist/composer) August 6; Theresa Cornelys (Italian soprano) August 19; Pietro Maria Crispi (Italian organist) June 16; Philip Hayes (British organist) March 19; Nicolas-Jean Le Froid de Méreaux (French organist/composer); Vasily Pashkevich (Russian violinist/composer) March 9; Johann Abraham Sixt (German organist/harpsichordist) January 30; Johann Baptist Wendling (German flutist/composer) November 27.
Others: Johann Friedrich Daube (German music theorist) September 19; William Mason (British musician/poet) April 5.

C. **Debuts**
Singers: Domenico Ronconi (Italian tenor—Venice); Giuseppe Siboni (Italian tenor—Florence).
Performers: Giovanni Battista Polledro (Italian violinist—Turin).

D. **New Positions**
Conductors: Franz von Destouches (music director, Erlangen); Johann Chrysostomus Drexel (kapellmeister, Augsburg Cathedral), Marco Santucci (maestro di cappella, S. Giovanni in Laterano, Rome); Anton Wranitzky (kapellmeister, Prince Lobkowitz).
Others: Bartolommeo Campagnoli (concertmaster, Leipzig Gewandhaus Concerts); William Crotch (organ, St. Johns College); Bernard Sarrette (director, Paris Conservatory).

F. **Biographical Highlights**
Ludwig van Beethoven begins teaching piano in Vienna; Gottlieb Graupner begins his music teaching career in Boston; Friedrich Heinrich Himmel begins a long concertizing tour through Russia

and Scandinavia; Joseph Boulogne Saint-Georges resigns his position as colonel in the French colored regiment and, retiring from his
army career, moves to Paris for the remainder of his life; Václav Jan
Tomásek switches his studies to law at the University of Prague but
continues his studies in music as well; Carl Maria von Weber enters
the Institute for Choir Boys in Salzburg and studies composition
with Michael Haydn.

G. **Cultural Beginnings**
Music Publications: *The Pianoforte Magazine* (London).
Performing Centers: Teatro Cerri (Bergamo).
Other: John Gelb and Co., organ builders (New York).

H. **Musical Literature**
John Aitken, *Scots Musical Museum*; Edward Bunting, *General Collec-
tion of Ancient Irish Music I*; Bartolomeo Campagnoli, *Metodo per Vio-
lino*; Johann F. Daube, *Anleitung zur Erfindung der Melodie und ihrer
Fortsetzung I*; Charles Gauzargues, *Traité de Composition*; Oliver
Holden, *The Worcester Collection*; George Vogler, *Organ School—
Method of Clavier and Thoroughbass*.

I. **Musical Compositions**
Chamber Music:
   String Quartets: Franz Joseph Haydn, *"Erdödy" Quartets, Opus 76:
   No. 1 in G–No. 2 in d, "Fifths"–No. 3 in C, "Emperor"–No. 4 in B♭,
   "Sunrise"–No. 5 in D–No. 6 in E♭*; Friedrich Hiller, *Three Quartets,
   Opus 3*; František Krommer, *Three Quartets, Opus 7*.
   Sonata/Solos: Ludwig van Beethoven, *Two Cello Sonatas (F, g), Opus
   5–Twelve Variations in G on Handel's "See, the Conquering Hero Comes"*
   (cello, piano); Luigi Boccherini, *Six Violin Duets (G, E, f, C, E, d)*.
   Ensembles: Ludwig van Beethoven, *String Serenade in D, Opus 8*
   (string trio)–*Quintet in E♭ for Piano and Woodwinds, Opus 16*; Luigi
   Boccherini, *Six Quintets for Flute (Oboe) and Strings (G, F, D, A, E♭,
   d), Opus 55–Six String Quintets (e, F, C, E♭, D, a), Opus 56*; Jan L.
   Dussek, *Two Trios, Opus 34* (harp, violin, cello); Adalbert Gyrowetz, *Three Piano Trios, Opus 18*; Augustus Kollmann, *The Shipwreck* (piano trio); František Krommer, *Three String Quintets, Opus
   8*; Ignace Pleyel, *Six Quartets (D, F, A, C, G, A), Ben. 387–92* (flute,
   violin, viola, cello)–*Three Keyboard Trios (B♭, A, C), Ben. 468–70–Six
   String Trios (D, F, G, B♭, G, A,), Ben. 410–15*.
   Piano: Ludwig van Beethoven, *Piano Sonata in D, Opus 6 (four
   hands)–Sonata No. 4 in E♭, Opus 7–No. 5 in c, Opus 10, No. 1–No. 6 in
   F, Opus 10, No. 2–Rondo in C, Opus 15, No. 1*; Muzio Clementi, *Six
   Progressive Sonatas (C, G, C, F, G, D), Opus 36*; Carl Ditters von Dit-

tersdorf, *Twelve Keyboard Sonatas, Four Hands*; Jan L. Dussek, *Three Sonatas (B♭, G, c), Opus 35*; Ignace A. Ladurner, *Three Sonatas, Opus 4*; Joseph Wölfl, *Three Sonatas, Opus 3*.

Choral/Vocal Music:

Choral: Domenico Cimarosa, *S Filippo Neri che risuscita Paolo Massimi* (oratorio); Franz Joseph Haydn, *Gott erhalte Franz den Kaiser* (Austrian National Anthem); Friedrich H. Himmel, *Trauer-Cantate–Das Vertrauen auf Gott* (cantata); Friedrich L. A. Kunzen, *The Hallelujah of Creation*; Giovanni Paisiello, *Silvio e Clori* (cantata); Niccolò Piccinni, *Arco di amore* (cantata); Ignace Playel, *Mass in G, Ben. 741*; Georg "Abbe" Vogler, *Te Deum in D*.

Vocal: Friedrich F. Hůrka, *Fifteen Deutsche Lieder*; Johann F. Reichardt, *Gesänge der klage und der trostes*.

Musical Stage: Thomas Attwood, *The Fairy Festival–Fast Asleep*; François Boieldieu, *La pari–La famille suisse–L'heureuse nouvelle*; Luigi Cherubini, *Médée*; Domenico Cimarosa, *L'imprudente fortunato–Achille all'assedio di Troja–Artemisia, regina di Caria*; Nicolas Dalayrac, *La leçon–La Maison isolée*; Carl Ditters von Dittersdorf, *Der Mädchenmarkt–Die lustigen Weiber von Windsor*; Pierre Gaveaux, *Le traité nul–Sophie et Moncars*; André Grétry, *Lisbeth–Le barbier du village–Anacréon chez Polycrate*; Nicolò Isouard, *I due avari–L'improvisata in campagna*; Friedrich A. Kunzen, *Dragedukken*; Jean F. Lesueur, *Artaxerse*; Étienne Méhul, *Le jeune Henri*; Wenzel Müller, *Das lustige Beilager*; Ferdinando Paër, *Tamarlane–Griselda*; Giovanni Paisiello, *Andromaca*; Victor Pelissier, *Ariadne Abandoned by Theseus*; Antonio Salieri, *I tre filosofo*; Johann Schmidt, *Der Schlaftrunk*; William Shield, *Love and Nature–The Italian Villagers*; Fernando Sor, *Telemaco nell'isola de Calipso*; Gaspare Spontini, *Adelina Senese*; Joseph Weigl, *I Solitari*; Joseph Wölfl, *Das schöne Milchmädchen*; Nicola Zingarelli, *La morte di Mitridate*.

Orchestra/Band Music:

Concerted Music:

Piano: François Boieldieu, *Concerto*.

Violin: Ignace Pleyel, *Clarinet/Flute/Violin Concerto in C, Ben. 106*.

Other: François Devienne, *Symphonie concertante in F* (flute, oboe, horn, bassoon); Jan Václav Stich, *Horn Concerto No. 5–No. 6*.

Ballet/Incidental Music: Domenico Mazzochi, *Pizarro* (B)–*Sapho et Phaeon* (B); Alexander Reinagle, *Columbus* (IM)–*The Savoyard* (IM); Joseph Weigl, *Alcina* (B).

Standard Works: Peter von Hagen, *Federal Overture*.

Symphonies: Joachim Albertini, *Symphony*; Johann A. André, *Symphony in D, "Zur Friedenfeier," Opus 7*.

1798

❄

Historical Highlights: The War of the Second Coalition begins; Napoleon Bonaparte begins his Egyptian Campaign; Admiral Nelson destroys the French fleet at Abukir Bay; the Pope is taken prisoner by the French revolutionary forces; in the United States, the Kentucky Resolutions and the Virginia Resolutions set forth the principles of State's Rights; Congress authorizes all-out naval war with France over her harassment of U.S. shipping.

Art and Literature Highlights: Births—artist Ferdinand Eugène Delacroix, writers August Hoffmann, Adam Mickiewicz; Deaths—artist Asmus Jacob Carstens, writer Jeremy Belknap. Art—Earl's *Looking East from Denny Hill*, Camuccini's *The Death of Julius Caesar*, Gérard's *Cupid and Psyche*; Literature—Brown's *Wieland*, Cowper's *The Castaways*, Rowson's *Reuben and Rachel: Tales of Old Time*.

Musical Highlights

A. **Births**

Composers: Engelbert Aigner (Austria) February 23; Désiré-Alexandre Batton (France) January 2; Josef Dessauer (Bohemia) May 28; Franz Glässer (Bohemia) April 19; John Henry Griesbach (England) June 20.

Conductors: Carl Gottlieb Reissiger (Germany) January 31.

Singers: James Bland (British bass) March 5; Jean-Baptiste Chollet (French tenor) May 20; Henriette Clémentine (Méric-) Lalande (French soprano).

Performers: Henri Bertini (British pianist/publisher) October 28; Aline Bertrand (French harpist); August Berwald (Swedish violinist) August 28; Paul Emile Johns (Polish-born pianist/publisher)(?); Alexei Feodorovich Lvov (Russian violinist/composer) June 5.

Others: Jean Andries (Belgian educator/music author) April 25; Jonas Chickering (American piano maker) April 5; Jean-Baptiste Vuillaume (French piano maker) October 7.

B. **Deaths**

Composers: Felice Alessandri (Italy) August 15; Damasus Brosmann (Moravia) September 16; Christian Cannabich (Germany) January 20; Giuseppe Giordani (Italy) January 4; Johann Georg Lang (Bohemia) July 17; Christian Gottlob Neefe (Germany) January 26.

Singers: Angelo (Maria) Amorevoli (Italian tenor) November 15.

Performers: Gaetano Brunetti (Italian violinist/composer) December 16; William Flackton (British organist/composer) January 5;

Aloisio Lodovico Fracassini (Italian violinist) October 9; Gaetano Pugnani (Italian violinist/composer) June 15; William Selby (British organist) December 12.

Others: Christoph Torricella (Swiss publisher) January 24; James Leach (British psalmodist) February 8; Johann Thomas Trattner (Hungarian-born violin maker) July 31.

C. Debuts

Singers: Thomas Bellamy (British bass—Dublin); Manuel García (Spanish tenor—Spain); Bianchi Jackson (Lacy) (British soprano—London).

Performers: Friedrich Dotzauer (German cellist—Hildburghausen).

D. New Positions

Conductors: Bernardo Bittoni (maestro di cappella/organ, Fabriano Cathedral); José Nunes García (mestre de capela, Cathedral, Rio de Janeiro); Jeronymo Francisco de Lima (mestre de capela, Lisbon Cathedral); Carl David Stegmann (Hamburg Theater); Peter von Winter (hofkapellmeister, Munich).

Others: Jean Paul Martini (inspector, Paris Conservatory); Johann Friedrich Rochlitz (founder/editor, *Allgemeine Musikalische Zeitung*); Ignaz Schuppanzigh (manager, Ausgarten Concerts, Vienna).

E. Prizes/Honors

Honors: Nicolas Dalayrac (Royal Academy of Sweden).

F. Biographical Highlights

Ludwig van Beethoven notices the first signs of his approaching deafness; Louis François Dauprat is the first to receive first prize in horn from the Paris Conservatory; James Hewitt buys out Carr's Musical Repository and begins publishing music; Konradin Kreutzer begins the study of law at the University of Freiburg; Rodolphe Kreutzer gets to meet Beethoven while in Vienna; Vincenzo Manfredini returns to Russia at the invitation of Czar Paul I, his former pupil; Pierre Monsigny, ruined by the revolution in France, is given a pension by the Paris Opéra-Comique; Niccolò Piccinni is released from home arrest and leaves for Paris.

G. Cultural Beginnings

Performing Groups—Choral: Concentores Sodales (London).

Performing Groups—Instrumental: Concerto de la Rue Cléry (Paris); United States Marine Fife and Drum Corps (beginning of the U.S. Marine Band).

Music Publishers: Broderip, Clementi and Co. (London); T. Mollo and Co. (Vienna).

Music Publications: *Allgemeine Musikalische Zeitung; Journal d'Apollon pour le Forte-Piano; Unpartheiische Kritik* (by C. G. Thomas).

Performing Centers: Astley's Royal Amphitheater (London); Park Theater (New York); Théâtre des Jeunes-Artistes (Paris).

Other: Accademia dei Costanti (Pisa); Nicolas Lupot, violin maker (Paris); Thomas Tomkison, piano maker (London).

H. Musical Literature

Antoine Bailleux, *Méthode raisonnée pour apprendre à jouer du Violin*; Domenico Corri, *A Musical Dictionary*; Jean B. Cartier, *L'Art du Violon*; William Jackson, *The Four Ages with Essays on Various Subjects*; Justin H. Knecht, *Vollständige Orgelschule für Anfänger und Geübtere III*; Ludwig Lachnith/J. L. Adam, *Méthode ou principe général du doigte pour le forte-piano*; Honoré Langlé, *Traité de la Basse sous le Chant précédé de toutes le règles de la composition*; John Relfe, *Guida Armonica*; Franz P. Rigler, *Anleitung zum gesange, und dem Klaviere oder die Orgel zu spielen*; Jan Václav Stich, *Hornschule*; Georg Vogler, *Système de simplification pour les orgues*; Michel Woldemar, *Méthode pour le violon*; M. Wright, *American Musical Miscellany*.

I. Musical Compositions

Chamber Music:

String Quartets: Johann G. Distler, *Six Quartets, Opus 6*; Adalbert Gyrowetz, *Three Quartets, Opus 21*; Rodolphe Kreutzer, *Six New Quartets, Opus 2*; František Krommer, *Three Quartets, Opus 11–Three Quartets, Opus 16*; Joseph Wölfl, *Three Quartets, Opus 4*.

Sonata/Solos: Ludwig van Beethoven, *Violin Sonatas No. 1–3 (D, A, E♭), Opus 12–Twelve Variations in F on Mozart's "Ein Mädchen oder Weibchen," Opus 66* (cello, piano); Jan L. Dussek, *Violin Sonata in C, Opus 36*.

Ensembles: Ludwig van Beethoven, *Three String Trios (G, D, c), Opus 9–Trio, Opus 11* (clarinet, cello, piano); Adalbert Gyrowetz, *Three Piano Trios, Opus 23–Divertimento, Opus 25* (piano trio); František Krommer, *Three String Quintets, Opus 11–Quartet No. 1 in f for Flute and Strings, Opus 13*; Franz C. Neubauer, *Piano Trio, Opus 20*; Ignace Pleyel, *Two Quartets (D, G), Ben. 393,4* (flute, strings)–*Three Keyboard Trios (B♭, D, E♭), Ben. 471–3*; Anton Reicha, *Flute Quartet in D, Opus 12–Sonata for Four Flutes, Opus 19*; Joseph Wölfl, *Three Piano Trios, Opus 5*.

Piano: Ludwig van Beethoven, *Sonata No. 7 in D, Opus 10, No. 3–Sonata No. 8 in c, "Pathétique," Opus 13*; Muzio Clementi, *Three Sonatas (C, G, D), Opus 37–Twelve Waltzes, Opus 38*; Carl Ditters von Dittersdorf, *Six Keyboard Sonatas on Ovid's "Metamorphoses"*; Jan L. Dussek, *Sonata in C* (piano, four hands); Friedrich H. Himmel, *Twelve Variations on "Marlborough's'en va-t-en guerre"*;

Domenico Mazzochi, *Sonata, Opus 36, "Lord Nelson's Victory"*; Ignace Pleyel, *Air with Variation in B♭, Ben. 615*; Joseph Wölfl, *Three Sonatas, Opus 6*.

Organ: August E. Müller, *Sammlung von Orgelstucken*.

Choral/Vocal Music:

Choral: Catterino Cavos, *L'Eroe* (cantata); Domenico Cimarosa, *Te Deum*; Franz Joseph Haydn, *The Creation* (oratorio)–*Missa solemnis in d, "Nelsonmesse"*; Friedrich H. Himmel, *Te Deum*; Johann G. Naumann, *I pellegrini al sepolcro* (oratorio); Niccolò Piccinni, *Psalm 87*.

Vocal: Luigi Boccherini, *Dramatic Scene, "Ynes de Castro"*; Adalbert Gyrowetz, *Seven German Songs, Opus 34*; Friedrich H. Himmel, *Deutsche Lieder: ein Neujahrsgeschenk*; William Jackson, *Six Epigrams, Opus 17–Six Madrigals, Opus 18*(?); Honoré Langlais, *Hymne à l'éternel*; Christian G. Neefe, *Bilder und Träume*; Johann Reichardt, *Lieder der Liebe und der Einsamkeit I–Wiegen lieder für gute deutscher Mütter*; Daniel Steibelt, *Six Romances–Five Airs d'Estelle*.

Musical Stage: Felice Alessandri, *I sposi burlati*; Thomas Attwood, *A Day at Rome*; François Boieldieu, *Zoraïme et Zulnar–La dot de Suzette*; Luigi Cherubini, *L'hôtellerie portugaise*; Domenico Cimarosa, *L'apprensivo raggirato*; Nicolas Dalayrac, *Gulnare–Alexis–Primerose*; Carl Ditters von Dittersdorf, *Die Opera buffa–Don Coribaldi*; Johann L. Dussek, *The Captive of Spilberg*; Pierre Gaveaux, *Léonore–Le diable couleur de Rose*; Antoine Gresnick, *La forêt de Sicile–La grotte des Cévennes*; Friedrich H. Himmel, *Alessandro*; Nicolò Isouard, *Ginevra di Scozia–Il barone d'Alba chiara*; Ferdinand Kauer, *Das Donauweibchen*; Friedrich A. Kunzen, *Erik Ejegod*; Louis S. Lebrun, *L' astronome–Le menteur maladroit–Un moment d'erreur*; Vicente Martín y Soler, *La festa del villagio*; Simon Mayr, *Che originale*; Wenzel Müller, *Der Sturm*; Marcos Portugal, *Fernando nel Messico*; Johann Reichardt, *Die Geisterinsel*; Giuseppe Sarti, *Andromeda*; Gaspare Spontini, *L'eroismo ridiculo–Il Teseo riconosciuto*; Daniel Steibelt, *Albert und Adelaide*; Franz X. Süssmayr, *Der Wildfang*; Joseph Weigl, *Das Dorf im Gebürge*; Peter Winter, *Der Sturm*; Joseph Wölfl, *Der kopf ohne mann*; Nicola Zingarelli, *Ines de Castro–Meleagro*; Johann Zumsteeg, *Die Geisterinsel*.

Orchestra/Band Music:

Concerted Music:

Piano: Jan L. Dussek, *Concerto in B♭, Opus 40, "Military"*; Franz C. Neubauer, *Concerto, Opus 21*; Johann Schmidt, *Concerto, Opus 1*; Daniel Steibelt, *Concerto No. 3, Opus 35*.

Other: Johann A. André, *Oboe Concerto in F, Opus 8*; Jan Václav Stich, *Horn Concerto No. 7*.

Ballet/Incidental Music: John Davy, *Alfred the Great* (B); Domenico Mazzochi, *Eliza, Opus 32* (B); Johann F. Reichardt, *Iphi-*

genia (IM); Alexander Reinagle, *The Italian Monk* (IM)–*The Gentle Shepherd* (IM).

Standard Works: Ludwig van Beethoven, *Twelve Minuets for Orchestra, Opus 139.*

Symphonies: Luigi Boccherini, *Symphony in C (with guitar);* Georg "Abbe" Vogler, *Symphony in C, "Scanlan";* Ernst von Wenczura, *No. 2, "Russian."*

1799

❉

Historical Highlights: Napoleon Bonaparte returns to France, overthrows the directory and makes himself first consul; France begins negotiations with the United States over the shipping problems; Russia withdraws from the Second Coalition; in the United States, Fries Rebellion, a revolt by the Pennsylvania Germans against the land tax, takes place; a National Quarantine Act is passed—Congress also standardizes all weights and measures.

Art and Literature Highlights: Births—writers Honoré de Balzac, Karl Nicander, Alexander Pushkin; Deaths—artist Ferdinand Kobell, writers Amos Bronson Alcott, Pierre Caron de Beaumarchais, Jean-François Marmontel. Art—David's *Rape of the Sabine Women,* Thorvaldsen's *Bacchus and Ariadne,* Turner's *Battle of the Nile;* Literature—Bocage's *Ormond,* Brown's *Arthur Merwyn,* Schiller's *Wallenstein Trilogy.*

Musical Highlights

A. Births

Composers: Vincenzo Fioravanti (Italy) April 5; Jacques Fromental Halévy (France) May 27; Giuseppe Persiani (Italy) September 11; Joseph Rastrelli (Italy-Germany) April 13; Alexei Vertovsky (Russia) March 1.

Conductors: Ferenc Bräuer (Hungary) October 20.

Performers: Jean Ancot, *fils* (Belgian pianist/composer) July 6; Heinrich Friedrich Enckhausen (German organist) August 28; Johann Heinrich Lübeck (Dutch violinist/conductor) February 11; Charles Mayer (German pianist/composer) March 21; Daniel Schlesinger (German-born pianist); Théophile (Alexandre) Tilmant (French violinist/conductor) July 8.

Others: Siegfried Dehn (German music theorist) February 24; Aloys Fuchs (Austrian musicologist) June 22; Edward Holmes (British music critic) November 10; John Antes Latrobe (British music author); Thomas Oliphant (Scottish music author/editor) December 25; Ludwig Rellstab (German music author) April 13.

B. Deaths

Composers: João de Sousa Carvalho (Portugal)(?); Narciso Casanovas (Spain) April 1; Carl Ditters von Dittersdorf (Austria) October 24; François Giroust (France) April 28; Antoine-Frédéric Gresnick (Belgium) October 16; Vincenzo Manfredini (Italy) August 16; Henri Joseph Riegel (France) May 2; Joseph Boulogne de Saint-Georges (France) June 9(?).

Singers: Joseph Friebert (Austrian tenor) August 6; Polly Young (British soprano) September 20.

Performers: Claude Balbastre (French organist/composer) May 9; Joah Bates (British organist) June 8; Wilhelm Cramer (German violinist/composer) October 5; Johann Georg Distler (Austrian violinist/composer) July 28; František Xaver Dušek (Bohemian pianist/composer) February 12; Pieter Hellendaal (Dutch-born organist/composer) April 19; Jan Kirkmann (Dutch organist/composer); David Traugott Nicolai (German organist/composer) December 20.

Others: Johann André (German publisher/composer) June 18; Esteban de Arteaga (Spanish music author) October 30; Gotthold Heinrich Donati (German organ builder) December 28; Jean-Henri Naderman (French harpsichord maker/publisher) February 4; Andrea Luigi Serassi (Italian organ builder).

D. New Positions

Conductors: Antonio Bartolomeo Bruni (Paris Opéra-Comique); Friedrich Adam Hiller (Königsberger Theater); Giovanni Liverati (kapellmeister, National Theater, Prague); Adamo Marcori (maestro di cappella, Pisa Cathedral); Giacomo Rampini (maestro di cappella, Udine Cathedral).

Others: William Francis Ayrton (organ, Ripon Cathedral); John Clarke (organ, Trinity and St. John's Colleges, Cambridge); Giacomo Tritto (director, Conservatorio della Pieta dei Turchini, Naples).

E. Prizes/Honors

Honors: François-Joseph Gossec (Royal Academy of Sweden); Stanislao Mattei (Accademia Filarmonica, Bologna).

F. Biographical Highlights

Domenico Cimarosa, sentenced to death for favoring the French occupation of Italy, is pardoned but banished from Naples; Jan L. Dussek, on the failure of the Corri publishing firm, flees to Germany leaving his wife and family behind; Anton Reicha goes to Paris with high hopes for performance of his operas but has little success; Louis Spohr's first tour is a failure but he is hired by the duke of Brunswick; Daniel Steibelt, pardoned for army desertion, returns to

Vienna and loses an improvising duel with Beethoven; Filippo Traetta escapes political prison and settles in Boston.

G. Cultural Beginnings
Music Publishers: Georges-Julien Sieber (Paris).
Performing Centers: Lübeck Opera House.

H. Musical Literature
Antonio Abreu, *Guitar Method*; Louis Adam, *Méthode générale du doigté*; Johann G. Albrechtsberger, *Anfangsgründe zur Klavierkunste*; Rudolph Z. Becker, *Mildheimisches Liederbuch*; Giuseppe M. Cambini, *Méthode pour le flûte traversière*; Joseph Corfe, *A Treatise on Singing*; Domenico Corri, *The Art of Fingering*; Augustus Kollmann, *An Essay on Practical Musical Composition*; Luigi Sabbatini, *La vera idea delle musicali numeriche signature*; William Shield, *An Introduction to Harmony*; Florido Tomeoni, *Théorie de la musique vocale*.

I. Musical Compositions
Chamber Music:
   String Quartets: Johann G. Albrechtsberger, *Three Quartets, Opus 19*; Luigi Boccherini, *Six Quartets (C, E, B♭, b, D, E♭), Opus 58*; Franz Joseph Haydn, *"Lobkowitz" Quartets, Opus 77: No. 1 in G–No. 2 in F*; Joseph Wölfl, *Six Quartets, Opus 10*.
   Sonata/Solos: François Boieldieu, *Three Violin Sonatas, Opus 3*; Margarete Danzi, *Violin Sonata*.
   Ensembles: Ludwig van Beethoven, *Septet in E♭, Opus 20*; Luigi Boccherini, *Six Piano Quintets (A, B♭, a, d, E, C), Opus 57*; Jan L. Dussek, *Sonata in E♭, Opus 37* (piano, violin, cello)–*Piano Quintet in f, Opus 41*; Adalbert Gyrowetz, *Quintet for Flute and String Quartet, Opus 27*–*Three Piano Trios, Opus 28*; Johann N. Hummel, *Piano Trio in F, Opus 22*; František Krommer, *Quartet No. 2 for Flute and Strings, Opus 17*; Franz C. Neubauer, *Three Trios, Opus 3* (flute, violin, viola); Ignace Pleyel, *Two Quartets (D, G), Ben. 393,4* (flute, strings).
   Piano: Johann G. Albrechtsberger, *Six Fugues, Opus 8* (harpsichord/organ); Ludwig van Beethoven, *Seven Ländler, Opus 168*–*Ten Variations, on Salieri's "La Stessa, La Stessissima," Opus 185*; Friedrich (W. H.) Benda, *Sonata for Piano, Four Hands, Opus 6*; François Boieldieu, *Two Sonatas, Opus 4*; Jan L. Dussek, *Three Sonatas (G, C, B♭), Opus 39*; Ignace Pleyel, *Seven Pieces, Ben. 618–24*; Samuel Wesley, *Twelve Sonatinas, Opus 4*.
   Organ: Johann Albrechtsberger, *Six Fugues, Opus 8*.
Choral/Vocal Music:
   Choral: Domenico Cimarosa, *Mass in c*–*Bella Italia–No che più lieto giorno* (cantatas); Franz Joseph Haydn, *Missa solennis in B♭, "Theresienmesse."*

Vocal: Adalbert Gyrowetz, *Six German Songs, Opus 38*; Friedrich H. Himmel, *Six romances françaises*; Johann G. Naumann, *Twenty-five neue Lieder verschiedenen Inhalts*; Johann Reichardt, *Lieder für die Jugend*.

Musical Stage: Thomas Attwood, *The Magic Oak*; Henri-Montan Berton, *Le délire–Montano et Stéphanie*; Francesco Bianchi, *Merope*; François Boieldieu, *Les méprises espagnoles–La prisonnière* (with Cherubini); Luigi Cherubini, *La punition*; Domenico Cimarosa, *Semiramide*; Nicolas Dalayrac, *Arnill–Adolphe et Clara*; Franz Danzi, *Der Kuss*; Carl Ditters von Dittersdorf, *25,000 Gulden*; Giacomo Ferrari, *I due Svizzeri*; Valentino Fioravanti, *Le cantatrici villane*; Antoine Gresnick, *Le tuteur original–Rencontre sur rencontre*; André Grétry, *Elisca*; James Hewitt, *Columbus–The Mysterious Marriage*; Friedrich A. Kunzen, *Naturens røst*; Louis S. Lebrun, *La veuve américaine–La maçon*; Simon Mayr, *Adelaide di Gueselino*; Étienne Méhul, *Adrien–Ariodant*; Ferdinando Paër, *Camilla–Il morto vivo*; Victor Pelissier, *The Vintage*; Anton Reicha, *Les Français en Egypte*; Vincenzo Righini, *La Gerusalemme liberata*; Antonio Salieri, *Falstaff*; Giuseppe Sarti, *Enea nel Lazio–La famille indienne en Angleterre*; Johann Schenk, *Die Jagd*; Gaspare Spontini, *La finta filosofa*; Franz X. Süssmayr, *Soliman II–Der Marktschreier*; Paul Wranitzky, *Der Schreiner–Johanna von Montfaucon*; Nicola Zingarelli, *Il ritratto*.

Orchestra/Band Music:
Concerted Music:
    Piano: John Field, *Concerto No. 1 in E♭*; Daniel Steibelt, *Concerto No. 3 in E, Opus 33, "L'orage"*; Joseph Wölfl, *Concerto, Opus 43, "Grand concerto militaire."*
    Other: François Devienne, *Symphonie concertante in G, Opus 76* (two flutes); Johann N. Hummel, *Mandolin Concerto*.
Ballet/Incidental Music: Catterino Cavos, *Il sotterraneo* (B); Johann L. Dussek, *Pizarro* (IM); Vicente Martín y Soler, *Tancrède* (B); Victor Pelissier, *The Fourth of July* (IM); Johann F. Reichardt, *Die Geisterinsel* (B); Joseph Weigl, *Clothilde, Prinzessin von Salerno* (B).
Symphonies: Ludwig van Beethoven, *No. 1 in C, Opus 21*; Ignace Pleyel, *Symphony in B♭, Ben. 150–Symphony in C, Ben. 151*.

1800

❄

Historical Highlights: The British capture the island of Malta; Napoleon Bonaparte conquers Italy and advances on Vienna; in another secret deal, Spain gives the Louisiana Territory in the New World back to France; in the United States, the census indicates a population of

5,308,000, a thirty-five percent increase in ten years; because of a tied electoral vote, the House of Representatives chooses Thomas Jefferson as third president; Washington, D.C., becomes the capital.
Art and Literature Highlights: Births—writer Anna Marie Halland, artists Emil Cauer, Louis Eugène Lami, Sarah M. Peale; Deaths—poet William Cowper, sculptor John Skillin. Art—Chalon's *Banditti at Their Repast*, Earl's *Looking East from Leicester Hill, Worcester*, Ingres' *Cincinnatus Receiving the Deputies*; Literature—Davis' *The Farmer of New Jersey*, Edgeworth's *Castle Rackrent*, Schiller's *Maria Stuart*.

Musical Highlights

A. Births

Composers: Józef Stefani (Poland) April 16; Nikolai Alexievich Titov (Russia) May 10.

Conductors: Heinrich Dorn (Germany) November 14; Louis Schlösser (Germany) November 17; Carl Friedrich Zöllner (Germany) March 17.

Singers: Giuseppina Ronzi de Begnis (Italian-born soprano) January 11; Maria Caradori-Allan (Italian soprano) December 27; Antonio Tamburini (Italian baritone) March 28; Harriett Waylett (British soprano) February 7.

Performers: Karl Drechsler (German cellist) May 27; John Goss (British organist) December 27; Eduard Grell (German organist/conductor) November 6; Georg Hellmesberger, Sr. (Austrian violinist/conductor) April 24; Christian Friedrich Nohr (German violinist) October 7; Henry Kemble Oliver (American organist/composer) November 24; Antonio James Oury (British violinist); Louis Schlösser (German violinist/composer) November 17.

Others: Raimondo Boucheron (Italian music theorist/conductor) March 15; William Dauney (Scottish music historian) October 27; Henry Erben (American organ builder) March 10; Ludwig Köchel (Austrian bibliographer) January 14; Philipp Wackernagel (German music scholar) June 28.

B. Deaths

Composers: Julije Bajamonti (Croatia) August 4; Gaudenzio Battistini (Italy) February 25; Dominique Della Maria (France) March 9; Evstigney Fomin (Russia) April 27; Niccolò Piccini (Italy) May 7; Johann Abraham Schulz (Germany) June 10; Johann Christoph Toeschi (Germany) March 3.

Singers: Antoine Albanese (French castrato) December 2; Margarethe Danzi (German soprano) June 11; Giambattista Mancini (Italian castrato) January 4(?).

Performers: Louis Aubert (French violinist/composer) December 2(?); Carl Friedrich Christian Fasch (German harpsichordist/conductor) August 3; Johann Chrtistian Fischer (German oboist/composer) April 29; Pierre Gaviniès (French violinist) September 8; Louis Granier (French violinist/conductor) December 2; Francis Linley (British organist/composer) September 14; Johan Wikmanson (Swedish organist/composer) December 28.

Others: Daines Barrington (British music author) March 14; Jorge Bosch Bernat-Veri (Spanish organ builder) December 2; Raimondo Boucheron (Italian music theorist/conductor) March 15; Christoph Gottlob Breitkopf (German publisher) April 4; William Jones (British music author/composer) January 6; Francisco Ignacio Solano (Portugese music theorist) September 18; Joseph Warton (British critic) February 23.

C. **Debuts**
   Performers: Carl Czerny (Austrian pianist—Vienna); Friedrich Fesca (German violinist—Magdeburg, age eleven); Joseph Mayseder (Austrian violinist—Vienna); Charles Neate (British pianist—London).

D. **New Positions**
   Conductors: Mateo Pérez de Albéniz (maestro de capilla, S. María la Redonda, San Sebastián); Ernst Häusler (cantor, St. Anne's, Augsburg); Marcos Antônio Portugal (San Carlo Theater—mestre de capela Royal Chapel, Lisbon); Carl Zelter (Berlin Singakademie).
   Others: Pierre-Alexandre Monsigny (Inspector of Music Education, Paris).

E. **Prizes/Honors**
   Honors: David Auguste von Apell (Order of the Golden Spur).

F. **Biographical Highlights**
   Ludwig van Beethoven meets Czerny and presents his first concert of his own works; Luigi Boccherini enters the service of Louis Bonaparte, Napoleon's ambassador to Madrid; Anton Diabelli continues his priesthood studies and enters the monastery at Raichenhaslach; Josephina Grassini becomes Napoleon's mistress and goes with him to Paris; Michael Haydn loses all his property when the French occupy Salzburg; Samuel Holyoke moves to Salem, Massachusetts, and continues to teach music; Konradin Kreutzer, on the death of his father, returns to the study of music; Daniel Steibelt, following his pianistic defeat by Beethoven, returns to Paris; Carl Maria von Weber fails in the lithography business in Frieberg and returns to composing.

G. **Cultural Beginnings**
   Performing Groups: Euterpean Society of New York.

Performing Groups—Instrumental: Philharmonic Society of New York; Société du Concert (Lille).
Educational: Library of Congress (Washington, D.C.).
Music Publishers: Graupner Music Store and Publishing House (Boston); Hoffmeister and Kühnel's Bureau de Musique (Leipzig—bought out, 1814, by C. F. Peters); Momigny Publishing House (Paris).
Music Publications: *Musical Journal for the Piano Forte.*
Other: Flight and Robinson, organ builders (London); Portable Grand (Upright) Piano (by J. I. Hawkins and M. Müller, working independently); Stockholm New Music Society.

H. **Musical Literature**
Joseph Corfe, *Sacred Music*; Johann F. Dalberg, *Untersuchungen über den Ursprung der Harmonie*; Fedele Fenaroli, *Partimento ossia Basso numerato–Studio del contrappunto*; Carlo Gervasoni, *La Scuola della Musica*; Oliver Holden, *Modern Collection of Sacred Music–Plain Psalmody and Sacred Dirges*; Samuel Holyoke, *Instrumental Assistant I*; Ferdinand Kauer, *Kurzegefasste Generalbass-Schule für Anfänger*; Jacob Kimball, *The Essex Harmony*; Matthew P. King, *A General Treatise on Music*; John Page, *Harmonia Sacra*; Timothy Swan, *The Songster's Assistant.*

I. **Musical Compositions**
Chamber Music:
  String Quartets: Ludwig van Beethoven, *String Quartets, Opus 18: No. 1 in F–No. 2 in G–No. 3 in D–No. 4 in c–No. 5 in A–No. 6 in B♭*; Luigi Boccherini, *Six Quartets (C, E♭, B♭, b, D, E♭), Opus 58*; Adalbert Gyrowetz, *Three Quartets, Opus 29*; František Krommer, *Three Quartets, Opus 18*; Niccolò Paganini, *Three Quartets (d, E♭, a)*; Samuel Wesley, *Quartet in E♭–Fugue in B♭*; Anton Wranitzky, *Six Quartets, Opus 4.*
  Sonata/Solos: Franz Neubauer, *Six Trios, Opus 6* (flute, violin, cello); Vincenzo Righini, *Partita in E♭* (woodwind octet); Joseph Boulogne de Saint-Georges, *Six Violin Sonatas*; Anton Wranitzky, *Two Violin Sonatas, Opus 6.*
  Ensembles: Johann G. Albrechtsberger, *Six Quartets with Fugues for Various Instruments, Opus 20*; François Boieldieu, *Piano Trio, Opus 5(?)*; Adalbert Gyrowetz, *String Quintet, Opus 45*; Domenico Mazzochi, *Concertante, Opus 42* (flute, piano, strings); Maria Theresia von Paradis, *Piano Trio*; Jan Václav Stich, *Twenty Trios for Three Horns.*
  Piano: Ludwig van Beethoven, *Sonata No. 11 in B♭, Opus 22*; François Boieldieu, *Sonata, Opus 6(?)*; Muzio Clementi, *Twelve Waltzes, Opus 39*; Jan L. Dussek, *Sonata in A, Opus 43–Sonata in E♭,*

"Farewell," Opus 44–Three Sonatas (B♭, G, D), Opus 45; Ignace Pleyel, Three Sonatas (a, F, G), Ben. 625–7; Carl Maria von Weber, Six Variations, Opus 2; Joseph Wölfl, Three Sonatas, Opus 7–Three Sonatas, Opus 11.

Organ: Johann Albrechtsberger, Six fughe colla cadenze, Opus 9; Samuel Wesley, Nine Organ Voluntaries, Opus 6.

Choral/Vocal Music:

Choral: David August von Apell, Missa pontificale; Ludwig van Beethoven, Christ on the Mount of Olives, Opus 85 (oratorio); Luigi Boccherini, Mass, Opus 59–Stabat Mater, Opus 61; Johann M. Dreyer, Te Deum; Franz Joseph Haydn, The Seasons (oratorio)–Te Deum in C; Étienne Méhul, Chant National du 14 Juillet, 1800; Johann Naumann, Il ritorno di figliolo prodigo (oratorio).

Vocal: Pierre Gaveaux, Recueil de canzonettes italiennes; Adalbert Gyrowetz, Six German Songs, Opus 44; Friedrich H. Himmel, Gesänge aus Tiedges Urania, Opus 18; Oliver Holden, From Vernon's Mount Behold the Hero Rise (song); Friedrich F. Hůrka, Der Sänger(?)–Das Strickerlied(?); Johann F. Reichardt, Twelve deutsche lieder; Johann Zumsteeg, Kleine Balladen und Lieder I, II.

Musical Stage: François Boieldieu, The Caliph of Bagdad; Luigi Cherubini, Les deux journées–Epicure (with Méhul); Nicolas Dalayrac, Maison à vendre; Evstigney Fomin, The Americans–The Golden Apple; Pietro Generali, Gli amanti ridicoli; James Hewitt, Robin Hood–Pizarro; Nicolò Isouard, Le Petit Page; Conradin Kreutzer, Die lächerliche Werbung; Louis S. Lebrun, Marcelin–Elénor et Dorval; Simon Mayr, Il carretto del venditore d'aceto; Domenico Mazzochi, Paul and Virginia, Opus 43; Étienne Méhul, Bion; Richard Mount-Edgcumbe, Zenobia; Anton Reicha, L'ouragan; Johann Reichardt, Lieb' und Treue–Lieb und Frieden–Der Jubel; Alexander Reinagle, The Castle Spectre–Pizarro; Vincenzo Righini, Tigrane; Antonio Salieri, L'Angiolina–Cesare di Farmacusa; Gaspare Spontini, La fuga in maschere–I quadri parlanti–Gli elisi delusi; Franz X. Süssmayr, Gülnare; Raynor Taylor, Pizarro; Carl Maria von Weber, Das Waldmädchen; Joseph Weigl, Die Uniform; Nicola Zingarelli, Clitennestra.

Orchestra/Band Music:

Concerted Music:

Piano: Ludwig van Beethoven, Concerto No. 3 in c, Opus 37; Adalbert Gyrowetz, Concerto No. 2, Opus 49; Daniel Steibelt, Concerto No. 4 in E♭.

Violin: Jean-Baptiste Davaux, Symphonie concertante in D, Opus 16 (two violins).

Other: François Boieldieu, Harp Concerto; Samuel Wesley, Organ Concerto No. 2 in D.

Ballet/Incidental Music: Vicente Martín y Soler, *Le retour de Poliocète* (B); Étienne Méhul, *La dansomanie* (B); Joseph Weigl, *Alceste* (B)–*Zulima und Azons* (B).
Standard Works: Alexander Reinagle, *Masonic Overture*.
Symphonies: Johann A. André, *Two Symphonies "d'une execution facile," Opus 11.*

1801

Historical Highlights: The Treaty of Luneville ends the outdated Holy Roman Empire; the Act of Union combines Ireland and Great Britain under one government; the British drive the French out of Cairo while the Turks regain control of Egypt; Czar Paul I of Russia is assassinated and succeeded by Alexander I; in the United States, the Tripoli Pirates demand tribute from all U.S. ships—Congress sends the U.S. Navy to the Mediterranean.

Art and Literature Highlights: Births—artists Thomas Cole, Henry Inman, John Quidor, writer Cardinal Newman; Deaths—artists Daniel Chodowiecki, Ralph Earl, writers Margaretta Fangeres, Novalis. Art— Canova's *Perseus with the Head of Medusa*, Ingres' *Envoys of Agamemnon*, Trumbull's *The Infant Jesus and St. John*; Literature—Brentano's *Godwi*, Brown's *Jane Talbot*, Chateaubriand's *Atala*, Schiller's *Die Jungfrau von Orleans*.

Musical Highlights

A. Births
Composers: Antonio d'Antoni (Italy) June 25; Vincenzo Bellini (Italy) November 3; John Hill Hewitt (U.S.A.) July 12; Johann Wenzel Kalliwoda (Bohemia) February 21; Adolf Fredrik Lindblad (Sweden) February 1; Gustav Albert Lortzing (Germany) October 23; Adolf Müller, Sr. (Hungary) October 7; Alexander Varlamov (Russia) November 27; Ramón Vilanova (Spain) January 21; Joseph A. Wade (Ireland)(?).
Conductors: František Jan Škroup (Bohemia) June 3.
Singers: Laure Cinte-Damoreau (French soprano) February 6; Giuseppe Concone (Italian singer/composer) September 12; Frances Corri (Scottish soprano)(?); Eduard Devrient (German baritone/author) August 11; Henry Phillips (British bass) August 13; Ann Maria Tree (British mezzo-soprano) August.
Performers: Johannes Bernardus van Bree (Dutch violinist/composer) January 29; Joseph Ghys (Belgian violinist); Joseph Lanner (Austrian violinist/conductor) April 12.

Others: Pietro Alfieri (Italian music scholar) June 29; Salvatore Cammarano (Italian librettist) March 19; Georges Chanot, Sr. (French violin maker) March 25; Gustav Theodore Fechner (German music theorist) April 19; Adrien (Juste) de La Fage (French music writer/composer) March 30; Joseph Mainzer (music educator/journalist) October 21.

B. **Deaths**
   Composers: Domenico Cimarosa (Italy) January 11; Andrea Lucchesi (Italy) March 21; Carlo Monza (Italy) December 19; Johann Gottlieb Naumann (Germany) October 23; Carl Philipp Stamitz (Germany) November 9.
   Singers: Nicholas Audinot (French bass/impresario) May 21; Catarina Cavalieri (Austrian soprano) June 30.
   Performers: Johann Altenburg (German trumpeter) May 14: Theodore Aylward (British organist) February 27; Jonathan Battishill (British organist) December 10; Johann Drexel (German organist/composer) February 8; Angelo Morini (Italian violinist).
   Others: Claude Cliquot (French organ maker) March 29; Angelo Mirigi (Italian music theorist) January 22; Nicola Sala (Italian music theorist) August 13.

C. **Debuts**
   Singers: Teresa Belloc-Giorgi (Italian mezzo-soprano—Turin); Isabella Colbran (Spanish soprano—Paris); Filippo Galli (Italian bass—Naples, as a tenor); Ignaz Schuster (Austrian bass—Vienna); Giovanni Battista Velluti (Italian castrato soprano—Forli).

D. **New Positions**
   Conductors: Franz Bühler (kapellmeister, Augsburg Cathedral); Heinrich K. Ebell (kapellmeister, Breslau); Valentino Fioravanti (St. Carlo Theater, Lisbon); Józef Kozlowski (Imperial Theaters, St. Petersburg); Domenico Rampini (maestro di capella, Teatro Nuovo, Trieste); Ignaz von Seyfried (Theater an der Wien, Vienna); Georg Friedrich Wolf (kapellmeister, Wernigerode).
   Others: Antonio Bruni (director, Opéra-Italienne, Paris); Antonio Calegari (organ, St. Antonio, Padua); Matthew Camidge (organ, St. Michael-le-Belfrey, York); Emanuel Schikaneder (manager, Theater an der Wien); John Stafford Smith (organ, Chapel Royal, London).

F. **Biographical Highlights**
   Maddalena Allegranti retires from the operatic stage; Ludwig van Beethoven's deafness becomes acute; Frédéric Kalkbrenner graduates from Paris Conservatory with first prizes in piano and harmony; Niccolò Paganini retires from public performance and begins an affair with a noblewoman of Tuscany; Anton Reicha settles in Vienna and renews his friendships with Beethoven, Haydn, and

Salieri; Ferdinand Ries begins piano study with Beethoven; Carl
Maria von Weber moves back to Salzburg and studies with Michael
Haydn.

G. **Cultural Beginnings**
Performing Groups—Choral: Trieste Opera Co.
Educational: American Conservatorio (Boston); Bavarian Academy
of Arts and Sciences (Munich); Mallet and Graupner Musical Acad-
emy (Boston).
Music Publishers: Michael Kelly (London); Kunst-und Industrie-
Comptoir (Vienna).
Performing Centers: Danziger Theater (Gdansk); Teatro de Circo
(Havana); Teatro Lentasio (Milan); Teatro Nuovo (Teatro Grande,
Trieste); Theater an der Wien (Vienna).

H. **Musical Literature**
Thomas Busby, *Complete Dictionary of Music*; Muzio Clementi, *Intro-
duction to the Art of Playing the Piano-Forte*; Johann Friedrich Dalberg,
Die Äolsharfe, Ein allegorischer Traum; Pietro Gianelli, *Dizionario della
Musica*; Uri K. Hill, *The Vermont Harmony*; Johann Christian Kittel,
Der angehende praktische Organist; Johann J. Klein, *Lehrbuchs der prak-
tischen Musik*; Augustus Kollmann, *A Practical Guide to Thoroughbass*;
Honoré Langlé, *Nouvelle méthode pour chiffrer les accords*; Nehemiah
Shumway, *American Harmony*; Timothy Swan, *New England Har-
mony*; Frédéric Thiemé, *Nouvelle théorie sur le difféns mouvemens des
airs*; George Vogler, *Data zur Akustik*.

I. **Musical Compositions**
Chamber Music:
String Quartets: Johann A. André, *Three Quartets, Opus 14*;
František Krommer, *Three Quartets, Opus 19*.
Sonata/Solos: Ludwig van Beethoven, *Violin Sonata No. 5 in F,
"Spring," Opus 24*; Francesco Petrini, *Four Harp Sonatas, Opus 40*;
Václav Pichl, *Twelve Capriccios, Opus 46, for Solo Violin*.
Ensembles: Johann Albrechtsberger, *Six Sonatas, Opus 21* (two vio-
lins, two cellos)–*Quintet for Flute and Strings*; Ludwig van
Beethoven, *String Quintet in C, Opus 29*; Luigi Boccherini, *Six
String Quintets (c, B♭, a, E♭, G, F), Opus 60*; François Devienne, *Three
Woodwind Trios, Opus 75* (two clarinets, bassoon); Adalbert Gy-
rowetz, *Three Piano Trios, Opus 35–Three Piano Trios, Opus 36*.
Piano: John Field, *Three Sonatas (E♭, A, c), Opus 1*; Ludwig van
Beethoven, *Sonata No. 12 in A♭, Opus 26–Sonata No. 13 in E♭, Opus
27, No. 1–Sonata No. 14 in c♯, "Moonlight," Opus 27, No. 2–Sonata
No. 15 in D, "Pastoral," Opus 28–Six Easy Variations in G, Opus*

188–Twenty-Four Variations on Righini's "Veni amore"; Jan L. Dussek, *Two Sonatas (D, G), Opus 47–Sonata in C, Opus 48* (four hands); James Hewitt, *The Fourth of July (A Grand Military Sonata)*; Friedrich Himmel, *Sonata for Two Pianos*; Johann N. Hummel, *Variations in G, Opus 8*; August E. Müller, *Three Sonatas, Opus 14(?)*; Carl Maria von Weber, *Six Easy Pieces, Opus 3* (piano, four hands)–*Twelve Allemandes, Opus 4*; Joseph Wölfl, *Three Sonatas, Opus 14, on Haydn's "Creation."*

Choral/Vocal Music:
Choral: Franz Joseph Haydn, *The Seven Last Words* (choral version)–*Missa solennis in B♭*, *"Schöpfungsmesse"*; Michael Haydn, *Missa sotto il titulo di Sancte Teresia–Te Deum VI*; Johann Naumann, *Mass in A♭*; Venanzio Rauzzini, *Requiem*; Giuseppe Sarti, *Oratorio for Catherine the Great*; Christian Weinlig, *Die Erlösung* (oratorio); Carl Friedrich Zelter, *Te Deum.*

Vocal: François Boieldieu, *Six Romances, Set XI–Four Romances, Set XII–Set XIV–Four Romances, Set XIV*; Luigi Cherubini, *La cintura d'Armida*; Johann Zumsteeg, *Kleine Balladen und Lieder III.*

Musical Stage: Ludwig Abeille, *Amor and Psyche*; Johann A. André, *Rinaldo und Alcina*; Thomas Attwood, *The Sea-Side Story*; Francesco Bianchi, *Alzira*; Domenico Cimarosa, *Artemisia* (unfinished); Nicolas Dalayrac, *Léhéman*; Anton Eberl, *Die Königin der Schwarzen Inseln*; André Grétry, *Le casque et les colombes*; Friedrich Himmel, *Vasco da Gama–Frohsinn und Schwärmerei*; E. T. A. Hoffmann, *Scherz, List und Rache*; Nicolò Isouard, *Flaminius à Corinthe–Le tonnelier–L'impromtu de campagne*; Daniil Kashin, *Natalia, the Boyard's Daughter*; Rodolphe Kreutzer, *Flaminius à Corinthe–Astyanax*; Simon Mayr, *Ginerva di Scozia*; Étienne Méhul, *L'irato*; Johann Naumann, *Aci e Galatea*; Ferdinando Paër, *Achille*; Marcos Portugal, *La morte de Semiramide*; Johann Reichardt, *Rosamonda*; Antonio Salieri, *Annibale in Capua*; Gaspare Spontini, *Gli amanti in cimento*; Franz Süssmayr, *Phasma*; Vittorio Trento, *Quanti casi in un sol giorno.*

Orchestra/Band Music:
Concerted Music:
Piano: Jan L. Dussek, *Concerto in g, Opus 49*; Joseph Wölfl, *Concerto No. 1 in G, Opus 20.*
Other: Joseph Wölfl, *Double Concerto for Violin and Piano.*
Ballet/Incidental Music: Ludwig van Beethoven, *The Creatures of Prometheus, Opus 43* (B); Alexander Reinagle, *Edwy and Elgiva* (IM); Joseph Weigl, *Die tänzerin von Athen* (B)–*Der spanier auf der insel Christina* (B).
Symphonies: Johann A. André, *Grande sinfonie, Opus 13*; Ignace Pleyel, *Symphony in E♭, Ben. 152–Symphony in f, Ben. 153(?).*

1802

Historical Highlights: Napoleon, made first consul for life by the French, annexes Parma, Piacenza, and Piedmont; the Treaty of Amiens gives France and England a fourteen-month breathing spell from the war; in the United States, Congress repeals several unpopular laws, which were causes of considerable political problems; West Point Military Academy is officially established in New York by Congressional action.

Art and Literature Highlights: American Academy of Fine Arts opens. Births—artists Richard Bonington, Edwin Landseer, Emil Wolff; Deaths—artists Thomas Girtin, George Romney, poet Marie Anne Boccage. Art—Guérin's *Phèdre and Hippolyte*, Turner's *Tenth Plague on Egypt*, West's *Death on a Pale Horse*; Literature—Chateaubriand's *Genius of Christianity*, Mme. De Staël's *Delphine*, Sarah Wood's *Amelia, or, The Influence of Virtue.*

Musical Highlights

A. Births

Composers: John Barnett (England) July 15; Louis Niedermeyer (Switzerland) April 27; Cesare Pugni (Italy) May 31.

Conductors: Joseph Labitzky (Bohemia-Germany) July 5.

Singers: Eugène Étienne Massol (French baritone) August 23; Adolphe Nourrit (French tenor) March 3; Mary Ann Paton (Scottish soprano) October 23; John Templeton (Scottish tenor) July 30; Mary Ann Wilson (British soprano) December 19.

Performers: Charles Auguste de Bériot (Belgian violinist) February 20; Charles Louis Hanssens (Belgian cellist) July 2; Ureli Corelli Hill (American violinist/composer)(?); Niels Peter Jensen (Danish organist) July 23; Wilhelm Bernhard Molique (German violinist/composer) October 7; Hubert Ries (German violinist) April 19; Eduard Rietz (German violinist/conductor) October 17; Friedrich Wilhelm Wieprecht (German trombonist/inventor) August 8.

Others: Moritz Wilhelm Drobisch (German mathematician/philosopher/author) August 16; John Ella (British violinist/composer) December 19; Joseph-Louis d'Ortigue (French music author) May 22.

B. Deaths

Composer: Antonio Lolli (Italy) August 10; Giuseppe Sarti (Italy) July 28; Johann Rudolf. Zumsteeg (Germany) January 27.

Singers: Madeleine Sophie Arnould (French soprano) October 22; Charlotte Brent (British soprano) April 10; Henri Larrivée (French baritone) August 7; Giuseppe Millico (Italian tenor/composer) Oc-

tober 23; Corona Elisabeth Schröter (German soprano) August 23; Johann Spangler (Austrian tenor) November 2.
Performers: Isidore Bertheaume (French violinist/composer) March 20; Carl Franz (German horn virtuoso) November 2; François Joseph Hérold (French pianist/composer) September 1; Hyacinthe Jadin (French pianist) September; Jacques-Philippe Lamoninary (French violinist) August 29; Bernhard Molique (German violinist) October 7; Joseph Barnabé Saint-Sevin (French violinist/composer) August 6.
Others: Franz Ambros Alexander (German instrument maker) December 1; Samuel Arnold (British music scholar) October 22; Johann J. Engel (German theorist) June 28.

C. Debuts
Singers: Josef Blahack (Hungarian tenor—Vienna).
Performers: Ludwig Maurer (German violinist—Berlin); Franz Xaver Pechaczek, Jr. (Austrian violinist—Prague).

D. New Positions
Conductors: Franz Clement (Theater an der Wien); Simon Mayr (maestro di capella, S. Maria Maggiore, Bergamo); Ferdinando Paër (kapellmeister, Dresden); Giovanni Paisiello (maître de chapelle, Napoleon in Paris); Friedrich Witt (kapellmeister, Würzburg).
Others: Robert Cooke (organ, Westminster Abbey); Charles Knyvett, Jr. (organ, St. George's, London).

E. Prizes and Honors
Honors: André Grétry (Legion of Honor).

F. Biographical Highlights
Daniel François Auber is sent to London by his father to study commerce; Ludwig van Beethoven, in despair over his growing deafness, writes his "Heiligenstadt Testament"; Fanny Burney and her husband are forced by the war into a ten-year stay in France; Muzio Clementi begins his third continental tour; John Field accompanies Clementi on his tour to Paris; Gioacchino Rossini, age ten, begins singing in local churches; Louis Spohr accompanies violinist Johann Friedrich Eck on his Russian tour, where he meets Clementi and Field.

G. Cultural Beginnings
Performing Groups—Choral: Leipzig Singakademie; Massachusetts Musical Society.
Performing Groups—Instrumental: St. Petersburg Philharmonic Society; United States Marine Band (full brass band).
Music Publishers: George E. Blake (Philadelphia); John Cole (Baltimore); Dalmas Music Publishing Co. (St. Petersburg); Hacker Music

Publishing Co. (Salzburg); C. Lose and Co. (Copenhagen); George Schetky (Philadelphia).
Music Publications: *Correspondence des Amateurs Musiciens* (Paris); *Edinburgh Review; Le Magasin de Musique* (Paris).
Performing Centers: Bamberg Theater (Germany).
Other: Claviola (by J. I. Hawkins); Miniature Scores (by Ignaz Pleyel); Order of the Legion of Honor (created by Napoleon); Staffless Music Notation (by Andrew Law); Nannette Streicher Piano Co. (Vienna).

H. Musical Literature
Mateo Albéniz, *Instrucción melódica, especulativa y prática para enseñar a cantar y a tañer la música antigua*; Antonio Calegari, *Gioco pittagorico musicale*; Charles Catel, *Traité d'harmonie*; Ernst Chladni, *Die Akustik*; James Hewitt, *Collection of the Most Favorite Country Dances*; Samuel Holyoke, *Columbian Repository of Sacred Harmony*; Edward Jones, *The Bardic Museum*; Heinrich Koch, *Musikalisches Lexikon*; Luigi Sabbatini, *Trattato sopra le fughe*; Georg Vogler, *Handbuch zur Harmonielehre und für den Generalbass*.

I. Musical Compositions
Chamber Music:
  String Quartets: Adalbert Gyrowetz, *Three Quartets, Opus 42*; František Krommer, *Quartet, Opus 23–Three Quartets, Opus 24*.
  Sonata/Solos: Ludwig van Beethoven, *Three Violin Sonatas (A, e, G), Opus 30–Seven Variations in E♭ on Mozart's "Bei Männern"* (cello, piano); Feliks Janiewicz, *Violin Sonata in A*.
  Ensembles: Johann Albrechtsberger, *Six String Sextets, Opus 12*(?); Ludwig van Beethoven, *Trio in E♭, Opus 38* (clarinet, viola, piano)–*Serenade, Opus 25* (flute, violin, piano); Luigi Boccherini, *Six String Quintets (c, E♭, F, B♭, D, E), Opus 62*; Friedrich Himmel, *Grand sestetto, Opus 18* (piano, two horns, strings); Johann N. Hummel, *Piano Quintet in E♭, Opus 87*; Jan Václav Stich, *Sextet, Opus 34*; Anton Wranitzky, *Three String Quintets, Opus 8*.
  Piano: Ludwig van Beethoven, *Sonata No. 16 in G, Opus 31/1–Sonata No. 17 in d, "The Tempest," Opus 31/2–Sonata No. 18 in E♭, Opus 31/3–Two Easy Sonatas (No. 19 in g–No. 20 in G), Opus 49–Seven Bagatelles, Opus 33–Six Variations in F, Opus 34–Fifteen Variations in E♭ on the Prometheus Theme, Opus 35*; Muzio Clementi, *Three Sonatas (G, b, d/D), Opus 40*; Johann Himmel, *Variation in E on a March by Cherubini, Opus 9*; August E. Müller, *Three Sonatas, Opus 18*(?); Carl Maria von Weber, *Six Ecossaises, Opus 29, 34*.

Organ: Johann Albrechtsberger, *Six Fugues, Opus 10–Six Fugues, Opus 11–Three Fugues, Opus 21.*

Choral/Vocal Music:

Choral: Ludwig van Beethoven, *Opferlied, Opus 121b*; Luigi Boccherini, *Christmas Cantata, Opus 63*; Franz Joseph Haydn, *Missa solennis, "Harmoniemesse"*; Nicolò Isouard, *La Paix* (cantata); Giovanni Paisiello, *Messa pastorale in G*; Carl Maria von Weber, *Mass in E♭, "Jugendmesse"*; Friedrich Witt, *Der Leidende Heiland* (oratorio).

Vocal: Johann Zumsteeg, *Kleine Balladen und Lieder IV–VI.*

Musical Stage: Samuel Arnold, *The Sixty Third Letter*; Bonifazio Asioli, *Gustava al Malabar*; Charles S. Catel, *Sémiramis*; Nicolas Dalayrac, *La Boucle de cheveux*; Franz Danzi, *El Bondocani*; Valentino Fioravanti, *La capricciosa pentita*; Pierre Gaveaux, *Le Retour inattendu*; Nicolò Isouard, *Michel-Ange–La statue*; Friedrich A. Kunzen, *The Homecoming*; Simon Mayr, *I Misteri eleusini*; Étienne Méhul, *Une folie–Joanna–Le Trésor supposé*; Ferdinando Paër, *Ginevra degli Almieri*; Marcos Portugal, *Zaira–Il trionfo di Clelia*; Johann F. Reichardt, *Das Zauberschloss–Herkules Tod*; Antonio Salieri, *La bella selvaggia*; Johann Schenk, *Der Fassbinder*; Gaspare Spontini, *Le metamorfosi di Pasquale*; Alexei Titov, *Andromeda and Perseus*; Giacomo Tritto, *Gli Americani*; Georg "Abbe" Vogler, *Der Koppengeist auf Reisen*; Nicola Zingarelli, *Edipo a Colono–La notte dell'armicizia*; Johann Zumsteeg, *Elbondocani.*

Orchestra/Band Music:

Concerted Music:

Piano: Auguste E. Müller, *Concerto No. 2, Opus 21*; Ignace Pleyel, *Symphonie concertante in F*; Daniel Steibelt, *Concerto No. 5 in E♭, "A la chasse," Opus 64.*

Violin: Rodolphe Kreutzer, *Concerto No. 9 in e, Opus 9–No. 10 in d, Opus 10–No. 11 in C, Opus 11*; Giovanni Viotti, *Concerto No. 28 in d.*

Other: François Devienne, *Flute Concerto No. 10 in D*; Rodolphe Kreutzer, *Symphonie concertante* (violin, cello); František Krommer, *Flute Concerto No. 1, Opus 30*; Franz Neubauer, *Variations for Flute and Orchestra, Opus 9*; Vincenzo Righini, *Flute Concerto– Oboe Concerto*; Jan Václav Stich, *Horn Concertos No. 8–10*; Peter von Winter, *Sinfonie Concertante in e.*

Ballet/Incidental Music: André Destouches, *Turandot* (IM); Johann Reichardt, *Die Kreutzfahrer* (IM); Daniel Steibelt, *Le Retour de Zéphyre* (B); Georg "Abbe" Vogler, *Die Kreutzfahrer* (IM).

Symphonies: Ludwig van Beethoven, *No. 2 in D, Opus 36*; James Hewitt, *Grand Sinfonie, Characteristic of the Peace of the French Republic*; Samuel Wesley, *Symphony in B♭.*

1803

❀

Historical Highlights: Napoleon sells the Louisiana Territory to the United States for $15,000,000, doubling the size of the country; France and Great Britain return to warfare over the Malta issue; the British turn Tasmania into a penal colony and put down an Irish independence uprising; in the United States, Lewis and Clark begin their expedition to the Northwest Territory; Fort Dearborn is built on the site of present-day Chicago.

Art and Literature Highlights: Births—writers Thomas Beddoes, Ralph Waldo Emerson, Prosper Mérimée, artists Alexandre Decamps, Paul Huet; Deaths—poets Vittorio Alfieri, James Beattie, Friedrich Klopstock, Nikolai Lvov. Art—Alston's *The Deluge*, Boilly's *The Arrival of the Statecoach*, Runge's *Morning*, Turner's *Calais Pier*; Literature—Porter's *Thaddeus of Warsaw*, Richter's *The Titan*, Schiller's *Die Braut von Messina*.

Musical Highlights

A. Births

Composers: Adolphe Charles Adam (France) July 24; Louis Hector Berlioz (France) December 11; Karl Ludwig Drobisch (Germany) December 24; Friedrich Theodor Frölich (Switzerland) February 20; Alexander Gurilyov (Russia) September 3; Johann Vesque von Püttlingen (Austrian composer) July 23.

Conductor: Franz Paul Lachner (Germany) April 2; Ferdinand Stegmayer (Austria) August 25.

Singers: Josephine Fröhlich (Austrian soprano) December 12; Caroline Unger (Austrian contralto) October 28.

Performers: Louis Ancot (Belgian pianist/composer) June 3; Jean-Désiré Artôt (French horn virtuoso) September 23; Henri Herz (German pianist/composer) January 6; Wojciech Albert Sowinski (Polish pianist) December 24; Joseph C. Taws (American pianist)(?); George James Webb (British-born organist/hymnist) June 24.

Others: Alfred Julius Becher (British critic/composer) April 27; François Durutte (Belgian music theorist) October 15; Eliza Flower (British hymnist) April 19; William Knabe (German piano maker) June 3; Gustav Schilling (German lexicographer) November 3; George Stevens (American organ builder) April 22.

B. Deaths

Composers: Gennaro Astarita (Italy) November 3; Angelo Baldan (Ireland) April 23; Gregorio Ballabene (Italy)(?); Candido Ruano (Spain) March 17; Esteban Salas y Castro (Cuba) July 14; Franz Süssmayr (Austria) September 17; Peter Van Hagen, Sr. (Holland-U.S.A.) August 20.

Performers: Pieter Joseph van den Bosch (Dutch organist) February 19; Charles Broche (French organist) September 30; John Camidge (British organist) April 25; Johann Georg Danner (German violinist) March 28; François Devienne (French bassoonist/composer) September 5; William Jackson (British organist) July 5; Jean-Baptiste Aimé Janson (French cellist) September 2; Johann Christoph Kellner (German organist) November 3; Richard Langdon (British organist) September 8; John Christoph Moller (German organist) September 21; Georg von Pasterwitz (Austrian organist) January 26; Jacob Schiller (Bohemian violinist); Jan Václav Stich (Punto) (Czech horn virtuoso) February 16; Armand-Emmanuel Trial (French pianist/composer) September 9; Pierre Vachon (French violinist) October 7.

Others: Domenico Gasparo Angiolini (Italian choreographer/composer) February 6; Giambattista Casti (Italian librettist) August 29; Henri Moreau (Belgian music theorist/composer) November 3; Baron Gottfried von Swieten (Dutch-born music patron) March 29.

C. Debuts

Singers: Henri Etienne Dérivis (French bass—Paris); (Pauline) Anna Milder-Hauptmann (German soprano—Vienna); Eliza Salmon (British soprano—London).

D. New Positions

Conductors: Guillaume Kennis (kapellmeister, Antwerp Cathedral); Peter Ritter (Mannheim Court Orchestra); Alessandro Rolla (La Scala Orchestra).

Others: François Boieldieu (composer, Imperial Court, St. Petersburg); Francis Jeffrey (editor, *Edinburgh Review*).

E. Prizes/Honors

Prizes: Albert Auguste Androt (Prix de Rome—first to be given).
Honors: John Andrew Stevenson (knighted).

F. Biographical Highlights

Daniel François Auber gives up on commerce and, with political tensions high between England and France, returns to Paris and music; Anton Diabelli, leaves the monastery when it is secularized by the Bavarian government, and returns to Vienna and music; Jacques-Pierre Rode travels to Russia with Boieldieu and begins a five-year stay; Gaspare Spontini decides to settle down in Paris but fails in his first two operatic tries; Carl Maria von Weber moves to Vienna to study with Abbé Vogler and meets Haydn and Beethoven.

G. Cultural Beginnings

Performing Groups—Instrumental: Prague Tonkünstler-Societät.
Educational: Prix de Rome in Music (French).
Music Publishers: Anton Böhm und Sohn (Augsburg); Chemische Druckerey (Haslinger Music Publishers, Vienna); Janiewicz's Music and Musical Instrument Warehouse (Liverpool); Thaddäus Weigl (Vienna).
Music Publications: *Répertoire des Clavecinistes* (Zurich).
Performing Centers: Teatro Carcano (Milan).
Other: Union of Musical Artists for the Support of Widows and Orphans (London).

H. Musical Literature

Anton Bemetzrieder, *Complete Treatise on Music*; Charles Dibdin, *The Professional Life of Mr. Dibdin*; Johann Eberhard, *Handbuch der Aesthetik I, II*; John Gunn, *An Introduction to Music* . . . ; Oliver Holden, *Charlestown Collection of Sacred Songs*; Johann Kittel, *Neues Choralbuch*; Justin Heinrich Knecht, *Allgemeiner musikalischer Katechismus*; Rodolphe Kreutzer, *Méthode de violon*; Andrew Law, *Musical Primer*; Jérôme de Momigny, *La Première Année de leçons de pianoforte*; Étienne Ozi, *Nouvelle méthode de basson*; Timothy Swan, *The Songster's Museum*.

I. Musical Compositions

Chamber Music:

String Quartets: Johann A. André, *Quartet, Opus 22, No. 1*; Franz Joseph Haydn, *Quartet in d, Opus 103* (unfinished); František Krommer, *Three Quartets, Opus 34*; Ignace Pleyel, *Three Quartets (C, B♭, f), Ben. 365–7*.

Sonata/Solos: Johann A. André, *Sonata, Opus 17* (violin, cello)–*Violin Sonata, Opus 21*; Ludwig van Beethoven, *Violin Sonata in a, Opus 47, "Kreutzer"*; François Boieldieu, *Air and Nine Variatiosn* (harp, piano); Antoine Reicha, *Violin Sonata in C, Opus 44–Flute Sonata in G, Opus 54–Two Violin Sonatas (B♭, E♭), Opus 55–Violin Sonata in A, Opus 62*.

Ensembles: Johann Albrechtsberger, *Six String Quintets, Opus 22*; Adalbert Gyrowetz, *Three Piano Trios, Opus 40*; Johann N. Hummel, *Piano Trio in E♭, Opus 12*; Rodolphe Kreutzer, *Three Trio Sonatas, Opus 16*; František Krommer, *Six String Quintets, Opus 25*; Franz Neubauer, *Three String Trios, Opus 8*(?); Ignace Pleyel, *Three Keyboard Trios (F, B♭, E♭), Ben. 474–6*; Joseph Wölfl, *Three Piano Trios, Opus 23*; Anton Wranitzky, *String Quintet, Opus 16*.

Piano: Ludwig van Beethoven, *Five Variations in D on "Rule, Britannia"–Seven Variations in C on "God Save the King"*; João Domingo Bomtempo, *Sonata No. 1 in f, Opus 1*; Ignace Pleyel, *Thirty-Six Ecossaises, Ben. 628–63*; Anton Reicha, *Sonata in E, Opus*

40; Joseph Wölfl, *Three Sonatas, Opus 19* (with violin); *Three Progressive Piano Sonatas, Opus 24–Three Sonatas, Opus 25* (with violin and cello).

Choral/Vocal Music:
Choral: Michael Haydn, *Missa sub Titulo Sancti Francisci Serephici–Te Deum*; Alexander Reinagle, *Masonic Ode*; Antonio Salieri, *Gesù al limbo* (oratorio).
Vocal: Ludwig van Beethoven, *Six Songs, Opus 48*; François Boieldieu, *Four Romances, Set XV*; Carl Friedrich Zelter, *Kleiner Balladen und Lieder*.

Musical Stage: Joachim Albertini, *Le Virgine vestale*; Henri Berton, *Aline, Reine de Golconde*; François Boieldieu, *Ma tante Aurora*; Catterino Cavos, *Rusalka*; Luigi Cherubini, *Anacréon*; François Gossec, *Les sabots et le cerisier*; André Grétry, *Delphis et Mopsa–Le Ménage*; E. T. A. Hoffmann, *Der Renegat*; Nicolò Isouard, *Le Baiser et la quittance–Les confidences–Le Médecin–Le déjeuner de Garçons*; Rodolphe Kreutzer, *Le baiser et la quittance*; Simon Mayr, *Alonso e Cora*; Étienne Méhul, *Hélèna–L'heureux malgré lui*; Ferdinando Paër, *Sargino*; Giovanni Paisiello, *Proserpine*; Johann Reichardt, *Kunst und Liebe*; Vincenzo Righini, *La selva incantata e Gerusalemme liberata*; Franz Süssmayr, *List und Zufall*; Vittorio Trento, *Ines de Castro*; Carl Maria von Weber, *Peter Schmoll*; Nicola Zingarelli, *Il bevitore fortunato*.

Orchestra/Band Music:
Concerted Music: Franz Danzi, *Symphonie concertante in B♭*.
Piano: Joseph Wölfl, *Concerto No. 2 in E, Opus 26*.
Violin: Rodolphe Kreutzer, *Concerto No. 12 in A, Opus 12–No. 13 in D, Opus A–No. 14 in e, Opus B–Sinfonie concertante No. 3 in E* (two violins); František Krommer, *Concerto No. 2, Opus 41–No. 3, Opus 42–No. 4, Opus 43–No. 5, Opus 44*; Louis Spohr, *Concerto No. 1 in A, Opus 1–Concertante in C*; Anton Wranitzky, *Concerto, Opus 11*.
Other: Johann N. Hummel, *Trumpet Concerto*; František Krommer, *Clarinet Concerto, Opus 36–Oboe Concerto No. 1, Opus 37*; Franz Neubauer, *Cello Concerto(?)*; Anton Reicha, *Cello Concerto in D*.

Ballet/Incidental Music: Franz von Destouches, *Die Braut von Messina* (IM)–*Die Jungfrau von Orleans* (IM); Étienne Méhul, *Daphnis et Pandrose* (B); Alexei Titov, *Blanka* (B).

Standard Works: Ludwig van Beethoven, *Twelve Contradances, Opus 141*.

Symphonies: Ludwig van Beethoven, *No. 3 in E♭, Opus 55, "Eroica"*; Marie-Alexandre Guénin (with Barrière) *Three Symphonies (A, d, C)*; František Krommer, *No. 2, Opus 40*; Ignace Pleyel, *Symphony in C, Ben. 154–Symphony In a, Ben. 155(?)*; Joseph Wölfl, *No. 1 in g, Opus 40*.

1804

❀

Historical Highlights: Napoleon is crowned emperor of France; the Code Napoleon goes into effect for all French-controlled lands; Spain declares war on Great Britain; the Haitians defeat the French army and declare independence; in the United States, Thomas Jefferson is re-elected president; the Twelfth Amendment on a separate vote for the vice-president is ratified; the Lewis and Clark Expedition reaches the Pacific; war with Tripoli accelerates.

Art and Literature Highlights: Births—writers Nathaniel Hawthorne, George Sand, Charles Sainte-Beuve, Eduard Mörike; Deaths—artists George Morland, Giovanni Tiepolo, philospher Immanuel Kant. Art— Turner's *Great Falls at Reichenbach*, Vanderlyn's *Death of Jane McCrea*, Vernet's *Battle of Marengo*; Literature—Blake's *Jerusalem*, Schiller's *William Tell*, Wood's *Ferdinand and Elmire: A Russian Story*.

Musical Highlights

A. Births

Composers: Per Conrad Boman (Sweden) June 6; Michel Ivanovich Glinka (Russia) June 1; Edward Sobolewski (Germany) October 1; Johann Strauss, Sr. (Austria) March 14.

Conductors: Julius Benedict (England) November 27; Carl August Krebs (Germany) January 16; Ernst Julius Otto (Germany) September 1.

Singers: Agostino Rovere (Italian bass); Wilhelmine Schröder-Devrient (German soprano) December 6.

Performers: Jeanne Louise Farrenc (French pianist/composer) May 31; Henry Forbes (British organist/composer); Hippolite Mompou (French organist/composer) January 12.

Others: Charles Spackman Barker (British organ builder) October 10; Théodore-Joseph Devroye (Belgian music scholar) August 19; Alphonse Leduc (French publisher) March 9; Julius Schuberth (German publisher) July 14.

B. Deaths

Composers: Albert Auguste Androt (France) August 19; Pietro Alessandro Guglielmi (Italy) November 19; Ivan Khandoshkin (Russia) March 28; Johann A. Miller (Germany) July 16; Carl Leopold Röllig (Austria) March 4; Johann Schwanenberger (Germany) April 5.

Singers: Valentin Adamberger (German tenor) August 24; Caterina Galli (Italian mezzo-soprano) December 23.

Performers: Philip Barth (German oboist/composer) December 22; Franz Eck (German violinist) December 22; Louis-Joseph Francœur (French violinist/conductor) March 10; Giovanni Giornovichi (Italian violinist/composer) November 23; Christian Ernst Graf (German violinist) July 17; John Moorehead (Irish violinist/composer) March 29; Jean Engelbert Pauwels (Belgian violinist/conductor) June 3; David Tannenberg (German-born organ builder) May 19.
Others: Benoit Andrez (Belgian publisher) December 12.

C. Debuts
Performers: George Augustus Kollmann (British pianist—London); Nicholas Mori (British violinist—London, age eight); Ferdinand Ries (German pianist—Vienna).

D. New Positions
Conductors: Charles S. Ashworth (U.S. Marine Band); Adalbert Gyrowetz (Vienna Hoftheater); Jean François Lesueur (maître de chapelle, Napoleon); August Müller (cantor, Thomasschule, Leipzig); Joseph Ignaz Schnabel (kapellmeister, Breslau Cathedral); Carl Maria von Weber (Breslau Opera); Anton Zingarelli (maestro di capella, Sistine Chapel, Rome).

E. Prizes/Honors
Honors: Nicolas Dalayrac (Legion of Honor); François Gossec (Legion of Honor); Franz Joseph Haydn (Honorary Citizen of Vienna); Michael Haydn (Swedish Royal Academy); Étienne Méhul (Legion of Honor), Pierre-Alexandre Monsigny (Legion of Honor).

F. Biographical Highlights
Ludwig van Beethoven, upon hearing that Napoleon crowned himself emperor, tears up the dedication of his Eroica Symphony in a fit of rage; E. T. A. Hoffmann begins a limited law practice in Poznan; Johann Hummel becomes assistant kapellmeister in the court of Prince Esterházy; Konradin Kreutzer moves to Vienna to study counterpoint with Albrechtsberger and there meets Franz Joseph Haydn; Louis Spohr makes his first official concert tour around Germany.

G. Institutional Openings
Performing Groups—Instrumental: New Ipswich Military Band.
Educational: Liceo Filarmonico (Bologna); Würzburg Institute of Music (Royal Music School in 1820).
Performance Centers: Coliseo Provisional (Theater Argentina, Buenos Aires); Koninklijke Schouwburg (Concert Hall, The Hague); Teatro Municipale (Piacenza); Teatro Porteño (Buenos Aires).
Other: Charles Challen Piano Co (London); William Goodrich, organ builder (Boston); Conrad Graf, piano builder (Vienna).

H. Musical Literature

Jean-Baptiste Bréval, *Traité du Violoncelle*; Ebenezer Child, *The Sacred Musician*; Kinsha Danilov, *Ancient Russian Poetry*; Charles Dibdin, *Music Epitomised*; Samuel Holyoke, *The Christian Harmonist*; George Jackson, *David's Psalms*; August E. Müller, *Klavier- und Fortepiano-Schule*; John Page, *Festive Harmony*; Johann Reichardt, *Vertraute Briefe aus Paris*; Franz X. Richter, *Traité d'harmonie et de composition*; Anton Wranitzky, *Violin Fondament*.

I. Musical Compositions

Chamber Music:

String Quartets: Luigi Boccherini, *Two Quartets (F, D), Opus 64*; Adalbert Gyrowetz, *Three Quartets, Opus 44*; František Krommer, *Three Quartets, Opus 48–Three Quartets, Opus 50–Three Quartets, Opus 53*; Antoine Reicha, *Three Quartets (C, G, E♭), Opus 48–Eighteen Variations and Fantasia on a Theme by Mozart, Opus 51* (flute, strings).

Ensembles: Ludwig van Beethoven, *Fourteen Variations in E♭, Opus 44, for Piano Trio*; Luigi Boccherini, *Two String Quintets (F, D), Opus 64* (unfinished); Jan L. Dussek, *Piano Quartet in E♭, Opus 56*; Józef Elsner, *String Quintet in c*; František Krommer, *Flute Quintet, Opus 49*; Gioacchino Rossini, *Six Sonata a Quattro for Strings*; Carl Maria von Weber, *Six Variations on Vogler's "Samori," Opus 6* (piano trio).

Piano: Ludwig van Beethoven, *Sonata No. 21 in C, "Waldstein," Opus 53–No. 22 in F, Opus 54–Three Grand Marches, Opus 45* (piano, four hands); Benjamin Carr, *The Siege of Tripoli: Historical Naval Sonata, Opus 4*; Muzio Clementi, *Sonata in E♭, Opus 41*; Jan L. Dussek, *Fantasia and Fugue in f, Opus 50*; Johann N. Hummel, *Variations in D on "God Save the King," Opus 10–Variations in A on a March by Dalyrac, Opus 15*; Sigismund von Neukomm, *Fantasy, Opus 1*; Anton Reicha, *Sonata in E♭, Opus 43–Three Sonatas (G, B♭, E), Opus 46*; Carl Maria von Weber, *Six Variations on Vogler's "Castor and Pollux," Opus 5*; Joseph Wölfl, *Three Sonatas, Opus 35*.

Organ: Johann Albrechtsberger, *Twelve New Easy Preludes*.

Choral/Vocal Music:

Choral: Franz Danzi, *Das Freudenfest* (cantata); Georg Druschetzky, *Mass No. 7 in C*; Friedrich H. Himmel, *Das Lob Gottes*; Johann N. Hummel, *Mass in E♭, Opus 80*; Giovanni Paisiello, *Mass in B♭ for Double Chorus*; Antonio Salieri, *Missa pro defunctis in c*; Joseph Weigl, *La passione di Gesù Cristo–La resurrezione di Gesù Cristo* (oratorios).

Vocal: Jan L. Dussek, *Six Canzonets, C.200–5*; Friedrich H. Himmel, *Twelve deutsche und französische Lieder*; Étienne Méhul, *Messe Solennelle in A♭*(?).

Musical Stage: Henry Bishop, *Angelina*; François Boieldieu, *Aline, reine de Golconde–Abderkan*; Nicolas Dalayrac, *La jeune prude–Une heure de mariage*; Pierre Gaveaux, *Un quart d'heure de silence–Le bouffe et le tailleur–Trop tôt*; Pietro Generali, *Pamela nubile*; Adalbert Gyrowetz, *Selico*; Friedrich Himmel, *Fanchon das Leiermädchen*; E. T. A. Hoffmann, *Die lustigen Musikanten*; Johann N. Hummel, *Le vicende d'amore*; Jean-François Lesueur, *Ossian, ou Les Bardes*; Simon Mayr, *Elisa–I due viaggiatori–Zamori*; Sigismund von Neukomm, *Alessander am Indus–Die Nachtwächte–Der schauspieldirektor*; Ferdinado Paër, *I Fuorusciti*; Marcos Portugal, *Argenide–L'oro non compra amore*; Antonio Salieri, *Die Neger*; Johann Schmidt, *Der Onkel*; Gaspere Spontini, *Milton–La petite maison*; Vittorio Trento, *Ifigenia in Aulide*; Georg "Abbe" Vogler, *Samori*; Carl Maria von Weber, *Rübezahl*; Joseph Wölfl, *L'amour romanesque*; Paul Wranitsky, *Mitgefühl*.

Orchestra/Band Music:

Concerted Works:

Piano: João Domingos Bomtempo, *Concerto No. 1 in E♭*; Anton Reicha, *Concerto No. 4 in E♭*.

Violin: Rodolphe Kreutzer, *Concerto No. 15 in A, Opus C–No. 16 in e, Opus D*; Louis Spohr, *Concerto No. 2 in d, Opus 2*; Giovanni B. Viotti, *Concerto No. 29 in e*.

Other: Ludwig van Beethoven, *Triple Concerto in C, Opus 56* (violin, cello, piano); Luigi Cherubini, *Two Sonatas for Horn and Orchestra*.

Ballet/Incidental Music: Luigi Cherubini, *Achille à Scyros* (B); André Destouches, *Wilhelm Tell* (B)–*Die Hussiten vor Naumburg* (IM); Etienne Méhul, *Les Hussites* (IM); Daniel Steibelt, *Le jugement du berger Paris* (B).

Standard Works: Johann A. André, *Ouverture militaire, Opus 24*.

Symphonies: Johann A. André, *Grosse Symphonie in E♭, Opus 25*; Franz Danzi, *No. 3 in C, Opus 20*; Anton Eberl, *No. 2, Opus 33*; Ignace Pleyel, *Symphony in G, Ben. 156*.

1805
❀

Historical Highlights: War of the Third Coalition—the battles of Ulm and Austerlitz—the Battle of Trafalgar establishes British naval supremacy; the Peace of Pressburg is signed by France and by Austria, who loses her Italian possessions; the United States breaks off relations with Great Britain over the West Indies trade problem; the official war with Tripoli ends; the Michigan Territory is formed out of former Indian territory.

Art and Literature Highlights: Births—writers Esteban Echeverría, Hans Christian Andersen, artists Horatio Greenough, Constantin Guys, Wilhelm von Kalmbach; Deaths—artists Jean-Baptiste Greuze, Louis Moreau, poets Friedrich von Schiller, Manuel de Bocage. Art—Alston's *Diana in the Chase*, Koch's *Landscape with Rainbow*, Turner's *The Shipwreck*; Literature—Davis' *The First Settlers of Virginia*, Scott's *Lay of the Last Minstrel*.

Musical Highlights

A. Births

Composers: Jacob Niklas Ahlström (Sweden) June 5; Louise-Angélique Bertin (France) February 15; Antoine Auguste de Bournonville (Denmark) August 21; Johan Peter Hartmann (Denmark) May 14; Luigi Ricci (Italy) June 8; John Thomson (Scotland) October 28.

Singers: Cesare Babiali (Italian bass) December 24; Carl Friedrich Curschmann (German singer/composer) June 21; Julie Dorus-Gras (Belgian soprano) September 7; Manuel Patricio García (Spanish vocal teacher) March 17; Mary Anne Goward (British soprano) November 22; Giuditta Grisi (Italian mezzo-soprano) July 28.

Performers: Jan N. Bobrowicz (Polish guitarist) May 12; John Balsir Chatterton (British harpist) December 24; Victor François Desvignes (French violinist/composer) June 5; Stephen Elvey (British organist) June 27; Fanny Mendelssohn Henselt (German pianist/composer) November 14; Théodore Labarre (French harpist) March 5; Sebastian Lee (German cellist) December 24; Julius Schneider (German organist) July 6.

Others: Ludwig Bausch (German violin maker) January 15; Edmond de Coussemaker (French music scholar) April 19; Dom Prosper-Louis Guéranger (French ecclesiastic scholar) April 4; John Thomas Hart (British violin maker) December 17; Adolf Reubke (German organ builder) December 6.

B. Deaths

Composers: Carl Joseph Birnbach (Germany) May 29; Luigi Boccherini (Italy) May 28; Giovanni Cimador (Italy) February 27; Friedrich Christoph Gestewitz (Germany) August 1.

Conductors: John Ashley (England) March 14; Johann Christoph Kühnau (Germany) October 13.

Singers: Anna Marie Crouch (British soprano) October 2; Friedrich Hürka (Czech tenor) December 10.

Performers: Franz Anton Ernst (German violinist/composer) January 13; Václav Pichl (Czech violinist/composer) January 23; Johann Georg Tromlitz (German flutist/composer) February 4.

C. Debuts
Singers: Louis Nourrit (French tenor—Paris).
Performers: Frédéric Wilhelm Kalkbrenner (French pianist—Berlin).

D. New Positions
Conductors: Bonifazio Asioli (maestro di cappella, Milan); Felice Blangini (kapellmeister, Saxe-Coburg, Munich); James Hewitt (municipal bands, New York); Niccolò Paganini (music director, Princess of Lucca); Johann Friedrich Rochlitz (Leipzig Gewandhaus Concerts); Gaetano Valeri (maestro di cappella, Padua Cathedral).
Others: Christoph Ernst Weyse (organ, Copenhagen Cathedral).

E. Prizes/Honors
Prizes: Victor Dourlen (Prix de Rome).
Honors: Joseph A. Elsner (Warsaw Society of Friends of Science).

F. Biographical Highlights
Ludwig van Beethoven, in another of his fits of rage, withdraws *Fidelio* after three performances—meets Cherubini who is visiting in Vienna; Franz Joseph Haydn completes the thematic catalogue of his own works; Anthony Philip Heinrich makes his first visit to the United States; after a year of serious practice, Niccolò Paganini makes a second debut causing enthusiastic responses everywhere he performs; Lorenzo Da Ponti emigrates to the United States with his mistress and their children; Gioacchino Rossini adds horn playing to singing in local theaters; Joseph Wölfl leaves Paris for London, where he becomes a fashionable teacher and performer.

G. Cultural Beginnings
Educational: Lezioni Caritatevoli di Musica (Istituto Musicale G. Donizetti, Bergamo); Pennsylvania Academy of Fine Arts (Philadelphia); Tausch School for Wind Performers (Berlin); Zürcherische Singinstitut (Zurich).
Music Publishers: Carli Music Publishers (Paris); Cramer and Keys (London); Kunst und Industrie Comptoir (Pest); Purday and Button (London); Charles S. Richault Publishing Co. (Paris).
Performing Centers: Teatro del Corso (Bologna).
Other: Melodion (by J. C. Dietz).

H. Musical Literature
Joseph Corfe, *Thorough Bass Simplified*; Georg Grosheim, *Über den verfall der Tonkunst*; Wilhelm Heinse, *Musical Dialogues*; Jeremiah Ingalls, *The Christian Harmony*; Stephen Jenks, *The Delight of Harmony*; Honoré Langlé, *Traité de la Fugue*; Joubert de La Salette, *Sténographie musicale*; Daniel Steibelt, *Méthode de pianoforte*; Johann Gottfried Vierling, *Allgemein fasslicher Unterricht in Generalbass*; Joseph Walker,

An Historical Account and Critical Essay on the Opera; Johann Werner, *Orgelschule*.

I. **Musical Compositions**
Chamber Music:
String Quartets: Johann Albrechtsberger, *Six Quartets, Opus 23*; František Krommer, *Three Quartets, Opus 54–Three Quartets, Opus 56*; Antoine Reicha, *Three Quartets (c, D, B), Opus 499–Quartet in A, Opus 58–Quartet in C, Opus 52*; Joseph Wölfl, *Three String Quartets, Opus 30*.
Sonata/Solos: Johann A. André, *Twelve Little Pieces for Two Horns, Opus 26*; Carl Czerny, *Twenty Variations Concertantes* (violin, piano); Józef Elsner, *Three Violin Sonatas (F, D, E♭), Opus 10*; Feliks Janiewicz, *Violin Sonata in F(?)–Sonata in A for Violin and Cello*; Louis Spohr, *Sonata in C for Harp and Violin*.
Ensembles: Józef Elsner, *Piano Quartet in E♭, Opus 15*; František Krommer, *Flute Quintet No. 2, Opus 55*.
Piano: Johann Albrechtsberger, *Prelude and Fugue* (four hands); Ludwig van Beethoven, *Air and Variations on "Ich denke dein"* (four hands); Józef Elsner, *Sonata in B♭, Opus 16* (four hands)–*Three Sonatas (B♭, D, F)*; Johann N. Hummel, *Sonata in E♭, Opus 13(?)–Fantasie in E♭, Opus 13*; Feliks Janiewicz, *Sonata in B♭(?)*; Anton Reicha, *Two Fantasias (C, F), Opus 59*; Daniel Steibelt, *Etude, Opus 78*.
Organ: Samuel Wesley, *Six Voluntaries, Opus 6, Book 1*.
Choral/Vocal Music:
Choral: Michael Haydn, *Leopoldmesse*; Johann N. Hummel, *Mass in d*; Giovanni Paisiello, *Il fonte prodigioso di Orebbe* (oratorio)–*Mass in B♭*; Antonio Salieri, *Missa in d*; Georg "Abbe" Vogler, *Vesperae de Paschate*; Anton Zingarelli, *Saul* (oratorio).
Vocal: Ludwig van Beethoven, *An die Hoffnung, Opus 32–Eight Songs, Opus 52*; George C. Grosheim, *Hektors Abschied*; Johann F. Reichardt, *Six Romances–Romantisch-Gesänge*; Johann Zumsteeg, *Kleine Balladen und Lieder VII*.
Musical Stage: Daniel Auber, *L'erreur d'un moment*; Ludwig van Beethoven, *Fidelio, Opus 72*; François Boieldieu, *La jeune femme colère–Amour et Mystère*; Catterino Cavos, *The Invisible Prince*; Nicolas Dalayrac, *Gulistan*; Franz von Destouches, *Das Missverständniss*; Pietro Generali, *Don Chisciotte*; E. T. A. Hoffmann, *Die ungebetenen Gäste*; Johann N. Hummel, *Die beiden Genies*; Nicolò Isouard, *L'intrigue aux fenêtres–Léonce–La ruse inutile*; Simon Mayr, *Eraldo ed Emma–L'amor cojugale*; Ferdinando Paër, *Leonora–Il maniscalco–Sofonisba*; Gaspare Spontini, *Julie*; Alexei Titov, *Yam*; Vittorio Trento, *Andromeda*; Joseph Weigl, *Vestas Feuer*; Peter von Winter, *Der Frauenbund*; Joseph Wölfl, *Fernando*; Paul Wranitzky, *Die Erkenntlichkeit*.

Orchestra/Band Music:
Concerted Music:
Piano: Ludwig van Beethoven, *Concerto No. 4 in G, Opus 58*; João Domingos Bomtempo, *Concerto No. 2 in f*; Anton Eberl, *Concerto No. 2, Opus 32*; Joseph Wölfl, *Concerto No. 2 in F, Opus 32*.
Violin: Etienne Barrière, *Premier air variée, Opus 14*; Ludwig van Beethoven, *Romance in G, Opus 40*; Rodolphe Kreutzer, *Concerto No. 17 in G, Opus E*; Louis Spohr, *Concerto No. 4 in b, Opus 10*; Giovanni Viotti, *Concerto No. 28 in d–No. 29 in e*.
Other: Johann N. Hummel, *Bassoon Concerto–Double Concerto in G, Opus 17* (violin, piano); František Krommer, *Oboe Concerto No. 2, Opus 52*.
Ballet/Incidental Music: Pierre Gaveaux, *L'amour à Cythère* (B); E. T. A. Hoffmann, *Das Kreuz an der Ostsee* (IM); Sigismund von Neukomm, *Die Braut von Messina* (IM)–*Sittah Man* (IM); Alexander Reinagle, *The Voice of Nature* (IM); Daniel Steibelt, *La belle laitière* (B); Alexei Titov, *The Judgment of Solomon* (IM); Joseph Wölfl, *La Surprise de Diane* (B).
Standard Works: Ludwig van Beethoven, *Leonore Overture No. 2*; Anton Reicha, *Overture to Maria Theresa*; Alexander Reinagle, *Overture, The Wife of Two Husbands*.
Symphonies: Anton Eberl, *No. 3, Opus 34*; Ignace Pleyel, *Sympony in C, Ben. 157*(?).

1806

❈

Historical Highlights: Napoleon crushes Prussia and enters Berlin; the Confederation of the Rhine is founded; Napoleon closes all continental ports to the British who in turn blockade the continent; in the United States, the Lewis and Clark Expedition returns to St. Louis; another explorer, Zebulon Pike, discovers Pike's Peak in Colorado; construction begins on the Cumberland Road, the first federal highway in the new nation.

Art and Literature Highlights: Births—writers Robert Montgomery Bird, Elizabeth Browning; Deaths—artists Honoré Fragonard, Hans Füseli, George Stubbs, poet Carlo Gozzi. Art—Gros' *The Battle of Aboukir*, Ingres' *Napoleon as Emperor*, C. W. Peale's *Exhumation of the Mastodon*; Literature—Arnim/Brentano's *Des Knaben Wunderhorn*, Goethe's *Faust I*, Kleist's *Der Zerbrochene Krug*, Webster's *Dictionnary of the English Language*.

Musical Highlights

A. **Births**
Composers: Juan Crisóstomo Arriaga (Spain) January 27; Albert Grisar (Belgium) December 26; Johann Friedrich Kittl (Bohemia) May 8.
Conductors: Michael Costa (Italy-England) February 4.
Singers: Fanny Ayton (British soprano); Gilbert (Louis) Duprez (French tenor) December 6; Eduard Mantius (German tenor) January 18; Elizabeth Masson (British soprano); Napoleone Moriani (Italian tenor) March 10; Nanette Schechner-Waagen (German soprano); Henriette Sontag (German soprano) January 3; Pierre-François Wartel (French tenor) April 3.
Performers: Napoléon Coste (French guitarist) June 28; Joseph Kasper Mertz (Austrian guitarist) August 17; August Friedrich Pott (German violinist) November 7; Josef Slavík (Bohemian violinist/composer) March 26.
Others: Pietro Scudo (Italian critic/author) June 8.

B. **Deaths**
Composers: Carl Cannabich (Germany) June 1; Tommaso Giordani (Italy) February 23/24; Michael Haydn (Austria) August 10; Christian Kalkbrenner (Germany) August 10; Vicente Martín y Soler (Spain) January 30; Franz Seydelmann (Germany) October 23.
Singers: Brigida Giorgi Banti (Italian soprano) February 18; Salomea Deszner (Polish soprano) March 20; Domenico Guardasoni (Italian tenor/impresario) June 14.
Performers: John Alcock, Sr. (British organist/composer) February 23; Johann Gottfried Arnold (German cellist/composer) July 6; Carl Cannabich (German violinist/composer) May 1; John Abraham Fisher (British violinist/composer); Antoine Lacroix (French violinist/publisher) June 18; William Shrubsole (British organist) January 18.
Others: Jean François Lirou (French music theorist); Richard Potter (British flute maker) December 3.

C. **Debuts**
Singers: Davidde Banderali (Italian tenor—Milan); Johanna Sophia Kollmann (British singer—London), Adelaide Malanotte (Italian contralto—Verona); Joseph August Röckel (German tenor—Vienna).

D. **New Positions**
Conductors: João José Baldi (mestre de capela, Lisbon Cathedral); Juan Bros y Bertomeu (maestro de capilla, Léon Cathedral); Ferdinand Fränzl (Munich Opera); François-Antoine Habeneck (Paris Conservatory Orchestra); Gabriele Prota (maestro de capela, Naples); Vittorio Trento (Italian Opera, Amsterdam).

Others: Vincenzo Camuccini (director, Academy of St. Luke, Rome); Jeremiah Clarke (organ, Worcester Cathedral).

E. Prizes/Honors
Honors: Charles Burney (government stipend); Giovanni Paisiello (Legion of Honor).

F. Biographical Highlights
Gaetano Donizetti enters Bergamo Free School to study music despite his father's wish that he become a lawyer; François Fétis marries into a fortune, which he proceeds to lose by 1811; Josephina Grassini returns to Paris and becomes court singer as well as mistress to Napoleon; Ferdinand Hérold enters Paris Conservatory for the serious study of music, which was delayed by his father's opposition; E. T. A. Hoffmann abandons civil service work for music; Gioacchino Rossini enters the Liceo Musicale in Bologna; Carl Maria von Weber resigns his Breslau post after troubles with management but fails to gain the coveted Karlsruhe appointment.

G. Cultural Beginnings
Performing Groups—Choral: Accademia Polimniaca (Bologna); Lukas-Bund (Vienna).
Performing Groups—Instrumental: Thubaneau Concert Society (Marseilles).
Educational: Arras Music Conservatory; Mannheim Conservatory of Music.
Music Publishers: Heinrichshofen Music Publishers (Germany); Antonio Pacini (Paris).
Music Publications: *Journal des Troubadours*; *Journal of National Music* (Moscow); *Wiener Theatre-Zeitung*.
Performing Centers: Adelphi Theater (Sans Pareil, London); Moscow Imperial Theater; Teatro dei Floridi (S. Marco).
Other: Karl Bochsa Music Store (Paris); Jürgen Marcussen (Marcussen and Reuter), organ builders (Copenhagen); Johann C. Schlimbach, organ and piano builder (Königshofen).

H. Musical Literature
David A. von Apell, *Galerie der vorzüglichsten Tonkünstler und merkwürdigsten Musik-Dilettanten in Cassel vom Anfang des XVI Jahrhunderts bis auf gegenwärtige Zeiten*; John Callcott, *A Musical Grammar*; Johann Dalberg, *Fantasien aus dem Reich der Töne*; Gottlieb Graupner, *Rudiments of the Art of Playing the Pianoforte*; Uri Hill, *The Sacred Minstrel*; Stephen Jenks, *Laus Deo*; Matthew Peter King, *Introduction to Sight Singing*; Augustus Kollmann, *A New Theory of Musical Harmony*; José Mauricio, *Metodo di musica*; Jérôme de Momigny, *Cours complet d'harmonie et de composition*.

I. Musical Compositions

Chamber Music:

String Quartets: Ludwig van Beethoven, *String Quartets No. 7–9 (F, e, C), Opus 59, "Razumovsky"*; Jan L. Dussek, *Three Quartets (G, B♭, E♭), Opus 60*; Józef Elsner, *Three Quartets (C, E♭, d), Opus 8*; Johann Wilhelm Wilms, *No. 1*; Anton Wranitzky, *Three String Quartets, Opus 13.*

Sonata/Solos: Louis Spohr, *Sonata in B♭, Opus 16–Sonata in E♭, Opus 113* (violin, harp); Joseph Wölfl, *Grand Duo, Opus 37, for Harp and Piano.*

Ensembles: Daniel Auber, *Piano Trio in D, Opus 1*(?); Johann Albrechtsberger, *Serenata for Wind Quintet.*

Piano: Jan L. Dussek, *Sonatina in C, C.207* (four hands); Anton Eberl, *Grand Sonata, Opus 39*; Johann N. Hummel, *Sonata in f, Opus 20*(?)*–Variations in B♭ on "Chanson hollandaise," Opus 21*; August E. Müller, *Sonata, Opus 26*(?).

Choral/Vocal Music:

Choral: Luigi Cherubini, *Credo for Eight Voices*; Michael Haydn, *Requiem in B♭* (unfinished); Johann N. Hummel, *Das Fest des Dankes un Freude–Diane ed Endimione* (cantatas)*–Te Deum in D–Missa Solemnis in D*; Christian Weinlig, *Mass in B♭*; Carl Zelter, *Die Gunst des A ugenblicks* (cantata).

Vocal: Luigi Cherubini, *Ten Vocal Canons*; Friedrich Kuhlau, *Three Songs, Opus 56*; Johann F. Reichardt, *Le troubadour italien, français et allemand.*

Musical Stage: Friedrich Benda, *Das Blumenmädchen*; Henry Bishop *Tamerlane et Bajazet*; François Boieldieu, *Télémaque*; Luigi Cherubini, *Faniska*; Domenico Corri, *The Travelers*; Nicolas Dalayrac, *Deux mots–Koulouf*; Edouard Dupuy, *Youth and Folly*; Pierre Gaveaux, *Monsieur Deschalumeaux*; Adalbert Gyrowetz, *Mirana, die Königin der Amazonen–Agnes Sorel*; Friedrich Himmel, *Die Sylphen*; Johann N. Hummel, *Die vereitelten Ränke*; Nicolò Isouard, *La prise de Passau–Idala*; Rodolphe Kreutzer, *Les surprises*; Simon Mayr, *Adelasia e Aleramo*; Etienne Méhul, *Les deux aveugles de Tolède–Gabrielle d'Estrées–Uthal*; Sigismund von Neukomm, *Musikalische malerei*; Johann Poissl, *Die Opernprobe*; Anton Reicha, *Argine, regina di Granata*; Gioacchino Rossini, *Demetrio e Polibro*; Johann Schmidt, *Eulenspiegel*; Louis Spohr, *Die Prüfung*; Gaspare Spontini, *Tout le monde a tort*; Daniel Steibelt, *La fête de Mars*; Alexei Titov, *The Hungarian*; Georg "Abbe" Vogler, *Epimenides*(?); Joseph Weigl, *Il principe invisibile*; Friedrich Witt, *Das Fischerweib.*

Orchestra/Band Music:

Concerted Music:

Piano: Jan. L. Dussek, *Concerto in B♭ for Two Pianos, Opus 63.*

Violin: Ludwig van Beethoven, *Concerto in D, Opus 61*; Louis Spohr, *Concerto No. 3 in C, Opus 7*.
Other: François Devienne, *Flute Concerto No. 11 in b–No. 12 in A/a*; Carl Maria von Weber, *Six Variations in C for Viola and Orchestra*, Opus 49.
Ballet/Incidental Music: Rodolphe Kreutzer, *Paul et Virginie* (B); Sigismund von Neukomm, *Totenfeier* (IM); Joseph Weigl, *Der vier Elemente* (B).
Standard Works: Ludwig van Beethoven, *Leonore Overture No. 3, Opus 72a*.
Symphonies: Ludwig van Beethoven, *No. 4 in B♭, Opus 60*; E. T. A. Hoffman, *Symphony in E♭*.

1807

Historical Highlights: War of the Third Coalition ends—Treaty of Tilsit signed by France, Russia, and Prussia; the French occupy Portugal—Portugese royal family flees to Brazil; Great Britain, France, Spain, and Portugal outlaw African slave trade; the Prussians free their serfs; in the United States, the Chesapeake Affair strains relations between the United States and England; Robert Fulton takes the steamship *Clermont* from Albany to New York.

Art and Literature Highlights: Births—writers Gabriel Legouvé, Henry Wadsworth Longfellow, John Greenleaf Whittier, artist Thomas Duncan; Deaths—artists Angelica Kauffman, John Opie, poet August Meissner. Art—Thorvaldsen's *Cupid and Psyche*, Turner's *Sun Rising in the Mist*, Vanderlyn's *Marius Amid the Ruins of Carthage*; Literature—Barlow, *The Columbiad*, Byron's *Hours of Idleness*, Oehlenschläger's *Baldur, the Good*.

Musical Highlights

A. **Births**
 Composers: Luigi Fernando Casamorata (Italy) May 15; Franz Pocci (Germany) March 7; Napoléon-Henri Reber (France) October 21.
 Conductors: Karl Albrecht (Germany) August 27; Ignaz Lachner (Germany) September 11; Henrik Rung (Denmark) March 3.
 Singers: Marietta Brambilla (Italian contralto) June 6; Osip Petrov (Russian bass) November 15; Joseph Staudigl, Sr. (Austrian bass) April 14; Joseph Tichatschek (Bohemian tenor) July 11.
 Performers: Ignacy Felix Dobrzynski (Polish pianist/composer) March 15; Julius Knorr (German pianist-pedagogue) September 22;

Heinrich Panofka (German violinist) October 3; Adrien-François Servais (Belgian cellist/composer) June 6.
Others: Hilarión Eslava (Spanish music scholar/composer) October 21; Gaetano Gaspari (Italian music historian/librarian) March 15; John W. Moore (American lexicographer) April 11; Giuseppe Rocca (Italian violin maker) April 27; Baltasar Saldoni (Spanish lexicographer) January 4; Michael Welte (German instrument maker) September 29.

B. Deaths
Singers: Sabina Hitzelberger (German soprano)(?).
Performers: Anton Eberl (Austrian pianist/composer) March 11; Edward Miller(British organist) September 12.
Others: Carl Friedrich Cramer (German music author) December 8; Carl Augustin Grenser (German woodwind maker) May 4; Friedrich Grimm (German music critic) December 19; Honoré Langlé (French music theorist/composer) September 20; John Mainwaring (British biographer) April 15; Paolo Morellati (Italian piano maker) February 16.

C. Debuts
Singers: Anton Forti (Austrian tenor/baritone—Esterháza).

D. New Positions
Conductors: Henri-Montan Berton (Opèra-Comique, Paris); Franz Danzi (kapellmeister, Stuttgart); Mariano Rodrigo de Ledesma (Madrid Opera); Ferdinando Paër (Opèra-Comique and maître de chapelle, Napoleon); Georg Vogler (kapellmeister, Darmstadt).
Others: Friedrich Wilhelm Riem (organ, Thomaskirche, Leipzig); Nicolas Séjan (organ, Les Invalides, Paris); Carl Maria von Weber (private secretary to Duke Louis of Württemburg).

E. Prizes/Honors
Honors: Franz Joseph Haydn (Société Academique des Enfans d'Apollon).

F. Biographical Highlights
The family of Jacques François Halévy changes their name officially from Levy; E. T. A. Hoffmann returns to Germany to pursue a musical career as conductor and composer; Carl Maria von Weber moves to Stuttgart, where his loose lifestyle puts him at odds with the authorities.

G. Cultural Beginnings
Performing Groups—Choral: Apollonian Society (Pittsburgh); Dreyssigsche Singakademie (Dresden).
Performing Groups—Instrumental: Gesellschaft für Privatkonzerte (Bremen).

Educational: Milan Conservatory of Music; Zelter Ripienschule (Berlin).
Music Publishers: Friedrich Hofmeister (Leipzig); Musik Hug (Zurich Publishing House); Penson, Robertson and Co., (Scotland); James Power (London).
Music Publications: *Salmagundi* (by Irving and Paulding).
Performing Centers: Boston Athenaeum; Teatro Diurno (Pisa); Theater of the States (German Opera, Prague); Theater Royal (Birmingham, England); Théâtre de la Porte-St.-Martin (Paris).
Other: Smollet Holden Music Shop (Dublin); Pleyel Piano Factory (Paris).

H. Musical Literature

Henri-Louis Blanchard, *Concise Introduction to . . . Music*; Charles Dibdin, *The Musical Master*; Heinrich Domnich, *Horn Method*; John Gunn, *An Historical Inquiry Respecting the Performance on the Harp in the Highlands of Scotland . . .*; Oliver Holden, *Vocal Companion*; Samuel Holyoke, *Instrumental Assistant II*; Augustus Kollmann, *A Second Practical Guide to Thorough Bass*; Andrew Law, *Harmonic Companion and Guide to Social Worship*; Peter Lichtenthal, *Der musikalische Arzt*; August E. Müller, *Kleines Elementarbuch für Klavierspielen*(?); Guillaume-André Villoteau, *Recherches sur l'analogie de la musique avec les arts qui ont pour object l'inmitation du langage*; George Vogler, *Gründliche Anleitung zum Clavierstimmen*.

I. Musical Compositions
Chamber Music:
String Quartets: Johann Albrechtsberger, *Six Quartets, Opus 24*; Jan L. Dussek, *Three Quartets (G, B♭, E♭), Opus 60*; Louis Spohr, *Two Quartets (C, g), Opus 4–Quartet in d, Opus 11*.
Ensembles: Jan L. Dussek, *Trio in F, Opus 65*; Anton Reicha, *Three String Quintets (F, D, E♭), Opus 92–Six String Quintets* (string quartets, two with solo violin, four with solo viola).
Piano: Johann A. André, *Instruktive Variationen über fünf tönen, Opus 31*; Ludwig van Beethoven, *Thirty-Two Variations in c*; Jan L. Dussek, *Sonata in f♯, Opus 61–Sonata in A♭, "Le retour à Paris," Opus 64*; Maria Theresia von Paradis, *Fantaisie I*; Carl Maria von Weber, *Seven Variations on a Theme of Bianchi, Opus 7*.
Chorus/Vocal Music:
Chorus: Ludwig van Beethoven, *Mass in C, Opus 86*; Jan L. Dussek, *Six Choral Canons, C.215–20*; Johann N. Hummel, *Lob der Freundschaft* (cantata); Francesco Morlacchi, *Miserere for Sixteen Voices*; Giovanni Paisiello, *Mass in C–Mass in D*; Carl Zelter, *Die Auferstehung und Himmelfahrt Jesu* (cantata).

Vocal: Luigi Cherubini, *Twelve Vocal Canons*; Friedrich H. Himmel, *Gedichte aus dem Kyllenion, Opus 20–Six Lieder, Opus 21*; Friedrich Kuhlau, *Die Blumen (Six Songs)*.

Musical Stage: Thomas Attwood, *The Curfew*; Gottlob Bierey, *Wladimir*; François Boieldieu, *Un tour de soubrette*; Charles S. Catel, *L'Auberge de Bagnères–Les artistes par occasion*; Catterino Cavos, *Ilya the Hero*; Nicolas Dalayrac, *Lina*; Franz Danzi, *Iphigenie in Aulis*; Józef Elsner, *Andromeda*; Valentino Fioravanti, *I Virtuosi ambulanti*; Adalbert Gyrowetz, *Ida, der büssende–Die Junggesellen–Emericke*; E. T. A. Hoffmann, *Liebe und Eifersucht*; Nicolò Isouard, *Les créanciers–Un Jour à Paris–Le rendez-vous bourgeois*; Friedrich A. Kunzen, *Gyrithe*; Rodolphe Kreutzer, *François I*; Jean Lesueur, *L'inauguration du temple de la Victoire–Le triomphe de Trajan*; Étienne Méhul, *Joseph und seine Brüder*; Francesco Morlacchi, *Il ritratto–Il poeta spiantata*; Bernhard Romberg, *Ulisse und Circe*; Gaspare Spontini, *La vestale*; Alexei Titov, *Nurzadakh*; Joseph Weigl, *Cleopatra–Kaiser Hadrian–Adrian von Ostade*.

Orchestra/Band Music:

Concerted Music:

    Piano: Jan L. Dussek, *Concerto in f for Two Pianos*; Anton Eberl, *Concerto No. 3, Opus 40*; Georg "Abbe" Vogler, *Variation on "Ah que dirais-je maman"*; Joseph Wölfl, *Concerto No. 4 in G, "La Calme," Opus 36*.

    Violin: Louis Spohr, *Concerto No. 5 in E♭, Opus 17*.

    Other: Daniel Steibelt, *Harp Concerto*.

Ballet/Incidental Music: Étienne Méhul, *Le retour d'Ulysse* (B); Joseph Weigl, *Das fest der bacchanten* (B); Joseph Wölfl, *Alzire* (B).

Standard Works: Ludwig van Beethoven, *Coriolanus Overture, Opus 62–Leonore Overture No. 1, Opus 138*; Louis Spohr, *Overture in c, Opus 12*; Carl Maria von Weber, *Grand Overture, Opus 8*.

Symphonies: Ludwig van Beethoven, *No. 5 in c, Opus 67*; Carl Maria von Weber, *No. 1 in C, Opus 50–No. 2 in C, Opus 51*.

1808

❊

Historical Highlights: Napoleon occupies the Iberian peninsula—Britain backs Spanish guerillas against Napoleon; the Congress of Erfurt strengthens Franco-Russian ties; in the United States, James Madison is elected as fourth president; Congress outlaws the importation of slaves from Africa; John Jacob Astor founds the American Fur Co.; *The American Law Journal*, the first legal journal in the New World, begins publication.

Art and Literature Highlights: Births—artists Honoré Daumier, Seth Eastman, Karl Lessing, poet Henrik Wergeland; Deaths—artist Hubert Robert, poets Melchiorre Cesarotti, Jonathan Sewall, Thomas Thorild. Art—Canova's *Pauline Borghese as Venus*, Ingres' *The Bather*, Rush's *Comedy* and *Tragedy*; Literature—Barker's *The Indian Princess*, Goethe's *Pandora*, Kleist's *Penthesilea*, Maturin's *The Wild Irish Boy*.

Musical Events

A. **Births**

Composers: Michael William Balfe (Ireland) May 15; Joaquim Casimiro Júnior (Portugal) May 30; Albert Grisar (Belgium) December 26.

Conductors: Frederick Nicholls Crouch (England) July 31; Louis Dietsch (France) March 17; Carl Liebig (Germany) July 25.

Singers: Prosper Dérivis (French bass) October 28; Wilhelm Dettmer (German bass) June 29; Maria Malibran (Spanish mezzo-soprano) March 24.

Performers: Carlo Bignami (Italian violinist) December 6; Antoine-Louis Clapisson (French violinist/composer) September 15; Auguste Franchomme (French cellist) April 10; Gottfried Hermann (German violinist) May 15; Adolph Hesse (German organist) August 30; Hyacinthe-Eléonore Klosé (French clarinetist) October 11; Joseph Menter (German cellist) January 23; Anna Caroline Ouri (German pianist) June 24.

Others: Giuseppe Curci (Italian music author/composer) June 15; Antoine Elwart (French music author/composer) November 18; J. B. Napoléon Fourneaux (French instrument maker) May 21; Franz Joseph Kunkel (German music theorist) August 20; Ernst Friedrich Richter (German music theorist) October 24; Carl Friedrich Weitzmann (German music theorist) August 10.

B. **Deaths**

Composers: Giuseppe Amendola (Italy); Filippo Maria Gherardeschi (Italy); Henri Hardouin (France) August 13.

Singers: Anton Fischer (German tenor) December 1; Regina Mingotti (Italian soprano) October 1.

Performers: Edmund Ayrton (British organist) May 22; Carlos Baguer (Spanish organist) February 29; François-Hippolyte Barthélemon (French violinist/composer) July 20; Joseph Anton Bauer (Bohemian trumpet virtuoso) August 30; Giovanni Battista Cirri (Italian cellist) June 11; François Cupis (French cellist) October 13; Thomas Haigh (British pianist) April; Alois Luigi Tomasini (Italian violinist/composer) April 25; Paul Wranitzky (Czech violinist/composer) September 26.

Others: John Avery (British organ builder); Johannes Theodorus Cuypers (Dutch violin maker) September; Antonio Eximeno (Spanish music author) June 9; William Forster, Sr. (British violin maker) December 14; Johann Jacob Schramm (German organ builder) June 7.

C. Debuts

Singers: Giulio Marco Bordogni (Italian tenor—Milan); Giovanni David (Italian tenor—Siena); Domenico Donzelli (Italian tenor—Bergamo); Joséphine Fodor-Mainvielle (French soprano—St. Petersburg); Johann Nepomuk Schelble (?German tenor/baritone—Stuttgart).

Performers: Ignaz Moscheles (Czech pianist—Prague).

D. New Positions

Conductors: Gottlob B. Bierey (kapellmeister, Breslau); José Nunes García (mestre de capela, Brazilian Court); E. T. A. Hoffmann (Bamberg Theater); Wenzel Müller (German Opera, Prague); Friedrich Ludwig Seidel (Berlin Royal Chapel); Daniel Steibelt (kapellmeister, Kassel Opera); Karl Jakob Wagner (kapellmeister, Darmstadt).

Others: Bonifazio Asioli (director, Milan Conservatory); John "Christmas" Beckwith (organ, Norwich Cathedral); Mateo Ferrer (organ, Barcelona Cathedral); Gottfried Wilhelm Fink (music critic, *Allgemeine Musikalische Zeitung*); Johann C. Haeffner (music director, Uppsala University); Giuseppe Sigismondi (librarian, Naples Conservatory); Christian Friedrich Uber (director, Kassel Opera).

E. Prizes/Honors

Prizes: Pierre-Auguste Blondeau (Prix de Rome).

F. Biographical Highlights

Gottlieb Graupner becomes a naturalized American citizen; Giuseppe Mercadante, over the age for entering the Collegio di San Sebastiano changes his name and birth records in order to gain entrance; Anton Reicha moves to Paris and gains a modest success with his operas; Franz Schubert enters the Imperial Chapel School in Vienna; Carl Maria von Weber is arrested, imprisoned for two weeks, and then expelled from Stuttgart for innocent involvement in a fraud scheme.

G. Cultural Beginnings

Performing Groups—Instrumental: Brno Philharmonic Society; Harvard College Orchestra (first in the U.S.A.); Liebhaberkonzerte (Cologne); Schuppanzigh (Razumovsky) String Quartet (Vienna); Schweizerische Musikgesellschaft (Lucerne).

Educational: Accademia dei Concordi (Bologna); Anschütz Vocal School (Koblenz); Koblenz Musikinstitut; Naples Conservatory of Music.

Music Publishers: Ricordi and Co. (Milan); Williams Music Publishers (London).
Music Publications: *Phöbus* (Dresden); *Protokoll der Schweizerischen Musikgesellschaft.*
Performing Centers: St. Phillippe Theater (New Orleans); Teatro della Concordia (Cremona).
Other: Belfast Harp Society; Familienkonzerte (Cologne); Pierian Sodality (Harvard Musical Association in 1837); Société de Musique Helvétique.

H. Musical Literature
Johann Albrechtsberger, *Clavierschule für Anfänger*; Daniel Auber, *Règles de contrepoint*; Alexandre Choron, *Principes de composition des écoles d'Italie*; Charles Dibdin, *The English Pythagoras*; Charles Favart, *Mémoires et Correspondance littéraires, dramatiques et Anecdotiques*; Karl Krause, *Vollständige Anweisung*; Jérôme de Momigny, *Le nouveau Solfège*; Thomas Moore, *Irish Melodies I*; Daniel Türk, *Anleitung zu Temperaturberechnungen.*

I. Musical Compositions
Chamber Music:
   String Quartets: Johann Albrechtsberger, *Six Quartets, Opus 26*; František Krommer, *Three Quartets, Opus 68–Three Quartets, Opus 72–Three Quartets, Opus 74(?)*; Anton Reicha, *Three Quartets, Opus 94–Three Quartets, Opus 95–Six Quartets (E♭, G, C, e, F, D), Opus 96*; Gioacchino Rossini, *Five Quartets* (published); Louis Spohr, *Two Quartets (E♭, D), Opus 15.*
   Sonata/Solos: Ludwig van Beethoven, *Cello Sonata in A, Opus 69*; Mauro Giuliani, *Guitar Sonata, Opus 15.*
   Ensembles: Daniel Auber, *Piano Quartet in e*; Ludwig van Beethoven, *Two Piano Trios (D, E♭), Opus 70*; František Krommer, *Flute Quintet No. 3, Opus 58–No. 4, Opus 63–Quartet for Flute and Strings, Opus 75*; Franz C. Neubauer, *Three String Trios, Opus 8–Variations, Opus 16* (flute, violin, viola).
   Piano: Luigi Cherubini, *Two Romances*; Johann N. Hummel, *Sonata in C, Opus 38*; August E. Müller, *Six Caprices, Opus 29(?)*; Carl Maria von Weber, *Grande Polonaise in E♭, Opus 21–Seven Variations, Opus 9*; Samuel Wesley, *Sonata in D (Fugue on Theme of Salomon).*
   Organ: Johann Albrechtsberger, *Six Fugues, Opus 18*; Joseph "Abbe" Vogler, *Preludes*; Samuel Wesley, *Six Voluntaries, Opus 6, Book II.*
Choral/Vocal Music:
   Choral: Ludwig van Beethoven, *Choral Fantasia in c, Opus 80* (piano, chorus, orchestra); Franz Danzi, *Abraham auf Moria* (oratorio); Johann N. Hummel, *Mass in D, Opus 111*; Anton Reicha,

Requiem; Johann F. Reichardt, *Miltons Morgensang;* Gioacchino Rossini, *Il pianto d'armonia* (cantata); Vittorio Trento, *The Deluge* (oratorio); Georg "Abbe" Vogler, *Laudate Dominum in B♭;* Carl Maria von Weber, *Der erste Ton, Opus 14* (cantata).

Vocal: Johann A. André, *Sprich wörter (Quartetto a canone), Opus 32;* Ludwig van Beethoven, *Arietta, In Questa Tomba Oscura;* Friedrich H. Himmel, *Twelve Lieder des Knaben Wunderhorn, Opus 27.*

Musical Stage: Barker/Bray, *The Indian Princess;* François Boieldieu, *La dame invisible–Les voitures versées;* Catterino Cavos, *Three Hunchback Brothers;* Pierre Gaveaux, *L'echelle du soie;* Pietro Generali, *Le lagrime d'una vedova–L'idolo cinese;* Georg C. Grosheim, *Les esclaves d'Alger;* Adalbert Gyrowetz, *Die Pagen des Herzogs von Vendôme;* E. T. A. Hoffmann, *Der Trank der Unsterblichkeit;* Nicolò Isouard, *Cimarosa;* Conradin Kreutzer, *Die Nacht im Walde–Aesop in Phrygien;* Rodolphe Kreutzer, *Aristippe–Jadis et aujour'hui;* Karol Kurpinski, *Pygmalion;* Francesco Morlacchi, *Il corradino–Oreste;* Sigismund Neukomm, *Arkona;* Ferdinando Paër, *Numa Pompilio;* Giovanni Paisiello, *I pittagorici;* Johann N. Poissl, *Antigonus;* Johann F. Reichardt, *L'heureux naufrage;* Louis Spohr, *Alruna, die Eulenkönigin;* Alexei Titov, *Le caverne orientale–The Wedding of Filatka;* Jaroslav Tomášek, *Serafine.*

Orchestra/Band Music:

Concerted Music:

Piano: Friedrich H. Himmel, *Concerto in D, Opus 25.*

Violin: Daniel Auber, *Concerto in D;* František Krommer, *Concerto No. 6, Opus 61–No. 7, Opus 64*(?); Louis Spohr, *Concerto No. 1 in A, Opus 48, for Two Violins and Orchestra;* Giovanni Viotti, *Concerto No. 26 in B♭.*

Other: Johann A. André, *Horn Concerto, Opus 33;* Mauro Giuliani, *Guitar Concerto No. 1, Opus 30;* Louis Spohr, *Clarinet Concerto No. 1 in c, Opus 26.*

Ballet/Incidental Music: François Boieldieu, *Athalie* (IM); Franz von Destouches, *Wanda* (IM); Adalbert Gyrowetz, *Harlekin als Papagei* (B); E. T. A. Hoffmann, *Arlequin* (B); Rodolphe Kreutzer, *Les amours d'Antoine et Cléopatre* (B).

Standard Works: Luigi Cherubini, *Six Contra Dances;* Franz C. Neubauer, *Variations for Orchestra, Opus 9;* Gioacchino Rossini, *Overture in D.*

Symphonies: Ludwig van Beethoven, *No. 6 in F, Opus 68, "Pastoral";* František Krommer, *No. 3, Opus 62;* Étienne Méhul, *No. 2 in D;* Anton Reicha, *No. 1 in E♭, Opus 41–No. 2 in E♭, Opus 42;* Joseph Wölfl, *No. 2 in D, Opus 41.*

1809

✻

Historical Highlights: Napoleon conquers Austria; Napoleon annexes the Papal States; Metternich becomes chief minister of Austria; Great Britain and Turkey sign the Treaty of the Dardanelles; in the United States, Congress passes the Non-Intercourse Act, which opens trade to all nations but France and Great Britain; the world's first ocean-going steamship, the *Phoenix*, makes its maiden voyage; the Illinois Territory is formed out of the Northwest Territory.

Art and Literature Highlights: Births—artist Karl Bodmer, writers Nikolai Gogol, Oliver Wendell Holmes, Edgar Allen Poe, Alfred Lord Tennyson; Deaths—artists Nicolai Abildgaard, Augustin Pajou, Johann Wagner. Art—Friedrich's *Landscape with Rainbow*, Rush's *Water Nymph and Bittern*; Literature—Fessenden's *Pills, Poetical, Political and Philosophical*, Irving's *The Knickerbocker's History of New York*, Knight's *The Cypriad*.

Musical Highlights

A. Births

Composers: Felix Mendelssohn-Bartholdy (Germany) February 3; Auguste-François Morel (France) November 26; Fredrik Pacius (Germany) March 19; Friedrich August Reissiger (Germany-Norway) July 26; Federico Ricci (Italy) October 22.

Conductors: Eugène-Prosper Prévost (France-U.S.A.) April 23; Friedrich August Reissiger (Germany-Norway) July 26; Anton Emil Titl (Bohemia) October 2.

Singers: Henry Robinson Allen (Irish baritone/composer) December 23; Francesco Chiarmonte (Italian tenor) July 20; Sabine Heinefetter (German soprano) August 19; Arthur P. Seguin (British bass) April 7; Eugenia Tadolini (Italian soprano).

Performers: Jean-Baptiste Willent-Bordogni (French bassoonist) December 8; John Leman Brownsmith (British organist); Eugène Sauzay (French violinist) July 14; Francesco Schirz (Italian double-bass virtuoso/composer) August 21.

Others: Alexandre-François Debain (French piano maker/inventor); Frederick Gye (British impresario); Friedrich Wilhelms Jahns (German vocal pedagogue/author) January 2; Wilhelm von Lenz (Russian music author) June 1; Gotthilf Körner (German publisher) June 3.

B. Deaths

Composers: Johann Georg Albrechtsberger (Austria) March 7; Francisco Azzopardi (Malta) February 6; Nicholas Dalayrac (France)

November 26; Francisco Javier García Fajer (Spain) February 26;
Franz Joseph Haydn (Austria) May 31; Joseph Aloys Schmittbaur
(Germany) October 24.
Singers: Bartolomeo Giacometti (Italian bass) January 4; Margarete
Schick (German soprano) April 29.
Performers: Christian Samuel Barth (German oboist) July 8; Franz
Beck (German violinist/composer) December 31; John "Christmas"
Beckwith (British organist) June 3; Johann Gottfried Eckard (German
pianist) July 24; Johann Christian Kittel (German organist/com-
poser) April 17; Jean Lebrun (French horn virtuoso); Jean-Pierre
Legrand (French organist) July 31; Alexander Reinagle (British-born
pianist/composer) September 21.
Others: Johann August Eberhardt (German aesthetician) January 6;
Luigi Antonio Sabbatini (Italian music theorist/composer) January 29.

C. Debuts
  Singers: Charles Edward Horn (British-born singer—London); Jacques
  Émile Lavigne (French tenor—Paris).
  Performers: Charles Franz Schoberlechner (Austrian pianist—
  Vienna).

D. New Positions
  Conductors: Joseph Preindl (kapellmeister, St. Stephen's, Vienna).
  Others: Domenico Barbaia (manager, Royal Opera Houses of
  Naples); William Gifford (editor, *Quarterly Review*); Carl Zelter (pro-
  fessor, Royal Academy of Arts, Berlin).

E. Prizes/Honors
  Prizes: Louis-Joseph Daussoigne-Méhul (Prix de Rome).

F. Biographical Highlights
  Ludwig van Beethoven gains powerful supporters in the Archduke
  Rudolph and princes Kinsky and Lobkowitz who are willing to
  overlook his boorishness in deference to his musical genius; Eliza-
  beth Billington, at the peak of her career, retires from the opera stage;
  Niccolò Paganini begins his career as a free concert artist; Fernando
  Sor travels to London, where he makes the guitar fashionable in
  society.

G. Cultural Beginnings
  Performing Groups—Choral: Berlin Liedertafel (male chorus); Psal-
  lonian Society (Providence); Società degli Esercizi Musicali (Livorno).
  Music Publishers: William Daler (London); Robert Purdie (Edin-
  burgh).
  Music Publications: *Quarterly Review* (London).

Performing Centers: Covent Garden Theater II (London); Théâtre d'Orléans (New Orleans).

Other: Piano Repetitive Action (perfected by S. Érard); Schiedmayer und Söhne, Piano Manufacturers (Stuttgart).

H. Musical Literature

Bonifazio Asioli, *Principi elementari di musica*; Marie-Désiré Beaulieu/ Étienne Méhul, *Cours de composition*(?); Edward Bunting, *Ancient Irish Airs II*; Xavier Désargus, *Traité général sur l'art de jouer la Harpe*; Alexis de Garaudé, *Méthode de chant*; Andrew Law, *The Art of Playing the Organ and Pianoforte*; Simon Mayr, *Breve notizii istoriche della vite e delle opere di G. Haydn*; Giuseppe Rossi, *Alli intendenti di Contrappunto*; George Thomson, *Select Collection of Original Welsh Airs*.

I. Musical Compositions

Chamber Music:

String Quartets: Ludwig van Beethoven, *No. 10 in E♭, Opus 74, "The Harp"*; František Krommer, *Three Quartets, Opus 85–Three Quartets, Opus 90*(?).

Sonata/Solos: Louis Spohr, *Sonata in E♭, Opus 115, for Harp and Violin*.

Ensembles: Jan L. Dussek, *Notturno concertante in E♭, Opus 68*; František Krommer, *Three String quintets, Opus 88–Flute Quintet No. 5, Opus 66*; Sigismund von Neukomm, *Clarinet Quintet, Opus 8*; Gioacchino Rossini, *Six Quartets for Woodwinds*; Carl Maria von Weber, *Piano Quartet in B♭, Opus 76*.

Piano: Ludwig van Beethoven, *Fantasia in B♭, Opus 77–Sonata No. 24 in F♯, Opus 78–No. 25 in G, Opus 79–No. 26 in E♭, Opus 81a, "Das Lebewohl, Abwesenheit und Wiedersehn"*; Friedrich Kuhlau, *Three Rondos, Opus 1–3–Sonata in E♭, Opus 4*; August E. Müller, *Three Caprices, Opus 31*(?); Carl Maria von Weber, *Six Pieces, Opus 10* (piano, 4 hands).

Organ: Johann Albrechtsberger, *Six Fugues, Opus 16*(?).

Choral/Vocal Music:

Choral: Luigi Cherubini, *Mass in F*; Louis-Sébastien Lebrun, *Te Deum*; Jean-François Lesueur, *La mort d'Adam* (oratorio); Giovanni Paisiello, *Mass in G*; Antonio *Salieri, Missa in B♭*; Georg "Abbe" Vogler, *Requiem in E♭*.

Vocal: Friedrich H. Himmel, *Three Gedichte, Opus 24–Six Gedichte, Opus 31*; Giovanni Paisiello, *Mass in G*; Louis Spohr, *Six German Songs, Opus 2*; Carl Maria von Weber, *Six Songs, Opus 15*.

Musical Stage: Ludwig Abeille, *Peter und Ännchenn*; Henri Berton, *Françoise de Foix*; Henry Bishop, *The Circassian Bride*; Luigi Cherubini, *Pygmalion*; Nicolas Dalayrac, *Le poète et le musicien–Le pavillon des fleurs–Elise-Hortense*; Anton Diabelli, *Adam in der Klemme*; Pierre Gaveaux, *La rose blanche et la rose rouge*; Pietro Generali, *La moglie di tre mariti–Amor vince lo Sdegno*; Adalbert Gyrowetz, *Der*

Sammtrock; Nicolò Isouard, *L'intrigue au sérail*; Daniil Kashin, *Fair Olga*; Simon Mayr, *Il matrimonio per concorso–Il ritorno di Ulisse*; Francesco Morlacchi, *Rinaldo d'Asti–La principessa per ripiego–La Simoncino–La avventure d'una giornata*; Sigismund Neukomm, *Niobé*; Ferdinando Paër, *Agnese*; Johann Reichardt, *Bradamante*; Gaspare Spontini, *Fernand Cortez*; Alexei Titov, *The Old Bachelor*; Sergei Titov, *The Meeting*; Joseph Weigl, *Die Schweitzerfamilie–Der Verwandlungen*; Christoph Weyse, *The Sleeping Potion*; Peter Winter, *Colmal*; Nicola Zingarelli, *Il ritorno di Serse*.

Orchestra/Band Music:
Concerted Music:
    Piano: Ludwig van Beethoven, *Concerto No. 5 in E♭, Opus 73, "Emperor"*; João Domingos Bomtempo, *Concerto No. 3 in g*; Anton Eberl, *Concerto, Opus 45, for Two Pianos*.
    Violin: Rodolphe Kreutzer, *Concerto No. 18 in a, Opus F*; Louis Spohr, *Concerto No. 6 in g, Opus 28*.
    Other: Carl Maria von Weber, *Andante and Hungarian Rondo in c, Opus 79* (viola, orchestra).
Ballet/Incidental Music: Adalbert Gyrowetz, *Deodata* (IM); Johann N. Hummel, *Das belebte Gemählde* (B); Daniel Steibelt, *La fête de l'Empereur* (B); Carl Maria von Weber, *Turandot, Opus 37* (IM).
Standard Works: Ludwig van Beethoven, *Military March, Opus 145*; Sigismund von Neukomm, *Fantasy No. 1, Opus 9*.
Symphonies: François Gossec, *Symphony in 17 parts in F*; Etienne Méhul, *No. 1 in g–No. 2 in D–No. 3 in C*; Anton Reicha, *No. 3 in F*.

1810
❄

Historical Highlights: Napoleon annexes Holland, Hanover, Bremen, and Lübeck; the Decree of Fontainbleau calls for the confiscation of all British possessions around the world; the Mexican Revolution begins; in the United States, the census shows a population of 7,240,000, a 36.4% increase in ten years; Congress annexes Florida when the Floridians revolt against Spanish rule; Yale Medical School opens.

Art and Literature Highlights: Births—artists Chauncey B. Ives, Clark Mills, writers Robert Griepenkerl, Elizabeth Gaskell, Alfred de Musset; Deaths—artists John Hoppner, Philipp Runge, Johann Zoffany. Art—Blake's *The Canterbury Pilgrims*, Gérard's *The Battle of Austerlitz*, Guérin's *Andromaque et Pyrrhus*; Literature—Crabbe's *The Borough*, Kleist's *Das Kathchen von Heilbronn*, Scott's *The Lady of the Lake*.

Musical Highlights

A. **Births**
Composers: Félicien David (France) April 13; Claudio S. Grafulla (Spain-U.S.A.); Johann Kinkel (Germany) July 8; Hans Christian Lumbye (Denmark) May 2; Otto Nicolai (Germany) June 9; Lauro Rossi (Italy) February 19; Robert Schumann (Germany) June 8.
Conductors: Franz Erkel (Hungary) November 7.
Singers: Anna Bishop (British soprano) January 9; Konstancja Gladkowska (Polish soprano) June 10; Nicolai Ivanov (Russian tenor) October 22; Giovanni Matteo Mario (Italian tenor) October 17; Giorgio Ronconi (Italian baritone) August 6; Lorenzo Salvi (Italian tenor) May 4.
Performers: Ole Bull (Norwegian violinist) February 5; Norbert Burgmüller (German pianist/composer) February 8; Frédéric Chopin (Polish pianist/composer) March 1; Ferdinand David (German violinist) January 19; Constantin Decker (German pianist/composer) December 29; Julian Fontana (Polish pianist); Julius Emil Leonhard (German pianist) June 13; Holger Simon Paulli (Danish violinist/composer) February 22; Johann Julius Seidel (German organist) July 14; Samuel Sebastian Wesley (British organist/composer) August 14.
Others: Alfred Day (British music theorist) January; Jean-Georges Kastner (French music theorist/composer) March 9; Alfred Novello (British publisher) August 12.

B. **Deaths**
Composers: Francesco Bianchi (Italy) November 27; Francesco Gnecco (Italy)(?); Franz Teyber (Austria) October 22.
Conductors: Jean-Baptiste Rey (France) July 15.
Singers: Venanzio Rauzzini (Italian castrato soprano/composer) April 18.
Performers: José Manuel Aldana (Mexican violinist) February 7; Johann Friedrich Kranz (German violinist) February 20; Samuel Porter (British organist) December 11; Franz Teyber (Austrian organist/conductor) October 22.
Others: Nicolas Étienne Framery (French music theorist) November 26; Johann Michel Götz (German publisher) February 15.

C. **Debuts**
Singers: John Sinclair (Scottish tenor—London).
Performers: Joachim Kaczkowski (Polish violinist—Warsaw); Maria Agate Szymanowska (Polish pianist—Warsaw).

D. New Positions
Conductors: Nicola Benvenuti (maestro di cappella, Pisa Cathedral); Henry Bishop (Covent Garden); Antonio Brunetti (maestro di cappella, Urbino Cathedral); Antonio Canova (director, Academy of St. Luke, Rome); Francesco Morlacchi (deputy kapellmeister, Italian Opera, Dresden); August Müller (kapellmeister, Weimar); Louis Luc de Persuis (Paris Opera); Friedrich Wilhelm Pixis, Jr. (Prague Theater Orchestra); Johann Gottfried Schicht (kantor, Thomasschule, Leipzig); Johann Philipp Schulz (Leipzig Gewandhaus and Singakademie).
Others: Gaspare Spontini (director, Théâtre-Italien, Paris); Franz Teyber (organ, Vienna Court).

E. Prizes/Honors
Prizes: Désiré Beaulieu (Prix de Rome).
Honors: Gian Francisco Fortunati (Institute of Sciences and Letters, Parma).

F. Biographical Highlights
Muzio Clementi, finished with his years of touring, settles in London and soon begins a business career; Anthony Heinrich emigrates to the United States and settles in Philadelphia; Rodolphe Kreutzer's concert career ends with a broken arm; Rossini's first commissioned opera, *La cambiale di matrimonio*, is staged in Venice; Fernando Sor is promoted to the rank of captain in the French army; Carl Maria von Weber, failing to gain a position at Mannheim, concertizes around Germany.

G. Cultural Beginnings
Performing Groups—Choral: Harmonischer Verein (Mannheim); Sons of Handel (Dublin); Worcester Glee Club (Massachusetts).
Performing Groups—Instrumental: Boston Philo-Harmonic Society.
Festivals: Thuringian Festival (Frankenhausen).
Educational: Conservatoire Secondaire de Paris.
Music Publishers: Chapell and Co., Ltd. (London); Janet et Cotelle (Paris); Ludwig Maisch (Vienna); Schlesingersche Buch- und Musikalienhandlung (Berlin).
Performing Centers: Grand Ducal Theater (Karlsruhe); Teatro del Campillo (Granada).
Other: Bass Trumpet (patent by L. Frichot); Harmonichord (by F. Kaufmann); Musikalske Lyceum (Oslo); Society for the Improvement of Musical Art in Bohemia; Guillaume Triebert, woodwind maker (Paris); William Whitley Instrument Shop (Utica, New York).

H. Musical Literature
Alexandre Choron/François Fayolle, *Dictionnaire des Musiciens I*; Joseph Corfe, *Church Music*; Domenico Corri, *The Singer's Preceptor*;

Charles Dignum, *Vocal Music*; Franz X. Glöggl, *Erklärung des musikalischen Hauptzirkels*; Karl Gottlieb Hering, *Praktische Violin-Schule*; Joubert de La Salette, *Considérations sur les divers systèmes de la musique ancienne et moderne*; Johann Nägeli, *Gesangsbildungslehre nach Pestalozzischen Grundsätzen*; Francesco Petrini, *Etude préliminaire de la composition, selon le nouveau systême de l'harmonie*; Johann Reichardt, *Briefe auf einer Reise nach Wien.*

I. Musical Compositions
Chamber Music:
String Quartets: Ludwig van Beethoven, *No. 11 in f, Opus 95, "Serioso"*; Ignace Pleyel, *Two Quartets (E♭, D), Ben. 368,9*; Franz Schubert, *String Quartet in G, D. 2*; Samuel Wesley, *String Quartet in E♭.*

Sonata/Solos: Ferdinand Ries, *Horn Sonata*; Carl Maria von Weber, *Six Progressive Violin Sonatas (F, G, d, E♭, F, C), Opus 10.*

Ensembles: Ludwig van Beethoven, *Sextet in E♭, Opus 71* (clarinet, horns, bassoons)–*Sextet in E♭, Opus 81b* (two horns, string quartet); John Field, *Divertimento No. 1 in E, Opus 13A.*

Piano: Johann Albrechtsberger, *Six Preludes*; Ludwig van Beethoven, *Six Variations in D, Opus 76–Bagatelle in a, "Fur Elise"*; Alexandre Boëly, *Two Sonatas, Opus 1*; Luigi Cherubini, *Fantasia in C*; Carl Czerny, *Sonata No. 1 in A♭, Opus 7*; Jan L. Dussek, *Sonata in E♭, Opus 72* (four hands); James Hewitt, *Yankee Doodle with Variations*; Johann N. Hummel, *Variations, Opus 34*; Franziszek Lessel, *Variations in a, Opus 15*; August E. Müller, *Variations on Mozart's "Ein Mädchen oder Weibchen," Opus 32*; André G. Onslow, *Sonata in e, for Four Hands*; Antoine Reicha, *Six Fugues, Opus 81*; Joseph Wölfl, *Three Piano Sonatas, Opus 48.*

Organ: Johann Albrechtsberger, *Six Fugues, Opus 17.*

Choral/Vocal Music:
Choral: Luigi Cherubini, *Litanie de la Sainte Vièrge*; Joseph Eybler, *Die vier letzten dinge* (oratorio); Friedrich H. Himmel, *Nater unser* (cantata); Johann N. Hummel, *Mass in B♭, Opus 77*; Jean-François Lesueur, *Ruth et Naomi* (oratorio); Etienne Méhul, *Cantata for Napoleon's Birthday*; Francesco Morlacchi, *Mass No. 1*; Vincenzo Righini, *Requiem–Te Deum*; Christian Weinlig, *Dem Chaos im dunkel der nacht* (cantata).

Vocal: Ludwig van Beethoven, *Six Songs, Opus 75–Three Songs, Opus 83*; Benjamin Carr, *Six Ballads from "The Lady of the Lake," Opus 7*; Georg C. Grosheim, *Teutschen Gedichte, Vol. 6–Vol. 7*; Friedrich H. Himmel, *Bewustseyn, Opus 33–Three Lieder, Opus 36*; Johann Reichardt, *Schiller Lyrische Gedichte*; Carl Maria von Weber, *Five Songs, Opus 13.*

Musical Stage: François Boieldieu, *Rien de trop*; Charles Catel, *Les bayadères*; Luigi Cherubini, *Le crescendo*; Pietro Generali, *Adelina*; Adalbert Gyrowetz, *Der betrogene Betrüger–Das augemauerte Fenster*; Johann N. Hummel, *Mathilde von Guise*; Nicolò Isouard, *Cendrillon–La fête du village–La Victime des arts*; Conradin Kreutzer, *Jery und Bätely–Panthea–Konradin von Schwaben*; Rodolphe Kreutzer, *Abel*; Friedrich A. Kunzen, *Love in the Country*; Francesco Morlacchi, *Le danaïdi*; Ferdinando Paër, *Didone abbandonata*; Anton Reicha, *Cagliostro*; Johann Reichardt, *Der Taucher*; Gioacchino Rossini, *La cambiale di matrimonio*; Louis Spohr, *Der Zweikampf mit der Geliebten*; Daniel Steibelt, *Cendrillon–Sargines*; George (Abbé) Vogler, *Der Admiral*; Carl Maria von Weber, *Silvana*; Joseph Weigl, *Der Einsiedler auf den Alpen*; Peter von Winter, *Die beiden Blinden*.

Orchestra/Band Music:
Concerted Music:
  Piano: João Domingos Bomtempo, *Concerto No. 4 in D*; Jan L. Dussek, *Concerto in E♭, Opus 70*; Friedrich Kuhlau, *Concerto in C, Opus 7*; Carl Maria von Weber, *Concerto No. 1 in C, Opus 11*; Joseph Wölfl, *Concerto in D, Opus 49*.
  Violin: Rodolphe Kreutzer, *Concerto No. 19 in d, Opus G*; Louis Spohr, *Violin Concerto No. 10 in A, Opus 62*.
  Other: Gioacchino Rossini, *Variations in C* (clarinet, orchestra); Louis Spohr, *Clarinet Concerto No. 2 in E♭, Opus 57*.
Ballet/Incidental Music: Ludwig van Beethoven, *Egmont, Opus 84* (IM); Adalbert Gyrowetz, *William Tell* (B); Heinrich Marschner, *Die stolze Bäuerin* (B); Etienne Méhul, *Persée et Andromède* (B); Giacomo Meyerbeer, *Der Fischer und das Milchmädchen* (IM); Daniel Steibelt, *Der blöde Ritter* (B).
Standard Works: Sigismund von Neukomm, *Fantasy No 2, Opus 11*.
Symphonies: João Domingos Bomtempo, *No. 1*; Etienne Méhul, *No. 4 in E–No. 5 in A* (unfinished).

1811
❄

Historical Highlights: The British take over the island of Java in the South Pacific; the Prince of Wales takes over as regent of Great Britain when the insanity of King George III becomes acute; Paraguay gains its independence; in the United States, William Henry Harrison defeats the Indian forces under Tecumseh at the Battle of Tippecanoe; the greatest earthquake in U.S. history takes place in the Mississippi Valley and covers 300,000 square miles.

Art and Literature Highlights: Births—artists George Bingham, Théophile Gautier, writers Harriet Beecher Stowe, William Thackeray; Deaths—artist James Sharples, writers Heinrich von Kleist, Thomas Percy. Art—Alston's *Poor Author and Rich Bookseller*, Thorvaldsen's *Procession of Alexander the Great*, Trumbull's *Lady of the Lake*; Literature— Austen's *Sense and Sensibility*, Brentano's *Gockel, Hinkel und Gackeleia*, Fouqué's *Undine*.

Musical Highlights

A. **Births**

Composers: Wilhelm Taubert (Germany) March 23; Ambroise-Charles Thomas (France) August 5; Friedrich Hieronymus Truhn (Germany) November 14.

Conductor: Ludwig Schindelmeisser (Germany) December 8; Pierre Joseph Varnay (France) December 1.

Singers: Filippo Coletti (Italian baritone) May 11; Giulia Grisi (Italian soprano) July 28; Francesco Lamperti (Italian vocal teacher) March 11; Ignacio Marini (Italian bass) November 28; Jane Shirreff (British soprano).

Performers: Gaetano Capocci (Italian organist) October 16; Pierre Alexandre Chevillard (French cellist) January 15; Ferdinand Hiller (German pianist/composer) October 24; Vincenz Lachner (German organist/composer) July 19; Samuel de Lange (Dutch organist) June 9; Franz Liszt (Hungarian pianist/composer/conductor) October 22; Lambert Massart (Belgian violinist) July 19; August Gottfried Ritter (German organist) August 25; Henri Rosellen (French pianist/ composer) October 13; Henry Christian Timm (German-born pianist) July 11.

Others: Franz Brendel (German music author) November 26; Angelo Catelani (Italian music historian) March 30; Oliver Ditson (American publisher) October 20; Tito Ricordi (Italian publisher) October 29.

B. **Deaths**

Composers: Guillaume Navoigille, *l'aîné* (France) November 11; Louis de Reigny (France) December 11; Christian Gotthilf Tag (Germany) June 19.

Singers: Sarah Bates (British soprano) December 11; Dorothea Wendling (German soprano) August 20.

Performers: Johann Braun (German violinist) January 1; Thomas Ebdon (British organist) September 23; Ignaz Fränzl (German violinist/composer) September 3; Joseph Ignaz Leutgeb (Austrian horn virutuoso) February 27; Julien-Amable Mathieu (French violinist) September 6; Giacomo Rampini (Italian organist) November 15; Jacques Tours (Dutch organist) March 11; Louis-Charles Rey (French cellist/composer) May 12; Johann Georg Voigt (German organist) February 24.

C. Debuts
Singers: Filippo Galli (Italian tenor—Padua, as a bass); Benedetta Rosmundo Pisaroni (Italian soprano—Bergamo); John Sinclair (Scottish tenor—London).

D. New Positions
Conductors: Giacomo Carcani (maestro di cappella, Piacenza Cathedral); Johann Henneberg (kapellmeister, Eisenstadt); Giuseppe Jannaconi (maestro di cappella, St. Peter's, Rome); Marcos Portugal (mestre de capela, Rio de Janeiro); Giovanni Tadolini (Théâtre-Italien, Paris). **Others:** Friedrich Dionys Weber (director, Prague Conservatory).

E. Prizes/Honors
Prizes: Hippolyte-André Chélard (Prix de Rome).
Honors: George Thomas Smart (knighted).

F. Biographical Highlights
François Boieldieu, despite a firm promise of a substantial pay raise, leaves Russia and returns to Paris; Johann N. Hummel leaves Eisenstadt and settles in Vienna as a piano teacher; Franz Schubert's songs attract the attention and interest of Antonio Salieri; Nicola Zingarelli is jailed for refusing to take part in a musical tribute to Napoleon's son and is sent to Paris, where he is freed by Napoleon himself.

G. Cultural Beginnings
Performing Groups—Choral: Birmingham Oratorio Society (England); Elberfelder Gesangverein (Wuppertal); Havana Opera Troupe; Musikalische Akademie (Munich).
Performing Groups—Instrumental: Möser String Quartet (Berlin); Orchestra of the National Guard (Krakow).
Educational: Istituto Filarmonico (Venice); Prague Conservatory of Music.
Music Publishers: Marco Berra Publishing House and Music Shop (Prague); Chiswick Press (London); Jacques-Joseph Frey, music publisher (Paris); Novello and Co., Ltd. (London); Edward Riley, music publisher and store (New York); B. G. Teubner Publishing House (Leipzig).
Performing Centers: Théâtre d'Orléans (New Orleans).
Other: Double-Action Harp (by Sébastien Érard); Thomas Hall, organ builder (Philadelphia).

H. Musical Literature

Luigi Angeloni, *Sopra la vita le opera ed il sapere di Guido d'Arezzo* . . . ; August Böckh, *De metris Pindari*; Bonaventura Furlanetto, *Trattato di contrappunto*; Stéphanie Genlis, *Harp Method*; Johann Friedrich Herbart, *Psychologische Bemerkungen zur Tonlehre*; Heinrich Koch, *Handbuch bei dem Studium der Harmonie*; Felix Lipowsky, *Baierisches Musiklexicon*; Victor Pelissier, *Columbian Melodies*; Francesco Pollini, *Metodo per Clavicembalo*; George "Abbé" Vogler, *System für den Fugenbau*; Christian Weinlig, *Vorlesungen über Grundbasse und Composition überhaupt*.

I. Musical Compositions

Chamber Music:

String Quartets: Franz Schubert, *Overture in c, D. 8–Overture in g/B♭, D. 18.*

Sonata/Solos: Jan L. Dussek, *Two Sonatas for Harp and Piano, Opus 69/1,2–Three Violin Sonatas (B♭, G, D), Opus 69*; Ferdinand Hérold, *Violin Sonata No. 1–No. 2*; Louis Spohr, *Sonata, Opus 114, for Violin and Harp*; Carl Maria von Weber, *Seven Variations on a Theme from "Silvana," Opus 33* (clarinet, piano).

Ensembles: Ludwig van Beethoven, *Piano Trio in B♭, Opus 97, "Archduke"*; John Field, *Divertissement No. 2 in A, Opus 14* (piano, string quartet)–*Serenade in E♭* (string sextet); Anton Reicha, *Six Wind Quintets.*

Piano: Johann A. André, *Six Progressive Sonatas, Opus 34*; João Domingos Bomtempo, *Two Sonatas (E♭, C), Opus 9*; Luigi Cherubini, *Romance, "Le mystère"*; Jan L. Dussek, *Three Sonatas (C, F, B♭) for Piano, Four Hands, Opus 66–Sonata in D, Opus 69/3–Sonata in B♭, Opus 74* (four hands)–*Fantasy in F, Opus 76–Sonata in f, "L'invocation," Opus 77*; Johann N. Hummel, *Choix des plus beaux morceaux de musique–Variations in C on a March by Isouard, Opus 40a*; Friedrich Kuhlau, *Four Sonata (d, a, D, F), Opus 5a–Ten Waltzes*; Maria Theresia von Paradis, *Fantaisie II.*

Choral/Vocal Music:

Choral: Hippolyte Chélard, *Ariana* (cantata); Luigi Cherubini, *Mass in d*; Jan L. Dussek, *Solemn Mass, C.256*; José Mauricio Nunes García, *Pastoral Mass*; Ferdinand Hérold, *Mlle. De la Vallière* (cantata); Friedrich H. Himmel, *Die Wanderer* (cantata); Jean François Lesueur, *Ruth et Boaz* (oratorio); Giacomo Meyerbeer, *Gott und die Natur* (oratorio)–*Geistliche Gesänge*; Francesco Morlacchi, *La Passione* (oratorio); Gioacchino Rossini, *La mort de Didone* (cantata).

Vocal: Ludwig van Beethoven, *Four Ariettas and Duets, Opus 82*; Ferdinand Hérold, *Lyrical Scene, Ariana*; Franz Schubert, *Hagar's*

Klage; Carl Maria von Weber, *Scene and Aria, "Signor se padre sei"–Scene and Aria, "Miséra me"–Three Songs, Opus 29–Three Duets, Opus 31.*

Musical Stage: Daniel Auber, *Julie*; Franz Danzi, *Dido*; Pierre Gaveaux, *L'enfant prodigue*; Pietro Generali, *La vedova delirante*; Adalbert Gyrowetz, *Der Augenarzt*; E. T. A. Hoffmann, *Aurora*; Nicoló Isouard, *Le magicien sans magic–Le billet de loterie*; Rodolphe Kreutzer, *Le triomphe du mois de Mars*; Karol Kurpinski, *Zwei hutten–Luzifers Palast*; Simon Mayr, *Ifigenia in Aulide–L'amor figliale*; Étienne Méhul, *Les amazones*; Francesco Morlacchi, *Raoul de Créqui*; Gioacchino Rossini, *L'equivoco stravagante–L'inganno felice*; Jaroslav Tomásek, *Seraphine*; Vittorio Trento, *Climène*; Carl Maria von Weber, *Abu Hassan*; Peter Winter, *Die Pantoffeln*; Nicola Zingarelli, *Baldovino–Berenice, regina d'Armenia.*

Orchestra/Band Music:
Concerted Music:
Piano: Johann N. Hummel, *Concerto in C, Opus 34a*; Giacomo Meyerbeer, *Concerto.*

Other: Carl Maria von Weber, *Clarinet Concerto No. 1 in f, Opus 114–No. 2 in E♭, Opus 118–Bassoon Concerto in F, Opus 127–Concertino in E♭, Opus 109* (clarinet)*–Adagio and Rondo in F, Opus 115* (harmonichord).

Ballet/Incidental Music: Ludwig van Beethoven, *The Ruins of Athens, Opus 113* (IM)*–King Stephen, Opus 117* (IM).

Standard Works: Carl Maria von Weber, *Overture, Der Beherrscher der Geister, Opus 8.*

Symphonies: Giacomo Meyerbeer, *No. 1 in E♭*; Anton Reicha, *No. 4*; Louis Spohr, *No. 1 in E♭, Opus 20.*

1812
❊

Historical Highlights: Napoleon is defeated by the Russian winter and retreats from Moscow—at home, he defeats a conspiracy to crown Louis XVIII; British Prime Minister Perceval is assassinated in the House of Commons; in the United States, James Madison is reelected president; Louisiana becomes the eighteenth state—the Missouri Territory is formed out of the remainder of the original Louisiana Purchase; the United States goes to war with Great Britain.

Art and Literature Highlights: Births—artists Pierre Rousseau, Johann August Tischbein, writers Robert Browning, Charles Dickens; Deaths—artist Johann Friedrich Tischbein, writers Joel Barlow, Gabriel Legouvé.

Art—Canova's *Italian Venus*, Morse's *The Dying Hercules*, Rush's *Nymph of the Schuylkill*, Turner's *Hannibal Crossing the Alps*; Literature—Baker's *Marmion*, DeQuincy's *Confessions of an English Opium Eater*.

Musical Highlights

A. **Births**
Composers: Wiktor Kazyński (Poland) December 30; Achille Peri (Italy) December 20; William (Vincent) Wallace (Ireland) March 11.
Conductors: Louis Jullien (France) April 23; Carl Kossmaly (Germany) July 29.
Singers: Isidor Dannström (Swedish baritone/composer) December 15; Julian Dobrski (Polish tenor) December 31(?); Fanny Persiani (Italian soprano) October 4; Henry Russell (British tenor) December 24.
Performers: Johannes Gijsbertus Bastiaans (Dutch organist) October 31; John Hullah (British organist) June 27; Théodore Nisard (Belgian organist/music author) January 27; Julius Rietz (German cellist/conductor) December 28; Joseph Schad (German pianist) March 6; Sigismond Thalberg (Swiss pianist/composer) January 8; Wilhelm Volckmar (German organist) December 26.
Others: Léon-Philippe Burbure de Wesembeek (Belgian music scholar) August 16; Jean-Louis-Félix Danjou (French music author/organist) June 21; Édouard (Louis) Fétis (Belgian music editor/librarian) May 16; Johann Adam Heckel (German musical instrument maker) July 14; Otto Kraushaar (German music theorist) May 31; Thomas D. Paine (American instrument maker) October 9; Carl Gottlieb Röder (German publisher) June 22.

B. **Deaths**
Composers: Joachim Albertini (Poland) March 27; Michel-Richard Delalande (France) December 23; Vincenzo Righini (Italy) August 19; Joseph Schuster (Germany) July 24.
Singers: Lorenzo Bibelli (Italian baritone) November 5; Johann Ernst Dauer (German tenor) September 12; Lorenzo Gibelli (Italian baritone/composer); Samuel Harrison (British tenor) June 25; John Page (British tenor) August 16; Antoinette Cécile Saint-Huberty (French soprano) July 22.
Performers: Joseph Beer (Bohemian clarinetist/composer) October 28; Eligio Celestino (Italian violinist) January 24; Johann Dalberg (German pianist/author) July 26; Johann Ladislaus Dussek (Bohemian pianist/composer) March 20; Friedrich Adam Hiller (German violinist/composer) November 23; Jean-Joseph Rodolphe

(French horn virtuoso) August 19; Anton Stadler (Austrian clarinetist) June 15; Joseph Wölfl (Austrian pianist/composer) May 21. **Others:** Franz Hoffmeister (German publisher) February 9; Emanuel Schikaneder (Austrian playwright/librettist) September 21.

C. Debuts
Singers: Luigi Lablache (Italian bass—Naples).

D. New Positions
Conductors: Ramón Félix Cuéllar y Altarriba (maestro de capilla, Saragona); Franz Danzi (kapellmeister, Karlsruhe); Conradin Kreutzer (hofkapellmeister, Stuttgart); Peter Joseph von Lindpaintner (Isarthor Theater, Munich).
Others: James Hewitt (organ, Trinity Church, Boston); Ferdinando Paër (director, Théâtre-Italien, Paris); Johann Christian Friedrich Schneider (organ, Thomaskirche, Leipzig).

E. Prizes/Honors
Prizes: Ferdinand Hérold (Prix de Rome).

F. Biographical Highlights
Ludwig van Beethoven meets Goethe; Franz Adolf Berwald begins playing violin and viola in the Stockholm Court Orchestra; Lowell Mason goes to Savannah, Georgia, and works as a sales clerk and bank clerk; Giacomo Meyerbeer quits his studies to embark on a performance career; Carl Maria von Weber begins several literary works and meets Goethe and Wieland.

G. Cultural Beginnings
Performing Groups—Choral: Allgemeine Musikgesellschaft (Zürich); Musikgesellschaft und Liedertafel (Worms).
Performing Groups—Instrumental: Arras Philharmonic Society; Lausanne Musical Society; Musikalische Gesellschaft (Cologne).
Educational: Alday Music Academy (Dublin); Brussels Conservatory of Music; Music Institute of Pest.
Music Publications: *Quarterly Music Register* (two issues only).
Performing Centers: Argyll Rooms (London); Drury Lane Theater II (London); Theater am Isartor (Munich); Town Theater (Pest).
Other: Gesellschaft der Musikfreunde (Vienna); Roxburghe Club (London); Trochléon (by J. C. Dietz).

H. Musical Literature
Giuseppe Carpani, *Le Haydine Ovvera Lettere sula vita e le opera del celebre Giuseppe Haydn*; William Crotch, *Elements of Musical Composition*; Alphonse Fortia de Piles, *Quelques Réflexions d'un Homme du Monde*; Ernst Gerber, *Neues historisches biographisches Lexikon der*

Tonkünstler I, II; Carlo Gervasoni, *Nuova Teoria de Musica;* Ambrogio Minoja, *Lettere sopra il canto;* Johann Gottfried Schicht, *Grundregeln der Harmonie nach dem Verwechslungssystem;* John Stafford Smith, ed., *Musical Antiqua I, II;* Georg Telemann, *Sammlung alter und neuer Kirchenmelodien.*

I. Musical Compositions

Chamber Music:

String Quartets: Franz Schubert, *Quartet in g, D. 18–in C, D. 32–in B♭, D. 36;* Louis Spohr, *Quartet in g, Opus 27.*

Sonata/Solos: Ludwig van Beethoven, *Violin Sonata in G, Opus 96.*

Ensembles: Ludwig van Beethoven, *Three Equali* (d, D, B♭) (four trombones); John Field, *Rondeau in A♭, Opus 18A* (piano quintet); Gioacchino Rossini, *Theme and Variations for Woodwind Quartet.*

Piano: John Field, *Sonata No. 4 in B–Nocturne No. 1 in E♭, H.24–No. 2 in c, H.25–No. 3 in A♭, H.26;* Friedrich Kuhlau, *Sonata in E♭, Opus 4–Sonata in d, Opus 5–Grand Sonata in a, Opus 8a;* August E. Müller, *Three Caprices, Opus 34;* Franz Schubert, *Six Variations in E♭, D. 21–Twelve Viennese German Dances, D. 128;* Carl Maria von Weber, *Sonata No. 1 in C, Opus 138–Seven Variations on a Theme of Méhul, Opus 141;* Samuel Wesley, *Sonata in D, "Siège of Badajoz."*

Organ: Franz Schubert, *Three Fugues (C, G, d), D .24;* Samuel Wesley, *Grand Duett in Three Movements.*

Choral/Vocal Music:

Choral: Daniel Auber, *Mass;* William Crotch, *Palestine* (oratorio); Giovanni Paisiello, *Mass in E♭;* Johann N. Poissl, *Mass in C;* Franz Schubert, *Namensfeier* (cantata); Louis Spohr, *Der jüngste Gericht* (oratorio); Carl Maria von Weber, *In Seinem Ordnung schafft der Herr* (cantata); Christian Weinlig, *Jesus Christus der Welterlöser* (oratorio); Nicola Zingarelli, *La Riedificazione di Gerusalemme* (oratorio).

Vocal: Johann F. Reichardt, *Lieder von C. L. Reissig;* Carl Maria von Weber, *Four Songs, Opus 23.*

Musical Stage: Daniel Auber, *Jean de Couvin;* François Boieldieu, *Jean de Paris;* Charles Catel, *Les aubergistes de qualité;* Franz Danzi, *Camilla und Eugen;* Friedrich von Drieberg, *Don Cocagno;* Pietro Generali, *Attila–La Vevoda stravagante;* Adalbert Gyrowetz, *Federica ed Adolfo–Das Winterguartier in America;* Ferdinand Hérold, *Madamoiselle de la Vallière;* Nicolò Isouard, *Le prince de Catane–Lulli et Quinault;* Conradin Kreutzer, *Feodora;* Rodolphe Kreutzer, *L'homme sans façon;* Giacomo Meyerbeer, *Jephtas Gelübde;* Ferdinando Paër, *Un passo ne fa cento;* Johann Poissl, *Ottaviano in Sicilia;* Gioacchino Rossini, *Ciro in Babilonia–Il Signor Bruschino–La scala di seta–La pietra del paragone–L'occasione fa il ladro;* Franz Schubert, *Der Spiegelritter* (operetta); Daniel Steibelt, *La princesse de Babylone;*

Alexei Titov, *Credulous Folk–Emmerich Tekkely*; Michael Umlauf, *Der Grenadier*; Joseph Weigl, *Franciska von Foix*; Christoph Weyse, *Faruk*.

Orchestra/Band Music:

Concerted Music:

Piano: Ferdinand Hérold, *Concerto No. 1 in E, Opus 25–Concerto No. 2 in E♭, Opus 26*; Carl Maria von Weber, *Concerto No. 2 in E♭, Opus 155*; Joseph Wölfl, *Concerto in E, Opus 64*.

Other: Mauro Giuliani, *Guitar Concerto No. 2, Opus 36*; Giacomo Meyerbeer, *Concerto for Violin, Piano and Orchestra*; Johann N. Poissl, *Clarinet Concerto*.

Ballet/Incidental Music: Johann N. Hummel, *Sappho von Mitilene* (B).

Standard Works: Johann Reichardt, *Sakuntala Overture*; Franz Schubert, *Overture, "Der Teufel als Hydraulicus."*

Symphonies: Ludwig van Beethoven, *No. 7 in A, Opus 92–No. 8 in F, Opus 93*.

1813

❄

Historical Highlights: Napoleon is decisively defeated at the Battle of the Nations—Wellington enters France—Ferdinand VII takes the Spanish throne away from Joseph Bonaparte; William of Orange returns to Holland after the French departure; Venezuela gains its independence—Simón Bolívar becomes dictator; in the United States, the British blockade on Lake Erie is broken; the U.S. invasion of Canada fails; the Creek War breaks out in Alabama.

Art and Literature Highlights: Births—artists George Healy, William Ranney, writers Friedrich Hebbel, Henry Tuckerman; Deaths—artists Anton Graff, Alessandro Longhi, writers Michel de Crèvecoeur, Christoph Wieland; Art—Krimmel's *Interior of an American Inn*, Raeburn's *The Macnab*, Sargent's *Landing of the Pilgrims*; Literature—Austen's *Pride and Prejudice*, Shelley's *Queen Mab*, Wyss' *Swiss Family Robinson*.

Musical Highlights

A. Births

Composers: Alexander Dargomijsky (Russia) February 14; Friedrich von Flotow (Germany) April 27; William Henry Fry (U.S.A.) August 10; George Macfarren (England) March 2; Carl Mangold (Germany)

October 8; Errico Petrella (Italy) December 10; Giuseppe Verdi (Italy) October 10; Richard Wagner (Germany) May 22.

Singers: Giovanni Battista Belletti (Italian tenor) February 17; Teresa Brambilla (Italian soprano) October 23; Semyon Stepanovich Gulak-Artemovsky (Russian baritone) February 16; William Harrison (British tenor) June 15; Anna-Maria Hasselt-Barth (Dutch soprano) July 15; Clara Heinefetter (German soprano) September 7; Agnes Schebest (Austrian mezzo-soprano) February 10; Felice Varesi (French-born baritone).

Performers: (Charles-Valentin) Alkan (French pianist/composer) November 30; Justin Cadaux (French pianist/composer) April 13; Ernst Haberbier (German pianist) October 5; Stephen Heller (Hungarian pianist) May 15; Matthias Keller (German-born violinist/composer) March 20; Jacob Rosenhain (German pianist) December 2; Prosper Sainton (French violinist) June 5; Henry Thomas Smart (British organist) October 26.

Others: Carl Hermann Bitter (German music author) February 27; Henri Blaze (French music critic) May 17; Franz Commer (German music historian) January 23; J. W. Davison (British music critic) October 5; John Sullivan Dwight (American critic/editor) May 13; Otto Jahn (German music scholar) June 16.

B. **Deaths**

Composers: Friedrich August Baumbach (Germany) November 30; Gotthilf von Baumgarten (Germany) October 1; Stepan Degtiarev (Russia) May 5; André Grétry (France) September 24; Johann Baptist Vanhal (Czechoslovakia) August 20.

Singers: Giuseppe Aprile (Italian castrato soprano) January 11; Richard Bellamy (British bass) September 11; Carl Stenborg (Swedish tenor/composer) August 1; Marianne de Tribolet (Austrian soprano) April 21.

Performers: Ferdinando Gioseffo Bertoni (Italian organist) December 1; Christian Danner (German violinist) April 29; Étienne Ozi (French bassoonist/composer) October 5; Johann Gottfried Palschau (German pianist/composer); Johann Friedrich Peter (Dutch-born violinist/organist/composer) July 13; Ignazio Raimondi (Italian violinist) January 14; Johann Joseph Rösler (Bohemian pianist/composer) January 28; William Russell (British organist) November 21; Daniel Gottlob Türk (German organist/ theorist) August 26; Johann Gottfried Vierling (German organist) November 22.

Others: Gaetano Callido (Italian organ builder) December 12; Johann Grenser (German woodwind maker) December 12; Johann Carl Rellstab (German publisher) August 19.

C. Debuts

Singers: Giuseppe de Begnis (Italian bass—Modena); Giovanni Bordogni (Italian tenor—Milan); Nicolas-Prosper Levasseur (French bass—Paris); Catherine Stephens (British soprano—London).

D. New Positions

Conductors: Friedrich Kuhlau (Copenhagen Court).
Others: William Ayrton (music critic, London *Morning Chronicle*); François-Joseph Fétis (organ, St. Pierre, Douai); Carl Maria von Weber (director, German Opera, Prague); Johann Rinck (organ, Darmstadt Court); Nicola Zingarelli (director, Royal College of Music, Naples).

E. Prizes/Honors

Prizes: Auguste-Mathieu Panseron (Prix de Rome).
Honors: Jean François Lesueur (French Institute); Pierre-Alexandre Monsigny (French Institute); Ferdinand Ries (Swedish Academy).

F. Biographical Highlights

Heinrich August Marschner goes to Leipzig to study law at the University but is encouraged to go into music by Johann Schicht at the Thomasschule; Benedetta Pisaroni contracts a serious illness, which forces her voice down to the alto range; Ferdinand Ries moves to London, where he concertizes and begins teaching piano; Pierre Joseph Rode arrives in Vienna and becomes associated with Beethoven.

G. Institutional Openings

Performing Groups—Choral: French Opera Co. (New Orleans).
Performing Groups—Instrumental: London Philharmonic Society; Urbany String Quartet (Pest).
Music Publishers/Dealers: Anton Paterno, music publisher (Vienna).
Music Publications: *Neujahrsgeschenk an die Züricherische Jugend von der Allgemeine Musikgesellschaft Zürich*; *Patterson's Church Music*.
Performing Centers: Real Teatro de São João (Rio de Janeiro); Teatro Re (Milan).

H. Musical Literature

Bonifazio Asioli, *Trattato d'armonia e d'accompagnamento*; Thomas Busby, *Dictionary of Music*; Alexandre Choron, *Traité général des voix et des instruments d'orchestre*; Alphonse Fortia de Piles, *A Bal les Masques!*; Ernst Gerber, *Neues historisch-biographisches Lexikon der Tonkünstler III*; Ignaz von Mosel, *Versuch einer Aesthetik des dramatischen Tonsatzes*; Bernhard Natorp, *Anleitung zur Unterweisung im Singen für Lehrer in Volksschulen*; George "Abbé" Vogler, *Über Choral-*

und Kirchengesänge; Solomon Warriner, *Springfield Collection of Sacred Music*.

I. **Musical Compositions**
    Chamber Music:
    String Quartets: Franz Schubert, *Quartets; in C, D. 46–in B♭, D. 68–in E♭, D. 87.*
    Ensembles: Anton Reicha, *Six Quartets, Opus 98* (flute, strings); Franz Schubert, *Octet in F for Woodwinds, D. 72–Nonet in e♭ for Winds, D 79*; Louis Spohr, *Nonet in F, Opus 31* (woodwind quintet, strings).
    Piano: Gaetano Donizetti, *Pastorale in E–Sinfonia in A*; Jan L. Dussek, *Sonata in F, Opus 73* (piano, four hands); John Field, *Sonata in B, H.17–Polonaise in E♭, H.21*; Friedrich Kuhlau, *Three Grande Sonaten (a, D, F), Opus 8*; August E. Müller, *Sonata, Opus 36*; Franz Schubert, *Twenty Minuets, D. 41.*
    Choral/Vocal Music:
    Choral: François Gossec, *Messes des Vivants*; Ferdinand Hérold, *Hymn sur la Transfiguration*; Francesco Morlacchi, *Russian Mass* (a capella chorus).
    Vocal: Friedrich H. Himmel, *Kriegslieder der Teutschen, Opus 21–Six Lieder, Opus 42–Romances françoises (5), Opus 44–Three Lieder, Opus 44*; Friedrich Kuhlau, *Six Songs, Opus 9–Ten German Songs, Opus 11*; Carl Maria von Weber, *Six Songs, Opus 30.*
    Musical Stage: Daniel Auber, *Le séjour militaire*; François Boieldieu, *Le nouveau seigneur du village*; Luigi Cherubini, *Les Abencérages*; Franz Danzi, *Rübezahl*; Józef Elsner, *The Cabalist*; Pietro Generali, *Eginardo e Lisbetta*; Friedrich Himmel, *Der Kobold*; Johann N. Hummel, *Der Junker in der Mühle*; Nicolò Isouard, *Le français à Venise*; Conradin Kreutzer, *Die Insulanerin–Der Taucher*; Rodolphe Kreutzer, *Le camp de Sobieski–Constance et Théodore*; Simon Mayr, *Medea in Corinto–La Rosa rossa e la Rosa bianca–Tamerlano*; Étienne Méhul, *Le prince troubadour*; Giacomo Meyerbeer, *Wirth und Gast*; Wenzel Müller, *Der Schlossgärtner und der Windmüller*; Giovanni Pacini, *Annetta e Lucindo*; Ferdinando Paër, *I Baccanti*; Charles Plantade, *Le Mari de circonstances*; Johann Poissl, *Aucassin und Nicolette*; Gioacchino Rossini, *Tancredi–L'italiana in Algieri–Aureliano in Palmira*; Johann Schmidt, *Der blinde Gärtner*; Louis Spohr, *Faust*; Alexei Titov, *An Old Fashioned Christmas*; Joseph Weigl, *Der Bergsturz.*
    Orchestra/Band Music:
    Concerted Music:
    Piano: Ferdinand Hérold, *Concerto No. 3 in A–Concerto No. 4 in e.*
    Violin: Nicolò Paganini, *Variations, "Le Streghe," for Violin and Orchestra, Opus 8*; Giovanni Viotti, *Concerto No. 27 in C.*

Other: Franz Danzi, *Symphonie concertante in B♭, Opus 41*; Carl Maria von Weber, *Andante and Hungarian Rondo, Opus 35* (bassoon, orchestra—arr. of *Opus 79*).

Program Music: Ludwig van Beethoven, *Wellington's Victory, Opus 91.*

Standard Works: Ludwig van Beethoven, *Triumphal March in C, Opus 143.*

Symphonies: Ferdinand Hérold, *No. 1 in C*; Franz Schubert, *No. 1 in D, D. 82.*

1814

Historical Highlights: England invades France—Napoleon is sent to the isle of Elba—Louis XVIII returns to the throne as king; the Congress of Vienna begins; Cape Town, South Africa, is ceded to the British; in the United States, the British set fire to Washington, D.C., but are defeated in their attempt to invade New York; Francis Scott Key, at Fort McHenry, writes the words of the "Star Spangled Banner"; the Treaty of Ghent officially ends the War of 1812.

Art and Literature Highlights: Births—artists Albertus de Browere, Jean-François Millet, writers Mikhail Lermontov, Aubrey de Vers; Deaths—sculptor Clodion, writers Charles Palissot de Montenoy, Mercy Otis Warren. Art—Géricault's *Wounded Cuirassier*, Ingres' *Grand Odalisque*, Vanderlyn's *Ariadne Asleep on the Island of Naxox*; Literature—Byron's *Le Corsair*, Hoffmann's *Phantasiestücke in Callots Manier*, Scott's *Waverley.*

Musical Highlights

A. Births

Composers: Mihály Mosonyi (Hungary) September 4; August Schäffer (Germany) August 25.

Conductors: August Röckel (Austria) December 1.

Singers: Emma Albertazzi (British contralto) May 11; Karl Beck (Austrian tenor)(?); Marie-Cornélie Falcon (French soprano) January 28; Franz Götze (German tenor) May 10; Adelaide Kemble (British soprano); Heinrich Kotzolt (Danish tenor) August 26; Jan Křtitel Pišek (Bohemian baritone) October 13; Elizabeth Rainforth (British soprano) November 23; Ludwika Rivoli (Polish soprano) March 3; Emma Romer (British soprano); Sebastiano Ronconi (Italian baritone) May; Mary Shaw (British contralto).

Performers: Arnold Joseph Blaes (Belgian clarinetist) December 1; Theodor Döhler (German pianist/composer) April 20; Heinrich Wilhelm Ernst (Czech violinist) May 6; Adolph Henselt (German pianist) May 9; Charles Salaman (British pianist) March 3.

Others: Alexander Ellis (British acoustician) June 14; August Gemünder (German-born violin maker) March 22; Prince Carl Lichnowsky (Austrian patron of the arts) April 15; Augustin Savard (French music educator/theorist) October 21; Adolphe Sax (Belgian instrument maker) November 6.

B. **Deaths**
Composers: Charles Dibdin (England) July 25; Johann Antonin Kozeluch (Bohemia) February 3; Johann Friedrich Reichardt (Germany) June 27; Angelo Tarchi (Italy) August 19; Maximilian Ulbrich (Austria) September 14; Georg "Abbé" Vogler (Germany) May 6.
Singers: Marianna Monti (Italian soprano).
Performers: Christoforo Babbi (Italian-born violinist) November 19; Friedrich Benda (German violinist) June 19; Franz Vollrath Buttstett (German organist) May 7; Friedrich Heinrich Himmel (German pianist/composer) June 8; Johann Gottfried Krebs (German organist) January 5; Johann Jacob Kriegk (German violinist/cellist) December 24.

C. **Debuts**
Singers: Eduard Franz Genast (German baritone—Weimar); Henriette Clémentine Lalande (French soprano—Naples); Geltrude Righetti-Giorgi (Italian contralto—Bologna).

D. **New Positions**
Conductor: Antonio Calegari (maestro di cappella, Padua); Bonaventura Furlanetto (maestro di cappella, St. Marks); Christian Friedrich Uber (kapellmeister, Mainz); Jan Vitásek (choirmaster, St. Vitus' Cathedral, Prague); Franz Volkert (assistant, Leopoldstadt Theater, Vienna); Christian Theodor Weinlig (cantor, Dresden Kreuzschule); Georg Friedrich Wolf (kapellmeister, Wernigerode); Anton Wranitzky (Theater an der Wien).
Others: Angelica Catalani (manager, Théâtre-Italien, Paris); Nicolas Séjan (organ, Royal Chapel, Paris); Thomas Forbes Walmisley (organ, St. Martin-in-the-Fields); George Ebenezer Williams (organ, Westminster Abbey).

E. **Prizes/Honors**
Honors: Luigi Cherubini (Legion of Honor); Jean Baptiste Davaux (Legion of Honor); Charles-Henri Plantade (Legion of Honor); Peter von Winter (ennobled).

F. Biographical Highlights

Gaetano Donizetti goes to Bologna to study composition with Padre Martini; E. T. A. Hoffmann, dismissed from his Leipzig position, settles permanently in Berlin; Anton Schindler meets Beethoven and soon becomes his personal secretary; Franz Schubert tries teaching in his father's school, a career definitely not to his liking; Gaspare Spontini is made court composer to Louis XVIII of France; Richard Wagner's mother moves to Dresden and marries actor Ludwig Geyer.

G. Cultural Beginnings

Performing Groups—Choral: Handel Society of Maine.

Performing Groups—Instrumental: Accademia Filarmonica (Turin); Anacreontic Society (Belfast Orchestra); Bordeaux Orchestre de Concert.

Educational: Cuban Academy of Music.

Music Publishers/Dealers: August Cranz, music publisher (Hamburg); C. F. Peters, music publisher (Leipzig).

Music Publications: *Galignani's Messenger.*

Performing Centers: Teatro Contavalli (Bologna); Theatrum Vlahicum Bucharestini.

Other: Chiroplast (patent by J. Logier); Claviharpe (keyed harp by J. C. Dietz); Clair Godefroy, woodwind manufacturer (Paris); Handelian Academy (New York); Michael Schnabel Piano Co. (Breslau); Society for Religious and National Music (Warsaw).

H. Musical Literature

Johann A. Apel, *Metrik I*; Alexandre Choron, *Méthode élémentaire de composition*; Ernst Gerber, *Neues historisch-biographisches Lexikon der Tonkunster IV*; Uri Hill, *The Handelian Repository*; Andrew Law, *Essays on Music*; John D. Loder, *General and Comprehensive Instruction Book for the Violin*; Étienne Ozi, *Méthode de serpent*; Anton Reicha, *Traité de mélodie*; Stendhal, *Vies de Haydn, Mozart et Métatase.*

I. Musical Compositions

Chamber Music:

String Quartets: Luigi Cherubini, *No. 1 in E♭*; Ferdinand Hérold, *Three Quartets (D, C, g)*; Franz Schubert, *Quartet No. 7 in D, D. 94–No. 8 in B♭, D. 112*; Louis Spohr, *Quartet in A, Opus 30.*

Ensembles: Adalbert Gyrowetz, *Three Piano Trios, Opus 60*; Louis Spohr, *Octet in E, Opus 32–Two String Quintets (E♭, G), Opus 33.*

Piano: Ludwig van Beethoven, *Sonata No. 27 in e, Opus 90*; John Field, *Rondo écossais in B, H.23E*; Ignaz Moscheles, *Sonata in B♭, "Caractéristique," Opus 27–Variations on a Theme of Handel, Opus 29.*

Choral/Vocal Music:
Choral: Ludwig van Beethoven, *Der Glorreiche Augenblick, Opus 136* (cantata)–*Germania, Opus 193*; Jacques-François Halévy, *La Mort* (cantata); Conradin Kreutzer, *Die Sendung Mosis* (oratorio); Francesco Morlacchi, *Mass for the King of Saxony*; Johann N. Poissl, *Der Sommertag* (cantata); Franz Schubert, *Mass No. 1 in D, D. 105.*
Vocal: Friedrich H. Himmel, *Alexis und Ida, Opus 43* (cycle); Franz Schubert, *Gretchen am Spinrade*; Georg "Abbe" Vogler, *Lied an den Rhein–Kriegslied*; Carl Maria von Weber, *Four Songs, Opus 41.*
Musical Stage: Henry Bishop, *The Maid of the Mill*; Adrien Boieldieu, *Angéla*; Luigi Cherubini, *Bayard à Mézières*; Franz Danzi, *Malvina*; Friedrich von Drieberg, *Der Sänger und der Schneider*; Pietro Generali, *Bajazet*; Johann N. Hummel, *Die Eselshaut, oder Die blaue Insel–Die Rückfahrt des Kaisers*; Nicolò Isouard, *Bayard à Mézières–Jeannot et Colin–Joconde*; Conradin Kreutzer, *Alimon und Zaide–Die Nachtmütze*; Rodolphe Kreutzer, *L'oriflamme–Le béarnais*; Friedrich Kuhlau, *Die Räuberburg*; Karol Kurpiński, *Jadwiga–Laska Imperatora*; Simon Mayr, *Atar–Elena*; Giacomo Meyerbeer, *Das Brandenburger Tor*; Giovanni Pacini, *L'ambizione delusa–L'escavazione del tesoro–La ballerina raggiratrice*; Ferdinando Paër, *L'oriflamme*; Johann Poissl, *Athalia*; Gioacchino Rossini, *Il turco in Italia–Sigismondo*; Franz Schubert, *Des teufels lustschloss*; Gaspare Spontini, *Pélage*; Giovanni Tadolini, *La fata Alcina*; Joseph Weigl, *Der jugend Peter des Gross.*
Orchestra/Band Music:
Concerted Music:
   Piano: John Field, *Concerto No. 2 in A♭*; Johann N. Hummel, *Concerto No. 3 in C, Opus 34a.*
   Violin: Louis Spohr, *Concerto No. 7 in e, Opus 38*; Peter von Winter, *Symphonie concertante in B♭, Opus 20.*
Ballets/Incidental Music: Conradin Kreutzer, *Antonio und Kleopatra* (B)–*Mirsile und Anteros* (B).
Standard Works: Ludwig van Beethoven, *Fidelio Overture, Opus 72b–Namensfeier Overture, Opus 115*; Johann Reichardt, *Overture to Vittoria.*
Symphonies: Ferdinand Hérold, *No. 2 in D*; Johann Reichardt, *Schlachtsymphonie.*

1815
❋

Historical Highlights: Napoleon, escaping from Elba, is defeated at the Battle of Waterloo—sent to St. Helena; the Congress of Vienna ends—a Confederation of German States plus Austrian and Prussia is established; the Fourth Partition of Poland greatly benefits Russia; in the

United States, a treaty of commerce is signed with England; Stephen Decatur decisively defeats the Barbary Pirates; the *USS Fulton* becomes the world's first steam-powered warship.

Art and Literature Highlights: Births—artists Thomas Couture, Adolf von Menzel, writers Richard Dana, Jr., Anthony Trollope; Deaths—artists John Singleton Copley, Robert Fulton, poets Richard Alsop, Charles Crawford. Art—Canova's *Three Graces*, King's *Poor Artist's Cupboard*, Goys' *Third of May, 1808*; Literary—Austen's *Emma*, Brackenridge's *Modern Chivalry*, Pellico's *Francesca da Rimini*, Scott's *Guy Mannering*.

Musical Highlights

A. Births

Composers: Giovanni Bajetti (Italy)(?); Antonio Buzzola (Italy) March 2; Robert Franz (Germany) June 28; Josephine Lang (Germany) March 14; Robert Volkmann (Germany) April 6.

Singers: Charlotte Ann Birch (British soprano)(?); Carl Johann Formes (German bass) August 7; Sophie (Johanna) Löwe (German soprano) March 24; Gustave-Hippolyte Roger (French tenor) December 17; Fanny Salvini-Donatelli (Italian soprano); Maschinka (Schneider) Schubert (Estonian soprano) August 25; Giorgio Stigelli (German tenor); Rosine Stoltz (Italian mezzo-soprano) February 13; Giuseppina Strepponi (Italian soprano) September 8.

Performers: Jean-Delphin Alard (French violinist) March 8; Alexandre-Joseph Artôt (Belgian violinist) January 25; Halfdan Kjerulf (Norwegian pianist/composer) September 17; Henry Lazarus (British clarinetist) January 1; Ernesto Camillo Sivori (Italian violinist/composer) October 25.

Others: J. Lathrop Allen (American instrument maker) September 24; Alfred G. Badger (American flute maker); Johann Gotthilf Bärmig (German organ builder) May 13; Bartholf Senff (German publisher) September 2.

B. Deaths

Composers: Daniel Belknap (U.S.A.) October 31; Prosper-Didier Deshayes (France); Franz Götz (Bohemia) December; Jakub Jan Ryba (Czechoslovakia) April 8; Johann Lukas Schubaur (Germany) November 15.

Singers: Luigi Asioli (Italian tenor) November 17; Robert Hudson (British tenor) December 19; Frederick Charles Reinhold (British bass) September 28.

Performers: William Reeve (British organist/composer) June 22; Johann Peter Salomon (German violinist/impresario) November 25; Michel Woldemar (French violinist) December 19.

Others: José Mauricio (Portugese music theorist/composer) September 12; Jean Baptiste Mercadier (French music theorist) January 14.

C. **Debuts**
Singers: Pierre Ignace Begrez (French tenor—Paris); Thomas S. Cooke (Irish tenor—London); Giuditta Pasta (Italian soprano—Milan); Lucia Elizabeth Vestris (British contralto—London).

D. **New Positions**
Conductors: Karl Ludwig Hellwig (kapellmeister, Berlin Cathedral); Felice Alessandro Radicati (Bologna Orchestra); Andreas Jakob Romberg (kapellmeister, Gotha); Christian Rummel (Wiesbaden Court Orchestra).
Others: Carl Friedrich Zelter (music director, Friedrich-Wilhelm University).

E. **Prizes/Honors**
Prizes: François Benoist (Prix de Rome).
Honors: Domingo Arquimbeau (Accademia Filarmonica, Bologna); Henri-Montan Berton (French Institute); Charles S. Catel (French Institute); Frédéric Duvernoy (Legion of Honor); Sigismund von Neukomm (Legion of Honor).

F. **Biographical Highlights**
Ludwig van Beethoven, on the death of his brother, takes over the care of his nephew; Hector Berlioz learns the rudiments of flute and guitar from his father and begins composing; Ferdinand Hérold leaves Italy, visits in Vienna before returning permanently to Paris; E. T. A. Hoffmann returns to his old civil service job in Berlin; Giacomo Meyerbeer, in Italy, becomes enamoured of Rossini's operas and begins writing in the Italian vein; Gioacchino Rossini is engaged by the impresario Barbaia with an exclusive contract to write operas for Naples.

G. **Cultural Beginnings**
Performing Groups—Choral: Boston Handel and Haydn Society; Bremen Singakademie; Practical Musical Society (Trondheim).
Performing Groups—Instrumental: Bernische Musikgesellschaft (Switzerland); Styrian Music Society (Graz).
Educational: Drechsler's Music School (Vienna); Scuola Canto Corale (Parma).
Music Publishers: Adam and William Geib (Manhattan); Charles H. Gilfert (Charleston, South Carolina); Giuseppe Girard (Naples).
Music Publications: *North American Review.*
Performing Centers: Teatro Fiando (Milan).
Other: Backofen Instrument Factory (Darmstadt); Louis Drouet, flute maker (London); John Firth (Firth, Hall and Pond) piano maker

(New York); John Osborne, piano maker (Boston); Jean H. Pape, piano maker (Paris); Piston Valve (probable date of invention); Charles-Joseph Sax, instrument maker (Brussels).

H. Musical Literature
Giuseppe Bertini, *Dizionario storico-critico degli scrittori di musica*; Alexandre Choron, *Principes d'accompagnement des écoles d'Italie*; Johann Cramer, *Grosses praktische Pianoforte Schule*; Bohumír Dlabac, *Allgemeines historisches Künstler-lexicon für Böhmen I*; William Gardiner, *Sacred Melodies*; August von Kotzebue, *Opera Almanach*; August E. Müller, *Elementarbuch für Flötenspieler*; Gaspard Prony, *Rapport sur la nouvelle harpe à double mouvement*; William Shield, *Rudiments of Thorough Bass*.

I. Musical Compositions
Chamber Music:
    String Quartets: Franz Schubert, *Quartet No. 9 in g, D. 173*; Louis Spohr, *Three Quartets (E♭, C, f), Opus 29*.
    Sonata/Solos: Ludwig van Beethoven, *Two Cello Sonatas (C, D), Opus 102*; Adalbert Gyrowetz, *Violin Sonata, Opus 61*; Rodolphe Kreutzer, *Eighteen New Caprices or Etudes* (violin solo); Antonio Salieri, *Variations on "La Folia di Spagna"* (violin, piano).
    Ensembles: John Field, *Piano Quintet in A♭, Opus 34*; Ignaz Moscheles, *Sextet in E♭, Opus 35*; Carl Maria von Weber, *Clarinet Quintet in B♭, Opus 182*.
    Piano: Friedrich Kuhlau, *Variations on a Norwegian Air, Opus 15–Fantasia and Variations on Swedish Airs and Dances, Opus 45*; Franz Schubert, *Sonata in E, D. 157–Ten Variations in F, D. 156–Sonata in C, D. 279–Twelve Ecossaises, D. 299–Twelve Ländler, D. 681*; Carl Maria von Weber, *Variations on a Russian Theme, Opus 179*.
    Organ: Samuel S. Wesley, *Twelve Short Pieces for Organ*.
Choral/Vocal Music:
    Choral: Ludwig van Beethoven, *Calm Sea and Prosperous Voyage, Opus 112*; Luigi Cherubini, *Hymn to Spring* (cantata); Louis-Sébastien Lebrun, *Missa solemnis*; Franz Schubert, *Mass No. 2 in G, D. 167–Mass No. 3, D. 324*; Carl Maria von Weber, *Kampf und Sieg, Opus 44* (cantata).
    Vocal: Ludwig van Beethoven, *Twelve Songs*; Franz Schubert, *Der Erlkönig–Heidenröslein*; Carl Maria von Weber, *Scene and Aria, "Non Paventar, " Opus 51–Scene and Aria, "Ah, se Edmondo," Opus 52*.
    Musical Stage: Catterino Cavos, *Ivan Sussanin*; Hippolyte Chélard, *La casa da vendere*; Pietro Generali, *L'impostre*; Adalbert Gyrowetz, *Robert, oder Die Prüfung*; Ferdinand Hérold, *La gioventù di Enrico Quinto*; Johann N. Hummel, *Pimmalione*; Conradin Kreutzer, *Die Alpenhütte–Der Herr und sein Diener*; Rodolphe Kreutzer, *La princesse*

de Babylone–La perruque et la redingote; Karol Kurpiński, *Nadgroda;* Giacomo Meyerbeer, *Le bachelier de Salamanque* (unfinished); Giovanni Pacini, *La Rosina–Bettina vedova;* Ferdinando Paër, *L'eroismo in amore;* Johann Poissl, *Der Wettkampf zu Olympia;* Gioacchino Rossini, *Elizabeth, Queen of England–Torvaldo e Dorliska;* Franz Schubert, *Der Vierjährige Posten–Der Freunde von Salamanka–Claudine von Villa Bella–Adrast* (unfinished); Gaspare Spontini, *Le roi et la paix;* Giovanni Tadolini, *Le bestie in uomini;* Christian Uber, *Der frohe Tag;* Nicola Vaccai, *I solitari di Scozia;* Joseph Weigl, *L'imboscata.*

Orchestra/Band Music:
Concerted Music:
    Piano: Ignaz Moscheles, *La marche d'Alexandre, Opus 32.*
    Violin: Niccolò Paganini, *Concerto in e*(?).
    Other: Anton Reicha, *Clarinet Concerto*(?); Carl Maria von Weber, *Concertino in e, Opus 45, for Horn and Orchestra, Opus 188.*
Ballet/Incidental Music: Rodolphe Kreutzer, *L'heureux retour* (B).
Standard Works: Luigi Cherubini, *Concert Overture in G;* Cipriani Potter, *Overture in e.*
Symphonies: Luigi Cherubini, *Symphony in D;* Franz Schubert, *No. 2 in B♭, D. 125–No. 3 in D, D .200.*

1816

❄

Historical Highlights: The first known constitution for a German state is drawn up by Saxe-Weimar; Louis XVIII dissolves the Chamber of Deputies; Argentina declares its independence from Spain; in the United States, James Monroe is elected fifth president; Indiana is admitted to the Union as state number nineteen; Congress passes the country's first protective tariff; Baltimore, Maryland, becomes the first American city to have coal gas street lights.

Art and Literature Highlights: Births—artists John Kensett, Emmanuel Leutze, writers Charlotte Brontë, Wolfgang Müller, Bernhard Malmström; Deaths—writers Hugh Brackenridge, Richard Sheridan. Art—Cornelius' *Joseph and His Brothers,* Jarvis' *Oliver Hazard Perry at the Battle of Lake Erie,* Trumbull's *Surrender of General Burgoyne at Saratoga;* Literature—Byron's *Siege of Corinth,* Niccolini's *Nabucco,* Shelley's *Alastor.*

Musical Highlights

A. Births
    Composers: François-Emmanuel-Joseph Bazin (France) September 4; Karl Binder (Austria) November 29; William B. Bradbury (U.S.A.)

October 6; Achille Graffigna (Italy) May 5; Józef Poniatowski (Poland) February 20.

Conductors: Gustav Schmidt (Germany) September 1; Johannes Verhulst (Holland) March 19.

Singers: Marius-Pierre Audran (French tenor) September 26; Charlotte Cushman (American contralto) July 23; Jenny Dingelstedt (Bohemian soprano) March 4; Gaetano Fraschini (Italian tenor) February 16; Johanna Sophie Lowe (German soprano) March 24; Francilla Göhringer Pixis (German contralto) May 15.

Performers: William Sterndale Bennett (British pianist/composer) April 13; George Elvey (British organist) March 27; Carl Haslinger (Austrian pianist/publisher) June 11; Antoine-François Marmontel (French pianist/pedagogue) July 16; Edward Rimbault (British organist/music scholar) June 13; Edward Roeckel (German pianist) November 26; Carl Schröder (I) (German violinist) March 17.

Others: August Wilhelm Ambros (Austrian music historian) November 17; John Curwen (British music theorist/educator) November 14; Georg Gemünder (German-born violin maker) April 13; William Allen Johnson (American organ builder) October 27.

B. Deaths

Composers: Joseph Arquier (France) October; João José Baldi (Portugal) May 18; Giuseppe Jannaconi (Italy) March 16; Blas de Laserna (Spain) August 8; Giovanni Paisiello (Italy) June 5; Angelo Tarchi (Italy) August 19.

Singers: Anna Lucia de Amicis (Italian soprano); Matteo Babbini (Italian tenor) September 22; Karl Fribert (Austrian tenor) August 6; Giovanni Valesi (German tenor) January 10.

Performers: Rafael Anglés (Spanish organist/composer) February 9; Robert Cooke (British organist) August 13; Joseph Fiala (Bohemian oboist/composer) July 31; William Mahon (British oboist/violinist) May 3; Jean Paul Martini (French organist) February 10; Samuel Webbe, Sr. (British organist) May 25.

Others: Johann August Apel (German music author) August 9; Pierre Louis Ginguené (French music author) November 16; Pierre Leduc (French publisher) October; Antoine-Marcel Lemoine (French publisher) April 10; Joseph Franz Lobkowitz (Bohemian patron of the arts) December 15.

C. Debuts

Singers: Laure Cinti-Damoreau (French soprano—Paris); Giuseppina Ronzi de Begnis (Italian soprano—Bologna); Harriett Waylett (British soprano—Bath).

Performers: Philip Cipriani Potter (British pianist—London).

D. New Positions

Conductors: Georg F. Bischoff (kapellmeister, Hildesheim); Valentino Fioravanti (maestro di capella, St. Peter's, Rome); Joseph A. Gürrlich (kapellmeister, Berlin); Johann Nepomuk Hummel (kapellmeister, Stuttgart); Charles Frédéric Kreubé (Opèra-Comique, Paris); Sigismund von Neukomm (kapellmeister, Brazilian Court, Rio de Janeiro); Charles-Henri Plantade (maître de chapelle, Royal Chapel, Paris); John Powley (U.S. Marine Band); Pietro Terziani (maestro di capella, St. John Lateran); Nicola Zingarelli (maestro di cappella, Naples Cathedral).

Others: August Wilhelm Bach (organ, Marienkirche, Berlin); Dmitri Bortniansky (censor of composition, Russian Orthodox Churches); Luigi Cherubini (composition, Paris Conservatory).

E. Prizes/Honors

Honors: Friedrich Herschel (knighted); Francesco Morlacchi (Order of the Golden Spur).

F. Biographical Highlights

Ludwig van Beethoven sues his brother's wife over the custody of his nephew; Johann Nepomuk Maelzel builds the metronome on an idea of Winkel; Felix Mendelssohn visits Paris and studies with Marie Bigot; Giacomo Meyerbeer turns a visit into a nine-year stay in Italy; Sigismund von Neukomm travels to Rio with the duke of Luxembourg and stays for five years; Anton Schindler moves in with Beethoven and becomes his secretary; Franz Schubert gives up on teaching for good.

G. Cultural Beginnings

Performing Groups—Choral: Augsburg Harmoniegesellschaft; Euterpian Society (Hartford); Rheinischer Musikverein (Mannheim); The Sons of Handel (Dublin).

Performing Groups—Instrumental: Essener Bergkapelle; Società Filarmonica (Cremona).

Educational: Fitzwilliam Collection and Museum (donated to Cambridge University by the 7th Viscount Fitzwilliam); Mees Music Academy (Brussels).

Music Publishers: Allyn and Bacon (Philadelphia); William Blackwood and Sons (Edinburgh); Thomas Boosey Publishing House (London).

Performing Centers: New San Carlo Theater (Naples).

H. Musical Literature

João D. Bomtempo, *Piano Method*; Alexander Campbell, *Albyn's Anthology I*; Alexandre Choron, *Le Musicien Pratique*; John C. Clifton, *Theory of Harmony Simplified*; Ananias Davisson, *Kentucky Harmony*;

Xavier Désargus, *Cours Complet de Harpe*; Henri Gérard, *Méthode de Chant*; Thomas Hastings/S. Warriner, *Musica Sacra*; Peter Lichtenthal, *Harmony Treatise*; Giuseppe Serassi, *Sugli Organi*; George Thomson, *Select Collection of Original Irish Airs*.

I. Musical Compositions

Chamber Music:

String Quartets: František Krommer, *Three Quartets, Opus 92*; Antoine Reicha, *Ouverture générale pour les séances des quatuors*; Franz Schubert, *Quartet in E, D. 353*.

Sonata/Solos: Niccolò Paganini, *Violin Sonata in E, "Maria Luisa"*; Franz Schubert, *Three Violin Sonatinas (D, a, g), Opus 137*.

Ensembles: John Field, *Piano Quintet in A♭*; Johann N. Hummel, *Septet in d, Opus 74*; Niccolò Paganini, *Three Quartets (c, a/C, A), Opus 4–Three Quartets (D,C,d), Opus 5* (guitar, strings).

Piano: Ludwig van Beethoven, *Sonata No. 28 in A, Opus 101*; Alexandre Boëly, *Thirty Caprices, Opus 2*; João Domingos Bomtempo, *Sonata No. 8 in G–No. 9 in f–No. 10 in E♭, Opus 18*; Ignaz Moscheles, *Grand Sonata, Opus 41–Sonata in E♭, Opus 47* (four hands); Franz Schubert, *Twelve German Dances, D. 420–Six Ecossaises, D. 421–Sonata in F, D. 459*; Carl Maria von Weber, *Sonata No. 2 in A♭, Opus 199–No. 3 in d, Opus 206*.

Organ: Samuel Wesley, *Twelve Short Pieces with Added Voluntary*.

Choral/Vocal Music:

Choral: Luigi Cherubini, *Messe Solemnelle in C–Requiem in c–Le mariage de Salomon* (cantata); José Nunes García, *Requiem*; Jacques Halévy, *Les dernier moments du Tasse* (cantata); Giovanni Pacini, *La felicitá del Lago* (cantata); Johann N. Poissl, *Mass in A♭*; Franz Schubert, *Mass No. 4, D. 452–Requiem in E♭, D. 453*.

Vocal: Ludwig van Beethoven, *An die Ferne Geliebte, Opus 98–Twenty-Five Scotch Songs, Opus 108–Seventy-Five Irish Songs, Opus 223, 224, 225*; Luigi Cherubini, *Ave Maria*.

Musical Stage: Henry Bishop, *The Slave*; François Boieldieu, *La fête du village voisin*; Gaetano Donizetti, *Il Pigmalione*; Adalbert Gyrowetz, *Helene–Die beiden Eremiten–Der Gemahl von ungefähr*; E. T. A. Hoffmann, *Undine*; Nicolò Isouard, *Les deux maris–L'une pour l'autre*; Rodolphe Kreutzer, *Le maître et le valet–Les dieux rivaux*; Karol Kurpiński, *Kleine Schule für Männer–Superstition*; Carl Loewe, *Die Alpenhütte*; Heinrich Marschner, *Titus*; Étienne Méhul, *La journée aux aventures*; Giacomo Meyerbeer, *Glimori di Teolindo*; Francesco Morlacchi, *Il barbiere di Siviglia–La capricciosa pentita*; Wenzel Müller, *Der Fiaker als Marquis*; Giovanni Pacini, *L'ingenua*; Johann N. Poissl, *Die wie mir oder Alle betrügen*; Anton Reicha, *Natalie*; Gioacchino Rossini, *Il barbiere di Siviglia–Othello–La gazzetta*;

Johann Schmidt, *Die Alpenhütte*; Franz Schubert, *Die Burgschaft*; Joseph Weigl, *Margaritta d'Anjou*.

Orchestra/Band Music:

Concerted Music:

Piano: John Field, *Concerto No. 3 in E♭, Opus 32–No. 4 in E♭, Opus 28*; Johann N. Hummel, *Concerto No. 4 in E, Opus 110–No. 5 in G, Opus 72–No. 6 in a, Opus 85*; Daniel Steibelt, *Concerto No. 6 in g, "Le voyage au Mont St. Bernard"–No. 7 in e, "Grand Military Concerto."*

Violin: Franz Berwald, *Theme and Variations for Violin and Orchestra*; Louis Spohr, *Concerto, Opus 47*.

Ballet/Incidental Music: Henry R. Bishop, *A Midsummer Night's Dream* (IM); Adalbert Gyrowetz, *Die Hochzeit der Thetis und des Peleus* (B); Rudolphe Kreutzer, *Le carnaval de Venise* (B).

Standard Works: Franz Schubert, *Overture in B♭*.

Symphonies: Gaetano Donizetti, *Two Sinfonias in C*; Franz Schubert, *No. 4 in c, D. 417, "Tragic"–No. 5 in B♭, D. 485*.

1817

❋

Historical Highlights: Great Britain signs the Rush-Bagot Treaty with the United States limiting Naval forces of both countries on the Great Lakes; Liberia is founded in Africa as a home for returned slaves from the United States; in the United States, the American Society for the Return of Negroes to Africa is founded; Mississippi becomes state number twenty; the Seminole War with the Indians begins in Florida; work begins on the Erie Canal.

Art and Literature Highlights: Amsterdam Rijksmuseum opens. Births—artists Charles-François Daubigny, Erastus Palmer, writers Henry Thoreau, Alexei Tolstoy; Deaths—writers Jane Austen, Fredrick Douglass, Timothy Dwight, Mme. de Staël. Art—Allston's *Uriel in the Sun*, David's *Cupid and Psyche*, Krafft's *Battle of Leipzig*; Literature—Byron's *Manfred–The Lament of Tasso*, Moore's *Lalla Rookh*, Scott's *Rob Roy*.

Musical Highlights

A. Births

Composers: Salvatore Agnelli (Italy); Anton Berlijn (Holland) May 2; Niels Gade (Denmark) February 22; Teodulo Mabellini (Italy) April 2; Aimé (Louis) Maillart (France) March 24; Carlo Pedrotti (Italy) November 12.

Conductors: Édouard Delvedez (France) May 31.

Singers: Aloys Anders (Bohemian tenor) October 13; Elisa Blaes (Belgian soprano) November 2.

Performers: Charles Dancla (French violinist/composer) December 19; Antoine de Kontski (Polish pianist) October 27; Hermann Küster (German organist/author) July 14; Louis James Lefébure-Wély (French organist/composer) November 13; Emile Prudent (French pianist) February 3; Henry Brinley Richards (British pianist) November 13; Robert Schaab (German organist) February 28; Hippolyte-Prosper Seligmann (French cellist) July 28; Eugène Vivier (French horn virtuoso) December 4.

Others: Theodore Heintzman (German-born piano maker) May 19; Léon Charles Kreutzer (French critic/composer) September 23; Gustav Nottebohm (German musicologist) November 12; Alexander Wheelock Thayer (American music scholar) October 22.

B. Deaths

Composers: Bonaventura Furlanetto (Italy) April 6; Pietro Carlo Guglielmi (Italy) February 21; Otto Carl Kospoth (Germany) June 23; Friedrich Ludwig Kunzen (Germany) January 28; Etienne-Nicolas Méhul (France) October 18; Pedro Etienne Solère (Spain); Giovanni Zanotti (Italy) November 1.

Singers: Nancy Storace (British soprano) August 24.

Performers: Joseph Augustin Gürrlich (German contrabassist/composer) June 27; Justin Heinrich Knecht (German organist/music theorist) December 1; Wenzel Krumpholz (Bohemian violinist/composer) May 2; Pierre-Alexandre Monsigny (French cellist/composer) January 14; August Eberhard Müller (German organist) December 3; Johann Franz Sterkel (German organist) October 12; Franz Tausch (German clarinetist/composer) February 9.

Others: Ernst Christoph Leuckart (German publisher) February 2; Giuseppe Serassi, Jr. ("Il Giovane") (Italian organ builder) May 13.

C. Debuts

Singers: Carlo Angrisani (Italian bass—London); Luigia Boccabadati (Italian soprano—Italy); Alberico Curioni (Italian tenor—Milan); Christian Wilhelm Fischer (German bass—Leipzig); Franz Hauser (Bohemian baritone—Prague).

Performers: Wilhelm Bernhard Molique (German violinist—Vienna); Giovanni Puzzi (Italian horn virtuoso—London).

D. New Positions

Conductors: Johannes Amon (kapellmeister, Prince of Oettingen-Wallerstein); Ramòn Félix Cuéllar y Altarriba (maestro de capilla, Ovieto Cathedral); Traugott Eberwein (kapellmeister, Rudolstadt); Pietro Generali (Teatro Santa Cruz, Barcelona); Giuseppe Mosca (Teatro Carolino, Palermo); Giovanni Agostino Perotti (St. Mark's, Venice); Friedrich Silcher (music director, University of Tübingen);

Louis Spohr (Frankfurt Opera); Carl Maria von Weber (German Opera, Dresden).
Others: François Boieldieu (composition, Paris Conservatory); Luigi Palmerini (organ, S. Petronio, Bologna).

E. Prizes/Honors
Prizes: Désiré-Alexandre Batton (Prix de Rome).
Honors: François Boieldieu (French Academy); William Shield (Master of the King's Music).

F. Biographical Highlights
Frédéric Chopin, age eight, makes his first appearance at a private recital playing a concerto by Gyrowetz; Gaetano Donizetti goes to Bergamo and begins writing opera; Mikhail Glinka is sent to the Pedagogic Institute in St. Petersburg; Anthony Heinrich moves to Kentucky; Felix Mendelssohn begins composition study with Zelter; Franz Schubert leaves home to follow the Bohemian lifestyle.

G. Cultural Beginnings
Performing Groups—Choral: German Opera of Dresden; Gesang-verein zu Danzig; Halifax Choral Society (England); Städischer Singverein Barmen (Wuppertal).
Performing Groups—Instrumental: Kraków Society of Friends of Music; Warsaw Amateur Music Society.
Educational: Conservatorium der Gesellschaft der Musikfreunde (Vienna); Institution Royale de Musique Classique et Religieuse (Paris).
Music Publications: *Edinburgh Monthly Magazine* (*Blackwood's Magazine*).
Other: Franz Feller and Sons, organ builders (Königswald); Franklin Music Warehouse (Boston); König and Bauer, steam press manufacturers (Würzburg).

H. Musical Literature
Alexandre Choron, *Méthode concertante de musique à plusiers parties*; Thomas Hastings, *The Musical Reader*; Friedrich Hofmeister, *Handbuch der musikalischen Literatur*; George K. Jackson, *The Choral Companion*; Joubert de La Salette, *De la notation musicale en général, et en particulier de celle du système grec*; Bernhard Natorp, *Über den Gesang in den Kirchen der Protestanten*; Karl G. Umbreit, *Die Evangelischen Kirchenmelodien . . .* ; Gottfried Weber, *Versuch einer geordneten Theorie der Tonsetzkunst I.*

I. Musical Compositions
Chamber Music:
   String Quartets: Gaetano Donizetti, *No. 1 in E♭*; Louis Spohr, *Quartet in F, "Quator brillant," Opus 43*.
   Sonata/Solos: Franz Schubert, *Violin Sonata in A, Opus 162*.

Ensembles: Ludwig van Beethoven, *String Quintet in c, Opus 104–Fugue in D, Opus 137* (string quintet); Gaetano Donizetti, *Piano Trio in E♭*; Ferdinand Hérold, *Caprice, Opus 8* (piano quintet); František Krommer, *2 String Quintets, Opus 70,80–Piano Quintet No. 1, Opus 95*; Anton Reicha, *Six Wind Quintets, Opus 88–Octet in E♭, Opus 96* (woodwinds, string quartet); Franz Schubert, *String Trio in B♭, D. 471.*

Piano: Frédéric Chopin, *Polonaise in g (No. 1)–Polonaise in B♭ (No. 2)*; Muzio Clementi, *Gradus ad Parnassum*; John Field, *Nocturnes No. 4 in A–No. 5 in B♭–No. 6 in F*; Johann N. Hummel, *Variations in A, Opus 76*; Carl Loewe, *Abend-Fantasie, Opus 11*; Franz Schubert, *Piano Sonata in a, D. 537–in A♭, D. 557–in e, D. 566–in E♭, D. 568–in B, D. 575*; Carl Maria von Weber, *Seven Variations on a Gypsy Song, Opus 55.*

Choral/Vocal Music:

Choral: Luigi Cherubini, *Requiem in c*; Jacques Halévy, *La mort d'Adonis* (cantata); Francesco Morlacchi, *Isaaco, Figura di Redentore* (oratorio); Johann N. Poissl, *Méhuls Gedächtnisfeyer–Mass in E♭*; Georg "Abbé" Vogler, *Veni sancte spiritus in B♭*; Carl Maria von Weber, *L'Accoglianza* (cantata).

Vocal: Ludwig van Beethoven, *Twenty-Six Welsh Songs, Opus 226*; Franz Schubert, *Die Forelle–Death and the Maiden*; Louis Spohr, *Six Songs for Male Voices, Opus 44.*

Musical Stage: Michele Carafa, *Ifigenia in Tauride*; Franz Danzi, *Turandot–L'Abbé di l'Attaignant*; Gaetano Donizetti, *Olimpiade–L'ira d'Achille*; Pietro Generali, *Rodrigo di Valenza*; Adalbert Gyrowetz, *Die beiden Savoyarden*; Ferdinand Hérold, *La clochette–Les rosières*; Daniil Kashin, *The One-day Reign of Nourmahal*; Friedrich Kuhlau, *Die Zauberharfe, Opus 27*; Karol Kurpiński, *Jan Kochanowski*; Etienne Méhul, *Valentine de Milan*; Giacomo Meyerbeer, *Romilda e Costanze*; Francesco Morlacchi, *La semplicetta di Pirna–Laodicea*; Giovanni Pacini, *Adelaide e Comingio–Il matrimonio per procra*; Johann Poissl, *Nittetis*; Bernhard Romberg, *Rittertreue*; Gioacchino Rossini, *La gazza ladra–Adelaide di Borgogna–La Cenerentola–Armida*; Peter Winter, *Maometto II.*

Orchestra/Band Music:

Concerted Music:

Piano: John Field, *Concerto No. 5 in C, "L'incendie par l'orage," Opus 39.*

Violin: Franz Berwald, *Concerto in E for Two Violins*; Niccolò Paganini, *No. 1 in E♭/D, Opus 6.*

Other: Gaetano Donizetti, *Concertino in G for English Horn and Orchestra*; Johann N. Poissl, *Cello Concerto.*

Ballet/Incidental Music: Carl Maria von Weber, *Donna Diana* (IM)–*König Yngurd* (IM).

Standard Works: Franz Schubert, *Overture in the Italian Style in D–Overture in the Italian Style in C–Overture in d.*
Symphonies: Franz Danzi, *No. 4 in B♭–No. 5 in D*; Gaetano Donizetti, *Three Sinfonias in D–Sinfonia in g.*

1818

Historical Highlights: San Martin leads Chile to independence from Spain; German states of Baden and Bavaria receive constitutional governments; all occupation troops are removed from France; in the United States, Congress approves the Stars and Stripes as the official U.S. flag—the Flag Act provides for an additional star for each new state; General Andrew Jackson puts down the Indian uprising ending the First Seminole War.

Art and Literature Highlights: Prado Museum opens in Madrid. Births—Wilhelm Camphausen, Charles Deas, writers Emily Brontë, Eliza Cook, Charles de Lisle, Ivan Turgenev; Deaths—writers David Humphreys, Matthew Lewis, artist Heinrich Füger. Art—Allston's *Elijah Fed by the Ravens*, Gericault's *Raft of the Medusa*; Literature—Keats' *Endymion*, Mary Shelley's *Frankenstein*, Percy Shelley's *Prometheus Unbound*.

Musical Highlights

A. Births
Composers: Charles Gounod (France) June 17; Jacob Axel Josephson (Sweden) March 27; Paul Mériel (France) January 4.
Conductors: Georges Bousquet (France) March 12; Heinrich Esser (Germany) July 15.
Singers: Marianna Barbieri-Nini (Italian soprano) February 18; Moritz Deutsch (German tenor) December 16; Livia Frege (German soprano) June 13; Erminia Frezzolini (Italian soprano) March 27; Anton Mittewurzer (Austrian baritone) April 12; Maria Dolores Nau (American soprano) March 18; Clara Novello (British soprano) June 10; Sims Reeves (British tenor) September 26.
Performers: Jacques Louis Battmann (French organist) August 25; Antonio Bazzini (Italian violinist) March 11; Giulio Briccialdi (Italian flutist/composer) March 2; Francis H. Brown (American pianist/composer) April 6; Alexander Dreyschock (Bohemian pianist) October 15; Félix Godefroid (Belgian harpist) July 24; Stefano Golinelli (Italian pianist) October 26; Edward John Hopkins (British organist) June 30; Samuel P. Jackson (American organist) February 5; Hubert Ferdinand Kufferath (German violinist/

conductor) June 11; Theodor Kullak (German pianist/conductor) September 12.

Others: Abramo Basevi (Italian music critic) November 29; Carl Engel (German music historian) July 6; Friedrich Ladegast (German organ builder) August 30; Henry Charles Litolff (British publisher) February 6.

B. Deaths

Composers: Agostino Accorimboni (Italy) August 13; Giuseppe Gazzaniga (Italy) February 1; Nicolò Isouard (France) March 23; José Pons (Spain) August 2.

Singers: Elizabeth Billington (British soprano) August 25; Marie-Jeanne Trial (French soprano) February 13.

Performers: Giuseppe Antonio Capuzzi (Italian violinist/composer) March 28; Jean-Pierre Duport (French cellist) December 31; Leopold Kozeluch (Bohemian pianist/composer) May 7; Pierre La Houssaye (French violinist).

Others: Johann Nikolaus Forkel (German music historian) March 20; John (Johann) Geib (German-born piano maker) October 30; Franz Gleissner (German lithographer) September 18.

C. Debuts

Singers: Jean Baptiste Chollet (French tenor—as baritone); Frances Corri (Scottish soprano—London); Antonio Tamburini (Italian baritone—Cento).

Performers: Felix Mendelssohn (German pianist—Berlin, age nine); Eduard Rietz (German violinist—Berlin); Charles Thibault (French-born pianist—New York).

D. New Positions

Conductors: Giuseppi Baini (maestro di cappella, St. Peter's, Rome); Theobald Böhm (Munich Court); Ramón Carnicer (Coliseo Theater Orchestra, Barcelona); Ferdinand Gassner (music director, Gneissen University); Johann August Heinroth (music director, University of Göttingen); Conradin Kreutzer (kapellmeister, Donaueschingen); Franz Krommer (kapellmeister, court composer, Vienna); Stefano Pavesi (maestro di capella, Crema Cathedral); Jan Václav Voříšek (Gesellschaft der Musikfreunde, Vienna).

E. Prizes/Honors

Honors: François Boieldieu (French Institute); Gaspare Spontini (State Pension by Louis XVIII).

F. Biographical Highlights

George Frederick Handel's *Messiah* receives its first American performance by the New York Handel and Haydn Society; Oliver

Holden is elected to the South Carolina House of Representatives; Frédéric Kalkbrenner simplifies and promotes Logier's Chiroplast; Lowell Mason founds the Savannah Missionary Society; Franz Schubert becomes music master to the Esterházy family during the summer months; Giovanni Viotti fails in the wine business and returns to Paris.

G. Cultural Beginnings
Performing Groups—Choral: Bavarian State Opera (Munich); Frankfurt Cäcilienverein; Königsberg Singverein.
Performing Groups—Instrumental: Bradford Harmonic Society.
Educational: Académie de Musique et de Chant (Brussels); Royal Harmonic Institution (London).
Music Publishers/Dealers: Cappi and Diabelli (Vienna); Dumont-Schauberg Verlag (Cologne).
Music Publications: *Amphion* (The Netherlands); *Quarterly Musical Magazine and Review.*
Performing Centers: National Theater (Munich); Teatro Nuovo (Pesaro); Théâtre d'Orléans (rebuilt—New Orleans).

H. Musical Literature
François Aimon, *Connaissances préliminaires de l'harmonie*; John Burrowes, *The Pianoforte Primer*; Thomas Busby, *A Grammar of Music*; Alexandre Choron, *Méthode de plain-chant*; Gottfried Dlabacz, *Allgemeines historisches Künstlerlexikon für Böhmen*; Giacomo G. Ferrari, *Breve trattato di canto italiano*; Pierre Galin, *Exposition d'une nouvelle méthode pour l'enseignement de la musique*; Johann Bernhard Logier, *Chiroplast Méthod de Piano*; Ignaz von Mosel, *Die Tonkunst in Wien während der letzten fünf Dezennien*; Anton Reicha, *Cours de composition musicale*; Isaac Watts, *The Psalms of David*; Johann Gottlob Werner, *Harmonielehre I.*

I. Musical Compositions
Chamber Music:
String Quartets: Gaetano Donizetti, *No. 2 in A–No. 3 in c–No. 4 in D*; Louis Spohr, *Three Quartets (C, e, f), Opus 45.*
Ensembles: Sigismund von Neukomm, *String Quintet, "Une fête de village en Suisse."*
Piano: Ludwig van Beethoven, *Piano Piece in B♭, Opus 172*; João Domingos Bomtempo, *Sonata No. 11 in E♭ (Grande Sonate)*; August E. Müller, *Three Caprices, Opus 41*; Cipriani Potter, *Sonata in C, Opus 1–in D, Opus 3–in e, Opus 4–Fantasia and Fugue in c, Opus 22* (two pianos); Franz Schubert, *Fantasy in C, "Grazer Fantasie," D. 605–Sonata in C, D .613–Sonata in f, D. 625*; Jan Václav Voříšek, *Twelve Rhapsodies, Opus 1.*

Choral/Vocal Music:
Choral: Ludwig van Beethoven, *O Hoffnung;* Vincenzo Bellini, *Magnificat;* Luigi Cherubini, *Messe Solemnelle in E;* Simon Mayr, *Samuele* (oratorio); Francesco Morlacchi, *Messa a capella;* Franz Schubert, *Deutsche Trauermesse, D. 621;* Carl Maria von Weber, *Missa Sancta No. 1–Natur und Liebe* (cantata)–*Jubilee Cantata, Opus 58.*
Vocal: Gaetano Donizetti, *Il ritorno di prima vera* (cantata); Georg C. Grosheim, *Teutscher Gedichte, Vol 8;* Franz Gruber, *Silent Night* (Christmas song); Carl Loewe, *Three Songs, Opus 1* (includes *The Erlking*); Carl Maria von Weber, *Scene and Aria, "Was sag ich," Opus 56–Six Songs, Opus 54.*
Musical Stage: François Boieldieu, *Le petit chaperon rouge;* Michele Carafa, *Berenice in Siria–Elisabetta in Derbyshire;* Catterino Cavos, *Dobrynia Nikitich;* Gaetano Donizetti, *Enrico di Borgogna–Una follia;* Józef Elsner, *King Lokietek;* Pietro Generali, *Il servo padrone–La cecchina sonatrice;* Adalbert Gyrowetz, *Il finto Stanislao;* Ferdinand Hérold, *Le premier venu;* Nicolò Isouard, *Aladin* (completed by A. Benincori)–*Une nuit de Gustave Waso* (finished by Gasse); Conradin Kreutzer, *Orestes;* Karol Kurpiński, *Der Prinz Czaromys;* Heinrich Marschner, *Heinrich IV;* Francesco Morlacchi, *Gianni di Parigi;* Giovanni Pacini, *Atala–Il barone di Dolsheim;* Johann Poissl, *Issipile;* Gioacchino Rossini, *Mosè in Egitto–Ricciardo e Zoraide–Adina;* Antonio Salieri, *Cyrus und Astyages;* Johann Schmidt, *Das Fischermädchen;* Giovanni Tadolini, *Tamerlano;* Nicola Vaccai, *Il lupo di Ostenda;* Joseph Weigl, *Die Nachtigall und die Rabe;* Peter Winter, *Etelinda.*
Orchestra/Band Music:
Concertos: Franz Danzi, *Symphonie concertante in B♭, Opus 47.*
Ballet/Incidental Music: Rodolphe Kreutzer, *La servante justifiée* (B); Saverio Mercadante, *Il servo balordo* (B)–*Il califfo generoso* (B)–*Il flauto incantato* (B); Bernhard Romberg, *Daphne und Agathokles* (B); Carl Maria von Weber, *Das Haus Anglade* (IM)–*König von Frankreich* (IM)–*Lieb' um Liebe* (IM).
Standard Works: Johann A. André, *Overture, Die Hussiten vor Naumburg, Opus 36;* Heinrich Marschner, *Overture on Hungarian National Airs;* Carl Maria von Weber, *Jubel Overture, Opus 59.*
Symphonies: Gaetano Donizetti, *Sinfonia in d;* Franz Schubert, *No. 6 in C, D. 589.*

1819

Historical Highlights: Singapore is founded by the British East India Co.; Simón Bolívar defeats the Spanish in Venezuela; the Carlsbad De-

crees attempt to bar liberalism from all European universities; in the United States, the Panic of 1819 brings on a four-year depression; Alabama becomes state number twenty-two; the Florida territory is bought from Spain for $5,000,000; Fort Snelling (Minneapolis) is built.
Art and Literature Highlights: Births—artists Gustave Courbet, Martin Heade, writers Georg Eliot, James Russell Lowell, Herman Melville, Walt Whitman; Deaths—artist Samuel Bird, writers August Kotzebue, John Ruskin, John Wolcot. Art—Sully's *Washington at the Passage of the Delaware*, Thorvaldsen's *Christ and the Apostles*; Literature—Byron's *Mazeppa–Don Juan*, Irving's *The Sketch Book*, Scott's *The Bride of Lammermoor*.

Musical Highlights

A. Births
Composers: Franz Abt (Germany) December 22; Théodore Gouvy (France) July 5; Stanislaw Moniuszko (Poland) May 5; Jacques Offenbach (Germany-France) June 20; Franz von Suppé (Austria) April 18; Isaac Baker Woodbury (U.S.A.) October 23.
Conductors: Charles Hallé (England) April 11; Jules-Étienne Pasdeloup (French conductor) September 15.
Singers: Giuseppina Brambilla (Italian contralto); Jeanne Anaïs Castellan (French soprano) October 26; Elizabeth Taylor Greenfield (American soprano)(?); Kathinka Heinefetter (German soprano) September 12; Henriette Nissen (Swedish soprano) March 12; Susan Sunderland (British soprano) April 30; Sophie Anne Thillon (British soprano).
Performers: Charles-Louis Hanon (French pianist/pedagogue) July 2; Anna Robena Laidlaw (British pianist) April 30; Hubert Léonard (Belgian violinist) April 7; Carl Mikuli (Polish pianist) October 20; Edwin George Monk (British organist) December 13; Clara (Wieck) Schumann (German pianist) September 13; Elizabeth Stirling (British organist/composer) February 26; Gustave J. Stoeckel (German-born organist/composer) November 9; Samuel Parkman Tuckerman (American organist/composer) February 11.
Others: Gustave Chouquet (Frenc music author) April 16; Ferdinand Peter Laurencin (Austrian music author) October 15; Carl Ferdinand Pohl (German music author) September 6; Heinrich Joseph Vincent (German music theorist) February 23; Richard Storrs Willis (American music author/composer) February 10.

B. Deaths
Composers: Georg Druschetzky (Bohemia) September 6; János Fusz (Hungary) March 9; Antonio-Leal Moreira (Portugal) November 21; Simon Peter (Holland-U.S.A.) May 29.

Singers: Franz Christian Hartig (German tenor); Josepha Weber (German soprano) December 29.
Performers: Josef Bähr (Austrian clarinetist) August 7; Jean-Louis Duport (French cellist) September 7; Charles H. Florio (British flutist); Casper Fürstenau (German flutist) May 11; Giovanni Battista Gaiani (Italian organist) October 13; Francisco Galeazzi (Italian violinist) January; Karl Haack (German violinist) September 28; Louis Luc Loiseau de Persuis (French violinist/composer) December 20; Francesco Petrini (French harpist); Nicolas Séjan (French organist/composer) March 16; Jean-François Tapray (French organist/composer).
Others: Robert Birchall (British publisher) December 19; Ernst Ludwig Gerber (German lexicographer) June 30; Carlo Gervasoni (Italian music theorist/historian) June 4; Giacomo Morelli (Italian musicologist) May 5.

C. **Debuts**
Singers: Eduard Devrient (German baritone—Berlin); Ann Maria Tree (British mezzo-soprano—London).
Performers: Ole Bull (Norwegian violinist—Bergen, age nine); Georg Hellmesberger, Sr. (Austrian violinist—Vienna); Luigi Legnani (Italian guitarist—Milan).

D. **New Positions**
Conductors: Francisco Andreví y Castellar (music director, Valencia Cathedral); Johan Fredrik Berwald (Stockholm Royal Orchestra); Pietro Generali (maestro di capella, Novara Cathedral); Johann N. Hummel (kapellmeister, Weimar); Karol Kurpiński (kapellmeister, Polish Royal Court); Peter Joseph von Lindpainter (Stuttgart Court Orchestra); Giuseppe Niccolini (maestro di cappella, Piacenza Cathedral).
Others: Thomas Greatorex (organ, Westminster Abbey); Hippolyte Mompou (organ, Tours Cathedral); François Louis Perne (librarian, Paris Conservatory); Giuseppe Siboni (director, Copenhagen Opera/Conservatory); Giovanni Battista Viotti (director, Paris Opera).

E. **Prizes/Honors**
Prizes: Jacques Halévy (Prix de Rome).

F. **Biographical Highlights**
Vincenzo Bellini enters Naples Conservatory for his first professional music instruction; August von Kotzebue is stabbed to death by a university student; Carl Loewe makes a concert tour of Germany before settling down in Stettin; Felix Mendelssohn, age ten, enters the Berlin Singakademie and begins composing; Franz Schubert fails to gain Goethe's approval for the setting of his poems;

Louis Spohr, following the great success of his opera *Zemire und Azor*, resigns his Frankfurt directorship.

G. Cultural Beginnings

Performing Groups—Choral: Freunde der Religiösen Gesanges (Hamburg Singakademie); Gotha Singverein; Neue Liedertafel von Berlin; Oxford Choral Society; Rostocker Singakademie; Spirituel-Concerte (Vienna).

Educational: Library of the Gesellschaft der Musik Freunde, Vienna; Pastou Sīnging School (Paris).

Music Publishers: Paterson and Sons (Edinburgh).

Music Publications: *The Indicator; London Magazine.*

Performing Centers: Darmstadt Theater (New).

Other: Beethoven Musical Society of Portland, Maine; Dubois and Stodart, piano manufacturers (New York); Haydn Society of Cincinnati; Irish Harp Society (Belfast); Klemm and Brother, instrument dealers (Philadelphia).

H. Musical Literature

John Burrowes, *The Thorough-bass Primer*; Thomas Busby, *General History of Music*; Alexandre Choron, *Exposition élémentaire des principes de la Musique*; Friedrich von Drieberg, *Aufschlüss über die musik der Griechen*; Henri Gérard, *Considérations sur la Musique . . .* ; Benjamin Jacob, *National Psalmody*; Jean Jousse, *Lectures on Thoroughbass*; Joseph Kemp, *A New System of Musical Education*; John Relfe, *Remarks on the Present State of Musical Instruction*; Félix Savart, *Mémoire sur la Construction des Instruments à Cordes et Archet*; Oliver Shaw, *Melodia Sacra*.

I. Musical Compositions

Chamber Music:

String Quartets: Gaetano Donizetti, *No. 5 in e–No. 6 in g–No. 7 in f–No. 8 in B♭*; Louis Spohr, *Quartet in b, Opus 61*.

Sonata/Solos: Ludwig van Beethoven, *Six Easy Variations, Opus 105* (violin/flute, piano); Alexandre Boëly, *Seven Variations, Opus 3* (cello, piano); Gaetano Donizetti, *Flute Sonata in d–Violin Sonata in f*; Ignaz Moscheles, *Flute Sonata in A, Opus 44*; Louis Spohr, *Sonata for Harp and Violin in A♭*.

Ensembles: Franz Berwald, *Quartet in E♭ for Piano and Winds*; Johann N. Hummel, *Piano Trio in E, Opus 83*; Anton Reicha, *Six Wind Quintets (C, a, D, g, A, c), Opus 91–Six Wind Quintets (C, f, F, D, E♭, G), Opus 99*; Franz Schubert, *Piano Quintet in A, "The Trout," D. 667*; Carl Maria von Weber, *Trio, Opus 259* (piano, flute, cello).

Piano: Ludwig van Beethoven, *Sonata No. 29 in B♭, Opus 106, "Hammerklavier"*; Gaetano Donizetti, *Three Sonatas (E♭, C, D)*; Johann N. Hummel, *Sonata in f♯, Opus 81*; Friedrich Kuhlau, *Three*

Sonatinas (C, G, F), Opus 20; Carl Loewe, Sonate brillante in E♭, Opus 41; Ignaz Moscheles, Französisches Rondo, Opus 48 (violin, piano)–Sonate Mélancholique in f♯, Opus 49; Franz Schubert, Sonata in c♯, D. 655–Sonata in A, D. 664; Carl Maria von Weber, Invitation to the Dance: Rondo Brillante (orchestrated 1841 by Berlioz)–Eight Pieces, Opus 6 (piano, four hands).

Choral/Vocal Music:
Choral: Johann A. André, Missa Solemnis, Opus 43; João Domingos Bomtempo, Requiem in c, "In Memory of Camöes"; Luigi Cherubini, Solemn Mass in G; Gaetano Donizetti, Magnificat in D; Jacques Halévy, Herminie (cantata—Prix de Rome); Gioacchino Rossini, Partenope (cantata); Antonio Salieri, Te Deum in C; Johann Schenk, Der Mai–Die Huldigung (cantatas); Carl Maria von Weber, Mass in G, Opus 76.

Vocal: Gaetano Donizetti, Salve Regina in F; Friedrich Kuhlau, Twelve Songs, Opus 23; Carl Maria von Weber, Fourteen Songs, Opus 64 and 71.

Musical Stage: Juan Arriaga, Les esclavos felices; Daniel Auber, Le testament et les billets-doux; Ramón Carnicer, Adele di Lusignano; Charles Catel, L'Officier enlevé; Gaetano Donizetti, Il falegname di Livónia; Pietro Generali, Adelaide di Borgogna; Adalbert Gyrowetz, Aladin; Ferdinand Hérold, L'amour platonique–Les troqueurs; Conradin Kreutzer, Cordelia; Karol Kurpiński, The Castle of Czorsztyn; Heinrich Marschner, Saidar und Zulima–Das stille Volk; Saverio Mercadante, L'apoteosi d'Ercole; Giacomo Meyerbeer, Semiramide Riconosciuta–Emma di Resburgo; Giovanni Pacini, La sposa fedele–L'omaggio più grato; Gioacchino Rossini, Ermione–La donna del lago–Bianca e Falliero–Eduardo e Cristina; Franz Schubert, Die Zwillingsbrüder; Louis Spohr, Zemire und Azor; Gaspare Spontini, Olimpie; Alexei Vertovsky, Grandmother's Parrot.

Orchestra/Band Music:
Concerted Music:
Piano: John Field, Concerto No. 6 in C, Opus 49; Johann H. Hummel, Concerto No. 7 in b, Opus 89; Conradin Kreutzer, Concerto No. 1 in B♭, Opus 42(?); Ignaz Moscheles, Concerto No. 1 in F, Opus 45.
Violin: Niccolò Paganini, Introduction and Variations on Rossini's "La Cenerentola," Opus 12–Introduction and Variations on Rossini's "Tancredi," Opus 13–Introduction and Variations on Rossini's "Mosè."
Other: Savierio Mercadante, Six Flute Concertos(?).
Ballet/Incidental Music: Henry R. Bishop, A Comedy of Errors (B); Saverio Mercadante, I portughesi nelle India (B).
Standard Works: Franz Schubert, Overture in e, D. 648; Louis Spohr, Concert Overture in F.

Symphonies: Muzio Clementi, *Symphony in D, Opus 44*; Cipriani Potter, *No. 1 in g.*

1820

❄

Historical Highlights: King George III of England dies and is succeeded by George IV; revolutions take place in Portugal and Spain—King Ferdinand VII restores the Spanish Constitution; the continent of Antartica is discovered; in the United States, the Census shows a population of 9,683,000, a thirty-three percent increase in ten years; James Monroe is reelected president; the Missouri Compromise limits slavery in the Louisiana Purchase Territory.

Art and Literature Highlights: Venus de Milo statue is discovered. Births—writers Charles M. Barras, Anne Brontë, artist Josef Mánes; Deaths—Ferdinand Jagerman, Benjamin West, writers William Hayley, James Ogilvie. Art—Fisher's *Great Horseshoe Falls, Niagara*, Goya's *The Giant*, Trumbull's *The Surrender of Cornwallis at Yorktown*; Literature—Blake's *Jerusalem*, Lamartine's *Méditations Poétiques*, Scott's *Ivanhoe*.

Musical Highlights

A. Births

Composers: Karl Eckert (Germany) December 7; Luther Orlando Emerson (U.S.A.) August 3; George Frederick Root (U.S.A.) August 30; Hans Schläger (Austria) December 5.

Conductors: Gustaf Adolf Heintze (Sweden) October 1; Friedrich Lux (Germany) November 24.

Singers: Édouard Gassier (French baritone); Lodovico Graziani (Italian tenor) November 14; Jenny Lind (Swedish soprano) October 6; Louis-Henri Obin (French bass) August 4; Elizabeth Poole (British mezzo-soprano) April 5; Enrico Tamberlik (Italian tenor) March 16; Willoughby Hunter Weiss (British tenor) April 2.

Performers: Jules Armingaud (French violinist) May 3; Michal Bergson (Polish pianist) May 20; Robert Burton (British organist/conductor) September 1; George Cooper (British organist) July 7; Alexander Fesca (German pianist/composer) May 22; Louis Köhler (German pianist) September 5; Ange-Conrad Prumier (French harpist) January 5; Georg Vierling (German organist) September 5; Henri Vieuxtemps (Belgian violinist) February 17.

Others: Gustav Auguste Besson (French instrument maker); Fanny Crosby (American hymn writer) March 24; George Grove (British musicographer) August 13; Hiram Murray Higgins (American publisher) October 13; Elias Howe (American publisher); Stéphen

Morelot (French church music scholar) January 12; Alexander Serov (Russian music critic/composer) January 23.

B. Deaths

Composers: Henri Hamal (Belgium) September 17; Samuel Holyoke (U.S.A.) February 7.

Singers: Giuseppe Naldi (Italian bass) December 14; Matthäus Stegmayer (Austrian singer/composer) May 10.

Performers: Josepha Barbara Auernhammer (Austrian pianist) January 30; Marie Bigot (French pianist/composer) September 16; Joseph Corfe (British organist) July 29; Joseph Gehot (Belgian violinist)(?); Anton Kraft (Austrian cellist) August 28; Ludwig Wenzel Lachnith (Bohemian horn virtuoso) October 3; János Lavotta (Hungarian violinist) August 11; Felice Alessandre Radicati (Italian violinist) March 19; Joseph Weigl, Sr. (German cellist/composer) January 25. Anton Wranitzky (Czech violinist) August 6.

Others: François Callinet (French organ builder) May 21; Bohumír Jan Dlabač (Bohemian music scholar) February 4.

C. Debuts

Performers: Aline Bertrand (French harpist—Paris); Franz Liszt (Hungarian pianist—Raiding, age nine).

D. New Positions

Conductors: Georg Abraham Schneider (Royal Theater, Berlin); Gaspare Spontini (Berlin); Henri-Justin Valentino (Paris Opera).

Others: William Beale (organ, Trinity College, Cambridge); Lowell Mason (organ, Independent Presbyterian Church, Savannah, Georgia).

E. Prizes/Honors

Prizes: Aimé Ambroise Leborne (Prix de Rome).

Honors: Franz S. Kandler (Accademia Filarmonica, Bologna).

F. Biographical Highlights

Ludwig van Beethoven wins his lawsuit against his sister-in-law for the custody of his nephew; Hector Berlioz, at his father's insistence, reluctantly begins the study of medicine; Franz Liszt begins piano study with Czerny and gives his first recital; Louis Spohr makes the first known use of the baton in a concert in London; Carl Maria von Weber makes a concert tour with his wife.

G. Cultural Beginnings

Performing Groups—Choral: Bamberg Musikverein; Cologne Singverein; Quebec Harmonic Society.

Performing Groups—Instrumental: Orchestra of the Militia of the Free Town of Kraków; Philharmonic Society of Bethlehem (Pennsylvania).
Educational: Musikalische Bildungsanstalt (Berlin); Toulouse Conservatory of Music.
Music Publishers: Elwer and Co. (London); Trautwein Music Publishers (Berlin).
Music Publications: *Euterpeiad, or Musical Intelligencer* (U.S.A.); *National Gazette and Literary Register*; *New Monthly Magazine and Literary Journal*; *The Scottish Minstrel*.
Other: Charles F. Gand, violin maker (Paris); William Hall, piano maker (Firth, Hall and Pond, New York); Musical Fund Society (Philadelphia); Eberhard Walcker, organ builder (Ludwigsburg).

H. Musical Literature

Dionysio Aguado, *Estudios para la Guitarra*; Carl Almenraeder, *Traité sur le perfectionnement du basson avec deux tableaux*; François Blaze, *De l'opéra en France*; Allen Carden, *Missouri Harmony*; James Carrell, *Songs of Zion*; Uri Hill, *Solfeggio Americano . . .*; Edward Jones, *Cambro-British Melodies*; Félix Savart, *Sur la communication des mouvements vibratoires entre les corps solides*; Friedrich Schneider, *Elementarbuch der Harmonie und Tonsetzkunst*.

I. Musical Compositions
Chamber Music:
> **String Quartets:** Franz Schubert, *No. 12 in c, "Quartettsatz," D. 703*.
> **Sonata/Solos:** Friedrich Kuhlau, *Violin Sonata No. 1 in f, Opus 33*; Felix Mendelssohn, *Violin Sonata No. 1 in F*; Niccolò Paganini, *Six Sonatas, Opus 2–Six Sonatas, Opus 3* (guitar, violin).
> **Ensembles:** František Krommer, *Quartet No. 5 for Flute and Strings, Opus 89–No. 6, Opus 90–No. 7, Opus 93–No. 8, Opus 54–Flute Quintet No. 7, Opus 101*; Friedrich Kuhlau, *Piano Quartet No. 1 in c, Opus 32*; Anton Reicha, *Six Wind Quintets (F, d, E♭, e, a, B♭), Opus 100*; Louis Spohr, *Woodwind Quintet in C, Opus 52*.
> **Piano:** Johann A. André, *Three Sonatas, Opus 46* (four hands); Ludwig van Beethoven, *Sonata No. 30 in E, Opus 109–Ten National Themes with Variations, Opus 107*; Frédéric Chopin, *Mazurka in D(?)*; Muzio Clementi, *Sonata in B♭, Opus 46*; Gaetano Donizetti, *Sonata in a*; Friedrich Kuhlau, *Variations on a Danish Songs, Opus 22–Variations on a Danish Folk Song, Opus 35–Sonata in B♭, Opus 30*; Felix Mendelssohn, *Three sonatas (f, a, e)–Presto in C*; Sigismund von Neukomm, *Sonata, "Le retour à la Vie," Opus 30*; Franz Schubert, *Six Ecossaises in A♭, D. 697*.
> **Organ:** Felix Mendelssohn, *Six Little Pieces*; Samuel Wesley, *Variations in E on "God Save the King."*

Choral/Vocal Music:
Choral: Luigi Cherubini, *In paradisum–Litanie della Vergine;* Jacques Halévy, *De Profundis;* Bernhard Klein, *Job* (oratorio); Felix Mendelssohn, *In feierlichen Tönen* (wedding cantata); Gioacchino Rossini, *Messe de Gloria–Messe Solennelle;* Friedrich Schneider, *Der Weltgericht* (oratorio); Franz Schubert, *Gesang der Geister über den Wassern, Opus 167;* Louis Spohr, *Mass in C, Opus 54;* Václav Tomášek, *Requiem in c;* Carl Maria von Weber, *Agnus Dei* (chorus and winds).
Vocal: Gaetano Donizetti, *Gloria Patri in F;* Anthony Heinrich, *The Dawning of Music in Kentucky, Opus 1–The Western Minstrel, Opus 2* (publication of earlier piano, vocal and instrumental works); Friedrich Kuhlau, *Three Poems, Opus 21–Twelve German Songs, Opus 23;* Carl Maria von Weber, *Six Songs, Opus 80.*
Musical Stage: Daniel Auber, *La bergère châtelaine;* Melchiore Balbi, *La notte perigliosa;* Gaetano Donizetti, *La nozze in Villa;* Jacques Halévy, *Les bohémiennes;* Ferdinand Hérold, *L'auteur mort et vivant;* Friedrich Kuhlau, *Elisa, Opus 29;* Karol Kurpiński, *Kalmora;* Felix Mendelssohn, *Die Soldaten liebschaft;* Saverio Mercadante, *Violenza e costanza–Il gelosa ravveduto–Scipione in Cartagine–Anacreonte in Samo;* Giacomo Meyerbeer, *Margherita d'Anjou;* Giovanni Pacini, *La gioventù di Enrico V–La schiava in Bagdad–La sacerdotessa d'Irminsu;* Johann Poissl, *La rappressaglia;* Gioacchino Rossini, *Maometto II;* Franz Schubert, *Sakuntala–Die Zauberharfe;* Giovanni Tadolini, *Il finto molinaro;* Alexei Vertovsky, *Quarantine;* Joseph Weigl, *Daniel in der Löwengrube;* Peter Winter, *Der Sänger un der Schneider.*
Orchestra/Band Music:
Concerted Music:
> **Piano:** Johann N. Hummel, *Variations in F, Opus 97;* Ignaz Moscheles, *Concerto No. 3 in g, Opus 60;* Daniel Steibelt, *Concerto No. 8 in E♭.*
> **Violin:** Franz A. Berwald, *Concerto in c♯;* Bartolomeo Campagnoli, *Concerto in B♭;* Louis Spohr, *Concerto No. 9 in d, Opus 55.*
> **Other:** Mauro Giuiliani, *Guitar Concerto No. 3, Opus 70;* Albert Lortzing, *Andante and Variations* (harp)–*Andante Maestoso con variazioni* (horn); Anton Reicha, *Rondo for Horn and Orchestra.*
Ballet/Incidental Music: Henry R. Bishop, *Twelfth Night* (IM); Rodolphe Kreutzer, *Clari* (B); Karol Kurpiński, *Mars i Flora* (B); Carl Maria von Weber, *Preciosa* (IM)–*Der Leuchtturm* (IM).
Standard Works: Luigi Cherubini, *Funeral March;* Conradin Kreutzer, *Scenes from Goethe's Faust.*
Symphonies: Anton André, *Grande Sinfonie, Opus 41;* František Krommer, *No. 5, Opus 105;* Louis Spohr, *No. 2 in d, Opus 49.*

1821

❋

Historical Highlights: Mexico declares its independence—Santa Anna becomes president; Guatamala, Panama, and Santo Domingo gain independence through the actions of San Martin; Greece begins a war of independence from Turkey; in the United States, Missouri joins the Union as state number twenty-four; the United States begins the official settlement of the Florida Territory; Texas, a state of Mexico, is opened to settlement by Moses Austin.

Art and Literature Highlights: Births—artists Joseph Paton, Anne Whitney, writers Champfleury, Feodor Dostoyevsky, Gustave Flaubert, Charles Baudelaire; Deaths—artists Richard Cosway, John Crome, poet John Keats. Art—Constable's *The Hay Wain*, Martin's *Belshazzar's Feast*, Morse's *Old House of Representatives*; Literature—Cooper's *The Spy*, Grillparzer's *The Golden Fleece*, Scott's *Kenilworth*, Shelley's *Adonais*.

Musical Highlights

A. **Births**

Composers: Friedrich Kiel (Germany) October 7; Auguste-Emmanuel Vaucorbeil (France) December 15; Jean-Baptiste Weckerlin (France) November 29.

Conductors: Mathilde (Angelo) Mariani (Italy) October 11; Emanuele Muzio (Italy) August 24.

Singers: Italo Gardoni (Italian tenor) March 12; Mathilde Marchesi (de Castrone) (German mezzo-soprano) March 24; Hans Feodor von Milde (Austria baritone) April 13; Ernst Pasqué (German baritone) September 3; Charlotte Sainton-Dolby (British contralto) May 17; Joseph Tagliafico (French bass-baritone) January 1; Pauline Viardot-García (French mezzo-soprano) July 28.

Performers: Nicolai Afanasyev (Russian violinist) January 12; Carl Bergmann (German cellist/conductor) April 12; Giovanni Bottesini (Italian contrabass virtuoso) December 22; Oscar Fredrik Byström (Swedish organist/composer) October 13; August Conradi (German organist/conductor) June 27; Albert (Franz) Doppler (Austrian flutist/composer) October 16; Arthur Saint-Léon (French violinist) September 17; Rudolf Joseph Schachner (German pianist/composer) December 31; Heinrich Rudolph Willmers (German pianist) October 31.

Others: Gustave-Alexandre Flaxland (French publisher) January 26; Hermann von Helmholtz (German acoustician) August 31; Henry Willis (British organ builder) April 27.

B. Deaths
Composers: Matthias Kasmienski (Poland) January 25.
Singers: Louise Dugazon (French soprano) September 22; Gasparo Pacchiarotti (Italian castrato soprano) October 28.
Performers: Angelo Maria Benincori (Italian violinist/composer) December 30; Antonio Bruni (Italian violinist/composer) August 5; John Wall Callcott (British organist) May 15; Georg Friedrich Fuchs (French clarinettist/composer) October 9; Charles Hague (British violinist) July 13; Georg Godfrey Müller (German-born violinist/composer) March 19; Andreas Jacob Romberg (German violinist) November 10; Bernard Anselm Weber (German pianist/conductor) March 23.
Others: Andrew Law (American music educator) April 21; Franciscus Geissenhof (Austrian violin maker) January 2.

C. Debuts
Singers: Josephine Fröhlich (Austrian soprano—Vienna); Anton Haizinger (Austrian tenor—Vienna); Adolphe Nourrit (French tenor—Paris); Wilhemine Schröder-Devrient (German soprano—Vienna); Henriette Sontag (German soprano—Prague); Mary Ann Wilson (British soprano—London).
Performers: Charles Auguste de Bériot (Belgian violinist—Paris); Ferdinand Hiller (German pianist—Frankfurt, age ten); Josef Slavík (Bohemian violinist—Prague).

D. New Positions
Conductors: Thomas (Simpson) Cook (Drury Lane, London); Friedrich Schneider (kapellmeister, Anhalt-Dessau).
Others: François Fétis (counterpoint, Paris Conservatory); Carl Loewe (music director, Stettin, and organ, St. Jacobus Cathedral).

E. Prizes/Honors
Honors: Edward Hodges Baily (Royal Academy); François Boieldieu (Legion of Honor); Andrew Law (honorary doctorate, Allegheny College); Félix Savart (French Academy).

F. Biographical Highlights
Ferdinand Hérold goes to Italy to recruit singers for Paris; Johann Wenzel Kalliwoda embarks on a European concert tour; Ignaz Moscheles settles in London and continues his concert tours from there; Sigismund von Neukomm arrives back in Paris following his South American visit; Louis Spohr settles temporarily in Dresden; Nicola Vaccai moves to Trieste for a two-year period as singing teacher; Carl Maria von Weber turns down a call to Kassel and establishes subscription concerts in Dresden.

G. Cultural Openings

Performing Groups—Choral: Accademie Filarmonica Romana (Rome); Bradford Musical Friendly Society; The Diligentia Music Society (The Hague).
Festivals: Niederrheinisches Musikfest (Cologne).
Educational: Free School of Music (Marseilles).
Music Publishers: Chelard Publishing Co. (Paris); Karl Heckelr (Mannheim); Carl August Klemm Publishing Co. (Leipzig); Ratti, Cencetti and Co. (Rome); Maurice Schlesinger (Paris).
Performing Centers: Diligentia Music Hall (The Hague); Kolozavár National Theater (Hungary); Neue Schausspielhaus (Berlin).
Other: Thomas Appleton, organ maker (Boston); Ophecleide (patented); Henry Smart, piano maker (England).

H. Musical Literature

François Blaze, *Dictionnaire de musique moderne*; Ernst Chladni, *Beiträge zur praktische Akustik*; Ananias Davisson, *An Introduction to Sacred Music*; Józef Elsner, *The Beginnings of Music, Especially of Singing*; Karl Friedrich Horn, *A Treatise on Harmony*; Jérôme de Momigny, *La seule vraie théorie de la Musique*; Peter Mortimer, *Choralgesang zur Zeit der Reformation*; John Relfe, *Lucidus Ordo*; Franz Stöpel, *Grundzuge der Geschichte der modernen Musik*; Georg Telemann, *Über die wahl der melodie eines Kirchenliedes*.

I. Musical Compositions

Chamber Music:

String Quartets: Gaetano Donizetti, *No. 9 in d–No. 10 in g–No. 11 in C–No. 12 in C–No. 13 in A*; František Krommer, *Three Quartets, Opus 103*; Carl Loewe, *Three Quartets (F, G, B♭), Opus 24*; Felix Mendelssohn, *Fifteen Fugues*.
Sonata/Solos: Franz Danzi, *Violin Sonata in f, Opus 33*; Ignaz Moscheles, *Introduction and Scottish Rondo, Opus 63* (horn, piano).
Ensembles: Franz Danzi, *Three Wind Quintets, Opus 56*; Johann N. Hummel, *Piano Trio in E♭, Opus 93*; František Krommer, *Flute Quintet No. 8, Opus 104*; Friedrich Kuhlau, *Piano Quartet in f, Opus 32*; Carl Loewe, *Piano Trio in g, Opus 12*.
Piano: Ludwig van Beethoven, *Sonata No. 3l in A♭, Opus 110*; Frédéric Chopin, *Polonaise in A♭ (No. 3)*; Muzio Clementi, *Two Capriccios (e, c), Opus 47–Fantasie with Variations on "Au clair de la lune," Opus 48–Three Sonatas (A, d, g), Opus 50*; John Field, *Nocturnes No. 7 in C–No. 8 in e*; Friedrich Kuhlau, *Sonata in G, Opus 34–Divertimento in E♭, Opus 37*; Felix Mendelssohn, *Sonata in g, Opus 105*; Ignaz Moscheles, *Fantaisie et variations sur "Au clair de la lune," Opus 50–Allegre de bravura, Opus 51*; Franz Schubert, *Twelve Waltzes, D. 145*.

Choral/Vocal Music:
Choral: Luigi Cherubini, *Solemn Mass in B♭*; Francesco Morlacchi, *La morte d'Abel* (oratorio); Gioacchino Rossini, *La riconoscenza* (cantata); Louis Spohr, *Mass in c*; Johann N. Poissl, *Stabat Mater*; C. P. E. Weyse, *Christmas Cantata No. 3*.
Vocal: Gaetano Donizetti, *Teresa e gianfaldoni*; Friedrich Kuhlau, *Die Feier des wohlwollens, Opus 36* (cantata); Carl Friedrich Zelter, *Neue Lieder*.
Musical Stage: Daniel Auber, *Emma*; François Benoist, *Léonore et Félix*; Michele Carafa, *Jeanne d'Arc à Orléans*; Ramón Carnicer, *Elena e Constantino*; Edouard Dupuy, *Felicie*; Pietro Generali, *Elena e Olfredo–La festa maraviglione*; Adalbert Gyrowetz, *La fête hongroise*; Rodolphe Kreutzer, *Le négociant de Hambourg*; Karol Kurpiński, *Kasimir der Grosse–Der schatten des fürsten Josef Poniátowski–Der Forster aus dem wald vor Kozienice*; Felix Mendelssohn, *Die beiden Pädagogen*; Saverio Mercadante, *Maria Stuarda regina di Scozia–Andronico–Elisa e Claudio*; Giacomo Meyerbeer, *L'esule di Granata*; Francesco Morlacchi, *Donna Aurora*; Giovanni Pacini, *Cesare in Egitto*; Ferdinando Paër, *Le Maître de Chapelle–Blanche de Provence*; Gioacchino Rossini, *Matilde di Shabran*; Gaspare Spontini, *Lalla Rookh*; Carl Maria von Weber, *Der Freischütz–Die Drei Pintos* (unfinished); Joseph Weigl, *König Waldemar–Edmund und Caroline*.
Orchestra/Band Music:
Concerted Music:
Piano: Carl Maria von Weber, *Konzertstücke in f, Opus 245*.
Violin: Johann Kalliwoda, *Concerto, Opus 9*.
Other: Friedrich Kuhlau, *Concertino, Opus 45* (two horns); Louis Spohr, *Clarinet Concerto No. 3 in f*.
Ballet/Incidental Music: Henry R. Bishop, *Two Gentlemen of Verona* (IM); Heinrich Marschner, *Prinz Friedrich von Homburg* (IM).
Standard Works: Albert Lortzing, *Overture alla Turca*; Sigismund von Neukomm, *Fantasy No. 3, Opus 27*; Carl Gottlieb Reissiger, *Overture, Das Rockenweibchen, Opus 10*.
Symphonies: Felix Mendelssohn, *String Symphonies 1–6 (C, D, e, c, B♭, E♭)*; Cipriano Potter, *No. 3 in B♭*; Franz Schubert, *No. 7 in E, D. 729* (sketches only); Jan Voříšek, *Symphony in D*.

1822

✤

Historical Highlights: Brazil wins its independence from Portugal and Peru from Spain; the Congress of Verona studies what they call the Spanish rebellion problem; Turkish troops invade Greece and massacre the Greek inhabitants of Chios; the Republic of Haiti is formed; Florida becomes a U.S. Territory; Congress establishes diplomatic relations with the two newly independent South American countries.

Art and Literature Highlights: Births—artist Rosa Bonheur, writers Matthew Arnold, Edward Everett Hale, Alfred von Meissner, Dmitri Grigorovich; Deaths—artists Arthur Devis, Franz Kobell, Antonio Canova. Art—Delacroix's *Dante and Virgil in Hell*, Doughty's *View of Baltimore from Beach Hill*, C. W. Peale's *The Artist in his Studio*; Literature—Nodler's *Trilby*, Pushkin's *Eugene Onegin*, Shelley's *The Triumph of Life*.

Musical Highlights

A. **Births**

Composers: Luigi Arditi (Italy) July 22; César Franck (Belgium-France) December 10; Rafael Hernándo (Spain) May 31; Victor Massé (France) March 7; Joseph Joachim Raff (Germany) May 27; Gaetano Valeri (Italy) April 13.

Conductors: Carlo Emanuele Barbieri (Italy) October 22; Henry Wylde (England) May 22.

Singers: Charles-Amable Battaille (French bass) September 30; Enrico Delle Sedie (Italian baritone) June 17; Louis Gueymard (French tenor) August 17; Salvatore Marchesi de Castrone (Italian baritone) January 15; Hermine Rudersdorff (Ukrainian soprano) December 12; Ferdinand Sieber (Austrian baritone) December 5; Anna Zerr (German soprano) July 26.

Performers: Félix Clément (French organist/music author) January 13; Cornelius Abrányi (Hungarian pianist/author) October 15; Baldassare Gamucci (Italian pianist/composer) December 14; Eugène Gautier (French violinist/composer) February 27; Charles Edward Horsley (British organist/composer) December 16; Theodore von La Hache (German-born pianist) March; Alfredo Piatti (Italian cellist) January 8; Karl Reinthaler (German organist/composer) October 13; Wilhelm Rust (German organist) August 15; Franz Strauss (German horn virtuoso) February 26.

B. **Deaths**

Composers: Jean-Baptiste Davaux (France) February 2; Albert Christoph Dies (Germany) December 29; E. T. A. Hoffman (Germany) July 24; George K. Jackson (England-U.S.A.) November 18; Gaetano Valeri (Italy) April 13.

Singers: Martin Joseph Adrien (Belgian bass) November 19; Joseph Carl Ambrosch (German tenor) September 8; Charles Duquesnoy (Belgian tenor) May 9; Charles Knyvett, Sr. (British tenor) January 19.

Performers: Christian Dieter (German violinist/composer) May 15; Jean-Baptiste-Edouard Dupuy (French violinist/composer) April 3; Franz Xaver Gebauer (German organist/conductor) December 13; Johann Wilhelm Hässler (German organist) March 29; Johann Baptist Henneberg (Austrian organist) November 26; Maria Hester Park (British pianist) August 15; Christian Friedrich Schwencke (German pianist) October 27; Anton Tayber (Austrian pianist) November 18; Christian Friedrich Uber (German violinist/conductor) March 2; Carl Jacob Wagner (German oboist/composer) November 24; Johann Gottlob Werner (German organist) July 19.

Others: Sir William Herschel (British astronomer/composer) August 25; François-Louis Pique (Grench violin maker) October 26.

C. Debuts

Singers: Maria Caradori-Allen (Italian soprano—London); Sabine Heinefetter (German soprano—Frankfurt); Mary Anne Paton (Scottish soprano—London).

Performers: Lambert Massart (Belgian violinist—Liège).

D. New Positions

Conductors: François Aimon (Théâtre-Française, Paris); José Elizaga (maestro de capilla, Mexico City Court); Johann Wenzel Kalliwoda (Prince Fürstenberg's orchestra, Donaueschingen); Conradin Kreutzer (kapellmeister, Kärnthnertor Theater, Vienna); George Frederick Perry (Haymarket Theatre, London); Friedrich Ludwig Seidel (kapellmeister, Berlin).

Others: François-Henri Blaze (music critic, *Journal des Débats*); George T. Smart (organ, Chapel Royal, London); Louis Spohr (kapellmeister, Kassel); Carl Friedrich Zelter (director, Royal Institute for Church Music, Berlin).

E. Prizes/Honors

Honors: Pierre N. Guérin (French Academy, Rome); François Habeneck (Legion of Honor), Niccolò Zingarelli (knighted).

F. Biographical Highlights

Hector Berlioz abandons medicine and begins the serious study of music with Lesueur; Frédéric Chopin begins the study of piano with Elsner; Mikhail Glinka leaves school and becomes a musical dilettante; Gioacchino Rossini finally marries soprano Isabella Colbran and meets with Beethoven; Anton Schindler gives up the study of law to devote full time to music and Beethoven; Franz Schubert finally gets to meet Beethoven and Weber; Filippo Traetta settles in Philadelphia as a private music teacher; Richard Wagner enters the Kreuzschule in Dresden.

G. Cultural Beginnings

Performing Groups—Choral: Jubal Society (Hartford).
Performing Groups—Instrumental: Sociedad Filarmónica (Buenos Aires); Sociedade Philarmonica (Lisbon); Società Filarmonica (Bergamo).
Educational: Akademie für Kirchenmusik (Berlin); American Conservatorio (Philadelphia); Escuela de Música y Canto (Buenos Aires); Linz Music Academy (Bruckner Conservatorium); Royal Academy of Music (London); Trieste Academy of Music.
Music Publishers: P. J. Tonger, music publisher and retailer (Cologne).
Music Publications: *Aurora* (Hungary).
Performing Centers: Cologne Theater; Theater in der Josefstadt (Vienna).
Other: Andreas Mollenhauer, woodwind maker (Vienna).

H. Musical Literature

Prosper-Didier Deshayes, *Idées générales sur l'Académie royale de musique*; Franz X. Glöggl, *Der musikalische Gottesdienst–Allgemeines musikalisches Lexikon*; Thomas Hastings, *Dissertation on Musical Tastes*; Charles Hempel, *Introduction to the Pianoforte . . .* ; Karl Gottlieb Hering, *Zittauer Choralbuch*; Lowell Mason, *Handel and Haydn Society's Collection of Church Music*; Bernhard Natorp, *Melodienbuch*; Etienne Pastou, *École de la lyre harmonique*; François Perne, *Cours d'harmonie et d'accompagnement*; Gottfried Weber, *Allgemeine Musiklehre zum Selbstunterrichte*.

I. Musical Compositions

Chamber Music:

String Quartets: Louis Spohr, *Three String Quartets (E♭, a, G), Opus 58.*
Ensembles: Johann N. Hummel, *Quintet in E♭, Opus 87–Piano Trio in E♭, Opus 96*; František Krommer, *Three String Quintets, Opus 100*; Friedrich Kuhlau, *Piano Quartet No. 2 in A, Opus 50–Three Flute Quintets (D, E, A), Opus 51*; Felix Mendelssohn, *Piano Quartet in d–Piano Quartet No. 1 in C, Opus 1.*
Piano: Ludwig van Beethoven, *Sonata No. 32 in c, Opus 111*; Frédéric Chopin, *Polonaise in g♯ (No. 4)*; John Field, *Rondo in C*; Mikhail Glinka, *Mozart Variations in E♭*; Friedrich Kuhlau, *Three Sonatas (G, d, C), Opus 46–Three Sonatas (F, B♭, A), Opus 52*; Franz Liszt, *Variations on a Diabelli Waltz*; Franz Schubert, *Fantasy in C, "Der Wanderer," D. 760*; Carl Maria von Weber, *Sonata No. 4 in e, Opus 70.*

Choral/Vocal Music:

Choral: Gaetano Donizetti, *L'assunzione di Maria Vergine*; Felix Mendelssohn, *Psalm LXVI–Magnificat in D*; Giovanni Pacini, *Mass for the Madonna del Castello–Il puro omaggio* (cantata); Franz Schubert, *Mass No. 5 in A♭, D. 678.*

Vocal: Ludwig van Beethoven, *Arietta, "The Kiss," Opus 128*; Felix Mendelssohn, *Salve Regina in E♭*; Franz Schubert, *Wanderer's Nachtlied, D. 768.*

Musical Stage: Daniel Auber, *Leicester*; Henry Bishop, *Maid Marion*; Michele Carafa, *Le solitaire*; Ramón Carnicer, *Don Giovanni Tenoria*; Catterino Cavos, *The Firebird*; Gaetano Donizetti, *La zingara–Zoriada di Granata–Chiara e Serafina–La lettera anonima*; Pietro Generali, *Argene e Alsindo–La sposa indiana*; Jacques Halévy, *Marco Curzio*; Conradin Kreutzer, *Libussa*; Rodolphe Kreutzer/Kreubé, C. F., *La paradies de Mahomet*; Felix Mendelssohn, *Die wandernden Komödianten*; Saverio Mercadante, *Amleto–Il posto abbandonato–Alfonso ed Elisa*; Giacomo Meyerbeer, *L'esule di Granata*; Francesco Morlacchi, *Tebaldo e Isolina–La gioventu di Enrico V*; Wenzel Müller, *Aline*; George Perry, *Morning, Noon and Night*; Anton Reicha, *Sapho*; Gioacchino Rossini, *Zelmira*; Franz Schubert, *Alfonso und Estrella*; Gaspare Spontini, *Nurmahal*; Alexei Vertovsky, *New Mischief–The Madhouse.*

Orchestra/Band Music:

Concerted Music:

Piano: John Field, *Concerto No. 7 in c, Opus 58*; Conradin Kreutzer, *Concerto No. 2 in C, Opus 50*(?); Felix Mendelssohn, *Concerto in g* (with strings).

Violin: Felix Mendelssohn, *Concerto in d* (with strings).

Ballet/Incidental Music: Karol Kurpiński, *Die drei Grazien* (B); Sigismund von Neukomm, *Athalie* (IM); Carl Maria von Weber, *Den Sachsen Sohn* (IM).

Orchestra/Band: Ludwig van Beethoven, *Consecration of the House Overture, Opus 124*; Carl Maria von Weber, *Marcia Vivace in D* (ten trumpets, orchestra).

Symphonies: František Krommer, *No. 6*; Felix Mendelssohn, *String Symphony No. 8 in D*; Sigismund von Neukomm, *No. 1–No. 2*; Franz Schubert, *No. 8 in b, "Unfinished," D. 759.*

1823

Historical Highlights: Several Latin American states unite to form the United Provinces of Central America; Ferdinand VII revokes the Spanish Constitution and, with French help, crushes the people's rebellion; the British Anti-Slavery Society is founded; President James Monroe proclaims his Monroe Doctrine warning the European nations to steer clear of the Americas; the steamboat *Virginia* becomes the first on the Mississippi River.

Art and Literature Highlights: Births—artist Coventry Patmore, writers Théodore de Banville, Mary B. Chesnut, Ned Buntline; Deaths—artists Joseph Nollekens, Henry Raeburn, Pierre-Paul Prud'hon. Art— Durand's *Signing of the Declaration of Independence,* Inman's *Rip Van Winkle Awakening,* Waldmüller's *Portrait of Ludwig van Beethoven;* Literature—Cooper's *The Pioneers,* Lamb's *Essays of Elia,* Scott's *Quentin Durward.*

Musical Highlights

A. Births

Composers: Pascual Juan Arrieta y Corera (Spain) October 21; Francisco Asenjo Barbieri (Spain) August 3; Vincenzo Battista (Italy) October 5; Édouard Lalo (France) January 27; Ernest Reyer (France) December 1.

Conductors: Richard Genée (Germany) February 7.

Singers: Achille Errani (Italian tenor); Marietta Alboni (Italian contralto) March 6; Thomas J. Bowers (American tenor)(?); Emilio Naudin (Italian-born tenor) October 23; Paulina Rivoli (Polish soprano) July 22; Wilhelm Troszel (Polish bass) August 26; Theodor Wachtel (German tenor) March 10.

Performers: Immanuel Faisst (German organist) October 13; Julius Hesse (German pianist/inventor) March 2; Theodor Fürchtegott Kirchner (German pianist/composer) December 10; William Henry Monk (British organist/composer) March 16; William Rockstro (British pianist/music author) January 5; Friedrich Gottlieb Schwencke (German organist/composer) December 15; Thomas Tellefsen (Norwegian pianist) November 26; Johann Vogt (German pianist) January 17.

Others: John Bacchus Dykes (British hymnist) March 10; Adolf Kullak (German music theorist/critic) February 23; William H. Simmonds (American organ builder).

B. Deaths

Composers: Thomas Hamly Butler (British composer); Luigi Caruso (Italy) November 15; Emanuel Aloys Förster (Germany) November 12; Nicolas-Joseph Hüllmandel (France) December 19; Josef Preindl (Austria) October 26; Johann Gottfried Schicht (Germany) February 16.

Singers: Pierre Jean Garat (French tenor/baritone) March 1.

Performers: Anton Felix Bečvařovský (Bohemian organist) May 15; Jean-Baptiste Sébastien Bréval (French cellist/composer) March 18; Philipp Christoph Kayser (German pianist) December 23; Jean Henri Levasseur (French cellist); Josef Preindl (Austrian organist/theorist) October 26; Theodor Schacht (German pianist/composer) June 20; Daniel Steibelt (German pianist) October 2.

Others: John Betts (British violin maker) March; Matthew Peter King (British music theorist) January; August Leduc (French publisher) May 25; Count Ferdinand Waldstein (German patron of the arts) August 29.

C. Debuts
Singers: Mary Anne Goward (British soprano—Dublin).
Performers: Michael William Balfe (Irish violinist—London).

D. New Positions
Conductors: Johann Gänsbacher (kapellmeister, Vienna Cathedral); Johann Hermann Kufferath (Bielefeld); Christian Theodor Weinlig (cantor, Thomasschule, Leipzig).
Others: William Ayrton (editor, *Harmonicon*); Jan Václav Voříšek (organ, Vienna Court).

E. Prizes/Honors
Honors: Józef A. Elsner (Order of St. Stanislaw).

F. Biographical Highlights
Heinrich Marschner joins Weber and Morlacchi as joint kapellmeisters in Dresden; Giacomo Meyerbeer tries unsuccessfully to have his operas performed in Berlin; Gioacchino Rossini moves to Paris and visits in London; Wilhemine Schröder marries actor Karl Devrient; Fernando Sor goes to Russia to oversee the production of his ballets; Carl Maria von Weber corresponds with Beethoven and finally gets to meet him in Baden.

G. Cultural Beginnings
Performing Groups—Choral: Freiberg Singakademie; New York Sacred Music Society.
Performing Groups—Instrumental: Geneva Musical Society; Lüneburg Musikverein.
Festivals: Yorkshire Music Festival (Bradford).
Educational: Accademie di Revvivati (Pisa); Agthe-Kräger Music Academy (Dresden).
Music Publishers: Robert Cocks and Co. (London); Ewer and Co. (London); Probst (Kistner's) Music Publishing Co. (Leipzig); Wessel and Stodart (London).
Music Publications: *Muse Française.*
Performing Centers: Zwickau Theater.
Other: Briedenstein's Musikalischer Apparet (University of Bonn); George Chanot Violin Co. (Paris); Hibernicon (patented by J. R. Cotter); R. and W. Nunns (Nunns and Clark), piano makers (New York); Jean Savary, bassoon maker (Paris); Stewart and Chickering, piano makers (Boston).

H. Musical Literature

Bonifazio Asioli, *Elementi di Contrabasso* . . . ; José Elizaga, *Elementos de música*; Nathaniel Gould, *Social Harmony*; Johann Heinroth, *Gesang-unterrichts-Methode*; Conrad Kocher, *Die Tonkunst in der Kirche*; Isaac Nathan, *An Essay on the History and Theory of Music, and on the Qualities, Capabilities and Management of the Human Voice*; Giacomo Tritto, *Scuola di contrappunto*; Christian Urban, *Über die Musik, deren theorie und den musikunterricht*; Johann Werner, *Orgelschule II.*

I. Musical Compositions
Chamber Music:

String Quartets: Felix Mendelssohn, *Quartet No. 1 in E♭*; Louis Spohr, *String Quartet in A, Opus 68–Double Quartet in d, Opus 65.*

Ensembles: Mikhail Glinka, *Septet in E♭* (oboe, bassoon, horn, strings); František Krommer, *Flute Quintet No. 6, Opus 92*(?); Friedrich Kuhlau, *Piano Quartet No. 2 in A, Opus 50–Three Quintets (D, E, A), Opus 51* (flute, strings); Franz Lachner, *Woodwind Quintet No. 1 in F*; Felix Mendelssohn, *Piano Quartet No. 2 in f, Opus 2.*

Piano: Ludwig van Beethoven, *Diabelli Variations, Opus 12–Seven Bagatelles, Opus 126*; Friedrich Kuhlau, *Variations on Weber's "Preciosa," Opus 53–Six Sonatinas (C, G, c, F, D, C), Opus 55*; Franz Schubert, *Sonata in a, D. 784–Twelve German Dances, D. 790*; Charles Thibault, *Rondo: Le Printemps, Opus 6–Variations: Le Souvenir, Opus 7.*

Organ: Felix Mendelssohn, *Chorale-Prelude, "Wie gross ist des Almächt'gen Güte"–Fantasia in g*(?); Samuel Wesley, *Three Volumes to J. Harding, Book I.*

Choral/Vocal Music:

Choral: Ludwig van Beethoven, *Missa Solemnis, Opus 123–Cantata, Opus 199–Bundeslied, Opus 122*; Hector Berlioz, *Le passage de la Mer rouge* (oratorio); Lowell Mason, *Missionary Hymn (From Greenland's Icy Mountains)*; Sigismund von Neukomm, *Der Ostermorgan* (cantata); Gioacchino Rossini, *La vera omaggio* (cantata); Friedrich Schneider, *The Deluge* (oratorio).

Vocal: Gaetano Donizetti, *A Silvio amante*; Friedrich Kuhlau, *Three Songs, Opus 72b*; Franz Schubert, *Die Schöne Müllerin, D. 795* (cycle).

Musical Stage: Daniel Auber, *La neige*; Hector Berlioz, *Estelle et Nemorin*; Henry Bishop, *Cortez–Clari*; François Boieldieu, *La France et l'Espagne*; Michele Carafa, *Le valet de chambre*; Gaetano Donizetti, *Alfredo il grande–Il fortunato inganno*; Pietro Generali, *Chiara di Rosembergh–Le nozze fra Nemici*; Adalbert Gyrowetz, *Das Ständchen*; Ferdinand Hérold, *Le muletier–Lasthénie–Vendôme en Espagne* (with Auber); Bernhard Klein, *Dido*; Conradin Kreutzer, *Siguna*; Jean François Lesueur, *Alexandre à Babylone*; Heinrich Marschner, *Der Holzdieb*; Felix Mendelssohn, *Der Onkel aus Boston*; Saverio Mercadante, *Didone abbandonata–Gli sciti–Costanza ed Almeriska*; Giacomo Meyerbeer, *Costanza ed Almeriska*; Giovanni Pacini, *La Vestale–Temistocle*; Luigi Ricci, *L'impresario in angustie*; Gioacchino Rossini, *Semiramide*; Franz Schubert, *Fierabras, D. 796–Der Häusliche Krieg, D. 787–Rüdiger, D. 791*; Fernando Sor, *Cendrillon*; Louis Spohr, *Jessonda*; Alexei Titov, *The Mogul's Feast*; Carl Maria von Weber, *Euryanthe*; Joseph Weigl, *Die eiserne Pforte*.

Orchestra/Band Music:

Concerted Music:

> **Piano:** Felix Mendelssohn, *Concerto No. 1 for Two Pianos in E*; Ignaz Moscheles, *Concerto No. 2 in E♭, Opus 56–No. 4 in F, Opus 64*.
> **Violin:** Josef Slavik, *Concerto*.
> **Other:** Karol Kurpiński, *Clarinet Concerto*.

Ballet/Incidental Music: Karol Kurpiński, *Krakauer hochzeit* (B); Heinrich Marschner, *Schön Ella* (IM)–*Ali Baba* (IM); Johann N. Poissl, *Renata* (IM); Franz Schubert, *Rosamunde, D. 797* (IM).

Standard Works: James Hemmenway, *The Philadelphia Grand March*; Anton Reicha, *Grand Overture in D*.

Symphonies: Ludwig van Beethoven, *No. 9 in d, "Choral," Opus 125*; Felix Mendelssohn, *String Symphony No. 9 in C–No. 10 in b–No. 11 in F–No. 12 in g*.

1824

❄

Historical Highlights: Colombia wins its independence from Spain; the first Burmese War begins—the British take Rangoon; Charles X becomes king of France; in the United States, none of the four presidental candidates have an electoral majority, so Congress picks John Quincy Adams as the sixth president; the Bureau of Indian Affairs is created in the War Department; frontiersman Jim Bridger becomes the first white man to visit the Great Salt Lake.

Art and Literature Highlights: Births—artists Pierre de Chavannes, William M. Hunt, Eastman Johnson, writer Alexander Dumas, *fils*; Deaths—artist Théodore Gèricault, writers Lord Byron, Susanna Rowson. Art—David's *Mars and Venus*, Delacroix's *Massacre of Chios*, Overbeck's *Christ Entering Jerusalem*; Literature—Irving's *Tales of a Traveller*, Scott's *Red Gauntlet*, Shelley's *The Witch of Atlas*, Tyler's *The Chestnut Tree*.

Musical Highlights

A. Births

> **Composers:** Anton Bruckner (Austria) September 4; Peter Cornelius (Germany) December 24; Edward Francis Fitzwilliams (England) Au-

gust 1; Francesco Malipiero (Italy) January 9; Carl Reinecke (Germany) June 23; Carlo Romani (Italy) May 24; Bedřich Smetana (Bohemia) March 2; Théophile Semet (France) September 6; Hermann Wichmann (Germany) October 24; Richard Wuerst (Germany) February 22.

Singers: Joseph-Théodore Barbot (French tenor) April 12; Eliza Biscaccianti (American soprano); Pasquale Brignoli (Italian tenor); Anne Charton-Demeur (French mezzo-soprano) March 5; Leone Giraldoni (French-born baritone).

Performers: Emanuel Abraham Aguilar (British pianist/composer) August 23; James Coward (British organist) January 25; Raimund Dreyschock (Belgian pianist) August 20; Julius Eichberg (German-born cellist) June 13; Moritz Fürstenau (German flutist) July 26.

Others: Thomas E. Chickering (American piano maker) October 22; Rudolf Genée (German music scholar) December 12; Antonio Ghislanzoni (Italian music author/editor) November 25; Otto Kornmüller (German music author) January 5; Vladimir Stasov (Russian music author) January 14.

B. Deaths

Composers: Alexander Campbell (Scotland) May 15; John Davy (England) February 22; Johann Melchior Dreyer (Germany) March 22; Santiago Ferrer (Spain) August 21; Luigi Mosca (Italy) November 30; Giacomo Tritto (Italy) September 16.

Singers: Francesco Benucci (Italian bass) April 5; Josefa Dušek (Czech soprano) January 8.

Performers: Karl Baumgarten (German organist); Johann August Burgmüller (German organist/conductor) August 21; Henry Condell (British violinist) June 24; Edward Jones (British harpist) April 18; Joseph Kemp (British organist) May 22; Marie Theresia von Paradies (Austrian pianist) February 1; Johann G. C. Schetky (German cellist/composer) November 29; Giovanni Battista Viotti (Italian violinist/composer) March 3.

Others: Jacques-Georges Cousineau (French harp maker); William Forster, Jr. (British violin maker) July 24; Nicolas Lupot (French violin maker) August 14.

C. Debuts

Singers: Matilde Palazzesi (Italian soprano—Dresden); Henry Phillips (British bass—London); Caroline Unger (Hungarian contralto—Vienna).

Performers: August Friedrich Pott (German violinist—Kassel).

D. New Positions

Conductors: Josef Blahack (kapellmeister, St. Peter's, Vienna), Carlo Coccia (King's Theatre, London); Joseph Leopold Eybler (hofkapell-

meister, Vienna); François-Antoine Habeneck (Paris Opera); Karol Kurpiński (Warsaw Opera); Giovanni Battista Polledro (maestro di cappella, Turin); Pietro Raimondi (Royal Theaters, Naples); Gioacchino Rossini (Théâtre-Italien, Paris).
Others: Adolf Marx (editor, *Allgemeine Musikalische Zeitung*); Gottfried Weber (editor, *Cäcilia*).

E. Prizes/Honors
Honors: Rodolphe Kreutzer (Legion of Honor); Stanislao Mattei (French Institute).

F. Biographical Highlights
Adolphe Adam receives honorable mention in the Prix de Rome competition; Mikhail Glinka takes a post in the Russian Ministry of Communications; Frèdèric Kalkbrenner becomes a partner in the Pleyel Piano Co. in Paris; Anton Schindler, accused of financial cheating, is thrown out of the house (temporarily) by Beethoven; Václav Tomášek marries Wilhelmine Ebert and opens his own music school; Richard Wagner takes some piano lessons, but finds the opera more interesting.

G. Cultural Beginnings
Performing Groups—Choral: Basler Gesangverein; Königsberg Liedertafel; Norwich Choral Society; Stuttgartner Liederkranz.
Performing Groups—Instrumental: Accademia Filarmonica (Cagliari); Athenaeum Club (London); Luxembourg Philharmonic Society; New Orleans Philharmonic Society; Sociedad Filharmónica (Mexico City).
Festivals: Norfolk and Norwich Triennial Music Festival.
Educational: Benvenuti Music School (Pisa); Mees Music Academy (Antwerp).
Music Publishers: Johann B. Cramer and Co., Ltd. (London).
Music Publications: *Berliner Allgemeine Musikalische Zeitung*; *Cäcilia* (Mannheim); *Westminster Review*.
Performing Centers: Camp Street Theater (New Orleans); Königstädtisches Theater (Berlin).

H. Musical Literature
Richard Bacon, *Elements of Vocal Science*; Giuseppe Carpani, *Lettere Musico-Teatrali*; François-Joseph Fétis, *Traité du contrepoint et de la fugue*; Joubert de La Salette, *De la fixité et de l'invariabilité des sons musicaux*; Richard Mount-Edgcumbe, *Musical Reminiscences*; Anton Reicha, *Traité de haute composition musicale I*; Johann Friedrich Rochlitz, *Für Freunde der Tonkunst I*; John H. Sainsbury, *A Dictionary of Musicians*; Christian Urban, *Theorie der Musik nach Rein Naturgemässen Grundsätzen*.

I. Musical Compositions
Chamber Music:
String Quartets: Ludwig van Beethoven, *No. 12 in E♭, Opus 127*; Mikhail Glinka, *No.1 in D*; Franz Schubert, *No. 13 in a, D. 804–No. 14 in d, "Death and the Maiden," D. 810*.
Sonata/Solos: Johann N. Hummel, *Cello Sonata in A, Opus 104*; Friedrich Kuhlau, *Variations on a Theme by Weber, Opus 68* (flute, piano)–*Flute Sonata in E♭*; Felix Mendelssohn, *Viola Sonata in c–Clarinet Sonata in E♭*; Franz Schubert, *Violin Sonata in a, "Arpeggione," D. 821*.
Ensembles: Ludwig van Beethoven, *Variations, Opus 121a* (violin, cello, piano); Franz Lachner, *Septet in E♭* (woodwinds, strings); Felix Mendelssohn, *Piano Sextet in D, Opus 110*; Cipriani Potter, *Three Grand Piano Trios (E♭, D, b♭), Opus 12*; Anton Reicha, *Quartet in E♭, Opus 104* (piano, woodwinds); Franz Schubert, *Octet in F, D. 803*.
Piano: Frédéric Chopin, *Mazurka in A♭, Opus 7, No. 4*; John Field, *Rondo brillant in C*; Mikhail Glinka, *Variations on an Original Theme in F*; Fanny Mendelssohn Hensel, *Sonata in c*; Johann N. Hummel, *Sonata in D, Opus 106*; Carl Loewe, *Tone Poem in Sonata Form, Opus 47, "Le Printemps"*; Felix Mendelssohn, *Rondo capriccioso in E, Opus 14*; Franz Schubert, *Sixteen German Dances, D. 783–Twenty Waltzes, D. 146–Thirty-Four Valses Sentimentales, D. 779*; Charles Thibault, *Variations: L'espérance, Opus 8–Variations: La Bretonne, Opus 9*.
Choral/Vocal Music:
Choral: Johann W. Poissl, *Judith* (oratorio)–*Miserere*; Václav Voříšek, *Mass in B♭*; Christian Weinlig, *Unser Vater in den seel'gen Höhen* (cantata).
Vocal: Gaetano Donizetti, *La fuga di Tisbe*; Friedrich Kuhlau, *Six Songs for Male Voices, Opus 67*; Carl Loewe, *Three Ballades, Opus 1–Three Ballades, Opus 2–Wallheide, Opus 6*.
Musical Stage: Daniel Auber, *Léocadie–Le concert à la cour–Les trois genres* (with Boieldieu); Michele Carafa, *L'auberge supposée*; Gaetano Donizetti, *Don Gregorio–Emilia di Liverpool*; Jacques Halévy, *Pygmalion*; Ferdinand Hérold, *Le roi René*; Conradin Kreutzer, *Erfüllte Hoffnung*; Rodolphe Kreutzer, *Ipsiboé*; Friedrich Kuhlau, *Lulu, Opus 65*; Albert Lortzing, *Ali Pascha von Janina*; Saverio Mercadante, *Nitocri–Doralice–Gli amici di Siracusa–Le nozze di Telemaco ed Antiope*; Giacomo Meyerbeer, *Il crociato in Egitto*; Francesco Morlacchi, *Ilda d'Avenel*; Giovanni Pacini, *Isabella ed Enrico–Alessandro nelle Indie*; Carl Reissiger, *Didone abbandonata*; Johann Schmidt, *Das verborgene Fenster*; Giovanni Tadolini, *Moctar*; Waldemar Thrane, *A Mountain Adventure*; Nicola Vaccai, *Pietro il grande–La pastorella feudataria*; Alexei Vertovsky, *Who Is Brother? Who Is Sister?–Teacher and Pupil–The Petitioner*.

Orchestra/Band Music:
Concerted Music:
Piano: Felix Mendelssohn, *Concerto No. 1 in A♭ for Two Pianos.*
Standard Works: Mikhail Glinka, *Overture in g–Overture in D– Andante and Rondo in d;* Felix Mendelssohn, *Overture in C for Winds, Opus 24;* Anton Reicha, *Grand Overture in E♭.*
Symphonies: Mikhail Glinka, *Symphony in B♭*(?); Felix Mendelssohn, *No. 1 in c, Opus 11;* Anton Reicha, *Chamber Symphony No. 1 in C.*

1825

❄

Historical Highlights: Bolivia gains its independence from Spain; trade unions are officially legalized in Europe; Nicholas I becomes Czar of Russia and crushes the Decembrists revolt; the Dutch put down revolts in Java and consolidate their control over the area; in the United States, the Erie Canal is officially opened for shipping by DeWitt Clinton, governor of New York; Congress seeks to move all Indians to reservations west of the Mississippi River.

Art and Literature Highlights: Births—artists George Inness, Richard Woodville, writers Robert Ballantyne, Richard Stoddard; Deaths—artist Jacques-Louis David, Henry Füseli, writers Giuseppe Carpani, Jean Paul Richter. Art—Cole's *Kaaterskill Falls,* Lawrence's *The Red Boy,* Sargent's *The Dinner Party;* Literature—Leggett's *Leisure Hours at Sea,* Pushkin's *Boris Godounov,* Scott's *The Talisman,* Woodworth's *The Forest Rose.*

Musical Highlights

A. Births
Composers: George Frederick Bristow (U.S.A.) December 19; Hervé (Florimond Ronger—France) June 30; Richard Hol (Holland) July 23; Frederick Gore Ouseley (England) August 12; Johann Strauss, Jr. (Austria) October 25.
Conductors: Hans Balatka (Czechoslovakia) February 26; Cristóbal Oudrid (Spain) February 7.
Singers: Giacomo Galvani (Italian tenor) November 1; Catherine Hayes (Irish soprano) October 25; Anne Caroline de La Grange (French soprano) July 24; Alexander Reichardt (Hungarian tenor) April 17; Malvina Schnorr von Carolsfeld (German soprano) December 7.
Performers: Jean-Baptiste Arban (French cornetist) February 28; Joseph Dachs (German pianist) September 30; Wulf Fries (German-born cellist) January 10; Mary Ann Gabriel (British pianist/composer) February 7; Joseph Goldberg (Austrian violinist) January 1;

Julius Schulhoff (Czech pianist/composer) August 2; John Wheeler Tufts (American organist) May 12.

Others: Léon Carvalho (French opera manager/baritone) January 18; Eduard Hanslick (Austrian music critic) September 11; August Reissmann (German music author) November 14.

B. Deaths

Composers: Inácio de Almeida (Portugal) October 25; Dmitri Bortniansky (Russia) October 10; Rodrigo Ferraira da Costa (Portugal) November 1; Domenico Corri (Italy) May 22; Stepan Ivanovich Davidov (Russia) May 22; Ambrogio Minoja (Italy) August 3; Giovanni Domenico Perotti (Italy) March 24; Antonio Salieri (Italy-Austria) May 7; Raynor Taylor (England-U.S.A.) August 17; Ján Vaclav Voříšek (Bohemia) November 19; Peter von Winter (Germany) October 17.

Conductors: Johannes Andreas Amon (Germany) March 29.

Singers: Luigi Bassi (Italian baritone) September 13; Ludwig Fischer (German bass) July 10; Pierre Gaveaux (French tenor) February 5.

Performers: Giuseppe Maria Cambini (Italian violinist/composer) December 29; Joseph-Denis Doche (French organist) July 20; François-Joseph Garnier (French oboist); Joseph Gelinek (Bohemian pianist/composer) April 13; Franz Lauska (Bohemian pianist) April 18; Richard Wainwright (British organist) August 20.

Others: Johann Simeon Buchholz (German organ builder) February 24; Giuseppe Carpani (Italian music author) January 22; François Chanot (French violin maker) November 12; Louis Alexandre Frichot (French inventor) April 9; Bernard Germain Lacépède (French theorist/composer) October 6.

C. Debuts

Singers: Julie Aimée Dorus-Gras (Belgian soprano—Brussels); Gilbert-Louis Duprez (French tenor—Paris); María Malibran (Spanish mezzo-soprano—London); Jean-Etienne Massol (French baritone—Paris).

Performers: Ferdinand David (German violinist—Leipzig); Antoine de Kontski (Polish pianist—Warsaw).

D. New Positions

Conductors: Henry Bishop (Drury Lane Theater); Jonathan Blewitt (Sadler's Wells Theater); Adolf Ganz (kapellmeister, Hessen-Darmstadt), Joseph Hartmann (Munich Opera); Karl August von Lichtenstein (Berlin Royal Opera); Feodor Lvov (Russian Imperial Chapel); Wilhelm Mangold (Darmstadt Court); Georg Abraham Schneider (kapellmeister, Berlin Royal Theater).

Others: John Lockhart (editor, *Quarterly Review*); Johann Schneider (organ, Dresden Court); Alexei Vertovsky (Inspector of Theaters, Moscow).

E. **Prizes/Honors**
Honors: Daniel-François Auber, Charles-Simon Catel, and Johann Hummel (Legion of Honor); Giovanni Tadolini (Accademia Filarmonica, Bologna).

F. **Biographical Highlights**
Charles Coussemaker begins the study of law; Joséphine Fodor-Mainville, losing her voice during a Paris performance, retires from the stage; John Hill Hewitt has his first songs published; Franz Liszt makes his second concert tour to London; Felix Mendelssohn, while visiting Paris, meets Cherubini, Rossini, and Meyerbeer.

G. **Cultural Beginnings**
Performing Groups—Choral: Breslau Singakademie; García Italian Opera Co. (New York).
Performing Groups—Instrumental: Joseph Labitzky Orchestra (Karlsbad); Société Philharmonique de Beauvais.
Educational: Elíazaga Conservatory of Music (Mexico City).
Music Publishers: Aibl Music Publishers (Munich); Edwin Ashdown, Ltd. (London); Lucca Music Publishing House (Milan); Eugéne Troupenas (Paris).
Performing Centers: Warsaw Grand Theater; Weimar National Theater.
Other: Buffet Auger Woodwind Co. (Buffet-Crampon et Cie., Paris); Hart and Sons, violin makers (London); J. F. Schulze and Sons, organ builders (Mühlhausen).

H. **Musical Literature**
Dionysio Aguado, *Escuela o Método de Guitarra*; Richard Bacon, *The Art of Improving the Voice and Ear*; Melchiore Balbi, *Grammatica ragionata della musica considerata sotto l'aspetto di lingua*; Thomas Busby, *Concert Room and Orchestral Anecdotes*; William Horsley, *An Explanation of the Musical Intervals*; Hans Nägeli, *Vorlesungen über Musik*; Félix Savart, *Sur la voix humaine*; Anton Thibaut, *Über Reinheit der Tonkunst*; Bernhard Tröstler, *Traité général et raisonné de Musique*; Peter Winter, *Vollständige singschule*.

I. **Musical Compositions**
Chamber Music:
   String Quartets: Carl Arnold, *Quartet*; Ludwig van Beethoven, *No. 13 in a, Opus 132–14 in B♭, Opus 130–Grosse Fuge in B♭, Opus 133*; Gaetano Donizetti, *No. 14 in D*.

Sonata/Solos: Johan P. Hartmann, *Sonata for flute/clarinet, Opus 1*; Friedrich Kuhlau, *Flute Sonata in G, Opus 69–Flute Sonata in e, Opus 71*; Felix Mendelssohn, *Violin Sonata No. 2 in f, Opus 4*.

Ensembles: Carl Arnold, *Sextet for Piano and Strings*; František Krommer, *Six String Quintets, Opus 106, 7*; Felix Mendelssohn, *Piano Quartet No. 3 in b, Opus 3–String Octet in E♭, Opus 20*; Anton Reicha, *Chamber Symphony No. 1*.

Piano: Frédéric Chopin, *Mazurka in A♭, B.7–Mazurka in a, B.8–Rondo in c, Opus 1–Polonaise in d, Opus 71/1*; Louise Farrenc, *Variations brillantes sur un thème d'Aristide Farrenc, Opus 2*; Carl Loewe, *Grand sonata élégique in f, Opus 32(?)*; Felix Mendelssohn, *Capriccio in f♯, Opus 5*; Cipriani Potter, *"Enigma" Variations, Opus 5*; Franz Schubert, *Sonatas in C, "Reliquie," D. 840–in a, D. 845–in D, D. 850*; Charles Thibault, *Three Waltzes, Opus 13*.

Organ: Samuel Wesley, *Four Short Preludes(?)–Three Volumes to J. Harding, Book II*.

Choral/Vocal Music:

Choral: Hector Berlioz, *Resurrexit–Messe Solennelle*; Luigi Cherubini, *Coronation Mass in A*; František Krommer, *Mass in C, Opus 108*; Giovanni Pacini, *Il felice ritorno* (cantata).

Vocal: Johann A. André, *Des sängers lied zu den sternen, Opus 47*; Franz Berwald, *Serenade*; Carl Loewe, *Hebrew Songs II, III, Opus 13–Six Serbian Songs, Opus 15*; Franz Schubert, *Ave Maria*.

Musical Stage: Daniel Auber, *Le maçon*; Vincenzo Bellini, *Adelson e Salvina*; Henry Bishop, *The Fall of Algiers*; François Boieldieu, *La dame blanche*; Ferdinand Hérold, *Le lapin blanc*; Franz Liszt, *Don Sanche*; Carl Loewe, *Rudolph der deutsche Herr*; Felix Mendelssohn, *Die Hochzeit des Camacho, Opus 10*; Saverio Mercadante, *Erode–Ipermestra*; Giacomo Meyerbeer, *Ines di Castro*; Louis Niedermeyer, *La casa nel bosco*; Giovanni Pacini, *L'ultimo giorno di Pompei–Amazilia*; Johann Poissl, *Die Prinzessin von Provence*; Gioacchino Rossini, *Il viaggio a Reims*; Louis Spohr, *Der Berggeist*; Gaspare Spontini, *Alcidor*; Nicola Vaccai, *Giulietta e Romeo*; Alexei Vertovsky, *The Caliph's Amusement–The Miraculous Nose*; Christoph Weyse, *Floribella*.

Orchestra/Band Music:

Concerted Music:

Piano: Conradin Kreutzer, *Concerto No. 3 in E♭, Opus 65*.

Violin: Louis Spohr, *Concerto No. 11 in G, Opus 70*.

Ballet/Incidental Music: Louis Spohr, *Macbeth* (IM).

Standard Works: Daniel Auber, *Pièce symphonique in A(?)*; Johann P. Hartmann, *Overture in d, Opus 3*; Anton Reicha, *Grand Overture in C*; Carl Reissiger, *Overture, Der Ahrenschatz, Opus 80*.

1826

❊

Historical Highlights: Saudi Arabia is formed from the conquests of Ibn Saud; the Treaty of Yandabu brings an end to the First Burmese War; the Russo-Persian War begins; the massacre of the Janissaries takes place in Constantinople; in the United States, Congress is cool to the Pan-American Conference meeting in Panamas; Kansas City is founded on the Missouri River; the internal combustion engine is patented by Samuel Morey.

Art and Literature Highlights: Births—artists Frederic E. Church, Silvestro Lega, Gustave Moreau, writer Charles M. Barras; Deaths—sculptor John Flaxman, writers Jens Baggesen, William Gifford, Johann Peter Hebel, Royall Tyler. Art—Cole's *The Falls of the Kaaterskill*, Goya's *The Butcher Table*, Martin's *The Deluge*; Literature—Cooper's *The Last of the Mohicans*, Disraeli's *Vivian Grey*, Nicander's *The Death of Tasso*.

Musical Highlights

A. Births

Composers: Vincenzo Federici (Italy) September 26; Stephen Foster (U.S.A.) July 4; Ivar Hallström (Sweden) June 5; Vladimir Kashperov (Russia) September 6; Albert Rubenson (Sweden) December 20.

Conductors: Francesco Cortesi (Italy) September 11; Frédéric Louis Ritter (Germany) June 22; Carl Zerrahn (Germany-U.S.A.) July 28.

Singers: Jenny Bürde-Ney (Austrian soprano) December 21; Jeanne Sophie Cruvelli (German soprano) March 12; Theodor Formes (German tenor) June 24; Julius Stockhausen (German baritone/conductor) July 22; Fortunata Tedesco (Italian soprano) December 14; Johanna Wagner (German soprano) October 13.

Performers: W. T. Best (British organist) August 13; Franz Coenen (Dutch violinist) December 26; Johann Decker-Schenk (Austrian guitarist); Otto Dresel (German-born pianist) December 20; Johann Carl Eschmann (Swiss pianist) April 12; Ivar Hallström (Swedish pianist) June 5; Léon Minkus (Austrian violinist/composer) March 23; Ernst Pauer (Austrian pianist/author) December 21; Lindsay Sloper (British pianist) June 14.

Others: Carl Bechstein (German piano maker) June 1; Friedrich Chrysander (German musicologist) July 8; Richard Pohl (German music author) September 12; Edmund Van der Straeten (Belgian music historian) December 3; Rudolf Westphal (German music scholar) July 3.

B. **Deaths**
   Composers: Gaetano Andreozzi (Italy) December 24(?); Juan Crisós-
   tomo Arriaga (Spain) January 17; Franz Ignaz Danzi (Germany)
   April 13; Jacob Kimball, Jr. (U.S.A.) February 6; Friedrich Christian
   Ruppe (Holland) May 25; Carl Maria von Weber (Germany) June 5.
   Singers: Giovanni Ansani (Italian tenor) July 15; Charles Incledon
   (British tenor) February 18; Michael Kelly (Irish tenor) October 9;
   Rosalie Levasseur (French soprano) May 6; Luise Reichardt (Ger-
   man soprano) November 17; Elizaveta Semyonova Sandunova
   (Russian mezzo-soprano) December 3; Benedikt Schack (Austrian
   tenor) December 10; Carl David Stegmann (German tenor/harpsi-
   chordist) May 27.
   Performers: Gervais Couperin (French organist) March 11; Friedrich
   Ludwig Dülon (German flutist) July 7; Friedrich Fesca (German vio-
   linist/composer) May 24; Joseph Graetz (German pianist) July 17;
   Jean Henri Levasseur (French cellist)(?).
   Others: Reginald Heber (British hymnist) April 3.

C. **Debuts**
   Singers: James Bland (British bass—London); Jean Baptiste Chollet
   (French tenor—Paris, as tenor); Giuditta Grisi (Italian mezzo-
   soprano—Vienna); Osip Petrov (Russian bass—Elizavetgrad); Agos-
   tino Rovere (Italian bass—Pavia).
   Performers: (Charles-Valentin) Alkan (French pianist—Paris); Henri
   Vieuxtemps (Belgian violinist—Viviers, age six).

D. **New Positions**
   Conductors: Johann Kaspar Aiblinger (hofkapellmeister, Munich);
   Carl Eberwein (Weimar Opera); Carl Gottlieb Reissiger (Dresden
   Court Opera); Eduard Rietz (Berlin Philharmonic Society).
   Others: Edward Holmes (music critic, *Atlas*); Jan A. Vitásek (direc-
   tor, Prague Organ School); Samuel Sebastien Wesley (organ, St.
   James', London).

E. **Prizes/Honors**
   Honors: Gioacchino Rossini (Composer to His Majesty and Inspector-General of Singing, Paris).

F. **Biographical Highlights**
   Hector Berlioz enters Paris Conservatory and fails in his attempt at
   the Prix de Rome; Rodolphe Kreutzer retires from active musical
   life; Gioacchino Rossini quits the Italian Theater in Paris leaving
   himself free to write for the Opera; Anton Schindler returns to care
   for Beethoven until his death; Richard Wagner, left in Dresden, be-

gins writing *Leubald*; Carl Maria von Weber, still suffering the effects of tuberculosis, travels to England where he dies.

G. Cultural Beginnings

Performing Groups—Choral: Cäcilien-Verein (Lvov); Munich Liederkranz; Sängerverein der Stadt Zurich.

Performing Groups—Instrumental: Berlin Philharmonic Society; Dublin Philharmonic Society; Gregorius Musis Sacrum (Leider Orchestra); Nantes Philharmonic Society; Salem Mozart Association; Johann Strauss Orchestra (Vienna).

Educational: Agthe Music Academy (Posen); Bibliographisches Institut (Gotha); Koninklijke Music School (The Hague); Carl Reissiger Conservatory of Music (The Hague); South African Academy of Music (Cape Town).

Music Publishers: Elíazaga Music Publishers (Mexico City); Eruditio Musica (Rotterdam); Hachette et Cie. (Paris); Friedrich Pustet (Regensburg); J. Schuberth and Co. (Hamburg).

Music Publications: *Atlas*.

Other: Bernardel Violin Shop (Paris); Meneely and Co., Bell Foundry (New York); Society for the Promotion of Church Music in Bohemia (Prague).

H. Musical Literature

Charles Baudiot, *Méthode de violoncelle I*; Henri Berton, *De la musique méchcanique et de la musique philosophique*; François Blaze, *De l'opéra en France II*; Frederick Crouch, *Complete Treatise on the Violoncello*; Michael Kelly, *Reminiscences of Michael Kelly, of the King's Theatre . . .* ; Raphael Kiesewetter, *Die Verdienste der Niederlander um die Tonkunst*; Peter Lichtenthal, *Dizionario e bibliografia della musica*; Carl Loewe, *Gesang-Lehre theoretisch und practisch*; Lowell Mason, *Address on Church Music*; Félix Savart, *Sur la communication des mouvements vibratoires par les liquides*.

I. Musical Compositions

Chamber Music:

String Quartets: Ludwig van Beethoven, *No. 15 in c♯, Opus 131–No. 16 in F, Opus 135*; Norbert Burgmüller, *No. 2 in d, Opus 17*; Franz Schubert, *Quartet in G, D. 887*; Louis Spohr, *Three Quartets (a, B♭, d), Opus 74*.

Sonata/Solos: Johan P. Hartmann, *Violin Sonata No. 1 in g, Opus 8*; Franz Schubert, *Rondo Brillant in b, D. 895* (violin, piano).

Ensembles: Felix Mendelssohn, *String Quintet No. 1 in A, Opus 18*; Anton Reicha, *Quintet in F, Opus 107–Quintet in A, Opus 105*; Franz Schubert, *Piano Trio in B♭, D. 898*; Louis Spohr, *String Quintet No. 3 in b, Opus 69*.

Piano: Ludwig van Beethoven, *Rondo a Capriccio in G, "Rage over a Lost Penny,"* Opus 129; Norbert Burgmüller, *Sonata, Opus 8*; Frédéric Chopin, *Three Ecossaises (D,G,D♭), Opus 72, No. 3–Two Mazurkas (G, B♭)–Introduction and Variations in E on a German Air–Polonaise in b♭, "Adieu"*; Felix Mendelssohn, *Sonata in E, Opus 6–Fugue in c♯*; Ignaz Moscheles, *Etudes, Opus 70*; Cipriani Potter, *Introduction and Rondo giocoso, Opus 20*; Franz Schubert, *Sonata in G, D. 894.*

Choral/Vocal Music:

Choral: Hector Berlioz, *La Revolution Grecque* (cantata); Mikhail Glinka, *Memorial Cantata*; Carl Loewe, *Six Songs for Male Chorus, Opus 19*; Felix Mendelssohn, *Te Deum in D*; Giovanni Pacini, *Partenope* (cantata); Johann N. Poissl, *Die Macht des Herrn* (cantata); Louis Spohr, *The Last Judgment* (oratorio).

Vocal: Johann A. André, *Auf der freude, Opus 48*; Luigi Cherubini, *O Salutaris*; Friedrich Kuhlau, *Two Poems, Opus 78–Eight Songs for Male Voices, Opus 89*; Carl Loewe, *Hebrew Songs IV, Opus 4–Two Ballads, Opus 5*; Franz Schubert, *Who Is Sylvia–Hark! Hark! the Lark*; Carl Zelter, *Six German Songs for Bass Voice.*

Musical Stage: Daniel Auber, *Fiorella–Le timide*; Vincenzo Bellini, *Bianca e Gernando*; Henry Bishop, *Knights of the Cross–Aladdin*; Gaetano Donizetti, *Elvida–Alahor di Granata*; Heinrich Dorn, *Rolands Knappen*; Adalbert Gyrowetz, *Des Kaisers Genesung*; Ferdinand Hérold, *Marie*; Conradin Kreutzer, *Die lustige Werbung–Der Besuch auf dem Lande*; Rodolphe Kreutzer, *Mathilde*; Friedrich Kuhlau, *Shakespeare, Opus 74*; Heinrich Marschner, *Lucretia*; Saverio Mercadante, *Caritea, regina di Spagna*; Giovanni Pacini, *Niobe–La gelosia corretta*; Gioacchino Rossini, *Le siège de Corinthe*; Giovanni Tadolini, *Mitridate*; Nicola Vaccai, *Bianca di Messina–Il precipizio*; Carl Maria von Weber, *Oberon.*

Orchestra/Band Music:

Concerted Music:

Piano: Ignaz Moscheles, *Souvenirs d'Irlande, Opus 69–Anklänge aus Schottland, Opus 75–Concerto No. 5 in C, Opus 87.*

Violin: Niccolò Paganini, *No. 2 in b, Opus 7–No. 3 in E*

Ballet/Incidental Music: Michael Balfe, *La Pérouse* (B); Johann N. Poissl, *Belisar* (B)–*Kaiser Ludwig's Traum* (IM); Cesare Pugni, *Elerz e Zulmida* (B).

Standard Works: Johann N. Hummel, *Overture in B♭, Opus 101*; Felix Mendelssohn, *Overture, Midsummer Night's Dream, Opus 21–Trumpet Overture in C, Opus 101*; Carl Maria von Weber, *March in C for Winds.*

Symphonies: Johann Kalliwoda, *No. 1 in f, Opus 7*; Carl Neuner, *Symphony in E♭*; Cipriani Potter, *No. 6 in c–No. 7 in F.*

1827

❄

Historical Highlights: Greek-Turkish War continues as Russia, France, and Great Britain enter the war against Turkey—Turkish fleet destroyed at the Battle of Navarino; the screw propellor is designed by Joseph Ressel; in the United States, the Baltimore and Ohio becomes the first passenger and freight railroad to be chartered; the Cherokee Nation forms a constitutional government in the Georgia Territory; the first Mardi Gras celebration takes place in New Orleans.

Art and Literature Highlights: Births—artists Arnold Böcklin, William Holman Hunt, Jean Baptiste Carpeaux; Deaths—poet/artist William Blake, artist Charles Willson Peale, writers Wilhelm Hauff, Wilhelm Müller, Ugo Foscolo. Art—Neagle's *Pat Lyon at the Forge*, Ingres' *Apotheosis of Homer*, Vanderlyn's *View of Niagara Falls*; Literature—Fairfield's *Cities of the Plain*, Forrester's *Absurdities in Prose and Verse*, Hugo's *Cromwell*.

Musical Highlights

A. **Births**

Composers: Emil Naumann (Germany) September 8; Lucien H. Southard (U.S.A.) February 4; Hugo Ulrich (Germany) November 26; Septimus Winner (U.S.A.) May 11.

Conductors: Carl Riedel (Germany) October 6; Josef Strauss (Austria) August 22; Julius Tausch (Germany) April 15.

Singers: Johann Nepomuk Beck (Hungarian baritone) May 5; Marie Cabel (Belgian soprano) January 31; Caroline Carvalho (French soprano) December 31; Antonio Giuglini (Italian tenor); Mary Caroline Richings (British-born soprano).

Performers: Ferdinando Bonamici (Italian pianist); Lisa Cristiani (French cellist) December 24; Alexander Wilhelm Gottschalg (German organist) February 14; Heinrich Maylath (Austrian-born pianist) December 4; Teresa Milanollo (Italian violinist) August 28; Eduard Mollenhauer (German-born violinist) April 12; Ellsworth C. Phelps (American organist/composer) August 11; Thomas Ryan (Irish clarinetist/violist); Edouard Silas (Dutch pianist) August 22; Hermann Adolf Wollenhaupt (German pianist/composer) September 27.

Others: Franz Magnus Böhme (German music author) March 11; Friedrich Ehrbar (German organ builder) April 26; Charles Eliot Norton (American educator/patron) November 16; Luigi Francesco Valdrighi (Italian music scholar) July 30.

B. Deaths

Composers: Ludwig van Beethoven (Germany) March 26; Pierre Joseph Candeille (France) April 24; James Hewitt (England-U.S.A.) August 2; Luigi Piccinni (Italy-France) July 31; Alexei Nikolaivich Titov (Russia) November 20.

Conductors: Johann Philipp Schulz (Germany) January 30.

Singers: Charles Dignum (Irish tenor) March 29; Franz Xaver Gerl (German bass) March 9.

Performers: Friedrich Wilhelm Berner (German organist) May 9; János Bihari (Hungarian violinist/conductor) April 26; Benjamin Blake (British violinist)(?); Bartolomeo Campagnoli (Italian violinist/composer) November 7; Franz Anton Dimmler (German horn virtuoso) February 7; James Hook (British organist); David Moritz Michael (German-born violinist/composer) February 27; Franz Anton Schubert (German doublebass virtuoso/composer) March 5.

Others: Ernest Chladni (German acoustician) April 3; Archibald Constable (Scottish publisher) July 21; Gottfried Christoph Härtel (German publisher) July 25; Carl Friedrich Peters (German publisher) November 20.

C. Debuts

Singers: Marietta Brambilla (Italian contralto—London); Alexandrine Duprez (French soprano—Paris).

Performers: Heinrich Panofka (German violinist—Vienna); Ernesto Camillo Sivori (Italian violinist—Genoa); Sigismond Thalberg (German pianist—Vienna).

D. New Positions

Conductors: John O. Curvillier (U.S. Marine Band); Mateo Ferrer (Teatro de la Cruz, Barcelona); Pietro Generali (maestro di cappella, Novara Cathedral); Ferdinand Hérold (chorus, Paris Opera); Carl August Krebs (kapellmeister, Hamburg Theater); Franz Lachner (Kärntnertor Theater, Vienna); Heinrich Marschner (kapellmeister Leipzig Stadttheater); Giuseppe Mosca (Messina Theater); Christian Pohlenz (Leipzig Gewandhaus).

Others: Francesco Basili (director, Milan Conservatory); Louis-Joseph Daussoigne-Méhul (director, Liège Conservatory); François Fétis (librarian, Paris Conservatory and editor, *La Revue Musicale*); Johann Lübeck (director, Conservatory of the Hague); Lowell Mason (president, Boston Handel and Haydn Society).

E. Prizes/Honors

Prizes: Jean Baptiste Guiraud (Prix de Rome).

Honors: Conrad Kocher (honorary doctorate, Tübingen University); Niccolò Paganini (Knight of the Golden Spur).

F. **Biographical Highlights**
Hector Berlioz falls in love with the British actress Henrietta Smithson and again fails to win the Prix de Rome; Alexander Dargomijsky enters the service of the Russian government; Anthony Heinrich travels to London, where he plays violin in a theater orchestra and studies music theory; Lowell Mason moves to Boston and begins supervision of church music and organ work; Karl Nicander, on winning the Swedish Academy Award, travels to Italy for further music study; Ferdinando Paër, blamed for the financial losses sustained, is forced to resign his post at the Italian Theater in Paris.

G. **Cultural Beginnings**
Performing Groups—Choral: Bonn Gesangverein; Bremen Liedertafel; Breslau Liedertafel; Hartford Choral Society; Leeds Amateur Society; Società Armonica (London).
Performing Groups—Instrumental: Portland (Maine) Civic Band; Santiago Symphony Orchestra (Chile); Zagreb Musikverein.
Educational: Académie de Chant (Strasbourg); Accademia Peloritana (Messina); Breslau Singakademie; Adolf Lindblad Music School (Sweden).
Music Publishers: Carl Baedeker (Koblenz).
Music Publications: *Constable's Miscellany; La Revue Musicale.*
Performing Centers: Bowery Theater (New York); Christiania National Theater (Oslo); Teatro delle Muse (Ancona); Theater am Dammtor (Hamburg); Tremont Theater (Boston).
Other: Accademia Filarmonica (Casale Monferrato); Thomas Glen, instrument maker (Edinburgh); August Guicharde, musical instruments (Paris); Hook and Hastings, organ builders (Salem); Niblo's Gardens (New York); Rotary Valve (probable date); Société de Chant Sacré (Geneva).

H. **Musical Literature**
François Aimon, *Sphère harmonique, tableau des accords*; François Alday, *Grande méthode pour l'alto*; Ernst Chladni, *Kurze Übersicht der Schall- und Klanglehre*; François Fétis, *Solfège progressifs*; John Goss, *Parochial Psalmody*; Friedrich Griepenkerl, *Lehrbuch der Aesthetik*; Thomas Hastings, *The Juvenile Psalmody*; Karl Krause, *Darstellung aus der geschichte der Musik*; Johann Logier, *System der Musikwissenschaft und der musikalischen Komposition*; Josef Preindl, *Wiener Ton-*

schule (posthumous publication); Friedrich Schneider, *Vorschule der Musik*.

I. **Musical Compositions**
   Chamber Music:
   String Quartets: Felix Mendelssohn, *No. 2 in A, Opus 13–Fugue in E♭, Opus 81/4*; Louis Spohr, *Double Quartet in d, Opus 65*.
   Sonata/Solos: Friedrich Kuhlau, *Three Violin Sonatas (F, a, C), Opus 79–Three Flute Sonatas (G, C, g), Opus 83–Flute Sonata in a, Opus 85*; Franz Schubert, *Fantasy in C, D .934–Fantasy in D, D. 929* (cello, piano).
   Ensembles: Cipriani Potter, *Sextet, Opus 11*; Franz Schubert, *Piano Trio in B♭, Opus 99*.
   Piano: Frédéric Chopin, *Nocturne in e, Opus 72/1–Funeral March in a, Opus 72/2–Variations in E on Rossini's "La Cenerentola"*; Friedrich Kuhlau, *Four Sonatinas (C, G, a, F), Opus 88*; Felix Mendelssohn, *Sonata in B♭, Opus 106–Seven Characteristic Pieces, Opus 7–Fantasia in E on "The Last Rose of Summer," Opus 15*; Ignaz Moscheles, *Fifty Preludes, Opus 73*; Cipriani Potter, *Rondeau brillant No. 2, Opus 21*; Franz Schubert, *Four Impromtus (c, E♭, G♭, A♭), D. 899–Four Impromtus (f, A♭, B♭, f), D. 935*.
   Choral/Vocal Music:
   Choral: Johann A. André, *Vater Unser, Opus 50*; Hector Berlioz, *La Mort d'Orphée* (cantata); Felix Mendelssohn, *Tu es Petrus, Opus 111* (cantata); Francesco Morlacchi, *Requiem for the King of Saxony*; Sigismund von Neukomm, *Christi Grablegung* (oratorio); Franz Schubert, *Deutsche Messe, D. 872–Nachtgesang in Walde, D. 913*; Joseph Weigl, Mass, *"Conceptione B.M.V."*
   Vocal: Friedrich Kuhlau, *Nine Songs for Male Voices, Opus 82*; Carl Loewe, *Two Ballads, Opus 8*; Franz Schubert, *Die Winterreise* (cycle); Carl Zelter, *Six German Songs for Alto Voice*.
   Musical Stage: Vincenzo Bellini, *Il pirata*; Louise Bertin, *Le loup-garou*; Franz Berwald, *Gustav Wasa*; Hippolyte Chélard, *Macbeth*; Gaetano Donizetti, *Olivo e Pasquale–Il borgomastro di Saardam–Otto mesi in due ore*; Heinrich Dorn, *Der Zauberer und das ungethüm–Die Bettlerin*; Adalbert Gyrowetz, *Der blinde Harfner*; Jacques Halévy, *L'artisan–Le roi et le batelier*; Johann Kalliwoda, *Blanda–Prinzessin Christine*; Conradin Kreutzer, *L'eau de jouvenance*; Rodolphe Kreutzer, *Matilde*; Friedrich Kuhlau, *Hugo und Adelheid, Opus 107*; Saverio Mercadante, *Ezio–Il montanaro–La testa di bronzo*; Giovanni Pacini, *Gli arabi nelle Gallie–Margherita regina d'Inghilterra*; Giuseppe Persiani, *Attila*; Carl Reissiger, *Yelva*; Gioacchino Rossini, *Moïse*; Louis Spohr, *Pietro von Abano, Opus 76*; Giovanni Tadolini, *Almanzor*; Nicola Vaccai, *Giovanna d'Arco*.

Orchestra/Band Music:
Concerted Music:
Piano: Frédéric Chopin, *Variations in B♭ on 'Là ci darem,"* Opus 2;
Johann N. Hummel, *Concerto No. 8 in A♭,* Opus 113; Cipriani Pot-
ter, *Introduction and Rondo "Alla militaire."*
Other: Franz Berwald, *Concertstücke in F for Bassoon and Orchestra.*
Ballet/Incidental Music: Ferdinand Hérold, *La Somnambule* (B)–
Astolphe et Joconde (B); Cesare Pugni, *Pellia e Mileto* (B); Fernando
Sor, *Le Sicilien* (B).
Standard Works: Johann P. Hartmann, *Overture in c, "Geistlig,"*
Opus 9.
Symphonies: Anton Reicha, *Chamber Symphony No. 1–No. 2.*

1828
❆

Historical Highlights: The British Parliament repeals the laws forbid-
ding Catholics and Nonconformists to hold public office; Treaty of Rio
de Janeiro makes Uruguay an independent state between Brazil and Argentina; in the United States, Andrew Jackson is elected president and
introduces the spoils system into Washington politics; Congress passes
the so-called Tariff of Abominations over the protests of the southern
states.
Arts and Literature Highlights: Births—artists Oscar Begas, Jules Delaunay, Dante Rossetti, writers George Meredith, Henrik Ibsen, Jules
Verne; Deaths—artists Jean Houdon, Francisco de Goya, Gilbert Stuart,
writer L. Fernández de Moratin. Art—Camuccini's *Judith*, Martin's *The
Fall of Ninevah*, Rush's *Schuykill Chained*; Literature—Hawthorne's *Fan-
shawe*, Porter's *The Field of Forty Footsteps*, Scott's *The Fair Maid of Perth*.

Musical Highlights

A. Births
Composers: Woldemar Bargiel (Germany) October 3; Grat-Norbert
Barthe (France) June 7; Antonio Cagnoni (Italy) February 8; Luigi
Luzzi (Italy) March 28; Pietro Platania (Italy) April 5; Ferdinand
Poise (France) June 3; Giovanni Rossi (Italy) August 5.
Singers: Francesco Graziani (Italian baritone) April 26; Luigi Van-
nuccini (Italian singing master) December 4; William Winn (British
bass) May 8.
Performers: Adolfo Fumagalli (Italian pianist) October 19; Joseph
Hellmesberger, Sr. (Austrian violinist/conductor) November 3;
Mathis Lussy (Swiss pianist/author) April 8; J. C. D. Parker (Ameri-

can organist/composer) June 2; Ede Reményi (Hungarian violinist) January 17; George William Warren (American organist) August 17. **Others:** Arrey von Dommer (German music historian) February 9; François Auguste Gevaert (Belgian musicologist) July 31; Luther Whiting Mason (American music educator) April 3; Juan Facundo Riaño (Spanish music scholar) November 24.

B. **Deaths**
Composers: Elizabeth Anspach (England) January 13; Antonio Calegari (Italy) July 22; Brizzio Petrucci (Italy) June 15; Franz Schubert (Austria) November 19.
Singers: Celeste Coltellini (Italian mezzo-soprano) July 28.
Performers: Josephus Andreas Fodor (Dutch violinist) October 3; Waldemar Thrane (Norwegian violinist/conductor) December 30.
Others: Antonio Calegari (Italian music theorist/composer) July 22.

C. **Debuts**
Singers: Luciano Fornasari (Italian bass—Italy); Eugenia Tadolini (Italian soprano—Florence).
Performers: Stephen Heller (Hungarian pianist—Vienna); Antonio James Oury (British violinist—London); Clara Wieck Schumann (German pianist—Leipzig); Wojciech A. Sowinski (Polish pianist—Vienna).

D. **New Positions**
Conductors: Ramón Carnicer (Royal Opera, Madrid); Heinrich Dorn (kapellmeister, Königsberg Theater); Friedrich Wilhelm Grund (Hamburg PO); François-Antoine Habeneck (Société des Concerts du Conservatoire de Paris); Adolf Müller, Sr. (Theater an der Wien, Vienna); Carl Gottlieb Reissiger (hofkapellmeister, Dresden); Ignaz Schuppanzigh (German Opera, Vienna).
Others: Ramón Félix Cuellar y Altarriba (principal organist, Santiago de Compostela); Gottfried Wilhelm Fink (editor, *Allgemeine Musikalische Zeitung*); Niels Peter Jensen (organ, St. Peter's, Copenhagen).

E. **Prizes/Honors**
Honors: Frédéric Kalkbrenner (Legion of Honor); Ferdinando Paër (Legion of Honor); Joseph Rastrelli (Knight of the Golden Spur).

F. **Biographical Highlights**
Hector Berlioz finally wins second prize in the Prix de Rome competition; Mikhail Glinka resigns his government post and begins studying composition with Zamboni; Ferdinand Hiller moves to Paris for a seven-year teaching stay; Niccolò Paganini, following his Vienna debut, becomes the idol of the Viennese public; Robert Schumann begins the study of law at Leipzig University but also studies piano

with his future father-in-law, Friedrich Wieck; Maria Szymanowska retires from performing and settles in St. Petersburg as a teacher.

G. **Cultural Beginnings**
Performing Groups—Choral: Bürgerlicher Gesangverein (Jena); Portland (Maine) Handel and Haydn Society; St. Martin's Church Music Society (Bratislava).
Performing Groups—Instrumental: Hamburg Philharmonic Concert Society; Société des Concerts du Conservatoire de Paris.
Educational: Brno Music Institute.
Music Publications: *Theatrical Censor and Musical Review.*
Performing Centers: Teatro Carlo Felice (Genoa).
Other: Boehm Flute Co. (Munich); Bösendorfer Piano Co. (Vienna); Music Lover's Society (St. Petersburg); New York Musical Fund Society; Polyplectron (by J. C. Dietz); Jean Vuillaume, violin maker (Paris).

H. **Musical Literature**
Tommaso Barsotti, *Méthode de musique;* František Blatt, *Clarinet Method;* Thomas Busby, *A Musical Manual;* Johann Heinroth, *Kurze Anleitung, das Klavier oder Forte-piano spielen zu lernen;* Edward Holmes, *A Ramble among the Musicians of Germany;* Johann Hummel, *Anweisung zum Piano-forte Spiel;* Adolf Marx, *Über Malerei in der Tonkunst;* Hans Georg Nägeli, *Musikalisches Tabellwerk für Volksschulen . . . ;* Johann Schiedermayer, *Theoretisch-praktische Chorallehre zum Gebrauch beim katholischen Kirchenritus;* Friedrich Dionys Weber, *Allgemeine theoretisch-praktische Vorschlule der Musik.*

I. **Musical Compositions**
Chamber Music:
String Quartets: Johann A. André, *Quartet, "Poissons d'avril," Opus 54/2(?).*
Sonata/Solos: Mikhail Glinka, *Viola Sonata in d;* Ignaz Moscheles, *Flute/Violin Sonata in G, Opus 79;* Niccolò Paganini, *Maestoso sonata sentimentale–Sonata and Variations on a Theme by Weigl;* Fernando Sor, *Guitar Etudes, Opus 6, 29 and 31.*
Ensembles: Franz Berwald, *Grand Septet in B♭;* Frédéric Chopin, *Piano Trio in g;* Franz Lachner, *Piano Trio No. 1 in E;* Franz Schubert, *String Quintet in C, D. 956.*
Piano: Alkan, *Variations on a Theme from Steibelt, Opus 1;* Frédéric Chopin, *Sonata in c, Opus 4–Two Polonaises (B♭, f), Opus 71/2,3–Rondo in C, Opus 73* (two pianos); Louise Farrenc, *Three Rondos faciles, Opus 8;* Friedrich Kihlau, *Variations on an Old Swedish Air, Opus 91–The Charms of Copenhagen, Opus 92–Fantasia on Swedish Airs, Opus 93;* Carl Loewe, *Alpenfantasie, Opus 53;* Franz Schubert, *Sonata*

in c, D. 958–Sonata in A, D. 959–Sonata in B♭, D. 960–Four Impromtus (c, E♭, G♭, A♭), Opus 90–Moments Musicaux (C, A♭, f, c♯, f, A♭), Opus 94.
Organ: Franz Schubert, *Fugue in e, D. 952* (four hands).
Choral/Vocal Music:
Choral: Hector Berlioz, *Herminie* (cantata)–*Eight Scenes from Faust, Opus 1*; Gaetano Donizetti, *Inno reale* (oratorio); Friedrich T. Fröhlich, *Christmas Mass*; Bernhard Klein, *Jephtha* (oratorio); Friedrich Kuhlau, *Elverhøj*; Albert Lortzing, *Die Himmelfahrt Jesu Christi* (oratorio); Felix Mendelssohn, *Grosse Festmusik zum Dürerfest*; Franz Schubert, *Mass No. 6 in E♭, D. 950–Glaube, Hoffnung und Liebe, D. 854*; Carl Zelter, *Six Songs for Male Chorus*.
Vocal: Johann A. André, *Ein alt lied von God, Opus 49*(?)–*Six Duets, Opus 51*(?); Carl Loewe, *Eleven Nachtgesänge, Opus 9 (i,ii)–Ten Gesänge der Sehnsucht, Opus 9 (iii,iv)–Ten Heitere Gesänge, Opus 9 (v,vi)–Eleven Gedichte, Opus 9 (vii,viii)–Twelve Lieder, Opus 9 (ix,x)*; Felix Mendelssohn, *Twelve Songs, Opus 8*; Franz Schubert, *Der Hirt auf dem Felsen, D. 965–Schwanengesang, D. 957* (cycle).
Musical Stage: Daniel Auber, *La muette de Portici*; Michele Carafa, *La violette*; Michael Costa, *Il carcere d'Ildegonda*; Gaetano Donizetti, *Alina, regina di Golconda–Gianni di Calais–L'esule di Roma*; Pietro Generali, *Il divorzio persiano*; Adalbert Gyrowetz, *Der Geburtstag*; Jacques Halévy, *Clari*; Franz Lachner, *Die Bürgschaft*; Heinrich Marschner, *Der Vampyr*; Saverio Mercadante, *Gabriella di Vergy– Francesca da Rimini–Adriano in Siria*; Francesco Morlacchi, *Colombo–I saraceni in Sicilia*; Wenzel Müller, *Der Alpenkönig und der Menschenfeind*; Giovanni Pacini, *I cavalieri de Valenza–I crociati à Tolemaide*; Carl Gottlieb Reissiger, *Libella*; Gioacchino Rossini, *Le Comte Ory*; Franz Schubert, *Der Graf von Gleicher*; Nicola Vaccai, *Saladino e Clotilde*; Alexei Vertovsky, *Pan Tsardovsky*.
Orchestra/Band Music:
Concerted Music:
Piano: Frédéric Chopin, *Grand Concert Rondo in F–Fantasia in A on Polish Airs, Opus 13*; Ignaz Moscheles, *Fantaisie sur des airs des bardes écossais, Opus 80*.
Violin: Louis Spohr, *Concerto No. 12 in A, Opus 79*.
Other: Franz Lachner, *Harp Concerto in c*.
Ballet/Incidental Music: Ferdinand Hérold, *Lydie* (B)–*La fille mal gardée* (B); Friedrich Kuhlau, *Der Elfenhügel* (IM); Albert Lortzing, *Die Hochfeuer* (IM); Heinrich Marschner, *Alexander und Darius* (IM); Cesare Pugni, *Agamemnone* (B).
Standard Works: Hector Berlioz, *Waverly Overture, Opus 1–Les Franc-Juges Overture, Opus 3*; Felix Mendelssohn, *Calm Sea and Prosperous Voyage Overture, Opus 27*.

Symphonies: Franz Lachner, *No. 1 in E♭, Opus 32*; George Mac-farren, *No. 1 in C*; Cipriani Potter, *No. 8 in E♭*; Franz Schubert, *No. 9 in C, "The Great," D. 944*; Louis Spohr, *Symphony No. 3 in c, Opus 78.*

1829

❀

Historical Highlights: Russia and Turkey sign the Peace of Adrianople; Greece, upon gaining her independence, becomes a republic; Swiss Constitution revision grants universal suffrage and freedom of the press; Catholic Emancipation Law is passed in Great Britain; Braille printing is invented; in the United States, the first steam locomotive, the "Tom Thumb" begins operation; the "Kitchen Cabinet" becomes a part of Andrew Jackson's presidency.

Art and Literature Highlights: Births—artists Albert Bellows, John Everett Millais, Johan Malmström, writers Victor Cherbuliez, Alexei Potemkin; Deaths—artist Johann Heinrich Tischbein, Jr., poet Karl von Schlegel. Art—Fisher's *Corn Husking Frolic*, Delacroix's *Death of Sardana-palus*, Turner's *Polyphemus Deriding Polyphemus*; Literature—Goethe's *Wilhelm Meisters Wanderjahre*, Hugo's *Les Orientales*, Scott's *Anne of Geierstein.*

Musical Highlights

A. Births

Composers: Domenico Bertini (Italy) June 26; Harrison Millard (U.S.A.) November 27; José Rogel (Spain) December 24; Anton Rubinstein (Russia) November 28.

Conductors: Frédéric Blasius (France); Albert Dietrich (Germany) August 28; Patrick S. Gilmore (U.S.A.) December 25.

Singers: Adelaide Borghi (Italian mezzo-soprano) August 9; August Gottfried Fricke (German bass) March 24; Darya Leonova (Russian contralto) March 9; Domenico Mustafà (Italian castrato soprano) April 14; Giovanni Sbriglia (Italian tenor) July 23; John Rogers Thomas (British-born baritone) March 26; Delphine Ugalde (French soprano) December 3.

Performers: Gaetano Braga (Italian cellist) June 9; Otto Goldschmidt (German pianist/conductor) August 21; Louis Moreau Gottschalk (American pianist/composer) May 8; Ernst Lübeck (Dutch pianist/composer) August 24; William Mason (American pianist/composer) January 24.

Others: Gustav Schirmer (German publisher) September 19.

B. **Deaths**
   Composers: Domingo Arquimbau (Spain) January 26; François-Joseph Gossec (Belgium) February 16; Bernardo Porta (Italy) June 11; Jan Stefani (Poland) February 24; Karl Gottlieb Umbreit (Germany) April 28.
   Conductors: Frédéric Blasius (France).
   Singers: Louis-Sébastien Lebrun (French tenor/composer) June 27; Luigi Marchesi (Italian castrato/composer) December 14; Giovanni Battista Rubinelli (Italian castrato contralto).
   Performers: Jean Ancot, *fils* (Belgian pianist/composer) June 5; Maurice Montagney Artôt (French horn virtuoso) January 8; Michael Gottard Fischer (German organist) January 12; Mauro Giuliani (Italian guitarist/composer) May 8; Benedikt Hacker (German violinist/composer) May 2; Benjamin Jacob (British organist) August 24; Johann Baptist Kucharz (Bohemian organist/composer) February 18; Jean Xavier Lefevre (Swiss-born clarinetist) November 9; Maria Anna Mozart (Austrian pianist) October 29; William Shield (British violinist/composer) January 25.
   Others: Augustus Frederic Kollmann (German music theorist/composer) April 19; Thomas Wright (British inventor) November 24.

C. **Debuts**
   Singers: Emma Albertazzi (British contralto—London); Giulia Grisi (Italian soprano—Milan); Domenico Reina (Italian tenor—Milan); Arthur P. Seguin (British bass—Exeter Festival).

D. **New Positions**
   Conductors: Antonio d'Antoni (Società Filarmonico-Dramatica, Trieste); Paolo Bonfichi (maestro di cappella, Santa Casa, Loreto); Raimondo Boucheron (maestro di cappella, Vigerano Cathedral); Conradin Kreutzer (Karnthnerthor Theater, Vienna); Franz Paul Lachner (Kärtnertor Theater); Adrien de La Fage (maître de chapelle, St. Étienne du Mont, Paris); Johann Heinrich Lübeck (hofkapellmeister, The Hague); Giovanni Tadolini (Théâtre-Italien, Paris).
   Others: Carlo Bignami (director, Teatro Sociale, Mantua); Samuel Sebastien Wesley (organ, St. Giles).

E. **Prizes/Honors**
   Honors: Daniel-François Auber (French Institute); Christian Kramer (Master of the King's Music); Gioacchino Rossini (Legion of Honor); Gustave Vogt (Legion of Honor).

F. **Biographical Highlights**
   Michael Costa is sent to England, where he remains for the rest of his life; Felix Mendelssohn conducts the revival of Bach's *St. Matthew Passion* and visits England and Scotland; Anton Reicha becomes a

naturalized French citizen; Robert Schumann gives up on law study and temporarily goes to Heidelberg to study music.

G. Cultural Beginnings

Performing Groups—Choral: Maatschappij tot Bervordering der Toonkunst (Amsterdam Choral Society); Mannheim Musikverein; Teatro Regio Opera Co. (Parma).

Performing Groups—Instrumental: Società Filarmonico-drammatica (Trieste).

Educational: Bartay-Menner Singing Academy (Pest); Paganini Music Conservatory (Genoa); Domenico Ronconi Singing School (Milan); Friedrich Schneider Music School (Dessau).

Music Publications: *Allgemeiner Musikalischer Anzeiger; Musikalisch-litterarischer Monatsbericht* (by F. Hofmeister); *La Revue de Paris.*

Other: Jacob Alexandre Harmonium Co. (Paris); Association for the Promotion of the Art of Music (Rotterdam); Concertina (by Charles Wheatstone); Asa Hopkins, woodwind maker (Litchfield, Connecticut); Conrad Meyer, piano maker (Philadelphia); Pierre Silvestre, violin maker (Lyons).

H. Musical Literature

Franz J. Antony, *Archäologisch-liturgisches Gesangbuch des . . . Kirchengesangs*; Antonio Calegari, *Sistema Armonico* (posthumous publication); Adolf B. Marx, *Über die Geltung Händelscher Sologesänge für unsere Zeit*; Lowell Mason, *The Juvenile Psalmist*; Bernhard Natorp, *Choralbuch für evangelische Kirchen*; Vincent Novello, *Purcell's Sacred Music*; Joseph d'Ortigue, *De la Guerre des Dilettanti*; Filippo Traetta, *Introduction to the Art and Science of Music*; Théodore de Vroye, *Vesperal.*

I. Musical Compositions

Chamber Music:

String Quartets: Luigi Cherubini, *No. 2 in C*; Ignacy F. Dobrzynski, *No. 1*; Louis Spohr, *Three Quartets (E, G, a), Opus 82–Double Quartet in E♭, Opus 77.*

Sonata/Solos: Frédéric Chopin, *Introduction and Polonaise in C, Opus 3* (cello, piano); Friedrich Kuhlau, *Variations on a Scottish Folksong, Opus 104–Variations on an Irish folksong, Opus 105* (flute, piano)–*Three Flute Sonatas, Opus 110*; Felix Mendelssohn, *Variations Concertantes, Opus 17* (cello, piano); Niccolò Paganini, *Variations on "God Save the King," Opus 9–Variations on "O mamma, mamma cara," Opus 10* (violin, piano); Fernan-do Sor, *Guitar Divertissements, Opus 1, 2, 8, 13, and 23–Guitar Etudes, Opus 35, 44, and 60–Six Guitar Pieces, Opus 48.*

Ensembles: Frédéric Chopin, *Piano Trio in g, Opus 8*; Józef Elsner, *Septet in D*; Ferdinand Hiller, *Piano Quartet No. 1, Opus 1*(?); Johann N. Hummel, *Septet Militaire in C, Opus 114*; Friedrich Kuhlau, *Piano Quartet No. 3 in g, Opus 108*; Franz Lachner, *Woodwind Quintet in E♭–Piano Trio No. 2 in c*; Robert Schumann, *Piano Quartet in c*.

Piano: Alkan, *Les Omnibus Variations, Opus 2*; Frédéric Chopin, *Four Etudes (F, f, A♭, E♭), Opus 10/8-11–Two Mazurkas (C, F), Opus 68–Waltz in b, Opus 69/2–Waltz in D♭, Opus 70/3–Variations in A, "Souvenir de Paganini"*; Stephen Heller, *Les charmes de Hambourg, Opus 2–Sonata No. 1 in d, Opus 9*; Carl Loewe, *Grosse sonate in E, Opus 16–Grand duo in F, Opus 18* (piano, four hands); Felix Mendelssohn, *Three Fantasies, Opus 16–Scherzo in b*.

Organ: Fanny Mendelssohn Hensel, *Three Organ Preludes (F, G, G)*.

Choral/Vocal Music:

Choral: Johann A. André, *Te Deum, Opus 60*; Hector Berlioz, *Cléopatre* (cantata); Franz Lachner, *Die vier menschenalter* (cantata); Carl Loewe, *Die Zerstörung Jerusalem, Opus 30* (oratorio); Giovanni Pacini, *L'annunzio felice*; Filippo Traetta, *Daughter of Zion* (oratorio); Joseph Weigl, *Mass, "Purificatione B.M.V."*

Vocal: Johann A. André, *Kleine Kantate, Opus 55*; Friedrich Kuhlau, *Six Songs, Opus 106*; Felix Mendelssohn, *Twelve Songs, Opus 9*.

Musical Stage: Adolphe Adam, *Pierre et Catherine*; Daniel Auber, *La fiancée*; Michael Balfe, *I rivali di se stressi*; Vincenzo Bellini, *Zaira–La straniera*; François Boieldieu, *Les deux nuits*; Michele Carafa, *Jenny*; Ramón Carnicer, *Elena e Malvina*; Hippolyte Chélard, *La table et le logement*; Michael Costa, *Malvina*; Gaetano Donizetti, *Il paria–Elisabetta*; Pietro Generali, *Francesca da Rimini*; Adalbert Gyrowetz, *Der dreizehnte Mantel*; Jacques Halévy, *La dilettante d'Avignon*; Ferdinand Hérold, *Emmaline–L'illusion*; Conradin Kreutzer, *Das Mädchen von Montfermeuil*; Heinrich Marschner, *Der Templer und die Jüdin*; Felix Mendelssohn, *Die Heimkehr aus der Fremde, Opus 89*; Saverio Mercadante, *Don Chisciotte–La rappresaglia*; Giovanni Pacini, *Il talismano–I fidanzati*; Errico Petella, *Il diavolo color di rosa*; Johann N. Poissl, *Der Untersberg*; Lauro Rossi, *Le contesse villane*; Gioacchino Rossini, *William Tell*; Gaspare Spontini, *Agnes von Hohenstaufen*; Nicola Vaccai, *Saul*.

Orchestra/Band Music:

Concerted Music:

Piano: Cipriani Potter, *Bravura Variation on a Theme by Rossini*.

Violin: Johann Kalliwoda, *Variations Brillantes, Opus 14* (two violins).

Ballet/Incidental Music: Louis Hérold, *La belle au bois dormant* (B); Albert Lortzing, *Don Juan and Faust* (IM); Cesare Pugni, *Adelaide di Franchia* (B).

Symphonies: Ferdinand Hiller, *No. 1*; Johann Kalliwoda, *No. 2 in Eᵇ, Opus 17*; Ignaz Moscheles, *No. 1 in C, Opus 81*; Georges Onslow, *No. 2 in d, Opus 42.*

1830
❄

Historical Highlights: July Revolution in France—Charles X abdicates in favor of Louis Philippe; the French invade Algeria; the Belgians revolt against the rule of the Netherlands; England's first railway begins operation; Ecuador and Venezuela gain independence; in the United States, the census shows a population of 12,866,000, a thirty-three percent increase in ten years; further U.S. colonization of Texas territory is forbidden by the Mexican government.

Art and Literature Highlights: Births—artists Albert Bierstadt, Camille Pissarro, writers Christina Rosetti, Jules Alfred de Goncourt, Frédéric Mistral; Deaths—artists Thomas Lawrence, Johann von Müller, Benjamin Constant. Art—Delacroix's *Liberty Guiding the People*, King's *Vanity of the Artist's Dream*, Palmer's *Coming from Evening Church*; Literature—Balzac's *La Vendetta*, Chamisso's *Frauenliebe und Leben*, Snelling's *Tales of the Northwest.*

Musical Highlights

A. Births
   Composers: Karl Goldmark (Hungary) May 18; Peter Heise (Denmark) February 11.
   Conductors: Hans von Bülow (Germany) January 8; Eduard Lassen (Denmark) April 13.
   Singers: Georg Ephraim Arlberg (Swedish baritone) March 21; Angiolina Bosio (Italian soprano) August 22; Clara M. Brinkerhoff (American soprano); Albert Eilers (German bass) December 21; Jean-Baptiste Faure (French baritone) January 15; Pietro Mongini (Italian tenor).
   Performers: August Adelburg (Austrian violinist/composer) November 1; Georg Hellmesberger, Jr. (Austrian violinist/composer) January 27; J. Sebastian Bach Hodges (British organist); Karl Klindworth (German pianist/conductor) September 25; Edmund Kretschmer (German organist) August 31; Theodor Leschetizky (Polish pianist/pedagogue) June 22; Franz Nachbaur (German tenor) March 25; Karl August Riccius (German violinist/conductor) July 26; Adolph Schlösser (German pianist) February 1.
   Others: Marie-Auguste Durand (French organist/publisher) July 18; Filippo Filippi (Italian critic) January 13; Karl Klindworth (German

pianist/conductor) September 25; Theodor Steingräber (German publisher) January 25; Wilhelm Tappert (German music scholar) February 19.

B. **Deaths**
Composers: Charles-Simon Catel (France) November 29; Stanilas Champein (France) September 19; José Mauricio Nunes García (Brazil) April 18; Marcos Antonio Portugal (Portugal) February 7.
Singers: Antonio Peregrino Benelli (Italian tenor) August 16; Giacomo Davide (Italian tenor) December 31; Therese Teyber (Austrian soprano) April 15.
Performers: Karl Friedrich Horn (German organist) August 5; Wenzel Thomas Matiegka (Austrian guitarist/composer) January 18; Carl Neuner (German violinist/composer) April 1; Peter Nikolaus Petersen (German flutist) August 19; Pierre Rode (French violinist/composer) November 25; Ignaz Schuppanzigh (Austrian violinist) March 2.

C. **Debuts**
Singers: Konstancja Gladkowska (Polish soprano—Warsaw); Eduard Mantius (German tenor—Berlin); Ludwika Rivoli (Polish soprano—Warsaw); Emma Romer (British soprano—London); Lorenzo Salvi (Italian tenor—Naples).

D. **New Positions**
Conductors: Henry Bishop (music director, Vauxhall); Johann Hermann Kufferath (Collegium Musicum/Gesangverein, Utrecht); Julius Otto (cantor, Kreuzkirche, Dresden); Joseph Rastrelli (Dresden Royal Opera); Ramón Vilanova (maestro de capilla, Barcelona Cathedral).
Others: Georg Hellmesberger (concertmaster, Vienna Opera Orchestra); Johann Gottlob Töpfer (town organist, Weimar); Louis Véron (director, Paris Opera); George James Webb (organist, Old South Church, Boston).

E. **Prizes/Honors**
Prizes: Hector Berlioz (Prix de Rome).

F. **Biographical Highlights**
Frédéric Chopin leaves Poland permanently; Muzio Clementi retires from the publishing business; Jenny Lind enrolls in the Swedish Royal Opera School; Felix Mendelssohn refuses the chair of music at Berlin University and visits Italy; Gioacchino Rossini loses his contract during the Revolution and writes his last opera; Robert Schumann returns to Leipzig, where he moves in with the Wiecks; Richard Wagner joins the Leipzig revolt and suffers a concert fiasco with his *Overture in B-flat*.

G. Cultural Beginnings

Performing Groups—Choral: Academic Music Society (Helsinki—continuation of Tuoku Student's Choral Society); Alte Hannoversche Liedertafel; Dresdner Liedertafel; Uppsala University Choral Union.

Performing Groups—Instrumental: Buffalo Philharmonic Society; Florence Philharmonic Society; Müller String Quartet I (Braunschweig); Union Alsacienne de Music (Strasbourg).

Educational: Madrid Royal Conservatory of Music; Proksch Music School (Prague); Städtische Singschule (Munich).

Music Publishers: Edward Moxon (London).

Music Publications: *Musikalisches Jugendblatt für Gesang, Clavier und Flöte* (Zittau).

Other: Philipp Furtwängler, organ builder (Hammer-Orgelbau); Samuel Graves and Co., instrument makers (New Hampshire); Urban Kreutzbach, organ builder (Borna); Telford and Telford, organ builders (Dublin).

H. Musical Literature

Prudent Aubéry du Boulley, *Grammaire Musicale*; Giacomo Ferrari, *Studio di musica teorica pratica–Anecdotti piacevole e interessanti accorsi nella vita di Giacomo Ferrari*; François Fétis, *Curiosités historiques de la Musique*; John Goss, *Piano Forte Student's Catechism*; Georg C. Grosheim, *Über pflege und Anwendung der Stimme*; Thomas Hastings, *The Union Minstrel*; Friedrich Kalkbrenner, *Méthode pour apprendre le piano-forte à l'aide du guide-mains*; Christian G. Körner, *Das deutsche evangeliche kirchenlied*; Emanuel Langbecker, *Das Deutsch-Evangelische Kirchenlied*; Gustav Schilling, *Musikalisches Handwörterbuch*; Friedrich Schneider, *Handbuch des Organisten*; Fernando Sor, *Méthode pour la Guitare*; Friedrich Weber, *Theoretisch-praktisches Lehrbuch der Harmonie I*.

I. Musical Compositions

Chamber Music:

String Quartets: Mikhail Glinka, *No. 2 in F*; Carl Loewe, *No. 4, "Spirituel."*

Sonata/Solos: Napoleon Costa, *Variations et Finale sur un Motif govori de la Fimilla Suisse de Weigl*, Opus 2 (guitar).

Ensembles: Ferdinand Hiller, *Piano Quartet No. 2, Opus 3*; Franz Lachner, *Trio in E♭* (horn, clarinet, piano); Ignaz Moscheles, *Piano Trio in c, Opus 84*.

Piano: Frédéric Chopin, *Four Polonaises (E♭, C, D, C), Opus 1– Nocturne in c♯, B.49–Four Mazurkas (f♯, c♯, E, e♭), Opus 6–Five Etudes (c, a, G♭, e♭, c), Opus 10/1,2,5,6,12*; Léon Boëly, *Thirty Etudes, Opus*

6(?); Carl Loewe, *Mazeppa, Opus 27–Der barmherzige Brüder, Opus 28*; Felix Mendelssohn, *Songs without Words, Book I, Opus 19*; Ignaz Moscheles, *Souvenirs de Danemarc, Opus 83*; Robert Schumann, *Abegg Variations, Opus 1*.

Choral/Vocal Music:

Choral: Hector Berlioz, *La Mort de Sardanapale* (cantata); Hippolyte Chélard, *Messe Solennelle*; Bernhard Klein, *David* (oratorio); Johann G. Lickl, *Requiem in C*; Felix Mendelssohn, *Jesu, meine Freuce–Psalm CXV, "Non nobis, Domine," Opus 31*; George Perry, *The Fall of Jerusalem* (oratorio); Joseph Weigl, *Mass, "Annuntiatione B.M.V."*

Vocal: Johann A. André, *Liederkranz, Opus 57*(?); Hector Berlioz, *Nine Irish Melodies, Opus 2*; Frédéric Chopin, *Four Songs, Opus 74*; Thomas Hastings, *Toplady* (hymn tune, "Rock of Ages"); Otto Nicolai, *Three Songs, Opus 3–Six Songs, Opus 6–Preussens Stimme, Opus 4*.

Musical Stage: Adolphe Adam, *Danilowa*; Daniel Auber, *Fra Diavolo–Le dieu et la bayadère*; Michael Balfe, *Un avertimento ai gelosi*; Vincenzo Bellini, *Il Capuleti e i Montecchi*; Henry Bishop, *Under the Oak*; Gaetano Donizetti, *Anna Bolena–Il diluvio universale–Imelda de' Lambertazzi–I pazzi per progetto*; Jacques Halévy, *La langue musicale*; Ferdinand Hérold, *L'auberge d'Auray*; Conradin Kreutzer, *Baron Luft*; Heinrich Marschner, *Des Falkners Braut*; Giovanni Pacini, *Giovanna d'Arc*; George Perry, *Family Jars*; Errico Petrella, *Il giorno delle nozze*; Lauro Rossi, *Costanza e Oringaldo*; Johann Schmidt, *Alfred der Grosse*; Louis Spohr, *Der Alchymist*; Gaspare Spontini, *Mignon's Lied*; Alexei Vertovsky, *Man and Wife*.

Orchestra/Band Music:

Concerted Music:

Piano: Frédéric Chopin, *Concerto No. 1 in e, Opus 11–No. 2 in f, Opus 13*; Friedrich Flotow, *Concerto No. 1*; Johann Kalliwoda, *Grosses Rondo, Opus 16*; Sigismond Thalberg, *Concerto in f, Opus 5*.

Violin: Niccolò Paganini, *Concerto No. 4 in d–No. 5 in a*.

Ballet/Incidental Music: Heinrich Dorn, *Amor's macht* (B); Jacques Halévy, *Manon Lescaut* (B); Ferdinand Hérold, *La Noce de village* (B); Friedrich Kuhlau, *The Triplet Brothers from Damascus* (IM); Franz Lachner, *Lanassa* (IM); Albert Lortzing, *Yelva* (IM).

Standard Works: Felix Mendelssohn, *Hebrides Overture, Opus 26*; Richard Wagner, *Overture in B♭*.

Symphonies: Hector Berlioz, *Fantastic Symphony, Opus 14*; Johann Kalliwoda, *Symphony No. 3 in d, Opus 32*; František Krommer, *No. 9*.

1831

❄

Historical Highlights: Leopold I becomes king of an independent Belgium; Austria tries unsuccessfully to stamp out Italian nationalism; the Polish Insurrection is crushed by Russian troops; in the United States, Turner's Rebellion in Virginia results in fifty whites killed—Turner is hanged; William Garrison begins publication of *The Liberator*; South Bend, Indiana, is founded; New York University is chartered; R. L. Stevens introduces the flanged railroad track.

Art and Literature Highlights: Births—artists Reinhold Degas, Jean Falguière, Constantin Meunier, writers Jane Austin, Victorien Sardou; Deaths—writers Achim von Arnim, Willem Bilderdijk, Friedrich von Klinger. Art—Cole's *Wild Scene*, Decamp's *The Turkish Patrol*, Lauder's *The Bride of Lammermoor*; Literature—Gogol's *Evenings on a Farm*, Hugo's *Notre Dame de Paris*, Whittier's *Legends of New England*.

Musical Highlights

A. Births

Composers: Fillippo Marchetti (Italy) February 26; Ludvig Norman (Sweden) August 28; Cipriano Pontoglio (Italy) December 25.

Conductors: Johann Herbeck (Austria) December 25; Salomon Jadassohn (German) August 13.

Singers: Antonio Cotogni (Italian baritone) August 1; Marie Luise Dustmann (German soprano) August 22; Constance Nantier-Didiée (French mezzo-soprano) November 16; Albert Niemann (German tenor) January 15; Bessie Palmer (British contralto) August 9; Antonio Sangiovanni (Italian singing master) September 14; Therese Tietjens (German soprano) July 17.

Performers: W. H. Cummings (British organist) August 22; Richard Hoffman (British-born pianist) May 24; Joseph Joachim (Hungarian violinist) June 28.

Others: Henry Charles Banister (British music theorist/composer) June 13; Georges Chanot, Jr. (French-born violin maker) January 11; Charles Meerens (Belgian acoustician/musicologist) December 26; Rudolph Wurlitzer (German-born organ builder) January 31.

B. Deaths

Composers: (Frans Fredric) Eduard Brendler (Sweden) August 16; Benjamin Carr (England-U.S.A.) May 24; Ferdinand Kauer (Austria) April 13; Józef Kozlowski (Poland) February 27; Georg Michael Telemann (Germany) March 4; Friedrich Wollanck (Germany) September 6.

Singers: François Lays (French tenor) March 30; Louis Nourrit (French tenor) September 23.

Performers: Mateo Pérez de Albéniz (Spanish organist) June 23; Traugott Eberwein (German violinist/composer) December 2; Peter Fuchs (Austrian violinist/composer) June 15; Thomas Greatorex (British organist) July 18; Peter Hänsel (German violinist) September 18; Franz Vincez Krommer (Czech violinist/conductor) January 8; Rodolphe Kreutzer (French violinist/conductor) January 6; Vincenz Mašek (Bohemian pianist) November 15; Pierre-Jean Porro (French guitarist) May 31; Friedrich Ludwig Seidel (German organist/conductor) May 5; Maria Agate Szymanowska (Polish pianist/composer) July 24.

Others: John Aitken (Scottish publisher) September 8; Sébastien Érard (French piano maker) August 5; Christian Gottfried Körner (German music theorist) May 13; Ignace Joseph Pleyel (Austrian-born piano maker/composer) November 14; Johann George Schetky (German-born cellist/composer/publisher) December 11.

C. **Debuts**

Singers: Anna Bishop (British soprano—London); Teresa Brambilla (Italian soprano—Milan); Prosper Dérivis (French bass—Paris); Anna Maria Hasselt-Barth (Dutch soprano—Trieste), Clara Heinefetter (German soprano—Vienna); Nicolai Ivanov (Russian tenor—Naples); Elizabeth Masson (British soprano—England), Giorgio Ronconi (Italian baritone—Pavia); Jane Shirreff (British soprano—London); John Templeton (Scottish tenor—London); Pierre-François Wartel (French tenor—Paris).

Performers: Jean-Delphin Alard (French violinist—Paris); Heinrich Wilhelm Ernst (Czech violinist—Paris); Julius Knorr (German pianist—Leipzig); Sebastian Lee (German cellist—Hamburg).

D. **New Positions**

Conductors: Francisco Andreví y Castellar (choirmaster, Madrid Royal Chapel); Heinrich Dorn (music director, St. Peter's Cathedral, Riga); Ignaz Lachner (hofkapellmeister, Stuttgart); Friedrich Müller (conductor, Royal Orchestra, Rudolstadt); Lauro Rossi (assistant, Teatro Valle, Rome); Anton Schindler (choirmaster, Münster Cathedral); Henri-Justin Valentino (Opéra-Comique, Paris).

Others: Auguste Bottée de Toulmon (librarian, Paris Conservatory); Henry F. Chorley (music critic, *London Athenaeum*); Johann T. Mosewius (director, Institute for Church Music, Breslau).

E. **Prizes/Honors**

Prizes: Eugène-Prosper Prévost (Prix de Rome).

Honors: Eduard Brendler (Swedish Royal Academy); Adolf Fredrik Lindblad (Swedish Royal Academy); Ferdinando Paër (French Academy); Anton Reicha (Legion of Honor).

F. **Biographical Highlights**
Frédéric Chopin moves to Paris; Alexander Dargomijsky enters the Russian Department of Justice; Félicien David leaves the Paris Conservatory and joins the Saint-Simonian cult; John Field, sick from cancer, returns to England; Niccolò Paganini makes highly successful debuts in London and Paris; Robert Schumann begins studying composition with Heinrich Dorn; Richard Wagner enters the University of Leipzig.

G. **Cultural Beginnings**
Performing Groups—Choral: Ansbach Choral Society; Bund der Nordwestdeutschen Liedertafeln; Darmstadt Musikverein; Glasgow Amateur Musical Society; Mainz Liedertafel; Newark (New Jersey) Handel and Haydn Society.
Performing Groups—Instrumental: Bradford Philharmonic Society.
Festivals: Dublin Music Festival.
Educational: Agthe Music Academy (Breslau).
Music Publications: *Charivari* (France); *Figaro in London*.
Performing Centers: Exeter Hall (London); Grand Theater (Lyons); Meiningen Hoftheater.
Other: Johann Heckel, instrument maker (Wiesbaden); Tulou-Nonon Flute Co. (Paris).

H. **Musical Literature**
François Aimon, *Abécédaire musical, principes élémentaires à l'usage des élèves*; Georg C. Grosheim, *Chronologisches Verzeichniss vorzüg ticher Beförder und Meister der Tonkunst*; August F. Haeser, *Chorgesangschule*; Thomas Hastings/Lowell Mason, *Spiritual Songs for Social Worship*; John A. Latrobe, *The Music of the Church in Its Various Branches, Congregational and Choral*; Peter Lichtenthal, *Estetica*; Joseph Mainzer, *Singschule*; Lowell Mason, *The Juvenile Lyre*; Jérôme-Joseph de Momigny, *A l'Académie des Beaux-Arts*; Louis Spohr, *Violin School*; José Virués y Spinola, *La Geneuphonia*; Théodore de Vroye, *Graduel*; Charles Zeuner, *Church Music*.

I. **Musical Compositions**
Chamber Music:
Piano: Frédéric Chopin, *Five Mazurkas (B♭, a, f, A♭, C), Opus 7–Three Nocturnes (b♭, E♭, B), Opus 9–Two Nocturnes (F, F♯), Opus 15/1,2–Waltze in E♭, Opus 18–Waltz in a, Opus 34/2*; John Field, *Pastorale in A–Grand Pastorale in E*; Stephen Heller, *Three Impromtus, Opus 7–Rondo Scherzo, Opus 8*; Friedrich Kuhlau, *Sonata in E♭, Opus 127*; Robert Schumann, *Papillons, Opus 2–Allegro, Opus 8*.

Organ: Camille Saint-Saëns, *Three Rhapsodies, Opus 7*; Samuel Wesley, *Six Introductory Movements and a Loud Voluntary with Introduction and Fugue.*
Choral/Vocal Music:
Choral: Hector Berlioz, *Meditation, Opus 18*; Fanny Mendelssohn Hensel, *Job–Lobegesang* (cantatas); Otto Nicolai, *Te Deum*(?); Carl Zelter, *Ten Songs for Male Chorus.*
Musical Stage: Daniel Auber, *Le philtre*; Vincenzo Bellini, *Norma–La sonnambula*; Louise-Angélique Bertin, *Fausto*; Michele Carafa, *Le lure de l'hermite*; Ramón Carnicer, *Cristoforo Colombo*; Hippolyte Chélard, *Mitternacht*; Gaetano Donizetti, *Gianni di Parigi–Francesca di Foix–La romanziera e l'uomo nero*; Heinrich Dorn, *Abu Kara*; Pietro Generali, *Il Romito di Provenza*; Adalbert Gyrowetz, *Felix und Adele*; Ferdinand Hérold, *Zampa*; Conradin Kreutzer, *Die Hochländerin–Die Jungfrau*; Saverio Mercadante, *Zaïra*; Giacomo Meyerbeer, *Robert, le diable*; Giovanni Pacini, *Il corsaro*; Cesare Pugni, *Il disertore svizzero*; Carl Reissiger, *Die Felsenmühle zu Estaliéres*; Luigi Ricci, *Chiara di Rosemberg*; Lauro Rossi, *Lo sposo al lotto–La casa in vendita*; Alexei Vertovsky, *The Old Hussar.*
Orchestra/Band Music:
Concerted Music:
Piano: Friedrich Flotow, *Concerto No. 2*; Felix Mendelssohn, *Concerto No. 1 in g, Opus 25.*
Violin: Johann Kalliwoda, *Concertante, Opus 20, for Two Violins and Orchestra.*
Other: Charles Zeuner, *Organ Concerto No. 2.*
Ballet/Incidental Music: Michael Costa, *Kenilworth* (B).
Standard Works: Hector Berlioz, *King Lear Overture, Opus 4–Le Corsaire Overture, Opus 21*; Anthony Heinrich, *Pushmataha*; Richard Wagner, *Overture in d–Overture in C.*
Symphonies: George Macfarren, *No. 2 in d*; Otto Nicolai, *No. 1 in c*; W. C. Peters, *Symphony in D*; Wilhelm Taubert, *Symphony No. 1.*

1832

Historical Highlights: Giuseppe Mazzini founds the Young Italy Society to help promote nationalism; the Egyptians defeat the Turks at the Battle of Konia; a major cholera epidemic sweeps around the world; in the United States, Andrew Jackson is reelected as president and proceeds to veto the National Bank Reform Bill; the Black Hawk Indian War takes place in Wisconsin; the first clipper ship, the *Ann McKim*, is launched.

Art and Literature Highlights: Births—writers Louisa May Alcott, Lewis Carroll, artists Gustav Doré, Édouard Manet, William Orchardson; Deaths—writers George Crabbe, Johann Wolfgang von Goethe, Sir Walter Scott. Art—Constable's *Waterloo Bridge*, Quidor's *Leatherstocking Meets the Law*, Turner's *Childe Harold's Pilgrimage*; Literature—Hugo's *Le Roi s'Amuse*, Paulding's *Westward Ho!*, Scott's *Castle Dangerous*.

Musical Highlights

A. Births
Composers: Charles (Alexandre) Lecocq (France) June 3; Henry Clay Work (U.S.A.) October 1.
Conductors: Leopold Damrosch (Germany-U.S.A.) October 22.
Singers: Ivan Melnikov (Russian baritone) March 4; Caroline Pruckner (Austrian soprano) November 4; Louisa Pyne (British soprano) August 27; Henri Warnots (Belgian tenor) July 11; Marie Wieck (German pianist) January 17.
Performers: Friedrich Grützmacher (German cellist) March 1; Alfred Jaëll (Austrian pianist) March 5; Wilhelm Langhans (German violinist/composer) September 21; Ferdinand Laub (Bohemian violinist) January 19; Johann Lauterbach (German violinist) July 24; Franz Wüllner (German pianist/composer) January 28.
Others: Heinrich Bellermann (German music theorist) March 10; Charles Converse (American hymnist) October 7; William H. Doane (American hymnist) February 3; Robert Eitner (German musicologist) October 22.

B. Deaths
Composers: David August von Apell (Germany) January 30; Bonifazio Asioli (Italy) May 18; Pietro Generali (Italy) November 3; Bernhard Klein (Germany) September 9; Henrik Klein (Moravia) August 26; Carl Friedrich Zelter (Germany) May 15.
Singers: Manuel García (Spanish tenor) June 9; Adelaide Malanotte (Italian contralto) December 31; Andrea Nozzari (Italian tenor) December 12.
Performers: Charles François Angelet (Belgian pianist) December 20; Henri Berton (French pianist/composer) July 19; Francisco Javier Cabo (Spanish organist) December 21; Muzio Clementi (Italian pianist/composer) March 10; Johann Sebastian Demar (German organist/composer)(?); Xavier Désargus (French harpist); Jean Imbault (French violinist/publisher) April 15; Jean Nicolas Kreutzer (French violinist) August 31; Friedrich Kuhlau (German-born pianist/composer) March 12; Eduard Rietz (German violinist/author) January 22.

Others: Karl C. F. Krause (German music author) September 27; François Louis Perne (French music historian) May 26; Nikolaus Simrock (German publisher) June 12.

C. **Debuts**
Singers: Julian Dobrski (Polish tenor—Warsaw); Marie-Cornélie Falcon (French soprano—Paris); Livia Frege (German soprano—Leipzig); Nicolai Ivanov (Russian tenor—Naples); Sophie Loewe (German soprano—Vienna); Clara Novello (British soprano—Windsor); Fanny Persiani (Italian soprano—Livorno); Maschinka Schneider Schubert (Estonian soprano—London); Rosine Stoltz (French mezzo-soprano—Brussels).
Performers: Hubert Léonard (Belgian violinist—Liège); Henry Charles Litolff (French pianist—London).

D. **New Positions**
Conductors: Michael Costa (King's Theater, London); Heinrich Dorn (Hamburg Opera); Hilarión Eslava (maestro de capilla, Seville Cathedral); Adolf Marx (music director, University of Berlin); Johann Theodor Mosewius (music director, University of Breslau); Ferdinando Paër (music director, Royal Chapel, Paris); Alexander Varlamov (kapellmeister, Moscow Imperial Theaters).
Others: August Wilhelm Bach (director, Royal Institute for Church Music, Berlin); Samuel Sebastian Wesley (organ, Hereford Cathedral).

E. **Prizes/Honors**
Prizes: Ambroise Thomas (Prix de Rome).
Honors: Giacomo Meyerbeer (Legion of Honor).

F. **Biographical Highlights**
Frédéric Chopin makes his Paris debut and meets John Field; Anthony Heinrich, returning once more to the United States, settles in Boston; Felix Mendelssohn makes his second trip to England; Niccolò Paganini returns to Italy and buys the Villa Gajona with his English fortune; Robert Schumann ruins his hand (and his concert career) by use of his so-called "strengthening apparatus"; Giuseppe Verdi is refused admittance to the Milan Conservatory after failing the entrance exams.

G. **Cultural Beginnings**
Performing Groups—Choral: Adelphi Glee Club (London); Sacred Harmony Society of London; Trotebau Male Choir (Marseilles).
Performing Groups—Instrumental: Glasgow Philoharmonic Society; New Haven Musical Society (Connecticut); Société Philharmonique (Dijon).

Educational: Boston Academy of Music; Brussels State Academy (Conservatory) of Music.
Music Publishers: J. Schuberth and Co., Leipzig branch; Ticknor and Fields Publishing House (Boston).
Music Publications: *De Muzen* (The Netherlands); *Revue Rétrospective*.
Performing Centers: San Juan Municipal Theater (Puerto Rico).
Other: Charles Barker, organ maker (Bath); Boehm Flute (first known).

H. Musical Literature

Johann A. André, *Lehrbuch der Tonsetzkunst I*; François Blaze, *Chapelle musique des Rois de France*; Friedrich Dotzauer, *Violoncellschule*; William Gardiner, *The Music of Nature*; Johann Häuser, *Neue pianoforte-schule*; Heinrich Hoffmann, *Geschichte des deutschen Kirchenlieds*; August Kahlert, *Blätter aus der Brieftasches eines Musikers*; Lowell Mason, *Lyra Sacra*; Gaspard Prony, *Instruction élémentaire sur les moyens de calculer les intervalles musicaux*; Johann Seyfried, *Wiener Tonschule*; Charles Zeuner, *The American Harp*.

I. Musical Compositions

Chamber Music:
String Quartets: Louis Spohr, *Three Quartets (d, A♭, b), Opus 84*.
Sonata/Solos: Frédéric Chopin, *Grand Duo in E on Meyerbeer's "Robert le diable"* (cello, piano).
Ensembles: John Field, *Grand Pastorale in E* (piano, string quartet); Mikhail Glinka, *Sextet in E♭, for Piano and Strings*; Ignaz Moscheles, *Grosses Septet in D, Opus 88*.
Piano: Frédéric Chopin, *Three Etudes (E, c♯, C), Opus 7–Introduction and Rondo, Opus 16–Scherzo in b, Opus 20*; Louise Farrenc, *Air suisse varié, Opus 7*; John Field, *Nocturne in E♭, "The Troubadour"*; Cipriani Potter, *Fifty-Four Impromtus, Opus 22*; Clara Schumann, *Caprices on forme de valse, Opus 2*; Robert Schumann, *Paganini Etudes I, Opus 3–Six Intermezzi, Opus 4*; Samuel Wesley, *Sonata in G, for Piano, Four Hands*.

Choral/Vocal Music:
Choral: Alkan, *Hermann et Ketty* (cantata); Hector Berlioz, *Lélio, ou Le Retour à la Vie, Opus 14*; Józef Elsner, *Passion of our Lord Jesus Christ*; Felix Mendelssohn, *Te Deum in A–Die Erste Walpurgisnacht, Opus 60*; Sigismund von Neukomm, *Das Besetz des alten Bundes* (oratorio); Otto Nicolai, *Mass in D*; Johann N. Poissl, *Vergangenheit und Zukunst*; Louis Spohr, *Three Psalms, Opus 85*; Joseph Weigl, *Mass, "In Nomine B.M.V."*
Vocal: Franz Lachner, *Sängerfahrt* (cycle); Carl Loewe, *Geistliche Gesänge I–Three Ballads, Opus 20*; Otto Nicolai, *Lieder und Gesänge, Opus 16*.

Musical Stage: Carl Arnold, *Irene*; Daniel Auber, *Le serment*; Gaetano Donizetti, *L'elisir d'amore–Fausta–Ugo, conte di Parigi*; Heinrich Dorn, *Das Schwarmermädchen*; Jacques Halévy, *La tentation–Yella*; Johan P. Hartmann, *The Raven*; Ferdinand Hérold, *Le pré aux clercs–La médecine sans médecin*; Conradin Kreutzer, *Der Lastträger an der Themse*; Carl Loewe, *Malekadhel*; Albert Lortzing, *Der Weihnachtsabend–Der Pole und sein kind–Andreas Hofer*; Saverio Mercadante, *I normanni a Parigi–Ismalia*; Giovanni Pacini, *Ivanhoe–Don Giovanni Tenorio*; Cesare Pugni, *La vendetta–Ricciarda di Edinburgh*; Lauro Rossi, *Baldorino, tiranno di Spoleto–Il maestro di scuola*; Alexei Vertovsky, *Vadim*; Richard Wagner, *Die Hochzeit* (unfinished).
Orchestra/Band Music:
Concerted Music:
    Piano: Alkan, *Concerto da Camera No. 1 in a*(?); William Sterndale Bennett, *Concerto No. 1 in d, Opus 1*; Felix Mendelssohn, *Capriccio Brillante in b, Opus 22*; Cipriani Potter, *Concerto No. 2 in d*.
    Other: Franz Lachner, *Flute Concerto in d*.
Ballet/Incidental Music: Michael Costa, *Une Heure à Naples* (B); Carl Loewe, *Das Märchen im Traum* (IM).
Orchestra/Band: William Sterndale Bennett, *Overture, the Tempest*; Hector Berlioz, *Rob Roy Overture*; George Macfarren, *Overture in E♭*; Felix Mendelssohn, *Calm Sea and Prosperous Voyage Overture, Opus 27*.
Symphonies: George Macfarren, *No. 3 in e*; Felix Mendelssohn, *No. 5 in d, "Reformation," Opus 107*; Cipriani Potter, *No. 10 in g*; Robert Schumann, *Symphony in g* (unpublished); Louis Spohr, *No. 4 in F, Opus 86, "Die Weihe der Töne"*; Richard Wagner, *Symphony in C*; Samuel Sebastian Wesley, *Symphony in c*(?).

1833

❄

Historical Highlights: The British Parliament bans slavery throughout the British Empire; the Factory Act improves the lot of children in English factories; the Ottoman Empire concludes a treaty with Russia in order to prevent an Egyptian takeover; in the United States, President Jackson withdraws all public funds from the Bank of the United States; the American Anti-Slavery Society is founded; Oberlin College becomes the first coed college in America.
Art and Literature Highlights: Births—artists Edward Burne-Jones, Henri M. Chapu, Launt Thompson, writers Pedro de Alarcón, Mary Abigail Dodge; Deaths—poet Charles Chenedollé, artists Pierre-Narcisse Guérin, William Rush. Art—Catlin's *Dying Buffalo*, Etex's *Cain Cursed by*

God, Morse's *Exhibition Gallery of the Louvre*; Literature—*Autobiography of Black Hawk*, Carlyle's *Sartor Resartus*, Lamb's *Last Essays of Elia*.

Musical Highlights

A. Births

Composers: Alexander Borodin (Russia) November 12; Johannes Brahms (Germany) May 7; Grenville Dean Wilson (U.S.A.) January 26.

Singers: Luigi Agnesi (Belgian bass) July 17; Giuseppe Fancelli (Italian tenor) November 24; Maria Charlotte Geistinger (Austrian soprano) July 26; Barbara Marchisio (Italian contralto) December 6; Adelaide Phillipps (British contralto) October 26; Hortense Schneider (French soprano) April 30; Genevieve Ward (American soprano) March 27; Marie Witt (Austrian-born soprano) January 30.

Performers: Francis Edward Bache (British pianist) September 14; Jean Becker (German violinist) May 11; Antonín Bennewitz (Bohemian violinist) March; Charles-Wilfride de Bériot (French pianist) February 21; William Cusins (British pianist/organist/conductor) October 14; Wilhelm Ganz (German-born pianist/conductor) November 6; Johannes Hobert (Bohemian organist) October 18; Robert Pflughaupt (German pianist) August 4; Alexander Ritter (German violinist/conductor) June 27; Josef Richard Rozkosný (Czech pianist) September 21.

Others: Adolph Fürstner (German publisher) April 2; August Robert Forberg (German publisher) May 18; Michael Hermesdorff (German musicologist/organist) March 4.

B. Deaths

Composers: Maria Rosa Coccia (Italy) November; Ferdinand Hérold (France) January 19; Prince Michael Cleofas Oginski (Poland) October 18; Vittorio Trento (Italy)(?).

Singers: Maria Dickons (British soprano); Gertrud Mara (German soprano) January 20; Luiza Rosa Todi (Portugese mezzo-soprano) October 1.

Performers: Philip Cogan (Irish organist) February 3; Ramón Félix Cuellar y Altarriba (Spanish organist) January 7; Joseph Valentin Dont (Austrian cellist) December 14; Jacob Eckhard (German-born organist) November 10; Ferdinand Fränzl (German violinist/conductor) November 19; Johann Christian Haeffner (Swedish organist/conductor) May 28; Johann Wilhelm von Königslow (German organist) May 14; Antonio da Silva Leite (Portuguese organist/composer) January 10; Josef Slavík (Czech violinist/composer) May 30.

Others: John Crosse (British musicologist) October 20; William Marcellus Goodrich (American organ maker) September 15; Joubert de La Salette (French music theorist) February 4; Prince Anton Heinrich Radziwill (Polish patron of the arts) April 7.

C. Debuts

Singers: Ignazio Marini (Italian bass—Milan); Napoleone Moriani (Italian tenor—Pavia).
Performers: Niels Gade (Danish violinist—Copenhagen); Otto Nicolai (German pianist—Berlin).

D. New Positions

Conductors: Conradin Kreutzer (kapellmeister, Josephstadt Theater, Vienna); Felix Mendelssohn (Düsseldorf SO); Giuseppe Saverio Mercadante (maestro di cappella, Novara Cathedral); Carl Friedrich Rungenhagen (Berlin Singakademie); Francesco Shira (San Carlos Theater, Lisbon).
Others: João Bomtempo (director, Lisbon Conservatory); François Fétis (director, Brussels Conservatory).

E. Prizes/Honors

Honors: Friedrich Berr (Legion of Honor); Hans Nägeli (honorary doctorate, Bonn University).

F. Biographical Highlights

Hector Berlioz marries British actress Henriette Smithson; César Franck, age eleven, makes his first tour of Belgium as a concert organist; William Knabe emigrates to the United States and settles in Baltimore; Alexis Lvov composes the Russian Czarist Anthem; Niccolò Paganini commissions a viola work from Berlioz; Robert Schumann founds his so-called Davidsbündler; Johann Strauss, Sr., begins touring with his orchestra; Henri Vieuxtemps begins a long German tour at the age of thirteen.

G. Cultural Beginnings

Performing Groups—Choral: Ansbach Male Chorus; Glasgow Choral Society; Lübeck Gesangverein (Singakademie); Warsaw Grand Opera; York Choral Society; Zöllner-Verein (Leipzig).
Performing Groups—Instrumental: Boston Academy Orchestra; Concerts Symphoniques (Lyons); Distin Family Brass Quartet (London); Kiev Philharmonic Society; Sociedade Beneficencia Musical (Rio de Janeiro); Société Philharmonique (Rheims).
Festivals: Cincinnati Music Festival.
Educational: Accademia Filo-Armonica di Messina.
Music Publishers: Coventry and Hollier (London).
Music Publications: *Gazette Musicale de la Belgique*; *Magasin Pittoresque*; *Le Ménestrel*; *Régolo* (Hungary).
Performing Centers: Mainz Stadttheater; Italian Opera House (New York); The Ossolineum (Lvov); Paris Orphéon; Small Opera Theater (St. Petersburg).

Other: C. J. Martin and Co., guitar makers (New York); Henry Pilcher and Sons, organ builders (Newark).

H. Musical Literature

François Fétis, *Universal Biography of Musicians and Music I*; Henri Gérard, *Traité méthodique d'harmonie*; Karl Gollmick, *Kritische terminologie*; John Goss, *Introduction to Harmony and Thoroughbass*; Johann Häuser, *Geschichte des christlichen evangelischen Kirchengesanges*; Joseph d'Ortigue, *Le Balcon de l'Opéra*; Anton Reicha, *L'Art du compositeur dramatique*; Gottfried Weber, *Generalbasslehre zum selbstunterrichte*.

I. Musical Compositions

Chamber Music:

String Quartets: Louis Spohr, *Double Quartet in e, Opus 87*; Ambroise Thomas, *Quartet in e, Opus 1*.

Ensembles: Friedrich Kuhlau, *Piano Quartet No. 3 in g, Opus 108*; Franz Lachner, *Andante in Aᵇ* (brass).

Piano: Alkan, *Rondo brillant, Opus 4(?)–Variations on Rossini's "Largo al factotum," Opus 5–Rondeau chromatique, Opus 12*; Frédéric Chopin, *Nocturne in g, Opus 13–Four Mazurkas (Bᵇ, e, Aᵇ, a), Opus 17–Bolero in C/A, Opus 19–Waltz in Gᵇ, Opus 70/1*; John Field, *Nocturne No. 11 in Eᵇ–Nouvelle Fantasie in G*; Felix Mendelssohn, *Fantasia (Sonata Ecossaise) in f♯, Opus 28*; Robert Schumann, *Impromtus on a Theme of Clara Wieck, Opus 5–Toccata in C, Opus 7–Paganini Etudes II, Opus 10*.

Organ: Samuel Wesley, *Three Introduction and Fugues (G, b, d-?)*.

Choral/Vocal Music:

Choral: Franz Lachner, *Moses* (oratorio); Carl Loewe, *Die sieben Schlafer, Opus 46–Die Walpurgisnacht*; Lauro Rossi, *Saul* (oratorio); Johann Schmidt, *Missa Solemnis in D*; Joseph Weigl, *Mass, "Nativitate B.M.V."*

Vocal: Carl Loewe, *(Twelve) Bilder des Orients–Geistliche Gesänge II*; Lowell Mason, *Olivet (hymn tune, "My Faith Looks Up to Thee")*.

Musical Stage: Daniel Auber, *Gustave III*; Michael Balfe, *Enrico IV*; Vincenzo Bellini, *Beatrice di Tenda*; Michele Carafa, *La prison d'Edimbourg*; Luigi Cherubini, *Ali Baba*; Gaetano Donizetti, *Lucrezia Borgia–Torquato Tasso–Parisina–Il furioso all'isola di San Domingo*; Friedrich von Flotow, *Die Bergknappen–Alfred der Grosse*; Jacques Halévy, *Les souvenirs de Lafleur*; Ferdinand Hérold, *Ludovic* (finished by Halévy); Jean-Georges Kastner, *Oskars Tod*; Conradin Kreutzer, *Melusina–Der Ring des Glückes*; Carl Loewe, *Neckereien*; Heinrich Marschner, *Hans Heiling*; Saverio Mercadante, *Il conte di Essex*; Giovanni Pacini, *Fernando duca di Valenza–Irene*; Vincenzo Pucitta, *Adolfo e Chiara*; Cesare Pugni, *Il contrabbandiere*; Luigi

Ricci, *I due sergenti*; Lauro Rossi, *La fucine di Bergen*; Friedrich von Sobolewski, *Imogen*; Richard Wagner, *Die Feen*.

Orchestra/Band Music:
Concerted Music:
Piano: Alkan, *Concerto No. 2, Opus 39*; William Sterndale Bennett, *Concerto No. 2 in E♭, Opus 4*; Johann N. Hummel, *Concerto No. 9 in F, Opus Posth.*; Ignaz Moscheles, *Concerto No. 6 in B♭, "Fantastique," Opus 90*; Cipriani Potter, *Concerto in E♭*.
Violin: Johann Kalliwoda, *Concertino, Opus 37*; Louis Spohr, *Concertante No. 2 in b, Opus 88* (two violins).
Other: Franz Lachner, *Harp Concerto No. 2 in d*.

Ballet/Incidental Music: Adolphe Adam, *Faust* (B); Michael Costa, *Sir Huon* (B); Felix Mendelssohn, *Der standhafte Prinz* (IM).

Orchestra/Band: Friedrich T. Fröhlich, *Concert Overture in B*; Felix Mendelssohn, *Beautiful Melusine Overture, Opus 32*.

Symphonies: Friedrich Flotow, *Symphony*; Johannes Fröhlich, *Symphony in E♭*; Franz Lachner, *No. 2 in F*; George Macfarren, *No. 4 in f–No. 5*; Felix Mendelssohn, *No. 4 in A, Opus 90, "Italian"*; Cipriani Potter, *No. 2 in D*.

1834

Historical Highlights: Robert Peel becomes the British prime minister; Civil War in Spain between the Constitutionalists and the Carlists; the Zollverein, the first step toward German unity, is formed; the South Australia Act opens the country for colonization—the city of Melbourne is founded; in the United States, the Whig Party is formed as an anti-Jackson political party; Anti-Abolitionist Riots take place in the North; Fort Laramie is built on the Oregon Trail.

Art and Literature Highlights: Births—artists Edgar Degas, James M. Whistler, writers George du Maurier, Jan Neruda, Charles F. Browne; Deaths—sculptor John H. I. Browere, writers Charles Lamb, Samuel Coleridge-Taylor. Art—Catlin's *Little Spaniard, a Warrior*, Delacroix's *Women of Algiers*, Turner's *The Burning of Parliament*; Literature—Bulwer-Lytton's *The Last Days of Pompeii*, Pushkin's *The Queen of Spades*, Sainte-Beuve's *Volupté*.

Musical Highlights

A. Births
Composers: Carlo Angeloni (Italy) June 16; Peter Benoit (Belgium) October 17; Wilhelm Blodek (Czechoslovakia) October 3; Hart P.

Danks (U.S.A.) April 6; Horatio R. Palmer (U.S.A.) April 26; Amil-
care Ponchielli (Italy) August 31.
Conductors: Rudolf Bial (Germany) August 26; Charles Lamoureux
(France) September 28.
Singers: Charles Adams (American tenor) February 9; Armand de
Castelmary (French bass) August 16; Helen Lemmens-Sherrington
(British soprano) October 4; Nicolini (Ernest-Nicolas) (French tenor)
February 23; Marietta (Maria) Piccolomini (Italian soprano) March
15; Charles Santley (British baritone) February 28; Teresa Stolz
(Bohemian soprano) June 5; Gustav Walter (Bohemian tenor) Febru-
ary 11.
Performers: Wilhemine Clauss-Szarvady (Bohemian pianist) De-
cember 13; Julius Reubke (German pianist) March 23.
Others: Henry Lee Higginson (American patron of the arts) Novem-
ber 18; Paul Jausions (French church music scholar) November 15;
Jan Pieter Land (Dutch musicologist) April 23; Arthur Pougin
(French music author) August 6; Eben Tourjée (American music educator) June 1; George P. Upton (American music critic/author) October 25.

B. **Deaths**
Composers: François Boieldieu (France) October 8; Silvestro (De)
Palma (Italy) August 8; Friedrich Christian Ruppe (Germany) Au-
gust 14.
Performers: Jacques-Marie Beauvarlet-Charpentier (French organ-
ist) September 7; Julie Candeille (French pianist) February 4; Au-
gust Duranowski (Polish violinist); John Mahon (British clarinetist/
composer) January; Charles Wesley (British organist/composer)
May 23.
Others: Alexandre Choron (French music theorist/editor) June 28.

C. **Debuts**
Singers: Filippo Coletti (Italian baritone—Naples); Francilla Göhringer Pixis (German contralto—Karlsruhe); Elizabeth Poole (British
mezzo-soprano—London); Mary Shaw (British contralto—London);
Giuseppina Strepponi (Italian soprano—Adria); Felice Varesi (French-
born baritone—Varese).
Performers: Arthur Saint-Léon (French violinist—Stuttgart).

D. **New Positions**
Conductors: Franz Lachner (Mannheim National Theater); Fran-
cisco Manuel da Silva (Sociedade Filarmônica, Rio de Janeiro);
Ferdinand Ries (Aachen Orchestra and Singakademie); Théophile
Tilmant (Théâtre-Italien, Paris); Richard Wagner (Heinrich Beth-
mann's theater company, Magdeburg).

Others: Pedro Albéniz y Basanta (organ, Royal Chapel, Madrid); William Ayrton (editor, *The Musical Library*); John Perry (music critic, *London Morning Post*).

E. **Prizes/Honors**
Prizes: Antoine-Aimable Elwart (Prix de Rome).
Honors: Henri-Montan Berton (Legion of Honor); Heinrich Marschner (doctorate, University of Leipzig); Giacomo Meyerbeer (French Institute).

F. **Biographical Highlights**
Mikhail Glinka, upon the death of his father, returns to Russia to take care of the family affairs; Franz Liszt goes to Geneva and moves in with the Countess d'Agoult by whom he has three children, one of them being Cosima; Niccolò Paganini, in failing health, returns to Italy and begins limiting his engagements; Richard Wagner, while conducting the orchestra with Bethmann's theater company in Magdeburg, meets actress Christine (Minna) Planer.

G. **Cultural Beginnings**
Performing Groups—Choral: Antient Concerts Society (Dublin); Mozart Sacred Society (Newark, New Jersey); Musikalischer Cirkel (Breslau).
Performing Groups—Instrumental: Helsinki City Orchestra; Maglioni Chamber Concerts (Florence); Société des Derniers Quators de Beethoven.
Educational: Orleans Institut Musical; Wyeth Music School (Chicago).
Music Publishers: Jacques Heugel and Co. (Paris).
Music Publications: *Le Franc-juge*; *Neue Zeitschrift für Musik*.
Performing Centers: Paradise Street Town Hall (Birmingham, England).
Other: A = 440 vps (decided by the Stuttgart Congress of Physicists); Alexandre Debain Instrument Co. (Paris); Maatschaplpij moor Tonkunst (Leiden music society); Society of British Musicians (London).

H. **Musical Literature**
Pierre Baillot, *L'Art du violon*; András Bartay, *Magyar Apollo*; Carl Czerny, *Lehrbuch der . . . Composition*; Józef Elsner, *School of Singing*; Georg C. Grosheim, *Versuch einer ästhetischen Darstellung mehrerer Werke dramatischer Tonmeister älterer und neuerer Zeit*; Raphael Kiesewetter, *Geschichte der europäisch-abendländischen, das ist unserer heutigen Musik*; Lowell Mason, *Manual of Instruction (Pestalozzian)*; Jérôme-Joseph de Momigny, *Cours général de musique*; Johann Scheibler, *Der physikalische und musikalische Tonmesser*; Carl von Winterfeld, *Johannes Gabrieli und sein zeitalter*.

I. Musical Compositions
Chamber Music:
String Quartets: Luigi Cherubini, *No. 3 in d*; Fanny Mendelssohn Hensel, *Quartet in E♭*; George Macfarren, *No. 1 in g(?)*.

Sonata/Solos: Norbert Burgmüller, *Duo for Clarinet and Piano, Opus 15*.

Ensembles: César Franck, *Grand Trio, Opus 6* (piano trio); Franz Lachner, *String Quintet in c, Opus 121*; Louis Spohr, *String Quintet No. 4 in a, Opus 91*.

Piano: Frédéric Chopin, *Seven Etudes (a, e, g♯, D♭, G♭, b, a), Opus 25/4–6, 8–11*; John Field, *Nocturen No. 12 in G–No. 13 in d*; Franz Liszt, *Harmonies poètique et religieuses–Apparitions*; Felix Mendelssohn, *Rondo Brillant, Opus 29*; Robert Schumann, *Etudes Symphoniques, Opus 13*; Samuel Wesley, *Variations in D on "God Save the King"* (four hands).

Choral/Vocal Music:
Choral: Alkan, *L'entrée en loge* (cantata); Henry Bishop, *The Seventh Day* (cantata); Carl Loewe, *Die eherne Schlange, Opus 40* (oratorio); Felix Mendelssohn, *Six Partsongs, Opus 41*; Sigismund von Neukomm, *David* (oratorio); Franz von Suppé, *Mass in F*; Joseph Weigl, *Mass in A*.

Vocal: Carl Loewe, *Three Legends, Opus 33–Der grosse Christoph, Opus 34–Two Legends, Opus 35–Three Legends, Opus 36–Three Legends, Opus 37–Der Bergman, Opus 39* (cycle); Felix Mendelssohn, *Infelice, Opus 94*; Lady Jane Scott, *Annie Laurie*.

Musical Stage: Adolphe Adam, *Le Châlet*; Daniel Auber, *Lestocq*; John Barnett, *The Mountain Sylph*; Gaetano Donizetti, *Maria Stuarda–Rosamonda d'Inghilterra–Gemma di Vergy*; Adalbert Gyrowetz, *Hans Sachs im vorgerückten Alter*; Jean-Georges Kastner, *Der Sarazene*; Conradin Kreutzer, *Tom Rick–Das Nachtlager in Granada–Der Verschwender*; Carl Loewe, *Die drei Wünsche*; Saverio Mercadante, *Emma d'Antiochia–La gioventù di Enrico V–Uggero il danese*; Stanislaw Moniuszko, *The Bureaucrats*; Giovanni Pacini, *Irene*; Ferdinando Paër, *Un caprice de femme*; Eugène Prévost, *Cosimo*; Cesare Pugni, *Un episodio di San Michele*; Luigi Ricci, *Chi dura vince–Un aventura di Scaramuccia*; Jacob Rosenhaim, *Der besuch im irrenhause*; Lauro Rossi, *Amelia–La casa disabitata*; Wilhelm Taubert, *Der Zigeuner*.

Orchestra/Band Music:
Concerted Music:
Piano: William Sterndale Bennett, *Concerto No. 3 in c, Opus 9*; Franz Liszt, *Grande Fantaisie Symphonique on Themes of Berlioz*.

Other: Johann Kallivoda, *Introduction and Rondo, Opus 51* (horn).

Ballet/Incidental Music: Herman S. Løvenskold, *Sylfiden* (B); Cesare Pugni, *Monsieur de Chalumeaux* (B).

Standard Works: William Sterndale Bennett, *Parisina Overture–Overture, Merry Wives of Windsor*; Hector Berlioz, *Harold in Italy, Opus*

16; Hippolyte Chélard, *Braveurstücke*; Louise Farrenc, *Overture, Opus 23–Overture, Opus 24*; Mikhail Glinka, *Overture-Symphony on Russian Themes*; Johann Kalliwoda, *Concert Overture No. 2 in F, Opus 44–Concert Overture No. 3 in C, Opus 55–Concert Overture No. 4 in E, Opus 56*; George Macfarren, *Overture, The Merchant of Venice*(?); Otto Nicolai, *Funeral March on the Death of Bellini*.

Symphonies: William Sterndale Bennett, *No. 4 in A*; Ferdinand Hiller, *No. 2, Opus 67*; Franz Lachner, *No. 3 in d, Opus 41–No. 4 in E*; Cipriani Potter, *No. 4 in D–No. 5 in c*.

1835
❉

Historical Highlights: Halley's Comet makes its scheduled appearance; the Municipal Corporations Act attempts to regulate and standardize all local governments in England; Turkey takes control over Tripoli; in the United States, President Andrew Jackson escapes harm when an assassin's pistol misfires; the Liberty Bell cracks during Justice Marshall's funeral; the Second Seminole War is fought in Florida; the Texas Revolution against Mexico begins.

Art and Literature Highlights: Births—artist John La Farge, Larkin Meade, writers Giosuè Carducci, Samuel Clemens (Mark Twain); Deaths—artist Antoine-Jean Gros, poets James Hogg, William Motherwell, August Platen. Art—Corot's *Hagar in the Desert*, Eakins' *The Swimming Hole*, Kaulbach's *Battle of the Huns*; Literature—Büchner's *Dantons Tod*, Bulwer-Lytton's *Rienzi*, Gogol's *Taras Bulba*, Simms' *The Yemassee*.

Musical Highlights

A. **Births**
Composers: Jules-Émile Cohen (France) November 2; César Cui (Russia) January 18; Felix Draeseke (Germany) October 7; Camille Saint-Saëns (France) October 9.
Conductors: Eduard Strauss (Austria) March 15; Theodore Thomas (Germany-U.S.A.) October 11.
Singers: Marguerite-Desirée Artôt (Belgian mezzo-soprano) July 21; Franz Betz (German baritone) March 19; Allen J. (Signor) Foli (Irish bass) August 7; Isabella Galletti-Gianoli (Italian soprano) November 11; Carlotta Marchisio (Italian soprano) December 8; John Patey (British baritone); Carlotta Patti (Italian soprano) October 30; Hans von Rokitansky (Austrian bass) March 6.
Performers: Vasili Bezekirsky (Russian violinist) January 26; Frederic Brandeis (Austrian-born pianist) July 5; Nicolai Rubinstein

(Russian pianist) June 14; Henryk Wieniawski (Polish violinist) July 10; August Winding (Danish pianist) March 24.
Others: Andrew Carnegie (American patron of the arts) November 25; George Sherburn Hutchings (American organ builder) December 9; Dom Joseph Pothier (French music scholar) December 7; Ebenezer Prout (British music theorist) March 1.

B. Deaths
Composers: Vincenzo Bellini (Italy) September 23; William Linley (England) May 6; Klaus Scholl (Denmark) August 10.
Conductors: Wenzel Müller (Austria) August 3.
Singers: Georgina Oldmixon (British-born soprano) February 3.
Performers: Olaf Ahlström (Swedish organist) August 11; Paul Alday (French violinist/composer); Aline Bertrand (French harpist) March 13; Marie-Alexandre Guénin (French violinist/composer) January 22; François-Joseph Nadermann (French harpist) April 2; Nicolas-Joseph Platel (French cellist/composer) August 25.
Others: John Osborne (American piano maker) May 27; François Tourte (French bow maker) April.

C. Debuts
Singers: Charlotte Cushman (American contralto—Boston); Adelaide Kemble (British soprano—London); Jan Křtitel Pišek (Bohemian baritone—Prague).
Performers: Henry Christian Timm (German-born pianist—New York).

D. New Positions
Conductors: Felix Mendelssohn (Leipzig Gewandhaus Orchestra); Hubert Ries (Berlin Philharmonic Society); Lauro Rossi (Italian Opera Co., Mexico); Francis Schenig (U.S. Marine Band); Giuseppe Verdi (maestro di musica, Busseto).
Others: Hector Berlioz (music critic, *Journal des Débats*); João Domingos Bomtempo (director, Lisbon Royal Conservatory); Victor François Desvignes (director, Metz Conservatory); Martin-Joseph Mengal (director, Ghent Conservatory); Samuel Sebastian Wesley (organ, Exeter Cathedral).

E. Prizes/Honors
Honors: Vincenzo Bellini (Legion of Honor); Lowell Mason (honorary doctorate, New York University); Anton Reicha (French Academy).

F. Biographical Highlights
Anton Bruckner begins some regular music instruction from his father and cousin; César Franck moves with his family to Paris and begins

organ lessons with Reicha; Felix Mendelssohn, accepting the position as conductor of the Gewandhaus Orchestra, soon turns it into one of the best on the continent; Georg K. Nagler begins publication of the monumental *Neues Allgemeines Künstlerlexikon*; William Vincent Wallace begins his travels to Australia, New Zealand, and the Americas.

G. Cultural Beginnings
Performing Groups—Choral: Gotha Liedertafel; Philadelphia Männerchor.
Performing Groups—Instrumental: Boston Brass Band; Carlsbad Symphony Orchestra (Germany); Philipp Fahrbach Orchestra (Vienna); Société de Musique de Chambre (Paris).
Educational: Conservatório Nacional (Lisbon); Geneva Conservatory of Music; Ghent Conservatory of Music; Metz Conservatory of Music; Whittlesey's Music School (Salem, Massachusetts).
Music Publishers: Giovanni Canti (Milan); C. A. Challier and Co. (Berlin); Oliver Ditson and Co. (Boston).
Music Publications: *Deutsche Revue; Gazette Musicale de Paris; Musical Magazine* (New York).
Performing Centers: St. James Hall (Buffalo, New York).
Other: Bass Tuba (by W. F. Wieprecht); Brinsmead Piano Co. (London).

H. Musical Literature
Pietro Alfieri, *Saggio storico teorio pratico del canto gregoriano*; William Ayrton, *Sacred Minstrelsy*; Luigi Cherubini, *Cours de contrepoint et de la fugue*; Friedrich von Drieberg, *Wörterbuch der grieschen Musik*; José Elizaga, *Principios de la harmonía y de la melodia*; George Hogarth, *Musical History, Biography and Criticism*; Lowell Mason, *Boston Academy Collection of Church Music*; Thomas Oliphant, *Brief Account of the Madrigal Society*; Gustav Schilling, *Enzyklopädie der gesamten musikalischen Wissenschaften I*; Simon Sechter, *Praktische Generalbass-Schule*; William Walker, *Southern Harmony*; Wesley Woolhouse, *Essay on Musical Intervals*.

I. Musical Compositions
Chamber Music:
   String Quartets: Norbert Burgmüller, *No. 4 in a, Opus 14*; Luigi Cherubini, *No. 4 in E–No. 5 in F*; Ferdinand Hiller, *No. 1, Opus 12–No. 2, Opus 13*(?); Johann Kalliwoda, *No. l in G, Opus 61*; Louis Spohr, *Quartet in A, Opus 93*.
   Sonata/Solos: Johann N. Hummel, *Rondo brillant in G, Opus 126* (violin, piano).
   Ensembles: Ferdinand Hiller, *Piano Trio No. 1, Opus 6–No. 2, Opus 7–No. 3, Opus 8*(?); Ambroise Thomas, *String Quintet*.

Piano: John Field, *Nocturne No. 14 in C*; Frédéric Chopin, *Ballade in g, Opus 23–Four Mazurkas (g, C, A♭, b♭), Opus 24–Two Polonaises (c♯, e♭), Opus 26–Two Nocturnes (c♯, E♭), Opus 27–Waltz in A♭, Opus 34/1–Fantaisie-Impromtu in c♯, Opus 66–Two Mazurkas (G, C), Opus 67/1,3*; César Franck, *Grande Sonate No. 1, Opus 10*; Felix Mendelssohn, *Three Capriccios, Opus 33–Songs without Words II, Opus 30*; Robert Schumann, *Carnaval, Opus 9–Sonata No. 1 in f♯, Opus 11.*

Choral/Vocal Music:

Choral: Gaetano Donizetti, *Requiem Mass in d (in memory of Bellini)*; Carl Loewe, *Die Apostel von Philippi, Opus 48* (oratorio); Johann N. Poissl, *Der Erntetag* (oratorio); Louis Spohr, *Des Heilands letzte Stunden* (oratorio).

Vocal: Hippolyte Chélard, *Musikalische Reise*; Carl Loewe, *Three Ballads, Opus 43–Three Ballads, Opus 44–Two Ballads, Opus 45–Three Ballads, Opus 49–Two Polish Ballads, Opus 50–Sängers Wanderlied*; Felix Mendelssohn, *Two Sacred Songs, Opus 112.*

Musical Stage: Daniel Auber, *Le cheval de bronze*; Michael Balfe, *The Siege of Rochelle*; Vincenzo Bellini, *I puritani*; Michele Carafa, *La grande duchesse*; Hippolyte Chélard, *Die Hermannsschlacht*; Gaetano Donizetti, *Lucia de Lammermoor–Marino Faliero*; Friedrich von Flotow, *Pierre et Catherine*; Jacques Halévy, *La juive–L'eclair*; Johan P. Hartmann, *The Corsairs, Opus 16*; Jean-Georges Kastner, *Die Königin der Sarmaten*; Conradin Kreutzer, *Der Bräutigam in der Klemme*; Adolf Lindblad, *Frondörerne*; Albert Lortzing, *Die beiden Schützen*; Saverio Mercadante, *I due Figaro–Francesco Donato*; Giovanni Pacini, *Carlo di Borgogna*; Giuseppe Persiani, *Ines de Castro*; Errico Petrella, *La Cimodocea*; Carl Reissiger, *Turandot*; Luigi Ricci, *Chiara di Montalbano–La donna colonello*; Lauro Rossi, *Leocadia*; Friedrich Truhn, *Trilby*; Alexei Vertovsky, *Askold's Grave*; Richard Wagner, *Das Liebesverbot*.

Orchestra/Band Music:

Concerted Music:

Piano: Ferdinand Hiller, *Concerto No. 1 in A♭, Opus 5*; Franz Liszt, *Concert No. 1 in E♭*; Cipriani Potter, *Concerto in E–Ricercara on a Favorite French Theme, Opus 24*; George Macfarren, *Concerto in c*.

Violin: Louis Spohr, *Concerto No. 13 in E, Opus 92.*

Standard Works: Friedrich T. Fröhlich, *Passion Music Overture*; Johann Kalliwoda, *Concert Overture No. 2 in F, Opus 44*; Ignaz Moscheles, *Overture, Joan of Arc, Opus 91*; Cipriani Potter, *Overture, Antony and Cleopatra*; Richard Wagner, *Columbus Overture*.

Symphonies: Johan P. Hartmann, *No. 1 in g, Opus 17*; Anthony Heinrich, *Gran sinfonia eroica*; Johann Kalliwoda, *No. 4 in C, Opus 60*; Franz Lachner, *No. 5 in c, "Preis-Symphnie," Opus 52*; Otto Nicolai, *No. 2 in D*.

1836

❄

Historical Highlights: The Boers begin their "Great Trek" out of South Africa in order to escape British rule; the University of London is founded; settlement of the city of Adelaide, Australia, begins; in the United States, Martin Van Buren is elected as the eighth president; Arkansas becomes state number twenty-five; the Texans are defeated at the Battle of the Alamo but defeat the Mexicans at the Battle of San Jacinto; President Andrew Jackson's *Specie Circular* causes a panic.

Art and Literature Highlights: Births—artists Lawrence Alma-Tadema, Winslow Homer, Edward Poynter, authors Thomas Bailey Aldrich, Bret Harte; Deaths—artists Ezra Ames, Carle Vernet, writers William Godwin, George Colman, Jr. Art—Cole's *The Course of Empire*, Corot's *Diana and Actaeon*, Overbeck's *Marriage of the Virgin*; Literature—Büchner's *Woyzeck*, Dickens's *Pickwick Papers*, Gogol's *The Inspector General*.

Musical Highlights

A. Births

Composers: Samuel David (France) November 12; Léo Delibes (France) February 21; Carlos Gomes (Brazil) July 11; Charles Jerome Hopkins (U.S.A.) April 4.

Singers: William Castle (British tenor) December 23; Thomas Aynsley Cook (British bass) July (1831?); Vincenzo Graziani (Italian baritone) February 16; Frederike Grün (German soprano) June 14; Elsie Hensler (American soprano); Jean Morère (French tenor) October 6; Ilma di Murska (Croatian soprano) January 4; Francesco Pandolfini (Italian baritone) November 22; Euphrosyne Parepa-Rosa (Scottish soprano) May 7; Ludwig Schnoor von Carolsfeld (German tenor) July 2; Myron Whitney (American bass) September 5.

Performers: Friedrich Baumfelder (German pianist) May 28; John Carrodus (British violinist) January 20; Adolf Friedrich Christiani (German-born pianist) March 8; Arabella Goddard (British pianist) January 12; Jesús de Monasterio (Spanish violinist) March 21; S. Austen Pearce (British-born organist) November 7; Thomas Philander Ryder (American organist) June 29.

Others: Mitrophan Belaiev (Russian publisher) February 22; Sir William S. Gilbert (British librettist) November 18; Oskar Kolbe (German music theorist/composer) August 10; Oscar Paul (German music scholar) April 8; Benjamin Edward Woolf (British-born music critic/composer) February 16.

B. Deaths

Composers: Carl Friedrich Ebers (Germany) September 19; Giuseppe Farinelli (Italy) December 12; Friedrich Theodor Fröhlich (Switzerland) October 16; José Melchor Gomis y Colomer (Spain) July 26; Gottlieb Graupner (Germany-U.S.A.) April 16; Christian Ignatius Latrobe (England) May 6; Vincenzo Lavigna (Italy) September 14; Daniel Read (U.S.A.) December 4; Anton Reicha (Bohemia) May 28; Claude-Joseph Rouget de Lisle (France) June 27; Johann Baptist Schenk (Austria) December 29.

Singers: Gaetano Crivelli (Italian tenor) July 16; Cecilia Davies (British soprano) July 3; Maria Malibran (Spanish mezzo-soprano) September 23.

Performers: Louis Ancot (Belgian pianist/composer) September; Richard G. Ashley (British violist) October 11; Norbert Burgmüller (German pianist/composer) May 7; William Crane Carl (American organist) December 8; John Clarke (British organist/composer) February 22; Friedrich Witt (German violinist/composer) January 3.

Others: Supply Belcher (American hymn writer) June 9; Jacques Cousineau (French harp maker) January 11; John Feltham Danneley (British music theorist); Hans Georg Nägeli (Swiss publisher/author) December 26; James Power (Irish publisher) August 26; Count Andreas Razumovsky (Russian patron of the arts); John Stafford Smith (Brtitish music scholar/composer) September 21.

C. Debuts

Singers: Kathinka Heinefetter (German soprano—Frankfurt); Maria Dolores Nau (American soprano—Paris); Elizabeth Rainforth (British soprano—London); Sebastiano Ronconi (Italian baritone—Lucca).

Performers: Teresa Milanollo (Italian violinist—Mondovi); Edward Roeckel (German pianist—London).

D. New Positions

Conductors: Franz Erkel (German Municipal Theater, Pest); Franz Lachner (hofkapellmeister, Munich); Luigi Ricci (maestro di cappella, Trieste); Ferdinand Ries (Frankfurt St. Cecilia Society); Raphael R. Triay (U.S. Marine Band).

Others: Thomas Attwood (organ, Royal Chapel, London); William Henry Fry (music critic, *Philadelphia National Gazette*); Louis Kufferath (director, Leeuwarden Conservatory).

E. Prizes/Honors

Prizes: Xavier Boisselot (Prix de Rome).

Honors: Jacques Halévy (French Institute); Frédéric Kalkbrenner (Order of Leopold); Clara Wieck (Imperial Chamber Virtuoso, Vienna).

F. **Biographical Highlights**
Ferdinand David, on the invitation of Mendelssohn, becomes concertmaster of the Leipzig Gewandhaus Orchestra; Franz Liszt defeats Sigismond Thalberg in their famous pianistic "duel"; Maria Malibran marries the violinist Charles de Bériot just six months before her death; Gioacchino Rossini, after winning his litigation suit against France, settles in Bologna; Richard Wagner marries Minna Planer but loses his position when the Magdeburg Opera group fails.

G. **Cultural Beginnings**
Performing Groups—Choral: Huddersfield Choral Society (England); Old Settler's Harmonic Society (Chicago); Portland Sacred Music Society (Maine); Toronto Musical Society.
Performing Groups—Instrumental: Boston Academy Orchestra; Dayton (Ohio) Philharmonic Society; Israel Broadcasting Authority Orchestra (Jerusalem Orchestra).
Music Publishers: Brainard and Son, publishers (Cleveland); J. F. Edelmann, music publisher (Havana); J. B. Lippincott and Co. (Philadelphia).
Music Publications: *Musical World*.
Other: Danish Musical Society (Copenhagen); Friedrich Haas, organ builder (Switzerland); Luigi Lambertini, piano maker (Lisbon); Mahillon Wind Instrument Co. (Brussels); Pestbuda Society of Musicians; Purcell Club (London); Samuel R. Warren, organ builder (Montreal).

H. **Musical Literature**
Bonifazio Asioli, *Il Maestro di composizione*; Friedrich Berr, *Traité complet de la clarinette à 14 clefs*; Antonio Calegari, *Modi generali del canto*; Julius Knorr, *Neue pianoforteschule*; Joseph Mainzer, *Méthode de chant pour voix d'hommes*; Lowell Mason, *Sabbath School Songs*; Thomas Oliphant, *A Short Account of Madrigals*; Jean-Louis Tulou, *Flute Method*; Peter Wolle, ed., *Moravian Tune Book*.

I. **Musical Compositions**
Chamber Music:
   String Quartets: Gaetano Donizetti, *No. 15 in e*.
   Sonata/Solos: Louise Farrenc, *Variations concertantes sur un air suisse Opus 20* (violin, piano).
   Ensembles: John Field, *Nocturne No. 16 in F, Opus 62A* (piano, string quartet); Cipriani Potter, *Sextet in E♭*.
   Piano: Frédéric Chopin, *Five Etudes (Nos. 1,2,3,7,12–A♭, f, F, c♯, g), Opus 25–No. 10 in E–No. ll in C–No. 15 in C*; John Field, *Nocturnes No. 14 in C–No. 15 in C*; Franz Liszt, *Grande Valse de Bravura–Fantaisie romantique sur deux mélodies suisses–Album d'un voyageur III*; Felix

Mendelssohn, *Scherzo à capriccio in f♯*; Ignaz Moscheles, *Characteristic Etudes, Opus 95*; Clara Schumann, *Four Characteristic Pieces, Opus 5*; Robert Schumann, *Piano Sonata in f, Opus 14–Fantasy in C, Opus 17.* **Organ:** Anton Bruckner, *Prelude in E♭*; Samuel Sebastian Wesley, *Six Organ Voluntaries, Opus 36.*

Choral/Vocal Music:
Choral: Luigi Cherubini, *Requiem No. 2 in d*; Carl Loewe, *Gutenberg, Opus 55–Die Festizeiten (Gospel according to St. John), Opus 66*; Felix Mendelssohn, *St. Paul, Opus 36* (oratorio); George Perry, *Belshazzar's Feast* (cantata); Johann Schmidt, *Rinaldo* (cantata); Franz von Suppé, *Mass in C*; C. P. E. Weyse, *Easter Cantata No. 1.*

Vocal: Frédéric Chopin, *Seventeen Polish Songs, Opus 74*; Gaetano Donizetti, *Nuits d'été à Pausilippe*; Carl Loewe, *Ester, Opus 52 (cycle)–Three Ballades, Opus 56–Five Odes for Male Voices, Opus 57–Three Ballads, Opus 59–Frauenliebe, Opus 60*; Felix Mendelssohn, *Six Songs, Opus 34*; Saverio Mercadante, *Les soirées italiennes.*

Musical Stage: Adolphe Adam, *Le Postillon de Longjumeau–La Fille du Danube*; Daniel Auber, *Actéon–L'ambassadrice–Les chaperons blanc*; Michael Balfe, *The Maid of Artois*; Louise Bertin, *Esmeralda*; Gaetano Donizetti, *Belisario–Il campanello di notte–L'assedio di Calais–Betly*; Friedrich von Flotow, *Sérafine*; Mikhail Glinka, *A Life for the Tsar*; Albert Grisar, *Sarah*; John Hullah, *The Village Coquette*; Albert Lortzing, *Die Schatzkammer des Ynka*; Heinrich Marschner, *Das Schloss am Aetna*; Saverio Mercadante, *I briganti*; Giacomo Meyerbeer, *Les Huguenots*; Hippolyte Monpou, *Le luthier de Vienne*; Otto Nicolai, *Enrico II*; Giovanni Pacini, *Belezza e cuor di ferro*; Lauro Rossi, *Giovanni Shore*; Friedrich von Sobolewski, *Velleda*; Joseph Strauss, *Armiodan*; Nicola Vaccai, *Giovanna Gray*; Christoph Weyse, *Festen paa Kenilworth.*

Orchestra/Band Music:
Concerted Music:
Piano: William Sterndale Bennett, *Concerto No. 4 in f*; Ignaz Moscheles, *Concerto No. 7 in c, "Pathétique," Opus 93*; Clara Schumann, *Concerto in a, Opus 7*; Ambroise Thomas, *Fantasie brillante, Opus 6.*
Violin:. Henri Vieuxtemps, *Concerto No. 2 in f♯, Opus 19.*
Other: George Macfarren, *Cello Concertino in A.*
Standard Works: William Sterndale Bennett, *The Naiads Overture*; George Macfarren, *Overture, Romeo and Juliet–Overture, Chevy Chace*; Felix Mendelssohn, *Trauermarsch, Opus 103, for Band*; Cipriani Potter, *Overture, Cymbeline*; Richard Wagner, *Polonia Overture–Rule, Britannia Overture.*

Symphonies: Johann P. Hartmann, *No. 1 in g, Opus 17*; Anthony Heinrich, *Symphony, "The Combat of the Condor"*; George Macfarren, *No. 6 in B♭*.

1837

❄

Historical Highlights: The Victorian Era begins with the accession of Queen Victoria to the British Throne; several unsuccessful rebellions against British rule take place in Canada; the American and Foreign Bible Society is founded; in the United States, the Panic of 1837 sweeps the country; Michigan becomes state number twenty-six; Atlanta, Georgia, is founded; the Chesapeake and Ohio Railroad is chartered; the Second Seminole War comes to an end in Florida.

Art and Literature Highlights: Births—artists Thomas Moran, Hans von Maurées, writers Edward Eggleston, William Dean Howells, Algernon Swinburne; Deaths—artists John Constable, François Gérard, writers Georg Büchner, Asa Breen, Alexander Pushkin. Art—Cole's *The Departure–The Return*, Watts' *The Wounded Heron*; Literature—Bertrand's *Gaspard de la Nuit*, Dickens' *Oliver Twist*, Hawthorne's *Twice-Told Tales*.

Musical Highlights

A. Births

Composers: Mily Balakirev (Russia) January 2; Eugène Diaz (de la Peña) (France) February 27; Albert Fäsy (Switzerland) April 1; Alfred R. Gaul (England) April 30; Charles Jean Grisart (France) September 29; Ernest Guiraud (France) June 23; William Shakespeare Hayes (U.S.A.) July 19; Hans Sommer (Germany) July 20; Emil Waldteufel (Germany) December 9.

Conductors: Auguste-Charles Vianesi (Italy-France) November 2.

Singers: Gustav Siehr (German bass) September 17; Georg Unger (German tenor) March 6; Georgina Weldon (British soprano) May 24; Louise Wippern (German soprano).

Performers: John Francis Barnett (British pianist) October 16; Charles-Alexis Chauvet (French organist/composer) July 7; Théodore Dubois (French organist/composer) August 24; Alexandre Guilmant (French organist/composer) March 12; Benjamin Lang (American pianist/conductor) December 28; W. S. B. Mathews (American organist/author) May 8; Józef Wieniawski (Polish pianist) May 23.

Others: Friedrich von Hausegger (Austrian musicologist) April 26; Marie Lipsius (La Mara) (German music author) December 30; Gustav Mollenhauer (German woodwind maker) February 7.

B. Deaths

Composers: August Bergt (Germany) February 10; Johann Evangelist Brandl (Germany) May 25; Valentino Fioravanti (Italy) June 16; Jean-François Le Sueur (France) October 6; Joseph Schubert (Bohemia) July 28; Nicola Antonio Zingarelli (Italy) May 5.

Singers: Jean-Blaise Martin (French baritone) October 28; Johann Nepomuk Schelble (German tenor) August 6; Luigi Zamboni (Italian bass) February 28.

Performers: Franz Joseph Antony (German organist/author) January 7; James Cervetto (British cellist) February 5; John Field (British pianist/composer) January 11; Ernst Häusler (German cellist) February 20; Johann N. Hummel (Austrian pianist) October 17; Joseph Lincke (German cellist) March 26; Charles Nicholson (British flutist) March 26; Samuel Wesley (British organist/composer) October 11.

Others: John Relfe (British music theorist/composer)(?); Johann Heinrich Scheibler (German music theorist) November 20; Friedric August Simrock (German publisher) January 2.

C. Debuts

Singers: Giovanni Battista Belletti (Italian baritone—Stockholm); Jeanne Anaïs Castellan (French soprano—Turin); Gaetano Fraschini (Italian tenor—Pavia); Paulina Rivoli (Polish soprano—Warsaw); Joseph Tichatschek (Bohemian tenor—Graz); Pauline Viardot-García (French mezzo-soprano—Brussels).

Performers: Joseph Goldberg (Austrian violinist—Vienna); Anna Robena Laidlaw (British pianist—Leipzig); Alfredo Piatti (Italian cellist—Milan).

D. New Positions

Conductors: Francesco Basili (maestro di cappella, St. Peter's, Rome); Carlo Bignami (Cremona Orchestra); Alexei Lvov (Imperial Chapel Choir, St. Petersburg); Otto Nicolai (Kärntnerthor Theater, Vienna); Heinrich Proch (Josephstadt Theater, Vienna); František Jan Skroup (Estate Theater, Prague); Richard Wagner (Riga Theater).

Others: William Ayrton (music critic, London *Examiner*); Constantin Julius Becker (editor, *Neue Zeitschrift für Musik*); Gaetano Donizetti (director, Naples Conservatory); Lowell Mason (superintendent of music, Boston Schools).

E. Prizes/Honors

Prizes: Louis-Désiré Besozzi (Prix de Rome).

Honors: Manuel Bretón de los Herreros (Spanish Academy); Michele Carafa de Colobrano (French Academy); Franz Cramer (Master of the King's Music); Johann Carl Loewe (Berlin Academy); Felix Mendelssohn (doctorate, Leipzig University).

F. Biographical Highlights

Frédéric Chopin breaks up with Marie Wodzinska and meets Aurora Dupin, who writes under the name George Sand; César Franck enters the Conservatory of Paris and is given a prize for his sight-reading ability; Charles Gounod wins the second Prix de Rome with his cantata *Maria Stuart et Rizzio*; Felix Mendelssohn marries Cécile Sophie Jeanrenaud and conducts at the Birmingham Festivals in England; Gioacchino Rossini leaves his wife Isabella and goes to live with Olympe Pélissier; Robert Schumann becomes engaged to Clara Wieck over her father's objections.

G. Cultural Beginnings

Performing Groups—Choral: Bristol Madrigal Society (England); Cleveland Harmonic Society; Concerts Valentino (Paris); Hanover Hofoper; Melophonic Society of London; Newark Amateur Glee Company; Regensburger Liederkranz; University of Dublin Choral Society.
Performing Groups—Instrumental: Philadelphia Philharmonic Society.
Educational: Kolozavár Music Conservatory (Hungary).
Music Publishers: Little, Brown and Co. (Boston); Tauchnitz Publishing House (Leipzig).
Music Publications: *La France Musicale.*
Performing Centers: Hungarian National Theater (Pest).
Other: Knabe and Gaehle, piano makers (Baltimore); Prague Mozart Society; Tiffany, Young and Ellis (New York—Tiffany and Co. by 1853).

H. Musical Literature

William Caldwell, *The Union Harmony*; Luigi Cherubini, *Traité de la Fugue*; Salvador Daniel, *Grammaire philharmonique*; François Fétis, *Traité du chant en choeur*; Jean-Georges Kastner, *Traité générale d'instrumentation*; Joseph Mainzer, *Abécédaire de chant*; Adolf Bernhard Marx, *Die lehre von der musikalischen Komposition I, II*; Lowell Mason, *The Sabbath School Harp*; Lowell Mason/George Webb, *The Odeon: A Collection of Secular Melodies*; Thomas Oliphant, *La Musa madrigalesca.*

I. Musical Compositions

Chamber Music:

String Quartets: Luigi Cherubini, *No. 6 in a*; Felix Mendelssohn, *No 3 in D–No. 4 in e, Opus 44.*
Sonata/Solos: Napoleon Coste, *Fantasy de Concert, Opus 6* (guitar).
Ensembles: Luigi Cherubini, *String Quintet in e.*
Piano: Alkan, *Three Improvisations dans le style brillant, Opus 12–Three Andantes romantiques, Opus 13–Three morceaux dans la*

genre pathétique, Opus 15–Three Scherzi, Opus 16; Frédéric Chopin, *Four Mazurkas (c, b, D♭, c♯), Opus 30–Scherzo in b♭/D♭, Opus 31–Two Nocturnes (B, A♭), Opus 32–Nocturne in c, B.108*; Franz Liszt, *Twenty-Four Grande Etudes*; Felix Mendelssohn, *Songs without Words III, Opus 38–Six Preludes and Fugues, Opus 35–Capriccio in E, Opus 48*; Ignaz Moscheles, *Charakterestisch studien, Opus 95*; Clara Schumann, *Concert Variations on a Cavatina by Bellini, Opus 8*; Robert Schumann, *Die Davidsbündler, Opus 6–Fantasiestücke, Opus 12.*

Organ: Felix Mendelssohn, *Three Preludes and Fugues (c, G, d), Opus 37*; Samuel Wesley, *Six Voluntaries for the Use of Young Organists, Opus 36.*

Choral/Vocal Music:

Choral: Hector Berlioz, *Requiem, Opus 5*; Gaetano Donizetti, *Requiem Mass (for Zingarelli)–Messa di Gloria in c*; Charles Gounod, *Marie Stuart* (cantata); Felix Mendelssohn, *Psalm XLII, Opus 42, "As Pants the Hart"*; Joseph Weigl, *Mass in E.*

Vocal: Gaetano Donizetti, *Soirées d'automne à l'infrascata*; Carl Loewe, *Two Poems, Opus 61–Twelve Poems, Opus 62–Two Songs, Opus 63–Four Fabellieder, Opus 64–Three Ballads, Opus 65–Three Historical Ballads, Opus 67*; Henry Russell, *Woodman, Spare That Tree!*; Louis Spohr, *Six German Songs, Opus 103*; George J. Webb, *Webb* (hymn tune, "Stand Up for Jesus").

Musical Stage: Daniel Auber, *Le domino noir*; Michael Balfe, *Joan of Arc–Catherine Grey*; Ramón Carnicer, *Ismalia*; Gaetano Donizetti, *Robert Devereux–Pia de'Tolomei*; Friedrich von Flotow, *Alice–Rob-Roy–La lettre du préfet*; John Hullah, *The Barber of Bassora*; Conradin Kreutzer, *Fridolin–Die Höhle bei Waverley*; Albert Lortzing, *Zar und Zimmerman–Le bourgmestre de Saardam*; Heinrich Marschner, *Der Bäbu*; Saverio Mercadante, *Il giuramento*; Hippolyte Monpou, *Piquillo*; Louis Niedermeyer, *Stradella*; Eugène Prévost, *Liebeszauber*; Franz von Suppé, *Virginia*; Ambroise Thomas, *La double échelle.*

Orchestra/Band Music:

Concerted Music:

Piano: Franz Liszt, *Hexameron for Piano and Orchestra*; Felix Mendelssohn, *Concerto No. 2 in d, Opus 40.*

Standard Works: Daniel Auber, *Fête Vénitienne*; Charles Gounod, *Scherzo for Orchestra*; Cipriani Potter, *Overture, The Tempest.*

Symphonies: Félicien David, *No. 1 in F*; Anthony Heinrich, *Grand American National Chivalrous Symphony*; Franz Lachner, *No. 6 in D, Opus 6(?)*; E. J. Moeran, *Symphony in g*; Louis Spohr, *No. 5 in c, Opus 102.*

1838

❄

Historical Highlights: The Chartist Movement in Great Britain seeks to increase the power of labor; steamship travel on the Atlantic is inaugurated on the steamship *Great Western*; in the United States, Personal Liberty Laws in the North try to offset the national Fugitive Slave Law—the Underground Railway is set up to aid the runaway slaves; the Cherokee Indians are forced to move to an Oklahoma reservation; Samuel F. B. Morse introduces the Morse Code.

Art and Literature Highlights: The London National Gallery opens. Births—artists Charles Carolus-Durand, Aimé-Jules Dalou, poet David Gray; Deaths—writers Adalbert von Chamisso, Anne McVickar Grant, Lorenzo da Ponte; Art—Deas' *Turkey Shooting*, Thorvaldsen's *Christ and the Apostles*; Literature—Bulwer-Lytton's *Lady of Lyons*, Hugo's *Ruy Blas*, Kennedy's *Rob of the Bowl*, Lee's *Recollection of a Southern Matron*.

Musical Highlights

A. Births

Composers: Karel Bendl (Czechoslovakia) April 16; Tommaso Benvenuti (Italy) February 4; Georges Bizet (France) October 25; David Braham (England-U.S.A.); Max Bruch (Germany) January 6; Frédéric Clay (England) August 3; Melesio Morales (Mexico) December 4.

Conductors: Édouard Colonne (France) July 23.

Singers: Emil Fischer (German bass) June 13; Leonard Labatt (Swedish tenor) December 4; Charles Lunn (British tenor) January 5; Angelo Neumann (Austrian tenor) August 18; Bernhard Pollini (German tenor) December 16; Emil Scaria (Austrian bass) September 18; Sophie Stehle (German soprano) May 15; Zélia Trebelli (French mezzo-soprano).

Performers: Frederick Archer (British-born organist) June 16; Joseph Barnby (British organist) August 12; Carl Davidov (Russian cellist) March 15; James Remington Fairlamb (American organist) January 23; Sebastian Bach Mills (British pianist) March 13; Wilma Neruda (Czech violinist) March 21; Alfred H. Pease (American pianist/composer) May 6; Whitney Eugene Thayer (American organist) December 11; David Duffle Wood (American organist) March 2.

Others: Philip Paul Bliss (American hymnwriter/singer) July 9; Ludwig Bussler (German music theorist) November 26; Alice Cunningham Fletcher (American ethnomusicologist) March 16; Emil Robert Lienau (German publisher) December 28; Ernst Mach (German physicist/acoustician) February 18.

B. **Deaths**
Composers: Charles-Louis-Joseph André (Belgium) April 8; Bernhard Henrik Crusell (Finland) July 28; Jeremiah Ingalls (U.S.A.) April 6; Franz Lessel (Poland) December 26; Giuseppe Pilotti (Italy) June 12.
Singers: Maria Therese Bland (British soprano) January 15; Anna (Pauline) Milder-Hauptmann (Austrian soprano) May 29.
Performers: Johann Ludwig Abeille (German organist) March 2; Andrew Ashe (Irish flutist); Thomas Attwood (British organist/ composer) March 24; Antoine Tranquille Berbiguie (French flutist/ composer) January 28; Friedrich Berr (French clarinetist/composer) September 24; Laurent-François Boutmy (Belgian organist) November 3; Bernhard Henrik Crusell (Finnish clarinetist) July 28; Frédéric Nicolas Duvernoy (French horn virtuoso) July 19; Friedrich Johann Eck (German violinist/composer) February 22; Karl Ludwig Hellwig (German organist) November 24; Pierre Louis Hus-Desforges (French cellist) January 20; Philippe Libon (French violinist) February 5; Ferdinand Ries (German pianist/composer) January 13; Adolph Martin Schlesinger (German-born publisher) January 8; Sophia Maria Westenholz (German pianist) October 4.
Others: Louis-François Beffara (French music author) February 2; Thomas Busby (British music author) May 28; Asa Hopkins (American woodwind maker) October 27; Johannes Nepomuk Maelzel (German inventer) July 31; Lorenzo da Ponte (Italian librettist) August 17.

C. **Debuts**
Singers: Erminia Frezzolini (Italian soprano—Florence); Heinrich Kotzolt (Danish tenor—Danzig); Jenny Lind (Swedish soprano—Stockholm); (Giovanni Matteo) Mario (Italian tenor—Paris); Sims Reeves (British tenor—Newcastle, as baritone); Gustave-Hippolyte Roger (French tenor—Paris); Sophie Anne Thillon (British soprano— Paris).
Performers: Henry Lazarus (British clarinetist—London).

D. **New Positions**
Conductors: Julius Benedict (Drury Lane Theatre); Franz Erkel (National Theater, Pest); Luigi Palmerini (maestro di cappella, S. Petronio, Bologna); Eugène-Prosper Prévost (Théâtre d'Orléan, New Orleans); August Roeckel (Weimar Theaters).
Others: Andreas Bartay (director, National Theater, Pest); John Goss (organ, St. Paul's Cathedral, London); Nicola Vaccai (director, Milan Conservatory).

E. **Prizes/Honors**
Prizes: Georges Bousquet (Prix de Rome).

F. Biographical Highlights

Alkan begins a six-year, self-imposed exile from the concert stage; Frédéric Chopin moves to Majorca with George Sand; Gaetano Donizetti, after the censor refuses his latest opera, goes to Paris; Louis Jullien, fleeing his creditors in France, goes to London; Felix Mendelssohn gives the premiere of Schubert's *Great C Major Symphony*, newly discovered by Robert Schumann; Niccolò Paganini belatedly pays Berlioz 20,000 francs for his *Harold in Italy*; William V. Wallace leaves his family and his debts behind in Sydney and begins a three-year stay in South America.

G. Cultural Beginnings

Performing Groups—Choral: English Opera Co. (by Edward Sequin); Essen Gesang-Musikverein; Norwich Madrigal Society.

Performing Groups—Instrumental: Königsberg Philharmonic Society; St. Louis Philharmonic Orchestra.

Educational: Liceo Filarmónico Dramático Barcelonés de S. M. Doña Isabel II; Krakow School of Singing and Music.

Music Publishers: Bote and Bock (Berlin); Jan Hoffman (Prague); Gotthilf Körner (Erfurt).

Music Publications: *Caricature* (Paris); *Nouvelle Gazette Musicale* (Paris).

Performing Centers: Teatro de la Victoria (Buenos Aires).

Other: Joseph Allen, brass instruments (Sturbridge, Massachusetts); Besson Instruments Co. (Paris); Daublaine et Cie., organ builders (Paris); Lambertini Piano Co. (Lisbon); London Promenade Concerts; St. Louis Musical Fund Society (St. Louis); The Sterling Club (London).

H. Musical Literature

August Bergt, *Briefwechsel eines alten und jungen Schulmeisters*; William Chappell, *National English Airs I*; William Gardiner, *Music and Friends I*; Ferdinand Gassner, *Ein Leitfaden zum Selbstunterricht*; George Hogarth, *Memoirs of the Musical Drama*; August Kahlert, *Tonleben*; Christian G. Körner, *Gesangblätter aus den 16. Jahrhundert*; Karl Krause, *Anfangsgründe der allgemeinen Theorie der Musik*; Lowell Mason, *The Boston Glee Book*; Gustav Schilling, *Versuch einer Philosophie des Schönen in der Musik*; Salomon Sulzer, *Schir Zion*.

I. Musical Compositions

Chamber Music:

String Quartets: Felix Mendelssohn, *Quartet No. 5, Opus 44, No. 3.*

Sonata/Solos: Felix Mendelssohn, *Cello Sonata No. 1 in B♭, Opus 45–Violin Sonata in F.*

Ensembles: Louis Spohr, *String Quintet No. 5 in g, Opus 106.*

Piano: Alkan, *Six Morceaux caractéristiques, Opus 16–Three Grand Etudes, Opus 76*(?); Frédéric Chopin, *Four Mazurkas (g♯, D, C, b), Opus 33–Polonaise in A, Opus 40/1–Waltz in F, Opus 34/2*; Franz Liszt, *Grand Galop chromatique–Etudes d'Exécution Transcendente d'apres Paganini*; Clara Schumann, *Souvenir de Vienne, Opus 9–Scherzo in d, Opus 10*; Robert Schumann, *Kinderszenen, Opus 15–Kreisleriana, Opus 16–Noveletten, Opus 21–Sonata No. 2, Opus 22* (final movement).

Organ: Johann P. Hartmann, *Fantasy in f, Opus 20*(?).

Choral/Vocal Music:

Choral: Gaetano Donizetti, *Colombo* (cantata); Felix Mendelssohn, *Psalm XCV–Im Freien zu singern, Opus 41*; Saverio Mercadante, *Seven Last Words of Christ*; Giovanni Pacini, *Il Trionfo della religione.*

Vocal: Carl Loewe, *Two Ballads, Opus 68*; James E. Spilman, *Flow Gently, Sweet Afton*; Louis Spohr, *Six Songs, Opus 105*; Giuseppe Verdi, *Six Romances.*

Musical Stage: Adolphe Adam, *Le fidèle berger–Le Brasseur de Preston*; Daniel Auber, *Margarethe von Gent*; Michael Balfe, *Falstaff–Diadeste*; Julius Benedict, *The Gypsy's Warning*; Hector Berlioz, *Benvenuto Cellini*; Michele Carafa, *Thérèse*; Gaetano Donizetti, *Maria di Rudenz*; Friedrich von Flotow, *Lady Melvil–Le comte de Saint-Mégrin*; Charles Gounod, *La Vendetta*; Jacques Halévy, *Guido et Ginevra*; John Hullah, *The Outpost*; Saverio Mercadante, *Elena da Feltre–Le due illustri rivali*; Stanislaw Moniuszko, *A Night in the Apennines*; Hippolyte Monpou, *Un conte d'autrefois*; Otto Nicolai, *Rosmonda d'Inghilterra*; Errico Petrella, *I pirati spagnuoli*; Józef Pontiatowski, *Giovanni da Procida*; Joseph Strauss, *Berthold der Zähringer*; Ambroise Thomas, *Le perruquier de la régence*; Nicola Vaccai, *Marco Visconti*; Johann Vesque von Püttlingen, *Turandot.*

Orchestra/Band Music:

Concerted Music:

Piano: Felix Mendelssohn, *Serenade and Allegro in b, Opus 43*; Ignaz Moscheles, *Concerto No. 8 in D,"Pastoral," Opus 96.*

Ballet/Incidental Music: Daniel Auber, *Le bourgeois gentilhomme* (IM); Johan P. Hartmann, *Olaf den Hellige, Opus 23* (IM); Hippolyte Monpou, *La Perugina* (IM).

Standard Works: Johann Kalliwoda, *Concert Overture No. 5 in f–No. 6 in E♭, Opus 76.*

Symphonies: David, Félicien, *No. 2 in E.*

1839

❀

Historical Highlights: The Opium War between China and Great Britain begins; Belgian independence is formally recognized by the Dutch government; the Central American Federation is dissolved and the countries of Guatamala, El Salvador, Costa Rica, Nicaragua, and Honduras become independent states; in the United States, the Aroostook War is averted by the settlement of the Maine-Canada boundary; Fort Sutter (Sacramento), California, is founded.

Art and Literature Highlights: Births—writers Henry George, Walter Pater, artists Paul Cézanne, Karl A. Oesterley, Alfred Sisley; Deaths—artist Joseph Anton Koch, writers Karl A. Nicander, Winthrop Praed. Art—Delacroix's *Jewish Wedding in Morocco*, Quidor's *Rip Van Winkle at Vedder's Tavern*, Turner's *The Fighting Temeraire*; Literature—Longfellow's *Voices of the Night*, Poe's *Tales of the Grotesque and Arebesque*, Slowacki's *Mazepa*.

Musical Highlights

A. Births

Composers: Dudley Buck (U.S.A.) March 10; Riccardo Gandolfi (Italy) February 16; Adolf Müller, Jr. (Austria) October 15; Modest Petrovich Mussorgsky (Russia) March 21; John Knowles Paine (U.S.A.) January 9.

Conductors: Hermann Levi (Germany) November 7; Eduard Nápravnik (Bohemia-Russia) August 24.

Singers: Valentina Bianchi (Russian soprano); Victor Capoul (French tenor) February 27; Caroline Ferni-Giraldoni (Italian soprano) August 20; Amalie Joachim (German mezzo-soprano) May 10; Minna Peschka-Leutner (Austrian soprano) October 25.

Performers: Henri Ghis (French pianist) May 17; Robert Goldbeck (American pianist/composer) April 19; François Jehin-Prume (Belgian-born violinist) April 18; Fritz Listeman (German violinist) March 25; Joseph Rheinberger (German organist/composer) March 17.

Others: George Hart (British violin maker) March 25; Nikolai Dmitrievich Kashkin (Russian critic) December 9.

B. Deaths

Composers: Charles-Louis André (Belgium) April 8; Wenzel Robert Gallinberg (Austria) November 2; Giuseppe Mosca (Italy) September 14; Ferdinando Paër (Italy) May 3; Charles-Henri Plantade (France) December 18; Jan August Vitásek (Bohemia) December 7.

Conductors: Franz Xaver Glöggl (Austria) July 16.

Singers: Violante Camporese (Italian soprano); Adolphe Nourrit (French tenor) March 8; Domenico Ronconi (Italian tenor) April 13; Giuseppe Siboni (Italian-born tenor) March 28; Aloysia Weber (German soprano) June 8.

Performers: Johann Georg Backofen (German harpist) July 10; Ludwig Berger (German pianist/composer) February 16; William Carnaby (British organist) November 13; Pierre Dalvimore (French harpist) June 13; Giuseppe Maria Festa (Italian violinist/conductor) April 7; Jean-Jacques Grasset (French violinist) Ausust 25; Ignaz-Antoine Ladurner (French pianist) March 4; Charles Philippe Lafont (French violinist) August 23; Heinrich Gerhard Lentz (German pianist) August 21; Nicolas Mori (British violinist/publisher) June 14; Georg Abraham Schneider (German horn virtuoso/conductor) January 19; Fernando Sor (Spanish guitarist/composer) July 10.

Others: Aloys Mooser (Swedish organ builder) December 19; Richard Mount-Edgcumbe (British music author/composer) Septermber 26; Gaspard-Claire Prony (French music theorist/harpist) July 29; Guillaume-André Villoteau (French music scholar) April 27; Gottfried Weber (German music theorist) September 21.

C. Debuts

Singers: Elisa Blaes (Belgian soprano—Leipzig); William Harrison (British tenor—London); Fanny Salvini-Donatelli (Italian soprano—Venice); Georgine Schubert (German mezzo-soprano—Hamburg); Anna Zerr (German soprano—Karlsruhe).

Performers: Alexandre-Joseph Artôt (Belgian violinist—London); Jacques Offenbach (French cellist—Paris).

D. New Positions

Conductor: Francisco Andreví y Castellar (maître de chapelle, Bordeaux Cathedral); Karl Binder (Josefstädter Theater, Vienna); Piero Antonio Coppola (Lisbon Royal Opera); Vincenzo Fioravanti (maestro di cappella, Abruzzi Cathedral).

Others: Gaetano Capocci (organ, S. Maria Maggiore, Rome); Joseph Hanisch (organ, Regensburg Cathedral); Edward Hodges (organ, Trinity Parish Church, New York).

E. Prizes/Honors

Prizes: Charles Gounod (Prix de Rome).
Honors: Gaspare Spontini (French Institute).

F. Biographical Highlights

Frédéric Chopin, his health deteriorating in the wet Majorcan climate, returns to Paris; George Grove graduates from the Institute of Civil Engineers in London; Franz Liszt begins his virtuoso career as a pianist; the Rainer Family from Switzerland begins a four-year tour of the United States; George Root begins his music teaching in Boston; Richard Wagner, fleeing his creditors, sails to England and France.

G. Cultural Beginnings

Performing Groups—Choral: Augsburg Musikliebhaberverein.
Performing Groups—Instrumental: Norwich Philharmonic Society.
Festivals: North German Music Festival (Lübeck).
Educational: John Reid Chair of Music (Edinburgh University); Scuola Musicale (Piacenza); Scuola Pubblica di Musica (Istituto Musicale in 1842, Lucca).
Music Publishers: Meissonier and Heugel (Paris); Nathaniel Philips (St. Louis).
Music Publications: *Musical Magazine, or Repository of Musical Science, Literature and Intelligence.*
Other: Bathyphon (by Wieprecht and Skorra); George Jadin and Son, organs (New York); George Reed Music Store (G. P. Reed and Co.—Boston); Royal Society of Female Musicians (London).

H. Musical Literature

Antoine Elwart, *Petit manuel d'harmonie*; Eduard Krüger, *Grundriss der Metrik*; Joseph Mainzer, *Esquisses musicales*; Adolf Marx, *Allgemeine Musiklehre*; Lowell Mason, *The Modern Psalmist*; Elizabeth Masson, *Original Jacobite Songs*; Ignaz von Mosel, *Über die Originalpartitur des Requiems von W. A. Mozart*; Joseph d'Ortigue, *De l'école musicale italienne*; Edward Taylor, *Vocal Schools of Italy in the 16th Century*; Théodore de Vroye, *Traité du plain-chant*.

I. Musical Compositions

Chamber Music:
String Quartets: Stanislaw Moniuszko, *No. 1 in d–No. 2 in G*(?); Otto Nicolai, *Quartet*(?).
Ensembles: William S. Bennett, *Piano Trio in A, Opus 26*; Félicien David, *Nonet No. 1 in F–No. 2 in c* (brass); Felix Mendelssohn, *Piano Trio No. 1 in d, Opus 49*.
Piano: Frédéric Chopin, *Twenty-Four Preludes, Opus 28* (publication)–*Sonata in b♭, Opus 35–Two Nocturnes (g, G), Opus 37–Three Mazurkas (E, B, A♭), Opus 41/1,3,4–Polonaise in c, Opus 40/2–Impromtu in F♯, Opus 36–Ballade in F/a, Opus 38–Scherzo in c♯, Opus 39*; Louise Farrenc, *Hymne russe varié, Opus 27*(?)–*Variation sur un thème allemand, Opus 28*(?); Mikhail Glinka, *Valse-fantasie in b*; Clara Schumann, *Three Romances (e♭, g, A♭), Opus 11*. Robert Schumann, *Nachtstücke, Opus 23–Faschingsschwank aus Wien, Opus 26–Three Romances, Opus 28–Four Pieces, Opus 32*.

Organ: Felix Mendelssohn, *Fugue in e–Fugue in f.*

Choral/Vocal Music:

Choral: Charles Gounod, *Fernand* (cantata); Felix Mendelssohn, *Psalm V, "Lord, Hear the Voice"–Die erste Frühlingstag, Opus 48–Psalm XXXI, "Defend Me, Lord"–Psalm CXIV, Opus 51, "When Israel Out of Egypt Came."*

Vocal: Gaetano Donizetti, *Un hiver à Paris*; Joseph P. Knight, *Rocked in the Cradle of the Deep*; Felix Mendelssohn, *Six Songs, Opus 47–Three Songs, Opus 48*; Giacomo Meyerbeer, *Six Elegies and Romances.*

Musical Stage: Adolphe Adam, *La reine d'un Jour*; Daniel Auber, *Le lac de fées*; John Barnett, *Farinelli*; Alexander Dargomijsky, *Esmeralda*; Gaetano Donizetti, *Gabriella di Vergy II*; Friedrich von Flotow, *L'eau merveilleuse–Le naufrage de la Méduse*; Jacques Halévy, *Le shérif–Les treize*; Ferdinand Hiller, *Romilda*; Franz Lachner, *Alidia*; Albert Lortzing, *Caramo*; George Macfarren, *Agnes Bernauer, the Maid of Augsburg*; Saverio Mercadante, *Il bravo*; Hippolyte Monpou, *Le planteur–La chaste Suzanne*; Francesco Morlacchi, *Francesco da Rimini*; Giovanni Pacini, *Furio Camillo*; Achille Peri, *Una visita a Bedlam*; Errico Petrella, *La miniere di Freinbergh*; Nicola Vaccai, *La sposa di Messina*; Giuseppe Verdi, *Oberto, Count of San Bonifacio*; Alexei Vertovsky, *Homesickness.*

Orchestra/Band Music:

Concerted Music:

Piano: Franz Liszt, *Concerto No. 2 in A.*

Violin: Hector Berlioz, *Reverie and Caprice, Opus 8*; Heinrich Ernst, *Concertino in D on Rossini's "Othello," Opus 11*; Johann Kalliwoda, *Concertino, Opus 100*; Louis Spohr, *Concerto No. 14 in a, Opus 110.*

Ballet/Incidental Music: Adolphe Adam, *La jolie fille de Gand* (B); Niels Gade, *Aladdin* (IM); Louis Spohr, *Der Matrose* (IM); Ambroise Thomas, *La gypsy* (B).

Standard Works: Hippolyte Chélard, *Variations*; Mikhail Glinka, *Polonaise in E*; Johann Kalliwoda, *Concert Overture No. 1 in d, Opus 38*; Felix Mendelssohn, *Ruy Blas Overture, Opus 95.*

Symphonies: Hector Berlioz, *Romeo and Juliet, Dramatic Symphony, Opus 17*; Franz Lachner, *No. 7 in d, Opus 58*; Adolf Lindblad, *Symphony No. 1 in C(?)*; Louis Spohr, *Symphony No. 6 in G, Opus 116, "Historische."*

1840

❁

Historical Highlights: Great Britain sets up the first postal system—the "Penny Black" becomes the first postage stamp; the Act of Union combines Upper and Lower Canada into one entity; Brazil becomes an empire under Pedro I; in the United States, William Henry Harrison is elected as the ninth president; Congress approves the ten-hour workday for all federal employees; the United States recognizes the Republic of Texas.

Art and Literature Highlights: Births—artists Thomas Hovenden, Claude Monet, Auguste Rodin, writers Alphonse Daudet, Thomas Hardy, Émile Zola; Deaths—artists Kasper Friedrich, Alexander Nasmyth, writers Louis S. Lemercier, Fanny Burney. Art—Dannhauser's *Franz Liszt at the Piano*; Martin's *The Eve of the Deluge*; Literature—Cooper's *The Pathfinder*, Dana's *Two Years before the Mast*, Dickens' *The Old Curiosity Shop*.

Musical Highlights

A. Births

Composers: Edmund Audran (France) April 12; Hermann Goetz (Germany) December 7; Christian Frederik Emil Horneman (Denmark) December 17; John Stainer (England) June 6; Johan Svendsen (Norway) September 30; Peter Ilyich Tchaikovsky (Russia) May 7.

Conductors: Jules Danbé (France) November 16; Franco Faccio (Italy) March 8.

Singers: William Candidus (American tenor) July 25; Bronislawa Dowiakowska-Klimowiczowa (Polish soprano) February 9; Célestine Galli-Marié (French mezzo-soprano) November; Georgine Schubert (German mezzo-soprano) October 28; Jennie Van Zandt (American soprano).

Performers: Carlo Andreoli (Italian pianist/conductor) January 8; Louis Brassin (French pianist) June 24; Filippo Capocci (Italian organist) May 11; Emil Krause (German pianist/critic) July 30; Charles Kunkel (German pianist/publisher) July 22; Barrett Isaac Poznanski (American violinist) December 11; George E. Whiting (American organist/composer) September 14.

Others: William Horatio Clarke (American organ builder) March 8; Antoine Dechevrens (Swiss musicologist) November 3; Franz Xaver Haberl (German music theorist/editor/historiographer) April 12; Ira D. Sankey (American hymnist/evangelist singer) August 28; Surindo Tagore (Indian musicologist).

B. Deaths

Composers: Catterino Cavos (Italy-Russia) May 10; Matthäus Fischer (Germany) May 5.

Conductors: Gottlob Benedikt Bierey (Germany) May 5.

Singers: Johann Friedrich Döring (German bass) August 27; Giuditta Grisi (Italian mezzo-soprano) May 1; Johann Michael Vogl (Austrian baritone/composer) November 19.

Performers: Paolo Bonfichi (Italian organist) December 29; Józef Jawurek (Polish pianist) July 22; Niccolò Paganini (Italian violinist/composer) May 27; Franz Pecháček (Bohemian violinist/composer) September 15; Johann Baptist Schiedermayer (German organist/composer) January 6.

Others: José Virués (Spanish music theorist) May 13.

C. Debuts

Singers: Marius-Pierre Audran (French tenor—Paris); Marianna Barbieri-Nini (Italian soprano—Milan); Italo Gardoni (Italian tenor—Italy); Hermine Rudersdorff (Russian soprano—Germany).

D. New Positions

Conductors: Henry Bishop (Covent Garden); Hippolyte-André Chélard (Weimar Court); Francisco da Costa (mestre de capela, Oporto Cathedral, Portugal); Carl Wilhelm Henning (kapellmeister, Berlin); Louis Jullien (Drury Lane Theater); Friedrich Klingenberg (cantor, Peterskirche, Görlitz); Conradin Kreutzer (municipal music director, Cologne); Heinrich Proch (Vienna Court Opera); Friedrich August Reissiger (Oslo Theater).

Others: William B. Bradbury (organ, Baptist Tabernacle, Boston); Jean-Louis Danjou (organ, Notre Dame, Paris); Saverio Mercadante (director, Naples Conservatory); Pierre Joseph Varney (director, French Opera Co., New Orleans).

E. Prizes/Honors

Prizes: François-Emmanuel Bazin (Prix de Rome).

Honors: Jenny Lind (Swedish Royal Academy).

F. Biographical Highlights

César Franck takes first prize for fugue at the Paris Conservatory; Franz Liszt concertizes for the Beethoven Bonn Memorial and performs for Queen Victoria; Stanislaw Moniuszko returns to Poland and settles in Vilnius as teacher and organist; Robert Schumann finally gets to marry Clara Wieck; Giuseppe Verdi loses his wife shortly after the death of their two children; Richard Wagner spends three weeks in a Paris debtor's prison and first meets Franz Liszt.

G. Cultural Beginnings

Performing Groups—Choral: Amsterdam Cecilia Society; Dortmünder Liedertafel; Mannheim Liedertafel; Munich Bürgersängerzunft; St. Cecilia Society of Prague; St. Louis Sacred Music Society.

Performing Groups—Instrumental: Liverpool Philharmonic Society.

Educational: Conservatory of the Pest-Buda Society of Music (National Conservatory in 1867); Zofín Academy of Music (Prague).
Music Publications: *Nouvelliste* (St. Petersburg).
Performing Centers: Belfast Music Hall; Gotha Hoftheater; Teatro Metastasio (Assisi).
Other: Aberdeen Haydn Society (Scotland); Cast-Iron Piano Frame (patented by Jonas Chickering); Musical Antiquarian Society (London); Saxophone (by Adolph Sax).

H. Musical Literature
Pedro Albéniz y Basanta, *Método completo para piano*; Carl Becker, *Die Hausmusik in Deutschland in 16., 17. und 18. Jahrhunderts*; Siegfried Dehn, *Theoretisch-praktische Harmonielehre*; Antoine Elwart, *Théorie musicale*; François Fétis, *Esquisse de l'histoire de l'harmonie*; Prosper Guéranger, *Institutions liturgiques I*; Florentius Kist, *Protestant Churchmusic in the Netherlands*; Gustav Schilling, *Lehrbuch der allgemeinen Musikwissenschaft*; Johann Gottlob Töpfer, *Anleitung zur erhaltung und stimmung der Orgel*; Carl von Winterfeld, *Martin Luthers deutsche geistliche Lieder*.

I. Musical Compositions
Chamber Music:
Sonata/Solos: Alkan, *Grand duo concertant, Opus 21* (violin, piano); Ferdinand Hiller, *Cello Sonata No. 1, Opus 22*.
Piano: Alkan, *Variations on a Theme from Donizetti's "Elixir d'amore"–Variations on a Theme from Donizetti's "Ugo conte di Parigi"*; Johann A. André, *Three sonatinas, Opus 71*(?); Frédéric Chopin, *Waltz in E♭, "Sostenuto"–Waltz in A♭, Opus 42–Mazurka in a, "Notre temps"*; Stephen Heller, *Rondo Valse, Opus 11*; Theodor Kullak, *Two Concert Etudes, Opus 2*; Franz Liszt, *Three Valse-Caprices–Album d'un voyageur I, II*; Otto Nicolai, *Three Etudes, Opus 40*.
Organ: Johann A. André, *Twenty-Five Organ Pieces, Opus 64–Ten Organ Pieces, Opus 68*(?).
Choral/Vocal Music:
Choral: George Elvey, *The Resurrection and Ascension* (oratorio); Charles Gounod, *"Roman" Mass*; Ferdinand Hiller, *Der zerstörung Jerusalems, Opus 24* (oratorio); Felix Mendelssohn, *Festgesang* (male voices)–*Geistliches Lied in E♭*; Saverio Mercadante, *Mass for Male Voices*(?); Otto Nicolai, *Pater noster*; Robert Schumann, *Six Songs for Male Chorus, Opus 33*; Simon Sechter, *Sodoms Untergang* (oratorio); Louis Spohr, *The Fall of Babylon* (oratorio).
Vocal: Frederick Crouch, *Kathleen Mavourneen*; Mikhail Glinka, *A Farewell to St. Petersburg* (cycle); Theodor Kullak, *Two Songs, Opus 1*; Carl Loewe, *Four Legends, Opus 75–Two Legends, Opus 76–Two Ballads, Opus 78*; Robert Schumann, *Liederkreis, Opus 24* (cycle after

Heine)–*Myrthen, Opus 25* (cycle)–*Lieder und Gesänge I, Opus 27–Three Poems, Opus 30–Three Ballads, Opus 31–Twelve Poems, Opus 35–Six Poems, Opus 36–Liebesfrühling, Opus 37* (cycle)–*Liederkreis, Opus 39* (cycle after Eichendorff)–*Five Songs, Opus 40–Frauenliebe und Leben, Opus 42* (cycle)–*Dichterliebe, Opus 48* (cycle).
Musical Stage: Daniel Auber, *Zanetta*; Gaetano Donizetti, *La fille du régiment–La favorite–Il duc d'Alba*; Jacques Halévy, *Le drapier*; Conradin Kreutzer, *Die beiden Figaro*; Albert Lortzing, *Hans Sachs*; Saverio Mercadante, *La vestale–La solitaria dell Asturie*; Hippolyte Monpou, *La reine Jeanne*; Otto Nicolai, *Il Templario*; Giovanni Pacini, *Saffo*; Carlo Pedrotti, *Lina–Clara di Mailand*; Józef Poniatowski, *Don Desiderio*; Joseph Strauss, *Der Währwolf*; Ambroise Thomas, *Carline*; Giuseppe Verdi, *Un giorno di Regno*; Johann Vesque von Püttlingen, *Jeanne d'Arc*; Richard Wagner, *Rienzi*.
Orchestra/Band Music:
Concerted Music:
  Piano: Franz Liszt, *Malédiction* (piano, strings).
  Violin: Henri Vieuxtemps, *Concerto No. 1 in E, Opus 10*.
  Others: Jacques Offenbach, *Prière et Boléro, Opus 22* (cello).
Standard Works: Niels Gade, *Echoes from Ossian Overture, Opus 1*; Richard Wagner, *A Faust Overture*.
Symphonies: Hector Berlioz, *Grande symphonie funèbre et triomphale, Opus 15*; Johann Kalliwoda, *No. 5 in b, Opus 106*; George Macfarren, *No. 7 in c♯*; Felix Mendelssohn, *No. 2 in B♭, "Hymn of Praise," Opus 52*.

1841

❄

Historical Highlights: The British seize the city of Hong Kong as a protectorate; New Zealand is made a British colony; explorer Ross claims the Antarctic for Great Britain; the European Nations agree to close the Dardanelles to all countries but Turkey; in the United States, President Harrison dies from pneumonia a month after his inauguration—John Tyler becomes the tenth president; the Whigs denounce Tyler, whose cabinet resigns en masse.
Art and Literature Highlights: Births—writers W. H. Hudson, Catulle Mendès, artists Jean Charles Cazin, Pierre-Auguste Renoir; Deaths—writers William Austin, Louis Bertrand, artists J. H. von Dannecker, David Wilkie. Art—Clonney's *Militia Training*, Greenough's *Venus Victrix*, Spitzweg's *Sunday Walk*, Turner's *Peace: Burial at Sea*; Literature—Cooper's *The Deerslayer*, Ingraham's *The Quadroon*, Lermontov's *The Demon*.

Musical Highlights

A. Births

Composers: Elfrida Andrée (Sweden) February 19; Giovanni Bolzoni (Italy) May 15; Emmanuel Chabrier (France) January 18; Antonin Dvořák (Bohemia) September 8; Victor E. Nessler (Germany) January 28.

Conductors: Enrico Bevignani (Italy) September 29.

Singers: Annie Louise Cary (American contralto) October 22; Daniel Filleborn (Polish tenor) November 7; Franz Krückl (Moravian baritone) November 10; Pauline Lucca (Austrian soprano) April 25; Aglaja Orgeni (Hungarian soprano) December 17; Giuseppe del Puente (Italian baritone) January 30; Anna Schimon-Regan (German soprano) September 18.

Performers: Edoardo Caudella (Romanian violinist/composer) June 3; Anton Franz Grunicke (German organist) January 23; Henri Kowalski (French-born pianist); Bernhard Listemann (German violinist) August 28; Walter Parratt (British organist) February 10; Giovanni Sgambati (Italian pianist/conductor/composer) May 28; Carl Tausig (Polish pianist/composer) November 4; Alfred Volkland (German pianist/conductor) April 10; Samuel Prowse Warren (American organist) February 18.

Others: Victor-Charles Mahillon (Belgian acoustician) March 10; Felipe Pedrell (Spanish musicologist) February 19; Julius Philipp Spitta (German music scholar) December 27; Emil Welte (German instrument maker) April 20.

B. Deaths

Composers: Felice Blangini (Italy) December 18; Karl Friedrich Curschmann (Germany) August 24; Ignacy Dobrzyński (Poland) August 16; Georg Christoph Grosheim (Germany) November 18; Daniil Nikitich Kashin (Russia) December 22; Francesco Morlacchi (Italy) October 28; John Thomson (Scotland) May 6.

Conductors: Ignaz Seyfried (Austria) August 27.

Performers: Jean-Baptiste Cartier (French violinist/composer); Ferdinando Carulli (Italian guitarist) February 17; Hippolyte Mompou (French organist) August 10; Alessandro Rolla (Italian violinist) September 15; Bernhard Heinrich Romberg (German cellist) August 13.

Others: Domenico Barbaja (Italian impresario) October 19; Félix Savart (French acoustician) March 17.

C. Debuts

Singers: Giuseppina Brambilla (Italian contralto—Trieste); Isidor Dannström (Swedish baritone—Stockholm); Malvina Schnorr von

Carolsfeld (German soprano—Breslau); Enrico Tamberlik (Italian tenor—Naples).
Performers: Ernest Lübeck (Dutch pianist—Holland); Thomas Tellefsen (Norwegian pianist—Trondheim).

D. New Positions

Conductors: Franz Abt (choral conductor, Zürich); Otto Nicolai (hofkapellmeister, Vienna); Carlo Pedrotti (Italian Opera, Amsterdam). **Others:** Robert Franz (organ, Ulrichskirche, Halle); Florentius C. Kist (editor, *Nederlandsch Musikaal Tijdschrift*); Karl Matthias Kudelski (director, Moscow Imperial Theater).

E. Prizes/Honors

Prizes: Louis-Aimé Maillart (Prix de Rome); Etienne Joseph Soubre (Prix de Rome).
Honors: Niels Gade (Copenhagen Musical Union).

F. Biographical Highlights

Hector Berlioz leaves Henrietta and moves in with Marie Recio; Anton Bruckner begins a short career as a school teacher in Windhaag; Luigi Cherubini retires from active musical life; Joseph Joachim is taken to Vienna for further music study at the Conservatory; Gaspare Spontini resigns his Berlin post after problems arise with his attitude toward the public and management; William V. Wallace leaves South America and arrives in New Orleans, where he stays for three years.

G. Cultural Beginnings

Performing Groups—Choral: Abbey Glee Club (London); Roland de Lattre Choral Society (Mons); Maatschappij Caecilia (Amsterdam Choral Society); The Motett Society (London); Munich Liedertafel.
Performing Groups—Instrumental: Mainz Instrumentalverein.
Educational: Hullah's Singing School for Schoolmasters (London).
Music Publishers: Alphonse Leduc Publishing Co. (Paris).
Music Publications: *Allgemeine Wiener Musik-Zeitung; Iberia Musical y Literaria; La Mélomanie Revue Musicale; Revue Indépendante* (Paris).
Performing Centers: Breslau Opera House; Internationale Stiftung Mozarteum (Salzburg); Kiel Stadttheater; Royal Saxon Opera House (Dresden); Teatro Comunale Nuovo (Modena).
Other: Austin Lyceum; Jacob Becker Piano Co. (St. Petersburg); John and James Hopkinson, piano makers.

H. Musical Literature

Pietro Alfieri, *Raccolta di musica sacra I*; Henry F. Chorley, *Music and Manners in France and Germany*; Antoine Elwart, *Feuille harmonique*; Edward Hodges, *An Essay on the Cultivation of Church Music*; Jan Karlovitch, *Theory of Composition*; Raphael Kiesewetter, *Schicksale und beschaffenheit des weltlichen Gesanges;* Adolf Marx, *Alte musiklehre im streit mit unserer Zeit;* Lowell Mason, *Carmina Sacra;* Sylvanus Pond, *The United States Psalmody;* Filippo Traetta, *Rudiments of Singing I;* Philipp Wackernagel, *Das deutsche Kirchenlied von der ältesten Zeit . . .*

I. **Musical Compositions**
   Chamber Music:
   String Quartets: Friedrich Kuhlau, *Quartet in g, Opus 122.*
   Ensembles: Alkan, *Piano Trio, Opus 30;* César Franck, *Three Piano Trios (f♯, B♭, b), Opus 1.*
   Piano: Frédéric Chopin, *Tarantelle in A♭, Opus 43–Polonaise in f♯, Opus 44–Prelude in c♯, Opus 45–Allegro de concert, Opus 46–Ballade in A♭, Opus 47–Two Nocturnes (c, f♯), Opus 48–Fantasie in f/A♭, Opus 49–Three Mazurkas (G, A♭, c♯), Opus 50;* Felix Mendelssohn, *Songs without Words IV, Opus 53–Serious Variations in d, Opus 54–Variations in E♭, Opus 82–Variations in B♭, Opus 83;* Otto Nicolai, *Sonata in d, Opus 27.*
   Organ: Felix Mendelssohn, *Prelude in c.*
   Choral/Vocal Music:
   Choral: Charles Gounod, *Requiem Mass;* Carl Loewe, *Palestrina* (oratorio)–*Johann Hus, Opus 82;* William Jackson, *Psalm 103;* Albert Lortzing, *Jubel-Kantate;* Francesco Morlacchi, *Mass No. 10;* Sigismund von Neukomm, *Christi Auferstehung* (oratorio); Gioacchino Rossini, *Stabat Mater.*
   Vocal: Hector Berlioz, *Nuits d'été, Opus 7;* Gaetano Donizetti, *Matinée musicale–Inspirations viennoises;* Clara Schumann, *Three Songs of Rückert, Opus 12.*
   Musical Stage: Adolphe Adam, *La Rose de Péronne;* Daniel Auber, *Les diamants de la couronne;* Michael Balfe, *Keolanthe;* Hippolyte Chélard, *Der Scheibentoni;* Gaetano Donizetti, *Maria Padilla–Rita–Adelia;* Heinrich Dorn, *Der Banner von England;* Hilarión Eslava, *Il solitario;* William Henry Fry, *Aurelia, the Vestal;* Jacques-François Halévy, *Le guitarrero–La reine de Chypre;* Jean-Georges Kastner, *La maschera;* Franz Lachner, *Catarina Cornaro;* Albert Lortzing, *Casanova;* Stanislaw Moniuszko, *Ideal–The New Don Quixote;* Otto Nicolai, *Il proscritto;* Giovanni Pacini, *L'uomo del mistero;* Carlo Pedrotti, *Matilde;* Achille Peri, *Il solitario;* Ambroise Thomas, *Le comte der Carmagnola;* Richard Wagner, *The Flying Dutchman.*
   Orchestra/Band Music:
   Concerted Music:
   Piano: William Sterndale Bennett, *Concert-Stück in A, Opus 22.*
   Ballet/Incidental Music: Adolphe Adam, *Giselle* (B); Felix Mendelssohn, *Antigone, Opus 55* (IM).

Standard Works: William Sterndale Bennett, *The Wood Nymphs Overture*; Felix Mendelssohn, *March in D, Opus 108*; Robert Schumann, *Overture, Scherzo and Finale in E, Opus 52*.

Symphonies: Jeanne Louise Farrenc, *No. 1 in c, Opus 32*; Niels Gade, *No. 1 in c, Opus 5*; Johann Kalliwoda, *No. 6 in g*; Robert Schumann, *No. 1 in B♭, Opus 38, "Spring"–No. 4 in d, Opus 120*; Louis Spohr, *No. 7 in C, Opus 121, "Earthly and Divine."*

1842
❋

Historical Highlights: By the Treaty of Nanking, China is forced to officially cede Hong Kong to the British; the British Mining Act prohibits women and children from working in the mines; in the United States, the Webster-Ashburton Treaty settles the northeastern boundary dispute between Canada and the United States; Massachusetts limits children's labor time to ten hours a day; Dorr's Rebellion in Rhode Island leads to universal male suffrage.

Art and Literature Highlights: Births—writers Ambrose Bierce, Sidney Lanier, Stéphane Mallarmé, artist Giovanni Boldini; Deaths—artists John Cotman, Louise Vigée-Lebrun, writers Clemens Brentano, Marie Stendhal. Art—Cole's *Voyage of Life Series*, Ingres' *Luigi Cherubini and the Muse of Poetry*, Turner's *Steamer in a Snow Storm*; Literature—W. C. Bryant's *The Fountain and Other Poems*, Dickens' *American Notes*, Gogol's *Dead Souls*.

Musical Highlights

A. Births

Composers: Arrigo Boito (Italy) February 24; Alphons Czibulka (Hungary) May 14; Jean-Baptiste van den Eeden (Belgium) December 26; Henri Maréchal (France) January 22; Jules Massenet (France) May 12; Rikard Nordraak (Norway) June 12; Arthur Sullivan (England) May 13.

Conductors: Gyula Erkel (Hungary) July 4; Johann Nepomuk Fuchs (Austria) May 5.

Singers: Marianne Brandt (Austrian contralto) September 12; Eugen Gura (German bass-baritone) November 8; Clara (Louise) Kellogg (American soprano) July 9; (Marie) Gabrielle Krauss (Austrian soprano) March 24; Stanislaw Niedzielski (Polish baritone) July 13; Melitta Otto (German soprano) December 16; Janet Patey (Scottish contralto) May 1; Heinrich Wiegand (German bass) September 9; Sarah Edith Wynne (British soprano) March 11.

Performers: Walter Bache (British pianist/conductor) June 19; Emile Bernard (French organist) November 28; Gustav Frieman (Polish violinist) October 29; Wilhelm Fritze (German pianist) February 17; Heinrich Hofmann (German pianist) January 13; Sidney Lanier (American flutist/poet) February 3; Edmund Neupert (Norwegian-born pianist) April 1; Carl Rosa (German violinist/impresario) March 22; Camilla Urso (French-born violinist) June 13; Samuel Brenton Whitney (American organist) June 4; Emanuel Wirth (Bohemian violinist) October 18.

Others: Wilhelm Bäumker (German music author) October 25; Vasili Bessel (Russian publisher) April 25.

B. Deaths

Composers: Luigi Cherubini (Italy-France) March 15; José Mariano Elízaga (Mexico) October 2; Giacomo Ferrari (Italy) December; Pehr Frigel (Sweden) November 24; Giuseppe Nicolini (Italy) December 18; Joseph Rastrelli (Italy-Germany) November 15; Timothy Swan (U.S.A.) July 23.

Singers: Jean Elleviou (French tenor) May 5.

Performers: Pierre Baillot (French violinist) September 15; João Domingos Bomtempo (Portugese pianist) August 18; Franz Clement (Austrian violinist/composer) November 3; Henri-Joseph de Croes (Belgian violinist) January 6; Timothy Swan (American organist) July 23; Michael Umlauf (Austrian violinist/conductor) June 20; Christoph Ernst Weyse (Danish organist/composer) October 8.

Others: Johann Anton André (Germany publisher) April 6; Alpheus Babcock (American piano maker) April 3; Tobias Haslinger (Austrian publisher) June 18; Felix Joseph Lipowsky (German lexicographer) March 21; Jérôme-Joseph de Momigny (Belgian music theorist/publisher) August 25; Friedrich Dionys Weber (Bohemian music author/composer) December 25; (Christian) Theodor Weinlig (German music theorist/composer) March 7; Guillaume-Louis Wilhem (French music educator) April 26.

C. Debuts

Singers: Marietta Alboni (Italian contralto—Bologna); Henry Robinson Allen (Irish baritone—London); Anne Charton-Demeur (French mezzo-soprano—Bordeaux); Karl Johann Formes (German bass—Cologne); Semyon Stepanovich Gulak-Artemovsky (Russian baritone—St. Petersburg); Anne Caroline de La Grange (French soprano—Italy); Charlotte Sainton-Dolby (British contralto—London); Willoughby Hunter Weiss (British tenor—Liverpool).

Performers: Julius Schulhoff (German pianist—Dresden).

D. New Positions
Conductors: Robert Franz (Halle Singakademie); Moritz Hauptmann (cantor, Thomasschule, Leipzig); Giacomo Meyerbeer (Berlin Court Opera).
Others: Daniel-Louis Auber (director, Paris Conservatory); Moritz Brosig (organ, Breslau Cathedral); Siegfried Dehn (music librarian, Royal Library, Berlin); Alexei Vertovsky (general manager, Moscow Opera); Samuel Sebastian Wesley (organ, Leeds' Parish Church).

E. Prizes/Honors
Honors: Henry Bishop (knighted); Giacomo Meyerbeer (Order of Paris); Georges Onslow (Institut de France); Edward Rimbault (Swedish Academy).

F. Biographical Highlights
J. Lathrop Allen moves his brass instrument business to Boston; George Bristow becomes violinist in the newly formed New York Philharmonic; Louis Moreau Gottschalk goes to Paris for further music study; Franz Liszt makes a concert tour of Russia; Felix Mendelssohn visits with Queen Victoria and organizes the Leipzig Conservatory; Robert Schumann suffers a nervous breakdown due to overwork; Richard Wagner returns to Dresden and begins sketches for *Tannhauser*.

G. Cultural Beginnings
Performing Groups—Choral: Cleveland Sacred Music Society; Cologne Männergesangverein; Galitzin Boys Choir (Moscow); Mannheim Liederkranz.
Performing Groups—Instrumental: Dando String Quartet (London); New York Philharmonic Orchestra; Vienna Philharmonic Orchestra.
Educational: Académie du Chant (Paris); École de Musique de la Ville d'Anvers (Belgium).
Music Publishers: Escudier Publishing House (Paris); Abraham Hirsch (Stockholm); A. and S. Nordheimer (Ontario).
Music Publications: *Ainsworth's Magazine*; *Florentine Gazzetta Musicale*; *Gazzetta Musicale di Milano*; *Musical Examiner*; *Le Musicien*.
Performing Centers: Crosby Hall (London); Thalia Theater (Hamburg); Vilnius Theater.
Other: Athens Fine Arts Society; Cervený Brass Instrument Co. (Königgratz); Chicago Musical Society; Harmonium (by Alexandre-François Debain); Elias Howe Music Store (Rhode Island); Mudie's Lending Library (London).

H. Musical Literature
Pietro Alfieri, *Accompagnamento coll'organo de' toni ecclesiatici*; Carl F. Becker, *Harmonielehre für dilettanten*; Heinrich A. Hoffmann, *Schles-*

ische volkslieder mit melodien; Louis Lambillotte, *Musée des Organistes I;* John D. Loder, *The Whole Modern Art of Bowing;* Joseph Mainzer, *The Musical Athenaeum;* John W. Moore, *Sacred Minstrel;* Gustav Schilling, *Die musikalische Europa;* Johann Gottlob Töpfer, *Die Scheibler'sche stimm-Methode–Abhandlung über den saitenbezug der Pianoforte.*

I. Musical Compositions
Chamber Music:
String Quartets: George Macfarren, *No. 2 in A;* Robert Schumann, *Three Quartets (a, F, A), Opus 41.*

Sonata/Solos: Niels Gade, *Violin Sonata No. 1 in A, Opus 6;* Camille Saint-Saëns, *Violin Sonata in B♭.*

Ensembles: Louise Farrenc, *Piano Quintet in a, Opus 80;* César Franck, *Piano Trio No. 4 in b, Opus 2;* Robert Schumann, *Piano Quintet in E♭, Opus 44–Piano Quartet in E♭, Opus 47.*

Piano: Frédéric Chopin, *Impromtu in G♭, Opus 51–Ballade in f, Opus 52–Polonaise in A♭, Opus 53–Scherzo in E, Opus 54;* Carl Loewe, *Ziguener-Sonate, Opus 107b;* George Macfarren, *Sonata No. 1 in E♭;* Joachim Raff, *Serenade, Opus 1–Three Characteristic Pieces, Opus 2–Scherzo, Opus 3–Fantasie brillante, Opus 4;* Clara Schumann, *Scherzo No. 2 in c, Opus 14–Sonata in g.*

Organ: Alexander Boëly, *Four Offertories, Opus 9–Recueil contenant 14 morceaux qui pourrent servir pendart l'office divin, Opus 10–Messe du jour de Noël, Opus 11.*

Choral/Vocal Music:
Choral: Anton Bruckner, *Mass in C;* František Krommer, *Mass in d;* Carl Loewe, *Te Deum, Opus 77–Gesang der geister über den wassern;* Felix Mendelssohn, *Psalm 100–Six Male Choruses, Opus 50–Nachtgesang;* Giacomo Meyerbeer, *Dem Vaterland–Freundschaft* (male voices); Mihály Mosonyi, *Mass No. 1 in C;* Sigismund von Neukomm, *Christi Himmelfahrt* (oratorio); Louis Spohr, *The Last Hours of the Saviour* (oratorio).

Vocal: Carl Loewe, *Six Songs, Opus 89;* George Macfarren, *Six Convivial Glees Illustrating the History of England;* Jacques Offenbach, *Six Fables de Lafontaine.*

Musical Stage: Adolphe Adam, *Le roi d'Yvetot;* Daniel Auber, *Le Duc d'Olonne;* Gaetano Donizetti, *Linda di Chamounix;* Mikhail Glinka, *Russlan und Ludmilla;* Hervé, *L'ours et la pacha;* Conradin Kreutzer, *Der Edelknecht;* Carl Loewe, *Emmy;* Albert Lortzing, *Der Wildschütz;* Saverio Mercadante, *Il proscritto;* Stanislaw Moniuszko, *The Lottery;* Giovanni Pacini, *La fidanzata corsa–Il duca d'Alba;* Ambroise Thomas, *La guerillero;* Giuseppe Verdi, *Nabucco.*

Orchestra/Band Music:
Concerted Music:
Violin: Heinrich Ernst, *Polonaise in D, Opus 17–Variations sur l'air hollandais, Opus 18.*
Other: Jacques Offenbach, *Air de ballet du 17me siècle, Opus 24* (cello).
Ballet/Incidental Music: Niels Gade, *Napoli* (B); Johan P. Hartmann, *Undine, Opus 33* (M); Felix Mendelssohn, *A Midsummer Night's Dream, Opus 61* (IM).
Program Music: Franz Berwald, *Memories of the Norwegian Alps.*
Standard Works: Mihály Mosonyi, *Overture in b, Opus 15*; Louis Spohr, *Concert Overture in D, Opus 126.*
Symphonies: Franz Berwald, *No. 1 in g, "Serieuse"–No. 2 in D, "Capricieuse"*; George Macfarren, *Overture, Don Carlos*; Felix Mendelssohn, *No. 3 in a, "Scotch," Opus 56.*

1843
❋

Historical Highlights: The First Maori War against British rule takes place in New Zealand; Louis Napoleon becomes head of the French Republic; the Spanish dictatorship is overthrown and Isabella II is declared Queen of Spain; in the United States, Mexican President Santa Anna warns the United States not to annex Texas; J. C. Fremont explores the Oregon Trail Territory and New Mexico; Dorothea Dix begins her campaign against prison and asylum conditions.

Art and Literature Highlights: Births—artist Alexandre Regnault, writers Henry James, Charles Stoddard; Deaths—artists Washington Allston, John Trumbull, writers Robert Southey, Friedrich La Motte-Focqué, Johann C. Hölderlin. Art—Chassériau's *The Two Sisters*, Corot's *Destruction of Sodom*, Powers' *The Greek Slave*; Literature—Auerbach's *Schwarzwälder Dorfgeschichten*, Dickens' *A Christmas Carol*, Gutiérrez's *Simón Boccanegra.*

Musical Highlights

A. Births
Composers: Caryl Florio (England-U.S.A.) November 13; Edvard Grieg (Norway) June 15; Asger Hamerik (Denmark) April 8; Heinrich Herzogenberger (Austria) June 10; Charles Édouard Lefebvre (France) June 19; Emile-Louis Pessard (France) May 29; William Sudds (England-U.S.A.) March 5.
Conductors: Gustave Huberti (Belgium) April 14; Adolph Neuendorff (Germany-U.S.A.) June 13; Hans Richter (Hungary-Germany)

April 4; George Stephănescu (Romania) December 13; Josef Sucher (Hungary) November 23.

Singers: Pierre-Léon Melchissédec (French baritone) May 7; Christine Nilsson (Swedish soprano) August 20; Adelina Patti (British soprano) February 19; Feodor Stravinsky (Russian bass) June 20.

Performers: Louis Diémer (French pianist) February 14; Alexis-Henri Fissot (French pianist) October 24; Anna Mehlig (German pianist) July 11; David Popper (Austrian cellist) November 9.

Others: Theodor Helm (Austrian music critic) April 9; Francis Hueffer (German-born music author) May 22; Romeo Orsi (Italian clarinetist/maker) October 18.

B. Deaths

Composers: Franz Xaver Gebel (Germany) May 3; Marco Santucci (Italy) November 29.

Conductors: Johann Georg Lickl (Austria) May 12; Christian August Pohlenz (Germany) March 10.

Singers: Thomas L. Bellamy (British bass) January 3; Domenico Reina (Italian tenor) July 29.

Performers: Charles Jane Ashley (British cellist) August 29; Joseph Lanner (Austrian violinist/conductor) April 11; Louis Barthólemy Pradher (French pianist) October; Charles Franz Schoberlechner (Austrian pianist) January 7; Joseph Sellner (German oboist) May 17; Samuel Webbe, Jr. (British organist/composer) November 25.

Others: Christian Frederick Albrecht (German-born piano maker) March; Johann Friedrich Kind (German librettist) June 25; Imanuel Langbecker (German music author) October 24.

C. Debuts

Singers: Emilio Naudin (French tenor—Cremona); Henrietta Nissen (Swedish soprano—Paris); Alexander Reichardt (Hungarian tenor—Lemberg); Wilhelm Troszel (Polish bass—Warsaw).

Performers: Alfred Jaëll (Austrian pianist—Venice, age eleven); Ernst Pauer (Austrian pianist—Vienna); Marie Wieck (German pianist—Leipzig).

D. New Positions

Conductors: Heinrich Dorn (Cologne Singverein and Musikalischen Gesellschaft); Ferdinand Hiller (Leipzig Gewandhaus Orchestra); Teodulo Mabellini (Florence PO); Alessandro Nini (maestro di cappella, Novara Cathedral); August Roeckel (kapellmeister, Dresden); Richard Wagner (assistant hofkapellmeister, Dresden).

Others: Johan Peter Hartmann (organ, Copenhagen Cathedral); Edward John Hopkins (organ, Temple Church, London); Johann Kittl (director, Prague Conservatory).

F. Biographical Highlights

Ole Bull begins his first American tour; Charles Hallé begins his series of concerts in London; Joseph Joachim, age twelve, goes to Leipzig, where he performs with the Gewandhaus Orchestra; Joseph Joachim Raff sends some piano works to Mendelssohn who recommends them to his publisher; Carl Reinecke makes his first concert tour of Scandinavia; Robert Schumann teaches in Leipzig and takes a hiatus from composing; Bedrich Smetana settles in Prague and teaches privately for the family of Count Thun; Henri Vieuxtemps undertakes his first American tour.

G. Cultural Beginnings

Performing Groups—Choral: Adelaide Choral Society (Australia); Augsburger Liedertafel; Berlin Männergesangverein; Darmstadt Mozartverein; St. Cecilia Society of Bordeaux; Société de Musique Vocale, Religieuse et Classique (Paris).

Performing Groups—Instrumental: Berlin Symphoniekapelle; Blagrove's Quartet Concerts (London); Bonn Orchesterverein.

Educational: Cambridge University (Peterhouse) Musical Society; Leipzig Conservatory of Music; Sinico Singing School (Trieste).

Music Publishers: Carl Warmuth (Oslo).

Music Publications: *L'Illustration; Musikalisch-Kritisches Repertorium; Signale für die Musikalische Welt* (Leipzig).

Other: Antoine Bord Piano Co. (Paris); Forster and Andrews, organ builders (Hull); Glasgow Musical Association; Malmsjö Piano Co. (Gothenburg); Joseph Merklin (Merklin, Schütze et Cie.), organ builders (Brussels); George Rogers and Sons, piano makers (London); Tivoli Gardens (Copenhagen).

H. Musical Literature

Raimondo Boucheron, *Filosofia della musica;* Gottfried Fink, *Musikalischer hausschatz;* John Hullah, *A Grammar of Vocal Music;* Jan Jarmusiewicz, *A New System of Music;* Gustav Schilling, *Musikalische dynamik;* Johann Seidel, *Die Orgel un ihr Bau;* Johann Gottlob Töpfer, *Die Orgel, Zweck und beschaffenheit Teile;* Samuel Sebastian Wesley, *The Psalter;* Carl von Winterfeld, *Der evangelische Kirchengesang I;* Wesley Woolhouse, *A Catechism of Music.*

I. Musical Compositions

Chamber Music:

String Quartets: Franz Lachner, *No. 1 in b, Opus 75–No. 2 in c, Opus 76–No. 3 in B♭, Opus 77;* Felix Mendelssohn, *Capriccio in e, Opus 81/3.*

Sonata/Solos: Felix Mendelssohn, *Cello Sonata No. 2 in D, Opus 58.*

Ensembles: César Franck, *Piano Trio No. 4 in b, Opus 2.*

Piano: Frédéric Chopin, *Two Nocturnes (f, e♭), Opus 55–Three Mazurkas (B, C, c), Opus 56*; César Franck, *Grande Caprice, Opus 5–Souvenirs d'Aix-la-chapelle, Opus 7*; Niels Gade, *Nine Songs in Folkstyle, Opus 9*; Johan P. Hartmann, *Sonata No. 1, Opus 34*; Fanny Mendelssohn Hensel, *Sonata in g*; Joachim Raff, *Four galops brillants, Opus 5–Fantaisie et variations brillantes, Opus 6–Rondo brillant, Opus 7–Twelve Romances, Opus 8*; Robert Schumann, *Andante and Variations in B♭, Opus 46* (two pianos); Louis Spohr, *Sonata in A♭, Opus 125*.

Organ: Alexandre Boëly, *Twenty-Four Pieces, Opus 12*.

Choral/Vocal Music:

Choral: Charles Gounod, *Vienna Mass–Un Hymne Français*; Johann Kalliwoda, *Mass No. 1, Opus 137*; Carl Loewe, *Der Meister von Avis* (oratorio); Felix Mendelssohn, *Three Psalms, Opus 78–Psalm XCVIII, Opus 91*; Sigismund von Neukomm, *Lobet de Herrn* (cantata); Otto Nicolai, *Mass to Friedrich Wilhelm IV*; Giovanni Pacini, *Requiem in c*; Robert Schumann, *Paradise and the Peri, Opus 50* (cantata); Richard Wagner, *The Love Feast of the Apostles* (cantata).

Vocal: Robert Franz, *Twelve Songs, Opus 1*; Carl Loewe, *Five Humoresken for Male Voices, Opus 84–Two Ballads, Opus 94*; Felix Mendelssohn, *Six Songs, Opus 57*.

Musical Stage: Daniel Auber, *La part du diable*; Michael Balfe, *Le puits d'amour–The Bohemian Girl*; Hippolyte Chélard, *Die Seekadetten*; Franz von Destouches, *Der Teufel un der Schneider*; Gaetano Donizetti, *Don Pasquale–Don Sébastien–Maria di Rohan*; Hilarión Eslava, *Pietro il crudele*; Friedrich von Flotow, *L'esclave de Camoëns*; Jacques Halévy, *Charles VI*; Heinrich Marschner, *Kaiser Adolf von Nassau*; Saverio Mercadante, *Il reggente*; Giacomo Meyerbeer, *Das Hoffest von Ferrara*; Hippolyte Monpou, *Lambert Simnel*; Giovanni Pacini, *Medea–Maria Regina d'inghilterra*; Achille Peri, *Ester d'Engaddi*; Giuseppe Persiani, *Il Fantasma*; Johann Poissl, *Zaide*; Józef Poniatowski, *Bonafazio de' Geremei*; Ambroise Thomas, *Mina–Angélique et Médor*; Giuseppe Verdi, *I Lombardi*.

Orchestra/Band Music:

Concerted Music:

Violin: Heinrich Ernst, *Bolero, Opus 16*.

Other: Jacques Offenbach, *Hommage à Rossini* (cello).

Ballet/Incidental Music: Cesare Pugni, *Ondine* (B).

Standard Works: Johann Kalliwoda, *Overture Pastorale in A, Opus 108*.

Symphonies: Niels Gade, *No. 2 in E, Opus 10*; Johann Kalliwoda, *No. 7 in F*.

1844

❄

Historical Highlights: The Young Men's Christian Association (YMCA) is founded in London; the Dominican Republic succeeds in gaining its independence from Haiti; the French defeat the Moroccans; in the United States, James K. Polk is elected as eleventh president; the first telegraph message is sent from Washington, D.C., to Baltimore; "Fifty-four Forty or Fight!" becomes the battle cry of settlers in Oregon in their border dispute with Canada.

Art and Literature Highlights: Births—artists Mary Cassatt, Thomas Eakins, Henri Rousseau, writers George Washington Cable, Anatole France, Friedrich Nietzsche; Deaths—sculptor Bertel Thorvaldsen, writers Thomas Campbell, Sándor Kisfaludy. Art—Bingham's *Mill Boy*, Landseer's *The Challenge*, Turner's *Rain, Steam and Speed*; Literature—Dickens' *Martin Chuzzlewit*, Dumas' *Three Musketeers*, Emerson's *Essays II*.

Musical Highlights

A. **Births**

Composers: Emile Paladilhe (France) June 3; Nicolai Rimsky-Korsakov (Russia) March 18.

Conductors: Thomas H. Rollinson (U.S.A.) January 4.

Singers: Alfred Arthur (American tenor) October 8; Julián Gayarre (Spanish tenor) January 9; Angelo Masini (Italian tenor) November 28; Amalie Materna (Austrian soprano) July 10; George Laurie Osgood (American tenor) April 3; Clara Kathleen Rogers (British-born soprano) January 14.

Performers: Oscar Beringer (German-born pianist) July 14; Karl Bohm (German pianist) September 11; Otis Bardwell Boise (American organist) August 13; Frederick Bridge (British organist) December 5; Edward Dannreuther (German-born pianist/music scholar) November 4; Amy Fay (American pianist) May 21; Eugène Gigout (French organist) March 23; Ernest Grosjean (French organist) December 18; Richard Hofmann (German violinist/publisher) April 30; Pablo de Sarasate (Spanish violinist/composer) March 10; Charles-Marie Widor (French organist/composer) February 21.

Others: Richard D'Oyly Carte (British impresario) May 3.

B. **Deaths**

Composers: Henri-Montan Berton (France) April 22; Franz von Destouches (Germany) December 10; Johann Baptist Gänsbacher (Austria) July 13; Frank Johnson (U.S.A.) April 6; André da Silva

Gomes (Brazil) June 17; August Ferdinand Häser (Germany) November 1; Uri Keeler Hill (U.S.A.) November 9; Oliver Holden (U.S.A.) September 4.

Conductors: Ignaz Franz von Mosel (Austria) April 18.

Performers: John Addison (British double bassist) January 30; Matthew Camidge (British organist) October 23; Heinrich Domnich (German horn virutoso/composer) July 19; Joseph Binns Hart (British organist/composer) December 10; Francis Johnson (American cornetist/conductor) April 6; Joseph Mazzinghi (British pianist/composer) January 15; Johann Christian Till (American organist) November 19.

Others: William MacKenzie Bacon (British music author) November 27; Giuseppe Baini (Italian music author) May 21; John Meacham, Jr. (American piano maker) December 8; Thaddäus Weigl (Austrian publisher/conductor) February 29.

C. Debuts

Singers: Mathilde Marchesi de Castrone (German mezzo-soprano—Frankfurt); Louis Henri Obin (French bass—Paris); Ernst Pasqué (German baritone—Mayence); Joseph Tagliafico (French bass-baritone—Paris); Fortunata Tedesco (Italian soprano—Milan); Johanna Wagner (German soprano—Dresden).

Performers: Heinrich (Rudolf) Willmers (Danish pianist—Berlin).

D. New Positions

Conductors: Joseph Drechsler (kapellmeister, St. Stephen's, Vienna); Hilarión Eslava (chapel master, Queen Isabella, Madrid Royal Chapel); Albert Lortzing (Leipzig Opera); Joseph Lucchesi (U.S. Marine Band); Francesco Shira (Drury Lane); Étienne-Joseph Soubre (Brussels PO).

Others: Margaret Fuller (music critic, *New York Tribune*); Ignace Leybach (organ, Toulouse Cathedral); Franz Mirecki (director, Kracow Opera); Gottfried von Preyer (director, Vienna Conservatory); August Gottfried Ritter (editor, *Urania*).

E. Prizes/Honors

Prizes: Victor Massé (Prix de Rome); Renaud de Vilback (Prix de Rome).

Honors: William Dyce (Royal Academy, London).

F. Biographical Highlights

Johannes Brahms, at the age of ten, performs for the first time in public with a chamber group; César Franck leaves Belgium to settle permanently in Paris; Niels Gade becomes assistant to Mendelssohn in Leipzig; Albert Lortzing begins a conducting career; Robert and

Clara Schumann tour Russia while Robert, suffering a second nervous breakdown, gives up his music paper; Mary Shaw, at the shock of her husband's sudden insanity, loses her voice; William V. Wallace returns to Europe and tours the continent.

G. Cultural Beginnings

Performing Groups—Choral: Berlin Kunstlerverein.
Performing Groups—Instrumental: Strauss Orchestra II (by Johann Strauss, Jr.).
Educational: Bressler's Conservatory of Music (Nantes).
Music Publishers: G. G. Guidi (Florence); Macmillan and Co. (Cambridge).
Music Publications: *Caecilia: Algemeen Musikaal Tijdschrift ver Nederlands; Hood's Magazine; Mainzer's Musical Times and Singing Circular; Orgel-Archiv; Vierteljahrsschrift für Musikwissenschaft.*
Performing Centers: Josef Kroll Theater (Berlin); Palmo's Opera House (New York); Teatro de la Victoria (Santiago, Chile); Teatro del Buen Orden (Buenos Aires); Wadsworth Atheneum (Hartford).

H. Musical Literature

Carl F. Becker, *Evangelischen choralbuch*; Hector Berlioz, *Traité d'instrumentation*; Emile Chevé, *Méthode élémentaire de la musique vocale*; François Fétis, *The Theory and Practice of Harmony*; Hyacinthe Klosé, *Grande Méthode pour la clarinette*; Juste de La Fage, *Histoire générale de la musique*; Johann Christian Lobe, *Compositionslehre*; Lowell Mason, *The Vocalist*; Joseph d'Ortigue, *Abécédaire du plain-chant*; Giovanni Pacini, *Corso teorico-pratico de lezioni di armonia*; Samuel Tuckerman, *Episcopal Harp*.

I. Musical Compositions

Chamber Music:
Ensembles: Mihály Mosonyi, *String Sextet*; George Macfarren, *Romance and Allegro in e* (piano trio)*–Piano Quintet*.
Piano: Alkan, *Le Preux, étude de concert, Opus 17–Nocturne, Opus 22–Saltarello, Opus 23–Variations-fantaisie on Mozart's "Don Giovanni," Opus 26–Le chemin de fer, Opus 27*; Frédéric Chopin, *Berceuse in D♭, Opus 57–Sonata in b, Opus 58*; César Franck, *Fantasia No. 1 on a Theme of Dalyrac, Opus 11–No. 2, Opus 12–Fantasie, Opus 13*; Stephen Heller, *Scherzo, Opus 24–Two Capriccio brillant, Opus 27–28–Twenty-Four Easy Etudes, Opus 45–Thirty Progressive Etudes, Opus 46–Four Arabesques, Opus 49–Scènes pastorales, Opus 50*; Carl Loewe, *Biblische Bilder, Opus 96*; Felix Mendelssohn, *Songs without Words V, Opus 62*; Joachim Raff, *Fantaisie gracieuse, Opus 12–Sonata*

with fugue, Opus 14–Six Poems, Opus 15–Fantaisie dramatique, Opus 19; Clara Schumann, *Four pièces fugitives (f, a, D, G), Opus 15*.

Organ: Alexandre Boëly, *Recueil de 12 morceaux, Opus 14*; Felix Mendelssohn, *Four Little Pieces–Chorale in A♭–Six Sonatas (f, c, A, B♭, D, d), Opus 44*.

Choral/Vocal Music:

Choral: Anton Bruckner, *Mass in F* (a capella chorus); Félicien, David, *Le désert* (ode-symphonie); William Jackson, *The Deliverance of Israel from Babylon* (oratorio); Joseph A. Josephson, *The Melting of the Ice*; Felix Mendelssohn, *Im Grünen, Opus 59–Three Psalms, Opus 78–Six Partsongs, Opus 88–Four Partsongs, Opus 100*; Saverio Mercadante, *De profundis*.

Vocal: Stephen Foster, *Open Thy Lattice, Love*; Robert Franz, *Schilflieder, Opus 2–Six Songs, Opus 3*; Carl Loewe, *Three Ballads, Opus 97–Der Graf von Habsburg, Opus 98–Kaiser Karl V, Opus 99–Three Songs, Opus 103*; Clara Schumann, *Six Lieder, Opus 13*.

Musical Stage: Adolphe Adam, *Richard in Palestine–Cagliostro*; Daniel Auber, *La sirène*; Michael Balfe, *The Enchantress–The Castle of Aymon*; Julius Benedict, *The Brides of Venice*; Michael Costa, *Don Carlos*; Gaetano Donizetti, *Catarina Cornaro*; Friedrich von Flotow, *Allessandro Stradella*; Jacques Halévy, *Le lazzarone*; Alexei Lvov, *Bianca*; Victor Massé, *Le renégat de Tanger*; Saverio Mercadante, *Leonora*; Giacomo Meyerbeer, *Ein Feldlager in Schlesien*; Louis Niedermeyer, *Marie Stuart*; Giovanni Pacini, *L'ebrea*; Carlo Pedrotti, *La figlia dell'arciere*; Lauro Rossi, *Il borgomastro di Schiedam*; Robert Schumann, *Der Corsar*; Giuseppe Verdi, *Ernani*.

Orchestra/Band Music:

Concerted Music:

Piano: William Sterndale Bennett, *Caprice in E, Opus 22*; Stephen Heller, *Concerto No. 2 in b, Opus 65*; Johann Kalliwoda, *Introduction and Variations, Opus 128*; Henry Litolff, *Concerto No. 2, Opus 22*; Mihály Mosonyi, *Concerto in e*.

Violin: Heinrich Ernst, *Le carnaval de Venise, Opus 18*; Felix Mendelssohn, *Concerto in e, Opus 64*; Louis Spohr, *Concerto No. 15 in e, Opus 128*; Henri Vieuxtemps, *Concerto No. 3 in a, Opus 25*.

Other: Johann Kalliwoda, *Concertina, Opus 110* (oboe, orchestra).

Ballet/Incidental Music: Friedrich von Flotow, *Lady Henrietta* (B); Cesare Pugni, *La Esmeralda* (B).

Standard Works: Hector Berlioz, *Overture, Roman Carnival, Opus 9*; Niels Gade, *In the Highlands Overture, Opus 7*; J. P. E. Hartmann, *Overture, Hakon Jarl*; Otto Nicolai, *Festival Overture, Ein Feste Burg, Opus 32*; Richard Wagner, *Trauermusik for Winds*.

Symphonies: Mihály Mosonyi, *No. 1 in D*.

1845

❖

Historical Highlights: The Second Maori War takes place in New Zealand; the Sikhs battle the British in India; more than a million people die in Ireland's Great Famine; the first underwater cable is laid across the English Channel; in the United States, Florida and Texas become states numbers twenty-seven and twenty-eight; Mexico snubs the envoys sent to settle the Texas-California questions; the term "Manifest Destiny" first appears in local politics.

Art and Literature Highlights: Births—sculptors Karl Begas, Jr., François Bosio; Deaths—artists Louis-Léopold Boilly, Thomas Duncan, Henry Sargent, writers János Bacsányi, August von Schlegel, Henrik Wergeland. Art—Bingham's *Fur Traders Descending the Missouri*, Deas' *The Death Struggle*, Menzel's *Room with a Balcony*; Literature—Dumas' *The Count of Monte Cristo*, Mérimée's *Carmen*, Poe's *The Raven and Other Poems*.

Musical Highlights

A. Births

Composers: Gabriel Fauré (France) May 12.

Conductors: Wilhelm Gericke (Austria) April 18.

Singers: Teresina Brambilla-Ponchielli (Italian soprano) April 15; Nellie E. Brown (American soprano); Italo Campanini (Italian tenor) June 30; Frank H. Celli (Brtitish baritone) April 9; Alfred-Auguste Giraudet (French bass) March 29; Nina (Hagerup) Grieg (Norwegian soprano) November 24; Heinrich Gudehus (German tenor) March 30; Thomas Koschat (Austrian bass) August 8; Elizaveta Andreievna Lavroskaya (Russian mezzo-soprano) October 18; Edward Lloyd (British tenor) March 7; Angela Peralta (Mexican soprano) July 6; Emma Thursby (American soprano) February 21; Vilma von Voggenhuber (Hungarian soprano); Heinrich Vogl (German tenor) January 15; Jeannie Winston (British-born soprano).

Performers: Anton Jörgen Andersen (Norwegian cellist) October 10; Richard Arnold (German-born violinist) January 10; Leopold Auer (Hungarian violinist/pedagogue) June 7; Beniamino Cesi (Italian pianist) November 6; James C. Culwick (British organist) April 28; Annie Curwen (Irish pianist) September 1; Carl Rafael Hennig (German organist/theorist) January 4; Friedrich Niecks (German violinist) February 3; John Nelson Pattison (American pianist) October 22; Ernst Perabo (American pianist) November 14; Madeline Schiller (British pianist); Charles Paul Turban (French clarinetist) October 3; August Wilhelmj (German violinist) September 21; Agnes Zimmermann (German-born pianist) July 5.

Others: Gustav Jacobsthal (German musicologist) March 14; Frederick Niecks (German-born music author) February 3; H. E. Woodridge (British musicologist) March 28; Bernard Ziehn (German-born music theorist) January 20.

B. **Deaths**
Composer: François René Gebauer (France) July 28; Simon Mayr (Germany) December 2; Francesco Ruggi (Italy) January 23; Joseph Augustine Wade (Ireland) July 15.
Singers: Isabella Colbran (Spanish soprano) October 7; François Foignet (French tenor) July 27.
Performers: Thaddäus Amadé (Hungarian pianist) May 17; Alexandre-Joseph Artôt (Belgian violinist) July 20; Wilhelm Friedrich Ernst Bach (German pianist/harpsichordist) December 25; Charles Duvernoy (French clarinetist/composer) February 28; Alexander Juhan (American violinist); George Augustus Kollmann (British pianist/inventor) March 19; Hieronymus Payer (Austrian organist/conductor) August 17; Chrétien Urhan (French violinist) November 2; Franz Volkert (Austrian organist/conductor).
Others: Louis Callinet (French organ builder); Charles François Gand, *père* (French violin maker) May 10; James Alexander Hamilton (British music theorist) August 2; Karl August Lichtenstein (German theater manager/conductor) September 16.

C. **Debuts**
Singers: Aloys Anders (Bohemian tenor—Vienna); Clara Brinkerhoff (British-born soprano—New York); Édouard Gassier (French baritone—Paris); Lodovico Graziani (Italian tenor—Bologna); Catherine Hayes (Irish soprano—Marseilles).
Performers: Jesús de Monasterio (Spanish violinist—Madrid).

D. **New Positions**
Conductors: Heinrich Esser (kapellmeister, Mainz); Franz von Suppé (Theater an der Wien); Wilhelm Taubert (Berlin Royal Opera and court kapellmeister).
Others: Karl Franz Brendel (editor, *Neue Zeitschrift für Musik*); Hervé (Florimond Rongé) (organ, St. Eustache, Paris).

E. **Prizes/Honors**
Prizes: Adolphe Samuel (Prix de Rome).
Honors: Ambroise Thomas (Legion of Honor); Alfred Victor Vigny (French Academy).

F. **Biographical Highlights**
Alkan (Charles-Henri Valentin) emerges from his self-imposed exile and resumes his concert career; Anton Bruckner begins teaching at

St. Florian; Gaetano Donizetti suffers a paralytic stroke that ends his composing career; William Henry Fry writes what is believed to be the first American opera, *Leonora*; Felix Mendelssohn resumes his teaching and conducting at Leipzig following his time in London; William V. Wallace finally returns to England.

G. Cultural Beginnings

Performing Groups—Choral: Artisans' Glee Society (Christiana); Berner Liedertafel; Birmingham Festival Choral Society; Gloucester Choral Society; Jähnsscher Gesangverein (Berlin); Linz Liedertafel "Frohsinn" (Sängerbund); Den Norske Studentersangforening (Norway).

Performing Groups—Instrumental: Aberdeen Euterpean Society; Dortmunder Musikverein; Helsinki Symphonic Society I; The Musical Union (London morning chamber series); Stuttgart Chamber Orchestra; Toronto Philharmonic Society.

Educational: Agthe School of Music (Berlin); Rheinische Musikschule (Cologne).

Music Publishers: Chouden's Music Publishing House (Paris).

Music Publications: *Boose's Military Band Journal*; *Jerrold's Magazine*; *Revue de la Musique Religieuse, Populaire et Classique*; *Table Book*.

Performing Centers: Teatro de la Federación (Buenos Aires); Tivoli Theater (Kiel).

Other: Beethoven Memorial (Bonn); Casavant Frères, organ builders (Canada); Castle Gordon (New York); Distin and Sons, music dealers (London); Franz Rieger, organ builder (Jägerndorf); William Benjamin Simmons, organ builder; Sociedad Filarmónica de Cuba; Henry Willis, organ builder (London).

H. Musical Literature

Carl F. Becker, *Die choralsammlungen der verschiedenen Christlichen Kirchen*; Heinrich Birnbach, *Der vollkommene Kapellmeister*; Alfred Day, *Treatise on Harmony*; Gilbert Duprez, *L'art du chant*; Antoine Elwart, *Traité de contrepoint et de la fugue*; Jacques F. Gallay, *Méthode compléte pour le cor*; Sarah A. Glover, *Manual of the Norwich Sol-Fa System*; Theodor Hagen, *Civilization and Music*; Léon Kreutzer, *Essai sur l'art lyrique au théâtre*; Julius Maier, *Klassische kirchenwerke alter Meister*; Lowell Mason, *The Psaltery*; Johann Gottlob Töpfer, *Theoretisch-praktische Orgelschule*; Theodor Weinlig, *Theoretisch-praktische Anleitung zur Fuge, für den Selbstunterricht*.

I. Musical Compositions

Chamber Music:

Sonata/Solos: Henri Vieuxtemps, *Variations on a Theme from Bellini, Opus 6–Three Romance sans paroles, Opus 7–Four Romance* *sans paroles, Opus 9* (violin, piano)–*Violin Sonata in D, Opus 12–Six Etudes de Concert, Opus 16* (solo violin).

Ensembles: Niels Gade, *String Quintet No. 1 in e, Opus 8*; Felix Mendelssohn, *Piano Trio No. 2 in c, Opus 66–String Quintet No. 2 in B♭, Opus 87*; Louis Spohr, *String Quintet No. 6 in e, Opus 129– Piano Quintet in D, Opus 130.*

Piano: Frédéric Chopin, *Three Mazurkas (a, f, A♭, f♯), Opus 59*; César Franck, *Fantasia on Polish Airs, Opus 15*; Stephen Heller, *Tarantelle No. 1, Opus 53–Scherzo fantastique, Opus 57–Valse brillante, Opus 59*; Theodor Kullak, *Grande sonatae, Opus 7 in f♯*(?); George Macfarren, *Sonata No. 2 in A*; Felix Mendelssohn, *Songs without Words VI, Opus 67–VII, Opus 85*; Ignaz Moscheles, *Grand Sonata Symphonique No. 2 in b, Opus 112* (four hands); Joachim Raff, *Trois pièces caractéristiques, Opus 23*; Clara Schumann, *Three Preludes and Fugues (g, B♭, D), Opus 16–Prelude and Fugue in f♯*; Robert Schumann, *Four Fugues, Opus 72–Six Etudes in Canonic Form, Opus 56.*

Organ: Felix Mendelssohn, *Six Organ Sonatas (f, c, A, B♭, D, d), Opus 65–Fugue in B♭b–Andante Sostenuto in D*; Robert Schumann, *Six Fugues on B-A-C-H, Opus 60–Four Sketches, Opus 60.*

Choral/Vocal Music:

Choral: Anton Bruckner, *Litany for Brass and Chorus–Vergissmeinnicht* (cantata); Antoine Elwart, *Noé* (oratorio); Carl Loewe, *Psalm 23–Psalm 33–Psalm 121*; Simon Sechter, *Der Offenbarung Johannes* (oratorio).

Vocal: Frédéric Chopin, *Two Songs, Opus 74*; Félicien David, *Les perles d'orient* (cycle); Robert Franz, *Twelve Songs, Opus 4*; Carl Loewe, *Three Historische Balladen*; Felix Mendelssohn, *Six Duets, Opus 63–Six Songs, Opus 99*; Ignaz Moscheles, *Six Songs, Opus 117–Six Songs, Opus 119*(?); Otto Nicolai, *Künstler Erdenwallen, Opus 31.*

Musical Stage: Daniel Auber, *La barcarolle*; Michael Balfe, *L'étoile de Séville*; Alexander Dargomijsky, *Der Triumph des Bacchus*; Ferdinand Hiller, *Ein traum in der Christnacht*; Albert Lortzing, *Undine*; Saverio Mercadante, *Il Vascello de Gama*; Giovanni Pacini, *Bondelmonte–Lorenzino de' Medici*; Louis Spohr, *Die Kreutzfahrer*; Anton Titl, *Das Wolkenkind*; Nicola Vaccai, *Virginia*; Giuseppe Verdi, *Giovanni d'Arco–Alzira*; Richard Wagner, *Tannhauser*; William V. Wallace, *Maritana.*

Orchestra/Band Music:

Concerted Music:

Piano: Robert Schumann, *Concerto in a, Opus 54.*

Violin: Henry Vieuxtemps, *Hommage à Paganini, Opus 9– Fantaisie-caprice, Opus 11.*

Other: Louis Spohr, *Concerto in a, Opus 131* (string quartet).

Ballet/Incidental Music: Felix Mendelssohn, *Athalie, Opus 74* (IM)–*Oedipus at Colonos, Opus 93* (IM); Cesare Pugni, *Eolina* (B)–*Kaya* (B); Wilhelm Taubert, *Blaubart* (IM).

Standard Works: Mikhail Glinka, *Valse-Fantasie for Orchestra*– *Spanish Overture No. 1, "Jota Aragonesa"*; Ferdinand Hiller, *Overture in d, Opus 32*.

Symphonies: Franz Berwald, *No. 3 in C, "Singuliere"*–*No. 4 in E♭*; Louise Farrenc, *No. 2 in D, Opus 35*; George Macfarren, *No. 8 in D*.

1846

❅

Historical Highlights: The Sikh War ends in India; Robert Peel is defeated as British Prime Minister; Europe's first cheap newspaper, the *London Daily News*, is founded; in the United States, the Mexican War breaks out over the annexation of Texas; an agreement is reached on the 49th Parallel as the border between Canada and the Oregon Territory; Iowa becomes state number twenty-nine; Milwaukee, Wisconsin, is incorporated; the Pennsylvania Railroad is chartered.

Art and Literature Highlights: The Smithsonian opens in Washington, D.C. Births—writers Holger Drachmann, Henryk Sienkiewicz, artist Francis Millet; Deaths—artist Henry Inman, writers Étienne Senáncour, George Darley. Art—Landseer's *Stag at Bay*, Ranney's *Hunting Wild Horses*, Schwind's *Singing Contest at the Wartburg*; Literature—Hawthorne's *Mosses from an Old Manse*, Melville's *Typee*, Mörike's *Idylle von Bodensee*.

Musical Highlights

A. Births

Composers: Federico Chucca (Spain) May 5; Arthur-Joseph Coquard (France) May 26; Luigi Denza (Italy) February 24; Riccardo Drigo (Italy) June 3; William Wallace Gilchrist (U.S.A.) January 8; Paul Kuczinski (Germany) November 10; Francesco Paolo Tosti (Italy) April 9; Joaquin Valverde (Spain) February 27; Martin Wegelius (Finland) November 10.

Conductors: Alexander Archangelski (Russia) October 23; Heinrich Adolf Köstler (Germany) October 4; Ernst von Schuch (Austria) November 23.

Singers: Marie Hangstängel (German soprano) April 30; Tom Karl (Irish tenor) January 19; Francis Alexander Korbay (Hungarian tenor) May 8; Marie-Hippolyte Rôze (French soprano) March 2; Anton Schott (German tenor) June 24.

Performers: Ignaz Brüll (Austrian pianist/composer) November 7; Carl Faelten (German-born pianist) December 21; Marie Trautmann Jaëll (French pianist) August 17; Julius Nicolaivich Melgunov (Russian pianist) September 11; Sophie Menter (German pianist) July 29; Louis Pabst (German pianist) July 18; Silas Gamaliel Pratt (American pianist/composer) August 4; Jacques E. Rensburg (Dutch cellist) May 22; Frederick W. Root (American organist/composer) June 13; Henry Schradieck (German violinist) April 29; Wilhelm Moritz Vogel (German organist/composer) July 9.

Others: William Henry Dana (American music educator) June 10; Oscar Hammerstein (American impresario) May 8; Albert Lavignac (French musicologist) January 21; Franz Ries (German publisher) April 7; Arthur P. Schmidt (German-born publisher) April 1; George C. Stebbins (American hymnist/organist) February 26.

B. **Deaths**

Composers: Giacomo Cordella (Italy) May 8(?); Joseph Leopold Eybler (Austria) July 24; Joseph Weigl (Austria) February 3.

Conductors: William Hawes (England) February 18; Charles Frédéric Kreubé (France).

Singers: Josef Blahack (Austrian tenor) December 15; Girolamo Crescentini (Italian castrato mezzo-soprano) April 24; Giovanni Liverati (Italian tenor) February 18.

Performers: Domentico Dragonetti (Italian doublebass virtuoso) April 16; Carolus Antonius Fodor (Dutch pianist/conductor) February 22; Johann Wilhelm Gabrielski (German flutist) September 18; Guillaume-Pierre Gatayes (French guitarist) October; Simon Hermstedt (German clarinetist) August 10; Niels Peter Jensen (Danish organist) October 19; Johann Bernhard Logier (German pianist) July 17; Francesco Pollini (Italian pianist) September 17; Franz (Anton) Ries (German violinist) November 1; Johann Christian Rinck (German organist) August 7; Peter Ritter (German cellist/composer) August 1; Josef Triebensee (Bohemian oboist) April 22.

Others: Gottfried Wilhelm Fink (German music author) August 27; Eliza Flower (British hymnist) December 12; J. B. Napoléon Fourneaux (French instrument builder) July 19; Johann August Heinroth (German music author) June 2.

C. **Debuts**

Singers: Adelaide Borghi (Italian mezzo-soprano—Urbino); Angiolina Bosio (Italian soprano—Milan); Theodor Formes (German tenor—Ofen); Antonio Ghislanzoni (Italian baritone—Lodi).

Performers: William Mason (American pianist—Boston); Wilma Maria Neruda (Moravian violinist—Vienna); Ede Reményi (Hungarian violinist—Pest); Camille Saint-Saëns (French pianist—Paris); Lindsay Sloper (British pianist—London).

D. **New Positions**
Conductors: José Bernardo Alcedo (maestro de capilla, Santiago Cathedral); Michael Balfe (Her Majesty's Theatre); Michael Costa (London PO and Royal Italian Opera); Prosper Sainton (London Philharmonic Society); Eduard Tauwitz (Prague Theater).
Others: William Henry Fry (European correspondant, New York *Tribune*); Franz Hauser (director, Munich Conservatory); George Hogarth (music critic, London *Daily News*); Johann Christian Lobe (editor, *Allgemeine Musikzeitung*).

E. **Prizes/Honors**
Prizes: Léon-Gustave Gastinel (Prix de Rome).
Honors: Anton Berlijn (Knight of the Crown of Oak, Holland).

F. **Biographical Highlights**
Gaetano Donizetti, now insane, is placed in a sanatorium in Ivey; Stephen Foster moves to Cincinnati to be the bookkeeper for his brother's business; Charles Gounod begins studies for the priesthood; Albert Lortzing, after failing as an impresario and conductor in Leipzig, moves to Vienna; Felix Mendelssohn again visits England to conduct his *Elijah*; Gioacchino Rossini, following the death of his wife, finally marries Olympe Pélissier; Henri Vieuxtemps begins a five-year stay in Russia; Richard Wagner meets Hans von Bülow.

G. **Cultural Beginnings**
Performing Groups—Choral: Bradford Liedertafel; Chicago Choral Union; Concordia Male Chorus (Bonn); Graz Männergesangverein; Nottingham Vocal Music Club (Sacred Harmonic Society).
Performing Groups—Instrumental: Bogota Philharmonic Orchestra (Colombia); Oslo Philharmonic Society; Regensburger Musikverein.
Educational: Munich Conservatory of Music; Zschocher'sches Musik-Institut (Leipzig).
Music Publishers: Baker and Scribner (New York); Brandus Music Publishers (Paris); Horneman and Erslev (Copenhagen); Peters and Co. (Peters, Field and Co.) (Cincinnati); Carl G. Röder, engraver (Leipzig); Carl F. W. Siegel Publishing Co. (Leipzig).
Music Publications: *La España Musical.*
Performing Centers: Seville Amfiteatro; Teatro de Tacón (Havana); Teatro Nuovo (Verona).
Other: Eugène Albert, woodwind maker (Brussels); Carhart and Needham, organ builders (New York); Estey Organ Co. (Vermont); August Gemünder Violin Shop (Springfield, Massachusetts); Fried-

rich Ladergast, organ builder (Weissenfels); Pierre Simon, bow-maker (Paris).

H. Musical Literature

Jesse B. Aikin, *The Christian Minstrel*; Émile Chevé, *Méthode élémentaire d'harmonie*; Moritz Drobisch, *Über die mathematische Bestimmung der musikalische Intervalle*; Hilarión Eslava, *Método de solféo sin acompañamiento*; Ferdinand S. Gassner, *Dirigent und Ripienist*; Christian Hohmann, *Lehrbuch der musikalischen Composition*; Johann Christian Lobe, *Die lehre von der thematischen Arbeit*; George Root, *The Young Ladies Choir*; Anton Schindler, *Aesthetik der tonkunst*; Christian Wilke, *Beiträge zur geschichte der neuen Orgelbaukunst*.

I. Musical Compositions

Chamber Music:

String Quartets: George Macfarren, *No. 3 in F, Opus 54*; Louis Spohr, *Quartet in A, Opus 132*.

Sonata/Solos: Frédéric Chopin, *Cello Sonata in g, Opus 65*; Johan P. Hartmann, *Violin Sonata No. 2 in C, Opus 39*.

Ensembles: Clara Schumann, *Piano Trio in g, Opus 17*; Louis Spohr, *Piano Trio No. 4 in B, Opus 133*.

Piano: Alkan, *Marche funèbre, Opus 26–Marche triomphale, Opus 27*; Alexandre Boëly, *Third Book of Etudes, Opus 13*; Frédéric Chopin, *Barcarolle in F♯, Opus 60–Polonaise-fantaisie in A♭, Opus 61–Two Nocturnes (B, E), Opus 62–Three Mazurkas (B, f, c♯), Opus 63–Mazurka in a, Opus 67/4*; Stephen Heller, *Tarentella No. 2, Opus 61–Two Valses, Opus 62–Capriccio brillant, Opus 63–Scherzo-Humoresque, Opus 64*; Franz Liszt, *Tre sonetti del Petrarca–Hungarian Rhapsody No. 1 in c♯*.

Organ: Anton Bruckner, *Prelude and Postlude in d*(?); Bedřich Smetana, *Six Preludes for Organ*.

Choral/Vocal Music:

Choral: Félicien David, *Moses at Sinai* (oratorio); César Franck, *Ruth* (oratorio); Niels Gade, *Comala, Opus 12* (cantata); Charles Gounod, *Messe brève et salut in G, Opus 1*; Jacques Halévy, *Les plages du Nil* (cantata); William Jackson, *Mass in E*; Felix Mendelssohn, *Elijah* (oratorio)–*Lauda Sion, Opus 73* (cantata)–*Four Part-songs, Opus 76, for Male Voices*; Sigismund von Neukomm, *Pfingstfeier* (cantata); Robert Schumann, *Ten Songs for Chorus, Opus 55, 59*.

Vocal: Stephen Foster, *There's a Good Time Coming*; Robert Franz, *Twelve Songs, Opus 5–Six Songs, Opus 6–Six Songs, Opus 7–Six Songs, Opus 8*; Carl Loewe, *Two Ballads, Opus 110*; Jacques Offenbach, *Le langage des fleurs*.

Musical Stage: Michael Balfe, *The Bondsman*; Julius Benedict, *The Crusaders*; Hector Berlioz, *The Damnation of Faust, Opus 24*;

Friedrich von Flotow, *L'âme en peine*; Jacques Halévy, *Les mousque-taires de la reine*; Johan P. Hartmann, *Liden Kirsten, Opus 44*; Con-radin Kreutzer, *Des Sängers Fluch–Die Hochländerin am Kaukasus*; Albert Lortzing, *Der Waffenschmied*; Friedrich Lux, *Die Kätchen von Heilbronn*; George Macfarren, *An Adventure of Don Quixote*; Carl Mangold, *Tannhäuser*; Saverio Mercadante, *Orazi e Curiazi*; Louis Niedermeyer, *Robert Bruce*; Giovanni Pacini, *La regina de Cipro*; Carlo Pedrotti, *Romea di Montfort*; Józef Poniatowski, *Malek Adel*; Carl Reissiger, *Der Schiffbruch der Medusa*; Lauro Rossi, *La figlia di Figaro*; Franz von Suppé, *Poet and Peasant*; Giuseppe Verdi, *Attila*.

Orchestra/Band Music:
Concerted Music:
  Piano: Henry Litolff, *Concerto No. 3, Opus 45*; Clara Schumann, *Concertsatz in f.*
  Violin: Heinrich Ernst, *Rondo Papageno, Opus 21.*
Ballet/Incidental Music: Giacomo Meyerbeer, *Struensee* (IM); Ce-sare Pugni, *Catarina* (B)–*Lalla Rook* (B)–*Le judgment de Paris* (B); Ambroise Thomas, *Betty* (B).
Standard Works: Johann Kalliwoda, *Overture No. 9 in C, "Solen-nelle," Opus 126–No. 10 in F, Opus 142–No. 11 in B♭, Opus 143.*
Symphonies: Félicien David, *No. 3 in E♭*; Georges Onslow *No. 4 in G, Opus 71*; Robert Schumann, *No. 2 in C, Opus 61.*

1847

Historical Highlights: Liberia, the first republic in Africa, is founded by freed American slaves; the British Factory Act further limits working hours for women and children; the Irish begin a giant migration to the United States following their great famine; in the United States, peace negotiations begin with Mexico; Congress approves adhesive postage stamps; the *Chicago Tribune* begins publication; the American Medical Association is founded.

Art and Literature Highlights: Births—artists Max Liebermann, Albert Ryder, writers Giuseppe Giacosa, Archibald Gunter; Deaths—artists William Collins, Georg Kersting, writers Frans M. Franzen. Art—Couture's *Romans of the Decadence*, Mount's *The Power of Music*, Weir's *The Embarkation of the Pilgrims*; Literature—C. Brontë's *Jane Eyre*, E. Brontë's *Wuthering Heights*, Longfellow's *Evangeline*, Melville's *Omoo*, Thackeray's *Vanity Fair*.

Musical Highlights

A. **Births**
Composers: Robert Fuchs (Austria) February 15; Augusta Holmès (France) December 16; Alexander Mackenzie (Scotland) August 22; Philipp Scharwenka (Poland) February 16.
Conductors: Ernst Frank (Germany) February 7; August Klughardt (Germany) November 30.
Singers: Emma Albani (Canadian soprano) November 1; Numa Auguez (French baritone); Fritz Friedrichs (German bass) January 13; Emmy Fursch-Madi (French soprano); Giuseppe Kaschmann (Italian baritone) July 14; Jean-Louis Lassalle (French baritone) December 14; Joseph Maas (British tenor) January 30; Mathilde Mallinger (Croatian soprano) February 17; Romilda Pantaleoni (Italian soprano); Ippolit Prianishnikov (Russian baritone) August 26; Luise Radecke (German soprano) June 27.
Performers: Carl Joachim Andersen (Danish flutist) April 29; Karl Heinrich Barth (German pianist) July 12; Agathe Grøndahl (Norwegian pianist/composer) December 1; Alma Haas (German pianist) January 31; Martin Marsick (Belgian violinist) March 9; Guido Papini (Italian violinist) August 1; Walton Perkins (American pianist) November 16; Joseph Rubinstein (Russian pianist) February 8.
Others: Walter Willson Cobbett (British patron of the arts) July 11; Lionel Dauriac (French psychologist/author) November 19; Ernest Eulenberg (German publisher) November 30; Carl Friedrich Glasenapp (German music scholar) October 3; Otakar Hostinský (Czech esthetician/critic) January 2.

B. **Deaths**
Composers: Felix Mendelssohn-Bartholdy (Germany) November 4; Mariano Rodrigues de Ledesma (Spain) March 28.
Singers: Emma Albertazzi (British contralto) December 25.
Performers: Heinrich Bäermann (German clarinetist) June 11; George Baker (British organist) February 19; William Crotch (British organist/composer) December 29; François-Joseph Dizi (French harpist) November; Casper Ett (German organist) May 16; Ernst Köhler (German organist/composer) May 26; Fanny Mendelssohn Hensel (German pianist/composer) May 14; William Thomas Parke (British oboist/composer) August 26; Jan Willem Wilms (Dutch pianist/composer) July 19.
Others: Carlantonio de Rosa (Italian music author) January 30.

C. **Debuts**
Singers: Eliza Biscaccianti (American soprano—New York); Jenny Bürde-Ney (Austrian soprano—Olmütz); Jeanne Sophie Cruvelli

(German soprano—Venice); Leone Giraldoni (Italian baritone— Lodi).
Performers: Adolph Schlösser (German pianist—Frankfurt).

D. **New Positions**
Conductors: Raimondo Boucheron (maestro di cappella, Milan Cathedral); George Bousquet (Paris Opera); Heinrich Esser (Vienna Court Opera); Niels Gade (Leipzig Gewandhaus Orchestra); Georg Hellmesberger (Vienna PO); Ferdinand Hiller (kapellmeister, Düsseldorf); Charles Edward Horn (Boston Handel and Haydn Society); Angelo Mariani (Copenhagen Court Theater); Ludwig Schindelmeisser (Hamburg); Eugenio Terziani (Apollo Theater, Rome).
Others: Manuel Bretón de los Herreros (director, Biblioteca Nacional, Spain); William Henry Fry (editor, *Philadelphia Ledger*); Louis Lefébure-Wély (organ, Madelaine, Paris).

E. **Prizes/Honors**
Prizes: Pierre-Louis Deffés (Prix de Rome); François Gevaert (Prix de Rome).
Honors: Johann Friedrich Bellermann (Gold Medal of Arts and Letters, Greece); William Horsley (Swedish Royal Academy).

F. **Biographical Highlights**
Frédéric Chopin breaks up with George Sand; Mikhail Glinka leaves Spain and returns to Russia; Franz Liszt gives his last concert appearance and meets the Princess Sayn-Wittgenstein; Felix Mendelssohn, broken by his sister's death, makes a last visit to England and Switzerland before his own death; Samuel Sebastian Wesley suffers a serious injury on a fishing trip.

G. **Cultural Beginnings**
Performing Groups: Aberdeen Harmonic Choir; Christiania Commercial Choral Society (Oslo); Deutsche Liederkranz (New York); Handelsstandens Sangforening (Norway); Royal Italian Opera (London); Salzburger Liedertafel; Sternscher Gesangverein (Berlin); Stuttgarter Oratorienchor.
Performing Groups—Instrumental: Mainz Philharmonische Verein; Sociedad Filarmonica (Bogota).
Educational: Conservatorio Imperial de Música (Rio de Janeiro); Faiszt Organ School (Stuttgart); Salzburger Singakademie.
Music Publishers: Durand et Cie. (Paris); Flaxland Music Publishers (Paris); Little, Brown and Co.; Bartolf Senff (Leipzig).
Music Publications: *Italia Musicale; Neue Berliner Musikzeitung.*
Performing Centers: Astor Place Opera House (New York); Carltheater (Vienna); Gran Teatro del Liceo (Barcelona); Teatro de la Zarzuela (Madrid); Teatro de San Fernando (Seville); Teatro Goldoni (Livorno).

Other: Gaveau Piano Co. (Paris); Hals Brothers, piano makers (Christiana); Steinmeyer Organ Co. (Oettingen).

H. Musical Literature

Jesse B. Aikin, *The Juvenile Minstrel*; Johann F. Bellermann, *Die Tonleitern und Musiknoten der Griechen*; Pierre Blondeau, *Histoire de la musique moderne*; Noël Brossard, *Théorie des sons musicaux*; Carl Czerny, *Method for the Piano*; William Horsley, *Introduction to Harmony and Modulation*; Eduard Emil Koch, *Geschichte des Kirchenliedes und Kirchengesanges, inbesondere der deutschen evangelischen Kirche*; Eduard Krüger, *Beiträge für leben und wissenschaft der Tonkunst*; Théodore Nisard, *La science et la pratique de plain-chant*; Peter Singer, *Metaphysische blicke in die Tonwelt*.

I. Musical Compositions

Chamber Music:

String Quartets: Felix Mendelssohn, *No. 6 in f, Opus 80–Andante (E) and Scherzo (a), Opus 81*; Louis Spohr, *Double Quartet in g, Opus 136*.

Sonata/Solos: Henri Vieuxtemps, *Six morceaux de salon, Opus 22* (violin, piano)(?); Henryk Wieniawski, *Grand caprice fantastique, Opus 1* (violin, piano).

Ensembles: Robert Schumann, *Piano Trio No. 1 in d, Opus 63–No 2 in F, Opus 80*.

Piano: Alkan, *Twenty-Five Preludes in all Keys, Opus 31*; Frédéric Chopin, *Three Waltzes (Db ["Minute"], c#, Ab), Opus 64*; Mikhail Glinka, *A Greeting to My Native Land*; Stephen Heller, *Twenty-Four New Etudes, Opus 90*; Franz Liszt, *Hungarian Rhapsody No. 2 in c#*; Felix Mendelssohn, *Kinderstücke, Opus 72*.

Organ: Alexandre Boëly, *Fourteen Préludes sur des cantiques de Denizot, Opus 15*; Anton Bruckner, *Prelude and Fugue in c*; Johann P. Hartmann, *Good Friday–Easter Morning, Opus 43*.

Choral/Vocal Music:

Choral: Félicien David, *Christophe Colomb*; Heinrich Dorn, *Das Hallelujah der Schöpfung* (oratorio); Ferdinand Hiller, *Gesang der Geister, Opus 36*; Felix Mendelssohn, *Three Motets, Opus 69–Christus, Opus 97* (unfinished oratorio)–*Four Male Choruses, Opus 120*.

Vocal: Stephen Foster, *Lou'siana Belle*; Carl Loewe, *Der Papagei, Opus 11* (male voices); Felix Mendelssohn, *Six Songs, Opus 71*; Robert Schumann, *Zum Abschied, Opus 84*.

Musical Stage: Daniel Auber, *Haidée*; Michael Balfe, *The Maid of Honour*; Giovanni Bottesini, *Cristoforo Colombo*; Antonio Buzzolla, *Amleto*; Antonio Cagnoni, *Don Bucefalo*; August Conradi, *Rübezahl*; Friedrich von Flotow, *Martha*; Ivar Hallström, *The White Lady of Drottningholm*; Ferdinand Hiller, *Konradin*; Johann Kalliwoda, *Blonda*; Henry C. Litolff, *Die Braut von Kynast*; Albert Lortzing, *Zum Grossadmiral*; Alexei Lvov, *Ondine*; Stanislaw Moniuszko,

Halka; Jacques Offenbach, *L'alcôve*; Giovanni Pacini, *Merope*; Achille Peri, *Tancreda*; Józef Poniatowski, *Esmeralda*; Federico Ricci, *Griselda*; Luigi Ricci, *Il birraio di Preston*; Lauro Rossi, *Bianca Contarini*; Franz von Suppé, *Das Mädchen vom Lande–Die Krämer und sein Kommis*; Giuseppe Verdi, *Macbeth–Jerusalem*; Charles L. Vogel, *Le Siège de Leyde*; William V. Wallace, *Matilda of Hungary*.

Orchestra/Band Music:
Ballet/Incidental Music: Cesare Pugni, *Coralia* (B)–Fiorita et la reine des elfrides (B).
Program Music: Niels Gade, *Siegfried und Brunhilde* (symphonic fragments).
Symphonies: Louise Farrenc, *No. 3 in g, Opus 36*; Niels Gade, *No. 3 in a, Opus 15*; Jacob A. Josephson, *Symphony, Opus 4*; Louis Spohr, *No. 8 in G, Opus 137*.

1848
❋

Historical Highlights: The "Year of Revolutions" in Europe; Louis Napoleon becomes president of the Second French Republic; Francis Joseph becomes emperor of Austria; Taiping Rebellion in China; in the United States, Zachary Taylor is elected twelfth president; the Treaty of Guadalpe-Hidalgo ends the Mexican War—Mexico cedes most of the present-day southwestern territory to the United States; Wisconsin becomes state number thirty; the California Gold Rush begins.

Art and Literature Highlights: Births—artists Jules Bastien-Lepage, Augustus Saint-Gaudens, writers Joel Chandler Harris, James Otis Kaler; Deaths—writers Emily Brontë, artists Thomas Cole, Benjamin Tanner. Art—Hick's *The Peaceable Kingdom*, Lanseer's *A Random Shot*, Millet's *The Winnower*, Woodville's *Politics in an Oysterhouse*; Literature—Dumas' *La Dame aux Camélias*, Gaskell's *Mary Barton*, Lowell's *Vision of Sir Launfal*.

Musical Highlights

A. Births
Composers: Henri Duparc (France) January 21; Otto Malling (Denmark) June 1; Charles Hubert Parry (England) February 27; Jean-Robert Planquette (France) July 31; Henri Viotta (Holland) July 16.
Conductors: Luigi Mancinelli (Italy) May 5.
Singers: Jacques-Joseph Bouhy (Belgian-born baritone) June 18; Lucien Fugère (French baritone) July 22; Pierre Gailhard (French bass/manager) August 1; Lilli Lehmann (German soprano) November 24; Victor Maurel (French baritone) June 17; Arthur W. Tams

(American baritone/manager) October 7; Alwina Valleria (American soprano) October 12.

Performers: Wilhelm Fitzenhagen (German cellist) September 15; Frederick Grant Gleason (American organist/composer) December 17; Camille Gurickx (Belgian pianist) December 29; Ferdinand Inten (German-born pianist) February 23; Horace Nicholl (British organist) March 17; Vladimir de Pachmann (Russian pianist) July 27; Karl Schröder (German cellist) December 18.

Others: William Foster Apthorp (American music critic) October 24; Heinrich Conried (Austrian impresario) September 13; Louis Elson (American music historian) April 17; Hermann Kretzschmar (German musicologist) January 19; Theodore Presser (American publisher) July 3; Paul Runge (German musicologist) January 2; Stepan Smolensky (Russian music scholar) October 20; Carl Stumpf (German acoustician/musicologist) April 21; Hans Wolzogen (German music author) November 13.

B. **Deaths**
Composers: Gaetano Donizetti (Italy) April 1; Henri-Philippe Gerard (Belgium) September 11; Nicola Vaccai (Italy) August 6; Alexander Egorovich Varlamov (Russia) October 27.
Conductors: Carl Guhr (Germany) July 22.
Singers: François van Campenhout (Belgian tenor/composer) April 24; Thomas (Simpson) Cooke (Irish tenor/composer) February 26.
Performers: Jean Ancot, *père* (Belgian violinist) July 12; Carlo Bignami (Italian violinist/composer) October 2; Franz Cramer (German violinist) August 1; Joseph Ghys (Belgian violinist) August 22; Feliks Janiewicz (Polish pianist/conductor) July 22; Louis Massonneau (German violinist) October 4; Oliver Shaw (American organist) December 31.
Others: Charles Albrecht (American piano maker) June 28; Alfred Julius Becher (British music critic/composer) November 23; Karl August Hüttenrauch (German organ builder) February 26; Christian Friedrich Wilke (German organ builder) June 31.

C. **Debuts**
Singers: Joseph-Théodore Barbot (French tenor—Paris); Charles-Amable Bataille (French bass—Paris); Louis Gueymard (French tenor—Paris); Delphine Ugalde (French soprano—Paris).
Performers: Adolfo Fumagalli (Italian pianist—Milan); Henryk Wieniawski (Polish violinist—Paris).

D. **New Positions**
Conductors: Vincenz Lachner (Frankfurt Opera); Franz Liszt (Weimar Orchestra); Carl Mangold (hofkapellmeister, Darmstadt);

Otto Nicolai (Berlin Royal Opera); Julius Rietz (Leipzig Gewand-haus Orchestra); Francesco Shira (Covent Garden).
Others: Henry Bishop (chair of music, Oxford); Eduard Hanslick (music critic, *Vienna Zeitung*).

E. **Prizes/Honors**
Prizes: Jules-Laurent Duprato (Prix de Rome).
Honors: George F. Anderson (Master of the Queen's Music); Jakob Blumenthal (pianist to the Queen).

F. **Biographical Highlights**
Johannes Brahms gives his first public recital in Hamburg, but under an assumed name; Frédéric Chopin concertizes in England and Scotland; Karl Goldmark is almost shot as a rebel while performing in Raab; Ede Reményi flees to the United States following his revolutionary activities; Bedřich Smetana opens his own school in Prague; Giuseppe Verdi buys his estate at Sant' Agata; Richard Wagner joins the revolutionary Vaterlandsverein.

G. **Cultural Beginnings:**
Performing Groups—Choral: Brno Male Choral Society; Buffalo (New York) Liedertafel; Dresden Cecilia Society; Société Ste.-Cécile (Brussels); Verein für Choralgesang (Dresden).
Performing Groups—Instrumental: Montreal Philharmonic Society I.
Educational: Royal Irish Academy of Music (Dublin).
Music Publishers: S. S. Griggs and Co. (Chicago); Lee and Walker Publishing Co. (Philadelphia); Sasseti and Co. (Lisbon).
Performing Centers: Balmer and Weber Music House (St. Louis); Bossel Theater (Bucharest); Deichmann (Friedrich-Wilhelmstad-tisches) Theater (Berlin).
Other: Holywell Hall (Oxford); Société Alard-Franchomme (Paris).

H. **Musical Literature**
Francisco Andreví y Castellar, *Traité d'harmonie et de composition*; Hector Berlioz, *Mémoires*; Franz Brendel, *Grundzüge der Geschichte der Musik*; Eduard Devrient, *Geschichte der deutschen Schausspielkunst*; François Fétis, *Les musiciens Belges*; Theodor Hagen, *Musikalisches novellen*; Samuel Jackson, *Sacred Harmony*; Raphael Kiesewetter, *Über die Octave des Pythagoras*; Joseph Mainzer, *Music and Education*; Henry Phillips, *Hints on Declamation*.

I. **Musical Compositions**
Chamber Music:
Sonata/Solos: Edouard Lalo, *Fantaisie, Opus 1–Allegro Maestoso, Opus 2–Two Impromtus* (violin, piano); Ludvig Norman, *Violin*

Sonata in d, Opus 3; Henryk Wieniawski, *Allegro de sonate, Opus 2* (violin, piano).

Ensembles: Niels Gade, *String Octet in F, Opus 17*; Anton Reicha, *Six Wind Quintets*; Louis Spohr, *String Sextet in C, Opus 140.*

Piano: Alkan, *Four Impromtus, Opus 32/1–Grand Sonata, "The Four Ages of Man," Opus 33–Tweve Etudes in all Major Keys, Opus 35d*; Theodor Kullak, *Symphony for Piano, Opus 27*(?)*–Schule des Octavenspiels, Opus 48*; Franz Liszt, *Sonetto 104 del Petrarco–Three Etudes de Concert (A♭, f, D♭)–Six Consolations*; Anton Rubinstein, *Tarantella in b, Opus 6–Two Nocturnes (F, G)*; Robert Schumann, *Album für die Jugend, Opus 68–Four Marches, Opus 76*; Bedřich Smetana, *Six Characteristic Pieces, Opus 1.*

Choral/Vocal Music:
  Choral: Hippolyte Chélard, *Le vieux drapeau*; Félicien David, *L'Eden* (oratorio); Franz Liszt, *St. Cecilia Mass–Hungaria* (cantata); Carl Loewe, *Hiob* (oratorio); Felix Mendelssohn, *Wandersmann, Opus 75–Four Male Choruses, Opus 76–Three Psalms, Opus 78–Six Anthems, Opus 79*; Stanislaw Moniuszko, *Milda* (cantata); Emil Naumann, *Christus der Friedensbote* (oratorio); Gioacchino Rossini, *Inno Nazionale–Inno Alla Pace* (cantatas).

  Vocal: Stephen Foster, *Oh Susanna–Old Uncle Ned*; Felix Mendelssohn, *Three Duets, Opus 77*; Joachim Raff, *Three Songs, Opus 47–Two Songs, Opus 48–Three Songs, Opus 49*; Anton Rubinstein, *Six Little Songs in Low German, Opus 1.*

  Musical Stage: François Benoist, *L'Apparition*; Heinrich Dorn, *Die musiker von Aix-la-Chapelle*; François Gevaert, *Hugues de Zomerghem–La comédie à la ville*; Jacques Halévy, *Le val d'Andorre*; Hervé, *Don Quichotte et Sancho Pança*; Albert Lortzing, *Regina*; Saverio Mercadante, *La schiava saracena*; Giovanni Pacini, *Allan Cameron–L'orfana svizzera*; Henri Reber, *La Nuit de Noël*; Robert Schumann, *Genoveva, Opus 81*; Friedrich von Sobolewski, *Salvator Rosa*; Franz von Suppé, *Der Bandit*; Giuseppe Verdi, *Il Corsaro.*

Orchestra/Band Music:
  Concerted Music:
    Piano: Joseph Joachim Raff, *Konzertstücke for Piano and Orchestra.*
    Violin: Johann Kalliwoda, *Concertino No. 6, Opus 151.*
    Other: Jacques Offenbach, *Concerto militaire* (cello).
  Ballet/Incidental Music: Robert Schumann, *Manfred, Opus 115* (IM).
  Program Music: Hippolyte Chélard, *La Symphonéide*; Franz Liszt, *Les Préludes*; Stanislaw Moniuszko, *Bajka Overture.*
  Standard Works: Mikhail Glinka, *Kamarinskaya*; Johann Strauss, Jr., *Radetsky March, Opus 228.*
  Symphonies: George Bristow, *No. 1 in E♭, Opus 10*; Johan P. Hartmann, *No. 2 in E, Opus 48b.*

1849

❊

Historical Highlights: Hungary, under the leadership of Lajos Kossuth, declares its independence—Russia helps Austria crush the rebellion; the British crush the second Sikh uprising in India and annex the Punjab state; Frederick IV of Prussia refuses the title "Emperor of the Germans"; in the United States, the California Gold Rush begins in earnest; the Department of the Interior is created; Elizabeth Blackwell is the first woman to receive an M.D. degree.

Art and Literature Highlights: Births—artist William Chase, writers Sarah Orne Jewett, James Whitcomb Riley, August Strindberg; Deaths—artist Edward Hicks, writers Maria Edgeworth, Eunice Pinney, Edgar Allen Poe. Art—Courbet's *The Stonebreakers*, Cole's *The Good Shepherd*, Ingres' *The Golden Age*; Literature—Cooper's *The Sea Lions*, Emerson's *Representative Men*, Scribe/Legouvé's *Adrienne Lecouvreur*, Thoreau's *Civil Disobedience*.

Musical Highlights

A. **Births**
Composers: Benjamin Godard (France) August 18.
Conductors: Willem De Haan (Holland) September 24.
Singers: Mathilde Bauermeister (German soprano); Franz Diener (German tenor) February 19; Mieczyslaw Apolinary Horbowski (Polish baritone) July 23; Emma Aline Osgood (American soprano); Eugenie Pappenheim (Austrian soprano); Theodor Reichmann (German baritone) March 15; Wladyslaw Seideman (Polish bass)(?); Rosa Sucher (German soprano) February 23; Hermann Winckelmann (German tenor) March 8.
Performers: Thomas Greene "Blind Tom" Bethune (American pianist/composer) May 25; Henri Dallier (French organist) March 20; Charles Harford Lloyd (British organist/composer) October 16.
Others: Carl Fischer (German-born publisher) December 7; Alphonse Goovaerts (Belgian musicologist) May 25; Mikhail Mikhailovich Ivanov (Russian music critic/composer) September 23; Dom André Mocquereau (French musicologist) June 6; Hugo Riemann (German musicologist) July 18.

B. **Deaths**
Composers: Charles Edward Horn (England-U.S.A.) November 21; Conradin Kreutzer (Germany) December 14; Otto Nicolai (Germany) May 11.

Conductors: François-Antoine Habeneck (France) February 8; Christian Rummel (Germany) February 13; Johann Strauss, Sr. (Austria) September 25.

Singers: Davidde Banderali (Italian tenor) June 13; Giuseppe de Begnis (Italian bass) August; Angelica Catalani (Italian soprano) June 12; Charles Edward Horn (British singer/composer) October 21; Johanna Sophia Kollmann (British soprano) May 14; Eliza Salmon (British soprano) June 5.

Performers: Dionysio Aguado (Spanish guitarist) December 29; Frédéric Chopin (Polish pianist/composer) October 17; Dorothea von Ertmann (German pianist) March 16; Alexander Fesca (German pianist/composer) February 22; Friedrich Griepenkerl (German music scholar) April 6; Frédéric Kalkbrenner (French pianist) June 10; Jacques-Féréol Mazas (French violinist/composer) August 26.

Others: Alfred Day (British music theorist) February 11.

C. Debuts

Singers: Marie Cabel (Belgian soprano—Paris); Caroline Carvalho (French soprano—Paris); Marie Luise Dustmann (German soprano—Breslau); Giacomo Galvani (Italian tenor—Spoleto); Antonio Giuglini (Italian tenor—Fermo); Albert Niemann (German tenor—Dessau); Louisa Pyne (British soprano—Bologne), Susan Sunderland (British soprano—London); John Rogers Thomas (British born baritone—New York); Therese Tietjens (German soprano—Altona); Theodor Wachtel (German tenor—Hamburg).

Performers: Wilhemine Clauss-Szarvady (Bohemian pianist—Prague); William George Cusins (British pianist—London).

D. New Positions

Conductors: Michael Costa (Birmingham Festivals); Louis Dietsch (maître de chapelle, Madeleine, Paris); Heinrich Dorn (kapellmeister, Berlin Royal Opera); Jacopo Foroni (Stockholm Court); Charles Hallé (Gentlemen's Concerts, Manchester); Jacques Offenbach (Théâtres Française, Paris); Ferdinando Taglioni (San Carlo Theater, Naples).

Others: Robert Burton (organ, Leeds Parish Church); William George Cushman (organ, Queen's Private Chapel); Frederick Gye (manager, Covent Garden); Heinrich Laube (director, Vienna Hofburgtheater); Samuel Sebastian Wesley (organ, Winchester Cathedral).

E. Prizes/Honors:

Prizes: Alexandre Stadtfeldt (Prix de Rome).

Honors: Petter Boman (Swedish Academy); Ferdinand Hiller (Berlin Academy); Otto Nicolai (Royal Academy, Berlin).

F. **Biographical Highlights**
Hans von Bülow enters Leipzig University to study law; Eduard Hanslick receives a doctorate in law from the Vienna University; Joseph Joachim becomes concertmaster in Liszt's Weimar orchestra; Jenny Lind retires from the opera stage; William Gregory Mason begins studying music in Leipzig; Alexander Serov leaves his government job for music; Henryk Wieniawski reenters Paris Conservatory to study composition.

G. **Cultural Beginnings**
Performing Groups—Choral: Aberdeen Choral Society; Cincinnati Männerchore; German Saengerbund of North America; Schwäbischer Sängerbund; Società Corale del Carmine (Florence); Société Ste. Cécillie (Paris).
Performing Groups—Instrumental: Bree String Quartet (Amsterdam); Detroit Harmonie; Filharmoniska Sällskapet (Uppsala); Hellmesberger String Quartet (Vienna); Mendelssohn Quintette Club (Boston); Wüppertal City Orchestra.
Festivals: Norwegian Choral Festival.
Educational: Istituto Musicale (Florence); National Conservatory of Music (Santiago, Chile).
Music Publishers: Carl Merseburger Music Publishing Co. (Leipzig); Jakob Rieter-Biedermann (Winterthur).
Performing Centers: Liverpool Philharmonic Hall.
Other: Chicago Mozart Society.

H. **Musical Literature**
Laure Cinti-Damoreau, *Méthode de chant*; Félix Clément, *Rapport . . . sur l'état de la musique religieuse en France*; Moritz Fürstenau, *Beiträge zur geschichte der königlich-sächsischen musikalischen Kapelle*; Christian Hohmann, *Praktische Violin-schule*; Frédéric Kalkbrenner, *Traité d'harmonie du pianiste*; Julius Knorr, *Methodischer leitfaden für Klavierlehrer*; Théodore de Vroye, *Manuale cantorum*; Richard Wagner, *Art and Revolution*; Carl Friedrich Weitzmann, *Geschichte der harmonie*; Samuel Sebastian Wesley, *A Few Words on Cathedral Music*.

I. **Musical Compositions**
Chamber Music:
String Quartets: Franz Berwald, *No. 2–No. 3*; Franz Lachner, *No. 4 in d, Opus 120–No. 5 in G, Opus 169*; George Macfarren, *No. 4 in G*; Louis Spohr, *String Quartet in C, Opus 141*.
Sonata/Solos: Neils Gade, *Violin Sonata No. 2 in d, Opus 21*; Robert Schumann, *Five Pieces, Opus 102* (cello, piano)–*Adagio and Allegro in A♭, Opus 70* (horn, piano)–*Fantasiestücke, Opus 73* (clarinet, piano).
Ensembles: Joachim Raff, *Piano Trio in g*.

Piano: Alkan, *Deuxième recueil d'impromptus, Opus 32/2*; Frédéric Chopin, *Mazurka in g, Opus 68/2–Mazurka in f, Opus 69/4*; Stephen Heller, *Sérènade, Opus 56–Three Pieces, Opus 73*; Franz Liszt, *Années de pélerinage II*; Robert Schumann, *Twelve Piano Pieces, Opus 85–Waldscenen, Opus 82, for Piano*.

Choral/Vocal Music:
Choral: Hector Berlioz, *Te Deum, Opus 22*; Anton Bruckner, *Requiem in d*; Heinrich Dorn, *Die Sündflut* (oratorio); Charles Gounod, *Messe solennelle*; Jacques Halévy, *Prométhée enchaîné*; Carl Loewe, *Psalm 51*; Mihály Mosonyi, *Mass No. 3 in F*; Robert Schumann, *Requiem für Mignon, Opus 98b*.
Vocal: Stephen Foster, *Nelly Bly–Nelly Was a Lady*; Edouard Lalo, *Six Popular Romances*; Joachim Raff, *Zwei italienische lieder, Opus 50–Zwei lieder vom Rhein, Opus 53*; Robert Schumann, *Spanische Liebeslieder, Opus 138*.
Musical Stage: Adolphe Adam, *Le Toréador*; Jacques Halévy, *La fée aux roses*; Conradin Kreutzer, *Aurelia*; Albert Lortzing, *Rolands-Knappen*; George A. Macfarren, *King Charles II*; Victor Massé, *La Chambre gothique*; Franz Lachner, *Benvenuto Cellini*; Giacomo Meyerbeer, *Le prophète*; Otto Nicolai, *The Merry Wives of Windsor*; Giovanni Pacini, *L'orfano svizzera*; Lauro Rossi, *Il domino nero*; Ambroise Thomas, *Le caïd*; Giuseppe Verdi, *Luisa Miller–La Battaglia di Legnano*.

Orchestra/Band Music:
Concerted Music:
   Piano: Franz Liszt, *Totentanz*; Anton Rubinstein, *Concerto in C* (based on *Octet in D*); Robert Schumann, *Concertpiece, Opus 92*.
   Other: Robert Schumann, *Concertpiece in F, Opus 86* (four horns).
Ballet/Incidental Music: Félicien David, *Le jugement dernier* (IM); Jacques Halévy, *Prométhée enchaîné* (IM); Albert Lortzing, *Vier wochen in Ischl* (IM).
Program Music: Franz Liszt, *Ce qu'on entend sur la montagne (Bergsymphonie)–Tasso*.
Standard Works: Johann Kalliwoda, *Concert Overture No. 13*; Franz Liszt, *Festival March* (for the Goethe Jubilee); Bedřich Smetana, *Overture in D*.
Symphonies: Félicien David, *No. 4 in c*.

1850

�֍

Historical Highlights: In the terms of the Peace of Berlin, Denmark and Prussia work out a compromise on the Schleswig-Holstein question; the Taiping Rebellion continues in China; the Great Kaffir War takes place in South Africa; in the United States, President Zachary Taylor dies—Millard Fillmore becomes the thirteenth president; California becomes state number thirty-one; the Compromise of 1850 settles the slavery question in new territories.

Art and Literature Highlights: Births—writers Guy de Maupassant, Robert Louis Stevenson, Max Kalbeck, sculptor Hamo Thornycroft; Deaths—writers Johann-Gottfried Schadow, Nikolaus Lenau, William Wordsworth. Art—Bingham's *Shooting for the Beef*, Delacroix's *Arab Attacked by a Lion*, Millet's *The Sower*; Literature—Browning's *Sonnets from the Portuguese*, Dickens' *David Copperfield*, Hawthorne's *The Scarlet Letter*.

Musical Highlights

A. Births

Composers: Tomás Bretón y Hernández (Spain) December 29; Zdeněk Fibich (Czechoslovakia) December 21; Jakob Adolf Hägg (Sweden) June 27; Peter Erasmus Lange-Müller (Denmark) December 1; Franz Xaver Scharwenka (Poland-Germany) January 6; Emma Steiner (U.S.A.); Alexander Taneiev (Russia) January 17; Francis Thomé (France) October 18.

Conductors: Francesco Fanciulli (Italy-U.S.A.) July 17; George Henschel (England) February 18; Gustav Hinrichs (Germany-U.S.A.) December 10; Anton Seidl (Austria) May 7.

Singers: Emma Abbott (American soprano) December 9; Jean De Reszke (Polish tenor) January 14; Marie Fillunger (Austrian soprano) January 27; Julia Gaylord (American soprano)(?); George Henschel (German baritone) February 18; Sofia Scalchi (Italian mezzo-soprano) November 29; Clementine Schuch-Proska (Hungarian soprano) February 12; Joseph Staudigl, Jr. (Austrian baritone) March 18; Antoinette Sterling (American contralto) January 23; Francesco Tamagno (Italian tenor) December 28; Edmund-Alphonse Vergnet (French tenor) July 4.

Performers: Richard Barth (German violinist/conductor) June 5; Eduard Herrmann (German-born violinist) December 18; Luise Adolpha Le Beau (French pianist/composer) April 25; Alexandre Luigini (French violinist/conductor) March 9; John Orth (American organist) December 2; Heinrich Reimann (German organist/music author) March 14; Joseph Servais (Belgian cellist) November 23; Anton Urspruch (German pianist/composer) February 17.

Others: Melville Clark (American organ/piano maker).

B. Deaths

Composers: Francesco Basili (Italy) March 25; Adalbert Gyrowetz (Bohemia) March 19; Steffano Pavasi (Italy) July 28; Louis Alexandre Piccinni (France) April 24; Václav Jan Tomášek (Bohemia) April 3.

Singers: Luigia Boccabadati (Italian soprano) October 12; Josephina Grassini (Italian contralto) January 3; Jeanne Charlotte Saint-Aubin (French soprano) September 11.
Performers: Charles-Nicolas Baudiot (French cellist) September 26; Joseph von Blumenthal (Belgian violinist) May 9.
Others: Auguste Bottée de Toulmon (French music author) March 22; Raphael George Kiesewetter (Austrian music author) January 1.

C. **Debuts**
Singers: Johann Nepomuk Beck (Hungarian baritone—Budapest); Constance Nantier-Didiée (French mezzo-soprano—Turin); Karoline Pruckner (Austrian soprano—Hanover).
Performers: Arabella Goddard (French-born pianist—London).

D. **New Positions**
Conductors: Hans Balatka (Milwaukee Musical Society); Pietro Antonio Coppola (Lisbon Royal Opera); Niels Gade (Copenhagen Musical Society Orchestra and Chorus); Gustav Adolf Heinze (German Opera, Amsterdam), Ferdinand Hiller (kapellmeister, Cologne); Carl August Krebs (kapellmeister, Dresden Court Opera); Constantin Liadov (St. Petersburg Imperial Opera).
Others: Ludwig F. Bischoff (editor, *Rheinische Review*); Lauro Rossi (director, Milan Conservatory); Samuel Sebastian Wesley (organ, Royal Academy, London); Isaac Baker Woodbury (editor, *American Monthly Musical Review*).

F. **Biographical Highlights**
Alexander Borodin enters medical school in St. Petersburg; Jenny Lind appears in the United States under the auspices of P. T. Barnum; Adolf Marx retires from teaching to concentrate on writing; Clara Novello returns to the operatic and recital stage; Richard Wagner again visits Paris and has a brief affair with Jennie Laussot; William V. Wallace marries his second wife, Helene Stoepel, in New York.

G. **Cultural Beginnings**
Performing Groups—Choral: Evangelical Sacred Choral Society (Frankfurt); Leeds Madrigal and Motet Society.
Performing Groups—Instrumental: Balatka String Quartet; Beethovenverein (Bonn); Chicago Philharmonic Society; Cleveland Mendelssohn Society; Washington Philharmonic Society (D.C.).
Educational: Duprez Vocal School (Paris); Musikakademie für Damen (Berlin); Stern Conservatory of Music (Berlin).
Music Publishers: Allen and Co. (Melbourne); Bach Gesellschaft (Germany); Rózsavölgyi and Fárza (Budapest).

Music Publications: *The Church Musician; Musical World and New York Musical Times; The New York Musical Review and Choral Advocate* (New York); *Rheinische Musik-Zeitung für Kunstfreunde und Künstler.* **Performing Centers:** Madrid Teatro Real; St. Martin's Hall (London); Tremont Music Hall (Chicago).

H. Musical Literature

Pierre Chevillard, *Méthode complète de violoncelle*; Sarah Anna Glover, *Manual Containing a Development of the Tetrachordal System*; Thomas Hastings, *Devotional Hymns and Religious Poems*; William Jackson, *A Singing Class Manual*; Johann Lobe, *Lehrbuch der musikalischen Composition*; Lowell Mason, *Cantica Laudis*; Pierre Scudo, *Critique et littérature musicale I*; Richard Wagner, *Kunst und Klima–Das Kunstwerke der Zukunft*; Richard S. Willis, *Church Chorals and Choir Studies*; Carl von Winterfeld, *Zur geschichte heiliger Tonkunst I.*

I. Musical Compositions
Chamber Music:

String Quartets: Franz Lachner, *No. 6 in e, Opus 173*; Carl Reinecke, *No. 1 in Eᵇ, Opus 16*(?).

Sonata/Solos: Joseph Joachim, Edouard Lalo, *Pastorale and Scherzo alla Pulcinella* (violin, piano); Carl Loewe, *Three Pieces, Opus 2* (clarinet, piano); *Schottische Bilder, Opus 112* (clarinet, piano); Emil Naumann, *Violin Sonata, Opus 1*(?); Henryk Wieniawski, *Fantaisie slave, Opus 27–Introduction and rondo in E, Opus 28*(?) (violin, piano).

Ensembles: Friedrich Kiel, *Piano Trio in D, Opus 3*; Franz Lachner, *Octet in Bᵇ, Opus 156* (woodwinds); Edouard Lalo, *Piano Trio No. 1 in c*(?); Louis Spohr, *String Quintet No. 7 in g, Opus 144.*

Piano: Franz Liszt, *Grand Solo de Concert–Liebesträume*; Carl Loewe, *Four Fantasies, Opus 137*; Felix Mendelssohn, *Songs without Words VIII, Opus 102*; Anton Rubinstein, *Six Studies, Opus 23–Two Fantasias on Russian Folksongs.*

Organ: Alkan, *Pro organo*; Franz Liszt, *Fantasy and Fugue, "Ad nos, ad salutarem undam."*

Choral/Vocal Music:

Choral: Anton Bruckner, *Psalm CXIV*; Charles Gounod, *Tobie* (oratorio); Jacques Halévy, *Ave Verum*; Carl Loewe, *Psalm 61*; George Macfarren, *The Sleeper Awakened*; Stanislaw Moniuszko, *Mass in d, "Funeral Mass"*; Carl Reissiger, *David* (oratorio); Robert Schumann, *Neujahrslied, Opus 144.*

Vocal: Hector Berlioz, *Fleurs des landes* (cycle); Stephen Foster, *Camptown Races*; Carl Loewe, *Three Ballads, Opus 116*; Felix Mendelssohn, *Three Songs, Opus 84*; Ignaz Moscheles, *Frühlingslied, Opus 125*(?); Thomas Oliphant, *Santa Lucia*; Joachim Raff, *Five Songs, Opus 51–Three Songs, Opus 52*; Anton Rubinstein, *Six Fables, Opus*

64–Six Songs, Opus 8; Robert Schumann, *Five Songs, Opus 77–Three Songs, Opus 83–Six Songs, Opus 89–Five Songs, Opus 96–Five Songs, Opus 127*; Richard S. Willis, *It Came Upon the Midnight Clear.*

Musical Stage: Adolphe Adam, *Giralda*; Pascual Arrieta y Corera, *La conquista de Granadas*; Daniel Auber, *L'enfant prodigue*; Francisco Barbieri, *Gloria y peluca*; Heinrich Dorn, *Artaxerxes*; Friedrich von Flotow, *Sophia Katherina*; Niels Gade, *Mariotta*; Jacques Halévy, *La tempestà–La dame de pique*; George Macfarren, *Allan of Aberfeldy*; Victor Massé, *La chanteuse voilée*; Stanislaw Moniuszko, *The Gypsies*; Joachim Raff, *König Alfred*; Federico Ricci, *I due ritratti*; Anton Rubinstein, *The Battle of Kulikovo*; Ambroise Thomas, *Le songe d'une nuit d'été*; Giuseppe Verdi, *Stiffelio*; Richard Wagner, *Lohengrin.*

Orchestra/Band Music:
Concerted Music:
  Piano: Theodor Kullak, *Concerto in c, Opus 55*(?); Anton Rubinstein, *Concerto No. 1 in e, Opus 25.*
  Violin: Heinrich Ernst, *Airs hongrois variés, Opus 22*; Henri Vieuxtemps, *Concerto No. 4 in d, Opus 31*(?).
  Other: Robert Schumann, *Cello Concerto in a, Opus 129.*
Ballet/Incidental Music: Albert Lortzing, *Eine Berliner Grisette* (IM)–*Ferdinand von Schill* (IM)–*Ein Nachmittag in Ischl* (IM); Cesare Pugni, *Les métamorphoses* (B)–*Stella* (B).
Program Music: Franz Liszt, *Heroïde Funèbre–Prometheus.*
Standard Works: Niels Gade, *Overture, Nordische Sehnfahrt*; Joseph A. Josephson, *Festive March in G*; Robert Schumann, *Overture, Die Braut von Messina, Opus 100.*
Symphonies: Niels Gade, *No. 4 in B♭, Opus 20*; Camille Saint-Saëns, *Symphony in A*(?); Robert Schumann, *No. 3 in E♭, Opus 97, "Rhenish"*; Louis Spohr, *No. 9 in b, Opus 143, "Die Jahrszeiten."*

1851
❄

Historical Highlights: Louis Napoleon forces a new constitution on France, paving the way for a new French empire; Cuba fails in an independence attempt; Victoria, Australia, is granted self-government status; in the United States, the *New York Times* begins publication; the Illinois Central Railroad is chartered; Des Moines, Iowa, and Portland, Oregon, are chartered; Isaac Singer patents the sewing machine; the clipper ship *Flying Cloud* is launched.

Art and Literature Highlights: Births—artist Samuel Robb, writer Kate O'Flaherty Chopin; Deaths—artists Thomas Birch, Alexei Egorov, Joseph Turner, writers James Fenimore Cooper, Mary Wollstonecraft Shelley.

Art—Landseer's *Monarch of the Glen*, Leutze's *Washington Crossing the Delaware*, Woodville's *Waiting for the Stage*; Literature—Hawthorne's *House of the Seven Gables*, Hoffmann's *Liebeslieder*, Melville's *Moby Dick*.

Musical Highlights

A. **Births**

Composers: Jan Blockx (Belgium) January 25; Guillaume Couture (Canada) October 23; Vincent d'Indy (France) March 27; Emile-Pierre Ratez (France) November 5; André Wormser (France) November 1.

Singers: Blanche Cole (British soprano); Phillipine Edwards (British-born soprano); Minnie Hauk (American mezzo-soprano) November 16; Marie Lehmann (German soprano) May 15; Pol-Henri Plançon (French bass) June 12.

Performers: Richard Andersson (Swedish pianist) August 22; Victor Emanuel Bendix (Danish pianist/composer) May 17; Adolf Brodsky (Russian violinist) March 21; Clarence Eddy (American organist) June 23; Anna Essipova (Russian pianist) February 12; Emil Liebling (German-born pianist) April 12; Alexander Michalowski (Polish pianist) May 5; Paul Étienne Wachs (French organist/composer) September 19; Frank Rush Webb (American organist/conductor) October 8.

Others: Theodore Baker (American compiler/author) June 3; W. C. Brownell (American music critic/author) August 30.

B. **Deaths**

Composers: Engelbert Aigner (Austria); Alexander Aliabiev (Russia) March 6; Gioseffo Catrufo (Italy) August 19; Josef Alois Ladurner (Austria) February 20; Gustav Albert Lortzing (Germany) January 21; Carl Friedrich Rungenhagen (Germany) December 21; Gaspare Spontini (Italy) January 24.

Conductors: Martin-Joseph Mengal (Belgium) July 4.

Singers: Harriett Waylett (British soprano) April 26.

Performers: Antoine-Charles Glachant (French violinist) April 9; Michael Henkel (German organist) March 4; Martin-Joseph Mengal (Belgian horn virtuoso/conductor) July 4; Karl Möser (German violinist/conductor) January 27.

Others: James Shudi Broadwood (British piano maker) August 8; Conrad Graf (Austrian piano maker) March 18; Joseph Mainzer (German musical journalist) November 10; John Parry (Welsh music author/composer) April 8; George Thomson (Scottish folk song collector) February 18.

C. Debuts

Singers: Enrico Delle Sedie (Italian baritone—San Casciano); Francesco Graziani (Italian baritone—Ascoli); Elizabeth Taylor Greenfield (American soprano—Buffalo, New York).
Performers: Frederic Brandeis (Austrian-born pianist—New York); Ernst Pauer (Austrian pianist—London).

D. New Positions

Conductors: George Bristow (New York Harmonic Society); Karl Eckert (Théâtre-Italien, Paris); Robert Franz (Halle University); Joseph Hellmesberger, Sr. (Gesellschaft der Musikfreunde, Vienna); Hervé (Palais Royal, Paris); Friedrich Wilhelm Kücken (kapellmeister, Stuttgart).
Others: Jean Andries (director, Ghent Conservatory); César Franck (organ, St. Jean-St. François); Carl Hennig (organ, Sophienkirche, Berlin); Richard Grant White (music critic, *New York Inquirer* and *The Morning Courier*).

E. Prizes/Honors

Prizes: Eduard Lassen (Prix de Rome).
Honors: Ambroise Thomas (French Academy).

F. Biographical Highlights

Hans von Bülow leaves Switzerland and goes to Weimar to study with Franz Liszt; Antoine de Kontski moves to Paris and concertizes throughout Europe; Ernst Pauer, after a successful London debut, decides to settle there; Cesare Pugni goes to St. Petersburg as ballet composer to the Imperial Theater; Alexander Serov begins his music criticism career; Henri Wieniawski begins his virtuoso career with two years in Russia.

G. Cultural Beginnings

Performing Groups—Choral: Cecilia Society of Copenhagen; Choral Institute of Dublin; Classical Harmonists (Belfast); Hannoverische Männergesangverein; Milwaukee Musikverein; Washington Sängerbund (D.C.).
Performing Groups—Instrumental: New York Philharmonic Society; Société des Jeunes Artistes du Conservatoire de Paris.
Educational: Boston Music School; Cologne Conservatory of Music; Grädener Vocal Academy (Hamburg); Karl Hering School of Music (Berlin); Städtische Akademie für Tonkunst (Darmstadt).
Music Publishers: Christian Kahnt Music Publishing Co. (Leipzig); W. C. Peters and Sons (Cincinnati); John L. Peters and Brother (St. Louis); Methven Simpson; Trübner and Co. (London).
Music Publications: *The Echo; Revue de Paris.*

Performing Centers: Crystal Palace (London); Fireman's Hall (Detroit); St. Lawrence Hall (Toronto); Teatro Sociale (Guillaume—Brescia); Théâtre-Lyrique (Paris).
Other: Feurich Piano Co. (Leipzig); Haines Brothers Piano Co. (East Rochester); Joseph Henry, bowmaker (Paris); Henri Herz, piano maker (Paris); William A. Johnson, organ builder (Hartford); Georg Kilgen and Son, organ builders (New York).

H. **Musical Literature**
Michael Balfe, *Indispensable Studies for a Bass Voice–Indispensable Studies for a Soprano Voice*; Carl Czerny, *Umriss der ganzen Musikgeschichte*; François Gevaert, *Rapport sur l'état de la musique en Espagne*; Wiktor Kazyński, *History of Italian Opera*; Louis Lambillotte, *Clef des mélodies grégoriennes*; Johann Christian Lobe, *Katechismus der musik*; Carl Loewe, *Musikalischer Gottesdienst: methodische anweisung zum kirchengesange und orgelspiel–Klavier- und General-Bass-Schule*; Lowell Mason, *The Glee Hive*; Friedrich Silcher, *Harmonie- und kompositionslehre*; William Spark, *A Lecture on Church Music*; Richard Wagner, *Oper und Drama*; Carl von Winterfeld, *Musiktreiben und Musikempfindungen im 16. und 17. Jahrhundert*.

I. **Musical Compositions**
Chamber Music:
Sonata/Solos: Ignaz Moscheles, *Cello Sonata in E, Opus 121*; Anton Rubinstein, *Violin Sonata in G, Opus 13*; Robert Schumann, *Violin Sonata No. 1 in a, Opus 105–No. 2 in d, Opus 121*.
Ensembles: Woldemar Bargiel, *Piano Trio No. 1, Opus 6*; Franz Berwald, *Piano Trio No. 2 in f*; Louise Farrenc, *Quintet in E for Piano and Strings, Opus 31*; Niels Gade, *String Quintet in f*; Anton Rubinstein, *Two Piano Trios (F, g), Opus 15*; Robert Schumann, *Piano Trio No. 3 in g, Opus 110*.
Piano: Johannes Brahms, *Scherzo in e♭, Opus 4*; Louis Moreau Gottschalk, *Fantasy on "God Save the Queen"–Souvenirs d'Andalousie*; Stephen Heller, *Spaziergänge eines einsamen, Opus 78–Traumbilder, Opus 79*; Franz Liszt, *Twelve Études d'exécution transcendante–Hungarian Rhapsody No. 15 in a, "Râkóczy March"–Grandes études de Paganini–Two Polonaises (c, E)*; Ludvig Norman, *Two Pieces*; Joachim Raff, *Schweizerweisen, Opus 60*; Robert Schumann, *Three Fantasiestücke, Opus 111*.
Organ: Niels Gade, *Three Pieces, Opus 22*; Joseph Rheinberger, *Three Fughettas*.
Choral/Vocal Music:
Choral: Anton Bruckner, *Entsagen in B♭* (cantata); Heinrich Dorn, *Missa pro Defunctis*; William Jackson, *Isaiah* (oratorio); Carl Loewe, *Die Hochzeit der Thetis, Opus 120a* (cantata); Emil Naumann, *Missa*

solennis; Joachim Raff, *Te Deum*; Camille Saint-Saëns, *Moïse sauvé des eaux* (oratorio); Robert Schumann, *Der Rose Pilgerfahrt, Opus 112–Der Königssohn, Opus 116*.

Vocal: Stephen Foster, *Laura Lee–Old Folks at Home–Ring de Banjo*; Felix Mendelssohn, *Six Songs, Opus 86*; Ludvig Norman, *Eight Songs, Opus 13*; Jacques Offenbach, *Les voix mystérieuses*; Anton Rubinstein, *Twelve Songs, Opus 36*; Robert Schumann, *Mädchenlieder, Opus 103–Seven Songs, Opus 104–Husarenlieder, Opus 117– Three Gedichte, Opus 119*.

Musical Stage: Daniel Auber, *Zerline*; Félicien David, *La perle di Brésil*; François Gevaert, *Les Empiriques*; Charles Gounod, *Sapho*; Albert Lortzing, *Die Opernprobe*; Heinrich Marschner, *Austin*; Saverio Mercadante, *Medea*; Carlo Pedrotti, *Fiorina–Zaffira–Malvina di Scozia*; Errico Petrella, *Il carnevale di Venezia*; Joseph Sigismond Thalberg, *Florinda*; Ambroise Thomas, *Raymond*; Giuseppe Verdi, *Rigoletto*.

Orchestra/Band Music:
Concerted Music:
    Violin: Heinrich Ernst, *Concerto pathétique in f♯, Opus 23*; Joseph Joachim, *Andantino and Allegro Scherzoso, Opus 1*.
    Other: Johann Joseph Albert, *Doublebass Concerto*; Jacques Offenbach, *Cello Concertino*.
Program Music: Franz Liszt, *Mazeppa*.
Standard Works: François Gevaert, *La Feria Andaluza*; Mikhail Glinka, *Spanish Overture No. 2, "Summer Night in Madrid"*; Robert Schumann, *Overture, Julius Caesar, Opus 128–Overture, Hermann und Dorothea, Opus 136*.
Symphonies: Franz Lachner, *No. 8 in g, Opus 100*; Anton Rubinstein, *No. 2 in C, "Ocean," Opus 42*.

1852
❄

Historical Highlights: Louis Napoleon declares himself emperor of the Second French Empire; the British enter into the Second Burmese War in Asia; a new constitutional government is provided for New Zealand; the Transvaal is founded in South Africa; in the United States, Franklin Pierce is elected fourteenth president; the Wells Fargo Co. opens offices in San Francisco; Massachusetts passes the first compulsory school attendance law for young people.

Art and Literature Highlights: Births—artists George Clausen, Jef Lambeaux, Theodore Robinson, writers Alfredo Oriani, Henry Van Dyke; Deaths—artists Horatio Greenough, John Vanderlyn, writers Nikolai Gogol, Ernst Raupach. Art—Bingham's *Daniel Boone Escorting Settlers in* *the Wilderness*, Menzel's *Flute Concert at Sans Souci*; Literature—Bouci-cault's *The Corsican Brothers*, Dumas' *Camille*, Stowe's *Uncle Tom's Cabin*.

Musical Highlights

A. **Births**

Composers: Josef Bayer (Austria) March 6; Frederic Hymen Cowen (England) January 29; Paul Joseph Hillemacher (France) November 29; Hans Huber (Switzerland) June 28; Charles Villiers Stanford (England) September 30.

Conductors: Gabriel Marie (France) January 8; Edoardo Mascheroni (Italy) September 4; Fritz Scheel (Germany) November 7.

Singers: Barton M'Guckin (Irish tenor) July 28; Antonia Mielke (German soprano)(?).

Performers: Hans Bischoff (German pianist) February 17; Rafael Jos-effy (Hungarian pianist) July 3; Johann Georg Leitert (German pianist) September 29; Antoine de Lhoyer (French guitarist); Louis Maas (German-born pianist/composer) June 21; Eugenio Pirani (Italian pianist) September 8; Raoul Pugno (French pianist) June 23; Vasili Safonov (Russian pianist/conductor) February 6; Emile Sauret (French violinist/composer) March 22; Otakar Ševček (Czech violin-ist/pedagogue) March 22; Constantin Sternberg (Russian-born pi-anist) July 9; Francisco Tárrega (Spanish guitarist) November 21; Max Vogrich (Austrian pianist) January 24.

Others: Max Friedlaender (German musicologist) October 12; Ben-jamin Ives Gilman (American ethnomusicologist) February 19; Au-gustus Harris (British impresario).

B. **Deaths**

Composers: Józef Damse (Poland) December 15; Joseph Dreschler (Bohemia) February 27; Johann Baptist Weigl (Germany) July 5.

Singers: Alexis de Garaudé (French singer) March 23; Thomas Moore (Irish singer/composer) February 25; Arthur P. Seguin (British bass) December 6.

Performers: John Burrowes (British organist) March 31; Anton B. Fürstenau (German flutist) November 18; Georg Hellmesberger, Jr. (Austrian violinist) November 12; August Alexander Klengel (Ger-man pianist/organist) November 22; Joseph Merk (Austrian cellist) June 16; Henri-Jean Rigel (French pianist/composer) December 16; Johann Friedrich Schwencke (German organist/composer) Septem-ber 28; Jean-Baptiste Willent-Bordogni (French bassoonist) May 11.

Others: Giuseppe Bertini (Italian musicographer) March 15; Salvatore Cammarano (Italian librettist) July 17; George Catlin (American in-strument maker) May 1; François Fayolle (French music author) De-cember 2; Carl von Winterfeld (German music author) February 19.

C. Debuts

Singers: Antonio Cotogni (Italian baritone—Rome); Jean-Baptiste Faure (French baritone—Paris); Darya Leonova (Russian contralto—St. Petersburg); Maria Piccolomini (Italian soprano—Florence); Caroline Richings (British-born soprano—Philadelphia).

Performers: Camilla Urso (French-born violinist—New York, age ten).

D. New Positions

Conductors: Julius Benedict (Her Majesty's Theater, London); Antonio Cagnoni (Cathedral of Vigevano); Theodor Eisfeld (New York PO); Charles Gounod (Orphéon Choral Society, Paris); Angelo Mariani (Teatro Carlo Felice, Genoa); Pietro Raimondi (St. Peter's, Rome).

Others: William Henry Fry (music critic, *New York Tribune*); Moritz Fürstenau (music librarian, Royal Library of Dresden); George Grove (secretary, Crystal Palace); Friedrich Gottlieb Schwencke (organ, Nikolai Kirche, Hamburg); Robert Stewart (organ, St. Patrick's Cathedral, Dublin); Richard S. Willis (editor, *Musical Times*).

E. Prizes/Honors

Honors: Charles Barry (knighted); Max Bruch (Mozart Scholarship); Camille Saint-Saëns (St. Cecilia, Bordeaux); Friedrich Silcher (doctorate, University of Tübingen).

F. Biographical Highlights

Michael Balfe begins a two-year tour of Russia and Austria; August and Georg Gemünder move their violin-making business from Boston to New York; Louis Moreau Gottschalk makes a very successful European concert tour; Charles Gounod decides against taking Holy Orders and marries Anna Zimmermann; Otto Jadassohn begins teaching music in Leipzig; Jenny Lind marries the American conductor Otto Goldschmidt.

G. Cultural Beginings

Performing Groups—Choral: Basler Liedertafel; Bucharest Deutsche Liedertafel; Chicago Männergesang-Verein; Cleveland St. Cecilia Society; Ludwig Erk Gesangverein (Berlin).

Performing Groups—Instrumental: Aachen Städtisches Orchester; Bonn Konzertverein; Melbourne Philharmonic Society (Australia); New Philharmonic Society (London); San Francisco Philharmonic Society.

Festivals: Westphalian Music Festival.

Educational: Bergen (Norway) Musical College; École Communale de Musique et de Déclamation (Marseilles).

Music Publishers: Joseph Atwill and Co. (San Francisco); De Santis Music Publishers (Rome); H. O. Houghton and Co. (Houghton-Mifflin Co. in 1880).

Music Publications: *Dwight's Journal of Music* (Boston); *Gazzetta Musical di Napoli; Neue Wiener Musik-Zeitung.*
Performing Centers: Boston Music Hall (Aquarius Theater); Bucharest National Theater; Graslin Theater (Nantes); Hanover State Opera House.
Other: Johannes Kleis, organ builder (Germany); Stieff Piano Co. (Baltimore); Weber Piano Co. (New York).

H. Musical Literature

Franz Brendel, *Geschichte der Musik in Italien, Deutschland und Frankreich von den ersten christlichen Zeiten bis auf die Gegenwart;* Charles Coussemaker, *Histoire de l'harmonie au Moyen-Age;* Moritz Drobisch, *Über musikalische Tonbestimmung und Temperatur;* John Hullah, *A Grammar of Harmony;* Otto Kraushaar, *Der accordliche Gegensatz und der Begründung der Scala;* Johann Christian Lobe, *Musikalische Briefe eines Wohlbekannten;* Lowell Mason, *New Carmina Sacra;* John Moore, *Complete Encyclopedia of Music, Elementary, Technical, Historical, Biographical, Vocal, and Instrumental;* Elise Polko, *Musikalische Märchen;* Lucien Southard, *Union Glee Book.*

I. Musical Compositions
Chamber Music:
String Quartets: Carl Reinecke, *No. 2 in F, Opus 30;* Anton Rubinstein, *Two quartets (G, a), Opus 17.*
Sonata/Solos: Anton Rubinstein, *Cello Sonata in D, Opus 18.*
Ensembles: Louise Farrenc, *Sextet in c, Opus 40, for Piano and Winds;* Edouard Lalo, *Piano Trio No. 2 in b.*
Piano: Johannes Brahms, *Sonata No. 2 in f♯, Opus 2;* George Frederick Bristow, *A Life on the Ocean Wave, Opus 21;* Louis Moreau Gottschalk, *Midnight in Seville;* Stephen Heller, *Wanderstunden, Opus 80;* Franz Liszt, *Fantasia on Beethoven's "Ruins of Athens"–Hungarian Rhapsody No. 16 in a–No. 17 in d;* Joachim Raff, *Frühlingsboten, Opus 55;* Anton Rubinstein, *Two Melodies (F, B), Opus 3–Three Pieces, Opus 5;* Camille Saint-Saëns, *Trois morceaux, Opus 1.*
Organ: Anton Bruckner, *Two Pieces in d.*
Choral/Vocal Music:
Choral: Anton Bruckner, *Psalm 114 in G–Zwei Totenlieder (E♭, F);* Peter Cornelius, *Requiem for Male Chorus;* Niels Gade, *Spring Fantasy, Opus 23* (cantata); George Frederick Root, *The Flower Queen* (cantata); Camille Saint-Saëns, *Ode to St. Cecilia;* Robert Schumann, *Requiem in D♭, Opus 148–Mass in C, Opus 147–Von Pagen und der Königstochter, Opus 140* (cantata).

Vocal: Stephen Foster, *Massa's in de Cold, Cold Ground*; Carl Loewe, *Three Songs, Opus 123*; Stanislaw Moniuszko, *Ninola* (cantata); Robert Schumann, *Five Poems of Queen Mary, Opus 135–Four Ballads, Opus 141–Four Songs, Opus 142*.

Musical Stage: Adolphe Adam, *If I Were a King–La poupée de Nuremberg*; Daniel Auber, *Marco Spada*; Michael Balfe, *The Sicilian Bride–The Devil's in It*; Friedrich von Flotow, *Rübezahl*; Jacques Halévy, *Le juif errant*; Louis Maillart, *La croix de Marie*; Victor Massé, *Galathée*; Stanislaw Moniuszko, *Bettly*; Errico Petrella, *Elena di Tolosa*; Giovanni Rossi, *Elena di Taranto*; Lauro Rossi, *Le sabine*; Anton Rubinstein, *The Siberian Hunters*.

Orchestra/Band Music:
Concerted Music:
   Piano: Mily Balakirev, *Grand Fantasy on Russian Folk Songs, Opus 4*; Franz Liszt, *Hungarian Fantasy*; Henry Litolff, *Concerto No. 4, Opus 102*(?).

Ballet/Incidental Music: Charles Gounod, *Ulysse* (IM)–*Le Bourgeois Gentilhomme* (B); Franz Lachner, *König Ödipus* (IM); Cesare Pugni, *Amazons of the 9th Century* (B).

Standard Works: Johann Peter Hartmann, *Concert Overture No. 3 in C, Opus 51*; Johann Strauss, Jr., *Annen Polka*.

Symphonies: Johann Joseph Albert, *No. 1*; William Henry Fry, *The Breaking Heart Symphony*; Niels Gade, *No. 5 in d, Opus 25*; Mikhail Glinka, *Ukranian Symphony* (1 movement only).

1853

❄

Historical Highlights: Commodore Perry sails the U.S. fleet into Tokyo bay and opens Japan to world trade; the Crimean War begins between Turkey and Russia; Great Britain becomes the first nation to require smallpox vaccinations for all its citizens; in the United States, the Gadsden Purchase from Mexico adds land to the Arizona and New Mexico territories; the Washington and Oregon Territories are separated into two separate entities.

Art and Literature Highlights: Births—artists John Twachtmann, Vincent Van Gogh, writers René Bazin, Irwin Russell; Deaths—artist Sarah Goodridge, writers Johann Tieck, Tommaso Grossi. Art—Bonheur's *The Horse Fair*, Courbet's *The Bathers*, Martin's *The Great Day of His Wrath*, Wimar's *Indians Pursued by American Dragoons*; Literature—Dickens' *Bleak House*, Hawthorne's *Tanglewood Tales*, Ruskin's *The Stones of Venice*.

Musical Highlights

A. **Births**

Composers: Arthur Foote (U.S.A.) March 5; Iwan Knorr (Germany) January 3; Hans Koessler (Germany) January 1; André Messager (France) December 30; Emil Sjögren (Sweden) June 16.

Conductors: Richard Henneberg (Germany) August 5.

Singers: Edouard De Reszke (Polish bass) December 22; Johannes Elmblad (Swedish bass) August 22; Hedwig Reicher-Kinderman (German soprano) July 15; Auguste Seidl-Kraus (German soprano) August 28; Gabriel Soulacroix (French baritone) December 11; Emil-Alexandre Taskin (French baritone) March 8.

Performers: Maria Teresa Carreño (Venzuelan pianist) December 22; Henry Morton Dunham (American organist/composer) July 29; Henry Granger Hanchett (American organist/inventor) August 29; Charles Henry Morse (American organist) January 5; Jean-Louis Nicodé (German pianist/conductor) August 12; Theodore Pfeiffer (German pianist) October 20; Laura Rappoldi (Austrian pianist) January 14; Alfonso Rendano (Italian pianist) April 5; Franz Rummel (German-born pianist) January 11.

Others: Theodore von Frimmel (Austrian music/art historian) December 15; Percy Goetschius (American music theorist/pedagogue) August 30; Charles Malherbe (French music author/composer) April 21.

B. **Deaths**

Composers: Francisco Andrevi y Castellar (Spain) November 23; Jonathan Blewitt (England) September 4; Carl Gottlieb Hering (Germany) January 4; Georges Onslow (France) October 3; Pietro Raimondi (Italy) October 30; Johann Philipp Schmidt (Germany) May 9.

Conductors: Edward Lannoy (Belgium-Austria) March 29.

Singers: Giuseppina Ronzi de Begnis (Italian soprano) June 7; Filippo Galli (Italian bass) June 3.

Performers: Lisa Cristiani (French cellist); Victor François Desvignes (French violinist/composer) December 30; Johann Leopold Fuchs (Germany) April 15; Louis Emmanuel Jadin (French pianist/pedagogue) April 11; Nicolaus Kraft (Hungarian cellist) May 18; Giovanni B. Polledro (Italian violin) August 15; Friedrich Schneider (German organist/conductor) November 23; Pierre-Joseph Zimmerman (French pianist/educator) October 29.

Others: Jonas Chickering (American piano maker) December 8; William Gardiner (British music author) November 16; Peter Lichtenthal (Austrian music author/composer) August 18; Giovanni Ricordi (Italian publisher) March 15.

C. Debuts

Singers: Pietro Mongini (Italian tenor—Genoa); Adelaide Phillipps (British contralto—Brescia); Jean-Baptiste (Giovanni) Sbriglia (Italian-born tenor—Naples); Hortense Schneider (French soprano—Agen). **Performers:** Josef Strauss (Austrian conductor—Vienna).

D. New Positions

Conductors: Karl Eckert (Vienna Court Opera); Franz Erkel (Budapest PO); Maurits Hagemann (Groningen); Joseph Joachim (Royal Music Director, Hanover); Ludwig Schindelmeisser (Darmstadt). **Others:** Johannes van Bree (director, Amsterdam Conservatory); César Franck (maître de chapelle, Ste. Clothilde); Johann Christian Lobe (editor, *Fliegende Blätter für Musik*).

E. Prizes/Honors

Honors: Henry Bishop (doctorate, Oxford); Aimé-Ambroise Leborne (Legion of Honor).

F. Biographical Highlights

Alkan begins a twenty-year withdrawal from public performance; Johannes Brahms accompanies Ede Reményi on his tour and meets Clara and Robert Schumann; Hans von Bülow makes his first concert tour as pianist; Louis Moreau Gottschalk returns to the United States for a long concert tour; Robert Schumann's mental illness deepens; Theodore Thomas, playing in Jullien's orchestra, gets his first taste of good music; Richard Wagner first meets the young Cosima Liszt and meets the Wesendoncks; Franz Wurlitzer emigrates to the United States.

G. Cultural Beginnings

Performing Groups—Choral: Belgrade Choral Society; Continental Vocalists (U.S.A.); London City Glee Club; Orphei Dränger (The Sons of Orpheus, Sweden).
Performing Groups—Instrumental: Budapest Philharmonic Orchestra; Jullien's Monster Concerts for the Masses (New York); London Concerti da Camera; Pest Philharmonic Society; Philharmonic Society of the Friends of Art (New Orleans); Royal Melbourne (Australia) Philharmonic Society; Toulouse Chamber Orchestra.
Educational: École Spéciale de Chant (Paris, by Gilbert Duprez); New York Normal Music Institute.
Music Publishers: Augener and Co. (London); Berry and Gordon (New York); Wilhelm Hansen Music Publishing Co. (Copenhagen); Miller and Beecham (Baltimore); P. F. Werlein (New Orleans).
Music Publications: *L'Arpa*; *Gazzetta Musicale di Firenze*; *Niederrheinische Musikzeitung* (Cologne); *Tonic Sol-Fa Reporter*.

Other: Bechstein Piano Co. (Berlin); Wilhelm Biese Piano Co. (Berlin); Blüthner Piano Co. (Leipzig); Merklin, Schütze et Cie., organ builders (Brussels); J. and P. Schiedmayer, piano makers (Stuttgart); Steinway and Sons (New York); Tonic Sol-Fa Association (London).

H. Musical Literature

Hector Berlioz, *Les soirées de l'orchestre*; Moritz Hauptmann, *Die natur der harmonik und der metrik*; William Horsley, *The Musical Treasury*; Lowell Mason, *Musical Letters from Abroad*; Richard Pohl, *Akustische Briefe . . .* ; Ernst Richter, *Lehrbuch der harmonie*; Augustin Savard, *Cours complet d'harmonie théorique et pratique*; Simon Sechter, *Die Grundsätze der musikalischen Komposition I, II*; Carl Weitzmann, *Der übermässige Dreiklang*; Friedrich Wiecks, *Clavier und gesang*.

I. Musical Compositions
Chamber Music:
String Quartets: Anton Rubinstein, *Quartet in F, Opus 17/3.*
Sonata/Solos: Edouard Lalo, *Violin Sonata, Opus 12*; Anton Rubinstein, *Violin Sonata No. 2 in a, Opus 19*; Henryk Wieniawski, *Adagio élégiaque in A, Opus 5* (violin, piano).
Ensembles: Franz Berwald, *Piano Quintet No. 1 in e*; Niels Gade, *Novelletten, Opus 29* (violin, cello, piano); Theodor Kullak, *Piano Trio in e, Opus 77*; Carl Reinecke, *Piano Quartet in E, Opus 34*; Camille Saint-Saëns, *Piano Quartet in E*; Robert Schumann, *Märchenerzählungen, Opus 132* (clarinet, viola, piano); Louis Spohr, *Septet in a, Opus 147.*
Piano: Johannes Brahms, *Sonata No. 1 in C, Opus 1–No. 3 in f, Opus 5–Variations in D on a Hungarian Song, Opus 21*; Stephen Heller, *Twenty-Four Preludes, Opus 81–Blumen-, Frucht- und Dornenstücken, Opus 82–Six feuillets d'album, Opus 83*; Ferdinand Hiller, *Sonata No. 1 in e, Opus 47(?)*; Franz Liszt, *Sonata in b–Hungarian Rhapsodies 4–14 (E♭, e, D♭, d, f♯, E♭, E, a, c♯, a, f)*; Ludvig Norman, *Four Fantasy Pieces, Opus 5*; Clara Schumann, *Variations on a Theme of Robert Schumann, Opus 20–Three Romances (D♭, g, B♭), Opus 22*; Robert Schumann, *Three Piano Sonatas for the Young (G, D, C), Opus 118–Seven Pieces in Fughetta Form, Opus 126.*
Organ: Camille Saint-Saëns, *Assai moderato in B♭.*
Choral/Vocal Music:
Choral: William Bradbury, *Daniel* (cantata); Anton Bruckner, *Magnificat*; Niels Gade, *Chorus, Opus 26*, (male chorus)–*Erlkönigs Tochter, Opus 30* (cantata); Charles Gounod, *Messe in c/C, "aux Orphéonistes"*; George Macfarren, *Lenora* (cantata); Giacomo Meyerbeer, *Psalm XCI*; George Frederick Root, *Daniel* (cantata); Robert Schumann, *Scenes from Goethe's Faust–Ballad, "Das Glück von Edenhall," Opus 143.*

Vocal: Johannes Brahms, *Six Songs, Opus 3–Six Songs, Opus 6–Six Songs, Opus 7*; Stephen Foster, *My Old Kentucky Home–Old Dog Tray*; Carl Loewe, *Two Ballads, Opus 121–Der Letzte Ritter, Opus 124* (three ballads); Clara Schumann, *Six Lieder aus Jucunde, Opus 23.*

Musical Stage: Adolphe Adam, *Le Sourd*; César Franck, *Le Valet de Ferme*; Jacques Halévy, *Le nabab*; Victor Massé, *Les noces de Jeannette*; Saverio Mercadante, *Statira–Violetta*; Louis Niedermeyer, *La Fronde*; Jacques Offenbach, *Pépito*; Giovanni Pacini, *Rodrigo di Valenza–El Cid–Lidia di Brabante*; Carlo Pedrotti, *Gelmina*; Lauro Rossi, *L'alchimista*; Anton Rubinstein, *Thomas, the Fool–Revenge*; Ambroise Thomas, *La Tonelli*; Giuseppe Verdi, *Il trovatore–La traviata*; Charles L. Vogel, *La moissonneuse.*

Orchestra/Band Music:
Concerted Music:
    Piano: Robert Schumann, *Introduction and Allegro in D/d, Opus 134.*
    Violin: Robert Schumann, *Fantasy in C, Opus 131*; Henri Wieniawski, *Concerto No. 1 in f♯, Opus 14– Polonaise No. 1 in D, Opus 4–Souvenir de Moscow, Opus 6.*

Program Music: Franz Liszt, *Festklänge.*

Standard Works: Anton Rubinstein, *Concert Overture in B♭, Opus 60*; Robert Schumann, *Festival Overture, "Rheinweinlied," Opus 123.*

Symphonies: George Bristow, *No. 2 in d, Opus 24, "Jullien"*; William Henry Fry, *Santa Claus Symphony*; Camille Saint-Saëns, *No. 1 in E♭, Opus 2.*

1854
❄

Historical Highlights: The Crimean War—France and Great Britain declare war on Russia; the Treaty of Kanagawa is signed by the United States and Japan; the Dogma of the Immaculate Conception is declared by Pope Pius IX; in the United States, the modern Republican Party is born in Wisconsin; the Kansas-Nebraska Act is passed while the provisions of the Missouri Compromise are repealed; the Ostend Manifesto on the buying or taking of Cuba is made public.

Art and Literature Highlights: Births—artist John Frederick Peto, writers Jean Rimbaud, Oscar Wilde; Deaths—artists Karl Begas, John J. Chalon, writers Albert Bitzius, Jeremias Gotthelf, Richard Penn Smith. Art—Barye's *War, Peace, Force, Order*, Millet's *The Reaper*, Tait's *Arguing the Point: Settling the Presidency*; Literature—Cummins' *The Lamplighter*, Patmore's *The Betrothal*, Thoreau's *Walden*, Tolstoy's *The Cossacks*.

Musical Highlights

A. Births

Composers: Alfredo Catalani (Italy) June 19; George Whitefield Chadwick (U.S.A.) November 13; Edmond-Marie Diet (France) September 25; Adolphe Martin Foerster (U.S.A.) February 2; Engelbert Humperdinck (Germany) September 1; Leoš Janáček (Czechoslovakia) July 3; Alexander Alexandrovich Kopylov (Russia) July 14; Jean Eugène Lemaire (France) September 9; Paul de Wailly (France) May 16.

Conductors: Frederick Neil Innes (U.S.A.) October 29; John Philip Sousa (U.S.A.) November 6.

Singers: Hypolite Belhomme (French bass); Heinrich Bötel (German tenor) March 6; Eugenie-Elise Colonne (French soprano); Maurice Devries (American baritone); Adèle Isaac (French soprano) January 8; Pavel Khokhlov (Russian baritone) August 2; George Sieglitz (German bass) April 26; Adolf Wallnöfer (Austrian tenor) April 26.

Performers: Alfredo Barili (Italian-born pianist/pedagogue) August 2; Emma Brandes (German pianist) January 30; Eugene Gruenberg (Austrian-born violinist) October 30; Moritz Moszkowski (German pianist/composer) August 23; Ovide Musin (Belgian violinist) September 22; Julie Rivé-King (American pianist) October 30; William Hall Sherwood (American pianist/pedagogue) January 31; Emile Wambach (Belgian violinist) November 26; Joseph Miroslav Weber (Czech violinist/composer) November 9; Julius Zarębskí (Polish pianist/composer) February 28.

Others: George Eastman (American patron of the arts) July 12; Henry T. Finck (American music critic/editor) September 22; Philip Hale (American music critic) March 5; Henry Krehbiel (American music critic) March 10; Philipp Wolfrum (German musicologist/conductor) December 17.

B. Deaths

Composers: Andreas Barthay (Hungary) October 4; Karl Ludwig Drobisch (Germany) August 20; Josef-Antoni Elsner (Poland) April 18; Filippo Traetta (Italy-U.S.A.) January 9.

Singers: Teresa Bertinotti (Italian soprano) February 12; Giovanni Battista Rubini (Italian tenor) March 3; Henriette Sontag (German soprano) June 17.

Performers: William Beale (British organist) May 8; Iwan Müller (German clarinetist) February 4; Heinrich Aloys Praeger (Dutch violinist) August 7; Gottlob Wiedebein (German organist) April 17.

Others: Georges Bosquet (French critic/conductor) June 15; Henri Lemoine (French publisher) May 18; Johannes Franciscus Pressenda (Italian violin maker) September 11.

C. Debuts

Singers: Albert Eilers (German bass—Dresden); Amalie Joachim (German mezzo-soprano—Vienna); Bessie Palmer (British contralto—London); Ludwig Schnorr von Carolsfeld (German tenor—Karlsruhe).

Performers: Guglielmo Andreoli (Italian pianist—London); August Wilhelmj (German violinist—Wiesbaden, age nine).

D. New Positions

Conductors: Melchiore Balbi (maestro di cappella, Basilica San Antonio, Padua); Charles Hallé (Manchester SO); Carl Reinecke (music director, Barmen); Max Seifriz (hofkapellmeister, Löwenberg).

Others: Jacques Halévy (secretary, Academy of Fine Arts, Paris); Josef Hasselmans (director, Strasbourg Conservatory); Hervé (founder/manager, Folies-Concertantes, Paris); Johann Georg Herzog (music director, Erlangen University).

E. Prizes/Honors

Prizes: Grat-Norbert Barthe (Prix de Rome).

Honors: Louis Clapisson (French Academy).

F. Biographical Highlights

Hector Berlioz, on the death of Henrietta, marries Marie Ricio; Mikhail Glinka, on the outbreak of the war, returns to Russia; Ebenezer Prout receives his B.A. degree in education from London University; Robert Schumann is placed in an institution after attempting suicide; Richard Wagner begins a liaison with Mathilde Wesendonck.

G. Cultural Beginnings

Performing Groups—Choral: Cleveland Gesangverein; Indianapolis Männerchor; Leipziger Riedel Verein; Linzer Männergesangverein (Sängerbund); Männersangverein Arion (New York); Munich Oratorio Society; Neu-Weimar-Verein; Teutonia Männerchor of Pittsburgh.

Performing Groups—Instrumental: Dresdner Tonkünstlerverein; Pittsburgh Orchestral Society; Sociedad de Mayo (Buenos Aires).

Educational: Birmingham and Midland Institute (School of Music in 1859); New York Academy of Music; Strasbourg Conservatory of Music.

Music Publishers: Faulds, Stone and Morse (Louisville, Kentucky); Joseph P. Shaw Music House and Publishing Co. (Rochester, New York).

Music Publications: *The Pioneer.*

Performing Centers: Boston Theater (New); St. George's Hall Concert Room (Liverpool).

Other: Bradbury's Piano-Forte Warehouse (New York); Conacher and Co., organ builders (Huddersfield); Félibrige Organization (Provençal); Mason and Hamlin Organ Co. (Boston); R. S. Williams and Sons (Toronto).

H. Musical Literature

Karl F. Brendel, *Die musik der Gegenwart und die Gesamtkunst der Zukunft*; Henry Chorley, *Modern German Music*; Félix Clément, *Introduction à une méthode complete de plain-chant d'après les règles du chant grégorien et traditionnel*; Eduard Hanslick, *Vom Musikalisch-Schönen*; Thomas Hastings, *History of Forty Choirs*; Julius Knorr, *Erklärendes Verzeichniss der hauptsächlichsten Musikkunstwörter*; L. Lucas, *L'acoustique nouvelle*; Lowell Mason, *Musical Notation in a Nutshell*; Théodore Nisard, *Dictionnaire litugique, historique et pratique du plainchant*; Heinrich Panofka, *L'art de chanter*.

I. Musical Compositions

Chamber Music:

Sonata/Solos: Edouard Lalo, *Chanson villageoise, Opus 14* (violin/cello, piano); Joachim Raff, *Violin Sonata No. 1 in e, Opus 73–Two Fantasiestücke, Opus 86* (cello, piano); Henri Vieuxtemps, *Three Fantasias on Themes from Verdi, Opus 29* (violin, piano)(?); Henryk Wieniawski, *L'école moderne (ten etudes), Opus 10* (solo violin)–*Caprice-Valse in E, Opus 7–Variations on an Original Theme, Opus 15* (violin, piano).

Ensembles: Alexander Borodin, *String Quintet*; Johannes Brahms, *Piano Trio No. 1 in B, Opus 8*; Ludvig Norman, *String Sextet in A, Opus 18*; Carl Reinecke, *Piano Trio No. 1 in D, Opus 38*.

Piano: Alexandre Boëly, *Four Suites dans le style des anciens maîtres, Opus 16*; Johannes Brahms, *Variations in f♯ on a Theme of Schumann, Opus 9–Four Ballades (d, D, b, B), Opus 10*; Anton Bruckner, *Three Pieces (G, G, F)* (four hands); Louis Moreau Gottschalk, *The Last Hope–El Cocoyé*; Stephen Heller, *Two Tarantellas, Opus 85–Im Walde, Opus 86*; Franz Liszt, *Années di pélerinage I*; Carl Loewe, *Auswanderer-Sonaten, Opus 137* (four Fantasias); Anton Rubinstein, *Kammini-Ostov, Opus 10–Sonata No. 1 in E, Opus 12–Sonata No. 2 in c, Opus 20*(?)–*Six Preludes (A♭, f, E, b, G, c), Opus 24*; Robert Schumann, *Albumblätter, Opus 124*.

Organ: Josef Rheinberger, *Three Preludes and Fugues*.

Choral/Vocal Music:

Choral: Hector Berlioz, *L'enfance du Christ, Opus 25*; Anton Bruckner, *Missa Solemnis in B♭*; Charles Gounod, *The Angel and Tobias* (oratorio); Ferdinand Hiller, *Psalm 25, Opus 60*; Carl Loewe, *Cantata for Male Voices*; Mihály Mosonyi, *Mass No. 4*; Giovanni Pacini, *Il trionfo di Giuditta* (oratorio); George Frederick Root, *The Pilgrim*

Fathers (cantata); Anton Rubinstein, *Six Songs for Male Voices, Opus 31–Twelve Songs, Opus 48*; Franz von Suppé, *Requiem*.

Vocal: Stephen Foster, *I Dream of Jeannie with the Light Brown Hair*; Joachim Raff, *Traumkönig un sein Lieb, Opus 66*; Anton Rubinstein, *Persian Songs, Opus 34*; Henry Clay Work, *We Are Coming, Sister Mary*.

Musical Stage: Michael Balfe, *Pittore e Duca*; Georges Bizet, *La Prêtresse*; Heinrich Dorn, *Die Nibelungen*; Charles Gounod, *La nonne sanglante*; Ferdinand Hiller, *Der Advokat*; Alexei Lvov, *Starosta Boris*; Victor Massé, *La fiancée du diable*; Giacomo Meyerbeer, *L'étoile du nord–Judith* (unfinished); Jacques Offenbach, *Luc et Lucette*; Giovanni Pacini, *La punizione–La donna delle isole*; Carlo Pedrotti, *Genoveffa del Brabante*; Achille Peri, *Orfano e diavolo*; Errico Petrella, *Marco Visconti*; Louis Reyer, *Maître Wolfram*; Richard Wagner, *Das Rheingold*.

Orchestra/Band Music:
Concerted Music:
  Piano: Anton Rubinstein, *Concerto No. 3 in G, Opus 45*.
  Violin: Joachim Raff, *La fée d'amour in a, Opus 67*.
Ballet/Incidental Music: Johan P. Hartmann, *A Folk Tale* (B); Cesare Pugni, *Faust* (B).
Program Music: Franz Liszt, *Orpheus–Hungaria*.
Standard Works: William Henry Fry, *Hagar in the Wilderness*; Karl Goldmark, *Overture*; Joseph Joachim, *Overture to a Comedy by Gozzi, Opus 8*.
Symphonies: William Henry Fry, *Niagara Symphony*; Charles Gounod, *No. 1 in D*; Franz Liszt, *A Faust Symphony*; Joachim Raff, *Symphony in E*; Anton Rubinstein, *No. 3 in A, Opus 56*; Bedřich Smetana, *Triumphal Symphony in E*.

1855
❄

Historical Highlights: Cyrus Field lays the first successful cable from Nova Scotia to Newfoundland; Townshend Harris becomes the first foreign minister to Japan; Czar Nicholas I dies—Alexander II takes the throne; the Young Women's Christian Association (YWCA) is founded in England; in the United States, the Pennsylvania Rock Oil Co. becomes the first to exploit the new resource; Northwestern University is established in Evanston, Illinois.

Art and Literature Highlights: Births—artists William Brymner, Homer Watson, writers Arthur Pinero, Agnes Repplier, Émile Verhaeren; Deaths—artists Wilhelm von Kobell, François Rude, writers Charlotte Brontë, Sarah S. B. Keating Wood. Art—Bingham's *The Verdict of the Peo-*

ple, Courbet's *The Painter's Studio*, Church's *The Andes of Ecuador*; Literature—Alarcón's *El Final de Norma*, Longfellow's *Hiawatha*, Whitman's
Leaves of Grass.

Musical Highlights

A. Births

Composers: Ernest Chausson (France) January 20; Julian Edwards
(U.S.A.) December 11; Anatole Liadov (Russia) May 11; Anton Rückauf (Bohemia) March 13.

Conductors: Joseph Hellmesberger, Jr. (Austria) April 9; Arthur
Nikisch (Hungary) October 12; Emil Paur (Austria) August 29; Fritz
Steinbach (Germany) June 17; Alexander Vinogradsky (Russian) Au-
gust 15.

Singers: Bianca Bianchi (German soprano) June 27; Giuseppe Campanari (Italian baritone) November 17; Mary Davies (British mezzo-
soprano) February 27; Josephine De Reszke (Polish soprano) June 4;
David Thomas Ffrangcon-Davies (British baritone) December 11;
Etelka Gerster (Hungarian soprano) June 15; Paul Kalisch (German
tenor) November 6; Katharina Klafsky (Hungarian soprano) Sep-
tember 19; Antonio Magini-Coletti (Italian baritone) February 17;
Therese Malten (German soprano) June 21; Fanny Moran-Olden
(German soprano) September 28; Francesco Navarini (Italian bass)
December 26; William Frye Parker (British violinist) September 10;
Giulia Valda (American soprano)(?).

Performers: Károly Agghâzy (Hungarian pianist) October 30; Joseph Kotek (Russian violinist) October 25; Emil Mollenhauer (American violinist/conductor) August 4; Edward Baxter Perry (American
pianist) February 14; Cornelius Rybner (Danish-born pianist) October 26; John White (American organist/composer) March 12.

Others: Guido Adler (Austrian musicologist) November 1; William
J. Henderson (American music critic) December 4.

B. Deaths

Composers: Désiré-Alexandre Batton (France) October 15; Ramón
Carnicer (Spain) March 17; Sir Henry Rowley Bishop (England)
April 30; Giovanni Agostino Perotti (Italy) June 28.

Singers: Teresa Belloc-Giorgi (Italian contralto) May 13; Jacques-
Émile Lavigne (French tenor).

Performers: Pedro Albéniz y Basenta (Spanish organist) April 12;
Charles William Hempel (British organist) March 14; Robert Lindley
(British cellist) June 13; Marie Leopoldine Pachler-Koschak (Aus-
trian pianist) April 10; Camille Pleyel (French pianist/piano maker)
May 4; John Pratt (British organist) March 9.

Others: Louis Lambillotte (French music author/organist) February 27.

C. **Debuts**

Singers: Valentina Bianchi (Russian soprano—Frankfurt); Elise Hensler (American soprano—Milan); Euphrosyne Parepa-Rosa (Scottish soprano—Malta); Gustav Walter (Bohemian tenor—Brünn); William Winn (British bass—London).

D. **New Positions**

Conductors: Franz Wilhelm Abt (Braunschweig Court); Carl Bergmann (New York PO); Antonio Buzzolla (maestro di cappella, St. Mark's, Venice); Julius Tausch (Music Society and Subscription Concerts, Düsseldorf).

Others: Gaetano Capocci (organ, St. John Lateran, Rome); Gaetano Gaspari (librarian, Bologna Liceo); Eduard Hanslick (music critic, *Wiener Presse*, Düsseldorf).

E. **Prizes/Honors**

Prizes: Pierre de Mol (Prix de Rome).
Honors: Henri Reber (Legion of Honor).

F. **Biographical Highlights**

Hector Berlioz, attending a festival of his own music at Weimar, meets Liszt; Anton Bruckner goes to Vienna to study harmony and counterpoint with Sechter; William Mason, after a concert tour of various American cities, settles in New York; Gioacchino Rossini moves permanently to Paris; Nicholai Rubinstein graduates with a law degree from the University of Moscow; Sigismond Thalberg begins an extended tour in South America and the United States; Richard Wagner conducts his music in London and meets with Queen Victoria.

G. **Cultural Beginnings**

Performing Groups—Choral: Birmingham Amateur Harmonic Association; Buffalo Sängerbund; Glasgow Choral Union; Göttingen Singakademie; Innsbruck Liedertafel; Old Folks Concert Troupe (Boston); Philadelphia Harmonie; Schlosskirchenchor (Schwerin).

Performing Groups—Instrumental: Christopher Bach Orchestra (Milwaukee); Detroit Philharmonic Society; Dodsworth Hall Matinee Concerts (by Theodore Thomas); Mason-Thomas Quintet; Müller String Quartet II (Meiningen); New Orleans Classical Music Society; Société de Musique de Chambre Armingaud (Armingaud-Jacquard Quartet); Stein and Buchheister Orchestra (Detroit).

Educational: Neue Akademie der Tonkunst (Berlin); Scuola Corale (Pisa); Yale University Music Classes.

Music Publishers: Higgins Brothers (Chicago); Mason Brothers (Boston).

Music Publications: *Blätter für Theater, Musik und Bildene Kunst; Gazeta Musical de Madrid; L'Orphéon.*

Performing Centers: Teatro Ginásio Dramático (Rio de Janeiro).

Other: American Steam Music Co. (Worcester—by the inventor of the Calliope); Berteling Woodwind Co. (Boston-New York); Holtkamp Organ Co. (Cleveland); Laryngoscope (by M. P. García); Melodina (by J. B. Fourneaux); Willem Paling Piano Co. (Sydney, Australia).

H. Musical Literature

Carl A. André, *Der klavierbau und seine geschichte;* Francesco Caffi, *Storia della musica sacra;* Henri-Louis Duvernoy, *Solfège des chanteurs;* Franz J. Kunkel, *Kleine Musiklehre;* Adrien (Juste) de La Fage, *Cours complet de plain-chant;* Adolf B. Marx, *Die Musik des 19. Jahrhundert und ihre Pflege;* Stéphan Morelot, *Manuel de Psalmodie;* Auguste Panseron, *Traité de l'harmonie;* C. D. Parker, *Manual of Harmony;* George F. Root/Lowell Mason, *Young Men's Singing Book;* Georges Schmitt, *Nouveau manuel complet de l'organiste I;* Lucien H. Southard, *A Course in Harmony.*

I. Musical Compositions

Chamber Music:

String Quartets: Mily Balakirev, *Quartet, "Original Russian," Opus 2;* Joachim Raff, *No. 1 in d, Opus 77.*

Sonata/Solos: Louise Farrenc, *Violin Sonata in c, Opus 37;* Joseph Joachim, *Three Pieces, Opus 5* (violin, piano)–*Hebräische melodien, Opus 9* (viola, piano); Carl Reinecke, *Cello Sonata in a, Opus 42;* Anton Rubinstein, *Viola Sonata in F, Opus 49;* Henri Vieuxtemps, *Trois morceaux de salon, Opus 32–Bouquet américain, Opus 33*(?).

Ensembles: Louise Farrenc, *Piano Trio in E♭, Opus 33–Piano Trio in d, Opus 34*(?); Ferdinand Hiller, *Piano Trio No. 4, Opus 64–Piano Trio No. 5, Opus 74*(?); Anton Rubinstein, *Quintet for Woodwinds and Piano in F, Opus 55;* Camille Saint-Saëns, *Piano Quintet in a, Opus 14*(?).

Piano: Alexandre Boëly, *Sonata, Opus 17* (four hands); Louise Farrenc, *Twenty Etudes, Opus 42;* Johan P. Hartmann, *Six Novelletten, Opus 55b;* Stephen Heller, *Tarantelle No. 5, "Scènes italiennes," Opus 87;* Anton Rubinstein, *Three Pieces (F, D, g), Opus 16–Three Caprices (F♯, D, E♭), Opus 21–Three Serenades (F, g, E♭), Opus 22– Suite, Opus 38–Sonata No. 3 in F, Opus 41;* Clara Schumann, *Three Romances (a, F, g), Opus 21;* Bedřich Smetana, *Three Polkas for Piano, Opus 7.*

Organ: Franz Liszt, *Prelude and Fugue on B-A-C-H–Fantasia on "Ad nos, as salutarem undam";* Camille Saint-Saëns, *Prelude in F*(?).

Choral/Vocal Music:

Choral: Hector Berlioz, *L'Imperiale, Opus 26* (cantata); Michael Costa, *Eli* (oratorio); William Henry Fry, *Stabat Mater*; Charles Gounod, *Ste. Cecilia Mass in G*; Johan P. Hartmann, *A Summer Day* (cantata); Franz Liszt, *Graner Mass–Psalm 13*; Stanislaw Moniuszko, *Mass No. 2 in e*; Emil Naumann, *Die Zerstörung Jerusalem durch Titus* (cantata); Frederick Ouseley, *The Martyrdom of St. Polycarp* (oratorio); Anton Rubinstein, *Das verlorene Paradies* (oratorio); Camille Saint-Saëns, *Mass, Opus 4.*

Vocal: Stephen Foster, *Come Where My Love Lies Dreaming*; Charles Gounod, *L'emploi de la journée* (cycle).

Musical Stage: Daniel Auber, *Jenny Bell*; George Frederick Bristow, *Rip Van Winkle*; Friedrich von Flotow, *Hilda–Albin*; François Gevaert, *Les lavandières de Santarem*; Mikhail Glinka, *The Bigamist*; Jacques Halévy, *Jaguarita l'indienne–L'inconsolable*; Victor Massé, *Les saisons–Miss Fauvette*; Jacques Offenbach, *Ba-ta-clan–Une nuit blanche–Les deux aveugles–Entrez, messieurs, mesdames*; Carl Reinecke, *Der vierjährige Posten*; Lauro Rossi, *La sirena*; Lucien Southard, *The Scarlet Letter*; Sigismond Thalberg, *Cristina de Svezia*; Ambroise Thomas, *La cour de Célimène*; Giuseppe Verdi, *Sicilian Vespers.*

Orchestra/Band Music:

Concerted Music:

Piano: Franz Berwald, *Concerto in D.*

Violin: Joseph Joachim, *Concerto in One Movement in g, Opus 3.*

Ballet/Incidental Music: Jacques Offenbach, *Arlequin barbier* (B)–*Pierrot clown* (B)–*Polichinelle dans le monde* (B).

Standard Works: Joseph Joachim, *Hamlet Overture, Opus 4–Demetrios Overture, Opus 6–Heinrich IV Overture, Opus 7*(?); Anton Rubinstein, *Triumphal Overture, Opus 43.*

Symphonies: Georges Bizet, *Symphony in C*; Charles Gounod, *No. 2 in E♭*; Adolf Lindblad, *No. 2 in D.*

1856

✴

Historical Highlights: The Crimean War ends with the Russian control of southeastern Europe broken—the Congress of Berlin settles the Eastern question and all points of international law that are involved; Great Britain goes to war with China; the Bessemer Process revolutionizes the processing of steel; in the United States, James Buchanan is elected fifteenth president; Bloody Kansas describes the Potawatomie Massacre over the slavery question.

Art and Literature Highlights: Births—artist John Singer Sargent, writers H. Rider Haggard, Arthur Rimbaud, George Bernard Shaw; Deaths—artists Theodore Chasseriau, Paul Delaroche, writers Heinrich Heine, James G. Percival. Art—Delacroix's *Sultan of Morocco*, Mount's *The Banjo Player*, Palmer's *The Indian Girl*; Literature—Aksakov's *Chronicles of a Russian Family*, Stowe's *Dred: A Tale of the Great Dismal Swamp*.

Musical Highlights

A. Births

Composers: Franz Xavier Arens (Germany-U.S.A.) October 28; Arthur Bird (U.S.A.) July 23; Charles H. Gabriel (U.S.A.) August 18; Giuseppe Martucci (Italy) January 6; William J. Scanlan (U.S.A.) February 14; Christian Sinding (Norway) January 11; George Templeton Strong (U.S.A.) May 26; Sergei Taniev (Russia) November 25.

Conductors: Robert Kajanus (Finland) December 2; Willem Kes (Holland) February 16; Felix Mottl (Austria) August 24.

Singers: Max Alvary (German tenor) May 3; Mattia Battistini (Italian baritone) February 27; Marie Brema (British mezzo-soprano) February 28; Alma Fohstrom (Finnish soprano) January 2; Emil Götze (German tenor) May 19; Marie Litta (American soprano) July 7; Giovanni Battista de Negri (Italian tenor) April 3; Mary Elizabeth Salter (American soprano/composer) March 15.

Performers: Arthur Bird (American pianist) July 23; Johan Hyatt Brewer (American organist/composer) January 18; Helen Hopekirk (Scottish pianist) May 2; Natalia Janotha (Polish pianist/composer) June 8; José Trago (Spanish pianist) September 25.

Others: Orville H. Gibson (American mandolin/guitar maker); Daniel Guggenheim (American patron of the arts) July 9; Oscar Fleisher (German musicologist) November 2; J. A. Fuller Maitland (British music scholarship) April 7; Wilhelm Heckel (instrument maker/inventor) January 25.

B. Deaths

Composers: Adolphe Charles Adam (France) May 3; František T. Blatt (Boheian clarinetist) March 9; Stephen Jenks (U.S.A.) June 5; Robert Lucas Pearsall (England) August 5; Robert Schumann (Germany) July 31; Peter Ivanovich Turchaninov (Russia) March 16.

Conductors: Peter Joseph von Lindpaintner (Germany) August 21; Philipp Jakob Riotte (Germany) August 20.

Singers: Giulio Marco Bordogni (Italian tenor) July 31; John Braham (British tenor) February 17; Henri-Etienne Dérivis (French bass) February 1; William Knyvett (British counter-tenor) November 17; Lucia Elizabeth Vestris (British contralto) August 8.

Performers: Nicholas-Charles Bochsa (French harpist) January 6; Theodor Döhler (Austrian pianist/composer) February 21; Adolfo Fumagali (Italian pianist) May 3; Joseph Menter (German cellist) April 18; Joseph Kasper Mertz (Austrian guitarist) October 14; Johann Julius Seidel (German organist) February 13.

Others: Friedrich von Drieberg (German music historian/composer) May 21; Friedrich Heinrich von der Hagen (German music scholar) June 11; Count Mikhail Wielhorsky (Russian patron of the arts) September 9.

C. **Debuts**
   Singers: Charles R. Adams (American tenor—Boston); Franz Betz (German baritone—Hanover); Thomas Ainsley Cook (British bass—Manchester); August Gottfried Fricke (German bass—Berlin); Helen Lemmens-Sherrington (British soprano—London); Barbara Marchisio (Italian contralto—Vicenza); Carlotta Marchisio (Italian soprano—Madrid); Minna Peschka-Leutner (Austrian soprano—Breslau); Hans von Rokitansky (Austrian bass—London); Henri Warnots (Belgian tenor—Liège).

D. **New Positions**
   Conductors: William Sterndale Bennett (London PO); Antonio Cagnoni (maestro di cappella, Vigevano); Ludwig Friedrich Hetsch (Mannheim Court Theater); Alexander Ritter (Stettin Opera).
   Others: Anton Bruckner (organ, Linz Cathedral); Edward Hanlick (professor of music ethics, Vienna University); Carl Reissiger (director, Dresden Conservatory).

E. **Prizes/Honors**
   Prizes: Jules Delaunay (Prix de Rome); Charles Lecocq (Offenbach); Arthur Sullivan (Mendelssohn).
   Honors: William Sterndale Bennett (doctorate, Cambridge); Hector Berlioz (French Institute); John Goss (Composer to the Chapel Royal, London); Victor Massé (Legion of Honor).

F. **Biographical Highlights**
   Alexander Borodin graduates with honors from the Academy of Medicine in St. Petersburg and immediately becomes a part of its staff; Louis Moreau Gottschalk begins a five-year tour of the West Indies; Jullien loses much of his music in a Covent Garden fire; Modeste Mussorgsky graduates from Cadet School and joins the regular guard;

Nicolai Rimsky-Korsakov enters the Naval College in St. Petersburg; Pablo de Sarasate is sent to Paris to study at the Conservatory.

G. Cultural Beginnings

Performing Groups—Choral: Cincinnati Cecilia Society; Nottingham Sacred Harmonic Society; Verein für Kirchlichen Gesang (Hanover).

Performing Groups—Instrumental: Cincinnati Philharmonic Orchestra; Coenen String Quartet (Holland); Germania Orchestra (Philadephia).

Educational: Dresden Conservatory of Music; École Saint Simeon (Le Havre); Royal Military School of Music (Twickenham, England).

Music Publishers: Casa Romero (Spain); Leuckart Publishing House (Germany); A. Lundquist (Stockholm).

Music Publications: *L'Armonia* (Italy); *Western Journal of Music* (Chicago).

Performing Centers: Bolshoi Opera Theater II (Moscow); Free Trade Hall (Manchester); Teatro de la Zarzuela (Madrid); Teatro Solis (Montevideo).

Others: American Music Association (New York); Decker and Son, pianos (Albany); Deutsche Händelgesellschaft; Mendelssohn Scholarship; Wutlitzer Organ Co. (Cincinnati); Jacob Zech, piano maker (San Francisco).

H. Musical Literature

August Ambros, *Die Grenzen der Musik und Poesie*; August Baumgartner, *Kurzgefasste geschichte der musikalischen notation*; François H. Blaze, *Sur l'opéra français*; Raimondo Boucheron, *La Scienza dell'armonia . . .* ; Thomas Hastings, *Sacred Praise*; Louis Köhler, *Systematische lehrmethode für klavierspiel und musik I*; Ferdinand Laurencin, *Zur geschichte der kirchenmusik bei den italienern un deutschen*; Stéphan Morelot, *De la musique au XV siècle*; Emil Naumann, *Über einführung des psalmengesanges in die evangelische kirche*.

I. Musical Compositions

Chamber Music:

String Quartets: Max Bruch, *Quartet No. 1 in c, Opus 9*; Anton Rubinstein, *Three Quartets (e, B♭, d), Opus 47*; Louis Spohr, *Quartet in E♭*.

Sonata/Solos: Edouard Lalo, *Allegro, Opus 16* (cello, piano)–*Cello Sonata*; Henryk Wieniawski, *Scherzo tarantelle in g, Opus 16* (violin, piano).

Ensembles: Mily Balakirev, *Octet, Opus 3, for Woodwinds and Strings*.

Piano: Johannes Brahms, *Variations on an Original Theme in D, Opus 21/1*; Anton Bruckner, *Klavierstück in E♭*; Stephen Heller,

Sonata No. 3 in C, Opus 88–Spaziergänge eines Einsamen III, Opus 89–Sérènade No. 2; Anton Rubinstein, *Two Pieces (G♭, E♭), Opus 28*; Camille Saint-Saëns, *Six Bagatelles*.

Organ: Alexander Boëly, *Twelve Pieces, Opus 18*; Johannes Brahms, *Chorale, Prelude and Fugue in a, "O Traurigkeit"–Fugue in a♭–Prelude and Fugue in a*; Camille Saint-Saëns, *Interlude fugué in g*.

Choral/Vocal Music:

Choral: George Bizet, *David* (cantata); William Bradbury, *Esther* (cantata); Johannes Brahms, *Geistliche Lied, Opus 30*; Charles Gounod, *Jésus de Nazareth* (cantata); William Jackson, *Psalm 103 II*.

Vocal: Peter Cornelius, *Brautlieder–Weihnachtslieder, Opus 8*; Stephen Foster, *Gentle Annie*; Edouard Lalo, *Six Melodies, Opus 17*; Robert Franz, *Six Songs, Opus 16*; Carl Loewe, *Three Ballads, Opus 125*; Anton Rubinstein, *Six Songs from Heine, Opus 32–Six German Songs, Opus 33*.

Musical Stage: Daniel Auber, *Manon Lescaut*; Peter Benoit, *A Mountain Village*; Alexander Dargomijsky, *Russalka*; Léo Delibes, *Deux sous de charbon–Deux vieilles gardes–Six demoiselles à marier*; Heinrich Dorn, *Ein Tag in Russland*; Friedrich von Flotow, *Albin*; Jacques Halévy, *Valentine d'Aubigny*; Charles Lecocq, *Le docteur Miracle*; Louis Maillart, *Les dragons de Villars*; Victor Massé, *La reine Topaze*; Jacques Offenbach, *Le savetier et le financier–La bonne d'enfants–Les Dragées du baptême*; Giovanni Pacini, *I portoghesi nel Brasile*; Carlo Pedrotti, *Tutti in maschera*; Achille Peri, *I fidanzati*; Errico Petrella, *L'assedio di Leida*; Amilcare Ponchielli, *I promessi sposi*; Richard Wagner, *Die Walküre*.

Orchestra/Band Music:

Concerted Music:

Piano: Mily Balakirev, *Concert Movement in f♯, Opus 1*.

Other: Johann Kalliwoda, *Variations and Rondo, Opus 57* (bassoon).

Ballet/Incidental Music: Adolphe Adam, *Le Corsaire* (B); Friedrich von Flotow, *Die Libelle* (B); Jacques Offenbach, *Les bergers de Watteau* (B).

Standard Works: George Bristow, *Overture, A Winter's Tale, Opus 70*; Johan P. Hartmann, *Overture, Axel og Valberg, Opus 57*; Johann Kalliwoda, *Concert Overture No. 14 in C, Opus 206*; Henry Litolff, *Overture, Maximilian Robespierre, Opus 55–Overture, Das Welflied von Gustav von Meyern, Opus 99*; George Macfarren, *Overture to Hamlet*; Stanislaw Moniuszko, *Kaim Overture*.

Symphonies: Niels Gade, *No. 6 in g, Opus 32*; Franz Liszt, *Dante Symphony*; Mihály Mosonyi, *No. 2 in a*; Camille Saint-Saëns, *Symphony in F, "Urbs Roma."*

1857

❄

Historical Highlights: The Sepoy Rebellion against British rule begins in India; Persia surrenders to the British; the French take over control of the North African country of Algieria; the Italian National Association is formed by Garibaldi in an attempt to unify the Italian peninsula; in the United States, overspeculation results in a severe financial panic on Wall Street; the Dred Scott decision is handed down by the Supreme Court.

Art and Literature Highlights: Births—artists Edward C. Potter, Max Klinger, writers Joseph Conrad, Hendrik von Pontoppidan; Deaths— artists Thomas Crawford, Johan Dahl, writers Joseph von Eichendorff, Alfred de Musset. Art—Bingham's *Jolly Flatboatmen in Port*, Courbet's *The Hunting Party*, Millais' *Escape of the Heretic*; Literature—Baudelaire's *Les Fleurs du Mal*, Flaubert's *Madame Bovary*, Hughes' *Tom Brown's Schooldays*.

Musical Highlights

A. Births

Composers: Edwin E. Bagley (U.S.A.); Alfred Bruneau (France) March 3; Cécile Chaminade (France) August 8; Edward Elgar (England) June 2; Edgar Stillman Kelley (U.S.A.) April 14; Wilhelm Kienzl (Austria) January 17; Sylvio Lazzari (Austria-France) December 30; Ruggiero Leoncavallo (Italy) April 23; Henry Schoenfeld (U.S.A.) October 4.

Singers: David Bispham (American baritone) January 5; Rose Lucille Caron (French soprano) November 17; Blanche Deschamps-Jehin (French contralto) September 18; Nicolai Figner (Russian tenor) February 21; Charles Manners (Irish bass/impresario) December 27; Lillian Nordica (American soprano) November 12; Herminie Spies (German contralto) February 25; Elena Teodorini (Romanian soprano) March 25.

Performers: Timothée Adamowski (Polish-born violinist) March 24; Leandro Campanari (Italian violinist/composer) October 20; Benjamin Cutter (American violinist/theorist) September 6; Jan Drozdowski (Polish pianist/educator) February 2; Sam Franko (American violinist) January 20; Clayton Johns (American pianist) November 24; Carl Lachmund (American pianist/conductor) March 27; August Spanuth (German pianist/conductor) March 15; César Thomson (Belgian violinist) March 7; Mary Knight Wood (American pianist/composer) April 7.

Others: James Gibbons Huneker (American music author) January 31; Gustav Kobbé (American music author) March 4; Eusebius Mandyczewski (Romanian musicologist) August 17; Waldo Selden

Pratt (American music historian) November 10; Julien Tiersot (French musicologist) July 5.

B. Deaths

Composers: Jacob Niklas Ahlström (Sweden) May 4; Edward Francis Fitzwilliams (England) January 20; Mikhail Ivanovich Glinka (Russia) February 15; Karol Kurpiński (Poland) September 18; Charles Zeuner (German-born organist) November 7.

Singers: Clara Heinefetter (German soprano) February 23; John Sinclair (Scottish tenor) September 23.

Performers: Johannes Bernardus van Bree (Dutch violinist/composer) February 14; Jan Bobrowicz (Polish guitarist); Carl Czerny (Austrian pianist/composer) July 15; Sebastian Ludwig Friedl (German cellist)(?); Friedrich Wilhelm Riem (German organist) April 20.

Others: François-Henri Blaze (French music author) December 11.

C. Debuts

Singers: Désirée Artôt (Belgian mezzo-soprano—Brussels); Bronislawa Dowiakowska-Klimowiczowa (Polish soprano—Warsaw); Emil Fischer (German bass—Graz); Franz Nachbaur (German tenor—Passau); Nicolini (Ernest Nicolas, French tenor—Paris); Bernhard Pollini (German tenor—Cologne); Charles Santley (British baritone—Pavia); Teresa Stolz (Bohemian soprano—Tiflis); Louise Wippern (German soprano—Berlin).

Performers: Friedrich Niecks (German violinist—Düsseldorf).

D. New Positions

Conductors: Jean Joseph Bott (Meiningen Court); Georg Aloys Schmitt (Schwerin Court); Karl Stör (Weimar Court).

Others: Alexandre Guilmant (organ, St. Nicholas, Boulogne); Hermann Küster (organ, Berlin Cathedral and Court); Hermann Langer (music director, Leipzig University); Camille Saint-Saëns (organ, Madeleine, Paris); Maurice Strakosch (director, New York Academy of Music).

E. Prizes/Honors

Prizes: Peter Benoit (Prix de Rome); George Bizet (Prix de Rome).

F. Biographical Highlights

Dudley Buck goes to Leipzig to study at the Conservatory; Hans von Bülow marries Cosima Liszt; Louis Moreau Gottschalk tours South America; Modest Mussorgsky, through Dargomijsky, meets Balakirev and Cui; Giuseppe Verdi leaves Paris to return to Italy; Henri Vieuxtemps, along with Sigismond Thalberg, makes a second tour of the United States; Richard Wagner moves to the Asyl on the Wesendonck's property.

G. Cultural Beginnings

Performing Groups—Choral: Adelaide Liedertafel (Australia); National Opera of Rio de Janeiro; Pine-Harrison English Opera Co. (London); Ullman and Strakosch Opera Co. (by merger).
Performing Groups—Instrumental: Brooklyn Philharmonic Orchestra; Chicago Musical Union; Gürzenichkonzerte (Cologne).
Festivals: Handel Festival (Crystal Palace, London).
Educational: American Academy of Music (Philadelphia); Imperial Academy of Music (Rio de Janeiro); Peabody Conservatory of Music (Baltimore); Stuttgart Musikschule.
Music Publishers: Forsyth Brothers, Ltd. (Manchester); Gebethner und Spólka (Warsaw); W. W. Kimball Co. (Chicago).
Music Publications: *La Maîtrese* (Paris); *Ruch Muzyczny* (Poland).
Performing Centers: Santiago (Chile) Municipal Theater; Teatro Colón (Buenos Aires).
Others: Friedrich Ehrbar Organ Factory (Vienna); Hohner Harmonica Factory (Trossingen); Keller's Patent Steam Violin Manufactory (Philadelphia); George Steck and Co., piano makers (New York); Charles Taphouse and Son, Ltd., music dealers (Oxford); John F. Stratton Brass Instrument Factory (New York).

H. Musical Literature

Michael Balfe, *A New Universal Method of Singing*; Francis J. Child, *English and Scottish Popular Ballads*; Luther Emerson, *The Golden Wreath*; Joséphine Fodor-Mainvielle, *Réflexions et conseils sur l'art du chant*; Jacques Halévy, *Leçons de lecture musicale*; Karl G. Hering, *Methodischer leitfaden für violinlehrer*, Louis Niedermeyer/Joseph d'Ortigue, *Traité théorique et pratique de l'accompagnement du plain-chant*; Josef Proksch, *Allgemeine musiklehre*; Edward Rimbault, *The Organ, Its History and Construction*; Wojciech Sowinski, *Musiciens polonais et slaves, anciens et modernes*; William Viner, *The Chanter's Companion*.

I. Musical Compositions

Chamber Music:
String Quartets: Alexander Boëly, *Four Quartets, Opus 27–30*; Joachim Raff, *No. 2 in A, Opus 90*; Louis Spohr, *Quartet in g, Opus 157*.
Sonata/Solos: Alkan, *Sonate de concert, Opus 47* (cello, piano); Alexander Boëly, *Two Violin Sonatas, Opus 32*; Anton Rubinstein, *Cello Sonata No. 2 in G, Opus 39*.
Ensembles: Franz Berwald, *Piano Quintet No. 2 in A*; Félicien David, *Three Piano Trios (E♭, d, c)*; Ludvig Norman, *Piano Quartet in E, Opus 10*; Anton Rubinstein, *Piano Trio in B♭, Opus 32*.
Piano: Alkan, *Twelve Etudes in Minor Keys, Opus 39–Three Marches, Opus 40* (four hands)–*Three Petite fantaisies, Opus 41–Réconciliation, Opus 42*; Alexander Boëly, *Twenty-Four Pieces, Opus 20*;

Félicien David, *Six esquisses symphoniques*; Louis Moreau Gottschalk, *Souvenir of Puerto Rico*; Modest Mussorgsky, *Souvenirs d'enfance*; Joachim Raff, *Suite in a, Opus 69–Suite in C, Opus 71– Suite in e, Opus 72*; Julius Reubke, *Sonata*; Anton Rubinstein, *Six Pieces (g, B♭, a, D♭, F, B♭), Opus 51–Six Preludes and Fugues in Free Style, Opus 53*.

Organ: Johannes Brahms, *Prelude and Fugue in g*; Julius Reubke, *Sonata*; Camille Saint-Saëns, *Fantaisie in E♭*.

Choral/Vocal Music:

Choral: Peter Benoit, *Le meurtre d'Abel* (cantata); Georges Bizet, *Cloris et Clothilde* (cantata); Franz Liszt, *The Legend of St. Elizabeth* (oratorio); Carl Loewe, *Der Friede–Regenlied*; George Macfarren, *May Day* (cantata); Giovanni Pacini, *Sant' Agnese* (oratorio); Carl Reinecke, *Ein geistliches Abendlied, Opus 50*(?); George Frederick Root, *The Haymakers* (cantata); Louis Spohr, *Requiem* (unfinished); Ambroise Thomas, *Messe Solennelle*.

Vocal: César Cui, *Three Songs, Opus 3*; J. H. Hopkins, *We Three Kings of Orient Are* (carol); Carl Loewe, *Three Ballads, Opus 129*; J. S. Pierpont, *Jingle Bells*; Richard Wagner, *Wesendonck Songs*.

Musical Stage: Michael Balfe, *The Rose of Castille*; George Bizet, *Doctor Miracle*; Félicien David, *Le fermier de Franconville*(?); Léo Delibes, *Maître Griffard*; Friedrich von Flotow, *Johann Albrecht bon Mechlenburg–Pianella*; Richard Genée, *Der Geiger aus Tirol*; Teodulo Mabellini, *Fiammetta*; Victor Massé, *Le cousin de Marivaux*; Saverio Mercadante, *Pelagio*; Mihály Mosonyi, *Kaiser Max auf der Martinswand*; Jacques Offenbach, *Croquefer–Dragonette–Une demoiselle en loterie–Les deux pêcheurs*; Giovanni Pacini, *Niccolò de Lapi*; Achille Peri, *Vittore Pisani*; Joachim Raff, *Samson*; Lucien Southard, *Omano*; Ambroise Thomas, *Psyché–Le carnaval de Venise*; Giuseppe Verdi, *Simon Boccanegra*.

Orchestra/Band Music:

Concerted Music:

Piano: Joachim Raff, *Ode au printemps in G, Opus 76*.

Violin: Joseph Joachim, *Concerto in d, "in ungarischer weise," Opus 11*; Anton Rubinstein, *Concerto in G, Opus 48*.

Program Music: Franz Liszt, *Die Ideale–The Battle of the Huns*; Bedřich Smetana, *Richard II, Opus 11*.

Standard Works: Mily Balakirev, *Overture on a Spanish March Theme*; Johannes Brahms, *Serenade No. 1 in D, Opus 11*; Friedrich von Flotow, *Jubel Overture*; William Henry Fry, *Overture, World's Own*; J. P. E. Hartmann, *Overture, Axel og Valborg*; Stanislaw Moniuszko, *Military Overture*; Carl Reinecke, *Dame Kobold Overture, Opus 51*.

Symphonies: Louis Spohr, *No. 10 in E♭*.

1858

❄

Historical Highlights: The India Act passed by the British Parliament makes India a Crown Colony—Sepoy Rebellion ceases; Cyrus Field lays the first Atlantic Cable, which soon breaks; the Treaties of Tientsin end the British-Chinese war and opens China for exploitation by the European powers; in the United States, Minnesota becomes state number thirty-two; Denver, Colorado, is founded; a stagecoach line is established between St. Louis and San Francisco.

Art and Literature Highlights: Births—artists Lovis Corinth, Robert W. Vonnoh, writers Selma Lagerlöf, Charles Chesnutt; Deaths—artist Hezekiah Auger, writers James Nelson Barker, Joseph B. Cobb, William Trotter Porter. Art—Bierstadt's *Yosemite Valley*, Daubigny's *Le Printemps*, Stanley's *Disputed Shot*; Literature—Busch's *Max und Moritz*, Holmes' *The Autocrat at the Breakfast Table*, Turgenev's *A Nest of Gentlefolk*.

Musical Highlights

A. Births

Composers: Paul Dresser (U.S.A.) April 22; Guy d'Hardelot (Mrs. W. I. Rhodes-France)(?); Georges Hüe (France) May 6; Frank Lynes (U.S.A.) May 16; Chauncey Olcott (U.S.A.) June 21; Giacomo Puccini (Italy) December 22; Ethel Smyth (England) April 22.

Conductors: Siegfried Ochs (Germany) April 19; E. T. Paull (U.S.A.); Karl Pohlig (Germany) February 10; Romualdo Sapio (Italy) September 8; Frank Van der Stucken (U.S.A.) October 15.

Singers: Emma Calvé (French soprano) August 15; Ben Grey Davies (British tenor) January 6; Hermann Devries (American bass) December 25; Wilhelm Grüning (German tenor) November 2; Medea Mei-Figner (Italian-born soprano) April 3; Alessandro Moreschi (Italian castrato soprano) November 11; Carl Nebe (German bass); Eugène Oudin (American baritone) February 24; Karl Perron (German bass-baritone) July 15; Antonio Pini-Corsi (Italian baritone) June; Marcella Sembrich (Polish soprano) February 15; Zaré Thalberg (British soprano) April 16; Marie Van Zandt (American soprano) October 8; Ludwig Wüllner (German vocalist) June 19.

Performers: Stanislaw Barcewicz (Polish violinist/conductor) April 16; Edward Shippen Barnes (American organist/composer) September 14; Jenö Hubay (Hungarian violinist) September 15; Bruno Oscar Klein (German-born pianist/organist) June 6; Peter Christian Lutkin (American organist) May 27; Tobias Matthay (British pianist) February 19; Harry Rowe Shelley (American organist) June 8; Eugène Ysaÿe (Belgian violinist) July 16.

Others: Camille Bellaigue (French music critic) May 24; Michel Brenet (French musicologist) April 12; Frank W. Burdett (American publisher) October 29; Arnold Dolmetsch (French-born music scholar/instrumentalist) February 24; Francis W. Galpin (British music author) December 25; Max Hesse (German publisher) February 18; Frank Holton (American brass instrument maker) March 10; Carl Stoeckel (American patron of the arts) December 7; Luigi Torchi (Italian musicologist) November 7.

B. **Deaths**

Composers: Pauline Duchambge (France) April 23; Alexander L. Gurilov (Russia) September 12; Johanna Kinkell (Germany) November 15; Joseph-Henri Mees (Belgium) December 18; Isaac Baker Woodbury (U.S.A.) October 26.

Conductors: Bernard Sarrette (France) April 11.

Singers: Kathinka Heinefetter (German soprano) December 20; Bianchi Jackson (Lacy) (British soprano) May 19; Luigi Lablache (Italian bass) January 23.

Performers: William Ayrton (British organist/critic) March 8; Francis Edward Bache (British pianist) August 24; Henri-Louis Blanchard (French violinist/critic) December 18; Alexandre Pierre Boëly (French organist/composer) December 27; Johann Baptist Cramer (German pianist) April 16; Karel Frant Pitsch (Bohemian organist) June 13; William Horsley (British organist) June 12; Sigismund von Neukomm (Austrian pianist) April 3; Julius Reubke (German pianist/composer) June 3.

Others: Siegfried Dehn (German music theorist) April 12; Anton Diabelli (Austrian publisher/composer) April 8; Johanna Theodor Mosewius (German musicologist/conductor) September 15; Alexander Dmitrievich Oulibicheff (Russian music author) February 5.

C. **Debuts**

Singers: Georg Ephraim Arlberg (Swedish baritone—Stockholm); Gabrielle Krauss (Austrian soprano—Berlin); John Patey (British baritone—London); Myron Whitney (American bass—Boston).

Performers: Carlo Andreoli (Italian pianist—Milan); Benjamin Lang (American pianist—Boston); Sebastian Bach Mills (British pianist—Leipzig); Raoul Pugno (French pianist—Paris); Carl Tausig (Polish pianist—Berlin).

D. **New Positions**

Conductors: Luigi Arditi (Her Majesty's Theatre, London); Leopold Damrosch (Breslau PO); Otto von Königslöw (Gürzenich Orchestra, Cologne); Ignaz Lachner (Stockholm Court); Eduard Lassen (kapellmeisgter, Weimar); Anton Rubinstein (St. Petersburg Court).

Others: Franz Espagne (head, music division, Berlin Royal Library); Filippo Filippi (editor, *Gazzetta Musicale*); César Franck (organ, Ste. Clothilde, Paris); Josef Krejči (director, Prague Organ School); Louis Lefébure-Wély (organ, St. Sulpice); Karl Mikuli (director, Lvov Conservatory); Carl Reinthaler (organ, Bremen Cathedral).

E. Prizes/Honors
Prizes: Samuel David (Prix de Rome).
Honors: Thomas Hastings (doctorate, New York University).

F. Biographical Highlights
Mily Balakirev suffers from encephalitis; Alexander Borodin receives his doctorate in chemistry from the St. Petersburg Academy of Medicine; Max Bruch begins teaching violin in Cologne; Edvard Grieg, on the advice of Ole Bull, goes to the Leipzig Conservatory for further music study; Modest Mussorgsky resigns his cadet commission in order to concentrate on music; John Knowles Paine studies music in Berlin; Richard Wagner goes to Venice as Minna leaves for Germany.

G. Cultural Beginnings
Performing Groups—Choral: Edinburgh Royal Choral Union; Metropolitan Choral Society of Toronto; Milwaukee Liedertafel; Vienna Singverein.
Performing Groups—Instrumental: Hallé Orchestra (Manchester); Popular Concerts of Chamber Music (London).
Festivals: Worcester Music Festival (Massachusetts).
Educational: Vienna Academy of Music.
Music Publishers: Matthias Gray Co. (San Francisco); Louis Grunewald (New Orleans); Root and Cady (Chicago); Russell and Tolman (Boston).
Music Publications: *Dalibor*.
Performing Centers: Covent Garden Theater III; St. James Hall (London).
Others: Musical Society of London.

H. Musical Literature
François Bazin, *Cours d'harmonie théorique et pratique*; Heinrich Bellermann, *Die Mensuralnoten und Taktzeichen*; William B. Bradbury, *The Jubilee*; François Fétis, *Mémoire sur l'harmonie simultanée*; Karl Gollmick, *Handlexicon der Tonkunst*; Louis Köhler, *Systematische Lehrmethode für Klavierspiel und Musik*; Carl Kosmaly, *Über die anwendung des programm mes zur erklärung musikalischen compositionen*; Adolph Kullak, *Das musikalisch-schöne*; Alexei Lvov, *On Free or Non-Symmetrical Rhythm*; Ferdinand Sieber, *Vollständiges lehrbuch der gesangkunst für Lehrer und Schüler*; Samuel Tuckerman, *A Collection of Cathedral Chants*.

I. Musical Compositions
Chamber Music:
String Quartets: Peter Benoit, *No. 4.*

Sonata/Solos: Joachim Raff, *Violin Sonata No. 2 in A, Opus 78;* Anton Rubinstein, *Cello Sonata No. 2 in G, Opus 39.*

Piano: Alexandre Boëly, *Twenty-Four Pieces, Opus 22;* Louise Farrenc, *Twelve Étude brillantes, Opus 41–Mélodie, Opus 43–Scherzo, Opus 47;* Stephen Heller, *Three Nocturnes, Opus 91–Three Eklogen, Opus 92;* Modeste Mussorgsky, *Scherzo in c♯;* Anton Rubinstein, *Six Characteristic Pictures, Opus 26* (four hands)–*Hungarian Fantasia.*

Organ: Louis Lefébure-Wély, *Meditaciones Religiosas;* César Franck, *Andantino in g–Five Pieces for Harmonium;* Camille Saint-Saëns, *Procession in C.*

Choral/Vocal Music:
Choral: Johannes Brahms, *Ave Maria, Opus 12–Begräbnisgesang, Opus 13;* Félicien David, *The Last Judgment* (oratorio); Samuel David, *Jephté* (cantata); César Franck, *Messe Solennelle in B;* Niels Gade, *Frühlings-Botschaft, Opus 35–Baldur's Dream* (cantatas); Johan P. Hartmann, *The Dryad's Wedding, Opus 60* (cantata); Ferdinand Hiller, *Saul, Opus 80* (oratorio); Giovanni Pacini, *La distruzione di Gerusalemme* (oratorio); Joachim Raff, *Wachet auf, Opus 80;* Anton Rubinstein, *Paradise* (oratorio); Camille Saint-Saëns, *Oratorio de Noël.*

Vocal: Johannes Brahms, *Eight Songs and Romances, Opus 15–Five Poems, Opus 19–Fourteen Children's Folksongs–Twenty-Eight German Folksongs.*

Musical Stage: Michael Balfe, *Satanella;* Hector Berlioz, *Les Troyens;* Max Bruch, *Scherz, List und Rache;* Peter Cornelius, *The Barber of Bagdad;* César Cui, *The Prisoner of the Caucasus;* François Gevaert, *Quentin Durward;* Charles Gounod, *Le médecin malgré lui;* Jacques Halévy, *La magicienne;* Heinrich Marschner, *Sangeskönig Hiarne;* Stanislaw Moniuszko, *The Raftsman;* Emil Naumann, *Judith;* Jacques Offenbach, *Orpheus in the Underworld–Mesdames de la Halle;* Giovanni Pacini, *Il saltimbanco;* Errico Petrella, *Jone;* Charles Vogel, *Le Nid de Cigognes.*

Orchestra/Band Music:
Concerted Music:
Piano: Johannes Brahms, *Concerto No. 1 in d, Opus 15;* Anton Rubinstein, *Concerto No. 2 in F, Opus 35;* Camille Saint-Saëns, *Concerto No. 1 in D, Opus 17.*

Violin: Camille Saint-Saëns, *Concerto No. 2 in C, Opus 58.*

Ballet/Incidental Music: Joachim Raff, *Barnhard von Weimar* (IM).

Program Music: Franz Liszt, *Hamlet.*

Standard Works: Mily Balakirev, *Overture on Three Russian Themes;* Peter Benoit, *Danses des spectres;* J. P. E. Hartmann, *Overture to Cor-*

reggio, Opus 59; Johann Kalliwoda, *Concert Overture No. 15 in E, Opus 226*; Franz Liszt, *Huldigungs Marsch*; Henri Litolff, *Overture, Chant des Belges, Opus 101*; Modeste Mussorgsky, *Scherzo in B♭*; Johann Strauss, Jr., *Tritsch-Tratsch Polka–Champagne Polka*.
Symphonies: George Frederick Bristow, *No. 3 in f♯*; Ludvig Norman, *No. 1 in F for Strings, Opus 22*.

1859
❅

Historical Highlights: The Franco-Italian War with Austria comes to an end; the German National Association seeks to form a Germany united under the leadership of Prussia; work begins on the Suez Canal; in the United States, the first successful oil well is drilled in Titusville, Pennsylvania; discovery of silver in Nevada and gold in Colorado causes a new rush for the West; Oregon becomes state number thirty-three; the Pawnee War takes place in the Nebraska Territory.

Art and Literature Highlights: Births—artists Childe Hassam, Maurice Prendergast, Georges Seurat, writers Arthur Conan Doyle, E. A. Housman; Deaths—writers Washington Irving, Alexis de Touqueville. Art—Bierstadt's *Thunderstorm in the Rockies*, Fantin-Latour's *The Two Sisters*, Miller's *The Indian Lodge*; Literature—Boucicault's *The Octaroon*, Dickens' *A Tale of Two Cities*, Eliot's *Adam Bede*, Tennyson's *Idylls of the King*.

Musical Highlights

A. Births
Composers: Reginald De Koven (U.S.A.) April 3; Josef Bohuslav Foerster (Czechoslovakia) December 30; Victor Herbert (U.S.A.) February 1; Mikhail Ippolitov-Ivanov (Russia) November 19; Nikolai Alexandrovich Sokolov (Russia) March 26.
Conductors: Camille Chevillard (France) October 14; Frank Damrosch (Germany) June 22; Karl Muck (Germany) October 22.
Singers: Francesco d'Andrade (Portugese baritone) January 11; Andrew Black (Scottish baritone) January 15; Léon Escalaïs (French tenor) August 8; Medea Figner (Italian soprano) April 4; Emilie Herzog (Swiss soprano) December 17; Emma Nevada (American soprano) February 7; Jean Noté (Belgian baritone) May 6; Karl Scheidemantel (German baritone) January 21; Juliette Simon-Girard (French soprano) May 8.
Performers: Charles Hubert Farnsworth (American organist) November 29; Arthur Friedheim (German pianist) October 26; Willy Hess (German violinist) July 14; Victor Küzdö (Hungarian violinist) September 19; Winthrop Smith Sterling (American organist) No-

vember 28; Bertha Feiring Tapper (Norwegian-born pianist) January 25; Richard Henry Warren (American organist/composer) September 17.

Others: Jules Combarieu (French music historian) February 4; W. H. Flood (Irish music historian) November 1; Hugo Goldschmidt (German musicologist) September 19; W. H. Hadow (British music author/composer) November 1; Robert Hope-Jones (British organ builder) February 9; Charles F. Lummis (American ethnomusicologist) March 1; Henry W. Savage (American impresario) March 21; Cecil Sharp (British folksong collector) November 22; Emil Vogel (German musicologist) January 21.

B. Deaths
Composers: Luigi Ricci (Italy) December 31; Carl Gottlob Reissiger (Germany) November 7; Louis Spohr (Germany) October 22.
Conductors: Antonio d'Antoni (Italy) August 18; Philippe Musard (France) March 30; Carl Gottlieb Reissiger (Germany) November 7; Joseph Hartmann Stuntz (Germany) June 18.
Singers: Angiolina Bosio (Italian soprano) April 13; Christian Wilhelm Fischer (German bass) November 4; Anton Forti (Austrian tenor/baritone) June 16; Nicola Tacchinardi (Italian tenor) March 14.
Performers: Henry Forbes (British organist) November 24; Charles Hart (British organist) March 29; Charles Knyvett, Jr. (British organist) November 2.
Others: John Abbey (British organ builder) February 19; Ignaz Bösendorfer (Austrian piano maker) April 14; Edward Holmes (British music critic) August 28.

C. Debuts
Singers: Marie Luise Dustmann (German soprano—Breslau); Célestine Galli-Marié (French mezzo-soprano—Strasbourg); Pauline Lucca (Austrian soprano—Olmütz); Danica Mastilović (Yugoslavian soprano—Frankfurt); Angelo Neumann Austrian tenor—Berlin); Francesco Pandolfini (Italian baritone—Pisa); Adelina Patti (Spanish soprano—New York); Zélia Trebelli (French mezzo-soprano—Madrid).

D. New Positions
Conductors: Johann Herbeck (Gesellschaft der Musikfreunde, Vienna); Hermann Levi (Saarbrücken); Anton Rubinstein (Russian Musical Society).
Others: Immanuel Faisst (director, Stuttgart Conservatory); Filippo Filippi (music critic, *Perseveranza*); Edwin Monk (organ, York Minster); Carl Reinecke (music director, Breslau University).

E. **Prizes/Honors**
Prizes: Ernest Guiraud (Prix de Rome); Jean-Théodore Radoux (Prix de Rome).

F. **Biographical Highlights**
Johannes Brahms, given a women's chorus to conduct in Hamburg, fails in his endeavor; Jullien, returning to Paris, is arrested and imprisoned for his outstanding debts—dies shortly thereafter in an insane asylum; Ebenezer Prout gives up teaching for music; Pablo Sarasate begins a concert tour of Europe; Peter Tchaikovsky graduates from the School of Jurisprudence in St. Petersburg and becomes a government clerk; Theodore Thomas begins his conducting career; Giuseppe Verdi and Giuseppina Strepponi are finally married; Richard Wagner, moving to Paris, is rejoined by Minna.

G. **Cultural Beginnings**
Performing Groups—Choral: French Opera Co. of New Orleans; Richings Grand Opera Co.
Performing Groups—Instrumental: Concerts Spirituales (Madrid); Gilmore's Grand Band (Boston); Imperial Russian Music Society (St. Petersburg).
Festivals: Welsh Music Festival (Aberdare).
Educational: Florentine Liceo Musicale; Tourjée Musical Institute (Rhode Island).
Music Publishers: John Church and Co. (Philadelphia); Elkan and Schildknecht (Stockholm); Gebauer Music Publishers (Bucharest); Giudici and Strada (Turin).
Music Publications: *Le Plain-Chant*; *Revue Fantaiste*; *Peter's Sax-Horn Journal*; *The Southern Musical Advocate and Singer's Friend*.
Performing Centers: Aberdeen Music Hall; French Opera House (New Orleans); Gothenburg Grand Theater; Viktoria Theater (Berlin).
Others: Förster Piano Co. (Lobau, Germany); Gutheil Music House (Moscow); J. H./C. S. Odell, organ builders (New York).

H. **Musical Literature**
Hector Berlioz, *Les Grotesques de la musique*; Jean G. Bertrand, *Histoire ecclésiastique de l'orgue*; Siegfried Dehn, *Lehre vom Kontrapunkt, dem Kanon und der Fuge*; Christian Hohmann, *Praktische Orgelschule*; Moritz Karasowski, *History of Polish Opera*; Julius Knorr, *Ausführliche Klaviermethode*; Franz Liszt, *Des bohémiens et de leur musique en Hongrie*; Johann C. Lobe, *Aus dem leben eines musikers*; Józef Poniatowski, *Le progrès de la musique dramatique*; Ernst F. Richter, *Lehrbuch der Fuge*; Eduard de Sobolewski, *Das Geheimnis der neuester Schule der Musik*.

I. Musical Compositions

Chamber Music:

String Quartets: Peter Benoit, *Quartet in D*; Edouard Lalo, *Quartet in E♭, Opus 19* (revised 1880 as *Opus 45*); John Knowles Paine, *Quartet in D, Opus 5*

Sonata/Solos: Henri Vieuxtemps, *Three Mährchen, Opus 34–Six Morceaux, Opus 85* (violin, piano).

Ensembles: Carl Goldmark, *Piano Trio No. 1 in B♭, Opus 6*; Anton Rubinstein, *String Quintet in F, Opus 59*.

Piano: Alkan, *Three Minuets, Opus 51–Paraphrase, Super flumina Babylonis, Opus 52–Two Nocturnes, Opus 57–Deux petites pièces, Opus 60–Nocturne No. 4, "Le grillon"*; Carl Goldmark, *Sturm und Drang, Nine Characteristic Pieces, Opus 5*; Louis Moreau Gottschalk, *Souvenir de la Havane*; Stephen Heller, *Two Waltzes, Opus 93*; Ferdinand Hiller, *Sonata No. 3 in g, Opus 78*; Franz Liszt, *Prelude, "Weinen, Klagen, Sorgen, Zagen"*; John Knowles Paine, *Sonata No. 1 in a, Opus 1*; Joachim Raff, *Twelve Pieces, Opus 75–Twelve morceaux, Opus 83* (four hands)–*Suite in D, Opus 91*.

Organ: Antonin Dvořák, *Preludes and Fugues*; César Franck, *Trois antiennes*; John Knowles Paine, *Prelude and Fugue in g*; Camille Saint-Saëns, *Bénédiction nuptiale, Opus 9–Six morceaux–Offertoire in D–Communion in E♭*.

Choral/Vocal Music:

Choral: Michael Balfe, *Nelly Grey* (cantata); Johannes Brahms, *Marienlieder, Opus 22*; Samuel David, *La Génie de la Terre*; Antonin Dvořák, *Mass in B♭*; Robert Franz, *Six Lieder for Male Voices, Opus 32*; Jacques Halévy, *Italie* (cantata); William Jackson, *The Year* (cantata); Franz Liszt, *The Beatitudes* (cantata)–*Psalm 23–Psalm 37*; Carl Loewe, *Das hohe lied von Salomonis* (oratorio); Stanislaw Moniuszko, *Ballad of Florian the Grey*.

Vocal: William B. Bradbury, *Sweet Hour of Prayer* (hymn); Johannes Brahms, *Five Songs, Opus 19*; Charles Gounod, *Ave Maria* (on Bach's *Prelude No. 1*); Carl Loewe, *Liedergabe, Opus 130–Five Songs, Opus 145*(?).

Musical Stage: Daniel Auber, *Magenta*; Peter Benoit, *Le roi des Aulnes*; Georges Bizet, *Don Procopio*; César Cui, *The Mandarin's Son*; Félicien David, *Herculanum*; Léo Delibes, *La fille du golfe–L'omeletté à la Follembuche*; Friedrich von Flotow, *La veuve Grapin*; François Gevaert, *Le diable au moulin*; Louis Moreau Gottschalk, *Escenas Campestres*; Charles Gounod, *Faust*; Giacomo Meyerbeer, *Le pardon de Ploërmel*; Jacques Offenbach, *Geneviève de Brabant–Un mari à la porte–Les vivandières de la grande armée*; Carlo Pedrotti, *Isabella d'Aragona*; Errico Petrella, *Il duca di Scilla*; Giuseppe Verdi, *The Masked Ball*; Richard Wagner, *Tristan und Isolde*.

Orchestra/Band Music:
Concerted Music:
  Violin: Camille Saint-Saëns, *Concerto No. 1 in A, Opus 20.*
Ballet/Incidental Music: Friedrich von Flotow, *Wintermärchen* (IM).
Program Music: George Bizet, *Vasco da Gama.*
Standard Works: Johannes Brahms, *Serenade No. 2 in A, Opus 16;*
César Cui, *Tarantella for Orchestra;* Giacomo Meyerbeer, *Schiller Centenary March.*
Symphonies: Louis Moreau Gottschalk, *No. 1, "A Night in the Tropics";* Camille Saint-Saëns, *No. 2 in a, Opus 55.*

1860
❄

Historical Highlights: The Second Maori War ushers in ten years of strife in New Zealand; Vladivostok, Siberia, is founded; the U.S. Census indicates a population of 31,443,000; Abraham Lincoln is elected as sixteenth president; the first and only convention of the Constitutional Union Party is held; the Pony Express begins its short life between St. Joseph, Missouri, and Sacramento, California.

Art and Literature Highlights: Births—writers James Barrie, Anton Chekhov, Hamlin Garland, Owen Wister; Deaths—artists Charles Fraser, Rembrandt Peale, authors James K. Paulding, Arthur Schopenhauer. Art—Manet's *The Spanish Guitar Player,* Blythe's *The Postoffice,* Johnson's *Corn Husking;* Literature—Eliot's *The Mill on the Floss,* Hawthorne's *Marble Faun,* Swinburne's *The Queen Mother,* Whittier's *Home Ballads, Poems and Lyrics.*

Musical Highlights

A. Births
  Composers: Isaac Albéniz (Spain) May 29; Gustave Charpentier (France) June 25; Pietro Floridia (Italy) May 5; Alberto Franchetti (Italy) September 18; Francesco Paolo Frontini (Italy) August 6; Céleste de Longpré Heckscher (U.S.A.) February 23; Gustav Mahler (Austria) July 7; Emil Nicolaus von Reznicek (Austria) May 4; William Wallace (Scotland) July 3; Hugo Wolf (Germany) March 13.
  Conductors: Cleofonte Campanini (Italy) September 1.
  Singers: Mario Ancona (Italian baritone) February 28; Alexander Bandrowski-Sas (Polish tenor) April 22; Lola Beeth (Polish-born soprano) November 23; Hariclea Darclée (Romanian soprano) June 10; Jessie Bartlett Davis (American contralto); Fernando De Lucia (Italian tenor) October 11; Pelagie Greef-Andriessen (Austrian soprano) June 20; Dora Henninges (American mezzo-soprano) Au-

gust 2; Lillian Bailey Henschel (American soprano) January 17; Vilém Hes (Czech bass) July 3; Félia Litvinne (Russian soprano) August 31; Eugenia Mantelli (Italian mezzo-soprano); Luise Reuss-Belce (Austrian soprano) October 24; Francisco Signorini (Italian tenor).

Performers: Laura Valborg Aulin (Swedish pianist) January 9; Otto Barblan (Swiss organist/conductor) March 22; Ludwig Holm (Danish violinist/composer); Edward MacDowell (American pianist/composer) December 18; Ignace Jan Paderewski (Polish pianist) November 18; Emilio Pente (Italian violinist) October 16; Alfred George Robyn (American organist) April 29; Wallace Arthur Sabin (British-born organist) December 15.

Others: Georges Houdard (French music author) March 30; Josef Mantuani (Austrian music scholar) March 28; Arthur Prüfer (German musicologist) July 7; Théodore Reinach (French musicologist) July 3; Heinrich Rietsch (Austrian musicologist) September 22; Richard Wallaschek (Austrian music theorist) November 16.

B. Deaths

Composers: Karl Binder (Austria) November 5; Friedrich Silcher (Germany) August 26.

Conductors: Louis Jullien (France) March 14; Carl Friedrich Zöllner (Germany) September 25.

Singers: Julius Cornet (Austrian tenor/author) October 2; Nanette Schechner-Waagen (German soprano) April 29; Wilhemine Schröder-Devrient (German soprano) Janury 26.

Performers: Ludwig Böhner (German pianist) March 28; George Bridgetower (Polish violinist) February 29; Céleste Couperin (French pianist/composer) February 14; Friedrich Dotzauer (German cellist) March 6; Stephen Elvey (British organist) October 6; Paul Emile Johns (Polish-born pianist/publisher) August 10.

Others: Ludwig Rellstab (German music author/poet) November 27.

C. Debuts

Singers: Peter van der Bilt (Dutch baritone—Amsterdam); Patricia Brooks (American soprano—New York); Viorica Cortez (Romanian soprano—Iasi); Isabella Galleti-Gianoli (Italian soprano—Brescia); Melitta Otto (German soprano-Dresden); Guido Papini (Italian violinist—Florence); Janet Patey Scottish contralto—Birmingham); Angela Peralta (Mexican soprano—Mexico City); Emil Scaria (Austrian bass—Pest); Sophie Stehle (German soprano—Munich).

D. New Positions

Conductors: Hans Balatka (Chicago Philharmonic Society); Joaquim Casimiro Júnior (mestre de capela, Lisbon Cathedral); Otto Dessoff

(Vienna Court Orchestra); Pierre-Louis Dietsch (Paris Opera); Karl Eckert (Stuttgart Court Opera); Julius Otto Grimm (Münster SO); Angelo Mariani (Teatro Communale, Bologna); Carl Reinecke (Leipzig Gewandhaus Orchestra); Théophile Tilmant (Concerts du Conservatoire de Paris); Johannes Verhulst (Diligentia Concerts, The Hague).

Others: Ernst Naumann (music director, University of Jena); Joseph Rheinberger (organ, St. Michael's, Munich); Otto Scherzer (music director, Tübinger University); Charles Marie Widor (organ, St. François, Lyons).

E. **Prizes/Honors**
   Prizes: Emile Paladilhe (Prix de Rome).

F. **Biographical Highlights**
   Edvard Grieg suffers a nervous breakdown and pleurisy, which leaves him a cripple for life; Clara Novello gives her farewell performance in London and retires to Italy; Giuseppe Verdi is elected a deputy to the first Italian National Parliament; Richard Wagner is given amnesty in all German states except Saxony—he writes his Paris version of *Tannhauser*.

G. **Cultural Beginnings**
   Performing Groups—Choral: Amateur Musical Society of Hawaii; Asociatión Artistico-Musical de Socorros Mutuos (Madrid); Canterbury Vocal Union (New Zealand); Duitse Opera (Rotterdam); Märkischen Zentral-Sängerbund (Berlin); Musik-Dilettantenverein (Bayreuth); San Francisco Oratorio Society; Société des Concerts de Chant Classique (Paris).
   Performing Groups—Instrumental: Boulogne Philharmonic Society; Dodsworth Band (Washington, D.C.); Newark Harmonic Society; St. Louis Philharmonic II; Seventh Regiment Band (New York); Vienna Orchesterverein.
   Educational: Frankfurt Musikschule.
   Music Publishers: Blackmar Brothers (New Orleans); Hopwood and Crew (London); Elias Howe Publishing Firm II (Boston).
   Music Publications: *Boston Musical Times*; *Deutsche Musikzeitung*; *Zenészeti Lapok* (Hungary).
   Performing Centers: Marjinsky (Kirov) Theater (St. Petersburg).
   Other: Heintzman and Co., Ltd., piano makers (Toronto); Russian Musical Society.

H. **Musical Literature**
   Félix Clément, *Histoire générale de la Musique religieuse–Des diverses réformes du chant grégorien*; Charles Coussemaker, *Drames liturgiques de moyen-âge*; Antoine Elwart, *Histoire de la Société des concerts du Con-*

servatoire; Luther Emerson, *The Golden Harp*; Julius Knorr, *Ausführliche klaviermethode: Schule der mechanik*; George Macfarren, *The Rudiments of Harmony*; Théodore Nisard, *Le vrais principes de l'accompagnement du plain-chant*; Henry Oliver, *Oliver's Collection of Hymn and Psalm Tunes*; Charles Poisot, *History of Music in France*; Edward Riombault, *The Pianoforte: Its Origin, Progress and Construction*; Carl Weitzmann, *Harmonie-system*.

I. **Musical Compositions:**
Chamber Music:
String Quartets: Max Bruch, *No. 2 in E, Opus 10*; Karl Goldmark, *Quartet in D, Opus 8*.
Sonata/Solos: Ferdinand Hiller, *Suite in Canonic Form, Opus 86* (violin, piano); Joseph Joachim, *Variations über ein eigenes Theme, Opus 10* (viola, piano)(?).
Ensembles: Woldemar Bargiel, *Piano Trio No. 2 in E♭, Opus 20*; Johannes Brahms, *String Sextet No. 1 in B♭, Opus 18*; Carl Goldmark, *Piano Quintet, Opus 54*.
Piano: Peter Benoit, *Sonata in G*; Louis Moreau Gottschalk, *Grand Tarentelle*; Stephen Heller, *Grande étude, Opus 96–Allegro pastorale, Opus 95–Twelve Ländler and Waltzes, Opus 97*; Anton Rubinstein, *Soirées à Saint-Petersbourg, Opus 44*.
Organ: Ferdinand Alday, *Fantaisie de Salon, Opus 16*; John Knowles Paine, *Concert Variations on the Austrian Hymn, Opus 3/1–Variations on the Star-Spangled Banner, Opus 3/2*.
Choral/Vocal Music:
Choral: Peter Benoit, *Cantate de Noël*; Johannes Brahms, *Four Part-Songs for Women's Voices, Opus 17–Two Motets, Opus 29*; Anton Bruckner, *Psalm CXLVI in A*; César Cui, *Two Choruses, Opus 4*; César Franck, *Mass, Opus 12*; Robert Franz, *Psalm CXVII, Opus 19*; Johan P. Hartmann, *Six Songs for Male Voices, Opus 61*; Franz Liszt, *Psalm 18*; Carl Loewe, *Polus von Atella* (oratorio); George Macfarren, *Christmas* (cantata); George Frederick Root, *Belshazzar's Feast* (cantata); Bedřich Smetana, *Song of the Czechs* (cantata).
Vocal: Daniel Aubert, *O salutaris*; Johannes Brahms, *Three Duets, Opus 20*; Stephen Foster, *Old Black Joe*; Robert Franz, *Six Songs, Opus 9–Six Songs, Opus 10–Six Songs, Opus 12–Six Songs, Opus 14–Six Songs, Opus 17–Six Songs, Opus 18*(?); Carl Loewe, *Der Asra, Opus 133–Two Ballads, Opus 135–Legend, Der Traum der Witwe, Opus 142*.
Musical Stage: Daniel Auber, *La circassienne*; Michael Balfe, *Bianca*; Léo Delibes, *Monsieur de Bonne-Etoile*; François Gevaert, *Le château trompette*; Charles Gounod, *Philémon et Baucis–La colombe*; George Macfarren, *Robin Hood*; Louis Maillart, *Les pêcheurs de Catane*; Giacomo Meyerbeer, *La jeunesse de Goethe*; Stanislaw Moniuszko,

Verbum nobile–The Countess; Jacques Offenbach, *Daphnis et Chloé–Le carnaval des revues–Barkouf*; Giovanni Pacini, *Gianni di Nisida*; Achille Peri, *Giuditta*; Errico Petrella. *Morasina*; Józef Poniatowski, *Pierre de Médicis*; Camille Saint-Saëns, *Macbeth*; Franz von Suppé, *Tannhäuser–Das Pensionat*; Ambroise Thomas, *Le roman d'Elvire*.

Orchestra/Band Music:
Concerted Music:
  Violin: Henri Vieuxtemps, *Fantasia appassionata, Opus 35–Ballade and Polonaise, Opus 38*; Henry Wieniawski, *Légende, Opus 17*.
Ballet/Incidental Music: Jacques Offenbach, *Le Papillon* (B).
Program Music: Bedřich Smetana, *Wallingstein's Camp, Opus 14*.
Standard Works: William Henry Fry, *Evangeline Overture*; Louis Moreau Gottschalk, *Grand March*; Franz Liszt, *Two Episodes from Lenau's "Faust"*; Mihály Mosonyi, *Festival Music*; Ivo Petrić, *Concert Overture*; Albert Rubenson, *Symphonic Intermezzo*; Johann Strauss, Jr., *Perpetual Motion*.
Symphonies: Karl Goldmark, *Symphony in C*; Asger Hamerik, *Symphony in c* (lost); Léon C. Kreutzer, *Symphony in f*.

1861

❊

Historical Highlights: Czar Alexander II emancipates the Russian serfs; Victor Emmanuel II of Sardinia is crowned King of Italy—Italian unification begins; the American Civil War begins—the Battle of Bull Run takes place; West Virginia chooses to stay with the Union and secedes from Virginia; Kansas becomes state number thirty-four; the Dakota Territory is formed; Yale University awards the first Ph.D. to be given in America.

Art and Literature Highlights: Births—artists Émile Bourdelle, Cyrus Dallin, Aristide Maillol, Frederic Remington, authors Charles Loomis, Rabindranath Tagore; Deaths—artists Bass Otis, Samuel L. Waldo, author Elizabeth Browning. Art—Delacroix's *Lion Hunt*, Inness' *Delaware Water Gap*, Rimmer's *The Dying Centaur*; Literature—Dickens' *Great Expectations*, Dostoyevsky's *The House of the Dead*, Eliot's *Silas Marner*, Tolstoy's *Don Juan*.

Musical Highlights

A. Births
  Composers: Anton Arensky (Russia) July 12; Georgi Lvovich Catoire (Russia) April 27; Charles Martin Loeffler (France-U.S.A.) January 30; Ludwig Thuille (Austria) November 30.
  Conductors: Theodor Gerlach (Germany) June 25; Váša Suk (Czechoslovakia) November 16.

Singers: Albert Alvarez (French tenor) May 16; Vittorio Arimondi (Italian bass); Teresa Arkel (Austria); Sigrid Arnoldson (Swedish soprano) March 20; Jean-François Delmas (French bass-baritone) April 14; Leopold Demuth (Austrian baritone) November 2; Selma Kronold (Polish-born soprano) August 18; Lise Landouzy (French soprano); Nellie Melba (Australian soprano) May 19; Cécile Merquillier (French soprano); Joseph O'Mara (Irish tenor) July 16; Maurice Renaud (French baritone) July 24; Ernestine Schumann-Heink (Austrian soprano) June 15; Ernest Van Dyck (Belgian tenor) April 2.

Performers: Gustave Louis Becker (American pianist) May 22; Fanny Davies (British pianist) June 27; Clifford Curzon (British pianist) July 6; Nahan Franko (American violinist/conductor) July 23; M. H. van't Kruis (Dutch organist) March 8; Arthur Battelle Whiting (American pianist/composer) June 20; Huntington Woodman (American organist/composer) January 18.

Others: William Arms Fisher (American music author/editor) April 27; Lionel de La Laurencie (French musicologist) July 24.

B. Deaths

Composers: Per Conrad Boman (Sweden) March 17; Franz Gläser (Bohemia) August 29; Heinrich Marschner (Germany) December 14; Abraham Louis Niedermeyer (Switzerland) March 14.

Conductors: August Neithardts (Germany) August 18.

Singers: James Bland (British bass) July 17; Giuseppe Concone (Italian singing teacher/composer) June 1; Catherine Hayes (Irish soprano) October 11; Joseph Staudigl, Sr. (Austrian bass) March 28; Giovanni Battista Vellutti (Italian castrato soprano) January 22.

Performers: Christian Frederik Barth (Danish oboist) July 17; Carl Gottlieb Bellman (German organist) December 26; Johann Fredrik Berwald (Swedish violinist) August 26; Alexandre-Jean Boucher (French violinist) December 29; Hippolyte-André Chélard (French violinist/composer) February 12; Anthony Philip Heinrich (Czech-born violinist/composer) May 3; Julius Knorr (Germany pianist/pedagogue) June 17; Carl Lipínski (Polish violinist) December 16.

Others: Horace Meacham (American piano maker); Vincent Novello (British publisher) August 9; Carl Proske (German music scholar) December 20; Abbate Fortunato Santini (Italian music scholar) September 14.

C. Debuts

Singers: Renata Bruson (Italian baritone—Spoleto); Victor Capoul (French tenor—Paris); William Castle (British-born tenor—New York); Clara Kellogg (American soprano—New York); Jean Morère (French tenor—Paris); Carlotta Patti (Italian soprano—New York); Genevieve Ward (American soprano—London).

Performers: John Francis Barnett (British pianist—London).

D. New Positions
Conductors: Hermann Levi (German Opera, Rotterdam); Ludvig Norman (Stockholm Royal Orchestra).
Others: Samuel P. Jackson (organ, Church of the Ascension, New York); Apollinaire de Kontski (director, Warsaw Conservatory); Wilhelm Rust (organ, St. Luke's, Leipzig); Camille Saint-Saëns (piano, École Niedermeyer); Arthur Sullivan (organ, St. Michael's, London).

E. Prizes/Honors
Prizes: Théodore Dubois (Prix de Rome).
Honors: Robert Franz (Mus.Doc., Halle University); Jacques Offenbach (Legion of Honor); William Spark (doctorate, Dublin University).

F. Biographical Highlights
Emmanuel Chabrier begins working in the French Ministry of the Interior; Louis Moreau Gottschalk leaves the West Indies for the United States when the Civil War begins; Edvard Grieg returns to Leipzig for further music study; Jacques Offenbach resigns his position as manager of the Théâtre de la Gaîte; Bedrich Smetana resigns his Göteborg post and returns to Prague to lead the Nationalist movement in music.

G. Cultural Beginnings
Performing Groups—Choral: Akademischer Gesangverein (Munich); Biscacciante Opera Co. (San Francisco); Hlahol Choral Society (Prague Male Chorus); Yale University Glee Club.
Performing Groups—Instrumental: Concerts Populaire de Musique Classique (Paris); Denver (Colorado) City Band; Heidelberg Kammerorchester; Music Society of Victoria (Melbourne); Società del Quartetto di Firenze (Florence); Wuppertal Konzertgesellschaft.
Educational: Brooklyn Academy of Music; Katski (Kontski) Music Conservatory (Warsaw); London Royal Academy of Music; Orpheon Free Schools (New York); University of Edinburgh Music Department.
Music Publishers: P. I. Jurgensen (Moscow); Schreiner Music Store and Publishing Co. (Savannah, Georgia).
Music Publications: *Revue Musicale Suisse* (*Schweizerische Musikzeitung*).
Performing Centers: Frankfurt Concert Hall.
Other: Allgemeiner Deutscher Musikverein; American Cabinet Organ; Collection Litolff; Harrison and Harrrison, organ builders (Rochdale); Morris and Co. (London); Prix Chartier (Paris).

H. Musical Literature

Charles Battaille, *Nouvelles recherches sur la phonation*; William B. Bradbury, *Golden Chain of Sabbath School Melodies*; John Ella, *Musical Sketches Abroad and at Home*; Hilarión Eslava, *Escuela de armonía y composición*; Adolph Kullak, *Die ästhetik des klavierspiels*; Ferdinand Laurencin, *Die Harmonik der Neuzeit*; Johann C. Lobe, *Vereinfachte harmonielehre*; Joseph d'Ortigue, *La musique à l'église*; F. Palgrave, *Golden Treasury of Songs and Lyrical Poems I*; August Reissmann, *Das deutsche Lied in seiner historischen Entwicklung*; Augustin Savard, *Principes de la musique*; Carl Weitzmann, *Die neue harmonielehre im Streit mit der Alten*.

I. Musical Compositions
Chamber Music:
String Quartets: Edvard Grieg, *Quartet in d*.

Sonata/Solos: Louise Farrenc, *Violin Sonata in B♭, Opus 46*; Friedrich von Flotow, *Violin Sonata in A, Opus 14*.

Ensembles: Johannes Brahms, *Piano Quartet No. 1 in g, Opus 25*; Antonin Dvořák, *String Quintet in a, Opus 1*; Louise Farrenc, *Clarinet Trio in E♭, Opus 44*; Theodore Gouvy, *Piano Quintet*; Joachim Raff, *Piano Trio No. 1 in c, Opus 102*.

Piano: Alkan, *Sonatine, Opus 61–Chants, Set III, Opus 65*; Johannes Brahms, *Variations on a Theme by Schumann, Opus 23* (four hands)–*Variations and Fugue in B♭ on a Theme by Handel, Opus 24*; Edvard Grieg, *Vier Stücke, Opus 1*; Stephen Heller, *Four Fantasiestücke, Opus 99–Jagdstück, Opus 102–Polonaise No. 1, Opus 104*; John Knowles Paine, *Sonata in a/F♯*.

Organ: Alkan, *Treize prières, Opus 64*; Anton Bruckner, *Fugue in d*; John Knowles Paine, *Concert Variation on Old Hundred*.

Choral/Vocal Music:
Choral: Peter Benoit, *Mass*; Johannes Brahms, *Three Songs for Male Voices, Opus 42*; George Bristow, *Praise to God* (oratorio); Anton Bruckner, *Ave Maria* (a capella chorus); Théodore Dubois, *Atala* (cantata); Robert Franz, *Six Heine Lieder–Six Lieder, Opus 24*; Niels Gade, *The Holy Night, Opus 40* (cantata); Carl Loewe, *Johannes der Täufer* (oratorio); Saverio Mercadante, *Mass No. 3 for Male Voices*; Stanislaw Moniuszko, *Madonna*.

Vocal: Daniel Auber, *Pie Jesu*; Johannes Brahms, *Magelone Romances*; César Cui, *Six Songs, Opus 5*; John Dykes, *Nicaea* (hymn tune, "Holy, Holy, Holy"); Edvard Grieg, *Four Songs, Opus 2*; George F. Root, *The Vacant Chair*; Anton Rubinstein, *Three Partsongs for Male Voices, Opus 61–Six Partsongs, Opus 62–The Water Sprite, Opus 63*.

Music Stage: Michael Balfe, *The Puritan's Daughter*; Tommaso Benvenuti, *Guglielmo Shakespeare*; Hippolyte Chélard, *L'Aquila romana*;

Léo Delibes, *Les musiciens de l'orchestre–Les eaux d'Ems*; Ferenc Erkel, *Bánk- Bán*; François Gevaert, *Les deux amours*; Carlos Gomes, *Noite do Castello*; Mosonyi, *Pretty Helen*; Emil Naumann, *Die Mühlenhexe*; Jacques Offenbach, *La chanson de Fortunio–Apothécaire et perruquier–Le pont des soupirs*; Giovanni Pacini, *Belfegor–Il mulattiere di Toledo*; Carlo Pedrotti, *Mazeppa–Guerra in quattro*; Achille Peri, *L'espiazione*; Errico Petrella, *Virginia*; Amilcare Ponchielli, *La savojarda*; Józef Poniatowski, *Au travers du mur*; Louis Reyer, *La statue*; Anton Rubinstein, *Die Kinder der Heide*; Ambroise Thomas, *Gille et Gillotin*; Vincent Wallace, *The Amber Witch*.

Orchestra/Band Music:

Concerted Music:

Piano: Ferdinand Hiller, *Concerto No. 2 in f♯, Opus 69.*

Violin: Joseph Joachim, *Concerto in Hungarian Style, Opus 11;* Henri Vieuxtemps, *Concerto No. 5 in a, Opus 37.*

Ballet/Incidental Music: Mily Balakirev, *King Lear* (IM); Friedrich von Flotow, *Der Tanzkönig* (B); Johan P. Hartmann, *Valkyrien, Opus 62* (B); Arthur Sullivan, *The Tempest* (IM).

Standard Works: Georges Bizet, *Overture, La chasse d'Ossian–Scherzo and Funeral March in f*; George Bristow, *Columbus Overture, Opus 32*; Niels Gade, *Hamlet Overture, Opus 37–Michelangelo Overture, Opus 39*; Franz Lachner, *Suite No. 1 in d, Opus 113*; Giacomo Meyerbeer, *Krönumgsmarsch*.

Symphonies: Albert Becker, *Symphony in g*; Eduard Nápravnik, *No. 1*(?); Joseph Joachim Raff, *No. 1 in D, Opus 96, "An das Vaterland."*

1862

❄

Historical Highlights: Otto von Bismarck becomes chancellor of the new Prussia; Otto I of Greece resigns following a revolution and is succeeded by George I; Jean B. Foucault succeeds in measuring the speed of light; in the United States, the Battles of Shiloh, Antietam, and Bull Run II take place; the Monitor and the Merrimac engage in the first battle between iron-clad boats; slavery is outlawed in the District of Columbia; Congress creates the Medal of Honor.

Art and Literature Highlights: Births—artists Arthur Davies, Gustav Klimt, Edmund Tarbell, writers Maurice Maeterlinck, William S. Porter, Edith Wharton; Deaths—artists Charles Bird King, Karl Wimar, writers Ludwig Fulda, Bernhard Ingemann, Fitz Hugh O'Brien. Art—Daumier's *Third-Class Carriage,* Homer's *The Sharpshooter;* Literature—Browne's *Artemus Ward: His Book,* Flaubert's *Salammbó,* Hugo's *Les Misérables.*

Musical Highlights

A. Births

Composers: Edward Behm (Germany) April 8; Arturo Berutti (Italy-Argentina) March 27; Carrie Jacobs Bond (U.S.A.) August 11; Claude Achille Debussy (France) August 22; Frederick Delius (England) January 29; Alphons Diepenbrock (Holland) September 2; Louis Gaston Ganne (France) April 5; Edward German (England) February 17; Robert A. King (U.S.A.) September 20; Ethelbert Nevin (U.S.A.) November 25; Edmund Severn (England-U.S.A.) December 10; Alberto Williams (Argentina) November 23.

Conductors: Carl Busch (Denmark-U.S.A.) March 29; Walter Damrosch (Germany-U.S.A.) January 30; Karel Kovařovic (Czechoslovakia) December 9.

Singers: George Anthes (German tenor) March 12; Perry Averill (American baritone) June 11; Alice Barbi (Italian mezzo-soprano) June 1; Lola Beeth (Polish-born soprano) November 23; Lawrence Kellie (British tenor) April 3; Liza Lehmann (British soprano) July 11; Juan Lurie (Polish baritone) December 20; Zélie de Lussan (American soprano) December 21; Eva Tetrazzini (Italian soprano) March; Helena Theodorini (Romanian soprano) March 25; Elly Elisabeth Warnots (Belgian soprano).

Performers: Joseph Adamowski (Polish-born cellist) July 4; Guglielmo Andreoli II (Italian pianist) January 9; Conrad Ansorge (German pianist) October 15; Léon Boëllmann (French organist/composer) September 25; Henry Holden Huss (American pianist/composer) June 21; Ernest Richard Kroeger (American organist) August 10; Alexander Lambert (Polish pianist) November 1; Moriz Rosenthal (Austrian pianist) December 17; Emil von Sauer (German pianist) October 8; Emily Shinner (Briths violinist) July 7; Leo Stern (British cellist) April 5; István Thomán (Hungarian pianist) November 4; Johan Wagenaar (Dutch organist/composer) November 1; Hans Wessely (Austrian violinist) December 23.

Others: Wilhelm Altmann (German music scholar) April 4; Arnaldo Bonaventura (Italian musicologist) July 28; Maurice Emmanuel (French music scholar/composer) May 2; Vasili Metalov (Russian musicologist) March 13.

B. Deaths

Composers: Ignaz Assmayer (Austria) August 31; Joaquim Casimiro Júnior (Portugal) December 28; Joseph Funk (U.S.A.) December 24; Jacques Halévy (France) March 27; George Frederick Perry (England) March 4; Alexei Vertovsky (Russia) November 17.

Conductors: František Jan Škroup (Bohemia) February 7.

Singers: Geltrude Righetti-Giorgi (Italian contralto); Ann Maria Tree (British mezzo-soprano) February 17.
Performers: Charles Mayer (German pianist) July 2.
Others: Joseph Fröhlich (German music theorist/composer) January 5; Adolf Kullak (German music theorist/critic) December 25; (Juste) Adrien de La Fage (French music author) March 8.

C. Debuts

Singers: Frank H. Celli (British bass—London); Carolina Ferni-Giraldoni (Italian soprano—Turin); Daniel Filleborn (Polish tenor—Warsaw); Allen James (Signor) Foli (Irish bass—Catania); Ilma di Murska (Croatian soprano—Florence); Allen James (Signor) Foli (Irish bass—Catania); Ilma di Murska (Croatian soprano—Florence); Vilma von Voggenhuber (Hungarian soprano—Budapest); Sarah Edith Wynne (British soprano—London).
Performers: Teresa Carreño (Venezuelan pianist—New York); Wilhelm Fitzenhagen (German cellist—Brunswick); Louis Pabst (German pianist—Königsberg); Madeline Schiller (British pianist—Leipzig); Eduard Strauss (Austian conductor—Vienna).

D. New Positions

Conductors: Carlo Emanuele Barbieri (National Theater, Buda); Leopold Damrosch (Breslau Orchestral Society); Theodore Thomas (Brooklyn Philharmonic Society).
Others: Filippo Filippi (editor, *La Perseveranza*); James H. Mapleson (manager, Her Majesty's Theater); John Knowles Paine (faculty, Harvard Music School); Anton Rubinstein (director, St. Petersburg Conservatory); Etienne-Joseph Soubre (director, Liège Conservatory).

E. Prizes/Honors

Prizes: Louis Bourgault-Ducoudray (Prix de Rome).
Honors: Arrigo Boito (Government stipend); Léon Burbure de Wesembeck (Belgian Royal Academy); Félicien David (Legion of Honor); Octave Feuillet (French Academy); Théodore Labarre (Legion of Honor); Joseph Mayseder (Order of Franz Joseph); Louis-Etienne Reyer (Legion of Honor).

F. Biographical Highlights

Johannes Brahms, on tour, visits Vienna for the first time; Dudley Buck returns to the United States and begins teaching in Hartford; Louis Moreau Gottschalk makes a second concert tour of the United States; Edvard Grieg graduates with honors and gives his first concert; Nicolai Rimsky-Korsakov begins a three-year cruise around the world with the Russian Navy; Richard Wagner is given amnesty by the Saxon government and breaks up with Minna.

G. Cultural Beginnings

Performing Groups—Choral: Berliner Bachverein; Berne Caecilienverein; Continental Singing Society (Buffalo, New York); Zürich Male Chorus.

Performing Groups—Instrumental: Breslau Orchestral Society; Brünner Musikverein (Brno); Eidgenössicher Musikverein (Switzerland); Società del Quartetto (Turin); Theodore Thomas Orchestra.

Educational: Eduard Ganz Music School (Berlin); Harvard Music School; St. Petersburg Conservatory of Music.

Music Publishers: Robert Forberg Music Publishing Co. (Leipzig).

Music Publications: *Journal des Maîtrises* (Paris); *Musical Standard*.

Performing Centers: Prague National Opera House; Salt Lake City Theater; Ulster Hall (Belfast).

Other: Balakirev Circle; D. H. Baldwin Piano Co. (Cincinnati); Decker Brothers, pianos (New York); Hall and Quimby Brass Instrument Factory (Boston).

H. Musical Literature

August Ambros, *History of Music I*; Heinrich Bellermann, *Der Kontrapunkt*; Henry Chorley, *Thirty Year's Musical Recollections*; Henry S. Edwards, *History of the Opera from Its Origin in Italy to the Present Time*; George Hogarth, *The Philharmonic Society of London*; John Hullah, *History of Modern Music*; Ludwig Köchel, *Chronologischthematisches Verzeichnis sämtlicherTonwerke Wolfgang Amade Mozarts*; Bernhard Kothe, *Die Musik in der katholischen Kirche*; Henri Reber, *Traité d'harmonie*; Albert Vivier, *Traité complet d'harmonie*.

I. Musical Compositions

Chamber Music:

String Quartets: Anton Bruckner, *Quartet in c*; Antonin Dvořák, *Quartet No. 1 in A, Opus 2*.

Sonata/Solos: Camille Saint-Saëns, *Suite, Opus 16, for Cello and Piano*.

Ensembles: Alexander Borodin, *Piano Quintet No. 1*; Johannes Brahms, *Piano Quartet No. 2 in A, Opus 26*; Louise Farrenc, *Flute Trio in e, Opus 45*; Karl Goldmark, *String Quintet No. 1 in a, Opus 9*; Joachim Raff, *Piano Quintet in a, Opus 107*; Friedrich A. Reissiger, *String Quintet*.

Piano: Anton Bruckner, *Adagio in F*; Niels Gade, *Four Fantastic Pieces, Opus 41*; Louis Moreau Gottschalk, *The Union*; Stephen Heller, *Three Lieder ohne wörter, Opus 105*; Camille Saint-Saëns, *Mazurka No. 1 in f, Opus 21*.

Organ: Charles-Alexis Chauvet, *Vingt Morceaux*; César Franck, *Fantasie in C, Opus 16–Prélude, Fugue and Variations in b, Opus 18–Pastorale in E, Opus 19–Prière in c♯, Opus 20–Finale in B♭, Opus 21*.

Choral/Vocal Music:

Choral: Michael Balfe, *Mazeppa* (cantata); Peter Benoit, *Te Deum*; Arrigo Boito, *Le Sorelle d'Italia* (cantata); Johannes Brahms, *Soldatenlieder, Opus 41*; Anton Bruckner, *Preiset den Herrn* (cantata); Franz Liszt, *Die Legende von der heiligen Elisabeth* (oratorio)–*Cantico del sol di S Francesco d'Assisi*; Eduard Nápravnik, *Cantata in C*; Giuseppe Verdi, *Hymn of the Nations*.

Vocal: Daniel Auber, *Benedictus in A♭*; Johannes Brahms, *Four Duets, Opus 28*; Robert Franz, *Six Songs, Opus 35*–*Six Songs, Opus 36*; George F. Root, *The Battle Cry of Freedom*; Julia Ward Howe, *The Battle Hymn of the Republic*.

Musical Stage: Michael Balfe, *Blanche de Nevers*; Julius Benedict, *The Lily of Killarney–The Lake of Glenaston*; Hector Berlioz, *Beatrice and Bénédict*; Georges Bizet, *La guzla de l'émir*; Félicien David, *Lalla Rookh*; Léo Delibes, *Mon ami Pierrot*; Julius Eichberg/B. E. Woolf, *The Doctor of Alcantara*; Charles Gounod, *La reine de Saba*; Jacques Halévy, *Noë* (finished by Bizet); Ferdinand Hiller, *Die Katakomben*; Victor Massé, *Mariette la promisse*; Jacques Offenbach, *Jacqueline–Les Bavards–Monsieur et Madame Denis–Le voyage de MM. Dunanan père et fils*; John Knowles Paine, *Il pesceballo*; Anton Rubinstein, *Feramors*; Franz von Suppé, *Zehn Mädchen und kein Mann–Die Kartenaufschlägerin–Voyage de Monsieur Dunanan*; Giuseppe Verdi, *La forza del destino*.

Orchestra/Band Music:

Concerted Music:

Violin: Henryk Wieniawski, *Concerto No. 2 in d, Opus 22*.

Ballet/Incidental Music: Friedrich von Flotow, *Wilhelm von Oranien* (IM); Cesare Pugni, *Théolinda l'orphelina* (B)–*Pharoah's Daughter* (B).

Program Music: Bedřich Smetana, *Hakon Jarl*.

Standard Works: Daniel Auber, *Grand Overture for the London Universal Exposition*; William Sterndale Bennett, *Overture-Fantasy, Paradise and the Peri*; Anton Bruckner, *Three Pieces for Orchestra*; William Henry Fry, *Overture to MacBeth*; Franz Lachner, *Suite No. 2 in e, Opus 115*; Giacomo Meyerbeer, *Fest-Ouverture in Marschstyl*; Joachim Raff, *Concert Overture in F, Opus 123*.

1863

❄

Historical Highlights: Maximilian is made emperor of an attempted French Empire in Mexico; the first subway begins operation in London; a severe epidemic of scarlet fever breaks out in Europe; in the United States, the Battle of Gettysburg takes place in July—President Lincoln gives his Gettysburg Address in November; the Emancipation Proclamation is made public; Thanksgiving is made a national holiday; West Virginia becomes state number thirty-five.

Art and Literature Highlights: Births—artists Frederick Macmonnies, Edvard Munch, writers Gabriele d'Annunzio, Anthony Hawkins, George Santayana, Gene Stratton Porter; Deaths—artists Eugène Delacroix, Horace Vernet, writers Christian Hebbel, William Thackeray, Alfred de Vigny. Art—Manet's *Dejeuner sur l'Herbe*, Vedder's *Questioner of the Sphinx*; Literature—Brown's *Marjorie Fleming*, Longfellow's *Tales of a Wayside Inn*.

Musical Highlights

A. Births

Composers: Helen Hood (U.S.A.) June 28; Xavier Leroux (France) October 11; Pietro Mascagni (Italy) December 7; Alexander Olenin (Russia) June 13; Horatio Parker (U.S.A.) September 15; Gabriel Pierné (France) August 16.

Conductors: Paul Henri Lebrun (Belgium) April 21; Franz Schalk (Austria) May 27; Felix Weingartner (Austria) June 2.

Singers: Cesira Ferrani (Italian soprano) May 8; Ellen Gulbranson (Swedish soprano) March 4; Bruno Heydrich (German tenor) February 23; Emma Juch (American soprano) July 4; Ernst Kraus (German tenor) June 8; Blanche Marchesi (French soprano) April 4; Marie Renard (Austrian soprano) January 18; Frances Saville (American soprano) January 6; Milka Ternina (Croatian soprano) December 19; Francisco Vignas (Spanish tenor) March 27.

Performers: Enrique Fernández Arbós (Spanish violinist/conductor) December 24; Hugo Becker (German cellist) February 13; Gilbert Raynolds Combs (American organist) January 5; Charles Dennée (American pianist) September 1; Adele Margulies (Austrian pianist) March 7; Isidore Philipp (Hungarian-born pianist) September 2; Carl Adolph Preyer (German-born pianist) July 28; Alfred Reisenauer (German pianist) November 1; Arnold Josef Rosé (Romanian violinist) October 24; Benno Schönberger (Austrian pianist) September 12; Alexander Siloti (Russian pianist) October 9; Robert Teichmüller (German pianist) May 4; Fannie Bloomfield Zeisler (Austrian-born pianist) July 16.

Others: Richard Aldrich (American music critic) July 31; Henry Expert (French musicologist) May 12; Willibald Nagel (German musicologist/pianist) January 12; Arthur Seidl (German musicologist) June 8.

B. Deaths

Composers: Marie-Désiré Beaulieu (France) December 21; Pierre-Auguste Blondeau (France) April 14.

Conductors: Karl Albrecht (Germany-Russia) March 8; Ferdinand Stegmeyer (Austria) May 6.

Singers: Pierre Ignace Begrez (French tenor) December 19; Laure Cinti-Damoreau (French soprano) February 25.

Performers: Arthur Thomas Corfe (British organist) January 28; Adolph Friedrich Hesse (German organist) August 5; Joseph Mayseder (Austrian violinist) November 21; Emile Prudent (French pianist) March 13; Hermann Wollenhaupt (German-born pianist/composer) September 18.

Others: Pietro Alfieri (Italian music scholar) June 12; Franz Gruber (Austrian clergyman/songwriter) June 7; Edward Taylor (British musician/author) March 12.

C. Debuts

Singers: Elizabeth Bainbridge (British mezzo-soprano—Glyndebourne); Teresa Brambilla-Ponchielli (Italian soprano—Odessa), Armand de Castelmary (French bass—Paris); Clara Kathleen Rogers (British-born soprano—Turin); Gustav Siehr (German bass—Neustrelitz).

Performers: John Carrodus (British violinist—London); Edward Dannreuther (German-born pianist—London); Joseph Hellmesberger II (Austrian violinist—Vienna?); Jerome Lowenthal (American pianist—New York); Agnes Zimmermann (German-born pianist—London).

D. New Positions

Conductors: Johannes Brahms (Vienna Singakademie); François Hainl (Paris Opéra); Holger Simon Paulli (Copenhagen Court Orchestra); Robert Radecke (Berlin Royal Opera).

Others: Yury Arnold (editor, *Neue Zeitschrift für Musik*); Marius-Pierre Audran (director, Marseilles Conservatory); Joseph Barnby (organ, St. Andrews, London); Eugène Gigout (organ, St. Augustin, Paris); Edmund Kretschmer (organ, Dresden Court); Joseph Louis d'Ortigue (editor, *Le Ménestral*); George P. Upton (music critic, Chicago *Tribune*); Henry C. Watson (music critic, the *New York Tribune*); Henry Clay Work (editor, the *Song Messenger*).

E. Prizes/Honors

Prizes: Jules Massenet (Prix de Rome).

F. Biographical Highlights

Alexandre Guilmant inaugurates the new organ at St. Sulpice in Paris; Modest Mussorgsky begins a four-year stint as a clerk in the Russian Ministry of Communications; Johann Strauss, Jr., is put in charge of all court balls in Vienna; Peter Ilyich Tchaikovsky quits his government post in order to devote full time to music.

G. Cultural Beginnings

Performing Groups—Choral: Buffalo (New York) St. Cecilia Society.
Performing Groups—Instrumental: Concerti Popolari a Grande Orchestra (Florence); Monte Carlo Opera Orchestra.
Educational: Civica Scuola di Musica (Casale Monferrato); Giorgio Ronconi Vocal School (Granada).
Music Publishers: John Curwen and Sons, Ltd. (London); Philip Phillips (Cincinnati).
Music Publications: *The Choir and Musical Record; Jahrbuch für Musikalische Wissenschaft; Song Messenger of the North-West* (U.S.A.).
Other: Albrecht and Co., piano makers (Philadelphia); Boston Musician's Union; Mathushek Piano Co. (New York); Henry F. Miller and Sons Piano Co. (Boston); Musical Mutual Protective Union of New York; Philadelphia Musical Association; Player Piano (by Tourneaux in France); Société des Compositeurs de Musique (Paris).

H. Musical Literature

Jean Andries, *Précis de l'histoire de la musique depuis les temps les plus reculés*; Charles A. Battaille, *De la physiologie appliquée au méchanisme du chant*; Francisco S. Daniel, *La musique arabe*; Luther Emerson, *The Harp of Judah*; François Gevaert, *Traité général d'instrumentation*; Johann C. Hauff, *Theorie der Tonsetskunst I*; Hermann von Helmholtz, *On the Sensations of Tone as a Physiological Basis for the Theory of Music*; Karl R. Köstlin, *Aesthetik I*; Franz J. Kunkel, *Die neue Harmonielehre . . .* ; Julius Maier, *Auswahl englischer Madrigale*; Giovanni Pacini, *Memoria sul migliore indirizzo degli studii musicali*; Prosper-Charles Simon, *Nouveau manuel complet de l'organiste II*; Carl Weitzmann, *Geschichte des Clavierspiele*.

I. Musical Compositions

Chamber Music:

String Quartets: Giovanni Pacini, *No. 4.*
Sonata/Solos: C. Hubert Parry, *Three Movements for Violin and Piano*; Henri Vieuxtemps, *Viola Sonata in B♭, Opus 36*; Henryk Wieniawski, *Eight Etudes-caprices, Opus 18* (violin, piano).
Ensembles: Johannes Brahms, *Piano Quintet in f, Opus 34*; Niels Gade, *Piano Trio in F, Opus 42–String Sextet in E♭, Opus 44*; Joachim Raff, *Piano Trio No. 2 in G, Opus 112*; Camille Saint-Saëns, *Piano Trio No. 1 in F, Opus 18*.
Piano: Johannes Brahms, *Variations in a on a Theme of Paganini, Opus 35*; Gabriel Fauré, *Three Romances sans Paroles, Opus 17*; Edvard Grieg, *Six Poetic Tone Pictures, Opus 3*; Stephen Heller, *Scherzo, Opus 106–Four Ländler, Opus 107*; Ferdinand Hiller, *Sonata No. 2 in A♭, Opus 9*; Franz Liszt, *Legendes*; John Knowles Paine, *A Christmas Gift, Opus 7*; Joachim Raff, *Hungarian Rhapsody, Opus 113.*

Organ: César Franck, *Forty-Four Little Pieces for Organ–Grande pièce symphonique, Opus 17.*

Choral/Vocal Music:

Choral: Julius Benedict, *Richard the Lion-Hearted* (cantata); Peter Benoit, *Requiem*; Johannes Brahms, *Twelve Songs and Romances, Opus 44–Three Sacred Choruses, Opus 37*; Anton Bruckner, *Psalm CXII for Double Chorus and Orchestra*; César Franck, *Ave Maria*; Carl Loewe, *Die auferweckung des Lazarus, Opus 132* (oratorio); Jules Massenet, *Requiem*; John Knowles Paine, *Domine salvum, Opus 8*; Joachim Raff, *Ten Songs for Male Voices, Opus 97–Deutschlands Auferstehung, Opus 100*; Gioacchino Rossini, *Petite Messe Solennelle.*

Vocal: Johannes Brahms, *Three Vocal Quartets, Opus 31*; Patrick Gilmore, *When Johnny Comes Marching Home Again.*

Musical Stage: Michael Balfe, *The Armourer of Nantes*; Georges Bizet, *The Pearl Fishers*; Max Bruch, *Die Loreley*; Léo Delibes, *Le jardinier et son seigneur*; William Henry Fry, *Notre Dame de Paris*; Hervé, *Les toréadors de Grenade*; George Macfarren, *Freya's Gift*; Giacomo Meyerbeer, *L'Africaine*; Jacques Offenbach, *Il Signor Fagotto–Lischen et Fritzchen*; Giovanni Pacini, *Carmelita*; Amilcare Ponchielli, *Roderico, re dei goti*; Alexander Serov, *Judith*; Franz von Suppé, *Flotte bursche–Das corps der rache*; Vincent Wallace, *The Desert Flower.*

Orchestra/Band Music:

Concerted Music:

Piano: Giovanni Pacini, *Sinfonia Dante.*

Violin: Camille Saint-Saëns, *Introduction and Rondo Capriccioso in a, Opus 28.*

Other: Karl Davidov, *Cello Concerto No. 2*; George Macfarren, *Cello Concerto in G.*

Standard Works: Anton Bruckner, *Overture in g*; Karl Goldmark, *Orchestral Scherzo No. 1, Opus 19*; Johan P. Hartmann, *Concert Overture No. 4, "An Autumn Hunt," Opus 63b*; Ferdinand Hiller, *Concert Overture in A, Opus 101*; Jules Massenet, *Ouverture de Concert, Opus 1*; Joachim Raff, *Suite No. 1 in C, Opus 101*; Camille Saint-Saëns, *Suite in D, Opus 49–Spartacus Overture in E♭*; Arthur Sullivan, *Procession March–Princess of Wales March.*

Symphonies: Anton Bruckner, *Symphony in f* (unpublished); Richard Hol, *No. 1.*

1864

❀

Historical Highlights: Chancellor Otto Bismarck leads Prussia against Denmark in a dispute over Schleswig-Holstein; Karl Marx helps to form the first International Workingmen's Association; the International Red Cross is formed in Geneva; in the United States, Civil War events include Sherman's March to the Sea—Ulysses S. Grant is appointed supreme commander of the Northen Army; Abraham Lincoln is re-elected as president; Nevada becomes state number thirty-six.

Art and Literature Highlights: Births—artists Charles M. Russell, Henri Toulouse-Lautrec, writers Henri de Régnier, Frank Wedekind, Israel Zangwill; Deaths—artist William Dyce, writers Jean Ampères, Nathaniel Hawthorne, Walter Landor. Art—Manet's *Battle of the Kearsarge and the Alabama*, Moreau's *Oedipus and the Sphinx*, Vedder's *Lair of the Sea Serpent*; Literature—Kivi's *Kullervo*, Marston's *Donna Diana*, Tennyson's *Enoch Arden*.

Musical Highlights

A. Births

Composers: Eleanor Freer (U.S.A.) May 14; Louis Glass (Denmark) March 23; Alexander Gretchaninov (Russia-U.S.A.) October 25; Johan Halvorsen (Norway) March 15; Sidney Homer (U.S.A.) December 9; Franco Leoni (Italy) October 24; Joseph Guy Ropartz (France) June 15; Richard Strauss (Germany) June 11.

Conductors: Hale A. VanderCook (U.S.A.) September 3; Max Zach (Austria-U.S.A.) August 31; Giovanni Tebaldini (Italy) September 7.

Singers: Gemma Bellincioni (Italian soprano) August 18; Francesco Daddi (Italian tenor); Anna Schoen-René (German-born soprano) January 12; Evgenia Mravina (Russian soprano) February 16; Ella Russell (American soprano) March 30.

Performers: Eugène d'Albert (Scottish-born pianist/composer) April 10; Philip H. Goepp (American organist/author) June 23; Jean Paul Kürsteiner (American pianist/pedagogue) July 8; Alessandro Longo (Italian pianist) December 30; Marie Soldat (Austrian violinist) March 25; Benjamin Lincoln Whelpley (American pianist).

Others: Oskar Bie (German music critic) February 9; Elizabeth Sprague Coolidge (American patron of the arts) October 30; William Sherman Haynes (American flute maker) July 27; Adolf Sandberger (German musicologist) December 19; Gustav Schirmer II (American publisher) February 18; Thomas Tapper (American music educator) January 28; Charles Sanford Terry (British music scholar) October 24.

B. Deaths

Composers: Moritz Dietrichstein (Austria) August 27; Victor Dourlen (France) January 8; Stephen Foster (U.S.A.) January 13; William Henry Fry (U.S.A.) December 21; Giacomo Meyerbeer (Germany) May 2; Isaac Nathan (England-Australia) January 15.

Conductors: Ludwig Schindelmeisser (Germany) March 30.

Singers: Aloys Anders (Bohemian tenor) December 3; Giovanni David (Italian tenor); Stephen Foster (U.S.A.) January 13; Mary Ann Paton (Scottish soprano) July 21.

Performers: Mateo Ferrer (Spanish organist) January 4; Jacques François Gallay (French horn virtuoso) October 18; Johann Hermann Kufferath (German violinist/conductor) July 28; Joseph Proksch (Bohemian pianist) December 20; Anton Felix Schindler (Moravian violinist/conductor) January 16; Johann Schneider (German organist) April 13.

Others: Nathan Adams (American instrument maker) March 16; Friedrich Hofmeister (German publisher) September 30; William Knabe (German-born piano maker) May 21; Luigi Lambertini (Italian piano maker) November 13; Pietro Scudo (Italian-born music author) October 14.

C. Debuts

Singers: Stafford Dean (British bass—Glyndebourne); Christine Nilsson (Swedish soprano—Paris); Anna Schimon-Regan (German soprano—Hannover); Arthur W. Tams (American baritone—Philadelphia); Jennie Van Zandt (American soprano—New York).

Performers: Julius Nicolaivich Melgunov (Russian pianist—St. Petersburg); Alfred H. Pease (American pianist—New York).

D. New Positions

Conductors: Kazuyoshi Akiyama (Tokyo Symphony); Hans von Bülow (Munich Royal Opera); Johann Nepomuk Fuchs (Pressburg Opera); Hermann Levi (Karlsruhe); Friedrich Marpurg (Sondershausen); Carl Millöcker (Graz Theater); Joseph Rheinberger (Munich Oratorio Society).

Others: James C. D. Parker (organ, Trinity Church, Boston); Giovanni Rossi (director, Parma Musical Institute); Samuel Tuckerman (organ, Trinity Church, New York).

E. Prizes/Honors

Honors: Franz Adolf Berwald (Swedish Royal Academy); Hyacinthe-Eléonore Klosé (Legion of Honor).

F. Biographical Highlights

Isaac Albéniz appears as a pianist at age four; Johannes Brahms gives up his post with the Vienna Singakademie; Cesar Cui begins a writing career as a critic and journalist; Alexander Dargomijsky makes his second European concert tour; Carlos Gomes begins study in Italy on a Brazilian government grant; Richard Wagner is befriended by Ludwig II of Bavaria and begins an affair with Cosima von Bülow.

G. Cultural Beginnings

Performing Groups—Choral: Barnby's Choir (London); Montreal Mendelssohn Choir.

Performing Groups—Instrumental: Düsseldorf Municipal Orchestra; Moscow Philharmonic Orchestra; Portland (Oregon) Mechanics Band; Sheffield Amateur Musical Society; Società del Quartetto (Milan).

Educational: Bucharest Conservatory of Music; Eitner Piano School (Berlin); Musical Institute of Providence (Rhode Island); Royal College of Organists (London); Scuola Comunale di Musica ("Orazio Vecchi," Modena); Yale University Fine Arts Department (first in the United States).

Music Publishers: J. Fischer and Brother (Dayton, Ohio).

Music Publications: *Orpheonist and Philharmonic Journal*; *Western (Brainard's) Musical World*.

Performing Centers: Music Hall (Academy of Music, Milwaukee); Thalia Theater (Graz); Ukrainian Theater (L'vov).

Other: Gilmore, Graves and Co., brass instruments (Boston); Irving Hall Symphonic Soirées (by Theodore Thomas); Kranich and Bach Piano Co. (New York); Gustav Mollenhauer, woodwind manufacturer (Kassel).

H. Musical Literature

Jean-Baptiste Arban, *Grande Méthode complète pour cornet à pistons et de saxhorn*; Antoine Elwart, *Petit Manuel d'Instrumentation*; Carl Engel, *Music of the Most Ancient Nations*; Edouard Gregoir, *Les Artistes-Musiciens Néerlandais*; Franz Xaver Haberl, *Theoretisch-praktische Anweisung zum harmonischen Kirchengesang*; Ferdinand Hiller, *Die Musik und das Publikum*; John Hullah, *A Grammar of Counterpoint*; Louis Köhler, *Die Neue Richtung in der Musik*; Charles Meerens, *Instruction élémentaire de calcul musical*; Giovanni Pacini, *Cenni storici sulla musical e trattado di contrappunto*; Henry Phillips, *Musical and Personal Recollections during Half a Century*; Samuel Tuckerman, *Trinity Collection of Church Music*.

I. Musical Compositions

Chamber Music:

String Quartets: Johan Svendsen, *Quartet, Opus 1*.

Sonata/Solos: Johan P. Hartmann, *Suite for violin/clarinet, Opus 66*; Henri Vieuxtemps, *Feuille d'album, Opus 40* (violin, piano).

Ensembles: Johannes Brahms, *String Sextet No. 2 in G, Opus 36*; Anton Rubinstein, *Piano Quartet in C, Opus 66*; Camille Saint-Saëns, *Piano Trio No. 1 in F, Opus 18*.

Piano: Johannes Brahms, *Sonata in f for Two Pianos, Opus 34b*; Louis Moreau Gottschalk, *The Dying Poet–The Maiden's Blush: Grande Valse de Concert*; Edvard Grieg, *Two Symphonic Pieces, Opus 14* (four hands); Stephen Heller, *Herbstblätter, Opus 109*; Anton Rubinstein, *Fantasia in f for Two Pianos, Opus 73*.

Organ: Franz Liszt, *Ora pro nobis, litany–Variations, "Weinen, Klagen, Sorgen, Zagen"*; Frederick Ouseley, *Thirty-One Preludes and Fugues, Set I*; John Knowles Paine, *Two Preludes, Opus 19*; C. Hubert Parry, *Grand Fugue with Three Subjects*.

Choral/Vocal Music:

Choral: Max Bruch, *Frithjof-Scenen, Opus 23*; Anton Bruckner, *Mass No. 1 in d*; William Henry Fry, *Kyrie Eleison–Mass in E♭*; Ernest Guiraud, *Bajazet et le joueur de flûte* (cantata); William Jackson, *Full Service in G*; George Macfarren, *Catholic Service in E♭*; Giovanni Pacini, *Rossini e la patria*; C. Hubert Parry, *Magnificat and Nunc Dimittis in A*; Anton Rubinstein, *Six Songs, Opus 67*; Arthur Sullivan, *Kenilworth* (oratorio).

Vocal: William B. Bradbury, *Aughton* (hymn tune, "He Leadeth Me"); Johannes Brahms, *Four Songs, Opus 46*; Stephen Foster, *Beautiful Dreamer*; Robert Franz, *Six Goethe Lieder, Opus 33*; Edvard Grieg, *Six Songs, Opus 4–The Heart's Melodies, Opus 5*; Joachim Raff, *Sangesfrühling, Opus 98–Twelve Duets, Opus 114*; Anton Rubinstein, *Six German Songs, Opus 57–Six German Songs, Opus 72*; George C. Stebbins, *Gordon* (hymn tune, "My Jesus, I Love Thee").

Musical Stage: Daniel Auber, *La fiancée du Roi de Garbe*; Michael Balfe, *The Sleeping Queen*; Julius Benedict, *The Bride of Song*; Tommaso Benvenuti, *La Stella de Toledo*; Franz Berwald, *The Queen of Golconda*; Félicien David, *La captive*; Léo Delibes, *Grande nouvelle–Le serpent à plumes*; François Gevaert, *Le Capitaine Henriot*; Charles Gounod, *Mireille*; Ernest Guiraud, *Sylvie*; Hervé, *Le joueur de flûte–La liberté des théâtres–La revue pour rire*; Charles Lecocq, *Liliane et Valentin–Le baiser à la porte*; George Macfarren, *She Stoops to Conquer–Helwellyn*; Stanislaw Moniuszko, *The Haunted Manor*; Jacques Offenbach, *L'amour chanteur–Die Rheinnixen–Les géorgiennes*; Errico Petrella, *La contessa d'Amalfi*; Bedřich Smetana, *The Brandenburgers in Bohemia*; Franz von Suppé, *Pique Dame–Franz Schubert*.

Orchestra/Band Music:

Concerted Music:

Piano: Peter Benoit, *Symphonic Ode, Opus 43b*; Anton Rubinstein, *Concerto No. 4 in d, Opus 70*.

Other: Anton Rubinstein, *Cello Concerto No. 1 in A, Opus 65*.

Ballet/Incidental Music: Friedrich von Flotow, *Der Königschuss* (B); Cesare Pugni, *The Little Hump-backed Horse* (B); Arthur Sullivan, *The Sapphire Necklace* (B).

Program Music: Anton Rubinstein, *Faust, Opus 68*.

Standard Works: Hermann Goetz, *Spring Overture*; Franz Lachner, *Suite No. 3 in f, Opus 122*; Emil Naumann, *Concert Overture, Loreley, Opus 25*; Joachim Raff, *Jubel Overture in C, Opus 103–Fest-Overture in A, Opus 117*; Bedřich Smetana, *Shakespearean Festival March*; Johann Strauss, Jr., *Morning Papers Waltz*; Peter Ilyich Tchaikovsky, *Overture to the Tempest*; Richard Wagner, *Huldigungsmarsch*.
Symphonies: John F. Barnett, *Symphony*; Anton Bruckner, *Symphony in d, "Die Nullte"* (revised 1869); Edvard Grieg, *Symphony in c.*

1865

❄

Historical Highlights: The War of the Triple Alliance in South America pits Argentina, Brazil, and Uruguay against Paraguay; Peru declares war on Spain; Leopold I of Belgium dies and is succeeded by Leopold II; in the United States, the Civil War ends—President Lincoln is assassinated—Andrew Johnson becomes seventeenth president; the Thirteenth Ammendment ends slavery in the United States and territories; work begins on the transcontinental railroad line.

Art and Literature Highlights: Births—artists Paul Barlett, Robert Henri, Henry Kitson, writers Baroness Emmuska Orczy, William Yeats; Deaths— artists John Neagle, Ferdinand Waldmüller, writers Elizabeth Gaskell, Bernhard Malmström. Art—Blythe's *Dry Goods and Notions*, Corot's *La Zingara*, Orchardson's *Challenged*; Literature—Carrol's *Alice's Adventures in Wonderland*, Dodge's *Hans Brinker*, Newman's *The Dream of Gerontius.*

Musical Highlights

A. Births
   Composers: Auguste De Boeck (Belgium) May 9; Paul Dukas (France) October 1; Giuseppe Ferrata (Italy-U.S.A.) January 1; Paul Gilson (Belgium) June 15; Alexander Glazunov (Russia) August 10; Harvey Worthington Loomis (U.S.A.) February 5; Albéric Magnard (France) June 9; Carl Nielsen (Denmark) June 9; Heinrich Reinhardt (Austria) April 13; Jan Sibelius (Finland) December 8.
   Conductors: Ferdinand Löwe (Austria) February 19.
   Singers: Blanche Arral (Belgian soprano); Lloyd d'Aubigné (American tenor)(?); Charles W. Clark (American baritone) October 15; John Coates (British tenor) June 29; Peter Cornelius (Danish tenor) January 4; Emma Eames (American soprano) August 13; Edoardo Garbin (Italian tenor) March 12; Marie Goetze (German mezzo-soprano) November 2; (Harry) Plunkett Greene (Irish baritone) June 24; Vilhelm Herold (Danish tenor) March 19; Paul Knüpfer (German bass)

June 21; Martha Leffler-Burckard (German soprano) June 16; Margaret Macintyre (British soprano); Franz Navál (Austrian tenor) October 20; Giulio Rossi (Italian bass) October 27; Therese Rothauser (Hungarian contralto) June 10; Sibyl Sanderson (American soprano) December 7.

Performers: Agnes Charlotte Adler (Danish pianist) February 19; Maurice Arnold (American violinist/composer) January 19; Herbert Brewer (British organist) June 21; William Crane Carl (American organist) March 2; Earl R. Drake (American violinist/composer) November 26; Franz Kniesel (German-born violinist) January 26; Edwin H. Lemare (British-born organist/composer) September 9; Georg Liebling (German-born pianist) January 22; Leo Schulz (German cellist) March 28; Henry Dike Sleeper (American organist) October 9; Joseph von Slivinski (Polish pianist) December 15.

Others: Charles Barnhouse (American publisher) March 20; Guido Gasperini (Italian musicologist) June 7; Margaret H. Glyn (British musicologist) February 28; Emile Jaques-Dalcroze (Swiss music educator) July 6; Stewart Macpherson (British music theorist) March 29; Edward B. Marks (American publisher) November 28; Frank J. Metcalf (American hymnist) April 4; Ernest C. Schirmer (American publisher) March 15; R. R. Terry (British music scholar/organist) January 3; Peter Wagner (German musicologsit) August 19.

B. Deaths

Composers: William (Vincent) Wallace (Ireland) October 12.

Conductors: Louis Dietsch (France) February 20; Francisco Manuel da Silva (Brazil) December 18; Henri-Justin-Armand Valentino (France) January 20.

Singers: Rovere Agostino (Italian bass) December 10; Cesare Badiali (Italian bass) November 17; Maria Caradori-Allen (Italian soprano) October 15; Antonio Giuglini (Italian tenor) October 12; Elizabeth Masson (British mezzo-soprano) January 9; Giuditta Pasta (Italian soprano) April 1; Ludwig Schnoor von Carolsfeld (German tenor) July 21.

Performers: Heinrich Wilhelm Ernst (Czech violinist) October 8; Aristide Farrenc (French flutist/editor) January 31; Julian Fontana (Polish pianist) December 24; Johann Heinrich Lübeck (Dutch violinist) February 7; Jean Louis Tulou (French flutist) July 23.

Others: Gotthilf Körner (German publisher) January 3; Giuseppe Rocca (Italian violin maker) January 17; Felice Romani (Italian librettist) January 28.

C. Debuts

Singers: Luigi Agnesi (Italian bass—London); Alfredo Barili (Italian bass—New York); Mathilde Bauermeister (German soprano—London); Eugen Gura (German bass-baritone—Munich); Francis Alexander Korbay (Hungarian tenor—Budapest); Lilli Lehmann (German soprano—Prague); Amalie Materna (Austrian soprano—Graz); Aglaja Orgeni (Hungarian soprano—Berlin); Marie-Hippolyte Rôze (French soprano—Paris); Heinrich Vogl (German tenor—Munich); Maria Waldmann (Austrian mezzo-soprano—Pressburg); Marie Wilt (Austrian-born soprano—Graz).

Performers: Johann Georg Leitert (German pianist—Dresden); Ernst Perabo (German-born pianist—Boston).

D. New Positions

Conductors: Adolf Emil Büchner (Meiningen); Karl Doppler (Stuttgart); Friedrich Hegar (Zürich Tonhalle Orchestra); Alfred Mellon (Liverpool PO); Franz von Suppé (Carl Theater, Vienna).

Others: Max Bruch (director, Koblenz Concert-Institute); Maurits Hagemann (director, Batavia Conservatory); Josef Krejčí (director, Prague Conservatory); Henri-Marie Lavoix (librarian, Bibliothèque Nationale, Paris); Samuel Sebastian Wesley (organ, Gloucester Cathedral).

E. Prizes/Honors

Prizes: Gustave-Léon Huberti (Prix de Rome); Charles Lenepveu (Prix de Rome).

Honors: Friedrich Kiel (Prussian Academy); Halfdan Kjerulf (Swedish Royal Academy).

F. Biographical Highlights

Louis Moreau Gottschalk, in trouble over a young lady in California, flees to Brazil; Franz Liszt suffers his first serious bout with dipsomania; Nicolai Rimsky-Korsakov returns from the Russian Navy world cruise and joins Balakirev's music circle; Giuseppe Verdi gives up his post in the Italian National Parliament; Richard Wagner is exiled to Switzerland by Ludwig II.

G. Cultural Beginnings

Performing Groups—Choral: Chicago Männerchor; Germania Men's Chorus (Newark, New Jersey); Oberösterreichischer und Salzburgischer Sängerbund.

Performing Groups—Instrumental: Christiania String Quartet; Concerts Populaires de Musique Classique (Brussels); Edinburgh University Musical Society; Euterpe Music Society (Denmark); Harvard Musical Association; Oxford Philharmonia Society; Quartetto Fiorentino (by Jean Becker); Städtisches Orchester (Augsburg).

Educational: London Organ School; Mollenhauer Studio of Music (Brooklyn, New York); Oberlin College Conservatory of Music; Ramann-Volkmann Music School (Nuremberg).

Music Publishers: Hawkes and Co., instrument makers and music publishers (merges with Boosey and Co. in 1930).
Performing Centers: Crosby Opera House (Chicago); Staatstheater am Gärtnerplatz (Munich).
Other: Charles Foetisch Music Co. (Lausanne); Moses Slater, brass instruments (New York).

H. Musical Literature

Karl Franz Brendel, *Die Organisation des Musikwesens . . .* ; Charles Coussemaker, *Les Harmonistes des XIIe et XIIIe Siècles*; Luther Emerson, *Merry Chimes*; Franz Haberl, *Magister Choralis*; Karl Kudelski, *Kurzgefasste Harmonielehre*; Ernst Mach, *Über musikalische Akustik*; Adolf Marx, *Erinnerungen: aus Meinem Leben*; August Reissmann, *Grundriss der Musikgeschichte*; Alexander Thayer, *Chronologisches Verzeichnis der Werke Ludwig von Beethoven*; Johann Vesque von Püttlingen, *Das musikalische Autorrecht*.

I. Musical Compositions

Chamber Music:
    String Quartets: Ferdinand Hiller, *No. 3, Opus 105*.
    Sonata/Solos: Johannes Brahms, *Cello Sonata No. 1 in e, Opus 38*; Edvard Grieg, *Violin Sonata No. 1 in F, Opus 8*; Joachim Raff, *Violin Sonata No. 3 in D, Opus 128*.
    Ensembles: Elfrieda Andrée, *Piano Quintet in e–Piano Quintet in a*; Johannes Brahms, *"Horn" Trio in E♭, Opus 40*; Camille Saint-Saëns, *Serenade in E♭, Opus 15*.
    Piano: Johannes Brahms, *Sixteen Waltzes, Opus 39* (piano duet); Zdeněk Fibich, *Le Printemps, Opus 1*; César Franck, *Les plaintes d'une poupée*; Edvard Grieg, *Sonata in E, Opus 7*; Stephen Heller, *Morceaux de ballet, Opus 111–Caprice humoristique, Opus 112–Fantasie-Caprice, Opus 113*; Modest Mussorgsky, *From Memories of Childhood*; John Knowles Paine, *Funeral March for Lincoln, Opus 9*; C. Hubert Parry, *Sonata in f for Two Pianos*; Joachim Raff, *Klavierstücken, Opus 126*; Peter Ilyich Tchaikovsky, *Sonata in c♯, Opus 37*.
Choral/Vocal Music:
    Choral: Daniel Auber, *Veni Ceator–Kyrie in C–Kyrie in a*; Peter Benoit, *Lucifer* (oratorio); César Franck, *The Tower of Babel* (oratorio); Charles Gounod, *Tobie* (oratorio); Franz Liszt, *Missa Choralis*; Carl Loewe, *Märznacht*; Stanislaw Moniuszko, *Mass No. 3 in E♭–Phantoms* (cantata); Carl Reinecke, *Belsazar, Opus 73* (oratorio).
    Vocal: Antonin Dvořák, *Cypresses*; John Dykes, *Lux Benigna* (hymn tune, "Lead, Kindly Light"); Robert Franz, *Six Songs, Opus 11(?)–Six Poems, Opus 13(?)–Six Songs, Opus 20(?)–Six Songs, Opus 21(?)*; Edvard Grieg, *Four Songs, Opus 9*; Ferdinand Hiller, *Christnacht, Opus 79*.

Musical Stage: Georges Bizet, *Ivan, the Terrible* (unfinished); Peter Cornelius, *Le Cid*; Ferdinand David, *Le Saphir*; Léo Delibes, *Le boeuf Apis*; Heinrich Dorn, *Der Botenläufer von Pirna–Gewitter bei Sonnenschein*; Friedrich von Flotow, *Naïde–La Châtelaine*; Hervé, *La biche au bois–Une fantasia*; Ferdinand Hiller, *Der deserteur*; Jules Massenet, *Esmeralda*; Jacques Offenbach, *Les Bergers–Les refrains des bouffes–Cascoletto*; Carlo Pedrotti, *Marion de Lorme*; Errico Petrella, *Celinda*: Józef Poniatowski, *L'aventurier*; Alexander Serov, *Rogneda*; Franz von Suppé, *Die schöne Galatea*.

Orchestra/Band Music:
  Concerted Music:
    Piano: Peter Benoit, *Concerto*; Ferdinand Hiller, *Concertstück, Opus 113*(?).
    Other: Peter Benoit, *Flute Concerto–Symphonic Tale, Opus 30* (flute).
  Ballet/Incidental Music: Zdeněk Fibich, *Romeo and Juliet* (IM).
  Standard Works: Mily Balakirev, *Overture No. 2 on Russian Themes, "Russia"*; Théodore Dubois, *Concert Overture in D*; Karl Goldmark, *Sakuntala Overture, Opus 13*; Franz Lachner, *Suite No. 4 in D♭, Opus 129*; Jules Massenet, *Suite No. 1 for Orchestra*; Carl Reinecke, *Overture, Alladin, Opus 70*; Peter Ilyich Tchaikovsky, *Concert Overture in F*.
  Symphonies: Antonin Dvořák, *No. 1 in c, Opus 31, "The Bells of Zlonice"–No. 2 in B♭, Opus 41*; Niels Gade, *No. 7 in F, Opus 45*; Giovanni Pacini, *Dante Symphony*; Nikolai Rimsky-Korsakov, *No. 1 in e♭, Opus 1*.

1866

❖

Historical Highlights: Cyrus Field succeeds in laying down a lasting Atlantic Cable; Alfred Nobel invents dynamite; the Seven Weeks War takes place between Prussia and Austria; in the United States, Congress passes the Civil Rights Act over President Johnson's veto; Ulysses S. Grant becomes the first American to be promoted to general; the nickel is approved for coining by the Treasury Department; the Grand Army of the Republic (GAR) is founded.

Art and Literature Highlights: Births—artists Jules Guerin, Wassily Kandinsky, writers Jacinto Benavante y Mártinez, Tristan Bernard, Philander C. Johnson; Deaths—writers Carl Almqvist, Roger de Beauvoir, Friedrich Rückert. Art—Daumier's *Don Quixote and the Windmills*, Manet's *The Fifer*, Weir's *The Gun Foundry*; Literature—Dostoyevsky's *Crime and Punishment*, Hugo's *Toilers of the Sea*, Tolstoy's *War and Peace*.

Musical Highlights

A. Births

Composers: Ferruccio Busoni (Italy) April 1; Francesco Cilèa (Italy) July 23; Arthur Mansfield Curry (U.S.A.) January 27; Gustave Doret (Switzerland) September 20; Hugo Felix (Austria-U.S.A.) November 19; Vasili Kalinnikov (Russia) January 13; Clara Anna Korn (Germany-U.S.A.) January 30; Ottokar Nováček (Czechoslovakia) May 13; Vladimir Rebikov (Russia) May 31; Erik Satie (France) May 17; Charles Wood (Ireland) June 15.

Conductors: Tor Aulin (Sweden) September 10; Viktor Hollaender (Germany) April 20.

Singers: Henri Albers (Dutch-born baritone) February 1; Ellen Brandt-Forster (Austrian soprano) October 11; Otto Briesemeister (German tenor) May 18; Henry Thacker Burleigh (American baritone/composer) December 2; Andreas Dippel (German-born tenor) November 30; Gervase Elwes (British tenor) November 15; Arthur van Eweyk (American baritone) May 27; Charles Gilibert (French baritone) November 29; Theodor Lierhammer (Austrian baritone) November 18; Maria Mikhailova (Russian soprano) June 3; Fanny Moody (British soprano) November 23; Antonio Scotti (Italian baritone) January 25.

Performers: Rossetter Gleason Cole (American organist/composer) February 5; David Mannes (American violinist) February 16; Max von Pauer (Austrian pianist) October 31.

Others: Clarence C. Birchard (American publisher) July 3; Théodore Gérold (French music scholar) October 26; Romain Rolland (French musicologist) January 29; Carl Emil Seashore (American musician/psychologist) January 28; Ernest M. Skinner (American organ builder) January 15; Henry B. Tremaine (American piano maker) July 20.

B. Deaths

Composers: Carl Jonas Almquist (Sweden) November 26; Johann Wenzel Kallivoda (Bohemia) December 3; Aimé-Ambroise Leborne (France) April 1; Rikard Nordraak (Norway) March 20.

Conductors: François Aimon (France) February 2.

Singers: Eduard Franz Genast (German baritone) August 4; Sophie (Johanna) Löwe (German soprano) November 28.

Performers: John Leman Brownsmith (British organist) September 14; Antoine-Louis Clapisson (French violinist/composer) March 19; Aloys Schmitt (German pianist/composer) July 25; (Adrien-) François Servais (Belgian cellist) November 26; Prosper-Charles Simon (French organist) May 31.

Others: Angelo Catelani (Italian music scholar) September 5; Jean-Louis-Félix Danjou (French music author) March 4; Charles Édouard

Delezenne (French acoustician) August 2; Otto Kraushaar (German music theorist) November 23; Adolf Bernhard Marx (German music theorist/author) May 17; Joseph-Louis d'Ortigue (French music author) November 20; Charles-Simon Richault (French publisher) February 20.

C. Debuts

Singers: Giuseppe Fancelli (Italian tenor—Milan); Minnie Hauk (American soprano—Brooklyn, age fourteen); Leonard Labatt (Swedish tenor—Stockholm); Mathilde Mallinger (Croatian soprano—Munich); Pierre Léon Melchissédec (French baritone—Paris); Stanislaw Niedzielski (Polish baritone—Kraków); Eugenie Pappenheim (Austrian soprano—Linz); Sofia Scalchi (Italian mezzo-soprano—Mantua).

Performers: Gustav Frieman (Polish violinist—Dresden); Anna Mehlig (German pianist—London); Emile Sauret (French violinist—London).

D. New Positions

Conductors: Théodore Dubois (maître de chapelle, Sainte-Clothilde, Paris); Edvard Grieg (Christiana Harmonic Society, Norway); Bedřich Smetana (Provisional Theater, Prague); Carl Zerrahn (Harvard Musical Association).

Others: William Sterndale Bennett (principal, Royal Academy of Music, London); Hilarión Eslava (director, Madrid Conservatory); Gabriel Fauré (organ, St. Sauveur, Rennes); Alphonse Goovaerts (archivist, Royal Archives, Brussels); Adolf L'Arronge (director, Kroll Opera, Berlin); Nicolai Rubinstein (director, Moscow Conservatory); Wilhelm Tappert (editor, *Allgemeine Deutsche Musikzeitung*); Peter Ilyich Tchaikovsky (Professor of Harmony, Moscow Conservatory).

E. Prizes/Honors

Prizes: Edvard Grieg (Stockholm Academy Prize); Emile-Louis Pessard (Prix de Rome); Alexandre Regnault (Prix de Rome).
Honors: Charles Gounod (French Institute).

F. Biographical Highlights

Johannes Brahms tours as accompanist with the violinist Joseph Joachim; Carl Loewe quits his Stettin post and settles in Kiel; Pablo de Sarasate acquires his famous Stradivarius violin; German publisher Arthur P. Schmidt settles in Boston; Theodore Thomas becomes sole conductor of the Brooklyn Philharmonic; Henri Vieuxtemps moves to Paris to escape political unrest.

G. Cultural Beginnings

Performing Groups—Choral: Augsburger Oratorienverein; Bedford Music Society (England); Mendelssohn Glee Club of New York; Muza (Kraków amateur music society).

Performing Groups—Instrumental: Istituto Filarmonico (Vicenza); Louisville (Kentucky) Philharmonic Society; Portland (Oregon) Philharmonic Music Society; Sociedad de Conciertos (Madrid); Sociedad de Música Clásica (Havana); Union Musicale de Québec.

Educational: Istituto Musicale Antonio Venturi (Brescia); Klavier-Schule Tausig (Berlin); Liceo Musicale (Turin); Moscow Conservatory of Music.

Music Publishers: Alsbach Music Publishers (Rotterdam); Georges Hartmann (Paris); G. Schirmer Publishing Co. (New York).

Music Publications: *Fliegende Blätter für Katholische Kirchenmusik*; *Musica Sacra*; *Il Secolo*.

Performing Centers: Continental Theatre (Boston); Düsseldorf Tonhalle; Greenlaw Opera House (Memphis); St. Paul (Minnesota) Opera House; Steinway Hall (New York).

Other: Domino Club (Bologna); Leypoldt and Holt, book publishers; G. P. Putnam and Son (New York); Schwartzer Zither Factory; Summer Terrace Garden Concerts (New York).

H. Musical Literature

Domenico Bertini, *Compendio de' principi di musica, secondo un nuovo sistema*; Jean G. Bertrand, *Les origines de l'harmonie*; Carl Engel, *An Introduction to the Study of National Music*; Otto Jahn, *Gesammelte Aufsätze über Musik*; Eduard Krüger *System der Tonkunst*; Ernst Mach, *Einleitung in die Helmholtz'sche musiktheorie*; Arthur von Oettingen, *Harmoniesystem in dualer Entwickelung*; Wilhelm Tappert, *Musik und musikalische Erziehung*; Théodore de Vroye, *De la musique religieuse*; William Walker, *The Christian Harmony*.

I. Musical Compositions

Chamber Music:

   String Quartets: Joachim Raff, *No. 3 in e, Opus 136*.

   Sonata/Solos: Anton Bruckner, *Abendklänge in e* (violin, piano); Joachim Raff, *Violin Sonata No. 4 in g, Opus 129*; Henri Vieuxtemps, *Old England, Opus 42* (violin, piano).

   Ensembles: Caryl Florio, *Piano Trio in D*; Carl Reinecke, *Piano Quintet in A, Opus 83*; Camille Saint-Saëns, *Romance in B♭, Opus 27*; Giovanni Sgambati, *Piano Quintet No. 1*.

   Piano: Zdeněk Fibich, *Albumblätter, Opus 2–Scherzo in e, Opus 4*; Stephen Heller, *Two Etudes, Opus 116–Three Ballades, Opus 113*; John Knowles Paine, *Four Character Pieces, Opus 11*; Silas G. Pratt, *Shakespearian Grand March*; Joachim Raff, *Blätter und Blüten, Opus*

135; Anton Rubinstein, *Album de Peterhof, Opus 75–Fantasia in e, Opus 77.*

Organ: Dudley Buck, *Grand Sonata in E♭*; Joachim Raff, *Introduction and Fugue in e*; Camille Saint-Saëns, *Three Rhapsodies on Breton Themes, Opus 7.*

Choral/Vocal Music:
Choral: Julius Benedict, *St. Cecilia* (oratorio); Johannes Brahms, *Twelve Songs and Romances, Opus 44*; George Frederick Bristow, *Daniel, Opus 42* (oratorio); Anton Bruckner, *Mass No. 2 in e*; Théodore Dubois, *Les sept Paroles du Christ*; César Franck, *Mass in e*; Niels Gade, *Die Kreuzfahrer, Opus 50* (cantata); Charles Gounod, *Tobie* (cantata); William Jackson, *Praise of Music*; Franz Liszt, *Christus*; Emil Naumann, *Dank- und Jubel-Cantate, Opus 30;* Giovanni Pacini, *Canto del prigionero*; Anton Rubinstein, *Morning, Opus 74* (cantata).
Vocal: John B. Dykes, *St. Agnes* (hymn tune, "Jesus, the Very Thought of Thee"); Robert Franz, *Six Songs, Opus 37*; Modest Mussorgsky, *Hopak*; Henry Clay Work, *Who Shall Rule This American Nation?*
Musical Stage: Friedrich von Flotow, *Zilda*; Hervé, *Les chevaliers de la Table Ronde–Les métamorphoses de Tartempion*; Edouard Lalo, *Fiesque*; Charles Lecocq, *Le Myosotis–Ondines au champagne*; Jules Massenet, *La coupe du roi de Thulé*; Saverios Mercadante, *Virginia*; Jacques Offenbach, *Barbe-bleue–La vie parisienne*; Errico Petrella, *Catarina Howard*; Franz von Suppé, *Light Cavalry–Freigeister*; Ambroise Thomas, *Mignon.*

Orchestra/Band Music:
Concerted Music:
   Violin: Camille Saint-Saëns, *Romance in E, Opus 67* (horn/cello).
   Other: Peter Benoit, *Symphonic Ode, Opus 30* (flute); Carl Reinecke, *Cello Concerto in d, Opus 82*; Arthur Sullivan, *Cello Concerto in D.*
Ballet/Incidental Music: Léo Delibes, *La source* (B); Stanislaw Moniuszko, *Monte Cristo* (B).
Standard Works: Edvard Grieg, *Concert Overture, "In Autumn," Opus 11*; Franz Liszt, *Trois odes funèbres*; Stanislaw Moniuszko, *Polonaise de Concert*; Eduard Nápravnik, *Solemn Overture, Opus 14*; Nikolai Rimsky-Korsakov, *Overture on Three Russian Themes, Opus 28*; Arthur Sullivan, *Overture, In Memoriam*; Peter Ilyich Tchaikovsky, *Festival Overture on Danish Hymn, Opus 15–Concert Overture in c.*
Symphonies: Mily Balakirev, *No. 1 in C*; Anton Bruckner, *No. 1 in c–No. 2 in c;* Joseph Joachim Raff, *No. 2 in C, Opus 140*; Arthur Sullivan, *Symphony in e, "Irish"*; Peter Ilyich Tchaikovsky, *No. 1 in g, Opus 13, "Winter Dreams."*

1867

❄

Historical Highlights: The Austrian-Hungarian Empire is formed with Joseph I as emperor; the French dream of a Mexican Empire comes to an end with the execution of Emperor Maximilian; the North German Federation is formed; Canada becomes a sovereign state in the British Commonwealth; "Seward's Folly"—the United States buys Alaska from Russia; Nebraska becomes state number thirty-seven; the Standard Oil Co. is founded by John D. Rockefeller.

Art and Literature Highlights: Births—artists Frank Brangwyn, George Luks, Emil Nolde, writers Léon Daudet, John Galsworthy, Luigi Pirandello, Laura Wilder; Deaths—artist Charles Deas, writers Charles Browne, Fitz-Greene Halleck. Art—Manet's *Execution of Emperor Maximilian*, Monet's *Ladies in a Garden*, Renoir's *Diana*, Weir's *Forging the Shaft*; Literature—Carré's *Mignon*, Ibsen's *Peer Gynt*, Zola's *Thérèse Raquin*.

Musical Highlights

A. Births

Composers: Amy (Mrs. H. H. A.) Beach (U.S.A.) September 5; Umberto Giordano (Italy) August 28; Enrique Granados (Spain) July 27; Charles Koechlin (France) November 27; Margaret Ruthven Lang (U.S.A.) November 27; Edward Maryon (England) April 3; Wilhelm Peterson-Berger (Sweden) February 27; Adolf Weidig (Germany-U.S.A.) November 28.

Conductors: Carl Wilhelm Henning (Germany) March; Emil Oberhoffer (Germany-U.S.A.) August 10; Vincent F. Safranek (U.S.A.) March 24; Roland Forrest Seitz (U.S.A.) June 14; Arturo Toscanini (Italy) March 25.

Singers: Josephine von Antner (Czech soprano) November 10; Robert Blass (American bass) October 27; Olimpia Boronat (Italian soprano); Edmond Clément (French tenor) March 28; Léon David (French tenor) December 18; Marie Dietrich (German soprano) January 1; Ivan Ershov (Russian tenor) November 20; Ida Hiedler (Austrian soprano) August 24; Laura Hilgermann (Austrian mezzo-soprano) October 13; William Wade Hinshaw (American baritone) November 3; Marcel Journet (French bass) July 23; Adolphe Maréchal (Belgian tenor) September 26; Alice Nielsen (American soprano)(?); Albert Saléza (French tenor) October 18; Laurent Swolfs (Belgian tenor); Thomas Salignac (French tenor) March 19; Sophie Traubmann (American soprano) May 12; Jacques Urlus (Dutch tenor) January 9; Edyth Walker (American mezzo-soprano) March 27; Harry Evan Williams (American tenor) September 7.

Performers: Herbert Clarke (American cornet virtuoso) September 12; Charles Winfred Douglas (American organist) February 15; Karl Fiqué (German-born organist) April 17; T. Tertius Noble (British-born organist/composer) May 5; William Orchard (British-born pianist/conductor) October 26; Vasili Sapelnikov (Russian pianist) November 2; Martinus Sieveking (Dutch-born pianist) March 24; John Winter Thompson (American organist) December 21; Teresina Tua (Italian violinist) May 22.

Others: Eduard Bernoulli (Swiss music scholar) November 6; Frances Densmore (American ethnomusicologist) May 21; Ferdinand Hoesick (Polish musicologist) October 16; Otto Hermann Kohn (German-born patron of the arts); John Avery Lomax (American folk music collector) September 23; Walter Naumburg (American patron of the arts) December 25; Henry Taylor Parker (American critic) April 29; Gertrude Clarke Whittall (American patron of the arts) October 7.

B. Deaths

Composers: György Adler (Hungary)(?); Nicola Benvenuti (Italy) August 14; John Fawcett (England) October 26; Wiktor Kazyński (Poland) March 18; Giovanni Pacini (Italy) December 6; Józef Stefani (Poland) March 19.

Conductors: Johann Kasper Aiblinger (Germany) May 6; Carlo Emanuele Barbieri (Italy) September 28.

Singers: Henriette Clementine Lalande (French soprano) September 7; Constance Nantier-Didiée (French mezzo-soprano) December 4; Fanny Persiani (Italian soprano) May 3; Willoughby-Hunter Weiss (British tenor) October 24; Mary Ann Wilson (British soprano) December 13.

Performers: Ignacy Felix Dobrzynski (Polish pianist/composer) October 10; Edward Hodges (British organist) September 1; Simon Sechter (Austrian organist/pedagogue) September 10; George T. Smart (British organist) February 23.

Others: Jean Georges Kastner (French music theorist/composer) December 19; William Letton Viner (British hymnist) July 24.

C. Debuts

Singers: Marianne Brandt (Austrian contralto—Olmütz); William Candidus (American tenor—New York); Annie Louise Cary (American contralto—Copenhagen); Pierre Gailhard (French bass—Paris); Marie Hanfstängel (German soprano—Paris); Elizaveta Andreievna Lavrovskaya (Russian mezzo-soprano—St. Petersburg); Marie Leh-

mann (German soprano—Leipzig); Angelo Masini (Italian tenor—Finale Emilia); Victor Maurel (French baritone—Marseilles); Ivan Melnikov (Russian baritone—St. Petersburg); Luise Radecke (German soprano—Cologne); Georg Unger (German tenor—Leipzig).
Performers: Sophie Menter (German pianist—Leipzig); Joseph Servais (Belgian cellist—Warsaw).

D. New Positions
Conductors: Johann Joseph Abert (Stuttgart Court Orchestra); Mily Balakirev (Musical Society Concerts, Moscow); Julius Benedict (Liverpool Philharmonic Society); George Frederick Bristow (New York Mendelssohn Society); Max Bruch (Sondershausen); William Cusins (London Philharmonic Society); Franz von Dingelstedt (Vienna Opera); François Gevaert (Paris Opera); Eugenio Terziani (La Scala, Milan).
Others: Elfrida Andrée (organ, Gothenburg Cathedral); Hans von Bülow (director, Munich Conservatory); Alexander Dargomijsky (President, Russian Musical Society); Julius Eichberg (director, Boston Conservatory); Niels Gade (director, Copenhagen Conservatory); Eben Tourjée (director, New England Conservatory).

E. Prizes/Honors
Prizes: Hendrik Waelput (Prix de Rome).

F. Biographical Highlights
Anton Bruckner suffers a nervous breakdown; Edvard Grieg, settling in Copenhagen to teach, marries Nina Hagerup; Modest Mussorgsky is dismissed from his ministry job; Vladimir Stasov, writing in a Russian journal, creates the name, "the mighty handful," in referring to the Balakirev circle; Johann Strauss takes his orchestra on their only English visit; Arthur Sullivan, in Vienna with Charles Grove, helps discover Schubert's lost manuscripts.

G. Cultural Beginnings
Performing Groups—Choral: Denver Musical Union; Hamburg Tonkünstlerverein; Hungarian Singer's Association (Budapest); Kiev Opera Co.; Manchester Vocal Union; Società dei Concerti Benedetto Marcello (Venice); Uppsala Cathedral Choir.
Performing Groups—Instrumental: Bilsesche Kapelle (Berlin); Chandler's Band (Portland, Maine); Florentine String Quartet; Knoxville (Tennessee) Philharmonic Society; Pest Philharmonic Society; Società Romana del Quartetto (Rome).
Educational: Basler Musikschule; Boston Conservatory of Music; Buda Music Academy; Chicago Musical College; Cincinnati Conservatory of Music; Flemish Music School (Antwerp); Free Music School (Vilnus); Melopea Accademia Filarmonica-Drammatica (Messina);

New England Music Conservatory; Norwegian Academy of Music; Tonic Sol-Fa College (Manchester).

Music Publishers: Bigelow and Main (New York); Enoch and Sons (London); Ginn and Co. (Boston); Smith, White and Perry (Boston).

Performing Centers: Augsburger Stadttheater; Colston Hall (Bristol, England); Pence Opera House (Minneapolis); Regio Teatro Nuovo (Pisa); St. George's Hall (London).

Other: Clube Mozart (Rio de Janeiro); Music Lover's Society of Pest; National Hungarian Association of Choral Societies; Pernerstorfer Circle (Vienna Conservatory); Schreiber Cornet Co. (New York); Turner and Steere Organ Co. (Westfield, Massachusetts); Working Men's Society of London.

H. Musical Literature

Johannes Bastiaans, *Treatise on Harmony*; William B. Bradbury, *Fresh Laurels for Sabbath School*; Ludwig Bussler, *Musikalische elementarlehre*; J. B. Fourneaux, *Instrumentologie: traité théorique et practique*; Gaetano Gaspari, *Recherche, documenti e memorie risquardanti la storia dell'arte musicale in Bologna*; George Macfarren, *Six Lectures on Harmony, Delivered at the Royal Institution*; Lucy McKim Garrison et al., *Slave Songs of the U.S.*; Adolf Marx, *Das ideal und die Gegenwart* (posthumous publication); William Mason, *A Method for the Piano*; William Mathews, *Outlines of Music Form*; Emil Naumann, *Das Alter des Psalmengesänge*; John Tyndall, *Sound*.

I. Musical Compositions

Chamber Music:

String Quartets: C. Hubert Parry, *No 1 in g*; Joachim Raff, *No. 5 in G, Opus 138*.

Sonata/Solos: Henri Duparc, *Cello Sonata in a*; Edvard Grieg, *Violin Sonata No. 2 in G, Opus 13*; Ludvig Norman, *Cello Sonata in D, Opus 28*; Carl Reinecke, *Cello Sonata in D, Opus 89*.

Ensembles: Ludvig Norman, *String Octet in C, Opus 30*.

Piano: George Frederick Bristow, *Raindrops, Opus 43*; Edvard Grieg, *Lyric Pieces, Book I, Opus 12*; Stephen Heller, *Three Preludes, Opus 117–Variétés, Opus 118–Thirty-Two Preludes "à Mlle Lili," Opus 119–Seven Lieder, Opus 120–Three morceaux, Opus 121*; Silas G. Pratt, *Grand March Heroique*; Anton Rubinstein, *Five Pieces (A♭, G, a, b, d), Opus 69–Three Pieces (A♭, f, D♭), Opus 71*; Charles M. Widor, *Concert Variations on an Original Theme*.

Choral/Vocal Music:

Choral: William Sterndale Bennett, *The Woman of Samaria* (oratorio); Peter Benoit, *Prometheus* (oratorio); Max Bruch, *Schön Ellen, Opus 21*; Théodore Dubois, *The Seven Last Words of Christ* (oratorio); Charles Gounod, *Stabat Mater*; Franz Liszt, *Hungarian Corona-*

tion Mass; Stanislaw Moniuszko, *Crimean Sonnets*; Modest Mussorgsky, *The Rout of Sennacherib* (cantata); Giovanni Pacini, *Il carcere Mamertino*; John Knowles Paine, *Mass in D, Opus 10*; Józef Poniatowski, *Messe solennelle*; Joachim Raff, *De profundis, Opus 141*; Camille Saint-Saëns, *Les noces de Prométhée, Opus 19* (cantata).
Vocal: Robert Franz, *Six Heine Lieder, Opus 38–Six Heine Lieder, Opus 39–Six Songs, Opus 40–Six Songs, Opus 41*; Ludvig Norman, *Forest Songs, Opus 31*; Anton Rubinstein, *Six German Songs, Opus 76*; Joseph P. Webster, *In the Sweet By and By.*
Musical Stage: Peter Benoit, *Isa*; Georges Bizet, *The Fair Maid of Perth*; Vilem Blodek, *In the Well*; Alexander Borodin, *The Bogatyrs*; Jules-Laurent Duprato, *La Fiancée de Corinthe*; Charles Gounod, *Romeo and Juliet*; Hervé, *Clodoche et Normande–L'oeil crevé*; Vladimir Kashperov, *The Storm*; Jules Massenet, *La grand'tante*; Victor Nessler, *Dornröschens Brautfahrt*; Jacques Offenbach, *Robinson Crusoé–La permission de dix heures–La Grande-Duchesse de Gérolstein*; Giovanni Pacini, *Don Diego di Mendoza*; Amilcare Ponchielli, *La stella del Monte*; Carl Reinecke, *König Manfred*; Lauro Rossi, *Lo Zingaro rivale–Il maestro e la cantante*; Bedřich Smetana, *Dalibor*; Gilbert/Sullivan, *Cox and Box–Contrabandista*; Franz von Suppé, *Banditenstreiche*; Giuseppe Verdi, *Don Carlo*; Pauline Viadot-Garcia, *Trop de Femmes.*
Orchestra/Band Music:
Concerted Music:
  Piano: Henry Litolff, *Concerto No. 5, Opus 123.*
Program Music: Modest Mussorgsky, *A Night on Bald Mountain.*
Standard Works: Mily Balakirev, *Overture on Czech Themes*; Franz Liszt, *Hungarian Crown March*; Nikolai Rimsky-Korsakov, *Fantasy on Serbian Themes*; Frédéric L. Ritter, *Overture to Othello*; Johann Strauss, Jr., *On the Beautiful Blue Danube.*
Symphonies: Alexander Borodin, *No. 1 in E♭*; Johan Svendsen, *No. 1 in D, Opus 4.*

1868

❄

Historical Highlights: The Burlingame Treaty opens the way for uninhibited immigration of cheap labor from the Orient; Cuba tries to gain her independence by going to war with Spain; William Gladstone becomes the new British Prime Minister; in the United States, the impeachment of President Andrew Johnson fails by one vote; Ulysses S. Grant is elected as eighteenth president; the Fourteenth Amendment is ratified.

Art and Literature Highlights: Births—artists Alfred Maurer, Édouard Vuillard, writers W. E. B. DuBois, Paul Claudel, Maxim Gorky, Wladyslaw Reymont; Deaths—artists Emmanuel Leutze, William S. Mount, writer Robert Griepenkerl. Art—Degas' *L'Orchestre*, Heade's *Storm Approaching Narragansett Bay*, Renoir's *The Skaters*, Literature—Alcott's *Little Women*, Dostoyevsky's *The Idiot*, Tolstoy's *Czar Feodor Ivanovich*.

Musical Highlights

A. Births

Composers: Julián Aguirre (Argentina) January 28; Granville Bantock (England) August 7; Ernst Ellberg (Sweden) December 14; Henry F. Gilbert (U.S.A.) September 26; Hamish MacCunn (Scotland) March 22; John (Blackwood) McEwen (Scotland) April 13; Lodewijk Mortelmans (Belgium) February 5; Leone Sinigaglia (Italy) August 14; Charles Sanford Skilton (U.S.A.) August 16.

Conductors: Max von Schillings (Germany) April 19.

Singers: Desider Aranyi (Hungarian tenor) August 18; Hans Breuer (German tenor) April 27; Irene von Chavanne (Austrian contralto) April 18; John Forsell (Swedish baritone) November 6; Ferruccio Giannini (Italian-born tenor) November 15; Sissieretta Jones (American soprano) January 5; Lev Klementyev (Russian tenor) April 1; Frieda Langendorff (German contralto) March 24; Alice Nielsen (American soprano) June 7(?); Denis O'Sullivan (American baritone) April 25; Thila Plaichinger (Austrian soprano) March 13; Mario Sammarco (Italian baritone) December 13; Erik Schmedes (Danish tenor) August 27; Ellison Van Hoose (American tenor) August 18; Erika Wedekind (German soprano) November 13; Marie Wittich (German soprano) May 27.

Performers: Leonard Borwick (British pianist) February 26; Franz Drdla (Hungarian violinist/composer) November 28; Scott Joplin (American pianist/composer) November 24(?); Frederic Lamond (Scottish pianist) January 28; Maud Powell (American violinist) August 22; Alfred Madeley Richardson (British organist) June 1; Louis Victor Saar (Dutch-born pianist) December 10; Antoinette Szumowska (Polish-born pianist) February 22.

Others: Paul Bergmans (Belgian musicologist) January 23; Nikolai Findeisen (Russian music historian/journalist) July 23; Giulio Gatti-Casazza (Italian impresario) February 3; Alfred Lorenz (Austrian musicologist/conductor) July 11; Ernest Newman (British critic/author) November 30; Max Seiffert (German musicologist) February 9; Heinrich Schenker (Austrian music theorist) June 9.

B. Deaths

Composers: Franz Berwald (Sweden) April 3; William Batchelder Bradbury (U.S.A.) January 7; Carlo Conti (Italy) July 10; Anselm

Huttenbrenner (Austria) June 5; Johann Friedrich Kittl (Bohemia) July 20; Gioacchino Rossini (Italy) November 13.

Singers: William Harrison (British tenor/impresario) November 9; Emma Romer (British soprano) April 11; Giorgio Stigelli (German tenor) July 3; William Winn (British bass) June 4.

Performers: Louis-François Dauprat (French horn virtuoso/composer) July 16; Carl Eberwein (German violinist) March 2; Carl Haslinger (Austrian pianist/publisher) December 26; Halfdan Kjerulf (Norwegian pianist/composer) October 11; Antoine Prumier (French harpist) January 20.

Others: Franz Brendel (German music author) November 25; Moritz Hauptman (German music theorist) January 3; Léon Charles Kreutzer (French critic/composer) October 6; Alphonse Leduc (French publisher) June 17; Jerome H. Remick (American publisher) November 15; Peter Joseph Simrock (German publisher) December 13; Alexandre-Joseph Vincent (French music theorist) November 26.

C. **Debuts**

Singers: Alfred-Auguste Giraudet (French bass—Paris); Emmy Fursch-Madi (French soprano—Paris); George Henschel (German baritone—Leipzig); Franz Krückl (Moravian baritone—Brünn); Jean Lassalle (French baritone—Liège); Romilda Pantaleoni (Italian soprano—Milan).

Performers: Alma Haas (German pianist—Leipzig); Ferdinand Inten (German-born pianist—New York); Natalia Janotha (Polish pianist—Warsaw); Laura Rappoldi (Austrian pianist—Vienna).

D. **New Positions**

Conductors: Ernst Frank (Würzburg Theater); Franz Richard Genée (Theater an der Wien, Vienna); Friedrich Marpurg (Darmstadt); Carlo Pedrotti (Teatro Regio, Turin).

Others: Mily Balakirev (director, Free School of Music, St. Petersburg); Anton Bruckner (professor of organ, theory and counterpoint, Vienna Conservatory); Alexandre Guilmant (organ, Notre Dame, Paris); John R. Hassard (music critic, the *New York Tribune*); Joseph Joachim (director, Berlin Hochschule); Otto Kitzler (director, Brünn Music School and Music Society); James H. Mapleson (manager, Drury Lane); Jules Pasdeloup (manager, Théâtre Lyrique, Paris); Carl Riedel (president, Allgemeiner Deutscher Musikverein); Theodore Seward (editor, *New York Musical Gazette*); Lucien Southard (director, Peabody Consevatory, Baltimore).

E. **Prizes/Honors**

Honors: Edvard Grieg (government life grant); Ferdinand Hiller (honorary doctorate, Bonn); Camille Saint-Saëns (Legion of Honor).

F. Biographical Highlights

Arrigo Boito suffers through the catastrophic premiere of his *Mephistopheles*; Robert Franz, due to increasing deafness and nervous disorders, retires; Richard Wagner begins a friendship with Nietzsche.

G. Cultural Beginnings

Performing Groups—Choral: Allgemeine Deutsche Caeciliaenverein (Bamberg); Apollo Club of Boston; Chicago Oratorio Society; Church Music Association (New York); Radecke Choral Society (Berlin); Société des Oratorios (Paris).

Performing Groups—Instrumental: Copenhagen Society of Chamber Music; Montevideo Philharmonic Society (Uruguay); Societatea Filarmonica Româna (Filarmonica George Enescŭ).

Educational: Academie de Musique (Quebec); Dreszer Music School (Halle); Goldbeck Conservatory of Music (Chicago); Orleans Municipal Music School; Peabody Institute (Baltimore); Royal Danish Music Conservatory (Copenhagen).

Music Publishers: Edition Peters (Leipzig); Fürstner Publishing Co. (Berlin); Gubrynowicz Publishing House (Lvov); Kunkel Brothers (St. Louis); Seyfarth Music (Lvov).

Music Publications: *The Musical Independent; New York Philharmonic Journal; Zeitschrift für Katholische Kirchenmusik.*

Performing Centers: Belgrade National Theater; Grand (Pike's) Opera House (New York); Powell Symphony Hall (St. Louis).

Other: Charles F. Albert Violin Shop (Philadelphia); Erben Organ (St. Patrick's, New York); Gesellschaft für Musikforschung (Berlin); Johann C. Neupert, piano and harpsichord maker; Société Bourgault-Ducoudray (Paris); Society for the History of Netherlands' Music; Tonhalle-Gesellschaft (Zürich).

H. Musical Literature

Félix Clément, *Les musiciens célèbres depuis le 16ème siècle jusqu'à nos jours*; Ferdinand Hiller, *Aus dem Tonleben unserer Zeit*; Rudolf Lotze, *Geschichte der Aesthetik in Deutschland*; Charles Meerens, *Phénomènes Musico-Physiologiques*; Frederick Ouseley, *Treatise on Harmony*; Oscar Paul, *Geschichte des Klaviers*; Edouard Schuré, *Histoire du Lied*; Wilhelm Tappert, *Musikalische Studien*; Otto Tiersch, *System und Methode der Harmonielehre*; Carl Weitzmann, *Der Letzte der Virtuosen.*

I. Musical Compositions

Chamber Music:

String Quartets: Félicien David, *Quartet in f*; Frederick Ouseley, *No. 1 in C–No. 2 in d*; C. Hubert Parry, *No. 2 in e.*

Sonata/Solos: Friedrich Kiel, *Cello Sonata in a*; Joachim Raff, *Violin Sonata No. 5 in g, Opus 145.*

Ensembles: Ferdinand Hiller, *Piano Quartet No. 3, Opus 133*; Franz Lachner, *Piano Quintet No. 1 in a, Opus 139*.

Piano: Anton Bruckner, *Fantasie in G*; Dudley Buck, *Concert Variations on "The Star-Spangled Banner"*; Zdeněk Fibich, *Fugato, Opus 24*; Hermann Goetz, *Sonata in g, Four Hands*; Stephen Heller, *Feuilles volantes, Opus 123–Kinderszenen, Opus 124–Twenty-four études d'expression et de rhythme, Opus 125*; John Knowles Paine, *Romance in c, Opus 12*.

Choral/Vocal Music:

Choral: Peter Benoit, *De schelde* (oratorio); Johannes Brahms, *Ein Deutsches Requiem, Opus 45–Rinaldo, Opus 50* (cantata); Anton Bruckner, *Mass No. 3 in f*; Ferdinand Hiller, *Ostermorgen, Opus 134*; Franz Liszt, *Requiem*; George Macfarren, *Songs in a Cornfield* (cantata); Saverio Mercadante, *Gran messa*; C. Hubert Parry, *Te Deum and Benedictus*; Bedřich Smetana, *Song of the Czechs II* (cantata).

Vocal: Alexander Borodin, *Five Songs* (includes *The Sea*); Johannes Brahms, *Seven Songs, Opus 48–Five Songs, Opus 49*; Charles Converse, *Converse* (hymn tune, "What a Friend We Have in Jesus"); Carl Goldmark, *Twelve Songs, Opus 18*; Jules Massenet, *Poème de Souvenir*; Horatio Palmer, *Hymn, "Yield Not to Temptation"*; Lewis H. Redner, *St. Louis* (hymn tune, "O Little Town of Bethlehem"); Anton Rubinstein, *Twelve Russian Songs, Opus 78*; Septimus Winner, *Whispering Hope*.

Musical Stage: Daniel Auber, *Le premier jour de bonheur*; Karel Bendl, *Lejla*; Georges Bizet, *Noé* (with Halévy); Arrigo Boito, *Mephistopheles*; Hervé, *Trombolina–Chilpéric–Le roi Amatibou*; Charles Lecocq, *Fleur-de-thé–L'amour et son carquois*; Modest Mussorgsky, *The Marriage*; Eduard Nápravník, *The Inhabitants of Nishij Novgorod, Opus 15*; Jacques Offenbach, *La Périchole–L'île de Tulipatan–Le château à toto*; Józef Poniatowski, *La Contessina*; Joachim Raff, *Die Parole*; Alexander Serov, *Taras Bulba* (unfinished); Franz von Suppé, *Die Frau Meisterin*; Peter Ilyich Tchaikovsky, *Pan Voyevoda, Opus 3*; Ambroise Thomas, *Hamlet*; Pauline Viardot-Garcia, *L'Ogre*; Richard Wagner, *Die Meistersinger von Nurnburg*.

Orchestra/Band Music:

Concerted Music:

Piano: Louis Moreau Gottschalk, *Grand Tarantelle*; Edvard Grieg, *Concerto in a, Opus 16*; Camille Saint-Saëns, *Concerto No. 2 in g, Opus 22*.

Violin: Max Bruch, *Concerto No. 1 in g, Opus 26*; Henryk Wieniawski, *Fantasy on Gounod's Faust, Opus 20*.

Ballet/Incidental Music: Johann P. Hartmann, *The Legend of Thrym, Opus 67* (B); Stanislaw Moniuszko, *In the Quarters* (B).

Program Music: Georges Bizet, *Roma*; Peter Ilyich Tchaikovsky, *Fatum, Opus 7*.

Standard Works: Louis Moreau Gottschalk, *Marche Solennelle*; Franz Lachner, *Suite No. 5 in c, Opus 135*; Saverio Mercadante, *Omaggio a Rossini*; Bedřich Smetana, *Festive Overture in C*; Johann Strauss, Jr., *Tales from the Vienna Woods–Thunder and Lightning Polka*.

Symphonies: Louis Moreau Gottschalk, *No. 2, "A Montevideo"*; Nikolai Rimsky-Korsakov, *No. 2, "Antar," Opus 9*.

1869

❄

Historical Highlights: The Suez Canal is officially opened to ocean-going traffic of all nations; the British Debtor's Act abolishes mandatory imprisonment for debt; Napoleon III gives France a parliamentary government; in the United States, the transcontinental railroad line is completed at Promontory Point, Utah; Black Friday marks the beginning of a Panic on Wall Street; the American Women Suffrage Association is founded.

Art and Literature Highlights: Births—artist Henri Matisse, writers André Gide, Edgar Lee Masters, Edwin Arlington Robinson, Booth Tarkington; Deaths—artists Paul Huet, Robert Lauder, writers Frederick Cozzens, Alphonse de Lamartine. Art—Carpeaux's *The Dance*, Manet's *The Balcony*, Moran's *The Spirit of the Indian*; Literature—Blackmore's *Lorna Doone*, Southworth's *The Fatal Marriage*, Twain's *Innocents Abroad*.

Musical Highlights

A. Births

Composers: Juan Bautista Fuentes (Mexico) March 16; Harry Lawrence Freeman (U.S.A.) October 9; Hans Pfitzner (Germany) May 5; Carl Prohaska (Austria) April 25; Albert Roussel (France) April 5; Siegfried Wagner (Germany) June 6.

Conductors: Armas Järnefelt (Finland) August 14; Arnold Volpe (Lithuania-U.S.A.) July 9; Henry Wood (England) March 3.

Singers: Theodor Bertram (German baritone) February 12; Richard Breitenfeld (Bohemian baritone) December 13; Lucienne Bréval (Swiss-born soprano) November 4; Susanne Dessoir (Germany soprano) July 23; Annie Dirkens (German soprano) September 25; Fritz Feinhals (German baritone) December 4; Berta Foersterova-Lautererová (Czech soprano) January 11; Marie Olenine d'Alheim

(Russian soprano) October 1; Jean Périer (French baritone) February 2; Joseph Sheehan (American tenor).

Performers: Hugh Percy Allen (British organist) December 23; Ivor Atkins (British organist) November 29; Clara Damrosch Mannes (German-born pianist) December 12; Karl Ekman (Finnish pianist/composer) December 18; Richard Epstein (Austrian pianist) January 26; Patty Stair (American organist/composer) November 12; George Waring Stebbins (American organist/composer) June 16; Sigismund Stojowski (Polish-born pianist/composer) May 14; Arnold Volpe (Russian violinist) July 9.

Others: John Turnell Austin (British-born organ builder) May 16; André Pirro (French musicologist) February 12; Johannes Wolf (German musicologist) April 17.

B. Deaths

Composers: Louis Hector Berlioz (France) March 8; Alexander Dargomijsky (Russia) January 17; Albert Grisar (Belgium) June 15; Carl Loewe (Germany) April 20; Giuseppe Persiani (Italy) August 14.

Singers: Giulia Grisi (Italian soprano) November 29; Anton Haizinger (Austrian tenor) December 31; Agnes Schebest (Austrian mezzo-soprano) December 22.

Performers: August Berwald (Swedish violinist) November 13; Alexander Dreyschock (Bohemian pianist) April 1; Raimund Dreyschock (Bohemian violinist) February 6; Louis Moreau Gottschalk (American pianist/composer) December 18; Ernst Haberbier (German pianist) March 12; Theodore von La Hache (German-born pianist/composer) November 21; Louis-James Léfebure-Wély (French organist) December 31; Wilhelm Molique (German violinist/composer) May 10.

Others: Otto Jahn (German music scholar) September 9; George Peabody (American patron of the arts) November 4.

C. Debuts

Singers: Marie Cabel (Belgian soprano—Paris); Giuseppe Kaschmann (Italian baritone—Zagreb); Theodor Reichmann (German baritone—Madgeburg); Francesco Tamagno (Italian tenor—Palermo).

Performers: Nahan Franko (American violinist—New York); Sam Franko (American violinist—New York); Alexander Michalowski (Polish pianist—Leipzig); Vladimir de Pachmann (Russian-born pianist—Odessa).

D. New Positions

Conductors: Karl Eckert (Berlin Royal Opera); Heinrich Laube (Leipzig Stadttheater); Carl Millöcker (Theater an der Wien); Eduard

Nápravník (Russian Imperial Opera and Russian Musical Society Orchestra).
Others: Charles-Alexis Chauvet (principal organ, La Trinité, Paris); Robert Eitner (editor, *Monatschefte für Musikgeschichte*); Hendrik Waelput (director, Bruges Conservatory).

E. **Prizes/Honors**
Prizes: Jan van den Eeden (Prix de Rome); Antoine Taudou (Prix de Rome).
Honors: Michael Costa (knighted); Félicien David (French Institute); Nicolas Levasseur (Legion of Honor); John Knowles Paine (M.A., Harvard); Eben Tourjée (Ph.D., Wesleyan University).

F. **Biographical Highlights**
Anton Bruckner makes his first appearance as an organ virtuoso in France; Cosima von Bülow divorces Hans and bears Wagner's son, Siegfried; Patrick S. Gilmore stages his mammoth National Peace Jubilee in Boston; Modest Mussorgsky reenters government service as a clerk in the Ministry of State Property; Theodore Thomas takes his orchestra on a national tour.

G. **Cultural Beginnings**
Performing Groups—Choral: Parepa-Rosa English Opera Co.; Schola Cantorum of San Salvatore (Lauro); Société Sainte-Cécile (Quebec); Vienna Staatsoper; Washington Choral Society (D.C.).
Performing Groups—Instrumental: Joachim String Quartet (Berlin); Nya Harmonska Sällskapet (Stockholm).
Educational: College of Organists (London); Czech Teacher's Institute; Dijon Conservatory of Music; Liceo Musicale "G. Frescobaldi" (Ferrara); Philadelphia Musical Academy; Radecke Music School (Berlin); Tonic Sol-Fa College (Curwen Institute); Wyman Music School (Claremont, New York).
Music Publishers: Bessel and Co. (St. Petersburg); Concordia Publishing House (St. Louis); Durand Schoenewerk and Cie. (A. Durand et Fils, 1891—Paris).
Music Publications: *L'Écho Musical*; *The Folio: A Journal of Music, Art and Literature*; *Monatschefte für Musikgeschichte*; *Organist's Quarterly Journal* (London); *Le Rappel*.
Performing Centers: Detroit Opera House; German Theater (San Francisco).
Other: Boston Musical Instrument Co.; J. H. Willcox Co. (Hutchings, Plaisted and Co.), organ builders (Boston).

H. **Musical Literature**
José Alcedo, *Filosofia elemental de la música*; Charles Coussemaker, *Les Harmonistes du XIV Siècle*; Carl Engel, *Musical Instruments of All*

Countries; Hilarión Eslava, *Lira Sacra-Hispana*; François-Joseph Fétis, *Histoire générale de la Musique I*; Gaetano Gaspari, *Ragguagli sulla cappella musicale della Basilica di S. Petronio in Bologna*; Otto Gumprecht, *Musikalische charakterbilder*; Eduard Hanslick, *Geschichte des Concertwesens in Wien*; Emil Krause, *Ergänzungen: Aufgabenbuch für die Harmonielehre*; Johann Christian Lobe, *Consonanzen und Dissonanzen*; Frederick Ouseley, *A Treatise on Counterpoint, Canon and Fugue, Based on Cherubini*; Richard Wagner, *Über das Dirigieren*.

I. Musical Compositions
Chamber Music:
String Quartets: Antonin Dvořák, *No. 2 in B♭–No. 3 in D*(?).

Sonata/Solos: Zdeněk Fibich, *Violin Sonatina in d, Opus 27*; Carl Goldmark, *Suite No. 1 in D, Opus 11* (violin, piano); Ludvig Norman, *Viola Sonata in G, Opus 32*; Carl Reinecke, *Cello Sonata No. 2 in D, Opus 89*(?).

Ensembles: Antonin Dvořák, *Clarinet Quintet in b♭*(?); Franz Lachner, *Piano Quintet No. 2 in c, Opus 145*; Ludvig Norman, *Sextet in a, Opus 29* (piano, strings).

Piano: Henri Duparc, *Feuilles Volantes, Opus 1*(?); Louis Moreau Gottschalk, *Fantasy on Brazilian National Anthem–The Dying Swan*; C. Hubert Parry, *Sonnets and Songs without Words I*.

Organ: George Macfarren, *Sonata in C*; Frederick Ouseley, *Six Short Preludes*.

Choral/Vocal Music:
Choral: Johannes Brahms, *Alto Rhapsody, Opus 53*; Niels Gade, *Festsang*; Charles Gounod, *Le temple de l'harmonie* (cantata); Franz Liszt, *Psalm 116*; Henry Litolff, *Ruth et Boaz* (oratorio); Arthur Sullivan, *The Prodigal Son* (oratorio).

Vocal: Johannes Brahms, *Liebeslieder, Opus 52*; César Cui, *Six Songs, Opus 7*; Niels Gade, *Denderliedeken* (cycle); Ferdinand Hiller, *Frühlingsnacht, Opus 139*; Carl Loewe, *Five Songs for Low Voice, Opus 145*; Anton Rubinstein, *Ten Songs, Opus 83*; William F. Sherwin, *Sound the Battle Cry* (hymn).

Musical Stage: Daniel Auber, *Rêve d'amour*; Karel Bendl, *Bretislav*; César Cui, *William Ratcliff*; Alexander Dargomijsky, *The Stone Guest* (unfinished); Léo Delibes, *L'ecossais de Chatou–La cour du roi Pétaud*; Ernest Guiraud, *En prison*; Hervé, *Le petit Faust–Les turcs*; Heinrich Hofmann, *Cartouche*; Charles Lecocq, *Gandolfo–Le rajah de Mysore*; Filippo Marchetti, *Ruy Blas*; Jules Massenet, *Manfred*; Stanislaw Moniuszko, *Paria*; Modest Mussorgsky, *Boris Goudonov*; Jacques Offenbach, *Vert-vert–La diva–Les brigands*; Errico Petrella, *Giovanni di Napoli–I promessi Sposi*; Joachim Raff, *Dame Kobold*; Josef Rheinberger, *Die sieben Raben*; Anton Rubinstein, *Der thurm* *zu Babel, Opus 80*; Franz von Suppé, *Isabella*; Peter Ilyich Tchaikovsky, *Undine*; Richard Wagner, *Siegfried*.

Orchestra/Band Music:

Concerted Music:

Piano: Anton Rubinstein, *Fantasia in C, Opus 84*; Camille Saint-Saëns, *Concerto No. 3 in E♭, Opus 29*.

Violin: Johan Svendsen, *Concerto in A, Opus 6*.

Program Music: Mily Balakirev, *Islamey*; Anton Rubinstein, *Ivan IV, Opus 79* (IM); Peter Ilyich Tchaikovsky, *Romeo and Juliet Fantasy Overture*.

Standard Works: Charles Converse, *American Concert Overture on "Hail Columbia"*; Melesio Morales, *La Locomotiva*; Johann Strauss, Jr., *Wine, Women and Song–Pizzicato Polka*.

Symphonies: Henry Cowell, *No. 1 in C*; Joseph Joachim Raff, *No. 3 in F, "Im Walde," Opus 153*.

1870

❄

Historical Highlights: The Franco-Prussian War begins in July—Napoleon III is deposed and the Third French Republic is proclaimed; the Doctrine of Papal Infallibility is proclaimed by Rome; in the United States, the census shows a population of 39,818,000; the Fifteenth Amendment on the right to vote is ratified; the symbol of the Democratic donkey first appears; the Department of Justice is created; the U.S. Weather Bureau is authorized.

Art and Literature Highlights: Births—artists Ernst Barlach, Hugh Breckenridge, Maurice Denis, writers Hilaire Belloc, Ivan Bunin, Pierre Louijs; Deaths—authors Charles Dickens, Alexander Dumas (père), Prosper Mérimée. Art—Alma-Tadema's *Un Jongleur*, Courbet's *The Wave*, Wood's *The Village Post Office*; Literature—Harte's *The Luck of Roaring Camp and Other Stories*, Tolstoy's *Tsar Boris*, Verne's *Twenty Thousand Leagues under the Sea*.

Musical Highlights

A. Births

Composers: Joseph Carl Breil (U.S.A.) June 29; Louis Coerne (U.S.A.) February 27; Mabel Wood Hill (U.S.A.) March 12; Lucius Hosmer (U.S.A.) August 14; Franz Lehár (Austria) April 30; Guillaume Lekeu (Belgium) January 20; Vitěslav Novák (Czechoslovakia) December 5; Joseph Ryelandt (Belgium) April 7; Florent Schmitt (France) September 28; Oscar Straus (Austria) March 6.

Conductors: Emil Mlynarski (Poland) July 18; Arthur Pryor (U.S.A.) September 22.

Singers: Alessandro Bonci (Italian tenor) February 10; Carl Burrian (Czech tenor) January 12; Mme. Charles Cahier (American contralto) January 8; Hector Dufranne (Belgian bass-baritone) October 25; Riza Eibenschütz (Hungarian contralto) February 17; Fiorello Giraud (Italian tenor) October 22; Heinrich Knote (German tenor) November 26; Felix von Kraus (Austrian bass) October 3; Max Lohfing (German bass) May 20; Matja von Niessen-Stone (Russian-born soprano) December 28; Antonio Paoli (Puerto Rican tenor); Aloys Pennarini (Austrian tenor); Albert Reiss (German tenor) February 2; Francis Rogers (American baritone) April 14; Robert Kennerley Rumford (British baritone) September 2; Susan Strong (American soprano) August 3; Minnie Tracey (?American soprano); Anton Van Rooy (Dutch bass-baritone) January 1.

Performers: August Johannes Biehle (German organist) June 18; Howard A. Brockway (American pianist/composer) November 22; Henry Eichheim (American violinist/composer) January 3; Leopold Godowsky (Polish-born pianist) February 13; August Schmid-Lindner (German pianist) July 15; Rose Laura Sutro (American pianist) September 15; Charles Tournemire (French organist/composer) January 22; Louis Vierne (French organist/composer) October 8; Hermann Wetzler (American organist/conductor) September 8; Theodor Wiehmayer (German pianist) January 7.

Others: Edmund H. Fellowes (British music scholar/editor) November 11; Cecil Forsyth (British music author/composer) November 30; Henryk Opieński (Polish music scholar/conductor) January 13; Dobroslav Orel (Czech music scholar) December 15; Anton Preobrazhensky (Russian musicologist) February 28; William Treat Upton (American musicologist/pianist/organist) December 17.

B. Deaths

Composers: Michael William Balfe (Ireland) October 20; Anton Berlijn (Holland) January 18; Erik Drake (Sweden) June 9; William Henry Havergal (England) April 19; Giuseppe Saverio Mercadante (Italy) December 17; Mihály Mosonyi (Hungary) October 31; Cesare Pugni (Italy) January 26; Ramon Vilanova (Spain) May.

Conductors: Josef Strauss (Austria) July 21.

Singers: Joséphine Fodor-Mainvielle (French soprano) August 14; Franz Hauser (Bohemian tenor) August 14; Arthur Saint-Léon (French violinist/conductor) September 2.

Performers: Charles Auguste de Bériot (Belgian violinist) April 8; Théodore Labarre (French harpist) March 8; Karl Leibl (German organist/conductor) October 4; Alexei Feodorevich Lvov (Russian violinist/composer) December 28; Ignaz Moscheles (Polish pianist/ composer) March 10; Johann Gottlob Töpfer (German organist) June 8; Gustave Vogt (French oboe virtuoso/composer) May 30.

Others: August Heinrich Cranz (German publisher); George Hogarth (Scottish music publisher) February 12; Dom Paul Jausions (French music author) September 9.

C. Debuts

Singers: Emma Albani (Canadian soprano—Messina); Georgina Weldon (British soprano—London); Heinrich Wiegand (German bass—Zürich).

Performers: Rafael Joseffy (Hungarian pianist—Berlin).

D. New Positions

Conductors: Johann Herbeck (Vienna Court Opera); Isodor Seiss (Musikalische Gesellschaft, Cologne); Auguste-Charles Vianesi (Covent Garden).

Others: Basil Köhner (director, Tiflis Conservatory); Hermann Mendel (editor, *Deutsche Musiker-Zeitung*); Lauro Rossi (director, Naples Conservatory); Charles Widor (organ, St. Sulpice).

E. Prizes/Honors

Prizes: Charles Édouard Lefebvre (Prix de Rome); Henri-Charles Maréchal (Prix de Rome).

Honors: William Sterndale Bennett (D.C.L. degree, Oxford); William George Cusins (Master of the Queen's Music).

F. Biographical Highlights

Charles Gounod visits London and forms his own concert choir; Vladimir Stasov donates his music collection to the St. Petersburg library; Henri Vieuxtemps makes his first concert tour of the United States; Richard Wagner marries Cosima von Bülow.

G. Cultural Beginnings

Performing Groups—Choral: Berner Männerchor; Denver Männerchor; Gounod's Choir (London); Société Chorale (Dijon); University Choral Society (Aberdeen); Worcester Musical (Festival Choral) Society; Zagreb Opera Co.

Performing Groups—Instrumental: Leeds Philharmonic Society; University Orchestral Society (Aberdeen).

Festivals: Brighton Festival (England).

Educational: Conservatorio Nacional de Música (Quito); Free School of Music (St. Petersburg); Nancy Conservatory of Music; Philadelphia Musical Academy; Salzburg Mozarteum; Warnot's Music School (St. Josseten-Noode).

Music Publishers: Durand and Schönewerk (successor to Flaxland); Stanislaw Krzyzanowski, bookseller and music publisher (Kraków).
Music Publications: *Deutsche Musiker-Zeitung; Musical Million and Fireside Friend; Scribner's Monthly.*
Performing Centers: Coates Opera House (Kansas City, Missouri); Gewerbehaussaal (Dresden Concert Hall); Horton Hall (San Diego, California); Merced Theater (Los Angeles).
Other: Internationale Mozart-Stiftung (Salzburg); Société Nationale de Musique (France); Wagner Tubas; Warsaw Music Society.

H. Musical Literature

Edgar Brinsmead, *History of the Pianoforte*; Hilarión Eslava, *Escuela de contrapunto, fuga y composición*; Gustavo Fechner, *Vorschule der Aesthetik*; Eduard Hanslick, *Aus dem Concertsaal*; Otto Kornmüller, *Lexikon der Kirchlichen Tonkunst*; Emil Naumann, *Die Tonkunst in der Culturgeschichte*; James Parker, *Theoretical and Practical Harmony*; Frédéric Ritter, *History of Music I*; Friedrich Stade, *Vom Musikalisch-Schönen*.

I. Musical Compositions
Chamber Music:

String Quartets: Antonin Dvořák, *No. 2 in B♭(?)–No. 3 in D(?)–No. 4 in e(?).*
Sonata/Solos: César Cui, *Violin Sonata, Opus 84*; Anton Rubinstein, *Piano Trio in A, Opus 85*; Henri Vieuxtemps, *Fantasia on Gounod's "Faust"* (violin, piano).
Ensembles: Woldemar Bargiel, *Piano Trio No. 3 in B♭, Opus 13*; Theodore Gouvy, *String Quintet in A*; Ludvig Norman, *String Quintet in c, Opus 35*; Joachim Raff, *Piano Trio No. 3 in g, Opus 155–Piano Trio No. 4 in D, Opus 158.*
Piano: Edvard Grieg, *Norwegian Songs and Dances, Opus 17*; Vincent d'Indy, *Three Romances san paroles, Opus 1*; Franz Liszt, *Élégie No. 2*; Joachim Raff, *Suite in g, Opus 162*; Anton Rubinstein, *Six Studies (G, A, g, E, d, E♭), Opus 81–Sonata in D for Piano, Four Hands, Opus 89.*

Choral/Vocal Music:

Choral: Joseph Barnby, *Rebekah* (oratorio); Julius Benedict, *St. Peter* (cantata); Théodore Dubois, *Solemn Mass*; Charles Gounod, *À la frontière* (cantata); Vincent d'Indy, *Chanson des aventuriers de la mer, Opus 2*; Stanislaw Moniuszko, *Mass No. 4 in a*; Joachim Raff, *Ten a Capella Songs for Male Voices, Opus 195*; Peter Ilyich Tchaikovsky, *Nature and Love* (cantata).
Vocal: César Franck, *Paris, a Patriotic Song*; Robert Franz, *Six Songs, Opus 22–Six Songs on German Folksong Texts, Opus 23–Six Heine Songs, Opus 25–Six Songs, Opus 26–Six Morike Songs, Opus 27–Eighteen Songs, Opus 28, 30, 31–Aus Osten, Opus 42–Twelve*

Songs, Opus 43, 44; Edvard Grieg, *Four Songs, Opus 21*; Edouard Lalo, *Three Melodies*(?); Joachim Raff, *Eight Songs, Opus 173*.

Musical Stage: Michael Balfe, *The Knight of the Leopard*; Georges Bizet, *Clarissa Harlowe*; Antonin Dvořák, *Alfred the Great*; Friedrich von Flotow, *L'ombre*; Antonio Gomes, *Il Guaraný*; Ernest Guiraud, *Le Kobold*; Hervé, *Aladdin the Second*; Jacques Offenbach, *La romance de la rose–Mam'zelle Moucheron*; Carlo Pedrotti, *Il Favorito–La vergine di Kermo*; Bedřich Smetana, *The Bartered Bride*; Franz von Suppé, *Lohengelb*.

Orchestra/Band Music:

Concerted Music:

Violin: Anton Rubinstein, *Romance and Caprice, Opus 86*; Henry Wieniawski, *Polonaise Brillante No. 2 in A, Opus 21*.

Other: Johan Svendsen, *Cello Concerto in d, Opus 7*.

Ballet/Incidental Music: Léo Delibes, *Coppélia* (B); Stanislaw Moniuszko, *The Devil's Joke* (B).

Program Music: Anton Rubinstein, *Don Quixote, Opus 87*.

Standard Works: Charles Converse, *Fest-Ouverture*; Antonin Dvořák, *Dramatic (Tragic) Overture, Opus 1*(?); Ferdinand Hiller, *Overture, Demetrius, Opus 145*; Franz Liszt, *Hungarian March*; Henry Litolff, *Overture, Die Girondisten, Opus 80*; Johann Strauss, Jr., *Wiener Blut*; Richard Wagner, *Siegfried Idyll*.

Symphonies: Max Bruch, *No. 1 in E♭, Opus 28–No. 2 in f, Opus 36*; Carl Reinecke, *No. 1 in A, Opus 79*; Charles M. Widor, *No. 1 in F, Opus 16*.

1871

✿

Historical Highlights: The Franco-Prussian War ends with the proclamation of a new German Empire; labor unions in England are authorized by the Parliament for the first time; explorer Henry Stanley finds David Livingston in Africa and begins his own exploration of the Dark Continent; in the United States, the Great Chicago Fire destroys much of downtown Chicago; the Treaty of Washington settles the disputes between the United States and Canadian fishermen.

Art and Literature Highlights: Births—artists Auguste Delacroix, Georges Rouault, John Sloan, writers Leonid Andreyev, Stephen Crane, Theodor Dreiser, Marcel Proust, J. M. Synge; Deaths—artists George Hayter, Alexandre Regnault, writers Henry Brackenridge, Emile Deschamps. Art—Johnson's *Old Stagecoach*, Millais' *Chill October*; Literature—Eggleston's *Hoosier Schoolmaster*, Rimbaud's *Les Illuminations*, Swinburne's *Songs before Sunrise*.

Musical Highlights

A. Births

Composers: Frederick Shepherd Converse (U.S.A.) January 5; Henry Hadley (U.S.A.) December 20; Arthur Nevin (U.S.A.) April 27; Zakhary Petrovich Paliashvili (Russia) August 16; Franklin Peale Patterson (U.S.A.) January 5; Daniel Alamias Robles (Peru) January 3; Wilhelm Stenhammar (Sweden) February 7; Alexander von Zemlinsky (Austria) October 14.

Conductors: Leo Blech (Germany) April 21; Ferenc Brauer (Hungary) April 15; F. Melius Christiansen (Norway-U.S.A.) April 1; Giuseppe Creatore (Italy) June 21; Willem Mengelberg (Holland) March 28.

Singers: Giuseppe Borgatti (Italian tenor) March 17; Alois Burgstaller (German tenor) September 21; Charles Dalmorès (French tenor) January 1; Olive Fremstad (Swedish-born mezzo-soprano) March 14; Eugenio Giraldoni (Italian baritone) May 20; Louise Homer (American contralto) April 30; Regina Pacini (Portugese soprano) January 6; Angelica Pandolfini (Italian soprano) August 21; Halfdan Rode (Norwegian baritone) June 20; Hermann Schramm (German tenor) February 7; Luisa Tetrazzini (Italian soprano) June 29; Friedrich Weidemann (German baritone) January 1; Clarence Whitehill (American bass-baritone) November 5.

Performers: P. Paul Bliss (American organist) November 25; Arthur Fickenscher (American pianist/composer) March 9; Wallace Goodrich (American organist/conductor) May 27; Ernest Hutcheson (Australian pianist/author) July 20; Bertram Shapleigh (American pianist/composer) January 15.

Others: Hermann Abert (German musicologist) March 25; Adolphe Boschot (French music critic) May 4; Karl Grunsky (German critic) March 5; Howard Eugene Wurlitzer (American instrument maker/dealer) September 5.

B. Deaths

Composers: Daniel-François Auber (France) May 24; Antonio Buzzola (Italy) March 20; Aimé (Louis) Maillart (France) May 26.

Conductors: Friedrich Müller (Germany) December 13; Heinrich Rung (Denmark) December 13.

Singers: Nicolas Levasseur (French bass) December 6.

Performers: John Balsir Chatterton (British harpist) April 9; Charles-Alexis Chauvet (French organist/composer) January 28; Charles-Louis Hanssens (Belgian cellist/conductor) April 8; Robert Pflughaupt (German pianist) June 12; (Philip) Cipriani Potter (British pianist) September 26; Carl Tausig (Polish pianist) July 17; Sigismond Thalberg (Swiss pianist/composer) April 27.

Others: Ludwig Bausch (German violin maker) May 26; François-Joseph Fétis (Belgian music theorist/historian) March 26; Thomas E. Chickering (American piano maker) February 14; Alexander Serov (Russian critic/composer) February 1; Heinrich Engelhard Steinweg (German-born piano maker) February 7; Sylvanus Billings Pond (American publisher/composer) March 12.

C. Debuts

Singers: Numa Auguez (French baritone—Paris); Jacques-Joseph Bouhy (Belgian baritone—Paris); Italo Campanini (Italian tenor—Bologna); Heinrich Gudehus (German tenor—Berlin); Virginia Gungl (Hungarian-born soprano—Munich); Adèle Isaac (French soprano—Paris); Edward Lloyd (Brtitish tenor—Gloucester); Joseph Maas (British tenor—London); Hedwig Reicher-Kinderman (German soprano—Karlsruhe); Anton Schott (German tenor—Munich); Rosa Sucher (German soprano—Munich); Alwina Valleria (American soprano—London).

Performers: Walter Bache (British pianist—London); William Frye Parker (British violinist—London).

D. New Positions

Conductors: Pietro Coppola (maestro di capella, Novara Cathedral); Michael Costa (Her Majesty's Opera, Haymarket); Max von Erdmannsdörfer (Sonderhausen Court); Franco Faccio (La Scala, Milan); Henry Fries (U.S. Marine Band); Franz Xaver Haberl (Regensburg Cathedral); Hans Richter (National Theater, Pest); Bernhard E. Scholz (Breslau SO); Franz Wüllner (Munich Court Opera).

Others: François Gevaert (director, Brussels Conservatory); Alexandre Guilmant (organ, Ste. Trinité, Paris); Asger Hamerik (director, Peabody Conservatory, Baltimore); Silas G. Pratt (organ, Church of the Messiah, Chicago); Ebenezer Prout (editor, *Monthly Musical Record*); Fenlon B. Rice (director, Oberlin Conservatory, Ohio); Adolphe Samuel (director, Ghent Conservatory); Ambroise Thomas (director, Paris Conservatory).

E. Prizes/Honors

Prizes: Gaston Serpette (Prix de Rome).
Honors: Julius Benedict (knighted); William Sterndale Bennett (knighted); George Elvey (knighted).

F. Biographical Highlights

Leopold and Walter Damrosch move to the United States; Léo Delibes quits his job, gets married, and devotes full time to music; William S. Gilbert begins a long-time collaboration with Arthur Sullivan; Edvard Grieg begins choral conducting for the Norwegian

Music Society; Root and Cady lose their publishing business to the Chicago fire.

G. Cultural Beginnings

Performing Groups—Choral: Boston Apollo Club; Royal (Albert Hall) Choral Society.

Performing Groups—Instrumental: Indianapolis Philharmonic Orchestra; Musical Society of Christiana (Oslo Musikforening, Norway); Oslo Philharmonic Orchestra; Schroeder String Quartet (Leipzig); Sociedad de Cuartetos Clásicos (Granada).

Educational: Athens Conservatory of Music; Beethoven Conservatory of Music (St. Louis, Missouri); Cleveland Conservatory of Music; Minneapolis Academy of Music; Petersilea Academy of Music (Boston).

Music Publishers: Conover Brothers (Kansas City, Missouri); Hubebni Matice (Czechoslovakia); Sherman and Hyde (Sherman, Clay and Co.); Society for the Publication of Danish Music.

Music Publications: *Church's Musical Visitor*; *Monthly Musical Record*.

Performing Centers: Grand Opera House (Milwaukee); Providence Opera House (Rhode Island); Royal Albert Hall (London).

Other: Musicians' National Protective Association; Packard Piano and Organ Co. (Ft. Wayne, Indiana).

H. Musical Literature

Raimondo Boucheron, *Esercizi d'Armonia*; Robert Eitner, *Hilfsbuch beim Klavierunterricht*; Henry Hiles, *The Harmony of Sounds*; Gustav Jacobsthal, *Die Mensuralnotenschrift des 12. und 13. Jahrhunderts*; Otto Kornmüller, *Die Musik beim liturgischen Hochamt*; Stanislaw Moniuszko, *Textbook on Harmony*; Emil Naumann, *Deutsche Tondichter*; Carl Pohl, *Die Gesellschaft der Musikfreunde und ihr Conservatorium in Wien*; John Stainer, *A Theory of Harmony*; Peter Ilyich Tchaikovsky, *Practical Study of Harmony*.

I. Musical Compositions

Chamber Music:

String Quartets: Anton Rubinstein, *No. 2 in e, Opus 90*; Peter Ilyich Tchaikovsky, *No. 1 in D, Opus 11*; Henri Vieuxtemps, *No. 1 in e, Opus 44*.

Sonata/Solos: Antonin Dvořák, *Cello Sonata in f*(?); Camille Saint-Saëns, *Berceuse in B♭, Opus 38* (violin, piano); Henri Vieuxtemps, *Suite in b, Opus 43* (violin, piano).

Piano: César Franck, *Offertoire sur un air breton*; Stephen Heller, *Im walde II, Opus 128–Impromtu No. 2, Opus 129*; Joachim Raff, *Suite in G, Opus 163–Fantaisie-Sonate, Opus 168*; Anton Rubinstein, *Theme* *and Variations in G, Opus 88*; Camille Saint-Saëns, *Mazurka No. 2 in g, Opus 24*; Peter Ilyich Tchaikovsky, *Three Piano Pieces, Opus 9– Two Pieces, Opus 10*.

Organ: Alkan, *Impromptu sur le choral de Luther, Opus 69*.

Choral/Vocal Music:

Choral: Peter Benoit, *Drama Christi* (oratorio); Johannes Brahms, *Schicksalslied, Opus 54–Triumphlied, Opus 55*; Max Bruch, *Odysseus* (oratorio); Niels Gade, *Kalanus* (cantata); Charles Gounod, *Messe brève in C– De Profundis–Gallia: lamentation*; Johan P. Hartmann, *Spring Songs, Opus 70* (cantata); Franz Liszt, *Mass for Male Voices– Psalm 114*; Giuseppe Martucci, *Messa di Gloria*; Stanislaw Moniuszko, *Beata*; Joachim Raff, *Two Songs, Opus 171*; Arthur Sullivan, *On the Shore and Sea* (oratorio).

Vocal: Johannes Brahms, *Eight Songs, Opus 57–Eight Songs, Opus 58*; Antonin Dvořák, *Four Songs, B.23–The Orphan, Opus 5*; Zdeněk Fibich, *Hildenbrandlied* (cycle); César Franck, *Panis Angelicus*; J. E. Gould, *Jesus, Saviour, Pilot Me* (hymn).

Musical Stage: Georges Bizet, *Djamileh–Numa*; Antonin Dvořák, *King and Charcoal Burner*; Zdeněk Fibich, *Bukovin*; Gilbert/Sullivan, *Thespis*; Ivar Hallström, *The Mountain King's Bride*; Charles Lecocq, *Le barbier de Trouville–Le Testament de M. de Crac*; Henry Litolff, *La boîte de Pandore*; Jacques Offenbach, *Boule de neige*; Giovanni Rossi, *La Contessa d'Alternberg*; Anton Rubinstein, *The Demon*; Johann Strauss, Jr., *Indigo und die Vierzig Rauber*; Giuseppe Verdi, *Aïda*.

Orchestra/Band Music:

Concerted Music:

Violin: Joseph Joachim Raff, *Concerto No. 1 in b, Opus 161*.

Other: Camille Saint-Saëns, *Romance in D♭, Opus 37* (flute/violin).

Ballet/Incidental Music: Stanislaw Moniuszko, *The Merchant of Venice* (IM)*–The Robbers* (IM)*–Hamlet* (IM); Carl Reinecke, *Wilhelm Tell, Opus 102* (IM); Arthur Sullivan, *The Merchant of Venice* (B).

Program Music: Camille Saint-Saëns, *Le Rouet d'Omphale, Opus 31*.

Standard Works: Antonin Dvořák, *Concert Overture in F*; Zdeněk Fibich, *Overture, Der Jude von Prag*; Ernest Guiraud, *Orchestral Suite No. 1*; Franz Lachner, *Suite No. 6 in C, Opus 150*; Jules Massenet, *Suite No. 2: Scènes hongroises*; Joseph Joachim Raff, *Suite No. 3, "Italian"*; Carl Reinecke, *Overture, Friedensfeier, Opus 105*; Albert Rubenson, *Trois pièce symphoniques*; Camille Saint-Saëns, *Marche héroïque, Opus 34*; Johann Strauss, Jr., *One Thousand and One Nights*; Richard Wagner, *Kaisermarsch*.

Symphonies: Niels Gade, *No. 8 in b♭, Opus 47*; Ludvig Norman, *No. 2 in E♭, Opus 40*; Joseph Joachim Raff, *No. 4 in g, Opus 167*.

1872

❄

Historical Highlights: The Spanish Civil War results in the defeat of the Carlists; Porfirio Diaz is elected president of the Mexican Republic; the British Ballot Act introduces the secret ballot in voting for public office; in the United States, President Ulysses S. Grant is reelected; the Credit Mobilier scandal breaks out; the Amnesty Act clears all Confederate leaders of treason; Arbor Day is inaugurated in Nebraska; Spokane, Washington, is founded.

Art and Literature Highlights: Births—artists Naoum Aronson, Max Beerbohm, Piet Mondriaan, Bessie Vonnoh, poet Félix Bataille; Deaths—authors Théophile Gautier, Franz Grillparzer, artists George Catlin, John Kensett, Thomas Sully. Art—Monet's *Impression: Sunrise*, Duveneck's *Whistling Boy*, Whistler's *The Artist's Mother*; Literature—Carroll's *Through the Looking Glass*, Daudet's *L'Arlesienne*, Twain's *Roughing It*.

Musical Highlights

A. Births

Composers: Hugo Alfvén (Sweden) May 1; Henri-Paul Busser (France) January 16; Arthur Farwell (U.S.A.) April 23; Rubin Goldmark (U.S.A.) August 15; Edward Burlingame Hill (U.S.A.) September 9; Paul Juon (Russia-Switzerland) March 6; William Kraft (U.S.A.) September 29; Alexander Scriabin (Russia) January 6; Déodat de Sévérac (France) July 20; Serge Vasilenko (Russia) March 30; Ralph Vaughan-Williams (England) October 12; Alexander Zemlinsky (Austria) October 4; Vasili Zolotarev (Russia) March 7.

Conductors: Siegmund von Hausegger (Austria) August 16; Alfred Hertz (Germany-U.S.A.) July 15; Juan Lamote de Grignon (Spain) July 7; Peter Raabe (Germany) November 27; Walter Henry Rothwell (England) September 22; Frederick Stock (Germany-U.S.A.) November 11; Josef Stransky (Bohemia) September 9.

Singers: Irene Abendroth (Austrian soprano) July 14; Suzanne Adams (American soprano) November 28; Frederic Austin (British baritone) March 30; Clara Butt (British contralto) February 1; Alexander Davidov (Russian tenor) September 4; Johanna Gadski (German soprano) June 15; Salomea Krushelnitska (Russian soprano) September 23; Otokar Mařák (Czech tenor) January 5; Anna Mildenburg (Austrian soprano) November 29; Lina Pasini (Italian soprano) November 8; Leonid Sobolov (Russian tenor) June 7; Anne Tariol-Baugé (French soprano) August 28.

Performers: Adelina DeLara (British pianist) January 23; Henry Purmort Eames (American pianist) September 12; Katherine Goodson

(British pianist) June 18; Caspar Koch (German-born organist) November 25; Joaquín Malats (Spanish pianist) March 4; Carl Rudolf Friedberg (German pianist) September 18; Edward Faber Schneider (American pianist) October 3; Ethel Sharpe (Irish pianist) November 28; Ottilie Sutro (American pianist) January 4; Frank Edwin Ward (American organist/composer) October 7.

Others: Felix Borowski (British-born critic/composer) March 10; Sergei Diaghilev (Russian ballet impresario) March 19; Rupert Hughes (American music author) January 31; Friedrich Ludwig (German musicologist) May 8.

B. Deaths

Composers: Michele Carafa (Italy) July 26; Conrad Kocher (Germany) March 12; Stanislaw Moniuszko (Poland) June 4; Edward Sobolewski (Germany-U.S.A.) May 17; Hugo Ulrich (Germany) May 23.

Conductors: Heinrich Esser (Germany) June 3; Carl Liebig (Germany) October 6; Eugène-Prosper Prévost (France) August 19.

Singers: Charles-Amable Battaille (French bass) May 2; Édouard Gassier (French baritone) December 18; Sabina Heinefetter (German soprano) November 18; Carlotta Marchisio (Italian soprano) June 28; Benedetta Rosamunda Pisaroni (Italian contralto) August 6; Mason (American music educator/composer) August 11.

Others: Jean Andries (Belgian violinist/educator/author) January 21; Thomas Appleton (American organ builder) July 11; Thomas Hastings (American hymnist) May 15; Lowell Mason (American music educator/composer) August 11; Eberhard Friedrich Walcker (German organ builder) October 2; Friedrich Wilhelm Wieprecht (German inventor/trombonist) August 4.

C. Debuts

Performers: Richard Andersson (Swedish pianist—Stockholm); Jacques E. Rensburg (Dutch cellist—Leipzig); Franz Rummel (German pianist—Antwerp).

D. New Positions

Conductors: Johannes Brahms (Gesellschaft der Musikfreunde, Vienna); Ernst Frank (kapellmeister, Mannheim); Andreas Hallén (Gothenburg); Hermann Levi (Munich Court Opera); Karl Schröder (Kroll Opera, Berlin); Ernst von Schuch (Dresden Court Opera).

Others: Constanz Berneker (director, Königsberg Singakademie); John Pyke Hullah (Inspector of Schools, London); Vincent d'Indy (organ, St. Leu-la-Forêt); Alberto Mazzucato (director, Milan Conservatory); Walter Parratt (organ, Magdalen College, Oxford); Jean-Théodore Radoux (director, Conservatoire Liège); John Stainer (organ, St. Paul's Cathedral, London).

E. Prizes/Honors

Prizes: Gaston Salvayre (Prix de Rome).

Honors: Edward Armitage (Royal Academy); François Bazin (French Academy); John Goss (knighted); Edvard Grieg (Swedish Academy); William Mason (D. Mus., Yale); Victor Massé (French Institute); Robert Stewart (knighted).

F. Biographical Highlights

Engelbert Humperdinck turns from architecture and enters Cologne Conservatory; Leoš Janáček graduates from Czech Teachers' Institute; Charles Lamoureux becomes assistant conductor of the Concerts du Conservatoire de Paris; Johann Strauss, Jr., visits the United States and conducts several "monster concerts"; Richard Wagner goes to Bayreuth for the cornerstone ceremonies for his Festspielhaus.

G. Cultural Beginnings

Performing Groups—Choral: Apollo Music Club (Chicago); Concerti Populari (Turin).

Performing Groups—Instrumental: Beau-Rivage Orchestra (Lausanne); Cincinnati Symphony Orchestra; Koblenz Verein der Musikfreunde; Royal Amateur Orchestral Society (London); St. Petersburg Society for Quartet (Chamber) Music; Symphonie- und Kurorchester (Baden-Baden).

Festivals: World Peace Jubilee and International Musical Festival.

Educational: Ducal Orchestral School (Liszt Hochschule, Weimar); St. Louis Conservatory of Music; Sainton-Dolby Vocal School (London); Scuola Gratuita de Canto (Turin); Trinity College of Music (London); Verein zur Erforschung alter Choralhandschriften.

Music Publishers: Carl Fischer, Inc. (New York); Ruebush, Kieffer and Co.; E. Schuberth (New York); Franz A. Urbánek Co. (Prague).

Music Publications: *Musical Leaflet*.

Performing Centers: Bösendorfer Saal (Vienna); Germania Theater (New York); Monte Carlo Concert Hall; Staub's Opera House (Knoxville); Teatro dela Opera (Buenos Aires); Theater in der Guckengasse (Cologne); Turnverein Hall (Los Angeles).

Other: Brisbane Musical Union (Australia); Moeller Organ Co. (Maryland); Oxford University Musical Club; Schwarzer Zither Factory (Washington, Missouri); Sohmer and Co., piano makers (New York); Wagner Society of London; Rudolf Wurlitzer and Brother (Cincinnati).

H. Musical Literature

August Ambros, *Bunte Blätter: Skizzen und Studien für freunde der Musik I*; Jean Bertrand, *Les Nationalities musicales étudiées du la Drame lyrique*; John Ella, *Lectures on Dramatic Music Abroad and at Home*; Henri Kowalski, *A Travers l'Amerique*; Hermann Küster, *Über die For-*

men in der Musik; Wilhelm Langhans, *Das musikalische Urteil und seine Ausbildung durch des Erziehung;* Johann Lobe, *Katechismus der Compositionslehre;* Ernst Mach, *Zur Theorie des Gehörorgans;* Friedrich Nietzsche, *Die Geburt der Tragödie aus dem Geiste der Musik;* Felipe Pedrell, *Gramática musical o manual expositivo de la teoria del solfeo, en forma de diálogo;* Karoline Pruckner, *Theorie und Praxis der Gesangskunst;* Ernst Richter, *Lehrbuch des einfachen und doppelten Kontrapunkts.*

I. **Musical Compositions**
    Chamber Music:
    Sonata/Solos: Elfrida Andrée, *Violin Sonata No. 1 in E♭–No. 2 in E♭;* C. Hubert Parry, *Freundschaftlieder* (violin, piano); Carl Reinecke, *Violin Sonata in e, Opus 116;* Camille Saint-Saëns, *Cello Sonata No. 1 in c, Opus 32.*
    Ensembles: Antonin Dvořák, *Piano Quintet in A, Opus 5;* Zdeněk Fibich, *Piano Trio in f;* Ludvig Norman, *Piano Trio in b, Opus 38;* Joachim Raff, *String Octet in c, Opus 176–String Sextet in g, Opus 178.*
    Piano: Alkan, *Les mois, 12 morceaux caractéristiqaues, Opus 74–Toccatina, Opus 75*(?); Georges Bizet, *Jeux d'enfants* (four hands); Charles Gounod, *Funeral March of a Marionette* (orchestrated 1879); Stephen Heller, *Polonaise No. 2, Opus 132–Kleines album, Opus 134;* C. Hubert Parry, *Seven Charakterbilder;* Joachim Raff, *Two Pieces, Opus 166–Orientales, Opus 175;* Charles M. Widor, *Six Salon Pieces, Opus 15.*
    Organ: Charles Widor, *Organ Symphonies No. 1, 2, 3, and 4.*
    Choral/Vocal Music:
    Choral: George Bristow, *The Pioneer, Opus 49* (cantata); Dudley Buck, *Festival Hymn, Opus 57;* Antonin Dvořák, *Heirs of the White Mountain, Opus 30* (cantata); Caryl Florio, *Song of the Elements* (cantata); César Franck, *Mass in Three Voices, Opus 12–Redemption* (oratorio); Robert Franz, *Six Lieder, Opus 45;* Charles Gounod, *Requiem in F–Morning Service–Evening Service;* Ferdinand Hiller, *Israels Siegesgesang, Opus 157;* Stanislaw Moniuszko, *Mass No. 5 in B♭;* John Knowles Paine, *St. Peter, Opus 20* (oratorio); Anton Rubinstein, *Songs and Requiem for Mignon, Opus 91;* Arthur Sullivan, *Festival Te Deum;* George E. Whiting, *Mass in c.*
    Vocal: Peter Benoit, *Liefdedrama* (cycle); Antonin Dvořák, *Four Serbian Folk Poems, Opus 6–Six Songs, Opus 7;* Zdeněk Fibich, *Der Asra* (cycle); Robert Fuchs, *Six Songs, Opus 3–Four Songs, Opus 6;* Modest Mussorgsky, *The Nursery* (cycle); Joachim Raff, *Maria Stuart, Opus 172* (cycle); Arthur Sullivan, *Onward, Christian Soldiers* (hymn).
    Musical Stage: Max Bruch, *Hermione;* Ernest Guiraud, *Madame Turlupin;* Heinrich Hofmann, *Armin, Opus 40;* Charles Lecocq, *La fille de Madame Angot;* Henry Litolff, *Heloïse et Abelard;* Jules

Massenet, *Don César de Bazan*; Jacques Offenbach, *Le Roi Carotte–Le corsaire noir–Fleurette–Fantasio*; Carlo Pedrotti, *Olema la schiava*; Errico Petrella, *Manfredo*; József Poniatowski, *Gelmina*; Nikolai Rimsky-Korsakov, *Ivan, the Terrible*; Camille Saint-Saëns, *La princesse Jaune*; Bedřich Smetana, *Libuse*; Peter Ilyich Tchaikovsky, *The Oprichnik*.

Orchestra/Band Music:
Concerted Music:
   Violin: Joachim Raff, *Concerto No. 1 in b, Opus 161*.
   Other: Camille Saint-Saëns, *Cello Concerto No. 1 in a, Opus 33*.
Ballet/Incidental Music: Georges Bizet, *L'Arlésienne* (IM); Charles Gounod, *Les deux reines* (IM); Edvard Grieg, *Sigurd Jorsalfar, Opus 22* (IM); Edouard Lalo, *Divertissement* (B).
Standard Works: Zdeněk Fibich, *Concert Overture in E*; Peter Ilyich Tchaikovsky, *Serenade for Nikolai Rubinstein's Name Day*.
Symphonies: George Frederick Bristow, *No. 4, "Arcadian," Opus 50*; Anton Bruckner, *No. 2 in c*; Henry Cowell, *No. 2 in f*; Vincent d'Indy, *No. 1 in A*; Joseph Joachim Raff, *No. 5 in E, "Lenore," Opus 177*; Peter Ilyich Tchaikovsky, *No. 2 in c, "Little Russian," Opus 17*.

1873

❀

Historical Highlights: Buda, Óbuda, and Pest unite to form the city of Budapest, Hungary; Spain begins a two-year experiment as a republic; the city of Zanzibar in Africa closes all slave markets and halts all slave trade in its territory; in the United States, financial panic ushers in a six-year depression; Jesse James and his gang rob their first train; the San Francisco cable cars make their debut; penny postcards make their appearance.

Art and Literature Highlights: Births—writers Valery V. Bryusov, Willa Cather, William Irwin, George Cabot Lodge; Deaths—artists William Jewett, Edwin Landseer, Hiram Powers, writers Edward Bulwer-Lytton, Manuel Bretón de los Herreros, Alessandro Manzoni. Art—Degas' *Cotton Market, New Orleans*, Hood's *Village Post Office*; Literature—Howell's *A Chance Acquaintance*, Verne's *Around the World in Eighty Days*.

Musical Highlights

A. Births
   Composers: W. H. Bell (England-South Africa) August 20; André Bloch (France) January 18; Eugen Haile (Germany-U.S.A.) February 21; Joseph Jongen (Belgium) December 14; Daniel Gregory Mason (U.S.A.) November 29; Mary Carr Moore (U.S.A.) August 6; Henri

Rabaud (France) November 10; Max Reger (Germany) March 19; Jean Roger-Ducasse (France) April 18.

Conductors: Bartolomeo Pérez-Casas (Spain) January 24; Giorgio Polacco (Italy) April 12; Landon Ronald (England) June 7; Egisto Tango (Italy) November 13; Nicolai Tcherepnin (Russia) May 15.

Singers: Alfred von Bury (German tenor) January 18; Enrico Caruso (Italian tenor) February 25; Feodor Chaliapin (Russian bass) February 13; Francesco Federici (Italian baritone); Otto Goritz (German baritone) June 8; Karl Jörn (Latvian-born tenor) January 5; Louise Kirkby-Lunn (British mezzo-soprano) November 8; Antonina Nezhdanova (Russian soprano) June 16; Rosa Olitzka (German-born contralto) September 6; Adrienne Osborne (American contralto) December 2; Jane Osborn-Hannah (American soprano) July 8; Anita Rio (American soprano) July 30; Edouard Risler (German pianist) February 23; Leo Slezak (Austrian tenor) August 18; Herbert Witherspoon (American bass) July 21.

Performers: Modest Altschuler (Russian-born cellist/conductor) February 15; Harold Bauer (British-born pianist) April 28; Adolfo Betti (Italian violinist) March 21; Clarence Dickinson (American organist) May 7; Carl Flesch (Hungarian violinist/pedagogue) October 9; Walter Keller (American organist) February 23; Franz Listemann (American cellist) December 17; Serge Rachmaninoff (Russian-born pianist/composer) April 1; Karl Straube (German organist/conductor) January 6; Anice Terhune (American pianist/composer) October 27; Henri Verbrugghen (Belgian violinist/conductor) August 1; T. Carl Whitmer (American organist/composer) June 24; Rudolph Henry Wurlitzer (American instrument maker) December 30.

Others: Peter Dykema (American music educator) November 25; Arthur Elson (American musicologist) November 18; Amédée Gastoué (French music scholar/organist) March 19; Max Graf (Austrian critic/musicologist) October 1; Theodor Kroyer (German musicologist) September 9; Thomas Oliphant (Scottish educator/music author) March 9; Oscar G. T. Sonneck (American musicologist) October 6; Karl Weinmann (German musicologist) December 22.

B. **Deaths**

Composers: Vincenzo Battista (Italy) November 14; Carlo Coccia (Italy) April 13; József Michal Poniatowski (Poland) July 3.

Conductors: Angelo Mariani (Italy) June 13.

Singers: Domenico Donzelli (Italian tenor) March 31; Semyon Stepanovich Gulak-Artemovsky (Russian baritone/composer) April 17; Ignazio Marini (Italian bass) April 29; Jan Křtitel Pišek (Bohemian baritone) February 16.

Performers: August Adelburg (Austrian violinist/composer) October 20; Albrecht Wilhelm Agthe (German pianist) October 8; August

Conradi (German organist/conductor) May 26; Ferdinand David (German violinist/composer) July 18; Louis François Drouet (French flutist/composer) September 30; Georg Hellmesberger, Sr. (Austrian violinist/conductor) August 16; Friedrich Wieck (German pianist/ pedagogue) October 6; Ernst Johann Wiedemann (German organist/conductor) December 7.

Others: Georges Chanot, Sr. (French violin maker) January 10; Ludovicus Coenen (Dutch organ builder) March 12; Théodore-Joseph Devroye (Belgian music scholar) July 19.

C. Debuts

Singers: Bianca Bianchi (German soprano—Karlsruhe); Mary Davies (British mezzo-soprano—London); Julián Sébastian Gayarre (Spanish tenor—Italy); Mieczyslaw Apolinary Horbowski (Polish baritone— Warsaw); Therese Malten (German soprano—Dresden); Clementine Schuch-Proska (Hungarian soprano—Dresden); Antoinette Sterling (American contralto—London); Feodor Stravinsky (Russian bass— Kiev).

Performers: Martin-Pierre Marsick (Belgian violinist—Paris); Moritz Moszkowski (German pianist—Berlin); Otakar Ševčik (Czech violinist—Vienna).

D. New Positions

Conductors: Antonio Cagnoni (maestro di capella, Novarra Cathedral); Leoš Janácek (choirmaster, Svatopluk Choral Society); Johann August Langert (Gotha Court); Friedrich Marpurg (Laibach Court); Giovanni Rossi (Teatro Carlo Felice, Genoa); Charles Villiers Stanford (Cambridge Musical Society).

Others: Theodor Kirchner (director, Würzburg Conservatory); Théodore de Lajante (archivist, Paris Opera); Charles Villiers Stanford (organ, Trinity College).

E. Prizes/Honors

Prizes: Paul-Charles Puget (Prix de Rome); François M. Servais (Prix de Rome).

Honors: Georges Bizet (Legion of Honor).

F. Biographical Highlights

Charles Grove begins work on the *Dictionary*; poet Sidney Lanier becomes first flutist with the Peabody Orchestra; John Knowles Paine becomes assistant professor at Harvard; Nikolai Rimsky-Korsakov becomes inspector of Naval Bands in Russia.

G. Cultural Beginnings

Performing Groups—Choral: Cleveland (Ohio) Vocal Society; English Opera Co.; Finnish National Opera Co.; Kellogg Opera Co.

(New York); Oratorio Society of New York; Orpheus Society of Springfield (Massachusetts); St. Cecilia Society of America; Société de l'Harmonie Sacrée (Paris).
Performing Groups—Instrumental: Beethoven String Quartet (Boston); Colonne Concerts (Paris); Concerts Symphoniques Populaires (Lyons); Pittsburgh Germania Orchestra; Stockley's Concerts (Birmingham).
Festivals: Bristol Music Festival (England); Cincinnati May Music Festival.
Educational: Augsburger Musikschule; Bernuth Music Conservatory (Hamburg); Hamburger Musikakademie; La Lira Conservatory (Montevideo); National Training School for Music (Royal College, London); Russian Musical Society Music School (Vilnius).
Music Publishers: Henry Holt and Co.
Music Publications: *The Kansas Folio: A Repertoire of Music, Art and Literature.*
Performing Centers: Grand Opera House (Little Rock, Arkansas); Macauleys' Theater (Louisville, Kentucky).

H. Musical Literature
Heinrich Bellermann, *Die Grösse der Intervalle als Grundlage der Harmonie*; Peter Benoit, *De Vlaamsche muziekschool van Antwerp*; Gustave Chouquet, *Histoire de la musique dramatique en France depuis ses origines jusqu'a nos jours*; William H. Dana, *Practical Thorough-Bass*; Charles Dancla, *Les compositeurs chefs d'orchestre*; Charles Hallé, *Pianoforte School*; Oskar Kolbe, *Handbuch der Harmonielehre*; Heinrich Köstlin, *Geschichte der Musik im Umriss*; Mathis Lussy, *Traité de l'expression musicale*; Charles Meerens, *Le diapason et la notation musicale simplifiée*; Oscar Paul, *Handlexicon der Tonkunst*; Hugo Riermann, *Über das musikalische Hören*; Ira Sankey, *Sacred Songs and Solos.*

I. Musical Compositions
Chamber Music:
   String Quartets: Johannes Brahms, *No. 1 in c, Opus 51, No. 1–No. 2 in a, Opus 51, No. 2*; Antonin Dvořák, *Andante in F–No. 5 in f, Opus 9–No. 6 in a, Opus 12*; Engelbert Humperdinck, *No. 1 in e*; Eduard Nápravnik, *No. 1 in E, Opus 16*; Giuseppe Verdi, *Quartet in a.*
   Sonata/Solos: Antonin Dvořák, *Violin Sonata in a*; Joachim Raff, *Cello Sonata in D, Opus 183.*
   Ensembles: Antonin Dvořák, *Octet (Serenade)*; Ferdinand Hiller, *Piano Quartet, Opus 156*; Alexander Mackenzie, *Piano Quartet in E♭, Opus 11*; Joachim Raff, *Sinfonietta in F for Woodwinds, Opus 188.*
   Piano: William Sterndale Bennett, *Sonata in A♭, Opus 46, "The Maid of Orleans"*; Stephen Heller, *Im walde III, Opus 136–Two Tarantellas, Opus 137*; John Knowles Paine, *Ten Sketches: In the Country, Opus*

26; C. Hubert Parry, *Two Short Pieces (C, F)*; Joachim Raff, *Variations on an Original Theme, Opus 179–Totentanz, Opus 181–Erinnerung an Venedig, Opus 187.*

Choral/Vocal Music:

Choral: Peter Benoit, *De oorlog*; George Frederick Bristow, *Morning Service, Opus 51*; Niels Gade, *Zion, Opus 49–The Mountain Thrall* (cantatas); Charles Gounod, *Missa angeli custodes in C*; Edvard Grieg, *Olaf Trygvason, Opus 50* (cantata); Ferdinand Hiller, *Loreley, Opus 70*(?); Stanislaw Moniuszko, *Funeral Mass in g*; Frederick Ouseley, *Hagar* (oratorio); C. Hubert Parry, *Te Deum in E♭*; Errico Petrella, *Messe funebre*; Józef Poniatowski, *Mass in F*; Joachim Raff, *Morgenlied, Opus 186a*; Charles V. Stanford, *Magnificat and Nunc Dimittis in E♭–Evening Service in E♭*; Arthur Sullivan, *The Light of the World* (oratorio); George E. Whiting, *Prologue to "The Golden Legend."*

Vocal: Johannes Brahms, *Eight Songs, Opus 59*; Zdeněk Fibich, *Four Balladen, Opus 7*; Joachim Raff, *Six Trios for Women's Voices, Opus 184.*

Musical Stage: Léo Delibes, *Le roi l'a dit*; Théodore Dubois, *La Guzla de l'Emir*; Hervé, *La veuve du Melabar*; Jules Massenet, *Marie-Magdeleine*; Jacques Offenbach, *Les braconniers–La jolie parfumeuse–Pomme d'api*; Amilcare Ponchielli, *Il parlatore eterno.*

Orchestra/Band Music:

Concerted Music:

Piano: Joachim Raff, *Concerto in c, Opus 185*; Carl Reinecke, *Concerto No. 2 in e, Opus 120.*

Violin: Edouard Lalo, *Concerto in F, Opus 20–Symphonie Espagnole, Opus 21*; Ivo Petrić, *Three Images*; Joachim Raff, *Suite in G, Opus 180.*

Ballet/Incidental Music: Charles Gounod, *Jeanne d'Arc* (IM); Ernest Guiraud, *Gretna Green* (B-band); Amilcare Ponchielli, *Clarina* (B); Peter Ilyich Tchaikovsky, *The Snow Maiden, Opus 12* (IM).

Program Music: Zdeněk Fibich, *Othello, Opus 6–Záboj, Opus 37*; Camille Saint-Saëns, *Phaeton, Opus 39*; Peter Ilyich Tchaikovsky, *The Tempest, Opus 18.*

Standard Works: Georges Bizet, *Patrie Overture*; Johannes Brahms, *Variations on a Theme by Haydn, Opus 56a*; Théodore Dubois, *Divertissement for Orchestra*; Antonin Dvořák, *Romeo and Juliet Overture*; Zdeněk Fibich, *Lustspiel Overture, Opus 35*; Heinrich Hofmann, *Hungarian Suite, Opus 16*; Jules Massenet, *Phèdre Overture–Suite No. 3: Scènes dramatiques*; C. Hubert Parry, *Overture, Vivien*; John Philip Sousa, *Salutation March–March, Review.*

Symphonies: Anton Bruckner, *No. 3 in d*; Antonin Dvořák, *No. 3 in E♭, Opus 10*; Eduard Nápravník, *No. 2 in C, Opus 17*; Joseph Joachim Raff, *No. 6 in d, Opus 189.*

1874

❊

Historical Highlights: Benjamin Disraeli becomes prime minister of Great Britain; Great Britain annexes the Fiji Islands; Henry Stanley begins exploring the African Congo region; the British Factory Act reduces the legal work week to fifty-six and a half hours; in the United States, the first electric-powered streetcar is demonstrated in New York City; the Republican elephant first appears in a Nast cartoon; barbed wire, a "revolution in ranching" is invented.

Art and Literature Highlights: Births—authors Robert Frost, Hugo von Hofmannsthal, Amy Lowell, W. Somerset Maugham, artists Romaine Brooks, Charles Despiau; Deaths—authors Sidney Dobell, Victor Séjour, artist Wilhelm von Kaulbach. Art—Barker's *Charge of the Light Brigade*, Hunt's *The Ball Players*, Renoir's *The Loge*; Literature—Alarcón's *Three Cornered Hat*, Hardy's *Far from the Madding Crowd*, Verlaine's *Romances sans Paroles*.

Musical Highlights

A. Births

Composers: Gustav Holst (England) September 21; Charles Ives (U.S.A.) October 20; William Landré (Holland) June 12; Arne Oldberg (U.S.A.) July 12; Franz Schmidt (Austria) December 22; Arnold Schoenberg (Austria-U.S.A.) September 13; Josef Suk (Czechoslovakia) January 4.

Conductors: Reynaldo Hahn (Venezuela-France) August 9; Serge Koussevitzky (Russia-U.S.A.) July 26.

Singers—Female: Lillian Evans Blauvelt (American soprano) March 16; Lina Cavalieri (Italian soprano) December 25; Clara Clemens (American contralto) June 8; Ada Crossley (Australian mezzo-soprano) March 3; Mary Garden (Scottish-born soprano) February 20; Marie Gutheil-Schroder (German soprano) February 16; Selma Kurz (Austrian soprano) October 15; Minnie Nast (German soprano) October 10; Minnie Saltzmann-Stevens (American soprano) March 17; Selma vom Scheidt (German soprano) June 26.

Singers—Male: Giuseppe Agostini (Italian-born tenor) July 21; Amadeo Bassi (Italian tenor) July 29; Rudolf Berger (Czech tenor) April 17; Johannes Bischoff (German baritone) March 19; Nikolai Bolshakov (Russian tenor) November 23; Adamo Didur (Polish bass) December 24; Emilio de Gogorza (American baritone) May 29; Heinrich Hensel (German tenor) October 29; Riccardo Martin (American tenor) November 18; Léon Rothier (French bass) December 26; Andrés de Segurola (Spanish bass-baritone) March 27; Oley Speaks (American baritone/composer) June 28.

Performers: Edward Bairstow (British organist) August 22; Glenn Dillard Gunn (American pianist/conductor) October 2; Charles Herbert Kitson (British organist/music theorist) November 13; Josef Lhévinne (Russian-born pianist) December 13; Leonard Liebling (American pianist/critic) February 7; Marguerite Long (French pianist) November 13; Henri Marteau (French violinist) March 31; Elizabeth Quaile (Irish-born pianist) January 20.

Others: Pierre Aubry (French music scholar) February 14; Hugo von Hofmannsthal (Austrian librettist) February 1; Mikhail Ivanov-Boretzky (Russian musicologist) June 16; Robert Lach (Austrian musicologist/composer) January 29; Hugo Leichtentritt (German-born music scholar) January 1; Charles Van den Borren (Belgian musicologist) November 17.

B. Deaths

Composers: Salvatore Agnelli (Italy)(?); Wilhelm Blodek (Czechoslovakia) May 1; Peter Cornelius (Germany) October 26.

Conductors: Friedrich Wilhelm Grund (Germany) November 24; Hans Christian Lumbye (Denmark) March 20.

Singers: Theodor Formes (German tenor) October 15; Eduard Mantius (German tenor) July 4; Pietro Mongini (Italian tenor) April 27; Euphrosyne Parepa-Rosa (Scottish soprano) January 21.

Performers: Friedrich August Belcke (German trombonist) December 10; Justin Cadaux (French pianist) November 8; Johann Peter Pixis (German pianist/composer) December 22; Thomas Tellefsen (Norwegian pianist/composer) October 6.

Others: Johann Friedrich Bellermann (German music scholar) February 5; Francesco Caffi (Italian music scholar) January 24; Thomas Hall (American organ builder) May 23; John Thomas Hart (British violin maker) January 1.

C. Debuts

Singers: Nellie E. Brown (American soprano—Boston); Jean De Reszke (Polish tenor—Venice, as baritone); Josephine De Reszke (Polish soprano—Venice); Blanche Deschamps-Jehin (French contralto—Brussels); Maurice Devries (American baritone—Liège), Medea Mei-Figner (Italian soprano—Sinaluga); Wladyslaw Seideman (Polish baritone—Vienna); Edmund-Alphonse Vergnet (French tenor—Paris).

Performers: Camille Gurickx (Belgian pianist—Paris); Luigi Mancinelli (Italian conductor—Perugia); August Spanuth (German pianist—Frankfurt).

D. New Positions

Conductors: William W. Gilchrist (Mendelssohn Glee Club, Philadelphia); B. J. Lang (Cecilia Society of Boston); Otto Malling (Copenhagen Concert Society); Luigi Mancinelli (Teatro Apollo, Rome); J. Gustav Stehle (music director, St. Gallen Cathedral).

Others: Gustave Huberti (director, Mons Conservatory of Music); Henry Krehbiel (critic, *Cincinnati Gazette*); André Messager (organ, St. Sulpice, Paris); Joseph Pembaur, Sr. (director, Innsbruck Music School).

E. Prizes/Honors

Prizes: Oskar Pasch (Meyerbeer).

Honors: Antonin Dvořák (Austrian State Prize); Edvard Grieg (government life stipend); Samuel Sebastian Wesley (civil pension).

F. Biographical Highlights

Zdeněk Fibich becomes second conductor at the National Theater of Prague; C. Hubert Parry leaves the business world for full time in music; Nikolai Rimsky-Korsakov debuts as a conductor in his own *Third Symphony*; Bedřich Smetana, becoming totally deaf in his left ear, resigns his conducting position; Giuseppe Verdi is elected to the Italian Senate as an honor member; Richard Wagner moves into his Villa Wahnfried in Bayreuth.

G. Cultural Beginnings

Performing Groups—Choral: Association Artistique des Concerts du Châtelet (Paris); Cecilia Society of Boston; Darmstadt Stadtkirchenchor; Komische Oper am Schottentor (Vienna); Leipziger Bach-Verein; Mendelssohn Glee Club of Philadelphia.

Performing Groups—Instrumental: Barmer Orchesterverein; Belfast Philharmonic Society; Copenhagen Koncertforeningen; Glasgow Choral Union Orchestra; Philharmonic Club of Boston; Romanian Orchestral Society.

Festivals: Chautauqua Summer Music Festival.

Educational: Akademie der Tonkunst (Munich); Chatauqua Institute (New York); Detroit Conservatory of Music; Kirchenburg Kirchenmusikschule; Künstler- und Dilettantenschule für Klavier (Stuttgart); Milwaukee (Wisconsin) College of Music; Olivet Conservatory of Music (Michigan); Ratisbon School of Church Music (Regensburg).

Music Publishers: J. and W. Chester (Brighton); Ernst Eulenburg (Leipzig); William Lewis and Son, violin dealers and publisher (Chicago).

Music Publications: *Deutsche Rundschau*; *Musica Sacra: Revue du Chant Liturgique et de la Musique Religieuse* (France).

Performing Centers: Toronto Grand Opera House.

Other: Sustaining Pedal for Piano (patented by Henry G. Hanchett).

H. Musical Literature

Kornél Abrányi, *Harmony*; August Ambros, *Bunte Blätter II*; Georges Becker, *La musique en Suisse*; Frederick Crowest, *The Great Tone Poets*; Bernhard Kothe, *Abriss der Musikgeschichte für Lehrerseminare und Dilettanten*; Charles Lunn, *Philosophy of Voice*; Victor C. Mahillon, *Les éléments d'acoustique musicale et instrumentale*; Oscar Paul, *Musikalische Instrumente*; John Tyndall, *On the Transmission of Sound by the Atmosphere*.

I. Musical Compositions
Chamber Music:

String Quartets: Antonin Dvořák, *No. 7 in a, Opus 16*; Zdeněk Fibich, *No. 1 in A*; Joachim Raff, *Three Quartets, Opus 192*; Carl Reinecke, *No. 3 in C, Opus 132*; Peter Ilyich Tchaikovsky, *No. 2 in F, Opus 22*.

Sonata/Solos: Zdeněk Fibich, *Violin Sonata No. 1 in c*; Carl Goldmark, *Violin Sonata in D, Opus 25*; Giuseppe Martucci, *Violin Sonata, Opus 22*.

Ensembles: Zdeněk Fibich, *Piano Quartet in e, Opus 11*; Heinrich Hofmann, *Piano Trio in A, Opus 18*; Alexander Mackenzie, *Piano Trio in D*; John Knowles Paine, *Piano Trio in d, Opus 22*.

Piano: Robert Fuchs, *Variations in d, Opus 10* (four hands?); Stephen Heller, *Notenbuch für klein und gross, Opus 138–Drei Etüden, Opus 139*; Modest Mussorgsky, *Pictures at an Exhibition*; Silas G. Pratt, *Fantasie Caprice–Grand Polonaise I*; Joachim Raff, *Feux follets, Opus 190*; Camille Saint-Saëns, *Variation on a Theme of Beethoven, Opus 35* (two pianos).

Organ: Alexandre Guilmant, *Sonata No. 1 in d, Opus 42*; Jacques-Nicolas Lemmens, *Organ Sonata No. 1, "Pontificale"–No. 2, "O filii"–No. 3, "Pascale."*

Choral/Vocal Music:

Choral: Johannes Brahms, *Seven Choral Songs for a capella Chorus, Opus 62*; Dudley Buck, *The Legend of Don Munio* (secular cantata); Zdeněk Fibich, *Three Lieder, Opus 46–Meluzina, Opus 55*; Hermann Goetz, *Nenie, Opus 9*; Franz Liszt, *The Legend of Ste. Cecilia* (oratorio)*–Die Glocken des Strassburger Münsters*; Stanislaw Moniuszko, *Mass No. 7 in D♭*; Joachim Raff, *Ten a Capella Songs for Male Voices, Opus 198*; Carl Reinecke, *Die flucht der heiligen familie, Opus 131*; Giuseppe Verdi, *Manzoni Requiem*; George E. Whiting, *Mass in f*.

Vocal: Johannes Brahms, *Four Duets, Opus 61–Nine Songs, Opus 63–Three Vocal Quartets, Opus 64–Neue Liebeslieder, Opus 65*; César Cui, *Six Songs, Opus 9*; Luigi Mancinelli, *Alchiaro di luna* (cycle); Modest Mussorgsky, *Sunless* (cycle); Joachim Raff, *Blumensprache,*

Opus 191; Ira Sankey, *The Ninety and Nine* (hymn); Peter Ilyich Tchaikovsky, *Six Songs, Opus 25.*

Musical Stage: Antonin Dvořák, *The Stubborn Lovers, Opus 12;* Friedrich von Flotow, *La fleur de Harlem;* Ivar Hallström, *Den Bergtagna;* Charles Lecocq, *Giroflé-Girofla–Les prés Saint-Gervais;* Henry Litolff, *La fiancée du roi de Garbe;* Jacques Offenbach, *Whittington–Madame l'archiduc–Bagetelle;* Errico Petrella, *Bianca Orsini;* Amilcare Ponchielli, *I lituani;* Carl Reinecke, *Ein Abenteur Händels, Opus 104;* Anton Rubinstein, *Die Maccabäer;* Johann Strauss, Jr., *Die Fledermaus;* Peter Ilyich Tchaikovsky, *Valkula the Smith;* Ambroise Thomas, *Gille et Gillotin;* Richard Wagner, *Götterdämmerung.*

Orchestra/Band Music:

Concerted Music:

Violin: George Macfarren, *Concerto in g;* Camille Saint-Saëns, *Romance in C, Opus 48.*

Other: Gottfried Mathison-Hansen, *Organ Concerto, Opus 15;* Joachim Raff, *Cello Concerto No. 1 in D, Opus 193;* Anton Rubinstein, *Cello Concerto No. 2 in d, Opus 96;* Camille Saint-Saëns, *Romance in F, Opus 36* (horn).

Program Music: Henri Duparc, *Poème Nocturne;* Antonin Dvořák, *Symphonic Poem in a, Opus 14;* Vincent d'Indy, *Max et Thécla;* Camille Saint-Saëns, *Danse Macabre, Opus 40;* Bedřich Smetana, *Vysehrad–The Moldau–Sarka* (Nos. 1, 2, 3 of *Ma Vlast*).

Standard Works: Emmanuel Chabrier, *Lamento for Orchestra;* Théodore Dubois, *Suite No. 1 for Orchestra;* Antonin Dvořák, *Rhapsody in a, Opus 15;* Robert Fuchs, *Serenade No. 1 in D, Opus 9* (strings); Ernest Guiraud, *Ouverture de Concert (d'Arteveld), Opus 10;* Ferdinand Hiller, *Dramatic Fantasy, Opus 166;* George Macfarren, *Festival Overture*(?); Jules Massenet, *Suite No. 4: Scènes pittoresques;* Joachim Raff, *Suite No. 2 in F, "In Hungarian Style," Opus 194;* Wolfgang Rihm, *Morphonie.*

Symphonies: George Bristow, *Arcadian Symphony;* Anton Bruckner, *No. 4 in E♭, "Romantic";* Antonin Dvořák, *No. 4 in d, Opus 13;* George Macfarren, *No. 9 in e;* Eduard Nápravnik, *No. 3 in c, "The Demon," Opus 18;* Nicolai Rimsky-Korsakov, *No. 3 in C.*

1875

❄

Historical Highlights: The Socialist Democratic Party is founded in Germany; Verney Cameron becomes the first white man to cross the African continent east to west; Captain M. Webb becomes the first person to swim the English Channel; in the United States, the new Civil

Rights Act forbids racial discrimination in public facilities; the Specie Resumption Act permits the redeeming of paper money on demand.

Art and Literature Highlights: Births—artist Carl Milles, writers Grazia Deledda, Wallace Irwin, Thomas Mann, Rainer Maria Rilke; Deaths—artists Antoine Louis Barye, Jean Baptiste Corot, Seth Eastman, writers Hans Christian Andersen, Edward Mörike, Alexei Tolstoy. Art—Eakins' *The Gross Clinic*, French's *The Minute Man*, Renoir's *Two Little Circus Girls*; Literature—Howell's *A Foregone Conclusion*, Miller's *The Ship in the Desert*.

Musical Highlights

A. Births

Composers: Franco Alfano (Italy) March 8; Julián Carrillo (Mexico) January 28; Mikolajus Karstantinas Čiurlionis (Lithuania) October 4; Samuel Coleridge-Taylor (England) August 15; Guido Alberto Fano (Italy) May 18; Henri Février (France) October 2; Reinhold Glière (Russia) January 11; Maurice Ravel (France) March 7; Richard Wetz (Germany) February 26.

Conductors: Paul Eisler (Austria) September 9; Agide Jacchia (Italy) January 5; Albert Ketèlby (England) August 9; Pierre Monteux (France) April 4; Max d'Ollone (France) June 13; Norman O'Neil (England) March 14; Ettore Panizza (Argentina) August 12.

Singers: Angelo Bada (Italian tenor); Paul Bender (German bass-baritone) July 28; Herminie Bosetti (Austrian-born soprano) September 28; Clotilde Bressler-Gianoli (Italian contralto) June 3; Marie Delna (French contralto) April 3; Ida Ekman (Finnish soprano) April 22; Katherina Fleischer-Edel (German soprano) September 25; Josephine Jacoby (American contralto); Putnam Griswold (American bass-baritone) December 23; Camilla Pasini (Italian soprano) November 6; Maria Philippi (Swiss contralto) July 26; Friedrich Plaschke (Czech bass-baritone) January 7; Riccardo Stracciari (Italian baritone) June 26.

Performers: Coenraad Valentin Bos (Dutch pianist) December 7; Gaston-Marie Déthier (Belgian-born organist) April 18; Alexander Goldenweiser (Russian pianist/composer) March 10; Fritz Kreisler (Austrian-born violinist) February 2; Ethel Newcomb (American pianist) October 30; Henriette Renié (French harpist) September 18; Cyril Rootham (British organist) October 5; Arthur Hilton Ryder (American organist) April 30; Albert Schweitzer (German organist) January 14; Józef Zygmunt Szule (Polish pianist/composer) April 4; Camille Zechwer (American pianist/composer) June 26.

Others: James Francis Cooke (American musicologist) November 14; Natalie Curtis (American folk music authority) April 26; Donald Tovey (British music scholar/pianist) July 17.

B. Deaths

Composers: Georges Bizet (France) June 3; Louis-Joseph Daussoigne-Méhul (France) March 10; John Henry Griesbach (England) January 9; William J. Hays (U.S.A.)(?); Carlo Romani (Italy) March 4; Nikolai Alexeievich Titov (Russia) December 22.

Singers: Luigi Agnesi (Belgian bass) February 2; Marietta Brambilla (Italian contralto) November 6; Alberico Curioni (Italian tenor) March.

Performers: Evangelista Andreoli (Italian pianist) June 16; Johannes Gijsbertus Bastiaans (Dutch organist/composer) February 16; Sir William Sterndale Bennett (British pianist/composer) February 1; Jeanne Louise Farrenc (French pianist/composer) September 15; Ureli Corelli Hill (American violinist) September 2; Matthias Keller (German-born violinist/composer) October 12; Ferdinand Laub (Czech violinist) March 18; Christian Friedrich Nohr (German violinist/composer) October 5.

Others: Gustav Auguste Besson (French instrument maker); Dom Prosper Louis Guéranger (French music scholar) January 30; Adolf Reubke (German organ builder) March 3; Julius Schuberth (German publisher) June 9; Jean-Baptiste Vuillaume (French violin maker) February 19.

C. Debuts

Singers: Julia Gaylord (American soprano—Dublin); Katharina Klafsky (Hungarian soprano—Salzburg); Joseph Staudigl, Jr. (Austrian baritone—Karlsruhe); Emile Alexandre Taskin (French baritone—Amiens); Zaré Thalberg (British soprano—London); Hermann Winkelmann (German tenor—Sondershausen).

Performers: Julie Rivé-King (American pianist—New York); Sergei Taneyev (Russian pianist—Moscow); Edmond Van der Straeten (German cellist—Cologne); Fannie Bloomfield Zeisler (American pianist—Chicago).

D. New Positions

Conductors: Joseph Barnby, (Eton); Otto Dessoff (Karlsruhe SO); Johann Herbeck (Gesellschaft der Musikfreunde, Vienna, second term); Hans Richter (Vienna Opera and PO).

Others: Anton Bruckner (music theory, Vienna Conservatory); Ferenc Erkel (director, Budapest Academy of Music); Max Kalbeck (music critic, *Schlesische Zeitung*); John Knowles Paine (first American to be appointed Professor of Music—at Harvard).

E. Prizes/Honors

Prizes: André Wormser (Prix de Rome).

Honors: Heinrich Bellermann (Berlin Academy of Arts); Georges Bizet (Legion of Honor); Franz Liszt (Hungarian Academy); Carl Reinecke (Berlin Academy of Arts).

F. Biographical Highlights

Dudley Buck moves to New York and becomes assistant to Theodore Thomas; Hans von Bülow makes a concert tour of the United States; Arthur Foote receives the first M.A. music degree to be given by an American university; Silas G. Pratt goes to Germany to study with Franz Liszt; Camille Saint-Saëns makes a concert tour of Russia; John Philip Sousa resigns from the U.S. Marine Corps and begins private teaching.

G. Cultural Beginnings

Performing Groups—Choral: Bach Choir of London; Johaniterne (Norwegian Choral Society); Kärntner Quintet; Ottawa Choral Union; Carl Rosa Opera Co.; Società Corale (Turin); Società del Quartetto Corale (Milan).

Performing Groups—Instrumental: Harmonie Cornet Band (San Diego, California); Springfield (Massachusetts) Orchestral Club; Winterthur Stadtorchester.

Festivals: Munich Opera Festival.

Educational: Hershey School of Musical Art (Chicago); Istituto Musicale Livornese; National Hungarian Royal Academy of Music (Budapest—Liszt Academy of Music, 1925); Potsday Musikschule.

Music Publishers: Will Thompson (East Liverpool, Ohio).

Music Publications: *The Music Trades Review (Musical and Dramatic Times)*; *Siona*.

Performing Centers: Paris Opera House; Palais Garnier (Paris); People's Theater (Budapest); Whitney's Grand Opera House (Detroit, Michigan).

Others: A. B. Chase Co. (Ohio); C. G. Conn Co. (Elkhart, Indiana); M. P. Möller, organ builder (Erie, Pennsylvania); Root and Sons Music Co. (Chicago).

H. Musical Literature

William H. Dana, *Orchestration*; Felix Draeseke, *Anweisung zum kunstgerechten Modulieren*; Gaetano Gaspari, *Memorie dell'arte musicale in Bologna a IXVI secolo*; François Gevaert, *Histoire et théorie de la musique de l'antiquité I*; Eduard Hanslick, *Die Moderne Oper I*; George Hart, *The Violin: Its Famous Makers and Their Imitators*; Nicolai Kashkin, *Elementary Music Theory*; Henri Lavoix, *La musique dans l'imagerie du moyen-âge*; Joseph Leibrock, *Musikalische Akkordenlehre*; Frederick Ouseley, *A Treatise on Musical Form and General Composition*; Hugo Riemann, *Die Hülfsmittel der modulation*; Edouard Schuré, *Le Drame Musical*.

I. Musical Compositions

Chamber Music:

String Quartets: Alexander Mackenzie, *Quartet in G.*

Sonata/Solos: Zdeněk Fibich, *Violin Sonata No. 2 in D*; Ferdinand Hiller, *Cello Sonata No. 2, Opus 172*(?); John Knowles Paine, *Violin Sonata in b, Opus 24*; Camille Saint-Saëns, *Allegro appassionato, in b, Opus 43* (violin, piano—also orchestrated).

Ensembles: Johannes Brahms, *Piano Quartet No. 3 in c, Opus 60*; Antonin Dvořák, *String Quintet in G, Opus 77–Piano Trio in B♭, Opus 21–Piano Quartet in D, Opus 23*; Heinrich Hofmann, *String Sextet, Opus 25*(?); Engelbert Humperdinck, *Piano Quintet in G*; Franz Lachner, *Nonet in F* (woodwind quintet, strings); John Knowles Paine, *Piano Trio No. 2 in B♭, Opus 22*; Camille Saint-Saëns, *Piano Quartet in B♭, Opus 41*; Charles M. Widor, *Piano Trio, Opus 19.*

Piano: Stephen Heller, *Voyage autour de ma chambre, Opus 140*; Ludvig Norman, *Concertpiece in F, Opus 54*; C. Hubert Parry, *Sonnets and Songs without Words II–Variations on an Air by Bach*; Joachim Raff, *Four Pieces, Opus 196–Capriccio, Opus 197.*

Organ: Alexandre Guilmant, *Pièces d'orgue dans differente styles*; Leoš Janáček, *Prelude–Chorale fantasia*; Camille Saint-Saëns, *Offertoire in e.*

Choral/Vocal Music:

Choral: Leopold Damrosch, *Ruth and Naomi* (oratorio); Gabriel Fauré, *Les Djins, Opus 12*; August Söderman, *Catholic Mass*; John Stainer, *Gideon* (oratorio); Charles Villiers Stanford, *The Golden Legend–The Resurrection* (oratorios).

Vocal: Antonin Dvořák, *Four Moravian Duets, Opus 20–Five Duets, Opus 66*; Robert Fuchs, *Five Songs, Opus 16*(?).

Musical Stage: Georges Bizet, *Carmen*; James A. Butterfield, *Ruth, the Gleaner*; Antonin Dvořák, *Vanda, Opus 25*; Gilbert/Sullivan, *Trial by Jury*; Karl Goldmark, *Die Königen von Saba*; Hervé, *La belle poule–Alice de Nevers*; Jacques Offenbach, *Voyage dans la lune–La boulangère a des écus–La créole*; Joseph Strauss, Jr., *Cagliostro in Wien*; Arthur Sullivan, *The Zoo.*

Orchestra/Band Music:

Concerted Music:

Piano: Joachim Raff, *Suite in E♭, Opus 200*; Anton Rubinstein, *Concerto No. 5 in E♭, Opus 94*; Camille Saint-Saëns, *Concerto No. 4 in c, Opus 44*; Peter Ilyich Tchaikovsky, *Concerto No. 1 in b♭, Opus 23.*

Violin: Ferdinand Hiller, *Fantasiestück, Opus 152b*; Peter Ilyich Tchaikovsky, *Serenade Melancholique, Opus 26.*

Other: Dudley Buck, *Romanza for Four Horns and Orchestra, Opus 71.*

Ballet/Incidental Music: Edvard Grieg, *Peer Gynt, Opus 23* (IM); Johan P. Hartmann, *Arcona, Opus 72* (B); Alexandre Luigini, *Ballet Egyptien* (B).

Program Music: Henri Duparc, *Lénore*; Zdeněk Fibich, *Toman and the Wood Nymphs, Opus 49*; Hermann Goetz, *Overture, Francesco da Rimini*; Bedřich Smetana, *From Bohemia's Wood and Meadows* (No. 4 of *Ma Vlast*).

Standard Works: Antonin Dvořák, *Serenade in E for Strings, Opus 22*; Gabriel Fauré, *Suite d'orchestre, Opus 20*; Edouard Lalo, *Allegro Symphonique*; Franz Liszt, *Hungarian Storm March*.

Symphonies: Antonin Dvořák, *No. 5 in F, Opus 76*; Vincent d'Indy, *Symphony, "Jean Huryade," Opus 5*; André Messager, *Symphony in A*; Silas G. Pratt, *No. 2, "The Prodigal Son"*; Joseph Joachim Raff, *No. 7 in B♭, "In Den Alpen," Opus 201*; Carl Reinecke, *No. 2 in c, "Hakon Jarl," Opus 134*; Anton Rubinstein, *No. 4 in d, "Dramatic," Opus 95*; Charles Villiers Stanford, *No. 1 in B♭*; Peter Ilyich Tchaikovsky, *No. 3 in D, "Polish," Opus 29*.

1876
❈

Historical Highlights: Porfirio Diaz seizes the Mexican government via revolution (not deposed until 1911); Korea is granted its independence by Japan; Serbia and Montenegro both declare war on Turkey; in the United States, Rutherford B. Hayes is elected as nineteenth president; Colorado becomes state number thirty-eight; the Battle of Little Big Horn results in the death of General Custer and all his troops; Alexander Bell patents the telephone.

Art and Literature Highlights: Pennsylvania Academy of Fine Arts created. Births—artists Maurice de Vlaminck, Raymond Duchamp-Villon, writers Sherwood Anderson, Jack London; Deaths—writers Irwin S. Cobb, Louis Colet, George Sand; Art—Degas' *The Absinthe Drinkers*, Homer's *Breezing Up*, Moreau's *L'Apparition*; Literature—James' *Roderick Hudson*, Mallarmé's *L'Après-midi d'un Faune*, Twain's *The Adventures of Tom Sawyer*.

Musical Highlights

A. Births

Composers: Flor Alpaerts (Belgium) September 12; Frederic Ayres (U.S.A.) March 17; Hakon Børresen (Denmark) June 2; Havergal Brian (England) January 29; John Alden Carpenter (U.S.A.) February 28; Jens Laursen Emborg (Denmark); Manuel de Falla (Spain) November 23; Jan Ingenhoven (Holland) May 29; Mieczyslaw Karlowicz (Poland) December 11; Carl Ruggles (U.S.A.) March 11; Ernest Schelling (U.S.A.) July 26; Walter William Stockhoff (U.S.A.) November 12; Ermanno Wolf-Ferrari (Italy) January 12.

Conductors: Bruno Walter (Germany-U.S.A.) September 15.

Singers: Aïno Ackté (Finnish soprano) April 23; Giuseppe Anselmi (Italian tenor) November 16; Lola Artôt de Padilla (Spanish soprano) October 5; Ernesto Badini (Italian baritone) September 14; Therese Behr (German contralto) September 12; Edmund Burke (Canadian bass) July 12; Horatio Connell (American baritone) March 15; Giuseppe De Luca (Italian baritone) December 25; Marya Freund (Polish soprano) December 12; Waldemar Henke (German tenor) March 24; Lucien Muratore (French tenor) August 29; Rosina Storchio (Italian soprano) May 19; Carrie Tubb (British soprano) May 17; Lucie Weidt (German-born soprano) May 11; Hermann Weil (German baritone) May 29; Giovanni Zenatello (Italian tenor) February 22.

Performers: Feodor Akimenko (Russian pianist/composer) February 20; Georges Barrère (French-born flutist) October 31; Pablo Casals (Spanish cellist) December 29; Josef Hofmann (Polish-born pianist) January 20; Ralph Kinder (British-born organist) January 27; Lionel Tertis (British violist) December 29.

Others: Mary Louise Curtis Bok (American patron of the arts) August 6; Walter Niemann (German music author) October 10; Ludwig Schiedermair (German musicologist) December 7.

B. Deaths

Composers: Giovanni Bajetti (Italy) April 28; Raimondo Boucheron (Italy) February 28; Félicien David (France) August 29; Josef Dessauer (Austria) July 8; Hermann Goetz (Germany) December 3; Luigi Luzzi (Italy) February 23; Franz Pocci (Germany) May 7.

Conductors: August Röckel (Austria) June 18.

Singers: Henry Robinson Allen (Irish baritone) November 27; Wilhelm Dettmer (German bass) May 28; Elizabeth Taylor Greenfield (American soprano) April; Anton Mitterwurzer (Austrian baritone) April 2; Henry Gene Phillips (British bass) November 8; Mary Shaw (British contralto) September 9; Antonio Tamburini (Italian baritone) November 8.

Performers: Carl Bergmann (German-born cellist/conductor) August 10; Henri Bertini (British-born pianist) October 1; Joseph Böhm (Hungarian violinist) March 28; George Cooper (British organist) October 2; Charles Edward Horsley (British organist) February 28; Ernst Lübeck (Dutch pianist/composer) September 17; Giovanni Puzzi (Italian horn viruoso) March 1; Henri Rosellen (French pianist/composer) March 18; Samuel Sebastian Wesley (British organist/composer) April 19.

Others: August Wilhelm Ambros (Austrian music historian) June 28; Philip Paul Bliss (American hymnwriter) December 29; Raimondo Boucheron (Italian music theorist/conductor) February 28; Edmond de Coussemaker (French music scholar) January 10; John Bacchus Dykes (British hymn composer) January 22; Edward Francis Rimbault (British music author/organist) September 26; William H. Simmonds (American organ builder) October 31.

C. Debuts

Singers: Emma Abbott (American soprano—London); Ada Adiny (American soprano—Varese); Eugènia Élise Colonne (French soprano—Paris); Edouard De Reszke (Polish bass—Paris); Etelka Gerster (Hungarian soprano—Venice); Lillian Bailey Henschel (American soprano—Boston); Marie Litta (American soprano—London); Francesco Navarrini (Italian bass—Ferrara); Lillian Nordica (American soprano—Boston); Ippolit Petrovich Prianishnikov (Russian baritone—Milan); Ernestine Schumann-Heink (Austrian-born mezzo-soprano—Graz).

Performers: Amy Fay (American pianist—Boston); Moriz Rosenthal (Austrian pianist—Vienna); Leo Schulz (German cellist—Berlin).

D. New Positions

Conductors: George Matzka (New York PO); Gustav Schmidt (hofkapellmeister, Darmstadt).

Others: William Foster Apthorp (music critic, *Atlantic Monthly*); Léon Carvalho (director, Opéra-Comique, Paris); Karl Davidov (director, St. Petersburg Conservatory); Friedrich Hegar (director, Zürich Conservatory); Angelo Neumann (manager, Leipzig Opera); Eban Tourjée (president, Music Teachers National Association, U.S.A.); Jean Baptiste Weckerlin (librarian, Paris Conservatory); Richard Zeckwer (director, Philadelphia Musical Academy).

E. Prizes/Honors

Prizes: Paul Hillemacher (Prix de Rome).

Honors: Niels Gade (government life stipend); John Goss (Mus. Doc., Cambridge); Jules Massenet (Legion of Honor); Herbert Oakley (knighted); Louis-Etienne Reyer (French Institute); John Steele (knighted).

F. Biographical Highlights

George W. Chadwick quits his father's business and begins teaching music theory at Olivet College in Michigan; Niels Gade visits England and conducts at the Birmingham Music Festival; Anatol Liadov is expelled from St. Petersburg Conservatory for failure to attend classes; Felix Mottl becomes assistant to Wagner at Bayreuth; Peter Ilyich Tchaikovsky begins correspondence with Mme. von Meck.

G. Cultural Beginnings

Performing Groups—Choral: Dresden Männergesangverein; Purcell Society of London.

Performing Groups—Instrumental: Basler Allgemeine Musikgesellschaft; Bernische Orchesterverein; Mainz Civic Orchestra; Music Society of Kraków; Prague Kammermusikverein.

Festivals: Silesian Music Festival; Wagner Festival (Bayreuth).

Educational: Conservatorio Benedetto Marcello (Venice); Music Teacher's National Association (MTNA); New York College of Music; Zürich Conservatory of Music.

Music Publishers: J. W. Pepper (Philadelphia); Arthur P. Schmidt Co. (Boston); Adam and Oliver Shattinger (St. Louis); Zimmermann Publishing Co. (St. Petersburg, Russia).

Music Publications: *Cäcilienkalendar*; *Der Heimgarten* (Graz).

Performing Centers: Evans Hall (Fort Worth, Texas); Wade's (Grand) Opera House (San Francisco).

Others: Sheffield Tonic Sol-Fa Association (Musical Union); Tremaine Brothers (Tremaine Piano Co.—New York); Wilcox and White, organ makers (Connecticut).

H. Musical Literature

Jesse B. Aikin, *The Imperial Harmony*; Luigi F. Casamorata, *Manuale di Armonia*; Félix Clément, *De la réédition du plain-chant romain traditionnel*; Enrico Delle Sedie, *L'art lyrique*; Carl Engel, *Musical Myths and Facts*; Alphonse Goovaerts, *La musique d'église*; Ferdinand Hiller, *Musikalisches und persönliches*; Charles E. Horsley, *Textbook of Harmony*; José Inzenga, *Impresiones de un artista en Italia*; Ebenezer Prout, *Instrumentation*; Emil Naumann, *Musikdrama oder Oper? Eine Beleuchtung der Bayreuther Bühnerfestspiele*; Nicolai Rimsky-Korsakov, *Autobiography*.

I. Musical Compositions

Chamber Music:

String Quartets: Johannes Brahms, *No. 3 in B♭, Opus 67*; Antonin Dvořák, *No. 8 in E, Opus 80*; Engelbert Humperdinck, *No. 2*; Bedřich Smetana, *No. 1 in e, "From My Life"*; Peter Ilyich Tchaikovsky, *No. 3 in e♭, Opus 30*.

Sonata/Solos: Gabriel Fauré, *Violin Sonata No. 1 in A, Opus 13*; Joachim Raff, *Voler, Opus 203* (violin, piano); Anton Rubinstein, *Violin Sonata No. 3 in b, Opus 98*; Henri Vieuxtemps, *Voix intimes, Opus 45*.

Ensembles: Antonin Dvořák, *Piano Trio in g, Opus 26*; Robert Fuchs, *Piano Quartet om g, Opus 15*; Eduard Nápravnik, *Piano Trio in g, Opus 24*; Joachim Raff, *Piano Quartet in C/c, Opus 202*; Anton Rubinstein, *String Sextet in D, Opus 97–Piano Quintet in g, Opus 99*.

Piano: Antonin Dvořák, *Theme and Variations in A♭, Opus 36*; Robert Fuchs, *Variations in g, Opus 13*(?); Carl Goldmark, *Hungarian Dances, Opus 22* (four hands); Anatol Liadov, *Biryulki (Fourteen Pieces), Opus 2*; Franz Liszt, *Weihnachtsbaum-Arbre de Noël*; Edward MacDowell, *Eight Chansons Fugitives, Opus 2–Three Petits morceaux, Opus 4–Suite, Opus 5*; Giuseppe Martucci, *Sonata, Opus 34*(?); John Knowles Paine, *Four Characteristic Pieces, Opus 25*; Joachim Raff, *Suite in B♭, Opus 204*; Julius Röntgen, *Introduction, Scherzo, Intermezzo and Finale, Opus 16* (four hands); Peter Ilyich Tchaikovsky, *The Seasons, Opus 37b*.

Organ: Charles Gounod, *Offertorium*; Charles M. Widor, *Organ Symphonies 1–4, Opus 13*.

Choral/Vocal Music:

Choral: Dudley Buck, *Centennial Meditation on Columbus*; Antonin Dvořák, *Four Partsongs, Opus 29*; Charles Gounod, *The Seven Last Words of Christ* (cantata); Ferdinand Hiller, *Bundeslied, Opus 174*; Heinrich Hofmann, *Das Märchen von der schönen Melusine, Opus 30*; Edouard Lalo, *Litanies de la sainte Vierge*; George Macfarren, *St. John the Baptist–The Resurrection* (oratorios); John Knowles Paine, *Centennial Hymn, Opus 27*; Silas G. Pratt, *Centennial Hymn*; Camille Saint-Saëns, *Le Déluge, Opus 45* (oratorio).

Vocal: César Cui, *Six Songs, Opus 10*; Antonin Dvořák, *Five Moravian Duets, Opus 29–Eight Moravian Duets, Opus 32*; Anatol Liadov, *Four Songs, Opus 1*; Alexander Mackenzie, *Two Songs, Opus 3*; Luigi Mancinelli, *Un'estate a Perugia* (cycle).

Musical Stage: Peter Benoit, *The Pacification of Ghent–Charlotte Corday*; César Cui, *Angelo*; Ernest Guirard, *Piccolino*; Hervé, *Estelle et Némorin*; Jules Massenet, *Bérangère et Anatole*; Victor Nessler, *Irmingard*; Jacques Offenbach, *Pierette et Jacquot–La boîte au lait*; Ole Olsen, *Stig Hvide*; Errico Petrella, *Diane*; Amilcare Ponchielli, *La Gioconda*; Bedřich Smetana, *The Kiss*; Franz von Suppé, *Fatinitza*.

Orchestra/Band Music:

Concerted Music:

Piano: Théodore Dubois, *Concerto Capriccioso*; Antonin Dvořák, *Concerto in g, Opus 33*(?); Charles M. Widor, *Concerto No. 1, Opus 39*.

Violin: Benjamin Godard, *Concerto Romantique*; Ferdinand Hiller, *Concerto, Opus 152*.

Other: Edouard Lalo, *Cello Concerto in D*; Joseph Joachim Raff, *Cello Concerto No. 2 in G*.

Ballet/Incidental Music: Léo Delibes, *Sylvia* (B); Alexandre Luigini, *Anges et Démons* (B); Luigi Mancinelli, *Messalina* (IM); Jules Massenet, *La Vie de Bohème* (IM); Peter Ilyich Tchaikovsky, *Swan Lake, Opus 20* (B).

Program Music: César Franck, *Les Eolides*; Vincent d'Indy, *Overture, Anthony and Cleopatra*; John Knowles Paine, *The Tempest, Opus 31*; Peter Ilyich Tchaikovsky, *Francesca da Rimini, Opus 32*.

Standard Works: Charles Gounod, *Marche religieuse in C*; Robert Fuchs, *Serenade No. 2 in C, Opus 14* (strings); Alexander Mackenzie, *Overture to a Comedy*; Jules Massenet, *Suite No. 5: Scènes napolitaines*; John Knowles Paine, *Overture, As You Like It, Opus 28*; Silas G. Pratt, *Centennial Overture*; Giacomo Puccini, *Preludio Sinfonico*; Peter Ilyich Tchaikovsky, *Marche Slav, Opus 31*; Richard Wagner, *Grosser Festmarsch* (for Philadelphia Centennial Celebration).

Symphonies: Alexander Borodin, *No. 2 in b*; Johannes Brahms, *No. 1 in c, Opus 68*; Anton Bruckner, *No. 5 in B♭*; Karl Goldmark, *Rustic Wedding Symphony, Opus 26*; Heinrich Hofmann, *Frithjof-Symphonie, Opus 22*; John Knowles Paine, *No. 1 in c*; Joseph Joachim Raff, *No. 8 in A, "Frühlingsklänge," Opus 205–No. 11 in a, "Der Winter," Opus 214*.

1877
❄

Historical Highlights: Romania becomes a full and independent state; Russia joins in the war against Turkey; in Africa, Henry Stanley founds Leopoldville in the Belgian Congo; Deimas and Phobos, two moons of Mars, are discovered; in the United States, the Nez Perce Indian War takes place; the Desert Land Act provides up to 640 acres of land at 25 cents an acre; the Bell Telephone Co. is founded; Thomas Edison patents the phonograph.

Art and Literature Highlights: Births—artists Raoul Dufy, Marsden Hartley, George Kolbe, Jacob Lawrence, writers Rex Beach, Lloyd C. Dounglas; Deaths—sculptor Joel T. Hart, writer William Hosmer. Art—Degas' *Dancers at the Bar*, Eakins' *William Rush Carving the Allegorical Figure of the Schuylkill River*, Monet's *Gare Saint-Lazare*; Literature—Carré's *Paul et Virginie*, James' *The American*, Tolstoy's *Anna Karenina*.

Musical Highlights

A. Births

Composers: Louis-François Aubert (France) February 19; John Parsons Beach (U.S.A.) October 11; Ernst von Dohnányi (Hungary-U.S.A.) July 27; Blair Fairchild (U.S.A.) June 23; Sigfrid Karg-Elert (Germany) November 21; Paul Ladmirault (France) December 8; Felix Nowowiejski (Poland) February 7; Pavel Tchesnokov (Russia) October 24.

Conductors: Artur Bodanzky (Austria) December 16; Jāzeps Mediņš (Latvia) February 13; David Stanley Smith (U.S.A.) July 6.

Singers: Morton Adkins (American baritone) November 25; Bella Alten (Polish soprano) June 30; Jane Bathori (French mezzo-soprano) June 14; Celestina Boninsegna (Italian soprano) February 26; Emma Carelli (Italian soprano) May 12; Karl Erb (German tenor) July 13; Allen C. Hinckley (American bass) October 11; Hermann Jadlowker (Latvian tenor) July 17; Vanni Marcoux (French baritone) June 12; Richard Mayr (Austrian bass) November 18; Agnes Nicholls (British soprano) July 14; Tina Poli-Randaccio (Italian soprano); Corinne Rider-Kelsey (American soprano) February 24; Titta Ruffo (Italian baritone) June 9; Oscar Seagle (American baritone) October 31; Marcia Van Dresser (American soprano) December 4; Domenico Viglione-Borghese (Italian baritone) July 3.

Performers: Sergei Bortkiewicz (Russian pianist) February 28; Alfred Cortot (French pianist) September 26; Angela Diller (American pianist) August 1; George Herbert Fryer (British pianist) May 21; Weston Gales (American organist/conductor) November 5; Rudolph Ganz (Swiss-born pianist/conductor) February 24; Jean Gérardy (Belgian cellist) December 6; Alexander Goedicke (Russian pianist/composer) March 4; Katherine Ruth Heyman (American pianist); Jean Huré (French organist) September 17; Isabelle Vengerova (Russian-born pianist) March 1; Harriet Ware (American pianist) August 26.

Others: Michel Dimitri Calvocoressi (Greek music author) October 2; Jean Chantavoine (French music author) May 17; Eric Eggen (Norwegian music scholar) November 17; Edwin A. Fischel (American patron of the arts) July 14; Alfred Heuss (Swiss-born critic) January 27; Erich Moritz von Hornbostel (Austrian musicologist) February 25; Arnold Schering (German music historian) April 2; Percy Scholes (British music author) July 24.

B. Deaths

Composers: Carl Arnold (Germany-Norway) November 11; Louise (Angelique) Bertin (France) April 26; Pietro Antonio Coppola (Italy) November 13; Vincenzo Fioravanti (Italy) March 28; Mary Ann Gabriel (England) August 7; Errico Petrella (Italy) April 7; Federico Ricci (Italy) December 10; Pietro Romini (Italy) January 11.

Conductors: Johann Herbeck (Austria) October 28; (Ernst) Julius Otto (Germany) March 5; Cristóbal Oudrid (Spain) March 12; Julius August Rietz (Germany) September 12.

Singers: Eduard Devrient (German baritone/author) October 4; Jenny Dingelstedt (Bohemian soprano) October 3; Elizabeth Rainforth (British soprano) September 22; Therese Tietjens (German soprano) October 3; Caroline Unger (Austrian contralto) March 23.

Performers: Pierre Alexandre Chevillard (Belgian cellist) December 18; Luigi Legnani (Italian guitarist/guitar maker) August 5; Charles

Neate (British pianist) March 30; Julius Rietz (German cellist/conductor) September 12.
Others: Giuseppe Curci (Italian music author/composer) August 5; Alexandre-François Debain (French piano maker/inventor) December 3; Antoine Elwart (French music author) October 14; Johann Adam Heckel (German instrument maker) April 13; Ludwig Köchel (Austrian music bibliographer) June 3; Philipp Wackernagel (German music scholar) June 20.

C. Debuts
Singers: Fanny Moran-Olden (German soprano—Leipzig); Lucien Fugère (French bass—Paris); Pol-Henri Plançon (French bass—Lyons); Marcella Sembrich (Polish-born soprano—Athens); Juliette Simon-Girard (French soprano—Paris).

D. New Positions
Conductors: Jules Danbé (Opéra-Comique, Paris); Théodore Dubois (maître de Chapele, Madeleine, Paris); Henryk Jarecki (Polish Theater, Posen); Charles Lamoureux (Paris Opera); Joseph Rheinberger (Munich Court); Theodore Thomas (New York PO).
Others: William Barrett (editor, *Monthly Music Record*); Frans Coenen (director, Amsterdam Conservatory); August Kretschmer (music director, Rostock University); Joseph Joaquim Raff (director, Frankfurt Conservatory); Franz Wüllner (director, Dresden Conservatory).

E. Prizes/Honors
Prizes: Edgar Tinel (Prix de Rome).
Honors: Joseph Joachim (doctorate, Cambridge).

F. Biographical Highlights
Ernest Chausson is sworn in as a lawyer but never takes up the practice; Peter Ilyich Tchaikovsky, after a week of marriage to Antonina Milyukov, attempts suicide and separates from her—he is given a yearly annuity by Mme. von Meck with the stipulation that they never meet.

G. Cultural Beginnings
Performing Groups—Choral: Romanian Opera Co.; Württemberg Evangelical Kirchengesangverein.
Performing Groups—Instrumental: Helsinki Concert Society; Ladies (Indiana) Matinee Musical (Indianapolis); Montreal Philharmonic Society (revival); Nyack Symphonic Society; Rostocker Konzertverein; Schubert String Quartet; Società dei Concerti Sinfonici Popolari (Milan).
Festivals: Salzburg Festival; Württemberg Evangelical Festival.

Educational: Academia de Belas Artas (Instituto de Música da Bahia); Instituto Nacional de Bellas Artes (Venezuela); Liceo Musicale (Rome); Morgan Conservatory of Music (Oakland, California); Philadelphia Conservatory of Music; Scuolo d'Arco (Verona).
Music Publishers: Francis, Day and Hunter (London); Julien Hamelle (Paris); I. K. Funk and Co. (Funk and Wagnalls), publishers.
Music Publications: *Journal de Musique*; *Musical Opinion*; *J. W. Pepper's Musical Times and Band Journal (Musical Times)*.
Performing Centers: Central City (Colorado) Opera House; Tivoli Opera House I (San Francisco).

H. Music Publications

Kornél Ábrányi, *Music Aesthetic*; William A. Barrett, *English Church Composers*; W. H. Cummings, *Primer of the Rudiments of Music*; Moritz Drobisch, *Über reine Stimmung und Temperatur der Töne*; Carl Grädener, *System der harmonielehre*; John Hullah, *Music in the House*; Francesco Lamperti, *Treatise on the Art of Singing*; Henri Lavoix, *La Musique dans la Nature*; Emil Naumann, *Zukunftsmusik und die Musik der Zukunft*; Ernst Pauer, *Elements of the Beautiful in Music–The Art of Pianoforte Playing*; Hugo Riemann, *Musikalische syntaxis: Grundriss einer harmonischen Satzbildungslehre*.

I. Musical Compositions

Chamber Music:

String Quartets: Johann H. Beck, *No. 1 in c*; Antonin Dvořák, *No. 9 in d, Opus 34*; Caryl Florio, *No. 1*.

Sonata/Solos: Camille Saint-Saëns, *Romance in D, Opus 51* (cello, piano).

Ensembles: Elfrieda Andrée, *Piano Trio in g*; C. Hubert Parry, *Nonet in B♭* (winds); Richard Strauss, *Piano Trio in A*.

Piano: Ferruccio Busoni, *Five Pieces, Opus 3*; Cesare Cui, *Three Pieces, Opus 8*; Antonin Dvořák, *Scottish Dances in d*; Zdeněk Fibich, *Suite in g–Variations in B♭*; Robert Fuchs, *Sonata No. 1 in G♭, Opus 19(?)*; Anatol Liadov, *Six Pieces (D, F, g, G, B, C), Opus 3*; Franz Liszt, *Années de pélerinage, Year III*; Arthur de Lulli, *The Celebrated Chop Waltz (Chopsticks)*; Alexander Mackenzie, *Five Pieces, Opus 13*; C. Hubert Parry, *Sonata No. 1 in F*; Joachim Raff, *Fantasie in g for Two Pianos, Opus 207*; Anton Rubinstein, *Sonata No. 4 in a, Opus 100*; Camille Saint-Saëns, *Six Etudes, Opus 52*; Charles M. Widor, *Six Valses caractéristiques, Opus 26–Twelve Feuillets d'album, Opus 31*.

Organ: Dudley Buck, *Organ Sonata No. 2 in g, Opus 77–Variations on "Sweet Bye and Bye"*; Franz Liszt, *Resignazione*; Frederick Ouseley, *Thirty-One Preludes and Fugues, Set II–Sonata No. 1*; Camille Saint-Saëns, *Prelude in A(?)*.

Choral/Vocal Music:

Choral: Max Bruch, *Arminius* (oratorio); Frédéric Clay, *Lalla Rookh* (cantata); Antonin Dvořák, *Three Songs, Opus 45–Stabat Mater, Opus 58–Bouquet of Czech Folk Songs, Opus 41*; Charles Gounod, *Messe du Sacré-Coeur de Jésus in C*; Franz Liszt, *Christus* (oratorio); George Macfarren, *Joseph* (oratorio)–*Lady of the Lake* (cantata); J. C. D. Parker, *Redemption Hymn*; Giacomo Puccini, *I Figli d'Italia* (cantata); Franz von Suppé, *Missa Dalmatica*; George E. Whiting, *Dream Pictures*.

Vocal: Johannes Brahms, *Nine Songs, Opus 69–Four Songs, Opus 70–Five Songs, Opus 71– Five Songs, Opus 72*; César Cui, *Six Songs, Opus 11*; Antonin Dvořák, *Four Moravian Duets, Opus 38*; Robert Fuchs, *Five Songs, Opus 189*; Annie F. Harrison, *In the Gloaming*; Modest Mussorgsky, *Songs and Dances of Death*; Anton Rubinstein, *Twelve Songs from Tolstoy, Opus 101–Ten Servian Songs, Opus 105*; Arthur Sullivan, *The Lost Chord*.

Musical Stage: Emmanuel Chabrier, *L'Étoile*; Antonin Dvořák, *The Cunning Peasant, Opus 37*; Zdeněk Fibich, *Blaník, Opus 50*; Gilbert/ Sullivan, *The Sorcerer*; Charles Gounod, *Cinq-Mars*; Ivar Hallström, *The Vikings' Voyage*; Charles Lecocq, *La Marjolaine*; Ruggero Leon-cavallo, *Chatterton*; Alexandre Luigini, *Les Caprices de Margot*; Jules Massenet, *Le Roi de Lahore*; Jacques Offenbach, *Le Docteur Ox–La Foire Saint-Laurent*; Jean Planquette, *Les Cloches de Corneville*; Lauro Rossi, *Biorn*; Anton Rubinstein, *Néron*; Camille Saint-Saëns, *Samson and Delilah–Le Timbre d'argent*; Johann Strauss, Jr., *Prinz Methusalem*.

Orchestra/Band Music:

Concerted Music:

Piano: Eduardo Nápravnik, *Concerto, Opus 27*.

Violin: Antonin Dvořák, *Romance in f, Opus 11*; Karl Goldmark, *Concerto in a, Opus 28*; Eduardo Nápravnik, *Two Ballades, Opus 26*; Joachim Raff, *Concerto No. 2 in a, Opus 206*; Carl Reinecke, *Concerto in g, Opus 141*; Peter Ilyich Tchaikovsky, *Valse Scherzo in C, Opus 34*.

Other: Edouard Lalo, *Cello Concerto in d*; John Knowles Paine, *Duo Concertante, Opus 33* (violin, cello); Nicolas Rimsky-Korsakov, *Trombone Concerto* (with band); Henry Vieuxtemps, *Cello Concerto in a, Opus 46*.

Ballet/Incidental Music: Luigi Mancinelli, *Cleopatra* (IM).

Program Music: Vincent d'Indy, *Antoine et Cléopâtre, Opus 6*; Camille Saint-Saëns, *La Jeunesse d'Hercule, Opus 50*.

Standard Works: Théodore Dubois, *Suite No. 2*; Antonin Dvořák, *Symphonic Variations, Opus 78*; Robert Fuchs, *Serenade No. 3 in e, Opus 21* (strings); Carl Goldmark, *Ländliche Hochzeit, Opus 26*; Leoš Janáček, *Suite for String Orchestra*; Alexander Mackenzie, *Cervantes Overture*; Silas G. Pratt, *Canon for String Orchestra*; Joachim Raff,

Suite No. 4, "Thüringer"; John Philip Sousa, *The Rivals Overture–Sardanapolis Waltzes–Blending of the Blue and Gray* (band); Charles Villiers Stanford, *Festival Overture*.

Symphonies: Johannes Brahms, *No. 2 in D, Opus 73*; Peter Ilyich Tchaikovsky, *No. 4 in f, Opus 36*.

1878

❋

Historical Highlights: The Congress of Berlin divides the Ottoman Empire among the European powers; Cuba once again fails to gain independence from Spain; in the United States, the first telephone exchange (listing of fifty names) is set up in New Haven, Connecticut; the Bland-Allison Act concerning the coining of silver is passed by Congress; a new gold strike in Arizona results in the founding of the town of Tombstone.

Art and Literature Highlights: Births—authors Émile Cammaerts, John Masefield, Ferenc Molnár, Carl Sandberg, sculptor Abastemia St. Leger Eberle; Deaths—artists George Cruikshank, Charles-François Daubigny, poet William Cullen Bryant; Art—Harnett's *Music and Literature,* Marées' *The Ages of Man*, Sargent's *The Oyster Gatherers*; Literature—Baumbach's *Lieder eines Fahrenden Gesellen*, Hardy's *Return of the Native*.

Musical Highlights

A. **Births**

Composers: Lionel Barrymore (U.S.A.) April 28; Fritz Brun (Switzerland) August 18; Conrado del Campo (Spain) October 28; George M. Cohan (U.S.A.) July 3; Mabel Wheeler Daniels (U.S.A.) November 27; Constantino Gaito (Argentina) August 13; Thurlow Lieurance (U.S.A.) March 21; Albert Mildenberg (U.S.A.) January 13; Selim Palmgren (Finland) February 16; Carlos Pedrell (Uruguay) October 16; Arrigo Pedrollo (Italy) December 5; Franz Schreker (Austria) March 23; Vincenzo Tommasini (Italy) September 17.

Conductors: Carl Ehrenberg (Germany) April 6; Edwin Franko Goldman (U.S.A.) January 1; Tullio Serafin (Italy) September 1.

Singers: Pasquale Amato (Italian baritone) March 21; Giannina Russ Cerri (Italian soprano); Eleanora de Cisneros (American mezzo-soprano) November 1; Emmy Destinn (Czech soprano) February 26; Maria Farneti (Italian soprano); Maude Fay (American soprano) April 18; Edoardo Ferrari-Fontana (Italian tenor) July 8; Rita Fornia-Labey (American mezzo-soprano) July 17; Hedwig Francillo-Kaufmann (Austrian soprano) September 30; Gustav Huberdeau (French bass-baritone)(?); Edward Johnson (Canadian tenor/administrator) August 22; Berta Morena (German soprano) January 27;

Amelia Pinto (Italian soprano); Paul Reimers (German tenor) March 14; Rudolf Ritter (Austrian tenor) January 19; Fritz Soot (German tenor) August 20; Valerie Thomán (Hungarian singer) August 16.

Performers: Augusta Cottlow (American pianist) April 2; Louis Fleury (French flutist) May 24; Ossip Gabrilowitsch (Russian pianist/conductor) February 7; Heinrich Gebhard (German-born pianist/composer) June 25; Percy Hull (British organist) October 27; Miguel Llobet (Spanish guitarist) October 18; Albert Riemenschneider (American organist) August 31.

Others: Fortune Galla (Italian-born impresario) May 9; Lawrence Gilman (American music critic) July 5; Kálmán Isoz (Hungarian musicologist) December 4; Otto Kinkeldey (American musicologist) November 27; Emile Vuillermoz (French critic) May 23.

B. Deaths

Composers: José Bernado Alcedo (Peru) December 28; François-Emmanuel-Joseph Bazin (France) July 2; Adolf Fredrik Lindblad (Sweden) August 23.

Conductors: Théophile Tilmant (France) May 7.

Singers: Elisa Blaes (Belgian soprano) November 6; Josephine Fröhlich (Austrian soprano) May 7; Napoleone Moriani (Italian tenor) March 4; Ossip A. Petrov (Russian bass) March 11; Ludwika Rivoli (Polish soprano) October 16; Georgine Schubert (German soprano) December 26; Louise Wippern (German soprano) October 5.

Performers: Lucy Anderson (British pianist) December 24; François Benoist (French organist) May 6; Constantin Decker (German pianist/composer) January 28; Eugène Gautier (French violinist/composer) April 1; Gotfried Hermann (German violinist) June 6; Hermann Küster (German organist/music author) March 17; Ludwig Maurer (German violinist) October 25; Wilhelm Speyer (German violinist) April 5; Théophile Tilmant (French violinist) May 7; Rudolf Willmers (Danish pianist) August 24.

Others: Carlo de Blasis (Italian choreographer) January 15; Hilarión Eslava (Spanish music scholar) July 23; Samuel Graves (American instrument maker) November 18; Frederick Gye (British impresario) December 4; Oskar Kolbe (German music theorist/composer) January 2; John Antes Latrobe (British music author).

C. Debuts

Singers: Mattia Battistini (Italian baritone—Rome); Alma Fohstrom (Finnish soprano—Berlin); Selma Kronold (Polish-born soprano—Leipzig); Antonia Kufferath (Belgian soprano—Berlin); Julius Lieban (German tenor—Leipzig); Zélie de Lussan (American soprano—New York); Barton M'Guckin (Irish tenor—Dublin); Carl Nebe (German bass—Wiesbaden); Giovanni Battista de Negri (Italian

tenor—Bergamo); Antonio Pini-Corsi (Italian baritone—Cremona); Gabriel Soulacroix (French baritone—Brussels); Fernando Valero (Spanish tenor—Spain); Adolf Wallnöfer (Austrian tenor—Olmütz); Elly Elisabeth Warnots (Belgian soprano—Brussels).
Performers: Helen Hopekirk (Scottish-born pianist—Leipzig); Benno Schönberger (Austrian pianist—Vienna).

D. New Positions
Conductors: Willem De Haan (Darmstadt); Joseph Mertens (Flemish Opera, Brussels); Artur Nikisch (Leipzig Opera); Karl Alexander Raida (Viktoria Theater, Berlin).
Others: Heinrich Conried (manager, Germania Theater, New York); Jan van den Eeden (director, Mons Musical Academy); Francis Hueffer (music critic, *London Times*); W. S. B. Mathews (music critic, *Chicago Tribune*); Ignace Jan Paderewski (piano faculty, Warsaw Conservatory).

E. Prizes/Honors
Prizes: Benjamin Godard (Prix de Rome).
Honors: Philip Calderon (Legion of Honor); Robert Franz (knighted, Bavaria); Charles Lamoureux (Legion of Honor); Jules Massenet (French Academy); Arthur Sullivan (Legion of Honor).

F. Biographical Highlights
Isaac Albéniz begins piano study with Franz Liszt; Antonin Dvořák enjoys his first publication, his *Slavonic Dances*; Minnie Hauk returns to the United States and sings the title role in the first American performance of Bizet's *Carmen*.

G. Cultural Beginnings
Performing Groups—Choral: Emma Abbott Opera Co.; Milwaukee Liederkranz; Moscow Choral Society; Munich Lehrergesangverein; Oratorio Society of Newark (New Jersey).
Performing Groups—Instrumental: Los Angeles Philharmonic Society; New York Symphony Orchestra; People's Concert Society (London); Philharmonic Quintet Club (St. Louis); Unión Artístico-Musical (Madrid).
Educational: Cincinnati College of Music; Doppler School of Music; Escuela de Música de la Provincia (Buenos Aires); Hegar Music School (Zürich); Instituto Musicale (Padua); Milwaukee (Wisconsin) Conservatory of Music; New York College of Music; Teodor Burada (Romanian Academy); Wellesley College School of Music.
Music Publishers: Eugene Ascherberg and Co.; Theodor Steingräber Publishing House (Hanover).

Music Publications: *Bayreuther Blätter; Boston Musical Record; Der Klavierlehrer; Kunkel's Music Review; Musical Critic and Trade Review.*
Performing Centers: Cincinnati Music Hall; Dresden Opera House; Monte Carlo Playhouse.
Other: Mechanical Orguinette Co. (Aeolian Organ Co.).

H. Music Publications

Francis Hueffer, *The Troubadours*; Heinrich Köstlin, *Die Tonkunst: Einführung in die Aesthetik der Musik*; Friedrich Langhans, *Musikgeschichte in zwölf Vorträgen*; Henri Lavoix, *Histoire de l'instrumentation*; Antoine Marmontel, *Les Pianistes célèbres*; William Mason, *Pianoforte Technics*; John Moore, *The Sentimental Songbook*; Ernst Pauer, *Musical Forms*; Hugo Riemann, *Studien zur geschichte der Notenschrift*; Wilhelm von Wasielewski, *Geschichte der Instrumental-Musik in SVI. Jahrhundert.*

I. Musical Compositions
Chamber Music:

String Quartets: George W. Chadwick, *No. 1 in g–No. 2 in C*; Felix Otto Dessoff, *Quartet in F*; Zdeněk Fibich, *No. 2 in G, Opus 8*; Caryl Florio, *No. 2*; Edvard Grieg, *Quartet in g, Opus 27*; George Macfarren, *No. 5 in f♯, Opus 20*; Eduard Nápravnik, *No. 2 in A, Opus 28.*

Sonata/Solos: Antonin Dvořák, *Capriccio* (violin, piano); Zdeněk Fibich, *Concert Polonaise*; Robert Fuchs, *Violin Sonata No. 1 in f♯, Opus 20*; Charles Gounod, *Cinq-Mars* (piano, violin); Asger Hamerik, *Concert-Romanze, Opus 27* (cello, piano); C. Hubert Parry, *Fantasie-Sonata in b* (violin, piano).

Ensemble: Antonin Dvořák, *String Sextet in A, Opus 48*; Vincent d'Indy, *Piano Quartet in a, Opus 7*; Giuseppe Martucci, *Piano Quintet, Opus 45*; C. Hubert Parry, *Piano Trio No. 1 in e*; Richard Strauss, *Piano Trio No. 2 in D.*

Piano: Arthur H. Bird, *French Overture* (piano, four hands); Johannes Brahms, *Eight Pieces, Opus 76*; Zdeněk Fibich, *Sonata in B♭*; Stephen Heller, *Sonata No. 4 in b♭, Opus 143–Sonatina No. 1, Opus 146–No. 2, Opus 147*; Anatol Liadov, *Arabesque, Opus 4*; Alexander Mackenzie, *Trois Morceaux, Opus 15*; C. Hubert Parry, *Sonata No. 2 in A*; Julius Röntgen, *Theme and Variations, Opus 17*; Bedřich Smetana, *Fourteen Czech Dances*; Ethel Smyth, *Variations on an Original Theme*; Peter Ilyich Tchaikovsky, *Children's Album, Opus 39–Twelve Pieces, Opus 40.*

Organ: César Franck, *Fantasie in A–Pièce Heroïque in b–Cantabile in B*; Josef Rheinberger, *Sonata No. 5.*

Choral/Vocal Music:

Choral: Dudley Buck, *The Nun of Nidaros* (cantata); Antonin Dvořák, *Five a Capella Partsongs, Opus 27*; Charles Gounod, *Jésus sur le lac de Tibériade*; Ferdinand Hiller, *Rebecca, Opus 182*; Joseph Rheinberger, *Mass in E♭ (cantus Missae), Opus 109*; Joachim Raff, *Die Tageszeiten, Opus 209*; George Frederick Root, *The Song Tournament* (cantata); Camille Saint-Saëns, *Requiem, Opus 54*; Peter Ilyich Tchaikovsky, *Liturgy of St. John Chrysostom, Opus 41.*

Vocal: Johannes Brahms, *Four Ballades and Romances, Opus 75*; César Cui, *Six Songs, Opus 13*; Claude Debussy, *Beau Soir*; Antonin Dvořák, *Three Modern Greek Poems, Opus 50*; Robert Franz, *Six Songs, Opus 48*; Queen Liliuokalani, *Aloha Oe*; Alexander Mackenzie, *Eight Songs, Opus 6–Three Songs, Opus 17.*

Musical Stage: Gilbert/Sullivan, *H. M. S. Pinafore*; Charles Gounod, *Polyeucte*; Heinrich Hofmann, *Ännchen von Tharau, Opus 44*; Jacques Offenbach, *Madame Favart–Maître Péronilla*; Joachim Raff, *Benedetto Marcello*; Nicolai Rimsky-Korsakov, *May Night*; Bedřich Smetana, *The Secret*; Peter Ilyich Tchaikovsky, *Eugene Onegin, Opus 24*; Ambroise Thomas, *Psyché.*

Orchestra/Band Music:

Concerted Music:

Piano: Giuseppe Martucci, *Concerto No. 1 in d*; Carl Reinecke, *Concerto No. 3 in C, Opus 144*; Anton Rubinstein, *Caprice Russe, Opus 120.*

Violin: Johannes Brahms, *Concerto in D, Opus 77*; Max Bruch, *Concerto No. 2 in d, Opus 44*; Edouard Lalo, *Norwegian Fantasy*; Eduardo Nápravnik, *Fantasy on Russian Themes, Opus 30*; Adolph Neuendorff, *No. 1*; Peter Ilyich Tchaikovsky, *Concerto in D, Opus 35.*

Other: Nicolai Rimsky-Korsakov, *Concerto for Clarinet and Band*; Anton Rubinstein, *Concertpiece for Clarinet and Band.*

Ballet/Incidental Music: Ferdinand Hiller, *Prinz Papagei, Opus 183* (IM); André Messager, *Fleur d'oranger* (B).

Program Music: Zdeněk Fibich, *Eternity*; Vincent d'Indy, *The Enchanted Forest, Opus 8*; Horace Nicholl, *Tartarus, Opus 11*; Bedřich Smetana, *Tabor* (No. 5 of *Ma Vlast*).

Standard Works: Dudley Buck, *Marmion Overture*; Antonin Dvořák, *Serenade in d, Opus 44–Three Slavonic Rhapsodies (D, g, a♭), Opus 45–Slavonic Dances, Series I, Opus 46*; Charles Gounod, *Marche Solennelle in E♭*; Carl Reinecke, *Fest-Ouvertüre, Opus 148*; Giovanni Rossi, *Overture, Saul*; John Philip Sousa, *March, Esprit de Corps*; Edgard Tinel, *Polyeucte Overture.*

Symphonies: Adolph Neuendorff, *No. 1*; Ole Olsen, *Symphony in G*; Joseph Joachim Raff, *No. 9 in e, "In Summer," Opus 208.*

1879

❈

Historical Highlights: The Belgian Congo is reorganized as the Congo Free State; the British fight the Zulu War in the Transvaal of South Africa; in South America, Chile defeats Bolivia and Peru in the War of the Pacific; first electric railway system is set up by Werner von Siemens; in the United States, the incandescent lightbulb is introduced; the Archeological Institute of America is founded; the Geological Survey Department is established.

Art and Literature Highlights: Births—artists Gifford Beall, Paul Klee, writers René Dumesnil, Vachel Lindsay, Wallace Stevens; Deaths—artists George Bingham, Honoré Daumier, William M. Hunt, Antoine Preault, writers Richard Henry Dana, Sr., Sarah Josepha Hale. Art—Manet's *In a Boat*, Moran's *The Mirage, Teton Range, Idaho*; Literature—Cable's *Old Creole Days*, Dostoyevsky's *The Brothers Karamozov*, Ibsen's *The Doll House.*

Musical Highlights

A. Births
Composers: Nathanael Berg (Sweden) February 9; Franz Carl Bornschein (U.S.A.) February 10; Frank Bridge (England) February 26; Joseph Canteloube (France) October 21; Jean Émile Cras (France) May 22; Maurice Delage (France) November 13; Joseph Haas (Germany) March 19; John Ireland (England) August 13; Eastwood Lane (U.S.A.) May 22; Otakar Ostrčil (Czechoslovakia) February 25; Ottorino Respighi (Italy) July 9; Jean Rogister (Belgium) October 25; Cyril Scott (England) September 27; Armen Tigranian (Armenia) December 26.
Conductors: Volkmar Andreae (Switzerland) July 5; Peter van Anrooy (Holland) October 13; Thomas Beecham (England) April 29; Philippe Gaubert (France) July 3; Hamilton Hardy (England) December 4.
Singers: Lina Abarbanell (German soprano) January 3; Julia Claussen (Swedish mezzo-soprano) June 11; Zdenka Fassbender (Bohemian soprano) December 12; Maria Gay (Spanish contralto) June 13; Mizzi Günther (Bohemian soprano) February 8; Francis Maclennan (American tenor) January 7; Aurelie Révy (Hungarian soprano); Fritzi Scheff (Austrian soprano) August 30; Karl Seydel (German tenor) December 14; Margarethe Siems (German soprano)

December 30; Geneviève Vix (French soprano) December 31; Hermann Wiedemann (German baritone).

Performers: André Benoist (French pianist) April 4; Joseph Canteloube (French pianist) October 21; John Erskine (American pianist/author) October 5; Ernst Isler (Swiss organist/critic) September 30; Frank La Forge (American pianist) October 22; Benjamin Lambord (American organist) June 10; Wanda Landowska (Polish harpsichordist) July 5; Heniot Lévy (Polish-born pianist) July 19; Otto Olsson (Swedish organist/composer) December 19; Jacob Weinberg (Russian-born pianist/composer) July 7; Julius Weismann (German pianist/composer) December 26.

Others: Daniel Fryklund (Swedish musicologist) May 4; Tobias Norlind (Swedish musicologist) May 6; Verne Q. Powell (American woodwind maker) April 7; Paul Stefan (Austrian music author) November 25; Fritz Stein (German musicologist) December 17; Otto Ursprung (German musicologist) January 16; Otokar Zich (Czech musicologist) March 25.

B. Deaths

Composers: Antoine Auguste de Bournonville (Denmark) November 30; Karl Eckert (Germany) October 14; Peter Heise (Denmark) September 12; August Schäffer (Germany) August 7.

Conductors: Pierre Joseph Varney (France) February 7.

Singers: Karl Beck (Austrian tenor) March 3; Franz Diener (German tenor) May 15; Barbara Fröhlich (Australian contralto) June 30; Adelaide Kemble (British soprano) August 4; Henriette Nissen (Swedish soprano) August 27; Gustave Hippolyte Roger (French tenor) September 12; Lorenzo Salvi (Italian tenor) January 16.

Performers: August Friedrich Kummer (German cellist) August 22; Joseph Schad (German pianist) July 4; Henry Thomas Smart (British organist/composer) July 6.

Others: Melchiore Balbi (Italian music theorist/composer) June 21; Charles Spackman Barker (British organ builder) November 26; Marie-Pierre Hamel (French organ builder) July 25; Ernst Friedrich Richter (German music theorist/organist) April 9.

C. Debuts

Singers: Max Alvary (German tenor—Weimar); Hypolite Belhomme (French bass—Paris); Jean De Reszke (Polish tenor—Madrid, as tenor); Hermann Devries (American bass—Paris); Paul Kalisch (German tenor—Rome); Pavel Khokhlov (Russian baritone—Moscow); Helena Theodorini (Romanian soprano—Cuneo); Giulia Valda (American soprano—Paris); Marie Van Zandt (American soprano—Turin).

Performers: Timothée Adamowski (Polish-born violinist—Boston); Adele Margulies (Austrian pianist—Vienna); Arnold Josef Rosé (Austrian violinist—Leipzig).

D. New Positions

Conductors: Riccardo Drigo (Italian Opera, St. Petersburg, Russia); Ernst Frank (Hanover Court Opera); Anton Seidl (Leipzig Opera). **Others:** Albert Peace (organ, Glasgow Cathedral).

E. Prizes/Honors

Prizes: Georges Hüe (Prix de Rome); Engelbert Humperdinck (Mendelssohn); Samuel-Alexandre Rosseau (Prix Cressent). **Honors:** Johannes Brahms (Ph.D., University of Breslau); Arthur Sullivan (Mus.Doc., Harvard).

F. Biographical Highlights

Edward Elgar becomes bandmaster at Worcester Lunatic Asylum; Engelbert Humperdinck, upon meeting Wagner in Berlin, soon becomes his disciple; Franz Liszt is made an honorary Canon of Albano; Edward MacDowell enters Frankfurt Conservatory in order to study with Raff; Henri Vieuxtemps, due to health problems, is forced to retire from public performance.

G. Cultural Beginnings

Performing Groups—Choral: Antwerp Lassallekring; Bloch'sche Verein (Berlin Opera Society); Boston Ideal Opera Co.; Brno Schubertbund; Geneva Grand Opera Co.; Opéra de Monte Carlo; Oslo Cecilia Society; Palestrina Society.
Performing Groups—Instrumental: Ganz Orchestral Concerts (London); Mozart Club of Pittsburgh; Neuer Orchesterverein (Munich); Sociedad de Música Clásica (Santiago); Società del Quartetto (Bologna); Società Orchestrale della Scala; Société des Quintettes pour Instruments à Vent (Paris); Shanghai Symphony Orchestra.
Festivals: Pittsburgh Music Festival.
Educational: Balatka Academy of Musical Art (Chicago); Choir School of Christchurch (New Zealand); Denver University School of Music; Lemmens Institute of Church Music (Mechelen); University of Michigan School of Music.
Music Publishers: Schroeder and Gunther (New York).
Music Publications: *Music Trade Journal*; *La nouvelle revue* (Paris); *Zeitschrift für Instrumentenbau*.
Performing Centers: Central Music Hall (Chicago); Geneva Grand Theater; Squire's Opera House (Seattle); Teatro Politeama (Buenos Aires, Argentina); Teatro San Felipe (Montevideo, Uruguay); Tivoli Theater II (San Francisco).

Other: Krzyzanowski Concert Bureau (Kraków).

H. Music Literature

Carl Engel, *The Literature of National Music*; George Grove, *Dictionary of Music and Musicians I*; Henry Hiles, *The Grammar of Music*; Otakar Hostinsky, *Die Lehre von den musikalischen Klängen*; Cyrill Kistler, *Harmonielehre*; William Pole, *Philosophy of Music*; August Reissmann, *Zur Aesthetik der tonkunst*; William Rockstro, *A History of Music*; John Stainer, *Music of the Bible*.

I. Musical Compositions

Chamber Music:

String Quartets: Alexander Borodin, *No. 1 in A*; Antonin Dvořák, *No. 10 in E♭, Opus 51*.

Sonata/Solos: Johannes Brahms, *Violin Sonata in G, Opus 78*; César Cui, *Petite Suite, Opus 14* (violin, piano); Zdeněk Fibich, *Romance in B♭, Opus 10* (violin, piano)–*Idyll, Opus 16* (violin/clarinet, piano); Eduard Nápravník, *Suite No. 1 in D, Opus 29* (cello, piano); Joachim Raff, *Suite, Opus 218* (violin, piano).

Ensembles: Anton Bruckner, *String Quintet in f*; Gabriel Fauré, *Piano Quartet No. 1 in c, Opus 15*; Caryl Florio, *Allegro de Concert* (saxophone quartet); César Franck, *Piano Quintet in f*; Robert Franz, *Piano Trio in C, Opus 22*; Heinrich von Herzogenberg, *String Trio, Opus 27/2*; Ferdinand Hiller, *Piano Trio No. 1, Opus 180*; Carl Goldmark, *String Quintet No. 2 in B♭, Opus 30*; C. Hubert Parry, *Piano Quartet in A*.

Piano: Johannes Brahms, *Two Rhapsodies, Opus 79*; Antonin Dvořák, *Silhouettes, Opus 8*; Stephen Heller, *Sonatina No. 3, Opus 149*–*Two Etudes, Opus 151*–*Twenty Preludes, Opus 156*–*Three Feuillets d'album, Opus 157*–*Four Mazurkas, Opus 148*–*Mazurka, Opus 158*; Alexander Mackenzie, *Six Compositions, Opus 20*; Ignace Jan Paderewski, *Suite in E♭*; Silas G. Pratt, *Caprice Fantastique–Nocturne Impromptu*; Joachim Raff, *Aus der adventzeit, Opus 216*; Anton Rubinstein, *Bal Costumé, Opus 103* (two pianos).

Organ: Franz Liszt, *Missa pro organo*; Giuseppe Martucci, *Sonata*.

Choral/Vocal Music:

Choral: George Bristow, *The Great Republic* (cantata); Max Bruch, *Das Lied von der Glocke* (oratorio); Dudley Buck, *Scenes from "The Golden Legend"*; Antonin Dvořák, *Psalm CXLX, Opus 79*; César Franck, *The Beatitudes* (oratorio); Robert Franz, *Six Lieder, Opus 49*; Vincent d'Indy, *La Chevauchée du cid, Opus 11*; Franz Liszt, *Cantantibus organis*; Charles V. Stanford, *Complete Service in B♭, Opus 10*.

Vocal: Johannes Brahms, *Six Songs, Opus 86*; César Cui, *Six Songs, Opus 16*; Robert Franz, *Six songs, Opus 50*–*Ten Songs, Opus 51*; Carl Goldmark, *Seven Songs, Opus 32*; Edouard Lalo, *Five Songs*; Alexander Mackenzie, *Seven Songs, Opus 8–Three Songs, Opus 14*; Modest Mussorgsky, *The Flea*; John Knowles Paine, *Four Songs, Opus 29*; Joachim Raff, *Frühlingslied*; Camille Saint-Saëns, *La Lyre et la Harpe, Opus 57*; Bedřich Smetana, *Evening Songs* (cycle); Peter Ilyich Tchaikovsky, *Seven Songs, Opus 47*; Henry Clay Work, *The Old Village Doctor*.

Musical Stage: Théodore Dubois, *Le Pain Bis*; Ernest Guiraud, *Le Feu*; Gilbert/Sullivan, *The Pirates of Penzance*; Hervé, *Panurge–La marquise des rues–La femme à papa*; Charles Lecocq, *La petite Mademoiselle*; Jacques Offenbach, *La Fille du Tambour-Major–La Marocaine*; Anton Rubinstein, *The Merchant Kalashnikov*; Camille Saint-Saëns, *Étienne Marcel*; Charles V. Stanford, *The Veiled Prophet of Khorassan*; Franz von Suppé, *Boccaccio*; Peter Ilyich Tchaikovsky, *The Maid of Orleans*.

Orchestra/Band Music:
Concerted Music:
   Piano: Charles Hubert Parry, *Concerto in F♯*; Carl Reinecke, *Concerto No. 1 in f♯, Opus 72*.
   Violin: Antonin Dvořák, *Mazurek, Opus 49*; Edouard Lalo, *Romance-sérénade–Concerto russe*; Gabriel Fauré, *Concerto, Opus 14*.
Ballet/Incidental Music: Jules Massenet, *Notre Dame de Paris* (IM); André Messager, *Les vins de France* (B)–*Mignons et vilains* (B).
Program Music: Niels Gade, *A Summer's Day in the Country, Opus 55*; Bedřich Smetana, *Blanik* (No. 6 of *Ma Vlast*).
Standard Works: Dudley Buck, *Festival Overture on "The Star-Spangled Banner"*; George Chadwick, *Overture, Rip Van Winkle*; Théodore Dubois, *Overture in C*; Antonin Dvořák, *Czech Suite, Opus 39–Festival March, Opus 54*; Benjamin Godard, *Scènes Poétiques*; Carl Goldmark, *Penthesilea Overture, Opus 31*; Hans Huber, *A Comedy Overture, Opus 50*; Edouard Lalo, *Norwegian Rhapsody*; Jules Massenet, *Suite No. 6: Scènes de féerie*; Joseph Joachim Raff, *Four Shakespeare Overtures: The Tempest–Macbeth–Romeo and Juliet–Othello*; Camille Saint-Saëns, *Suite Algérienne, Opus 60*; John Philip Sousa, *Globe and Eagle March*; Peter Ilyich Tchaikovsky, *Suite No. 1 in D, Opus 43*.
Symphonies: Pietro Mascagni, *Symphony in c*; Eduard Nápravnik, *No. 4 in d, Opus 32*; Joseph Joachim Raff, *No. 10 in f, "Zur Herbstzeit," Opus 213*.

1880

❄

Historical Highlights: William Gladstone begins his second term as prime minister of Great Britain; the British Parliament votes free and compulsory education up to age ten; the Irish Insurrection against British rule begins; in the United States, James A. Garfield is elected twentieth president; the census shows a population of 50,189,000—New York City's population passes the one million mark; Cleveland, Ohio, becomes the first city to be lit by electricity.

Art and Literature Highlights: Births—authors Guillaume Apollinaire, Kathleen Norris, Alfred Noyes, artists André Derain, Jacob Epstein, Hans Hofmann, Ernst Kirchner, Walt Kuhn; Deaths—authors George Eliot, Gustave Flaubert, artists Anselm Feuerbach, Karl Lessing. Art—Böcklin's *Isle of the Dead*, Rodin's *The Thinker*, Ryder's *Mending the Harness*; Literature—Cable's *The Grandissimes*, Wallace's *Ben Hur*, Zola's *Nana*.

Musical Highlights

A. Births

Composers: Edgar Leslie Bainton (England-Australia) February 4; Ernest Bloch (Switzerland-U.S.A.) July 24; Ernst Boehe (Germany) December 27; Rudolf Karol (Czechoslovakia) November 9; Jaime Pahissa (Spain-Argentina) October 7; Ildebrando Pizzetti (Italy) September 20; Francis George Scott (England) January 25; Arthur Shepherd (U.S.A.) February 19; Healey Willan (Canada) October 12.

Conductors: D. E. Ingelbrecht (France) September 17; Bernardino Molinari (Italy) April 11; Robert Stolz (Austria) August 25.

Singers: Elsa Alsen (German-born contralto) April 7; Marguerite Carré (French soprano) August 16; Julia Culp (Dutch contralto) October 6; Eduard Habich (German baritone) September 3; Melanie Kurt (Austrian soprano) January 8; Maria Labia (Italian soprano) February 14; Estelle Liebling (American soprano) April 21; Theodor Scheidl (Austria baritone) August 3; Florence Wickham (American contralto/composer).

Performers: Joseph-Ermend Bonnal (French organist/composer); Richard Buhlig (American pianist) December 21; Eric De Lamarter (American organist/conductor) February 18; Albert von Doenhoff (American pianist) March 16; Jan Kubelík (Czech-born violinist) July 5; Nicolai Medtner (Russian pianist/composer) January 5; Alberto Randegger (Italian violinist) August 3; Alexander Russell (American organist) October 2; Joseph Schwarz (Latvian-born baritone); Jacques Thibaud (French violinist) September 27; Clarence Cameron White (American violinist/composer) August 10.

Others: Bruno Barilli (Italian music author/composer) December 14; Raffaele Casimiro Casimiri (Italian musicologist) November 3; Adolf Chybiński (Polish musicologist) April 29; Henry S. Drinker (American music scholar) September 15; Alfred Einstein (German musicologist) December 30; John Foulds (British musicologist/composer) November 2; Edgar Istel (German musicologist) February 23; Nemesio Otaño (Spanish musicologist/composer) December 19; Carl Van Vechten (American music author) June 17.

B. **Deaths**

Composers: Jacob Axel Josephson (Sweden) March 29; George Jackson Lambert (England) January 24; Josephine Lang (Germany) December 2; Jacques Offenbach (Germany-France) October 5; Achille Peri (Italy) March 28; Napoléon-Henri Reber (France) November 24.

Conductors: Claudio S. Grafullo (Spain) December 2; Carl August Krebs (Germany) May 16.

Singers: Prosper Dérivis (French bass) December 11; Louis Gueymard (French tenor) July; Anna Fröhlich (Austrian soprano) March 11; Nicolai Ivanov (Russian tenor) July 7.

Performers: Ole Bull (Norwegian violinist) August 17; James Coward (British organist) January 22; Sir John Goss (British organist) May 10; Hyacinthe-Eléonore Klosé (French clarinetist) August 29; Anna Caroline Oury (German pianist) July 22; Wojciech Albert Sowinski (Polish pianist) March 5; Henryk Wieniawski (Polish violinist) March 31.

Others: John Curwen (British music theorist) May 26; August Robert Forberg (German publisher) October 10; Franz Joseph Kunkel (German music theorist) December 31; Gustav Schilling (German lexicographer) March; Carl Friedrich Weitzmann (German music theorist) November 7; Michael Welte (German instrument maker) January 17.

C. **Debuts**

Singers: Blanche Arral (Belgian soprano—Paris); Gemma Bellincioni (Italian soprano—Naples); Emilie Herzog (Swiss soprano—Munich); Vilém Heš (Czech bass—Brno); Antonio Magini-Coletti (Italian baritone—Italy); Emma Nevada (American soprano—London); George Sieglitz (German bass—Hamburg); Elena Teodorini (Romanian soprano—Milan).

Performers: Karl Muck (German pianist—Leipzig); Vasili Safonov (Russian pianist—St. Petersburg); Alexander Siloti (Russian pianist—Moscow); José Tragó (Spanish pianist—Paris).

D. **New Positions**

Conductors: Max Bruch (Liverpool PO); Hans von Bülow (Meiningen); Gustave Kerker (H. V. B. Mann Opera Co.); Emil Paur (Mannheim Court); John Philip Sousa (U.S. Marine Band); Theodore Thomas (New York Philharmonic Society).

Others: Otto Floersheim (editor, *Musical Courier*); Henry Krehbiel (critic, *New York Tribune*).

E. **Prizes/Honors**

Prizes: Lucien Hillemacher (Prix de Rome).

Honors: Leopold Damrosch (D. Mus., Columbia); Charles Gounod (Legion of Honor).

F. Biographical Highlights
Emmanuel Chabrier resigns his post to devote full time to composition; Ernest Chausson enters the Paris Conservatory to study with Massenet but soon leaves to study privately with Franck; Claude Debussy becomes accompanist and tutor for the von Meck family; Modest Mussorgsky is permanently dismissed from government service.

G. Cultural Beginnings
Performing Groups—Choral: Archangelsky Chorus (Russia); St. Louis Choral Society (Choral Symphony Society in 1890).

Performing Groups—Instrumental: Birmingham Musical Association (England); Dimitrescu String Quartet (Bucharest); Messina Società del Quartetto; Newcastle Chamber Music Society; St. Louis Symphony Orchestra; Società del Quartetto (Naples); Società Orchestrale (Naples); Société Populaires des Concerts de Musique Classiques (Marseille).

Festivals: National Eisteddfod Association (Welsh Festival).

Educational: Ann Arbor School of Music (part of the University of Michigan, 1892); Cardiff Choir School; Conservatorio Nacional de Música (Buenos Aires); Guildhall School of Music and Drama (London); Horneman Conservatory (Copenhagen); St. Louis College of Music; Scuola Gregoriana (Rome); University of Nebraska School of Music.

Music Publishers: Enoch Frère et Costallat (Paris); Max Hesse Publishing House (Leipzig).

Music Publications: *The Musical Courier*; *Musical Harp*; *Musical Herald*; *Neue Musikzeitung* (Stuttgart).

Performing Centers: Haymarket Theatre II (London); Teatro Municipal (Caracas, Venezuela).

Other: Fairbanks and Cole, banjo makers (Boston); W. W. Kimball Organ Co.

H. Musical Literature
César Cui, *Music in Russia*; James C. Culwick, *The Rudiments of Music*; Gilbert-Louis Duprez, *Souvenirs d'un chanteur*; Louis Elson, *Curiosities of Music*; Edmund Gurney, *The Power of Sound*; Eduard Hanslick, *Musikalische Stationen*; Ferdinand Hiller, *Künstlerleben*; Francis Hueffer, *Musical Studies*; Cyrill Kistler, *Musikalische elementarlehre*; William Mathews, *How to Understand Music I*; Emil Naumann, *Der moderne musikalishe Zopf–Illustrierte Musikgeschichte I*; Hugo Riemann, *Skizze einer neuen Methode der Harmonielehre*; George Upton, *Woman in Music*.

I. Musical Compositions
Chamber Music:
String Quartets: Johann H. Beck, *No. 4*; Antonin Dvořák, *Two Waltzes, Opus 59*; Edwin A. Jones, *No. 1, Opus 18*; Edgar Stillman Kelley, *Theme and Variations, Opus 1*; C. Hubert Parry, *No. 3 in G*; Anton Rubinstein, *Two Quartets (A♭, f), Opus 106*; Hugo Wolf, *Quartet in d*.

Sonata/Solos: Antonin Dvořák, *Violin Sonata in F, Opus 57*; Heinrich Hofmann, *Romance, Opus 48* (cello, piano); Giuseppe Martucci, *Cello Sonata in f♯, Opus 52*; Ignace Jan Paderewski, *Violin Sonata in a, Opus 13*.

Ensembles: Claude Debussy, *Piano Trio No. 1 in G*; Heinrich Hofmann, *Piano Quartet, Opus 50*; Carl Goldmark, *Piano Trio No. 2 in e, Opus 33*; Edouard Lalo, *Piano Trio No. 3 in a*; Sergei Lyapunov, *Rêverie du soir, Opus 3*; Camille Saint-Saëns, *Septet in E♭, Opus 65*; Richard Strauss, *Serenade, Opus 7, for Winds*; Sergei Taneyev, *String Trio No. 1 in D*.

Piano: Emanuel Chabrier, *Ten pièces pittoresques*; Antonin Dvořák, *Six Pieces, Opus 52–Eight Waltzes, Opus 54–Six Mazurkas, Opus 56*; Vincent d'Indy, *Petite sonate, Opus 9*; Leoš Janáček, *Variations for Zdenka, Opus 1*; George Macfarren, *Sonata No. 3 in g*; Alexander Mackenzie, *In the Scottish Highlands, Opus 23*.

Organ: Josef Rheinberger, *Sonata No. 6*; Charles M. Widor, *Organ Symphonies 5–8, Opus 42*.

Choral/Vocal Music:
Choral: Dudley Buck, *Midnight Service for New Year's Eve*; Charles Gounod, *The Redemption* (oratorio); Gustav Mahler, *Das Klagende Lied*; Jules Massenet, *La Vierge*; André Messager, *Don Juan et Haydée* (cantata); Giacomo Puccini, *Mass in A♭*; George Frederick Root, *Under the Palms* (cantata); Charles V. Stanford, *Complete Service in A, Opus 12*; Arthur Sullivan, *The Martyr of Antioch* (oratorio); Sergei Taneyev, *John of Damascus*.

Vocal: Luigi Denza, *Funiculi, Funiculà*; Antonin Dvořák, *Seven Gypsy Songs, Opus 55*; Gabriel Fauré, *Three Songs, Opus 18*; Robert Fuchs, *Five Songs, Opus 26*(?); Carl Goldmark, *Four Songs, Opus 34*(?); Edvard Grieg, *Twelve Songs, Opus 18*; Joachim Raff, *Blondel de Nesle, Opus 211* (cycle); John R. Sweeney, *Tell Me the Story of Jesus*.

Musical Stage: Dudley Buck, *Deseret*; Léo Delibes, *Jean de Nivelle*; Hervé, *Le voyage en Amérique–La mère des compagnons*; George Macfarren, *Kenilworth*; Pietro Mascagni, *Pinota*(?); Jules Massenet, *Robert de France*; Modest Mussorgsky, *Khovant-china* (unfinished); Adolph Neuendorff, *Der Rattenfänger von Hameln*; Jacques Offenbach, *Belle Lusette*; Amilcare Ponchielli, *Il figliuol prodigo*; Charles-Marie Widor, *La Korrigane*.

Orchestra/Band Music:
Concerted Music:
Piano: Robert Fuchs, *Concerto in b♭, Opus 27*; Peter Ilyich Tchaikovsky, *Concerto No. 2 in G, Opus 44*.
Violin: Max Bruch, *Scottish Rhapsody*; Antonin Dvořák, *Concerto in a, Opus 53*; Gabriel Fauré, *Berceuse, Opus 16*; Niels Gade, *Concerto in d, Opus 56*; Heinrich Hofmann, *Concerto in d, Opus 31*; Camille Saint-Saëns, *Morceau de Concert in G, Opus 62*.
Ballet/Incidental Music: Luigi Mancinelli, *Tizianello* (IM).
Program Music: Alexander Borodin, *In the Steppes of Central Asia*; Zdeněk Fibich, *The Tempest, Opus 46*; Vincent d'Indy, *Wallenstein's Camp*; Peter Ilyich Tchaikovsky, *Overture Solennelle 1812, Opus 49*.
Standard Works: Johannes Brahms, *Academic Festival Overture, Opus 80*; Ion Ivanovici, *Waves of the Danube (Anniversary Waltz)*; Alexander Mackenzie, *Scottish Rhapsody No. 2, Opus 21–Scenes in the Scottish Highland*; André Messager, *Loreley*; Johann Strauss, Jr., *Roses from the South*; Peter Ilyich Tchaikovsky, *Serenade for Strings in C, Opus 48*.
Symphonies: Claude Debussy, *Symphony in g*; Antonin Dvořák, *No. 6 in D, Opus 60*; Asger Hamerik, *No. 1 in F, "Poétique," Opus 26*; Adolph Neuendorff, *No. 2*; John Knowles Paine, *No. 2 in A, "In Spring," Opus 34*; Anton Rubinstein, *No. 5 in g, Opus 107*.

1881

Historical Highlights: Czar Alexander II of Russia is assassinated—Alexander III becomes czar; France takes over control of the North African port of Tunis; Louis Pasteur manages to isolate the rabies virus; in the United States, President James Garfield is assassinated—Chester Arthur becomes the twenty-first president; the International Red Cross is founded by Clara Barton; the Federation of Organized Trades and Labor Unions is organized.

Art and Literature Highlights: Births—artists George Braque, Fernand Léger, Pablo Picasso, Max Weber, writers Sidney Lanier, Stefan Zweig; Deaths—artist John Quidor, writers Feodor Dostoyevsky, Sidney Lanier, Giovanni Ruffini. Art—Marées' *Judgment of Paris*, Renoir's *Luncheon of the Boating Party*, Repin's *Portrait of Modest Mussorgsky*; Literature—Collodi's *Pinocchio*, James' *Portrait of a Lady*, Spyri's *Heidi*, Verlaine's *Sagesse*.

Musical Highlights

A. Births
Composers: Béla Bartók (Hungary) March 25; Gena Branscombe (U.S.A.) November 4; Charles Wakefield Cadman (U.S.A.) Decem-

ber 24; Arne Eggen (Norway) August 28; George Enescu (Romania) August 19; Harvey B. Gaul (U.S.A.) April 1l; Jan van Gilse (Holland) May 11; Edvin Kallstenius (Sweden) August 29; Nicolai Miaskovsky (Russia) April 20; Nikolai Andreyevich Roslavets (Russia) January 5; Karl Weigl (Austria-U.S.A.) February 6.

Conductors: Theodor Blumer (Germany) March 24; Henry Fillmore (U.S.A.) December 3; Gaetano Merola (Italy-U.S.A.) January 4; Václav Vačkář (Czechoslovakia) August 12; William C. White (U.S.A.) September 29.

Singers: George Baklanov (Russian baritone) January 17; Marthe Chenal (French soprano) August 24; Nazzareno De Angelis (Italian bass) November 7; Erna Denera (German soprano) September 4; Ilona Durigo (Hungarian soprano) May 13; Povla Frijsch (Danish-born soprano) August 3; Albert Huberty (Belgian bass; Barbara Kemp (German soprano) December 12; Morgan Kingston (British tenor) March 16; Forrest Lamont (Canadian tenor); Margarete Matzenauer (Hungarian soprano) June 1; Frank Mullings (British tenor) March 10; Eva von der Osten (German soprano) August 19; Oscar Ralf (Swedish tenor) October 3; Yvonne de Tréville (American soprano) August 25.

Performers: Fannie Charles Dillon (American pianist) March 16; Arthur Hartmann (American violinist) July 22; Ferencz Hegedus (Hungarian violinist) February 26; Paolo Martucci (Italian-born pianist) October 5; Egon Petri (German pianist) March 23; Lev Tseitlin (Russian violinist) March 15.

Others: Domenico Alaleona (Italian music theorist) November 16; Jean-Baptiste Beck (Alsatian-born musicologist) August 14; Rudolf Bode (German acoustician) February 3; Paul Hirsch (German born music bibliographer/collector) February 24; Arthur Judson (American concert manager) February 17; Curt Sachs (German musicologist) June 29; H. J. W. Tillyard (British musicologist) November 18.

B. **Deaths**

Composers: Luigi Fernando Casamorata (Italy) September 24; Auguste-François Morel (France) April 22; Modest Petrovich Mussorgsky (Russia) March 28; Lucien H. Southard (U.S.A.) January 10; Richard Wüerst (Germany) October 9.

Conductors: Rudolf Bial (Germany) November 26; Joseph Labitzky (Bohemia-Germany) August 19.

Singers: Anna Maria Hasselt-Barth (Dutch soprano) January 6; Heinrich Kotzolt (Danish tenor) July 2; Paulina Rivoli (Polish soprano) October 12; Anna Zerr (German soprano) June 14.

Performers: Theobald Böhm (German flutist/inventor) November 25; Giulio Briccildi (Italian flutist) December 17; Wilhelm Fritze (German pianist/composer) October 7; Julius Hesse (German pianist/

inventor) April 5; Sidney Lanier (American flutist/poet) September 7; Nicolai Rubinstein (Russian pianist) March 23; Henry Vieuxtemps (Belgian violinist/composer) June 6.

Others: François Camille Durutte (Belgian music theorist) September 21; Gaetano Gaspari (Italian librarian/historiographer) March 31; Johann Christian Lobe (German music author) July 27; Augustin Savard (French music educator/theorist) June 7.

C. Debuts

Singers: Alexander Bandrowski-Sas (Polish tenor—Lemberg, as baritone); Emma Calvé (French soprano—Brussels); Ben Grey Davies (British tenor—Birmingham); Wilhelm Grüning (German tenor—Danzig); Emma Juch (American soprano—Detroit); Luise Reuss-Belce (Austrian soprano—Karlsruhe).

Performers: Eugène d'Albert (Scottish-born pianist—London); Alfred Reisenauer (German pianist—Rome); Emily Shinner (British violinist—London).

D. New Positions

Conductors: Otto Dessoff (Frankfurt Opera); George Henschel (Boston SO); Gustav Mahler (Ljubljana Theater).

Others: William F. Apthorp (critic, *Boston Evening Transcript*); Léon Boëllmann (organ, St. Vincent de Paul, Paris); James Culwick (organ, Chapel Royal, Dublin); Henry T. Finck (critic, *New York Evening Post*); Nicolai Hubert (director, Moscow Conservatory); Leoš Janáček (director, Brno Organ School); Theodore Seward (editor, *Tonic Sol-Fa Advocate*).

E. Prizes/Honors

Prizes: Eugène d'Albert (Mendelssohn); Alfred Bruneau (Prix de Rome); Sylvain Dupuis (Prix de Rome); Georges-Adolphe Hüe (Prix Crescent); Engelbert Humperdinck (Meyerbeer).

Honors: Edward M. Bowman (Royal College of Organists, London); Camille Saint-Saëns (French Institute).

F. Biographical Highlights

Edward Bowman becomes the first American to be taken into the prestigious Royal College of Organists; Walter Damrosch leads a 250 piece orchestra and a 1,200 member choir in a New York Festival; Claude Debussy visits Russia with the von Meck family; Ignace Jan Paderewski, on his wife's death, goes to Berlin for further music study; Horatio Parker enters the Royal Conservatory in Munich; Felix Weingartner begins the study of philosophy at Leipzig University.

G. Cultural Beginnings

Performing Groups—Choral: Church Choral Union (New York); Hosmer Hall Choral Union (Hartford, Connecticut); Royal Welsh Ladies' Choir; St. Gregorius Vereniging (Antwerp).

Performing Groups—Instrumental: Boston Symphony Orchestra; Cleveland Philharmonic Society; Concerts Lamoureux (Paris); Heckmann String Quartet (Germany); Quintetto dell Regina (Rome).

Educational: Kraków Conservatory of Music; Scharwenka Conservatory of Music (Berlin); Schumacher Conservatory of Music (Mainz).

Music Publishers: Harms Music Publishers (New York); Ries and Erler (Berlin).

Music Publications: *Bulletin Critique de Littérature, d'Histoire et de Théologie; Chicago Musical Times; La Jeune Belgique; Perry's Musical Magazine; Tonic Sol-Fa Advocate.*

Performing Centers: Denver Tabor (Grand) Opera House; National Theater of Prague; Savoy Theatre (London).

Other: Cincinnati Musicians' Protective Union; François Lorée, woodwind maker (Paris); St. Louis Musical Union; Società Artistico-Filarmonica (Modena); Hermann Wolff Concert Management (Berlin).

H. Musical Literature

Guido Adler, *Studie zur Geschichte der Harmonie;* Félix Clément, *Observations sur un nouveau projet de restauration de mélodies grégoriennes;* Henry S. Edwards, *The Lyric Drama I, II;* Amy Fay, *Music Study in Germany;* Louis Moreau Gottschalk, *Notes of a Pianist;* Ferdinand Hiller, *Wie hören wir Musik?;* Ernst Pauer, *The Birthday Book of Musicians and Composers;* Hugo Riemann, *Die Entwickelung unserer Notenschrift;* William Rockstro, *Practical Harmony;* Otakar Ševčík, *Schule der Violine-Technik;* Henri Viotta, *Lexicon der toonkunst I.*

I. Musical Compositions

Chamber Music:

String Quartets: Ferruccio Busoni, *No. 1 in c, Opus 19;* Antonin Dvořák, *No. 11 in C, Opus 61–Quartet Movement in F.*

Sonata/Solos: Robert Fuchs, *Cello Sonata No. 1 in d, Opus 29;* Eduard Nápravník, *Suite No. 2 in A for Cello and Piano, Opus 36;* Charles-Marie Widor, *Violin Sonata No. 1, Opus 50.*

Ensembles: Cécile Chaminade, *Piano Trio No. 1;* Camille Saint-Saëns, *Septet in E♭, Opus 65* (trumpet, piano, strings).

Piano: Antonin Dvořák, *Ten Legends for Piano, Four Hands, Opus 59;* Gabriel Fauré, *Impromtu No. 1, Opus 25;* Edvard Grieg, *Norwegian Dances, Opus 35* (piano duet); Heinrich Hofmann, *Two Serenades, Opus 54;* Vincent d'Indy, *Poème des montagnes, Opus 15;* Anatol Liadov, *Two Intermezzos (D, F), Opus 7*; Ignace Paderewski, *Trois morceaux, Opus 2*; Joachim Raff, *Von der schwäbischen Alb, Opus 215*.

Choral/Vocal Music:
Choral: Joseph Barnby, *Magnificat*; Johannes Brahms, *Nänie, Opus 82*; Anton Bruckner, *Te Deum*; George W. Chadwick, *The Viking's Last Voyage*; Zdeněk Fibich, *The Romance of Spring, Opus 23* (cantata); César Franck, *Rebecca* (oratorio); Charles Gounod, *Mors et vita* (oratorio); Ferdinand Hiller, *Es fürchte des Götter das Menschen geschlecht, Opus 193*; Heinrich Hofmann, *Aschenbrödel, Opus 45*; Franz Liszt, *Psalm 129*; Alexander Mackenzie, *The Bride, Opus 25* (cantata); Luigi Mancinelli, *Credo in e–Gloria in f♮*; Giuseppe Martucci, *Samuel* (oratorio); Joachim Raff, *Weltende, Gericht, Neue Welt, Opus 212*; Carl Reinecke, *Sommertagsbilder, Opus 161*.

Vocal: Johannes Brahms, *Five Songs and Romances, Opus 84*; César Cui, *Bolero, Opus 17–Seven Songs and Duets, Opus 19*; Zdeněk Fibich, *Six Songs, Opus 12*; Horatio Parker, *Five Part Songs, Opus 2*.

Musical Stage: Antonin Dvořák, *The Pig-Headed Peasants*; Friedrich von Flotow, *Sakuntala* (unfinished); Gilbert/Sullivan, *Patience*; Charles Gounod, *Le tribut de Zamore*; Charles Lecocq, *Le jour et la nuit*; Jules Massenet, *Hérodiade–Les Girondins*; Modest Mussorgsky, *The Fair at Sorochinsk* (unfinished); Victor Nessler, *Der Wilde Jäger*; Jacques Offenbach, *Les contes d'Hoffmann*; Nikolai Rimsky-Korsakov, *The Snow Maiden*; William J. Scanlan, *Friend and Foe*; Johann Strauss, Jr., *Der Lustige Krieg*; Franz von Suppé, *Der Gascogner*; Giuseppe Verdi, *Simon Boccanegra*.

Orchestra/Band Music:
Concerted Music:
Piano: Johannes Brahms, *Concerto No. 2 in B♭, Opus 83*; Gabriel Fauré, *Ballade, Opus 19*; Eduard Nápravnik, *Fantasy on Russian Themes, Opus 39*.
Violin: Camille Saint-Saëns, *Concerto No. 3 in b, Opus 61*.
Other: Max Bruch, *Kol Nidrei* (cello).

Ballet/Incidental Music: John Knowles Paine, *Oedipus Tyrannus, Opus 35* (IM).

Program Music: Mily Balakirev, *Thamar*; Zdeněk Fibich, *Spring, Opus 13*; Eduard Nápravnik, *Vostok, Opus 40*; Ludvig Norman, *Anthony and Cleopatra Overture, Opus 57*.

Standard Works: Johannes Brahms, *Tragic Overture, Opus 81*; César Cui, *Marche Solennelle, Opus 18*; Théodore Dubois, *Frithiof Overture*; Antonin Dvořák, *Overture, My Home, Opus 62*; Edward Elgar, *Three Little Pieces for Orchestra, Opus 10*; J. P. E. Hartmann, *Overture, Yrsa*; Franz Lachner, *Suite No. 7 in d, Opus 190*; Franz Liszt, *Mephisto Waltz No. 2*; Jules Massenet, *Suite No. 7: Scènes alsaciennes*; Eduard Nápravnik, *Suite in A, Opus 49*; Camille Saint-

Saëns, *A Night in Lisbon, Opus 63–Jota aragonese, Opus 64*; Richard Strauss, *Concert Overture in c, Opus 4*.

Symphonies: Anton Bruckner, *No. 6 in A*; Alexander Glazunov, *No. 1 in E, Opus 5*; Pietro Mascagni, *No. 2 in F*; Ludvig Norman, *No. 3 in d, Opus 58*; Giovanni Sgambati, *No. 1 in d, Opus 16*; Richard Strauss, *Symphony in d*.

1882

❈

Historical Highlights: The Triple Alliance is formed between Germany, Italy, and the Austro-Hungarian Empire; Great Britain occupies Egypt and proclaims it a protectorate; in the United States, the world's first hydroelectric plant is built in Appleton, Wisconsin; Labor Day observance begins with the New York Central Labor Union; the Chinese Exclusion Act is passed by Congress; Dow Jones and Co. is founded.

Art and Literature Highlights: Births—artists George Bellows, Georges Braques, Elie Nadelman, writers Susan Glaspell, James Joyce, Wyndham Lewis, Virginia Woolf; Deaths—artist Dante Rosetti, writers Berthold Auerbach, Henry James, Henry Wadsworth Longfellow, Anthony Trollope. Art—Manet's *Bar at the Follies Bergère*, Sargent's *El Jaleo*; Literature—Howell's *A Modern Instance*, Twain's *The Prince and the Pauper*.

Musical Highlights

A. Births

Composers: Walter Braunfels (Germany) December 19; R. Nathaniel Dett (U.S.A.) August 11; Carl Eppert (U.S.A.) November 5; Richard Hageman (Holland-U.S.A.) July 9; Zoltán Kodály (Hungary) December 16; Gian Francesco Malipiero (Italy) March 18; Geoffrey O'Hara (U.S.A.) February 2; Marcel Rousseau (France) August 18; Mart Saar (Estonia) September 16; Lazzare Saminsky (Russia-U.S.A.) November 8; Igor Stravinsky (Russia-France) June 17; Karol Szymanowski (Poland) October 6; Joaquín Turina (Spain) December 9; Haydn Wood (England) March 25.

Conductors: Albert Coates (England) April 23; Ralph Lyford (U.S.A.) February 22; Gino Marinuzzi (Italy) March 24; Manuel María Ponce (Mexico) December 8; Leopold Stokowski (England-U.S.A.) April 18.

Singers: Karl Arnster (German baritone) December 4; Lucca Botta (Italian tenor) April 16; Claire Croiza (French mezzo-soprano) September 14; Pauline Donalda (Canadian soprano) March 5; Florence Easton (British soprano) October 25; Geraldine Farrar (American soprano) February 28; Carlo Galeffi (Italian baritone) June 4; Amelita Galli-Curci (Italian soprano) November 18; Jeanne Gerville-Réache

(French contralto) March 26; Lydia Lipkovska (Russian soprano) May 10; Pavel Ludikar (Czech bass-baritone) March 3; Maurice d'Oisly (British tenor) November 2; Emil Schipper (Austrian bass-baritone) August 19; Alfons Schützendorf (German baritone) May 25; Dmitri Smirnov (Russian tenor) November 19; Alfio Tedeschi (Italian tenor) January 4; Fritz Vogelstrom (German tenor) November 4; Helene Wildbrunn (Austrian soprano) April 8.

Performers: Alberto Bimboni (Italian-born pianist) August 24; Seth Bingham (American organist/composer) April 16; Adolphe Borchard (French pianist) June 30; Vladimir Cernikof (French pianist) May 2; Percy Grainger (Australian pianist/composer) July 8; Mary Howe (American pianist/composer) April 4; Bronislaw Huberman (Polish violinist) December 19; Alf Hurum (Norwegian pianist/composer) September 21; Hendrik Melcher Melchers (Swedish violinist) May 30; Elly Ney (German pianist) September 27; Emanuel Ondříček (Czech violinist) December 6; John Powell (American pianist/composer/ethnomusicologist) September 6; Olga Samaroff (American pianist) August 8; Artur Schnabel (Austrian pianist) April 17; Carl H. Tollefsen (British-born violinist) August 15; Michael Zadora (American pianist) June 14.

Others: Paul Bekker (German-born music author) September 11; Donald Ferguson (American music educator/author) June 30; Karl Gehrkens (American music educator) April 19; Abraham Zevi Idelsohn (Latvian musicologist) July 13; Paul-Marie Masson (French musicologist) September 19; Eugene Schmitz (German musicologist) July 12.

B. **Deaths**
   Composers: Joseph Joachim Raff (Germany) June 24.
   Conductors: Gustav Schmidt (Germany) February 11; Anton Emil Titl (Bohemia) January 21.
   Singers: Italo Gardoni (Italian tenor) March 26; Adelaide Phillipps (British contralto) October 3; Mary Caroline Richings (British-born pianist/soprano) January 14; Hermine Rudersdorff (Russian soprano) February 26; Maschinka (Schneider) Schubert (Estonian-born soprano) September 20; Catherine Stephens (British soprano) February 22; Pierre-François Wartel (French tenor) August 3.
   Performers: Johann Carl Eschmann (Swiss pianist) October 27; Alfred Jaëll (Austrian pianist) February 27; Theodor Kullak (German pianist) March 1; Alfred H. Pease (American pianist/composer) July 12; Hippolyte-Prosper Seligmann (French cellist) February 5.
   Others: Carl Engel (German music historian) November 17; Gustav Nottebohm (German musicologist) October 29.

C. Debuts

Singers: Francesco d'Andrade (Portugese baritone—San Remo); Alice Barbi (Italian mezzo-soprano—Milan); Lola Beeth (Polish-born soprano—Berlin); Nikolai Figner (Russian tenor—Naples); Félia Litvinne (Russian soprano—Paris); Charles Manners (Irish bass—London); Marie Renard (Austrian soprano—Graz); Francesco Signorini (Italian tenor—Florence); Hermine Spies (German contralto—Berlin); Milka Ternina (Croatian soprano—Zagreb); Eva Tetrazzini (Italian soprano—Florence); Marie Wittich (German soprano—Magdeburg).
Performers: Agnes Charlotte Adler (Danish pianist—Copenhagen); Cleofonte Campanini (Italian conductor—Parma); Franz Kniesel (German violinist—Vienna); Victor Küzdö (Hungarian-born violinist—Budapest).

D. New Positions

Conductors: Robert Kajanus (Helsinki PO); Richard Kleinmichel (Leipzig Municipal Theater); Gustav Mahler (Olmütz Theater); Franz Wüllner (Berlin PO).
Others: Antonio Bazzini (director, Milan Conservatory); Antonín Bennewitz (director, Prague Conservatory); George Grove (director, Royal College of Music); Mikhail Ippolitov-Ivanov (director, Tiflis Music School); John Fuller Maitland (critic, *Pall Mall Gazette*); Angelo Neumann (manager, Bremen Opera); William Parratt (organ, St. George's Chapel, Windsor); Carlo Pedrotti (director, Liceo Musicale, Pesaro); Martin Wegelius (director, Helsinki College of Music).

E. Prizes/Honors

Prizes: Gabriel Pierné (Prix de Rome); Marie Soldat (Mendelssohn).
Honors: Peter Benoit (Belgian Royal Academy); Heinrich Hofmann (German Royal Academy); Thomas Hovenden (National Academy); Carl Reinthaler (Berlin Academy).

F. Biographical Highlights

Fritz Kreisler, age seven, is admitted to the Vienna Conservatory; Edward MacDowell, at the invitation of Liszt, plays his *First Piano Concerto* at a Zurich music convention; Sergei Rachmaninoff, at his parents' separation, follows his mother to St. Petersburg and enters the Conservatory; Erik Satie is dismissed from the conservatory for failing to reach required standards.

G. Cultural Beginnings

Performing Groups—Choral: Bethlehem (Pennsylvania) Choral Union; Bohnscher Gesangverein (Breslau); Bradford St. Cecilia Society; Handel Society of London; Siegfried Ochs Choral Union (Berlin); Oratorio Society of Baltimore.

Performing Groups—Instrumental: Berlin Philharmonic Orchestra; Helsinki New Philharmonic Society; Rosé String Quartet (Vienna); St. Paul Schubert Club; Strolling Players Amateur Orchestral Society. **Educational:** Academia Nacional de Música (Bogota); Akademie für Dramatische Gesang (Berlin); Bengal Conservatory of Music (India); Brno Organ School; Helsinki College of Music (Sibelius Academy); Liceo Musicale (Pesaro); Prang Educational Co. (Boston); Seville Conservatory of Music.
Music Publications: *Grimaces; Music and Drama; Notas Musicales y Literarias* (Barcelona); *Salterio Sacro-hispano* (Barcelona).
Performing Centers: Arena Peloro (Messina); Brno German Theater; Schwerin Landestheater; Teatro Nacional (Buenos Aires).
Other: Incorporated Society of Musicians (Manchester, England); Johannes Klais Organ Co. (Bonn); Ladies' Morning Musical Club (Montreal); Mason and Hamlin Piano Co. (Boston); John Stark and Son, pianos (Sedalia, Missouri).

H. Musical Literature

Eugen Albrecht, *Orchestral Music in Russia*; Jules Armingaud, *Consonances et dissonances*; Michel Brenet, *Histoire de la Symphonie à Orchestre*; Félix Clément, *Les grands musiciens*; Clarence Eddy, *The Church and Concert Organist I*; Percy Goetschius, *The Material Used in Musical Composition*; Eugen Krantz, *Lehrgang im Klavierunterricht*; Friedrich Langhans, *Die Geschichte der musik des 17., 18., und 19. Jahrhunderts I*; Albert Lavignac, *Cours complet théorique de dictée musicale*; Mathis Lussy/E. David, *Histoire de la notation musicale*; Hugo Riemann, *Musiklexikon*; William Rockstro, *Rules of Counterpoint*.

I. Musical Compositions
Chamber Music:

String Quartets: Alexander Glazunov, *No. 1 in D, Opus 1*; Theodore Gouvy, *No. 5*; Giovanni Sgambati, *Quartet in c♯*.
Sonata/Solos: César Cui, *Twelve Miniatures, Opus 20* (violin, piano); Heinrich Hofmann, *Serenade in F, Opus 63* (cello, piano); Carl Nielsen, *Violin Sonata No. 1 in G*; Jan Sibelius, *Violin Sonata in d*; Henri Vieuxtemps, *Thirty-Six Etudes, Opus 48* (solo violin).
Ensembles: Johannes Brahms, *Piano Trio No. 2 in C, Opus 87–String Quintet No. 1 in F, Opus 88*; Arthur Foote, *Piano Trio No. 1, Opus 5*; Giuseppe Martucci, *Piano Trio No. 1 in C, Opus 59*; Eduard Nápravník, *Piano Quartet in a, Opus 42*; Jan Sibelius, *Piano Trio in a–Piano Quartet in e*; Peter Ilyich Tchaikovsky, *Piano Trio in a, Opus 50*.
Piano: Arthur H. Bird, *Three Pieces, Opus 2*; Gabriel Fauré, *Valse-caprice No. 1, Opus 30–Nocturne No. 3, Opus 33, No. 3*; Vincent d'Indy, *Four Pieces, Opus 16–Helvetia, Opus 17*; Edward MacDowell, *Modern Suite No. 2 in a, Opus 14–Serenade, Opus 16*; John

Knowles Paine, *Romance in D♭, Opus 39*; Camille Saint-Saëns, *Mazurka No. 3 in b, Opus 66*.

Organ: Arthur H. Bird, *Four Sonatas*; František Musil, *Sonata Solemnis*; Camille Saint-Saëns, *Offertoire in F.*

Choral/Vocal Music:

Choral: Johannes Brahms, *Gesang der Parzen, Opus 89*; Claude Debussy, *Printemps*; Antonin Dvořák, *In Nature's Realm, Opus 63*; Charles Gounod, *La redemption*(?)–*Messe aux communautés religieuses*; Alexander Mackenzie, *Jason, Opus 26* (cantata); John Knowles Paine, *The Realm of Fancy, Opus 36*–*Phoebus, Arise, Opus 37* (cantatas); George Frederick Root, *David, the Shepherd Boy* (cantata); Peter Ilyich Tchaikovsky, *Russian Vesper Service, Opus 52.*

Vocal: Antonin Dvořák, *Four Songs, Opus 2*–*Evening Songs, Opus 3*; Gabriel Fauré, *Three Songs, Opus 23*; William J. Kirkpatrick, *Redeemed, How I Love to Proclaim It* (hymn); Pietro Mascagni, *Motetto in modo dorico*; Horatio Parker, *Five Songs, Opus 2*; Christian Sinding, *Songs for the Arabian Tale of Antar and Alba*; Samuel A. Ward, *Materna* (tune for "America the Beautiful").

Musical Stage: Léo Delibes, *Le roi s'amuse*; Antonin Dvořák, *Dimitri, Opus 64*; Gilbert/Sullivan, *Iolanthe*; Ernest Guiraud, *Galante aventure*; Hervé, *Lili*; Heinrich Hofmann, *Wilhelm von Oranien, Opus 56*; Vincent d'Indy, *Attendez-moi sous l'orme, Opus 14*; Carl Millöcker, *Bettelstudent*; Adolph Neuendorff, *Don Quixote*; Silas G. Pratt, *Zenobia, Queen of Palmyra*; Raoul Pugno, *Ninetta*; Joachim Raff, *Die eifersüchtigen*; Bedřich Smetana, *The Devil's Wall*; John Philip Sousa, *The Smugglers*; Ambroise Thomas, *Francesco de Rimini*; Richard Wagner, *Parsifal.*

Orchestra/Band Music:

Concerted Music:

Piano: Anton Arensky, *Concerto in f.*

Violin: Gabriel Fauré, *Romance, Opus 28*; Joseph Joachim, *Variations in e*; Richard Strauss, *Concerto*; Henri Vieuxtemps, *Concerto No. 6 in G, Opus 47*–*No. 7 in g, Opus 49*; Charles-Marie Widor, *Concerto, Opus 41.*

Ballet/Incidental Music: Antonin Dvořák, *Josef Kajétan Tyl* (IM); Édouard Lalo, *Namouna* (B); George Macfarren, *Ajax* (IM); Ole Olsen, *King Erik VIV* (IM); Frank Van der Stucken, *The Tempest* (IM).

Program Music: Ernest Chausson, *Vivianne, Opus 5*; César Franck, *Le Chasseur Maudit*; Vincent d'Indy, *La Mort de Wallenstein*; Anton Rubinstein, *Russia.*

Standard Works: Arthur H. Bird, *Suite in E for Strings, Opus 1*; Patrick S. Gilmore, *Famous Twenty-Second Regiment March*; Ernest Guiraud, *Overture Artevalde*; Alexander Glazunov, *Overture No. 1 in g on Greek Themes, Opus 3*; Mikhail Ippolitov-Ivanov, *Symphonic*

Scherzo; Joachim Raff, *Grosse fuge*; Carl Reinecke, *Overture, Zur Jubelfeier, Opus 166*; Charles V. Stanford, *Serenade for Orchestra, Opus 18*; Johann Strauss, Jr., *Voices of Spring Waltz*.
Symphonies: George W. Chadwick, *No. 1 in C*; Louis Maas, *Symphony, "On the Prairies"*; Charles Hubert Parry, *No. 1 in G*; Charles Villiers Stanford, *No. 2 in d, "Elegiac."*

1883
❄

Historical Highlights: The South Pacific volcano, Krakatoa, erupts with great loss of life and causing worldwide weather problems; the famous Orient Express makes its first run across Europe; synthetic rayon is discovered; in the United States, the New York Brooklyn Bridge opens to traffic in May; the Pendleton Act establishes the second Civil Service Commission; William "Buffalo Bill" Cody takes his Wild West Show to audiences on the east coast.

Art and Literature Highlights: Births—artists Charles Demuth, José Orozco, Maurice Utrillo, writers Lord Berners, Franz Kafka, Alexei Tolstoy, William C. Williams; Deaths—artists Oscar Begas, Paul Doré, Édouard Manet, author Ivan Turgenev. Art—Eakins' *The Swimming Hole*, Homer's *Inside the Bar*, Renoir's *By the Seashore*; Literature—Harris' *Nights with Uncle Remus*, Nietzsche's *Also Sprach Zarathustra*, Stevenson's *Treasure Island*.

Musical Highlights

A. Births
Composers: Alexander Alexandrov (Russia) April 13; Harry Alford (U.S.A.); Paul Hastings Allen (U.S.A.) November 28; Hubert Bath (England) November 6; Arnold Bax (England) November 8; Alfredo Casella (Italy) July 25; Bainbridge Crist (U.S.A.) February 13; Arnold Ebel (Germany) August 15; Josef Hauer (Austria) March 19; Judge Jackson (U.S.A.) March 12; Petar Konjovic (Serbia) May 6; Alexander Krein (Russia) October 20; Toivo Kuula (Finland) July 7; Andrei Pashchenko (Russia) August 15; Luigi Perrachio (Italy) May 28; Edgard Varése (France-U.S.A.) December 22; Anton Webern (Austria) December 3; Riccardo Zandonai (Italy) May 30.
Conductors: Hermann Abendroth (Germany) January 19; Ernest Ansermet (Switzerland) November 11; Nikolai Malko (Russia-U.S.A.) May 4; Fritz Stiedry (Austria-U.S.A.) October 11; Václav Talich (Czechoslovakia) May 28.
Singers: Frances Alda (New Zealand soprano) May 31; Ramón Blanchart (Spanish baritone)(?); Armand Crabbé (Belgian baritone) April

23; Giuseppe Danise (Italian baritone) January 11; Elena Gerhardt (German mezzo-soprano) November 11; Percy Hemming (British baritone) September 6; Gustav Schützendorf (German baritone); Reinald Werrenrath (American baritone) August 7.

Performers: Augustin Barie (French organist) November 15; Alexander Barjansky (Russian cellist) December 16; Giannotto Bastianelli (Italian pianist) June 20; Carl Deis (American organist/editor) March 7; William H. Harris (British organist) March 28; Hazel Harrison (American pianist) May 12; Gustave Langenus (Belgian-born clarinetist) August 6; Juan Manén (Spanish violinist/composer) March 14; Enrico Toselli (Italian pianist/composer) March 13.

Others: Melville Antone Clark (American harpsichord maker) September 12; A. T. Davison (American music educator) October 11; Otto Erich Deutsch (Austrian musicologist) September 5; Carl Engel (German-born musicologist) July 21; Friedrich Gennrich (German musicologist) March 27; Julius Kapp (German music author) October 1; Hisao Tanabe (Japanese musicologist) August 16; Fausto Torrefranca (Italian musicologist) February 1; Francis Toye (British musical author) January 27; Max Unger (German musicologist/conductor) May 28.

B. Deaths

Composers: Friedrich von Flotow (Germany) January 24; Johann Vesque von Püttlingen (Austria) October 29; Robert Volkmann (Germany) October 29; Richard Wagner (Germany) February 13.

Conductors: Friedrich August Reissiger (Germany-Norway) March 2.

Singers: Marie Litta (American soprano); (Giovanni Matteo) Mario (Italian tenor) December 11; Hedwig Reicher-Kindermann (German soprano) June 2; Angela Peralta (Mexican soprano) August 30; Jane Shirreff (British soprano) December 23.

Performers: Napoléon Coste (French guitarist) February 17; (Albert) Franz Doppler (Austrian flutist/composer) July 27; Julius Emil Leonhard (German pianist); Heinrich Maylath (Austrian-born pianist) December 31; Antonio James Oury (British violinist) July 25; August Friedrich Pott (German violinist) August 27; Francesco Schira (Italian contrabass virtuoso) October 15.

Others: Wilhelm von Lenz (Russian music author) January 31; Carl Gottlieb Röder (German publisher) October 29.

C. Debuts

Singers: Vittorio Arimondi (Italian bass—Varese); Heinrich Bötel (German tenor—Hamburg); Rose Lucille Caron (French soprano—Brussels); Léon Escalaïs (French tenor—Paris); Marguerite Long (French pianist—Nimes); Eugenia Mantelli (Italian mezzo-soprano—Treviso); Jean Noté (Belgian baritone—Ghent); Maurice Renaud

(French baritone—Brussels); Hermine Spies (German contralto—Germany); Ernest Van Dyck (Belgian tenor—Paris).
Performers: Amy (Mrs. H. H. A.) Beach (American pianist—Boston); Romualdo Sapio (Italian conductor—Milan).

D. New Positions
Conductors: Max Bruch (Breslau SO); Adolf Cech (Prague Opera); Charles Hallé (Liverpool PO); Wilhelm Kienzl (German Opera, Amsterdam); Anton Seidl (Bremen Opera); Johan Svendsen (Royal Opera, Copenhagen).
Others: Henry Abbey (general manager, Metropolitan Opera); Ludwig Bussler (music critic, *Berlin National-Zeitung*); Max Kalbeck (music critic, *Neue Freie Presse*).

E. Prizes/Honors
Prizes: Paul Vidal (Prix de Rome).
Honors: Xavier van Elewyck (Belgian Royal Academy); Edvard Grieg (Leyden Musical Academy); Sir George Grove (knighted); George Macfarren (knighted); Henry Oliver (Mus.Doc., Darmouth); Sir Charles Hubert Parry (doctorates, Cambridge); Sir Arthur Sullivan (knighted).

F. Biographical Highlights
Walter Damrosch takes the New York Symphony Orchestra on a tour of the western United States; Claude Debussy takes the second Prix de Rome; Alwina Valleria becomes the first Native American to appear at the Metropolitan Opera; Felix Weingartner becomes an assistant to Liszt in Weimar.

G. Cultural Beginnings
Performing Groups—Choral: Apollo Club of Portland, Oregon; Birmingham (England) Choral Association; Boston Bach Club; Metropolitan Opera Association; Stock Exchange Choral Society (London).
Performing Groups—Instrumental: Amsterdam Concertgebouw Society; Birmingham (England) Orchestra Association; Clube Haydn (São Paulo); Darmstadt Instrumentalverein; Moscow Philharmonic Society; Sociedade de Concertos Clássicos (Rio de Janeiro); Stock Exchange Orchestral Society (London).
Educational: Adelaide College of Music (Australia); Christiania Organ School (Conservatory in 1894); Los Angeles Conservatory of Music; University of Southern California School of the Performing Arts.
Music Publishers: Couesnon et Cie. (Paris, by merger); Theodore Presser.
Music Publications: *Echo: A Music Journal*; *Keynote*.

Performing Centers: Buffalo Music Hall; Dallas Opera House; Fort Worth Opera House; New National Opera House (Prague); Weber Hall (Chicago).

Other: Allgemeiner Richard-Wagner-Verband (Bayreuth); Crane Memorial Library (Boston); Everett Piano Co. (Boston); Fred Gretsch Mfg. Co. (Brooklyn); Emmons Howard, organ builder (Westfield); Springfield (Massachusetts) Tonic Sol-Fa Association; Vienna Schubertbund.

H. Musical Literature

Wilhelm Bäumker, *Das katholische deutsche Kirchenlied in seinen Singweisen*; Carl Engel, *Early History of the Violin Family*; Henry Gadsby, *Harmony*; Otto Gumprecht, *Unsere Klassischen Meister I*; Salomon Jadassohn, *Harmonielehre*; Louis Köhler, *Allgemeine Musiklehre*; Hugo Riemann, *Elementar-musiklehre–Neue schule der melodik: Entwerf einer lehre des kontrapunkts nach einer neuen method*; Frédéric Ritter, *Music in America*; Carl Stumpf, *Tonpsychologie I*; Albert Tottmann, *Abriss der Musikgeschichte*.

I. Musical Compositions

Chamber Music:

String Quartets: Zdeněk Fibich, *Theme and Variations in B♭*; Arthur Foote, *No. 1 in g, Opus 4*; Carl Nielsen, *No. 1 in f*; Giacomo Puccini, *Quartet in D*; Bedřich Smetana, *No. 2*.

Sonata/Solos: Edvard Grieg, *Cello Sonata in A*; Heinrich Hofmann, *Violin Sonata, Opus 67*; Horace Nicholl, *Violin Sonata in A, Opus 13*; C. Hubert Parry, *Cello Sonata in A*; Henri Vieuxtemps, *Voies du Coeur, Opus 53–Three fantaisies brillantes, Opus 54–Greetings to America, Opus 56–Impressions et réminiscences de Pologne, Opus 57* (violin, piano).

Ensembles: Antonin Dvořák, *Piano Trio in f, Opus 65*; Josef B. Foerster, *Piano Trio No. 1 in f, Opus 8*; Robert Fuchs, *Violin Sonata No. 2 in D, Opus 33*; Edward German, *Piano Trio in D*; Heinrich Hofmann, *Octet, Opus 80*; Giuseppe Martucci, *Piano Trio No. 2 in E♭, Opus 62*; Carl Nielsen, *Piano Trio in G*; Anton Rubinstein, *Piano Trio in c, Opus 108*.

Piano: Ferruccio Busoni, *Six Etudes*; César Cui, *Suite, Opus 21–Quatro morceaux, Opus 22*; Gabriel Fauré, *Impromptu No. 2, Opus 31–Impromtu No. 3, Opus 34*; Edvard Grieg, *Lyric Pieces, Book II, Opus 37*; Anatol Liadov, *Two Intermezzos, Opus 8–Two Pieces (f♯, A♭), Opus 8*; Franz Liszt, *Mephisto Waltz No. 3*; George Macfarren, *Sonata in B♭*; Ignace Jan Paderewski, *Elégie, Opus 4–Danses polonaises, Opus 5–Tatra Album, Opus 12*; Josef Suk, *Sonata*.

Organ: Franz Liszt, *Requiem für die Orgel–Am Grabe Richard Wagners*; Frederick Ouseley, *Sonata No. 2*; Josef Rheinberger, *Twelve fughette in Strict Style*.

Choral/Vocal Music:

Choral: Charles Gounod, *Messe funèbre in F–Messe solennelle de Pâques in Eᵇ*; Ferdinand Hiller, *Richard Löwenherz, Opus 200*; Heinrich Hofmann, *Sinn und Minnin, Opus 68*; Engelbert Humperdinck, *Das Glück von Edenhall*; George Macfarren, *King David* (oratorio); Pietro Mascagni, *Mass*; John Knowles Paine, *The Nativity, Opus 38* (cantata); Horatio Parker, *The Lord Is My Shepherd, Opus 3*; J. C. D. Parker, *The Blind King*; George Frederick Root, *The Choicest Gift* (cantata).

Vocal: Claude Debussy, *La Belle au bois dormant*; Alexander MacKenzie, *Three Songs, Opus 18*; Gustav Mahler, *Songs of a Wayfarer*; Arthur Messiter, *Marion* (hymn, "Rejoice, Ye Pure in Heart"); Henry Clay Work, *The Lost Letter*.

Musical Stage: Léo Delibes, *Lakmé*; Ludwig Englander, *The Prince Consort*; Zdeněk Fibich, *The Bride of Messina, Opus 18*; Hervé, *Mam'zelle Nitouche–Le vertigo*; Vincent d'Indy, *Le chant de la cloche, Opus 18*; Alexander Mackenzie, *Colomba, Opus 28*; André Messager, *François-les-Bas-Bleus*; Carl Reinecke, *Glückskind und Pechvogel, Opus 117*; Anton Rubinstein, *Sulamith–Unter Räubern*; Camille Saint-Saëns, *Henry VIII*; William J. Scanlan, *The Irish Minstrel*; John Philip Sousa, *Désirée*; Johann Strauss, Jr., *A Night in Venice*; Peter Ilyich Tchaikovsky, *Mazeppa*.

Orchestra/Band Music:

Concerted Music:

Piano: Nicolai Rimsky-Korsakov, *Concerto in c♯, Opus 30*.

Violin: César Cui, *Suite Concertante, Opus 25*; Richard Strauss, *Concerto in d, Opus 8*.

Other: Henry Vieuxtemps, *Cello Concerto No. 2 in b, Opus 50*.

Ballet/Incidental Music: Johan P. Hartmann, *Yrsa, Opus 78* (IM); Engelbert Humperdinck, *Der richter von Zalamea* (IM); C. Hubert Parry, *The Birds* (IM).

Program Music: Zdeněk Fibich, *The Water Sprite*; Mikhail Ippolitov-Ivanov, *Yar-Khmel*; Franz Liszt, *From the Cradle to the Grave*.

Standard Works: Emmanuel Chabrier, *España Rhapsody*; George W. Chadwick, *Overture, Thalia*; Paul Dukas, *King Lear Overture*; Antonin Dvořák, *Hussite Overture, Opus 67–Scherzo Capriccioso, Opus 66*; Alexander Glazunov, *Overture No. 2 in D on Greek Themes, Opus 6–Orchestra Serenade No. 1 in A, Opus 7*; Sergei Lyapunov, *Ballad in c♯, Opus 2*; Horatio Parker, *Concert Overture in Eᵇ*; Giacomo Puccini, *Capriccio Sinfonico*; Bedřich Smetana, *Prague Carnival*; Peter Ilyich Tchaikovsky, *Suite No. 2 in C, Opus 53*; Frank Van der Stucken, *Prologue to William Ratcliffe*.

Symphonies: Anton Arensky, *No. 1 in b*; Johannes Brahms, *No. 3 in F, Opus 90*; Anton Bruckner, *No. 7 in E*; Zdeněk Fibich, *No. 1 in F, Opus 17*; Benjamin Godard, *No. 1, "Gothique"*; Asger Hamerik, *No.*

2 in c, "Tragique", Opus 32; Louis Maas, *No. 2, "American"*; C. Hubert Parry, *No. 2 in F, "Cambridge"*; Frederick Zech, Jr., *No. 1.*

1884

❋

Historical Highlights: The Berlin West German Conference meets while Germany begins annexing several South-West African states; Sir Hiram Maxim invents the Machine Gun, a "weapon so terrible, it will wipe out warfare"; the first modern bicycle appears in England; in the United States, Grover Cleveland is elected for his first of two separate terms as twenty-second president; American Historical Association is founded; National Cash Register Co. founded.

Art and Literature Highlights: Births—artists Max Beckmann, Amedeo Modigliani, writers Sean O'Casey, Sara Teasdale, Hugh Walpole; Deaths—artist Jules Bastien-Lepage, writers Charles Calverley, William Channing, Heinrich Laube. Art—Rodin's *Burghers of Calais*, Ryder's *Toilers of the Sea*, Sargent's *Portrait of Madame X*; Literature—Jewett's *A Country Doctor*, Twain's *Adventures of Huckleberry Finn*, Verga's *Cavalleria Rusticana*.

Musical Highlights

A. Births

Composers: Ralph Benatzky (Czechoslovakia) June 5; York Bowen (England) February 22; Albert Elkus (U.S.A.) April 30; Charles Tomlinson Griffes (U.S.A.) September 17; Louis Gruenberg (Russia-U.S.A.) August 3; Léon Jongen (Belgium) March 2; Edward Kilenyi, Sr. (Hungary-U.S.A.) January 25; John F. Larchet (Ireland) July 13; Arthur Meulemans (Belgium) May 19; Ture Rangström (Sweden) November 30; Piotr Rytel (Poland) September 20; Apolinary Szeluto (Russia-Poland) July 23; Wintter Watts (U.S.A.) March 14; Emerson Whithorne (U.S.A.) September 6.

Conductors: Willem van Hoogstraten (Holland) March 18; Albert Wolff (France) January 19.

Singers: Norman Allin (British bass) November 19; Maria Barrientos (Spanish soprano) March 10; Rafaelo Diaz (American tenor); Werner Engel (German baritone); Helen Forti German soprano) April 25; Alma Gluck (Romanian-born soprano) May 11; Lillian Hannah von Granfelt (Finnish soprano) June 2; Joseph Hislop (Scottish tenor) April 5; Kathleen Howard (Canadian-born soprano) July 17; Gertrude Kappel (German soprano) September 1; Nanny Larsen-Todsen (Swedish soprano) August 2; John McCormack (Irish tenor) June 14; Eidé Norena (Norwegian soprano) April 26; Alfred Piccaver (British tenor) February 15; Marie Sundelius (Swedish soprano) February 4.

Performers: Florence Austin (American violinist) March 11; Wilhelm Backhaus (German pianist) March 26; Joseph Bonnet (French organist) March 17; Ruth Lynda Deyo (American pianist) April 20; Edwin Grasse (American violinist) August 13; Marie Hall (British violinist) April 18; Edwin Hughes (American pianist) August 15; Hans Lange (German violinist/conductor) February 17; John M. Williams (American pianist/pedagogue) January 1.

Others: Boris Asafiev (Russian musicologist/composer) July 29; Aladár Sendrey (Hungarian-born musicologist) February 29; Alceo Toni (Italian musicologist/composer) May 22.

B. Deaths

Composers: Sir Michael Costa (Italy-England) April 29; Victor Massé (France) July 5; Bedřich Smetana (Bohemia) May 12; Auguste-Emmanuel Vaucorbeil (France) November 2; Henry Clay Work (U.S.A.) June 8.

Singers: Valentina Bianchi (French pianist) March 11; Anna Bishop (British soprano) March 18; Pasquale Brignoli (Italian tenor) October 30; Erminia Frezzolini (Italian soprano) November 5.

Performers: Jean Becker (German violinist) October 10; Louis Brassin (French pianist) May 17; Auguste Franchomme (French cellist) January 21; John Hullah (British organist) February 21; Samuel de Lange (Dutch organist) May 15; Ange-Conrad Prumier (French harpist) April 3; Joseph Rubinstein (Russian pianist) September 15.

Others: Henry Erben (American organ builder) May 7.

C. Debuts

Singers: Teresa Arkel (Austrian soprano—Lemberg); Fritz Friedrichs (German bass—Nuremberg); Marie Goetze (German mezzo-soprano—Kroll); Pelagie Greef-Andriessen (Austrian soprano—Leipzig); Nellie Melba (Australian soprano—Melbourne); Karl Perron (German bass-baritone—Leipzig).

Performers: Leopold Godowsky (Polish-born pianist—Boston); Henri Marteau (Swedish violinist—Vienna, age ten); Richard Strauss (German conductor—Meiningen); Felix Weingartner (Austrian conductor—Weimar).

D. New Positions

Conductors: Giuseppe Gallignani (maestro di cappella, Milan Cathedral); Wilhelm Gericke (Boston Symphony); Franz Wüllner (Gürzenich Concerts, Cologne and director Cologne Conservatory of Music).

Others: John Comfort Fillmore (director, Milwaukee School of Music); John Fuller Maitland (critic, *London Guardian*); Pierre Gailhard (co-manager with M. Ritt, Paris Opera); Frederick Gleason (critic, *Chicago Tribune*); Hendrik Waelput (director, Ghent Conservatory); Hugo Wolf (critic, Vienna *Salonblatt*).

E. Prizes/Honors
Prizes: Claude Debussy (Prix de Rome); Max Puchat (Mendelssohn). **Honors:** Léo Delibes (French Institute); C. Hubert Parry (honorary doctorate, Oxford).

F. Biographical Highlights
Frederick Delius leaves for his Florida orange plantation but meets Thomas Ward, Jacksonville organist; Edward MacDowell returns to the United States to marry Marian Nevins, then goes back to Frankfurt; Pietro Mascagni is dismissed from Milan Conservatory for failure to apply himself to his studies; Bedřich Smetana is committed to an insane asylum just before his death; Richard Strauss leaves Munich University to concentrate on music.

G. Cultural Beginnings
Performing Groups—Choral: Berliner Liedertafel; Treble Clef Club (Philadelphia).
Performing Groups—Instrumental: Beethoven String Quartet (New York); Boston Orchestral Club; Concerts Symphonique du Grand Theater (Lyons); Kunkel's Popular Concerts (St. Louis); Orquestra da Real Academia de Amadores de Música (Lisbon); Oxford Musical Union; Société des Concerts Populaires (Orleans).
Educational: American College of Musicians; Amsterdam Conservatorium; Charleston Conservatory of Music (South Carolina); Chicago Conservatory of Music; Grand Ducal Conservatory (Badisches Konservatorium für Musik); Klindworth Klavierschule (Berlin); Krüss-Färber Konservatorium (Hamburg); Milwaukee School of Music.
Music Publications: *American (Music Journal)*; *Vierteljahrsschrift für Musikwissenschaft*.
Performing Centers: Brünn-Brno Opera House; Child's Grand Opera House (Los Angeles); Frye's Opera House (Seattle, Washington); Krueger Auditorium (Newark, New Jersey); Provisional Theater (National Theater, Brno); Royal Hungarian Opera House (Budapest).
Other: Amsterdam Wagner-Vereniging; Cercle des Vingts (Libre Esthétique, Brussels); Henry Distin, instrument maker (Philadelphia); John Friedrich and Brother, violin makers (New York); John Spencer Murdoch, piano maker (London).

H. Musical Literature
Henry Banister, *Some Musical Ethics and Analogies*; William H. Dana, *Practical Harmony*; Francis Davenport, *Elements of Music*; Heinrich Ehrlich, *Lebenskunst und Kunstleben*; Henry Hiles, *Part-Writing or*

Modern Counterpoint; Ferdinand Hiller, *Erinnerungsblätter*; Salomon Jadassohn, *Kontrapunkt*; Antoine Marmontel, *Éléments d'aesthétique musicale*; Friedrich Niecks, *Concise Dictionary of Musical Terms*; Hugo Riemann, *Musikalische dynamik und agogik: Lehrbuch der musikalischen Phrasierung*; Nicolai Rimsky-Korsakov, *Textbook on Harmony*.

I. **Musical Compositions**
    Chamber Music:
    String Quartets: Alexander Glazunov, *No. 2 in F, Opus 10*; Henri Vieuxtemps, *No. 2 in c, Opus 51–No. 3 in B♭, Opus 52*.
    Sonata/Solos: Antoni Dvořák, *Ballad in d* (violin, piano); Henri Vieuxtemps, *Allegro de Concert, Opus 59–Allegro and Scherzo, Opus 60* (violin, piano).
    Ensembles: Ferdinand Hiller, *Capriccio for Four Violins, Opus 203*; C. Hubert Parry, *String Quintet in E♭–Piano Trio No. 2 in b*.
    Piano: Antonin Dvořák, *Humoresque in F♯–From the Bohemian Mountains, Opus 68* (four hands); Gabriel Fauré, *Nocturne No. 4 in E♭, Opus 36–Nocturne No. 5, Opus 37–Valse-caprice No. 2, Opus 38*; César Franck, *Prelude, Chorale and Fugue*; Edward German, *Sonata in G*; Edvard Grieg, *Holberg Suite, Opus 40* (also orchestral version); Anatol Liadov, *Three Pieces (D♭, C, D), Opus 10*; Edward Mac-Dowell, *Forest Idyls, Opus 19*; Ignace Jan Paderewski, *Introduction and Toccata, Opus(?)–Album de mai, Opus 10–Variation and Fugue in a, Opus 11*; John Knowles Paine, *Three Pieces, Opus 41*; Anton Rubinstein, *Soirées musicales, Opus 109*.
    Organ: Anton Bruckner, *Prelude in C*; Johan P. Hartmann, *Sonata in g, Opus 58*; Franz Liszt, *Vortragstücke*.
    Choral/Vocal Music:
    Choral: Johannes Brahms, *Six Songs and Romances, Opus 93a* (a capella chorus)–*Tafellied, Opus 93b*; Anton Bruckner, *Te Deum in C*; Claude Debussy, *L'enfant prodigue* (cantata); Antonin Dvořák, *The Spectre's Bride, Opus 69* (cantata); César Franck, *Psalm 150*; George Macfarren, *St. George's Te Deum*; Alexander Mackenzie, *The Rose of Sharon, Opus 30* (oratorio); Ole Olsen, *Ludvig Holberg* (cantata); Horatio Parker, *Psalm, The Lord Is My Shepherd, Opus 3–Ballade, Opus 6*.
    Vocal: Johannes Brahms, *Five Songs, Opus 91–Six Vocal Quartets, Opus 92–Five Songs, Opus 94–Seven Songs, Opus 95–Four Songs, Opus 96*; César Cui, *Six Songs, Opus 27*; Claude Debussy, *Claire de Lune* (song); Robert Franz, *Six Songs, Opus 52*; John Knowles Paine, *Four Songs, Opus 40*; Peter Ilyich Tchaikovsky, *Six Songs, Opus 57*.
    Musical Stage: Ernest Chausson, *Les Caprices de Marianne–Hélène*; Théodore Dubois, *Aben-Hamlet*; Joseph K. Emmett, *Fritz, the Bohemian*; Gilbert/Sullivan, *Princess Ida*; Hervé, *Le cosaque–La nuit aux*

soufflets; Jules Massenet, *Manon*; Victor Nessler, *Der Trompeter von Säkkingen*; Giacomo Puccini, *Le Villi*; Anton Rubinstein, *Der Papagei*; Charles Villiers Stanford, *Savonarola–The Canterbury Pilgrims*; Felix Weingartner, *Sakuntala*.

Orchestra/Band Music:

Concerted Music:

Piano: Eugène d'Albert, *Concerto No. 1 in b*; Camille Saint-Saëns, *Rhapsodie d'Aubergne in C, Opus 73–Allegro appassionato, Opus 70*; Peter Ilyich Tchaikovsky, *Concert Fantasy, Opus 56*.

Violin: César Cui, *Deux morceaux, Opus 24–Suite concertante, Opus 25*.

Other: Josef Rheinberger, *Organ Concerto No. 1 in F, Opus 137*; Richard Strauss, *Horn Concerto No. 1 in E♭, Opus 11*.

Ballet/Incidental Music: Edgar Stillman Kelley, *Macbeth* (IM).

Program Music: Antonin Dvořák, *From the Bohemian Forest, Opus 68*; Josef Bohuslav Foerster, *In the Mountains*; César Franck, *Les Djinns*.

Standard Works: Paul Dukas, *Gotz von Berlichingen Overture*; Niels Gade, *Holbergiana, Opus 61*; Alexander Glazunov, *Serenade No. 2 in F, Opus 11*; Édouard Lalo, *Scherzo for Orchestra, Opus 13*; Horatio Parker, *Concert Overture in E♭, Opus 4–Overture, Regulus, Opus 5–Venetian Overture, Opus 12–Scherzo in g*; Anton Rubinstein, *Fantasie eroica, Opus 110*; Peter Ilyich Tchaikovsky, *Suite No. 3 in G, Opus 55*.

Symphonies: Gabriel Fauré, *Symphony in d, Opus 40*; Robert Fuchs, *No. 1 in C, Opus 37* (1886 Beethoven Prize); Benjamin Godard, *No. 2, "Orientale," Opus 84*; Asger Hamerik, *No. 3, "Lyrique"*; Richard Hol, *No. 3*; Richard Strauss, *Symphony in f, Opus 12*.

1885

Historical Highlights: William Gladstone is ousted as British prime minister by the Marquess of Salisbury; Louis Pasteur succeeds in giving the first successful rabies inoculation; Belgium takes over control of the Congo region of Central Africa; in the United States, the Washington Monument is dedicated in the nation's capital; American Telephone and Telegraph Co. is incorporated; the Sault-Ste. Marie Locks are opened between the Great Lakes.

Art and Literature Highlights: Births—artists Robert Delauney, Paul Manship, Hugh Robus, writers Sinclair Lewis, Ezra Pound, Elinor Wylie; Deaths—authors Per Atterbom, Victor Hugo, Helen Hunt Jackson. Art—Harnett's *After the Hunt*, Peto's *The Poor Man's Store*, Van Gogh's *The Potato Eaters*; Literature—Haggard's *King Solomon's Mines*,

William D. Howells' *The Rise of Silas Lapham*, Stevenson's *A Child's Garden of Verse*.

Musical Highlights

A. Births

Composers: Humberto Allende (Chile) June 29; Alban Berg (Austria) February 9; Cecil Burleigh (U.S.A.) April 17; George Butterworth (England) July 12; Thomas Hartmann (Russia-U.S.A.) September 21; Henri-Georges d'Hoedt (Belgium) May 14; Stevan Hristić (Yugoslavia) June 19; Eduard Künneke (Germany) January 27; Wallingford Riegger (U.S.A.) April 29; Deems Taylor (U.S.A.) December 22; Trygve Torjussen (Norway) November 14; Egon Wellesz (Austria-England) October 21.

Conductors: Walerian Bierdiajew (Poland) March 7; Désiré Defauw (Belgium) September 5; Vittorio Gui (Italy) September 14; Artur Holde (Germany) October 16; Werner Josten (Germany-U.S.A.) June 12; Otto Klemperer (Germany) May 14; Artur Rothier (Germany) October 12; Erwin Stein (Austria) November 7.

Singers: Margarethe Arndt-Ober (German contralto) April 15; Giulio Crimi (Italian tenor) May 10; Claire Dux (German-born soprano) August 2; Eva Gauthier (Canadian mezzo-soprano) September 20; Frieda Hempel (German soprano) June 26; Ludwig Hoffmann (German bass) January 14; Lucille Marcel (American soprano); Elfriede Marherr (German soprano); Giovanni Martinelli (Italian tenor) October 22; Carmen Melis (Italian soprano) April 14; Aureliano Pertile (Italian tenor) November 9; Richard Schubert (German tenor) December 15; Ferenc Szekelyhidy (Hungarian tenor) April 4; Giuseppe Taccani (Italian tenor); Curt Taucher (German tenor) October 25; Luisa Villani (Italian soprano); Martha Winternitz-Dorda (Austrian soprano); Eric Wirl (Austrian tenor).

Performers: Hermann Keller (German organist/musicologist) November 20; Lea Luboshutz (Russian-born violinist) February 22; Francis Macmillen (American violinist) October 14; Augustin Barrios Mangore (Paraguayan guitarist); Carlos Salzédo (French harpist) April 6.

Others: Maud Karpeles (British ethnomusicologist) November 12; Rudolph Réti (Serbian-born music theorist/composer) November 27; Sigmund Spaeth (American music author) April 10.

B. Deaths

Composers: Franz Abt (Germany) March 31; Ludvig Norman (Sweden) March 28; Lauro Rossi (Italy) May 5.

Conductors: Sir Julius Benedict (Germany-England) June 5; Leopold Damrosch (Germany-U.S.A.) February 15; Hans Schläger (Austria) May 17.

Singers: Thomas J. Bowers (American tenor) October 3; Marie Cabel (Belgian soprano) May 23; Lodovico Graziani (Italian tenor) May 15; Alexander Reichardt (Hungarian tenor) March 14; Charlotte Sainton-Dolby (British contralto) February 18.

Performers: Adolf Friedrich Christiani (German-born pianist) February 16; Félix Clément (French organist/music author) January 23; Heinrich F. Enckhausen (German organist) January 15; Ferdinand Hiller (German pianist/composer) May 10; Samuel P. Jackson (British-born organist) July 27; Friedrich Kiel (German violinist/composer) September 13; Joseph Kotek (Russian violinist) January 4; Henry Kemble Oliver (American organist/hymnist) August 12; (Henry) Brinley Richards (British pianist) May 1; August Gottfried Ritter (German organist) August 26; Julius Schneider (German organist) April 3; Joseph Servais (Belgian cellist) August 29; Juliusz Zarębski (Polish pianist/composer) September 15.

Others: Abramo Basevi (Italian critic) November 25; Carl Hermann Bitter (German music author) September 12; J. W. Davison (British critic) March 24; Michael Hermesdorff (German musicologist/organist) January 17.

C. Debuts

Singers: Sigrid Arnoldson (Swedish soprano—Prague); Ramon Blanchart (Spanish baritone—Barcelona); Ellen Brandt-Forster (Austrian soprano—Danzig); Irene von Chavanne (Austrian contralto—Dresden); Fernando De Lucia (Italian tenor—Naples); Guerrina Fabbri (Italian contralto—Viadana); Laura Hilgermann (Austrian mezzo-soprano—Prague); Paul Knüpfer (German bass—Sondershausen); Liza Lehmann (British soprano—London); Juan Luria (Polish baritone—Stuttgart); Fanny Moody (British soprano—London); Sophie Traubmann (American soprano—New York).

Performers: Fanny Davies (British pianist—London); Frederic Lamond (Scottish pianist—Berlin).

D. New Positions

Conductors: Cosme Damián José de Benito (maestro de capilla, Royal Chapel, Madrid); Walter Damrosch (New York Symphony Society); Andreas Hallén (Stockholm PO); Richard Henneberg (Stockholm Opera); Anton Seidl (Metropolitan Opera).

Others: Richard Aldrich (music critic, *Providence Journal*, Rhode Island); Jacques-Joseph Bouhy (director, New York Conservatory); Edward Elgar (organ, St. Georges Catholic Church, Worcester); Henry Hiles (editor, *Quarterly Musical Review*); Alexander Taneyev (director, Moscow Conservatory).

E. Prizes/Honors

Prizes: Léon Dubois (Prix de Rome); Vincent d'Indy (City of Paris); Lucien Lambert (Rossini); Xavier Leroux (Prix de Rome).
Honors: César Franck (Legion of Honor); Vladimir de Pachmann (knighted, Denmark).

F. Biographical Highlights

Frederick Delius abandons his Florida orange farm and begins music teaching in Jacksonville; Edvard Grieg builds his villa, Trold-haugen, in Norway; Lillian Nordica, following her husband's death, re-debuts in Boston; Jan Sibelius enters Helsinki University Law School but soon switches to music; Richard Strauss becomes assistant to Hans von Bülow at Meiningen.

G. Cultural Beginnings

Performing Groups—Choral: American (National) Opera Co. (New York); Heidelberg Bachverein; Nice Opera.
Performing Groups—Instrumental: Boston Pops Orchestra; Filhar-moniska Sällskapet (Stockholm); Glauchau Konzertverein; Russian Public Symphony Concerts (St. Petersburg).
Educational: Cleveland School of Music; Combs Conservatory (Philadelphia); Conservatorio Nacional (Havana); Forest Gate College of Music (London); Melbourne Academy of Music (Australia); National Conservatory of Music (New York); Newark College of Music; Northwestern Conservatory of Music (Minneapolis).
Music Publishers: Belaiev Publishing House (St. Petersburg); Boston Music Co.; Silver Burdett Co. (Boston); Josef Weinberger (Vienna); M. Witmark (New York).
Music Publications: *Die Gesellschaft; Kastner's Wiener Musikalische Zeitung; The Metronome; Revue Félibré-anne; Russian Musical Review.*
Performing Centers: Bijou Theater (Boston); Chestnut Street Opera House (Philadelphia); Smetana Theater (Prague).
Other: Estey Piano Co. (Vermont); Listemann Concert Co. (Boston); Musicians Mutual Benefit Association (St. Louis); Schimmel Piano Factory (Leipzig); Ernst Hubertus Seifert, organ builder (Cologne); Henri Selmer et Cie. (Paris).

H. Musical Literature

Kornél Ábrányi, *History of Music;* Félix Clément, *Histoire de la musique depuis les temps ancien jusqu'à nos jours;* Clarence Eddy, *The Church and Concert Organist II;* Friedrich von Hausegger, *Musik als ausdruck;* Julius Hey, *Deutscher Gesangunterricht;* Engelbert Humper-dinck, *Essayo de un metodo de armonia;* Antoine Marmontel, *Histoire du piano et ses origines;* Emil Naumann, *Illustrierte Musikgeschichte II;* John Knowles Paine, *Lecture Notes;* Camille Saint-Saëns, *Harmonie et mélodie*; Heinrich Vincent, *Die Zwölfzahl in der Tonwelt*; Henri Viotta, *Lexicon der Toonkunst II*; Wilhelm Volckmar, *Handbuch der Musik*.

I. **Musical Compositions**
    Chamber Music:
    String Quartets: George W. Chadwick, *No. 3 in D*; Horatio Parker, *Quartet in F, Opus 11*; Julius Röntgen, *Quartet in a*.
    Sonata/Solos: Ferruccio Busoni, *Kleine Suite, Opus 23* (cello, piano); Niels Gade, *Sonata No. 3 in B♭, Opus 59*; Carl Nielsen, *Fantasy Piece in g* (clarinet, piano); Carl Reinecke, *Flute Sonata, "Undine," Opus 167*; Camille Saint-Saëns, *Violin Sonata No. 1 in d, Opus 75–Romance in E, Opus 57* (horn, piano).
    Ensembles: Richard Strauss, *Piano Quartet in c*.
    Piano: Léon Böellmann, *Three Pieces–Prélude et Fuge*; George Frederick Bristow, *Dreamland, Opus 59*; Gabriel Fauré, *Barcarolle No. 2, Opus 41–Barcarolle No 3, Opus 42*; Zdeněk Fibich, *Two Rondinos (F, G)–Kolovil* (four hands); Johan P. Hartmann, *Sonata No. 2, Opus 80*; Anatol Liadov, *Three Pieces (b, a, f♯), Opus 11*; Franz Liszt, *Hungarian Rhapsody No. 18 in c♯–No. 19 in d*; Edward MacDowell, *Three Poesien, Opus 20* (four hands); Ignace Jan Paderewski, *Two Intermezzi (g, c)*; C. Hubert Parry, *Theme and Variations in d*; Anton Rubinstein, *Six Pieces, Opus 104*; Alexander Scriabin, *Valse in f, Opus 1*; Charles-Marie Widor, *Suite polonaise, Opus 51*.
    Organ: George W. Chadwich, *Ten Canonic Studies for Organ*.
    Choral/Vocal Music:
    Choral: George Frederick Bristow, *Mass in C, Opus 57*; Max Bruch, *Achilleus* (oratorio); Dudley Buck, *The Voyage of Columbus* (cantata); Emmanuel Chabrier, *La Sulamite* (cantata); César Cui, *Seven Choruses, Opus 28*; Antonin Dvořák, *Hymn of the Czech Peasants, Opus 28*; George Elvey, *Mount Carmel* (oratorio); Zdeněk Fibich, *Missa brevis in F, Opus 21*; Arthur Foote, *The Farewell of Hiawatha, Opus 11*; Edward German, *Te Deum in F*; Charles Gounod, *Mors et vita(?)*; Heinrich Hofmann, *Nornengesang, Opus 21–Festgesang, Opus 74*; Vincent d'Indy, *Ste. Marie-Magdeleine, Opus 23* (cantata); Hamish MacCunn, *The Moss Rose*; Horatio Parker, *König Trojan, Opus 8*; Richard Strauss, *Wanderer's Sturmlied, Opus 14*.
    Vocal: Johannes Brahms, *Six Songs, Opus 90*; Ferruccio Busoni, *Unter den Linden*; Antonin Dvořák, *In Folk Tone, Opus 73*; William W. Gilchrist, *Eight Songs*; Alexander Glazunov, *Five Romances, Opus 4*; Alexander Mackenzie, *Three Songs, Opus 16–Ten Songs, Opus 31*; F. E. Meacham, *American Patrol*; André Messager, *Nouveau printemps*; Ignace Jan Paderewski, *Four Songs, Opus 7(?)*.
    Musical Stage: César Franck, *Hulda*; Gilbert/Sullivan, *The Mikado*; Frederick Gleason, *Montezuma*; Hervé, *Mam'zelle Gavroche*; Luigi

Mancinelli, *Isora di Provenza*; Pietro Mascagni, *Guglielmo Ratcliff*; Jules Massenet, *Le Cid*; André Messager, *La fauvette du temple–La béarnaise*; John Philip Sousa, *The Queen of Hearts*; Johann Strauss, Jr., *The Gypsy Baron*.

Orchestra/Band Music:
Concerted Music:

> **Piano:** César Franck, *Symphonic Variations*; Henry Huss, *Rhapsody for Piano and Orchestra*; Vincent d'Indy, *Symphony on a French Mountain Air*; Edward MacDowell, *Concerto No. 1 in a, Opus 15*; Giuseppe Martucci, *Concerto No. 2 in b♭, Opus 66*.
> **Violin:** Alexander Mackenzie, *Concerto in c♯, Opus 32*.
> **Other:** César Cui, *Deux morceaux, Opus 36* (cello); Vincent d'Indy, *Lied, Opus 19* (cello); Carl Reinecke, *Harp Concerto in e, Opus 182*.

Ballet/Incidental Music: André Messager, *Le petit poucet* (IM); Charles Villiers Stanford, *The Euminides* (IM); Charles-Marie Widor, *Les Jacobites* (IM).

Program Music: Alexander Glazounov, *Stenka Razin, Opus 13*; Edward MacDowell, *Hamlet–Ophelia*; Vincent d'Indy, *Saugefleurie, Opus 21*.

Standard Works: Arthur H. Bird, *Little Suite II, Opus 6*; Alexander Borodin, *Scherzo for Orchestra*; Edward Elgar, *The Wand of Youth Suite No. 1, Opus 1a*; Hamish MacCunn, *Cior Mhor Overture*; John Philip Sousa, *Sound Off March*.

Symphonies: Arthur H. Bird, *Symphony in A, Opus 8*; Johannes Brahms, *No. 4 in e, Opus 98*; Antonin Dvořák, *No. 7 in d, Opus 70*; Asger Hamerik, *Symphonie Lyrique in E, Opus 33*; Jenö Hubay, *No. 1 in B♭, Opus 26*; Horatio Parker, *Symphony in C, Opus 7*; Xaver Scharwenka, *Symphony*; Peter Ilyich Tchaikovsky, *Manfred Symphony, Opus 58*.

1886
❀

Historical Highlights: Portugal claims the territory in Africa located between Angola and Mozambique; Vancouver, British Columbia, is incorporated in Canada; in the United States, Samuel Gompers becomes the first president of the reorganized American Federation of Labor; the Haymarket Square Riots take place in Chicago; the Statue of Liberty is unveiled; Apache leader Geronimo is captured in the Arizona Territory.

Art and Literature Highlights: Births—artists Oscar Kokoschka, Antoine Pevsner, Diego Rivera, writers Nikolai Gumilyov, Alfred Joyce Kilmer; Deaths—authors Mary B. Chesnut, Emily Dickinson, artists Asher Durand, Jerome Thompson. Art—Harnett's *The Old Violin*,

Rodin's *The Kiss*, Seurat's *Sunday Afternoon, Grande Jatte*; Literature—Burnett's *Little Lord Fauntleroy*, Rimbaud's *Les Illuminations*, Stevenson's *Dr. Jekyll and Mr. Hyde*.

Musical Highlights

A. Births

Composers: Edward Ballantine (U.S.A.) August 6; John J. Becker (U.S.A.) January 22; Gustav Adolf Bengtsson (Sweden) March 29; Eric Coates (England) August 27; George Foote (U.S.A.) February 19; L. Wolfe Gilbert (U.S.A.) August 31; Jésus Guridi (Spain) September 25; Jef van Hoof (Belgium) May 8; Gustaf Nordqvist (Sweden) February 12; Daniel Ruyneman (Holland) August 8.

Conductors: Gustav Adolf Bengtsson (Sweden) March 29; Wilhelm Furtwängler (Germany) January 25; Robert Heger (Germany) August 19; Gennaro Papi (Italy-U.S.A.) December 21; Paul Paray (France) May 24; Nicolai Alexandrovich Sokoloff (Russia-U.S.A.) May 28; Ole Windingstad (Norway-U.S.A.) May 18; Kōsaku Yamada (Japan) June 9.

Singers: Mária Basilides (Hungarian contralto) November 11; Guerrina Fabbri (Italian contralto); Hermann Gallos (Austrian tenor) January 21; Fraser Gange (Scottish-born baritone) June 17; Mabel Garrison (American soprano) April 24; Apollo Granforte (Italian baritone) July 20; Mignon Nevada (American soprano) August 14; Nadezhda Obukhova (Russian mezzo-soprano) March 6; Gabriella Ritter-Ciampi (French soprano) November 2; Ada Sari (Polish soprano) June 29; Leo Schützendorf (German bass) May 7; César Vezzani (Italian tenor) August 8; Carolina White (American soprano) November 23.

Performers: Joseph Achron (Lithuanian-born violinist/composer) May 13; Clarence Adler (American pianist) March 10; Paul Bazelaire (French cellist) March 4; George Frederick Boyle (Australian-born pianist) June 29; Edouard Déthier (Belgian-born violinist) April 25; Marcel Dupré (French organist) May 3; Edwin Fischer (Swiss pianist/conductor) October 6; Fay Foster (American pianist) November 8; James Friskin (Scottish-born pianist) March 3; Ethel Leginska (British pianist/composer) April 13; Frank Merrick (British pianist) April 30; George Oldroyd (British organist) December 1; Othmar Schoeck (Swiss pianist/composer) September 1; Pietro Alessandro Yon (Italian organist/composer) August 8.

Others: Dirk Jacobus Balfoort (Dutch musicologist) July 19; Olin Downes (American music critic) January 27; Oscar Esplá (Spanish music educator/composer) August 5; Wilhelm Fischer (Austrian musicologist) April 19; Robert Haas (Austrian musicologist) August 15; Jacques Handschin (Swiss musicologist/organist) April 5; Ernst Kurth (Austrian-born musicologist) June 1; Armand Machabey

(French musicologist) May 7; Henry Prunières (French musicologist) May 24; Charles Seeger (American musicologist) December 14; André Tessier (French musicologist) March 8.

B. Deaths

Composers: Adolf Müller, Sr. (Austria) July 29; Amilcare Ponchielli (Italy) January 15; Giovanni Rossi (Italy) March 30; Friedrich Hieronymus Truhn (Germany) April 30.

Conductors: Louis Schlösser (Germany) November 17.

Singers: Jenny Bürde-Ney (Austrian soprano) May 17; Francesco Chiarmonte (Italian tenor/composer) October 15; Charlotte Cushman (American contralto) February 18; Julian Dobrski (Polish tenor) May 2; Joseph Maas (British tenor) January 16; Emil Scaria (Austrian bass) July 22; John Templeton (Scottish tenor) July 2; Joseph Tichatschek (Bohemian tenor) January 18.

Performers: Jacques-Louis Battman (French organist) July 7; August Edward Grell (German organist/composer) August 10; Louis Köhler (German pianist) February 16; Franz Liszt (Hungarian pianist/ composer) July 31; (Pieter) Hubert Ries (German violinist) September 14.

Others: Gustave Chouquet (French music author) January 30.

C. Debuts

Singers: Olimpia Boronat (Italian soprano—Naples); Jean-François Delmas (French bass-baritone—Paris); Ellen Gulbranson (Swedish soprano—Stockholm); Lawrence Kellie (British tenor—London); Eugène Oudin (American baritone—New York).

Performers: Arthur Bird (American pianist—Berlin); Josef Hofmann (Polish-born pianist—Berlin, age ten); Franz Schalk (Austrian conductor—Liberec); Arturo Toscanini (Italian conductor—Rio de Janeiro); Benjamin Lincoln Whelpley (American pianist—Boston).

D. New Positions

Conductors: Stanislaw Barcewicz (Warsaw Opera); Riccardo Drigo (Russian Imperial Ballet); Antonio Gagnoni (maestro di cappella, S. Maria Maggiore); Wilhelm Kienzl (director, Steiermärkischer Musikverein, Graz); Karl Muck (Deutsches Landestheater, Prague); Karl Schröder (German Opera, Rotterdam); Fritz Steinbach (hofkapellmeister, Meiningen).

Others: Louis C. Elson (music critic, *Boston Advertiser*); Francis Hueffer (editor, *Musical World*); Max Kalbeck (critic, *Neues Wiener Tageblatt*); Filippo Marchesi (director, Liceo Musicale, Rome); Giuseppe Martucci (director, Bologna Conservatory).

E. Prizes/Honors

Prizes: Robert Fuchs (Beethoven); Marie-Emmanuel Savard (Prix de Rome).

Honors: Anton Bruckner (Order of Franz Josef—government stipend); Niels Gade (Order of Daneborg); Pierre Gailhard (Legion of Honor); Ernesto C. Sivori (Legion of Honor).

F. Biographical Highlights

Claude Debussy deserts Rome but is talked into returning; Gustav Mahler begins a two-year stint as assistant to Nikisch at Leipzig; Joseph Guy Ropartz leaves the Conservatory to study with Franck; Richard Strauss leaves Meiningen to become third conductor at the Munich Court Opera.

G. Cultural Beginnings

Performing Groups—Choral: Austin (Texas) Musical Union; Berliner Lehrergesangverein; Church Choral Society (New York); Eurydice Chorus of Philadelphia.

Performing Groups—Instrumental: Andreyev Balalaika Orchestra (St. Petersburg); Concerts Classiques (Marseilles); Kneisel String Quartet (Boston); London Symphony Concerts; Sociedad del Cuarteto (Santiago); Società Orchestrale l'Avenire (Messina).

Festivals: Norfolk Choral Festival.

Educational: American Conservatory of Music (Chicago); American Institute of Applied Music (Metropolitan Conservatory, New York); Richard Anderssons Music School (Sweden); Minneapolis School of Fine Arts; Musikalische Akademie (Cologne); Toronto Royal Conservatory of Music.

Music Publications: *Het Orgal*; *La Wallonie*.

Performing Centers: Grand Opera House (San Antonio, Texas); Slovak National Theater (Bratislava).

Other: American Academy and Institute of Fine Arts; American Publisher's Copyright League; Berne Convention for the Protection of Literary and Artistic Works; Celeste (patented); National League of Composers.

H. Musical Literature

Adolf Christiani, *Principles of Musical Expression in Piano Playing*; Annie Curwen, *Mrs. Curwen's Pianoforte Method*; Francis W. Davenport, *Elements of Harmony, Counterpoint*; Eduard Hanslick, *Konzerte, komponisten und virtuosen des letzten 15 Jahre*; Eduard von Hartmann, *Philosophie des Schönen*; Charles Nuitter/Ernest Thoinan, *Origines de l'Opéra français*; C. Hubert Parry, *Studies of the Great Composers*; Carl Reinecke, *Was sollen wir spielen?*; William Rockstro, *General History of*

Music; Julius Stockhausen, *Gesangsmethode I*; Richard Wallaschek, *Ästhetik der Tonkunst*.

I. **Musical Compositions**
    Chamber Music:
    String Quartets: Alexander Glazunov, *Five Novelettes, Opus 15*; Hans Pfitzner, *Quartet in d*.
    Sonata/Solos: Johannes Brahms, *Cello Sonata No. 2 in F, Opus 99– Violin Sonata No. 2 in A, Opus 100*; César Franck, *Violin Sonata in A*; Johan P. Hartmann, *Violin Sonata No. 3 in g, Opus 83*; Giuseppe Martucci, *Three Pezzi, Opus 67* (violin, piano).
    Ensembles: Johann H. Beck, *String Sextet in d*; Jan Blockx, *Piano Quintet*; Johannes Brahms, *Piano Trio No. 3 in c, Opus 101*; Max Bruch, *Piano Quintet*; Gabriel Fauré, *Piano Quartet No. 2 in g, Opus 45*; Josef B. Foerster, *String Quinter, Opus 3*.
    Piano: Arthur H. Bird, *Eight Pieces, Opus 15*; César Cui, *Deux polonaises, Opus 50–Trois valses, Opus 31–Trois impromtus, Opus 35*; Zdeněk Fibich, *Sonata in B♭, Opus 28* (four hands); Edvard Grieg, *Lyric Pieces, Book III, Opus 43–Reminincences: From Mountain and Fjord, Opus 44*; Edward MacDowell, *Four Pieces, Opus 24*; Ignace Jan Paderewski, *Two Pieces, Opus 1*(?); Horatio Parker, *Five Characteristic Pieces, Opus 9*; Alexander Scriabin, *Two Valses (g♯, D♭)– Sonate-fantaisie in g♯*; Peter Ilyich Tchaikovsky, *Dumka, Opus 59*.
    Organ: Alexandre Guilmant, *Noëls, Opus 60*.
    Choral/Vocal Music:
    Choral: Dudley Buck, *The Light of Asia* (cantata); Ernest Chausson, *Hymne védique, Opus 9*; Antonin Dvořák, *St. Ludmilla, Opus 71* (oratorio); Robert Franz, *Trinkspruch*; Heinrich Hofmann, *Rattanfängerlieder, Opus 62a*; Franz Liszt, *Missa Choralis*; Alexander Mackenzie, *The Story of Seyid, Opus 34* (cantata); Horatio Parker, *Idylle, Opus 15* (cantata after Goethe); George F. Root, *Faith Triumphant* (cantata).
    Vocal: Edwin Barnes, *Southampton* (hymn tune, "O Worship the Lord")–*Morton* (hymn tune, "O Let Me Walk With Thee"); Amy (Mrs. H. H. A.) Beach, *Four Songs, Opus 1*; Johannes Brahms, *Five Songs, Opus 105–Five Songs, Opus 106–Five Songs, Opus 107*; César Cui, *Seven Poems, Opus 33–Three Songs, Opus 37*; Antonin Dvořák, *In Folk Tone, Opus 73*; Robert Fuchs, *Six Songs, Opus 41*; Horatio Parker, *Three Love Songs, Opus 10*.
    Musical Stage: Emmanuel Chabrier, *Gwendoline*; Hervé, *Flafla–Frivoli*; Heinrich Hofmann, *Donna Diana, Opus 75*; Henry Litolff, *Les templiers*; Alexander Mackenzie, *The Troubador, Opus 33*; Eduard Nápravník, *Harold, Opus 45*; Victor Nessler, *Otto der Schütz*; C. Hubert Parry, *Guinevere*; Carl Reinecke, *Auf hohen befehl, Opus 184*; Charles-Marie Widor, *Maître Ambros*.

Orchestra/Band Music:
Concerted Music:
Piano: Caryl Florio, *Concerto in A♭*; Charles Gounod, *Fantasy on the Russian National Hymn*; Vincent d'Indy, *Symphony on a French Mountain Air*; Edward MacDowell, *Concerto No. 2 in d.*
Violin: Nicolai Rimsky-Korsakov, *Fantasia on Russian Themes, Opus 33.*
Other: Arthur H. Bird, *Introduction and Fugue in d, Opus 16* (organ).
Ballet/Incidental Music: Peter E. Lange-Müller, *Once Upon a Time* (IM); André Messager, *Le deux pigeons* (B).
Program Music: Arthur Foote, *Overture: In the Mountains, Opus 14*; Edward MacDowell, *Lancelot and Elaine, Opus 25*; Camille Saint-Saëns, *Carnival of the Animals* (not performed till 1922); Richard Strauss, *Aus Italien, Opus 16.*
Standard Works: Mily Balakirev, *Spanish Overture*; George W. Chadwick, *Overture, The Miller's Daughter*; Zdeněk Fibich, *Overture: A Night in Karlštijn Castle, Opus 26*; Emil Naumann, *Overture, Käthchen von Heilbronn, Opus 40*; C. Hubert Parry, *Suite Moderne*; John Philip Sousa, *The Gladiator March*; Arthur B. Whiting, *Concert Overture.*
Symphonies: Eugène d'Albert, *Symphony in F*; George W. Chadwick, *No. 2 in B♭, Opus 21*; Felix Draeseke, *No. 3*; Alberto Franchetti, *Symphony in e*; Alexander Glazunov, *No. 2 in f♯, Opus 16*; Benjamin Godard, *No. 3, "Symphonie légendaire"*; Édouard Lalo, *Symphony in g*; Anton Rubinstein, *No. 6 in a, Opus 111*; Camille Saint-Saëns, *No. 3 in c, Opus 78, "Organ"*; Charles-Marie Widor, *No. 2 in A, Opus 54.*

1887

Historical Highlights: The first World Colonial Conference opens in London; the southeast Asian states of Vietnam, Cambodia, and Laos are combined by France to form French Indo-China; working-model internal combustion cars are developed by both Gottlieb Daimler and Karl Benz; in the United States, free mail delivery service begins in larger towns and cities; first electric trolley set up in Richmond, Virginia; the U.S. Navy leases Pearl Harbor in Hawaii.

Art and Literature Highlights: Births—artists Jean Arp, Marc Chagall, Georgia O'Keeffe, William Zorach, writers Rupert Brooke, Blaise Cendars, Edna Ferber; Deaths—artist Mans von Marée, writers Albertus de Browere, Alfred Domett, Emma Lazarus, Marianne Moore. Art—Bartlett's *Bohemian Bear Tamer*, Renoir's *The Bathers*, Ryder's *The Flying Dutchman*; Literature—Sardou's *La Tosca*, Wilde's *The Canterbury Ghost*.

Musical Highlights

A. Births

Composers: Willem Andriessen (Holland) October 25; Kurt Atterberg (Sweden) December 12; Marion Bauer (U.S.A.) August 15; Nicolae Bretan (Romania) April 6; Clara Edwards (U.S.A.) April 18; Heino Eller (Estonia) March 7; Louis Hirsch (U.S.A.) November 28; Oskar Lindberg (Sweden) February 3; Ernest Pingoud (Russia-Finland) October 14; Sigmund Romberg (Hungary-U.S.A.) July 29; Yuri Shaporin (Russia) November 8; Lily Strickland (U.S.A.) January 28; Ernst Toch (Austria-U.S.A.) December 7; Max Trapp (Germany) November 1; José María Usandizaga (Basque) March 31; Fartein Valen (Norway) August 25; Heitor Villa-Lobos (Brazil) March 5; Percy Wenrich (U.S.A.) January 23.

Conductors: Lawrence Collingwood (England) March 14; Ariy Pazovsky (Russia) February 2; Heinz Tiessen (Germany) April 10; John Finley Williamson (U.S.A.) June 23.

Singers—Female: Lucrezia Bori (Spanish soprano) December 24; Elvira Casazza (Italian mezzo-soprano) November 15; Florica Cristoforeanu (Romanian mezzo-soprano) August 16; Maria Jeritza (Czech soprano) October 6; Ingeborg Liljeblad (Finnish soprano) October 17; Felice Lyne (American soprano) March 28; Irma Tervani (Finnish mezzo-soprano) June 4.

Singers—Male: Michael Bohnen (German bass-baritone) May 2; Richard Bonelli (American baritone) February 6; William Gustafson (American bass) November 23; Roland Hayes (American tenor) June 3; Oszkár Kálman (Hungarian bass) June 18; Hippolito Lazaro (Spanish tenor) October 13; Virgilio Lazzari (Italian-born bass) April 20; Francesco Merli (Italian tenor) January 27; Luigi Montesanto (Italian baritone) November 23; Giuseppe Nessi (Italian tenor) September 25; Wilhelm Rode (German bass-baritone) February 17; Manuel Salazar (Costa Rican tenor) January 3.

Performers: Edward Shippen Barnes (American organist/composer) September 14; Alice Ehlers (Austrian-born harpsichordist) April 16; Walter Golde (American pianist) January 4; Paul Kochánski (Polish-born violinist) September 14; Yolanda Merö-Irion (Hungarian-born pianist) August 30; Boris Ord (British organist/conductor) July 9; Louis Persinger (American violinist) February 11; Artur Rubinstein (Polish-born pianist) January 28; Walter Morse Rummel (German pianist) July 19; Gino Tagliapietra (Italian pianist/composer) May 30; Paul Wittgenstein (Austrian pianist) November 5; Nándon Zsolt (Hungarian violinist/conductor) May 12.

Others: Josef Bartoš (Czech music author) March 4; Nadia Boulanger (French educator/composer) September 16; Anthony van Hoboken

(Dutch collector/biliographer) March 23; Bernhard Paumgartner (Austrian musicologist/conductor) November 14; Oscar Thompson (American music critic/editor) October 10.

B. **Deaths**

Composers: Alexander Borodin (Russia) February 27; Sir George Macfarren (England) October 31; Francesco Malipiero (Italy) May 12.

Conductors: Jules-Étienne Pasdeloup (France) August 13.

Singers: Marius-Pierre Audran (French tenor) January 9; Marianna Barbieri-Nini (Italian soprano) November 27; Gaetano Fraschini (Italian tenor) May 23; Jenny Lind (Swedish soprano) November 2; Jean Étienne Massol (French baritone) October 31; Jean Morère (French tenor) February; Wilhelm Troszel (Polish bass) March 2; Georg Unger (German tenor) February 2.

Performers: Jean-Désiré Artôt (Belgian horn virtuoso) March 25; Sebastian Lee (German cellist) January 4; Heinrich Panofka (German violinist) November 18; Thomas Philander Ryder (American organist) December 2; Robert Schaab (German organist) March 18; Lindsay Sloper (British pianist) July 3; Wilhelm Volckmar (German organist) August 27; George James Webb (British-born organist/hymnist) October 7.

Others: Franz Commer (German music historian) August 17; Gustav Theodor Fechner (German music theorist) November 19; Filippo Filippi (Italian critic) June 24; Carl Ferdinand Pohl (German music author) April 28.

C. **Debuts**

Singers: Andrew Black (Scottish baritone—London); Andreas Dippel (German-born tenor—Bremen); Cesira Ferrani (Italian soprano—Turin); Berta Foersterová-Lautererová (Czech soprano—Prague); Bruno Heydrich (German tenor—Sondershausen); Ida Hiedler (Austrian soprano—Berlin); Giulio Rossi (Italian bass—Parma); Therese Rothauser (Hungarian contralto—Leipzig); Anna Schoen-René (German- born soprano—Altenburg).

Performers: Arthur Hartmann (American violinist—Philadelphia, age six).

D. **New Positions**

Conductors: Gabriel Marie (Société Nationale de Musique, Paris); Auguste-Charles Vianesi (Paris Opéra); Felix Weingartner (Hamburg).

Others: Otto Barblan (organ, St. Pierre, Geneva); William Barrett (editor, *Musical Times*); Giovanni Bolzoni (director, Turin Conservatory); Carl Fuchs (music critic, *Danziger Zeitung*); William J. Henderson (music critic, *New York Times*); Anton Rubinstein (director, St.

Petersburg Conservatory); Johan Wagenaar (director, Utrecht Music School and organist, Utrecht Cathedral).

E. Prizes/Honors
Prizes: Gustave Charpentier (Prix de Rome).
Honors: Stephen Heller (Legion of Honor); Salomon Jadassohn (Ph.D., Leipzig); Charles Lenepveu (Legion of Honor); John F. Murphy (National Academy); Joseph Rheinberger (Berlin Royal Academy); Charles Santley (Order of St. Gregory); Marcus Stone (Royal Academy, London).

F. Biographical Highlights
Emil Berliner introduces the flat phono disc; Claude Debussy joins Mallarmé's circle; Frederick Delius visits Norway and meets Grieg; Victor Herbert plays his own *Cello Concerto* with the New York Philharmonic; Leoš Janáček joins František Bartoš in investigating Moravian folk music; Albert Roussel is admitted to the École Navale as a cadet; Peter Ilyich Tchaikovsky debuts as a conductor.

G. Cultural Beginnings
Performing Groups—Choral: Bostonian's Light Opera Group; Corale Rossini (Modena).
Performing Groups—Instrumental: Aulin String Quartet (Sweden); Dallas Philharmonic Society; Fremantle Orchestral Society (Perth); Shinner String Quartet (London); Marie Soldat String Quartet I (Vienna).
Festivals: Hovingham Music Festival.
Educational: Denver Music Conservatory; Halifax Ladies' College Music Department; Liceo Musicale (Trieste); London College of Music; Maritime Conservatory of Music (Halifax); Tokyo Music School.
Music Publishers: Carisch Music Publishers (Milan).
Music Publications: *Scribner's Magazine.*
Performing Centers: Louis Opera House (San Diego); Théâtre Libre (Paris).
Other: American Gramophone Co. (Washington, D.C.); Berlin Gesellschaft der Opernfreunde; Edinburgh Society of Musicians; North American Phonograph Co.; Società Wagneriana (Bologna); South Place Sunday Concerts (London); Yamaha Co. (Japan).

H. Musical Literature
Henry Banister, *Lectures on Music Analysis*; Camille Benoît, *Musiciens, poètes et philosophes*; Heinrich Bulthaupt, *Dramaturgie der oper*; Clarence Eddy, *The Organ in Church*; Ferdinand Hiller, *Briefe an eine Ungenannte* (posthumous publication); Cyrill Kistler, *Volksschul-*

lehrer-Tonkünstlerlexicon; August Kretzschmar, *Führer durch den Konzert-Saal*; Charles Malherbe/Albert Soubies, *Précis d'histoire de l'Opéra-Comique*; Juan Facundo Riaño, *Critical and Bibliographical Notes on Early Spanish Music*; Hugo Riemann, *Opern-Handbuch–Systematische modulationslehre als grundlage der musikalischen formenhehre*; Martin Wegelius, *Foundations of General Music Science*.

I. Musical Compositions
Chamber Music:
String Quartets: Ferruccio Busoni, *No. 2*; Antonin Dvořák, *Cypresses*; Edwin A. Jones, *No. 2*; Carl Nielsen, *No. 1 in g, Opus 13*.

Sonata/Solos: Felix Draeseke, *Clarinet Sonata in B♭, Opus 38*; Antonin Dvořák, *Four Romantic Pieces, Opus 75* (violin, piano); Alexander Glazunov, *Elegy in D♭, Opus 17* (cello, piano); Edvard Grieg, *Violin Sonata No. 3 in c, Opus 45*; George Macfarren, *Violin Sonata No. 1 in e*; Wilhelm Peterson-Berger, *Violin Sonata No. 1 in e, Opus 1*; Richard Strauss, *Violin Sonata in E♭, Opus 18*.

Ensembles: Arthur H. Bird, *Nonet for Woodwinds*; Cécile Chaminade, *Piano Trio No. 2*; Antonin Dvořák, *Piano Quintet in A, Opus 81*; Carl Reinecke, *Trio for Oboe, Horn and Piano, Opus 188*.

Piano: Arthur H. Bird, *Ten Pieces, Opus 20 and 21*; Zdeněk Fibich, *From the Mountains, Opus 29*; César Franck, *Prelude, Aria and Finale*; Anatol Liadov, *Four Preludes (G, B♭, A) Opus 13–Two Mazurkas (A, d), Opus 15–Two Bagatelles, Opus 17*; Edward MacDowell, *Six Idyls after Goethe, Opus 28–Six Poems after Heine, Opus 31*; Ignace Jan Paderewski, *Humoresque de concert à l'antique, Opus 14, No. 1*; Gabriel Pierné, *March of the Little Lead Soldiers, Opus 14* (also for orchestra); Sergei Rachmaninoff, *Nocturne in f♯–Nocturne in F*; Camille Saint-Saëns, *Souvenir d'Italie, Opus 80*; Erik Satie, *Three Sarabandes*; Charles-Marie Widor, *Suite, Opus 58*.

Organ: Charles-Marie Widor, *Organ Symphony No. 5–No. 6–No. 7*.

Choral/Vocal Music:
Choral: Antonin Dvořák, *Mass in D, Opus 86*; Gabriel Fauré, *Requiem, Opus 48–Pavane, Opus 50* (chorus, ad libitum); Charles Gounod, *Messe à la mémoire de Jeanne d'Arc in F*; Asger Hamerik, *Requiem in c, Opus 34*; George Macfarren, *Around the Hearth* (cantata); Luigi Mancinelli, *Isaias*; Pietro Mascagni, *Requiem Mass*; C. Hubert Parry, *Blest Pair of Sirens*; George F. Root, *The Pillar of Fire* (cantata); Charles M. Widor, *La nuit de Walpurgis, Opus 60*.

Vocal: Amy (Mrs. H. H. A.) Beach, *Three Songs on Burns, Opus 12*; Johannes Brahms, *Zigeunerlieder, Opus 103*; Anatol Liadov, *Six Children's Songs, Opus 14–Six Children's Songs, Opus 18*; Alexander Mackenzie, *Three Shakespeare Songs, Opus 35*; Giuseppe Martucci,

La canzona dei ricordi; James McGranahan, *I Will Sing of My Redeemer* (hymn); C. Hubert Parry, *Four Sonnets from Shakespeare*; Hans Pfitzner, *Sechs Jugendlieder*; John R. Sweney, *There Is Sunshine in the Soul Today* (hymn); Peter Ilyich Tchaikovsky, *Six Songs, Opus 63*; Daniel Towner, *Trust and Obey* (hymn); Anton Urspruch, *Lieder, Opus 25*.

Musical Stage: Alexander Borodin, *Prince Igor* (unfinished); Emmanuel Chabrier, *Le roi malgré lui*; Friedrich von Flotow, *La jeunesse de Mozart*; Mikhail Ippolitov-Ivanov, *Ruth*; Edgar Stillman Kelley, *Pompeiian Picnic, Opus 9*; André Messager, *Le bourgeois de Calais*; Adolph Neuendorff, *Prince Waldmeister*; Silas G. Pratt, *Lucille*; Emil von Rezniček, *Die Jungfrau von Orleans*; Camille Saint-Saëns, *Proserpine*; Giuseppe Verdi, *Othello*.

Orchestra/Band Music:
Concerted Music:
 Piano: Gabriel Pierné, *Concerto in c, Opus 12*; José Vianna de Mota, *Concerto in A*.
 Violin: Dudley Buck, *Canzonetta and Bolero*; Camille Saint-Saëns, *Havanaise in E, Opus 83*.
 Other: Arthur H. Bird, *Oriental Scene and Caprice, Opus 17* (flute); Johannes Brahms, *Double Concerto in a, Opus 102* (violin, cello); Edward MacDowell, *Romanze, Opus 35* (cello); Camille Saint-Saëns, *Morceau de concert in f, Opus 94* (horn).

Program Music: Alexander Glazunov, *The Forest, Opus 19*; Ernest Guiraud, *Chasse fantastique*; Hamish MacCunn, *Overture, Land of the Mountains and the Flood, Opus 3*; Edward MacDowell, *Lamia, Opus 29*; Richard Strauss, *MacBeth, Opus 23*.

Standard Works: George W. Chadwick, *Overture, Melpomene*; César Cui, *Orchestral No. 2, Opus 38–Suite No. 4, Opus 40, "A Argenteau"*; Claude Debussy, *Printemps*; Frederick Delius, *Florida Suite*; Antonin Dvořák, *Slavonic Dances, Series 2, Opus 72*; Alexander Glazunov, *Characteristic Suite in D, Opus 9*; Sergei Rachmaninoff, *Scherzo in d*; Carl Reinecke, *Overture, Zur Reformationfeier, Opus 191–Zenobia Overture, Opus 193*; Nicolai Rimsky-Korsakov, *Capriccio Espagnole, Opus 34*; Philipp Scharwenka, *Arkadische Suite*; Peter Ilyich Tchaikovsky, *Suite No. 4 in G, "Mozartiana," Opus 61*.

Symphonies: Alexander Borodin, *No. 3 in a* (unfinished); Max Bruch, *No. 3 in e, Opus 51*; Anton Bruckner, *No. 8 in c*; Caryl Florio, *No. 1 in G–No. 2 in C*; Robert Fuchs, *No. 2 in E♭, Opus 45*; Edward German, *No. 1 in e*; Karl Goldmark, *No. 2 in E♭, Opus 35*; Sergei Liapunov, *Symphony in b, Opus 12*; Charles Villiers Stanford, *No. 3 in f, "Irish," Opus 28*.

1888

❋

Historical Highlights: Kaiser Wilhelm II of Prussia becomes emperor of Austria as well; Cecil Rhodes makes himself a virtual dictator in South Africa; all the European powers agree on the neutrality of the Suez Canal; France annexes the Island of Tahiti in the South Pacific; in the United States, Benjamin Harrison is elected twenty-third president despite his losing in the popular vote; Charles M. Hall introduces a cheaper method for producing aluminum.

Art and Literature Highlights: Births—artists Josef Albers, Giorgio de Chirico, writers Maxwell Anderson, T. S. Eliot, Eugene O'Neill; Deaths—sculptor Antoine Étex, writers Louisa May Alcott, Matthew Arnold, Edward Lear. Art—Bierstadt's *Last of the Buffalo*, Gogh's *L'Arlesienne*, Renoir's *After the Bath*, Weir's *Idle Hours*; Literature—Hardy's *Tess of the d'Urbervilles*, Seaman's *Ten Days in a Madhouse*, Stevenson's *Master of Ballantrae*.

Musical Highlights

A. Births

Composers: Anatoli Alexandrov (Russia) May 25; Johanna Beyer (Germany-U.S.A.) July 4; Philip Greeley Clapp (U.S.A.) August 4; Felix Deyo (U.S.A.) April 21; Louis Durey (France) May 27; Hugo Kauder (Austria-U.S.A.) June 9; Krsto Odak (Croatia) March 20; Florence Beatrice Price (U.S.A.) April 9; Poul Schierbeck (Denmark) June 8; Cristòfor Taltabull (Spain) July 28; Burnet Corwin Tuthill (U.S.A.) November 16; Matthijs Vermeulen (Holland) February 8; Gabriel von Wayditch (Hungary-U.S.A.) December 28; Roy Webb (U.S.A.) October 3.

Conductors: Emil Ábrányi (Hungary) September 22; Vincenzo Bellezza (Italy) February 17; Hans von Benda (Germany) November 22; Eugène Bigot (France) February 28; Piero Coppola (Italy) October 11; Hans Knappertsbusch (Germany) March 12; Ion Otescu (Romania) December 15; Fritz Reiner (Hungary) December 19.

Singers: Louis d'Angelo (Italian-born baritone) May 6; Gabriella Besanzoni (Italian mezzo-soprano) September 20; Alice Gentle (American mezzo-soprano) June 30; Louis Graveure (British baritone) March 18; Lillian Grenville (American soprano) November 20; Lotte Lehmann (German soprano) February 27; Frida Leider (German soprano) April 18; Emanuel List (Austrian-born bass) March 22; George Meader (American tenor) July 6; Elisabeth Ohms (Dutch soprano) May 17; Graziella Pareto (Spanish soprano) March 6; Poul Schierbeck (Danish organst) June 8; Tito Schipa (Italian tenor) Janu-

ary 2; Heinrich Schlusnus (German baritone) August 6; Friedrich
Schorr (Hungarian-born bass-baritone) September 2; Elisabeth Schumann (German soprano) June 13; Oda Slobodskaya (Russian soprano) December 10; Mariano Stabile (Italian baritone) May 12;
Maggie Teyte (British soprano) April 17.

Performers: Steffi Geyer (Hungarian violinist) January 28; Julius Isserlis (Russian pianist) November 7; Heinrich Neuhaus (Russian pianist) April 12; Rudolph Ernst Reuter (American pianist) September
21; Felix Salmond (British-born cellist) November 19; Albert Spalding (American violinist) August 15; Guilhermina Suggia (Portuguese cellist) June 27.

Others: Higini Anglès (Spanish musicologist) January 1; Victor Be-
laiev (Russian music author) February 6; Johanna Magdalena
Beyer (German-born musicologist/composer) July 11; Antoine-
Élisée Cherbuliez (Swiss musicologist) August 22; George Sher-
man Dickinson (American music educator/author) February 9;
Sophie Drinker (American music author) August 24; John Hays
Hammond, Jr. (American organ builder) April 13; Sol Hurok
(Russian born impresario/manager) April 9; Lauri Ikonen
(Finnish musicologist) August 16; Ernst C. Krohn (American mu-
sicologist) December 23; Marc Pincherle (French musicologist)
June 13.

B. Deaths

Composers: Rafael Hernándo (Spain) July 10; Emil Naumann (Germany) June 23; Théophile Semet (France) April 15.

Conductors: Carl Riedel (Germany) June 3.

Singers: Anne Childe (British soprano) August; Blanche Cole
(British soprano) August 31; Giuseppe Fancelli (Italian tenor) Janu-
ary 22; Franz Götze (German tenor) April 2; Vilma von Voggenhuber
(Hungarian soprano) January 11.

Performers: Jean-Delphin Alard (French violinist) February 22;
(Charles-Valentin) Alkan (French pianist/composer) March 29; Walter Bache (British pianist/conductor) March 26; John Ella (British vi-
olinist/conductor) October 2; Stephen Heller (Hungarian pianist/
composer) January 14; Henri Herz (Austrian pianist/composer) January 5; Edmund Neupert (Norwegian-born pianist) June 22; Théodore Nisard (Belgian organist/music author) February 29; Johann
Vogt (German pianist/composer) July 31.

Others: Henri Blaze (French music critic) March 15; Oliver Ditson
(American publisher) December 21; Friedrich Wilhelm Jähns (German pedagogue/music author) October 8; Tito Ricordi (Italian publisher) September 7.

C. Debuts

Singers: Josephine von Artner (Czech soprano—Leipzig); Hariclea Darclée (Romanian soprano—Paris); Marie Dietrich (German soprano—Stuttgart); Charles Gilibert (French baritone—Paris); (Harry) Plunket Greene (Irish bass-baritone—Stepney); Sissieretta Jones (American soprano—New York); Lev Klementyev (Russian tenor—Kiev); Martha Leffler-Burckard (German soprano—Strasbourg); Margaret Macintyre (British soprano—London); Franz Navál (Austrian tenor—Frankfurt); Regina Pacini (Portugese soprano—Lisbon); Albert Saléza (French tenor—Paris); Mario Sammarco (Italian baritone—Palermo); Sybil Sanderson (American soprano—The Hague); Francisco Vignas (Spanish tenor—Barcelona).
Performers: Ignace Jan Paderewski (Polish pianist—Vienna); Vasili Sapelnikov (Russian pianist—Hamburg).

D. New Positions

Conductors: Federic Cowen (London Philharmonic Society); Edward German (Globe Theater); Willem Kes (Amsterdam Concertgebouw Orchestra); Gustav Mahler (Budapest Royal Opera); Luigi Mancinelli (Covent Garden); Horatio R. Palmer (Chautauqua); Josef Sucher (Berlin Royal Opera).
Others: Charles H. Farnsworth (music director, Colorado University); Augustus Harris (manager, Covent Garden); Alexander C. Mackenzie (principal, Royal Academy, London); Horatio Parker (organ, Holy Trinity Church, Boston); Hans Bronsort von Schellendorf (president, Allgemeiner Deutscher Musikverein).

E. Prizes/Honors

Prizes: Camille Erlanger (Prix de Rome).
Honors: Louis Bourgault-Ducoudray (Legion of Honor); Charles Hallé (knighted); Edouard Lalo (Legion of Honor); John Stainer (knighted); Peter Ilyich Tchaikovsky (government pension).

F. Biographical Highlights

Johannes Brahms again tours Italy, where he meets Tchaikovsky; Claude Debussy visits Bayreuth and begins a liaison with Gaby Dupont; Frederick Delius begins serious music study with his father's permission; Edvard Grieg meets Tchaikovsky and conducts at the Birmingham Festival; Edward MacDowell returns to the United States and settles in Boston; John Stainer resigns his organ post because of increasing blindness.

G. Cultural Beginnings

Performing Groups—Choral: Hinrichs Opera Co. (Philadelphia); Los Angeles Ellis Clubs; Newcastle and Gateshead Choral Union.

Performing Groups—Instrumental: Adamowski String Quartet (Boston); Amsterdam Concertgebouw Orchestra; Athens Philharmonic Society; Fadette Ladies' Orchestra (Boston); Nouveaux Concerts Symphoniques (Belgium).

Educational: Artist-Artisan Institute (New York); Des Moines (Iowa) Musical College; Karl Mikuli School of Music (Lvov); Toronto College of Music.

Music Publishers: Clayton F. Summy Co. (Chicago).

Music Publications: *La Ilustración Musical Hispano-Americana; Music Review Weekly* (St. Petersburg); *Musica Romana.*

Performing Centers: Amsterdam Concertgebouw; Ateneul Román (Bucharest Concert Hall); German Theater (Prague); Harlem Opera House (New York); Lessing Theater (Berlin); Odd-Fellow Palace (Copenhagen Concert Hall); Philadelphia Grand Opera House; Teatro Costanzi (Rome); Theater am Brausenwerth (Wuppertal).

Other: Boston Manuscript Club; Mechanical Organette and Music Co. (New York); Mozart Musical and Literary Society (Dayton, Ohio); Plainsong and Medieval Music Society (London); Carmen Primavera, violin maker (Philadelphia); Società Vincenzo Bellini (Ancona).

H. Musical Literature

Hugh A. Clarke, *Manual of Orchestration*; Henry Edwards, *The Prima Donna I, II*; Louis C. Elson, *History of German Song*; Alfred Goodrich, *The Art of Song*; Eduard Hanslick, *Musikalisches Skizzenbuch*; Alfred Hipkins, *Musical Instruments, Historic, Rare and Unique*; Friedrich Nietzsche, *Der Fall Wagner*; Ludvig Norman, *Musikaliska uppsatser och Kritiker*; Hugo Riemann, *Lehrbuch des einfachen, doppelten und imitierenden Kontrapunkts–Katechismus der musik–Katechismus der musikgeschichte–Katechismus der musikinstrumente–Katechismus der Orgel–Katechismus der klavierspiels–Wie hören wir musik? Drei vorträge*; Martin Wegelius, *Treatise on General Musical Science and Analysis I*.

I. Musical Compositions
Chamber Music:

String Quartets: Frederick Delius, *No. 1* (unfinished); Josef B. Foerster, *No. 1 in E, Opus 15*; Alexander Glazunov, *No. 3 in G, "Quartuor Slave"*; Carl Nielsen, *No. 2 in g, Opus 13*; Josef Suk, *Quartet*.

Sonata/Solos: Johannes Brahms, *Violin Sonata No. 3 in d, Opus 108*; Louis Glass, *Cello Sonata in G, Opus 5*; Alexander Mackenzie, *Six Pieces, Opus 37* (violin, piano); Giuseppe Martucci, *Drei Pezzi, Opus 69* (cello, piano); Richard Strauss, *Andante* (horn, piano).

Ensembles: George W. Chadwick, *Piano Quintet in E♭*; Charles Gounod, *Little Symphony* (woodwinds); Vincent d'Indy, *Trio, Opus 29* (clarinet, cello, piano); Carl Nielsen, *String Quintet in G*; Jan

Sibelius, *Piano Trio in C, "Loviisa"*; Ludwig Thuille, *Sextet for Piano and Winds, Opus 6*.

Piano: Arthur H. Bird, *Four Pieces, Opus 26*; Claude Debussy, *Deux Arabesques*; Alexander Glazunov, *Prelude and Two Mazurkas, Opus 25*; Edvard Grieg, *Lyric Pieces, Book IV, Opus 47*; Sergei Liapunov, *Three Pieces, Opus 1*; Albéric Magnard, *Three Pieces, Opus 1*; Edward MacDowell, *Les Orientales, Opus 37–Marionetten, Opus 38*; Ignace Jan Paderewski, *Humoresque de concert moderne, Opus 14, No. 2–Dans le désert: tableau musical en forme d'une toccata, Opus 15*; Sergei Rachmaninoff, *Three Nocturnes (f♯, F, c)*; Erik Satie, *Three Gymnopedies*.

Organ: Dudley Buck, *Variations on "Old Folks at Home"*; Alexander Mackenzie, *Three Pieces, Opus 27*.

Choral/Vocal Music:

Choral: Johannes Brahms, *Five Songs, Opus 104*; Rosetter G. Cole, *The Passing of Summer* (cantata); Paul Dukas, *Vélléda* (cantata); Arthur Foote, *The Wreck of the Hesperus, Opus 17*; Charles Gounod, *Messe solennelle sur l'intonation de la liturgie catholique–Te Deum in C*; Heinrich Hofmann, *Harald's Brautfahrt, Opus 90*; Vincent d'Indy, *Sur la mer, Opus 32*; Charles Ives, *Psalm XLII*; Pietro Mascagni, *Messa di Gloria in F*; Hamish MacCunn, *Lay of the Last Minstrel, Opus 7*; John Knowles Paine, *Song of Promise, Opus 43* (cantata); Horatio Parker, *Normannenzug, Opus 16* (cantata); C. Hubert Parry, *Judith* (oratorio); George F. Root, *The Coming of the Flowers* (cantata).

Vocal: Antonin Dvořák, *Four Songs, Opus 82–Love Songs, Opus 83*; Carl Goldmark, *Eight Songs, Opus 37*; Victor Herbert, *Three Songs, Opus 15*; Edward MacDowell, *Three Songs, Opus 33*.

Musical Stage: Reginald De Koven, *The Begum*; Antonin Dvořák, *The Jacobin, Opus 84*; Gilbert/Sullivan, *Yeoman of the Guard*; Benjamin Godard, *Jocelyn*; Edouard Lalo, *Le roi d'Ys*; Henry Litolff, *L'escadron volant de la reine*; André Messager, *Isoline*; Anton Rubinstein, *The Doleful One*; John Philip Sousa, *The Wolf*.

Orchestra/Band Music:

Concerted Music:

Piano: Horace Nicholl, *Concerto in d, Opus 10*; Ignace Jan Paderewski, *Concerto in a, Opus 17*; Arthur B. Whiting, *Concerto in d*.

Violin: Charles V. Stanford, *Suite*.

Other: Heinrich Hofmann, *Konzertstück, Opus 98* (flute); Vincent d'Indy, *Fantaisie, Opus 31* (oboe); Arthur B. Whiting, *Suite for Four Horns and Strings, Opus 6*.

Ballet/Incidental Music: Ernest Chausson, *The Tempest* (IM); Frederick Delius, *Zanoni* (IM); Gabriel Fauré, *Caligula* (IM).

Program Music: Frederick Delius, *Hiawatha*; Zdeněk Fibich, *Hákon*; César Franck, *Psyché*; Carl Goldmark, *Overture, In Spring,*

Opus 36; John Knowles Paine, *An Island Fantasy, Opus 44*; Nicolai Rimsky-Korsakov, *Scheherazade, Opus 35–Russian Easter Overture, Opus 36*; Richard Strauss, *Don Juan, Opus 20*; Peter Ilyich Tchaikovsky, *Hamlet, Opus 67a*.

Standard Works: Eugène d'Albert, *Esther Overture*; Arthur H. Bird, *Two Episodes for Orchestra–Two Poems, Opus 25*; Ferruccio Busoni, *Symphonic Suite, Opus 25*; Alexander Mackenzie, *Twelfth Night Overture*; Albéric Magnard, *Suite in Olden Style in g, Opus 2*; Carl Nielsen, *Little Suite, Opus 1* (strings); Frederick Ouseley, *Overture in D*; John Philip Sousa, *Semper Fidelis March–National Fencibles March*; Johann Strauss, Jr., *Emperor Waltz*.

Symphonies: Josef Bohuslav Foerster, *No. 1 in d, Opus 9*; César Franck, *Symphony in d*; Gustav Mahler, *No. 1 in D, "Titan"*; George Templeton Strong, *No. 2, "Sintram"*; Peter Ilyich Tchaikovsky, *No. 5 in e, Opus 64*.

1889

❄

Historical Highlights: The first International American Conference is held; a Parliamentary Government is introduced into Japan; the Eiffel Tower becomes a significant feature of the great Paris Exposition; British South Africa Co. is incorporated; in the United States, North and South Dakota, Montana, and Washington become states thirty-nine through forty-two; the Oklahoma Territory is opened—Oklahoma City is built up overnight; the great Johnstown Flood occurs in Pennsylvania.

Art and Literature Highlights: Births—writers George Abbott, Tristan Derème, Arnold Toynbee, artists Willi Baumeister; Thomas Hart Benton; Deaths—authors Robert Browning, Champfleury, William C. Faulkner. Art—Liebermann's *Mending the Nets*, Macmonnies' *Diana*, Rodin's *The Thinker*; Literature—Twain's *A Connecticut Yankee in King Arthur's Court*, Heidenstram's *Endymion*, Nietzsche's *Götzendämmerung*.

Musical Highlights

A. Births

Composers: Fritz Behrend (Germany) March 3; Edward Joseph Collins (U.S.A.) November 10; Cecil Armstrong Gibbs (England) August 10; Ethel Glenn Hier (U.S.A.) June 25; José Padilla (Spain) May 28; Rudolph Simonsen (Denmark) March 30; Max Wald (U.S.A.) July 14.

Conductors: F. Charles Adler (England) July 2; Adrien Boult (England) April 8; Alexander Smallens (Russia-U.S.A.) January 1; Phil Spitalny (Russia-U.S.A.) November 7.

Singers: Paul Althouse (American tenor) December 2; Juanita Caracciolo (Italian soprano); Anna Case (American soprano) October 29; Xeniya Derzhinskaya (Russian soprano) February 6; Charles Hackett (American tenor) November 4; Alfred Jerger (Austrian bass-baritone) June 9; Claudia Muzio (Italian soprano) February 7; Karl Oestvig (Norwegian tenor) May 17; Sigrid Onégin (Swedish-born contralto) June 1; Margaret Sheridan (Irish soprano) October 15; Hertha Stolzenberg (German soprano); Giulia Tess (Italian mezzo-soprano) February 9.

Performers: Alexander Borovsky (Russian pianist) March 18; Samuel Chotzinoff (Russian-born pianist/critic) July 4; Grigoras Dinicu (Romanian violinist/composer) April 3; Clarence Loomis (American pianist/composer) December 13; David Saperton (American pianist) October 29; Elie Robert Schmitz (French-born pianist) February 8; Frederick Preston Search (American cellist/composer) July 22; John Sylvanus Thompson (American pianist/pedagogue) March 8; Efrem Zimbalist (Russian-born violinist) April 21.

Others: Peter Dinev (Bulgarian musicologist); Harold Flammer (American publisher) September 19; Willibald Gurlitt (German musicologist/editor) March 1; Dom Anselm Hughes (British musicologist) April 15; Franz Ludwig (Bohemian musicologist/composer) July 7; Hans Joachim Moser (German musicologist) May 25; Paul Nettl (Czech-born musicologist) Janaury 10; Alfred Orel (Austrian musicologist) July 3.

B. Deaths

Composers: Frédéric Clay (England) November 24; Carl Mangold (Germany) August 5; Sir Frederick Gore Ouseley (England) April 6.
Conductors: Ernst Frank (Germany) August 17.
Singers: Karl Johann Formes (German bass) October 15; Giacomo Galvani (Italian tenor) May 7; Konstancja Gladkowska (Polish soprano) December 20; Ilma di Murska (Croatian soprano) January 14; Carlotta Patti (German soprano) June 27; Enrico Tamberlik (Italian tenor) March 13; Felice Varesi (French-born baritone) March 13.
Performers: Jean Baptiste Arban (French cornetist/pedagogue) April 9; Hans Bischoff (German pianist) June 12; Giovanni Bottesini (Italian contrabass virtuoso/conductor) July 7; Carl Davidov (Russian cellist) February 26; Moritz Fürstenau (German flutist) March 25; Adolph Henselt (German pianist) October 10; Louis Maas (German-born pianist/composer) September 17; William Henry Monk (British organist/composer) March 1; Carl Rosa (German violinist/impresario) April 30; Eugene Thayer (American organist) June 27.
Others: Léon-Philippe Burbure de Wesembeek (Belgian music scholar) December 8; Francis Hueffer (German-born music author) January 19;

John W. Moore (American musicologist/lexicographer) March 23; Baltasar Saldoni (Spanish lexicographer/composer) December 3.

C. Debuts

Singers: Henri Albers (Dutch-born baritone—Amsterdam); Mario Ancona (Italian baritone—Trieste); Georg Anthes (German tenor—Dresden); Theodor Bertram (German baritone—Ulm); Edmond Clément (French tenor—Paris); Leopold Demuth (Austrian baritone—Halle); Emma Eames (American soprano—Paris); Johanna Gadski (German soprano—Berlin); Líse Landouzy (French soprano—Paris); Antonio Scotti (Italian baritone—Naples).

Performers: Leonard Borwick (British pianist—Frankfurt); George Enescu (Romanian violinist—Slánic, Moldavia).

D. New Positions

Conductors: Arthur Nikisch (conductor, Boston SO).

Others: Richard Aldrich (music critic, *Washington Evening Star*); Arrigo Boito (director, Parma Conservatory); Giovanni Bottesini (director, Parma Conservatory); Ernest Chausson (secretary, Société Nationale de Musique); Henri de Curzon (music critic, *Gazette de France*); Reginald DeKoven (music critic, *Chicago Evening Post*); Albert Fuchs (director, Wiesbaden Conservatory); John Fuller-Maitland (music critic, London *Times*); Raoul Gunsbourg (director, Nice Opera); Vasily Safonov (director, Moscow Conservatory).

E. Prizes/Honors

Prizes: Paul Gilson (Prix de Rome); August Schmid-Lindner (Mendelssohn); Charles Smulders (Prix de Rome).

Honors: Johannes Brahms (Order of Leopold); Louis Diemer (Legion of Honor); Benjamin Godard (Legion of Honor); Franz Haberl (Dr.Theol., Würzburg); Jean Louis Meissonier (Legion of Honor).

F. Biographical Highlights

Claude Debussy makes his second Bayreuth pilgrimage, hears Javanese music at the Exposition, and is introduced to Mussorgsky's *Boris Godunov*; Alexander Glazunov conducts his own works in Paris; Alexander Gretchaninov enters St. Petersburg Conservatory; Vitěslav Novák begins the study of law and music in Prague; Richard Strauss leaves Munich and works summers in Bayreuth; Bruno Walter decides on a conducting career.

G. Cultural Beginnings

Performing Groups—Choral: Bristol Choral Society; Church Choral Society of New York; Euterpe Choral Society of New York; Emma Juch Grand Opera Co.; Kansas City Apollo Club; Norwegian Male

Chorus (Seattle); Orpheus Club of Newark, New Jersey; Treble Clef (later: Lyric Club, Los Angeles).
Performing Groups—Instrumental: Arnhem Philharmonic Orchestra; Brooklyn Symphony Orchestra; Nahan Franko Orchestra; Heidelberg Stadtisches Orchester; Marie Soldat String Quartet II.
Educational: Associated Board of the Royal Schools of Music (London); Coblenz Music Conservatory; Metropolitan College of Music (London); Rauchenecker Music School (Elberfeld).
Music Publishers: Károly Rozsnyai (Budapest); Carlo Schmidl (Trieste).
Music Publications: *Ethnographical Review; Le Monde Musical.*
Performing Centers: Chicago Auditorium Theater; Teatro Principal (Lima, Peru); Verein Beethovenhaus (Bonn).
Other: Columbia Phonograph Co. (Washington, D.C.); Crosby Brown Instrumental Collection (Metropolitan Museum, New York); Freie Bühne (Theater Co.); Hamilton Organ Co. (Chicago); Manuscript Society of New York (Society of American Musicians and Composers, 1899).

H. Musical Literature

Carl/Reinhold Faelten, *Conservatory Course for Pianists*; Henry T. Finck, *Chopin and Other Musical Essays*; Alfred Goodrich, *Complete Musical Analysis*; Eduard Hanslick, *Musikalisches und Literarisches*; Henry Hiles, *Harmony or Counterpoint?*; Francis Hueffer, *Half a Century of Music in England*; Salomon Jadassohn, *Die Formen in den Werken der Tonkunst–Lehrbuch der Instrumentation*; William Mathews, *A Hundred Years of Music in America*; Ebenezer Prout, *Harmony, Its Theory and Practice*; Hugo Riemann, *Katechismus den kompositionslehre–Katechismus des generalbass-spiels–Katechismus des musik-diktats.*

I. Musical Compositions
Chamber Music:

String Quartets: César Franck, *Quartet in D*; Niels Gade, *Quartet in D, Opus 63*; Charles Martin Loeffler, *Quartet in a*; Jan Sibelius, *Quartet in E♭, Opus 4–Theme and Variations in c♯*.
Sonata/Solos: Frederick Delius, *Romance* (violin, piano); Gabriel Fauré, *Petite Pièce, Opus 49* (cello, piano); Josef Bohuslav Foerster, *Violin Sonata No. 1 in b, Opus 10*; Arthur Foote, *Violin Sonata in g, Opus 20*; Louis Glass, *Cello Sonata*; Carl Nielsen, *Two Fantasy Pieces, Opus 2* (oboe, piano); C. Hubert Parry, *Violin Sonata in D*; Jan Sibelius, *Violin Sonata in F–Two Pieces, Opus 2* (violin, piano).
Ensembles: Antonin Dvořák, *Piano Quartet in E♭, Opus 87*; Otto Malling, *Piano Trio*.
Piano: Amy (Mrs. H. H. A.) Beach, *Valse-caprice, Opus 4*; Arthur H. Bird, *Theme and Variations, Opus 27–Four Romances, Opus 29*;

Claude Debussy, *Petite Suite*; Antonin Dvořák, *Poetic Tone Pictures, Opus 85*; Alexander Glazunov, *Two Pieces, Opus 22*; Henry H. Huss, *Three Bagatelles*; Anatol Liadov, *Three Pieces (A♭, C, F), Opus 33*; Horace Nicholl, *Eight Character Pieces, Opus 23* (four hands); John Knowles Paine, *Nocturne in B♭, Opus 45*; Camille Saint-Saëns, *Les cloches du soir in E♭, Opus 85*; Alexander Scriabin, *Sonata in e♭–Three Pieces, Opus 2–Ten Mazurkas, Opus 3*.

Organ: Edward Elgar, *Eleven Vesper Voluntaries, Opus 14*; Vincent d'Indy, *Vêpres du Commun d'un Martyr, Opus 31*.

Choral/Vocal Music:

Choral: Peter Benoit, *De Rhijn* (oratorio); Johannes Brahms, *Three Motets, Opus 110*; Max Bruch, *Das Feuer Kreus* (oratorio); Paul Dukas, *Sémélé* (cantata); Henry H. Huss, *Festival Sanctus*; Alexander Mackenzie, *The Dream of Jubal* (cantata); George F. Root, *The Building of the Temple–Bethlehem* (cantatas); Josef Suk, *Křečovics Mass*; Hugo Wolf, *Christnacht* (cantata).

Vocal: Amy (Mrs. H. H. A.) Beach, *Three Songs, Opus 11*; Reginald De Koven, *Oh, Promise Me*; Frederick Delius, *Sakuntala*; Robert Fuchs, *Die Königsbraut, Opus 46*; Edvard Grieg, *Six Songs, Opus 48–Six Poems, Opus 49*; Victor Herbert, *Eight Songs, Opus 10, 13 and 14*; Ethelbert Nevin, *Five Songs, Opus 5*; Hans Pfitzner, *Seven Songs, Opus 2–Three Songs, Opus 3–Four Songs, Opus 4–Three Songs, Opus 5–Six Songs, Opus 6–Five Songs, Opus 7–Five Songs, Opus 9*; Charles M. Widor, *Solis d'été, Opus 63*; Hugo Wolf, *Spanisches Liederbuch*.

Musical Stage: Tomas Bretón y Hernández, *Los Amantes de Teruel*; Dudley Buck, *Serapis*; Reginald De Koven, *Don Quixote*; Zdeněk Fibich, *Hippodamia I: The Courtship of Pelops, Opus 31*; Josef Bohuslav Foerster, *Drei Ritter, Opus 21*; Gilbert/Sullivan, *The Gondoliers*; Henry Hadley, *Happy Jack*; Jules Massenet, *Escarmonde*; André Messager, *Le mari de la reine*; Emil Naumann, *Loreley*; Anton Rubinstein, *Moses, Opus 112*.

Orchestra/Band Music:

Concerted Music:

Piano: Claude Debussy, *Fantasy for Piano and Orchestra*; Édouard Lalo, *Concerto in f*; Anton Rubinstein, *Concertstück in A♭, Opus 113*; Charles M. Widor, *Fantaisie, Opus 62*.

Violin: Alexander Mackenzie, *Pibroch-Suite for Violin and Orchestra, Opus 42*.

Other: Ernest Chausson, *Concerto for Piano, Violin and String Quartet, Opus 21*; Théodore Dubois, *Triumphant Fantasy for Organ and Orchestra*.

Ballet/Incidental Music: Gabriel Fauré, *Shylock, Opus 57* (IM); Edward German, *Richard III* (IM); Christian F. E. Horneman, *Esther*

(IM)–*Le bleuets* (B); André Messager, *Colibri* (IM); Peter Ilyich Tchaikovsky, *The Sleeping Beauty, Opus 66* (B).

Program Music: Alexander Glazunov, *The Sea, Opus 28*; Richard Strauss, *Death and Transfiguration, Opus 24*.

Standard Works: George Bristow, *Overture Jibbenainosay, Opus 64*; Frederick Delius, *Petite Suite–Idylle de Printemp*; Arthur Foote, *Suite in E for Strings, Opus 63*; Carl Goldmark, *Der gefesselte Prometheus Overture, Opus 38–Oriental Rhapsody in G, Opus 18*; Victor Herbert, *Serenade for Strings, Opus 12*; Carl Nielsen, *Symphonic Rhapsody in F, Opus 7*; John Philip Sousa, *Washington Post March– Thunderer March*.

Symphonies: Elfrieda Andrée, *No. 1 in C*; Anton Arensky, *No. 2 in A*; Antonin Dvořák, *No. 8 in G, Opus 88*; Asger Hamerik, *No. 4 in C, "Symphonie Majesteuse," Opus 35*; Horace Nicholl, *No. 2 in C, Opus 12*; Wilhelm Peterson-Berger, *No. 1 in B♭, "The Banner"*; Charles Villiers Stanford, *No. 4 in F, Opus 31*.

1890
❖

Historical Highlights: Otto Bismarck is forced to resign as German chancellor; the Duchy of Luxembourg becomes independent; Wilhemina becomes Queen of the Netherlands; in the United States, the Census shows a population of 62,980,000; Idaho and Wyoming become states number forty-three and number forty-four; the last major Indian war, the Ghost Dance War, is fought; Sitting Bull is killed in a skirmish with soldiers in South Dakota; the U.S. Weather Bureau is created.

Art and Literature Highlights: Births—artists Naum Gabo, Man Ray, Franz Werfel, writers Boris Pasternak, Katherine Anne Porter; Deaths—artists Vincent van Gogh, Thomas Hicks, writers George Henry Boker, Octave Feuillet. Art—Poynter's *Queen of Sheba Visiting Solomon*, Remington's *The Buffalo Hunt*; Literature—France's *Thaïs*, Hovenden's *Breaking Home Ties*, Tolstoy's *The Kreutzer Sonata*, Wilde's *The Picture of Dorian Gray*.

Musical Highlights

A. Births

Composers: René Barbier (Belgium) July 12; Hans Gál (Austria) August 5; Jacques Ibert (France) August 15; Frank Martin (Switzerland) September 15; Bohuslav Martinů (Bohemia) December 8; Gösta Nystroem (Sweden) October 13; Anthony Louis Scarmolin (Italy-U.S.A.) July 30; Victor Schertzinger (U.S.A.) April 8; Edwin John Stringham (U.S.A.) July 11; Gizella Augusta Zuckermann (Mana-Zucca—December 25).

Conductors: Giuseppe Bamboschek (Italy-U.S.A.) June 12; Fritz Busch (Germany) March 13; Erich Kleiber (Austria) August 5; Michael Taube (Poland) March 13; Geoffrey Toye (England) February 17; Paul Whiteman (U.S.A.) March 28.

Singers: Fernand Ansseau (Belgian tenor) November 6; Robert Berg (Czech baritone) March 29; Thomas Burke (British tenor) March 2; Hans Clemens (German tenor) July 27; Beniamino Gigli (Italian tenor) March 20; Maria Kurenko (Russian soprano) August 16; Germaine Lubin (French soprano) February 1; Giuseppe Lugo (Italian tenor); Joseph von Manowarda (Austrian bass) July 3; Lauritz Melchior (Danish tenor) March 20; Tino Pattiera (Croatian tenor) June 27; José Riavez (Italian tenor); Marcella Roeseler (German soprano); Vladimir Rosing (Russian tenor) January 23; Vilem Zitek (Czech bass) September 9.

Performers: Joseph Waddell Clokey (American organist/composer) August 28; Arcady Dubensky (Russian violinist) October 15; Zbigniew Drzewiecki (Polish pianist) April 8; Carl Hugo Grimm (American organist/composer) October 31; Myra Hess (British pianist) February 25; Philip James (American organist/composer) May 17; Benno Moiseiwitsch (Russian-born pianist) February 22; Harold Morris (American pianist/composer) March 17; Kathleen Parlow (Canadian violinist) September 20; Lee Pattison (American pianist) July 22; Powell Weaver (American organist/composer) June 10; George Anson Wedge (American organist/author) January 15.

Others: Semyon Bogatyrev (Russian musicologist) February 15; Hugo Holle (German music scholar) January 25; John Tasker Howard (American music author) November 30; A. Walter Kramer (American critic/publisher) September 23; Antal Molnár (Hungarian musicologist/composer) January 7; Vaclav Nijinsky (Russian ballet star) February 28; Paul Leopold Rosenfeld (American music critic/author) May 4; Gustav Schirmer III (American publisher) December 29; Alfred Swan (Russian-born musicologist) February 15; Willy Tappolet (Swiss music author) August 6.

B. Deaths

Composers: John Barnett (England) April 17; Domenico Bertini (Italy) September 7; César Franck (Belgium-France) November 8; Niels Gade (Denmark) December 21; John Hill Hewitt (U.S.A.) October 7; Victor E. Nessler (Germany) May 28.

Conductors: Franz Paul Lachner (Germany) January 20; Emanuele Muzio (Italy) November 27; Henry Wilde (England) March 13.

Singers: Giovanni Battista Belletti (Italian baritone) December 27; Julián Sebástian Gayarre (Spanish tenor) January 2; Emilio Naudin (Italian-born tenor) May 5; Minna Peschka-Lautner (Austrian soprano) January 12; Giorgio Ronconi (Italian baritone) January 8.

Performers: Otto Dresel (German-born pianist) July 26; Wilhelm Fitzenhagen (German cellist) February 14; Joseph Goldberg (Austrian violinist) December 20; Hubert Léonard (Belgian violinist/composer) May 6; Prosper Sainton (French violinist) October 17; Karl Schröder (I) (German violinist) April 21; Samuel Parkman Tuckerman (American organist) June 30.

Others: Alexander Ellis (British acoustician) October 28; Ferdinand Peter Laurencin (Austrian music author) February 5.

C. Debuts

Singers: Desider Aranyi (Hungarian tenor—Brünn); Hermann Bachmann (German baritone—Halle); Annie Dirkens (German soprano—Berlin); David Thomas Frangcon-Davies (British baritone—Manchester); Matja von Niessen-Stone (Russian soprano—Dresden); Luisa Tetrazzini (Italian soprano—Florence).

Performers: Jean Gerárdy (Belgian cellist—London); Enrique Granados (Spanish pianist—Barcelona); Bronislav Huberman (Polish violinist—age seven); Artur Schnabel (Austrian pianist—Vienna, age eight); Joseph von Slivinski (Polish pianist—Warsaw); Theodor Wiehmayer (German pianist—Leipzig).

D. New Positions

Conductors: Henry T. Fleck (Harlem Philharmonic Society, New York); Joseph Hellmesberger, Jr. (Vienna Court Opera); Wilhelm Kienzl (Hamburg Opera).

Others: Carl Faelten (director, New England Conservatory); Philip Hale (music critic, *Boston Post*); Konrad Heubner (director, Koblenz Conservatory); Engelbert Humperdinck (music critic, *Frankfurter Zeitung*); Max Kalbeck (critic, *Wiener Monats-Revue*); Eugen Krantz (director, Dresden Conservatory); Gabriel Pierné (organ, Ste. Clothilde, Paris); Karl Schröder (director, Soderhausen Conservatory).

E. Prizes/Honors

Prizes: Ferruccio Busoni (Rubinstein); Michel-Gaston Carraud (Prix de Rome); Bernhard Stavenhagen (Mendelssohn).

Honors: Richard Andersson (Swedish Royal Academy); Anton Bruckner (government stipend); Edvard Grieg (French Academy); Alexander Mackenzie (honorary doctorate, Edinburgh); Pietro Mascagni (Knight of the Crown, Italy); John Knowles Paine (Ph.D., Yale); Christian Sinding (government stipend).

F. Biographical Highlights

Isaac Albéniz retires from active musical life; Frederick Delius moves to Paris and meets Ravel, Schmitt, and Gauguin; Percy Goetschius returns to the United States and teaches at Syracuse University; Wilhelm Stenhammar passes the organ exam on his own initiative; Peter Ilyich Tchaikovsky loses the support of Mme. von Meck.

G. Cultural Beginning

Performing Groups—Choral: Amsterdam A Capella Choir; Capilla Catalana (Spain); Denver Choral Society.

Performing Groups—Instrumental: Harlem Philharmonic Society (New York).

Educational: Athenaeum School (Royal Scottish Academy) of Music; Chicago National College of Music; Dublin Municipal School (College) of Music; Hanover Conservatory of Music; Hartford (Connecticut) School of Music; Spangenberg Music Conservatory (Wiesbaden); Sternberg School of Music (Philadelphia).

Music Publishers: Curtis Publishing Co.; Lorenz Publishing Co. (Dayton, Ohio); Frederick A. Stokes Co. (New York).

Music Publications: *Mercure de France*; *Music Trades* (New York); *Musikinstrumenten-Zeitung*; *Organ*; *Paléographic Musicale*.

Performing Centers: Marquam Grand Theater (Portland, Oregon); Netherlands Lyric Theater (Flemish Opera); Théâtre des Arts (Paris); Tivoli Opera House III (San Francisco).

Other: Contrabass clarinet; Annibale Fagnola, violin maker (Turin); Heckel-Clarina; Magulies Trio; Metzler und Söhne, organ builders (Switzerland); Verdi Institute (Montevideo); Virgil Practic Clavier Co. (New York).

H. Musical Literature

Louis Elson, *The Theory of Music*; François-Auguste Gevaert, *Cours méthodique d'orchestration*; Hugo Goldschmidt, *Die italienische Gesangmethode des 17. Jahrhunderts*; Salomon Jadassohn, *Die Kunst zu Modulieren und Präludieren*; Franz Krenn, *Musik- und Harmonielehre*; William Mathews, *Primer of Musical Forms*; Charles Meerens, *La gamme musicale majeure et mineure*; Ebenezer Prout, *Counterpoint, Strict and Free*; Carl Reinecke, *Rathschläge und Winke für Clavierschüler*; Hugo Riemann, *Katechismus der fugen-composition–Katechismus der harmonie- und modulationslehre–Katechismus der phrasierung* (with C. Fuchs); John Philip Sousa, *National, Patriotic and Typical Airs of All Countries*.

I. Musical Compositions

Chamber Music:

String Quartets: César Cui, *No. 1 in c*; Carl Nielsen, *No. 3 in f, Opus 5*; Ottokar Nováček, *No. 1*; Jan Sibelius, *Quartet in B♭, Opus 4*.

Sonata/Solos: Ferruccio Busoni, *Violin Sonata No. 1 in e, Opus 29*; Felix Draeseke, *Cello Sonata No. 1 in c*; Louis Glass, *Violin Sonata*

No. 1, Opus 7; Alexander Glazunov, *Rêverie in D♭, Opus 24* (horn, piano); Heinrich von Herzogenberg, *Legends, Opus 63* (cello, piano); Hans Pfitzner, *Cello Sonata in f♯, Opus 1*; Sergei Rachmaninoff, *Romance in f* (cello, piano); Max Reger, *Violin Sonata in d, Opus 1*; Alexander Scriabin, *Romance* (horn, piano).

Ensembles: Léon Böellmann, *Piano Quartet, Opus 10*; Johannes Brahms, *String Quintet No. 2 in G, Opus 111*; Arthur Foote, *Piano Quartet in C, Opus 23*; C. Hubert Parry, *Piano Trio No. 3 in G*(?); Hans Pfitzner, *Piano Trio in F, Opus 8*; Charles M. Widor, *Piano Quintet No. 1, Opus 7*.

Piano: George F. Bristow, *Marche-Caprice, Opus 51*; Claude Debussy, *Rêverie*; Anatol Liadov, *Two Pieces, Opus 24*; Edward MacDowell, *Twelve Piano Studies, Opus 39*; Ethelbert Nevin, *Three Duets, Opus 4–Four Pieces, Opus 7*; Carl Nielsen, *Five Pieces, Opus 3*; Horatio Parker, *Four Sketches, Opus 19*; Camille Saint-Saëns, *Scherzo for Two Pianos, Opus 87*; Alexander Scriabin, *Two Nocturnes, Opus 5*.

Organ: Léon Böellmann, *Twelve Pieces, Opus 16*; César Franck, *L'Organiste–Three Chorales (B, b, a)*; Horatio Parker, *Four Compositions, Opus 17*; Ralph Vaughan-Williams, *Organ Overture*; Charles M. Widor, *Symphony No. 7, Opus 42, No. 3–Symphony No. 8, Opus 42, No. 4*.

Choral/Vocal Music:

Choral: Amy Beach, *Mass in E♭, Opus 5*; Antonin Dvořák, *Requiem Mass, Opus 89*; Charles Gounod, *Messe brève aux chapelles in C– Messe aux cathédrales in G*; Stanislaw Moniuszko, *Requiem*; Horatio Parker, *The Kobolds, Opus 21* (cantata)–*Magnificat in E♭–Te Deum in B♭*; J. C. D. Parker, *St. John* (cantata); Joseph Rheinberger, *The Star of Bethlehem* (cantata); George F. Root, *Florens, the Pilgrim–Jacob and Esau* (cantatas); Charles M. Widor, *Mass, Opus 35*(?).

Vocal: César Cui, *Les deux ménétrier, Opus 42–Vingt poèmes de Jean Richepin, Opus 44*; Frederick Delius, *Seven Songs from the Norwegian*; Alexander Glazunov, *Two Songs, Opus 27*; Victor Herbert, *Die Versunkenen, Opus 20*; William Kirkpatrick, *He Hideth My Soul* (hymn); Anatol Liadov, *Six Children's Songs, Opus 22*; Edward MacDowell, *Six Love Songs, Opus 40*; Alexander Mackenzie, *Spring Songs, Opus 44*; Anton Rubinstein, *Ten Songs, Opus 115*.

Musical Stage: Reginald De Koven, *Robin Hood*; Zdeněk Fibich, *Hippodamia II: The Atonement of Tantalus, Opus 32*; Frederick Gleason, *Otho Visconti, Opus 7*; Mikhail Ippolitov-Ivanov, *Azra*; Charles Lecocq, *L'egyptienne*; Hamish MacCunn, *The Cameronian's Dream, Opus 10*; Pietro Mascagni, *Cavalleria Rusticana*; André Messager, *La basoche*; Victor Nessler, *Die Rose von Strassburg*; Ernest Reyer, *Salammbô*; Nicolai Rimsky-Korsakov, *Mlada*.

Orchestra/Band Music:
Concerted Music:
    Piano: Ferruccio Busoni, *Concertstücke, Opus 31a*; Sergei Liapunov, *Concerto No. 1 in e♭, Opus 4*; Otto Malling, *Concerto.*
    Violin: Léon Böellmann, *Fantasy on Hungarian Airs, Opus 7*; Charles Martin Loeffler, *Les Veillées de l'Ukraine.*
Ballet/Incidental Music: Gabriel Fauré, *La Passion* (IM); Alexander Mackenzie, *Ravenswood, Opus 45* (IM); Ole Olsen, *Svein Uraed* (IM); Charles M. Widor, *Jeanne d'Arc* (B).
Program Music: Frederick Delius, *Three Small Tone Poems*; Arthur Foote, *Francesca da Rimini, Opus 24*; Alexander Glazunov, *The Kremlin, Opus 30*; Jules Massenet, *Visions*; Sergei Rachmaninoff, *Manfred*; Anton Rubinstein, *Antony and Cleopatra, Opus 116.*
Standard Works: Arthur H. Bird, *Little Suite III, "Souvenirs of Summer Saturdays," Opus 32*; George W. Chadwick, *Serenade in F Major for Strings*; Edward Elgar, *Froissart Overture, Opus 19*; Alexander Glazunov, *Oriental Rhapsody, Opus 29*; Armas Järnefelt, *Lyrical Overture*; Horatio Parker, *Overture, Count Robert of Paris, Opus 24b*; Wilhelm Peterson-Berger, *Oriental Dance*; Max Reger, *Symphonic Movement in d*; Ethel Smyth, *Serenade*; John Philip Sousa, *High School Cadets March.*
Symphonies: Ernest Chausson, *Symphony in B♭, Opus 20*; Alexander Glazunov, *No. 3 in D, Opus 33*; Albéric Magnard, *No. 1 in c, Opus 4.*

1891

❋

Historical Highlights: The United States of Brazil is established; the Triple Alliance of Italy, Austria, and Germany is renewed; the Duomintang is formed to promote democracy and social reforms in China; work begins on the Trans-Siberian Railway; in the United States, the U.S. Court of Appeals is formed to relieve the pressure on the Supreme Court; the Populist party is formed by disgruntled farmers in Ohio; the International Copyright Law is passed by Congress.

Art and Literature Highlights: Births—artists Otto Dix, Max Ernst, writers Jean Cocteau, Zora Neale Hurston, Pär Lagerkvist; Deaths—artist Georges Seurat, writers James Russell Lowell, Herman Melville, Jan Neruda. Art—Cézanne's *The Card Players*, Ryder's *Siegfried and the Rhinemaidens*; Literature—Doyle's *The Adventures of Sherlock Holmes*, Garland's *Main-Travelled Roads*, Maurier's *Peter Ibbetson.*

Musical Highlights

A. Births

Composers: Arthur Bliss (England) August 2; Claude Champagne (Canada) May 27; Ruy Coelho (Portugal) March 3; Frederick Jacobi (U.S.A.) May 4; K. B. Jirák (Czechoslovakia-U.S.A.) January 28; Marinus de Jong (Belgium) August 14; Morfydd Llywn Owen (England) October 1; Athos Palma (Argentina) June 7; Serge Prokofiev (Russia) April 24; Timothy Mather Spelman (U.S.A.) January 21; Bengt von Törne (Finland) November 22; Adolph Weiss (U.S.A.) September 12.

Conductors: Issay (Alexandrovich) Dobrowen (Russia) February 27; Karl Elmendorff (Germany) October 25; Karl L. King (U.S.A.) February 21; Charles Munch (France) September 26; Holger Simon Paulli (Denmark) December 23; Erno Rapee (Hungary-U.S.A.) June 4; Hermann Scherchen (Germany) June 21; Eugen Szenkar (Hungary) August 9.

Singers—Female: Giannina Arangi-Lombardi (Italian soprano) June 20; Karin Maria Branzell (Swedish contralto) September 24; Käthe Herwig (German soprano) December 9; Felice Hüni-Mihacsek (Hungarian soprano) April 3; Maria Ivogün (Hungarian soprano) November 18; Florence Macbeth (American soprano) January 12; Dorothée Manski (German-born soprano) March 11; Lotte Schöne (Austrian-born soprano) December 15; Violetta de Strozzi (Yugoslavian soprano).

Singers—Male: Dino Borgioli (Italian tenor) February 15; Antonio Cortis (Spanish tenor) August 12; Benvenuto Franci (Italian baritone) July 1; Parry Jones (Welsh tenor) February 14; Alexander Kipnis (Russian-born bass) February 13; Jaro Prohaska (Austrian bass-baritone) January 24; Richard Tauber (Austrian-born tenor) May 16; John Charles Thomas (American baritone) September 6.

Performers: Emmanuel Bay (Russian pianist) January 20; Josef Blatný (Czech organist) March 19; Adolf Busch (German-born violinist) August 8; Richard Frank Donovan (American organist/conductor) November 29; Samuel Dushkin (Polish-born violinist) December 13; Mischa Elman (Russian-born violinist) January 20; Samuel Gardner (Russian-born violinist/composer) August 25; Marcel Granjany (French harpist) September 3; Pierre Luboshutz (Russian-born pianist) June 17; Guy Maier (American pianist) August 15; Czeslaw Marek (Polish-born pianist/composer) September 16; Georges Migot (French organist) February 27; Mishel Piastro (Russian-born violinist) July 1; Ferdinand Timmermans (Dutch organist) September 7.

Others: Lucien Cailliet (French-born arranger) May 22; Joseph Maddy (American music educator) October 14; Hans Mersmann (German musicologist) October 6; Guido Pannain (Italian musicologist) November 17.

B. Deaths

Composers: Léo Delibes (France) January 16; Fredrik Pacius (Germany) January 8; Wilhelm Taubert (Germany) January 7.

Conductors: Franco Faccio (Italy) July 21; Frédéric Louis Ritter (Germany-U.S.A.) July 4; Johannes Verhulst (Holland) January 17.

Singers: Emma Abbott (American soprano) January 5; Livia Frege (German soprano) August 22; Josephine De Reszke (Polish soprano) February 22; Marie Dolores Nau (American soprano); Fanny Salvini-Donatelli (Italian soprano) June; Marie Witt (Austrian-born soprano) September 24.

Performers: Francis H. Brown (American pianist/composer) June 23; Stefano Golinelli (Italian pianist) July 3; Holger Simon Paulli (Danish violinist/composer) December 23.

Others: George Hart (British violin maker) April 25; Henry Charles Litolff (British publisher) August 6; Eben Tourjée (American music educator) April 12.

C. Debuts

Singers: David Bispham (American baritone—London); Lillian Evans Blauvelt (American soprano—Brussels); Marie Brema (British mezzo-soprano—London); Karl Burian (Czech tenor—Brno); Francesco Daddi (Italian tenor—Milan); Arthur van Eweyk (American baritone—Berlin); Edoardo Garbin (Italian tenor—Vicenza); Ferruccio Giannini (Italian-born tenor—Boston); Eugenio Giraldoni (Italian baritone—Barcelona); Fiorello Giraud (Italian tenor—Vercelli); Marie Gutheil-Schoder (German mezzo-soprano—Weimar); Marcel Journet (French bass—Montpellier); Adolphe Maréchal (Belgian tenor—Tournai); Rosa Olitzka (German contralto—Berlin); Joseph O'Mara (Irish tenor—London); Selma von Scheidt (German soprano—Elberfeld); Erik Schmedes (Danish tenor—Wiesbaden, as baritone); Minnie Tracey (American soprano—Geneva).

Performers: Pablo Casals (Spanish cellist—Barcelona); Adelina De-Lara (British pianist—London); Ethel Sharpe (Irish pianist—London).

D. New Positions

Conductors: Gustav Mahler (Hamburg Opera); Willem Mengelberg (municipal music director, Lucerne); Anton Seidl (New York PO); Theodore Thomas (Chicago Symphony); Felix Weingartner (Berlin Court).

Others: Richard Aldrich (music critic, *New York Times*); Giuseppe Gallignani (director, Parma Cons.); Philip Hale (music critic, *Boston Journal*); James G. Huneker (music critic, *New York Recorder*); August Winding (director, Copenhagen Conservatory).

E. Prizes/Honors

Prizes: Paul Henri Lebrun (Prix de Rome); Charles Silver (Prix de Rome).

Honors: Anton Bruckner (honorary doctorate, Vienna); Victor Duvernoy (Legion of Honor); Antonin Dvořák (Ph.D., Cambridge and Prague); Augustus Harris (knighted); Gustave-Léon Huberti (Belgian Academy); Charles Hubert Parry (Mus.D., Dublin).

F. Biographical Highlights

Adolf Brodsky moves to the United States and becomes concertmaster of the New York Symphony; Anton Bruckner retires from teaching at the Vienna Conservatory; Hubert Parry becomes examiner for the London University Music Department; Peter Ilyich Tchaikovsky visits the United States at the opening of Carnegie Hall.

G. Cultural Beginnings

Performing Groups—Choral: Bellmanska Söllskapet (Stockholm choir); Cleveland Singers' Club; Lehrergesangverein (Zürich); Leipziger Männerchor; Zürich Opera.

Performing Groups—Instrumental: Chicago Symphony Orchestra; Czech String Quartet; Orfeó Català (Barcelona); Scottish Orchestra (Glasgow).

Festivals: Fiesta San Jacinto (San Antonio,Texas).

Educational: Melbourne University Chair of Music; Scharwenka Conservatory, New York Branch.

Music Publications: *Il Corriere di Napoli; Music; The Musical Messenger: A Monthly Magazine* (Cincinnati, Ohio); *Nuevo Teatro Crítico* (Madrid).

Performing Centers: Carnegie Hall (New York); Palace Theatre (London); Vancouver Opera House; Zürich Opera House.

Other: Independent Theatre Society (London); International Copyright Agreement.

H. Musical Literature

Jesse B. Aikin, *True Principles of the Science of Music*; Lionel Dauriac, *Introduction à la psychologie du musicien*; Théodore Dubois, *87 Leçons d'harmonie*; Heinrich Ehrlich, *Musikstudium und Klavierspiel*; Adolphe Jullien, *Musiciens d'Aujourd'hui I*; Nicolai Kashkin, *First Twenty-Five Years of the Moscow Conservatory*; Felipe Pedrell, *Por nuestra música*; Ebenezer Prout, *Double Counterpoint, Canon and Fugue*; Hugo Riemann, *Katechismus der akustik–Katechismus der gesangskompositon*; Frédéric Ritter, *Music in Its Relation to Intellectual Life*; Anton Rubinstein, *A Conversation on Music: Music and Its Masters*; Thomas Tapper, *The Music Life*; Richard Wallaschek, *On the Origin of Music*.

I. Musical Compositions

Chamber Music:

String Quartets: Alexander Glazunov, *Suite in C, Opus 35*; Edvard Grieg, *String Quartet in F* (unfinished); Vincent d'Indy, *No. 1, Opus 35*; Carl Reinecke, *No. 4 in D, Opus 211–No. 5 in g, Opus 287*(?).

Sonata/Solos: Antonin Dvořák, *Silent Woods, Opus 68/5–Rondo in g, Opus 94* (cello, piano); Alexander Glazunov, *Meditation in D, Opus 32* (violin, piano); Vitěslav Novák, *Violin Sonata in d*; Max Reger, *Violin Sonata in D, Opus 3*; Arthur B. Whiting, *Violin Sonata*.

Ensembles: Johannes Brahms, *Trio in a, Opus 114* (clarinet, violin, piano)–*Clarinet Quintet in b, Opus 115*; Antonin Dvořák, *Piano Trio, Opus 90, "Dumky"*; Charles Martin Loeffler, *String Sextet*(?); Max Reger, *Piano Trio in b, Opus 2*; Josef Suk, *Piano Quartet, Opus 1–Piano Trio, Opus 2*; Charles-Marie Widor, *Piano Quartet, Opus 66*.

Piano: Emmanuel Chabrier, *Bourrée Fantasque*; Gabriel Fauré, *Valse-Caprice No. 3, Opus 59*; Alexander Glazunov, *Three Etudes, Opus 31*; Edvard Grieg, *Lyric Pieces, Book V, Opus 54*; Heinrich Hofmann, *Zum Wiegenfeste, Opus 109* (four hands); Edgar Stillman Kelley, *Three Pieces, Opus 2*; Guillaume Lekeu, *Sonata*; Anatol Liadov, *Three Preludes (E♭, B, G♭), Opus 27*; Ethelbert Nevin, *Water Scenes, Opus 13*; Horatio Parker, *Six Lyrics, Opus 23*; Camille Saint-Saëns, *Suite in F, Opus 90*.

Organ: Charles Ives, *Variations on "America"*; Horatio Parker, *Four Pieces, Opus 20–Four Pieces, Opus 28*.

Choral/Vocal Music:

Choral: Amy Beach, *Festival Jubilate, Opus 17*; Dudley Buck, *The Story of the Cross* (cantata); George W. Chadwick, *The Pilgrims–Phoenix Expirans* (cantatas); Arthur Foote, *The Skeleton in Armor, Opus 28*; Victor Herbert, *The Captive* (cantata); Anatol Liadov, *Final Scene, Die Braut von Messina, Opus 28*; Edward MacDowell, *Two Northern Songs, Opus 43*; Alexander Mackenzie, *Veni, creator spiritus, Opus 46–Two Choral Odes, Opus 48*; Horatio Parker, *Dream King and His Love–Te Deum in A*; Hans Pfitzner, *Columbus, Opus 16–Herr Oluf, Opus 17*; Silas G. Pratt, *The Incas's Farewell* (cantata).

Vocal: Amy Beach, *Three Songs, Opus 2–Four Songs, Opus 14*; Arthur H. Bird, *Frau Holde, Opus 30* (cycle); Frederick Delius, *Three English Songs*; Albéric Magnard, *Six Poèmes in musique, Opus 3*; Ethelbert Nevin, *Five Songs, Opus 12*; Carl Nielsen, *Ten Songs, on P. J. Jacobsen Opus 4–Viser og vers, Opus 6*; Horatio Parker, *Three Sacred Songs, Opus 22–Three Songs, Opus 23–Six Songs, Opus 24*; Max Reger, *Six Songs, Opus 4*; Hugo Wolf, *Italianisches Lieder-buch*.

Musical Stage: Zdeněk Fibich, *Hippodamia: Hippodamia's Death, Opus 33*; Joseph Bohuslav Foerster, *Deborah, Opus 41*; Albéric Magnard, *Yolande, Opus 5*; Pietro Mascagni, *L'amico Fritz*; Jules Massenet, *Le Mage*; Carl Reinecke, *Der Gouverneur von Tours*; Arthur Sullivan, *Ivanhoe*; Peter Ilyich Tchaikovsky, *Iolanthe, Opus 69*.

Orchestra/Band Music:
Concerted Works:
   Piano: Sergei Rachmaninoff, *Concerto No. 1 in f♯, Opus 1*; Camille Saint-Saëns, *Africa (in g), Opus 89*.
   Violin: Anton Arensky, *Concerto*; Max Bruch, *Concerto No. 3 in d, Opus 58*; Harry B. Shelley, *Concerto*.
   Other: Victor Herbert, *Fantasy on a Schubert Theme* (cello).
Ballet/Incidental Music: Vincent d'Indy, *Karadee, Opus 34* (IM); Leoš Janáček, *Rakos Rakoczy* (B); Edgar Stillman Kelley, *Prometheus Bound, Opus 16* (IM); Édouard Lalo, *Néron* (B); André Messager, *Scaramouche* (B)–*Hélène* (IM); Éduard Nápravnik, *Don Juan* (IM); C. Hubert Parry, *The Frogs* (IM).
Program Music: Antonin Dvořák, *Overture, In Nature's Realm, Opus 91–Carnaval Overture, Opus 92*; Alexander Glazunov, *Spring, Opus 34*; Sergei Rachmaninoff, *Prince Rostislav*; Philipp Scharwenka, *Frühlingswagen*; Peter Ilyich Tchaikovsky, *The Voyvoda, Opus 78*.
Standard Works: Emmanuel Chabrier, *Marche Joyeuse*; Paul Dukas, *Polyeuchte Overture*; Joseph Bohuslav Foerster, *Orchestral Suite in C*; Vincent d'Indy, *Tableaux de voyage, Opus 36*; Edward MacDowell, *Suite No. 1 in a, Opus 42*; Camille Saint-Saëns, *Rapsodie bretonne*; Jan Sibelius, *Overture in E*; Richard Strauss, *Overture in c*.
Symphonies: Theodor Gerlach, *Epic Symphony*; William W. Gilchrist, *No. 1 in C*; Asger Hamerik, *Simphonie Sérieuse in g, Opus 36*.

1892
❄

Historical Highlights: William Gladstone begins his last term as prime minister of Great Britain; Rudolph Diesel patents the diesel engine; the Gilbert and Ellis islands are taken over as a protectorate of Great Britain; in the United States, Grover Cleveland is elected for a second non-consecutive term; Charles Duryea and Henry Ford both enter the automobile business; the General Electric Co. is incorporated; W. S. Burroughs patents the adding machine.

Art and Literature Highlights: Births—artist Grant Wood, writers Richard Aldington, Pearl Buck, J. R. R. Tolkien; Deaths—sculptor Jean Bonnasieux, writers Alfred Lord Tennyson, Walt Whitman, John Greenleaf Whittier. Art—Clarke's *Night Market, Morocco*, Chase's *Pulling for Shore*, Eakin's *The Concert Singer*; Literature—Harrison's *A Daughter of the South*, Maeterlinck's *Pelléas et Mélisande*, Wilde's *Lady Windemere's Fan*.

Musical Highlights

A. Births

Composers: Fred E. Ahlert (U.S.A.) September 19; Hendrik Andriessen (Holland) September 17; Samuel Barlow (U.S.A.) June 1; Giorgio Federico Ghedini (Italy) July 11; Ferde Grofé (U.S.A.) March 27; David Guion (U.S.A.) December 15; Charles Haubiel (U.S.A.) January 30; Oscar van Hemel (Holland) August 3; Arthur Honegger (Switzerland) March 10; Herbert Howells (England) October 17; Otakar Jeremiáš (Czechoslovakia) October 17; Arthur Vincent Lourié (Russia-U.S.A.) May 14; Darius Milhaud (France-U.S.A.) September 4; Rudolf Moser (Switzerland) January 7; Nicolai Obukhov (Russia) April 22; Petros Petridis (Greece) July 23; John Donald Robb (U.S.A.) June 12; Hilding Constantin Rosenberg (Sweden) June 21; Germaine Tailleferre (France) April 19.

Conductors: Howard Barlow (U.S.A.) May 1; Hans Kindler (Holland-U.S.A.) January 8; Artur Rodzinski (Poland) January 1; Victor de Sabata (Italy) April 10.

Singers—Female: Florence Austral (Australian soprano) April 26; Valeriya Barsova (Russian soprano) June 13; Sophie Braslau (American contralto) August 16; Gilda Dalla Rizza (Italian soprano) October 2; Elvira de Hidalgo (Spanish soprano) December 27; Miriam Licette (British-born soprano) September 9; Ruth Miller (American soprano) July 1; Minghini-Cattaneo (Italian contralto) April 12; Gladys Moncrieff (Austrian soprano) April 13; Maria Olczewska (German mezzo-soprano) August 12; Carmela Ponselle (American mezzo-soprano) June 7; Delia Reinhardt (German soprano) April 27; Eva Turner (British soprano) March 10.

Singers—Male: Mario Basiola (Italian baritone) July 12; Rudolf Bockelmann (German bass-baritone) April 2; George Cehanovsky (Russian baritone) April 14; Mario Chamlee (American tenor) May 29; Herbert Janssen (German-born baritone) September 22; Giacomo Lauri-Volpi (Italian tenor) December 11; Ezio Pinza (Italian baritone) May 18; Rudolf Watzke (German bass) April 5; Walter Widdop (British tenor) April 19; Renato Zanelli (Chilean baritone) April 1; Erich Zimmermann (German tenor) November 29.

Performers: Isidor Achron (Lithuanian-born pianist) November 24; Richard Burgin (Polish-born violinist) October 11; Fredric Fradkin (American violinist) April 2; Harold Gleason (American organist/musicologist) April 26; Beatrice Harrison (British cellist) December 9; Mieczyslaw Horszowski (Polish pianist) June 23; Nikolai Orlov (Russian pianist) February 26; Leo Ornstein (Russian-born pianist) December 11; K. S. Sorabji (British pianist/composer) August 14; Edward Steuermann (Polish pianist/composer) June 18; Joseph Szigeti

(Hungarian violinist) September 5; Emil Telmányi (Hungarian-born violinist/conductor) June 22.

Others: Guido M. Gatti (Italian music critic/author) May 30; Knud Jeppesen (Danish musicologist/composer) August 15; Robert Lachmann (German musicologist) November 28; John Jacob Niles (American folk-music collector/singer) April 28.

B. Deaths

Composers: Robert Franz (Germany) October 24; Ernest Guiraud (France) May 6; Hervé (Florimond Ronger (France) November 3; Édouard Lalo (France) April 22; Wilhelm Langhans (Germany) June 9; Ferdinand Poise (France) May 13; Cipriano Pontoglio (Italy) February 22.

Conductors: Heinrich Dorn (Germany) January 10; Patrick S. Gilmore (U.S.A.) September 24.

Singers: Anne Charton-Demeur (French mezzo-soprano) November 30; Jean-Baptiste Chollet (French tenor) January 10; Moritz Deutsch (German tenor) February 27; Francesco Lamperti (Italian vocalist/educator) May 1; Ernst Pasqué (German baritone) March 20; Antonio Sangiovanni (Italian singing master) January 6; Zélia Trebelli (French mezzo-soprano) August 18.

Performers: Arnold Joseph Blaes (Belgian clarinetist) January 11; Robert Burton (British organist) August 2; Baldassare Gamucci (Italian pianist) January 8; Lambert Massart (Belgian violinist/pedagogue) February 13; Wilhelm Rust (German organist) May 2; Henry Christian Timm (German-born organist/pianist) September 5.

Others: Alfred G. Badger (American flute maker) November 8; Rudolf Westphal (German music scholar) July 10.

C. Debuts

Singers: Alberto Alvarez (French tenor—Paris); Robert Blass (American bass—Weimar); Giuseppe Borgatti (Italian tenor—Castelfranco Veneto); Lucienne Bréval (Swiss-born soprano—Paris); Clara Butt (British contralto—London); Peter Cornelius (Danish tenor—Copenhagen); Ada Crossley (Australian mezzo-soprano—Melbourne); Léon David (French tenor—Paris); Marie Delna (French contralto—Paris); Olive Fremstad (Swedish-born soprano—Boston); Heinrich Knote (German tenor—Munich); Salomea Krushelnitskaya (Russian soprano—Lvov); Maria Mikhailova (Russian soprano—St. Petersburg); Jean Alexis Périer (French baritone—Paris); Frances Saville (American soprano—Brussels); Rosina Storchio (Italian soprano—Milan).

Performers: Wilhelm Backhaus (German pianist—Leipzig); Carl Friedberg (German pianist—Vienna).

D. New Positions

Conductors: Édouard Colonne (Paris Opéra); Andreas Hallén (Stockholm Royal Opera); Alexander Mackenzie (London Philharmonic Society); Karl Muck (Berlin Royal Opera).

Others: Theodore Baker (literary editor, G. Schirmer); Joseph Barnby (principal, Guildhall School); Arrigo Boito (Inspector-General, Italian Conservatories); Alfred J. Caldicott (director, London College of Music); Antonin Dvořák (director, National Conservatory, New York); Gabriel Fauré (Inspector of Fine Arts, Paris); Louis Glass (director, Glass Conservatory, Copenhagen).

E. Prizes/Honors

Prizes: Samuel-Alexandre Rousseau (City of Paris).

Honors: Joseph Barnby (knighted); Francisco A. Barbieri (Spanish Royal Academy); William Cusins (knighted); Hans Huber (Dr.Phil., Basel); Vincent d'Indy (Legion of Honor); William Leibl (Berlin Academy); Emile Paladilhe (French Institute); Walter Parratt (knighted); Camille Saint-Saëns (Mus.D., Cambridge).

F. Biographical Highlights

Nicolai Rimsky-Korsakov suffers a nervous breakdown; John Phillip Sousa retires from the Marines to form his own band; Ermanno Wolf-Ferrari transfers to Munich's Akademie der Tonkunst.

G. Cultural Beginnings

Performing Groups—Choral: Association des Chanteurs de St. Gervais; Orpheus Club of Oakland (California); People's Choral Union of New York.

Performing Groups—Instrumental: Barcewicz String Quartet (Warsaw); Bohemian String Quartet (Prague); Lehman String Quartet; Parent String Quartet (Paris); Societatea Simfonică "Buciumul" (Bucharest); Societatea Simfonică "Lyra" (Bucharest); John Phillip Sousa Band; Syracuse (New York) Symphony Orchestra; Utah Symphony Orchestra I; Wellington Orchestra Society (New Zealand).

Festivals: Cardiff Triennial Festival.

Educational: Ithaca Conservatory of Music; Kühner Music School (St. Petersburg).

Music Publishers: Boosey and Co. (Boosey and Hawkes, 1930—New York); Charles K. Harris (New York); Hope Publishing Co. (Chicago); Jakubowski Publishing House (Lvov).

Music Publications: *School Music Review.*

Performing Centers: Fisher Opera House (San Francisco); Joseph Meyerhoff Symphony Hall (Baltimore, Maryland); New York Public Library; Slovene Regional Theater (Ljubljana).

Other: Bibliographical Society of London; Bühnen der Stadt Essen; Circolo Scarlatti (Naples); Manuscript Music Society (Philadelphia); Semaines Saintes de St. Gervais (Paris).

H. Musical Literature

Hugh A. Clarke, *Theory Explained*; W. H. Cummings, *Biographical Dictionary of Musicians*; Oskar Fleischer, *Führer durch die Sammlung alter Musikinstrumente*; François-Auguste Gevaert, *Abrégé du nouveau traité d'instrumentation*; Percy Goetschius, *The Theory and Practice of Tone Relations*; W. H. Hadow, *Studies in Modern Music I*; Eduard Hanslick, *Aus dem Tagebuch eines Musikers*; Ernst Mach, *Beitrag zur geschichte der Musik*; Charles Meerens, *Acoustique musicale*; Moriz Rosenthal/L. Schytte, *Schule des höheren klavierspiel*; John Stainer, *Music in Relation to the Intellect and Emotions*.

I. Musical Compositions
Chamber Music:

String Quartets: Vasili Wrangell, *Quartet.*

Sonata/Solos: Rosetter Gleason Cole, *Violin Sonata in D, Opus 8*; Felix Draeseke, *Viola Sonata No. 1 in c*; Carl Goldmark, *Cello Sonata in F, Opus 39–Suite No. 2 in E♭, Opus 43* (violin, piano); Eduard Nápranik, *Violin Sonata in G, Opus 52*; Sergei Rachmaninoff, *Two Pieces, Opus 2* (cello, piano); Max Reger, *Cello Sonata in f, Opus 5*; Camille Saint-Saëns, *Chant saphique, Opus 91*; Franz Schmidt, *Three kleine phantasiestücke nach ungarischen Nationalmelodien* (cello, piano).

Ensembles: Alexander Glazunov, *Brass Quartet, "In modo religioso," Opus 38–String Quintet in A, Opus 39*; Vitěslav Novák, *Piano Trio in g, Opus 1*; Sergei Rachmaninoff, *Trio élégiaque in g*; Carl Reinecke, *Wind Octet, Opus 216*(?); Camille Saint-Saëns, *Piano Trio No. 2 in e, Opus 92*.

Piano: Amy Beach, *Four Sketches, Opus 15*; Johannes Brahms, *Fantasien, Opus 116–Three Intermezzi (E♭, b♭, c♯), Opus 117–Six Pieces, Opus 118–Four Pieces, Opus 119*; Anatol Lyadov, *Marionettes, Opus 29*; Ethelbert Nevin, *In Arcady, Opus 16–Two Etudes, Opus 18*; Sergei Rachmaninoff, *Five Pieces, Opus 3*; Max Reger, *Twelve Waltz-Caprices for Two Pianos, Opus 9*; Alexander Scriabin, *Sonata No. 1 in f, Opus 6–Sonata No. 2, Opus 19–Two Impromtus, Opus 7*.

Organ: Max Reger, *Three Organ Pieces, Opus 7*.

Choral/Vocal Music:

Choral: Anton Bruckner, *Psalm 150 in C*; Dudley Buck, *The Triumph of David* (cantata); George W. Chadwick, *Ode for the Opening of the Chicago World's Fair*; Gustave Charpentier, *La Vie du Poète* (cantata); Antonin Dvořák, *Te Deum, Opus 103*; Josef B. Foerster, *Stabat Mater, Opus 56*; Heinrich Hofmann, *Prometheus, Opus 110*; John Knowles Paine, *Columbus March and Hymn*; Charles Hubert Parry, *Job* (oratorio); Silas G. Pratt, *The Triumph of Columbus*; Max Reger, *Three Choruses, Opus 6*; Jan Sibelius, *Kullervo, Opus 7* (oratorio).

Vocal: Amy Beach, *Eilende Wolken, Segler die Lüfte* (alto, orchestra); William Kirkpatrick, *Lord, I'm Coming Home* (hymn); Ernest Chausson, *Poème de l'Amour et de la Mer, Opus 19*; Claude Debussy, *Fêtes Galantes, Set I*; Gabriel Fauré, *La Bonne Chanson, Opus 61* (cycle); Ethelbert Nevin, *Three Songs, Opus 17 (The Rosary)*; Horatio Parker, *Two Part-Songs, Opus 27–Six Songs, Opus 29*; Wilhelm Peterson-Berger, *Four Folk Ballads, Opus 5*; Jan Sibelius, *Seven Runeberg Songs, Opus 13*; George W. Warren, *National Hymn (God of Our Fathers)*.

Musical Stage: Granville Bantock, *Caedmar*; George W. Chadwick, *The Quiet Lodging*; Reginald De Koven, *The Fencing Master*; Frederick Delius, *Irmelin*; Umberto Giordano, *Mala Vita*; Ernest Guiraud, *Frédégonde* (completed by Saint-Saëns and Dukas); Hervé, *Bacchanale*; Edgar Stillman Kelley, *Puritania*; Ruggero Leoncavallo, *I Pagliacci*; Hamish MacCunn, *Queen Hynde of Calefon, Opus 13*; Pietro Mascagni, *I Rantzau*; Jules Massenet, *Werther*; Adolph Neuendorff, *The Minstrel*; Sergei Rachmaninoff, *Aleko*.

Orchestra/Band Music:
Concerted Music:
   Other: Louis A. Coerne, *Organ Concerto in E*.
Ballet/Incidental Music: Granville Bantock, *Egypt* (B); Ernest Chausson, *La Légende de Sainte Cécilia* (IM); Edward German, *Henry VIII* (IM); Jules Massenet, *Le carillon* (B); Peter Ilyich Tchaikovsky, *The Nutcracker, Opus 71* (B).
Program Music: Frederick Delius, *Paa Vidderne*; Antonin Dvořák, *Othello, Opus 93*; Alexander Glazounov, *Le Printemps, Opus 34*; Jan Sibelius, *En Saga, Opus 9*; William Wallace, *The Passing of Beatrice*.
Standard Works: Louis A. Coerne, *Suite in d for Strings*; Edward Elgar, *Serenade in e, Opus 20, for String Orchestra*; Zdeněk Fibich, *Festival Overture, Komenský, Opus 34*; Alexander Glazunov, *Carnival Overture in F, Opus 45–Triumphal March in E♭, Opus 46*; Victor Herbert, *Irish Rhapsody*; Charles Ives, *Three Marches for Band*; Vitěslav Nóvak, *Corsaire Overture*; John Knowles Paine, *Columbus March and Hymn*; Carl Reinecke, *Overture, Opus 218*; John Philip Sousa, *On Parade March*; Josef Suk, *Serenade for Strings, Opus 6–Dramatic Overture, Opus 4*.
Symphonies: Carl Nielsen, *No. 1 in g, Opus 7*.

1893

Historical Highlights: Hawaii becomes an independent republic when the first treaty of annexation is withdrawn by the United States; New

Zealand becomes the first country to allow women's suffrage; France takes over the Asian country of Laos as a protectorate; in the United States, a financial panic ushers in a four-year depression; the Cimarron Strip opens in the Oklahoma Territory; Sears, Roebuck and Co. is founded; the Columbian Exposition is held in Chicago.

Art and Literature Highlights: Births—writers Faith Baldwin, J. P. Marquand, Wilfred Owen, artists Milton Avery, George Grosz, Joan Miró; Deaths—writers Lucy Larcom, Guy de Maupassant, artists Karl Bodmer, Robert Cauer. Art—Barnard's *Struggle of the Two Natures in Man,* Munch's *The Scream,* Tanner's *The Banjo Lesson*; Literature—Crane's *Maggie: A Girl of the Streets,* Garland's *Prairie Folks,* Stevenson's *David Balfour.*

Musical Highlights

A. Births

Composers: Jean Absil (Belgium) October 23; Milton Ager (U.S.A.) October 6; Alfred Alessandrescu (Romania) August 14; Arthur Benjamin (Australia-England) September 18; Jean Binet (Switzerland) October 17; Lili Boulanger (France) August 21; Godfried Devreese (Belgium) January 22; Walter Donaldson (U.S.A.) February 15; Alois Hába (Czechoslovakia) June 21; Rued Langgaard (Denmark) July 23; Ernest MacMillan (Canada) August 18; Frederico Mompou (Spain) April 16; Douglas Moore (U.S.A.) August 10; Manuel Palau Boix (Spain) January 4; Evgeni Tikotsky (Russia) December 25; Moses Pergament (Finland-Sweden) September 21; Paul Amadeus Pisk (Austria-U.S.A.) May 16; Bernard Rogers (U.S.A.) February 4.

Conductors: Franz André (Belgium) June 10; Anthony Collins (England) September 3; Alexander Gauk (Russia) August 15; Vladimir Golschman (France-U.S.A.) December 16; Eugene Goosens (England) May 26; Clemens Krauss (Austria) March 31; Fabian Sevitsky (Russia-U.S.A.) September 29; Fritz Zweig (Bohemia-U.S.A.) September 8.

Singers: Toti Dal Monte (Italian soprano) June 27; Astra Desmond (British contralto) April 10; Irene Eden (German soprano); Miguel Fleta (Spanish tenor) December 28; Göta Ljungberg (Swedish soprano) October 4; Edith Mason (American soprano) March 22; Hans Hermann Nissen (German baritone) May 20; Carl Norbert (Czech bass) October 3; Tancredi Pasero (Italian bass) January 11; Nino Piccaluga (Italian tenor); Rosa Raisa (Polish soprano) May 23.

Performers: Jelly d'Aranyi (Hungarian-born violinist) May 30; Emmanuel Durlet (Belgian pianist/composer) October 11; Elliot Griffes (American pianist/composer) January 28; Michel Gusikoff (American violinist) May 15; Páll Ísólfsson (Icelandic organist/composer) October 12; Ilona Kabós (Hungarian pianist) December 7; Isolde

Menges (British violinist) May 16; Andrés Segovia (Spanish guitarist) February 21; Magda Tagliaferro (Brazilian pianist) January 19. **Others:** Willi Apel (German music scholar/encyclopedist) October 10; Friedrich Blume (German musicologist/editor) January 5; Kurt Huber (German musicologist) October 24; Willi Kahl (German musicologist) July 18; Edwin F. Kalmus (Austrian-born publisher) December 15; Josef Rufer (Austrian music scholar) December 18; Hans Schnoor (German music author) October 4.

B. Deaths

Composers: Alfredo Catalani (Italy) August 7; Charles Gounod (France) October 18; Carlo Pedrotti (Italy) October 16; Peter Ilyich Tchaikovsky (Russia) November 6.

Conductors: Franz Erkel (Hungary) June 15; Carl Kossmaly (Germany) December 1.

Singers: Melitta Otto (German soprano) January 13; Hermine Spies (German contralto) February 26; Theodor Wachtel (German tenor) November 14; Henri Warnots (Belgian tenor) February 27.

Performers: Sir William (George) Cusins (British pianist/organist/conductor) August 31; Julius Eichberg (German-born violinist) January 19; Sir George Elvey (British organist) December 9; Joseph Hellmesberger, Sr. (Austrian violinist) October 24; Vincenz Lachner (German organist) January 22; Julius N. Melgunov (Russian pianist) March 31; Karl August Riccius (German violinist/conductor) July 8.

Others: Georges Chanot, Jr. (French violin maker) March 11; John Sullivan Dwight (American music critic/editor) September 5; Antonio Ghislanzoni (Italian music author/editor) July 16; Gustav Schirmer (American publisher) August 5.

C. Debuts

Singers: Lillian Evans Blauvelt (American soprano—Brussels); Otto Briesemeister (German tenor—Dessau); Giuseppe Campanari (Italian baritone—New York); Alexander Davidov (Russian tenor—Tiflis); Ivan Ershov (Russian tenor—St. Petersburg); Vilhelm Herold (Danish tenor—Copenhagen); Louise Kirkby-Lunn (British mezzo-soprano—London); Ernst Kraus (German tenor—Munich); Adrienne Osborne (American-contralto—Leipzig); Lina Pasini (Italian soprano—Milan); Aloys Pennarini (Austrian tenor—Pressburg); Thila Plaichinger (Austrian soprano—Hamburg); Thomas Salignac (French tenor—Paris); Susan Strong (American soprano—London).

Performers: Joseph Achron (Lithuanian-born violinist—Warsaw?); Harold Bauer (British-born pianist—Paris); Ruth Linda Deyo (American pianist—Chicago); Egisto Tango (Italian conductor—Venice).

D. New Positions

Conductors: Dan Godfrey (Bournemouth SO); Raoul Gunsbourg (Monte Carlo Opera); Johan Halvorsen (Bergen PO); Victor Herbert (Twenty Second Regiment Band); Felix Mottl (general music director, Karlsruhe); Arthur Nikisch (Budapest Royal Opera); Emil Paur (Boston SO).

Others: Granville Bantock (editor, *New Quarterly Musical Review*); Nikolai Findeisen (editor, *Russian Musical Gazette*); Charles Ives (organ, St. Thomas Episcopal Church, New Haven, Connecticut); Edgar Stillman Kelley (music critic, *San Francisco Examiner*); Heinrich Reimann (curator, Berlin Royal Library).

E. Prizes/Honors

Prizes: André Bloch (Prix de Rome); Henri Büsser (Prix de Rome); Lodewijk Mortelmans (Prix de Rome).

Honors: Arrigo Boito (D. Mus., Cambridge); Max Bruch (D. Mus., Cambridge); Francesco Cilea (Crown of Italy); Walter Parratt (Master of the Queen's Music).

F. Biographical Highlights

Isaac Albéniz settles permanently in Paris; Antonin Dvořák discovers the Bohemian colony at Spilsville, Iowa; Horatio Parker resigns his posts in New York and moves to Boston; Bruno Walter becomes a coach at the Cologne Opera.

G. Cultural Beginnings

Performing Groups—Choral: Brooklyn Oratorio Society; Royal Flemish Opera Company.

Performing Groups—Instrumental: Bournemouth Symphony Orchestra; Capet String Quartet I (Paris); Kaim Orchestra (Munich); Munich Philharmonic Orchestra; Newark (New Jersey) Symphony Orchestra; Saint Louis Amateur (Philharmonic Society III) Orchestra.

Educational: Royal Manchester College of Music; Schweizerische Musikpädagogische Verband (Zürich); Alberto Williams Conservatory of Music (Argentina).

Music Publishers: Brockhaus Publishing Co. (Leipzig); Karl Gehrman (Sweden); Lengnick Music Publishers (London); B. F. Wood.

Music Publications: *The Etude*; *Gazeta Musicale* (Brazil); *Music Trades*; *The New Quarterly Musical Review* (England); *Russian Musical Gazette*.

Performing Centers: Cape Town Opera House; Colonial Theater (Boston); Empire Theater (New York); Gray's Armory (Cleveland); Queen's Hall (London); Raimundtheater (Vienna).

Other: King Musical Instrument Co. (Cleveland); National Federation of Music Clubs; North Tonawanda Barrel Organ Works (De-

Kleist Musical Instrument Co.); Popular Concerts (St. Petersburg); Sociedad de Autores, Compositores y Editores de Música (Madrid); Stein Organ Works (New York); Tamburini Organ Co. (Crema).

H. Musical Literature

Enrico Bossi/Giovanni Tebaldini, *Metodo di studio per l'organo moderno*; Henri de Curzon, *Musiciens du temps passé*; Edward Dannreuther, *Musical Ornamentation I*; Heinrich Ehrlich, *Celebrated Pianists, Past and Present*; Niels Gade, *Aufzeichnen und Briefe* (posthumous publication); Friedrich von Hausegger, *Vom jenseits des Kunstlers*; C. Hubert Parry, *The Art of Music–Summary of the History and Development of Mediaeval and Modern European Music*; Ebenezer Prout, *Musical Form*; Hugo Riemann, *Vereinfachte harmonielehre*; Richard Wallaschek, *Primitive Music*; C. Willerby, *Masters of English Music*.

I. Musical Compositions
Chamber Music:

String Quartets: Louis A. Coerne, *Quartet in c, Opus 19*; Claude Debussy, *Quartet in g, Opus 10*; Frederick Delius, *No. 2*; Antonin Dvořák, *No. 12 in F, Opus 96*; Josef B. Foerster, *No. 2 in D, Opus 39*; Arthur Foote, *No. 2 in E, Opus 32*; Guy Ropartz, *No. 1*.

Sonata/Solos: César Cui, *Kaleidoscope, Opus 50* (violin, piano); Antonin Dvořák, *Violin Sonatina in G, Opus 100*; Alexander Glazunov, *Elegy in g, Opus 44* (viola, piano); Victor Herbert, *Mélodie* (cello, piano); Sergei Rachmaninoff, *Two Pieces, Opus 6* (violin, piano); Camille Saint-Saëns, *Fantasy, Opus 95* (harp); Charles V. Stanford, *Cello Sonata No. 2, Opus 93*; Charles Tournemire, *Violin Sonata, Opus 1*.

Ensembles: Antonin Dvořák, *String Quintet in E♭, Opus 97*; Zdeněk Fibich, *Piano Quintet in D, Opus 42*; Horatio Parker, *Suite, Opus 35* (piano trio); Josef Suk, *Piano Quintet*.

Piano: Alexander Glazunov, *Valse de Concert, Opus 41–Three Miniatures, Opus 42*; Edvard Grieg, *Lyric pieces, Book VI, Opus 57*; Anatol Liadov, *Two Pieces (G, b♭), Opus 31–A Musical Snuffbox, Opus 32*; Edward MacDowell, *Piano Sonata No. 1, "Tragica"*; Albéric Magnard, *Promenades, Opus 7*; Vitěslav Nóvak, *Variations on a Theme by Schumann–Balata in e, Opus 2*; Ignace Jan Paderewski, *Fantasie Polonaise, Opus 19*; Sergei Rachmininoff, *Suite No. 1 for Two Pianos, Opus 5*; Max Reger, *Twenty German Dances for Two Pianos, Opus 10–Seven Waltzes, Opus 11*; Jan Sibelius, *Six Impromtus, Opus 5–Sonata in F, Opus 12*; Josef Suk, *Six Pieces, Opus 7*.

Organ: Vincent d'Indy, *Prélude et petit canon, Opus 88*; Horatio Parker, *Five Sketches for Organ, Opus 32–Four Pieces, Opus 36*.

Choral/Vocal Music:
   Choral: Anton Bruckner, *Helgoland*; George W. Chadwick, *The Lily Nymph* (cantata); Antonin Dvořák, *The American Flag, Opus 102*; Edward Elgar, *The Black Knight, Opus 25* (cantata); Arthur Foote, *The Skeleton in Armor, Opus 28*; Alexander Glazunov, *Triumphal March for the Chicago Columbian Exposition*; Charles Gounod, *Requiem*; Heinrich Hofmann, *Waldfräulein, Opus 111*; Luigi Mancinelli, *Salve Regina*; Horatio Parker, *Hora Novissima, Opus 30* (oratorio)–*Three Male Choruses, Opus 33*–*The Holy Child, Opus 37* (cantata)–*Four Male Choruses, Opus 39*; Harry R. Shelley, *Vexilla regis* (cantata).
   Vocal: Amy Beach, *Six Songs, Opus 19 and 21*; César Cui, *Five Songs "Der maner Franz Schuberts"*; Zdeněk Fibich, *Frühlingsstrahlen, Opus 36*; Robert Fuchs, *Die Teufelsglacke*; Edward MacDowell, *Eight Songs, Opus 47*; Horatio Parker, *Three Songs, Opus 34*–*Cáhal Mór of the Wine-Red Hand, Opus 40*; Wilhelm Peterson-Berger, *Jämtland Memories, Opus 4*; Sergei Rachmaninoff, *Six Songs, Opus 4*–*Six Songs, Opus 8*; Christian Sinding, *Madmen's Songs*.
   Musical Stage: Reginald De Koven, *The Knickerbockers*–*The Algerian*; Julian Edwards, *King René's Daughter*; Gilbert/Sullivan, *Utopia Unlimited*; Engelbert Humperdinck, *Hansel und Gretel*; Paul Ladmirault, *Gilles de Retz*; André Messager, *Madame Chrysanthème*–*Miss Dollar*; Ole Olsen, *Lajta*; Giacomo Puccini, *Manon Lescaut*; Anton Rubinstein, *Christus, Opus 117*; Wilhelm Stenhammar, *Gildet på Solhaug*; Giuseppe Verdi, *Falstaff*; George E. Whiting, *Lenora*.
Orchestra/Band Music:
   Concerted Music:
      Piano: Eugen d'Albert, *Concerto No. 2 in E♭*; Ignace Jan Paderewski, *Polish Fantasy, Opus 19*; Wilhelm Stenhammar, *Concerto No. 1 in b♭*; Peter Ilyich Tchaikovsky, *Concerto No. 3 in E♭, Opus 75*; José Vianna de Motta, *Fantasia dramatica*; Vasili Wrangell, *Fantasy*.
      Other: Léon Böellmann, *Variations symphoniques, Opus 23* (cello); Antonin Dvořák, *Rondo in g, Opus 94* (cello); Arthur Foote, *Cello Concerto, Opus 33*; Charles Martin Loeffler, *Morceau fantastique* (cello); Josef Rheinberger, *Organ Concerto No. 2*.
   Ballet/Incidental Music: Gabriel Fauré, *Le Bourgeois Gentilhomme* (IM); Zdeněk Fibich, *At Twilight, Opus 39*; André Messager, *Amants éternels* (B); C. Hubert Parry, *Hypatia* (IM); Jan Sibelius, *Karelia, Opus 11* (IM).
   Program Music: Louis A. Coerne, *Hiawatha*; Sergei Rachmaninoff, *The Rock, Opus 7*; Jan Sibelius, *The Swan of Tuonela, Opus 22*.
   Standard Works: Amy Beach, *Bal masqué*; Alexander Glazunov, *Chopiniana, Opus 44*–*Concert Waltz No. 1 in D, Opus 47*; Karl Goldmark, *Sappho Overture, Opus 44*; Victor Herbert, *The Vision of*

Columbus; Margaret R. Lang, *Dramatic Overture, Opus 12–Witichis Overture*; C. Hubert Parry, *Overture to an Unwritten Tragedy*; Harry R. Shelley, *Carnival Overture*; John Philip Sousa, *Liberty Bell March–Manhattan Beach March*.

Symphonies: Elfrieda Andrée, *No. 2 in e*; George Bristow, *No. 5, "Niagara," Opus 62*; Antonin Dvořák, *No. 9 in e, "From the New World"*; Zdeněk Fibich, *No. 2 in E♭, Opus 38*; Josef Bohuslav Foerster, *No. 2 in F, Opus 29*; Edward German, *No. 2 in a, "Norwich."*; Albéric Magnard, *No. 2 in E, Opus 6*; Henri Rabaud, *No. 1 in d, Opus 1*; Henry Schoenefeld, *No. 1, "Rural"*; Peter Ilyich Tchaikovsky, *No. 6 in b, "Pathétique," Opus 74*.

1894

❊

Historical Highlights: The Sino-Japanese War begins; the Dreyfus Affair begins in France with the conviction of Captain Alfred Dreyfus of treason; the Turks begin the eradication of the Armenians; in the United States, Jacob Coxey leads an "army" of unemployed in a march on Washington, D.C.; a bitter Pullman Strike spreads throughout the nation; Labor Day is made an official government holiday; a graduated income tax law is passed by Congress.

Art and Literature Highlights: Births—authors e. e. cummings, Aldous Huxley, J. B. Priestley, James Thurber, artists Wäinö Aaltonen, Stuart Davis; Deaths—writers Oliver Wendell Holmes, Christina Rossetti, Robert Louis Stevenson, artists George Inness, Launt Thompson. Art—Fraser's *End of the Trail*, Monet's *Rouen Cathedral, Early Morning*; Literature—Hawkins' *Prisoner of Zenda*, Kipling's *Jungle Book*, Maurier's *Trilby*.

Musical Highlights

A. Births
Composers: Mihail G. Andricu (Romania) December 22; Aaron Avshalomov (Russia-U.S.A.) November 11; Krešimir Baranović (Croatia) July 25; Robert Russell Bennett (U.S.A.) June 15; Pavel Bořkovec (Czechoslovakia) June 10; Ricardo Castillo (Guatemala) October 1; Paul Dessau (Germany) December 19; Ludvig Irgens-Jenson (Norway) April 13; Ernest Kanitz (Austria-U.S.A.) April 9; Wesley La Violette (U.S.A.) January 4; E. J. Moeran (England) December 31; Willem Pijper (Holland) September 8; Walter Piston (U.S.A.) January 20; Bernard Wagenaar (Holland-U.S.A.) July 25; Peter Warlock (Philip Heseltine) (England) October 30; Marc Wessel (U.S.A.) March 26; Eugene Zador (Hungary-U.S.A.) November 5.

Conductors: Frank Black (U.S.A.) November 28; Karl Böhm (Austria) August 28; Heinz Bongartz (Germany) July 31; Arthur Fiedler (U.S.A.) December 17; Guy Fraser Harrison (England-U.S.A.) November 6; Reginald Jacques (England) January 13; Karl Krueger (U.S.A.) January 19.

Singers: Gertrud Bindernagel (German soprano) January 4; Maria Carena (Italian soprano); Maria Hussa (Austrian soprano) December 7; Giovanni Inghilleri (Italian baritone) March 9; Nina Koshetz (Russian soprano) December 30; Rosa Pauly (Hungarian soprano) May 15; Laura Pasini (Italian soprano) January 28; André Pernet (French bass) January 6; Heinrich Rehkemper (German bass-baritone) May 23; Elizabeth Rethburg (German soprano) September 22; Bianca Scacciati (Italian soprano) July 3; Christy Solari (Turkish-born tenor); Viorica Ursuleae (Romanian soprano) March 26; Fritz Wolff (German tenor) October 28.

Performers: Mildred Dilling (American harpist) February 23; Arthur Loesser (American pianist) August 26; André Marchal (French organist) February 6; Albert Frederic Stoessel (American violinist/conductor/composer) October 11.

Others: Gustav Becking (German musicologist) March 4; Nicholas Bessaraboff (Russian music author) February 12; Hans Engel (German musicologist) December 20; Jacob Kwalwasser (American music psychologist) February 2; Roland Tenschert (Austrian musicologist) April 5.

B. **Deaths**

Composers: Pascual Juan Arrieta y Corera (Spain) February 11; Francisco Asenjo Barbieri (Spain) February 19; Emmanuel Chabrier (France) September 13; Alphons Czibulka (Hungary) October 27; Vladimir Kashperov (Russia) July 8; Guillaume Lekeu (Belgium) January 21; Anton Rubinstein (Russia) November 20.

Conductors: Hans von Bülow (Germany) February 12.

Singers: Marietta Alboni (Italian contralto) June 23; Filippo Coletti (Italian baritone) June 13; Thomas Aynsley Cook (British bass) February 16; August Gottfried Fricke (German bass) June 27; Emma Fürsch-Madi (French soprano) September 19; Julia Gaylord (American soprano); Eugène Oudin (American baritone) November 4; Janet Patey (Scottish contralto) February 28; Johanna Wagner (German soprano) October 16.

Performers: Immanuel Faisst (German organist) June 5; Jacob Rosenhain (German pianist) March 21; Ernesto Camillo Sivori (Italian violinist/composer) February 19.

Others: Hermann von Helmholtz (German acoustician) September 8; Adolphe Sax (Belgian instrumental inventor) February 4; Julius

Philipp Spitta (German music scholar) April 12; George Stevens (American organ builder) August 15.

C. Debuts

Singers: Lina Abarbanell (German soprano—Berlin); Enrico Caruso (Italian tenor—Naples); Feodor Chaliapin (Russian bass—St. Petersburg); John Coates (British tenor—London); Adamo Didur (Polish bass—Milan); Katharina Fleischer-Edel (German soprano—Dresden); Theodor Lierhammer (Austrian baritone—Vienna); Max Lohfing (German bass—Metz); Vanni Marcoux (French bass-baritone—Turin); Angelica Pandolfini (Italian soprano—Modena); Halfdan Rode (Norwegian baritone—London); Jacques Urlus (Dutch tenor—Amsterdam); Edyth Walker (American mezzo-soprano—Berlin); Erika Wedekind (German soprano—Dresden).

Performers: Edouard Risler (German pianist—Paris); Ottilie and Rose Sutro (American duo-pianists—London).

D. New Positions

Conductors: José Eibenschütz (Abo Symphony, Finland); Sam Franko (American SO); Don Lorenzo Perosi (maestro di cappella, San Marco, Venice); Richard Strauss (assistant conductor, Munich Opera and conductor, Berlin PO).

Others: Johann Fuchs (director, Vienna Conservatory); Gustav Hollaender (director, Stern Conservatory); Korbay Edmundo Pallemaerts (director, Conservatorio Argentino); Horatio Parker (head, Yale University Music Department); C. Hubert Parry (director, Royal College, London); Guy Ropartz (director, Nancy Conservatory); John F. Runciman (music critic, *Saturday Review*); Luigi Torchi (editor, *Rivista Musicale Italiana*).

E. Prizes/Honors

Prizes: Ossip Gabrilowitsch (Rubinstein Prize); Henri Rabaud (Prix de Rome); Carl Thiel (Mendelssohn).

Honors: Théodore Dubois (French Academy); Edvard Grieg (Mus. Doc., Cambridge); Walter Parratt (D. Mus., Oxford); Felipe Pedrell (Royal Academy, Madrid).

F. Biographical Highlights

Anton Bruckner, because of his poor health, retires from public life; Rubin Goldmark, for health reasons, leaves New York for Colorado; Albert Roussel resigns his navy commission to devote full time to music; Ralph Vaughan-Williams receives his B.M. degree from Trinity College; Bruno Walter begins working as an assistant to Mahler in Hamburg.

G. Cultural Beginnings

Performing Groups—Choral: Apollo Club of St. Louis; Damrosch Opera Co.; Goosens Male-Voice Choir (Liverpool); Ladies Choral Union of Budapest; Musical Art Society of New York; Schola Cantorum of Paris; Toronto Mendelssohn Choir.

Performing Groups—Instrumental: American Symphony Orchestra; Cincinnati Orchestra Association; Czech Philharmonic Orchestra; Czech Society of Chamber Music; Fitzner String Quartet (Austria); New Haven (Connecticut) Symphony Orchestra; Maud Powell String Quartet; Societana Filarmonică Română (II).

Festivals: Ann Arbor May Festival.

Educational: Conservatorio Santa Cecilia (Buenos Aires); Dominion College of Music (Montreal); Heidelberg Conservatory of Music; Lawrence College Conservatory of Music (Wisconsin); Yale Universtiy School of Music.

Music Publishers: Joseph Stern and Co. (Edward B. Marks Music Co., 1923).

Music Publications: *The Billboard*; *The Cadenza*; *The Organist and Choirmaster*; *Revista Musicale Italiana*; *Weekblad voor Musiek* (Holland).

Performing Centers: Abbey Theatre (Ireland); Kansas City Athenaeum; Lyric Theater (Baltimore); Massey Hall (Toronto).

Other: British Chamber Music Concerts; Foster-Armstrong Piano Co. (Rochester, New York); Hope-Jones Organ Co. (Birkenhead); Nicodé Concerts (Dresden); Philharmonische Populäre Künstlerkonzerte (Dresden); Peter's Music Library (Leipzig).

H. Musical Literature

Georgi Conus, *Manual of Harmony*; Henry Expert, *Les Maîtres-Musiciens de la Renaissance française I*; J. A. Fuller-Maitland, *Masters of German Music*; Eduard Hanslick, *Aus meinem Leben*; Henry Hiles, *Harmony, Chordal or Contrapuntal*; Cyrill Kistler, *Über originalität in Tonkunst*; Stewart Macpherson, *Practical Harmony*; Charles Meerens, *L'avenir de la science musicale*; Camille Saint-Saëns, *Problèmes et mystères*; Giovanni Tebaldini/Enrico Bossi, *La musica sacra in Italia*.

I. Musical Compositions

Chamber Music:

String Quartets: Alexander Glazunov, *No. 4 in a, Opus 64*; Joseph Jongen, *No. 1, Opus 3*; Louis Vierne, *Quartet*.

Sonata/Solos: Johannes Brahms, *Two Clarinet (Viola) Sonatas (f, E♭), Opus 120*; Horatio Parker, *Suite in e, Opus 41* (violin, piano); Joseph Rheinberger, *Horn Sonata, Opus 178*.

Ensembles: Josef B. Foerster, *Piano Trio No. 2 in B, Opus 38*; Albéric Magnard, *Quintet in d, Opus 8 for Piano and Woodwinds*; Vitěslav

Novák, *Piano Quartet in c, Opus 7*; Horatio Parker, *String Quintet in d, Opus 38*; Ermanno Wolf-Ferrari, *String Trio in b*.

Piano: Amy Beach, *Three Morceaux caractéristiques, Opus 28*; George F. Bristow, *Plantation Pleasures, Opus 82*; Antonin Dvořák, *American Suite in A, Opus 98–Eight Humoresques, Opus 101*; Alexander Glazunov, *Three Morceaux, Opus 49*; Anatol Liadov, *Variations on a Theme by Glinka, Opus 35*; Edward MacDowell, *Twelve Virtuoso Etudes, Opus 46*; Carl Nielsen, *Symphonic Suite, Opus 8*; Vitěslav Novák, *Reminiscences, Opus 6*; Sergei Rachmaninoff, *Seven Concert Pieces, Opus 10–Six Duets, Opus 11*; Alexander Scriabin, *Twelve Etudes, Opus 8–Two Pieces for Left Hand, Opus 9–Two Impromtus, Opus 10*.

Organ: Carl Nielsen, *Symphonic Suite, Opus 8*; Joseph-Guy Ropartz, *Trois pièces*; Camille Saint-Saëns, *Three Preludes and Fugues, Opus 99*.

Choral/Vocal Music:

Choral: Heinrich Hofmann, *Nordische Meerfahrt, Opus 113*; Henry H. Huss, *Cleopatra's Death*; Charles Ives, *Psalm 150–Psalm 67–Psalm 54–Psalm 40*; Alexander Mackenzie, *Bethlehem, Opus 49* (oratorio); J. C. D. Parker, *The Life of Man* (oratorio); C. Hubert Parry, *King Saul, Opus 6* (oratorio)(?); Silas G. Pratt, *America* (cantata); Henri Rabaud, *Daphne* (cantata); George F. Root, *Plough and Sickle* (cantata); Charles Tournemire, *Andantino, Opus 2–Sontie, Opus 3*.

Vocal: Antonin Dvořák, *Ten Biblical Songs, Opus 99*; Edvard Grieg, *Norway, Opus 58* (cycle); Franz Lehar, *Karst-Lieder*; Alexander Mackenzie, *Three Shakespeare Sonnets, Opus 50–Three Songs, Opus 54*; Carl Nielsen, *Six Songs, Opus 1*; Ignace Jan Paderewski, *Six Songs, Opus 18*; Horatio Parker, *Two Shakespeare Songs*; Max Reger, *Ten Songs, Opus 15*.

Musical Stage: Granville Bantock, *The Pearl of Iran*; George W. Chadwick, *Tabasco*; Reginald De Koven, *Rob Roy*; Julian Edwards, *Madeleine*; Zdeněk Fibich, *The Tempest, Opus 40*; Victor Herbert, *Prince Ananias*; Jules Massenet, *Thaïs–Le portrait de Manon*; Hamish MacCunn, *Jeanie Deans*; André Messager, *Mirette*; Emil von Reznicek, *Donna Diana*; Arthur Sullivan, *The Chieftain*.

Orchestra/Band Music:

Concerted Music:

Piano: Helen Hopekirk, *Concertstück in d*; Henry H. Huss, *Concerto in B, Opus 10*; Charles V. Stanford, *Concerto No. 1 in G, Opus 59*.

Violin: Charles Martin Loeffler, *Divertimento in a, Opus 1*.

Other: Victor Herbert, *Cello Concerto No. 2, Opus 30*; Josef Rheinberger, *Organ Concerto No. 2 in g, Opus 177*.

Ballet: Claude Debussy, *Prélude à l'après-midi d'un faun* (B).

Program Music: Arthur Farwell, *The Death of Virginia, Opus 4*; Alexander Glazunov, *From Darkness to Light, Opus 53*; Henry Hadley, *Overture, Hector and Andromache*; Florent Schmitt, *En été, Opus 10.*
Standard Works: George W. Chadwick, *A Pastoral Prelude*; Alexander Glazunov, *Cortège solennel in D, Opus 50–Concert Waltz No. 2 in F, Opus 51–Scenes de Ballet, Opus 52*; Carl Goldmark, *Scherzo No. 2 in A, Opus 45*; Charles Ives, *Circus Band March*; Edgar Stillman Kelley, *Aladdin Suite Opus 10*; Alexander Mackenzie, *Britannia Overture, Opus 52*; C. Hubert Parry, *Lady Radnor's Suite* (strings); Sergei Rachmaninoff, *Caprice bohémien, Opus 12*; Anton Rubinstein, *Suite in E♭, Opus 119*; Jan Sibelius, *Spring Song, Opus 16*; Josef Suk, *A Winter's Tale, Opus 9.*
Symphonies: Amy Beach, *Symphony in e, "Gaelic"*; Léon Böellmann, *Symphony, Opus 24*(?); Anton Bruckner, *No. 9 in d*; George W. Chadwick, *No. 3 in F*; Alexander Glazunov, *No. 4 in E♭, Opus 48*; Alexander Gretchaninov, *No. 1*; Gustav Mahler, *No. 2 in c, "Resurrection"*; Luigi Mancinelli, *Symphony* (unfinished); Guy Ropartz, *No. 1*; Charles V. Stanford, *No. 5 in D, Opus 56*; Vasili Wrangell, *Symphony in D.*

1895

❄

Historical Highlights: The Sino-Japanese War comes to an end as the Japanese defeat China; Guglielmo Marconi sends the first telegraph message on a one-mile long wire; the Lumiere Brothers, in Paris, present the first moving pictures; W. K. Roentgen discovers X-rays; the Monroe Doctrine is given its first big test by the Venezuela-British dispute; the first auto race takes place between Chicago and Waukegan, Illinois—average speed of 7½ mph.
Art and Literature Highlights: Births—authors Paul Éluard, Robert Graves, László Moholy-Nagy, novelist Liam O'Flaherty; Deaths—writers Alexander Dumas, *fils*, Thomas Huxley, artists Thomas Hovenden, Silvestro Lega. Art—Degas' *Dancer Looking at Her Foot*, Munch's *The Scream*, Remington's *Bronco Buster*; Literature—Crane's *Red Badge of Courage*, Sienkiewicz's *Quo Vadis?*, Wilde's *The Importance of Being Ernest.*

Musical Highlights

A. Births
Composers: August Baeyens (Belgium) June 5; Henriëtta Bosmans (Holland) December 5; Bjarne Brustad (Norway) March 4; Mario Castelnuovo-Tedesco (Italy-U.S.A.) April 3; Juan José Castro (Argentina) March 7; Ernest Charles (U.S.A.) November 21; Viking Dahl

(Sweden) October 8; Johann N. David (Austria) November 30; Granville English (U.S.A.) January 27; Paul Hindemith (Germany) November 16; Gordon Jacob (England) July 5; Alexander László (Hungary) November 20; Albert Hay Malotte (U.S.A.) May 19; Shukichi Mitsukuri (Japan) October 21; Carl Orff (Germany) July 10; Slavko Osterc (Slovenia) June 17; Karol Rathaus (Poland-U.S.A.) September 16; Dane Rudhyar (France-U.S.A.) March 23; William Grant Still (U.S.A.) May 11; Ivo Tijardović (Croatia) September 18.

Conductors: Malcolm Sargent (England) April 29; Moshe Paranov (U.S.A.) October 28; Hans Rosbaud (Austria) July 22; Joseph Rosenstock (Poland-U.S.A.) January 27; Nathaniel Shilkret (U.S.A.) January 1; Heinz Unger (Germany-Canada) December 14.

Singers: Dame Isobel Baillie (Scottish soprano) March 9; Kirsten Flagstad (Norwegian soprano) July 12; Karl Hartmann (German tenor) May 2; Fritzi Jokl (Austrian soprano) March 23; René Maison (Belgian tenor) November 24; Ella Némethy (Hungarian mezzo-soprano) April 5; Ettore Parmeggiani (Italian tenor) August 15; Hans Reinmar (Austrian baritone) April 11; Meta Seinemeyer (German soprano) September 5; Grete Stückgold (German soprano) June 6; Conchita Supervia (Spanish mezzo-soprano) December 9.

Performers: Zlatko Baloković (Croatian violinist) March 21; Eddy Brown (American violinist) July 15; Walter Gieseking (German pianist) November 5; Clara Haskil (Romanian-born pianist) January 7; José Iturbi (Spanish-born pianist/conductor) November 28; Wilhelm Kempff (German pianist) November 25; William Kincaid (American flutist) April 26; Wiktor Labunski (Russian pianist) April 14; Carl McKinley (American organist/composer) October 9; Mischa Mischakoff (Russian-born violinist) April 3; Guiomar Novães (Brazilian pianist) February 28; Moshe Paranov (American pianist/conductor) October 28; Mark Reyzen (Russian bass) July 3; Leo Sowerby (American organist/composer) May 1; Eduardo Toldrá (Spanish violinist/composer) April 7; Victor Trambitsky (Russian pianist/conductor) February 12.

Others: Martha Baird (American patron of the arts/pianist); Cecil Gray (Scottish music author) May 19; Laurens Hammond (American electric organ maker) January 11; Joseph Müller-Blattau (German musicologist) May 21; Fernando Sacconi (Italian-born violin maker) May 30; André Schaeffner (French musicologist) February 7; Joseph Schillinger (Russian-born music theorist/composer) August 31; Shōichi Tsuji (Japanese musicologist) December 20.

B. Deaths

Composers: Samuel David (France) October 3; Benjamin Godard (France) January 10; Harrison Millard (U.S.A.) September 10; George

Frederick Root (U.S.A.) August 6; Joseph P. Skelley (Ireland-U.S.A.) June 23; Franz von Suppé (Austria) May 21.

Conductors: Richard Genée (Germany) June 15; Charles Hallé (England) October 25; Ignaz Lachner (Germany) February 24; Friedrich Lux (Germany) July 9; Julius Tausch (Germany) November 11.

Singers: Teresa Brambilla (Italian soprano) July 15; Caroline Carvalho (French soprano) July 10; Stanislaw Niedzielski (Polish baritone) March 4; Louis-Henri Obin (French bass) November 11; Ferdinand Sieber (Austrian baritone) February 19.

Performers: John Carrodus (British violinist/conductor) July 12; Henry Lazarus (British clarinetist) May 6; William Rockstro (British pianist) July 2; Elizabeth Sterling (British organist) March 25; Paul White (American violinist/composer) August 22.

Others: Gustave-Alexandre Flaxland (French publisher) November 11; August Gemünder (German-born violin maker) September 7; Elias Howe (American publisher) July 6; Thomas D. Paine (American instrument maker/inventor) June 1; Edmond Van der Straeten (Belgian music historian) November 26.

C. Debuts

Singers: Suzanne Adams (American soprano—Paris); Giuseppe Agostini (Italian tenor—Nuovi Ligure); Lloyd d'Aubigné (American tenor—New York); Perry Averill (American baritone—Boston); Ernesto Badini (Italian baritone—Milan); Clotilde Bressler-Gianoli (Italian contralto—Geneva); Riza Eibenschütz (Hungarian contralto—Leipzig); Fritz Feinhals (German baritone—Essen); Otto Goritz (German baritone—Neustrelitz); Selma Kurz (Austrian soprano—Hamburg); Blanche Marchesi (French soprano—Berlin); Anna Mildenburg (Austrian soprano—Hamburg); Agnes Nicholls (British soprano—Manchester); Denis O'Sullivan (American baritone—London); Hermann Schramm (German tenor—Breslau); Joseph Sheehan (American tenor—Boston).

Performers: Carl Flesch (Hungarian violinist—Vienna); Frank Merrick (British pianist—Bristol); Emilio Pente (Italian violinist—Florence).

D. New Positions

Conductors: Anton Arensky (Imperial Chapel Choir, St. Petersburg); Johann H. Beck (Detroit SO); Alfred Hertz (Barmen-Elberfeld Opera); Willem Kes (Scottish SO, Glasgow); Ernst Kunwald (Rockstock Opera); Benjamin Lang (Boston Handel and Haydn Society); Willem Mengelberg (Amsterdam Concertgebouw Orchestra); Arthur Nikisch (Leipzig Gewandhaus Orchestra); Fritz Scheel (San Francisco SO); Frank Van der Stucken (Cincinnati SO); Arturo Toscanini (Turin Opera).

Others: Leopold Godowsky (piano director, Chicago Conservatory); Henry Hadley (director, St. Paul's School, Garden City); Daniel de Lange (director, Amsterdam Conservatory); Peter Lutkin (Dean of Music, Northwestern University); Pietro Mascagni (director, Rossini Conservatory).

E. Prizes/Honors

Prizes: Omer Letorey (Prix de Rome); Martin Lunssens (Prix de Rome); Josef Lhevinne (Rubinstein).

Honors: Arrigo Boito (Legion of Honor); Edward German (Royal Academy, London); Alexander C. Mackenzie (knighted); Ebenezer Prout (Mus.Doc, Dublin, Edinburgh).

F. Biographical Highlights

Edward Hanslick retires from active music life; Sergei Rachmaninoff tours Russia with violinist Teresina Tua; Maurice Ravel leaves Paris Conservatory for a two-year study break; Frederick Stock moves to the United States and begins playing in Theodore Thomas' orchestra.

G. Cultural Beginnings

Performing Groups—Choral: Henry Savage Grand Opera Co. (Boston).

Performing Groups—Instrumental: Bournemouth Symphony Orchestra; Bruges Concert Society; Cincinnati Symphony Orchestra Association; Pittsburgh Symphony Orchestra; San Francisco Symphony Orchestra.

Festivals: Sheffield Music Festival.

Educational: American School of Classical Studies (Rome); Bendix Music Conservatory (San Francisco); Melbourne Memorial Conservatorium (Australia); Metropolitan School of Music.

Music Publishers: Bobbs-Merrill Co.; Leo Feist; Hall, Mack Co. (Philadelphia); Music Publisher's Association of the United States; Shapiro, Bernstein and Co. (New York).

Music Publications: *The Baton: A Monthly Journal Devoted to Western Music Matters; Musical Canada; The Musical Leader and Concertgoer; Le Passe-temps* (Canada).

Performing Centers: Beethoven Concert Hall (San Antonio, Texas); Belfast Grand Opera House; Carnegie Music Hall (Pittsburgh); Zagreb Opera House.

Other: Murray M. Harris Organ Factory (Los Angeles); Museo Naciónal de Bellas Artes (Buenos Aires); Promenade Concerts (New York); Queen's Hall Promenade Concerts (London); Société des Instruments Anciens (Paris); Société Moderne d'Instruments à Vent (Paris); M. H. de Young Memorial Museum (San Francisco).

H. Musical Literature

Theobold Baker, *Dictionary of Musical Terms*; Henry Davey, *History of English Music*; W. H. Flood, *History of Irish Music*; George Gow, *The Structure of Music*; Louis Lacombe, *Philosophie et Musique*; Albert Lavignac, *La Musique et les musiciens*; Ernst Pauer, *A Dictionary of Pianists and Composers for the Pianoforte, with an Appendix of Manufacturers of the Instrument*; Ebenezer Prout, *Applied Forms*; Hugo Riemann, *Präludien und Studien: gesammelte aufsätz zur ästhetik, theorie und geschichte der musik*; Felix Weingartner, *Über das Dirigieren*.

I. Musical Compositions

Chamber Music:

String Quartets: Teresa Carreño, *Quartet*; Antonin Dvořák, *No. 13 in G, Opus 106–No. 14 in A♭, Opus 105*; Henry Eichheim, *Quartet*; Robert Fuchs, *Quartet in E, Opus 58*; Charles Gounod, *No. 3 in a*; John Ireland, *No. 1 in d*; Alexander Zemlinsky, *No. 1(?)*.

Sonata/Solos: Henry Eichheim, *Violin Sonata No. 1*; Alexander Mackenzie, *From the North, Opus 53* (violin, piano); Carl Nielsen, *Violin Sonata No. 2 in A, Opus 9*; C. Hubert Parry, *Twelve Short Pieces* (violin, piano); Charles Tournemire, *Cello Sonata, Opus 5*.

Ensembles: Léon Böellmann, *Piano Trio, Opus 19(?)*; Ernst von Dohnányi, *Piano Quintet in C, Opus 1*; Georges Enescu, *Piano Quintet No. 1*; Gabriel Fauré, *Piano Quintet No. 1, Opus 59*; Carl Reinecke, *Piano Trio No. 2 in c, Opus 230(?)*.

Piano: George F. Bristow, *Plantation Memories I, II*; Gabriel Fauré, *Theme and Variations, Opus 73*; Alexander Glazunov, *Two Impromptus, Opus 54*; Edvard Grieg, *Lyric Pieces, Book VII, Opus 62*; Victor Herbert, *The Belle of Pittsburgh*; Anatol Liadov, *Variations on a Theme in B♭ by Glinka, Opus 35–Three Preludes (F♯, b♭, G), Opus 36*; Sergei Liapunov, *Three Preludes (F♯, b♭, G), Opus 6*; Edward MacDowell, *Piano Sonata No. 2 in g, "Eroica," Opus 50*; Daniel Gregory Mason, *Sonata*; Alexander Scriabin, *Two Impromtus, Opus 12–Six Preludes, Opus 13–Two Impromtus, Opus 13–Five Preludes, Opus 15*; Clara Kathleen Rogers, *Scherzo in D, Opus 32*.

Organ: Léon Boëllmann, *Suite Gothique, Opus 25–Ten Improvisations, Opus 28(?)*; Edward Elgar, *Sonata in G, Opus 28*; Max Reger, *Suite "Den Manen J. S. Bachs," Opus 16*; Camille Saint-Saëns, *Fantaisie in D♭, Opus 101*; Charles Tournemire, *Offertoire, Opus 10*; Charles Widor, *Symphonie Gothique, Opus 70*.

Choral/Vocal Music:

Choral: Max Bruch, *Moses* (oratorio); Dudley Buck, *The Coming of the King* (cantata); César Cui, *Six Choruses, Opus 53*; Charles Gounod, *Messe dite de Clovis in C–Requiem in C–Coronation Cantata*; Heinrich von Herzogenberg, *Mass in e, Opus 87*; Horatio Parker,

Ode for Commencement Day at Yale; C. Hubert Parry, *Invocation to Music, Opus 42*; Henri Rabaud, *L'été*; Harry R. Shelley, *The Inheritance Divine* (cantata); Charles S. Skilton, *Lenore* (cantata after Poe).
Vocal: Amy Beach, *Four Songs, Opus 49*; Frederick Delius, *Two Songs of Verlaine*; Robert Fuchs, *Seven Songs, Opus 82*(?); Edvard Grieg, *Haugtussa Songs, Opus 67*; Wilhelm Peterson-Berger, *Two Oriental Songs, Opus 8–Three Songs, Opus 10*.
Musical Stage: Tomas Bretón, *La Dolores*; Reginald De Koven, *The Tzigane*; Frederick Delius, *The Magic Fountain*; Zdeněk Fibich, *Hedy, Opus 43*; Victor Herbert, *The Wizard of the Nile*; Vincent d'Indy, *Fervaal*; Pietro Mascagni, *Silvano*; Jules Massenet, *Amadis*; Edvard Nápravnik, *Dubrovsky, Opus 58*; Hans Pfitzner, *Der Arme Heinrich*; Nicolai Rimsky-Korsakov, *Christmas Eve*; Alexander Zelinsky, *Sarema, the Rose of the Caucasus*.
Orchestra/Band Music:
  Concerted Music:
    Piano: Vitěslav Novák, *Concerto in e*.
    Violin: Frederick Delius, *Légende*; Ottokar Novácek, *Perpetuum Mobile*; Philipp Scharwenka, *Concerto*.
    Other: Antonin Dvořák, *Cello Concerto in b, Opus 104*; Alexander Gretchaninov, *Cello Concerto*.
  Ballet/Incidental Music: Edward German, *Romeo and Juliet* (IM).
  Program Music: Mikhail Ippolitov-Ivanov, *Caucasian Sketches, Opus 10*; Lodewijk Meulemans, *The Myth of Spring*; Jan Sibelius, *The Wood Nymph–Three Legends for Orchestra, Opus 22*; Richard Strauss, *Till Eulenspiegel's Merry Pranks, Opus 28*; Siegfried Wagner, *Sehnsucht*.
  Standard Works: Arthur H. Bird, *Suite No. 3*; Ferruccio Busoni, *Orchestral Suite No. 2, Opus 34a*; Antonin Dvořák, *Suite in A, Opus 98b*; Georges Enescu, *Tragic Overture–Triumphant Overture*; Arthur Foote, *Suite No. 3 in d, Opus 36*; Robert Fuchs, *Serenade No. 4 in g, Opus 51* (strings)–*No. 5 in D, Opus 53*(?); Edward German, *Symphonic Suite in d*; Alexander Glazunov, *Oriental Suite*; Victor Herbert, *Badinage*; Sergei Liapunov, *Solemn Overture in C on Russian Themes, Opus 7*; Edward MacDowell, *Suite No. 2 in e, "Indian," Opus 48*; Albéric Magnard, *Chant funébre, Opus 9–Overture, Opus 10*; Vitěslav Novák, *Serenade in F*; John Philip Sousa, *King Cotton March*.
  Symphonies: Howard A. Brockway, *Symphony in D*; Josef Bohuslav Foerster, *No. 3 in D, Opus 36*; Alexander Glazunov, *No. 5 in B♭, Opus 55*; Vasili Kalinnikov, *No. 1 in g*; Giuseppe Martucci, *No. 1 in d, Opus 75*; Sergei Rachmaninoff, *No. 1 in d, Opus 13*; Carl Reinecke, *No. 3 in g, Opus 227*(?); Charles-Marie Widor, *No. 3, Opus 69* (with organ).

1896

❅

Historical Highlights: The Young Turks are formed to further the cause of Turkish independence; the island of Madagascar is annexed by France; Italian troops, defeated by the Abyssinians, withdraw from their self-proclaimed protectorate of that country; in the United States, William McKinley is elected as forty-fifth president; Utah becomes state number twenty-five; Miami, Florida, is incorporated; William Jennings Bryan gives his "Cross of Gold" speech.

Art and Literature Highlights: Births—art figures Allyn Cox, Morris Kantor, André Masson, writers A. J. Cronin, John Dos Passos, F. Scott Fitzgerald; Deaths—artists John-Everett Millais, Henry Moore, writers Mary A. Dodge, Harriet B. Stowe, Paul Verlaine. Art—Homer's *All's Well*, Rodin's *The Kiss*, Tanner's *Daniel in the Lion's Den*; Literature—Chekhov's *The Sea Gull*, Hardy's *Jude, the Obscure*, Wilde's *Salome*.

Musical Highlights

A. Births

Composers: Roberto Gerhard (Spain-England) September 25; Howard Hanson (U.S.A.) October 28; Walter Helfer (U.S.A.) September 30; Leroy Robertson (U.S.A.) December 21; Roger Sessions (U.S.A.) December 28; Josip Slavenski (Croatia) May 11; Virgil Thomson (U.S.A.) November 25; Jaroslav Tomásek (Czechoslovakia) April 10; Jaromir Weinberger (Czechoslovakia-U.S.A.) January 8.

Conductors: Jenö Adám (Hungary) December 12; Warwick Braithwaite (England); Tauno Hannikainen (Finland) February 26; Serge Jaroff (Russia) March 20; Richard Kountz (U.S.A.) July 8; Dimitri Mitropoulos (Greece) March 1; Wilfrid Pelletier (Canada) June 30.

Singers: Mathieu Ahlersmeyer (German baritone) June 29; Ivar Andrésen (Norwegian bass) July 27; Xenia Belmas (Ukrainian soprano)(?); Res Fischer (German contralto) November 8; Madeline Grey (French soprano) June 11; Queena Mario (American soprano) August 21; Galliano Masini (Italian tenor); Heddle Nash (British tenor) June 14; Rosetta Pampanini (Italian soprano) September 2; Charles Panzéra (Swiss-born baritone) February 16; Kálmán Pataky (Hungarian tenor) November 14; Ivan Patorzhinsky (Ukrainian bass) March 3; Hina Spani (Argentine soprano) February 15; Kerstin Thorborg (Swedish contralto) May 19; Lawrence Tibbett (American baritone) November 16; Armand Tokatyan (Bulgarian-born tenor) February 12.

Performers: Simon Barere (Russian pianist) September 1; Alexander Brailowsky (Russian pianist) February 16; Aurelio Giorni (Italian-born pianist) September 15; Nicolai Graudan (Russian cellist) September 5; Adolph Hallis (South African pianist) July 4; Rudolf Kolisch (Austrian-born violinist) July 20; Ernesto Lecuona (Cuban pianist/composer) August 7; Kathleen Long (British pianist) July 7; Bernard Shore (British violist) March 17; Jacques Wolfe (Romanian-born pianist/composer) April 29.

Others: Erwin Bodky (German-born music scholar) March 17; Glen Haydon (American musicologist) December 9; Helmuth Osthoff (German musicologist) August 13; Leon Theremin (Russian inventor) August 15.

B. Deaths

Composers: Anton Bruckner (Austria) October 11; Antonio Cagnoni (Italy) April 30; Richard Flury (Switzerland) March 26; Percy Gaunt (U.S.A.); Carlos Gomes (Brazil) September 16; Achille Graffigna (Italy) July 19; Charles-Ambroise Thomas (France) February 12.

Conductors: Frederick Nicholls Crouch (England) August 18.

Singers: Georg Ephraim Arlberg (Swedish baritone) February 21; Eliza Biscaccianti (American soprano); Italo Campanini (Italian tenor) November 22: Julie Dorus-Gras (Belgian soprano) February 6; Gilbert-Louis Duprez (French tenor) September 23; Albert Eilers (German bass) September 4; Katharina Klafsky (Hungarian soprano) September 22; Darya Leonova (Russian contralto) February 6; Gustav Siehr (German bass) May 18; John Rogers Thomas (British-born baritone) April 5.

Performers: Sir Joseph Barnby (British organist/composer) January 28; Joseph Dachs (German pianist) June 6; Alexis-Henri Fissot (French pianist) January 28; Hubert Ferdinand Kufferath (German violinist/conductor) June 11; Barrett Isaac Poznanski (American violinist) June 23; Carl Reinthaler (German organist/composer) February 13; Alexander Ritter (German violinist/composer) April 12; Rudolf Joseph Schachner (German pianist) August 15; Clara (Wieck) Schumann (German pianist/composer) May 20; Friedrich Gottlieb Schwenke (German organist/composer) June 24.

Others: Moritz Wilhelm Drobisch (German music scholar) September 30; Sir Augustus Harris (British impresario) June 22; Luther Whiting Mason (American music educator) July 4; Alfred Novello (British publisher) July 16; Richard Pohl (German music author) December 17.

C. Debuts

Singers: Giuseppe Anselmi (Italian tenor—Athens); Alessandro Bonci (Italian tenor—Parma); Celestina Boninsegna (Italian soprano—Fano); Hans Breuer (German tenor—Bayreuth); Alois Burgstaller (German tenor—Bayreuth); Hector Dufranne (Belgian bass-baritone—Brussels); John Forsell (Swedish baritone—Stockholm); Karl Jörn (Latvian tenor—Breigau); Felix von Kraus (Austrian bass—Vienna); Marie Olenine d'Alheim (Russian soprano—Paris); Fritzi Scheff (Austrian soprano—Frankfurt); Oscar Seagle (American baritone—New York); Leo Slezak (Austrian tenor—Brünn); Harry Evan Williams (American tenor—Worcester).

Performers: Alfred Cortot (French pianist—Paris); Ossip Gabrilowitsch (Russian-born pianist—Berlin); Friedrich Weidemann (German baritone—Brieg).

D. New Positions

Conductors: Frederick Archer (Pittsburgh SO); Herbert Brewer (Gloucester Cathedral); Frederic Cowen (Liverpool PO and Manchester Concerts); Oskar Nedbal (Czech PO); Emil von Reznicek (Mannheim Court).

Others: Théodore Dubois (director, Paris Conservatory); Hans Huber (director, Basel Conservatory); Edward MacDowell (head, Columbia University Music Department); Henri Viotta (director, The Hague Conservatory).

E. Prizes/Honors

Prizes: Jules Mocquet (Prix de Rome).

Honors: Nikolai Afanasiev (Russian Musical Society); Karl Goldmark (Order of Leopold); Louis Gouvy (Legion of Honor); Edvard Grieg (Legion of Honor); Charles Lenepveu (French Academy); Edward MacDowel (Mus.D., Princeton).

F. Biographical Highlights

Emma Albani retires from the stage; Alexander Glazunov travels to England on a conducting engagement; Percy Goetschius resigns his conservatory post and begins teaching privately in Boston; Engelbert Humperdinck, in ill health, retires from active music life; Alexander Scriabin, sponsored by Belaiev Publishing House, makes a grand concert tour of Europe.

G. Cultural Beginnings

Performing Groups—Choral: Catalunya Nova (Barcelona Choral Society); Nicodé Chorus (Dresden); Oxford Bach Choir.

Performing Groups—Instrumental: Adamowski Trio; Indianapolis Symphony Orchestra I; Portland Symphony Orchestra (Oregon Symphony Orchestra, 1967); Winderstein Orchestra (Leipzig); Women's String Orchestra of New York.

Music Publishers: Editions Salabert (Paris).

Music Publications: *La Cronaca Musical* (Italy); *The Etude*; *Die Jugend*; *Monatschrift für Gottesdienst und Kirchliche Kunst*; *The Musician*.

Performing Centers: Steinert Hall (Boston); Theater des Westens (Berlin).

Other: American Federation of Musicians; American Guild of Organists; Genossenschaft Deutscher Tonsetzen (Munich); Knudsen Piano Factory (Bergen); Joseph Koening, Piano Builder (Caen); Ignace Jan Paderewski Foundation; Russian Music Circle (Moscow); Sociedade de Concertos Populares (Rio de Janeiro); Theatrical Syndicate (New York).

H. **Musical Literature**
Theodor Billroth, *Wer ist musikalische?*; César Cui, *The Russian Song: a Study of its Development*; François-Auguste Gevaert, *La Mélopée antique dans l'église latine*; Philip H. Goepp, *Annals of Music in Philadelphia*; W. H. Hadow, *Sonata Form*; Carl Hennig, *Aesthetik der Tonkunst*; Alfred Hipkins, *Description and History of the Pianoforte*; Max Kalbeck, *Humoresken und Fantasien*; Henry Krehbiel, *How to Listen to Music*; William Mathews, *Dictionary of Music Terms*; Anton Preobrazhensky, *Dictionary of Russian Church Chant*; Nicolai Rimsky-Korsakov, *Principles of Orchestration*.

I. **Musical Compositions**
Chamber Music:
String Quartets: George W. Chadwick, *No. 4 in e*; Charles Ives, *String Quartet No. 1, "Revival Service"*; Alexander Zemlinsky, *No. 1.*
Sonata/Solos: Amy Beach, *Violin Sonata in a, Opus 34*; Frederick Delius, *Romance for Cello and Piano*; Arthur de Greef, *Violin Sonata No. 1*; Wilhelm Peterson-Berger, *Suite, Opus 15* (violin, piano); Carl Reinecke, *Cello Sonata No. 3 in G, Opus 238*; Camille Saint-Saëns, *Violin Sonata No. 2 in E♭, Opus 102*; Charles Tournemire, *Andante* (horn, piano).
Ensembles: Vitěslav Novák, *Piano Quintet in a, Opus 12*; Hans Pfitzner, *Piano Trio in F, Opus 8*; Charles M. Widor, *Piano Quintet No. 2, Opus 68*; Alexander Zemlinsky, *Clarinet Trio, Opus 3.*
Piano: Léon Böellmann, *Nocturne, Opus 36–Rondo francaise, Opus 37*; Gabriel Fauré, *Dolly, Opus 56* (four hands); Edvard Grieg, *Lyric Pieces, Book VIII, Opus 65*; Anatol Liadov, *Four Preludes (A♭, c, B, f♯), Opus 39*; Edward MacDowell, *Woodland Sketches, Opus 51*; Ethelbert Nevin, *La Guitare, Maggio in Toscana* (suite); Vitěslav Novák, *Ecology, Opus 11–At Dusk, Opus 13*; Wilhelm Peterson-Berger, *Tone Pictures, Opus 11*; Sergei Rachmaninoff, *Moments musicaux, Opus 16*; Max Reger, *Improvisation, Opus 18–Humoresques, Opus 20*; Alexander Scriabin, *Twenty-Four Preludes, Opus 11* (completion)– *Five Preludes, Opus 15–Seven Preludes, Opus 16–Allegro de Concert, Opus 18*; Josef Suk, *Eight Pieces, Opus 12*; Charles Tournemire, *Serenade, Opus 9.*

Organ: Léon Böellmann, *Suite No. 2, Opus 27*; Johannes Brahms, *Eleven Chorale Preludes, Opus 122* (opus posthumous); Josef B. Foerster, *Fantasy in C, Opus 14*.

Choral/Vocal Music:

Choral: Dudley Buck, *Christ, the Victor* (cantata); Edward Elgar, *The Light of Life, Opus 29* (oratorio); Alexander Glazunov, *Coronation Cantata, Opus 56*; Vincent d'Indy, *Motet: Deus Israel*; Sergei Rachmaninoff, *Six Choruses, Opus 15*; George F. Root, *The Star of Light* (cantata); Florent Schmitt, *Mélusine* (cantata); Jan Sibelius, *Coronation Cantata*; Charles V. Stanford, *Requiem*.

Vocal: Amy Beach, *Three Songs, Opus 31–Four Songs, Opus 35*; Arthur H. Bird, *Five Songs, Opus 36*; Johannes Brahms, *Four Serious Songs, Opus 121*; Vítěslav Novák, *A Tale of the Heart, Opus 8*; Wilhelm Peterson-Berger, *Two Songs, Opus 9–Marit's Songs, Opus 12–Fröseblomster I, Opus 16*; Sergei Rachmaninoff, *Twelve Songs, Opus 14*; Charles Tournemire, *Three Melodies, Opus 7*; Vasili Wrangell, *Three Romances, Opus 20*; Alexander Zemlinsky, *Forest Talk*.

Musical Stage: Walter Damrosch, *The Scarlet Letter*; Gilbert/Sullivan, *The Grand Duke*; Umberto Giordano, *Andrea Chenier*; Luigi Mancinelli, *Ero e Leandro*; Pietro Mascagni, *Zanetto*; André Messager, *La fiancée en loterie–Le chavalier d'Harmentel*; Giacomo Puccini, *La Bohème*; Nicolai Rimsky-Korsakov, *Sadko*; John Philip Sousa, *El Capitán*; Charles Villiers Stanford, *Shamus O'Brien, Opus 61*; Hugo Wolf, *Der Corregidor*.

Orchestra/Band Music:

Concerted Music:

Piano: Georges Enescu, *Fantasie*; Victor Herbert, *The Veiled Prophet* (piano, band); Camille Saint-Saëns, *Concerto No. 5 in F "Egyptian," Opus 103*; Alexander Scriabin, *Concerto in f♯, Opus 20*; Charles V. Stanford, *Concerto No. 1*; Frederick Zech, Jr., *Concerto No. 4*.

Violin: Ernest Chausson, *Poème, Opus 25*; Georges Enescu, *Concerto*; Yuly Konyus, *Concerto in e*.

Ballet/Incidental Music: John Alden Carpenter, *Branglebrink* (IM); Edward German, *As You Like It* (IM); André Messager, *Le procès des roses* (B).

Program Music: Frederick Delius, *Appalachia*; Frederick Gleason, *Edris*; Antonin Dvořák, *The Water-Sprite, Opus 107–The Midday Witch, Opus 108–The Golden Spinning Wheel, Opus 109–The Wood Dove, Opus 110*; Richard Strauss, *Also Sprach Zarathustra, Opus 30*.

Standard Works: George W. Chadwick, *Symphonic Sketches*; Arthur Foote, *Suite in d, Opus 36*; Vincent d'Indy, *Ishtar Variations, Opus 42*; Sergei Liapunov, *Solemn Overture on Russian Themes, Opus 7*; John Philip Sousa, *Stars and Stripes Forever*.

Symphonies: August de Boeck, *Symphony in G*; Samuel Coleridge-Taylor, *Symphony in A*; Paul Dukas, *Symphony in C*; Alexander Glazounov, *No. 6 in c, Opus 58*; Albéric Magnard, *No. 3 in b♭, Opus 11*; Gustav Mahler, *No. 3 in d*.

1897
❊

Historical Highlights: The Peace of Constantinople marks the end of the Greek-Turkish War; Russia occupies Port Arthur in China; the first Zionist Congress seeks ways to make Palestine a Jewish state; in the United States, the Klondike Gold Rush takes place in the Alaskan Territory; P. K. Kellogg Brothers introduce corn flakes—C. W. Post introduces his new cereal, Grape Nuts; the Katzenjammer Kids becomes the first American comic strip.

Art and Literature Highlights: Births—artists Paul Delvaux, Ivan Albright, writers William Faulkner, Thorrnton Wilder; Deaths—artists Homer Martin, Charles Nahl, writers Alphonse Daudet, Margaret J. Preston. Art—La Farge's *The Strange Thing Little Kiosai Saw in the River*, Pissarro's *Boulevard Montmartre*, Rousseau's *The Sleeping Gypsy*; Literature—Kipling's *Captains Courageous*, Rostand's *Cyrano de Bergerac*, Shaw's *Candide*.

Musical Highlights

A. Births
Composers: Paul Ben Haim (Germany-Israel) July 5; Jørgen Bentzon (Denmark) February 14; Manuel Blancafort (Spain) August 12; Henry Cowell (U.S.A.) March 11; Oscar Lorenzo Fernandez (Brazil) November 4; John Fernström (Sweden) December 6; Harrison Kerr (U.S.A.) October 13; Erich Wolfgang Korngold (Bohemia-U.S.A.) May 29; Francisco Mignone (Brazil) September 3; Fernando Obradors (Spain); (William) Quincy Porter (U.S.A.) February 7; Knudåge Riisager (Denmark) March 6; Lamar Edwin Stringfield (U.S.A.) October 10; Margaret Sutherland (Australia) November 20; Alexandre Tansman (Poland) June 12.
Conductors: Břetislav Bakala (Czechoslovakia) February 12; Quinto Maganini (U.S.A.) November 30; Henry Swoboda (Czechoslovakia) October 29; George Szell (Hungary-U.S.A.) June 7; Mogens Wöldike (Denmark) July 5.
Singers—Female: Marian Anderson (American contralto) February 17; Conchita Badia (Spanish soprano) November 14; Eva Bandrowska-Turska (Polish soprano) May 20; Mercedes Capsir (Spanish soprano) July 20; Tiana Luise Lemnitz (German soprano) August 26;

Mária Németh (Hungarian soprano) March 13; Maria Nezadál (Czech soprano) February 21; Rosa Ponselle (American soprano) January 22; Marian Telva (American contralto) December 26; Gertrud Wettergren (Swedish contralto) February 17.

Singers—Male: Willi Domgraf-Fassbänder (German baritone) February 9; Frederick Jagel (American tenor) June 10; Carlo Morelli (Chilean baritone) December 25; Helge Rosvaenge (Danish tenor) August 29; Paul Schöffler (German bass-baritone) September 15; Hans Tänzler (German tenor); Georges Thill (French tenor) December 14; Adolf Vogel (German bass-baritone) August 18; Lazar Weiner (Russian-born pianist/composer).

Performers: Hans Barth (German-born pianist/composer) June 25; John Fernström (Swedish violinist/composer) December 6; Alexander Hilsberg (Polish violinist/conductor) March 24; György Kósa (Hungarian pianist/composer) April 24; Lazar Weiner (Russian pianist) October 24.

Others: J. Murray Barbour (American musicologist) March 31; Karel Philippus Bernet-Kempers (Dutch musicologist) September 20; Henri Elkan (Belgian publisher) November 23; Gotthold Frotscher (German musicologist) December 6; Herbert Eimert (German musicologist) April 8; Oswald Jonas (Austrian-born musicologist) January 10; Donald Wales MacArdle (American musicologist) July 3.

B. **Deaths**

Composers: Woldemar Bargiel (Germany) February 23; Karel Bendl (Czechoslovakia) September 20; Johannes Brahms (Germany) April 3; Paul Kuczinski (Germany) October 21; Teodulo Mabellini (Italy) March 10; Paul Mériel (France) February 24; Grenville Dean Wilson (U.S.A.) September 20.

Conductors: Edouard Deldevez (France) November 6; Adolph Neuendorff (Germany-U.S.A.) December 4.

Singers: Joseph-Théodore Barbot (French tenor) January 1; (Armand de) Castelmary (French bass) February 10; Isidor Dannström (Swedish baritone/composer) October 17; Achille Errani (Italian-born tenor) January 6; Marie-Cornélie Falcon (French soprano) February 25; Leone Giraldoni (Italian baritone) October 1; Leonard Labatt (Swedish tenor) March 7; Bernhard Pollini (German tenor) November 27; Giuseppina Strepponi (Italian soprano) November 14; Alexandre Taskin (French baritone) October 5; Sarah Edith Wynne (British soprano) January 24.

Performers: Antonio Bazzini (Italian violinist) February 10; W. T. Best (British organist) May 10; Léon Boëllmann (French organist/composer) October 11; Félix Godefroid (Belgian harpist) July 12; Carl Mikuli (Polish pianist) May 21.

Others: Henry Charles Banister (British music theorist/composer) November 20; Léon Carvalho (French impresario/opera manager) December 29; H. Murray Higgins (American publisher) July 13; Jan Pieter Land (Dutch musicologist) April 30; Alexander Wheelock Thayer (American music scholar) July 15.

C. Debuts

Singers: Aïno Ackté (Finnish soprano—Paris); Bella Alten (Polish soprano—Leipzig); Richard Breitenfeld (Bohemian baritone—Cologne); Charles W. Clark (American baritone—New York); Giuseppe De Luca (Italian baritone—Piacenza); Emilio de Gogorza (American baritone—New York); Mizzi Günther (Bohemian soprano—Hermannstadt); Heinrich Hensel (German tenor—Freiburg); Hermann Jadlowker (Latvian tenor—Cologne); Minnie Nast (German soprano—Aachen); Albert Reiss (German tenor—Königsberg); Aurelie Révy (Hungarian soprano—Budapest); Corinne Rider-Kelsey (American soprano—Rockford, Illinois); Leonid Sobinov (Russian tenor—Moscow); Ellison Van Hoose (American tenor—Philadelphia); Anton Van Rooy (Dutch bass-baritone—Bayreuth).

Performers: Ernst von Dohnányi (Hungarian pianist—Berlin); Katherine Goodson (British pianist—London); Louis Persinger (American violinist—Colorado).

D. New Positions

Conductors: Cleofonte Campanini (Covent Garden); Ernst Kunwald (Sondershausen Opera); Alexander Luigini (Opéra-Comique, Paris); Gustav Mahler (Vienna Opera); Emil Mlynarski (Warsaw Opera); Hans Richter (Hallé Orchestra, Manchester).

Others: Ivor Adkins (organist, Worcester Cathedral); Joseph-Amédée Capoul (manager, Paris Opera); George W. Chadwick (director, New England Conservatory); Frank Damrosch (music supervisor, New York Public Schools); Frederick Edwards (editor, *Musical Times*); William Fisher (editor, Oliver Ditson and Co.); Giuseppe Gallignani (director, Milan Conservatory); Robert Kajanus (music director, Helsinki University); Carl Reinecke (director, Leipzig Conservatory); Giovanni Tebaldini (director, Parma Conservatory).

E. Prizes/Honors

Prizes: Joseph Jongen (Prix de Rome); Max d'Ollone (Prix de Rome).

Honors: Frederick Bridge (knighted); George C. Martin (knighted); Emile Paladilhe (Legion of Honor); Jan Sibelius (life pension, Finland).

F. Biographical Highlights

John Alden Carpenter graduates from Harvard and enters his father's business; Ernst von Dohnányi begins his conducting career; Maurice Ravel begins the study of composition with Fauré; Ralph

Vaughan Williams travels to Berlin to study with Max Bruch; Hugo Wolf, suffering from recurring illness, finally goes mad.

G. Cultural Beginnings

Performing Groups—Choral: Castle Square Opera Co. (Boston); Hausermann Privatchor (Zürich); Kansas City (Missouri) Oratorio Society; Moody-Manners Opera Co.; Palermo Opera; Philadelphia Choral Society.

Performing Groups—Instrumental: Beethoven Society of Montevideo (Uruguay); Bournemouth Municipal Orchestra; Copenhagen Philharmonic Concerts; Rostock Stadt- und Theaterorchester; Société Avignonase des Concerts Symphoniques.

Festivals: Feis Ceoil (Irish Festival); Maine Music Festival (Portland).

Educational: Adelaide University Chair of Music; Faelten Piano School (Boston); Library of Congress Division of Music; Sherwood Piano School (Chicago); Stierlin Music School (Münster).

Music Publishers: Doubleday and McClure Co.; Geibel and Lehmann; Gesellschaft der Autoren, Komponisten und Musikverleger (Vienna); Morse Music Co. (New York).

Music Publications: *The Musical Herald.*

Performing Centers: Providence (Rhode Island) Opera House; Teatro Massimo (Palermo); Théâtre Antoine (Paris).

Other: Museo Donizettiano (Bergamo); National Piano Manufacturer's Association.

H. Musical Literature

Kornél Ábrányi, *From My Life and Memories*; Henry Banister, *The Harmonising of Melodies*; George W. Chadwick, *Harmony, A Course of Study*; Lionel Dauriac, *La Psychologie dans l'opéra français*; Victor Maurel, *L'Art du Chant*; Willibald Nagel, *History of Music in England II*; Felipe Pedrell, *Diccionario biográfico y bibliográfico de músicos y escritores de música españolas, portugueses y hispano-americanos antiguos y modernos*; Hermann von der Pfordten, *Musikalische Essays I*; Anton Preobrazhensky, *On Church Chant*; Giovanni Tebaldini/E. Bossi, *Metodo teorico pratico per organo*; Martin Wegelius, *Homophonic Writing*; Hans von Wolzogen, *Grossmeister deutscher Musik.*

I. Musical Compositions

Chamber Music:

    String Quartets: Carl Busch, *String Quartet*; Robert Fuchs, *No. 1 in E, Opus 58*; John Ireland, *No. 2 in C*; Eduard Nápravnik, *No. 3 in C, Opus 65*; Frederick Zech, Jr., *No. 1.*

    Sonata/Solos: Léon Böellmann, *Cello Sonata, Opus 40*; Georges Enescu, *Violin Sonata No. 1, Opus 2*; André Messager, *Trois pièces* (violin, piano); Eduard Nápravnik, *Four Pieces for Cello and Piano,*

Opus 64; Maurice Ravel, *Violin Sonata*; Philipp Scharwenka, *Violin Sonata in b, Opus 110*; Charles S. Skilton, *Violin Sonata No. 1 in g*; Charles Tournemire, *Suite, Opus 11* (viola, piano).

Ensembles: Ernest Chausson, *Piano Quartet, Opus 30*; Arthur Foote, *Piano Quintet in a, Opus 38*; Robert Fuchs, *Seven Fantasy Pieces, Opus 57* (violin, viola, piano); Heinrich von Herzogenberg, *Piano Quartet in Bb, Opus 95*; Charles Ives, *Fugue in Four Keys on the Shining Shore*; Joseph Jongen, *Piano Trio, Opus 10*; Eduard Nápravnik, *Piano Trio No. 2 in d, Opus 62*; Philipp Scharwenka, *Piano Trio in cb, Opus 100*.

Piano: Amy Beach, *Children's Album, Opus 36*; Léon Böellmann, *Sur la mer, Opus 38*; John Alden Carpenter, *Sonata No. 1*; Ernst von Dohnányi, *Four Pieces, Opus 2*; Georges Enescu, *Suite "dans le style ancien," Opus 3*; Anatol Liadov, *Etude in c♯–Three Preludes (C, d, Db), Opus 40–Two Fugues (f♯, D), Opus 41*; Nicolai Medtner, *Eight Stimmensbilder, Opus 1*; Alexander Scriabin, *Allegro de Concert, Opus 18– Sonata No. 3, Opus 23–Polonaise, Opus 21–Four Preludes, Opus 22*.

Organ: Camille Saint-Saëns, *Marche religieuse, Opus 107*.

Choral/Vocal Music:

Choral: Amy Beach, *Three Shakespeare Choruses, Opus 39*; Edward Elgar, *The Banner of St. George, Opus 33* (cantata); Robert Fuchs, *Mass in F*; Carl Nielsen, *Hymnus amoris, Opus 12*; Ole Olsen, *Griffenfeldt* (cantata)–*Nidaros* (oratorio); Horatio Parker, *The Legend of St. Christopher, Opus 43* (oratorio); C. Hubert Parry, *Magnificat in F*; Wilhelm Peterson-Berger, *Sveagaldrar* (cantata); Florent Schmitt, *Frédégonde* (cantata); Alexander von Zemlinsky, *Burial of Spring* (cantata).

Vocal: Amy Beach, *Three Shakespeare Songs, Opus 37*; George W. Chadwick, *Lochinvar*; Claude Debussy, *Chansons de Bilitis*; Robert Fuchs, *Four Songs, Opus 56*(?); Vitěslav Novák, *Gypsy Melodies, Opus 14* (cycle)–*Songs on Moravian Folk Texts I, II, Opus 17*; Nicolai Rimsky-Korsakov, *By the Sea* (cycle); Richard Strauss, *Three Songs, Opus 31–Five Songs, Opus 32–Four Songs, Opus 33*.

Musical Stage: Meliton Balanchivadze, *Tamara the Treacherous*; Arthur H. Bird, *Daphne*; Francesco Cilèa, *L'arlésiana*; Louis A. Coerne, *A Woman of Marblehead*; Frederick Delius, *Koanga*; Julian Edwards, *The Wedding Day*; Zdeněk Fibich, *Sarka, Opus 51*; Josef Bohuslav Foerster, *Eva, Opus 50*; Victor Herbert, *The Idol's Eye*; Hervé, *Le cabinet Piperlin*; Reginald De Koven, *The Highwayman*; Ruggero Leoncavallo, *La Bohème*; Hamish MacCunn, *Diarmid, Opus 34*; Alexander Mackenzie, *His Majesty, Opus 56–The Little Minister, Opus 57*; Jules Massenet, *Sapho*; André Messager, *Les P'tites michu*.

Orchestra/Band Music:
Concerted Music:
Piano: Frederick Delius, *Concerto in c*; Théodore Dubois, *Concerto No. 2*; Alexander MacKenzie, *Concerto, "Scottish," Opus 55*; Arthur B. Whiting, *Fantasia in b♭, Opus 11*; Camille Zeckwer, *Concerto*.
Violin: Ferruccio Busoni, *Concerto in D, Opus 35a*.
Other: Léon Böellmann, *Fantaisie dialoguée* (organ); Charles Martin Loeffler, *La Mort de Tintagiles* (two violas d'amore).
Ballet/Incidental Music: Alexander Glazunov, *Raymonda, Opus 57* (B); Christian F. E. Horneman, *The Struggle with the Muses* (IM); Engelbert Humperdinck, *Königskinder* (IM); André Messager, *La montagne enchantée* (IM)–*Le chevalier aux fleurs* (B); Arthur Sullivan, *Victoria and Merrie England* (B).
Program Music: Paul Dukas, *The Sorcerer's Apprentice*; Antonin Dvořák, *The Hero's Song, Opus 111*; Edward German, *Hamlet*; Richard Strauss, *Don Quixote*.
Standard Works: Ernest Chausson, *Chant Funèbre*; Frederick Converse, *Overture, Youth*; Frederick Delius, *Over the Hills and Far Away*; Edward Elgar, *Imperial March, Opus 32*; Robert Fuchs, *Overture, Des Meeres un de Liebe Wellen, Opus 59*; Hamish MacCunn, *Highland Memories Suite Opus 30*; Arthur Nevin, *Lorna Doone Suite*; Richard Ohlsson, *Swedish Dances* (strings); C. Hubert Parry, *Symphonic Variations–Elegy for Brahms*; Ralph Vaughan-Williams, *Serenade in A*.
Symphonies: Hugo Alfvén, *No. 1 in f, Opus 7*; Ernst von Dohnányi, *No. 1 in d, Opus 9*; Henry Hadley, *No. 1 in d, "Youth and Life," Opus 25*; Asger Hamerik, *No. 6, "Spirituelle," Opus 38*; Hans Huber, *No. 2 in e, "Böcklin," Opus 115*; Ernst Mielk, *Symphony in f*; Joseph Ryelandt, *No. 1*; Harry R. Shelley, *Symphony in E♭*.

1898

Historical Highlights: The Empress Elizabeth of Austria is murdered in Geneva; the Paris Metro begins operation; Count von Zeppelin invents the motor-driven airship named after him; the Curies discover the existence of radium; in U.S. history, the U.S.S. *Maine* blows up in Havana harbor precipitating the Spanish-American War; by the Treaty of Paris, the United States gives Spain $20,000,000 for Guam, Hawaii, Puerto Rico, and the Philippines.

Art and Literature Highlights: Births—artists Alexander Calder, René Magritte, Ben Shahn, writers Bertold Brecht, Federico García-Lorca; Deaths—authors Stephen Vincent Benét, Lewis Carroll, Stéphane Mallarmé, artists Edward Burne-Jones, Gustave Moreau. Art—Adam's *Winged Victory*, Eakins' *Agnew Clinic*, Rodin's *The Hand of God*; Literature—Chekhov's *Uncle Vanya*, Long's *Madame Butterflly*, Wells' *The War of the Worlds*.

Musical Highlights

A. Births

Composers: Alexander Abramsky (Russia) January 22; Salvador Bacarisse (Spain) September 12; Ernest Bacon (U.S.A.) May 26; Gérard Bertouille (Belgium) May 26; Louis Cheslock (England-U.S.A.) September 9; William Levi Dawson (U.S.A.) September 26; Norman Demuth (England) July 15; Hanns Eisler (Germany) July 6; Herbert Elwell (U.S.A.) May 10; George Gershwin (U.S.A.) September 26; Ebbe Hamerik (Denmark) September 5; Roy Harris (U.S.A.) February 12; Tibor Harsányi (Hungary-France) June 27; Lev Knipper (Russia) December 3; Gustaf Paulson (Sweden) January 22; Vittorio Rieti (Italy) January 28.

Conductors: Luc Balmer (Switzerland) July 13; Wheeler Beckett (U.S.A.) March 7; Roger Désormière (France) September 13; Jascha Horenstein (Russia) May 6; Paul Müller-Zürich (Switzerland) June 19; Hugh Ross (England-U.S.A.) August 21.

Singers: Joseph Bentonelli (American tenor) September 10; Jules Bledsoe (American baritone) December 29; Armando Borgioli (Italian baritone) March 19; Giuseppina Cobelli (Italian soprano) August 1; Robert Easton (British bass) June 8; Deszö Ernster (Hungarian bass) November 23; Marta Fuchs (German soprano) January 1; Grace Moore (American soprano) December 5; Maria Müller (Czech soprano) January 29; Augusta Oltrabella (Italian soprano); Iva Pacetti (Italian soprano) December 13; Alessio de Paolis (Italian tenor) March 5; Julius Patzak (Austrian tenor) April 9; Lily Pons (French soprano) April 12; Paul Robeson (American baritone) April 9; Erna Sack (German soprano) February 6; Carlo Tagliabue (Italian baritone) January 12; Maria Zamboni (Italian soprano) July 25.

Performers: Charles Barkel (Swedish violinist-conductor) February 6; Emil Frey (Swiss pianist) January 26; Mischa Levitzki (American pianist) May 25; Beryl Rubinstein (American pianist) October 26; Bronislaw Rutkowski (Polish organist) February 27; Alfred Wallenstein (American cellist/composer) October 7.

Others: Albert Goldberg (American music critic) June 2; Maurice Martenot (French electronic inventor) October 4; Willi Reich (Austrian-born musicologist/critic) May 27; Shin'ichi Suzuki (Japanese violin method originator) October 18; Aladár Tóth (Hungarian music author/administrator) February 4; Emanuel Winternitz (Austrian-born musicologist) August 4; Hermann Zenck (German musicologist) March 19.

B. **Deaths**
   Composers: Grat-Norbert Barthe (France) August 13; George Frederick Bristow (U.S.A.) December 13; Louis-Théodore Gouvy (France) April 21.
   Conductors: Anton Seidl (Hungary) March 28.
   Singers: Max Alvary (German tenor) November 7; Nicolini (Ernest Nicolas—French tenor) January 19.
   Performers: Nicolai Afanasyev (Russian violinist/composer) June 3; Michal Bergson (Polish pianist) March 9; Gaetano Capocci (Italian organist) January 11; Georg Kulenkampff (German violinist) January 23; Antoine-François Marmontel (French pianist/pedagogue) January 17; Sebastian Bach Mills (British pianist) December 21; Ede Reményi (Hungarian violinist) May 15; Julius Schulhoff (Bohemian pianist/composer) March 13.
   Others: Charles Jerome Hopkins (American music author/composer) November 4; Franz Magnus Böhme (German music author) October 18; Oscar Paul (German music scholar) April 18.

C. **Debuts**
   Singers: Angelo Bada (Italian tenor—Novara); Maria Barrientos (Spanish soprano—Barcelona); Therese Behr (German contralto—Germany); Hermine Bosetti (Austrian-born soprano—Wiesbaden); Eleanora de Cisneros (American mezzo-soprano—New York); Emmy Destinn (Czech soprano—Berlin); Maria Farneti (Italian soprano—Milan)(?); Francesco Federici (Italian baritone—Italy); Waldemar Henke (German tenor—Posen), Louise Homer (American contralto—Vichy); Gustav Huberdeau (French bass-baritone—Paris); Estelle Liebling (American soprano—Dresden); Berta Morena (German soprano—Munich); Francis Rogers (American baritone—Boston); Titta Ruffo (Italian baritone—Rome); Erik Schmedes (Danish tenor—Vienna, as tenor); Riccardo Stracciari (Italian baritone—Bologna); Yvonne de Tréville (American soprano—New York); Clarence Whitehill (American baritone—Brussels); Herbert Witherspoon (American bass—New York); Giovanni Zenatello (Italian tenor—Vienna, as baritone).
   Performers: George Herbert Fryer (British pianist—London); Jan Kubelík (Czech violinist—Prague); Tullio Serafin (Italian conductor—Ferrara); Jacques Thibaud (French violinist—Paris).

D. New Positions

Conductors: Wilhelm Gericke (Boston SO); Victor Herbert (Pittsburgh SO); Armas Järneffelt (Vyberg Municipal Orchestra); Ernst Kunwald (Essen Opera); Ferdinand Löwe (Vienna Opera); André Messager (Opéra-Comique, Paris); Emil Paur (New York PO); Don Lorenzo Perosi (Sistine Chapel); Josef Stransky (Landestheater, Prague); Richard Strauss (Berlin Royal Opera); Arturo Toscanini (La Scala, Milan).

Others: Marcel Dupré (organ, St. Vivien, Rouen); John Freund (editor, *Musical America*); Giulio Gatti-Casazza (general manager, La Scala, Milan); Harold Randolph (director, Peabody Institute); Charles Tournemire (organ, Sainte Clotilde, Paris).

E. Prizes/Honors

Prizes: Emil Mlynarski (Paderewski).

Honors: Max Bruch (French Academy); Francesco Cilea (Royal Academy, Florence); Reginald De Koven (National Institute of Arts and Letters); Ernst von Dohnányi (Hungarian Millennium Prize); Friedrich Niecks (Mus.Doc., Dublin University); Charles Hubert Parry (knighted).

F. Biographical Highlights

Charles Ives graduates from Yale; Albert Roussel begins study with Vincent d'Indy; Josef Suk marries Antonin Dvořák's daughter, Otilie; Donald Tovey graduates with honors from Oxford; Hugo Wolf, released from the asylum, tries to drown himself and is readmitted to the asylum.

G. Cultural Beginnings

Performing Groups—Choral: Bethlehem Bach Choir (Pennsylvania); Maurice Grau Opera Co.; New Brighton Choral Society; Stockholm Opera Co.; Vienna Volksoper.

Performing Groups—Instrumental: Los Angeles Symphony Orchestra; Società del Quartetto (Ferrara); Société Symphonique Lyonnaise; Worchestershire Philharmonic Society; York Symphony Orchestra.

Educational: Fox-Buonameci School (Boston); Mu Alpha Sinfonia Fraternity (Boston); Musikwissenschaftliches Institut (University of Vienna); Phi Mu Gamma Sorority.

Music Publishers: Theodore Morse (New York).

Music Publications: *Musical America*.

Performing Centers: Manhattan Opera House I; Metropol Theater (Berlin); Moscow Art Theater; Royal Opera House (Stockholm).

Other: Collection of Ancient Musical Instruments (Copenhagen); Deutsche Gramophon Gesellschaft; English Folk Song Society; National Federation of Music Clubs; National Institute of Arts and Letters; Rosenfeld Musical Press Bureau (New York); Young People's Concerts (by Frank Damrosch—New York).

H. Musical Literature

Arnaldo Bonaventura, *Manuale distoria della musica*; Antoine Dechevrens, *Études de Science Musicale*; Philip H. Goepp, *Symphonies and Their Meaning I*; Percy Goetschius, *Homophonic Forms of Musical Composition*; Salomon Jadassohn, *Methodik des Musiktheoretisches Unterrichts*; Max Kalbeck, *Opernabende I, II*; Franz Kullak, *Der Vortrag in der Musik am Ende des 19 Jahrhunderts*; Ebenezer Prout, *The Orchestra I*; Hugo Riemann, *Geschichte der Musiktheorie im IX.-XIX. Jahrhundert*; George Bernard Shaw, *The Perfect Wagnerite*; F. W. Shinn, *Musical Memory and Its Cultivations*; Hans Sommer, *Genossenschaft Deutscher Komponisten*.

I. Musical Compositions
Chamber Music:

String Quartets: Volkmar Andreae, *Quartet in E♭*; George W. Chadwick, *No. 5 in d*; Vincent d'Indy, *No. 2, Opus 45*; Alexander Glazunov, *No. 5 in d, Opus 70*; Carl Nielsen, *No. 4 in E♭, Opus 14*; Ottokar Nováček, *No. 2*; Richard Ohlsson, *No. 1 in e*; Henry Rabaud, *Quartet in g, Opus 3*; Vincenzo Tomasini, *No. 1*; Ralph Vaughan-Williams, *String Quartet in C*.

Sonata/Solos: Ferruccio Busoni, *Violin Sonata No. 2*; Georges Enescu, *Cello Sonata No. 1, Opus 26*; Arthur Farwell, *Ballade, Opus 1* (violin, piano); Josef Foerster, *Cello Sonata No. 1 in f, Opus 45*; Max Reger, *Cello Sonata in g, Opus 28–Violin Sonata in a, Opus 41*; Charles M. Widor, *Introduction and Rondo, Opus 72* (clarinet, piano).

Ensembles: Béla Bartók, *Piano Quartet in c, Opus 20*; Arthur H. Bird, *Serenade for Nineteen Wind Instruments, Opus 40*; Victor Herbert, *Humoresque for Woodwinds*; Hans Huber, *Sextet for Piano and Wind Quintet*; John Ireland, *Sextet* (clarinet, horn, string quartet); Max Reger, *Piano Quintet in e*; Carl Reinecke, *String Trio in E♭, Opus 249*; Charles Tournemire, *Piano Quintet, Opus 15*.

Piano: Arnold Bax, *Sonata No. 1*; Georges Enescu, *Variations on an Original Theme, Opus 5* (two, pianos); Gabriel Fauré, *Nocturne No. 7 in c♯, Opus 74*; Edvard Grieg, *Lyric Pieces, Book IX, Opus 68*; Anatol Liadov, *Two Preludes (B♭, B)–Mazurka in A on Polish Themes, Opus 42*; Sergei Liapunov, *Nocturne in D♭, Opus 8–Two Mazurkas, Opus 9*; Edward MacDowell, *Sea Pieces, Opus 55*; Ethelbert Nevin, *A Day in Venice, Opus 25*; Camille Saint-Saëns, *Caprice Héroïque, Opus 106* (two pianos).

Organ: Arthur H. Bird, *Three Oriental Sketches, Opus 42*; Léon Böellmann, *Offertoire sur des Noëls*; Max Reger, *Chorale Fantasia, "Ein' feste Berg," Opus 27–Fantasia and Fugue in f, Opus 29–Choral*

Fantasy, "Freudich sehr, o meine seele," Opus 30; Camille Saint-Saëns, *Three Preludes and Fugues, Opus 109.*

Choral/Vocal Music:

Choral: Max Bruch, *Gustav Adolf* (oratorio); Samuel Coleridge-Taylor, *Hiawatha's Wedding Feast* (cantata, part I); Dudley Buck, *Paul Revere's Ride* (male chorus, orchestra); Edward Elgar, *Caractacus, Opus 35* (cantata); Charles Ives, *Psalm 67*; Luigi Mancinelli, *La cantata del lavoro*; Vitěslav Novák, *Two Ballads on Polk Poetry, Opus 19*; C. Hubert Parry, *A Song of Darkness and Light*; Florent Schmitt, *Radegonde* (cantata); Harry R. Shelley, *Death and Life* (cantata); Giuseppe Verdi, *Four Sacred Pieces.*

Vocal: Amy Beach, *Three Songs, Opus 41*; Ernest Chausson, *Chanson perpétuelle*; Frederick Delius, *Mitternachtslied*; Alexander Glazunov, *Six Songs, Opus 59–Six Songs, Opus 60*; Charles Horwitz, *Because*; Engelbert Humperdinck, *Junge Lieder* (cycle); Edward MacDowell, *Four Songs, Opus 56*; Alexander Mackenzie, *Six Rustic Songs, Opus 66*; Max Reger, *Four Songs, Opus 23–Six Songs of Anna Ritter, Opus 21*; Richard Strauss, *Four Songs, Opus 36–Six Songs, Opus 37–Five Songs, Opus 39.*

Musical Stage: Isaac Albéniz, *Merlin*; Eugène d'Albert, *Die Abreise*; George Bristow, *Niagara*; Victor Herbert, *The Fortune Teller*; Pietro Mascagni, *Iris*; André Messager, *Véronique*; John Knowles Paine, *Azara*; Nicolai Rimsky-Korsakov, *The Tsar's Bride–Mozart and Salieri*; John Philip Sousa, *The Charlatan–The Bride Elect*; Wilhelm Stenhammar, *Tirfing, Opus 15.*

Orchestra/Band Music:

Concerted Music:

Piano: Volkmar Andreae, *Concerto in d*; Ernst von Dohnányi, *Concerto No. 1 in e, Opus 5*; Ernst Mielck, *Concert Piece.*

Other: Eduard Nápravnik, *Suite for Cello and Orchestra, Opus 60.*

Ballet/Incidental Music: Gabriel Fauré, *Pelléas et Mélisande, Opus 80* (IM); Edward German, *Much Ado about Nothing* (IM); Alexander Glazounov, *Les ruses d'amour, Opus 61* (B); Vincent d'Indy, *Médée, Opus 47* (IM); Alexander Mackenzie, *Manfred, Opus 58* (IM); Camille Saint-Saëns, *Déjanire* (IM); Jan Sibelius, *King Christian II, Opus 27* (IM).

Program Music: Zdeněk Fibich, *Impressions: From the Countryside*; Richard Strauss, *Ein Heldenleben, Opus 40.*

Standard Works: Ernest Chausson, *Soir de Fête, Opus 32*; Georges Enescu, *Poème roumain, Opus 1*; Zdeněk Fibich, *Overture, Oldřich e Božena*; Edvard Grieg, *Symphonic Dances, Opus 64*; Victor Herbert, *American Fantasia*; Vitěslav Novák, *Overture Maryša, Opus 18*; Ottokar Ostrčil, *Village Fête, Opus 1–Suite No. 2 in G*; Maurice Ravel, *Shéhérazade Overture*; Charles M. Widor, *Ouverture espagnole.*

Symphonies: Hugo Alfvén, *No. 2 in D, Opus 11*; Frederick Converse, *No. 1 in d*; Zdeněk Fibich, *No. 3 in e, Opus 53*; Charles Ives, *No. 1*; Vasili Kalinnikov, *No. 2 in A*; Hugo Kaun, *Symphony*.

1899
❁

Historical Highlights: The First Hague Conference sets up a Permanent Court of Arbitration to settle disputes between nations; the Boer War between the Dutch and British breaks out in South Africa; Friedrich Bayer and Co. introduces aspirin; in U.S. history, Cuba, Puerto Rico, and Guam become U.S. protectorates—the Philippines begin their revolt for independence from the United States; John Hay proclaims the Open Door Policy for trade with China.

Art and Literature Highlights: Births—artists Moses and Raphael Soyer, writers Noel Coward, C. S. Forester, Ernest Hemingway; Deaths—artists Rosa Bonheur, Alfred Sisley, writers Horatio Alger, E.D.E.N. Southworth. Art—Homer's *The Gulf Stream*, Prendergast's *Umbrellas in the Rain*; Literature—Chekhov's *The Three Sisters*, Chesnutt's *The Conjure Woman*, Fitch's *The Cowboy and the Lady*, Reymont's *Promised Land*.

Musical Highlights

A. Births
Composers: Georges Auric (France) February 15; Alan Bush (England) December 22; Carlos Chávez (Mexico) June 13; Pavel Haas (Czechoslovakia) June 21; Anthon van der Horst (Holland) June 20; Jón Leifs (Iceland) May 1; Harl McDonald (U.S.A.) July 27; George Frederick McKay (U.S.A.) June 11; Francis Poulenc (France) January 7; Silvestre Revueltas (Mexico) December 31; Alexander Tcherepnin (Russia) January 20; Randall Thompson (U.S.A.) April 21; Pantcho Vladigerov (Bulgaria) March 13.

Conductors: Peter Herman Adler (Czechoslovakia-U.S.A.) December 2; John Barbirolli (England) December 2; Zdeněk Chalabala (Czechoslovakia) April 18; Werner Janssen (U.S.A.) June 1; Lovro von Matačić (Yugoslavia) February 14; Eugene Ormandy (Hungary-U.S.A.) November 18; William Steinberg (Germany-U.S.A.) August 1; Hans Swarowsky (Austria) September 16.

Singers: Pierre Bernac (French baritone) January 12; Roy Henderson (Scottish baritone) July 4; Dorothea Dix Lawrence (American soprano) September 22; Dennis Noble (British baritone) September 25; Alexander Pirogov (Russian bass) July 4; Gertrude Rünger (German contralto); Joachim Sattler (German tenor) August 21; Helen Traubel

(American soprano) June 20; Franz Völker (German tenor) March 31; Ludwig Weber (Austrian bass) July 29.

Performers: Robert Casadesus (French pianist) April 7; Wilbur Chenoweth (American pianist) June 4; Ania Dorfman (Russian-born pianist) July 9; S-C "Sonia" Eckhardt-Gramatté (Russian-born violinist) January 6; Jascha Heifetz (Russian-born violinist) February 2; Henry Holst (Danish violinist) July 25; Alton Jones (American pianist) August 3; Leopold Mannes (American pianist/educator) December 26; Gerald Moore (British pianist) July 30; Feri Roth (Hungarian-born violinist) July 18; Toscha Seidel (Russian-born violinist) November 17; Mária Thomán (Hungarian violinist) July 12.

Others: Otto Edwin Albrecht (American musicologist) July 8; Claudia Cassidy (American critic) November 15; Karl Geiringer (Austrian-born musicologist) April 26; Rudolf Gerber (German musicologist) April 15; Gustav Reese (American musicologist) November 29; André Souris (Belgian musicologist) July 10.

B. Deaths

Composers: Ernest Chausson (France) June 10; Johann Strauss, Jr., (Austria) June 3.

Conductors: Hans Balatka (Czechoslovakia-U.S.A.) April 17; Johann Nepomuk Fuchs (Austria) October 5; Charles Lamoureux (France) December 21.

Singers: Marie Luise Dustmann (German soprano) March 2; A. J. (Signor) Foli (American bass) October 20; Mary Anne Goward (British soprano) March 12; Amalie Joachim (German mezzo-soprano) February 3; Franz Krückl (Moravian baritone) January 13; Hans Feodor von Milde (Austrian baritone) December 10; Maria Piccolomini (Italian soprano) December 23; Heinrich Wiegand (German bass) May 28.

Performers: Frederic Brandeis (Austrian-born pianist) May 14; Johann Decker-Schenk (Austrian guitarist) September 4; François Jehin-Prume (Belgian-born violinist) May 29; Antoine de Kontski (Polish pianist) December 7; Edward Roeckel (German pianist) November 2; August Winding (Danish pianist) June 16.

Others: Johann Gotthilf Bärmig (German organ builder) October 26; George Gemünder (German-born violin maker) January 15; Friedrich von Hausegger (Austrian musicologist) February 23; Theodore Heintzman (German-born piano maker) July 25; Stéphen Morelot (French church music scholar) October 7; Luigi Francesco Valdrighi (Italian music scholar) April 20.

C. Debuts

Singers: Amadeo Bassi (Italian tenor—Florence); Johannes Bischoff (German baritone—Cologne); Nicolai Bolshakov (Russian tenor—St. Petersburg); Eleanor Broadfoot (American mezzo-soprano—New

York); Eugenia Burzio (Italian soprano—Turin); Marquerite Carré (French soprano—Nantes); Charles Dalmorès (French tenor—Rouen); Zdenka Fassbender (Bohemian soprano—Karlsruhe); Jeanne Gerville-Réache (French contralto—Paris); William Wade Hinshaw (American baritone—St. Louis); Otokar Marák (Czech tenor—Brünn); Amelia Pinto (Italian soprano—Brescia); Léon Rothier (French bass—Paris); Domenico Viglione-Borghese (Italian baritone—Lodi).

Performers: Rudolph Ganz (Swiss-born pianist—Berlin); Heinrich Gebhard (German-born pianist—Boston); Katherine Ruth Heyman (American pianist—Boston); Heniot Lévy (Polish-born pianist—Berlin); Sergei Rachmaninoff (Russian pianist/conductor—London).

D. New Positions

Conductors: Leo Blech (German Theater, Prague); Camille Chevillard (Lamoureux Concerts, Paris); Jules Danbé (Théátre Lyrique, Paris); Michele Esposito (Dublin Orchestral Society); Johan Halvorsen (Oslo National Theater); Alfred Hertz (Breslau Opera); Peter Raabe (Netherlands Opera, Amsterdam).

Others: Oskar Fleischer (president, International Music Society); Otto Malling (director, Copenhagen Conservatory); Emil Paur (director, National Conservatory, New York); Richard von Preger (director, Vienna Conservatory).

E. Prizes/Honors

Prizes: Charles Levadé (Prix de Rome); Léon Moreau (Prix de Rome); François Rasse (Prix de Rome); Benno Moiseiwitsch (Rubinstein).

Honors: Moritz Moszkowsky (Berlin Academy); Joseph Rheinberger (Dr.Phil., Munich); Hugo Riemann (Mus.Doc., Edinburgh U.).

F. Biographical Highlights

Feodor Chaliapin becomes a regular member of the Bolshoi Opera; Arthur Farwell returns to the United States and begins lecturing at Cornell; Nicolas Miaskovsky enters the Academy of Military Engineering but also studies music; Jan Sibelius visits Italy and Bayreuth, where his anti-Wagner feelings begin to emerge; Frederick Stock becomes assistant to Theodore Thomas at the Chicago Symphony.

G. Cultural Beginnings

Performing Groups—Choral: Litchfield County Choral Union (Connecticut); Orpheus Choral Society of Dublin; Schola Cantorum d'Avignon; Washington Permanent Chorus (D.C.).

Performing Groups—Instrumental: Dublin Orchestral Society; Essen Symphony Orchestra; Hartford (Connecticut) Philharmonic Orchestra.

Festivals: Norfolk Chamber Music Festival.

Educational: Conservatorio de Música y Declamación (Havana); Guilmant Organ School (New York); Heidingsfeld Conservatory of

Music (Danzig); Mokranjac (Serbian) Music School (Belgrade); Vogt'sche Konservatorium (Hamburg); Wiest Conservatory of Music (Bucharest).
Music Publishers: Willis Music Co. (Cincinnati).
Music Publications: *Bollettino Bibliografico Musicale; Brainard's Musical; Choir: A Monthly Journal of Church Music; Die Fackel.*
Performing Centers: Olympia Music Hall (New York).
Other: Austin Organ Co. (Hartford, Connecticut); Cambridge University Musical Club; International Music Society (Berlin); Kansas City Musical Club; Lyon and Healy Harp Co. (Chicago); Swiss Musicological Society.

H. Musical Literature

Robert Eitner, *Quellenlexicon der Musiker I;* Louis Elson, *National Music of America and Its Sources;* Juan Bautista Fuentes, *Teoria de la Música;* J. A. Fuller-Maitland, *Musician's Pilgrimage;* Guido Gasperini, *Storia della Musica;* Eduard Hanslick, *Am ende des Jahrhunders;* Salomon Jadassohn, *Das Wesen der melodie in der Tonkunst;* Pierre Lalo, *La musique;* Dobroslav Orel, *A Theoretical and Practical Manuel of Roman Plainsong;* Camille Saint-Saëns, *Portraits et souvenirs;* Max Seiffert, *Geschichte der Klaviermusik;* J. E. West, *Catholic Organs Past and Present.*

I. Musical Compositions
Chamber Music:
String Quartets: Vitěslav Novák, *No. 1 in G, Opus 22;* Richard Ohlsson, *No. 2 in D;* Ottokar Ostrčil, *Quartet in B, Opus 4;* Robert Fuchs, *No. 2 in a, Opus 62;* Camille Saint-Saëns, *No. 1 in e, Opus 112;* Richard Tobias, *No. 1.*
Sonata/Solos: Georges Enescu, *Violin Sonata No. 2, Opus 6.*
Ensembles: Volkmar Andreae, *Piano Trio No. 1 in f, Opus 1;* André Caplet, *Quintet for Piano and Winds;* Manuel de Falla, *Piano Quartet;* Vincent d'Indy, *Chansons et Danses, Opus 50.*
Piano: Manuel de Falla, *Serenata andaluza;* Arthur Farwell, *Owasco Memories, Opus 8;* Alexander Glazunov, *Prelude and Fugue, Opus 62;* Anatol Liadov, *Four Preludes (B♭, g, G, e) Opus 46;* Edward MacDowell, *Sonata No. 3 in d, "Norse," Opus 57;* Horace Nicholl, *Twelve Etudes Mélodiques, Opus 26;* Vitěslav Novák, *Four Pieces, Opus 20;* Horatio Parker, *Three Characteristic Pieces, Opus 49;* Maurice Ravel, *Pavane for a Dead Princess* (orchestrated 1912); Camille Saint-Saëns, *Six Etudes, Opus 111;* Alexander Scriabin, *Nine Mazurkas, Opus 25;* Charles Tournemire, *Sonata, Opus 17.*
Organ: Max Reger, *Sonata No. 1 in f♯, Opus 37–Two Choral Fantasias, Opus 40;* Florent Schmitt, *Preludes, Opus 11;* Charles Tournemire, *Pièce symphonique, Opus 16;* Louis Vierne, *Organ Symphony No. 1;* Charles-Marie Widor, *Symphony No. 10, "Romane."*

Choral/Vocal Music:

Choral: Hugo Alfven, *Cantata of the Turn of the Century*; Samuel Coleridge-Taylor, *The Death of Minnehaha* (cantata); Alexander Glazunov, *Cantata for Pushkin's 100ᵗʰ Birthday, Opus 65*; Henry Hadley, *In Music's Praise*; Charles Ives, *The Celestial Country* (cantata); Margaret R. Lang, *Te Deum, Opus 34*; Luigi Mancinelli, *Missa in auxilium Christianorum in e*; Zakhary Paliashvili, *Mass in E♭*; Horatio Parker, *Adstant angelorum chori, Opus 45*; Max Reger, *Seven Male Choruses, Opus 38*; Nicolai Rimsky-Korsakov, *Song of Oleg, the Wise, Opus 58*; Florent Schmitt, *Callirhoé* (cantata); Ralph Vaughan-Williams, *Mass*; Ermanno Wolf-Ferrari, *La Sulamite* (oratorio).

Vocal: Amy Beach, *Five Songs on Burns, Opus 43*; César Cui, *Twenty-Five Pushkin Poems, Opus 57*; Edward Elgar, *Sea Pictures* (cycle); Edward MacDowell, *Three Songs, Opus 58*; Ethelbert Nevin, *Songs from Vineacre, Opus 28–Captive Memories, Opus 29* (cycle); Horatio Parker, *Six Old English Songs, Opus 47*; Wilhelm Peterson-Berger, *The River to the Girl–The Wood Spirit*; Maurice Ravel, *Deux épigrammes de Clément Marot*; Max Reger, *Six Songs, Opus 35–Five Songs, Opus 37*; Jan Sibelius, *Seven Songs, Opus 17– Six Songs, Opus 36*.

Musical Stage: Elfrieda Andrée, *Fritiofs Saga*; Reginald De Koven, *The Three Dragoons*; Antonin Dvořák, *The Devil and Kate, Opus 112*; Victor Herbert, *Cyrano de Bergerac–The Ameer*; John Philip Sousa, *Chris and the Wonderful Lamp*; Wilhelm Stenhammar, *Das Fest auf Solhaug*.

Orchestra/Band Music:

Concerted Music:

Piano: Amy Beach, *Concerto in c♯, Opus 45*.

Violin: Ludwig Holm, *Concerto No. 2*; Joseph Joachim, *Concerto in G, Opus 17*.

Ballet/Incidental Music: Alexander Glazunov, *The Seasons* (B); Frederick Gleason, *The Song of Life* (B); Gustav Holst, *Suite de Ballet, Opus 10* (B); C. Hubert Parry, *A Repentance* (IM); Edgar Stillman Kelley, *Ben Hur* (IM).

Program Music: Claude Debussy, *Three Nocturnes*; Frederick Delius, *Paris: Song of a Great City*; Arne Oldberg, *Paolo and Francesca*; Ottokar Ostrčil, *The Tale of Šemik, Opus 3*; Horatio Parker, *A Northern Ballad, Opus 46*; Franz Schmidt, *Eglogue, poème vigilien*; Arnold Schoenberg, *Transfigured Night, Opus 4*; Jan Sibelius, *Finlandia, Opus 26*; William Wallace, *Sister Helen*.

Standard Works: George W. Chadwick, *Overture, Adonais*; Edward Elgar, *Enigma Variations, Opus 36*; Georges Enescu, *Pastorale-Fantasie*; Edward German, *The Seasons* (symphonic suite); Hugo Kaun, *Overture, Der Mahler von Antwerp*; Jules Massenet, *Overture, Brumaire*;

Alexander Scriabin, *Reverie for Orchestra, Opus 24*; Jan Sibelius, *Scènes Historiques I, Opus 25*; John Philip Sousa, *March, Hands across the Sea*. **Symphonies:** Volkmar Andreae, *Symphony in F*; W. H. Bell, *Walt Whitman Symphony*; Joseph Jongen, *Symphony, Opus 15*; Henri Rabaud, *No. 2 in e, Opus 5*; Franz Schmidt, *No. 1 in E*; Jan Sibelius, *No. 1 in e, Opus 39*; Josef Suk, *Symphony in E, Opus 14*.

1900
❉

Historical Highlights: The Boxer Rebellion comes to an end in China with help from the Western powers; Victor Emanuel III becomes king of Italy; Ibn Saud forms the Kingdom of Saudi Arabia; the Paris Universal Exposition draws worldwide crowds; the British Labour Party is formed; in the United States, William McKinley is reelected president; Hawaii officially becomes a U.S. territory; Carrie Nation begins her hachet crusade against liquor.

Art and Literature Highlights: Births—writers James Hilton, Laura Hobson, Thomas Wolfe, artists Louise Nevelson, Yves Tanguy; Deaths—writers Stephen Crane, Oscar Wilde, artists Frederic Church, Jean Falguière, Wilhelm Leibl. Art—Bourdelle's *Head of Apollo*, Pendergast's *Central Park*, Toulouse-Lautrec's *La Modiste*; Literature—Conrad's *Lord Jim*, Dreiser's *Sister Carrie*, Shaw's *Caesar and Cleopatra*, Tarkington's *Monsieur Beaucaire*.

Musical Highlights

A. Births
Composers: George Antheil (U.S.A.) July 8; Nicolai Berezowsky (Russia-U.S.A.) May 17; Robert Blum (Switzerland) November 27; Willy Burkhard (Switzerland) April 17; Aaron Copland (U.S.A.) November 14; Gunnar Ek (Sweden) June 21; Pierre-Octave Ferroud (France) January 6; Isadore Freed (U.S.A.) March 26; Boyan Georgiev Ikonomov (Bulgaria) December 14; Ernst Krenek (Austria-U.S.A.) August 23; Achille Longo (Italy) March 28; Otto Luening (U.S.A.) June 15; Colin McPhee (Canada-U.S.A.) March 15; Alexander Mossolov (Russia) August 11; Robert Oboussier (Switzerland) July 9; Leo Smit (Holland) May 14; Joseph Frederick Wagner (U.S.A.) January 9; Kurt Weill (Germany) March 2.
Conductors: Leon Barzin (U.S.A.) November 27; Edward van Beinum (Holland) September 3; Paul Kletzki (Poland-Switzerland) March 21; Efrem Kurtz (Russia-Germany) November 7; Charles O'Connell (U.S.A.) April 22; Jonel Perlea (Romania-U.S.A.) December 13; Karl Ristenpart (Germany) January 26; Hans Schmidt-Isserstedt (Germany) May 5; Tibor Serly (Hungary) November 25;

Reginald Stewart (Scotland-U.S.A.) April 20; Fred Waring (U.S.A.) June 9.

Singers: Salvatore Baccaloni (Italian bass) April 14; Erna Berger (German soprano) October 19; Roger Bourdin (French baritone) June 14; Vina Bovy (Belgian soprano) May 22; John Brownlee (American baritone) January 7; Arthur Carron (British tenor) December 12; Gina Cigna (Italian soprano) March 6; Richard Crooks (American tenor) June 26; Henri-Bertrand Etcheverry (French bass-baritone) March 29; Ella Flesch (Hungarian soprano) June 16; Dusolina Giannini (American soprano) December 19; August Griebel (German bass) July 2; Ivan Kozlovsky (Russian tenor) March 24; Mary Lewis (American soprano) January 7; Karl Schmitt-Walter (German baritone) December 23; Gladys Swarthout (American mezzo-soprano) December 25; Jennie Tourel (Russian-born mezzo-soprano) June 22.

Performers: Maurice Eisenberg (German-born cellist) February 24; Jacques Février (French pianist) July 26; Joseph Fuchs (American violinist) April 26; Anis Fuleihan (Cyprus-born pianist) April 2; Florence Grandland Galajikian (American pianist) July 29; Mieczyslaw Munz (Polish-born pianist) October 31; Solomon Pimsleur (Austrian-born pianist) September 19; Max Rosen (Polish-born violinist) April 11; Alexander Tcherepnin (Russian-born pianist/composer) January 20; Elinor Remick Warren (American pianist/composer) February 23.

Others: Heinrich Besseler (German musicologist) April 2; Werner Danckert (German musicologist) June 22; Helen Hewitt (American musicologist) May 2.

B. Deaths

Composers: Zdeněk Fibich (Czechoslovakia) October 15; Johann Peter Hartmann (Denmark) March 10; Heinrich Herzogenberger (Austrian) October 9; Ottokar Nováček (Czechoslovakia) February 3; Arthur Sullivan (England) November 22.

Conductors: Hermann Levi (Germany) May 13.

Singers: Charles Adams (American tenor) July 4; Franz Betz (German baritone) August 11; Giuseppe del Puente (Italian baritone) May 25; Sims Reeves (Brtiish tenor) October 25; Sebastiano Ronconi (Italian baritone) February 6; Henry Russell (British tenor) December 8; Joseph Tagliafico (French bass) January 27; Heinrich Vogl (German tenor) April 21.

Performers: Jules Armingaud (French violinist) February 27; Charles-Louis Hanon (French pianist/pedagogue) March 19; Edwin George Monk (British organist) January 3; S. Austen Pearce (British-born organist/composer) April 9; Eugène Vivier (French horn virtuoso) February 24.

Others: Carl Bechstein (German piano maker) March 6; Ludwig Bussler (German music theorist) January 18; Sir George Grove (British musicographer) May 28; Bartholf Senff (German publisher) June 25; Richard Storrs Willis (American music author/composer) May 7.

C. Debuts

Singers: Elsa Alsen (German-born soprano—Breslau, as alto); Pasquale Amato (Italian baritone—Naples); Jane Bathori (French mezzo-soprano—Nantes); Paul Bender (German bass-baritone—Breslau); Anna Case (American soprano—New York); Lina Cavalieri (Italian soprano—Naples); Povla Frijsh (Danish-born soprano—Paris); Mary Garden (Scottish-born soprano—Paris); Friedrich Plaschke (Czech bass-baritone—Dresden); Joseph Schwarz (Latvian-born baritone—Linz).

Performers: Nicolai Medtner (Russian pianist—Vienna); Artur Rubinstein (Polish pianist—Potsdam); David Saperton (American pianist—Pittsburgh).

D. New Positions

Conductors: Frederic Cowen (London Philharmonic Society and Glascow Scottish Orchestra); Karel Kovařovic (National Theater, Prague); Ferdinand Löwe (Vienna Gesellschaftkonzerte); Fritz Scheel (Philadelphia Orchestra); Gustav Strube (Boston Pops Orchestra); Alexander von Zemlinsky (Karlstheater, Vienna).

Others: Wilhelm Altman (librarian, Prussian State Library, Berlin); Granville Bantock (music director, Birmingham Institute); Frederick Gleason (director, Chicago Conservatory); James G. Huneker (music/art critic, *New York Sun*); Samuel de Lange (director, Stuttgart Conservatory); John J. McClellan (organ, Mormon Tabernacle, Utah); Henry Newbolt (editor, *Monthly Review*); Louis Vierne (organ, Notre Dame, Paris).

E. Prizes/Honors

Prizes: Alexander Goedicke (Rubinstein); Paul M. Lanowski (Prix de Rome); Florent Schmitt (Prix de Rome).

Honors: Gustav Charpentier (Legion of Honor); W. H. Cummings (D. Mus., Trinity College, Dublin); Edward Elgar (Mus.Doc., Cambridge).

F. Biographical Highlights

Manuel de Falla's family loses a fortune and moves to Madrid; John Philip Sousa takes his band on a highly successful first European tour; Moritz Steiner donates his famous instrument collection to Yale University; Eduard Strauss takes his Vienna Orchestra on a tour of the United States.

G. Cultural Beginnings

Performing Groups—Choral: Filharmoniska Sällskapet (Stockholm chorus).

Performing Groups—Instrumental: Amateur Symphony Orchestra (Denver, Colorado); Cherniavsky Trio; Dallas Symphony Orchestra; Honolulu Symphony Orchestra; Huddersfield Chamber Music Society; Philadelphia Orchestra; Vienna Symphony Orchestra.

Festivals: Bethlehem Bach Festival (Pennsylvania).

Educational: Drake School of Music (Chicago); Matthay Piano School (London); Seminar für Schulgesang (Berlin); West Side Musical College (Cleveland).

Music Publishers: Casa Dotesio (Unión Musical Española) Publishing Co. (Spain).

Music Publications: *American Music Journal* (Cleveland); *The Violinist*; *Weiner Konzerthausgesellschaft*.

Performing Centers: Boston Symphony Hall; Butler Standard Theater (Kansas City, Missouri).

Others: Melville Clark Piano Co.; Hall of Fame for Great Americans; "His Master's Voice" (patent by Emil Berliner); Leedy Manufacturing Co. (Indianapolis); People's Symphony Concerts (New York); Society of Classical Concerts (Barcelona); Tonal Art Club (London).

H. Music Literature

Kornél Abrányi, *Hungarian Music in the 19th Century*; Theodore Baker, *Baker's Biographical Dictionary of Musicians*; Robert Eitner, *Biographisch-Bibliographisches Quellen-Lexicon der Musiker . . .* (ten volumes by 1904); Amintore Galli, *Estetica della musica*; Eduard Hanslick, *Aus Neuer und Neuster Zeit*; Rupert Hughes, *Contemporary American Composers*; Stewart MacPherson, *Practical Counterpoint*; Carl Reinecke, *Und manche liebe Schatten steigen auf: Gedenkblätter an berühmte Musiker*; Hugo Riemann, *Die elemente der musikalischen Ästhetic*; Richard Specht, *Kritisches Skizzenbuch*.

I. Musical Compositions

Chamber Music:

String Quartets: Franz Bornschein, *Quartet*; Ernst von Dohnányi, *No. 1, Opus 7*; Reinhold Glière, *No. 1, Opus 2*; Ludolf Nielsen, *No. 1 in A, Opus 1*; Arne Oldberg, *Quartet in c*; Max Reger, *Two Quartets (g, A), Opus 52*; Guy Ropartz, *No. 2*; Alexander Scriabin, *Variations in G*.

Sonata/Solos: Joseph Joachim, *Romanze in C* (violin, piano); Max Reger, *Four Violin Sonatas (d, A, b, g), Opus 42–Clarinet (Viola) Sonata No. 1–No. 2, Opus 49*; Julius Röntgen, *Cello Sonata, Opus 41*; Jan Sibelius, *Fantasia* (cello, piano); Josef Suk, *Four Pieces, Opus 17* (violin, piano).

Ensembles: Georgi Catoire, *Piano Trio in f*; Georges Enescu, *Octet for Strings, Opus 7*; Reinhold Glière, *String Sextet, Opus 1–Octet, Opus 5*.
Piano: César Cui, *Five Pieces, Opus 52*(?); Arthur Farwell, *American Indian Melodies, Opus 11*; Alexander Glazunov, *Theme and Variations, Opus 72*; Victor Herbert, *Six Pieces for Piano, Set I*; Edward MacDowell, *Sonata No. 4 in e, "Keltic"*; Vitěslav Novák, *Sonata eroica, Opus 24*; Alexander Scriabin, *Two Preludes, Opus 25–Fantaisie, Opus 28*; Karol Szymanowski, *Nine Preludes, Opus 1*; Charles Tournemire, *Six Little Pieces, Opus 20*; Louis Vierne, *Suite bourguignonne*.
Organ: Horace Nicholl, *Twelve Symphonic Preludes and Fugues, Opus 30*; Felix Nowowiejski, *Easy Pieces I*; Max Reger, *Fantasy and Fugue on B-A-C-H, Opus 46–Six Trios, Opus 47–Three Chorale Fantasias, Opus 52*; Charles M. Widor, *Symphonie Romaine, Opus 73*.

Choral/Vocal Music:
Choral: Hugo Alfven, *The Bells*; Léon Böellmann, *Laudate Dominum–Veni Creator*; Samuel Coleridge-Taylor, *Hiawatha's Departure* (cantata); Antonin Dvořák, *Festival Song, Opus 113*; Edward Elgar, *The Dream of Gerontius, Opus 38* (oratorio); Victor Herbert, *The Viceroy* (cantata); Charles Ives, *Psalm 135*; Ruggero Leoncavallo, *Requiem for King Umberto I*; Pietro Mascagni, *Requiem in Memory of King Umberto I*; Jules Massenet, *La terre Promise* (oratorio); Vitěslav Novák, *Two Ballads, Opus 23*; Horatio Parker, *A Wanderer's Psalm, Opus 50*; C. Hubert Parry, *Te Deum in F*; Henri Rabaud, *Job, Opus 9*; Max Reger, *Three Choruses, Opus 39*; Louis Vierne, *Messe Solennelle*.
Vocal: Amy Beach, *Three (Robert) Browning Songs, Opus 44*; Charles Gabriel, *The Glory Song*; Edvard Grieg, *Five Songs, Opus 69–Five Songs, Opus 70*; Sergei Liapunov, *Four Songs, Opus 14*(?); Vitěslav Novák, *Spring Moods*; Horatio Parker, *Three Songs, Opus 52*; Wilhelm Peterson-Berger, *Frösöblomster II*; Max Reger, *Eight Songs, Opus 43–Seven Songs, Opus 48–Twelve Songs "An Hugo Wolf," Opus 51*; Richard Strauss, *Five Songs, Opus 46–Five Songs, Opus 47–Five Songs, Opus 48*; Vasili Wrangell, *Eight Songs, Opus 37*.
Musical Stage: George W. Chadwick, *Judith*; Gustave Charpentier, *Louise*; César Cui, *Mam'zelle Fifi*; Antonin Dvořák, *Rusalka, Opus 114*; Gabriel Fauré, *Prométhée, Opus 82*; Zdeněk Fibich, *The Fall of Arkun*; Mikhail Ippolitov-Ivanov, *Asya*; Charles Lecocq, *La Belle au Bois Dormant*; Ruggero Leoncavallo, *Zaza*; Hamish MacCunn, *The Masque of War and Peace*; Alexander Mackenzie, *The Cricket on the Hearth*; Albéric Magnard, *Guercoeur, Opus 12*; Ignace Jan Paderewski, *Manru*; Wilhelm Peterson-Berger, *Ran*; Giacomo Puccini, *Tosca*; Nicolai Rimsky-Korsakov, *Tsar Saltan*; Humphrey Stewart, *The Conspirators*; Arthur Sullivan, *The Rose of Persia*; Ermano Wolf-Ferrari, *Cenerentola*.

Orchestra/Band Music:
  Concerted Music:
    Piano: Volkmar Andreae, *Concertpiece in b*; Helen Hopekirk, *Concerto in D*; Carl Reinecke, *Concerto No. 4 in b, Opus 254*(?).
    Violin: Max Reger, *Two Romances (G, D)*; Charles V. Stanford, *Concerto in D*.
    Other: Alexander Glazunov, *Chant du Ménéstrel, Opus 71* (cello); Joseph Jongen, *Cello Concerto, Opus 18*; Charles Martin Loeffler, *Divertissement espagnol* (saxophone); Charles M. Widor, *Choral et variations* (harp).
  Ballet/Incidental Music: Anton Arensky, *Egyptian Nights* (B); Riccardo Drigo, *Les Millions d'Arlequin* (B); Alexander Glazunov, *Ruses d'Amour* (B); Johan Halvorsen, *Gurre* (IM); Jules Massenet, *Phèdre* (IM); André Messager, *Une aventure de la guimard* (B); John Knowles Paine, *The Birds* (IM); C. Hubert Parry, *Agamemnon* (IM).
  Program Music: Granville Bantock, *Thalaba, the Destroyer*; Ernest Bloch, *Vivre-aimer*; Frederick Converse, *The Festival of Pan*; Zdeněk Fibich, *The Submerged Bell*; Josef Bohuslav Foerster, *My Youth, Opus 44*; Rubin Goldmark, *Hiawatha*; Josef Suk, *Pohádka, Opus 16*; Frank Van der Stucken, *Pax Triumphans*.
  Standard Works: Arthur Farwell, *Academic Overture, "Cornell," Opus 9*; Arthur Foote, *Four Character Pieces after the Rubáiyát of Omar Khayyám*; Julius Fučik, *Entry of the Gladiators*; Carl Goldmark, *Ouverture solennelle, Opus 73*; Henry Hadley, *Overture, In Bohemia, Opus 28*; Jakob A. Hägg, *Amerikanische Festklänge*; Philipp Scharwenka, *Dramatische Fantasie*; Harry R. Shelley, *Santa Claus Overture*; Ralph Vaughan-Williams, *Bucolic Suite*.
  Symphonies: Reinhold Glière, *No. 1 in E♭, Opus 8*; Edgar Stillman Kelley, *No. 1, "Gulliver: His Voyage to Lilliput"*; Gustave Mahler, *No. 4*; Jaime Pahissa, *No. 1 for Strings*; Alexander Scriabin, *No. 1 in E, Opus 26*.

Composition Index

Aaltonen, Erkki: *Piano Concerto No. 1*, 1948I; *Piano Concerto No. 2*, 1954I; *Symphony No. 1*, 1947I; *Symphony No. 2, "Hiroshima,"* 1949I; *Symphony No. 3, "Popular,"* 1952I; *Symphony No. 4*, 1959I; *Symphony No. 5*, 1964I

Aav, Evald: *The Vikings*, 1928I

Abbado, Marcello: *String Quartet No. 1*, 1947I; *String Quartet No. 2*, 1953I; *String Quartet No. 3*, 1969I

Abe, Kōmei: *String Quartet No. 1*, 1934I; *String Quartet No. 2*, 1937I; *String Quartet No. 3*, 1939I

Abeille, Ludwig: *Peter und Ännchen*, 1809I

Abel, Carl F.: *Flute Trios (4), Opus 16*, 1783I; *String Trios (6), Opus 16*, 1783I; *Symphonies (6) in Four Parts, Opus 1*, 1759I; *Symphonies No. 7-12, Opus 4*, 1762I; *Symphonies No. 13-18, Opus 7*, 1767I; *Symphonies No. 19-24, Opus 10*, 1773I; *Symphonies No. 31-36*, 1783I

Abos, Girolamo: *Erifile*, 1752I; *Lucio Vero*, 1752I; *Tito Manlio*, 1751I

Abrahamsen, Hans: *Cello Concerto*, 1987I; *Stratification*, 1975I; *Symphony in C*, 1972I; *Symphony No. 1*, 1974I; *Symphony No. 2*, 1982I; *Walden*, 1978I

Absil, Jean: *Piano Concerto No. 1*, 1937I; *Symphony No. 1*, 1920I; *Symphony No. 2*, 1936I

Accorimboni, Agostino: *L'amante nel sacco*, 1772I; *L'amor artigiano*, 1777I; *Le contadine astute*, 1770I; *Le finte zingarelle*, 1774I; *Il finto cavaliere*, 1777I; *Giuseppe riconosciuto*, 1757I; *Il Governatore delle Isole Canarie*, 1785I; *Il marchese di Castelverde*, 1779I; *Nitteti*, 1777I; *Il podestà di Tufo antico*, 1780I; *Il Regno delle Amazzoni*, 1783I; *Le scaltre contedine de Montegelato*, 1768I; *Lo schiavo fortunato*, 1783I; *Le virtuose bizzarre*, 1778I

Achron, Isadore: *Piano Concerto No. 1*, 1937I; *Piano Concerto No. 2*, 1942I

Achron, Joseph: *Violin Concerto No. 1, Opus 60*, 1925I; *Violin Concerto No. 2, Opus 68*, 1933I; *Violin Sonata*, 1910I

Acker, Dieter: *Arcades*, 1995I; *Bassoon Concerto*, 1980I; *Piano Concerto*, 1984I; *Piano Sonata No. 2*, 1993I; *Piano Sonata for Two Pianos*, 1993I; *String Quartet No. 1*, 1964I; *String Quartet No. 2*, 1966I; *String Quartet No. 3*, 1968I; *String Quartet No. 4*, 1975I; *String Quartet No. 5*, 1995I; *Symphony No. 1, "Lebenslaufe,"* 1978I; *Symphony No. 2*, 1982I

Adam, Adolphe: *Le brasseur de Preston*, 1838I; *Cagliostro*, 1844I; *Le châlet*, 1834I; *Le corsaire*, 1856I; *Danilowa*, 1830I; *Faust*, 1833I; *Le fidèle berger*, 1838I; *Giralda*, 1850I; *Giselle*, 1841I; *If I Were a King*, 1852I; 1836I; *La jolie fille de Gand*, 1840I; *Le lac des fées*, 1839I; *Pierre et Catherine*, 1829I; *Le postillon de Longjumeau*, 1836I; *La poupée de Nuremberg*, 1852I; *La reine d'un jour*, 1839I; *La rose de Péronne*, 1841I; *Le sourd*, 1853I; *Le toréador*, 1849I

Adam, Claus: *Cello Concerto*, 1973I; *String Quartet No. 1*, 1975I; *String Trio*, 1967I

Adams, Daniel: *Quandary*, 2000I

Adams, John: *American Standard*, 1973I; *The Chairman Dances*, 1986I; *China Gates*, 1977I; *Common Tones in Simple Time*, 1979I; *Death of Klinghoffer*, 1991I; *El Dorado*, 1991I; *Eros Piano* (piano, orchestra), 1989I; *Fearful Symmetries*, 1988I; *Grand Pianola Music*, 1982I; *Grounding*, 1975I; *Harmonielehre*, 1985I; *Harmonium*, 1980I; *Lollapalooza*, 1995I; *Naive & Sentimental Music*, 1998I; *El Niño*, 2000I; *Nixon in China*, 1987I; *Onyx*, 1976I; *Phrygian Gates*, 1977I; *Piano Concerto, "Century Rolls"* (piano), 1996I; *Piano Quintet*, 1970I; *Shaker Loops*, 1978I; *Slonimsky's Earbox*, 1996I; *The Wound Dresser*, 1989I

Adams, Mark: *Little Women*, 1998I

Adams, Stephen: *The Holy City*, 1905I

Addinsell, Richard: *Warsaw Concerto*, 1942I

Adès, Thomas: *America*, 1999I; *Asyla*, 1997I; *"but all shall be well,"* 1993I; *Chamber Symphony*, 1990I; *Concerto Conciso*, 1998I; *Eliot Landscapes (5), Opus 1*, 1990I; *January Writ*, 1999I; *Living Toys*, 1993I; *Powder Her Face*, 1995I; *String Quartet Arcadiana, Opus 12*, 1994I

Adler, Richard: *The Lady Remembers*, 1985I; *Wilderness Suite*, 1982I; *Yellowstone Overture*, 1980I

Adler, Samuel: *Aeolus, God of the Winds*, 1977I; *Behold Your God*, 1966I; *The Binding*, 1967I; *Cello Concerto*, 1995I; *Cello Sonata*, 1966I; *Choose Life*, 1986I; *Concertino No. 2*, 1976I; *Concerto for Orchestra*, 1971I; *Concerto for Woodwind Quintet*, 1991I; *The Disappointment*, 1974I; *Elegy for String Orchestra*, 1962I; *Festive Prelude* (band), 1962I; *Flute Concerto*, 1977I; *Flute Sonata*, 1981I; *From Out of Bondage*, 1968I; *Guitar Concerto*, 1994I; *Guitar Sonata*, 1985I; *Harpsichord Sonata*, 1982I; *Histrionics*, 1971I; *Horn Sonata*, 1948I; *Introduction & Capriccio for Harp*, 1964I; *A Little Night & Day Music* (band), 1978I; *The Lodge of Shadows*, 1973I; *Oboe Sonata*, 1985I; *Of Musique, Poetrie, Nature & Love*, 1978I; *Organ Concerto*, 1970I;

Adler, Samuel: *(cont.)*
Organ Sonata "Epistrophe," 1990I; *The Outcasts of Poker Flat,* 1959I; *Piano Concerto,* 1983I; *Piano Concerto No. 2,* 1996I; *Piano Sonatina,* 1979I; *Piano Trio No. 1,* 1964I; *Piano Trio No. 2,* 1978I; *Requiescat in pace,* 1963I; *Sonata Breve for Piano,* 1963I; *Southwestern Sketches,* 1960I; *Stars in the Dust,* 1988I; *String Quartet No. 1,* 1945I; *String Quartet No. 2,* 1950I; *String Quartet No. 3,* 1953I; *String Quartet No. 4,* 1963I; *String Quartet No. 5,* 1969I; *String Quartet No. 6,* 1975I; *String Quartet No. 7,* 1981I; *String Quartet No. 8,* 1990I; *Symphony No. 1,* 1953I; *Symphony No. 2,* 1957I; *Symphony No. 3, "Diptych,"* 1960I; *Symphony No. 4, "Geometrics,"* 1967I; *Symphony No. 5, "We Are the Echoes,"* 1975I; *Symphony No. 6,* 1985I; *Toccata for Orchestra,* 1954I; *Toccata Recitation & Postlude,* 1959I; *Viola Sonata,* 1984I; *Violin Sonata No. 1,* 1948I; *Violin Sonata No. 2,* 1956I; *Violin Sonata No. 3,* 1965I; *Vision in Twilight,* 1995I; *Vision of Isaiah,* 1962I; *The Waking,* 1978I; *A Whole Bunch of Fun,* 1969I; *The Wrestler,* 1971I; *Zeami,* 1995I
Adlgasser, Anton C.: *Abraham und Isaak,* 1768I; *Amysis,* 1875I; *Bela Hungariae Princeps,* 1763I; *Christ on the Mount of Olives,* 1754I; *Esther,* 1611I; *Die gereinigte Magdalena,* 1770I; *Hannibal, Capuanae urbis hospes,* 1767I; *Iphigenia mactata,* 1875I; *Kampf der Busse und Bekehrung,* 1768I; *Mercurius,* 1772I; *La nitteti,* 1766I; *Ochus regnana (Samuel und Heli),* 1763I; *Philemon und Baucis,* 1768I; *Pietas in hospitem,* 1772O; *Der wirkende Gnade Gottes,* 1756I
Adma, Adolphe: *Le roi d'Yvetot,* 1842I
Adolfati, Andrea: *Adriano in Siria,* 1751I; *La clemenza di Tito,* 1753I; *Ipermestra,* 1752I; *Sesostri, re d'Egitto,* 1755I; *Vologeso,* 1752I
Adorno, Theodor: *String Quartet Studies (6),* 1920I; *String Quartet 1921, Opus 2,* 1921I
Adriessen, Hendrik: *Organ Concerto,* 1950I
Agnesi, Maria Teresa: *Ciro in Armenia,* 1753I; *Insubria consolata,* 1766I; *Nitocri,* 1771I; *Sofonisba,* 1765I
Agrell, Johan J.: *Harpsichord Concertos (3), Opus 3,* 1751; *Harpsichord Concertos (3), Opus 4,* 1753I; *Trio Sonatas (6), Opus 2,* 1757I
Agricola, Johann F.: *Achille in Sciro,* 1765I; *Amor e Psiche,* 1767I; *Die Auferstehung des Erlösers,* 1758I; *Cleofide,* 1754I; *La nobilitá delusa,* 1754I; *Oreste e Pilade,* 1772I; *Psalm 21,* 1757I; *Il re pastore,* 1770I; *La ricamatrice divenuta dama,* 1751I; *Il tempio d'amore,* 1755I; *Trauerkantate,* 1757I; *Triumphlied bei der Rùckkehr Friedrichs II,* 1763I; *Les voeux de Berlin,* 1770I
Agthe, Carl Christian; *Lieder eines leichten und fliessenden Gesangs,* 1782I; *Die Morgen, Mittag, Abend Und Nacht,* 1784I; *Der Spiegelritter,* 1795I
Aguila, Miguel del: *Pacific Serenade,* 1998I
Agus, Giuseppe: *Notturnos for Strings (6), Opus 4,* 1770I; *String Trios (6), Opus 3,* 1764I; *Violin Duets (12),* 1772I
Aho, Kalevi: *Before We Are All Drowned,* 1999I; *The Book of Secrets,* 1998I; *Cello Concerto,* 1984I; *Chamber Symphony No. 2,* 1992I; *Chamber Symphony No. 3,* 1996I; *Chamber Symphony No. 4,* 1976I; *Chinese Songs (6),* 1997I; *A Cynic's Paradise,* 1991I; *The Frost,* 1992I; *In Memoriam,* 1980I; *Insect Life,* 1987I; *Interludes (3) for Organ,* 1993I; *Inventions & Postlude (7),* 1998I; *Joy & Asymmetry,* 1996I; *Ludus solemnis for Organ,* 1978I; *A Mystery,* 1994I; *Oboe Quintet,* 1973I; *Oboe Sonata,* 1985I; *Piano Concerto,* 1989I; *Piano Sonata,* 1980I; *Prelude, Toccata & Postlude,* 1974I; *Quintet for Clarinet & String Quartet,* 1999I; *Rejoicing of the Deep Waters,* 1995I; *Saxophone Quintet,* 1994I; *Solo I,* 1975I; *Solo III,* 1991I; *Solo IV,* 1997I; *Solo V,* 1999I; *Solo VI,* 1999I; *Sonatina for Piano,* 1993I; *Songs (3) on Life,* 1977I; *String Quartet No. 2,* 1970I; *String Quartet No. 3,* 1971I; *Symphony No. 1,* 1969I; *Symphony No. 2,* 1970I; *Symphony No. 3, "Sinfonia concertante,"* 1973I; *Symphony No.4,* 1973I; *Symphony No. 5,* 1976I; *Symphony No. 6,* 1980I; *Symphony No. 7, "Insect Life,"* 1988I; *Symphony No. 8,* 1993I; *Symphony No. 9,* 1994I; *Symphony No. 10,* 1996I; *Symphony No. 11,* 1998I; *Violin Sonata,* 1973I
Ahrens, Joseph: *Cantata No. 1,* 1958I; *Cantiones gregorianae,* 1957I; *The Christian Year,* 1952I; *Organ Mass,* 1945I; *Triptychon on B-A-C-H,* 1949I
Aitken, Joseph: *Cantata No. 4,* 1961I; *Cantata No. 5,* 1961I; *Cantata No. 6,* 1981I; *Mass,* 1950I; *Mass II,* 1964I; *Piano Concerto,* 1953I; *Piano Fantasy,* 1966I; *Quartet for Clarinet & Strings,* 1959I; *Quintet for Oboe & String Quartet,* 1957I; *Serenade for Ten Instruments,* 1958I; *Toccata for Orchestra,* 1950I; *The Revelation of St. John, Part I,* 1965I; *The Revelation of St. John, Part II,* 1986I
Akutagawa, Yasushi: *Rhapsody for Orchestra,* 1971I
Alain, Jehan: *Ballade en mode phrygien,* 1930I; *Cantique en mode phrygien,* 1932I; *Chorale cistercienne pour une élévation,* 1934I; *Danses à Agni Yavishta (2),* 1934I; *Fantasy I,* 1934I; *Fantasy II,* 1936I; *Grave for Organ,* 1932I; *Intermezzo,* 1935I; *Introduction & Variations, Scherzo, Choral,* 1936I; *Le jardin suspendu,* 1934I; *Messe brève,* 1938I; *Messe de Requiem,* 1938I; *Messe grégorienne de mariage,* 1938I; *Monodia,* 1938I; *Organ Lamento,* 1930I; *Organ Litanies,* 1937I; *Organ Variations sur Lucis creator,* 1932I; *Petite Pièce for Organ,* 1932I; *Postlude pour l'office de Complies,* 1930I; *Prélude et fugue,* 1935I; *Prélude profane (12),* 1933I; *Premier prélude profane,* 1933I; *Variation on a Theme by Clément Jannequin,* 1937I

A *Births*   B *Deaths*   C *Debuts*   D *New Positions*
E *Prizes/Honors*

Albéniz, Isaac: *Iberia*, 1909I; *Merlin*, 1898I

Alberghi, Paolo T.: *Magnificat*, 1780I; *Mass*, 1763I

Albert, Eugène d': *Die Abreise*, 1898I; *Suite for Orchestra*, 1924I; *Symphony in F*, 1886I; *Die toten Augen*, 1916I

Albert, Johann Joseph: *Doublebass Concerto*, 1851I; *Symphony No. 1*, 1852I

Albert, Stephen: *Anthems & Processionals*, 1988I; *Canons for String Quartet*, 1964I; *Cathedral Music*, 1971I; *Cello Concerto*, 1990I; *Ecce Puer*, 1992I; *Flower of the Mountain*, 1985I; *Illuminations*, 1962I; *Into Eclipse*, 1981I; *Leaves from the Golden Notebook*, 1971I; *Music from the Stone Harp*, 1980I; *Rilke Song*, 1991O; *String Quartet Imitations*, 1964I; *Symphony: RiverRun*, 1984I; *Symphony No. 2*, 1992I; *To Wake the Dead*, 1977I; *Vox Femina*, 1984I; *Wedding Songs*, 1965I; *Winter Songs*, 1965I

Albertini, Joachim: *Circe und Ulisses*, 1785I; *Don Juan*, 1783I; *Missa solemnis*, 1782I; *Scipione africano*, 1786I; *Symphony*, 1796I; *Le virgine vestale*, 1803I; *Virginia*, 1786I

Albrechtsberger, Johann: *Christo Kreutz-Erfindung*, 1757I; *Fuga sopra do, re, mi, fa, sol, la, Opus 5*, 1789I; *Fughe (6) colla cadenze, Opus 9*, 1800I; *Harp Concerto*, 1773I; *New Easy Preludes (12) for Organ*, 1804I; *Oratorium de nativitate Jesu*, 1772I; *Oratorium de Passione Domini*, 1762I; *Organ Fugue in C, Opus 4 (?)*, 1786I; *Organ Fugues (6), Opus 8*, 1799I; *Organ Fugues (6), Opus 10, 11*, 1802I; *Organ Fugues (6), Opus 16*, 1809I; *Organ Fugues (6), Opus 17*, 1810I; *Organ Fugues (6), Opus 18*, 1808I; *Organ Fugues (3), Opus 21*, 1802I; *Organ Fugues (6) & Preludes (2), Opus 6 (?)*, 1787I; *Organ/Harpsichord Fugues (12), Opus 1*, 1783I; *Organ/Harpsichord Fugues (6), Opus 7*, 1796I; *Organ Concerto*, 1762I; *Organ Preludes & Fugues (6), Opus 15*, 1795I; *Die Pilgrime auf Golgotha*, 1781I; *Preludes & Fugues, Opus 3*, 1781I; *Quatuors en fugues (6), Opus 2*, 1782I; *Quatuors en fugues (6)*, 1780I; *Quatuors en Fugues (6), Opus 20*, 1800I; *Sonatas (6) for 2 Violins, Opus 8*, 1789I; *String Quartets (3), Opus 19*, 1799I; *Symphony No. 1 in F*, 1768I; *Symphony No. 2 in C*, 1768I; *Symphony No. 3 in D*, 1770I; *Symphony No. 4 in D*, 1772I; *Trio Sonatas (6), Opus 11b*, 1795I; *Trombone Concerto*, 1769I

Albright, William: *Abiding Passions*, 1988I; *Alliance*, 1970I; *Bacchanal* (organ concerto), 1981I; *Chasm: Symphonic Fragment*, 1988I; *Chicester Mass*, 1974I; *Chromatic Dances (5) for Piano*, 1976I; *Clarinet Quintet*, 1987I; *The Enigma Syncopations*, 1982I; *Flights of Fancy for Organ*, 1992I; *The King of Instruments*, 1978I; *Mass in D*, 1974I; *Organbook I*, 1967I; *Organbook II*, 1971I; *Organbook III*, 1978I; *Saxophone Sonata*, 1984I; *The Seven Deadly Sins*, 1974I; *Shaera*, 1985I; *Sweet Sixteenths for Piano*, 1975I; *Symphony for Organ*, 1987I; *That Sinking Feeling for Organ*, 1982I; *Whistler Nocturnes for Organ*, 1989I

Alcorn, Michael: *In-Flame*, 1999I; *Patina*, 1998I

Alday, Ferdinand: *Fantaisie de Salon, Opus 16*, 1860I; *Geneviève de Brabant*, 1791I

Alessandri, Felice: *Adriano in Siria*, 1779I; *Al villanella rapita*, 1784I; *Alcina e Ruggero*, 1775I; *Argea*, 1773I; *L'Argentino*, 1768I; *Armida*, 1794I; *Attalo re di Bitinia*, 1780I; *Bethulia liberata*, 1781I; *Calliroe*, 1778I; *La cariera per amore*, 1774I; *Creso*, 1774I; *Dario*, 1791I; *L'enlèvement des Sabines*, 1779I; *Erifile*, 1780I; *La finta principessa*, 1782I; *Il matrimonio per concorso*, 1767I; *Il medonte re d'Epiro*, 1774I; *La Moglie fedele*, 1768I; *La novita*, 1775I; *L'ouverture du grand opéra italien à Nankin*, 1790I; *I puntigli gelosi*, 1783I; *Il re alla caccia*, 1769I; *Sandrina*, 1775I; *La sposa persiana*, 1775I; *I sposi burlatti*, 1798I; *Il tempio della fama*, 1782I; *Il tobia*, 1767I; *Il vecchio geloso*, 1781I; *Venere in Cipro*, 1779I; *Virginia*, 1793I; *La virtu rivali*, 1783I; *Zemira*, 1794I

Alessandro, Rafaelle d': *Piano Concerto No. 1*, 1939I; *Piano Concerto No. 2*, 1945I; *Piano Concerto No. 3*, 1951I; *Piano Preludes (24)*, 1940I; *Serenade for English Horn & Strings*, 1936I; *Symphony No. 1*, 1948I

Alexander, Charles: *Out of the Ivory Palaces*, 1915I

Alexander, Josef: *Piano Bagatelles, (10)*, 1967I; *Piano Etudes (9)*, 1979I; *Piano Pieces in the Attic*, 1972I; *Piano Sonata No. 1*, 1936I; *Piano Sonata No. 2*, 1943I; *Songs of Eve*, 1957I; *Symphony No. 1, "Clockwork,"* 1949I; *Symphony No. 2*, 1954I; *Symphony No. 3*, 1961I; *Symphony No. 4*, 1968I; *The Twelve Signs of the Zodiac*, 1974I

Alexander, Peter: *Symphony No. 1*, 1994I

Alexander, Russell: *Colossus of Columbia March*, 1901I; *Embossing the Emblem March*, 1902I

Alexandre, Charles G.: *L'esprit du jour*, 1767I; *Georget et Georgette*, 1761I; *String Quartets (6)*, 1778I; *Symphonies (6) "à 8," Opus 6*, 1766I; *Le tonnelier*, 1765I; *Trios (6), Opus 4*, 1762I; *Violin Duets (6), Opus 8*, 1775I

Alford, Kenneth: *Colonel Bogey March*, 1914I

Alfvén, Hugo: *The Bells*, 1900I; *Cantata of the Turn of the Century*, 1899I; *Gustav II, Opus 49*, 1932I; *The Prodigal Son*, 1957I; *Swedish Rhapsody, No. 1, "Midsummer Vigil," Opus 19*, 1904I; *Swedish Rhapsody No. 2, "Uppsala," Opus 24*, 1907I; *Swedish Rhapsody No. 3, Opus 47*, 1931I; *Symphony No. 1 in f, Opus 7*, 1897I; *Symphony No. 2 in D, Opus 11*, 1898I; *Symphony No. 3 in E, Opus 23*, 1905I; *Symphony No. 4 in c, Opus 39*, 1919I; *Symphony No. 5 in a, Opus 54*, 1953I

Alkan (Charles Valentin): *Chants, Set II, Opus 65*, 1861I; *Le chemin de fer, Opus 27*, 1844I; *L'entrée en loge, Opus 17*, 1844I; *Étude de concert, Opus 17*, 1844I; *Etudes (12) in All Major Keys, Opus 35*, 1848I; *Etudes (12) in*

Alkan (Charles Valentin): (*cont.*)
   Minor Keys, Opus 39, 1857I; *Grand Sonata, "Four Ages of Man,"* 1848I; *Hermann et Kitty,* 1832I;
   Impromptu sur le choral de Luther, Opus 69, 1871I; *Marche funèbre, Opus 26,* 1846I; *Marche triomphale,*
   Opus 27, 1846I; *Les mois, Opus 74,* 1872I; *Nocturne, Opus 22,* 1844I; *Paraphrase, "Super flumina*
   Babylonis," Opus 52, 1859I; *Piano Concerto No. 1,* 1931I; *Piano Concerto da Camera No. 1 in a* (?), 1832I;
   Piano Concerto No. 2, Opus 39, 1833I; *Piano Sonatine, Opus 61,* 1891I; *Preludes (25) in all Keys, Opus 31,*
   1847I; *Pro organo,* 1850I; *Recueil d'impromptus,Opus 32/2,* 1849I; *Treize prières, Opus 64,* 1861I;
   Variations-fantaisie, Opus 26, 1844I
Allen Paul H.: *Pilgrim Symphony,* 1910I
Almeida, Francisco de: *L'Ippolito,* 1752I
Alpaerts, Flor: *James Ensor Suite,* 1931I
Alpher, David: *Pathways,* 2000I
Alwyn, William: *String Quartet No. 1 in d,* 1955I; *String Trio,* 1962I
Alyabiev, Alexander: *Piano Quintet in E♭,* 1949I; *Piano Trio in a,* 1947I; *Violin Sonata in e,* 1950I
Amendola, Giuseppe: *Ordeo,* 1788I
Amirkhanian, Charles: *Bajanoom,* 1990I; *Beemsterboer,* 1975I; *Chu Lu Lu,* 1992I; *Dog of Stravinsky,* 1982I;
   Dreams Freud Dreamed, 1979I; *Mahogany Ballpark,* 1976I; *Martinque & the Course of Abstraction,* 1984I;
   Seatbelt Seatbelt, 1973I; *She, She & She,* 1974I; *Sound Nutrition,* 1972I; *Vers les anges,* 1990I; *Walking*
   Tune, 1987I
Amirov, Fikret: *Azerbaijan Capriccio,* 1961I
Amram, David: *Bassoon Concerto,* 1971I; *Brazilian Memories,* 1973I; *The Final Ingredient,* 1965I; *Horn*
   Concerto, 1966I; *King Lear Variations,* 1967I; *Landscapes,* 1980I; *Overture for Brass & Percussion,* 1977I;
   Piano Sonata, 1960I; *Piano Trio, "Dirge & Variations,"* 1962I; *String Quartet No. 1,* 1961I; *The Trail of*
   Beauty, 1976I; *Twelfth Night,* 1968I; *Violin Sonata,* 1964I; *The Wind & the Rain,* 1963I; *Wind Quintet,*
   1968I
Anderson, Beth: *Dreaming Fields,* 1987I; *Joan,* 1974I; *Morning View & Maiden Spring,* 1978I; *Overture for*
   Band, Revelation, 1981I; *Soap Tuning,* 1976I
Anderson, Douglas: *Medea in Exile,* 2000I
Anderson, Julian: *Alhambra Fantasy,* 2000I; *The Crazed Moon,* 1996I; *Pavillons en l'air,* 1995I; *Piano Etude*
   No. 1, 1995I; *Piano Etude No. 2,* 1996I; *Piano Etude No. 3,* 1998I; *The Stations of the Sun,* 1998I
Anderson, Leroy: *Fiddle Faddle,* 1947I; *Jazz Pizzicato,* 1938I; *Sleigh Ride,* 1950I; *The Typewriter,* 1950I
Anderson, Laurie: *Americans on the Move,* 1979I; *United States,* 1983I
Anderson, Ruth: *Centering,* 1979I; *Communications,* 1980I; *Sound Environment,* 1975I; *Time & Tempo,*
   1984I
Anderson, T. J.: *Beyond Silence,* 1973I; *Introduction & Allegro,* 1959I; *Soldier Boy, Soldier,* 1982I; *String*
   Quartet No. 1, 1958I; *Symphony in Three Movements,* 1964I; *Watermelon for Piano,* 1971I
André, Anton: *Grand Sinfonie, Opus 44,* 1820I; *Symphony No. 4 in C, Opus 4,* 1795I; *Symphony No. 5 in F,*
   Opus 5, 1795I; *Symphony No. 6 in C, Opus 6,* 1795I
André, Johann A.: *Der Alchymist,* 1778I; *Alt lied von Gott, Ein, Opus 49,* 1828I; *Der Alte Freyer,* 1776I; *Auf*
   der Freude, Opus 48, 1826I; *Auserlesene Scherzhafte und Zärtliche lieder,* 1774I; *Der Barbier von Bagdad,*
   1783I; *Der Barbier von Sevilien,* 1776I; *Die Bezauberten,* 1777I; *Der Bräutigam in der Klemme,* 1796I;
   Elmine, 1782I; *Die Entführung aus dem Serail,* 1781I; *Erwin und Elmire,* 1775I; *Flute Concerto, Opus 10,*
   1796I; *Flute Concerto in c, Opus 13,* 1795I; *Grande sinfonie, Opus 13,* 1801I; *Grosse Symphonie in E♭, Opus*
   25, 1804I; *Horn Concerto, Opus 33,* 1808I; *Instruktive Variations über fünf tönen, Opus 31,* 1807I; *Kleine*
   Kantate, Opus 55, 1829I; *Liederkranz, Opus 57* (?), 1830I; *Little Pieces (12) for 2 Horns, Opus 26,* 1805I;
   Missa solemnis, Opus 43, 1819I; *Musikalischer Blumenstrauss,* 1776I; *Neue Sammlung von Liedern,* 1784I;
   Oboe Concerto in F, Opus 8, 1798I; *Organ Pieces (25), Opus 64,* 1840I; *Organ Pieces (10), Opus 68* (?),
   1840I; *Ouverture militaire, Opus 24,* 1804I; *Overture, Die Hussiten vor Naumburg, Opus 36,* 1818I; *Piano*
   Sonatinas (3), Opus 71, 1840I; *Piano Sonatas (6), Progressive, Opus 34,* 1811I; *Piano Sonatas (3), Opus 46,*
   1820I; *Rinaldo und Alcina,* 1801I; *Des Sängers lied zu den sternen, Opus 47,* 1825I; *Scherzhafte lieder,*
   1774I; *String Quartets (3), Opus 14,* 1801I; *String Quartet, Opus 22/1,* 1803I; *Sprich wörter (Quartetto a*
   canone), Opus 32, 1808I; *String Quartet, "Poissons d'avril," Opus 54/2,* 1828I; *Symphony in D, "Zur*
   Friedenfeier," Opus 7, 1797I; *Symphonies (2) "d'une exécution facile," Opus 11,* 1800I; *Te Deum, Opus 60,*
   1829I; *Der Topfer,* 1773I; *Trio Sonatas (3), Opus 1,* 1776I; *Vater Unser, Opus 50,* 1827I; *Violin Sonata, Opus*
   21, 1803I; *Violin/Cello Sonata, Opus 17,* 1803I; *Die Werbung aus Liebe,* 1782I
Andreae, Volkmar: *Abenteur des Casanova, Opus 34,* 1924I; *Charons Nachen, Opus 3,* 1901; *Magentalied,*
   Opus 28, 1917I; *Oboe Concertino, Opus 442,* 1947I; *Piano Concerto in d,* 1898I; *Piano Concertpiece in b,*
   1900I; *Piano Trio No. 1 in f, Opus 1,* 1899I; *Piano Trio No. 2 in E♭, Opus 14,* 1908I; *Ratcliff, Opus 25,* 1914I;
   Rhapsodie, Opus 32 (violin), 1920I; *Sinfonische fantasie, Opus 7,* 1903I; *String Quartet in E♭,* 1898I; *String*

❈

A   *Births*   B *Deaths*   C *Debuts*   D *New Positions*
E *Prizes/Honors*

Quartet No. 1, Opus 9, 1905I; String Quartet No. 2 in e, Opus 33, 1921I; String Trio in d, Opus 29, 1917I; Symphony in C, Opus 31, 1919I; Symphony in F, 1899I; Vater unser, Opus 19, 1917I; Violin Concerto in f, Opus 40, 1936I

Andrée, Elfrieda: Fritiofs Saga, 1899I; Piano Quintets in a & e, 1865I; Piano Trio in g, 1877I; Swedish Mass, 1902I; Symphony No. 1 in C, 1889I; Symphony No. 2 in e, 1893I; Violin Sonata No. 1 in E♭, 1872I; Violin Sonata No. 2 in E♭, 1872I

Andriessen, Hendrik: Organ Theme & Variations, 1949I; Philomela, 1950I; Piano Sonata No. 1, 1934I; Piano Sonata No. 2, 1966I; Sinfonia for Organ, 1940I; Symphony No. 1, 1930I; Symphony No. 2, 1937I; Symphony No. 3, 1946I; Symphony No. 4, 1954I; Wind Quintet, 1951I

Andriessen, Jurriaan: Piano Concerto, 1948I; Symphony No. 1, "Berkshire Symphonies," 1949I; Symphony No. 2, 1962I; Symphony No. 3, 1963I; Symphony No. 4, 1963I; Symphony No. 5, "Time Spirit," 1970I

Andriessen, Louis: De Materie, 1988I; De Stilj, 1985I; Rosa–The Death of a Composer, 1994I; Writing to Vermeer, 1996I

Andriessen, Willem: Piano Concerto, 1908I; Piano Sonata, 1938I

Anfossi, Pasquale: Alessandro nell'Indie, 1772I; L'amante confuso, 1772I; Antigono, 1773I; Armida, 1770I; Artaserse, 1788I; L'avaro, 1775I; Il Barone di Rocca Antica, 1771I; Cajo Mario, 1770I; Cleopatra, 1779I; Il curioso indiscreto, 1777I; Demofoonte, 1773I; Didone abbandonata, 1775I; Ezio, 1778I; Fiammetta generosa, 1766I; La finta giardiniera, 1774I; La finta cingara per amore, 1780I; Il finto medico, 1764I; La forza della donne, 1778I; Le gelosie fortunate, 1783I; Gengis-Kan, 1777I; L'incognita perseguitata, 1773I; L'Inglese in Italia, 1786I; Lucio Silla, 1774I; La Maga Circe, 1788I; Il Matrimonio per inganno, 1779I; I Matrimoni per dispetto, 1767I; Montezuma, 1776I; Olimpiade, 1774I; Quinto Fabio, 1771I; La serva spiritosa, 1763I; Lo sposo per equivoco, 1781I; Lo sposo di tre e marito de nessuna, 1763I; Tito nelle Gallie, 1780I; Il trionfo d'Arianna, 1781I; Il trionfo della costanze, 1782I; I vecchi burlati, 1783I; La vera costanza, 1776I; Zemira, 1782I

Antes, John: String Trios (3), 1769I

Antheil, George: Ballet mécanique, 1925I; The Capital of the World, 1952I; Capriccio, 1930I; La femme 100 têtes, 1933I; Fragments from Shelley (8), 1951I; Helen Retires, 1931I; Little Pieces (6), String Quartet, 1931I; McKonkey's Ferry, 1948I; Piano Concerto No. 1, 1922I; Piano Concerto No. 2, 1926I; Piano Sonata No. 1, "Airplane," 1921I; Piano Sonata No. 2, "Sauvage," 1923I; Piano Sonata No. 3, "Dreams of Machines," 1923I; Piano Sonata No. 4, 1948I; Piano Sonata No. 5, 1950I; Songs of Experience, 1948I; String Quartet No. 1, 1924I; String Quartet No. 2, 1928I; String Quartet No. 3, 1948I; Symphony No. 1 in F, 1926I; Symphony No. 2, 1937I; Symphony No. 3, "American," 1939I; Symphony No. 4, "1942," 1942I; Symphony No. 5, "Joyous," 1948I; Symphony No. 6, "After Delacroix," 1948I; Transatlantic, 1928I; Violin Concerto, 1946I; Violin Sonata No. 1, 1923I; Violin Sonata No. 2, 1923I; Violin Sonata No. 3, 1924I; Volpone, 1952I

Antoniou, Theodore: Circle of Accusation, 1975I; Circle of Thanatos & Genesis, 1978I; Periander, 1979I; Piano Prelude & Toccata, 1982I; Prometheus, 1983I

Apell, David August von: Euthyme und Lysis, 1782I; Missa pontificale, 1800I

Appledorn, Mary Jean van: Galilean Galaxies, 1999I; Melora, a Fanfare for Orchestra, 2000I

Araja, Francesco: Alessandro nell'Indie, 1755I; Eudossa incoronata, 1751I

Arel, Bülent: Capriccio for TV, 1969I; Electronic Music I, 1960I; For Violin & Piano, 1966I; Music for String Quartet & Tape, 1957I; Stereo Electronic Music I, 1961I; Stereo Electronic Music II, 1970I

Arensky, Anton: Egyptian Nights, 1900I; Nal and Damayanti, Opus 47, 1904I; Piano Concerto in f, 1882I; Symphony No. 1 in b, 1883I; Symphony No. 2 in A, 1889I

Argento, Dominick: The André Expedition, 1982I; The Aspern Papers, 1988I; The Boor, 1957I; Casanova's Homecoming, 1984I; Colonel Jonathan the Saint, 1961I; The Dread of Valentino, 1993I; Elizabethan Songs (6), 1958I; A Few Words about Chekhov, 1996I; Fire Variations, 1981I; From the Diary of Virginia Woolf, 1974I; I Hate & I Lovev, 1981I; In Praise of Music, 1977I; Jonah & the Whale, 1973I; Letters of Elizabeth Browning, 1983I; Letters from Composers, 1968I; The Masque of Angels, 1963I; Miss Havisham's Fire, 1978I; Miss Havisham's Wedding Night, 1980I; Ode to the West Wind, 1956I; Oresteia, 1967I; Postcard from Morocco, 1971I; The resurrection of Don Juan, 1956I; Reverie–Reflections on a Hymn Tune, 1997I; The Revelation of St. John the Divine, 1966I; A Ring of Time, 1972I; St. Joan, 1964I; Songs about Spring, 1951I; String Quartet No. 1, 1956I; Te Deum, 1987I; To Be Sung upon the Water, 1972I; Variations for Orchestra: The Mask of Night, 1965I; Volpone, 1964I; The Voyage of Edgar Allen Poe, 1976I

Arne, Michael: The Artifice, 1780I; The Choice of Harlequin, 1781I; Cymon, 1767I; Edgar and Emmeline, 1761I; Hymen, 1764I; Vertumus and Pomona, 1782I

Arne, Thomas: The Arcadian Nuptials, 1764I; Artaxerxes, 1762I; Bacchus and Ariadne, 1765I; Beauty and Virtue, 1762I; The Birth of Hercules, 1763I; Britannia, 1755I; Caractacus, 1775I; The Cooper, 1772I; The Country Lasses, 1751I; Eliza, 1754I; The Fairy Prince, 1771I; Favorite Concertos (6) for Keyboard, 1787I;

Arne, Thomas: (*cont.*)
  Florizel and Perdita, 1761I; *The Guardian Outwitted*, 1764I; *Harlequin Sorcerer*, 1752I; *Injured Honor*,
  1756I; *Isabella*, 1757I; *Judith*, 1761I; *The Ladies' Frolick*, 1770I; *Lethe*, 1753I; *Love in a Village*, 1762I; *May
  Day*, 1776I; *The Oracle*, 1752I; *Overtures (8)*, 1751I; *Phoebe at Court*, 1777I; *The Pincushion*, 1756I; *The
  Prophetess*, 1758I; *The Sultan*, 1758I; *Thomas and Sally*, 1760I
Arnold, Carl: *Irene*, 1832I; *Sextet for Piano & Strings*, 1825I; *String Quartet*, 1825I
Arnold, Malcolm: *Cello Concerto*, 1989I; *Clarinet Concerto No. 1, Opus 20*, 1948I; *Clarinet Concerto No. 2,
  Opus 115*, 1974I; *Concerto for Piano, Four Hands, Opus 32*, 1951I; *Cornish Dances (4), Opus 91*, 1966I; *The
  Dancing Master, Opus 34*, 1951I; *Electra, Opus 79*, 1963I; *English Dances, Set I, Opus 27*, 1950I; *English
  Dances, Set II, Opus 33*, 1951I; *Fantasy on a Theme of John Field, Opus 116*, 1975I; *Flute Concerto No. 1,
  Opus 45*, 1954I; *Flute Concerto No. 2, Opus 111*, 1972I; *Guitar Concerto, Opus 67*, 1959I; *Harmonica
  Concerto, Opus 46*, 1954I; *Horn Concerto No. 1*, 1945I; *Horn Concerto No. 2, Opus 59*, 1956I; *Oboe
  Concerto, Opus 39*, 1952I; *The Open Window, Opus 56*, 1956I; *Overture, Beckus, the Dandipratt*, 1943I;
  Peterloo Overture, 1968I; *Rinaldo & Armida, Opus 49*, 1954I; *Scottish Dances, Four, Opus 59*, 1957I;
  String Quartet No. 1, Opus 23, 1949I; *String Quartet No. 2*, 1976I; *Sweeney Todd, Opus 68*, 1959I;
  Symphony for Strings, Opus 11, 1946I; *Symphony No. 1, Opus 22*, 1949I; *Symphony No. 2, Opus 40*, 1953I;
  Symphony No. 3, Opus 63, 1957I; *Symphony No. 4, Opus 71*, 1960I; *Symphony No. 5, Opus 74*, 1961I;
  Symphony No. 6, Opus 95, 1967I; *Symphony No. 7, Opus 113*, 1973I; *Symphony No. 8*, 1979I; *Symphony
  No. 9*, 1987I; *Tam O'Shanter Overture*, 1955I; *Violin Sonata No. 1, Opus 15*, 1947I; *Violin Sonata No. 2,
  Opus 43*, 1953I
Arnold, Samuel: *The Cure of Saul*, 1767I; *Elisha*, 1795I; *The Enchanted Wood*, 1792I; *The Gnome*, 1788I;
  Harlequin Dr. Faustus 1766I; *The Magnet*, 1771I; *New Spain*, 1790I; *The Sixty Third Letter*, 1802I; *The
  Surrender of Calais*, 1791I; *The Royal Garland*, 1768I
Arrego-Salas, Juan: *The Days of God*, 1976I; *Violin Sonata*, 1945I
Arriaga, Juan: *Les esclavos felices*, 1819I
Arrieta y Corera, Pascual: *La conquista de Granadas*, 1850I
Arutiunian, Alexander: *Trombone Concerto*, 1991I; *Trumpet Concerto*, 1950I
Asafiev, Boris: *The Bronze Horseman*, 1401; *Cinderella*, 1906I; *The Ice Maiden*, 1918I; *Symphony No. 1 in b*,
  "In Memory of Lermontov," 1938I; *Symphony No. 2 in f#*, 1938I; *Symphony No. 3 in C*, 1942I; *Symphony
  No. 4 in B♭*, 1942I; *Symphony No. 5, "The Seasons,"* 1942I; *The White Lily*, 1910I
Ashley, Robert: *# + Heat*, 1961I; *Atalanta*, 1982I; *Atalanta Strategy*, 1984I; *Balseros*, 1997I; *Dust*, 1999I;
  Fancy Free, 1970I; *Fives*, 1961I; *It's There*, 1970I; *Kitty Hawk*, 1964I; *Night Train*, 1965I; *Orange Dessert*,
  1965I; *Outcome Inevitable*, 1992I; *Perfect Lives*, 1983I; *Piano Sonata*, 1959I; *She Was a Visitor*, 1967I;
  Superior Seven, 1986I; *That Morning Thing*, 1967I; *The Wolfman Motorcity Revue*, 1969I; *The Wolfman
  Tapes*, 1964I
Asia, Daniel: *Black Light*, 1990I; *Breath in a Ram's Horn*, 1995I; *Cello Concerto*, 1997I; *Cello Sonata*, 1989I;
  Piano Concerto, 1994I; *Piano Set I*, 1975I; *Piano Set II*, 1976I; *Pines Songs*, 1984I; *Sacred Songs*, 1989I;
  Sand II, 1978I; *Scherzo Sonata for Piano*, 1987I; *Songs from the Page of Swords*, 1987I; *String Quartet No.
  1*, 1976I; *String Quartet No. 2*, 1985I; *Symphony No. 1*, 1987I; *Symphony No. 2*, 1990I; *Symphony No. 3*,
  1992I; *Symphony No. 4*, 1993I
Asioli, Bonifazio: *Cinna*, 1793I; *Gustava al Malabar*, 1802I
Asplmayr, Franz: *Acis et Galathée*, 1773I; *Alexandre et Campaspe de Larisse*, 1773I; *Ifigenia*, 1772I
Atterberg, Kurt: *Aladdin, Opus 43*, 1941I; *Cello Concerto*, 1922I; *Concert Overture in a, Opus 4*, 1910I;
  Concert Overture, Opus 41, 1940I; *Double Concerto in g/c* (violin, cello), 1960I; *Foolish Virgins, Opus 17*,
  1920I; *Horn Concerto in A, Opus 20*, 1926I; *Piano Concerto in b♭, Opus 37*, 1935I; *Piano Quintet*, 1927I;
  Piano Rhapsody, Opus 1, 1909I; *Requiem, Opus 8*, 1914I; *The River, Opus 33*, 1929I; *String Quartet No. 1
  in D, Opus 2*, 1909I; *String Quartet No. 2, Opus 11*, 1918I; *String Quartet No. 3, Opus 39*, 1937I; *Suite No.
  1, "Oriental,"* 1913I; *Suite No. 2*, 1915I; *Suite No. 3, Opus 19/1*, 1917I; *Suite No. 4, "Turandot," Opus
  19/2*, 1920I; *Suite No. 5, Opus 23*, 1923I; *Suite No. 6, "Oriental legend," Opus 30*, 1924I; *Suite No. 7, Opus
  29*, 1926I; *Suite No. 8, Opus 34, "Pastorale,"* 1931I; *Suite No. 9 "Drammatica," Opus 47*, 1944I; *Swedish
  Summer Festival*, 1957I; *Symphony No. 1 in b, Opus 3*, 1911I; *Symphony No. 2 in F, Opus 6*, 1913I;
  Symphony No. 3, Opus 10, 1916I; *Symphony No. 4 in g, "Sinfonia picola," Opus 14*, 1918I; *Symphony No.
  5, "Sinfonia funèbre,"* 1922I; *Symphony No. 6 in C, "Dollar," Opus 31*, 1928I; *Symphony No. 7,
  "Romantic," Opus 45*, 1942I; *Symphony No. 8 in e, Opus 48*, 1944I; *Symphony No. 9, "Visionary," Opus
  54*, 1956I; *Variations & Fugue, Opus 46*, 1944I; *Violin Concerto in e, Opus 7*, 1913I; *The White Horse, Opus
  24*, 1924I
Attwood, Thomas: *Cello Sonatas (3), Opus 2*, 1791I; *The Curfew*, 1807I; *A Day at Rome*, 1798I; *The Fairy
  Festival*, 1797I; *Fast Asleep*, 1797I; *The Magic Oak*, 1799I; *The Mariners*, 1793I; *The Packet Boat*, 1794I;
  Piano Trios (3), Opus 1, 1787I; *The Sea-Side Story*, 1801I; *The Smugglers*, 1796I

❄

A *Births*   B *Deaths*   C *Debuts*   D *New Positions*
E *Prizes/Honors*

Auber, Daniel: *Actéon*, 1836I; *L'ambassadrice*, 1836I; *La barcarolle*, 1845I; *Benedictus in A*♭, 1862I; *La bergère châtelaine*, 1820I; *Le bourgeois gentilhomme*, 1838I; *Les chaperons blanc*, 1836I; *Le cheval de bronze*, 1835I; *La circassienne*, 1860I; *Le concert à la cour*, 1824I; *Les diamants de la couronne*, 1841I; *Le Dieu et la bayadère*, 1830I; *Le domino noir*, 1837I; *Le duc d'Olonne*, 1842I; *Emma*, 1821I; *L'enfant prodigue*, 1850I; *fête Vénitienne*, 1837I; *La fiancée*, 1829I; *La fiancée du Roi de Garbe*, 1864I; *Fiorelle*, 1826I; *Fra Diavolo*, 1830I; *Grand Overture, London Universal Exposition*, 1862I; *Gustave III*, 1833I; *Haidée*, 1847I; *Jean de Couvin*, 1812I; *Jenny Bell*, 1855I; *Julie*, 1811I; *Kyrie in C, Kyrie in a*, 1865I; *Le lac des fées*, 1839I; *Leicester*, 1822I; *Léocadie*, 1824I; *Lestocq*, 1834I; *Le maçon*, 1825I; *Magenta*, 1859I; *Manon Lescaut*, 1856I; *Marco Spada*, 1852I; *Margarethe von Gent*, 1838I; *Mass*, 1812I; *La muette de Portici*, 1828I; *La neige*, 1823I; *O salutaris*, 1860I; *La part du diable*, 1843I; *Le philtre*, 1831I; *Pie Jesu*, 1861I; *Pièce symphonique in A*, 1825I; *Le premier Jour de bonheur*, 1868I; *Rêve d'amour*, 1869I; *Le séjour militaire*, 1813I; *Le serment*, 1832I; *La sirène*, 1844I; *Le testament et les billets-doux*, 1819I; *Le timide*, 1826I; *Les trois genres*, 1824I; *Veni Creator*, 1865I; *Violin Concerto in D*, 1808I; *Zanetta*, 1840I; *Zerline*, 1851I

Aubert Louis: *Symphonies (6), Opus 2*, 1755I

Aulette Pietro: *Didone*, 1759I

Auric, Georges: *Alphabet*, 1920I; *Interludes*, 1914I; *Joues en feu*, 1920I

Austin, Larry: *Blues Ax*, 1995I; *The Maze*, 1965I; *Sin-Edo: Cityscape Set*, 1996I; *Transmission Two: The Great Excursion*, 1990I; *Variations . . . Beyond Pierrot*, 1995I; *Violet's Invention for Piano*, 1988I

Avalon, Robert: *Concerto for Flute, Harp & Strings, Opus 31*, 1998I; *Sextet to Julia de Burgos, Opus 21*, 1989I; *Flute Sonata, Opus 26*, 1991I; *Piano Concerto, Opus 10*, 1986I; *Violin Sonata, Opus 6*, 1983I

Avison, Charles: *Concertos (6) in Seven Parts, Opus 3*, 1751I; *Concertos (8) in Seven Parts, Opus 4*, 1755I; *Concertos (6) in Seven Parts, Opus 10*, 1769I; *Harpsichord Concertos (6), Opus 6*, 1758I; *Trio Sonatas (6), Opus 5*, 1756I; *Trio Sonatas (6), Opus 7*, 1760I; *Trio Sonatas (6), Opus 8*, 1764I

Avshalomov, Aaron: *Flute Concerto*, 1948I; *Piano Concerto*, 1935I; *Symphony No. 1 (?)*, 1940I; *Symphony No. 2*, 1949I; *Symphony No. 3*, 1950I; *Symphony No. 4*, 1951I

Avshalomov, David: *Songs for Alyce*, 1976I

Avshalomov, Jacob: *How Long, Oh Lord*, 1948I; *Inscriptions at the City of Brass*, 1957I; *Symphony No. 1, "The Oregon,"* 1962I; *Symphony No. 2*, 1985I; *Symphony No. 3*, 1993I; *Tom O'Bedlam*, 1953I

Ayres, Frederick: *Cello Sonata*, 1926I; *String Quartet*, 1916I; *Violin Sonata No. 2*, 1926I

Azais Hyacinthe: *Symphonies (6)*, 1782I

Azevedo, Sérgio: *Atlas' Journey*,1998I; *Clarinet Quintet*, 1996I; *Concerto for Two Pianos*, 2000I; *Festa*, 1998I; *Retabulo de Brecht*, 1998I

Azzopardi, Francesco: *La Passione di Cristo*, 1782I

Baaren, Kees van: *Piano Concerto*, 1964I; *String Quartet No. 1*, 1932I; *String Quartet No. 2*, 1933I

Babadjanian, Arno: *Heroic Ballad*, 1951I; *Piano Trio in f*♯, 1952I; *Violin Concerto*, 1949I; *Violin Sonata in b*♭, 1959I

Babbitt, Milton: *Allegro Penserosa for Piano*, 1999I; *Around the Horn*, 1993I; *Canonical Form for Piano*, 1983I; *Cavalier Settings (4)*, 1991I; *Clarinet Quintet*, 1996I; *Composition for Four Instruments*, 1948I; *Composition for Tenor & Six Instruments*, 1960I; *Composition for Synthesizer*, 1961I; *Composition for Viola & Piano*, 1950I; *Cultivated Choruses (3)*, 1987I; *Du*, 1951I; *Emblems for Piano*, 1989I; *Envoi for Piano*, 1990I; *The Head of the Bed*, 1982I; *Joy of More Sextets*, 1986I; *Lagniappe for Piano*, 1985I; *Manifold Music for Organ*, 1995I; *Music for the Mass*, 1941I; *No Longer Very Clear*, 1994I; *None But the Lonely Flute*, 1991I; *Partitions*, 1957I; *Philomel*, 1964I; *Phonemena*, 1970I; *Piano Compositions (3)*, 1947I; *Piano Concerto*, 1985I; *Piano Concerto No. 2*, 1998I; *Piano Quartet*, 1995I; *Playing for Time for Piano*, 1983I; *Preludes, Interludes & Postlude for Piano*, 1991I; *Quatrains*, 1993I; *Reflections for Piano & Tape*, 1974I; *Relata I*, 1965I; *Relata II*, 1968I; *Sheer Pluck*, 1984I; *A Solo Requiem*, 1977I; *String Quartet No. 1*, 1948I; *String Quartet No. 2*, 1954I; *String Quartet No. 3*, 1970I; *String Quartet No. 4*, 1970I; *String Quartet No. 5*, 1982I; *String Trio*, 1941I; *Tutte le Corde for Piano*, 1994I; *Woodwind Quartet*, 1953I

Bacarisse, Salvador: *Charlot*, 1933I; *Corrido de Feria*, 1930I; *Fuenteovejuna*, 1962I; *Piano Concerto No. 1*, 1933I; *Piano Concerto No. 2*, 1957I; *Piano Concerto No. 3*, 1958I; *El Tesoro de Boabdil*, 1958I; *La tragedia de Doña Ajada*, 1929I

Bacewicz, Grażyna: *Cello Concerto No. 1*, 1951I; *Cello Concerto No. 2*, 1963I; *Desire*, 1968I; *Erik in Ostend*, 1964I; *Esquisse for Organ*, 1966I; *The Peasant King*, 1953I; *Piano Concerto*, 1949I; *Piano Sonata No. 1*, 1930I; *Piano Sonata No. 2*, 1935I; *Piano Sonata No. 3*, 1938I; *Piano Sonata No. 4*, 1942I; *Piano Sonata No. 5*, 1949I; *Piano Sonata No. 6*, 1953I; *String Quartet No. 2*, 1942I; *String Quartet No. 3*, 1947I; *String Quartet No 4*, 1951I; *String Quartet No. 5*, 1955II; *String Quartet No. 6*, 1960I; *String Quartet No. 7*, 1965I; *Symphony for Strings*, 1946I; *Symphony No. 1*, 1945I; *Symphony No. 2*, 1951I; *Symphony No. 3*, 1952I; *Symphony No. 4*, 1953I; *Violin Concerto No. 1*, 1937I; *Violin Concerto No. 2*, 1945I; *Violin Concerto No. 3*, 1948I; *Violin Concerto No. 4*, 1951I; *Violin Concerto No. 5*, 1954I; *Violin Concerto No. 6*, 1957I

Bach, Carl Phillip Emanuel: *Auferstehung und Himmelfahrt Jesu, H. 777*, 1780I; *Bachus und Venus*, H.698, 1766I; *Concertos (6) H.471-6*, 1771I; *Double Concerto in E♭, H.479*, 1778I; *Flute Sonata in G*, H.564, 1786I; *Geistliche oden und lieder (12), H.696*, 1764I; *Geistliche Oden und Lieder, H.686*, 1757I; *Geistliche gesänge I, H.749*, 1780I; *Geistliche gesänge II, H.752*, 1781I; *Geistliche oden und lieder (12), H. 696*, 1764I; *Hamburg Symphonies (4), Wg, 183*, 1780I; *Harpsichord Concerto in B♭, H.447*, 1762I; *Harpsichord Concerto in B♭, H.465*, 1765I; *Harpsichord Concerto in E♭, H.469*, 1769I; *Harpsichord Concerto in F, H.454*, 1763I; *Harpsichord Concerto in B♭, H.434*, 1751I; *Harpsichord Concerto in F, H.470*, 1770I; *Harpsichord Concerto in A, H.437*, 1753I; *Harpsichord/Organ Concerto in E♭, H.446*, 1759I; *Harpsichord Sonata in G, H.563*, 1762I; *Heilig, H. 778*, 1778I; *The Israelites in the wilderness*, 1775I; *Die letzten Leiden des Erlösers, H. 776*, 1770I; *Masonic Songs (12), H.704*, 1788I; *Morgengesang am Schöpfungsfaste, H. 779*, 1783I; *Organ Sonatas (4), H.84-87*, 1755I; *Organ/Harpsichord Concerto in G, H.464*, 1755; *Oster-Musik, H. 803*, 1756I; *Oster-Musik, H. 804*, 1778I; *Oster-Musik, H. 805*, 1778I; *Oster-Musik, H. 806*, 1780I; *Oster-Musik, H. 807*, 1784I; *Phillis un Thirsis, H.697*, 1765I; *Preludio in D, H. 108*, 1756I; *Psalm 2, H.773, Psalm 4, H. 774*, 1761I; *Der Rerechte, H. 818*, 1774I; *Simphonies (6) H. 657-662*, 1773I; *St. John Passion I, H. 787*, 1771I; *St. John Passion II, H. 789*, 1776I I; *St. John Passion III, H. 791*, 1780I; *St. John Passion IV, H. 797*, 1788I; *St. John Passion V, H. 801*, 1788I; *St. Luke Passion I, H. 782*, 1769I; *St. Luke Passion II, H. 784*, 1771I; *St. Luke Passion III, H. 791*, 1779I; *St. Luke Passion IV, H. 96*, 1783I; *St. Luke Passion V, H.800*, 1787I; *St. Mark Passion I, H. 783*, 1770I; *St. Mark Passion II, H. 787*, 1774I; *St. Mark Passion III, H. 791*, 1778I; *St. Mark Passion IV, H. 795*, 1782I; *St. Mark Passion V, H. 1799*, 1786I; *St. Matthew Passion I, H. 782*, 1769I; *St. Matthew Passion II, H. 786*, 1772I; *St. Matthew Passion III, H. 790*, 1777I; *St. Matthew Passion IV, H.794*, 1781I; *St. Matthew Passion V, H. 798*, 1785I; *St. Matthew Passion VI, H. 802*, 1788I; *Symphonies (3), H.648-650*, 1755I; *Symphonies (3) K.654-656*, 1762I; *Symphonies (4) in Twelve Voices, H.663-6*, 1776I; *Symphony in e, H. 652*, 1756I; *Symphony in e, H. 653*, 1756I; *Trio Sonata in E♭, H.584*, 1754I; *Trio Sonata in G, H.583*, 1754I; *Trio Sonatas (6), T.317*, 1766I; *Trio Sonata in B♭, H.587*, 1755I; *Trio Sonata in F, H.590*, 1756I; *Weihnachts-Musik, H. 815*, 1775I; *Der Wirth und die Gäste, H.699*, 1766I

Bach, Jan: *Horn Concerto*, 1983I; *Piano Concerto*, 1975I

Bach, Johann Christian: *Adriano in Siria*, 1765I; *Alessandro nell'Indie*, 1762I; *Amadis de Gaule*, 1779I; *Amor vincitore*, 1774I; *Artaserse*, 1760I; *Canzonettes (6), Opus 4*, 1765I; *Carattaco*, 1767I; *Catone in Ituca*, 1761I; *Clavecin Concertos, (6), Opus 1*, 1763I; *La clemenza di Scipione, Opus 14*, 1778I; *Endimione*, 1772I; *Flute Quartets (4), Opus 19*, 1784I; *Flute Quintets (6), Opus 8*, 1772I; *Gioas, re di Guida*, 1770I; *Grand Overtures (6), Opus 18*, 1781I; *Instrumental Quartets (6), Opus 11*, 1777I; *Keyboard Concertos (6), Opus 13*, 1777I; *Lucio Silla*, 1774I; *Magnificat in C, T.207*, 1758I; *Quartets (6), T.309*, 1775I; *Quintets (6), Opus 11*, 1774I; *Quintets (2), Opus 22*, 1785I; *Requiem in F*, 1757I; *Sextet in C, T.302*, 1783I; *Sinfonias (6), Opus 18*, 1782I; *Sinfonia (6), Woodwind Quintet, T.285*, 1782I; *String Quintet in B♭, T.305*, 1770I; *Symphonie concertante in A, T. 284*, 1773I; *Symphonies (6), Opus 3*, 1765I; *Symphonies (6), Opus 6*, 1770I; *Symphonies (3), Opus 9*, 1775I; *Symphonies (3), Opus 9*, 1773I; *Symphonies (2), Opus 18*, 1785I; *Symphonies périodiques (6), Opus 8*, 1770I; *Symphony in B♭, Opus 9*, 1763I; *Symphony in E♭, Opus 18, No. 1*, 1763I; *Te Deum in D, T.210*, 1762I; *Themistocle*, 1772I; *Trio Sonatas (6), Opus 6*, 1767I; *Trio Sonatas (4), Opus 15*, 1779I; *Trios (6), Opus 2*, 1763I; *Violin Sonatas (6), Opus 2*, 1764I; *Violin Sonatas (6), Opus 10*, 1773I; *Violin Sonatas (4), Opus 18*, 1781I; *Violin Sonatas (6), Opus 16*, 1779I; *Zanaida*, 1763I

Bach, Johann Christoph Friedrich: *Die Auferstehung und Himmelfahrt Jesu*, 1773I; *Brutus*, 1774I; *Gott wird deinen Fuss nicht gleiten lassen*, 1787I; *Die Hirten bei der Krippe Jesu*, 1785I; *Die Kindheit Jesu*, 1773I; *Michaels Sieg*, 1775I; *Pygmalion*, 1786I; *Septet in E♭ for Winds*, 1794I; *Singet dem Herrn ein neues Lied*, 1785I; *Symphonies No. 1-3*, 1768I; *Symphony No. 4 in E*, 1769I; *Symphony No. 10 in E♭*, 1772I; *Symphony No. 20 in B♭*, 1794I; *Der Tod Jesu*, 1769I

Bach, Wilhelm Friedmann: *Halleluja, wohl diesen volk*, 1757I; *Ja, Ja, es hat mein Gott*, 1757I; *Lobe den Herrn in seinem Heiligtum*, 1762I

Bäck, Sven-Erik: *Cat's Journey*, 1969I; *Ikaros*, 1963I; *Movements*, 1966I; *String Quartet No. 1*, 1945I; *String Quartet No. 2*, 1947I; *String Quartet No. 3*, 1962I; *String Quartet No. 4*, 1981I; *Te Deum*, 1980I

Backers, Cor: *Missa Sancta*, 1974I

Bacon, Ernst: *Elegy* (oboe & strings concerto), 1957I; *Erie Waters*, 1961I; *Fantasy & Fugue*, 1926I; *Ford's Theater*, 1946I; *From These States*, 1951I; *On Ecclesiastes*, 1936I; *Over the Waters Overture*, 1977I; *Piano Concerto No. 1, "Riolama,"* 1963I; *Piano Concerto No. 2*, 1982I; *Piano Trio*, 1981I; *Requiem, "The Last Invocations,"* 1971I; *String Quintet*, 1950I; *Symphony No. 1*, 1932I; *Symphony No. 2*, 1937I; *Violin Sonata*, 1982I

Bacon, Samuel: *From Emily's Diary*, 1947I

Bacri, Nicolas: *Cello Suite No. 4*, 1996I

❄

A   *Births*   B   *Deaths*   C   *Debuts*   D   *New Positions*

E   *Prizes/Honors*

Baden, Conrad: *Concerto for Orchestra*, 1968I; *Mass*, 1949I; *Piano Concerto*, 1979I; *Symphony No. 1*, 1952I; *Symphony No. 2*, 1958I; *Symphony No. 3, "Sinfonia Piccola,"* 1959I; *Symphony No. 4*, 1970I; *Symphony No. 5, "Sinfonia voluntatis,"* 1976I; *Symphony No. 6, "Sinfonia Espressiva,"* 1980I; *String Quartet No. 1*, 1944I; *String Quartet No. 2*, 1946I; *String Quartet No. 3*, 1961I; *Viola Concerto*, 1973I

Badings, Henk: *American Folk Song Suite*, 1975I; *Concerto for Harp & Winds*, 1967I; *String Quartet No. 1*, 1931I; *String Quartet No. 2*, 1936I; *String Quartet No. 3*, 1944I; *String Quartet No. 4*, 1966I; *String Quartet No. 5*, 1980I; *String Quartet No. 6*, 1984I; *Symphonic Variations*, 1937I; *Symphony No. 1*, 1932I; *Symphony No. 2*, 1932I; *Symphony No. 3*, 1934I; *Symphony No. 4*, 1943I; *Symphony No. 5*, 1949I; *Symphony No. 6, "Symphony of Psalms,"* 1953I; *Symphony No. 7, "Louisville,"* 1954I; *Symphony No. 8, "Hannover,"* 1956I; *Symphony No. 9*, 1959I; *Symphony No. 10*, 1961I; *Symphony No. 11, "Giocosa,"* 1964I; *Symphony No. 12*, 1964I; *Symphony No. 13 (band)*, 1966I; *Symphony No. 14*, 1968I; *Violin Concerto No. 1*, 1928I; *Violin Concerto No. 2*, 1935I

Badinski, Nicolai: *Luftmusik*, 1981I; *Traumvisionen*, 1982I

Baeyens, August: *String Quartet No. 1*, 1922I; *String Quartet No. 2*, 1925I; *String Quartet No. 3*, 1927I; *String Quartet No. 4*, 1949I; *String Quartet No. 5*, 1951I; *String Quartet No. 6*, 1962I; *Symphony No. 1*, 1923I; *Symphony No. 2*, 1939I; *Symphony No. 3*, 1949I; *Symphony No. 4*, 1952I; *Symphony No. 5*, 1954I; *Symphony No. 6*, 1955I; *Symphony No. 7*, 1958I; *Symphony No. 8*, 1961I

Bagley, E. E.: *National Emblem March*, 1906I

Bainbridge, Simon: *Ad Ora Incerta*, 1994I; *Caliban Fragments & Aria*, 1991I; *Clarinet Quintet*, 1993I; *Double Concerto*, 1990I; *Pieces (3) for Orchestra*, 1998I; *Primo Levi Settings (4)*, 1996I; *A Song from Michelangelo*, 1989I; *String Quartet*, 1972I; *Viola Concerto*, 1976I

Bainton, Edgar L.: *Parecelsus*, 1921I; *The Pearl Tree*, 1944I; *Symphony No. 2 in d*, 1933I

Bainville, François: *Nouvelles pièces d'orgue composées sur différents tons*, 1767I

Baird, Tadeusz: *Erotyki*, 1962I; *Love Sonnets from Shakespeare*, 1956I

Baird, Takeusz: *Lyrical Suite*, 1953I; *Piano Concerto*, 1949I; *String Quartet*, 1957I; *String Quartet Play*, 1971I; *Symphony No. 1*, 1950I; *Symphony No. 2*, 1952I; *Symphony No. 3*, 1969I; *Variations in Rondo Form*, 1978I; *Voices from Afar*, 1981I

Bairstow, Edward: *Organ Sonata*, 1937I

Bajamonti, Julije: *La traslazione di San Domino*, 1770I

Bajoras, Feliksas: *Legends*, 1969I; *Pieces (4) for String Quartet*, 1968I; *String Quartet No. 1*, 1974I; *String Quartet No. 2*, 1975I; *Symphony No. 1*, 1964I; *Symphony No. 2, "Stalactites,"* 1970I; *Symphony No. 3*, 1972I; *Violin Sonata*, 1979I

Baker, Claude: *Fantasy Variations, String Quartet*, 1986I; *String Quartet*, 1969I

Baker, David: *Tuba Concerto*, 1998I

Baker, Michael: *String Quartet*, 1969I

Baksa, Robert: *Clarinet Quintet*, 1973I

Balada, Leonardo: *Auroris*, 1973I; *Cervantinas (3)*, 1967I; *Christopher Columbus*, 1989I; *Concerto for Four Guitars*, 1976I; *The Death of Columbus*, 1992I; *Geometria No. 1*, 1966I; *Geometria II*, 1967I; *Guernica*, 1966I; *Guitar Concerto*, 1965I; *Hangman, Hangman!*, 1982I; *Homage to Casals*, 1975I; *Homage to Sarasate*, 1975I; *Maria Sabina*, 1969I; *Mosaico*, 1970I; *Music for Oboe & Orchestra*, 1993I; *Piano Concerto*, 1964I; *Piano Persistencies*, 1978I; *The Seven Last Words*, 1963I; *Sonata for Ten Wind Instruments*, 1980I; *Symphony No. 1, "Sinfonia en Negro,"* 1968I; *Symphony No. 2*, 1971I; *Symphony No. 3, "Steel,"* 1972I; *Symphony No. 4, "Lausanne,"* 1992I; *Thunderous Scenes*, 1992I; *Violin Sonata*, 1960I; *Zapata!*, 1982I

Balakauskas, Ostvaldas: *Concerto for Oboe & Harpsichord*, 1981I; *Cracow Rain*, 1991I; *Ludus Moderum*, 1972I; *Macbeth*, 1988I; *Organ Sonata No. 1*, 1965I; *Organ Sonata No. 2*, 1980I; *Piano Caprices (3)*, 1964I; *Requiem*, 1995I; *String Quartet No. 1*, 1971I; *String Quartet No. 2*, 1971I; *String Quartet No. 3*, 1998I; *Symphony No. 1*, 1973I; *Symphony No. 2*, 1979I; *Symphony No. 3*, 1989I; *Symphony No. 4*, 1998I; *To the Blue Flowers*, 1976I; *Tristan*, 1998I; *Violin Sonata*, 1969I

Balakirev, Mily: *Grand Fantasy on Russian Folk Songs, Opus 4*, 1852I; *Islamey*, 1869I; *King Lear*, 1861I; *Octet, Opus 3*, 1856I; *Overture on a Spanish March Theme*, 1857I; *Overture on Czech Themes*, 1867I; *Overture on Three Russian Themes*, 1858I; *Overture No. 2 on Russian Themes, "Russia,"* 1865I; *Piano Concert Movement in f♯, Opus 1*, 1856I; *Piano Sonata No. 2*, 1905I; *Spanish Overture*, 1886I; *String Quartet "Original Russian," Opus 2*, 1855I; *Symphony No. 1 in C*, 1866I; *Symphony No. 2 in C*, 1908I; *Thamar*, 1881I

Balanchivadze, Andrei: *The Heart of the Mountain*, 1936I; *Piano Concerto No. 1*, 1944I; *Piano Concerto No. 2*, 1946I; *Piano Concerto No. 3*, 1952I; *Piano Concerto No. 4*, 1968I; *Symphony No. 1*, 1944I; *Symphony No. 2*, 1959I; *Symphony No. 3*, 1984I

Balanchivadze, Meliton: *Tamara the Treacherous*, 1897I

Balbi, Melchiore: *The Armourer of Nantes*, 1863I; *Un avertimento ai gelosi*, 1830I; *Bianca*, 1860I; *Blanche de Nevers*, 1862I; *The Bohemian Girl*, 1843I; *The Bondsman*, 1846I; *The Castle of Aymon*, 1844I; *Catherine Grey*, 1837I; *The Devil's in It*, 1852I; *Diadeste*, 1838I; *The Enchantress*, 1844I; *Enrico IV*, 1833I; *L'étoile de Séville*, 1845I; *Falstaff*, 1838I; *Joan of Arc*, 1837I; *Keolanthe*, 1841I; *The Knight of the Leopard*, 1870I; *The Maid of Honour*, 1847I; *The Maid of Artois*, 1836I; *Mazeppa*, 1862I; *Nelly Grey*, 1859I; *La notte perigliosa*, 1820I; *La Pérouse*, 1826I; *Pittore e Duca*, 1854I; *Le puits d'amour*, 1843I; *The Puritan's Daughter*, 1861I; *I revali di se stressi*, 1829I; *The Rose of Castille*, 1857I; *Satanella*, 1858I; *The Sicilian Bride*, 1852I; *The Siege of Rochelle*, 1835I; *The Sleeping Queen*, 1864I

Bales, Richard: *The Confederacy*, 1953I; *The Republic*, 1955I; *The Union*, 1956I

Baley, Virko: *Dreamtime*, 1996I; *Hunger*, 1990I; *A Journey after Loves*, 1999I; *Klytemnestra*, 1998I; *Nocturnal No. 1*, "*Mirrors*," 1958I; *Nocturnal No. 2*, "*Tears*," 1960I; *Nocturnal No. 3 for Three Pianos*, 1960I; *Partita No. 2*, 1992I; *Piano Concerto No. 1*, 1993I; *Piano Concerto No. 2*, "*Favola in musica*," 1988I; *Piano Nocturne No. 5*, 1980I; *Piano Nocturne No. 6*, 1980I; *Symphony No. 1*, "*Sacred monuments*," 1985I

Ballantine, Edward: *By a Lake in Russia*, 1922I; *The Eve of St. Agnes*, 1917I

Ballard, Louis: *Portrait of Will Rogers*, 1972I

Ballif, Claude: *Flute Sonata*, 1958I; *Organ Sonatas (4)*, 1956I; *String Quartet No. 1*, 1955I; *String Quartet No. 2*, 1958I; *String Quartet No. 3*, 1959I; *String Quartet No. 4*, 1987I; *String Quartet No. 5*, 1989I; *Violin Sonata*, 1957I

Ballou, Esther: *Guitar Concerto*, 1964I; *Konzertstück (viola concerto)*, 1969I; *Piano Concerto No. 1*, 1945I; *Piano Concerto No. 2*, 1964I; *Piano Sonata*, 1955I; *Sonata No. 1 for Two Pianos*, 1943I; *Sonata No. 2 for Two Pianos*, 1958I; *Variations, Scherzo & Fugue*, 1959I

Balmer, Luc: *Chorale Preludes (6) for Organ*, 1978I

Balsach, Llorenc: *String Trio*, 1992I

Banks, Ján: *Benedictus*, 1976I

Banshchikov, Gennadi: *Accordion Sonata*, 1977I; *Cello Sonata*, 1970I; *Clarinet Sonata*, 1972I; *Flute Sonata*, 1975I; *Piano Concerto*, 1963I; *Symphony No. 1*, 1967I; *Symphony No. 2*, 1977I; *Vestris*, 1969I

Bantock, Granville: *Atalanta in Calydon*, 1911I; *Caedmar*, 1892I; *Celtic Symphony*, 1940I; *Dante*, 1901I; *Egypt*, 1892I; *Fifine at the Fair*, 1901I; *The Great God Pan*, 1920I; *The Great God Pan*, 1902I; *The Hebridean Symphony*, 1916I; *Hudibras*, 1902I; *Lalla Rookh*, 1902I; *Omar Khayyám*, 1909I; *Overture, Pierrot of the Minute*, 1908I; *Pagan Symphony*, 1928I; *A Pageant of Human Life*, 1913I; *The Pilgrim's Progress*, 1928I; *Prometheus Unbound*, 1936I; *Sapphic Poem (cello)*, 1908I; *Sappho*, 1907I; *The Sea Wanderers*, 1906I; *The Seal Woman*, 1924I; *The Song of Songs*, 1922I; *Thalaba, the Destroyer*, 1900I; *The Time Spirit*, 1902I; *Vanity of Vanities*, 1913I; *The Witch of Atlas*, 1902I

Barab, Seymour: *String Quartet No. 1*, 1977I

Barati, George: *Branches of Time* (concerto, 2 pianos), 1981I; *B.U.D. Sonata for Piano*, 1984I; *Cello Concerto*, 1953I; *Chamber Concerto for Woodwind Quaartet*, 1952I; *Clarinet Trio*, 1988I; *Guitar Concerto*, 1976I; *Harpsichord Quartet*, 1964I; *The Love of Don Perlimplin*, 1947I; *Noelani*, 1968I; *String Quartet, No. 1*, 1944I; *String Quartet No. 2*, 1961I; *String Quartet No. 3*, 1991I; *Symphony*, 1963I

Barber, Samuel: *Adagio for Strings, Opus 11*, 1936I; *Andromache's Farewell*, 1962I; *Anthony & Cleopatra*, 1966I; *Capricorn Concerto, Opus 21*, 1944I; *Cello Concerto, Opus 22*, 1945I; *Cello Sonata, Opus 6*, 1932I; *Commando March*, 1943I; *Despite & Still*, 1969I; *Dover Beach, Opus 3*, 1931I; *Essay No. 1, Opus 12*, 1937I; *Essay No. 2, Opus 17*, 1942I; *Essay No. 3*, 1978I; *Excursions (4)*, 1944I; *A Hand of Bridge*, 1953I; *Hermit Songs*, 1953I; *Knoxville: Summer of 1915*, 1947I; *The Lovers, Opus 43*, 1971I; *Medea*, 1946I; *Medea's Meditation & Dance of Vengeance*, 1956I; *Music for a Scene from Shelley*, 1933I; *Nocturne: Homage to John Fields*, 1959I; *Nursery Songs (7)*, 1923I; *Overture to "A School for Scandal*," 1933I; *Piano Concerto*, 1962I; *Piano Interludes*, 1932I; *Prayers of Kierkegård, Opus 30*, 1954I; *Sonata, Opus 26*, 1949I; *Songs (3), Opus 45*; *Souvenirs, Opus 28* 1952I; *A Stopwatch and an Ordnance Map*, 1940I; *String Quartet*, 1936I; *Summer Music for Woodwind Quintet*, 1955I; *Symphony No. 1, Opus 9*, 1936I; *Symphony No. 2, Opus 19*, 1944I; *Toccata Festiva, Opus 36*, 1960I; *Vanessa*, 1957I; *Violin Concerto, Opus 14*, 1939I; *Violin Sonata*, 1928I

Barbier, René: *Les génies du sommeil*, 1923I; *Piano Quintet*, 1915I; *Les pierres magiques*, 1957I; *String Quartet*, 1939I; *Viola Sonata*, 1916I; *Violin Sonata*, 1914I

Barbieri, Francisco: *Gloria y peluca*, 1850I

Bargiel, Woldemar: *Piano Trio No. 1, Opus 6*, 1851I; *Piano Trio No. 2, Opus 20*, 1860I; *Piano Trio No. 3, Opus 13*, 1870I

Bark, Jan: *Bar*, 1967I

Barkauskas, Vytautas: *Credo for Organ*, 1989I; *Gloria Urbi for Organ*, 1972I; *Legend about Love*, 1975I; *Piano Concerto*, 1992I; *The Rebirth of Hope*, 1989I; *The Sun*, 1983I; *Symphony No. 1*, 1962I; *Symphony No. 2*, 1971I; *Symphony No. 3*, 1979I; *Symphony No. 4*, 1984I; *Symphony No. 5*, 1986I; *Violin Sonata No. 1*,

---

A   *Births*   B   *Deaths*   C   *Debuts*   D   *New Positions*
E   *Prizes/Honors*

"*Sonata Subita*," 1976I; *Violin Sonata No. 2*, "*Dialogue*," 1978I; *Violin Sonata No. 3*, 1984I; *Zodiac for Organ*, 1980I

Barker, Bray: *The Indian Princess*, 1808I

Barkin, Elaine: *At the Piano*, 1982I; *Inward & Outward Bound*, 1975I; *Pieces for Piano (6)*, 1969I; *String Quartet No. 1*, 1969I; *String Trio*, 1976I; *To Whom It May Concern*, 1989I

Barlow, David: *String Quartet*, 1969I

Barlow, Fred: *Gladys*, 1916I; *La Grand Jatte*, 1938I; *Polichinelle et Colombina*, 1927I

Barlow, Samuel: *Alba*, 1927I; *Amanda*, 1936I; *Ballad & Scherzo, String Quartet*, 1933I; *Ballo sardo*, 1928I; *Mon ami Pierrot*, 1934I; *Piano Concerto*, 1931I; *Songs from the Chinese (3)*, 1924I

Barlow, Wayne: *Hampton Beach Overture*, 1971I; *Images* (harp concerto), 1961I; *Mass in G*, 1951I; *Missa Sancti Thomae*, 1959I; *Moonflight*, 1970I; *Night Song*, 1957I; *Psalm 23*, 1944I; *Soundprints in Concrete*, 1975I; *Soundscapes*, 1972I; *Study in Electronic Sounds*, 1965I; *Voices of Faith*, 1975I; *Wait for the Promise of the Father*, 1968I

Barnby, Joseph: *Magnificat*, 1881I; *Rebekah*, 1870I

Barnes, Edwin: *Morton* (O Let Me Walk With Thee), 1886I; *Southampton* (O Worship the Lord), 1886I

Barnes, Milton: *Amber Garden*, 1972I

Barnett, John: *Farinelli*, 1839I; *The Mountain Sylph*, 1834I; *Symphony*, 1864I

Barolsky, Michael: *The Book of Changes*, 1983I; *Cries & Whispers*, 1975I; *Ein Stück aus der Nacht*, 1978I; *Stück-Mund-Stück*, 1983; *Tonos*, 1979I; *Violin Sonata*, 1964I; *Woodwind Quartet*, 1965I

Barraqué, Jean: *Piano Sonata No. 1*, 1952I

Barrière, Etienne: *Premier air varié, Opus 14*, 1805I; *Quartets (6) for Strings, Opus 3*, 1778I; *Symphonies concertantes (2), Opus 8*, 1776I; *Symphonies (3), Opus 10*, 1785I; *Violin Concerto in A, Opus 5*, 1778I; *Violin Concerto in D, Opus 7*, 1780I

Barry, Gerald: *String Quartet No. 2*, 1999I

Bárta, Josef: *La diavolessa*, 1772I

Bárta, Lubor: *Piano Sonata No. 1*, 1956I; *Piano Sonata No. 2*, 1961I; *Piano Sonata No. 3*, 1971I

Barth, Hans: *Concerto for Quarter-Tone Piano, Opus 15*, 1930I; *Piano Concerto, Opus 11*, 1928I; *Piano Sonata No. 1*, 1929I; *Piano Sonata No. 2*, 1932I; *Piano Suite No. 1, Opus 20*, 1938I; *Piano Suite No. 2*, 1941; *Quintet for Quarter-tone Piano & Strings*, 1930I; *Suite for Quarter-Tone Strings, Brass & Timpani*, 1930I; *Symphony, "Prince of Peace," Opus 25*, 1940I; *Symphony No. 2*, 1948I

Barthélémon, François: *The Judgment of Paris*, 1768I; *The Maid of the Oaks*, 1774I; *Organ Voluntaries (6), Opus 2*, 1782I; *Overtures (6), Opus 6*, 1776I; *Pelopida*, 1766I; *String Quartets (6), Opus 12*, 1790I; *Symphonies (6), Opus 3*, 1769I; *Violin Sonatas (6), Opus 9*, 1785I; *Violin Sonatas (6), Opus 10*, 1785I

Bartók, Béla: *Allegro Barbaro*, 1911I; *Bluebeard's Castle*, 1911I; *Cantata Profana*, 1930I; *Concerto for Orchestra*, 1943I; *Dance Suite*, 1923I; *Divertimento for Strings*, 1939I; *Kossuth*, 1903I; *Mikrokosmos* (completed), 1939I; *The Miraculous Mandarin, Opus 19*, 1919I; *Music for Strings, Percussion & Celesta*, 1936I; *Piano Concerto No. 1*, 1926I; *Piano Concerto No. 2*, 1931I; *Piano Concerto No. 3*, 1945I; *Piano Quartet in c, Opus 20*, 1898I; *Piano Quintet*, 1904I; *Piano Rhapsody, Opus 1*, 1904I; *Piano Sonatina*, 1915I; *Piano Studies (3), Opus 18*, 1918I; *Piano Suite, Opus 14*, 1916I; *Pictures (2), Opus 10*, 1910I; *Pieces (4), Opus 12*, 1912I; *Portraits (2), Opus 5*, 1907I; *Rhapsody for Cello & Orchestra*, 1928I; *Rhapsody No. 1* (violin, orch), 1928I; *Rhapsody No. 2* (violin, orch), 1928I; *Romanian Dances, Opus 8a*, 1910I; *Scherzo for Piano & Orchestra, Opus 2*, 1904I; *Scherzo for Orchestra*, 1902I; *Sonata for Two Pianos & Percussion*, 1937I; *String Quartet No. 1, Opus 7*, 1908I; *String Quartet No. 2, Opus 17*, 1917I; *String Quartet No. 3*, 1927I; *String Quartet No. 4*, 1928I; *String Quartet No. 5*, 1934I; *String Quartet No. 6*, 1939I; *String Quartet Studies, (3), Opus 18*, 1918I; *Suite No. 1, Opus 3*, 1905I; *Suite No. 2, Opus 4*, 1906I; *Viola Concerto*, 1945I; *Violin Concerto No. 1*, 1908I; *Violin Concerto No. 2*, 1938I; *Violin Sonata in e*, 1903I; *Violin Sonata No. 1*, 1921I; *Violin Sonata No. 2*, 1922I; *The Wooden Prince*, 1916I

Bartolozzi, Bruno: *Concerto for Orchestra*, 1952I; *String Quartet No. 2*, 1979I; *Violin Concerto No. 1*, 1957I

Barto, Jan: *Cello Sonata*, 1938I; *Horn Concerto*, 1967I; *King of the Manège*, 1963I; *Manuhan*, 1941I; *Song of St. Matthias*, 1945I; *String Quartet No. 1*, 1940I; *String Quartet No. 2*, 1946I; *String Quartet No. 3*, 1948I; *String Quartet No 4*, 1951I; *String Quartet No 5*, 1952I; *String Quartet No. 6*, 1956I; *String Quartet No. 7*, 1960I; *String Quartet No. 8*, 1963I; *String Quartet No. 9*, 1970I; *String Quartet No. 10*, 1971I; *String Quartet No. 11*, 1973I; *Symphony No. 1*, 1952I; *Symphony No. 2*, 1956I; *Symphony No. 3*, 1965I; *Symphony No. 4*, 1968I; *Symphony No. 5*, 1974I; *Symphony No. 6*, 1977I; *Symphony No. 7*, 1978I; *Trombone Sonata*, 1978I

Bartow, Nevett: *Harpsichord Concerto*, 1955I; *Mass of the Bells*, 1957I

Bassett, Leslie: *Brass Quintet*, 1988I; *Collect*, 1969I; *Colloquy for Orchestra*, 1969I; *Colors & Contours*, 1984I; *Concerti Lyrico*, 1983I; *Concerto for Orchestra*, 1991I; *Concerto for Orchestra*, 1993I; *Concerto for Two Pianos*, 1976I; *Configurations (5) for Piano*, 1987I; *Echoes from an Invisible World*, 1975I; *For City,*

F *Biographical*   G *Cultural Beginnings*   H *Musical Literature*
I *Musical Compositions*

Bassett, Leslie: (*cont.*)
   Nation, World, 1959I; *Forces* (violin, cello & Piano concerto), 1972I; *Horn Sonata*, 1952I; *The Jade Garden*, 1973I; *Liturgies for Organ*, 1980I; *Movements (5) for Orchestra*, 1961I; *Nonet*, 1967I; *Organ Voluntaries*, 1958I; *Piano Preludes (7)*, 1984I; *Piano Quintet*, 1962I; *Pierrot Songs*, 1988I; *Sextet* (piano, strings), 1971I; *Sextet* (woodwinds, strings), 1979I; *Sounds, Shapes & Symbols* (band), 1977I; *Statements (4) for Organ*, 1964I; *String Quartet No. 1*, 1951I; *String Quartet No. 2*, 1957I; *String Quartet No. 3*, 1962I; *String Quartet No. 4*, 1978I; *String Quintet*, 1954I; *Suite in G*, 1946I; *Things that Sing, Burn & Breathe*, 1997I; *Three Studies in Electronic Sounds*, 1965I; *Triform*, 1966I; *Trio* (clarinet, clarinet, piano), 1980I; *Trio for Viola, Clarinet & Piano*, 1953I; *Trombone Concerto Lirico*, 1984I; *Variations for Orchestra*, 1963I; *Viola Sonata*, 1956I; *Violin Sonata*, 1959I; *Wind Music*, 1975I; *Woodwind Quintet*, 1958I

Bate, Jennifer: *Canone Inglese for Organ*, 1996I; *Il filataio*, 1988I; *French Carol Variations*, 1982I; *Homage to 1685*, 1985I; *Lament for Organ*, 1997I; *Reflections (4) for Organ*, 1986I; *Toccata on a Theme of Martin Shaw*, 1972I; *Variations on a Gregorian Theme*, 1997I

Bate, Stanley: *Eros*, 1935I

Bath, Hubert: *Bubbles*, 1923I

Bauer, Marion: *China, Opus 38*, 1944I; *Dance Sonata*, 1932I; *From the New Hampshire Woods*, 1921I; *Indian Pipes*, 1927I; *In the Country*, 1913I; *Lament of African Themes*, 1928I; *Orientale*, 1914I; *Piano Concerto, "American Youth," Opus 36*, 1943I; *Piano Pieces (4), Opus 17*, 1930I; *Pieces (5), String Quartet*, 1949I; *Ragpicker's Love*, 1935I; *Songs for Soprano & String Quartet (4)*, 1936I; *Sun Splendor*, 1926I; *String Quartet*, 1928I; *Symphony No. 1*, 1950I; *Viola (Clarinet) Sonata*, 1935I; *Violin Sonata No. 1*, 1922I

Baumann, Herbert: *Guitar Concerto*, 1958I; *Mandolin Concerto*, 1996I

Baumann, Max: *Organ Pieces (3)*, 1963I

Baur, Jürg: *Sonata for Solo Viola*, 1969I; *Sonata for Solo Violin*, 1962I; *Vom tiéfinnern Sang*, 1957I

Bautista, Julián: *Juerga*, 1921I

Bax, Arnold: *Between Dusk & Dawn*, 1917I; *Cello Concerto*, 1932I; *Cello Sonata*, 1923I; *Christmas Eve on the Mountains*, 1911I; *Clarinet Sonata*, 1934I; *Concertante for Piano, Left Hand & Orchestra*, 1948I; *Concerto for Flute, Oboe, Harp & Strings*, 1936I; *Eire: Into the Twilight*, 1908I; *Elegiac Trio for Flute, Viola & Harp*, 1916I; *Enchanted Summer*, 1910I; *The Garden of Fand*, 1916I; *Gloria*, 1945I; *The Happy Forest*, 1921I; *In Memoriam*, 1916I; *In the Fairy Hills*, 1909I; *A Legend*, 1944I; *Legend-Sonata for Cello & Piano*, 1943I; *Magnificat*, 1948I; *Nonet*, 1930I; *November Woods*, 1917I; *Nympholept*, 1915I; *Oboe Quintet*, 1922I; *Overture to Adventure*, 1936I; *Phantasy (viola)*, 1920I; *Piano Quintet No. 1*, 1915I; *Piano Quintet No. 2*, 1922I; *Piano Sonata No. 1*, 1898I; *Piano Sonata No. 2*, 1919I; *Piano Sonata No. 3*, 1926I; *Piano Sonata No. 4*, 1932I; *Piano Trio No. 1*, 1906I; *Piano Trio No. 2*, 1946I; *Quintet for Harp & Strings*, 1919I; *A Song of Life & Love*, 1905I; *A Song of War & Victory*, 1905I; *String Quartet No. 1*, 1916I; *String Quartet No. 2*, 1925I; *String Quartet No. 3*, 1936I; *String Quintet No. 1*, 1908I; *String Quintet No. 2*, 1933I; *Symphonic Variations*, 1917I; *Symphony No. 1 in E♭*, 1921I; *Symphony No. 2 in e/C*, 1924I; *Symphony No. 3*, 1928I; *Symphony No. 4*, 1930I; *Symphony No. 5*, 1931I; *Symphony No. 6*, 1934I; *Symphony No. 7*, 1939I; *The Tale the Pine Trees Knew*, 1931I; *Te Deum*, 1944I; *Tintagel*, 1919I; *Viola Sonata*, 1922I; *Violin Concerto*, 1938I; *Violin Sonata No. 1*, 1910I; *Violin Sonata No. 2*, 1915I; *Violin Sonata No. 3*, 1927I

Bayle, François: *L'archipel*, 1963I; *Aér*, 1987I; *Aéroformes*, 1984I; *Erosphère*, 1980I; *Espaces inhabitables*, 1967I; *Fabulae*, 1991I; *Lumière*, 1983I; *Motion-Emotion*, 1986I; *Muriel*, 1963I; *Portraits (3) d'un oiseau qui n'existe pas*, 1962I; *Rêves d'oiseau (3)*, 1972I; *Son vitesse*, 1983I; *Théâtre d'ombres*, 1989I; *Vibrations composées*, 1973I

Bazelon, Irwin: *Ballet Suite*, 1949I; *Brass Quintet*, 1963I; *Early American Suite*, 1965I; *Entre nous*, 1992I; *Excursions*, 1965I; *Four . . . Parts of a World*, 1991I; *Junctures*, 1979I; *Legends & Love Letters*, 1987I; *Overture, The Taming of the Shrew*, 1959I; *Piano Concerto, "Trajectories,"* 1985I; *Piano Pieces (5)*, 1950I; *Piano Re-Percussions*, 1982I; *A Quiet Piece for a Violent Time*, 1975I; *Quintessentials*, 1983I; *Sound Dreams*, 1977I; *Spirits of the Night*, 1976I; *String Quartet No. 2*, 1947I; *String Quartet No. 3*, 1995I; *Suite for Young People*, 1950I; *Sunday Silence for Piano*, 1990I; *Symphony No. 1*, 1960I; *Symphony No. 2, "A Short Symphony,"* 1962I; *Symphony No. 3*, 1963I; *Symphony No. 4*, 1965I; *Symphony No. 5*, 1966I; *Symphony No. 6*, 1969I; *Symphony No. 7, "Ballet for Orchestra,"* 1980I; *Symphony No. 8 for Strings*, 1986I; *Symphony No. 8 H*, 1988I; *Symphony No. 9, "Sunday Silence,"* 1992I; *Symphony No. 10*, 1995I; *Trajectories*, 1985I; *Woodwind Quintet*, 975I

Bazelaire, Paul: *Cléopâtre*, 1908I

Beach, Amy (Mrs. H. H. A.): *Bal masqué*, 1893I; *Browning Songs (3), Opus 44*, 1900I; *Cabildo, Opus 149*, 1932I; *The Canticle of the Sun, Opus 123*, 1925I; *The Chambered Nautilus, Opus 66*, 1907I; *Children's Album, Opus 36*, 1897I; *Christ in the Universe, Opus 139*, 1931I; *Eilende Wilken, Seglerdie Lüfte*, 1892I; *Eskimos: Four Characteristic Pieces, Opus 64*, 1907I; *The Fair Hills of Eire*, 1922I; *Festival Jubilate, Opus 17*, 1891I; *From Six to Twelve, Opus 119*, 1927I; *A Hymn of Freedom: America*, 1903I; *Improvisations (5),*

Opus 148, 1938I; *Jephthah's Daughter, Opus 53*, 1903I; *Mass in E♭, Opus 5*, 1890I; *Morceaux caractéristiques (3), Opus 28*, 1894I; *Pastorale for Woodwind Quintet, Opus 151*, 1942I; *Piano Compositions (2), Opus 102*, 1924I; *Piano Concerto in c♯, Opus 45*, 1899I; *Piano Pieces (3), Opus 128*, 1932I; *Piano Quintet in a, Opus 34*, 1908I; *Piano Quintet in f♯, Opus 67*, 1907I; *Piano Suite française, Opus 65*, 1905I; *Piano Trio in a, Opus 150*, 1938I; *Shakespeare Choruses (3), Opus 39*, 1897I; *Shakespeare Songs (3), Opus 37*, 1897I; *Sketches (4), Opus 15*, 1892I; *Songs (3) on Burns, Opus 12*, 1887I; *Songs (4), Opus 1*, 1886I; *Songs (3), Opus 11*, 1889I; *Songs (7), Opus 2, 14*, 1891I; *Songs (6), Opus 19, 21*, 1893I; *Songs (4), Opus 35*, 1896I; *Songs (3), Opus 41*, 1898I; *Songs (5) on Burns, Opus 43*, 1899I; *Songs (4), Opus 49*, 1895I; *Songs (4), Opus 48*, 1902I; *Songs (4), Opus 51*, 1903I; *Songs (4), Opus 56*, 1904I; *Songs (8), Opus 72, 73, 75, 76*, 1914I; *Songs (2), Opus 77*, 1915I; *Songs (3), Opus 78*, 1917I; *Songs: When Mama Sings (4), Opus 99*, 1923I; *Songs: A Mirage (2), Opus 100*, 1924I; *Songs (3), Opus 117*, 1925I; *String Quartet No. 1*, 1929I; *Sylvania: A Wedding Cantata*, 1901I; *Symphony in e, "Gaelic,"* 1894I; *Theme & Variations, Opus 80*, 1916I; *Valse-caprice, Opus 4*, 1889I; *Variations in a, Opus 80*, 1920I; *Variations on Balkan Themes, Opus 60*, 1904I; *Violin Sonata in a, Opus 34*, 1896I

Beach, John Parsons: *Mardi Gras*, 1926I; *Poem for String Quartet*, 1920I

Beamish, Sally: *Black, White, Blue*, 1997I; *Burns Songs (2)*, 1996I; *Cello Concerto*, 1996I; *Magnificat*, 1992I; *Piano Sonata*, 1996I; *Rive*, 1997I; *Songs (7) for Girl's Voices*, 1990I; *Symphony No. 1*, 1992I; *Symphony No. 2*, 1998I; *Violin Sonata*, 1976I; *The Wedding at Cana*, 1991I

Beane, Raymond: *Brown Studies* (string quartet), 1998I

Beaser, Robert: *Central Park: The Food of Love*, 1999I

Becerra, Gustave: *Piano Concerto*, 1958I; *Violin Concerto*, 1950I

Beck, Conrad: *Choral Sonata*, 1947I; *Organ Sonatina*, 1927I; *Piano Concerto*, 1933I; *Requiem*, 1930I; *String Quartet No. 1*, 1922I; *String Quartet No. 2*, 1924I; *String Quartet No. 3*, 1926I; *String Quartet No. 4*, 1934I; *Symphony No. 1*, 1925I; *Symphony No. 2, "Sinfonietta,"* 1926I; *Symphony No. 3*, 1927I; *Violin Concerto*, 1940I

Beck, Franz Ignaz: *Overtures (6), Opus 1*, 1758I; *Stabat Mater*, 1789I

Beck, Jan: *People of Note*, 1993I

Beck, Johann H.: *String Quartet No. 4*, 1880I; *String Quartet No. 1 in c*, 1877I; *String Sextet in d*, 1886I

Becker, Albert: *Symphony in g*, 1861I

Becker, John J.: *Abongo, a Primitive Dance: Stagework No. 2*, 1933I; *Antigone*, 1944I; *Architectural Impressions (2)*, 1924I; *The City of Shagpat*, 1927I; *Concerto Arabesque*, 1930I; *Dance Figure: Stagework No. 4*, 1932I; *Deirdre: Stagework No. 6*, 1945I; *Faust: A Television Opera*, 1951I; *A Heine Song Cycle*, 1924I; *Horn Concerto*, 1933I; *Improvisation*, 1960I; *Madeleine et Judas*, 1958I; *A Marriage with Space: Stagework No. 3*, 1935I; *Missa Symphonica*, 1933I; *Out of the Cradle Endlessly Rocking*, 1929I; *Piano Concerto No. 2, "Satirico,"* 1938I; *Privilege & Privation: Stagework No. 5c*, 1939I; *Rain Down Death: Stagework No. 5a*, 1939I; *Sonata American for Violin & Piano*, 1925I; *Sonata for Flute & Clarinet: Soundpiece No. 6*, 1942I; *Songs for Soprano & String Quartet (4)*, 1919I; *Soundpiece No. 1 for Piano & String Quartet*, 1932I; *Soundpiece No. 3: Violin Sonata*, 1936I; *Soundpiece No. 5: Piano Sonata*, 1937I; *Soundpiece No. 7: Two Piano Sonata*, 1949I; *String Quartet No. 1, "Homage to Haydn,"* 1936I; *String Quartet No. 2*, 1937I; *String Quartet No. 3*, 1959I; *Symphony No. 1 "Etude primitive,"* 1912I; *Symphony No. 2, "Fantasia tragica,"* 1920I; *Symphony No. 3, "Symphonia brevis,"* 1929I; *Symphony No. 4*, 1938I; *Symphony No. 5, "Homage to Mozart,"* 1942I; *Symphony No. 6, "Out of Bondage,"* 1942I; *Symphony No. 7, "Sermon on the Mount,"* 1954I; *Viola Concerto*, 1937I; *Violin Concerto*, 1948I; *When the Willow Nods: Stagework No. 5b*, 1940I

Beckwith, John, *Crazy to Kill*, 1989I; *The Shivaree*, 1982I

Bedford, David: *Symphony No. 1*, 1984I; *Symphony No. 2* (band), 1987I

Beecroft, Norma: *Evocations: Images of Canada*, 1991I; *Hedda*, 1982I

Beeson, Jack: *Captain Jinks of the Horse Marines*, 1975I; *Cyrano*, 1990I; *Dr. Heidegger's Fountain of Youth*, 1978I; *From a Watchtower*, 1976I; *Hello, Out There*, 1954I; *Lizzie Borden*, 1965I; *Lyrics on English & American Poets (6)*, 1952I; *My Heart's in the Highlands*, 1969I; *Old Hundredth: Prelude & Doxology for Organ*, 1972I; *Piano Sonata No. 4*, 1945I; *Piano Sonata No. 5*, 1946I; *String Quartet*, 1948I; *The Sweet Bye & Bye*, 1956I; *Symphony No. 1 in A*, 1959I; *Viola Sonata*, 1953I

Beethoven, Ludwig van: *"Ah, perfido," Opus 65*, 1796I; *Adelaide, Opus 46*, 1795I; *Air & Variations, "Ich denke dein," 1805I; *An die Hoffnung, Opus 32*, 1805I; *An die Ferne Geliebte, Opus 98*, 1816I; *Arietta, "The Kiss," Opus 128*, 1822I; *Arietta, In Questa Tomba Oscura*, 1808I; *Ariettas and Duets (4), Opus 82*, 1811I; *Bagatelle in a,"Für Elise,"* 1810I; *Bagatelles (7), Opus 33*, 1802I; *Bagatelles (7), Opus 126*, 1823I; *Bundeslied, Opus 122*, 1823I; *Calm Sea & Prosperous Voyage, Opus 112*, 1815I; *Cantata on the Death of Joseph II*, 1790I; *Cello Sonatas (2), Opus 5*, 1797I; *Cello Sonatas (2), Opus 102*, 1815I; *Cello Sonata, Opus 69*, 1808I; *Choral Fantasia in c, Opus 80*, 1808I; *Christ on the Mount of Olives, Opus 85*, 1800I; *Clarinet*

Beethoven, Ludwig van: *(cont.)*
Trio, *Opus 11*, 1798I; *Contradances (12), Opus 141*, 1803I; *Coriolanus Overture, Opus 62*, 1807I; *The Creatures of Prometheus, Opus 43 1*, 1801I; *Diabelli Variations, Opus 12*, 1823I; *Egmont, Opus 84*, 1810I; *Equali (3) for Trombones*, 1812I; *Fidelio, Opus 72*, 1805I; *Fidelio Overture, Opus 72b*, 1814I; *Fugue in D, Opus 137*, 1817I; *German Dances (12), Opus 140*, 1795I; *Der glorreiche Augenblick, Opus 136*, 1814I; *Grand Marches (3), Opus 45*, 1804I; *Grosse Fuge, Opus 133*, 1825I; *Irish Songs (75), Opus 223, 224, 225*, 1816I; *King Stephen, Opus 117*, 1811I; *Leonore Overture No. 1, Opus 138*, 1807I; *Leonore Overture No. 2*, 1805I; *Leonore Overture No. 3, Opus 72a*, 1806I; *Mass in C, Opus 86*, 1807I; *Minuets (12), Opus 139*, 1798I; *Missa Solemnis, Opus 123*, 1823I; *Namensfeier Overture, Opus 115*, 1814I; *National Themes with Variations, Opus 107*, 1820I; *O Hoffnung*, 1818I; *Opferlied, Opus 121b*, 1802I; *Piano Concerto No. 1 in C, Opus 15*, 1795I; *Piano Concerto No. 2 in B♭, Opus 19*, 1795I; *Piano Concerto No. 3 in c, Opus 37*, 1800I; *Piano Concerto No. 4 in g, Opus 58*, 1805I; *Piano Concerto No. 5 in E♭, "Emperor,"* 1809I; *Piano Fantasia in B♭, Opus 77*, 1809I; *Piano Sonata No. 12 in A♭, Opus 26*, 1801I; *Piano Sonata No. 13 in E♭, Opus 27/1*, 1801I; *Piano Sonata No. 14 in c♯, "Moonlight," Opus 272*, 1801I; *Piano Sonata No. 15 in D, "Pastoral," Opus 28*, 1801I; *Piano Sonata No. 21, "Waldstein," Opus 53*, 1804I; *Piano Sonata No. 22 in F, Opus 54*, 1804I; *Piano Sonata No. 24 in F♯, Opus 78*, 1809I; *Piano Sonata No. 25 in G, Opus 79*, 1809I; *Piano Sonata No. 26, Opus 81a*, 1809I; *Piano Sonata No. 27 in e, Opus 90*, 1814I; *Piano Sonata No. 28 in A, Opus 101*, 1816I; *Piano Sonata No. 29, "Hammerklavier,"* 1819I; *Piano Sonata No. 30 in E, Opus 109*, 1820I; *Piano Sonata No. 31 in A♭, Opus 110*, 1821I; *Piano Sonata No. 32 in c, Opus 111*, 1822I; *Piano Sonatas (3) Opus 31*, 1802I; *Piano Sonatas, Easy (2), Opus 49*, 1802I; *Pianostücke in B♭, Opus 172*, 1818I; *Piano Trios (3) Opus 1*, 1795I; *Piano Trios (2), Opus 70*, 1808I; *Quintet in E♭, Opus16*, 1797I; *Romance in G, Opus 40*, 1804I; *Rondo a Capriccio in G, Opus 129*, 1826I; *Rondo in B♭*, 1793I; *The Ruins of Athens, Opus 113*, 1811I; *Scotch Songs (25), Opus 108*, 1816I; *Septet in E♭, Opus 20*, 1799I; *Serenade in D, Opus 8*, 1797I; *Sextet in E♭, Opus 71*, 1810I; *Songs (6), Opus 48*, 1803I; *Songs (8), Opus 52*, 1805I; *Songs (9), Opus 75, 83*, 1810I; *Songs (12), Opus 228*, 1815I; *String Quartets(6), Opus 18*, 1800I; *String Quartets(3), "Razumovsky," Opus 59*, 1806I; *String Quartet No. 10 in E♭, Opus 74, "The Harp,"* 1809I; *String Quartet No. 11 in f, Opus 95, "Serioso,"* 1810I; *String Quartet No. 12 in E♭, Opus 127*, 1824I; *String Quartet No. 13 in a, Opus 132*, 1825I; *String Quartet No. 14 in B♭, Opus 130*, 1825I; *String Quartet No. 15 in c♯, Opus 131*, 1826I; *String Quartet No. 16 in F, Opus 135*, 1826I; *String Quintet in E♭, Opus 4*, 1795I; *String Quintet in C, Opus 29*, 1801I; *String Trios (3), Opus 9*, 1798I; *String Quintet in c, Opus 104*, 1817I; *Symphony No. 1 in C, Opus 21*, 1799I; *Symphony No. 2 in D, Opus 36*, 1802I; *Symphony No. 3 in E♭, Opus 55, "Eroica,"* 1803I; *Symphony No. 4 in B♭, Opus 60*, 1806I; *Symphony No. 5 in c, Opus 67*, 1807I; *Symphony No. 6 in F, Opus 68,"Pastoral,"* 1808I; *Symphony No. 7 in A, Opus 92*, 1812I; *Symphony No. 8 in F, Opus 93*, 1812I; *Symphony No. 9 in d, "Choral," Opus 125*, 1823I; *Triple Concerto in C, Opus 56*, 1804I; *Trio in E♭, Opus 38*, 1802I; *Trio, "Archduke," Opus 97*, 1811I; *Variations (6) in F, Opus 34*, 1802I; *Variations (15), "Prometheus," Opus 35*, 1802I; *Variations (5) on "Rule, Britannia,"* 1803I; *Variations (7) on "God Save the King,"* 1803I; *Variations (14) in E♭, Opus 44*, 1804I; *Variations (32) in c*, 1807I; *Variations (6) in D, Opus 76*, 1810I; *Variations, 6 Easy, Opus 105*, 1818I; *Variations, Opus 121a*, 1824I; *Variations (6) in G, Opus 188*, 1801I; *Variations (24) on Righini*, 1801I; *Variations in F on Mozart, Opus 66*, 1798I; *Variations on Mozart, Opus 156*, 1793I; *Violin Sonata in a, Opus 24*, 1801I; *Violin Sonata in a, "Kreutzer,"* 1803I; *Violin Sonata in G, Opus 96*, 1812I; *Violin Sonatas (3), Opus 12*, 1798I; *Violin Sonatas (3), Opus 30*, 1802I; *Violin Concerto in D, Opus 61*, 1806I; *Wellington's Victory, Opus 91*, 1814I; *Welsh Songs 26), Opus 226*, 1817I; *Woodwind Trio, Opus 87*, 1794I
Beglarian, Grant: *Organ Suite*, 1956I; *Violin Sonata*, 1949I; *Women of Troy*, 1949I
Behrend, Fritz: *Almansor*, 1931I; *Cello Sonata*, 1925I; *Dornröschen*, 1934I; *König Renés Tochter*, 1919I; *Die lächerlichen Presiösen*, 1928I; *Piano Trio No. 1*, 1923I; *Piano Trio No. 2*, 1929I; *Der schwangerer Bauer*, 1927I; *Der Spiegel*, 1950I; *Violin Sonata*, 1925I; *Wind Quintet*, 1951I; *Der Wunderdoktor*, 1947I
Behrman, David: *On the Other Ocean*, 1977I
Bekku, Sadao: *Flute Sonata*, 1954I; *Piano Concerto*, 1981I; *Violin Sonata*, 1967I
Bell, Elizabeth: *Perne in a Gyre*, 1984I; *String Quartet No. 1*, 1957I; *Symphony No. 1*, 1971I
Bell, Larry Thomas: *Reminiscences & Reflections*, 1998I
Bell, W. H.: *Hippolytus*, 1914I; *South African Symphony*, 1927I; *Symphony No. 2*, 1918I; *Symphony No. 3*, 1919I; *Symphony in f*, 1932I; *Walt Whitman Symphony*, 1899I
Bellini, Vincenzo: *Adelson e Salvina*, 1825I; *Beatrice di Tenda*, 1833I; *Bianca e Gernando*, 1826I; *Il Capuleti e i Montecchi*, 1830I; *Magnificat*, 1818I; *Norma*, 1831I; *Il pirata*, 1827I; *I puritani*, 1835I; *La sonnambula*, 1831I; *La straniera*, 1829I; *Zaira*, 1829I
Belmont, Jean: *Remembrance*, 1997I
Benda, Franz: *Violin Sonatas (6), Opus 1*, 1763I

❄

A   *Births*   B   *Deaths*   C   *Debuts*   D   *New Positions*
E   *Prizes/Honors*

Benda, Friedrich (Wilhelm Heinrich): *Alceste*, 1786I; *Das Blumenmädchen*, 1806I; *Flute Concertos (2), Opus 2*, 1779I; *Die Grazien*, 1789I; *Die Jungen am Grabe des Auferstandenen*, 1792I; *Orpheus*, 1785H; *Pygmalion*, 1784I; *Trio Sonatas (6), Opus 1*, 1778I; *Violin Sonatas (3), Opus 3*, 1781I

Benda, Friedrich Ludwig: *Der Barbier von Sevilla*, 1776I; *Louise*, 1791I; *Mariechen*, 1792I; *Narren ballett*, 1779I; *Psalm 97*, 1786I; *Der Tod*, 1788I; *Trauercantate*, 1785I; *Der Verlobung*, 1790I; *Violin Sonata*, 1782I

Benda, Georg Anton: *Amynts Klagen über die Flucht der Lalage*, 1772I; *Ariadne auf Naxos*, 1775I; *Bendas Klagen*, 1792I; *Il buon marito*, 1766I; *Cephalus und Aurore*, 1789I; *Der Dorfjahrmarkt*, 1775I; *Der Holzhauer*, 1778I; *Medea*, 1775I; *Il mestro di capella*, 1767I; *Philon und Theone*, 1779I; *Pygmalion*, 1779I; *Romeo und Juliet*, 1776I; *Der sterbende Jesus*, 1757I; *Das Tartarische Gesetz*, 1780I (87?); *Walden*, 1776I; *Xindo riconnosciuto*, 1765I; *Die Zurückkunst der Lalage*, 1772I

Bendl, Karel:; *Bretislav*, 1869I; *Lejla*, 1868I

Benedict, Julius: *The Bride of Song*, 1864I; *The Brides of Venice*, 1844I; *The Crusaders*, 1846I; *The Gypsy's Warning*, 1838I; *The Lake of Glenaston*, 1862I; *The Lily of Killarney*, 1862I; *Richard the Lion-Hearted*, 1863I; *St. Peter*, 1870I; *St. Cecilia*, 1866I; *Caprice in E, Opus 22*, 1844I; *Concert-Stück in a, Opus 22*, 1841I; *The Naiads Overture*, 1836I; *Overture, Merry Wives of Windsor*, 1834I; *Overture-Fantasy, Paradise & the Peri*, 1862I; *Parisina Overture*, 1834I; *Piano Sonata in A♭, Opus 46*, 1873I; *Piano Trio in A, Opus 26*, 1839I; *Piano Concerto No. 1 in d, Opus 1*, 1832I; *Piano Concerto No. 2 in E♭, Opus 4*, 1833I; *Piano Concerto No. 3 in c, Opus 9*, 1834I; *Piano Concerto No. 4 in f*, 1836I; *Symphony No. 4 in A*, 1834I; *The Woman of Samaria*, 1867I; *The Wood Nymphs Overture*, 1841I

Bengtsson, Gustav: *Piano Trio*, 1916I; *String Quartet*, 1907I; *Symphony No. 1 in c*, 1908I; *Symphony No. 2*, 1910I; *Symphony No. 3*, 1921I; *Vettern*, 1950I

Ben-Haim, Paul: *Capriccio for Piano & Orchestra*, 1960I; *Cello Concerto*, 1962I; *Pan*, 1931I; *Piano Concerto*, 1949I; *Pieces (3) for Cello*, 1973I; *Sonata for Solo Violin*, 1953I; *String Quartet*, 1937I; *Symphony No. 1*, 1940I; *Symphony No. 2*, 1945I; *Violin Concerto*, 1960I

Benjamin, Arthur: *Concerto Quasi Una Fantasia*, 1950I; *The Devil Take Her*, 1931I; *Harmonica Concerto*, 1953I; *Piano Concertino*, 1927I; *String Quartet No. 1*, 1924I; *String Quartet No. 2*, 1959I; *Symphony No. 1*, 1945I; *Violin Concerto*, 1932I

Benjamin, George: *Antara*, 1987I; *Panorama*, 1985I; *Upon Silence*, 1990I

Bennett, Richard Rodney: *Capriccio*, 1990I; *Clarinet Concerto*, 1987I; *Clarinet Quintet*, 1992I; *Concerto for Orchestra*, 1973I; *Diversions*, 1990I; *Doublebass Concerto*, 1978I; *Guitar Sonata*, 1983I; *Harpsichord Concerto*, 1980I; *Horn Sonata*, 1978I; *Impromptus (5)*, 1968I; *Lamente d'Arianna*, 1986I; *Love Songs*, 1984I; *Missa Brevis*, 1990I; *Piano Concerto*, 1968I; *Piano Sonata*, 1954I; *Romances*, 1985I; *Sonata for Solo Violin*, 1964I; *String Quartet Music*, 1981I; *String Quartet No. 1*, 1952I; *String Quartet No. 2*, 1953I; *String Quartet No. 3*, 1960I; *String Quartet No. 4*, 1964I; *Summer Music*, 1982I; *Symphony No. 1*, 1966I; *Symphony No. 2*, 1968I; *Symphony No. 3*, 1987I; *Travel Notes I (String Quartet)*, 1975I; *Viola Concerto*, 1973I; *Violin Sonata*, 1978I

Bennett, Robert Russell: *Armed Forces Suite*, 1959I; *Clarinet Quintet*, 1941I; *Columbine*, 1916I; *Concerto for Harp & Cello*, 1960I; *Crystal*, 1972I; *Double Concerto* (violin & piano), 1958I; *The Enchanted Kiss*, 1945I; *Endimion*, 1926I; *Four Freedoms Symphony*, 1943I; *Hexapoda for Violin & Piano*, 1940I; *Horn Concerto*, 1956I; *Maria Malibran*, 1934I; *Organ Sonata*, 1929I; *Overture to an Imaginary Opera*, 1946I; *Piano Concerto*, 1947I; *String Quartet*, 1956I; *Suite of Old American Dances*, 1949I; *Symphonic Songs*, 1957I; *Violin Concerto*, 1941I; *Symphony No. 1*, 1926I; *Symphony No. 2, "Abraham Lincoln,"* 1929I; *Symphony No. 3 in D, "For the Dodgers,"* 1941I; *Symphony No. 6*, 1946I; *Commemoration Symphony*, 1959I; *Symphony No. 7*, 1962I

Benoist, François: *L'apparition*, 1848I; *Léonore et Félix*, 1821I

Benoit, Peter: *Cantate de Noël*, 1860I; *Charlotte Corday*, 1876I; *Danses des spectres*, 1858I; *De liefde in het level*, 1870I; *De Rhijn*, 1889I; *De oorlog*, 1873I; *De schelde*, 1868I; *Drama Christi*, 1871I; *Flute Concerto*, 1865I; *Isa*, 1867I; *Liefdedrama*, 1872I; *Lucifer*, 1865I; *Le meurtre d'Abel*, 1857I; *A Mountain Village*, 1856I; *The Pacification of Ghent*, 1876I; *Piano Sonata in G*, 1860I; *Piano Concerto*, 1865I; *Prometheus*, 1867I; *Requiem*, 1863I; *Le roi des Aulnes*, 1859I; *String Quartet in D*, 1859I; *Symphonic Ode, Opus 30*, 1866I; *Symphonic Ode, Opus 43b*, 1864I; *Te Deum*, 1862I

Benson, Warren: *Bailando*, 1965I; *Horn Concerto*, 1971I; *Songs for the End of the World*, 1980I; *String Quartet No. 1*, 1969I; *String Quartet No. 2*, 1985I; *Symphony No. 2, "Lost Songs"* (band), 1982I

Bentock, Granville: *The Pearl of Iran*, 1894I

Bentoiu, Pascal: *Symphony No. 1*, 1965I; *Symphony No. 2*, 1974I; *Symphony No. 3*, 1976I; *Symphony No. 4*, 1978I; *Symphony No. 5*, 1979I; *Symphony No. 6*, 1985I; *Symphony No. 7*, 1986I; *Symphony No. 8*, 1987I; *Violin Sonata*, 1962I

Bentzon, Jørgen: *Mikrofoni No. 1*, 1939I; *Saturnalia*, 1944I; *Sonatina for Wind Trio*, 1924I; *Symphony No. 1*, 1940I; *Symphony No. 2*, 1947I; *Variazioni interrotti*, 1926I

    F *Biographical*   G *Cultural Beginnings*   H *Musical Literature*
                 I *Musical Compositions*

Bentzon, Niels Viggo: *Clarinet Sonata*, 1950I; *Concerto for Two Pianos, Opus 482*, 1985I; *Duel, Opus 404*, 1977I; *Flute Concerto*, 1963I; *Piano Concerto No. 1, Opus 49*, 1948I; *Piano Concerto No. 4, Opus 96*, 1954I; *Piano Concerto No. 5, Opus 149*, 1963I; *Savonarola, Opus 500*, 1986I; *Symphony No. 10, Opus 105*, 1963I; *The Tempered Piano I, Opus 157*, 1964I; *The Tempered Piano II, Opus 379*, 1976I; *The Tempered Piano III, Opus 400*, 1977I; *The Tempered Piano IV, Opus 409*, 1978I; *The Tempered Piano VI, Opus 470*, 1985I; *The Tempered Piano VII, Opus 530*, 1989I; *The Tempered Piano VIII, Opus 532*, 1989I; *The Tempered Piano IX, Opus 541*, 1989I; *The Tempered Piano X, Opus 542*, 1990I; *The Tempered Piano XI, Opus 546*, 1990I; *The Tempered Piano XII, Opus 554*, 1991I; *The Tempered Piano XIII, Opus 633*, 1996I; *Violin Concerto No. 1, Opus 106*, 1956I

Benvenuti, Tommaso: *Guglielmo Shakespeare*, 1861I; *La stella de Toledo*, 1864I

Beran, Jan: *Piano Concerto No. 1, "Immaculate Conception,"* 1992I; *Piano Concerto No. 2*, 1999I

Berezovsky, Maximus: *Demofoonte*, 1773I

Berezowsky, Nicolai: *Gilgamesh*, 1947I; *Introduction & Allegro, Opus 8*, 1945I; *String Quartet No. 1*, 1931I; *String Quartet No. 2*, 1934I; *Symphony No. 1, Opus 12*, 1931I; *Symphony No. 3, Opus 21*, 1937I; *Symphony No. 4, Opus 27*, 1943I; *Symphony No. 5, Opus 18*, 1934I; *Viola Concerto, Opus 28*, 1941I; *Violin Concerto*, 1930I; *Woodwind Quintet No. 1*, 1937I; *Woodwind Quintet No. 2*, 1928I

Berg, Alban: *Lulu*, 1935I; *Lyric Suite*, 1926I; *Orchestral Songs (5), Opus 4*, 1912I; *Pieces (4) for Clarinet & Piano, Opus 5*, 1913I; *Sonata, Opus 1*, 1908I; *Songs (4), Opus 2*, 1909I; *String Quartet, Opus 3*, 1910I; *Three Pieces, Opus 6*, 1915I; *Ke Vin*, 1929I; *Violin Concerto*, 1935I; *Wozzeck*, 1921I

Berg, Gerald: *Odd Trio*, 1991I

Berg, Gunnar: *Melos II for Organ*, 1979I; *Moulture*, 1953I; *Pour orgue*, 1960I; *Pour piano et orchestre*, 1959I; *String Quartet Mouvements*, 1979I; *Tantum ergo*, 1978I

Berg, Josef: *Organ Music on a Theme of Gilles Binchois*, 1964I; *String Quartet*, 1966I

Berg, Natanael: *Alvorna*, 1914I; *Brigitta*, 1941I; *The Duchess's Suitors*, 1920I; *Genoveva*, 1946I; *Judith*, 1935I; *Leila*, 1910I; *Piano Concerto*, 1931I; *Piano Quintet*, 1917I; *Sensitive*, 1919I; *The Song of Solomon*, 1925I; *String Quartet No. 1*, 1917I; *String Quartet No. 2*, 1919I; *Symphony No. 1*, 1913I; *Symphony No. 2*, 1916I; *Symphony No. 3*, 1917I; *Symphony No. 4, "Pezzo sinfonico,"* 1918I; *Symphony No. 5*, 1922I

Berge, Sigurd: *Wind*, 1981I

Berger, Arthur: *Chamber Music for Thirteen Instruments*, 1956I; *Piano Fantasy*, 1942I; *Piano Perspectives III*, 1982I; *Piano Pieces (5)*, 1969I; *Piano Trio*, 1980I; *Pieces for Two Pianos (3)* 1961I; *Septet*, 1966I; *String Quartet No. 1*, 1958I; *Wind Quintet*, 1984I; *Woodwind Quartet*, 1941I

Berger, Jean: *Caribbean Cruise* (two pianos), 1958I; *The Cherry Tree Carol*, 1975I; *Creole Overture*, 1949I; *Diversion for Strings*, 1977I; *Divertissement for Strings*, 1970I; *The Fiery Furnace*, 1962I; *Piano Compositions (5)*, 1944I; *Pied Piper*, 1968I; *Short Overture*, 1958I; *Sonatina*, 1952I; *Songs after Hughes*, 1950I; *Yiphth & His Daughter*, 1972I

Berger, Roman: *Exodus for Organ*, 1982I

Berger, Theodor: *Heiratsannoncen*, 1958I; *String Quartet No. 1*, 1930I; *String Quartet No. 2*, 1931I; *Violin Concerto*, 1954I

Berger, Wilhelm G.: *Horia*, 1985I

Bergman, Erik: *Exsultate*, 1954I; *The Singing Tree*, 1988I; *String Quartet*, 1982I; *Violin Sonata*, 1943I

Bergsma, William: *A Carol on Twelfth Night*, 1974I; *Chameleon Variations*, 1960I; *Changes*, 1971I; *Concerto for Wind Quintet*, 1958I; *The Fortunate Islands*, 1947I; *Gold & the Señor Commandante*, 1941I; *In Celebration*, 1963I; *The Murder of Comrade Sharik*, 1973I; *Music on a Quiet Theme*, 1943I; *Paul Bunyan*, 1939I; *String Quartet No. 1*, 1942I; *String Quartet No. 2*, 1944I; *String Quartet No. 3*, 1953I; *String Quartet No. 4*, 1970I; *String Quartet No. 5*, 1982I; *String Quartet No. 6*, 1991I; *Sweet Was the Song the Virgin Sung: Tristan Revisited*, 1977I; *Symphony No. 1*, 1949I; *Symphony No. 2, "Voyages,"* 1976I; *Tangents*, 1951I; *Variations for Piano*, 1984I; *The Wife of Martin Guerre*, 1956I

Berio, Luciano: *Accordo*, 1981I; *Alternatim* (concerto for viola & clarinet), 1997I; *Cello Concerto*, 1976I; *Chamber Music*, 1953I; *Circles*, 1960I; *Concerto for Two Pianos*, 1973I; *Coro*, 1976I; *Cries of London*, 1974I; *Ekphasis*, 1996I; *Encore*, 1978I; *Epiphanies*, 1991I; *Fa–Si for Organ*, 1975I; *Memory for Piano*, 1971I; *Momenti*, 1957I; *Mutazioni*, 1954I; *Nones*, 1956I; *Opera*, 1969I; *Perspectives*, 1957I; *Piano Sequenze IV*, 1966I; *Piano Variations*, 1952I; *Points on the Curve to Find . . .* (concerto), 1974I; *Un re in Ascolto*, 1983I; *Ricorrenze*, 1985I; *Sequenza II*, 1963I; *Sequenze III*, 1966I; *Sequenze V*, 1966I; *Sequenza VI*, 1967I; *Sequenze VII*, 1969I; *Sequenza XIII*, 1995I; *Sincronie* (String Quartet), 1964I; *Sinfonia*, 1969I; *String Quartet No. 1*, 1955I; *String Quartet No. 2*, 1993I; *Thema (Omaggio a Joyce)*, 1958I; *La vera storia*, 1982I; *Visage*, 1961I; *Voci* (viola concerto), 1984I

Berkeley, Lennox: *Concerto for Piano & Double String Orchestra*, 1958I; *Dinner Engagement, A*, 1954I; *Flute Concerto*, 1952I; *Flute Sonata No. 2 (?)*, 1933I; *Jonah*, 1935I; *The Judgment of Paris*, 1938I; *Legend-Sonata for Cello & Piano*, 1943I; *Magnificat*, 1968I; *Nelson*, 1954I; *Piano Concerto*, 1947I; *Ronsard Sonnets*

A   *Births*   B   *Deaths*   C   *Debuts*   D   *New Positions*

E   *Prizes/Honors*

I (4), 1952I; *Ronsard Sonnets II, (4)*, 1963I; *Ruth*, 1956I; *String Quartet No. 1*, 1935I; *String Quartet No. 2*, 1942I; *String Quartet No. 3*, 1970I; *Suite No. 1*, 1927I; *Suite No. 2*, 1953I; *Symphony for Strings*, 1931I; *Symphony No. 1*, 1940I; *Symphony No. 2*, 1958I; *Symphony No. 3*, 1969I; *Symphony No. 4*, 1978I; *Violin Sonata No. 1*, 1931I

Berkeley, Michael: *Baa, Baa, Black Sheep*, 1993I; *Cello Concerto*, 1983I; *Clarinet Quintet*,1983I; *Gregorian Variations*, 1982I; *Horn Concerto*, 1984I; *Jane Eyre*, 1998I; *Oboe Concerto*, 1977I; *Organ Concerto*, 1987I; *Organ Sonata*, 1979I; *Piano Trio*, 1982I; *The Secret Garden*, 1997I; *Songs of Awakening Love*, 1996I; *String Quartet No. 1*, 1981I; *String Quartet No. 2*, 1984I; *String Quartet No. 3*, 1987I; *String Quartet No. 4*, 1995I; *String Trio*, 1978I, 1978I; *Violin Sonata*, 1979I; *The Wild Wings*, 1978I; *Wild Bells* (organ), 1987I; *Winter Fragments*, 1996I

Berlin, Irving: *God Bless America*, 1918I

Berlinski, Herman: *The Burning Bush*, 1956I; *Return*, 1950I; *Sinfonia No. 1*, 1956I; *Sinfonia No. 10 for Cello & Organ*, 1977I; *Sinfonia No. 11 for Organ*, 1978I; *String Quartet*, 1953I

Berlioz, Hector: *Béatrice and Bénédict*, 1862I; *Benvenuto Cellini*, 1838I; *Cléopatre*, 1829I; *Le corsaire Overture, Opus 21*, 1831I; *The Damnation of Faust, Opus 24*, 1846I; *Eight Scenes from Faust, Opus I*, 1828I; *L'enfance du Christ, Opus 25*, 1854I; *Estelle et Nemorin*, 1823I; *Fantastic Symphony, Opus 14*, 1830I; *Fleurs des Landes*, 1850I; *Les franc-juges Overture, Opus 3*, 1828I; *Grande symphonie funèbre et triomphale, Opus 15*, 1840I; *Harold in Italy, Opus 16*, 1834I; *Herminie*, 1828I; *L'imperiale, Opus 26*, 1855I; *Irish Melodies (9), Opus 2*, 1830I; *King Lear Overture, Opus 4*, 1831I; *Lélio, ou le retour à la vie, Opus 14*, 1832I; *La mort d'Orphée, Opus 18*, 1827I; *La mort de Sardanapale*, 1830I; *Les nuits d'été, Opus 7*, 1841I; *Overture, Roman Carnival, Opus 9*, 1844I; *Le passage de la mer rouge*, 1823I; *Requiem, Opus 5*, 1837I; *Resurrexit*, 1825I; *Rêverie and Caprice, Opus 8*, 1839I; *La révolution grecque*, 1825I; *Romeo and Juliet, Dramatic Symphony, Opus 17*, 1839I; *Te Deum, Opus 22*, 1849I; *Les Troyens*, 1858I; *Waverly Overture, Opus 1*, 1828I

Bernard, George: *The Old Rugged Cross*, 1913I

Bernasconi, Andrea: *Adriano in Siria*, 1755I; *Artaserse*, 1763I; *Didone abandonata*, 1756I; *L'huomo*, 1754I; *Olimpiade*, 1764I

Berners, Lord: *The Triumph of Neptune*, 1926I

Bernier, René: *Le bal des ombres*, 1954I

Bernstein, Leonard: *Airs & Barcarolles*, 1989I; *Anniversaries (5) for Piano*, 1964I; *The Birds*, 1939I; *Candide*, 1956I; *Chichester Psalms*, 1965I; *Clarinet Sonata*, 1941I; *Divertimento for Orchestra*, 1980I; *The Dybbuk*, 1974I; *Facsimile*, 1946I; *Fancy Free*, 1944I; *Harvard Choruses*, 1957I; *Jubilee Games*, 1986I; *Kid Songs (5)*, 1943I; *Mass*, 1971I; *On the Town*, 1944I; *Overture, Slava!*, 1977I; *Peter Pan*, 1950I; *Piano Sonata*, 1938I; *Piano Touches*, 1980I; *A Quiet Place*, 1983I; *Salmoe*, 1955I; *Serenade*, 1954I; *Song Fest*, 1977I; *Symphony No. 1, "Jeremiah,"* 1942I; *Symphony No. 2, "The Age of Anxiety,"* 1949I; *Symphony No. 3, "Kaddish,"* 1963I; *Trouble in Tahiti*, 1951I; *Violin Sonata*, 1940I; *West Side Story*, 1957I; *Wonderful Town*, 1953I

Berry, Wallace: *Spoon River*, 1952I; *String Quartet No. 1*, 1960I; *String Quartet No. 2*, 1964I; *String Quartet No. 3*, 1966I; *String Quartet No. 4*, 1982I

Bertheaume, Isidore: *Violin Concertos (2), Opus 5*, 1787I; *Violin Sonata (6), Opus 1*, 1769I; *Violin Sonatas (2), Opus 2*, 1786I; *Violin Sonatas (2), Opus 4*, 1787I

Bertin, Louise: *Angélique*, 1831I; *Esmeralda*, 1836I; *Fausto*, 1831I; *Le loup-garou*, 1827I

Bertino, Ferdinando: *I bagni d'Abano*, 1753I; *Ginevra*, 1753I

Berton, Henri-Montan: *Aline, reine de Golconde*, 1803I; *Le délire*, 1799I; *Françoise de Foix*, 1809I; *Montano et Stéphanie*, 1799I

Bertoni, Ferdinando: *Antigono*, 1752I; *La bella Cirometta*, 1761I; *Ezio*, 1781I; *Lucio Vero*, 1757I; *La moda*, 1754I; *Orfeo*, 1776I; *Le pescatrici*, 1751I; *Sesostri*, 1754I; *Il vologeso*, 1759I

Bertouille, Gérard: *Violin Concerto No. 1*, 1942I; *Violin Sonata No. 1*, 1936I; *Violin Sonata No. 2*, 1942I; *Violin Sonata No. 3*, 1946I; *Violin Sonata No. 4*, 1953I; *Violin Sonata No. 5*, 1971I

Berwald, Franz: *Concerto in F for Two Violins*, 1817I; *Concertstücke in F for Bassoon*, 1827I; *Estrella de soria*, 1841I; *Grand Septet in B♭*, 1828I; *Gustav Wasa*, 1827I; *Memories of the Norwegian Alps*, 1842I; *Piano Concerto in D*, 1855I; *Piano Quintet No. 1 in e*, 1853I; *Piano Quintet No. 2 in A*, 1857I; *Piano Trio No. 2 in f*, 1851I; *Quartet in E♭, Piano & Winds*, 1819I; *The Queen of Golconda*, 1864I; *Serenade*, 1825I; *String Quartet No. 2*, 1849I; *String Quartet No. 3*, 1849I; *Symphony No. 1 in g, "Serieuse,"* 1842I; *Symphony No. 2 in D, "Capricieuse,"* 1842I; *Symphony No. 3 in C, "Singuliere,"* 1845I; *Symphony No. 4 in E♭*, 1845I; *Violin Concerto in c♯*, 1820I

Bettinelli, Bruno: *Cello Sonata*, 1951I; *Concerto for Orchestra No. 1*, 1940I; *Concerto for Orchestra No. 2*, 1951I; *Concerto for Orchestra No. 3*, 1964I; *Messa di Requiem*, 1943I; *Piano Concerto No. 1*, 1953I; *Piano Concerto No. 2*, 1968I; *Violin Sonata*, 1980I

Betts, Lorne: *Piano Concerto No. 1*, 1955I; *Piano Concerto No. 2*, 1957I; *Violin Sonata*, 1948I

❈

F   *Biographical*   G   *Cultural Beginnings*   H   *Musical Literature*

I   *Musical Compositions*

Beveridge, Thomas: *Yizkor Requiem*, 1994I

Beversdorf, Thomas: *Cello Sonata* (concerto), 1969I; *Radha Sings*, 1985I; *Sonata for Violin & Harp*, 1977I; *Violin Concerto, "Danforth,"* 1959I

Beyer, Frank M.: *Concerto for Orchestra*, 1957I

Bezanson, Philip: *Overture, Cyrano de Bergerac*, 1949I; *Songs of Innocence*, 1959I; *The Word of Love*, 1956I

Bialas, Günter: *Bagatelles (9)*, 1984I; *Cello Concerto No. 1*, 1962I; *Cello Concerto No. 2*, 1993I; *Clarinet Concerto*, 1961I; *Flute Sonata*, 1946I; *Piano Concerto Lirico*, 1967I; *Quintet for Harp & String Quartet*, 1983I; *String Quartet No. 1*, 1936I; *String Quartet No. 2*, 1949I; *String Quartet No. 3*, 1969I; *Viola Concerto*, 1940I; *Viola Sonata*, 1946I; *Violin Concerto*, 1949I; *Violin Sonata*, 1946I

Bianchi, Francesco: *Alzira*, 1801I; *Antigona*, 1796I; *Il Grand Cidde*, 1773I; *Les méprises espagnoles*, 1799I; *La prisonnière*, 1799I; *La réduction de Paris*, 1775I; *La vendetta de Nino*, 1790I

Biarent, Adolphe: *Poème héroïque*, 1907I; *Rapsodie wallonne*, 1910I

Bibalo, Antonio: *Concerto Allegorico* (violin), 1957I; *Fantasia* (violin concerto), 1954I; *Macbeth*, 1989I; *Piano Concerto No. 1*, 1955I; *Piano Concerto No. 2*, 1971I; *Prelude & Elegy for Organ*, 1989I; *Sonata for Solo Violin*, 1978I; *String Quartet*, 1972I; *Symphony No. 1*, 1968I; *Symphony No. 2*, 1979I

Bierey, Gottlob: *Wladimir*, 1807I

Bigelow, F. E.: *Our Director March*, 1926I

Biggs, John: *Oboe Concerto*, 1958I; *Triple Concerto*, 1962I

Bingham, Seth: *Baroques*, 1943I; *Carillon de Château-Thierry*, 1936I; *Harmonies of Florence*, 1929I; *He Is Risen: Fantasy-Toccata*, 1962I; *Hymn & Carol Canons (36)*, 1952I; *Hymn-Preludes (12)*, 1942I; *Organ Concerto*, 1946I; *Organ Suite*, 1926I; *Pastoral Psalms*, 1938I; *Pièce gothique (organ)*, 1908I; *Pioneer America*, 1928I; *Sonata for Prayer & Praise*, 1960I; *String Quartet*, 1916I; *Suite for Nine Wind Instruments*, 1915I; *Ut Queant Lasix: Hymn to John the Baptist*, 1962I; *Variation Studies*, 1950I; *Wall Street Fantasy*, 1916I; *Wilderness Stone*, 1933I

Binkerd, Gordon: *Cello Sonata*, 1952I; *Organ Service*, 1957I; *Piano Miscellany*, 1969I; *Piano Sonata No. 1*, 1955I; *Piano Sonata No. 2*, 1981I; *Piano Sonata No. 3*, 1982I; *Piano Sonata No. 4*, 1983I; *Piano Trio*, 1979I; *Piano Concert Set*, 1969I; *String Quartet No. 1*, 1956I; *String Quartet No. 2*, 1961I; *Symphony No. 1*, 1955I; *Symphony No. 2*, 1957I; *Symphony No. 3*, 1959I; *Symphony No. 4*, 1963I; *Trio for Clarinet, Viola & Cello*, 1955I; *Violin Sonata*, 1977I

Bird, Arthur H.: *Concert Fantasia*, 1904I; *Daphne*, 1897I; *Episodes (2) for Orchestra*, 1888I; *Frau Holde, Opus 30*, 1891I; *French Overture for Piano*, 1878I; *Introduction & Fugue in d, Opus 16*, 1886I; *Little Suite II, Opus 6*, 1885I; *Little Suite III, "Summer Saturdays," Opus 19*, 1890I; *Nonet for Woodwinds*, 1887I; *Organ Sonatas (4)*, 1882I; *Oriental Scene & Caprice, Opus 17*, 1887I; *Oriental Sketches (3), Opus 42*, 1898I; *Oriental Sketches (3)*, 1903I; *Piano Pieces (4), Opus 26*, 1888I; *Piano Pieces (3), Opus 2*, 1882I; *Poems (2), Opus 25*, 1888I; *Serenade for 19 Instruments, Opus 40*, 1898I; *Songs (5), Opus 36*, 1896I; *Suite in E for Strings, Opus 1*, 1882I; *Suite No. 3*, 1895I; *Symphony in A, Opus 8*, 1885I; *Theme & Variations, Opus 27*, 1889I

Birtwistle, Harrison: *Antiphonies*, 1992I; *Clarinet Quintet*, 1980I; *Exody*, 1997I; *Gawain*, 1991I; *The Mask of Orpheus*, 1975I; *Movements (3) for String Quartet*, 1993I; *Nenie: The Death of Orpheus*, 1970I; *Night*, 1992I; *Poems (4) of Juan Kaplinski*, 1991I; *Pulse Field: Frames, Pulses & Interruptions*, 1977I; *Punch & Judy*, 1967I; *The Second Mrs. Kong*, 1994I; *Songs of Autumn (4)*, 1987I; *The Triumph of Time*, 1972I; *Words Overheard*, 1985I; *Yan, Tan, Tethera*, 1984I

Biscardi, Chester: *Piano Concerto*, 1983I; *Piano Sonata*, 1986I; *Piano Trio*, 1976I; *Saphic Lyrics (5)*, 1974I

Bischof, Rainer: *String Quartet*, 1986I

Bishop, Henry: *Aladdin*, 1826I; *Angelina*, 1804I; *The Circassian Bride*, 1809I; *Clari*, 1823I; *A Comedy of Errors*, 1819I; *Cortez*, 1823I; *The Fall of Algiers*, 1825I; *Knights of the Cross*, 1826I; *Maid Marion*, 1822I; *The Maid of the Mill*, 1814I; *A Midsummer Night's Dream*, 1816I; *The Seventh Day*, 1834I; *The Slave*, 1816I; *Tamerlane et Bajazet*, 1806I; *Twelfth Night,,* 1820I; *Two Gentlemen of Verona*, 1821I; *Under the Oak*, 1830I

Bittner, Julius: *Cello Sonata*, 1915I; *String Quartet No. 1*, 1913I; *String Quartet No. 2*, 1917I; *Symphony No. 1*, 1918I; *Symphony No. 2*, 1934I

Bizet, Georges: *L'arlésienne*, 1872I; *Carmen*, 1875I; *Clarissa Harlowe*, 1870I; *Cloris et Clothilde*, 1857I; *David*, 1856I; *Djamileh*, 1871I; *Doctor Miracle*, 1857I; *Don Procopio*, 1859I; *The Fair Maid of Perth*, 1867I; *La Guzla de l'émir*, 1862I; *Ivan, the Terrible*, 1865I; *Jeux d'enfants*, 1872I; *Noé*, 1868I; *Numa*, 1871; *Overture, La chasse d'Ossian*, 1861I; *Patri Overture*, 1873I; *The Pearl Fishers*, 1863I; *La prêtresse*, 1854I; *Roma*, 1868I; *Scherzo and Funeral March in f*, 1861I; *Symphony in C*, 1855I; *Vasco da Gama*, 1859I

Bjelinski, Bruno: *Clarinet Sonata*, 1966I

Bjerre, Jens: *Toccata with Fughetta & Chaconne*, 1956I

Blacher, Boris: *200,000 Thaler*, 1969I; *Ariadne*, 1971I; *Cello Sonata*, 1940I; *Clarinet Concerto*, 1971I; *Concert Overture*, 1931I; *Concertante Music*, 1937I; *Elecktronische studie über ein posaunenglissando*, 1962I;

A *Births*   B *Deaths*   C *Debuts*   D *New Positions*
E *Prizes/Honors*

Geigenmusik (violin concerto), 1936I; *Der Grossinquisitor*, 1942I; *Hamlet*, 1940I; *Henry IV*, 1970I; *Lulu*, 1952I; *Multiple Raumperspektiven*, 1962I; *Music for Cleveland*, 1957I; *Orchestral Fantasy*, 1956I; *Piano Concerto*, 1935I; *Piano Concerto No. 1, Opus 28*, 1948I; *Piano Concerto No. 2, "Variable Meters,"* 1952I; *Requiem*, 1958I; *Robespierre*, 1963I; *Romeo & Juliet*, 1951I; *String Quartet No. 1*, 1930I; *String Quartet No. 2*, 1940I; *String Quartet No. 3*, 1944I; *String Quartet No. 4*, 1951I; *String Quartet No. 5*, 1967I; *Symphony*, 1938I; *Tristan & isolde*, 1965I; *Trumpet Concerto*, 1979I; *Viola Concerto*, 1955I; *Violin Concerto*, 1948I; *Violin Sonata*, 1951I; *War & Peace*, 1955I

Blackwood, Easley: *Cello Sonata*, 1985I; *Clarinet Concerto, Opus 13*, 1964I; *Clarinet Sonata in a, Opus 37*, 1994I; *Experimental Pieces (10)*, 1948I; *Flute Concerto*, 1968I; *Flute Sonata, Opus 12*, 1962I; *Guitar Sonata, Opus 29*, 1983I; *Nocturnes, (2), Opus 41*, 1996I; *Oboe Concerto, Opus 19*, 1965I; *Pastorale & Variations, Opus 11*, 1961III; *Piano Concerto*, 1970I; *Piano Trio, Opus 22*, 1967I; *Sonata, Opus 40*, 1996I; *Sonatina for Piccolo Clarinet, Opus 38*, 1994I; *String Quartet No. 1, Opus 4*, 1957I; *String Quartet No. 2, Opus 6*, 1959I; *String Quartet No. 3*, 1998I; *Symphonic Fantasy, Opus 17*, 1965I; *Symphonic Movement, Opus 18*, 1966I; *Symphony No. 1, Opus 3*, 1955I; *Symphony No. 2, Opus 9*, 1960I; *Symphony No. 3, Opus 14*, 1964I; *Symphony No. 4*, 1973I; *Symphony No. 5*, 1978I; *Twelve Microtonal Etudes, Opus 28*, 1982I; *Viola Sonata*, 1953I; *Violin Sonata No. 1*, 1960I; *Violin Sonata No. 2, Opus 26*, 1973I; *Violin Sonata No. 3, Opus 32*, 1986I

Bláha, Ivo: *Cello Sonata*, 1972I; *Hymnus*, 1980I; *Vaults*, 1986I

Blainville, Charles de: *Symphonies (6), Opus 2*, 1751I

Blake, Benjamin: *Divertimentos (9), Opus 5*, 1795I; *Duets (6), Violin & Viola, Opus 2*, 1782I; *Duets (6), Violin & Viola, Opus 3*, 1785I; *Duets, Violin & Viola (6)*, 1781I; *Violin Sonatas (3), Opus 4*, 1794I

Blatn, Pavel: *Concerto for Orchestra*, 1956I

Blašek, Zdeněk: *Violin Sonata*, 1982I

Blavet, Michel: *La fête de Cythère*, 1753I; *Floriane, ou La grotte des spectacles*, 1752I

Bliss, Arthur: *Adam Zero*, 1946I; *Angels of the Mind*, 1968I; *As You Like It*, 1919I; *The Ballads of the Four Seasons*, 1923I; *The Beatitudes*, 1961I; *Cello Concerto*, 1970I; *Checkmate*, 1937I; *Clarinet Quintet*, 1932I; *A Colour Symphony*, 1922I; *Concerto for Two Pianos*, 1933I; *Discourse*, 1957I; *Edinburgh Overture*, 1956I; *Elizabethan Suite*, 1923I; *Introduction & Allegro*, 1926I; *Kenilworth Suite*, 1936I; *King Solomon*, 1924I; *A Knot of Riddles*, 1963I; *The Lady of Shalott*, 1958I; *Mary of Magdala*, 1962I; *Metamorphic Variations*, 1972I; *Miracle in the Gorbals*, 1944I; *Music for Strings*, 1935I; *Oboe Quintet*, 1927I; *The Olympians*, 1949I; *Piano Concerto*, 1939I; *Piano Quartet*, 1915I; *Piano Quintet*, 1919I; *Piano Sonata*, 1952I; *String Quartet No. 1*, 1940I; *String Quartet No. 2*, 1950I; *String Quartet No. 3*, 1941I; *The Tempest*, 1921I; *Tobias & the Angel*, 1959I; *Two Studies for Orchestra*, 1921I; *Violin Concerto*, 1954I; *Viola Sonata*, 1933I; *Violin Sonata (?)*, 1914I

Blitzstein, Marc: *Androcles & the Lion*, 1946I; *Another Part of the Forest*, 1946I; *The Cradle Will Rock*, 1937I; *Juno*, 1959I; *King Lear*, 1950I; *The Little Foxes*, 1948I; *A Midsummer's Night Dream*, 1958I; *No for an Answer*, 1940I; *Parabola & Circula*, 1929I; *Piano Sonata*, 1927I; *Piano Suite*, 1933I; *Regina*, 1949I; *Sacco & Vanzetti*, 1964I; *String Quartet No. 1*, 1930I; *Symphony: The Airbourne*, 1946I; *Toys in the Attic*, 1960I; *Variations for Orchestra*, 1934I; *Volpone*, 1956I; *Whitman Songs (4)*, 1928I

Bloch, Augustyn: *Forte, piano e forte*, 1985I; *Jubilato for Organ*, 1974I; *Organ Fantasia*, 1953I; *Organ Sonata*, 1954I

Bloch, Ernest: *Alpenkönig und Menschenfeind*, 1903I; *America: An Epic Rhapsody*, 1926I; *Baal Shem for Violin & Piano*, 1923I; *Circus Pieces (4)*, 1922I; *Concertino for Flute, Viola & Strings*, 1950I; *Concerto Grosso No. 1*, 1925I; *Concerto Grosso No. 2*, 1952I; *Concerto Symphonique*, 1948I; *Evocations*, 1937I; *From Jewish Life for Cello and Piano*, 1925I; *Helvetia: Land of Mountains & Its People*, 1929I; *Hiver*, 1905I; *Hiver-printemps*, 1905I; *In Memoriam*, 1952I; *In the Night*, 1922I; *Israel Symphony*, 1916I; *Jewish Poems (3)*, 1913I; *Last Poems (2)*, 1958I; *Macbeth*, 1909I; *Méditation Hébraïque for Cello and Piano*, 1925I; *Organ Preludes (6)*, 1949I; *Piano Quintet No. 1*, 1923I; *Piano Quintet No. 2*, 1957I; *Piano Sonata*, 1935I; *Poèmes d'automne*, 1906I; *Poems of the Sea*, 1922I; *Psalm XXII*, 1914I; *Sacred Service*, 1933I; *Schelomo (cello)*, 1916I; *Sinfonia Brève*, 1953I; *String Quartet No. 1*, 1916I; *String Quartet No. 2*, 1946I; *String Quartet No. 3*, 1951I; *String Quartet No. 4*, 1953I; *String Quartet No. 5*, 1956I; *Suite for Viola & Orchestra*, 1919I; *Suite Hébraïque* (viola/violin concerto), 1951I; *Suite Modale* (flute & strings concerto), 1956I; *Suite No. 1 for Solo Cello*, 1956I; *Suite No. 2 for Solo Cello*, 1956I; *Suite No. 3 for Solo Cello*, 1957I; *Suite Symphonique*, 1944I; *Symphony for Trombone & Orchestra*, 1954I; *Symphony in E♭*, 1955I; *Symphony No. 1 in c♯*, 1902I; *Violin Concerto*, 1938I; *Violin Sonata No. 1*, 1920I; *Violin Sonata No. 2, "Poème Mystique,"* 1924I; *Visions & Prophecies*, 1936I; *Vivre-aimer*, 1900I; *The Voice in the Wilderness*, 1936I

Block, Jan: *Piano Quintet*, 1886I

Blodek, Vilem: *In the Well*, 1867I

Blomberg, Erik: *Symphony No. 1*, 1966I; *Symphony No. 2*, 1968I; *Symphony No. 3*, 1971I; *Symphony No. 4*, 1973I; *Symphony No. 5*, 1974I; *Symphony No. 6*, 1982I; *Symphony No. 7*, 1984I; *Symphony No. 8, "Liten,"* 1992I

Blomdahl, Karl-Birger: *Altisonans*, 1966I; *Aniara*, 1959I; *Concert Overture*, 1942I; *Dance Suite No. 1*,
1948I; *Game for Eight*, 1962I; *Herr von Hancken*, 1965I; *Little Suite for Bassoon & Piano*, 1945I;
Minotaurus, 1958I; *Polyphonic Pieces (3)*, 1945I; *Sisyphos*, 1954I; *String Quartet No. 1*, 1939I; *String
Quartet No. 2*, 1948I; *String Trio*, 1945I; *Suite for Cello & Piano*, 1944I; *Symphony No. 1*, 1943I; *Symphony
No. 2*, 1947I; *Symphony No. 3, "Facetter,"* 1950I; *Viola concerto*, 1944I; *Violin Concerto*, 1947I
Blumenfeld, Harold: *Seasons in Hell*, 1995I
Boatwright, Howard: *Adoration & Longing*, 1991I; *Clarinet Sonata*, 1983I; *Piano Sonata*, 1956I; *Piano
Suite*, 1959I; *Pieces (12) for Solo Violin*, 1978I; *Poems (5) of Sylvia Plath*, 1993I; *String Quartet No. 1*,
1947I; *String Quartet No. 2*, 1975I; *Symphony No. 1*, 1976I
Boccherini, Luigi: *Ballet espagnolo*, 1773I; *Cefalo e Procri*, 1778I; *Cello Sonatas (4)*, 1767I; *Cello Sonata in B♭*,
1773I; *Cello Sonata in C*, 1783I; *Cello Sonatas (4)*, 1762I; *Cello Sonatas (3)*, 1763I; *Cello Sonatas (3)*, 1764I;
Cello Sonatas (4), 1766I; *Cello Sonatas (4)*, 1768I; *Cello Concerto in C*, 1766I; *Cello Concerto in c*, 1770I;
Cello Concerto in D, 1782I; *Cello Concertos (2)*, 1763I; *Cello Concertos (3))*, 1767I; *Cello Concertos (4)*,
1771I; *Christmas Cantata, Opus 63*, 1802I; *Concert Arias (12)*, 1792I; *Concerto for Harpsichord in E♭*,
1768I; *Concerto for Two Violins, Opus 7*, 1779I; *Confederazioni dei Sabini con Roma*, 1765I; *Dramatic
Scene, "Ynes de Castro,"* 1798I; *Flute Quintets (6), Opus 17*, 1773I; *Flute Quintets (6), Opus 19*, 1774I;
Flute Quintets (6), Opus 55, 1797I; *Flute Sextets (6), Opus 16*, 1773I; *Gioas, re di Giudea*, 1765I; *Il
Giuseppe riconosciuto*, 1765I; *Mass, Opus 59*, 1800I; *Octet in G, Opus 38*, 1787I; *Piano Quintets (6), Opus
57*, 1799I; *Quintets (4), Opus 45*, 1792I; *Serenade in D*, 1777I; *Serenade in D*, 1776I; *Sextets (5), Opus 38*,
1787I; *Sonata in C, Two Cellos*, 1762I; *Stabat Mater*, 1781I; *Stabat Mater, Opus 61*, 1800I; *String Quartets
(6), Opus 2*, 1761I; *String Quartets (6), Opus 8*, 1769I; *String Quartets (6), Opus 9*, 1770I; *String Quartets
(6), Opus 15*, 1772I; *String Quartets (6), Opus 22*, 1775I; *String Quartets (6), Opus 24*, 1777I; *String
Quartets (6), Opus 26*, 1778I; *String Quartets (6), Opus 32*, 1780I; *String Quartets (6), Opus 33*, 1781I;
String Quartets (6), Opus 36, 1786I; *String Quartets (3), Opus 39*, 1787I; *String Quartets (2), Opus 41*,
1788I; *String Quartets (2), Opus 42*, 1789I; *String Quartets (2), Opus 43*, 1790I; *String Quartets (6), Opus
44*, 1792I; *String Quartets (4), Opus 45*, 1792I; *String Quartets (6), Opus 48*, 1794I; *String Quartets (4),
Opus 52*, 1795I; *String Quartets (6), Opus 53*, 1796I; *String Quartets (6), Opus 58*, 1799I; *String Quintets
(6), Opus 9*, 1771I; *String Quintets (6), Opus 11*, 1771I; *String Quintets (6), Opus 13*, 1772I; *String
Quintets (6), Opus 18*, 1774I; *String Quintets (6), Opus 20*, 1775I; *String Quintets (6), Opus 25*, 1778I;
String Quintets (6), Opus 27, 1779I; *String Quintets (6), Opus 29*, 1779I; *String Quintets (6), Opus 30*,
1780I; *String Quintets (6), Opus 31*, 1780I; *String Quintets (6), Opus 36*, 1784I; *String Quintets (3), Opus
39*, 1787I; *String Quintets (6), Opus 40*, 1788I; *String Quintets (4), Opus 42*, 1789I; *String Quintets (3),
Opus 43*, 1790I; *String Quintets (6), Opus 46*, 1793I; *String Quintets (5), Opus 49*, 1794I; *String Quintets
(6), Opus 50*, 1795I; *String Quintets (2), Opus 51*, 1795I; *String Quintets (6), Opus 56*, 1797I; *String
Quintets (6), Opus 60*, 1801I; *String Quintets (6), Opus 62*, 1802I; *String Quintets (2), Opus 64*, 1804I;
String Sextets (6) Opus 23, 1776I; *String Trios (6), Opus 1*, 1760I; *String Trios (6), Opus 4*, 1766I; *String
Trios (6), Opus 6*, 1769I; *String Trios (6), Opus 14*, 1772I; *String Trios (6), Opus 34*, 1781I; *String Trios (3),
Opus 47*, 1793I; *Symphony in c, Opus 41*, 1788I; *Symphony in D, Opus 42*, 1789I; *Symphony in D, Opus
43*, 1790I; *Symphony in d, Opus 45*, 1792I; *Symphony in C (with guitar)*, 1798I; *Symphonies (6), Opus 12*,
1771I; *Symphonies (6), Opus 21*, 1775I; *Symphonies (6), Opus 35*, 1782I; *Symphonies (4), Opus 37/1,2,5,6*,
1786I; *Symphonies (2), Opus 37/3,4*, 1787I; *Villancios (4)*, 1783I; *Violin Duets (6)*, 1797I; *Violin Duets (6)*,
Opus 3, 17; *Violin Concerto in F*, 1767I
Bodin, Lars-Gunnar: *For Jon II: Retrospective Episodes*, 1986I
Body, Jack: *Fanfares*, 1981I; *Jankrik Genggong*, 1985I; *Krytophones*, 1973I; *Mouth Music*, 1989I
Boëllmann, Léon: *Cello Sonata, Opus 40*, 1897I; *Fantaisie dialoguée*, 1897I; *Fantasy on Hungarian airs, Opus
7*, 1890I; *Nocturne, Opus 36*, 1896I; *Offertoire sur des Noëls*, 1898I; *Organ Improvisations (10), Opus 28*,
1895I; *Organ Pieces (12), Opus 16*, 1890I; *Organ Suite No. 2, Opus 27* 1896I; *Piano Quartet, Opus 10*,
1890I; *Piano Trio, Opus 19*, 1895I; *Suite Gothique, Opus 25*, 1895I; *Sur la mer, Opus 38*, 1897I; *Symphony,
Opus 24 (?)*, 1894I; *Variations symphoniques, Opus 23*, 1893I; *Veni Creator*, 1900I
Boëly, Alexandre: *Etudes, Book III, Opus 13*, 1846I; *Messe du jour de Noël, Opus 11*, 1842I; *Offertories (4)*,
Opus 9, 1842I; *Organ Pieces (12), Opus 18*, 1856I; *Organ Pieces (24), Opus 12*, 1843I; *Piano Caprices (30)*,
Opus 2, 1816I; *Piano Pieces (24), Opus 20*, 1857I; *Piano Pieces (24), Opus 22*, 1858I; *Piano Sonatas (2)*,
Opus 1, 1810I; *Piano Sonata (4 hands), Opus 17*, 1855I; *Piano Suites (4), Opus 16*, 1854I; *Préludes (14) sur
des cantiques de Denizot, Opus 15*, 1847I; *Recueil de 12 morceaus, Opus 14*, 1844I; *Recueil contenant 14
morceaux . . . Opus 10*, 1842I; *String Quartets (4), Opus 27, 30*, 1857I; *Variations (7), Opus 3*, 1819I; *Violin
Sonatas (2), Opus 32*, 1857I
Boëly, Léon: *Etudes (30), Opus 6*, 1830I
Boesmans, Philippe: *Fanfare II for Organ*, 1972I; *Fly & Driving*, 1989I; *Intervalles I*, 1972I; *Intervalles II*,
1973I; *Piano Concerto*, 1978I; *Piano Concerto*, 1979I; *Reigen*, 1992I; *Ricercar sconvolto for Organ*, 1983I;

    A *Births*   B *Deaths*   C *Debuts*   D *New Positions*
                  E *Prizes/Honors*

String Quartet, 1988I; *String Quartet No. 2*, 1995I; *Symphony for Piano & Orchestra*, 1966I; *Violin Concerto*, 1980I; *Wintermärchen*, 1999I
Boguslawski, Edward: *Piano Concerto*, 1981I
Boháč, Josef: *Cello Sonata*, 1954I; *Concerto for Orchestra*, 1983I; *Goya*, 1977I
Boieldieu, François: *Abderkan*, 1804I; *Aline, reine de Golconde*, 1804I; *Amour et mystère*, 1805I; *Angéla*, 1814I; *Athalie*, 1808I; *The Caliph of Bagdad*, 1800I; *Chant populaire pour la fête de la raison*, 1793I; *Clarinet Concerto No. 1*, 1795I; *La dame blanche*, 1825I; *La dame invisible*, 1808I; *Les deux nuits*, 1829I; *Les deux lettres*, 1796I; *La dot de Suzette*, 1798I; *La famille suisse*, 1797I; *La fête du village voisin*, 1816I; *La fille coupable*, 1793I; *La France et l'Espagne*, 1823I; *Harp Concerto*, 1800I; *L'heureuse nouvelle*, 1797I; *Jean de Paris*, 1812I; *La jeune femme en colère*, 1805I; *Ma tante aurora*, 1803I; *Le nouveau seigneur du village*, 1813I; *Le petit chaperon rouge*, 1818I; *Piano Concerto*, 1795I; *Piano Trio, Opus 3*, 1800I; *Rien de trop*, 1811I; *Romances (18), Sets XI, Set XIV*, 1801I; *Romances (4), Set XV*, 1803I; *Rosalie et Myrza*, 1795I; *Télémaque*, 1806I; *Un tour de soubrette*, 1806I; *Violin Sonatas (3), Opus 3*, 1799I; *Les voitures versées*, 1808I; *Zoraïme et Zulnar*, 1798I
Boito, Arrigo: *Mephistopheles*, 1868I; *Nerone*, 1918I; *Le sorelle d'Italia*, 1862I
Bolcom, William: *Brass Quintet*, 1980I; *Cello Sonata*, 1989I; *Chorale & Prelude,"Abide with Me,"* 1970I; *Commedia for Chamber Orchestra*, 1971I; *Concerto for Two Pianos, Left Hand*, 1995I; *Dream Music 1 for Piano*, 1965I; *Etudes, (12)*, 1960I; *Etudes for Orchestra*, 1989I; *Five Fold Five*, 1987I; *Gaea* (piano concerto), 1996I; *Garden of Eden Suite for Piano*, 1968I; *Gospel Preludes (3) for Organ*, 1979I; *Gospel Preludes for Organ II*, 1982I; *Gospel Preludes for Organ III*, 1982I; *Hydraulis for Organ*, 1971I; *Let Evening Come*, 1994I; *Lyric Concerto*, 1993I; *McTeague*, 1992I; *Monsterpieces for Piano*, 1980I; *Morning & Evening Songs*, 1966I; *Mysteries for Organ*, 1976I; *New Etudes (12) for Piano*, 1987I; *Octet*, 1962I; *Open House*, 1975I; *Piano Concerto*, 1976I; *Piano Fantasy Sonata No. 1*, 1961I; *Piano Quartet*, 1976I; *Recuerdos for Piano*, 1991I; *Romantic Pieces*, 1959I; *Seattle Slew Suite*, 1977I; *Songs of Innocence & Experience*, 1984I; *String Quartet No. 8*, 1965I; *String Quartet No. 9*, 1972I; *String Quartet No. 10*, 1988I; *Summer Divertimento*, 1973I; *Symphony, "Oracles,"* 1965I; *Symphony No. 1*, 1957I; *Symphony No. 3*, 1979I; *Symphony No. 4*, 1987I; *Symphony No. 5*, 1989I; *Symphony No. 6*, 1997I; *A View from the Bridge*, 1999I; *A Walt Whitman Triptych*, 1995I
Bomtempo, João D.: *Piano Sonata No. 1 in f, Opus 1*, 1803I; *Piano Sonatas (2), Opus 9*, 1811I; *Piano Sonatas 8-9, Opus 18*, 1816I; *Piano Sonata No. 11 in E♭*, 1818I; *Piano Concerto No. 1 in E♭*, 1804I; *Piano Concerto No. 2 in f*, 1805I; *Piano Concerto No. 3 in g*, 1809I; *Piano Concerto No. 4 in D*, 1810I; *Requiem in c, "In Memory of Camões,"* 1819I; *Symphony No. 1*, 1810I
Bond, Carrie Jacobs: *I Love You Truly*, 1901I; *A Perfect Day*, 1910I
Bond, Victoria: *Cello Sonata*, 1971I; *Dreams of Flying*, 1994I; *Equinox*, 1977I; *A Modest Proposal*, 1999I; *Other Selves*, 1979I; *Travels*, 1995I; *Variations on a Theme of Brahms*, 1998I
Bonds, Margaret: *Mass in d*, 1959I
Bonner, Eugene M.: *The Gods of the Mountain*, 1936I
Bonno, Giuseppe: *Colloquio amoroso fra Piramo e Tisba*, 1757I; *Didone abbandonata*, 1752I; *L'eroe cinese*, 1752I; *Il Giuseppe riconosciuto*, 1744I; *Isacco figura del redentore*, 1759I; *L'isola disabitata*, 1754I; *Latenaide*, 1762I; *Il re pastore*, 1751I; *Il sogno di Scipione*, 1763I
Borck, Edmund von: *Concerto for Orchestra*, 1936I; *Piano Concerto*, 1941I
Boretz, Benjamin: *music/consciousness/gender*, 1994I; *String Quartet No. 1*, 1958I; *Violin Concerto*, 1956I
Bořkovec, Pavel: *Love Songs*, 1932I; *Piano Quartet*, 1922I; *The Satyr*, 1938I; *String Quartet No. 1*, 1924I; *String Quartet No. 2*, 1928I; *String Quartet No. 3*, 1940I; *String Quartet No. 4*, 1947I; *String Quartet No. 5*, 1962I; *Symphonietta I*, 1968I; *Symphony No. 1*, 1927I; *Symphony No. 2*, 1955I; *Symphony No. 3*, 1959I; *Tom Thumb*, 1947I; *Twilight*, 1920I; *Violin Concerto*, 1933I; *Violin Sonata No. 1*, 1934I; *Violin Sonata No. 2*, 1956I
Bornschein, Franz C.: *Onawa*, 1916I; *The Phantom Canoe*, 1916I; *The Sea God's Daughter*, 1924I; *String Quartet*, 1900I
Borodin, Alexander: *The Bogatyrs*, 1867I; *Prince Igor*, 1887I; *In the Steppes of Central Asia*, 1880I; *Scherzo for Orchestra*, 1885I; *Symphony No. 3 in a*, 1887I; *Songs (5)*, 1868I; *Piano Quintet No. 1*, 1862I; *String Quartet No. 1 in A*, 1879I; *Symphony No. 1 in E♭*, 1867I; *Symphony No. 2 in b*, 1876I
Boroni, Antonio: *L'amore in musica*, 1763I; *Artaserse*, 1769I; *Il carnevale*, 1769I; *Le déserteur*, 1775I; *Didone*, 1768I; *L'isola disabitata*, 1775I; *Le moda*, 1761I; *La notte critica*, 1766I; *Le organe svizzeri*, 1770I; *La pupilla rapito*, 1763I; *Siroe*, 1764I; *Sofonisba*, 1764I; *Symphony*, 1772I; *Le villeggiatrici ridicolo*, 1765I; *Zémire et Azor*, 1775I
Bořovec, Pavel: *Te Deum*, 1968I
Borowski, Felix: *Allegro de Concert (organ)*, 1915I; *Piano Concerto*, 1914I; *Semiramis*, 1925I; *Symphony No. 1*, 1933I; *Symphony No. 2*, 1936I; *Symphony No. 3*, 1939I

❀

F *Biographical*   G *Cultural Beginnings*   H *Musical Literature*
I *Musical Compositions*

Børresen, Hakon: *Serenade for Horn, Strings & Timpani*, 1944I; *String Quartet No. 1 in e, Opus 18*, 1913I; *String Quartet No. 2 in c*, 1939I; *String Sextet in B, Opus 5*, 1901I; *Symphony No. 1 in c*, 1901I; *Symphony No. 2 in A, "The Sea," Opus 7*, 1904I; *Symphony No. 3 in C, Opus 21*, 1926I; *Violin Concerto in G, Opus 11*, 1904I; *Violin Sonata in a, Opus 9*, 1907I

Bortkiewicz, Sergei: *Piano Preludes (10), Opus 33*, 1926I

Bortniansky, Dmitri: *Alcide*, 1778I; *Alexseyevna Songs (8)*, 1792I; *Creonte*, 1776I; *Le faucon*, 1786I; *La fête du seigneur*, 1786I; *Quintet in C*, 1787I; *Quinto Fabio*, 1778I

Bortoni, Ferdinando: *Nitteti*, 1789I

Börtz, Daniel: *Marie Antoinette*, 1997I; *Preludes (5) for Flute*, 1964I; *Symphony No. 1*, 1973I; *Symphony No. 2*, 1975I; *Symphony No. 3*, 1976I; *Symphony No. 4*, 1977I; *Symphony No. 5*, 1981I; *Symphony No. 6*, 1983I; *Symphony No. 7*, 1986I; *Symphony No. 8*, 1988I; *Symphony No. 9*, 1991I; *Symphony No. 10*, 1992I; *Symphony No. 11*, 1994I

Bose, Hans-Jürgen von: *The Sorrows of Young Werther*, 1986I

Bottesini, Giovanni: *Cristoforo Colombo*, 1847I

Boulanger, Lili: *Clairières dans le ciel*, 1914I; *Faust et Hélène*, 1913I; *Psalm 24*, 1916I

Boulez, Pierre: *Dérive I*, 1984I; *Doubles*, 1958I; *Éclat*, 1965I; *. . . explosante fixe . . .*, 1974I; *Figures-doubles-prismes*, 1964I; *Le marteau sans maître*, 1955I; *Multiples*, 1970I; *Notations*, 1978I; *Piano Notations (12)*, 1945I; *Piano Sonata No. 1*, 1946I; *Piano Sonata No. 2*, 1952I; *Piano Sonata No. 3*, 1957I; *Piano Structures, Book II*, 1961I; *Pli Selon Pli*, 1960I; *Polyphonie for 18 Instruments*, 1951I; *Le soleil des eaux*, 1948I; *Structures I for Two Pianos*, 1952I; *Sur incises*, 1998I; *Le visage nuptial*, 1950I

Bowles, Paul: *Concerto for Two Pianos*, 1947I; *Latin-American Pieces (6)*, 1948I; *Piano Preludes (6)*, 1945I; *Piano Sonatina*, 1933I; *Sonata for Two Pianos*, 1947I; *Suite for Small Orchestra*, 1933I

Boyar, Peter: *Three Olympians for String Orchestra*, 2000I

Boyce, William: *Harlequin's Invasion*, 1759I; *Lyra britannica*, 1755I; *Ode in Commemoration of Shakespeare*, 1757I; *Ode to the New Year*, 1758I; *The Shepherd's Lottery*, 1751I

Boydell, Brian: *Megalithic Ritual Dance*, 1956I; *Violin Concerto*, 1954I

Boyer, Peter: *Celebration Overture*, 1997I; *Ghosts of Troy*, 2000I; *Titanic*, 1996I

Boykan, Martin: *Clarinet Sonata*, 1992I; *Elegy*, 1982I; *Epithalamion*, 1987I; *Piano Sonata No. 1*, 1986; *Piano Sonata No. 2*, 1990I; *Piano Trio No. 1*, 1975I; *Piano Trio No. 2*, 1997I; *Psalm 21*, 1997I; *Sea Gardens*, 1993I; *Shakespeare Songs, (3)*, 1996I; *String Quartet No. 1*, 1967I; *String Quartet No. 2*, 1974I; *String Quartet No. 3*, 1984I; *String Quartet No. 5*, 1996I; *Symphony*, 1989I; *Violin Sonata*, 1994I

Bradbury, William B.: *Aughton* (He Leadeth Me), 1864I; *Daniel*, 1853I; *Esther*, 1856I; *Sweet Hour of Prayer*, 1859I

Brahms, Johannes: *Academic Festival Overture, Opus 80*, 1880I; *Alto Rhapsody, Opus 53*, 1869I; *Ave Maria, Opus 12*, 1858I; *Ballades (4), Opus 10*, 1854I; *Ballades & Romances (4), Opus 75*, 1878I; *Begräbnisgesang, Opus 13*, 1858I; *Cello Sonata No. 1 in e, Opus 38*, 1865I; *Cello Sonata No. 2 in F, Opus 99*, 1886I; *Children's Folksongs (14)*, 1858I; *Choral Songs (7), a Capella Chorus, Opus 62*, 1874I; *Choral Preludes (11), Opus 122*, 1896I; *Chorale, Prelude & Fugue in a, "O Traurigkeit,"* 1856I; *Clarinet Quintet in b, Opus 115*, 1891I; *Clarinet (Viola) Sonatas (2), Opus 120*, 1894I; *Deutsches Requiem, Ein, Opus 45*, 1868I; *Double Concerto in a, Opus 102*, 1887I; *Duets (3), Opus 20*, 1860I; *Duets (4), Opus 28*, 1862I; *Duets (4), Opus 61*, 1874I; *Fantasien (3), Opus 116*, 1892I; *Geistliche Lied, Opus 30*, 185; *German Folksongs (28)*, 1858I; *Gesang der Parzen, Opus 89*, 1882I; *Intermezzi (3), Opus 117*, 1892I; *Liebeslieder, Opus 52*, 1869I; *Magelone Romances*, 1861I; *Marienlieder, Opus 22* 1859I; *Motets (3), Opus 110*, 1889I; *Nänie, Opus 82*, 1881I; *Neue Liebeslieder, Opus 65*, 1874I; *Piano Concerto No. 1 in d, Opus 15*, 1858I; *Piano Concerto No. 2 in B♭, Opus 83*, 1881I; *Piano Pieces (8), Opus 76*, 1878I; *Piano Pieces (6), Opus 118*, 1892I; *Piano Pieces (4), Opus 119*, 1892I; *Piano Quartet No. 1 in g, Opus 25*, 1861I; *Piano Quartet No. 2 in A, Opus 26*, 1862I; *Piano Quartet No. 3 in c, Opus 60*, 1875I; *Piano Quintet in f, Opus 34*, 1863I; *Piano Trio No. 1 in B, Opus 8*, 1854I; *Piano Trio No. 2 in C, Opus 87*, 1882I; *Piano Trio No. 3 in c, Opus 101*, 1886I; *Piano Sonata No. 1, Opus 1*, '1853I; *Piano Sonata No. 2, Opus 2*, 1852I; *Piano Sonata No. 3 in f for Two Pianos, Opus 34b*, 1864I; *Poems (5), Opus 19*, 1858I; *Prelude & Fugue in a*, 1856I; *Prelude & Fugue in g*, 1857I; *Rhapsodies (2), Opus 79*, 1879I; *Rinaldo, Opus 50*, 1868I; *Sacred Choruses (3), Opus 37*, 1863I; *Scherzo in e♭, Opus 4*, 1851I; *Schicksalslied, Opus 54*, 1871I; *Serenade, No. 1 in D, Opus 11*, 1857I; *Serenade No. 2 in A, Opus 16*, 1859I; *Serious Songs (4), Opus 121*, 1896I; *Soldatenlied, Opus 41*, 1862I; *Songs (18), Opus 3, 6, 7*, 1853I; *Songs (5), Opus 19*, 1859I; *Songs (4), Opus 46*, 1864I; *Songs (12), Opus 48, 49*, 1868I; *Songs (16), Opus 57, 58*, 1871I; *Songs (8), Opus 59*, 1873I; *Songs (9), Opus 63*, 1874I; *Songs (23), Opus 69, 70, 71, 72*, 1877I; *Songs (6), Opus 86*, 1878I; *Songs (6), Opus 90*, 1885I; *Songs (10), Opus 91, 94*, 1884I; *Songs (11), Opus 95, 96*, 1884I; *Songs (15), Opus 105, 106, 107*, 1886I; *Songs & Romances (8), Opus 15*, 1858I; *Songs & Romances (12), Opus 44*, 1863I; *Songs & Romances (8), Opus 84*, 1881I; *Songs & Romances (6), Opus 93a*, 1884I; *String Quartet No. 1 in c, Opus 51/1*, 1873I; *String Quartet No. 2 in a, Opus 51/2*, 1873I;

❋

A *Births*   B *Deaths*   C *Debuts*   D *New Positions*
                    E *Prizes/Honors*

String Quartet No. 3 in B♭, Opus 67, 1876I; *String Quintet No. 1in F, Opus 88*, 1882I; *String Quintet No. 2 in G, Opus 111*, 1890I; *String Sextet No. 1, Opus 18*, 1860I; *String Sextet No. 2 in G, Opus 36*, 1864I; *Symphony No. 1 in c, Opus 68*, 1876I; *Symphony No. 2 in D, Opus 73*, 1877I; *Symphony No. 3 in F, Opus 90*, 1883I; *Symphony No. 4 in e, Opus 98*, 1885I; *Tragic Overture, Opus 81*, 1881I; *Trio in a, "Clarinet," Opus 114*, 1891I; *Trio in E♭, "Horn," Opus 40*, 1865I; *Triumphlied, Opus 55*, 1871I; *Variations on Theme of Schuman, Opus 9*, 1854I; *Variations on an Original Theme, Opus 21/1*, 1856; *Variations on a Hungarian Song, Opus 21*, 1853I; *Variations on . . . Schumann, Opus 23*, 1861I; *Variations & Fugue on . . . Handel, Opus 24*, 1861I; *Variations on . . . Paganini, Opus 35*, 1863I; *Variations on a Theme by Haydn, Opus 56a*, 1873I; *Violin Sonata No. 1 in G, Opus 78*, 1879I; *Violin Sonata No. 2 in A, Opus 100*, 1886I; *Violin Sonata No. 3 in d, Opus 108*, 1888I; *Violin Concerto in F, Opus 77*, 1878I; *Vocal Quartets (3), Opus 31*, 1863I; *Vocal Quartets (3), Opus 64*, 1874I; *Vocal Quartets (6), Opus 92*, 1884I; *Waltzes (16), Opus 39*, 1865I; *Zigeunerlieder, Opus 103*, 1887I

Brant, Henry: *500: Hidden Hemisphere*, 1992I; *An American Requiem*, 1973I; *Antiphony I*, 1953I; *Clarinet Concerto*, 1938I; *Desert Forest*, 1983I; *Desert Music*, 1985I; *Down Town Suite*, 1942I; *Encephalograms II*, 1955I; *Fisherman's Overture*, 1938I; *Hieroglyphics I*, 1957I; *Hieroglyphics II*, 1966I; *Hieroglyphics III*, 1958I; *In Praise of Learning*, 1958I; *Inside Track* (piano concerto), 1982I; *Labyrinth I, II*, 1955I; *Plowshares & Swords*, 1995I; *Prisons of the Mind*, 1990I; *Spatial Concerto* (piano), 1979I; *Spatial Symphony*, 1990I; *A Trinity of Spheres*, 1978I; *Violin Concerto*, 1940I; *Voyage Four*, 1963I; *Western Springs: A Spatial Assembly*, 1984I

Braunfels, Walter: *String Quartet No. 1, Opus 60*, 1944I; *String Quartet No. 2, Opus 61*, 1944I; *String Quartet No. 3, Opus 67*, 1946I; *Die Vögel*, 1920I

Bretan, Nicolae: *Arald*, 1942I; *Golem*, 1924I; *Luceafǎl*, 1921I

Bretón y Hernández, Tomas: *Los amantes de Teruel*, 1889I; *La Dolores*, 1895I

Bréval, Jean-Baptiste: *Cello Concerto No. 1 in A, Opus 14*, 1784I ; *Cello Concerto No. 2 in G, Opus 17*, 1784I; *Cello Concerto No. 3, Opus 20*, 1785I; *Cello Concerto No. 4 in C, Opus 22*, 1786I; *Cello Concerto No. 5, Opus 24*, 1786I; *Cello Concerto No. 6 in C, Opus 26*, 1786I; *Cello concerto No. 7 in a, Opus 35*, 1794I; *Cello Sonatas (6), Opus 12*, 1783U; *Cello Sonatas (6), Opus 28*, 1787I; *Cello Sonatas (6), Opus 40*, 1795I; *Ines et Leonore*, 1788I; *Quatuors Concertants (6), Opus 1*, 1775I; *Quatuors concertante (6), Opus 5*, 1778I; *Quatuors concertante, Opus 7*, 1781I; *Quatuors concertante, Opus 18*, 1785I; *String Trios (6), Opus 3*, 1777I; *String Trios (6), Opus 27*, 1786I; *Symphonic Concertos, Opus 11*, 1783I; *Symphonie concertante, Opus 33*, 1792I; *Symphonie concertante, Opus 38*, 1795I; *Symphonies concertante (2), Opus 4*, 1777I; *Trios (6), Flute & Strings, Opus 8*, 1782I

Brewaeys, Luc: *Antigone*, 1991I; *Réquialm*, 1989I; *Symphony No. 5*, 1993I

Brewbaker, Daniel: *Cincinnatus Psalm*, 2000I

Brian, Havergal: *Cello Concerto*, 1964I; *Concerto for Orchestra*, 1964I; *Elegy*, 1954I; *In Memoriam*, 1910I; *Symphony No. 1, "Gothic,"* 1927I; *Symphony No. 2*, 1931I; *Symphony No. 3*, 1932I; *Symphony No. 4*, 1933I; *Symphony No. 5, "Wine of Summer,"* 1937I; *Symphony No. 6, "Tragica,"* 1948I; *Symphony No. 7*, 1948I; *Symphony No. 8*, 1949I; *Symphony No. 9*, 1951I; *Symphony No. 10*, 1954I; *Symphony No. 11*, 1954I; *Symphony No. 12*, 1957I; *Symphony No. 13*, 1959I; *Symphony No. 14*, 1960I; *Symphony No. 15*, 1960I; *Symphony No. 16*, 1960I; *Symphony No.17*, 1961I; *Symphony No. 18*, 1961I; *Symphony No. 19*, 1961I; *Symphony No. 20*, 1962I; *Symphony No. 21*, 1963I; *Symphony No. 22*, 1965i; *Symphony No. 23*, 1965I; *Symphony No. 24*, 1965I; *Symphony No. 25*, 1966I; *Symphony No. 26*, 1966I; *Symphony No. 27*, 1966I; *Symphony No. 28*, 1967I; *Symphony No. 29*, 1967I; *Symphony No. 30*, 1967I; *Symphony No. 31*, 1968I; *Symphony No. 32*, 1968I; *Violin Concerto in C*, 1935I

Briccetti, Thomas: *Overture, The Fountain of Youth*, 1972I

Bridge, Frank: *Cello Sonata*, 1917I; *Fantasy* (String Quartet), 1905I; *Idylls (3) for String Quartet*, 1907I; *In Memoriam C. H. H. P.*, 1918I; *Organ Pieces (3)*, 1905I; *Organ Pieces, Book 1*, 1905I; *Organ Pieces, Book II*, 1912I; *Phantasm*, 1934I; *Piano Trio No. 1 in c, "Phantasie,"* 1907I; *Piano Trio No. 2*, 1929I; *The Sea-Suite*, 1910I; *String Quartet No. 1*, 1901I; *String Quartet No. 2*, 1915I; *String Quartet No. 3*, 1927I; *String Quartet No. 4*, 1937I; *String Quintet in e*, 1901I; *String Sextet*, 1912I; *Summer*, 1914I

Bristow, George Frederick: *Arcadian Symphony*, 1874I; *Columbus Overture, Opus 32*, 1861I; *Daniel, Opus 42*, 1866I; *The Great Republic*, 1879I; *A Life on the Ocean Waves, Opus 21*, 1852I; *Marche-Caprice, Opus 51*, 1890I; *Mass in C, Opus 57*, 1885I; *Morning Service, Opus 51*, 1873I; *Overture Jibbenainosay, Opus 64*, 1889I; *Overture, A Winter's Tale, Opus 70*, 1856I; *The Pioneer, Opus 49*, 1872I; *Plantation Memories I, II*, 1895I; *Plantation Pleasures, Opus 82*, 1894I; *Raindrops, Opus 43*, 1867I; *Rip Van Winkle*, 1855I; *Symphony No. 1 in E♭, Opus 10*, 1848I; *Symphony No. 2 in d, Opus 24, "Jullien,"* 1853I; *Symphony No. 3 in f♯*, 1858I; *Symphony No. 4, "Arcadian," Opus 50*, 1872I; *Symphony No. 5, "Niagara," Opus 62*, 1893I

Britten, Benjamin: *Albert Herring*, 1947I; *The Beggar's Opera*, 1948I; *Billy Budd*, 1951I; *The Burning Fiery Furnace*, 1966I; *Cabaret Songs*, 1937I; *Canticle No. 4, "Journey of the Magi,"* 1971I; *Cello Sonata in C*,

---

❈

Britten, Benjamin: (*cont.*)
Opus 65, 1961I; *A Ceremony of Carols*, 1942I; *Death in Venice*, 1973I; *Divertimenti (3)* (String Quartet), 1936I; *English folk song Suite*, 1974I; *Festival Te Deum*, 1945I; *Gloriana*, 1953I; *Les illuminations*, 1939I; *Midsummer Night's Dream*, 1960I; *Nocturne*, 1958I; *Noye's Fludde*, 1957I; *Owen Wingrave*, 1970I; *Peter Grimes*, 1945I; *Piano Concerto No. 1*, 1938I; *Prince of the Pagodas*, 1956I; *The Rape of Lucrecia*, 1946I; *Serenade for Tenor, Horn & Strings*, 1943I; *Simple Symphony*, 1934I; *Sinfonia da Requiem*, 1940I; *Sinfonietta*, 1932I; *Spring Symphony*, 1949I; *String Quartet No. 1 in D, Opus 25*, 1941I; *String Quartet No. 2 in C, Opus 36*, 1945I; *String Quartet No. 3*, 1975I; *Suite No. 2 for Solo Cello*, 1967I; *Symphony for Violin, Cello & Orchestra*, 1964I; *Variations on a Theme of Frank Bridge*, 1937I; *A War Requiem*, 1962I; *Young Person's Guide to the Orchestra*, 1946I
Brockway, Howard A.: *Symphony in D*, 1895I
Brooks, Richard: *Moby Dick*, 1987I
Brotons, Salvador: *Soliloquy* (guitar), 1996I; *Stabat Mater*, 1997I; *Symphony No. 3*, 1992I; *Trombone Concerto*, 1995I; *Violin Sonata*, 1994I
Broughton, Rutland: *Concerto for String Orchestra*, 1937I; *Flute Concerto*, 1937I; *Folk Dances (3)*, 1911I; *Oboe Quintet No. 1*, 1930I; *String Quartet No. 1 in A, "On Greek Folk Songs,"* 1923I; *String Quartet No. 2 in F, "From the Welsh Hills,"* 1923I
Brouwer, Leo: *Concierto de Volos*, 1996I; *Hika*, 1996I; *Toronto Concerto*, 1987I
Brouwer, Margaret: *Crosswinds* (string quartet), 1995I ; *Horn Sonata*, 1996I
Brown, Earle: *25 Pages for 1 to 25 Pianos*, 1953I; *Available Forms I*, 1961I; *Available Forms II*, 1962I; *Cross Sections & Color Fields*, 1975I; *Event: Synergy II*, 1968I; *Folio II*, 1981I; *Four Systems*, 1954I; *From Here*, 1963I; *Modules I*, 1966I; *Modules II*, 1966I; *Music for Violin, Cello & Piano*, 1952I; *Octet 1*, 1953I; *Piano Corroboree*, 1964I; *Sounder Rounds*, 1982I; *String Quartet 1965*, 1965I; *Syntagm III*, 1970I; *Time Spans*, 1972I; *Tracking Pierrot*, 1992I; *Windsor Jambs*, 1980I
Brubeck, Dave: *To Hope*, 1980I
Bruch, Max: *Achilleus*, 1885I; *Arminius*, 1877I; *Concerto for Two Pianos, Opus 88a*, 1912I; *Das Feuer Kreus*, 1889I; *Frithjof-Scenen, Opus 23*, 1864I; *Gustav Adolf*, 1898I; *Hermione*, 1872I; *Das Lied von der Glocke*, 1879I; *Die Loreley*, 1863I; *Moses*, 1895I; *Odysseus*, 1871I; *Piano Quintet*, 1886I; *Scherz, List und Rache*, 1858I; *Schön Ellen, Opus 21*, 1867I; *Scottish Rhapsody*, 1880I; *String Quartet No. 1 in c, Opus 9*, 1856I; *String Quartet No. 2 in E, Opus 10*, 1860I; *String Octet*, 1919I; *String Quintet in a*, 1918I; *Symphony No. 1 in E♭, Opus 28*, 1870I; *Symphony No. 2 in f, Opus 36*, 1870I; *Symphony No. 3 in e, Opus 51*, 1887I; *Violin Concerto No. 2 in d, Opus 44*, 1878I; *Violin Concerto No. 1 in g, Opus 26*, 1868I
Bruckner, Anton: *Helgoland*, 1893I; *Litany for Brass and Chorus*, 1845I; *Magnificat*, 1853I; *Mass in C*, 1842I; *Mass in F*, 1844I; *Mass No. I in d*, 1864I; *Mass No. 2 in e*, 1866I; *Mass No. 3 in f*, 1868I; *Missa Solemnis in B♭*, 1854I; *Organ Fugue in d*, 1861I; *Organ Pieces (2) in d*, 1852I; *Organ Prelude in E♭*, 1836I; *Overture in g*, 1863I; *Piano Pieces, Four Hands (3)*, 1854I; *Pieces (3) for Orchestra*, 1862I; *Preiset den Herrn*, 1862I; *Prelude in C*, 1884I; *Prelude & Fugue in c*, 1847I; *Prelude & Postlude in d*, 1846I; *Psalm 112*, 1863I; *Psalm 114*, 1850I; *Psalm 146 in A*, 1860I; *Psalm 150 in C*, 1892I; *Requiem in d*, 1849I; *String Quartet in C*, 1862I; *String Quintet in F*, 1879I; *Symphony in f* (unpublished), 1863I; *Symphony in d, "Die Nullte"* (revised 1869), 1864I; *Symphony No. 1 in c*, 1855I; *Symphony No. 2 in c*, 1872I; *Symphony No. 3 in d*, 1873I; *Symphony No. 4 in E♭, "Romantic,"* 1874I; *Symphony No. 5 in B♭*, 1876I; *Symphony No. 6 in A*, 1881I; *Symphony No. 7 in E*, 1883I; *Symphony No. 8 in c*, 1887I; *Symphony No. 9 in d*, 1894I; *Te Deum*, 1881I; *Te Deum in C*, 1884I; *Totenlieder (2)*, 1852I; *Vergissmeinnicht*, 1845I
Brun, Fritz: *Symphony No. 2*, 1911I
Brunetti, Gaetano: *Concert Aria, "E ver' por troppo,"* 1783I; *Miserere*, 1794I; *Overtures (Symphonies 1-6)*, 1772I; *Sextets (6), Oboe & Strings*, 1776I; *String Quintets (6), Opus 1*, 1771I; *String Trios (6), Opus 1*, 1776I; *String Trios (6), Opus 2*, 1776I; *String Trios (6), Opus 3*, 1782I; *String Sextets (6)*, 1776I; *Symphonies No. 14, 15*, 1779I; *Symphonies No. 16, 17, 28*, 1789I; *Symphonies No 18-20*, 1780I; *Symphony No. 21 in E♭*, 1784I; *Symphonies No. 22, 25*, 1783I; *Symphony No. 26 in B♭*, 1782I; *Symphony No. 27 in B♭*, 1787I; *Symphonies No. 29*, 1783I; *Symphony No. 34 in F*, 1790I; *Viola Sonata in b*, 1789I
Bruzdowicz, Joanna: *Violin Sonata, "Spring in America,"* 1994I
Bryars, Gavin: *Adnan Songbook*, 1996I; *Cadman Requiem*, 1989I; *Cello Concerto, "Farewell to Philosophy,"* 1995I; *Dr. Ox's Experiment*, 1998I; *Elegies (3) for Nine Clarinets*, 1993I; *The First Book of Madrigals*, 2000I; *String Quartet No. 2*, 1990I; *Super Flumina*, 2000I; *Violin Concerto, "Farewell to Philosophy,"* 1995I; *String Quartet No. 3*, 1998I
Bubalo, Rudolph: *Cello Concerto*, 1992I
Buchholz, Thomas: *Chamber Symphony No. 6, "Todesfuge,"* 1994I
Buck, Dudley: *Centennial Meditation on Columbus*, 1876I; *Christ, the Victor*, 1896I; *The Coming of the King*, 1895I; *Deseret*, 1880I; *Festival Overture on "The Star-Spangled Banner,"* 1879I; *Festival Hymn, Opus 57*,

1872I; *Grand Organ Sonata (No. 1) in E♭, Opus 22*, 1866I; *The Legend of don Munio*, 1874I; *The Light of Asia*, 1886I; *Marmion Overture*, 1878I; *Midnight Service for New Year's Eve*, 1880I; *The Nun of Nidaros*, 1878I; *Organ Sonata No. 2 in g, Opus 77*, 1877I; *Paul Revere's Ride*, 1898I; *Romanza for Four Horns and Orchestra, Opus 71*, 1875I; *Scenes from "The Golden Legend,"* 1879I; *Serapis*, 1889I; *The Story of the Cross*, 1891I; *The Triumph of David*, 1892I; *Variations on "Old folks at Home,"* 1888I; *Variations on Star Spangled Banner*, 1868I; *Variations on "Sweet Bye and Bye,"* 1877I; *The Voyage of Columbus*, 1885I

Buck, Ole: *Felix luna*, 1971I; *Landscapes*, 1995I

Buckley, John: *Airflow*, 1998I; *Alto Saxophone Concerto*, 1997I; *Arabesque for Solo Sax*, 1990I; *In Lines of Dazzling Light*, 1995I; *Organ Concerto*, 1992I; *Piano Preludes (3)*, 1995I; *Maynooth Te Deum*, 1995I; *Sonata for Solo Horn*, 1993I; *Symphony No. 1*, 1988I; *The Words upon the Window Pane*, 1991I

Buechner, Margaret: *Elizabeth* (B), 1990I; *Trilogy: The American Civil War*, 1992I; *The Old Swedes Church*, 1987I

Bunin, Revol: *Symphony No. 6*, 1966I

Burge, David: *Piano Eclipse II*, 1964I; *Piano Variations on "Simple Gifts,"* 1980I

Burgon, Geoffrey: *The Calm*, 1974I; *Requiem*, 1976I; *A Vision*, 1991I

Burian, Emil F.: *String Quartet No. 1*, 1927I; *String Quartet No. 2*, 1929I; *String Quartet No. 3*, 1940I; *String Quartet No. 4*, 1947I; *String Quartet No. 5*, 1947I; *String Quartet No. 6*, 1948I; *String Quartet No. 7*, 1949I; *String Quartet No. 8*, 1951I

Burkhard, Willy: *Chorale Triptychon, Opus 91*, 1953I; *Fantasia & Chorale, "Ein Feste Berg,"* 1939I; *Organ Concerto, Opus 74*, 1945I; *Prelude & Fugue*, 1932I; *String Quartet*, 1943I

Burleigh, Cecil: *A Ballad of Early New England, Opus 58*, 1924I

  Essays: Illusion, Transition, 1945I; *Evangeline, Opus 41*, 1929I; *Four Prairie Sketches, Opus 13*, 1916I; *Four Rocky Mountain Sketches*, 1914I; *Hymn to the Ancients for Piano Quintet*, 1940I; *Mood Pictures (3), Opus 56*, 1926I; *Mountain Pictures*, 1917I; *Sketches from the Orient, Opus 55*, 1926I; *Violin Concerto No. 1, Opus 25*, 1912I; *Violin Concerto No. 2, Opus 43*, 1918I; *Violin Concerto No. 3, Opus 60*, 1927I; *Violin Sonata No. 1, "The Ascension,"* 1914I; *Violin Sonata No. 2, "From the Life of St. Paul,"* 1926I

Burleigh, Henry T.: *From the Southland*, 1914I; *Passionale*, 1915I; *Saracen Songs*, 1914I; *Songs of Laurence Hope (5)*, 1915I

Burrs, Savoy: *Vanqui*, 1999I

Busch, Carl: *Cello Concerto*, 1919I; *Minnehaha's Vision*, 1914I; *String Quartet*, 1897I; *Violin Concerto*, 1919I

Bush, Alan: *Dialectic* (string quartet), 1929I

Bush, Geoffrey: *Music for Orchestra*, 1967I

Busoni, Ferruccio: *Arlecchino, Opus 50*, 1916I; *Die Brautwahl*, 1911I; *Christmas Sonatina*, 1917I; *Divertimento for Flute & Orchestra*, 1920I; *Doktor Faust*, 1924I; *Elegies*, 1908I; *Fantasia Contrapuntistica*, 1910I; *Indian Diary, Opus 47*, 1915I; *Indian Fantasy, Opus 44*, 1913I; *Kleine Suite, Opus 23*, 1885I; *Orchestral Suite No. 2, Opus 34a*, 1895I; *Piano Concerto, Opus 39*, 1904I; *Piano Concertstücke, Opus 31a*, 1890I; *Piano Etudes (6)*, 1883I; *Piano Pieces (5), Opus 3*, 1877I; *Piano Sonatina No. 2*, 1912I; *Piano Toccata*, 1920I; *Rondo Arlecchinesco, Opus 46*, 1915I; *Sarabande & Cortège, Opus 51*, 1922I; *String Quartet No. 1 in c, Opus 19*, 1881I; *String Quartet No. 2*, 1887I; *Symphonic Nocturne*, 1912I; *Symphonic Suite, Opus 25*, 1888I; *Turandot*, 1917I; *Turandot Suite, Opus 41*, 1904I; *Unter den Linden*, 1885I; *Violin Sonata No. 1 in e*, 1890 I; *Violin Sonata No. 2*, 1898I; *Violin Concerto in D, Opus 35a*, 1897I

Butterfield, James A.: *Ruth, the Gleaner*, 1875I

Butterworth, Arthur: *Symphony No. 1*, 1957I

Butterworth, George: *A Shropshire Lad*, 1913I

Buzzolla, Antonio: *Amleto*, 1847I

Cadman, Charles W.: *American Folksong Suite*, 1937I; *American Indian Songs (4)*, 1907I; *At Dawning*, 1906I; *Aurora Borealis*, 1942I; *The Belle of Havana*, 1928I; *Dark Dancers of the Mardi Gras*, 1933I; *The Father of Waters*, 1928I; *From the Land of Sky-blue Water*, 1908I; *From Wigwam & Tepee*, 1914I; *Garden of Mystery*, 1915I; *Irish Songs (4)*, 1909I; *Joshua*, 1909I; *A Mad Empress Remembers* (cello concerto), 1944I; *Oriental Suite*, 1921I; *Oriental Rhapsody*, 1917I; *Overture, Huckleberry Finn Goes Fishing*, 1945I; *Piano Quintet in g*, 1937I; *Piano Sonata in A*, 1915I; *Piano Trio in D, Opus 36*, 1914I; *Prairie Sketches*, 1906I; *The Rubaiyat of Omar Khayyám*, 1921I; *Sayonara*, 1913I; *Shanewis*, 1918I; *The Sunset Trail*, 1922I; *Symphony*, 1939I; *Symphony in e, "Pennsylvania,"* 1940I; *Thunderbird Suite*, 1914I; *Violin Sonata in G*, 1932I; *The Vision of Sir Launfal*, 1909I; *The Willow Tree*, 1925I; *Willow Wind*, 1922I; *A Witch of Salem*, 1926I

Cafano, Pasquale: *Antigono*, 1770I; *L'incendio di Troia*, 1757I; *Ipermestra*, 1751I; *Ladisfatta di Dario*, 1755I; *L'Olimpiade*, 1769I

Cage, John: *34'46.776,"* 1954I; *4'3,"* 1952I; *Bacchanale*, 1938I; *Clarinet Sonata*, 1933I; *Concerto for Prepared Piano*, 1951I; *Europeras I, II*, 1987I; *Fontana Mix*, 1958I; *Four*, 1989I; *Four Walls*, 1944I; *HPSCHD*, 1969I; *Music for Piano, 1952*, 1952I; *Music for Piano, 1953*, 1953I; *Music of Changes*, 1951I; *Percussion Quartet*,

---

Cage, John: (*cont.*)
1935I; *Piano Concerto*, 1958I; *Pieces (30), String Quartet*, 1983I; *The Seasons*, 1947I; *Seventy-Four* (piano concerto), 1992I; *Sonatas & Interludes*, 1948I; *Songs on e. e. cummings (5)*, 1938I; *Songs on Gertrude Stein (3)*, 1932I; *String Quartet*, 1936I; *String Quartet in Four Parts*, 1950I; *Thirteen*, 1992I; *Thirty Pieces for Five Orchestras*, 1981I; *Twenty-Three*, 1989I; *Two²* for *Piano, 1989I*; *Variations I, 1961I*; *Winter Music, 1957I*

Calegari, Antonio: *L'amor soldato*, 1786I; *Don Bucefalo*, 1847I; *Le sorelle rivali*, 1784I

Caltabiano, Ronald: *Hexagons*, 1994I; *Prelude & Fugue for Organ*, 1981I; *Sonata for Solo Cello*, 1982I; *String Quartet No. 1*, 1981I; *String Quartet No. 2*, 1987I

Camacho, Marvin: *Danzas Primitivas* (organ), 1992I

Cambini, Giuseppe M.: *Adele et Edwin*, 1791I; *Aleidas*, 1789I; *Aleméon*, 1789I; *Le bon père*, 1788I; *Colas et Colette*, 1788I; *Cora*, 1789I; *La croisée*, 1787I; *Nantilde et Dagobert*, 1791I; *Les romains*, 1776I; *Rose d'amour*, 1777I; *Rose et carloman*, 1779I; *La statue*, 1784I; *Symphonies (3), Opus 5*, 1776I; *Symphonies in F, e, D*, 1787I; *Symphonies (3)*, 1788I; *Les trois garçons*, 1793I; *Le tuteur avare*, 1787I

Camilleri, Charles: *Concerto for Organ, Strings & Timpani*, 1983I

Campagnoli, Bartolomeo: *Violin Concerto in B♭*, 1820I

Canavas, Jean B.: *Cello Sonatas I (6)*, 1767I; *Cello Sonatas II (6)*, 1773I

Cannabich, Christian: *Achille reconnu*, 1774I; *Acis et Galathée*, 1768I; *L'amour espagnol*, 1766I; *L'amour jardinier*, 1766I; *Les amours de Télémaque*, 1765I; *Angélique et Médor*, 1770I; *Azakia*, 1778I; *Bacchus et Ariadne*, 1770I; *Cephales et Procrid*, 1787I; *Ceyx et Alcyone*, 1763I; *Corésus et Callihoé*, 1784I; *Cortez et Thélaire*, 1794I; *La croisée*, 1788I; *La descente d'Hercule*, 1780I; *Electro*, 1781I; *L'embarquement pour Cythère*, 1775I; *L'enlèvement de Proserpine*, 1767I; *La fête marine*, 1774I; *Les filets de Vulcain*, 1768I; *Ippolito e Aricia*, 1759I; *Le jugement de Paris*, 1764I; *Das Liebes des Cortes*, 1778I; *Les mariages de Samnites*, 1772I; *Médée et Jason*, 1772I; *Mirtil et Amarilis*, 1767I; *Persée et Andromède*, 1784I; *Renaud et Armide*, 1769I; *Roland furieux*, 1768I; *Symphonia concertantes (6), Opus 7*, 1769I; *Symphonies (6) for Large Orchestra*, 1766I; *Symphonies (6), Opus 4*, 1767I; *Symphonies (6), Opus 10*, 1778I; *Symphony No. 25 in C*, 1762I; *Symphony (No. 5) in G*, 1760I; *Symphony No. 26 in F*, 1763I; *Trio Sonatas (6), Opus 3*, 1766I; *Ulisse et Circée*, 1765I

Caplet, André: *Quintet for Piano & Winds*, 1899I

Capron, Nicolas: *Quartets (6), Opus 1*, 1772I; *Quartets (6), Opus 2*, 1772I; *Violin Sonatas, Book I, Opus 1*, 1768I

Capuzzi, Giuseppe A.: *Quartets (6), Opus 1*, 1780I; *Quartets (6), Opus 2*, 1780I; *String Quartets (6), Opus 6*, 1787I

Carafa, Michele: *L'auberge supposée*, 1824I; *Berenice in Siria*, 1818I; *Elisabetta in Derbyshire*, 1818I; *La grande duchesse*, 1835I; *Ifigenia in Tauride*, 1817I; *Jeanne d'Arc à Orléans*, 1821I; *Jenny*, 1829I; *Le lure de l'hermite*, 1831I; *La prison d'Edimbourg*, 1833I; *Le solitaire*, 1822I; *Thérèse*, 1838I; *Le valet de chambre*, 1823I; *La violette*, 1828I

Cardonne, Jean-Baptiste: *Symphony in G*, 1781I

Carlson, David: *Cello Concerto No. 1*, 1979I; *Cello Sonata*, 1992I; *Dreamkeepers*, 1996I; *The Midnight Angel*, 1993I; *Quixotic Variations*, 1978I

Carnicer, Ramón: *Adele di Lusignano*, 1819I; *Cristoforo Colombo*, 1831I; *Don Giovanni Tenoria*, 1822I; *Elena e Constantino*, 1821I; *Elena e Malvina*, 1829I; *Ismalia*, 1837I

Carpenter, John Alden: *Adventures in a Perambulator*, 1914I; *The Anxious Bugler*, 1943I; *The Birthday of the Infanta*, 1917I; *Branglebrink*, 1896I; *Carmel Concerto*, 1948I; *Gitanjali*, 1913I; *Krazy Kat*, 1921I; *Patterns*, 1932I; *Piano Concertino*, 1915I; *Piano Quintet*, 1934I; *Piano Sonata No. 1*, 1897I; *A Pilgrim Vision*, 1920I; *Polonaise américaine*, 1912I; *Sea Drift*, 1933I; *The Seven Ages Suite*, 1945I; *Skyscrapers*, 1924I; *Song of Faith*, 1931I; *Song of Freedom*, 1941I; *String Quartet No. 1*, 1927I; *Suite for Orchestra*, 1909I; *Symphony No. 1, "Sermons in Stones,"* 1917I; *Symphony No. 2*, 1940I, 1942I; *Symphony No. 3*, 1941I; *Tango amércaine*, 1920I; *Violin Concerto*, 1936I; *Violin Sonata*, 1911I; *Water-Colors*, 1916I

Carr, Benjamin: *Ballads (6) from "The Lady of the Lake," Opus 7*, 1810I; *Federal Overture*, 1795I; *The Mountaineers of Switzerland*, 1796I; *Philander and Silvia*, 1792I; *The Siege of Tripoli, Opus 4*, 1804I

Carter, Elliott: *90+ for Piano*, 1994I; *Adagio Tenebroso*, 1995I; *Allegro Scorrevole*, 1997I; *Anniversary*, 1991I; *A Celebration of Some 100 x 150 Notes*, 1986I; *Cello Sonata*, 1948I; *Clarinet Concerto*, 1996I; *Concerto for Orchestra*, 1969I; *Double Concerto*, 1961I; *Eight Etudes & a Fantasy for Woodwind Quartet*, 1950I; *Enchanted Preludes*, 1988I; *Holiday Overture*, 1945I; *In Challenge & in Love*, 1994I; *In Sleep, In Thunder*, 1981I; *The Minotaur*, 1947I; *Mirror on Which to Dwell*, 1975I; *Night Fantasies for Piano*, 1980I; *Oboe Concerto*, 1988I; *Occasions (3) for Orchestra*, 1989I; *Partita*, 1994I; *Pastorale for Clarinet & Piano*, 1940I; *Penthode*, 1985I; *Piano Concerto*, 1965I; *Piano Quintet*, 1997I; *Piano Sonata*, 1946I; *Pocahontas*, 1939I; *Quintet for Piano & Winds*, 1991I; *Remembrance*, 1988I; *Retrouvailles for Piano*, 2000I; *Rhapsodic Musings*

❊

A   *Births*   B   *Deaths*   C   *Debuts*   D   *New Positions*
E   *Prizes/Honors*

(String Quartet), 2000I; *Scrivo in vento*, 1991I; *Shard*, 1997I; *Sonata for Flute, Oboe, Cello & Harpsichord*, 1952I; *String Quartet Fragment II*, 1999I; *String Quartet No. 1*, 1951I; *String Quartet No. 2*, 1959I; *String Quartet No. 3*, 1971I; *String Quartet No. 4*, 1986I; *String Quartet No. 5*, 1995I; *Symphonia: Sum fluxae pratium spei*, 1998I; *A Symphony for Three Orchestras*, 1976I; *Symphony No. 1*, 1942I; *Syringa*, 1978I; *Trilogy*, 1992I; *Variations for Orchestra*, 1955I; *What Next?*, 1999I; *Woodwind Quintet*, 1948I

Carvalho, João de Sousa: *Adrasto rè degli Argivi*, 1784I; *L'amore industrica*, 1769I; *L'angelica*, 1778I; *L'Endimione*, 1783I; *L'Eumene*, 1773I; *Everado Il rè di Lituania*, 1782I; *Leleuco, rè di Siria*, 1781I; *Nettuno ed Eglé*, 1785H; *La nitteti*, 1766I; *Numa Pompilio, Il rè dei romans*, 1789I; *Penelope nella partenza da Sparta*, 1782I; *Perseo*, 1779I; *Testoride argonauta*, 1780I

Carwithen, Doreen: *Bishop Rock Overture*, 1952I; *Suffolk Suite*, 1964I

Casals, Pablo: *El Pessebre*, 1960I

Casella, Alfredo: *Cello Concerto*, 1935I; *Cello Sonata in C, Opus 45*, 1927I; *Children's Pieces (11)*, 1920I; *Concerto Romano (organ)*, 1926I; *Il convento Veneziano*, 1912I; *La donna serpente*, 1931I; *Elegia Eroica*, 1916I; *La giara*, 1924I; *Italie, Opus 11*, 1909I; *Orchestral Suite in C*, 1909I; *Paganiniana*, 1942I; *Pagine di Guerra*, 1918I; *Piano Pieces (9), Opus 24*, 1914I; *Pupazzetti*, 1918I; *Scarlattiana*, 1926I; *Serenata*, 1927I; *Sonata a Tre*, 1938I; *Symphony No. 1*, 1905I; *Symphony No. 2 in c*, 1909I; *Symphony No. 3, Opus 63*, 1940I; *Triple Concerto for Violin, Cello & Piano, Opus 56*, 1933I

Castelnuovo-Tedesco, Mario: *An American Rhapsody*, 1943I; *Anthony & Cleopatra Overture*, 1947I; *Capricios de Goya (24)*, 1961I; *Cello Concerto*, 1935I; *Cello Sonata, Opus 50*, 1928I; *Clarinet Sonata*, 1945I; *Concerto in E for Two Guitars*, 1962I; *Coplan*, 1915I; *Fantastic Variations, Opus 47*, 1927I; *Guitar Concerto No. 1 in D, Opus 99*, 1939I; *Guitar Concerto No. 2 in C, Opus 160*, 1953I; *Introduction, Aria & Fugue*, 1967I; *The Merchant of Venice*, 1961I; *Midsummer Night's Dream Overture*, 1940I; *Overture: As you Like It*, 1953I; *Overture: Julius Caesar*, 1934I; *Overture: The Merchant of Venice*, 1933I; *Overture: Much Ado about Nothing*, 1953I; *Overture, The Taming of the Shrew*, 1930I; *Overture, The Tragedy of Coriolanus*, 1948I; *Overture: Twelfth Night*, 1933I; *Piano Concerto No. 1*, 1928I; *Piano Concerto No. 2*, 1939I; *Piano Quintet No. 1*, 1932I; *Piano Quintet No. 2*, 1951I; *Piano Sonata*, 1928I; *Piano Trio No. 1*, 1928I; *Piano Trio No. 2*, 1932I; *The Princess & the Pea*, 1943I; *Quintet for Guitar & Strings*, 1950I; *Ricercare on the Name of Luigi Dallapiccolo*, 1958I; *Romancero Gitano*, 1953I; *Sephardic Songs (3)*, 1947I; *Sonata quasi una fantasia for Violin & Piano*, 1929I; *Sonatina zoologica, Opus 187*, 1960I; *The Song of Songs*, 1963I; *String Quartet No. 1*, 1929I; *String Quartet No. 2*, 1948I; *String Quartet No. 3*, 1964I; *Symphonic Variations (violin)*, 1930I; *Violin Concerto No. 1, "Concerto italiano,"* 1926I; *Violin Concerto No. 2, "The Prophet,"* 1933I; *Violin Concerto No. 3*, 1939I

Castillo, David: *Cello Concerto No. 2*, 1997I; *Festive Overture*, 1998I; *Resurrection*, 1989I; *String Quartet*, 1992I

Castillo, Manuel: *Preludio, Diferencias y Toccata*, 1959I

Catán, Daniel: *Florencia en la Amazonos*, 1996I; *La hija de Tappacini*, 1991I

Catel, Charles S.: *Les artistes par occasion*, 1807I; *L'auberge de Bagnères*, 1807I; *Les aubergistes de qualité*, 1812I; *Les bayadères*, 1810I; *L'officier enlevé*, 1819I; *Sémiramis*, 1802I

Catoire, Georgi: *Piano Trio in f*, 1900I

Catoire, Jean: *Requiem*, 1991I

Cavos, Catterino: *Dobrynia Nikitich*, 1818I; *L'eroe*, 1798I; *The Firebird*, 1822I; *Ilya the Hero*, 1807I; *The Invisible Prince*, 1805I; *Ivan Sussanin*, 1815I; *Rusalka*, 1803I; *Il sotterraneo*, 1799I; *Three Hunchback Brothers*, 1808I

Cazden, Norman: *Piano Trio*, 1969I

Chabrier, Emmanuel: *España Rhapsody*, 1883I; *L'étoile*, 1877I; *Gwendoline*, 1886I; *Lamento for Orchestra*, 1874I; *Marche Joyeuse*, 1891I; *Pièces pittoresques (10)*, 1880I; *Le roi malgré lui*, 1887I; *La Sulamite*, 1885I

Chadabe, Joel: *Piano Variations*, 1983I

Chadwick, George W.: *Angel of Death*, 1919I; *Anniversary Overture*, 1922I; *Aphrodite*, 1912I; *Canonic Studies (10)*, 1885I; *Cleopatra*, 1904I; *Elegy in Memoriam, Horatio Parker*, 1920I; *Judith*, 1900I; *The Lily Nymph*, 1893I; *Lochinvar*, 1897I; *The Miller's Daughter*, 1886I; *Ode for the Opening of the Chicago world's Fair*, 1892I; *Overture, Adonais*, 1899I; *Overture, Euterpe*, 1906I; *Overture, Melpomene*, 1887I; *Overture, Rip Van Winkle*, 1879I; *Overture, Thalia*, 1883I; *The Padrone*, 1015I; *A Pastoral Prelude*, 1894I; *Piano Pieces (5)*, 1905I; *Piano Quintet in E♭*, 1888I; *The Quiet Lodging*, 1892I; *Serenade in F Major for Strings*, 1890I; *Sinfonietta in D*, 1904I; *String Quartet No. 1 in g*, 1878I; *String Quartet No. 2 in C*, 1878I; *String Quartet No. 3 in D*, 1885I; *String Quartet No. 4 in e*, 1896I; *String Quartet No. 5 in d*, 1898I; *Suite in Variation Form*, 1923I; *Suite Symphonique in E♭*, 1911I; *Symphonic Sketches*, 1904I; *Symphony No. 1 in C*, 1882I; *Symphony No. 2 in B♭, Opus 21*, 1886I; *Symphony No. 3 in F*, 1894I; *Tabasco*, 1894I; *Tam O'Shanter*, 1915I; *Theme, Variations & Fugue*, 1908I; *The Viking's Last Voyage*, 1881I

Chaitkin, David: *Quintet*, 1985I

❈

F *Biographical*   G *Cultural Beginnings*   H *Musical Literature*
I *Musical Compositions*

Chaminade, Cécile: *Piano Trio No. 1*, 1881I; *Piano Trio No. 2*, 1887I

Champein, Stanislas: *Le nouveau Don Quichotte*, 1789I

Chance, John B.: *Symphony No. 1*, 1956I; *Symphony No. 2* (band), 1975I

Chanler Theodor: *Epitaphs*, 1937

Charpentier, Gustave: *Louise*, 1900I; *La vie du poète*, 1892I

Charpentier Jacques: *Concerto No. 1 for Organ & Strings*, 1969I; *Concerto No. 2 for Guitar & Strings*, 1970I; *Concerto No. 3 for Harpsichord & Strings*, 1971I; *Concerto No. 4 for Piano & Strings*, 1971I; *Concerto No. 5 for Saxophone & Orchestra*, 1975I; *Concerto No. 6 for Oboe & Strings*, 1975I; *Concerto No. 7 for Trumpet & Strings*, 1975I; *Concerto No. 8 for Horn & Strings*, 1976I; *Concerto No. 9 for Horn & Strings*, 1976I; *Concerto No. 10 for Clarinet & Strings*, 1983I; *Impressions d'Italie*, 1913I; *Symphony No. 1, "Breve,"* 1958I; *Symphony No. 2, "Sinfonia sacra,"* 1965I; *Symphony No. 3, "Shiva Nataraja,"* 1969I; *Symphony No. 4, "Brazil,"* 1973I; *Symphony No. 5*, 1977I; *Symphony No. 6 with Organ*, 1979I; *Symphony No. 7, "Acropolis,"* 1985I

Chasins, Abram: *Piano Concerto*, 1929I; *Piano Preludes (24)*, 1928I

Chausson, Ernest: *Les caprices de Marianne*, 1884I; *Chanson perpétuelle*, 1898I; *Chant Funèbre*, 1897I; *Concerto for Piano, Violin & String Quartet, Opus 21*, 1891I; *Hélène*, 1884I; *Hymne védique, Opus 9*, 1886I; *La légende de Sainte Cécilia*, 1892I; *Poème, Opus 25, for Violin & Orchestra*, 1896I; *Poème de l'amour et de la mer, Opus 19*, 1892I; *Le roi Arthur Opus23*, 1903I; *Soir de Fête, Opus 32*, 1898I; *Symphony in B♭, Opus 20*, 1890I; *The Tempest*, 1888I; *Vivianne, Opus 5*, 1882I

Chauvet, Charles-Alexis: *Morceaux (20)*, 1862I

Chávez, Carlos: *Antigone*, 1932I; *Clio*, 1970I; *Concerto for Four Horns*, 1937I; *Los cuatro soles*, 1926I; *Daughter of Collquide*, 1944I; *Discovery*, 1969I; *Elatio for Orchestra*, 1967I; *Energia for Nine Instruments*, 1925I; *El Fuego Nuevo*, 1921I; *Fuego Olimpico Suite*, 1969I; *HP*, 1927I; *Obertura Republicana*, 1935I; *Piano Concerto*, 1940I; *Resonancias for Orchestra*, 1964I; *String Quartet No. 1*, 1921I; *String Quartet No. 2*, 1932I; *String Quartet No. 3*, 1944I; *Symphony No. 1, "Antigone,"* 1933I; *Symphony No. 2, "Sinfonia India,"* 1936I; *Symphony No. 3*, 1951I; *Symphony No. 4, "Romantic,"* 1952I; *Symphony No. 5 for Strings*, 1953I; *Symphony No. 6*, 1961I; *Toccata*, 1947I; *Toccata for Percussion*, 1942I; *Violin Concerto*, 1948I

Chaynes, Charles: *String Quartet*, 1971I; *Visages mycéniens*, 1983I

Chélard, Hippolyte:; *L'aquila romana*, 1861I; *Ariana*, 1811I; *Braveurstücke*, 1834I; *La casa da vendere*, 1815I; *Die Hermannsschlacht*, 1835I; *Macbeth*, 1827I; *Messe solennelle*, 1830I; *Musikalische Reise*, 1835I; *Der Scheibentoni*, 1841I; *Die Seekadetten*, 1842I; *La symphonéide*, 1848I; *La table et le logement*, 1829I; *Le vieux drapeau*, 1848I

Chen Yi: *Symphony No. 2*, 1993I

Cherubini, Luigi: *Les abencérages*, 1813I; *Achille à Scyros*, 1804I; *Adriano in Siria*, 1782I; *Alessandro nell'Indie*, 1784I; *Ali Baba*, 1833I; *Amphion* (Freemason cantata), 1787I; *Anacréon*, 1803I; *Armida abbandonata*, 1782I; *Ave Maria*, 1816I; *Bayard à Mézières*, 1814I; *La cintura d'Armida*, 1801I; *Circé*, 1789I; *Clytemnestre*, 1794I; *Concert Overture in G*, 1815I; *Contra Dances (6)*, 1808I; *Coronation Mass in A*, 1825I; *Credo for Eight voices*, 1806I; *Le Crescendo*, 1810I; *Demophon*, 1788I; *Les deux journées*, 1800I; *Eliza*, 1794I; *Epicure*, 1800I; *Faniska*, 1806I; *La finta principessa*, 1785H; *Funeral March*, 1820I; *Il Giulio Sabino*, 1786I; *L'hôtellerie portugaise*, 1798I; *Hymn to spring*, 1815I; *L'Idalide*, 1784I; *Ifigenia in Aulide*, 1788I; *Koukourgi*, 1793I; *Litanie della Vergine*, 1820I; *Litanie de la Sainte Vièrge*, 1810I; *Lodoïska*, 1791I; *Marguerite d'Anjou*, 1790I; *Le mariage de Salomon*, 1816I; *Mass in F*, 1809I; *Mass No. 1 in C*, 1774I; *Mass No. 2 in C*, 1775I; *Mass "Te laudamus domine,"* 1779I; *Médée*, 1797I; *Il messenzio*, 1782I; *O Salutaris*, 1826I; *Piano Fantasia in C*, 1810I; *La pubblica felicità*, 1774I; *La punition*, 1799I; *Pygmalion*, 1809I; *Il quinto Fabio*, 1780I; *Requiem in c*, 1817I; *Requiem No. 2 in d*, 1836I; *Solemn Mass in G*, 1819I; *Solemn Mass in C*, 1816I; *Solemn Mass in E*, 1818I; *Sonata for Two Organs*, 1780I; *Sonatas (2) for Horn & Orchestra*, 1804I; *Lo sopso de tre e martia di nessuna*, 1783I; *String Quartet No. 1 in E♭*, 1814I; *String Quartet No. 2 in C*, 1829I; *String Quartet No. 3 in d*, 1834I; *String Quartet No. 4, 5*, 1835I; *String Quartet No. 6 in a*, 1837I; *String Quintet in e*, 1837I; *Symphony in D*, 1815I; *Te Deum*, 1777I; *Vocal Canons (10)*, 1806I; *Vocal Canons (12)*, 1807I

Chihara, Paul: *Ceremony I*, 1971I; *Ceremony II*, 1972I; *Ceremony III*, 1973I; *Ceremony IV*, 1974I; *Forest Music*, 1968I; *Missa Carminum*, 1976I; *Saxophone Concerto*, 1981I; *Symphony No. 1*, 1975I; *Symphony No. 2*, 1982I

Childs, Barney: *Clarinet Concerto*, 1970I; *Symphony No. 1*, 1954I; *Symphony No. 2*, 1956I; *Timpani Concerto*, 1989I

Ching, Michael:; *Buoso's Ghost*, 1998I

Chizy, Edith Canat de: *Cello Concerto, "Moira,"* 1998I

Chopin, Frédéric: *Allegro de Concert, Opus 46*, 1832I; *Ballade in f, Opus 52*, 1842I; *Cello Sonata in g, Opus 65*, 1846I; *Ecossaises (3), Opus 72/3*, 1826I; *Etudes (12), Opus 10*, 1832I; *Etudes (12), Opus 25*, 1836I;

A *Births*   B *Deaths*   C *Debuts*   D *New Positions*
E *Prizes/Honors*

Fantasia in A on Polish Airs, Opus 13, 1828I; *Fantasie in f/A♭, Opus 49,* 1841I; *Funeral March, Opus 72/2,* 1827I; *Funeral March in b♭ (from Sonata, Opus 35),* 1837I; *Grand Concert Rondo in F,* 1828I; *Impromtu in f♯, Opus 36,* 1839I; *Impromtu in G♭, Opus 51,* 1842I; *Introduction & Rondo, Opus 16,* 1832I; *Mazurka in A♭, Opus 7/4,* 1824I; *Mazurka in g, Opus 67/2,* 1849I; *Mazurka in f, Opus 69/4,* 1849I; *Mazurkas (2),* 1826I; *Mazurkas (4), Opus 17,* 1833I; *Mazurkas (4), Opus 30,* 1837I; *Mazurkas (4), Opus 33,* 1838I; *Mazurkas (3), Opus 41,* 1839I; *Mazurkas (3), Opus 50,* 1841I; *Mazurkas (3), Opus 56,* 1843I; *Mazurkas (3), Opus 59,* 1845I; *Mazurkas, Opus 63 (3),* 1846I; *Mazurkas (2), Opus 68,* 1829I; *Nocturne in g, Opus 15,* 1833I; *Nocturnes (2), Opus 32,* 1837I; *Nocturnes (2), Opus 48,* 1841I; *Nocturnes (2), Opus 55,* 1843I; *Nocturnes (2), Opus 62,* 1846I; *Nocturne in e, Opus 72/1,* 1827I; *Piano Concerto No. 1 in e, Opus 11,* 1830I; *Piano Concerto No. 2 in f, Opus 13,* 1830I; *Piano Pieces (3), Opus 70,* 1829I; *Piano Sonata in c, Opus 4,* 1828I; *Piano Sonata in b, Opus 58,* 1844I; *Piano Trio in g, Opus 8,* 1829I; *Polish Songs (17), Opus 74,* 1836I; *Polonaise in C, Opus 3,* 1829I; *Polonaise in A, Opus 40,* 1838I; *Polonaise in c, Opus 40/2,* 1839I; *Polonaise in A♭, Opus 53,* 1842I; *Polonaise in f♯, Opus 44,* 1841I; *Polonaise, Opus 71/1,* 1825I; *Polonaises (2), Opus 71/2,3,* 1828I; *Prelude in c♯, Opus 45,* 1841I; *Rondo in c, Opus 1,* 1825I; *Scherzo in b, Opus 20,* 1832I; *Scherzo in b♭, Opus 31,* 1837I; *Scherzo in c♯, Opus 39,* 1839I; *Scherzo in E, Opus 54,* 1842I; *Songs (6), Opus 74,* 1845I; *Variations on German National Air,* 1826I; *Variations, "Souvenir de Paganini,"* 1829I; *Variations in B♭ on "Làci darem," Opus 2,* 1827I; *Waltz in A♭, Opus 42,* 1840I; *Waltzes (3), Opus 64,* 1847I

Chou Wen-Chung: *Clouds* (string quartet), 1996I; *Beijing in the Mist,* 1985I; *Echoes from the Gorge,* 1989I

Christoff, Dimiter: *Piano Sonata No. 1,* 1962I; *Piano Sonata No. 2,* 1974I; *Piano Sonata No. 3,* 1974I; *Piano Sonata No. 4,* 1974I; *Piano Sonata No. 5,* 1992I; *Piano Sonata No. 6,* 1992I

Christoskov, Peter: *Bulgarian Caprices (24),* 1977I

Churches, Richard: *Requiem Mass,* 1999I

Ciampi, Vincenzo: *Arsinoe,* 1758I; *Antigona,* 1762I; *Arias* (12) Six with Recitative, 1754I; *Armore in caricatura,* 1761I; *Catone in Utica,* 1756I; *Il chimico,* 1757I; *Il clemenza di Tito,* 1757I; *Didone,* 1754I; *Gianguir,* 1759I; *Missa solemnis,* 1758I; *Te Deum,* 1758I; *Vexillum fidei,* 1759I; *Virgines prudentes et fatuae,* 1760I

Cilèa, Francesco: *Adriana Lecouveur,* 1902I; *L'Arlésiana,* 1897I

Cimadoro, Giovanni Battista: *Pimmaglione,* 1790I

Cimarosa, Domenico: *Absolamo,* 1782I; *Achille all'assedio diTroja,* 1797I; *Alessandro nell'Indie,* 1781I; *L'amor constante,* 1782I; *Amor rende sagace,* 1793I; *Angelica et Medoro,* 1783I; *L'apprensivo raggirato,* 1798I; *L'armida immaginaria,* 1777I; *Artaserse,* 1781I; *Artemisia, regina di Caria,* 1797I; *Le astuzie femminili,* 1794I; *Atene edificata,* 1788I; *La ballerina amonte,* 1782I; *La bella greca,* 1784I; *Bella Italia,* 1799I; *Cajo Mario,* 1780I; *La Cleopatra,* 1789I; *Concerto in G for Two Flutes,* 1793I; *Il credulo,* 1786I; *Le donne rivali,* 1780I; *La ergine del sole,* 1788I; *L'eroe cinese,* 1782I; *Il falegname,* 1780I; *Il fanatico per gli antichi romani,* 1777I; *La finta parigina,* 1773I; *I finti nobili,* 1780I; *La frascatana nobile,* 1776I; *Giannina e Bernardone,* 1781I; *Il giorno felice,* 1775I; *Giuditta,* 1782I; *Gli Orazi ed i Curiazi,* 1796I; *Gli amanti comici,* 1778I; *Gloria parti,* 1769I; *L'impegno superato,* 1795I; *L'impresario in angustie,* 1786I; *L'imprudente fortunato,* 1797I; *L'infedeltà fedele,* 1779I; *L'italiana in Londra,* 1779I; *Magnificat,* 1769I; *Il marito disperato,* 1785I; *Mass in F* (male voices), 1765I; *Mass in C,* 1772I; *Mass in D,* 1776I; *Mass in G,* 1782I; *Mass in E♭,* 1796I; *Mass in c,* 1799I; *Il matirio,* 1795I; *I matrimoni in burla,* 1776I; *Il matrimonio segreto,* 1792I; *I nemici generosi,* 1796I; *Nina e Martuffo,* 1783I; *Le nozze in garboglio,* 1795I; *L'Olimpiade,* 1784I; *Penelope,* 1795I; *Requiem pro defunctis in g,* 1787I; *Il retorno di Don Caladrino,* 1778I; *Il sacrificio d'Abramo,* 1786I; *Il secreto,* 1798I; *Semiramide,* 1799I; *La serenata non preveduta,* 1791I; *Le stravaganze del conte,* 1772I; *Le stravaganze d'amore,* 1778I; *Te Deum,* 1798I; *I traci amanti,* 1793I; *I tre amanti,* 1777I; *Il trionfo della fede,* 1794I; *La vanità delusa,* 1784I; *La villana riconosciuta,* 1783I

Claflin, Avery: *Hester Prynne,* 1933I; *Lament for April 15,* 1955I; *Uncle Tom's Cabin,* 1964I

Clapp, Philip G.: *String Quartet in c,* 1909I; *Symphony No. 1 in E,* 1910; *Symphony No. 2 in e,* 1914I; *Symphony No. 3 in E♭,* 1917I; *Symphony No. 4 in A,* 1919I; *Symphony No. 5 in D,* 1926I; *Symphony No. 6 in B, "Golden Gate,"* 1926I; *Symphony No. 7 in A,* 1928I; *Symphony No. 8 in C,* 1930I; *Symphony No. 9 in e, "Pioneers,"* 1931I; *Symphony No. 10 in F, "Heroic,"* 1935I; *Symphony No. 11 in in C,* 1942I; *Symphony No. 12 in B♭,* 1944I

Clay, Frédéric: *Lalla Rookh,* 1877I

Cleary, David: *String Quartet No. 1,* 1988I; *String Quartet No. 2,* 1991I

Clementi, Muzio: *Capriccios (2), Opus 47,* 1821I; *Fantasie with Variations, Opus 48,* 1821I; *Gradus ad Parnassum,* 1817I; *Piano Sonatas (3), Opus 50,* 1821I; *Piano Sonatas (3), Opus 40,* 1802I; *Piano Concerto in C,* 1796I; *Piano Sonata in E♭, Opus 41,* 1804I; *Piano Trios (3), Opus 27,* 1791I; *Piano Sonata in B♭, Opus 46,* 1820I; *Symphonies (2), Opus 18,* 1787I; *Symphony in D, Opus 44,* 1819I

Clifford, Hubert: *Symphony 1940,* 1940I

❀

F *Biographical*   G *Cultural Beginnings*   H *Musical Literature*
I *Musical Compositions*

Cloidt, Jay: *Karoshi*, 1995I
Coates, Eric: *Four Ways Suite*, 1928I; *London Suite*, 1933I; *Sleepy Lagoon*, 1930I
Coates, Gloria: *Homage to Van Gogh*, 1993I; *Indian Sounds*, 1991I; *Leonardo da Vinci*, 1979I; *Natural Voice & Electronic Sound*, 1973I; *Piano Structures*, 1972I; *The Planets*, 1974I; *String Quartet No. 1*, 1966I; *String Quartet No. 2*, 1972I; *String Quartet No. 3*, 1976I; *String Quartet No. 4*, 1977I; *String Quartet No. 5*, 1988I; *Symphony No. 1, "Music on Open Strings,"* 1973I; *Symphony No. 2, "Music in Abstract Lines,"* 1987I; *Symphony No. 3, "Nocturne for Strings,"* 1978I; *Symphony No. 3, "Symphony Nocturne,"* 1985I; *Symphony No. 4, " Chiaroscuro,"* 1990I; *Symphony No. 5*, 1985I; *Symphony No. 6, "Music in Microtones,"* 1986I; *Symphony No. 7*, 1991I; *Symphony No. 8, "Indian Sounds,"* 1991I; *Symphony No. 9*, 1994I; *Symphony No. 10*, 1994I; *Symphony No. 11, "Philomen & Baucis,"* 1998I
Cocchi, Gioacchino: *Demetrios*, 1757I; *Il pazzo glorioso*, 1753I; *I semiramide*, 1757I; *Il tutore*, 1752I
Cochereau, Pierre: *Improvisations on St. Matthew*, 1984I; *Variations on a Chromatic Theme*, 1963I
Coelho, Ruy: *String Quartet No. 1*, 1910I; *String Quartet No. 2*, 1923I
Coerne, Louis A.: *Excalibur*, 1921I; *Hiawatha*, 1893I; *Organ Concerto in E*, 1892I; *String Quartet in c, Opus 19*, 1893I; *Suite in d for Strings*, 1892I; *The Trojan Women*, 1917I; *A Woman of Marblehead*, 1897I; *Zenobia*, 1902I
Cogan, Philip: *The Contract*, 1782I
Cohan, George M.: *Over There*, 1917I
Cohen, Fred: *Woodwind Trio*, 1992I
Cohen, Steve: *Sax Quartet No. 2*, 1998I
Cohn, Arthur: *String Quartet No. 1, "Four Preludes,"* 1928I; *String Quartet No. 2*, 1930I; *String Quartet No. 3*, 1932I; *String Quartet No. 4*, 1935I; *String Quartet No. 5*, 1935I; *String Quartet No. 6*, 1945I
Cohn, James: *Piano Trio*, 1990I; *Wind Quintet No. 2*, 1992I
Cole, Rosetter G.: *The Broken Troth, Opus 32*, 1917I; *The Maypole Lovers*, 1931I; *Meditation, Opus 29*, 1914I; *Overture, Pioneer, Opus 35*, 1918I; *The Passing of Summer*, 1888I; *Rhapsody, Opus 30*, 1914I; *The Rock of Liberty, Opus 36*, 1920I; *Symphonic Prelude, Opus 28*, 1914I; *Violin Sonata in D, Opus 8*, 1892I
Cole, Ulric: *Fantasy Sonata*, 1933I; *Piano Concerto No. 1*, 1930I; *Piano Concerto No. 2*, 1942I
Coleridge-Taylor, Samuel: *The Blind Girl of Castel Cuille*, 1901I; *The Death of Minnehaha*, 1899I; *Endymion's Dream*, 1909I; *Hiawatha's Departure*, 1900I; *Hiawatha's Wedding Feast*, 1898I; *Meg Blane*, 1902I; *Symphony in A*, 1896I; *Toussaint l'Ouverture*, 1901I
Colgrass, Michael: *Arctic Dreams* (band), 1991I; *As Quiet As*, 1966I; *Concerto for Two Pianos*, 1982I; *Déjà Vu*, 1977I; *The Earth's a Baked Apple*, 1968I; *Letters from Mozart* (piano, orchestra), 1976I; *New People*, 1969I; *Piano Metamusic*, 1981I; *The Schubert Birds*, 1989I; *Snow Walker*, 1990I; *Theater of the Universe*, 1977I
Collett, John: *Symphonies (6), Opus 2*, 1766I; *Violin Solos (6), Opus 1*, 1758I
Collins, Edward J.: *Mardi Gras*, 1923I; *A Tragic Overture*, 1923I
Cone, Edward T.: *New Weather*, 1933I; *Philomela*, 1954I; *Prelude, Passacaglia & Fugue*, 1957I; *Serenade*, 1975I
Connolly, Justin: *Symphony*, 1991I
Conradi, August: *Rübezahl*, 1847I
Consoli, Marc-Antonio: *Afterimages*, 1982I; *Cello Concerto*, 1988I; *Greek Lyrics*, 1988I; *Naked Masks*, 1980I; *Odefonia*, 1976I; *Pensieri Sosposi*, 1997I; *String Quartet No. 1*, 1983I; *String Quartet No. 2*, 1990I; *Varie Azioni for Piano*, 1995I; *Vicu Siculani*, 1979I; *Violin Concerto*, 1988I
Constant, Franz: *Concertino Solstice*, 1994I
Constantinides, Dinos: *Antigone*, 1993I
Converse, Charles: *American Concert Overture on "Hail Columbia,"* 1869I; *Converse* (What a Friend We Have in Jesus), 1868I; *Fest-Ouverture*, 1870I
Converse, Frederick: *American Sketches*, 1935I; *Ave atque vale*, 1917I; *La belle dame sans merci*, 1902I; *Elegiac Poem*, 1928I; *Endymion's Narrative*, 1901I; *Euphrosyne Overture*, 1903I; *The Festival of Pan*, 1900I; *Flivver Ten Million*, 1927I; *Job*, 1906I; *Night & Day, Two Poems after Whitman*, 1901I; *Ormazd*, 1912I; *Overture, Youth*, 1897I; *The Peace Pipe*, 1914I; *Piano Sonata*, 1935I; *Piano Trio in e*, 1932I; *The Pipe of Desire*, 1905I; *Prophecy*, 1932I; *Song of the Sea*, 1924I; *String Quartet No. 1 in e*, 1935I; *String Quartet No. 2 in a*, 1904I; *Symphony No. 1*, 1920I; *Symphony No.1 in d*, 1898I; *Symphony No. 2*, 1921I; *Symphony No. 3 in F*, 1936I; *Violin Concerto*, 1902I
Cooke, Arnold: *Clarinet Sonata*, 1955I
Cooke, Francis J.: *Piano Variations in G*, 1982I; *Symphony 1994*, 1994I; *Symphony 1990*, 1990I
Cooper, Paul: *Piano Frescoes*, 1994I; *Piano Intermezzi, (4)*, 1980I; *Piano Sonata No. 1*, 1949I; *Piano Sonata No. 2*, 1963I; *Sinfonia for Piano*, 1989I; *String Quartet No. 1*, 1952I; *String Quartet No. 2*, 1954I; *String Quartet No. 3*, 1959I; *String Quartet No. 4*, 1964I; *String Quartet No. 5*, 1975I; *String Quartet No. 6*,

---

❈

1977I; *Symphony No. 1*, 1954I; *Symphony No. 2*, 1956I; *Symphony No. 3 for Strings*, 1971I; *Symphony No. 4*, 1975I

Cope, David: *Arena*, 1974I; *Glassworks*, 1979I; *Piano Sonata No. 1*, 1960I; *Piano Sonata No. 4*, 1967I; *Spirals*, 1972I; *String Quartet, In Memoriam*, 1991I; *String Quartet No. 1*, 1961I; *String Quartet No. 2*, 1963I

Copland, Aaron: *Appalachian Spring*, 1944I; *Billy the Kid*, 1938I; *Canticle of Freedom*, 1955I; *The Cat & the Mouse*, 1920I; *Clarinet Concerto*, 1948I; *Connotations for Orchestra*, 1962I; *Dance Symphony*, 1925I; *Danzon Cubano for Two Pianos*, 1942I; *Grogh*, 1925I; *In the Beginning*, 1947I; *Inscape*, 1967I; *A Lincoln Portrait*, 1942I; *Moods (3)*, 1926I; *Music for a Great City*, 1964I; *Music for Radio*, 1937I; *Music for the Theater*, 1925I; *Nonet*, 1960I; *Old American Songs, Set I*, 1950I; *Old American Songs, Set II*, 1952I; *Orchestral Variations*, 1957I; *Our Town*, 1940I; *Outdoor Overture*, 1938I; *Piano Concerto*, 1926I; *Piano Fantasy*, 1957I; *Piano Sonata*, 1941I; *Piano Variations*, 1930I; *Poems by Emily Dickinson (12)*, 1950I; *Proclamation for Piano*, 1973I; *The Quiet City*, 1939I; *Rodeo*, 1942I; *El salón México*, 1936I; *The Second Hurricane*, 1937I; *A Short Symphony*, 1933I; *Statements for Orchestra*, 1934I; *Symphonic Ode*, 1929I; *Symphony for Organ & Orchestra*, 1924I; *Symphony No. 3*, 1946I; *The Tender Land*, 1954I; *Threnody I (Igor Stravinsky: In Memoriam)*, 1971I; *Threnody II (Beatrice Cunningham: In Memoriam)*, 1973I; *Violin Sonata*, 1943I; *Vitebsk for Piano Trio*, 1929I

Coppola, Anton: *Sacco & Vanzetti*, 2000I

Cordero, Roque: *Centennial Symphonic Tribute*, 1997I; *Meditaciones Poéticas (3)*, 1995I; *Piano Concerto*, 1944I; *Piano Sonata*, 1985I; *Piano Sonata breve*, 1966I

Corghi: *Divara–Wasser & Blut*, 1993I

Corigliano, John: *Chiaroscuro for Piano*, 1997I; *Clarinet Concerto*, 1977I; *The Cloisters*, 1965I; *Dylan Thomas Trilogy I*, 1961I; *Dylan Thomas Trilogy II*, 1970I; *Dylan Thomas Trilogy III*, 1976I; *Fantasia on an Ostinato*, 1986I; *A Figaro for Antonia*, 1986I; *Gazebo Dances for Piano*, 1972I; *The Ghosts of Versailles*, 1991I; *Kaleidoscope for Two Pianos*, 1959I; *Oboe Concerto*, 1975I; *Of Rage & Remembrance*, 1991I; *Phantasmagoria*, 1993I; *Piano Concerto*, 1968I; *Piano Etude Fantasy*, 1977I; *Piano Fantasia on an Ostinato*, 1985I; *Pied Piper Fantasy* (flute concerto), 1982I; *Promenade Overture*, 1981I; *The Red Violin*, 1998I; *String Quartet No. 1*, 1995I; *Symphony No. 1*, 1989I, 1990I; *Symphony No. 2*, 2000I; *Three Hallucinations*, 1982I; *To Music*, 1995I; *Troubadours* (guitar concerto), 1993I; *Violin Sonata*, 1963I; *Vocalise*, 1999I; *Voyage*, 1988I

Cornelius, Peter: *The Barber of Bagdad*, 1858I; *Brautlieder*, 1856I; *Le Cid*, 1865I; *Requiem for Male Chorus*, 1852I; *Weihnachtslieder, Opus 8*, 1856I

Corrette, Michel: *Livre d'orgue*, 1756I; *Noëls with Variations*, 1783I; *Pièces pour l'orgue dans un genre nouveau*, 1787I; *Tenebrae Lessons*, 1784I

Corri, Domenico: *The Travelers*, 1806I

Cortez, Luis Jaime: *Flute Sonata*, 1992I; *String Quarteto X*; *Symphony No. 1, "Lluvias,"* 1991I; *Symphony No. 2, "En blanco y negro,"* 1995I; *Las Tentaciones de San Antonio*, 1996I

Costa, Michael: *Malina*, 1829I; *Il carcere d'Ildegonda*, 1828I; *Don Carlos*, 1844I; *Eli*, 1855I; *Une heure à Naples*, 1832I; *Kenilworth*, 1831I; *Sir Huon*, 1833I

Coste, Napoleon: *Fantasy de Concert, Opus 6*, 1837I; *Variations and Finale, Opus 2*, 1830I

Coulthard, Jean: *Piano Sonata No. 1*, 1948I

Cowell, Henry: *American Pipers*, 1943I; *Ancient Desert Drone*, 1940I; *The Banshee*, 1925I; *Harmonica Concerto*, 1960I; *Harp Concerto*, 1965I; *Percussion Concerto*, 1958I; *Piano Concerto*, 1928I; *Quartet Euphometric*, 1919I; *Sinister Resonance*, 1935I; *String Quartet No. 1, "Pedantic,"* 1916I; *String Quartet No. 2, "Movement,"* 1928I; *String Quartet No. 3, "Mosaic,"* 1935I; *String Quartet No. 4, "United,"* 1936I; *String Quartet No. 5*, 1956I; *Symphony No. 1 in b*, 1918I; *Symphony No. 1 in C*, 1869I; *Symphony No. 2 in f*, 1872I; *Symphony No. 2, "Anthropos,"* 1938I; *Symphony No. 3, "Gallic,"* 1942I; *Symphony No. 4, "Short Symphony,"* 1946I; *Symphony No. 5*, 1948I; *Symphony No. 6*, 1955I; *Symphony No. 7*, 1952I; *Symphony No. 8*, 1952I; *Symphony No. 9*, 1953I; *Symphony No. 10*, 1953I; *Symphony No. 11*, 1953I; *Symphony No. 12*, 1956I; *Symphony No. 13, "Madras,"* 1958I; *Symphony No. 14*, 1960I; *Symphony No. 15*, 1960I; *Symphony No. 16, "Icelandic,"* 1962I; *Symphony No. 17*, 1963I; *Symphony No. 18*, 1964I; *Symphony No. 19*, 1965I; *Symphony No. 20*, 1965I; *Symphony No. 21*, 1965I; *Synchrony*, 1931I; *The Tides of Manaunaun*, 1912I; *Variations for Orchestra*, 1956I

Crawford-Seeger, Ruth: *String Quartet No. 1*, 1931I

Creston, Paul: *Accordion Concerto*, 1958I; *Ceremonial*, 1972I; *Concerto for Two Pianos*, 1951I; *Dance Overture*, 1954I; *Dance Variations*, 1942I; *Dances (5), Opus 1*, 1932I; *Frontiers*, 1943I; *Lydian Ode*, 1956I; *Metamorphoses, Opus 84*, 1964I; *Narratives (3), Opus 79*, 1962I; *The Northwest*, 1969I; *Out of the Cradle Endlessly Rocking*, 1934I; *Piano Concerto*, 1949I; *Piano Preludes (6), Opus 38*, 1945I; *Piano Sonata, Opus 9*, 1936I; *Piano Trio*, 1979I; *Saxophone Concerto*, 1941I; *Saxophone Sonata, Opus 19*, 1939I; *String Quartet*

Creston, Paul: (*cont.*)
No. 1, Opus 8, 1936I; *Suite for Saxophone Quartet,* 1979I; *Symphony No. 1,* 1941I; *Symphony No. 2, Opus 35,* 1945I; *Symphony No. 3, Opus 48,* 1950I; *Symphony No. 4,* 1952I; *Symphony No. 5,* 1956I; *Symphony No. 6, "Organ,"* 1982I; *Thanatopsis,* 1971I; *Two-Part Inventions, Opus 14,* 1937I; *Violin Concerto No. 1,* 1956I; *Violin Concerto No. 2,* 1960I
Crist, Bainbridge: *Colored Stars,* 1921I
Crockett, Donald: *Celestial Mechanics,* 1990I; *Ecstatic Songs I,* 1989I; *Ecstatic Songs II,* 1995I; *Horn Quintet, "Barca,"* 1999I; *Short Stories,* 1995I; *String Quartet No. 1, "Array,"* 1987I; *String Quartet No. 2,* 1993I; *The Tenth Muse,* 1986I; *Whistling in the Dark,* 1999I
Cross, Gordon: *Cello Concerto,* 1976I
Crotch, William: *Palestine,* 1812I
Crouce, Frederick: *Kathleen Mavourneen,* 1840I
Crumb, George: *Ancient Voices of Children,* 1970I; *Apparition: Elegiac Songs & Vocalises,* 1979I; *Black Angels,* 1970I; *Cello Sonata,* 1955I; *Drones & Refrains of Death,* 1968I; *Early Songs (3),* 1947I; *Echoes of Time & the River,* 1967I; *Eleven Echoes of Autumn, 1965,* 1965I; *Gnomic Variations for Piano,* 1981I; *A Haunted Landscape,* 1984I; *Lux Aeterna for Five Masked Players,* 1971I; *Madrigals, Book I,* 1965I; *Madrigals, Book II,* 1965I; *Madrigals, Book III,* 1969I; *Madrigals, Book IV,* 1969I; *Makrokosmos I for Piano,* 1972I; *Makrokosmos II for Piano,* 1973I; *Makrokosmos III for Piano,* 1974I; *Makrokosmos IV for Piano,* 1978I; *Mundus Canis: Five Humoresques,* 1998I; *Night Music I,* 1963I; *Night Music II,* 1963I; *Night of the Four Moons,* 1969I; *Nocturnes (4),* 1964I; *Pastoral Drone for Organ,* 1982I; *Piano Pieces (5),* 1962I; *Star Child,* 1977I; *Variazioni,* 1959I; *Zeitgeist for Piano,* 1987I
Cui, César: *Angelo,* 1876I; *Barcarolle, Opus 81,* 1910I; *Bolero, Opus 17,* 1811I; *The Captain's Daughter,* 1909I; *Choruses (2), Opus 4,* 1860I; *Choruses (7), Opus 28,* 1885I; *Choruses (6), Opus 53,* 1895I; *Choruses (6), Opus 63,* 1903I; *Choruses (7), Opus 77,* 1908I; *Les deux ménétriers, Opus 42,* 1890I; *Echoes of War, Opus 66,* 1905I; *Kaleidoscope, Opus 50,* 1893I; *Mam'zelle Fifi,* 1900I; *The Mandarin's Son,* 1859I; *Marche Solennelle, Opus 18,* 1881I; *Matteo Falcone,* 1901I; *Mickiewicz Songs (6), Opus 71,* 1907I; *Miniatures (12), Opus 20,* 1882I; *Morceaux (2), Opus 36,* 1885I; *Nekrasov Poems (21), Opus 72,* 1902I; *Orchestral No. 2, Opus 38,* 1887I; *Petite Suite, Opus 14,* 1879I; *Piano Pieces (3), Opus 8,* 1877I; *Piano Pieces (5), Opus 52,* 1900I; *Piano Pieces (4), Opus 60,* 1901I; *Piano Pieces (5), Opus 83,* 1911I; *Piano Preludes (21), Opus 62,* 1903I; *Piano Preludes (25), Opus 64,* 1902I; *Piano Suite, Opus 21,* 1883I; *Piano Variations (18), Opus 100,* 1916I; *Pieces (3) for Two Pianos, Opus 69,* 1907I; *Poèmes (20) de Jean Richepin, Opus 44,* 1890I; *Poems (7), Opus 33,* 1886I; *The Prisoner of the Caucasus,* 1858I; *Psalms, (3), Opus 80,* 1910I; *Pushkin Poems (25), Opus 57,* 1899I; *Scherzos (3), Opus 81,* 1910I; *Sonatina, Opus 106,* 1916I; *Songs (3), Opus 3,* 1857I; *Songs (6), Opus 5,* 1861I; *Songs (6), Opus 7,* 1869I; *Songs (6), Opus 9,* 1874I; *Songs (6), Opus 10,* 1876I; *Songs (6), Opus 11,* 1877I; *Songs (6), Opus 13,* 1878I; *Songs (6), Opus 16,* 1879I; *Songs (6), Opus 27,* 1884I; *Songs (5),"Der maner Franz Schuberts,"* 1893I; *Songs & Duets (7), Opus 19,* 1881I; *Songs for Male Voices (2), Opus 58,* 1901I; *String Quartet No. 1 in c,* 1890I; *String Quartet No. 2 in D, Opus 68,* 1907I; *String Quartet No. 3 in E♭,* 1913I; *Suite No. 4, Opus 40, "A Argenteau,"* 1887I; *Suite Concertante, Opus 25,* 1883I; *Tarantella for Orchestra,* 1859I; *Theme & Variations, Opus 61,* 1901I; *Theme, Variations & Prelude, Opus 104,* 1916I; *Tolstoy Songs (18), Opus 67,* 1904I; *Violin Sonata, Opus 84,* 1870I; *William Ratcliff,* 1869I
Cumming, Richard: *Silhouettes for Piano,* 1993I; *We Happy Few,* 1963I
Cummings, Conrad: *Dinosaur Music,* 1981I; *endangered species,* 1977I; *Subway Songs,* 1974I; *Tonkin,* 1993I
Currier, Nathan: *From the Grotto,* 1995I; *A Musical Banquet,* 1987I
Currier, Sebastian: *Theo's Notebook,* 1992I; *Vocalissimus,* 1991I
Curtis-Smith, Curtis: *Clarinet Trio,* 2000I; *Concerto for Piano, Left Hand,* 1990I; *Fantasy Pieces for Piano,* 1987I; *Great American Symphony-GAS!,* 1982I; *Masada for Piano,* 1973I; *Masquerades for Organ,* 1978I; *The Mystic Trumpeter,* 1991I; *Piano Etudes (12),* 2000I; *Piano Trio No. 2,* 1992I; *Symphony No. 2, "African Laughter,"* 1996I; *Unisonics,* 1976I
Czerny, Carl: *Piano Sonata No. 1 in A♭, Opus 7,* 1810I; *Variations Concertantes (20),* 1805I
Dahl, Ingolf: *Concerto A Tre for Clarinet, Violin & Cello,* 1947I; *Concerto for Saxophone &Wind Orchestra,* 1949I; *Piano Quintet,* 1957I; *Piano Sonata seria,* 1953I; *Piano Trio,*1962I; *Prelude & Fugue,* 1939I; *Sinfonietta,* 1961I; *Sonata Pastorale,* 1959I; *String Quartet No. 2,* 1958I; *Tower of Santa Barbara,* 1955I
Dahl, Viking: *Maison de fous,* 1920I
Dalayrac, Nicolas: *Adèle et Dorsan,* 1795I; *Adolphe et Clara,* 1799I; *Agnès et Olivier,* 1791I; *Alexis,* 1798I; *L'amant-statue,* 1785I; *Ambroise,* 1793I; *Arnill,* 1799I; *Azémia,* 1786I; *Laboucle de cheveux,* 1802I; *Camille,* 1791I; *Le chêne patriotique,* 1790I; *Le chevalier à lamode,* 1811I; *Le corsaire,* 1783I; *Deux mots,* 1806I; *Les deux petits savoyards,* 1789I; *Les deux sérénades,* 1788I; *Les deux soupers,* 1783I; *Les deux tuteurs,* 1784I; *L'éclipsetotale,* 1782I; *Elise-Hortense,* 1809I; *La famille américaine,* 1796I; *Fanchette,* 1788I; *Gulistan,* 1805I; *Gulnare,* 1798I; *Une heure de mariage,* 1804I; *La jeune prude,* 1804I; *Koulouf,* 1806I; *La leçon,* 1797I;

A *Births*   B *Deaths*   C *Debuts*   D *New Positions*
E *Prizes/Honors*

Léhéman, 1801I; *Lina*, 1807I; *La maison isolée*, 179I; *Maison à vendre*, 1800I; *Marianne*, 1796I; *Nina*, 1786I; *La pauvre femme*, 1795I; *Lepavillon des fleurs*, 1809I; *Le petit souper*, 1781I; *Philippe et Georgette*, 1791I; *Le poèteet le musicien*, 1809I; *Primerose*, 1798I; *La prise de Toulon*, 1794I; *Raoul, sire decrequi*, 1789I; *Sargines*, 1788I; *La soirée orageuse*, 1790I; *String Quartets (6)*, 1781I; *Urgande et Merlin*, 1793I; *Vert-Vert*, 1790I

Dalbavie, Marc-André: *Diademes*, 1986I

Dallapiccola, Luigi: *Canti di Liberazione*, 1955I; *Canti di Prigoniera*, 1941I; *Odysseus*, 1968I; *Ilprigioniero*, 1948I; *Quanderno Musicale di Annalibera*, 1952I; *Sonatina Canonica onPaganini Caprices*, 1943I; *Variations for Orchestra*, 1954I; *Marsia*, 1942I

Damase, Jean-Michael: *Ochelata's Wedding*, 1999I; *Pastorales (4) for Organ*, 1993I; *Rhapsodie* (horn concerto), 1986I; *Theme & Variations*, 1994I; *Variation on a Theme by Mozart*, 1994I

Damrosch, Leopold: *Ruth and Naomi*, 1875I

Damrosch, Walter: *Cyrano de Bergerac*, 1913I; *The Man Without a Country*, 1937I; *The OperaClerk*, 1942I; *The Scarlet Letter*, 1896I

Danielpour, Richard: *Anima Mundi*, 1995I; *Canticle of Peace*, 1995I; *Celestial Night*, 1997I; *Cello Concerto*, 1994I; *Concerto for Orchestra*, "Zorastrian Riddles," 1996I; *Elegy: Symphony in Five Movements*, 1997I; *The Enchanted Garden*, 1992I; *Metamorphosis* (piano), 1993I; *Piano Concerto No. 1*, 1981I; *Piano Concerto No. 2*, 1993I; *PianoQuintet*, 1988I; *Piano Sonata*, 1986I; *Prologue & Prayer*, 1982I; *Song of Remembrance*,1991I; *Songs of the Night*, 1993I; *Sonnets to Orpheus*, 1992I; *Sonnets to Orpheus II*,1994I; *Spirits in the Well*, 1998I; *String Quartet No. 1*, 1983I; *String Quartet No. 2,*"Shadow Dances," 1993I; *String Quartet No. 3*, "Psalms of Sorrow," 1994I; *Sweet Talk*, 1996I; *Symphony No. 1*, "Dona nobis pacem," 1985I; *Symphony No. 2*, "Visions," 1986I; *Symphony No. 3*, 1989I; *Symphony No. 3*, "Journey without Distance," 1989I; *Towardthe Splendid City*, 1992I; *Urban Dances*, 1997I

Daniels, Mabel Wheeler: *The Desolate City*, 1913I; *The Holy Star*, 1928I; *Song of Jael*, 1939I; *Songs of Elfland*, 1924I

Dankner, Stephen: *String Quartet No. 3*, 1992I; *String Quartet No. 4*, 1993I; *String Quartet No. 5*, 1993I

Danner, Christian: *Violin Concerto*, 1785I

Danzi, Franz: *L'Abbé di l'Attaignant*, 1817I; *Abraham auf Moria*, 1808I; *Azakia*, 1780I; *LeBondocani*, 1802I; *Camille und Eugen*, 1812I; *Cleopatra*, 1780I; *Deucalion et Pirrha*,1795I; *Dido*, 1811I; *Das Freudenfest*, 1804I; *Iphigenie in Aulis*, 1807I; *Der Kuss*, 1799I; *Laura Rosetti*, 1781I; *Malina*, 1814I; *Die Mitternachtstunde*, 1799I; *Der Quasi-Mann*,1789I; *Rübezahl*, 1813I; *Der Sylphe*, 1788I; *Symphonie concertante in B♭, Opus 41*,1813I; *Symphonie concertante in B♭, Opus 47*, 1818I; *Symphony No. 1 in D* (?), 1790I; *Symphony No. 2 in d, Opus 19* (?), 1796I; *Symphony No. 3 in C, Opus 20*, 1804I; *Symphonies No. 4 & 5*, 1817I; *Der Triumph der Treue*, 1789I; *Turandot*, 1817I; *ViolinSonata in f, Opus 33*, 1821I; *Wind Quintets (3), Opus 56*, 1821I

Danzi, Margarete: *Violin Sonata*, 1799I

Dargomijsky, Alexander: *Esmeralda*, 1839I; *Russalka*, 1856I; *The Stone Guest*, 1869I; *DerTriumph des Bacchus*, 1845I

Dashow, James: *Far Sounds, Broken Cries*, 1999I; *Media Survival Kit*, 1996I; *Songs from a Spiral Tree*, 1986I; *Sul Filo dei Tramonti*, 2000I

Daugherty, Michael: *Jackie O*, 1997I; *Niagara Falls*, 1997I; *Sing Sing: J. Edgar Hoover*, 1992I

Dauvergne, Antoine: *Alphée et Aréthuse*, 1762I; *Les amours de Tempe*, 1752I; *Canente*, 1760I; *La coquette trompée*, 1753I; *Enée et Lavinie*, 1758I; *Les fêtes d'Euterpe*, 1758; *Herculemourant*, 1761I; *Polyxene*, 1763I; *Le prix de la valeur*, 1771I; *La sibylle*, 1753I; *Lesicilien*, 1780I; *La tour enchantée*, 1770I; *Les troqueurs*, 1753I

Davaux, Jean-Baptiste: *Cécilia*, 1786I; *Quartets (6), Opus 6*, 1773I; *Symphonies (2), Opus 8*,1775I; *Symphonies (3), Opus 11*, 1784I; *Symphonies concertantes (2), Opus 7*, 1773I; *Symphonies concertantes (2), Opus 8*, 1776I; *Symphonies concertantes (2), Opus 5*, 1772I; *Symphonies concertante (2), Opus 12*, 1784I; *Symphonies concertante (2), Opus 13*, 1787I; *Théodore*, 1785I; *Trios (6) for Strings, Opus 15*, 1792I

David, Félicien: *La captive*, 1864I; *Christophe Colomb*, 1847I; *Le désert*, 1844I; *L'eden*, 1848I; *Esquisses symphoniques (6)*, 1857I; *Le fermier de Franconville*, 1857I; *Herculanum*,1859I; *Le jugement dernier*, 1849I; *Lalla Rookh*, 1862I; *The Last Judgment*, 1858I; *Moses at Sinai*, 1846I; *La Perle de Brésel*, 1851I; *Les perles d'orient*, 1845I; *Symphony No. 1 in F*, 1837I; *Symphony No. 3 in E♭*, 1846I; *Symphony No. 4 in c*, 1849I

David, Ferdinand: *Le saphir*, 1865I

David, Johann N.: *Chaconne & Fugue for Organ*, 1962I; *Chaconne in a*, 1927I; *Fantasia super"L'homme armé*," 1929I

David, Johann Nepomuk: *Flute Concerto*, 1934I; *Organ Concerto*, 1965I; *Partita on B-A-C-H for Organ*, 1964I; *Passacaglia & Fugue in g*, 1928I; *Ricercare in c*, 1925I; *Toccata &Fugue for Organ*, 1962I; *Twelve Fugues in All Keys, Opus 66*, 1968I; *Violin ConcertoNo. 1*, 1952I; *Violin Concerto No. 2*, 1957I

❊

F   *Biographical*   G   *Cultural Beginnings*   H   *Musical Literature*
I   *Musical Compositions*

David, Samuel: *Le génie de la terre*, 1859I; *Jephté*, 1858I
Davidov, Karl: *Cello Concerto No. 2*, 1863I
Davidovsky, Mario: *Biblical Songs*, 1990I; *Concerto for String Quartet*, 1989I; *Divertimento for Cello & Orchestra*, 1985I; *Electronic Study I*, 1961I; *Electronic Study II*, 1962I; *Festino*, 1994I; *Flashbacks*, 1995I; *Quartetto*, 1993I; *Quartetto for Oboe & String Trio*, 1996I; *Songs from Shir-ha-shirim*, 1977I; *String Quartet No. 1*, 1954I; *String Quartet No. 2*, 1958I; *String Quartet No. 3*, 1976I; *String Quartet No. 4*, 1980I; *String Trio*, 1982I; *Synchronism No. 1*, 1963I; *Synchronism No. 2*, 1964I; *Synchronism No. 3*, 1965I; *Synchronism No. 4*, 1967I; *Synchronism No. 6*, 1970I; *Synchronism No. 7*, 1973I; *Synchronism No. 8*, 1974I; *Synchronisms No. 10*, 1992I
Davidson, Tina: *Billy & Zelda*, 1998I; *Bleached Thread, Sister Thread*, 1991I; *Fire on the Mountain*, 1993I
Davies, Peter Maxwell: *The Beltane Fire*, 1995I; *Blind Man's Buff*, 1972I; *Caroline Mathilde*, 1990I; *Dark Angels*, 1974I; *The Doctors of Myddgai*, 1996I; *Fantasia on "O Magnummysterium,"* 1960I; *Job*, 1997I; *The Lighthouse*, 1979I; *The Martyrdom of St. Magnus*, 1976I; *The Medium*, 1981I; *A Mirror of Whitening Light*, 1977I; *Miss Donnithorne's Maggot*, 1974I; *Nocturnal Dances*, 1970I; *Notre Dame des Fleurs*, 1966I; *O Magnum Mysterium*, 1960I; *Organ Sonata*, 1982I; *Orkney Saga I*, 1997I; *Peliqui domum meum*, 1996I; *Piano Concerto*, 1997I; *Piano Sonata*, 1981I; *Piccolo Concerto*, 1997I; *Revelation & Fall*, 1965I; *Richard II*, 1961I; *The Road to Colonnus*, 1991I; *Salome*, 1978I; *Secret Songs (6) for Piano*, 1993I; *Solstice of Light*, 1979I; *Songs for a Mad King (8)*, 1969I; *A Stone Litany*, 1975I; *Strathclyde Concerto No. 1*, 1986I; *StrathclydeConcerto No. 2*, 1987I; *Strathclyde Concerto No. 8* (orchestra), 1996I; *Symphony No. 1*, 1976I; *Symphony No. 2*, 1980I; *Symphony No. 3*, 1984I; *Symphony No. 4*, 1989I; *Symphony No. 5*, 1994I; *Symphony No. 6*, 1996I; *Taverner*, 1968I; *Thaw*, 1995I; *Time & the Raven*, 1995I; *Trumpet Concerto*, 1988I; *Voluntaries (3) for Organ*, 1976I; *The Well*, 1981I; *Witch*, 1992I
Davis, Anthony: *Armistad*, 1997I; *X*, 1985I; *Tania*, 1991I; *Under the Double Moon*, 1989I
Davy, John: *Alfred the Great*, 1798I
Dawson, Ted: *Dragon Songs*, 1998I; *Symphony No. 1*, 1996I
Dawson, William: *Negro Folk Symphony*, 1931I; *Piano Trio*, 1925I; *Violin Sonata*, 1927I
Deák, Csaba: *Anemones de Felix*, 1994I; *Symphony for Wind Orchestra*, 1995I
Deane, Raymond: *After-Pieces for Piano*, 1990I; *Macabre Trilogy I: Marche Oubilés for Piano*, 1996I; *Macabre Trilogy II: Catacombs*, 1994I; *Macabre Trilogy III: Seachange*,1994I; *The Wall of Cloud*, 1997I
Debussy, Claude: *Arabesques (2)*, 1888I; *Ballades de François Villon (3)*, 1910I; *Beau Soir*, 1878I; *La belle au bois dormant*, 1883I; *Cello Sonata No. 1*, 1915I; *Chansons de Bilitis*, 1897I; *Children's Corner*, 1908I; *Claire de lune* (song), 1884I; *Danses sacrée et profane*, 1904I; *L'enfant prodigue*, 1884I; *Estampes*, 1903I; *Etudes, Book I*, 1915I; *Etudes, Book II*, 1915I; *Fantasy for Piano and Orchestra*, 1889I; *Fêtes Galantes, Set I*, 1892I; *Fêtesgalantes, Set II*, 1904I; *Iberia* 1908I; *Images, Book 1*, 1905I; *Images, Book II*, 1907I; *Jeux*, 1912I; *The Martyrdom of St. Sebastian*, 1911I; *Masques*, 1904I; *La mer*, 1905I; *Pelleas et Mélisande*, 1902I; *Petite suite*, 1889I; *Piano Preludes, Book 1*, 1910I; *Piano Préludes, Book II*, 1913I; *Piano Trio No. 1 in G*, 1880I; *Poems of Mallarmé (3)*, 1913I; *Pour le piano*, 1901I; *Prélude à l'après-midi d'un faune*, 1894I; *Printemps*, 1887I; *Printemps* (song), 1882I; *Rêverie*, 1890I; *Rhapsody for Saxophone & Orchestra*, 1905I; *Rhapsody No. 1 for Clarinet*, 1910I; *Rondes de printemps*, 1909I; *Sonata for Flute, Violaand Harp*, 1916I; *String Quartet in g, Opus 10*, 1893I; *Symphony in g*, 1880I; *Syrinx forSolo Flute*, 1912I; *Three Nocturnes*, 1899I; *Violin Sonata No. 3*, 1917I
Decker, Pamela: *Flores del desierto*, 1998I; *Kairos*, 1996I; *Nightsong & Ostinato Dances*, 1992I; *Retablos*, 1997I
Decoust, Michel: *A jamais d'ombre*, 1997I; *Cabaret X*, 1998I; *Cello Octet*, 1996I; *Homage to Maurice Ravel*, 1987I; *Les mains déliées*, 1998I; *Les pas du temps*, 2000I
DeFesch, Willem: *Mr. Defesch's Songs Sung at Marybone Gardens*, 1753I
De Koven, Reginald: *The Algerian*, 1893I; *The Begum*, 1888I; *The Canterbury Pilgrims*, 1917I; *Don Quixote*, 1889I; *The Fencing Master*, 1892I; *The Highwayman*, 1897I; *The Knickerbockers*, 1893I; *The Little Duchess*, 1901I; *Oh, Promise Me*, 1889; *The Red Feather*, 1903I; *Rip Van Winkle*, 1920I; *Rob Roy*, 1894I; *Robin Hood*, 1890I; *The Student King*, 1906I; *The Three Dragoons*, 1899I; *The Tzigane*, 1895I; *The Wedding Trip*, 1911I
De Lamarter, Eric: *Masquerade Overture*, 1916I; *Organ Concerto No. 1 in E*, 1920I; *Organ Concerto No. 2 in A*, 1922I
Delage, Maurice: *Contrerimes*, 1927I; *Haiku (7)*, 1925I; *Poèmes hindous (4)*, 1921I; *String Quartet in d*, 1949I
Delaney, Robert: *John Brown's Song*, 1931I
Delgado, Alexandre: *String Quartet No. 1*, 1991I; *Tresvariacoes*, 1999I
Delibes, Léo: *Le boeuf Apis*, 1865I; *Coppélia*, 1870I; *La cour du roi Pétaud*, 1869I; *Deux sousde charbon*, 1856I; *Deux vieilles gardes*, 1856I; *Les eaux d'Ems*, 1861I; *L'écossais de Chatou*, 1869I; *La fille du golfe,*

A   *Births*   B   *Deaths*   C   *Debuts*   D   *New Positions*
               E   *Prizes/Honors*

1859I; *Grande nouvelle*, 1864I; *Le jardinier et sonseigneur*, 1863I; *Jean de Nivelle*, 1880I; *Lakmé*, 1883I; *Maître Griffard*, 1857I; *Mon ami Pierrot*, 1862I; *Monsieur de Bonne-Etoile*, 1860I; *Les musiciens de l'orchestre*, 1861I; *L'omelette à la Follembuche*, 1859I; *Le roi s'amuse*, 1882I; *Le roi l'a dit*, 1873I; *Leserpent à plumes*, 1864I; *Six demoiselles à marier*, 1856I; *La source*, 1866I; *Sylvia*, 1876I

DeLio, Thomas: *as though*, 1994I; *not*, 1992I; *though, on*, 1996I

Delius, Frederick: *Appalachia*, 1896I, 1902I; *Brigg Fair: An English Rhapsody*, 1907I; *Caprice & Elegy (cello)*, 1930I; *Cello Concerto*, 1921I; *Cello Sonata*, 1916I; *Dance Rhapsody No. 1*, 1908I; *Dance Rhapsody No. 2*, 1916I; *Double Concerto for Violin & Cello*, 1916I; *English Songs (3)*, 1891I; *Eventyr*, 1917I; *Fantastic Dance*, 1931I; *Fennimore & Gerda*,1910I; *Florida* (suite), 1886I; *Florida Suite*, 1887I; *Hassan*, 1923I; *Hiawatha*, 1888I; *Idylle de Printemps*, 1889I; *In a Summer Garden*, 1908I; *Irmelin*, 1892I; *Irmelin Prelude*, 1931I; *Koanga*, 1897I; *A Late Lark*, 1925I; *Légende* (violin), 1895I; *La lune blanche*,1910I; *The Magic Fountain*, 1895I; *Margot la rouge*, 1902I; *A Mass of Life*, 1905I; *Midsummer Song*, 1908I; *Mitternachslied*, 1898I; *North Country Sketches*, 1914I; *Old English Lyrics (4)*, 1915I; *On Craig Dhu*, 1907I; *On Hearing the First Cuckoo in Spring*, 1912I; *Over the Hills and Far Away*, 1897I; *Paa Vidderne*, 1892I; *Paris: Song of a GreatCity*, 1899I; *Petite Suite*, 1889I; *Piano Concerto in c*, 1897I; *Piano Pieces (5)*, 1923I; *Piano Preludes (3)*, 1923I; *A Poem of Life & Love*, 1919I; *Requiem*, 1916I; *Romance for Violin & Piano*, 1889I; *Romance for Cello & Piano*, 1896I; *Sakuntala*, 1889I; *Sea Drift*,1904I; *A Song before Sunrise*, 1918I; *A Song of Summer*, 1929I; *Song of the High Hills*,1912I; *Songs (2) of Verlaine*, 1895I; *Songs of Farewell*, 1930I; *Songs of Sunset*, 1907I; *Songs (7) from the Norwegian*, 1890I; *Songs to be Sung of a Summer Night on the Water (2)*, 1917I; *The Splendor Falls on Castle Wells*, 1923I I; *String Quartet No. 1*, 1888I; *String Quartet No. 2*, 1893I; *String Quartet No. 3*, 1916I; *Summer Landscape*, 1902I; *Summer Night on the River*, 1911I; *Three Small Tone Poems*, 1890I; *A Village Romeo & Juliet*, 1901I; *Violin Concerto*, 1916I; *Violin Sonata No. 1*, 1905I; *Violin Sonata No. 2*,1923I; *Violin Sonata No. 3*, 1930I; *Wanderer's Song*, 1908I; *Zanoni*, 1888I

Della Maria, Dominique: *Il maestro di cappella*, 1792I

Dello Joio, Norman: *Air Power* (MT), 1957I; *Blood Moon*, 1961I; *Colonial Variants*, 1976I; *Concert Music*, 1945I; *Concert Variations for Piano*, 1980I; *Concertato for Clarinet & Orchestra*, 1949I; *Concerto for Two Pianos*, 1941I; *Divertimento*, 1997I; *The Duke of Sacramento*, 1942I; *Evocations*, 1970I; *Fantasy & Variations for Piano*, 1962I; *The Glass Heart*, 1968I; *Harp Concerto*, 1947I; *Introduction & Fantasies on a Chorale Theme*, 1986I; *Lyric Piano Pieces*, 1971I; *Mass*, 1976I; *Meditations on Ecclesiastes*, 1956I; *The Mystic Trumpeter*, 1943I; *Nativity*, 1987I; *New York Profiles*, 1949I; *Nocturnes (2)*, 1946I; *Piano Diversions*, 1975I; *Piano Images (5)*, 1967I; *Piano Ricercari*, 1946I; *Piano Sonata No. 1*, 1933I; *Piano Sonata No. 2*, 1944I; *Piano Sonata No. 3*, 1948I; *Piano Suite*, 1940I; *Prairie*, 1942I; *Short Intervallic Etudes for Piano*, 1988I; *Sinfonietta*, 1941I; *String Quartet No. 1*, 1974I; *String Quartet No. 2, "Lyrical Interludes,"* 1997I; *Symphony: The Triumph of St. Joan*, 1951I; *A Time of Snow*, 1968I; *The Trial at Rouen*, 1956I; *Trumpet Sonata*, 1979I; *Variations & Capriccio*, 1947I; *Variations, Chaconne & Finale*, 1947I

Del Tredici, David: *Adventures Underground*, 1971I; *An Alice Symphony*, 1969I; *All In the Golden Afternoon*, 1981I; *Annotated Alice*, 1976I; *Baritone Songs (3)*, 1999I; *Brother*, 1997I; *Child Alice*, 1986I; *Final Alice*, 1976I; *In Memory of a Summer Day*, 1980I; *In Wonderland*, 1975I; *Lobster-Quadrille*, 1969I; *March to Tonality*, 1985I; *Quaint Events*, 1982I; *The Spider & the Fly*, 1998I; *Syzygy*, 1966I; *Tattoo*, 1988I; *Vintage Alice*, 1972I

Delz, Christoph: *Nocturnes (2)*, 1986I; *Piano Concerto*, 1985I

Demenga, Thomas: *Concerto for Two Cellos*, 1990I

Denisov, Edison: *Alto Sax Sonata*, 1970I; *Chamber Symphony No. 2*, 1994I; *L'écume des jours*, 1985I; *Peinture*, 1970I; *Piano Concerto*, 1975I; *Piano Variations 1961*, 1961I; *PianoVariations on a Theme by Handel*, 1986I; *Pictures of Paul Klee (3)*, 1985I; *Signes enblanc for Piano*, 1974I; *Sonata for Alto Sax & Cello*, 1994I; *Sun of the Incas*, 1964I; *Sun of the Incas*, 1964I

Denza, Luigi: *Funiculi, Funiculà*, 1880I

Deparc, Henri: *Poème Nocturne*, 1874I

De Plessis, Hubert: *Symphony No. 1*, 1954I

Deshayes, Prosper-Didier: *Bello*, 1795 I; *Jepthé*, 1786I; *Les macchabées*, 1780I; *Zelia*, 1791I

Dessau, Paul: *Einstein*, 1973I; *Little Piano Pieces (4)*, 1955I; *Piano Etudes (12)*, 1932I; *Piano Sonata*, 1914I; *String Quartet No. 1*, 1932I; *String Quartet No. 2*, 1943I; *String Quartet No. 3*, 1946I; *String Quartet No. 4*, 1948I; *String Quartet No. 5*, 1955I; *Suite No. 3,"Lenin,"* 1969I; *Symphony No. 1*, 1926I; *Symphony No. 2*, 1934I

Dessoff, Felix: *String Quartet in F*, 1878I

Destouches, André: *Die Hussiten vor Naumburg*, 1804I; *Turandot*, 1802I; *Wilhelm Tell*, 1804I

Destouches, Franz von: *Die Braut von Messino*, 1803I; *Die Jungfrau von Orleans*, 1803I; *Das Missverständniss*, 1805I; *Der Teufel und der Schneider*, 1843I; *Die Thomasnacht*, 1792I; *Wanda*, 1808I

Dett, R. Nathanie: *Bible Vignettes (8)*, 1943I; *The Chariot Jubilee*, 1921I; *The Cinnamon Grove Suite*, 1928I; *Enchantment Suite*, 1922I; *In the Bottoms Suite*, 1912I; *Magnolia Suite*, 1911I; *Music in the Mine*, 1916I; *The Ordering of Moses*, 1937I; *Tropic Winter Suite*, 1938I

Devienne, François: *Bassoon Concerto No. 1 in C*, 1785I; *Bassoon Concerto No. 2*, 1794I; *Bassoon Concerto No. 3 in F*, 1790I; *Bassoon Concerto No. 4 in C*, 1793I; *Flute Concerto No. 1 in D*, 1782I; *Flute Concerto No. 2 in D*, 1783I; *Flute Concerto No. 3 in G*, 1784I; *Flute Concerto No. 6 in D*, 1794I; *Flute Concerto No. 7 in e*, 1787I; *Flute Concerto No. 8 in G*, 1794I; *Flute Concerto, No. 9 in e*, 1793I; *Flute Concerto, No. 10 in D*, 1802I; *Flute Concerto No. 11 in b*, 1806I; *Flute Concerto No. 12 in A/a*, 1806I; *Grand Symphony in D, "La Bataille de Gemmapp,"* 1794I; *Horn Concerto No. 1 in C*, 1785I; *Mariage clandestin*, 1790I; *Ouverture* (wind band), 1794I; *Overture, La bataille de Gemmapp*, 1794I; *Quartets (6), Flute & Strings, Book I*, 1783I; *Quartets (6), Flute &Strings, Book II*, 1786I; *Quartets (3), Flute & Strings, Book III*, 1791I; *Quartets (6), Flute & Strings, Book IV*, 1793I; *Quartets (6), Flute & Strings, Book V*, 1793I; *Symphonie concertante No. 1 in F*, 1785I; *Symphonie concertante No. 2 in C*, 1785I; *Symphonie concertante No. 3 in F, Opus 22*, 1788I; *Symphonie concertante No. 4 in B♭,Opus 25*, 1788I; *Symphonie concertante No. 5 in F*, 1791I; *Symphonie concertante in G,*1794I; *Symphonie concertante in F*, 1797I; *Symphonie concertante in G, Opus 76*, 1799I; *Trios (6), Opus 17*, 1782I; *Trios (6), Flutes, Cello, Opus 19*, 1787I; *Woodwind Trios (6), Opus 6*, 1795I; *Woodwind Trios (6), Opus 27*, 1790I

De Vocht, Lodewijk: *Cello Concerto*, 1956I

Devreese, Frédéric: *Overture for Large Orchestra*, 1983I; *Piano Concerto No. 1*, 1949I

Dezede, Nicolas: *Alexis et Justine*, 1785I; *Auguste et Théodore*, 1789I; *Balise et Babet*, 1783I; *Cécile*, 1780I; *L'erreur d'un moment*, 1773I; *Fatmé*, 1777I; *Julie*, 1772I; *Mélito Cécile etErmance*, 1792I; *Paulin et clairette*, 1792I; *Péronne sauvée*, 1783I; *Le porteur de chaise*, 1778I; *Le stratagème découvert*, 1773I; *Les trois fermiers*, 1777I; *A Trompeur, trompeuret demi*, 1780I; *Zulima*, 1778I

Dhomont, Francis: *AvatArsSon*, 1998I; *Convulsive*, 1995I; *Frankenstein Symphony*, 1997I; *Lettrede Sarajevo*, 1996I; *Les moirures du temps*, 1999I; *Objets retrouvés, "In MemorianPierre Schaeffer,"* 1996I; *Ricercare*, 1998I; *Studio de Nuit*, 1992I; *Vol d'arondes*, 1999I

Di Domenica, Robert: *Dream Journeys*, 1984I; *Variations & Soliloquies*, 1988I

Diabelli, Anton: *Adam in der Klemme*, 1809I

Diamond, David: *Cello Concerto*, 1938I; *Cello Sonata No. 1*, 1938I; *Cello Sonata No. 2*, 1987I; *Clarinet Trio*, 1994I; *Concert Piece for Orchestra*, 1940I; *Concerto for Two Pianos,*1942I; *Flute Concerto*, 1985I; *Kaddish* (cello concerto), 1989I; *Organ Symphony*, 1987I; *Partita for Oboe, Bassoon & Piano*, 1935I; *Piano Concerto*, 1950I; *Piano Prelude, Fantasy & Fugue*, 1983I; *Piano Quartet*, 1936I; *Piano Quartet No. 2*, 1972I; *Piano Quintet No. 1*, 1972I; *Piano Quintet No. 2*, 1996I; *Piano Sonata No. 1*, 1947I; *Piano Sonata No. 2*, 1972I; *Piano Sonatina No. 1*, 1935I; *Piano Sonatina No. 2*, 1987I; *Piano Trio*, 1932I; *Psalm Ninety-Eight*, 1991I; *Quintet in b for Flute, Piano & String Trio*, 1937I; *Romeo & Juliet*, 1947I; *Rounds*, 1944I; *String Quartet No. 1*, 1940I; *String Quartet No. 2*, 1943I; *String Quartet No. 3*, 1946I; *String Quartet No. 4*, 1951I; *String Quartet No. 5*, 1960I; *String Quartet No. 6*, 1962I; *String Quartet No. 7*, 1963I; *String Quartet No. 8*, 1964I; *String Quartet No. 9*, 1966I; *String Quartet No. 10*, 1966I; *String Trio*, 1937I; *Symphony No. 1*, 1941I; *Symphony No. 2*, 1942I; *Symphony No. 3*, 1945I; *Symphony No. 4*, 1945I; *Symphony No. 5*, 1951I; *Symphony No. 6*, 1954I; *Symphony No. 7*, 1962I; *Symphony No. 8*, 1960I; *Symphony No. 9*, 1985I; *Symphony No. 11*, 1992I; *Violin Concerto No. 1*, 1936I; *Violin Concerto No. 2*, 1947I; *Violin Concerto No. 3*, 1960I; *Violin Sonata No. 1*, 1945I; *Violin Sonata No. 2*, 1981I; *The World of Paul Klee*, 1957I

Diazmuñoz, Eduardo: *Zonante*, 1980I

Dibdin, Charles: *The Shepherd's Artifice*, 1764I

Dickinson, Peter: *Comic Songs (3)*, 1960I; *A Dylan Thomas Song Cycle*, 1959I; *Organ Concerto*, 1971I; *Outcry*, 1969I; *Piano Concerto*, 1984I; *Surrealistic Landscape*, 1973I; *W. H. Auden Songs*, 1956I

Dickman, Stephen: *Cyrano*, 1997I; *Four for Tom*, 1997I; *King Arthur*, 1996I; *Maximus Song Cycle*, 1987I; *The Music of Eric Zann*, 1998I; *Pieces (4) for Piano*, 1971I; *Rabbi Nathan's Prayer*, 1995I; *Real Magic in New York*, 1971I; *Seven Dancing Princesses*, 1994I; *String Trio No. 1*, 1965I; *String Trio No. 2*, 1971I; *String Quartet No. 1*, 1967I; *String Quartet No. 2*, 1978I; *String Quartet No. 3*, 1978I; *String Quartet No. 4*, 1978I; *Tibetan Dreams*, 1990I; *Trees & Other Inclinations*, 1983I; *Winter Song*, 1989I; *Words No More*, 1993I

Diemer, Emma Lou: *Biblical Settings (4) for Organ*, 1993I; *Celebration for Organ*, 1970I; *Christmas Cantata*, 1988I; *Declarations for Organ*, 1973I; *Gloria*, 1996I; *Hymn Preludes (10)*, 1960I; *Kyrie*, 1993I; *Little Suite for Organ*, 1985I; *Marimba Concerto,*1990I; *Peace Cantata*, 1986I; *Piano Concerto*, 1991I; *Piano Pieces (3)*, 1991I; *Piano Variations*, 1987I; *Preludes to the Past for Orgn*, 1989I; *Santa Barbara Overture*, 1996I; *Serenade for String Orchestra*, 1988I; *Sextet*, 1992I; *Space Suite for Piano*, 1988I; *String Quartet No. 1*,

---

❄

A *Births*   B *Deaths*   C *Debuts*   D *New Positions*
E *Prizes/Honors*

1989I; *Symphony No. 1*, 1952I; *Symphony No. 2*, 1959I; *Symphony No.3*, *"Antique,"* 1961I; *Toccata & Fugue for Organ*, 1969I; *Toccata for Organ*, 1964I; *Trumpet Concerto*, 1983I; *Variation on "Rendez à Dieu" for Organ*, 1999I

Dijk, Jan van: *String Quartet No. 1*, 1940I; *String Quartet No. 2*, 1941I; *String Quartet No. 3*,1942I; *String Quartet No. 4*, 1965I; *String Quartet No. 5*, 1974I; *String Quartet No. 6*, 1994I

Dillon, James: *String Quartet No. 1*, 1983I; *String Quartet No. 2*, 1991

Dimas de Melo Pimenta, Emanuel: *Andromeda*, 1997I; *Area*, 1996I; *Gravitational Sounds*,1992I; *Olivestone*, 1999I; *Voglio Meere le Mia Montagne*, 1999I

Dinicu, Grigoras: *Hora Staccato*, 1906I

Distler, Hugo: *Kleine Organchoralbearbeitung (7)*, 1938I; *Organ Partita No. 1, Opus 8*, 1933I; *Organ Partita No. 2*, 1935I; *Organ Sonata, Opus 18*, 1939I

Distler, Johann G.: *String Quartets (3), Opus 1*, 1791I; *String Quartets (3), Opus 2*, 1795I; *String Quartets (6), Opus 6*, 1798I; *Violin Concerto*, 1791I

Dittersdorf, Carl Ditters von: *L'amore disprezzato*, 1771I; *L'arcifanfano, re de'matti*, 1776I; *Ilbarone di rocca antica*, 1776I; *Betrug durch Aberglauben*, 1786I; *La contadina fedele*,1776I; *Doktor und Apotheker*, 1786I; *Don Coribaldi* 1798I; *Don Quixotte der Zweite*,1795I; *L'Esther*, 1773I; *Il finto opazzo per amore*, 1772I; *Flute Concerto in e*, 1763I; *Das Gespenst mit der Trommel*, 1794I; *Giobbe*, 1786I; *Gott Mars und der Hauptmannvon Bärenzahm*, 1795I; *Harpsichord Concerto in B♭*, 1773I; *Hieronymus Knicker*,1789I; *Hokus-Pokus*, 1790I; *Isaac, figura del redentore*, 1766I; *Job*, 1780I; *Die lustigenWeiber von Windsor*, 1797I; *Der Mädchenmarkt*, 1797I; *Die Opera buffa*, 1798I; *Das Reich der toten*, 1767I; *Das Rote Käppchen*, 1788I; *Der Schachvan Schivas*, 1795I; *Der Schiffspatron*, 1789I; *Der schöne Herbsttag*, 1796I; *Six Symphonies, Opus 1*, 1766I; *Six Symphonies, Opus 4*, 1767I; *Lo sposo burlato*, 1775I; *String Quintets (6)*, 1782I; *String Quartets (6)*, 1788I; *String Quintets (6)*, 1789I; *Symphony in E♭, Opus 8/1*, 1766I; *Symphony in B♭, Opus 8/2*, 1767I; *Symphony in E♭,Opus 8, No. 3*, 1773I; *Symphonies (3), Opus 5*, 1769I; *Symphonies (3), Opus 6*, 1770I; *Symphonies (3), Opus 7*, 1773I; *Symphonies (6), Opus 13*, 1811I; *Symphonies (5)*, 1788I; *Der Teufel ein Hydraulikus*, 1790I; *Il tribunale di Giove*, 1774I; *Il tutore e la pupilla*, 1773I; *25,000 Gulden*, 1799I; *Ugolino*, 1796I; *Il viaggiatore americano in Joannesberg*, 1771I; *Viola Concertos (3)*, 1777I; *Violin Concertos (4)*, 1766I

Dlugoszewski, Lucia: *Fire Fragile Flight*, 1976I; *The Heidi Songs*, 1970I; *Music for the LeftEar*, 1958I; *Piano Sonata No. 1*, 1949I

Dobrzynski, Ignacy: *String Quartet No. 1*, 1829I

Dockstader, Tod: *Quartermass*, 1964I; *Two Moons of Quartermass*, 1964I; *Water Music*, 1963I

Dohnányi, Ernst von: *American Rhapsody, Opus 47*, 1953I; *Concert Etudes (6), Opus 28*, 1916I; *Harp Concerto*, 1952I; *Piano Concerto No. 1 in e, Opus 5*, 1898I; *Piano Concerto No. 2in b, Opus 42*, 1947I; *Piano Pieces, (4), Opus 2*, 1897I; *Piano Pieces (6), Opus 41*, 1945I; *Piano Quintet in C, Opus 1*, 1895I; *Piano Quintet No. 2 in E♭, Opus 26*, 1914I; *Piano Suite im alten Stil, Opus 24*, 1913I; *Rhapsodies (4), Opus 11*, 1903I; *Ruralia Hungarica*, 1924I; *Serenade in C, Opus 10*, 1902I; *Sextet for Clarinet, Horn, Piano &Strings*, 1933I; *String Quartet No. 1, Opus 7*, 1900I; *String Quartet No. 2, Opus 15*,1906I; *String Quartet No. 3 in a, Opus 33*, 1926I; *Suite en valse for Two Pianos, Opus 39a*, 1945I; *Suite in f♯, Opus 19*, 1909I; *Symphonic Minutes, Opus 36*, 1933I; *Symphony No. 1 in d, Opus 9*, 1897I; *Variations on a Nursery Song*, 1913I; *Variations on a Hungarian Folk Song, Opus 29*, 1917I; *Violin Concerto No. 1 in d*, 1915I; *Violin Concerto No. 2 in c, Opus 43*, 1950I; *Violin Sonata*, 1912I

Donatoni, Franco: *Esa*, 2000I

Donizetti, Gaetano: *Alahor di Granata*, 1826I; *A Silvio amante*, 1823I; *Alfredo il grande*, 1823I; *Alina, regina di Golconda*, 1828I; *Anna Bolena*, 1830I; *L'assedio di Calais*, 1836I; *L'Assunzione di Maria Vergine*, 1822I; *Belisario*, 1836I; *Betly*, 1836I; *Il borgomastro di Saardam*, 1827I; *Il campanello di notte*, 1836I; *Catarina Cornaro*, 1844I; *Chiara eserafina*, 1822I; *Colombo*, 1838I; *Daelia*, 1841I; *Il diluvio universale*, 1830I; *Don Gregorio*, 1824I; *Don Pasquale*, 1843I; *Don Sébastien*, 1843I; *Il duc d'Alba*, 1840I; *Elisabetta*, 1829I; *L'elisir d'amore*, 1832I; *Elvida*, 1826I; *Emilia di Liverpool*, 1824I; *English Horn Concertino in G*, 1817I; *Enrico di Borgogna*, 1818I; *L'esule di Roma*,1828I; *Il falegnamedi Livónia*, 1819I; *Fausta*, 1832I; *La favorite*, 1840I; *La fille durégiment*, 1840I; *Flute Sonata in d*, 1819I; *Follia, Una*, 1818I; *Il fortunato inganno*,1823I; *Francesca di Foix*, 1831I; *La fuga di Tisbe*, 1824I; *Il furioso all'isola di SanDomingo*, 1833I; *Gabriella de Vergy II*, 1839I; *Gemma di Vergy*, 1834I; *Gianni di Parigi*, 1831I; *Gloria Patri in F*, 1820I; *Un hiver à Paris*, 1839I; *Imelda di Lambertazzi*,1830I; *Inno reale*, 1828I; *L'ira d'Achille*, 1817I; *La lettera anonima*, 1822I; *Linda diChamounix*, 1842I; *Lucia di Lammermoor*, 1835I; *Lucrezia Borgia*, 1833I; *Magnificat in D*, 1819I; *Maria di Rohan*, 1843I; *Maria di Rudenz*, 1838I; *Maria Padilla*, 1841I; *Maria Stuarda*, 1834I; *Marino Faliero*, 1835I; *Matinée musicale*, 1841I; *Messa di Gloria in c*,1837I; *Le nozze in villa*, 1820I; *Nuits d'été à Pausilippe*, 1836I; *Olimpiade*, 1817I; *Olivoe Pasquale*, 1827I; *Otto mesi in due ore*, 1827I; *Il Paria*, 1829I;

Donizetti, Gaetano: (*cont.*)
  Parisina, 1833I; *Pastorale in E*, 1813I; *I pazzi per progetto*, 1830I; *Pia de'Tolomei*, 1837I; *Piano Sonatain a*,
  1820I; *Piano Sonatas (3, E♭, C,D)*, 1819I; *Piano Trio in E♭*, 1817I; *Il Pigmalione*, 1816I; *Requiem Mass (for
  Zingarelli)*, 1835I; *Rita*, 1841I; *Il ritorno di prima vera*, 1818I; *Robert Devereux*, 1837I; *La romanziera e
  l'uomo nero*, 1831I; *Rosamondad'Inghilterra*, 1834I; *Salve Regina in F*, 1819I; *Sinfonia in A*, 1813I; *Sinfonia
  in d*,1818I; *Sinfonias (3) in D, Sinfonia in g*, 1817I; *Sinfonias (2) in C*, 1816I; *Soiréesd'automne à
  l'infrascata*, 1837I; *String Quartet No. 2, 4*, 1818I; *String Quartet No. 5, 8*, 1819I; *String Quartet No. 15 in
  e*, 1836I; *String Quartets No. 9, 13*, 1821I; *String Quartet No. 14 in D*, 1825I; *String Quartet No. 1 in E♭*,
  1817I; *Teresa e Gianfaldoni*,1821I; *Torquato Tasso*, 1833I; *Ugo, conte di Parigi*, 1832I; *Violin Sonata in f*,
  1819I; *Lazingara*, 1822I; *Zoriada di Granata*, 1822I
Donovan, Richard: *Elizabethan Lyrics (5)*, 1957I; *Passacaglia on Vermont Folk Tunes*, 1949I; *Piano Suite No.
  1*, 1933I; *Songs for Soprano & String Quartet (4)*, 1933I
Dorati, Antal: *Piano Concerto*, 1974I; *Symphony No. 1*, 1957I; *Symphony No. 2, "Querela pacis,"* 1985I
Dorn, Heinrich: *Abu Kara*, 1831I; *Amour's macht*, 1830I; *Artaxerxes*, 1850I; *Der Banner von England*, 1841I;
  Die Bettlerin, 1827I; *Der Botenläufer von Pirna*, 1865I; *Gewitter bei Sonnenschein*, 1865I; *Das Hallelujah
  der Schöphfun*, 1847I; *Missa pro Deufunctis*,1851I; *Die Musiker von Aix-la-Chapelle*, 1848I; *Die
  Nibelungen*, 1854I; *Rolands Knappen*, 1826I; *Das Schwarmermädchen*, 1832I; *Die Sündflut*, 1849I; *Ein Tag
  in Russland*, 1856I; *Der Zauberer und das Ungethüm*, 1827I
Draeseke, Felix: *Cello Sonata No. 1 in c*, 1890I; *Symphony No. 3*, 1886I; *Viola Sonata No. 1 inc*, 1892I; *Viola
  Sonata No. 2 in F*, 1902I
Drattell, Deborah: *Central Park: Festival of Regrets*, 1999I
Dresher, Paul: *Are Are*, 1983I; *Awed Behavior*, 1993I; *Blue Diamonds*, 1995I; *Channels Passing/Study for
  Variations*, 1982I; *Dark Blue Circumstance*, 1983I; *Industrial Strength Music*, 1982I; *Other Fire*, 1984I;
  Power Failure, 1989I; *Race*, 1998I; *re: act: ion*, 1984I; *See Hear*, 1984I; *Slow Fire*, 1985I; *Stretch*, 1995I;
  Water Dreams, 1986I
Dreyer, Johann M.: *Te Deum*, 1800I
Drieberg, Friedrich von: *Don Cocagno*, 1812I; *Der Sänger und der Schneider*, 1814I
Drigo, Riccardo: *Les millions d'Arlequin*, 1900I
Druckman, Jacob: *Animus I*, 1966I; *Animus II*, 1968I; *Animus III*, 1969I; *Animus IV*, 1977I; *Athanor*, 1986I;
  Aureola, 1979I; *Brangle*, 1989I; *Chiaroscuro*, 1977I; *Counterpoise*, 1994I
Druschetzky, Georg: *Mass No. 7 in C*, 1804I
Dubensky, Arcady: *Russian Bells*, 1928I; *String Quartet No. 1 in C*, 1932I; *String Sextet in C*, 1933I;
  Symphony in g, 1916I; *Tom Sawyer Overture*, 1935I
Dubois, Théodore: *Aben-Hamlet*, 1884I; *Concert Overture in D*, 1865I; *Divertissement for Orchestra*, 1873I;
  Frithiof Overture, 1881I; *La guzla de l'Emir*, 1873I; *Overture in C*, 1879I; *Le pain bis*, 1879I; *Piano Concerto
  No. 2*, 1897I; *Piano Concerto Capriccioso*,1876I; *Les sept paroles du Christ*, 1867I; *Solemn Mass*, 1870I;
  Suite No. 2, 1877I; *Suite No. 1 for Orchestra*, 1874I; *Symphonie Française*, 1908I; *Trimphant Fantasy for
  Organ & Orchestra*, 1889I
Ducasse, Jean-Roger: *Motets (3)*, 1911I
Duckworth, William: *Mysterious Numbers*, 1996I; *The Time Curve Preludes*, 1978I
Duffy, John: *Symphony No. 1, "Utah,"* 1989I
Dukas, Paul: *Ariadne et Barbe-Bleu*, 1907I; *Götz von Berlichingen Overture*, 1884I; *King Lear Overture*,
  1883I; *La Peri*, 1912I; *Polyeuchte Overture*, 1891I; *Sémélé*, 1889I; *The Sorcerer's Apprentice*, 1897I;
  Symphony in C, 1896I; *Velléda*, 1888I; *Villanelle for Horn& Piano*, 1906I
Dukelsky, Vladimir: *Cello Concerto*, 1943I; *Epitaphs*, 1931I; *Symphony No. 1*, 1928I; *Symphony No. 2*,
  1929I; *Symphony No. 3*, 1947I; *Violin Concerto*, 1942I; *Zéphyr et Flore*, 1925I
Duni, Egidio: *La bonne fille*, 1761I; *La boutique de poète*, 1760I; *La buona figliuola*, 1756I; *Laclochette*, 1766I;
  Les deux chasseurs et la laitière, 1763I; *Le docteur Sangrado*, 1758I; *L'école de la jeunesse*, 1765I; *La fille mal
  gardée*, 1758I; *L'isle des foux*, 1760I; *Mazet*, 1761I; *Les moissonneurs*, 1768I; *Nina et Lindor*, 1758I;
  Olimpiade, 1755I; *Le peintreamoureux de son modèle*, 1757I; *Le rendez-vous*, 1763I; *Les sabots*, 1768I; *La
  semplicecuriosa*, 1751I; *Themire*, 1770I; *La veuve indécise*, 1759I
Duparc, Henri: *Aux Étoiles*, 1911I; *Feuilles volantes, Opus 1*, 1869I; *Lénore*, 1875I
Duprato, Jules-Laurent: *La fiancée de Corinthe*, 1867I
Dupré, Marcel: *Angélus, Opus 34*, 1936I; *L'annonciation, Opus 56*, 1956I; *Annunciation: In Memoriam, Opus
  61*, 1961I; *Antiennes pour le temps de Noël (6), Opus 48*, 1952I; *Lechemin de la croix, Opus 29*, 1931I;
  Chorale & Fugue, Opus 57, 1957I; *Chorales (2),Opus 59*, 1959I; *Chorales (79), Opus 28*, 1931I; *Cortège et
  Litanie, Opus 19*, 1921I; *Élévations, (3), Opus 32*, 1935I; *Entrée, Méditation, Sortie, Opus 62*, 1967I;
  Epithalame, 1948I; *Esquisses, (2), Opus 41*, 1945I; *Evocation, Opus 37*, 1941I; *La France au Calvaire, Opus*

A   *Births*   B   *Deaths*   C   *Debuts*   D   *New Positions*
             E   *Prizes/Honors*

49, 1953I; *Fugues modales (4), Opus 63*, 1968I; *Gregorian Preludes (8)*,1948I; *Hymnes, (3), Opus 58*, 1958I; *Inventions (24), Opus 50*, 1956I; *Lamento, Opus 24*,1926I; *Meditation for Organ*, 1966I; *Misere Mei, Opus 46*, 1948I; *Les nympheas, Opus 54*, 1959I; *Offrande à la Vierge, Opus 40*, 1944I; *Organ Concerto (Symphony) No. 1 in g, Opus 25*, 1928I; *Organ Concerto No. 2 in e, Opus 31*, 1934I; *Organ Pieces (7), Opus 27*, 1931I; *Organ Suite, Opus 39*, 1944I; *Organ Symphony No. 1*, 1928I; *Organ Symphony No. 2, Opus 26*, 1946I; *Piano Pieces (4), Opus 19*, 1921I; *Poème héroïque, Opus 33*, 1936I; *Préludes et Fugues (3), Opus 7*, 1912I; *Préludes & Fugues (3)*, Opus 36, 1938I; *Psalm XVIII, Opus 47*, 1949I; *Regina Coeli for Organ*, 1969I; *Scherzo, Opus 16*, 1919I; *Sonata for Cello & Organ*, 1964I; *Suite bretonne, Opus 21*, 1923I; *Symphonie-Passion, Opus 23*, 1924I; *Symphony No. 2, Opus 26*, 1925I; *Te Deum Paraphrase*, 1946I; *Letombeau de Titelouze, Opus 38*, 1943I; *Triptyque, Opus 51*, 1951I; *Variations in c♯, Opus 22*, 1924I; *Variations sur un vieux noël, Opus 20*, 1922I; *Les vêpres de la Vierge, Opus 18*, 1919I; *Vision, Opus 44*, 1947I; *The Way of the Cross, Opus 29*, 1932I
Dupuy, Edouard: *Felicie*, 1821I; *Youth and Folly*, 1806I
Durante, Francesco: *Mass in A*, 1753I; *S. Antonio de Padua*, 1754I
Duruflé, Maurice: *Mass*, 1967I; *Requiem, Opus 9*, 1947I
Dussek, Jan Ladislav: *Canzonets (6), C.200-5*, 1804I; *The Captive of Spillberg*, 1798I; *Choral Canons (6), C.215-20*, 1807I; *Fantasia & Fugue in f, Opus 50*, 1804I; *Flute/Violin Sonatas (3), Opus 4*, 1786I; *Flute Sonatas (3), Opus 7*, 1789I; *In Folk Tone, Opus 73*,1886I; *Notturno concertante in E♭, Opus 68*, 1809I; *Piano Concerto in E♭, Opus 3*,1787I; *Piano Concerto in F, Opus 14*, 1791I; *Piano Concerto in F, Opus 17*, 1792I; *Piano Concerto in B♭, Opus 22*, 1793I; *Piano Concerto in F, Opus 27*, 1794I; *Piano Concerto in C, Opus 29*, 1795I; *Piano Concerto in G, Opus 30*, 1795I; *Piano Concerto in B♭, Opus 40, "Military,"* 1798I; *Piano Concerto in g, Opus 49*, 1801I; *Piano Concerto in E♭, Opus 70*, 1810I; *Piano Concerto in B♭ for Two Pianos, Opus 63*, 1806I; *Concerto in f for Two Pianos*, 1807I; *Piano Fantasy in F, Opus 76*, 1811I; *Piano Quartet in E♭, Opus 56*, 1804I; *Piano Quintet in f, Opus 41*, 1799I; *Piano Sonatas (3), 4 Hands, Opus66*, 1811I; *Piano Sonata in F, 4 Hands, Opus 73*, 1813I; *Piano Sonatas (2), Opus 47*, 1801I; *Piano Sonata in C, Opus 48*, 1801I; *Piano Sonata in f♯, Opus 61*, 1807I; *Piano Sonata in E♭, Opus 72*, 1810I; *Piano Sonata in f, Opus 77*, 1811I; *Piano Sonata in D,Opus 69/3*, 1811I; *Piano Sonata, "Le retour à Paris," Opus 64*, 1807I; *Piano Sonata in B♭, 4 Hands, Opus 74*, 1811I; *Piano Sonatina in C, C.207*, 1806I; *Pizarro*, 1799I; *Solemn Mass, C.256*, 1811I; *Sonata in e♭, Opus 37*, 1799I; *Sonata in C for Flute andCello*, 1793I; *String Quartets (3), Opus 60*, 1806I; *Trio in F, Opus 65*, 1807I; *Trios (2), Harp, Violin, Cello, Opus 34*, 1797I; *Violin Sonatas (3), Opus 1*, 1782I; *Violin Sonatas (6), Opus 2*, 1786I; *Violin Sonatas (3), Opus 4*, 1787I; *Violin Sonatas (2), Opus 5*, 1788I; *Violin Sonatas (3), Opus 9*, 1789I; *Violin Sonatas (3), Opus 10*, 1789I; *Violin Sonatas(3), Opus 12*, 1790I; *Violin Sonatas (3), Opus 13*, 1790I; *Violin Sonatas (3), Opus 14*, 1791I; *Violin Sonatas (3), Opus 16*, 1791I; *Violin Sonatas (3), Opus 18*, 1792I; *Violin Sonatas (2), Opus 25/1,3*, 1795I; *Violin Sonatas (6), Opus 28*, 1795I; *Violin Sonatas (2), Opus 31/1,3*, 1795I; *Violin Sonata in C, Opus 36*, 1798I; *Violin Sonatas (3), Opus 69*,1811I
Dutilleux, Henri: *Le loup*, 1953I; *Métaboles*, 1964I; *Mystère de l'instant*, 1989I; *Piano Sonata*, 1948I; *Sarabande*, 1941I; *Shadows of Time: Five Episodes for Orchestra*, 1997I; *String Quartet "Ainsi la nuit,"* 1977I; *Summer's End*, 1981I; *Symphony No. 1*, 1951I; *Symphony No. 2, "Le double,"* 1959I; *Timbres, espace, mouvement*, 1978I; *Tout un monde lointain (cello & orchestra)*, 1970I; *Viola Concerto*, 1978I
Dvořáček, Jiří: *Organ Sonata*, 1979I
Dvořák, Antonin: *Alfred the Great*, 1870I; *The American Flag, Opus 102*, 1893I; *American Suitein A, Opus 98*, 1894I; *Armida, Opus 115*, 1903I; *Biblical Songs (10), Opus 99*, 1894I; *Carnaval Overture, Opus 92*, 1891I; *Cello Concerto in b, Opus 104*, 1895I; *Cello Sonata in f*, 1871I; *Clarinet Quintet in b♭*, 1869I; *Concert Overture in F*, 1871I; *The Cunning Peasant, Opus 37*, 1877I; *Cypresses*, 1865I; *Czech Suite, Opus 39*, 1879I; *The Devil and Kate, Opus 112*, 1899I; *Dimitri, Opus 64*, 1882I; *Dramatic (Tragic) Overture, Opus 1*, 1870I; *Duets (5), Opus 66*, 1875I; *Evening Songs, Opus 3*, 1882I; *Festival Song, Opus 113*, 1900I; *From the Bohemian Forests, Opus 68*, 1884I; *The Golden Spinning Wheel, Opus 109*, 1896I; *Gypsy Songs (7), Opus 55*, 1880I; *Heirs of the White Mountain, Opus 30*, 1872I; *The Hero's Song, Opus 111*, 1897I; *Humoresque in F♯*, 1884I; *Humoresques (8), Opus 101*, 1894I; *Hussite Overture, Opus 67*, 1883I; *Hymn of the Czech Peasants, Opus 28*, 1885I; *In Folk Tone, Opus 73*, 1885I; *In Nature's Realm, Opus 63*, 1882I; *The Jacobin, Opus 84*, 1888I; *Josef Kajétan Tyl*, 1882I; *King and Charcoal Burner*, 1871I; *Legends (10), Opus 59*, 1881I; *Love Songs, Opus 83*, 1888I; *Mass in D, Opus 86*, 1887I; *The Midday Witch, Opus 108*, 1896I; *Modern Greek Poems (3), Opus 50*, 1878I; *Moravian Duets (4), Opus 20*, 1875I; *Moravian Duets (13), Opus 29, 32*, 1876I; *Moravian Duets (4), Opus 38*, 1877I; *The Orphan, Opus 5*, 1871I; *Othello, Opus 93*, 1892I; *Overture, My Home, Opus 62*, 1881I; *Overture, In Nature's Realm, Opus 91*, 1891I; *Partsongs (5) A Capella, Opus 27*, 1878I; *Partsongs,(4), Opus 29*, 1876I; *Piano Concerto in g, Opus 33*, 1876I; *Piano Pieces, Opus 52*, 1880I; *Piano Quartet in D, Opus 23*, 1875I; *Piano Quartet in E♭, Opus 87*, 1889I; *Piano Quintet in A, Opus 5*, 1872I; *Piano Quintet in A, Opus 81*, 1887I; *Piano Trio in B♭, Opus 21*, 1875I; *Piano Trio in g,*

❖

F *Biographical*   G *Cultural Beginnings*   H *Musical Literature*
I *Musical Compositions*

Dvořák, Antonin: (cont.)
  Opus 26, 1876I; Piano Trio in f, Opus 65, 1883I; Piano Trio "Dumky," Opus 90, 1891I; The Pig-Headed
  Peasants, 1881I; Poetic Tone Pictures, Opus 85, 1889I; Preludes &Fugues, 1859I; Psalm 49, Opus 79, 1879I;
  Requiem Mass, Opus 89, 1890I; Rhapsody in a, Opus 15, 1874I; Romantic Pieces (4), Opus 75, 1887I;
  Romeo & Juliet Overture, 1873I; Rondo in g, Opus 94, 1891I; Rusalka, Opus 114, 1990I; Scherzo
  Capriccioso, Opus 66, 1883I; Serbian Folk Poems (4), Opus 6, 1872I; Serenade in E for Strings, Opus 22,
  1875I; Serenade in d, Opus 44, 1878I; Silhouettes (12), Opus 8, 1879I; Slavonic Dances, Series I, Opus 46,
  1878I; Slavonic Dances, Series 2, Opus 72, 1887I; Slavonic Rhapsodies (3), Opus 45, 1878I; Songs (4), Opus
  2, 1882I; Songs (6), Opus 7, 1872I; Songs (4), Opus 23, 1871I; Songs (3), Opus 45, 1877I; Songs (4), Opus
  82, 1888I; The Spectre's Bride, Opus 69, 1884I; St. Ludmilla, Opus 71, 1886I; Stabat Mater, Opus 58,1877I;
  String Quartet Movement in F, 1881I; String Quartet No. 1 in A, Opus 2, 1862I; String Quartet No. 2 in
  B♭, 1869I; String Quartet No.3 in D, 1869I; String Quartet No. 4 in e, 1870I; String Quartet No. 5 in f,
  Opus 9, 1873I; String Quartet No.6 in a, Opus 12, 1873I; String Quartet No. 7 in a, Opus 16, 1874I; String
  Quartet No. 8 in E, Opus 80, 1876I; String Quartet No. 9 in d, Opus 34, 1877I; String Quartet No. 10 in E♭,
  Opus 51, 1879I; String Quartet No. 11 in C, Opus 61, 1881I; String Quartet No. 12 in F, Opus 96,1893I;
  String Quartet No. 13 in G, Opus 106, 1895I; String Quartet No. 14 in A♭, Opus 105, 1895I; String Quintet
  in G, Opus 18/77, 1875I; String Quintet in a, Opus 1, 1861I; String Sextet in A, Opus 48, 1878I; The
  Stubborn Lovers, Opus 12, 1874I; Suite in A, Opus 98b, 1895I; Symphonic Poem in a, Opus 14, 1874I;
  Symphonic Variations, Opus 78, 1877I; Symphony No. 1 in c, Opus 31, "Bells of Zlonice," 1865I; Symphony
  No. 2 inB♭, Opus 41, 1865I; Symphony No. 3 in E♭, Opus 10, 1873I; Symphony No. 4 in d, Opus 13, 1874I;
  Symphony No. 5 in F, Opus 76, 1875I; Symphony No. 6 in D, Opus 60, 1880I; Symphony No. 7 in D, Opus
  70, 1885I; Symphony No. 8 in G, Opus 88, 1889I; SymphonyNo. 9 in e, "From the New World," 1893I; Te
  Deum, Opus 103, 1892I; Theme &Variations in A♭, Opus 36, 1876I; Vanda, Opus 25, 1875I; Violin Concerto
  in a, Opus 53, 1880I; Violin Sonata in a, 1873I; Violin Sonata in F, Opus 57, 1880I; Violin Sonatinain g,
  Opus 100, 1893I; Waltzes (8), Opus 54, 1880I; The Water-Sprite, Opus 107, 1896I; The Wood Dove, Opus
  110, 1896I
Dykes, John: Lux Benigna (Lead, Kindly Light), 1865I; Nicaea (Holy, Holy, Holy), 1861I; St.Agnes (Jesus,
  the Very Thought of Thee), 1866I
Dyson, George: The Canterbury Pilgrims, 1930I; In Honour of the City, 1928I
Dzubay, David: Cello Sonata, 1992I
Eaton, John: Ajax, 1972I; Concert Music for Clarinet, 1961I; Concert-Piece No. 2 for Synket,1966I; The Cry of
  Clytaemnestra, 1980I; Danton & Robespierre, 1978I; Duet for Syn-Ket & Synthesizer, 1968I; Genesis,
  1992I; Heracles, 1964I; Ma Barker, 1957I; Mass, 1970I; Microtonal Fantasy for Two Pianos, 1965I;
  Myshkin, 1971I; Peer Gynt, 1991I; Piano Trio: in Memoriam Mario Cristini, 1971I; Piano Variations, 1957I;
  Soliloquy, 1967I; Sonority Movement, 1971I; String Quartet No. 1, 1958I; Symphony No. 2, 1981I; The
  Tempest, 1985I; Tertullian Overture, 1958I; The Three Graces, 1972I
Eben, Petr: Annon Domini, 1999I; Biblical Dances for Organ, 1991I; Chorale Fantasias (2) for Organ, 1972I;
  Chorale Overtures (10) for Organ, 1971I; Faust for Organ, 1980I; Festive Preludes (2) for Organ, 1992I;
  Hommage à Dietrich Buxtehude, 1987I; Jeremias, 1997I; Job for Organ, 1987I; Laudes for Organ, 1964I;
  Love Songs (6), 1951I; Momentid'Organa, 1994I; The Most Secret Songs, 1952I; Organ Concerto No. 2,
  1983I; Piano Concerto, 1961I; Piano Quintet, 1992I; Prague Te Deum, 1990; Sunday Music, 1959I; Versetti,
  1982I; Versio ritmica for Organ, 1995I
Eberl, Anton: Concerto, Opus 45, for 2 Pianos, 1809I; Grand Piano Sonata, Opus 39, 1806I; Die Königin der
  Schwarzen Inseln, 1801I; La marchande des modes, 1787I; Piano Concerto No. 2, Opus 32, 1805I; Piano
  Concerto No. 3, Opus 40, 1807I; Symphony No.2, Opus 33, 1804I; Die Zigeuner, 1793I
Eckerberg, Sixten: Piano Concerto No. 1, 1943I; Piano Concerto No. 2, 1949I; Piano Concerto No. 3, 1971I
Eckert, Rinde: Dry Land Divine, 1988I
Edelmann, Jean-Frédéric: Clavecin Concerto, Opus 12, 1782I; Clavecin Sonatas (4), 1784I; Concerts (3),
  Clavecin & Strings, 1785I; Divertissements (2), Opus 3, 1776I; Esther, 1781I; Quartets (4), Opus 9, 1781I;
  Sinfonie pour le clavecin, Opus 4, 1776I; ViolinSonatas (6), Opus 1, 1775I; Violin Sonatas (6), Opus 2,
  1776I
Eder, Helmut: Organ Concerto "L'homme armé," Opus 50, 1969I; Partita on a Theme from J.N. David's Opus
  42, 1965I; String Quartet, 1985I; Vox media for Organ, 1969I
Edgar, Edward: Polonia, Opus 76, 1915I
Edlund, Lars: String Quartet No. 1, 1981I; String Quartet No. 2, 1993I
Edwards, George: Draconian Measures for Piano, 1976I; String Quartet No. 1, 1967I; String Quartet No. 2,
  1982I
Edwards, Julian: King Rene's Daughter, 1893I; Lazarus, 1907I; Madeleine, 1894I; The Wedding Day, 1897I
Edwards, Ross: Piano Concerto, 1982I; String Quartet, Enyato I, 1994I; Symphony Da Pacem Domine, 1991I

--- ❊ ---

    A   Births   B   Deaths   C   Debuts   D   New Positions
                    E   Prizes/Honors

Effinger, Cecil: *Cantata, Opus 111: From Ancient Prophets*, 1983I; *Cyrano de Bergerac*, 1965I; *Flute Sonata*, 1985I; *The Invisible Fire*, 1957I; *Landscape I*, 1966I; *Paul of Tarsus*,1968I; *Piano Concerto*, 1946I; *String Quartet No. 1*, 1943I; *String Quartet No. 3*, 1944I; *String Quartet No. 4*, 1947I; *String Quartet No. 5*, 1963I; *String Quartet No. 6*, 1985I; *Symphony No. 2*, 1946I; *Symphony No. 3*, 1954I; *Symphony No. 4*, 1952I; *Viola Sonata*,1944I; *Western Overture*, 1942I

Egge, Klaus: *Cello Concerto*, 1966I; *Piano Concerto No. 1, Opus 9*, 1937I; *Piano Concerto No. 2*, 1946I; *Piano Concerto No. 3*, 1974I; *Sonata No. 1, "Draumkvaedet," Opus 4*, 1933I; *Sonata No. 2, Opus 27*, 1955I; *Symphony No. 1, Opus 17*, 1942I; *Symphony No. 2, Opus 22*, 1947I; *Symphony No. 3, Opus 28*, 1957I; *Symphony No. 4*, 1968I; *Symphony No. 5*, 1969I; *Violin Concerto*, 1953I

Eggen, Arne: *Chaconne*, 1917I; *Symphony*, 1920I

Egk, Werner: *Abraxas*, 1947I; *Casanova in London*, 1969I; *The Chinese Nightingale*, 1953I; *Circe*, 1945I; *Columbus*, 1932I; *French Suite*, 1949I; *Irisch Legende*, 1955I; *Joan von Zarissa*, 1940I; *Kleine Symphonie*, 1926I; *Moria*, 1973I; *Peer Gynt*, 1938I; *Piano Sonata*,1947I; *Der Revisor*, 1957I; *String Quartet No. 1*, 1923I; *String Quintet*, 1924I; *Die Zaubergeige*, 1935I

Egli, Heinrich: *Lieder des Weisheit un Tugend*, 1790I; *Schweizerlieder*, 1787I

Ehrenberg, Carl: *Anneliese*, 1922I

Ehrlich, Abel: *Job*, 1990I; *Let Us Proclaim*, 1982I

Eichberg, Julius/Woolf, B.E.: *The Doctor of Alcantara*, 1862I

Eichheim, Henry: *The Rivals*, 1924I; *String Quartet*, 1895I; *Violin Sonata No. 2*, 1934I

Eiler, Heino: *Symphony No. 3*, 1961I

Einem, Gottfried von: *Der Besuch der Alten Dame*, 1971I; *Bruckner Dialogue*, 1971I; *Cello Sonata*, 1987I; *Concerto for Orchestra*, 1944I; *Dantons Tod, Opus 6*, 1946I; *Kabale und Liebe*, 1976I; *Medusa*, 1957I; *Nachtstücke*, 1962I; *Orchestra Music, Opus 9*, 1948I; *Pasde coeur*, 1952I; *Philharmonic Symphony*, 1961I; *Piano Concerto, Opus 20*, 1955I; *Prinzessin Turandot*, 1843I; *Der Prozess*, 1952I; *Sonata for Solo Double Bass*, 1982I; *Sonata for Solo Viola*, 1980I; *Sonata for Solo Violin*, 1975I; *Steinbeis Serenade*, 1981I; *String Quartet No. 1*, 1975I; *String Quartet No. 2*, 1977I; *String Quartet No. 3*, 1980I; *String Quartet No. 4*, 1981I; *String Quartet No. 5*, 1991I; *Symphony No. 2, "Wiener,"* 1976I; *Symphony No. 3, "Münchner,"* 1985I; *Symphony No. 4*, 1988I; *Tulifant*, 1990I; *Violin Sonata*, 1947I; *Wiener Symphonie*, 1977I; *Wind Quintet*, 1976I

Eisler, Hanns: *Chamber Cantatas (9)*, 1937I; *Johannes Faustus*, 1953I; *Kleine Sinfonie*, 1932I; *Lenin Requiem*, 1946I; *Pieces for Orchestra, Five*, 1938I; *The Storm*, 1957I; *String Quartet 1938, Opus 75*, 1938I; *Violin Sonata*, 1937I

Eisma, Will: *Concerto for Orchestra I*, 1958I; *Concerto for Orchestra II*, 1959I; *Concerto for Orchestra III*, 1960I; *String Quartet*, 1961I

Ek, Gunnar: *Doomsday Cantata*, 1946I; *Fantasy* (violin & orchestra), 1936I; *Piano Concerto*, 1944I; *Suite for Organ*, 1966I; *Symphony No. 1*, 1924I; *Symphony No. 2*, 1930I; *Symphony No. 5*, 1932I

Eklund, Hans: *Requiem*, 1979I

El-Dabh, Halim: *Rhapsodia Egyptia-Brasileira*, 1985I; *Symphony No. 1*, 1950I; *Symphony No. 2*, 1952I; *Symphony No. 3*, 1956I

Elgar, Edward: *The Apostles*, 1903I; *The Banner of St. George, Opus 33*, 1897I; *Beau Brummel*, 1929I; *The Black Knight, Opus 25*, 1893I; *Caractacus, Opus 35*, 1898I; *Cello Concerto, Opus 85*, 1919I; *Cello Sonata in e, Opus 85*, 1919I; *Cockaigne Overture, Opus 40*, 1901I; *Coronation March, Opus 65*, 1911I; *Coronation Ode*, 1902I; *The Crown of India, Opus 66* (masque), 1912I; *The Dream of Gerontius, Opus 38*, 1900I; *Elegy for Strings, Opus 58*, 1909I; *Enigma Variations, Opus 36*, 1899I; *Falstaff, A symphonic Study, Opus 68*, 1913I; *Froissart Overture, Opus 19*, 1890I; *Grania & Diarmid, Opus 42*, 1901I; *Imperial March, Opus 32*, 1897I; *Introduction & Allegro for Strings, Opus 47*, 1905I; *King Arthur*, 1923I; *The Kingdom, Opus 51*, 1906I; *The Light of Life, Opus 29*, 1896I; *Little Pieces (3) for Orchestra, Opus 10*, 1881I; *The Music Makers, Opus 69*, 1912I; *Organ Sonata in G, Opus 28*, 1895I; *Overture, in the South, Opus 50*, 1904I; *Piano Quintet in a, Opus 84*, 1919I; *Pomp & Circumstance March No. 1 in D*, 1901I; *Pomp & Circumstance March No. 2 in A*, 1901I; *Pomp & Circumstance March No. 3*, 1905I; *Pomp & Circumstance March No. 4 in G*, 1907I; *Pomp & Circumstance March No. 5*,1930I; *The Sanguine Fan, Opus 81*, 1917I; *Sea Pictures*, 1899I; *Serenade in e, Opus 20, for Strings*, 1892I; *String Quartet No. 1 in e, Opus 83*, 1918I; *Symphony No. 1 in A♭, Opus 55*, 1908I; *Symphony No. 2 in E♭, Opus 63*, 1910I; *Vesper Voluntaries (11), Opus 14*, 1889I; *Violin Concerto, Opus 61*, 1910I; *Violin Sonata in e, Opus 82*, 1918I; *TheWand of Youth Suite No. 1, Opus 1a*, 1885I; *The Wand of Youth Suites (2)*, 1907I

Elias, Alfonso de: *Organ Sonata*, 1963I; *Violin Sonata*, 1932I

Eliasson, Anders: *String Quartet*, 1970I; *Symphony No. 1*, 1986I; *Symphony No. 3*, 1989I

Elizalde, Federico: *Piano Concerto*, 1947I; *Violin Concerto*, 1943I

Elkus, Albert I.: *Serenade for String Quartet*, 1921I

Elkus, Jonathan: *The Outcasts of Poker Flat*, 1959I; *Will of Stratford*, 1964I

Eller, Heino: *Dawn*, 1918I; *Fantasy for Violin & Orchestra*, 1916I; *Nocturnal Sounds*, 1919I; *Phantoms*, 1924I; *Piano Sonata No. 4*, 1958I; *String Quartet No. 1*, 1925I; *String Quartet No. 2*, 1930I; *Symphony No. 1*, 1936I; *Symphony No. 2*, 1947I; *Twilight*, 1918I; *Violin Concerto*, 1933I; *Violin Sonata No. 1*, 1922I; *Violin Sonata No. 2*, 1946I

Eloy, Jean-Claude: *. . . d'une étoile oubliée*, 1986I; *Étude IV: Points-lignes-paysages*, 1980I; *Gaku-no-Michi*, 1978I; *Poème Picasso*, 1978I

Elsner, Józef: *Andromeda*, 1807I; *The Cabalist*, 1813I; *King Lokietek*, 1818I; *Passion of Our Lord Jesus Christ*, 1832I

Elvey, George: *Mount Carmel*, 1885I; *The Resurrection and Ascension*, 1840I

Elwart, Antoine: *Noé*, 1845I

Elwell, Herbert: *Blue Symphony*, 1944I; *Divertimento* (string quartet), 1929I; *Lincoln: Requiem Aeternam*, 1946I; *Orchestral Sketches*, 1937I; *Piano Preludes (3)*, 1930I; *Piano Quintet*, 1923I; *Piano Sonata*, 1926I; *String Quartet No. 1 in e*, 1937I

Emborg, Jens L.: *Violin Concerto*, 1926I

Emmett, Joseph K.: *Fritz, the Bohemian*, 1884I

Enescu, Georges: *Cello Sonata No. 1, Opus 26*, 1898I; *Cello Sonata No. 2*, 1937I; *Concert Overture, Opus 32*, 1948I; *Fantasie*, 1896I; *Impressions d'Enfance*, 1940I; *Octet for Strings, Opus 7*, 1900I; *Orchestral Suite No. 1*, 1903I; *Orchestral Suite No. 2, Opus 20*, 1915I; *Orchestral Suite No. 3, "Villageoise," Opus 27*, 1938I; *Pastorale-Fantasie*, 1899I; *Piano Quartet No. 1, Opus 16*, 1909I; *Piano Quartet No. 2, Opus 30*, 1944I; *Piano Quintet No. 1*, 1895I; *Piano Quintet No. 2, Opus 29*, 1940I; *Piano Sonata No. 1, Opus 24*, 1924I; *Piano Sonata No. 2, Opus 24*, 1935I; *Piano Suite No. 2, Opus 10*, 1903I; *Piano Suite No. 3, Opus 18*, 1916I; *Poème roumain, Opus 1*, 1898I; *Romanian Rhapsody No. 1*, 1901I; *Romanian Rhapsody No. 2*, 1902I; *String Quartet No. 1, Opus 22*, 1920I; *String Quartet No. 2, Opus 22*, 1953I; *Suite "dans le style ancien,"* 1897I; *Symphonie Concertante, Opus 88 (cello)*, 1901I; *Symphonie de chambre, Opus 33*, 1954I; *Symphony No. 1 in E♭, Opus 13*, 1906I; *Symphony No. 2*, 1913I; *Symphony No. 3*, 1919I; *Symphony No. 4* (unfinished), 1934I; *Symphony No. 5*, 1941I; *Tragic Overture*, 1895I; *Variations on an Original Theme, Opus 5*, 1898I; *Violin Concerto*, 1896I; *Violin Sonata No. 1, Opus 2*, 1897I; *Violin Sonata No. 2, Opus 6*, 1899I; *Violin Sonata No. 3*, 1926I; *Triumphant Overture*, 1895I

Englander, Ludwig: *The Prince Consort*, 1883I

Englund, Einar: *Cello Concerto*, 1954I; *Clarinet Concerto*, 1991I; *Flute Concerto*, 1985I; *Marcia funebre for Organ*, 1976I; *Passacaglia for Organ*, 1971I; *Piano Concerto No. 1*, 1955I; *String Quartet*, 1985I; *Symphony No. 1*, 1946I; *Symphony No. 2*, 1947I; *Symphony No. 3*, 1971I; *Symphony No. 4, "Nostalgic,"* 1976I; *Symphony No. 5, "Fennica,"* 1977I; *Symphony No. 6, "Aphorisms,"* 1984I; *Symphony No. 7*, 1988I; *Wind Quintet*, 1989I

Eötvös, Peter: *As I Crossed a Bridge of Dreams*, 1999I; *Der Blick*, 1997I; *Marchen*, 1968I; *Monologues (2)*, 1998I; *Radames*, 1975I; *String Quartet,"Korrespondenz,"* 1992I; *Three Sisters*, 1997I

Eppert, Carl: *String Quartet No. 1 in e*, 1927I

Epstein, David: *Fancies*, 1966I; *Piano Variations*, 1961I; *The Seasons*, 1955I; *Sonority Variations*, 1967I; *String Quartet No. 1*, 1952I; *String Quartet No. 2*, 1971I

Erb, Donald: *Cello Concerto*, 1976I; *Changes*, 1995I; *Clarinet Concerto*, 1984I; *Concerto for Brass & Orchestra*, 1987I; *Concerto for Orchestra*, 1985I; *Concerto for Solo Percussionist & Orchestra*, 1966I; *Contrabass Concerto*, 1984I; *Cummings Cycle*, 1963I; *Dance, You Monster*, 1998I; *Drawing Down the Moon*, 1991I; *Evensong*, 1993I; *Fanfare for Brass & Percussion*, 1971I; *Hair of the Wolf-full Moon*, 1981I; *Harp Sonata*, 1995I; *Music for a Festive Occasion*, 1975I; *New England's Prospect*, 1974I; *Piano Nightmusic II*, 1979I; *Pieces (3) for Brass Quintet & Piano*, 1968I; *Pieces (3) for Solo Doublebass*, 1999I; *Prismatic Variations*, 1983I; *Ritual Observances*, 1991I; *The Seventh Trumpet*,1969I; *Solstice*, 1988I; *Sonneries*, 1981I; *String Quartet No. 1*, 1960I; *String Quartet No. 2*, 1989I; *String Quartet No. 3*, 1995I; *Symphony for Winds*, 1989I; *Symphony of Overtures*, 1964I; *Trombone Concerto*, 1976I; *Trumpet Concerto*, 1980I; *Views of Space & Time*, 1987I; *Violin Sonata*, 1994I

Erdmann, Dietrich: *Piano Sonata No. 1*, 1939I

Erickson, Robert: *Aurora*, 1982I; *Fantasy* (cello & orchestra), 1953I; *Piano Sonata*, 1948I; *Rainbow Rising*, 1974I; *Solstice*, 1985I; *String Quartet No. 1*, 1950I; *String Quartet No. 2*, 1956I; *Variations for Orchestra*, 1957I

Erkel, Ferenc: *Bánk-Bán*, 1861I

Ernst, Heinrich: *Airs hongrois variés, Opus 22*, 1850I; *Bolero, Opus 16*, 1843I; *Le carnaval de Venise, Opus 18*, 1844I; *Concerto pathétique in f♯, Opus 23*, 1851I; *Rondo Papageno,Opus 21*, 1846I; *Variations sur l'air hollandais, Opus 18*, 1842I; *Violin Concertino on Rossini's "Othello," Opus 11*, 1839I

Erskine, Thomas A.: *Overtures (6) in Eight Parts, Opus 1*, 1761I; *Trio Sonatas (6)*, 1769I

A   *Births*   B   *Deaths*   C   *Debuts*   D   *New Positions*
E   *Prizes/Honors*

Escot, Pozzi: *Jubilation for String Quartet*, 1991I; *Symphony No. 6*, 1999I
Eshpai, Andrei: *Concerto for Orchestra*, 1967I; *Doublebass Concerto*, 1995I; *Piano Concerto No. 2*, 1972I; *Songs of the Mountain & Meadow Mari*, 1981I; *String Quartet*, 1992I; *Symphonic Dances*, 1952I; *Symphony No. 1*, 1959I; *Symphony No. 2, "Praise to Light,"* 1962I; *Symphony No. 3*, 1964I; *Symphony No. 4*, 1982I; *Symphony No. 5*, 1986I; *Symphony No. 6*, 1989I; *Symphony No. 7*, 1991I
Eslava, Hilarión: *Pietro il crudele*, 1843I; *Il solitario*, 1841I
Esplá, Oscar: *Piano Pieces (3)*, 1930I; *Piano Sonata Española*, 1949I
Etler, Alvin: *Clarinet Sonata No. 2*, 1969I; *Concerto for Orchestra*, 1957I; *Concerto for Violin & Wind Quintet*, 1958I; *Passacaglia & Fugue*, 1947I; *String Quartet No. 1*, 1963I; *String Quartet No. 2*, 1965I
Evett, Robert: *Cello Concerto*, 1954I; *Piano Concerto*, 1957I; *Piano Quartet*, 1961I; *Piano Quintet*, 1954I; *Piano Sonata No. 1*, 1945I; *Piano Sonata No. 2*, 1952I; *Piano Sonata No. 3*, 1953I; *Piano Sonata No. 4*, 1956I; *Symphony No. 1*, 1960I; *Symphony No. 2*, 1965I; *Symphony No. 3*, 1965I
Eybler, Joseph L.: *Christmas Oratorio*, 1784I; *Der Hirten bei der Krippe*, 1794I; *Die vier letztenDinge*, 1810I; *Das Zauberschwert*, 1794I
Eyerly, Scott: *The House of the Seven Gables*, 2000I
Fairchild, Blair: *Psalms (6)*, 1913I; *String Quartet No. 1*, 1909I; *String Quartet No. 2*, 1911I
Falla, Manuel de: *El amor Brujo*, 1915I; *Allegro de Concert*, 1903I; *Master Peter's Puppet Show*, 1923I; *Nights in the Gardens of Spain*, 1915I; *Piano Quartet*, 1899I; *Serenataandaluza*, 1899I; *The Three Cornered Hat*, 1919I; *La vida breve*, 1905I
Fano, Guido A.: *Piano Quintet*, 1917I; *String Quartet*, 1942I
Farago, Marcel: *Freedom Symphony*, 1991I
Farberman, Harold: *Concerto for Alto Saxophone*, 1965I; *Evolution* (percussion), 1954I; *Millenium Concerto*, 2000I; *String Quartet No. 1*, 1960I; *Symphony No. 1*, 1957I; *Timpani Concerto*, 1958I; *Violin Concerto*, 1974I
Faria, Alexandre de: *Eyes of a Recollection*, 1996I
Farinelli, Giuseppe: *Il dottorato di Pulcinella*, 1792I
Farquhar, David: *Symphony No. 1*, 1959I
Farr, Garath: *Aikoi*, 1998I; *From the Depths Sound the Great Sea Gongs*, 1996I; *Mousehole*, 1998I; *Still Sounds Lie*, 1996I; *String Quartet No. 1, "Owhiro,"* 1993I; *String QuartetNo. 2, "Mondo Rondo,"* 1997I
Farrenc, Jeanne Louise: *Études (20), Opus 42*, 1855I; *Études brillantes (12), Opus 41*, 1858I; *Overture, Opus 23*, 1834I; *Overture, Opus 24*, 1834I; *Symphony No. 1 in c, Opus 32*, 1841I; *Symphony No. 2 in D, Opus 35*, 1845I; *Symphony No. 3 in g, Opus 36*, 1847I
Farwell, Arthur: *Academic Overture, "Cornell," Opus 9*, 1900I; *American Indian Melodies, Opus 11*, 1900I; *Americana, Opus 78*, 1927I; *Ballade for Violin & Piano, Opus 1*, 1898I; *Cello Sonata, Opus 116*, 1950I; *Dawn, Fantasy on Two Indian Themes, Opus 12*, 1901I; *The Death of Virginia, Opus 4*, 1894I; *The Domain of Hurakan, Opus 15*, 1902I; *Emily Dickinson Songs (4), Opus 101*, 1936I; *Emily Dickinson Songs (12), Opus 107*, 1944I; *Emily Dickinson Songs (10), Opus 112*, 1949I; *From Mesa & Plain, Opus 20*, 1905I; *Fugue Fantasy for String Quartet*, 1914I; *The Gods of the Mountains*, 1927I; *Impressions of the Wa-Wan Ceremony of the Omaha Indians, Opus 21*, 1905I; *In the Tetons, Opus 86*,1930I; *Indian Coruses (2), Opus 111*, 1946I; *Indian Songs (3), Opus 32*, 1912I; *Indian Songs (4), Opus 102*, 1937I; *Indian Suite, Opus 110*, 1944I; *Modal Invention in theDorian Mode, Opus 68*, 1923I; *Owasco Memories, Opus 8*, 1899I; *Piano Quintet in e, Opus 103*, 1937I; *Polytonal Studies, Opus 109*, 1952I; *Prelude & Fugue, Opus 94*, 1936I; *Prelude to a Spiritual Drama*, 1932I; *Rudolph Gott Symphony, Opus 95*, 1934I; *Sonata, Opus 113*, 1949I; *String Quartet "The Hako," Opus 65*, 1922I; *Symbolist Study No. 1, "Toward the Dream," Opus 16*, 1901I; *Symbolist Study No. 2, "Perhelion," Opus 18*, 1905I; *Symbolist Study No. 3, "After Whitman," Opus 18*, 1905I; *Symbolist Study No. 5, Opus 27*, 1906I; *Symbolist Study No. 6, "Mountain Vision," Opus 27*, 1912I; *Tone Pictures(2), Opus 101*,1936I; *Violin Sonata in g, Opus 80*, 1927I
Fasch, Johann F.: *Der Fremdling auf Golgotha*, 1776I
Fauré, Gabriel: *Ballade, Opus 19*, 1881I; *Barcarolles No. 2, 3 Opus 41, 42*, 1885I; *Berceuse,Opus 16* (violin), 1880I; *La bonne chanson, Opus 61* (cycle), 1892I; *Le bourgeois gentilhomme*, 1893I; *Caligula*, 1888I; *Cello Sonata No. 1, Opus 109*, 1917I; *Cello Sonata No. 2, Opus 117*, 1921I; *La chanson d'Eve, Opus 95*, 1910I; *Les djins, Opus 12*, 1875I; *Dolly*, 1897I; *Impromptu No. 1, Opus 25*, 1881I; *Impromptus No. 2 & 3, Opus 31, 34*, 1883I; *Le jardin clos, Opus 106*, 1918I; *Masque et bergamasque, Opus 112*, 1919I; *Nocturne No. 3, Opus 33/3*, 1882I; *Nocturnes No. 4 & 5, Opus 36, 37*, 1884I; *Nocturne No. 7, Opus 74*, 1898I; *La Passion*, 1890I; *Pavane, Opus 50*, 1887I; *Pelléas et Mélisande, Opus 80*, 1898I; *Penelope*, 1913I; *Petite pièce, Opus 49*, 1889I; *Piano Fantasie, Opus 111*, 1919I; *Piano Preludes (9), Opus 101*, 1910I; *Piano Preludes (9), Opus 103*, 1911I; *Piano Quartet No. 1 in c, Opus 15*, 1879I; *Piano Quartet No. 2 in g, Opus 45*, 1886I; *Piano Quintet No. 1, Opus 59*, 1895I; *Piano Quintet No. 1, Opus 89*, 1906I; *Piano Quintet No. 2, Opus 115*, 1921I; *Pièces Brèves (8), Opus 84*, 1902I; *Prométhée, Opus 82*, 1900I; *Requiem, Opus 48*, 1877I; *Romance, Opus 28* (violin), 1882I;

❈

F   *Biographical*   G   *Cultural Beginnings*   H   *Musical Literature*
I   *Musical Compositions*

Fauré, Gabriel: (*cont.*)
  Romances sans paroles (3), *Opus 17*, 1863I; *Serenade, Opus 98*, 1908I; *Shylock, Opus 57*, 1889I; *Songs (3)*,
  Opus 18, 1880I; *Songs (3), Opus 23*, 1882I; *Songs (3), Opus 85*, 1903I; *String Quartet, Opus 121*, 1924I;
  Suite d'orchestre, Opus 20, 1875I; *Symphony in d, Opus 40*, 1884I; *Theme & Variations, Opus 73*, 1895I;
  Valse-Caprice No. 1, Opus 30, 1882I; *Valse-Caprice No. 2, Opus 38*, 1884I; *Valse-Caprice No. 3, Opus 59*,
  1891I; *Laviole du bonheur, Opus 88*, 1901I; *Violin Concerto, Opus 14*, 1879I; *Violin Sonata No. 1 in A*,
  Opus 13, 1876I; *Violin Sonata No. 2, Opus 108*, 1917I
Feigin, Joel: *Poems (4) of Wallace Stevens*, 1985I; *First Tragedy*, 1982I
Fekete, Gyula: *Roman Fever*, 1995I
Felciano, Richard: *The Captives*, 1965I; *Contractions*, 1965I; *Crystal* (string quartet), 1981I; *Galactic
  Rounds*, 1972I; *Glossolalia*, 1967I; *In Celebration of Golden Rain*, 1978I; *Kindertotenlieder*, 1984I;
  Mutations, 1966I; *On the Divine Presence*, 1968I; *On the Heart of the Earth*, 1976I; *Orchestra*, 1980I;
  Organ Concerto, 1986I; *Piano Gravities*, 1965I; *Poems from the Japanese (4)*, 1964I; *Short Pieces (5) for
  Piano*, 1986I; *Sir Gawain & the Green Knight*, 1964I; *Soundings for Mozart*, 1970I
Felder, David: *a pressure triggering dream*, 1997I; *In Between* (percussion concerto), 1999I
Feldman, Barbara: *The Immutable Silence*, 1990I; *Infinite Other*, 1992I; *Pure Difference*, 1991I; *Variations for
  String Quartet & Chorus*, 1987I
Feldman, Morton: *Beckett*, 1987I; *Cello & Orchestra Concerto*, 1972I; *Chorus & Instruments I*, 1963I; *Chorus
  & Instruments II*, 1967I; *Chorus & Orchestra I*, 1971I; *Chorus & Orchestra II*, 1972I; *Concerto for String
  Quartet & Orchestra*, 1973I; *Coptic Light*, 1986I; *Crippled Symmetry*, 1984I; *Durations III*, 1961I; *Durations
  IV*, 1961I; *Durations V*, 1961I; *Flute & Orchestra*, 1978I; *For Bunita Marcus for Piano*, 1985I; *For John Cage*,
  1982I; *For Philip Guston*, 1984I; *Instruments I*, 1974I; *Instruments II*, 1974I; *Last Pieces*, 1959I; *Madame
  Press Died Last Week at Ninety*, 1970I; *On Time & the Instrumental Factor*, 1969I; *Orchestra*, 1976I; *Palais
  de Mari for Piano*, 1986I; *Piano & Orchestra*, 1975I; *Piano & String Quartet*, 1985I; *Piano*, 1977I; *Piano
  Piece*, 1964I; *Piece for Four Pianos*, 1957I; *Pieces (2) for Clarinet & String Quartet*, 1961I; *Pieces for Three
  Pianos (2)*, 1966I; *Principal Sound for Organ*, 1980I; *Projections I-IV*, 1951I; *String Quartet No. 1*, 1979I;
  String Quartet No. 2, 1983I; *Structures* (string quartet), 1951I; *Triadic Memories for Piano*, 1981I; *The
  Turfan Fragments*, 1980I; *Vertical Thoughts I for Piano*, 1963I; *Vertical Thoughts II*, 1963I; *Vertical Thoughts
  III*, 1963I; *Vertical Thoughts III*, 1963I; *Vertical Thoughts IV*, 1963I; *Vertical Thoughts IV*, 1963I; *Vertical
  Thoughts IV for Piano*, 1963I; *The Viola in My Life IV* (viola concerto), 1971I; *The Viola in My Life, I*,
  1970I; *The Viola in My Life III*, 1970I; *Voice, Violin & Piano*, 1976I; *Voice & Instruments I*, 1972I; *Voice &
  Instruments II*, 1974I; *Voices & Instruments I, II*, 1972I; *Why Patterns*, 1978I
Felton, William: *Organ/Harpsichord Concertos (6), Opus 4*, 1752I; *Organ/HarpsichordConcertos (6), Opus 5*,
  1755I; *Organ/Harpsichord Concertos (8), Opus 7*, 1760I
Fennelly, Brian: *Concerto for Sax & Strings*, 1984I; *In Wildness Is the Preservation of the World*, 1975I;
  String Quartet No. 1, 1974I; *SUNYATA*, 1970I; *Spring of Andromeda*, 1991I; *A Thoreau Symphony*, 1993I
Ferko, Frank: *Stabat Mater*, 1999I
Fernandez, Oscar: *Malazarte*, 1933I
Ferneyhough, Brian: *String Quartet No. 1*, 1967I; *String Quartet No. 2*, 1980I; *String Quartet No. 3*, 1987I;
  String Quartet No. 4, 1990I; *La terre est un homme*, 1978I
Fernström, John: *Bassoon Concerto*, 1947I; *Symphonic Prologue, Opus 88*, 1949I; *Symphony No. 6, Opus 40*,
  1939I
Ferrandini, Giovanni: *Catone in Utica*, 1753I; *Demetrio*, 1758I; *Diana placata*, 1755I
Ferrari, Giacomo: *I due Svizzeri*, 1799I
Ferrari, Luc: *Antisonate*, 1953I; *Comme une fantaisie dite des réminiscences for Piano*, 1991I
Ferroud, Pierre-Octave: *Jeunesse*, 1933I; *Serenade*, 1927I; *Symphony in A*, 1930I
Festinger, Richard: *String Quartet*, 1994I; *Tapestries*, 1997I
Fibich, Zdeněk: *Albumblätter, Opus 2*, 1866I; *Der Asra*, 1872I; *At Twilight, Opus 39*, 1893I; *Balladen (4)*,
  Opus 7, 1873I; *Blanik, Opus 50*, 1877I; *The Bride of Messina, Opus 18*, 1883I; *Bukovin*, 1871I; *Concert
  Overture in E*, 1872I; *Eternity*, 1878I; *The Fall of Arkun*, 1899I; *Festival Overture, Komensk, Opus 34*,
  1892I; *Frühlingsstrahlen, Opus 36*, 1893I; *Hákon*, 1888I; *Hedy, Opus 43*, 1895I; *Hildenbrandlied*, 1871I;
  Hippodamia I: The Courtship of Pelops, Opus 31, 1889I; *Hippodamia II: Atonement of Tantalus, Opus 32*,
  1890I; *Hippodamia III: Hippodamia's Death, Opus 33*, 1891I; *Impressions: From the Countryside*, 1898I;
  Lieder (3), Opus 46, 1874I; *Lustspiel Overture, Opus 35*, 1873I; *Meluzina, Opus 55*, 1874I; *Missa brevis in
  F, Opus 21*, 1885I; *Othello, Opus 6*, 1873I; *Overture: A Night in Karltijn Castle, Opus 26*, 1886I; *Overture,
  Der Jude von Prag*,1871I; *Overture, Oldřich e Bošena*, 1898I; *Piano Quartet*, 1874I; *Piano Quintet*, 1893I;
  Piano Sonata in B♭, 1876I; *Piano Suite in g*, 1877I; *Piano Trio*, 1872I; *Le printemps, Opus 1*, 1865I; *The
  Romance of Spring, Opus 23*, 1881I; *Romeo and Juliet*, 1865I; *Sarka, Opus 51*, 1897I; *Songs (6), Opus 12*,
  1881I; *Spring, Opus 13*, 1881I; *String Quartet No. 1 in A*, 1874I; *String Quartet No. 2 in G, Opus 8*, 1878I;
  The Submerged Bell, 1900I; *Symphony No. 1 in F, Opus 17*, 1883I; *Symphony No. 2 in E♭, Opus 38*, 1893I;

❁

A   *Births*   B   *Deaths*   C   *Debuts*   D   *New Positions*
                  E   *Prizes/Honors*

Symphony No. 3 in e, Opus 53, 1898I; *The Tempest, Opus 46,* 1880I; *The Tempest, Opus 40* (opera), 1894I;
  Toman and the Wood Nymphs, Opus 49, 1875I; *Violin Sonata No. 1,* 1874I; *Violin Sonata No. 2,* 1875I; *The
  Water Sprite,* 1883I; *Záboj, Opus 37,* 1873I
Fickénscher, Arthur: *Piano Quintet,* 1939I
Field, John: *Exercise Nouveau in C,* 1821I; *Grand Pastorale in E,* 1832I; *Nocturnes 1-3,* 1814I; *Nocturnes 4-6,*
  1817I; *Nocturnes 7, 8 (c,e),* 1821I; *Nocturne, "The Troubadour,"* 1832I; *Nocturne No. 11 in E♭,* 1833I;
  Nocturne No. 14 in C, 1836I; *Nocturne No. 15 in C,* 1836I; *Nouvelle Fantasie in G,* 1833I; *Piano Concerto
  No. 1 in E♭,* 1799I; *Piano Concerto No. 2 in A♭,* 1814I; *Piano Concerto No. 3 in E♭, Opus 32,* 1816I; *Piano
  Concerto No. 4 in E♭, Opus 28,* 1816I; *Piano Concerto No. 5 in C, Opus 39,* 1817I; *Piano Concerto No. 7 in c,
  Opus 58,* 1822I; *Piano Quintet in A♭,* 1816I; *Piano Sonatas(3), Opus 1,* 1801I; *Piano Sonata No. 4,* 1812I;
  Polonaise in E♭, 1813I
Fine, Irving: *Blue Towers,* 1959I; *Childhood Fables for Grownups,* 1954I; *The Choral New Yorker,* 1944I;
  Choruses (3) from "Alice in Wonderland," 1942I; *Diversions for Orchestra,* 1960I; *Fantasia for String Trio,*
  1956I; *Notturno for Harp & Strings,* 1951I; *Partita for Wind Quintet,* 1948I; *Serious Song: A Lament for
  Strings,* 1955I; *String Quartet No. 1,* 1952I; *Symphony 1962,* 1962I; *Violin Concerto,* 1946I; *Violin Sonata,*
  1946I
Fine, Vivian: *Alcestis,* 1960I; *Brass Quintet,* 1978I; *Chamber Voncerto,* 1966I; *Concertante,*1944I; *Concertino
  for Piano & Percussion,* 1965I; *Double Variations for Piano,* 1982I; *Drama for Orchestra,* 1982I;
  Dreamscape, 1964I; *Momenti for Piano,* 1978I; *My Son, My Enemy,* 1965I; *Piano Pieces (4),* 1966I; *Piano
  Preludes (5),* 1941I; *Piano Suite in E♭,* 1940I; *Piano Trio,* 1980I; *Piano Variations,* 1952I; *Poetic Fires* (piano
  concerto), 1984I; *Polyphonic Pieces (4),* 1932I; *Quintet* (piano, strings, woodwinds), 1967I;
  Quintet(strings, trumpet, piano), 1984I; *The Song of Persephone,* 1964I; *Sonnets (3) from Keats,* 1976I;
  Sounds of the Nightingale, 1971I; *String Quartet No. 1,* 1957I; *Violin Sonata,* 1952I; *The Women in the
  Garden,* 1972I
Finkbeiner, Reinhold: *Piano Suite,* 1954I
Finke, David: *Viola Concerto,* 1971I
Finney, Ross Lee: *Alto Saxophone Concerto,* 1974I; *Cello Sonata No. 2 in C,* 1949I; *Chamber Music,* 1950I;
  Concerto for Percussion, 1965I; *Computer Marriage,* 1987I; *Earthrise, Part 1: Still Are New Worlds,* 1962I;
  Earthrise, Part III, 1978I; *Inventions,* 1956I; *Piano Concerto No. 1,* 1948I; *Piano Concerto No. 2,* 1968I; *Piano
  Fantasy (Sonata No. 2),*1939I; *Piano Games (32),* 1968I; *Piano Narrative in Argument,* 1991I; *Piano Quintet
  No.1,* 1953I; *Piano Quintet No. 2,* 1961I; *Piano Sonata in d,* 1933I; *Piano Sonata No. 3,* 1942I; *Piano Sonata
  No. 4, "Christmastime,"* 1945I; *Piano Sonata quasi una Fantasia,* 1961I; *Piano Trio No. 2,* 1954I; *Poor
  Richard,* 1946I; *The Remorseless Rush of Time,*1969I; *Seventeenth Century Lyrics (3),* 1938I; *Spaces,* 1971I;
  String Quartet No. 1, 1935I; *String Quartet No. 2,* 1937I; *String Quartet No. 3,* 1940I; *String Quartet No. 4,*
  1947I; *String Quartet No. 5,* 1949I; *String Quartet No. 6,* 1950I; *String Quartet No. 7,* 1955I; *String Quartet
  No. 8,* 1960I; *String Quintet,* 1958I; *Symphony No. 1,"Communiqué,"* 1942I; *Symphony No. 2,* 1958I;
  Symphony No. 3, 1960I; *Symphony No. 4,* 1972I; *Variations for Orchestra,* 1957I; *Variations, Fuguing &
  Holiday,* 1943I; *Variations on a Theme by Alban Berg,* 1952I; *Viola Sonata No. 1,* 1937I; *Violin Concerto No.
  1,* 1933I; *Violin Sonata No. 1,* 1934I; *Weep, Torn Land,* 1984I; *Youth's Companion for Piano,* 1980I
Finnissy, Michael: *Anima Christi,* 1991I; *English Country-Tunes for Piano,* 1977I; *The Liturgy of St. Paul,*
  1995I; *North American Spirituals for Piano,* 1998I; *String Quartet,* 1984I; *Therese Raquin,* 1993I
Finsterer, Maru: *Madame He,* 1988I
Finzi, Gerald: *Clarinet Concerto,* 1949I; *Dies Natalis,* 1940I
Fioravanti, Valentino: *Le avventure di Bertoldino,* 1784I; *Le cantatrici villane,* 1799I; *Lacapricciosa pentita,*
  1802I; *Il furbo contro al furbo,* 1796I; *I virtuosi ambulanti,* 1807I
Fischer, Edwin: *Piano Sketches (5),* 1914I
Fisher, John Abraham: *Judith,* 1761I; *Providence,* 1777I; *Symphonies (4),* 1767I; *Symphonies in Eight Parts
  (6),* 1770I
Fitelberg, Jerzy: *String Quartet No. 1,* 1926I; *String Quartet No. 2,* 1928I; *String Quartet No. 3,* 1936I;
  String Quartet No. 4, 1936I; *String Quartet No. 5,* 1945I
Fitkin, Graham: *Servant* (string quartet), 1992I
Flagello, Nicolas: *A Goldoni Overture,* 1969I; *The Land,* 1954I; *Overture Burlesca,* 1952I; *Piano Concerto
  No. 1,* 1950I; *Piano Concerto No. 2,* 1956I; *Piano Concerto No. 3,* 1962I; *Piano Concerto No. 4,* 1975I; *Piano
  Sonata, Opus 38,* 1962I; *Prelude, Ostinato & Fugue,Opus 30,* 1960I; *Serenata,* 1968I; *Symphony No. 1,*
  1967I; *Symphony No. 2, "Symphony of the Winds,"* 1970I; *Te Deum for Mankind,* 1968I; *Violin Concerto,*
  1955I; *Violin Sonata, Opus 41,* 1963I
Flanagan, William: *Chapter from Ecclesiastes,* 1962I; *A Concert Ode,* 1951I; *A Concert Overture,* 1948I;
  Divertimento (string quartet), 1947I; *The Lady of Tearful Regret,* 1959I; *Narrative for Orchestra,* 1964I;
  Piano Sonata, 1950I
Fleischmann, Alois: *Piano Quintet,* 1938I

❉

F *Biographical*   G *Cultural Beginnings*   H *Musical Literature*
           I *Musical Compositions*

Fleury, André: *Organ Symphony No. 1,* 1947I; *Organ Symphony No. 2,* 1949I
Florio, Caryl: *Allegro de Concert, Sax Quartet,* 1879I; *Piano Concerto in A♭,* 1886I; *Piano Trioin D,* 1866I; *Song of the Elements,* 1872I; *String Quartet No. 1,* 1877I; *String Quartet No. 2,* 1878I; *Symphonies No. 1, 2,* 1887I
Flotow, Friedrich von: *Albin,* 1856I; *Alessandro Stradella,* 1844I; *Alfred der Grosse,* 1833I; *Alice,* 1837I; *L'âme en peine,* 1846I; *Die Bergknappen,* 1833I; *La châtelaine,* 1865I; *Lecomte de Saint-Mégrin,* 1838I; *L'eau merveilleuse,* 1839I; *L'esclave de Camoëns,* 1843I; *La fleur de Harlem,* 1874I; *Hilda, Albin,* 1855I; *La jeunesse de Mozart,* 1887I; *Johann Albrecht bon Mechlenburg,* 1857I; *Jubel Overture,* 1857I; *Der Königschuss,* 1864I; *Lady Henrietta,* 1844I; *Lady Melvil,* 1838I; *La lettre du préfet,* 1837I; *Die Libelle,* 1856I; *Martha,* 1847I; *Naida,* 1865I; *Le naufrage de la Méduse,* 1839I; *L'ombre,* 1870I; *Pianella,* 1857I; *Piano Concerto No. 1,* 1830I; *Piano Concerto No. 2,* 1831I; *Pierre et Cathérine,* 1835I; *Rob-Roy,* 1837I; *Rübezahl,* 1852I; *Sakuntala,* 1811I; *Sérafine,* 1836I; *Sophia Katherina* 1850I; *Symphony,* 1833I; *Der Tanskönig,* 1861I; *La veuve Grapin,*1859I; *Violin Sonata in A, Opus 14,* 1861I; *Wilhelm von Oranien,* 1862I; *Wintermärchen,*1859I; *Zilda,* 1866I
Floyd, Carlisle: *Bilby's Doll,* 1976I; *Citizen of Paradise,* 1983I; *Cold, Sassy Tree,* 1999I; *Flower& Hawk,* 1972I; *Fugitives,* 1951I; *Introductions, Aria & Dance,* 1967I; *Markheim,* 1966I; *The Mystery,* 1962I; *Of Mice & Men,* 1969I; *Out of the CradleEndlessly Rocking,* 1952I; *Overture, In Celebration,* 1971I; *The Passion of JonathanWade,* 1962I; *Piano Sonata,* 1957I; *Pilgrimage,* 1956I; *Slow Dusk,* 1949I; *The Sojourner & Mollie Sinclair,* 1963I; *Susannah,* 1954I; *Willie Stark,* 1980I; *Wuthering Heights,* 1958I
Flury, Richard: *Romantic Pieces (50),* 1949I
Foerster, Josef Bohuslav: *Cello Concerto,* 1931I; *Cello Sonata No. 1 in f, Opus 45,* 1898I; *Cello Sonata No. 2 in c, Opus 130,* 1926I; *The Conquerors,* 1918I; *Cyrano de Bergerac, Opus 55,* 1903I; *Debora, Opus 4,* 1891I; *Drei Ritter, Opus 21,* 1889I; *Eva, Opus 50,* 1897I; *Enigma, Opus 99,* 1909I; *From Shakespeare, Opus 76,* 1908I; *In the Mountains,* 1884I; *Jessica, Opus 60,* 1905I; *My Youth, Opus 44,* 1900I; *Orchestral Suite in C,* 1891I; *OrganFantasy in C, Opus 14,* 1896I; *Sonata quasi fantasia, opus 177,* 1943I; *Stabat Mataer, Opus 56,* 1892I; *Symphony No. 1 in d, Opus 9,* 1888I; *Symphony No. 2 in F, Opus 29,* 1893I; *Symphony No. 3 in D, Opus 36,* 1895I; *Symphony No. 4, "Easter," Opus 54,*1905I; *Symphony No. 5, Opus 141,* 1929I; *Violin Concerto No. 1,* 1911I; *Violin Sonata No. 1 in b, Opus 10,* 1889I
Fomin, Evstigney: *The Americans,* 1800I; *The Golden Apple,* 1800I; *Magician, Fortune-Teller& Matchmaker,* 1791I; *Melnik,* 1779I; *Novgorod Hero Vassily Boyeslavich,* 1786I; *Orpheus and Eurydice,* 1792I
Foote, Arthur: *Cello Concerto, Opus 33,* 1893I; *Character Pieces (4) after Omar Kháyám, Opus48,* 1912I; *Character Pieces (4) after the Rubáiyát . . . ,* 1900I; *The Farewell of Hiawatha, Opus 11,* 1885I; *Francesca de Rimini, Opus 24,* 1890I; *Lygeia,* 1906I; *Night Piece for Solo Flute,* 1914I; *Nocturne & Scherzo for Flute & String Quartet,* 1918I; *Organ Suite in D,* 1904I; *Overture: In the Mountains, Opus 14,* 1886I; *Piano Quartet in C, Opus 23,* 1890I; *Piano Quintet in a, Opus 38,* 1897I; *Piano Trio No. 1, Opus 5,* 1882I; *Piano TrioNo. 2 in B♭, Opus 65,* 1908I; *The Skeleton in Armor, Opus 28,* 1891I; *String Quartet No.1 in g, Opus 4,* 1883I; *String Quartet No. 2 in E, Opus 32,* 1893I; *String Quartet No. 3 in D, Opus 70,* 1911I; *Suite in d, Opus 36,* 1896I; *Suite in E for Strings, Opus 63,* 1907I; *Suite No. 3 in d, Opus 36,* 1895I; *Violin Sonata in g, Opus 20,* 1889I; *The Wreck of theHesperus, Opus 17,* 1888I
Fortner, Wolfgang: *Die Bluthochzeit,* 1956I; *Capriccio & Finale,* 1939I; *Cello Concerto,* 1951I; *Cello Sonata,* 1948I; *Concerto for Organ & Strings,* 1932I; *Corinna,* 1958I; *The Creation,* 1954I; *Dedications,* 1981I; *Elegies (7),* 1950I; *Elisabeth Tudor,* 1971I; *Ernste Musik,* 1940I; *Farewell,* 1981I; *Flute Sonata,* 1947I; *Hoffmansthal Songs (4),* 1961I; *Holderlin Songs (4),* 1933I; *In seinem Garten liebt Don Perlimlin Belisa,* 1962I; *Kammermusik,* 1944I; *Mouvements for Piano,* 1953I; *Piano Concerto,* 1942I; *Preamble & Fugue,* 1935I; *Shakespeare-Songs,* 1946I; *String Quartet No. 1,* 1929I; *String Quartet No. 2,* 1938I; *String Quartet No. 4,* 1975I; *Symphony No. 1,* 1947I; *That Time,* 1977I; *Toccata & Fugue in d,* 1930I; *Violin Concerto,* 1946I; *Violin Sonata,* 1945I; *The White Rose,* 1950I; *Die Witwe von Ephesus,* 1952I
Foss, Lukas: *American Cantata,* 1977I; *Baroque Variations,* 1967I; *Brass Quintet,* 1978I; *The Cave of Winds,* 1972I; *Celebration,* 1990I; *Cello concerto,* 1967I; *Clarinet Concerto No.1,* 1941I; *Clarinet Concerto No. 2,* 1988I; *Concerto for Improvising Instruments & Orchestra,* 1960I; *Concerto for the Lest Hand* (piano), 1994I; *Echoi,* 1963I; *Exeunt,* 1982I; *Geod,* 1969I; *The Gift of the Magi,* 1945I; *Horn Trio,* 1984I; *The Jumping Frog of Calaveras County,* 1949I; *MAP,* 1970I; *A Parable of Death,* 1952I; *Percussion Quartet,* 1983I; *Piano Concerto No. 1,* 1943I; *Piano Concerto No. 2,* 1951I; *The Prairie,* 1942I; *Renaissance Concerto,* 1986I; *Solo Transformed* (piano concerto), 2000I; *The Song of Songs,* 1946I; *String Quartet No. 1 in G,* 1947I; *String Quartet No. 2, "Divertissement'pour Mica,' "* 1973I; *String Quartet No. 3,* 1975I; *String Quartet No. 4,* 1998I; *Symphony in G,* 1945I; *Time Cycle,* 1960I; *With Music Strong,* 1988I
Foster, Stephen: *Beautiful Dreamer,* 1864I; *Camptown Races,* 1854I; *Come Where My Love Lies Dreaming,* 1855I; *Gentle Annie,* 1856I; *I Dream of Jeannie with the Light Brown Hair,* 1854I; *Lou'siana Belle,* 1847I;

Massa's in de Cold, Cold Ground, 1852I; *My Old Kentucky Home*, 1853I; *Nelly Bly, Nelly Was a Lady*, 1849I; *Oh Susanna*, 1848I; *Old Black Joe*, 1860I; *Old Dog Tray*, 1853I; *Old Folks at Home*, 1851I; *Open The Lattice, Love*, 1844I; *There's a Good Time Coming*, 1846I

Foulds, John: *Cello Sonata*, 1905I; *Essays in the Modes*, 1928I; *World Requiem*, 1921I

Frackenpohl, Arthur: *Brass Quartet*, 1950I; *String Quartet No. 1*, 1971I; *Tuba Sonata*, 1983I

Françaix, Jean: *Bagatelles (8)* (string quartet), 1980I; *Bassoon Concerto*, 1980I; *Cassazione for Three Orchestras*, 1975I; *Clarinet Quintet*, 1977I; *Flute Concerto*, 1967I; *Flute Sonata*,1996I; *L'heure du berger for Woodwind Quintet*, 1947I; *Les malheurs de Sophie*, 1935I; *La princesse de Clèves*, 1965I; *Quintet No. 1 for Flute, Horn & String Trio*, 1934I; *Quintet No. 2*, 1989I; *String Quartet*, 1937I; *Symphony for Strings*, 1948I; *Symphony in G*, 1953I; *Wind Quintet No. 1*, 1948I; *Wind Quintet No. 2*, 1987I; *Wind Sextet*, 1991I

Franchetti, Alberto: *Symphony in e*, 1886I

Franck, César: *Antiennes (3)*, 1859I; *Ave Maria*, 1863I; *The Beatitudes*, 1879I; *Cantabile in B*, 1878I; *Le chasseur maudit*, 1882I; *Les djinns*, 1884I; *Les Eolides*, 1876I; *Fantasia No. 1, Opus 11*, 1844I; *Fantasia No. 2, Opus 12*, 1844I; *Fantasia No. 3, Opus 13*, 1844I; *Fantasia on Polish Airs, Opus 15*, 1845I; *Fantasie in A*, 1878I; *Fantasie in C, Opus 16*, 1862I; *Finale in B♭, Opus 21*, 1864I; *Grande Pièce Symphonique, Opus 17*, 1863I; *Grande Caprice, Opus 5*, 1843I; *Hulda*, 1885I; *L'organiste*, 1890I; *Little Pieces (44)*, 1863I; *Mass in Three Voices, Opus 12*, 1872I; *Mass in e*, 1866I; *Organ Chorales (B,b,a)*,1890I; *Panis Angelicus*, 1871I; *Paris, a Patriotic Song*, 1870I; *Pastorale in E, Opus 19*,1862I; *Piano Quintet in f*, 1879I; *Piano Trios (3), Opus 1*, 1841I; *Piano Trio No. 4, Opus 2*, 1843I; *Pièce Heroïque in b*, 1878I; *Prelude, aria et final*, 1887I; *Prelude, Chorale &Fugue*, 1884I; *Prélude, Fugue & Variations in b, Opus 18*, 1862I; *Prière in c♯, Opus 20*, 1862I; *Psalm 150*, 1884I; *Psyché*, 1888I; *Rebecca*, 1881I; *Redemption*, 1872I; *Ruth*, 1846I; *Solemn Mass in B*, 1858I; *Souvenirs d'Aix-la-chapelle, Opus 7*, 1843I; *String Quartet in D*, 1889I; *Symphonic Variations*, 1885I; *Symphony in d*, 1888I; *The Tower of Babel*, 1865I; *Le valet de ferme*, 1853I; *Violin Sonata in A*, 1886I

Frankel, Benjamin: *Viola Concerto, Opus 45*, 1967I; *Violin Concerto*, 1951I

Franz, Robert: *Aus Osten, Opus 42*, 1870I; *Goethe Lieder (6), Opus 33*, 1864I; *Heine Songs (6), Opus 25*, 1870I; *Heine Lieder (12), Opus 38, 39*, 1867I; *Lieder (6) for Male Voices, Opus 32*, 1859I; *Lieder (6), Opus 45*, 1872I; *Lieder (6), Opus 49*, 1879I; *Morike Songs (6), Opus 27*, 1870I; *Poems (6), Opus 13*, 1865I; *Schliflieder, Opus 2*, 1844I; *Songs (12), Opus 1*, 1843I; *Songs (6), Opus 3*, 1844I; *Songs (12), Opus 4*, 1845I; *Songs (30), Opus 5, 6, 7, 8*, 1846I; *Six Songs (24), Opus 9, 10, 12, 14*, 1860I; *Songs (12), Opus 11, 21*, 1865I; *Songs (6), Opus 16*, 1856I; *Songs (12), Opus 17, 18*, 1860I; *Songs (12), Opus 40, 41*, 1867I; *Songs (12), Opus 22, 23*, 1870I; *Songs (36), Opus 26, 28, 30, 31, 43, 44*, 1870I; *Songs (12), Opus 35, 36*, 1862I; *Songs (6), Opus 37*, 1866I; *Songs (6), Opus 48*, 1878I; *Songs (16), Opus 50, 51*, 1879I; *Songs (6), Opus 52*, 1884I; *Trinkspruch*, 1886I

Fränzel, Ignaz: *Symphony in C (?)*, 1764I; *Symphony in F*, 1767I; *Symphonies in D & C*, 1775I

Franzetti, Carlos: *Piano Concerto No. 2*, 1996I; *Symphony No. 1*, 1995I

Freed, Isadore: *Lyrical Sonorities*, 1934I; *Piano Sonata*, 1933I; *Sonorités rhythmiques*, 1931I; *String Quartet No. 1*, 1925I; *String Quartet No. 2*, 1930I; *String Quartet No. 3*, 1936I; *Symphony No. 2*, 1951I

Freeman, Harry L.: *Athalia*, 1916I; *Touchings*, 1989I; *Zululand*, 1944I

Freer, Eleanor: *Sonnets from the Portugese*, 1939I

Fricker, Peter Racine: *Laudi Concertati*, 1979I

Friml, Rudolf: *The Donkey Serenade*, 1937I; *The Firefly*, 1912I; *Gloriana*, 1918I; *High Jinks*, 1913I; *The Wild Rose*, 1926I

Fröhlich, Friedrich T.: *Christmas Mass*, 1828I; *Passion Music Overture*, 1835I

Fröhlich, Johannes: *Symphony in E♭*, 1833I

Fry, William Henry: *Aurelia, the Vestal*, 1841I; *Evangeline Overture*, 1860I; *Hagar in the Wilderness*, 1854I; *Kyrie Eleison*, 1864I; *Mass in E♭*, 1864I; *Niagara Symphony*, 1854I; *Notre Dame de Paris*, 1863I; *Overture to MacBeth*, 1862I; *Overture, World's Own*, 1857I; *Stabat Mater*, 1855I; *Symphony, the Breaking Heart*, 1852I; *Symphony, Santa Claus*, 1853I

Fuchs, Kenneth: *String Quartet No. 2, "Where Have You Been?,"* 1995I

Fuchs, Robert: *Cello Sonata No. 2 in e♭, Opus 83*, 1908I; *Clarinet Quintet in E♭, Opus 102*,1917I; *Doublebass Sonata in g, Opus 97*, 1913I; *Die Königsbraut, Opus 46*, 1889I; *Massin F*, 1897I; *Mass No. 3, Opus 116*, 1926I; *Overture, Des Meeres & Liebe Wellen, Opus 59*, 1897I; *Piano Concerto in b, Opus 27*, 1880I; *Piano Quartet No. 2 in b, Opus 75*,1905I; *Piano Sonata No. 1 in G♭, Opus 19*, 1877I; *Piano Trio No. 2 in B♭, Opus 72*, 1905I; *Piano Variations in d, Opus 10*, 1874I; *Piano Variations in g, Opus 13*, 1876I; *Serenade No. 1 in D, Opus 9*, 1874I; *Serenade No. 2 in C, Opus 14*, 1876I; *Serenade No. 3 in e, Opus 21*, 1877I; *Serenade No. 4 in g, Opus 51*, 1895I; *Serenade No. 5 in D, Opus 53*, 1895I; *Sonata No. 2 in g, Opus 88*, 1910I; *Sonata No. 3 in D♭, Opus 109*, 1923I; *Songs (10), Opus 3, 6*, 1872I; *Songs (5), Opus 16*, 1875I; *Songs (5), Opus 26*, 1880I; *Songs (6), Opus 41*, 1886I; *Songs (4), Opus 56*, 1897I; *Songs (6), Opus 73*, 1903I; *Songs(7), Opus 81*, 1907I; *Songs (7), Opus 82*, 1895I; *Songs (5), Opus 89*, 1877I; *String Quartet No. 3 in C, Opus 71*, 1903I;

※

F   *Biographical*   G   *Cultural Beginnings*   H   *Musical Literature*
I   *Musical Compositions*

Fuchs, Robert: (*cont.*)
  String Quartet No. 4 in A, Opus 106, 1934I; *String Trio*, 1910I; *String Trio in A, Opus 94*, 1912I;
  Symphony No. 1 in C, Opus 37, 1884I; *Symphony No. 2 in E♭, Opus 45*, 1887I; *Die Teufelsglacke*, 1893I;
  Trio in f♯, Opus 115,1926I; *Viola Sonata in d, Opus 86*, 1909I; *Violin Sonata No. 1*, 1878I; *Violin Sonata No. 3 in d, Opus 68*, 1902I; *Violin Sonata No. 4 in E, Opus 77*, 1905I; *Violin Sonata No. 5 in A, Opus 95*, 1913I;
  Violin Sonata No. 6 in g, Opus 103 (?), 1923I
Fučik, Julius: *Entry of the Gladiators*, 1900I
Fuleihan, Anis: *Concerto for Two Pianos*, 1940I; *Piano Concerto No. 1*, 1937I; *Piano Concerto No. 2*, 1937I;
  Symphony No. 2, 1967I; *Vasco*, 1960I
Funk, Eric: *Symphony No. 1, "Emily,"* 1978I; *Lidice*, 1973I; *String Quartet, "In Memoriam Shostakovich,"*
  1993I
Furlanetto, Bonaventura: *David Goliath triumphator*, 1781I; *David in Siceleg*, 1776I; *De solemninuptiae in
  domum Lebani*, 1788I; *Dies extreme mundi*, 1781I; *Gideon*, 1792I; *Israelisliberatio*, 1777I; *Jerico*, 1775I;
  Judith triumphans, 1787I; *Melior fiducia vos ergo*, 1775I; *Mors Adam*, 1777I; *Moyses in Nilo*, 1771I;
  Triumphus Jephte, 1789I
Furrer, Beat: *Die Blinden*, 1991I; *String Quartet No. 1*, 1984I
Gabichvadze, Revaz: *Symphony No. 1*, 1963I
Gabriel, Charles H.: *The Glory Song*, 1900I; *His Eye Is On the Sparrow*, 1905I
Gaburo, Kenneth: *Antiphony I*, 1958I; *Antiphony II, III*, 1962I; *Antiphony IV*, 1967I; *Antiphony V*, 1968I;
  Antiphony VI, 1971I; *Antiphony VII*, 1974I; *Antiphony VIII, "Revolution,"*1984I; *Fat Millie's Lament*,
  1964I; *Lemon Drops*, 1965I; *My, My, My, What a Wonderful Fall*, 1975I; *On a Quiet Theme*, 1950I;
  Wasting of Lucrezia, 1964I
Gade, Niels: *Aladin*, 1840I; *Baldur's Dream*, 1858I; *Chorus, Opus 26*, 1853I; *Comala, Opus 12*, 1846I;
  Denderliedeken, 1869I; *Echoes from Ossian Overture, Opus 1*, 1840I; *Erlkönigs Tochter, Opus 30*, 1853I;
  Fantastic Pieces (4), Opus 41, 1862I; *Festsang*, 1869I; *Frühlings-Botschaft, Opus 35*, 1858I; *Hamlet
  Overture, Opus 37*, 1861I; *Holbergiana, Opus 61*, 1884I; *In the Highlands Overture, Opus 7*, 1844I;
  Kalanus, 1871I; *Die Kreuzfahrer, Opus 50*, 1866I; *Mariotta*, 1850I; *Michelangelo Overture, Opus 39*, 1861I;
  The Mountain Thrall, 1873I; *Napoli*, 1842I; *Novelletten, Opus 29*, 1883I; *Organ Pieces (3), Opus 22*, 1851I;
  Overture, Nordische Sehnfahrt, 1850I; *Piano Trio in F, Opus 42*, 1863I; *Siegfried und Brunhilde*, 1847I;
  Sonata No. 3 in B♭, Opus 59, 1885I; *Songs inFolkstyle (9), Opus 9*, 1843I; *Spring Fantasy, Opus 23*, 1852I;
  String Octet in F, Opus 17, 1848I; *String Quartet in D, Opus 63*, 1889I; *String Quintet No. 1, Opus 8*,
  1845I; *String Quintet in f*, 1851I; *String Sextet in E♭, Opus 44*, 1863I; *A Summer's Day in the Country,
  Opus 55*, 1879I; *Symphony No. 1 in c, Opus 5*, 1841I; *Symphony No. 2 in E,Opus 10*, 1843I; *Symphony No.
  3 in a, Opus 15*, 1847I; *Symphony No. 4 in B♭, Opus 20*, 1850I; *Symphony No. 5 in d, Opus 25*, 1852I;
  Symphony No. 6 in g, Opus 32, 1856I; *Symphony No. 7 in F, Opus 45*, 1865I; *Symphony No. 8 in b♭, Opus
  47*, 1871I; *Violin Concerto in d, Opus 56*, 1880I; *Zion, Opus 49*, 1873I
Gagneux, Renaud: *Triptyque*, 1993I
Gaines, David R.: *Symphony No. 1*, 2000I
Gaito, Constantino: *Cello Sonata*, 1918I
Gallico, Paul: *The Apocalypse*, 1922I
Galuppi, Baldassare: *Amor lunatico*, 1770I; *Adam*, 1771I; *Adriano in Siria*, 1758I; *Alessandronelle Indie*,
  1754I; *L'amante ditutte*, 1760I; *L'anfione*, 1780I; *Antigona* 1751I; *Artaserse*,1751I; *Arianna e Teseo*, 1763I;
  Attalo, 1754I; *Il caffe di campagna*, 1761I; *Cajo Mario*, 1764I; *La calamita de' cuori*, 1752I; *La cameriera
  spiritosa*, 1766I; *La cantarina*, 1756I; *La clemenze di Tito*, 1760I; *Dario*, 1751I; *Debbora prophetissa*, 1772I;
  Demetrio, 1761I; *Demofoonte*, 1758I; *La diavolessa*, 1755I; *Didone abbandonato*, 1751I; *La donna digoverno*,
  1763I; *L'eroe cinese*, 1753I; *Exitus Israelis de Aegypto*, 1775I; *Ezio*, 1757I; *Ilfilosofo di compagna*, 1754I;
  Flora, Apollo, Medoaco, 1769II; *Gl'intrighi amorosi*,1772; *Gloria*, 1761I; *Idomeneo*, 1756I; *Ifigenia in
  Tauride*, 1768I; *L'inimico delle donne*, 1771I; *Ipermestra*, 1758I; *Lucio Papirio*, 1751I; *Il marchese villano*,
  1762I; *Maria Magdalena*, 1763I; *Melite riconosciuto*, 1759I; *Montezuma*, 1772I; *Moyses de Synairevertens*,
  1776I; *Mundi salus*, 1776I; *Le nozze di Paaride*, 1756I; *Il nozze*, 1755I; *L'organa onorata*, 1762I; *La Pace tra
  la Virtu e la Bellezza*, 1766I; *La partenza ilritorno de' marinari*, 1764I; *Le pescatrici*, 1756I; *Il poverto
  superbo*, 1755I; *Il re allacaccia*, 1763I; *La ritornata di Londra*, 1759I; *Il ritorno di Tobia*, 1782I; *Sacrificium
  Abraham*, 1764I; *La serva per amore*, 1757I; *Sesostri*, 1757I; *Siroe*, 1754I; *Sofonisba*,1753I; *Solimano*, 1760I;
  Li tre amanti ridicoli, 1761I; *Tres Mariae ad sepulchrum Christi*, 1769I; *Tres pueri hebraei in captivitate
  Babylonis*, 1774I; *Triumphus diviniamoris*, 1765I; *Venere al tempio*, 1775I; *Il villano geloso*, 1769I; *Viriate*,
  1762I; *La virtuliberata*, 1765I; *Le virtuose ridicole* 1752I
Gandolfi, Michael: *Freshman Theory*, 2000I; *Of Memories Lost*, 1989I; *Piano Concerto*, 1989I; *Piano Etudes*,
  1998I; *Piano Preludes*, 1999I; *Transfiguration*, 1987I; *Two Studies of theSun*, 1981I; *UFO*, 2000I
Gann, Kyle: *Desert Sonata for Piano*, 1994I

❉

    A *Births*   B *Deaths*   C *Debuts*   D *New Positions*
                E *Prizes/Honors*

Ganne, Louis: *Les ailes,* 1910I
Ganz, Rudolf: *Piano Concerto in E♭, Opus 32,* 1940I
García, José Manuel: *Le finta schiava,* 1754I; *Sinfonia funebre,* 1790I; *Pompeo Magno in Armenia,* 1755I; *La Pulilla,* 1755I
Garcia, José Nunes: *Pastoral Mass,* 1811I; *Requiem,* 1816I
Garcia Fajer, Francisco: *Lo scultore deluso,* 1756I
Gardner, John: *The Ballad of the White House,* 1959I; *Bel & the Dragon,* 1973I; *Cantata for St. Cecilia, Opus 195,* 1991I; *Cantiones Sacrae, Opus 12,* 1952I; *Fantasy & Fugue on a Prelude of Bruckner, Opus 185,* 1988I; *Half Holiday Overture,* 1962I; *Herrick Cantata,* 1961I; *Irish Suite, Opus 231,* 1996I; *Mass in D, Opus 159,* 1983I; *The Moon & the Sixpence, Opus 32,* 1957I; *The Noble Heart, Opus 59,* 1964I; *Oboe Concerto, Opus 193,* 1990I; *Oboe Sonata No. 2,* 1986I; *Overture, Midsummer Ale, Opus 73,* 1965I; *Piano Concerto No. 1, Opus 34,* 1957I; *Piano Sonata, Opus 204,* 1992I; *Reflections at Edinburgh,* 1952I; *Sextet for Piano & Winds, Opus 223,* 1995I; *Sinfonia Piccolo,* 1960I; *Stabat Mater,* 1993I; *String Quartet No. 2, Opus 148,* 1978I; *String Quartet No. 3 in D, Opus 176,* 1987I; *Symphony No. 1, Opus 2,* 1951I; *Symphony No. 2, in E♭, Opus 166,* 1985I; *Symphony No. 3,* 1989I; *Trumpet Concerto,* 1962I; *Variations on a Waltz by Carl Nielsen, Opus 13,* 1952I; *The Visitors, Opus 14,* 1972I
Gardner, Maurice: *Piano Quintet,* 1991I; *String Quartet No. 2,* 1994I
Gardner, Samuel: *Broadway,* 1924I; *Piano Quintet, "To a Soldier,"* 1918I; *String Quartet No. 1 in d,* 1918I; *Variations for String Quartet,* 1919I
Gasparini, Quirino: *Artaserse,* 1756I
Gassmann, Florian: *Achille in Sciro,* 1766I; *L'amore artigiano,* 1767I; *Amore e Psyche,* 1767I; *Catone in Utica,* 1761I; *La contessina,* 1770I; *Ezio,* 1770I; *Filosofia ed amore,* 1760I; *Il filosofo inamorato,* 1771I; *Gli Uccellatori,* 1759I; *Issipile,* 1758I; *Merope,* 1757I; *Lanotte critica,* 1768I; *L'Olimpiade,* 1764I; *Un Pazzo ne fa Cento,* 1762I; *Le pescatrici,* 1771I; *Quartets (6), Flute & Strings, Opus 1,* 1769I; *Rovinati, I,* 1772I; *String Quartets(6), Opus 1,* 1771I; *String Quartets (6), Opus 2,* 1773I; *String Quintets (6),* 1766I; *Il trionfo d'amore,* 1765I; *Trios (5), Flute, Violin, Bass,* 1773I; *Il viaggiatori ridicolo,*1766I
Gatti, Luigi: *Antigono,* 1781I; *Virgilio e Manto (cantata),* 1769I
Gaubert, Philippe: *Flute Sonata No. 1,* 1917I; *Flute Sonata No. 2,* 1924I
Gaveaux, Pierre: *L'amour à Cythère,* 1805I; *Le bouffe et le tailleur,* 1804I; *Cêliane,* 1796I; *Les deux ermites,* 1793I; *Les deux suisses,* 1792; *Le diable couleur de rose,* 1798I; *L'échellede soie,* 1808I; *L'enfant prodigue,* 1811I; *La famille indigente,* 1793I; *La gasconade,* 1795I; *Léonore,* 1798I; *Lise et Colin,* 1796I; *Monsieur Deschalumeaux,* 1806I; *Le paria,* 1792I; *Le petit matelot,* 1796I; *Un quart d'heure de silence,* 1804I; *Recueil decanzonettes italiennes,* 1800I; *Le retour inattendu,* 1802I; *La rose blanche et la roserouge,* 1809I; *Sophia et Moncar,* 1797I; *Le traité nul,* 1797I; *Trop tôt,* 1804I
Gazzaniga, Giuseppe: *Amore per oro,* 1782I; *Il calandrino,* 1771I; *La distatta dei Mori,* 1791I; *La fedeltà d'amore alla pruova,* 1776I; *La Locanda,* 1771I; *I profeti al Calvario,* 1781I; *La stravagante,* 1781I
Gehlhaar, Rolf: *Cusps, Swallowtails & Butterflies for Piano,* 1983I; *Tokamak (piano &orchestra),*1982I
Genée, Richard: ; *Der Geiger aus Tirol,* 1857I
Generali, Pietro: *Adelaide di Borgogna,* 1819I; *Adelina,* 1810I; *Amor vince lo Sdegno,* 1809I; *Argene e alsindo,* 1822I; *Attila,* 1812I; *Bajazet,* 1814I; *La cecchina sonatrice,* 1818I; *Chiara di Rosemberg,* 1823I; *Don Chisciotte,* 1805I; *Il divorzio persiano,* 1828I; *Eginardo e Lisbetta,* 1813I; *La festa maraviglione,* 1821I; *Francesca da Rimini,* 1829I; *Gli amanti ridicoli,* 1800I; *L'idolo cinese,* 1808I; *L'imposte,* 1815I; *Le lagrime d'unavedova,* 1808I; *La moglie di tre mariti,* 1809I; *Le nozze fra Nemici,* 1823I; *Pamelanubile,* 1804I; *Rodrigo di Valenza,* 1817I; *Il romito di Provenza,* 1831I; *Il servopadrone,* 1818I; *La sposa indiana,* 1822I; *La vedova delirante,* 1811I
Genzmer, Hans: *Piano Preludes (10),* 1963I; *Piano Sonata No. 5,* 1985I
Genzmer, Harald: *Easter Concerto for Organ,* 1980I; *Organ Sonata No. 2,* 1956I; *Organ Sonata No. 3,* 1963I; *Piano Concerto No. 3,* 1974I; *Piano Sonata No. 1,* 1952I; *The Times of Day, for Organ,* 1968I
Gerber, Steven: *Cello Concerto,* 1994I; *Symphony No. 1,* 1989I; *Viola Concerto,* 1996I
Gerhard, Roberto: *Cello Sonata,* 1956I; *Chaconne for Solo Violin,* 1959I; *Concerto for Orchestra,* 1965I; *Concerto for Piano & String Orchestra,* 1951I; *Epithalamion,* 1966I; *Gemini,* 1966I; *Harpsichord Concerto,* 1956I; *Impromtus, (3),* 1950I; *Leo,* 1969I; *Libra,*1968I; *Nonet,* 1957I; *Pandora,* 1943I; *Piano Trio,* 1918I; *String Quartet No. 1,* 1955I; *String Quartet No. 2,* 1962I; *Symphony No. 1,* 1953I; *Symphony No. 2,* 1959I; *Symphony No. 3,* 1961I; *Symphony No. 4, "New York,"* 1967I; *Violin Concerto,* 1945I
Gerlach, Theodor: *Epic Symphony,* 1891I
German, Edward: *As You Like It,* 1896I; *Hamlet,* 1897I; *Henry VIII,* 1892I; *Merrie England,*1902I; *Much Ado about Nothing,* 1898I; *Piano Sonata in G,* 1884I; *The Princess of Kensington,* 1903I; *Richard III,* 1889I; *Romeo and Juliet,* 1895I; *The Seasons,* 1899I; *Symphonic Suite in d,* 1895I; *Symphony No. 1 in e,* 1887I; *Symphony No. 2 in a,"Norwich,"* 1893I; *Te Deum in F,* 1885I; *Tom Jones,* 1907I

❄

F   *Biographical*   G   *Cultural Beginnings*   H   *Musical Literature*
I   *Musical Compositions*

Gerschefski, Edwin: *Piano Sonatina*, 1933I
Gershwin, George: *An American in Paris*, 1928I; *Cuban Overture*, 1932I; *Piano Concerto in F*, 1925I; *Piano Preludes (3)*, 1926I; *Porgy & Bess*, 1935I; *Rhapsody in Blue*, 1924I; *Rhapsody No. 2*, 1931I; *Variations on "I Got Rhythm,"* 1934I
Gevaert, François: *Le capitaine Henriot*, 1864I; *Le château trompette*, 1860I; *Les deux amours*,1861I; *Le diable au moulin*, 1859I; *Les empiriques*, 1851I; *La feria Andaluza*, 1851I; *Hugues de Zomerghem*, 1848I; *Les lavandières de Santarem*, 1855I; *Quentin Durward*, 1858I
Giannini, Vittorio: *Beauty & the Beast*, 1938I; *Blennerhasset*, 1939I; *The Harvest*, 1961I; *IBM Symphony*, 1939I; *Piano Sonata*, 1963I; *Requiem*, 1936I; *The Scarlet Letter*, 1937I; *Symphony: In Memoriam Theodore Roosevelt*, 1935I; *Symphony No. 4*, 1960I ; *Violin Concerto*, 1944I
Giardini, Felice de': *Elfrida*, 1774I; *Enea e Lavinia*, 1764I; *Guitar Trios (6), Opus 18*, 1780I; *Harpsichord Quartets (6), Opus 21*, 1780I; *Italian Hymn*, 1769I; *Olimpiade*, 1756I; *Quintets (6), Opus 11*, 1770I; *Il re-pastore*, 1765I; *Rosmira*, 1757I; *Ruth*, 1765I; *Sappho*, 1778I; *Siroe*, 1763I; *String Quartets (6), Opus 29*, 1790I; *String Trios (6), Opus 17*, 1775I; *String Trios (6), Opus 20*, 1779I; *String Trios (6), Opus 26*, 1784I; *String Trios(6), Opus 30*, 1790I; *Violin Concertos (6), Opus 15*, 1775I; *Violin Sonatas (6), Opus 1*, 1751I
Gibson, Robert: *Ex Machina for Computer Generated Tape*, 1995I
Gideon, Miriam: *Biblical Masks (3)*, 1958I; *The Condemned Playground*, 1963I; *Creature to Creature*, 1985I; *Epitaphs for Robert Burns*, 1952I; *Morning Star*, 1980I; *Piano Sonata*,1977I; *Piano Suite No. 1, "Three-Cornered Pieces,"* 1935I; *Piano Suite No. 2,"Sketches,"* 1940I; *Piano Suite No. 3*, 1951I; *Questions on Nature*, 1964I; *Rhymes from the Hills*, 1966I; *The Resounding Lyre*, 1979I; *Six Cuckoos in Quest of a Composer*, 1953I; *Songs of Voyage*, 1961I; *Songs of Youth & Madness*, 1977I; *Sonnets from "Fatal Interview,"* 1952I; *Spirit Above the Dust*, 1980I; *String Quartet No. 1*, 1946I; *Voices from Elysium*, 1979I; *Wing'd Hour*, 1983I; *A Woman of Valor*, 1981I
Gilbert, Henry F.: *American Dances (3)*, 1911I; *Celtic Songs*, 1905I; *Comedy Overture on Negro Themes*, 1905I; *Dance in the Place Congo*, 1906I; *Indian Sketches.*, 1914I; *Island of the Fay*, 1904I; *The Island of the Fay*, 1923I; *Negro Dances*, 1914I; *Negro Rhapsody*, 1912I; *Piano Pieces (6), Opus 19*, 1927I; *Symphonic Piece*, 1925I; *Uncle Remus*, 1906I; *Verlaine Moods (2), Opus 8*, 1903I
Gilbert/Sullivan: *Contrabandista*, 1867I; *Cox and Box*, 1867I; *The Gondoliers*, 1889I; *The Grand Duke*, 1896I; *H. M. S. Pinafore*, 1878I; *Iolanthe*, 1882I; *The Mikado*, 1885I; *Patience*, 1881I; *The Pirates of Penzance*, 1879I; *Princess Ida*, 1884I; *The Sorcerer*, 1877I; *Thespis*, 1871I; *Trial by Jury*, 1875I; *Utopia Unlimited*, 1893I; *Yeoman of the Guard*, 1888I
Gilchrist, William W.: *The Lamb of God*, 1909I; *Songs (8)*, 1885I; *Symphony No. 1 in C*, 1891I
Gilles, Joseph: *Organ Symphony in E*, 1937I
Gillis, Don: *The Alamo*, 1944I; *Symphony No. 1, "An American Symphony,"* 1940I; *Symphony No. 1*, 1939I; *Symphony No. 2, "Symphony of Faith,"* 1940I; *Symphony No. 3, "of Free Men,"* 1941I; *Symphony No. 4*, 1943I; *Symphony No. 5*, 1945I; *Symphony No. 5H,"Symphony For Fun,"* 1947I; *Symphony No. 6*, 1947I; *Symphony No. 10*, 1967I; *Tulsa, A Symphonic Portrait*, 1950I
Gilmore, Patrick S.: *Famous Twenty-Second Regiment March*, 1882I; *When Johnny Comes Marching Home*, 1863I
Gilse, Jan van: *Nonet*, 1916I; *String Quartet in f*, 1922I; *Trio for Flute, Violin & Viola*, 1927I
Ginastera, Alberto: *American Preludes (12)*, 1944I; *Beatrix Cenci*, 1971I; *Bomarzo*, 1967I; *Cantata para América Magica*, 1960I; *Cello Concerto*, 1968I; *Concert Variations*, 1953I; *Concerto for Strings*, 1965I; *Estancia*, 1941I; *Harp Concerto*, 1957I; *Iubilum: Celebración Sinfonica*, 1980I; *Panambi*, 1940I; *Piano Concerto No. 1*, 1961I; *Piano Concerto No. 2*, 1972I; *String Quartet No. 1*, 1948I; *String Quartet No. 2*, 1958I; *String Quartet No. 3*, 1973I; *String Quartet No. 4*, 1974I
Giordani, Giuseppe: *L'astuto in imbroglio*, 1771I; *Atalanta*, 1792I; *Caio Ostilio*, 1788I; *Caio Mario*, 1790I; *Don Mitrillo contrastato*, 1791I; *Elpinice*, 1781I; *Epponina*, 1779I; *Erifile*, 1783I; *La fuga in Egitto*, 1775I; *Good Friday Passion*, 1776I; *Ifigenia in Aulide*,1786I; *Medonte*, 1791I; *La morte di Abelle*, 1786I; *Osmano*, 1785I; *Pizarro nell'Indie*,1784I; *Ritorno d'Ulisse*, 1782I; *Scipione*, 1788I; *Tito Manlio*, 1784I; *La vestale*, 1786I
Giordani, Tommaso: *Aci e Galatea*, 1777I; *Antigono*, 1774I; *Artaserse*, 1772I; *Il Bacio*, 1782I; *Calypso*, 1785I; *The Castle Ode*, 1769I; *Chamber Concertos (6)*, 1775I; *La comediantefatta cantatrice*, 1756I; *The Cottage Festival*, 1796I; *The Distressed Knight*, 1791I; *Don Fulminone*, 1765I; *The Elopement*, 1768I; *The Enchanter*, 1765I; *L'eroe cinese*, 1766I; *Flute Concertos (6), Opus 19*, 1780I; *Gibraltar*, 1784I; *Gretna Green*, 1785I; *Harpsichord Quintets (6), Opus 1*, 1771I; *The Haunted Castle*, 1784I; *The Hypochondriac*, 1785I; *Isaac*, 1767I; *Love in Disguise*, 1765I; *Il padre e il figlio rivali*, 1770I; *Perserverance*, 1789I; *Phyllis at Court*, 1767I; *Quartets (3)*, 1775I; *Il re pastore*, 1778I; *String Quartets (6), Opus 18*, 1785I; *Violin Sonatas (3), Opus 34*, 1788I
Giordano, Umberto: *Andrea Chenier*, 1896I; *Fedora*, 1906I; *Giove a Pompei*, 1921I; *Madame Sans-Gene*, 1915I; *Mala Vita*, 1892I; *Marcella*, 1907I; *Mese Mariano*, 1910I; *Il re*, 1929I; *Siberia*, 1904I

❋

A *Births*   B *Deaths*   C *Debuts*   D *New Positions*
E *Prizes/Honors*

Gipps, Ruth: *Horn Concerto*, 1997I; *Symphony No. 2*, 1946I; *Symphony No. 4, Opus 61*, 1972I; *Symphony No. 5, Opus 64*, 1982I

Giraud, François: *Acanthe et Cydippe*, 1764I; *Deucalion et Pyrrha*, 1755I; *La gageure de village*, 1756I; *Les hommes*, 1753I

Giroust, François: *Rosemonde*, 1781I

Giuliani, Mauro: *Guitar Concerto No. l, Opus 30*, 1808I; *Guitar Concerto No. 2, Opus 36*, 1812I; *Guitar Concerto No. 3, Opus 70*, 1820I; *Guitar Sonata, Opus 15*, 1808I

Glanville-Hicks, Peggy: *Beckett*, 1990I; *Sappho*, 1963I; *Saul & the Witch of Endor*, 1959I; *Tapestry*, 1956I; *Thomsoniana*, 1949I; *The Transposed Heads*, 1953I

Glass, Louis: *Cello Sonata in G, Opus 5*, 1888I; *String Quartet No. 3*, 1907I; *String Quartet No. 4*, 1907I; *Symphony No. 5 in C, "Sinfonia Svastica," Opus 57*, 1916I; *Violin Sonata No. 1, Opus 7*, 1890I; *Violin Sonata No. 2*, 1904I

Glass, Philip: *Akhnaton*, 1984I; *La belle et la bête*, 1994I; *The Canyon*, 1988I; *Concert Fantasy for Two Timpanists & Orchestra*, 2000I; *Concerto for Saxophone Quartet*, 1995I; *A Descent into the Maelstrom*, 1986I; *Dracula*, 1999I; *Einstein on the Beach*, 1975I; *The Fall of the House of Usher*, 1989I; *Hydrogen Jukebox*, 1990I; *Hydrogen Jukebox*, 1992I; *Itaipu*, 1989I; *The Light*, 1987I; *Low Symphony*, 1992I; *Making of the Representative for Planet 8*, 1988I; *Music in Contrary Motion for Organ*, 1969I; *Music in Eight Parts*, 1969I; *Music in Similar Motion*, 1969I; *Music in Twelve Parts*, 1974I; *Music with Changing Parts*, 1970I; *1000 Airplanes on the Roof*, 1988I; *Orphée*, 1993I; *The Photographer*, 1982I; *Pieces in the Shape of a Square*, 1968I; *Satyagraha*, 1980I; *String Quartet No. 2*, 1983I; *String Quartet No. 3, "Mishima,"* 1985I; *String Quartet No. 4: Boczak*, 1989I; *Symphony No. 2*, 1994I; *Symphony No. 3*, 1995I; *Symphony No. 5*, 1999I; *Trumpet Concerto*, 2000I; *The Voyage*, 1992I

Glazunov, Alexander: *Ballade in F for Orchestra*, 1902I; *Cantata, Praise the Lord*, 1914I; *Cantata for Pushkin's 100SUPth/SUP Birthday, Opus 65*, 1899I; *Carnival Overture in F, Opus 45*,1892I; *Le chant de destin, Overture*, 1907I; *Chant du Ménéstrel, Opus 71*, 1900I; *Characteristic Suite in D, Opus 9*, 1887I; *Chopiniana, Opus 44*, 1893I; *Concert WaltzNo. 1 in D, Opus 47*, 1893I; *Concert Waltz No. 2 in F, Opus 51*, 1894I; *Concerto Ballatain C, Opus 108 (cello)*, 1931I; *Coronation Cantata, Opus 56*, 1896I; *Cortège solennel*, 1910I; *Cortège solennel in D, Opus 50*, 1894I; *Finnish Fantasy in C, Opus 88*, 1909I; *The Forest, Opus 19*, 1887I; *From Darkness to Light, Opus 53*, 1894I; *From the Middle Ages, Opus 79*, 1902I; *In Modo Religioso for Brass*, 1886I; *Karelische Legende*, 1915I; *The Kremlin, Opus 30*, 1890I; *March on a Russian Theme, Opus 76*, 1901I; *Orchestra Serenade No. 1 in A, Opus 7*, 1883I; *Oriental Rhapsody, Opus 29*, 1890I; *Oriental Suite*, 1895I; *Overture No. 2 in D on Greek Themes, Opus 6*, 1883I; *Petite suite de Ballet*, 1910I; *Piano Concerto No. 1 in f, Opus 92*, 1911I; *Piano Concerto No. 2 in B, Opus 100*,1917I; *Prelude & Fugue in D, Opus 39*, 1907I; *Prelude & Fugue No. 2 in d, Opus 98*, 1914I; *Le printemps, Opus 34*, 1892I; *Raymonda, Opus 57*, 1897I; *Romances (5), Opus 40* 1885I; *Les ruses d'amour, Opus 61*, 1898I; *Saxophone Concerto in Eᵇ, Opus 109*,1934I; *Scenes de Ballet, Opus 52*, 1894I; *The Sea, Opus 28*, 1889I; *The Seasons*, 1899I; *Serenade No. 2 in F, Opus 11*, 1884I; *Songs (2), Opus 27*, 1890I; *Songs (12), Opus 59, 60*, 1898I; *Spring, Opus 34*, 1891I; *Stenka Razin, Opus 13*, 1885I; *String Quartet No. 3 in G, Opus 26*, 1889I; *Symphony No. 1 in E, Opus 5*, 1881I; *Symphony No. 2 in f♯, Opus 16*, 1886I; *Symphony No. 3 in D, Opus 33*, 1890I; *Symphony No. 4 in Eᵇ, Opus 48*, 1894I; *Symphony No. 5 in Bᵇ, Opus 55*, 1895I; *Symphony No. 6 in c, Opus 58*, 1896I; *Symphony No. 7 in F, Opus 77*, 1902I; *Symphony No. 8 in Eᵇ, Opus 83*, 1906I; *Symphony No. 9*, 1910I; *Theme & Variations, Opus 72*, 1900I; *Triumphal March in Eᵇ, Opus 46*, 1892I; *Triumphal March, Chicago Columbian Exposition*, 1893I; *Violin Concerto, Opus 82*, 1904I

Gleason, Frederick: *Edris*, 1896I; *Montezuma*, 1885I; *Otho Visconti, Opus 7*, 1890I; *The Song of Life*, 1899I

Glebov, Evgeny: *Cello Concerto*, 1991I; *The Coliseum*, 1995I; *The Master and Margarita*,1990I; *Memories of Till*, 1977I; *Symphony No. 1*, 1958I; *Symphony No. 2*, 1963I; *Symphony No.3*, 1964I; *Symphony No. 4*, 1968I; *Symphony No. 5*, 1985I; *Symphony No. 6*, 1994I

Glière, Reinhold: *Bronze Horseman*, 1949I; *Chrysis*, 1912I; *Concerto for Soprano & Orchestra*, 1942I; *The Cossacks of Zaporozh*, 1921I; *Harp Concerto*, 1938I; *Poems for Soprano & Orchestra (2), Opus 60*, 1924I; *The Red Poppy*, 1927I; *The Sirens, Opus 33*, 1908I; *String Quartet No. 2*, 1905I; *String Quartet No. 3*, 1928I; *String Quartet No. 4*, 1948I; *Symphony No. 1 in Eᵇ, Opus 8*, 1900I; *Symphony No. 2 inc, Opus 25*, 1907I; *Symphony No. 3, "Ilya Mourometz," Opus 42*, 1911I; *Taras Bulba*, 1952I; *Trizna, Opus 66*, 1915I

Glinka, Mikhail: *Andante and Rondo in d*, 1824I; *The Bigamist*, 1855I; *A Farewell to St. Petersburg*, 1840I; *A Greeting to My Native Land*, 1847I; *Kamarinskaya*, 1848I; *A Life for the Tsar*, 1836I; *Memorial Cantata*, 1826I; *Mozart Variations in Eᵇ*, 1822I; *Overtures in D & g*, 1824I; *Overture-Symphony on Russian Themes*, 1834I; *Russlan und Ludmilla*, 1842I; *Sextet in Eᵇ, Piano & Strings*, 1832I; *Spanish Overture 1, "Jota Aragonesa,"* 1845I; *Spanish Overture 2, "Summer Night in Madrid,"* 1851I; *String Quartet No. 1 in D*, 1824I; *String Quartet No. 2 in F*, 1830I; *Symphony in Bᵇ*, 1824I; *Ukranian Symphony*, 1852I; *Valse-fantasie in b*, 1839I; *Viola Sonata in d*, 1828I

Gluck, Christoph Willibald: *Alceste*, 1767I; *Alessandro*, 1764I; *Antigono*, 1756I; *L'arbreenchanté*, 1759I; *Armide*, 1777I; *Le cadi dupé*, 1761I; *Le Cinesi*, 1754I; *La clemenza diTito*, 1752I; *La corona*, 1765I; *La Cythère assiégée*, 1759I; *La danza*, 1755I; *DeProfundis*, 1782I; *Le diable à quatre*, 1759I; *Don Juan*, 1761I; *Echo et Narcisse*, 1779I; *La fausse esclave*, 1758I; *Le feste d'Apollo*, 1769I; *Flute Concerto in G*, 1752I; *L'Ile de Merlin*, 1758I; *L'innocenza giustificata*, 1755I; *Iphigenie en Aulide*, 1774I; *Iphigenie enTauride*, 1778I; *Issipile*, 1752I; *L'ivrogne corrigé*, 1760I; *Ode an der Tod*, 1783I; *Orfeoed Euridice* 1762I; *Paride ed Elena*, 1770I; *Il Prologo*, 1767I; *Il re pastore*, 1756I; *Larencontre imprévue*, 1764I; *Semiramis*, 1765I; *Telemaco*, 1765I; *Tetide*, 1760I; *Il trionfodi Clelia*, 1763I

Gnazzo, Anthony: *The Art of Canning Music*, 1976I; *Compound Skull Fracture*, 1975I; *Gigin Again*, 1977I

Godard, Benjamin: *Concerto romantique*, 1876I; *Jocelyn*, 1888I; *Scènes poétiques*, 1879I; *Symphony No. 1, "Gothique,"* 1883I; *Symphony No. 2, "Orientale," Opus 84*, 1884I; *Symphony No. 3, "Symphonie légendaire,"*1886I

Godowsky, Leopold: *Java Suite for Piano*, 1925I

Goeb, Roger: *Symphony No. 2*, 1945I; *Symphony No. 3*, 1952I; *Symphony No. 4*, 1954I; *Violin Concerto*, 1953I

Goebbels, Heiner: *Surrogate Cities*, 2000I

Goehr, Alexander: *Arden muss sterben, Opus 21*, 1966I; *Arianna*, 1995I; *Behold the Sun, Opus 44*, 1984I; *Cello Sonata, Opus 45*, 1984I; *The Death of Moses, Opus 53*, 1992I; *Eve Dreams in Paradise*, 1988I; *Kantan & Damask*, 1998I; *Konzertstück, Opus 20*, 1969I; *Piano Concerto, Opus 33*, 1972I; *Schlussgesang, Opus 61*, 1996I; *String Quartet No. 1*, 1957I; *String Quartet No. 3*, 1976I; *String Quartet No. 4, "In Memoriam John Ogdon,"* 1990I; *Symphony in One Movement*, 1969I; *Symphony with Chaconne, Opus 48*, 1986I; *Violin Concerto*, 1962I

Goemanne, Noel: *Fantasia 2000—The Millenium*, 2000I

Goetz, Hermann: *Nenie, Opus 9*, 1874I; *Overture, Francesco da Rimini*, 1875I; *Piano Sonata in g (4 hands)*, 1868I; *Spring Overture*, 1864I

Goeyvaerts, Karel: *Litany I for Piano*, 1979I; *Sonata for Two Pianos*, 1951I; *String Quartet No.1*, 1986I; *String Quartet No. 2*, 1992I

Goldenthal, Elliot: *Fire Water Paper: A Vietnam Oratorio*, 1995I

Goldenweiser, Alexander: *Piano Trio in e*, 1943I

Goldman, Edwin Franko: *On the Mall*, 1923I; *The Pride of America March*, 1911I

Goldmark, Carl: *Characteristic Pieces (9), Opus 5*, 1859I; *Der Gefesselte Prometheus Overture,Opus 38*, 1889I; *Götz von Berlichingen*, 1902I; *Hungarian Dances, Opus 22*, 1876I; *Die Königen von Saba*, 1875I; *Ländliche Hochzeit, Opus 26*, 1877I; *Orchestral Scherzo No. 1, Opus 19*, 1863I; *Oriental Rhapsody in G, Opus 18*, 1889I; *Ouverture solennelle, opus 73*, 1900I; *Overture, In Spring, Opus 36*, 1888I; *Overture*, 1854I; *Penthesilea Overture, Opus 31*, 1879I; *Sakuntala Overture, Opus 13*, 1865I; *Sappho Overture, Opus 44*, 1893I; *Scherzo No. 2 in A, Opus 45*, 1894I; *Songs (7), Opus 32*, 1879I; *Songs (12), Opus 18*,1868I; *Songs (4), Opus 34*, 1880I; *Songs (8), Opus 37*, 1888I; *String Quartet in a, Opus 9*, 1862I; *String Quartet in D, Opus 8*, 1860I; *Symphony in C*, 1860I; *Symphony No. 1,"Rustic Wedding," Opus 26*, 1876I; *Symphony No. 2 in E♭, Opus 45*, 1887I; *Violin Concerto in a, Opus 28*, 1877I; *Ein Wintermärchen*, 1908I

Goldmark, Rubin: *Hiawatha*, 1900I; *A Negro Rhapsody*, 1922I; *Piano Quintet*, 1909I; *Requiem*,1919I; *Samson*, 1914I

Goldschmidt, Berthold: *Chronica*, 1939I; *Clarinet Quartet*, 1982I; *Overture to A Comedy of Errors*, 1925I; *Passacaglia*, 1925I; *Piano Sonata*, 1926I; *String Quartet No. 1*, 1925I; *String Quartet No. 2*, 1936I

Goleminov, Marin: *Diptych* (flute concerto), 1982I; *Oboe Concerto*, 1984I

Golijov, Osvaldo: *St. Mark Passion*, 2000I

Gomes, André de Silva: *Christmas Matins*, 1774I

Gomes, (Antonio) Carlos: *Il Guaran*, 1870I; *Noite do Castello*, 1861I

Gómez-Martinez, Miguel: *Songs (5) on Poems of Alfonso Gama*, 1995I; *Symphony of Discovery*, 1987I

Goosens, Eugene: *Symphony No. 1*, 2000I

Gorecki, Hendrik: *Kleines Requiem für ein Polka, Opus 66*, 1993I; *Lerchenmusik, Opus 53*,1985I

Gossec, François: *Les agréments d'Hylas et Silvie*, 1768I; *Alexis et Daphne*, 1775I; *Annette et Lubin*, 1778I; *Athalie*, 1785I; *Le chant du 14 juillet*, 1791I; *Chant martial pour la fête dela victoire*, 1796I; *Le double déguisement*, 1767I; *Electre*, 1782I; *Le faux lord*, 1765I; *La fête de village*, 1778I; *La fête de Mirza*, 1781I; *Grand Symphonies (3), Opus 8*, 1765I; *Hymne à la nature*, 1793I; *Hymne à la statue de la liberté*, 1793I; *Hymne à l'égalité*,1793I; *Hymne à liberté*, 1792I; *Messe de morts*, 1760I; *Messe des vivants*, 1813I; *Mirza*, 1779I; *La nativité*, 1774I; *Les pêcheurs*, 1766I; *Le périgourdin*, 1761I; *Philémon et Baucis*, 1775I; *Le pied de boeuf*, 1787I; *La reprise de Toulon*, 1796I; *Sabvinus*, 1774I; *Les sabots et le cerisier*, 1803I; *Les Scythes enchaînés*, 1779I; *String Quartets (6), Opus 14*, 1769I; *String Quartets (6), Opus 15*, 1772I; *String Trios (6), Opus 9*, 1766I; *Symphony in D (Périodique No. 48)*, 1763I; *Symphony in F, "Tobia,"* 1774I; *Symphonyin 17 Parts in F*, 1809I; *Symphonie concertante No. 2 in F Major*, 1778I; *Symphonie dechasses*

(In D), 1776I; *Symphonies (6), Opus 3*, 1756I; *Symphonies (6), Opus 4*, 1758I; *Symphonies (6), Opus 5*, 1762I; *Symphonies (6) Opus 6*, 1762I; *Symphonies (6) for Large Orchestra, Opus 12*, 1769I; *Symphonies (3) for Large Orchestra*, 1773I; *Symphonies in C& F*, 1794I; *Te Deum* (male voices), 1790I; *Thésée*, 1782I; *Toinon et Toinette*, 1767I

Gotkovsky, Ida: *Clarinet Concerto*, 1968I; *Concerto lyrique for Clarinet*, 1982I; *Hommage à Jean de la Fontaine*, 1995I; *Oratorio Olympique*, 1992I

Gottlieb, Jack: *String Quartet No. 1*, 1954I

Gottschalk, Louis M.: *El Cocoyé*, 1854I; *The Dying Swan*, 1869I; *The Dying Poet*, 1864I; *Escenas Campestres*, 1859I; *Fantasy on God Save the Queen*, 1851I; *Fantasy on Brazilian Nat'l Anthem*, 1869I; *Grand March*, 1860I; *Grand Tarantelle*, 1860I; *The LastHope*, 1854I; *The Maiden's Blush*, 1864I; *Marche Solennelle*, 1868I; *Midnight in Seville*,1852I; *Souvenir de la Havane*, 1859I; *Souvenir de Puerto Rico*, 1857I; *Souvenirs d'Andalousie*, 1851I; *Symphony No. 1, "A Night in the Tropics,"* 1859I; *Symphony No. 2,"A Montevideo,"* 1868I; *The Union*, 1862I

Gould, J. E.: *Jesus, Savior, Pilot Me*, 1871I

Gould, Morton: *American Salute*, 1943I; *American Symphonette No. 4, "Latin-American,"* 1940I; *Burchfield Gallery*, 1979I; *Concerto for Tap Dancer & Orchestra*, 1952I; *Diversions* (tenor sax concerto), 1990I; *Fall River Legend* 1947I; *Flute Concerto*, 1984I; *Housewarming*, 1982I; *Interplay*, 1945I; *Jekyll & Hyde Variations*, 1955I; *Piano Concerto*, 1938I; *Showpiece for Orchestra*, 1954I; *Soundings*, 1969I; *Spirituals for Orchestra*, 1940I; *Stringmusic*, 1994I; *Symphony No. 1*, 1942I; *Symphony No. 2*, 1944I; *Symphony No. 3*, 1947I; *Symphony of Spirituals*, 1976I; *Venice*, 1966I; *Vivaldi Gallery*, 1967I

Gounod, Charles: *A la frontière*, 1870I; *The Angel & Tobias*, 1854I; *Ave Maria*, 1859I; *Lebourgeois gentilhomme*, 1852I; *Cinq-Mars*, 1877I; *La colombe*, 1860I; *Les deux reines*, 1872I; *L'emploi de la journée*, 1855I; *Fantasy on the Russian National Hymn*, 1886I; *Faust*, 1859I; *Fernand*, 1839I; *Funeral March of a Marionette*, 1872I; *Gallia: lamentation*, 1871I; *Jeanne d'Arc*, 1873I; *Jésus sur le lac de Tibériade*, 1878I; *Jésus de Nazareth*, 1856I; *Little Symphony* (woodwinds), 1888I; *Marche Solennelle in E♭*, 1878I; *Marche religieuse in C*, 1876I; *Marie Stuart*, 1837I; *Le médecin malgré lui*, 1858I; *Messeaux cathédrales in G*, 1890I; *Messe aux communautés religieuses*, 1882I; *Messe brève inC*, 1871I; *Messe brève aux chapelles in C*, 1890I; *Messe brève et salut in G, Opus 1*,1846I; *Messe dite de Clovis in C*, 1895I; *Messe du Sacré-Coeur de Jésus in C*, 1877I; *Messe funèbre in F*, 1855I; *Messe à la mémoire de Jeanne d'Arc in F*, 1887I; *Messe in c/C, "aux Orphéonistes,"* 1853I; *Messe solennelle*, 1849I; *Messe solennelle de Pâques inE♭*, 1883I; *Messe solennelle sur l'intonation de la liturgie . . .* , 1881I; *Mireille*, 1864I; *Missa angeli custodes in C*, 1873I; *Mors et Vita*, 1885I; *La nonne sanglante*, 1854I; *Offertorium*, 1876I; *Philémon et Baucis*, 1860I; *Polyeucte*, 1878I; *The Redemption*, 1880I; *La reine de Saba*, 1862I; *Requiem Mass*, 1841I; *Requiem in F*, 1872I; *Requiem*,1893I; *Romeo and Juliet*, 1867I; *Sapho*, 1851I; *Scherzo for Orchestra*, 1837I; *The Seven Last Words of Christ*, 1876I; *Stabat Mater*, 1867I; *Ste. Cecilia Mass in G*, 1855I; *Symphony No. 1 in D*, 1854I; *Symphony No. 2 in E♭*, 1855I; *Te Deum in C*, 1888I; *Letemple de Pharmonie*, 1869I; *Le tribut de Zamore*, 1811I; *Ulysse*, 1852I; *La Vendetta*,1838I; *Vienna Mass*, 1843I

Gouvy, Theodore: *Piano Quintet*, 1861I; *String Quartet No. 5*, 1882I

Grabner, Hermann: *Media vitae in morte sumus*, 1957I; *Psalm 66*, 1957I

Graf, Christian: *Symphonies (6), Opus 9*, 1769I

Grainger, Percy: *Handel in the Strand*, 1930I; *Shepherd's Hey*, 1922I; *Suite, "In a Nutshell,"* 1916I

Granados, Enrique: *Goyescas*, 1911I

Granier, François: *Cello Solos (6)*, 1754I

Grant, James: *Piano Concerto*, 1995I

Grant, Parks: *Symphony No. 1 in d*, 1938I; *Symphony No. 2*, 1941I

Graun, Carl H.: *L'Armida*, 1751I; *Britannico* 1751I; *I fratelli nemici*, 1756I; *Il giudicio di Paride*, 1752I; *Ezio*, 1755I; *La Merope*, 1756I; *Montezuma*, 1755I; *L'Orfeo*, 1752I; *Semiramide*, 1754I; *Silla*, 1753I; *Te Deum*, 1756I; *Te Deum Laudemus*, 1757I; *Der Tod Jesu*, 1755I

Greef, Arthur de: *Violin Sonata No. 1*, 1896I

Greenleaf, Robert: *Under the Arbor*, 1992I

Greef, Arthur de: *Violin Sonata No. 2*, 1933I

Gresnick, Antoine: *Le baiser donné et rendu*, 1796I; *La forêt de Sicile*, 1798I; *La grotte des Cévennes*, 1798I; *Rencontre sur rencontre*, 1799I; *Le tuteur original*, 1799I

Gretchaninov, Alexander: *Cello Concerto*, 1895I; *Clarinet Sonata No. 1*, 1939I; *Clarinet Sonata No. 2*, 1943I; *Festival Overture, Opus 178*, 1946I; *Liturgia Domestica, Opus 79*, 1917I; *The Marriage*, 1946I; *Mass, "Et in terra pax,"* 1942I; *Missa Festiva*, 1937I; *Missaoecumenica*, 1944I; *Piano Sonata No. 2*, 1944I; *Piano Trio No. 1 in c*, 1906I; *Piano Trio No. 2 in G*, 1931I; *Praise the Lord*, 1915I; *Rhapsody on a Russian Theme, Opus 147*, 1940I; *Seven Days of Passion, Opus 58*, 1911I; *Snowflakes*, 1910I; *Symphony No. 1*, 1894I; *Symphony No. 2, "Pastoral,"* 1909I; *Symphony No. 3, Opus 100*, 1923I; *Symphony No. 4*, 1927I; *Symphony No. 5*, 1936I I; *Vespers, Opus 59*, 1912I

❀

F   *Biographical*   G   *Cultural Beginnings*   H   *Musical Literature*
          I   *Musical Compositions*

Grétry, André: *L'amant jaloux*, 1778I; *L'ami de la maison*, 1771I; *L'amitié à l'épreuve*, 1770I; *Amphitryon*, 1786I; *Anacréon chez Polycrate*, 1797I; *Andromaque*, 1780I; *Aspasie*, 1789I; *Aucassin et Nicolette*, 1779I; *Le barbier du village*, 1797I; *Basile*, 1792I; *Lacaravane du Caire*, 1783I; *Le casque et les colombes*, 1801I; *Cephale et Procris*, 1773I; *Le comte d'Albert*, 1786I; *Delphis et Mopsa*, 1803I; *Denys le tyran*, 1794I; *Les deuxavares*, 1770I; *Les deux couvents*, 1792I; *La double épreuve*, 1782I; *Elisca*, 1799I; *L'embarras des richesses*, 1782I; *Emilie*, 1781I; *L'épreuve villageoise*, 1784I; *Lesévénements imprévus*, 1779I; *La fausse magie*, 1775I; *Guillaume Tell*, 1791I; *Le huron*, 1768I; *Isabelle et Gertrude*, 1766I; *Joseph Barra*, 1794I; *Le jugement de Midas*, 1778I; *Lucile*, 1769I; *Le magnifique*, 1773I; *Les mariages samnites*, 1768I; *Matroco*, 1777I; *Leménage*, 1803I; *Messe solennelle*, 1759I; *Panurge dans l'ile des lanternes*, 1785I; *Pierrele Grand*, 1790I; *Raoul Barbebleue*, 1789I; *Richard Coeur-de-Lion*, 1784I; *Le rivalconfident*, 1788I; *La rosière de Salency*, 1773I; *La rosière républicaine*, 1794I; *Silvain*, 1770I; *Small Symphonies (6)*, 1758I; *Le tableau parlant*, 1769I; *Théodore et Paulin*, 1784I; *Les trois âges de l'opéra*, 1778I; *La Vendemmiatrice*, 1765I; *Zémire et Azor*, 1771I

Grieg, Edvard: *Around the Curve of the World*, 1999I; *Cello Sonata in A*, 1883I; *ConcertOverture, "In Autumn,"* Opus 11, 1866I; *From Mountain and Fjord*, Opus 44, 1886I; *Haugtussa Songs*, Opus 67, 1895I; *The Heart's Melodies*, Opus 5, 1864I; *Holberg Suite*, Opus 40, 1884I; *Lyric Pieces, Book I*, Opus 12, 1867I; *Lyric Pieces, Book II*, Opus 37, 1883I; *Lyric Pieces, Book III*, Opus 43, 1886I; *Lyric Pieces, Book IV*, Opus 47, 1888I; *Lyric Pieces, Book V*, Opus 54, 1891I; *Lyric Pieces, Book VI*, Opus 57, 1893I; *Lyric Pieces, Book VII*, Opus 62, 1895I; *Lyric Pieces, Book VIII*, Opus 65, 1896I; *Lyric Pieces, Book IX*, Opus 68, 1898I; *Lyric Pieces X*, Opus 71, 1901I; *Norway*, Opus 58, 1894I; *Norwegian Dances*, Opus 35, 1881I; *Norwegian Peasant Dances*, Opus 72, 1902I; *Norwegian Songs & Dances*, Opus 17, 1870I; *Olaf Trygvason*, Opus 50, 1873I; *Peer Gynt*, Opus 23 1875I; *Piano Pieces (4)*, Opus 1, 1861I; *Piano Sonata in E*, Opus 7, 1865I; *Piano Sonata in F*, 1918I; *Poem for Flute & Orchestra*, 1919I; *Poems ((6)*, Opus49, 1889I; *Poetic Tone Pictures (6)*, Opus 3, 1863I; *Sigurd Jorsalfar*, Opus 22, 1872I; *Songs (4)*, Opus 2, 1861I; *Songs (6)*, Opus 4, 1864I; *Songs (4)*, Opus 9, 1865I; *Songs (12)*, Opus 18, 1880I; *Songs (4)*, Opus 21, 1870I; *Songs (4)*, Opus 48, 1889I; *Songs (10)*, Opus 69, 70, 1900I; *String Quartet in d*, 1861I; *String Quartet in g*, Opus 27, 1878I; *String Quartet in F*, 1891I; *Symphonic Pieces (2)*, Opus 14, 1864I; *Symphonic Dances*, Opus 64, 1898I; *Symphony in c*, 1864I; *Violin Sonata No. 1 in F*, Opus 8, 1865I; *Violin Sonata No. 2 in G*, Opus 13, 1867I; *Violin Sonata No. 3 in c*, Opus 45, 1887I

Grier, Lita: *Flute Sonata*, 1956I

Griffes, Charles T.: *Fantasy Pieces*, Opus 6, 1915I; *Piano Preludes (3)*, 1919I; *Piano Sonata*, 1918I; *The Pleasure Dome of Kubla Khan*, 1920I; *Poem for Flute & Orchestra*, 1918I; *Poems (3)*, Opus 9, 1916I; *Poems by MacLeod (3)*, Opus 11, 1918I; *Poems of Ancient China & Japan (5)*, Opus 10, 1917I; *Roman, Sketches*, Opus 7, 1915I; *Songs (5)*, Opus 10, 1916I; *Symphonische Phantasie*, 1907I; *Tone Pictures (3)*, Opus 5, 1914I

Griffis, Elliot: *Piano Sonata*, 1919I; *String Quartet No. 2*, 1930I; *Symphony No. 1*, 1932I; *Violin Sonata*, 1931I

Grisar, Albert: *Sarah*, 1836I

Grofé, Ferde: *Death Valley Suite*, 1957I; *Grand Canyon Suite*, 1931I; *Mississippi Suite*, 1925I Grøndahl, Launy: *Violin Concerto*, 1917I

Grosheim, Georg C.: *Les esclaves d'Alger*, 1808I; *Das heilige Kleeblatt*, 1794I; *Hektors Abschied*, 1805I; *Hessische kadettenlieder*, 1782I; *Teutschen Gedichte, Vol. 6, Vol. 7*, 1810I; *Teutscher Gedichte, Vol. 8*, 1818I; *Titania*, 1792I

Grove, Stefan: *String Quartet*, 1993I

Gruber, Franz: *Silent Night*, 1818I

Gruber, H. K.: *Cello Concerto*, 1989I; *Frankenstein*, 1978I; *Gomorra*, 1976I; *Trumpet Concerto, "Ariel,"* 1999I; *Violin Concerto No. 1*, 1978I

Gruenberg, Louis: *Antony & Cleopatra*, 1955I; *The Bride of the Gods*, 1913I; *Cello Concerto*, Opus 58, 1949I; *Creation*, 1926I; *The Daniel Jazz*, 1923I; *Diversions (4)*, Opus 32 (string quartet), 1930I; *The Emperor Jones*, 1932I; *The Enchanted Isle*, Opus 11, 1927I; *Green Mansions*, 1937I; *The Hill of Dreams*, 1920I; *Jack & the Beanstalk*, 1931I; *Piano Concerto No. 1*, 1914I; *Piano Concerto No. 2*, 1938I; *Piano Quintet No. 1*, 1929I; *Piano Quintet No. 2*, 1937I; *String Quartet No. 1*, 1937I; *String Quartet No. 2*, 1938I; *Symphony No. 1*, 1919I; *Symphony No. 2*, Opus 43, 1941I; *Symphony No. 3*, Opus 44,1942I; *Symphony No. 4*, Opus 50, 1946I; *Violin Concerto*, 1944I; *Violin Sonata No. 1*, 1912I; *Violin Sonata No. 2*, 1919I; *Violin Sonata No. 3*, 1950I; *Volpone*, 1945I

Guarnieri, Camargo: *Brazilian Dance*, 1941I; *Pedro Malazarte*, 1931I; *Piano Concerto No. 1*, 1936I; *Piano Concerto No. 2*, 1946I; *Piano Concerto No. 3*, 1964I; *Piano Concerto No. 4*, 1967I; *Piano Concerto No. 5*, 1970I; *String Quartet No. 1*, 1932I; *String Quartet No. 2*, 1944I; *String Quartet No. 3*, 1962I; *Symphony No. 1*, 1944I; *Symphony No. 2*, 1946I; *Symphony No. 3*, 1952I; *Symphony No. 4*, 1963I; *Trionfo della Notte*, 1987I; *Violin Concerto No. 1*, 1940I; *Violin Concerto No. 2*, 1953I; *Violin Sonata No. 2*, 1933I

Gubaidulina, Sofia: *Double Bass Sonata*, 1975I; *The Feast is in Full Progress* (cello concerto),1993I; *Figures of Time*, 1994I; *In the Shadow of the Tree*, 1998I; *Night in Memphis*, 1968I; *Piano Chaconne*, 1963I; *Piano*

A *Births*   B *Deaths*   C *Debuts*   D *New Positions*
E *Prizes/Honors*

Introitus, 1978I; *Piano Sonata*, 1965I; *Pre et Contra*, 1989I; *Stimmen verstummen*, 1986I; *String Quartet No. 1*, 1971I; *String Quartet No. 2*, 1987I; *String Quartet No. 3*, 1987I; *String Trio*, 1988I; *Two Paths*, 1999I; *Viola Concerto*, 1997I

Guénin, Marie-Alexandre: *Symphonies (3), Opus 4*, 1776I; *Symphonies (3), Opus 6*, 1778I

Guglielmi, Alessandro: *Concerti da Camera (6), Opus 1*, 1768I

Guglielmi, Pietro: *I capricci di una vedova*, 1759I; *Enea e Lavinia*, 1786I; *Il filosofo burlato*, 1758I; *La francese brillante*, 1763I; *L'impresa d'opera*, 1769I; *L'inganno amoroso*, 1786I; *La moglie imperiosa*, 1759I; *L'Olimpiade*, 1763I; *L'Ottavia*, 1760I; *Le pazzie di Orlando*, 1771I; *La ricca locandiera*, 1759I; *Li rivali placati*, 1764I; *Ruggiero*, 1769I; *Laserva innamorata*, 1790I; *Siroe re de Persia*, 1764I; *Lo solachianello 'mbroglione*, 1757I; *Tito Manlio*, 1763I

Guilmant, Alexandre: *Noëls, Opus 60*, 1886I; *Organ Sonata No. 1 in d, Opus 42*, 1874I; *Piano Sonata No. 7*, 1902I; *Pièces d'orgue dans différente styles*, 1875I

Guion, David: *Shingandi*, 1832; *Southern Nights Suite*, 1922I

Guiraud, Ernest: *Bajazet et le joueur de flûte*, 1864I; *Chasse fantastique*, 1887I; *En prison*, 1869I; *Le feu*, 1879I; *Frédégonde*, 1892I; *Galanteaventure*, 1882I; *Gretna Green* (band), 1873I; *Le Kobold*, 1870I; *Madame Turlupin*, 1872I; *Orchestral Suite No. 1*, 1871I; *Ouverture de concert (d'Arteveld), Opus 10*, 1874I; *Overture Artevalde*, 1882I; *Piccolino*, 1876I; *Sylvie*, 1864I

Guridi, Jesús: *Una aventura de don Quixote*, 1916I; *Basque Impressions*, 1922; *Hommage to Walt Disney*, 1956I

Gurlitt, Manfred: *Soldaten*, 1926I; *Wozzeck, Opus 16*, 1925I

Gutchë, Gene: *Ghenghis Khan*, 1963I; *Perseus & Andromeda XX*, 1977I; *Piano Concerto*, 1955I; *String Quartet No. 3*, 1950I; *Symphony No. 1*, 1950I; *Symphony No. 2*, 1950I; *Symphony No. 3*, 1952I; *Symphony No. 4*, 1959I; *Symphony No. 5 for Strings*, 1962I

Gyger, Elliott: *And I Heard a Voice Out of Heaven*, 1997I; *Compass Variations for Piano*, 1993I; *The Hammer That Shapes*, 1989I

Gyrowetz, Adalbert: *Agnes Sorel*, 1806I; *Aladin*, 1819I; *Der Augenarzt*, 1811I; *Die beiden Eremiten*, 1816I; *Die beiden Savoyarden*, 1817I; *Der betrogene Betrüger*, 1810I; *Der blinde Harfner*, 1827I; *Deodata*, 1809I; *Divertimento, Opus 25*, 1798I; *Der dreizehnte Mantel*, 1829I; *Emericke*, 1807I; *Federica ed Adolfo*, 1812I; *Felix und Adele*, 1831I; *Lafête hongroise*, 1821I; *Il finto Stanislao*, 1818I; *Der Geburtstag*, 1828I; *Der Gemahl vonungefähr*, 1816I; *German Songs (8), Opus 22*, 1794I; *German Songs (7), Opus 34*, 1798I; *German Songs (6), Opus 38*, 1799I; *German Songs (6), Opus 44*, 1800I; *Hans Sachs imvorgerückten Alter*, 1834I; *Harlekin als Papagei*, 1808I; *Helene*, 1816I; *Die Hochzeit der Thetis und des Peleus*, 1816I; *Ida, der büssende*, 1807I; *Italian Ariettas (6), Opus 6*, 1793I; *Italian Ariettas (8), Opus 17*, 1796I; *Die Junggesellen*, 1807I; *Mirana, die Königin der Amazonen*, 1806I; *Die Pagen des Herzogs von Vendôme*, 1808I; *Piano Concerto No. 1, Opus 26*, 1796I; *Piano Concerto No. 2, Opus 49*, 1800I; *Piano Trios (6), Opus 4*, 1790I; *Piano Trios (3), Opus 8*, 1793I; *Piano Trios (3), Opus 9*, 1793I; *Piano Trios (3), Opus 10*, 1795I; *Piano Trios (3), Opus 12*, 1795I; *Piano Trios (2), Opus 14*, 1796I; *Piano Trios (2), Opus 15*, 1796I; *Piano Trios (3), Opus 18*, 1797I; *Piano Trios (3), Opus 23*, 1798I; *Piano Trios (3), Opus 28*, 1799I; *Piano Trios (3), Opus 35*, 1801I; *Piano Trios (3), Opus 36*, 1801I; *Piano Trios (3), Opus 40*, 1803I; *Piano Trios (3), Opus 60*, 1814I; *Quartets (3), Flutes & Strings, Opus 11*, 1795I; *Quintet, Flute & Strings, Opus 27*, 1799I; *Robert, oder Die Prüfung*, 1815I; *Der Sammtrock*, 1809I; *Selico*, 1804I; *Das Ständchen*, 1823I; *String Quartets (6), Opus 2*, 1789I; *String Quartets (6), Opus 3*, 1790I; *String Quartets (3), Opus 5*, 1793I; *String Quartets (3), Opus 9*, 1794I; *String Quartets (3), "Prince of Wales,"* 1795I; *String Quartets (3), Opus 13*, 1796I; *String Quartets (3), Opus 16*, 1796I; *String Quartets (3), Opus 29*, 1800I; *String Quartets (3), Opus 42*, 1802I; *String Quartets (3), Opus 44*, 1804I; *String Quintet, Opus 45*, 1800I; *Violin Sonata, Opus 61*, 1815I; *William Tell*, 1810I; *Das Winterguartier in America*, 1812I

Haas, Joseph: *Church Sonata No. 1 in F*, 1926I; *Church Sonata No. 2 in d*, 1926I; *Variations on an Original Theme, Opus 31*, 1911I

Haas, Pavel: *Charlatan*, 1936I; *Songs on Chinese Poetry (4)*, 1942I; *String Quartet No. 1*, 1919I; *String Quartet No. 2*, 1920I; *String Quartet No. 3*, 1922I; *Wind Quintet, Opus 10*, 1929I

Hába, Alois: *For Peace*, 1950I; *Fugue Suite*, 1918I; *Moods (6) for Piano*, 1971I; *Mother*, 1929I; *The New Land*, 1936I; *Piano Pieces (6)*, 1920I; *Piano Sonata, Opus 62*, 1947I; *Sonata for Piano, Opus 3*, 1918I; *String Quartet No. 4*, 1922I; *String Quartet No. 5*, 1923I; *String Quartet No. 6*, 1950I; *String Quartet No. 7*, 1957I; *String Quartet No. 8*, 1957I; *String Quartet No. 9*, 1958I; *String Quartet No. 10*, 1952I; *String Quartet No. 11*, 1958I; *String Quartet No. 12*, 1960I; *String Quartet No. 13, "Astronautic,"* 1961I; *String Quartet No. 14*, 1963I; *String Quartet No. 15*, 1964I; *String Quartet No. 16*, 1967I; *Suite No. 1 for Quarter-Tone Piano*, 1922I; *Suite No. 2 for Quarter-Tone Piano*, 1922I; *Suite No. 3 for Quarter-Tone Piano*, 1923I; *Suite No. 4 for Quarter-Tone Piano*, 1924I; *Suite No. 5 for Quarter-Tone Piano*, 1925I; *Suite No. 6 for Quarter-Tone Piano*, 1959I; *Suite, Opus 103*, 1972I; *Symphonic Fantasy*, 1921I; *Toccata quasi una Fantasia*, 1931I; *Variations on a Canon by Schumann*, 1918I; *Viola Concerto*, 1957I; *Violin Concerto*, 1955I; *Violin Sonata*, 1915I

F *Biographical*   G *Cultural Beginnings*   H *Musical Literature*
I *Musical Compositions*

Hadjidakis, Manos: *Ilya Darling*, 1967I
Hadley, Henry: *Alma Mater Overture*, 1932I; *Atonement of Pan*, 1912I; *Aurora Borealis Overture*, 1931I; *Azora, Daughter of Montezuma*, 1915I; *Belshazzar, Opus 112*, 1932I; *Bianca*, 1917I; *Christmas Cantata, Opus 91*, 1922I; *Cleopatra's Night*, 1918I; *The Culprit Fay, Opus 62*, 1909I; *The Enchanted Castle Overture*, 1933I; *The Golden Prince*, 1914I; *Happy Jack*, 1889I; *In Music's Praise*, 1899I; *Lucifer*, 1913I; *Merlin & Vivian, Opus 52*, 1906I; *Nancy Brown*, 1903I; *The New Earth, Opus 85*, 1919I; *A Night in Old Paris*, 1925I; *The Nightingale and the Rose, Opus 54*, 1911I; *The Ocean, Opus 99*, 1920I; *Ode to Music*, 1917I; *Oriental Suite, Opus 32*, 1903I; *Othello Overture, Opus 96*, 1919I; *Overture, Hector and Andromache*, 1894I; *Overture, In Bohemia, Opus 28*, 1901I; *Piano Quintet, Opus 50*, 1919I; *Piano Trio, Opus 132*, 1932I; *The Princess of Y's, Opus 34*, 1903I; *Resurgam, Opus 98*, 1922I; *Safié*, 1909I; *Salome, Opus 55*, 1905I; *San Francisco*, 1931I; *Scherzo Diabolique, Opus 135*, 1934I; *Silhouettes*, 1932I; *String Quartet No. 2, Opus 132*, 1934I; *Suite ancienne*, 1926I; *Symphony No. 1 in d, "Youth and Life," Opus 25*, 1897I; *Symphony No. 2, "The Four Seasons," Opus 30*, 1901I; *Symphony No. 3 in b*, 1906I; *Symphony No. 4, "North, East, South, West,"* 1911I; *Symphony No. 5, "Connecticut," Opus 140*, 1935I
Hageman, Richard: *Caponsacchi*, 1931I
Hagen, Daron: *Bandana*, 1999i; *Blake Poems (4)*, 1994I; *Built up Dark* (piano concerto), 1995I; *Cello Concerto*, 1995I; *Dear Youth*, 1991I; *Duo for Violin & Cello*, 1997I; *Echo's Songs*, 1983I; *Fire Music*, 1991I; *Flute sonata*, 1998SI; *Higher, Louder, Faster*, 1987I; *J'entends*, 1986I; *Joyful Music*, 1993I; *Litany of Reconciliation*, 1996I; *Lost in Translation*, 1994I; *Love Scene from"Romeo & Juliet,"* 1996I; *Love Songs*, 1986I; *Merrill Songs*, 1995I; *Occasional Notes for Organ*, 1985I; *Overture to Vera*, 1995I; *Postcards from America*, 1996I; *Shining Brow*, 1992I; *Songs of Madness & Sorrow*, 1996I; *A Stillness at Appomatox*, 1982I; *String Quartet No. 2*, 1985I; *Suite for Solo Cello*, 1985I; *Suite for Solo Violin*, 1984I; *Symphony No. 1*, 1988I; *Symphony No. 2*, 1990I; *Symphony No. 3*, 1996I; *Symphony No. 3*, 1997I; *Three Silent Things*, 1984I; *Trio Concertante*, 1984I; *Vera of Las Vegas*, 1995I; *The Waking Father*, 1994I; *A Walt Whitman Requiem*, 1984I
Hägg, Jakob A.: *Amerikanische Festklänge*, 1900I
Hahn, Reynaldo: *Angelo*, 1905I; *Askeladden*, 1930I; *Le bal de Béatrice*, 1909I; *Le bois sacré*, 1912I; *Ciboulette*, 1923I; *Les deux courtisanes*, 1902I; *Le dieu bleu*, 1912I; *Esther*, 1905I; *La fête chez Thérèse*, 1909I; *Fête triomphale*, 1919I; *Lucrèce Borgia*, 1911I; *Le marchand de Venise*, 1935I; *Méduse*, 1911I; *Piano Concerto in E♭*, 1931I; *Piano Quintet in f*, 1921I; *Prométhée triomphant*, 1908I; *String Quartet No. 1*, 1939I; *String Quartet No. 2*, 1943I; *Violin Concerto*, 1927I
Haieff, Alexei: *Ballet in E*, 1955I; *Caligula*, 1971I; *Cello Sonata*, 1963I; *Piano Concerto No. 1*, 1950I; *Piano Sonata*, 1955I; *Sonata for Two Pianos*, 1945I; *String Quartet No. 1*, 1951I; *Symphony No. 1*, 1942I; *Symphony No. 2*, 1957I; *Symphony No. 3*, 1961I; *Violin Concerto*, 1948I; *Wind Quintet*, 1983I
Hailstork, Adolphus: *Piano Sonata*, 1980I
Haim, Paul Ben: *Evocation* (violin & orchestra), 1942I
Haimo, Ethan: *Symphony for Strings*, 1990I
Halévy, Jacques: *L'artisan*, 1827I; *Ave Verum*, 1850I; *Les bohémiennes*, 1820I; *Charles VI*, 1843I; *Clari*, 1828I; *La dame de pique*, 1850I; *De Profundis*, 1820I; *Les derniers moments du Tasse*, 1816I; *La Dilettante d'Avignon*, 1829I; *Le drapier*, 1840I; *L'éclair*, 1835I; *La fée aux roses*, 1849I; *Guido et Ginevra*, 1838I; *Le guitarrero*, 1841I; *Herminie*, 1819I; *L'inconsolable*, 1855I; *Italie*, 1819I; *Jaguarita indienne*, 1855I; *Le juif errant*, 1852I; *La juive*, 1835I; *La langue musicale*, 1830I; *Le Lazzarone*, 1844I; *La magicienne*, 1858I; *Manon Lescaut*, 1830I; *Marco Curzio*, 1822I; *La mort*, 1814I; *La mort d'Adonis*, 1817I; *Les mousquetaires de la reine*, 1846I; *Le Nabab*, 1853I; *Les plages du Nil*, 1846I; *Prométhée enchaîné*, 1849I; *Pygmalion*, 1824I; *La reine de Chypre*, 1841I; *Le roi et le batelier*, 1827I; *Le shérif*, 1839I; *Les souvenirs de Lafleur*, 1833I; *La tempestà*, 1850I; *La tentation*, 1832I; *Les treize*, 1839I; *Le val d'Andorre*, 1848I; *Valentine d'Aubigny*, 1856I; *Yella*, 1832I
Halffter, Cristóbal: *Cello Concerto No. 1*, 1974I; *Cello Concerto No. 2*, 1985I; *Daliniana*, 1994I; *Don Quichotte*, 1970I; *Fantasia on a Sonority of Handel*, 1981I; *Mural sonante*, 1993I; *Piano Concerto*, 1988I; *String Quartet No. 2, "Memories, 1970,"* 1970I; *String Quartet No. 3*, 1978I; *Tiento del premer tono y Batalla Imperial*, 1998SI; *Veni Creator Spiritus*, 1992I
Halffter, Ernesto: *Guitar Concerto*, 1968I; *Rapsodia portuguesa*, 1962I; *Sonatina*, 1927I; *Symphonic Sketches (2)*, 1925I
Halffter, Rodolfo: *Don Lindo de Almeria*, 1936I; *Marinero en tierra*, 1925I; *Piano Sonata No. 1*, 1947I; *Piano Sonata No. 2*, 1951I; *Piano Sonata No. 3*, 1967I; *Violin Concerto*, 1940I
Hall, Charles John: *A Celebration Overture*, 1983I; *A Psalmic Symphony*, 1986I
Hallgrimsson, Haflidi: *String Quartet No. 1*, 1962I; *String Quartet No. 2*, 1964I
Hallström, Ivar:; *Den Bergtagna*, 1874I; *The Mountain King's Bride*, 1871I; *The Vikings' Voyage*, 1877I; *The White Lady of Drottningholm*, 1847I

✿

A   *Births*   B   *Deaths*   C   *Debuts*   D   *New Positions*
E   *Prizes/Honors*

Halvorsen, Johan: *Gurre*, 1900I; *The Merchant of Venice*, 1922I; *Symphony No. 1, "Fatum,"* 1923I; *Symphony No. 2*, 1924I; *Symphony No. 3, "Summer,"* 1929I

Hambraeus, Bengt: *Antiphonie for Organ*, 1977I; *Apocalipsis cum figuri secundum Dürer*, 1987I; *Après Sheng*, 1988I; *Cadenza for Organ*, 1988I; *FM642765*, 1997I; *Livre d'orgue*, 1981I; *Meteros*, 1993I; *Missa pro organo: In Memoriam Olivier Messiaen*, 1992I; *Motetum Archangelski Michaelis*, 1967I; *Organum Sancti Jacobi*, 1993I; *Piano Concerto*, 1992I; *Rhapsodies (2) for Piano*, 1994I; *Ricercare*, 1974I; *Toccata pro organo: Monumentum per Max Reger*, 1973I; *Trytique for Organ*, 1994I; *Variations sur un thème de Gilles Vigneault for Organ*, 1984I

Hamerik, Asger: *Concert-Romance, Opus 27*, 1878I; *Requiem in c, Opus 34*, 1887I; *Symphony in c* (lost), 1860I; *Symphony No. 1 in F, "Poétique," Opus 26*, 1880I; *Symphony No. 2 in c, "Tragique," Opus 32*, 1883I; *Symphony No. 3, "Lyrique," Opus 33*, 1884I; *Symphony No. 4 in C, "Majesteuse," Opus 35*, 1889I; *Symphony No. 5 in g, "Sérieuse," Opus 36*, 1891I; *Symphony No. 6, "Spirituelle," Opus 38*, 1897I

Hamilton, Iain: *Anna Karenina*, 1978I; *Aurora*, 1972I; *Bulgaria*, 1999I; *The Cataline Conspiracy*, 1973I; *Clarinet Concerto*, 1950I; *Commedia* (orchestra concerto), 1972I; *Lancelot*, 1983I; *On the Eve*, 1996I; *Passion According to St. Mark*, 1982I; *Piano Concerto No. 1*, 1949I; *Piano Concerto No. 2*, 1960I; *Requiem*, 1979I; *Scottish Dances (5)*, 1956I; *Symphonic Variations*, 1953I; *Symphony No. 1*, 1948I; *Symphony No. 2*, 1951I; *Symphony No. 3 in G, "Spring,"* 1981I; *Symphony No. 4 in B*, 1981I; *Threnos–In Time of War*, 1966I; *Le tombeau de Bach*, 1986I; *Violin Concerto No. 1*, 1952I

Hamilton, Lou: *Symphony in G*, 1949I

Hampton, Calvin: *Prelude & Variations on Old 100th*, 1970I; *Transformation & Despair*, 1971I

Handel, George F.: *Jephtha*, 1751I; *The Triumph of Time & Truth*, 1757I

Hanson, Howard: *Before the Dawn*, 1920I; *Bold Island Suite*, 1961I; *Cherubic Hymn*, 1949I; *Chorale & Alleluia*, 1954I; *Concerto for Organ, Harp & Orchestra*, 1921I; *Dies Natalis*, 1967I; *Elegy in Memory of Serge Koussevitzky*, 1956I; *Exultation*, 1920I; *Fantasy-Variations on a Theme of Youth, Opus 40*, 1951I; *The Lament for Beowulf*, 1925I; *Lux Aeterna, Opus 24*, 1923I; *Merry Mount, Opus 31*, 1933I; *Miniatures (3), Opus 12*, 1919I; *Mosaics*, 1957I; *The Mystic Trumpeter*, 1969I; *Organ Concerto, Opus 27*, 1926I; *Pan & the Priest, Opus 26*, 1926I; *Piano Concerto*, 1948I; *Piano Quintet*, 1916I; *Piano Sonata, Opus 11*, 1918I; *Psalm 121*, 1968I; *Psalm 150*, 1968I; *Scandinavian Suite, Opus 13*, 1919I; *Song of Democracy*, 1957I; *Songs from "Drum Taps" (3)*, 1935I; *Summer Seascapes*, 1959I; *Symphonic Legend*, 1917I; *Symphonic Prelude, Opus 6*, 1916I; *Symphonic Rhapsody, Opus 14*, 1918I; *Symphony No. 1, "Nordic,"* 1922I; *Symphony No. 2, "Romantic," Opus 30*, 1930I; *Symphony No. 3, Opus 33*, 1938I; *Symphony No. 4, "Sinfonia da Requiem,"* 1943I; *Symphony No. 5, "Sinfonia sacra,"* 1954I; *Symphony No. 5, "Sinfonia Sacra,"* 1955I; *Symphony No. 6*, 1967I; *Symphony No. 7, "A Sea Symphony,"* 1977I

Harbison, John: *Cello Concerto*, 1994I; *Chorale Cantata*, 1994I; *Concerto for Double Brass Choir*, 1988I; *Concerto for Oboe, Clarinet & Strings*, 1985I; *Double Concerto*, 1984I; *Doublebass Concerto*, 1990I; *Elegiac Songs*, 1974I; *Fantasy Duo*, 1987I; *The Flight into Egypt*, 1986I; *The Flower-Fed Buffaloes*, 1976I; *Flute Concerto*, 1994I; *Full Moon in March*, 1977I; *Gli accordi piu usati*, 1993I; *The Great Gatsby*, 1999I; *Mirabai Songs*, 1982I; *The Most Often Used Chords*, 1992I; *The Natural World*, 1987I; *Oboe Concerto*, 1991I; *Partita*, 2000I; *Piano Concerto*, 1978I; *Piano Quintet*, 1981I; *Piano Sonata No. 1, "Roger Sessions: In Memoriam,"* 1985I; *Piano Trio*, 1969I; *Psalms (4)*, 1999I; *Quintet for Winds*, 1978I; *The Rewaking*, 1991I; *Simple Daylight*, 1988I; *Songs of Experience (5)*, 1971I; *String Quartet No. 1*, 1985I; *String Quartet No. 2*, 1987I; *Symphony No. 1*, 1981I; *Symphony No. 2*, 1987I; *Symphony No. 3*, 1990I, 1998I; *Three City Blocks* (band), 1993I; *Twilight Music*, 1984I; *Ulysses Bow*, 1983I; *Ulysses Raft*, 1983I; *Viola Concerto*, 1989I; *Winter's Tale*, 1974I; *Woodwind Quintet*, 1979I; *Words from Paterson*, 1989I

Harper, William: *El Greco*, 1993I

Harrington, Karl: *There's a Song in the Air*, 1904I

Harris, Donald: *Mermaid Variations*, 1992I

Harris, Roy: *Abraham Lincoln Walks at Midnight*, 1953I; *Accordion Concerto*, 1946I; *Canticle to the Sun*, 1960I; *Concert Piece*, 1930I; *Concerto for Amplified Piano*, 1968I; *Concerto for Two Pianos*, 1946I; *Cumberland Concerto*, 1951I; *Epilogue to Profiles in Courage*, 1964I; *Give Me the Splendid, Silent Sun*, 1959I; *Little Suite*, 1938I; *Piano Concerto No. 1*, 1944I; *Piano Concerto No. 2*, 1953I; *Piano Quintet*, 1936I; *Piano Sonata*, 1928I; *String Quartet No. 1*, 1930I; *String Quartet No. 2*, 1933I; *String Quartet No. 3*, 1939I; *String Quintet*, 1940I; *Symphony: 1933 (No. 1)*, 1933I; *Symphony No. 2*, 1934I; *Symphony No. 3*, 1939I; *Symphony No. 4, "Folksong,"* 1940I; *Symphony No. 5*, 1942I; *Symphony No. 6, "Gettysburg Address,"* 1944I; *Symphony No. 7*, 1952I; *Symphony No. 8, "San Francisco,"* 1961I; *Symphony No. 9*, 1962I; *Symphony No. 10, "Abraham Lincoln,"* 1965I; *Symphony No. 11*, 1967I; *Symphony No. 12, "Pere Marquette,"* 1969I; *Symphony No. 13, "Bicentennial,"* 1976I; *Toccata*, 1949I; *Toccata for Orchestra*, 1931I; *Variations on an Irish Theme*, 1938I; *Violin Concerto No. 2*, 1949I; *When Johnny Comes Marching Home: an American Overture*, 1934I

❄

F *Biographical*   G *Cultural Beginnings*   H *Musical Literature*
I *Musical Compositions*

Harrison, Annie F.: *In the Gloaming*, 1877I
Harrison, Jonty: *Unsound Objects*, 1996I
Harrison, Lou: *Almanac of the Seasons*, 1950I; *Concerto for Organ, Percussion & Orchestra*, 1973I; *Concerto No. 1 for Flute & Percussion*, 1939I; *Easter Cantata*, 1946I; *Green Mansions*, 1939I; *Johnny Appleseed*, 1940I; *Piano Trio*, 1990I; *String Quartet Set*, 1979I; *Suite for Violin & American Gamelan*, 1973I; *Suite No. 2 for Strings*, 1948I; *A Summerfield Set, for Piano*, 1988I; *Symphony on G*, 1966I; *Symphony No. 3*, 1995I; *Symphony No. 4*, 1990I; *Symphony on G*, 1961I; *Violin Concerto*, 1959I
Harrison, Sadie: *Arcosolia*, 1999I
Harsányi, Tibor: *Rhythmic Etudes (5)*, 1934I; *String Quartet No. 1*, 1918I; *String Quartet No. 2*, 1935I
Hartke, Stephen: *Ascent of the Equestrian in a Balloon*, 1995I; *Piano Sonata*, 1998I
Hartmann, Johan P.: *Songs (6) for Male Voices, Opus 61*, 1860I
Hartmann, Johann Peter Emilius: *Arcona, Opus 62*, 1875I; *Concert Overture No. 3 in C, Opus 51*, 1852I; *Concert Overture No. 4, Opus 63b*, 1863I; *The Corsairs, Opus 16*, 1835I; *The Dryad's Wedding, Opus 60*, 1858I; *A Folk Tale*, 1854I; *Good Friday, Easter Morning, Opus 43*, 1847I; *The Legend of Thrym, Opus 67*, 1868I; *Liden Kirsten, Opus 44*, 1846I; *Olaf den Hellige, Opus 23*, 1838I; *Organ Fantasy in f, Opus 20* (?), 1838I; *Organ Sonata in g, Opus 58*, 1884I; *Overture, Axel of Valborg, Opus 57*, 1856I; *Overture, Correggio, Opus 59*, 1858I; *Overture, Hakon Jarl*, 1844I; *Overture, Yrsa*, 1881I; *Overture in d, Opus 3*, 1825I; *Overture in c, "Geistlig," Opus 9*, 1827I; *Piano Sonata No. 2, Opus 80*, 1885I; *The Raven*, 1832I; *Spring Songs, Opus 70*, 1871I; *A Summer Day*, 1855I; *Symphony No. 1 in g, Opus 17*, 1835I; *Symphony No. 2 in E, Opus 48b*, 1848I; *Undine, Opus 33* (IM), 1842I; *Valkyrien, Opus 62*, 1861I; *Yrsa, Opus 78*, 1883I
Hartmann, Karl Amadeus: *Concerto Funebre* (violin), 1939I; *Miserere*, 1935I; *Symphony No. 1*, 1936I; *Symphony No. 2*, 1946I; *Symphony No. 3*, 1949I; *Symphony No. 4*, 1947I; *Symphony No. 5, "Sinfonie Concertante,"* 1951I; *Symphony No. 6*, 1953I; *Symphony No. 7*, 1958I; *Symphony No. 8*, 1963I; *Violin Sonata No. 1*, 1927I; *Violin Sonata No. 2*, 1927I
Harvey, Jonathan: *Fantasia for Organ*, 1991I; *Madonna of Winter & Spring*, 1986I; *Percussion Concerto*, 1997I; *Song Offerings*, 1985I; *String Quartet No. 1*, 1977I; *String Quartet No. 2*, 1988I
Hasse, Johann A.: *Achille in Sciro*, 1759I; *Adriano in Siria*, 1752I; *Alcide al bivio*, 1760I; *Artaserse II*, 1760I; *Artemisia*, 1754I; *Il calandrano*, 1755I; *Ciro riconosciuto*, 1751I; *Concertos (12) in Six Parts, Opus 3*, 1760I; *Demofoonte II*, 1758I; *Egeria*, 1764I; *L'eroe cinese*, 1753I; *Ezio II*, 1755I; *Mass in E♭*, 1779I; *Mass in d*, 1751I; *Nitteti*, 1758I; *L'Olimpiade*, 1756I; *Partenope*, 1767I; *Piramo e Tisbe*, 1768I; *Il re pastore*, 1755I; *Requiem in C*, 1763I; *Romolo ed Ersilia*, 1765I; *Il Ruggiero*, 1771I; *Salve Regina in E♭*, 1767I; *Il sogno di Scipione*, 1758I; *Solimano*, 1753I; *Te Deum in D*, 1751I; *Il trionfo di Clelia*, 1762I; *Zenobia*, 1761I
Hastings, Thomas: *Toplady* (Rock of Ages), 1930I
Haubenstock-Ramati, Roman: *Liasons for Solo Percussionist*, 1958I; *Mobile for Shakespeare*, 1958I; *String Quartet No. 1*, 1977I; *String Trio No. 1*, 1948I; *String Trio No. 2*, 1985I
Hauer, Josef M.: *Nomos I, Opus 1*, 1901I; *Nomos II, Opus 2*, 1913I; *Nomos III, Opus 19*, 1919I; *Symphony No. 1, "Nomos,"* 1913I; *Symphony No. 3*, 1914I
Haug, Halvor: *Insignia*, 1993I; *Symphony No. 3*, 1993I
Haven, Peter von: *Federal Overture*, 1797I
Hawkins, Malcolm: *Rasmandala*, 1996I
Haydn, Franz Joseph: *Acide*, 1762I; *Acide II*, 1773I; *Alfred, König der Angelsachsen*, 1796I; *L'anima del filosofo*, 1791I; *Arianna a Naxos*, 1789I; *Armida*, 1783I; *Austrian National Anthem*, 1797I; *Cacilienmesse in C*, 1766I; *Cello Concerto No. 2 in D*, 1783I; *The Creation*, 1798I; *Divertimento in E♭* (horn), 1767I; *Divertimentos (6), Opus 1*, 1759I; *Divertimentos, (4), Opus 2*, 1762I; *Divertimentos (6), Opus 9*, 1769I; *Il Dottore*, 1762I; *English Ballads (12)*, 1792I; *L'incontro improvviso*, 1775I; *L'infedelta delusa*, 1773I; *L'isola disabitata*, 1779I; *Keyboard Concerto No. 5 in C*, 1767I; *Keyboard Concerto No. 8 in G*, 1770I; *Der krumme Teufel*, 1752I; *La Marchesa Nespola*, 1762I; *Missa St. Nicolai in G*, 1772I; *Missa solennis, "Harmoniemesse,"* 1802I; *Missa brevis Sancti Joannis de Deo in B♭*, 1775I; *Missa St. Johannis de Deo in B♭*, 1778I; *Missa Sancti Bernardi ("Heiligmesse"),* 1796I; *Missa honorem Beata Maria virgine in B♭*, 1769I; *Missa Cellensis in C (Mariazeller-Messe)*, 1782I; *Missa solennis in B♭, "Theresienmesse,"* 1799I; *Missa solennis, "Nelsonmesse,"* 1798I; *Missa Sancti Josephi in E♭*, 1774I; *Il mondo della luna*, 1777I; *Der neue krumme Teufel*, 1758I; *Organ Concerto in C, H. XVII/8*, 1766I; *Organ Concerto No. 1 in C, H.SVIII/I*, 1756I; *Organ Concerto No. 2 in D*, 1767I; *Orlando paladino*, 1782I; *Le pescatrici*, 1769I; *Philemon und Baucis*, 1773I; *Piano Trios No.1 & 2*, 1784I; *Piano Trios No. 3, 7*, 1785I; *Piano Trios No. 11-14*, 1790I; *Piano Trio No. 14 in F*, 1768I; *Piano Trios No. 15, 18*, 1794I; *Piano Trios No. 19, 24*, 1795I; *Il ritorno di Tobia*, 1775I; *Salve Regina in E*, 1756I; *Salve Regina in g*, 1771I; *Il scanarella*, 1762I; *The Seasons*, 1800; *The Seven Last Words*, 1796I; *Sinfonia Concertante in B♭, Opus 84*, 1792I; *Six Songs, Set I, Six Songs, Set II*, 1781I; *Lo speziale*, 1768I; *Stabat Mater in g*, 1767I; *String Quartets (6), Opus 2*, 1762I; *String Quartets (6), Opus 8*, 1772I; *String Quartets (6), Opus 9*, 1771I; *String Quartets (6),*

❖

A   *Births*   B   *Deaths*   C   *Debuts*   D   *New Positions*
E   *Prizes/Honors*

"Russian," Opus 33, 1781I; String Quartet in d, Opus 42, 1785I; String Quartets (6),"Prussian," Opus 50, 1787I; String Quartets (3),"Tost," Opus 54, 1788I; String Quartets (3), "Tost," Opus 64, 1790I; String Quartets (3),"Apponyi," Opus 71, 1793I; String Quartets (3), "Apponyi," Opus 74, 1793I; String Quartets (6),"Erdödy," Opus 76, 1797I; String Quartets (2),"Lobkowitz," Opus 77, 1799I; String Quartet in d, Opus 103, 1803I; Symphony No. 1 in D, 1759I; Symphony No. 2 in C, 1760I; Symphonies No. 3, 5, 1762I; Symphony No. 6 in D, "Le matin," 1761I; Symphony No. 7 in C, "Le midi," 1761I; Symphony No. 8 in G, "Le soir," 1761I; Symphony No. 9 in C, 1762I; Symphony No. 10 in D, 1761I; Symphony No. 12 in E, 1763I; Symphony No. 13 in D, 1763I; Symphony No. 14 in A, 1764I; Symphony No. 15 in D, 1764I; Symphonies No. 16, 20, 25, 27, 1766I; Symphony No. 21 in A, 1764I; Symphony No. 22 in E♭, "Philosopher," 1764I; Symphony No. 23 in G, 1764I; Symphony No. 24 in D, 1764I; Symphony No. 26 in d, "Lamentatione," 1770I; Symphony No. 28 in A, 1765I; Symphony No. 29 in E, 1765I; Symphony No. 30 in C, "Alleluia," 1765I; Symphony No. 31 in d, "Hornsignal," 1765I; Symphony No. 32 in C, 1766I; Symphony No. 36 in E♭, 1769I; Symphony No. 38 in C, 1769I; Symphony No. 39 in g, 1770I; Symphony No. 40 in F, 1763I; Symphony No. 41 in C, 1770I; Symphony No. 42 in D, 1771I; Symphony No. 43 in E♭, "Mercury," 1772I; Symphony No. 44 in e, "Trauersinfonie," 1772I; Symphony No. 45 in f♯, "Farewell," 1772I; Symphony No. 46 in D, 1772I; Symphony No. 47 in G, 1772I; Symphony No. 49 in f, "La passione," 1768I; Symphony No. 50 in C, 1773I; Symphony No. 51 in B♭, 1774I; Symphony No. 52 in c, 1774I; Symphony No. 53 in D, 1778I; Symphony No. 54 in G, 1774I; Symphony No. 55 in E♭, "Schoolmaster," 1774I; Symphony No. 56 in C, 1774I; Symphony No. 57 in D, 1774I; Symphony No. 58 in F, 1775I; Symphony No. 59 in A, "Fire," 1769I; Symphony No. 60 in C, "Il Distratto," 1774I; Symphony No. 61 in D, 1776I; Symphony No. 64 in A, "Tempora mutantur," 1788I; Symphony No. 65 in A, 1778I; Symphony No. 66 in B♭, 1779I; Symphony No. 67 in F, 1779I; Symphony No. 68 in B♭, 1779I; Symphony No. 69 in C, "Laudon," 1779I; Symphony No. 70 in D, 1779I; Symphony No. 71 in B♭, 1780I; Symphony No. 72 in D, 1781I; Symphony No. 73 in D, "La Chasse," 1782I; Symphony No. 74 in E♭, 1781I; Symphony No. 75 in D, 1781I; Symphony No 76 in B♭, 1782I; Symphony No. 77 in B♭, 1782I; Symphony No. 78 in c, 1782I; Symphony No. 79 in F, 1784I; Symphony No. 80 in d, 1784I; Symphony No. 81 in G, 1784I; Symphony No. 82 in C, "The Bear" (Paris No. 1), 1786I; Symphony No. 83 in g, "La poule," 1785I; Symphony No. 84 in E♭, "La reine"(3), 1786I; Symphony No. 85 in B♭, 1785I; Symphony No. 86 in D (Paris No. 5), 1786I; Symphony No. 87 in A, 1785I; Symphony No. 88 in G, 1787I; Symphony No. 89 in F, 1787I; Symphony No. 90 in C, 1788I; Symphony No. 91 in E♭, 1788I; Symphony No. 92 in G, "Oxford," 1789I; Symphony No. 93 in D, 1791I; Symphony No. 94 in G, "Surprise," 1791I; Symphony No. 95 in c, 1797I; Symphony No. 96 in D, "Miracle," 1791I; Symphony No. 97 in C, 1792I; Symphony No. 98 in B♭, 1792I; Symphony No. 99 in E♭, 1793I; Symphony No. 100 in G, "Military," 1794I; Symphony No. 101 in D, "The Clock," 1794I; Symphony No. 102 in B♭, 1794I; Symphony No. 103 in E♭, "Drum Roll,"; Symphony No. 104 in F, "London," 1795I; Te Deum in C, 1800I; Te Deum in C, 1765I; Trios (4), Flutes & Cello, 1794I; Trumpet Concerto in E♭, 1796I; La vedova, 1762I; La vera costanza, 1779I; Violin Concerto No. 1 in C, 1765I; Violin Concerto No. 2 in D, 1765I; Violin Concerto No. 3 in A, 1770I; Violin Concerto No. 4 in G, 1769I; Der Zerstreute, 1774I

Haydn, Michael: Abels Tod, 1778I; Die Ährenleserin, 1788I; Der Büssende sünder, 1771I; Der Englishche Patriot, 1779I; Flute Concerto No. 1, 1766I; Flute Concerto No. 2, 1771I; Der fröhliche Wiederschein, 1791I; Die Hochzeit auf der Alm, 1768I; Horn Concerto, 1764I; Jubelfeier, 1787I; Der Kampf der Busse und Bekerung, 1768I; Leopoldmesse, 1805I; Missa hispanica in C, 1786I; Missa in Honorum Sancte Gotthardi, 1788I; Missa proquadregesimae sec cantum choralem, 1794I; Missa S. Aloysli, 1779I; Missa Sancte Crucis, 1792I; Missa Sancte Hieronyni, 1777I; Missa Sancte Ruperti, 1782I; Missa sotto il titulo di Sancte Teresia, 1801I; Missa sub Titulo Sancti Francisci Serephici, 1803I; Missa tempore quadragesimae, 1794I; Oratorium de Passione Domini nostra Jesu Christi, 1775I; Quintet in E♭, 1790I; Rebekka als Braut, 1766I; Requiem in c, 1771I; Requiem in B♭ (unfinished), 1806I; Der Reumütige Petrus, 1770I; Sanctificatio Julilaei, 1782I; Symphony in G (old Mozart No. 37), 1783I; Te Deum, 1803I; Te Deum VI, 1801I; Titus, 1774I; Trumpet Concerto, 1764I; Violin Concerto No. 1, 1761I; Violin Concerto No. 2 in B♭, 1760I; Violin Concerto No. 3, 1776I; Die Wahrheit der Natur, 1769I; Zaire, 1777I

Hays, Sorrell: Love in Space, 1986I

Headington, Christopher: A Bradfield Mass, 1977I; Cinquanta for Piano, 1986I; The Healing Fountain, 1978I; Piano Concerto, 1990I; Piano Preludes (5), 1953I; Piano Quartet, 1978I; Piano Sonata No. 1, 1955I; Piano Sonata No. 2, 1974I; Piano Sonata No. 3, 1985I; Shrewsbury Variations, 1981I; String Quartet No. 1, 1953I; String Quartet No. 2, 1972I; String Quartet No. 3, 1982I; String Quartet No. 4, 1985I; Symphony, 1996I; Violin Concerto, 1959I

Healey, Derek: Organ Sonata, 1961I; Variants for Organ, 1964I

Hedwall, Lennart: Organ Sonata, 1971I; Suite No. 2 for Organ, 1971I; Triptyk for Organ, 1984I

Heggie, Jake: Anna Madrigal Remembers, 1999I; Dead Man Walking, 2000I; Paper Wings, 1997I

❀

F Biographical G Cultural Beginnings H Musical Literature
I Musical Compositions

Heiden, Barnhard: *A Bestiary*, 1986I; *Clarinet Quintet*, 1955I; *Piano Sonata, Four Hands*, 1946I; *Voyage* (band), 1991I

Heininen, Paavo: *Cello Concerto*, 1986I; *Piano Concerto No. 1*, 1964I; *Piano Concerto No. 2*, 1966I; *Piano Concerto No. 3*, 1981I; *Saxophone Concerto*, 1983I; *The Silken Drum*, 1983I; *String Quartet No. 1*, 1974I; *Symphony No. 1*, 1958I; *Symphony No. 2, "Petite symphonie joyeuse,"* 1962I; *Symphony No. 3*, 1969I; *Symphony No. 4*, 1971I

Heiniö, Mikko: *Concerto for Orchestra*, 1982I; *Piano Concerto No. 1*, 1972I; *Piano Concerto No. 2*, 1973I; *Piano Concerto No. 3*, 1981I; *Piano Concerto No. 4*, 1986I; *Piano Concerto No. 5*, 1989I

Heinrich, Anthony: *Gran sinfonia eroica*, 1835I; *Grand American National Chivalrous Symphony*, 1837I; *Pushmataka*, 1831I. *Symphony, "The Combat of the Condor,"* 1836I

Heller, Alfred: *Cello Concerto*, 1999I; *Cello Sonata No. 2, "In the Sistine Chapel,"* 1999I; *From the Proverbs*, 1977I

Heller, Stephen: *Ballades (3), Opus 113*, 1866I; *Etudes (24), New, Opus 90*, 1847I; *Études (2), Opus 116*, 1866I; *Etudes (3), Opus 139*, 1874I; *Fantasiestücke (4), Opus 99*, 1861I; *Grande étude, Opus 96*, 1860I; *Herbstblätter, Opus 109*, 1864I; *Im Walde, Opus 86*, 1854I; *Im Walde II, Opus 128*, 1871I; *Im Walde III, Opus 136*, 1873I; *Jagdstück, Opus 102*, 1861I; *Kleines Album, Opus 134*, 1872I; *Nocturnes (3), Opus 91*, 1858I; *Piano Concerto No. 2 in b, Opus 65*, 1844I; *Piano Pieces (3), Opus 73*, 1849I; *Piano Preludes (24), Opus 81*, 1853I; *Piano Preludes (3) Opus 117*, 1867I; *Piano Preludes (32), Opus 119*, 1867I; *Piano Preludes (20), Opus 156*, 1879I; *Piano Sonata No. 3 in C, Opus 88*, 1856I; *Piano Sonata No. 4 in b♭, Opus 143*, 1878I; *Piano Sonatina No. 1, Opus 146*, 1878I; *Piano Sonatina No. 2, Opus 147*, 1878I; *Piano Sonatina No. 3, Opus 149*, 1879I; *Spaziergänge eines Einsamen II, Opus 89*, 1856I; *Wanderstunden, Opus 80*, 1852I

Helm, Everett: *Piano Concerto No. 1*, 1951I; *Piano Sonata Brevis*, 1942I; *Requiem*, 1942I

Helps, Robert: *Etudes (3)*, 1956I; *Gossamer Noons*, 1977I; *Hommages (3) for Piano*, 1973I; *Piano Concerto No. 1*, 1969I; *Piano Concerto No. 2*, 1976I; *Piano Trio No. 1*, 1957I; *Piano Trio No. 2*, 1997I; *Starscape*, 1958I; *String Quartet No. 1*, 1951I; *Symphony No. 1*, 1955I

Helweg, Kim: *The Return of Don Juan*, 1999I; *Trumpet Concerto, "Il Madrigale di Giovanni,"* 1998I

Hemmenway, James: *The Philadelphia Grand March*, 1823I

Henneberg, Johann B.: *Die Waldmänner*, 1793I

Hensel, Fanny Mendelssohn; *Job*, 1831I; *Lobegesang*, 1831I; *Organ Preludes (F,G,G)*, 1829I; *Piano Sonata in c*, 1824I; *Piano Sonata in g*, 1843I; *String Quartet in E♭*, 1834I

Henze, Hans Werner: *Auden Songs (3)*, 1983I; *L'autunno*, 1977I; *Ballet-Variations*, 1949I; *The Bassarids*, 1964I; *Boulevard Solitude*, 1951I; *El Cimarron*, 1969I; *Doublebass Concerto*, 1966I; *Elegie für Junge Liebende*, 1961I; *The English Cat*, 1983I; *Le fils de l'air*, 1995I; *Flute Sonatina*, 1947I; *Fraternity, Air for Orchestra*, 1999I; *Guitar Concerto*, 1986I; *Heliogabalus Imperator*, 1972I; *Der Idiot*, 1952I; *Der Junge Lord*, 1964I; *König Hirsch*, 1956I; *Labyrinth*, 1951I; *Moralities*, 1967I; *The Muses of Sicily*, 1966I; *Ode an den Westwind*, 1953I; *Orpheus*, 1978I; *Piano Concerto No. 1*, 1950I; *Piano Concerto No. 2*, 1967I; *Piano Quintet*, 1993I; *Pollicino*, 1979I; *Der Prinz von Homburg*, 1958I; *The Raft of the "Medusa,"* 1968I; *Serenade for Solo Cello*, 1950I; *Six Songs from the Arabic*, 1997I; *String Quartet No. 1*, 1947I; *String Quartet No. 2*, 1952I; *String Quartet No. 3*, 1975I; *String Quartet No. 4*, 1976I; *String Quartet No. 5*, 1976I; *Symphony No. 1*, 1947I; *Symphony No. 2*, 1948I; *Symphony No. 3*, 1949I; *Symphony No. 4*, 1955I; *Symphony No. 5*, 1962I; *Symphony No. 6*, 1969I; *Symphony No. 7*, 1984I; *Symphony No. 9, "Choral,"* 1997I; *Symphony No. 9*, 1999I; *Tancredi*, 1964I; *The Tedious Way to the Apartment of Natasha Ungeheuer*, 1971I; *Tristan* (piano, tape, orchestra), 1973I; *Undine*, 1956I; *Variations*, 1949I; *Venus und Adonis*, 1995I; *Das Verraiene Meer*, 1989I; *Versuch über schweine*, 1968I; *Viola Sonata*, 1978I; *Violin Concerto No. 1*, 1947I; *Violin Sonata*, 1946I; *Violin Sonatina*, 1979I; *We Come to the River*, 1976I; *Whispers from Heavenly Death*, 1984I; *Wind Quintet*, 1952I

Herbert, Victor: *The Ameer*, 1899I; *American Fantasia*, 1898I; *Angel Face*, 1919I; *Babes in Toyland*, 1903I; *Babette*, 1903I; *Badinage*, 1895I; *The Captive*, 1891I; *Cello Concerto No. 2, Opus 30*, 1894I; *Chant d'Amour*, 1924I; *Columbus*, 1903I; *Cosmopolitan*, 1923I; *Cyrano de Bergerac*, 1899I; *The Debutante*, 1914I; *Dream City*, 1906I; *The Dream Girl*, 1924I; *The Duchess*, 1911I; *Eileen*, 1917I; *The Enchantress*, 1911I; *Fantasy on a Schubert Theme*, 1891I; *Festival March*, 1935I; *The Fortune Teller*, 1898I; *The Girl in the Spotlight*, 1920I; *Hero & Leander*, 1901I; *Humoresque for Woodwinds*, 1898I; *The Idol's Eye*, 1897I; *Indian Summer*, 1939I; *Irish Rhapsody*, 1892I; *It Happened in Nordland*, 1904I; *The Lady of the Slipper*, 1912I; *Little Nemo*, 1908I; *Madeleine*, 1913I; *Mélodie for Cello & Piano*, 1893I; *Miss Dolly Dollars*, 1905I; *Mlle. Modiste*, 1905I; *Natoma*, 1911I; *Naughty Marietta*, 1910I; *Old Dutch*, 1909I; *The Only Girl*, 1914I; *Orange Blossoms*, 1922I; *Piano Pieces (6), Set I*, 1900I; *Prince Ananias*, 1894I; *The Princess Pat*, 1915I; *The Red Mill*, 1906I; *Romance for Cello & Piano*, 1906I; *The Rose of Algeria*, 1908I; *Rosemary*, 1917I; *Serenade for Strings, Opus 12*, 1889I; *Songs (8), Opus 10, 13, 14*, 1889I; *Songs (3), Opus 15*, 1888I; *Spanish Rhapsody*, 1905I; *Sweethearts*, 1913I; *The Tatooed Man*, 1907I; *The Veiled Prophet*, 1896I; *Die Versunkenen, Opus 20*, 1890I;

❈

A   *Births*   B   *Deaths*   C   *Debuts*   D   *New Positions*

E   *Prizes/Honors*

The Viceroy, 1900I; *The Vision of Columbus*, 1893I; *Western Overture*, 1906I; *The Wizard of the Nile*, 1895I; *Wonderland*, 1905I; *Woodland Fancies*, 1901I

Herbing, August B.: *Musikalische Belustigungen I*, 1758I; *Musikalische Belustigungen II*, 1767I; *Musikalischer Besuch*, 1759I

Herbolsheimer, Bern: *Mark Me Twain*, 1993I

Herman, Martin: *Arena for Piano*, 1991I

Hérold, Ferdinand: *L'amour platonique*, 1819I; *Ariana, Lyrical Scene*, 1811I; *Astolphe et Joconde*, 1827I; *L'auberge d'Auray*, 1830I; *L'auteur mort et vivant*, 1820I; *La clochette*, 1817I; *Emmaline*, 1829I; *La fille mal gardée*, 1828I; *La Gioventù di Enrico Quinto*, 1815I; *Hymn sur la Transfiguration*, 1813I; *L'illusion*, 1829I; *Le lapin blanc*, 1825I; *Lasthénie*, 1823I; *Ludovic*, 1833I; *Lydie*, 1828I; *Mademoiselle de la Vallière*, 1812I; *Marie*, 1826I; *La médecine sans médecin*, 1832I; *Le muletier*, 1823I; *La noce de village*, 1830I; *Piano Concerto No. 1 in e, Opus 25*, 1812I; *Piano Concerto No. 2 in E♭, Opus 26*, 1812I; *Piano Concerto No. 3 in A*, 1813I; *Piano Concerto No. 4 in e*, 1813I; *Le pré aux clercs*, 1832I; *Le premier venu*, 1818I; *Les rosières*, 1817I; *La somnambule*, 1827I; *Symphony No. 1 in C*, 1813I; *Symphony No. 2 in D*, 1814I; *Les troqueurs*, 1819I; *Vendôme en Espagne*, 1823I; *Zampa*, 1831I

Hérold, Louis: *La belle au bois dormant*, 1829I

Herrmann, Bernard: *Souvenir de Voyage*, 1967I; *String Quartet, "Echoes,"* 1965I

Herschel, William: *Symphonies (6)*, 1760I; *Symphonies (6)*, 1761I; *Symphonies (7)*, 1762I; *Symphonies (3)*, 1763I; *Symphonies (D,C,e)*, 1764I

Hervé: *Aladdin the Second*, 1870I; *Alice de Nevers*, 1875I; *Bacchanale*, 1892I; *La belle poule*, 1875I; *La biche au bois*, 1865I; *Le cabinet Piperlin*, 1897I; *Les chevaliers de la table ronde*, 1866I; *Chilpéric*, 1868I; *Don Quichotte et Sancho Pança*, 1848I; *Le Ertigo*, 1883I; *Estelle et Némorin*, 1876I; *Une fantasia*, 1865I; *La femme à papa*, 1879I; *Le joueur de flûte*, 1864I; *La liberté des théâtres*, 1864I; *Lili*, 1882I; *Mam'zelle Gavroch*, 1884I; *Mam'zelle Nitouche*, 1883I; *La mère des compagnons*, 1880I; *Les métamorphoses de Tartempion*, 1866I; *La nuit aux soufflets*, 1884I; *L'oeil crevé*, 1867I; *L'ours et la pacha*, 1842I; *Panurge*, 1879I; *Le petit Faust*, 1869I; *La revue pour rire*, 1864I; *Le roi Amatibou*, 1868I; *Les toréadors de Grenade*, 1863I; *Trombolina*, 1868I; *Les turcs*, 1869I; *La veuve du Melabar*, 1873I; *Le voyage en Amérique*, 1880I

Hervelois, Louis de Caix d': *Pièces di viole, Book 5*, 1752I

Hervig, Richard: *Off Center*, 1991I

Herzogenberg, Heinrich von: *Mass in e, Opus 87*, 1895I

Hessenberg, Kurt: *Concerto for Orchestra*, 1958I; *Symphony No. 1*, 1936I; *Symphony No. 2*, 1943I; *Symphony No. 3*, 1954I

Hétu, Pierre: *Piano Concerto*, 1969I

Hewitt, James: *Columbus*, 1799I; *The Fourth of July*, 1801I; *Grand Sinfonie, Characteristic of the Peace of the; French Republic*, 1802I; *The Mysterious Marriage*, 1799I; *Overture, Expressive of a Battle (Trenton)*, 1792I; *The Patriots*, 1794I; *Pizarro*, 1800I; *Robin Hood*, 1800I; *Tammany*, 1794I; *Yankee Doodle with Variations*, 1810I

Hill, Alfred: *String Quartet No. 2*, 1907I; *String Quartet No. 5, "The Allies,"* 1920I; *String Quartet No. 6, "The Kids,"* 1927I; *String Quartet No. 11*, 1935I

Hill, Edward Burlingame: *A Child's Garden of Verse*, 1918I; *Clarinet Quintet*, 1945I; *Clarinet Sonata*, 1927I; *Fall of the House of Usher*, 1920I; *Lilacs*, 1927I; *Nuns of the Perpetual Adorations*, 1907I; *Pan the Star*, 1914I; *The Parting of Lancelot & Guinevere*, 1915I; *Piano Quartet*, 1937I; *Sextet for Piano & Winds*, 1934I; *String Quartet No. 1*, 1935I; *Symphony No. 1 in B*, 1927I; *Symphony No. 2 in C*, 1929I; *Symphony No. 3 in G*, 1936I; *Violin Concerto*, 1934I

Hillborg, Anders: *Meltdown Variations*, 1997I

Hiller, Ferdinand: *Der Advokat*, 1854I; *Bundeslied, Opus 174*, 1876I; *Christnacht, Opus 79*, 1865I; *Concert Overture in A, Opus 101*, 1863I; *Concertstück, Opus 113*, 1865I; *Der Deserteur*, 1865I; *Dramatic Fantasy, Opus 166*, 1874I; *Es fürchte des Götter das Menschen geschlecht, Opus 193*, 1881I; *Fantasiestück, Opus 152b*, 1875I; *Frühlingsnacht, Opus 139*, 1869I; *Gesang der Geister, Opus 36*, 1847I; *Israels Stegesgesang, Opus 157*, 1872I; *Die Katakomben*, 1862I; *Konradin*, 1847I; *Loreley, Opus 7*, 1873I; *Ostermorgan, Opus 134*, 1868I; *Overture in d, Opus 32*, 1845I; *Overture, Demetrius, Opus 145*, 1870I; *Piano Concerto No. 1 in A♭, Opus 5*, 1835I; *Piano Concerto No. 2 in F♯, Opus 69*, 1861I; *Piano Sonata No. 1, Opus 47*, 1853I; *Piano Sonata No. 2 in A♭, Opus 59*, 1863I; *Piano Sonata No. 3 in g, Opus 78*, 1859I; *Prinz Papagei, Opus 183*, 1878I; *Psalm 25, Opus 60*, 1854I; *Rebecca, Opus 182*, 1878I; *Richard Löwenherz, Opus 200*, 1883I; *Romilda*, 1839I; *Saul, Opus 80* (cantata), 1858I; *Symphony No. 1*, 1829I; *Symphony No. 3, Opus 67*, 1834I; *Ein Traum in der Christnacht*, 1845I; *Violin Concerto, Opus 152*, 1876I; *Der Zerstörung Jerusalems, Opus 24*, 1840I

Hiller, Friedrich Adam: *String Quartets (3), Opus 1*, 1795I; *String Quartets (3), Opus 3*, 1795I

Hiller, Johann Adam: *Cantata Profana*, 1770I; *La Didone abbandonata*, 1770I; *Das Grab des Mufti*, 1779I; *Der greis Mann und Jungling*, 1778I; *Die Jubelhochzeit*, 1773I; *Der Krieg*, 1772I; *Die Liebe auf dem Lande*,

Hiller, Johann Adam: (*cont.*)
    1768I; *Lottchen am Hofe*, 1767I; *Die Muse*, 1767I; *Der Teufel ist los*, 1766I; *Die Verwandelter weiber*, 1764I
Hiller, Lejaren: *Computer Cantata*, 1963I; *Electronic Sonata*, 1976I; *Nightmare Music*, 1961I; *Piano Sonata No. 1*, 1946I; *Piano Sonata No. 2*, 1947I; *Piano Sonata No. 3*, 1950I; *Piano Sonata No. 4*, 1950I; *Piano Sonata No. 5*, 1961I; *Piano Sonata No. 6*, 1972I; *Seven Electronic Studies*, 1963I; *String Quartet No. 2*, 1951I; *String Quartet No. 3*, 1953I; *String Quartet No. 4*, 1957I; *String Quartet No. 5*, 1962I; *String Quartet No. 7*, 1979I; *Symphony No. 1*, 1954I; *Symphony No. 2*, 1960I; *Symphony No. 6*, 1972I
Himmel, Friedrich Heinrich: *Alessandro*, 1798I; *Alexis und Ida, Opus 43*, 1814I; *Bewustseyn, Opus 33*, 1810I; *La danza*, 1792I; *Deutsche Lieder: ein Naujahrsgeschenk*, 1798I; *Deutsche und französische Lieder (12)*, 1804I; *Fanchon das leiermädchen*, 1804I; *Frohsinn und Schwärmerei*, 1801I; *Gedichte (9), Opus 24, 31*, 1809I; *Gedichte aus dem Kyllenion, Opus 20*, 1807I; *Gesänge aus Tiedges Urania, Opus 18*, 1800I; *Grand Sestetto, Opus 18*, 1802I; *Isacco figura del redentore*, 1792I; *Der Kobold*, 1813I; *Kriegslieder der Teutschen, Opus 21*, 1813I; *Lieder (6), Opus 21*, 1807I; *Lieder (12), Knaben Wunderhorn, Opus 27*, 1808I; *Lieder (3), Opus 36*, 1810I; *Lieder (9), Opus 42, 44*, 1813I; *Das Lob Gottes*, 1804I; *La morte di Semiramide*, 1795I; *Piano Concerto in D, Opus 25*, 1808I; *Il primo navigatore*, 1794I; *Romances françaises (6)*, 1799I; *Romances françoises (5), Opus 44*, 1813I; *Sonata for Two Pianos*, 1801I; *Die Sylphen*, 1806I; *Te Deum*, 1798I; *Trauer-Cantate*, 1797I; *Vasco da Gama*, 1801I; *Vater unser*, 1810I; *Das Vertrauen auf Gott*, 1797I; *Die Wanderer*, 1811I
Hindemith, Paul: *Bass Sonata*, 1949I; *Cardillac*, 1926I; *Cello Concerto in E♭, Opus 3*, 1916I; *Cello Concerto No. 2*, 1940I; *Cello Sonata, Opus 11*, 1919I; *Clarinet Concerto*, 1947I; *Clarinet Quartet*, 1938I; *Clarinet Quintet*, 1923I; *Clarinet Sonata*, 1939I; *Concert Music for Harp, Piano & Brass, Opus 49*, 1931I; *Concert Music for Strings & Brass, Opus 50*, 1930I; *Concert Music for Viola & Orchestra*, 1930I; *Concert Music for Winds, Opus 41*, 1926I; *Concerto for Organ & Chamber Orchestra, Opus 46/2*, 1927I; *Der Dämon, Opus 28*, 1922I; *Easy Pieces (3) for Cello & Piano*, 1938I; *The Four Temperaments*, 1940I; *Die Harmonie der Welt*, 1957I; *Hin und Zurück*, 1927I; *Horn Concerto*, 1949I; *Horn Sonata in F*, 1939I; *Die Jung magd, Opus 23/2*, 1922I; *Kleine Kammermusik I, Opus 24/2*, 1922I; *Ludus Tonalis*, 1943I; *Madrigals (12)*, 1958I; *Das Marienleben*, 1923I; *Mass*, 1963I; *Mathis der Maler*, 1934I; *Morder, Hoffnung der Frauen*, 1921I; *Morgenmusik for Brass Quintet*, 1932I; *Neues von Tagen*, 1929I; *Nobilissima Visione*, 1937I; *Organ Concerto*, 1962I; *Organ Sonata No. 1*, 1937I; *Organ Sonata No. 2*, 1937I; *Organ Sonata No. 3*, 1940I; *Philharmonic Concert*, 1932I; *Piano Concerto*, 1945I; *Pittsburgh Symphony*, 1958I; *Sancta Susanna*, 1921I; *Der Schwanendreher* (violin concerto), 1935I; *Songs for Soprano (8), Opus 18*, 1920I; *Songs on Olden Tests (6), Opus 33*, 1923I; *String Quartet No. 1 in f, Opus 10*, 1915I; *String Quartet No. 2 in C, Opus 16*, 1921I; *String Quartet No. 3, Opus 22*, 1922I; *String Quartet No. 4, Opus 32*, 1923I; *String Quartet No. 5 in E♭*, 1943I; *String Quartet No. 6*, 1943I; *String Quartet No. 7*, 1945I; *Symphonia Serena*, 1946I; *Symphonic Dances*, 1938I; *Symphonic Metamorphosis on Themes of Carl Maria von Weber*, 1943I; *Symphony: Harmonie der Welt*, 1951I; *Symphony in B♭ for Band*, 1951I; *Symphony in E♭*, 1940I; *Das Unaufhörliche*, 1931I; *Violin Concerto*, 1939I; *Violin Sonata*, 1939I; *When Lilacs Last in the Dooryard Bloomed*, 1946I
Hirose, Ryohei: *Flute Sonata*, 1964I; *Shakuhachi Concerto*, 1976I
Hobson, Bruce: *Songs (3) of e. e. cummings*, 1987I
Hoch, James: *Symphony No. 1*, 2000I
Hodkinson, Sydney: *Alte Liebeslieder*, 1982I
Hoffman, Joel: *Millennium Dances*, 1997I; *Self-Portrait with Gebirtig*, 1998I
Hoffmann, E. T. A.: *Arlequin*, 1808I; *Aurora*, 1811I; *Das Kreuz an der Ostsee*, 1805I; *Liebe und Eifersucht*, 1807I; *Die lustigen Musikanten*, 1804I; *Der Renegat*, 1803I; *Scherz, List und Rache*, 1801I; *Symphony in E♭*, 1806I; *Der Trank der Unsterblichkeit*, 1808I; *Undine*, 1816I; *Die ungebetenen Gäste*, 1805I
Hofmann, Heinrich: *Ännchen von Tharau, Opus 44*, 1878I; *Armin, Opus 40*, 1872I; *Aschenbrödel, Opus 45*, 1881I; *Cartouche*, 1869I; *Donna Diana, Opus 75*, 1886I; *Festgesang, Opus 74*, 1885I; *Frithjof-Symphonie, Opus 22*, 1876I; *Harald's Brautfahrt, Opus 90*, 1888I; *Hungarian Suite, Opus 16*, 1873I; *Konzertstück, Opus 98*, 1888I; *Das Märchen von der schönen Melusine, Opus 30*, 1876I; *Nordische Meerfahrt, Opus 113*, 1894I; *Nornengesang, Opus 21*, 1885I; *Prometheus, Opus 110*, 1892I; *Rattanfänger, Opus 62a*, 1886I; *Sinn und Minnin, Opus 68*, 1883I; *Violin Concerto in d, Opus 31*, 1880I; *Weldfräulein, Opus 111*, 1893I; *Wilhelm von Oranien, Opus 56*, 1882I
Hoffmeister, Franz A.: *Grand Symphonie, Opus 14, "La chasse,"* 1784I
Hoiby, Lee: *After Eden*, 1966I; *Bon Appetit*, 1989I; *Cello Sonata, Opus 59*, 1993I; *Dona nobis pacem, Opus 55*, 1983I; *The English Painter*, 1983I; *For You, O Democracy, Opus 57*, 1993I; *Galileo Galilei*, 1975I; *I Have a Dream*, 1988I; *I Was There*, 1995I; *The Italian Lesson*, 1980I; *Landscape*, 1967I; *Magnificat, Opus 38*, 1983I; *Measureless Love*, 1995I; *Music for Celebration, Opus 30*, 1975I; *Natalia Petrovna*, 1964I; *Night Songs*, 1950I; *Piano Concerto No. 1*, 1958I; *Piano Concerto No. 2*, 1979I; *Piano Narrative*, 1983I; *Preludes*,

(5), *Opus 7*, 1952I; *Psalm Ninety-Three*, 1985I; *Rainforest, Opus 65*, 1996I; *St. Mary Magdalene*, 1995I; *The Scarf*, 1958I; *Schubert Variations for Piano*, 1981I; *Something New for the Zoo*, 1979I; *A Song of Joys*, 1991I; *Suite No. 2, Opus 8*, 1953I; *Southern Voices, Opus 53*, 1990I; *Summer & Smoke*, 1970I; *The Tempest*, 1986I; *Theme & Variations, Opus 61*, 1994I; *Three Ages of Women, Opus 31*, 1990I; *Violin Sonata*, 1952I; *What Is This Light?*, 1995I

Hol, Richard: *Symphony No. 1*, 1863I; *Symphony No. 3*, 1884I

Holbrook, Joseph: *Piano Concerto No. 1, "Song of Gwynn ap Nudd,"* 1907I

Holden, Oliver: *Coronation (All Hail the Power)*, 1792I; *From Vernon's Mount Behold the Hero Rise*, 1800I;

Höller, York: *Der Meister und Margarita*, 1989I

Holm, Ludwig: *Violin Concerto No. 2*, 1899I

Holmboe, Vagn: *Brass Quintet*, 1978I; *Concerto for Orchestra No. 8*, 1945I; *Concerto for Piano, Strings & Timpani, Opus 17*, 1939I; *Chamber Concerto No. 1*, 1939I; *Chamber Concerto No. 2, Opus 20*, 1940I; *Chamber Concerto No. 3, Opus 21*, 1942I; *Chamber Concerto No. 4, "Triple Concerto,"* 1942I; *Chamber Concerto No. 5*, 1943I; *Chamber Concerto No. 6*, 1943I; *Chamber Concerto No. 7*, 1945I; *Chamber Concerto No. 8*, 1945I; *Chamber Concerto No. 9*, 1946I; *Chamber Concerto No. 10*, 1946I; *Chamber Concerto No. 11, Opus 44*, 1948I; *Chamber Concerto No. 12, Opus 52*, 1950I; *Epilog, Opus 80*, 1962I; *Epitaph*, 1954I; *Epitaph, Opus 68*, 1956I; *Flute Concerto*, 1976I; *String Quartet No. 1*, 1949I; *String Quartet No. 2*, 1949I; *String Quartet No. 3*, 1950I; *String Quartet No. 4*, 1954I; *String Quartet No. 5*, 1955I; *String Quartet No. 6*, 1961I; *String Quartet No. 7*, 1965I; *String Quartet No. 8*, 1965I; *String Quartet No. 9*, 1966I; *String Quartet No. 10*, 1969I; *String Quartet No. 11*, 1971I; *String Quartet No. 12*, 1973I; *Symphony No. 1*, 1935I; *Symphony No. 2*, 1939I; *Symphony No. 3, "Sinfonia Rustica,"* 1941I; *Symphony No. 4, "Sinfonia Sacra,"* 1941I; *Symphony No. 5*, 1944I; *Symphony No. 6*, 1947I; *Symphony No. 7*, 1950I; *Symphony No. 8, "Sinfonia Boreale,"* 1952I; *Symphony No. 9*, 1968I; *Symphony No. 10*, 1971I; *Symphony No. 11*, 1980I; *Symphony No. 12, Opus 175*, 1989I; *Symphony No. 13, Opus 192*, 1993I; *Tempo Variable*, 1972I; *Tuba Concerto, Opus 127*, 1976I; *Violin Concerto No. 1, Opus 14*, 1938I

Holst, Gustav: *At the Boar's Head*, 1925I; *Choral Fantasia, Opus 51*, 1930I; *Cotswold Symphony, Opus 8*, 1902I; *Egdon Heath*, 1928I; *Hammersmith: Prelude & Scherzo, Opus 52*, 1930I; *The Hymn of Jesus*, 1917I; *Hymns from the Rig Veda*, 1912I; *Japanese Suite*, 1915I; *The Perfect Fool*, 1921I; *The Planets*, 1914I; *Savitri*, 1916I; *Somerset Rhapsody, A, Opus 21*, 1910I; *St. Paul's Suite*, 1913I; *Suite de Ballet, Opus 10*, 1899I; *Suite No. 1 for Band*, 1909I; *Suite No. 2 for Band*, 1911I

Holyoke, Samuel: *Hark from the Tombs*, 1800I; *Washington*, 1790I

Holzbauer, Ignaz: *Adriano in Siria*, 1768I; *Alessandro nell'Indie*, 1759I; *Le Betulia Liberata*, 1760I; *La clemenza de Tito*, 1757I; *Don Chisciotte*, 1757I; *Il figlio delle selve*, 1753I; *Il filosofo di campagna*, 1756I; *Il Guidizio di Salomone*, 1766I; *Günther von Schwarzburg*, 1776I; *Ippolito ed Aricia*, 1759I; *Isacco*, 1757I; *L'isola disabitata*, 1754I; *L'issipile*, 1754I; *La morte di Didone*, 1779I; *Nitteti*, 1758I; *Le nozze d'Arianna*, 1756I; *La Passione de Gesu Christo*, 1754I; *Symphonies (6) in Four Parts, Opus 2*, 1757I; *Symphonies (6) in 8 Parts, Opus 3e*, 1769I; *Tancredi*, 1783I

Homer, Sidney: *String Quartet*, 1937I; *Piano Quintet*, 1932I; *Piano Sonata*, 1922I

Homilius, Gottfried: *Die Freude der Kirten uber die Geburt Jesu*, 1777I

Homs, Joaquín: *Catalan Variations*, 1943I

Honegger, Artur: *Antigone*, 1927I; *Cello Concerto*, 1929I; *Chant de Joie*, 1923I; *Christmas Cantata*, 1953I; *Les cris du Monde*, 1931I; *Fugue in c♯*, 1917I; *Horace Victorieux*, 1920I; *Joan of Arc at the Stake*, 1935I; *Judith*, 1925I; *King David*, 1921I; *Pacific 231*, 1923I; *Pastorale d'Été*, 1920I; *Piano Concertino*, 1925I; *Prelude to the Tempest*, 1923I; *Rugby, Symphonic Movement No. 2*, 1928I; *Sèmirámis*, 1934I; *The Skating Rink*, 1921I; *Symphonic Movement No. 3*, 1933I; *Symphony No. 1*, 1930I; *Symphony No. 2*, 1941I; *Symphony No. 3, "Liturgique,"* 1946I; *Symphony No. 4, "Deliciae Basiliensis,"* 1947I; *Symphony No. 5, "Di Tre Re,"* 1950I

Hoof, Jef van: *Meivuur*, 1915I; *Small Quartet in C for Strings*, 1919I; *Symphony No. 1 in A*, 1938I; *Symphony No. 2*, 1941I; *Symphony No. 3*, 1945I; *Symphony No. 4 in B*, 1951I; *Symphony No. 5*, 1956I; *Tycho-Brahe*, 1911I; *William, the Silent, Overture*, 1910I

Hoover, Katherine: *Canyon Echoes*, 1991I; *Eleni: A Greek Tragedy*, 1987I; *Quintet*, 1989I

Hopekirk, Helen: *Piano Concertstück in d*, 1894I; *Piano Concerto in D*, 1900I

Hopkins, J. H.: *We Three Kings of Orient Are*, 1857I

Hopkinson, Francis: *My Days Have Been So wondrous Free . . .*, 1759I; *Ode to Music*, 1754I; *The Temple of Minerva*, 1781I

Horne, David: *Broken Instruments*, 2000I; *Friend of the People, Opus 3*, 1999I; *Pensive*, 1998I; *Phantom Moon*, 1993I; *Piano Concerto*, 1992I; *String Quartet No. 1, "Surrendering to the Stream,"* 1993I; *String Quartet No. 2, "Undulations,"* 1995I

Horneman, Christian F. E.: *Les bleuets*, 1889I; *Esther*, 1889I; *The Struggle with the Muses*, 1897I

Horovitz, Joseph: *Oboe Concerto*, 1993I; *Trumpet Concerto*, 1963I
Horwitz, Charles: *Because*, 1898I
Hovhaness, Alan: *And God Created Great Whales*, 1970I; *Blue Job Mountain Sonata for Piano*, 1986I; *Concerto No. 1 for Orchestra*, 1951I; *Concerto No. 2 for Violin*, 1957I; *Concerto No. 3 for Trombone*, 1948I; *Concerto No. 4 for Orchestra*, 1952I; *Concerto No. 5 for Piano*, 1952I; *Concerto No. 6 for Harmonica*, 1953I; *Concerto No. 7 for Orchestra*, 1953I; *Concerto No. 8 for Orchestra*, 1953I; *Concerto No. 9 for Piano*, 1954I; *Concerto No. 10*, 1988I; *Guitar Concerto*, 1979I; *Guitar Concerto No. 2, Opus 394*, 1985I; *Harp Sonata*, 1954I; *The Holy City*, 1967I; *Magnificat*, 1959I; *Mount Katahdin for Piano*, 1987I; *Piano Sonata Ananda*, 1977I; *Piano Sonata Fred the Cat*, 1977I; *Piano Sonata Mt. Chocorua*, 1982I; *Piano Sonata Mt. Ossipee*, 1977I; *Prelude & Quadruple Fugue*, 1936I; *Revelations of St. Paul*, 1981I; *Sonata for Harp & Guitar, Opus 374*, 1983I; *Symphony No. 1, "Exile," Opus 17*, 1937I; *Symphony No. 2, "Mysterious Mountain,"* 1954I; *Symphony No. 3*, 1956I; *Symphony No. 4*, 1959I; *Symphony No. 5, Opus 170*, 1953I; *Symphony No. 6, "Celestial Gate,"* 1959I; *Symphony No. 7*, 1959I; *Symphony No. 8, "Arjuna,"* 1947I; *Symphony No. 9, "St. Vartan," Opus 80*, 1950I; *Symphony No. 10*, 1959I; *Symphony No. 11*, 1960I; *Symphony No. 12*, 1960I; *Symphony No. 13*, 1953I; *Symphony No. 14, "Ararat," Opus 194*, 1961I; *Symphony No. 15, "Silver Pilgrimage,"* 1962I; *Symphony No. 16, Opus 202*, 1962I; *Symphony No. 17*, 1963I; *Symphony No. 18, "Circe,"* 1964I; *Symphony No. 19, "Vishnu," Opus 217*, 1966I; *Symphony No. 20, "Three Journeys to a Holy Mountain," Opus 223*, 1968I; *Symphony No. 21, "Etchmiadzin," Opus 234*, 1970I; *Symphony No. 22, "City of Light," Opus 236*, 1971I; *Symphony No. 23, "Ani," Opus 249*, 1972I; *Symphony No. 24, "Majnun,"* 1973I; *Symphony No. 25, "Odysseus,"* 1973I; *Symphony No. 26, "Consolation," Opus 280*, 1975I; *Symphony No. 27*, 1975I; *Symphony No. 28*, 1976I; *Symphony No. 29*, 1976I; *Symphony No. 30*, 1976I; *Symphony No. 31*, 1976I; *Symphony No. 32*, 1977I; *Symphony No. 33*, 1977I; *Symphony No. 34*, 1977I; *Symphony No. 35*, 1978I; *Symphony No. 36*, 1979I; *Symphony No. 37*, 1978I; *Symphony No. 38*, 1978I; *Symphony No. 39*, 1978I; *Symphony No. 40*, 1978I; *Symphony No. 41*, 1978I; *Symphony No. 42*, 1978I; *Symphony No. 44, Opus 339*, 1980I; *Symphony No. 45*, 1978I; *Symphony No. 46*, 1981I; *Symphony No. 47*, 1981I; *Symphony No. 48*, 1982I; *Symphony No. 49*, 1981I; *Symphony No. 50*, 1982I; *Symphony No. 51*, 1982I; *Symphony No. 52*, 1982I; *Symphony No. 53*, 1982I; *Symphony No. 54*, 1982I; *Symphony No. 55*, 1982I; *Symphony No. 56*, 1982I; *Symphony No. 57*, 1982I; *Symphony No. 58*, 1982I; *Ukiyo, Floating World*, 1964I
Hovhannessian, Edgar S.: *Marmar*, 1956I; *Symphony No. 3*, 1983I
Hovland, Egil: *Trombone Concerto*, 1972I
Howe, Julia Ward: *Battle Hymn of the Republic*, 1862I
Howe, Mary: *Piano Quintet*, 1923I
Howells, Herbert: *An English Mass*, 1955I; *Fantasia for Cello & Orchestra*, 1937I; *Hymus Paradisi*, 1938I; *Piano Concerto No. 1 in c, Opus 4*, 1913I; *Piano Concerto No. 2 in C, Opus 29*, 1924I; *Requiem*, 1936I; *Rhapsody No. 3*, 1918I
Hristić, Stevan: *The Legend of Okhrid*, 1933I
Hubarenko, Vitali: *Monologues of Juliet*, 1998I
Hubay, Jenö: *Anna Karenina*, 1915I; *Symphony No. 1 in B♭, Opus 26*, 1885I; *Symphony No. 2, Opus 93*, 1915I
Huber, Hans: *A Comedy Overture, Opus 50*, 1879I; *Sextet for Piano and Winds*, 1898I; *Symphony No. 2 in e, "Böcklin," Opus 115*, 1897I
Hullah, John: *The Barber of Bassora*, 1937I; *The Outpost*, 1838I; *The Village Coquette*, 1836I
Hummel, Berthold: *Hallelujah for Organ*, 1972I; *Marian Frescoes (3)*, 1970I; *Percussion Concerto*, 1982I
Hummel, Johann Nepomuk: *Bassoon Concerto*, 1803I; *Das belebte Gemählde*, 1809I; *Die beiden Genies*, 1805I; *Cello Sonata in A, Opus 104*, 1824I; *Choix des plus beaux morceaux de musique*, 1811I; *Diane ed Endimione*, 1806I; *Die Eselshaut, oder Die blaue Insel*, 1814I; *Das Fest des Dankes un Freude*, 1806I; *Der Junker in der Mühle*, 1813I; *Lob der Freundschaft*, 1807I; *Mandolin Concerto*, 1799I; *Mass in E♭, Opus 80*, 1804I; *Mass in d*, 1805I; *Mass in D, Opus 111*, 1808I; *Mass in B♭, Opus 77*, 1810I; *Mathilde von Guise*, 1810I; *Missa Solemnis in D*, 1806I; *Oboe Concerto No. 1, Opus 37*, 1803I; *Overture in B♭, Opus 101*, 1826I; *Piano Concerto No. 3 in C, Opus 34a*, 1814I; *Piano Concerto No. 4 in E, Opus 110*, 1816I; *Piano Concerto No. 5 in G, Opus 72*, 1816I; *Piano Concerto No. 6 in a, Opus 85*, 1816I; *Piano Concerto No. 7 in b, Opus 89*, 1819I; *Piano Concerto No. 8 in A♭, Opus 113*, 1827I; *Piano Concerto No. 9 in F, Opus Posth.*, 1833I; *Piano Fantasie in E♭, Opus 13*, 1805I; *Piano Sonata in E♭, Opus 13*, 1805I; *Piano Sonata in f, Opus 20*, 1806I; *Piano Sonata in C, Opus 38*, 1808I; *Piano Sonata in f♯, Opus 81*, 1819I; *Piano Trio in E♭, Opus 12*, 1803I; *Piano Trio in F, Opus 22*, 1799I; *Piano Trio in E, Opus 83*, 1819I; *Piano Trio in E♭, Opus 93*, 1821I; *Piano Trio in E♭, Opus 96*, 1822I; *Pimmalione*, 1815I; *Quintet in E♭, Opus 87*, 1822I; *Rondo brillant in G, Opus 126*, 1835I; *Die Rückfahrt des Kaisers*, 1814I; *Sappho von Mitilene*, 1812I; *Septet Militaire in C, Opus 114*, 1829I; *Septet in d, Opus 74*, 1816I; *Te Deum in D*, 1806I; *Trumpet Concerto*, 1803I; *Variations on a March*

❈

A *Births*   B *Deaths*   C *Debuts*   D *New Positions*
E *Prizes/Honors*

by Dalyrac, Opus 15, 1804I; *Variations on a March by Isouard, Opus 40a*, 1811I; *Variations, Opus 34*, 1810I; *Variations in F on a Theme from Vogler, Opus 6*, 1792I; *Variations in G, Opus 8*, 1801I; *Variations in E on Cherubini March, Opus 9*, 1802I; *Variations in A, Opus 76*, 1817I; *Variations in F, Opus 97*, 1820I; *Variations on "Chanson hollandaise," Opus 21*, 1806I; *Variations on "God Save the King," Opus 10*, 1804I; *Die vereitelten Ränke*, 1806I; *Le vicende d'amore*, 1804I

Humperdinck, Engelbert: *As You Like It*, 1907I; *Bluebeard*, 1910I; *Dornröschen*, 1902I; *Gaudeamus*, 1919I; *Das Glück on Edenhall*, 1883I; *Hansel und Gretel*, 1893I; *Jung Lieder*, 1898I; *Königskinder* (IM), 1897I; *Königskinder* (opera), 1910I; *Lysistrata*, 1908I; *Die Marketenderin*, 1914I; *Der Richter von Zalamea*, 1883I; *String Quartet No. 3 in C*, 1920I; *The Tempest*, 1906I; *The Winter's Tale*, 1906I

Hůrka, Friedrich F.: *Deutsche Lieder (12) I*, 1793I; *Deutsche Lieder (12) II*, 1794I; *Deutsche Lieder (15)III*, 1797I; *Ehelicher guter Morgen und gute Nacht*, 1796I; *Die Geburtstagfeier*, 1795I; *Schez und Ernst in zwölf Liedern*, 1787I; *Das Strickerlied*, 1800I

Hurum, Alf: *String Quartet, Opus 6*, 1913I; *Symphony in d*, 1927I

Husa, Karel: *Cello Concerto*, 1988I; *Concerto for Brass Quintet*, 1965I; *Concerto for Orchestra*, 1986I; *Concerto for Wind Ensemble*, 1983I; *Divertimento for Brass & Percussion*, 1958I; *Fantasies for Orchestra*, 1956I; *Frammenti for Organ*, 1987I; *Mosaïques*, 1960I; *Music for Prague* (band), 1968I; *Piano Sonata No. 1*, 1950I; *Piano Sonata No. 2*, 1975I; *String Quartet No. 1*, 1948I; *String Quartet No. 2*, 1953I; *String Quartet No. 3*, 1968I; *String Quartet No. 4, "Poems,"* 1990I; *Symphonic Suite*, 1984I; *Symphony No. 1*, 1953I; *Symphony No. 2, "Reflections,"* 1983I; *The Trojan Women*, 1980I; *Trumpet Concerto*, 1987I; *Violin Sonata*, 1973I

Huss, Henry Holden: *Cleopatra's Death*, 1894I; *Festival Sanctus*, 1889I; *Life's Conflicts*, 1921I; *La nuit*, 1902I; *Piano Concerto in B, Opus 10*, 1894I; *Pieces (6), Opus 23*, 1912I; *Rhapsody for Piano and Orchestra*, 1885I; *Sketches (7), Opus 32*, 1927I; *Songs (4), Opus 22*, 1907I; *String Quartet No. 3 in b*, 1918I; *String Quartet No. 4 in g, Opus 31*, 1921I; *Violin Concerto*, 1906I; *Violin Sonata, Opus 19*, 1903I

Huston, Scott: *Diorama for Organ*, 1968I; *For Our Times*, 1974I; *Organ Sonata*, 1960I; *Symphony No. 4 for Strings*, 1972I; *Symphony No. 5*, 1975I; *Symphony No. 6, "The Human Condition,"* 1981I

Indy, Vincent d': *Antoine et Cléopâtre, Opus 6*, 1877I; *Attendez-moi sous l'orme, Opus 14*, 1882I; *Chanson des aventuriers de la mer, Opus 2*, 1870I; *Le chant de la cloche, Opus 18*, 1883I; *La chevauchée du Cid, Opus 11*, 1879I; *The Enchanted Forest, Opus 8*, 1878I; *Fervaal*, 1895I; *Ishtar Variations, Opus 42*, 1896I; *Karadee, Opus 34*, 1891I; *Max et Thécla*, 1874I; *Médée, Opus 47*, 1898I; *La mort de Wallenstein*, 1882I; *Motet: Deus Israel*, 1896I; *Overture, Anthony and Cleopatra*, 1876I; *Petit Sonata, Opus 9*, 1880I; *Piano Quartet in A, Opus 7*, 1888I; *Poème des montagnes, Opus 15*, 1811I; *Prélude et petit canon, Opus 88*, 1893I; *Romances sans paroles (3), Opus 1*, 1870I; *Sauge fleurie, Opus 21*, 1885I; *Ste. Marie-Magdeleine, Opus 23*, 1885I; *Sur la mer, Opus 32*, 1888I; *Symphony No. 1 in A*, 1872I; *Symphony, "Jean Huryade," Opus 5*, 1875I; *Symphony on a French Mountain Air*, 1886I; *Tableaux de voyage, Opus 36*, 1891I; *Vêpres du commun des Martyrs, Opus 31*, 1889I; *Wallenstein's Camp*, 1880I

Iannaccone, Anthony: *Magnificat*, 1963I; *Piano Keyboard Essays*, 1972I; *Piano Trio*, 1959I; *Remembrances*, 1968I; *String Quartet No. 1*, 1965I; *String Quartet No. 3*, 1999I; *Symphony No. 1*, 1965I; *Symphony No. 2*, 1966I; *Symphony No. 3*, 1992I; *Two-Piano Inventions*, 1985I; *Variations for Organ*, 1983I; *Viola Sonata*, 1961I; *Violin Sonata No. 1*, 1964I; *Violin Sonata No. 2*, 1971I; *Whispers of Heavenly Death*, 1989I

Ibert, Jacques: *Les amours de Jupiter*, 1946I; *Angélique*, 1927I; *Bacchanale*, 1958I; *The Ballad of Reading Gaol*, 1922I; *Barbebleue*, 1943I; *Bostoniana*, 1961I; *Capriccio*, 1938I; *Chansons de C. Vidrac (3)*, 1923I; *Chansons de don Quichotte (4)*, 1932I; *Chant de folie*, 1924I; *Le chevalier errant*, 1950I; *Concertino da Camaera for Saxophone & Orchestra*, 1935I; *Concerto for Cello & Wind Instruments*, 1926I; *Conzague*, 1931I; *Diane de Poitiers*, 1934I; *Divertissement*, 1930I; *Excales*, 1922I; *Féerique*, 1925I; *Flute Sonatina, "Jeux,"* 1924I; *Louisville Concerto*, 1954I; *Noël et Picardie*, 1914I; *Ouverture de fête*, 1942I; *Persée et Andromède*, 1921I; *Pieces (6) for Harp*, 1017I; *Le poète et la fée*, 1919I; *Les rencontres*, 1925I; *Le roi d'Yvetot*, 1930I; *String Quartet*, 1944I; *Suite élisabéthaine*, 1944I; *Suite symphonique*, 1932I; *Tropisms for Imaginary Loves*, 1957I

Ichiyanagi, Toshi: *Dimensions for Organ*, 1990I; *Parallel Music*, 1962I; *Piano Concerto No. 1, "Reminiscence of Space,"* 1981I; *Piano Concerto No. 2, "Winter Portrait,"* 1987I; *Piano Concerto No. 3, "Cross Water Roads,"* 1991I; *Requiem*, 1985I; *String Quartet*, 1957I; *String Quartet No. 1*, 1964I; *String Quartet, No. 2, "Interspace,"* 1986I; *String Quartet No. 3*, 1994i; *Symphony: Reinkagu*, 1987I; *Symphony: Berlin Renshi*, 1988I; *Symphony: Time Perspection*, 1997I; *Violin Sonata*, 1954I

Ifukube, Akira: *Piano Concerto*, 1941I; *Violin Concerto No. 1*, 1947I

Ikebe, Shin-Ichiro: *Dimorphism* (organ), 1974I; *For a Beautiful Star*, 1990I; *Hokkat Swells*, 1992I; *Movements (2) for Orchestra*, 1966I; *Piano Concerto No. 1*, 1967I; *Piano Concerto No. 2, "Tu M',"* 1987I; *Quatrevalence*, 1996I; *Strata I* (string quartet), 1988I; *Strata III*, 1989I; *Strata IV*, 1994I; *Strata V* (string quartet), 1995I; *Symphony for Green & Friendship*, 1987I; *Symphony No. 1*, 1967I; *Symphony No. 2*,

---

F *Biographical*   G *Cultural Beginnings*   H *Musical Literature*
I *Musical Compositions*

Ikebe, Shin-Ichiro: (cont.)
1979I; *Symphony No. 3, "Egō Phanō,"* 1989AI; *Symphony No. 4,* 1990I; *Symphony No. 5,* 1990I; *Symphony No. 6,* 1993I; *Violin Concerto, "Almost a Tree,"* 1996I; *Violin Sonata,* 1965I

Ikenouchi, Tomojirô: *Flute Sonata,* 1946I; *String Quartet No. 1,* 1937I; *String Quartet No. 2,* 1945I; *String Quartet No. 3,* 1946I; *Violin Sonata,* 1946I

Ikonen, Lauri: *Symphony No. 1, "Sinfonia inornata,"* 1922I; *Symphony No. 2,* 1937I; *Symphony No. 3,* 1941I; *Symphony No. 4,* 1942I; *Symphony No. 5,* 1943I; *Symphony No. 6,* 1956I; *Violin Concerto,* 1939I

Imbrie, Andrew: *Angle of Repose,* 1976I; *Cello Concerto,* 1972I; *Cello Sonata,* 1966I; *Daedalus for Piano,* 1986I; *Dream Sequence,* 1986I; *Drumtaps,* 1960I; *Flute Concerto,* 1977I; *Legend,* 1959I; *On the Beach at Night,* 1948I; *Organ Prelude,* 1987I; *Piano Concerto No. 1,* 1973I; *Piano Concerto No. 2,* 1974I; *Piano Concerto No. 3,* 1992I; *Piano Sonata,* 1947I; *Piano Trio,* 1946I; *Piano Trio No. 2,* 1989I; *Requiem,* 1984I; *Serenade for Flute, Violin & Piano,* 1952I; *String Quartet No. 1,* 1942I; *String Quartet No. 2,* 1953I; *String Quartet No. 3,* 1957I; *String Quartet No. 4,* 1969I; *String Quartet No. 5,* 1987I; *Symphony No. 1,* 1965I; *Symphony No. 2,* 1970I; *Symphony No. 3,* 1970I; *Three Against Christmas,* 1963I; *Three Piece Suite for Piano,* 1987I; *Violin Concerto,* 1954I

Ince, Kamran: *The Blue Journey,* 1982I; *Curve,* 1997I; *Evil Eye,* 1996I; *Fantasy of a Sudden Turtle,* 1991I; *Hot, Red, Cold, Vibrant,* 1992I; *Lines,* 1997I; *Piano Concerto,* 1984I; *Remembering Lycia,* 1996I; *Symphony No. 1,* 1989I; *Symphony No. 2, "Fall of Constantinople,"* 1994I; *Tracing,* 1994I; *Turquoise,* 1996I; *An Unavoidable Obsession,* 1988I

Inch, Herbert: *Piano Concerto,* 1940I; *Piano Quintet,* 1930I; *Symphony,* 1932I; *Violin Concerto,* 1947I

Indy, Vincent d': *Cello Sonata,* 1926I; *Choral Varié,* 1995I; *Diptyque méditerranéen,* 1926I; *L'étranger,* 1903I; *Jour d'été à la montagne, Opus 61,* 1905I; *La légende de Saint-Christophe,* 1920I; *Organ Prélude,* 1913I; *Piano Quintet,* 1925I; *Piano Trio,* 1929I; *Le poème des rivages, Opus 77,* 1921I; *Le rêve de Cynias,* 1927I; *Souvenirs, Opus 62,* 1907I; *String Sextet,* 1928I; *Symphony No. 2 in B♭,* 1903I; *Symphony No. 3, "Sinfonia brevis de bello gallico,"* 1917I; *Violin Sonata,* 1905I

Ingenhoven, Jan: *Cello Sonata No. 1,* 1919I; *Cello Sonata No. 2,* 1922I; *Clarinet Sonata,* 1917I; *String Quartet No. 1,* 1908I; *String Quartet No. 2,* 1911I; *String Quartet No. 3,* 1912I; *Violin Sonata No. 1,* 1920I; *Violin Sonata No. 2,* 1921I; *Woodwind Quintet,* 1911I

Inghelbrecht, D. E.: *La nuit vénitienne,* 1908I; *Requiem,* 1940I; *Virage sur l'aile,* 1947I

Ingolfsson, Atli: *String Quartet No. 1, "HZH,"* 1999I

Insanguine, Giacomo: *Adriano in Siria,* 1773I; *Arianna e Teseo,* 1773I; *Le astuzie per amore,* 1777I; *Calipso,* 1782I; *Didone abbandonata,* 1772I; *Der Dorfbarbier,* 1770I; *Eumene,* 1778I; *La finta semplice,* 1769I; *Lo funnaco revotato,* 1756I; *Die Jagd,* 1770I; *La Matilde generosa,* 1757I; *Medonte,* 1779I; *Merope,* 1772I; *Montezuma,* 1780I; *Il nuovo Belisario,* 1765I; *Pulcinella,* 1777I; *Le quattro mal maritate,* 1766I; *La vedova capricciosa,* 1765I

Ippolitov-Ivanov, Mikhail: *Asya,* 1900I; *Azra,* 1890I; *Caucasian Sketches, Opus 10,* 1895I; *In the Steppes of Turkmenistan,* 1935I; *Izmena,* 1909I; *Karelia Suite,* 1935I; *The Last Barricade,* 1933I; *Mtzyri,* 1922I; *Ole from Nordland,* 1916I; *Ruth,* 1887I; *String Quartet No. 2,* 1924I; *Symphonic Scherzo,* 1882I; *Symphony,* 1908I; *Yar-Khmel,* 1883I

Ireland, John: *Cello Sonata in g,* 1923I; *The Forgotten Rite,* 1913I; *Julius Caesar,* 1942I; *The Land of Lost Content,* 1921I; *Legend,* 1933I; *Mai-Dun,* 1921I; *Miniature Suite,* 1943I; *Piano Concerto,* 1930I; *Piano Rhapsody No. 1,* 1906I; *Piano Rhapsody No. 2,* 1915I; *Piano Trio No. 1, "Phantasie,"* 1906I; *Piano Trio No. 2 in E,* 1917I; *Piano Trio No. 3 in E,* 1918I; *Sextet for Clarinet, Horn & Strings,* 1898I; *String Quartet No. 1 in d, No. 2 in C,* 1897I; *Violin Sonata No. 1,* 1909I; *Violin Sonata No. 2,* 1917I

Ishii, Maki: *String Quartet, "West-Gold-Autumn,"* 1992I

Isouard, Nicolò: *Aladin,* 1818I; *Artaserse,* 1794I; *L'avviso ai maritati,* 1795I; *Le baiser et la quittance,* 1803I; *Il barbiere di Siviglia,* 1796I; *Il barone d'Alba chiara,* 1798I; *Bayard à Mézières,* 1814I; *Le billet de loterie,* 1811I; *Cendrillon,* 1810I; *Cimarosa,* 1808I; *Les confidences,* 1803I; *Les créanciers,* 1807I; *Le déjeuner de garçons,* 1803I; *Les deux maris,* 1816I; *I due avari,* 1797I; *La fête du village,* 1810I; *Flaminius à Corinthe,* 1801I; *Le français à Venise,* 1813I; *Ginevra di Scozia,* 1798I; *Idala,* 1806I; *L'impromptu de campagne,* 1801I; *L'improvisata in campagna,* 1797I; *L'intrigue aux fenêtres,* 1805I; *L'intrigue au sérail,* 1809I; *Jeannot et Colin,* 1814I; *Joconde,* 1814I; *Un jour à Paris,* 1807I; *Léonce,* 1805I; *Lulli et Quinault,* 1812I; *Le magicien sans magique,* 1811I; *Le médecin,* 1803I; *Michel-Ange,* 1802I; *La paix,* 1802I; *Le petit page,* 1800I; *Le prince de Catane,* 1812I; *La prise de Passau,* 1806I; *Le rendez-vous bourgeois,* 1807I; *Rinaldo d' Asti,* 1796I; *La ruse inutile,* 1805I; *La statue,* 1802I; *Le tonnelier,* 1801I; *L'une pour l'autre,* 1816I; *La victime des arts,* 1810I

Israel, Brian: *Alto Sax Sonata,* 1980I; *Clarinet Sonata,* 1969I; *Oboe Sonata,* 1972I; *Piano Concerto (with band),* 1979I; *Piano Quintet,* 1973I; *Sonata for Two Horns,* 1980I; *String Quartet No. 1, "Canonic Variations,"* 1971I; *String Quartet No. 2,* 1976I; *String Quartet No. 3,* 1978I; *Symphony No. 1 (band),*

1974I; *Symphony No. 2*, 1974I; *Symphony No. 3* (band), 1981I; *Symphony No. 4*, 1984I; *Symphony No. 5* (band), 1984I; *Symphony No. 6*, 1985I; *Viola Concerto*, 1974I

Istvánffy, Benedek: *Missa sanctificabis annum quinquagesium*, 1774I

Ivanovici, Ion: *Waves of the Danube (Anniversary Waltz)*, 1880I

Ivanovs, Janis: *Cello Concerto*, 1938I; *Hill Above the Clouds*, 1938I; *Mountain Under the Sky*, 1939I; *Piano Concerto*, 1959I; *Piano Trio*, 1976I; *Rainbow*, 1938I; *Sonata Brevis for Piano*, 1962I; *String Quartet No. 1*, 1933I; *String Quartet No. 2*, 1946I; *String Quartet No. 3*, 1961I; *Symphony No. 1*, 1933I; *Symphony No. 2 in d*, 1937I; *Symphony No. 3 in f*, 1938I; *Symphony No. 4, "Atalantida,"* 1941I; *Symphony No. 5 in C*, 1945I; *Symphony No. 6, "Latvian,"* 1949I; *Symphony No. 7*, 1953I; *Symphony No. 8*, 1956I; *Symphony No. 9 (?)*, 1960I; *Symphony No. 10*, 1963I; *Symphony No. 11*, 1965I; *Symphony No. 12, "Sinfonia Energica,"* 1967I; *Symphony No. 13, "Symphonia humana,"* 1969I; *Symphony No. 14, "Sinfonia da camera,"* 1971I; *Symphony No. 15, "Symphonia ipsa,"* 1972I; *Symphony No. 16*, 1974I; *Symphony No. 17*, 1976I; *Violin Concerto*, 1951I

Ives, Charles: *The Anti-Abolitionist Riots*, 1908I; *Calcium Light Night*, 1907I; *The Celestial Country*, 1899I; *Central Park in the Dark*, 1907I; *Charlie Rutledge*, 1921I; *Children's Hour*, 1901I; *Chrômatimelôdtune*, 1919I; *Circus Band March*, 1894I; *Country Band March*, 1903I; *Decoration Day*, 1912I; *Emerson Overture*, 1907I; *The Fourth of July*, 1913I; *From the Steeples & Mountains*, 1901I; *Fugue in Four Keys, "Shining Shore,"* 1897I; *General William Booth Enters into Heaven*, 1914I; *The Gong on the Hook & Ladder*, 1912I; *Hallowe'en*, 1906I; *Harvest Home Chorales (3)*, 1901I; *Lincoln, the Great Commoner*, 1912I; *Marches (3) for Band*, 1892I; *Orchestral Set No. 2*, 1915I; *Overture & March "1776,"* 1903I; *Piano Sonata No. 1*, 1909I; *Piano Sonata No. 2, "Concord Sonata,"* 1915I; *Piano Trio*, 1911I; *The Pond*, 1906I; *Psalm 25*, 1901I; *Psalm 40*, 1894I; *Psalm 42*, 1888I; *Psalm 54*, 1894I; *Psalm 67*, 1898I; *Psalm 135*, 1900I; *Psalm 150*, 1894I; *Putnam's Camp*, 1912I; *Quarter-Tone Pieces (3)*, 1924I; *Robert Browning Overture*, 1911I; *Set No. 3 for Small Orchestra*, 1918I; *Some South-paw Pitching*, 1908I; *String Quartet No. 1*, 1896I; *String Quartet No. 2*, 1914I; *Symphony No. 1*, 1898I; *Symphony No. 2*, 1902I; *Symphony No. 3, "Camp meeting,"* 1904I; *Symphony No. 4*, 1916I; *Thanksgiving, and/or Forefather's Day*, 1904I; *Theater Orchestra Set*, 1911I; *Three Page Sonata*, 1905I; *Tone Roads No. 1*, 1911I; *The Unanswered Question*, 1906I; *Variations on "America,"* 1891I; *Violin Sonata (KW. 4)*, 1902I; *Violin Sonata No. 1*, 1908I; *Violin Sonata No. 2*, 1910I; *Violin Sonata No. 3*, 1914I; *Violin Sonata No. 4*, 1915I; *Washington's Birthday*, 1909I

Ivey, Jean Eichelberger: *Cello Concerto*, 1985I; *Forms in Motion*, 1972I; *Piano Sonata*, 1957I; *Songs of the Night (3)*, 1971I; *String Quartet No. 1*, 1960I; *Theme & Variations*, 1952I; *Voyager*, 1991I; *Woman's Love*, 1962I

Jackson, Francis: *Organ Sonata No. 1*, 1969I; *Organ Sonata No. 2*, 1972I; *Organ Sonata No. 3*, 1979I

Jackson, Nicholas: *Organ Sonata da Chiesa*, 1989I; *Organ Sonata No. 4*, 1985I

Jackson, William: *Canzonets (12), Opus 9*, 1770I; *Canzonets (12), Opus 13*, 1782I; *The Deliverance of Israel from Babylon*, 1844I; *Elegies (6), Opus 3*, 1760I; *Epigrams (6), Opus 17*, 1798I; *Isaiah*, 1851I; *Madrigals (6), Opus 18*, 1798I; *Mass in E*, 1846I; *The Metamorphosis*, 1783I; *Pastorals (12), Opus 15*, 1786I; *Praise of Music*, 1866I; *Psalm 103*, 1841I; *Psalm 103 II*, 1856I; *Songs (12), Opus 1*, 1755I; *Songs (12), Opus 4*, 1765I; *Songs (12), Opus 7*, 1770I; *Songs (12), Opus 17*, 1790I; *The Year*, 1859I

Jacob, Gordon: *Clarinet Quintet*, 1942I; *Little Symphony*, 1957I; *Mini Concerto*, 1980I

Jacob, Jeffrey: *De Profundis*, 1996I; *Piano Concerto No. 1*, 1991I

Jacobi, Frederick: *Cello Concerto*, 1932I; *Fantasy for Viola & Piano*, 1941I; *Piano Pieces (6)*, 1921I; *The Poet in the Desert*, 1925I; *The Prodigal Son*, 1944I; *String Quartet No. 1 on Indian Themes*, 1924I; *String Quartet No. 2*, 1933I; *String Quartet No. 3*, 1945I; *Symphony No. 1, "Assyrian,"* 1924I; *Symphony No. 2*, 1948I

Jacobs, Jeffrey: *Symphony No. 2*, 1996I

Jadin, Louis E.: *Symphony* (band), 1794I

Jaffe, David A.: *Silicon Valley Breakdown*, 1982I

Jaffe, Stephen: *Double Sonata for Piano*, 1989I; *Fort Juniper Songs*, 1989I; *Four Songs with Ensemble*, 1988I; *Pedal Point*, 1992I; *The Rhythm of the Running Plough*, 1985I; *Songs of Turning*, 1996I; *String Quartet No. 1*, 1991I; *Triptych*, 1992I

Jager, Robert: *The Wall*, 1997I

James, Charles: *The Seasons*, 1959I

James, Philip: *Organ Sonata*, 1929I; *Serenade*, 1931I; *Song of the Night*, 1931I; *Station WGZBX*, 1931I

Janáček, Leo: *The Ballad of Blanik*, 1920I; *Chorale fantasia*, 1875I; *The Cunning Little Vixen*, 1924I; *The Diary of One Who Vanished*, 1916I; *The Eternal Gospel*, 1916I; *The Excursions of Mr. Brouček*, 1914I; *From the House of the Dean*, 1928I; *Glagolithic Mass*, 1926I; *Jenufa*, 1903I; *Kata Kabanova*, 1921I; *The Makropoulos Affair*, 1925I; *Piano Concertino*, 1925I; *Prelude*, 1875I; *Rakos Rakoczy* 1891I; *Sinfonietta*, 1926I; *String Quartet No. 1, "Kreutzer Sonata,"* 1923I; *String Quartet No. 2, "Intimate Letters,"* 1928I; *Suite for String Orchestra*, 1877I; *Taras Bulba*, 1918I; *Violin Sonata*, 1921I

❈

F *Biographical*   G *Cultural Beginnings*   H *Musical Literature*

I *Musical Compositions*

Janiewicz, Feliks: *Piano Sonata in B♭*, 1805I; *Violin/Cello Sonata*, 1805I; *Violin Sonata in A*, 1802I; *Violin Sonata in F*, 1805I

Janitsch, Johann Gottlieb: *Organ Sonata*, 1760I

Janssen, Werner: *Louisiana Symphony*, 1932I; *String Quartet No. 1*, 1934I; *String Quartet No. 2*, 1935I

Jaques-Dalcroze, Emile: *Violin Concerto No. 1*, 1902I; *Violin Concerto No. 2*, 1911I

Järnefelt, Armas: *Lyrical Overture*, 1890I

Jaroch, Jiří: *String Quartet No. 2*, 1970I

Jeppesen, Knud: *Symphony*, 1939I

Jerusalem, Ignacio de: *Matins for the Virgin of Guadalupe*, 1764I

Jeth, William: *Fas/Nefas* (piano concerto), 1997I; *Flux/Redux*, 1998I; *Piano Concerto*, 1994I

Ješek, Jaroslav: *Piano Concerto*, 1927I

Jiménez-Mabarak, Carlos: *Portrait Gallery*, 1993I; *Symphony No. 1*, 1945I; *Symphony No. 2, "In One Movement,"* 1961I; *Ballad of the Deer & the Moon*, 1948I; *Ballad of the Rivers of Tabasco*, 1900I

Joachim, Joseph: *Andantino & Allegro Scherzoso, Opus 1*, 1851I; *Demetrios Overture, Opus 6*, 1855I; *Hamlet Overture, Opus 4*, 1855I; *Heinrich IV Overture, Opus 7*, 1855I; *Overture to a Comedy by Gozzi, Opus 8*, 1854I; *Overture zu einem gozzi'schen lustspiel, Opus 8*, 1902I; *Variations in c*, 1882I; *Violin Concerto in One Movement in g, Opus 3*, 1855I; *Violin Concerto "in ungarischer weise," Opus 11*, 1857I; *Violin Concerto No. 3 in G, Opus 17*, 1864I

Johnsen, Hinrich P.: *Church Music for Easter Sunday*, 1757I

Johnson, David: *Cello Sonata*, 1993I; *Piano Concerto*, 1987I; *Preludes & Fugues (12) for Piano*, 1995I; *Violin Sonata—Trumpet Sonata*, 1992I

Johnson, Hunter: *The Scarlet Letter*, 1975I; *Symphony No. 1*, 1931I

Johnston, Ben: *Piano Sonata*, 1964I; *Saint Joan*, 1955I; *Sonata for Microtonal Piano*, 1965I; *String Quartet No. 2*, 1964I; *String Quartet No. 3*, 1973I; *String Quartet No. 4*, 1973I; *String Quartet No. 5*, 1980I; *String Quartet No. 6*, 1980I; *String Quartet No. 7*, 1985I; *String Quartet No. 8*, 1986I; *String Quartet No. 9*, 1988I; *Suite for Microtonal Piano*, 1977I

Jolivet, André: *Ariadne*, 1964I; *Antigone*, 1951I; *Cello Concerto No. 1*, 1962I; *Cello Concerto No. 2*, 1966I; *Chansons de ménestrels (3)*, 1943I; *Chants des hommes (3)*, 1937I; *Le coeur et la matière*, 1965I; *Concerto for Ondes Martinot*, 1947I; *Coriolan*, 1956I; *Défilé*, 1936I; *Dolorès*, 1942I; *Flute Concerto No. 1*, 1949I; *Flute Sonata*, 1958I; *Guignol et Pandore*, 1943I; *Hymne à l'univers for Organ*, 1962I; *L'inconnue*, 1950I; *Iphigénie en Aulide*, 1949I; *Mandala for Organ*, 1969I; *Marines*, 1961I; *Mass, "Uxon tua,"* 1961I; *Messe pour le jour de la paix*, 1940I; *Pastoral de Noël*, 1943I; *Percussion Concerto*, 1958I; *Piano Concerto*, 1950I; *Piano Sonata No. 1*, 1945I; *Piano Sonata No. 2*, 1957I; *Poèmes (3)*, 1935I; *Poèmes intime*, 1944I; *Prelude, Cosmogonie*, 1938I; *Prométhée enchaîné*, 1954I; *Les quatre vérités*, 1941I; *Soir*, 1936I; *String Quartet*, 1934I; *Suite delphique*, 1943I; *Suite française*, 1957I; *Symphony for Strings*, 1961I; *Symphony No. 1*, 1953I; *Symphony No. 2*, 1959I; *Symphony No. 3*, 1964I; *La tentation dernière*, 1941I; *Transoceanic Suite*, 1955i; *Les trois complaintes du soldat*, 1940I; *La vérité de Jeanne*, 1956I

Jommelli, Niccolò: *Achille in Sciro*, 1771I; *Gerusalemme convertita*, 1755I; *La critica*, 1766I; *Ifigenia in Tauride*, 1771I; *Alessandro nell'Indie*, 1760I; *Armida Abbandonata*, 1770I; *Artaserse II*, 1756I; *L'asilo d'amore*, 1758I; *Le avventure di Cleomede*, 1772I; *Bajazette*, 1753I; *Caio Fabrizio*, 1760I; *Catine in Utica*, 1754I; *Cerere placata*, 1772I; *Cesare in Egitto*, 1751I; *La clemenza di Tito* 1753I; *Creso*, 1757I; *Demetrio*, 1753I; *Demofoonte II*, 1753I; *Demofoonte III*, 1764I; *Didone abbandonata*, 1763I; *Don Falcone*, 1754I; *Endimione*, 1759I; *Enea nel Lazio*, 1755I; *Ezio III*, 1758I; *Fetonte*, 1753I; *Il giardino incanto*, 1755I; *Ifigenia in Aulide*, 1751I; *Imeneo in Atene*, 1765I; *Ipermestra*, 1751I; *L'isola disabitata*, 1761I; *Lucio Vero*, 1754I; *Missa Solemnis in D*, 1766I; *Il matrimonio concorso*, 1766I; *Miserere*, 1774I; *Missa pro defunctis in E♭*, 1756I; *La Nativita della beatissima Vergine*, 1752I; *Nitteti*, 1759I; *L'Olimpiade*, 1761I; *La pastorella illustre*, 1763I; *Pelope*, 1755I; *I ravali delusi*, 1752I; *Il re pastore*, 1764I; *La reconciliazione della virtú e della Gloria*, 1754I; *La schiava liberata*, 1768I; *La Semiramide in Bernesco*, 1767I; *Talestri*, 1751I; *Temistocle*, 1757I; *Tito Manlio*, 1758I; *Il trionfo d'amore*, 1763I; *Il trionfo di Clelia*, 1774I; *L'uccellatrice*, 1751I; *L'unione coronata*, 1768I; *Vologeso*, 1766I

Jones, Charles: *Emblemate for Organ*, 1994I; *The Fond Observer*, 1978I; *Noël for Organ*, 1983I; *Sonata for Piano, Four Hands*, 1984I; *String Quartet No. 1*, 1936I; *String Quartet No. 2*, 1944I; *String Quartet No. 3*, 1951I; *String Quartet No. 4*, 1954I; *String Quartet No. 5*, 1961I; *String Quartet No. 6*, 1976I; *String Quartet No. 7*, 1978I; *String Quartet No. 8*, 1984I; *Violin Sonatina*, 1942I

Jones, Daniel: *String Quartet No. 1*, 1948I; *String Quartet No. 2*, 1957I; *String Quartet No. 3*, 1975I; *String Quartet No. 4*, 1978I; *String Quartet No. 5*, 1980I; *String Quartet No. 6*, 1982I; *String Quartet No. 7*, 1987I; *String Quartet No. 8*, 1993I

Jones, Edwin A.: *String Quartet No. 1, Opus 18*, 1880I; *String Quartet No. 2*, 1887I

Jones, Samuel: *Rounding*, 2000I

A   *Births*   B   *Deaths*   C   *Debuts*   D   *New Positions*
E   *Prizes/Honors*

Jong, Marinus de: *Horn Concerto*, 1966I; *String Quartet No. 1*, 1923I; *String Quartet No. 2*, 1926I; *String Quartet No. 3*, 1947I; *String Quartet No. 4*, 1956I; *String Quartet No. 5*, 1956I; *String Quartet No. 6*, 1962I

Jongen, Joseph: *Allegro appassionato, Opus 79 (viola)*, 1928I; *Alleluia, Opus 112*, 1940I; *Cello Concerto, Opus 18*, 1900I; *Cello Sonata, Opus 39*, 1912I; *Chant de May, Opus 53*, 1917I; *Concertino, Opus 111*, 1940I; *Concerto à cinque, Opus 71*, 1923I; *Concerto for Wind Quintet, Opus 124*, 1942I; *Elegy for Three Flutes, Opus 114*, 1941I; *Fantaisie Rhapsodique, Opus 74 (cello)*, 1925I; *Flute Sonata, Opus 77*, 1924I; *Harp Concerto, Opus 129*, 1944I; *Humoresque for Cello & Organ, Opus 92*, 1930I; *Impressions d'Ardennes, Opus 44*, 1913I; *Lalla-Roukh, Opus 28*, 1904I; *Little Preludes, (24), Opus 116*, 1941I; *Mass, Opus 130*, 1946I; *Oberon*, 1946I; *Organ Pieces, (2), Opus 108*, 1938I; *Ouverture de fête, Opus 117*, 1941I; *Passacaglia & Gigue*, 1929I; *Piano Concerto, Opus 127*, 1943I; *Piano Pieces (2), Opus 33*, 1908I; *Piano Pieces (10), Opus 96*, 1932I; *Piano Preludes (13), Opus 69*, 1922I; *Piano Quartet, Opus 23*, 1902I; *Piano Trio, Opus 95*, 1931I; *Pieces (2) for Wind Quintet, Opus 98*, 1933I; *Pièces en trio (2), Opus 80*, 1925I; *Poem No. 2, Opus 46 (cello)*, 1916I; *Poème heroïque, Opus 62 (violin)*, 1920I; *Prelude & Chaconne, Opus 101*, 1934I; *Sonata heroica, Opus 94*, 1930I; *Songs (6), Opus 25*, 1902I; *String Quartet No. 2, Opus 50*, 1916I; *String Trio, Opus 135*, 1948I; *Suite, Opus 48 (viola)*, 1919I; *Symphonic Adagio, Opus 20*, 1901I; *Symphonic Movements, Three, Opus 137*, 1951I; *Symphonic Piece, Opus 84*, 1928I; *Symphonie concertante, Opus 81 (organ)*, 1926I; *Symphony, Opus 15*, 1899I; *Tableaux pittoresques, Opus 56*, 1917I; *Trio, Opus 30*, 1907I; *Tryptique, Opus 103*, 1937I; *Violin Sonata No. 1 in D, Opus 27*, 1902I; *Violin Sonata No. 2 in E, Opus 34*, 1909I

Jongen, Léon: *L'ardennaise*, 1909I; *Masque of the Red Death*, 1956I; *Music for a Ballet*, 1954I; *Le rêve d'une nuit de noël*, 1917I; *Rhapsodia belgica*, 1948I; *Thomas l'Agnelet*, 1923I

Joplin, Scott: *The Entertainer*, 1902I; *The Guest of Honor*, 1903I; *Treemonisha*, 1911I

Jordanova, Victoria: *Preludes (4) for Harp*, 1993I; *Variations for Harp*, 1993I

José, Antonio: *Guitar Sonata*, 1990I

Josephson, Joseph Axel: *The Melting of the Ice*, 1844I; *Symphony, Opus 4*, 1847I

Josten, Werner: *Horn Sonata*, 1944I; *Piano Sonata*, 1937I; *String Quartet No. 1 in A*, 1934I; *Symphony No. 1*, 1935I; *Symphony No. 2*, 1936I

Juon, Paul: *Cello Sonata No. 2*, 1912I; *Divertimento for Piano & Wind Quintet*, 1912I; *Wind Quintet*, 1928I

Just, Justin A.: *Piano Trios (6), Opus 2*, 1770I

Kabalevsky, Dmitri: *Cello Concerto No. 1*, 1949I; *Cello Concerto No. 2*, 1964I; *Colas Breugnon*, 1938I; *The Comedians, Opus 26*, 1940I; *The Family of Taras*, 1950I; *Master of Clamency*, 1937I; *The Motherland*, 1966I; *Nikita Vershinin*, 1955I; *Piano Concerto No. 1*, 1929I; *Piano Concerto No. 2*, 1936I; *Piano Concerto No. 3*, 1952I; *Piano Preludes (24)*, 1943I; *Requiem*, 1963I; *Sisters*, 1969I; *Symphony No. 1, "Proletarians, Unite,"* 1932I; *Symphony No. 2*, 1933I; *Symphony No. 3, "Requiem for Lenin,"* 1934I; *Symphony No. 4*, 1939I; *Symphony No. 4*, 1956I; *Violin Concerto*, 1948I

Kabeláč, Miloslav: *Inventions (8) for Percussion Ensemble*, 1962I; *Reflections*, 1964I; *Symphony No. 3*, 1957I; *Symphony No. 4, "Camarata,"* 1958I

Kagel, Mauricio: *Kidnapping in the Concert Hall*, 2000I; *Tanz-Schul*, 1988I

Kahn, Erich Itor: *Actus Tragicus*, 1946I

Kaipainen, Jouni: *Clarinet Concerto, "Carpe Diem,"* 1990I; *Oboe Concerto*, 1994I; *Sisyphus Dreams*, 1994I; *Symphony No. 1, Opus 20*, 1985I; *Symphony No. 2, Opus 44*, 1994I

Kalinnikov, Vasili: *Symphony No. 1 in g*, 1895I; *Symphony No. 2 in A*, 1898I

Kalliwoda, Johann Wenzel: *Blanda*, 1827I; *Concert Overture No. 1 in d, Opus 38*, 1839I; *Concert Overture No. 2 in F, Opus 44*, 1834I; *Concert Overture No. 3 in C, Opus 55*, 1834I; *Concert Overture No. 5 in f, Opus 56*, 1834I; *Concert Overture No. 5 in f, Opus 38*, 1838I; *Concert Overture No. 6 in E♭, Opus 76*, 1838I; *Concert Overture No. 9,"Solennelle," Opus 126*, 1846I; *Concert Overture No. 10 in F, Opus 142*, 1846I; *Concert Overture No. 11 in B♭, Opus 143*, 1846I; *Concert Overture No. 13*, 1849I; *Concert Overture No. 14 in C, Opus 206*, 1856I; *Concert Overture No. 15 in E, Opus 226*, 1858I; *Concertante, Opus 20, for Two Violins*, 1831I; *Concertina, Opus 110*, 1844I; *Grosses Rondo, Opus 16*, 1830I; *Introduction & Variations, Opus 128*, 1844I; *Introduction & Rondo, Opus 51*, 1834I; *Mass No. 1, Opus 137*, 1843I; *Overture Pastorale in A, Opus 108*, 1843I; *Prinzessin Christine*, 1827I; *String Quartet No. 1 in G, Opus 61*, 1835I; *Symphony No. 1 in f, Opus 7*, 1826I; *Symphony No. 2 in E♭, Opus 17*, 1829I; *Symphony No. 3, Opus 32*, 1830I; *Symphony No. 4 in C, Opus 60*, 1835I; *Symphony No. 5, Opus 106*, 1840I; *Symphony No. 6 in g*, 1841I; *Symphony No. 7 in F*, 1843I; *Variations and Rondo, Opus 57*, 1857I; *Variations Brillantes, Opus 14*, 1829I; *Violin Concertino, Opus 37*, 1833I; *Violin Concertino, Opus 100*, 1839I; *Violin Concertino No. 6, Opus 151*, 1848I; *Violin Concerto, Opus 9*, 1821I

Kallstenius, Edvin: *Dalecarian Rhapsody*, 1931I; *Song Offering*, 1944I; *Symphony No. 2*, 1935I

Kálmán, Emmerich: *The Bayadere*, 1921I; *The Duchess of Chicago*, 1929I

❆

Kaminski, Heinrich: *Chorale Sonata*, 1926I; *Toccata on "Wie Schön leucht uns der morganstern,"* 1923I

Kancheli, Giya: *Bright Sorrow*, 1985I; *Light Sorrow*, 1984I

Kangro, Raimo: *Concerto for Two*, 1993I; *Concerto No. 2 for Two Pianos*, 1988I; *Display VIII: Portrait of Schubert*, 1998I; *Gaudio*, 1987I; *Piano Concerto No. 2*, 1999I

Karamanov, Alemdar: *Symphony No. 3*, 1964I

Karchin, Louis: *Cello Sonata*, 1989I; *Songs of Distance & Light*, 1988I; *String Quartet No. 2*, 1994I

Karg-Elert, Sigfrid: *Alto Clarinet Sonata in c♯, Opus 110*, 1924I; *An die Getrennet, Opus 20*, 1902I; *Aus meiner Schwabenheimat, Opus 38*, 1906I; *Bagatelles (5), Opus 17*, 1902I; *Bassoon Sonata*, 1926I; *Catholic Windows, Opus 106*, 1923I; *Cello Sonata in A, Opus 71*, 1907I; *Choral-Improvisations (66), Opus 65*, 1910I; *Clarinet Sonata No. 1 in b♭*, 1917I; *Clarinet Sonata No. 2*, 1926I; *Diverse Pieces, Opus 75*, 1910I; *Fantasia & Fugue in D, Opus 39b*, 1905I; *Flute Sonata in B, Opus 121*, 1918I; *Homage to Handel, Opus 75b*, 1914I; *Impressions (3), Opus 72*, 1911I; *Impressions exotiques, Opus 134*, 1919I; *Kaleidoscope, Opus 144*, 1930I; *Die Kunstreiterin, Opus 19*, 1905I; *Lieder im Volkston (6), Opus 12*, 1901I; *Little Sonata in C, Opus 68*, 1914I; *Male Choruses, (5), Opus 55*, 1907I; *Mass in b*, 1924I; *Organ Pastels (3), Opus 92*, 1912I; *Organ Pieces (3), Opus 142*, 1932I; *Organ Preludes & Postludes (20), Opus 78*, 1912I; *Organ Sonata No. 1 in b, Opus 36*, 1905I; *Organ Sonata No. 2 in a, Opus 74*, 1909I; *Partita in D for Solo Violin, Opus 89*, 1912I; *Passacaglia & Fugue on B-A-C-H, Opus 150*, 1932I; *Passacaglia in e♭, Opus 25b*, 1908I; *Pastels (7) from Lake Constance, Opus 96*, 1919I; *Pedalstudien, Opus 83*, 1913I; *Piano Concerto No. 1 in d, Opus 6*, 1901I; *Piano Concerto No. 2 in D♭*, 1913I; *Piano Sonata No. 1 in f♯, Opus 50*, 1904I; *Piano Sonata No. 2 in b♭, Opus 80*, 1912I; *Piano Sonata No. 3 in c♯, "Patetica," Opus 105*, 1920I; *Piano Sonata No. 4*, 1919I; *Piano Sonatinas (3), Opus 74*, 1909I; *Piano Symphony in E*, 1927I; *Poems (8), Opus 52*, 1905I; *Poems (7), Opus 62*, 1908I; *Poems (10), Opus 63*, 1908I; *Preludes (50) on Gregorian Themes & English Hymns*, 1927I; *Requiem aeternam, Opus 109*, 1913I; *Sanctus & Pastorale, Opus 48*, 1903I; *Schöne Augen, Opus 24*, 1904I; *Sequenz No. 1 in a*, 1908I; *Sequenz, No. 2 in c*, 1910I; *Sketches (5), Opus 10*, 1904I; *Sonata appasionata in f♯, Opus 140*, 1919I; *Songs (2), Opus 43*, 1908I; *Songs (2), Opus 98*, 1914I; *Songs (6), Opus 111*, 1914I; *Spiritual Songs for Women's Voices (15), Opus 44*, 1908I; *Stimmungen und betrachtungen, Opus 53*, 1905I; *Suite pointillistique, Opus 135*, 1919I; *Symphonic Chorales (3), Opus 87*, 1913I; *Triptych, Opus 141*, 1930I; *Triumph, Opus 79*, 1912I; *Variations on a Theme of Brahms, Opus 8*, 1902I; *Die Verhüllten*, 1914I; *Violin Sonata in e, Opus 88*, 1912I; *Woodwind Quintet in e, Opus 30*, 1904I; *Woodwind Trio in d, Opus 49*, 1902I

Karpen, Richard: *Dénouement*, 1992I

Kashin, Daniil: *Fair Olga*, 1809I; *Natalia, the Boyard's Daughter*, 1801I; *The One-day Reign of Nourmahal*, 1817I; *Piano Concerto*, 1790I

Kashkin, Nikita: *The Prince's Toys*, 1980I

Kashperov, Vladimir: *The Storm*, 1867I

Kastner, Jean-Georges: *Die Königin der Sarmaten*, 1835I; *La Maschera*, 1841I; *Oskars Tod*, 1833I; *Der Sarazene*, 1834I

Kauer, Ferdinand: *Das Donauweibchen*, 1798I

Kaun, Hugo: *Overture, Der Mahler von Antwerp*, 1899I; *Symphony*, 1898I

Kay, Hersey: *L'inconnue*, 1965I

Kay, Ulysses: *The Boor*, 1955I; *The Capitoline Venus*, 1970I; *Choral Triptych*, 1962I; *Concerto for Orchestra*, 1948I; *Concerto for Orchestra*, 1953I; *Fantasy Variations*, 1963I; *Frederick Douglass*, 1983I; *Jubilee*, 1976I; *The Juggler of Our Lady*, 1956I; *Oboe Concerto*, 1940I; *Overture, Of New Horizons*, 1944I; *Pieces after Blake (3)*, 1952I; *Serenade*, 1954I; *A Short Overture*, 1946I; *Song of Jeremiah*, 1945I; *String Quartet No. 1*, 1949I; *String Quartet No. 2*, 1956I; *String Quartet No. 3*, 1961I; *Suite for Orchestra*, 1945I; *Symphony No. 1*, 1967I

Keats, Donald: *String Quartet No. 1*, 1951I; *String Quartet No. 2*, 1965I

Kee, Piet: *Triptych on Psalm 86*, 1960I; *Variations on a Carol*, 1954I

Kelemen, Milko: *Apocalyptica*, 1975I; *Drammatico*, 1991I; *Nonet*, 1993I

Keller, Homer: *Cello Sonata*, 1977I; *Piano Concerto*, 1949I; *Piano Sonata*, 1972I; *String Quartet No. 1*, 1935I

Kelley, Edgar Stillman: *Alice in Wonderland Suite*, 1919I; *Ben Hur*, 1899I; *Macbeth*, 1884I; *Piano Pieces (30, Opus 2*, 1891I; *Piano Quintet, Opus 20*, 1901I; *The Pilgrim's Progress, Opus 37*, 1917I; *The Pit & the Pendulum Suite*, 1930I; *Pompeiian Picnic, Opus 9*, 1887I; *Prometheus Bound, Opus 16*, 1891I; *Puritania*, 1892I; *Quartet, Opus 25*, 1907I; *Symphony No. 1, "Gulliver,"* 1900I; *Symphony No. 2, "New England," Opus 33*, 1913I

Kelly, Bryan: *Pastorale & Paean*, 1973I; *Piano Sonata*, 1971I

Kelly, Robert: *Cello Concerto*, 1974I; *Rural Songs*, 1980I

Kenins, Talivaldis: *Cello Sonata*, 1950I; *Concertante*, 1966I; *Piano Quartet No. 2*, 1979I; *Piano Sonata No. 1*, 1961I

A *Births*   B *Deaths*   C *Debuts*   D *New Positions*

E *Prizes/Honors*

Kennan, Kent: *Night Soliloquy*, 1936I; *Piano Preludes (3)*, 1939I; *Piano Preludes (2)*, 1951I; *Sea Sonata for Violin & Piano*, 1939I; *Symphony*, 1938I

Kern, Jerome: *Mark Twain Suite*, 1942I

Kernis, Aaron Jay: *America(n) (Day) Dreams*, 1984I; *Before Sleep & Dreams*, 1990I; *Brilliant Sky, Infinite sky*, 1990I; *Colored Field*, 1994I; *Goblin Market*, 1995I; *How God Answers the Soul*, 1996I; *Invisible Mosaic II*, 1988I; *Love Scenes*, 1987I; *Morningsongs*, 1983I; *Poisoned Nocturnes*, 1987I; *Simple Songs*, 1991I; *Songs of Innocents I*, 1989I; *Songs of Innocents II*, 1991I; *Still Movement with Hymn*, 1993I; *String Quartet No. 1, "Musica Celestis,"* 1990I; *String Quartet No. 2, "musica instrumentalis,"* 1997I; *Superstar Etude No. 1*, 1992I; *Symphony in Waves*, 1989I; *Symphony No. 2*, 1991I

Kerr, Harrison: *Piano Sonata No. 1*, 1929I; *Piano Sonata No. 2*, 1943I; *String Quartet No. 1*, 1935I; *String Quartet No. 2*, 1937I; *Symphony No. 1*, 1929I; *Symphony No. 2*, 1937I; *Symphony No. 2*, 1945I; *Symphony No. 3*, 1954I; *The Tower of Kel*, 1960I; *Violin Concerto*, 1951I

Keuris, Tristan:*Concerto for Two Cellos*, 1992I; *Organ Concerto*, 1993I; *Sinfonia*, 1974I; *String Quartet No. 1*, 1982I; *String Quartet No. 2*, 1985I; *Symphony in D*, 1995I; *Violin Concerto No. 1*, 1984I; *Violin Concerto No. 2*, 1995U

Keyes, Christopher: *Ballade for the Children of a Modern Age*, 1990I; *Bartók Variations for Piano*, 1991I; *Compuintro-Music*, 1996I; *Descant of a Sonic Pendulum*, 1997I

Khachaturian Aram: *Cello Concerto in e*, 1946I; *Concert-Rhapsody in D♭*, 1955I; *Concert-Rhapsody*, 1963I; *Gayne*, 1942I; *Masquerade*, 1944I; *Piano Concerto in D♭*, 1936I; *Piano Sonata*, 1961I; *Spartacus*, 1953I; *Suite No. 4*, 1966I; *Symphony No. 1*, 1934I; *Symphony No. 2*, 1943I; *Symphony No. 3*, 1947I; *Violin Concerto*, 1940I

Khrennikov, Tikhon: *Piano Concerto*, 1933I; *Symphony No. 2*, 1942I; *Violin Concerto No. 1*, 1959I; *Violin Concerto No. 2*, 1975I

Kiel, Friedrich: *Cello Sonata in a*, 1868I

Kilpinen, Yrjö: *Kanteletav Songs, Opus 100*, 1954I

Kilstofte, Mark: *Recurring Dreams: Variations for Orchestra*, 1997I

Kim, Earl: *Dear Linda*, 1992I; *Footfalls*, 1983I; *Where Grief Slumbers*, 1982I

Kimper, Paula M.: *Patience & Sarah*, 1998I

King, Karl: *Barnum & Bailey's Favorite March*, 1913I; *March, Invictus*, 1921I

Kinsella, John: *Cello Concerto*, 1967I; *Festive Overture*, 1995I; *Music for Cello & Chamber Orchestra*, 1971I; *Piano Sonata No. 2*, 1971I; *String Quartet No. 1*, 1960I; *String Quartet No. 2*, 1968I; *String Quartet No. 3*, 1977I; *String Quartet No. 4*, 1993I; *Symphony No. 1*, 1984I; *Symphony No. 2*, 1988I; *Symphony No. 3*, 1990I; *Symphony No. 4, "The Four Provinces,"* 1991I; *Symphony No. 5*, 1992I; *Symphony No. 6*, 1993I; *Symphony No. 7*, 1997I; *Symphony No. 8*, 1999I

Kirchner, Leon: *Belshazzar*, 1985I; *Cello Concerto*, 1992I; *Kaleidoscope*, 1989I; *Lily*, 1976I; *Little Suite*, 1949I; *Music for Cello & Orchestra*, 1994I; *Music for Flute & Orchestra*, 1978I; *Music for Orchestra*, 1969I; *Of Things Exactly As They Are*, 1996I; *Piano Concerto No. 1*, 1953I; *Piano Concerto No. 2*, 1963I; *Piano Pieces (5)*, 1984I; *Piano Pieces (5)*, 1987I; *Piano Pieces (5)*, 1997I; *Piano Sonata*, 1948I; *Piano Trio*, 1954I; *Sinfonia for Orchestra*, 1952I; *String Quartet No. 1*, 1949I; *String Quartet No. 2*, 1958I; *String Quartet No. 3*, 1966I; *Variations on "L'homme armé,"* 1947I

Kirkpartick, William: *He Hideth My Soul*, 1890I; *Lord, I'm Coming Home*, 1892I; *Redeemed, How I Love to Proclaim It*, 1882I

Kiss, Janos: *Quo Vadis*, 1982I

Klami, Uuno: *King Lear Overture*, 1945I; *Symphony No. 1*, 1938I; *Symphony No. 2*, 1944I; *Violin Concerto*, 1940I

Klebe, Giselher: *Jakobowsky und der Oberst*, 1965I; *Sonata for Two Pianos*, 1949I

Klein, Bernhard (Joseph): *David*, 1830I; *Dido*, 1823I; *Jephtha*, 1828I; *Job*, 1820I

Klein, Gideon: *Piano Sonata*, 1943I; *String Trio*, 1944I

Kletzki, Paul: *Symphony No. 2 in g*, 1928I

Klohr, John N.: *The Billboard March*, 1901I

Klusák, Jan: *Count of Monte Cristo*, 1993I; *Invention V, "Game of Chess,"* 1965I; *Invention VI*, 1960I; *String Quartet No. 1*, 1956I; *String Quartet No. 2*, 1962I; *String Quartet No. 3*, 1975I; *String Quartet No. 4*, 1990I; *String Quartet No. 5*, 1994I; *Symphony No. 1 in C*, 1956I; *Symphony No. 2*, 1956I; *Symphony No. 3*, 1960I

Knight, Edward: *Big Shoulders*, 1991I

Knight, Joseph P.: *Rocked in the Cradle of the Deep*, 1839I

Knussen, Oliver: *Horn Concerto, Opus 28*, 1994I; *The Rajah's Diamond*, 1979I; *Symphony No. 3*, 1979I; *Where the Wild Things Are*, 1980I

Koch, Frederick: *Piano Trio No. 1*, 1998I

❄

F *Biographical*   G *Cultural Beginnings*   H *Musical Literature*
I *Musical Compositions*

Koch, Sigurd von: *Violin Sonata*, 1913I
Kochan, Günter: *Cello Concerto No. 1*, 1967I; *Cello Concerto No. 2*, 1976I; *Cello Sonata*, 1960I; *Concerto for Orchestra I*, 1962I; *Concerto for Orchestra II*, 1990I; *Five Movements for String Quartet*, 1961I; *Piano Concerto*, 1958I; *String Quartet*, 1974I; *Symphony No. 1*, 1964I; *Symphony No. 2*, 1968I; *Symphony No. 3*, 1972I; *Symphony No. 4*, 1984I; *Symphony No. 5*, 1987I; *Violin Concerto No. 1*, 1952I; *Violin Sonata*, 1985I
Kodály, Zoltán: *Ballet Music for Orchestra*, 1925I; *Concerto for Orchestra*, 1939I; *Dances of Galanta*, 1933I; *Háry János*, 1926I; *Laudes organi*, 1966I; *Marosszék Dances*, 1930I; *Missa Brevis*, 1945I; *Peacock Variations*, 1939I; *Psalmus Hungaricus, Opus 13*, 1923I; *Sonata for Solo Cello, Opus 8*, 1915I; *Stille Messe*, 1942I; *String Quartet No. 1*, 1909I; *String Quartet No. 2*, 1918I; *Summer Evening*, 1906I; *Symphony in C*, 1961I; *Te Deum*, 1936I; *Theatre Overture*, 1927I
Koechlin, Charles: *Les Bandar-Log, Opus 176*, 1940I; *Cello Sonata*, 1917I; *Motets in the Archaic Style (15)*, 1950I
Koetsiers, Jan: *Symphony for Brass*, 1987I
Kohn, Karl: *Impromtus*, 1969I; *Interlude I*, 1969I; *Interlude II*, 1969I; *Piano Recreations*, 1968I
Kohs, Ellis: *Automatic Pistol*, 1943I; *Cello Concerto*, 1947I; *Concerto for Orchestra*, 1941I; *Passacaglia for Organ & Strings*, 1946I; *String Quartet No. 1*, 1940I; *String Quartet No. 2, "A Short Concert,"* 1948I; *String Quartet No. 3*, 1984I; *Symphony No. 1*, 1950I; *Symphony No. 2*, 1957I; *Violin Sonatina*, 1948I
Kokkonen, Joonas: *The Last Temptation*, 1975I; *Requiem*, 1981I; *Symphony No. 1*, 1960I; *Symphony No. 2*, 1961I; *Symphony No. 3*, 1967I; *Symphony No. 4*, 1970I
Kolb, Barbara: *All in Good Time*, 1994I; *Appello for Piano*, 1976I; *The Enchanted Loom*, 1989I; *Extremes*, 1989I; *Grisaille*, 1979I; *Soundings*, 1972I; *Trobar Clus*, 1970I
Kolessa, Mykola: *Symphony No. 1*, 1950I
Kollmann, Augustus: *The Shipwreck*, 1797I
Konyus, Yuly: *Violin Concerto in e*, 1896I
Koppel, Herman: *Moses*, 1963I
Koppel, Norman D.: *MacBeth, Opus 79*, 1968I
Korf, Anthony: *Requiem*, 1989I
Korn, Peter Jona: *Horn Sonata*, 1952I; *Saxophone Concerto*, 1956I; *String Quartet No. 1*, 1950I; *String Quartet No. 2*, 1963I; *Symphony No. 1*, 1946I; *Symphony No. 2*, 1951I; *Symphony No. 2*, 1956I; *Symphony No. 3*, 1977I; *Trumpet concerto*, 1979I
Korndorf, Nikolai: *Hymn II*, 1987I; *Hymn III*, 1990I
Korngold, Erich: *Cello Concerto in C, Opus 37*, 1946I; *Concerto in D, Opus 35*, 1945I; *The Dead City*, 1920I; *Die Kathrin*, 1939I; *The Miracle of Heliane*, 1927I; *Passover Psalm*, 1941I; *Piano Concerto in c♯ for the Left Hand*, 1924I; *Piano Quintet, Opus 15*, 1921I; *Piano Sonata No. 1*, 1909I; *Piano Sonata No. 2*, 1911I; *Der Ring des Polykrates*, 1916I; *Der Schneeman*, 1908I; *Songs, (5), Opus 38*, 1947I; *Songs of the Clowns, Opus 29*, 1939I; *String Quartet No. 1*, 1922I; *String Quartet No. 2 in E, Opus 26*, 1935I; *String Quartet No. 3 in D, Opus 34*, 1945I; *String Sextet*, 1916I; *Symphony in F♯, Opus 40*, 1950I; *Tomorrow, Opus 33*, 1942I; *Die töte Stadt*, 1920I; *Violanta*, 1916I; *Violin Sonata in G, Opus 6*, 1912I
Korte, Karl: *Epigrams for Piano*, 1993I; *Hill Country Birds*, 1982I; *New Zealand Songs*, 1986I; *Piano Concerto*, 1977I; *Piano Trio*, 1979I; *Symphony No. 2*, 1963I; *Symphony No. 3*, 1968I
Koshkin, Nikita: *Fall of Birds*, 1978I
Koskinan, Jukka: *String Quartet*, 1987I
Kotavičius, Bronius: *Epitaph to Passing Time*, 1998I
Kounova, Penka: *String Quartet No. 1*, 1995I
Koussevitzky, Serge: *Doublebass Concerto*, 1905I
Koutzen, Boris: *String Quartet No. 2*, 1936I; *String Quartet No. 3*, 1944I
Kozarenko, Oleksandr: *Don Juan from Kolimiya*, 1994; *The Oresteia*, 1996I
Kozeluch, Leopold: *Didone abbandonata*, 1790I; *Piano Concerto No. 7*, 1784I
Kozeluhova, Jitka: *Songs (6) on Emily Dickinson*, 1992I
Kraft, Leo: *Concerto No. 2 for Thirteen Instruments*, 1966I; *Concerto No. 3 for Cello, Winds & Percussion*, 1968I; *Concerto No. 5 for Oboe & Strings*, 1986I; *Concerto No. 6 for Clarinet & Orchestra*, 1986I; *Partita No. 1*, 1958I; *Piano Sonata*, 1956I; *Piano Statements & Commentaries*, 1965I; *Piano Variations*, 1951I; *Pieces (3) for Orchestra*, 1963I; *Short Pieces (10) for Piano*, 1976I; *String Quartet No. 1*, 1950I; *String Quartet No. 2*, 1959I; *String Quartet No. 3*, 1966I; *Symphony No. 1*, 1985I; *Variations for Orchestra*, 1958I
Kraft, William: *American Carnival Overture*, 1962I; *Andirivieni*, 1978I; *Contextures II: The Final Beast*, 1989I; *Interplay for Cello & Orchestra*, 1982I; *Melange*, 1985I; *Of Ceremonies, Pageants & Celebrations*, 1986I; *Piano Concerto*, 1973I; *Quartet for Percussion*, 1988I; *Quartet for the Love of Time*, 1987I; *Silent Boughs*, 1963I; *The Sublime & the Beautiful*, 1979I; *Timpani Concerto*, 1983I; *Veils & Variations*, 1988I; *Vintage 1990-1991*, 1990I; *Vintage Renaissance*, 1989I; *Weavings*, 1984I

❀

A *Births*   B *Deaths*   C *Debuts*   D *New Positions*
E *Prizes/Honors*

Kramer, Jonathan: *Notta Sonata for Piano*, 1993I
Krása, Hans: *Betrothal in a Dream*, 1930I; *Symphony*, 1923I
Kraus, Joseph M.: *Funeral Cantata*, 1792I; *Requiem*, 1775I
Krček, Jaroslav: *Symphony No. 3*, 1990I
Kreek, Cyrillus: *Estonian Requiem*, 1927I
Krein, Alexander: *Jewish Sketches for Clarinet Quintet*, 1910I; *Piano Sonata*, 1922I; *Symphony No. 1*, 1925I
Krein, Yulian: *Piano Concerto No. 1*, 1929I; *Piano Concerto No. 2*, 1942I; *Piano Concerto No. 3*, 1943I; *String Quartet No. 1*, 1925I; *String Quartet No. 2*, 1927I; *Violin Concerto*, 1959I
Kreisler, Fritz: *Liebesfreud for Violin*, 1910I; *Liebeslied for Violin*, 1910I
Krenek, Ernst: *Cello Concerto No. 1, Opus 133*, 1953I; *Cello Concerto No. 2, Opus 236*, 1982I; *Changing Settings*, 1965I; *Concerto for Two Pianos*, 1951I; *Dopelfuge, Opus 1*, 1918I; *The Four Winds, for Organ*, 1975I; *Johnny spielt auf, Opus 45*, 1926I; *Karl V*, 1934I; *Opus Sine Nomine*, 1990I; *Organ Concerto*, 1982I; *Organ Sonata, Opus 92*, 1941I; *Piano Concerto No. 1, Opus 18*, 1923I; *Piano Concerto No. 3*, 1946I; *Piano Concerto No. 4*, 1950I; *Piano Sonata No. 1*, 1919I; *Piano Sonata No. 2*, 1928I; *Piano Sonata No. 3*, 1943I; *Piano Sonata No. 4, Opus 114*, 1948I; *Piano Sonata No. 5, Opus 121*, 1950I; *Piano Sonata No. 6, Opus 128*, 1951I; *Piano Sonata No. 7*, 1988I; *Short Pieces, (12)*, 1938I; *Songs (3), Opus 216*, 1972I; *Songs of Franz Kafka (5)*, 1938I; *String Quartet No. 1*, 1921I; *String Quartet No. 2*, 1921I; *String Quartet No. 3*, 1923I; *String Quartet No. 4*, 1924I; *String Quartet No. 5*, 1930I; *String Quartet No. 6*, 1937I; *String Quartet No. 7*, 1943I; *String Quartet No. 8*, 1952I; *String Trio in Twelve Stations, Opus 237*, 1988I; *Study for Guitar*, 1957I; *Symphony, Opus 34*, 1925I; *Symphony No. 1, Opus 7*, 1921I; *Symphony No. 2*, 1922I; *Symphony No. 3*, 1922I; *Symphony No. 4*, 1947I; *Symphony No. 5*, 1949I; *Violin Concerto No. 1*, 1952I; *Violin Concerto No. 2*, 1954I; *Zeitleider (2), Opus 215*, 1972I
Kreutz, Arthur: *Hamlet*, 1949I; *Symphony No. 2*, 1946I
Kreutzer, Conradin: *Aesop in Phrygien*, 1808I; *Alimon und Zaide*, 1814I; *Die Alpenhütte*, 1815I; *Antonio und Kleopatre*, 1814I; *Aurelia*, 1849I; *Baron Luft*, 1830I; *Die beiden Figaro*, 1840I; *Der Bräutigam in der Klemme*, 1835I; *Cordelia*, 1819I; *L'eau de jouvenance*, 1827I; *Der Edelknecht*, 1842I; *Erfüllte Hoffnung*, 1824I; *Feodora*, 1812I; *Fridolin*, 1837I; *Der Herr und sein Diener*, 1815I; *Die Hochländerin am Kaukasus*, 1846I; *Die Hochländerin*, 1831I; *Die Insulanerin*, 1813I; *Jery und Bätely*, 1810I; *Die Jungfrau*, 1831I; *Konradin von Schwaben*, 1810I; *Die lächerliche Werbung*, 1800I; *Der Lastträger an der themse*, 1832I; *Libussa*, 1822I; *Die lustige Werbung*, 1826I; *Das Mädchen von Montfermeuil*, 1829I; *Melusina*, 1833I; *Mirsile und anteros*, 1814I; *Die Nacht im Walde*, 1808I; *Das Nachtlager in Granada*, 1834I; *Die Nachtmütze*, 1814I; *Orestes*, 1818I; *Panthea*, 1810I; *Piano Concerto No. 1 in B♭, Opus 43*, 1819I; *Piano Concerto No. 2 in C, Opus 50* (?), 1822I; *Piano Concerto No. 3 in E♭, Opus 65*, 1825I; *Der Ring des Glückes*, 1833I; *Des Sängers Fluch*, 1846I; *Scenes from Goethe's Faust*, 1820I; *Das Sendung Mosis*, 1814I; *Siguna*, 1823I; *Der Taucher*, 1813I; *Tom Rick*, 1834I; *Der Verschwender*, 1834I; *Der Besuch auf dem Lande*, 1826I
Kreutzer, Léon: *Symphony in f*, 1860I
Kreutzer, Rodolphe: *Abel*, 1810I; *Les amours d'Antoine et Cléopatre*, 1808I; *Astyanax*, 1801I; *Le baiser et la quittance*, 1803I; *Le béarnais*, 1814I; *Le camp de Sobieski*, 1813I; *Le carnaval de Venise* 1816I; *Charlotte et Worther*, 1792I; *Clari*, 1820I; *Le congrès des rois*, 1794I; *Constance et Théodore*, 1813I; *Le déserteur*, 1793I; *Les dieux rivaux*, 1816I; *Etudes (42) for Solo Violin*, 1796I; *Le Feme brators*, 1791I; *Flaminius à Corinthe*, 1801I; *François I*, 1807I; *L'heureux retour*, 1815I; *L'homme sans façon*, 1812I; *Imogène*, 1796I; *Ipsiboé*, 1824I; *Jeanne d'Arc*, 1790I; *La journée de Marathon*, 1792I; *La journée du 10 août 1792*, 1795I; *Lodoïska*, 1791I; *Le maître et le valet*, 1816I; *Malide*, 1827I; *Le négociant de Hambourg*, 1821I; *New Caprices (18 Etudes)*, 1815I; *L'oriflamme*, 1814I; *Overture, La journée de Marathon*, 1794I; *Paul et Virginie (opera)*, 1791I; *Paul et Virginie (ballet)*, 1806I; *La perruque et la redingote*, 1815I; *La servante justifiée*, 1818I; *Le siège de Lille*, 1792I; *String Quartets (3), Opus 2*, 1795I; *Les surprises*, 1804I; *Symphonie concertante (violin, cello)*, 1802I; *Symphonie concertante No. 2 in F*, 1794I; *Symphonie concertante No. 3 in E*, 1803I; *Le triomphe du mois de Mars*, 1811I; *Violin Concerto in G, Opus 1*, 1783I; *Violin Concerto No. 2 in A, Opus 2*, 1784I; *Violin Concerto No. 3 in E♭, Opus 3*, 1785I; *Violin Concerto No. 4 in C, Opus 4*, 1786I; *Violin Concerto No. 5 in A, Opus 5*, 1787I; *Violin Concerto No. 6 in e, Opus 6*, 1788I; *Violin Concerto No. 7 in A, Opus 7*, 1790I; *Violin Concerto No. 8 in d, Opus 8*, 1795I; *Violin Concerto No. 9 in e, Opus 9*, 1802I; *Violin Concerto No. 10 in d, Opus 10*, 1802I; *Violin Concerto No. 11 in C, Opus 11*, 1802I; *Violin Concerto No. 12 in A, Opus 12*, 1802I; *Violin Concerto No. 13 in D, Opus A*, 1803I; *Violin Concerto No. 14 in E, Opus B*, 1803I; *Violin Concerto No. 15 in A, Opus C*, 1804I; *Violin Concerto No. 16 in e, Opus D*, 1804I; *Violin Concerto No. 17 in G, Opus E*, 1805I; *Violin Concerto No. 18 in a, Opus F*, 1809I; *Violin Concerto No. 19 in d, Opus G*, 1810I
Krommer, Frantiek: *Clarinet concerto, Opus 36*, 1803I; *Flute Concerto No. 1, Opus 30*, 1802I; *Flute Quartet No. 2, Opus 17*, 1799I; *Mass in C, Opus 108*, 1825I; *Mass in d*, 1842I; *Oboe Concerto No. 1, Opus 37*, 1803I; *Oboe Concerto No. 2, Opus 52*, 1805I; *Quartet No. 1, Flute & Strings*, 1798I; *String Quartets (3)*,

***

F   *Biographical*   G   *Cultural Beginnings*   H   *Musical Literature*
I   *Musical Compositions*

Krommer, Frantiek: (*cont.*)
Opus 1, 1793I; *String Quartets (3), Opus 3*, 1793I; *String Quartets (3), Opus 4*, 1794I; *String Quartets (3), Opus 5*, 1796I; *String Quartets (3), Opus 7*, 1797I; *String Quintets (3), Opus 8*, 1797I; *String Quartets (3), Opus 10*, 1798I; *String Quintets (3), Opus 11*, 1798I; *String Quartets (3), Opus 16*, 1798I; *String Quartets (3), Opus 18*, 1800I; *Symphony No. 2, Opus 40*, 1803I; *Symphony No. 3, Opus 62*, 1808I; *Symphony No. 5, Opus 105*, 1820I; *Symphony No. 6, Opus 11* 1822I; *Symphony No. 9*, 1830I; *Violin Concerto No. 2, Opus 41*, 1803I; *Violin Concerto No. 3, Opus 42*, 1803I; *Violin Concerto No. 4, Opus 43*, 1803I; *Violin Concerto No. 5, Opus 44*, 1803I; *Violin Concerto No. 6, Opus 61*, 1808I; *Violin Concerto No. 7, Opus 64*, 1808I

Krumpholz, Johann: *Harp Symphony No. 2, Opus 11*, 1784I; *Variations on Mozart, Opus 10*, 1783I

Krzywicki, Jan: *Songs (4) after Rexroth*, 1995I; *Starscape*, 1983I; *String Quartet*, 1994I; *Trumpet Sonata*, 1994I

Kubelik, Raphael: *Orphikon: Symphony in Three Movements*, 1981I

Kubik, Gail: *Orchestral Suite*, 1935I; *Piano Concerto*, 1983I; *Piano Sonata*, 1947I; *Symphony Concertante*, 1951I; *Symphony No. 1*, 1949I; *Symphony No. 2*, 1955I; *Symphony No. 3*, 1956I; *Violin Concerto*, 1941I

Kuhlau, Friedrich: *Die Blumen*, 1807I; *Concertino, Opus 45, for Two Horns*, 1821I; *Die Drillingsbrüder von Damaskus*, 1830I; *Der Elfenhügel*, 1828I; *Elisa, Opus 29*, 1820I; *Elverhøj*, 1828I; *Die Feier des wohlwollens, Opus 36*, 1821I; *German Songs (3), Opus 11*, 1813I; *German Songs (6), Opus 23*, 1820I; *Hugo und Adelheid, Opus 107*, 1827I; *Lulu, Opus 65*, 1824I; *Piano Concerto in C, Opus 7*, 1810I; *Piano Quartet No. 1 in f, Opus 32*, 1821I; *Piano Quartet No. 2 in A, Opus 50*, 1823I; *Piano Quartet No. 3 in g, Opus 108*, 1829I; *Piano Sonata in E♭, Opus 4*, 1812I; *Piano Sonata in d, Opus 5*, 1812I; *Piano Sonatas (3), Opus 26*, 1820I; *Piano Sonata in G, Opus 34*, 1821I; *Piano Sonatas (3), Opus 8*, 1813I; *Piano Sonatinas (3), Opus 20*, 1820I; *Poems (2), Opus 78*, 1826I; *Poems (3), Opus 21*, 1820I; *Quintets (#) for Flute & Strings, Opus 51*, 1823I; *Die Räuberburg*, 1814I; *Shakespeare, Opus 74*, 1826I; *Songs (6), Opus 9*, 1813I; *Songs (12), Opus 23*, 1819I; *Songs (3), Opus 72b*, 1823I; *Songs (6), Opus 106*, 1829I; *Songs (6), Male Voices, Opus 67*, 1824I; *Songs (9), Male Voices, Opus 82*, 1827I; *Songs (8), Male Voices, Opus 89*, 1826I; *Songs (3), Opus 56*, 1806I; *The Triplet Brothers from Damascus*, 1830I; *Violin Sonata No. 1 in f*, 1820I; *Die Zauberharfe, Opus 27*, 1817I

Kuhn, Max: *Tenerif Concerto for Piano*, 1964I

Kullak, Theodor: *Grande sonate in f♯, Opus 7*, 1845I; *Piano Concerto in c, Opus 55* (?), 1850I; *Songs (2), Opus 1*, 1840I; *Symphony for Piano, Opus 27*, 1848I

Kun Hu: *Symphony*, 1984I

Künneke, Eduard: *Die lockende Plamme*, 1933I; *Der Vetter aus Dingsda*, 1921I

Kunzen, Friedrich Ludwig: *Die Auferstehung*, 1796I; *Dragedukken*, 1797I; *Erik Ejegad*, 1798I; *Das Fest der Winzer*, 1793I; *Festen i Valhal*, 1796I; *Gyrithe*, 1807I; *The Hallelujah of Creation*, 1797I; *Hemmeligheden*, 1796I; *Holger Danske*, 1789I; *The Homecoming*, 1802I; *Love in the Country*, 1810I; *Weisen und lyrische Gesänge*, 1788I

Kupferman, Meyer: *Banners*, 1994I; *Cello Concerto*, 1974I; *Chaconne Sonata*, 1993I; *Clarinet Concerto*, 1984I; *Concerto Brevis*, 1997I; *Concerto for Four Guitars & Orchestra*, 1998I; *A Crucible for the Moon*, 1986I; *Echoes from Barcelona*, 1977I; *A Faust Concerto*, 1997I; *The Fires of Prometheus*, 1986I; *Guitar Concerto*, 1993I; *Ice Cream Concerto*, 1992I; *Infinity No. 8* (string quartet), 1963I; *Little Symphony*, 1952I; *Lunar Symphony*, 1998I; *Moonfingers Demon for Piano*, 1998I; *A Nietzsche Cycle*, 1979I; *O North Star*, 1997I; *Piano Concerto No. 2*, 1978I; *The Proscenium*, 1992I; *Quasar Symphony*, 1996I; *Rhapsody for Guitar & Orchestra*, 1980I; *Savage Landscape*, 1988I; *A Soul for the Moon*, 1990I; *Sound Phantoms No. 6* (string quartet), 1980I; *Strata*, 1997I; *String Quartet No. 4*, 1958I; *String Quartet No. 5*, 1959I; *Summer Music*, 1987I; *Symphonic Odyssey*, 1990I; *Symphony for Six*, 1984I; *Symphony No. 1*, 1950I; *Symphony No. 2*, 1950I; *Symphony No. 3*, 1952I; *Symphony No. 4*, 1955I; *Symphony No. 6, "Yin-Yang,"* 1972I; *Symphony No. 7*, 1974I; *Symphony No. 8*, 1975I; *Symphony No. 9*, 1979I; *Symphony No. 10, "F.D.R.,"* 1981I; *Symphony No. 11*, 1983I; *The Three Faces of Electra*, 1995I; *Tinker Hill* (also sax concerto), 1999I; *Variations for Orchestra*, 1959I; *Winter Symphony*, 1997I

Kupper, Leo: *Inflexions Vocales*, 1982I

Kurka, Robert: *Suite, The Good Soldier Schweik*, 1956I

Kurpinski, Karol: *The Castle of Czorsztyn*, 1819I; *Clarinet Concerto*, 1823I; *Die drei Grazien*, 1822I; *Der Forster aus dem wald vor Kozienice*, 1821I; *Jadwiga*, 1814I; *Jan Kochanowski*, 1817I; *Kalmora*, 1820I; *Kasimir der Grosse*, 1821I; *Kleine Schule für Männer*, 1816I; *Krakauer hochzeit*, 1823I; *Laska Imperatora*, 1814I; *Luzifers Palast*, 1811I; *Mars i Flora*, 1808I; *Nadgroda*, 1815I; *Der Prinz Czaromysl*, 1818I; *Der Schatten des fürsten Josef Poniatowski*, 1821I; *Superstition*, 1816I; *Zwei hutten*, 1811I

Kurtág, György: *Microludes (12), Opus 13*, 1978I; *Officium Breve in Memoriam Andreae Szervánsky*, 1988I; *Stele, Opus 38*, 1994I; *String Quartet No. 1, Opus 1*, 1959I; *String Quartet No. 3, Opus 28*, 1989I

Kuzmenko, Larysa: *In Memoriam to the Victims of Chernobyl for Piano*, 1997I

Kvandal, Johan: *Variations & Fugue*, 1954I

La Barbara, Joan: *L'Alberto Della Foglie Azzure*, 1989I; *Autumn Signal*, 1982I; *Awakenings*, 1991I; *Events in the Elsewhere*, 1990I; *The Executioner's Bracelet*, 1979I; *Helga's Lied*, 1986I; *In the Dreamtime*, 1990I; *Loose Tongues*, 1985I; *October Music: Star Showers & Extreterrestrials*, 1980I; *Time(d) Trials & Unscheduled Events*, 1984I; *Urban Tropics*, 1988I

Labunski, Felix: *Songs without Words*, 1946I; *Symphony No. 2 in D*, 1954I; *Variations for Orchestra*, 1947I

Labunski, Wiktor: *Piano Concerto in C*, 1937I; *Variations on a Theme of Paganini*, 1943I

Lachner, Franz Paul: *Alidia*, 1839I; *Benvenuto Cellini*, 1849I; *Die Bürgschaft*, 1828I; *Catarina Cornaro*, 1841I; *Flute Concerto in d*, 1832I; *Harp Concerto in c*, 1828I; *Harp Concerto No. 2 in d*, 1833I; *König Odipus*, 1852I; *Lanassa*, 1830I; *Moses*, 1833I; *Sängerfahrt*, 1832I; *Suite No. 1 in D, Opus 113*, 1861I; *Suite No. 2 in e, Opus 115*, 1862I; *Suite No. 3 in f, Opus 122*, 1864I; *Suite No. 4 in D♭, Opus 129*, 1865I; *Suite No. 5 in c, Opus 135*, 1868I; *Suite No. 6 in C, Opus 150*, 1871I; *Suite No. 7 in d, Opus 190*, 1881I; *Symphony No. 1 in E♭, Opus 32*, 1828I; *Symphony No. 2 in F*, 1833I; *Symphony No. 3 in d, Opus 41*, 1834I; *Symphony No. 4 in E*, 1834I; *Symphony No. 5 in c, "Preis-Sympnie," Opus 52*, 1835I; *Symphony No. 6 in D, Opus 6*, 1837I; *Symphony No. 7 in d, Opus 58*, 1839I; *Symphony No. 8 in g, Opus 100*, 1851I; *Die vier menschenalter*, 1829I

Lachnith, Ludwig Wenzel: *Harpsichord/Piano Concertos (3), Opus 9*, 1785I; *Harpsichord/Piano Concertos (3), Opus 10*, 1785I; *Harpsichord Concertos (6), Opus 18*, 1786I; *L'heureuse réconciliation*, 1785I; *Sonates concertantes (6), Opus 14*, 1788I; *String Quartets (6), Opus 7*, 1782I; *Symphonies (6), Opus 1*, 1779I; *Symphonies (3), Opus 3*, 1784I; *Symphonies (3), Opus 4*, 1783I; *Symphonies (3), Opus 6*, 1781I; *Symphonies (3), Opus 11*, 1786I; *Symphonies (3), Opus 12*, 1786I; *Trio Sonatas (6), Opus 5*, 1782I

Laderman, Ezra: *And David Wept*, 1970I; *Cello Concerto*, 1984I; *Concerto for Flute & Bassoon*, 1982I; *Concerto for String Quartet*, 1981I; *Concerto for Violin, Cello & Orchestra*, 1987I; *Double Helix*, 1968I; *Double String Quartet*, 1983I; *Fantasy*, 1998I; *Flute Concerto, "Celestial Bodies,"* 1968I; *Flute Concerto*, 1985I; *Galileo Galilei*, 1978I; *Marilyn*, 1993I; *A Mass for Cain*, 1983I; *Momenti for Piano*, 1974I; *Pentimento*, 1989I; *Piano Concerto No. 1*, 1978I; *Piano Concerto No. 2*, 1989I; *Piano Pieces (3)*, 1956I; *Piano Sonata No. 1*, 1952I; *Piano Sonata No. 2*, 1955I; *Preludes (25) in Different Forms for Organ*, 1975I; *The Questions of Abraham*, 1973I; *String Quartet No. 1*, 1959I; *String Quartet No. 2*, 1962I; *String Quartet No. 3*, 1966I; *String Quartet no. 4*, 1974I; *String Quartet No. 5*, 1976I; *String Quartet No. 6*, 1980I; *String Quartet No. 7*, 1983I; *String Quartet No. 8*, 1986I; *Summer Solstice*, 1980I; *Symphony No. 1*, 1964I; *Symphony No. 2, "Luther,"* 1969I; *Symphony No. 3, "Jerusalem,"* 1973I; *Symphony No. 4*, 1980I; *Symphony No. 5, "Isaiah,"* 1982I; *Symphony No. 6*, 1983I; *Symphony No. 7*, 1984I; *Viola Concerto*, 1977I

Ladmirault, Paul: *Gilles de Tetz*, 1893I; *Myrdhin*, 1902I; *La prêtresse de Korydwen*, 1925I

Ladurner, Ignace Antoine: *Les vieux faux*, 1796I; *Wenzel*, 1793II

Laitman, Lori: *Days & Nights*, 1995I; *Love Poems of Marichiko*, 1994I; *Mystery*, 1998I

Lajtha, László: *The Grove of Four Gods*, 1943I; *Harp Quintet*, 1948I; *In Memorium*, 1941I; *Lysistrata*, 1933I; *Mass in Days of Tribulation*, 1950I; *Nocturnes*, 1941I; *Piano Trio*, 1928I; *Symphony No. 1*, 1936I; *Symphony No. 2*, 1938I; *Symphony No. 3*, 1949I; *Symphony No. 4*, 1951I; *Symphony No. 5*, 1952I; *Symphony No. 6*, 1955I; *Variations*, 1947I; *Violin Sonatina*, 1930I

Lalo, Édouard: *Allegro Symphonique*, 1875I; *Cello Concerto in D*, 1877I; *Concerto russe, Opus 29* (violin), 1879I; *Divertissement*, 1872I; *Fiesque*, 1866I; *Litanies de la sainte Vierge*, 1876I; *Melodies (6), Opus 17*, 1856I; *Melodies (3)*, 1870I; *Namouna*, 1882I; *Néron*, 1891I; *Norwegian Fantasy*, 1878I; *Norwegian Rhapsody*, 1879I; *Piano Concerto in f*, 1889I; *Popular Romances (6)*, 1849I; *Le Roi d'Ys*, 1888I; *Scherzo for Orchestra, Opus 13*, 1884I; *Songs (5)*, 1879I; *String Quartet in E♭, Opus 19/45*, 1859I; *Symphonie espagnole, Opus 21*, 1873I; *Symphony in g*, 1886I; *Violin Concerto in F, Opus 20*, 1873I

Lambert, Constant: *Horoscope*, 1937I; *Piano Sonata*, 1929I; *Pomona*, 1927I; *Prize Fight*, 1924I; *The Rio Grande*, 1929I; *Romeo & Juliet*, 1926I; *Tiresias*, 1951I

La Montaine, John: *Be Glad Then, America*, 1974I; *Birds of Paradise* (piano, orchestra), 1964I; *Erode, the Great*, 1969I; *The Marshes of Glynn*, 1984I; *Mass of Nature*, 1974I; *Piano Concerto No. 1*, 1958I; *Piano Concerto No. 2*, 1987I; *Piano Concerto No. 3*, 1987I; *Piano Concerto No. 4, Opus 59*, 1989I; *Piano Sonata*, 1942I; *String Quartet No. 1, Opus 16*, 1957I; *Symphonic Variations, Opus 50*, 1982I; *Symphony No. 1*, 1957I; *Wilderness Journal*, 1972I

Lampugnani, Giovanni: *Amor cantadina*, 1760I; *Le cantatrici*, 1758I; *Enea in Italia*, 1763I; *Ezio III*, 1758I; *Giulia*, 1760I; *Siroe*, 1755I; *Vologeso*, 1753I

Landowski, Marcel: *Bassoon Concerto*, 1957I; *The Clock*, 1982I; *Concerto for Ondes Martinot*, 1955I; *Edina*, 1946I; *Flute Concerto*, 1995I; *Galina*, 1996I; *Les nois Magas*, 1994I; *The Storm*, 1961I

Lane, Eastwood: *Adirondack Sketches*, 1922I; *American Dances (5)*, 1919I; *Eastern Sea Suite for Piano*, 1925I; *The Fourth of July*, 1935I; *In Sleepy Hollow*, 1913I; *Sold Down the River*, 1928I

Lang, David: *Hecuba*, 1994I; *International Business Machine*, 1990I; *Judith & Holofernes*, 1989I; *Modern Painters*, 1995I; *Orpheus Over & Under*, 1989I; *The Tempest*, 1995I

❈

F   *Biographical*   G   *Cultural Beginnings*   H   *Musical Literature*
I   *Musical Compositions*

Lang, Dorothy: *Life Cycle*, 1994I
Lang, Margaret Ruthven: *Dramatic Overture, Opus 12*, 1893I; *The Heavenly Noël, Opus 57*, 1916I; *The Lonely Rose*, 1906I; *The Night of the Star, Opus 52*, 1913I; *The Spirit of the Old House, Opus 58*, 1917I; *Te Deum, Opus 34*, 1899I; *Witichis Overture*, 1893I
Lange-Müller, Peter Erasmus: *Once Upon a Time* 1886I
Langgaard, Rued: *Antikrist*, 1923I; *Insektarium*, 1917I; *Music of the Spheres*, 1918I; *Piano Sonata No. 3*, 1987I; *Sinfonia interna*, 1915I; *Song of Solomon*, 1949I; *String Quartet No. 2*, 1918I; *String Quartet No. 3*, 1924I; *Tone Pictures (4)*, 1917I; *Violin Concerto*, 1943I
Langlais, Honoré: *Hymne à l'éternel*, 1798I
Langlais, Jean: *American Suite*, 1959I; *Canticle of the Sun*, 1968I; *Characteristic Pieces (3)*, 1957I; *Chorales (5) for Organ*, 1971I; *Ecumenical Book*, 1968I; *Esquisses gothiques(3)*, 1975I; *Esquisses romanes (3)*, 1976I; *Festival Alleluia*, 1971I; *Hommage à Frescobaldi*, 1951I; *Implorations (3)*, 1970I; *In Memoriam*, 1986I; *Incantation*, 1949I; *Mass, "Salve regina,"* 1954I; *Meditations (3) on the Trinity*, 1962I; *Méditations (5) sur L'apocalypse*, 1974I; *Messe Solennelle*, 1951I; *Modal Pieces (8)*, 1956I; *Mort et Resurrection*, 1990I; *Mosaique*, 1977I; *Office pour la Sainte Trinité*, 1958I; *Office pour la Sainte Familie*, 1957I; *Offrandes à Marie*, 1972I; *Organ Book*, 1956I; *Organ Concerto No. 1*, 1949I; *Organ Concerto No. 2*, 1961I; *Organ Concerto No. 3*, 1971I; *Organ Pieces (9)*, 1943I; *Organ Postludes (4)*, 1950I; *Organ Suite Brève*, 1947I; *Organ Suite Medievale*, 1947I; *Organ Symphony No. 1*, 1942I; *Organ Symphony No. 2*, 1959I; *Organ Symphony No. 3*, 1977I; *Paraphrases grégoriennes (3)*, 1934I; *Petite Pièces (12)*, 1962I; *Poèmes évangéliques (3)*, 1932I; *Progressions*, 1979I; *Solemn Mass, "Orbis factor,"* 1969I; *Suite baroque*, 1973I; *Suite folklorique*, 1952I; *Suite française*, 1948I; *Suite médiévale*, 1950I; *Supplication*, 1972I; *Triptyque, Opus 51*, 1957I
Langlé, Honoré: *Antiochus et Stratonice*, 1786I; *Corisandre*, 1791I; *Hymne à le Liberté*, 1795I; *Military Symphonies (6), Opus 1* (winds), 1776I
Lansky, Paul: *Fantasies (6) on a Poem of Thomas Campion*, 1979I; *Idle Chatter*, 1985I; *Idle Chatter Junior*, 1999I; *Just More Idle Chatter*, 1987I; *Not so Heavy Metal*, 1989I; *Notjustmoreidlechatter*, 1988I; *Quaker Bridge*, 1990I; *The Things She Carried*, 1996I
Larsen, Libby: *Aspects of Glory*, 1990I; *The Atmosphere as a Fluid System*, 1992I; *Beauty & the Beast*, 1989I; *Coming Forth into Day*, 1986I; *Concerto: Cold, Silent Snow*, 1989I; *Eric Hermannsons' Soul*, 1998I; *Frankenstein: the Modern Prometheus*, 1990I; *Ghosts of an Old Ceremony*, 1991I; *Marimba Concerto*, 1992I; *Mrs. Dalloway*, 1993I; *Overture: Parachute Dancing*, 1984I; *Piano Concerto: Since Armstrong* (piano), 1991I; *Solo Symphony*, 1999I; *Songs from Letters*, 1989I; *Songs of Light & Love*, 1998I; *String Quartet Schoenberg, Schenker, Schillinger*, 1991I; *Symphony No. 1, "Water Music,"* 1984I; *Symphony No. 4, "String Symphony,"* 1998I; *Three Summer Scenes*, 1988I; *Trumpet Concerto*, 1988I; *What the Monster Saw*, 1987I; *The Words upon the Windowpane*, 1978I; *A Wrinkle in Time*, 1992I
Larsson, Lars Erik: *Croquiser: Suite*, 1948I; *Little Fugues (7) with Preludes in the Olden Style*, 1969I; *Music for Orchestra*, 1950I; *Orchestral Variations*, 1962I; *Piano Sonatina No. 1*, 1936I; *Piano Sonatina No. 2*, 1947I; *Piano Sonatina No. 3*, 1950I; *Violin Concerto*, 1952I
Laufer, Beatrice: *Symphony No. 1*, 1944I; *Symphony No. 2*, 1962I
La Violette, Wesley: *Concerto for String Quartet*, 1939I; *Piano Concerto*, 1937I; *Piano Quintet*, 1927I; *Quintet for Flute & String Quartet*, 1943I; *String Quartet No. 1*, 1926I; *String Quartet No. 2*, 1933I; *String Quartet No. 3*, 1936I; *Symphony No. 1*, 1936I; *Symphony No. 2*, 1939I; *Symphony No. 3*, 1952I; *Violin Concerto No. 1*, 1929I; *Violin Concerto No. 2*, 1938I
Layton, Billy Jim: *Dylan Thomas Poems (3)*, 1956I
Lazarof, Henri: *Cello Concerto*, 1968I; *Chamber Concerto No. 3*, 1974I; *Chamber Symphony*, 1976I; *Clarinet Concerto*, 1989I; *Concerto for Orchestra*, 1977I; *Flute Concerto*, 1973I; *Impromtus for String Quartet*, 1995I; *Lamenti for Organ*, 1965I; *Largo for Organ*, 1963I; *Mirrors, Mirrors . . .*, 1980I; *Mutazione*, 1967I; *Piano Cadence IV*, 1970I; *Piano Concerto*, 1961I; *Piano Trio*, 1988I; *String Quartet No. 2*, 1962I; *String Quartet No. 3*, 1980I; *String Quartet No. 4*, 1996I; *String Quintet*, 1997I; *Structures sonores*, 1966I; *Symphony No. 2*, 1991I; *Symphony No. 3*, 1994I; *Symphony No. 4, "In Celebration,"* 1998I; *Viola Concerto*, 1960I; *String Quartet No. 1*, 1956I
Lazzari, Silvio: *The Lighthouse*, 1928I; *Symphony*, 1907I
LeBaron, Anne: *The E and O Line*, 1989I; *Metamorphosis*, 1977I
Lebrun, Louis-Sébastien: *L'art d'aimer, ou L'amour au village*, 1790I; *L'astronome*, 1798I; *Le bon fils*, 1795I; *Elénor de Dorval*, 1800I; *Emilie et Melcour*, 1795I; *Marcelin*, 1800I; *Le menteur maladroit*, 1798I; *Un moment d'erreur*, 1798I; *Montansier*, 1791I; *Missa solemnis*, 1815I; *Te Deum*, 1809I; *La veuve américaine*, 1799I
Leclair, Jean-Marie, *l'aîné: Ouvertures (3) et sonates en trio, Opus 13*, 1753I
Lecocq, (Alexandre) Charles: *L'amour et son carquois*, 1868I; *Le baiser à la porte*, 1864I; *Le barbier de Trouville*, 1871I; *La belle au bois Dormant*, 1900I; *Le docteur Miracle*, 1856I; *L'égyptienne*, 1890I; *La fille de Madame Angot*, 1872I; *Fleur-de-thé*, 1868I; *Gandolfo*, 1869I; *Giroflé-Girofla*, 1874I; *Le jour et la nuit*, 1881I;

A *Births*   B *Deaths*   C *Debuts*   D *New Positions*
E *Prizes/Honors*

Liliane et Valentin, 1864I; *La marjolaine,* 1877I; *Le myosotis,* 1866I; *Ondines au champagne,* 1866I; *La petite mademoiselle,* 1879I; *Les prés Saint-Gervais,* 1874I; *Le rajah de Mysore,* 1869I; *Le testament de M. de Crac,* 1871I

Lecuona, Ernesto: *Rapsodia Negra,* 1943I

Le Duc, Simon: *Trio divertimenti (6), Opus 5,* 1776I

Lee, Hyla: *String Quartet No. 1,* 1975I; *String Quartet No. 2,* 1985I; *String Quartet No. 3,* 1989I

Lee, Noel: *Dialogs for Violin & Piano,* 1958I; *Piano Caprices on the Name Schoenberg,* 1975I; *Preludes (5) Prolonged for Piano,* 1992I

Lee, Thomas O.: *String Quartet No. 2,* 1983I

Lees, Benjamin: *Collage,* 1973I; *Concerto for Brass Choir,* 1983I; *Concerto for Orchestra,* 1959I; *Concerto for Piano & Cello,* 1982I; *Concerto for String Quartet & Orchestra,* 1964I; *Concerto for Woodwind Quintet,* 1976I; *Etudes for Piano & orchestra,* 1974I; *Fantasy Variations for Piano,* 1983I; *Horn Concerto,* 1991I; *Kaleidoscopes,* 1959I; *Mirrors for Piano,* 1992I; *Mobiles for Orchestra,* 1979I; *Oboe Concerto,* 1963I; *Ornamental Etudes (6),* 1957I; *Passacaglia for Orchestra,* 1976I; *Piano Concerto No. 1,* 1955I; *Piano Concerto No. 2,* 1966I; *Piano Pieces (10),* 1954I; *Piano Preludes (3),* 1962I; *Piano Sonata No. 1,* 1949I; *Piano Sonata No. 2,* 1950I; *Piano Sonata No. 3, "Breve,"* 1956I; *Piano Sonata No. 4,* 1963I I; *Sonata for Two Pianos,* 1951I; *String Quartet No. 1,* 1952I; *String Quartet No. 2,* 1955I; *String Quartet No. 3,* 1981I; *String Quartet No. 4,* 1989I; *Symphony No. 1,* 1953I; *Symphony No. 2,* 1958I; *Symphony No. 3,* 1968I; *Symphony No. 4, "Memorial Candles,"* 1985I; *Symphony No. 5,* 1986I; *The Trumpet of the Swan,* 1972I; *Viola Concerto,* 1977I; *Violin Concerto,* 1958I; *Violin Sonata No. 1,* 1953I; *Violin Sonata No. 2,* 1973I; *Violin Sonata No. 3,* 1989I

Leeuw, Ton de: *Antigone,* 1991I

Lefebre-Wely: *L'organiste moderne,* 1967I

Lefébure-Wély, Louis James: *Meditaciones Religiosas,* 1858I

Lehar, Franz: *The Count of Luxembourg,* 1909I; *Karst-Lieder,* 1894I; *The Merry Widow,* 1905I; *Wiener Frauen,* 1902I; *Wo die Lerche Singt,* 1918I

Lehman, Mark Louis: *Pilgrim Songs,* 1989I

Lehrdahl, Fred: *Fantasy Etudes,* 1995I; *String Quartet No. 2,* 1982I

Lehrman, Leonard: *Suppose a Wedding,* 1997I

Leibowitz, René: *Piano Concerto,* 1954I; *Ricardo Gonfolano,* 1953I; *La rumeur de l'espace,* 1950I; *Symphony No. 4,* 1941I; *Trauersymphonie,* 1955I

Leifs, Jón: *Deltifoss, Opus 52,* 1964I; *Fine I* (vibraphone, strings), 1963I; *Fine II* (vibraphone, strings), 1963I; *Galdra-Loftr,* 1925I; *Groa's Spell,* 1965I; *Iceland Cantata,* 1930I; *Icelandic Overture, Opus 9,* 1926I; *Lay of Gudrun,* 1940I; *Night,* 1964I; *Organ Concerto,* 1930I; *Pastoral Variations, Opus 8,* 1920I; *Requiem, Opus 33b,* 1947I

Leighton, Kenneth: *Columba,* 1980I; *Martyrs for Organ,* 1976I

Lekeu, Guillaume: *Piano Sonata,* 1891I

Lemeland, Aubert: *Laure,* 1995I

Lemmens, Jacques-Nicolas: *Organ Sonata No. 1, "Pontificale,"* 1874I; *Organ Sonata No. 2, " O filii,"* 1874I; *Organ Sonata No. 3, "Pascale,"* 1874I

Lendvay, Kamilló: *Double Concerto,* 1991I; *Rhapsody for Orchestra,* 1997I; *Soprano Saxophone Concerto,* 1996I;*Stabat Mater,* 1992I; *Trumpet Concerto,* 1990I; *Via Crucis,* 1989I

Lennon, John Anthony: *Ghostfires,* 1989I

León, Tania: *Scourge of Hyacinths,* 1994I

Leoncavallo, Ruggero: *La bohème,* 1897I; *Chatterton,* 1877I; *Goffredo Mameli,* 1916I; *I Pagliacci,* 1892I; *Requiem for King Umberto I,* 1900I; *Roland,* 1904I; *Zaza,* 1900I; *Zingari,* 1912I

Leoni, Franco: *L'Oracolo,* 1904I

Lerdahl, Fred: *Quiet Music,* 1994I; *String Quartet No. 1,* 1978I

Lerman, Richard: *Kristallnacht Music,* 1992I; *A Matter of Scale,* 1986I; *A Matter of Scale II,* 1993I; *Sonic Journeys with Pitch to Midi,* 1995I

Lessel, Franciszek: *Variations in a, Opus 15,* 1810I

Lesueur, Jean-François: *Alexandre à Babylone,* 1815I; *Artaxerse,* 1797I; *La caverne,* 1793I; *L'inauguration du temple de la Victoire,* 1807I; *Paul et Virginie,* 1794I; *Ruth et Boaz,* 1811I; *Télémaque,* 1796I; *Le triomphe de Trajan,* 1807I; *Tyrté,* 1794I; *La mort d'Adam,* 1809I; *Ossian, ou Les bardes,* 1804I; *Ruth et Naomi,* 1810I

Levine, D.: *Anna Karenina,* 1992I

Levinson, Gerald: *Dreamlight,* 1990I; *Morning Star for Piano,* 1989I; *Symphony No. 2,* 1994I

Levy, Ernst: *Suite No. 3,* 1957I; *Symphony No. 11,* 1949I

Levy, Marvin David: *Arrows of Time,* 1988I; *The Balcony,* 1978I; *Escorial,* 1958I; *Masada,* 1973I; *Mourning Becomes Electra,* 1967I; *Piano Concerto,* 1970I; *String Quartet No. 1,* 1955I; *Symphony No. 1,* 1960I; *The Tower,* 1957I

❊

F   *Biographical*   G   *Cultural Beginnings*   H   *Musical Literature*
I   *Musical Compositions*

Lewin, Frank: *Burning Bright*, 1993I
Lewis, Robert Hall: *Kantaten*, 1990I; *Nuances II*, 1975I; *Piano Serenade I*, 1970I; *String Quartet No. 1*, 1956I; *String Quartet No. 2*, 1962I; *String Quartet No. 3*, 1981I; *String Quartet No. 4*, 1993I; *Symphony No. 1*, 1964I; *Symphony No. 2*, 1971I; *Symphony No. 3*, 1985I; *Symphony No. 4*, 1990I; *Three Pieces for Orchestra*, 1965I
Liadov, Anatol: *Baba-Yaga*, 1904I; *Bagatelles (3), Opus 53*, 1906I; *Biryulki, Opus 2*, 1876I; *Children's Songs (6), Opus 22*, 1890I; *Children's Songs (12), Opus 14, 18*, 1887I; *Danse de'Amazone, Opus 65*, 1910I; *The Enchanted Lake, Opus 62*, 1909I; *Final Scene, Die Braut von Messina, Opus 28*, 1891I; *Kikimora, Opus 63*, 1909I; *A Musical Snuffbox, Opus 32*, 1893I; *Nénié, Opus 67*, 1914I; *Piano Pieces (6), Opus 3*, 1877I; *Piano Pieces (3), Opus 33*, 1889I; *Piano Pieces (3), Opus 57*, 1906I; *Piano Pieces (4), Opus 64*, 1910I; *Piano Pieces (3), Opus 57*, 1905I; *Piano Preludes (4), Opus 13*, 1887I; *Piano Preludes (3), Opus 27*, 1891I; *Piano Preludes (3), Opus 36*, 1895I; *Piano Preludes (4), Opus 39*, 1896I; *Piano Preludes (3), Opus 40*, 1897I; *Piano Preludes (4), Opus 46*, 1899I; *Polonaise in D, Opus 55*, 1902I; *Russian Folksongs (8), Opus 58*, 1906I; *Sister Beatrice, Opus 60*, 1906I; *Songs (4), Opus 1*, 1876I; *Variations on a Polish Folk Theme in A♭, Opus 51*, 1901I; *Variations on a Theme of Glinka, Opus 35*, 1895I
Liapunov, Sergei: *Ballad in c♯, Opus 2*, 1883I; *Divertissements (6), Opus 35*, 1909I; *Easy Pieces (6), Opus 59*, 1914I; *Evening Songs, Opus 68*, 1920I; *Fêtes de Noël, Opus 41*, 1910I; *Hashish, Opus 53*, 1913I; *Male Quartets (5), Opus 47*, 1912I; *Male Quartets (5), Opus 48*, 1912I; *Mazurka No. 3 in e♭, Opus 17*, 1902I; *Mazurka No. 4 in A♭, Opus 19*, 1903I; *Mazurka No. 5 in b♭, Opus 21*, 1903I; *Mazurka, No. 7 in g♯, Opus 31*, 1908I; *Mazurka No. 8, Opus 36*, 1909I; *Organ Prelude & Pastorale, Opus 38*, 1909I; *Piano Concerto No. 1 in e, Opus 4*, 1890I; *Piano Concerto No. 2 in E, Opus 38*, 1909I; *Piano Pieces (3), Opus 1*, 1888I; *Piano Pieces (3), Opus 40*, 1910I; *Piano Studies (12), Opus 11*, 1905I; *Polonaise in D♭, Opus 16*, 1902I; *Psalm 140, Opus 64*, 1916I; *Rêverie du soir, Opus 3*, 1880I; *Rhapsody on Ukrainian Themes in f♯, Opus 28*, 1907I; *Russian Folksongs (30), Opus 10*, 1901I; *Sextet for Piano & Strings*, 1915I; *Solemn Overture in C on Russian Themes, Opus 7*, 1895I, 1896I; *Sonata in f, Opus 27*, 1908I; *Sonatina in D♭, Opus 65*, 1917I; *Songs (4), Opus 14 (?)*, 1900I; *Songs (4), Opus 30*, 1908I; *Songs (4), Opus 32*, 1908I; *Songs (3), Opus 39*, 1909I; *Songs (3), Opus 42*, 1911I; *Songs (7), Opus 43*, 1911I; *Songs (3), Opus 44*, 1911I; *Songs (4), Opus 50*, 1912I; *Songs (4), Opus 51*, 1912I; *Songs (4), Opus 52*, 1912I; *Songs (4), Opus 56*, 1913I; *Songs (4), Opus 61*, 1919I; *Songs (4), Opus 71*, 1920I; *Symphony No. 1 in b, Opus 12*, 1887I; *Symphony No. 2 in b♭, Opus 66*, 1917I; *Toccata & Fugue in C*, 1920I; *Violin Concerto in d, Opus 61*, 1915I; *Zhelyazova Volya, Opus 37*, 1909I
Lickl, Johann G.: *Requiem in C*, 1830I
Lidholm, Ingvar: *Dream Play*, 1992I
Lie, Harald: *The Bat's Letter*, 1939I; *Symphony No. 1*, 1934I; *Symphony No. 2*, 1937I
Liebermann, Lowell: *Album for the Young*, 1994I; *Appalachian Lieberstieder, Opus 54*, 1996I; *Cello Sonata No. 2, Opus 61*, 1998I; *De Profundis for Organ*, 1985I; *Flute Sonata*, 1987I; *Nocturne No. 1, Opus 20*, 1986I; *Nocturne No. 2, Opus 31*, 1990I; *Nocturne No. 3, Opus 35*, 1991I; *Nocturne No. 4, Opus 38*, 1992I; *Nocturne No. 5, Opus 55*, 1996I; *Out of the Cradle Endlessly Rocking*, 1993I; *Piano Concerto No. 1, Opus 12*, 1983I; *Piano Concerto No. 2, Opus 36*, 1992I; *Piano Concerto*, 1996I; *Piano Quintet, Opus 34*, 1990I; *Piano Trio, Opus 32*, 1990I; *Piccolo Concerto, Opus 50*, 1996I; *The Picture of Dorian Gray*, 1994I; *A Poet to His Beloved*, 1992I; *Six Songs after Longfellow, Opus 57*, 1997I; *Sonata for Flute & Harp, Opus 56*, 1996I; *String Quartet No. 1*, 1979I; *String Quartet No. 2, Opus 60*, 1998I; *Symphony No. 1, Opus 9*, 1982I; *Symphony No. 2*, 1999I; *Variations on a Theme of Mozart, Opus 42*, 1993I; *Viola Sonata*, 1984I; *Violin Sonata, Opus 46*, 1994I
Liebermann, Rolf: *Enigma*, 1994I; *Furioso*, 1945I; *Piano Concerto*, 1995I; *Symphony*, 1950I
Lieberson, Peter: *Ashoka's Dream*, 1997I; *Cello Concerto*, 1974I; *Horn Concerto*, 1999I; *The Ocean that Has No West & No East*, 1997I; *Piano Concerto No. 1*, 1983I; *Piano Concerto No. 2*, 1999I; *Piano Fantasy*, 1975I; *Red Garuda*, 1999I; *Rilke Song Cycle*, 2000I; *Stiller Freund*, 1997I; *String Quartet*, 1994I; *Symphony Drala*, 1996I; *Symphony No. 1*, 1986I; *Tashi Quartet*, 1979I; *Viola Concerto*, 1994I; *World's Turning*, 1991I
Ligeti, György: *Aventures*, 1962I; *Atmosphères*, 1961I; *Bagatelles (6) for Woodwind Quintet*, 1953I; *Chamber concerto*, 1970I; *Clocks & Clouds*, 1973I; *Coulée for Organ*, 1969I; *Double Concerto*, 1972i; *The Grand Macabre*, 1977I; *Harmonies: Two Studies for Organ*, 1967I; *Horn Trio*, 1982I; *Kylwiria*, 1972I; *Musica Recerata*, 1953I; *Nouvelle aventures*, 1965I; *Piano Concerto*, 1988I; *Piano Etudes, Book I*, 1985I; *Piano Etudes, Book II*, 1993I; *Piano Pieces (10)*, 1968I; *Pieces (3) for Two Pianos*, 1976I; *Requiem*, 1965I; *San Francisco Polyphony*, 1974I; *Sonata for Solo Viola*, 1994I; *String Quartet No. 1, "Métamorphoses Nocturnes,"* 1954I; *String Quartet No. 2, "Hommage à Hilding Rosenberg,"* 1968I; *Volumina for Organ*, 1962I
Liliuokalani, Queen: *Aloha Oe*, 1878I
Lim, Liza: *Garden of Earthly Desire*, 1988I; *The Oresteia*, 1993I

❁

A   *Births*   B   *Deaths*   C   *Debuts*   D   *New Positions*

E   *Prizes/Honors*

Lindberg, Magnus: *Arena*, 1995I; *Auro*, 1994I; *Cantigas*, 1999I; *Cello Concerto*, 1999I; *Clarinet Quintet*, 1992I; *Corrente II*, 1992I; *Engine*, 1996I; *Feria*, 1997I; *Fresco*, 1998I; *Piano Concerto*, 1991I; *Twine*, 1988I
Lindblad, Adolf Fredrik: *Frondörerne*, 1835I; *Symphony No. 1 in C*, 1839I; *Symphony No. 2 in D*, 1855I
Lindley, Thomas: *Let God Arise*, 1773I; *The Song of Moses*, 1777I; *A Shakespeare Ode*, 1776I
Lindroth, Scott: *Light*, 1993I; *String Quartet*, 1997I; *Terza Rima*, 1995I
Lipper, Binnette: *Horizons*, 1999I
Liszt, Franz: *Album d'un voyageur I, II*, 1840I; *Album d'un voyageur III*, 1836I; *Am Grabe Richard Wagners*, 1883I; *Années de pélerinage I*, 1854I; *Années de pélerinage II*, 1849I; *Années de pélerinage III*, 1877I; *Apparitions*, 1834I; *The Battle of the Huns*, 1857I; *The Beatitudes*, 1859I; *Cantantibus organis*, 1879I; *Cantico del sol di S. Francesco d'Assisi*, 1862I; *Ce qu'on entend sur la montagne*, 1849I; *Christus*, 1859I; *Consolations (6)*, 1848I; *Dante Symphony*, 1856I; *Don Sanche*, 1825I; *Élégie No. 2*, 1870I; *Episodes (2) from Lenau's "Faust,"* 1860I; *Etudes d'Exécution transcendante . . . Paganini*, 1838I; *Etudes de Concert (3)*, 1848I; *Études (12) d'exécution transcendante*, 1851I; *Fantaisie romantique sur deux mélodies suisses*, 1836I; *Fantasia on "Ad nos, as salutarem undam,"* 1855I; *Fantasia on Beethoven's "Ruins of Athens,"* 1852I; *Fantasy & Fugue, "Ad nos, ad salutarem undam,"* 1850I; *Faust Symphony*, 1854I; *Festival March*, 1849I; *Festklänge*, 1853I; *From the Cradle to the Grave*, 1883I; *Die Glocken des Strassburger Münsters*, 1874I; *Grand galop chromatique*, 1838I; *Grand Solo de Concert*, 1850I; *Grande etudes (24)*, 1837I; *Grandes études de Paganini*, 1851I; *Grande Fantaisie Symphonique on . . . Berlioz*, 1834I; *Grande Valse de Bravura*, 1836I; *Graner Mass*, 1855I; *Hamlet*, 1858I; *Harmonies poètique et religieuse*, 1834I; *Heroïde Funèbre*, 1850I; *Hexameron for Piano and Orchestra*, 1837I; *Huldigungs Marsch*, 1858I; *Hungaria*, 1854I; *Hungarian Crown March*, 1867I; *Hungarian Coronation Mass*, 1867I; *Hungarian Fantasy*, 1852I; *Hungarian March*, 1870I; *Hungarian Rhapsody No. 1 in c♯*, 1846I; *Hungarian Rhapsody No. 2 in c♯*, 1847I; *Hungarian Rhapsodies 4, 14*, 1853I; *Hungarian Rhapsody No. 15*, 1851I; *Hungarian Rhapsodies No. 18, 19*, 1885I; *Hungarian Storm March*, 1875I; *Die Ideale*, 1857I; *The Legend of St. Elisabeth*, 1862I; *The Legend of Ste. Cecilia*, 1874I; *Legendes*, 1863I; *Liebesträume*, 1850I; *Malédiction*, 1840I; *Mass for Male Voices*, 1871I; *Mazeppa*, 1851I; *Mephisto Waltz No. 2*, 1881I; *Mephisto Waltz No. 3*, 1883I; *Missa pro organo*, 1879I; *Missa Choralis*, 1865I; *Ora pro nobis, litany*, 1864I; *Orpheus*, 1854I; *Piano Concerto No. 1 in E♭*, 1835I; *Piano Concerto No. 2 in A*, 1839I; *Piano Sonata in b*, 1853I; *Prelude & Fugue on B-A-C-H*, 1855I; *Prelude, "Weinen, Klagen, Sorgen, Zagen,"* 1859I; *Les préludes*, 1850I; *Prometheus*, 1850I; *Psalm 13*, 1855I; *Psalm 18*, 1860I; *Psalm 23*, 1859I; *Psalm 37*, 1859I; *Psalm 114*, 1871I; *Psalm 116*, 1869I; *Psalm 129*, 1881I; *Râkóczy March*, 1851I; *Requiem*, 1868I; *Requiem für die Orgel*, 1883I; *Resignazione*, 1877I; *Sonetto 104 del Petrarco*, 1848I; *St. Cecilia Mass*, 1848I; *Tasso*, 1849I; *Totentanz*, 1849I; *Tre sonetti del Petrarca*, 1846I; *Trois odes funèbres*, 1866I; *Valse-Caprices (3)*, 1840I; *Variations on a Diabelli Waltz*, 1822I; *Variations, "Weinen, Klagen, Sorgen, Zagen,"* 1864I; *Vortragstücke*, 1884I; *Weihnachtsbaum*, 1876I
Litolff, Henry Charles: *La boîte de Pandore*, 1871I; *Die Braut von Kynast*, 1847I; *L'escadron volant de la reine*, 1888I; *La fiancée du roi de Garbe*, 1874I; *Heloïse et Abelard*, 1872I; *Overture, Chant des Belges, Opus 101*, 1858I; *Overture, Die Girondisten, Opus 80*, 1870I; *Over., Welflied von Gustav von Meyern, Opus 99*, 1856I; *Overture, Maximilian Robespierre, Opus 55*, 1856I; *Piano Concerto No. 2, 1844I; *Piano Concerto No. 3, Opus 45*, 1846I; *Piano Concerto No. 4, Opus 102 (?)*, 1852I; *Piano Concerto No. 5, Opus 123*, 1867I; *Ruth et Boaz*, 1869I; *Les templiers*, 1886I
Lloyd, George: *Pervigilium Veneris*, 1979I; *Symphony No. 7*, 1988I; *Symphony No. 12*, 1990I
Locklair, Dan: *Brief Mass*, 1994I; *Creation's Seeing Order*, 1987I; *Fantasy Brings the Day*, 1989I; *Hues for Orchestra*, 1994I; *Organ Concerto, " . . . Ere long we thee see . . . ,"* 1996I; *Reynalda Reflections*, 2000I; *Voyage for Organ*, 1991I
Lockwood, Normand: *Piano Sonata*, 1944I
Loeffler, Charles Martin: *Divertimento in a, Opus 1*, 1894I; *Divertissement espagnol*, 1900I; *Evocation*, 1930I; *Hora mystica*, 1915I; *Irish Fantasies (5)*, 1920I; *Memories of My Childhood*, 1924I; *Morceau fantastique*, 1893I; *La mort de Tintagiles*, 1897I; *A Pagan Poem*, 1906I; *Poems (4), Opus 15*, 1905I; *String Sextet*, 1891I; *String Quartet in a*, 1889I; *Les veillées de l'Ukraine*, 1890I
Loewe, Carl: *Die Alpenhütte*, 1816I; *Alperfantasie, Opus 3*, 1828I; *Die Apostel von Philippi, Opus 48*, 1835I; *Der Asra, Opus 133*, 1860I; *Die Auferweckung des Lazarus, Opus 132*, 1863I; *Auswanderer-Sonaten, Opus 137*, 1854I; *Ballads (3), Opus 125*, 1856I; *Ballads (6), Opus 1, 2*, 1824I; *Ballads (2), Opus 5*, 1826I; *Ballads (2), Opus 8*, 1827I; *Ballads (3), Opus 20*, 1832I; *Ballads (13), Opus 43, 44, 45, 49, 50*, 1835I; *Ballads (3), Opus 56*, 1836I; *Ballads (6), Opus 65, 67*, 1837I; *Ballads (2), Opus 68*, 1838I; *Ballads (2), Opus 78*, 1840I; *Ballads (2), Opus 94*, 1843I; *Ballads (3), Opus 97*, 1844I; *Ballads (2), Opus 110*, 1846I; *Ballads (3), Opus 116*, 1850I; *Ballads (2), Opus 121*, 1853I; *Ballads (3), Opus 129*, 1857I; *Ballads (2), Opus 135*, 1860I; *Ballads (3), Historical*, 1845I; *Der Bergman, Opus 39*, 1834I; *Biblische Bilder (4), Opus 96*, 1844I; *Bilder der Orients (12)*, 1833I; *Cantata for Male Voices*, 1854I; *Die drei Wünsche*, 1834I; *Die eherne Schlange, Opus 40*, 1834I; *Emmy*, 1842I; *Ester, Opus 52*, 1836I; *Fantasies (4), Opus 137*, 1850I; *Febellieder (4), Opus 64,*

F *Biographical*   G *Cultural Beginnings*   H *Musical Literature*
I *Musical Compositions*

Loewe, Carl: (cont.)
1837I; *Die Festizeiten, Opus 66*, 1836I; *Frauenliebe, Opus 60*, 1836I; *Der Friede*, 1857I; *Geistliche Gesänge I*, 1832I; *Geistliche Gesänge II*, 1833I; *Gesang der geister über den wassern*, 1842I; *Gesänge (10), Opus 9*, 1828I; *Der Graf von Habsburg, Opus 98*, 1844I; *Grand Duo in F, Opus 18*, 1829I; *Grande Sonata brillante, Opus 41*, 1819I; *Grande Sonata élégique, Opus 32*, 1825I; *Der grosse Christoph, Opus 34*, 1834I; *Grosse Sonata in E, Opus 16*, 1829I; *Hebrew Songs II, III, Opus 13*, 1825I; *Hebrew Songs IV, Opus 36*, 1826I; *Hiob*, 1848I; *Die Hochzeit der Thetis, Opus 120a*, 1851I; *Das Hohe lied von Saolmonis*, 1859I; *Humoresken (5), Male Voices, Opus 84*, 1843I; *Johann Hus, Opus 82*, 1841I; *Kaiser Karl V, Opus 99*, 1844I; *Legend, Der Traum der Witwe, Opus 142*, 1860I; *Legends (11), Opus 33, 35, 36, 37*, 1834I; *Legends (6), Opus 75, 76*, 1840I; *Der letzte Ritter, Opus 124*, 1853I; *Liedergabe, Opus 130*, 1859I; *Malekadhel*, 1832I; *Das Märchen im Traum*, 1832I; *Märznacht*, 1865; *Mazeppa, Opus 27*, 1830I; *Der Meister von Avis*, 1843I; *Nachtgesänge (11), Opus 9*, 1828I; *Neckereien*, 1833I; *Odes (5), Male Voices, Opus 57*, 1836I; *Palestrina*, 1841I; *Der Papagei, Opus 11*, 1847I; *Poems (14), Opus 61, 62*, 1837I; *Poems (11), Opus 9*, 1828O; *Polus von Atella*, 1860I; *Psalm 23*, 1845I; *Psalm 33*, 1845I; *Psalm 51*, 1849I; *Psalm 61*, 1850I; *Psalm 121*, 1845I; *Regenlied*, 1857I; *Rudolph der deutsche Herr*, 1825I; *Sängers Wanderlied*, 1835I; *Serbian Songs (6), Opus 15*, 1825I; *Die sieben Schlafer, Opus 46*, 1833I; *Songs (3), Opus 1*, 1818I; *Songs (12), Opus 9*, 1828I; *Songs (6) for Male Chorus, Opus 19*, 1826I; *Songs (2), Opus 63*, 1837I; *Songs (3), Opus 89*, 1842I; *Songs (3), Opus 103*, 1844I; *Songs (3), Opus 123*, 1852I; *Songs (5), Opus 145*, 1859I; *Te Deum, Opus 77*, 1842I; *Tone Poem in Sonata Form, Opus 47*, 1824I; *Die Walpurgisnacht*, 1833I; *Die Zerstörung Jerusalem, Opus 30*, 1829I; *Zigeuner-Sonate, Opus 107*, 1842I
Logroscino, Nicola Bonifacio: *Amore figlio del piacere*, 1751I; *I disturbi*, 1756I; *Elmire generosa*, 1753I; *Ester*, 1761I; *La finta frascatana*, 1751I; *Le finte magie*, 1756I; *Lo finto Perziano*, 1752I; *La Friselda*, 1752I; *La Gelosia*, 1765I; *Il natale de Achille*, 1760I; *Olimpiade*, 1753I; *La pastorella scaltra*, 1753I; *La spedizione di Giosue contro gli Amalechiti*, 1763I; *Stabat Mater in E*♭, 1760I; *Il tempo del onore*, 1765I; *Il vecchio marito*, 1760I; *La viaggiatrice de bell'umore*, 1762I
Lombardini-Sirmen, Maddalena Laura: *Harpsichord Concertos (6)*, 1773I; *Violin Concertos (6)*, 1770I
London, Edward: *The Death of Lincoln*, 1976I
Loomis, Clarence: *Fall of the House of Usher*, 1941I; *Piano Concerto*, 1915I; *String Quartet No. 1*, 1953I; *String Quartet No. 2*, 1963I; *String Quartet No. 3*, 1965I
Lopatnikoff, Nikolai: *Cello Sonata*, 1929I; *Concerto for Orchestra*, 1964I; *Concerto for Two Pianos, Opus 33*, 1951I; *Festival Overture, Opus 40*, 1960I; *Melting Pot*, 1976I; *Music for Orchestra, Opus 39*, 1958I; *Piano Concerto No. 1, Opus 5*, 1921I; *Piano Concerto No. 2, Opus 15*, 1930I; *Piano Sonata in E*, 1943I; *Piano Trio*, 1935I; *Small Pieces (4)*, 1920I; *String Quartet No. 1*, 1920I; *String Quartet No. 2*, 1928I; *String Quartet No. 3, Opus 36*, 1955I; *Symphony No. 1, Opus 12*, 1928I; *Symphony No. 2, Opus 24*, 1939I; *Symphony No. 3, Opus 35*, 1954I; *Symphony No. 4, Opus 46*, 1971I; *Variations for Piano*, 1932I; *Violin Concerto, Opus 26*, 1941I; *Violin Sonata No. 1*, 1927I; *Violin Sonata No. 2*, 1948I
Lo Presti, Ronald: *Requiem*, 1975I
Lorman, Richard: *Cold Storage*, 1994I
Lortzing, (Gustav) Albert: *Ali Pascha von Janina*, 1824I; *Andreas Hofer*, 1832I; *Die beiden Schützen*, 1835I; *Eine Berliner Grisette*, 1850I; *Le bourgmestre de Saardam*, 1837I; *Caramo*, 1839I; *Casanova*, 1841I; *Don Juan and Faust*, 1829I; *Ferdinand von Schill*, 1850I; *Hans Sachs*, 1840I; *Die Himmelfahrt Jesu Christ*, 1828I; *Die Hochfeuer*, 1828I; *Jubel-Kantate*, 1841I; *Ein Nachmittag in Ischl*, 1850I; *Die Opernprobe*, 1851I; *Overture alla Turca*, 1821I; *Der Pole und sein kind*, 1832I; *Regina*, 1848I; *Rolands-Knappen*, 1849I; *Die Schatzkammer des Ynka*, 1836I; *Undine*, 1845I; *Vier wochen im Ischl*, 1849I (?); *Der Waffenschmied*, 1846I; *Der Weihnachtsabend*, 1832I; *Der Wildschütz*, 1842I; *Yelva*, 1830I; *Zar und Zimmerman*, 1837I; *Zum Grossadmiral*, 1847I
Loudova, Ivana: *Chorale*, 1971I
Lourié, Arthur V.: *String Quartet No. 1*, 1921I; *String Quartet No. 2*, 1923I; *String Quartet No. 3*, 1924I
Løvenskold, Herman: *Sylfiden*, 1834I
Lucier, Alvin: *Amplifiers & Reflectors*, 1990I; *Ghosts*, 1978I; *Music for Gamelan Instruments, Microphones, Amplifiers & Loud-speakers*, 1994I; *Music for Piano & Amplified Sonorous Vessels*, 1990I; *Music for Piano with Magnetic Strings*, 1995I; *Music for Pure Waves*, 1980I; *Music on a Long Thin Wire*, 1977I; *Seesaw*, 1983I; *Serenade*, 1985I; *Silver Streetcar*, 1988I; *Solar Sounder*, 1979I; *Spinner*, 1984I; *Whistlers*, 1967I; *Windshadows*, 1994I
Ludwig, Thomas: *Symphony No. 1*, 1979I
Luening, Otto: *Dynamophonic Suite*, 1958I; *Gargoyles*, 1960I; *Joyce Cycle*, 1993I; *Louisville Concerto*, 1951I; *Music for Orchestra*, 1923I; *Piano Sonata in Memorium Ferruccio Busoni*, 1966I; *Piano Sonority Forms I*, 1983I; *Piano Trio No. 1*, 1921I; *A Poem in Cycles & Bells (tape)*, 1954I; *Short Sonata No. 5 for Piano*, 1979I; *Short Sonata No. 6 for Piano*, 1979I; *Short Sonata No. 7 for Piano*, 1979I; *String Quartet No. 1*, 1920I;

❄

A　*Births*　　B　*Deaths*　　C　*Debuts*　　D　*New Positions*

E　*Prizes/Honors*

String Quartet No. 2, 1923I; *String Quartet No. 3*, 1928I; *Symphonic Fantasia I*, 1924I; *Symphonic Fantasia II*, 1939I; *Symphonic Fantasia III*, 1982I; *Symphonic Fantasia IV*, 1982I; *Symphonic Fantasias V, VI*, 1985I; *Symphonic Fantasias VII*, 1986I; *Symphonic Fantasias VIII*, 1986I; *Symphonic Fantasy IX*, 1988I; *Symphonic Fantasia X*, 1990I; *Symphonic Fantasia XI*, 1991I; *Symphonic Interlude III*, 1975I; *Symphonic Interlude IV*, 1985I; *Symphonic Interlude V*, 1986I; *Symphonic Interludes, Two*, 1935I; *Theater Piece No. 2*, 1956I; *Wisconsin Symphony*, 1975I

Luigini, Alexandre: *Agnes et Démons*, 1876I; *Ballet Egyptien*, 1875I; *Les caprices de Margot*, 1877I

Luke, Ray: *Medea*, 1979I; *Piano Concerto*, 1969I; *Suite No. 1*, 1958I; *Symphony No. 1*, 1959I; *Symphony No. 2*, 1963I; *Symphony No. 3*, 1964I; *Symphony No. 4*, 1970I

Lumsdaine, David: *A Garden of Earthly Delights*, 1991I

Lundquist, Torbjörn: *Arktis*, 1984I; *Evocation*, 1964I; *Siebenmal Rilke*, 1989I; *Symphony No. 1*, 1956I

Lutoslawski, Witold: *Cello Concerto*, 1970I; *Chantefleurs et Chantefables*, 1990I; *Concerto for Oboe, Harp & Chamber Orchestra*, 1980I; *Concerto for Orchestra*, 1954I; *Les espaces du sommeil*, 1975I; *Funeral Music*, 1958I; *Jeux Vénitiens*, 1961I; *Livre Pour Orchestre*, 1968I; *Mi-parti*, 1976I; *Novelette*, 1979I; *Overture for Strings*, 1949I; *Paroles Tissées*, 1965I; *Piano Concerto No. 1*, 1988I; *Poems by Henri Michaux (3)*, 1963I; *Preludes & Fugues*, 1972I; *Songs (5)*, 1957I; *String Quartet*, 1964I; *Symphonic Variations*, 1938I; *Symphony No. 1*, 1947I; *Symphony No. 2*, 1967I; *Symphony No. 3*, 1982I; *Symphony No. 4*, 1992I

Lutyens, Elisabeth: *Lament of Isis*, 1969I; *The Valley of Hatsu-Se*, 1965I

Lux Friedrich: *Die Kätchen von Heilbronn*, 1846I

Lvov, Alexei: *Bianca*, 1844I; *Ondine*, 1847I; *Starosta Boris*, 1854I

Lyatoshinsky, Boris: *The Golden Ring, Opus 23*, 1929I; *Grazhyna, Opus 58*, 1955I; *On the Banks of the Vistula, Opus 59*, 1958I; *Overture on Ukrainian Folk Themes, Opus 20*, 1927I; *Piano Concerto, Opus 54*, 1953I; *Piano Quintet, Opus 42*, 1942I; *Piano Trio No. 1, Opus 7*, 1922I; *Piano Trio No. 2, Opus 41*, 1942I; *Poem of the Unification, Opus 49*, 1950I; *Romeo & Juliet*, 1954I; *Shchors, Opus 29*, 1937I; *Solemn Overture, Opus 70*, 1967I; *Sonata No. 1, Opus 13*, 1924I; *Sonata No. 2, Opus 18*, 1925I; *String Quartet No. 1 in d, Opus 1*, 1915I; *String Quartet No. 2 in A, Opus 4*, 1922I; *String Quartet No. 3, Opus 21*, 1928I; *String Quartet No. 4, Opus 43*, 1943I; *Suite for Woodwind Quartet*, 1944I; *Suite on Ukrainian Folk Themes* (string quartet), 1944I; *Symphony No. 1 in A, Opus 2*, 1919I; *Symphony No. 2 in b, Opus 26*, 1936I; *Symphony No. 3 in b, Opus 50*, 1951I; *Symphony No. 4 in b♭, Opus 63*, 1963I; *Symphony No. 5 in C, Opus 67*, 1966I; *Taras Schevchenko, Opus 51*, 1950I; *Violin Sonata, Opus 19*, 1926I

Lybbert, Donald: *Monica*, 1952I; *The Scarlet Letter*, 1965I

Maas, Louis: *Symphony, "On the Prairies,"* 1882I; *Symphony No. 2, "American,"* 1883I

Maazel, Lorin: *Music for Cello & Orchestra*, 1996I; *Music for Violin, Cello & Orchestra*, 1994I

Mabellini, Teodulo: *Fiammetta*, 1857I

MacBeth, W. Francis: *Piano Pieces (3)*, 1958I; *Symphony No. 1*, 1955I; *Symphony No. 3*, 1963I; *Symphony No. 4*, 1970I

McBride, David: *Chartres for Piano*, 1989I; *Dances (3) for String Quartet*, 1987I; *Mexican Rhapsody*, 1934I; *Pumpkin Eater's Little Fugue*, 1952I; *Symphonic Melody*, 1968I

McCabe, John: *Chagall Windows*, 1975I; *Clarinet Concerto*, 1977I; *Concerto for Orchestra*, 1982I; *Edward II*, 1994I; *Fire at Drilgai*, 1988I; *Mary Queen of Scots*, 1975I; *Notturni ed Alba*, 1970I; *Piano Fantasy on a Theme of Liszt*, 1967I; *The Shadow of Light*, 1979I; *String Quartet No. 1*, 1960I; *String Quartet No. 2*, 1972I; *String Quartet No. 3*, 1979I; *String Quartet No. 4*, 1982I; *String Quartet No. 5*, 1989I; *Symphony for Organ*, 1961I; *Symphony No. 1*, 1965I; *Symphony No. 2*, 1971I; *Symphony No. 3, "Hommages,"* 1978I; *Symphony No. 4*, 1994I; *The Teaching of Don Juan*, 1973I; *Variation on a Theme of Hartmann*, 1964I

McColl, Hugh F.: *String Quartet No. 1*, 1928I

McCollin, Frances: *Piano Variations on an Original Theme*, 1934I

MacCunn, Hamish: *The Cameronian's Dream, Opus 10*, 1890I; *Cior Mhor Overture*, 1885I; *Diarmid, Opus 34*, 1897I; *The Golden Girl*, 1905I; *Highland Memories Suite, Opus 30*, 1897I; *Jeanie Deans*, 1894I; *The Lay of the Last Minstrel, Opus 7*, 1888I; *The Masque of War and Peace*, 1900I; *The Moss Rose*, 1885I; *Overture, Land of the Mountains . . . Opus 3*, 1887I; *The Pageant of Darkness & Light*, 1908I; *Psalm 8*, 1901I; *Queen Hynde of Calefon, Opus 13*, 1892I; *The Wreck of the Hesperus*, 1905I

MacDonald, Andrew P.: *Pleiades Variations for Piano*, 1998I

MacDonald, Harl: *Concerto for Two Pianos*, 1936I; *Legend of the Arkansas Traveller*, 1939I; *My Country at War*, 1943I; *Piano Trio No. 1*, 1931I; *Piano Trio No. 2*, 1932I; *Song of the Nations*, 1945I; *String Quartet Fantasy*, 1932I; *String Quartet on Negro Themes*, 1933I; *Symphony No. 1, "The Santa Fe Trail,"* 1932I; *Symphony No. 2, "Rhumba,"* 1934I; *Symphony No. 3, "Lamentations of Fu Hsuan,"* 1935I; *Symphony No. 4, "Festival of the Workers,"* 1937I; *Violin Concerto*, 1943I

MacDowell, Edward: *Chansons fugitives (8), Opus 2*, 1876I; *Fireside Tales, Opus 61*, 1902I; *Forest Idyls,Opus 19*, 1884I; *Hamlet*, 1851I; *Idyls (6) after Goethe Opus 28*, 1887I; *Lamia, Opus 29*, 1889I;

❋

F *Biographical*   G *Cultural Beginnings*   H *Musical Literature*
I *Musical Compositions*

MacDowell, Edward: (*cont.*)
Lancelot & Elaine, Opus 25, 1886I; Love Songs (6), Opus 40, 1890I; Marionetten, Opus 38, 1888I; Modern Suite No. 2, Opus 14, 1882I; New England Idylls, Opus 62, 1902I; Northern Songs (2), Opus 43, 1891I; Ophelia, 1885I; Les orientales, Opus 37, 1888I; Piano Concerto No. 1 in a, Opus 15, 1885I; Piano Concerto No. 2 in d, 1886I; Piano Pieces (4), Opus 24, 1886I; Piano Poems (3), Opus 20, 1885I; Piano Sonata No. 1, "Tragica," 1893I; Piano Sonata No. 2, "Eroica," Opus 50, 1895I; Piano Sonata No. 3, "Norse," 1899I; Piano Sonata No. 4 in e, "Keltic" Opus 59, 1900I, 1901I; Piano Suite, Opus 5, 1876I; Piano Studies (12), Opus 39, 1890I; Poems (6) after Heine, Opus 31, 1887I; Sea Pieces, Opus 55, 1898I; Serenade, Opus 16, 1882I; Songs (8), Opus 47, 1893I; Songs (3), Opus 33, 1888I; Songs (4), Opus 56, 1898I; Songs (3), Opus 58, 1899I; Songs (3), Opus 60, 1901I; Suite No. 1 in a, Opus 42, 1891I; Suite No. 2 in e, "Indian," Opus 48, 1895I; Virtuoso Etudes (12), Opus 46, 1894I; Woodland Sketches, Opus 51, 1896I
McEwen, John: Fantasy for String Quintet, 1911I; Hills o' Heather (cello), 1918I; Hymn on the Morning of Christ's Nativity, 1905I; Piano Trio in a, 1937I; Scottish Rhapsody, "Prince Charlie," 1915I; String Quartet No. 3 in e, 1901I; String Quartet No. 4 in c, 1905I; String Quartet No. 5, "Nugae," 1912I; String Quartet No. 6 in A, "Biscay," 1913I; String Quartet No. 7 in E♭ "Threnody," 1916I; String Quartet No. 8 in E♭, 1918I; String Quartet No. 9 in b, 1920I; String Quartet No. 10, 1920I; String Quartet No. 12, "National Dances," 1923I; String Quartet No. 13 in c, 1928I; String Quartet No. 14 in d, 1936I; String Quartet No. 15, "In modo scotico," 1936I; String Quartet No. 16 in G, 1936I; Suite No. 2, "Ballet Suite," 1935I; Suite No. 3 in G, 1935I; Suite No. 4 in D, 1941I; Symphony No. 2 in c♯, "Solway," 1911I; Viola Concerto, 1901I; Violin Sonata No. 1 in E♭, 1913I; Violin Sonata No. 2 in f, 1913I; Violin Sonata No. 3 in G, 1913I; Violin Sonata No. 4 in A, 1913I
Macfarren, George: An Adventure of Don Quixote, 1846I; Agnes Bernauer, the Maid of Augsburg, 1839I; Akax, 1882I; Allan of Aberfeldy, 1850I; Around the Hearth, 1887I; Catholic Service in E♭, 1864I; Cello Concertino in A, 1836I; Cello Concerto in G, 1863I; Christmas, 1860I; Convivial Glees Illustrating the History of England, 1842I; Festival Overture (?), 1874I; Freya's Gift, 1863I; Helwellyn, 1864I; Joseph, 1877I; Kenilworth, 1880I; King David, 1883I; King Charles II, 1849I; Lady of the Lake, 1877I; Lenora, 1853I; May Day, 1857I; Organ Sonata in C, 1869I; Overture, Chevy Chace, 1836I; Overture, Don Carlos, 1842I; Overture, Hamlet, 1856I; Overture, Romeo and Juliet, 1836I; Overture, The Merchant of Venice, 1834I; Piano Sonata No. 1, 1842I; Piano Sonata No. 2 in A, 1845I; Piano Sonata No. 3 in g, 1880I; Piano Concerto in c, 1835I; The Resurrection, 1876I; Robin Hood, 1860I; She Stooops to Conquer, 1864I; The Sleeper Awakened, 1850I; Songs in a Cornfield, 1868I; St. John the Baptist, 1876I; Symphony No. 1 in C, 1828I; Symphony No. 2 in d, 1831I; Symphony No 3 in e, 1832I; Symphony No. 4 in f, 1833I; Symphony No. 5, 1833I; Symphony No. 6 in B♭, 1836I; Symphony No. 7 in c♯, 1840I; Symphony No. 8 in D, 1845I; Symphony No. 9 in e, 1874I; Violin Concerto in g, 1874I
McGranahan, James: I Will Sing of My Redeemer, 1887I
Machover, Tod: Bounce, 1992I; Desires, 1989I; Electronic Etudes, 1983I; Forever & Ever, 1993I; Nature's Breath, 1984I; Resurrection, 1999I; Spectres Parisiens, 1984I; String Quartet No. 1, 1981I; Valis, 1987I
McKay, George F.: Cello Concerto, 1942I; Organ Sonata No. 1, 1930I; Suite on 16th Century Hymns, 1960I; Violin Concerto, 1940I
Mackenzie, Alexander: Bethlehem, Opus 49, 1894I; The Bride, Opus 25, 1881I; Britannia Overture, Opus 52, 1894I; Canadian Rhapsody, Opus 67, 1905I; Cervantes Overture, 1877I; Choral Odes (2), Opus 48, 1891I; Colomba, Opus 28, 1883I; Compositions, (6), Opus 20, 1879I; Coriolanus, 1901I; Coronation March, Opus 63, 1902I; The Cricket on the Hearth, 1900I; The Dream of Jubal, 1889I; The Eve of St. John, Opus 87, 1924I; From the North, Opus 53, 1895I; His Majesty, Opus 56, 1897I; In the Scottish Highlands, Opus 23, 1880I; In Varying Moods, Opus 88, 1921I; Jason, Opus 26, 1882I; Jottings, Opus 84, 1916I; The Knights of the Road, Opus 65, 1905I; The Little Minister, Opus 57, 1897I; Manfred, Opus 58, 1898I; Moreaux (3), Opus 15, 1878I; Old English Air with Variations, Opus 81, 1915I; Organ Pieces (3), Opus 27, 1888I; Overture to a Comedy, 1876I; Overture, Youth, Sport & Loyalty, Opus 90, 1922I; Part Songs (4), Opus 71, 1912I; Piano Concerto, "Scottish," Opus 55, 1897I; Piano Pieces (5), Opus 13, 1877I; Piano Quartet in E♭, Opus 11, 1873I; Piano Trio in D, 1874I; Pibroch-Suite, Opus 42, 1889I; Pieces (6), Violin & Piano, Opus 37, 1888I; Ravenswood, Opus 45, 1890I; The Rose of Sharon, Opus 30, 1884I; Rustic Songs (6), Opus 66, 1898I; Scenes in the Scottish Highland, 1880I; School Songs (3), Opus 85, 1918I; Scottish Rhapsody No. 2, Opus 21, 1880I; Shakespeare Songs (3), Opus 35, 1887I; Shakespeare Sonnets (3), Opus 50, 1894I; Songs (2), Opus 3, 1876I; Songs (11), Opus 6, 17, 1878I; Songs (10), Opus 8, 14, 1879I; Songs (13), Opus 16, 31, 1885I; Songs (3), Opus 18, 1883I; Songs (3), Opus 54, 1894I; Spring Songs, Opus 44, 1890I; The Story of Seyid, Opus 34, 1886I; String Quartet in G, 1875I; Suite for Violin & Orchestra, Opus 68, 1907I; Suite, London Day by Day, Opus 64, 1902I; The Sun-God's Return, 1910I; Tam O'Shanter, Opus 74, 1911I; The Temptation, 1914I; Tennyson Songs (4), Opus 79, 1913I; The Troubador, Opus 33, 1886I; Twelfth Night Overture, 1888I; Veni, creator spriitus, Opus 46, 1891I; Violin Concerto in c♯, Opus 32, 1885I; The Witche's Daughter, Opus 66, 1904I

❈

A *Births*   B *Deaths*   C *Debuts*   D *New Positions*
E *Prizes/Honors*

Mackey, Steven: *Banana/Dump Truck*, 1994I; *Deal*, 1995I; *Eating Greens*, 1993I; *Fumeux Fume*, 1986I; *Lost & Found*, 1996I; *No Two Breaths*, 1995I; *ON ALL FOURS*, 1990I; *Physical Property*, 1992I; *Ravenhead*, 1998I; *String Quartet*, 1983I; *String Theory*, 1997I; *TILT*, 1992I; *Tuck & Roll*, 2000I
McKinley, Carl: *String Quartet in One Movement*, 1942I
McKinley, William Thomas: *Boston Overture*, 1986I; *Clarinet Concerto No. 3, "The Alchemical,"* 1992I; *Concerto for the New World*, 1991I; *Concerto for Orchestra III*, 1993I; *Concerto Domestica*, 1991I; *Concert Variations*, 1993I; *Lightning Overture*, 1993I; *Piano Concerto No. 1*, 1974I; *Piano Concerto No. 2*, 1987I; *Piano Concerto No. 3*, 1994I; *Piano Quartet No. 1*, 1988I; *Symphony No. 4*, 1985I; *Viola Concerto No. 3*, 1992I; *Viola Concerto No. 3*, 1993I
McLean, Barton: *The Electric Sinfonia*, 1982I; *Genesis*, 1973I; *The Sorcerer Revisited*, 1975I
McLean, Priscilla: *Dance of Dawn*, 1974I; *Invisible Chariots*, 977I; *Night Images*, 1973I; *Sage Songs of Life & Thyme*, 1992I; *Spectra I*, 1971I; *Spectra II*, 1972I
MacMillan, James: *Angels*, 1993I; *Beatus Vir*, 1983I; *The Beserking* (piano concerto), 1990I; *Cecilian Variations for JFK*, 1991I; *Cello Concerto*, 1996I; *Cello Sonata*, 1999I; *Concerto for Orchestra*, 1996I; *English Horn Concerto, "The World's Ransoming,"* 1996I; *Gusqueda*, 1988I; *Ines de Castro*, 1995I; *Kiss on Wood*, 1994I; *Little Preludes (14)*, 1997I; *Lumen Christi for Piano*, 1997I; *Mass*, 2000I; *Momento* (string quartet), 1994I; *Ninian* (clarinet concerto), 1996I; *Piano Sonata*, 1985I; *Raising Sparks*, 1997I; *Seven Last Words from the Cross*, 1993I; *St. Anne's Mass*, 1985I; *Symphony, "Vigil,"* 1997I; *Symphony No. 2, "Vigil,"* 1999I; *Tryst*, 1989I; *Veni, Veni, Emanuel*, 1992I; *Visitatio sepulchri*, 1993I; *Wedding Introit for Organ*, 1983I; *White Note Paraphrase for Organ*, 1994I; *Why Is This Night Different?*, 1997I
McNabb, Michael: *Love in an Asylum*, 1981I
McPhee, Colin: *Kinesis*, 1930I; *Piano Concerto No. 1, "La mort d'Arthur,"* 1920I; *Piano Concerto No. 2*, 1923I; *Sea Chanty Suite*, 1929I; *Sketches (4), Opus 1*, 1916I; *Symphony No. 1*, 1930I; *Symphony No. 2, "Pastorale,"* 1957I; *Symphony No. 3*, 1962I; *Tabuh-Tabuhan*, 1936I; *Transitions*, 1954I
McPherson, Gordan: *Resurrection Day*, 1992I; *Rimas*, 1993I; *String Quartet No. 1*, 1989I; *String Quartet No. 2, "Dead Roses,"* 1990I; *String Quartet No. 3, "Original Soundtrack,"* 1999I
Madarasz, Ivan: *Lot*, 1986I; *The Woman & the Devil*, 1973I
Maderna, Bruno: *Concerto for Two Pianos, Percussion and Harps*, 1948I; *Juilliard Serenade*, 1971I; *Musica per Due Dimensioni*, 1952I; *Oboe Concerto*, 1962I; *Piano Concerto*, 1959I; *String Quartet in Two Tempos*, 1955I
Madetoja, Leevi: *Comedy Overture, Opus 53*, 1923I; *Juha, Opus 74*, 1934I; *Okon Fuoko, Opus 58*, 1930I; *The Ostrobothians, Opus 45*, 1923I; *Symphonic Suite, Opus 4*, 1910I; *Symphony No. 1 in G, Opus 29*, 1916I; *Symphony No. 2 in Eᵇ, Opus 35*, 1918I; *Symphony No. 3 in A, Opus 55*, 1926I
Maeda, Katsuji: *Reflections for Orchestra with Two Pianos*, 2000I
Maganini, Quinto: *The Argonauts*, 1935I; *Symphony in g*, 1932I
Magnard, Albéric: *Bérénice, Opus 10*, 1909I; *Cello Sonata in A, Opus 10*, 1910I; *Chant funèbre, Opus 9*, 1895I; *Guercoeur, Opus 12*, 1900I; *Hymn to Venus, Opus 17*, 1906I; *Overture, Opus 10*, 1895I; *Piano Pieces (3), Opus 1*, 1888I; *Piano Trio in f, Opus 18*, 1904I; *Poèmes in musique (6), Opus 3*, 1891I; *Sonata in f for Piano, Violin & Cello, Opus 18*, 1905I; *String Quartet in e, Opus 16*, 1903I; *Suite in Olden Style in g, Opus 2*, 1888I; *Symphony No. 1 in c, Opus 4*, 1890I; *Symphony No. 2 in E, Opus 6*, 1893I; *Symphony No. 3 in bᵇ, Opus 11*, 1896I; *Symphony No. 3, Opus 11*, 1902I; *Symphony No. 4*, 1913I; *Violin Sonata in G, Opus 13*, 1901I; *Yolande, Opus 5*, 1891I
Mahler, Gustav: *Kindertotenlieder*, 1902I; *Das klagende Lied*, 1880I; *Das Lied von der Erde*, 1908I; *Rückert Songs (5)*, 1902I; *Songs of a Wayfarer*, 1883I; *Symphony No. 1 in D, "Titan,"* 1888I; *Symphony No. 2 in c, "Resurrection,"* 1894I; *Symphony No. 3 in d*, 1896I; *Symphony No. 4*, 1900I; *Symphony No. 5 in cᵇ*, 1902I; *Symphony No. 6*, 1904I; *Symphony No. 7*, 1905I; *Symphony No. 8 in Eᵇ, "Symphony of a Thousand,"* 1907I; *Symphony No. 9*, 1909I; *Symphony No. 10*, 1910I
Maillart, Louis: *La croix de Marie*, 1852I; *Les dragons de Villars*, 1856I; *Les pêcheurs de Catane*, 1860I
Mailman, Martin: *String Quartet No. 1*, 1962I; *Symphony No. 1*, 1969I; *Symphony No. 2*, 1979I; *Symphony No. 3*, 1983I
Majo, Giovan di: *L'Almeria*, 1761I; *Ricimero redei Goti*, 1758I
Maleingreau, Paul de: *Organ Suite, Opus 14*, 1919I
Malipiero, Gian: *Antonio e Cleopatra*, 1938I; *Cimarosiana*, 1922I; *Ditirambo Tragico*, 1917I; *Flute Concerto*, 1968I; *Grottesco for Orchestra*, 1918I; *Pause del Silenzio*, 1923I; *Piano Concerto No. 1*, 1934I; *Piano Concerto No. 2*, 1935I; *Piano Concerto No. 3*, 1948I; *Piano Concerto No. 4*, 1950I; *Piano Concerto No. 5*, 1958I; *Piano Concerto No. 6, "Delle Machine,"* 1966I; *Sinfonia del Mare*, 1906I; *String Quartet No. 1, "Rispetti e Strombotti,"* 1920I; *String Quartet No. 2, "Stornelli e Ballate,"* 1923I; *String Quartet No. 3, "Cantari alla madrigalesca,"* 1931I; *String Quartet No. 4*, 1934I; *String Quartet No. 5, "Dei capricci,"* 1940I; *String Quartet No. 6, "L'arca di Noé,"* 1947I; *String Quartet No. 7*, 1950I; *String Quartet No. 8, "Per Elisabetta,"* 1964I; *Symphony No. 3*, 1945I; *Symphony No. 5*, 1947I; *Symphony No. 8, "Sinfonia Brevis,"* 1964I; *Symphony No. 10, "Atropo,"* 1967I; *Symphony No. 11, "Dalla Cornamuse,"* 1970I

❖

F   *Biographical*   G   *Cultural Beginnings*   H   *Musical Literature*

I   *Musical Compositions*

Malling, Otto: *Piano Concerto*, 1890I; *Piano Trio*, 1889I
Malotte, Albert Hay: *The Lord's Prayer*, 1935I
Mamlok, Ursula: *2000 Notes for Piano*, 2000I; *Der Andreas Garten*, 1987I; *Constellations*, 1993I; *Girasol* (string quartet), 1990I; *Mosaics*, 1969I; *Oboe Concerto*, 1976I; *Panta Rhei*, 1981I; *Polarities*, 1995I; *Sonar Trajectory*, 1966I; *String Quartet No. 1*, 1962I; *String Quartet No. 2*, 1998I; *Woodwind Quintet*, 1981I
Mana-Zucca: *Piano Concerto, Opus 49*, 1919I
Mancinelli, Luigi: *Alchiaro di luna*, 1874I; *La cantata del lavoro*, 1898I; *Cleopatra*, 1877I; *Credo in e*, 1881I; *Ero e Leandro*, 1896I; *Gloria in f♯*, 1881I; *Isaias*, 1887I; *Isora di Provenza*, 1885I; *Messalina*, 1876I; *Missa in auxilium Christianorum in e*, 1899I; *Paolo e Francesca*, 1907I; *Salve Regina*, 1893I; *Sancta Agnes*, 1905I; *Sogno di una notta d'estate*, 1917I; *Symphony* (unfinished), 1894I; *Tizianello*, 1880I; *Un'estate a Perugia*, 1876I
Manfredini, Vincenzo: *Les amants réchappés du naufrage*, 1766I; *Armida*, 1770I; *Armour et Psyche*, 1762I; *Artaserse*, 1772I; *Carlo Magno*, 1763I; *La constance récompensée*, 1767I; *La finta ammalata*, 1763I; *Harpsichord Concerto in B♭*, 1769I; *L'Olimpiade*, 1762I; *La pace degli eroi*, 1762I; *Le pupilla*, 1763I; *Pygmalion*, 1763I; *Requiem for Empress Elizabeth*, 1762I; *Le sculpteur de Carthage*, 1766I; *Semiramide*, 1760I; *String Quartets (6)*, 1781I; *Symphonies (6)*, 1776I
Mangold, Carl: *Tannhäuser*, 1846I
Mannes, Leopold D.: *String Quartet No. 1*, 1927I
Mansoury, Philippe: *60th Parallel*, 1997I; *Pluton*, 1988I
Marchand, Jacques: *Guitar Concerto*, 2000I
Marchetti, Filippo: *Ruy Blas*, 1869I
Marco, Tomas: *Tarots*, 1991I
Marek, Czeslaw: *Ballade, Opus 7*, 1912I; *Echos de la jeunesse, Opus 9*, 1913I; *Morceaus (2), Opus 4*, 1911I; *Rural Scenes*, 1929I; *Serenade*, 1918I; *Sinfonia, Opus 28*, 1928I; *Sinfonietta*, 1916I; *Songs (6), Opus 1*, 1911I; *Suite for Violin & Piano*, 1918I; *Suite, Opus 40*, 1958I; *Triptychon, Opus 8*, 1913I; *Variations (12) on an Original Theme, Opus 3*, 1911I; *Village Songs*, 1934I
Marinuzzi, Gino: *Jacquerie*, 1918I
Markevitch, Igor: *Cinéma Overture*, 1930I; *The Flight of Icarus*, 1832I; *Lorenzo il Magnifico*, 1940I; *Le nouvel Âge*, 1937I; *Ouverture symphonique*, 1931I; *Paradise Lost*, 1934I; *Piano Concerto*, 1929I; *Rébus*, 1931I; *Sinfonietta*, 1929I; *Variations, Fugue & Envoi on a Theme of Handel*, 1941I
Marsalis, Wynton: *Ghost Story*, 1998I; *In This House, On This Morning*, 1994I; *String Quartet, "At the Octaroon Ball,"* 1995I; *Sweet Release*, 1998I
Marschner, Heinrich: *Alexander und Darius*, 1828I; *Ali Baba*, 1823I; *Austin*, 1851I; *Der Bäbu*, 1837I; *Des Falkners Braut*, 1830I; *Hans Heiling*, 1833I; *Heinrich IV*, 1818I; *Der Holzdieb*, 1823I; *Kaiser Adolf von Nassau*, 1843I; *Lucretia*, 1826I; *Overture on Hungarian National Airs*, 1818I; *Prinz Friedrich von Homburg*, 1821I; *Saidar und Zulima*; *Sangeskönig Hiarne*, 1858I; *Das Schloss am Aetna*, 1836I; *Schön Ella*, 1823I; *Das stille Volk*, 1819I; *Die stolze Bäuerin*, 1810I; *Der Templer und die Jüdin*, 1829I; *Titus*, 1816I; *Der Vampyr*, 1828I
Martin, François: *Symphonies (6), Opus 4*, 1751I
Martin, Frank: *Ballade for Piano*, 1939I; *Les dithyrambes*, 1918I; *The Four Elements*, 1964I; *Golgotha*, 1949I; *Harpsichord Concerto*, 1952I; *In terra pax*, 1944I; *Maria-Triptychon*, 1968I; *Mass*, 1926I; *Mass for Double Choir*, 1922I; *Mystère de la Nativité*, 1959I; *Ode to Music*, 1961I; *Passacaglia*, 1944I; *Piano Concerto No. 1*, 1934I; *Piano Concerto No. 2*, 1968I; *Piano Preludes (8)*, 1948I; *Piano Quintet*, 1919I; *Pilate*, 1964I; *Quatre Pièces Brèves for Guitar*, 1933I; *Requiem*, 1972I; *Sonnets to Cassandra (4)*, 1921I; *String Quartet*, 1967I; *String Trio*, 1936I; *Symphony*, 1937I; *The Tempest*, 1955I; *Trio on Irish Folk Tunes for Piano*, 1925I; *Le vin herbé, Part I*, 1938I; *Le vin herbé, Part II, III*, 1941I; *Violin Concerto*, 1951I; *Violin Sonata No. 1, Opus 1*, 1913I; *Violin Sonata No. 2*, 1932I
Martin, Laurent: *Leucade*, 1996I; *Paysages habitables*, 1994I; *Serai*, 1997I
Martin, Philip: *Piano Concerto No. 2, "A Day in the City,"* 1991I
Martino, Donald: *Alto Saxophone Concerto*, 1987I; *Augenmusik*, 1972I; *Cello Concerto*, 1972I; *Clarinet Sonata*, 1951I; *From the Other Side*, 1988I; *Notturno*, 1973I; *Octet*, 1998I; *Paradiso Choruses*, 1974I; *Pianisissimo*, 1970I; *Piano Concerto*, 1965I; *Piano Fantasies & Impromptus*, 1981I; *Piano Fantasy*, 1958I; *Piano Preludes (12)*, 1991I; *Quodlibets II*, 1979I; *A Set for Clarinet*, 1954I; *String Quartet No. 1*, 1983I; *Triple Concerto*, 1977I; *Violin Sonata*, 1952I; *The White Island*, 1985I
Martinon, Jean: *Cello Concerto*, 1965I; *Symphony No. 1*, 1936I; *Symphony No. 4, "Altitudes,"* 1965I
Martinů, Bohuslav: *Butterfly That Stamped*, 1926I; *Cello Concerto No. 1*, 1930I; *Cello Concerto No. 2*, 1945I; *Cello Sonata No. 1*, 1939I; *Cello Sonata No. 2*, 1941I; *Cello Sonata No. 3*, 1952I; *Clarinet Sonatina*, 1956I; *Concerto for Orchestra*, 1949I; *Concerto for String Quartet*, 1931I; *Concerto for Two Pianos*, 1943I; *Czech Rhapsody for Violin & Piano*, 1945I; *Double Concerto*, 1938I; *Double Violin Concerto No. 2*, 1950I; *Elegy for*

❊

A *Births*   B *Deaths*   C *Debuts*   D *New Positions*
E *Prizes/Honors*

Violin & Piano, 1909I; *Estampes*, 1958I; *Greek Passion*, 1957I; *Harpsichord Concerto*, 1935I; *Istar*, 1921I; *The Knife's Tears*, 1928I; *Magic Night*, 1918I; *The Marriage*, 1952I; *Memorial to Lidice*, 1943I; *Oiseaux exotiques*, 1956I; *Overture to a Comedy*, 1935I; *The Parables*, 1958I; *Piano Concerto No. 2*, 1935I; *Piano Concerto No. 3*, 1948I; *Piano Concerto No. 4*, 1956I; *Piano Quartet No. 1*, 1942I; *Piano Trio No. 1*, 1930I; *Piano Trio No. 2*, 1950I; *Piano Trio No. 3*, 1951I; *Quartet for Clarinet, Horn, Cello & Side-drum*, 1924I; *Quartet for Oboe & Piano Trio*, 1947I; *La revue de cuisine*, 1927I; *Rhythmic Etudes for Violin & Piano*, 1931I; *Short Pieces (5) for Violin & Piano*, 1929I; *Sinfonia for Two Orchestras*, 1932I; *Sinfonietta Giocoso*, 1940I; *Sonata for Two Violins*, 1923I; *String Quartet No. 1*, 1918I; *String Quartet No. 2*, 1925I; *String Quartet No. 3*, 1929I; *String Quartet No. 4*, 1937I; *String Quartet No. 5*, 1938I; *String Quartet No. 6*, 1946I; *String Quartet No. 7, "Concerto da Camera,"* 1947I; *String Quintet*, 1927I; *Symphony No. 1*, 1942I; *Symphony No. 2*, 1943I; *Symphony No. 3*, 1944I; *Symphony No. 4*, 1945I; *Symphony No. 5*, 1946I; *Symphony No. 6, "Fantaisies Symphoniques,"* 1953I; *The Three Wishes*, 1929I; *Vanishing Midnight*, 1922I; *Variations on a Slovak Theme for Cello & Piano*, 1059I; *Viola Sonata*, 1955I; *Violin Sonata No. 1*, 1929I; *Violin Sonata No. 2*, 1931I; *Violin Sonata No. 3*, 1944I; *The Voice of the Forest*, 1935I

Martin y Soler, Vicente: *Aci e Galatea*, 1784I; *L'amore geloso*, 1782I; *Amour et Psyche*, 1793I; *Andromaca*, 1780I; *Astartea*, 1781I; *La bella Arsene*, 1780I; *Il burbero di buon cuore*, 1786I; *Le burle per amore*, 1784I; *Il castello d'Atlante*, 1791I; *Cosa rara, Una*, 1786I; *Cristiano II, rè di Danimarca*, 1782I; *Didon abandonée*, 1792I; *La festa del villagio*, 1798I; *Ifigenia in Aulide*, 1779I; *Ipermestra*, 1780I; *L'isola del piacere*, 1795I; *La Madrileña*, 1776I; *Le melomania*, 1790I; *L'oracle*, 1793I; *Partenope*, 1782I; *I ratti Sabini*, 1780I; *La regina di Golconda*, 1811I; *Le retour de Poliocète*, 1800I; *La scuola dei maritati*, 1795I; *Tancrède* 1799I; *La vedova spiritosa*, 1785I; *Vologeso*, 1783I

Martirano, Salvatore: *The Cherry Orchard*, 1949I; *Fast Forward*, 1977I; *Fifty One*, 1978I; *Isabela*, 1992I; *LON/dons*, 1989I; *The Magic Stone*, 1951I; *O, O, O, O, That Shakespeherian Rag*, 1958I; *She Spoke*, 1979I *Shop Talk*, 1974I; *Three Electronic Dances*, 1963I; *Underworld*, 1965I

Martucci, Giuseppe: *Cello Sonata in f♯, Opus 52*, 1880I; *La canzona dei ricordi*, 1887I; *Messa di Gloria*, 1871I; *Organ Sonata*, 1879I; *Piano Concerto No. 1 in d*, 1878I; *Piano Concerto No. 2 in b♭, Opus 66*, 1885I; *Piano Sonata, Opus 34*, 1876I; *Piano Trio No. 1*, 1882I; *Piano Trio No. 2*, 1883I; *Samuel*, 1881I; *Symphony No. 1 in d, Opus 75*, 1895I

Marx, Joseph: *Piano Concerto in E*, 1919I; *String Quartet No. 1, "in modo chromatico,"* 1937I; *String Quartet No. 2, "in modo antico,"* 1938I; *String Quartet No. 3, "in modo classico,"* 1941I

Mascagni, Pietro: *L'amico Fritz*, 1891I; *Cavalleria Rusticana*, 1890I; *Guglielmo Ratcliff*, 1885I; *Iris*, 1898I; *Mass*, 1883I; *Messa di Gloria in F*, 1888I; *Motetto in modo dorico*, 1882I; *Pinota*, 1880I; *Rantzau I*, 1892I; *Requiem Mass*, 1887I; *Requiem in Memory of King Umberto I*, 1900I; *Silvano*, 1895I; *Symphony in c*, 1879I; *Symphony No. 2 in F*, 1881I; *Zanetto*, 1896I

Mascagni, Pietro: *Amica*, 1905I; *The Eternal City*, 1902I; *Isabeau*, 1911I; *Lodoletta*, 1917I; *La Maschere*, 1901I; *Nerone*, 1935I; *Parisina*, 1913I; *Il piccolo Marat*, 1921I; *Sì*, 1919I

Maslanka, David: *A Child's Garden of Dreams*, 1981I; *Mountain Roads*, 1997I; *Symphony No. 1 (band)*, 1970I; *Symphony No. 2 (band)*, 1987I; *Symphony No. 2 (band)*, 1983I; *Symphony No. 3 (band)*, 1991I; *Symphony No. 4 (band)*, 1993I; *Woodwind Quintet No. 2*, 1986I

Mason, Daniel Gregory: *Chanticleer Overture, Opus 27*, 1926I; *Clarinet Sonata, Opus 14*, 1923I; *Divertimento for Five Winds, Opus 26*, 1927I; *Folk Song Fantasy, Opus 28*, 1929I; *Love Songs (4), Opus 4*, 1906I; *Love Songs (6), Opus 15*, 1915I; *Nautical Songs (3), Opus 38*, 1941I; *Piano Quartet, Opus 7*, 1911I; *Piano Sonata*, 1895I; *Pieces (3) for Flute, Harp & String Quartet, Opus 13*, 1922I; *Prelude & Fugue, Opus 20*, 1919I; *Prelude & Fugue for Strings, Opus 37*, 1939I; *Prelude & Fugue, Opus 12*, 1914I; *Russians, Opus 18*, 1917I; *Sentimental Sketches for Piano Trio*, 1935I; *Serenade (string quartet)*, 1931I; *Soldiers, Opus 42*, 1949I; *Songs of the Countryside, Opus 23*, 1923I; *String Quartet on Negro Themes, Opus 19*, 1919I; *Symphony No. 1, Opus 11*, 1914I; *Symphony No. 2 in A, Opus 30*, 1929I; *Symphony No. 3, "Lincoln," Opus 35*, 1936I; *Variations on a Quiet Theme, Opus 40*, 1939I; *Variations on a Theme of John Powell*, 1925I; *Violin Sonata*, 1908I

Mason, Lowell: *Missionary Hymn*, 1823I; *Oliver (My Faith Looks Up to Thee)*, 1833I

Massé, Victor: *La chambre gothique*, 1849I; *La chanteuse voilée*, 1850I; *Le cousin de Marivaux*, 1857I; *La fiancée du diable*, 1854I; *Galathée*, 1852I; *Mariette la promisse*, 1862I; *Miss Fauvette*, 1855I; *Les noces de Jeannette*, 1853I; *La reine Topaze*, 1856I; *Le renégat de Tanger*, 1844I; *Les saisons*, 1855I

Massenet, Jules: *Amadis*, 1895I; *Ariane*, 1906I; *Bacchus*, 1909I; *Bérangère et Anatole*, 1876I; *Le carillon*, 1892I; *Chérubin*, 1905I; *Le Cid*, 1885I; *La cigale*, 1904I; *Cléopatre*, 1914I; *La coupe du roi de Thulé*, 1866I; *Don César de Bazan*, 1872I; *Don Quichotte*, 1910I; *Escarmonde*, 1889I; *Esmeralda*, 1865I; *Espade*, 1908I; *Les girondius*, 1881I; *La grand'tante*, 1867I; *Le grillon du foyer*, 1904I; *Grisélidis*, 1901I; *Hérodiade*, 1881I; *Jerusalem*, 1914I; *Le jongleur de Notre Dame*, 1902I; *Le mage*, 1891I; *Manfred*, 1869I; *Manon*, 1884I; *Le manteau du roi*, 1907I; *Marie-Magdeleine*, 1873I; *Notre Dame de Paris*, 1879I; *Ouverture de Concert*,

Massenet, Jules: (*cont.*)
  Opus 1, 1863I; *Overture, Brumaire*, 1899I; *Panis Angelicus*, 1910I; *Panurge*, 1913I; *Phèdre*, 1900I; *Phèdre Overture*, 1873I; *Piano Concerto*, 1903I; *Poème des fleurs*, 1908I; *Poèmes chastes (3)*, 1903I; *Poème de Souvenir*, 1868I; *Quelques chansons mauves*, 1902I; *Requiem*, 1863I; *Roma*, 1912I; *Robert de France*, 1880I; *Le roi de Lahore*, 1877I; *Sapho*, 1897I; *Suite No. 1 for Orchestra*, 1865I; *Suite No. 2: Scènes hongroises*, 1871I; *Suite No. 3: Scènes dramatiques*, 1873I; *Suite No. 4: Scènes pittoresques*, 1874I; *Suite No. 5: Scénes napolitaines*, 1876I; *Suite No. 6: Scènes de féerie*, 1879I; *Suite No. 7: Scènes alsaciennes*, 1881I; *La terre promise*, 1900I; *Thaïs*, 1894I; *Thérèsa*, 1907I; *La vie de bohème*, 1876I; *La Vierge*, 1880I; *Visions*, 1890I; *Werther*, 1892I
Másson, Áskell: *Black & White*, 1975I; *Elegie for Organ*, 1981I; *The Elements*, 1974I; *The Fire Troll*, 1974I; *Meditation for Organ*, 1992I; *Organ Sonata*, 1986I; *Piano Concerto*, 1985I; *Wedding March*, 1984I
Massoneau, Louis: *Symphonies (2), Opus 3*, 1792I; *Symphony No. 3 in c, Opus 5*, 1794I
Matej, Daniel: *Lumina*, 1996I
Mathias, William: *Capriccio, Opus 46/2*, 1969I; *Chorale for Organ*, 1966I; *Clarinet Concerto*, 1975I; *Concerto for Orchestra*, 1964I; *Dance Overture, Opus 16*, 1961I; *Fantasy, Opus 78*, 1978I; *Festival Te Deum, Opus 28*, 1964I; *The Fields of Praise*, 1977I; *Gloria, Opus 52*, 1970I; *Harp Concerto*, 1970I; *Harp Sonata, Opus 66*, 1974I; *Holiday Overture*, 1971I; *Invocation, Opus 35*, 1967I; *Jubilate, Opus 67*, 1974I; *A May Magnificat, Opus 79*, 1978I; *Missa Brevis, Opus 64*, 1973I; *Piano Concerto No. 1, Opus 2*, 1955I; *Piano Concerto No. 2, Opus 13*, 1960I; *Piano Concerto No. 3, Opus 40*, 1968I; *Piano Sonata No. 1*, 1963I; *Piano Trio, Opus 30*, 1965I; *Processional for Organ*, 1964I; *Serenade, Opus 18*, 1961I; *The Servants*, 1980I; *Sextet, Opus 8*, 1958I; *Shakespeare Songs (8), Opus 80*, 1978I; *Sonata No. 2, Opus 46/1*, 1969I; *String Quartet, Opus 38*, 1967I; *Symphony No. 1, Opus 31*, 1966I; *Symphony No. 2, Opus 90*, 1983; *Symphony No. 3*, 1991I; *Toccata Giocosa, Opus 36*, 1967I; *Veni Sancte Spiritus*, 1985I; *Violin Sonata No. 1*, 1961I; *Vision of Time & Eternity, Opus 61*, 1972I; *Wind Quintet, Opus 22*, 1963I; *Zodiac Trio, Opus 70*, 1975I
Mathison-Hansen, Gottfried: *Organ Concerto, Opus 15*, 1874I
Matsumura, Teizo: *Piano Concerto No. 2*, 1978I; *Symphony No. 1*, 1965I
Mattheson, Johann: *Das Fröliche Sterbelied*, 1760I
Matthews, Colin: *Studies (11) in Velocity*, 1987I
Matthus, Siegfried: *Crown Prince Friedrich*, 1999I; *Farinelli, or The Power of Song*, 1998I; *Judith*, 1985I; *Mirabeau*, 1989I
Matti, Veli: *String Quartet No. 1 Puumala*, 1994I
Maw, Nicholas: *American Games*, 1991I; *Essay for Organ*, 1961I; *Ghost Dances*, 1988I; *Hymnus*, 1996I; *Life Studies*, 1977I; *Odyssey*, 1994I; *Piano Trio*, 1991I; *The Rising of the Moon*, 1970I; *Roman Canticle*, 1989I; *Shahname*, 1992I; *Sonata Notturna (cello & orchestra)*, 1985I; *String Quartet No. 1*, 1965I; *String Quartet No. 2*, 1982I; *String Quartet No. 3*, 1995I; *Variations in Old Style*, 1995I; *Violin Sonata*, 1997I; *The World in the Evening*, 1988I
Maxfield, Richard: *Amazing Grace*, 1960I; *Bacchanale*, 1963I; *Five Movements*, 1959I; *Pastoral Symphony*, 1960I
Mayer, William: *A Death in the Family*, 1983I; *Enter Ariel*, 1980I; *The Eve of St. Agnes*, 1967I; *Octagon, (piano concerto)*, 1971I; *Of Rivers & Trains*, 1988I; *Overture for an American*, 1958I; *The Snow Queen*, 1963I; *Unlikely Neighbors*, 2000I
Mayr, Simon: *Adelaide di Gueselino*, 1799I; *Adelasia e Aleramo*, 1806I; *Alonso e Cora*, 1803I; *L'amor figliale*, 1811I; *L'amor cojugale*, 1805I; *Atar*, 1814I; *Il carretto del venditore d'aceto*, 1800I; *Che originale*, 1798I; *I due viaggiatori Zamori*, 1804I; *Elena*, 1814I; *Elisa*, 1804I; *Eraldo ed Emma*, 1805I; *Ginevra di Scozia*, 1801I; *Ifigenia in Aulike*, 1811I; *La Lodoiska*, 1796I; *Il matrimonio per concorso*, 1809I; *Medea in Corinto*, 1813I; *I misteri eleusini*, 1802I; *Il ritorno di Ulisse*, 1809I; *La Rosa rossa e la Rosa bianca*, 1813I; *Saffo*, 1794I; *Samuele*, 1818I; *Tamerlano*, 1813I
Mayuzumi, Toshiro: *Bacchanale*, 1954I; *Companologie*, 1957I; *Kinkakuji*, 1976I; *Kojiki*, 1996I; *Mandala Symphony*, 1960I; *Nirvana Symphony*, 1958I
Mazzochi, Domenico: *Admète*, 1789I; *L'amour et Psisché*, 1788I; *L'amour jardinier*, 1786I; *Le bouquet, Opus 22*, 1796I; *Les caprices de Galatée*, 1789I; *Concertante, Opus 42*, 1800I; *Les deux solitaires*, 1786I; *Eliza, Opus 32*, 1798I; *La fête marine*, 1786I; *Les fêtes de Tempe*, 1788I; *La foire de Smirne*, 1792I; *L'heureux événement*, 1787I; *Les offrandes à l'amour*, 1787I; *Paul and Virginia, Op. 43*, 1800I; *Pizarro*, 1797I; *Le premier navigateur*, 1786I; *Quartets (3)*, 1789I; *Sapho et Phaeon*, 1797I; *Les trois sultanes, Opus 20*, 1796I; *Le volage fixé*, 1792I; *Zémire et Azor*, 1787I
Meacham, F. E.: *American Patrol*, 1885I
Meale, Richard: *Piano Concerto*, 1983I; *Symphony No. 1*, 1994I
Mechem, Kirke: *Symphony No. 2*, 1967I
Medtner, Nicolai: *Dithyrambes (3), Opus 10*, 1906I; *Fairy Tales (2), Opus 8*, 1905I; *Fairy Tales (3), Opus 9*, 1906I; *Gedichte von Heine (3), Opus 12*, 1908I; *Goethe-Lieder (9), Opus 6*, 1905I; *Goethe-Lieder (12), Opus*

❀

A *Births*   B *Deaths*   C *Debuts*   D *New Positions*
E *Prizes/Honors*

15, 1908I; *Goethe Poems (6), Opus 18,* 1909I; *Nietzsche gedichte (5), Opus 19,* 1910I; *Nocturnes (3), Opus 16,* 1908I; *Piano Concerto No. 1 in c, Opus 33,* 1918I; *Piano Concerto No. 2 in c, Opus 50,* 1927I; *Piano Concerto No. 3 in e, Opus 60,* 1943I; *Piano Quintet in C, Opus posth.,* 1949I; *Piano Sonata No. 2,* 1926I; *Piano Sonata-Ballade,* 1913I; *Poèmes (7), Opus 28,* 1914I; *Poems (5), Opus 37,* 1918I; *Poems (8), Opus 24,* 1911I; *Pushkin Poems (7), Opus 29,* 1913I; *Pushkin Poems (6), Opus 32,* 1915I; *Pushkin Poems (6), Opus 36,* 1918I; *Romansa (3), Opus 3,* 1903I; *Sonata in g, Opus 22,* 1910I; *Sonata minacciosa in f, Opus 53,* 1932I; *Sonata romantica in b♭,* 1932I; *Sonata-Idylle in G, Opus 56,* 1937I; *Sonaten-Triade, Opus 11,* 1908I; *Songs (4), Opus 45,* 1924I; *Songs (7), Opus 46,* 1926I; *Stimmensbilder (8), Opus 1,* 1897I; *Violin Sonata No. 1 in b, Opus 21,* 1910I; *Violin Sonata, No, 2 in G, Opus 44,* 1926I; *Violin Sonata No. 3 in e, "Epica," Opus 57,* 1938I

Méhul, Étienne-Nicolas: *Adrien,* 1799I; *Alonzo et Cora,* 1785I; *Les amazones,* 1811I; *Ariodant,* 1799I; *Bion,* 1800I; *Cantata for Napoleon's Birthday,* 1810I; *La caverne,* 1795I; *Chant National du 14 Juillet, 1800,* 1800I; *Cora,* 1791I; *La dansomanie,* 1800I; *Daphnis et Pandrose,* 1803I; *Les deux aveugles de Tolède,* 1806I; *Doria,* 1795I; *Euphrosine,* 1790I; *Une folie,* 1802I; *Gabrielle d'Estrées,* 1806I; *Hèléna,* 1803I; *L'heureux malgré lui,* 1803I; *Horatius Coclès,* 1794I; *Les hussites,* 1804I; *Hymne à la raison,* 1793I; *L'irato,* 1801I; *Le jeune Henri,* 1797I; *Le jeune sage et le vieux fou,* 1793I; *Joanna,* 1802I; *Joseph und seine Brüder,* 1807I; *La journée aux aventures,* 1816I; *Le jugement de Paris,* 1793I; *Mélidore et Phrosine,* 1794I; *Messe Solennelle in A♭,* 1804I; *Ode Sacree,* 1782I; *Persée et Andromède,* 1810I; *Le prince troubadour,* 1813I; *Retour d'Ulysse,* 1807I; *Stratonice,* 1792I; *Symphonies No. 1, 3,* 1809I; *Symphony No. 4 in E,* 1810I; *Tancrède et Chlorinde,* 1796I; *Timolén,* 1794I; *Le trésor supposé,* 1802I; *Uthal,* 1806I; *Valentine de Milan,* 1817I

Meier, Jost: *The Dreyfus Affair,* 1994I

Melartin, Erkki: *Lyric Suite No. 3, "Impressions of Belgium,"* 1914I; *Sleeping Beauty,* 1911I; *Violin Concerto,* 1913I

Melchers, H. Melcher: *Violin Sonata,* 1928I

Méller, Gottfired: *Symphony, "Dürer,"* 1963I

Mendelssohn, Felix: *Andante & Scherzo, Opus 81,* 1847I; *Andante Sostenuto in D,* 1845I; *Anthems(6), Opus 79,* 1848I; *Antigone, Opus 55,* 1841I; *Athalie, Opus 74,* 1845I; *Die beiden Pädagogen,* 1821I; *Calm Sea & Prosperous Voyage, Opus 27,* 1828I; *Capriccio in f♯, Opus 5,* 1825I; *Capriccio in E, Opus 48,* 1837I; *Capriccio in e, Opus 81/3,* 1843I; *Capriccio Brillante in b, Opus 22,* 1832I; *Capriccios (3), Opus 33,* 1835I; *Cello Sonata No. 1 in B♭, Opus 45,* 1838I; *Cello Sonata No. 2 in D, Opus 58,* 1843I; *Characteristic Pieces (7), Opus 7,* 1827I; *Christus, Opus 97,* 1847I; *Chorale-Prelude, "Wie gross . . . Almächt'gen Güte,"* 1823I; *Clarinet Sonata in E♭,* 1824I; *Concerto No. 1 for Two Pianos in E,* 1823I; *Concerto No. 2 in A♭ for Two Pianos,* 1824I; *Duets (6), Opus 63,* 1845I; *Duets (3), Opus 77,* 1848I; *Elijah,* 1846I; *Die erste Frühlingstag, Opus 48,* 1839I; *Die erste Walpurgisnacht, Opus 60,* 1832I; *Fantasia in E, "Last Rose of Summer,"* 1827I; *Fantasia in f♯, Opus 28,* 1833I; *Fantasies (3), Opus 16,* 1829I; *Festgesang,* 1840I; *Fugue in c♯,* 1826I; *Fugue in E♭, Opus 81/4,* 1827I; *Fugues (15) for SQ,* 1821I; *Geistliches Lied in E♭,* 1840I; *Hebrides Overture, Opus 26,* 1830I; *Die Heimkehr aus der Frende, Opus 89,* 1829I; *Die Hochzeit des Camacho, Opus 10,* 1825I; *Im Freien zu singern, Opus 41,* 1838I; *Infelice, Opus 94,* 1843I; *Kinderstücke, Opus 72,* 1847I; *Lauda Sion, Opus 73,* 1846I; *Little Pieces (6) for Organ,* 1820I; *Little Pieces (4) for Organ,* 1844I; *Magnificat in D,* 1822I; *Male Choruses (4), Opus 76,* 1848I; *Male Choruses (4), Opus 120,* 1847I; *A Midsummer Night's Dream, Opus 61,* 1842; *Motets (3), Opus 69,* 1847I; *Nachtgesang,* 1842I; *Oedipus at Colonos, Opus 93,* 1845; *Der Onkel aus Boston,* 1823I; *Organ Sonatas (6), Opus 44,* 1844I; *Organ Sonatas (6), Opus 65,* 1845I; *Overture in C for Winds, Opus 24,* 1824I; *Overture, Midsummer Night's Dream, Opus 21,* 1826I; *Piano Concerto in g (strings),* 1822I; *Piano Concerto No. l in g, Opus 25,* 1831I; *Piano Concerto No. 2 in d, Opus 40,* 1837I; *Piano Quartet No. 1, Opus 1,* 1822I; *Piano Quartet No. 2, Opus 2,* 1823I; *Piano Quartet No. 3, Opus 3,* 1825I; *Piano Quartet No. 1, Opus 1,* 1822I; *Piano Sextet in D, Opus 110,* 1824I; *Piano Sonatas (3), f,a,e),* 1820I; *Piano Sonata in g, Opus 105,* 1821I; *Piano Sonata in E, Opus 6,* 1826I; *Piano Sonata in B♭, Opus 106,* 1827I; *Piano Trio No. 1, Opus 49,* 1839I; *Piano Trio No. 2, Opus 66,* 1845I; *Piano Variations in E♭, Opus 82,* 1841I; *Piano Variations in B♭, Opus 83,* 1841I; *Preludes and Fugues (6), Opus 35,* 1837I; *Preludes & Fugues (c, G, d), Opus 37,* 1837I; *Presto in C,* 1820I; *Psalm 42, Opus 42,* 1837I; *Psalm 66,* 1822I; *Psalm 95,* 1838I; *Psalm 100,* 1842I; *Psalm 31,* 1839I; *Psalm 114, Opus 51,* 1839I; *Psalm 115, Opus 31,* 1830I; *Psalms (3), Opus 78,* 1843I; *Rondo capricciosao in E, Opus 14,* 1824I; *Rondo Brillant, Opus 29,* 1834I; *Ruy Blas Overture, Opus 95,* 1839I; *Sacred Songs (2), Opus 112,* 1835I; *Salve Regina in E♭,* 1822I; *Scherzo in b,* 1829I; *Scherzo à capriccio in f♯,* 1836I; *Serenade and Allegro in b, Opus 43,* 1838I; *Serious Variations in E♭, Opus 54,* 1841I; *Die Soldaten liebschaft,* 1820I; *Songs (12), Opus 8,* 1828I; *Songs (12), Opus 9,* 1829I; *Songs (9), Opus 47, 48,* 1839I; *Songs (6), Opus 57,* 1843I; *Songs (6), Opus 71,* 1847I; *Songs (3), Opus 84,* 1850I; *Songs (6), Opus 86,* 1851I; *Songs (6), Opus 99,* 1845I; *Songs (6), Opus 34,* 1836I; *Songs without Words I, Opus 19,* 1830I; *Songs without Words II, Opus 30,* 1835I; *Songs without Words III, Opus 38,* 1837I; *Songs without Words IV, Opus 53,* 1841I; *Songs without Words V, Opus 62,* 1844I; *Songs without Words VI, Opus 67,* 1845I; *Songs without Words VII, Opus 85,* 1845I; *Songs without Words VIII, Opus 102,* 1850I;

✵

F   *Biographical*   G   *Cultural Beginnings*   H   *Musical Literature*

I   *Musical Compositions*

Mendelssohn, Felix: (*cont.*)
St. Paul, Opus 36, 1836I; Der Standhafte Prinz, 1833I; String Octet in E♭, Opus 20, 1825I; String Quartet No. 1 in E♭, Opus 12, 1829I; String Quartet No. 2 in A, Opus 13, 1827I; String Quartet No. 3 in D, 1837I; String Quartet No. 4 in e, Opus 44, 1837I; String Quartet No. 5, Opus 44/3, 1838I; String Quartet No. 6 in f, Opus 80, 1847I; String Quintet No. 1 in A, Opus 18, 1826I; String Quintet No. 2 in c, Opus 87, 1845I; String Symphonies 1, 6, 1821I; String Symphony No. 8 in D, 1822I; String Symphonies No. 9 & 10, 1823I; String Symphonies No. 11 & 12, 1823I; Symphony No. 1 in c, Opus 11, 1824I; Symphony No. 2 in B♭, "Hymn of Praise," Opus 52, 1840I; Symphony No. 3 in a, "Scotch," Opus 56, 1842I; Symphony No. 4 in A, Opus 90, "Italian," 1833I; Symphony No. 5 in d, "Reformation," Opus 107, 1832I; Te Deum in A, 1832I; Te Deum in D, 1826I; Trauermarsch, Opus 103, for Band, 1836I; Trumpet Overture in C, Opus 101, 1826I; Tu es Petrus, Opus 111, 1827I; Variations Concertantes, Opus 17, 1829I; Violin Concerto in d, 1822I; Violin Concerto in e, Opus 65, 1844I; Viola Sonata in c, 1824I; Violin Sonata No. 1 in F, 1820I; Violin Sonata No. 2 in f, Opus 4, 1825I; Violin Sonata in F, 1838I; Die Wandernden Komödianten, 1822I; Wandersmann, Opus 75, 1848I
Menken, Alan: Beauty & the Beast, 1994I
Mennin, Peter: Cantata de Virtue: The Pied Piper of Hamelin, 1969I; Canto for Orchestra, 1964I; Cello Concerto, 1956I; Chinese Poems (4), 1948I; Concertato, Moby Dick, 1952I; Concerto for Orchestra, 1944I; Flute Concerto, 1983I; Folk Overture, 1945I; Organ Sonata, 1941I; Piano Concerto, 1958I; Piano Pieces (5), 1949I; Piano Sonata, 1963I; Sinfonia for Large Orchestra, 1970I; Songs on Dickinson (4), 1941I; String Quartet No. 1, 1941I; String Quartet No. 2, 1951I; Symphony No. 1, 1941I; Symphony No. 2, 1944I; Symphony No. 3, 1946I; Symphony No. 4, "The Cycle," 1948I; Symphony No. 5, 1950I; Symphony No. 6, 1953I; Symphony No. 7, "Variation Symphony," 1963I; Symphony No. 8, 1973I; Symphony No. 9, "Sinfonia capricciosa," 1980I
Mennini, Louis: Mass, 1953I; The Rope, 1955I; String Quartet, 1961I; Symphony No. 1, "La Chiesa," 1960I; Symphony No. 2, "Da Festa," 1963I
Menotti, Gian Carlo: Amahl & the Night Visitors, 1951I; Amelia Goes to the Ball, 1936I; Apocalypse, 1951I; A Bride from Pluto, 1982I; Canti della lontananza, 1967I; Clarinet Trio, 1996I; The Consul, 1949I; Death of the Bishop of Brindisi, 1963I; Doublebass Concerto, 1983I; The Egg, 1976I; Errand into the Maze, 1947I; For the Death of Orpheus, 1990I; Goya, 1986I; Help! Help! The Globolinks, 1968I; The Hero, 1976I; The Island God, 1942I; Labyrinth, 1963I; Landscapes & Remembrances, 1976I; The Last Savage, 1963I; La Loca, 1979I; Maria Golovin, 1958I; Martin's Lie, 1964I; The Medium, 1945I; The Most Important Man, 1971I; The Old Maid & the Thief, 1939I; Piano Concerto No. 1 in F, 1945I; Piano Concerto No. 2, 1982I; Pieces (4) for String Quartet, 1936I; The Saint of Bleecker Street, 1954I; Sebastian, 1944I; Singing Child, 1993I; Suite for Two Cellos & Piano, 1973I; Symphony No. 1, "The Halcyon," 1976I; Tamu-Tamu, 1973I; The Telephone, 1946I; The Trial of the Gypsy, 1978I; Triple Concerto a tre, 1970I; The Unicorn, the Gorgon & the Manicore, 1956I; Variations on a Theme of Schumann, 1931I; Violin Concerto in a, 1952I
Mercadante, Saverio: Adriano in Siria, 1828I; Alfonso ed Elisa, 1822I; Amleto, 1822I; Anacreonte in Samo, 1820I; Andronico, 1821I; L'apoteosi d'Ercole, 1819I; Il bravo, 1839I; I Briganti, 1836I; Il califfo generoso, 1818I; Caritea, regina di Spagna, 1826I; Il conte di Essex, 1833I; Costanza ed Almeriska, 1823I; De profundis, 1844I; Didone abbandonata, 1823I; Don Chisciotte, 1829I; Doralice, 1824I; Le due illustri rivali, 1838I; I due Figaro, 1835I; Elena da Feltre, 1838I; Emma d'Antiochia, 1834I; Erode, 1825I; Ezio, 1827I; Il flauto incantato, 1818I; Flute Concerts (6), 1819I; Francesca da Rimini, 1828I; Francesco Donato, 1835I; Gabriella di Vergy, 1828I; Il gelosa ravveduto, 1820I; La Gioventù di Enrico V, 1834I; Il giuramento, 1837I; Gli sciti, 1823I; Gli amici di Siracusa, 1824I; Gran messa, 1868I; Ipermestra, 1825I; Ismalia, 1832I; Leonora, 1844I; Maria Stuarda regina di Scozia, 1821I; Mass for Male Voices, 1840I; Medea, 1851I; Il Montanaro, 1827I; Nitocri, 1824I; Il Normanni a Parigi, 1832I; Le nozze di Telemaco ed Antiope, 1824I; Omaggio a Rossini, 1868I; Orazi e Curiazi, 1846I; Pelagio, 1857I; I Portughesi nelle India, 1819I; I posto abbandonato, 1822I; Il Proscritto, 1842I; La rappresaglia, 1829I; Il reggente, 1843I; La shiava saracena, 1848I; Scipione in Cartagine, 1820I; Il servo balordo, 1818I; Seven Last Words of Christ, 1838I; Les soirées italiennes, 1836I; La solitaria dell'Asturie, 1840I; Statira, 1853I; La testa di bronzo, 1827I; Uggero il danese, 1834I; Il Vascello de Gama, 1845I; La vestale, 1840I; Violenza e costanza, 1820I; Violetta, 1853I; Virginia, 1866I; Zaïra, 1831I
Merikanto, Aarre: The Abduction of Kyllikki, 1930I; Ekho, 1922I; Piano Concerto No. 1, 1913I; Piano Concerto No. 2, 1937I; Piano Concerto No. 3, 1955I; String Sextet, 1932I; Cello concerto No. 1, 1919I; Cello Concerto No. 2, 1944I; Dance Suite, 1934I; Julia, 1922I; Lemminkäinen, 1916I; Nonetto for Mixed Ensemble, 1926I; Pan, 1924I; Partita, 1931I; Symphony No. 1, 1916I; Symphony No. 2, 1918I; Symphony No. 3, 1952I; Violin Concerto No. 1, 1916I; Violin Concerto No. 2, 1925I; Violin Concerto No. 3, 1931I; Violin Concerto No. 4, 1954
Meriläinen, Usko: Piano Sonata No. 1, 1960I; Piano Sonata No. 2, 1966I; Piano Sonata No. 3, 1972I; Piano Sonata No. 4, 1974I; Piano Sonata No. 5, 1992I

❄

A   Births　　B   Deaths　　C   Debuts　　D   New Positions
E   Prizes/Honors

Messager, André: *Amants éternels*, 1893I; *L'amour masqué*, 1923I; *Une aventure de la guimard*, 1900I; *La basoche*, 1890I; *La béarnaise*, 1885I; *Béatrice*, 1914I; *Le bourgeois de Calais*, 1887I; *Le chevalier d'Harmental*, 1896I; *Le chevalier aux fleurs*, 1897I; *Colibri*, 1889I; *Coups de noulis*, 1928I; *Les deux pigeons*, 1886I; *Don Juan et Haydée*, 1880I; *La fauvette du Temple*, 1885I; *La fiancée en Loterie*, 1896I; *Fleur d'oranger*, 1878I; *Fortunio*, 1907I; *François-les-Bas-Bleus*, 1883I; *Hélène*, 1891I; *Isoline*, 1888I; *Loreley*, 1880I; *Madame Chrysanthème*, 1893I; *Le mari de la reine*, 1889I; *Mignons et villains*, 1879I; *Mirette*, 1894I; *Miss Dollar*, 1893I; *Monsieur Beaucaire*, 1919I; *La montagne enchantée*, 1897I; *Nouveau printemps*, 1885I; *Passionnément*, 1926I; *Les p'tites michu*, 1897I; *Le Petit Poucet*, 1885I; *Le procès des roses*, 1896I; *Scaramouche*, 1891I; *Symphony in A*, 1875I; *Véronique*, 1898I; *Les vins de France*, 1879I
Messiaen, Olivier: *Apparition de l'église éternelle*, 1932I; *L'ascension*, 1933I; *Banquet céleste*, 1928I; *Le banquet eucharistique*, 1928I; *Cantéyodjayá*, 1948I; *Des canyons aux étoiles*, 1974I; *Catalogue d'Oiseaux*, 1958I; *Chants de Terre et de Ciel*, 1936I; *Chronochromie*, 1960I; *Le corps glorieux, sept visions brèves de la vie des ressuscités*, 1938I; *Diptyque, essai sur la vie terrestre et l'éternité bienheureuse*, 1930I; *Esquisse modale*, 1927I; *La fauvette des jardins*, 1971I; *Fugue in d*, 1928I; *Harawi, Chant d'amour et de mort*, 1945I; *L'hôte aimable des âmes*, 1928I; *Hymne au Saint Sacrement*, 1932I; *Le livre d'orgue*, 1951I; *Livre du Saint Sacrement for Organ*, 1984I; *Méditations sur le mystère de la Sainte Trinité*, 1969I; *Messe de la Pentecôte*, 1950I; *La Nativité du Seigneur*, 1935I; *Les offrandes oubliées*, 1930I; *Petite liturgies de la Présence Divine (3)*, 1944I; *Piano Preludes*, 1929I; *Pièce pour le tombeau de Paul Dukas*, 1935I; *Poèmes pour Mi*, 1935I; *Quartet for the End of Time*, 1940I; *Rechants (5)*, 1949I; *Réveil des oiseaux*, 1953I; *St. Francis of Assisi*, 1983I; *Theme & Variations*, 1932I; *Le tombeau respendissant*, 1931I; *La Transfiguration de Notre Seigneur Jésus-Christ*, 1969I; *La tristesse d'un grand ciel blanc*, 1925I; *Turangalila Symphony*, 1948I; *Variations écossaises*, 1928I; *Verset pour la fête de la dédicace*, 1960I; *Vingt Regards sur l'enfant Jésus*, 1944I; *Visions de l'amen*, 1943I
Messiter, Arthur: *Marion* (Rejoice, Ye Pure in Heart), 1883I
Mettraux, Laurent: *Fantasia*, 1995I; *Piano Trio No. 2*, 1996I; *String Quartet*, 1997I; *String Trio*, 1998I
Meulemans, Arthur: *Adriaen Brouwer*, 1926I; *Cello Concerto No. 1*, 1920I; *Cello Sonata*, 1953I; *Egmont*, 1944I; *Flute Concerto*, 1942I; *Harp Concerto*, 1953I; *Horn Concerto No. 1*, 1940I; *Oboe Concerto*, 1942I; *Organ Concerto No. 1*, 1942I; *Organ Concerto No. 2*, 1942I; *Organ Pieces (7)*, 1959I; *Organ Sonata*, 1915I; *Organ Symphony No. 1*, 1949I; *Organ Symphony No. 2*, 1949I; *Piano Concerto No. 1*, 1941I; *Piano Concerto No. 2*, 1956I; *Piano Concerto No. 3*, 1960I; *Piano Quartet*, 1915I; *Piano Sonata No. 1*, 1916I; *Piano Sonata No. 2*, 1917I; *Piano Sonata No. 3*, 1951I; *Pièce heroïque*, 1959I; *Pliny's Fountain*, 1913I; *String Quartet No. 1*, 1915I; *String Quartet No. 2*, 1932I; *String Quartet No. 3*, 1933I; *String Quartet No. 4*, 1944I; *String Quartet No. 5*, 1952I; *Symphony No. 1*, 1931I; *Symphony No. 2*, 1933I; *Symphony No. 3, "Dennen-Symphonie,"* 1933I; *Symphony No. 4*, 1934I; *Symphony No. 5*, 1939I; *Symphony No. 6*, 1940I; *Symphony No. 7*, 1942I; *Symphony No. 8*, 1942I; *Symphony No. 9*, 1943I; *Symphony No. 10*, 1943I; *Symphony No. 11*, 1946I; *Symphony No. 12*, 1948I; *Symphony No. 13, "Rembrandt,"* 1950I; *Symphony No. 14*, 1954I; *Symphony No. 15*, 1960I; *Trumpet Concerto*, 1943I; *Vikings*, 1919I; *Viola Concerto*, 1942I; *Viola Sonata*, 1953I; *Violin Concerto No. 1*, 1942I; *Violin Concerto No. 2*, 1946I; *Violin Concerto No. 3*, 1950I; *Violin Sonata No. 1*, 1915I; *Violin Sonata No. 2*, 1953I
Meulemans, Lodewijk: *The Myth of Spring*, 1895I
Meyer, Edgar: *Quintet for String Quartet & Double Bass*, 1995I
Meyer, Krzysztof: *Canti Amadei*, 1984I; *Symphony No. 1*, 1964I; *Symphony No. 2, "In Memoriam Stansilaw Wiechovicz,"* 1967I; *Symphony No. 3, "Symphonie d'Orphée,"* 1968I; *Symphony No. 4*, 1973I; *Symphony No. 5*, 1979I; *Symphony No. 6, "Polish,"* 1981I
Meyerbeer, Giacomo: *L'africaine*, 1863I; *Le bachelier de Salamanque*, 1815I; *Das Brandenburger Tor*, 1814I; *Concerto for Violin, Piano and Orchestra*, 1812I; *Costanza ed Almeriska*, 1823I; *Il crociato in Egitto*, 1824I; *Dem Vaterland*, 1842I; *Elegies and Romances (6)*, 1839I; *Emma di Resburgo*, 1819I; *L'esule di Granata*, 1822I; *L'étoile du nord*, 1854I; *Ein Feldlager in Schlesien*, 1844I; *Der Fischer und das Milchmädchen*, 1810I (Ballet); *Freundschaft*, 1842I; *Geistliche Gesänge*, 1811I; *Glimori di Teolindo*, 1816I; *Gott und die Natur*, 1811I; *Das Hoffest von Ferrara*, 1843I; *Les huguenots*, 1836I; *Ines di Castro*, 1825I; *Jephtas Gelübde*, 1812I; *La jeunesse de Goethe*, 1860I; *Judith*, 1854I; *Krönumgsmarsch*, 1861I; *Margherita d'Anjou*, 1820I; *Le pardon de Ploërmel*, 1859I; *Piano Concerto*, 1811I; *Le prophète*, 1849I; *Psalm XCI*, 1853I; *Robert, le diable*, 1831I; *Romilda e Costanze*, 1817I; *Schiller Centenary March*, 1859I; *Semiramide Riconosciuta*, 1819I; *Struensee*, 1846I; *Symphony No. 1 in E♭*, 1811I; *Wirth und Gast*, 1813I
Miaskovsky, Nikolai: *Alastor, Opus 14*, 1913I; *At Close of Day, Opus 21*, 1922I; *Cello Concerto in c, Opus 66*, 1945I; *Dramatic Overture in g, Opus 60*, 1942I; *From Youthful Years, Opus 2*, 1906I; *Kremlin at Night, Opus 75*, 1947I; *Lermontov Romances (12), Opus 40*, 1936I; *Meditations, Opus 1*, 1907I; *Piano Sonata No. 1 in d, Opus 6*, 1909I; *Piano Sonata No. 2 in f♯, Opus 13*, 1912I; *Piano Sonata No. 3 in c, Opus 19*, 1920I; *Piano Sonata No. 4 in c, Opus 27*, 1924I; *Piano Sonata No. 5, Opus 64/1*, 1944I; *Piano Sonata No. 6, Opus*

❖

F *Biographical*   G *Cultural Beginnings*   H *Musical Literature*
I *Musical Compositions*

Miaskovsky, Nikolai: (*cont.*)
64/2, 1944I; *Piano Sonata No. 7 in C, Opus 82*, 1949I; *Piano Sonata No. 8 in d, Opus 83*, 1949I; *Piano Sonata No. 9 in F, Opus 84*, 1949I; *Premonitions, Opus 16*, 1914I; *Reminiscences, Opus 29*, 1927I; *Silence, Opus 9*, 1908I; *Slavonic Rhapsody, Opus 71*, 1946I; *Songs of the Arctic Explorers (3)*, 1939I; *String Quartet (3), Opus 33*, 1930I; *String Quartet No. 4 in f, Opus 33/4*, 1937I; *String Quartet No. 5 in e, Opus 47*, 1939I; *String Quartet No. 6 in g, Opus 49*, 1940I; *String Quartet No. 7 in F, Opus 55*, 1941I; *String Quartet No. 8 in f♯, Opus 59*, 1942I; *String Quartet No. 9 in d, Opus 62*, 1943I; *String Quartet (No. 10 & 11), Opus 67*, 1945I; *String Quartet No 12 in G, Opus 77*, 1947I; *String Quartet No. 13 in a, Opus 86*, 1949I; *Symphony No. 1 in c, Opus 3*, 1908I; *Symphony No. 2 in c♯, Opus 11*, 1911I; *Symphony No. 3 in a, Opus 15*, 1914I; *Symphony No. 4 in e, Opus 17*, 1918I; *Symphony No. 5 in D, Opus 18*, 1918I; *Symphony No. 6 in e♭, Opus 23*, 1923I; *Symphony No. 7 in b, Opus 24*, 1923I; *Symphony No. 8 in A, Opus 64*, 1925I; *Symphony No. 9 in e, Opus 28*, 1927I; *Symphony No. 10 in f, Opus 30*, 1927I; *Symphony No. 11 in b♭, Opus 34*, 1932I; *Symphony No. 12 in g, Opus 35*, 1932I; *Symphony No. 13 in b♭, Opus 36*, 1933I; *Symphony No. 14 in C, Opus 37*, 1933I; *Symphony No. 15 in d, Opus 38*, 1934I; *Symphony No. 16 in F, Opus 39*, 1936I; *Symphony No. 17 in g♯, Opus 41*, 1937I; *Symphony No. 18 in c, Opus 42*, 1937I; *Symphony No. 19 in E♭, Opus 46*, 1938I; *Symphony No. 20 in e, Opus 50*, 1940I; *Symphony No. 21 in f♯, Opus 51*, 1940I; *Symphony No. 22 in b, "Ballad of the Patriotic War," Opus 54*, 1941I; *Symphony No. 23 in a, Opus 56*, 1941I; *Symphony No. 24 in f, Opus 63*, 1943I; *Symphony No. 25 in D♭, Opus 85*, 1950I; *Violin Concerto in d, Opus 44*, 1937I
Micheelsen, Hans F.: *Organ Concerto, "Is sungen drei Engel,"* 1943I; *Organ Concerto No. 3*, 1946I; *Organ Concerto No. 5*, 1954I; *Organ Concerto No. 6*, 1961I; *Organ Concerto No. 7, "Der Morgenstern,"* 1963I
Mielck, Ernst: *Piano Concert Piece*, 1898I; *Symphony in f*, 1897I
Migot, Georges: *Organ Book I*, 1933I; *De Grigny Tombeau*, 1938I
Miki, Minoru: *The Tale of Jenji*, 1999I; *Wakahimi*, 1991I
Mikolaiev, Alexei: *That Time in Seville*, 1973I
Milburn, Ellsworth: *The Stone Forest*, 1989I; *String Quartet No. 1*, 1974I; *String Quartet No. 2*, 1988I
Miles, C. A.: *I Come to the Garden Alone*, 1912I
Milhaud, Darius: *L'abandon d'Ariane, Opus 98*, 1927I; *Adieu, Opus 410*, 1964I; *Agamemnon*, 1913I; *Alissa, Opus 9*, 1913I; *Les amours de Ronsard, Opus 132*, 1934I; *L'apothéose de Molière, Opus 286*, 1948I; *Aspen Serenade, Opus 361*, 1957I; *Aubade, opus 387*, 1960I; *L'automne, Opus 115*, 1932I; *Le bal martiniquais, Opus 249*, 1944I; *Ballade for Piano & Orchestra, Opus 59*, 1920I; *Le boeuf sur le toit, Opus 58*, 1919I; *Bolivar, Opus 236*, 1943I; *Le candélabre à sept branches, Opus 315*, 1951I; *Cantate de Job, Opus 413*, 1965I; *Cantate de l'initiation, Opus 388*, 1960I; *Cantate de proverbes, Opus 310*, 1950I; *Cantate de Psaumes, Opus 425*, 1967I; *Cantate Nuptiale, Opus 168*, 1937I; *Cantate sur des textes de Chaucer, Opus 386*, 1960I; *Carnaval à Nouvelle Orléans, Opus 275*, 1947I; *Le carnaval d'Aix, Opus 83b*, 1926I; *Caroles, Opus 402*, 1963I; *Catalogue de fleurs, Opus 60*, 1920I; *Cello Concerto No. 1, Opus 136*, 1934I; *Cello Concerto No. 2, Opus 263*, 1946I; *Cello Sonata, Opus 377*, 1959I; *Chamber Symphony No. 1, "Printemps," Opus 43*, 1917I; *Chamber Symphony No. 2, "Pastorale," Opus 49*, 1918I; *Chamber Symphony No. 3, "Serenade," Opus 71*, 1921I; *Chamber Symphony No. 4, Opus 74*, 1921I; *Chamber Symphony No. 5, Opus 75*, 1922I; *Chansons (5), Opus 167*, 1935I; *Chansons bas, Opus 44*, 1917I; *Chansons de Négresse (3), Opus 148b*, 1936I; *Chansons de Ronsard*, 1941I; *Chants populaires hébraïques (6), Opus 86*, 1925I; *Chants de Misère (6), Opus 265*, 1946I; *Le château de feu, Opus 338*, 1954I; *La cheminée du roi René, Opus 205*, 1939I; *Les Choéphores, Opus 24*, 1915I; *Christopher Columbus, Opus 102*, 1928I; *Clarinet Concerto, Opus 230*, 1941I; *Concerto for Flute & Violin, Opus 197*, 1939I; *Concerto for Marimba & Vibe, Opus 278*, 1947I; *Concerto for Percussion & Small Orchestra*, 1930I; *Concerto for Two Pianos, Opus 228*, 1942I; *Concerto for Two Pianos & Four Percussionists, Opus 394*, 1961I; *Couronne de gloire, Opus 211*, 1940I; *La couronne de Marguerite, Opus 353*, 1956I; *La création du monde, Opus 81*, 1923I; *David, Opus 320*, 1952I; *La délivrance de Thésée, Opus 99*, 1927I; *Élégies (3), Opus 199*, 1939I; *L'enlèvement d'Europe, Opus 94*, 1927I; *Esquisses, (4), Opus 227*, 1941I; *Esther de Carpentras, Opus 89*, 1925I; *Etudes (5) for Piano & Orchestra, Opus 63*, 1920I; *Les Eumenides, Opus 41*, 1922I; *Fantaisie pastorale, Opus 188*, 1938I; *Fiesta, Opus 370*, 1958I; *Le globe-trotter, Opus 358*, 1956I; *Harp Concerto, Opus 323*, 1953I; *Harp Sonata, Opus 437*, 1971I; *Harpsichord Concerto, Opus 407*, 1964I; *L'homme et son désir, Opus 48*, 1918I; *Hymne de glorification, Opus 331*, 1954I; *Le jeu de Robin et de Marion*, 1948I; *Jewish Poems (8), Opus 34*, 1916I; *Une journée, Opus 269*, 1946I; *Kentuckiana, Opus 287*, 1948I; *Machines agricoles, Opus 56*, 1919I; *Les malheurs d'Orphée, Opus 24*, 1924I; *Maximilien, Opus 110*, 1930I; *Médée, Opus 191*, 1938I; *Mélodies: Pourquoi? (3), Opus 265*, 1930I; *La mère coupable, Opus 412*, 1964I; *Les miracles de la foi, Opus 324*, 1951I; *La muse ménagère, Opus 245*, 1945I; *Music for Boston, Opus 414*, 1965I; *Music for Graz, Opus 424*, 1969I; *Music for Indiana, Opus 418*, 1966I; *Music for Lisbon, Opus 420*, 1966I; *Music for New Orleans, Opus 422*, 1966I; *Music for Prague, Opus 415*, 1965I; *Music for San Francisco, Opus 436*, 1971I; *Naissance de Vénus, Opus 298*, 1949I; *Oboe Concerto, Opus 365*, 1957I; *Organ

---

A   *Births*   B   *Deaths*   C   *Debuts*   D   *New Positions*
E   *Prizes/Honors*

Preludes, (9), Opus 231b, 1942I; *Organ Sonata,* 1931I; *Ouverture méditerranéene, Opus 330,* 1953I;
Ouverture philharmonique, Opus 397, 1962I; *Pacem in terris, Opus 404,* 1963I; *Pastorale, Opus 229,* 1941I;
Le pauvre Matelot, Opus 92, 1926I; *Petite Suite, Opus 348,* 1955I; *Petites Légende, Opus 319,* 1952I; *Piano
Concerto No. 1, Opus 127,* 1933I; *Piano Concerto No. 2, Opus 225,* 1941I; *Piano Concerto No. 3, Opus 270,*
1946I; *Piano Concerto No. 4, Opus 295,* 1949I; *Piano Concerto No. 5, Opus 346,* 1955I; *Piano Quartet,
Opus 417,* 1966I; *Piano Trio, Opus 428,* 1968I; *Poème sur un cantique de Camarque, Opus 13,* 1914I;
Poèmes (8), Opus 37, 1916I; *Poèmes (3), Opus 276,* 1947I; *Poèmes de Catulle (4), Opus 80,* 1923I; *Poèmes de
Francis Jammes, Opus 50,* 1918I; *Poèmes de Jean Cocteau (3), Opus 59,* 1920I; *Poèmes de Jorge Guillen (8),
Opus 371,* 1958I; *Poems of Claudel (7), Opus 7,* 1913I; *Prière pour les morts, Opus 250,* 1945I; *Prières (5),
Opus 231c,* 1942I; *Le printemps, Opus 18,* 1914I; *Le printemps, Opus 25,* 1919I; *Psalm 129, Opus 53,*
1919I; *Psalme 136, Opus 53,* 1919I; *Psalmes de David (3), Opus 339,* 1954I; *Les quatre éléments, Opus 189,*
1938I; *Quintet No. 3, Opus 325,* 1953I; *Quintet No. 4 for Cello & String Quartet, Opus 350,* 1956I; *Rag
Caprices (3), Opus 78,* 1922I; *Le retour de l'enfant prodigue, Opus 42,* 1917I; *Le rêve de Jacob, Opus 294,*
1949I; *Sacred Service, Opus 279,* 1947I; *Saint Louis, roi de France,* 1970I; *Salade, Opus 83,* 1924I; *Saudades
do Brasil, Opus 67,* 1921I; *Scaramouch Suite for Two Pianos, Opus 165b,* 1937I; *Ségoviana for Guitar, Opus
366,* 1957I; *Les soirées de Pétrograd,* 1919I; *Sonata for Two Violins, Opus 15,* 1914I; *Sonata for Violin &
Harpsichord, Opus 257,* 1945I; *Sonata No. 1, Opus 33,* 1916I; *Sonata No. 2, Opus 293,* 1949I; *Sonatina,
Opus 354,* 1956I; *String Quartet No. 1, Opus 5,* 1912I; *String Quartet No. 2, Opus 16,* 1915I; *String
Quartet No. 3, Opus 22,* 1916I; *String Quartet No. 4, Opus 46,* 1918I; *String Quartet No. 5, Opus 64,*
1920I; *String Quartet No. 6, Opus 77,* 1922I; *String Quartet No. 7, Opus 87,* 1925I; *String Quartet No. 8,
Opus 121,* 1932I; *String Quartet No. 9, Opus 140,* 1934I; *String Quartet No. 10, Opus 218,* 1940I; *String
Quartet No. 11, Opus 232,* 1942I; *String Quartet No. 12, Opus 252,* 1945I; *String Quartet No. 13, Opus
268,* 1946I; *String Quartet No. 14, Opus 291,* 1949I; *String Quartet No. 15, Opus 291,* 1949I; *String
Quartet No. 16, Opus 303,* 1950I; *String Quartet No. 17, Opus 307,* 1950I; *String Quartet No. 18, Opus
308,* 1950I; *String Quintet, Opus 316,* 1952I; *String Septet, Opus 468,* 1964I; *String Sextet, Opus 368,*
1958I; *String Trio, Opus 274,* 1947I; *Suite campagnarde, Opus 329,* 1953I; *Suite de sonnets, Opus 401,*
1963I; *Suite for Two Pianos & Orchestra, Opus 300,* 1950I; *Suite Française, Opus 248,* 1944I; *Suite in G,
Opus 431,* 1969I; *Suite No. 1, Opus 12,* 1914I; *Suite Provençale, Opus 152b,* 1936I; *Symphonic Suite No. 2,
"Protée," Opus 57,* 1919I; *Symphony No. 1, Opus 210,* 1940I; *Symphony No. 2, Opus 247,* 1944I;
Symphony No. 3, Opus 271, 1946I; *Symphony No. 4, Opus 281,* 1947I; *Symphony No. 5, Opus 322,*
1953I; *Symphony No. 6, Opus 343,* 1955; *Symphony No. 7, Opus 344,* 1955I; *Symphony No. 8,
"Rhodanienne," Opus 362,* 1957I; *Symphony No. 9, Opus 380,* 1959I; *Symphony No. 10, Opus 382,*
1960I; *Symphony No. 11, "Romantique," Opus 384,* 1960I; *Symphony No. 12, "Rurale," Opus 390,*
1961I; *La tragédie humaine, Opus 369,* 1958I; *Le train bleu, Opus 84,* 1924I; *Variations on a Theme by
Cliquet, Opus 23,* 1915I; *Viola Concerto No. 1, Opus 108,* 1929I; *Viola Concerto No. 2, Opus 340,* 1955I;
Viola Sonata No. 1, Opus 240, 1944I; *Viola Sonata No. 2, Opus 244,* 1944I; *Violin Concerto No. 1, Opus
93,* 1927I; *Violin Concerto No. 2,* 1948I; *Violin Concerto No. 3,* 1958I; *Violin Sonata No. 1, Opus 3,*
1911I; *Violin Sonata No. 2, Opus 40,* 1917I; *Le voyage d'été, Opus 216,* 1946I; *West Point Suite, Opus
313,* 1951I; *Wind Quintet,* 1973I
Millöcker, Carl: *Bettelstudent,* 1882I
Mills, Charles: *String Quartet No. 1,* 1939I; *Symphony No. 5,* 1980I
Mills, Robert: *Symphonic Ode,* 1976I
Mimaroglu, Ilhan: *Agony,* 1965I; *Piano Preludes (12),* 1967I
Minchev, Georgi: *Fahrenheit 451,* 1993I; *SentiMetal Cello Concerto,* 1993I
Mirzoyan, Edvard: *String Quartet,* 1947I; *Symphony for Strings & Timpani,* 1962I
Miyoshi, Akira: *Concerto for Orchestra,* 1964I; *Ouverture de Fête,* 1973I; *Symphonic Movements (3),* 1960I
Mobberley, James: *Piano Concerto,* 1994I
Moeran, E. J.: *Cello Concerto,* 1945I; *Cello Sonata,* 1947I; *English Lyrics (4),* 1933I; *Fantasy-Quartet for Oboe
& Strings,* 1946I; *Phyllide & Corydon,* 1934I; *Piano Pieces (3),* 1919I; *Piano Trio in D,* 1920I; *Poems of
James Joyce (7),* 1927I; *Shakespeare Songs (4),* 1940I; *Sonata for Two Violins,* 1930I; *Songs of Springtime,*
1934I; *String Quartet,* 1921I; *String Trio in G,* 1931I; *Suffolk Folksongs (6),* 1931I; *Symphony in g,* 1837I;
Violin Sonata in e, 1923I
Moevs, Robert: *Endymion,* 1948I; *Main-Travelled Roads* (Sym. Piece No. 6), 1973I; *Pandora: Music for
Small Orchestra II,* 1983I; *Piano Sonata,* 1950I; *Piano Sonatina,* 1947I; *Prometheus: Music for Small
Orchestra I,* 1980I; *String Quartet No. 1,* 1957I; *Symphonic Pieces (3),* 1955I; *Symphonic Piece No. 5,*
1984I; *Variations for Orchestra (14),* 1952I
Mohr, Christopher: *From the Realm of the shadow,* 1991I
Moineau, Georges: *Messe Solennelle de Saint Remi,* 1958I
Mollicone, Henry: *Coyote Tales,* 1997I

❈

Mondonville, Jean-Joseph de: *Daphnis et Alcimadure*, 1754I; *Les fêtes de Paphos*, 1762I; *Les fureurs de Saul*, 1759I; *Les israelites au Mont Oreb*, 1758I; *Les projets de l'amour*, 1771I; *Psyche*, 1762I; *Thesee*, 1765I; *Les Titans*, 1761I; *Titon et 'Aurore*, 1753I; *Venus et Adonis*, 1752I

Moniuszko, Stanislaw: *Bajka Overture*, 1848I; *Ballad of Florian the Grey*, 1859I; *Beata*, 1871I; *Bettly*, 1852I; *The Bureaucrats*, 1834I; *The Countess*, 1860I; *Crimean Sonnets*, 1867I; *The Devil's Joke*, 1870I; *Funeral Mass in g*, 1873I; *The Gypsies*, 1850I; *Halka*, 1847I; *Hamlet*, 1871I; *The Haunted Manor*, 1864I; *Ideal*, 1841I; *In the Quarters*, 1868I; *Kaim Overture*, 1856I; *The Lottery*, 1842I; *Mass in d, "Funeral Mass,"* 1850I; *Mass No. 2 in e*, 1855I; *Mass No. 3 in E♭*, 1865I; *Mass No. 4 in a*, 1870I; *Mass No. 5 in B♭*, 1872I; *Mass No. 7 in D♭*, 1874I; *The Merchant of Venice*, 1871I; *Milda*, 1848I; *Military Overture*, 1857I; *Monte Cristo*, 1866I; *The New Don Quixote*, 1841I; *A Night in the Apennines*, 1838I; *Ninola*, 1852I; *Paria*, 1869I; *Phantoms*, 1865I; *Polonaise de concert*, 1866I; *The Raftsman*, 1858I; *Requiem*, 1890I; *The Robbers*, 1871I; *Verbum nobile*, 1860I

Monk, Meredith: *Atlas*, 1992I

Monpou, Hippolyte: *La chaste Suzanne*, 1839I; *Un conte d'autrefois*, 1838I; *Lambert Simnel*, 1843I; *Le luthier de Vienne*, 1836I; *La perugina*, 1838I; *Piquillo*, 1837I; *Le planteur*, 1839I; *La reine Jeanne*, 1840I

Monsigny, Pierre: *Aline, reine de Golconde*, 1766I; *Les aveux indiscrets*, 1759I; *Le belle Arsène*, 1773I; *Le bouquet de Thalie*, 1764I; *Le cadi dupé*, 1761I; *Le déserteur*, 1769I; *Le faucon*, 1771I; *Félix, ou l'enfant trouvé*, 1777I; *L'isle sonnante*, 1767I; *Le maître en droit*, 1760I; *Le nouveau monde*, 1763I; *On ne s'avise jamais de tout*, 1761I; *Pagamin da Monègue*, 1770I; *Le rendez-vous bien employé*, 1774I; *Le roi et le fermier*, 1762I; *Rose et Colas*, 1764I; *La rosiére de Salency*, 1769I

Monsonyi Mihály: *Pretty Helen*, 1861I

Montague, Stephen: *Behold a Pale Horse*, 1991I; *Piano Concerto*, 1997I; *Silence: John, Yvar & Tim*, 1994I; *Snakebite*, 1995I; *String Quartet No. 1, No. 2, "Shaman,"* 1993I; *Southern Lament*, 1997I; *Vlug*, 1992I

Monti, Gaetano: *L'Adriano in Siria*, 1775I; *La Contadina accorta*, 1781I; *La donna fedele*, 1784I; *Le donne vendicate*, 1781I; *Il gelosa sincerato*, 1779I; *Lo studente*, 1783I

Montsalvatge, Xavier: *Laberinto*, 1971I; *Sortilegis*, 1992I

Moore, Douglas: *The Ballad of Baby Doe*, 1956I; *Carrie Nation*, 1966I; *The Devil & Daniel Webster*, 1938I; *The Emperor's New Clothes*, 1948I; *Farm Journal*, 1947I; *Gallantry*, 1958I; *Giants in the Earth*, 1949I; *The Headless Horseman*, 1936I; *In Memoriam*, 1943I; *Moby Dick*, 1928I; *Overture on an American Tune*, 1932I; *The Pageant of P. T. Barnum*, 1924I; *Passacaglia*, 1939I; *Piano Pieces (4)*, 1955I; *Piano Suite*, 1948I; *String Quartet No. 1*, 1933I; *A Symphony of Autumn*, 1930I; *Symphony No. 2 in A*, 1945I; *White Wings*, 1935I; *The Wings of the Dove*, 1961I

Moore, Mary Carr: *Beyond These Hills*, 1924I; *Narcissa*, 1911I; *Piano Concerto*, 1934I; *String Quartet in f*, 1930I; *String Quartet in g*, 1926I

Morales, Melesio: *La locomotiva*, 1869I

Moran, Robert: *Desert of Roses*, 1992I; *The Dracula Diary*, 1994I; *From the Towers of the Moon*, 1991I

Moravec, Paul: *Missa Miserere*, 1981I

Morlacchi, Francesco: *Le avventure d'una giornata*, 1809I; *Il barbiere di Siviglia*, 1816I; *La capricciosa pentita*, 1816I; *Colombo*, 1828I; *Il corradino*, 1808I; *Le Danaïdi*, 1810I; *Donna Aurora*, 1821I; *Francesco da Rimini*, 1839I; *Gianni di Parigi*, 1818I; *La gioventu di Enrico V*, 1822I; *Ilda d'Avenel*, 1824I; *Isaaco, Figura di Redentroe*, 1817I; *Laodicea*, 1817I; *Mass No. 1*, 1801I; *Mass for the King of Saxony*, 1814I; *Mass No. 10*, 1841I; *Messe a capella*, 1818I; *Miserere for Sixteen Voices*, 1807I; *La Morte d'Abel*, 1821I; *Oreste*, 1808I; *La passione*, 1811I; *Il poeta spiantata*, 1807I; *La principessa per ripiego*, 1809I; *Raoul de Créqui*, 1811I; *Requiem for the King of Saxony*, 1827I; *Rinaldo d'Asti*, 1809I; *Il ritratto*, 1807I; *Russian Mass*, 1813I; *I saraceni in Sicilia*, 1828I; *La semplicetta di Pirna*, 1817I; *La simoncino*, 1809I; *Tebaldo e Isolina*, 1822I

Moross, Jerome: *The Last Judgment*, 1953I; *Sonata for Piano, Four Hands*, 1975I; *Sorry, Wrong Number*, 1977I

Morris, Harold: *String Quartet No. 1*, 1928I; *Symphony No. 2, "Prospice,"* 1925I

Morris, Kenneth: *Just a Closer Walk with Thee*, 1940I

Morse, Theodore: *M-O-T-H-E-R*, 1915I

Mortensen, Finn: *Wind Quintet*, 1944I

Moscheles, Ignaz: *Anklänge aus Schottland, Opus 75*, 1826I; *Etudes, Opus 70*, 1826I; *Études caractteristic, Opus 95*, 1836I; *Fantaisie sur des airs des bardes écossais, Opus 80*, 1828I; *Frühlingslied, Opus 125*, 1850I; *Grand sonata concertante, Opus 44*, 1819I; *Grand sonata symphonique No. 2*, 1845I; *Introduction & Scottish Rondo, Opus 93*, 1821I; *La marche d'Alexandre, Opus 32*, 1815I; *Overture, Joan of Arc, Opus 91*, 1835I; *Piano Concerto No. 1 in F, Opus 45*, 1819I; *Piano Concerto No. 2 in E♭, Opus 56*, 1823I; *Piano Concerto No. 3 in g, Opus 60*, 1820I; *Piano Concerto No. 4 in F, Opus 64*, 1823I; *Piano Concerto No. 5 in C, Opus 87*, 1826I; *Piano Concerto No. 6 in B♭, Opus 90*, 1833I; *Piano Concerto No. 7 in c, "Pathétique," Opus 93*, 1836I; *Piano Concerto No. 8 in D, "Pastoral," Opus 96*, 1838I; *Piano Sonata, "Caractéristique." Opus*

❖

A   *Births*   B   *Deaths*   C   *Debuts*   D   *New Positions*
E   *Prizes/Honors*

27, 1814I; *Piano Sonata, Opus 41*, 1816I; *Piano Sonata, Opus 47*, 1816I; *Preludes (50), Opus 73*, 1827I;
Septet in D, Opus 88, 1832I; *Sextet, Opus 35*, 1815I; *Songs (12), Opus 117, 119*, 1845I; *Souvenirs d'Irlande,
Opus 69*, 1826I; *Symphony No. 1 in C, Opus 81*, 1829I
Mosolov, Alexander: *Cello Concerto*, 1946I; *The Iron Foundry*, 1927I; *String Quartet No. 1*, 1926I; *String
Quartet No. 2*, 1942I
Mosonyi, Mihály: *Festival Music*, 1860I; *Kaiser Max auf der Martinswand*, 1857I; *Mass No. 1 in C*, 1842I;
Mass No. 3 in F, 1849I; *Mass No. 4*, 1854I; *Overture in b, Opus 15*, 1842I; *Piano Concerto in e*, 1844I;
Pretty Helen, 1861I; *String Sextet*, 1844I; *Symphony No. 1 in D*, 1844I; *Symphony No. 2 in a*, 1856I
Mostad, John: *Cello Concerto*, 1990I
Mount-Edgcumbe, Richard: *Zenobia*, 1800I
Moyzes, Alexander: *Symphony No. 1*, 1929I; *Symphony No. 2*, 1932I
Mozart, Wolfgang Amadeus: *The Abduction from the Seraglio*, 1782I; *Adagio & Allegro, K. 594, for
Mechanical Organ*, 1790I; *Adagio & Fugue in c, K. 546*, 1788I; *Adagio & Rondo in c, K. 617*, 1791I; *Apollo
et Hyacinthus*, 1767I; *Ascanio in Alba*, 1771I; *Bassoon Concerto in B♭, K. 191*, 1774I; *Bastien und Bastienne,
K. 50*, 1768I; *La Betulia liberata, K. 188*, 1771I; *Clarinet Concerto in A, K. 622*, 1791I; *Clarinet Quintet in
A, K. 581*, 1789I; *La clemenze di Tito, K. 621*, 1791I; *Concerto for Flute and Harp in C, K. 299*, 1778I;
Concerto Rondo, K. 371, for Horn, 1781I; *Concerto No. 7 in F for Three Pianos, K. 242*, 1776I; *Concerto No.
10 in E♭ for Two Pianos, K. 365*, 1779I; *Cosi fan tutti, K. 588*, 1790I; *Dixit Dominus, Magnificat in C., K.
193*, 1774I; *La finta giardiniera*, 1775I; *La finta semplice, K. 51*, 1768I; *Flute Concerto in G, K. 313*, 1778I;
Flute Concerto in D, K. 314, 1778I; *Grabmusik, K. 42*, 1767I; *Horn Concerto No. 2 in E♭, K. 417*, 1783I;
Horn Concerto No. 3 in E♭, K. 495, 1786I; *Horn Concerto No. 4 in E♭, K. 447*, 1787I; *Idomeneo, K. 366*,
1781I; *Lucio Silla, K. 135*, 1772I; *The Magic Flute, K. 620*, 1791I; *Marriage of Figaro, The, K 492*, 1786I;
Masonic Funeral Music in c, K. 477, 1785I; *Mass in C, "Dominicus," K. 66*, 1769I; *Mass in C., K. 167
"Trinitatis,"* 1773I; *Mass in C, K. 257 "Credo,"* 1776I; *Mass in C,"Coronation," K. 317*, 1779I; *Die
Mauerfreude, K. 471*, 1785I; *Miserere in a, K. 85*, 1770I; *Missa Brevis in D, K. 65*, 1769I; *Missa Brevis in g,
K. 140*, 1773I; *Missa Brevis in D., K. 194*, 1774I; *Missa Brevis in F, K. 192*, 1774I; *Missa Brevis in G, K.
220*, 1775I; *Missa Brevis in C, K. 258 "Spaur,"* 1776I; *Missa Brevis in C, K. 259 "Organ Solo," 176*II; *Missa
Brevis in B♭, K. 275*, 1777I; *Missa Longa in C, K .62*, 1775I; *Mitridate*, 1770I; *Motet, "Ave verum corpus," K.
618*, 1791I; *Motet in F, K. 165 "Exultate Jubilate,"* 1773I; *Musical Joke, A, K. 522*, 1787I; *L'oca del Cairo*,
1783I; *Organ Sonatas No. 1-3*, 1767I; *Organ Sonata No. 6, K. 212*, 1775I; *Piano Concerto No. 5 in D, K. 175*,
1773I; *Piano Concerto No. 6 in B♭, K. 238*, 1776I; *Piano Concerto No. 8 in C, K. 246*, 1776I; *Piano Concerto
No. 9 in E♭, K. 271*, 1777I; *Piano Concerto No. 11 in F, K. 413*, 1783I; *Piano Concerto No. 12 in A, K. 414*,
1782I; *Piano Concerto No. 13 in C, K. 415*, 1783I; *Piano Concerto No. 14 in E♭, K. 449*, 1784I; *Piano Concerto
No. 15 in B♭, K. 450*, 1784I; *Piano Concerto No. 16 in D, K. 451*, 1784I; *Piano Concerto No. 17 in G, K. 453*,
1784I; *Piano Concerto No. 18 in B♭, K. 456*, 1784I; *Piano Concerto No. 19 in F, K. 459*, 1784I; *Piano Concerto
No. 20 in d, K. 466*, 1785I; *Piano Concerto No. 21 in C, K. 467*, 1785I; *Piano Concerto No. 22 in E♭, K. 482*,
1785I; *Piano Concerto No. 23 in E, K. 488*, 1786I; *Piano Concerto No. 24 in c, K. 491*, 1786I; *Piano Concerto
No. 25 in C, K. 503*, 1786I; *Piano Concerto No. 26 in D, K. 537, "Coronation,"* 1788I; *Piano Concerto No. 27
in B♭, K. 595*, 1791I; *Piano Quartet in g, K. 478*, 1785I; *Piano Quartet in E♭, K. 493*, 1786I; *Piano Trio in d, K.
442*, 1783I; *Piano Trios (G,E♭,B♭) K. 496,498,502*, 1786I; *Piano Trios No. 8-10, K. 542,548,564*, 1788I; *Quartet,
Flute & Strings, K. 198*, 1778I; *Quartet, Flute & Strings, K. 278*, 1777I; *Quartet, Flute & Strings, K. 285b*,
1781I; *Quartet, Oboe & Strings, K. 370*, 1781I; *Quintet in E♭, Piano & Winds, K. 452*, 1784I; *Il re pastore*,
1775I; *Requiem in d, H.626*, 1791I; *Die Schauspieldirektor K. 486*, 1786I; *Die Schuldigheit des ersten Gebots*,
1767I; *Serenade in c, K. 388*, 1782I; *Serenade in D, "Haeffner," K. 250*, 1776I; *Serenade in D, "Notturna," K.
239*, 1776I; *Serenade, K. 525, "Eine kleine Nachtmusik"* 1787I; *Serenade in D, K. 203*, 1774I; *Serenade in D, K.
204*, 1775I; *Serenade in D, K. 320, "Posthorn,"* 1779I; *Serenades, K. 361*, 1781I; *Serenades, K. 375 for Winds*,
1781I; *Sinfonia Concertante in E♭, K. 364*, 1779I; *Il sogno di scipione*, 1772I; *Solemn Mass in C, K. 337*, 1780I;
Lo sposo deluso, 1783I; *Stabat Mater, K. 33c*, 1766I; *String Quartet in G, K .80*, 1770I; *String Quartet in D,
K. 155*, 1772I; *String Quartet in C, K. 157*, 1773I; *String Quartet in F, K. 158*, 1773I; *String Quartet in B♭, K.
159*, 1773I; *String Quartet in E♭, K 160*, 1773I; *String Quartet in F, K. 168*, 1773I; *String Quartet in A, K. 169*,
1773I; *String Quartet in C, K. 170*, 1773I; *String Quartet in E♭, K. 171*, 1773I; *String Quartet in B♭, K. 172*,
1773I; *String Quartet in d, K. 173*, 1773I; *String Quartet in G, K. 387*, 1782I; *String Quartet in D, K. 421*,
1783I; *String Quartet in E♭, K. 428*, 1783I; *String Quartet in B♭, K. 458*, 1784I; *String Quartet in A, K. 464*,
1785I; *String Quartet in C, K. 465*, 1785I; *String Quartet in D Major, K. 499*, 1786I; *String
Quartet,"Prussian I," K. 575*, 1789I; *String Quartets (2) "Prussian II, III," K. 589, 590*, 1790I; *String Quintet
in B♭, K. 174*, 1773I; *String Quintet in C, K. 515*, 1787I; *String Quintet in g, K. 516*, 1787I; *String Quintet in
D, K. 593*, 1790I; *String Quintet in E♭, K. 614*, 1791I; *String Trio in E♭, K. 547*, 1788I; *String Trio in E♭, K. 563*,
1788I; *Symphonie concertante in E♭, K. 364*, 1779I; *Symphony (No. 42) in B♭, K. 75*, 1771I; *Symphony (No.
43) in F, K. 76*, 1767I; *Symphony (No. 44) in D, K. 81*, 1770I; *Symphony (No.45) in D,*

❆

F   *Biographical*   G   *Cultural Beginnings*   H   *Musical Literature*
                I   *Musical Compositions*

Mozart, Wolfgang Amadeus: (cont.)
   K. 95, 1770I; Symphony (No. 46) in D, K. 96, 1771I; Symphony (No. 47) in D, K. 97, 1770I; Symphony (No.
   50) in D, K. 161,3, 1774I; Symphony (No. 55) in B♭, K. a214, 1768I; Symphony in B♭, K. a217, 1769I;
   Symphony in B♭, K. a218, 1769I; Symphony in C, K. a222, 1765I; Symphony in F, K. a223, 1765I; Symphony
   No. 1 in E♭, K. 16, 1764I; Symphony No. 4 in D, K. 19, 1765I; Symphony No. 5 in B♭, K. 22, 1765I; Symphony
   No. 6 in F, K. 43, 1767I; Symphony No. 7 in d, K. 45, 1768I; Symphony No. 8 in D. K. 48, 1768I; Symphony
   No. 9 in C, K. 73, 1772I; Symphony No. 10 in G, K. 74, 1770I; Symphony No. 11, K. 84, 1770I; Symphony
   No. 12 in G, K. 110, 1771I; Symphony No. 13 in F K. 112, 1771I; Symphony No. 14 in A, K. 114, 1771I;
   Symphony No. 15 in G, K. 124, 1772I; Symphony No. 16 in C, K. 128, 1772I; Symphony No. 17 in G, K. 129,
   1772I; Symphony No. 18 in F, K. 130, 1772I; Symphony No. 19 in E♭, K. 132, 1772I; Symphony No. 20 in D,
   K. 133, 1772I; Symphony No. 21 in A, K. 134, 1772I; Symphony No. 22 in c, K. 162, 1773I; Symphony No. 23
   in D, K. 181, 1773I; Symphony No. 24 in B♭, K. 182, 1773I; Symphony No. 25 in g, K. 183, 1773I; Symphony
   No. 26 in E♭, K. 184, 1773I; Symphony No. 27 in G, K. 199, 1773I; Symphony No. 28 in C, K. 200, 1774I;
   Symphony No. 29 in A, K. 201, 1774I; Symphony No. 30 in D, K. 202, 1774I; Symphony No. 31, "Paris," K.
   297, 1778I; Symphoniy No. 32 in G, K. 318, 1779I; Symphony No. 33 in B♭, K. 319, 1779I; Symphony No. 34
   in C, K. 338, 1780I; Symphony No. 35 in E, "Haffner," K. 385, 1782I; Symphony No. 36 in C, K. 425, "Linz,"
   1783I; Symphony No. 38 in D, K. 504 "Prague," 1786I; Symphony No. 39 in E♭, 1788I; Symphony No. 40 in
   g, K. 550, 1788I; Symphony No. 41 in C, "Jupiter," K. 551, 1788I; Te Deum in C, K. 141, 1769I; Variations,
   "Ah vous dirai-je, Maman," K. 265, 1782I; Variations in G, K. 359, in g, K. 360, 1781I; Vesper Service in C.,
   K. 321, 1779I; Vespers in C, K. 339, 1780I; Violin Concerto No. 2 in D, K. 211, 1775I; Violin Concerto No 3 in
   G, K. 126, 1775I; Violin Concerto No. 4 in D, K. 218, 1775I; Violin Concerto No. 5 in A, K. 219, 1775I; Violin
   Sonatas (10), K. 6-15, 1764I; Violin Sonatas (6), K. 26-31, 1766I; Violin Sonatas (4), K. 376,7, 379, 380,
   1781I; Violin Sonata in A, K. 402, 1782I; Violin Sonata in C, K. 404, 1782I; Violin Sonata in B♭, K. 454,
   1784I; Violin Sonata in E♭, K. 481, 1785I; Violin Sonata in A, K. 526, 1787I; Zaide, K. 344, 1779I
Muczynski, Robert: Cello Sonata, Opus 25, 1968I; Dream Cycle, Opus 44, 1983I; Masks, Opus 40, 1980I;
   Maverick Pieces for Piano, 1976I; Moments, 1992I; Piano Concerto, Opus 7, 1954I; Saxophone Concerto,
   Opus 41, 1981I; Saxophone Sonata, 1970I; Sketches (5), Opus 3, 1952I; Sonata No. 1, Opus 9, 1957I; Sonata
   No. 2, Opus 22, 1966I; Sonata No. 3, Opus 35, 1974I; Summer Journal, A, Opus 19, 1964I; Symphonic
   Dialogues, Opus 20, 1965I; Woodwind Quintet, Opus 45, 1985I
Müller, August E.: Caprices (6), Opus 29, 1808I; Caprices (3), Opus 31, 1809I; Caprices (3), Opus 34, 1812I;
   Caprices (3), Opus 41, 1818I; German Songs (12), Volume 1, 1796I; Piano Concerto No. 1, Opus 1, 1792I;
   Piano Concerto No. 2, Opus 21, 1802I; Piano Sonatas (3), Opus 18, 1802I; Piano Sonata, Opus 26, 1806I;
   Piano Sonata, Opus 36, 1813I; Piano Sonatinas (3), Opus 14, 1801I; Sammlung von Orgelstücken, 1798I;
   Variations on Mozart, Opus 32, 1810I
Müller, Gottfried: Concerto for Orchestra, 1937I
Müller (-Zürich) Paul: Trio in c for Piano, Clarinet & Strings, 1937I; Viola Concerto, 1934I; Violin Sonata,
   1941I
Müller, Wenzel: Aline, 1822I; Der Alpenkönig und der Menschenfeind, 1828I; Der Fagottist, 1792I; Der
   Fiaker als Marquis, 1816I; Das lustige Beilager, 1797I; Der Schlossgärtner und der Windmüller, 1813I; Die
   Schwestern von Prag, 1794I; Der Sonnofest der Braminen, 1790I; Der Sturm, 1798I
Mumma, Gordon: Aleutian Displacement, 1987I; Begault Meandown Sketches, 1987I; Conspiracy 8, 1970I;
   Cybersonic Cantilevers, 1973I; Echo, 1978I; Epoxy, 1962I; Hornpipe, 1967I; Le Corbusier, 1965I; Megaton
   for Wm. Burroughs, 1963I; Mesa, 1966I; Music from the Venezia Space Theater, 1964I; Passenger Pigeon
   1776, 1976I; Piano Gestures II, 1962I; Sinfonia, 1960I
Musgrave, Thea: Beauty & the Beast, 1969I; Chamber Concerto No. 1, 1962I; A Christmas Carol, 1979I;
   Concerto for Orchestra, 1967I; The Decision, 1965I; Festival Overture, 1965I; The Five Ages of Man, 1963I;
   Harriet, The Woman Called Moses, 1984; Horn Concerto, 1971I; Mary, Queen of Scots, 1977I; Music for
   Horn & Piano, 1967I; Nocturne & Arias, 1966I; An Occurrence at Owl Creek Bridge, 1981I; Orfeo II, 1975I;
   Peripateia, 1981I; The Phoenix & the Turtle, 1962I; Piano Sonata No. 2, 1956I; Simón Bolivar, 1994I; Space
   Play, 1974I; String Quartet, 1958I; Viola Concerto, 1973I; The Voice of Ariadne, 1973I
Musil, Frantiek: Sonata solemnis, 1882I
Mussorgsky, Modest: Boris Goudonov, 1869I; The Fair at Sorochinski, 1881I; The Flea, 1879I; From
   Memories of Childhood, 1865I; Hopak, 1866I; Khovantchina, 1880I; The Marriage, 1868I; A Night on Bald
   Mountain, 1867I; The Nursery, 1872I; The Rout of Sennacherib, 1867I; Songs and Dances of Death, 1877I;
   Pictures at an Exhibition, 1874I; Scherzo in c♯, 1858I; Scherzo in B♭, 1858I; Souvenirs d'enfance, 1857I;
   Sunless, 1874I
Mustonen, Olli: Fantasia (piano, strings), 1985I
Myers, Theldon: Symphony 1969, 1969I
Mykietyn, Pawel: Cello Concerto, 1998I; Eine Kleine Herbstmusik, 1995I; String Quartet, 1998I; Piano
   Concerto, 1996I; Violin Concerto, 1998I

❁

A   Births   B   Deaths   C   Debuts   D   New Positions
E   Prizes/Honors

Myron, Tom: *Symphony No. 2*, 2000I
Mysliveček, Josef: *Adamo ed Eva*, 1771I; *Adriano in Siria*, 1776I; *Antigona*, 1774I; *Antigono*, 1780I; *Armida*, 1779I; *Artaserse*, 1774I; *Atide*, 1774I
Mysliveček Josef: *Il Bellerofonte*, 1767I; *La Calliroe*, 1778I; *La Circe*, 1779I; *La clemenza di Tito*, 1773I; *Il Demetrio, I*, 1779I; *Il Demetrio, II*, 1773I; *Il Demofoonte, I*, 1769I; *Ezio*, 1775I; *La famiglia di Tobia*, 1769I; *Farnace*, 1767I; *Giuseppe riconosciuto*, 1771I; *Il Gran Tamerlano*, 1771I; *L'ipermestra*, 1769I; *Isaaco Figura del Redentore*, 1776I; *La liberazione d' Israele*, 1775I; *Medea*, 1764I; *Medonte*, 1780I; *Merope*, 1775I; *Montezuma*, 1771I; *La nitteti*, 1770I; *L'Olimpiade*, 1778I; *Orchestral Trios (4) for Strings* 1772I; *Overtures (6)*, 1775I; *La Passione di Gesù Cristo*, 1773I; *Romolo ed Ersillia*, 1773I; *Sinfonia concertante (6), Opus 2*, 1768I; *Sinfonie a quatre, Opus 1*, 1763I; *String Quartets (6), Opus 2*, 1781I; *String Quartets (6), Opus 1*, 1780I; *Il tempio d'eternita*, 1777I; *Trio Sonatas (6), Opus 1*, 1768I; *Trionfo di Clelia, Il*, 1767I; *Trios (6), Flute, Violin, Cello*, 1795I
Nabokov, Nicolas: *Bassoon Sonata*, 1941I; *Canzone, Introduzione e Allegro*, 1950I; *Cello Concerto, "Les hommages,"* 1953I; *Concerto corale* (flute, piano, strings), 1950I; *Don Quixote*, 1965I; *Flute Concerto*, 1948I; *The Holy Devil*, 1958I; *Job*, 1933I; *The Last Flower*, 1941I; *Love's Labour Lost*, 1973I; *Lyric Songs (6)*, 1966I; *Ode: Méditation sur la majesté de Dieu*, 1928I; *Piano Concerto*, 1932I; *Piano Sonata No. 1*, 1926I; *Piano Sonata No. 2*, 1940I; *Poems (4) by Boris Pasternak*, 1961I; *Poems by Anna Akhmatova (5)*, 1964I; *The Return of Pushkin*, 1947I; *Samson Agonistes*, 1938I; *Serenata estiva*, 1937I; *Symphonic Variations*, 1967I; *Symphony No. 1, "Symphonie lyrique,"* 1930I; *Symphony No. 2, "Biblica,"* 1940I; *Symphony No. 3*, 1967I; *Union Pacific*, 1934I; *La vie de Polichinelle*, 1934I
Nadarejshuili, Zurab: *String Quartet No. 1*, 1987I
Nancarrow, Conlon: *String Quartet No. 1*, 1945I; *String Quartet No. 3*, 1988I
Nápravník, Eduard: *Ballades (2), Opus 26* (violin), 1877I; *Cantata in C*, 1862I; *Cello Suite No. 1 in D, Opus 29*, 1879I; *Cello Suite No. 2 in A, Opus 36*, 1881I; *Don Juan*, 1891; *Dubrovsky, Opus 58*, 1895I; *Fantasy on Russian Themes, Opus 30*, 1878I; *Fantasy on Russian Themes, Opus 39*, 1881I; *Francesca da Rimini*, 1903I; *Harold, Opus 45*, 1886I; *The Inhabitants of Nishij Novgorod, Opus 15*, 1868I; *Piano Concerto, Opus 27*, 1877I; *Piano Quartet in a, Opus 42*, 1882I; *Piano Trio No. 1 in g, Opus 24*, 1876I; *Piano Trio No. 2 in d, Opus 62*, 1897I; *Pieces (4) for Cello & Piano, Opus 64*, 1897I; *Solemn Overture, Opus 14*, 1866I; *String Quartet No. 1 in E, Opus 16*, 1873I; *String Quartet No. 2 in A*, 1878I; *String Quartet No. 3 in C, Opus 65*, 1897I; *Suite in A for Cello, Opus 49*, 1881I; *Suite for Cello & Orchestra, Opus 60*, 1898I; *Symphony No. 1*, 1861I; *Symphony No. 2 in C, Opus 17*, 1873I; *Symphony No. 3 in c, "The Demon," Opus 18*, 1874I; *Symphony No. 4 in d, Opus 32*, 1879I; *Violin Sonata in G, Opus 52*, 1892I; *Vostok, Opus 40*, 1881I
Nardini, Pietro: *Flute/Violin Sonatas (6)*, 1765I; *String Quartets (6)*, 1782I; *Violin Concertos (6), Opus 1*(?), 1765I; *Violin Sonatas (6), Opus 2*, 1770I; *Violin Sonatas (6), Opus 5*, 1769I
Nash, Gary Powell: *In Memoriam: Sojourner Truth*, 1992I
Nash, Peter Paul: *Symphony No. 1*, 1991I
Naumann, Emil: *Christus der Friedensbote*, 1848I; *Concert Overture, Loreley, Opus 25*, 1864I; *Dank- und Jubel-Cantate, Opus 30*, 1866I; *Judith*, 1858I; *Loreley*, 1889I; *Missa solemnis*, 1851I; *Die Mühlenhexe*, 1861I; *Overture, Käthchen von Heilbronn, Opus 40*, 1886I; *Violin Sonata No. 1*, 1850I; *Die Zerstörung Jerusalem durch Titus*, 1855I
Naumann, Johann Gottlieb: *L'Achille in Sciro*, 1767I; *Aci e Galatea*, 1801I; *Alessandro nelle Indie*, 1768I; *Amore Giustificato*, 1792I; *Amphion*, 1778I; *Armida*, 1773I; *La Clemenza di Tito*, 1769I; *Concerto for Harpsichord/Piano*, 1792I; *Creduti spiriti, Li*, 1764I; *Davide in Terebinto, figura del Salvatore*, 1794I; *Elisa*, 1781I; *Elisens geistlichen liedern (12)*, 1787I; *Giuseppe riconosciuto*, 1777I; *Gottes Wege*, 1795I; *Gustaf Wasa*, 1786I; *Ipermestra*, 1774I; *L'ipocondriaco*, 1776I; *Isacco, Figura del Redentore*, 1772I; *L'isola disabitata*, 1773I; *Mass in A*, 1774I; *Mass in A♭*, 1801I; *Mass in d, "Pastoralmesse,"* 1778I; *Mass in A*, 1791I; *Medea in Colchide*, 1788I; *La Morte d'Abel*, 1790I; *Neue Lieder verschiedenen Inhalts (25)*, 1799I; *O Cora och Alonzo*, 1782I; *L'olimpiade*, 1791I; *Orpheus og Eurydike*, 1786I; *Osiride*, 1781I; *La Passione di Gesù Christo, I*, 1767I; *La Passione di Gesù Christo, II*, 1787I; *Pellegrini al sepolcro, I*, 1798I; *Piano Concerto*, 1794I; *Psalm 103, Lobe den Herrn, Meine Seele*, 1790I; *Quartets, Opus 1*, 1786I; *Il Ritorno del figliolo prodigo, I*, 1785I; *Il Ritorno di figliolo prodigo, II*, 1800I; *S. Elena al calvario*, 1775I; *Sechs neue lieder*, 1795I; *Solimano*, 1773I; *Il Tesoro insidiato*, 1762I; *Tutto per amore*, 1785I; *Unserer Brüder*, 1785I; *La Villanella incostante*, 1774I; *Il Villano geloso*, 1770I; *Zeit und Ewigkeit*, 1783I
Naumann, Siegfried: *Il Cantico del Sole, Opus 8*, 1963I; *Estate, Opus 21*, 1969I; *Ljudposter*, 1970I; *Missa in onore della Madonna di Loreto, Opus 11*, 1965I; *Musica Sacra No. 4*, 1951I; *Phaedri: Four Fables, Opus 3*, 1960I; *Sonnets from Petrarch (7), Opus 2*, 1959I; *Spettecolo II, Opus 19*, 1967I; *Strutture per Giovanni, Opus 9*, 1963I; *Transformazioni, Opus 5*, 1962I
Navoigille, Guillaume: *Symphonies (6), Opus 5*, 1775I; *Symphonies (3), Opus 87*, 1776I
Navok, Lior: *Meditations Over Shore*, 1997I; *Sea of Sunset*, 1997I

F   *Biographical*   G   *Cultural Beginnings*   H   *Musical Literature*
I   *Musical Compositions*

Nebra, José: *Mass, "Jubilate in conspectu Regis,"* 1756I; *Mass in B♭*, 1753I; *Mass in D*, 1757I; *Missa, benedicamus Domino*, 1764I; *Missa de difuntos*, 1765I; *Missa, de profundis clamavi*, 1766I; *Missa, "Domino exaudi ocem meam,"* 1758I; *Missa, In viam pacis*, 1760I; *Missa, per singules dies*, 1763I; *Missa Pro de functis*, 1758I; *Missa, Sie benedicam Domino*, 1759I

Neefe, Christian G.: *Adelheit von Veltheim*, 1780I; *Amors guckkasten*, 1772I; *Die Apotheke*, 1771I; *Bilder und Träume*, 1798I; *Der Dorf-barbier*, 1771I; *Der Einsprüch*, 1772I; *Freimaurerlieder*, 1774I; *Heinrich und Lyda*, 1776I; *Klopstock Odes*, 1776I; *Lessings Totenfeier-Overture*, 1781I; *Macbeth*, 1779I; *Piano (Harpsichord) Concerto*, 1782I; *Sophonisbe*, 1778I; *Violin Sonata*, 1780I; *Zemire und Azor*, 1776I; *Die Zigeuner*, 1777I

Neikrug, Marc: *Concerto for String Quartet & Orchestra*, 1987I; *Cycle of Seven for Piano*, 1978I; *Flute Concerto*, 1989I; *Los Alamos*, 1988I; *Modile for Orchestra*, 1981I; *Nachtlieder*, 1988I; *Piano Concerto*, 1966I; *Stars the Mirror* (string quartet), 1988I; *String Quartet No. 1*, 1969I; *String Quartet No. 2*, 1972I; *Symphony No. 1*, 1991I; *Viola Concerto*, 1974I

Nelson, Robert: *Christmas Cantata*, 1994I; *A Room with a View*, 1993I

Nelson, Ron: *Aspen Jubilee*, 1984I; *Hamaguchi*, 1981I; *Pieces (5) after Paintings by Andrew Wyeth*, 1976I; *Savannah River Holiday*, 1953I

Nessler, Victor: *Dornröschens Brautfahrt*, 1867I; *Irmingard*, 1876I; *Otto der Schütz*, 1886I; *Dir Rose von Strassburg*, 1890I; *Der Trompeter von Säkkingen*, 1884I; *Der Wilde Jäger*, 1881I

Neubauer, Franz Christoph: *Cello Concerto*, 1803I; *Fernando und Yariko*, 1788I; *Flute Concerto, Opus 13*, 1795I; *Flute Trios (3), Opus 3*, 1799I; *Flute Trios (6), Opus 6*, 1800I; *Hymne auf die Natur*, 1787I; *Piano Concerto, Opus 21*, 1798I; *Piano Trio, Opus 20*, 1798I; *Quartets (6), Flute & Strings*, 1788I; *String Quartets, Early (3)*, 1785I; *String Quartets (6), (no Opus #)*, 1792I; *String Quartets (3), Opus 3*, 1792I; *String Quartets (4), Opus 6*, 1792I; *String Quartets (3), Opus 7*, 1793I; *String Trios (3), Opus 8*, 1808I; *Symphony, Opus 1*, 1791I; *Symphonies (3), Opus 4*, 1792I; *Symphonies (3), Opus 8*, 1793I; *Symphonies (3), Opus 12*, 1795I; *Trios (3), Flute & Strings, Opus 14*, 1793I; *Variations for Flute & Orchestra, Opus 9*, 1802I; *Variations for Orchestra, Opus 9*, 1808I; *Variations, Opus 16*, 1808I; *Violin Sonata*, 1791I

Neuendorff, Adolph: *Don Quixote*, 1882I; *The Minstrel*, 1892I; *Prince Waldmeister*, 1887I; *Der Rattenfänger von Hameln*, 1880I; *Symphony No. 1*, 1878I; *Symphony No. 2*, 1880I; *Violin Concerto No. 1*, 1878I

Neukomm, Sigismond: *Arkona*, 1808I; *Alessander am Indus*, 1804I; *Athalie*, 1822I; *Das Besetz des alten Bundes*, 1832I; *Dir Braut von Messina*, 1805I; *Christi Grablegung*, 1827I; *Christi Himmelfahrt*, 1842I; *Christi Auferstehung*, 1841I; *Clarinet Quintet, Opus 8*, 1809I; *David*, 1834I; *Fantasy No. 1, Opus 9*, 1809I; *Fantasy, No. 2, Opus 11*, 1810I; *Fantasy No. 3, Opus 27*, 1821I; *Lobet de Herrn*, 1843I; *Musikalische malerei*, 1806I; *Die Nachtwächte*, 1804I; *Niobé*, 1809I; *Ostermorgan. Der*, 1823I; *Pfingstfeier*, 1846I; *Piano Fantasy, Opus 1*, 1804I; *Piano Sonata, "Le retour à la vie,"* 1820I; *Der Schauspieldirektor*, 1804I; *Sittah Man*, 1805I; *String Quartet, "Une fête en Suisse,"* 1818I; *Symphonies No. 1 & 2*, 1822I; *Totenfeier*, 1806I

Neuner, Carl: *Symphony in E♭*, 1826I

Neuwirth, Olga: *Anaptykis*, 2000I; *Clinamen/Nodus*, 1999I; *Nova Mob*, 1997I

Nevin, Arthur: *Arizona*, 1935I; *A Daughter of the Forest*, 1918I; *The Djinns*, 1913I; *Lorna Doone Suite*, 1897I; *Miniature Suite*, 1902I; *String Quartet No. 1 in d*, 1929I

Nevin, Ethelbert: *Captive Memories, Opus 29*, 1899I; *Mighty Lak a Rose*, 1901I; *O'er Hill and Dale*, 1902I; *The Quest*, 1902I; *Songs from Vineacre, Opus 28*, 1899I; *Songs (5), Opus 5*, 1889I; *Songs (5), Opus 12*, 1891I; *Songs (3), Opus 17 (The Rosary)*, 1892I; *Water Scenes, Opus 13* 1891I

Niblock, James: *Ruth*, 2000I

Nicholl, Horace: *Character Pieces (8), Opus 23*, 1889I; *Concert Preludes & Fugues, Opus 31*, 1923I; *Études mélodiques (12), Opus 26*, 1899I; *Life, Opus 50*, 1902I; *Piano Concerto in d, Opus 10*, 1888I; *Piano Trio in b*, 1901I; *String Quartet in c, Opus 39*, 1901I; *Symphonic Preludes & Fugues (12), Opus 30*, 1900I; *Symphony No. 2 in C, Opus 12*, 1889I; *Tartarus, Opus 11*, 1878I; *Violin Sonata in A, Opus 13*, 1883I

Nichols, Jeff: *Chelsea Square*, 1999I

Nicolai, David T.: *Organ Fantasy & Fugue*, 1789I

Nicolai, Otto: *Enrico II*, 1836I; *Etudes (3), Opus 40*, 1840I; *Festival Overture, Ein Feste Burg, Opus 32*, 1844I; *Funeral March on the Death of Bellini*, 1834I; *Künster Erdenwallen, Opus 31*, 1845I; *Lieder und Gesänge, Opus 16*, 1832I; *Mass in D*, 1832I; *Mass to Friedrich Wilhelm IV*, 1843I; *The Merry Wives of Windsor*, 1849I; *Pater noster*, 1840I; *Piano Sonata in d, Opus 27*, 1841I; *Preussens Stimme, Opus 4*, 1830I; *Il Proscritto*, 1841I; *Rosmonda d'Inghilterra*, 1838I; *Songs (9), Opus 3, 6*, 1830I; *String Quartet*, 1839I; *Symphony No. 1 in c*, 1831I; *Symphony No. 2 in D*, 1835I; *Te Deum*, 1831I; *Il templario*, 1840I

Niedermeyer, Louis: *La Casa nel bosco*, 1825I; *La Fronde*, 1853I; *Marie Stuart*, 1844I; *Robert Bruce*, 1846I; *Stradella*, 1837I

Nielsen, Carl: *Aladdin, Opus 34*, 1919I; *Atalanta*, 1901I; *Chaconne, Opus 32*, 1916I; *Clarinet Concerto, Opus 57*, 1928I; *Commotio, Opus 58*, 1931I; *Flute Concerto*, 1926I; *Helios Overture, Opus 17*, 1903I; *Hymnus*

---

amoris, Opus 12, 1897I; *Little Preludes (29), Opus 51,* 1929I; *Little Suite, Opus 1,* 1888I; *Masquerade,* 1906I; *Motets (3), Opus 55,* 1929I; *Organ Preludes (2),* 1930I; *Pan & Syrinx, Opus 49,* 1918I; *Piano Pieces (5), Opus 3,* 1890I; *Piano Pieces (3), Opus 59,* 1928I; *Piano Trio in G,* 1883I; *Saga-Drøm, Opus 39,* 1908I; *Saul og David,* 1901I; *Songs (6), Opus 1,* 1894I; *Songs (10), Opus 4 on P. J. Jacobsen,* 1891I; *String Quartet No. 1,* 1883I; *String Quartet No. 2, Opus 13,* 1887I; *String Quartet No. 3, Opus 5,* 1890I; *String Quartet No. 4, Opus 14,* 1898I; *String Quartet No. 5, "Piacevolezza," Opus 19,* 1906I; *String Quintet in G,* 1888I; *Symphonic Rhapsody in F, Opus 7,* 1889I; *Symphonic Suite for Piano, Opus 8,* 1894I; *Symphony No. 1 in g, Opus 7,* 1892I; *Symphony No. 2, "The Four Temperaments," Opus 16,* 1902I; *Symphony No. 3, "Sinfonia Expansiva," Opus 27,* 1911I; *Symphony No. 4, "Inextinguishable," Opus 29,* 1916I; *Symphony No. 5, Opus 50,* 1922I; *Symphony No. 6, "Sinfonia Semplice," Opus 116,* 1925I; *Theme & Variations, Opus 40,* 1917I; *Tove,* 1906I; *Violin Concerto, Opus 33,* 1911I; *Violin Sonata in G,* 1882I; *Violin Sonata in A, Opus 9,* 1895I; *Violin Sonata No. 3, Opus 35,* 1912I; *Viser og vers, Opus 6,* 1891I; *Wind Quintet, Opus 43,* 1922I

Nielsen, Ludolf: *Berceuse, Opus 9* (violin), 1904I; *Hjortholm,* 1923I; *Lola,* 1920I; *Regnar Lodbrog, Opus 2,* 1901I; *Romance, Opus 11* (cello), 1906I; *String Quartet No. 1 in A, Opus 1,* 1900I; *String Quartet No. 2, Opus 5,* 1904I; *String Quartet No. 3 in C, Opus 41,* 1920I; *Symphony No. 1 in b, Opus 3,* 1903I; *Symphony No. 2 in E, Opus 19,* 1909I; *Symphony No. 3 in C, Opus 32,* 1913I; *Uhret, Opus 16,* 1913I

Nielsen, Ludvig: *Benedicamus, Opus 31,* 1972I; *Chorales (9), Opus 5,* 1942I; *Chorales, Opus 24a,* 1967I; *Christmas Fantasy, Opus 12,* 1949I; *Concerto for Organ & Strings, Opus 25,* 1965I; *Fantasy on Three Old Christmas Melodies, Opus 10,* 1946I; *Fantasy on Two Old St. Olaf Melodies, Opus 4,* 1941I; *Hymns (7), Opus 32,* 1972I; *Intrada gotica, Opus 14,* 1952I; *Intrada solemnis, Opus 17,* 1958I; *Introduction & Fugue, Opus 6,* 1943I; *The Kingdom of God, Opus 8,* 1943I; *Mass No. 1, Opus 20a,* 1960I; *Mass No. 2, Opus 20a,* 1962I; *Mass No. 3, Opus 20a,* 1964I; *Mass, Opus 11,* 1948I; *Meditations, Opus 27,* 1968I; *Organ Pieces (2), Opus 29,* 1970I; *Organ Variations, Opus 2,* 1941I; *Passacaglia on Draumkvedet, Opus 23,* 1963I; *Songs, (6), Opus 22,* 1963I; *Suite, Opus 19,* 1960I; *Te Deum, Opus 9,* 1945I

Nielsen, Riccardo: *Concerto for Orchestra,* 1936I; *Symphony No. 1,* 1933I; *Symphony No. 2,* 1935I; *Violin Concerto,* 1932I

Nielsen, Svend: *Into the Black,* 1994I

Nielsen, Tage: *Five Romantic Songs,* 1994I

Nielson, Lewis: *Crosscurrents on the Vertical River,* 1992I

Nikolaiev, Alexei: *Festive Suite,* 1958I; *Grief-not misfortune,* 1961I; *Lunoglazka,* 1961I; *Symphony No. 1,* 1960I; *Symphony No. 2,* 1961I; *Symphony No. 3,* 1962I; *Symphony No. 4,* 1968I; *Symphony No. 5,* 1971I; *The Value of Life,* 1964I

Nin-Culmell, Joaquin: *Danzas Española, (3),* 1938I; *Danza Ibérica,* 1925I; *Don Juan,* 1959I; *Piano Concerto,* 1946I; *Piano Quintet,* 1936I; *Le rêve de Cyrano,* 1978I

Nishimura, Akira: *Alto Saxophone Concerto, "Esse in anima,"* 1999I; *Astral Concerto, "A Mirror of Light,"* 1992I; *Cello Concerto,* 1990I; *Concerto for Flute, Winds & Percussion,* 1997I; *Double Concerto, "A Ring of Lights,"* 1991I; *Heterophony,* 1987I; *Meditation of Vishnu,* 1985I; *Mutazione,* 1977I; *Nirvana,* 1997I; *The Painter,* 199I; *Piano Concerto No. 1, "Given,"* 1979I; *Piano Concerto No. 2,* 1982I; *Piano Sonata,* 1972I; *Poem of Water,* 1996I; *Prelude, "Vision in Flames,"* 1996I; *Silence & Light,* 1996I; *String Quartet No. 1, "Heterophony,"* 1975I; *String Quartet No. 2, "Pulses of Light,"* 1992I; *String Quartet No. 3, "Avian,"* 1997I; *Symphony No. 1,* 1976I; *Symphony No. 2,* 1979I; *Three Visions,* 1994I; *Timpani Concerto,* 1988I; *Viola concerto, "Flame & Shadow,"* 1996I; *Zeami,* 1995I

Nixon, Roger: *A Bride Comes to Yellow Sky,* 1967I; *Chinese Seasons,* 1942I; *Moods of Love Songs (6),* 1950I; *A Narrative of Tides,* 1984I

Nono, Luigi: *Canciones for Guiomar,* 1963I; *Fragmente-Stille* (string quartet), 1980I; *Intolleranza,* 1960I; *Piano Concerto No. 1,* 1972I; *Piano Concerto No. 2,* 1975I; *Polifonia-Monodia-Ritmica,* 1951I; *Sul Ponte di Hiroshima,* 1962I

Norby, Erik: *The Rainbow Serpent,* 1975I; *Södergran-Lieder (5),* 1992I

Nordentoft, Anders: *Cello Concerto, "Sweet Kindness,"* 1996I; *The City of Threads,* 1994I; *Distant Night Ship,* 1996I; *Entgegen,* 1985I; *Hymne,* 1995I; *String Sextet,* 1998I

Nordgren, Pehr: *Agnus Dei, Opus 15,* 1970I; *Alex,* 1983I; *The Black Monk,* 1981I; *Cello Concerto No. 1,* 1980I; *Cello Concerto No. 2,* 1984I; *Cello Concerto No. 3,* 1992I; *Cronaca, Opus 79,* 1991I; *Euphonie I, Opus 1,* 1967I; *Euphonie 2, Opus 5,* 1967I; *Euphonie 3,* 1975I; *Piano Concerto,* 1975I; *Piano Quintet,* 1978I; *Sonata for Solo Cello,* 1992I; *String Quartet No. 1,* 1967I; *String Quartet No. 2,* 1968I; *String Quartet No. 3,* 1976I; *String Quartet No. 4,* 1983I; *String Quartet No. 5,* 1986I; *String Quartet No. 6,* 1989I; *String Quartet No. 7,* 1992I; *Symphony No. 1,* 1974I; *Symphony No. 2,* 1990I; *Symphony No. 3, Opus 88,* 1993I; *Symphony No. 5, Opus 103,* 1998I; *Viola Concerto No. 1, Opus 12,* 1970I; *Viola Concerto No. 2,* 1979I; *Viola Concerto No. 3,* 1986I; *Violin Sonata,* 1993I

Nordheim, Arne: *Ariadne*, 1977I; *Canzona*, 1960I; *Cello Concerto*, 1982I; *Colorazione*, 1968I; *Eco*, 1967I; *Epitaffio*, 1963I; *Evolution*, 1966I; *Floating*, 1970I; *Greening*, 1973I; *Katharsis*, 1962I; *Lux et tenebrae*, 1970I; *Osak-Music*, 1970I; *Solitaire*, 1968I; *The Tempest*, 1979I; *Warszawa*, 1967I

Nordoff, Paul: *Symphony No. 1, "Winter,"* 1954I; *Violin Sonata No. 1*, 1932I; *Violin Sonata No. 2*, 1952I

Nørgård, Per: *Calendar Music*, 1972I; *Choral Preludes (3)*, 1955I; *Chorales (5), Opus 12*, 1953I; *Constellations*, 1958I; *Fragment VI*, 1961I; *Gilgamesh*, 1972I; *Iris*, 1967I; *Labyrinten*, 1963I; *Luna*, 1967I; *Partita concertante, Opus 23*, 1958I; *Secret Melody Sonata*, 1992I; *Siddharta*, 1979I; *Sonata in One Movement*, 1951I; *Sonata No. 2, Opus 20*, 1957I; *String Quartet No. 1, "Quarteto brioso," Opus 21*, 1958I; *String Quartet No. 2, "In three Spheres,"* 1965I; *String Quartet No. 3, "Inscape,"* 1969I; *Symphony No. 1, "Symphonie austera,"* 1954I; *Symphony No. 2*, 1970I; *Symphony No. 3*, 1974I; *Symphony No. 3*, 1975I; *Symphony No. 4*, 1981I; *Symphony No. 5*, 1990I; *Twilight*, 1977I

Nørholm, Ib: *Accordian Sonata, Opus 41*, 1967I; *After Icarus, Opus 39*, 1967I; *Apocryphal Songs, Opus 24*, 1960I; *The Birds, Opus 129*, 1994I; *Concertino, Opus 17*, 1958I; *Elverspejl, Opus 141*, 1996I; *Five Songs, Opus 139*, 1995I; *Flowers from the Floras of Danish Poetry, Opus 36*, 1966I; *The Funen Cataracts, Opus 66*, 1976I; *The Garden Wall, Opus 68*, 1976I; *The Garden with Paths that Part, Opus 86*, 1982I; *Guitar Sonata No. 1, Opus 69*, 1976I; *Guitar Sonata No. 2, Opus 110*, 1989I; *Inquiries for Organ, Opus 69*, 1969I; *Lerchenborg akrostikon, Opus 98*, 1986I; *Light & Praise, Opus 55*, 1971I; *Light & Shade, Opus 111*, 1989I; *Madrigals (3), Opus 11*, 1957I; *Organ Concerto No. 2, "Olympiade," Opus 142*, 1996I; *Organ Sonata, Opus 127*, 1993I; *Organ Sonata, Opus 9*, 1956I; *Persuasions, Opus 49*, 1970I; *Piano Trio, Opus 22*, 1959I; *Songs (4), Opus 3a*, 1955I; *Songs (3), Opus 3b*, 1955I; *Songs (6), Opus 6*, 1955I; *Songs, (3), Opus 8a*, 1956I; *Songs (3), Opus 14*, 1957I; *Songs (3), Opus 30*, 1965I; *Songs (5), Opus 44*, 1968I; *Songs (3), Opus 46*, 1969I; *Songs (6), Opus 64*, 1975I; *String Quartet No. 1, "In Vere," Opus 4*, 1955I; *String Quartet No. 2, "Five Impromtus," Opus 31*, 1965I; *String Quartet No. 3, "From y Green Herbarium," Opus 35*, 1966I; *String Quartet No. 4, "September–October–November," Opus 38*, 1966I; *String Quartet No. 5*, 1976I; *String Quartet No. 6, Opus 65*, 1976I; *String Quartet No. 7, "En passant," Opus 94*, 1985I; *String Quartet No. 8, Opus 107*, 1988I; *String Trio No. 2, "Essai prismatique,"* 1979I; *Symphony No. 1, Opus 10*, 1958I; *Symphony No. 2, "Isola bella," Opus 50*, 1971I; *Symphony No. 3, "A Day's Nightmare,"* 1973I; *Symphony No. 4*, 1979I; *Symphony No. 5, "The Elements," Opus 80*, 1980I; *Symphony No. 6, "Moralities," Opus 35*, 1981I; *Symphony No. 7, Opus 88*, 1982I; *Symphony No. 8, Opus 114*, 1990I; *Symphony No. 9, Opus 116*, 1990I; *Theme & Variations, Opus 1*, 1955I; *Theme & Five Variations, Opus 61*, 1971I; *Tombeau, Opus 7*, 1956I; *Trio, Opus 13 for Clarinet, Violin & Piano*, 1957I; *Variants, Opus 19*, 1959I; *Viola Concerto, Opus 130*, 1995I; *Violin Sonata, Opus 12*, 1957I; *Whispers of Heavenly Death, Opus 103*, 1987I; *The Young Park, Opus 48*, 1970I

Norman, Ludvig: *Anthony & Cleopatra Overture, Opus 57*, 1881I; *Cello Sonata in D, Opus 28*, 1867I; *Concertpiece in F, Opus 54*, 1875I; *Fantasy Pieces (4), Opus 5*, 1853I; *Forest Songs, Opus 31* 1867I; *Piano Pieces (2), Opus 10*, 1857I; *Piano Trio in b, Opus 38*, 1872I; *Sextet in a, Opus 29*, 1869I; *Songs (8), Opus 13*, 1851I; *String Octet in C, Opus 30*, 1867I; *String Quintet in c, Opus 35*, 1870I; *String Sextet in A, Opus 18*, 1854I; *Symphony No. 1 in F for Strings, Opus 22*, 1858I; *Symphony No. 2 in E♭, Opus 40*, 1871I; *Symphony No. 3 in d, Opus 58*, 1881I; *Viola Sonata in G, Opus 32*, 1869I; *Violin Sonata in d, Opus 3*, 1848I

North, Alex: *Symphony No. 2*, 1968I; *Symphony No. 3*, 1971I

Nováček, Ottokar: *Perpetuum Mobile*, 1895I; *String Quartet No. 1*, 1890I; *String Quartet No. 2*, 1898I

Novak, Lionel: *String Quartet No. 1*, 1938I; *Violin Sonatina*, 1944I

Novák, Vítéslav: *Autumn Symphony, Opus 62*, 1934I; *Ballads (2), Opus 28*, 1902I; *Ballads (2) on Folk Poetry, Opus 19*, 1898I; *Ballads (2), Opus 23*, 1900I; *Cello Sonata, Opus 68*, 1941I; *Corsaire Overture*, 1892I; *Czech Songs (3), Opus 53*, 1918I; *De Profundis, Opus 67*, 1941I; *Eternal Longing, Opus 33*, 1905I; *Exoticon, Opus 45*, 1911I; *From Life, Opus 60*, 1932I; *Grandfather's Legacy, Opus 57*, 1925I; *Gypsy Melodies, Opus 14* (cycle); *Home, Opus 69*, 1941I; *In Memoriam, Opus 65*, 1937I; *In the Tatras, Opus 26*, 1902I; *Karltejn, Opus 50*, 1915I; *The Lantern, Opus 56*, 1922I; *Legends on Moravian Poetry (2), Opus 76*, 1944I; *Lullabies on Moravian Texts (12), Opus 61*, 1932I; *Male Choruses (6), Opus 37*, 1906I; *May Symphony, Opus 73*, 1943I; *Melancholy, Opus 25*, 1901I; *Melancholy Love Songs, Opus 38*, 1906I; *Nikotina*, 1929I; *Notturna, Opus 39*, 1908I; *On Native Soil, Opus 44*, 1911I; *Overture, Lady Godiva*, 1907I; *Overture Marya, Opus 18*, 1898I; *Pan, Opus 43*, 1910I; *Piano Concerto in e*, 1895I; *Piano Pieces (4), Opus 20*, 1899I; *Piano Quartet in c, Opus 7*, 1884I; *Piano Quintet in a, Opus 12*, 1896I; *Piano Trio in g, Opus 1*, 1892I; *Piano Trio No. 1 in d, Opus 27*, 1902I; *Poems, (4), Opus 47*, 1912I; *Reminiscences, Opus 6*, 1894I; *St. Wenceslas Triptych, Opus 70*, 1941I; *Serenade in D, Opus 36*, 1905I; *Serenade in F*, 1895I; *Signorina Gioventu, Opus 58*, 1927I; *Slovak Suite, Opus 32*, 1903I; *Sonata eroica, Opus 24*, 1900I; *Sonatinas (6), Opus 54*, 1920I; *The Song of the Zlin Workers, Opus 79*, 1948I; *Songs on Moravian Folk Texts, I, II, Opus 17*, 1897I; *Songs on Southern Bohemian Motifs (5), Opus 77*, 1947I; *Songs on Winter Nights*, 1903I; *South*

Bohemian Suite, Opus 64, 1937I; *Spring, Opus 52*, 1918I; *Spring Moods*, 1900I; *Stars*, 1949I; *The Storm*, 1910I; *Strength & Defiance, Opus 51*, 1917I; *String Quartet No. 1 in G, Opus 22*, 1899I; *String Quartet No. 2 in D, Opus 35*, 1905I; *String Quartet No. 3 in G, Opus 66*, 1938I; *A Tale of the Heart, Opus 8*, 1896I; *Toman & the Wood Nymph, Opus 40*, 1907I; *Valley of the New Kingdom, Opus 31*, 1903I; *Variations on a Theme by Schumann*, 1893I; *Violin Sonata in d*, 1891I; *The Wedding Shift, Opus 48*, 1913I; *Youth, Opus 55*, 1920I; *řiška, Opus 78*, 1948I; *The Zvikov Imp, Opus 49*, 1914I

Nowka, Dieter: *Eine Bauernlegende*, 1958I; *Oboe Concerto*, 1953I; *Piano Concerto No. 1*, 1963I; *Piano Concerto No. 2 for Left Hand*, 1971I; *Piano Sonata No. 1*, 1953I; *String Quartet No. 1*, 1954I; *String Quartet No. 2*, 1956I; *String Quartet No. 3*, 1960I; *String Quartet No. 4*, 1972I; *Symphony No. 1*, 1958I; *Symphony No. 2*, 1963I; *Symphony No. 3*, 1969I; *Violin Concerto No. 1*, 1956I

Nowowiejski, Felix: *Beatrice*, 1903I; *Cello Concerto*, 1938I; *Easy Pieces I*, 1900I; *Easy Pieces II*, 1902I; *Ellenai*, 1915I; *The Emigrants*, 1917I; *Entrée solennelle*, 1911I; *In paradisium*, 1911I; *The Invention of the Cross*, 1905I; *Kosiusko*, 1924I; *Legenda Baltyku*, 1924I; *Leluja*, 1927I; *Meditation in E*, 1911I; *Missa pro pace*, 1941I; *Organ Concerto No. 1*, 1938I; *Organ Concerto No. 2*, 1939I; *Organ Concerto No. 3*, 1940I; *Organ Concerto No. 4*, 1941I; *Organ Symphonies (9), Opus 45*, 1931I; *Piano Concerto*, 1941I; *Quo Vadis?*, 1903I; *Return of the Prodigal Son*, 1901I; *Symphony (No. 1)*, 1903I; *Symphony No. 2 (original No. 3)*, "*Rhythm & Work*," 1937I; *Symphony No. 4*, 1941I

Nyman, Michael: *Concerto for Harpsichord & Strings*, 1995I; *Double Concerto*, 1997I; *String Quartet In Re Don Giovanni*, 1991I; *String Quartet No. 2*, 1988I; *String Quartet No. 3*, 1990I; *String Quartet No. 4*, 1995I; *Trombone Concerto*, 1995I; *Yamamoto Perpetuo*, 1993I

Nystedt, Knut: *The Burnt Sacrifice, Opus 36*, 1954I; *Canticles of Praise*, 1995I; *De Profundis, Opus 54*, 1964I; *Deus Sancta Trinitas, Opus 28*, 1951I; *Entrada festivo, Opus 60* (band), 1969I; *Fantasia trionfale, Opus 37*, 1955I; *Horn Concerto*, 1987I; *Introduction & Passacaglia, Opus 7*, 1940I; *Lucis creator optime, Opus 58*, 1968I; *Magnificate for the New Millennium*, 2000I; *Miserere, Opus 140*, 1993I; *O Crux*, 1977I; *Organ Suite, Opus 84*, 1978I; *Pia Memoria*, 1971I; *Pietà, Opus 50*, 1961I; *Resurrexit, Opus 68*, 1973I; *The Seven Seals, Opus 46*, 1960I; *String Quartet No. 1, Opus 1*, 1938I; *String Quartet No. 2, Opus 23*, 1948I; *String Quartet No. 3, Opus 40*, 1956I; *String Quartet No. 4, Opus 56*, 1966I; *Symphony for Strings, Opus 26*, 1950I; *Tu es Petrus, Opus 69*, 1973I

Nystroem, Gösta: *The Arctic Ocean*, 1925I; *Concerto No. 1 for Strings*, 1930I; *Concerto No. 2 for Strings*, 1955I; *Concerto ricercante*, 1959I; *The Executioner*, 1934I; *Herr Arne's Money*, 1958I; *The King*, 1933I; *Madame Bovary*, 1938I; *The Merchant of Venice*, 1936I; *Overture, Le fiancé*, 1934I; *Prélude pastorale*, 1960I; *Rondo capriccioso (violin)*, 1917I; *Sea Visions (3)*, 1956I; *Sinfonia di lontano*, 1963I; *Songs by the Sea*, 1943I; *String Quartet No. 1*, 1956I; *String Quartet No. 2*, 1961I; *Symphonic Overture*, 1945I; *Symphony No. 1, "Breve,"* 1931I; *Symphony No. 2, "Espressiva,"* 1935I; *Symphony No. 3, "Sinfonia del mare,"* 1948I; *Symphony No. 4, "Shakespeariana,"* 1952I; *Symphony No. 5, "Sinfonia seria,"* 1963I; *Symphony No. 6, "Traumontana,"* 1965I; *The Tempest*, 1934I; *The Tower of Babel*, 1925I; *Viola Concerto, "Hommage à la France,"* 1940I; *Violin Concerto*, 1954I; *Young Gentleman & the Six Princesses*, 1951I

Nyvang, Michael: *Movements for a Monument to the Loneliness of Our World*, 1993I

Obradors, Fernando: *The Jungle Book*, 1938I

Obradović, Alexander: *Cello Concerto*, 1979I

O'Brien, Eugene: *Tristan's Lament*, 1969I

Obukhov, Nikolai: *Création de l'or*, 1916I; *Invocations*, 1916I; *Piano Preludes (6)*, 1915I; *Tableaux (10) psychologiques*, 1915I

Oehlenschlägel, Jan: *Captiva filia Sion*, 1757I; *Innocentia de pietas*, 1760I; *Justitia et clementia*, 1759I; *Patientia et humilitas*, 1761I; *Penitentia victrix*, 1763I; *Vox filiae Sion*, 1762I

Offenbach, Jacques: *Air de ballet du 17me siècle, Opus 24*, 1842; *L'alcôve*, 1847I; *L'amour chanteur*, 1864I; *Apothécaire et perruquier*, 1861I; *Arlequin Barbier*, 1855I; *Ba-ta-clan*, 1855I; *Bagatelle*, 1874I; *Barbe-bleue*, 1866I; *Barkouf*, 1860I; *Les bavards*, 1862I; *Belle Lusette*, 1880I; *Les bergers*, 1865I; *Les bergers de Watteau*, 1856I; *La boîte au lait*, 1876I; *La bonne d'enfants*, 1856I; *La boulangère a des écus*, 1875I; *Boule de neige*, 1871I; *Les braconniers*, 1873; *Les brigands*, 1869I; *Le carnaval des revues*, 1860I; *Cascoletto*, 1865I; *Cello Concertino*, 1851I; *La chanson de Fortunio*, 1861I; *Le château à toto*, 1868I; *Concerto militaire* (cello), 1848I; *Les contes d'Hoffmann*, 1881I; *Le corsaire noir*, 1872I; *La créole*, 1875I; *Croquefer*, 1857I; *Daphnis et Chloé*, 1860I; *Une demoiselle en loterie*, 1857I; *Les deux pêcheurs*, 1857I; *Les deux aveugles*, 1855I; *La Diva*, 1869I; *Le docteur Ox*, 1877I; *Les dragées du baptême*, 1856I; *Dragonette*, 1857I; *Entrez, messieurs, mesdames*, 1855I; *Fables de Lafontaine (6)*, 1842I; *Fantasio*, 1872I; *La fille du Tambour-Major*, 1879I; *Fleurette*, 1872I; *La foire Saint-Laurent*, 1877I; *Geneviève de Brabant*, 1859I; *Les géorgiennes*, 1864I; *La grande-duchesse de Gérolstein*, 1867I; *L'île de tulipatan*, 1868I; *Jacqueline*, 1862I; *La jolie parfumeuse*, 1873I; *Le langage des fleurs*, 1846I; *Lischen et Fritzchen*, 1863I; *Luc et Lucette*, 1854I; *Madame l'archiduc*, 1874I; *Madame Favart*, 1878I; *Maître Péronilla*, 1878I; *Mam'zelle Moucheron*, 1870I; *Un mari à la porte*, 1859I; *La marocaine*,

---

❈

F *Biographical*   G *Cultural Beginnings*   H *Musical Literature*
I *Musical Compositions*

Offenbach, Jacques: (*cont.*)
    1879I; *Mesdames de la Halle*, 1858I; *Monsieur et Madame Denis*, 1862I; *Une nuit blanche*, 1855I; *Orpheus in the Underworld*, 1858I; *Le papillon*, 1860I; *Pépito*, 1853I; *Le périchole*, 1868I; *Le permission de dix heures*, 1867I; *Pierette et Jacquot*, 1876I; *Pierrot clown*, 1855I; *Polichinelle dans le monde*, 1855I; *Pomme d' api*, 1873I; *Le pont des soupirs*, 1861I; *Prière et Boléro, Opus 22*, 1840I; *Les refrains des bouffes*, 1865I; *Die Rheinnixen*, 1864I; *Robinson Crusoé*, 1867I; *Le roi carotte*, 1872I; *La romance de la rose*, 1870I; *Le savetier et le financier*, 1856I; *Il Signor Fagotto*, 1863I; *Vert-vert*, 1869I; *La vie parisienne*, 1866I; *Les vivandières de la grande armée*, 1859I; *Les voix mystérieuses*, 1851I; *Le voyage de MM. Dunanan père et fils*, 1862I; *Voyage dans la lune*, 1875I; *Whittington*, 1874I
Ogden, Will: *Summer Images & Reflections*, 1985I
Ohana, Maurice: *Messe*, 1977I; *Office des Oracles*, 1974I; *Piano Concerto*, 1981I
Ohlsson, Richard: *Konzertstück in C (violin)*, 1918I; *String Quartet No. 2 in D*, 1899I; *String Quartet No. 3 in A♭*, 1914I; *Swedish Dances (strings)*, 1897I
Olah, Tiberiu: *String Quartet*, 1952I
Oldberg, Arne: *Academic Overture*, 1909I; *Paolo & Francesca*, 1908I; *Piano Concerto No. 2*, 1931I; *The Sea*, 1934I; *Sonata, Opus 28*, 1909I; *String Quartet in c*, 1900I; *Violin Concerto*, 1933I
Oliphant, Thomas: *Santa Lucia*, 1850I
Oliver, Stephen: *Beauty & the Beast*, 1984I; *Festal Magnificat & Nunc Dimittis*, 1986I; *Guitar Sonata*, 1979I; *The Lord of the Rings*, 1981I; *Nicholas Nickleby*, 1980I; *Peter Pan*, 1982I; *The Ring*, 1984I; *Tom Jones*, 1975I; *The Vessel*, 1990I
Oliverio, James: *Concerto for Orchestra*, 1990I; *Timpani Concerto*, 1990I
Oliveros, Pauline: *Beautiful Soop*, 1967I; *Big Mother is Watching You*, 1966I; *Gone with the Wind*, 1980I; *In Memoriam Mr. Whitney*, 1991I; *Sound Patterns*, 1961I; *Variations for Piano Sextet*, 1960I
Ollone, Max d': *George Dandin*, 1930I; *Le retour*, 1913I; *La samaritaine*, 1937I; *Les uns et les autres*, 1922I
Olsen, Ole: *Griffenfeldt*, 1897I; *Horn Concerto*, 1905I; *King Erik VIV*, 1882I; *Klippeøerne*, 1910I; *Lajta*, 1893I; *Ludvig Holberg*, 1884I; *Nidaros*, 1897I; *Petite Suite*, 1902I; *Sein Uraed*, 1890I; *Stallo*, 1902I; *Stig Hvide*, 1876I; *Symphony in G*, 1878I
Olsen, Poul: *Belisa, Opus 50*, 1964I; *La création*, 1952I; *Etudes (3), Opus 63*, 1969I; *Images, Opus 51*, 1965I; *Inventions (5), Opus 38*, 1957I; *Light Songs (4), Opus 19*, 1951I; *Little Pieces (6), Opus 5*, 1946I; *Piano Concerto, Opus 31*, 1954I; *The Planets*, 1978I; *Schicksalieder, Opus 28*, 1953I; *Songs after Blake (4), Opus 7*, 1947I; *Songs for Male Chorus (4), Opus 43*, 1959I; *The Stranger*, 1969I; *String Quartet No. 1*, 1948I; *String Quartet No. 2, Opus 62*, 1969I; *Symphonic Variations, Opus 27*, 1953I; *Violin Sonata, Opus 4*, 1946I; *The Wedding*, 1966I
Olsen, Sparre: *De profundis*, 1946I; *Kleine Overture, Opus 7*, 1932I; *Old Lom Folktunes (6), Opus 2*, 1929I; *The Spark, Opus 16*, 1933I; *String Quartet*, 1972I; *Sursum corda, Opus 34*, 1946I; *Symphonic Fantasy No. 2, Opus 47*, 1960I; *Symphonic Fantasy No. 3*, 1974I; *Symphonic Fantasy No. 2*, 1939 (?); *Theme & Variations, Opus 6*, 1947I; *Vers sanctum, Opus 30*, 1943I; *The Voices, Opus 21*, 1935I; *Wind Quintet*, 1950I
Olsson, Otto: *Credo Symphoniacum, Opus 50*, 1925I; *Gregorian Melodies, Opus 30*, 1910I; *Introduction & Scherzo*, 1905I; *Latin Hymns (6), Opus 40*, 1919I; *Organ Symphony No. 1*, 1903I; *Organ Symphony No. 2*, 1918I; *Preludes & Fugues I*, 1911I; *Prelude & Fugue III*, 1935I; *Prelude & Fugues II for Organ*, 1918I; *Requiem*, 1903I; *String Quartet No. 1*, 1903I; *String Quartet No. 2*, 1906I; *String Quartet No. 3*, 1947I; *Symphony in g*, 1902I; *Te Deum, Opus 25*, 1906I
Onslow, (André) Georges: *Piano Sonata, Four Hands, in e*, 1810I; *Symphony No. 2 in d, Opus 42*, 1829I; *Symphony No. 4 in G, Opus 71*, 1846I
Opieński, Henryk: *Maria*, 1904I; *The Prodigal Son*, 1930I
Orbán, György: *Bassoon Sonata*, 1987I; *Sonata for Solo Violin*, 1970I
Orbón, Julián: *Danzas sinfónicas*, 1955I; *Symphony*, 1945I
Orcharenko, Halyne: *Transformations*, 1997I
Orchinnikov, Viacheslav: *Sulamith*, 1961I
Ore, Cécile: *Etapper*, 1988I; *Vacuus*, 1986I
Orff, Carl: *Antigonae*, 1948I; *Astutuli*, 1946I; *Die Bernauderin*, 1945I; *Carmina Burana*, 1937I; *Catulli Carmina*, 1943I; *Comoedia de Christi Resurrectione*, 1955I; *De Temporum fine comoedia*, 1971I; *Joan von Zarissa*, 1939I; *Die Kluge*, 1942I; *Der Mond*, 1938I; *Oedipus der Tyrann*, 1958I; *Prometheus*, 1967I; *Rota*, 1973I; *Ein Sommernachtstraum*, 1932I; *The Triumph of Aphrodite*, 1951I; *The Vigil*, 1973I
Orgitano, Vincenzo: *Le Passie per amore*, 1761I; *Il Finto partorello*, 1759I
Ornstein, Leo: *A La Mexicana*, 1920I; *À la chinoise*, 1918I; *Biography in Sonata Form for Piano*, 1974I; *Cello Sonata No. 1, Opus 42*, 1918I; *Cello Sonata No. 2*, 1920I; *Dwarf Suite, Opus 9 "Messe Noire," Opus 68*, 1913I; *The Fog*, 1915I; *Hebraic Fantasy*, 1975I; *Imp on Notre Dame*, 1914I; *Impression of Chinatown*, 1917I; *Lysistrata Suite*, 1930I; *New York Scenes for Piano*, 1971I; *Nocturne & Dance of the Fates*, 1937I; *Piano*

A   *Births*   B   *Deaths*   C   *Debuts*   D   *New Positions*
E   *Prizes/Honors*

Concerto, 1923I; *Piano Quintet*, 1927I; *Piano Sonata*, 1913I; *Piano Sonata No. 4*, 1924I; *Piano Sonata No. 6*, 1981I; *Piano Sonata No. 7*, 1983I; *Piano Sonata No. 8*, 1990I; *Poems of 1917 (10)*, 1918I; *Preludes (6), Cello & Piano*, 1931I; *Songs (5), Opus 17*, 1928I; *String Quartet No. 2*, 1929I; *String Quartet No. 3*, 1976I; *Symphony No. 1*, 1934I; *Three Moods: Anger, Peace, Joy*, 1914I; *Three Russian Impressions*, 1916I; *Violin Sonata No. 1 (?)*, 1915I; *Violin Sonata No. 2*, 1918I; *Water Colors (5)*, 1935I

Orr, Buxton: *Celtic Suite*, 1968I

Orr, Robin: *Deirdre of the Sorrows*, 1951I; *Elegy for Organ*, 1968I; *From the Book of Philip Sparrow*, 1969I; *Oedipus et Colonus*, 1950I; *Preludes (3) on a Scottish Psalm Tune*, 1958I; *Toccata alla Marcia*, 1937I; *Viola Sonata*, 1947I; *A Winter's Tale*, 1947I

Orrega-Salas, Juan: *Quintet for Flute, Piano & Strings*, 1937I; *Sextet in B♭, Opus 38*, 1954I; *Sonata, Opus 60*, 1967I; *String Quartet No. 1*, 1957I; *Symphony No. 4, "Of the Distant Answer," Opus 59*, 1966I

Orthel, Léon: *Cello Sonata No. 1*, 1925I; *Cello Sonata No. 2*, 1965I; *Concertstücke (violin)*, 1924I

Osborne, Nigel: *Heaventree*, 1973I

Osterc, Slavko: *Symphony*, 1922I

Ostrčil, Ottokar: *The Bud, Opus 12*, 1910I; *Czech Christmas Legend, Opus 15*, 1912I; *Honza's Kingdom, Opus 25*, 1933I; *Kunála's Eyes, Opus 11*, 1908I; *The Legend of Erin, Opus 19*, 1919I; *The Legend of St. Zita, Opus 17*, 1913I; *Léto, Opus 23*, 1926I; *Masque of the Red Death*, 1930I; *The Orphan, Opus 10*, 1906I; *Saxophone Sonata*, 1935I; *Songs (3), Opus 18*, 1913I; *Sonatina, Opus 22*, 1925I; *Strange Guest, Opus 16*, 1913I; *String Quartet in B, Opus 4*, 1899I; *String Quartet No. 1*, 1927I; *String Quartet No. 2*, 1934I; *Suite in c, Opus 14*, 1912I; *Suite No. 2 in G, Opus 20*, 1921I; *Symphony in A, Opus 7*, 1905I; *Symfonietta, Opus 20*, 1921I; *Symphony in A, Opus 7*, 1905I; *The Tale of emik, Opus 3*, 1899I; *Village Fête, Opus 1*, 1898I; *Vlasia's Passing, Opus 5*, 1903I; *The Way of the Cross*, 1928I

Otaka, Hisatada: *Piano Rhapsody*, 1943I; *String Quartet No. 1*, 1938I; *String Quartet No. 2*, 1943I

Oteri, Frank: *Two Transfers*, 1985I

Otescu, Ion: *Les enchantements d'Armida (violin)*, 1915I; *Ileana Cosinzeana*, 1918I; *La légende de la rose rouge*, 1910I; *The Miraculous Roby*, 1919I; *Narcis*, 1911I; *Since Times of Old*, 1912I; *Le temple du guide*, 1908I

Ott, David: *Cello Concerto*, 1985I; *Concerto for Alto Flute & Strings*, 1989I; *Interludes (5)*, 1990I; *Lucinda Hero*, 1985I; *Music of the Canvas*, 1990I; *Piano Concerto*, 1983I; *Piano Concerto*, 1994I; *String Quartet No. 1*, 1989I; *Symphony No. 1, "Short,"* 1984I; *Symphony No. 2*, 1990I; *Symphony No. 3*, 1991I; *Symphony No. 4*, 1994I; *Triple Concerto*, 1993I; *Viola Sonata*, 1982I; *Visions: The Isle of Patmos*, 1988I

Otte, Hans: *minimum: maximum*, 1973I; *Sounds for Organ*, 1992I; *Touches for Organ*, 1965I

Ouseley, Frederick: *Hagar*, 1873I; *The Martyrdom of St. Polycarp*, 1855I; *Organ Sonata No. 1*, 1877I; *Organ Sonata No. 2*, 1883I; *Overture in D*, 1888I; *Preludes and Fugues (31), Set I*, 1864I; *Preludes and Fugues (31), Set II*, 1877I; *Short Preludes (6)*, 1869I; *String Quartet No. 1 in C*, 1868I; *String Quartet No. 2 in d*, 1868I

Ovcharenko, Halyna: *Moods*, 1997I; *Negative of Sketch*, 1996I; *String Quartet*, 1996I; *The Sun-Scorched Mallow*, 1992I

Overton, Hall: *Cello Sonata*, 1960I; *Piano Polarities No. 1*, 1959I; *Piano Polarities No. 2*, 1971I; *Piano Sonata*, 1963I; *Sonorities*, 1964I; *String Quartet No. 1*, 1950I; *String Quartet No. 2*, 1954I; *String Quartet No. 3*, 1967I; *Symphony No. 2*, 1962I; *Viola Sonata*, 1960I

Owen, Richard: *Abigail Adams*, 1987I; *Tom Sawyer*, 1989I

Ozi, Étienne: *Symphonie concertante No. 1 in B♭, Opus 5*, 1785I

Pablo, Luis de: *Chamán*, 1976I; *Llanto*, 1987I; *Piano Concerto No. 1*, 1979I; *Piano Concerto No. 2*, 1980I; *Soledad interrumpida*, 1971I; *Tamaño*, 1970I

Paccagnini, Angelo: *Bivio*, 1968I; *Brevi canti*, 1958I; *Concerto No. 3 for Soprano & Orchestra*, 1965I; *Cori di Euripides (5)*, 1952I; *Flou I*, 1971I; *Flou II*, 1972I; *I dispersi*, 1961I; *Musica da camera*, 1960I; *Partner*, 1969I; *Sequenze e strutture*, 1962I; *Stimmen*, 1969I; *String Quartet*, 1956I

Pacini, Giovanni: *Adelaide e Comingio*, 1817I; *Alessandro nelle Indie*, 1824I; *Allan Cameron*, 1848I; *Amazilia*, 1825I; *L'ambizione delusa*, 1814I; *Annetta e Lucindo*, 1813I; *L'annunzio felice*, 1829I; *Atala*, 1818I; *La ballerina raggiratrice*, 1814I; *Il barone di Dolsheim*, 1818I; *Belezza e cuor di ferro*, 1836I; *Belfegor*, 1861I; *Bettina vedova*, 1815I; *Bondelmonte*, 1845I; *Canto del prigionero*, 1866I; *Il Carcere Mamertino*, 1867I; *Carlo di Borgogna*, 1835I; *Carmelita*, 1863I; *I Cavalieri di Valenza*, 1828I; *Cesare in Egitto*, 1821I; *El Cid*, 1853I; *Il Corsaro*, 1831I; *I Crociati a Tolemaide*, 1828I; *Dante Symphony*, 1865I; *La distruzione di Gerusalemme*, 1858I; *Don Giovanni Tenorio*, 1832I; *Don Diego di Mendoza*, 1867I; *La donna delle isole*, 1854I; *Il Duca d'Alba*, 1842I; *L'ebrea*, 1844I; *L'escavazione del tesoro*, 1814I; *Il felice ritorno*, 1825I; *La felicitá del Lago*, 1816I; *Fernando duca di Valenza*, 1833I; *La fidanzata corsa*, 1842I; *I fidanzati*, 1829I; *Furio Camillo*, 1839I; *La gelosia corretta*, 1826I; *Gianni di Nisida*, 1860I; *Giovanna d'Arc*, 1830I; *La gioventù di Enrico V*, 1820I; *Gli arabi nelle Gallie*, 1827I; *L'ingenua*, 1816I; *Irene*, 1833I; *Isabella ed Enrico*, 1824I;

Pacini, Giovanni: (*cont.*)
Ivanhoe, 1832I; *Lidia di Brabante,* 1853I; *Lorenzino de' Medici,* 1845I; *Margherita regina d'Inghilterra,* 1827I; *Maria Regina d'inghilterra,* 1843I; *Mass for the Madonna del Castello,* 1822I; *Il matrimonio per procra,* 1817I; *Medea,* 1843I; *Merope,* 1847I; *Il mulattiere di Toledo,* 1861I; *Niccolò de' Lapi,* 1855I; *Niobe,* 1826I; *L'imaggio più grato,* 1819I; *L'orfana svizzera,* 1848I; *Partenope,* 1826I; *I Portoghesi nel Braile,* 1856I; *La punizione,* 1854I; *Il puro omaggio,* 1822I; *La regina de Cipro,* 1846I; *Requiem in c,* 1843I; *Rodrigo di Valenza,* 1853I; *La rosina,* 1815I; *Rossini e la patria,* 1864I; *La sacerdotessa d'Irminsu,* 1820I; *Saffo,* 1840I; *Il saltimbanco,* 1858I; *Sant'Agnese,* 1857I; *La schiava in Bagdad,* 1820I; *Sinfonia Dante,* 1863I; *La sposa fedele,* 1819I; *String Quartet No. 4,* 1863I; *Il talismano,* 1829I; *Temistocle,* 1823I; *Il trionfo di giuditta,* 1854I; *Il trionfo della religione,* 1838I; *L'ultimo giorno di Pompei,* 1825I; *L'uomo del mistero,* 1841I; *La vestale,* 1823I
Paciorkiewicz, Tadeusz: *Capriccios (4),* Clarinet & Piano, 1960I; *Cello Sonata,* 1975I; *Horn Concerto,* 1986I; *Improvisations (2) for Organ,* 1968I; *Music for Soprano & String Orchestra,* 1967I; *Oboe Concerto,* 1982I; *Organ Concerto No. 1,* 1967I; *Organ Concerto No. 2,* 1988I; *Organ Sonata,* 1947I; *Organ Sonata No. 2,* 1976I; *Phantasy for Violin & Piano,* 1957I; *Piano Concerto No. 1,* 1952I; *Piano Concerto No. 2,* 1954I; *Piano Quintet,* 1972I; *String Quartet No. 1,* 1960I; *String Quartet No. 2,* 1982I; *Symphony No. 1,* 1953I; *Symphony No. 2,* 1957I; *Symphony No. 3,* 1989I; *Symphony No. 4,* 1992I; *Trombone Concerto,* 1971I; *Violin Concerto,* 1955I; *Violin Sonata,* 1954I; *Warsaw Legend,* 1959I; *Weight of the World,* 1965I; *Wind Quintet,* 1951I
Paderewski, Ignace Jan: *Album de Mai, Opus 10,* 1884I; *Dans le désert, Opus 15,* 1888I; *Fantasie Polonaise, Opus 19,* 1893I; *Humoresque de Concert II, Opus 14,* 1888I; *Intermezzi (2–g,c),* 1885I; *Manru,* 1900I; *Mélodies (12), Opus 22,* 1903I; *Piano Suite in E♭,* 1879I; *Piano Concerto in a, Opus 17,* 1888I; *Piano Sonata in e♭, Opus 14,* 1903I; *Polish Fantasy, Opus 19,* 1893I; *Songs (4), Opus 7,* 1885I; *Songs (6), Opus 18,* 1894I; *Symphony in b, "Polonia,"* 1907I; *Tatra Album, Opus 12,* 1883I; *Variation and Fugue in a, Opus 11,* 1884I; *Violin Sonata in a, Opus 13,* 1880I
Paër, Ferdinando: *Achille,* 1801I; *Agnese,* 1809I; *I baccanti,* 1813I; *Blanche de Provence,* 1821I; *Camilla,* 1799I; *Un caprice de femme,* 1834I; *Circe,* 1791I; *Didone abbandonata,* 1810I; *L'eroismo in amore,* 1815I; *I fuorusciti,* 1804I; *Ginevra degli almieri,* 1802I; *Griselda,* 1797I; *Leonora,* 1805I; *Le maître de chapelle,* 1821I; *Il maniscalco,* 1805I; *I molinari,* 1793I; *Numa Pompilio,* 1808I; *L'Oriflamme,* 1814I; *Un passo ne fa cento,* 1812I; *Le selva incantata e Gerusalemme liberata,* 1803I; *Sofonisba,* 1805I; *Tamarlane,* 1797I; *Una in bene e una in male,,* 1794I
Paganini, Niccolò: *Introduction & Variations on Rossini's "Mosè,"* 1819I; *Introduction & Variations on Rossini's "La Cenerentola," Opus 12,* 1819I; *Introduction & Variations on Rossini, Opus 13,* 1819I; *Maestoso sonata sentimentale,* 1828I; *Quartets (3) for Guitar& Strings, Opus 4,* 1816I; *Quartets (3) for Guitar & Strings, Opus 5,* 1816I; *Sonata and Variations on a Theme of Weigl,* 1828I; *Sonatas (6), Opus 2,* 1820I; *Sonatas (6), Opus 3,* 1820I; *Variations on "O mamma, mamma caro," Opus 10,* 1829I; *Variations on "God Save the King," Opus 9,* 1829I; *Variations on "La carmagnola,"* 1795I; *Variations, "Le Streghe," Opus 8,* 1813I; *Violin Sonata in E, "Maria Luisa,"* 1816I; *Violin Concerto in e, Opus 15,* 1815I; *Violin Concerto No. 1 in E♭/D, Opus 6,* 1817I; *Violin Concerto No. 2 in b, Opus 7,* 1826I; *Violin Concerto No. 3 in E,* 1826I; *Violin Concerto No. 4 in d,* 1830I; *Violin Concerto No. 5 in a,* 1830I
Pahissa, Jaime: *Angélica,* 1938I; *Bodas en Montaña,* 1946I; *El cami,* 1909I; *Cañigó,* 1910I; *Don Gilde las calzas verdes,* 1955I; *Galla Placidia,* 1913I; *Marianela,* 1923I; *La Morisca,* 1919I; *Nit de somnis,* 1921I; *Overture, En las costas mediterráneas,* 1904I; *La Princesa Margarida,* 1906I; *Symphony No. 1 for Strings,* 1900I; *Symphony No. 2,* 1921I
Paine, John Knowles: *Azara,* 1898I; *The Birds,* 1900I; *Centennial Hymn, Opus 27,* 1876I; *Character Pieces (4), Opus 11,* 1866I; *Columbus March & Hymn,* 1892I; *Concert Variations, Austrian Hymn, Opus 3/1,* 1860I; *Concert Variation on Old Hundred,* 1861I; *Domine salvum, Opus 8,* 1863I; *In the Country, Opus 26,* 1873I; *An Island Fantasy, Opus 44,* 1888I; *Mass in D, Opus 10,* 1867I; *The Nativity, Opus 38,* 1883I; *Nocturne in B♭, Opus 45,* 1889I; *Oedipus Tyrannus, Opus 35,* 1881I; *Organ Preludes (2), Opus 19,* 1864I; *Overture, As you Like It, Opus 28,* 1876I; *Il pesceballo, Opus 37,* 1862I; *Phoebus, Arise, Opus 37,* 1882I; *Piano Sonata No. 1 in a, Opus 1,* 1859I; *Piano Trio in d, Opus 22,* 1874I; *Piano Sonata in a/F♯, Opus 22,* 1861I; *Poseidon & Amphitrite,* 1903I; *Prelude & Fugue in g, Opus 22,* 1859I; *The Realm of Fancy, Opus 36,* 1882I; *Song of Promise, Opus 43,* 1888I; *Song of the West,* 1903I; *Songs (4), Opus 29,* 1879I; *Songs (4), Opus 40,* 1884I; *St. Peter, Opus 20,* 1872I; *String Quartet in D, Opus 5,* 1859I; *Symphony No. 1 in c, Opus 23,* 1875I; *Symphony No. 2 in A, "In Spring," Opus 34,* 1880I; *The Tempest, Opus 31,* 1876I; *Variations on . . . Star-Spangled Banner, Opus 3/2,* 1860I; *Violin Sonata in b, Opus 24,* 1875I
Paisiello, Giovanni: *Achille in Sciro,* 1778I; *Alcide al bivio,* 1780I; *L'amor contrastato,* 1788I; *Amore vendicato,* 1786I; *L'amore in ballo,* 1765I; *Andromaca,* 1797I; *Andromeda,* 1774I; *Le ane gelosie,* 1790I; *Annibale in Torino,* 1771I; *Antigono,* 1784I; *Artaserse,* 1771I; *Le astuzie amoroso,* 1775I; *I bagni d'Abano,* 1765I; *Baldassare,* 1878I; *Il barbiere di Siviglia,* 1782I; *Cantata epitalamica,* 1791I; *Cantata per la sollennità*

del S. Corpo dei Cristo, 1790I; Catone in Utica, 1789I; Christus, 1794I; Il ciarlone, 1764I; Il credulo deluso, 1774I; La dardane, 1772I; Demetrio, 1765I; Demofoonte, 1775I; Didone abbandonate, 1792I; La Disfatta di Dario, 1776I; Don Chisciotte della Mancia, 1769I; Le due contesse, 1776I; Il duello, 1774I; Elfrida, 1792I; Elira, 1794I; Fedra, 1788I; La finta amante, 1780I; Le finta maga per vendetta, 1768I; Le finte contesse, 1766I; Il fonte prodigioso di Orebbe, 1805I; I francesi brillanti, 1764I; Il furbo malacorte, 1767I; Le gare generose, 1786I; Gli astrologi immaginari, 1779I; L'idolo cinese, 1767I; L'innocente fortunata, 1772I; Ipermestra, 1791I; Lavedova a bel genio, 1766I; Le nozze di Bacco ed Arianna, 1765I; Lucinda e Armidore, 1777I; Lucio Papirio dittatore 1767I; La luna abitata 1768I; Madama l'umorista, 1765I; Mass in B♭ for Double Chorus, 1804I; Mass in C, 1807I; Mass in B♭, 1805I; Mass in G, 1809I; Mass in E♭, 1812I; Mass in G, 1809I; Mass in D, 1807I; Il matrimonio inaspettato, 1779I; Il mondo della luna, 1782I; Montezuma, 1772I; Nina, 1789I; Nitteti, 1777I; Olimpia, 1768I; Olimpiade II, 1786I; La Passione de Gesù Cristo, 1783I; I pittagorici, 1808I; Il re Teodoro in Venezia, 1784I; Requiem in c for Double Choir, 1789I; Il ritorno di Perseo, 1785I; Il ritorno d'Idomeneo in Creta, 1792I; I scherzi d'amore e di fortuna, 1771I; La serva padrona, 1781I; Silvio e Clori, 1797I; Lo sposo burlato, 1778I; String Quartets (6), 1780I; Te Deum, 1791I; Le trame per amore, 1770I; La zelmira, 1769I; Zenobia in Palmire, 1790I; I zingari in fiera, 1789I

Pakhmutova, Alexandra: Lucid Vision, 1973I; Trumpet Concerto, 1955I

Palella, Antonio: Il geloso, 1751I

Paliashvili, Zakhary: Abesalom & Eteri, 1918I; Festival Cantata, 1927I; Georgian Suite, 1928I; Latavra, 1927I; Mass in E♭, 1899I; Tbilisi, 1919I; Twilight, 1923I

Palma, Athos: Cello Sonata, 1912I; Los hijos de sol, 1929I; Jardines, 1926I; Violin Sonata, 1924I

Palmer, Horatio: Hymn, "Yield Not to Temptation," 1868I

Palmer, Robert: Cello Sonata No. 1, 1978I; Cello Sonata No. 2, 1983I; A Centennial Overture, 1965I; Concerto for Orchestra, 1943I; Evening Music, 1956I; Morning Music for Piano, 1973I; Of Night and the Sea, 1956I; Piano Concerto, 1971I; Piano Preludes (3), 1941I; Piano Quartet, 1973I; Piano Quartet No. 1, 1947I; Piano Quartet No. 2, 1973I; Piano Quintet, 1950I; Piano Sonata No. 1, 1938I; Piano Sonata No. 2, 1942I; Piano Sonata No. 3, 1979I; Piano Trio, 1958I; Quintet (piano, strings, clarinet), 1952I; Sonata for Piano, Four Hands, 1952I; Sonata for Two Pianos, 1944I; String Quartet No. 1, 1939I; String Quartet No. 2, 1943I; String Quartet No. 3, 1954I; String Quartet No. 4, 1959I; Symphony No. 1, 1953I; Symphony No. 2, 1966I; Toccata Ostinato, 1945I; Variations, Chorale & Fugue, 1947I; Viola Sonata, 1951I; Violin Sonata, 1956I; Wind Quintet, 1951I

Palmgren, Selim: Concerto Fantasy, Opus 104, 1945I; Daniel Hjort, 1910I; Piano Concerto No. 1, 1903I; Piano Concerto No. 2, Opus 33, "The Stream," 1913I; Piano Concerto No. 3, "Metamorphoses," 1915I; Piano Concerto No. 4, "Huhtikuu," 1926I; Piano Concerto No. 5, Opus 99, 1941I; The Seasons, Opus 24, 1910I

Palombo, Paul: Cello Sonata, 1966I; Crystals, 1971I; Etcetera, 1973I; Laser Music, 1975I; Morphosis, 1970I; Music for Tricerapops Americus, 1977I; Piano Sonata, 1965I; Stegowagenvolkssaurus, 1974I; String Quartet, 1967I

Pampini, Antonio: Amor divino e urbana, 1768I; Antigono, 1756I; Artaserse, 1756I; Astianatte, 1755I; Carmine complexum, 1754I; Demofoonte, 1757I; Eurione, 1754I; Madama Dulcinea, 1753I; Magnificat III, 1753I; Magnificat IV, 1756I; Magnificat V, 1757I; Magnificat VI, 1761I; Magnificat VII, 1764I; Messa a più voci, 1764I; Messiea praeconium, 1754I; Olimpiade, 1766I; Pro solemni die BVM, 1764I; Prophetiae evangelicae ac mors Isaiae, 1760I; Sofonea id est Joseph pro Rex Aegypti, 1755I; Triumphus Judith, 1757I; Venceslao, 1752I

Panufnik, Andrzej: Autumn Music, 1962I; Bassoon Concerto, 1985I; Cello Concerto, 1991I; Concertino for Timpani, Percussion & Strings, 1980I; Concerto Festivo, 1979I; Dreamscape, 1977I; Heroic Overture, 1952I; Metasymphonie (organ, timpani & strings), 1978I; Pantasonata for Piano, 1984I; Piano Concerto, 1962I; Prayer to the Virgin of Skempe, 1990I; String Quartet No. 1, 1976I; String Quartet No. 2, "Messages," 1980I; String Quartet No. 3, "Wycinanki," 1990I; String Sextet, "Trains of Thought," 1987I; Symphony No. 1, "Sinfonia Rustica," 1948I; Symphony No. 2, 1957I; Symphony No. 3, "Sinfonia-Sacra," 1963I; Symphony No. 4, "Sinfonia concertante," 1973I; Symphony No. 5, "Sinfonia di Sfere," 1975I; Symphony No. 6, "Sinfonia Mistica," 1977I; Symphony No. 7, "Metasinfonia," 1978I; Symphony No. 8, "Sinfonia Votiva," 1981I; Symphony No. 9, "Sinfonia di Speranza," 1986I; Symphony No. 10, 1989I; Tragic Overture, 1942I; Winter Solstice, 1972I

Panufnik, Roxanna: Westminster Mass, 1998I

Papaioannou, Yannis: Concerto for Orchestra, 1954I; The Corsair, 1940I; Hellas, 1956I; Inventions (12), 1958I; Piano Concerto, 1950I; Piano Pieces (7), 1967I; Piano Preludes, (12), 1938I; Piano Sonata, 1958I; Piano Suite No. 2, 1960I; Piano Trio, 1977I; Poem of the Forest, 1942I; Pygmalion, 1951I; String Quartet, 1959I; Suite for Guitar, 1960I; Symphonic Tableaux, 1968I; Symphony No. 1, 1946I; Symphony No. 2, 1947I; Symphony No. 3, 1953I; Symphony No. 4, 1963I; Symphony No. 5, 1964I; Violin Sonata, 1947I

❋

F *Biographical*   G *Cultural Beginnings*   H *Musical Literature*
I *Musical Compositions*

Papandopulo, Boris: *Beatrice Cenci*, 1959I; *Concerto for Four Timpani*, 1969I; *Doktor Atom*, 1966I; *Gitanella*, 1965I; *Harpsichord Concerto*, 1962I; *Passion of Our Lord Jesus Christ*, 1935I; *People in a Hotel*, 1967I; *Piano Concerto No. 1*, 1938I; *Piano Concerto No. 2*, 1942I; *Piano Concerto No. 3*, 1947I; *Piano Concerto No. 4*, 1958; *String Quartet No. 1*, 1927I I; *String Quartet No. 2*, 1933I; *String Quartet No. 3*, 1945I; *String Quartet No. 4*, 1950I; *String Quartet No. 5*, 1970I; *Symphony No. 1*, 1930I; *Symphony No. 2*, 1945I; *Teuta*, 1973I; *Trumpet Concerto*, 1952I; *Viola Concerto*, 1956I; *Violin Concerto No. 1*, 1944I

Papavoine: *Symphonies (6), Opus 1*, 1751I; *Symphonies (6), Opus 3*, 1755I; *Symphonies (6), Opus 4*, 1756I; *Symphony No. 1*, 1764I; *Symphony No. 2*, 1765I

Pape, Gerard: *The Burning Thing*, 1989I; *Electro-Acoustic Songs, (2)*, 1993I; *Feu Toujours Vivant*, 1997I; *Pieces (5) for Saxophone & Piano*, 1989I; *Prélude Electronique*, 1992I; *String Quartet No. 2*, 1988I; *Varesia Variations*, 1992I; *Weaveworld*, 1991I

Papineau-Couture, Jean: *Autour de Dies Irae*, 1991I; *C'est bref for Organ*, 1991I; *Courbes for Organ*, 1988I; *Nuit for Piano*, 1978I; *Oboe Quartet*, 1998I; *Papotages*, 1949I; *Piano Concerto*, 1965I; *Piano Trio*, 1997I; *Psalm 150*, 1954I; *Quasapassacaille for Organ*, 1988I; *Septet*, 1997I; *Sextet*, 1967I; *Slano*, 1976I; *String Quartet No. 1*, 1953I; *String Quartet No. 2*, 1967I; *Suite for Solo Violin*, 1956I; *Symphony No. 1 in C*, 1948I; *Tournants for Organ*, 1992I; *Vers l'extinction*, 1987I; *Verségères*, 1975I; *Viole d'amour*, 1966I; *Violin Concerto*, 1952I; *Violin Sonata in G*, 1944I

Paradies, Domenico: *La forza d'amore*, 1751I

Paradis, Maria Theresia von: *Leonore*, 1790I; *Lieder (12)*, 1786I; *Piano Fantaisie I*, 1807I; *Piano Fantaisie II*, 1811I; *Piano Trio*, 1800I; *Trauerkantate*, 1792I

Paray, Paul: *Mass for the 500ᵗʰ Anniversary of the Death of Joan of; Arc, 1931I;* Symphony No. 1 in C, 1934I

Parik, Ivan: *Cello Sonata*, 1967I; *Flute Sonata*, 1962I; *Fragment*, 1969I; *Hommage à Hummel*, 1980I; *Hommage to William Croft*, 1969I; *Sonata-Canon*, 1971I; *Tower Music*, 1971I; *Trumpet Sonata*, 1965I

Parker, Horatio: *A.D. 1919*, 1919I; *Adstant angelorum chori, Opus 45*, 1899I; *Cáhal Mór of the Wine-Red Hand, Opus 40*, 1893I; *Alice Brand, Opus 76*, 1913I; *Characteristic Pieces (5), Opus 9*, 1886I; *Characteristic Pieces (3), Opus 49*, 1899I; *Collegiate Overture, Opus 72*, 1911I; *Concerto Overture in E♭, Opus 4*, 1883I; *Concert Overture in E, Opus 4*, 1884I; *Crépuscule, Opus 62*, 1907I; *Cupid & Psyche, Opus 80*, 1916I; *Dream King and His Love, Opus*, 1891I; *The Dream of Mary, Opus 82*, 1918I; *Fairyland, Opus 77*, 1914I; *Greek Pastoral Scenes (7), Opus 74*, 1912I; *The Holy Child, Opus 37*, 1893I; *Hora Novissima*, 1893I; *Idylle, Opus 15*, 1886I; *Introduction & Fugue in e*, 1916I; *King Gorm, the Grim, Opus 64*, 1907I; *The Kobolds, Opus 21*, 1890I; *König Trojan, Opus 8*, 1885I; *The Leap of Roushan Beg, Opus 75*, 1913I; *The Legend of St. Christopher, Opus 43*, 1897I; *Love Songs (3), Opus 10*, 1886I; *Magnificat in E♭*, 1890I; *Male Choruses (3), Opus 33*, 1893I; *Male Choruses (4), Opus 39*, 1893I; *Mona, Opus 71*, 1910I; *Morven and the Grail, Opus 79*, 1915I; *Normannenzug, Opus 16*, 1888I; *Northern Ballad, A, Opus 46*, 1899I; *Ode for Commencement Day at Yale*, 1895I; *Office for the Holy Communion, Opus 57*, 1904I; *Old English Songs (6), Opus 47*, 1899I; *Organ Compositions (4), Opus 17*, 1890I; *Organ Concerto, Opus 55*, 1902I; *Organ Pieces (4), Opus 20*, 1891I; *Organ Pieces (4), Opus 28*, 1891I; *Organ Pieces (4), Opus 36*, 1893I; *Organ Sketches (5), Opus 32*, 1893I; *Organ Sonata in E♭, Opus 65*, 1908I; *Overture, Count Robert of Paris, Opus 24b*, 1890I; *Overture, Regulus, Opus 5*, 1884I; *Part Songs (5), Opus 2*, 1881I; *Part-Songs (2), Opus 27*, 1892I; *Part Songs (3), Opus 48*, 1901I; *Part Songs (4), Opus 51*, 1901I; *Part Songs for Male Voices (3), Opus 48*, 1901I; *Piano Compositions (4), Opus 67*, 1910I; *Piano Sketches, Opus 19*, 1890I; *The Prince of India*, 1905I; *Psalm, The Lord Is My Shepherd, Opus 3*, 1884I; *Sacred Songs (3), Opus 22*, 1891I; *Sacred Songs (3), Opus 58*, 1905I; *Shakespeare Songs (2), Opus 73*, 1911I; *The Shepherd's Vision, Opus 63*, 1906I; *Short Pieces (5), Opus 68*, 1908I; *Song of Times, A, Opus 73*, 1911I; *Songs (5), Opus 2*, 1882I; *Songs (9), Opus 23, 24*, 1891I; *Songs (6), Opus 29*, 1892I; *Songs (3), Opus 34*, 1893I; *Songs (3), Opus 52*, 1900I; *Songs (4), Opus 59*, 1904I; *Songs (7), Opus 70*, 1910I; *Spirit of Beauty, Opus 61*, 1905I; *Star Song, A, Opus 54*, 1901I; *String Quartet in F, Opus 11*, 1885I; *String Quintet in d, Opus 38*, 1894I; *Suite for Piano Trio, Opus 35*, 1893I; *Symphony in C, Opus 7*, 1885I; *Te Deum in A, Opus 56*, 1903I; *Te Deum in B♭*, 1890I; *Te Deum in A*, 1891I; *Union & Liberty, Opus 60*, 1905I; *Vathek, Opus 56*, 1903I; *Venetian Overture, Opus 12*, 1884I; *A Wanderer's Psalm, Opus 50*, 1900I

Parker, J. C. D.: *The Blind King*, 1883I; *The Life of Man*, 1894I; *Redemption Hymn*, 1877I; *St. John*, 1890I

Parker, Jon: *Pan Dreams*, 1989I

Parris, Robert: *Angels*, 1974I; *The Book of Imaginary Beings*, 1972I; *Flute Concerto*, 1964I; *Hymn for the Nativity*, 1962I; *Piano Concerto*, 1954I; *Quintet for Strings, & Woodwinds*, 1957I; *Sonata for Solo Violin*, 1965I; *String Quartet No. 1*, 1951I; *String Quartet No. 2*, 1952I; *String Trio No. 1*, 1947I; *String Trio No. 2*, 1951I; *Symphonic Variations*, 1987I; *Symphony*, 1952I; *Trombone Concerto*, 1964I; *Viola Concerto*, 1956I; *Viola Sonata*, 1957I; *Violin Sonata*, 1956I

Parrott, Ian: *Agincourt*, 1948I; *Eastern Wisdom*, 1987I; *Elegy*, 1957I; *Fantasia for Organ*, 1974I; *Mosaics for Organ*, 1968I; *Organ Sonata*, 1933I; *String Quartet No. 1*, 1946I; *String Quartet No. 2*, 1955I; *String*

A　*Births*　　B　*Deaths*　　C　*Debuts*　　D　*New Positions*
E　*Prizes/Honors*

Quartet No. 3, 1957I; *String Quartet No. 4*, 1963I; *String Quartet No. 5*, 1994I; *Suite No. 1 for Organ*, 1977I; *Suite No. 2 for Organ*, 1991I; *Symphony No. 1*, 1946I; *Symphony No. 2, "Round the World,"* 1961I; *Symphony No. 3*, 1966I; *Symphony No. 4, "Sinfonietta,"* 1978I; *Symphony No. 5*, 1979I; *Toccata for Organ*, 1962I

Parry, C. Hubert: *The Acharians*, 1914I; *Agamemnon*, 1900I; *The Birds*, 1883I; *Blest Pair of Sirens*, 1887I; *Cello Sonata in A*, 1883I; *Charakterbilder (7)*, 1872I; *The Chivalry of the Sea*, 1916I; *Choral Fantasies (3)*, 1915I; *Chorale Preludes (7) I*, 1912I; *Chorale Preludes (7) II*, 1916I; *The Clouds*, 1905I; *Elegy for Brahms*, 1897I; *Elegy in aᵇ*, 1913I; *Fantasie-Sonata in b*, 1878I; *Freundschaftlieder*, 1872I; *The Frogs*, 1891I; *From Death to Life*, 1914I; *Grand Fugue with Three Subjects*, 1864I; *Guinevere*, 1886I; *Hands Across the Centuries*, 1918I; *Hypatia*, 1893I; *In Praise of Song*, 1904I; *Invocation to Music, Opus 42*, 1895I; *Job*, 1892I; *King Saul, Opus 6*, 1894I; *Lady Radnor's Suite*, 1894I; *Magnificat & Nunc dimittis in A*, 1864I; *Magnificat in F*, 1897I; *Miniatures (5)*, 1926I; *Movements (3) for Violin & Piano*, 1863I; *Nonet in Bᵇ for Winds*, 1877I; *Organ Fantasia & Fugue in G*, 1913I; *Overture, Vivian*, 1873I; *Overture to an Unwritten Tragedy*, 1893I; *Piano Concerto in F♯*, 1879I; *Piano Quartet in A*, 1879I; *Piano Sonata No. 1 in F*, 1877I; *Piano Sonata No. 2 in A*, 1878I; *Piano Trio No. 1 in e*, 1878I; *Piano Trio No. 2 in Bᵇ*, 1884I; *Piano Trio No. 3 in G*, 1890I; *Proserpina*, 1912I; *A Repentance*, 1899I; *Short Pieces (12) for Violin & Piano*, 1895I; *Sonata for Two Pianos*, 1865I; *A Song of Darkness and Light*, 1898I; *Sonnets (4) from Shakespeare*, 1887I; *Sonnets & Songs without Words I*, 1869I; *Sonnets & Songs without Words II*, 1875I; *String Quartet No. 1 in g*, 1867I; *String Quartet No. 2 in e*, 1868I; *String Quartet No. 3 in G*, 1880I; *String Quintet in Eᵇ*, 1884I; *Suite in D*, 1907I; *Suite in F for Violin, & Piano*, 1907I; *Suite Moderne*, 1886I; *Symphonic Fantasia "1912" in b*, 1912I; *Symphonic Variations*, 1897I; *Symphony No 1 in G*, 1882I; *Symphony No. 2 in F, "Cambridge,"* 1883I; *Symphony No. 5*, 1912I; *Te Deum in D*, 1911I; *Te Deum in Eᵇ*, 1873I; *Te Deum in F*, 1900I; *Te Deum and Benedictus*, 1868I; *Toccata & Fugue in G, "Wanderer,"* 1921I; *Variations on an Air by Bach*, 1875I; *Violin Sonata in D*, 1889I; *A Vision of Life*, 1907I; *War & Peace*, 1903I

Parsch, Arnot: *Organ Sonata*, 1968I; *Rotae Rotarum Prologos*, 1971I

Pärt, Arvo: *Annum per annum*, 1980I; *Beatitudes*, 1991I; *Como anhela la cierva*, 1998I; *Litany: Prayers of St. Chrysostom . . .*, 1994I; *Magnificat*, 1989I; *Magnificat Anthems (7)*, 1988I; *Mein weg hat gipfel und wellentäler*, 1985I; *Missa Sillabica*, 1977I; *Neikrolog*, 1960I; *Pari intervallo, Version B*, 1980I; *Symphony No. 3*, 1971I; *Trivium*, 1976I

Pasatieri, Thomas: *Before Breakfast*, 1980I; *The Black Widow*, 1972I; *Calvary*, 1971I; *La Divina*, 1966I; *Heloise & Abelard*, 1971I; *Inez de Castro*, 1976I; *Invocations*, 1968I; *Maria Elena*, 1983I; *Mass*, 1983I; *Padrevia*, 1967I; *The Penitentes*, 1974I; *Rites of Passage*, 1974I; *The Seagull*, 1974I; *Signor Deluso*, 1974I; *Songs (3) of James Agee*, 1974I; *Three Sisters*, 1979I; *The Trial of Mary Lincoln*, 1972I; *The Trysting Place*, 1964I; *The Women*, 1965I

Pasquali, Niccolò: *Overtures (12)*, 1751I

Patachich, Iván: *Symphony No. 1*, 1965I; *Symphony No. 2*, 1966I; *Viola Sonata*, 1962I

Patterson, David: *Last Words*, 1980I; *Saving Daylight Time*, 1995I

Patterson, Paul: *Concerto for Orchestra*, 1981I; *Conversations for Clarinet & Piano*, 1974I; *Fluorescence for Organ*, 1973I; *Games for Organ*, 1977I; *Interludium for Organ*, 1972I; *Intrada for Organ*, 1969I; *Jubilate for Organ*, 1969I; *Magnificat & Nunc Dimittis*, 1986I; *Mass of the Sea*, 1983I; *Suite for Solo Cello*, 1987I; *Te Deum*, 1988I; *Upside-Down-Under-Variations*, 1985I; *Visions for Organ*, 1972I

Pauer, Jiří: *Bassoon Concerto*, 1949I; *Horn Concerto*, 1958I; *Oboe Concerto*, 1954I; *Piano Trio*, 1963I; *String Quartet No. 1*, 1960I; *String Quartet No. 2*, 1970I; *Symphony*, 1964I; *Violin Concerto*, 1959I; *Wind Quintet*, 1961I

Paulson, Gustaf: *Piano Concerto No. 1*, 1940I; *Piano Concerto No. 2*, 1961I; *Symphony No. 1*, 1928; *Symphony No. 2*, 1933I; *Symphony No. 3*, 1945I; *Violin Concerto*, 1960I

Paulus, Stephen: *American Vignettes*, 1988I; *Bagatelles*, 1990I; *Canticles: Songs & Rituals for Eaters & the May*, 1977I; *Concerto for Orchestra*, 1983I; *Double Concerto, "The Veil of Illusion,"* 1994I; *Elizabethan Songs (3)*, 1973I; *Harmoonia*, 1991I; *Ice Fields (guitar concerto)*, 1990I; *Letters for the Times*, 1980I; *Ordway Overture*, 1984I; *Organ Concerto*, 1991I; *Piano Preludes*, 1992I; *The Postman Always Rings Twice*, 1981I; *Seven Short Pieces for Orchestra*, 1983I; *Spectra*, 1981I; *Street Music*, 1990I; *String Quartet No. 1, "Music for Contrasts,"* 1980I; *String Quartet No. 2*, 1987I; *String Quartet Quartessence*, 1990I; *Summer*, 1999I; *Symphony in Three Movements, "Soliloquy,"* 1985I; *The Three Hermits*, 1997I; *Translucent Landscapes (5)*, 1978I; *Translucent Landscapes*, 1982I; *Triumph of the Saints*, 1994I; *Trumpet Concerto*, 1991I; *The Village Singer*, 1977I; *Voices*, 1988I; *The Woman at Otowi Crossing*, 1995I; *The Woodlanders*, 1984I

Pauly, Francis: *Piano Concerto in Eᵇ*, 1914I

Paur, Emil: *An Easter Idyll*, 1907I; *Symphony in A, "In der Natur,"* 1909I

Pavlica, Jir: *Missa Brevis*, 1997I

Pavlova, Atla: *Elegy* (piano concerto), 1998I; *Symphony No. 2, "For the New Millennium,"* 1998I
Pax, Juan Carlos: *Galaxia for Organ,* 1964I; *Música para piano y orquesta,* 1964I; *String Quartet No. 1,* 1938I; *String Quartet No. 2,* 1943I
Payne, Anthony: *String Quartet,* 1978I; *Symphonies of Wind & Rain,* 1993I
Payne, Maggie: *Aeolian Confluence,* 1993I
Pedrollo, Arrigo: *L'amante in trappola,* 1936I; *Delitto e Castigo,* 1926I; *Juana,* 1914I; *Maria di Magdala,* 1924I; *Terre promessa,* 1908I; *La veglia,* 1919I
Pedrotti, Carlo: *Clara di Mailand,* 1840I; *Il favorito,* 1870I; *La figlia dell'arciere,* 1844I; *Fiorina,* 1851I; *Gelmina,* 1853I; *Genoveffa del Brabante,* 1854I; *Guerra in quattro,* 1861I; *Isabella d' Aragona,* 1859I; *Lina,* 1840I; *Malina di Scozia,* 1851I; *Marion de Lorme,* 1865I; *Matilde,* 1841I; *Mazeppa,* 1861I; *Olema la schiava,* 1872I; *Romeo di Montfort,* 1846I; *Tutti in maschera,* 1856I; *La Vergine di Kermo,* 1870I; *Zaffira,* 1851I
Peeters, Flor: *Lied Symphony,* 1948I; *Lyrical Pieces (6),* 1966I; *Organ Concerto,* 1944I; *Passacaglia & Fugue,* 1938I; *Short Chorale Preludes (30),* 1959I; *Sinfonia,* 1940I
Peiko, Nikolai: *String Quartet No. 1,* 1964I; *String Quartet No. 2,* 1965I; *String Quartet No. 3,* 1966I; *Violin Sonata,* 1976I
Pelemans, Willem: *Piano Concerto No. 1,* 1945I; *Piano Concerto No. 2,* 1950I; *Piano Concerto No. 3,* 1967I; *Violin Concerto,* 1954I
Pelissier, Victor: *Ariadne Abandoned by Theseus,* 1797I; *Edwin and Angelina,* 1796I; *The Fourth of July,* 1799I; *The Vintage,* 1799I
Pellegrini, Ferdinando: *Harp Sonatas (6), Opus 16,* 1766I; *Harpsichord Sonatas (6), Opus 6,* 1763I; *Italian Songs (8),* 1760I
Penderecki, Krzysztof: *Anaklasis,* 1960I; *The Black Mask,* 1986I; *Brigade of Death,* 1963I; *Capriccio for Solo Cello,* 1968I; *Cello Concerto No. 1,* 1972I; *Cello Concerto No. 2,* 1982I; *Cello Sonata,* 1964I; *Clarinet Quartet,* 1993I; *Credo,* 1998I; *De Natura Sonoris I,* 1966I; *De Natura Sonoris II,* 1971I; *The Devils of Loudon,* 1969I; *Dies Irae,* 1967I; *Dimensions of Time and Silence,* 1960I; *The Dream of Jacob,* 1974I; *Emanationen,* 1958I; *Fluorescences,* 1961I; *Flute Concerto,* 1992I; *Fonogranni,* 1961I; *Koenig Ubu,* 1984I; *Kosmogonia,* 1970I; *Magnificat,* 1974I; *Mensura sortis* (two pianos), 1963I; *Paradise Lost,* 1978I; *Partita,* 1972I; *Passion According to St. Luke,* 1966I; *Per Slava,* 1986I; *Polymorphia,* 1961I; *Praeludium,* 1971I; *Psalms of David,* 1958I; *Psalmus,* 1961I; *Seven Gates of Jerusalem,* 1997I; *Song of Solomon,* 1973I; *Stabat Mater,* 1962I; *String Quartet No. 1,* 1960I; *String Quartet No. 2,* 1968I; *String Trio,* 1991I; *Symphony No. 1,* 1973I; *Symphony No. 2, "Christmas,"* 1980I; *Symphony No. 3,* 1995I; *Symphony No. 4,* 1989I; *Symphony No. 5,* 1992I; *Te Deum,* 1979I; *Threnody for the Victims of Hiroshima,* 1960I; *Utrenja,* 1971I; *Violin Sonata,* 1953I
Pentland, Barbara: *Cello Sonata,* 1943I; *Concerto for Organ & Strings,* 1949I; *Concerto for Piano & Strings,* 1956I; *Ice Age,* 1986I; *The Lake,* 1952I; *Mutations,* 1972I; *Piano Preludes (5),* 1938I; *Piano Quartet,* 1939I; *Piano Quintet,* 1983I; *Piano Sonata,* 1945I; *Piano Trio,* 1963I; *Piano Variations,* 1942I; *Rhapsody,* 1939I; *Septet,* 1967I; *Sonata for Two Pianos,* 1953I; *Song Cycle,* 1945I; *String Quartet No. 1,* 1944I; *String Quartet No. 2,* 1953I; *String Quartet No. 3,* 1969I; *Symphony for Ten Parts,* 1957I; *Symphony No. 1,* 1948I; *Symphony No. 2,* 1950I; *Violin Sonata,* 1946I; *Wind Octet,* 1948I
Pépin, Clermont: *Cycle-Éluard,* 1949I; *Guernica,* 1952I; *Merchant of Venice,* 1964I; *Monade I,* 1964I; *Monade IV,* 1973I; *Monade VI,* 1976I; *L'oiseau-phénix,* 1956I; *Passacaglia,* 1950I; *Piano Concerto No. 1 in c♯,* 1946I; *Piano Concerto No. 2,* 1948I; *Porte-rêve,* 1958I; *Le rite du soleil noir,* 1955I; *String Quartet No. 1,* 1948I; *String Quartet No. 2, "Variations,"* 1956I; *String Quartet No. 3, "Adagio and Fugue,"* 1959I; *String Quartet No. 4, "Hyperpoles,"* 1960I; *String Quartet No. 5,* 1976I; *Symphonic Variations,* 1947I; *Symphony No. 1 in b,* 1948I; *Symphony No. 2,* 1957I; *Symphony No. 3, "Quasars,"* 1967I; *Symphony No. 4, "La messe sur le monde,"* 1975I; *Symphony No. 5, "Implosion,"* 1983I
Pepping, Ernst: *Böhmisches Orgelbuch,* 1953I; *Chorale Partita No. 3, "Mit fried und freud,"* 1953I; *Kleines Orgelbuch,* 1940I; *Chorale Partita No. 1, "Ach wie flüchtig,"* 1953I; *Chorale Partita No. 2,* 1953I; *Choral Preludes (12),* 1958I; *Choral Vespers,* 1961I; *Deutsche choralmesse,* 1938I; *Flute Sonata,* 1958I; *Fugues (4),* 1942I; *Fugues on BACH (3),* 1943I; *Grosses Orgelbuch,* 1939I; *Das Gute Leben,* 1936I; *Hymnen,* 1954I; *Kleine Messe,* 1929I; *Missa, "Dona nobis pacem,"* 1948I; *Das Morgen,* 1942I; *Organ Concerto No. 1,* 1941I; *Organ Concerto No. 2,* 1941I; *Organ Sonata,* 1958I; *Partita, "Wer nur den lieben Gott lässt walten,"* 1932I; *Partita, "Wie schön leuchtet der morgenstern,"* 1933I; *Piano Concerto,* 1950I; *Piano Sonata No. 4,* 1945I; *Piano Sonatine,* 1931I; *Prelude,* 1929I; *Psalm CXXXIX,* 1964I; *St. Matthew Passion,* 1950I; *Sprüche und Lieder,* 1930I; *String Quartet,* 1943I; *Symphony No. 1,* 1939I; *Symphony No. 2,* 1942I; *Symphony No. 3, "Die Tageszeiten,"* 1944I; *Te Deum,* 1956I; *Toccata & Fugue, "Mitten wir im Leben sind,"* 1941I; *Variations,* 1949I; *Vaterland,* 1946I
Peragallo, Mario: *Concerto for Orchestra,* 1939I; *Violin Concerto,* 1954I
Perera, Ronald: *Earthsongs,* 1983I; *Summer Songs (5),* 1972I; *The White Whale,* 1981I; *The Yellow Wallpaper,* 1989I

❊

A *Births*   B *Deaths*   C *Debuts*   D *New Positions*
E *Prizes/Honors*

Perez, David: *Adriano in Siria*, 1752I; *Alessandro nell'Indie*, 1755I; *La Berenice*, 1762I; *Il Cinese*, 1769I; *Creusa in Delfo*, 1774I; *Demetrio*, 1766I; *Demofoonte*, 1752I; *La Didone*, 1751I; *Enea in Italie*, 1759I; *L'eroe cinese*, 1753I; *L'eroe coronato*, 1775I; *Ezio*, 1751I; *Giulio Cesare*, 1762I; *L'ipermestra*, 1754I; *L'isola disabitata*, 1767I; *Lucio Vero*, 1754I; *Olimpiade*, 1753I; *La pace fra la virtù la Bellezza*, 1777I; *Il ritorno di Ulisse in Itaca*, 1774I; *Solimano*, 1757I; *La zenobia*, 1751I

Pergament, Moses: *Dybbuk*, 1935I; *Krelantems & Eldeling*, 1927I; *Sonata for Solo Violin*, 1961I; *String Quartet No. 1*, 1922I; *String Quartet No. 2*, 1952I; *String Quartet No. 3*, 1956I; *Violin Concerto*, 1948I; *Violin Sonata*, 1920I

Peri, Achille: *L'espiazione*, 1861I; *Ester d'Engaddi*, 1843I; *I fidanzati*, 1856I; *Giuditta*, 1860I; *Orfano e diavolo*, 1854I; *Il solitario*, 1841I; *Tancreda*, 1847I; *Una visita a Bedlam*, 1839I; *Vittore Pisani*, 1857I

Perkowski, Piotr: *String Quartet No. 1*, 1930I; *String Quartet No. 2*, 1977I

Perle, George: *The Birds*, 1961I; *Brief Encounters* (string quartet), 1999I; *Cello Sonata*, 1985I; *Critical Moments*, 1997I; *Dance Overture*, 1987I; *Dickinson Songs (13)*, 1978I; *Dickinson Songs (3)*, 1979I; *Lyric Intermezzo*, 1987I; *New Etudes (6) for Piano*, 1984I; *Nightsong*, 1987I; *Piano Concerto No. 1*, 1990I; *Piano Concerto No. 2*, 1991I; *Piano Etudes (6)*, 1976I; *Piano Sonata, Opus 27*, 1950I; *Piano Sonatina*, 1986I; *Rhapsody for Orchestra*, 1954I; *Serenade No. 1*, 1962I; *Serenade No. 2*, 1968I; *Serenade No. 3*, 1983I; *Short Sonata for Piano*, 1964I; *Short Symphony, A*, 1980I; *Sinfonietta II*, 1990I; *Sonata quasi una fantasia*, 1972I; *Sonnets of Praise & Lamentation*, 1974I; *String Quartet No. 5*, 1960I; *String Quartet No. 6*, 1969I; *String Quartet No. 7*, 1973I; *String Quartet No. 8, "Windows of Order,"* 1989I; *String Quintet No. 2*, 1989I; *String Quintet, Opus 35*, 1958I; *Suite in C for Piano*, 1970I; *Symphony No. 2*, 1950I; *Three Movements*, 1960I; *Transcendental Modulations*, 1996I; *Wind Quintet No. 1*, 1959I; *Wind Quintet No. 2*, 1960I; *Wind Quintet No. 3*, 1967I; *Wind Quintet No. 4*, 1984I

Perlea, Jonel: *String Quartet*, 1922I; *Symphony*, 1951I

Perlongo, Daniel: *Piano Concerto*, 1992I; *Songs (3)*, 1994I; *String Quartet No. 1*, 1973I; *String Quartet No. 2*, 1983I; *Tapestry for Organ*, 1981I

Perosi, Lorenzo: *The Last Judgment*, 1904I; *Moses*, 1901I; *Seven Last Words of Christ*, 1913I

Perrachio, Luigi: *La calumia*, 1952I; *Il creato*, 1961I; *Mirtilla*, 1940I; *Notturni a G. Verdi (3)*, 1929I; *Piano Concerto*, 1932I; *Piano Preludes (25)*, 1927I; *Piano Quintet*, 1919I; *String Quartet No. 1*, 1910I; *String Quartet No. 2*, 1930I; *Violin Concerto*, 1932I; *Violin Sonata*, 1936I

Perrin, Jean: *String Quartet*, 1988I; *Symphony No. 3*, 1966I

Perry, George: *Belshazzaar's Feast*, 1836I; *The Fall of Jerusalem*, 1830I; *Family Jars*, 1830I; *Morning, Noon and Night*, 1822I

Perry, Julia: *Symphony No. 6*, 1966I

Persiani, Giuseppe: *Artaserse*, 1751I; *Attila*, 1827I; *Il fantasma*, 1843I; *Ines de Castro*, 1835I; *Tamerlano*, 1754I; *Zenobia*, 1761I

Persichetti, Vincent: *Concerto for Piano, Four Hands*, 1951I; *The Creation*, 1969I; *Dryden Liturgical Suite*, 1980I; *English Horn Concerto, Opus 137*, 1977I; *Fairy Tale, Opus 48*, 1950I; *Harmonium, Opus 51*, 1951I; *Mass, Opus 84*, 1960I; *A Net of Fireflies, Opus 115*, 1970I; *Organ Sonata, Opus 86*, 1960I; *Parable VI, Opus 117*, 1971I; *Piano Concerto, Opus 90*, 1962I; *Piano Quintet, Opus 66*, 1956I; *Piano Sonata No. 1*, 1939I; *Piano Sonata No. 2*, 1939I; *Piano Sonata No. 3*, 1943I; *Piano Sonata No. 4*, 1949I; *Piano Sonata No. 5*, 1949I; *Piano Sonata No. 6*, 1950I; *Piano Sonata No. 7*, 1950I; *Piano Sonata No. 8*, 1950I; *Piano Sonata No. 9, Opus 50*, 1952I; *Piano Sonata No. 10, Opus 67*, 1955I; *Piano Sonata No. 11, Opus 101*, 1965I; *Piano Sonata No. 12, opus 145*, 1980I; *Serenade No. 3 for Piano Trio*, 1943I; *Sonata for Two Pianos*, 1940I; *Sonatina No. 1-3*, 1950I; *Sonatina No. 4-6*, 1954I; *String Quartet No. 1, Opus 7*, 1939I; *String Quartet No. 2, Opus 24*, 1944I; *String Quartet No. 3, Opus 81*, 1959I; *String Quartet No. 4*, 1972I; *Symphony No. 1, Opus 18*, 1942I; *Symphony No. 2, Opus 19*, 1942I; *Symphony No. 3, Opus 30*, 1946I; *Symphony No. 4, Opus 51*, 1951I; *Symphony No. 5, "For Strings," Opus 61*, 1953I; *Symphony No. 6, "For Band," 1956I; *Symphony No. 7*, 1958I; *Symphony No. 8, Opus 106*, 1967I; *Symphony No. 9, "Sinfonia Janiculum," Opus 113*, 1970I

Peter, Johann E.: *String Quintets (6)*, 1789I

Peters, Randolph: *The Golden Ass*, 1998I

Peters, W. C.: *Symphony in D*, 1831I

Peterson, Wayne: *Capriccio for Flute & Piano*, 1972I; *Duodecaphony*, 1988I; *The Face of the Night, The Heart of the Dark*, 1991I; *String Quartet No. 1*, 1984I; *String Quartet No. 2*, 1992I; *Trilogy*, 1987I; *The Widening Gyre*, 1990I

Peterson-Berger, Wilhelm: *Arnljot*, 1909I; *Folk Ballads (4), Opus 5*, 1892I; *Frösöblomster I, Opus 16*, 1896I; *Frösöblomster II*, 1900I; *Frösöblomster III*, 1914I; *The Happiness*, 1903I; *Italian Suite*, 1922I; *Jämtland Memories, Opus 4*, 1893I; *Marit's Songs, Opus 12*, 1896I; *Oriental Songs (2), Opus 8*, 1895I; *Oriental Dance*, 1890I; *The Prophets of Doom*, 1917I; *Ran*, 1900I; *The River to the Girl*, 1899I; *Songs (2), Opus 9*,

---

F   *Biographical*   G   *Cultural Beginnings*   H   *Musical Literature*

I   *Musical Compositions*

Peterson-Berger, Wilhelm: (*cont.*)
1896I; *Songs (3), Opus 10*, 1895I; *Suite, Opus 15*, 1896I; *Suite, Last Summer*, 1903I; *Suite: Spring*, 1917I; *Sveagaldrar*, 1897I; *Symphony No. 1 in B♭, "The Banner,"* 1889I; *Symphony No. 2 in E♭, "Journey to the South,"* 1910I; *Symphony No. 3 in f, "Lappland,"* 1915I; *Symphony No. 4 in A*, 1929I; *Symphony No. 5 in b, "Solitude,"* 1933I; *Tone Pictures, Opus 11*, 1896I; *Violin Concerto in c♯*, 1928I; *Violin Sonata No. 1 in e, Opus 1*, 1887I; *Violin Sonata No. 2 in G*, 1910I; *The Wood Spirit*, 1899I
Petitgirard, Laurent: *Joseph Merrick Called Elephant Man*, 1998I
Petrassi, Goffredo: *Concerto I (orchestra)*, 1934I; *Concerto for Orchestra No. 2*, 1951I; *Concerto for Orchestra No. 3*, 1953I; *Concerto for Orchestra No. 4* (strings), 1954I; *Concerto for Orchestra No. 5*, 1955I; *Concerto for Orchestra No. 6*, 1957I; *Concerto for Orchestra No. 7*, 1962I; *Concerto for Orchestra No. 8*, 1972I; *Il cordovano*, 1948I; *Flute Concerto*, 1960I; *La folia di Orlando*, 1943I; *Introduzione e allegro for Violin & Piano*, 1933I; *Magnificat*, 1940I; *Morte dell'aria*, 1950I; *Noche oscura*, 1951I; *Nunc*, 1971I; *Orationes Christi*, 1975I; *Piano Concerto*, 1939I; *Preludio, aria e finale for Cello & Piano*, 1933I; *Ritratto di Don Chisciotte*, 1945I; *Sinfonia, siciliana e fuge* (string quartet), 1929I; *String Quartet*, 1958I; *Suoni notturni for Guitar*, 1959I
Petrella, Errico: *L'assedio di Leida*, 1856I; *Bianca Orsini*, 1874I; *Il carnevale di Venezia*, 1851I; *Catarina Howard*, 1866I; *Celinda*, 1865I; *La cimodocea*, 1835I; *La contessa d'Amalfi*, 1864I; *Diane*, 1876I; *Il diavolo color di rosa*, 1829I; *Il duca di Scilla*, 1859I; *Elena di Tolosa*, 1852I; *Il giorno delle nozze*, 1830I; *Giovanni di Napoli*, 1869I; *Jone*, 1858I; *Manfredo*, 1872I; *Marco Visconti*, 1854I; *Messe funebre*, 1873I; *La miniere di Freinbergh*, 1839I; *Morasina*, 1860I; *I pirati spagnuoli*, 1838I; *I promessi Sposi*, 1869I; *Virginia*, 1861I
Petrić, Ivo: *Bassoon Sonata*, 1954I; *Clarinet Concerto*, 1958I; *Clarinet Sonata*, 1957I; *Concerto for Harp & Strings*, 1959I; *Concert Overture*, 1860I; *Dialogues concertante*, 1972I; *Epitaph*, 1966I; *Flute Concerto*, 1957I; *Flute Sonata*, 1955I; *Gemini Music*, 1971I; *Horn Sonata*, 1960I; *Horn Sonatina*, 1961I; *Images (3)* (violin), 1873I; *Musique concertante* (piano), 1971I; *Oboe Sonatina*, 1955I; *Pieces (6), for Flute & Piano*, 1961I; *String Quartet*, 1956I; *Summer Music*, 1973I; *Symphonic Mutations*, 1964I; *Symphony No. 1, "Goga,"* 1954I; *Symphony No. 2*, 1957I; *Symphony No. 3*, 1960I; *Variations on a Theme of Bartók*, 1955I; *Wind Quintet No. 2*, 1959I; *Wind Quintet No. 3*, 1974I
Petridis, Petros: *Cello Concerto*, 1936I; *Concerto for Two Pianos*, 1972I; *Greek Melodies (4)*, 1922I; *Iphiginia in Tauris*, 1941I; *The Pedlar*, 1942I; *Piano Concerto No. 1 in C*, 1934I; *Piano Concerto No. 2 in D*, 1937I; *Symphony No. 1 in G, "Greek,"* 1929I; *Symphony No. 2, "Lyric,"* 1941I; *Symphony No. 3 in D, "Rarisian,"* 1946I; *Symphony No. 4 in C, "Doric,"* 1943I; *Symphony No. 5 in F, "Pastoral,"* 1951I; *Zefyra*, 1925I
Petrini, Francesco: *Harp Concertos (2), Opus 18*, 1782I; *Harp Concerto No. 3 & 4, Opus 27, 29*, 1793I; *Harp Sonatas (6), Opus 1*, 1769I; *Harp Sonatas (6), Opus 3*, 1780I; *Harp Sonatas (2), Opus 4*, 1780I
Petrovics, Emil: *String Quartet No. 1*, 1958I
Petsalis, Vanghelis: *Symphony No. 1*, 1995I
Pettersson, Allan: *Barefoot Songs*, 1945I; *Concerto for Violin & String Quartet*, 1949I; *Concerto No. 1 for Strings*, 1950I; *Concerto No. 2 for Strings*, 1956I; *Concerto No. 3 for Strings*, 1957I; *Sonata for Two Violins*, 1951I; *String Trio*, 1936I; *Symphonic Movement*, 1973I; *Symphony No. 1*, 1953I; *Symphony No. 2*, 1955I; *Symphony No. 3*, 1954I, 1959I; *Symphony No. 4*, 1962I; *Symphony No. 5*, 1961I; *Symphony No. 6*, 1967I; *Symphony No. 7*, 1969I; *Symphony No. 8*, 1970I; *Symphony No. 9*, 1970I; *Symphony No. 10*, 1972I; *Symphony No. 11*, 1973I; *Symphony No. 12, "The Dead in the Square,"* 1974I; *Symphony No. 13*, 1976I; *Symphony No. 14*, 1978I; *Symphony No. 15*, 1978I; *Symphony No. 16*, 1979I; *Vox Humana*, 1974I
Petukhov, Mikhail: *Piano Sonata*, 1990I
Petyrek, Felix: *Concerto in F for Two Pianos*, 1931I; *Piano Trio*, 1921I; *Sextet for Clarinet, Piano & Strings*, 1922I; *String Quartet in E*, 1913I; *Symphony in b*, 1919I; *Violin Sonata in e*, 1913I
Peyton, Malcolm: *String Quartet*, 1993I
Pfitzner, Hans: *Alte Weisen, Opus 33*, 1923I; *An den Mond, Opus 18*, 1906I; *Der arme Heinrich*, 1895I; *Cantata after Goethe*, 1949I; *Cello Concerto in a, Opus 52*, 1944I; *Cello Concerto in G, Opus 42*, 1935I; *Cello Sonata in f♯, Opus 1*, 1890I; *Das Christ-Elflein, Opus 20*, 1906I; *Columbus, Opus 16*, 1891I ,1905I ; *Concerto in b, Opus 34*, 1939I; *Das dunkle Reich, Opus 38*, 1929I; *Die Heinzelmännchen, Opus 14*, 1903I; *Herr Oluf, Opus 17*, 1891I; *Das Herz, Opus 39*, 1931I; *Jugendlieder (6)*, 1887I; *Das Käthchen von Heilbronn, Opus 17*, 1905I; *Kleine Symphonie in G, Opus 44*, 1939I; *Lethe, Opus 37*, 1926I; *Love Songs (6), Opus 35*, 1924I; *Palestrina*, 1915I; *Piano Concerto in E♭, Opus 31*, 1921I; *Piano Pieces, (5), Opus 47*; *Piano Quintet in C, Opus 23*, 1908I; *Piano Studies (6), Opus 51*, 1943I; *Piano Trio in F, Opus 8*, 1890I; *Die Rose vom Liebesgarten*, 1901I; *Songs (14), Opus 2, 3, 4*, 1889I; *Songs (19), Opus 5, 6, 7, 9*, 1889I; *Songs (8), Opus 10, 11*, 1901I; *Songs (4), Opus 15*, 1904I; *Songs (2), Opus 19*, 1905I; *Songs (7), Opus 21, 22*, 1907I; *Songs (4), Opus 24*, 1909I; *Songs (5), Opus 26*, 1916I; *Songs (8), Opus 29, 30*, 1922I; *Songs (4), Opus 32*, 1923I; *Songs (6), Opus 40*, 1931I; *Songs for Male Chorus (3), Opus 53*, 1944I; *String Quartet in d*, 1886I; *String Quartet No. 2 in D*, 1903I; *String Quartet No. 3 in c♯, Opus 36*, 1925I; *String Quartet No. 4 in c*,

---

A *Births*   B *Deaths*   C *Debuts*   D *New Positions*
E *Prizes/Honors*

Opus 50, 1942I; *Symphony in c♯*, 1931I; *Symphony No. 2 in C, Opus 46*, 1940I; *Two Male Chorus, Opus 48*, 1941I; *Violin Concerto in b, Opus 34*, 1923I; *Violin Sonata in e, Opus 27*, 1918I; *Von Deutscher Seele, Opus 28*, 1921I

Pfügen, Hans Georg: *Piano Concerto*, 1991I

Phan, P. Q.: *Banana Trumpet Games*, 1993I; *Beyond the Mountains*, 1995I; *Unexpected Desire*, 1997I

Philidor, François: *L'amant déguisé*, 1769I; *L'amitié au village*, 1785I; *Bélisaire*, 1795I; *Berthe*, 1775I; *Blaise le savetier*, 1759I; *Le bon fils*, 1773I; *Le bûcheron*, 1763I; *Carmen saeculare*, 1779I; *Le diable à quatre*, 1756I; *Ernelinde princesse de Norvège*, 1767I; *Les femmes vengées*, 1775I; *Les fêtes de la paix*, 1763I; *L'huître et les plaideurs*, 1759I; *Le jardinier de Sidon*, 1768I; *Le jardinier et son seigneur*, 1761I; *Le maréchal ferrant*, 1761I; *Le mari comme il les faudrait tous*, 1788I; *Mote, Laude Jerusalem*, 1754I; *La nouvelle école des femmes*, 1770I; *Le nozze disturbate*, 1766I; *Persée*, 1780I; *Quartets (6), Oboe & Strings*, 1755I; *Requiem in Memory of Rameau*, 1764I; *Le retour de printemps*, 1756I; *La rosière de Salency*, 1769I; *Sancho Pança dans son isle*, 1762I; *Le soldat magicien*, 1760I; *Le sorcier*, 1764I; *Te Deum*, 1786I; *Thémistocle*, 1785I; *Tom Jones*, 1765H; *Le volage fixé*, 1760I; *Zémire et Mélinde*, 1773I

Phillips, Burrill: *Cello Sonata*, 1948I; *Concerto Grosso (string quartet)*, 1949I; *Don't We All*, 1947I; *Dr. Faustus*, 1957I; *Organ Sonata*, 1964I; *Piano Commentaries*, 1983I; *Piano Concerto*, 1942I; *Piano Sonata No. 1*, 1942I; *Piano Sonata No. 4*, 1960I; *La piñata*, 1969I; *Princess & Puppet*, 1933I; *The Return of Odysseus*, 1956I; *Scherzo*, 1944I; *Selections from McGuffey's Reader*, 1933I; *Sinfonia Brevis*, 1959I; *Sonata for Violin & Harpsichord*, 1965I; *String Quartet No. 1*, 1940I; *String Quartet No. 2*, 1958I; *Tom Paine Overture*, 1946I; *Triple Concerto (clarinet, viola, piano)*, 1952I; *The Unforgiven*, 1981I; *Violin Sonata*, 1941I

Piccinni, Niccolò: *Adèle de Ponthieu*, 1781I; *Alessandro nelle Indie I*, 1758I; *Alessandro nelle Indie II*, 1774I; *L'amante ridicolo deluso*, 1757I; *L'Americano*, 1772I; *Amor senza malizia*, 1762I; *Antigono*, 1762I; *Antigono II*, 1771I; *Arco di amore*, 1797I; *Artaserse*, 1762I; *L'astratto*, 1772I; *Atys*, 1780I; *Il barone di Torreforte*, 1765I; *Berenice*, 1764I; *La buona figliuola maritata*, 1761I; *Caio Mario*, 1757I; *Catone in Utica*, 1770I; *Il cavaliere per amore*, 1763I; *La cecchina*, 1759I; *Cesare e Cleopatra*, 1770I; *Ciro riconosciuto*, 1759I; *Clytemnestra*, 1787I; *Le contadine bizzarre*, 1763I; *La contessina*, 1775I; *La corsala*, 1771I; *Il curioso del suo proprio danno*, 1756I; *Demetrio*, 1769I; *Demofoonte*, 1761I; *Diane et Endymion*, 1784I; *Didon*, 1783I; *Didone abbandonata*, 1770I; *La donna di bell'umore*, 1771I; *Le donne vendicate*, 1763I; *Le donne dispettose*, 1754I; *Le dormeur éveillé*, 1783I; *Le faux lord*, 1783I; *La finta baronessa*, 1767I; *La finta ciarlatana*, 1769I; *Le finte gemelle*, 1771I; *La furba burlata*, 1760I; *Le gelosie*, 1755I; *Gioas, re di Giuda*, 1752I; *Gionata*, 1792I; *Giove piacevole nella regia di Partenope*, 1771I; *Giove revotato*, 1790I; *Gli amanti mascherati*, 1774I; *Gli uccellatori*, 1758I; *Gli stravaganti*, 1764I; *Il gran Cid*, 1766I; *La griselda*, 1793I; *L'ignorante astuto*, 1775I; *L'innocenza riconosciuta*, 1769I; *Ipermestra*, 1772I; *Iphigénie en Tauride*, 1781I; *La locandiera di spirito*, 1768I; *Lucette*, 1784I; *Madame Arrighetta* 1758I; *La molinarella*, 1766I; *La morte di Abele*, 1758I; *Il napoletani in America*I, 1768I; *La notte critica*, 1767I; *Il nuovo Orlando*, 1764I; *L'origille*, 1760I; *Pace fra Giunone ed Alcide*, 1765I; *Pénélope*, 1785I; *La pescatrice*, 1766I; *Phaon*, 1778I; *Psalm 87*, 1798I; *Le quattro nazioni*, 1773I; *Radamisto*, 1776I; *Roland*, 1778I; *Sara*, 1769I; *La scaltra letterata* 1758I; *La schiaitù per more*, 1761I; *La schiava seria*, 1757I; *Scipione in Cartagena*, 1772I; *La serva onorata*, 1792I; *Il serva padrone*, 1794I; *Siroe rè di Persia*, 1759I; *Lo sposo burlato*, 1768I; *Lo stravaganti*, 1761I; *I vagabondo fortunato*, 1773I; *Il vago disprezzato*, 1799I; *I viaggiatori*, 1775I; *Vittorina*, 1777I; *Zenobia*, 1756I

Pichl, Václav: *Capriccios (12), Opus 46*, 1801I; *Capriccios (12) for Solo Violin*, 1796I; *Quartets (3), Clarinet & Strings, Opus 16*, 1790I; *Quartets (3), Flute & Strings, Opus 12*, 1787I; *String Quartets (6), Opus 2*, 1779I; *String Quartets (3), Opus 13*, 1788I; *String Trios (6), Opus 4*, 1785I; *String Trios (6), Opus 7*, 1783I; *Variations (100) for Solo Violin, Opus 11*, 1787I; *Violin Concertos (3), Opus 3*, 1779I

Pickard, John: *Piano Sonata*, 1987I; *A Starlight Dome*, 1995I

Picker, Tobias: *Emmeline*, 1996I; *Fantastic Mr. Fox*, 1998I; *The Rain in the Trees*, 1993I; *Invisible Lilacs*, 1991I; *Piano Concerto No. 1*, 1980I; *Piano Concerto No. 2, "Keys to the City,"* 1983I; *Piano Concerto No. 3, "Kilauea,"* 1986I; *Piano Quintet*, 1988I; *Piano-o-rama*, 1984I; *Remembering*, 1987I; *Run*, 1992I; *String Quartet, "New Memories,"* 1987I; *Suite for Cello & Piano*, 1998I; *Symphony No. 1*, 1982I; *Symphony No. 2*, 1986I; *Symphony No. 3*, 1989I; *Viola Concerto*, 1991I

Pierné, Gabriel: *Cello Sonata*, 1902I; *The Children's Crusade*, 1904I; *Concertstücke for Harp & Orchestra*, 1901I; *Cydalise et le Chèvre-Pied*, 1923I; *March of the Little Lead Soldiers, Opus 14*, 1887I; *On ne Badine pas avec l'Amour*, 1910I; *Piano Concerto in c, Opus 12*, 1887I; *Saint François d'Assise*, 1912I

Pierpont, J. S.: *Jingle Bells*, 1857I

Pijper, Willem: *Antigone*, 1922I; *De Bacchanten*, 1924I; *Cello Concerto*, 1936I; *Cello Sonata No. 1*, 1919I; *The Cyclops*, 1925I; *Flute Sonata*, 1925I; *Halewijn*, 1933I; *Phaëton*, 1937I; *Piano Concerto*, 1927I; *Piano Sonata*, 1930I; *Piano Sonatina No. 1*, 1918I; *Piano Trio No. 1*, 1914I; *Piano Trio No. 2*, 1921I; *Rhapsody for Piano & Orchestra*, 1915I; *Septet for Wind Quintet, Piano & Bass*, 1920I; *Sonata for Two Pianos*, 1935I; *Sonatina No. 2*, 1925I; *Sonatina No. 3*, 1925I; *String Quartet No. 2*, 1920I; *String Quartet No. 3*, 1923I; *String*

Pijper, Willem: (*cont.*)
   Quartet No. 4, 1928I; *String Quartet No. 5*, 1946I; *Symphonic Epigrams (6)*, 1928I; *Symphony No. 1*, "*Pan*," 1917I; *Symphony No. 2*, 1921I; *Symphony No. 3*, 1926I; *The Tempest*, 1930I; *Violin Concerto*, 1939I; *Violin Sonata No. 1*, 1919I; *Wind Quintet*, 1929I; *Woodwind Trio*, 192I
Pingoud, Ernest: *The Fetish*, 1917I; *Prophet*, 1921I; *Song of Space*, 1938I
Pinkham, Daniel: *Advent Cantata*, 1991I; *Ascension Cantata*, 1970I; *Blessings for Organ*, 1977I; *Christmas Cantata*, 1957I; *Christmas Symphony*, 1992I; *The Conversion of Saul*, 1981I; *Daniel in the Lion's Den*, 1973I; *The Dreadful Dining Car*, 1982I; *Easter Cantata*, 1957I; *Epiphanies*, 1978I; *Hezekiah*, 1979I; *Jonah*, 1966I; *Organ Concerto*, 1970I; *Overture Concertana*, 1992I; *The Passion of Judas*, 1976I; *Piano Preludes*, 1997I; *Requiem*, 1963I; *Shards for Piano*, 2001I; *St. Mark Passion*, 1965I; *String Quartet No. 1*, 1990I; *Symphony No. 1*, 1961I; *Symphony No. 2*, 1963I; *Symphony No. 3*, 1985I; *Symphony No. 4*, 1990I; *Weather Report for Piano*, 1999I; *When God Arose*, 1979I
Pintscher, Matthias: *Gesprungene Glocken*, 1994I; *Herodiade-Franmente*, 1999I; *Orchestral Pieces (5)*, 1997I; *String Quartet No. 2*, 1990I; *String Quartet No. 4*, 1992I; *Thomas Chatterton, Opus 2*, 1997I; *A Twilight's Song*, 1997I
Piston, Walter: *Capriccio for Harp & Strings*, 1963I; *Ceremonial Fanfare*, 1969I; *Chromatic Study of the Name of Bach*, 1940I; *Clarinet Concerto*, 1967I; *Concerto for Orchestra*, 1933I; *Concerto for String Quartet, Woodwinds & Percussion*, 1976I; *Concerto for Two Pianos*, 1959I; *Divetimento for Woodwinds & Strings*, 1946I; *Fantasy* (English horn & harp concerto), 1952I; *Flute Concerto*, 1971I; *Flute Sonata*, 1930I; *The Incredible Flutist*, 1938I; *Interlude for Viola & Piano*, 1942I; *Lincoln Center Festival Overture*, 1962I; *New England Sketches*, 1959I; *Orchestral Suite No. 1*, 1929I; *Orchestral Suite No. 2*, 1948; *Passacaglia*, 1943I; *Piano Concertino*, 1937I; *Piano Quartet*, 1964I; *Piano Quintet*, 1949I; *Piano Trio No. 1*, 1935I; *Piano Trio No. 2*, 1966I; *Pine Tree Fantasy*, 1965I; *Prelude & Allelgro* (organ & strings concerto), 1943I; *Prelude & Fugue*, 1934I; *Psalm & Prayer of David*, 1958I; *Quintet for Flute & String Quartet*, 1942I; *Sinfonietta*, 1941I; *String Quartet No. 1*, 1933I; *String Quartet No. 2*, 1935I; *String Quartet No. 3*, 1947I; *String Quartet No. 4*, 1951I; *String Quartet No. 5*, 1962I; *String Sextet*, 1964I; *Suite for Oboe & Piano*, 1931I; *Symphonic Piece*, 1927I; *Symphonic Prelude*, 1961I; *Symphony No. 1*, 1937I; *Symphony No. 2*, 1943I; *Symphony No. 3*, 1947I; *Symphony No. 4*, 1950I; *Symphony No. 5*, 1954I; *Symphony No. 6*, 1955I; *Symphony No. 7*, 1960I; *Symphony No. 8*, 1965I; *Toccata*, 1948I; *Turnbridge Fair*, 1950I; *Variations for Cello & Orchestra*, 1966I; *Variations on a Theme by Edward B. Hill*, 1963I; *Viola Concerto*, 1957I; *Violin Concerto No. 1*, 1939I; *Violin Concerto No. 2*, 1960I; *Violin Sonata*, 1939I; *Wind Quintet*, 1956I
Pizzetti, Ildebrando: *Agamemnone*, 1930I; *Assassinio nella cattedrale*, 1957I; *Cagliostro*, 1952I; *Il calzare d'argento*, 1961I; *Cello Concerto in C*, 1934I; *Cello Sonata in F*, 1921I; *Clitennestra*, 1964I; *Concerto dell'estate*, 1928I; *Debora e Jaele*, 1921I; *Ecclesiates*, 1958I; *Edipo a Colono*, 1936I; *Epithalamium*, 1939I; *Fedra*, 1912I; *La festa delle Panatenee*, 1935I; *Figlia di Iorio*, 1954I; *Fire Symphony*, 1914I; *Foglio d'album*, 1906I; *Fra Gherardo*, 1927I; *Gigliola*, 1915I; *Harp Concerto in B*♭, 1960I; *Ifigenia*, 1950I; *Lo Straniero*, 1925I; *La nave*, 1907I; *L'oro*, 1942I; *Orséolo*, 1935I; *Overture for a Tragic Farce*, 1911I; *Piano Concerto, "Songs of the High Season,"* 1930I; *Piano Sonata*, 1942I; *Piano Trio in A*, 1925I; *La pisanelle*, 1913I; *Poema emiliano* (violin), 1914I; *Poemetto romantico*, 1909I; *La rappresentazione de S Uliva*, 1933I; *Requiem Mass*, 1922I; *Rondo veneziano*, 1929I; *La sacra Rappresentazione d'Abraham ed Isaac*, 1917I; *Song of Songs*, 1966I; *Sonnets by Petrarch (3)*, 1922I; *String Quartet No. 1 in A*, 1906I; *String Quartet No. 2 in D*, 1933I; *Symphonic Preludes (3) on Sophocles*, 1904I; *Symphony in A*, 1940I; *Le Trachiniae*, 1932I; *Vanna Lupa*, 1949I; *Violin Concerto in A*, 1944I; *Violin Sonata in A*, 1919I
Planquette, Jean: *Les cloches de Corneville*, 1877I
Plantade, Charles: *Le mari de circonstances*, 1813I
Pleskow, Raoul: *Bagatelles (4) for Orchestra*, 1981I; *Cantata No. 1*, 1975I; *Cantata No. 2*, 1978I; *Epigrams (6) for Orchestra*, 1985I; *Music for Orchestra*, 1980I; *Music for Two Pianos*, 1965I; *Piano Bagatelles (3)*, 1969I; *Piano Sonata*, 1990I; *String Quartet No. 1*, 1979I; *Three Pieces*, 1974I
Plessis, Hubert du: *String Quartet*, 1951I
Pleyel, Ignace: *Cello Concertos (2), Ben. 101,2*, 1784I; *Cello Concerto in C, Ben. 106*, 1795I; *Ecossaises (36), Ben. 628-63*, 1803I; *Flute Quartets (6), Ben. 387-92*, 1797I; *Ifigenia in Aulide*, 1785I; *Keyboard Trios (3), Ben. 410-15*, 1797I; *Keyboard Trios (3), Ben. 428-430*, 1784I; *Keyboard Trios (6), Ben. 431-6*, 1788I; *Keyboard Trios (3), Ben. 437-9*, 1790I; *Keyboard Trios (3), Ben. 440-2*, 1791I; *Keyboard Trios (3), Ben. 443-5*, 1793I; *Keyboard Trios (6), Ben. 446-51*, 1794I; *Keyboard Trios (3), Ben. 452-4*, 1795I; *Keyboard Trios (13), Ben. 455-67*, 1796I; *Keyboard Trios (3), Ben. 471-3*, 1798I; *Keyboard Trios (3), Ben. 474-6*, 1803I; *Mass in G, Ben. 741*, 1797I; *Quartets (2), Flute & Strings, Ben. 393,4*, 1798I; *Serenade in F, Ben. 216*, 1790I; *String Quartets (6), Ben. 301-6*, 1783I; *String Quartets (6), Ben. 307-12*, 1784I; *String Quartets (6), Ben. 313-18*, 1785I; *String Quartets (6), Ben. 319-24*, 1786I; *String Quartets (6), Ben. 325-31*, 1787I; *String Quartets (12), Ben. 331-342*, 1787I; *String Quartets (10), Ben. 343-52*, 1788I; *String Quartets (6), Ben. 353-8*, 1791I;

❋

A *Births*   B *Deaths*   C *Debuts*   D *New Positions*
E *Prizes/Honors*

String Quartets (6), Ben. 359-364, 1792I; *String Quartets (3), Ben. 368,9,* 1810I; *String Quartets (6), Ben. 381-6,* 1789I; *String Quartets (6), Ben. 387-92,* 1797I; *String Quartets (2), Ben. 393-4,* 1799I; *String Quintets (2), Ben. 271,2,* 1785I; *String Quintets (2), Ben. 274,5,* 1787I; *String Quintets (2), Ben. 278,9,* 1789I; *String Quintets (5), Ben. 280-84,* 1788I; *String Septet in E♭, Ben. 251,* 1787I; *String Sextet in F, Ben. 261,* 1791I; *String Trios (3), Ben. 4012-3,* 1787I; *String Trios (6), Ben. 404-9,* 1789I; *Symphonie concertante in E♭, Opus 111,* 1786I; *Symphonie concertante in B♭, Ben. 112,* 1791I; *Symphonie concertante in F, Ben. 115,* 1792I; *Symphonie concertante in F,* 1802I; *Symphonies (2) Ben. 121, 2,* 1778I; *Symphonies (3), Ben. 123-25,* 1784I; *Symphonies (6), Ben. 127-32,* 1786I; *Symphonies (6), Ben. 133-38,* 1786I; *Symphonies (3), Ben. 139-41,* 1789I; *Symphonies (5) Ben. 142-46,* 1790I; *Symphonies in B♭ & C, Ben. 150,1,* 1799I; *Symphonies in E♭ & f, Ben. 152,3,* 1801I; *Symphonies in C & a, Ben. 154,5,* 1803I; *Symphony in D, Ben. 126,* 1785I; *Symphony in d, Ben. 147,* 1791I; *Symphony in E♭, Ben. 148,* 1793I; *Symphony in B♭, Ben. 149,* 1794I; *Symphony in C, B. 157,* 1805I; *Symphony in G, B. 156,* 1804I; *Viola/Cello Concerto in D, Ben. 105,* 1790I; *Violin Concerto in C, B. 101,* 1784I; *Violin Concerto in D, B. 102,* 1784I; *Violin Concerto in D, Ben. 103,* 1788I; *Violin Concerto in C, Ben. 104,* 1788I
Podgaits, Ephrem: *Missa Veris,* 1997I
Pohjannovo, Hannu: *String Quartet "The Poem of Autumn,"* 1997I
Pohjola, Seppo: *Piano Quartet,* 1996I; *String Quartet No. 1,* 1991I; *String Quartet No. 2,* 1995I; *Taika,* 1999I
Poissl, Johann: *Antigonus,* 1808I; *Athalia,* 1814I; *Aucassin und Nicolette,* 1813I; *Belisar,* 1826I; *Cello Concerto,* 1817I; *Clarinet Concerto,* 1812I; *Der Erntetag,* 1835I; *Judith,* 1824I; *Kaiser Ludwig's Traum,* 1826I; *Die Macht des Herrn,* 1826I; *Mass in C,* 1812I; *Mass in A♭,* 1816I; *Mass in E♭,* 1817I; *Méhuls Gedächtnisfeyer,* 1817I; *Nittetis,* 1817I; *Die Opernprobe,* 1806I; *Ottaviano in Sicilia,* 1812I; *Die Prinzessin von Provence,* 1825I; *La Rappressaglia,* 1820I; *Renata,* 1823I; *Der Sommertog,* 1814I; *Stabat Mater,* 1821I; *Der Untersberg,* 1829I; *Vergangenheit und Zukunst,* 1832I; *Der Wettkampf von Olympiar,* 1815I; *Die wie mir oder Alle betrügen,* 1816I; *Zaide,* 1843I
Ponce, Manuel: *Concierto del Sur (guitar),* 1941I; *Estrelitta,* 1914I; *Folia de España,* 1930I; *Guitar Preludes (24),* 1929I; *Guitar Sonata,* 1931I; *Piano Concerto,* 1910I; *Violin Concerto,* 1942I
Ponchielli, Amilcare: *Clarina,* 1873I; *Il figliuol prodigo,* 1880I; *La Gioconda,* 1876I; *Lituani, I,* 1874I; *Il parlatore eterno,* 1873I; *I promessi sposi,* 1856I; *Roderico, re dei goti,* 1863I; *La savojarda,* 1861I; *La stella del Monte,* 1867I
Poné, Gundaris: *American Portraits,* 1984I; *Avanti!,* 1975I; *Horn Concerto,* 1976I; *Overture, La Bella Veneziana,* 1987I; *La serenissima,* 1981I; *Titzarin,* 1986I; *Violin Concerto,* 1959I
Poniatowski, Józef: *Au travers du mur,* 1861I; *L'aventurier,* 1865I; *Bonafazio de' Geremei,* 1843I; *La contessina,* 1868I; *Don Desiderio,* 1840I; *Esmeralda,* 1847I; *Gelmina,* 1872I; *Giovanni da Procida,* 1838I; *Malek Adel,* 1846I; *Mass in F,* 1873I; *Messe solennelle,* 1867I; *Pierre de Médicis,* 1860I
Poole, Geoffrey: *Chamber Concerto, "The Second Coming,"* 1979I; *The Impersonal Touch,* 1995I; *Mosaics (organ),* 1973I; *String Quartet No. 1,* 1983I; *String Quartet No. 2,* 1990I; *String Quartet No. 3,* 1997I; *Ten,* 1981I; *The Net & Aphrodite,* 1982I; *Tibetan Book of the Dead,* 1993I
Poot, Marcel: *Cheerful Overture,* 1934I; *Pygmalion,* 1957I; *Symphony No. 6,* 1978I; *Symphony No. 1,* 1934I; *Symphony No. 2, "Motherland,"* 1943I
Porpora, Nicola: *Israel ad Aegyptiis liberatu,* 1759I; *Ouverture Royale in D,* 1763I; *Te Deum I,* 1756I; *Te Deum II,* 1757I; *Il trionfo di Camilla II,* 1760I; *Violin Sonatas (12),* 1754I
Porter, Quincy: *Antony & Cleopatra,* 1934I; *Canon & Fugue,* 1941I; *Clarinet Quintet,* 1929I; *Concerto for Two Pianos,* 1953I; *Dance in Three Time,* 1937I; *The Desolate City,* 1950I; *Harpsichord Concerto,* 1959I; *Horn Sonata,* 1946I; *The Mad Woman of Chaillot,* 1957I; *The Merry Wives of Windsor,* 1954I; *A Midsummer Night's Dream,* 1926I; *Miniatures (6),* 1943I; *Music for Strings,* 1941I; *Piano Quintet,* 1927I; *Piano Sonata,* 1930I; *Pieces (4), Violin & Piano,* 1947I; *Poem & Dance,* 1931I; *Quintet for Flute & Strings,* 1940I; *String Quartet No. 1,* 1923I; *String Quartet No. 2,* 1925I; *String Quartet No. 3,* 1930I; *String Quartet No. 4,* 1931I; *String Quartet No. 5,* 1935I; *String Quartet No. 6,* 1937I; *String Quartet No. 7,* 1943I; *String Quartet No. 8,* 1950I; *String Quartet no. 9,* 1958I; *String Sextet on Slavic Folk Songs,* 1947I; *Suite in c,* 1926I; *Symphony No. 1,* 1934I; *Symphony No. 2,* 1962I I; *Symptoms of Love,* 1961I; *Ukrainian Suite,* 1925I; *Viola Concerto,* 1948I; *Violin Sonata No. 1 in e,* 1926I; *Violin Sonata No. 2,* 1929I
Portugal, Marcos: *Argenide,* 1804I; *La donna di genio volubile,* 1796I; *Fernando nel Messico,* 1798I; *La morte de Semiramide,* 1801I; *L'oro non compra amore,* 1804I; *Zaira,* 1802I; *Zulima,* 1796I; *Il trionfo di Clelia,* 1802I
Post, David: *Symphony No. 1,* 1995I
Potter, Cipriani: *Bravura Variations on Rossini,* 1829I; *Enigma Variations, Opus 5,* 1825I; *Fanasia & Fugue in c, Opus 22,* 1818I; *Impromtus (54), Opus 22,* 1832I; *Introduction & Rondo "Alla militaire,"* 1827I; *Overture in e,* 1815I; *Overture, Antony and Cleopatra,* 1835I; *Overture, Cymbeline,* 1836I; *Overture, The*

Potter, Cipriani: (cont.)
   Tempest, 1837I; *Piano Concerto No. 2 in d*, 1832I; *Piano Concerto in E♭*, 1833I; *Piano Concerto in E*, 1835I; *Piano Sonata in C, Opus 1*, 1818I; *Piano Sonata in D, Opus 3*, 1818I; *Piano Sonata in e, Opus 4*, 1818I; *Piano Trios (3), Opus 12*, 1824I; *Ricercata on a Favorite French Theme, Opus 24*, 1835I; *Rondeau brillant No. 2, Opus 21*, 1827I; *Sextet, Opus 11*, 1827I; *Sextet in E♭*, 1836I; *Symphony No. 1 in g*, 1819I; *Symphony No. 2 in D*, 1833I; *Symphony No. 3 in B♭*, 1821I; *Symphony No. 4 in D*, 1834I; *Symphony No. 5 in c*, 1834I; *Symphonies No. 6 & 7*, 1826I; *Symphony No. 8 in E♭*, 1828I; *Symphony No. 10 in g*, 1832I

Poulenc, Francis: *Airs chantés*, 1928I; *Amphitryon* 1947I; *Les animaux modèles*, 1941I; *Aubade*, 1929I; *Le bal masqué*, 1932I; *Banalités*, 1940I; *La belle au bois dormant*, 1935I; *Le bestiaire*, 1919I; *Les biches*, 1923I; *Calligrammes*, 1948I; *Cello Sonata*, 1948I; *Chansons (7)*, 1936I; *Chansons de Lorca (3)*, 1947I; *Chansons françaises*, 1946I; *Chansons gaillardes*, 1926I; *Chansons polonaises (8)*, 1934I ; *Chansons pour enfants (4)*, 1934I; *Chansons villageoises*, 1941I; *Clarinet Sonata*, 1962I; *Cocardes*, 1919I; *Concerto Champêtre (harpsichord or piano & orchestra)*, 1928I; *Concerto in d for Two Pianos*, 1932I; *Concerto in g for Organ, Strings & Timpani*, 1938I; *La courte paille*, 1960I; *La dame de Monte Carlo*, 1961I; *Dialogues of the Carmelites*, 1957I; *La duchesse de Langeais*, 1942I; *Elégie for Horn & Piano*, 1957I; *Exultate Deo*, 1941I; *Feuillets d'album*, 1933I; *Figure humaine*, 1943I; *Flute Sonata*, 1956I; *La fraîcheur et le feu*, 1950I; *Le gendarme incompris*, 1921I; *Gloria*, 1959I; *Improvisations 1, 6*, 1932I; *Improvisations No. 8*, 1934I; *Improvisations No. 9*, 1934I; *Improvisations No. 10*, 1934I; *Improvisation No. 11*, 1941I; *Improvisation No. 12*, 1941I; *Improvisations 13, 14*, 1958I; *Intermezzo*, 1933I; *Léocadia*, 1940I; *Litanies à la vierge noire*, 1936I; *Mass in G*, 1937I; *Métamorphoses*, 1943I; *Motets for a Time of Penitence (4)*, 1939I; *Motets pour le temp de Noël (4)*, 1952I; *Mouvements Perpétuels*, 1918I; *Napoli*, 1925I; *Nocturne No. 1 in C*, 1929I; *Nocturne No. 2 in A*, 1933I; *Nocturne No. 3 in F*, 1934I; *Nocturne No. 4 in c*, 1934I; *Nocturne No. 5 in d*, 1934I; *Nocturne No. 6 in G*, 1934I; *Nocturne No. 7 in E♭*, 1935I; *Nocturne No. 8*, 1938I; *La nuit de la Saint-Jean*, 1944I; *Oboe Concerto*, 1961I; *Oboe Sonata*, 1962I; *Piano Concerto*, 1949I; *Piano Pieces (3)*, 1928I; *Piano Suite in C*, 1920I; *Poèmes de Apollinaire (4)*, 1931I; *Poèmes d'Eluard (5)*, 1935I; *Poèmes de Louise Lalanne (3)*, 1931I; *Poèmes de Ronsard*, 1925I; *Promenades*, 1921I; *Rapsodie Nègre*, 1917I; *La reine Margot*, 1935I; *Renaud et Armide*, 1962I; *Répons des ténèbres (7)*, 1961I; *Salve Regina*, 1941I; *Sécheresses*, 1937I; *Sextet for Piano & Winds*, 1939I; *Les soirées de Nazelles*, 1936I; *Le Soldat et la sorcière*, 1945I; *Sonata for Two Clarinets*, 1918I; *Sonata for Two Pianos*, 1953I; *Stabat Mater*, 1951I; *Suite Française*, 1935I; *Tel Jour Telle Nuit*, 1937I; *Le travail du peintre*, 1956I; *Trio for Oboe, Bassoon & Piano*, 1926I; *Un soir de neige*, 1944I; *Villageoises*, 1933I; *Violin Sonata*, 1943I; *La voix humaine*, 1958I; *Le voyage en Amérique*, 1951I; *Le voyageur sans bagages*, 1944I

Pousseur, Henri: *Dichterliebesreigentraum*, 1993I

Powell, John: *The Babe of Bethlehem*, 1934I; *In Old Virginia, Opus 28*, 1921I; *In the South, Opus 16*, 1906I; *Natchez on the Hill*, 1931I; *Piano Sonata No. 3, "Teutonica,"* 1913I; *Rapsodie Nègre*, 1917I; *A Set of Three*, 1935I; *Sonata Noble, Opus 21*, 1907I; *Sonata Virginanesque*, 1919I; *String Quartet No. 1*, 1907I; *String Quartet No. 2*, 1922I; *Violin Concerto*, 1910I; *Violin Sonata*, 1918I

Powell, Mel: *Cantilena*, 1970I; *Computer Prelude*, 1988I; *Duplicates* (piano concerto), 1990I; *Electronic Setting No. 1*, 1961I; *Electronic Setting No. 2*, 1962I; *Events*, 1963I; *Filigree Settings* (string quartet), 1959I; *Modules*, 1989I; *Piano Quintet*, 1957I; *Piano Trio*, 1957I; *Settings for Small Orchestra*, 1992I; *Settings for Soprano & Chamber Group*, 1979I; *Sonatina*, 1953I; *Strand Settings: Darker*, 1983I; *String Quartet No. 1, "Beethoven Analogs,"* 1949I; *String Quartet No. 2, "1982,"* 1982I; *Three Synthesizer Settings*, 1981I; *Trio '94*, 1994I

Pratt, Silas Gamaliel; *Canon for String Orchestra*, 1877I; *Centennial Hymn*, 1876I; *Centennial Overture*, 1876I; *Fantasie Caprice*, 1874I; *Grand March Heroique*, 1867I; *The Inca's Farewell*, 1891I; *Lucille*, 1887I; *Shakespearean Grand March*, 1866I; *Symphony No. 2, "The Prodigal Son,"* 1875I; *The Trimph of Columbus*, 1892I; *Zenobia, Queen of Palmyra*, 1882I

Previn, André: *Guitar Concerto*, 1971I; *Honey & Rue*, 1992I; *Piano Concerto*, 1987I; *Piano Variations on a Theme by Haydn*, 1988I; *A Streetcar Named Desire*, 1998I; *Trio for Piano, Oboe & Bassoon*, 1994I

Prevost, André: *Choregraphie I*, 1972I; *Choregraphie II, III*, 1974I; *Cosmophonie*, 1985I; *Oboe Concerto*, 1993I; *String Quartet No. 4*, 1992I; *String Quartet No. 2, "Ad pacem,"* 1972I; *String Quartet No. 3*, 1989I

Prévost, Eugène: *Cosimo*, 1834I; *Liebeszauber*, 1837I

Price, Florence: *Mississippi River Symphony*, 1934I; *Piano Concerto in f*, 1934I; *Piano Sonata in e*, 1932I; *Songs to the Dark Virgin*, 1941I; *Symphony No. 1 in e*, 1932I; *Violin Concerto No. 2*, 1952I

Pritsker, Gene: *Adversaries*, 1995I

Prokofiev, Sergei: *Alexander Nevsky, Opus 78*, 1938I; *American Overture, Opus 42*, 1926I; *Autumn Sketch*, 1910I; *Balmont Poems (5), Opus 36*, 1921I; *Betrothal in a Convent, Opus 86*, 1940I; *Cello Concerto in e, Opus 59*, 1938I; *Cello Sonata in C, Opus 119*, 1949I; *Chout, Opus 21*, 1915I; *Cinderella, Opus 87*, 1944I; *Divertimento, Opus 43*, 1929I; *The Duenna, Opus 86*, 1941I; *A Feast in Time of Plague*, 1903I; *The Flaming*

A *Births*   B *Deaths*   C *Debuts*   D *New Positions*
E *Prizes/Honors*

Angel, Opus 37, 1923I; *Flute Sonata in D, Opus 94,* 1943I; *The Gambler, Opus 24,* 1916I; *Ivan, the Terrible I,* 1942I; *Lermontov,* 1941I; *Lieutenant Kijé,* 1933I; *The Love of Three Oranges, Opus 33,* 1919I; *Maddelena, Opus 13,* 1913I; *The Meeting of the Volga & the Don, Opus 130,* 1951I; *On the Dnieper, Opus 51,* 1931I; *Overture on Hebrew Themes, Opus 34,* 1919I; *Le pas d'acier, Opus 41,* 1925I; *Peter & the Wolf, Opue 67,* 1936I; *Piano Concerto No. 1 in D♭, Opus 10,* 1911I; *Piano Concerto No. 2 in g, Opus 16,* 1913I; *Piano Concerto No. 3 in C, Opus 26,* 1921I; *Piano Concerto No. 4 in B♭ for piano, Left Hand, Opus 53,* 1931I; *Piano Concerto No. 5 in G, Opus 55,* 1932I; *Piano Etudes (4), Opus 2,* 1909I; *Piano Pieces (4), Opus 32,* 1918II; *Piano Sonata No. 1 in f, Opus 1,* 1909I; *Piano Sonata No. 10,* 1953I; *Piano Sonata No. 2 in d, Opus 36,* 1912I; *Piano Sonata No. 3 in a, Opus 28,* 1917I; *Piano Sonata No. 4 in c, Opus 29,* 1917I; *Piano Sonata No. 5 in C, Opus 38,* 1923I; *Piano Sonata No. 6 in A, Opus 82,* 1940I; *Piano Sonata No. 7 in B♭, Opus 83,* 1942I; *Piano Sonata No. 8 in B♭, Opus 84,* 1944I; *Piano Sonata No. 9 in C, Opus 103,* 1947I; *Piano Sonatinas (2), Opus 54,* 1932I; *Poems(2), Opus 9,* 1911I; *Poems by Akamatova (5), Opus 27,* 1916I; *The Prodigal Son, Opus 46,* 1929I; *Queen of Spades, Opus 70,* 1936I; *Quintet in g, Opus 39,* 1024I; *Romeo & Juliet, Opus 64,* 1935I; *Russian Folksongs (12), Opus 104,* 1944I; *Russian Overture, Opus 72,* 1936I; *Sarcasms, Opus 17,* 1912I; *Scythian Suite,* 1915I; *Scythian Suite, Opus 20,* 1914I; *Semyon Kotko, Opus 81,* 1939I; *Sonata for Two Violins in C, Opus 56,* 1932I; *Sonata in D for Solo Violin, Opus 115,* 1947I; *Songs (6), Opus 23,* 1915I; *Songs (4), Opus 66b,* 1935I; *Songs (7) & a March, Opus 89,* 1942I; *Songs (7), Opus 79,* 1939I; *Songs of Our Times, Opus 76,* 1937I; *The Stone Flower,* 1950I; *String Quartet No. 1 in b, Opus 50,* 1930I; *String Quartet No. 2 in F, Opus 92,* 1941I; *Suggestion Diabolique,* 1908I; *Symphonic Suite, 1941, Opus 90,* 1941I; *Symphony-Concerto in e, Opus 125,* 1951I; *Symphony in G,* 1902I; *Symphony in e,* 1908I; *Symphony No. 1, "Classical Symphony," Opus 25,* 1917I; *Symphony No. 2 in d, Opus 40,* 1924I; *Symphony No. 3 in c, "The Fiery Angel," Opus 44,* 1928I; *Symphony No. 4 in C, Opus 47 (revised as Opus 112),* 1930I; *Symphony No. 5 in B♭, Opus 100,* 1944I; *Symphony No. 6 in E♭, Opus 111,* 1946I; *Symphony No. 7 in c♯, Opus 131,* 1952I; *A Tale of a Real Man, Opus 117,* 1948I; *They Are Seven,* 1918I; *Toccata, Opus 11,* 1912I; *Trapeze, Opus 39,* 1924I; *Violin Concerto No. 1 in D, Opus 19,* 1917I; *Violin Concerto No. 2 in g, Opus 63,* 1935I; *Violin Sonata No. 1 in f,* 1946I; *Visions Fugitive, Opus 22,* 1917I; *War & Peace,* 1942I

Pruitt, Keith: *Movement for Orchestra,* 1993I

Pryor, Arthur: *The Whistler & His Dog,* 1905I

Puccini, Giacomo: *La bohème,* 1896I; *Capriccio Sinfonico,* 1883I; *I figli d'Italia,* 1877I; *Gianni Schicchi,* 1918I; *The Girl of the Golden West,* 1910I; *Madame Butterfly,* 1904I; *Manon Lescaut,* 1893I; *Mass in A♭,* 1880I; *Preludio sinfonico,* 1876I; *Requiem,* 1905I; *String Quartet in D,* 1883I; *Il tabarro,* 1918I; *Tosca,* 1900I; *Turandot,* 1924I; *Le villi,* 1884I

Pucitta, Vincenzo: *Adolfo e Chiara,* 1833I

Pugnani, Gaetano: *Achille in Scito,* 1785H; *Adone e Venere,* 1784I; *Correso e Calliroe,* 1792I; *Demetrio a Rodi,* 1789I; *Demofoönte,* 1788I; *Issea,* 1771I; *Nanetta e Lubino,* 1769I; *Sonatas (6) for Two Violins, Opus 4,* 1770I; *Tamas Kouli,* 1772I; *Trio Sonatas (6), Opus 2,* 1765I; *Trio Sonatas, Opus 6,* 1767I; *Trio Sonatas (6), Opus 9,* 1771I; *Violin Sonatas (6), Opus 3,* 1760I; *Violin Sonatas (6), Opus 7,* 1770I; *Werther,* 1796I

Pugni, Cesare: *Adelaide di Francia,* 1829I; *Agamemnone,* 1828I; *Amazons of the 9th Century,* 1852I; *Catarina,* 1846I; *Il contrabbandiere,* 1833I; *Coralia,* 1847I; *Il disertore svizzero,* 1831I; *Elerz e Zulmida,* 1826I; *Eolina, Kaya,* 1845I; *Un episodio di San Michele,* 1834I; *La esmeralda,* 1845I; *Faust,* 1854I; *Fiorita et la reine des elfrides,* 1847I; *Le jugment de Paris,* 1846I; *Lalla Rook,* 1846I; *The Little Hump-backed Horse,* 1864I; *Les métamorphoses,* 1850I; *Monsieur de Chalumeaux,* 1834I; *Ondine,* 1843I; *Pellia e Mileto,* 1827I; *Pharoah's Daughter,* 1862I; *Ricciarda di Edinburgh,* 1832I; *Stella,* 1850I; *Théolinda l'orphelina,* 1862I; *La vendetta,* 1832I

Pugno, Raoul: *Ninetta,* 1882I

Purcell, Kevin J.: *Symphony No. 1,* 1990I; *Symphony No. 2,* 1992I

Quantz, Johann Joachim: *Flute Duets (6), Opus 2,* 1759I

Quintanar, Héctor: *Sideral II,* 1969I

Quintón, José: *String Quintet in D,* 1913I

Rabaud, Henri: *L'appel de la mer,* 1924I; *Daphné,* 1894I; *L'été,* 1895I; *La fille de Roland,* 1904I; *Le jeu de l'amour et du hasard,* 1948I; *Job, Opus 9,* 1900I; *Job II, Opus 11,* 1905I; *Marouf, savetier du Caire,* 1914I; *Martine,* 1947I; *La procession nocturne,* 1910I; *Rolande et le mauvais garçon,* 1934I; *Symphony No. 1 in d, Opus 1,* 1893I; *Symphony No. 2 in e, Opus 5,* 1899I

Rabinovitch, Alexandre: *Schwanengesang an Apollo,* 1996I; *Sinfonia, "L'oeuvre,"* 2000I; *Symphony, "Six états intermédiaires,"* 1998I; *Die Zeit,* 2000I

Rachmaninoff, Sergei: *Aleko,* 1892I; *The Bells, Opus 35,* 1913I; *Caprice bohémien, Opus 12,* 1894I; *Cello Sonata in g, Opus 19,* 1901I; *Choruses (6), Opus 15,* 1896I; *Concert Pieces (7), Opus 10,* 1894I; *Etudes-Tableaus, Opus 33,* 1911I; *Etudes-Tableaux, Opus 39,* 1917I; *Francesca da Rimini, Opus 25,* 1905I; *The Isle*

❖

F *Biographical* G *Cultural Beginnings* H *Musical Literature*
I *Musical Compositions*

Rachmaninoff, Sergei: (cont.)
of the Dead, Opus 29, 1909I; *Liturgy of St. John Chrysostom, Opus 31,* 1910I; *Manfred,* 1890I; *The Miserly Knight, Opus 24,* 1905I; *Moments musicaux, Opus 16,* 1896I; *Nocturnes (2–f♯,F),* 1887I; *Nocturnes (3),* 1888I; *Piano Concerto No. 1 in f♯, Opus 1,* 1889I; *Piano Concerto No. 2 in c, Opus 18,* 1901I; *Piano Concerto No. 3 in d, Opus 30,* 1909I; *Piano Concerto No. 4 in g, Opus 40,* 1926I; *Piano Pieces (5), Opus 3,* 1892I; *Piano Preludes (10), Opus 23,* 1903I; *Piano Preludes (13), Opus 32,* 1910I; *Piano Sonata No. 1 in d, Opus 28,* 1907I; *Piano Sonata No. 2 in b♭, Opus 36,* 1913I; *Pieces (2) for Cello & Piano, Opus 2,* 1892I; *Pieces (2) for Violin & Piano, Opus 6,* 1893I; *Prince Rostislav,* 1891I; *Rhapsody on a Theme of Paganini, Opus 43,* 1934I; *The Rock, Opus 7,* 1893I; *Romance in f for Cello & Piano,* 1890I; *Russian Songs (3), Opus 41,* 1926I; *Scherzo in d,* 1887I; *Songs (12), Opus 4, 8,* 1893I; *Songs (12), Opus 14,* 1896I; *Songs (12), Opus 21,* 1902I; *Songs (15), Opus 26,* 1906I; *Songs (14), Opus 34,* 1912I; *Songs (6), Opus 38,* 1916I; *The Spring, Opus 20,* 1902I; *Suite No. 1 for 2 Pianos, Opus 5,* 1893I; *Suite No. 2 for Two Pianos, Opus 17,* 1901I; *Symphonic Dances, Opus 45,* 1940I; *Symphony No. 1 in d, Opus 13,* 1895I; *Symphony No. 2 in e, Opus 27,* 1907I; *Symphony No. 3,* 1936I; *Trio élégiaque in g,* 1892I; *Variations on a Theme of Corelli, Opus 42,* 1931I; *Variations on a Theme of Chopin, Opus 22,* 1903I; *Vesper Mass, Opus 37,* 1915I
Raff, Joachim: *A Capella Songs (10), Male Voices, Opus 198,* 1874I; *A Capella Songs (10), Male Voices, Opus 195,* 1870I; *Barnhard von Weimar,* 1858I; *Benedetto Marcello,* 1878I; *Blätter und Blüten, Opus 135,* 1866I; *Blondel de Nesle, Opus 211,* 1880I; *Blumensprache, Opus 191,* 1874I; *Cello Sonata in g, Opus 145,* 1868I; *Cello Sonata in D, Opus 183,* 1873I; *Cello Concerto No. 1 in D, Opus 193,* 1874I; *Cello Concerto No. 2 in G,* 1876I; *Characteristic Pieces (3), Opus 2,* 1842I; *Characteristic Pieces (3), Opus 23,* 1845I; *Concert Overture in F, Opus 123,* 1862I; *Dame Kobold,* 1869I; *De profundis, Opus 141,* 1867I; *Deutschlands Aufserstehung, Opus 100,* 1863I; *Duets (12), Opus 114,* 1864I; *Die Eifersüchtigen,* 1882I; *Fantasie brillante, Opus 4,* 1842I; *Fantaisie dramatique, Opus 19,* 1844I; *Fantaisie et variations, Opus 6,* 1843I; *Fantaisie gracieuse, Opus 12,* 1844I; *Fantasie-Sonate, Opus 168,* 1871I; *Fantasiestücke (2), Opus 86,* 1853I; *La fête d'amour in a, Opus 67,* 1854I; *Fest-Overture in A, Opus 117,* 1864I; *Frühlingslied,* 1879I; *Galops brillants (4), Opus 5,* 1843I; *Grosse fuge,* 1882I; *Hungarian Rhapsody, Opus 113,* 1863I; *Introduction and Fugue in e,* 1866I; *Italian Songs (2), Opus 50,* 1849I; *Jubel Overture in C, Opus 103,* 1864I; *Klavierstücken, Opus 126,* 1865I; *König Alfred,* 1850I; *Konzertstücke for Piano and Orchestra, Opus 48,* 1848I; *Lieder (2 vom Rhein, Opus 53,* 1849I; *Maria Stuart, Opus 172* (cycle); *Morceaux (12), Opus 83,* 1859I; *Morgenlied, Opus 186a,* 1873I; *Ode au printemps in G, Opus 76,* 1857I; *Orientales, Opus 175,* 1872I; *Die Parole,* 1868I; *Piano Concerto in c, Opus 185,* 1873I; *Piano Pieces (12), Opus 75,* 1859I; *Piano Quartet in C/c, Opus 202,* 1876I; *Piano Quintet in a, Opus 107,* 1862I; *Piano Scherzo, Opus 3,* 1842I; *Piano Serenade, Opus 1,* 1842I; *Piano Sonata with Fugue, Opus 14,* 1844I; *Piano Suite in a, Opus 69,* 1857I; *Piano Suite in c, Opus 71,* 1857I; *Piano Suite in e, Opus 72,* 1857I; *Piano Suite in e, Opus 90,* 1871I; *Piano Suite in D, Opus 91,* 1859I; *Piano Suite in g, Opus 162,* 1870I; *Piano Trio in g,* 1849I; *Piano Trio No. 1, Opus 102,* 1861I; *Piano Trio in G, Opus 112,* 1863I; *Piano Trio in g, Opus 155,* 1870I; *Piano Trio in D, Opus 158,* 1870I; *Piano Variations, Opus 179,* 1873I; *Poems (6) for piano, Opus 15,* 1844I; *Romances (12), Opus 8,* 1843I; *Samson,* 1857I; *Sangesfrühling, Opus 98,* 1864I; *Schweizerweisen, Opus 60,* 1851I; *Shakespeare Overtures: The Tempest, Macbeth; Shakespeare Overtures: Romeo & Juliet, Othello,* 1879I; *Sinfonietta in F, Opus 188,* 1873I; *Songs (8), Opus 47, 48, 49,* 1848I; *Songs (8), Opus 51, 52,* 1850I; *Songs (10), Male Voices, Opus 97,* 1863I; *Songs (8), Opus 173,* 1870I; *String Octet in c, Opus 176,* 1872I; *String Quartet No. 4 in G, Opus 138,* 1867I; *String Quartet No. 1 in d, Opus 77,* 1855I; *String Quartet No. 2 in A, Opus 90,* 1857I; *String Quartet No. 3 in e, Opus 136,* 1866I; *String Quartets (3), Opus 192,* 1874I; *String Sextet in g, Opus 178,* 1872I; *Suite No. 1 in G, Opus 180,* 1873I; *Suite No. 2, "Italian,"* 1871I; *Suite No. 3 in F, "In Hungarian Style," Opus 194,* 1874I; *Suite No. 4, "Thüringer,"* 1877I; *Suite for Violin, Opus 218,* 1879I; *Symphony in E,* 1854I; *Symphony No. 1 in D, Opus 96,* 1861I; *Symphony No. 2 in C, Opus 140,* 1866I; *Symphony No. 3 in F, "Im Walde," Opus 153,* 1869I; *Symphony No. 4 in g, Opus 167,* 1871I; *Symphony No. 5 in E, "Lenore," Opus 177,* 1872I; *Symphony No. 6 in d, Opus 189,* 1873I; *Symphony No. 7 in B♭, "In Den Alpen," Opus 201,* 1875I; *Symphony No. 8 in A, "Frühlingsklänge," Opus 205,* 1876I; *Symphony No. 9 in e, "In Summer," Opus 208,* 1878I; *Symphony No. 10 in f, "Zur Herbstzeit," Opus 213,* 1879I; *Symphony No. 11 in a, "Der Winter," Opus 214,* 1876I; *Die Tageszeiten, Opus 209,* 1878I; *Te Deum,* 1851I; *Todtentanz, Opus 181,* 1873I; *Traumkönig un sein Lieb, Opus 66,* 1854I; *Trios (6), Women's Voices, Opus 184,* 1873I; *Violin Concerto No. 1 in b, Opus 161,* 1872I; *Violin Sonata No. 1 in e, Opus 73,* 1854I; *Violin Sonata No. 2 in A, Opus 78,* 1858I; *Violin Sonata No. 3 in D, Opus 128,* 1865I; *Violin Sonata No. 4 in g, Opus 129,* 1866I; *Voler, Opus 203,* 1876I; *Von der schwäbischen Alb, Opus 215,* 1881I; *Wachet auf, Opus 80,* 1858I; *Weltende, Gericht, Neue Welt, Opus 212,* 1881I
Rahn, John: *Kali,* 1986I; *Miranda,* 1990I
Raid, Kaljo: *Little Quintet for Clarinet & String Quartet,* 1945I; *String Quartet,* 1942I
Raimondi, Ignazio: *Symphony: Les aventures de Télémaque,* 1777I; *Symphony, The Battle,* 1785I

❊

A *Births*   B *Deaths*   C *Debuts*   D *New Positions*
E *Prizes/Honors*

Rakov, Nicolai: *Symphony for Strings*, 1967I; *Symphony No. 1*, 1940I; *Symphony No. 2*, 1957I; *Violin Concerto No. 1*, 1947I

Raksin, David: *Laura*, 1945I

Rameau, Jean-Philippe: *Abaris*, 1764I; *Acante et Céphise*, 1751I; *Anacreon I*, 1754I; *Anacreon II*, 1757I; *Daphnis et Egle*, 1753I; *Lag Guirlande*, 1751I; *Linus*, 1751I; *Lysis e Délie*, 1753I; *La naissance d'Osiris*, 1754I; *Les paladins*, 1760I; *Le procureur dupe sans le savoir*, 1759I; *Les sybarites*, 1753I; *Zéphyre*, 1757I

Ran, Shulamit: *Between Two Worlds*, 1997I; *Capriccio for Piano & Orchestra*, 1963I; *Concert piece for Piano & Orchestra*, 1971I; *Legends*, 1993I; *Piano Concerto*, 1977I; *String Quartet No. 1*, 1984I; *Symphonic Poem for Piano & Orchestra*, 1967I; *Symphony No. 1*, 1990I

Rands, Bernard: *Belladonna*, 1999I; *Body and Shadow . . .* , 1988I; *Canti del Sole*, 1982I; *Canti lunatici*, 1980I; *Canzoni per orchestra*, 1995I; *Cello Concerto*, 1996I; *Ceremonial I*, 1985I; *Ceremonial II for Orchestra*, 1990I; *Ceremonial Three*, 1991I; *Concerto for Cello, Piano, Percussion & Orchestra*, 1998I; *Hiraeth (cello concerto)*, 1987I; *. . . in the receding mist . . .* , 1988I; *Madrigali*, 1977I; *Mésalliance* (piano concerto), 1972I; *Metalepsis II*, 1971I; *Requiescant*, 1986I; *Songs of the Eclipse*, 1993I; *Symphony No. 1*, 1993I; *Le tambourin Suites I, II*, 1984I; *Triple Concerto*, 1997I; *where the Murmurs die . . .* , 1993I; *Wildtrack 2*, 1973I

Rangström, Ture: *The Crown Bride*, 1919I; *Dithyramb*, 1910I; *Festival Prelude*, 1944I; *The Middle Ages*, 1921I; *A Midsummer Piece*, 1911I; *Ode to Autumn*, 1912I; *The Sea Sings*, 1914I; *Sotto Voce*, 1923I; *Symphony No. 1*, *"In Memoriam August Strindberg,"* 1915I; *Symphony No. 2*, *"My Country,"* 1919I; *Symphony No. 3*, *"Song under the Stars,"* 1929I; *Symphony No. 4*, *"Invocations,"* 1936I

Rapchak, Lawrence: *The Lifework of Juan Diaz*, 1988I; *Sinfonia antiqua*, 1989I

Raphael, Günter: *Cello Sonata No. 1 in b, Opus 14*, 1925I; *Choral Preludes (Five), Opus 1*, 1922I; *Choral Preludes, (12), Opus 37*, 1935I; *Clarinet Sonata, Opus 7 (?)*, 1925I; *Fantasia, "Christus, der ist mein Leben,"* 1945I; *Flute Sonata in e, Opus 8*, 1925I; *Galgenlieder (6), Opus 76*, 1956I; *Kleine Partita Herr Jesu Christ*, 1958I; *Marienlieder, Opus 15*, 1925I; *Oboe Sonata in b, Opus 32*, 1933I; *Organ Pièces (3), Opus 27*, 1934I; *Organ Pieces on Finnish Chorale (2), Opus 41*, 1939I; *Organ Preludes on Finnish Chorales (7) Opus 42*, 1939I; *Organ Sonata, Opus 68*, 1949I; *Piano Pieces (3), Opus 22*, 1930I; *Piano Sonatas (2), Opus 38*, 1939I; *Requiem, Opus 20*, 1928I; *Sacred Songs (3), Opus 31*, 1932I; *Sonata for Violin & Organ, Opus 36*, 1934I; *String Quartet No. 1, Opus 5*, 1926I; *String Quartet No. 2 in C, Opus 9*, 1926I; *String Quartet No. 3 in A, Opus 28 (?)*, 1930I; *String Quartet No. 4 in F, Opus 54*, 1945I; *String Quintet in f♯, Opus 17*, 1927I; *Symphony No. 1 in a, Opus 16*, 1926I; *Symphony No. 2 in b, Opus 34*, 1932I; *Symphony No. 3 in F, Opus 60*, 1942I; *Symphony No. 4 in C, Opus 62*, 1947I; *Symphony No. 5 in B♭, Opus 75*, 1953I; *Te Deum in D, Opus 26*, 1930I; *Toccata, Chorale & Variations, Opus 53*, 1944I; *Viola Sonata No. 1 in E♭, Opus 13*, 1926I; *Violin Sonata No. 2, Opus 80*, 1954I

Rapport, Evan: *String Quartet No. 2*, 2000I

Rasbach, Oscar: *Trees*, 1921I

Rathaus, Karol: *Fremde Erde*, 1930I; *The Last Pierrot*, 1926I; *Piano Concerto*, 1939I; *Suite for Orchestra, Opus 27*, 1930I; *Suite for Violin & Orchestra*, 1929I; *Symphony No. 1*, 1922I; *Symphony No. 2*, 1923I *Symphony No. 3*, 1943I; *Uriel Acosta*, 1936I; *Vision dramatique*, 1945I

Rautavaara, Einojuhani: *Angel of Dusk*, 1980I; *Angels & Visitations*, 1978I; *Autumn Gardens*, 1999I; *Harp Concerto*, 2000I; *Icons, Opus 6*, 1955I; *Isle of Bliss*, 1995I; *Magnificat*, 1979I; *Missa Duodecanonica*, 1963I; *Piano Concerto No. 1*, 1969I; *Piano Concerto No. 2*, 1989I; *Piano Concerto No. 3*, 1999I; *Preludes, (7), Opus 7*, 1956I; *Requiem in Our Time for Brass Ensemble*, 1953I; *String Quartet No. 1*, 1952I; *String Quartet No. 2*, 1958I; *String Quartet No. 3*, 1965I; *String Quartet No. 4*, 1975I; *String Quintet*, 1997I; *Studies (6), Opus 62*, 1969I; *Symphony No. 1*, 1956I; *Symphony No. 2*, 1957I; *Symphony No. 3*, 1960I; *Symphony No. 4*, 1962I; *Symphony No. 5*, 1985I; *Symphony No. 6*, 1992I; *Symphony No. 7*, 1994I; *Symphony No. 8*, 1999I; *Thomas*, 1985I; *Vigilia I: Morning Service*, 1971I; *Vigilia II: Evening Service*, 1972I; *Vincent*, 1990I; *Wind Octet*, 1962I

Rauzzini, Venanzio: *L'ali d'amore*, 1776I; *Alina*, 1784I; *Creusa in Delfo*, 1783I; *La Partenza*, 1777I; *Old Oliver, or The Dying Shepherd*, 1796I; *L'omaggio de paesani al signore del contado*, 1781I; *Piramo e Tisbe*, 1769I; *Requiem*, 1801I; *La vestale*, 1787I

Ravel, Maurice: *Alborado del gracioso*, 1918I; *Alcyone*, 1902I; *Berceuse sur le nom de Gabriel Fauré for Violin & Piano*, 1922I; *Bolero*, 1928I; *Chansons Madécasses*, 1925I; *Cinq mélodies populaires grecques*, 1906I; *Daphnis et Chloé*, 1912I; *Don Quichotte à Dulcinée*, 1932I; *L'enfant et les sortilèges*, 1925I; *Epigrammes de Clément Marot (2)*, 1899I; *Gaspard de la Nuit*, 1908I; *L'heure espagnole*, 1909I; *Histoire Naturelle*, 1906I; *Introduction and Allegro*, 1905I (ensemble); *Jeux d'eau*, 1901I; *Ma Mère l'Oye*, 1908I; *Mélodies Hébraïques (2)*, 1914I; *Miroirs*, 1905I; *Mother Goose Suite*, 1911I; *Myrrha*, 1901I; *Pavane for a Dead Princess*, 1899I; *Piano Concerto in D for Left Hand*, 1930I; *Piano Concerto in G*, 1931I; *Piano Sonatine*, 1905I; *Piano Trio in a*, 1914I; *Poèmes de Mallarmé (3)*, 1913I; *Rhapsodie Espagnole*, 1907I; *Schéhérazade*, 1903I; *Shéhérazade Overture*, 1898I; *String Quartet in F*, 1903I; *Sur l'herbe*, 1907I; *Le Tombeau de Couperin*, 1917I; *Tzigane for*

Ravel, Maurice: (*cont.*)
   Violin & Piano, 1924I; *La valse*, 1920I; *Valses nobles et sentimentales*, 1911I; *Violin Sonata*, 1927I; *Violin Sonata*, 1897I
Rawsthorne, Alan: *A Canticle of Man*, 1952I; *Cello Concerto*, 1965I; *Clarinet Quartet*, 1948I; *Concerto for Clarinet & Strings*, 1936I; *Concerto for Ten Instruments*, 1961I; *Concerto for Two Pianos*, 1968I; *Elegiac Rhapsody*, 1963I; *Elegie*, 1971I; *Fantasy Overture*, 1945I; *Madame Chrysanthéme*, 1955I; *Oboe Concerto*, 1947I; *Piano Concerto No. 1*, 1939I; *Piano Concerto No. 2*, 1951I; *Piano Quintet*, 1968I; *Piano Trio*, 1962I; *Quintet for Piano & Woodwinds*, 1963I; *String Quartet No. 1*, 1939I; *String Quartet No. 2*, 1954I; *String Quartet No. 3*, 1965I; *Suite for Flute, Viola & Harp*, 1958I; *Symphonic Studies*, 1938I; *Symphony No. 1*, 1950I; *Symphony No. 2, "Pastoral,"* 1959I; *Symphony No. 3*, 1964I; *Theme & Variations* (string quartet), 1939I; *Viola Sonata*, 1935I; *Violin Concerto No. 1*, 1948I; *Violin Concerto No. 2*, 1956I; *Violin Sonata*, 1958I
Read, Alfred: *Symphony No. 4* (band), 1993I; *Symphony No. 5* (band), 1994I
Read, Gardner: *and there appeared unto them tongues as of fire, Opus 134*, 1976I; *Aphorisms (5)*, 1991I; *Driftwood Suite, Opus 54*, 1942I; *Epistle to the Corinthians*, 1985I; *A Lute of Jade, Opus 36*, 1936I; *Night Flight*, 1936I; *Night Flight*, 1942I; *Nocturnal Visions, Opus 145*, 1985I; *Nocturnes (4), Opus 23*, 1934I; *Organ Suite, Opus 81*, 1949I; *Overture No. 1, Opus 58*, 1943I; *The Painted Desert, Opus 22*, 1933I; *Passacaglia & Fugue in d, Opus 34*, 1936I; *Piano Concerto, Opus 130*, 1977I; *Piano Quintet*, 1945I; *Piano Sonata da Chiesa*, 1944I; *Polytonal Etudes (5), Opus 116*, 1964I; *Prelude & Toccata*, 1936I; *Preludes (8) on Old Southern Hymns, Opus 90*, 1950I; *Preludes on Old Southern Hymns (6)*, 1960I; *The Prophet*, 1960I; *Satirical Sarcasms (3), Opus 29*, 1935I; *A Sheaf of Songs, Opus 84*, 1950I; *Sketches of the City, Opus 26*, 1933I; *Sonata da Ciiesa, Opus 61*, 1945I; *Songs (3), Opus 68*, 1946I; *Songs for a Rainy Night, Opus 48*, 1940I; *Songs to Children, Opus 76*, 1949I; *Sonoric Fantasia No. 4 for Organ*, 1975I; *String Quartet No. 1, Opus 100*, 1957I; *Symphony No. 1 in a, Opus 30*, 1936I; *Symphony No. 2*, 1943I; *Symphony No. 2 in e♭, Opus 45*, 1942I; *Symphony No. 3, Opus 75*, 1948I; *Symphony No. 4*, 1958I, 1959I; *Symphony No. 4, Opus 92*, 1951I; *Toccata Giocosa, Opus 94*, 1953I; *Villon*, 1965I; *Violin Concerto, Opus 55*, 1945I
Reale, Paul: *Piano Sonata Brahmsiana*, 1986I
Reber, Henri: *La nuit de Noël*, 1848I
Reda, Siegfried: *Organ Concerto No. 1*, 1947I
Redner, Lewis H.: *O Little Town of Bethlehem*, 1868I
Reed, H. Owen: *Earth Trapped*, 1960I; *La fiesta Mexicana*, 1949I; *For the Unfortunate* (band), 1972I; *Peter Homan's Dream*, 1955I; *A Tabernacle for the Sun*, 1963I; *The Turning Mind*, 1968I
Reger, Max: *Caprice in a for Cello & Piano*, 1901I; *Cello Sonata in g, Opus 28*, 1898I; *Cello Sonata in f, Opus 5*, 1892I; *Cello Sonata No. 1 in F, Opus 78*, 1904I; *Cello Sonata No. 2 in a, Opus 116*, 1910I; *Chorale Fantasis, "Ein 'feste Berg," Opus 27*, 1898I; *Choral Fantasy, "Freudich sehr . . . ," Opus 30*, 1898I; *Choral Fantasias (2), Opus 40*, 1889I; *Chorale Fantasias (3), Opus 52*; *Chorale Preludes (13), Opus 79b*, 1903I; *Choruses (3), Opus 6*, 1892I; *Choruses (3), Opus 39*, 1900I; *Clarinet (Viola) Sonata (2), Opus 49*, 1900I; *Clarinet (Viola) Sonata, No. 3, Opus 107*, 1908I; *Clarinet Quintet in A, Opus 146*, 1915I; *Clarinet/Viola Sonata No. 2 in B♭, Opus 107*, 1909I; *Easy Chorale Preludes (56), Opus 67*, 1902I; *Easy Preludes (52) to Protestant Chorales, Opus 67*, 1903I; *Eine ballettsuite, Opus 130*, 1913I; *Eine Lustspielouvertüre, Opus 120*, 1911I; *Fantasia & Fugue in d, Opus 135b*, 1916I; *Fantasia and Fugue in f, Opus 29*, 1898I; *Fantasy and Fugue on B-A-C-H, Opus 46*, 1900I; *Four Tone-paintings after Böcklin, Opus 128*, 1913I; *German Dances (29), Opus 10*, 1893I; *Gesang der Verklärten, Opus 7*, 1903I; *Introduction, Passacaglia & Fugue in b, Opus 96*, 1906I; *Little Chorale Preludes (30), Opus 135b*, 1914I; *Male Choruses (7), Opus 38*, 1899I; *Monologue, Twelve Pieces, Opus 63*, 1902I; *Mozart Variations*, 1915I; *The Nuns, Opus 112*, 1909I; *Organ Pieces (3), Opus 7*, 1892I; *Organ Pieces (12), Opus 80*, 1904I; *Organ Pieces (12), Opus 65*, 1902I; *Organ Pieces (9), Opus 129*, 1913I; *Organ Sonata No. 1 in f♯, Opus 37*, 1899I; *Organ Suite in g, Opus 92*, 1905I; *Organ Trios (6), Opus 47*, 1900I; *Piano Concerto in f, Opus 114*, 1910I; *Piano Pieces (12), Opus 59*, 1901I; *Piano Pieces (7), Opus 145*, 1916I; *Piano Quartet in d, Opus 113*, 1910I; *Piano Quartet No. 1*, 1912I; *Piano Quartet No. 2 in a, Opus 133*, 1914I; *Piano Quintet in c, Opus 64*, 1902I; *Piano Quintet in e, Opus 64*, 1898I; *Piano Sonata No. 2 in d, Opus 60*, 1901I; *Piano Sonatinas (4), Opus 89*, 1903I; *Piano Trio in b, Opus 2*, 1891I; *Piano Trio in e, Opus 102*, 1908I; *Pieces (12), Opus 80*, 1904I; *Pieces (6) for Piano Duet, Opus 94*, 1906I; *Prelude, Passacaglia & Fugue in e, Opus 127*, 1913I; *Preludes & Fugues (4), Opus 85*, 1904I; *Preludes & Fugues (6), Opus 99*, 1907I; *Psalm 100, Opus 106*, 1909I; *Quartet in E♭, Opus 109*, 1909I; *Romances (2) for Violin*, 1900I; *Eine Romantische Suite, Opus 125*, 1912I; *Römischer Triumphgesang, Opus 126*, 1912I; *Serenade in G, Opus 95*, 1906I; *Serenade, Opus 77a*, 1904I; *Sextet in F, Opus 118*, 1910I; *Sinfonietta, Opus 90*, 1905I; *Sonata No. 9 in c, Opus 139*, 1915I; *Sonatas (7) for Solo Violin, Opus 81*, 1905I; *Songs (6), Opus 4*, 1891I; *Songs (10), Opus 15*, 1894I; *Songs (10), Opus 21, 23*, 1898I; *Songs (11), Opus 35, 37*, 1899I; *Songs (27), Opus 43, 48, 51*, 1900I; *Songs (12), Opus 66*, 1902I; *Songs (15), Opus 55*, 1901I; *Songs (16), Opus 62*, 1901I; *Songs (17), Opus 70*, 1903I; *Songs (18), Opus 75*, 1903I; *Songs (2), Opus 144*, 1915I; *Songs (4),*

Opus 88, 1905I; *Songs (4), Opus 97*, 1906I; *Songs (5), Opus 98*, 1906I; *Songs (6), Opus 104*, 1907I; *Songs (6), Opus 68*, 1902I; *Songs for Male Voices (10), Opus 83*, 1904I; *Spiritual Songs (8), Opus 138*, 1914I; *Spiritual Songs, Opus 110*, 1912I; *String Quartets (2), Opus 52*, 1900I; *String Quartet in d, Opus 74* 1904I; *String Quartet in F♯, Opus 121*, 1911I; *String Trio in d, Opus 141b*, 1915I; *String Trio, Opus 77b*, 1904I; *Suite "Den Manen J.S. Bachs," Opus 16*, 1895I; *Suite in alten Stil in F, Opus 92*, 1906I; *Symphonic Fantasia & Fugue, Opus 57*, 1901I; *Symphonic Movement in d*, 1890I; *Symphonic Prologue to a Tragedy, Opus 108*, 1908I; *Träume am Kamin, Twelve Little Pieces, Opus 143*, 1915I; *Variations & Fugue on a Theme of G. P. Telemann: Opus 134*, 1914I; *Variations & Fugue on a Theme of Beethoven, Opus; 86*, 1904I; *Variations & Fugue on a Theme by Mozart, Opus; 132b*, 1914I; *Variations & Fugue on a Theme by J. S. Bach, Opus; 81*, 1904I; *Variations & Fugue on an Original Theme in f♯: Opus 73*, 1903I; *Variations & Fugue on a Theme by Hiller, Opus; 100*, 1907I; *Vaterländische Ouvertüre in F, Eine, Opus 140*, 1914I; *Violin Concerto in A, Opus 101*, 1908I; *Violin Sonata in d, Opus 1*, 1909I; *Violin Sonata in D, Opus 3*, 1891I; *Violin Sonata in a, Opus 41*, 1898I; *Violin Sonata No. 1 in C, Opus 72*, 1903I; *Violin Sonata No. 2 in f♯, Opus 84*, 1905I; *Violin Sonata No. 3 in e, Opus 122*, 1911I; *Violin Sonata No. 4 in c, Opus 139*, 1915I; *Waltz-Caprices (12), Opus 9*, 1892I; *Waltzes (7), Opus 11*, 1893I; *Die Weihe der Nacht, Opus 119*, 1911I
Reich, Steve: *The Cave*, 1993I; *The Desert Music*, 1983I; *Different Trains* (string quartet & tape), 1988I; *Drumming*, 1971I; *Electric Counterpoint*, 1987I; *Four Log Drums*, 1969I; *Four Organs*, 1970I; *The Four Sections*, 1987I; *Music for a Large Ensemble*, 1978I; *Music for Eighteen Musicians*, 1976I; *New York Counterpoint*, 1985I; *Pendulum Music*, 1968I; *Proverb*, 1995I; *Sextet*, 1985I; *Six Pianos*, 1973I; *Tehilim*, 1981I; *Three Movements for Orchestra*, 1986I; *Variations for Winds, Strings & Keyboard*, 1979I; *Vermont Counterpoint*, 1982I
Reicha, Anton: *Argine, regina de Granata*, 1806I; *Cagliostro*, 1810I; *Cello Concerto in D*, 1803I; *Clarinet Concerto*, 1815I; *Flute Quartet in D, Opus 12*, 1798I; *Flute Sonata in G, Opus 54*, 1803I; *Fugues (6) for Piano, Opus 81*, 1810I; *Les français en Egypte*, 1799I; *Grand Overture in D*, 1823I; *Grand Overture in E♭*, 1824I; *Grand Overture in C*, 1825I; *Natalie*, 1816I; *Octet in E♭, Opus 96*, 1817I; *L'ouragan*, 1800I; *Ouverture générale pour les séances des quatuors*, 1816I; *Overture to Maria Theresa*, 1805I; *Piano Concerto No. 4 in E♭*, 1804I; *Piano Fantasias (1), Opus 59*, 1805I; *Piano Sonatas (3), Opus 46*, 1804I; *Piano Sonata in E♭, Opus 43*, 1804I; *Piano Sonata in E, Opus 40*, 1803I; *Quartet in E♭, Opus 104*, 1824I; *Quartets (6), Flute and Strings, Opus 98*, 1813I; *Quintet in A, Opus 105*, 1826I; *Quintet in F, Opus 107*, 1826I; *Requiem*, 1808I; *Sapho*, 1822I; *Sonata for Four Flutes, Opus 19*, 1798I; *String Quartet in C, Opus 52*, 1805I; *String Quartet in A, Opus 58*, 1805I; *String Quartets (3), Opus 48*, 1805I; *String Quartets (3), Opus 94*, 1808I; *String Quartets (3), Opus 95*, 1808I; *String Quartets (6), Opus 96*, 1808I; *String Quintets (3), Opus 92*, 1807I; *Symphony No. 1 in E♭, Opus 41*, 1808I; *Symphony No. 2 in E♭, Opus 42*, 1808I; *Symphony No. 3 in F*, 1809I; *Symphony No. 4*, 1811I; *Variations (18) & Fantasia on Mozart, Opus 51*, 1805I; *Violin Sonata in C, Opus 44*, 1803I; *Violin Sonata in A, Opus 62*, 1803I; *Violin Sonatas (2), Opus 55*, 1803I; *Wind Quintets (6)*, 1811I; *Wind Quintets (6)*, 1848I; *Wind Quintets (6), Opus 88*, 1817I; *Wind Quintets (6), Opus 91*, 1819I; *Wind Quintets (6), Opus 99*, 1819I; *Wind Quintets (6), Opus 100*, 1820I
Reichardt, Johann: *Amore Gückkaston*, 1772I; *Andromeda*, 1788I; *Der Ariadne auf Naxos, May*, 1780I (?); *Auferstehungs-oratorium*, 1785I; *Bradamante*, 1809I; *Brenno*, 1789I; *Claudine von Villa Bella*, 1789I; *Concerto for Two Pianos*, 1773I; *Deutsche gesänge*, 1787I; *Deutsche gesänge von Matthisson*, 1794I; *Deutsche lieder (12)*, 1800I; *Egmont*, 1791I; *Erwin und Elmire*, 1791I; *Faust 1*, 1798I; *Le feste galanti*, 1775I; *Flute Sonata No. 1 in D*, 1787I; *Flute Sonata No. 2 in C*, 1787I; *Frohe lieder für deutsche männer*, 1779I; *Gedichte von R.C.I. Rudolphi . . .*, 1781I; *Die Geisterinsel*, 1798I, 1799I; *Geistliche Gesänge von Lavater*, 1790I; *Gesänge für Schöne Geschlecht*, 1775I; *Gesänge der klage und der trostes*, 1797I; *Goethes' lyrische Gedichte*, 1794I; *Gott ist unser Gesang*, 1778I; *Hänschen und Gretchen*, 1772I; *Harpsichord Sonatas (6), Opus 2*, 1777I; *Herkules Tod*, 1802I; *L'heureux Naufrage*, 1808I; *Der Holzbauer*, 1775I; *Ino*, 1779I; *Iphigenia*, 1798I; *Jery und Bätely*, 1789I; *Der Jubel*, 1800I; *Keyboard Concertos (6), Opus 1*, 1774I; *Die Kreutzfahrer*, 1802I; *Liebe nur begluckt*, 1780I; *Lieb und Frieden*, 1800I; *Lieb und Treue*, 1800I; *Lieder der Liebe und der Eisamkeit I*, 1798I; *Lieder für die Jugend*, 1799I; *Lieder von Gleim und Jacobi*, 1784I; *Lieder von C. L. Reissig*, 1812I; *Macbeth*, 1795I; *Miltons Morgensang*, 1808I; *Oden und Lieder I*, 1779I; *Oden und Lieder II*, 1780I; *Oden und Lieder III*, 1781I; *Oden und Lieder von Kleist und Hagedorn*, 1782I; *L'Olimpiade*, 1790I; *Overture to Vittoria*, 1814I; *Panthée*, 1786; *La Passione di Gesu Cristo*, 1783I; *Piano Concerto No. 8 in G*, 1772I; *Romances (6)*, 1805I; *Rosamonda*, 1801I; *Sakuntala Overture*, 1812I; *Schiller Lyrische Gedichte*, 1810I; *Schlachtsymphonie*, 1814I; *Symphonies No. 1, 2*, 1773I; *Symphonies No. 3, 4*, 1774I; *Symphony No. 6*, 1776I; *Tamerlan*, 1786I; *Der Taucher*, 1810I; *Te Deum laudamus*, 1786I; *Trio Sonatas (6), Opus 1*, 1778I; *Le troubadour italien, français et allemand*, 1806I; *Vermischte Musicalien*, 1773I; *Violin Concerto No. 7 in B♭*, 1773I; *Violin Sonatas (6)*, 1778I; *Weihnachts-Cantilene*, 1786I; *Wiegen lieder für gute deutscher Mütter*, 1798I; *Das Zauberschloss*, 1802I
Reid, Michael: *Different Fields*, 1995I

❄

F *Biographical*   G *Cultural Beginnings*   H *Musical Literature*
I *Musical Compositions*

Reimann, Aribert: *Gespenstersonate,* 1984I; *Lear,* 1978I; *Troades,* 1986I
Reinagle, Alexander: *The Castle Spectre,* 1800I; *Columbus,* 1797I; *Edwy and Elgiva,* 1801I; *The Gentle Shepherd,* 1798I; *The Italian Monk,* 1798I; *Masonic Ode,* 1803I; *Masonic Overture,* 1800I; *Overture, The Wife of Two Husbands,* 1805I; *Piano Concerto,* 1794I; *Pizarro,* 1800I; *The Savoyard,* 1797I; *Slaves in Algiers,* 1794I; *The Voice of Nature,* 1805I; *The Witches of the Rock,* 1796I
Reinecke, Carl: *Ein Abenteur Händels, Opus 104,* 1874I; *Auf hohen behehl, Opus 184,* 1886I; *Belsazar, Opus 73,* 1865I; *Cello Concerto in d, Opus 82,* 1866I; *Cello Sonata No. 1 in a, Opus 42,* 1855I; *Cello Sonata No. 2 in D, Opus 89,* 1869I; *Cello Sonata No. 3 in G, Opus 238,* 1896I; *Dame Kobold Overture, Opus 51,* 1857I; *Fest-Ouvertüre, Opus 148,* 1878I; *Flute Concerto in D, Opus 283,* 1908I; *Flute Sonata, "Undine," Opus 167,* 1885I; *Ein Geistliches Abendlied, Opus 50* (?), 1857I; *Glückskind und Pechvogel, Opus 117,* 1883I; *Der Gouverneur von Tours,* 1891I; *Harp Concerto in e, Opus 182,* 1885I; *König Manfred,* 1867I; *Overture, Opus 218,* 1892I; *Overture, Alladin, Opus 70,* 1865I; *Overture, Friedensfeier, Opus 105,* 1871I; *Overture, Zur Jubelfeier, Opus 166,* 1882I; *Overture, Zur Reformationfeier, Opus 191,* 1887I; *Piano Concerto No. 1 in e, Opus 120,* 1873I; *Piano Concerto No. 2 in C, Opus 144,* 1878I; *Piano Concerto No. 3 in f♯, Opus 72,* 1879I; *Piano Concerto No. 4 in b, Opus 254* (?), 1900I; *Piano Quartet in E♭, Opus 34,* 1853I; *Piano Quintet in A, Opus 83,* 1866I; *Piano Trio No. 1, Opus 38,* 1854I; *Piano Trio No. 2 in c, Opus 230,* 1895I; *Sommertagsbilder, Opus 161,* 1881I; *String Quartet No. 1 in E♭, Opus 31,* 1850I; *String Quartet No. 2 in F, Opus 30,* 1852I; *String Quartet No. 3 in C, Opus 132,* 1874I; *String Quartet No. 4 in D, Opus 211,* 1891I; *String Quartet No. 5 in g, Opus 287,* 1891I; *String Trio,* 1898I; *Symphony No. 1 in A, Opus 79,* 1870I; *Symphony No. 2 in c, "Hakon Jarl," Opus 134,* 1875I; *Symphony No. 3 in g, Opus 227* (?), 1895I; *Trio, Opus 188 for Oboe Horn & Piano,* 1887I; *Trio for Clarinet, Horn & Piano,* 1906I; *Trio for Piano, Clarinet & Viola, Opus 26d,* 1903I (?); *Der Vierjährige Posten,* 1855I; *Violin Concerto in g, Opus 141,* 1877I; *Violin Sonata in e, Opus 116,* 1872I; *Wilhelm Tell, Opus 102,* 1871I; *Wind Octet, Opus 216,* 1892I; *Zenobia Overture, Opus 193,* 1887I
Reise, Jay: *Rasputin,* 1988I
Reissiger, Carl Gottlieb: *David,* 1850I; *Didone abbandonata,* 1824I; *Die Felsenmühle zu Estaliéres,* 1831I; *Libella,* 1828I; *Overture, Das Rockenweibchen, Opus 10,* 1821I; *Overture, Der Ahrenschatz, Opus 80,* 1825; *Der Schiffbruch der Medusa,* 1846I; *String Quintet,* 1862I; *Turandot,* 1835I; *Yelva,* 1827I
Reizenstein, Franz: *Cello Sonata,* 1947I
Renié, Henriette: *Ballade Fantastique for Harp,* 1913I; *Danse des Lutins for Harp,* 1911I; *Harp,* 1901I
Respighi, Ottorino: *La boutique fantasque,* 1918I; *Brazilian Impressions,* 1927I; *Church Windows,* 1927I; *Concerto Gregoriano,* 1922I; *The Fountains of Rome,* 1917I; *Gods of the Woods,* 1917I; *Lauda per la Nativita del Signore,* 1930I; *Little Pieces for Two Pianos* (6), 1926I; *Lucrezia,* 1935I; *Maria Egiziaca,* 1932I; *Metamorphosen,* 1930I; *Piano Concerto,* 1902I; *La primavera,* 1923I; *Quartetto dorico,* 1924I; *Quattro liriche,* 1920I; *Re Enzo,* 1905I; *Roman Festivals,* 1929I; *Sei Lirische I,* 1909I; *Sei Melodie,* 1909I; *Semirama,* 1910I; *Sinfonia Drammatica,* 1915I; *String Quartet in D,* 1907I; *Trittico Botticelliano,* 1926I; *Violin Sonata,* 1917I
Reubke, Julius: *Organ Sonata,* 1857I; *Piano Sonata,* 1857I
Reutter, Georg: *La corona,* 1754I; *La gara,* 1755I; *Le grazie vendicate,* 1758I; *Il sogno,* 1757I; *Il tributo di Rispetto e d'Amore,* 1754I; *La virtuosa emulazione,* 1751I
Revueltas, Silvestre: *Colorines,* 1932I; *Cuauhnahuac,* 1930I; *La noche de los Mayas,* 1939I; *Sensemayá,* 1938I
Reyer, Ernest: *Salammbô,* 1890I; *Maître Wolfram,* 1854I
Reyer, Louis: *La statue,* 1861I
Reynolds, Roger: *Archipelago,* 1982I; *Ariadne's Thread* (string quartet), 1994I; *Ariadne's Thread,* 1994I; *The Bacchae,* 1991I; *The Behavior of Mirrors,* 1986I; *Canon in c* (string quartet), 1985I; *Dionysus,* 1990I; *The Ivanov Suite,* 1991I; *Last things, I think, to think about . . . ,* 1994I; *Odyssey,* 1993I; *Piano Variations,* 1988I; *The Red Act Arias,* 1997I; *Symphony, "The Stages of Life,"* 1992I, 1993I; *Symphony: Myths,* 1990I; *Symphony: Vertigo,* 1987I; *Transfigured Wind II,* 1984I; *The Vanity of Words: Voicespace V,* 1986I; *Versions/Stages I,* 1988I; *Versions/Stages II,* 1988I; *Versions/Stages III,* 1988I; *Versions/Stages IV,* 1991I; *Vertigo,* 1986I; *Voicespace I, "Still,"* 1975I; *Voicespace II, "A Merciful Coincidence,"* 1976I; *Voicespace III, "Eclipse,"* 1980I; *Watershed III,* 1995I; *Whispers Out of Time,* 1988I
Rezniček, Emil von: *A Comedy Overture,* 1903I; *Donna Diana,* 1894I; *Eros & Psyche,* 1917I; *Holofernes,* 1923I; *Die Jungfrau von Orleans,* 1887I; *Ritter Blaubart,* 1920I; *Symphony No. 1, "Tragic,"* 1904I; *Symphony No. 2, "Ironic,"* 1905I; *Symphony No. 3, "Schön,"* 1918I; *Symphony No. 4,* 1919I; *Til Eulenspiegel,* 1902I
Rheinberger, Joseph: *Fughettas* (3), 1851I; *Fughettas in Strict Style* (12), 1883I; *Mass in E♭ (cantus Missae), Opus 109,* 1878I; *Organ Concerto No. 1 in F, Opus 137,* 1884I; *Organ Concerto No. 2 in g, Opus 177,* 1894I; *Organ Sonata No. 5,* 1878I; *Organ Sonata No. 6,* 1880I; *Organ Sonata No. 20,* 1901I; *Preludes & Fugues* (3), 1854I; *Die Sieben Raber,* 1869I; *The Star of Bethlehem,* 1890I
Rhodes, Philip: *Visions of Remembrances,* 1979I

❀

A *Births* B *Deaths* C *Debuts* D *New Positions*
E *Prizes/Honors*

Ricci, Federico: *I due ritratti*, 1850I; *Griselda*, 1847I
Ricci, Luigi: *Un aventura di scaramuccia*, 1834I; *Il Birraio di Preston*, 1847I; *Chi dura vince*, 1834I; *Chiara di Montalbano*, 1835I; *Chiara di Rosemberg*, 1831I; *La donna colonello*, 1835I; *I due sergenti*, 1833I; *L'impresario in angustie*, 1823I
Richter, Franz X.: *Cello Concerto in G*, 1766I; *Horn Concertos (6)*, 1754I; *Periodic Overture No. 18*, 1767I; *Simphonie Periodique No. 49*, 1763I (?); *Sinfonia Periodique No. 61*, 1764I; *Sinfonias (No. 12-14) a piu stromenti obbligati*, 1763I; *Sonatas (6) da camera*, 1764I; *String Quartets (6), Opus 5*, 1768I; *Symphonies (6), Opus 2*, 1760I; *Symphonies (6), Opus 3*, 1760I; *Symphonies (6), Opus 4*, 1765I; *Symphonies (6), Opus 7*, 1767I; *Symphonies (3), Opus 10*, 1758I; *Trio Sonatas (6), Opus 3*, 1764I
Riegger, Wallingford: *La belle dame sans merci*, 1924I; *Candide, Opus 24*, 1937I; *Canon & Fugue in d for Strings, Opus 33*, 1941I; *Cantata, In Certainty of Song, Opus 46*, 1950I; *Concerto for Piano & Woodwind Quintet*, 1953I; *Dance Rhythms, Opus 58*, 1955I; *Dichotomy, Opus 12*; *Evocation*, 1933I; *Fantasy & Fugue, Opus 10*, 1931I; *Festival Overture, Opus 68*, 1957I; *Holiday Sketches (violin)*, 1927I; *Machine Ballet, Opus 28*, 1938I; *Music for Brass Choir, Opus 45*, 1949I; *New & Old: Twelve Pieces, Opus 38*, 1944I; *Overture, Opus 60*, 1955I; *Passacaglia & Fugue, Opus 34*, 1942I; *Piano Quintet, Opus 47*, 1951I; *Piano Trio*, 1920I; *Rhapsody for Orchestra, Opus 5*, 1926I; *A Shakespeare Sonnet*, 1956I; *String Quartet No. 1, Opus 30*, 1939I; *String Quartet No. 2*, 1947I; *String Quartet No. 3*, 1948I; *Study in Sonority, Opus 7*, 1927I; *Symphony No. 2, Opus 41*, 1945I; *Symphony No. 4, Opus 63*, 1956I; *Symphony No. 3, Opus 42*, 1947I; *Tone Pictures (4), Opus 14*, 1932I; *Variations for Piano & Orchestra*, 1953I; *Variations for Violin & Orchestra*, 1959I; *Woodwind Quintet, Opus 51*, 1952I
Ries, Ferdinand: *Horn Sonata*, 1810I
Rieti, Vittorio: *Cello Concerto No. 2*, 1953I; *Concerto for Two Pianos*, 1951I; *Piano Concerto No. 1*, 1926I; *Piano Concerto No. 2*, 1937I; *Piano Concerto No. 3*, 1955I; *Piano Preludes (12)*, 1979I; *Piano Sonata in A♭*, 1938I; *Piano Suite*, 1926I; *Short Pieces (6)*, 1932I; *Sonatina*, 1925I; *String Quartet No. 1*, 1926I; *String Quartet No. 2*, 1941I; *String Quartet no. 3*, 1951I; *String Quartet No. 4*, 1960I; *Symphony No. 1*, 1929I; *Symphony No. 2*, 1930I; *Symphony No. 2*, 1932I; *Symphony No. 4, "Tripartita,"* 1942I; *Symphony No. 5*, 1945I; *Symphony No. 6*, 1973I; *Symphony No. 7*, 1977I; *Symphony No. 8*, 1981I; *Symphony No. 9*, 1984I
Righini, Vincenzo: *Alcide al Bivio*, 1790I; *Armida*, 1782I; *Il bottegha del caffe*, 1775I; *Il convite di pietra*, 1776I; *Enea nel Lazio*, 1793I; *Flute Concerto*, 1802I; *La Gerusalemme liberata*, 1799I; *Mass in D, "Krönungsmesse,"* 1790I; *Il natal d'Apollo*, 1788I; *Oboe Concerto*, 1802I; *Partita in E♭ (ww octet)*, 1800I; *Requiem*, 1810I; *La sorpresa amorosa*, 1780I; *Te Deum*, 1810II; *Tigrano*, 1800I; *La vedova scaltra*, 1774I
Rihm, Wolfgang: *Deus Passus–St. Luke Passion*, 2000I; *Die Eroberung von Mexico*, 1992I; *Klangbeschreibung*, 1987I; *Lowry-Lieder*, 1987I; *Morponie*, 1874I; *Music for Three Strings*, 1977I; *Neue Alexanderlieder*, 1979I; *Das Rot*, 1990I; *Songs, (13), Opus 1*, 1970I; *Symphony No. 1*, 1976I; *Symphony No. 2, " Sub-Kontar,"* 1976I; *Symphony No. 3*, 1979I
Riisager, Knudåge: *Concertino for Trumpet & Strings*, 1933I; *Darduse*, 1936I; *Erastus Montanus Overture*, 1920I; *Etudes*, 1948I; *Qarrtsiluni*, 1938I; *Slaraffenland*, 1936I; *Twelve by the Mall*, 1939I
Riley, Terry: *Cadenza on the Night Plain*, 1984I; *Embroidery*, 1980I; *The Ethereal Time Shadow*, 1983I; *G-Song*, 1981I; *The Harp of New Albion, for Piano*, 1984I; *The Medicine Wheel*, 1983I; *Mescalin Mix*, 1963I; *Offering to Chief Crazy Horse*, 1983I; *A Rainbow in the Curved Air*, 1968I; *The Sands*, 1992I; *Song of the Emerald Runner*, 1983I; *Spectra*, 1959I; *String Quartet No. 1*, 1960I; *String Trio*, 1961I; *Sunrise of the Planetary Dream Collector*, 1981I
Rimsky-Korsakov, Nicolai: *By the Sea*, 1897I; *Capriccio Espagnole, Opus 34*, 1887I; *Christmas Eve*, 1895I; *Concerto for Clarinet & Band*, 1878I; *Le coq d'or*, 1907I; *Dubinuska*, 1905I; *Fantasia on Russian Themes, Opus 33*, 1886I; *Fantasy on Serbian Themes*, 1867I; *Ivan, the Terrible*, 1872I; *The Invisible City of Kitezh*, 1904I; *Kaschei, the Immortal*, 1902I; *May Night*, 1878I; *Mlada*, 1890I; *Mozart and Salieri*, 1898I; *Overture on Three Russian Themes, Opus 28*, 1866I; *Pan Voyevoda*, 1903I; *Piano Concerto in c♯, Opus 30*, 1883I; *Russian Easter Overture, Opus 36*, 1888I; *Sadko*, 1896I; *Scheherazade, Opus 35*, 1811I; *Sevilia*, 1901I; *The Snow Maiden*, 1881I; *Song of Oleg, the Wise, Opus 58*, 1899I; *Symphony No. 1 in e♭, Opus 1*, 1865I; *Symphony No. 2, "Antar," Opus 9*, 1868I; *Symphony No. 3 in C*, 1874I; *Trombone Concerto*, 1877I; *Tsar Saltan*, 1900I; *The Tsar's Bride*, 1898I
Rinaldo di Capua: *Adriano in Siria*, 1758I; *L'amante deluso*, 1753I; *Attalo*, 1754I; *Il caffe di campagna*, 1764I; *Il capitano napolitano*, 1756I; *La chiavarina*, 1754I; *La donna superba*, 1752I; *La donna vindicativa*, 1771I; *Le donne ridicole*, 1759I; *I finti pazzi per amore*, 1770I; *La forza della pace*, 1752I; *Gli impostori*, 1751I; *Il ripiego in amore di Flaminia*, 1751I; *La serva sposa*, 1753I; *La zingara*, 1753I
Ristori, Giovanni Alberto: *Mass in C*, 1752I
Ritter, Frédéric Louis: *Overture to Othello*, 1867I
Robertson, Leroy: *American Serenade*, 1944I; *The Book of Mormon*, 1953I; *Piano Quintet*, 1933I; *Punch & Judy Overture*, 1945I; *Rhapsody for Piano & Orchestra*, 1944I; *String Quartet*, 1940I

F   *Biographical*   G   *Cultural Beginnings*   H   *Musical Literature*
I   *Musical Compositions*

Robinson, Earl: *Ballad for Americans*, 1938I
Rochberg, George: *The Alchemist*, 1965I; *Bagatelles (12)*, 1952I; *Bartókiana*, 1959I; *Between Two Worlds*, 1982I; *Black Sounds*, 1966I; *Caprice Variations*, 1970I; *Carnival Music*, 1971I; *Chamber Symphony*, 1953I; *Circles of Fire*, 1997I; *Clarinet Concerto*, 1995I; *The Confidence Man*, 1981I; *David, the Psalmist*, 1954I; *Imago mundi*, 1973I; *Night Music*, 1948I; *Oboe Concerto*, 1984I; *Octet: A Grand Fantasia*, 1980I; *Partita Variations for Piano*, 1976I; *Piano Quartet*, 1983I; *Piano Quintet*, 1975I; *Piano Trio No. 1*, 1963I; *Piano Trio No. 2*, 1985I; *Short Sonatas (4) for Piano*, 1984I; *Sonata-Aria*, 1992I; *Sonata-fantasia*, 1956I; *Songs of Solomon*, 1946I; *String Quartet No. 1*, 1952I; *String Quartet No. 2*, 1961I; *String Quartet No. 3*, 1972I; *String Quartet No. 4*, 1978I; *String Quartet No. 5*, 1978I; *String Quartet No. 6*, 1978I; *String Quartet No. 7*, 1979I; *String Quintet*, 1982I; *Symphony No. 1*, 1955I; *Symphony No. 2*, 1956I; *Symphony No. 3*, 1968I; *Symphony No. 4*, 1975I; *Symphony No. 5*, 1984I; *Symphony No. 6*, 1987I; *Tableaux*, 1968I; *Time Span I*, 1960I; *Time-Span II*, 1962I; *To the Dark Wood*, 1985I; *Viola Sonata*, 1979I; *Violin Sonata*, 1988I
Rodó, Gabriel: *Symphony No. 2*, 1957I
Rodrigo, Joaquín: *Concierto en modo galante*, 1946I; *Concierto heroico*, 1933I; *Concierto pastorale*, 1978I; *Elogio de la Guitarra*, 1971I; *In Search of the Beyond*, 1976I; *Pequeñas Piezas (3)*, 1963I; *Sonata giocosa for Guitar*, 1961I
Rodriguez, Carlos: *Fábulas*, 1995I
Rodriguez, Robert X.: *A Colorful Symphony*, 1988I; *Con Flor y Canto*, 1994I; *Forbidden Fire*, 1998I; *Frida*, 1990I; *Piano Concerto No. 1*, 1968I; *Piano Concerto No. 2*, 1972I; *Piano Concerto No. 3*, 1974I; *Ursa: Four Seasons*, 1990I
Rodriguez de Hita, Antonio: *Briseida*, 1768I; *Missa del Pange Lingua*, 1772I; *Las segadores de Vallecas*, 1768I
Rogers, Bernard: *Amphitryon Overture*, 1946I; *Colors of War*, 1939I; *Dance of Salome*, 1940I; *Deirdre*, 1922I; *Japanese Dances, Three*, 1933I; *Leaves from the Tale of Pinocchio*, 1951I; *The Light of Man*, 1964I; *The Marriage of Aude*, 1931I; *The Nightingale*, 1954I; *Once Upon a Time*, 1934I; *Overture, The Faithful*, 1922I; *The Passion*, 1942I; *Prelude to Hamlet*, 1925I; *The Prophet Isaiah*, 1950I; *The Raising of Lazarus*, 1929I; *Soliloquy No. 2 (flute, strings)*, 1922I; *The Song of the Nightingale*, 1939I; *String Quartet No. 1*, 1918I; *String Quartet No. 2*, 1925I; *Symphony No. 1, "Adonais,"* 1925I; *Symphony No. 2 in A♭*, 1928I; *Symphony No. 3, "On a Thanksgiving Soong,"* 1936I; *Symphony No. 4 in g*, 1940I; *Symphony No. 5, "Africa,"* 1959I; *To the Fallen*, 1918I; *The Veil*, 1950I; *Violin Sonata*, 1962I; *The Warrior*, 1944I
Rogers, James H.: *In Memoriam*, 1919I
Rogers, Miguel: *String Quartet No. 2*, 1994I
Rogister, Jean: *String Quartet No. 1*, 1902I; *String Quartet No. 2*, 1914I; *String Quartet No. 3*, 1921I; *String Quartet No. 4*, 1926I; *String Quartet No. 5*, 1927I; *String Quartet No. 6*, 1928I; *String Quartet No. 7*, 1931I; *String Quartet No. 8*, 1940I; *Symphony in E*, 1943I
Rohde, Kurt: *Pieces (5) for Orchestra*, 2000I
Rolle, Johann Heinrich: *Christmas Oratori*, 1769I; *Thirza und ihre söhne*, 1779I
Rolnick, Neil: *Dogs of Desire*, 1994I; *ElectriCity*, 1991I
Roman, Johan Helmich: *Swedish Mass*, 1752I
Romberg, Andreas: *Der Rabe*, 1794I
Romberg, Bernhard: *Daphen und Agathokles*, 1818I; *Rittertreue*, 1817I; *Ulisse und Circe*, 1807I
Romberg, Sigmund: *Blossom Time*, 1921I; *The Blue Paradise*, 1915I; *The Desert Song*, 1926I; *Katinka*, 1915I; *May Wine*, 1935I; *The New Moon*, 1928I; *Robinson Crusoe, Jr.*, 1916I; *The Student Prince*, 1924I
Romig, James: *Variations for String Quartet*, 1999I
Röntgen, Julius: *Cello Sonata, Opus 41*, 1900I; *Introduction, Scherzo, Intermezzo & Finale*, 1876I; *Oboe Sonata No. 1*, 1918I; *Serenade for Seven Winds, Opus 14*, 1914I; *String Quartet in a*, 1885I; *Symphony in c♯*, 1930I; *Theme & Variations, Opus 17*, 1878I
Roosenschoon, Hans: *Narcissus*, 1985I
Root, George Frederick: *The Battle Cry of Freedom*, 1862I; *Belshazzar's Feast*, 1860I; *Bethlehem*, 1889I; *The Building of the Temple*, 1889I; *The Choicest Gift*, 1883I; *The Coming of the Flowers*, 1888I; *Daniel*, 1853I; *David, the Shepherd Boy*, 1882I; *Faith Triumphant*, 1886I; *Florens, the Pilgrim*, 1890I; *The Flower Queen*, 1852I; *The Haymakers*, 1857I; *Jacob and Esau*, 1890I; *The Pilgrim Fathers*, 1854I; *The Pillar of Fire*, 1887I; *Plough and Sickle*, 1894I; *The Song Tournament*, 1878I; *The Star of Light*, 1896I; *Under the Palms*, 1880I
Ropartz, Guy: *Cello Sonata No. 1*, 1904I; *Cello Sonata No. 2*, 1918I; *Concerto for Orchestra*, 1930I; *Le pays*, 1910I; *Organ Pieces (3)*, 1894I; *Rapsodie (cello)*, 1928I; *Requiem*, 1939I; *String Quartet No. 2*, 1912I; *String Quartet No. 3*, 1925I; *String Quartet No. 4*, 1934I; *String Quartet No. 5*, 1940I; *String Quartet No. 6*, 1951I; *String Trio*, 1918I; *Symphony No. 1*, 1894I; *Symphony No. 3*, 1905I; *Symphony No. 4*, 1910I; *Symphony No. 5*, 1944I; *Violin Sonata No. 1*, 1907I; *Violin Sonata No. 2*, 1917I; *Violin Sonata No. 3*, 1927I

❀

A *Births*   B *Deaths*   C *Debuts*   D *New Positions*
E *Prizes/Honors*

Rorem, Ned: *After Long Silence*, 1982I; *After Reading Shakespeare*, 1979I; *Air Music*, 1974I; *An American Oratorio*, 1984I; *The Anniversay*, 1962I; *Ariel*, 1971I; *The Auden Poems*, 1989I; *Ballet for Jerry*, 1951I; *Bertha*, 1968I; *The Book of Hours*, 1975I; *Bright Music*, 1987I; *Cain & Abel*, 1946I; *A Childhood Miracle*, 1952I; *Concerto for Cello, Piano & Orchestra*, 1979I; *Cycle of Holy Songs*, 1951I; *Dance Suite for Two Pianos*, 1949I; *Dorian Gray*, 1952I; *English Horn Concerto*, 1993I; *Excursions*, 1965I; *Fables*, 1970I; *Fantasy & Toccata*, 1946I; *Goodbye, My Fancy*, 1988I; *Hearing*, 1966I; *Irish Poems (6)*, 1950I; *King Midas*, 1961I; *Last Poems of Wallace Stevens*, 1972I; *Lions*, 1963I; *Lost in Fear*, 1945I; *Madrigals (4)*, 1947I; *Melos*, 1951I; *Miss Julie*, 1965I; *More Than a Day*, 1995I; *Nantucket Songs*, 1979I; *Night Music*, 1972I; *Organ Concerto*, 1984I; *Organbook I*, 1989I; *Organbook II*, 1989I; *Organbook III*, 1989I; *Overture in C*, 1948I; *Pastorale*, 1950I; *Piano Concerto for the Left Hand* (piano), 1991I; *Piano Concerto No. 2*, 1950I; *Piano Concerto No. 3 in Six Movements*, 1969I; *Piano Etudes (8)*, 1975I; *Piano Sonata No. 1*, 1948I; *Piano Sonata No. 2*, 1949I; *Piano Sonata No. 3*, 1954I; *Poèmes pour la Paix*, 1953I; *Poems by Whitman (8)*, 1954I; *Poems of Love & the Rain*, 1963I; *The Poet's Requiem*, 1955I; *Present Laughter*, 1995I; *A Quaker Reader*, 1976I; *Quintet*, 1981I; *The Robbers*, 1956I; *Romeo & Juliet*, 1975I; *Santa Fe Songs*, 1980I; *Schuyler Songs*, 1990I; *Septet: Scenes from Childhood*, 1985I; *Serenade on Five English Poems*, 1975I; *Some Trees*, 1968I; *Sonata for Piano, Four Hands*, 1952I; *Songs for High Voice & Orchestra (5)*, 1953I; *Songs of Sadness*, 1994I; *String Quartet No. 2*, 1950I; *String Quartet No. 3*, 1990I; *String Quartet No. 4*, 1995I; *Sun*, 1966I; *Sunday Morning*, 1977I; *Symphony No. 1*, 1950I; *Symphony No. 2*, 1956I; *Symphony No. 3*, 1958I; *Trio for Flute, Clarinet & Piano*, 1960I; *Variations (6) for Two Pianos*, 1995I; *Views from the Oldest House for Organ*, 1981I; *Violin Sonata*, 1949I; *Voyagers*, 1959I; *War Scenes*, 1969I; *Women's Voices*, 1976I
Rose, David: *Holiday for Strings*, 1943I
Rosell, Lars-Erik: *Overture for Organ*, 1993I
Rosenberg, Hilding: *Calvary*, 1938I; *Cello Concerto No. 1*, 1939I; *Cello Concerto No. 2*, 1953I; *Chorale Concerto, "Christ, unser Herr zum Jordan Kam,"* 1948I; *Concerto for Strings I*, 1946I; *Concerto for Strings IV*, 1966I
Rosenberg, Hilding: *The Holy Night*, 1936I; *The Isle of Bliss*, 1943I; *Joseph & His Brothers*, 1948I; *Journey to America*, 1932I; *Kasper's Shrove Tuesday*, 1953I; *Louisville Concerto*, 1954I; *Orpheus in Town*, 1938I; *Piano Concerto No. 1*, 1930I; *Piano Concerto No. 2*, 1950I; *Piano Sonata No. 1*, 1923I; *Piano Sonata No. 3*, 1926I; *Plastic Scenes*, 1921I; *The Portrait*, 1955I; *Salome*, 1963I; *Sonata for Solo Clarinet*, 1960I; *String Quartet No. 1*, 1920I; *String Quartet No. 2*, 1924I; *String Quartet No. 3 "Pastoral,"* 1926I; *String Quartet No. 4*, 1939I; *String Quartet No. 5*, 1949I; *String Quartet No. 6*, 1954I; *String Quartet No. 7*, 1956I; *String Quartet No. 8*, 1956I; *String Quartet No. 9*, 1956I; *String Quartet No. 10*, 1956I; *String Quartet No. 11*, 1956I; *String Quartet No. 12*, 1956I; *Swedish Suite*, 1927I; *Symphony No. 1*, 1917I; *Symphony No. 2, "Sinfonia grave,"* 1935I; *Symphony No. 3*, 1939I; *Symphony No. 4, "Revelation of St. John,"* 1940I; *Symphony No. 5, "Keeper of the Garden,"* 1944I; *Symphony No. 6, "Sinfonia semplice,"* 1951I; *Symphony No. 7*, 1968I; *Symphony No. 8, "In Candidum,"* 1974I; *Trumpet Concerto*, 1928I; *Viola Concerto*, 1942I; *Violin Concerto No. 1*, 1924I; *Violin Concerto No. 2*, 1951I; *Violin Sonata No. 1*, 1926I; *Violin Sonata No. 2*, 1940I; *Wind Quintet*, 1959I; *Wind Quintet*, 1959I
Rosenbloom, David: *Brave New World: Music for the Play*, 1995I; *Extended Trio*, 1992I; *Predictions, Conformations & Disconfirmations*, 1991I
Rosenblum, Mathew: *Ancient Eyes*, 1990I; *Nü Kuan Tzu*, 1996I
Rosenhaim, Jacob: *Der Besuch im Irrenhause*, 1834I
Rosenzweig, Morris: *Angels, Emeralds & the Towers*, 1992I; *On the Wings of the Wind*, 1994I; *Roman Passacaglias*, 1992I; *String Quartet No. 1*, 1997I
Rosetti, Francesco: *Das Winterfest der Hirten*, 1789I
Roslavetz, Nicolai: *End of the World*, 1922I; *String Quartet No. 1*, 1913I; *String Quartet No. 2*, 1916I; *String Quartet No. 3*, 1920I; *Symphony*, 1922I; *Viola Sonata No. 1*, 1926I; *Violin Concerto*, 1925I
Rosner, Arnold: *Oboe Sonata*, 1972I; *String Quartet No. 1*, 1962I; *String Quartet No. 2, Opus 19*, 1963I; *String Quartet No. 3, Opus 32*, 1965I; *String Quartet No. 4*, 1972I; *String Quartet No. 5*, 1977I; *Trinity* (band), 1988I
Rosseau, Norbert: *Concerto for Orchestra No. 1*, 1948I; *Concerto for Orchestra No. 2*, 1963I; *HSUB2/SUB0*, 1938I
Rossi, Giovanni: *La contessa d'Alternberg*, 1871I; *Elena di Taranto*, 1852I; *L'impresario delle Smirne*, 1793I (?); *Overture, Saul*, 1878I; *Pietro il grande*, 1793I; *Piramo e Tisbe*, 1792I
Rossi, Lauro: *L'alchimista*, 1853I; *Amelia*, 1834I; *Baldorino, tiranno di Spoleto*, 1832I; *Bianca Contarini*, 1847I; *Biorn*, 1877I; *Il borgomastro di Schiedam*, 1844I; *La casa disabitata*, 1834I; *La casa in vendita*, 1831I; *Constanza e Oringaldo*, 1830I; *Le contesse villane*, 1829I; *Il domino nero*, 1849I; *La figlia di Figaro*, 1846I; *La fucine di Bergen*, 1833I; *Giovanni Shore*, 1836I; *Leocadia*, 1835I; *Il maestro di scuola*, 1832I; *Il maestro e*

❈

    F *Biographical*   G *Cultural Beginnings*   H *Musical Literature*
              I *Musical Compositions*

Rossi, Lauro: (*cont.*)
la cantante, 1867I; *Le Sabine*, 1852I; *Saul*, 1833I; *La sirena*, 1855I; *Lo sposo al lotto*, 1831I; *Lo zingaro rivale*, 1867I
Rossini, Gioacchino: *Adelaide di Borgogna*, 1817I; *Adina*, 1818I; *Armida*, 1917I; *Aureliano in Palmira*, 1813I; *Il barbiere di Siviglia*, 1816I; *Bianca e Falliero*, 1819I; *La cambiale di matrimonio*, 1810I; *La cenerentola*, 1817I; *Ciro in Babilonia*, 1812I; *Le Comte Ory*, 1828I; *Demetrio e Polibro*, 1806I; *La donna del lago*, 1819I; *Eduardo e Cristina*, 1819I; *Elizabeth, Queen of England*, 1815I; *L'equivoco stravagante*, 1811I; *Ermoine*, 1819I; *La gazza ladra*, 1817I; *La gazzetta*, 1816I; *L'italiana in Algeri*, 1813I; *L'inganno felice*, 1811I; *Inno Nazionale*, 1848I; *Inno Alla Pace*, 1848I; *Il Maometto*, 1820I; *Matilde di Shabran*, 1821I; *Messe de Gloria*, 1820I; *Messe Solennelle*, 1820I; *Moïse*, 1827I; *La mort de Didone*, 1811I; *Mosè in Egitto*, 1818I; *L'occasione fa il ladro*, 1812I; *Othello*, 1816I; *Overture in D*, 1808I; *Partenope*, 1819I; *La peitra del paragone*, 1812I; *Petite Messe Solennelle*, 1863I; *Il pianto d'armonia*, 1808I; *Quartets (6) for Woodwinds*, 1809I; *Ricciardo e Zoraide*, 1818I; *La riconoscenze*, 1821I; *La scala di seta*, 1812I; *Semiramide*, 1823I; *Le siège de Corinthe*, 1826I; *Sigismondo*, 1814I; *Il signor Bruschino*, 1812I; *Sonata a Quattro (6–strs)*, 1804I; *Stabat Mater*, 1841I; *String Quartets (5)*, 1808I; *Tancredi*, 1813I; *Theme and Variations, WW Quartet*, 1812I; *Torvaldo e Dorliska*, 1815I; *Il Turco in Italia*, 1814I; *La vera omaggio*, 1823I; *Il viaggio a Reims*, 1825I; *William Tell*, 1829I; *Zelmire*, 1822I
Rota, Nino: *Aladino e la lampada magica*, 1968I; *Il cappello di paglio di Firenzi*, 1946I; *Cello Concerto No. 1*, 1972; *Cello Concerto No. 2*, 1973I; *Clarinet Trio*, 1958I; *Concerto in C, "Piccolo mondo antico,"* 1979I; *Concert-Soirée* (piano, orchestra), 1961I; *Le Molière imaginaire*, 1976I; *Napoli milionaria*, 1977I; *Nonet*, 1977I; *Organ Sonata*, 1965I; *Piano Concerto No. 1 in C*, 1960I; *Piano Concerto No. 2 in E, "Piccolo mondo antico,"* 1978I; *Piano Preludes (15)*, 1966I; *Il principe porcaro*, 1925I; *Quintet for Flute, Oboe, Viola, Cello & Harp*, 1935I; *Lo scoiattolo in gamba*, 1959I; *La scuola di guida*, 1959I; *Sonata for Flute & Harp*, 1937I; *String Quartet No. 1*, 1954I; *Symphony No. 1*, 1939I; *Symphony No. 2*, 1943I; *Symphony No. 3*, 1957I; *Torquemada*, 1943I; *Trio for Flute, Violin & Piano*, 1958I; *Trombone Concerto*, 1969I; *La visita meravigliosa*, 1970I
Röttger, Heinz: *Piano Concerto*, 1950I; *Symphony No. 1*, 1939I; *Symphony No. 2, "Dessauer,"* 1967I; *Violin Concerto No. 1*, 1942I
Rouget de L'Isle, Claude: *La Marseillaise*, 1792I
Rouse, Christopher: *Cello Concerto*, 1992I; *Clarinet Concerto*, 2000I; *Concerto for String Orchestra*, 1990I; *Doublebass Concerto*, 1985I; *Flute Concerto*, 1993I; *Der gerettete Alberich* (solo percussion concerto), 1997I; *Gorgon*, 1984I; *Guitar Concerto*, 1999I; *The Infernal Machine*, 1981I; *Iscariot*, 1989I; *Kabir Padavali*, 1997I; *Kabir Songbook*, 1998I; *Karolju*, 1990I; *Mitternachtlieder*, 1979I; *Phaeton*, 1986I; *Phantasmata*, 1985I; *Rotae Passionis*, 1983I; *Seeing* (piano concerto), 1998I; *String Quartet No. 1*, 1982I; *String Quartet No. 2*, 1988I; *Symphony No. 1*, 1986I ,1987I; *Symphony No. 2*, 1994I; *Trombone Concerto*, 1991I
Roussakis, Nicolas: *Fire & Earth & Water & Air*, 1983I; *Ode & Cataclysm*, 1975I; *To Dementer*, 1994I
Rousseau, Jean-Jacques: *Le devin du village*, 1752I; *Pygmalion*, 1775I
Roussel, Albert: *Bacchus et Ariane*, 1930I; *Cello Concertino*, 1936I; *Concerto for Small Orchestra*, 1927I; *Evocations*, 1911I; *Horn Quintet*, 1901I; *Padmâvatî, Opus 18*, 1918I; *Petite Suite, Opus 39*, 1929I; *Piano Concerto, Opus 36*, 1927I; *Piano Suite, Opus 14*, 1933I; *Piano Trio*, 1902I; *Pour une Fête de Printemps, Opus 22*, 1920I; *Prelude & Fughetto*, 1929I; *Psalm LXXX*, 1928I; *Résurrection, Opus 4*, 1903I; *Sinfonietta for String Orchestra, Opus 52*, 1934I; *String Quartet*, 1932I; *String Trio*, 1937I; *Suite in F, Opus 33*, 1926I; *Symphony No. l, "Le poème de la Forêt," Opus 7*, 1906I; *Symphony No. 2, Opus 23*, 1921I; *Symphony No. 3, Opus 42*, 1922; *Symphony No. 4, Opus 53*, 1930I; *Le testament de la Tante Caroline*, 1933I; *Violin Sonata No. 1*, 1908I; *Violin Sonata No. 2*, 1924I
Routh, Francis: *Divertimento for String Quartet*, 1998I; *Piano Concerto*, 1976I; *Sacred Tetralogy I: The Manger Throne*, 1959I; *Sacred Tetralogy II: Lumen Christi for Organ*, 1968I; *Sacred Tetralogy III: Aeterne Rex altissime*, 1970I; *Sacred Tetralogy IV: Gloria tibi Trinitas for Organ*, 1974I
Rovics, Howard: *My State Is Tied to Heaven*, 1996I; *Songs on Chinese Poetry*, 1982I; *Tangere*, 1996I; *Do You Not See*, 1978I
Royer, Joseph-Nicolas: *Pandore*, 1752I
Rózsa, Miklós: *Cello Concerto, Opus 32*, 1969I; *Piano Concerto, Opus 31*, 1966I; *Piano Sonata*, 1948I; *Sinfonia Concertante*, 1966I; *Sonata for Solo Violin*, 1986I; *String Quartet No. 1*, 1950I; *String Quartet No. 2*, 1981I; *Tripartita*, 1972I; *Variations on the Vintner's Daughter*, 1952I; *Viola concerto*, 1979I; *Violin Concerto*, 1954I
Rubbra, Edmund: *Cello Sonata*, 1946I; *Double Fugue*, 1924I; *Festival Overture, Opus 62*, 1947I; *Inscape*, 1964I; *Mass in Honour of St. Theresa*, 1981I; *Oboe Sonata*, 1958I; *Piano Concerto*, 1956I; *Piano Trio No. 1*, 1950I; *Piano Trio No. 2*, 1970I; *Rhapsody for Violin & Orchestra, I* 934I; *Sinfonia Concertante*, 1934I; *String Quartet No. 1*, 1933I; *String Quartet No. 2*, 1952I; *String Quartet No. 3*, 1963I; *String Quartet No. 4*, 1977I; *Symphony No. 1*, 1936I, 1937I; *Symphony No. 2*, 1957I; *Symphony No. 2, Opus 45*, 1937I;

❧

A *Births*   B *Deaths*   C *Debuts*   D *New Positions*
E *Prizes/Honors*

Symphony No. 3, 1939I; *Symphony No. 4*, 1941I; *Symphony No. 5*, 1949I; *Symphony No. 6*, 1954I; *Symphony No. 8, "Hommage à Teilhard de Chardin,"* 1968I; *Symphony No. 8*, 1971I; *Symphony No. 9, "Sinfonia Sacra,"* 1972I; *Symphony No. 10, "Sinfonia da Camera,"* 1974I; *Symphony No. 11*, 1979I; *Triple Fugue*, 1929I; *Veni, Creator Spiritus*, 1966I; *Violin Concerto*, 1959I; *Violin Sonata No. 1*, 1925I; *Violin Sonata No. 2*, 1931I; *Violin Sonata No. 3*, 1967I

Rubenson, Albert: *Symphonic Intermezzo*, 1860I; *Trois pièce symphoniques*, 1871I

Rubin, Marcel: *String Quartet No. 1*, 1926I; *Violin Sonata*, 1974I

Rubinstein, Anton: *Album de Peterhof, Opus 75*, 1866I; *Antony and Cleopatra, Opus 116*, 1890I; *The Battle of Kulikovo*, 1850I; *Caprice Russe, Opus 120*, 1878I; *Cello Concerto No. 1 in A, Opus 65*, 1864I; *Cello Concerto No. 2 in d, Opus 96*, 1874I; *Cello Sonata No. 1 in D, Opus 18*, 1852I; *Cello Sonata No. 2 in G, Opus 39*, 1858I; *Characteristic Pieces (6), Opus 26*, 1858I; *Christus, Opus 117*, 1893I; *Concert Overture in B♭, Opus 60*, 1853I; *Concertpiece for Clarinet & Band, 1878I; The Demon*, 1871I; *The Doleful One*, 1888I; *Don Quixote, Opus 87*, 1870I; *Fables, (6), Opus 64*, 1850I; *Fantasia in f, Opus 73*, 1864I; *Fantasia in C, Opus 84*, 1869I; *Fantasie eroica, Opus 110*, 1884I; *Faust, Opus 68*, 1864I; *Feramors*, 1862I; *German Songs (12), Opus 57, 72*, 1864I; *German Songs (6), Opus 76*, 1867I; *Hungarian Fantasia*, 1858I; *Ivan IV, Opus 79 (IM)*, 1869I; *Kammini-Ostrov, Opus 10*, 1854I; *Die Kinder der Heide*, 1861I; *Little Songs (6) in Low German, Opus 1*, 1848I; *Die Maccabäer*, 1874I; *Melodies (2), Opus 3*, 1852I; *The Merchant Kalashnikov*, 1879I; *Morning, Opus 74*, 1866I; *Moses, Opus 112*, 1889I; *Néron*, 1877I; *Nocturnes (2)*, 1848I; *Der Papagei*, 1884I; *Paradise*, 1858I; *Partsongs (9) Opus 61, 62*, 1861I; *Persian Songs, Opus 34*, 1854I; *Piano Sonata No. 1 in E, Opus 12*, 1854I; *Piano Concerto in C*, 1849I; *Piano Concerto No. 1 in e, Opus 25*, 1850I; *Piano Concerto No. 2 in F, Opus 35*, 1858I; *Piano Concerto No. 3 in G, Opus 45*, 1854I; *Piano Concerto No. 4 in d, Opus 70*, 1864I; *Piano Concerto No. 5 in E♭, Opus 94*, 1875I; *Piano Concertstück in A♭, Opus 113*, 1889I; *Piano Pieces (3), Opus 5*, 1852I; *Piano Pieces (6), Opus 51*, 1857I; *Piano Pieces (5), Opus 69*, 1867I; *Piano Pieces (3), Opus 71*, 1867I; *Piano Pieces (6),Opus 104*, 1885I; *Piano Preludes (6), Opus 24*, 1854I; *Piano Sonata No. 2 in c, Opus 20*, 1854I; *Piano Sonata No. 3 in D, Opus 89*, 1870I; *Piano Sonata No. 4 in a, Opus 100*, 1877I; *Piano Suite, Opus 38*, 1855I; *Piano Suite No. 3 in F, Opus 41*, 1855I; *Preludes & Fugues, Opus 53*, 1857I; *Revenge*, 1853I; *Romance & Caprice, Opus 86*, 1870I; *Russia*, 1882I; *Russian Songs (12), Opus 78*, 1868I; *Serenades (3), Opus 22*, 1855I; *Servian Songs (10), Opus 105*, 1877I; *The Siberian Hunters*, 1852I; *Soirées musicales, Opus 109*, 1884I; *Soirées à Saint-Petersbourg, Opus 44*, 1860I; *Songs (6), Opus 8*, 1850I; *Songs (6), Male Voices, Opus 31*, 1854I; *Songs (12) Opus 32, 33*, 1856I; *Songs (12), Opus 36*, 1851I; *Songs (12), Opus 48*, 1854I; *Songs (6), Opus 67*, 1864I; *Songs (10), Opus 83*, 1869I; *Songs (12) from Tolstoy, Opus 101*, 1877I; *Songs (10), Opus 115*, 1890I; *Songs & Requiem for Mignon, Opus 91*, 1872I; *String Quartet No. 1 in g*, 1871I; *String Quartet No. 2 in e, Opus 90*, 1871I; *Studies (6), Opus 8*, 1870I; *Suite in E♭, Opus 119*, 1894I; *Sulamith*, 1883I; *Symphony No. 2 in C, "Ocean," Opus 42*, 1851I; *Symphony No. 3 in A, Opus 56*, 1854I; *Symphony No. 4 in d, "Dramatic," Opus 95*, 1875I; *Symphony No. 5 in g, Opus 107*, 1880I; *Symphony No. 6 in a, Opus 111*, 1886I; *Theme & Variations in G, Opus 88*, 1871I; *Thomas, the Fool*, 1853I; *The Tower of Babel, Opus 80*, 1869I; *Triumphal Overture, Opus 43*, 1855I; *Unter Räubern*, 1883I; *Das Verlorene Paradies, Opus 54*, 1856I; *Viola Sonata in F*, 1855I; *Violin Concerto in G, Opus 48*, 1857I; *The Water Sprite, Opus 63*, 1861I

Rubinstein, Beryl: *Piano Concerto*, 1936I

Ruders, Poul: *Anima, Cello Concerto No. 2*, 1993I; *The Bells*, 1993I; *Concerto in Pieces*, 1995I; *Drama Trilogy I: Dramaphonia (piano concerto)*, 1987I; *Drama Trilogy II, Monodrama*, 1988I; *Drama Trilogy III, Polydrama*, 1988I; *gloria*, 1981I; *The Handmaid's Tale*, 1998I; *Horn Trio*, 1998I; *Manhattan Abstraction*, 1982I; *Oboe Concerto*, 1998I; *Piano Concerto*, 1995I; *Piano Postludes (13)*, 1988I; *Piano Recitatives (7)*, 1977I; *Piano Sonata No. 1, "Dante,"* 1970I; *Piano Sonata No. 2*, 1982I; *Requiem*, 1968I; *Solar Trilogy I: Gong*, 1992I; *Solar Trilogy II: Zenith*, 1993I; *Solar Trilogy III: Corona*, 1995I; *Stabat mater*, 1973I; *Star-Prelude & Love-Fugue for Piano*, 1990I; *String Quartet No. 1*, 1972I; *String Quartet No. 2*, 1979I; *String Quartet No. 3, "Motet,"* 1979I; *Symphony No. 1*, 1989I; *Symphony No. 2, "Symphony & Transformation,"* 1996I; *Thus Saw Saint John*, 1984I; *Towards the Precipice*, 1990I; *Tycho*, 1986I; *Variations for Solo Violin*, 1989I; *Viola Concerto*, 1995I

Rudhyar, Dane: *Chansons de Bilitis (3)*, 1918I; *Mosaics*, 1918I; *Piano Paeans (3)*, 1925I; *Piano Quintet*, 1950I; *Piano Transmutation*, 1976I; *String Quartet No. 1, "Advent,"* 1978I; *String Quartet No. 2, "Crisis & Overcoming,"* 1979I; *Symphony No. 1*, 1928I; *Symphony No. 5*, 1954I; *Three Poems for Violin & Piano*, 1920I; *The Warrior*, 1921I

Rudziński, Witold: *Piano Concerto*, 1936I; *String Quartet No. 1*, 1935I; *String Quartet No. 2*, 1943I; *Symphony No. 1*, 1938I; *Symphony No. 2*, 1944I; *Viola Sonata*, 1946I; *Violin Sonata*, 1937I

Ruggi, Francesco: *L'ombra di Nino*, 1795I

Ruggles, Carl: *Angels*, 1921I; *Evocations*, 1943I; *Men & Mountains*, 1924I; *Mood for Violin & Piano*, 1918I; *Organum*, 1947I; *Portals for Thirteen Strings*, 1925I; *Sun-Treader*, 1931I; *Toys*, 1919I; *Vox clamans in deserto*, 1923I

❉

F *Biographical*   G *Cultural Beginnings*   H *Musical Literature*
I *Musical Compositions*

Ruiters, Wim de: *Thick & Thin for Organ*, 1975I
Rush, Loren: *The Digital Domain*, 1983I; *A Little Travelling Music*, 1973I; *Piano Hexahedron*, 1963I; *Soft Music, Hard Music for Piano*, 1970
Russell, Craig: *Horn Rhapsody* (concerto), 2000I
Russell, Henry: *Woodman, Spare That Tree!*, 1837I
Russo, William: *Violin Sonata*, 1986I
Rutini, Giovanni Marco: *Il finta amante*, 1776I; *La Nitteti*, 1769I; *Semiramide*, 1753I
Rutter, John: *Magnificat*, 1990I; *Requiem*, 1985I
Ruyneman, Daniel: *Clarinet Sonata*, 1936I; *Concerto for Orchestra*, 1937I; *Piano Concerto*, 1939I; *Piano Sonata*, 1931I; *String Quartet No. 1*, 1914I; *Symphony No. 1, "Symphonie breve,"* 1927I; *Symphony No. 2, "Symphony 1953,"* 1953I; *Violin Concerto*, 1940I
Ruzicka, Peter: *Bewegung*, 1972I; *Fragment* (string quartet), 1970I; *Introspezione* (string quartet), 1969I; *Sonata for Solo Cello*, 1969I; *String Quartet No. 2*, 1970I; *String Quartet No. 3, "Über ein Verschwinden,"* 1992I; *String Quartet No. 4, "Sich Verlierend,"* 1996I; *String Quartet Klangschatten*, 1991I; *Z-Zeit for Organ*, 1975I; *Zeit for Organ*, 1975I
Ruzzini, Venanzio: *Italian Duettinos (12), Opus 5*, 1778I
Ryabov, Vladimir: *Symphony No. 1*, 1983I
Ryelandt, Joseph: *Gethsemane*, 1908I; *Mass for Six Voices*, 1934I; *Missa 6 Vocibus, Opus 111*, 1935I; *Oratorio No. 1, "Purgatorium,"* 1904I; *Oratorio No. 2, "De Komst der Herrn,"* 1907I; *Oratorio No. 3, "Maria,"* 1910I; *Oratorio No. 4, "Agnus Dei,"* 1915I; *Oratorio No. 5, "Chrisus Rex,"* 1922I; *Symphony No. 1*, 1897I; *Symphony No. 2*, 1904I; *Symphony No. 3*, 1908I; *Symphony No. 4*, 1913I; *Symphony No. 5*, 1934I
Rytel, Piotr: *The Corsair*, 1911I; *The Dream of Dante*, 1911I; *Grazyna*, 1908I; *Legend of St. George*, 1918I; *Piano Concerto*, 1907I; *Poemat*, 1910I; *Symphony No. 1*, 1909I; *Violin Concerto*, 1950I
Rzewski, Frederic: *Antigone-Legend*, 1982I; *Crusoe*, 1993I; *Down By the River Side*, 1979I; *Four North American Ballads*, 1979I; *Impersonation*, 1967I; *A Machine*, 1984I; *Night Crossing with Fisherman*, 1994I; *The People United Will Never Be Defeated*, 1975I; *Piano Ludes*, 1991I; *Piano Sonata*, 1991I; *The Road*, 1996I; *Squares*, 1978I; *Symphony*, 1968I; *Whangdoodles*, 1990I
Saariaho, Kaija: *L'amour de loin*, 2000I; *NoaNoa*, 1991I; *Oltra Mar, Seven Preludes for the New Millenium*, 1999I; *L'amour de loin*, 2000I; *Château d'âme*, 1996I; *From the Grammar of Dreams*, 1988I; *Jardin Secret I*, 1985I; *Lonh*, 1996I; *Maa*, 1991I
Sacchini, Antonio: *Adriano in Siria*, 1771I; *Alessandro nell'Indie*, 1763I; *L'amore in campo*, 1762I; *L'amore soldato*, 1778I; *Andromaca*, 1761I; *Armida*, 1772I; *Artaserse*, 1768I; *Arvire et Evelina*, 1788I; *L'avaro deluso*, 1778I; *Calliroe*, 1770I; *Chimène*, 1783I; *Il Cidde*, 1773I; *La contadina in Corte*, 1765I; *Il copista burlato*, 1759I; *Il creso*, 1765I; *Dardanue*, 1784I; *I due fratelli Beffati*, 1760I; *Enea e Lavinia*, 1779I; *Erifile*, 1778I; *L'eroe cinese*, 1770I; *Esther*, 1786I; *Eumene*, 1764I; *Ezio*, 1771I; *La finta contessa*, 1761I; *Fra Donata*, 1756I; *Gesù presentato al tempio*, 1761I; *Gioas*, 1767I; *Il giocatore*, 1757I; *Il gran Cidde*, 1764I; *L'isola d'amore*, 1766I; *Jephtes Sacrificium*, 1771; *Lucio Vero* 1764I; *Machabaeorum mater*, 1770I; *Mitridate*, 1781I; *Montezuma*, 1775I; *Nicoraste, Il Cidde*, 1769I; *Nitetti*, 1774I; *Nuptiae Ruth*, 1772I; *Oedipe à Colone*, 1786I; *Olimpiade*, 1763I; *Perseo*, 1774I; *Il popolo di Giuda, liberto della morte . . .* , 1768I; *Renaud*, 1783I; *S. Filippo Neri*, 1765I; *Scipiono in Cartogina*, 1770I; *Semiramide riconosciuta*, 1764I; *Tamerlano*, 1773I; *Il testaccio*, 1760I; *Trio Sonatas (6) Opus 1*, 1775I; *La vendemmia*, 1760I; *Violin Sonatas (6), Opus 3*, 1779I; *Vologeso*, 1772I
Sacco, Peter: *Piano Concerto No. 1*, 1964I
Saeverud, Harald: *Bassoon Concerto, Opus 44*, 1963I; *Bird Call Variations for Piano*, 1968I; *Cello Concerto*, 1931I; *Divertimento No. 1, Opus 13*, 1939I; *East Pieces for Piano*, 1939I; *Galdreslåtten*, 1943I; *Knight Bluebeard's Nightmare*, 1960I; *Oboe Concerto, Opus 12*, 1938I; *Peer Gynt, Opus 28*, 1947I; *Piano Concerto, Opus 31*, 1950I; *Piano Suite, Opus 6*, 1931I; *The Rape of Lucretia*, 1935I; *String Quartet No. 1, Opus 49*, 1970I; *String Quartet No. 2, Opus 52*, 1975I; *String Quartet No. 3, Opus 55*, 1978I; *Symphony No. 1, Opus 2*, 1920I; *Symphony No. 2*, 1922I; *Symphony No. 3 in b♭, Opus 5*, 1926I; *Symphony No. 4, Opus 11*, 1937I; *Symphony No. 5, "Quasi una fantasia," Opus 16*, 1941I; *Symphony No. 6, "Dolorosa," Opus 19*, 1942I; *Symphony No. 7, "Salme," Opus 40*, 1945I; *Symphony No. 8, "Minnesota," Opus 40*, 1958I; *Symphony No. 9, Opus 45*, 1965I; *Viola Sonatina*, 1989I; *Violin Concerto No. 1, Opus 7*, 1930I; *Violin Concerto No. 2, Opus 37*, 1956I; *Wind Quintet No. 2, Opus 56*, 1982I
Saint-Georges, Joseph Boulogne de: *L'amant anonyme*, 1780I; *Ernestine*, 1777I; *Europa riconosciuta*, 1778I; *Harpsichord Sonatas (3)*, 1781I; *Le marchand de marrons*, 1788I; *String Quartets (6), Opus 1*, 1773I; *Symphonies (2), Opus 11*, 1779I; *Symphonies concertante (2), Opus 6*, 1775I; *Symphonies concertante (2), Opus 10*, 1780I; *Symphonies concertante (2), Opus 13*, 1782I; *Violin Concertos (2), Opus 2*, 1773I; *Violin Concertos (2), Opus 3*, 1774I; *Violin Concerto in D, Opus 4*, 1774I; *Violin Concertos (2), Opus 5*, 1775I; *Violin Concertos (2), Opus 7*, 1779I; *Violin Concerto No. 9, Opus 8*, 1776I; *Violin Sonatas (6)*, 1800I

❈

A *Births* B *Deaths* C *Debuts* D *New Positions*
E *Prizes/Honors*

Saint-Saëns, Camille: *Africa, Opus 89*, 1891I; *Allegro appassionato in b, Opus 43*, 1875I; *Allegro de Concert in b*, 1913I; *L'ancêtre*, 1906I; *Assai moderato in B♭*, 1853I; *Les barbares*, 1901I; *Bassoon Sonata in G, Opus 168*, 1921I; *Caprice Héroïque, Opus 106*, 1898I; *Carnival of the Animals*, 1886I; *Cello Concerto No. 1 in a, Opus 33*, 1872I; *Cello Concerto No. 2 in d, Opus 119*, 1902I; *Cello Sonata No. 1 in c, Opus 32*, 1872I; *Cello Sonata No. 2 in F, Opus 123*, 1905I; *Clarinet Sonata in e♭, Opus 167*, 1921I; *Les cloches du soir, Opus 85*, 1889I; *Communion in E♭*, 1859I; *Cyprès et lauriers, Opus 156 (organ)*, 1919I; *Danse Macabre, Opus 40*, 1874I; *Déjanire*, 1898I; *Déjanire*, 1911I; *Le déluge, Opus 45*, 1876I; *Elévation ou Communion, Opus 13*, 1865I; *Étienne Marcel*, 1879I; *Etudes (6), Opus 52*, 1877I; *Etudes (6), Opus 111*, 1899I; *Etudes (6), Opus 135*, 1912I; *Fantaisie in A, Opus 124*, 1907I; *Fantaisie in E♭*, 1857I; *Fantasy for Harp, Opus 95*, 1893I; *Fantasia No. 3 in C, Opus 157*, 1919I; *Fugues (6), Opus 161*, 1920I; *Hélène*, 1904I; *Henry VIII*, 1883I; *Interlude fugué in g*, 1856I; *Introduction & Rondo Capriccioso in a, Opus 28*, 1863I; *La jeunesse d'Hercule, Opus 50*, 1877I; *Jota aragonese, Opus 64*, 1881I; *La lyre et la harpe, Opus 57*, 1879I; *Macbeth*, 1860I; *Marche du couronnement in E♭, Opus 117*, 1902I; *Marche héroïque, Opus 34*, 1871I; *Marche religieuse, Opus 107*, 1897I; *Mazurka in f, Opus 21*, 1862I; *Moïse sauvé des eaux*, 1851I; *Morceau de concert, Opus 154, for Harp &; Orchestra*, 1919I; *Morceau de concert in G, Opus 62*, 1880I; *Morceau de concert in g, Opus 154*, 1918I; *Morceau de concert in f, Opus 94*, 1887I; *Morceaux (3), Opus 1*, 1852I; *Morceaux (6)*, 1859I; *A Night in Lisbon, Opus 63*, 1881I; *Les noces de Prométhée, Opus 19*, 1867I; *Oboe Sonata in D, Opus 166*, 1921I; *Ode to St. Cecilia*, 1852I; *Offertoire in F*, 1882I; *Oratorio de Noël, Opus 12*, 1858I; *Organ Fantaisie in D♭, Opus 101*, 1895I; *Organ Improvisations (7), Opus 150*, 1917I; *Organ Rhapsodies (3), Opus 7*, 1831I; *Ouverture de Fête, Opus 133*, 1910I; *Phaeton, Opus 39*, 1873I; *Piano Concerto No. 1 in D, Opus 17*, 1858I; *Piano Concerto No. 3 in E♭, Opus 29*, 1869I; *Piano Concerto No. 4 in c, Opus 44*, 1875I; *Piano Concerto No. 5 in F "Egyptian," Opus 103*, 1896I; *Piano Quartet in E♭*, 1853I; *Piano Quartet in B♭, Opus 41*, 1875I; *Piano Quintet in a, Opus 14*, 1855I; *Piano Suite in F, Opus 90*, 1891I; *Piano Trio No. 1 in F, Opus 18*, 1863I; *Piano Trio No. 2 in e, Opus 92*, 1892I; *Prelude in F (?)*, 1855I; *Preludes and Fugues (3), Opus 99*, 1894I; *Preludes & Fugues (3), Opus 109*, 1898I; *La princesse Jaune*, 1872I; *Procession in C*, 1858I; *Prosperine*, 1887I; *Psalm CL*, 1906I; *Rapsodie bretonne*, 1891I; *Requiem, Opus 54*, 1787I; *Rhapsodie d'Aubergne in C, Opus 73*, 1884I; *Rhapsodies (3) on Breton Themes, Opus 7*, 1866I; *Romance in F, Opus 36*, 1874I; *Romance in D♭, Opus 37*, 1871I; *Romance in C, Opus 48*, 1874I; *Romance for Horn in E, Opus 57*, 1885I; *Le rouet d'Omphale, Opus 31*, 1871I; *Samson and Delilah*, 1877I; *Septet in E♭, Opus 65*, 1881I; *Souvenir d'Italie, Opus 80*, 1887I; *Spartacus Overture in E♭*, 1863I; *String Quartet No. 1 in e, Opus 112*, 1899I; *String Quartet No. 2 in G, Opus 153*, 1918I; *Suite Algérienne, Opus 60*, 1879I; *Suite for Cello, Opus 16*, 1862I; *Suite in D, Opus 49*, 1863I; *Symphony in A*, 1850I; *Symphony in F, "Urbs Roma,"* 1856I; *Symphony No. 1 in E♭, Opus 2*, 1853I; *Symphony No. 2 in a, Opus 55*, 1859I; *Symphony No. 3 in c, Opus 78, "Organ,"* 1886I; *Le timbre d'argent*, 1877I; *Variations on a Theme of Beethoven*, 1874I; *Violin Concerto No. 1 in A, Opus 20*, 1859I; *Violin Concerto No. 2 in C, opus 58*, 1858I; *Violin Concerto No. 3 in b, Opus 61*, 1881I; *Violin Sonata No. 1 in d, Opus 75*, 1885I; *Violin Sonata No. 2 in E♭, Opus 102*, 1896I

Sala, Oskar: *Electronic Impressions*, 1977I

Salieri, Antonio: *L'amore innocente*, 1770I; *L'angiolina*, 1800I; *Annibale in Capua*, 1801I; *Armida*, 1771I; *Il barone di Rocca antica*, 1772I; *La bella selvaggia*, 1802I; *La calamita de' Cuori*, 1774I; *Catilino*, 1790I; *Cesare di Farmacusa*, 1800I; *Le cifra*, 1789I; *Concertino for Flute and Strings*, 1777I; *Concerto for Oboe and Strings*, 1774I; *Cyrus und Astyages*, 1818I; *Daliso e Delmita*, 1776I; *Les Danaïdes*, 1784I; *Don Chisciotte alle nozze di Gamace*, 1771I; *Le donne letterate*, 1770I; *Eraclito et Democrito*, 1795I; *L'Europa riconosciuta*, 1778I; *Falstaff*, 1799I; *La fiera de Venezia*, 1772I; *La finta scema*, 1775I; *Gesùal limbo*, 1803I; *Grand Mass in D, "Kaisermesse,"* 1788I; *La grotta di Trofonio*, 1785I; *Les Horaces*, 1786I; *Il pastor fido*, 1789I; *Le jugement dernier*, 1787I; *La locandiera*, 1773I; *Missa pro defunctis in c*, 1804I; *Missa in d*, 1805I; *Missa in B♭*, 1809I; *La moda*, 1771I; *Il mondo alla rovescia*, 1795I; *Il moro*, 1796I; *Die Neger*, 1804I; *Organ Concerto*, 1773I; *Palmira Regina di Pergia*, 1795I; *La partenza inaspettata*, 1777I; *La Passione de Gésu Cristo*, 1776I; *Piano Concertos No. 1 & 2*, 1773I; *Der Rauchfangkehrer*, 1781I; *Il ricco d'un giorno*, 1784I; *La scofitta di Borea*, 1774I; *La scuola de' gelosim*, 1778I; *La secchia rapita*, 1772I; *Semiramide*, 1782I; *String Quartets (6), Opus 20*, 1772I; *Symphony in D, "Il giorno o nomastice,"* 1775I; *Il talismano*, 1788I; *Te Deum de incoronazione*, 1790I; *Te Deum in C*, 1819I; *I tre filosofo*, 1797I; *Il triofa della gloria e della virtù*, 1774I; *Triple Concerto in C (violin, oboe, cello)*, 1770I; *Variations on "La Folia,"* 1815I

Sallinen, Aulis: *Cello Concerto*, 1976I; *Cello Sonata*, 1971I; *Chamber Music I*, 1975I; *Chamber Music II*, 1976I; *Dies Irae*, 1978I; *Flute Concerto*, 1995I; *The Horseman*, 1974I; *Iron Age Suite*, 1982I; *The King Goes Forth to France*, 1983I; *Kullervo*, 1988I; *The Palace*, 1993I; *Quatro per quattro*, 1965I; *The Red Line*, 1978I; *Shadows*, 1982I; *Songs of Life & Death*, 1995I; *String Quartet No. 1*, 1958I; *String Quartet No. 2*, 1960I; *String Quartet No. 3*, 1971I; *String Quartet no. 4, "Quiet Songs,"* 1971I; *String Quartet No. 5, "Pieces of Mosaic,"* 1983I; *Symphony No. 1*, 1971I; *Symphony No. 2, "Symphonie Dialogue,"* 1972I; *Symphony No. 3,*

❖

F   *Biographical*   G   *Cultural Beginnings*   H   *Musical Literature*
I   *Musical Compositions*

Sallinen, Aulis: (*cont.*)
　1975I; *Symphony No. 4*, 1979I; *Symphony No. 5, "Washington Mosaics,"* 1985I; *Symphony No. 6*, 1990I;
　Variations (cello concerto), 1961I; *Variations sur Mallarmé*, 1967I
Salmanov, Vadim: *Cello Sonata*, 1963I; *The Forest*, 1948I; *Hero*, 1957I; *Piano Quartet*, 1947I; *Songs about
　Loneliness*, 1967I; *String Quartet No. 1*, 1945I; *String Quartet No. 2*, 1958I; *String Quartet No. 3*, 1961I;
　String Quartet No. 4, 1963I; *String Quartet No. 5*, 1968I; *String Quartet No. 6*, 1971I; *Symphony No. 1*,
　1952I; *Symphony No. 2*, 1959I; *Symphony No. 3*, 1963I; *Symphony No. 4*, 1974I; *Violin Sonata No. 1*, 1945I
Salonen, Esa-Pekka: *Five Images after Sappho*, 1999I; *LA Variations*, 1996I; *Mania*, 1999I
Salter, Mary E.: *Songs (5), Opus 34*, 1916I
Salzedo, Carlos: *The Enchanted Isle (harp)*, 1918I; *Harp Sonata*, 1922I; *Poetical Studies (5) for Harp*, 1918I
Salzman, Eric: *Civilization and Its Discontents*, 1977I; *The Conjurer*, 1974I; *Cummings Set*, 1954I; *Feedback*,
　1968I; *Flute Sonata*, 1956I; *In Praise of the Owl & the Cuckoo*, 1964I; *Lazarus*, 1973I; *Noah*, 1978I; *String
　Quartet No. 1*, 1955I
Saminsky, Lazare: *The Daughter of Jephtha*, 1928I; *Requiem*, 1945I; *Symphony No. 1*, 1914I; *Symphony No.
　2*, 1918I; *Symphony No. 3, "Symphony of the Seas,"* 1924I; *Symphony No. 4*, 1926I; *Symphony No. 5,
　"Jerusalem,"* 1930I; *The Vow (Concerto)*, 1943I
Sammartini, Giovanni: *Concerti grossi (6), Opus 6*, 1757I; *Pastorale offerta*, 1753I; *La reggia de'fati*, 1753I
Samuel, Gerhard: *AGAM*, 1983I; *String Quartet No. 1*, 1978I; *String Quartet No. 2*, 1981I; *Symphony: Out
　of Time*, 1978I
Sandby, Herman: *Symphony No. 4*, 1955I
Sanders, Robert: *Violin Sonata*, 1928I
Sandstrom, Sven-David: *Wind Pieces*, 1996I
Sandström, Jan: *Macbeth*, 1996I; *Surge aquilo*, 1998I; *Trumpet Concerto No. 2*, 1996I
Sankey, Ira: *The Ninety and Nine*, 1874I
Santos, Joly Braga: *Concerto in D for Strings*, 1951I; *Symphony No. 1*, 1946I; *Symphony No. 2*, 1947I;
　Symphony No. 3, 1949I; *Symphony No. 4*, 1950I; *Symphony No. 5*, 1966I
Sapp, Allan: *The Four Seasons – A Concerto for Chamber Orchestra*, 1994I
Sarti, Giuseppe: *Astrea splacata*, 1760I; *Achille in Schiro*, 1759I; *Adrianno in Sciro*, 1779I; *Alessandro e
　Timoteo*, 1782I; *Anagilda*, 1758I; *Andromaca*, 1760I; *Andromeda*, 1798I; *Antigono*, 1754I; *Arianna e Teseo*,
　1756I; *Armida e Rinaldo*, 1786I; *Armida abbandonata*, 1759I; *L'asile de l'amour*, 1769I; *Attalo, Re di Bitinia*,
　1782I; *La calzolaia di Strasburg*, 1768I; *Cesare in Egitto*, 1763I; *Ciro riconosciuto*, 1754I; *La clemenze di
　Tito*, 1771I; *Cleomene*, 1788I; *La contadina fedele*, 1771I; *I contrattempi*, 1778I; *Deucalion og Pyrrha*, 1772I;
　Didone abbandonata I, 1762I; *Didone abbandonata II*, 1784I; *Enea nel Lazio*, 1799I; *Farnace*, 1776I; *I finti
　eredi*, 1785H; *Fra i due litiganti il terzo gode*, 1782I; *Le gelosie villane*, 1776I; *La giardiniera brillante*, 1768I;
　Giulio Sabino, 1781I; *Gli amanti consolati*, 1784I; *Il gran Tamerlano*, 1764I; *Idalide*, 1783I; *Ifigenia*, 1777I;
　Ipermestra, 1766I; *Issipile*, 1761I; *Medonte*, 1777I; *Il militare bizarro*, 1777I; *Mithridate*, 1765I; *Il narciso*,
　1763I; *Il naufragio di Cipro*, 1764I; *Nitteti*, 1761I; *Olimpiade I*, 1778I; *Olimpiade II*, 1783I; *Oratorio for
　Catherine the Great*, 1801I; *Pompeo in Armenia*, 1752I; *Il re pastore*, 1753I; *Requiem for Ludwig XVI*, 1793I;
　Der Ruhm des Nordens, 1794I; *Scipione*, 1778I; *Semiramide*, 1762I; *Siroe*, 1779I; *Soliman II*, 1770I; *Lo
　stravagante inglese*, 1792I; *Te Deum*, 1789I; *Il testaccio*, 1760I; *Il trionfo della pace*, 1783I; *Il trionfo
　d'Atalanta*, 1791I; *Vologeso*, 1754I
Satie, Erik: *La Belle Excentrique*, 1920I; *Cinq Grimaces pour le Songe d'une nuit d'été*, 1914I; *Descriptions
　Automatiques*, 1913I; *Disagreeable Impressions*, 1908I; *Embryons Desséchés*, 1913I; *Gymnopedie (3)*, 1888I;
　En Habit de cheval, 1911I; *Parade*, 1917I; *Pousse l'Amour*, 1905I; *Quatre petites pièces Montées*, 1919I;
　Socrates, 1918I; *Sports et divertissements*, 1914I; *Three Pieces in the Shape of a Pear*, 1903I; *Véritables
　Préludes flasques (3)*, 1912I
Saunders, Rebecca: *String Quartet*, 1997I
Savage, Robert: *An Eye-Sky Symphony*, 1988I; *Florida Poems*, 1984I
Saxton, Robert: *Chacony for Left Hand for Piano*, 1988I; *Piano Sonata*, 1981I
Saygun, Ahmet: *Symphony No. 1*, 1953I
Saylor, Bruce: *Orpheus Descending*, 1994I
Scanlan, William J.: *Friend & Foe*, 1881I; *The Irish Minstrel*, 1883I
Scarlatti, Domenico: *Salve Regina*, 1756I
Scarlatti, Giuseppe: *Adriano in Siria*, 1752I; *Alessandro nell'Indie*, 1753I; *L'amor della Patia*, 1752I;
　Antigono, 1754I; *Armida*, 1766I; *Caio Mario*, 1754I; *La clemenza di Tito*, 1760I; *De gustibus non est
　disputandum*, 1753I; *Demetrio* 1752I; *L'impostore*, 1752I; *L'isola disabitata*, 1757I; *L'issipile*, 1760I; *La
　madamigella*, 1754I; *Il mercato di Malmantile*, 1757I; *Pelopida*, 1763I; *I portentosi effetti della Madre
　Natura*, 1752I; *La serva scaltra*, 1759I
Scarmolin, Anthony Louis: *Symphony No. 1 in e*, 1937I; *Symphony No. 2*, 1946I; *Symphony No. 3,
　"Sinfonia breve,"* 1952I

※

A　*Births*　　B　*Deaths*　　C　*Debuts*　　D　*New Positions*
E　*Prizes/Honors*

Scelsi, Giacinto: *Pranam*, 1961I; *Quatro pezzi*, 1959I
Schaefer, Peter: *See*, 1983I
Schaeffer, Boguslaw: *Doublebass Concerto*, 1979I; *Symphony No. 10*, 1979I
Schaeuble, Hans: *Piano Concerto*, 1967I
Schafer, R. Murray: *Requiem for the Party Girl*, 1966I
Scharwenka, Philipp: *Arkadische Suite*, 1887I; *Dramatische Fantasie*, 1900I; *Frühlingswagen*, 1891I; *Piano Trio, Opus 100*, 1897I; *Symphony*, 1885I; *Violin Concerto*, 1895I; *Violin Sonata in b, Opus 110*, 1897I
Schat, Peter: *Etudes*, 1992I; *Houdini Symphony*, 1976I; *Symphony No. 1*, 1978I; *Symphony No. 2*, 1983I
Schelb, Joseph: *English Horn Concerto*, 1970I
Schelle, Michael: *Concerto for Two Pianos*, 1987I
Schelling, Ernest: *Divertimento for Piano Quintet*, 1925I; *Fantastic Suite*, 1905I; *Impressions from an Artist's Life*, 1913I; *Suite Fantastique* (piano), 1906I; *A Victory Ball*, 1923I; *Violin Concerto*, 1916I
Schenk, Johann: *Achmet und Almanzine*, 1795I; *Der Dorfbarbier*, 1796I; *Der Erntekranz*, 1791I; *Der Fassbinder*, 1802I; *Die Huldigung*, 1819I; *Die Jagd*, 1799I; *Der Mai*, 1819I
Schetky, Johann G.: *Cello Sonatas (6), Opus 4*, 1776I; *Duets (6), Violin & Cello, Opus 2*, 1775I; *Flute Duets (6), Opus 5*, 1777I; *Piano Trios (6), Opus 3*, 1775I; *String Quartets (6)*, 1777I; *String Trios (6), Opus 1*, 1773I; *Symphonies in C & D*, 1765I
Schickele, Peter: *String Quartet No. 1*, 1983I; *String Quartet No. 2*, 1987I; *String Quartet No. 3*, 1988I; *String Quartet No. 4*, 1992I; *String Quartet No. 5*, 1998I; *Symphony No. 1*, 2000I
Schierbeck, Poul: *Piano Concerto No. 1*, 1938I; *Symphony*, 1921I; *Violin Sonata*, 1912I; *Wind Quintet*, 1941I
Schiff, David: *Gimpel, the Fool*, 1980I; *My Ladye Jane's Booke for Piano*, 1992I
Schiffman, Harold: *Piano Concerto*, 1982I; *Rhapsody for Guitar*, 1991I; *Spectrum Symphony*, 1961I
Schifrin, Lalo: *Concerto of the Americas* (piano), 1992I
Schifrin, Seymour: *Pieces, Three*, 1958I
Schillings, Max von: *Glockenlieder*, 1908I
Schlaepfer, Jean-Claude: *L'Ile de Re*, 1996I; *Missa brevis*, 1996I; *Stabat Mater*, 1990I
Schmid, Johann: *Tod un Begrabnis Jesu*, 1761I
Schmidt, Franz: *Das Buch mit Sieben Siegeln*, 1937I; *Chaconne in c♯*, 1925I; *Eglogue, Poème vigilien*, 1899I; *Fantasia & Fugue in D*, 1924I; *Fugue in F*, 1927I; *Kleine choralvorspiele (4)*, 1926I; *Königsfanfaren I*, 1916I; *Königsfanfaren II*, 1925I; *Little Preludes & Fugues (4)*, 1928I; *Notre Dame*, 1904I; *Piano Concerto in E♭ for the Left Hand*, 1934I; *Piano Concerto No. 2 for the Left Hand*, 1935I; *Piano Quintet in G*, 1925I; *Prelude & Fugue in E♭*, 1924I; *Prelude & Fugue in C*, 1927I; *Prelude & Fugue in A*, 1934I; *Quintet in A for Clarinet & Piano Quartet*, 1938I; *Quintet in B♭ for Clarinet & Piano Quartet*, 1932I; *String Quartet No. 1 in A*, 1925I; *String Quartet No. 2 in G*, 1929I; *Symphony No. 1 in E*, 1899I; *Symphony No. 2 in E♭*, 1913I; *Symphony No. 3 in A*, 1928I; *Symphony No. 4 in C*, 1933I; *Toccata & Fugue in A♭*, 1935I; *Toccata in C*, 1924I; *Variations on a Hussar Song*, 1930I; *Variations on a Theme of Beethoven*, 1923I
Schmidt, Johann: *Alfred der Grosse*, 1830I; *Die Alpenhütte*, 1816I; *Der blinde Gärtner*, 1813I; *Eulenspiegel*, 1806I; *Das Fischermädchen*, 1818I; *Missa Solemnis in D*, 1833I; *Der Onkel*, 1804I; *Piano Concerto, Opus 1*, 1798I; *Rinaldo*, 1836I; *Der Schlaftrunk*, 1797I; *Das verborgene Fenster*, 1824I
Schmidt, Ole: *Concert Overture*, 1966I; *Concerto for Flute & Strings*, 1984I; *Flute Concerto*, 1985I; *Horn Concerto*, 1966I; *Øresund Symphony*, 1993I; *Passion of Joan of Arc*, 1983I; *Piano Concerto No. 1*, 1951I; *Piano Concerto No. 2*, 1954I; *String Quartet No. 1*, 1954I; *String Quartet No. 2*, 1963I; *String Quartet No. 3*, 1965I; *String Quartet No. 4*, 1969I; *String Quartet No. 5*, 1977I; *Symphony No. 1*, 1956I; *Tuba Concerto*, 1975I; *Viola Sonata*, 1993I; *Wind Quintet*, 1991I
Schmitt, Florent: *Antoine et Cléopâtre*, 1920I; *L'arbre entre tous*, 1939I; *Callirhoé*, 1899I; *Le chant de la nuit, Opus 120*, 1951I; *Choruses (6), Opus 81*, 1931I; *Danses des Devadasis, Opus 47*, 1908I; *En bonnes voix, Opus 9*, 1938I; *En été, Opus 10*, 1894I; *Fête de la lumière, Opus 88*, 1936I; *Frédégonde*, 1897I; *Hasard for Piano Quartet, Opus 96*, 1944I; *Jardin Secret*, 1953I; *Marche nuptiale, Opus 108*, 1951I; *Mass, Opus 138*, 1958I; *Mélusine*, 1896I; *Musiques intimes II, Opus 29*, 1904I; *Nuits romaines, Opus 23*, 1901I; *Oriane et le prince d'amour*, 1933I; *Le palais hanté, Opus 49*, 1904I; *Le petit elfe ferme-l'oeil*, 1923I; *Piano Quintet, Opus 51*, 1908I; *Poèmes de Ronsard (4), Opus 100*, 1942I; *Psalm XLVII, Opus 38*, 1904I; *Quartet for Four Flutes, Opus 106*, 1949I; *Quintet for Brass, Opus 109*, 1946I; *Radegonde*, 1898I; *Salammbo, Opus 76*, 1925I; *Scènes de la vie moyenne, Opus 124*, 1952I; *Sělamlik*, 1906I; *String Quartet in G, Opus 112*, 1947I; *Symphonie Concertante, Opus 82*, 1930I; *Symphony No. 2, Opus 137*, 1956I; *The Tragedy of Salome, Opus 50*, 1907I
Schnabel, Artur: *Dance Suite*, 1921I; *Piano Piece in Seven Movements*, 1936I; *Piano Pieces (7)*, 1947I; *Piano Sonata*, 1922I; *Sonata for Solo Cello*, 1931I; *Sonata for Solo Violin*, 1919I; *Violin Sonata*, 1934I
Schneider, Friedrich: *The Deluge*, 1823I; *Der Weltgericht*, 1820I
Schnittke, Alfred: *Canon in Memoriam Igor Stravinsky*, 1971I; *Cello Concerto*, 1986I; *Cello Concerto No. 2*, 1990I; *Cello Sonata*, 1978I; *Cello Sonata No. 2*, 1993I; *Concerto for Piano & Strings*, 1979I; *Concerto for*

❄

F *Biographical*   G *Cultural Beginnings*   H *Musical Literature*
I *Musical Compositions*

Schnittke, Alfred: (*cont.*)
   Piano, Four Hands, 1987I; *Concerto Grosso No. 2*, 1981I; *Concerto Grosso No. 3*, 1985I; *Concerto Grosso No. 4*, 1985I; *Concerto Grosso No. 5* (piano), 1991I; *Concerto Grosso No. 6*, 1993I; *Gesualdo*, 1994I; *Gogol Suite*, 1991I; *The History of Dr. Johann Faust*, 1982I; *Labyrinths*, 1971I; *Life with an Idiot*, 1991I; *Peer Gynt*, 1986I; *Piano Concerto*, 1960I; *Piano Quartet*, 1989I; *Piano Quintet*, 1976I; *Piano Sonata No. 1*, 1987I; *Piano Sonata No. 2*, 1990I; *Piano Sonata No. 3*, 1992I; *Piano Trio*, 1993I; *Psalms of Repentance*, 1988I; *Requiem*, 1975I; *Septet*, 1981I; *Sketches*, 1985I; *String Quartet No. 1*, 1966I; *String Quartet No. 2*, 1980I; *String Quartet No. 3*, 1983I; *String Quartet No. 4*, 1989I; *String Trio*, 1985I; *Suite in Old Style*, 1972I; *Symphony No. 1*, 1972I; *Symphony No. 2*, 1979I; *Symphony No. 2*, 1980I; *Symphony No. 4*, 1983I, 1984I; *Symphony No. 5*, 1988I; *Symphony No. 6*, 1992I; *Symphony No. 7*, 1993I, 1997I; *Symphony No. 8*, 1994I; *Symphony No. 9*, 1985I; *Variations for String Quartet*, 1995I; *Viola Concerto*, 1985I; *Viola Concerto*, 1989I; *Violin Concerto No. 1*, 1957I; *Violin Sonata No. 1*, 1963I; *Violin Sonata No. 2*, 1968I; *Violin Sonata No. 3*, 1994I
Schoben, Brian: *Stabat Mater*, 1994I; *Te Deum*, 1994I
Schobert, Johann: *Le garde-chasse et le braconnier*, 1765I
Schoeck, Othmar: *Elegie*, 1922I; *Horn Concerto, Opus 65*, 1951I; *Legendig begraben*, 1926I; *Penthesilea*, 1927I; *Prelude for Orchestra*, 1932I; *Violin Sonata No. 1 in D, Opus 16*, 1908I; *Violin Sonata No. 2 in D*, 1909I; *Violin Sonata No. 3 in E*, 1931I
Schoenberg, Arnold: *Ballads (2), Opus 12*, 1907I; *Begleitungsmusik, Opus 34*, 1930I; *Das Buch der Hängenden Gärten*, 1909I; *Chamber Symphony No. 1, Opus 9*, 1906I; *Chamber Symphony No. 2, Opus 38*, 1939I; *De Profundis, Opus 50b*, 1950I; *Dreimal Tausend Jahre, Opus 50a*, 1949I; *Erwartung, Opus 17*, 1909I; *Fantasia, Opus 47*, 1949I; *Folksongs (3), Opus 49*, 1948I; *Friede auf Erden, Opus 13*, 1907I; *Die glückliche Hande, Opus 18*, 1913I; *Gurre-Lieder*, 1901I; *Herzgewächse, Opus 20*, 1911I; *Kol Nidre, Opus 39*, 1938I; *Little Pieces (6), Opus 19*, 1911I; *Moses & Aaron*, 1932I; *Ode to Napoleon*, 1942I; *Orchestral Songs (6), Opus 8*, 1905I; *Orchestral Songs (4), Opus 22*, 1916I; *Pelleas und Mélisande*, 1903I; *Piano Concerto, Opus 42*, 1942I; *Piano Pieces (3), Opus 11*, 1909I; *Piano Pieces (5), Opus 23*, 1923I; *Piano Suite, Opus 25*, 1923I; *Pieces (4), Opus 27*, 1925I; *Pieces (6), Opus 35*, 1930I; *Pieces for Orchestra (4), Opus 16*, 1909I; *Pierrot Lunaire, Opus 21*, 1912I; *Prelude for Orchestra, Opus 44*, 1946I; *Satires (3), Opus 28*, 1925I; *Serenade, Opus 24*, 1923I; *Songs (6), Opus 3*, 1903I; *Songs (8), Opus 6*, 1905I; *Songs (2), Opus 14*, 1908I; *Songs (3), Opus 48*, 1933I; *String Quartet No. 1, Opus 7*, 1905I; *String Quartet No. 2, Opus 15*, 1908I; *String Quartet No. 3*, 1927I; *String Quartet No. 4, Opus 37*, 1936I; *String Trio, Opus 45*, 1946I; *Suite, Opus 29*, 1925I; *A Survivor from Warsaw*, 1947I; *Theme & Variations, Opus 43a*, 1943I; *Transfigured Night, Opus 4*, 1899I; *Variations for Orchestra, Opus 31*, 1928I; *Variations on a Recitative, Opus 40*, 1941I; *Violin Concerto, Opus 36*, 1936I; *Von Heute auf Morgan, Opus 32*, 1929I; *Wind Quintet, Opus 26*, 1924I
Schoenefeld, Henry: *Symphony No. 1, "Rural,"* 1893I
Schoenfeld, Paul: *Piano Concerto, "The Four Parables,"* 1983I; *The Merchant & the Pauper*, 1999I; *Song of Deborah*, 1998I
Schonthal, Ruth: *Piano Reverberations*, 1964I
Schreker, Franz: *Birthday of the Infanta*, 1908I; *Ekkehard, Opus 12*, 1903I; *Fantastic Overture, Opus 15*, 1904I; *From Eternal Life*, 1927I; *Prelude to a Drama*, 1913I; *Prelude to a Grand Opera*, 1932I; *Romantic suite*, 1902I; *Der Schatzgräber*, 1918I
Schroeder, Hermann: *Sonata in b*, 1957I
Schubert, Franz: *Adrast*, 1815I; *Alfonso und Estrella*, 1822I; *Ave Maria*, 1825I; *Die Burgschaft*, 1816I; *Claudine von Villa Bella*, 1815I; *Death and the Maiden*, 1817I; *Deutsche Trauermesse, D. 621*, 1818I; *Deutsche Messe, D. 872*, 1827I; *Ecossaises (12), D. 299*, 1815I; *Ecossaises (6), D. 421*, 1816I; *Ecossaises (6), D. 697*, 1820I; *Der Erlkönig*, 1815I; *Fantasy in C, D. 605*, 1818I; *Fantasy in C, "Wanderer," D. 760*, 1822I; *Fantasy in C, D. 934*, 1827I; *Fierabras, D. 796*, 1823I; *Die Forelle*, 1817I; *Der Freunde von Salamanka*, 1815I; *German Dances (12), D. 420*, 1816I; *German Dances (16), D. 783*, 1824I; *German Dances (12), D. 790*, 1823I; *Gesang der Geister über den Wassern, Opus 167*, 1820I; *Glaube, Hoffnung und Liebe, D. 854*, 1828I; *Der Graf von Gleicher*, 1828I; *Gretchen am Spinrade*, 1814I; *Hagar's Klage*, 1811I; *Hark! Hark! The Lark*, 1826I; *Der häusliche Krieg, D. 87*, 1823I; *Der Hirt auf dem Felsen, C. 965*, 1828I; *Impromtus (4), Opus 90*, 1828I; *Impromtus (4), D. 899*, 1827I; *Impromtus (4), D. 935*, 1827I; *Ländler (12), D. 681*, 1815I; *Mass No. 1 in D, D. 105*, 1814I; *Mass No. 2 in G, D. 167*, 1815I; *Mass No. 3, De. 324*, 1815I; *Mass No. 4, D. 452*, 1816I; *Mass No. 6 in E♭, D. 950*, 1828I; *Minuets (20), D. 41*, 1813I; *Moments musicaux (6), Opus 94*, 1828I; *Nachtgesang in Walde, D. 913*, 1827I; *Namensfeier*, 1812I; *Octet in F, D. 803*, 1824I; *Organ Fugues (C,G,d), D. 24*, 1812I; *Overtures in c & g, D. 8,18*, 1811I; *Overture, "Der Teufel als Hydraulicus,"* 1812I; *Overtures in Italian Style in C &D*, 1817I; *Overture in B♭*, 1816I; *Overture in d*, 1817I; *Overture in e, D. 648*, 1819I; *Piano Quintet, "Trout,"* 1819I; *Piano Sonata in E, D. 157*, 1815I; *Piano Sonata in C, D. 279*, 1815I; *Piano*

A   *Births*   B   *Deaths*   C   *Debuts*   D   *New Positions*
              E   *Prizes/Honors*

Sonata in F, D. 459, 1816I; *Piano Sonata in a, D. 537*, 1817I; *Piano Sonata in A♭, D. 557*, 1817I; *Piano Sonata in e, D. 566*, 1817I; *Piano Sonata in D♭, D. 567*, 1817I; *Piano Sonata in E♭, D. 568*, 1817I; *Piano Sonata in B, D. 575*, 1817I; *Piano Sonata in C, D. 613*, 1818I; *Piano Sonata in f, D. 625*, 1818I; *Piano Sonata in c♯, D. 655*, 1819I; *Piano Sonata in A, D. 664*, 1819I; *Piano Sonata in a, D. 784*, 1823I; *Piano Sonata in C, D. 840*, 1825I; *Piano Sonata in a, D. 845*, 1825I; *Piano Sonata in D, D. 850*, 1825I; *Piano Sonata in G, D. 894*, 1826I; *Piano Sonata in c, D. 958*, 1828I; *Piano Sonata in A, D. 959*, 1828I; *Piano Sonata in B♭, D. 960*, 1828I; *Piano Trio in B♭, D. 898*, 1826I; *Piano Trio in B♭, D. 929*, 1827I; *Requiem in E♭, D. 453*, 1816I; *Rondo Brillant in b, D. 895*, 1826I; *Rosamunde, D. 797*, 1823I; *Rüdiger, D. 791*, 1823I; *Sakuntala*, 1820I; *Die schöne Müllerin, D. 795*, 1823I; *Schwanengesang, D. 957*, 1828I; *Der Spiegelritter*, 1812I; *String Quartet in G, D.2*, 1810I; *String Quartet in g, D. 18*, 1811I; *String Quartet in C, D. 32*, 1811I; *String Quartet in B♭, D. 36*, 1811I; *String Quartet in C, D. 46*, 1813I; *String Quartet in B♭, D. 68*, 1813I; *String Quartet in E♭, D. 87*, 1813I; *String Quartet in D, D. 94*, 1812II; *String Quartet in B♭, D. 112*, 1814I; *String Quartet in g, D. 173*, 1815I; *String Quartet in E, D. 353*, 1816I; *String Quartet in c, "Quartettsatz," D. 703*, 1820I; *String Quartet in a, D. 804*, 1824I; *String Quartet "Death and the Maiden," D. 810*, 1824I; *String Quartet in G, D. 887*, 1826I; *String Quintet in C, D. 956*, 1828I; *String Trio in B♭, D. 471*, 1817I; *Symphony No. 1 in D, D. 82*, 1813I; *Symphony No. 2 in B♭, D. 125*, 1815I; *Symphony No. 3 in D, D. 200*, 1815I; *Symphony No. 4 in c, D. 417, "Tragic,"* 1816I; *Symphony No. 5 in B♭, D. 485*, 1816I; *Symphony No. 6 in C, D. 589*, 1818I; *Symphony No. 7 in E, D. 729*, 1821I; *Symphony No. 8 in b, "Unfinished," D. 759*, 1822I; *Symphony No. 9 in C, "The Great," D. 944*, 1828I; *Valses Sentimentales, 34), D. 779*, 1824I; *Variations (6) in E♭, D. 21*, 1812I; *Variations (10) in F, D. 156*, 1815I; *Viennese Dances (12), D. 128*, 1812I; *Der vierjährige Posten*, 1815I; *Violin Sonata in A, Opus 162*, 1817I; *Violin Sonatinas (3), Opus 137*, 1816I; *Waltzes (12), D. 145*, 1821I; *Waltzes (20), D. 146*, 1824I; *Wanderer's Nachtlied, D. 768*, 1822I; *Die Winterreise*, 1827I; *Die Zauberharfe*, 1820I; *Die Zwillingsbrüder*, 1819I

Schubert, Franz Anton: *Symphony da camera in D.*, 1788I

Schulhoff, Ervin: *Cello Sonata*, 1914I; *Double Concerto (flute, piano)*, 1927I; *Flammen*, 1929I; *Flute Sonata*, 1927I; *Ogelala*, 1925I; *Piano Concerto No. 2*, 1923I; *Piano Sonata No. 1*, 1924I; *Piano Sonata No. 2*, 1927I; *Pieces (5) for String Quartet*, 1923I; *String Quartet in G*, 1918I; *String Quartet No. 2*, 1925I; *String Sextet*, 1924I; *Symphony No. 1*, 1925I; *Symphony No. 2*, 1932I; *Symphony No. 3*, 1935I; *Symphony No. 4*, 1937I; *Symphony No. 5*, 1938I; *Symphony No. 6, "of Freedom,"* 1940I; *Violin Sonata No. 1*, 1913I; *Violin Sonata No. 2*, 1927I

Schuller, Gunther: *Brass Quintet No. 2*, 1993I; *Cello Concerto*, 1945I; *Concerto for Orchestra II*, 1976I; *Concerto for Orchestra III, "Farbenspiel,"* 1985I; *Concerto for Orchestra No. 1, "Gala Music,"* 1966I; *Contrabasson Concerto*, 1978I; *Contrasts for Orchestra*, 1961I; *Contrasts for Wind Quintet & Orchestra*, 1960I; *Deai*, 1978I; *Double Bass Concerto*, 1968I; *Dramatic Overture*, 1951I; *Fantasy-Suite*, 1994I; *Flute Concerto*, 1988I; *Four Soundscapes*, 1974I; *Horn Concerto No. 1*, 1944I; *Horn Concerto No. 2*, 1976I; *Organ Concerto*, 1994I; *Piano Concerto No. 1*, 1962I; *Piano Concerto No. 2*, 1981I; *Piano Sonata/Fantasia*, 1993I; *Piano Trio*, 1984I; *Saxophone Concerto*, 1983I; *Seven Studies on Themes of Paul Klee*, 1959I; *Shapes & Designs*, 1969I; *String Quartet No. 1*, 1957I; *String Quartet No. 2*, 1965I; *String Quartet No. 3*, 1987I; *Symphonic Study*, 1948I; *Symphony No. 1*, 1965I; *Thou Art the Son of God*, 1987I; *Triplum for Orchestra*, 1967I; *Trumpet Concerto*, 1979I; *The Visitation*, 1966I

Schuman, William: *Amaryllis*, 1976I; *American Festival Overture*, 1939I; *Canonic Choruses (4)*, 1933I; *Carols of Death*, 1958I; *Casey at the Bat*, 1976I; *Chester Overture*, 1956I; *Choral Étude*, 1937I; *Circus Overture*, 1944I; *Colloquies (3) for Horn & Orchestra*, 1979I; *Concerto on Old English Rounds*, 1973I; *Credendum, Article of Faith*, 1955I; *Dances: Divertimento for Woodwind Quintet & Percussion*, 1985I; *George Washington Bridge*, 1950I; *In Praise of Shahn*, 1969I; *Judith*, 1949I; *Mail Order Madrigals*, 1971I; *Mighty Casey*, 1953I; *New England Triptych*, 1956I; *Newsreel for Orchestra*, 1941I; *Night Journey*, 1947I; *On Freedom's Ground: An American Cantata*, 1985I; *The Orchestra Song*, 1963I; *Philharmonic Fanfare*, 1965I; *Piano Concerto*, 1942I; *Piano Moods (3)*, 1958I; *Pioneers*, 1937I; *Prayer in Time of War*, 1943I; *Prelude & Fugue for Orchestra*, 1937I; *Prelude for a Great Occasion*, 1974I; *Prologue*, 1939I; *A Question of Taste*, 1989I; *Secular Cantata No. 2: A Free Song*, 1942I; *The Song of Orpheus (cello concerto)*, 1961I; *Steel Town*, 1944I; *String Quartet No. 1*, 1936I; *String Quartet No. 2*, 1937I; *String Quartet No. 3*, 1939I; *String Quartet No. 4*, 1950I; *String Quartet No. 5*, 1988I; *Symphony No. 1*, 1935I, 1936I; *Symphony No. 2*, 1937I; *Symphony No. 3*, 1941I, 1943I; *Symphony No. 4*, 1941I, 1942I; *Symphony No. 6*, 1946I, 1948I; *Symphony No. 7*, 1960I; *Symphony No. 8*, 1962I; *Symphony No. 9, "Le fosse ardeatine,"* 1968I; *Symphony No. 10, "American Muse,"* 1975I; *Te Deum*, 1944I; *This Is Our Time*, 1940I; *Three Score Set*, 1943I; *Time to the Old*, 1979I; *To Thee, Old Cause*, 1968I; *Undertow*, 1945I; *Violin Concerto*, 1947I; *Voyage*, 1953I; *Voyage for Orchestra*, 1972I; *William Billings Overture*, 1943i; *The Witch of Endor*, 1965I; *The Young Dead Soldiers*, 1975I

Schumann, Clara: *Concertsatz in f*, 1846I; *Piano Concerto in a, Opus 7*, 1836I; *Piano Scherzo No. 2, Opus 14*, 1842I; *Piano Trio in g, Opus 17*, 1846I; *Pièces Fugitives (4), Opus 15*, 1844I; *Preludes & Fugues (3), Opus*

F   *Biographical*   G   *Cultural Beginnings*   H   *Musical Literature*
I   *Musical Compositions*

Schumann, Clara: (*cont.*)
  16, 1845I; *Romances (3), Opus 21*, 1855I; *Songs (6), Opus 13*, 1844I; *Songs (6) of Jucunde, Opus 23*, 1853I;
  Songs (3) of Rückert, Opus 12, 1841I; *Variations on a Theme of R. S., Opus 20*, 1853I
Schumann, Robert: *Abegg Variations, Opus 1*, 1830I; *Adagio and Allegro in A♭, Opus 70*, 1849I; *Album für
  die Jugend, Opus 68*, 1848I; *Albumblätter, Opus 124*, 1854I; *Allegro, Opus 8*, 1831I; *Andante & Variations,
  Opus 46*, 1843I; *Ballads (3), Opus 31*, 1840I; *Ballads (4), Opus 141*, 1852I; *Carnaval, Opus 9*, 1835I; *Cello
  Concerto in a, Opus 129*, 1850I; *Concertpiece in F, Opus 86*, 1849I; *Concertpiece, Opus 92*, 1849I; *Der
  Corsar*, 1844I; *Davidsbündler, Opus 6*, 1837I; *Dichterliebe, Opus 48*, 1840I; *Etudes in Canonic Form (6),
  Opus 56*, 1845I; *Etudes Symphoniques, Opus 13*, 1834I; *Fantasiestücke, Opus 12*, 1837I; *Fantasiestücke,
  Opus 73*, 1849I; *Fantasiestücke (3), Opus 111*, 1851I; *Fantasy in C, Opus 17*, 1836I; *Fantasy in C, Opus
  131*, 1853I; *Faschingsschwank aus Wien, Opus 26*, 1839I; *Festival Overture, "Rheinweinlied," Opus 123*,
  1853I; *Frauenliebe und Leben, Opus 42*, 1840I; *Fugues (6) on B-A-C-H, Opus 60*, 1845I; *Genoveva, Opus
  81*, 1848I; *Das Glück von Edenhall, Opus 143*, 1853I; *Husarenlieder, Opus 177*, 1851I; *Impromtus on Theme
  of Clara Vieck, Opus 5*, 1833I; *Intermezzi (6), Opus 4*, 1832I; *Introduction & Allegro in D/d, Opus 134*,
  1853I; *Kinderszenen, Opus 15*, 1838I; *Der Königssohn, Opus 116*, 1851I; *Kreisleriana, Opus 16*, 1838I;
  Liebesfrühling, Opus 37, 1840I; *Lieder und Gesänge I, Opus 27*, 1840I; *Liederkreis, Opus 24* (Heine), 1840I;
  Liederkreis, Opus 39 (Eichendorff), 1840I; *Mädchenlieder, Opus 103*, 1851I; *Manfred, Opus 115*, 1848I;
  Märchenerzählungen, Opus 132, 1853I; *Mass in C, Opus 147*, 1852I; *Myrthen, Opus 25*, 1840I;
  Nachtstücke, Opus 23, 1839I; *Neujahrslied, Opus 144*, 1850I; *Noveletten, Opus 21*, 1838I; *Organ Sketches
  (4), Opus 58*, 1845I; *Overture, Die Braut von Messina, Opus 100*, 1850I; *Overture, Hermann und Dorothea,
  Opus 136*, 1851I; *Overture, Julius Caesar, Opus 128*, 1851I; *Overture, Scherzo & Finale in E, Opus 52*,
  1841I; *Paganini Etudes I, Opus 3*, 1832I; *Paganini Etudes II, Opus 10*, 1833I; *Papillons, Opus 2*, 1831I;
  Paradise and the Peri, Opus 50, 1843I; *Piano Concerto in a, Opus 54*, 1845I; *Piano Pieces (4), Opus 32*,
  1839I; *Piano Pieces (12), Opus 85*, 1849I; *Piano Pieces (7) in Fughetta Form, Opus 126*, 1853I; *Piano Sonata
  in f♯, Opus 11*, 1835I; *Piano Sonata in f, Opus 14*, 1836I; *Piano Sonata in g, Opus 22*, 1838I; *Piano Sonatas (3)
  for the Young, Opus 118*, 1853I; *Piano Quartet in c*, 1829I; *Piano Quartet in E♭, Opus 47*, 1842I; *Piano Quintet in E♭,
  Opus 44*, 1842I; *Piano Trio No. 1 in d, Opus 63*, 1847I; *Piano Trio No. 2 in F, Opus 80*, 1847I; *Piano Trio
  No. 3, Opus 110*, 1851I; *Poems (21), Opus 30, 35, 36*, 1840I; *Poems (3), Opus 119*, 1851I; *Poems (5) of
  Queen Mary, Opus 135*, 1852I; *Requiem für Mignon, Opus 98b*, 1849I; *Requiem in D, Opus 148*, 1852I;
  Romances (3), Opus 28, 1839I; *Der Rose Pilgerfahrt, Opus 112*, 1851I; *Scenes from Goethe's Faust*, 1853I;
  Songs (6), Male Chorus, Opus 33, 1840I; *Songs (5), Opus 40*, 1840I; *Songs (10) for Chorus, Opus 55, 59*,
  1846I; *Songs (19), Opus 77, 83, 89, 127*, 1850I; *Songs (7), Opus 104*, 1851I; *Songs (4), Opus 142*, 1852I;
  Spanische Liedeslieder, Opus 138, 1849I; *String Quartets (3), Opus 41*, 1842I; *Spring in g*, 1823I;
  Symphony No. 1 in B♭, Opus 38, "Spring," 1841I; *Symphony No. 2 in C, Opus 61*, 1846I; *Symphony No. 3
  in E♭, Opus 97, "Rhenish,"* 1850I; *Symphony No. 4 in d, Opus 120*, 1841I; *Toccata in C, Opus 7*, 1833I;
  Violin Sonata in a, Opus 105, 1851I; *Violin Sonata in d, Opus 121*, 1851I; *Von Pagen und der Königstochter,
  Opus 140*, 1852I; *Waldscenen, Opus 82*, 1849I; *Zum Abschied, Opus 84*, 1847I
Schurig, Wolfram: *Blendung/Light Sturz for Organ*, 1990I; *MAUERWERK*, 1994I; *SCHLEIFE SIMULTON
  SOLO*, 1995I; *String Quartet No. 2*, 1998I; *Hot, Powdery Snow*, 1995I
Schurmann, Gerard: *Piano Quartet No. 2*, 1998I; *Studies of Francis Bacon (6)*, 1968I
Schuster, Joseph: *Der Alchymist*, 1778I; *Rübezahl*, 1789I
Schwanenberg, Johann: *Adriano in Siria*, 1762I; *Antigono*, 1768I; *L'Olimpiade*, 1782I
Schwantner, Joseph: *Aftertones of Infinity*, 1978I; *Autumn Canticles*, 1974I; *Canticle of the Evening Bells*,
  1975I; *Concerto for Percussionist & Orchestra*, 1991I; *Consortium I*, 1970I; *Consortium II*, 1971I; *Diaphonia
  Intervallum*, 1965I; *Distant Runes & Incantations*, 1983I; *Evening Land*, 1995I; *First Morning of the World*
  (band), 1980I; *Freeflight*, 1989I; *In Aeternum*, 1973I; *Magabunda: Four Poems of Agueda Pizarro*, 1982I;
  Music of Amber, 1981I; *Piano Concerto*, 1988I; *A Play of Shadows*, 1990I; *Sparrows*, 1979I; *A Sudden
  Rainbow*, 1984I; *Through Interior Worlds*, 1981I; *Toward Light*, 1987I; *Wind Willow, Whisper*, 1980I
Schwartz, Elliott: *California Games*, 1978I; *Celebrations/Reflections: A Time Warp*, 1985I; *Dream Overture*,
  1972I; *Island*, 1970I; *Music for Orchestra*, 1965I; *Phoenix*, 1995I; *Rows Garden*, 1995I; *Spaces*, 1974I;
  Vienna Dreams, 1998I
Schweinitz, Wolfang von: *Helmholtz-Funk*, 1997I
Schweitzer, Anton: *Rosamunde*, 1780I
Schweizer, Heinrich: *East-West Symphony*, 1997I
Scott, Lady Jane: *Annie Laurie*, 1834I
Scott, Raymond: *The Toy Trumpet*, 1937I
Scott, Steve: *Brass Quartet*, 1995I
Scriabin, Alexander: *Allegro de Concert, Opus 18*, 1896I; *Dances (2), Opus 73*, 1914I; *Etudes (8), Opus 42*,
  1903I; *Etudes (3), Opus 65*, 1912I; *Feuillet d'album, Opus 58*, 1910I; *Mazurkas (10), Opus 3*, 1889I;

❖

  A *Births*   B *Deaths*   C *Debuts*   D *New Positions*
                      E *Prizes/Honors*

Mazurkas (9), Opus 25, 1899I; *Mazurkas (2), Opus 40,* 1903I; *Nocturnes (2),Opus 5,* 1890I; *Piano Concerto in f♯, Opue 20,* 1896I; *Piano Etudes (12), Opus 8; Piano Pieces(3), Opus 45,* 1905I; *Piano Pieces (3), Opus 49,* 1905I; *Piano Pieces (4), Opus 51,* 196I; *Piano Pieces (3), Opus 52,* 1906I; *Piano Pieces (4), Opus 56,* 1907I; *Piano Pieces (2), Opus 57,* 1907I; *Piano Pieces (2), Opus 59,* 1910I; *Piano Preludes, Opus 13,* 1895I; *Piano Preludes (5), Opus 15,* 1896I; *Piano Preludes (7), Opus 16,* 1896I; *Piano Preludes (4), Opus 22,* 1897I; *Piano Preludes (2), Opus 25,* 1900I; *Piano Preludes (2), Opus 27,* 1901I; *Piano Preludes (4), Opus 31,* 1903I; *Piano Preludes(4), Opus 33,* 1903I; *Piano Preludes (3), Opus 35,* 1903I; *Piano Preludes (4), Opus 37,* 1903I; *Piano Preludes (4), Opus 39,* 1903I; *Piano Preludes (4), Opus 48,* 1905I; *Piano Preludes (2), Opus 67,* 1913I; *Piano Preludes (5), Opus 74,* 1914I; *Piano Sonata in e♭,* 1889I; *Piano Sonata No. 1 in f, Opus 6,* 1892I; *Piano Sonata No. 2, Opus 19,* 1892I; *Piano Sonata No. 3 in f♯, Opus 23,* 1897I; *Poem of Ecstasy,* 1908I; *Poème, Opus 41,* 1903I; *Poème satanique, Opus 36,* 1903I; *Poème tragique, Opus 34,* 1903I; *Poems (2), Opus 32,* 1903I; *Poems (2), Opus 44,* 1905I; *Poems (2), Opus 69,* 1913I; *Poems (2), Opus 71,* 1914I; *Prometheus: Poem of Fire, Opus 60,* 1910I; *Reverie for Orchestra, Opus 24,* 1899I; *Romance for Horn & Piano,* 1890I; *Scherzo, Opus 46,* 1905I; *Sonata No. 4 in F♯, Opus 30,* 1903I; *Sonata No. 5, Opus 53,* 1907I; *Sonata No. 6, Opus 62,* 1911I; *Sonata No. 7, "Messe blanche," Opus 64,* 1911I; *Sonata No. 8, Opus 66,* 1913I; *Sonata No. 9, "Messe Noire," Opus 68,* 1913I; *Sonata No. 10, Opus 70,* 1913I; *Sonate-fantaisie in g♯,* 1886I; *Symphony No. 1 in E, Opus 26,* 1900I; *Symphony No. 2 in c, Opus 29,* 1901I; *Symphony No. 3, "The Divine Poem,"* 1904I; *Valse, Opus 38,* 1903I; *Valse in f, Opus 1,* 1885I; *Vers la Flamme, Opus 72,* 1914I
Sculthorpe, Peter: *Little Serenade,* 1977I; *Music for Japan,* 1970I; *Night Song,* 1976I; *Piano Concerto,* 1983I; *String Quartet No. 1,* 1947I; *String Quartet No. 2,* 1948I; *String Quartet No. 3,* 1949I; *String Quartet No. 4,* 1950I; *String Quartet No. 5,* 1959I; *String Quartet No. 6,* 1964I; *String Quartet No. 7, "Red Landscape,"* 1966I; *String Quartet No. 8,* 1968I; *String Quartet No. 9,* 1975I; *String Quartet No. 10,* 1983I; *String Quartet No. 11, "Jabiru Dreaming,"* 1990I; *String Quartet No. 12,* 1994I; *String Quartet No. 13,* 1996I; *String Quartet No. 14,* 1998I; *Sun,* 1960I; *Sun Music I,* 1965I; *Sun Music II,* 1966I; *Sun Music III,* 1967I; *Sun Music IV,* 1967I
Search, Frederick: *String Quartet No. 1,* 1910I; *String Quartet No. 2,* 1915I; *String Quartet No. 3,* 1932I; *String Quartet No. 4,* 1935I; *Symphony No. 1,* 1913I; *Symphony No. 2,* 1938I
Searle, Humphrey: *Hamlet,* 1969I; *Night Music, Opus 2,* 1943I; *Overture to a Drama,* 1949I; *Symphony No. 1,* 1952I; *Symphony No. 2, Opus 33,* 1958I; *Symphony No. 3, Opus 36,* 1959I; *Symphony No. 4,* 1962I; *Symphony No. 5, "to . . . Webern," Opus 43,* 1964I
Sechter, Simon: *Der Offenbarung Johannes,* 1845I; *Sodoms Untergang,* 1840I
Seeger, Charles: *String Quartet,* 1913I; *Violin Sonata,* 1913I
Seeger, Ruth Crawford: *Kaleidoscopic Changes on an Original Theme ending; with a Fugue,* 1924I; *Piano Preludes (5),* 1925I; *Piano Preludes (9),* 1926I; *Suite for Piano & Strings,* 1929I; *Suite for Piano & Winds,* 1927I; *Suite for Wind Quintet,* 1952I; *Violin Sonata,* 1926I
Segerstam, Leif: *Piano Concerto No. 1,* 1977I; *Symphony No. 1,* 1977I; *Symphony No. 2,* 1980I; *Symphony No. 3,* 1981I; *Symphony No. 4,* 1981I; *Symphony No. 5,* 1982I; *Symphony No. 6,* 1982I; *Symphony No. 7,* 1982I; *Symphony No. 8,* 1984I; *Symphony No. 9,* 1985I; *Symphony No. 10,* 1987I; *Symphony No. 11,* 1986I; *Symphony No. 12,* 1987I; *Symphony No. 14,* 1987I; *Symphony No. 15,* 1990I; *Symphony No. 16,* 1990I; *Symphony No. 18,* 1993I
Sellars, James: *The World Is Round,* 1993I
Serebrier, José: *Saxophone Quartet,* 1955I; *Sonata for Solo Violin, Opus 1,* 1948I; *Symphony No. 2, "Partita,"* 1958I
Serly, Tibor: *Concerto for Two Pianos,* 1958I; *The Pagan City,* 1938I; *Piano Sonata in Modus Lascivus,* 1946I; *String Quartet,* 1924I; *Symphony No. 1,* 1931I; *Symphony No. 2,* 1932I; *Viola Concerto,* 1929I
Serov, Alexander: *Judith,* 1863I; *Rogneda,* 1865I; *Taras Bulba,* 1868I
Sessions, Roger: *The Black Maskers,* 1923I; *Chorale Preludes (3),* 1926I; *Concertino,* 1972I; *Concerto for Orchestra,* 1981I; *Concerto for Violin, Cello & Orchestra,* 1971I; *Divertimento for Orchestra,* 1959I; *Idyll of Theocritus,* 1954I; *Montezuma,* 1963I; *Pages from My Diary,* 1939I; *Piano Concerto,* 1956I; *Piano Pieces (5),* 1975I; *Piano Sonata No. 1,* 1930I; *Piano Sonata No. 2,* 1946I; *Piano Sonata No. 3,* 1965I; *Psalm 140,* 1963I; *Rhapsody for Orchestra,* 1970I; *String Quartet No. 1,* 1936I; *String Quartet No. 2,* 1951I; *String Quintet,* 1958I; *Symphony in D,* 1917I; *Symphony No. 1,* 1927I; *Symphony No. 2,* 1946I; *Symphony No. 3,* 1957I; *Symphony No. 4,* 1958I; *Symphony No. 5,* 1964I; *Symphony No. 6,* 1966I; *Symphony No. 7,* 1967I; *Symphony No. 8,* 1968I; *Symphony No. 9,* 1978I; *The Trial of Lucullus,* 1947I; *Turandot,* 1925I; *Violin Concerto,* 1935I; *When Lilacs Last in the Dooryard Bloom'd,* 1970I
Seyfert, Johann: *Der Sterbentag Jesu,* 1757I
Sgambati, Giovanni: *Piano Quintet No. 1,* 1866I; *Symphony No. 1 in d, Opus 16,* 1881I
Shapero, Harold: *American Variations,* 1950I; *Credo,* 1955I; *Hebrew Cantata,* 1954I; *Nine-Minute Overture,* 1940I; *Piano Sonata No. 1,* 1944I; *Piano Sonata No. 2,* 1944I; *Piano Sonata No. 3,* 1944I; *Piano Sonata No. 4*

❀

F   *Biographical*   G   *Cultural Beginnings*   H   *Musical Literature*
I   *Musical Compositions*

Shapero, Harold: (*cont.*)
   in f, 1948I; *Piano Variations in c*, 1947I; *Six for Five*, 1994I; *Sonata for Piano, Four Hands*, 1941I; *String Quartet No. 1*, 1941I; *Symphony for Classical Orchestra*, 1947I; *Trumpet Concerto*, 1995I
Shapey, Ralph: *Cello Sonata*, 1954I; *Centennial Celebration*, 1991I; *Concerto Fantastique* (orchestra), 1991I; *Concerto for Piano, Cello & String Orchestra*, 1986I; *The Covenant*, 1977I; *Dinosaur Annex*, 1993I; *Evocations IV*, 1994I; *The Family of Man*, 1955I; *Fantasy for Orchestra*, 1951I; *Fromm Variations*, 1973I; *Kroslian Sonata*, 1985I; *Mutations*, 1956I; *Mutations II*, 1966I; *Piano Quintet*, 1947I; *Piano Sonata No. 1*, 1946I; *Piano Suite*, 1952I; *Piano Variations (21)*, 1978I; *Rhapsody*, 1993I; *Rituals*, 1959I; *Sonata Appassionata*, 1995I; *Sonata Profonde for Piano*, 1995I; *Sonata Variations*, 1954I; *Songs of Joy*, 1987I; *Songs of Life*, 1988I; *Songs of Love*, 1989I; *String Quartet No. 1*, 1946I; *String Quartet No. 2*, 1949I; *String Quartet No. 3*, 1951I; *String Quartet No. 4*, 1953I; *String Quartet No. 5*, 1958I; *String Quartet No. 6*, 1963I; *String Quartet No. 7*, 1972I; *String Quartet No. 8*, 1992I; *String Quartet No. 9*, 1995I; *Symphony No. 1*, 1952I; *Trio 1992*, 1992I; *Trio Concertante*, 1992I; *Variations for Organ*, 1998I
Shapiro, Gerald: *For Nancy*, 1977I; *Piano Trio*, 1993I; *Serenade No. 3*, 1983I; *String Quartet No. 2*, 1994I
Shapiro, Theodore: *Piano Concerto*, 1999I
Shchedrin, Rodion: *Akho Sonata*, 1984I; *Anna Karenina*, 1971I; *Cello Concerto*, 1994I; *Cello Sonata*, 1996I; *Chimes*, 1968I; *Concerto for Orchestra No. 1, "Naughty Limericks,"* 1963I; *Concerto for Orchestra No. 2, "Chimes,"* 1967I; *Concerto for Orchestra No. 3*, 1989I; *Concerto for Orchestra No. 4*, 1989I; *Concerto for Orchestra No. 5*, 1993I; *Dead Souls*, 1976I; *The Humpback Horse*, 1955I; *The Lady with a Lapdog*, 1985I; *Merry Pieces (3)*, 1997I; *Not for Love Alone*, 1971I; *Piano Concerto*, 1976I; *Piano Concerto No. 1*, 1954I; *Piano Concerto No. 2*, 1966I; *Piano Concerto No. 3*, 1973I; *Piano Concerto No. 4, "Sharp Keys,"* 1991I; *Piano Concerto No. 5*, 1999I; *Piano Notebook for Young People*, 1981I; *Piano Preludes & Fugues (24)*, 1964I; *Piano Quintet*, 1952I; *Piano Sonata No. 1*, 1961I; *Polyphonic Notebook for Piano*, 1971I; *The Seagull*, 1979I; *The Sealed Angel*, 1988I; *Symphony No. 1*, 1958I; *Symphony No. 2, "Twenty-Five Preludes,"* 1965I; *Telegramma for Organ*, 1986I; *Viola Concerto*, 1997I
Shebalin, Vissarion: *Cello Sonata, Opus 54/1*, 1960I; *The Lark, Opus 37*, 1943I; *Moscow*, 1946I; *Overture on March Themes in D, Opus 25*, 1936I; *Russian Overture, Opus 31*, 1941I; *String Quartet No. 1, Opus 2*, 1923I; *String Quartet No. 2, Opus 19*, 1934I; *String Quartet No. 3 in G, Opus 66*, 1938I; *String Quartet No. 4, Opus 29*, 1940I; *String Quartet No. 5 "Slavonica," Opus 33*, 1942I; *String Quartet No. 6, Opus 34*, 1943I; *String Quartet No. 7*, 1948I; *String Quartet No. 8*, 1960I; *String Quartet No. 9*, 1963I; *The Sun over the Steppes, Opus 27*, 1939I; *Symphony No. 1 in f, Opus 6*, 1925I; *Symphony No. 2 in c♯, Opus 11*, 1929I; *Symphony No. 3 in C, Opus 17*, 1934I; *Symphony No. 4 in B♭, "Heroes of Perekop," Opus 24*, 1935I; *Symphony No. 5 in C, Opus 56*, 1962I; *The Taming of the Shrew, Opus 46*, 1946I; *Viola Sonata, Opus 51/2*, 1954I; *Violin Concerto in G, Opus 21*, 1925I; *Violin Sonata, Opus 51/1*, 1958I
Shelley, Harry R.: *Carnival Overture*, 1893I; *Death and Life*, 1898I; *The Inheritance Divine*, 1895I; *Lochinvar's Ride*, 1915I; *The Pilgrims*, 1903I; *Santa Claus Overture*, 1900I; *The Soul Triumphant*, 1905I; *Symphony in E♭*,1897I; *Vexilla regis*, 1893I
Sheng, Bright: *China Dreams*, 1995I; *Flute Moon*, 1999I; *H'UN (Lacerations): In Memoriam 1966-1976*, 1987I; *Red Silk Dance* (piano concerto), 1991I; *The Silver River*, 1997I; *The Song of Majnun*, 1992I; *Spring Dreams*, 1998I; *String Quartet No. 1*, 1984I; *String Quartet No. 2*, 1985I
Shepherd, Arthur: *The Ballad of Trees & the Master*, 1934I; *Capriccio No. 1*, 1938I; *Capriccio No. 2*, 1941I; *The City in the Sea*, 1913I; *Divertissement for Wind Quintet*, 1943I; *Eclogue*, 1931I; *Fantasie Humoreske*, 1916I; *Fantasy Concertante on "The Garden Hymn,"* 1943I; *Fantasy Overture on Down East Spirituals*, 1946I; *Fugue in C♯*, 1920I; *Hilaritas*, 1942I; *Invitation to the Dance*, 1936I; *Movements (2) for String Quartet*, 1951I; *Nocturne in b*, 1908I; *Nocturne in f*, 1940I; *Organ Prelude in b*, 1904I; *Organ Prelude in e*, 1923I; *Ouverture Joyeuse, Opus 3*, 1901I; *Overture, The Festival of Youth*, 1915I; *Overture to a Drama*, 1919I; *Piano Quintet*, 1940I; *Piano Sonata No. 1 in f, Opus 4*, 1907I; *Piano Sonata No. 2*, 1930I; *Psalm 42*, 1944I; *A Psalm of the Mountains*, 1956I; *The Song of the Pilgrims*, 1932I; *Song of the Sea Wind*, 1915I; *Songs on James Russell Lowell (5), Opus 7*, 1909I; *String Quartet No. 1 in g*, 1926I; *String Quartet No. 2 in e*, 1933I; *String Quartet No. 3 in d*, 1936I; *String Quartet No. 4 in d*, 1944I; *String Quartet No. 5 in C*, 1955I; *Symphony No. 1, "Horizons,"* 1927I; *Symphony No. 2*, 1938I; *Triptych for High Voice & String Quartet*, 1925I; *Variations on an Original Theme*, 1952I; *Violin Concerto*, 1946I
Sherwin, William F.: *Sound the Battle Cry*, 1869I
Shield, William: *Alladin*, 1788I; *The Choleric Fathers*, 1785I; *The Cobbler of Casterbury*, 1779I; *The Czar Peter*, 1790I; *The Deaf Lover*, 1780I; *The Enchanted Castle*, 1786I; *The Flitch of Bacon*, 1778I; *Frederick in Prussia*, 1785I; *Friar Bacon*, 1782I; *Hartford Bridge*, 1792I; *The Irish Mimic*, 1795I; *The Italian Villagers*, 1797I; *Lock and Key*, 1796I; *Lord Mayor's Day*, 1782I; *Love and Nature*, 1797I; *The Midnight Wanderers*, 1793I; *The Mysteries of the Castle*, 1795I; *Netley Abbey*, 1794I; *The Noble Peasant*, 1784I; *The Relief of Williamsburg*, 1793I; *Richard Coeur de Lion*, 1786I; *Robin Hood*, 1784I; *Robinson Crusoe*, 1781I; *Rosina*, 1783I; *The Siege of Gibraltar*, 1780I; *The Travellers in Switzerland*, 1794I; *The Woodman*, 1791I

———————————————— ❈ ————————————————

A *Births*   B *Deaths*   C *Debuts*   D *New Positions*
E *Prizes/Honors*

Shifrin, Lalo: *Songs of the Aztecs*, 1988I
Shifrin, Seymour: *Cello Sonata*, 1948I; *Chronicles*, 1970I; *Five Last Songs*, 1979I; *Music for Orchestra*, 1948I; *Piano Trio*, 1974I; *Satires of Circumstance*, 1964I; *Serenade for Five Instruments*, 1956I; *String Quartet No. 1*, 1949I; *String Quartet No. 2*, 1962I; *String Quartet No. 3*, 1966I; *String Quartet No. 4*, 1967I; *String Quartet no. 5*, 1972I
Shostakovich, Dmitri: *Aphorisms*, Opus 13, 1927I; *The Bolt*, Opus 27, 1931I; *Cello Concerto No. 1 in E♭*, Opus 107, 1959I; *Cello Concerto No. 2*, Opus 126, 1966I; *Cello Sonata in d*, Opus 40, 1934I; *Children's Pieces (6)*, Opus 69, 1955I; *The Dreamers*, 1975I; *The Execution of Stepan Razin*, Opus 119, 1964I; *Faithfulness, Ballads for Male Voices*, Opus 136, 1970I; *Fantastic Dances*, Opus 5, 1922I; *Festive Overture*, Opus 96, 1954I; *Five Days–Five Nights*, Opus 111, 1960I; *From Jewish Folk Poetry*, Opus 79, 1948I; *The Gadfly*, Opus 97, 1955I; *The Golden Age*, Opus 22, 1930I; *The Golden Hills*, Opus 30, 1931I; *Hamlet*, 1932I; *The Human Comedy*, 1934I; *King Lear*, 1940I; *Lady MacBeth of Minsk*, Opus 29, 1932I; *Lermontov Songs (2)*, Opus 84, 1950I; *Michurin*, Opus 78, 1948I; *Monologues from Pushkin (4)*, Opus 91, 1952I; *The Nose*, Opus 15, 1928I; *October*, 1967I; *Overture on Russian & Kirghiz Folk Songs*, Opus 115, 1963I; *Piano Concerto No. 1 in c*, Opus 35, 1933I; *Piano Concerto No. 2 in F*, Opus 102, 1957I; *Piano Preludes (8)*, Opus 2, 1920I; *Piano Preludes (24)*, Opus 34, 1933I; *Piano Quintet in g*, Opus 57, 1940I; *Piano Sonata No. 1*, Opus 12, 1926I; *Piano Sonata No. 2*, Opus 61, 1942I; *Piano Trio No. 1*, Opus 8, 1923I; *Piano Trio No. 2 in e*, Opus 67, 1944I; *Pieces (2) for String Octet*, Opus 11, 1925I; *Pieces (3), Cello & Piano*, Opus 9, 1924I; *Pirogov*, 1947I; *Poem on the Homeland*, Opus 74, 1947I; *Poems by M. Tsvetsyeva*, Opus 143, 1973I; *Preludes & Fugues*, Opus 87 (24), 1951I; *Pushkin Songs (4)*, Opus 46, 1936I; *Revolutionary Choruses (10)*, Opus 88, 1951I; *Romances (6)*, Opus 62, 1942I; *Romances on Verses by Alexander Blok (7)*, Opus 127, 1967I; *Satires: Pictures of the Past*, Opus 109, 1960I; *Scherzo in B♭*, Opus 7, 1924I; *Scherzo in f♯, "Ironic,"* 1919I; *Song of the Forests*, Opus 81, 1949I; *Songs (2)*, Opus 72, 1945I; *Songs (4)*, Opus 86, 1951I; *Songs (5)*, Opus 98, 1954I; *Songs (5)*, Opus 121, 1965I; *Spanish Songs*, Opus 100, 1956I; *String Quartet No. 1 in c*, Opus 49, 1935I; *String Quartet No. 2 in A*, Opus 68, 1944I; *String Quartet No. 3 in F*, Opus 73, 1946I; *String Quartet No. 4 in D*, Opus 83, 1949I; *String Quartet No. 5 in B♭*, Opus 92, 1952I; *String Quartet No. 6 in G*, Opus 101, 1956I; *String Quartet No. 7 in f♯*, Opus 108, 1960I; *String Quartet No. 8 in c*, Opus 110, 1960I; *String Quartet No. 9 in E♭*, Opus 117, 1964I; *String Quartet No. 10 in A♭*, Opus 118, 1964I; *String Quartet No. 11 in f*, Opus 122, 1966I; *String Quartet No. 12 in D♭*, Opus 133, 1968I; *String Quartet No. 13 in b♭*, Opus 138, 1970I; *String Quartet No. 14 in F♯*, Opus 142, 1973I; *String Quartet No. 15 in e♭*, Opus 144, 1974I; *Suite for Two Pianos*, Opus 6, 1922I; *The Sun Shines on Our Motherland*, Opus 90, 1952I; *Symphony No. 1 in f*, Opus 10, 1925I; *Symphony No. 2, "To October,"* Opus 14, 1927I; *Symphony No. 3, "May Day,"* Opus 20, 1929I; *Symphony No. 4 in c*, Opus 43, 1936I; *Symphony No. 5 in d*, Opus 47, 1937I; *Symphony No. 6 in b*, Opus 54, 1939I; *Symphony No. 7 in C, "Leningrad,"* Opus 60, 1942I; *Symphony No. 8 in c*, Opus 65, 1943I; *Symphony No. 9 in E♭*, Opus 70, 1945I; *Symphony No. 10 in e*, Opus 93, 1953I; *Symphony No. 11 in g, "1905,"* 1957I; *Symphony No. 12 in d*, Opus 112, 1961I; *Symphony No. 13 in b♭*, Opus 113, "Babi Yar," 1962I; *Symphony No. 14*, Opus 135, 1969I; *Symphony No. 15 in A*, Opus 141, 1971I; *Theme & Variations in B♭*, Opus 3, 1922I; *Verses (4) of Captain Lebyadkin*, 1975I; *Viola Sonata*, Opus 147, 1975I; *Violin Concerto No. 1 in a*, Opus 77, 1948I; *Violin Concerto No. 2*, Opus 129, 1955I; *Violin sonata*, Opus 134, 1968I; *The Young Guard*, Opus 75, 1948I
Sibelius, Jan: *Bagatelles (6)*, Opus 97, 1920I; *The Bard*, Opus 64, 1913I; *Belshazzar's Feast*, 1906I; *Coronation Cantata*, 1896I; *The Dryad*, Opus 45, 1910I; *En Saga*, Opus 9, 1892I; *Finlandia*, Opus 26, 1899I; *Humoresques (2)*, Opus 87 (violin), 1917I; *Humoresques (4)*, Opus 89 (violin), 1917I; *Hymn of the Earth*, Opus 95, 1920I; *Impromtus (6)*, Opus 5, 1893I; *In Memoriam*, Opus 59, 1909I; *Jedermann*, Opus 83, 1916I; *Karelia*, Opus 11, 1893I; *King Christian II*, Opus 27, 1998I; *Kullervo*, Opus 7, 1892I; *Kuolema*, Opus 44, 1903I; *Legends (3) for Orchestra*, Ous 22, 1895I; *The Lizard*, 1909I; *Luonnotar*, Opus 70, 1913I; *Lyric Pieces (4)*, Opus 74, 1914I; *Night Ride & Sunrise*, Opus 55, 1907I; *The Oceanides*, Opus 73, 1914I; *Organ Pieces (2)*, Opus 111, 1925I; *The Origin of Fire*, Opus 72, 1902I; *Our Native Land*, Opus 92, 1918I; *Overture in a*, 1902I; *Overture in E*, 1891I; *Part Songs (2)*, Opus 65, 1912I; *Partsongs for Male Voices (9)*, Opus 18, 1904I; *Partsongs for Male Voices (5)*, Opus 84, 1915I; *Partsongs for Male Voices (2)*, Opus 108, 1925I; *Pelléas und Mélisande*, Opus 46, 1905I; *Piano Pieces (10)*, Opus 58, 1909I; *Piano Pieces (10)*, Opus 34, 1916I; *Piano Pieces (5)*, Opus 75, 1914I; *Piano Pieces (13)*, Opus 85, 1914I; *Piano Pieces (5)*, Opus 103, 1924I; *Piano Pieces (8)*, Opus 99, 1922I; *Piano Sonata in F*, Opus 12, 1893I; *Piano Quartet in e*, 1882I; *Piano Trio in a*, 1882I; *Piano Trio in C, "Loviisa,"* 1888I; *Pieces (4)*, Opus 115, 1929I; *Pieces (3)*, Opus 116, 1929I; *Pieces (6), Violin & Piano*, Opus 79, 1915I; *Pieces (2) for Violin & Piano*, 1889I; *Pieces for Orchestra (3)*, Opus 96, 1920I; *Pohjola's Daughter*, Opus 49, 1906I; *Romance in C*, Opus 42, for Strings, 1903I; *Romantic Pieces (5)*, Opus 101, 1923I; *Runeberg Songs (7)*, Opus 13, 1892I; *Scènes Historiques I*, Opus 25, 1899I; *Scènes Historiques, Suite II*, Opus 66, 1912I; *Serenades (D,g)*, Opus 69 (violin), 1913I; *Sonatinas (3)*, Opus 67, 1912I; *Song of the Earth*, Opus 93, 1919I; *Songs (13)*, Opus 17, 36, 1899I; *Songs (2)*, Opus 53, 1907I; *Songs (2)from "Twelfth Night,"* Opus 60, 1909I; *Songs (5)*, Opus 37, 1902I; *Songs (5)*, Opus 38, 1904I; *Songs (6)*,

---

❄

Sibelius, Jan: (cont.)
Opus 50, 1906I; Songs (8), Opus 57, 1909I; Songs (8), Opus 61, 1910I; Songs (6), Opus 72, 1915I; Songs (6), Opus 86, 1916I; Songs (6), Opus 88, 1917I; Songs (6), Opus 90, 1917I; Songs for American Schools, 1913I; Spring Song, Opus 16, 1894I; String Quartet in B♭, Opus 4, 1890I; String Quartet No. 2 in d, "Voces intimae," Opus 56, 1909I; Suite caractéristique, Opus 100 (harp, strings), 1922I; Surusiotto, 1931I; The Swan of Tuonela, Opus 22, 1893I; Swanwhite, Opus 52, 1908I; Symphony No. 1 in e, Opus 39, 1899I; Symphony No. 2 in D, Opus 43, 1901I; Symphony No. 3 in C, Opus 52, 1907I; Symphony No. 4 in a, Opus 63, 1911I; Symphony No. 5 in E♭, Opus 82, 1915I; Symphony No. 6 in d, Opus 104, 1923I; Symphony No. 7 in C, Opus 105, 1924I; Tapiola, Opus 112, 1925I; The Tempest, Opus 109, 1925I; Violin Concerto in d, Opus 47, 1903I; Violin Sonata in d, 1882I; Violin Sonata in F, 1889II; Violin Sonatina in E, Opus 80, 1915I; The Wood Nymph, 1895I
Sicilianos, Yorgos: Ballade for Large Orchestra, 1994I; Concerto for Orchestra, 1961I; Mellichomeide, 1980I
Sicong, Ma: Song of the Mountain Forest, 1953I; Symphony No. 2, 1959I
Sieber, Mátyás: Ulysses, 1949I
Siegmeister, Elie: Abraham Lincoln Walks at Midnight, 1937I; American Holiday, 1933I; Clarinet Concerto, 1955I; A Cycle of Cities, 1974I; Double Concerto for Violin & Piano, 1976I; The Face of War, 1966I; Fantasies in Line & Color: Five American Paintings, 1981I; Figures in the Wind, 1990I; Flute Concerto, 1960I; Lady of the Lake, 1985I; Moods (3), 1959I; Night of the Moonspell, 1976I; Ozark Set, 1943I; Piano Concerto, 1974I; Piano Sonata No. 1, "American," 1944I; Piano Sonata No. 2, 1964I; Piano Sonata No. 3, 1979I; Piano Sonata No. 4, "Prelude, Blues & Toccata," 1980I; Piano Studies (3), 1982I; The Plough & the Stars, 1963I; Robert Frost Songs (4), 1930I; Shadows & Light: Homage to 5 Paintings, 1975I; Songs of Innocence (6), 1972I; String Quartet No. 1, 1935I; String Quartet No. 2, 1960I; String Quartet No. 3, 1973I; Symphony No. 1, 1947I; Symphony No. 2, 1950I; Symphony No. 3, 1957I; Symphony No. 4, 1970I; Symphony No. 5, "Visions of Time," 1975I; Symphony No. 6, 1983I; Symphony No. 7, 1986I; Symphony No. 8, 1989I; Theme & Variations 1, 1932I; Theme & Variations II, 1967I; Ways of Love, 1983I; Western Suite, 1945I
Sierra, Roberto: Of Discoveries (guitar concerto), 1992I; Silver Messenger, 1986I; Tropicalia, 1991I
Sigurbjörnsson, Thorkell: Copenhagen Quartet, 1978I; Hässelby Quartet, 1968I
Silver, Sheila: Piano Concerto, 1996I; Piano Preludes (6), 1991I; String Quartet No. 1, 1977I; String Quartet No. 2, 1996I; The Thief of Love, 2000I
Silvestrov, Valentin: Cantata No. 1, 1973I; Cantata No. 2, 1977I; Dedication Symphony, 1991I; Diptych, 1995I; Ode to a Nightingale, 1983I
Simonsen, Rudolf: Symphony No. 2, "Hellas," 1921I
Simpson, Robert: Clarinet Quintet, 1968I; Eppur si muove: Ricercar e Passacaglia, 1985I; Media morte in vita jumus, 1975I; Piano Sonata, 1946I; String Quartet No. 1, 1952I; String Quartet No. 2, 1953I; String Quartet No. 3, 1954I; String Quartet No. 4, 1973I; String Quartet No. 5, 1974I; String Quartet No. 6, 1975I; String Quartet No. 7, 1977I; String Quartet No. 8, 1979I; String Quartet No. 9 -1982I; String Quartet No. 10, 1983I; String Quartet No. 11, 1984I; String Quartet No. 12, 1987I; String Quartet No. 13, 1989I; String Quartet No. 14, 1990I; String Quartet No. 15, 1991I; String Quintet No. 1, 1987I; String Quintet No. 2, 1994I; Symphony No. 1, 1951I; Symphony No. 2, 1955I; Symphony No. 3, 1962I; Symphony No. 4, 1972I; Symphony No. 5, 1972I; Symphony No. 6, 1976I; Symphony No. 7, 1977I; Symphony No. 8, 1981I; Symphony No. 9, 1985I; Symphony No. 10, 1988I; Symphony No. 11, 1990I; Tempi, 1988I; Variations & Finale on a Theme of Haydn, 1948I; Variations & Finale on a Theme of Beethoven, 1990I
Sims, Ezra: Clarinet Quintet, 1987I; Flight, 1989I; Four Dented Interludes & Coda, 1969I; String Quartet No. 1, 1959I; String Quartet No. 2, 1961I; String Quartet No. 3, 1962I; String Quartet No. 4, 1984I; Thirty Years Later, 1972I; Wall to Wall, 1972I
Sinding, Christian: Madmen's Songs, 1983I; Songs for the Tale of Antar & Alba, 1882I; Symphony No. 2, 1904I; Symphony No. 3, Opus 121, 1920I; Violin Concerto No. 2, 1901I; Violin Concerto No. 3, Opus 119, 1917I
Sitsky, Larry: Concerto for Violin, Orchestra & Female Voices, 1972I
Sjögren, Emil: Cello Sonata, 1912I
Skalkottas, Nikos: Greek Dances (9), 1947I; Greek Dances for Orchestra (36), 1936I; Kleine Tanz Suite, 1949I; Largo Sinfonico, 1944I; The Maiden & Death, 1938I; Orchestral Suite No. 1, 1939I; Orchestral Suite No. 2, 1943I; Ouvertüre Concertante, 1945I; Piano Concerto No. 1, 1931I; Piano Concerto No. 2, 1938I; Sonata for Solo Violin, 1925I; String Quartet No. 1, Opus 32, 1928I; String Quartet No. 2, Opus 33, 1929I; String Quartet No. 3, Opus 34, 1935I; String Quartet No. 4, Opus 35, 1940I; Violin Concerto, 1938I; Violin Sonata No. 1, 1928I; Violin Sonata No. 2, 1940I
Skilton, Charles S.: American Indian Fantasy, 1926I; Communion Service in C, 1937I; From Forest & Stream, 1930I; The Guardian Angel, 1925I; Indian Sketches (3), 1919I; Kalopin, 1927I; Lenore, 1895I; Mass in D,

1930I; *Miniatures (5)*, 1940I; *Mount Oread Overture*, 1928I; *Overture in E*, 1931I; *Perviglium Veneris*, 1916I; *String Quartet No. 1 in b*, 1938I; *The Sun Bride*, 1930I; *Ticonderoga*, 1932I; *Violin Sonata No. 1 in g*, 1897I; *Violin Sonata No. 2 in g*, 1922I; *The Witch's Daughter*, 1918I

Skrowaczewski, Stanislav: *Clarinet Concerto*, 1981I; *Concerto for Orchestra*, 1986I; *English Horn Concerto*, 1969I; *String Trio*, 1991I

Skrzyrczak, Bettina: *Piano Concerto*, 1998I

Slavenski, Josip: *Balkanophonia*, 1927I

Slavik, Josef: *Violin Concerto*, 1823I

Sleeper, Thomas: *Piano Concerto No. 1*, 1986I

Slonimsky, Sergei: *Chromatic Poem for Organ*, 1969I; *Pastorale & Toccata*, 1961I; *Piano Preludes & Fugues (24), Book I*, 1993I; *Piano Sonata*, 1962I; *Rondo-Humoresque*, 1979I; *Round Dance & Fugue*, 1976I

Small, Haskell: *Symphony for Solo Piano*, 1999I

Smetana, Bedřich: *The Bartered Bride*, 1870I; *Blanik* (No. 6 of *Ma Vlast*), 1879I; *The Brandenburgers in Bohemia*, 1864I; *Characteristic Pieces (6)*, Opus 1, 1848I; *Czech Dances (14)*, 1878I; *Dalibor*, 1867I; *The Devil's Wall*, 1882I; *Evening Songs*, 1879I; *Festive Overture in C*, 1868I; *From Bohemia's Wood & Meadows* (*Ma Vlast*), 1875I; *Hakon Jarl*, 1862I; *The Kiss*, 1876I; *Libue*, 1872I; *Organ Preludes (6)*, 1846I; *Overture in D*, 1849I; *Piano Polkas (3)*, Opus 7, 1855I; *Prague Carnival*, 1883I; *Richard II*, Opus 11, 1857I; *Sarka* (Nos. 1, 2, 3 of *Ma Vlast*), 1874I; *The Secret*, 1878I; *Shakespearean Festival March*, 1864I; *Song of the Czechs*, 1860I; *Song of the Czechs II*, 1868I; *String Quartet No. 1,"From My Life,"* 1876I; *Tabor* (No. 5 of *Ma Vlast*), 1878I; *Triumphal Symphony in E*, 1854I; *Vysehrad*, 1874I; *Wallingstein's Camp*, Opus 14, 1860I; *The Moldau*, 1874I

Smit, Leo: *The Alchemy of Love*, 1969I; *Characteristic Pieces (7)*, 1949I; *Concerto for Piano & Wind Orchestra*, 1937I; *Martha Through the Looking Glass for Piano*, 1974I; *Piano Concerto*, 1968I; *Quintet for Flute, Harp & Strings*, 1928I; *Rural Elegy*, 1948I; *Sextet for Clarinet, Bassoon & Strings*, 1940I; *Sonata in One Movement*, 1955I; *Symphony in C*, 1936I; *Symphony No. 1 in E♭*, 1955I; *Symphony No. 2*, 1965I; *Symphony No. 3*, 1981I; *Trio for Clarinet, Viola & Piano*, 1928I

Smith, David Stanley: *Cello Sonata*, 1928I; *Oboe Sonata*, Opus 43, 1918I; *Piano Sonata in A♭*, Opus 61, 1929I; *Piano Sonata No. 2*, 1940I; *Songs of Three Ages*, 1936I; *String Quartet No. 3 in C, "Gregorian,"* 1920I; *String Quartet No. 6 in C*, 1934I; *String Quartet No. 8 in A*, 1936I; *String Quartet No. 10*, 1944I; *String Sextet*, 1931I; *Symphony No. 2 in D*, 1917I; *Symphony No. 3 in c*, 1928I; *Symphony No. 4*, Opus 78, 1937I; *Symphony No. 5*, 1949I; *Triumph & Peace*, 1943I; *Violin Concerto No. 2*, 1942I; *Violin Sonata*, Opus 51, 1921I; *The Vision of Isaiah*, 1926I

Smith, Hale: *Toussaint L'Ouverture 1803*, 1977I

Smith, John Christopher: *The Fairies*, 1755I; *Judith*, 1758I; *Paradise Lost*, 1758I; *The Tempest*, 1756I

Smith, John Stafford: *To Anacreon in Heaven*, 1778I

Smith-Brindle, Reginald: *Symphony No. 1*, 1954I; *Symphony No. 2*, 1990I

Smyth, Ethel: *Concerto for Violin & Horn*, 1927I; *Serenade*, 1890I; *Variations on an Original Theme*, 1878I

Sobolewski, Friedrich von: *Imogen*, 1833I; *Salvator Rosa*, 1848I; *Velleda*, 1836I

Sokolov, Ivan: *Volokas for Piano*, 1988I

Soldier, David: *Ultraviolet Railroad*, 1992I; *War Prayer*, 1993I

Soler, Josep: *String Quartet No. 1*, 1966I; *String Quartet No. 2*, 1971I; *String Quartet No. 3*, 1975I; *String Quartet No. 5*, 1995I

Sollberger, Harvey: *Chamber Variations*, 1964I; *Divertimento*, 1970I; *Flute & Drums*, 1977I; *The Humble Heart*, 1983I

Somers, Harry: *Kyrie*, 1970I; *Piano Concerto No. 1*, 1949I; *Piano Concerto No. 2*, 1956I; *Piano Concerto No. 3*, 1995I; *Picasso Suite*, 1964I; *Songs for Dark Voices (5)*, 1956I; *String Quartet No. 1*, 1943I; *String Quartet No. 2*, 1950I; *String Quartet No. 3*, 1959I

Sommer, Vladimir: *String Quartet No. 1*, 1950I; *String Quartet No. 2*, 1987I

Sor, Fernando: *Cendrillon*, 1823I; *Guitar Divertissements*, Op. 1, 2, 8, 13, 23, 1829I; *Guitar Etudes*, Op. 35, 44, 60, 1829I; *Guitar Pieces (6)*, Opus 48, 1829I; *Le sicilien*, 1827I; *Telemaco nell'isola de Calipso*, 1797I

Sorabji, Kaikhosru: *Gullistān*, 1940I; *Opus clavicembalisticum*, 1930I; *Piano Quintet No. 1*, 1920I; *Prelude, Interlude & Fugue*, 1922I; *Symphonic Variations*, 1937I

Sørensen, Bent: *The Echoing Garden*, 1993I

Sousa, John Philip: *The American Maid*, 1909I; *Black Horse Troop March*, 1924I; *Blending of the Blue & Gray*, 1877I; *The Bride Elect*, 1898I; *El Capitán*, 1896I; *The Charlatan*, 1898I; *Chris and the Wonderful Lamp*, 1899I; *Désirée*, 1883I; *The Freelance*, 1905I; *The Gladiator March*, 1886I; *Globe and Eagle March*, 1879I; *High School Cadets March*, 1890I; *Invincible Eagle March*, 1901I; *The Irish Dragoon*, 1915I; *King Cotton March*, 1895I; *Liberty Bell March*, 1893I; *Manhattan Beach March*, 193I; *March, Esprit de Corps*, 1878I; *March, Fairest of the Fair*, 1908I; *March, Hands Across the Sea*, 1899I; *March, Nobles of the Mystic

Sousa, John Philip: (*cont.*)
   Shrine, 1923I; *National Fencibles Marach*, 1888I; *On Parade March*, 1892I; *The Queen of Hearts*, 1885I;
   The Rivals Overture, 1877I; *Salutation March*, 1873I; *Sardanapolis Waltzes*, 1877I; *Semper Fidelis March*,
   1888I; *The Smugglers*, 1882I; *Sound Off March*, 1885I; *Stars and Stripes Forever*, 1896I; *Thunderer*
   March, 1889I; *United States Field Artillery March*, 1917I; *Washington Post March*, 1889I; *The Wolf*,
   1888I
Sousa Carvalho, João de: *Alcione*, 1787I
Southard, Lucien: *Omano*, 1857I; *The Scarlet Letter*, 1855I
Sowerby, Leo: *All on a Summer's Day*, 1954I; *Autumn Time*, 1916I; *Ballad of King Estmere*, 1922I; *Bright*,
   Blithe & Brisk, 1962I; *Canticle of the Sun*, 1944I; *Cello Concerto No. 1*, 1917I; *Cello Concerto No. 2*, 1934I;
   Cello Sonata, 1921I; *Clarinet Sonata*, 1938I; *Classic Concerto*, 1944I; *Comes Autumn Time*, 1916I; *The Edge*
   of Darkness, 1920I; *Florida Suite*, 1929I; *From the Northland*, 1922I; *Harp Concerto*, 1916I; *A Liturgy of*
   Hope, 1917I; *Medieval Poem (organ)*, 1926I; *Organ Concerto in C*, 1936I; *Organ Suite*, 1937I; *Organ*
   Symphony in G, 1930I; *Pageant*, 1931I; *Passacaglia for Organ*, 1967I; *Passacaglia, Interlude & Fugue*,
   1932I; *Piano Concerto No. 1*, 1916I; *Piano Concerto No. 2*, 1932I; *Piano Sonata in D*, 1948I; *Prairie*, 1929I;
   Requiescat in Pace, 1920I; *Serenade for String Quartet*, 1917I; *Sinfonia Brevis for Organ*, 1965I; *Solomon's*
   Garden, 1965I; *Song of America*, 1942I; *String Quartet No. 1*, 1923I; *String Quartet No. 2*, 1935I;
   Symphony No. 1, 1921I; *Symphony No. 2*, 1928I; *Symphony No. 3*, 1940I; *Symphony No. 4*, 1947I;
   Symphony No. 5, 1964I; *Theme in Yellow*, 1937I; *The Throne of God*, 1956I; *Trio for Flute, Viola & Piano*,
   1919I; *Violin Concerto in G*, 1913I; *Violin Sonata No. 1*, 1922I; *The Vision of Sir Launfal*, 1925I; *Whimsical*
   Variations, 1950I; *Woodwind Quintet*, 1916I
Speaks, Oley: *Morning*, 1910I; *On the Road to Mandalay*, 1907I; *The Perfect Prayer*, 1930I
Speight, John: *Symphony No. 1*, 1984I; *Symphony No. 2*, 1991I
Spelman, Timothy: *Courtship of Miles Standish*, 1943I
Spilman, James E.: *Flow Gentley, Sweet Afton*, 1838I
Spohr, Louis: *Der Alchymist*, 1830I; *Alruna, die Eulenkönigin*, 1808I; *Der Berggeist*, 1825I; *Clarinet*
   Concerto No. 1 in c, Opus 26, 1808I; *Clarinet Concerto No. 2 in E♭, Opus 57*, 1810I; *Clarinet Concerto No. 3*
   in f, 1821I; *Concert Overture in F*, 1819I; *Concert Overture in D, Opus 126*, 1842I; *Concertante No. 2 in b*,
   Opus 88, 1833I; *Concerto for String Quartet, Opus 13*, 1845I; *Concerto No. 1 in A, Opus 48 for Two*
   Violins, 1808I; *Double Quartet in d, Opus 65*, 1823I; *Double Quartet in E♭, Opus 77*, 1829I; *Double Quartet*
   in e, Opus 87, 1833I; *Double Quartet in g, Opus 136*, 1847I; *The Fall of Babylon*, 1840I; *Faust*, 1813I;
   German Songs (6), Opus 2, 1809I; *German Songs, (6), Opus 103*, 1837I; *Des Heilands Letzte Stunden*,
   1835I; *Jessonda*, 1823I; *Der jüngste Gericht*, 1812I; *Die Kreutzfahrer*, 1845I; *The Last Judgment*, 1826I; *The*
   Last Hours of the Saviour, 1842I; *Macbeth*, 1825I; *Mass in C, Opus 54*, 1820I; *Mass in e*, 1821I; *Der*
   Matrose, 1840I; *Octet in E, Opus 32*, 1814I; *Overture in c, Opus 12*, 1807I; *Piano Quintet in D, Opus 130*,
   1845I; *Piano Sonata in A♭, Opus 125*, 1843I; *Piano Trio No. 4 in B, Opus 133*, 1846I; *Pietro von Abano*,
   Opus 76, 1827I; *Die Prüfung*, 1806I; *Psalms (3), Opus 85*, 1832I; *Requiem*, 1857I; *Septet in a, Opus 147*,
   1853I; *Sonata for Harp & Violin in C*, 1805I; *Sonata for Harp & Violin, Opus 16*, 1806I; *Sonata for Harp &*
   Violin, Opus 114, 1811I; *Sonata for Harp & Violin, Opus 115*, 1809I; *Sonata for Harp & Violin in A♭*, 1819I;
   Songs (6), Opus 105, 1838I; *Songs (6), Male Voices, Opus 44*, 1817I; *String Quartets (2), Opus 4*, 1805I;
   String Quartet in d, Opus 11, 1807I; *String Quartets (2), Opus 15*, 1808I; *String Quartet in g, Opus 27*,
   1812I; *String Quartets (3), Opus 29*, 1815I; *String Quartet in A, Opus 30*, 1814I; *String Quartet in F, Opus*
   43, 1817I; *String Quartets (3), Opus 45*, 1818I; *String Quartets (3), Opus 58*, 1822I; *String Quartet in b*,
   Opus 61, 1819I; *String Quartet in A, Opus 68*, 1823I; *String Quartets (3), Opus 74*, 1826I; *String Quartets*
   (3), Opus 82, 1829I; *String Quartets (3), Opus 84*, 1832I; *String Quartet in A, Opus 93*, 1835I; *String*
   Quartet in A, Opus 132, 1846I; *String Quartet in C, Opus 141*, 1849I; *String Quartet in g, Opus 157*,
   1857I; *String Quartet in E♭*, 1856I; *String Quintets (2), Opus 33*, 1814I; *String Quintet No. 3 in b, Opus 69*,
   1826I; *String Quintet No. 4 in a, Opus 91*, 1834I; *String Quintet No. 5 in g, Opus 106*, 1838I; *String*
   Quintet No. 6 in e, Opus 129, 1845I; *String Quintet No. 7 in g, Opus 144*, 1850I; *String Sextet in C, Opus*
   140, 1848I; *Symphony No. 1 in E♭, Opus 20*, 1811I; *Symphony No. 2 in d, Opus 49*, 1820I; *Symphony No. 3*
   in c, Opus 78, 1828I; *Symphony No. 4 in F, Opus 86*, 1832I; *Symphony No. 5 in c, Opus 102*, 1837I;
   Symphony No. 6 in G, Opus 116, "Historische," 1839I; *Symphony No. 7 in C, Opus 121*, 1841I; *Symphony*
   No. 8 in G, Opus 137, 1847I; *Symphony No. 9 in b, Opus 143, "Die Jahrzeiten,"* 1850I; *Symphony No. 10*
   in F♭, 1857I; *Violin Concertante in C*, 1803I; *Violin Concerto No. 1 in A, Opus 1*, 1803I; *Violin Concerto No.*
   2 in d, Opus 2, 1804I; *Violin Concerto No. 3 in C, Opus 7*, 1806I; *Violin Concerto No. 4 in b, Opus 10*,
   1805I; *Violin Concerto No. 5 in E♭, Opus 17*, 1807I; *Violin Concerto No. 6 in g, Opus 28*, 1809I; *Violin*
   Concerto No. 7 in e, Opus 38, 1814I; *Violin Concerto No. 8, Opus 47*, 1816I; *Violin Concerto No. 9 in d*,
   Opus 55, 1820I; *Violin Concerto No. 10 in A, Opus 62*, 1810I; *Violin Concerto No. 11 in G, Opus 70*, 1825I;
   Violin Concerto No. 12 in A, Opus 79, 1828I; *Violin Concerto No. 13 in E, Opus 92*, 1835I; *Violin Concerto*

❊

    A   *Births*   B   *Deaths*   C   *Debuts*   D   *New Positions*
               E   *Prizes/Honors*

No. 14 in a, Opus 110, 1839I; *Violin Concerto No. 15 in c, Opus 128,* 1844I; *Woodwind Quintet in C, Opus 52,* 1820I; *Zemire und Azor,* 1819I; *Der Zweikampf mit der Geliebten,* 1810I

Spontini, Gaspare: *Adelina Senese,* 1797I; *Agnes von Hohenstaufen,* 1829I; *Alcidor,* 1825I; *L'eroismo ridiculo,* 1798I; *Fernand Cortez,* 1809I; *La finta filosofa,* 1799I; *La fuga in maschere,* 1800I; *Gli amanti in cimento,* 1801I; *Gli elisi delusi,* 1800I; *Julie,* 1805I; *Lalla Rookh,* 1821I; *le metamorfosi di Pasquale,* 1802I; *Mignon's Lied,* 1830I; *Milton,* 1804I; *Nurmahal,* 1822I; *Olimpie,* 1819I; *La petite maison,* 1804I; *Li puntigli delle donne,* 1796I; *I quadri parlanti,* 1800I; *Le roi et la paix,* 1815I; *Tout le monde a tort,* 1806I; *La vestale,* 1807I

Spratlan Lewis: *Life is a Dream,* 1978I

Stainer, John: *Gideon,* 1875I

Stamitz, Johann: *Symphonies (6), Opus 2,* 1757I; *Symphonies (4), Opus 4,* 1758I

Stanford, Charles Villiers: *Bible Songs & Hymns, Opus 113,* 1909I; *The Canterbury Pilgrims,* 1884I; *Cello Sonata No. 2, Opus 93,* 1893I; *Complete service in B♭, Opus 10,* 1879I; *Complete Service in A, Opus 12,* 1880I; *Complete Service in G, Opus 81,* 1904I; *Complete Service in C, Opus 115,* 1909I; *The Critic,* 1916I; *The Eumenides,* 1885I; *Evening Service in E♭,* 1873I; *Festival Overture,* 1877I; *Gloria in Excelsis in B♭, Opus 128,* 1911I; *The Golden Legend,* 1875I; *Magnificat,* 1907I; *Magnificat & Nunc Dimittis in E♭,* 1873I; *Much Ado About Nothing,* 1901I; *Nunc Dimittis, Opus 98,* 1907I; *Piano Concerto No. 1 in B, Opus 59,* 1896I; *Piano Concerto No. 2,* 1915I; *Piano Concerto No. 3, Opus 171,* 1919I; *Requiem,* 1896I; *The Resurrection,* 1875I; *Savonarola,* 1884I; *Serenade for Orchestra, Opus 18,* 1882I; *Shamus O'Brien, Opus 61,* 1896I; *Stabat Mater,* 1907I; *Suite (violin),* 1888I; *Symphony No. 1 in B♭,* 1875I; *Symphony No. 2 in d,* 1882I; *Symphony No. 3 in f, "Irish," Opus 28,* 1887I; *Symphony No. 4 in F, Opus 31,* 1889I; *Symphony No. 5 in d, Opus 56,* 1894I; *Symphony No. 6, Opus 94,* 1905I; *Thanksgiving Te Deum in E♭, Opus 143,* 1914I; *The Veiled Prophet of Khorassan,* 1879I; *Violin Concerto in D,* 1900I; *Violin Concerto No. 1 in D,* 1901I; *Violin Concerto No. 2,* 1918I

Stanhope, Paul: *String Quartet Morning Star,* 1992I

Stankovich, Evgeny: *Symphony No. 2, "Heroic,"* 1975I; *Symphony No. 4, "Sinfonia Lirica,"* 1976I; *Symphony No. 6,* 1973I

Stankovich, Yevhan: *Rasputin,* 1990I

Stanley, John: *Organ Concertos (6), Opus 10,* 1775I

Starer, Robert: *Apollonia,* 1978I; *Ariel: Visions of Isaiah,* 1959I; *Cello Concerto,* 1988I; *Clarinet Concerto,* 1988I; *Concerto for Orchestra,* 1950I; *Concerto for Two Pianos,* 1996I; *The Contemporary Virtuoso, for Piano,* 1996I; *Double Concerto for Violin & Cello,* 1967I; *The Dybbuk,* 1960I; *Excursions for a Pianist,* 1991I; *Fantasia concertante,* 1959I; *Holy Jungle,* 1974I; *Hudson Valley Suite,* 1984I; *Images of Man,* 1973I; *Joseph & His Brothers,* 1966I; *Kaaterskill Quartet,* 1987I; *Kohelet,* 1952I; *The Lady of the House of Sleep,* 1968I; *The Last Lover,* 1974I; *Mutabili,* 1965I; *Nishmat Adam,* 1992I; *Pantagleize,* 1966?I; *Phaedra,* 1962I; *Piano Concerto No. 1,* 1947I; *Piano Concerto No. 2,* 1953I; *Piano Concerto No. 3,* 1972I; *Piano Preludes (5),* 1952I; *Piano Quartet,* 1977I; *Piano Quintet,* 1997I; *Piano Sketches in Color,* 1963I; *Piano Sonata No. 1,* 1949I; *Piano Sonata No. 2,* 1965I; *Piano Sonata No. 3,* 1993I; *Prelude & Dance,* 1949I; *Samson Agonistes,* 1961I; *Seasonal Pieces (4) for Piano,* 1985I; *The Sense of Touch,* 1967I; *Stone Ridge Set for Piano,* 1973I; *String Quartet No. 1,* 1947I; *String Quartet No. 2,* 1995I; *String Quartet No. 3,* 1996I; *Symphonic Prelude,* 1984I; *Symphony No. 1,* 1950I; *Symphony No. 3,* 1969I; *Transformation,* 1978I; *Variations (6) with Twelve Tones,* 1967I; *Violin Concerto,* 1958I

Stebbins, George: *Gordon* (My Jesus, I Love Thee), 1864I

Steibelt, Daniel: *Airs (5) d'Estelle,* 1798I; *Albert und Adelaide,* 1798I; *La belle laitère,* 1805I; *Der blöde Ritter,* 1810I; *Cendrillon,* 1810I; *Etude for Piano, Opus 78,* 1805I; *La fête for mars,* 1806I; *La fête de l'empereur,* 1809I; *Harp Concerto,* 1807I; *Le jugement du berger Paris,* 1804I; *Piano Concerto No. 1 in C,* 1796I; *Piano Concerto No. 2 in e,* 1796I; *Piano Concerto No. 3, Opus 33, "L'orage,"* 1799I; *Piano Concerto No. 4, Opus 35,* 1798I; *Piano Concerto No. 5 in E♭, Opus 64,* 1802I; *Piano Concerto No. 6 in g,* 1816I; *Piano Concerto No. 7 in e,* 1816I; *Piano Concerto No. 8 in E♭,* 1820I; *La princesse de Babylone,* 1812I; *Le retour de Zéphyre,* 1802I; *Romances (6),* 1798I; *Roméo et Juliette,* 1793I; *Sargines,* 1810I; *Mélanges d'airs et chansons . . . , Opus 10,* 1794I

Stein, Leon: *Quintet for Clarinet & String Quartet,* 1993I; *String Quartet No. 1,* 1933I; *String Quartet No. 2,* 1962I; *String Quartet No. 3,* 1964I; *String Quartet No. 4,* 1965I; *String Quartet No. 5,* 1967I; *Symphony No. 1 in C,* 1940I; *Symphony No. 2 in E,* 1942I; *Symphony No. 4,* 1974I

Stenhammar, Wilhelm: *Das Fest auf solhaug,* 1899I; *Gildet på Solhaug,* 1893I; *Piano Concerto No. 1 in b♭,* 1893I; *Piano Concerto No. 2,* 1907I; *Serenade, Opus 31,* 1913I; *Symphony No. 2 in g,* 1915I; *Tirfing,* 1898I

Stephan, Rudi: *Music for Violin & Orchestra,* 1913I

Steptoe, Roger: *Clarinet Concerto,* 1989I; *King of Macedon,* 1979I; *Sinfonia Concertante,* 1981I; *Symphony No. 1,* 1988I

❄

F   *Biographical*   G   *Cultural Beginnings*   H   *Musical Literature*
I   *Musical Compositions*

Sternefeld, Daniel: *Pierlala*, 1942I; *Symphony No. 1*, 1943I; *Symphony No. 2*, *"Breughel,"* 1983I
Stevens, Halsey: *Bassoon Sonata*, 1949I; *Canciones (7)*, 1964I; *Cello Concerto*, 1964I; *Cello Sonata*, 1965I;
   Clarinet Concerto, 1969I; *Double Concerto*, 1973I; *A Green Mountain Adventure*, 1948I; *Horn Sonata*,
   1953I; *Magnificat*, 1962I; *Millay Songs (6)*, 1949I; *Music for String Orchestra*, 1957I; *Organ Pieces (3)*,
   1962I; *Piano Fantasia*, 1961I; *Piano Preludes (6)*, 1956I; *Piano Quartet*, 1946I; *Piano Sonata No. 1*,
   1933I; *Piano Sonata No. 2*, 1937I; *Piano Trio No. 3*, 1954I; *Pieces (5) for Orchestra*, 1958I; *Portraits for
   Piano*, 1960I; *Quintet for Flute, Strings & Piano*, 1945I; *Septet for Winds & Strings*, 1957I; *Short Pieces
   (4) for Orchestra*, 1954I; *Short Preludes (3)*, 1956I; *Songs of Love & Death*, 1953I; *String Quartet No. 3*,
   1949I; *Symphony No. 2*, 1945I; *Symphony No. 3*, 1946I; *Te Deum*, 1967I; *A Testament of Life*, 1959I;
   Threnos: In Memoriam Quincy Porter, 1968I; *Triskelion*, 1953I; *Trumpet Sonata*, 1956I; *Viola Concerto*,
   1975I
Stevenson, Ronald: *Borger Boyhood*, 1970I; *A Child's Garden of Verses*, 1984I; *Haiku (9)*, 1971I
Stewart, Humphrey: *The Conspirators*, 1900I; *Cortège Triumphal*, 1929I; *Mass in d*, 1907I; *Missa pro
   defunctis*, 1931I; *Piano Sonata, "The Chambered Nautilus,"* 1922I
Stich, Jan Václav: *Horn Concerto No. 5 & 6*, 1797I; *Horn Concerto No. 7*, 1798I; *Horn Concertos No. 8-10*,
   1802I; *Quartets (3), Horn & Strings, Opus 18*, 1796I; *Sextet, Opus 34*, 1802I; *Trios (12) for Three Horns*,
   1793I; *Trios (20) for Three Horns*, 1800I
Still, Robert: *Symphony No. 4*, 1964I
Still, William Grant: *Archaic Ritual*, 1946I; *Blue Steel*, 1934I; *Costaso*, 1950I; *Darker America*, 1924I; *Dismal
   Swamp*, 1936I; *Festive Overture*, 1944I; *From the Black Belt*, 1963I; *From the Hearts of Women*, 1961I; *La guiablesse*, 1927I; *Highway I, USA*, 1962I; *Kaintuck*, 1935I; *Lenox Avenue*,
   1937I; *Levee Land*, 1925I; *Old California*, 1941I; *The Peaceful Land*, 1960I; *A Psalm for Living*, 1954I;
   Sahdji, 1930I; *Songs of Separation*, 1949I; *A Southern Interlude*, 1943I; *Suite, A Deserted Plantation*, 1933I;
   Symphony No. 1, "Afro-American," 1930I; *Symphony No. 2 in g*, 1937I; *Symphony No. 3, "Sunday
   Afternoon,"* 1958I; *Symphony No. 4, "Autochthonous,"* 1949I; *Symphony No. 5, "Western Hemisphere,"*
   1945I; *Troubled Island–A Bayou Legend*, 1941I
Stiller, Andrew: *A Periodic Table of Elements*, 1988I; *The Water is Wide, Daisy Bell*, 1987I
Stock, David: *Violin Concerto*, 1995I
Stock, Frederick: *Overture to a Romantic Comedy*, 1918I; *Symphonic Variations*, 1904I; *Violin Concerto*,
   1915I
Stockhausen, Karlheinz: *Adieu*, 1966I; *Aus den Sieben Tagen*, 1968I; *Carré*, 1960I; *Donnerstag -1980I*;
   Fresco, 1969I; *Gesang der Jünglinge*, 1956I; *Gruppen for Three Orchestras*, 1957I; *Helikopter-quartett*,
   1993I; *Herbstmusik*, 1974I; *Kontakte*, 1960I; *Kontra-Punkt*, 1954I; *Kreuzspiel*, 1951I; *Kurzwellen*, 1968I;
   Mantra, 1994I; *Mikrophonie I*, 1964I; *Mikrophonie II*, 1965I; *Momente*, 1962I; *Montag aus Licht*, 1988I;
   Plus-Minus, 1963I; *Punkte for Ten Instruments*, 1953I; *Samstag aus Licht*, 1984I; *Sirius*, 1977I; *Spiel*,
   1952I; *Sternklang*, 1971I; *Stop*, 1965I; *Trans*, 1972I; *Zeitmesse*, 1956I; *Zyklus for Percussion*, 1959I
Stockmeier Wolfgang: *Organ Concerto No. 1*, 1962I; *Organ Concerto No. 2*, 1973I; *Organ Pieces*, 1967I;
   Organ Sonata No. 1, 1961I; *Organ Sonata No. 2*, 1966I; *Organ Sonata No. 3*, 1970I; *Organ Sonata No. 4*,
   1973I; *Symphonia sacra for Organ*, 1969I; *Toccata No. 1 for Organ*, 1963I; *Toccata No. 2 for Organ*, 1970I;
   Variations on a Theme by Kuhnau for Organ, 1961I; *Variations on a Theme by Schoenberg for Organ*,
   1977I
Stoessel, Albert: *Cyrano de Bergerac*, 1922I; *Violin Sonata in G*, 1921I
Stokes Eric: *Apollonia's Circus*, 1994I; *Horsfal*, 1969I; *The Jealous Cellist*, 1977I; *The Phonic Paradigm*,
   1980I; *Symphony, Book I*, 1979I
Stolz, Robert: *Blumenlieder, Opus 500*, 1928I
Stone, Carl: *Audible Structures*, 1987I; *Ho Ban*, 1984I; *Hop Ken*, 1991I; *Mae Ploy*, 1994I; *Maneeya*, 1976I;
   Samanluang, 1986I; *Sudi Mampir*, 1995I; *Wei-fun*, 1996I
Storace, Stephen: *The Haunted Tower*, 1789I; *The Iron Chest*, 1796I; *The Pirates*, 1792I
Stout, Alan: *Clarinet Quintet*, 1958I; *Nocturnes*, 1970I; *Passion*, 1975I; *Sonata for Two Pianos*, 1975I; *String
   Quartet No. 1*, 1953I; *String Quartet No. 2*, 1953I; *String Quartet No. 3*, 1954I; *String Quartet No. 4*,
   1955I; *String Quartet No. 5*, 1957I; *String Quartet No. 6*, 1959I; *String Quartet No. 7*, 1960I; *String
   Quartet No. 8*, 1961I; *String Quartet No. 9*, 1962I; *String Quartet No. 10*, 1962I; *Symphony No. 1*, 1959I;
   Symphony No. 2, 1966I; *Symphony No. 3*, 1962I; *Symphony No. 4*, 1971I
Strang, Gerald: *Clarinet Quintet*, 1933I; *Mirrorrim*, 1931I; *String Quartet No. 1*, 1934I
Strange, Allen: *The Hairbreath Ring Screamers*, 1969I; *The Second Book of Angels*, 1979I; *Shaman: Sisters of
   Dreamtime*, 1994I; *Soundbeams*, 1977I; *Switchcraft*, 1971I
Straus, Oscar: *The Chocolate Soldier*, 1908I
Strauss, Johann, Jr.: *Annen Polka*, 1852I; *Champagne Polka*, 1858I; *Emperor Waltz*, 1888I; *Die Fledermaus*,
   1874I; *The Gypsy Baron*, 1885I; *Indigo und die Vierzig Rauber*, 1871I; *Der Lustige Krieg*, 1881I; *Morning*

❈

A *Births*   B *Deaths*   C *Debuts*   D *New Positions*
E *Prizes/Honors*

Papers Waltz, 1864I; A Night in Venice, 1883I; On the Beautiful Blue Danube, 1867I; One Thousand & One Nights, 1871I; Perpetual Motion, 1860I; Pizzicato Polka, 1869I; Prinz Methusalem, 1877I; Radetsky, March, Opus 228, 1848I; Roses for the South, 1880I; Tales from the Vienna Woods, 1868I; Thunder and Lightning Polka, 1868I; Tritsch-Tratsch Polka, 1858I; Voices of Spring Waltz, 1882I; Wiener Blut, 1870I; Wine, Women and Song, 1869I

Strauss, Joseph: Armiodan, 1836I; Berthold der Zähringer, 1838I; Der Währwolf, 1840I

Strauss, Joseph, Jr.: Cagliostro in Wien, 1875I

Strauss, Richard: Alpensinfonie, Eine, Opus 64, 1915I; Also Sprach Zarathustra, Opus 3, 1896I; Andante for Horn & Piano, 1888I; Arabella, 1932I; Ariadne auf Naxos, 1912I; Aus Italien, Opus 16, 1886I; Le bourgeois gentilhomme, 1918I; Capriccio, 1941I; Concert Overture in c, Opus 4, 1881I; Daphne, 1937I; Death and Transfiguration, Opus 24, 1889I; Domestic Symphony, Opus 53, 1903I; Don Quixote, 1897I; Don Juan, Opus 20, 1888I; Ein Heldenleben, Opus 40, 1898I; Elektra, 1909I; Festive Prelude (organ), 1913I; Feuersnot, 1901I; Die Frau ohne Schatten, 1919I; Der Friedenstag, 1938I; Gesäng des Orients, Opus 77, 1929I; Die gyptische Helena, 1927I; Horn Concerto No. 1 in E♭, Opus 11, 1884I; Horn Concerto No. 2, 1942I; Intermezzo, 1925I; Joseph Legende, 1914I; Die Liebe de Danae, 1940I; Little Songs (5), Opus 69, 1918I; MacBeth, Opus 23, 1887I; Metamorphosen, 1945I; Oboe Concerto in D, 1946I; Overture in c, 1891I; Piano Quartet in c, 1885I; Piano Trio in A, 1877I; Piano Trio No. 2 in D, 1878I; Der Rosenkavalier, 1910I; Salomé, 1905I; Schlagobers, 1924I; Die Schweigsame Frau, 1935I; Serenade for Winds, Opus 7, 1880I; Sonatina No. 1 in F for Sixteen Winds, 1943I; Sonatina No. 2 in E♭ for Sixteen Winds, 1945I; Songs (12), Opus 31, 32, 33, 1897I; Songs (15), Opus 36, 37, 39, 1898I; Songs (15), Opus 46, 47, 48, 1900I; Songs (6), Opus 67, 1918I; Songs (6), Opus 68, 1918I; Symphony in d, 1881I; Symphony in f, Opus 12, 1884I; Taillefer, Opus 5, 1903I; Till Eulenspiegel's Merry Pranks, Opus 28, 1895I; Violin Concerto in d, Opus 8, 1883I; Violin Sonata in E♭, Opus 18, 1887I; Wanderer's Sturmlied, Opus 14, 1885I

Stravinsky, Igor: Abraham & Isaac, 1963I; Agon, 1957I; Apollon Musagètes, 1927I; Le baiser de la fée, 1922I; Berceuse du Chat, 1916I; Cantata, 1952I; Canticum sacrum ad honorem Sancti Marci nominis, 1955I; Capriccio for Piano & Orchestra, 1928I; The Card Game, 1936I; Chorale Variations on "Von Himmel Hoch," 1956I; Circus Polka, 1942I; Concerto for Piano & Winds, 1924I; Concerto for Two Pianos, 1935I; Concerto in D for String Orchestra, 1946I; Danses Concertantes, 1942I; Double Canon for String Quartet, 1959I; The Dove Descending, 1962I; Dumbarton Oaks Concerto, 1938I; Ebony Concerto, 1945I; Elegy for John F. Kennedy, 1963I; Etudes for Orchestra (4), 1929I; The Firebird, 1910I; Fireworks, Opus 4, 1908I; The Flood, 1962I; Greetings Prelude, 1955I; L'histoire du soldat, 1918I; In Memoriam: Dylan Thomas, 1954I; Instrumental Miniatures (8), 1962I; Introitus, 1965I; Mass, 1948I; Mavra, 1922I; Monumentum pro Gesualdo, 1960I; Movements for Piano & Orchestra, 1959I; Les noces, 1917I; Norwegian Moods (4), 1942I; Octet for Winds, 1923I; Oedipus Rex, 1927I; Orchestra Variations, 1964I; Orpheus, 1947I; Petrouchka, 1911I; Piano Etudes (4), Opus 7, 1907I; Piano Rag Music, 1919I; Piano Sonata, 1904I; Pieces (3) for String Quartet, 1914I; Pulcinella, 1919I; Ragtime for Eleven Instruments, 1918I; The Rake's Progress, 1950I; Renard, 1917I; Requiem Canticles, 1966I; Le roi des étoiles, 1911I; Le rossignol, 1914I; Le sacre du printemps, Opus 61, 1913I; Scenes de Ballet, 1944I; Scherzo à la Russe, 1944I; Scherzo Fantastique, Opus 3, 1908I; Septet for Piano, Winds & Strings, 1952I; A Sermon, a Narrative and a Prayer, 1961I; Sonata for Two Pianos, 1944I; Suite No. 2 for Small Orchestra, 1921I; Symphonies of Wind Instruments, 1920I; Symphony in C, 1940I; Symphony in E♭, Opus 1, 1907I; Symphony in Three Movements, 1945I; Symphony of Psalms, 1930I; Tango, 1940I; Threni: id est Lamentationes Jeremiae prophetae, 1958I; Violin Concerto, 1931I

Stringfield, Lamar: At the Factory, 1929I; From the Blue Ridge, 1936I; From the Southern Mountains, 1927I; Indian Legend, 1923I; String Quartet, "A Mountain Episode," 1933I

Stringham, Edwin John: The Phantom, 1916I; The Pilgrim Fathers, 1931I; String Quartet No. 2 in f, 1935I; Symphony No. 1, "Italian," 1929I

Strong, George Templeton: Symphony No 2, "Sintram," 1888I

Strube Gustav: Cello Sonata, 1925I; Echo, 1913I; Lanier Symphony, 1923I; Lazarus, 1926I; Loreley, 1913I; Narcissus, 1913I; Piano Trio, 1923I; Preludes for Orchestra (4), 1920I; Rhapsody for Orchestra, 1901I; String Quartet No. 1, 1923I; String Quartet No. 2, 1936I; Symphony in b, 1909I; Viola Sonata, 1924I; Violin Concerto No. 1, 1924I; Violin Concerto No. 2, 1930I; Violin Sonata No. 1, 1923I; Violin Sonata No. 2, 1923I; Wind Quintet, 1930I

Stucky, Steven: American Muse, 1999I; Concerto for Orchestra, 1987I; Double Concerto, 1985I; Double Flute Concerto, 1994I; Four Poems of A. R. Ammons, 1992I; Symphony No. 1, 1972I; Symphony No. 2, 1974I; Symphony No. 4, 1978I; Subotnick, Morton: All My Hummingbirds Have Alibis, 1991I; And the Butterflies Began to Sing, 1989I; The Balcony, 1960I; Danton's Death, 1966I; A Desert Flower, 1988I; Galileo, 1964I; Intimate Immensity, 1997I; Jacob's Room, 1993I; The Key to Songs, 1985I; Lamination, 1968I; Liquid Strata, 1982I; Serenade No. 3, 1965I; Sidewinder, 1970I; Silver Apples of the Moon, 1967I; Two Butterflies, 1975I; The Wild Bull, 1968I

❈

F   *Biographical*   G   *Cultural Beginnings*   H   *Musical Literature*

I   *Musical Compositions*

Suderburg, Robert: *Chamber Music II*, 1967I; *Harp Concerto*, 1981I; *Orchestra Music I*, 1969I; *Percussion Concerto*, 1977I; *Piano Concerto, "Within the Mirror of Time,"* 1974I; *Piano Moments (6)*, 1962I; *Solo Music I*, 1970I; *Solo Music II*, 1990I

Süderman, August: *Catholic Mass*, 1875I

Suk, Josef: *Dramatic Overture, Opus 4*, 1892I; *Epilogue*, 1933I; *Fantasie, Opus 24* (violin), 1903I; *Fantastic Scherzo*, 1903I; *Křečovics Mass*, 1889I; *Mass in B♭*, 1931I; *Meditation on "St. Wenceslas," Opus 35a*, 1914I; *Piano Pieces (8), Opus 12*, 1896I; *Piano Sonata*, 1883I; *Pohádka, Opus 16*, 1900I; *Prague, Opus 26*, 1904I; *The Ripening, Opus 34*, 1917I; *Serenade for Strings, Opus 6*, 1892I; *String Quartet No. 2, Opus 31*, 1911I; *A Summer Fairy Tale, Opus 29*, 1909I; *Symphony in E, Opus 14*, 1899I; *Symphony No. 2, "Asrael," Opus 27*, 1906I; *Under the Apple Trees, Opus 20*, 1902I; *A Winter's Tale, Opus 9*, 1894I

Sullivan, Arthur: *Cello Concerto in D*, 1866I; *The Chieftain*, 1894I; *The Emerald Isle*, 1901I; *Festival Te Deum*, 1872I; *Ivanhoe*, 1891I; *Kenilworth*, 1864I; *The Light of the World*, 1873I; *The Lost Chord*, 1877I; *The Martyr of Antioch*, 1880I; *The Merchant of Venice*, 1871I; *On the Shore & Sea*, 1871I; *Onward, Christian Soldiers*, 1872I; *Overture, In Memoriam*, 1866I; *Princess of Wales March*, 1863I; *Procession March*, 1863I; *The Prodigal Son*, 1869I; *The Rose of Persia*, 1900I; *The Sapphire Necklace*, 1864I; *Symphony in e, "Irish,"* 1866I; *The Tempest*, 1861I; *Victoria & Merrie England*, 1897I; *The Zoo*, 1875I

Sumera, Lepo: *Piano Concerto*, 1989I; *Symphony No. 1*, 1980I; *Symphony No. 2*, 1984I; *Symphony No. 3*, 1988I; *Symphony No. 4, "Serena borealis,"* 1992I; *Symphony No. 5*, 1995I; *Symphony No. 6*, 2000I

Suppé, Franz von: *Der Bandit*, 1848I; *Benditenstreiche*, 1867I; *Boccaccio*, 1879I; *Das Corps der rache*, 1863I; *Fatinitza*, 1876I; *Flotte bursche*, 1863I; *Franz Schubert*, 1864I; *Die Frau Meisterin*, 1868I; *Freigeister*, 1866I; *Der Gascogner*, 1881I; *Isabella*, 1869I; *Die Kartenaufschlägerin*, 1862I; *Die Krämer und sein Kommis*, 1847I; *Light Cavalry*, 1866I; *Lohengelb*, 1870I; *Das Mädchen om Lande*, 1847I; *Mass in F*, 1834I; *Mass in C*, 1836I; *Missa Dalmatica*, 1877I; *Das Pensionat*, 1860I; *Pique Dame*, 1864I; *Poet and Peasant*, 1846I; *Requiem*, 1854I; *Die schöne Galatea*, 1865I; *Tannhäuser*, 1860I; *Virginia*, 1837I; *Voyage de Monsieur Dunanan*, 1862I; *Zehn Mädchen und kein Mann*, 1862I

Surinach, Carlos: *Agathe's Tale*, 1967I; *Chronique*, 1974I; *Concerto for Orchestra*, 1959I; *Double Concerto* (flute, doublebass), 1990I; *Feast of Ashes*, 1962I; *Harp Concerto*, 1978I; *The Owl & the Pussycat*, 1978I; *Piano Concerto*, 1974I; *String Quartet No. 1*, 1974I; *Symphonic Melismas*, 1993I; *Symphonic Variations*, 1963I; *Symphony No. 2*, 1949I

Susa, Conrad: *The Love of Don Perlimplin*, 1983I; *The Dangerous Liaisons*, 1994I; *Transformations*, 1973I

Süssmayr, Franz X.: *Die Drillinge*, 1786I; *Die edle Rache*, 1795I; *Die Freiwilligen*, 1796I; *Gülnare*, 1800I; *Idris und Zenide*, 1795I; *L'incanto superato*, 1793I; *Karl Stuart*, 1785I; *Die Liebe auf dem Lande*, 1789I; *List und Zufall*, 1803I; *Moses*, 1792I; *Piramo e Tisbe*, 1793I; *Quanti cast in un sol giorno*, 1801I; *Der rauschige Hans*, 1791I; *Der Ritter in Gefahr*, 1796I; *Soliman II*, 1799I; *Der Spiegel von Arkadien*, 1794I; *Il turco in Italia*, 1794I; *Die väterliche Rache*, 1789I; *Der Wildfang*, 1798I

Suter, Robert: *Geisha-Lieder*, 1943I

Sutermeister, Heinrich: *Inventions (12)*, 1934I; *Piano Concerto No. 1*, 1943I; *Piano Concerto No. 2*, 1953I

Sutherland, Margaret: *House Quartet for Clarinet, Horn, Viola & Piano*, 1936I; *Rhapsody* (violin concerto), 1938I; *String Quartet No. 1*, 1939I; *String Quartet No. 2, "Discussion,"* 1954I; *String Quartet No. 3*, 1967I

Sveinsson, Atli: *Flute Concerto*, 1975I

Svendsen, Johan: *Cello Concerto in d, Opus 7*, 1870I; *String Quartet, Opus 1*, 1864I; *Symphony No. 1 in D, Opus 4*, 1867I; *Violin Concerto in A, Opus 6*, 1869I

Svete, Tomaz: *Evocazione*, 1995I; *Requiem*, 1991I; *String Quartet*, 1992I

Svetlanov, Evgeni: *Symphony*, 1956I

Sviridov, Georgi: *Russia Adrift*, 1977I; *Children's Album*, 1948I; *Piano Sonata*, 1944I

Svoboda, Tomáš: *Concerto for Chamber Orchestra*, 1986I; *Etudes in Fugue Style, Opus 44*, 1966I; *Guitar Sonata*, 1980I; *Overture of the Season, Opus 89*, 1978I; *Piano Concerto No. 1*, 1974I; *Piano Concerto No. 2*, 1989I; *Piano Sonata No. 2 - Suite for Piano, Four Hands, Opus 124*, 1985I; *Piano Sonata No. 1, Opus 49*, 1967I; *Sonata for Two Pianos, Opus 55*, 1972I; *Piano Trio, "Van Gogh,"* 1986I; *String Quartet No. 1*, 1960I; *String Quartet No. 2*, 1995I; *Symphony No. 1, "Of Nature," Opus 20*, 1956I; *Symphony No. 3, Opus 43*, 1965I; *Symphony No. 6, Opus 137*, 1991I; *Symphony No. 4, "Apocalyptic," Opus 69*, 1975I; *Symphony No. 5, "In Unison," Opus 92*, 1978I; *Symphony No. 2, Opus 41*, 1964I; *Violin Sonata*, 1984I

Swack, Irwin: *Symphony No. 2*, 1988I

Swafford, Jan: *They Who Hunger*, 1989I

Swanson, Howard: *Cello Sonata*, 1973I; *Concerto for Orchestra*, 1954I; *Piano Concerto*, 1956I; *Piano Sonata No. 1*, 1948I; *Piano Sonata No. 2*, 1970I; *Piano Sonata No. 3*, 1978I; *Songs for Patricia*, 1951I; *Symphony No. 1*, 1945I; *Symphony No. 2, "Short Symphony,"* 1948I; *Symphony No. 3*, 1970I

Sweeney, John R.: *Tell Me the Story of Jesus*, 1880I; *There Is Sunshine in the Soul Today*, 1887I

Swinnen, Peter: *The Black Lark's Ballad*, 1995I; *JoenRuni*, 1993I

A   *Births*   B   *Deaths*   C   *Debuts*   D   *New Positions*

E   *Prizes/Honors*

Syberg, Franz: *Quintet for Flute, Clarinet & String Trio*, 1931I; *String Quartet*, 1931I; *String Trio*, 1933I; *Symphony*, 1939I
Sydeman, William: *Concerto da Camera No. 1*, 1958I; *Piano Sonata*, 1961I; *Piano Variations*, 1958I; *Projections No. 1*, 1968I; *Short Piano Pieces*, 1980I; *Study for Orchestra I*, 1959I; *Study for Orchestra II*, 1963I; *Study for Orchestra III*, 1965I; *Woodwind Quintet*, 1955I; *Woodwind Quintet No. 2*, 1961I
Szalowski, Antoni: *Symphony*, 1939I; *Violin Concerto*, 1954I
Székely, Endre: *Chamber Music for Eight*, 1863I; *String Quartet, No. 1*, 1953I; *String Quartet No. 2*, 1958I; *String Quartet No. 3*, 1962I; *String Quartet No. 4*, 1972I; *String Quartet No. 5*, 1981I; *String Trio*, 1943I; *Symphony*, 1956I
Szeligowski, Tadeusz: *Concerto (orchestra)*, 1932I; *Piano Concerto*, 1941I; *Wind Quintet*, 1950I
Szeluto, Apolinary: *Violin Concerto*, 1948I
Szervánszky, Endre: *Symphony*, 1948I
Szokolay, Sándor: *Concerto for Orchestra*, 1982I; *Concerto for Two Violins*, 1933I; *Piano Concerto*, 1958I; *Sonata for Solo Cello*, 1979I; *Sonata for Solo Violin*, 1956I; *Sonata No. 2 for Solo Violin*, 1996I; *String Quartet No. 1*, 1972I; *String Quartet No. 2*, 1982I; *Violin Concerto*, 1957I
Szőllősy, András: *String Quartet*, 1988I
Szymanowski, Karol: *Concert Overture, Opus 12*, 1905I; *Fantasy, Opus 14*, 1905I; *Hagith, Opus 25*, 1913I; *Harnasie, Opus 55*, 1931I; *King Roger, Opus 46*, 1924I; *The Lottery for Men*, 1909I; *Love Songs of Hafiz, Opus 26*, 1914I; *Mandragora, Opus 43*, 1920I; *Masques, Opus 34*, 1916I; *Mazurkas (2), Opus 62*, 1934I; *Paganini Caprices (3), Opus 40*, 1918I; *Penthesilea, Opus 18*, 1918I; *Piano Preludes (9), Opus 1*, 1900I; *Piano Sonata No. 1, Opus 8*, 1904I; *Piano Sonata No. 2, Opus 21*, 1911I; *Piano Sonata No. 3, Opus 36*, 1917I; *Piano Studies (4), Opus 4*, 1902I; *Piano Studies (12), Opus 33*, 1916I; *Piano Variations, Opus 3*, 1903I; *Prince Potemkin, Opus 51*, 1925I; *Romance, Opus 23*, 1910I; *Salome, Opus 6*, 1907I; *Songs of a Fairy-Tale Princess, Opus 31*, 1933I; *Stabat Mater, Opus 53*, 1926I; *String Quartet No. I, Opus 37*, 1917I; *String Quartet No. 2, Opus 56*, 1927I; *Symphony No. 1 in f, Opus 15*, 1907I; *Symphony No. 2, Opus 19*, 1910I; *Symphony No. 3, "Song of the Night," Opus 27*, 1916I; *Variations on a Polish Theme, Opus 10*, 1904I; *Veni Creator, Opus 57*, 1930I; *Violin Concerto No. 1, Opus 35*, 1916I; *Violin Concerto No. 2, Opus 61*, 1933I; *Violin Sonata, Opus 9*, 1904I
Tabachnik, Michel: *Gospel of St. Thomas*, 1985I; *La Légende de Haisha*, 1989I; *Piano Concerto*, 1989I
Tadolini, Giovanni: *Almanzor*, 1827I; *Le bestie in uomini*, 1815I; *La fata Alcina*, 1814I; *Il finto molinaro*, 1820I; *Mitridate*, 1826I; *Moctar*, 1824I; *Tamerlano*, 1818I
Tahourdin, Peter: *Symphony No. 1*, 1960I; *Symphony No. 2*, 1969I; *Symphony No. 3*, 1979I; *Symphony No. 4*, 1987I; *Symphony No. 5*, 1994I
Tailleferre, Germaine: *Concertino for Flute & Piano*, 1952I; *Concertino for Harp & Orchestra*, 1927I; *Harp Sonata*, 1954I; *Piano Concerto*, 1919I; *String Quartet*, 1918I; *Violin Sonata No. 1*, 1921I; *Violin Sonata No. 2*, 1951I
Takács, Jenő: *Piano Concerto No. 1*, 1932I; *Piano Concerto No. 2*, 1937I; *Songs of Silence*, 1967I
Takahashi, Yuri: *Tadori*, 1972I
Takata, Saburôn: *Wordless Tears*, 1963I
Takemitsu, Toru: *Asterism*, 1969I; *Autumn*, 1973I; *Coral Island*, 1962I; *Dorian Horizon*, 1966I; *A Flock Descends into the Pentagonal Garden*, 1977I; *Green, November Steps II*, 1967I; *Ki No. Kyoku*, 1961I; *Les yeux clos I*, 1979I; *Les yeux clos II*, 1988I; *Piano Distance*, 1961I; *Quiet Design*, 1960I; *Rain Tree Sketches I for Piano*, 1982I; *Rain Tree Sketches II for Piano*, 1992I; *Sky, Horse & Death*, 1954I; *Star Isle*, 1984I; *Static Relief*, 1955I; *String Quartet No. 1, "A Way a Lone,"* 1980I; *Textures*, 1964I; *Vocalism A-1*, 1956I; *Water Music*, 1960I; *Winter*, 1971I
Taktakishvili, Otar: *Cello Concerto*, 1947I; *Symphony No. 1*, 1949I; *Symphony No. 2*, 1953I
Tal, Josef: *String Quartet No. 1*, 1959I; *String Quartet No. 2*, 1964I; *String Quartet No. 3*, 1976I; *Symphony No. 1*, 1953I; *Symphony No. 2*, 1960I; *Symphony No. 3*, 1978I; *Symphony No. 4, "Jubilee,"* 1985I; *Symphony No. 5*, 1991I; *Symphony No. 6*, 1991I; *The Tower*, 1983I; *Viola Sonata*, 1960I
Talma, Louise: *The Alcestiad*, 1958I; *Conversations*, 1987I; *Dialogues for Piano & Orchestra*, 1964I; *The Divine Flame*, 1948I; *Episodes (7)*, 1987I; *Etudes (6)*, 1954I; *The Hound of Heaven*, 1938I; *Passacaglia & Fugue*, 1961I; *Piano Sonata No. 1*, 1943I; *Piano Sonata No. 2*, 1955I; *Piano Textures*, 1977I; *String Quartet No. 1*, 1954I; *Terre de France*, 1945I; *A Time to Remember*, 1967I; *Tocccata*, 1944I; *The Tolling Bell*, 1969I; *Violin Sonata*, 1962I; *Voices of Peace*, 1973I
Talon, Pierre: *Symphonies (6), Opus 1*, 1753I; *Symphonies (6), Opus 2*, 1761I; *Symphonies (6), Opus 5*, 1767I
Tamberg, Eino: *Cyrano de Bergerac*, 1974I; *Flight*, 1982I; *The House of Iron*, 1965I; *Saxophone Concerto*, 1987I; *String Quartet*, 1958II; *Symphony No. 1*, 1978I; *Symphony No. 2*, 1986I; *Symphony No. 3*, 1989I
Tan, Dun: *Deaths & Fire*, 1990I; *Eight Colors*, 1988I; *Feng Ya Son*, 1982I; *The Map*, 1999I; *Marco Polo*, 1994I; *Piano Concerto*, 1983I; *Symphony in Two Movements*, 1985I; *Symphony 1997, "Heaven Earth Mankind,"* 1997I; *2000 Today: A World Symphony for the Millennium*, 1999I

❋

F *Biographical*   G *Cultural Beginnings*   H *Musical Literature*
I *Musical Compositions*

Tanaka, Karen: *At the Grave of Beethoven,* 1999I; *Children of Light,* 1999I; *Crystalline I for Piano,* 1996I; *Departure,* 1999I; *Metallic Chrystal,* 1992I; *Metal Strings,* 1996I; *Questions of Nature,* 1998I; *The Zoo in the Sky,* 1995I

Taneyev, Sergei: *John of Damascus,* 1880I; *String Trio No. 2 in D, Opus 21,* 1908I; *String Trio No. 3, Opus 31,* 1911I; *String Trio No. 4 in B,* 1913I

Tanguy, Eric: *Célébration de Marie Madeleine,* 1995I; *Cello Concerto,* 1995I; *Litanies (5) for Organ,* 1996I; *Piano Preludes (5),* 1997I; *Piano Sonata,* 1996I; *Ricercaré for Organ,* 1994I; *String Quartet No. 1,* 1993I; *Tableaux (8) pour Orpheo,* 1997I

Tannenbaum, Elias: *Last Letters from Stalingrad,* 1981I

Tansman, Alexandre: *Bric-à- Brac,* 1937I; *Cello Concerto,* 1963I; *Cello Fantaisie for Cello & Piano,* 1936I; *Cello Sonata,* 1930I; *Clarinet Concerto,* 1958I; *Concerto for Orchestra,* 1954I; *Etudes for Orchestra,* 1962I; *Five Pieces (violin),* 1930I; *Flute Sonata,* 1925I; *La grande ville,* 1932I; *Les habits neufs du roi,* 1959I; *Partita,* 1955I; *Partita for Cello & Piano,* 1955I; *Piano Concerto No. 1,* 1926I; *Piano Concerto No. 2,* 1927I; *Resurrection,* 1962I; *Sextuor,* 1924I; *String Sextet,* 1940I; *Suite for Two Pianos & Orchestra,* 1928I; *Symphony No. 1,* 1925I; *Symphony No. 2,* 1926I; *Symphony No. 3, "Symphonie concertante,"* 1931I; *Symphony No. 4 in b,* 1939I; *Symphony No. 5,* 1942I; *Symphony No. 6, "In Memoriam,"* 1943I; *Symphony No. 7,* 1944I; *Viola Concerto,* 1936I; *Violin Concerto,* 1937I; *Violin Sonata,* 1919I

Tapray, Jean-François: *Organ Concertos (6),* 1758I

Taranov, Gleb: *String Quartet No. 1,* 1929I; *String Quartet No. 2,* 1945I

Tăranu, Cornel: *Cello Sonata,* 1960I; *Flute Sonata,* 1961I; *Piano Concerto,* 1966I; *Sonata for Solo Cello,* 1992I; *Sonata for Solo Viola,* 1990I; *Symphony No. 1,* 1962I; *Symphony No. 3, "Signes,"* 1984I; *Symphony No. 4, "Ritornele,"* 1987I

Tarchi, Angelo: *Ademira,* 1783I; *Le danaidi,* 1792I

Tardos, Béla: *Piano Concerto,* 1954I; *String Quartet No. 1,* 1947I; *String Quartet No. 2,* 1949I; *String Quartet No. 3,* 1963I; *Violin Sonata,* 1965I

Tartini, Giuseppe: *Trio Sonatas (6) II,* 1755I; *Trio Sonatas (12), Opus 3,* 1756I (?); *Trio Sonatas (6), Opus 9,* 1761I

Taubert, Wilhelm: *Blaubart,* 1845I; *Symphony No. 1,* 1831I; *Der Zigeuner,* 1834I

Tavener, John: *The Apocalypse,* 1994I; *Agraphon,* 1995I; *Akhmatova: Requiem,* 1980I; *Celtic Requiem,* 1969I; *Eternity's Sunrise,* 1998I; *Funeral Canticle,* 1996I; *A Gentle Spirit,* 1977I; *The Hidden Treasure,* 1989I; *Hymns of Paradise,* 1993I; *Ikon the Trinity,* 1990I; *Innocence,* 1995I; *Liturgy of St. John Chrysostem,* 1978I; *The Lord's Prayer,* 1982I; *Magnificat & Nunc Dimittis,* 1986I; *Mandelion for Organ,* 1981I; *Mini Song Cycle for Gina,* 1984I; *Palintropes,* 1979I; *Piano Concerto,* 1963I; *The Protecting Veil,* 1987I; *Psalm 121,* 1989I; *Resurrection,* 1989I; *Risen!,* 1981I; *Sappho,* 1981I; *Song of the Angel,* 1995I; *Theophony,* 1994I; *Thérèse,* 1972I

Taylor, Clifford: *The Freak Show,* 1975I; *Ideas (30) for Piano,* 1973I; *Theme & Variations,* 1952I; *More Ideas (36) for Piano,* 1976I; *Piano Studies (9),* 1962I; *String Quartet No. 1,* 1960I; *String Quartet No. 2,* 1978I; *Symphony No. 2,* 1965I; *Symphony No. 3,* 1978I; *Violin Sonata,* 1952I

Taylor, Deems: *The Chambered Nautilus, Opus 7,* 1914I; *The City of Joy, Opus 9,* 1916I; *The Highwayman, Opus 8,* 1914I; *Jurgen, Opus 17,* 1925I; *The King's Henchman, Opus 19,* 1926I; *Peter Ibbetson, Opus 20,* 1930I; *Piano Inventions (5),* 1926I; *Ramuntcho, Opus 23,* 1942I; *Songs (3), Opus 13,* 1920I; *Through the Looking Glass, Opus 12,* 1919I

Taylor, Raynor: *Pizarro,* 1800I

Tchaikovsky, Boris: *Cello Sonata,* 1957I; *Piano Trio,* 1953I; *Sextet,* 1990I; *String Quartet No. 1,* 1954I; *String Quartet No. 2,* 1961I; *String Quartet No. 3,* 1967I; *String Quartet No. 4,* 1972I; *String Quartet No. 5,* 1974I; *String Quartet No. 6,* 1976I; *Symphony No. 1,* 1947I; *Symphony No. 2,* 1967I; *Symphony No. 3,* 1980I

Tchaikovsky, Peter Ilyich: *Children's Album, Opus 39,* 1878I; *Concert Fantasy, Opus 56,* 1884I; *Concert Overture in F,* 1865I; *Concert Overture in c,* 1866I; *Dumka, Opus 59,* 1886I; *Eugene Onegin, Opus 24,* 1878I; *Fatum, Opus 7,* 1868I; *Festival Overture on Danish Hymn, Opus 15,* 1866I; *Francesca da Rimini, Opus 32,* 1876I; *Hamlet, Opus 67a,* 1888I; *Iolanthe, Opus 69,* 1891I; *Liturgy of St. John Chrysostom, Opus 41,* 1878I; *The Maid of Orleans,* 1879I; *Manfred Symphony, Opus 58* 1885I; *Marche Slav, Opus 31,* 1876I; *Mazeppa,* 1883I; *Nature and Love,* 1870I; *The Nutcracker, Opus 71,* 1892I; *The Oprichnik,* 1872I,; *Overture to the Tempest,* 1864I; *Overture Solennelle 1812, Opus 49,* 1880I; *Pan Voyevoda, Opus 3,* 1868I; *Piano Concerto No. 1 in b♭, Opus 23,* 1865I; *Piano Concerto No. 2 in G, Opus 44,* 1880I; *Piano Concerto No. 3 in E♭, Opus 75,* 1893I; *Piano Pieces (3), Opus 9,* 1871I; *Piano Pieces (12), Opus 40,* 1878I; *Piano Sonata in c♯, Opus 37,* 1865I; *Piano Trio in a, Opus 50,* 1882I; *Romeo and Juliet Fantasy Overture,* 1869I; *Russian Vesper Service, Opus 52,* 1882I; *The Seasons,* 1876I; *Serenade for Nikolai Rubinstein's Name Day,* 1872I; *Serenade for Strings in C, Opus 48,* 1880I; *Serenade Melancholique, Opus 26,* 1875I; *The Sleeping Beauty, Opus 66,*

❧

A *Births*   B *Deaths*   C *Debuts*   D *New Positions*
E *Prizes/Honors*

1889I; *The Snow Maiden, Opus 12*, 1873I; *Songs (6), Opus 25*, 1874I; *Songs (7), Opus 47*, 1879I; *Songs (6), Opus 57*, 1884I; *Songs (6), Opus 63*, 1887I; *String Quartet No. 1 in D, Opus 11*, 1871I; *String Quartet No. 2 in F, Opus 22*, 1874I; *String Quartet No. 3 in e♭, Opus 30*, 1876I; *Suite No. 1 in D, Opus 43*, 1879I; *Suite No. 2 in C, Opus 53*, 1883I; *Suite No. 3 in G, Opus 55*, 1884I; *Suite No. 4 in G, "Mozartiana," Opus 61*, 1887I; *Swan Lake, Opus 20*, 1876I; *Symphony No. 1 in g, Opus 13, "Winter Dreams,"* 1866I; *Symphony No. 2 in c, "Little Russian," Opus 17*, 1872I; *Symphony No. 3 in D, "Polish," Opus 29*, 1875I; *Symphony No. 4 in f, Opus 36*, 1877I; *Symphony No. 5 in e, Opus 64*, 1888I; *Symphony No. 6 in b, "Pathétique," Opus 74*, 1893I; *The Tempest, Opus 18*, 1873I; *Undine*, 1869I; *Valkula the Smith*, 1874I; *Valse Scherzo in C, Opus 34*, 1877I; *Violin Concerto in D, Opus 35*, 1878I; *The Voyvoda, Opus 78*, 1891I
Tcherepnin, Alexander: *Ajanta's Frescoes*, 1923I; *The Farmer & the Fairy*, 1952I; *The Lost Flute*, 1955I; *Piano Concerto No. 1*, 1920I; *Piano Concerto No. 2*, 1923I; *Piano Concerto No. 3*, 1932I; *Piano Concerto No. 4, "Fantasia,"* 1947I; *Piano Concerto No. 5, Opus 96*, 1963I; *Piano Concerto No. 6, Opus 99*, 1965I; *Piano Pieces (8)*, 1955I; *Piano Preludes (12)*, 1952I; *Piano Quintet*, 1927I; *Piano Sonata No. 1*, 1918I; *Piano Sonata No. 2, Opus 94*, 1961I; *Russian Sketches, Opus 106*, 1971I; *String Quartet No. 1*, 1922I; *String Quartet No. 2*, 1926I; *Symphonic Prayer, Opus 93*, 1959I; *Symphony No. 1*, 1927I; *Symphony No. 2 in E♭, Opus 77*, 1951I; *Symphony No. 3, Opus 83*, 1952I; *Symphony No. 4 in E, Opus 91*, 1957I; *Woodwind Quintet*, 1976I
Tcherepnin, Ivan: *Bachamatics*, 1985I; *The Creative Act*, 1990I; *Double Concerto*, 1995I; *Ring*, 1969I; *Set, Hold, Clear & Squelch*, 1976I
Tcherepnin, Nicolai: *Dionysus*, 1922I; *Masque de la mort rouge*, 1911I; *Narcisse et Echo*, 1911I; *Le pavilion d'Armide*, 1907I; *Piano Concerto*, 1907I; *Romance of the Mummy*, 1924I; *Russian Fairy Tale*, 1923I; *Two Tapes: Giuseppe's Background Music*, 1966I; *Two More Tapes: Additions & Subtraction*, 1966I
Teirilä, Tuomao Juhani: *Introitus, Kyrie & Gloria*, 1977I
Teitelbaum, Richard: *Digital Piano Music*, 1983I; *In Tune*, 1966I
Telemann, Georg Philipp: *Das Befreite Israel*, 1759I; *Cantata for the Birthday of King Friedrich V*, 1757I; *The Day of Judgment*, 1762I; *Don Quichotte der Lowenritter*, 1761I; *Flute Duets (7)*, 1752I; *DervHerr hat offenbart*, 1762I; *Die Hirten bei der Krippe zu Bethlehem*, 1759I; *Miriam und deine Wehmut*, 1759I; *Passion According to John V*, 1757I; *Passion According to John VI*, 1761I; *Passion According to Luke IV*, 1760I; *Passion According to Luke V*, 1764I; *Passion According to Mark I*, 1759I; *Passion According to St. Mark II*, 1767I; *Passion According to Matthew IV*, 1758I; *Passion According to Matthew V*, 1762I; *The Resurrection and Ascension of Jesus*, 1760I; *Siehe, ich verhùundige Euch*, 1761I; *Der Tod Jesu*, 1756I
Tenney, James: *Analog No. 1: Noise Study*, 1961I; *Collage No. 1: Blue Suede*, 1961I; *Dialogue*, 1963I; *Ergodos II*, 1964I; *Fabric for Che*, 1967I; *For Ann*, 1969I
Terényi, Ede: *Sonata for Solo Violin*, 1985I
Terradellas Domingo: *Sesostri*, 1751I
Terterian, Avet: *Symphony No. 3*, 1975I
Terzakis, Dimitri: *Daphnis & Chloe*, 1994I; *Des sechte Siegel*, 1987I; *Der Hölle Nachklang II*, 1993I; *Ichochrones I*, 1967I; *Passionen*, 1979I; *String Quartet No. 1*, 1969I; *String Quartet No. 2*, 1976I; *String Quartet No. 3*, 1982I; *String Quartet No. 4*, 1990I
Tessarini, Carlo: *Grande Overtures (6), Opus 18*, 1764I; *Grande Overtures (6), Opus 20*, 1765I; *Trio Sonatas (6), Opus 16*, 1753I
Testi, Flavio: *Riccardo III*, 1987I
Thalberg Sigismond: *Cristina de Svezia*, 1855I; *Florinda*, 1851I; *Piano Concerto in f, Opus 5*, 1830I
Theodorakis, Mikis: *Les amants de Teruel*, 1958I; *Antigone*, 1958I; *Antigone II*, 1971I; *Electra* (ballet), 1976I; *Electra* (opera), 1993I; *Mauthausen*, 1965I; *Medea*, 1990I; *Piano Concerto*, 1957I; *Sadoukeon Passion*, 1982I; *Symphony No. 1*, 1950I; *Symphony No. 2*, 1958I; *Symphony No. 3*, 1980I; *Symphony No. 4*, 1986I; *Symphony No. 7, "Spring,"* 1983I; *Symphony No. 8, "Canto Olympico,"* 1991I; *Zorba* (ballet), 1976I; *Zorbas* (opera), 1988I
Theofanidis, Christopher: *Statues for Piano*, 1992I
Thibault, Charles: *Rondo: Le printemps, Opus 6*, 1823I; *Variations: Le souvenir, Opus 7*, 1823I; *Variations: L'espérance, Opus 8*, 1824I; *Variations: La bretonne, Opus 9*, 1824I; *Waltzes (3), Opus 13*, 1825I
Thiriet, Maurice: *Flute Concerto*, 1959I
Thomas, Ambroise: *Angélique et Médor*, 1843I; *Betty*, 1846I; *Le caïd*, 1849I; *Carline*, 1840I; *Le carnaval de Venise*, 1857I; *Le comte der Carmagnola*, 1841I; *La cour de Célimène*, 1855I; *La double échelle*, 1837I; *Fantasie brillante, Opus 6*, 1836I; *Francesco de Rimini*, 1882I; *Gille et Gillotin*, 1874I; *La guerillero*, 1842I; *La gypsy*, 1840I; *Hamlet*, 1868I; *Messe Solennelle*, 1857I; *Mignon*, 1866I; *Mina*, 1843I; *Le perruquier de la régence*, 1838I; *Psyché*, 1857I; *Raymond*, 1851I; *Le roman d'Elvire*, 1860I; *String Quartet in e, Opus 1*, 1833I; *String Quintet*, 1835I; *La Tonelli*, 1853I

❉

F   *Biographical*   G   *Cultural Beginnings*   H   *Musical Literature*

I   *Musical Compositions*

Thomas, Augusta Read: *Ancient Chimes*, 1995I; *Air & Angels*, 1992I; *Angel Chant*, 1991I; *Aurora* (piano concerto), 1999I; *Ceremonial*, 1999I; *Chanson* (cello concerto), 1996I; *Concerto for Orchestra: Orbital Beacons*, 1998I; *Conquering the Fury of Oblivion*, 1995I; *Enchanted Orbits*, 1997I; *Fantasy* (piano concerto), 1994I; *Fantasy on Two Klee Studies*, 1988I; *Glass Moon*, 1988I; *Incantation*, 1995I; *Ligeia*, 1994I; *Night's Midsummer Blaze* (triple concerto), 1993I; *Nocturne*, 1994I; *Orbital Beacons*, 1998I; *Passions*, 1998I; *Ritual Incantation*, 1999I; . . . *Song in Sorrow* . . . , 2000I; *Spring Song*, 1995I; *Symphony No. 1*, 1992I; *Trumpet Sonata*, 1989I; *Tunnel at the End of Light* (piano concerto), 1984I; *Whites for Piano*, 1988I; *Whites II for Piano*, 1989I; . . . *words of the sea* . . . , 1996I
Thome, Diane: *Masks of Eternity*, 1994I; *The Palaces of Memory*, 1993I; *Ringing, Stillness, Pearl Light*, 1987I; *The Ruins of the Heart*, 1990I
Thompson, Randall: *Alleluia*, 1940I; *Americana*, 1932I; *Canticles (12)*, 1983I; *A Concord Cantata*, 1975I; *A Feast of Praise*, 1963I; *Frostiana*, 1959I; *Indianola Variations for Two Pianos*, 1918I; *Jabberwocky*, 1951I; *Jazz Poem*, 1928I; *The Last Words of David*, 1949I; *The Nativity According to St. Luke*, 1961I; *Odes of Horace (5)*, 1924I; *The Passion According to St. Luke*, 1965I; *The Peaceable Kingdom*, 1936I; *Piano Sonata in c*, 1923I; *Piano Sonata in g*, 1922I; *A Psalm of Thanksgiving*, 1967I; *Requiem*, 1958I; *Solomon & Belkis*, 1942I; *String Quartet No. 1*, 1941I; *String Quartet No. 2 in G*, 1967I; *Symphonic Fantasy: A Trip to Nahant*, 1954I; *Symphonic Prelude, The Piper at the Gates of Dawn*, 1924I; *Symphony No. 1*, 1929I; *Symphony No. 2*, 1931I; *Symphony No. 3*, 1949I; *The Testament of Freedom*, 1943I
Thomson, Virgil: *Agnus Dei*, 1925I; *Androcles & the Lion*, 1938I; *Antony & Cleopatra*, 1937I; *La belle en dormant*, 1931I; *A Bride for the Unicorn*, 1934I; *Cantata on Poems of Edward Lear*, 1973I; *Capital, Capitals*, 1927I; *Cello Concerto*, 1949I; *Choruses (7) from Euripides' "Medea,"* 1934I; *Concerto for Flute, Harp, Strings & Percussion*, 1954I; *De Profundis*, 1920I; *Etudes (10)*, 1944I; *Filling Station*, 1937I; *Four Saints in Three Acts*, 1934I; *The Grass Harp*, 1953I; *King Lear*, 1952I; *Kyrie*, 1953I; *Lord Byron*, 1968I; *Louisiana Story* 1948I; *Missa Brevis*, 1924I; *Missa pro defunctis*, 1960I; *The Mother of Us All*, 1947I; *Oedipus Tyrannus*, 1941I; *Passacaglia*, 1922I; *Piano Portraits, 5 Vols.*, 1945I; *Piano Sonata No. 1*, 1929I; *Piano Sonata No. 2*, 1929I; *Piano Sonata No. 3*, 1930I; *Piano Sonata No. 4*, 1940I; *The Plow That Broke the Plains*, 1936I; *Poèmes de la Duchesse de Rohan (3)*, 1928I; *Portraits (5) for Four Clarinets*, 1929I; *Psalm 123*, 1922I; *Psalm 133*, 1922I; *Psalm 135*, 1924I; *The River*, 1937I; *Sanctus*, 1926I; *Serenade for Flute & Violin*, 1931I; *Les soirées bagnolaises*, 1928I; *Solemn Music*, 1949I; *Sonata da Chiesa for Winds*, 1926I; *Sonata for Flute Alone*, 1943I; *Songs to Poems of William Blake (5)*, 1951I; *Songs to Poems of Thomas Campion (4)*, 1951I; *Stabat Mater*, 1931I; *String Quartet No. 1*, 1931I; *String Quartet No. 2*, 1932I; *Suite No. 2, "Portraits,"* 1944I; *Symphony No. 2*, 1931I; *Symphony No. 3*, 1972I; *Symphony on a Hymn Tune*, 1928I; *The Trojan Women*, 1940I; *Variations & Fugue on Sunday School Themes*, 1927I; *Violin Sonata No. 1*, 1930I; *Voluntaries (3) for Organ*, 1985I
Thórarinsson, Leifur: *Sonata for Manuela*, 1978I; *Symphony No. 1*, 1963I; *Symphony No. 2*, 1975I
Thorne, Francis: *Burlesque Overture*, 1964I; *Cello Concerto*, 1974I; *Echoes of Spoon River*, 1976I; *Elegy for Orchestra*, 1963I; *Gemini Variations*, 1968I; *Lyric Variations*, 1967I; *Lyric Variations II, III*, 1972I; *Money Matters*, 1988I; *Piano Concerto No. 1*, 1965I; *Piano Concerto No. 2*, 1973I; *Piano Concerto No. 3*, 1990I; *Piano Sonata*, 1972I; *Pop Partita*, 1976I; *Rhapsodic Variations*, 1965I; *Spoon River Overture*, 1977I; *String Quartet No. 1*, 1960I; *String Quartet No. 2*, 1967I; *String Quartet No. 3*, 1975I; *String Quartet No. 4*, 1983I; *Symphony in One Movement (No. 1)*, 1961I; *Symphony No. 1*, 1960I; *Symphony No. 2*, 1964I; *Symphony No. 3*, 1969I; *Symphony No. 4*, 1977I; *Symphony No. 5*, 1984I; *Symphony No. 6*, 1992I; *Symphony No. 7*, 1995I
Thrane Waldemar: *A Mountain Adventure*, 1824I
Thuille, Ludwig: *Cello Sonata*, 1902I; *Sextet for Piano & Winds, Opus 6*, 1888I
Thybo, Leif: *Cello Sonata*, 1950I; *Markus-Passionen*, 1964I; *Piano Concerto*, 1963I; *Piano Trio No. 1*, 1976I; *String Quartet No. 1*, 1963I; *String Quartet No. 2*, 1990I; *Violin Sonata No. 1*, 1953I; *Violin Sonata No. 2*, 1960I
Tibbits, George: *Fantasy on the ABC*, 1975I
Tichel, Frank: *Radiant Voices*, 1993I
Tiensuu, Jukka: *Ai*, 1994I; *Sound of Life*, 1993I
Tiessen, Heinz: *Symphony No. 1*, 1911I; *Symphony No. 2*, 1912I
Tigranian, Arman: *Anush*, 1912I; *David-bek*, 1949I
Tijardović, Ivo: *Marco Polo*, 1960I
Tinel, Edgard: *Polyeucte Overture*, 1878I
Tippett, Michael: *Byzantium*, 1990I; *A Child of Our Time*, 1941I; *Concerto for Double String Orchestra*, 1939I; *Concerto for Orchestra*, 1963I; *Concerto for String Trio*, 1979I; *The Heart's Assurance*, 1950I; *The Ice Break*, 1977I; *Horn Quartet No. 1*, 1957I; *King Priam*, 1961I; *The Knot Garden*, 1970I; *Magnificat & Nunc Dimittis*, 1961I; *The Mask of Time*, 1983I; *The Midsummer Marriage*, 1952I; *New Year*, 1989I; *Piano*

A *Births*   B *Deaths*   C *Debuts*   D *New Positions*
E *Prizes/Honors*

Concerto, 1955I; *Piano Sonata No. 1*, 1942I; *Piano Sonata No. 2*, 1962I; *Piano Sonata No. 3*, 1972I; *Piano Sonata No. 4*, 1984I; *Preludio al Vespro de Monteverdi*, 1946I; *String Quartet No. 1 in A*, 1935I; *String Quartet No. 2*, 1944I; *String Quartet No. 3*, 1945I; *String Quartet No. 4*, 1978I; *String Quartet No. 5*, 1991I; *Suite in D for Orchestra*, 1948I; *Symphony No. 1*, 1945I; *Symphony No. 2*, 1958I; *Symphony No. 3*, 1972I; *Symphony No. 4*, 1977I; *The Vision of St. Augustine*, 1966I; *The Weeping Babe*, 1944I

Tishchenko, Boris: *Inventions (12) for Organ*, 1964I; *Piano Concerto*, 1962I; *Portraits (12) for Organ*, 1992I; *Sonata No. 1 for Solo Violin*, 1957I; *Sonata No. 2 for Solo Violin*, 1976I; *Sonata No. 9, Opus 114*, 1992I; *String Quartet No. 1*, 1957I; *String Quartet No. 2*, 1959I; *String Quartet No. 3*, 1969I; *String Quartet No. 4*, 1980I; *String Quartet No. 5*, 1984I; *Violin Concerto No. 1*, 1958I

Tisné, Antoine: *Altimira*, 1975I; *Luminescenes*, 1974I; *Preludes for Organ*, 1989I; *Processional*, 1993I

Titov, Anton: *Andromeda and Perseus*, 1802I; *Blanka*, 1803I; *The Brewer*, 1796I; *La caverne orientale, The Wedding of Filatka*, 1808I; *Credulous Folk*, 1812I; *Emmerich Tekkely*, 1812I; *The Hungarian*, 1806I; *The Judgment of Solomon*, 1805I; *The Mogul's Feast*, 1823I; *Nurzadakh*, 1807I; *The Old Bachelor*, 1809I; *An Old Fashioned Christmas*, 1813I; *The Wedding of Filatka*, 1808I; *Das Wolkenkind*, 1845I; *Yam*, 1805I

Tobias, Richard: *String Quartet No. 1*, 1899I; *Violin Concerto in B♭*, 1769I; *Concertos (6) for German Flute*, 1770I

Toch, Ernst: *Big Ben, Opus 62*, 1934I; *Dance Suite*, 1923I; *Egon & Emilie, Opus 46*, 1928I; *Der Fächer*, 1930I; *The Idle Stroller Suite*, 1938I; *The Last Tale*, 1962I; *Piano Concerto*, 1926I; *Piano Profiles*, 1946I; *Piano Quintet, Opus 64*, 1938I; *Piano Sonata No. 2*, 1962I; *Pinocchio*, 1935I; *String Quartet No. 6*, 1905I; *String Quartet No. 7*, 1908I; *String Quartet No. 8*, 1910I; *String Quartet No. 9*, 1919I; *String Quartet No. 10*, 1921I; *String Quartet No. 11*, 1924I; *String Quartet No. 12, Opus 70*, 1946I; *String Quartet No. 13*, 1953I; *String Trio*, 1936I; *Symphony No. 1, Opus 72*, 1950I; *Symphony No. 2, Opus 73*, 1951I; *Symphony No. 3*, 1955I; *Symphony No. 4, Opus 80*, 1957I; *Symphony No. 5, "Jephtha,"* 1961I; *Symphony No. 6*, 1963I; *Symphony No. 7*, 1964I; *Violin Sonata No. 1*, 1913I; *Violin Sonata No. 2*, 1928I; *Wegwende*, 1925I

Toda, Kunio: *Bassoon Concerto*, 1966I; *Passacaglia & Fugue*, 1994I; *Symphony*, 1956I

Toebosch, Louis: *Movements (3) for Organ*, 1986I; *Orgelspeil*, 1975I; *Postludia (2) for Organ*, 1964I; *Preludium et Fuga super*, 1954I; *Te Deum laudemus*, 1954I; *Tryptique*, 1939I

Toeschi, Carlo: *Die Americaner*, 1784I; *Feste del seraglio*, 1763I; *Florine*, 1784I; *Flute Concertos (4)*, 1763I; *Grandes Symphonies (3), Opus 8*, 1769I; *Symphonies (6), Opus 1*, 1762I; *Symphonies (6), Opus 6*, 1769I; *Symphonies (6), Opus 7*, 1773I; *Symphonies (3), Opus 10*, 1773I; *Symphonies (6), Opus 12*, 1777I; *Symphonies (6), Opus 30*, 1765I; *Telemaque*, 1762I; *Violin Concerto in D*, 1770I

Togni, Camille: *Recitative*, 1962I

Tokuhide, Niimi: *Concerto No. 1 for Organ*, 1991I; *Piano Concerto No. 1*, 1984I; *Piano Concerto No. 2, "Eyes of the Creator,"* 1993I; *String Quartet*, 1994I; *Wind Spiral*, 1991I

Toldrá, Eduard: *String Quartet, "Views of the Sea,"* 1921I

Tole, Vasíl S.: *Concerto for Orchestra*, 1990I; *Dichotomy*, 2000I; *Violin Sonata*, 1988I

Tomásek, Jaroslav: *Seraphine*, 1811I

Tomaek, Václav: *Requiem in c*, 1820I

Tomasi, Henri: *Les barbaresques*, 1960I; *La Grisi*, 1935I; *Nana*, 1962I

Tommasini, Vincenzo: *Concerto for String Quartet*, 1939I; *Harp Sonata*, 1938I; *String Quartet No. 2*, 1909I; *String Quartet No. 3*, 1926I; *String Quartet No. 4*, 1943I; *Violin Concerto*, 1932I; *Violin Sonata*, 1917I

Toradze, David: *Symphony No. 1*, 1946I; *Symphony No. 2*, 1968I

Torke, Michael: *Adjustable Wrench*, 1987I; *Black & White*, 1988I; *Bone*, 1994I; *The Book of Proverbs*, 1996I; *Brick-Symphony*, 1997I; *Bright Blue Music*, 1985I; *Bronze* (piano concerto), 1990I; *Central Park; Chalk* (string quartet), 1992I; *December*, 1995I; *Ecstatic Orange*, 1988I; *Four Proverbs*, 1993I; *Four Seasons*, 1999I; *Green*, 1986I; *Javelin*, 1994I; *King of Hearts*, 1995I; *Mass*, 1990I; *Music on the Floor*, 1992I; *Nylon*, 1994I; *Overnight Mail*, 1997I; *Piano Concerto*, 1993I; *Purple*, 1987I; *Red*, 1991I; *Rust*, 1989I; *Slate*, 1989I; *Strawberry Fields*, 1999I; *String Quartet July 19*, 1996I; *The Telephone Book*, 1995I; *White Pages*, 1995I; *The Yellow Pages*, 1985I

Tormis, Veljo: *Estonian Ballads*, 1980I; *Estonian Calendar Songs*, 1967I; *Ingrain Evenings*, 1979I; *Izhorian Epic*, 1975I; *Karelian Destiny*, 1989I; *Livonian Heritage*, 1970I; *Songs of the Ancient Sea*, 1979I; *Votic Wedding Songs*, 1971I; *Vepsian Paths*, 1983I

Tortelier, Paul: *Double Concerto for Two Cellos*, 1950I; *Suite for Solo Cello*, 1944I

Tournemire, Charles: *Apocalypse de St. Jean, Opus 63*, 1935I; *Cello Sonata, Opus 5*, 1895I; *Chorals-poèmes (7), Opus 67*, 1935I; *Cloches de Châteauneuf-du-Faou, Opus 62*, 1933I; *Dialogue sacré, Opus 50*, 1919I; *Les dieux sont morts, Opus 42*, 1912I; *Fantaisie symphonique, Opus 64*, 1934I; *Fresque symphonique sacrée 1*, 1938I; *Fresque symphonique sacrée II*, 1939I; *La légende de Tristan, Opus 53*, 1926I; *Melodies (3), Opus 7*, 1896I; *Musique orante, Opus 61*, 1933I; *Nittetis, Opus 30*, 1907I; *Offertoire, Opus 10*, 1895I; *L'orgue mystique, Opus 55-57*, 1932I; *La Passion du Christ*, 1937I; *Petites fleurs musicales, Opus 66*, 1934I; *Piano*

❋

F *Biographical*   G *Cultural Beginnings*   H *Musical Literature*
    I *Musical Compositions*

Tournemire, Charles: (*cont.*)
Pieces, Little (6), Opus 20, 1900I; *Piano Quintet, Opus 15*, 1898I; *Piano Serenade, Opus 9*, 1896I; *Piano Sonata, Opus 17*, 1899I; *Piano Trio, Opus 22*, 1901I; *Pièce symphonique, Opus 16*, 1899I; *Poème (organ)*, 1910I; *Poème for Cello & Piano*, 1908I; *Poème mystique, Opus 33*, 1908I; *Poèmes (3), Opus 59*, 1932I; *Postludes libres, Opus 68*, 1935I; *Il poverello di Assisi, Opus 73*, 1938I; *Préludes-poèmes, Opus 58*, 1932I; *Psalm LVII, Opus 37*, 1909I; *Psalm XLVI, Opus 45*, 1913I; *La Queste du Saint Graal, Opus 54*, 1927I; *Rhapsodie, Opus 29*, 1904I; *Sagesse, Opus 34*, 1908I; *Le sang de la sirène, Opus 27*, 1903I; *Sonata-poème for Violin & Piano*, 1935I; *Songs (3), Opus 46*, 1912I; *Suite de morceau I, Opus 19*, 1901I; *Suite de morceau II, Opus 24*, 1902I; *Suite évocatrice, Opus 74*, 1938I; *Symphonie sacrée, Opus 71*, 1936I; *Symphonie-Choral, Opus 69*, 1935I; *Symphony No. 2, "Ouessant," Opus 36*, 1909I; *Symphony No. 3, "Moscow," Opus 43*, 1913I; *Symphony No. 4, "Symphonic Pages," Opus 44*, 1913I; *Symphony No. 5, Opus 47*, 1914I; *Symphony No. 6, Opus 48*, 1918I; *Symphony No. 7, "Les danses de la vie," Opus 49*, 1922I; *Symphony No. 8, "La symphonie du triomphe de la mort," Opus 51*, 1924I; *Triptyque, Opus 39*, 1910I; *Viola Suite, Opus 11*, 1897I; *Violin Sonata, Opus 1*, 1893I
Tovey, Donald: *The Bride of Dionysus*, 1929I; *Cello Concerto*, 1934I; *Piano Concerto*, 1903I; *Sonata for Solo Cello*, 1913I; *Symphony*, 1913I; *Variations on a Theme by Gluck for Flute & String; Quartet*, 1913I
Tower, Joan: *Amazon I*, 1977I; *Amazon II*, 1979I; *Amazon III*, 1982I; *Ascent for Organ*, 1996I; *Cello Concerto*, 1984I; *Clarinet Concerto*, 1988I; *Concerto for Orchestra*, 1991I; *Duets*, 1994I; *Fanfare for the Uncommon Woman I*, 1986I; *Flute Concerto*, 1989I; *Island Prelude*, 1989I; *Island Rhythms Overture*, 1985I; *Night Fields*, 1994I; *Percussion Quartet*, 1963I; *Petroushskates*, 1980I; *Piano Concerto No. 1, "Homage to Beethoven,"* 1985I; *Platinum Spirals*, 1976I; *Rapids (Piano Concerto No. 2)*, 1996I; *Sequoia*, 1981I; *Silver Ladders*, 1986I; *Sonata Profonde*, 1995I; *Stepping Stones*, 1993I; *Stepping Stones for Piano*, 1993I; *Tambour*, 1998I; *Très lent, "In Memoriam Olivier Messiaen,"* 1994I; *Valentine Trills*, 1996I
Towner, Daniel: *Trust and Obey*, 1887I
Tozzi Antonio: *Il re pastore*, 1767I
Traetta, Filippo: *The Daughters of Zion*, 1829I
Traetta, Tommaso: *Alessandro nelle Indie*, 1762I; *Amor in trappola*, 1768I; *Amore e Psyche*, 1773I; *Antigona*, 1772I; *Antigono*, 1764I; *Armida*, 1761I; *Artenice*, 1778I; *Buono d'Antona*, 1756I; *Il cavaliere errante*, 1777I; *Demofoonte*, 1758I; *La Didone abbandonata*, 1757I; *La disfatta di Dario*, 1778I; *Enea e Lavinia*, 1761I; *Enea nel Lazio*, 1760I; *Ezio*, 1757I; *La fante furba*, 1756I; *Il farnace*, 1751I; *Germondo*, 1776I; *Ifigenia in Aulide*, 1759I; *Ifigenia in Tauride*, 1763I; *L'incredulo*, 1755I; *Ippolito ed Aricia*, 1759I; *L'isola disabitata*, 1768I; *I lindaridi*, 1760I; *Lucio Vero*, 1774I; *La merope*, 1776I; *La nitteti*, 1757I; *Le nozze contrastate*, 1754I; *Olimpiade*, 1758I; *The Passion According to St. John*, 1779I; *I pastori felici*, 1753I; *Rex Salomone*, 1766I; *Semiramide*, 1765I; *Le serve rivali*, 1766I; *Siroe re di Persia*, 1767I; *Sofonisba*, 1762I; *Solimano*, 1759I; *Symphony in D*, 1776I; *Telemacco*, 1777I; *Zenobia*, 1762I
Trambitsky, Victor: *Violin Concerto*, 1921I
Trapp, Max: *Piano Concerto*, 1930I; *Violin Concerto*, 1922I
Tremblay, George: *Chaparral Symphony*, 1938I; *Double Bass Sonata*, 1967I; *Exercises*, 1959I; *Exercise II*, 1960I; *Musique de feu*, 1991I; *The Phoenix: a Dance Symphony*, 1982I; *Piano Sonata No. 1*, 1938I; *Piano Sonata No. 2*, 1938I; *Piano Sonata No. 3*, 1957I; *String Quartet No. 1*, 1936I; *String Quartet No. 2*, 1962I; *String Quartet No. 4*, 1963I; *Symphony No. 1*, 1949I; *Symphony No. 2*, 1952I; *Symphony No. 3*, 1973I; *Wind Quintet*, 1940I
Trento, Vittorio: *Andromeda*, 1805I; *Climène*, 1811I; *The Deluge*, 1808I; *La finta ammalata*, 1793I; *Ifigenia in Aulide*, 1804I; *Ines de Castro*, 1803I
Trial, Armand E.: *La cause et les effets*, 1793I; *Le siège de Lille*, 1793I
Trial, Jean-Claude: *Esope a Cythere*, 1766I
Trifunović, Vitomir: *Violin Sonata*, 1958I
Trimble, Lester: *Boccaccio's Nightingale*, 1962I; *Episodes (5) for Piano & Orchestra*, 1962I; *Panels for Orchestra*, 1976I; *Panels I*, 1970I; *Panels II*, 1972I; *Panels III*, 1973I; *Panels IV*, 1974I; *Panel VI*, 1975I; *String Quartet No. 1*, 1950I; *String Quartet No. 2, "Pastorale,"* 1955I; *String Quartet No. 3*, 1975I; *Symphony No. 1*, 1951I; *Symphony No. 2*, 1968I; *Symphony No. 3, "The Tricentennial,"* 1985I
Tritto Giacomo: *Gli Americani*, 1802I
Trojahn, Manfred: *Cello Sonata*, 1983I; *Fantasia*, 1979I; *Requiem*, 1985I; *String Quartet No. 1*, 1976I; *String Quartet No. 2*, 1980I; *String Quartet No. 3*, 1983I; *Variations for Orchestra*, 1988I; *Violin Sonata*, 19893I
Trojan, Václav: *String Quartet No. 1*, 1929I
Truax, Barry: *Divan*, 1985I; *Dominion*, 1991I; *Song of Songs*, 1993I; *Sonic Landscape No. 1*, 1970I; *Sonic Landscape No. 4 for Organ*, 1977I; *Wings of Nike*, 1987I
Truhn, Friedrich: *Trilby*, 1835I

✷

A   *Births*   B   *Deaths*   C   *Debuts*   D   *New Positions*

E   *Prizes/Honors*

Trythall, Gil: *The Electric Womb*, 1969I; *Flute Sonata*, 1964I; *Harp Concerto*, 1963I; *Luxikon I*, 1978I; *Luxikon II*, 1981I; *The Music Lesson*, 1960I; *The Pastimes of Lord Caitanya*, 1992I; *Symphony*, 1958I; *The Terminal Opera*, 1982I

Trythall, Richard: *Piano Concerto "Composition,"* 1965I; *Piano Pieces (12)*, 1980I; *Symphony*, 1961I

Tsintsadze, Sulkhan: *Violin Concerto No. 1*, 1947I

Tsitsaros, Christos: *Piano Tales (9)*, 1993I

Tsontakis, George: *Bagatelles*, 1997I; *Birdwing Quintet*, 1983I; *Dust*, 1998I; *Eclipse*, 1995I; *The Epistle of James, Chapter I*, 1980I; *Erotokritos*, 1982I; *Five Sighs & a Fantasy*, 1984I; *Four Symphonic Quartets*, 1996I; *Galway Kinnell songs*, 1987I; *Gemini*, 1996I; *Ghost Variations for Piano*, 1991I; *Let the River Be Unbroken*, 1994I; *Mercurial Etudes*, 1988I; *Mood Sketches (3)*, 1988I; *October*, 2000I; *The Past, The Passion*, 1987I; *Requiescat*, 1996I; *Scenes from the Apocalypse*, 1978I; *Stabat Mater*, 1990I; *String Quartet No. 1*, 1980I; *String Quartet No. 2, "Emerson,"* 1984I; *String Quartet No. 3, "Coraggio,"* 1986I; *String Quartet No. 4*, 1989I; *Three Sighs, Three Variations*, 1981I

Tsvetanov, Tsvetan: *Cello Sonata*, 1973I; *Variations for String Quartet*, 1953I; *Violin Sonata*, 1955I

Tubin, Eduard: *Balakaika Concerto*, 1964I; *Double Bass Concerto*, 1948I; *Flute Sonata*, 1979I; *Kratt*, 1941I; *Piano Concerto*, 1946I; *Quartet on Estonian Motifs*, 1979I; *Saxophone Concerto*, 1951I; *Sonata for Solo Violin*, 1962I; *Symphony No. 1*, 1934I; *Symphony No. 2, "Legendary,"* 1937I; *Symphony No. 4, "Lyrical,"* 1943I; *Symphony No. 5*, 1946I; *Symphony No. 6*, 1954I; *Symphony No. 7*, 1958I; *Symphony No. 8*, 1966I; *Symphony No. 9, "Semplice,"* 1969I; *Symphony No. 10*, 1973I; *Viola Sonata*, 1965I; *Violin Concerto No. 1*, 1942I; *Violin Concerto No. 2*, 1945I; *Violin Sonata No. 1*, 1936I; *Violin Sonata No. 2*, 1949I

Tučapsky, Antonin: *Lauds*, 1976I; *Lenten Motets, (5)*, 1977I; *The Seven Sorrows*, 1989I

Tudor, David: *Electronic Web*, 1987I; *Electronics with Talking Shrimp*, 1986I; *Fluorescent Sound*, 1964I; *Forest Speech*, 1976I; *Hedgehog*, 1985I; *Island Eye Island Ear*, 1978I; *Neural Symtheses 6-9*, 1992I; *Neural Synthesis II*, 1993I; *Phonemes*, 1981I; *Pulsars*, 1976I; *Pulsars II*, 1978I; *RainForest III*, 1972I; *RainForest IV*, 1973I; *Sea Tails*, 1983I; *Tailing Dream*, 1985I; *Volatils with Sonic Reflection*, 1988I; *Web for J. C. I*, 1987I; *Web for J. C. II*, 1987I

Tull, Fisher: *Dialogues for Solo Percussionists & Orchestra*, 1988I; *Trumpet Concerto*, 1965I

Tuomela, Tapio: *Symphony No. 1*, 1991I

Turina, Joaquín: *El castillo de Almodóvar*, 1931I; *Cuentos de España, Set 1*, 1918I; *Cuentos de España, Set II*, 1928I; *Danzas Fantásticas*, 1920I; *Evangelio*, 1915I; *Evocaciones, Opus 46*, 1929I

Turina, Joachín: *Guitar Sonata*, 1932I; *Homenaje a Tárrega for Guitar*, 1935I; *Jardin de Oriente*, 1923I; *Margot*, 1914I; *Musette*, 1915I; *Navidad*, 1916I; *Organ Prelude*, 1914I; *Piano Quartet*, 1931I; *Piano Quintet*, 1907I; *La Procesión del rocío*, 1913I; *Rapsodia Sinfónica*, 1931I; *Sevillana for Guitar*, 1923I; *Sinfonia Sevillana*, 1920I; *String Quartet*, 1911I; *Violin Sonata No. 1*, 1929I; *Violin Sonata No. 2*, 1934I

Turnage, Mark-Anthony: *Blood on the Floor*, 1996I; *The Country of the Blind*, 1997I; *Greek*, 1988I; *Killing Time*, 1991I; *Kai (cello concerto)*, 1990I; *The Silber Tassie*, 1999I; *String Quartet, "Are You Sure?,"* 1990I; *Three Screaming Popes*, 1989I

Turner, Robert: *Voluntaries (6)*, 1959I

Turok, Paul: *Richard III*, 1975I; *String Quartet, No. 1*, 1955I; *String Quartet No. 2*, 1969I; *String Quartet No. 3*, 1980I; *Symphony*, 1955I; *Transcendental Etudes (3)*, 1970I; *Ultima Thule*, 1981I; *Variations on a Theme by Schoenberg*, 1952I; *Violin Concerto*, 1953I

Tuthill, Burnet: *Clarinet Quintet*, 1936I; *Nocturne for Flute & String Quartet*, 1933I; *Requiem, Opus 38*, 1960I; *String Quartet No. 1, Opus 34*, 1953I; *Symphony in C, Opus 21*, 1940I; *Trombone Concerto*, 1967I; *Tuba Concerto*, 1975I

Tuukkanen, Kalervo: *Violin Concerto No. 1*, 1943I; *Violin Concerto No. 2*, 1956I

Tüür, Erkki-Sven: *Crystallisatio*, 1995I; *Excitato ad contemplandum*, 1995I; *Exodus*, 1998I; *Glamour of the Game*, 1995I; *Requiem*, 1994I; *Symphony No. 1*, 1984I; *Symphony No. 2*, 1987I; *Symphony No. 3*, 1997I; *Tropic of Capricorn*, 1991I; *Zeitraum*, 1992I

Tveitt, Geirr: *Piano Concerto No. 1*, 1930I; *Piano Concerto No. 2*, 1933I; *Piano Concerto No. 3*, 1947I; *Piano Concerto No. 4*, 1947I; *Piano Concerto No. 5*, 1954I; *Piano Concerto No. 6*, 1960I; *Violin Concerto*, 1939I

Twardowski, Romuald: *Concerto for Orchestra*, 1957I; *The Naked Prince*, 1960I; *Piano Concerto No. 1*, 1956I; *Piano Concerto No. 2*, 1984I; *The Magician's Statues*, 1963I

Uber, Christian: *Der frohe Tag*, 1815I

Uliyanich, Victor: *Sacred Sounding of Light*, 1992I; *The Star Wind of Casseopeia*, 1990I

Ullmann, Victor: *The Fall of the Antichrist*, 1935I; *Piano Concerto*, 1939; *Slavonic Rhapsody*, 1940I; *String Quartet No. 3*, 1943I; *Der zerbrochene Krug*, 1942I

Umlauf, Michael: *Der Grenadier*, 1812I

Ung, Chinary: *Antiphonal Spirals*, 1995I; *Grand Spiral (band)*, 1990I; *Inner Voices*, 1986I; *Luminous Spirals*, 1997I; *Mirrors (7) for Piano*, 1997I; *Rising Light*, 1998I; *Rising Spirals*, 1996I; *Spiral I*, 1987I;

F *Biographical*   G *Cultural Beginnings*   H *Musical Literature*
I *Musical Compositions*

Ung, Chinary: (cont.)
   Spiral II, 1989I; *Spiral III* (string quartet), 1990I; *Spiral VI*, 1992I; *Spiral VII*, 1994I; *String Quartet No. 1*, 1991I; *Triple Concerto*, 1992I
Uny, Isang: *Clarinet Quintet No. 2*, 1994I
Urspruch, Anton: *Lieder, Opus 25*, 1887I
Ussachevsky, Vladimir: *Computer Piece No. 1*, 1968I; *Conflict*, 1971I; *Creation Prologue*, 1961I; *Dances & Fanfares for a Festive Occasion*, 1980I; *Jubilee Cantata*, 1938I; *Missa Brevis*, 1972I; *Of Wood & Brass*, 1965I; *A Poem in Cycles & Bells (tape)*, 1954I; *Studies in Sound Plus*, 1958I
Ustvolskaya, Galina: *Piano Concerto*, 1946I; *Piano Sonata No. 1*, 1947I; *Piano Sonata No. 2*, 1949I; *Piano Sonata No. 3*, 1952I; *Piano Sonata No. 4*, 1957I; *Piano Sonata No. 5*, 1986I; *Piano Sonata No. 6*, 1988I; *Symphony No. 1*, 1955I; *Symphony No. 2*, 1979I; *Symphony No. 3*, 1983I; *Symphony No. 4*, 1987I; *Violin Sonata*, 1952I
Uttini, Francesco: *Aline Queen of Golconda*, 1776I; *Il re pastore*, 1755I; *Thetis och Pelee*, 1773I; *Violin Trios (6), Opus 1*, 1768I
Vaccai, Nicola: *Bianca di Messina*, 1826I; *Giovanna Gray*, 1836I; *Giovanna d'Arco*, 1827I; *Giulietta e Romeo*, 1825I; *Il lupo di Ostenda*, 1818I; *Marco Visconti*, 1838I; *La pastorella feudataria*, 1824I; *Pietro il grande*, 1824I; *Il precipizio*, 1826I; *Saladino e Clotilde*, 1828I; *Saul*, 1829I; *I solitari di Scozia*, 1815I; *La sposa di Messina*, 1839I; *Virginia*, 1845I
Vachon, Pierre: *Les femmes et le secret*, 1767I; *Hippomène et Atalante*, 1769I; *Sara*, 1773I; *String Quartets (6), Opus 5*, 1775I; *String Quartets (6), Opus 6*, 1773I; *String Quartets (6), Opus 7*, 1773I; *String Quartets (6), Opus 9*, 1774I; *String Quartets (6), Opus 11*, 1872I; *String Trios (6), Opus 5*, 1772I; *String Trios (6), Opus 6*, 1772I; *Symphonies (6), Opus 2*, 1761I; *Violin Sonatas (6), Opus 1*, 1760I; *Violin Sonatas (6), Opus 3*, 1769I
Vadé, Jean-Joseph: *Il était temps*, 1754I; *La fileuse*, 1752I; *L'impromptu du coeur*, 1757I; *Le mauvais plaisant*, 1757I; *Le poirier*, 1752I; *Les raccoleurs*, 1756I; *Le rien*, 1753I; *Le suffisant*, 1753I; *Le trompeur trompé*, 1754I
Vainberg, Mosei: *Easy Pieces (17)*, 1946I; *Piano Sonata No. 1*, 1940I; *Symphony No. 4*, 1957I; *Trumpet Concerto*, 1967I; *Violin Concerto*, 1960I
Valen, Fartein: *String Quartet*, 1932I; *Violin Concerto*, 1940I
Vainberg, Mosei: *Easy Pieces (17)*, 1946I; *Piano Sonata No. 1*, 1940I; *Symphony No. 4*, 1957I; *Trumpet Concerto*, 1967I; *Violin Concerto*, 1960I
Valen, Fartein: *String Quartet*, 1932I; *Violin Concerto*, 1940I
Valentino Fioravanti: *Gl' inganni fortunati*, 1786I
Van der Stucken, Frank: *Pax Triumphans*, 1900I; *Prologue to William Ratcliffe*, 1883I; *The Tempest*, 1882I
Vanhal, Johan Baptist: *String Quartets (6), Opus 3*, 1776I; *String Quartets (6), Opus 4*, 1780I; *String Quartets (6), Opus 33*, 1785I; *Viola Sonatas (4), Opus 51*, 1781I; *Viola Sonata No. 5 in E♭*, 1787I
Van Vactor, David: *Etudes (24) for Flute*, 1933I; *Flute Concerto*, 1932I; *The Masque of the Red Death*, 1952I; *Overture to a Comedy I*, 1934I; *Overture to a Comedy II*, 1941I; *Piano Pieces (5)*, 1962I; *Quintet for Flute & String Quartet*, 1932I; *Sinfonia Breve*, 1966I; *String Quartet No. 1*, 1940I; *String Quartet No. 2*, 1950I; *Symphony No. 1*, 1937I; *Symphony No. 2, "Music for the Marines,"* 1943I; *Symphony No. 3*, 1958I; *Symphony No. 4, "Walden,"* 1971I; *Symphony No. 5*, 1975I; *Symphony No. 6*, 1980I; *Symphony No. 7*, 1983I; *Symphony No. 8*, 1984I; *Viola Concerto*, 1940I; *Violin Concerto*, 1951I
Van de Vate, Nancy: *All Quiet on the Western Front*, 1998I; *Chernobyl*, 1987I; *Dark Nebulae*, 1981I; *Der Herrscher und Das Mädchen*, 1995I; *Krakow Concerto*, 1988I; *Night Journey*, 1996I; *Piano Concerto*, 1968I; *Piano Preludes (9)*, 1978I; *Piano Sonata No. 1*, 1978I; *Piano Sonata No. 2*, 1983I; *Pieces (12) on One to Twelve Notes for Piano*, 1986I; *Viola Concerto*, 1990I; *Violin Concerto No. 2*, 1996I
Vantus, Istvan: *The Golden Coffin*, 1975I
Varèse, Edgard: *Amériques*, 1921I; *Arcana*, 1927I; *Bourgogne*, 1910I; *Density 21.5*, 1936I; *Déserts (orchestra & tape)*, 1954I; *Ecuatorial*, 1934I; *Étude pour Espace*, 1947I; *Hyperprisms*, 1923I; *Intégrales*, 1925I; *Ionisation for Percussion*, 1931I; *Nocturnal*, 1961I; *Octandre*, 1924I; *Offrandes*, 1922I; *Poème Electronique*, 1958I
Vasks, Pēteris: *Cello Concerto*, 1994I; *Musica Dolorosa*, 1983I; *Symphony No. 3 for Strings, "Voices,"* 1991I
Vaughan Williams, Ralph: *Along the Field*, 1927I; *Benedicite*, 1929I; *Blake Songs (10)*, 1958I; *Bucolic Suite*, 1900I; *Communion Service in g*, 1922I; *Concerto Accademico (violin)*, 1925I; *Concerto Grosso for Strings*, 1950I; *A Cotswold Romance*, 1951I; *Dona Nobis Pacem*, 1936I; *English Folk Song Suite*, 1923I; *Fantasia on "Old 104" Psalm Tune*, 1949I; *Fantasia on a Theme by Thomas Tallis*, 1910I; *Fantasia on Christmas Carols*, 1912I; *Fen & Flood*, 1956I; *Festival Te Deum*, 1937I; *Flos Campi*, 1925I; *Hodie*, 1954I; *The House of Life*, 1904I; *Hugh, the Drover*, 1924I; *In the Fen Country*, 1904I; *Job, A Masque for Dancing* 1930I; *The Lark Ascending (violin)*, 1920I; *Last Songs (4)*, 1958I; *Magnificat*, 1932I; *Mass*, 1899I; *Mass in g*, 1922I; *Mystical Songs (5)*, 1911I; *Nocturnes (3)*, 1908I; *Norfolk Rhapsody No. 1*, 1906I; *Norfolk Rhapsodies II, III,*

A   *Births*   B   *Deaths*   C   *Debuts*   D   *New Positions*
E   *Prizes/Honors*

1907I; *Old King Cole,* 1923I; *On Wenlock Edge,* 1909I; *Organ Overture,* 1890I; *An Oxford Elegy,* 1949I; *Partita for Double String Orchestra,* 1938I; *Piano Concerto,* 1931I; *The Pilgrim's Progress,* 1951I; *Prelude & Fugue in c,* 1921I; *Riders to the Sea,* 1936I; *Sancta Civitas,* 1925I; *Scott of the Antarctic,* 1948I; *A Sea Symphony (No. 1),* 1909I; *Serenade in A,* 1897I; *Serenade for Small Orchestra,* 1901I; *Serenade to Music,* 1938I; *The Shepherds on the Delectable Mountains,* 1922I; *Sir John in Love,* 1928I; *Songs of Travel,* 1904I; *String Quartet in C,* 1898I; *Suite for Viola & Orchestra,* 1934I; *Symphony No. 2, "London,"* 1913I; *Symphony No. 3, "A Pastoral Symphony,"* 1921I; *Symphony No. 4 in c,* 1934I; *Symphony No. 5,* 1943I; *Symphony No. 6 in e,* 1947I; *Symphony No. 7, "Sinfonia Antarctica,"* 1952I; *Symphony No. 8,* 1955I; *Symphony No. 9,* 1957I; *Te Deum,* 1928I; *Toward the Unknown Region,* 1907I; *Tuba Concerto,* 1954I; *Variants of "Dives & Lazarus," Five,* 1939I; *The Wasps,* 1909I
Vega, Aurelio de la: *Adiós,* 1977I; *Quintet for Winds,* 1959I; *String Quartet No. 1, "In Memoriam Alban Berg,"* 1957I
Vejvodová, Hana: *Pathways of Love,* 1990I; *Piano Concerto,* 1993I
Veltman, Michael: *Ja,* 1995I
Verdi, Giuseppe: *Aïda,* 1871I; *Alzira,* 1845I; *Attila,* 1846I; *La Battaglia di Legnano,* 1849I; *Il corsaro,* 1848I; *Don Carlo,* 1867I; *Ernani,* 1844I; *Falstaff,* 1893I; *La Forza del destino,* 1862I; *Un giorno di Regno,* 1840I; *Giovanni d'Arco,* 1845I; *Hymn of the Nations,* 1862I; *Jerusalem,* 1847I; *I Lombardi,* 1843I; *Luisa Miller,* 1849I; *Macbeth,* 1847I; *Manzoni Requiem,* 1874I; *The Masked Ball,* 1859I; *Nabucco,*1842I; *Obert, Count of San Bonifacio,* 1839I; *Othello,* 1887I; *Rigoletto,* 1851I; *Romances (6),* 1838I; *Sacred Pieces (4),* 1898I; *Sicilian Vespers,* 1855I; *Simon Boccanegra,* 1857I; *Stiffelio,* 1850I; *String Quartet in a,* 1873I; *La traviata,* 1853I; *Il Trovatore,* 1853I
Vereshchagin, Jaroslav: *Piano Sonata No. 1,* 1970I; *Piano Sonata No. 2,* 1975I; *String Quartet No. 2,* 1981I; *Violin Sonata,* 1993I
Veress, Sándor: *Clarinet Concerto,* 1982I; *Concerto for Piano, Strings & Percussion,* 1952I; *Csárdás (6),* 1938I; *Hommage à Paul Klee for Two Pianos,* 1951I; *Threnos,* 1945I; *Violin Sonata,* 1935I
Vermeulen, Matthijs: *Cello Sonata No. 2,* 1938I; *String Quartet,* 1961I; *Symphony No. 1,* 1914I; *Symphony No. 2,* 1920I; *Symphony No. 3,* 1922I; *Symphony No. 4,* 1941I; *Symphony No. 5,* 1945I; *Symphony No. 6,* 1958I; *Symphony No. 7,* 1965I
Verrall, John: *Piano Concerto,* 1959I; *Piano Sonata,* 1951I; *Songs of Nature,* 1979I; *String Quartet No. 1,* 1941I; *String Quartet No. 2,* 1942I; *String Quartet No. 3,* 1948I; *String Quartet No. 4,* 1949I; *String Quartet No. 5,* 1952I; *String Quartet No. 6,* 1956I; *String Quartet No. 7,* 1961I; *Symphony No. 1,* 1939I; *Symphony No. 2,* 1948I; *Symphony No. 3,* 1968I; *Viola Concerto,* 1968I; *Violin Concerto,* 1947I
Vertovsky, Alexei: *Askold's Grave,* 1835I; *The Caliph's Amusement,* 1825I; *Grandmother's Parrot,* 1819I; *Homesickness,* 1839I; *The Madhouse,* 1822I; *Man and Wife,* 1830I; *The Miraculous Nose,* 1825I; *New Mischief,* 1822I; *The Old Hussar,* 1831I; *Pan Tsardovsky,* 1828I; *The Petitioner,* 1824I; *Quarantine,* 1820I; *Teacher and Pupil,* 1824I; *Vadim,* 1832I; *Who Is Brother? Who Is Sister?,* 1824I
Vesque von Püttlingen Johann: *Jeanne d'Arc,* 1840I; *Turandot,* 1838I
Viadot-Garcia Pauline: *Cendrillon,* 1904I; *L'ogre,* 1868I; *Trop de femmes,* 1867I
Vianna de Motta, José: *Fantasia dramatica,* 1893I; *Piano Concerto in A,* 1887I
Vibert, Mathieu: *Symphonie Funèbre,* 1948I
Victory, Gerald: *Irish Pictures (3),* 1980I
Vierne, Louis: *Baudelaire Poems (4),* 1924I; *Les Djinns,* 1925I; *Eros,* 1916I; *Messe basse,* 1913I; *Messe basse pour les défunts,* 1936I; *Messe Solennelle,* 1900I; *Organ Pieces (24) in Free Style,* 1913I; *Organ Symphony No. 1,* 1899I; *Organ Symphony No. 2,* 1903I; *Organ Symphony No. 3, Opus 28,* 1912I; *Organ Symphony No. 4,* 1914I; *Organ Symphony No. 5,* 1924I; *Organ Symphony No. 6,* 1930I; *Piano Preludes (12),* 1921I; *Piano Quintet,* 1917I; *Poem for Piano & Orchestra,* 1922I; *Psyché,* 1926I; *Spleens et Détresses,* 1917I; *Suite bourguignonne,* 1900I; *Symphony,* 1908I; *Violin Sonata,* 1906I
Vieru, Anatol: *Cello Concerto,* 1962I; *Cello Sonata,* 1963I; *Clarinet Concerto,* 1975I; *Concerto for Orchestra,* 1955I; *Flute Concerto,* 1958I; *In the Sea of Sunsets,* 1998I; *Iona, Opus 1,* 1975I; *Kaleidoscope,* 1993I; *The Last Days,* 1995I; *Narration for Organ,* 1973I; *Piano Sonata No. 1,* 1976I; *Piano Sonata No. 2,* 1994I; *Piano Trio,* 1997I; *Saxophone Quartet,* 1990I; *String Quartet No. 1,* 1955I; *String Quartet No. 2,* 1956I; *String Quartet No. 3,* 1973I; *String Quartet No. 4,* 1980I; *String Quartet No. 5,* 1982I; *String Quartet No. 6,* 1986I; *String Quartet No. 7,* 1987I; *String Quartet No. 8,* 1991I; *Symphony No. 1, "Ode to Silence,"* 1967I; *Symphony No. 2,* 1973I; *Symphony No. 3, "An Earthquake Symphony,"* 1978I; *Symphony No. 4,* 1982I; *Symphony No. 5,* 1985I; *Symphony No. 6, "Exodus,"* 1989I; *Symphony No. 7, "Year of the Silent Sun,"* 1993I
Vieuxtemps, Henri: *Allegro & Scherzo, Opus 60,* 1884; *Allegro de Concert, Opus 59,* 1884I; *Ballade & Polonaise, Opus 38,* 1860I; *Bouquet américain, Opus 33,* 1855I; *Cello Concerto in a, Opus 46,* 1877I; *Etudes (36), Opus 48,* 1882I; *Etudes de Concert (6), Opus 16,* 1845I; *Fantaisie-caprice, Opus 11,* 1845I; *Fantaisies*

❈

Vieuxtemps, Henri: (*cont.*)
  brillantes (3), Opus 54, 1883I; *Fantasia appassionata, Opus 35*, 1860I; *Fantasia on Gounod's "Faust,"* 1870I;
  Fantasias (3) on Themes of Verdi, Opus 29, 1854I; *Feuille d'album, Opus 40*, 1864I; *Greetings to America,
  Opus 56*, 1883I; *Hommage à Paganini, Opus 9*, 1845I; *Impressions et réminiscences de Pologne, Opus 57*,
  1883I; *Mährchen (3), Opus 34*, 1859I; *Morceaux (6), Opus 85*, 1859I; *Morceaux de salon (6), Opus 22*,
  1847I; *Morceaux de salon (3), Opus 32*, 1855I; *Old England, Opus 42*, 1866I; *Romance (3) sans paroles,
  Opus 7*, 1845I; *Romance (4) sans paroles, Opus 9*, 1845I; *String Quartet No. 1 in e, Opus 44*, 1871I; *String
  Quartet No. 2 in c, Opus 51*, 1884I; *String Quartet No. 3 in B♭, Opus 52*, 1884I; *Suite for Violin in b, Opus
  43*, 1871I; *Variations on a Theme of Bellini, Opus 6*, 1845I; *Viola Sonata in B♭, Opus 36*, 1863I; *Violin
  Concerto No. 1 in E, Opus 10*, 1840I; *Violin Concerto No. 2 in f♯, Opus 19*, 1836I; *Violin Concerto No. 3 in a,
  Opus 25*, 1844I; *Violin Concerto No. 4 in d, Opus 31*, 1850I; *Violin Concerto No. 5 in a, Opus 37*, 1861I;
  Violin Concerto, No. 6 in G, Opus 47, 1882I; *Violin Concerto No. 7 in g, Opus 49*, 1882I; *Violin Sonata in
  D, Opus 12*, 1845I; *Voies du Coeur, Opus 53*, 1883I; *Voix intimes, Opus 45*, 1876I
Vigeland, Nils: *Eleven Pages for Piano*, 1984I
Villa-Lobos, Heitor: *A Prole do Bebé*, 1918I; *African Dances*, 1914I; *Amazonas*, 1917I; *Bachianas Brasileiras
  No. 1 for Eight Celli*, 1930I; *Bachianas Brasileiras No. 2*, 1930I; *Bachianas Brasileiras No. 3*, 1938I;
  Bachianas Brasileiras No. 5, 1938I; *Bachianas Brasileiras No. 7*, 1942I; *Bachianas Brasileiras No. 8*, 1944I;
  Brazilian Children's Carnival, 1920I; *Cello Concerto No. 1*, 1915I; *Cello Concerto No. 2*, 1953I; *Choros No. 1
  for Guitar*, 1920I; *Chôros No. 9*, 1929I; *Ciclo Brasileiro*, 1937I; *Cirandas*, 1926I; *Cirandinhas*, 1925I;
  Emperor Jones, 1956I; *Erosion of the Amazon*, 1950I; *Fantasia for Cello & Orchestra*, 1945I; *Frencette et Pia*,
  1929I; *Harmonica Concerto*, 1955I; *Malazarte*, 1921I; *Piano Concerto No. 1*, 1945I; *Piano Concerto No. 2*,
  1948I; *Piano Concerto No. 3*, 1957I; *Piano Concerto No. 4*, 1952I; *Piano Concerto No. 5*, 1954I; *Rudá–God
  of Love*, 1951I; *String Quartet No. 1*, 1915I; *String Quartet No. 2*, 1915I; *String Quartet No. 3*, 1916I;
  String Quartet No. 4, 1917I; *String Quartet No. 5*, 1931I; *String Quartet No. 6*, 1938I; *String Quartet No.
  7*, 1942I; *String Quartet No. 8*, 1944I; *String Quartet No. 9*, 1945I; *String Quartet No. 10*, 1946I; *String
  Quartet No. 11*, 1948I; *String Quartet No. 12*, 1950I; *String Quartet No. 13*, 1952I; *String Quartet No. 14*,
  1953I; *String Quartet No. 15*, 1954I; *String Quartet No. 16*, 1955I; *String Quartet No. 17*, 1958I; *Studies
  (12) for the Guitar*, 1929I; *Symphony No. 1, "The Unforeseen,"* 1916I; *Symphony No. 2, "Ascension,"*
  1917I; *Symphony No. 3, "The War,"* 1919I; *Symphony No. 4, "The Victory,"* 1919I; *Symphony No. 5, "The
  Peace,"* 1920I; *Symphony No. 6, "On the Outline of the Mountains of Brazil,"* 1944I; *Symphony No. 7*,
  1945I; *Symphony No. 8*, 1950I; *Symphony No. 9*, 1951I; *Symphony No. 10, "Amerinda,"* 1952I; *Symphony
  No. 11*, 1955I; *Symphony No. 12*, 1956I; *Uirapuru*, 1917I; *Violin Sonata No. 1*, 1913I; *Violin Sonata No. 2*,
  1914I
Vincent, John: *Symphony Poem after Descartes*, 1959I
Vine, Carl: *Flute Sonata*, 1992I; *Oboe Concerto*, 1996I; *Piano Concerto*, 1997I; *Piano Sonata No. 1*, 1987I;
  Piano Sonata No. 2, 1990I; *String Quartet No. 2*, 1984I; *String Quartet No. 3*, 1994I; *Symphony No. 2*,
  1988I; *Symphony No. 3*, 1990I; *Symphony No. 4*, 1993I; *Symphony No. 5*, 1995I; *Symphony No. 6*,
  "Choral," 1996I
Viotti, Giovanni Battista: *Violin Concerto No. 1 in C*, 1782I; *Violin Concerto No. 2 in E*, 1782I; *Violin
  Concerto No. 3 in A*, 1782I; *Violin Concerto No. 4 in D*, 1782I; *Violin Concerto No. 5 in C*, 1782I; *Violin
  Concerto No. 6 in E*, 1782I; *Violin Concerto No. 11 in A*, 1787I; *Violin Concerto No. 12 in B♭*, 1787I; *Violin
  Concerto No. 13 in A*, 1788I; *Violin Concerto No. 14 in a*, 1788I; *Violin Concerto No. 15 in B♭*, 1789I; *Violin
  Concerto No. 16 in e*, 1789I; *Violin Concerto No. 17 in d*, 1790I; *Violin Concerto No. 18 in e*, 1790I; *Violin
  Concerto No. 19 in g*, 1791I; *Violin Concerto No. 20*, 1792I; *Violin Concerto No. 21*, 1793I; *Violin Concerto
  No. 22 in a*, 1793I; *Violin Concerto No. 23*, 1793I; *Violin Concerto No. 24*, 1795I; *Violin Concerto No. 26 in
  B♭*, 1808I; *Violin Concerto No. 27 in C*, 1813I; *Violin Concerto No. 28 in d*, 1804I; *Violin Concerto No. 29 in
  e*, 1802I; *Violin Sonatas (6), Opus 4*, 1788I
Vito-Delvaux, Berthe di: *Horn Sonata*, 1966I
Vivier, Claude: *Siddartha*, 1977I
Vladigerov, Pancho: *Piano Concerto No. 1*, 1918I; *Piano Concerto No. 2*, 1930I; *Piano Concerto No. 3*, 1937I;
  Piano Concerto No. 4, 1953I; *Piano Concerto No. 5*, 1963I
Vlijmen Jan van: *A Wretch Clad in Black*, 1990I
Vogel, Charles Louis: *La moissonneuse*, 1853I; *Le nid de cigognes*, 1858I; *Le siège de Leyde*, 1847I
Vogel Johann Christoph: *Démophon*, 1788I; *Jepthe*, 1781I; *La toison d'or*, 1786I; *Violin Concerto*, 1782I
Vogler, George "Abbe": *Der Admiral*, 1810I; *Albert III on Baiern*, 1781I; *Der Auferstehung Jesu*, 1777I;
  Castor e Polluce, 1784I; *Deutsche Kirchenmusik*, 1777I; *Epimenides (?)*, 1806I; *Gustav Adolph*, 1792I;
  Hamlet, 1778I; *La kermesse*, 1783I; *Der Koppengeist auf Reisen*, 1802I; *Die Kreutz Fahrer*, 1802I; *Kriegslied*,
  1814I; *Laudate Dominum in B♭*, 1808I; *Lied an den Rhein*, 1814I; *Miserere in E♭*, 1789I; *Missa pasatorita in
  D*, 1768I; *Missa pastoritia in F*, 1775I; *Missa de quadragesima in F*, 1784I; *Missa solemnis in d*, 1784I;

❉

A *Births*   B *Deaths*   C *Debuts*   D *New Positions*

E *Prizes/Honors*

Organ Preludes, 1808I; *Piano Quartet in E*, 1778I; *Piano Trios (6), Opus 1*, 1776I; *Le rendez-vous de chasse*, 1772I; *Requiem in g*, 1776I; *Requiem in E♭*, 1809I; *Samori*, 1804I; *Symphonie concertante in E♭*, 1811I; *Symphony in G*, 1779I; *Symphony in d, "Pariser,"* 1782I; *Symphony in C, "Scanlan,"* 1798I; *Te Deum in D*, 1775I; *Te Deum in D*, 1797I; *Trauermusik auf Ludwig XVI*, 1793I; *Trio Sonatas (6), Opus 6*, 1782I; *Trio Sonatas (6), Opus 7*, 1783I; *Variation on "Ah, que dirais-je maman,"* 1808I; *Variations on Air de Marlborough*, 1791I; *Veni sancti spiritus in B♭*, 1817I

Volans, Kevin: *Cicada for Piano*, 1994I; *White Man Sleeps*, 1985I

Von Koch, Erland: *Symphony No. 2, "Sinfonia Dalecarlica,"* 1945I; *Viola Concerto*, 1946I

Voříek, Jan Vaclav: *Mass in B♭*, 1824I; *Rhapsodies (12), Opus 1*, 1818I; *Symphony in D*, 1821I

Wachner, Julian: *War Songs*, 1998I

Wächner, Wayne: *String Quartet No. 1*, 1992I

Wagenaar, Bernard: *Divertissement*, 1927I; *From a Very Little Sphinx*, 1921I; *Piano Sonata*, 1928I; *Pieces of Eight*, 1944I; *String Quartet No. 1*, 1926I; *String Quartet No. 2*, 1932I; *String Quartet No. 3*, 1936I; *String Quartet No. 4*, 1960I; *Symphony No. 1*, 1926I; *Symphony No. 2*, 1930I; *Symphony No. 3*, 1936I; *Symphony No. 4*, 1946I; *Triple Concerto*, 1935I; *Violin Concerto*, 1940I; *Violin Sonata*, 1925I

Wagenseil Georg Christoph: *Le cacciatrici amanti*, 1755I; *Demetrio*, 1760I; *Gioas, re di Giuda*, 1755I; *Prometeo Assoluto*, 1762I; *La redenzione*, 1755I; *Il roveto di Mose*, 1756I; *Symphonies (3), Opus 1*, 1755I; *Symphonies (6), Opus 2*, 1756I; *Symphonies (6), Opus 3*, 1760I

Wagner, Joseph F.: *Concert Preludes (12) for Organ*, 1974I; *Hudson River Legend*, 1941I; *Organ Concerto*, 1963I; *Piano Concerto*, 1929I; *Piano Sonata*, 1946I; *String Quartet No. 1*, 1940I; *Symphony No. 1*, 1934I; *Symphony No. 3*, 1951I; *Violin Concerto No. 1*, 1930I; *Violin Concerto No. 2*, 1956I

Wagner, Melinda: *Concerto for Flute, String & Percussion*, 1998I

Wagner, Richard: *Columbus Overture*, 1835I; *A Faust Overture*, 1840I; *Die Feen*, 1833I; *The Flying Dutchman*, 1841I; *Götterdämmerung*, 1874I; *Grosser Festmarsch*, 1876I; *Die Hochzeit*, 1832I; *Huldigungsmarsch*, 1864I; *Kaisermarsch*, 1871I; *Das Liebesverbot*, 1835I; *Lohengrin*, 1850I; *The Love Feast of the Apostles*, 1843I; *Die Meistersinger von Nurnburg*, 1868I; *Overture in B♭*, 1830I; *Overture in d*, 1831I; *Parsifal*, 1882I; *Polonia Overture*, 1836I; *Des Rheingold*, 1854I; *Rienzi*, 1840I; *Rule, Britannia Overture*, 1836I; *Sehnsucht*, 1895I; *Siegfried Ikyll*, 1870I; *Siegfried*, 1869I; *Symphony in C*, 1832I; *Tannhauser*, 1845I; *Trauermusik for Winds*, 1844I; *Tristan und Isolde*, 1859I; *Die Walküre*, 1856I; *Wesendonck Songs*, 1857I

Wagner, Siegfried: *Glück*, 1923I; *Scherzo*, 1922I; *Symphony in C*, 1925I

Walker, George: *Cello Concerto*, 1982I; *Folksongs for Orchestra*, 1990I; *Lilacs*, 1996I; *Mass*, 1978I; *Orpheus*, 1994I; *Piano Concerto*, 1975I; *Piano Sonata No. 1*, 1953I; *Piano Sonata No. 2*, 1957I; *Piano Sonata No. 3*, 1975I; *Piano Sonata No. 4*, 1985I; *Piano Variations*, 1953I; *Sinfonia, No. 2*, 1990I; *String Quartet No. 1*, 1946I; *String Quartet No. 2*, 1968I; *Symphony No. 1*, 1984I; *Violin Sonata No. 1*, 1957I; *Violin Sonata No. 2*, 1979I; *Wind Set*, 1999I

Walker, William: *Triple Concerto*, 1995I

Wallace, Stewart: *Hopper's Wife*, 1997I; *Peter Pan*, 2000I

Wallace, (William) Vincent: *The Amber Witch*, 1861I; *The Desert Flower*, 1863I; *Matilda of Hungary*, 1847I; *Maritana*, 1845I

Wallace, William: *The Passing of Beatrice*, 1892I; *Piano Concerto No. 2*, 1999I; *Sir William Wallace*, 1905I; *Sister Helen*, 1899I; *Villon*, 1909I

Wallach, Joelle: *Quartet 1999*, 1999I; *String Quartet 1986*, 1986I; *String Quartet 1995*, 1995I

Walton, William: *The Bear*, 1967I; *Belshazzar's Feast*, 1931I; *Capriccio Burlesco*, 1968I; *Cello Concerto*, 1956I; *Façade*, 1923I; *Gloria*, 1961I; *Magnificat*, 1974I; *Missa Brevis*, 1966I; *Orb & Scepter*, 1953I; *Partita for Orchestra*, 1957I; *Portsmouth Point Overture*, 1925I; *Scapino, a Comedy Overture*, 1940I; *String Quartet No. 1*, 1922I; *Symphony No. 1*, 1935I; *Symphony No. 2*, 1960I; *Troilus & Cressida*, 1954I; *Variations on a Theme of Hindemith*, 1963I; *Viola Concerto*, 1929I; *Violin Concerto*, 1939I

Ward, Robert: *Abelard & Heloise*, 1981I; *Appalachian Ditties & Dances*, 1989I; *Byways of Memories*, 1991I; *Celebrations of God in Nature*, 1980I; *Claudia Legare*, 1973I; *Concert Piece*, 1948I; *The Crucible*, 1961I; *Fatal Interview*, 1937I; *He Who Gets Slapped*, 1955I; *Invocation & Toccata*, 1963I; *Jubilation Overture*, 1948I; *The Lady from Colorado*, 1964I; *Minutes till Midnight*, 1982I; *Ode for Orchestra*, 1939I; *Piano Concerto*, 1968I; *Roman Fever*, 1993I; *Sacred Songs for Pantheists*, 1951I; *Saxophone Concerto*, 1984I; *The Scarlet Letter*, 1990I; *Songs for Ravenscroft*, 1993I; *Sonic Structures*, 1980I; *String Quartet No. 1*, 1966I; *Sweet Freedom's Song*, 1965I; *Symphony No. 1*, 1941I; *Symphony No. 2*, 1947I; *Symphony No. 3*, 1950I; *Symphony No. 4*, 1958I; *Symphony No. 6*, 1989I; *Violin Sonata No. 1*, 1950; *Violin Sonata No. 2*, 1990I

Ward, Samuel Augustus: *Materna (America the Beautiful)*, 1882I

Ward-Steinman, David: *Arcturus*, 1972I; *Cello Concerto*, 1966I; *Intersections*, 1982I; *Kaleidoscope*, 1971I; *Now Music*, 1967I; *Olympics Overture*, 1984I; *Piano Sonata*, 1957I; *Prisms & Reflections for Piano*, 1996I; *Sonata for Fortified Piano*, 1972I; *Song of Moses*, 1964I; *Symphony No. 1*, 1959I; *Western Orpheus*, 1964I

❈

F *Biographical*   G *Cultural Beginnings*   H *Musical Literature*
I *Musical Compositions*

Warren, Elinor Remick: *Abram in Egypt*, 1960I
Warren, George William: *National Hymn (God of Our Fathers)*, 1892I
Warren, Stanley: *Kafka: Letter to My Father*, 1996I
Washburn, Robert: *North Country Sketch*, 1969I; *Pieces for Orchestra (3)*, 1959I; *St. Lawrence Overture*, 1962I; *Symphony No. 1*, 1959I
Watts, Wintter: *Circles*, 1932I; *Vignettes of Italy*, 1919I; *Young Blood*, 1919I
Wayditch, Gabriel von: *The Caliph's Magician*, 1917I
Wayne, Hayden: *Symphony No. 4, "Funk,"* 1991I
Weaver, Powell: *Plantation Overture*, 1925I; *Violin Sonata*, 1945I
Webb, George James: *Webb* (Stand Up for Jesus), 1837I
Webber, Andrew Lloyd: *Requiem*, 1984I
Weber, Ben: *Episodes*, 1950I; *Lyric Piece, Opus 7* (string quartet), 1940I; *Piano Concerto, Opus 52*, 1961I; *Piano Suite No. 1, Opus 8*, 1941I; *Piano Suite No. 2, Opus 27*, 1948I; *Prelude & Passacaglia*, 1954I; *Rapsodie concertante* (viola concerto), 1957I; *Songs (5), Opus 15*, 1941I; *String Quartet No. 1, Opus 12*, 1942I; *String Quartet No. 2, Opus 35*, 1951I; *String Trio No. 1*, 1943I; *String Trio No. 2*, 1946I; *Symphony in Four Movements*, 1951I; *Symphony on Poems of William Blake*, 1950I; *Violin Concerto*, 1954I; *The Ways*, 1961I
Weber, Carl Maria von: *Abu Hassan*, 1811I; *L'accoglianza*, 1817I; *Adagio & Rondo in F, Opus 115*, 1811I; *Agnus Dei*, 1820I; *Allemandes (12), Opus 4*, 1801I; *Andante & Hungarian Rondo, Opus 35*, 1813I; *Andante & Hungarian Rondo in c, Opus 79*, 1809I; *Bassoon Concerto in F, Opus 127*, 1811I; *Clarinet Concerto No. 1 in f, Opus 114*, 1811I; *Clarinet Concerto No. 2 in E♭, Opus 118*, 1811I; *Clarinet Concertino in E♭, Opus 109*, 1811I; *Clarinet Quintet in B♭, Opus 182*, 1815I; *Donna Diana*, 1817I; *Die drei Pintos*, 1821I; *Duets (3), Opus 31*; *Easy Pieces (6), Opus 3*, 1801I; *Ecossaises (6), Opus 29, 34*, 1802I; *Der erste Ton, Opus 14*, 1808I; *Euryanthe*, 1823I; *Der Freischütz*, 1821I; *Grand Overture, Opus 8*, 1807I; *Grande Polonaise in E♭, Opus 21*, 1808I; *Das Haus Anglade*, 1818I; *Horn Concertino in e, Opus 45, Opus 188*, 1815I; *In Seinem Ordnung schafft der Herr*, 1812I; *Invitation to the Dance*, 1819I; *Jubel Overture, Opus 59*, 1818I; *Jubilee Cantata, Opus 58*, 1818I; *Kampf und Sieg, Opus 44*, 1815I; *König von Frankreich*, 1818I; *König Yngurd*, 1817I; *Konzertstücke in f, Opus 245*, 1821I; *Der Leuchtturm*, 1820I; *Lieb' um Liebe*, 1818I; *Mass in E♭, "Jugendmesse,"* 1802I; *Mass in G, Opus 76*, 1819I; *Missa Sancta No. 1*, 1818I; *Natur und Liebe*, 1818I; *Oberon*, 1826I; *Overture, Der Beherrscher der Geister, Opus 8*, 1811I; *Peter Schmoll*, 1803I; *Piano Concerto No. 1 in C, Opus 11*, 1810I; *Piano Concerto No. 2 in E♭, Opus 155*, 1812I; *Piano Pieces (8), Opus 6*, 1819I; *Piano Pieces (6), Opus 10*, 1809I; *Piano Quartet in B♭, Opus 76*, 1809I; *Piano Sonata No. 1 in C, Opus 138*, 1812I; *Piano Sonata No. 2 in A♭, Opus 199*, 1816I; *Piano Sonata No. 3 in d, Ous 206*, 1816I; *Piano Sonata No. 4 in e, Opus 70*, 1822I; *Preciosa*, 1820I; *Rübezahl*, 1804I; *Den Sachsen Sohn*, 1822I; *Scene & Aria, "Oh, se Edmondo," Opus 52*; *Scene & Aria, "Signor se padre sei,"* 1811I; *Scene &Aria, "Non paventar," Opus 51*, 1815I; *Silvana*, 1810I; *Songs (5), Opus 13*, 1810I; *Songs (6), Opus 15*, 1809I; *Songs (4), Opus 23*, 1812I; *Songs (3), Opus 29*, 1811I; *Songs (6), Opus 30*, 1813I; *Songs (4), Opus 41*, 1814I; *Songs (6), Opus 54*, 1818I; *Songs (14), Opus 64, 71*, 1819I; *Songs (6), Opus 80*, 1820I; *Symphonies No. 1 & 2, Opus 50, 51*, 1807I; *Trio, Opus 259*, 1819I; *Turandot, Opus 37*, 1809I; *Variations (7), Opus 9*, 1808I; *Variations (7), Opus 33*, 1811I; *Variations (6) in C, Opus 49*, 1806I; *Variations (7) on Bianchi, Opus 7*, 1807I; *Variations (6) on "Castor & Pollux," Opus 5*, 1804I; *Variations (7) on Méhul, Opus 14*, 1812I; *Variations (6) on Vogler, Opus 6*, 1804I; *Variations (7) on a Gypsy Song, Opus 55*, 1817I; *Variations on a Russian Theme, Opus 179*, 1815I; *Violin Sonatas, Progressive (6), Opus 10*, 1810I; *Das Waldmädchen*, 1800I
Webern, Anton: *Das Augenlicht, Opus 26*, 1935I; *Bagatelles (6), Opus 9*, 1913I; *Canons (5), Opus 16*, 1924I; *Cantata No. 1, Opus 29*, 1939I; *Cantata No. 2, Opus 31*, 1943I; *Concerto for Nine Instruments, Opus 24* 0 1934I; *Im Sommerwind*, 1904I; *Little Pieces (3), Cello & Piano*, 1914I; *Movements (5), Opus 5*, 1909I; *Passacaglia, Opus 1*, 1908I; *Pieces (4), Violin & Piano, Opus 7*, 1910I; *Quartet, Opus 22*, 1930I; *Sacred Folksongs (3), Opus 17*, 1924I; *Sacred Songs (5), Opus 15*, 1923I; *Six Pieces for Orchestra, Opus 6*, 1909I; *Songs (5), Opus 4*, 1909I; *Songs (2), Opus 8*, 1912I; *Songs (5), Opus 12*, 1917I; *Songs (5), Opus 13*, 1916I; *Songs (6), Opus 14*, 1921I; *Songs (3), Opus 18*, 1925I; *Songs (3), Opus 23*, 1934I; *Songs (3), Opus 25*, 1935I; *Songs (5) from "Der siebente Ring," Opus 3*, 1909I; *Songs for Chorus (2), Opus 19*, 1926I; *String Quartet, Opus 28*, 1938I; *String Trio, Opus 20*, 1927I; *Symphony, Opus 21*, 1928I; *Variations for Orchestra, Opus 30*, 1940I; *Variations for Piano, Opus 27*, 1936I
Webster, Joseph P.: *In the Sweet By and By*, 1867I
Weigl, Joseph: *Adrian von Ostade*, 1807I; *Alceste*, 1800I; *Alcina*, 1797I; *Alonzo e Cora*, 1796I; *L'amor marinaro*, 1796I; *Der Bergsturz*, 1813I; *Cleopatra*, 1807I; *Clothilde, Prinzzessin von Salerno*, 1799I; *Daniel in der Löwengrube*, 1820I; *Das Dorf im Gebürge*, 1798I; *Edmund und Caroline*, 1821I; *Der Einsiedler auf den Alpen*, 1810I; *Die eiserne Pforte*, 1823I; *Das Fest der bacchanten*, 1807I; *Franciska von Foix*, 1812I; *L'imboscata*, 1815I; *Der Jugend Peter des Gross*, 1814I; *Kaiser Hadrian*, 1807I; *König Waldemar*, 1821I;

❄

A   *Births*   B   *Deaths*   C   *Debuts*   D   *New Positions*

E   *Prizes/Honors*

Margaritta d'Anjou, 1816I; *Mass in E♭*, 1783I; *Mass in F*, 1784I; *Mass in A*, 1834I; *Mass in E*, 1837I; *Mass, "Annuntiatione B.M.V.,"* 1830I; *Mass, "Conceptione B.M.V.,"* 1827I; *Mass, "In Nomine B.M.V.,"* 1832I; *Mass, "Nativitate B.M.V.,"* 1833I; *Mass, "Purificatione B.M.V.,* 1829I; *Die Nachtigall und die Rabe*, 1818I; *La Passione di Gesù Cristo*, 1804I; *Das Petermännchen*, 1794I; *Il principe invisibile*, 1806I; *Der Raub der Helena*, 1795I; *La resurrezione di Gesù Cristo*, 1804I; *Die Schweitzerfamilie*, 1809I; *I solitari*, 1797I; *Der Spanier auf der insel Christina*, 1801I; *Der Strassensammler*, 1792I; *Die Tänzerin von Athen* 1801I; *Die Uniform*, 1800I; *Der Verwandlungen*, 1809I; *Vestas Feuer*, 1805I; *Der Vier Elemente*, 1806I; *Zulima und Azons*, 1800I

Weigl, Karl: *Festival Overture*, 1938I; *Piano Trio*, 1939I; *Rhapsody for Piano & Orchestra*, 1940I; *String Quartet No. 5*, 1933I; *String Quartet No. 6*, 1939I; *String Quartet No. 7 in f*, 1942I; *String Quartet No. 8*, 1949I

Weill, Kurt: *The Ballad of Magna Carta*, 1939I; *Die Bürgschaft*, 1932I; *Down in the Valley*, 1948I; *Lady in the Dark*, 1941I; *One Touch of Venus*, 1943I; *Der Protagonist*, 1926I; *The Rise & Fall of the City of Mahagonny*, 1927I; *String Quartet*, 1923I; *Symphony No. 1*, 1921I; *Symphony No. 2*, 1933I; *The Three Penny Opera*, 1928I; *Walt Whitman Songs (3)*, 1942I; *Der Weg der Verheissung*, 1935I

Weinberger, Jaromir: *Bible Poems*, 1939I; *Czech Rhapsody*, 1941I; *Dedications*, 1954I; *Lincoln Symphony*, 1941I; *Organ Preludes (5)*, 1954I; *Organ Sonata*, 1941I; *The Outcasts of Poker Flat*, 1932I; *Prelude & Fugue on a Southern Folktune*, 1940I; *Religious Preludes (6)*, 1946I; *Schwanda, the Bagpiper*, 1927I; *Variations & Fugue, "Under the Spreading Chestnut Tree,"* 1939I

Weiner, Lazar: *The Golem*, 1956I

Weiner, Leó: *Hungarian Folk Dances*, 1931I; *String Trio, Opus 6*, 1908I; *Csongor und Tünde*, 1913I; *Piano Concertino*, 1926I; *String Quartet No. 1*, 1906I; *String Quartet No. 2*, 1921I; *String Quartet No. 3*, 1938I

Weingartner, Felix: *Cain & Abel*, 1914I; *Dorfschule*, 1920I; *Meister Andrea*, 1920I; *Sakuntala*, 1884I

Weinlig, Christian Ehregott: *Dem Chaos im dunkel der nacht*, 1810I; *Der Christ am Kreuze Jesu*, 1793I; *Die Erlösung*, 1801I; *Die Feier des Todes Jesu*, 1789I; *Jesus Christus der Welterlöser*, 1812I; *Mass in B♭*, 1806I; *Unser Vater in den seel'gen Höhen*, 1824I

Weir, Judith: *A Night at the Chinese Opera*, 1987I

Weisberg, Arthur: *Concerto for Two Pianos & Two Percussionists*, 1997I

Weisgall Hugo: *Athaliah*, 1963I; *Esther*, 1992I, 1993I; *Fancies & Inventions*, 1970I; *The Garden of Adonis*, 1959I; *Impressions (4)*, 1931I; *Jennie, or, The Hundred Nights*, 1976I; *Lillith*, 1934I; *Lyrical Interval*, 1985I; *Nine Rivers from Jordan*, 1968I; *Outpost*, 1947I; *Overture in F*, 1943I; *Piano Sonata No. 1 in f♯*, 1931I; *Piano Sonata No. 2*, 1982I; *Piano Variations*, 1939I; *Prospect*, 1983I; *Purgatory*, 1958I; *Quest*, 1938I; *Six Characters in Search of an Author*, 1956I; *Soldier Songs*, 1946I; *A Song of Celebration*, 1975I; *Songs (4), Opus 1*, 1934I; *The Stranger*, 1952I; *Tekiator*, 1985I; *The Tenor*, 1950I; *Translations*, 1972I

Weisman, Julius: *Concertino for Horn & Orchestra*, 1935I; *Piano Pieces (4), Opus 78*, 1915I; *Suite, Opus 95*, 1927I

Weiss, Adolph: *Piano Preludes (12)*, 1927I; *Piano Sonata*, 1932I; *Scherzo, American Life*, 1928I; *Sextet for Piano & Winds*, 1947I; *Songs by Dickinson (7)*, 1928I; *String Quartet No. 1*, 1925I; *String Quartet No. 2*, 1926I; *String Quartet No. 3*, 1929I; *String Quartet No. 4*, 1932I; *Trumpet Concerto*, 1952I; *Violin Sonata*, 1941I

Welcher, Dan: *Brass Quintet*, 1982I; *Bright Wings*, 1996I; *Chameleon Music*, 1987I; *Clarinet Concerto*, 1987I; *Concerto da Camera*, 1975I; *Dance Variations for Piano*, 1979I; *Dante Dances*, 1996I; *Della's Gift*, 1986I; *Dervishes*, 1976I; *Evening Scenes*, 1985I; *Flute Concerto*, 1974I; *Phaedrus*, 1996I; *Piano Concerto, "Shiva's Drums"* (piano), 1994I; *Songs (3) of e. e. cummings*, 1990I; *String Quartet No. 1*, 1988I; *String Quartet No. 2, "Harbor Music,"* 1992I; *Symphony No. 1*, 1992I; *Symphony No. 2 "Night Watchers,"* 1994I; *Symphony No. 3, "Shaker Life,"* 1997I; *Visions of Merlin*, 1980I; *Walls & Fences* (band), 1970I; *Wind Quintet No. 1*, 1967I; *Wind Quintet No. 2*, 1977I; *Zion*, 1994I

Wellesz, Egon: *Die Bacchantinnen*, 1931I; *Piano Concerto*, 1934I; *Prospero's Spell, Opus 53*, 1935I; *Sketches (3), Opus 6*, 1911I; *Suite for Violin & Orchestra*, 1924I; *Tryptich, Opus 98*, 1966I

Wenczura, Ernest von: *Symphony No. 2, "Russian,"* 1798I

Wernick, Richard: *Cello Concerto*, 1980I; *The Emperor's Nightingale*, 1958I; *Haiku of Basho*, 1967I; *Maggie*, 1959I; *Moonsongs from the Japanese*, 1969I; *Piano Concerto*, 1990I; *Pieces (4) for String Quartet*, 1955I; *A Prayer for Jerusalem*, 1971I; *Saxophone Quartet*, 1992I; *Song of Remembrance*, 1974I; *String Quartet No. 1*, 1963I; *String Quartet No. 2*, 1973I; *String Quartet No. 3*, 1988I; *String Quartet No. 4*, 1990I; *String Quartet No. 5*, 1995I; *String Sextet*, 1989I; *Symphony No. 1*, 1987I; *Symphony No. 2*, 1994I; *The Trojan Women*, 1953I; *Viola Concerto*, 1986I; *Visions of Terror & Wonder*, 1976I

Wesley, Samuel: *Grand Duett in Three Movements*, 1812I; *Harpsichord Concertos (2)*, 1774I; *Introduction & Fugues (3)*, 1833I; *Introductory Movements (6)*, 1831I; *Organ Concerto No. 1 in A*, 1787I; *Organ Concerto No. 2 in D*, 1800I; *Organ Voluntaries (9), Opus 6*, 1800I; *Organ Voluntaries (6), Opus 6, Book II*, 1808I;

Wesley, Samuel: (*cont.*)
   Overture No. 2 in D, 1778I; *Overture No. 3 in C*, 1780I; *Piano Sonata in D*, 1808I; *Piano Sonata, "Siege of Badajoz*," 1812I; *Short Pieces (6) with Added Voluntary*, 1816I; *Short Preludes (4)*, 1825I; *Sonata in G, Piano, 4 Hands*, 1832I; *String Quartet No. 1 in G*, 1779I; *String Quartet No. 2 in c*, 1780I; *String Quartets (3)*, 1800I; *String Quartet in E♭*, 1810I; *Symphonies No. 1, 3*, 1784I; *Symphony in A*, 1811I; *Symphony in B♭*, 1802I; *Trio Sonata in G*, 1774I; *Variations in E on "God Save the King,"* 1820I; *Variations on "God Save the King,"* 1834I; *Violin Concerto No. 1 in C*, 1779I; *Violin Concerto No. 2 in D*, 1811I; *Violin Concerto No. 3 in A*, 1782I; *Violin Concerto No. 4 in B♭*, 1782I; *Violin Concerto No. 5 in C (?)*, 1782I; *Violin Concerto No. 6 in G*, 1783I; *Violin Concerto No. 7 in B♭*, 1785I; *Voluntaries (6) for . . . Young Organists, Opus 36*, 1837I; *Voluntaries (6), Opus 6, Book I*, 1805I

Wesley, Samuel Sebastian: *Organ Voluntaries (6), Opus 36*, 1836I; *Short Pieces (12) for Organ*, 1815I; *Symphony in c*, 1832I

Wessel, Mark: *Prelude & Fugue* (string quartet), 1931I; *String Quartet No. 1*, 1931I

Westergaard, Peter: *Cantata No. III: Leda & the Swan*, 1961I; *Mr. & Mrs. Discobolos*, 1966I; *String Quartet No. 1*, 1957I; *The Tempest*, 1990I

Wetz, Richard: *Kleist Overture, Opus 16*, 1907I; *Symphony No. 1*, 1917I; *Symphony No. 2*, 1919I; *Symphony No. 3*, 1922I

Weyse, Christoph: *Faruk*, 1812I; *Festen paa Kenilworth*, 1836I; *Floribella*, 1825I; *The Sleeping Potion*, 1809I

Weyse, C.P.E.: *Christmas Cantata No. 3*, 1821I; *Easter Cantata, No. 1*, 1836I

Whitaker, Howard: *Prayers of Habakkuk*, 1993I

White, Clarence: *Ouanga*, 1932I; *String Quartet No. 1*, 1931I; *String Quartet No. 2*, 1931I

White, Michael: *Songs from Another Time*, 1985I

White, Paul: *String Quartet*, 1925I

Whiteley, John Scott: *Fantasia Espansiva*, 1997I

Whithorne, Emerson: *Adventures of a Samurai*, 1919I; *The Aeroplane*, 1920I; *El Camino Real*, 1937I; *Greek Impressions* (string quartet), 1917I; *The Grim Troubadour*, 1927I; *New York Days & Nights*, 1922I; *Piano Quintet*, 1928I; *Poem, Opus 43 (piano, orchestra)*, 1927I; *Saturday's Child*, 1926I; *String Quartet No. 2*, 1930I; *Symphony No. 1*, 1929I; *Symphony No. 2*, 1935I; *Symphony No. 3*, 1937I; *Violin Concerto*, 1931I; *Violin Sonata*, 1932I

Whiting, Arthur Battelle: *Concert Overture*, 1886I; *Fantasia in b♭/f, Opus 11*, 1897I; *Piano Concerto in d*, 1888I; *Rubaiyát of Omar Khayyám, Opus 18*, 1901I; *Suite for Four Horns & Strings, Ous 6*, 1888I; *Violin Sonata*, 1891I

Whiting, George E.: *Dream Pictures*, 1877I; *Lenora*, 1893I; *Mass in c*, 1872I; *Mass in f*, 1874I; *Prologue, "The Golden Legend,"* 1873I

Whitlock, Percy: *Organ Extemporisations (4)*, 1933I; *Plymouth Suite*, 1937I; *Short Pieces (5)*, 1929I

Widdoes, Lawrence: *How to Make Love*, 1993I

Widor, Charles-Marie: *Choral et variations*, 1900I; *Concert Variations*, 1867I; *Fantaisie, Opus 62*, 1889I; *Feuillets d'album (12), Opus 31*, 1877I; *Introduction and Rondo, Opus 72*, 1898I; *Les Jacobites*, 1885I; *Jeanne d'Arc*, 1890I; *La Korrigane*, 1880I; *Maître Ambros*, 1886I; *Mass, Opus 35 (?)*, 1890I; *Nerto*, 1924I; *Nouvelles pièces (3)*, 1934I; *La nuit de Walpurgis, Opus 60*, 1887I; *Organ Suite Latine*, 1927I; *Organ symphonies 1-4, Opus 13*, 1876I; *Organ Symphonies 5-8, Opus 42*, 1880I; *Organ, Symphonie Gothique, Opus 70*, 1895I; *Organ Symphony No. 10, "Romane,"* 1899I; *Ouverture espagnole*, 1898I; *Les pêcheurs de Saint-Jean*, 1905I; *Piano Concerto No. 1, Opus 39*, 1876I; *Piano Quartet, Opus 66*, 1891I; *Piano Quintet No. 1, Opus 7*, 1890I; *Piano Quintet No. 2, Opus 68*, 1896I; *Piano Suite, Opus 58*, 1887I; *Piano Trio, Opus 19*, 1875I; *Salon Pieces (6), Opus 15*, 1872I; *Sinfonia Sacra for Organ & Orchestra*, 1908I; *Solis d'été, Opus 63*, 1889I; *Suite écossaise, Opus 78*, 1905I; *Suite Florentine for Violin & Piano*, 1919I; *Suite polonaise, Opus 51*, 1885I; *Symphonie antique*, 1911I; *Symphony in F, Opus 16*, 1870I; *Symphony No. 2 in A, Opus 54*, 1886I; *Symphony No. 3, Opus 69*, 1895I; *Symphony No. 7, Opus 42, No. 3*, 1890I; *Symphony No. 8, Opus 42, No. 4*, 1890I; *Valses caractéristiques (6), Opus 26*, 1877I; *Violin Concerto, Opus 41*, 1882I; *Violin Sonata No. 2, Opus 79*, 1907I

Wieniawski, Henryk: *Adagio élégiaque in A, Opus 5*, 1853I; *Allegro de sonate, Opus 2*, 1848I; *Caprice-Valse in E, Opus 7*, 1854I; *Etudes-caprices (8), Opus 18*, 1863I; *Fantaisie slave, Opus 27*, 1850I; *Fantasy on Gounod's Faust, Opus 2*, 1868I; *Grand caprice fantastique, Opus 1*, 1847I; *Introduction & rondo in E, Opus 28*, 1854I; *L'école moderne, Opus 10*, 1864I; *Légende, Opus 17*, 1860I; *Polonaise Brillante No. 2 in A, Opus 21*, 1870I; *Scherzo-tarantelle in g, Opus 16*, 1856I; *Souvenir de Moscow, Opus 6*, 1853I; *Variations on an Original Theme, Opus 15*, 1854I; *Violin Concerto No. 1 in f♯, Opus 14*, 1853I; *Violin Concerto No. 2 in d, Opus 22*, 1862I

Wigglesworth, Frank: *Aurora*, 1983I; *Portraits (3) for Strings*, 1970I; *Sea Winds*, 1984I; *A Short Mass*, 1970I; *Symphony No. 1*, 1953I; *Symphony No. 2*, 1958I; *Symphony No. 3*, 1960I; *Telesis*, 1951I; *The Willowdale Handcar*, 1969I; *Woodwind Quintet*, 1975I

❋

A   *Births*   B   *Deaths*   C   *Debuts*   D   *New Positions*
E   *Prizes/Honors*

Willan, Healey: *Andante, Fugue & Chorale, Opus 184*, 1965I; *Choral Preludes (6), Opus 155*, 1950I; *Choral Preludes (6), Opus 156*, 1951I; *Communion Service in D, Opus 244*, 1954I; *Communion Service in D, Opus 246*, 1955I; *A Fugal Trilogy, Opus 176*, 1958I; *Hymn Preludes (10), Opus 169*, 1956I; *Hymn Preludes (10), Opus 174*, 1958I; *Hymn Preludes (10), Opus 173*, 1957I; *Introduction, Passacaglia & Fugue, Opus 149*, 1916I; *Mass of St. Hugh, Opus 243*, 1935I; *Missa brevis in G/g, Opus 245*, 1954I; *Motets (6), Opus 303-8*, 1924I; *Order of Holy Communion, Opus 247*, 1955I; *Organ Pieces, (5), Opus 177*, 1958I; *Overture to an Unwritten Comedy*, 1951I; *Passacaglia & Fugue No. 2 in e, Opus 178*, 1959I; *Piano Concerto in c, Opus 76*, 1944I; *Prelude & Fugue in c, Opus 146*, 1908I; *Prelude & Fugue in b, Opus 147*, 1909I; *Preludes (5) on Plainchant Melodies, Opus 157*, 1951I; *Short Preludes & Postludes on Well-Known Hymn Tunes (36)*, 1960O; *Symphony No. 1 in d, Opus 70*, 1936I; *Symphony No. 2 in c, Opus 74*, 1941I; *Te Deum in B♭, Opus 53*, 1937I; *The Trumpet Call, Opus 53*, 1941I
Willey, James: *String Quartet No. 1*, 1975I; *String Quartet No. 2*, 1979I; *String Quartet No. 6*, 1989I
Williams, Grace: *Ballads for Orchestra*, 1968I; *The Dancers*, 1951I; *Songs of Gerard Manley Hopkins (6)*, 1958I; *Symphony No. 2*, 1956I
Williams, John: *Bassoon Concerto*, 1995I
Williamson, Malcolm: *Fanfarade*, 1979I; *Mass of Christ, the King*, 1978I; *Ode to Music*, 1973I; *Symphony No. 4*, 1977I; *Symphony No. 5, "Aquerò,"* 1980I; *The Stone Wall*, 1971I
Willis, Richard S.: *It Came Upon the Midnight Clear*, 1850I
Willson, Meredith: *Symphony No. 1*, 1936I; *Symphony No. 2*, 1940I
Wilms, Johann W.: *String Quartet No. 1*, 1806I
Wilson, Ian: *The Machine's Dream*, 1993I; *String Quartet No. 1*, 1992I; *String Quartet No. 2*, 1994I; *String Quartet No. 3*, 1996I; *Who's Afraid of Red, Yellow & Blue*, 1998I
Wilson, Olly: *A City Called Heaven*, 1989I; *Expansions III*, 1993I; *I Shall Not Be Moved*, 1993I; *Lumina*, 1981I; *Piano Trio*, 1976I; *Sinfonia*, 1984I; *Spirit Song*, 1974I
Wilson, Richard: *Aethelred the Unready*, 1994I; *Affirmations*, 1990I; *Articulations*, 1989I; *Bassoon Concerto*, 1983I; *Eclogue for Piano*, 1974I; *Fixations for Piano*, 1985I; *Intercalation for Piano*, 1985I; *Piano Concerto*, 1991I; *String Quartet No. 1*, 1968I; *String Quartet No. 2*, 1977I; *String Quartet No. 3*, 1982I; *String Quartet No. 4*, 1997I; *Symphony No. 1*, 1984I; *Symphony No. 2*, 1985I, 1986I; *Tribulations*, 1988I; *Triple Concerto*, 1998I; *Viola Sonata*, 1989I; *Wind Quintet*, 1974I
Winbeck, Heinz: *Symphony No. 1, "Tu Solus,"* 1983I
Winner, Septimus: *Whispering Hope*, 1868I
Winslow, Walter: *Concertati Veneziani*, 1996I; *Six Paripari*, 1995I; *A Voice from Elysium*, 1995I
Winter, Peter (von): *Armida*, 1778I; *Die beiden Blinden*, 1810I; *Bellerophon*, 1782I; *Der Bettelstudent*, 1785I; *Colmal*, 1809I; *Etelinda*, 1818I; *Der Frauenbund*, 1805I; *Il Maometto*, 1817I; *Die Pantoffeln*, 1811I; *Psyche*, 1793I; *Der Sänder un der Schneider*, 1820I; *Scherz, List und Rache*, 1784I; *Sinfonie concertante in e*, 1802I; *Der Sturm*, 1798I; *Symphonie concertante in B♭, Opus 20*, 1814I; *Symphonies in D & F*, 1780I
Wirén, Dag: *Cello Concerto, Opus 10*, 1936I; *Concert Overture No. 1*, 1931I; *Concerto Overture No. 2*, 1940I; *Flute Concertina*, 1972I; *Little Suite for Piano*, 1971I; *The Merchant of Venice*, 1943I; *Midsummer Nights Dream, A, Opus 30*, 1955I; *Piano Improvisations*, 1963I; *Piano Sonatine*, 1950I; *Serenade for Strings*, 1937I; *String Quartet No. 1*, 1929I; *String Quartet No 2, Opus 9*, 1935I; *String Quartet No. 3, Opus 18*, 1945I; *String Quartet No. 4, Opus 28*, 1953I; *String Quartet No. 5, Opus 41*, 1970I; *Symphony No. 1, Opus 3*, 1934; *Symphony No. 2, Opus 14*, 1939I; *Symphony No. 3*, 1944I; *Symphony No. 4*, 1952I; *Symphony No. 5, Opus 38*, 1964I; *Violin Concerto, Opus 23*, 1946I; *The Wicked Queen*, 1960I
Wissmer, Pierre: *Symphony No. 1*, 1938I; *Symphony No. 2*, 1951I; *Symphony No. 3*, 1955I; *Symphony No. 4*, 1962I; *Symphony No. 5*, 1969I; *Symphony No. 6*, 1977I; *Symphony No. 7*, 1983I; *Symphony No. 8*, 1986I; *Symphony No. 9*, 1989I
Witt, Friedrich: *Das Fischerweib*, 1806I; *Der leidende Heiland*, 1802I
Wolf, Ernst Wilhelm: *Der Abend im Walde*, 1773I; *Alcesta*, 1780I; *Die Dorfdeputierten*, 1772I; *Das Gärtnermädchen*, 1769I; *Die treuen Köhler*, 1772I
Wolf, Hugo: *Christnacht*, 1889I; *Der Corregidor*, 1896I; *Italienisches Liederbuch*, 1891I; *Spanisches Liederbuch*, 1890I; *String Quartet in d*, 1880I
Wolf-Ferrari, Ermanno: *Cello Concerto in C*, 1945I; *Cenerentola*, 1900I; *Le donne curiose*, 1903I; *Himmelskleid*, 1925I; *I Quattro Rustighi*, 1906I; *The Jewels of the Madonna*, 1911I; *The Secret of Suzanne*, 1909I; *Sinfonia brevis*, 1944I; *String Trio in a, Opus 32*, 1945I; *String Trio in b*, 1894I; *La sulamite*, 1899I; *La Vedove Scaltra*, 1931I; *Violin Concerto*, 1944I
Wolff, Christian: *For One, Two or Three People*, 1964I
Wölfl, Joseph: *Alzire*, 1807I; *L'amour romanesque*, 1804I; *Double Concerto for Violin and Piano*, 1801I; *Fernando*, 1805I; *Grand Duo, Opus 37*, 1806I; *Der Höllenberg*, 1795I; *Der Kopf ohne mann*, 1798I; *Piano Concerto, "Grand concerto militaire,"* 1799I; *Piano Sonatas (3), Opus 14*, 1801I; *Piano Sonatas (3), Opus 19*, 1803I; *Piano Sonatas (3), Opus 25*, 1803I; *Piano Sonatas (3), Opus 35*, 1804I; *Piano Sonatas (3), Opus*

❄

F *Biographical*   G *Cultural Beginnings*   H *Musical Literature*
I *Musical Compositions*

Wólfl, Joseph: (*cont.*)
   48, 1810I; *Piano Sonatas, Progressive (3), Opus 24*, 1803I; *Piano Trios (3), Opus 5*, 1798I; *Piano Trios (3), Opus 23*, 1803I; *Piano Concerto No. 2 in E, Opus 26*, 1803I; *Piano Concerto No. 3 in F, Opus 32* 1805I; *Piano Concerto No. 4 in G, "La Calme," Opus 36*, 1807I; *Piano Concerto in D, Opus 49*, 1810I; *Piano Concerto in E, Opus 64*, 1812I; *Piano Concerto No. 1 in G, Opus 20*, 1801I; *Das schöne Milchmädchen*, 1797I; *String Quartets (3), Opus 4*, 1798I; *String Quartets (6), Opus 10*, 1799I; *String Quartets (3), Opus 30*, 1805I; *La surprise de Diane*, 1805I; *Symphony No. 1 in g, Opus 40*, 1803I; *Symphony No. 2 in D, Opus 41*, 1808I
Wolpe, Michael: *Piano Trio*, 1996I; *String Quartet No. 2*, 1995I
Wolpe, Stefan: *Battle Piece*, 1947I; *Cantata for Voice, Voices & Instruments*, 1963I; *Chamber Piece No. 1*, 1964I; *Chamber Piece No. 2*, 1967I; *Enchantments*, 1953I; *Form*, 1959I; *The Man from Midian* 1942I; *Music for a Dancer*, 1950I; *Piano Pieces (7)*, 1951I; *Piano Studies in Basic Rows (4)*, 1936I; *Quartet for Oboe, Cello, Piano & Percussionist*, 1951I; *Quartet for Oboe, Cello, Piano & Percussion*, 1955I; *String Quartet No. 2*, 1969I; *Studies for Piano*, 1948I; *Symphony No. 1*, 1956I, 1964I; *Toccata*, 1941I; *Unnamed Lands*, 1940I; *Violin Sonata*, 1949I; *Zeus und Elida*, 1928I
Wood, Haydn: *Piano Concerto in d*, 1909I
Wood, Joseph: *String Quartet No. 1*, 1938I; *String Quartet No. 2*, 1941I; *Symphony No. 2*, 1952I
Woolf, B.E./Eichberg, Julius: *The Doctor of Alcantara*, 1862I
Woolf, Randall: *New Dancétudes for Piano*, 1988I
Woolrich, John: *Five Concert Arias*, 1994I
Wordsworth, William: *Symphony No. 1 in f, Opus 23*, 1944I; *Symphony No. 2 in D, Opus 34*, 1948I; *Symphony No. 3 in C, Opus 48*, 1951I; *Symphony No. 4 in E♭, Opus 54*, 1953I ; *Symphony No. 5 in a, Opus 68*, 1960I; *Symphony No. 6, "Eligiaca," Opus 102*, 1977I; *Symphony No. 7*, 1981I; *Symphony No. 8*, 1986I
Work, Henry Clay: *The Lost Letter*, 1883I; *The Old Village Doctor*, 1879I; *We Are Coming, Sister Mary*, 1854I; *Who Shall Rule This American Nation?*, 1866I
Wrangell, Vasili: *Fantasy for Piano and Orchestra*, 1893I; *Romances (3), Opus 20*, 1896I; *Songs (8), Opus 37*, 1900I; *String Quartet*, 1892I; *Symphony in D*, 1894I
Wranitzky, Anton: *String Quartets (6), Opus 1*, 1791I; *String Quartets (3), Opus 2*, 1792I; *String Quartets (3), Opus 4*, 1800I; *String Quartets (3), Opus 13*, 1806I; *String Quintets (3), Opus 8*, 1802I; *String Quintet, Opus 16*, 1803I; *Violin Concerto, Opus 11*, 1803I; *Violin Sonatas (2), Opus 6*, 1800I
Wranitsky, Paul: *Die Erkenntlichkeit*, 1805I; *Das Fest der Lassaronen*, 1794I; *Die Gute Mutter*, 1795I; *Johanna von Montfaucon*, 1799I; *Merkur, der heurat-stifter*, 1793I; *Mitgefühl*, 1804I; *Oberon, Konig der Elfen*, 1789I; *Rudolf von Felseck*, 1792I; *Der Schreiner*, 1799I
Wuorinen, Charles: *Astra*, 1990I; *The Celestial Sphere*, 1980I; *Chamber Concerto*, 1963I; *Concerto for Saxophone Quartet*, 1993I; *Concerto No. 2 for Amplified Piano*, 1973I; *Evolution Organ*, 1961I; *Five* (cello concerto), 1987I; *Genesis*, 1989I; *Grand Bamboula*, 1971I; *Horn Trio*, 1981I; *Horn Trio Continued*, 1985I; *Mass*, 1982I; *Movers & Shakers*, 1984I; *Music for Orchestra*, 1956I; *Natural Fantasy*, 1985I; *Orchestral & Electronic Exchanges*, 1965I; *Overture: Bamboula Beach*, 1987I; *Percussion Symphony*, 1978I; *Piano Concerto No. 1*, 1965I; *Piano Concerto No. 3*, 1983I; *Piano Quintet*, 1994I; *Piano Sonata No. 1*, 1969I; *Piano Sonata No. 2*, 1976I; *Piano Sonata No. 3*, 1986I; *Piano Variations*, 1963I; *Prelude to Kullervo*, 1985I; *A Reliquary for Igor Stravinsky*, 1975I; *Ringing Changes*, 1963I; *Saxophone Quartet*, 1992I; *Second Trio: Pieces for Stefan Wolpe*, 1962I; *Short Pieces (12) for Piano*, 1973I; *String Quartet No. 1*, 1971I; *String Quartet No. 2*, 1979I; *String Quartet No. 3*, 1987I; *String Sextet*, 1989I; *Symphony No. 1*, 1958I; *Symphony No. 2*, 1959I; *Symphony No. 3*, 1959I; *Time's Encomium*, 1969I; *Tuba Concerto*, 1970I; *Two-Part Symphony*, 1978I; *Violin Variations*, 1972I; *The W. of Babylon*, 1975I; *A Winter's Tale*, 1991I
Wykes, Robert A.: *Piano Quintet*, 1961I
Wyner, Yehudi: *Leonardo Vincitore*, 1988I; *On This Most Voluptuous Night*, 1982I; *String Quartet*, 1985I
Xenakis, Iannis: *Akanthos*, 1977I; *Anaktoria*, 1969I; *Antikhthon* 1971I; *Cendrées*, 1974I; *A Colonne*, 1977I; *Dok-Orkh*, 1991I; *Dual*, 1959I; *Eonta*, 1964I; *Epei*, 1976I; *Eridanos*, 1972I; *Erikhthon* (piano concerto), 1974I; *Evryal*, 1979I; *Hibiki-Hana-Ma*, 1970I; *Hiketides*, 1964I; *Ioolkos*, 1996I; *Kraanerg*, 1969I; *La légende d'Eer*, 1977I; *Metastasis*, 1954I; *Nomos Gamma*, 1968I; *Nuits*, 1967I; *Palimpsest*, 1979I; *Persépolis*, 1971I; *Piano Concerto, "Synaphai,"* 1969I; *Pithroprakta*, 1956I; *Sea-Change*, 1997I; *ST/10*, 1962I; *Strategie*, 1963I; *Terrêtektorh*, 1959I; *Violin Sonata*, 1958I; *Voyage Absolu des Unari vers Andromede*, 1989I; *Waarg*, 1988I
Yannatos, James: *Concerto for String Quartet*, 1995I; *Piano Concerto*, 1993I; *Symphony No. 3, "Prisms,"* 1988I; *Symphony No. 4*, 1990I
Yannay, Yehuda: *Clarinet Trio*, 1982I; *Late Spring Pieces (7) for Piano*, 1973I
Yardumian, Richard: *Passacaglia, Recitatives & Fugue (Concerto)*, 1957I; *Piano Fantasy No. 2*, 1974I; *Symphony No. 1*, 1961I; *Symphony No. 2, "Psalms,"* 964I; *Symphony No. 3*, 1981I
Yi, Chen: *Piano Concerto*, 1994I

A *Births*   B *Deaths*   C *Debuts*   D *New Positions*

E *Prizes/Honors*

Yim, Jan Alan: *Autumn Rhythm*, 1985I
Yon, Pietro: *Gesú Bambino*, 1917I; *The Triumph of St. Patrick*, 1934I
Yoshimatsu, Takashi: *Ode to Birds & Rainbow*, 1993I
Young, Victor: *String Quartet No. 5*, 1969I
Yttrehus, Rolv: *Symphony No. 1*, 1998I
Yun, Isang: *Clarinet Quintet No. 1*, 1984I; *Resonant Pipes*, 1967I; *String Quartet No. 3*, 1959I; *String Quartet No. 4*, 1988I; *String Quartet No. 5*, 1990I; *String Quartet No. 6*, 1992I; *Symphony No. 1*, 1983I; *Symphony No. 2*, 1984I; *Symphony No. 3*, 1985I
Zador, Eugene: *Christoph Columbus*, 1939I; *Festival Overture*, 1964I; *Symphony No. 4, "Children's,"* 1941I
Zaimont, Judith Lang: *Greyed Sonnets*, 1975I; *Hidden Heritage: A Dance Symphony*, 1987I; *Sacred Service for the Sabbath Evening*, 1976I; *Snazzy Sonata for Piano*, 1972I; *Songs of Innocence*, 1974I; *Symphony No. 1*, 1994I, 1995I; *Two Songs for Soprano & Harp*, 1978I
Zakaryan, Suren: *Instatu nascendi*, 1996I; *Piano Concerto No. 1*, 1985I; *Piano Concerto No. 2*, 1992I
Zech, Frederick, Jr.: *Cello Concerto*, 1907I; *Flute Sonata*, 1906I; *Piano Concerto No. 4*, 1896I; *Piano Quintet*, 1903I; *String Quartet No. 1*, 1897I; *String Quartet No. 2*, 1902I; *Symphony No. 1*, 1883I; *Symphony No. 3*, 1906I
Zechlin, Ruth: *Dies Irae*, 1999I; *In Memoriam Witold Lutoslawski*, 1995I; *Die Reise*, 1992I; *Stabat Mater*, 1999I; *String Quartet No. 1*, 1959I; *String Quartet No. 2*, 1965I; *String Quartet No. 3*, 1970I; *String Quartet No. 4*, 1971I; *String Quartet No. 5*, 1971I; *String Quartet No. 6*, 1977I; *String Quartet No. 7*, 1995I; *Triptychon 2000*, 2000I
Zeckwer, Camille: *Piano Concerto*, 1897I
Zeisl, Eric: *Requiem Ebraico*, 1944I
Zelter, Carl Friedrich: *Die Auferstehung und Himmelfahrt Jesu*, 1807I; *German Songs (6), Bass Voice*, 1826I; *German Songs (6), Alto Voice*, 1827I; *Die Gunst des Augenblicks*, 1806I; *Kleiner Balladen und Lieder*, 1803I; *Neue Lieder*, 1821I; *Songs (6), Male Chorus*, 1828I; *Songs (10), Male Chorus*, 1831I; *Te Deum*, 1801I
Zemlinsky, Alexander (von): *Burial of Spring*, 1897I; *Clarinet Trio, Opus 3*, 1896I; *Cymbeline*, 1914I; *Der Florentinische Tragödie*, 1916I; *Forest Talk*, 1896I; *Kleider Machen Leute*, 1910I; *Der König Kandaules*, 1936I; *Der Kreidekreis*, 1932I; *Lied der Circe*, 1939I; *Maeterlinck Songs (6), Opus 13*, 1913I; *May Flowers Were Blooming Everywhere*, 1904I; *Sarema, The Rose of the Caucasus*, 1895I; *Sinfonietta*, 1934I; *Songs (12)*, 1937I; *String Quartet No. 1*, 1896I; *String Quartet No. 2*, 1915I; *String Quartet No. 3*, 1924I; *String Quartet No. 4*, 1936I; *Symphonische Gesänge*, 1929I; *Ein Tanzpoem*, 1904I; *Der Traumgörge*, 1906I; *Der Zwerg*, 1921I
Zender, Hans: *Hölderlin lesen II*, 1987I; *Hölderlin lesen III*, 1991I
Zeuner, Charles: *Organ Concerto No. 2*, 1831I
Zhelobinsky, Valeri: *Piano Concerto No. 1*, 1933I; *Piano Concerto No. 2*, 1934I; *Piano Concerto No. 3*, 1939I; *Violin Concerto*, 1934I
Ziffrin, Marilyn: *Symphony for Voice & Orchestra*, 1990I
Zimbalist, Efrem: *Cello Concerto*, 1969I; *Violin Concerto*, 1947I
Zimmer, Ján: *Concerto for Two Pianos*, 1967I; *Death Shall Have No Dominion*, 1968I; *Flute Sonata*, 1978I; *Organ Sonata No. 1*, 1970I; *Organ Sonata No. 2*, 1981I; *Piano Concerto No. 1*, 1949I; *Piano Concerto No. 2*, 1952I; *Piano Concerto No. 3*, 1958I; *Piano Concerto No. 4*, 1960I; *Piano Concert No. 5 for the Left Hand*, 1964I; *Piano Concerto No. 6*, 1972I; *Piano Concerto No. 7*, 1985I; *Prelude & Fugue*, 1952I; *Small Preludes (3) for Organ*, 1977I; *Symphony No. 6, "Improvisata,"* 1965I; *Symphony No. 7*, 1966I; *Symphony No. 8*, 1971I; *Symphony No. 9*, 1973I; *Symphony No. 11, Opus 98*, 1981I; *Symphony No. 12*, 1986I; *Violin Concerto*, 1953I
Zimmermann, Bernd: *Cante di speranza*, 1957I; *Cello Concerto*, 1966I; *Dialogue (2 pianos)*, 1960I; *Oboe Concerto*, 1952I; *Phototosis*, 1968I; *Sonata for Solo Cello*, 1960I; *Sonata for Solo Viola*, 1955I; *Sonata for Solo Violin*, 1951I; *Symphony*, 1952I; *Violin Concerto*, 1950I
Zimmermann Udo: *Dans la marche: Hommage à Witold Lutoslawski*, 1994I; *Episoden*, 1971I; *Gantenbein*, 1998I; *Kettledrum Concerto*, 1966I; *Levins Mühle*, 1973I; *Der Mensch*, 1970I; *Neruda-Lieder*, 1965I; *Nouveaux divertissements d'après Rameau* (horn concerto), 1987I; *Ode an das Leben*, 1974I; *Piano Sonata*, 1967I; *Der Schuhu und die fliegende Prinzessin*, 1976I; *Die Sündflut*, 1991I; *Viola Concerto*, 1986I; *Violin Sonatina*, 1964I; *Der weisse Rose*, 1967I; *Der weisse Rose II*, 1985I; *Wenn ein Wintervogel . . .*, 1991I; *Die Wundersame Schustersfrau*, 1981I; *Ein Zeuge der Liebe besingt den Tod*, 1973I; *Die zweite Entscheidung*, 1969I
Zingarelli, Nicola Antonio: *Alsinda*, 1785I; *Andromeda*, 1796I; *Annibale in Torino*, 1792I; *Antigone*, 1789I; *Antigono*, 1786I; *Armida*, 1786I; *Artaserse*, 1789I; *Atalanta*, 1792I; *Baldovino*, 1811I; *Berenice, regina d'Armenia*, 1811I; *Il beritore fortunato*, 1803I; *Clitennestra*, 1800I; *La distruzione di Gerusalemme*, 1803I; *Edipo a Colono; Gerusalemme distrutta*, 1794I; *Giulietta e Tomeo*, 1796I; *Gli orazi e curiazi*, 1795I; *Ines de*

F *Biographical*   G *Cultural Beginnings*   H *Musical Literature*
I *Musical Compositions*

Castro, 1798I; *Meleagro*, 1798I; *Il mercate di Monfregoso*, 1792I; *Montezuma*, 1781I; *La morte de Cesare*, 1790I; *La morte di Mitridate*, 1797I; *La motte dell'armicizia*, 1802I; *Pirro, Ré d'Epiro*, 1791I; *I quattro pazzi*, 1768I; *Ricimero*, 1785I; *La riedificazione di Gerusalemme*, 1812I; *Il ritorno di Serse*, 1809I; *Il ritratto*, 1799I; *La Rossana*, 1793I; *Saul*, 1805I; *La secchia rapita*, 1793I

Zorn, John: *The Deadman*, 1990I
Zorzor, Ştefan: *Concerto for Orchestra*, 1965I
Zsolt, Nándor: *Symphony*, 1918I; *Violin Concerto*, 1906I
Zumsteeg, Johann Rudolf: *Armide*, 1785I; *Cello Concerto No. 1*, 1788I; *Elbondocani*, 1802I; *Die Geisterinsel*, 1798I; *Kleine Balladen und Lieder I, II*, 1800I; *Kleine Balladen und Lieder III*, 1801I; *Kleine Balladen und Lieder IV-VI*, 1802I; *Kleine Balladen und Lieder VII*, 1805I; *Tamira*, 1788I; *Das tartarische Gesetz*, 1780I
Zupko, Ramon: *Canti terrae*, 1982I; *Radiants*, 1971I; *Rituals & Dances*, 1981I; *Symphony No. 1, "Earth & Sky"* (band), 1984I; *Symphony No. 2, "Blue Roots,"* 1989I; *Te Deum Trilogy*, 1984I; *Violin Sonata*, 1958I; *Voices*, 1972I; *Windsongs*, 1979I
Zwilich, Ellen Taaffe: *American Concerto*, 1994I; *Bassoon Concerto*, 1992I; *Celebration*, 1984I; *Chamber Symphony*, 1979I; *Clarinet Quintet*, 1990I; *Concerto for Bass Trombone, Strings, Timpany & Cymbals*, 1989I; *Concerto Grosso 1985*, 1985I; *Double Concerto*, 1994I; *Double Quartet for Strings*, 1984I; *Flute Concerto*, 1989I; *Horn Concerto*, 1993I; *Jubilation*, 1996I; *Millennium Fantasy*, 2000I; *Motets for the liturgical Year (7)*, 1986I; *Oboe Concerto*, 1990I; *Passages*, 1981I; *Peanuts Gallery* (piano concerto), 1996I; *Piano Concerto*, 1986I; *Piano Trio*, 1987I; *Praeludium*, 1987I; *Prologue & Variations*, 1983I; *Sonata in Three Movements*, 1974I; *String Quartet No. 1*, 1974I; *String Quartet No. 2*, 1998I; *String Trio*, 1982I; *Symbolon*, 1988I; *Symphony for Winds*, 1989I; *Symphony No. 1: Three Movements for Orchestra*, 1982I; *Symphony No. 2*, 1985I; *Symphony No. 3*, 1992I; *Symphony No. 4, "The Gardens,"* 1999I; *Symposium for Orchestra*, 1973I; *Tanzspiel*, 1987I; *Triple Concerto*, 1996I; *Trombone Concerto*, 1988I

❄

A *Births*   B *Deaths*   C *Debuts*   D *New Positions*
E *Prizes/Honors*

Historical Index

A-R Editions, 1962G
Aalborg Symphony Orchestra, 1943G
Aaltonen, Erkki, 1910A
Aaquist, Johansen, 1948A
Aargau Symphony Orchestra, 1962G
Aarhus (Denmark): Concert Hall, 1982G; Symphony Orchestra, 1935G
Aarne, Els, 1917A
Aav, Evald, 1939B
Aavik, Juhan, 1925D, 1982B
Abaco, Joseph dall', 1766E
Abarbanell, Lina, 1879A, 1894C, 1963B
Abbado, Marcello, 1926A, 1958D, 1966D, 1972D
Abbado, Claudio, 1933A, 1958CE, 1963E, 1973E, 1979D, 1982F, 1985E 1986DE, 1989D
Abbado, Roberto, 1954A, 1977C, 1991D
Abbey, Henry, 1883D
Abbey, John, 1785A, 1859B
Abbey Theatre (Dublin, Ireland), 1894G, 1904G
Abbott, Emma, 1850A, 1876C, 1891B
Abbott, Emma, Opera Co., 1878G
Abe, Kōmei, 1911A
Abegg Trio, 1976G
Abeille, Johann Ludwig, 1761A, 1838B
Abel, Carl F., 1758F, 1759C, 1760F, 1764EF, 1782F, 1787B
Abel, Jenny, 1942A
Abel, Leopold Auguste, 1794B
Abel, Yves, 1968A, 1990D
Abel-Steinbeg-Winant Trio, 1984G
Abendroth, Hermann, 1883A, 1915D, 1918D, 1934D, 1946D, 1949D, 1953D, 1956B
Abendroth, Irene, 1932B
Aberg, Thomas Harald, 1952A
Abert, Hermann, 1871A, 1927B
Abert, Johann Joseph, 1867D
Åbo Musical Society, 1790G
Abraham, Gerald, 1904A, 1961E, 1972E, 1988B; *A Hundred Years of Music*, 1938H; *Masters of Russian Music*, 1936H; *Studies in Russian Music*, 1935H; *This Modern Stuff*, 1933H
Abrahamsen, Hans, 1952A
Abramowitz, Jonathan, 1947A
Abramsky, Alexander, 1898A, 1985B
Abrányi, Cornelius, 1822A, 1903B; *From My Life and Memories*, 1897H; *History of Music*, 1885H; *Hungarian Music in the 19th Century*, 1900H
Ábrányi, Emil, 1888A, 1911D, 1970B
Abravanel, Maurice, 1903A, 1924C, 1947D, 1961E, 1971E, 1976F, 1979F, 1981E, 1991E, 1993BF
Abreu, Antonio: *Guitar Method*, 1799H
Abreu, Eduardo, 1949A, 1963C
Abreu, Sergio, 1948A, 1963C

Absil, Jean, 1893A, 1921E, 1922D, 1974B
Abt, Franz W., 1819A, 1841D, 1855D, 1865B
AC Classics Record Label, 1994G
Academia de Belas Artas (Bahia), 1877G
Academia Musical Napoletana, 1933G
Academia de Musica Euterpe (Costa Rica), 1934G
Academy of St. Martin-in-the-Fields, 1959G
Accademia dei Dilettanti di Musica, 1928G
Accademia Daniel, 1995G
Accademia Monteverdiana, 1961G
Accardo, Salvatore, 1941A, 1956E, 1958E, 1993D
Accone, Frank A d'., 1931A
Accorimboni, Agostino, 1818B
Aceto, Raymond, 1992C
Achron, Isidor, 1892A, 1948B
Achron, Joseph, 1886A, 1893C, 1943B
Achucarro, Joaquín, 1936A, 1948C, 1959E
Acker, Dieter, 1940A
Ackley, Alfred, 1887A, 1960B
Ackté, Aïno, 1876A, 1897C, 1944B
Acosta, Adolovni, 1946A
Acs, Janos, 1952A
Adachi, Motohiko, 1940A
Adam, Adolphe, 1803A, 1824F, 1856B
Adam, Claus, 1917A
Adám, Jenö, 1896A
Adam, Johann, 1779B
Adam, Louis: *Méthode générale de doigté*, 1799H
Adam, Mariella, 1934A
Adam, Claus, 1983B
Adám, Jenö, 1957E, 1982B
Adam, Theo, 1926A, 1949C
Adamberger, Josef V., 1762C, 1792F, 1804B
Adamonti, 1762C
Adamowski, Joseph, 1862A, 1930B
Adamowski, Timothée, 1857A, 1879C, 1943B
Adamowski String Quartet, 1888G
Adamowski Trio, 1896G
Adams, Byron, 1955A
Adams, Charles, 1834A, 1856C, 1900B
Adams, Harriett, 1775C
Adams, John, 1947A, 1977E
Adams, Joseph, 1993D
Adams, Nathan, 1783A, 1864B
Adams, Richard E., 1988D
Adams, Suzanne, 1872A, 1895C, 1953B
Adams, Thomas, 1785A, 1858B
Addinsel, Richard, 1904A, 1977B
Addison, Adele, 1925A, 1948C
Addison, John, 1766A, 1844B
Adelaide, Australia: Festival of Arts, 1960G; Intimate Opera Group, 1957G; Singers, 1936G; Wind Quintet, 1964G
Adelburg, August, 1830A, 1873B

Adés, Thomas, 1971A, 1998D, 1999E
Adesi Chorus, 1924G
Adgate, Andrew, 1762A, 1793B; *Lessons for the Uranian Society*, 1785H; *Philadelphia Harmony*, 1789H; *The Rudiments of Music*, 1788H
Adiny, Ada, 1876C
Adkins, Anthony, 1973C
Adkins, Ivor, 1897D
Adkins, Morton, 1877A, 1909C, 1926B
Adlam-Burnett, Keyboard Maker, 1971G
Adler, Agnes Charlotte, 1865A, 1882C
Adler, Clarence, 1886A, 1969B
Adler, F. Charles, 1889A, 1959B
Adler, Guido, 1855A, 1941B; *Der Stil in der Musik*, 1911H; *Studie zur Geschichte der Harmonie*, 1881H
Adler, György, 1789A, 1867B
Adler, Kurt, 1907A, 1935D, 1943D, 1977B; *The Art of Accompanying & Coaching*, 1965H
Adler, Kurt Herbert, 1905A, 1925C, 1938D, 1943D, 1953D, 1988B
Adler, Larry, 1914A
Adler, Peter Herman, 1899A, 1959D, 1969D, 1973D, 1990B
Adler, Richard, 1921A
Adler, Samuel, 1928A, 1952D, 1964E, 1969E; *Singing & Hearing*, 1979H; *The Study of Orchestration*, 1982H
Adlgasser, Anton Cajetan, 1764F
Adlgasser, Johann Cajetan, 1777B
Adlung, Jakob, 1762B; *Anleitung zu der musikalischen Gelehrtheit*, 1758H; *Musica mechanica organoedi*, 1768H; *Musikalisches siebengestirn*, 1768H
Adni, Daniel, 1951A, 1964C
Adolphe, Bruce: *Of Mozart, Parrots & Cherry Blossoms*, 1999H
Adolfati, Andrea, 1760F
Adorno, Theodor: *Dissonanzen: Musik in der verwalteten Welt*, 1956H; *Einleitung in die Musiksoziologie*, 1962H; *Gesammelte Schriften I*, 1971H; *Klangfiguren*, 1959H
Adrien, Martin J., 1767A, 1781C, 1822B
Aeolian American Corporation, 1932G
Aeolian Chamber Players, 1961G
Aeolian Organ Co., 1878G
Aeolian-Skinner Organ Co., 1931G
Aeolian String Quartet, 1927G
Aeolian Weber Piano & Pianola Co., 1903G
Afanassiev, Valery, 1972E
Afanasyev, Nicolai, 1821A, 1896E, 1898B
Afanasyeva, Veronika, 1960A
Affiliate Artists, Inc., 1966G
Affiliate Artists' Exxon/Arts Endowment Conductors Program, 1972G
African Music, 1954G
Agache, Alexandru, 1955A, 1979C
Agay, Dénes, 1911A; *Teaching Piano*, 1981H
Agazhanov, Artyom, 1958A

Aggh ázy, Károly, 1855A, 1918B
Agnelli, Salvatore, 1817A, 1874B
Agnesi, Luigi, 1833A, 1865C, 1875B
Agnesi, Maria Teresa, 1795B
Agnew, Paul, 1964A
Agostini, Giuseppe, 1874A, 1895C, 1951B
Agrell, Johan Joachim, 1765B
Agricola, Benedetta Emilia, 1780B
Agricola, Johann Friedrich, 1751E, 1759D, 1774B; *Anleitung zur Singekunst*, 1757H
Agriris, Spiro, 1985D
Agrupación Coral Nuestra Señora, 1959G
Agthe, Carl Christian, 1762A, 1782D, 1797B
Agthe, Albrecht Wilhelm, 1790A, 1873B
Aguado, Dionisio (y García), 1784A, 1849B; *Escuela o Método de Guitarra*, 1825H; *Estudios para la Guitarra*, 1820H
Aguiari, Lucrezia, 1764C, 1768E
Aguila, Miguel del, 1957A
Aguilar, Emanuel A., 1824A, 1904B
Aguirre, Julián, 1868A, 1924B
Agujari, Lucrezia, 1783B
Ahern, David, 1947A, 1988B
Ahlersmeyer, Mathieu, 1896A, 1929C, 1979B
Ahlert, Fred, 1953B
Ahlstedt, Douglas, 1945A, 1971C
Ahlström, Jacob Niklas, 1805A, 1857B
Åhlström, Olof, 1756A, 1777D, 1786D, 1788F, 1792E, 1835B; *Musikaliskt tidsfördrif*, 1789H; *Skaldestycken satte i musik*, 1790H
Ahnsjö, Claes, 1942A, 1969C
Aho, Kalevi, 1949A; *Art & Reality*, 1997H; *Finnish Composers*, 1996H; *Mission of the Artist in the Postmodern Society*, 1992H
Ahrend & Burnzema, Organ Builders, 1954G
Ahrens, Joseph Johannes, 1904A
Ahronovich, Yuri, 1932A, 1964D, 1975D, 1984E, 1985D
Aibl Music Publishers, 1825G
Aiblinger, Johann Kaspar, 1779A, 1826D, 1867B
Aiello, Rita: *Musical Perceptions*, 1993H
Aigner, Engelbert, 1798A, 1851B
Aiken Jesse B.: *The Christian Minstrel*, 1846H; *The Imperial Harmony*, 1875H; *The Juvenile Minstrel*, 1847H; *True Principles of the Science of Music*, 1891H
Aikin, Laura, 1965A, 1992C
Aimon, François, 1779A, 1822D, 1866B; *Abécédaire musical, principes élémentaires...*, 1831H; *Connaissances préliminaires de l'harmonie*, 1818H; *Sphère harmonique, tableau des accords*, 1827H
Ainsley, John Mark, 1963A
Ainsworth's Magazine, 1842G
Aitken, Hugh, 1924A, 1970D, 1987E
Aitken, John, 1787F, 1831B; *Compilation of Litanies, Vespers, Hymns, Anthems*, 1787H; *Scots Musical Museum*, 1797H
Aitken, Robert, 1939A

✤

A *Births*   B *Deaths*   C *Debuts*   D *New Positions*
E *Prizes/Honors*

Aitken, Webster, 1908A, 1929C, 1981B
Ajmone-Marsan, Guido, 1947A, 1973E, 1986D
Akimenko, Feodor, 1876A, 1945B
Akiyama, Kazuyoshi, 1864D, 1941A, 1972D, 1973D, 1985D, 1988D
Akses, Necil Kazim, 1999B
Akutagawa, Yasushi, 1925A, 1989B
Alabama: Mobile Opera Guild, 1946G; Symphony Orchestra, 1997G
Alagna, Robert, 1963A, 1988CE
Alaimo, Simone, 1950A, 1977C
Alain, Jehan, 1911A, 1935D, 1936E, 1940B
Alain, Marie-Claire, 1926A, 1937C
Alaleona, Domenico, 1881A, 1928B
Alard, Jean-Delphin, 1815A, 1831C, 1888B
Alarie, Pierette, 1921A, 1940C
Alaska (*see also* Anchorage): Conservatory of Music, 1982G; Festival of Music, 1956G
Alaska New Music Forum, 1980G
Albanese, Antoine, 1800B
Albanese, Cecilia, 1937A
Albanese, Licia, 1909A, 1934C, 1995E
Albani, Emma, 1847A, 1870C, 1896F, 1925E, 1930B
Albany, New York: Electronic Music Foundation, 1994G; Symphony Orchestra, 1930G
Albeneri Trio, 1944G
Albéniz, Isaac, 1860A, 1864F, 1878F, 1890F, 1893F, 1909B
Albéniz, Mateo Pérez de, 1755A, 1800D, 1831B; *Instrucción melódica, especulativa y prática...*, 1802H
Albéniz y Basanta, Pedro, 1795A, 1834D, 1855B; *Método completo para piano*, 1840H
Alberghetti, Anna Maria, 1936A
Alberghi, Ignazio, 1787D
Alberghi, Paolo Tommaso, 1760D, 1785B
Albers, Henri, 1866A, 1889C, 1926B
Albert, Charles F., Violin Shop, 1868G
Albert, Eugèn d', 1864A, 1932B
Albert, Eugène, Woodwind Maker, 1846G, 1881CE
Albert, Stephen, 1941A, 1965E, 1992B
Albertarelli, Francesco, 1788C
Albertazzi, Emma, 1814A, 1829C, 1847B
Alberti, Giuseppe Matteo, 1751B
Albertini, Joachim, 1782D, 1794E, 1796F, 1812B
Albinoni, Tomaso, 1751B
Alboni, Marietta, 1823A, 1842C, 1894B
Albos, Girolamo, 1760B
Albrecht, Charles, Piano Maker, 1759A, 1789G, 1848B
Albrecht, Christian F., 1788A, 1843B
Albrecht, Eugen: *Orchestral Music in Russia*, 1882H
Albrecht, Gerd, 1935A, 1956C, 1957E, 1963D, 1966D, 1972D, 1975D, 1988D, 1991D, 1994D, 2000D

Albrecht, Hans, 1902A, 1941D, 1947D, 1948D, 1961B
Albrecht, Karl, 1807A, 1863B
Albrecht, Johann L.: *Gründliche Einleitung in ...der Tonkunst*, 1761H; *Vom Hasse der Musik*, 1765H
Albrecht, Otto Edwin, 1899A, 1984B
Albrecht & Co., Piano Makers, 1863G
Albrechtsberger, Johann G., 1759D, 1765F, 1768F, 1772D, 1791DF, 1793D, 1809B; *Anfangsgründe zur Klavierkunste*, 1799H; *Clavierschule für Anfänger*, 1808H; *Gründliche Anweisung zur Composition*, 1790H; *Kurzegefassie methode...General bass zu erlernen*, 1792H
Albright, William Hugh, 1944A, 1970E, 1998B
Albulescu, Eugene, 1970A
L'album musical, 1905G
Albuquerque, New Mexico: Civic Light Opera Co., 1967G; Civic Symphony Orchestra, 1931G; June Music Festival, 1940G; Opera Theater, 1973G
Alcaide, Tomáz, 1901A, 1925C, 1967B
Alcantara, Theo, 1941A, 1978D, 1987D
Alcedo, José Bernardo, 1788A, 1846D, 1878B; *Filosofia elemental de la música*, 1869H
Alcock, John, Jr., 1791B
Alcock, John, Sr., 1806B; *An Instructive and Entertaining Companion*, 1779H
Alcorn, Michael, 1962A
Alda, Frances, 1883A, 1904C, 1952B; *Men, Women & Tenors*, 1937H
Aldana, José Manuel, 1758A, 1810B
Alday, François, 1761A; *Grande méthode pour l'alto*, 1827H
Alday, Paul, 1763A, 1835B
Aldeburgh Festival, 1948G
Aldiss, John, Choir, 1962G
Aldrich, Richard, 1863A, 1885D, 1889D, 1891D, 1902D, 1937B; *Concert Life in New York, 1902-23*, 1941H
Alea Electronic Music Group, 1968G
Alejandro, Sergio, 1964A
Alembert, Jean le Rond d', 1783B; *De la Liberté de la musique*, 1759H; *The Elements of Music*, 1752H; *Réflexions sur la musique en général*, 1754H; *Réflexions sur la théorie de la musique*, 1777H; *Treatise on Rameau's Theories*, 1752H
Aler, David, 1959A
Aler, John, 1949A, 1977C
Alessandrescu, Alfred, 1893A, 1921D, 1926D, 1933D, 1959B
Alessandri, Felice, 1798B, 1777F, 1789F, 1792F
Alessandri & Scattaglia, Publishers, 1770G
Alessandro, Victor, 1915A, 1938D, 1951D, 1976B
Alexander, Christian, 1964A
Alexander, Franz Ambros, 1753A, 1802A
Alexander, John, 1923A, 1952C, 1990B

❀

F *Biographical*   G *Cultural Beginnings*   H *Musical Literature*
I *Musical Compositions*

Alexander, Josef, 1907A, 1992B
Alexander, Roberta, 1949A, 1980C
Alexander, Russell, 1915B
Alexander Brothers, Instrument Makers
(Mainz), 1782G
Alexander String Quartet, 1981G
Alexandra, Liana, 1947A
Alexandre, Charles-Guillaume, 1787B
Alexandre, Jacob, Harmonium Co., 1829G
Alexandrov, Alexander, 1883A, 1946B
Alexandrov, Anatoli, 1888A, 1982B
Alexandrov, Boris A., 1905A, 1994B
Alexeev, Dmitri, 1947A, 1975E
Alfano, Franco, 1875A
Alfieri, Pietro, 1801A, 1863B; *Accompagna,
coll'organo de' toni ecclesiatici,* 1842H; *Raccolta
di musica sacra I,* 1841H; *Saggio storico teorio
pratico del canto gregoriano,* 1835H
Alfven, Hugo, 1917E, 1960B
Algano, Franco, 1954B
Algarotti, Francesco, 1764B; *Saggio sopra l'opéra
in musica,* 1755H
Alheim, Marie Olenine d', 1869A
Aliabiev, Alexander, 1787A, 1851B
Aliberti, Lucia, 1957A, 1978C
Aliénor Harpsichord Composition Awards,
1920G
Alin, Cecilia Rydinger, 1961A, 1994D
Aliprandi, Bernardo, 1792B
Alkan (Charles-Valentin), 1813A, 1826C, 1838F,
1845F, 1853F, 1888B
All-American Youth Orchestra, 1939G
Alldis, John, Choir, 1962G
Allegranti, Maddalena, 1754A, 1779C, 1801F
Allegri String Quartet, 1953G
Allen, Betty, 1930A, 1954C, 1979D
Allen, Gregory, 1949A, 1980E
Allen, Henry Robinson, 1809A, 1842C, 1876B
Allen, Hugh Percy, 1869A, 1918D, 1920E, 1946B
Allen, J. Lathrop, 1815A, 1842F, 1905B
Allen, Joseph, Brass Instruments, 1838G
Allen, Paul H., 1883A, 1910E, 1952B
Allen, Thomas, 1944A, 1969C, 1090E
Allen, Warren: *Philosophies of Music History,*
1939H
Allen & Co., Publishers, 1850G
Allen Organ Co., 1939G
Allende, Humberto, 1885A, 1959B
Allgemeine Deutsche Bibliothek, 1765G
Allgemeine Musikalische Zeitung, 1798G
Allgemeine Wiener Musik-Zeitung, 1841G
Allgemeiner Deutscher Musikverein, 1861G
Allgemeiner Musikalischer Anzeiger, 1829G
Allin, Norman, 1884A, 1916C, 1973B
Allyn and Bacon, Publishers, 1816G
Allman, Ludwig, 1952D
Almeida, Antonia de, 1928A, 1957D, 1960D,
1976D, 1977E, 1997B
Almeida, Francisco António de, 1755B

Almeida, Inácio António de, 1760A, 1790D,
1825B
Almeida, Renato: *Historia da musica Brasileira,*
1926H
Ameln, Konrad: *Handbuch der deutschen
Evangelischen Kirchenmusik,* 1935H
Almenräder, Carl: *Traité sur le perfectionnement
du basson...,* 1820H
Almerares, Paula, 1967A, 1990C
Almquist, Carl Jonas, 1793A, 1866B
Alonso-Crespo, Eduardo, 1956A
Alotin, Yardena, 1930A, 1994B
Alpaerts, Flor, 1876A, 1934D, 1954B
Alsbach Music Publishers, 1866G
Alsen, Elsa, 1880A, 1900C, 1902C
Alsen, Herbert, 1906A, 1929C, 1978B
Alsop, Marin, 1989E, 1990D, 1993D, 1999F
Altamont Festival, 1969G
Alten, Bella, 1877A, 1897C, 1962B
Altenburg, Johann, 1801B; *Lebens-Umstande des
Organisten Altenburg,* 1769H
Altenburger, Christian, 1957A, 1976C
Altglass, Max, 1952B
Althouse, Paul, 1889A, 1913CF, 1954B
Altman, Elizabeth, 1948A, 1975C
Altman, Ludwig, 1910A, 1990B
Altmann, Wilhelm, 1862A, 1900D, 1951B
Altmeyer, Jeannine, 1948A, 1971C
Altmeyer, Theo, 1931A
Altnikol, Johann Christoph, 1759B
Altrichter, Peter (Petr), 1951A, 1983D, 1995D
Altschuler, Modest, 1873A, 1963B
Alva, Luigi, 1927A, 1950C
Alvares, Eduardo, 1947A, 1970C
Alvarez, Albert, 1861A, 1892C, 1933B
Alvarez, Carlos, 1963A
Alvary, Lorenzo, 1909A, 1934C, 1996B
Alvary, Max, 1856A, 1879C, 1898B
Alwyn, William, 1905A, 1978E, 1985B
Am, Magnar, 1952A
Amadé, Thaddäus, 1782A, 1845B
Amadé Trio, 1974G
Amadeus Festival (NJ), 1995G
Amadeus Kammerorchester, 1991G
Amadeus String Quartet, 1947G
Amadeus Trio, 1988G
Amaize, Odekhiren, 1953A
Amalia, Anna, 1787B
Amapola Records, 1998G
Amara, Lucine, 1927A, 1946C
Amason, Kristinn, 1963A
Amato, Pasquale, 1878A, 1900C, 1942B
Ambassador Duo, 1990G
Ambros, August Wilhelm, 1816A, 1876B; *Bunte
Blätter I,* 1872H; *Bunte Blätter II,* 1874H; *Die
Grenzen der Musik und Poesie,* 1856H; *History
of Music I,* 1862H
Ambrosch, Joseph Carl, 1759A, 1784C, 1822B
Amdré, Martin, 1960A

❄

A *Births*   B *Deaths*   C *Debuts*   D *New Positions*
E *Prizes/Honors*

Ameling, Elly, 1938A, 1958E, 1961C, 1995F
Amendola, Giuseppe, 1808B
American Academy & Institute of Fine Arts,
    1886G
American Academy of Arts and Letters, 1904G
American Academy of Conducting, 2000G
American Academy of Teachers of Singing,
    1922G
American Academy in Rome, 1921G
American Accordionists' Association, 1938G
American Artists International Foundation,
    1977G
American Arts Orchestra, 1950G
American Association of University Professors,
    1915G
American Ballad Singers, 1939G
American Ballet Caravan, 1941G
American Bandmasters Association, 1929G
American Berlin Opera Foundation, 1986G
American Brass Quintet, 1960G
American Cabinet Organ, 1861G
American Chamber Trio, 1972G
American Choral Director's Association,
    1959G
American Choral Foundation, 1954G
American Choral Review, 1958G
American Classical Musical Hall of Fame,
    1998G
American Classics Series (Naxos), 1998G
American College of Musicians, 1884G
American Composers Alliance, 1937G
American Composer's Orchestra, 1976G
American Composer's Project, 1925G
American Conservatory at Fontainebleau,
    1921G
American Council of Learned Societies, 1975G
American Federation of Musicians, 1896G
American Folksong Festival, 1930G
American Gramophone Co., 1887G
American Guild of Musical Artists, 1936G
American Guild of Organists, 1896G
American Harp Journal, 1967G
American Harp Society, 1962G
American Institute for Verdi Studies, 1976G
American Institute of Musicology
    (Cambridge), 1945G
American International Artists, 1978G
American Library of Musicology, 1932G
American Liszt Society, 1967G
American Music, 1983G
American Music Editions, 1951G
American Music Ensemble Vienna, 1987G
American Music Journal, 1884G, 1900G
The American Music Lover, 1935G
American Music Theater Festival, 1983G
American Music/Theater Group, 1977G
American Music Week, 1985G
American Musical Instrument, 1971G
American Musical Instrument Society, 1971G

American Musical Magazine, 1786G
American Musicological Society, 1934G
American National Orchestra, 1923G
American Opera Project, 1979G
American Opera Society, 1951G
American Orchestral Society, 1920G
The American Organist, 1918G
American Piano Co., 1908G
American Prix de Rome, 1905G
American Publisher's Copyright League,
    1886G
The American Recorder, 1960G
American Recorder Society, 1939G
American Repertory Singers, 1994G
American School Band Directors' Association,
    1953G
American Society for Jewish Music, 1974G
American Society of Ancient Instruments,
    1925G
American Society of Composers, Authors &
    Publishers (ASCAP), 1914G
American Society of Piano Technicians, 1940G
American Society of University Composers,
    1966G
American Steam Music Co., 1855G
American String Quartet, 1974G
The American String Teacher, 1951G
American String Teachers Association, 1946G
American Symphony Orchestra, 1894G, 1915G
American Symphony Orchestra (Stokowski),
    1962G
American Symphony Orchestra League, 1942G
American Women Composers, 1976G
American Youth Symphony Orchestra (LA),
    1964G
Americus Records, 1996G
Amherst Saxophone Quartet, 1977G
Amici della Musica (Ancona), 1914G
Amicis, Anna Lucia de, 1754C, 1816B
Amigos de Musica (Mexico), 1939G
Amiot, Jean-Joseph, 1793B; *Mémoire sur la
    musique des Chinois*, 1779H
Amirkhanian, Charles, 1945A
Amirov, Fikret, 1922A, 1984B
Amon, Johannes A., 1763A, 1817D, 1825B
Amor Artis Chorale (Yale), 1961G
Amor Artis Orchestra (Yale), 1961G
Amorevoli, Angelo (Maria), 1798B
Amoyal, Pierre, 1949A, 1963E, 1964E, 1970E,
    1971C
Ampex Co., 1944G
Amphion, 1818G
Amsellen, Norah, 1995C
Amsterdam, Netherlands: Cellokwartet
    Amsterdam, 1996G; Chamber Orchestra,
    1957G; Holland Festival, 1947G
Amundrud, Lawrence, 1954A, 1972C
Amy, Gilbert, 1936A, 1973D
An, Ning, 1976A, 2000E

❋

F *Biographical*   G *Cultural Beginnings*   H *Musical Literature*
        I *Musical Compositions*

An, Youngshin, 1983E
An Die Musik (NY), 1976G
Anapolis Brass Quintet, 1971G
Ančerl, Karel, 1908A, 1933D, 1945D, 1950D, 1969D, 1973B
Anchorage, Alaska: Civic Opera, 1955G; Community Chorus, 1947G; Symphony Orchestra, 1946G
Ancona, Mario, 1860A, 1889C, 1931B
Ancot, Jean, *pére*, 1779A, 1848B
Ancot, Jean, *fils*, 1799A, 1829B
Ancot, Louis, 1803A, 1836B
Anda, Géza, 1921A, 1938C, 1940E, 1976B
Anday, Rosette, 1903A, 1920C
Anders, Aloys, 1817A, 1845C, 1864B
Anders, Peter, 1908A, 1931C, 1954B
Andersen, Anton J., 1845A
Andersen, Arthur: *Practical Orchestration*, 1929H
Andersen, Bo, 1963A
Andersen, Carl J., 1847A, 1909B
Andersen, Karsten, 1964D
Anderson, Allen, 1951A
Anderson, Avril, 1953A
Anderson, Beth, 1950A
Anderson, David Maxwell, 1964A, 1990C
Anderson, Julian, 1967A
Anderson, Laurie, 1947A
Anderson, Leroy, 1975B
Anderson, Lorna, 1962A, 1988C
Anderson, Marian, 1897A, 1902A, 1925C, 1955F, 1963E, 1965G, 1978E, 1986E, 1993B
Anderson, Marian, Award for American Singers, 1988G
Anderson, Marian, Fellowship, 1972G
Anderson, George F, 1848E
Anderson, Lucy, 1797A, 1878B
Anderson Mark, 1963A, 1988C, 1993E, 1994E
Anderson, Sylvia, 1938A, 1962C
Anderson, T. J., 1972D
Anderson, Valdine, 1965A
Anderssen, B. Tommy, 1964A, 1992C
Andersson, Richard, 1851A, 1872C, 1890E, 1918B
Andersson, Richard, Music School, 1886G
Anderszewski, Piotr, 1969A, 1991C
Andorra Chamber Orchestra, 1993G
Andrade, Francesco d', 1859A, 1882C, 1921B
Andrade, Rosario, 1951A, 1974C
André, Carl A.: *Der Klavierbau und seine geschichte*, 1855H
André, Charles-Louis, 1765A, 1839B
André, Franz, 1893A, 1935D, 1952E, 1975B
André, Johann, 1799B
André, Johann, Publishing Co., 1774G
André, Johann Anton, 1775A, 1842B; *Lehrbuch der Tonsetzkunst I*, 1832H
André, Maurice, 1933A, 1954C, 1955E, 1963E
Andreae, Volkmar, 1906D, 1914D, 1962B

Andrée, Elfrida, 1841A, 1867D, 1929B
Andreescu, Horia, 1946A
Andreoli, Carlo, 1840A, 1858C, 1908B
Andreoli, Evangelista, 1875B
Andreoli, Guglielmo, 1854C
Andreoli, Guglielmo, II, 1862A, 1932B
Andreoni, Giovanni Battista, 1797A
Andreozzi, Gaetano, 1755A, 1826B
Andrésen, Ivar, 1896A, 1919C, 1940B
Andreszewski, Piotr, 1991C
Andrevi y Castellar, Francisco, 1786A, 1819D, 1831D, 1839D, 1853B; *Traité d'harmonie et de composition*, 1848H
Andrez, Benoit, 1804B
Andriasova, Marta, 1941A
Andricu, Mihail, 1894A, 1974B
Andries, Jean, 1798A, 1851D, 1872B; *Précis de l'histoire de la musique...*, 1863H
Andriessen, Hendrik, 1892A, 1937D, 1949D, 1981B
Andriessen, Jurriaan, 1925A, 1996B
Andriessen, Louis, 1939A
Andriessen, Willem, 1887A, 1937D, 1964B
Androt, Albert A., 1781A, 1803E, 1804B
Andsnes, Leif Ove, 1970A, 1987C, 1990E, 1998E
Anet, Jean-Baptiste, 1755B
Anfossi, Pasquale, 1763F, 1790F, 1791D, 1797B
Angas, Richard, 1942A, 1962E
Angel, Marie, 1953A
Angel, Ryland, 1966A
Angeles, Victoria de los, 1947E
Angelet, Charles François, 1797A, 1832B
Angelich, Nicholas, 1994
Angelici, Marta, 1938C
Angelo, Louis d', 1888A, 1917C, 1958B
Angeloni, Carlo, 1834A, 1901B
Angermüller, Rudolph, 1940A
Angiolini, Domenico Gasparo, 1803B
Angeloni, Luigi: *Sopra la vita le opera...de Guido d'Arezzo*, 1811H
Anglès, Higini, 1888A, 1917D, 1943D, 1969B; *Studio musicologia*, 1959H
Anglés, Rafael, 1762D, 1816B
Angrisani, Carlo, 1817C
Anichanov, André, 1991D
Anievas, Augustin, 1934A, 1952C, 1961E
Anisimova, Tania, 1966A
Annibali, Dominico, 1779B
Anonymous Four, 1995G
Anrooy, Peter van, 1879A, 1917D, 1954B
Ansani, Giovanni, 1826B
Ansbach, Germany: Bach Festival, 1948G; Choral Society, 1831G; Male Chorus, 1833G
Ansell, Gillian, 1968B
Anselmi, Giuseppe, 1876A, 1896C, 1929B
Ansermet, Ernest, 1883A, 1915D, 1918D, 1969B; *Débat sur l'art contemporain*, 1948H; *Fundamentals of Music in Human*

A *Births*   B *Deaths*   C *Debuts*   D *New Positions*
E *Prizes/Honors*

Consciousness, 1961H; *Le geste du chef d'orchestre*, 1943H
Ansorge, Conrad, 1862A, 1930B
Anspach, Elizabeth, 1828B
Ansseau, Fernand, 1890A, 1913C, 1972B
Antheil, George, 1959B; *Bad Boy of Music*, 1945H
Anthes, George, 1862A, 1889C, 1922B, 1988C
Anthologie Sonore, 1934G
Anthony, James R., 1922A
Antner, Josephine von, 1867A
Antoine, Anne-Marie, 1944A
Antonacci, Anna Caterina, 1961A, 1986C
Antoni, Antonio d', 1801A, 1829D, 1859B
Antonioli, Jean François, 1982C
Antoniotto, Giorgio, 1776B; *Treatise on the Composition of Music*, 1760H
Antoniozzo, Alfonso, 1963A
Antonucci, Stefano, 1955A, 1986C
Antony, Franz Joseph, 1790A, 1837B; *Archäologisch-liturgisches...Kirchengesangs*, 1829H
Antwerp Philharmonic Orchestra, 1955G
Aotea Centre for the Performing Arts (NZ), 1990G
Aparicio, José de Orejón, 1765B
Apel, Johann August, 1771A, 1816B; *Metrik I*, 1814H
Apel, Willi, 1893A, 1988B; *Der Fuge*, 1932H; *Gregorian Chant*, 1957H; *The Harvard Dictionary of Music*, 1944H; *Historical Anthology of Music I*, 1946H; *History of Organ & Clavier Music*, 1967H; *Die Italienische Violinmusik im 17. Jahrhundert*, 1983H; *Masters of the Keyboard*, 1947H; *Musik aus Früher Zeit I, II*, 1934H; *The Notation of Polyphonic Music, 900-1600*, 1942H
APELAC (Belgian Electronic Studio), 1958G
Apell, David August von, 1754A, 1800E
Aperghis, Georges, 1945A
Apollo's Fire, 1992G
Apostel, Hans Erich, 1901A, 1972B
Appel Toby, 1952A
Appelgren, Richard, 1997E
Appia, Edmond, 1952E
Appleton, Jon, 1939A; *The Development & Practice of Electronic Music*, 1975H; *Twenty-First Century Musical Instruments: Hardware & Software*, 1989H
Appleton, Thomas, 1785A, 1872B
Appleton, Thomas, Organ Maker, 1821G
Aprahamian, Felix: *Essays on Music*, 1967H
Aprile, Giuseppe, 1753C, 1813B; *The Modern Italian Method of Singing*, 1791H
Apthorp, William F, 1848A, 1876D, 1881D, 1913B; *Opera, Past & Present*, 1901H
Arad, Avner, 1988E
Aragall, Giacomo, 1939A, 1963CE
Araia, Francesco, 1755F, 1770B

Araiza, Francisco, 1950A, 1969C
Aranaz y Vides, Pedro, 1769D
Arangi-Lombardi, Giannina, 1891A, 1920C, 1951B
Aranyi, Desider, 1868A, 1890C, 1923B
Aranyi, Jelly d', 1893A, 1909C, 1966B
Arban, Jean-Baptiste, 1825A, 1889B; *Méthode complète pour cornet à pistons*, 1864H
Arbós, Enrique Fernández, 1863A, 1939B
Arcangelo, Ildebrando d', 1969B
Archangelski, Alexander, 1924B
Archangelsky Chorus (Russia), 1880G
Archer, Frederick, 1838A, 1896D, 1901B
Archer, Neill, 1961A
Archibald, Ann, 1967A
Archiv für Musikwissenschaft (Revival), 1952G
Archive of American Folksong, 1928G
Archives of Folk & Primitive Music (Columbia), 1936G
Arcy, Amelia d', 1997C
Ardaez, Igor, 1967A
Arden-Griffith, Paul, 1952A, 1973C
Arditi, Luigi, 1822A, 1858D, 1903B
Ardoin, John: *Philadelphia Orchestra: A Century of Music*, 1999H
Ardova, Asya, 1996C, 1972A
Arel, Bülent, 1959F
Arena, Giuseppe, 1784B
Arens, Franz Xavier, 1856A
Arensky, Anton, 1861A, 1895D, 1906B
Arenx, Franz Xavier, 1932B
Arevalo, Octavio, 1963A, 1989C
Argenta, Atáulfo, 1913A, 1945D, 1958B
Argenta, Nancy, 1957A
Argento, Dominick, 1927A, 1976E, 1980E, 1993E, 1998E
Argerich, Martha, 1941A, 1949C, 1957E, 1965E, 1980F
Argiris, Spiros, 1948A, 1986D, 1987D, 1988D, 1996B
Ariel Ensemble, 1976G
Arimondi, Vittorio, 1861A, 1883C, 1928B
Arioso String Quartet, 1986G
Arista Trio, 1987G
Arkansas (*see also* Little Rock): Ashley Slave Band, 1836G; Folk Festival, 1963G; Music Festival, 1982G; Opera Theater, 1973G; Symphony Orchestra, 1966G
Arkel, Teresa, 1861A, 1884C, 1929B
Arker, André d', 1924C
Arkhipova, Irina, 1925A, 1954C
Arkor, André d', 1901A, 1925C, 1945D, 1971B
Arlberg, Georg E., 1830A, 1858C, 1896B
Arlen, Harold, 1905A
Armilato, Fabio, 1963A, 1986CE
Armingaud, Jules, 1820A, 1900B; *Consonances et dissonances*, 1882H
Armingaud-Jacquard Quartet, 1855G

❈

F *Biographical*   G *Cultural Beginnings*   H *Musical Literature*
I *Musical Compositions*

Armitage, Edward, 1872E
L'armonia, 1856G
Armster, Karl, 1906C, 1943B
Armstrong, Karan, 1941A, 1969C
Armstrong, Richard, 1943A, 1973D, 1993D
Armstrong, Sheila, 1942A, 1965CE
Arndt-Ober, Margarethe, 1885A, 1906C, 1971B
Arne, Michael, 1786B
Arne, Thomas, 1755F, 1759E, 1767F, 1778B;
   Agreeable Musical Choice I, 1753H; *Agreeable*
   Musical Choice II, 1754H; *Vocal Melody III*,
   1751H; *Vocal Melody IV*, 1752H
Arnold, Carl, 1794A, 1877B
Arnold, David, 1949A, 1985C; *New Oxford*
   Companion to Music, 1983H
Arnold, Denis, 1926A, 1986B
Arnold, Johann Gottfried, 1773A, 1806B
Arnold, John: *Church Music Reformed*, 1765H;
   The Essex Harmony, 1767H
Arnold, Malcolm, 1921A, 1993E
Arnold, Maurice, 1865A, 1937B
Arnold, Richard, 1845A, 1918B
Arnold, Samuel, 1793D, 1802B
Arnold, Yury, 1863D
Arnoldson, Sigrid, 1861A, 1885C, 1943B
Arnould, Sophie, 1757C, 1802B
Arnster, Karl, 1882A
Aronica, Roberto, 1992C
Aronov, Arkady, 1929A, 1963C
Aronson, Naoum, 1943B
ARP Instruments, 1970G
L'Arpa, 1853G
Arquier, Joseph, 1763A, 1816B
Arquimbau, Domingo, 1758A, 1795D, 1815E,
   1829B
Arral, Blanche, 1865A, 1880C, 1945B
Arriaga, Juan Crisostomo, 1806A, 1826B
Arrieta y Corera, Pascual Juan, 1823A, 1894B
Arrau, Claudio, 1903A, 1914C, 1927E, 1984E,
   1991B
Arrau, Claudio, Fund for Young Musicians,
   1967G
Arrow Music Press, 1938G
Arroyo, Martina, 1936A, 1958C
Ars Nova Orchestra, 1974G
Ars Organi, 1952G
Ars Poetica Chamber Orchestra, 1990G
Ars Viva, Publisher, 1950
Art & Literature, 1873G
Artaria, Giovanni, and Co., 1765G
Arteaga, Esteban de, 1799B; *Del ritmo sonoro e*
   del ritmo muto..., 1796H; *Investigaciones*
   filósoficas sobre la belleza ideal..., 1789H;
   Rivoluzioni del teatro musicale italiano I,
   1783H; *Rivoluzioni del teatro musicale italiano*
   IV, 1788H
Arte Nova, 1995G
L'Arte Pianistica, 1914G
Artegna, Francesco Ellero d', 1948A, 1981C

Arthur, Alfred, 1844A, 1918B
Artist Led Recording Label, 1997G
Artistic (Ondříček) String Quartet, 1921G
Artistic Ambassador Program, 1982G
Artner, Josephine von, 1888C, 1932B
Artôt, Alexandre J., 1815A, 1839C, 1845B
Artôt, Désirée, 1857C, 1907B
Artôt, Jean-Désiré, 1803A, 1887B
Artôt, Marguerite-Desirée, 1835A
Artôt, Maurice M., 1772A, 1829B
Artôt de Padilla, Lola, 1933B
Artpark Festival, 1974G
ARTS (Munich), 1993G
Arts Council of Australia (Sydney), 1944G
Artzt, Alice, 1943A, 1969C
Arutiunian, Alexander, 1920A
Arvin, Gary, 1954A
Asafiev, Boris, 1884A, 1949B; *Composers of the*
   First Half of the 19th Century, 1945H; *Musical*
   Form as Process I, 1930H; *Russian Classical*
   Music, 1945H; *Russian Music from the*
   Beginning,...19th Century, 1930H; *Russian*
   Poets in Russian Music, 1921H
Asawa, Brian, 1966A, 1995C
Asbury, Stefan, 1965A
Asbury Brass Quintet, 1982G
ASCAP Foundation Grants to Young
   Composers, 1978G
Aschaffenbrug, Walter, 1966E
Ascherberg, Eugene, & Co., Publishers, 1878G
Ascoli, Bernard d', 1958A, 1981C
Ashdown, Edwin, Ltd., Publishers, 1825G
Ashe, Andrew, 1759A, 1792C, 1838B
Asheville Mountain Dance & Folk Festival,
   1928G
Ashkenazy, Dimitri, 1969A
Ashkenazy, Vesko, 1970A
Ashkenazy, Vladimir, 1937A, 1956E, 1962E,
   1981F, 1998D
Ashkenazy, Vovka, 1961A, 1983C
Ashley, Charles Jane, 1772A, 1843B
Ashley, John, 1805B
Ashley, Richard G, 1775A
Ashley, Robert, 1930A
Ashworth, Charles S., 1804D
Ashworth, Valerie, 1956A, 1969C
Asia, Daniel, 1953A, 1988D, 1991F
Asian American Arts Alliance, 1992G
Asian Music, 1968G
Asian Music Festival (Tokyo), 1990G
Asian Music Forum, 1969G (UNESCO)
Asioli, Bonifacio, 1769A, 1805D, 1808D, 1832B;
   Elementi de Contrabasso..., 1823H; *Il maestro de*
   composizione, 1836H; *Principi elementari di*
   musica, 1809H; *Trattato d'armonia e*
   d'accompagnamento, 1814H
Asioli, Luigi, 1767A, 1815B
Aspen, Colorado: Center for Advanced
   Quartet Studies, 1982G; Festival Piano

❄

A   *Births*   B   *Deaths*   C   *Debuts*   D   *New Positions*
E   *Prizes/Honors*

Quartet, 1955G; Harris Concert Hall, 1993G;
Music Festival, 1949G,1950G; Symphony
Orchestra, 1914G
Asplmayr, Franz, 1786B
Associated Councils of the Arts, 1960G
Associated Glee Clubs of America, 1924G
Associated Music Publishers, 1927G
Association des Amis d'Henry Expert..., 1952G
Association des Chanteurs de St. Gervais,
1892G
Association for Classical Music, 1982
Association for Recorded Sound Collections,
1966G
Association for the Advancement of Creative
Musicians (AACM), 1965G
Association of American Women Composers,
1926G
Association of Concert Bands, 1977G
Association of Independent Composers &
Performers, 1969G
Association of Italian Musicologists, 1908G
Association of Professional Vocal Ensembles,
1977G
Assmayer, Ignaz, 1790A, 1862B
Ast, Jochen van, 1970A
Astarita, Gennaro, 1803B
Aston Magna Foundation for Music, 1972G
Aston Magna Baroque Festival, 1972G
Astor, J. J., Music Shop, 1786G
Astor and Co., Flute Manufacturers, 1778G
Astreya Ensemble, 1975G
Atamian, Dickran, 1975E
Athene Records, 1991G
Atherton, David, 1967D, 1968CD, 1980D,
1981D, 1989D
Atherton, James, 1943A, 1971C, 1987B
Atherton, Joan, 1948A
Athinäos, Nikos, 1990D
Atkins, Ivor, 1869A, 1921E, 1953B
Atlanta, Georgia: Choral Guild, 1940G;
Viennese Summerfest, 1989G
Atlas, 1826G
Atlantic Brass Quintet, 1985G
Atlantic City Auditorium, 1967G
Atlantov, Vladimir, 1939A, 1963C
Atlas, Allan W., 1943A
Atlas, Dalia, 1933A, 1964E, 1978E
Atterberg, Kurt, 1887A, 1913D, 1974B
Attwood, Thomas, 1765A, 1775F, 1783F 1836D,
1838B
Atwill, Joseph, & Co., 1852G
Atzmon, Moshe, 1969D, 1972D
Auber, Daniel-Louis, 1842D
Auber, Daniel François, 1782A, 1802F, 1803F,
1825E, 1829E, 1842D, 1871B; Règles de
contrepoint, 1808H
Aubert, Jacques, 1753B
Aubert, Louis-François, 1877A, 1800B, 1968B
Aubigné, Lloyd d', 1865A, 1895C, 1930B

Aubry, Pierre, 1874A, 1910B
Auda, Antoine, 1964B; Les modes et les tons,
1931H
Audeyeva, Larisa, 1925A
Audiffren, Jean, 1762B
Audiffren, Joseph-Lazare, 1771D
Audinot, Nicholas, 1801B
Audran, Edmund, 1840A, 1901B
Audran, Marius-Pierre, 1816A, 1840C, 1863D,
1887B
Audsley, George A.: The Art of Organ Building,
1905H
Audubon String Quartet, 1974G
Auer, Edward, 1967E, 1968E
Auer, Leopold, 1845A, 1930B; Violin Master
Works & Their Interpretations, 1925H; Violin
Playing as I Teach It, 1921H
Auernhammer, Josepha B., 1758A, 1820B
Augener & Co., Publisher, 1853G
Augér, Arleen, 1939A, 1967C, 1993B
Auguez, Numa, 1847A, 1871C, 1903B
Augusta (Georgia) Opera, 1967G
Auletta, Pietro, 1771B
Aulin, Laura Valborg, 1860A, 1928B
Aulin, Tor, 1914B
Aulin String Quartet, 1887G
Auriacombe, Louis, 1917A, 1982B
Auric, Georges, 1899A, 1920F, 1983B
Aurisicchio, Antonio, 1756D, 1781B
Aurora (Hungary), 1822G
Auryn String Quartet, 1982G
Austin, Florence, 1884A, 1901C, 1927B
Austin, Frederic, 1872A, 1902C
Austin, John Turnell, 1869A, 1948B
Austin, Larry, 1930A, 1966D; Learning to
Compose, 1988H
Austin, William W., 1920A; Music in the
Twentieth Century, 1966H; New Looks at Italian
Opera, 1968H
Austin Organ Co., 1899G
Austral, Florence, 1892A, 1922C, 1968B
Austral String Quartet (Sydney), 1958G
Australia Music Center, 1976G
Australian Broadcasting Commission, 1932G
Australian Journal of Music Education, 1967G
Australian Opera Co., 1956G
Australian String Quartet, 1985G
Australian Youth Orchestra, 1957G
Austrian Radio Symphony Orchestra, 1969G
Autori, Franco, 1936D
Avalon, Robert, 1955A
Avalon Wind Quintet, 1991G
Avanti Chamber Orchestra, 1982G
Avedis Zildjian Co., 1929G
Averill, Perry, 1862A, 1895C
Avery, John, 1807B
Avila, M. Romero de, 1779B
Avison, Charles, 1770B; Essay on Musical
Expression, 1752H

F *Biographical*   G *Cultural Beginnings*   H *Musical Literature*
I *Musical Compositions*

Avondano, Pedro Antonio, 1782B
Avossa, Guiseppe d', 1796B
Avshalomov, Aaron, 1894A, 1965B
Avshalomov, Jacob, 1919A, 1965E
Ax, Emanuel, 1949A, 1974E, 1979E
Ax-Kim-Ma Trio, 1980G
Aydin, Özgür, 1972A
Aylward, Theodore, 1760D, 1788D, 1801B
Ayres, Frederic, 1876A, 1926B
Ayrton, Edmund, 1784E, 1808B
Ayrton, William, 1777A, 1799D, 1813D, 1823D, 1834D, 1837D, 1858B; *Sacred Minstrelsy*, 1835H
Ayton, Fanny, 1806A
Azaïs, Hyacinthe, 1796B; *Méthode de musique sur un nouveau plan*, 1776H
Azevedo, Luiz Heitor de, 1905A
Azevedo, Sérgio, *A invencao des sons*, 1998H
Azocar, José, 1961A
Azuma, Atsuko, 1939A, 1963C
Azzopardi, Francesco, 1809B
Baader, J. A., & Co, Zither Maker, 1790G
Baaren, Kees van, 1906A, 1948D, 1953D, 1958D, 1970B
Babadzhanian, Arno, 1921A, 1983B
Babayan, Sergei, 1990E
Babak, Renate, 1939A, 1958C
Babbi, Gregori, 1768B
Babbi, Christofore B., 1774E, 1775D, 1814B
Babbini, Matteo, 1754A, 1780C, 1816B
Babbitt, Milton, 1916A, 1931F, 1959D, 1965E, 1970E, 1982E, 1983E, 1986E; *The Function of Set Structure in the Twelve Tone System*, 1946H; *Words about Music*, 1987H
Babcock, Alpheus, 1785A, 1842B
Babiali, Cesare, 1805A
Babier, René, 1923D
Babikian, Virginia, 1957C
Babin, Victor, 1908A, 1961D, 1972B
Babin, Vitya Vronsky, 1992B
Bacarisse, Salvador, 1898A, 1963B
Baccaloni, Salvatore, 1900A, 1922C, 1969B
Bacewicz, Grazyna, 1909A, 1969B
Bach, Andreas, 1968A, 1984C
Bach, August Wilhelm, 1816D, 1832D
Bach, Conrad, 1977D
Bach, C. P. E., 1768D, 1788B; *Proper Method of Playing Keyboard Instruments I*, 1753H; *Proper Method of Playing Keyboard Instruments II*, 1762H
Bach, Erik, 1946A
Bach, Jan, 1961E
Bach, Johann Christian, 1754F, 1760DF, 1762F, 1764EF, 1772F, 1782B
Bach, Johann Christoph Friedrich, 1795B
Bach, Johann Ernst, 1756B, 1777B
Bach, Johann Nicolaus, 1753B
Bach, Wilhelm Friedemann, 1762F, 1764F, 1774F, 1784B

Bach, Wilhelm Friedrich Ernest, 1759A, 1845B
Bach, Vincent, Corporation, 1919G
Bach Aria Festival & Institute, 1981G
Bach Choir of Philadelphia, 1934G
Bach Choir of Pittsburgh, 1934G
Bach Festival, Krakow-Katowice, 1985G
Bach Gesellschaft (Germany), 1850G
Bach Home & Museum, 1907G
Bach Society of Chile, 1917G
Bach Society of St. Louis, 1942G
Bachauer, Gina, 1913A, 1933E, 1935C, 1976B
Bachauer, Gina, International Piano Competition, 1976G
Bache, Francis Edward, 1833A, 1858B
Bache, Walter, 1842A, 1871C, 1888B
Bachlund, Gary, 1958A
Bachmann, Alberto: *Encyclopedia of the Violin*, 1925H; *Les grands violonistes du passé*, 1913H; *Gymnastique à l'usage des violonistes*, 1914H; *Le violon*, 1906H
Bachmann, Hermann, 1890C
Bachmann, Rhonda, 1952A
Bachmann, Maria, 1983E
Bachofen, Johann C., 1755B
Bachorek, Milan, 1939A
Bachschmidt, Anton, 1797B
Bacilli, Monica, 1987C
Back Bay Brass Quintet, 1982G
Bäck, Sven-Erik, 1919A, 1961E, 1994B
Backers, Cor, 1910A
Backhaus, Wilhelm, 1884A, 1892C, 1969B
Backofen, Johann Georg, 1768A, 1839B
Backofen Instrument Factory, 1815G
Backus, John: *The Acoustical Foundations of Music*, 1969H
Bacon, Ernst, 1898A, 1932E, 1934D, 1945D, 1962E, 1990B; *Notes on the Piano*, 1963H; *Our Musical Idiom*, 1917H; *Words on Music*, 1960H
Bacon, Richard Mackenzie, 1776A, 1844B; *The Art of Improving the Voice and Ear*, 1825H; *Elements of Vocal Science*, 1824H
Bacon Piano Co., 1789G
Bacquier, Gabriel, 1924A, 1950C
Baculewski, Krzysztof, 1950A
Bad Godesberg Concert Society, 1918G
Bada, Angelo, 1875A, 1898C, 1908C, 1941B
Badea, Christian, 1947A, 1976D, 1983D
Baden, Conrad, 1908A, 1989B
Baden-Baden, Germany: Symphonie und Kurorchester, 1872G
Badescu, Dinu, 1904A, 1931C
Badger, Alfred G., 1815A, 1892B
Badia, Conchita, 1897A, 1913C, 1975B
Badiali, Cesare, 1865B
Badings, Henk, 1907A, 1987B
Badini, Ernesto, 1876A, 1895C, 1937B
Badinski, Nicolai, 1937A, 1979E
Badisches Konservatorium für Music, 1884G
Badisches Stattstheater (Karlsruhe), 1975G

A *Births*   B *Deaths*   C *Debuts*   D *New Positions*
E *Prizes/Honors*

Badura-Skoda, Paul, 1927A, 1947E, 1948C
Baedeker, Carl, Publisher, 18l27G
Bäermann, Heinrich, 1784A, 1847B
Baervoets, Raymond, 1930A, 1989B
Baeyens, August, 1895A, 1944D, 1953D, 1966B
Bagiatuni, Suren, 1976C
Bagley, Edwin E., 1922B
Baglioni, Bruna, 1970C
Bagratuni, Suren, 1963A
Baguer, Carlos, 1768A, 1789D, 18088B
Bahia Composers' Group, 1966G
Bahk, Jehi, 1971A, 1995C
Bahner, Gert, 1930A, 1965D, 1973D
Bähr, Josef, 1770A, 1819B
Bahr-Mildenburg, Anna, 1947B
Baildon, Joseph, 1774B
Bailey, Norman, 1933A, 1959C, 1977E, 1981E
Bailey Concert Hall (Fort Lauderdale), 1979G
Bailleux, Antoine: *Méthode...pour apprendre à
   jouer du violon*, 1798H
Baillie, Alexander, 1956A
Baillie, Isobel, 1895A, 1921C, 1978E, 1983B
Baillot, Pierre, 1771A, 1842B; *L'art du violon*,
   1834H
Baily, Edward Hodges, 1821E
Bain, Wilfred C., 1938D, 1947D
Bainbridge, Elizabeth, 1863C, 1936A, 1963C
Bainbridge, Simon, 1952A
Baines, Anthony, 1912A; *Bagpipes*, 1960H; *Brass
   Instruments*, 1976H; *Musical Instruments
   through the Ages*, 1961H; *The Oxford
   Companion to Musical Instruments*, 1992H;
   Woodwind Instruments & Their History, 1957H
Baini, Giuseppe, 1775A, 1818D, 1844B
Bainton, Edgar Leslie, 1880A, 1934D, 1956B
Bainville, François, 1763D, 1788B
Baird, Martha, 1895A, 1971B
Baird, Tadeusz, 1928A, 1958E, 1981B
Baird Music Hall (Buffalo), 1981G
Bairstow, Edward, 1874A, 1932E, 1946B;
   Counterpoint & Harmony, 1937H; *The
   Evolution of Musical Form*, 1943H
Bajamonti, Julije, 1800B
Bajetti, Giovanni, 1815A, 1876B
Bajoras, Feliksas, 1934A
Bakala, Břetislav, 1897A, 1929D, 1937D, 1956D,
   1958B
Bakaleinikov, Vladimir: *Elementary Rules of
   Conducting*, 1937H; *The Instruments of the
   Band & Orchestra*, 1940H
Bakels, Kees, 1998D
Baker, Alice, 1961A, 1986C
Baker, Alison Ruth, 1962A, 1977C
Baker, Claude, 1948A
Baker, David: *Techniques of Improvisation*,
   1971H
Baker, George, 1773A, 1847B
Baker, Gregg, 1955A, 1985C
Baker, Israel, 1921A

Baker, Janet, 1933A, 1953C, 1956E, 1976E,
   1982F
Baker, Julius, 1915A
Baker, Mark, 1953A, 1986C
Baker, Michael, 1937A
Baker, Theodore, 1851A, 1892D, 1934B; *Baker's
   Biographical Dictionary of Musicians*, 1900H;
   Dictionary of Musical Terms*, 1895H;
   Pronouncing Pocket Manual of Musical Terms,
   1905H
Baker & Scribner, Publishers, 1846G
Bakkegard, Benjamin, 1951A
Baklanov, George, 1881A, 1903C, 1938B
Baks, Richard, 1999B
Bakst, James: *A History of Russian Soviet Music*,
   1977H
Bakst, Lawrence, 1955A
Balada, Leonardo, 1933A
Balakauskas, Osvaldas, 1937A, 1992F, 1996E
Balakirev, Mily, 1837A, 1858F, 1867D, 1868D,
   1910B
Balakirev Circle, 1862G
Balanchine, George, 1933F, 1973E, 1983B;
   Complete Stories of Great Ballets, 1954H
Balanchivadze, Andrei, 1906A
Balasanian, Sergei, 1902A, 1982B
Balassa, Sandor, 1935A, 1972E, 1983E, 1988E
Balatka, Hans, 1825A, 1850D, 1860D, 1899B
Balatka Academy of Musical Art, 1879G
Balatka String Quartet, 1850G
Balban, Angelo, 1803B
Balbastre, Claude, 1799B
Balbi, Melchiore, 1796A, 1854D, 1879B;
   Grammatica ragionata della musica, 1825H
Baldan, Angelo, 1753A, 1803B
Baldi, João José, 1770A, 1789D, 1794D, 1806D,
   1816B
Baldwin, Dalton, 1931A
Baldwin, Marcia, 1939A
Baldwin, Samuel, 1949B
Baldwin, D. H., Piano Co., 1862G
Baldwin-Wallace Bach Festival (Ohio), 1932G
Baldwin-Wallace Conservatory of Music,
   1913G
Bales, Richard, 1915A, 1960E, 1985F
Baley, Virko, 1938A
Balfe, Michael, 1808A, 1823C, 1846D, 1852F,
   1870B; *Indispensable Studies for a Bass Voice*,
   1851H; *Indispensable Studies for a Soprano
   Voice*, 1851H; *A New Universal Method of
   Singing*, 1857H
Balfoort, Dirk Jacobus, 1886A, 1964B; *Het
   musiekleven in Nederland in de 17e en 18e eeuw*,
   1938H; *De Hollandsche Vioolmakers*, 1931H
Balkanska, Mimi, 1902A, 1919C
Balkwill, Bryan, 1922A
Ball, Ernest R., 1927B
Ball, Michael, 1946A
Ballabene, Gregorio, 1754E, 1803B

❈

F   *Biographical*   G   *Cultural Beginnings*   H   *Musical Literature*
   I   *Musical Compositions*

Ballantine, Christopher: *Twentieth Century Symphony*, 1983H
Ballantine, Edward, 1886A, 1971B
Ballard, Christophe, 1765B
Ballard, Louis W., 1931A; *Music of North American Indians*, 1975H
Ballet Russe de Monte Carlo, 1932G
Ballet Russe (Diaghilev), 1909G
Balletti, Giovanni Battista, 1813A
Ballif, Claude, 1924A; *Introduction à la métatonalité*, 1956H
Ballista, Antonio, 1936A
Ballo, Pietro, 1952A, 1977C
Ballou, Esther Williamson, 1915A, 1962F, 1973B; *Creative Explorations of Musical Elements*, 1971H
Balmer, Luc, 1898A, 1932D, 1935D, 1941D
Balogh, Endre, 1954A, 1971C
Balogh, Ernö, 1989B
Baloković, Zlatko, 1895A, 1965B
Balsach, Llorenc, 1953B
Balsam, Artur, 1906A, 1918C, 1930E, 1994B
Balsam, Artur, Foundation for Chamber Music, 1996G
Balslev, Lisbeth, 1945A, 1976C
Balsys, Eduardas, 1919A, 1984B
Balthrop Carmen, 1948A, 1973C
Baltimore, Maryland: Chamber Society, 1948G; Kraushaar Auditorium, 1962G; Lyric Theater, 1894G; Meyerhoff Symphony Hall, 1892G; Oratorio Society, 1882G; Peabody Conservatory of Music, 1857G; Peabody Institute, 1868G
Baltsa, Agnes, 1944A, 1964E, 1968C
Bal y Gay, Jesús, 1905A; *Trientos ensayos de estética musical*, 1960H
Bamberg, Germany: Allgemeine deutsche Caeciliaenverein, 1868G; Bamberg Theater, 1802G; Musikverein, 1820G
Bamberger, Carl, 1902A, 1924D, 1927D, 1987B; *The Conductor's Art*, 1965H
Bamboschek, Giuseppe, 1890A, 1918D, 1969B
Bamert, Matthias, 1942A, 1977D, 1985F, 1993D
Bampton, Rose, 1908A, 1929C
Band of the Royal Regiment of Artillery, 1762G
Banderali, Davidde, 1789A, 1806C, 1849B
Bandrowska-Turska, Eva, 1897A, 1919C, 1979B
Bandrowski-Sas, Alexander, 1881C, 1913B
Banff, Canada: Centre & School of Fine Arts, 1933G; Festival of the Arts, 1971G
Bang on a Can Festival, 1987G
Bangkok Opera, 1970G
Banister, Henry C., 1831A, 1897B; *The Art of Modulating*, 1901H; *The Harmonising of Melodies*, 1897H; *Lectures on Music Analysis*, 1887H; *Some Musical Ethics and Analogies*, 1884H
Banks, Barry, 1960A, 1989C
Banks, Benjamin, 1795B

Banks, Don, 1980BE
Banks, Jacques, 1943A
Bannatyne-Scott-Brian, 1955A, 1981C
Bannister Harpsichord Co., 1959G
Banse, Juliane, 1969A, 1989C
Banshchikov, Gennadi, 1943A
Banti, Brigida Giorgi, 1759A, 1776C, 1806B
Bantock, Granville, 1868A, 1893D, 1900D, 1946B
Bär, Olaf, 1957A, 1981C, 1982E
Barab, Seymour, 1921A
Baracewicz, Stanislaw, 1929B
Baracza, Peter, 1972C
Baranović, Kreimir, 1929D, 1952D, 1975B
Barantschik, Alexander, 1963A
Barati, George, 1913A, 1950D, 1959E, 1962E, 1996B
Barati Ensemble, 1989G
Barba, Daniel Dal, 1770D
Barbacino, Paolo, 1946A
Barbaja, Domenico, 1778A, 1809D, 1841B
Barbato, Elisabetta, 1944C
Barbaux, Christine, 1955A, 1977C
Barbe, Helmut, 1927A
Barbella, Emanuele, 1777B
Barber, Kimberley, 1961A, 1985C
Barber, Samuel, 1910A, 1928EF, 1928E, 1935E, 1941E, 1958E, 1976E, 1980E, 1981B
Barber Institute of Fine Arts (Birmingham), 1939G
Barbi, Alice, 1862A, 1882C, 1948B
Barbican Centre for Arts & Conferences, 1982G
Barbier, René, 1890A, 1981B
Barbieri, Carlo E., 1822A, 1862D, 1867B
Barbieri, Fedora, 1920A, 1940C
Barbieri, Francisco A., 1823A, 1892E, 1894B
Barbieri-Nini, Marianna, 1818A, 1840C, 1887B
Barbirolli, Evelyn: *Oboe Technique*, 1953H
Barbirolli, John, 1899A, 1926D, 1929D, 1933D, 1937D, 1943D, 1949E, 1961D, 1970B
Barbirolli Chamber Orchestra (Chelsea), 1925G
Barblan, Guglielmo, 1906A, 1978B
Barblan, Otto, 1860A, 1887D, 1943B
Barbosa-Lima, Carlos, 1944A, 1957C
Barbot, Joseph-Théodore, 1824A, 1848C, 1897B
Barbour, J. Murray, 1897A, 1970B; *Trumpets, Horns & Music*, 1964H; *Tuning & Temperament*, 1951H
Barcelona, Spain: Catalunya Nova, 1896G; Gran Teatro del Liceo, 1847G; Liceo Filarmónico Dramático, 1838G; Orfeó Catalâ, 1891G; Society of Classical Concerts, 1900G; Teatre Liceu, 1999G
Barcewicz, Stanislaw, 1858A, 1886D
Barcewicz String Quartet, 1892G
Barcza, Peter, 1949A
Barenboim, Daniel, 1942A, 1955C, 1975D, 1991D, 1992D
Bärenreiter-Verlag, 1923G

❊

A *Births*   B *Deaths*   C *Debuts*   D *New Positions*
E *Prizes/Honors*

Barere, Simon 1896A, 1951B
Bargiel, Woldemar, 1828A, 1897B
Bar Harbor Music Festival, 1964G
Bari Symphony Orchestra, 1967G
Barie, Augustin, 1883A, 1915B
Barili, Alfredo, 1854A, 1865C, 1935B
Bar-Illan, David, 1930A, 1946C
Barilli, Bruno, 1880A, 1952B; *Il paese del melodramma*, 1929H; *Il sorcio nel violino*, 1926H
Barjansky, Alexander, 1883A, 1961B
Bark, Jan, 1934A
Barkauskas, Vytautas, 1931A
Barkel, Charles, 1898A, 1942D, 1973B
Barkel String Quartet, 1928G
Barker, Charles, Organ Maker, 1832G
Barker, Charles Spackman, 1804A, 1879B
Barker, Jennifer Margaret, 1965A
Barker, John, 1781B
Barker, Paul, 1956A
Barkin, Elaine R., 1932A, 1964D
Barlow, Clara, 1928A, 1962C
Barlow, David, 1927A, 1975B
Barlow, Harold: *A Dictionary of Musical Themes*, 1948H; *A Dictionary of Vocal Themes*, 1950H
Barlow, Howard, 1892A, 1923D, 1927D, 1972B
Barlow, Samuel, 1892A, 1982B
Barlow, Stephen, 1954A
Barlow, Wayne, 1912A, 1996B; *Foundations of Music*, 1963H
Barlow Endowment for Music Composition, 1983G
Barmer Orchesterverein, 1874G
Bärmig, Johann Gotthilf, 1815A, 1899B
Barnby, Joseph (Sir), 1838A, 1863D, 1875D, 1892DE, 1896B
Barnes, Edward Shippen, 1858A, 1887A, 1958B
Barnett, Alice, 1975B
Barnett, John, 1802A, 1890B, 1917A, 1947D, 1953D, 1958D, 1979D
Barnett, John Francis, 1837A, 1861C, 1916B
Barnhouse, Charles, 1865A, 1929B
Barolsky, Michael, 1947A
Baron, Ernst Gottlieb, 1760B; *Abriss einer Abhandlung von der melodie*, 1756H
Baron, Samuel, 1925A; *Chamber Music for Winds*, 1969H
Baronesi, Debora, 1988C
Barraqué, Jean, 1928A, 1973B
Barrel Organ, 1772G
Barrère, Georges, 1876A, 1944B
Barrère-Britt-Salzedo Trio, 1932G
Barrère Little Symphony, 1914G
Barrère Ensemble of Wind Instruments, 1910G
Barrett, William, 1877D, 1887D; *English Church Composers*, 1877H
Barrie, James M., 1913E
Barrientos, Maria, 1884A, 1898C, 1946B
Barrière, Etienne J., 1767C, 1818B

Barrière, Jean-Baptiste, 1958A
Barrington, Daines, 1800B
Barrows, John, 1913A, 1974B
Barrueco, Manuel, 1952A, 1974C
Barry, Charles, 1852E
Barry, Gerald, 1952A
Barry, Jerome, 1939A
Barrymore, Lionel, 1878A
Barsanti, Francesco, 1772B
Barshai, Rudolf, 1924A
Barsotti, Tommaso Gaspara, 1786A; *Méthode de musique*, 1828H
Barsova, Valeriya, 1892A, 1920C, 1967B
Barstow, Josephine, 1940A, 1964C, 1995E
Bart, Lionel, 1999B
Barta, Ales, 1960A, 1984C
Bárta, Joseph, 1787B
Barta, Michael, 1954A, 1973CE
Bartay, András, 1799A, 1838D, 1854B; *Magyar Apollo*, 1834H
Barth, Christian Frederik, 1787A, 1861B
Barth, Christian Samuel, 1809B
Barth, Hans, 1897A, 1908C, 1956B
Barth, Karl Heinrich, 1847A, 1922B
Barth, Philip, 1774A, 1804B
Barth, Richard, 1850A, 1923B
Bartha, Clarry, 1958A, 1981C
Bartha, Denés, 1908A, 1993B
Barthe, Grat-Norbert, 1828A, 1854E, 1898B
Barthélemon, François-Hippolyte, 1808B
Bartholomée, Pierre, 1937A, 1977D
Bartini, Gary, 1976D
Bartlett, Homer Newton, 1920B
Barto, Tzimon, 1963A, 1983E, 1985C
Bartók, Béla, 1881A, 1903F, 1905F, 1926F, 1927F, 1931E, 1935E, 1937F, 1940E, 1943F, 1945B
Bartók String Quartet, 1957G
Bartoldi, Cecilia, 1966A, 1986C
Bartoletti, Bruno, 1926A
Bartolini, Lando, 1937A, 1973C
Bartolozzi, Bruno, 1911A, 1980B; *New Sounds for Woodwind*, 1967H
Barto, Frantiek, 1887F, 1905A, 1973B
Barto, Josef, 1887A, 1952B
Bartow, Nevett, 1934A, 1973B
Baryshnikov, Mikhail, 1989F
Barzin, Leon, 1900A, 1930D, 1960E, 1999B
Barzun, Jacques: *Berlioz & the Romantic Century*, 1950H; *Critical Questions on Music & Letters, Culture & Biography*, 1982H; *Music in American Life*, 1956H
Basel, Switzerland: Allgemeine Musikgesellschaft, 1876G; Chamber Orchestra, 1926G; Gesangverein, 1824G; Gesellschaft zur Beförderung des Guten, 1777G; Liedertafel, 1852G; Musikschule, 1867G
Basevi, Abramo, 1818A, 1885B
Bashkirov, Dmitri, 1931A, 1970E

❋

F *Biographical*   G *Cultural Beginnings*   H *Musical Literature*
I *Musical Compositions*

Bashmakov, Leonid, 1927A, 19779D
Bashmet, Yuri, 1953A, 1976E
Basically Bach Festival, 1978G
Basili, Andrea, 1777B
Basili, Francesco, 1767A, 1827D, 1837D, 1850B
Basilides, Mária, 1886A, 1915C, 1946B
Bainskas, Justinas, 1923A
Basiola, Mario, 1892A, 1918C, 1965B
Basquin, Peter: *Explorations in the Arts*, 1985H
Basrak, Cathy, 1995E
Bass Trumpet, 1810G
Bass Tuba, 1835G
Bassaraboff, Nicholas, 1973B
Bassett, Leslie, 1961E, 1923A, 1964E, 1976E
Bassi, Amadeo, 1874A, 1899C, 1949B
Bassi, Luigi, 1766A, 1779C, 1784C, 1825B
Bastiaans, Johannes Gijsbertus, 1812A, 1875B;
   Treatise on Harmony, 1867H
Bastianelli, Giannotto, 1883A, 1927B
Bastianini, Ettore, 1922A, 1945C, 1967B
Bastin, Jules, 1933A
Basto, Carla, 1956A, 1982C
Bate, Jennifer, 1944A, 1957C
Bate, Philip, 1909A; *The Flute: A Study of Its*
   History, Development & Construction, 1969H
Bate, Stanley, 1911A, 1959B
Bates, Joah, 1776D, 1799B
Bates, Leon, 1949A
Bates, Sarah, 1755A, 1777C, 1811B
Bath, Hubert, 1883A, 1945B
Bath Assembly Rooms ("The Upper Room"),
   1771G
Bathori, Jane, 1877A, 1900C, 1970B
Báthy, Anna, 1901A, 1928C, 1962B
Bathyphon, 1839G
Bátiz, Enrique, 1942A, 1969C, 1971D, 1983D,
   1984F, 1990D
Batjer, Margaret, 1959A, 1974C
The Baton: A Monthly Journal, 1895G
Baton Rouge, Louisiana: Lyric Opera Theater,
   1985G; Opera Co., 1982G
Bator, Tamas, 1989C
Battel, Giovanni, 1956A
Battaille, Charles-Amable, 1822A, 1848C,
   1872B; *Nouvelles recherches sur la phonation*,
   1861H; *De la Physiologie appliquée au...chant*,
   1863H
Batterham, Maurizio, 1968A
Battishill, Jonathan, 1801B
Battista, Vincenzo, 1823A, 1873B
Battista de Negri, Giovanni, 1923B
Battistini, Gaudenzio, 1800B
Battistini, Mattia, 1856A, 1878C, 1928B
Battle, Kathleen, 1948A, 1972C, 1994F
Battmann, Jacques Louis, 1818A, 1886B
Batton, Désiré-Alexandre, 1798A, 1817E,
   1855B
Baud-Bovy, Samuel: *Essai sur la chanson*
   populaire grecque, 1983H

Baudiot, Charles-Nicolas, 1773A, 1850B;
   Méthode de violoncelle I, 1826H
Baudo, Serge, 1927A, 1952C, 1959D, 1962D,
   1967D, 1969D, 1971D
Baudrier, Yves, 1906A, 1988B
Bauer, Harold, 1873A, 1893C, 1951B
Bauer, Joseph Anton, 1808B
Bauer, Marion, 1887A, 1955B; *Music Through*
   the Ages, 1932H; *Questions & Quizzes*, 1941H;
   Twentieth Century Music, 1933H
Bauer-Theussl, Franz, 1928A, 1957D, 1960D
Bauermeister, Mathilde, 1849A, 1865C, 1926B
Baugé, Anne Tariol, 1872A
Bauld, Alison, 1944A
Baum, Kurt, 1908A, 1933CE, 1989B
Baumann, Herbert, 1925A
Baumann, Hermann, 1934A
Baumann, Heinrich, 1964E
Baumbach, Friedrich A., 1753A, 1777D, 1813B;
   Kurzgefassies Handwörterbuch über
   die...Künste, 1794H
Baumfelder, Friedrich, 1836A, 1916B
Baumgarten, Alexander: *Aesthetica*, 1758H
Baumgarten, Gotthilf von, 1813B
Baumgarten, Karl, 1824B
Baumgartner, August: *Kurzgefasste geschichte*
   der musik...notation, 1856H
Baumgartner, Johann Baptist, 1776E, 1782B
Baumgartner, Paul, 1903A, 1976B
Baumgartner, Rudolf, 1917A, 1960D
Bäumker, Wilhelm, 1842A, 1905B; *Das*
   Katholische deutsche Kirchenlied..., 1883H
Baur, Jürg, 1918A, 1957E, 1965D
Bausch, Ludwig, 1805A, 1871B
Bautista, Julián, 1901A, 1961B
Bavarian Radio Symphony Orchestra, 1949G
Bavouzet, Jean-Efflam, 1962A
Bax, Arnold, 1883A, 1934E, 1937E, 1941E,
   1953B
Bay, Emmanuel, 1891A, 1967B
Bayer, Josef, 1852A, 1913B
Bayle, François, 1932A, 1990E
Bayly, Anselm: *The Alliance of Musick, Poetry*
   and Oratory, 1789H; *The Sacred Singer*, 1771H
Bayo, Maria, 1962A
Bayrakdanian, Isobel, 2000E
Bayreuth, Germany: Allgemeiner Richard-
   Wagner-Verband, 1883G; Musik-
   Dilettantenverein, 1860G; Wagner Festival,
   1876G
Bayreuther Blätter, 1878G
Bazelaire, Paul, 1886A, 1958B
Bazelon, Irwin, 1922A, 1995B; *Knowing the*
   Score, 1975H
Bazin, Emmanuel-Joseph, 1816A, 1878B
Bazin, François E., 1840E, 1872E; *Cours*
   d'harmonie, théorique et pratique, 1858H
Bazola, François, 1965A
Bazzini, Antonio, 1818A, 1882D, 1897B

BBC: Legends, 1998G; National Chorus of
Wales, 1983G; Northern Symphony
Orchestra, 1934G; Scottish Symphony
Orchestra, 1935G; Symphony Orchestra,
1930G; Welsh Symphony Orchestra, 1936G
Beach, Amy (Mrs. H. H. A.), 1867A, 1883C,
1926D, 1944B
Beach, John Parsons, 1877A, 1953B
Beale, William, 1784A, 1820D, 1854B
Beamish, Sally, 1956A, 1995C
Beard, John, 1751E, 1761D, 1767F, 1791B
Beardsley, Bethany, 1927A, 1949C
Bearns, Joseph H., Prize, 1928G
Beasser, Robert, 1954A, 1977E
Beattie, Herbert, 1926A, 1957C
Beattie, James: *The Minstrel I*, 1771H; *On Poetry
and Music*, 1762H
Beauchamp, Pierre François de, 1761B
Beaulieu, Marie-Désiré, 1791A, 1810E, 1863B;
Cours de composition, 1809H
Beauvais Société de Musique, 1766G
Beauvarlet-Charpentier, Jacques M., 1766A,
1834B
Beauvarlet-Charpentier, Jean J., 1771D, 1783D,
1794B
Beaux Arts Trio, 1955G
Beccaria, Bruno, 1957A, 1986C
Becerra, Gustavo, 1925A
Becher, Alfred Julius, 1803A, 1848B
Bechi, Gino, 1913A, 1936C
Bechly, Daniela, 1958A, 1984C
Bechstein, Karl, 1826A, 1900B
Bechstein Piano Co., 1853G
Beck, Conrad, 1901A, 1989B
Beck, Franz, 1809B
Beck, Gottfried Joseph, 1787B
Beck, Jean-Baptiste, 1881A, 1943B; *Die Melodien
der Troubadours & Trouvéres*, 1908H
Beck, Johann N., 1827A, 1850C, 1904B
Beck, John Ness, 1930A, 1987B
Beck, Karl, 1814A, 1879B
Becker, Carl F.: *Die Choralsammlungen
der...Christlichen Kirchen*, 1845H;
Evangelischen choralbuch, 1844H;
Harmonielehre für dilettanten, 1842H; *Die
Hausmusik in...16. 17. und 18 Jahrhunderts*,
1840H
Becker, Constantin J., 1837D
Becker, Frank, 1944A
Becker, Georges: *La musique en Suisse*, 1874H
Becker, Günther, 1924A
Becker, Gustave Louis, 1861A, 1959B
Becker, Heinz, 1922A; *Beiträge zur geschichte der
musikkritik*, 1965H; *Geschichte der
Instrumentation*, 1964H
Mechanik & Ästhetik des Violoncellspiels, 1929H
Becker, Hugo, 1863A, 1961A
Becker, Jacob, Piano Co., 1841G
Becker, Jean, 1833A, 1884B

Becker, John Joseph, 1886A, 1917D, 1929D,
1961B
Becker, Marcus, 1963A
Becker, Rudolph Z.: *Mildheimisches Liederbuch*,
1799H
Becker, Rudolph, Publishing House, 1795G
Becker-Bender, Tanja, 1978A
Beckett, Wheeler, 1898A, 1986B
Becking, Gustav, 1894A, 1945B; *Der
musikalische Rhythmus als Erkenntnisquelle*,
1928H
Beckmann, Johann Friedrich, 1792B
Beckwith, John, 1928A, 1950C
Beckwith, John "Christmas," 1808D, 1809B
Bečvařovsk, Anton Felix, 1754A, 1823B
Bedford, Steuart, 1939A, 1981D
Bedford Music Society, 1866G
Bedient, Gene R., Organ Co., 1969G
Bedos de Celles, François, 1759E
Beecham, Thomas, 1879A, 1905C, 1916E,
1941D, 1947F, 1961B; *A Mingled Chime*,
1943H
Beecham Opera Co., 1910G
Beecroft, Norma, 1934A
Beer, Joseph, 1812B
Beeson, Jack, 1921A, 1968D, 1976E
Beeth, Lola, 1862A, 1882C, 1940B
Beethoven, Ludwig van, 1770A, 1775F, 1778CF,
1779F, 1781F, 1782F, 1783F, 1784F, 1785F,
1787F, 1788F, 1790F, 1792F, 1793F, 1794F,
1795F, 1797F, 1799F, 1800F, 1801F, 1802F,
1804F, 1805F, 1809F, 1812F, 1815F, 1816F,
1820F, 1827B
Beethoven Archives Research Institute, 1927G
Beethoven Association of New York, 1918G
Beethoven by the Beach, 1997G
Beethoven String Quartet, 1873G, 1884G
Beethoven Trio, 1985G
Beffara, Louis-François, 1751A, 1838B
Begg, Heather, 1954C
Beglarian, Eve, 1958A
Beglarian, Grant, 1958E, 1969D
Begley, Kim, 1952A, 1983C
Begnis, Giuseppe de, 1793A, 1813C, 1849B
Begnis, Giuseppina Ronzi de, 1800A, 1853B
Begrez, Pierre Ignace, 1787A, 1815C, 1863B
Béhague, Gerard, 1937A, 1974D; *The Beginnings
of Musical Nationalism in Brazil*, 1971H; *Music
in Latin America: An Introduction*, 1977H;
*Performance Practice: Ethnomusico-logical
Perspectives*, 1984H
Behm, Eduard, 1946B
Behnke, Anna-Katharina, 1964A, 1986C
Běhohlák, Jiří, 1945A
Behr, Jan, 1996B
Behr, Therese, 1876A, 1898C, 1959B
Behren, Fritz, 1972B
Behrend, Jeanne, 1911A, 1988B
Behrend, Siegfried, 1933A, 1952C, 1990B

✳

F   *Biographical*   G   *Cultural Beginnings*   H   *Musical Literature*
I   *Musical Compositions*

Behrends, Jack, 1935A
Behrens, Hildegard, 1937A, 1971C
Behrent, John, 1775F
Beijing, China: Beijing University Computer
  Music Center, 1986G; Central Philharmonic
  Society, 1956G; Concert Hall, 1986G;
  International Youth Violin Competition,
  1986G
Beilman, Douglas, 1988C
Beinum, Edward van, 1900A, 1945D, 1956D,
  1959B
Beissel, Conrad, 1768B
Bekker, Paul, 1882A, 1911D, 1937B; *Das
  deutsche Musikleben, Versuch einer sozio-
  logischen Musikbetrachtung*, 1916H; *Kunst und
  Revolution*, 1919H; *Das Musikdrama der
  gegenward*, 1909H; *Musikgeschichte als
  geschichte der musikalischen formwandlungen*,
  1926H; *Das Operntheater*, 1930H; *Die Sinfonie
  von Beethoven bis Mahler*, 1918H; *The Story of
  Music*, 1927H; *The Story of the Orchestra*,
  1936H; *Von den Naturreichen des Klanges*,
  1924H; *Wandlungen der Oper*, 1934H; *Die
  Weltgeltung der deutschen Musik*, 1920H
Bekku, Sadao, 1922A
Belaiev, Mitrophan, 1836A, 1904B
Belaiev, Victor, 1888A, 1944E, 1968B
Belaiev Publishing House, 1885G
Belcanto Strings (Germany), 1993G
Belcher, Supply, 1751A, 1836B; *The Harmony of
  Maine*, 1794H
Belcke, Friedrich August, 1795A, 1874B
Belezza, Vincenzo, 1964B
Belfast, Ireland: Anacreontic Society, 1814G;
  Assembly Rooms, 1776G; Choral Society,
  1853G; Classical Harmonists, 1851G; Grand
  Opera House, 1895G; Harp Festival, 1792G;
  Harp Society, 1808G; Irish Harp Society,
  1819G; Music Hall, 1840G; National Theater,
  1868G; Orchestra, 1814G; Philharmonic
  Society, 1874G; Ulster Hall, 1862G
Belgian Radio Orchestra, 1923G
Belgrade, Yugoslavia: Mokranjac (Serbian)
  Music School, 1899G
Belhomme, Hypolite, 1854A, 1879C, 1923B
Belissen, Laurent, 1762B
Belkin, Boris, 1948A
Belknap, Daniel, 1771A, 1815B
Bell, Christopher, 1961A
Bell, Clive, 1964B
Bell, Donald, 1934A, 1955C
Bell, Joshua, 1967A, 1975C
Bell, Larry, 1983E
Bell, W. H., 1912D, 1873A, 1919D, 1946B
Bell Telephone Laboratories Computer Music
  Studio, 1957G
Bellaigue, Camille, 1858A, 1930B
Bellamy, Richard, 1813B
Bellamy, Thomas L., 1770A, 1798C, 1843B

Bellermann, Heinrich, 1832A, 1847E, 1875E;
  *Grösse der Intervalle als Grundlage der
  Harmonie*, 1873H; *Der Kontrapunkt*, 1862H;
  Die Mensuralnoten und Taktzeichen, 1858H
Bellermann, Heinrich, 1903B
Bellermann, Johann F., 1795A, 1874B;
  Bemerkungen über Russland, 1788H; *Die
  Tonleitern und Musiknoten der Griechen*, 1847H
Belletti, Giovanni B., 1837C, 1890B
Bellezza, Vincenzo, 1888A, 1908C
Bellincioni, Gemma, 1864A, 1880C, 1950B
Bellini, Vincenzo, 1801A, 1819F, 1835E, 1844B
Bellinzani, Paolo Benedetto, 1757B
Bellman, Carl Gottlieb, 1772A, 1861B
Bellman, Carl Michael, 1795B
Belloc-Giorgi, Teresa, 1784A, 1801C, 1855B
Bellosio, Alselmo, 1793B
Bellows, G. K.: *A Short History of Music in
  America*, 1957H
Bellugi, Piero, 1959D
Belmas, Xenia, 1896A, 1917C, 1926C, 1981B
Belohlávek, Jiri, 1946A, 1972D, 1977D, 1990D,
  1995D, 1996D
Belonogov, Svyatoslav, 1965A
Beltran, Tito, 1969A
Belwin, Inc, Publisher, 1918G
Belwin-Mills Corp., 1969G
Bemetzrieder, Anton: *Complete Treatise on
  Music*, 1803H; *Leçons de Clavecin et prinipes
  d'harmonie*, 1771H; *Réflexions sur les leçons de
  musique*, 1778H; *Le tolérantisme musical*,
  1779H; *Traité de musique*, 1776H;
Beňačková, Gabriela, 1947A, 1969E, 1970C
Benaroya Concert Hall, 1998G
Benatzky, Ralph, 1957B
Bencini, Peitro Paolo, 1755B
Benda, Franz, 1786B
Benda, Friedrich, 1814B
Benda, Friedrich Ludwig, 1752A, 1792B
Benda, Georg Anton, 1795B
Benda, Hans von, 1972B
Benda, Johann Ludwig, 1752B
Bender, Paul, 1875A, 1900C, 1947B
Bendix, Victor Emanuel, 1851A, 1926B
Bendl, Karel, 1838A, 1897B
Ben-Dor, Gisèle, 1955A, 1982C, 1986E, 1994D
Bene, Adriana Ferraresi del, 1786C
Benedict, Julius, 1804A, 1838D, 1852D, 1867D,
  1871E, 1885B
Benelli, Antonio P., 1771A, 1790C, 1830B
Benestad, Finn, 1929A, 1979E
Bengal Cons. of Music, 1882G
Bengraf, Joseph, 1791B
Bengtsson, Gustaf Adolf, 1965B
Bengtsson, Ingmar, 1920A, 1989B
Ben-Haim, Paul, 1897A, 1949D, 1957E, 1984B
Benincori, Angelo Maris, 1779A, 1821B
Benito, Cosme Damián José de, 1885D
Benjamin, Arthur, 1893A, 1924E, 1960B

❄

A *Births*   B *Deaths*   C *Debuts*   D *New Positions*
E *Prizes/Honors*

Benjamin, George, 1960A, 1979C
Benjamin, Thomas: *The Craft of Modal Counterpoint*, 1979H; *Modal Counterpoint*, 1976H; *Techniques & Materials of Tonal Music*, 1975H
Benjamin, William E., 1944A
Bennett, Elinor, 1943A
Bennett, John, 1784B
Bennett, Joseph: *Forty Years of Music*, 1908H
Bennett, Richard Rodney, 1936A, 1977E, 1998E
Bennett, Robert Russell, 1894A, 1981B; *Instrumentally Speaking*, 1975H
Bennett, William S., 1816A, 1856DE, 1866D, 1870E, 1871E, 1875B
Bennet-Kempers, Karel P., 1897A
Bennewitz, Antonin, 1833A, 1882D, 1926B
Benoist, André, 1879A, 1953B
Benoist, François, 1794A, 1815E, 1878B
Benoît, Camille: *Musiciens, poètes et philosophes*, 1887H
Benoit, Peter, 1834A, 1857E, 1882E; *De Vlaamsche Muziekschool van Antwerp*, 1873H
Benoit, Pierre, 1901B
Benson, Joan, 1929A
Benson, Warren, 1924A; *Compositional Process & Writing Skills*, 1974H
Bent, Ian D., 1938A; *Music Analysis*, 1987H; *Music Analysis in the Nineteenth Century*, 1994H; *Source Materials & the Interpretation of Music I*, 1981H
Bent, Margaret, 1940A
Bentoiu, Pascal, 1927A
Benton, Rita, 1918A, 1980B
Bentonelli, Joseph, 1898A, 1925C, 1975B
Bentzon, Jørgen, 1897A, 1951B
Bentzon, Niels Viggo, 1919A, 1943C, 2000B
Benucci, Francesco, 1769C, 1824B
Benvenuti, Nicola, 1783A, 1810D, 1867B
Benvenuti, Tommaso, 1838A, 1906B
Ben-Yohanan, Asher, 1929A
Benz, Robert, 1974E
Benzell, Mimi, 1922A, 1944C, 1970B
Benzi, Robert, 1989D
Bérard, Jean Antoine, 1772B; *L'art du chant*, 1755H
Berberian, Cathy, 1925A, 1983B, 1957C
Berbié, Jane, 1958C
Berbiguier, Antoine T., 1782A, 1838B
Berdar, Alexander, 1967A
Berens, Barbara, 1988C
Berezovsky, Boris, 1965A
Berezovsky, Maximus, 1777B
Berezowsky, Nicolai, 1900A, 1953B
Berg, Alban, 1885A, 1904F, 1935B
Berg, Gerald, 1954A
Berg, Gunnar, 1909A, 1989B
Berg, Josef, 1927A, 1971B
Berg, Nathan, 1968A
Berg, Natanael, 1932E, 1957B

Berg, Robert, 1890A
Bergamo, Italy: Istituto Musicale G. Donizetti, 1805G; Lezioni Caritatevolide Musica, 1805G; Museo Donizettiano, 1897G; Società Filarmonica, 1822G; Teatro Cerri, 1797G; Teatro delle Novita, 1937G; Teatro Riccardi, 1791G
Berganza, Teresa, 1935A, 1955C
Berge, Sigurd, 1929A
Bergel, Erich, 1930A, 1959D, 1998B
Bergen, Norway: Grieg Hall, 1978G; Harmonic Society, 1765G; Musical College, 1852G
Berger, Arthur, 1912A, 1943D, 1960E
Berger, Erna, 1900A, 1925C, 1990B
Berger, Jean, 1909A
Berger, Ludwig, 1777A, 1839B
Berger, Roman, 1930A
Berger, Rudolf, 1874A, 1915B
Berger, Theodor, 1905A, 1992B
Berger, Wilhelm Georg, 1929A, 1993B
Bergié, Jane, 1931A
Bergiron, Nicolas-Antoine, 1768B
Berglund, Ingela, 1959A, 1988C
Berglund Joel, 1903A, 1928C, 1949D, 1985B
Berglund, Paavo, 1929A, 1952D, 1962D, 1972DE, 1975D, 1981F, 1987D, 1993D
Bergman, Erik, 1911A, 1961E
Bergman, Heidi S., 1958A
Bergman, Marilyn, 1994D
Bergmann, Carl, 1821A, 1855D, 1876B
Bergmans, Paul, 1868A, 1935B; *Mélanges iconographiques, bibliographiques et historiques*, 1912H
Bergonzi, Carlo, 1924A, 1948C, 1951C
Bergsma, William, 1921A, 1945E, 1963D, 1967E, 1994B
Bergson, Michal, 1820A, 1898B
Bergt, C. G. August, 1771A, 1837B; *Briefwechseleines alten und jungen Schulmeisters*, 1838H
Beringer, Oscar, 1844A, 1922B
Berio, Ernest, 1951F
Berio, Luciano, 1925A
Bériot, Charles A. de, 1802A, 1821C, 1836F, 1870B
Bériot, Charles-Wilfride de, 1833A, 1914B
Berkeley, Lennox, 1903A, 1957E, 1970E, 1974E, 1989B
Berkeley, Michael, 1948A
Berkeley, California: Commedia dell'Opera, 1979G; Festival & Exhibition, 1989G; Symphony Orchestra, 1969G
Berkshire (Tanglewood) Music Center (Lenox, Massachusetts), 1940G
Berkshire Music Festival (Massachusetts), 1934G
Berkshire Festival of Contemporary Music, 1964G
Berlijn, Anton, 1817A, 1846E, 1870B

❊

F *Biographical*   G *Cultural Beginnings*   H *Musical Literature*
I *Musical Compositions*

Berlin, Irving, 1989B
Berlin, Irving, Music, Inc., Publisher, 1919G
Berlin, Johan Daniel, 1787B
Berlin, Germany: Agthe School of Music,
  1845G; Akademie für Dramatische Gesang,
  1882G; Akademie für Kirchenmusik, 1822G;
  Bachverein, 1862G; Bilsesche Kapelle, 1867G;
  Bloch'sche Verein, 1879G; Blüthner
  Orchestra, 1907G; Concerts Spirituels,
  1783G; Deichmann Theater, 1848G; Deutsche
  Hochschule für Musik (East Berlin), 1950G;
  Deutsche Oper, 1910G; Eitner Piano School,
  1864G; Erk Gesangverein, 1852G; Ganz
  Music School, 1862G; Gastpieloper, 1928G;
  Gesellschaft der Opernfreunde, 1887G;
  Gesellschaft für Musikforschung, 1868G;
  Hering School of Music, 1851G; Institut
  Biehle, 1927G; International Music Society,
  1899G; Jähnsscher Gesangverein, 1845G;
  Kammermusiksaal, 1987G; Klavier-Schule
  Tausig, 1866G; Klindworth Klavierschule,
  1884G; Königstädtisches Theater, 1824G;
  Kroll Theater, 1844G; Kunstlerverein, 1844G;
  Lehrergesangverein, 1886G; Lessing Theater,
  1888G; Liebhaber Konzerte, 1770G;
  Liedertafel (male chorus), 1809G;
  Liedertafel, 1884G; Liedertafel, Neue, 1819G;
  Männergesangverein, 1843G; Märkischen
  Zentral-Sängerbund, 1860G; Metropol
  Theater, 1898G; Möser String Quartet,
  1811G; Musikakademie für Damen, 1850G;
  Musikalische Bildungsanstalt, 1820G;
  Nationaltheater, 1786G; Neue Akademie der
  Tonkunst, 1855G; Ochs Choral Union,
  1882G; Old French Theater, 1786G;
  Philharmonic Society, 1826G; Philharmonic
  Orchestra, 1822G; Radecke Choral Society,
  1868G; Radecke Music School, 1869G; Royal
  Opera Co., 1792G; Scharwenka
  Conservatory, 1881G; Schausspielhaus II,
  1821G; Seminar für Schulgesang, 1900G;
  Singakademie, 1791G; Stern Conservatory of
  Music, 1850G; Sternscher Gesangverein,
  1847G; Symphoniekapelle, 1843G; Tausch
  School for Wind Performers, 1805G; Theater
  des Westens, 1896G; Viktoria Theater, 1859G;
  Zelter Ripienschule, 1807G
Berliner, Emil, 1887F
Berliner Allgemeine Musikalische Zeitung, 1824G
Berliner Ensemble (Brecht), 1949G
Berlinski, Dmitri, 1987E
Berlinski, Herman, 1910A
Berlioz, Hector, 1803A, 1815F, 1820F, 1822F,
  1826F, 1827F, 1828F, 1830E, 1833F, 1835D,
  1841F, 1854F, 1855F 1856E, 1869B; *Les
  grotesques de la musique*, 1859H; *Mémoires*,
  1848H; *Les soirées de l'orchestre*, 1853H; *Traité
  d'instrumentation*, 1844H
Berlioz Festival (Lyon), 1979G

Berman, Boris, 1948A, 1965C
Berman, Lazar, 1930A, 1940C
Berman, Pavel, 1990E
Bern, Germany: Municipal Theater, 1903G
Bernac, Pierre, 1899A, 1926C, 1979B; *The
  Interpretation of French Song I*, 1970H
Bernacchi, Antonio Maria, 1756B
Bernandi, Mario, 1930A
Bernard, Emile, 1902B
Bernardel Violin Shop (Paris), 1826G
Bernardi, Mario, 1969D, 1983D, 1984D
Bernasconi, Andrea, 1755D, 1784B
Bernasconi, Antonia, 1762C
Berne, Switzerland: Caecilienverein, 1862G;
  Hôtel de Musique, 1769G; Liedertafel,
  1845G; Männerchor, 1870G;
  Musikgesellschaft, 1815G; Orchesterverein,
  1876G
Berneker, Constanz, 1872D
Berner, Friedrich Wilhelm, 1780A, 1827B
Berners, Gerald (Lord), 1919E
Bernhard, Arnold, Arts-Humanities Center,
  1972G
Bernhardt, Robert, 1995D
Bernheimer, Martin, 1965D, 1981E
Bernier, René, 1905A, 1963E, 1984B
Bernoulli, Daniel, 1782B; *Essai théorique sur les
  vibrations des plaques*, 1787H
Bernoulli, Eduard, 1867A, 1927B
Bernstein, Elmer, 1922A
Bernstein, Lawrence F., 1939A, 1974D,
Bernstein, Leonard, 1918A, 1943C, 1944F,
  1945D, 1953G, 1958DEF, 1959F, 1960E,
  1961E, 1968E, 1969F, 1980E, 1981E, 1987E,
  1989E, 1999B; *Findings*, 1982H; *The Infinite
  Variety of Music*, 1966H; *The Joy of Music*,
  1959H; *The Unanswered Question*, 1976H
Bernstein, Louis, 1962B
Bernstein, Martin, 1904A, 1943C, 1945D,
  1958D; *An Introduction to Music*, 1937H; *Score
  Reading*, 1932H
Bernstein Center for Education Through the
  Arts, 1991G
Bernstein International Conducting
  Competition, 1995G
Bernuth Music Cons., 1873G
Béroff, Michel, 1950A, 1967CE
Beronesi, Debora, 1965A, 1988C
Berr, Friedrich, 1794A, 1833E, 1838B; *Traité
  complet de la clarinette à 14 clefs*, 1836H
Berra, Marco, Publishing House, 1811G
Berry, Walter, 1929A, 1950C, 2000B
Berry, Wallace, 1978E; *Eighteenth Century
  Imitative Counterpoint: Music for Analysis*,
  1969H; *Form in Music*, 1966H; *Musical
  Structure & Performance*, 1989H; *Structural
  Functions in Music*, 1976H; *Die Musik des
  Mittelalters und der Renaissance*, 1931H
Berry, Judy, 1992E

❊

A *Births*   B *Deaths*   C *Debuts*   D *New Positions*
E *Prizes/Honors*

Berry & Gordon, Publisher, 1853G
Berteau, Martin, 1771B
Berteling Woodwind Co., 1855G
Bertezen, Salvatore: *Principi della musica teorico-prattica*, 1781H
Bertheaume, Isidore, 1752A, 1802B
Berthold, Beatrice, 1964A, 1978C, 1983C
Bertin, Louise-Angélique, 1805A, 1877B
Bertini, Auguste, 1780A, 1793C
Bertini, Domenico, 1829A, 1890B; *Compendio de'principidi musica, secondo*, 1866H
Bertini, Gary, 1927A, 1965D, 1978D, 1983D, 1987D, 1994D
Bertini, Giuseppe, 1759A, 1852B; *Dizionario storico-critico degli scrittori di musica*, 1815H
Bertini, Henri, 1795A, 1876B
Bertini, Salvatore, 1794B
Bertinotti, Teresa, 1776A, 1854B
Bertolino, Mario, 1934A, 1955C
Bertolli, Francesca, 1767B
Bertolo, Aldo, 1949A, 1978C
Berton, Henri, 1784A, 1832B; *De la musique mécanique et...philosophique*, 1826H
Berton, Henri-Montan, 1767A, 1807D, 1815E, 1834E, 1844B
Berton, Pierre-Montan, 1754D, 1775D, 1780B
Bertoni, Ferdinando, 1752D, 1773E, 1785D, 1813B
Bertouille, Gérard, 1981B
Bertram, Theodor, 1869A, 1889C, 1907B
Bertrand, Aline, 1798A, 1802C, 1835B
Bertrand, Jean G.: *Histoire ecclésiastique de l'orgue*, 1859H; *Les nationalités musicales étudées dans le drame lyrique*, 1872H; *Les origines de l'harmonie*, 1866H
Berutti, Arturo, 1938B
Berwald, August, 1798A, 1869B
Berwald, Franz, 1796A, 1812F, 1864E, 1868B
Berwald, Johann Fredrik, 1787A, 1793C, 1819D, 1861B
Berwald Hall (Stockholm), 1979G
Besa, Alexander, 1971A, 1990C
Besançon, France: International Music Festival, 1948G; Opera House, 1786G
Besanzoni, Gabriella, 1888A, 1911C
Besozzi, Alessandro, 1793B
Besozzi, Carlo, 1791B
Besozzi, Gaetano, 1794B
Besozzi, Louis-Désiré, 1837E
Bessaraboff, Nicholas, 1894A
Bessel, Vasili, 1842A, 1907B
Bessel & Co., Publishers, 1869G
Besseler, Heinrich, 1900A, 1969B
Besson Instruments Co., 1838G
Besson, Gabriel, 1765B
Besson, Gabriel-Louis, 1785B
Besson, Gustav Auguste, 1820A, 1875B
Best, Matthew, 1957A
Best, W. T., 1826A, 1897B

Béthizy, Jean Laurent de, 1781B; *Exposition de la théorie et...pratique de la musique*, 1754H; *Betrachtungen der Mannheimer Tonschule*, 1778G
Bethlehem, Pennsylvania: Bach Choir, 1898G; Bach Festival, 1900G; Choral Union, 1882G; Philharmonic Society, 1820G
Bethune, "Blind Tom," 1908B
Betti, Adolfo, 1873A, 1933E, 1950B
Bettinelli, Bruno, 1913A
Betts, Lorne, 1918A, 1985B
Betz, Franz, 1835A, 1856C, 1900B, 1906B
Betts, John, Violin Maker, 1755A, 1780G, 1823B
Beudert, Mark, 1961A
Bevan, Clifford: *The Tuba Family*, 1978H
Beversdorf, Thomas, 1924A, 1981B
Bevignani, Enrico, 1841A, 1803B
Bevington & Sons Organ Co. (London), 1794G
Beyer, Frank, 1928A
Beyer, Johanna Magdalena, 1888A, 1944B
Beyschlag, Adolf: *Die Ornamentik der Musik*, 1908H
Bezanson, Philip, 1916A, 1964D, 1975B
Bezekirsky, Vasili, 1835A, 1919B
Bial, Rudolf, 1834A, 1881B
Bialas, Günter, 1907A, 1995B
Bianchi, Antonio, 1758A, 1772E,
Bianchi, Bianca, 1855A, 1873C, 1947A
Bianchi, Francesco, 1752A, 1776E, 1794D, 1810B
Bianchi, Valentina, 1839A, 1855C, 1884B
Bianconi, Philippe, 1981E
Biarent, Adolphe, 1916B
Bibalo, Antonio, 1922A
Bible, Frances, 1927A, 1948C
Bicentennial Convocation & Music Festival (Aspen Music Festival), 1949G
Bickley, Susan, 1955A
Bie, Oskar, 1864A, 1938B; *Intime musik*, 1904H; *Die Oper*, 1913H; *Das Rätsel der musik*, 1922H; *Tanzmusik*, 1905H
Biehle, August Johannes, 1870A
Biehle, Johannes, 1941B
Biel, Ann-Christin, 1958A, 1981C
Bielawa, Herbert, 1930A
Bielman, Douglas, 1965A
Bierdiajew, Walerian, 1956B
Bierey, Gottlob B., 1772A, 1808D, 1840B
Bieses, Wilhelm, Piano Co., 1853G
Bigelow & Main, Publishers, 1867G
Biggs, E. Power, 1906A, 1932C, 1977B
Biggs, John, 1932A
Bignami, Carlo, 1808A, 1829D, 1837D, 1848B
Bigot Eugéne, 1935D, 1936D, 1947D, 1965B
Bigot, Marie (de Morogues), 1786A, 1820B
Bihari, János, 1764A, 1827B
Bijvanck, Henk, 1909A, 1969B
Bilbao Festival (Spain), 1951G
Bílek, Zdeněk, 1969D, 1975D

The Billboard, 1894G
Billings, William, 1760F; *The Continental Harmony*, 1794H; *Music in Miniature*, 1779; *New England Psalmsinger*, 1770H; *Psalm Singer's Amusement*, 1781H; *The Singing Master's Assistant*, 1778H; *The Suffolk Harmony*, 1786H
Billington, Elizabeth, 1765A, 1784C, 1809F, 1818B
Billroth, Theodor: *Wer ist musikalische?*, 1896H
Bilson, Malcolm, 1935A
Bilt, Peter van der, 1860C, 1936A, 1960C, 1983B
Bimberg, Guido, 1954A; *Music of Russian & German Composers*, 1990H; *Die Musicalische Temperatur*, 1996H
Bimboni, Alberto, 1882A, 1960B
Binder, Christlieb S., 1753D, 1789B
Binder, Karl, 1816A, 1839D, 1860B
Bindernagel, Gertrud, 1894A, 1921C, 1932B
Binet, Jean, 1893A, 1960B
Bing, Rudolf, 1902A, 1935D, 1950D, 1971E, 1973E, 1997B; *5000 Nights at the Opera*, 1972H
Bingham, Seth, 1882A, 1972B
Bini, Carlo, 1947A, 1969C
Bini, Pasquale, 1770B
Binkerd, Gordon, 1916A, 1964E
Binkley, Thomas, 1931A, 1960D, 1995B
Binns, John: *Dictionary of Musical Terms*, 1770H
Binns, Malcolm, 1936A, 1957C
Birch, Charlotte Ann, 1815A
Birchall, Robert, 1750A, 1819B
Birchard, Clarence C., 1866A, 1946B
Birchard, C. C. Co., Publisher, 1901G
Bird, Arthur, 1856A, 1886C, 1923B
Birmingham, Alabama: Philharmonic Strings, 1927G; Symphony Orchestra, 1916G
Birmingham, England: Barber Institute of Fine Arts, 1939G; Choir, 1921G ; Music Festival, 1768G; New Street Theater, 1774G; Paradise Street Town Hall, 1834G; Stockley's Concerts, 1873G; Theater Royal, 1807G
Birmingham & Midland Institute (School of Music), 1854G
Birnbach, Carl Joseph, 1751A, 1805B
Birnbach, Heinrich: *Der Vollkommene Kapellmeister*, 1845H
Biriukov, Yuri, 1908A, 1976B
Birkeland, Oystein, 1958A
Birnbach Music Publishers, 1911G
Birtwistle, Harrison, 1934A, 1987E, 1988E
Biscaccianti, Eliza, 1824A, 1847C, 1896B
Biscardi, Chester, 1948A
Biscay Conservatory of Music, 1927G
Bischoff, Georg F., 1816D
Bischoff, Hans, 1852A, 1889B
Bischoff, Ludwig F, 1850D
Bischoff, Johannes, 1874A, 1899C, 1904C, 1936B

Bisengeliev, Marat, 1962A, 1991E
Bishop, Anne, 1810A, 1831C, 1884B
Bishop, Henry R., 17786A, 1810D, 1825D, 1830D, 1840D, 1842E, 1848D, 1853E, 1855B
Bishop-Kovacevich, Stephen, 1951C
Bispham, David, 1857A, 1891C, 1921B
Bispham Medal, 1921G
Bissell, Keith, 1912A, 1992B
BIT 20 Ensemble (Norway), 1989G
Bitetti, Ernesto, 1943A, 1958C
Bitter, Carl Hermann, 1813A, 1885B
Bittgood, Roberta, 1975D
Bittoni, Bernardo, 1779D, 1798D
Bizet, Georges, 1838A, 1857E, 1873E, 1875E, 1875B
Bjelinski, Bruno, 1909A
Bjerno, Majken, 1989C
Bjerre, Jens, 1903A, 1986B
Bjoner, Ingrid, 1927A, 1956C
Björlin, Ulf, 1933A, 1993B
Björling, Jussi, 1911A, 1930C, 1960B
Björling, Sigurd, 1907A, 1934C, 1983B
Blacher, Boris, 1903A, 1953D, 1975B
Blachut, Beno, 1913A, 1938C, 1985B
Black, Andrew, 1859A, 1887C, 1920B
Black, Christopher, 1958A
Black, Frank, 1894A, 1928D, 1968B
Black, Jeffrey, 1962A, 1986C
Black, Robert, 1950A
Black, Stanley, 1913B, 1959D
Black, Steven (David), 1952A
Black, William David, 1952A, 1977C
Black Artist Group, 1972G
Black Mountain Review, 1954G
Black Music Colloquium, 1980G
Black Music Research Journal, 1980G
Blackburn, Bonnie, 1939A
Blackmar Brothers, Publishers, 1860G
Blackshaw, Christian, 1949A, 1974E
Blackwell, Harolyn, 1960A
Blackwood, Alan: *Encyclopedia of Music*, 1979H
Blackwood, Easley, 1933A, 1960E
Blackwood, William, & Sons, Publishers, 1816G
Blackwood's Magazine, 1817G
Blaes, Arnold Joseph, 1814A, 1892B
Blaes, Elisa, 1817A, 1839C, 1878B
Blaha, Vladislav, 1957A, 1976C
Blahack, Josef, 1779A, 1802C, 1824D, 1846B
Blainville, Charles-Henri de, 1769B; *Essai sur un troisième mode*, 1751H; *Harmonie théoretico-pratique*, 1766H; *L'esprit de l'art musical*, 1754H; *Histoire générale, critique et philologique*, 1767H
Blaisdell Memorial Center (Honolulu), 1964G
Blaisdell Wind Quartet, 1938G
Blake, Benjamin, 1751A, 1827B
Blake, David, 1936A
Blake, Rockwell, 1951A, 1976C, 1978E

❄

A   *Births*   B   *Deaths*   C   *Debuts*   D   *New Positions*
E   *Prizes/Honors*

Blake, George E, Publishers, 1802G
Blamont, François Colin de, 1760B; *Essai sur les gôuts anciens et moderne*, 1754H
Blancafort, Manuel, 1897A, 1987B
Blanchard, Esprit Joseph, 1761D, 1770B
Blanchard, Henri-Louis, 1791A, 1858B; *Concise Introduction to...Music*, 1807H
Blanchart, Ramón, 1883A, 1885C, 1934B
Blanchet, François Etienne, *pére*, 1761B
Blanchet, François Etienne, *fils*, 1766B
Blanchet, Joseph: *L'art ou les principes philosophiques du chant*, 1756H
Blanck, Kirsten, 1965A, 1986C
Bland, James, 1798A, 1826C, 1861B
Bland, Maria Therese, 1769A, 1786C, 1838B
Bland and Weller, Instrument Makers, 1784G
Blangini, Felice, 1781A, 1805D, 1841B
Blankenburg, Walter, 1903A, 1986B
Blankenship Rebecca, 1954A
Blasco de Nebri, Maneul, 1784B
Blasi, Angela-Maria, 1956A
Blasis, Carlo de, 1797A, 1878B
Blasis, James de, 1988D
Blasius, Frédéric, 1758A, 1790D, 1829B *Clarinet Method*, 1796H
Blass, Robert, 1867A, 1892C, 1930B
Blatn, Josef, 1980B
Blatn, Pavel, 1931A
Blatt, Frantiek Tadeá, 1793A, 1856B; *Clarinet Method*, 1828H
Blatter, Alfred: *Instrumentation/Orchestration*, 1980H
Blätter für Theater, Musik un Bildene Kunst, 1855G
Blaukopf, Kurt, 1914A, 1999B; *Grosse Dirigenten*, 1953H; *Grosse Virtuosen*, 1954H; *Musiksoziologie*, 1952H; *Die Wiener Philharmoniker*, 1986H
Blauvelt, Lillian E., 1874A, 1891C, 1893C, 1947B
Blavet, Michel, 1768B
Blaze, François-Henri, 1784A, 1822D, 1857B; *Chapelle musique des Rois de France*, 1832H; *De l'opéra en France I*, 1820H; *De l'opéra en France II*, 1826H; *Dictionnaire de musique moderne*, 1821H; *Sur l'opéra français*, 1856H
Blaze, Henri, 1813A, 1888B
Blaze, Robin, 1971A
Blašek, Zdeněk, 1905A, 1988B
Blazekovic, Zdravdo, 1956A
Blech, Harry, 1910A, 1984E, 1999B
Blech, Leo, 1871A, 1899D, 1906D, 1926D, 1937D, 1958B
Blech String Quartet, 1933G
Bledsoe, Jules, 1898A, 1924C, 1943B
Blegen, Judith, 1940A, 1963C
Blewitt, Jonathan, 1782A, 1825D, 1853B; *Complete Treatise on the Organ*, 1795H
Bliss, Anthony, 1913A, 1981D, 1991B

Bliss, Arthur, 1891A, 1923F, 1950E, 1953E, 1975B; *As I Remember*, 1970H
Bliss, P. Paul, 1871A, 1904D, 1911D, 1933B
Bliss, Philip Paul, 1838A, 1876B
Blitz, Julian Paul, 1913D
Blitzstein, Marc, 1905A, 1946E, 1959E, 1964B
Blitzstein, Marc, Award, 1965G
Bloch, André, 1893E, 1960B
Bloch, Augustyn, 1929A
Bloch, Boris, 1978E
Bloch, Ernest, 1880A, 1916F, 1920D, 1925D, 1937E, 1943E, 1947E, 1959BE; *Zur Philosophie der Musik*, 1974H
Bloch, Ernest, Society, 1968G
Blochwitz, Hans Peter, 1949A, 1984C
Block, Michel, 1937A, 1953C, 1962E
Der Blockflötenspiegel, 1931G
Blockx, Jan, 1851A, 1912B
Blodek, Wilhelm, 1834A, 1874B
Blom, Eric, 1923D, 1931D, 1955E; *Classics, Major and Minor*, 1958H; *Everyman's Dictionary of Music*, 1946H; *The Limitations of Music*, 1928H; *Music in England*, 1942H; *A Musical Postbag*, 1941H; *The Romance of the Piano*, 1927H
Blomdahl, Karl-Birger, 1916A, 1953E, 1964D, 1968B
Blomstedt, Herbert, 1927A, 1953E, 1954D, 1962D, 1967D, 1971E, 1975D, 1978E, 1985D, 1996D, 1998D
Blondeau, Pierre-Auguste, 1784A, 1808E, 1863B; *Histoire de la musique moderne*, 1847H
Bloomfield, Theodor, 1923A, 1955D, 1959D, 1964D, 1966D, 1975D, 1998B
Blossom Music Center, 1968G
Blossom Music Festival, 1968G
Bluebird Records, 1932G
Blum, Robert, 1994B
Blume, Friedrich, 1893A, 1975B; *Die Evangelische Kirchenmusik*, 1931H; *Musik in Geschichte und Gegenwart I*, 1949H; *Was ist Musik?*, 1959H; *Wesen und Werden deutscher Musik*, 1944H
Blumenfeld, Harold, 1923A, 1963D
Blumental, Felicja, 1911A, 1991B
Blumenthal, Jakob, 1848E
Blumenthal, Joseph von, 1782A, 1850B
Blumer, Theodor, 1964B
Blüthner Piano Co., 1853G
Blythe, Stephanie, 1970A, 1994C, 1999E
BMI: the Magazine about Music, 1962G
BMI Student Composer Awards, 1951G
Boatwright, Helen, 1916A, 1942C
Boatwright, Howard, 1918A, 1935C, 1964D, 1999B; *Introduction to the Theory of Music*, 1956H
Boatwright, McHenry, 1928A, 1953E, 1956C, 1994B
Bobbs-Merrill Co., 1895G

❄

F   *Biographical*   G   *Cultural Beginnings*   H   *Musical Literature*
I   *Musical Compositions*

Bobrick, James, 1967A
Bobrowicz, Jan N., 1805A, 1857B
Boccabadati, Luigia, 1797A, 1817C, 1850B
Boccherini, Luigi, 1756C, 1761F, 1766F, 1769F,
   1800F, 1805B
Boccherini Quintet, 1949G
Bochsa, Karl, Music Store, 1806G
Bochsa, Nicolas-Charles, 1789A, 1865B
Böck, Ignaz, 1754A
Bockelmann, Rudolf, 1922C, 1958B
Böckh, August: *De Metris Pindari*, 1811H
Böcklin, Franz F.: *Beyträge zur Geschichte der
   Musik...Deutschland*, 1790H
Boda, Rudolf, 1970B
Bodanzky, Artur, 1877A, 1909D,1915D, 1916D,
   1919D, 1939B
Bode, Johann Joachim, 1793B
Bode, Rudolf: *Austruckgymnastik*, 1922H;
   Energie und Rhythmus, 1939H; *Musik und
   bewegung*, 1930H; *Der Rhythmus & seine
   bedeutung für die Erziehng*, 1920H
Bodin, Lars-Gunnar, 1935A, 1978D
Bodky, Erwin, 1896A, 1958B; *Das
   Charakterstück*, 1933H; *Der Vortag alter
   Klaviermusik*, 1932H
Bodley, Seóirse, 1933A
Body, Jack, 1944A
Boehe, Ernest, 1938B
Boehm Flute, 1832G
Boehm Flute Co. (Munich), 1828G
Boelke, Walter R., 1987B
Boelke-Bomart, Publishers, 1948G
Boëllmann, Léon, 1862A, 1881D, 1897B
Boëly, Alexandre Pierre, 1785A, 1858B
Boelza, Igor, 1994B
Boer, Berlil Van, 1952A
Boesch, Christian, 1941A, 1966C
Boesmans, Philippe, 1936A
Boettcher, Wolfgang, 1914A
Boettcher, Wolfgang: *Geschichte der Motette*,
   1989H
Boettcher, Wilfried, 1929A, 1967D, 1970D,
   1975D, 1994B
Bogard, Carol, 1930A
Bogatyrev, Semyon, 1960B
Bogdanov-Berezovsky, Valerian, 1903A, 1951D,
   1971B
Bogota, Colombia: Academia Nacional de
   Música, 1882G; Ibero-American Music
   Festival, 1938G; National Symphony
   Orchestra of Colombia, 1936G; Philharmonic
   Orchestra, 1846G; Sociedad Filarmonica,
   1847G
Boguslawski, Edward, 1940A
Boháč, Josef, 1928A
Boheme Quartet, 1986G
Bohemian String Quartet, 1892G
Böhm, Anton, und Sohn, Publishers
   (Augsburg), 1803G

Böhm, Elisabeth, 1797B
Böhm, Joseph, 1795A, 1876B
Böhm, Karl, 1894A, 1917C, 1920D, 1921D,
   1927D, 1934D, 1943D, 1950D, 1954D, 1981BE
Böhm, Theobald, 1794A, 1818D, 1881B
Böhm, Theobald, Archives, 1980G
Böhme, Franz Magnus, 1827A, 1898B
Böhme, Kurt, 1908A, 1930C, 1989B
Bohnen, Michael, 1887A, 1910C, 1965B
Böhner, Ludwig, 1787A, 1860B
Bohy, Jacques-Joseph, 1871C
Boieldieu, François, 1775A, 1803D, 1811F,
   1817DE, 1818E, 1821E, 1834B
Boiko, Rostislav, 1931A
Bois, Rob du, 1934A
Boise, Otis Bardwell, 1844A, 1912B; *Music & Its
   Masters*, 1902H
Boismortier, Joseph Bodin de, 1755B
Boisselot, Xavier, 1836E
Boito, Arrigo, 1842A, 1868F, 1889D, 1892D,
   1893E, 1895E, 1918B
Bok, Mary Louise Custis, 1876A, 1970B
Bokemeyer, Heinrich, 1751B
Bolcom, William, 1938A, 1993E; *Aesthetics of
   Survival*, 1984H
Bolet, Jorge, 1914A, 1935C, 1937E, 1938E,
   1990B
Bolívar, Simón, Symphony Orchestre, 1975G
Bolivian National Orchestra (La Paz), 1940G
Bolkvadze, Eliso, 1967A
Bollettino Bibliografico Musicale, 1899G
Bolliger, Phillip John, 1963A
Bollon, Fabrice, 1994D
Bologna, Italy: Accademia dei Concordi,
   1808G; Accademia Polimniaca, 1806G;
   Armonici Uniti, 1784G; Casino dei Nobili,
   1787G; Domino Club, 1855G; Liceo
   Filarmonico, 1796G, 1804G; Società
   Wagneriana, 1887G; Teatro Communale,
   1757G; Teatro Contavalli, 1814G; Teatro del
   Corso, 1805G
Bolshakov, Nikolai, 1874A, 1899C, 1958B
Bolshoi String Quartet, 1931G
Bolzoni, Giovanni, 1841A, 1887D, 1919B
Boman, Per Conrad, 1804A, 1849E, 1861B
Bombay Symphony Orchestra, 1935G
Bomtempo, João Domingos, 1775A, 1833D,
   1842B; *Piano Method*, 1816H
Bon, Maarten, 1933A
Bon, Willem Frederik, 1940A, 1983B
Bonamici, Ferdinando, 1827A, 1905B
Bonaventura, Anthony di, 1930A
Bonaventura, Arnaldo, 1952B; *Elementi di
   estetica musicale*, 1905H; *Manuale di cultura
   musicale*, 1924H; *Manuale dsitoria dolla musica*,
   1898H; *L'opera italiana*, 1928H; *Saggio storico
   sul teatre musicale italiano*, 1913H; *Storia degli
   stromenti musicali*, 1908H; *Storia e letteratura
   del pianoforte*, 1918H

❄

A *Births*   B *Deaths*   C *Debuts*   D *New Positions*
E *Prizes/Honors*

Bonaventura, Mario di, 1924A
Bonazzi, Elaine, 1936A
Bonci, Alessandro, 1870A, 1896C, 1940B
Bond, Carrie Jacobs, 1862A, 1946B
Bond, Chapel, 1752D, 1790B
Bond, Victoria, 1945A, 1977F, 1998D
Bondini, Pasquale, 1789B
Bonell, Carlos, 1949A
Bonelli, Richard, 1887A, 1915C, 1980B
Bonetti, Antoni, 1952A
Bongartz, Heinz, 1947D, 1978B
Bonfichi, Paolo, 1769A, 1829D, 1840B
Boninsegna, Celestina, 1877A, 1896C, 1947B
Bónis, Ferenc, 1932A
Bonn, Germany: Beethoven Halle, 1959G;
    Beethoven Memorial, 1845;
    Beethovenverein, 1850G; Concordia Male
    Chorus, 1846G; Gesangverein, 1827G;
    Konzertverein, 1852G; Nationaltheater,
    1778G; Orchesterverein, 1843G; Symphony
    Orchestra, 1911G; Theater der Stadt Bonn,
    1953G; Verein Beethovenhaus, 1889G
Bonnal, Joseph-Ermend, 1880A, 1944B
Bonnet, Joseph, 1884A, 1944B
Bonney, Barbara, 1956A, 1979C
Bonno, Giuseppe, 1774D, 1788B
Bonynge, Richard, 1930A, 1976D, 1977E
Bookspan, Martin, 1984E; *Masterpieces of Music
    & Their Composers*, 1968H
Boone, Charles, 1939A
Booren, Jo van den, 1936A
Boose's Military Band Journal, 1845G
Boosey, Thomas, Publishing House, 1816G
Boosey & Co. Music Publisher, 1892G
Boosey & Hawkes, Ltd., 1930G
Boosley, Thomas, Book Store (London), 1795G
Booth, John E.: *The Critic, Power, and the
    Performing Arts*, 1991H
Booth, Juliet, 1961A, 1987C
Boozer, Brenda, 1948A, 1978C
Borchard, Adolphe, 1882A, 1967B
Borck, Edmund von, 1944B
Bord, Antoine, Piano Co., 1843G
Bordeaux, France: Chamber Music Society,
    1926G; Grand Theater, 1780G; May Festival,
    1950G; Orchestre de Concert, 1814G; Saint
    Cecilia Society, 1843G
Bordogni, Giulio M., 1789A, 1808C, 1856B
Bordogni, Giovanni, 1813C
Bordoni, Faustina, 1751F, 1773F, 1781B
Bordsky, Jascha, 1997B
Borealis Wind Quintet, 1976G
Boretz, Benjamin, 1934A; *Perspectives on
    Contemporary Music Theory*, 1972H;
    Perspectives on Performance & Notation, 1976H
Boreyko, Andrei, 1957A, 1990D, 1992D, 1998D
Borg, Kim, 1919A, 1947C, 2000B
Borgatti, Giuseppe, 1871A, 1950B
Borge, Victor, 1909A, 1953F, 2000B

Borghi, Adelaide, 1826A, 1846C, 1901B
Borghi, Giovanni Battista, 1759D, 1778D, 1796B
Borgioli, Armando, 1925C
Borgioli, Dino, 1891A, 1914C, 1960B
Bori, Lucrezia, 1887A, 1908C, 1960B
Borkh, Inge, 1917A, 1940C
Borkiewicz, Sergei, 1952B
Bořkovec, Pavel, 1894A, 1972B
Bornefeld, Helmut, 1906A, 1990B
Bornschein, Franz Carl, 1879A, 1948B
Borodin, Alexander, 1833A, 1850F, 1856F,
    1858F, 1887B
Borodin String Quartet, 1955G
Borodina, Olga, 1963A
Boronat, Olimpia, 1867A, 1886C, 1934B
Boroni, Antonio, 1770D, 1778D, 1792B
Borovsky, Alexander, 1889A, 1912E, 1968B
Borowski, Felix, 1872A, 1916D, 1956B
Borren, Charles van den, 1939E
Børresen, Hakon, 1954B
Borroff, Edith, 1925A; *American Opera: A
    Checklist*, 1992H; *Music in Europe and the
    United States: A History*, 1971H; *Music in
    Perspective*, 1976H; *Music Melting Round: A
    History of Music in the United States*, 1995H;
    Music of the Baroque, 1968H
Borris, Siegfried: *Eingühren in die moderne
    Musik*, 1951H; *Der Schlüssel zur Musik von
    Heute*, 1967H
Borromeo String Quartet, 1989G
Bortkiewicz, Sergei, 1877A, 1902C
Bortniansky, Dmitri, 1751A, 1769F, 1779DF,
    1796D, 1816D, 1825B
Börtz, Daniel, 1943A
Borwick, Leonard, 1868A, 1889C, 1925B
Bos, Coenraad Valentyn, 1955B
Bosabalian, Luisa, 1936A, 1964C, 1998B
Bosch Bernat-Veri, Jorge, 1800B
Bosch, Pieter Joseph van den, 1765D, 1803B
Boschot, Adolphe: *Entretiens sur la beauté*,
    1927H; *Musiciens-Poètes*, 1937H
Bose, Fritz, 1906A, 1975B; *Musikalische
    Vöokerkunde*, 1953H
Bösendorfer, Ignaz, 1794A, 1859B
Bösendorfer Piano Co., 1828G
Bosetti, Hermine, 1875A, 1898C, 1936A
Bosio, Angiolina, 1830A, 1846C, 1859B
Bosmans, Henriëtte, 1895A, 1952B
Bosquet, Georges, 1854B
Bosse Music Book Publishers, 1912G
Bossler, Heinrich, Co., 1781G
Bostock, Douglas, 1991D
Boston, Massachusetts: Academy of Music,
    1832G; Academy Orchestra, 1833G;
    American Conservatorio, 1801G; Apollo
    Club, 1868G; Aquarius Theater, 1852G;
    Athenaeum, 1807G; Bach Club, 1883G;
    Berklee School of Music, 1945G; Bijou
    Theater, 1885G; Boston Theater I, 1793G;

✥

F *Biographical*   G *Cultural Beginnings*   H *Musical Literature*
                I *Musical Compositions*

Boston Theater II, 1854G; Brass Band, 1835G; Castle Square Opera Co., 1897G; Cecilia Society, 1874G; Choral Arts Society, 1901G; Colonial Theater, 1893G; Conservatory of Music, 1867G; Continental Theater, 1866G; Crane Memorial Library, 1883G; Fadette Ladies Orchestra, 1888G; Faelten Piano School, 1897G; Federal Street Theater, 1794G; Fox-Buonameci School, 1898G; Gilmore's Grand Band, 1859G; Handel and Haydn Society, 1815G; Haymarket Theater, 1796G; Ideal Opera Co., 1879G; Light Opera Group, 1887G; Longy School of Music, 1916G; Malkin Conservatory, 1933G; Mallet & Graupner Musical Academy, 1801G; Manuscript Club, 1888G; Mendelssohn Quintette Club, 1849G; Music Hall, 1852G; Music School, 1851G; Musician's Union, 1863G; New Orchestra of Boston, 1984G; Old Folks Concert Troupe, 1855G; Orchestral Club, 1884G; People's Symphony Orchestra, 1920G; Petersilea Academy of Music, 1871G; Philhamonic Club, 1874G; Philo-Harmonic Society, 1791G; Pops Orchestra, 1885G; Savage Grand Opera Co., 1895G; Steinert Hall, 1896G; Symphony Hall, 1900G; Symphony Orchestra, 1881G; Tremont Theater, 1827G; Zimbler Sinfonietta, 1946G
Boston Music Co., 1885G
Boston Musical Instrument Co., 1869G
Boston Musical Record, 1878G
Boston Musical Times, 1860G
Bostridge, Ian, 1965A, 1993C
Botazzi, Ana Maria de, 1958E
Bote & Bock, Publishers, 1838G
Bötel, Heinrich, 1854A, 1883C, 1938B
Botes, Christine, 1964A
Botha, Johan, 1965A, 1988C
Botnen, Geir, 1959A, 1859C
Botstein, Leon, 1975D, 1992D; *Music & Its Public*, 2000H
Bott, Jean Joseph, 1857D
Botta, Lucca, 1882A, 1911C, 1917B
Bottée de Toulmon, Auguste, 1797A, 1831D, 1850B
Bottesini, Giovanni, 1889D
Bottesini, Giovanni, 1821A, 1889BD
Bottomley, Sally Ann, 1959A, 1980C
Boucher, Alexandre-Jean, 1778A, 1786C, 1861B
Boucher, Gene, 1933A, 1958C, 1994B
Boucheron, Raimondo, 1800A, 1829D, 1847D, 1876B; *Esercizi d'Armonia*, 1871H; *Filosofia della musica*, 1843H; *La scienza dell'armonia*, 1856H
Boucourechliev, André, 1925A, 1997B
Boufferdin, Pierre-Gabriel, 1768B
Bouhy, Jacques, 1848A, 1885D, 1929B
Boulanger, Lili, 1893A, 1913E, 1918B

Boulanger, Nadia, 1887A, 1979B
Boulder, Colorado: Bach Festival, 1974G; College Music Society, 1957G
Boulez, Pierre, 1925A, 1942F, 1971D, 1972E, 2000E; *Penser la musique aujourd'hui*, 1963H; *Relevés d'apprenti*, 1966H; *Werkstatt-Texte*, 1972H
Boulogne Philharmonic Society, 1860G
Boult, Adrien, 1889A, 1918C, 1924D, 1937E, 1983B, 1950D; *Handbook on Technique of Conducting*, 1921H
Boulton, Laura: *Musical Instruments of World Cultures*, 1972H
Bourdin, Roger, 1900A, 1922C, 1973B
Bourgault-Ducoudray, Louis, 1862E, 1888E
Bournemouth, England: Municipal Orchestra, 1897G; Symphony Orchestra, 1895G
Bournonville, Antoine de, 1805A, 1879B
Bournonville, Jacques de, 1754B
Bousquet, George, 1838E, 1847D
Bousset, René Drouard de, 1760B
Boutmy, Guillaume, 1791B
Boutmy, Jean-Joseph, 1757D; *Traité abrégé de la basse continuo*, 1760H
Boutmy, Josse, 1779B
Boutmy, Laurent-François, 1756A, 1838B
Boutry, Roger, 1932A, 1954E
Bouvard, François, 1760B
Bovy, Vina, 1900A, 1917C, 1947D, 1983B
Bowdoin College Music Press, 1964G
Bowdoin Summer Music Festival, 1965G
Bowen, Geraint, 1963A
Bowen, John, 1968A
Bowen, York, 1884A, 1961B
Bowers, Thomas J., 1823A, 1885B
Bowles, Paul, 1910A, 1999B
Bowling Green Musical Arts Center, 1979G
Bowman, Edward M, 1881EF
Bowman, James, 1941A, 1967C
Boyce, William, 1759E, 1768F, 1779B; *Cathedral Music I*, 1760H
Boyd, Charles: *Elements of Music Theory I, II*, 1938H; *Lectures on Church Music*, 1912H
Boyde, Andreas, 1967A, 1989C
Boydell, Brian, 1917A, 2000B
Boyden, David Dodge, 1910A, 1986B; *The History & Literature of Music, 1750 to the Present*, 1948H; *The History of Violin Playing from Its Origins to 1761*, 1965H; *An Introduction to Music*, 1956H; *A Manual of Counterpoint Based on Sixteenth-Century Practice*, 1944H
Boyer, Pascal, 1759D, 1794B
Boykan, Martin, 1931A
Boylan, Orla, 1971A
Boyle, George Frederick, 1886A, 1948B
Bozza, Eugène, 1934E
Brabec, Lubomir, 1953A
Braccini, Luigi, 1755A, 1779D, 1791B

❈

A *Births*   B *Deaths*   C *Debuts*   D *New Positions*
E *Prizes/Honors*

Bradbury, William B., 1816A, 1840D, 1868B; *Fresh Laurels for Sabbath School*, 1867H; *Golden Chain of Sabbath School Melodies*, 1861H; *The Jubliee*, 1858H

Bradbury's Piano-Forte Warehouse, 1854G

Bradford, England: British National Opera Co., 1922G; Harmonic Society, 1818G; Liedertafel, 1846G; Musical Friendly Society, 1821G; Philharmonic Society, 1831G; St. Cecilia Society, 1882G; Yorkshire Music Festival, 1823G

Bradley, Gwendolyn, 1952A, 1976C

Bradshaw, Claire, 1976A

Braga, Gaetano, 1829A, 1907B

Braham, David, 1905B

Braham, John, 1774A, 1787C, 1856B

Brahms, Johannes, 1833A, 1844F, 1848F, 1853F, 1859F, 1862F, 1863D, 1864F, 1866F, 1872D, 1879E, 1888F, 1889E, 1897B

Brailowsky, Alexander, 1896A, 1919C, 1976B

Brain, Dennis, 1921A

Brainard & Son, Puslishers, 1836G

Brainard's Musical, 1899G

Braithwaite, Nicholas, 1939A, 1966C, 1981D, 1984D, 1987D, 1988D, 1991D

Braithwaite, Warwick, 1896A, 1956D, 1971B; *The Conductor's Art*, 1952H

Brambilla, Giuseppina, 1819A, 1841C, 1903B

Brambilla, Marietta, 1807A, 1827C, 1875B

Brambilla, Teresa, 1813A, 1831C, 1895B

Brambilla-Ponchielli, Teresina, 1845A, 1863C, 1921B

Brandeis, Frederic, 1835A, 1851C, 1899B

Brandenstein, Johann Konrad, 1757B

Brandes, Emma, 1854A

Brandl, Johann Evangelist, 1760A, 1847B

Brandrowski-Sas, Alexander, 1860A

Brandt, Marianne, 1842A, 1867C, 1921B

Brandt-Forster, Ellen, 1866A, 1885C, 1921B

Brandus Music Publishers (Paris), 1846G

Brankovic, Senka, 1975A

Brannigan, Owen, 1908A, 1943C, 1973B

Branscombe, Gena, 1881A, 1977B

Branscombe Ensemble, 1934G

Brant, Per, 1767B

Brant, Henry, 1913A, 1955E, 1979E

Branzell, Karin Maria, 1891A, 1912C, 1974B

Braslau, Sophie, 1892A, 1913C, 1935B

Brass Chamber Music Society of Annapolis, 1979G

Brass Partout, 1991G

Brassin, Louis, 1840A, 1884B

Bratislava, Slovakia: Boys Choir, 1982G; Bratislava Theater, 1764G; Festival, 1965G; National Opera, 1919G; Opera House, 1776G; Radio Orchestra, 1926G; Saint Martin's Church Music Society, 1828G; Slovak National Theater, 1886G

Brattleboro Music Center, 1951G

Bräuer, Ferenc, 1799A, 1871B

Braun, Hans, 1938C

Braun, Johann, 1753A, 1811B

Braun, Russell, 1968A, 1994E

Braun, Victor, 1935A

Braun Music Center, 1984G

Braunfels, Walter, 1882A, 1954B

Braunstein, Joseph, 1996B

Braunstein, Ronald, 1955A, 1979E

Braxton, Anthony, 1994E

Brazil: Academy of Music, 1945G; Brotherhood of St. Cecilia, 1784G; Conservatory of Music, 1936G; Grupo Renovacíon, 1929G; Symphony Orchestra, 1940G; Theatro Pedro II, 1930G

Bream, Julian, 1933A, 1985E

Bree, Johannes B. van, 1801A, 1853D, 1857B

Bree String Quartet, 1849G

Breil, Joseph Carl, 1870A, 1926B

Breitenfeld, Richard, 1869A, 1897C, 1943B

Breitkopf, Bernhardt Christoph, 1777B

Breitkopf, Christoph, 1800B

Breitkopf, Johann Gottlob, 1794B

Breitkopf und Hartel, 1756G

Brema, Marie, 1856A, 1891C, 1925B

Bremen, Germany: Gesellschaft fúr Privatkonzerte, 1807G; Liedertafel, 1827G; Singakademie, 1815G

Bremner, Robert, Publisher, 1754G, 1762F, 1789B; *Instructions for the Guitar*, 1758H; *The Rudiments of Music*, 1756H

Bremner Publishers, London Branch, 1762G

Brendel, Alfred, 1931A, 1948C, 1949E; *Musical Thoughts & Afterthoughts*, 1976H

Brendel, Franz, 1811A, 1845D, 1868B; *Geschichte der Musik....*, 1852H; *Grundzüge der Geschichte der Musik*, 1848H; *Die Musik der Gegenwart und...der Zukunft*, 1854H; *Die Organisation des Musikwesens...*, 1865H

Brendel, Wolfgang, 1947A

Brendler, Eduard, 1800A, 1831BE

Brenet, Michel, 1858A, 1918B; *Histoire de la symphonie à orchestre*, 1882H

Brent, Charlotte, 1755CF, 1802B

Brentano String Quartet, 1992G

Brentón y Hernández, Tomas, 1923B

Brescia, Italy: Istituto Musicale Antonio Venture, 1866G; Teatro Guillaume, 1851G; Teatro Sociale, 1851G

Brescianello, Giuseppe Antonio, 1758B

Breslau, Poland: Agthe Music Academy, 1831G; Bohnscher Gesangverein, 1882G; Liedertafel, 1827G; Musikalischer Cirkel, 1834G; Opera House, 1841G; Orchestral Society, 1862G; Singakademie, 1825G

Bresnick, Martin, 1946A, 1975E, 1998E

Bressler, Charles, 1926A, 1996B

Bressler-Gianoli, Clotilde, 1875A, 1895C, 1912B

Bretan, Nicolae, 1887A,1944D, 1968B

❖

F *Biographical*   G *Cultural Beginnings*   H *Musical Literature*
I *Musical Compositions*

Bretón de los Herreros, Manuel, 1847D
Bretón y Hernández, Tomás, 1850A
Breuer, Hans, 1868A, 1896C, 1929B
Breval, Jean-Baptiste, 1753A, 1778C, 1823B;
 Traité du Violoncelle, 1804H
Bréval, Lucienne, 1869A, 1892C, 1935B
Brewacys, Luc, 1959A
Brewer, Christine, 1960A
Brewer, Herbert, 1865A, 1896D, 1926E, 1928B
Brewer, Johan Hyatt, 1856A, 1931B
Brey, Carter, 1978E
Brezina, Alec, 1965A
Brian, Dennis, 1957B
Brian, Havergal, 1876A, 1972B
Briccetti, Thomas, 1936A
Briccialdi, Giulio, 1818A, 1881B
Brice, Carol, 1918A, 1943EF, 1985B
Bricetti, Thomas, 1963D, 1968D, 1970D, 1975D,
 1988D
Brico, Antonia, 1902A, 1934D, 1938F, 1948D,
 1989B
Bridge, Frank, 1879A, 1941B
Bridge, Frederick, 1844A, 1897E, 1924B
Bridge, Richard, 1758B
Bridge Records, 1981G
Bridgehampton Chamber Music Festival,
 1983G (NY)
Bridgetower, George, 1778A, 1789C, 1860B
Briedenstein's Musikalischer Apparet, 1823G
Briesemeister, Otto, 1866A, 1893C, 1910B
Briggs, Robert, 1979E
Briggs, Sarah Beth, 1972A
Brighton, England: Choral Society, 1898G;
 Festival, 1870G; Music Festival, 1967G
Brignoli, Pasquale, 1824A, 1884B
Brilioth, Helge, 1931A, 1958C, 1965C
Brindisi String Quartet, 1984G
Brindle, Reginald Smith: *Musical Composition*,
 1986H
Brinegar, Donald, Singers, 1996G
Brings, Allen, 1934A
Brinkerhoff, Clara M., 1830A, 1845C
Brinsmead, Edgar: *History of the Pianoforte*,
 1870H
Brinsmead Piano Co., 1835G
Brisbane, Australia: Musical Union, 1872G;
 Brisbane Conservatory of Music, 1956G
Bristol, England: Choral Society, 1898G;
 Festival, 1870G; Choral Society, 1889G;
 Madrigal Society, 1837G; Music Festival,
 1873G; Prince's Street Rooms, 1756G
Bristow, George F., 1825A, 1842F, 1851D,
 1867D, 1898B
British Arts Council, 1946G
British Chamber Music Concerts, 1894G
British Institute of Recorded Sound, 1951G
British Liszt Piano Competition, 1961G
British Music Information Centre, 1967G
British Sinfonietta, 1967G

Britt Festival, 1963G
Britten, Benjamin, 1913A, 1964E, 1965E,
 1976BE
Britten String Quartet, 1987G
Brixi, Franz Xaver, 1756D, 1759D, 1771B
Brno, Czech Republic: Brünner Musikverein,
 1862G; German Theater, 1882G; Janáček
 Academy of the Arts, 1947G; Janáček String
 Quartet, 1947G; Male Choral Society, 1848G;
 Club of Moravian Composers, 1922G; Music
 Institute, 1828G; National Theater, 1884G;
 Opera House, 1884G; Organ School, 1882G;
 Philharmonic Society, 1808G; Provisional
 Theater, 1884G; Redoutensale Theater,
 1785G; Schubertbund, 1879G
Broadcast Music, Inc. (BMI), 1939G
Broadfoot, Eleanor, 1899C
Broadwood Grand Piano, 1781G
Broadwood, James Shudi, 1772A, 1851B
Broche, Charles, 1752A, 1777D, 1803B
Brockhaus Publishing Co., 1893G
Brockway, Howard A., 1870A, 1910E, 1951B
Brockway, W.: *Men of Music*, 1939H; *Opera: A
 History of Its Creation & Performance*, 1941H
Broder, Nathan, 1905A, 1963D, 1967B;
 Contemporary Music in Europe, 1965H
Broderip, Clementi & Co., Publishers
 (London), 1798G
Broderip, Edmund, 1764D, 1779B
Broderip, John, 1770B
Broderip, Robert, 1780D, 1793D
Brødsgaard, Anders, 1955A
Brodsky, Adolf, 1851A, 1891F, 1929B
Brodsky, Joseph, 1972F
Bronfman, Yefim, 1958A, 1973F, 1976C, 1981E
Brönner, Heidi, 1989C
Bronx Opera Co., 1967G
Brook, Barry S., 1918A; *Musicology & the
 Computer*, 1970H; *Musicology 1960-2000: A
 Practical Program*, 1970H; *Perspectives in
 Musicology*, 1972H; *La symphonie française
 dans la second moitié du XVIIIe siècle*, 1962H
Brook Mays Music Store (Dallas), 1901G
Brooklyn, New York: Academy of Music,
 1861G; Chamber Music Society, 1939G;
 Oratorio Society, 1893G; Philharmonic
 Orchestra, 1857G, 1955G; Symphony
 Orchestra, 1889G
Brooks, Iris: *New Music Across America*, 1993H
Brooks, Patricia, 1860C, 1937A, 1960C, 1993B
Brophy, Gerard, 1953A
Bros, José, 1963A, 1987C
Bros (y Bertomue), Juan, 1776A, 1806D
Broschi, Riccardo, 1756B
Brosig, Moritz, 1842D
Brosmann, Damasus, 1798B
Brossard, Noël: *Théorie des sons musicaux*,
 1847H
Brotons, Salvador, 1959A, 1991D, 1997D

�✣

A   *Births*   B   *Deaths*   C   *Debuts*   D   *New Positions*
       E   *Prizes/Honors*

Brott, Alexander, 1915A
Broude, Alexander, 1909A
Broude, Alexander, Inc., Publisher, 1954G
Broude Brothers Publishers, 1929G
Broude Trust for the Publication of
  Musicological Editions, 1981G
Broughton, William, 1985D, 1989D
Brouwenstijn, Gré, 1915A, 1940C, 1999B
Brouwer, Leo, 1939A, 1955C
Broward Center for the Performing Arts,
  1991G
Brown, Crosby, Instrumental Collection, 1889G
Brown, Earle, 1926A, 1972E, 1986D
Brown, Eddy, 1895A, 1974B
Brown, Eddy, String Quartet, 1922G
Brown, Francis H., 1818A, 1891B
Brown, Iona, 1980F, 1997D
Brown, John, 1766B
Brown, Nellie E., 1845A, 1874B, 1874C, 1924B
Brown, Rayner, 1912A
Brown, William, 1783C
Brownell, W. C. 1851A
Browning, John, 1933A, 1954E, 1955E, 1956C
Brownlee, John, 1900A, 1901A, 1926C, 1953D,
  1956D, 1969B
Brownsmith, John Leman, 1809A, 1866B
Bruch, Max, 1838A, 1852E, 1858F, 1865D,
  1867D, 1880D, 1883D, 1893E, 1898E, 1918E,
  1920B
Bruck, Charles, 1955D
Bruckner, Anton, 1824A, 1835F, 1841F, 1845F,
  1855F, 1856D, 1867F, 1868D, 1869F, 1875D,
  1886E, 1890E, 1891EF, 1894F, 1896B
Bruckner Society of America, 1931G
Bruges, Belgium: Concert Society, 1895G
Bruins, Theo, 1929A, 1993B
Brüll, Ignaz, 1846A, 1907B
Brun, Fritz, 1878A, 1959B
Bruneau, (Louis) Alfred, 1857A, 1881E, 1934B
Brunetti, Antonio, 1790D, 1810D
Brunetti, Gaetano, 1798B
Brunetti, Giovan, 1754D, 1788D
Brunetti, Giovan Gualberto, 1756E, 1787B
Bruni, Antonio B., 1757A, 1780C, 1799D, 1821B
Brunner, Evelyn, 1949A
Brunswick, Mark, 1902A, 1946D, 1971B
Brunswick Records, 1921G
Brunswick Staatsmusikschule, 1939G
Brusilow, Anshel, 1928A, 1944C, 1970D
Bruson, Renata, 1861C, 1936A, 1961C
Brussels, Belgium: Académie de Musique et de
  Chant, 1818G; Cercle des Vingts, 1884G;
  Concerts Populaires de Musique Classique,
  1865G; Conservatory of Music, 1812G;
  Jeunesses Musicales, 1946G; Libre
  Esthétique, 1884G; Philharmonic Society,
  1927G; Société Ste. Cécile, 1848G; State
  Academy (Conservatory), 1832G; String
  Quartet, 1926G; Symphony Orchestra, 1931G

Brustad, Bjarne, 1895A, 1978B
Bryars, Gavin, 1943A; *Experimental Music,*
  1974H
Bryden, John, 1947A, 1971C
Brydenfelt, Michael, 1966A, 1994C
Bryn-Julson, Phyllis, 1945A, 1966C
Buchanan, Isobel, 1954A, 1976C
Buchanin, Alison, 1969A
Bucharest, Romania: Ateneul Román, 1888G;
  Bossel Theater, 1848G; Buda Music
  Academy, 1867G; Conservatory of Music,
  1864G; Deutsche Liedertafel, 1852G;
  Filarmonica George Enescû, 1868G; National
  Theater, 1852G; Philharmonic Society,
  1853G; Societatea Simfonicã "Lyra," 1892G;
  Theatrum Vlahicum Bucharestini, 1814;
  Wiest Conservatory of Music, 1899G
Buchholz, Johann Simeon, 1758A, 1825B
Buchla, Donald, 1937A
Buchla Associates (Berkeley), 1966G
Büchner, Adolf Emil, 1865D
Buck, Dudley, 1839A, 1857F, 1862F, 1875F,
  1909B
Buck, Ole, 1945A
Buckley, Emerson, 1916A, 1950D, 1963D,
  1963E, 1964D, 1989B
Buckley, John, 1951A
Buckley, Richard, 1953A, 1983D
Buckman, Rosina, 1948B
Budai, Livia, 1950A, 1973C
Budapest, Hungary: Bartay-Menner Singing
  Academy, 1829G; Conservatory of Pest-Buda
  Society, 1840G; Hungarian National Theater,
  1837G; Hungarian Singer's Ass'n, 1867G;
  Ladies Choral Union, 1894G; Music Institute
  of Pest, 1812G; Music Lover's Society of
  Pest, 1867G; National Conservatory, 1840G;
  National Royal Academy of Music, 1875G;
  People's Theater, 1875; Pestbuda Society of
  Musicians, 1836G; Royal Hungarian Opera
  House, 1884G; String Quartet, 1917G; Town
  Theater, 1812G
Buechner, David, 1959A, 1984E
Buechner, Margaret, 1922A, 1998B
Buelow, George J., 1929A
Buenos Aires, Argentina: Coliseo Provisional,
  1804G; Conservatorio Nacional, 1880G;
  Conservatorio Santa Cecilia, 1894G; Escuela
  de Música de la Provincie, 1878G; Escuela de
  Música y Canto, 1822G; Grupo de Acción
  Instrumental, 1970G; Museo Naciónal de
  Bellas Artes, 1895G; Sociedad de Mayo,
  1854G; Sociedad Filarmónica, 1822G; Teatro
  Argentina, 1804G; Teatro Colón, 1857G,
  1908G; Teatro de la Federación, 1845G;
  Teatro de la Opera, 1872G; Teatro de la
  Rancheria, 1783G; Teatro de la Victoria,
  1838G; Teatro de Operas y Comedians,
  1757G; Teatro del Buen Orden, 1844G;

❊

F *Biographical*   G *Cultural Beginnings*   H *Musical Literature*
       I *Musical Compositions*

Buenos Aires, Argentina: (*cont.*)
  Teatro Nacional, 1882G; Teatro Politeama,
  1879G; Teatro Porteño, 1804G
Buffalo, New York: Baird Music Hall, 1981G;
  Continental Singing Society, 1862G; June in
  Buffalo Festival, 1975G; Kleinhaus Music
  Hall, 1940G; Liedertafel, 1848G; Music Hall,
  1883G; Philharmonic Society, 1830G;
  Philharmonic Society II, 1908G; St. Cecilia
  Society, 1863G; St. James Hall, 1835G;
  Sängerbund, 1855G
Buffet Auger Woodwind Co., 1825G
Buffet-Crampton et Cie., 1825G
Bühler, Franz, 1801D
Buhlig, Richard, 1880A, 1901C, 1952B
Bühnen der Stadt Bielefeld Opera House,
  1904G
Buketoff, Igor, 1915A, 1942E, 1948D, 1968D
Bukofzer, Manfred, 1910A, 1955B; *Music of the
  Baroque Era*, 1947H; *The Place of Musicology in
  American Institutions of Higher Learning*,
  1957H; *Studies in Medieval & Renaissance
  Music*, 1950H
Bulgaria (*see also* Sofia): Bulgarian (Aramov)
  String Quartet, 1938G; Bulgarian Radio &
  Television Symphony Orchestra, 1949G;
  National Philharmonic Orchestra, 1914G;
  State Folksong & Dance Ensemble, 1951G;
  State Music Academy, 1921G
Bull, Ole, 1810A, 1819C, 1843F, 1880B
The Bulletin, 1965G
Bulletin Critique de Littérature, d'Histoire...,
  1881G
Bulletin of the American Composers' Alliance,
  1952G
Bullock, Ernest, 1951E
Bülow, Cosima von, 1864F, 1869F, 1870F
Bülow, Hans von, 1830A, 1849F, 1851F, 1853F,
  1857f, 1864D, 1867D, 1869F, 1875F, 1880D,
  1885F, 1894B
Bulthaupt, Heinrich: *Dramaturgie der Oper*,
  1887H
Bulychev-Okser, Michael, 1980A
Bumbry, Grace, 1937A, 1960C, 1961F, 1990E
Bunger, Richard Joseph, 1942A; *The Well-
  Prepared Piano*, 1973H
Bunin, Revol, 1924A, 1976B
Bunin, Stanislav, 1985E
Bunini, Maurizio, 1968A
Bunting, Edward: *Ancient Irish Airs II*, 1809H;
  General Collection of Ancient Irish Music I,
  1797H
Buranskas, Karen, 1950A
Burbank, Richard: *Twentieth Century Music*,
  1984H
Burbure de Wesembeek, Léon, 1812A, 1862E,
  1889B
Burchinal, Frederick, 1948A, 1976C
Burchuladze, Paata, 1951A, 1975C, 1986E

Bürde-Ney, Jenny, 1826A, 1847C, 1886B
Burdett, Frank W., 1858A, 1919B
Bureau, Karen, 1951A
Bureau de Musique (Paris), 1966G
Burg, Robert, 1915C, 1846B
Burge, David, 1930A
Burgess, Sally, 1953A, 1976C
Burgess, David, 1953A
Burghauser, Jarmil, 1921A, 1997B
Burgin, Richard, 1892A, 1903C, 1981B
Burgmüller, Johann A., 1766A, 1824B
Burgmüller, Norbert, 1810A, 1836B
Burgon, Geoffrey, 1941A
Burgstaller, Alois, 1871A, 1896C, 1945B
Burian, Emil Frantiek, 1904A, 1959B
Burian, Karl, 1891C
Burke, Edmund, 1876A, 1905C, 1970B
Burke, Thomas, 1890A, 1917C, 1969B
Burkhard, Willy, 1900A, 1955B
Burleigh, Cecil, 1885A, 1980B
Burleigh, Henry Thacker, 1866A, 1917E, 1949B;
  Jubilee Songs of the U.S.A., 1916H
Burmeister, Annelies, 1956C
Burmester, Pedro, 1963A
Burney, Charles, 1751DF, 1764EF, 1769F, 1770F,
  1772F, 1806E; *General History of Music I*,
  1776H; *The Present State of Music in France
  and Italy*, 1771H; *The Present State of Music in
  Germany...*, 1773H
Burney, Fanny, 1802F
Burrian, Carl, 1870A, 1924B
Burrowes, John, 1787A, 1852B; *The Pianoforte
  Primer*, 1818H; *The Thorough-bass Primer*,
  1819H
Burrowes, Norma, 1944A, 1970C
Burrows, Stuart, 1933A, 1963C
Burton, Frederick: *American Primitive Music*,
  1909H; *Songs of the Ojibway Indians*, 1903H
Burton, John, 1782B
Burton, Robert, 1820A, 1849D, 1892B
Burton, Stephen: *Orchestration*, 1982H
Burton, Stephen Douglas, 1943A
Bury, Alfred von, 1903C, 1926B
Bury, Bernard de, 1785BE
Bury, Grzegorz, 1961A
Burzio, Eugenia, 1899C
Busby, Thomas, 1755A, 1838B; *Complete
  Dictionary of Music*, 1801H; *Concert Room and
  Orchestral Anecdotes*, 1825H; *Dictionary of
  Music*, 1813H; *The Divine Harmonist*, 1788H;
  General History of Music, 1819H; *A Grammar
  of Music*, 1818H; *A Musical Manuel*, 1828H
Busch, Adolf, 1891A, 1952B
Busch, Carl, 1862A, 1911D, 1943B
Busch, Fritz, 1890A, 1912D, 1918D, 1922D,
  1951B
Busch, William, 1901A, 1927C, 1945B
Busch String Quartet, 1919G
Bush, Alan, 1899A, 1995B

A   *Births*   B   *Deaths*   C   *Debuts*   D   *New Positions*
         E   *Prizes/Honors*

Bush, Geoffrey, 1998B
Busoni, Ferruccio, 1866A, 1890E, 1913DE,
  1924B; *Toward a New Esthetic of Music*,
  1907H
Busoni International Piano Competition,
  1940G
Bussani, Dorothea, 1763A, 1786C
Bussani, Francesco, 1763C
Busse, Barry, 1946A
Busser, Henri-Paul, 1872A, 1893E, 1902D,
  1905D, 1938E, 1973B
Bussler, Ludwig, 1838A, 1883D, 1900B;
  Musikalische elementarlehr, 1867H
Bussotti, Sylvano, 1931A
Bustelli, Giuseppe, 1781D
Bustini, Alessandro: *La Sinfonia in Italia*, 1904H
Buswell, James Oliver, III, 1963C
Buswell, James Oliver, IV, 1946A
Butler, Thomas Hamly, 1755A, 1823B
Butt, Clara, 1872A, 1892C, 1920E, 1936B
Butterworth, Arthur, 1923A
Butterworth, George, 1885A, 1916B
Butterworth, Neil: *Dictionary of American
  Composers*, 1985H
Buttstett, Franz Vollrath, 1776D, 1814B
Buzzola, Antonio, 1815A, 1855D, 1871B
Bybee, Luretta, 1965A
Bychkov, Semyon, 1952A, 1985DF, 1989D,
  1992F, 1998D
Byfield, John, Jr., 1774B
Byfield, John, Sr., 1756B
Byrd, William, Singers, 1970G
Byström, Oscar Fredrik, 1821A, 1909B
Caballé, Monserrat, 1933A, 1953C, 1984B
Caballero, Jorge, 1996E
Cabasa Percussion Quartet, 1983G
Cabel, Marie, 1827A, 1869C, 1885B
Cabo, Francisco Javier, 1768A, 1832B
Cabrillo Music Festival, 1963G
Cacavas, John: *Music Arranging &
  Orchestration*, 1975H
Cäcilia, 1824G
Cäcilienkalendar, 1876G
Cadaux, Justin, 1813A, 1874B
Cadek School of Music (Chattanooga), 1904G
The Cadenza, 1894G
Cadman, Charles Wakefield, 1881A
Cadman, George W., 1908E, 1924E, 1926E,
  1928E, 1946B
*Caecilia: Algemeen Musikaal Tijdschrift ver
  Nederlands*, 1844G
Caesar, Irving, 1895A
Cafaro, Pasquale, 1787B
Caffarelli, 1756F, 1783B
Caffi, Francesco, 1778A, 1874B; *Storia della
  musica sacra*, 1855H
Caffiaux, Philippe: *Histoire de la musique*,
  1755H; *Nouvelle méthode de solfier la musique*,
  1756H

Cage, John, 1912A, 1968E, 1978E, 1989E, 1992B;
  Notations, 1969H; *Silence*, 1961H; *Themes &
  Variations*, 1982H; *Writings '67-'72*, 1973H
Cage, John, Award for Music, 1992G
Cagliari Accademia Filarmonica, 1824G
Cagnoni, Antonio, 1828A, 1852D, 1873D,
  1896B
Cahier, Mme. Charles, 1870A, 1904C, 1951B
Cahill, Teresa (Mary), 1944A, 1967C
Cahova, Monica, 1966A, 1988C
Cahusec, Thomas, Publisher, 1755G
Cailin String Quartet, 1993G
Cailliet, Lucien, 1891A, 1957D, 1985B
Cairns, Christine, 1959A
Caix d'Hervelois, Louis de, 1760B
Calderon, Philip, 1878E
Caldicott, Alfred J., 1892D
Caldwell, John: *Medieval Music*, 1978H
Caldwell, Sarah, 1924A, 1947F, 1952D, 1974E,
  1981F, 1983D
Caldwell, Tracey, 1996B
Caldwell, William: *The Union Harmony*,
  1837H
Calegari, Antonio, 1757A, 1791E, 1814D,
  1828B; *Cioco pittagorico musicale*, 1802H; *Modi
  generali del canto*, 1836H; *Sistema Armonico*,
  1829H
Calfaro, Pasquale, 1771D
Calgary, Canada: Center for the Performing
  Arts, 1985G; Philharmonic Orchestra, 1955G
Cali Conservatory & School of the Fine Arts,
  1933G
California: Baroque Virtuosi, 1981G; Chamber
  Symphony Orchestra, 1961G; Choral Society
  of Southern California, 1982G; Hall Johnson
  Choir, 1925G; Institute of the Arts, 1961G;
  Ojai Festival, 1947G; State University
  Electronic Center, 1961G
Callas, Maria, 1923A, 1938C, 1977B
Callas, Maria, International Club, 1989G
Callaway, Paul, 1909A
Callcott, John Wall, 1766A, 1821B; *A Musical
  Grammar*, 1806H
Callido, Gaetano, 1813B
Callinet, François, 1754A, 1820B
Callinet, Louis, 1786A, 1845B
Calori, Angiola, 1756C, 1790B
Caltabiano, Ronald, 1959A
Calvé, Emma, 1858A, 1881C, 1942B
Calvesi, Vincenzo, 1785C
Calvet String Quartet, 1926G
Calvocoressi, Michel Dimitri, 1877A, 1944B;
  Masters of Russian Music, 1936H; *La musique
  russe*, 1907H; *Musical Taste & How to Form It*,
  1925H; *Principles & Methods of Musical
  Criticism*, 1923H
Calzabigi, Ranieri, 1795B; *Su le poesie
  drammatiche del Sig...Metastasio*, 1755H
Camacho, Marvin, 1966A

❉

F *Biographical*   G *Cultural Beginnings*   H *Musical Literature*
        I *Musical Compositions*

Cambini, Giuseppe Maria, 1825B; *Nouvelle Méthode...pour le violon*, 1796H; *Méthode pour la flûte traversière*, 1799H
Cambreling, Sylvain, 1948A, 1981D
Cambridge Collegium Musicum, 1942G
Cambridge Singers, 1981G
Cambridge Summer School of Music, 1946G
Cambridge University: Musical Society, 1843G; Musical Club, 1899G
Camerata Helvetica, 1962G
Camerata Köln, 1979G
Camerata Singers (NY), 1960G
Camerloher, Placidus, 1782B
Cameron, Basil, 1932D
Camidge, John, 1803B; *Six Easy Lessons for the Harpsichord*, 1764H
Camidge, Matthew, 1764A, 1844B
Camilieri, Lorenzo, 1956B
Camilli, Camillus, 1754B
Cammarano, Salvatore, 1801A, 1852B
Campagnoli, Bartolomeo, 1751A, 1827B; *Metodo per Violino*, 1797H; *Nouvelle méthode de...violon*, 1791H
Campanari, Giuseppe, 1855A, 1893C, 1927B
Campanari, Leandro, 1857A, 1939B
Campanella, Michele, 1947A, 1966E
Campanini, Cleofonte, 1860A, 1882C, 1897D, 1906D, 1910D, 1913D, 1919B
Campanini, Italo, 1845A, 1871C, 1896B
Campbell, Alexander, 1764A, 1824B; *Albyn's Anthology I*, 1816H
Campbell, O.: *English Folksongs from the Southern Appalachians*, 1917H
Campbell-Watson, Frank: *Modern Elementary Harmony*, 1930H
Campenhout, François van, 1779A, 1848B
Campina, Fidela, 1983B
Campioni, Carlo Antonio, 1763D, 1788B
Campo, Conrado del, 1878A, 1953B
Campo, Régis, 1968A
Campora, Giuseppe, 1923A, 1949C
Camporese, Violante, 1785A, 1839B
Camuccini, Vincenzo, 1806D
The Canada Music Book, 1979G
Canada (*see also* Banff, Calgary, Montreal, Ottawa, Quebec, Toronto, Vancouver, Winnipeg): Academy of Music, 1911G; Broadcasting Co. Symphony, 1952G; Festival Singers of Canada, 1954G; Folk Music Society, 1956G; League of Composers, 1951G; Music Centre, 1959G; Opera Company, 1950G; National Youth Orchestra of Canada, 1960G; Orchestre Symphonique Régional d'Abitibi Témiscamingue, 1985G; Performing Rights Society, 1925G; Quartet Canada, 1975G
Canat de Chizy, Edith, 1950A
Canavas, Jean-Baptiste, 1784B
Canavas, Joseph, 1776B

Canberra Conservatory of Music, 1964G
Candeille, Julie, 1767A, 1782C, 834B
Candeille, Pierre Joseph, 1827B
Candidus, William, 1840A, 1867C, 1910B
Caniglia, Maria, 1905A, 1930C, 1979B
Canin, Stuart, 1959E
Canonici, Luca, 1961A, 1986C
Cannabich, Carl, 1771A, 1806B
Cannabich, Christian, 1774D, 1798B
Canova, Antonio, 1810D
Cantelli, Guido, 1920A, 1956B
Canteloube, Joseph, 1879A, 1957B
Canterbury, England: Vocal Union, 1860G
Canti, Giovanni, Publisher, 1835G
Cape, Jonathan, Publisher, 1921G
Cape & Islands Chamber Music Festival, 1980G (NY)
Cape Town, South Africa: Opera House, 1893G; Philharmonic Orchestra, 1997G; South African Academy of Music, 1826G; Symphony Orchestra, 1914G
Capecchi, Renato, 1923A, 1948C, 1998B
Capella Classica (Spain), 1932G
Capella Rojal de Catalunyz, 1987G
Capellen, George: *Der Musikalische Akustik als Grundlage der Harmonik & Melodik*, 1903H; *Ein Neuer exotischer musikstil*, 1906H
Capet String Quartet I, 1893G
Capet String Quartet II (Paris), 1903G
Capet String Quartet III (Paris), 1910G
Capilla Catalana, 1890G
Capital Hill Choral Society, 1983G
Capocci, Filippo, 1840A, 1911B
Capocci, Gaetano, 1811A, 1839D, 1855D, 1898B
Capoul, Joseph-Amédée, 1897D
Capoul, Victor, 1839A, 1861C, 1924B
Cappella Figuralis, 1989G
Cappelletti, Andrea, 1961A
Cappello, Roberto, 1976E
Cappi and Diabelli (Vienna), 1818G
Cappoletti, Andrea, 1984C
Cappuccilli, Piero, 1929A, 1957C
Caprioli, Alberto, 1956A
Capron, Nicolas, 1761C, 1784B
Capsir, Mercedes, 1897A, 1914C, 1969B
Capuzzi, Giuseppe Antonio, 1755A, 1818B
Carabella, John, 1930D
Caracas, Venezuela: Academy of Music, 1783G; Teatro Municipal, 1880G
Caracciolo, Juanita, 1889A, 1924B
Caradori-Allan, Maria, 1800A, 1822C, 1865B
Carafa, Michele, 1787A, 1872B
Caraffe, Charles-Placide, 1756B
Caramoor Festival (Katonah, N.Y.), 1946G
Carapetyan, Armen, 1908A, 1992B
Carcani, Giacomo, 1759D, 1811D
Card, June, 1942A, 1959C
Carden, Allen: *Missouri Harmony*, 1820H
Carden, Joan, 1937A, 1963C

A *Births*   B *Deaths*   C *Debuts*   D *New Positions*
E *Prizes/Honors*

Cardenas, Sergio, 1951A
Cardew, Cornelius, 1936A, 1981B
Cardiff, England: Cardiff Municipal Choir,
    1942G; Choir School, 1880G; National
    Eisteddfod Ass'n, 1880G; Triennial Festival,
    1892G; Ware, Henry, Symphony Orchestra,
    1918G
Cardon, Jean-Baptiste, 1788B
Carduff, Sylvia, 1966E
Carelli, Gabor, 1915A, 1999B
Carelli, Emma, 1877A
Carena, Maria, 1894A, 1917C
Carestini, Giovanni, 1760B
Carhart & Needham, Organ Builders, 1846G
Caricature, 1838G
Caridia, Miltiades, 1960D, 1962D, 1969D,
    1974D, 1979D, 1998B
Carisch Music Publishers, 1887G
Carl, William Crane, 1836B, 1865A, 1936B
Carli Music Publishers (Paris), 1805G
Carlsbad Symphony Orchestra, 1835G
Carlson, Claudine, 1937A, 1968C
Carlson, David, 1952A
Carlson, Lenus, 1945A, 1967C
Carlstedt, Jan, 1926A
Carlyle, Joan, 1931A, 1955C
Carmel Bach Festival, 1935G
Carmina String Quartet, 1984G
Carmirelli, Pina, 1914A, 1937C, 1993B
Carmirelli String Quartet, 1954G
Carnaby, Willaim, 1772A, 1839B
Carnegie, Andrew, 1835A, 1919B
Carner, Mosco, 1904A, 1985B
Carner, Mosco: On Men and Music, 1944H;
    Study in Twentieth Century Harmony, 1942H
Carnicer, Ramón, 1789A, 1818D, 1828D 1855B
Caroli, Angelo Antonio, 1778B
Carolsfeld, Ludwig Schnoor von, 1865B
Caron, Rose Lucille, 1857A, 1883C, 1930B
Carosio, Margherita, 1908A, 1927C
Carpani, Giuseppe, 1752A, 1825B; Lettere
    Musico-Teatrali, 1824H; Le Haydine Ovvera
    Lettere...Giuseppe Haydn, 1812H
Carpenter, John Alden, 1876A, 1897F, 1906F,
    1909F,1918E, 1921E, 1933E, 1942E, 1947E,
    1951B
Carpenter Performing Arts Center, 1997G
Carr, Benjamin, 1768A, 1793F, 1794F, 1831B
Carr, Colin, 1957A, 1981E
Carr, Joseph, Publishing House (Baltimore),
    1794G
Carr's Musical Repository, 1793G
Carraud, Michel-Gaston, 1890E
Carré, Marguerite, 1880A, 1899C, 1947B
Carrell, James: Songs of Zion, 1820H
Carreño, Cayetano, 1789D
Carreño, (Maria) Teresa, 1853A, 1862C, 1917B
Carreño, Teresa, Arts Center, 1983G
Carreño, Teresa, Conservatory of Music, 1951G

Carreras, José, 1946A, 1970C, 1971E
Carretti, Giuseppe Maria, 1756D
Carrick, Richard, 1971A
Carrillo, José, 1920D
Carrillo, Julián, 1875A, 1913D, 1965B; Tratado
    Sintético de Harmonia, 1914H
Carrodus, John, 1836A, 1863C, 1895B
Carrol, Silvano, 1939A, 1963C
Carron, Arthur, 1900A, 1929C, 1967B
Carse, Adam: Harmony Exercises, 1923H;
    Musical Wind Instruments, 1939H; The
    Orchestra from Beethoven to Berlioz, 1948H;
    The Orchestra of the 18th Century, 1940H;
    Orchestral Conducting, 1929H
Carte, Richard D'Oyly, 1844A, 1901B
Carter, Barbara, 1958A, 1980C
Carter, Elliott, 1908A, 1932F, 1953E, 1956E,
    1965E, 1983EF, 1985E, 1992E; The Writings of
    Elliott Carter: an American Composer Looks at
    Modern Music, 1977H
Carter, John, 1988B
Cartier, Jean-Baptiste, 1765A, 1841B; L'art du
    violon, 1798H
Cartledge, Nicholas Haydn, 1994C
Carulli, Ferdinando, 1770A, 1841B
Caruso, Enrico, 1873A, 1894C, 1904F, 1921B;
    How to Sing, 1923H
Caruso, Luigi, 1754A, 1790D, 1823B
Carvalho, Caroline, 1827A, 1895B
Carvalho, Eleazar de, 1912A, 1963D, 1996B
Carvalho, Léon, 1825A, 1876D, 1897B
Carvalho, João de Sousa, 1761F, 1767F, 1773D,
    1799B
Carwithen, Doreen, 1922A
Cary, Annie Louise, 1841A, 1867C, 1921B
Caryll, Ivan, 1921B
Casadesus, Gaby, 1901A, 1999B
Casadesus, Jean, 1927A, 1972B
Casadesus, Robert, 1899A, 1972B
Casadesus, Robert, Piano Competition,
    1975G
Casa Dotesio, Publishing Co., 1900G
Casagrande International Piano Competition,
    1966G
Casale Monferrato, Italy: Accademia
    Filarmonica, 1827G; Civica Scuola de
    Musica, 1863G; Teatro della Società, 1784G
Casali, Giovanni B., 1759D, 1792B
Casals, Marta, 1992D
Casals, Pablo, 1876A, 1891C, 1973B
Casals Festival (Puerto Rico), 1957G
Casamorata, Luigi Fernando, 1807A, 1881B;
    Manuale di Armonia, 1876H
Casanovas, Narciso, 1799B
Casa Romero, Publisher, 1856G
Casavant Frères, Organ Builders, 1845G
Casazza, Elvira, 1887A, 1909C, 1965B
Cascioli, Gianluca, 1979A, 1994C
Case, Anna, 1889A, 1900C, 1909C, 1984B

❈

F *Biographical*   G *Cultural Beginnings*   H *Musical Literature*
            I *Musical Compositions*

Casella, Alfredo, 1883A, 1947B; *Il Pianoforte*, 1938H
Casella, Alfredo, Competition, 1952G
Casella, Pietro, 1769A
Casellas, Jaime de, 1764B
Casimiri, Raffaele Casimiro, 1880A, 1943B
Cassard, Philippe, 1990C
Cassel, Walter, 1910A
Cassel, Walter, 1938C, 2000B
Cassello, Kathleen, 1958A, 1985C
Cassidy, Claudia, 1899A, 1942D, 1996B
Cassilly, Richard, 1927A, 1955C, 1998B
Cassuto, Álvaro, 1938A, 1970D, 1981D, 1993D
Castagna, Bruna, 1905A, 1925C, 1983B
Castel, Louis Bertrand, 1757B
Castellan, Jeanne A., 1819A, 1837C
Castellar, Francisco Andrevi y, 1786A
Castello Svevo International Festival, 1984G
Castelmary, (Armand de), 1834A, 1863C, 1897B
Castelnuovo-Tedesco, Mario, 1895A, 1968B, 1999F
Casti, Giambattista, 1803B
Castiglioni, Niccolò, 1932A, 1996B
Castillo, Ricardo, 1894A, 1966B
Cast-Iron Piano Frame, 1840G
Castle, Joyce, 1944A, 1970C
Castle, William, 1836A, 1861C, 1909B
Castle Hill Baroque & Classical Music Festival, 1972G
Castleman, Charles, 1941A, 1950C
Caston, Saul, 1901A, 1944D, 1970B
Castro, Juan José, 1895A, 1968B
Castro-Aberty, Margarita, 1947A, 1978C
Castrucci, Pietro, 1752B
Catalani, Alfredo, 1854A, 1893B
Catalani, Angelica, 1780A, 1841D, 1849B
Catalani, Angelina, 1795 C
Catel, Charles-Simon, 1773A, 1815E, 1825E, 1830B; *Traité d'harmonie*, 1802H
Catelani, Angelo, 1811A, 1866B
Cathedral Choir, Cathedral of St. Peter & St. Paul, 1912G
Cathedral Symphony Orchestra, 1982G
The Catholic Choirmaster, 1915G
Catley, Anne, 1762C, 1789B
Catlin, George, 1777A, 1852B
Catoire, Georgi Lvovich, 1861A, 1926B
Catrufo, Gioseffo, 1771A, 1851B
Catterall String Quartet, 1910G
Caudella, Edoardo, 1841A, 1924B
Cavalieri, Catarina, 1760A, 1775C, 1801B
Cavalieri, Lina, 1874A, 1900C, 1944B
Cavallier, Nicolas, 1964A, 1987C
Cavani String Quartet, 1984G
Cavos, Catterino, 1775A, 1840B
Caylus, Anne Claude Philippe, 1765B
Cazden, Norman, 1914A, 1980B; *Musical Consonance & Dissonance*, 1948H

Cebotari, Maria, 1910A, 1931C, 1949B
Ceccarini, Giancarlo, 1951A, 1975C
Ceccato, Aldo, 1934A, 1964C, 1973D, 1975D, 1985D, 1990D, 1991D
Cecchele, Gianfranco, 1940A, 1964C
Cecere, Carlo, 1761B
Cech, Adolf, 1883D
Cecil, Winifred, 1907A, 1935C, 1985B
Cedille Records, 1989G
Ceely, Robert, 1930A; *The Electronic Music Resource Book*, 1981H
Cehanovsky, George, 1892A, 1921C, 1986B
Celes, Dom François Bedos de, 1779B
Celeste, 1886G
Celestina, 1772G
Celestino, Eligio, 1812B
Celles, François Bedos de: *L'art du facteur d'orgues I*, 1766H; *L'art du facteur d'orgues III*, 1778H
Celli, Frank H., 1845A, 1862C, 1904B
Center for Black Music Research, 1983G
Center for Chinese Folk Music Research, 1967G
Center for Music Experiment, UC, San Diego, 1971G
Central City Opera House, 1877G
Central City Opera Festival, 1932G
Central Opera Service (Met), 1954G
Centre Belge de Documentation Musicale, 1951G
Centre de Documentation de Musique Internationale, 1949G
Centre de Recherches Musicales de Wallonie, 1970G
Centre Français d'Humanisme Musical, 1959G
Centre International De Recherches Musicales, 1968G
Centre Lyrique de Wallonie, 1974G
Centro dell'Oratorio Musicale (Rome), 1949G
Century Opera Co. of New York, 1913G
Century II Concert Hall (Wichita), 1969G
Cerar, Maja, 1972A
Cernikof, Vladimir, 1882A, 1905C, 1940B
Cerny, Paul, 1970A
Cerone, David, 1985D
Cerovsek, Corey, 1972A 1981C
Cerquetti, Anita, 1931A, 1951C
Cerri, Giannina Russ, 1878A
Ceruti, Roque, 1760B
Cerven Brass Instrument Co., 1842G
Cervetto, Giacomo Basevidetto, 1783B
Cervetto, James, 1760C, 1837B
Cesi, Beniamino, 1845A, 1907B
Chabanon, Michel de: *Musique considérée en elle-même et...*, 1785H; *Observations sur la musique...*, 1779H
Chabrier, Emmanuel, 1841A, 1861F, 1880F, 1894B

�֎

A   *Births*   B   *Deaths*   C   *Debuts*   D   *New Positions*
E   *Prizes/Honors*

Chadwick, George W, 1854A, 1876F, 1897D, 1905E, 1909E, 1928E, 1931B; *Harmony: A Course of Study*, 1897H
Chailly, Lucian, 1920A, 1968D, 1989D
Chailly, Riccardo, 1953A, 1982DF, 1986D, 1988D
Chalabala, Zdeněk, 1899A, 1925D, 1936D, 1945D, 1953D, 1962B
Chaliapin, Feodor, 1873A, 1894C, 1899F, 1901F, 1938B; *Man and Mask*, 1932H; *Pages from My Life*, 1927H
Challen, Charles, Piano Co (London), 1804G
Challender, Stuart, 1988F
Challenger, Robert, 1967A
Challier, C. A., & Co., Publisher, 1835G
Challis, John, 1907A, 1974B
Challis, John, Harpsichord Co., 1930G
Chalmeau-Damonte, Magali, 1978C
Chamber Music America, 1977G
Chamber Music in Historic Sites, 1981G
Chamber Music Magazine, 1984G
Chamber Music Northwest Summer Festival, 1971G
Chamber Music Plus, 1980G
Chamber Music Quarterly, 1982G
Chamber Music Society of America, 1932G
Chamber Music West, 1977G
Chamber Orchestra of Europe, 1981G
Chamber Players, League of Composers, 1983G
Chaminade, Cécile, 1857A, 1944B
Chamlee, Mario, 1892A, 1916C, 1966B
Champagne, Claude, 1891A, 1965B
Champein, Stanislas, 1753A, 1830B
Chan, Susan, 1964A, 1986C
Chance, John Barnes, 1932A, 1972B
Chandler, Dorothy Buffum, 1901A, 1997B
Chandler, Dorothy, Pavilion, 1964G
Chandos Recording Co., 1977G
Chang, Han-No, 1994E
Chang, Lynn, 1974E
Chang, Sarah, 1980A, 1988C, 1998E, 2000E
Chang, Yuan-Chih Beryl, 1980C
Chanler, Theodore Ward, 1902A, 1957E, 1961B
Chanot, François, 1788A, 1825B
Chanot, Georges, Jr., 1831A, 1893B
Chanot, Georges, Sr., 1801A, 1873B
Chanot, George, Violin Co., 1823G
Chantavoine, Jean, 1877A, 1952B; *Musiciens et poètes*, 1912H; *Petit guide de l'auditeur de musique*, 1947H; *The Symphonic Poem*, 1950H
Chanterie de La Renaissance, 1903G
Chanticleer, 1978G
Chanticleer Orchestra, 1961G
Chapin, Schuyler, 1923A, 1972D, 1976D; *Musical Chairs: A Life in the Arts*, 1977H
Chaplet, André, 1901E
Chappell, William: *National English Airs I*, 1838H

Chapell and Co., Ltd., 1810G
Chappell Music Publishers, U.S. Branch, 1935G
Chardiny, Louis, 1755A, 1780C, 1793B
Charivari (France), 1831G
Charles, Ernest, 1895A, 1984B
Charleston, South Carolina: Choral Society, 1944G; Conservatory of Music, 1884G; Philharmonic Orchestra, 1925G; Saint Cecilia Society, 1761G
Charpentier, Gustave, 1860A, 1887E, 1900E, 1912E, 1956B
Charpentier, Jacques, 1933B
Charton-Demeur, Anne, 1824A, 1842C, 1892B
Chase, A. B., Co., 1875G
Chase, Gilbert, 1906A, 1955D, 1961D, 1992B; *The American Composer Speaks*, 1966H; *America's Music: From the Pilgrims to the Present*, 1955H; *A Guide to the Music of Latin America*, 1962H; *The Music of Spain*, 1941H
Chasins, Abram, 1903A, 1929C, 1947D, 1987B; *The Appreciation of Music*, 1966H; *Music at the Crossroads*, 1972H; *Speaking of Pianists*, 1957H
Chaslin, Frederic, 1963A, 1991D
Chatauqua, New York: Institute, 1874G; Summer Music Festival, 1874G
Chatham, Rhys, 1952A, 1971D
Chatman, Stephen, 1950A
Chattanooga Symphony Orchestra, 1935G
Chatterton, John Balsir, 1805A, 1871B
Chausson, Ernest, 1855C, 1877F, 1880F, 1889D, 1899B
Chauvet, Charles-Alexis, 1837A, 1869D, 1871B
Chauvet, Guy, 1933A, 1959C
Chavanne, Irene von, 1868A, 1885C, 1939B
Chávez, Carlos, 1899A, 1928D, 1978B; *Musical Thought*, 1960H; *Toward a New Music*, 1937H
Cheek, John, 1948A, 1975C
Chélard, Hippolyte-André, 1789A, 1811E, 1840D, 1861B
Chelard Publishing Co., 1821G
Chelleri, Fortunato, 1757B
Chelsea Opera Group, 1950G
Chelsea Symphony Orchestra, 1944G
Cheltenham Music Festival, 1945G
Chemische Druckerey, Publishers (Vienna) 1803G
Chen, Leland, 1965A
Chen, Hung-Kuan, 1982E, 1983E, 1990C
Chen, Zuohuane, 1947A, 1987D, 1992D, 1996D, 1996D
Chenal, Marthe, 1881A, 1905C, 1947B
Cheng, Edmund Chung-kei, 1971A
Cheng, Wendy Fang, 1970A
Chenoweth, Wilbur, 1899A, 1980B
Chen Yi, 1986F, 2000F
Cherbuliez, Antoine-Élisée, 1888A, 1964B; *Gedankliche Grundlagen der Musikbetrachtung*, 1924H; *Die Schweiz in der deutschen Musikgeschichte*, 1926H; *Zum problem der religiösen Musik*, 1924H

❖

F *Biographical*   G *Cultural Beginnings*   H *Musical Literature*
I *Musical Compositions*

Cherkassky, Shura, 1911A, 1995A
Cherniavsky Trio, 1900G
Chernov, Vladimir, 1953A, 1983C
Chernykh, Pavel, 1960A, 1989C
Chéron, André, 1766B
Cherubini, Luigi, 1760A, 1778F, 1784F, 1786F,
  1814E, 1816D, 1841F, 1842B; *Cours de*
  contrepoint et de la fugue, 1835H; *Traité de la*
  fugue, 1837H
Cheslock, Louis, 1898A, 1981B
Chester, J. & W., Publishers, 1874G
Chestnut Brass Company, 1977G
Chevé, Emile: *Méthode élémentaire d'harmonie*,
  1846H; *Méthode élémentaire de la musique*
  vocale, 1844H
Chevillard, Camille, 1859A, 1899D, 1914D,
  1923B
Chevillard, Pierre Alexandre, 1811A, 1877B;
  Méthode complète de violoncelle, 1850H
Chiabrano, Carlo F., 1751C; *Compleat*
  Instructions for the Spanish Guitar, 1795H
Chiang Kai-Shek Cultural Center, 1987G
Chiara, Maria, 1965C
Chiarmonte, Francesco, 1809A, 1886B
Chiavari Agréable, 1993G
Chicago, Illinois: Apollo Music Club, 1872G;
  Auditorium Theater, 1889G; Central Music
  Hall, 1879G; Choral Union, 1846G; Civic
  Orchestra, 1919G; Civic Music Association,
  1913G; Conservatory of Music, 1884G;
  Crosby Opera House, 1865G; Drake School
  of Music, 1900G; Goldbeck Conservatory,
  1868G; Grand Opera Co. II, 1933G; Hershey
  School of Musical Art, 1875G; His Majesties
  Clerkes, 1982G (Chicago); International
  Grand Opera Co., 1909G; Little Symphony,
  1959G; Lyric Opera, 1954G; Männerchor,
  1865G; Männergesang-Verein, 1852G;
  Mozart Society, 1849G; Musical College,
  1867G; Musical Society, 1842G; Musical
  Union, 1857G; National College of Music,
  1890G; North Shore Festival, 1909G; Old
  Settler's Harmonic Society, 1836G; Opera
  House, 1929G; Oratorio Society, 1868G;
  Orchestra Hall of Chicago, 1904G;
  Philharmonic Society, 1850G; Pocket Opera
  Co., 1993G; Ravinia Festival, 1936G; Ravinia
  Opera, 1911G; Sherwood Piano School,
  1897G; Sinfonietta, 1987G; Symphony
  Chorus, 1957G; Symphony Orchestra,
  1891G; Tremont Music Hall, 1850G; Weber
  Hall, 1883G; Women's String Quartet,
  1926G; Women's Symphony Orchestra,
  1925G; Wyeth Music School, 1834G
Chicago Musical Times, 1881G
Chicago-Philadelphia Opera Co., 1910G
Chickering, Jonas, 1798A, 1853B
Chickering, Julius E., 1824A
Chickering, Thomas E., 1824A, 1871B

Chien, Alec, 1986E
Chigi Quintet (Siena), 1939G
Chigiana Ressegna annuale de Studi Musicologie,
  1964G
Chihara, Paul, 1938A, 1979E
Child, Ebenezer: *The Sacred Musician*, 1804H
Child Francis J.: *English & Scottish Popular*
  Ballads, 1857H
Childe, Anne, 1834C, 1888B
Childs, Barney, 1926A; *Contemporary Composers*
  on Contemporary Music, 1967H
Chili: Academy of Fine Arts, 1964G; Bach
  Society, 1917G
Chiroplast, 1814G
Chiswick Press (London), 1811G
Chiu, Frederic, 1964A, 1978C
Chladni, Ernest, 1756A, 1827B; *Die Akustik*,
  1802H; *Beiträge zur praktischen Akustik*,
  1821H; *Entdeckungen über der Theorie des*
  Klanges, 1787H; *Kurze Übersicht der Schall-*
  und Klanglehre, 1827H
Chlitsios, George, 1969A, 1989C, 1997D, 1993D
Choi, Hans, 1991E
Choir: A Monthly Journal of Church Music, 1899G
The Choir & Musical Record, 1863G
Choir of the Orchestra of St. John's, 1994G
Cho-Liang, Lin, 1960A, 1976C
Chollet, Jean-Baptist, 1798A, 1818C, 1826C,
  1892B
Chomiński, Jósef: *History of Harmony &*
  Counterpoint, 1958H
Choo, David Ik-Sung, 1962A
Chookasian, Lili, 1921A, 1957C
Chopin, Frédéric, 1810A, 1817F, 1822F, 1830F,
  1831F, 1832F, 1837F, 1838F, 1839F, 1847F,
  1848F, 1849B
Chopin, Frederick, Institute (Warsaw), 1934G
Chopin Piano Competition (Warsaw), 1949G
Chor, 1934G
Choral Arts Society of Washington, 1965G
Choral Club of Hartford, 1907G
The Choral Journal, 1959G
Chord and Discord, 1932G
Chorley, Henry F., 1831D; *Modern German*
  Music, 1854H; *Music and Manners in France*
  and Germany, 1841H; *Thirty Year's Musical*
  Recollections, 1862H
Choron, Alexandre, 1771A, 1834B; *Dictionnaire*
  des musiciens I, 1810H; *Exposition élémentaire*
  des principes...Musique, 1819H; *Méthode*
  d'accompagnement..., 1815H; *Méthode*
  concertante de musique à plusiers parties,
  1817H; *Méthode de plain-chant*, 1818H;
  Méthode élémentaire de composition, 1814H; *Le*
  musicien pratique, 1816H; *Principes de*
  composition des écoles d'Italie, 1808H; *Traité*
  général des voix et des instruments, 1813H
Chorus, Teatro Nacional de São Carlos, 1943G
Das Chorwerk, 1929G

     A *Births*   B *Deaths*   C *Debuts*   D *New Positions*
                        E *Prizes/Honors*

Chorzempa, Daniel, 1944A
Chotzinoff, Samuel, 1889A, 1925D, 1934D, 1936D, 1964B; *A Little Nightmusic*, 1964H; *A Lost Paradise: Early Reminiscences*, 1955H
Chouden's Publishing House, 1845G
Chouquet, Gustave, 1819A, 1886B; *Histoire de la musique dramatique en France...*, 1873H
Chou Wen-Chung, 1923A, 1946F, 1963E, 1982E
Chrétien, Jean-Baptiste, 1760B
Chretien, Raphaël, 1972A
Chribkova, Irene, 1959A
Chrismann, Franz, 1774F
Christ, Rudolf, 1941C
Christchurch Choir School, 1879G
Christensen, Mogens, 1955A
Christian Kahnt Music Publishing Co., 1851G
Christiani, Adolf Friedrich, 1836A, 1885B; *Principles of Musical Expression in Piano Playing*, 1886H
Christiania (*see* Oslo)
Christiania String Quartet, 1865G
Christiansen, Olaf, 1901A, 1984B
Christiansen, F. Melius, 1871A, 1903D, 1955B; *Practical Modulation*, 1916H
Christie, Michael, 1975A
Christie, William, 1944A
Christmann, Franz Xavier, 1795B
Christmann, Johann F.: *Elementarbuch der Tonkunst*, 1782H
Christodoulou, Nikos, 1959A
Christoff, Boris, 1914A, 1944F, 1946C, 1993B
Christoff, Dimiter, 1933B
Chromatic Trumpet and French Horn, 1788G
Chrysander, Friedrich, 1826A, 1901B
Chrysler Hall (Norfolk), 1972G
Chumley, Robert, 1954A
Chung, Kyung-Wha, 1948A, 1967E
Chung, Mia, 1964A, 1983C
Chung, Myung-Wha, 1944A, 1957C
Chung, Myung-Whun, 1953A, 1960C, 1971CE, 1984D, 1989DE
Chung-Kei, Edmund, 1986C
Church Music Review, 1901G
The Church Musician, 1850G, 1950G
Church, John, & Co., Publishers, 1859G
Church's Musical Visitor, 1871G
Chusid, Martin, 1925A
Chybiński, Adolf, 1880A, 1952B; *On Polish Folk Music*, 1961H
Ciaia, Azzolino Bernardino Della, 1755B
Ciampi, Giorgio, 1935C
Ciampi, Francesco, 1765B
Ciampi, Vincenzo, 1762B
Ciani, Dino, 1941A, 1974B
Ciani, Dino, Competition, 1975G
Ciannella, Giuliano, 1943A, 1976C
Cibber, Susanne Maria, 1766B
Ciccolini, Aldo, 1925A, 1942C
Ciesinki, Kristine, 1952A, 1977CE

Ciesinki, Katherine, 1950A, 1974C, 1976E, 1977E
Cigna, Gina, 1900A, 1927C
Cikker, Ján, 1911A, 1989B
Cilèa, Francesco, 1866A, 1893E, 1898E, 1913D, 1916D, 1950B
Cimadoro, Giovanni Battista, 1761A, 1805B
Cimarosa, Domenico, 1761F, 1771F, 1782F, 1785F, 1787DF, 1791DF, 1793DF, 1796D, 1799F, 1801B
Cincinnati, Ohio: Ballet Co., 1970G; Cecilia Society, 1856G; Chamber Music Society, 1929G; Chamber Orchestra, 1974G; College of Music, 1878G; Composer's Guild, 1978G; Conservatory of Music, 1867G; Haydn Society, 1819G; Institute of Fine Arts, 1928G; Männerchore, 1849G; May Music Festival, 1873G; Music Festival, 1833G; Music Hall, 1878G; Musician's Protective Union, 1881G; Opera Association & Festival, 1920G; Philharmonic Orchestra, 1856G; Pops Orchestra, 1977G; Symphony Orchestra, 1872G; Symphony Orchestra Ass'n, 1895G
Cinte-Damoreau, Laure, 1801A, 1816C, 1863B; *Méthode de chant*, 1849H
Ciormila, Mariana, 1956A, 1982C
Cirri, Giovanni B., 1759E, 1808B
Cisneros, Eleanora de, 1878A, 1898C, 1934B
Ciurca, Cleopatra, 1954A
Čiurlionis, Mikolajus, 1875A, 1911B
Civil, Alan, 1929A, 1989B
Clairbert, Clara, 1924C, 1970B
Clapisson, Antoine-Louis, 1808A, 1854E, 1866B
Clapp, Philip G., 1888A, 1919D, 1954B
Clarey, Cynthia, 1949A, 1977C
Clari, Giovanni Carlo Maria, 1754B
Clarinet, Contrabass, 1890G
Clarion Wind, 1997G
Clark, Charles W., 1865A, 1897C, 1925B
Clark, Graham, 1941A, 1975C
Clark, Henry Leland, 1907A
Clark, Herbert, 1945B
Clark, John, 1755B, 1799D
Clark, Melville, 1850A, 1918B
Clark, Melville, Piano Co., 1900G
Clark, Melville Antone, 1883A, 1953B
Clark, T.: *Learning to Compose: Modes, Materials & Models of Musical Invention*, 1987H
Clark Harp Co., 1913G
Clarke, Herbert, 1867A
Clarke Hugh A.: *Highways & By-ways of Music*, 1901H; *Manual of Orchestration*, 1888H; *Theory Explained*, 1892H
Clarke, Jeremiah, 1806D
Clarke, John, 1770A, 1836B
Clarke, Stephen, 1797B, 1964A
Clarke, William Horatio, 1840A, 1913B
Classical Band of New York, 1989G

❊

F *Biographical*   G *Cultural Beginnings*   H *Musical Literature*
I *Musical Compositions*

Classical Philharmonic Orchestra of Stuttgart, 1966G
Clauss-Szarvady, Wilhemine, 1834A, 1907B
Claussen, Julia, 1879A, 1903C, 1941B
Clavier, 1962G
Claviharpe, 1814G
Claviola, 1802G
Clay, Frédéric, 1838A, 1889B
Clayton, Beth, 1996C
The Clef, 1913G
Clef Club, 1910G
Clemens, Clara, 1874A, 1904C, 1962B
Clemens, Hans, 1890A, 1958B
Clément, Charles: *Essai sur la basse fondamentale*, 1762H
Clément, Edmond, 1867A, 1889C, 1928B
Clément, Félix, 1822A, 1885B; *L'accompagnement du clavecin*, 1758H; *Des Diverses Réformes du chant grégorien*, 1860H; *Les grands musiciens*, 1882H; *Histoire de la musique...jusqu'à nos jours*, 1885H; *Histoire générale de la musique religieuse*, 1860H; *Introduction à une méthode...de plain-chant*, 1854H; *Les musiciens célèbres...jusqu'à nos jours*, 1868H; *Rapport...l'état de la musique religieuse en France*, 1849H; *Réédition du plain-chant romain traditionnel*, 1876H
Clement, Franz, 1780A, 1802D, 1842B
Clement, Johann Georg, 1794B
Clement Music School (San Francisco), 1917G
Clementi, Muzio, 1752A, 1780F, 1786F, 1790F, 1802F, 1810F, 1830F, 1832B; *Introduction to the Art of Playing the Piano-Forte*, 1801H
Clemm, Johann G., 1757F, 1762B
Cleobury, Stephen, 1982D
Clérambault, César François, 1760B
Cleva, Fausto, 1902A, 1920C, 1942D, 1951D, 1971B
Cleveland, Ohio: Ballet, 1974G; Chamber Music Society, 1949G; Chamber Orchestra, 1923G; Conservatory of Music, 1871G; Gesangverein, 1854G; Grand Orchestra, 1902G; Gray's Armory, 1893G; Harmonic Society, 1837G; Institute of Music, 1920G; Lyric Opera, 1973G; Mendelssohn Society, 1850G; Messiah Chorus, 1921G; Musical Arts Association, 1915G; Music School Settlement, 1912G; Opera (New), 1976G; Opera Theater, 1973G; Orchestra Chorus, 1955G; Philharmonic Society, 1881G; Quartet Award, 1996G; Sacred Music Society, 18442G; St. Cecilia Society, 1852G; School of Music, 1885G; Severance Hall, 1931G; Singers' Club, 1891G; Symphony Orchestra, 1918G; Vocal Society, 1873G; West Side Musical College, 1900G; Women's Orchestra, 1935G; Youth Orchestra, 1986G
Cliburn, Van, 1934A, 1952E, 1954E, 1958E, 1974E, 1989F

Cliburn, Van, Piano Competition, 1962G
Clicquot, François-Henri, 1790B; *Théorie pratique de la facture de l'orgue*, 1789H
Clicquot, Louis-Alexandre, 1760B
Clifford, Herbert, 1959B
Clifton, John Charles, 1781A, 1841B; *Theory of Harmony Simplified*, 1816H
Cliquot, Claude, 1801B
Clive, Catherine "Kitty," 1785B
Clokey, Joseph Waddell, 1890A, 1939D, 1960B
Clowes Memorial Hall, 1963G
Cluytens, André, 1905A, 1927C, 1932D, 1935D, 1949D, 1960D, 1967B
Coates, Albert, 1882A, 1905D, 1911D, 1919D, 1946D, 1953B
Coates, Edith, 1908A, 1924C, 1983B
Coates, Eric, 1957B
Coates, George, Performance Works, 1977G
Coates, Gloria, 1938A
Coates, John, 1865A, 1894C, 1941B
Cobbett, Walter Willson, 1847A, 1937B; *Cyclopaedia of Chamber Music*, 1929H
Cobelli, Giuseppina, 1898A, 1924C, 1948B
Coblenz Music Conservatory, 1889G
Coburn, Pamela, 1955A, 1982C
Cocchi, Gioacchino, 1753D, 1757D
Coccia, Carlo, 1782A, 1824D, 1873B
Coccia, Maria Rosa, 1759A, 1833B
Cochereau, Pierre, 1924A, 1950D, 1955D, 1961D, 1980D, 1984B
Cochran, William, 1943A, 1968C, 1969E
Coci, Claire, 1912A, 1978B
Cocks, Robert, & Co., 1823G
Codreanu-Mihalcea, Claudia, 1969B
Coelho, Ruy, 1891A, 1986B
Coenen, Franz, 1826A, 1877D, 1904B
Coenen, Ludovicus, 1797A, 1873B
Coenen String Quartet, 1856G
Coerne, Louis, 1870A, 1905F, 1910D, 1922B; *The Evolution of Modern Orchestration*, 1905H
Coertse, Mimi, 1932A, 1955C
Coeuroy, André: *Dictionaire critique de la musique ancienne et moderne*, 1956H; *Musique et littérature comparées*, 1923H; *La musique française moderne*, 1922H
Cogan, Philip, 1780D, 1833B
Cognoni, Antonio, 1856D
Coh, James, 1928A
Cohan, George M., 1942B
Cohen, Aaron: *International Encyclopedia of Women Composers*, 1981H
Cohen, Alex, String Quartet, 1932G
Cohen, Arnaldo, 1948A, 1972E
Cohen, Joel, 1942A, 1968D
Cohen, Jules-Émile, 1835A, 1901B
Cohen, Robert, 1959A, 1971C, 1978E
Cohn, Arthur, 1910A, 1934D, 1998B; *Encyclopedia of Chamber Music*, 1990H; *The Literature of Chamber Music (4 Vols.)*, 1998H;

❄

A *Births*   B *Deaths*   C *Debuts*   D *New Positions*
E *Prizes/Honors*

Twentieth Century Music in Western Europe,
1965H
Colbran, Isabella, 1785A, 1801C, 1822F, 1845B
Cold, Ulrik, 1939A, 1963C, 1975D
Cole, Blanche, 1851A, 1888B
Cole, Hugo: *The Changing Face of Music*, 1978H
Cole, John, Publishers (Baltimore), 1802G
Cole, Maggie, 1952C
Cole, Rossetter Gleason, 1866A, 1952B; *Choral and Church Music*, 1916H
Coleridge-Taylor, Samuel, 1875A, 1912B
Coletti, Agostino Bonaventura, 1752B
Coletti, Filippo, 1811A, 1834C, 1894B
Colgrass, Michael, 1932A
Coliban, Sorin, 1970A, 1993C
Colin de Blamont, François, 1751E
Colla, Giuseppe, 1766D
Collard, Jean-Philippe, 1948A, 1973C
Collection Litolff, 1861G
College Band Director's National Ass'n, 1941G
Collegium Aureum, 1964G
Collegium Musicum 90, 1990G
Collegium Musicum Antwerpiense, 1938G
Collegium Records, 1984G
Collet, Henri, 1920F
Collett, John, 1775B
Collier, Marie, 1926A, 1954C, 1971B
Collinge, Robert, 1970D
Collings, Edward Joseph, 1889A
Collingwood, Lawrance, 1887A, 1982B
Collins, Anthony, 1893A, 1963B
Collins, Edward, 1912C, 1951B
Collins, Michael, 1962A, 1984C
Colloredo, Hieronymus, 1772F
Colobrano, Michele Carafa de, 1837E
Cologne, Germany: Bach Choir, 1931G; Chamber Orchestra, 1923G; Conservatory of Music, 1851G; Familienkonzerte, 1808G; Gurzenichkonzerte, 1857G; Haydn Institut, 1955G; Liebhaberkonzerte, 1808G; Männergesangverein, 1842G; Musikalische Akademie, 1886G; Musikalische Gesellschaft, 1812G; Musikhistorisches Museum, 1906G; Opera House, 1957G; Philharmonic Hall, 1986G; Rheinische Musikschule, 1845G; Singverein, 1820G; Theater, 1822G; Theater am Habsburger (Cologne), 1902G; Theater in der Guckengasse, 1872G
Colombara, Carlo, 1964A, 1985C
Colombo, Scipio, 1937C
Colonne, Edouard, 1838A, 1892D, 1910B
Colonne, Eugenie E., 1854A, 1876C
Colorado (*see also* Aspen; Boulder; Denver): Bravo! Colorado Music Festival, 1988G; Experimental Music Center, 1964G; Mahlerfest, 1988G; Music Festival, 1977G
Coltellini, Celeste, 1760A, 1780C, 1828B
Columbia Concerts Corporation, 1932G

Columbia Broadcasting Symphony, 1927G
Columbia Phonograph Co., 1889G
Columbia Record Co., 1903G
Columbian Magazine, 1786G
Columbia-Princeton Electronic Music Center, 1959G
La Columbina (Spain), 1990G
Columbo, Scipio, 1913A
Colzani, Anselmo, 1918A, 1947C
Combarieu, Jules, 1859A, 1916B; *Éléments de grammaire musicale historique*, 1906H; *Histoire de la Musique I, II*, 1913H; *La musique, ses lois, son évolution*, 1907H
Combs, Gilbert Raynolds, 1863A
Comet, Catherine, 1986F, 1990D
Comissiona, Sergiu, 1928A, 1946C, 1955DE, 1960D, 1966D, 1967D, 1969D, 1978D, 1979E, 1980D, 1987D
Commanday, Robert, 1964D
Commer, Franz, 1813A, 1887B
Commission des Orgues des Monuments Historiques, 1932G
Committee for the Promotion of New Music, 1943G
Community Artist Residency Training, 1978G
Compact Disc, 1982G
Compagnia dei Giovanni, 1954G
Composer's Facsimile Editions, 1952G
Composer's Forum-Laboratory (N.Y.), 1935G
Composer's Guild, Inc., 1985G
Composer's Guild of Great Britain, 1944G
Composers in Red Sneakers, 1981G
Composers Inside Electronics, 1973G
Composer's Press (N.Y.), 1935G
Composer's Recordings, Inc. (N.Y.), 1954G
Composer's String Quartet, 1963G
Composers Theater, 1964G
Composium, 1970G
Computer Music Journal, 1977G
Computer Music Project, 1970G
Concentus Musicus of Vienna, 1953G
Concert Artists Guild (NY), 1951G
Concert des Nations, 1989G
Concert Opera Association of San Francisco, 1984G
Concertina, 1829G
Concerts of British Chamber Music, 1907G
Concone, Giuseppe, 1801A, 1861B
Concord String Quartet, 1971G
Concord Summer School of Music, 1914G
Concorde East/West, 1987G
Concordia, 1984G
Concordia Publishing House, 1869G
Concours Gèza Anda, 1972G
Concours International de Montreal, 1965G
Concours Marguerite Long-Jacques Thibaud, 1943G
Concours Musical Reine Elisabeth (Belgium), 1937G

F *Biographical*   G *Cultural Beginnings*   H *Musical Literature*
I *Musical Compositions*

Condell, Henry, 1757A, 1824B
Condie, Richard P., 1985B
Conducting Institute, 1980G (S.C.)
Conductor's Guild, 1975G
Conductor's Institute, 1981G (W.V.)
Cone, Edward T., 1917A, 1966D; *The Composer's Voice*, 1974H; *Musical Form & Musical Performance*, 1968H; *Perspectives on Contemporary Music Theory*, 1972H; *Perspectives on Performance & Notation*, 1076H
Congrès International de Organologie (Strasbourg), 1932G
Conley, Eugene, 1908A, 1940C, 1981B
Conlon, James, 1950A, 1979F, 1983D, 1989D, 1995D, 1999E
Conn, C. G., Co., 1875G
Connecticut (*see also* Hartford; New Haven; New London): Early Music Festival, 1983G; Harp Festival, 1980G; Opera Association, 1942G; String Quartet, 1968G
Connell, Elizabeth, 1946A, 1972CE
Connell, Horatio, 1876A, 1904C
Conner, Nadine, 1913A, 1940C
Connoisseur Society (Record Co.), 1961G
Conover Brothers, Publishers, 1871G
Conrad, Barbara, 1945A, 1982C
Conradi, August, 1821A, 1873B
Conried, Heinrich, 1848A, 1878D, 1909B
Conservatoire de musique et de l'art dramatique, 1942G
Conservatorio Nacional de Música (Venezuela), 1972G
Consoli, Marc-Antonio, 1941A, 1975E
Consoni, Giovanni A., 1758E
Consoni, Giovanni B., 1758E
Consoni, Giuseppe Antonio, 1765B
The Consort, 1929G
Consortium Antiquum, 1964G
Constable, Archibald, 1774A, 1827B
Constable's Miscellany, 1827G
Constant, Franz, 1910A, 1996B
Constant, Marius, 1945E, 1962E, 1993E
Constantine, Alexander, 1964A
Constantinescu, Paul, 1909A, 1963B
Contemporary Chamber Ensemble of New York, 1960G
Contemporary Music Society (ONCE), 1960G
Conti, Carlo, 1796A, 1868B
Conti, Gioacchino, 1755F, 1761B
Conti, Ignazio Maria, 1759B
Conti, Nicoletta, 1957A, 1984C
Conti, Paolo, 1957A, 1984C
Continental Vocalists, 1853G
Continuum, 1967G
Conus, George: *Manual of Harmony*, 1894H
Converse, Charles, 1832A, 1918B
Converse, Frederick, 1871A, 1905E, 1908E, 1937E, 1940B
Cook, Gary: *Teaching Percussion*, 1988H

Cook, Nicholas: *A Guide to Musical Analysis*, 1987H; *Music, Imagination & Culture*, 1989H
Cook, Terry, 1956A, 1980C
Cook, Thomas A., 1836A, 1856C, 1894B
Cooke, Benjamin, 1752D, 1762D, 1775F, 1782D, 1793B
Cooke, Deryck, 1919A, 1960F, 1976B; *The Language of Music*, 1959H; *Variations: Essays on Romantic Music*, 1982H
Cooke, Francis Judd, 1910A, 1995B
Cooke, James F., 1875A, 1908D, 1960B; *Great Men & Famous Musicians*, 1925H; *Great Singers on the Art of Singing*, 1921H; *A Standard History of Music*, 1910H
Cooke, Merwyn, 1963A
Cooke, Robert, 1768A, 1793D, 1802D, 1816B
Cooke, Thomas (Simpson), 1782A, 1815 C, 1821D, 1848B
Coolidge, Elizabeth Sprague, 1864A, 1953B
Coolidge, Elizabeth Sprague, Foundation, 1925G
Coolidge Auditorium (Library of Congress), 1925G
Coolidge Chamber Music Festival, 1918G
Cooper, Anna, 1965A
Cooper, George, 1820A, 1876B
Cooper, Grosvenor: *The Rhythmic Structure of Music*, 1960H
Cooper, Imogen, 1949A, 1969E, 1973C
Cooper, Kenneth, 1941A, 1965C
Cooper, Martin: *British Musicians of Today*, 1952H
Cooper, Paul, 1926A, 1977E, 1999B; *Perspectives in Music Theory*, 1973H
Cooperative Studio for Electronic Music, 1958G
Coopersmith, J. M., 1903A, 1968B
Cooperstock, Andrew Bryan, 1960A, 1989C
Coote, Alice, 1968B
Cope, David, 1941A; *The Algorithmic Composers*, 2000H; *Computer Analysis of Musical Style*, 1990H; *Computers & Musical Style*, 1991H; *Experiments in Musical Intelligence*, 1996H; *New Directions in Music*, 1971H; *New Music Composition*, 1977H; *New Music Notation*, 1976H; *Notes in Discontinuum*, 1970H; *Techniques of the Contemporary Composer*, 1997H; *Virtual Music*, 2000H
Copeland, George, 1971B
Copenhagen, Denmark: Boys' Choir, 1924G; Cecilia Society, 1851G; Collection, Ancient Musical Instr., 1898G; Musical Society, 1836G; Horneman Conservatory, 1880G; Koncertforeningen, 1874G; Odd-Fellow Palace, 1888G; Philharmonic Concerts, 1897G; Royal Danish Music Conservatory, 1868G; Schola Cantorum, 1953G; Society of Chamber Music, 1868G; Tivoli Gardens, 1843G

A　*Births*　　B　*Deaths*　　C　*Debuts*　　D　*New Positions*
E　*Prizes/Honors*

Copenhagen Classic, 1997G
Copland, Aaron, 1900A, 1941F, 1947F, 1956E,
 1960E, 1961E, 1964E, 1978E, 1979E, 1986E,
 1990B, 1991E; *Copland on Music*, 1960H;
 Music and Imagination, 1952H; *Our New
 Music*, 1941H; *What to Listen for in Music*,
 1939H
Copland Association, 1993G
Copland Awards, 1998G
Copland Fund for Music, 1992G
Copland Society, 1996G
Coppola, Piero, 1971B
Coppola, Pietro Antonio, 1793A, 1839D, 1850D,
 1871D, 1877B
Coquard, Arthur-Joseph, 1846A, 1910B
Corbelli, Alessandro, 1952A, 1974C
Corbett, Patricia, Pavilion, 1972G
Corbett, Sidney, 1960A
Corbisieri, Francesco, 1771D
Corcoran, Frank, 1944A
Cordans, Bartolomeo, 1757B
Cordella, Giacomo, 1786A, 1846B
Cordero, Roque, 1917A, 1953D
Cordes, Marcel, 1941C
Cordon, Norman, 1904A, 1933C, 1964B
Cordonne, Jean Baptiste, 1788E
Corelli, Emma, 1928B
Corelli, Franco, 1921A, 1952C
Corena, Fernando, 1916A, 1937C, 1984B
Corfe, Arthur Thomas, 1773A, 1863B
Corfe, Joseph, 1792D, 1820B; *Church Music*,
 1810H; *Sacred Music*, 1800H; *Thorough Bass
 Simplified*, 1805H; *A Treatise on Singing*,
 1799H
Corfu Festival, 1981G
Corigliano, John, Jr., 1938A, 1991E
Corigliano, John, Sr., 1901A, 1919C, 1943F,
 1975B
Corigliano String Quartet, 1996G
Cork International Choral Festival, 1954G
Corn, Edward, 1977D
Cornelius, Peter (tenor), 1865A, 1892C, 1934B
Cornelius, Peter (composer), 1824A, 1874B
Cornelys, Theresa, 1797B
Cornet, Julius, 1793A, 1860B
Cornish Institute of the Performing & Visual
 Arts, 1914G
Cornwell, Joseph, 1959A, 1982C
Corporazione della Nuove Musiche, 1923G
Correspondence des Amateurs Musiciens (Paris),
 1802G
Corrette, Michel, 1795B; *Le maître de clavecin*,
 1753H; *Method for the Doublebass*, 1773H;
 Method for Mandolins, 1772H; *Le parfait maître
 à chanter*, 1758H
Corri, Domenico, 1781D, 1825B; *The Art of
 Fingering*, 1799H; *A Musical Dictionary*,
 1798H; *The Singer's Preceptor*, 1810H
Corri, Frances, 1795A, 1818C

Corri, Sophia Giustina, 1775A, 1791C
Il Corriere de Napoli, 1891G
Cors, Jacob Eckhard, 1786D
Corselli, Francesco, 1778B
Cortesi, Francesco, 1826A, 1904B
Cortez, Luis Jaime, 1963A
Cortez, Miguel, 1952A
Cortez, Viorica, 1860C, 1935A, 1960C
Cortis, Antonio, 1891A, 1915C, 1952B
Cortot, Alfred, 1877A, 1896C, 1934E, 1962B
Cory, Eleanor, 1943A
Cos-Cob (Arrow) Press, 1929G
Cosmoquintet, 1988G
Cossa, Dominic, 1935A, 1961C
Cossotto, Fiorenza, 1935A, 1957C
Cossutta, Carlo, 1932A, 1956C, 2000B
Costa, Francisco da, 1840D
Costa, Mary, 1932A, 1958C
Costa, Michael, 1806A, 1829F, 1832D, 1846D,
 1849D, 1869E, 1871D, 1884B
Costa, Rodrigo Ferreira da, 1776A, 1825B
Costanze, Giuseppe, 1958A, 1983C
Costanzi, Giovanni Battista, 1755D, 1778B
Coste, Napoléon, 1806A, 1883B
Cotogni, Antonia, 1831A, 1852C, 1918B
Cotrubas, Ileana, 1939A, 1964C
Cottlow, Augusta, 1878A, 1954B
Cotton Club (NY), 1918G
Cotumacci, Carlo, 1785B
Couesnon et Cie., Publisher, 1883G
Coulthard, Jean, 2000B
Council for the Encouragement of Music & the
 Arts, 1940G
Council for Young Musicians, 1982G
Council of Creative Artists, Libraries &
 Museums, 1970G
Couperin, Armand-Louis, 1770E, 1789B
Couperin, Celeste, 1793A,
Couperin, Gervais-François, 1759A, 1789D,
 1826B
Couperin, Pierre-Louis, 1755A, 1789BDE
Couroux, Marc, 1970A
Court-Circuit Ensemble, 1991G
Cousineau, Jacques-Georges, 1760A, 1836B
Coussemaker, Charles, 1825F; *Drames
 liturgiques de moyen-âge*, 1860H; *Les
 harmonistes des XIIe et XIIIe siècles*, 1865H; *Les
 harmonistes du XIV siècle*, 1869H; *Histoire de
 l'harmonie au moyen-âge*, 1852H
Coussemaker, Edmond de, 1805A, 1876B
Couture, Guillaume, 1851A, 1915B
Covent Garden Journal, 1752G
Coventry & Hollier, Publishers (London),
 1833G
Cowan, Richard, 1957A, 1983C
Cowan, Sigmund, 1948A, 1974C
Coward, James, 1824A, 1880B
Cowell, Henry, 1897A, 1912F, 1918F, 1929F,
 1936F, 1951E, 1965B; *American Composers on*

※

Cowell, Henry, (cont.)
American Music, 1933H; *New Musical Resources*, 1919H
Cowen, Frederic, 1852A, 1888D, 1896D, 1900D, 1911E, 1935B
Cox, Jean, 1922A, 1951C
Coxon, Richard, 1993C
Crabbé, Armand, 1883A, 1904C, 1947B
Craft, Robert, 1923A; *Conversations with Igor Stravinsky*, 1959H; *Current Convictions-1976H*; *Dialogues and a Diary*, 1963H; *Expositions & Developments*, 1962H; *Memories & Commentaries*, 1960H; *Themes & Episodes*, 1967H; *Prejudices in Disguise*, 1974H; *Present Perspectives*, 1984H; *Retrospections & Conclusions*, 1969H; *Stravinsky: Chronicle of a Friendship*, 1972H
Craig, Charles, 1919A, 1959C, 1997B
Cramer, Carl Friedrich, 1752A, 1807B
Cramer, Frank, 1954A
Cramer, Franz, 1772A, 1837E, 1848B
Cramer, Johann B., 1771A, 1781C, 1858B; *Grosses praktische Pianoforte Schule*, 1815H
Cramer, Johann B., & Co. Ltd., 1824G
Cramer, Wilhelm, 1799B
Cramer & Keys, Publishers (London), 1805G
Cramer Publishing House (Paris), 1795G
Crans, August, Publisher, 1814G
Cranz, August Heinrich, 1789A, 1870B
Cras, Jean Émile, 1879A, 1932B
Crass, Franz, 1928A, 1954C
Craven, Robert R.: *Symphony Orchestras of the U.S.*, 1986H
Crawford, Bruce, 1984D
Crawford, Ruth, 1901A, 1953B
Creatore, Giuseppe, 1871A, 1952B
Creatore Band (NY), 1902G
Creech, Philip, 1950A
Cremona, Italy: Società Filarmonica, 1816G; Teatro della Concordia, 1808G
Crescentini, Girolamo, 1762A, 1782C, 1846B
Creshevsky, Noah, 1945A
Crespin, Régine, 1927A, 1950C
Creston, Paul, 1906A, 1943E, 1956D, 1960D, 1985B; *Creative Harmony*, 1970H; *Principles of Rhythm*, 1964H; *Rational Metric Notation*, 1979H
Creswell, Lyell, 1944A
Crider, Michele, 1963A, 1989C
Crimi, Giulio, 1885A, 1910C, 1939B
Crispi, Pietro Maria, 1772D, 1778D, 1797B
Crist, Bainbridge, 1883A, 1969B; *The Art of Setting Words to Music*, 1944H
Cristiani, Lisa, 1827A, 1853B
Cristoff, Boris, 1942F
Cristoforeanu, Florica, 1887A, 1908C, 1960B
La critica musicale, 1918G
Crivelli, Gaetano, 1768A, 1794C, 1836B
Crocker, Richard, 1927A

Crockett, Donald, 1951A, 1991E, 1998E
Croes, Henri-Jacques de, 1786B
Croes, Henri-Joseph de, 1758A, 1776D, 1842B
Crofoot, Alan, 1979B
Croft, Dwayne, 1996E
Croiza, Claire, 1882A, 1905C, 1946B
La cronaca musical (Italy), 1896G
Crooks, Richard, 1900A, 1922C, 1972B
Crosby, Fanny, 1820A, 1915B
Crosby, John, 1926A, 1957D, 1975D, 1976D
Cross, Gregory, 1960A, 1992C
Cross, Lowell: *A Bibliography of Electronic Music*, 1967H
Cross, Milton, 1975B
Crosse, Gordon, 1937A
Crosse, John, 1786A, 1833B
Crossley, Ada, 1874A, 1892C, 1929B
Crossley, Paul, 1944A, 1968C, 1993E
Crossley-Holland, Peter: *Musical Learning & Creativity*, 1997H; *Some Musical Traditions of the Celtic-Speaking Peoples*, 1996H
Crotch, William, 1775A, 1779C, 1790D, 1797D, 1847B; *Elements of Musical Composition*, 1812H
Crouch, Anna Marie, 1763A, 1805B
Crouch Frederick; *Complete Treatise on the Violoncello*, 1826H
Crouse-Hinds Concert Theater, 1976G
Crowest Frederick; *The Great Tone Poets*, 1874H
Crozier, Catharine, 1914A, 1941C
Crumb, George, 1929A, 1967E, 1975E
Crusell, Bernhard Henrik, 1775A, 1838B
Cruvelli, Jeanne S., 1826A, 1847C, 1907B
Cruz-Romo, Gilda, 1962C
Cuberli, Lella, 1945A, 1975C
Cuellar y Altarriba, Ramón F., 1777A, 1812D, 1817D, 1828D, 1833B
Cuénod, Hugues, 1902A, 1928C
Cui, César, 1835A, 1864F, 1918B; *Music in Russia*, 1880H; *The Russian Song: A Study of its Development*, 1896H
Cullowhee Music Festival, 1975G
Culp, Julia, 1880A, 1901C, 1970B
Culwick, James C., 1845A, 1881D, 1907B; *The Rudiments of Music*, 1880H
Cumberland, David, 1945A
Cumberland County Civic Center, 1977G
Cummings, Claudia, 1941A, 1971C
Cummings, W. H. 1831A, 1900E, 1915B; *Biographical Dictionary of Musicians*, 1892H; *Primer of the Rudiments of Music*, 1877H
Cundick, Robert, 1965D
Cunitz, Maud, 1911A, 1934C
Cunningham, Merce, Dance Co., 1953G
Cunningham, Merce, School of Dance, 1959G
Cupido, Alberto, 1948A, 1977C
Cupis, Jean-Baptiste, 1773E, 1788B
Cupis, François, 1808B
Cura, José, 1962A

❉

A   *Births*   B   *Deaths*   C   *Debuts*   D   *New Positions*
               E   *Prizes/Honors*

Curci, Giuseppe, 1808A, 1877B
Curioni, Alberico, 1785A, 1817C, 1875B
Curioni, Rosa, 1754C
Curran, Pearl G., 1941B
Currant Musicology, 1965G
Currier, Sebastian, 1959A
Curry, Arthur Mansfield, 1866A, 1953B
Curry, Carrel A., 1969C
Curry, William, 1987E, 1988E
Curshmann, Karl Friedrich, 1805A, 1841B
Curtin, Phyllis, 1921A, 1983D, 1984F, 1987F
Curtis, Alan, 1934A
Curtis Edgar, 1948D
Curtis, Natalie, 1875A, 1921B; *The Indian's Book*,
    1907H; *Songs of Ancient America*, 1905H
Curtis Institute of Music, 1924G
Curtis Publishing Co., 1890G
Curtis String Quartet, 1932G
Curtis-Smith, Curtis, 1941A, 1972E, 1978E
Curtis-Verna, Mary, 1927A, 1949C
Curvillier, John O., 1827D
Curwen, Annie, 1845A, 1932B; *Mrs. Curwen's
    Pianoforte Method*, 1886H
Curwen, John, 1816A, 1880B
Curwen, John, & Sons, Ltd., Publishers, 1863G
Curwen Institute, 1869G
Curzon, Clifford, 1907A, 1923C, 1970E, 1977E,
    1982B
Curzon, Henri de, 1889D; *Musiciens du temps
    passé*, 1893H
Curzon, Clifford, 1861A
Cushman, Charlotte, 1816A, 1835C, 1886B
Cushman, William George, 1849D
Cusins, William, 1833A, 1849D, 1867D, 1870E,
    1892E, 1893B
Cutter, Benjamin, 1857A, 1910A; *Harmonic
    Analysis*, 1902H
Cuyler, Louise, 1908A, 1998B
Cuypers, Johannes Theodorus, 1808B
Cuzzoni, Francesca, 1778B
Czech Music Society of St. Louis, 1986G
Czech National Symphony Orchestra, 1993G
Czech Philharmonic Orchestra, 1894G,
    1901G
Czech Society of Chamber Music, 1894G
Czech String Quartet, 1891G
Czech Teacher's Institute, 1869G
Czecho-Slovak Radio Orchestra (Ostrava),
    1929G
Czechoslovak State Philharmonic Orchestra,
    1968G
Czejič, Biserka, 1923A, 1951C
Czerny, Carl, 1791A, 1795F, 1800C, 1857B;
    Lehrbuch der...Composition, 1834H; *Method for
    the Piano*, 1847H; *Umriss der ganzen
    Musikgeschichte*, 1851H
Czerwenka, Oscar, 1924A, 1947C, 2000B
Czibulka, Alphons, 1842A, 1894B
Cziffra, György, 1921A, 1956C, 1994B

Czyż, Henry, 1923A, 1948C, 1952D, 1953D,
    1957D, 1964D, 1971D, 1973D
da capo, 1989G
Da Capo Chamber Players, 1969G
Da Vinci String Quartet, 1980G
Dachs, Joseph, 1825A, 1896B
Dacosta, Janine, 1951E
Dadák, Jaromir, 1930A
Daddi, Francesco, 1864A, 1891C, 1945B
Dae Woo Chorale, 1983G
Daetwyler, Jean, 1907A, 1994B
Dagincour, François, 1758B
Dahl, Ingolf, 1912A, 1954E, 1964E, 1970B
Dahl, Tracy, 1964A
Dahl, Viking, 1895A, 1945B
Dahlhaus, Carl, 1989B: *Contemplating Music:
    Source Readings in the Aesthetics of Music*,
    1987H
Dala Sinfoniette, 1988G
Dalayman, Katarina, 1968A, 1991C
Dalayrac, Nicolas, 1753A, 1774F, 1798E, 1804E,
    1804E, 1809B
Dalberg, Frederick, 1908A, 1931C
Dalberg, Johann, 1760A, 1812B; *Die Äolsharfe,
    Ein allegorischer Traum*, 1801H; *Blicke eines
    Tonkünstlers in die Musik der Geister*, 1787H;
    Fantasien aus dem Reich der Töne, 1806H;
    *Untersuchungen über den ursprung der
    harmonie*, 1800H; *Vom Erfinden und Bilden*,
    1791H
Dalberto, Michel, 1955A, 1975E, 1978E, 1980C
Dalby, Martin, 1942A
Dale, Clamma, 1948A, 1973C, 1975E
Dale, Joseph, Publisher, 1783G
Dale, Laurence, 1957A, 1981C
Daler, William, Publisher, 1809G
Dalibor, 1858G
Dalis, Irene, 1925A, 1953C
Dallapiccola, Luigi, 1904A, 1972E, 1975B
Dallapozza, Adolf, 1962C
Dalla Rizza, Gilda, 1892A, 1912C, 1975B
Dallas, Texas: Chamber Music Society, 1942G;
    Civic Chorus, 1960G; Civic Music
    Association, 1930G; Civic Opera Co., 1957G;
    Dealy, G.B., Award Competition, 1931G;
    Grand Opera Association, 1939G;
    International Organ Competition, 1996G;
    Meyerson Symphony Center, 1989G; Opera
    House, 1883G, 1964G; Philharmonic Society,
    1887G; Symphony Chorus, 1964G;
    Symphony Orchestra, 1900G
Dallery, Charles, 1770B
Dallier, Henri, 1849A
Dallin, Leon: *Foundations in Music Theory*,
    1962H; *Techniques of 20th Century
    Composition*, 1957H
Dalmas Music Publishing Co., 1802G
Dal Monte, Toti, 1893A, 1916C, 1975B
Dalmorès, Charles, 1871A, 1899C, 1939B

❄

F *Biographical*   G *Cultural Beginnings*   H *Musical Literature*
            I *Musical Compositions*

Dalvimare, Pierre, 1772A, 1839B
Damonte, Magali, 1960A
Damrosch, Frank, 1859A, 1897D, 1904E, 1937B
Damrosch, Leopold, 1832A, 1858D, 1862D, 1871F, 1880E, 1885B
Damrosch, Walter, 1862A, 1871F, 1881F, 1883F, 1885D, 1902D, 1920F, 1927D, 1932E, 1938E, 1950B; *My Musical Life*, 1923H
Damse, Joseph, 1789A, 1852B
Dana, William Henry, 1846A, 1916B; *Orchestration*, 1875H; *Practical Harmony*, 1884H; *Practical Thorough-Bass*, 1873H
Danbé, Jules, 1840A, 1877D, 1899D, 1905B
Danckert, Werner, 1900A, 1970B; *Grundriss der Volksliedkunde*, 1939H; *Symbol, Metaphor, Allegorie in Lied der Völker*, 1077H; *Tonreich und symbolzahl in Hoghkulturen und in der Primitivenwelt*, 1966H; *Das Volkslied in Abendland*, 1966H
Dancla, Charles, 1817A, 1907B; *Les compositeurs chefs d'orchestre*, 1873H
Danco, Suzanne, 1911A, 1941C, 2000B
Dandara, Liviu, 1991B
Dando String Quartet, 1842G
Dang, Thai Son, 1980E
Daniel, Francisco S.; *La musique arabe*, 1863H
Daniel, Oliver, 1911A, 1990B
Daniel, Paul, 1958A, 1990D, 1997D
Daniel, Salvador; *Grammaire philharmonique*, 1837H
Daniélou, Alain, 1907A, 1994B
Danielpour, Richard, 1956A
Daniels, Barbara, 1946A, 1973C
Daniels, David, 1966A, 1990B, 1994C, 1997E
Daniels, Mabel Wheeler, 1878A, 1939E, 1971B
Danilov, Kinsha: *Ancient Russian Poetry*, 1804H
Danilova, Alexandra, 1997B
Danise, Giuseppe, 1883A, 1906C, 1963B
Dankner, Stephen, 1944A
Danks, Dan, 1923A
Danks, Hart P., 1834A, 1903B
Danneley, John Feltham, 1786A, 1836B
Danner, Christian, 1757A, 1813B
Danner, Johann G., 1803B
Dannreuther, Edward, 1844A, 1863C, 1905B; *Musical Ornamentation I*, 1893H
Dannström, Isidor, 1812A, 1841C, 1897B
Danuser, Hermann: *Die Klassizistiche Moderne in der Musik des 20, Jahrhundert*, 1997H; *Musikalische Interpretation*, 1992H
Danzi, Franz, 1763A, 1807D, 1812D, 1826B
Danzi, Margarethe, 1768A, 1787C, 1800B
Daquin, Louis-Claude, 1772B
Dara, Enzo, 1938A, 1960C
Darclée, Hariclea, 1860A, 1888C, 1939B
Dargomijsky, Alexander, 1813A, 1827F, 1831F, 1864F, 1867D, 1869B
Darmstadt, Germany: Contemporary Music Festival & Center, 1946G; Darmstadt

Theater, 1819G; Instrumentverein, 1831G; Mozartverein, 1843G; Musikverein, 1831G; Städtische Akademie für Tonkunst, 1851G; Stadtkirchenchor, 1874G
Darré, Jeanne-Marie, 1999B
Darrell, David, 1962A
Dart, Thurston, 1921A, 1947D, 1971B; *The Interpretation of Music*, 1954H
Daube, Johann Friedrich, 1797B; *Anteitung zur Erfindung der Melodie...I*, 1797H; *Der Musikalische Dillettant I*, 1770H; *Der Musikalische Dillettant II*, 1771H; *Der Musikalische Dillettant III*, 1773H
Daublaine et Cie., Organ Builders, 1838G
Dauer, Johann E., 1768C, 1812B
Daugherty, Michael, 1954A
Dauney, William, 1800B
Dauprat, Louis-François, 1781A, 1798F, 1868B
Dauriac, Lionel, 1847A; *Introduction à la psychologie du musicien*, 1891H; *La psychologie dans l'opéra français*, 1897H
Dauriac, Lionel A., 1923B; *Essai sur l'esprit musical*, 1904H
Dausgaard, Thomas, 1963A
Daussoigne-Méhul, Louis J., 1790A, 1809E, 1827D, 1875B
Dauvergne, Antoine, 1755E, 1762D, 1769D, 1780D, 1797B
Davaux, Jean Baptiste, 1814E, 1822B
Davey, Henry: *History of English Music*, 1895H
Davisson Ananias: *An Introduction to Sacred Music*, 1821H
Davia, Federico, 1933A, 1956C, 1997B
Davisson Ananias: *Kentucky Harmony*, 1816H; *Elements of Harmony, Counterpoint*, 1886H; *Elements of Music*, 1884H
David, Colin, 1950D
David, Gyula, 1913A. 1952E, 1957E, 1977B
David, Hans T., 1902A, 1967B
David, Johann N., 1945D, 1977B; *Der Musikalische Satz in Spiegel der Zeit*, 1963H
David, Léon, 1892C, 1962B
David, Félicien, 1810A, 1831F, 1862E, 1869E, 1876B
David, Ferdinand, 1810A, 1825C, 1836F, 1873B
David, Giovanni, 1790A, 1808C, 1864B
David, Johann N., 1895A
David, Léon, 1867A
David, Samuel, 1836A, 1858E, 1895B
Davide, Giacomo, 1773C, 1830B
Davidov, Alexander, 1872A, 1893C, 1944B
Davidov, Carl, 1838A, 1876D, 1889B
Davidov, Stepan Ivanovich, 1777A, 1825B
Davidovich, Bella, 1949E, 1978F
Davidovici, Robert, 1946A, 1972CE
Davidovsky, Mario, 1934A, 1965D, 1982E
Davidson, Lawrence, 1917A, 1942C
Davidson, Robert, 1965A
Davidson, Tina, 1952A

A *Births*   B *Deaths*   C *Debuts*   D *New Positions*
E *Prizes/Honors*

Davie, Cedric Thorpe, 1913A; *Musical Structure and Design*, 1953H
Davies, Ben Grey, 1858A, 1881C, 1943B
Davies, Catrin Wyn, 1994C
Davies, Cecilia, 1756A, 1836B
Davies, Dennis Russell, 1944A, 1961C, 1972D, 1977D, 1980D, 1987DE, 1989D
Davies, Fanny, 1861A, 1885C, 1934B
Davies, Henry W., 1934E
Davies, Louise M., Symphony Hall, 1980G
Davies, Mary, 1855A, 1873C, 1930B
Davies, Noel A., 1945A, 1967C, 1974D
Davies, Peter Maxwell, 1964E, 1979E, 1987E, 1988F, 1992D
Davies, Ryland, 1943A, 1964C
Davies, Wyn, 1952A
Davin, Patrick, 1962A
Davis, Andrew, 1944A, 1970C, 1975D, 1988D, 1992E, 2000D
Davis, Colin, 1927A, 1965E, 1967D, 1971D, 1972F, 1974F, 1977F, 1980E, 1983D, 1995D, 1998F
Davis, Ellabelle, 1960B
Davis, Ivan, 1932A, 1958E, 1959C, 1960E
Davis, Jessie Bartlett, 1860A, 1905B
Davislim, Steve, 1967A
Davison, A. T., 1883A, 1961B
Davison, Archibald: *Church Music, Illusion and Reality*, 1952H; *Choral Conducting*, 1940H; *Historical Anthology of Music I*, 1946H; *Music Education in America*, 1926H; *Protestant Church Music in America*, 1920H; *Technique of Choral Composition*, 1946H
Davison, J. W., 1813A, 1885B
Davisson, Ananias: *An Introduction to Sacred Music*, 1821H; *Kentucky Harmony*, 1816H
Davy, Charles: *Essay upon...Vocal and Instrumental Music*, 1768H
Davy, Gloria, 1931A, 1953C
Davy, John, 1763A, 1824B
Dawson, Anne, 1959A, 1978C
Dawson, Ted, 1951A
Dawson, William Levi, 1898A, 1927F, 1930D, 1954F, 1956F, 1976E, 1990B
Day, Alfred, 1810A, 1849B; *Treatise on Harmony*, 1845H
Dayton, Ohio: Bach Society, 1974G; Civic Ballet Co., 1937G; Mozart Musical & Literary Society, 1888G; Music Appreciation Choral Club, 1934G; Opera Association, 1960G; Philharmonic Orchestra, 1933G; Philharmonic Society, 1836G; Philharmonic Youth Orchestra, 1937G
Deák, Csaba, 1932A
Dealy, G. B., Award Competition (Dallas), 1931G
Dean, Stafford, 1864C, 1937A
De Angelis, Nazzareno, 1881A, 1903C, 1962B
Debain, Alexandre, Instrument Co., 1834G

Debain, Alexandre-François, 1809A, 1877B
De Boeck, Auguste, 1865A, 1937B
Debussy, Claude, 1862A, 1880F, 1883F, 1884EF, 1886F, 1887F, 1888F, 1889F, 1901D, 1918B
De Carolis, Natale, 1957A
Decca/London's Entartete Music Series, 1993G
Decca Portable Gramophone Co., 1913G
Decca Record Co. (U.S. branch), 1934G
Dechevrens, Antoine, 1840A, 1912B; *Composition musicale et composition littéraire*, 1911H; *Études de science musicale*, 1898H
Decker, Constantin, 1810A, 1878B
Decker, Franz-Paul, 1967D, 1989D, 1994D
Decker & Son, Pianos, 1856G
Decker Brothers, Pianos, 1862G
Decker-Schenk, Johann, 1826A, 1899B
De Clara, Roberto, 1955A, 1990D
Decoust, Michel, 19779D
Deer Valley International Chamber Music Festival, 1985G
DeFabritiis, Oliviero, 1920C, 1982B
Defauw, Désiré, 1885A, 1937D, 1941D, 1943D, 1960B
De Fesch, Willem, 1761B
Deffés, Pierre-Louis, 1847E
DeGaetani, Jan, 1933A, 1958C, 1989B
De Groote, Steven, 1989B
Degtiarev, Stepan A., 1766A, 1813B
De Haan, Willem, 1849A, 1878D, 1930B
Dehn, Siegfried, 1799A, 1842D, 1858B; *Lehre vom Kontrapunkt, dem Kanon und der Fuge*, 1859H; *Theoretisch-praktische Harmonielehre*, 1840H
Deichel, Joseph Christoph, 1753B
Deis, Carl, 1883A, 1917D, 1960B
DeKleist Musical Instrument Co., 1893G
Deko Publishers, 1981G
De Koven, Reginald, 1859A, 1889D, 1898E, 1920B
Delage, Maurice, 1879A, 1961B
Delalande, Michel Richard, 1761D, 1812B
Delamain, Henry, 1762D, 1796B
De Lamarter, Eric, 1880A, 1918D, 1953B
Delaney, Robert, 1903A, 1956B
DeLara, Adelina, 1872A, 1891C, 1961B
Delaunay, Jules, 1856E
DeLay, Dorothy, 1917A
Delden, Lex van, 1919A, 1988B
Delezenne, Charles Édouard, 1776A, 1866B
Delfs, Andreas, 1997D
Delibes, Léo, 1836A, 1871F, 1884E, 1891B
DeLio, Thomas, 1951A
Delius, Frederick, 1862A, 1884F, 1885F, 1887F, 1888F, 1890F, 1907F, 1934B
Delius Association of Florida, 1962G
Della Casa, Lisa, 1919A, 1941C
Della-Maria, Dominique, 1769A, 1800B
Deller, Alfred, 1912A, 1970E, 1979B
Deller, Florian Johann, 1773B

F *Biographical*   G *Cultural Beginnings*   H *Musical Literature*
I *Musical Compositions*

Delle Sedie, Enrico, 1822A, 1851C; *L'art lyrique*, 1876H
Dello Joio, Norman, 1913A, 1942E, 1946E, 1961E, 1972D
Dell'orifice, Luigi Eduardo, 1909A, 1998B
Del Mar, Jonathan, 1951A, 1984CE
Del Mar, Norman, 1919A, 1975E, 1985D, 1994B; *The Anatomy of the Orchestra*, 1981H; *A Companion to the Orchestra*, 1987H
Delmas, Jean-François, 1861A, 1886C, 1933B
Delmas, Marc Jean, 1920E
Del Monaco, Mario, 1915A, 1939C, 1982B
Delna, Marie, 1875A, 1892C, 1932B
Delone, Richard: *Aspects of Twentieth Century Music*, 1975H
Delta Omicron International Music Fraternity, 1909G
Del Tredici, David, 1968E, 1984E
De Luca, Giuseppe, 1876A, 1897C
De Lucia, Fernando, 1885C, 1925B
Delvedez, Edouard, 1817A, 1897B
Delz, Christoph, 1993B
De Main, John, 1978D, 1997D
Demar, Johann Sébastian, 1763A, 1832B
DeMarinis, Paul, 1948A
Demars, Jean Odo, 1756B
Demenga, Thomas, 1954A
Demessieux, Jeanne, 1921A, 1968B
Demeterova, Gabriela, 1971A
Demidenki, Nikolai, 1955A, 1985C
De Mille, Agnes, 1909A, 1980E, 1993B
Demmler, Johann Michael, 1774D, 1785B
Dempsey, Gregory, 1954C
Demus, Jörg, 1928A, 1943C, 1956E; *Abenteuer der Interpretation*, 1967H
Demuth, Leopold, 1861A, 1889C, 1910B
Demuth, Norman, 1898A, 1954E, 1968B; *French Opera*, 1963H; *The Symphony*, 1950H
Demuynck, Charles Michael, 1968A, 1995D
De Muzen, 1832G
Dencke, Jeremiah, 1795B
Denera, Erna, 1881A, 1906C, 1938B
Denhof (Beecham) Opera Co., 1910G
Denishawn School of Dancing & Related Arts, 1915G
Denisov, Edison, 1929A, 1996B
Denmark (see also Aarhus, Copenhagen): Danish Hymn Society, 1922G; Music Information Center, 1980G; Musicological Society, 1921G; National Radio Orchestra, 1925G; National Record Collection, 1911G; Danish Philharmonic (Jutland), 1963G; Society for Music Therapy, 1969G; Young Composer's Society of Denmark, 1920G
Dennée, Charles, 1863A, 1946B
Denney, William, 1910A
Dennis Noble, 1966B
Dennison, Robert, 1960A, 1971C
Denniston, Patrick, 1965A, 1994E

Den Norske Studentersangforening, 1845G
Denny, William D., 1980B
Dens, Michel, 1914A, 1938C
Densmore, Frances, 1867A, 1957B; *The American Indians and Their Music*, 1926H
Denver, Colorado: Amateur Symphony Orchestra, 1900G; Arion Singing Society, 1904G; Center for the Performing Arts, 1978G; Children's Chorale, 1974G; Choral Society, 1890G; City Band, 1861G; Civic Symphony Orchestra, 1921G; College of Music, 1925G; Early Music Consort, 1976G; Grand Opera Co., 1915G; Greater Denver Opera Co., 1955G; Lyric Theater, 1958G; Männerchor, 1870G; Music Conservatory, 1887G; Musical Union, 1867G; Philharmonic Orchestra, 1948G; String Quartet, 1921G; Tabor (Grand) Opera House, 1881G; University School of Music, 1879G; Wollcott Music Conservatory, 1920G
Denza, Luigi, 1846A, 1922B
De Peyer, Gervase, 1926A
DePlessis, Christian, 1944A, 1967C
De Ponti, Lorenzo, 1805F
DePrè, Jacqueline, 1979E, 1987B
DePreist, James, 1936A, 1962F, 1964EF, 1971F, 1976D, 1980D, 1990D, 1991D, 1994D, 2000E
DeQing, Wen, 1958A
De Reszke, Edouard, 1876C, 1917B
De Reszke, Jean, 1874C, 1879C, 1925B
De Reszke, Josephine, 1874C, 1891B
Dérivis, Henri F., 1780A, 1803C, 1856B
Dérivis, Prosper, 1808A, 1831C, 1880B
Dermota, Anton, 1910A, 1934C, 1989A
Dernesch, Helga, 1939A, 1961C
Derngate Centre for the Performing Arts, 1983G
De Rose, Peter, 1953B
Dervaux, Pierre, 1992B
Derzhinskaya, Xeniya, 1889A, 1913C
De Santis Music Publishers, 1852G
Désargus, Xavier, 1768A, 1832B; *Cours complet de harpe*, 1816H; *Traité général sur l'art de jouer la harpe*, 1809H
Desarzens, Victor, 1986B
Désaugiers, Marc-Antoine, 1793B
Deschamps-Jehin, Blanche, 1857A, 1874C, 1923B
Desderi, Claudio, 1945A, 1969C
Deshayes, Prosper-Didier, 1815B; *Idées générales sur l'Académie royale de musique*, 1822H
Des Marais, Paul, 1920A
Desmazures, Laurent, 1758D, 1777D, 1778B
Des Moines, Iowa: Ballet Co., 1970G; Drake-Des Moines Symphony Orchestra, 1937G; Metro Festival, 1972G; Metro Opera & Festival, 1973G; Music College, 1888G
Desmond, Astra, 1893A, 1915C, 1973B
Desormière, Roger, 1863B, 1898A, 1963B

A   *Births*   B   *Deaths*   C   *Debuts*   D   *New Positions*
E   *Prizes/Honors*

Despréauz Louis F.: *Cours d'éducation de Clavecin ou Pianoforte*, 1785H
Dessau, Paul, 1894A, 1919D, 1925D, 1979B; *Notizen und Noten*, 1974H
Dessau, Germany: Schneider Music School, 1829G
Dessauer, Josef, 1798A, 1876B
Dessay, Natalie, 1965A, 1990CE,
Dessi, Daniela, 1957A, 1979C
Dessoff, Otto, 1860D, 1875D, 1881D
Dessoff A Capella Singers, 1928G
Dessoff Madrigal Singers, 1916G
Dessoir, Max: *Aesthetik und allgemeine Kunstwissenschaft*, 1906H
Dessoir, Susanne, 1869A, 1953B
Destinn, Emmy, 1878A, 1898C, 1930B
Destouches, Franz von, 1772A, 1787D, 1844B
Desvignes, Victor François, 1805A, 1835D, 1853B
Deszner, Salomea, 1759A, 1778C, 1806B
Dethier, Christine, 1995B
Déthier, Edouard, 1886A, 1962B
Déthier, Gaston-Marie, 1875A, 1958B
Detroit, Michigan: Civic Opera Co., 1928G; Conservatory of Music, 1874G; Fireman's Hall, 1851G; Ford Auditorium, 1956G; Harmonie, 1849G; Institute of Musical Arts, 1914G; Masonic Auditorium, 1928G; Music Settlement School, 1926G; Opera House, 1869G; Orchestra Hall, 1919G; Philharmonic Society, 1855G; Piccola Opera Co., 1961G; Stein & Buchheister Orchestra, 1855G; Symphony Choir, 1921G; Symphony Chorus, 1985G; Symphony Orchestra, 1914G; Symphony Youth Orchestra, 1970G
Dett, R. Nathaniel, 1882A, 1943B
Dettmer, Wilhelm, 1808A, 1876B
Deuteukom, Cristina, 1931A, 1962C
Deutsch, Diana: *Music Perception*, 1983H; *The Psychology of Music*, 1982H
Deutsch, Max, 1982B
Deutsch, Moritz, 1818A, 1892B
Deutsch, Otto: *Franz Schubert: Die Dokuments Seines Lebens und Schaffens*, 1913H; *Handel: Documentary History*, 1954H; *Schubert: A Documentary Biography*, 1946H; *Schubert: Thematic Catalogue*, 1951H
Deutsch, Otto Erich, 1883A, 1967B
Deutsche Akademie für Musik (Prague), 1920G
Deutsche Brahmsgesellschaft, 1906G
Deutsche Chronik, 1774G
Deutsche Gesellschaft für Musik des Orients, 1966G
Deutsche Gramophon Gesellschaft, 1898G
Deutsche Händelgesellschaft, 1856G
Deutsche Musikzeitung, 1860G
Deutsche Musiker-Zeitung, 1870G
Deutsche Oper am Rhein (Düsseldorf), 1956G
Deutsche Revue, 1835G

Deutsche Rundschau, 1874G
Deutscher Verlag für Musik, 1954G
De Vaughn, Alteouise, 1984C
Devenney, David: *Nineteenth-Century American Choral Music*, 1987H; *Source Readings in American Choral Music*, 1995H
Devia, Mariella, 1948A, 1972C
Devienne, François, 1759A, 1782C, 1803B; *Méthode de flûte*, 1795H
Devlin, Michael, 1942A, 1963C
Devol, Luana, 1983C
De Vos Hall for the Performing Arts, 1980G
DeVoto, Mark, 1940A
Devoyon, Pascal, 1953A
Devreese, Frédéric, 1929A
Devreese, Godfried, 1893A, 1972B
Devrient, Eduard, 1801A, 1891C, 1877B; *Geschichte der deutschen Schausspielkunst*, 1848H
Devrient, Karl, 1823F
Devries, Hermann, 1858A, 1879C, 1949B
Devries, Maurice, 1854A, 1874C, 1919B
Devroye, Théodore-Joseph, 1804A, 1873B
De Waal, Rian, 1958A
Deyo, Felix, 1888A, 1939D, 1959B
Deyo, Ruth Lynda, 1884A, 1893C, 1904C, 1960B
DeYoung, Michelle, 1969A, 1995E
Dezéde, Nicolas, 1792B
Dia Center for the Arts, 1993G
Diabelli, Anton, 1781A, 1800F, 1803F, 1858B
Diaghilev, Sergei, 1872A, 1929B
Diamond, David, 1915A, 1943E, 1944E, 1966E, 1985E, 1995E
Diamov String Quartet, 1956G
Diaz, Andrés, 1964A, 1986E
Diaz, Eugène, 1837A, 1901B
Diaz, Justino, 1940A, 1957C
Diaz, Rafaelo, 1884A, 1911C, 1943B
Dibdin, Charles, 1778F, 1789F, 1792F, 1814B; *The English Pythagoras*, 1808H; *History of the Stage*, 1795H; *Music Epitomised*, 1804H; *The Musical Master*, 1807H; *The Professional Life of Mr. Dibdin*, 1803H; *The Musical Tour of Mr. Dibdin*, 1788H
Dichter, Mischa, 1945A, 1966CF
Dickinson, Clarence, 1873A, 1969B; *Excursions in Musical History*, 1917H; *Troubadour Songs*, 1920H
Dickinson, Edward, 1946B; *The Education of the Music Lover*, 1911H; *Music & Higher Education*, 1915H; *Music in the History of the Western Church*, 1902H; *The Spirit of Music*, 1925H
Dickinson, George S., 1888A, 1964B; *Classification of Musical Compositions*, 1938H; *Foretokens of the Tonal Principle*, 1923H; *The Growth & Use of Harmony*, 1927H; *A Handbook of Style in Music*, 1965H; *The Pattern of Music*,

---

F *Biographical*   G *Cultural Beginnings*   H *Musical Literature*
I *Musical Compositions*

Dickinson, George S., (*cont.*)
  1939H; *The Study of Music as Liberal Art*,
  1953H
Dickinson, Peter, 1934A
Dickinson, Thomas G., 1954A
Dickman, Stephen, 1943A, 1967E
Dickons, Marie, 1770A, 1833B
Dicterow, Glenn, 1948A
Diderot, Denis, 1784B
Didonato, Joyce, 1970A, 1996C
Didur, Adamo, 1874A, 1894C, 1946B
Diemer, Emma Lou, 1927A
Diémer, Louis, 1843A, 1889E, 1919B
Diener, Franz, 1849A, 1879B
Diener, Melanie, 1967A
Diepenbrock, Alphons, 1862A,1921B
Dierich, Carl, 1852A, 1928B
Dies, Albert Christoph, 1755A, 1822B
Diet, Edmond-Marie, 1854A, 1924B
Dieter, Christian, 1757A, 1822B
Dietrich, Albert, 1829A, 1908B
Dietrich, Marie, 1867A, 1888C, 1940B
Dietrichstein, Moritz, 1775A, 1864B
Dietsch, Louis, 1808A, 1849D, 1860D, 1865B
Di Giuseppe, Enrico, 1932A, 1959C
Dignum, Charles, 1765A, 1784C, 1827B; *Vocal
  Music*, 1810H
Dijk, Jan van, 1918A
Dijon, France: Conservatory of Music, 1869G;
  Société Chorale, 1870G; Société
  Philharmonique, 1832G
Diller, Angela, 1877A, 1921D, 1968B; *First
  Theory Book*, 1921H; *Keyboard Harmony I*,
  1936H; *Keyboard Harmony II*, 1937H; *Keyboard
  Harmony III*, 1943H; *Keyboard Harmony IV*,
  1949H; *The Splendor of Music*, 1957H
Diller-Quaile School of Music, 1921G
Dilling, Mildred, 1894A, 1911C, 1942E, 1982B
Dillon, Fannie Charles, 1881A, 1908C, 1947B
Dillon, James, 1950A
Dimitrescu String Quartet, 1880G
Dimitrova, Ghena, 1941A, 1965C, 1970E
Dimmler, Anton, 1783A, 1795C
Dimmler, Franz Anton, 1752A, 1827B
Dinant Saxophone Quartet, 1973G
Dineşcu, Violeta, 1953A
Dinev, Peter, 1889A, 1980B
Dingelder, Ingrid, 1941A
Dingelstedt, Franz von, 1867D
Dingelstedt, Jenny, 1816A, 1877B
Dinicu, Grigoras, 1889A, 1949B
Diocesan Choir School, 1953G
Dippel, Andreas, 1866A, 1887C, 1910D, 1932B
Dirkens, Annie, 1869A, 1890C, 1942B
Disney, Walt, 1940F
Dispeker, Thea, 2000B
Di Stefano, Giuseppe, 1946C
Distin, Henry, Instrument Maker, 1884G
Distin & Sons, Music Dealers, 1845G

Distin Family Brass Quartet, 1833G
Distler, Hugo, 1908A, 1942B
Distler, Johann Georg, 1760A, 1799B
Ditson, Alice M., Fund, 1940G
Ditson, Oliver, 1811A, 1888B
Ditson, Oliver, & Co., Publisher, 1835G
Dittersdorf, Carl D. von, 1751F, 1763F, 1765D,
  1770DE, 1773E, 1795F, 1799B
Divine Arts Record Label, 1994G
Dix, Barbara, 1944A, 1973C
Dixon, Dean, 1915A, 1938C, 1941F, 1948E,
  1953D, 1961D, 1964D, 1976B
Dixon, James, 1928A, 1963E
Dizi, François-Joseph, 1780A, 1847B
Dizikes, John: *Opera In America: A Cultural
  History*, 1993H
Dlabač, Bohumir Jan, 1758A, 1820B;
  Allgemeines...Künstlerlexicon für Böhman I,
  1815H; *Allgemeines...Künstlerlexikon für
  Böhmen III*, 1818H
Dlugoszewski, Lucia, 1931A, 2000B
Dmitriev, Georgy, 1942A
Doane, William H., 1832A, 1915B
Dobanzky, Artur, 1939A
Dobbs, Mattiwilda, 1925A, 1948CE, 1953F
Dobiá, Václav, 1909A, 1978B
Döbricht, Johanna Elisabeth, 1786B
Dobrowen, Issay, 1891A, 1936D, 1941D, 1948D,
  1953B
Dobrski, Julian, 1812A, 1832C, 1886B
Dobrzynski, Ignacy Felix, 1807A, 1779A, 1841B
  1867B
Dobson, Frank, 1953E
Doche, Joseph-Denis, 1766A, 1825B
Dodge, Charles, 1942A, 1971D, 1979D;
  *Computer Music: Synthesis, Composition &
  Performance*, 1985H
Dodgson, Stephen, 1924A
Doenhoff, Albert von, 1880A, 1905C, 1940B
Doese, Helena, 1946A, 1971C
Döhler, Theodor, 1814A, 1856B
Dohnányi, Christoph von, 1929A, 1951E,
  1957D, 1963D, 1964D, 1968D, 1977D, 1984D,
  1997D, 1999E
Dohnányi, Ernst von, 1877A, 1897CF, 1898E,
  1919DF, 1931D, 1934D, 1949F, 1960B
Dohnányi, Oliver von, 1955A, 1979D, 1993D
Doi, Chean See, 1997D
Doktor, Paul, 1919A, 1989B
Doles, Johann Friedrich, 1756D, 1797B
Dolge, Alfred: *Pianos & Their Makers*, 1911H;
  Pianos & Their Makers II, 1913H
Dolmetsch, Arnold, 1858A, 1938E, 1940B; *The
  Interpretation of Music of the 17th & 18th
  Centuries, 1915H*
Dolmetsch Foundation, 1929G
Dolukhanova, Zara, 1918A, 1939C, 1966E
Domaine Musical Concerts, 1954G
Domarkas, Juozas, 1964D

❊

A *Births*   B *Deaths*   C *Debuts*   D *New Positions*
E *Prizes/Honors*

Domenica, Robert De, 1927A
Domgraf-Fassbänder, Willi, 1897A, 1922C, 1978B
Dominant Symphony Orchestra, 1995G
Domingo, Plácido, 1941A, 1959C, 1977E, 1984F, 1996D
Dominguez, Guillermo, 1961A, 1984C
Dommer, Arrey von, 1828A, 1905B
Domnich, Heinrich, 1767A, 1781C, 1844B; *Horn Method*, 1807H
Donalda, Pauline, 1882A, 1904C, 1970B
Donat, Zdislawa, 1939A, 1964C
Donath, Helen, 1940A, 1960C
Donati, August Friedrich, 1773A
Donati, Christian Gottlob, 1795B
Donati, Gotthold Heinrich, 1799B
Donati, Johann C., 1756B
Donato, August, 1909A
Donatoni, Franco, 2000B
Donaueschingen Concert Hall, 1960G
Donaueschingen Contemporary Festival, 1921G
Donaueschingen Gesellschaft für Musik Freunde, 1913G
Donberger, Georg, 1768B
Dönch, Carl, 1915A, 1936C, 1994B
Donington, Robert, 1907A, 1990B; *Baroque Music, Style & Performance: A History*, 1982H; *Interpretation of Early Music*, 1963H; *A Performer's Guide to Baroque Music*, 1973H
Donington Consort, 1956G
Donizetti, Gaetano, 1797A, 1806F, 1814F, 1817F, 1837D, 1838F, 1845F, 1846F, 1848B,
Donizetti, Giuseppe, 1788A
Donizetti Society of London, 1973G
Donnelly, Patrick, 1958A
Donnington, Robert, 1979E
Donnini, Girolamo, 1752B
Donose, Ruxandra, 1991C
Donovan, Richard Frank, 1891A, 1936D, 1970B
Dont, Joseph Valentin, 1776A, 1833B
Donzelli, Domenico, 1790A, 1808C, 1873B
Dooley, William, 1932A, 1957C
Doppler School of Music, 1878G
Doppler, (Albert) Franz, 1821A, 1883B
Doppler, Karl, 1865D
Dorati, Antal, 1906A, 1925C, 1945D, 1949D, 1963D, 1966D, 1970D, 1977D, 1979F, 1981F, 1982F, 1984EF, 1988B
Doret, Gustave, 1866A, 1943B
Dorfman, Ania, 1899A, 1984B
Dorian, Frederick, 1902A, 1991B; *Commitment to Culture*, 1964H; *Hausmusik alter Meister*, 1933H; *History of Music in Performance*, 1942H; *The Musical Workshop*, 1947H
Dorian Wind Quintet, 1961G
Döring, Johann Friedrich, 1766A, 1840B
Dorn, Heinrich, 1800A, 1828D, 1831D, 1832D, 1843D, 1849D, 1892B

Dorn, Reinhard, 1957A
Dornel, Louis Antoine, 1765B
Dornemann, Joan, 1987D
Dortmund, Germany: Liedertafel, 1840G; Musikverein, 1845G
Dorus-Gras, Julie, 1805A, 1825C, 1896B
Dossenbach-Klingenberg School of Music, 1913G
Dotzauer, Friedrich, 1783A, 1798C, 1860B; *Violoncellschule*, 1832H
Double-Action Harp, 1811G
Doubleday & McClure Co., 1897G
Dougherty, Celius, 1902A, 1986B
Douglas, Barry, 1960A, 1981C, 1986EF
Douglas, Charles Winfred, 1867A, 1944B
Dourlen, Victor-Charles, 1780A, 1805E, 1864B
Dow, Daniel, 1783B
Dow, Dorothy, 1920A, 1946C
Dowd, William R., 1922A
Dowiakowska-Kilmowiczowa, Bronislawa, 1840A, 1857C, 1910B
Dowling, L.: *The Schillinger System of Musical Composition*, 1941H
Dowling, Richard William, 1962A, 1981C
Downes, Edward, 1924A, 1952D, 1972D, 1980D, 1986E, 1991E
Downes, Edward O. D., 1911A; *Adventures in Symphonic Music*, 1944H; *Perspectives in Musicology*, 1972H
Downes, Olin, 1886A, 1906D, 1924D, 1939E, 1955B; *The Lure of Music*, 1918H
Downes, Ralph, 1969E; *Baroque Tricks: Adventures with the Organ Builders*, 1983H
Downtown Glee Club (NY), 1927G
Draeseke, Felix, 1835A, 1913B; *Anweisung zum kunstgerechten Modulieren*, 1875H
Dragon, Carmen, 1914A
Dragonetti, Domenico, 1763A, 1776F, 1846B
Dragonette, Jessica, 1980B
Dragoni, Maria, 1958A, 1984C
Drahos, Béla, 1955A
Drake, Earl R., 1865A, 1916B
Drake, Erik, 1788A, 1870B
Drake University Auditorium, 1905G
Drake-Des Moines Symphony Orchestra, 1937G
Drakos, Bila, 1985E, 1993D
Dranoff, Murray, International Two Piano Competition (Miami), 1987G
Drath, Nina, 1954A, 1968C
Drdla, Franz, 1868A, 1944B
Drechsler, Joseph, 1782A, 1844D, 1852B
Drei Masken Verlag, 1910G
Dreier, Per, 1953C, 1957D
Der Dreiklang, 1937G
Dresden, Germany: Agthe-Kräger Music Academy, 1823G; Cecilia Society, 1848G; Conservatory of Music, 1856G; Dreyssigsche Singakademie, 1807G; German Opera,

Dresden, Germany: (cont.)
1817G; Gewerbehaussaal, 1870G;
Kammerchor, 1985G; Kammermusik der
Staats-Kapelle Dresden, 1952G; Liedertafel,
1830G; Männergesangverein, 1876G; Nicodé
Concerts, 1894G; Nicodé Chorus, 1896G;
Opera Festival, 1978G; Opera House, 1878G;
Palace of Culture, 1969G; Philharmonische
Populäre Künstlerkonzerte, 1894G; Royal
Saxon Opera House, 1841G; Societäts-
Theater, 1776G; Studio Neue Musik, 1974G;
Symphoniker, 1998G; Tonkünstlerverein,
1854G; Verein für Choralgesang, 1848G
Drechsler, Karl, 1800A
Dresel, Otto, 1826A, 1890B
Dresher, Paul Joseph, 1951A
Dresher, Paul, Ensemble, 1984G
Dressler, Marie, 1869A
Dressler, Ernst Christoph 1779B; Theater-Schule
für die Deutschen, das, 1777H
Dreszer, Anastasius, 1907B
Dreszer Music School (Halle), 1868G
Dretzel, Cornelius H., 1764D, 1775D
Dreves, Guido M.: Psalteria Rhythmica, 1901H
Drexel, Johann C., 1758A, 1797D, 1801B
Dreyer, Giovanni, 1772B
Dreyer, Johann Melchior, 1824B
Dreyschock, Alexander, 1818A, 1869B
Dreyschock, Raimund, 1824A, 1869B
Drieberg, Friedrich von, 1780A, 1856B;
Aufschlüss über die musik der Griechen, 1819H;
Wörterbuch der grieschen Musik, 1835H
Driesten, Roelof van, 1986D
Drigo, Riccardo, 1879D, 1846A, 1886D,
1930B
Dring, Madelein, 1923A, 1977B
Drinker, Henry S., 1880A, 1965B
Drinker, Henry S., Music Center, 1962G
Drinker, Sophie, 1888A, 1967B; Music &
Women, 1948H
Drinker Library of Choral Music, 1938G
Driscoll, Loren, 1928A, 1954C
Drivala, Jenny, 1965A, 1985C
Drobisch, Karl Ludwig, 1803A, 1854B
Drobisch, Moritz Wilhelm, 1802A, 1896B; Über
die...Bestimmung der musikalische Intervalle,
1846H; Über musikalische Tonbestimmung &
Temperatur, 1852H; Über reine Stimmung und
Temperature der Töne, 1877H
Drouet, Louis François, 1792A, 1873B
Drouet, Louis, Flute Maker, 1815G
Drozdowski, Jan, 1857A, 1918B
Drucker, Stanley, 1929A
Druckman, Jacob, 1928A, 1969E, 1975E, 1976D,
1978E, 1996B
Drury, Stephen, 1955A
Druschetzky, Georg, 1819B
Drzewiecki, Zbigniew, 1916C, 1971B, 1890A
Dubensky, Arcady, 1890A, 1966B

Dublin, Ireland: Abbey Theatre, 1894G, 1904G;
Adare Festival, 1990G; Alday Music
Academy, 1812G; Antient Concerts Society,
1834G; Arts Council of Ireland, 1951G;
Choral Institute, 1851G; Crow Street Theater,
1758G; Festival of 20th Century Music,
1969G; Grand Opera Society, 1941G; Irish
Music Fund, 1787G; Mornington, Lord,
Musical Academy, 1757G; Municipal School
of Music, 1890G; Music Association of
Ireland, 1948G; Music Festival, 1831G;
National Symphony of Ireland, 1947G;
Orchestral Players, 1939G; Orchestral
Society, 1899G; Orpheus Choral Society,
1899G; Philharmonic Society, 1826G;
Rotunda, 1764G; Royal Irish Academy of
Music, 1848G; Sons of Handel (Dublin),
1810G, 1816G; University Chair of Music,
1764G; University Choral Society, 1837G
Dubois & Stodart, Piano Manufacturers, 1819G
Dubois, Léon, 1885E
Dubois, Pierre, 1955E, 1995B
Dubois, Théodore, 1837A, 1861E, 1866D,
1877D, 1894E, 1896D, 1924B; 87 Leçons
d'harmonie, 1891H; Traité de Contrepoint et de
Fugue, 1901H
Dubourg, Matthew, 1761E, 1767B
Dubreuil, Jean, 1775B; Dictionnaire lyrique
portatif, 1766H
Duchambge, Pauline, 1778A, 1858B
Duckles, Vincent H., 1913A, 1985B; Music
Reference & Research Materials, 1964H
Duckworth, William, 1943A; The Language of
Experimental Music, 1981H; Talking Music:
Conversations with Five Generations of
American Experimental Composers, 1995H;
Theoretical Foundations of Music, 1978H
Ducloux, Paul, 1997B
Dudarova, Veronika, 1991D
Duerkson, George: Teaching Instrumental Music,
1972H
Duesing, Dale, 1947A, 1972C
Dufallo, Richard, 1933A, 2000B; Trackings:
Composers Speak..., 1989H
Duff, Arthur, 1956A
Dufourcq, Norbert, 1904A, 1990B
Dufranne, Hector, 1870A, 1896C, 1951B
Dugazon, Louise, 1755A, 1774C, 1821B
Duinn, Proinnsías Ó, 1966D, 1978D
Dukas, Paul, 1865A, 1934E, 1935B
Duke Symphony Orchestra, 1985G
Dukelsky, Vladimir, 1903A, 1969B
Dulon, Friedrich L., 1769A, 1779C, 1826B
Dumas, Jean, 1770B
Dumage, Pierre, 1751B
Dumay, Augustin, 1949A, 1963C
Dumesnil, René: L'envers de la musique, 1949H;
Histoire illustrée de la musique, 1934H; Le
monde des musiciens, 1924H; Music in France

A *Births*   B *Deaths*   C *Debuts*   D *New Positions*

E *Prizes/Honors*

between the Wars, 1946H; *Musiciens romantiques*, 1928H; *Musique contemporaine en France*, 1930H; *La musique romantique française*, 1944H
Duminy, Phillippe, 1973C
Dumont-Schauberg Verlag (Cologne), 1818G
Dun, Tan, 1957A
Duncan, Isadore, School of Dancing, 1904G
Duncan, Todd, 1903A, 1934C, 1998B
Duncan, William: *Encyclopedia of Musical Terms*, 1914H; *Fundamentals of Music Theory*, 1983H; *The Story of the Carol*, 1911H; *Ultra-Modernism in Music*, 1917H
Duncan Phyfe Shop (New York), 1795G
Dunham, Henry Morton, 1853A, 1929B
Duni, Egidio Romualdo, 1761D, 1775B
Dunn, Mignon, 1931A, 1955C
Dunn, Susan, 1954A, 1982C, 1983E
Dunsby, Jonathan: *Music Analysis in Theory & Practice*, 1987H
Duo-Art Reproducing Piano, 1913G
Duparc, Elisabeth, 1751F, 1773B
Duparc, Henri, 1848A, 1933B
Duphley, Jacques, 1789B
Dupin, Aurora. See Sand, George
Dupont, Gaby, 1888F
Dupont, Stephen, 1957A, 1984C
Duport, Jean L., 1768C
Duport, Jean-Pierre, 1761C, 1818B
Duprato, Jules-Laurent, 1848E
Dupré, Jacqueline, 1945A, 1961C
Dupré, Marcel, 1886A, 1898D, 1914E, 1954D, 1971B; *Manuel d'accompagnement du plainchant grégorien*, 1937H; *Méthode d'orgue*, 1927H; *Traité d'improvisation à l'orgue*, 1926H
Duprez, Alexandrine, 1827C
Duprez, Gilbert (Louis), 1806A, 1825C, 1896B; *L'art du chant*, 1845H; *Souvenirs d'un chanteur*, 1880H
Dupuis, Albert, 1903E
Dupuis, Sylvain, 1881E, 1911D
Dupuis, Thomas, 1758E, 1779D
Dupuy, Jean-Baptiste-Edouard, 1770A, 1822B
Dupuy, Martine, 1952A, 1975C
Duquesnoy, Charles, 1759A, 1822B
Duran, José, 1755D
Durand, Marie-Auguste, 1830A, 1909B
Durand and Schönewerk Publishers, 1870G
Durand et Cie., Publishers, 1847G
Duranowski, August, 1770A, 1834B
Durante, Francesco, 1755B
Durazzo Giacomo: *Lettre sur le mécanisme de l'opéra italien*, 1756H
Durey, Louis, 1888A, 1920F, 1979B
Durigo, Ilona, 1881A, 1906C, 1943B
Durkó, Zsolt, 1978E, 1983E
Durlet, Emmanuel, 1893A
Duruflé, Marie-Madeleine, 1999B

Duruflé, Maurice, 1902A, 1930D, 1986B
Durutte, François, 1803A, 1881B
Duek, Frantiek Xaver, 1799B
Duek, Josefa, 1754A, 1842B
Dushkin, Samuel, 1891A, 1918C, 1976B
Dussek, Johann Ladislaus, 1760A, 1779C, 1784F, 1786F, 1789F, 1790F, 1799F, 1812B; *Instructions on the Art of Playing the Pianoforte...*, 1796H
Dustmann, Marie Luise, 1831A, 1859C, 1899B
Dutilleux, Henri, 1916A, 1938E
Dutoit, Charles, 1936A, 1963C, 1967D, 1973D, 1975D, 1977D, 1983F, 1990D
Dutton, Lawrence, 1954A
Duval, Denise, 1921A, 1941C
Duvernoy, Charles, 1766A, 1845b
Duvernoy, Frédéric N., 1765A, 1815E, 1838B
Duvernoy Henri-Louis: *Solfège des chanteurs*, 1855H
Duvernoy, Victor, 1891E
Dux, Claire, 1885A, 1906C, 1967B
Dvořák, Antonín, 1841A, 1874E, 1878F, 1891E, 1892D, 1893F, 1904B
Dvořák, Otilie, 1898F
Dvořák String Quartet, 1951G
Dvořákova, Karolina, 1964A
Dvořáková, Ludmila, 1923A, 1949C
Dvorsk, Peter, 1951A, 1973C, 1975E
Dwight, John Sullivan, 1813A, 1893B
Dwight's Journal of Music, 1852G
Dworchak, Harry, 1976C, 1987E
Dyachkov, Yegor, 1974A
Dyce, William, 1844E
Dyk, Frantiek, 1929D
Dykema, Peter, 1873A, 1951B; *Music for School Administrators*, 1931H; *Music Tests*, 1929H; *School Music Handbook*, 1923H; *Teaching & Administration of High School Music*, 1941H
Dykes, John Bacchus, 1823A, 1876B
Dynamic Records, 1978G
Dyson, George, 1941E; *The New Music*, 1924H
Dyson, Ruth, 1997B
Dzelowski, Antoni, 1973B
Dziadek, Magdalena, 1961A
Dzubay, David, 1964A
Eaglen, Jane, 1960A, 1984C
Eames, Emma, 1865A, 1889C, 1952B
Eames, Henry P., 1872A, 1950B
E.A.R., 1981G
Ear Magazine, 1975G
Earhart, Will: *Elements of Music Theory I, II*, 1938H; *The Meaning and Teaching of Music*, 1935H; *Music in Secondary Schools*, 1917H; *Music in the Public Schools*, 1914H; *Music to the Listening Ear*, 1932H
Earle, Hobart, 1992D, 1993F
Early Music, 1976G
Easdale, Brian, 1909A, 1995B
East, Angela, 1949A, 1972C

F   *Biographical*   G   *Cultural Beginnings*   H   *Musical Literature*
I   *Musical Compositions*

Eastern Music Festival (N.C.), 1962G
Eastman, George, 1854A, 1932B
Eastman, George, Prize, 1982G
Eastman Wind Ensemble, 1952G
Easton, Florence, 1882A, 1903C, 1955B
Easton, Robert, 1898A
East-West Festival (Tokyo), 1961G
Eaton, John, 1935A, 1959E, 1972E, 1990E;
   Involvement with Music: New Music since
   1950, 1976H
Ebbecke, Michael, 1955A
Ebdon, Thomas, 1763D, 1811B
Ebel, Arnold, 1963B
Ebell, Heinrich K., 1801D
Eben, Petr, 1929A
Eberhardt, Johann August, 1809B; *Handbuch*
   der Aesthetik I, II, 1803H; *Théorie der Schönen*
   Wissenschaften, 1783H
Eberhart, Siegfried: *Der Beseelte Violinton*,
   1910H; *Virtuose Violin-Technik*, 1921H
Eberl, Anton, 1765A, 1784C, 1796D, 1807B
Eberlin, Johann Ernst, 1762B
Ebers, Carl Friedrich, 1770A, 1836B
Ebert, Wilhelmine, 1824F
Eberwein, Carl, 1786A, 1826D, 1868B
Eberwein, Traugott, 1775A, 1817D, 1831B
L'écho musical, 1869G
Echo: A Music Journal, 1883G
The Echo, 1851G
Eck, Franz, 1774A, 1804B
Eck, Friedrich Johann, 1767A, 1802F, 1838B
Eckard, Johann Gottfried, 1809B
Eckardt, Hans, 1904A, 1969B
Eckerberg, Sixten, 1909A, 1937D, 1991B
Eckert, Karl, 1820A, 1851D, 1853D, 1860D,
   1869D, 1879B
Eckert, Rinde, 1951A
Eckhard, Jacob, 1757A, 1833B
Eckhardt-Gramatté, S. C. "Sonia," 1899A,
   1974B
Eckhart, Janis (Gail), 1953A, 1981C
Eckstein, Pavel, 1911A, 1969D; *The Czechoslovak*
   Contemporary Opera, 1976H; *Czechoslovak*
   Opera, 1964H
École de Musique de la Ville d'Anvers, 1842G
École Normale pour Pianistes, 1912G
Eda-Pierre, Christiane, 1932A, 1958C
Eddy, Clarence, 1851A, 1937B; *The Church &*
   Concert Organist I, 1882H; *The Church &*
   Concert Organist II, 1885H; *A Method for Pipe*
   Organ, 1917H; *The Organ in Church*, 1887H
Eddy, Nelson, 1901A, 1967B
Edelman, Otto, 1917A, 1937C
Edelmann, J. F., Publisher, 1794B, 1836G
Edelmann, Sergei, 1960A, 1970C, 1978F
Eden, Irene, 1893A, 1915C
Eden-Tamir Piano Duo, 1952G
Eder, Helmut, 1916B, 1962E
Éder String Quartet, 1972G

Edinburgh, Scotland: Athenaeum School of
   Music, 1890G; Experimental Arts Society,
   1972G; Festival Chorus, 1965G; Music
   Festival, 1947G; Royal Choral Union, 1858G;
   Royal Scottish Academy, 1890G; Saint
   Cecilia Hall, 1762G; Society of Musicians,
   1887G; University Music Dept., 1861G;
   University Music Society, 1865G
Edinburgh Monthly Magazine, 1817G
Edinburgh Review, 1802G
Edinger, Christine, 1945A
Edition Peters (Leipzig), 1868G
Editions Russes de Musique, 1909G
Editions Salabert, Publisher (Paris), 1896G
Edlinger, Richard, 1958A
Edlund, Lars, 1922A
Edmonton Symphony Orchestra, 1952G
Educational Media Associates of American,
   Inc., 1968G
Educazione Musicale, 1964G
Edvaldsdóttir, Sigrún, 1967A
Edwards, Clara, 1887A, 1974B
Edwards, Frederick, 1897D
Edwards, Gus, 1945B
Edwards, Henry S.: *History of the Opera...to the*
   Present Time, 1862H; *The Lyric Drama I, II*,
   1881H; *The Prima Donna I, II*, 1888H
Edwards, John S., 1967D, 1975E
Edwards, Julian, 1855A, 1910B
Edwards, Phillipine, 1851A
Edwards, Sian, 1959A, 1986C, 1988F, 1993D
Edwards, Phillipine, 1930B
Edwards, Ross, 1943A
Eeden, Jan van den, 1869E, 1878D
Eeden, Jean-Baptiste van den, 1842A, 1917B
Effinger, Cecil, 1914A, 1990B
Efraty, Anat, 1970A, 1993C
Egge, Klaus, 1906A, 1945D, 1949E, 1958E,
   1979B
Eggebrecht, Hans Heinrich, 1919A;
   Musikalische Denken: Aufsätze zur Theorie und
   Ästhetic der Musik, 1977H; *Orgelbau &*
   Orgelmusik in Russland, 1991H; *Die*
   Orgelbewegung, 1967H
Eggebrecht, James, 1964D
Eggen, Arne, 1955B
Eggen, Erik, 1877A, 1957B
Egk, Werner, 1901A, 1983B
Egmond, Max von, 1936A
Egorov, Yuri, 1954A, 1975F, 1976F, 1988B
Egri, Monika, 1966A
Ehde, John, 1962A, 1987C
Ehlers, Alice, 1887A, 1981B
Ehmann, Wilhelm, 1989B; *Alte Musik in der*
   neuen Welt, 1961H; *Die Chorführung*, 1949H;
   Erziehung zur Kirchenmusik, 1951H;
   Kirchenmusik, Vermächtnis & Aufgabe, 1958H
Ehrbar, Friedrich, 1827A, 1905B
Ehrbar, Friedrich, Organ Factory, 1857G

❈

A *Births*   B *Deaths*   C *Debuts*   D *New Positions*
E *Prizes/Honors*

Ehrenberg, Carl, 1962B
Ehrlich, Abel, 1915A
Ehrlich Heinrich: *Celebrated Pianists, Past and Present*, 1893H; *Lebenskunst und Kunstleben*, 1884H; *Musikstudium und Klavierspiel*, 1891H
Ehrling, Sixten, 1918A, 1940C, 1953D, 1963D, 1993D
Eibenschütz, José, 1894D
Eibenschütz, Riza, 1870A, 1895C, 1946B
Eichberg, Julius, 1824A, 1867D, 1893B
Eichheim, Henry, 1870A, 1942B
Eichheim, Kurt, 1967D
Eichhorn, Kurt, 1908A, 1941D, 1967D, 1994B
Eichner, Adelheid, 1762A, 1787B
Eichner, Ernst, 1777B
Eidgenössicher Musikverein, 1862G
Eilers, Albert, 1830A, 1854C, 1896B
Eimert, Herbert, 1897A, 1972B; *Atonale musiklehre*, 1924H; *Grundlagen der musikalischern Reihhen technik*, 1963H; *Lehrbuch der Zwölftontechnik*, 1950H
Einem, Gottfried von, 1918A, 1941F, 1996B; *Komponist & Gesellschaft*, 1967H; *Musikalische Selbstporträt...von...unserer Zeit*, 1963H
Einstein Alfred, 1880A, 1952B; *Geschichte der Music*, 1917H; *Greatness in Music*, 1941H; *The Italian Madrigal*, 1949H; *Music in the Romantic Era*, 1947H; *A Short History of Music*, 1936H; *Lexikon der elektronishchen Musik*, 1973H
Einwald, Carl Joseph, 1753B
Eisenberg, Maurice, 1900A, 1916C, 1972B
Eisenbrandt, C. H., 1790B
Eisfeld, Theodor, 1852D
Eisinger, Irene, 1903A, 1926C, 1994B
Eisler, Hanns, 1962B
Eisler, Paul: *World Chronology of Music*, 1978H
Eisma, Will, 1929A
Eitner, Robert, 1832A, 1869D, 1905B; *Biographisch-Bibliographisches Quellen-Lexicon I*, 1900H; *Hilfsbuch beim Klavierunterricht*, 1871H; *Quellenlexicon der Musiker I*, 1899H
Ek, Gunnar, 1981B
Ekman, Karl, 1869A, 1907D, 1947B
Eklund, Anna, 1964A
Eklund, Hans, 1927A, 1975E
Ekman, Ida, 1875A
Elberfeld, Germany: Rauchenecker Music School, 1889G
El-Dabh, Halim, 1921A; *Derabucca: Hand Techniques in the Art of Drumming, The*, 1965H
Elder, Mark Philip, 1948A, 1974D, 1986D, 1989DE, 1992F, 1999D
Electric Metronome, 1939G
Electric Piano, 1937G
Electroacoustic Music Association of Great Britain, 1980G
Electronic Music Center at Columbia-Princeton, 1953G

Electronic Music Studio of the West German Radio, 1951G
Electronic Weasel Ensemble, 1974G
Elektra Womens' Choir, 1987G
Elewyck, Xavier van, 1883E
Elgar, Edward, 1857A, 1879F, 1885D, 1900E, 1904E, 1905EF, 1906E, 1907F, 1911E, 1924E, 1931E, 1934B
Elias, Manuel Jorge de, 1939A, 1973B
Elias, Rosalind, 1930A, 1954C
Eliasson, Anders, 1947A
Eliazaga Music Publishers, 1826G
Elizaga, José Mariano, 1786A, 1822D, 1842B; *Elementos de música*, 1823H; *Principios de la harmonia y de la melodia*, 1835H
Elizalde, Federico, 1908A, 1930D, 1979B
Elkan, Henri, 1897A, 1903G, 1926G, 1928D, 1960G, 1980B
Elkan & Schildknecht, Publishers, 1859G
Elkus, Albert, 1884A, 1962B
Elkus, Jonathan, 1931A
Ella, John, 1802A, 1888B; *Lectures on Dramatic Music Abroad and at Home*, 1872H; *Musical Sketches Abroad and at Home*, 1861H
Ellberg, Ernst, 1912E
Eller, Heino, 1970B
Elleviou, Jean, 1769A, 1790C, 1842B
Ellingwood, Leonard, 1905A, 1994B; *The History of American Church Music*, 1953H
Elliott, K.: *A History of Scottish Music*, 1973H
Elliott, Paul, 1950A
Ellis, Alexander, 1814A, 1890B
Ellis, Brent, 1946A, 1965C
Ellis, Ossian: *The Story of the Harp in Wales*, 1991H
Ellsasser, Richard, 1926A, 1972B
Ellsworth, Warren, 1954A
Elman, Mischa, 1891A, 1904C, 1967B
Elman String Quartet, 1926G
Elmblad, Johannes, 1853A
Elmendorff, Carl, 1891A, 1916C, 1925D, 1937D, 1942D, 1962B
Elming, Poul, 1989C
Elmo, Cloe, 1910A, 1932E, 1934C, 1962B
Eloy, Jean-Claude, 1938
El Paso, Texas: Chamber Music Festival, 1991G; Pro-Musica, 1977G
Elsner, Joseph, 1769A, 1792D, 1805E, 1823E, 1854B; *The Beginnings of Music, Especially of Singing*, 1821H; *School of Singing*, 1834H
Elson, Arthur, 1873A, 1920D, 1940B; *The Book of Musical Knowledge*, 1915H; *A Critical History of Opera*, 1901H; *Modern Composers of Europe*, 1905H; *The Musician's Guide*, 1913H; *Orchestra Instruments & Their Use*, 1902H; *Pioneer School Music Course*, 1917H; *Women's Work in Music*, 1903H
Elson, Louis C., 1848A, 1886D, 1920B; *Curiosities of Music*, 1880H; *Elson's Music*

❂

F *Biographical*   G *Cultural Beginnings*   H *Musical Literature*
I *Musical Compositions*

Elson, Louis C., (cont.)
Dictionary, 1905H; The History of American
Music, 1904H; History of German Song,
1888H; Mistakes & Disputed Points in Music,
1910H; Modern Music & Musicians, 1912H;
National Music of America and Its Sources,
1899H; Shakespeare in Music, 1901H; The
Theory of Music, 1890H; Women in Music,
1918H
Elston, Arnold, 1907A, 1971B
Elvey, George, 1816A, 1871E, 1893B
Elvey, Stephen, 1805A, 1860B
Elvira, Pablo, 1937A, 1968C, 2000B
Elwart, Antoine-Aimable, 1808A, 1834E,
1877B; Feuille harmonique, 1841H; Histoire de
la Société...du Conservatoire, 1860H; Petit
manuel d'harmonie, 1839H; Petit manuel
d'instrumentation, 1864H; Théorie musicale,
1840H; Traité de contrepoint et de la fugue,
1845H
Elwell, Herbert, 1898A, 1923E, 1932D, 1974B
Elwer and Co., Publishers, 1820G
Elwes, Gervase, 1866A, 1921B
Elysium Recordings, Inc., 1995G
Emblad, Johannes, 1910B
Emborg, Jens Laursen, 1876A, 1957B
Emerson, Luther Orlando, 1820A, 1915B; The
Golden Harp, 1860H; The Golden Wreath,
1857H; The Harp of Judah, 1863H; Merry
Chimes, 1865H
Emerson String Quartet, 1976G
Emmanuel, Maurice, 1862A, 1938B; La
polyphonie sacrée, 1923H
Emmett, Daniel, 1904B
Empire Brass Quintet, 1971G
Empire State Musical Festival, 1955G
Enckhausen, Heinrich Friedrich, 1799A, 1885B
Endelion String Quartet, 1979G
Enderle, Wilhelm Gottfired, 1790B
Endler, Johann Samuel, 1760D, 1762B
Endo, Akira, 1938A, 1969D, 1975D, 1980D
Enescu, Georges, 1881A, 1889C, 1923F, 1932E,
1937F, 1954F, 1955B
Enescu Festival, 1958G
Enescu Prize in Composition, 1912G
Enescu Symphony Orchestra, 1917G
Engel, Carl (I), 1818A, 1882B; Early History of
the Violin Family, 1883H; An Introduction to
the Study of National Music, 1866H; The
Literature of National Music, 1879H; Music of
the Most Ancient Nations, 1864H; Musical
Instruments of All Countries, 1869H; Musical
Myths and Facts, 1876H
Engel, Carl (II), 1883A, 1909D, 1922D, 1929D,
1934E, 1935E, 1944B; Alla Breve: Bach to
Debussy, 1921H; Discords Mingled, 1931H
Engel, Hans, 1894A, 1970B; Deutschland &
Italien in ihren musikgeschichtlichen
Beziehungen, 1944H; Musik der Völker &
Zeiten, 1951H

Engel, Johann J., 1802B; Über die musikalische
Malerei, 1780H
Engel, Lehman, 1910A, 1982B
Engel, Werner, 1884A, 1906C
England (see also Birmingham, Bournemouth,
Bradford, Brighton, Bristol, Canterbury,
Cardiff, Huddersfield, Leeds, Liverpool,
London, Manchester, Newcastle, Norwich,
Nottingham, Sheffield, Winchester,
Worcester, York): Buxton Festival
(Derbyshire), 1979G; Centre for American
Music, 1974G; Dorian Singers, 1945G;
National Central Library of England, 1916G;
Society for the Promotion of New Music,
1942G; Sonic Arts Society, 1980G
Englert, Anton, 1751B
English, Granville, 1895A, 1968B
English Bach Festival, 1963G
English Baroque Soloists, 1977G
English Chamber Orchestra, 1960G
English Concert, 1973G
English Consort of Viols, 1935G
English Folk Dance Society, 1911G
English Folk Song Society, 1898G
English Horn, 1760G
English Madrigal Singers, 1920G
English National Opera, 1931G
English Opera Co. (I), 1838G
English Opera Co. (II), 1873G
English Opera Group, 1947G
English String Quartet, 1909G
English String Orchestra, 1980G
English Symphony Orchestra, 1989G
Englund, Einer, 1916A, 1999B
Engramelle Marie: La tonotechnie, 1775H
Enoch & Sons, Publishers, 1867G
Enriquez, Manuel, 1994B
Ens, Phillip, 1962A, 1985C
Ensemble Capriccio, 1982G
Ensemble Concertant Frankfurt, 1987G
Ensemble Grupo Novo Horizonte, 1988G
Ensemble for Contemporary Music, 1977G
Ensemble for Early Music, 1974G
Ensemble for Viennese Music, 19987G
Ensemble Kalinda Chicago, 1994G
Ensemble Louis Berger, 1994G
Ensemble Mobile, 1989G
Ensemble Nipponia, 1964G
Ensemble Organum, 1982G
Ensemble TRA I TEMPI, 1992G
Enthoven, Emile, 1903A, 1950B
Entremont, Philippe, 1934A, 1951CE, 1976D,
1979D, 1987D, 1988D
Eolian Review, 1921G
Eötvös, Peter, 1944A, 1979D, 1997E
Eppert, Carl, 1882A, 1961B
Epstein, David M., 1930A; Beyond Orpheus:
Studies in Musical Structure, 1979H; Shaping
Time: Music, the Brain, & Performance, 1995H
Epstein, Richard, 1869A, 1919B

�֎

A   Births   B   Deaths   C   Debuts   D   New Positions
E   Prizes/Honors

Epstein Award for Archival & Library
  Research in American Music, 1997G
Equinox 1992, 1992G
Erard Piano and Harp Manufacturers (Paris),
  1779G
Érard, Sébastien, 1752A, 1777F, 1780F, 1831B
Erato String Quartet, 1983G
Erb, Donald, 1927A, 1982D, 1985E
Erb, John Lawrence, 1905D, 1914D, 1950B
Erb, Karl, 1877A, 1907C, 1958B
Erben, Henry, 1800A, 1884B
Erben Organ (St. Patrick's), 1868G
Erdélyi, Miklós, 1993B
Erdmannsdörfer, Max von, 1871D
Erdödy Chamber Orchestra, 1994G
Erede, Alberto, 1908A, 1930C
Erevan Theater of Opera & Ballet, 1933G
Erickson, Frank, 1923A, 1996B
Erickson, Kaaren, 1953A, 1982E, 1997B
Erickson, Robert, 1917A, 1981E, 1997B; *Sound
  Structures in Music*, 1975H; *The Structure of
  Music*, 1955H
Ericson, Eric, 1951D
Erkel, Franz, 1809A, 1836D, 1838D, 1853D,
  1875D, 1893B
Erkel, Gyula, 1842A, 1909A
Erlanger, Camille, 1888E
Ermedahl, Mattias, 1971A, 1994C
Ernst, Heinrich W., 1814A, 1831C, 1865B
Ernst, Franz Anton, 1805B
Ernster, Deszö, 1898A, 1926C, 1981B
Eroica String Quartet, 1993G
Erös, Peter, 1972D
Errani, Achille, 1823A, 1897B
Errecart, Héctor Tosar, 1923A
Ershov, Ivan, 1867A, 1893C, 1943B
Erskine, John, 1879A, 1928D, 1951B; *A Musical
  Companion*, 1935H; *The Philharmonic-
  Symphony Society of New York*, 1943H; *What is
  Music?*, 1944H
Erskine, Thomas Alexander, 1781B
Ertmann, Dorothea von, 1781A, 1849B
Escalaïs, Léon, 1859A, 1883C, 1941B
Eschenbach, Christoph, 1940A, 1952E, 1965E,
  1966D, 1979D, 1981D, 1988D, 1994F, 1995D,
  1998D
Escher, Rudolf (George), 1980B
Eschig, Max, Publishing Co., 1907G
Eschmann, Johann Carl, 1826A, 1882B
Eschmann, Karl: *Changing Forms in Modern
  Music*, 1945H
Escot, Pozzi: *The Poetics of Simple Mathematics
  in Music*, 1999H
Escudier Publishing House, 1842G
Escuela moderna de musica, 1940G
Esham, Faith, 1948A, 1977C
Eshpai, Andrei, 1925A
Eslava, Hilarión, 1807A, 1832D, 1844D, 1866D,
  1878B; *Escuela de armonía y composición*,
  1861H; *Escuela de contrapunto, fuga y*

composición, 1870H; *Método de solféo sin
  acompaña-miento*, 1846H; *Lira Sacra-Hispana*,
  1869H
Espace Musique Contemporary, 1984G
Espagne, Franz, 1858D
La España, 1846G
Esperian, Kallen, 1961A, 1985E
Esplá, Oscar, 1886A, 1976B
Esposito, Michele, 1899D
Esposito, Valeria, 1961A, 1986C
Essays on Modern Music, 1984G
Essen, Germany: Bergkapelle, 1816G; Bühnen
  der Stadt Essen, 1892G; Gesang-
  Musikverein, 1838G; Opera House, 1950G;
  Symphony Orchestra, 1899G
Essential Music, 1987G
Esser, Heinrich, 1818A, 1845D, 1847D, 1872B
Esser, Michael, 1772E
Essipova, Anna, 1851A, 1914B
Esswood, Paul, 1965C
Estel, Edgar: *Die Entstehung der deutschen
  Melodramas*, 1906H; *Die komische Oper*, 1906H
Esterhazy, Nicholas, 1790B
Esterhazy Opera House I, 1768G
Esterházy Opera House II, 1781G
Estes, Simon, 1938A, 1965CE, 1966F, 1978F
Estes, Richard, 1948A, 1980C
Esteve, Pierre: *Dialogue sur les arts*, 1756H;
  L'esprit des beaux-arts, 1753H; *Nouvelle
  découverte du principe de l'harmonie*, 1751H
Esteve y Grimau, Pablo, 1794B
Estey Piano Co., 1885G
Estey Organ Co., 1846G
Estienne, Françjois, 1755B
Estonian State Symphony Orchestra, 1926G
Estrada, Julio, 1943A
Etcheverry, Henri-Bertrand, 1900A, 1932C,
  1960B
Ethnographical Review, 1889G
Ethnomusicology, 1953G
Etler, Alvin, 1913A, 1973B; *Making Music: An
  Introduction to Theory*, 1974H
Ett, Caspar, 1788A, 1847B
The Etude, 1893G, 1896G
Eulenberg, Ernest, 1926B
Eulenburg, Ernst, Publisher, 1847A, 1874G
Euler, Leonhardt, 1783B; *Conjecture sur la raison
  de quelques dissonances*, 1764H; *Lettres à une
  princess d'Allemagne*, 1774H
Europa Galante, 1989G
Europe, James Reese, 1919B
European Community Youth Orchestra, 1978G
European Soloists Ensemble, 1992G
Euterpeiad, or Musical Intelligencer, 1820G
Evans, Anne, 1941A, 1968C
Evans, Damon, 1960A, 1985C
Evans, Joseph, 1950A, 1976C
Evans, Geraint, 1922A, 1948C, 1959E, 1969E,
  1992B
Evans, Nancy, 1915A, 1933C, 2000B

❊

F   *Biographical*   G   *Cultural Beginnings*   H   *Musical Literature*
           I   *Musical Compositions*

Evanti, Lillian, 1926C, 1934F
Everest Records, Inc., 1962G
Everett Piano Co. (Boston), 1883G
Evett, Robert, 1922A, 1975B
Evstatieva, Stefka, 1947A, 1971C
Ewen, David, 1907A, 1985B; *American Composers: A Biographical Dictionary*, 1982H; *The Book of Modern Composers*, 1942H; *Dictators of the Baton*, 1943H; *Modern Music*, 1962H; *Music Comes to America*, 1942H; *New Encyclopedia of the Opera*, 1971H
Ewer & Co., 1823G
Eweyk, Arthur van, 1866A, 1891C
Ewing, Maria, 1950A, 1973C, 1987F
EXASTUD, 1971G
Eximeno, Antonio, 1808B; *Dell'origine e delle regole della musica...*, 1774H
Experimental Music Center (Colorado), 1964G
Experimental Music Studio (Illinois), 1958G
Experimental Music Studio (MIT), 1973G
Expert, Henri, 1863A, 1909D, 1921D, 1952B; *Maître-Musiciens de la renaissance française*, 1894H, 1908H; *Monuments de la musique française au temps de la renaissance I*, 1924H
Exposition (Civic) Auditorium (San Francisco), 1915G
Express Yourself Festival, 1995G
Eybler, Joseph L., 1765A, 1824D, 1846B
Fabbri, Guerrina, 1886A, 1885C, 1946B
Fabbri, Inez, 1909B
Fabbricini, Tiziana, 1961A
Faber & Faber, 1964G
Fabri, Annibale Pio, 1760B
Fabritiis, Olivero De, 1902A
Faccio, Franco, 1840A, 1871D, 1891B
Facco, Giacomo, 1753B
Die Fackel, 1899G
Faelten, Carl, 1846A, 1890D, 1925B; *Conservatory Course for Pianists*, 1889H
Faelten, Reinhold, 1949B
Faenza Teatro Communale, 1788G
Fagan, Gideon, 1904A, 1980B
Fagnola, Annibale, Violin Maker, 1890G
Fairbanks & Cole, Banjo Makers, 1880G
Fairchild, Blair, 1877A, 1933B
Fairlamb, James Remington, 1838A, 1908B
Fair Park Music Hall, 1925G
Faisst, Immanuel, 1823A, 1859D, 1894B
Faitello, Vigilio Blasio, 1768B
Fajer, Francisco Javier García, 1756D
Falckenhagen, Adam, 1754B
Falcon, Marie-Cornélie, 1814A, 1832C, 1897B
Falcon, Ruth, 1946A, 1974C
Falkoner Center Theater, 1959G
Falla, Manuel de, 1876A, 1900F, 1946B
Falletta, JoAnn, 1954A, 1978D, 1985E, 1986D, 1989D, 1991D, 1998D
Falsenreitschule, 1933G
Falter und Sohn, Publishers (Munich), 1796G

Famous Music Corporation, 1928G
Fanciulli, Francesco, 1850A, 1915B
Fancelli, Giuseppe, 1833A, 1866C, 1888B
Fanfare, 1977G
Fanneti, Maria, 1955B
Fano, Guido Alberto, 1875A, 1905D, 1912D, 1916D, 1961B; *Nella vita del ritmo*, 1916H; *Pensieri sulla musica*, 1903H; *Lo studio del pianoforte*, 1923H
Farago, Marcel, 1924A
Farbach, Kent, 1961A
Farberman, Harold, 1929A
Farinelli (Carlo Broschi), 1761F, 1782B
Farinelli, Giuseppe, 1769A, 1836B
Farington, Joseph, 1785E
Farkas, Philip, 1914A, 1992B; *The Art of Brass Playing*, 1962H; *The Art of French Horn Playing*, 1956H
Farley, Carole Ann, 1946A, 1969C
Farmer, Henry: *Heresy in Art*, 1918H; *History of Music in Scotland*, 1908H; *Oriental Studies, Mainly Musical*, 1953H
Farnadi, Edith, 1921A, 1933C, 1973B
Farneti, Maria, 1878A, 1898C
Farnham Festival, 1961G
Farnsworth, Charles H., 1888D, 1947B; *Education Through Music*, 1909H
Farr, Gareth, 1968A
Farrar, Geraldine, 1882A, 1901C; *Such Sweet Compulsion*, 1938H
Farrell, Eileen, 1920A, 1940C
Farrenc, Aristide, 1794A, 1865B
Farrenc, Jeanne Louise, 1804A, 1875B
Farta, Alexandre de, 1972B
Farwell, Arthur, 1872A, 1899F, 1909D, 1910F, 1952B; *A Letter to American Composers*, 1903H
Fasch, Carl Friedrich, 1774D, 1800B
Fasch, Johann Friedrich, 1758B
Fassbaender, Brigitte, 1939A, 1961C
Fassbender, Zdenka, 1879A, 1899C, 1954B
Fäsy, Albert, 1837A, 1891B
Faulds, Stone & Morse, Publishers, 1854G
Faull, Ellen, 1918A, 1947C
Faure, Jean-Baptiste, 1830A, 1852C, 1914B
Fauré, Gabriel, 1845A, 1866D, 1892D, 1903D, 1905D, 1909E, 1920E, 1924B
Faust, Isabelle, 1972A, 1993E
Favero, Mafalda, 1903A, 1926C, 1981B
Favart, Charles-Simon, 1758D, 1792B; *Mémoires...littéraires, dramatiques*, 1808H
Favart, Marie, 1772B
Fävrier, Henry, 1957B
Fawcett, John, 1789A, 1867B
Fay, Amy, 1844A, 1876C, 1928B; *Music Study in Germany*, 1881H
Fay, Maude, 1878A, 1906C, 1964B
Fayolle, François Joseph, 1774A, 1852B; *Dictionnaire des musiciens I*, 1810H
Fazioli Piano Co., 1981G

❄

A   *Births*   B   *Deaths*   C   *Debuts*   D   *New Positions*
E   *Prizes/Honors*

Fechner, Gustav, 1801A, 1887B; *Vorschule der Aesthetik*, 1870H
Federal Music Project of the Works Progress Administration, 1935G
Federal Arts Project, 1933G
Fédération Internationale des Jeunesses Musicales, 1945G
Federici, Francesco, 1873A, 1898C, 1934B
Federici, Vincenzo, 1764A, 1826B
Fedoseyev, Vladimir, 1932A, 1974D
Feghali, José, 1985E
Feigin, Joel, 1951A
Feinhals, Fritz, 1869A, 1895C, 1940B
Feinstein, Martin, 1972D
Feis Ceoil (Irish Festival), 1897G
Feist, Leo, Publisher, 1895G
Fel, Antoine, 1771B
Fel, Marie, 1794B
Felciano, Richard, 1930A, 1974E; *Orchestration*, 1980H
Feldhoff, Gerd, 1931A, 1959C
Feldman, Jill, 1952A, 1979C
Feldman, Morton, 1926A, 1970E, 1987B; *Essays*, 1985H; *Illusions*, 1949H
Félibrige Organization, 1854G
Felici, Alessandro, 1772B
Felici, Bartolomeo, 1776B
Felix, Hugo, 1866A, 1934B
Feller, Franz, and Sons, Organ Builders, 1817G
Fellner, Till, 1972A
Fellowes, Edmund H., 1870A, 1951B; *English Cathedral Music from Edward VI to Edward VII*, 1941H; *The English Madrigal*, 1925H; *English Madrigal Composers*, 1921H; *The English Madrigal School I*, 1913H
Felton, William, 1769B
Feltsman, Vladimir, 1952A, 1963C, 1971E, 1979F, 1987F
Female Composers of America, 1976G
Fenaroli, Fedele, 1777D; *Partimento ossia Basso numerato*, 1800H; *Regole musicali per i principianti de cembalo*, 1775H; *Studio del contrappunto*, 1800H
Fenby, Eric, 1906A, 1997B
Fender Electric Instruments Co., 1946G
Fenlon, Iain: *The Renaissance*, 1990H
Fennell, Frederick, 1914A; *Time & the Winds*, 1954H
Fennelly, Brian, 1937A
Feo, Francesco, 1761B
Ferencsik, János, 1907A, 1945D, 1951E, 1952D, 1953D, 1984B
Ferguson, Donald, 1882A, 1985B; *A History of Musical Thought*, 1935H; *Image & Structure in chamber music*, 1964H; *Masterworks of the Orchestral Repertoire*, 1954H; *On the elements of Expression in Music*, 1944H; *A Short History of Music*, 1943H

Ferguson, Howard: *Keyboard Interpretation*, 1975H
Fernandez, Oscar Lorenzo, 1897A, 1948B
Fernandez, Wilhelmina, 1949A, 1977C
Ferneyhough, Brian, 1943A
Ferni-Giraldoni, Carolina, 1839A, 1862C, 1926B
Fernström, John, 1897A, 1953E, 1961B
Ferrandini, Giovanni Battista, 1791B
Ferrani, Cesira, 1863A, 1887C, 1943B
Ferrar Geraldine, 1967B
Ferrara, Lawrence, 1949A
Ferrara, Italy: Liceo Musicale "G. Frescobaldi," 1869G; Società dell Quartetto, 1898G
Ferraresi del Bene, Adriana, 1755A, 1788F, 1791F
Ferrari, Carlo, 1790B
Ferrari, Domenico, 1780B
Ferrari, Giacomo, 1763A, 1842B; *Anecdotti piacevole...accorsi nella vita di G. F.*, 1830H; *Breve trattato di canto italiano*, 1818H; *Studio di musica teorica pratica*, 1830H
Ferrari-Fontana, Edoardo, 1878A, 1909C, 1936B
Ferras, Christian, 1933A, 1942C, 1982B
Ferrata, Giuseppe, 1865A, 1928B
Ferrer, Mateo, 1788A, 1808D, 1827D, 1864B
Ferrer, Santiago, 1762A, 1824B
Ferretti, Paolo: *Il cursus metrico e il ritmo delle melodie del Canto Gregoriano*, 1913H; *Estètica gregoriana I*, 1934H
Ferreyra, Beatriz, 1937A
Ferrier, Karhleen, 1912A, 1943C, 1953B
Ferris, William, 2000B
Ferro, Gabriele, 1992D
Ferroud, Pierre-Octave, 1900A, 1936B
Fesca, Alexander, 1820A, 1849B
Fesca, Friedrich, 1789A, 1800C, 1826B
Festa, Giuseppe Maria, 1771A, 1839B
Festing, Michael, 1752B
Festinger, Richard, 1948A
Festival Internacional Cervantino, 1973G
Festival-Institute at Round Top, 1971G
Festival of a Thousand Oaks, 1978G
Festival of Two Worlds (Spoleto), 1958G
Festival of Two Worlds, U.S.A., 1977G
Festival of Venetian Music of the 17th & 18th Centuries, 1975G
Fétis, Édouard (-Louis), 1812A, 1909B
Fétis, François, 1784A, 1800F, 1806F, 1813D, 1821D, 1827D, 1833D, 1871B; *Curiosités historiques de la musique*, 1830H; *Esquisse de l'histoire de l'harmonie*, 1840H; *Histoire générale de la Musique I*, 1869H; *Mémoire sur l'harmonie simultanée*, 1858H; *Les musiciens belges*, 1848H; *Solfège progressif*, 1827H; *The Theory & Practice of Harmony*, 1844H; *Traité du chant en choeur*, 1837H; *Traité du contrepoint et de la fugue*, 1824H; *Universal Biography of Musicians and Music I*, 1833H
Feuermann, Emanuel, 1902A, 1913C, 1942B

※

F *Biographical*   G *Cultural Beginnings*   H *Musical Literature*
I *Musical Compositions*

Feuillet, Octave, 1862E
Feurich Piano Co., 1851G
Février, Henri, 1875A
Février, Jacques, 1900A
Ffrangcon-Davies, David Thomas, 1855A, 1890C, 1918B
Fiala, Joseph, 1816B
Fialkowska, Janina, 1951A
Fibich, Zdeněk, 1850A, 1874F, 1900B
Fickénscher, Arthur, 1871A, 1920D, 1954B
Fiedler, Arthur, 1894A, 1930D, 1976E, 1977E, 1979B
Fiedler, Max, 1908D
Field, John, 1782A, 1792C, 1802F, 1831F, 1837B
Field-Hyde, Margaret, 1905A, 1928C
Fields, James, 1948A
Fields, Lew, 1867A
Fields, Matthew H., 1961A
Figaro in London, 1831G
Figner, Medea, 1859A
Figner, Nikolai, 1857A, 1882C, 1918B
Figueredo, Carlos, 1986A
Figueroa, Rafael, 1961A
Filas, Juraj, 1959A
Filene Center (Wolf Trap), 1984G
Filharmonica della Scala, 1982G
Filharmoniska Sällskapet, 1849G, 1885G, 1900G
Filipova, Elena, 1957A, 1981C
Filippeschi, Mario, 1907A, 1937C, 1980B
Filippi, Filippo, 1830A, 1858D, 1859D, 1862D, 1887B
Filleborn, Daniel, 1841A, 1862C, 1904B
Fillmore, John Comfort, 1884D
Fillmore, Henry, 1881A, 1956B
Fillmore Band, 1915G
Fillunger, Marie, 1850A, 1930B
Filtz, Anton, 1760B
Finazzi, Filippo, 1776B
Finck, Henry T., 1854A, 1881D, 1926B; *Chopin and Other Musical Essays*, 1889H; *Musical Laughs*, 1924H; *Musical Progress*, 1923H; *My Adventures in the Golden Age*, 1926H
Findeisen, Nikolai, 1868A, 1893D, 1928B; *A History of Russian Music*, 1928H; *Musical Antiquity*, 1910H
Fine, Irving, 1914A, 1955E, 1962B
Fine, Vivian, 1913A, 1979E, 2000B
Fine Arts String Quartet, 1946G
Fingerhut, Margaret, 1955A
Fink, Gottfried W., 1783A, 1808D, 1828D, 1846B; *Musikalischer hausschatz*, 1843H
Fink, Michael Jon, 1954A
Fink, Myron S., 1932A
Finko, David, 1936A
Finley, Gerald, 1960A, 1986C
Finney, Ross Lee, 1906A, 1943F, 1956E, 1962E, 1967E, 1997B; *Thinking About Music: Collected Writings*, 1990H

Finney, Theodore, 1902A, 1978B; *A History of Music*, 1935H; *We Have Made Music*, 1955H
Finnie, Linda, 1952A, 1976C
Finnilä, Birgit, 1931A, 1963C
Finland (*see also* Helsinki, Kuhmo, Jyväskylä, Lahti, Tampere): Finnish Composer's Union, 1917G; Music Information Center, 1963G; Finnish Musicological Society, 1916G; National Opera Co., 1873G; Opera Co., 1911G; Philharmonic Choir, 1979G; Radio Chamber Choir, 1962G; Royal Orchestra, 1927G
Finnissy, Michael, 1946A
Finscher, Ludwig: *Musik in Geschichte und Gegenwart I, 2nd Ed.*, 1994H
Finzi, Gerald, 1901A, 1956B
Fioravanti, Valentino, 1764A, 1801D, 1816D, 1837B
Fioravanti, Vincenzo, 1799A, 1839D, 1877B
Fiore, John, 1991C
Fiorenza, Nicola, 1764B
Fiorillo, Federigo, 1755A, 1783D
Fiorillo, Ignazio, 1754D, 1762D, 1787B
Fioroni, Giovanni, 1765E, 1778B
Fiqué, Karl, 1867A, 1930B
Firberth, Karl, 1796E
Firenze, Italy: Società del Quartetto, 1861G; Teatro Communale di Firenze, 1928G
Firkun, Rudolf, 1912A, 1920C, 1994B
Firth, John, Piano Maker, 1815G
Firth, Hall & Pond, Piano Makers, 1815G, 1820G
Fischel, Edwin A., 1877A
Fischer, Ádám, 1949A, 1949A
Fischer, Annie, 1914A, 1922C, 1930E, 1995B
Fischer, Anton, 1778A, 1808B
Fisher, Avery, 1906A, 1977E, 1994B
Fisher, Avery, Competition, 1975G
Fischer, Carl, 1849A, 1923B
Fischer, Carl, Inc., Publisher, 1872G
Fischer, Carl, Los Angeles Branch, 1935G
Fischer, Carl, San Francisco Branch, 1969G
Fischer, Christian W., 1789A, 1817C, 1859B
Fischer, Edwin, 1886A, 1960B; *Musikalische Betrachtungen*, 1949H; *Von den Aufgaben des Musikers*, 1960H
Fischer, Emil, 1838A, 1857C, 1914B
Fischer, Hanne, 1968A, 1993C
Fischer, Irwin, 1903A, 1974D, 1977B; *A Handbook of Modal Counterpoint*, 1967H
Fischer, Iván, 1951A, 1984D
Fischer, Johann Christian, 1800B
Fischer, J., & Brother, 1864G
Fischer, Ludwig, 1825B
Fischer, Matthäus, 1763A, 1840B
Fischer, Michael Gottard, 1773A, 1829B
Fischer, Res, 1896A, 1927C, 1974B
Fischer, Wilhelm, 1886A, 1962B; *Zur Entwicklungsgeschichte des Wiener klassischen Stils*, 1915H

❄

A   *Births*   B   *Deaths*   C   *Debuts*   D   *New Positions*
E   *Prizes/Honors*

Fischer-Dieskau, Dietrich, 1925A, 1947C
Fischietti, Domenico, 1766D, 1772D
Fisher, Nina, 1940A
Fisher, John Abraham, 1806B
Fisher, Norma, 1956C
Fisher, Suzanne, 1990B
Fisher, Sylvia, 1910A, 1932C, 1996B
Fisher, William Arms, 1861A, 1897D, 1948B;
    Notes on Music in Old Boston, 1918H; Ye Olde
    New England Psalm Tunes (1620-1820) with
    Historical Sketches, 1930H
Fisk, Charles Benton, 1925A, 1983B
Fisk, C. B., Inc., Organ Builders, 1955G
Fisk, Eliot, 1954A, 1976C
Fissot, Alexis-Henri, 1843A, 1896B
Fistoulari, Anatole, 1907A, 1995B
Fitelberg, Jerzy, 1903A, 1951B
Fitzenhagen, Wilhelm, 1848A, 1862C, 1890B
Fitzner String Quartet, 1894G
Fitzpatrick, Robert, 1986D
Fizdale, Robert, 1944C, 1995B
Fitzwilliam Collection and Museum, 1816G
Fitzwilliams, Edward Francis, 1824A, 1857B
Fjeldstad, Øivin, 1903A, 1931C, 1946D, 1962D,
    1983B
Flackton, William, 1798B
Flagello, Nicolas, 1928A, 1994B
Flagello, Ezio, 1931A, 1952C
Flagg, Josiah, 1794B; Collection of the Best Psalm
    Tunes, 1764H; Sixteen Anthems...Added a Few
    Psalm Tunes, 1766H
Flagstad, Kirsten, 1895A, 1913C, 1958D, 1962B
Flagstad, Kirsten, International Society,
    1975G
Flagstaff Festival of the Arts, 1966G
Flammer, Harold, 1889A, 1939B
Flammer, Harold, Inc., Publisher, 1917G
Flanagan, William, Jr., 1923A, 1968E, 1969B
Flaxland, Gustave-Alexandre, 1821A, 1895B
Flaxland Music Publishers, 1847G
Fleck, Henry R., 1890D
Fleetwood, James, 1935A
Fleischer, Leon, 1928A, 1973D
Fleischer, Oskar, 1856A, 1899D, 1933B; Führer
    durch die...alter Musikinstrumente, 1892H
Fleischer, Tsippi, 1946A
Fleischer-Edel, Katharina, 1875A, 1894C, 1928B
Fleischman, Aloys, 1910A, 1934D, 1992B
Fleisher, Edwin A., 1959B
Fleisher, Leon, 1943C, 1952E, 1964F, 1982F,
    1985D, 1992E
Fleming, Shirley, 1964D
Fleming, Renée, 1959A, 1986C, 1990E
Flemish Opera, 1890G
Flenthrop Organ Co., 1903G
Flesch, Carl, 1873A, 1895C, 1944B; Der Beseelte
    Violinton, 1910H
Flesch, Ella, 1900A, 1920C, 1957B
Fleta, Miguel, 1893A, 1919C, 1938B
Fleta, Pierre, 1925A, 1949C

Fletcher, Alice Cunningham, 1838A, 1923B
Fletcher, Grant, 1913A
Fletzberger, Matthias, 1965A
Fleury, André, 1903A, 1995B
Fleury, Louis, 1878A, 1926B
Fliegende Blätter für Katholische Kirchenmusik,
    1866G
Flight & Robinson, Organ Builders (London),
    1800G
Floersheim, Otto, 1880D
Flonzaley String Quartet (New York), 1902G
Flood, W. H., 1859A, 1928B; History of Irish
    Music, 1895H, 1927H
Floquet, Étienne Joseph, 1785B
Flor, Claus Peter, 1953A, 1984D
Florence, Italy: Concerti Popolari a Grande
    Orchestra, 1863G; Istituto Musicale, 1849G,
    1860G; Liceo Musicale, 1859G; Maglioni
    Chamber Concerts, 1834G; Music Festival,
    1933G; Philharmonic Society, 1830G; Società
    Coprale del Carnine, 1849G
Florentine Gazzetta Musical, 1842G
Florentine String Quartet, 1867G
Florentine Wind Sextet, 1925G
Florida (see also Jacksonville; Miami): Delius
    Association, 1962G; International Festival,
    1966G; Key West Music Festival, 1997G;
    Orchestra, 1968G
Floridia, Pietro, 1860A, 1932B
Florio, Caryl, 1843A, 1920B
Florio, Charles H., 1782C, 1819B
Florio, Pietro Grassi, 1795B
Flotow, Friedrich von, 1813A, 1883B
Flower, Eliza, 1803A, 1846B
Flower, Newman, 1938E
Floyd, Carlisle, 1926A
Flummerfelt, Joseph, 1837A
Flury, Richard, 1896B, 1967B
Fodor, Carolus Antoinus, 1768A, 1846B
Fodor, Carolus Emanuel, 1759A
Fodor, Eugene, 1950A, 1972E, 1974F, 1989F
Fodor, Josephus Andreas, 1751A, 1828B
Fodor-Mainvielle, Joséphine, 1789A, 1808C,
    1825F, 1870B; Réflexions et conseils sur l'art du
    chant, 1857H
Foerster, Adolphe Martin, 1854A, 1927B
Foerster, Josef Bohuslav, 1859A, 1918F, 1951B
Foerstrová-Lautererová, Berta, 1869A, 1887C,
    1936B
Foetisch, Charles, Music Co., 1865G
Fohstrom, Alma, 1856A, 1936A
Foignet, François, 1782A, 1845B
Fokine, Michel, 1909F
Foland, Nicolle, 1968A
Foldes, Andor, 1913A, 1921C, 1933E, 1992B
Foldi, Andrew, 1981D
Foli, Allen J. (Signor), 1835A, 1862C, 1899B
The Folio: A Journal of Music, Art & Literature,
    1869G
Folkways Records, 1948G

❈

F *Biographical*   G *Cultural Beginnings*   H *Musical Literature*
I *Musical Compositions*

Fomin, Evstigney Ipatovich, 1761A, 1785E, 1800B
Fomina, Nina, 1972C
Fondary, Alain, 1932A, 1968C
Fontana, Julian, 1810A, 1865B
Fonteyn, Margot, 1919A
Foote, Arthur, 1853A, 1875F, 1909D, 1937B; *Modern Harmony in Its Theory & Practice*, 1905H; *Modulation & Related Harmonic Questions*, 1919H
Foote, George, 1886A, 1956B
Forare, Sten Erik, 1955A
Forberg, August Robert, 1833A, 1880B
Forberg, Robert, Music Publishing Co., 1862G
Forbes, Elliot, 1917A
Forbes, Henry, 1804A, 1859B
Ford, Bruce, 1956A, 1981C
Forkel, Johann N., 1778D, 1818B; *Allgemeine geschichte der musik I*, 1788H; *Allgemeine literature der Musik*, 1792H; *Genauere Bestimmung...musikalischer Begriffe*, 1780H; *Geschichte der italienischen Oper*, 1789H; *Musikalisch-kritischen Bibliothek I*, 1778H; *Über die Theorie der Musik*, 1777H
Formes, Carl Johann, 1815A, 1842C, 1889B
Formes, Theodor, 1826A, 1846C, 1874B
Fornasari, Luciano, 1828C
Fornia (-Labey), Rita, 1878A, 1901C, 1922B
Foroni, Jacopo, 1849D
Forqueray, Jean-Baptiste, 1782B
Forqueray, Nicolas-Gilles, 1761B
Forqueray, Michel, 1757B
Forrester, Maureen, 1930A, 1951C
Forsell, John, 1868A, 1896C, 1941B
Forsman, John, 1924A
Förster, Emanuel Aloys, 1823B
Förster, Horst, 1964D
Forster, William, Jr., 1764A, 1824B
Forster, William, Sr., 1808B, 1824B
Forster, William, Publishing Co, 1781G
Forster & Andrews, Organ Builders, 1843G
Förster Piano Co., 1859G
Forstrom, Alma, 1878C
Forsyth, Cecil, 1941B; *Choral Orchestration*, 1920H; *Clashpans*, 1933H; *A History of Music*, 1916H; *Music & Nationalism*, 1911H; *Orchestration*, 1914H
Forsyth Brothers, Ltd., Publishers, 1857G
Forsyth, Cecil, 1870A
Forti, Anton, 1790A, 1807C, 1859B
Forti, Helen, 1884A
Fortunati, Gian Francisco, 1810E
Fort Wayne, Indiana: Fine Arts Festival, 1958G; Philharmonic Orchestra, 1944G
Fort Worth, Texas: Bass Performance Hall, 1998G; Civic Opera Association, 1946G; Evans Hall, 1876G; Kennedy, John F., Theater, 1968G; Opera House, 1883G; Schola

Cantorum, 1964G; Texas Boys Choir, 1946G; Symphony Orchestra, 1913G
Forte, Allen, 1926A, 1960D, 1977D; *The Compositional Matrix*, 1961H; *Contemporary Tone Structures*, 1955H; *The Structure of Atonal Music*, 1973H; *Tonal Harmony in Concept & Practice*, 1962H
Forti, Helena, 1906C, 1942B
Fortner, Wolfgang, 1907A, 1987B
Fortunato, D'Anna, 1945A, 1980C
Fortune, George, 1935A, 1960C
Forum, 1931G
Forum Musik Jakarta, 1990G
Foss, Hubert: *Music in My Time*, 1933H
Foss, Lukas, 1922A, 1964D, 1971D, 1981D, 1983E, 1984E, 2000E
Foster, Catherine, 1975A
Foster, Fay, 1886A
Foster, Lawrence, 1941A, 1960C, 1966E, 1971D, 1979D, 1985D, 1988D, 1990D, 1992D, 1996D
Foster, Sidney, 1917A, 1940E, 1977B
Foster, Stephen, 1826A, 1846F, 1864B, 1940E
Foster-Armstrong Piano Co., 1894G
Foucquet, Pierre-Claude, 1758D
Foulds, John, 1880A, 1939B
Foundation for the Advancement of Education in Music, 1985G
Fountain, Ian, 1969A, 1989E
Fountain, Primous, III, 1949A
Fouquet, Pierre-Claude, 1772B
Four Corners Opera Association (N.M.), 1978G
Four Nations Ensemble, 1986G
Fourneaux, J. B. Napoléon, 1808A, 1846B; *Instrumentologie: traité théorique et practique*, 1867H
Fournet, Jean, 1913A, 1944D, 1961D, 1968D, 1973D,
Fournier, Pierre, 1906A, 1925C, 1953E, 1986B
Fournier, Pierre-Simon, 1768B
Fourth Dimension String Quartet, 1994G
Fowke, Philip Francis, 1950A, 1974C
Fox, Carol, 1954D
Fox, Charles Warren, 1904A, 1983B
Fox, Felix, 1947B
Fox, Sam, Publisher, 1906G
Fox, Sarah, 1973A, 1997E, 1998C
Fox, Virgil, 1912A, 1946D, 1980B
Fracassini, Aloisio Lodovico, 1798B
Frackenpohl, Arthur R.:*Harmonization at the Piano*, 1962H
Fradkin, Fredric, 1892A, 1911C, 1963B
Fraeg, Johann, Publisher (Vienna), 1794G
Frager, Malcolm, 1935A, 1955E, 1959E, 1960E, 1991B
Framery, Nicolas, 1770D, 1810B
Françaix, Jean, 1912A, 1997B
La France musicale, 1837G
France (*see also* Besançon, Bordeaux, Dijon, Le Havre, Lyon, Marseille, Nancy, Nantes,

A *Births*   B *Deaths*   C *Debuts*   D *New Positions*
E *Prizes/Honors*

Orleans, Paris, Reims, Rouen, Saint Gervais,
Toulouse, Strasbourg): Orchestre de l'Ile-de-
France, 1974G; Orchestre National de la
Radiodiffusion Française, 1934G
Francescatti, Zino, 1902A, 1918C, 1991B
Franchetti, Alberto, 1860A, 1942B
Franchetti, Arnold, 1909A, 1993B
Franchi, Sergio, 1990B
Franchomme, Auguste, 1808A, 1884B
Franci, Benvenuto, 1891A, 1918C, 1985B
Francillo-Kaufmann, Edoardo, 1878A
Francillo-Kaufmann, Hedwig, 1948B
Francis, Alun, 1966D, 1989D, 2000E
Francis, David Edward, 1980C
Francis, Day & Hunter, Publishers, 1877G
Franciscan String Quartet, 1983G
Le Franc-juge, 1834G
Franck, César, 1822A, 1833F, 1835F, 1837F,
1840F, 1844F, 1851D, 1853D, 1858D, 1885E,
1890B
Franck, Mikko, 1980A
Franco-American Musical Society (N.Y.),
1920G
Francoeur, François, 1757D, 1760E, 1787B
Francoeur, Louis-Joseph, 1767D, 1794D, 1804B;
Diapason général de tous les instruments à vent,
1772H
François, Samson, 1924A, 1943E, 1970B
Frandsen, John, 1956A
Frank, Alan: *The Clarinet*, 1939H
Frank, Claude, 1925A, 1947C
Frank, Ernst, 1847A, 1868D, 1872D, 1879D,
1889B
Frank, Hans-Peter, 1988D
Frank, Pamela, 1998E, 2000E
Frank Music Corporation, Publisher, 1949G
Frankenhausen, Germany: Thuringian
Festival, 1810G
Frankenpohl, Arthur, 1924A
Frankenstein, Alfred, 1906A, 1935D, 1981B;
Modern Guide to Symphonic Music, 1967H
Frankfurt, Germany: Cäcilienverein, 1818G;
Concert Hall, 1861G; Ensemble Concertant,
1987G; Evangelical Sacred Choral Society,
1850G; La Staglione, 1988G; Musikschule,
1860G; Philharmonic Orchestra, 1971G
Frankl, Peter, 1935A, 1957E, 1958E, 1962C
Frankl-Pauk-Kirshbaum Trio, 1969G
Franklin Music Warehouse, 1817G
Franko, Nahan, 1869C, 1930B
Franko, Nahan, Orchestra, 1889G
Franko, Sam, 1857A, 1869C, 1894D, 1937B
Frantini, Francesco Paolo, 1939B
Frantz, Ferdinand, 1906A, 1927C, 1959B
Franz, Carl, 1802B
Franz, Robert, 1815A, 1841D, 1842D, 1851D,
1861E, 1868F, 1878E, 1892B
Franzetti, Carlos, 1948A
Fränzl, Ferdinand, 1767A, 1806D, 1833B

Fränzl, Ignaz, 1778D, 1811B
Fraschini, Gaetano, 1816A, 1837C, 1887B
Fraser, Janet, 1911A
Fraser, Malcolm, 1945C
Frasi, Giulia, 1772B
Fraternity for the Creation of Opera in the
Georgian Language, 1906G
Freccia, Massimo, 1906A, 1939D, 1944D,
1952D, 1959D
Frederick the Great, 1786B
Frederiksson, Karl-Magnus, 1968A, 1996C
Free Academy of Music (Sao Paulo), 1952G
Freed, Isadore, 1900A, 1944D, 1960B
Freed, Richard, 1984E
Freeman, Betty, 1921A, 1987E
Freeman, Carroll B., 1951A
Freeman, Harry Lawrence, 1869A, 1954B
Freeman, Paul, 1936A. 1970D, 1979D, 1989D,
1996D
Freeman, Robert, 1935A, 1997D
Freeman School of Music, 1911G
Freer, Eleanor, 1864A, 1942B
Frege, Livia, 1818A, 1832C, 1891B
Frei, Andrea, 1990C
Freiberg Singakademie, 1823G
Freie Bühne (Theater Co.), 1889G
Freire, Nelson, 1944A, 1959C
Freithoff, Johan Henrik, 1767B
Fremantle Orchestra Society, 1887G
Frémaux, Louis, 1969D
Fremstad, Olive, 1871A, 1892C, 1951B
French Jacob: *New American Melody*, 1789H; *The
Psalmodist's Companion*, 1793H
French, Tania Gabrielle, 1963A
French Society of Musicology, 1904G
French Symphony Orchestra, 1989G
French Wind Quintet, 1945G
Freni, Mirella, 1935A, 1955C, 1957E, 1958E
Frenklova, Jane, 1947A, 1956C
Frère, Enoch, et Costallat, Publisher, 1880G
Fresk String Quartet, 1965G
Freo, Tibor, 1942D
Freudenthal, Heinz, 1936D
Freund, Etelka, 1901C
Freund, John, 1898D
Freund, Marya, 1876A, 1909C, 1966B
Frey, Alexander, 1961A
Frey, Emil, 1898A, 1946B
Frey, Jacques-Joseph, Publisher, 1811G
Frey-Rabine, Lia, 1950A, 1973C
Frezzolini, Erminia, 1838C, 1884B
Fribert, Karl, 1816B
Frichot, Louis Alexandre, 1760A, 1825B
Frick, Gottlob, 1906A, 1934C, 1994B
Frick, Philipp J.: *The Art of Musical Modulation*,
1780H; *Treatise on Thorough-Bass*, 1786H
Fricke, August Gottfried, 1829A, 1856C, 1894B
Fricker, Peter Racine, 1920A, 1952D, 1970D,
1990B

❁

F   *Biographical*   G   *Cultural Beginnings*   H   *Musical Literature*
I   *Musical Compositions*

Fricsay, Ferenc, 1914A, 1939D, 1945D, 1948D,
 1949D, 1954D, 1956D, 1963B
Friebert, Joseph, 1799B
Fried, Joel E., 1954A
Fried, Miriam, 1946A, 1968E, 1969C, 1971E
Friedberg, Carl Rudolf, 1892C, 1955B
Friede, Stefanie, 1959A, 1985C
Friedheim, Arthur, 1859A, 1932B
Friedheim Awards, 1978G
Friedl, Sebastian Ludwig, 1768A, 1857B
Friedlaender, Max, 1852A, 1934B; *Das deutsch
 Lied in 18. Jahrhundert*, 1902H
Friedman, Erick, 1939A, 1953C
Friedman, Richard, 1944A
Friedrich, John, & Brother, Violin Makers,
 1884G
Friedrichs, Fritz, 1847A, 1884C, 1918B
Frieman, Gustav, 1842A, 1866C, 1902B
Friend, Lionel, 1977D
Friend, Rodney, 1939A
Friends & Enemies of Modern Music, 1929G
Friends of Modern Music Orchestra, 1986G
Friends of the Gamelan, Inc., 1981G
Fries, Henry, 1871D
Fries, Wulf, 1825A, 1902B
Frigel, Pehr, 1778E, 1842B
Frijsch, Povla, 1881A, 1900C, 1960B
Friml, Rudolf, 1879A, 1972B
Frimmel, Theodore von, 1853A, 1928B
Friskin, James, 1886A, 1967B; *The Principles of
 Pianoforte Practice*, 1921H
Frith, Benjamin, 1957A, 1961C, 1986E, 1989E
Frittoli, Barbara, 1967A
Fritz, Barthold, 1766B; *Tuning of Keyboard
 Instruments*, 1756H
Fritz, Gaspard, 1783B
Fritze, Wilhelm, 1842A, 1881B
Fritzsch, Johannes, 1960A
Frobenius Organ Co., 1909G
Fröhlich, Anna, 1793A. 1880B
Fröhlich, Barbara, 1797A, 1879B
Fröhlich, Joseph, 1780A, 1862B
Fröhlich, Josephine, 1803A, 1821C, 1878B
Frölich, (Friedrich) Theodor, 1803A, 1836B
Fromm, Paul, 1906A, 1983E, 1986E, 1987B
Fromm Music Foundation (Harvard), 1952G
Frontini, Francesco Paolo, 1860A
Frotscher, Gotthold, 1897A,1967B
Frühbeck de Burgos, Rafael, 1933A, 1959D,
 1962D, 1974D, 1980D, 1990D, 1992D
Frusta Litteraria, 1763G
Fry, William Henry, 1813A, 1836D, 1845F,
 1846D, 1847D, 1852D, 1864B
Fryer, George H., 1877A, 1898C, 1957B
Fryklund, Daniel, 1879A, 1965B
Fuchs, Albert, 1889D
Fuchs, Aloys, 1799A
Fuchs, Carl, 1887D
Fuchs, Georg-Friedrich, 1752A, 1821B

Fuchs, Joseph, 1900A, 1920C, 1943C, 1997B
Fuchs, Johann Leopold, 1785A, 1853B
Fuchs, Johann Nepomuk, 1842A, 1864D,
 1894D, 1899B
Fuchs, Lillian, 1903A, 1926C, 1995B
Fuchs, Marta, 1898A, 1928C, 1974B
Fuchs, Peter, 1753A, 1831B
Fuchs, Robert, 1847A, 1886E, 1927B
Fuentes, Juan Bautista, 1869A, 1955B; *Teoria de
 la Música*, 1899H
Fuentes, Pascual, 1757D, 1768B
Fugère, Lucien, 1848A, 1877C, 1935B
Fujikawa, Mayumi, 1971E
Fujioka, Sachio, 1962A
Fuleihan, Anis, 1900A, 1919C, 1953D, 1963D,
 1970B
Fulgoni, Sarah, 1970A, 1994C
Fulkerson, Gregory, 1950A
Fuller, Margaret, 1844D
Fuller-Maitland, John, 1889D; *English Music in
 the Nineteenth Century*, 1902H; *Masters of
 German Music*, 1894H; *Musician's Pilgrimage*,
 1899H
Fulton, Thomas, 1949A, 1994B
Fumagalli, Adolfo, 1828A, 1848C, 1856B
Funk, Eric, 1949A
Funk, Joseph, 1778A, 1862B
Furlanetto, Bonaventura, 1814D, 1817B; *Lezioni
 de contrappunto*, 1789H; *Trattato di
 contrappunto*, 1811H
Furlanetto, Ferruccio, 1949A, 1974C
Furrer, Beat, 1954A
Fursch-Madi, Emmy, 1847A, 1868C, 1894B
Fúrstenau, Anton B., 1792A, 1852B
Fürstenau, Casper, 1772A, 1819B
Fürstenau, Moritz, 1824A, 1852D, 1889B
Fürstner, Adolph, 1833A, 1908B
Fürstner Publishing Co., 1868G
Furtwängler, Philipp, Organ Builder, 1830G
Furtwängler, Wilhelm, 1886A, 1911D, 1915D,
 1922D, 1954B; *Gespräche über Musik*, 1948H
Fussell, Charles, 1938A
Fusz, János, 1777A, 1819B
Futral, Elizabeth, 1992C
Futrell, Jon: *The Illustrated Encyclopedia of Black
 Music*, 1982H
Fux, Johann Joseph, Society (Graz), 1955G
Fuzelier, Louis, 1752B
Gabichvadze, Revaz, 1913A
Gabler, Joseph, 1771B
Gabos, Gabor, 1930A, 1952C
Gabriel, Charles H., 1856A, 1932B
Gabriel, Mary Ann, 1825A, 1877B
Gabrieli, Caterina, 1758F, 1796B
Gabrieli, Francesca, 1755A, 1786C
Gabrieli Consort & Players, 1981G
Gabrieli Ensemble, 1963G
Gabrieli String Quartet, 1966G
Gabrielski, Johann Wilhelm, 1791A, 1846B

❖

A   *Births*   B   *Deaths*   C   *Debuts*   D   *New Positions*
            E   *Prizes/Honors*

Gabrilowitsch, Ossip, 1878A, 1894E, 1896C, 1918D, 1936B
Gaburo, Kenneth, 1926A, 1993B
Gaceta Musical de Madrid, 1855G
Gaddes Fund for Young Singers, 1986G
Gade, Niels, 1817A, 1833C, 1841E, 1844F, 1847D, 1850D, 1867D, 1876EF, 1886E, 1890B
Gadsby Henry: *Harmony*, 1883H
Gadski, Johanna, 1872A, 1889C, 1932B
Gagneux, Renaud, 1947A
Gagnoni, Antonio, 1886D
Gaiani, Giovanni B., 1757A, 1781E, 1819B
Gail, Edmée Sophie, 1775A
Gailhard, André, 1908E
Gailhard, Pierre, 1848A, 1867C, 1884D, 1886E, 1918B
Gaither Music Co., 1961G
Gaito, Constantino, 1878A, 1945B
Gál, Hans, 1890A, 1987B; *The Musician's World*, 1965H
Galajikian, Florence Grandland, 1900A, 1970B
Galamian, Ivan, 1903A, 1924C; *Contemporary Violin Techniques I*, 1966H; *Contemporary Violin Technique II*, 1977H; *Principles of Violin Playing & Teaching*, 1962H
Galas, Diamanda, 1955A
Galaxy Music Corporation, 1931G
Galbraith, Nancy, 1951A
Galbraith, Paul, 1964A, 1982C
Galeazzi, Francisco, 1758A, 1819B; *Elementi teorico-pratici di Musica I*, 1791H; *Elementi teorico-pratici de Musica II*, 1796H
Galeffi, Carlo, 1882A, 1903C, 1961B
Gales, Weston, 1877A, 1914D, 1939B
Galignani's Messenger, 1814G
Galimir String Quartet II, 1938G
Galin Pierre: *Nouvelle méthode pour l'enseignement...musique*, 1818H
Galindo, Blas, 1910A, 1947D, 1993B
Galkin, Elliott W., 1921A, 1960D, 1962D, 1972E, 1975E, 1977D, 1982E, 1990B; *A History of Orchestral Conducting*, 1988H
Gall, Jeffrey, 1950A, 1980C
Galla, Fortune, 1878A
Gallardo-Domas, Cristina, 1968A
Gallay, Jacques François, 1795A, 1864B; *Méthode complète pour le cor*, 1845H
Galleberg, Wenzel Robert, 1783A, 1839B
Galletti-Gianoli, Isabella, 1835A, 1860C, 1901B
Galli, Amintore: *Estetica della musica*, 1900H; *Storia e teoria del sistemes musicale*, 1901H
Galli, Caterina, 1804B
Galli, Filippo, 1783A, 1801C, 1811C, 1853B
Galli-Curci, Amelita, 1882A, 1906C, 1963B
Galli-Marié, Célestine, 1840A, 1859C, 1905B
Galliard Harpsichord Trio, 1966G
Gallico, Paul, 1922E
Gallignani, Giuseppe, 1884D, 1891D, 1897D
Gallo, Fortune, 1970B

Gallo, Lucio, 1958A
Gallo, Pietro Antonio, 1777B
Gallois-Montbrun, Raymond, 1944E
Gallos, Hermann, 1886A, 1915C, 1957B
Galmian, Ivan, 1981B
Galpin, Francis W., 1858A, 1945B; *The Music of Electricity*, 1938H; *Music of the Sumerians, Babylonians and Assyrians*, 1937H; *Old English Instruments of Music*, 1910H; *A Textbook of European Musical Instruments*, 1937H
Galpin Society Journal, 1947G
Galpin Society of London, 1946G
Galsenapp, Carl Friedrich, 1847A
Galstian, Juliette, 1970A
Galston, Gottfried, 1950B
Galucci, Giovanni, 1931A
Galuppi, Baldassare, 1762D, 1765DF, 1768F, 1785B
Galvani, Giacomo, 1825A, 1889B
Galvany, Marisa, 1936A, 1968C
Gamba, Piero, 1936A, 1945C, 1962E, 1970D, 1982D
Gambarini, Elisabetta de, 1765A
Gamberoni, Kathryn, 1955A, 1981C
Gambill, Robert, 1955A, 1981C
Gamble Hinged Music Co., 1909G
Gamelan Galak Tika, 1993G
Gamucci, Baldassare, 1822A, 1892B
Ganassi, Sonia, 1967A, 1991C
Gand, Charles François, *père*, 1787A, 1845B
Gand, Charles F., Violin Maker, 1820G
Gand, Guillaume C., 1792A
Gandolfi, Michael, 1956A
Gandolfi, Riccardo, 1839A, 1920B
Ganer, Christopher, Piano Maker, 1774G
Gange, Fraser, 1886A, 1902C, 1962B
Gann, Kyle, 1955A; *American Music in the Twentieth Century*, 1997H
Ganne, Louis Gaston, 1862A, 1923B
Gänsbacher, Johann B., 1778A, 1823D, 1844B
Ganz, Adolf, 1825D
Ganz, Rudolph, 1877A, 1899C, 1929D, 1972B
Ganz, Wilhelm, 1833A, 1914B; *Memories of a Musician*, 1913H
Garaguly, Carl von, 1959D
Garat, Pierre Jean, 1762A, 1794C, 1823B
Gárate, Jesús Arámbarri, 1902A, 1960B
Garaudé, Alexis de, 1779A, 1852B; *Méthode de chant*, 1809H
Garbin, Edoardo, 1865A, 1891C, 1943B
Garbousova, Raya, 1905A, 1923C, 1997B
Garbuzov, Nicolai: *Musical Acoustics*, 1940H
García, Manuel Patricio, 1906B
Garcia, José Nunes, 1767A, 1798D, 1808, 1830B
García, Manuel, 1775A, 1798C, 1832B
García, Manuel Patricio, 1805A
Garcia Italian Opera Co., 1825G
García Fajer, Francisco Javier, 1755D, 1809B

❀

F *Biographical*   G *Cultural Beginnings*   H *Musical Literature*
I *Musical Compositions*

Gardelli, Lamberto, 1915A, 1944C, 1955D, 1965E, 1968D, 1983D, 1986D, 1998B
Garden, Mary, 1874A, 1900C, 1921D, 1967B
Gardes, Roger, 1922A, 1954C
Gardiner, John Eliot, 1943A, 1980D, 1983D, 1991D, 1998E
Gardiner, William, 1770A, 1853B; *Music and Friends I*, 1838H; *The Music of Nature*, 1832H; *Sacred Melodies*, 1815H
Gardner, John, 1917A
Gardner, Samuel, 1891A, 1918E, 1984B
Gardoni, Italo, 1821A, 1840C, 1882B
Gari, Giulio, 1994B
Garland, Peter, 1952A
Garnier, François-Joseph, 1755A, 1825B
Garrett, David, 1980A, 1993C
Garrett, Leslie, 1979E
Garrison, Jon, 1944A
Garrison, Mabel, 1886A, 1912C, 1963B
Garrison Lucy McKim: *Slave Songs of the U. S.*, 1867H
Gasdia, Cecilia, 1960A, 1981CE
Gaspari, Gaetano, 1807A, 1855D, 1881B; *Memorie dell'arte musicale in Bologna...*, 1875H; *Ragguagli sulla cappella musicale della Basilica di S. Petronio in Bologna*, 1869H; *Recherche, documenti e memorie risquardanti la storia dell'arte musicale in Bologna*, 1867H
Gasparik, Robert, 1961A
Gasperini, Guido, 1865A, 1942B; *I caratteri peculiari del Melodramma italiano*, 1913H; *Storia della Musica*, 1899H; *Storia della semiographica musicale*, 1905H
Gasparini, Quirino, 1751E, 1760D, 1778B
Gassier, Édouard, 1820A, 1845C, 1872B
Gassmann, Florien, 1774B
Gassner, Ferdinand, 1818D; *Dirigent und Ripienist*, 1846H; *Ein Leitfaden zum Selbstunterricht*, 1838H
Gasteen, Lisa, 1957A, 1985C
Gastinel, Léon-Gustave, 1846E
Gaston, E. Thayer: *Music in Therapy*, 1968H
Gastoué, Amédée, 1873A, 1943B; *L'art grégorien*, 1911H; *La liturgie et la musique*, 1931H; *L'orgue en France de l'antiquité au début de la période classique*, 1921H; *Les primitifs de la musique française*, 1922H; *La vie musicale de l'église*, 1929H
Gasull, Feliu, 1959A
Gatayes, Guillaume-Pierre, 1774A, 1846B; *Guitar Method*, 1790H; *Harp Method*, 1795H
Gatti, Daniele, 1961A, 1982C, 1996D
Gatti, Gabriela, 1916A, 1934C
Gatti, Guido M., 1892A, 1973B; *Cinquanta anni di opera a balletto in Italia*, 1954H; *Dizionario di musica*, 1925H; *Musicisti moderni d'Italia e di fuori*, 1920H
Gatti, Luigi, 1783D

Gatti-Casazza, Giulio, 1868A, 1898D, 1908D, 1940B; *Memories of the Opera*, 1941H
Gaubert, Philippe, 1879A, 1919D, 1941B
Gaudeamus Foundation, 1945G
Gaudeamus String Quartet, 1954G
Gauk, Alexander, 1893A, 1930D, 1936D, 1953D, 1963B
Gaul, Alfred R., 1837A, 1913B
Gaul, Harvey B., 1914D, 1945B
Gauldin, Robert: *A Practical Approach to Sixteenth-Century Counterpoint*, 1985H; *A Practical Approach to Eighteenth-Century Counterpoint*, 1987H
Gauthier, Eva, 1885A, 1902C, 1958B
Gauthier, Jacques, 1953A, 1982C
Gautier, Eugène, 1822A, 1878B
Gauzargues, Charles, 1758D; *Traité de Composition*, 1797H
Gavanelli, Paolo, 1959A, 1985C
Gaveau Piano Co., 1847G
Gaveaux, Pierre, 1760A, 1825B
Gaveaux Music Publishing Co., 1793G
Gavezzeni, Gianandrea, 1909A, 1940C, 1965D, 1996B
Gavazzeni, Gianandrea: *Carta da musica*, 1968H; *Le fests musicali*, 1944H; *I nemeci della musica*, 1965H; *La morte dell'opera*, 1954H; *La musica e il teatro*, 1954H; *Musicisti d'Europa*, 1954H; *Quaderno del musicista*, 1952H; *Trent'anni di musica*, 1958H
Gaviniés, Pierre, 1773D, 1800B
Gävleborg Symphony Orchestra, 1912G
Gavrilov, Andrei, 1955A, 1972E, 1976C
Gay, Maria, 1879A, 1902C, 1943B
Gayer, Catherine, 1937A, 1961C
Gayford, Christopher, 1963A, 1989E
Gaylord, Julia, 1850A, 1875C, 1894B
Gaylord, Monica, 1948A
Gaylord Music Library (Washington U.), 1960G
Gaytan y Arteaga, Manuel, 1751D
Gazeta Musicale, 1893G
Gazette Musicale de la Belgique, 1833G
Gazette Musicale de Paris, 1835G
Gazzaniga, Giuseppe, 1775D, 1791D, 1818B
Gazzelloni, Severino, 1919A, 1945C, 1992B
Gazzetta Musicale de Napoli, 1852G, 1955G
Gazzetta Musicale de Firenze, 1853G
Gazzetta Musicale di Milano, 1842G
Gdansk (Danzig), Poland: Danziger Theater, 1801G; Gesangverein zu Danzig, 1817G; Heidingsfeld Conservatory, 1899G
Gebauer Music Publishers, 1859G
Gebauer, François René, 1773A, 1845
Gebauer, Franz Xaver, 1784A, 1822B
Gebel, Franz Xaver, 1787A, 1843B
Gebel, Georg, Jr., 1755B
Gebethner & Spólka, Publishers, 1857G

❉

A　*Births*　　B　*Deaths*　　C　*Debuts*　　D　*New Positions*
E　*Prizes/Honors*

Gebhard, Heinrich, 1878A, 1899C, 1963B
Gèdalge, André, 1926B; *L'enseignement de la musique par l'éducation méthodique de l'Oreille,* 1920H; *Traité de la Fugue,* 1901H
Gedda, Nicolai, 1925A, 1952C
Gedge, Nicholas Paul, 1968A, 1994C
Gehann, Ada Beate, 1957A
Gehlhaar, Rolf, 1943A
Gehot, Jean (Joseph), 1756A, 1820B; *The Art of Bowing the Violin,* 1790H; *Complete Instructions,...Every Musical Instrument,* 1790H; *A Treatise on the Theory and Practice of Music,* 1784H
Gehrkens, Karl, 1882A, 1975B; *Essentials in Conducting,* 1919H; *Introduction to School Music Teaching,* 1919H; *Music Notation & Terminology,* 1914H
Gehrman, Karl, Publisher, 1893G
Geib, Adam & William, Publishers, 1815G
Geib, John (Joahnn), 1818B
Geibel & Lehmann, Publishers, 1897G
Geimeinhardt, K. G., Co., 1948G
Geiringer, Karl, 1899A, 1959E, 1989B; *Instruments in the History of Western Music,* 1978H; *Musical Instruments, Their History,* 1943H; *Vorgeschichte und Geschichte der europäischen Läute,* 1928H
Geissenhof, Franciscus, 1753A, 1821B
Geistinger, Maria Charlotte, 1833A, 1903B
Gelb, John, & Co, Organ Builders (New York), 1797G
Gellman, Steven D., 1947A
Gelinek, Joseph, 1758A, 1825B
Gemini Piano Trio, 1994G
Geminiani, Francesco, 1762B; *The Art of Accompaniment,* 1755H; *The Art of Playing the Guitar,* 1760H; *The Art of Playing the Violin,* 1751H; *Guida Armonica,* 1754H; *The Harmonical Miscellany,* 1758H
Gemret, Jiri, 1957A
Gemünder, August, Violin Shop, 1846G
Gemünder, August, 1814A, 1852F, 1895B
Gemünder, Georg, 1816A, 1852F, 1899B
Gena, Peter, 1947A
Genast, Eduard F., 1797A, 1814C, 1866B
Gencer, Leyla, 1924A, 1950C
Gendille, José-André, 1986D
Gendron, Maurice, 1920A, 1945C, 1990B
Genée, Franz Richard, 1868D
Genée, Richard, 1823A, 1895B
Genée, Rudolf, 1824A, 1914B
Generali, Pietro, 1773A, 1817D, 1819D, 1832B
Geneva, Switzerland: Conservatory of Music, 1835G; Grand Opera Co., 1879G; Grand Theater, 1879G; International Competition, Performers, 1939G; Music Society, 1823; Société de Chant Sacré, 1827G
Genlis Stéphanie: *Harp Method,* 1811H

Gennrich, Friedrich, 1883A, 1967B; *Musikwissenschaft und Romanische Philologie,* 1918H
Genoa, Italy: Paganini Music Conservatory, 1829G; Teatro Carlo Felice, 1828G; Teatro Comunale dell'Opera, 1936G; Teatro Marguerita, 1948G
Genossenschaft Deutscher Tonsetzen, 1896G
Gens, Véronique, 1966A, 1986C
Gentele, Goeren, 1917A, 1972B
Gentile, Louis, 1957A
Gentle, Alice, 1888A, 1909C, 1958B
Gentleman and Lady's Musical Companion, 1774G
The Gentleman's Musical Magazine, 1788G
Gentlemen's Private Concerts, 1788G
Genzmer, Hans (Harald), 1909A
George, Earl, 1924A
George, Lloyd, 1913A
George, Mechthild, 1956A
George, Thom Ritter, 1942A
Georghiu, Angela, 1990C
Georgia Woodwind Quartet, 1967G
Georgiades, Thrasybulos, 1907A, 1977B; *Musik und Sprache,* 1954H; *Das musikalische Theater,* 1965H
Georgian Philharmonic Society, 1905G
Gérard, Henri-Philippe, 1760A, 1848B; *Considérations sur la musique...,* 1819H; *Méthode de Chant,* 1816H; *Traité méthodique d'harmonie,* 1833H
Gérardy, Jean, 1877A, 1890C, 1929B
Gerber, Ernst Ludwig, 1775D, 1819B; *Historisch-biographisches Lexikon I,* 1790H; *Historisch-biographisches Lexicon II,* 1792H; *Neues historisch biographisches Lexikon I, II,* 1812H; *Neues historisch-biographisches Lexikon III,* 1813H; *Neues Historisch-biographisches Lexikon IV,* 1814H
Gerber, Heinrich Nikolaus, 1775B
Gerber, Rudolf, 1899A, 1957B
Gerbert, Martin, 1793D; *De cantu et musica sacra,* 1774H; *Monumenta veteris liturgiae alemannicae,* 1777H; *Scriptores ecclesiastici de musica sacra,* 1784H
Gergiev, Valery, 1953A, 1980D, 1988D, 1998F
Gerhard, Roberto, 1896A, 1970B
Gerhardt, Elena, 1883A, 1903C, 1961B
Gericke, Wilhelm, 1884D, 1844A, 1898D, 1925B
Gerl, Franz Xaver, 1764A, 1785C, 1827B
Gerlach, Theodor, 1861A, 1940B
German, Edward, 1862A, 1888D, 1895E, 1928E, 1934E, 1936B
German National Singspiel Co, 1778G
German Saengerbund of North America, 1849G
German Symphony Orchestra, 1946G
Germantown Conservatory of Music, 1906G
Germany (*see also* Ansbach, Bamberg, Bayreuth, Berlin, Bonn, Bremen, Cologne,

---

❋

F *Biographical*   G *Cultural Beginnings*   H *Musical Literature*
I *Musical Compositions*

Germany (*cont.*)
  Darmstadt, Dessau, Dortmund, Dresden,
    Essen, Frankfurt, Gotha, Hamburg,
    Hanover, Heidelberg, Kassel, Kiel, Koblenz,
    Königsberg, Leipzig, Lübeck, Mainz,
    Mannheim, Munich, Münster, Nurenberg,
    Regensburg, Rostock, Stuttgart, Weimar,
    Worms, Wüppertal, Württemberg,
    Würzburg): Bach Gesellschaft, 1850G;
    Belcanto Strings, 1993G; Bern Municipal
    Theater, 1903G; Mozart Gesellschaft, 1951G;
    Symphonie- und Kurorchester (Baden-
    Baden), 1872G
Gérold, Théodore, 1866A, 1956B; *L'art du chant
  en France au XVIIIe siècle*, 1921H; *Histoire de la
  musique des origines à la fin du XIVe siècle*,
  1936H; *La musicologie médiévale*, 1921H; *La
  musique au moyen âge*, 1932H; *Les pères de
  l'église et la musique*, 1931H
Gerschefski, Edwin, 1909A, 1992B
Gershwin, George, 1898A, 1937B
Gershwin, George, Award, 1945G
Gerstenberg, Johann, Music Store, 1792G
Gerstenberg, Johann D., Publisher, 1794G
Gerstenberg, Walter, 1904A, 1988B
Gerster, Etelka, 1855A, 1876C, 1920B
Gertler String Quartet, 1931G
Gervasoni, Carlo, 1762A, 1819B; *Nuova Teoria
  de Musica*, 1812H; *La scuola della musica*,
  1800H
Gervasoni, Stefano, 1962A
Gerville-Réache, Jeanne, 1882A, 1899C, 1915B
Gesangverein zu Danzig, 1817G
Der Gesellschaft, 1885G
Gessendorff, Mechthild, 1937A, 1961C
Gestewitz, Friedrich C., 1753A, 1805B
Geszty, Sylvia, 1934A, 1959C
Getzen Brass Instrument Co., 1939G
Gevaert, François Auguste, 1828A, 1867D,
  1847E, 1871D, 1908B; *Abrégé du nouveau traité
  d'instrumentation*, 1892H; *Cours méthodique
  d'orchestration*, 1890H; *La mélopée antique dans
  l'église latine*, 1896H; *Histoire et théorie de la
  musique de l'antiquité I*, 1875H; *Rapport sur
  l'état de la musique en Espagne*, 1851H; *Traité
  d'Harmonie théorique et pratique*, 1905H; *Traité
  général d'instrumentation*, 1863H
Geyer, Steffie, 1956B
Geyer, Ludwig, 1814F
Geyer, Steffi, 1888A
Ghazarian, Sonya, 1945A
Ghedini, Giorgio Federico, 1892A, 1951D,
  1965B
Ghent, Belgium: Conservatory of Music,
  1835G; Institute for Psychoacoustics &
  Electronic Music, 1962G
Gheorghiu, Angela, 1965A, 1990C
Ghera, C. G., Publisher, 1772G
Gherardeschi, Filippo, 1761DE, 1763D, 1766D,
  1768D, 1808B

Gheyn, Matthias van den, 1785B
Ghiaurov, Nicolai, 1929A, 1955CE
Ghiglia, Oscar, 1938A
Ghis, Henri, 1839A, 1908B
Ghisi, Federico, 1901A, 1975B
Ghislanzoni, Antonio, 1824A, 1846C, 1893B
Ghiuselev, Nicola, 1936A, 1961C
Ghys, Joseph, 1801A, 1848B
Giacometti, Bartolomeo, 1809B
Giai, Giovanni Antonio, 1764B
Giaiotti, Bonaldo, 1932A, 1958C
Gialidis, Elfrosini, 1966A; *Style & Idea in Greek
  Contemporary Musical Thought*, 1999H
Gianelli, Pietro: *Dizionario della Musica*, 1801H
Giannini, Dusolina, 1900A, 1902A, 1920C,
  1986B
Giannini, Ferruccio, 1868A, 1891C, 1948B
Gianinni, Vittorio, 1903A, 1932E, 1965D, 1966B
Gianotti, Pietro, 1765B; *Abrégé du nouveau traité
  d'instrumentation*, 1892H; *Le guide du
  compositeur I*, 1759H; *Le Guide du compositeur
  II*, 1775H; *Méthode...d'accompagnement à la
  harpe et clavecin*, 1764H
Giardini, Felice de', 1755D
Gibbons, Jack, 1962A, 1979C
Gibbs, Cecil Armstrong, 1889A, 1960B
Gibbs, Christoher, 1958A
Gibbs, Joseph, 1788B
Gibbs, Robert W., 1965A
Gibelli, Lorenzo, 1812A
Gibert, Paul-César, 1787B; *Mélange musical:
  premier recueil*, 1775H; *Solfèges ou leçons de
  musique*, 1769H
Gibson, Alexander, 1926A, 1952C, 1958D,
  1962D, 1977E, 1991D, 1995B
Gibson, Orville H., 1856A
Gideon, Miriam, 1906A, 1975E, 1996B
Giebel, Agnes, 1921A, 1947C
Gielen, Michael, 1927A, 1960D, 1969D, 1972D,
  1977D, 1980D, 1986D
Gieseking, Walter, 1895A, 1912C, 1956B
Gietz, Gordon, 1968A
Gietzen, Herbert, 1973C
Gifford, William, 1809D
Giger, Paul, 1952A
Gigli, Beniamino, 1890A, 1914CE, 1957B
Gigout, Eugène, 1844A, 1863D, 1925B
Gilad, Jonathan, 1980A
Gilbert, Alan, 1965A, 1993E, 2000D
Gilbert, Henry F., 1868A, 1928B
Gilbert, Jane, 1969A, 1993C
Gilbert, William S., 1836A, 1871F, 1911B
Gilberté, Hallett, 1946B
Gilchrist, Diana, 1989C
Gilchrist, William W., 1846A, 1874D, 1916B
Gilels, Emil, 1916A, 1929C, 1938E, 1985B
Giles, Christopher, 1977E
Giles, Joseph, 1903A
Gilfert, Charles H., Publishers, 1815G
Gilfry, Rodney, 1959A

A *Births*   B *Deaths*   C *Debuts*   D *New Positions*
E *Prizes/Honors*

Gilibert, Charles, 1866A, 1888C, 1910B
Gilles, Joseph, 1942B
Gillis, Don, 1912A, 1977B
Gillis Opera House (Kansas City, Kansas), 1902G
Gilman, Benjamin Ives, 1852A, 1933B
Gilman, Lawrence, 1878A, 1901D, 1915D, 1923D, 1939B; *Aspects of Modern Opera,* 1909H; *The Music of Tomorrow & Other Studies,* 1907H; *Phases of Modern Music,* 1904H
Gilmore, Gail, 1950A, 1975C
Gilmore, Patrick S., 1829A, 1869F, 1892B
Gilmore, Partick S., Band, 1858G
Gilmore Artist Award, 1991G
Gilmore, Graves & Co., Brass Instruments, 1864G
Gilse, Jan van, 1881A, 1933D, 1944B
Gilson, Paul, 1865A, 1889E, 1942B
Gimell Records, 1981G
Gimpel, Bronislaw, 1911A, 1979B
Gimpel, Jakob, 1906A, 1923C, 1989B
Gimse, Havard, 1966A, 1981C, 1995E, 1996E
Ginastera, Alberto, 1916A, 1945F, 1958D, 1962D, 1983B
Gingold, Josef, 1909A, 1995B
Ginguené, Pierre Louis, 1816B
Ginn & Co., Publishers, 1867G
Giordani, Giuseppe, 1791D, 1798B
Giordani, Marcello, 1963A, 1988C
Giordano, Maria, 1985E
Giordani, Tommaso, 1752F, 1753F, 1806B
Giordano, Umberto, 1867A, 1948B
Giorgi, Giovanni, 1762B
Giorni, Aurelio, 1896A, 1938B
Giornovichi, Giovanni M., 1773C, 1804B
Gipps, Ruth Dorothy, 1921A, 1981E, 1999B
Giraldoni, Eugenio, 1871A, 1891C, 1924B
Giraldoni, Leone, 1847A
Giraldoni, Leone, 1824A, 1847A, 1897B
Girard, Giuseppe, Publisher, 1815G
Giraud, Fiorello, 1870A, 1891C, 1928B
Giraud, Suzanne, 1958A
Giraudet, Alfred-Auguste, 1845A, 1868C, 1911B
Girelli, Antonia Maria, 1759C
Giroust, François, 1756D, 1769D, 1796E, 1799B
Gischer, Annie, 1933E
Giteck, Janice, 1946A
Giudici & Strada, Publishers, 1859G
Giuglini, Antonio, 1827A, 1865B
Giuliani, Mauro, 1781A, 1829B
Giulini, Carlo Maria, 1914A, 1944C, 1946D, 1950D, 1954D, 1969F, 1973D, 1978D
Giulini, Johann, 1755D, 1772B
Giuseppe Verdi Choir, 1961G
Gizzi, Domenico, 1758B
Gjeldstad, Øivin, 1921C
Gjevang, Anne, 1948A, 1972C
Glachant, Antoine-Charles, 1770A, 1885B

Glade, Coe, 1985B
Gladkowska, Konstancja, 1810A, 1830C, 1889B
Glaneur Lyrique, 1795G
Glanville, Mark, 1959A, 1987C
Glanville-Hicks, Peggy, 1912A, 1948D, 1953E, 1990B
Glasenapp, Carl Friedrich, 1915B
Gläser, Franz, 1798A, 1861B
Glasgow, Scotland: Amateur Musical Society, 1831G; Choral Society, 1833G; Choral Union, 1855G; Choral Union Orchestra, 1874G; Gentlemen's Private Concerts, 1788G; Grand Opera Co., 1905G; Orpheus Chorus, 1901G; Musical Association, 1843G; Philoharmonic Society, 1832G; Scottish Orchestra, 1891G; Symphony Orchestra, 1919G
Glass, Louis, 1864A, 1892D, 1936B
Glass, Philip, 1937A, 1982F
Glass, Philip, Ensemble, 1968G
Glassman, Allan, 1950A, 1975C
Glassychord (Glass Harmonica), 1761G
Glauchau Konzertverein, 1885G
Glaz, Herta, 1908A, 1931C
Glazunov, Alexander, 1865A, 1889F, 1896F, 1905D, 1907E, 1936B
Glazunov String Quartet, 1985G
Gleason, Frederick, 1848A, 1884D, 1900D
Gleason, Harold, 1892A, 1921D, 1980B; *Examples of Music Before 1400,* 1942H; *Method of Organ Playing,* 1937H; *Music Literature Outlines,* 1949H
Gleissner, Franz, 1759A, 1818B
Glen, Thomas, Instrument Maker, 1827G
Glenn, Bonita, 19960A
Glenn, Carroll, 1918A, 1938CE, 1983B
Glenn, Mabelle: *The Psychology of School Music Teaching,* 1931H
Glennon, Jean, 1960A
Glière, Reinhold, 1875A, 1914D, 1956B
Glimmerglass Opera Co., 1975G
Glinka, Mikhail, 1804A, 1817F, 1822F, 1824F, 1828F, 1834F, 1847F, 1854F, 1857B
Glissando Records, 1998G
Glöggl, Franz Xaver, 1764A, 1790D, 1839B
Gloriae Dei Cantores, 1971G
Glossop, Peter, 1928A, 1952C
Gloucester Choral Society, 1845G
Glover, Jane, 1975C, 1994F
Glover, Sarah Anna: *Manual...Development of the Tetrachordal System,* 1850H; *Manual of the Norwich Sol-Fa System,* 1845H
Gluck, Alma, 1884A, 1909C, 1938B
Gluck, Christoph Willbald, 1752F, 1755F, 1756EF, 1773F, 1774E, 1777F, 1778F, 1781F, 1779F, 1783F, 1787B; *Preface to Alceste,* 1769H
Gluschenko, Feodor, 1971D
Glydenfeldt, Graciela von, 1958A
Glyn, Margaret H., 1865A, 1946B
Glyndebourne Opera Festival, 1934G
Gmirya, Boris, 1903A, 1936C

❄

F *Biographical*   G *Cultural Beginnings*   H *Musical Literature*
I *Musical Compositions*

Gnattali, Radamés, 1906A, 1988B
Gnazzo, Anthony J., 1936A
Gnecco, Francesco, 1769A, 1810B
Gnocchi, Pietro, 1762D, 1771B
Gobbi, Tito, 1913A, 1935C, 1984B
Goble, Theresa, 1970A
Godard, Benjamin, 1849A, 1878E, 1889E, 1895B
Goddard, Arabella, 1836A, 1850C, 1922B
Godefroid, Félix, 1818A, 1897B
Godefroy, Clair, Woodwind Maker, 1814G
Godowsky, Leopold, 1870A, 1884C, 1895D, 1938B
Goeb, Roger, 1914A, 1953E, 1997B
Goebbels, Heiner, 1952A
Goedicke, Alexander, 1877A, 1900E, 1957B
Goehr, Alexander, 1932A; *Finding the Key*, 1998H
Goehr, Walter, 1903A, 1960B
Goepp, Philip H., 1864A, 1936B; *Annals of Music in Philadelphia*, 1896H; *Symphonies and Their Meaning I*, 1898H
Goerke, Christine, 1997E
Goerne, Matthias, 1967A, 1987C
Goetschius, Percy, 1853A, 1890F, 1896F, 1943B; *Applied Counterpoint*, 1902H; *Elementary Counterpoint*, 1909H; *Essentials of Music History*, 1913H; *Homophonic forms of Musical Composition*, 1898H; *The Larger Forms of Musical Composition*, 1915H; *Lessons in Music Form*, 1904H; *Masters of the Symphony*, 1929H; *The Material Used in Musical Composition*, 1882H; *The Structure of Music*, 1934H; *The Theory and Practice of Tone Relations*, 1892H
Goetz, Hermann, 1840A, 1876B
Goetze, Marie, 1865A, 1884C, 1922B
Goeyvaerts, Karel, 1923A, 1993B
Gogorza, Emilio de, 1874A, 1897C, 1949B
Gold, Arthur, 1917A, 1944C, 1990B
Gold, Ernest, 1999B
Gold Baton Award, 1983G
Goldbeck, Robert, 1839A, 1908B; *Encyclopedia of Music Education*, 1903H
Goldbeck Cons. of Music, 1868G
Goldberg, Albert, 1898A, 1925D, 1943D, 1990B
Goldberg, Johann Gottlieb, 1756B
Goldberg, Joseph, 1825A, 1837C, 1890B
Goldberg, Reiner, 1939A, 1966C
Goldberg, Szymon, 1909A, 1921C, 1990D, 1993B
Golde, Walter, 1887A, 1963B
Golden Age Singers, 1950G
Goldenweiser, Alexander, 1875A, 1961B
Goldman, Edwin Franko, 1878A, 1956B; *Band Guide & Aid to Teachers*, 1916H; *The Goldman Band System*, 1935H
Goldman, Richard Franko, 1910A, 1968D, 1980B; *The Band's Music*, 1938H; *The Concert Band*, 1946H; *The Wind Band*, 1961H

Goldman Band (N.Y.), 1911G
Goldmark, Karl, 1830A, 1848F, 1896E, 1915B
Goldmark, Rubin, 1872A, 1894F, 1909E, 1936B
Goldner String Quartet, 1995G
Goldovsky, Boris, 1908A, 1921C, 1942D, 1986E; *Accents of Opera*, 1953H; *Bringing Opera to Life*, 1968H; *Good Afternoon, Ladies & Gentlemen*, 1984H
Goldsbrough Orchestra, 1948G
Goldschmidt, Berthold, 1903A, 1996B
Goldschmidt, Hugo, 1859A, 1920B; *Italienische Gesangmethode des 17. Jahrhunderts*, 1890H; *Der Musikästhetik des 18. Jahrhunderts*, 1915H
Goldschmidt, Otto, 1829A, 1852F, 1907B
Goldschmidt, Walter, 1917A
Goldsmith, Barry, 1959A, 1982C
Goldstein, Ella, 1953E
Golianek, Ryszard Daniel, 1963A
Golinelli, Stefano, 1818A, 1891B
Gollmick Karl: *Handlexicon der Tonkunst*, 1858H; *Kritische terminologie*, 1833H
Golovanov, Nikolai, 1937D
Golovschin, Igor, 1956A
Golschmann, Vladimir, 1893A, 1928D, 1931D, 1958D, 1964D, 1972B
Golub, David, 1950A, 1964C, 2000B
Gombosi, Otto, 1902A, 1955B; *Tonarten und Stimmungen der antiken Musik*, 1939H
Gomes, André da Silva, 1752A, 1774D, 1844B
Gomes, Carlos, 1836A, 1864F, 1896B
Gomez-Martinez, Miguel-Angel, 1949A
Gomis y Colomer, José Melchor, 1791A, 1836B
Gondek, Juliana, 1953A, 1979C, 1983E
Gonley, Stephanie, 1966A
Goodall, Reginald, 1901A, 1936C, 1946D, 1975E, 1985E, 1990B
Goode, Richard, 1943A, 1962C, 1973E, 1980E
Goodman, Craig, 1957A, 1975C
Goodrich Alfred: *The Art of Song*, 1888H; *Complete Musical Analysis*, 1889H
Goodrich, William Marcellus, 1777A, 1833B
Goodrich, William, Organ Builder (Boston), 1804G
Goodrich, (John) Wallace, 1871A, 1907D, 1931D, 1952B; *The Organ in France*, 1917H
Goodson, Katharine, 1872A, 1897C, 1958B
Goosens, Eugene, 1893A, 1923D, 1931D, 1934E, 1947D, 1955E, 1962B
Goovaerts, Alphonse, 1849A, 1866D, 1922B; *La musique d'église*, 1876H
Gorchakova, Galina, 1962A, 1988C
Gordon, Alexander, 1755B
Gordon, Peter, 1951A
Gordon, Michael, 1956A
Gordon String Quartet, 1930G
Górecki, Henryk Mikolaj, 1933A
Gorin, Igor, 1908A, 1930C, 1982B
Goritz, Otto, 1873A, 1895C, 1929B
Gormley, Clare, 1969A

�֎

A *Births*   B *Deaths*   C *Debuts*   D *New Positions*
E *Prizes/Honors*

Görner, Johann Gottlieb, 1764D, 1778B
Görner, Johann Valentin, 1756D, 1762B
Gorno, Albin, 1945B
Gorodnitzki, Sascha, 1904A, 1930E, 1931C, 1986B
Gorr, Rita, 1926A, 1949C
Gorrara, Riccardo, 1964A
Gorzynska, Barbara, 1953A, 1974E
Gospel Workshop of America, 1968G
Goss, Adrian, 1956A
Goss, John, 1800A, 1838D, 1856E, 1872E, 1876E, 1880B; *Introduction to Harmony and Thoroughbass*, 1833H; *Parochial Psalmody*, 1827H; *Piano Forte Student's Catechism*, 1830H
Gossec, François-Joseph, 1751F, 1773D, 1780F, 1784D, 1795E, 1799E, 1804E, 1829B
Gossett, Philip, 1941A
Gotha, Germany: Bibliographisches Institut, 1826G; Court Theater, 1775G; Hoftheater, 1840G; Liedertafel, 1835G; Singverein, 1819G
Gothenberg Concert Hall, 1934G
Gothenberg School of Music, 1954G
Gothenberg Symphony Orchestra, 1905G
Gothenburg Grand Theater, 1859G
Gothoni, Rolf, 1994E
Gotkovsky, Ida, 1933A
Gotkovsky, Nell, 1939A, 1962C
Göttingen Singakademie, 1855G
Gottlieb, Jack, 1930A
Gottlieb, Jay (Mitchell), 1954A
Gottlieb, Johann, 1777F
Gottschalg, Alexander Wilhelm, 1827A
Gottschalk, Louis Moreau, 1829A, 1842F, 1852F, 1853F, 1856F, 1857F, 1861F, 1862F, 1865F, 1869B; *Notes of a Pianist*, 1881H
Götz, Franz, 1755A, 1788D, 1815B
Gotz, Johann, Publisher (Mannheim), 1768G
Götz, Johann Michel, 1810B
Götze, Emil, 1856A, 1901B
Götze, Franz, 1814A, 1888B
Gough, John, 1957A
Gould, Glenn, 1932A, 1946C, 1964F, 1982B
Gould, Glenn, Memorial Foundation, 1985G
Gould, Glenn, Prize, 1987G
Gould, Morton, 1913A, 1964, 1983E, 1986DE, 1994D, 1996B
Gould, Morton, Award, 1994G
Gould Nathaniel: *Social Harmony*, 1823H
Goulding, George, and Co., Publishers, 1786G
Gounod, Charles, 1818A, 1837F, 1839E, 1846F, 1852DF, 1866E, 1870F, 1889E, 1893B
Gourari, Anna, 1972A
Gouvy, Louis, 1896E
Gouvy, Théodore, 1819A, 1898B
Governor's State University Center for Arts & Technology, 1995G
Gow George: *The Structure of Music*, 1895H
Gow, Nathaniel, Music Shop, 1788G

Goward, Mary Anne, 1805A, 1823C, 1899B
Goy, Pierre, 1961A, 1983C
Grabner, Hermann: *Anleitung zur Fugen-composition*, 1934H; *Der Lineare Satz*, 1930H
Grädener Carl: *System der harmonielehre*, 1877H
Graetz, Joseph, 1760A, 1826B
Graf, Christian Ernst, 1804B; *Thoroughbass Method*, 1782H
Graf, Conrad, 1782A, 1851B
Graf, Conrad, Piano Builder (Vienna), 1804G
Graf, Friedrich H., 1772D, 1779E, 1795B
Graf, Hans, 1995D
Graf, Herbert, 1965D
Graf, Max, 1873A, 1958B; *From Beethoven to Shostakovich*, 1947H; *Geschichte & Geist der modernen Musik*, 1953H; *Die innere Werkstatt des Musikers*, 1910H; *Legend of a Musical City*, 1945H; *Modern Music—Composer & Critic*, 1946H
Graf, Walter, 1903A, 1982B
Gräfe, Johann Friedrich, 1787B
Graffigna, Achille, 1816A, 1896B
Graffman, Gary, 1928A, 1946E, 1847C, 1949E
Grafulla, Claudio S., 1810A, 1880B
Graham, Jean, 1948E
Graham, Martha, 1950F, 1974E, 1979E, 1985E, 1991B
Graham, Susan, 1960A
Grainger, Percy, 1882A, 1901C, 1950E, 1961B
Gramm, Donald, 1927A, 1944C, 1983B
Grammy Awards, 1958G
The Gramophone, 1923G
Granada, Spain: Ronconi Vocal School, 1829G; Sociedad de Cuartetos Clásicos, 1871G; Teatro del Campillo, 1810G
Granados, Enrique, 1867A, 1890C, 1914E, 1916B
Grand Canyon Chamber Music Festival, 1984G
Grand Ducal Conservatory, 1884G
Grandis, Franco de, 1984C
Grandison, Mark, 1965A
Grandjany, Marcel, 1909C, 1975B
Grand Teton Music Festival, 1962G
Grandval, Nicolas Recot de, 1753B
Granfelt, Lillian Hannah von, 1884A, 1908C
Granforte, Apollo, 1886A, 1914C
Grange, Anne Caroline de la, 1825A
Granier, François, 1779B
Granier, Louis, 1800B
Granjany, Marcel, 1891A
Grant, Frederick, 1903B
Grant, Mark N.: *Maestros of the Pen*, 1998H
Grant, Parks, 1910A
Grant, Degens & Bradbeer, Organ Builders, 1959G
Grantham, Donald, 1947A
Grasse, Edwin, 1884A, 1902C, 1954B
Grasset, Jean-Jacques, 1769A, 1839B
Grassi, Cecilia, 1760C, 1782B

❊

F *Biographical*   G *Cultural Beginnings*   H *Musical Literature*
I *Musical Compositions*

Grassineau, James, 1767B
Grassini Josephina, 1773A, 1789C, 1800F, 1806F, 1850B
Grau, Maurice, Opera Co., 1898G
Graudan, Nicolai, 1896A, 1964B
Graun, Carl Heinrich, 1759B
Graun, Johann Gottlieb, 1771B
Graupner, Christoph, 1760B
Graupner, Gottlieb, 1767A, 1795F, 1796F, 1788F, 1797F, 1808F, 1836B; *Rudiments of the Art of Playing the Pianoforte,* 1806H
Graupner Music Store & Publishing House (Boston), 1800G
Graves, Denyce, 1991E
Graves, Samuel, 1794A, 1878B
Graves, Samuel, & Co., Instrument Makers, 1830G
Graveure, Louis, 1888A, 1914C, 1965B
Grawemeyer Award, 1984G
Gray, Cecil, 1895A; *A Survey of Contemporary Music,* 1924H
Gray, H. Willard, 1950B
Gray, H. W., Co., Inc., Publisher, 1906G
Gray, Linda Esther, 1948A, 1969CE, 1973E
Gray, Matthias, Co., Publishers, 1858G
Gray and Davison, Organ Builders, 1774G
Gray's Inn Journal, 1752G
Graz, Austria: Fux, Johann Joseph, Society, 1955G; Männergesangverein, 1846G; Styrian Music Society, 1815G; Thalia Theater, 1864G
Graziani, Carlo, 1787B
Graziani, Francesco, 1828A, 1851C, 1901B
Graziani, Lodovico, 1820A, 1845C, 1885B
Graziani, Vincenzo, 1836A, 1906B
Grazioli, Giovanni Battista, 1782D
Greatorex, Thomas, 1758A, 1781D, 1786F, 1788F, 1819D, 1831B
Great Plains Chamber Music Institute, 1982G
Great Woods Center for the Performing Arts, 1986G
Greef-Andriessen, Pelagie, 1860A, 1884C, 1937B
Greek Royal Palace Boys' Choir, 1950G
Greek Society for Contemporary Music, 1966G
Green, Adolph, 1991E
Green, Barton, 1994E
Green, Elizabeth: *Principles of Violin Playing & Teaching,* 1962H
Green, Samuel, 1796B
Greenawald, Sheri, 1947A, 1974C
Greenbaum, Stuart, 1966A
Greenberg, Noah, 1919A, 1966B
Greenberg, Noah, Award, 1978G
Greene, Adam, 1970A
Greene, Arthur, 1978E, 1986E
Greene, David M.: *Greene's Biographical Encyclopedia of Composers,* 1985H
Greene, Harry Plunkett, 1936B
Greene, Maurice, 1755B

Greene, Plunkett, 1865A, 1888C
Greene, Susan, 1955A
Greene, Thomas "Blind Tom," 1849A
Greenfield, Elizabeth T., 1809A, 1851C, 1876B
Greenhouse, Bernard, 1916A, 1946C
Greensboro Opera Co., 1981G
Greenwich House Music School, 1906G
Gregoir Edouard: *Les artistes-musiciens néerlandais,* 1864H
Gregor Christian F.: *Choralbuch* (Moravian), 1784H
Gregor, Jószef, 1940A, 1964C
Gregorian, Leon, 1943A
Greindl, Josef, 1912A, 1936C, 1993B
Grell, (August Edward), 1800A, 1886B
Grenet, Francois-Lupien, 1753B
Grenser, Carl Augustin, 1756A, 1807B
Grenser, Johann Heinrich, 1764A, 1813B
Grenville, Lillian, 1888A, 1906C, 1928B
Gresnick, Antoine-Frédéric, 1755A, 1799B
Gretchaninov, Alexander, 1864A, 1889F, 1956B
Grétry, André, 1753F, 1759F, 1766F, 1767F, 1795E, 1802E, 1813B; *Mémoires,* 1789H
Gretsch, Fred, Mfg. Co. (Brooklyn), 1883G
Grey, Cecil, 1951B
Grey, Madeline, 1896A, 1919C, 1979B
Griebel, August, 1900A, 1922C
Grieg, Edvard, 1843A, 1858F, 1860F, 1861F, 1862F, 1866DE, 1867F, 1871F, 1872E, 1874E, !883E, 1885F, 1888F, 1890E, 1894E, 1896E, 1906E, 1907B
Grieg, Nina (Hagerup), 1845A, 1935B
Griepenkerl, Friedrich, 1782A, 1849B; *Lehrbuch der Aesthetik,* 1827H
Grier, Francis, 1956A
Griesbach, John Henry, 1798A, 1875B
Griesbacher, Peter: *Lehrbuch des Kontrapunkts,* 1910H
Griffel, Kay, 1940A, 1960C
Griffes, Charles Tomlinson, 1884A, 1903F, 1907D, 1920B
Griffes, Elliot, 1893A, 1967B
Griffith, David, 1939A
Griffith, Lisa, 1984C
Griffith Music Foundation, 1938G
Griffiths, Howard, 1950A
Griffiths, Paul, 1958A
Griffiths, Paul: *A Concise History of Music,* 1977H; *A Guide to Electronic Music,* 1979H; *Morder Music: The Avant Garde since 1945,* 1981H; *New Sounds, New Personalities: British Composers of the 1980s,* 1985H; *The Thames & Hudson Encyclopedia of 20th Century Music,* 1986H
Griggs, S. S., & Co, Publishers, 1848G
Grignon, Juan Lemote de, 1943D
Grigorian, Gegam, 1951A, 1971C
Griller String Quartet, 1928G
Grillo, Joan, 1939A, 1962C, 1999B

❄

A   *Births*   B   *Deaths*   C   *Debuts*   D   *New Positions*
E   *Prizes/Honors*

Grimaces, 1882G
Grimaud, Hélène, 1964A, 1969A, 1988C
Grimm, Carl Hugo, 1890A, 1978B
Grimm, Friedrich, 1807B; Le petit prophète de
    Boemisch-Broda, 1753H
Grimm, Julius Otto, 1860D
Grimsley, Greer, 1962A
Grin, Leonid, 1990D
Gringolts, Ilya, 1981A, 1998E
Grisar, Albert, 1808A, 1869B
Grisart, Charles-Jean, 1837A, 1904B
Grisi, Giuditta, 1805A, 1826C, 1840B
Grisi, Giulia, 1811A, 1829C, 1869B
Grist, Reri, 1934A, 1959C
Griswold, Putnam, 1875A, 1904C, 1914B
Grob-Prandl, Gertrud, 1917A, 1938C, 1995B
Grobe, Donald, 1929A, 1952C, 1986B
Groben, Françoise, 1965A
Grofé, Ferde, 1892A, 1972B
Grøndahl, Agathe, 1847A, 1907B
Grøndahl, Launy, 1925D
Gronemann, Albertus, 1778B
Groop, Monica, 1958A, 1986C
Groote, André de, 1940A, 1955C
Groote, Steven de, 1953A, 1977E
Grosheim, Georg Christoph, 1764A, 1841B;
    Über den verall der Tonkunst, 1805H; Über
    pflege und Anwendung der Stimme, 1830H;
    Versuch einer ästhetischen Darstellung...,
    1834H
Grosjean, Ernest, 1844A, 1936B
Groton Academy (New Hampshire), 1793G
Group for Contemporary Music, 1962G
Group for New Music (Mass.), 1974G
Group 49 (Poland), 1949G
Groupe de Recherches Théâtrales et
    Musicologiques, 1967G
Groupe d'Étude et de Realisation Musicales,
    1966G
Groupe Musiques Nouvelles, 1962G
Grout, Donald Jay, 1902A, 1987B; A History of
    Western Music, 1960H; A Short History of the
    Opera, 1947H
Groves, Charles, 1867F, 1873F, 1915A, 1973E,
    1992B
Grove, George, 1820A, 1839F, 1852D, 1882D,
    1883E, 1900B; Dictionary of Music and
    Musicians I, 1879H
Groves, Paul, 1964A, 1992C
Grua, Carlo Pietro, 1773B
Grua, Franz Paul, 1784D
Grube, Michael, 1954A, 1964C
Gruber, Andrea, 1965A, 1990C
Gruber, Franz, 1787A, 1863B
Gruber, Georg Wilhelm, 1765D, 1796B
Gruber, Johann S.: Beyträge zue literature der
    musik I, 1785H; Biographien einiger
    Tonkünstler, 1786H; Literatur der Musik,
    1783H

Gruberová, Edita, 1946A, 1968C
Gruenberg, Eugene, 1854A, 1928B
Gruenberg, Louis, 1884A, 1912C, 1964B
Grumiaux, Arthur, 1921A, 1939E, 1940CE,
    1973E, 1986B
Grümmer, Elisabeth, 1911A, 1941C, 1968B
Grün, Frederike, 1836A, 1917B
Grund, Friedrich Wilhelm, 1791A, 1828D,
    1873B
Gruner, Nathanael Gottfried, 1792B
Grunewald, Louis, Publisher, 1858G
Grunicke, Anton Franz, 1841A, 1913B
Grüning, Wilhelm, 1858A, 1881C
Grünner-Hegge, Odd, 1931D
Grünning, Wilhelm, 1942B
Grunsky, Karl, 1871A, 1943B; Der Kampf um
    deutsche Musik, 1933H; Musikästhetik, 1907H;
    Musikgeschichte des 17. Jahrhunderts, 1905H;
    Musikgeschichte des 18. Jahrhunderts, 1905H;
    Musikgeschichte des 19. Jahrhunderts, 1902H
Gruppe, Paulo, 1907C
Gruppo Team Roma, 1972G
Grützmacher, Friedrich, 1832A, 1903B
Gstaad Festival (Switzerland), 1956G
Guadagni, Gaetano, 1792B
Guadagnini, Giovanni, 1786B
Gualdo, Giovanni, 1771B
Guaneri, Pietro, 1762B
Guanieri, Camargo, 1907A, 1993B
Guardasoni, Domenico, 1806B
Guarducci, Tommaso, 1766C
Guarneri String Quartet, 1964G
Guarnieri Trio of Prague, 1986G
Guarrera, Frank, 1923A, 1948C
Guastavino, Carlos, 1912A, 2000B
Gubaidulina, Sofia, 1931A
Gubjornsson, Gunnar, 1988C
Gubrud, Irene, 1947A, 1972F, 1980E, 19981C
Gubrynowicz Publishing House, 1868G
Gudehus, Heinrich, 1845A, 1871C, 1909B
Gueden, Hilde, 1917A, 1939C, 1988B
Guelfi, Giangiacomo, 1924A, 1950C
Gueller, Bernhard, 1997D
Guénin, Marie-Alexandre, 1773C, 1835B
Guéranger, Dom Prosper-Louis, 1805A, 1875B;
    Institutions liturgiques I, 1840H
Guérin, Pierre N, 1822E
Guerrero, Antonio, 1776B
Guerrero, Manuela, 1773C
Guerrero, Rosalia, 1756C
Guest, Douglas, 1963D
Gueymard, Louis, 1822A, 1848C, 1880B
Guggenheim, Daniel, 1856A, 1930B
Guggenheim Fellowships, 1925G
Guggenheim Foundation, 1924G
Guglielmi, Pietro Alessandra, 1767F, 1793D,
    1804B
Guglielmi, Pietro Carlo, 1763A, 1817B
Guhr, Carl, 1787A, 1848B

❉

F   *Biographical*   G   *Cultural Beginnings*   H   *Musical Literature*
I   *Musical Compositions*

Gui, Vittorio, 1885A, 1907C, 1975B
Guichard, Louis J., 1775C
Guicharde, August, Musical Instruments, 1827G
Guidi, G. G., Publisher, 1844G
Guigui, Efrain, 1987E
Guignon, Jean-Pierre, 1774B
Guillaume, Edith, 1943A, 1970C
Guillemain, Louis-Gabriel, 1770B
Guilmant, Alexandre, 1837A, 1857D, 1863F, 1868D, 1871D, 1910E, 1911B
Guion, David, 1892A, 1962A, 1981B
Guiraud, Ernest, 1837A, 1859E, 1892B
Guiraud, Jean Baptiste, 1827E
Gulak-Artemovsky, Semyon S., 1813A, 1842C, 1873B
Gulbenkian Foundation, 1956G
Gulbranson, Ellen, 1863A, 1886C, 1947B
Gulbranson Piano Co., 1906G
Gulda, Friedrich, 1930A, 1944C, 1946E, 2000B
Guleghina, Maria, 1959A, 1984C
Gulin, Angeles, 1943A, 1963C
Gülke, Peter, 1986D
Gulli, Franco, 1926A, 1933C
Gulyás, Dénes, 1954A, 1978C
Gumprecht Otto: *Musikalische charakterbilder*, 1869H; *Unsere Klassischen Meister I*, 1883H
Gunge, Bo, 1964A
Gungl, Virginia, 1871C
GunMar Music, 1979G
Gunn, Barnabas, 1753B
Gunn, Glenn Dillard, 1874A, 1910D, 1922D, 1940D, 1963B; *A Course on the History & Esthetics of Music*, 1912H; *Music: Its History & Enjoyment*, 1939H
Gunn, John: *The Art of Playing the German Flute*, 1793H; *A Historical Inquiry...on the Harp in...Scotland...*, 1807H; *An Introduction to Music*, 1803H; *School of the German Flute*, 1796H; *Theory and Practice of Fingering the Violoncello*, 1789H
Gunn, Nathan, 1996E
Gunn School of Music & Dramatic Art, 1922G
Gunsbourg, Raoul, 1889D, 1893D, 1955B
Günther, Bernhard: *Dictionary of Contemporary Music from Austria*, 1997H
Günther, Mizzi, 1879A, 1897C, 1961B
Gunzenhauser, Stephen, 1942A, 1978D
Gura, Eugen, 1842A, 1865C, 1906B
Gurickx, Camille, 1848A, 1874C, 1937B
Guridi, Jésus, 1886A, 1961B
Gurilyov, Alexander, 1803A, 1858B
Gurlitt, Manfred, 1914D
Gurlitt, Willibald, 1889A, 1963B
Gurney Edmund: *The Power of Sound*, 1880H
Gurney, John, 1997B
Gürrlich, Joseph A., 1761A, 1816D, 1817B
Gurt, Michael, 1959A, 1982E
Guschlbauer, Theodor, 1969D, 1983D

Gusikoff, Michel, 1893A, 1978B
Gusman, Maurice, Philharmonic Hall, 1972G
Gustafsen, William, 1887A, 1920C, 1931B
Gustafson, Nancy, 1956A
Gustin, Denis-Pierre, 1971A
Gutchē, Gene, 1907A; *Music of the People*, 1978H
Gutheil Music House, 1859G
Gutheil-Schroder, Marie, 1874A, 1891C, 1935B
Gutiérrez, Horacio, 1948A, 1960C, 1970F, 1982E
Gutman, Natalia, 1942A, 1951C
Gutnikov, Boris, 1962E
Gutstein, Ernst, 1948C, 1998B
Guyer, Joyce, 1982E
Gwizdalanka, Danuta, 1955A
Gye, Frederick, 1809A, 1849D, 1878B
Gyldenfeldt, Graciela von, 1979C
Gyrowetz, Adalbert, 1763A, 1804D, 1850B
Gyurkovics, Mária, 1937C
Haack, Karl, 1751A, 1819B
Haar, James, 1929A
Haas, Alma, 1847A, 1868C, 1932B
Haas, Ernst Johann, 1792B
Haas, Friedrich, Organ Builder, 1836G
Haas, Joseph, 1879A, 1945D, 1960B
Haas, Pavel, 1899A, 1944B
Haas, Robert, 1886A, 1960B; *Auffuhrungspraxis der Musik*, 1931H; *Die Musik des Barocks*, 1928H; *Die Wiener Oper*, 1926H
Haas, Wolf Wilhelm, 1760B
Hába, Alois, 1893A, 1973B; *The Harmonic Foundations of the Quarter-tone System*, 1922H; *Mein Weg zur Viertel- und Sechsteltonmusik*, 1971H; *Neue Harmonielehre des diatonischen...*, 1927H; *Von der Psychologie der musikalischen Gestaltung*, 1925H
Habeneck, François-Antoine, 1781A, 1806D, 1822E, 1824D, 1828D, 1849B
Haberbier, Ernst, 1813A, 1869B
Haberl, Franz Xaver, 1840A, 1871D, 1889E, 1910B; *Magister Choralis*, 1865H; *Theoretisch-praktische Anweisung...Kirchengesang*, 1864H
Haberman, Michael, 1950A, 1977C
Habermann, Franz, 1783B
Habich, Eduard, 1880A, 1904C, 1960B
Hachette et Cie., Publishers, 1826G
Hacker, Benedikt, 1769A, 1829B
Hackett, Charles, 1889A, 1914C, 1942B
Hackley, Emma Azalia, 1922B
Hadden, James: *Modern Musicians*, 1914H
Haddock, Marcus, 1957A
Hadley, Henry, 1871A, 1895D, 1909D, 1911D, 1920D, 1924E, 1925E, 1929D, 1937B
Hadley, Henry, Foundation, 1938G
Hadley, Jerry, 1952A, 1976C, 1993E
Hadley, Vernon, 1986D
Hadow, W. H., 1859A, 1918E, 1937B; *Church Music*, 1926H; *Collected Essays*, 1928H; *English Music*, 1931H; *Music*, 1924H; *The*

❈

A   *Births*   B   *Deaths*   C   *Debuts*   D   *New Positions*
E   *Prizes/Honors*

Place of Music Among the Arts, 1933H; *Sonata Form*, 1896H; *Studies in Modern Music I*, 1892H
Haebler, Ingrid, 1954E
Haeffner, Johann Christian, 1759A, 1792D, 1808D, 1833B
Haefliger, Ernst, 1919A, 1942C; *Die Singstimme*, 1983H
Haendel, Ida, 1923A, 1937C, 1991E
Haeser August F.: *Chorgensangschule*, 1831H
Haffner, Johann, 1758G, 1767B
Hagegård, Håkan, 1945A, 1968C
Hageman, Richard, 1966B
Hagemann, Maurits, 1853D, 1865D
Hagen, Betty Jean, 1955E
Hagen, Daron, 1961A, 1985E, 1994E
Hagen, Friedrich Heinrich von der, 1780A, 1856B
Hagen Theodor: *Civilization and Music*, 1845H; *Musikalisches novellen*, 1848H
Hagerup (Grieg), Nina, 1867F
Hägg, Jakob Adolf, 1850A, 1928B
Häggander, Mari Anne, 1951A, 1977C
Hague, Charles, 1769A, 1821B
Hague, The, Holland: Concert Hall, The, 1987G; Diligentia Music Society and Hall, 1821G; Koninklijke Schouwberg, 1804G; Koninklijke Music School, 1826G; Reissiger Conservatory of Music, 1826G; Residentie Orchestra (The Hague), 1903G, 1904G
Hahn, Georg J.: *Wohl unterweisene General-Bass Schuler*, 1751H
Hahn, Hilary, 1981A, 1991C
Hahn, Reynaldo, 1874A, 1934D, 1947B; *Du Chant*, 1920H; *L'oreille au guet*, 1937H; *Thèmes variés*, 1946H
Haieff, Alexei, 1914A, 1947E, 1994B
Haigh, Thomas, 1769A, 1808B
Haijing, Fu, 1960A
Haile, Eugen, 1873A, 1933B
Haimovitz, Matt, 1970A, 1985C
Haines, Edmund, 1974B
Haines Brothers Piano Co., 1851G
Hainl, François, 1863D
Haitink, Bernard, 1929A, 1957D, 1961D, 1967D, 1987D
Haizinger, Anton, 1796A, 1821C, 1869B
Halász, László, 1905A, 1933C, 1965D
Halász, Michael, 1938A
Hale, Philip, 1854A, 1890D, 1891D, 1904D, 1934B
Hale, Robert, 1943A, 1965C
Hálek, Václav, 1937A
Hales William: *Sonorum doctrina rationalis et experimentalis*, 1778H
Halévy, Jacques, 1799A, 1807F, 1819E, 1826B, 1836E, 1854D; *Leçons de lecture musicale*, 1857H
Halffter, Cristóbal, 1930A

Halffter, Ernesto, 1905A, 1989B
Halfvarson, Eric, 1953A, 1977C
Halgrimson, Cindy, 1984E
Halifax, Nova Scotia: Atlantic Symphony Orchestra, 1968G; Choral Society, 1817G; Ladies College Music Dept., 1887G; Maritime Conservatory of Music, 1887G
Hall, Charles John, 1925A; *A Eighteenth Century Musical Chronicle*, 1990H; *A Nineteenth Century Musical Chronicle*, 1989H; *A Twentieth Century Musical Chronicle*, 1989H
Hall, David, 1916A, 1957D
Hall, Janice, 1953A
Hall, Marie, 1884A, 1902C, 1956B
Hall, Peter, 1977E, 1984D
Hall, Thomas, 1791A, 1874B
Hall & Quimby Brass Instrument Factory, 1862G
Hall, Mack, Co., 1895G
Hall, Thomas, Organ Builder, 1811G
Hall, William, Piano Maker, 1820G
Hall of Fame for Great Americans, 1900G
Hallé, Charles, 1819A, 1843F, 1849D, 1854D, 1883D, 1888E, 1895B; *Pianoforte School*, 1873H
Hallé Handel Festival, 1952G
Halle Hochschule für Theater & Musik, 1945G
Halle Madrigalists, 1963G
Hallén, Andreas, 1872D, 1885D, 1892D
Hallgrimsson, Haflidi, 1941A
Hallin, Margareta, 1931A, 1954C
Hallis, Adolph, 1896A, 1919C
Hallstein, Ingeborg, 1937A, 1956C
Hallström, Ivar, 1826A, 1901B
Halm, August: *Harmonielehre*, 1905H; *Von Grenzen und Ländern der Musik*, 1916H; *Von zwei Kulturen der Musik*, 1913H
Hals Brothers, Piano Makers, 1847G
Halvorsen, Johan, 1864A, 1893D, 1899D, 1935B
Hamal, Henri, 1820B
Hamal, Henri-Guillaume, 1752B
Hamal, Jean-Noël, 1778B
Hamari, Julia, 1942A, 1964E, 1966C
Hamblin, Pamela, 1954A, 1980C
Hambraeus, Bengt, 1928A
Hambro, Leonid, 1946E
Hamburg, Germany: Ackermann Theater, 1765G; Freunde der Religiösen Gesanges, 1819G; Grädener Vocal Academy, 1851G; Harmonic Gesellschaft, 1789G; Konzertsaal auf dem Kamp, 1761G; Krüss-Färber Konservatorium, 1884G; Musikakademie, 1873G; North German Symphony, 1945G; Opera House, 1926G; Philharmonic Concert Society, 1828G; Singakademie, 1819G; Thalia Theater, 1842G; Theater am Dammtor, 1827G; Tonkünstlerverein, 1867G; Vogt'sche Konservatorium, 1899G
Hamel, Marie-Pierre, 1786A, 1879B

❊

F *Biographical*   G *Cultural Beginnings*   H *Musical Literature*
I *Musical Compositions*

Hamelin, Marc-André, 1985E
Hamelle, Julien, Publisher, 1877G
Hamerik, Asger, 1843A, 1871D, 1923B
Hamerik, Ebbe, 1898A, 1951B
Hamilton, Catherine, 1782B
Hamilton, Clarence: *Epochs in Musical Progress*, 1926H; *Outlines of Music History*, 1908H; *Piano Music, Its Composers & Characteristics*, 1925H; *Piano Teaching*, 1910H; *Sound & Its Relationship to Music*, 1911H
Hamilton, David (critic), 1935A, 1965D; *The Listener's Guide to Great Instrumentalists*, 1981H
Hamilton, David (tenor), 1960A, 1984E
Hamilton, Iain, 1922A, 2000B
Hamilton, James A., 1785A, 1845B
Hamilton Organ Co., 1889G
Hamm, Charles, 1925A; *Music in the New World*, 1983H; *Opera*, 1966H
Hammer, Heinrich, 1954B
Hammerstein, Oscar, I, 1846A, 1919B
Hammond, Frederick, 1937A
Hammond, Joan, 1912D, 1929C, 1974E, 1996B
Hammond, John Hays, Jr., 1888A, 1965B
Hammond, Laurens, 1895A, 1973B
Hammond Chord Organ, 1950G
Hammond Instrument Co., 1929G
Hammond Organ Co., 1934G
Hampel, Anton Joseph, 1771B
Hampson, Thomas, 1955A, 1978E, 1981C
Hampton, Calvin, 1938A, 1984B
Hamvasi, Sylvia, 1972A
Han, Derek, 1957A
Han, Tong Il, 1965E
Hanani, Yehudi, 1943A
Hanchett, Henry Granger, 1853A, 1918B; *The Art of the Musician*, 1905H; *An Introduction to the Theory of Music*, 1918H
Handel, Georg Frederick, 1751F, 1759B, 1818F
Handel Opera Society of London, 1955G
Handel Society of Maine, 1814G
Handelsstandens Sangforening, 1847G
Handley, Vernon, 1962E, 1985D
Handschin, Jacques, 1886A, 1955B; *La musique de l'antiquité*, 1946H; *Der Toncharakter*, 1948H
Handt, Herbert, 1926A, 1949C
Handy, William C.: *Negro Authors & Composers of the United States*, 1935H
Hanfstängel, Marie, 1846A, 1867C, 1917B
Hanisch, Joseph, 1839D
Hanke, Karl, 1778D, 1781D
Hanks, Nancy, 1974E
Hanlick, Edward, 1848D, 1855D, 1856D
Hanlon, Kevin, 1953A, 1981E
Hannay, Roger D., 1930A
Hannikainen, Tauno, 1896A, 1942D, 1968B
Hanoi Conservatory of Music, 1956G
Hanon, Charles-Louis, 1819A, 1900B

Hanover, Germany: Alte Hannoversche Liedertafel, 1830G; Band, 1980G; Conservatory of Music, 1890G; Hofoper, 1837G; Männergesangverein, 1851G; State Opera House, 1852G; Verein Für Kirchlichen Gesang, 1856G
Hänsel, Peter, 1770A, 1831B
Hansen, Wilhelm, Music Publishing Co., 1853G
Hansford, Andrew, 1973A
Hanslick, Eduard, 1825A, 1849F, 1895F, 1904B; *Am ende des Jahrhunders*, 1899H; *Aus dem Concertsaal*, 1870H; *Aus dem Tagebuch eines Musikers*, 1892H; *Aus meinem Leben*, 1894H; *Aus Neuer und Neuster Zeit*, 1900H; *Geschichte des Concertwessens in Wian*, 1869H; *Konzerte, Komponisten...des letzten 15 Jahre*, 1886H; *Die Moderne Oper I*, 1875H; *Musikalische Stationen*, 1880H; *Musikalisches Skissenbuch*, 1888H; *Musikalisches und Literarisches*, 1889H; *Vom Musikalisch-Schönen*, 1854H
Hanson, George, 1989E, 1998D
Hanson, Howard, 1896A, 1921E, 1924D, 1935E, 1945E, 1946E, 1979E, 1981B; *Harmonic Materials of Modern Music*, 1960H; *Music in Contemporary American Civilization*, 1951H
Hanson, Peter S.: *Introduction to Twentieth Century Music*, 1967H
Hanssens, Charles-Louis, 1802A, 1871B
Hanssler Music Publishers, 1919G
Harasiewicz, Adam, 1955E
Harbison, John, 1938A, 1972E, 1980E, 1992E, 1998E
Harborfront Dance Theater, 1983G
Harburg, Edgar Y., 1898A
Harcourt, Brace & Co., 1919G
Hardelot, Guy d', 1858A, 1936B
Harder, Paul: *Basic Contrapuntal Techniques*, 1964H; *Music Manuscript Technique*, 1984H
Harding, Daniel, 1975A
Harding, Rosamond: *The Piano-Forte*, 1973H
Hardouin, Henri, 1808B; *Bréviaire du Diocese de Reims*, 1759H; *Méthode nouvelle pour apprendre le plain-chant*, 1762H
Hardy, Hamilton, 1879A, 1925E
Hargail Music Publishers, 1941G
Harker Music Publishing Co. (Salzburg), 1802G
Harlem School of the Arts, 1963G
Harmati, Sándor, 1936B
Harmon Fine Arts Center, 1973G
Harmonia Opera, 1983G
Harmonichord, 1810G
Harmonium, 1842G
Harmonizer The, 1940G
Harms Music Publishers, 1881G
Harney, Benjamin R., 1871A
Harnoy Ofra: 1965A, 1975C
Harp Pedal System, 1762G

A   *Births*   B   *Deaths*   C   *Debuts*   D   *New Positions*
                   E   *Prizes/Honors*

Harper, Edward, 1941A
Harper, Heather, 1930A, 1954C
Harper, Thomas, 1950A, 1982C
Harpsichord Music Society: 1957G
Harrap, George G. & Co., Ltd., 1901G
Harrell, Lynn, 1944A, 1957C, 1961C, 1971F, 1975E
Harrell, Mack, 1909A, 1938C, 1960B
Harrer, Gottlob, 1755B
Harries, Kathryn, 1951A, 1977C
Harris, Augustus, 1852A, 1888D, 1891E, 1896B
Harris, Charles K., Publisher, 1892G
Harris Donald, 1931A
Harris, Ernest: *Music Education*, 1978H
Harris, Margaret, 1971F
Harris, Murray M., Organ Factory, 1895G
Harris, Richard, 1956A
Harris Roy: 1898A, 1929F, 1942E, 1944E, 1973E, 1979B
Harris, Roy, Archive, 1973G
Harris Roy, Society: 1979G
Harris, William Henry: 1883A, 1929D, 1933D, 1956D, 1973B
Harris Concert Hall (Aspen), 1993G
Harrison, Beatrice, 1892A, 1907C, 1965B
Harrison, Guy Fraser, 1894A, 1930D, 1951D, 1965B
Harrison, Hazel, 1883A, 1969B
Harrison, Lou, 1917A, 1948E, 1973E
Harrison, Sadie, 1965A
Harrison, Samuel, 1760A, 1781C, 1812B
Harrison, Stanley C., Opera House, 1993G
Harrison, William, 1813A, 1839C, 1868B
Harrison & Harrison, Organ Builders, 1861G
Harrison's New German Flute Magazine, 1787G
Harsanyi, Janice, 1929A
Harsányi, Tibor, 1898A
Harshaw, Margaret, 1909A, 1942C, 1997B
Hart, Charles, 1797A, 1859B
Hart, George, 1839A, 1891B; *The Violin: Its famous Makers & Their Imitators*, 1875H
Hart, John Thomas, 1805A, 1874B
Hart, Joseph Binns, 1794A, 1844B
Hart, Weldon, 1911A, 1957B
Hart & Sons, Violin Makers, 1825G
Hart House String Quartet, 1924G
Härtel, Gottfried Christoph, 1763A, 1827B
Harteros, Anja, 1972A, 1996C
Hartford, Connecticut: Bushnell, Howard, Memorial Hall, 1930G; Chamber Orchestra, 1973G; Choral Club, 1907G; Choral Society, 1827G; Chorale, 1972G; Civic Center, 1975G; Euterpian Society, 1816G; Greater Hartford Arts Council, 1971G; Hosmer Hall Choral Union, 1881G; Jubal Society, 1822G; Oratorio Society, 1920G; Philharmonic Society, 1899G; School of Music, 1890G; Symphony Orchestra, 1934G; Wadsworth Atheneum, 1844G, 1934G

Harth, Sidney, 1925A, 1948E, 1949C
Hartig, Franz C., 1772C, 1819B
Hartke, Stephen, 1952A
Hartknoch, Johann Friedrich, 1789B
Hartknoch, Johann, Publisher, 1763G
Hartley, Walter S., 1927A
Hartman, Vernon, 1952A, 1977C
Hartmann, Arthur, 1881A, 1887C, 1956B
Hartmann, Carl, 1928C, 1969B
Hartmann Eduard von: *Philosophie des Schönen*, 1886H
Hartmann, Georges, Publisher, 1866G
Hartmann, Johann Ernst, 1768D, 1793B
Hartmann, Johann Peter, 1805A, 1843D, 1900B
Hartmann, Joseph, 1825D
Hartmann, Karl, 1895A
Hartmann, Karl Amadeus, 1905A, 1963B
Hartmann, Thomas, 1885A, 1956B
Hartt Opera Theater, 1942G
Hartt School of Music, 1920G
Harty, Hamilton, 1920D, 1941B
Harvard Musical Review, 1912G
Harvard University: College Orchestra, 1808G; Music School, 1862G; Musical Ass'n, 1808G; Pierian Society, 1808G
Harvey, Jonathan, 1939A
Harwood, Elizabeth, 1938A, 1960CE, 1963E, 1990B
Harwood, Richard, 1979A, 1990C
Harwood C. William, 1948A
Harwood C. William, 1982E
Häser, August Ferdinand, 1779A, 1844B
Haskell, Harry: *The Attentive Listener*, 1996H
Haskil, Clara, 1895A, 1903C, 1960B
Haslinger Music Publishers (Vienna), 1803G
Haslinger, Carl, 1816A, 1868B
Haslinger, Tobias, 1787A, 1842B
Hassard, John R., 1868D
Hasse, Hans: *Aufsätze zur harmonikalen Naturphilosophie*, 1974H
Hasse, Johann A., 1760F, 1763F, 1772F, 1773F, 1783B
Hasselmans, Josef, 1854D
Hasselmans, Louis, 1921D
Hasselt-Barth, Anna-Maria, 1813A, 1831C, 1881B
Hässler, Johann Wilhelm, 1822B
Hastings, Thomas, 1784A, 1858E, 1872B; *Devotional Hymns and Religious Poems*, 1850H; *Dissertation on Musical Tastes*, 1822H; *History of Forty Choirs*, 1854H; *The Juvenile Psalmody*, 1827H; *Musica Sacra*, 1816H; *The Musical Reader*, 1817H; *Sacred praise*, 1856H; *Spriritual Songs for Social Worship*, 1831H; *The Union Minstrel*, 1830H
Hataová, Anna Franziska, 1781B
Hattorri, Joji, 1969A
Haubenstock-Ramati, Roman, 1919A, 1994B
Haubiel, Charles, 1892A, 1977B

❈

F *Biographical*   G *Cultural Beginnings*   H *Musical Literature*
        I *Musical Compositions*

Hauer, Josef Matthias, 1883A, 1959B; *Deutung des Melos: Eine Frage an die Künstler und Denker unserer Zeit*, 1923H; *Über die Klangfarbe*, 1918H; *Vom Melos zur Pauke: Eine Einführung in die Zwölfton-musik*, 1925H; *Zwöltontechnik: Die Lehre vonden Tropen*, 1926H

Hauff Johann C.: *Theorie der Tonsetskunst I*, 1863H

Haug, Halvor: 1952A

Haugland, Aage, 1944A, 1968C, 2000B

Hauk, Minnie, 1851A, 1866C, 1878F, 1929B

Hauptmann, Moritz, 1792A, 1842D, 1868B; *Die Nature der Harmonik und der Metrik*, 1853H

Hausegger, Friedrich von, 1837A, 1899B; *Musik als ausdruch*, 1885H; *Vom jenseits des Kunstlers*, 1893H

Hausegger, Siegmund von, 1872A, 1918D, 1920D, 1948B

Hauser, Franz, 1794A, 1817C, 1846D, 1870B

Häuser, Johann: *Geschichte des christlichen...Kirchengesanges*, 1833H; *Neue pianoforte-schule*, 1832H

Häusler, Ernst, 1761A, 1800D, 1837B

Hausmusik, 1986G

Hausswald Günther: 1908A, 1974B; *Die deutsche Oper*, 1941H; *Dirigenten: Bild und Schrift*, 1966H; *Das neue Opernbuch*, 1951H

Hautzig, Walter, 1921A, 1943C

Havana, Cuba: Conservatorio de Música y Declamatión, 1899G; Conservatorio Nacional, 1885G; Cuban Academy of Music, 1814G; Festival of Contemporary Music, 1984G; National Symphony Orchestra, 1960G; Opera Troupe, 1811G; Sociedad de Música Clásica, 1866G; String Quartet, 1927G; Symphony Orchestra, 1910G; Teatro Coliseo, 1776G; Teatro de Circo, 1801G; Teatro de Tacón, 1846G

Havergal, William Henry, 1793A, 1870B

Haviland F. B., Publishing Co., 1904G

Havingha, Gerhardus, 1753B

Hawaii Opera Theater, 1960G

Hawdon, Matthias, 1787B

Hawes, William, 1785A, 1846B

Hawkes and Co., Music Publishers, 1865G

Hawkins, John, 1753F, 1771E, 1789B, 1944A; *General History of the Science & Practice of Music*, 1776H; *An Account of the Institution & Progress of the Academy of Ancient Music*, 1770H

Hawlata, Franz, 1963A, 1986C

Haxby, Thomas, 1796B

Haxby, Thomas, Instrument Maker, 1756G

Hayasaka, Fumio, 1914A, 1955B

Hayashi, Henzō, 1976B

Haydn, Franz J., 1752F, 1753F, 1754F, 1756F, 1761F, 1762F, 1766F, 1768F, 1769F, 1773F,

1776F, 1780E, 1784E, 1786F, 1790F, 1791EF, 1792F, 1793F, 1794, 1804E, 1805F, 1809B

Haydn, Michael, 1755F, 1762D, 1757D, 1798F, 1800F, 1804E, 1806B

Haydn, Nicholas, 1973B

Haydn Festival Choir (Indianapolis), 1932G

Haydn Institut (Cologne), 1955G

Haydn Male Chorus (Kansas City), 1925G

Haydn Monument (Rohrau), 1793G

Haydn Orchestra of London, 1949G

Haydon, Glen, 1896A, 1934D, 1966B; *Introduction to Musicology*, 1941H

Hayes, Catherine, 1825A, 1845C, 1861B

Hayes, Philip, 1776D, 1790D, 1797B

Hayes, Roland, 1887A, 1917C, 1925E, 1977B

Hayes, William, 1777B; *Anecdotes of the Five Music Meetings*, 1786H; *Art of Composing Music by a Method Entirely New*, 1751H; *Remarks on Avison's Essay on Musical Expression*, 1753H

Hayman, Cynthia, 1958A, 1984C

Hayman, Richard, 1951A

Haynes, William Sherman, 1864A, 1939B

Hays, William Shakespeare, 1907B

Hays, Sorrel, 1941A

Haywood, Lorna Marie, 1939A, 1964C

Headington Christopher, 1930A, 1996B; *The Bodley Head History of Western Music*, 1974H; *Illustrated Dictionary of Musical Terms*, 1980H; *Listener's Guide to Chamber Music*, 1982H; *Opera: A History*, 1987H; *The Orchestra & Its Instruments*, 1965H; *The Performing World of the Musician*, 1981H

Healey, Derek, 1936A

Heber, Reginald, 1783A, 1826B

Hebert, Pamela, 1946A, 1972C

Hebrew University Symphony Orchestra, 1955G

Heck John C.: *The Art of Fingering*, 1766H; *The Art of Playing the Harpsichord*, 1770H; *The Art of Playing Thorough Bass*, 1777H; *A Complete system of Harmony*, 1768H

Heckel, Clarina, 1890G

Heckel, Johann Adam, 1812A, 1877B

Heckel, Johann, Instrument Maker, 1831G

Heckel, Karl, Publisher (Mannheim), 1821G

Heckel, Wilhelm, 1856A, 1909B

Heckelphone, 1904G

Heckelphone-Clarinet, 1907G

Heckmann String Quartet, 1881G

Heckscher, Céleste de Longpré, 1860A, 1928B

Hedges Anthony, 1931A; *Basic Tonal Harmony*, 1987H

Hegar, Friedrich, 1865D, 1876D

Hege, Daniel, 1996F

Hegedüs, Ferenc, 1881A, 1944B

Heger, Robert, 1886A, 1913D, 1925D, 1933D, 1950D, 1978B

Hegyi, Julius, 1965D, 1983E

A   *Births*   B   *Deaths*   C   *Debuts*   D   *New Positions*

E   *Prizes/Honors*

Heidelberg, Germany: Bachverein, 1885G; Conservatory of Music, 1894G; Kammerorchester, 1861G; Stadtisches Orchester, 1889G
Heiden, Bernhard, 1910A
Heidler Ida, 1932B
Heifetz, Daniel, 1948A, 1970C
Heifetz Jascha, 1899A, 1911C, 1972F, 1987B
Heifetz, Robin, 1951A
Heifetz-Piatigorsky Concerts, 1961G
Heifetz-Piatigorsky-Rubinstein Trio, 1949G
Heighington, Musgrave, 1764D
Heilmann Uwe, 1960A, 1981C
Heim, Sean, 1999E
Der Heimgarten, 1876G
Heinefetter, Clara, 1813A, 1831C, 1857B
Heinefetter, Kathinka, 1819A, 1836C, 1858B
Heinefetter, Sabine, 1809A, 1822C, 1872B
Heiniö, Mikko, 1948A; *Contemporary Music, A History of Finnish Music*, 1995H
Heinitz Wilhelm, 1963B; *Instrumentenkunde*, 1929H
Heinrich, Anthony, 1781A, 1805F, 1810F, 1817F, 1827F, 1832F, 1861B
Heinrichshofen Publishers (Germany), 1806G
Heinroth, Johann August, 1780A, 1818D, 1846A; *Gesangunterrichts-Methode*, 1823H; *Kurze Anleitung, das Klavier...spielen zu lernen*, 1828H
Heinse Wilhelm: *Musical Dialogues*, 1805H
Heintzman & Co., Ltd., Piano Makers, 1860G
Heintzman, Theodore, 1817A, 1899B
Heinz, Hans, 1982B
Heinz Hall for the Performing Arts, 1927G
Heinze, Bernard, 1949E
Heinze, Gustav Adolf, 1850D, 1904B
Heise, Michael, 1940A, 1966C
Heise, Peter, 1830A, 1879B
Heja, Domonkos, 1974A, 1993C
Helfer, Walter, 1896A, 1959B
Helffer Claude, 1922A, 1948C
Hellendaal, Pieter, 1799B
Hellenic Conservatory of Music, 1919G
Hellenic Group of Contemporary Music, 1967G
Heller, Richard, 1954A
Heller, Stephen, 1813A, 1828C, 1887E, 1888B
Hellman Ivar, 1914D
Hellmesberger, Georg, 1830D, 1847D
Hellmesberger, Joseph, II, 1907B
Hellmann, Maximilian Joseph, 1763B
Hellmesberger String Quartet, 1849G
Hellmesberger, Georg, Jr., 1830A, 1852B
Hellmesberger, Georg, Sr., 1800A, 1819C, 1873B
Hellmesberger, Joseph, Jr., 1855A, 1863C, 1890D
Hellmesberger, Joseph, Sr., 1828A, 1851D, 1893B

Hellwig, Karl Ludwig, 1773A, 1815D, 1838B
Helm, Everett, 1913A; *Composer, Performer, Public*, 1970H; *Music & Tomorrow's Public*, 1981H
Helm, Theodor, 1843A, 1920B
Helmholtz, Hermann von, 1821A, 1894B; *On the Sensations of Tone as a Physiological Basis for the Theory of Music*, 1863H
Helmont, Charles-Joseph van, 1790B
Helps, Robert, 1928A, 1976E
Helsinki, Finland: Academic Choral Society, 1953G; Academic Music Society, 1830G; Chamber Orchestra, 1952G; City Orchestra, 1834G; College of Music, 1882G; Concert Society, 1877G; Festival of Contemporary Music, 1981G; Finlandia Hall, 1971G; Folk Conservatory, 1922G; Music Festival, 1968G; National Theater, 1902G; New Philharmonic Society, 1882G; Sibelius Academy, 1882G; Symphonic Society, 1845G
Helweg, Kim, 1956A
Hely-Hutchinson, Victor, 1901A, 1947B
Hemel, Oscar van, 1892A, 1981B
Heming, Percy, 1883A, 1915C, 1956B
Hemke, Frederick, 1935A
Hemm, Manfred, 1961A, 1984C
Hempel Freida, 1905C, 1955B
Hempel, Charles William, 1777A, 1855B; *Introduction to the Pianoforte...*, 1822H
Hempel, Frieda, 1885A
Hemsley Thomas, 1927A, 1951C
Henahan, Donald, 1947D, 1967D, 1979D
Hencke, Johann, 1766B
Henderson, Katherine, 1994C
Henderson, Roy, 1899A, 1925C
Henderson, William J., 1855A, 1887D, 1902D, 1937B; *Modern Musical Drift*, 1904H
Hendl, Walter, 1917A, 1949D, 1964D
Hendley, Vernon, 1998F
Hendricks, Barbara, 1948A, 1971E, 1972E, 1973CE, 2000E
Henke, Waldemar, 1876A, 1898C, 1946A
Henkel, Michael, 1780A, 1851B
Henle G. Verlag (Munich): 1947G
Henneberg, Johann Baptist, 1768A, 1790D, 1811D, 1822B
Henneberg, Richard, 1885D, 1925B
Hennig, Carl Rafael, 1845A, 1851D, 1914B; *Aesthetik der Tonkunst*, 1896H; *Einführung in das Wesen der Musik*, 1906H
Henning, Carl Wilhelm, 1784A, 1840D, 1867B
Henninges, Dora, 1860A
Henried, Robert, 1951B
Henriot, Nicole, 1925A
Henry, Joseph, Bowmaker, 1851G
Henschel, Jane, 1952A
Henschel, Lillian Bailey, 1860A, 1876C, 1901B

※

F   *Biographical*   G   *Cultural Beginnings*   H   *Musical Literature*
I   *Musical Compositions*

Henschel, George, 1850A, 1868C, 1881D, 1914E, 1934B; *Musings & Memories of a Musician*, 1918H
Hensel, Heinrich, 1874A, 1897C, 1935B
Henselt, Adolph, 1814A, 1889B
Henselt, Fanny Mandelssohn, 1805A, 1847B
Hensler, Elsie, 1836A, 1855C, 1929B
Hentzmann Erich, 1902A
Henze, Hans Werner, 1926A, 1963F, 1968F, 1969F, 2000E; *Essays*, 1964H; *Music & Politics*, 1982H
Heppner, Ben, 1988CE
Herbain, Chevalier d', 1769B
Herbart Johann Friedrich: *Psychologische Bemerkungen zur Tonlehre*, 1811H
Herbeck, Johann, 1831A, 1859D, 1870D, 1875D, 1877B
Herbert, Victor, 1859A, 1887F, 1893D, 1898D, 1908E, 194F, 1924B
Herbert, Victor, Orchestra, 1904G
Herbert, Walter, 1943D, 1975B
Herbig, Günther, 1931A, 1966D, 1972D, 1977D, 1981F, 1984D, 1990D
Herbig, Richard, 1917A
Herbing, August Bernhard, 1764D, 1766B
Hering, Karl Gottlieb, 1765A, 1853B; *Praktisches handbuch zur...des Klavier-Spielens*, 1796H; *Praktische Violin-Schule*, 1810H; *Zittauer Choralbuch*, 1822H
Hermann, Gottfried, 1808A, 1878B
Hermesdorff, Michael, 1833A, 1885B
Hermstedt, Simon, 1778A, 1846B
Hernándo, Rafael, 1822A, 1888B
Herold, Vilhelm, 1865A, 1893C, 1937B
Hérold, Ferdinand, 1791A, 1806F, 1812E, 1815F, 1821F, 1827D, 1833B
Hérold, François Joseph, 1755A, 1802B
Heroux, Magdalena, 1769C
Herrera de la Fuente, Luis, 1955D
Herreros, Manuel Bretón de los, 1837E
Herrmann, Bernard, 1911A, 1942E, 1943D, 1975B
Herrmann, Eduard, 1850A, 1937B
Herschel, William, 1757F, 1762D, 1780F, 1782F, 1816E, 1822B
Hertel, Johann Christian, 1754B
Hertel, Johann Wilhelm, 1789B
Hertz, Alfred, 1895D, 1872A, 1899D, 1902D, 1915D, 1942B
Hertz, Erich, Harpsichords, Inc., 1954G
Hertzmann, Erich, 1963B
Hervé (Florimond Ronger), 1825A, 1845D, 1851D, 1854D 1892B
Hervey, Arthur: *French Music in the Nineteenth Century*, 1904H
Herwig Käthe, 1914C, 1953B
Herz, Henri, Piano Maker, 1803, 1851G, 1888B
Herzog, Emilie, 1859A, 1880C, 1923B
Herzog, Johann Georg, 1854D

Herzogenberger, Heinrich, 1843A, 1900B
He, Vilém, 1869A, 1880C, 1908B
Heseltine, James, 1763B
Heseltine, Peter, 1894A
Hesperion XX, 1974G
Hess, Myra, 1890A, 1907C, 1941E, 1965B
Hess, Nigel, 1953A
Hess, Willy, 1859A, 1939B
Hesse, Adolph F., 1808A, 1863B
Hesse, Ernst C., 1762B
Hesse, Johann Heinrich, 1778B; *Kurze doch...answeisung zum General-Basse*, 1776H
Hesse, Julius, 1823A, 1881B
Hesse, Max, 1858A, 1907B
Hesse, Max, Publishing House, 1880G
Hessenberg, Kurt, 1908A, 1994B
Hester Mark Bowman, 1956A
Hetsch, Ludwig F., 1856D
Hétu Jacques, 1938A
Hétu, Pierre, 1936A
Heubner, Konrad, 1890D
Heugel, Jacques, & Co. (Paris), 1834G
Heuss, Alfred, 1877A, 1934B
Heussenstamm, George: *The Norton Manual of Music Notation*, 1987H
Hewitt, Helen, 1900A, 1977B
Hewitt, James, 1770A,1792F, 1798F, 1805D, 1812D, 1827B; *Collection of the Most Favorite Country Dances*, 1802H
Hewitt, John Hill, 1801A, 1825F, 1890B
Hewitt String Quartet, 1928G
Hey, Julius: *Deutscher Gesangunterricht*, 1885H
Heydrich, Bruno, 1863A, 1887C
Heyman, Katherine Ruth, 1877A, 1899C, 1944B
Hibernicon, 1823G
Hidalgo, Elvira de, 1892A, 1908C, 1980B
Hidas, Frigyes, 1928A, 1951D
Hiedler, Ida, 1867A, 1887C
Hier, Ethel Glenn, 1971B
Hiestermann, Horst, 1934A, 1957C, 1976F
Higgins, H. Murray, 1820A, 1897B
Higgins Brothers, Publishers, 1855G
Higginson, Henry Lee, 1834A, 1919B
High Anxiety Bones, 1991G
High Tor Opera Co., 1963G
Hildebrandt, Johann, 1775B
Hildebrandt, Zacharias, 1757B
Hiles, Henry, 1885D; *The Grammar of Music*, 1879H; *The Harmony of Sounds*, 1871H; *Harmony, Chordal or Contrapuntal*, 1894H; *Harmony or Counterpoint?*, 1889H; *Part-Writing or Modern Counterpoint*, 1884H
Hiley, David: *Western Plainchant, A Handbook*, 1993H
Hilger Trio, 1916G
Hilgermann, Laura, 1867A, 1885C, 1937B
Hill, Edward Burlingame, 1872A, 1916E, 1960B; *Modern French Music*, 1924H
Hill, Jenny, 1944A

❄

A *Births*   B *Deaths*   C *Debuts*   D *New Positions*
E *Prizes/Honors*

Hill, John, 1797B
Hill, Mabel Wood, 1870A
Hill, Norman & Beard, Organ Makers: 1916G
Hill, Ureli Corelli, 1802A, 1875B
Hill, Uri Keeler, 1780A, 1844B; *Solfeggio
Americano...*, 1820H; *The Handelian Repository*,
1814H; *The Sacred Minstrel*, 1806H; *The
Vermont Harmony*, 1801H
Hill, William, & Son, Organ Builders, 1755G
Hillard, Claire Fox, 1958A
Hillegas, Michael, Music Shop, 1759G
Hillemacher, Lucien, 1880E
Hillemacher, Paul Joseph, 1852A, 1876E, 1933B
Hiller, Ferdinand, 1811A, 1821C, 1828F, 1843D,
1847D, 1849E, 1850D, 1868E, 1885B; *Aus dem
Tonleben unserer Zeit*, 1868H; *Briefe an eine
Ungenannte*, 1887H; *Erinnerungsblätter*,
1884H; *Künstlerleben*, 1880H; *Die Musik und
das Publikum*, 1864H; *Musikalisches und
persönliches*, 1876H; *Wie hören wir Musik?*,
1881H
Hiller, Friedrich Adam, 1768A, 1799D, 1812B
Hiller, Johann A., 1751F, 1758F, 1787D, 1789D;
*Abhandlung über...achahmung der Natur in
Musik*, 1754H; *Allgemeines Choral-
Melodienbuch*, 1793H; *Anekdoten zur
lebensgeschichte grosser Regenten und
berühmter Staatsmänner*, 1772H; *Anweisung
zum musikalisch-richtigen gesange*, 1774H;
Anweisung zum musikalisch-zierlichen Gesang,
1780H; *Anweisung zur Singekunst in der
deutschen und italienischen Sprache*, 1773H;
Anweisung zum Violinspiel, 1792H;
*Lebensbeschreibungen berühmter
Musikgelehrten und Tonkunstler*, 1784H; *Über
alt und neu in der Musik*, 1787H; *Über die
Musik und deren werkungen*, 1781H; *Über
Metastasio und seine Werke*, 1786H; *Wer ist
wahre Kirchenmusik?*, 1789H
Hiller, Johann A., Singing School, 1771G
Hiller, Lejaren, 1924A, 1994B; *Experimental
Music*, 1959H; *Informations-theorie &
Computermusik*, 1964H
Hilliard Ensemble, 1974G
Hillis, Margaret, 1921A, 1955D, 1957D, 1972E,
1998B
Hillyer International Concert Arts Society,
1976G
Hilsberg, Alexander, 1897A, 1952D, 1961B
Hilt, Brian, 1956A, 1993B
Hime, Maurice, Publisher, 1790G
Himmel, Friedrich H., 1765A, 1785F, 1786F,
1793F, 11795D, 1797F, 1800F, 1814B
Hinckley, Allen C., 1877A, 1903C, 1954B
Hind, Rolf, 1964B
Hindemith, Paul, 1895A, 1917F, 1935DF, 1940F,
1953F, 1954E, 1963B; *A Composer's World*,
1952H; *Concentrated Course in Traditional
Harmony I*, 1943H; *Concentrated Course in

Traditional Harmony II, 1948H; *The Craft of
Musical Composition I*, 1937H; *The Craft of
Musical Composition II*, 1939H; *Elementary
Training for Musicians*, 1946H
Hinderas Natalie, 1927A, 1954C, 1987B
Hindsley, Mark, 1905A
Hines, Jerome, 1921A, 1941C, 1946E, 1962F;
Great Singers on Great Singing, 1984H; *This Is
My Story, This Is My Song*, 1968H
Hinrichs, Gustav, 1850A, 1942B
Hinrichsen Walter, 1907A, 1969B
Hinrichson's Musical Year Book, 1944G
Hinshaw, William Wade, 1867A, 1899C, 1903D,
1947B
Hinshaw School of Music, 1903G
Hipkins Alfred, *Description and History of the
Pianoforte*, 1896H; *Musical Instruments,
Historic, Rare and Unique*, 1888H
Hirokami, Jun'ichi, 1984E, 1991D
Hirose, Ryohei, 1930A
Hirsch Louis, 1924B
Hirsch, Paul, 1881A, 1951B
Hirsch, Abraham, Publishers, 1842G
Hirsch String Quartet, 1925G
Hirshhorn, Philippe, 1946A, 1967E, 1996B
Hirst Grayson, 1939A, 1969C
His Master's Voice, 1900G
Hislop, Joseph, 1884A, 1914C
*Historisch-Kritische Beytrage zur Aufnahme der
Musik*, 1754G
Hita, Antonio Rodriguez de, 1787B
Hitchcock, H. Wiley, 1923A; *Music in the United
States: A Historical Introduction*, 1969H; *New
Grove Dictionary of American Music*, 1986H
Hitzelberger, Sabina, 1755A, 1807B
Ho, Albert Benedict, 1955A
Ho, Sylvia, 1952A
Hobert, Johannes, 1833A
Hoboken, Anthony van, 1887A, 1983B
Hobson, Ian, 1952A, 1979C, 1981E
Hochschule für Kirchenmusik, 1948G
Höckh, Carl, 1773B
Hodges, Donald A.: *Handbook of Music
Psychology*, 1980H
Hodges, Edward, 1796A, 1839D, 1867B; *An
Essay on the Cultivation of Church Music*,
1841H
Hodges, J. Sebastian, B., 1830A, 1915B
Hodgkinson, Randall, 1955A
Hodkinson, Juliana, 1971A
Hodkinson Sydney P., 1934A
Hoedt, Henri-Georges d', 1885A, 1936B
Hoelstraete, Herman, 1985B
Hoesick, Ferdinand, 1867A, 1941B
Hoey Choo, 1958C, 1979D
Hoff, Jef van, 1959B
Höffgen, Marga, 1921A, 1952C, 1995B
Hoffman, Grace, 1925A, 1952C
Hoffman School of the Fine Arts (N.Y.), 1934G

❈

F *Biographical*   G *Cultural Beginnings*   H *Musical Literature*
I *Musical Compositions*

Hoffman, Richard, 1831A, 1909B
Hoffmann Ernst, 1935D
Hoffmann, E.T.A., 1776A, 1795F, 1804F, 1806F, 1807F, 1814F, 1815F, 1822B
Hoffmann Frank, 1990C
Hoffmann, Ludwig, 1885A, 1918C, 1964B
Hoffmeister, Franz Anton, 1754A, 1812B
Hoffmeister, Franz Anton, Publisher, 1783G
Hoffmeister & Kühnel's Bureau de Musique, 1800G
Hoffmann, Heinrich, 1842A, 1902B; *Geschichte des deutschen Kirchenlieds*, 1832H; *Schlesische volkslieder mit melodien*, 1842H
Hofmann, Josef, 1876A, 1886C, 1926D, 1957B; *Piano Questions Answered*, 1909H
Hofmann, Leopold, 1793B
Hofmann Peter, 1944A, 1972C
Hofmann Richard, 1844A, 1918B; *Katechismus der Musikinstrumente*, 1909H
Hofmannsthal, Hugo von, 1874A, 1929B
Hofmeister, Friedrich, 1782A, 1864B; *Handbuch der musikalischen Literatur*, 1817H
Hofmeister, Friedrich, Publishers, 1807G
Hogarth, George, 1783A, 1846D, 1870B; *Memoirs of the Musical Drama*, 1838H; *Musical History, Biography and Criticism*, 1835H; *The Philharmonic Society of London*, 1862H
Hogenson, R.: *Basics of Music*, 1987H
Hogwood Christopher, 1941A, 1985F, 1986D, 1988D
Hohenloher String Quartet, 1991G
Hohmann Christian: *Lehrbuch der musikalischen Composition*, 1846H; *Praktische Violin-schule*, 1849H; *Praktische Orgelschule*, 1859H
Hohner Harmonica Factory, 1857G
Hoiby, Lee, 1926A, 1957E
Hol, Richard, 1904B
Holand, Egil, 1924A
Holde Artur, 1885A, 1962B; *Jews in Music*, 1959H
Holden John: *An Essay towards a Rational System of Music*, 1770H
Holden, Oliver, 1765A, 1787F, 1818F, 1844B; *American Harmony*, 1792H; *Charlestown Collection of Sacred Songs*, 1803H; *Massachusetts Compiler*, 1795H; *Modern Collection of Sacred Music*, 1800H; *Plain Psalmody and Sacred Dirges*, 1800H; *Union Harmony*, 1793H; *Vocal Companion*, 1807H; *The Worcester Collection*, 1797H
Holden, Smollet, Music Shop (Dublin), 1807G
Hollaender, Gustav, 1894D
Hollaender, Viktor, 1866A, 1940B
Holland, Charles, 1909A, 1954C, 1987B
Holland, James: *Percussion*, 1978H
Hollander Lorin, 1944A, 1955C
Holle, Hugo, 1890A, 1942B
Hölle, Matthias, 1951A, 1976C
Holliday, Melanie, 1951A, 1973C

Holliger, Heinz, 1939A
Hollister Carroll, 1901A, 1925C, 1983B
Hollister, Frederick, 1761A
Hollister, Philip, 1760B
Holloway David, 1942A, 1968C
Hollreiser, Heinrich, 1913A, 1933D, 1952D, 1961D
Hollweg, Ilse, 1922A, 1942C, 1990B
Hollweg Werner, 1936A, 1962C
Hollywood, California: Bowl Concerts, 1922G; Bowl Orchestra, 1990G; String Quartet, 1947G
Holm, Ludvig, 1860A, 1921B
Holm Richard, 1912A, 1937C, 1988B
Holmboe, Vagn, 1909A, 1996B
Holmès, Augusta, 1903B
Holmes, Edward, 1797A, 1826D, 1859B; *A Ramble among the Musicians of Germany*, 1828H
Holmès, Augusta, 1847A
Holmquist, John E., 1955A, 1979C
Holoman, D. Kern: *Evenings with the Orchestra*, 1992H; *Writing about Music*, 1988H
Holst, Gustav, 1874A, 1923F, 1934B
Holst, Henry, 1899A, 1919C, 1991B
Holst, Imogen, 1984B
Holt Henry, 1934A, 1961C, 1966D, 1997B
Holt, Henry, & Co., Publishers, 1873G
Holtkamp Organ Co., 1855G
Holtman, Heidrun, 1961A
Holton, Frank, 1858A, 1918F, 1942B
Holton Julian, 1991C
Hol, Ondřej Frantiek, 1783B
Holyoke, Samuel, 1762A, 1789F, 1800F, 1820B; *The Christian Harmonist*, 1804H; *Columbian Repository of Sacred Harmony*, 1802H; *Harmonia Americana*, 1791H; *Instrumental Assistant I*, 1800H; *Instrumental Assistant II*, 1807H
Holzbauer, Ignaz, 1751D, 1753D, 1783B
Holzbogen, Johann Georg, 1775B
Holzer, Ruth, 1963A
Holzmair, Wolfgang, 1951A
Homer, Louise, 1871A, 1898C, 1947B
Homer, Sidney, 1864A, 1953B
Homilius, Gottffried A., 1755D, 1785B
Homs, Joaquín, 1906A
Honeck Manfred, 1958A
Honegger Artur, 1892A, 1920F, 1938E, 1955B; *Je suis compositeur*, 1951H
Honegger, Marc, 1926A; *Dictionnaire de la musique*, 1970H; *Dictionnaire des oeuvres de la musique*, 1992H; *Science de la musique*, 1976H
Honeybourne, Duncan John, 1977A, 1993C
Hong, Hei-Kyung, 1958A, 1983C
Hong Kong: Academy for the Performing Arts, 1986G; Cultural Centre, 1989G; Philharmonic Orchestra, 1974G
Hong-Shen, Li, 1960A

※

A *Births*   B *Deaths*   C *Debuts*   D *New Positions*
E *Prizes/Honors*

Höngen, Elisabeth, 1906A, 1933C, 1997B
Honolulu, Hawaii: Amateur Music Society,
1860G; Blaisdell Memorial Center, 1964G;
Symphony Chorus, 1978G; Symphony
Orchestra, 1900G, 1978G
Hood, Helen, 1863A, 1949B
Hood, Mantle: *The Ethnomusicologist*, 1971H
Hood's Magazine, 1844G
Hoof, Jef van, 1886A
Hoogstraten, Willem van, 1884A, 1914D,
1925D, 1939D, 1965B
Hook & Hastings, Organ Builders, 1827G
Hook, James, 1774D, 1827B; *Guida de Musica I*,
1785H; *Guida de Musica II*, 1794H; *New Guida
de Musica*, 1796H
Hoover, Katherine, 1937A
Hope Publishing Co., 1892G
Hope-Jones, Henry, 1859A
Hope-Jones, Robert, 1914B
Hope-Jones Organ Co., 1894G, 1907G
Hopekirk, Helen, 1856A, 1878C, 1945B
Hopf, Hans, 1916A, 1936C, 1993B
Hopkins, Asa, 1779A, 1838B
Hopkins, Asa, Woodwind Maker, 1829G
Hopkins, Charles Jerome, 1836A, 1898B
Hopkins, Edward John, 1818A, 1843D, 1901B
Hopkins, John, 1957D
Hopkinson, John & James, Piano Makers,
1841G
Hopkinson, Francis, 1754F, 1759F, 1791B; *A
Collection of Psalm Tunes with a Few Anthems*,
1763H; *The Psalms of David*, 1767H
Hoppin, Richard H., 1913A, 1991B; *Medieval
Music*, 1978H
Hopwood & Crew, Publishers, 1860G
Horbowski, Mieczyslaw Apolinary, 1849A,
1873C, 1937B
Horenstein, Jascha, 1898A, 1923C, 1925D,
1929D, 1973B
Hori, K.: *Japanese Compositions in the 20th
Century*, 2000H
Höricke Friedrich, 1963A
Horigome, Yuzuko, 1960A, 1980E
Horizon, 1939G
Horn, Charles E., 1786A, 1809C, 1847D,
1849B
Horn, Karl Friedrich, 1762A, 1830B; *A Treatise
on Harmony*, 1821H
Horn, Peter J.: 1922A
Hornbostel, Erich Moritz von, 1877A, 1935B
Horne Marilyn, 1934A, 1957C, 1982E, 1993E,
1995DE, 1999F
Horne, William, 1983B
Horneman, Christian F. E., 1840A, 1906B
Horneman & Erslev, 1846G
Horner Institute of Fine Arts, 1914G
Hornik, Gottfried, 1940A
Horowitz, Vladimir, 1903A, 1920C, 1965E,
1986F, 1988F, 1989BE

Horsley, Charles Edward, 1822A, 1876B;
Textbook of Harmony, 1876H
Horsley Colin, 1920A, 1943C
Horsley, Imogene: *The Fugue*, 1966H
Horsley, William, 1774A, 1847E, 1858B; *An
Explanation of the Musical Intervals*, 1825H;
Introduction to Harmony and Modulation,
1847H; *The Musical Treasury*, 1853H
Horst, Anthon van der, 1899A, 1931D, 1965B
Horszowski, Mieczyslaw, 1892A, 1902C,
1993B
Horvat, Milan, 1919A, 1958D, 1969D, 1975D;
Techniques & Materials of Tonal Music, 1975H
Holer, Zdeněk, 1951D
Hosmer, Lucius, 1870A, 1935B
Hostinsk, Otakar, 1847A, 1910B; *Die Lehre von
den musikalischen Klängen*, 1879H
Hotter Hans, 1909A, 1929C
Hotteterre, Jacques, "le Romain," 1762B
Hotteterre, Louis, 1761B
Houdard, Georges, 1860A, 1913B
Hough, Stephen, 1961A, 1982CE, 1983E
Houghton, H. O., & Co. (Houghton-Mifflin
Co.), 1852G
Houston, Texas: Ballet Academy, 1959G; Ballet
Co., 1955G; Civic Symphony, 1968G;
Cultural Arts Council, 1978G; Friends of
Music, 1959G; Gilbert & Sullivan Society,
1952G; Grand Opera Co., 1955G;
Harpsichord Society, 1967G; Lyric Theater
Center, 1985G; Moores School of Music
Building (U. of Houston), 1997G; Pops
Orchestra, 1971G; Symphony Orchestra,
1913G; Symphony Chorale, 1947G
Houtmann, Jacques, 1986D
Hovenden, Thomas, 1882E
Hovhaness, Alan, 1911A, 2000B
Hovingham Music Festival, 1887G
Howard, Ann, 1936A, 1964C
Howard, Emmons, 1931B
Howard, Emmons, Organ Builder (Westfield),
1883G
Howard, John Tasker, 1890A, 1964B; *Modern
Music*, 1957H; *Our American Music*, 1931H;
Our Contemporary Composers, 1941H; *A Short
History of Music in America*, 1957H; *This
Modern Music*, 1942H
Howard, Kathleen, 1884A, 1907C, 1956B;
Confessions of an Opera Singer, 1918H
Howard, Leslie, 1948A, 1967C
Howard, Samuel, 1760A, 1782B
Howarth, Judith, 1962A, 1984C
Howe, Elias, 1820A, 1895B
Howe, Elias, Music Store, 1842G
Howe, Elias, Publishing Firm II, 1860G
Howe, Mary, 1882A, 1964B
Howell, Gwynne, 1938A, 1968C, 1998E
Howells, Anne, 1941A, 1966C
Howells, Herbert, 1892A, 1983B

❖

F   *Biographical*   G   *Cultural Beginnings*   H   *Musical Literature*
I   *Musical Compositions*

Howes, Frank: *The Borderland of Music &*
Psychology, 1926H; *The English Musical*
Renaissance, 1966H; *Folk Music of Britain &*
Beyond, 1969H
Hristić, Stevan, 1885A, 1958B
Hruby Conservatory of Music, 1918G
Hsu, Hsin-Ay, 1997E
Hsu Tsang-houei: *Essays on the History of*
Music, 1996H; *The Music of China*, 1991H
Hu, Kun, 1979C
Hu, Nai-Yuan, 1985E
Hubay, Jenö, 1858A, 1937B
Hubbard, William: *The American History &*
Encyclopedia of Music, 1910H
Hubebni Matice, Publisher, 1871G
Huber, Hans, 1852A, 1892E, 1896D, 1905D,
1921B
Huber, Kurt, 1893A, 1943B
Huberdeau, Gustav, 1874A, 1898C
Huberman, Bronislaw, 1882A, 1890C, 1947B;
Aus der Werkstatt des Virtuosen, 1912H
Hubert, Charles, 1859A
Hubert, Christian Gottlob, 1793B
Hubert, Nicolai, 1881D
Huberti, Gustave-Léon, 1874D, 1865E, 1891E,
1910B
Huberty, Albert, 1881A, 1903C
Huddersfield, England: Chamber Music
Society, 1900G; Choral Society, 1836G
Hudecek, Václav, 1952A, 1967C
Hudson, Robert, 1815B
Hüe, Adolphe, 1881E
Hüe, Georges, 1858A, 1879E, 1922E, 1948B
Hueffer, Francis, 1843A, 1878D, 1886D, 1889B;
Half a Century of Music in England, 1889H;
Musical Studies, 1880H; *The Troubadours*,
1877H
Huehn, Julius, 1904A, 1935C, 1971B
Huet, Jean Baptiste, 1769E
Huffstodt Karen, 1954A, 1982C
Hug and Co., Music House, 1791G
Hugard, Pierre, 1761B
Hughes, Anselm, 1889A, 1974B
Hughes, Edwin, 1884A, 1912C, 1965B
Hughes, Herbert, 1912D
Hughes, Owain Arwel, 1942A, 1995D
Hughes, Rupert, 1872A, 1956B; *American*
Music, 1914H; *Contemporary American*
Composers, 1900H; *The Musical Guide (Music*
Lover's Encyclopedia), 1903H; *The Music-*
Lover's Encyclopedia, 1912H
Hugo, John Adam, 1945B
Huhn, Bruno, 1950B
Hulbert, Duane, 1980E
Hull, Arthur: *Modern Harmony*, 1914H; *Modern*
Musical Styles, 1916H
Hull, Percy C., 1878A, 1947E, 1968B
Hullah, John, 1812A, 1872D, 1884B; *A Grammar*
of Counterpoint, 1864H; *A Grammar of*

Harmony, 1852H; *A Grammar of Vocal Music*,
1843H; *History of Modern Music*, 1862H;
Music in the House, 1877H
Hüllmandel, Nicolas-Joseph, 1756A, 1823B;
Principles of Music...for the Pianoforte, 1795H
Hult Center for the Performing Arts, 1982G
Hume, Paul, 1915A, 1946D; *Catholic Church*
Music, 1956H; *Our Music, Our Schools & Our*
Culture, 1957H
Hummel, Johann Nepomuk, 1778A, 1787C,
1788F, 1790F, 1793F, 1804F, 1811F, 1816D,
1819D, 1825E 1837B; *Anweisung zum Piano-*
forte spiel, 1828H
Hummel Music Publishing Co., 1753G
Humperdinck, Engelbert, 1854A, 1872F,
1879EF, 1881E, 1890D, 1896F, 1921B; *Essayo*
de un metodo de armonia, 1885H
Humpert, H.: *Lexikon der elektronishchen Musik*,
1973H
Humphreys, Douglas, 1976E
Huneker, James G., 1857A, 1891D, 1900D,
1919D, 1921B; *Iconoclasts*, 1905H; *Ivory Apes*
& Peacocks, 1915H; *Melomaniacs*, 1902H;
Overtones: A Book of Temperaments, 1904H;
The Philharmonic Society of New York & Its
75th Anniversary, 1917H
Hungarian Music, 1960G
Hungary: Chamber Orchestra, 1957G; Radio &
TV Symphony Orchestra, 1945G; Hungarian
Recording Co., 1951G; State Folk Ensemble,
1950G; State Philharmonic Orchestra, 1949G;
State Symphony Orchestra, 1923G; String
Quartet, 1935G; Wind Quintet, 1961G
Hungerford, Bruce, 1922A, 1951C, 1977B
Hüni-Mihacsek, Felice, 1891A, 1919C, 1976B
Hunt, Alexandra, 1940A, 1971C
Hunt-Lieberson, Lorraine, 1954A
Hunter, Rita, 1933A, 1956C
Huré, Jean, 1877A, 1925D, 1930B; *La technique*
de l'orgue, 1918H
Hůrka, Friedrich, 1762A, 1784C, 1805B
Hurley, Laurel, 1927A, 1943C
Hurok, Sol, 1888A, 1974B·
Hurst, John, 1996C
Hurum, Alf, 1882A, 1972A
Husa, Karel, 1921A, 1950E, 1994E
Hüsch, Gerhard, 1901A, 1923C, 1984B
Hus-Desforges, Pierre-Louis, 1773A, 1838B
Huss, Henry Holden, 1862A, 1953B
Hussa, Maria, 1894A, 1917C
Huston, Scott, 1916A, 1991B
Hutcheson, Ernest, 1871A,
Hutcheson, Jere, 1937D, 1951B; *Musical Form &*
Analysis, 1972H
Hutchings, George Sherburn, 1835A, 1913B
Hutchings, Plaisted & Co., Organ Builders,
1869G
Hutchinson, Nigel, 1988C
Hutchinson, Stuart, 1956A

❋

A *Births*   B *Deaths*   C *Debuts*   D *New Positions*
E *Prizes/Honors*

Hüttenbrenner, Anselm, 1794A, 1868B
Hüttenrauch, Carl August, 1794A, 1848B
Huybrechts, Albert, 1926E
Huybrechts, François, 1946A, 1968E, 1979D
Hvorostovsky, Dmitri, 1962A, 1986C, 1987E
Hykes, David, 1953A
Hykryn, Jan, 1974A
Hyla, Lee, 1952A
Hymn Society of America, 1922G
The Hymn, 1949G
Hynes, Elizabeth, 1947A
Hynninen, Jorma, 1941A, 1970C, 1984D
Iannacone, Anthony, 1943A
Iberia Musical y Literaria, 1841G
Ibert, Jacques, 1890A, 1919E, 1937D, 1956E, 1962B
Iceland (*see also* Reykjavick): Opera Co., 1982G; Society of Musical Artists, 1940G; Schola Cantorum, 1996G; Symphony Orchestra, 1950G
Ichiyanagi, Toshi, 1933A, 1989D; *Music & the Contemporary Age*, 1998H
ICM Artists, 1976G
Idaho Falls Opera Theater, 1978G
Idelsohn, Abraham Zevi, 1882A, 1938B; *The Ceremonies of Judaism*, 1929H; *A History of Jewish Music*, 1924H; *Jewish Liturgy & its Development*, 1932H; *Jewish Music in its Historical Development*, 1929H; *Thesaurus of Hebrew-Oriental Melodies*, 1914H
Idelsohn Music School, 1919G
Idyllwild School of Music, 1950G
Ifukube, Akira, 1915A; *The Work of Music and the Problem of its Identity*, 1986H
Igloi, Thomas, 1947A, 1969C, 1971E
Ikebe, Shin-Ichiro, 1943A, 1976E, 1991E
Ikenouchi, Tomojirô, 1906A, 1991B
Ikonen, Lauri, 1888A, 1966B
Ikonomou, Katharina, 1957A, 1984C
Ikonomov, Boyen Georgiev, 1973B
Iliev, Konstantin, 1924A, 1956D, 1988B
Ilitsch, Daniza, 1914A, 1936C, 1965B
Illinois Chamber Orchestra, 1986G
Illustración Musical Hispano-Americana, 1888G
L'illustration, 1843G
Ilosfalvy, Robert, 1927A, 1954C
Imbault, Jean-Joseph, 1753A, 1770C, 1823B
Imbault, Jean, Publisher, 1783G
Imbrie, Andrew, 1921A, 1947E, 1950E, 1969E, 1980E
Improvisation Chamber Ensemble, 1957G
INA Memoire Vive, 1992G
Inbal, Eliahu, 1936A, 1956C, 1963E, 1974D, 1983D, 2000D
Ince, Kamran, 1960A, 1987E
Inch, Herbert, 1988B
Inchihara, Taro, 1950A, 1980C
Incledon, Charles, 1763A, 1784C, 1826B
Incontri Musicali, 1953G

Incorporated Association of Organists, 1913G
Indiana (*see also* Indianapolis; Lafayette): College of Music & Fine Arts, 1907G; Opera Theater, 1983G; State U. Contemporary Music Festival, 1967G; University Folklore Archives, 1956G; University Musical Arts Center, 1972G
Indianapolis, Indiana: Circle Theater, 1984G; Haydn Festival Choir, 1932G; Ladies Matinee Musical, 1877G; Männerchor, 1854G; Mendelssohn Choir, 1916G; Opera, 1975G; Orchestral Association, 1911G; Philharmonic Orchestra, 1871G; Symphony Orchestra I, 1896G; Symphony Orchestra II, 1910G; Symphony Orchestra III, 1930G; Violin Competition, 1982G
Indy, Vincent d', 1851A, 1872D, 1885E, 1892E, 1931B
Infantino, Luigi, 1921A, 1943C, 1991B
Ingalls, Jeremiah, 1764A, 1838B; *The Christian Harmony*, 1805H
Ingelbrecht, D. E., 1880A, 1908D, 1934, 1945D
Ingenhoven, Jan, 1951B
Ingham, Steve, 1951A
Inghelbrecht, D. E., 1965B; *Le chef d'orchestre parle au public*, 1957H; *Diabolus in musica*, 1933H; *Mouvement contraire: Souvenirs d'un musician*, 1947H
Inghilleri, Giovanni, 1894A, 1919C, 1959B
Ingolfsson, Judith, 1998E, 2000C
Innes, Frederick Neil, 1854A, 1926B
Innes School of Music, 1916G
Innisfree Festival Opera, 1986G
Innsbruck, Austria: Liedertafel, 1855G; Redoutengebäude, 1773G
Inoue, Michiyoshi, 1946A, 1983D, 1990D
Insanguine, Giacomo A., 1781D, 1785D, 1795B
Inspiration Point Fine Arts Colony, 1950G
Institut für Neue Musik & Musikerziehung, 1947G
Institut de Recherche...Acoustique/Musique, 1977G
Institute for Jewish Music, 1910G
Institute for Psychoacoustics & Electronic Music, 1962G
Institute for the History of Music, 1919G
Institute for Twentieth Century Music (Tokyo), 1957G
Institute Jaques-Dalcroze, 1915G
Institute of American Music, 1964G
Institute of Medieval Music, 1957G
Institute of Puerto Rican Culture, 1955G
Institution for the Encouragement of Church Music, 1784G
Instituto de Música da Bahia, 1877G
Instituto di Storia della Musica dell'Università, 1957G
Instituto Español de Musicologia, 1943G

※

F *Biographical*   G *Cultural Beginnings*   H *Musical Literature*
I *Musical Compositions*

Instituto Interamericano de Musicologia, 1938G
Instituto Nacional de Bellas Artes, 1877G
Instituto Superior de Arte, 1976G
Instrumentalist, The 1946G; Brass Anthology, 1984H; Percussion Anthology, 1984H
Inten, Ferdinand, 1848A, 1868C, 1918B
Inter-American Music Review, 1978G
InterArts Summer Festival, 1979G
Interlochen Arts Academy, 1962G
International Academy of Fine Arts, 1923G
International Arbeitsgemeinschaft für Hymnologie, 1959G
International Association of Music Libraries, 1950G
International Bach Institute, 1966G
International Beethoven Piano Competition, 1961G
International Berg Society, 1966G
International Brass Quintet Festival, 1980G
International Brass Society, 1975G
International Brucker Society, 1929G
International Carillon Festival, 1962G
International Chopin Piano Competition, 1927G
International Composers Guild, 1921G
International Conference of Symphony & Opera Musicians, 1962G
International Congress of Strings, 1959G
International Copyright Agreement, 1891G
International Electro-Acoustic Music Festival, 1970G
International Electronic Music Competition, 1968G
International Eotvos Institut, 1992G
International Federation of Choral Music, 1982G
International Festival-Institute, Round Top, 1970G
International Festival of Music at Purgatory, 1987G
International Festival of the Americas, 1984G
International Festival of the Art song, 1981G
International Folk Music Council, 1947G
International Index of Dissertations, 1977G
International Institute for Comparative Studies & Documentation, 1963G
International Institute for the String Bass, 1967G
International League of Women Composers, 1975G
International Library for African Music, 1953G
International Liszt Piano Competition, 1933G
International Liszt-Bartók Competition, 1956G
International Mahler Society (Vienna), 1955G
International Music Center (Vienna), 1961G
International Music Co., Publishers, 1941G
International Music Council (UNESCO), 1949G
International Musician, 1901G

International New Music Composer's Group, 1987G
International Record Critics Awards, 1968G
International Rostrum for Composers (UNESCO), 1954G
International Schoenberg Piano Concours, 1977G
International Soc., Contemporary Music (Salzburg), 1922G
International Soc. for Contemporary Music (U.S.A.), 1923G
International Society for Jazz Research, 1969G
International Society for Music Education, 1953G
International Society for Musicology, 1927G
International Society of Organ Builders, 1957G
International Student Music Council, 1930G
International Youth Philharmonic, 1987G
International Wolf-Ferrari Society, 1986G
Internationale Stifung Mozarteum, 1841G
Internationales Musiker-Brief-Archiv, 1945G
Intino, Luciana d', 1959A, 1983C
Inventionshorn, 1754G
Inzenga José: Impresiones de un artista en Italia, 1876H
Ioannidis, Yannis, 1930A
Iokeles, Alexander, 1912A, 1978B
Ippolitov-Ivanov, Mikhail, 1859A, 1882D, 1906D, 1925C, 1935B; Fifty Years of Russian Music, 1934H
Ippolitov-Boretzky, Mikhail, 1936B
Ireland, John, 1879A, 1904D, 1932E, 1962B
Ireland (see also Belfast, Dublin): National Chamber Choir of Ireland, 1991G; Wexford Festival, 1951G
Irgens-Jensen, Ludvig, 1946E, 1969B
Iribarren, Jaun F. de, 1767B
Irino, Yoshirō, 1960D
Irish Folk Song Society, 1904G
Irish Music Fund, 1787G
Irvine, Robert, 1963A
Irving, Robert, 1913A, 1948D, 1958D, 1991B
Irwin, Jane, 1991E
Irwin, Phyllis A.: Music Fundamentals, 1982H
Isaac, Adèle, 1854A, 1871C, 1915B
Isaac, Merle, 1996B
Isaacson, L.: Experimental Music, 1959H
Isbin, Sharon, 1956A, 1975E, 1976E, 1977C
Iseler, Elmer, 1927A, 1964D
Iseler, Elmer, Singers, 1978G
Isepp, Martin, 1930A
Isham, Mark, 1951A
Ishii, Maki, 1936A
Ishikawa, Shizuka, 1954A
Isler, Ernst, 1879A, 1902D, 1910D; Das Zürichische Musikleben sei' der neuen Tonhalle I (1895), 1935H
Isnard, Jean-Esprit, 1781B
Isoir, André, 1935A

❋

A   *Births*   B   *Deaths*   C   *Debuts*   D   *New Positions*
E   *Prizes/Honors*

I Solisti di Zagreb, 1950G
I Solisti Veneti (Padua), 1959G
Ísólfsson, Páll, 1893A, 1930D, 1956E
ISOS Quartet, 1995G
Isouard, Nicolò, 1775A, 1789F, 1795D, 1799F, 1818B
Isoz, Kálmám, 1878A; *The Musical Culture of Buda & Pest I: 1686-1873*, 1926H; *The Musical Society of Pest-Buda and its Public Concerts*, 1934H; *Past & Present of the Philharmonic Society, 1853-1903*, 1903H
Israel (*see also* Jerusalem, Tel Aviv): Academy of Music, 1945G; Broadcasting Authority Symphony, 1936G; Chamber Ensemble, 1965G; Chamber Orchestra, 1960G; Haifa Symphony Orchestra, 1951G; International Harp Contest, 1959G; New Opera Co. of Israel, 1985G; Opera Co., 1923G; String Quartet, 1939G; Vocal Arts Institute, 1988G; Woodwind Quintet, 1963G
Israeli Music Publications, 1949G
Isserlis, Julius, 1888A, 1968B
Isserlis, Steven, 1958A, 1977C, 1993E, 1998E
Istel, Edgar, 1880A, 1948B; *Blütezeit der Musikalischen Romantik in Deutschland*, 1909H; *Das Buch der Oper: Die deutschen Meister von Gluck bis Wagner*, 1919H; *Das deutsche Weihnachtsspiel und seine wiedergeburt aus dem geists der musik*, 1901H; *Die Moderne Oper vom tode Wagners bis zum Weltkrieg*, 1915H; *Revolution und Oper*, 1919H
Istomin, Eugene, 1925A, 1943CE
Istomin, Marta, 1980D
Itvan, Miroslav, 1961E
Istvánffy, Benedek, 1766D, 1778B
Italia Musicale, 1847G
Ithaca Cons. of Music, 1892G
Itin, Ilya, 1970A
Ito, Ryûta, 1922A
Iturbi, José, 1895A, 1929F, 1933C, 1936D, 1980B
Ivanov, Emil, 1960A, 1987C
Ivanov, Georgi, 1924A
Ivanov, Konstantin, 1907A, 1941D, 1946D, 1984B
Ivanov, Mikhail M., 1849A, 1927B; *Historical Development of Music in Russia I*, 1910H
Ivanov, Nicolai, 1810A, 1832C, 1880B
Ivanov-Boretzky Mikhail, 1874A
Ivanov-Radkevitch, Nikolai, 1904A, 1962B
Ivanovs, Janis, 1906A, 1983B
Ives, Burl: *The Burl Ives Book of Irish Songs*, 1958H; *Wayfaring Stranger*, 1948H
Ives, Charles, 1874A, 1893D, 1898F, 1908F, 1918F, 1922F
Ives, Charles, Living Award, 1998G
Ives Center for American Music, 1980G
Ives Oral History Project, 1968G
Ivey, Jean Eichelberger, 1923A
Ivogün, Maria, 1891A, 1913C, 1987B

Ivory Classics, 1997G
Iwaki, Hiroyuki, 1932A, 1964D, 1969D, 1974D, 1988D
Izzo d'Amico, Fiamma, 1964A, 1984C
Jablonski, Edward: *Encyclopedia of American Music*, 1980H
Jablonski, Krzysztof, 1965A
Jablonski, Marek, 1999B
Jablonski, Peter, 1971A, 1990C
Jacchia, Agide, 1932B
Jachimecki, Zdzislaw: *The History of Polish Music in Outline*, 1919H
Jackendorff, Ray: *A Generative Theory of Tonal Music*, 1983H
Jackson (Lacy), Bianchi, 1776A, 1798C, 1858B
Jackson, Carl A., 1958A
Jackson, George P.: *White Spirituals in the Southern Uplands*, 1933H
Jackson, George K., 1757A, 1822B; *The Choral Companion*, 1817H; *David's Psalms*, 1804H; *First Principles...on Practical Thorough Bass*, 1795H
Jackson, Isaiah, 1945A
Jackson, Judge, 1883A, 1958B; *The Colored Sacred Harp*, 1934H
Jackson, Laurence, 1967A
Jackson, Samuel P., 1818A, 1861D, 1885B; *Sacred Harmony*, 1848H
Jackson, William, 1777D, 1803B; *The Four Ages with Essays on Various Subjects*, 1798H; *Observations on the...State of Music in London*, 1791H; *A Singing Class Manual*, 1850H; *Thirty Letters on Various Subjects*, 1782H
Jackson Arts Center, 1977G
Jackson, Andrew, Hall, 1980G
Jacksonville, Florida: Civic Music Association, 1930G; College of Music, 1926G; Symphony Orchestra, 1950G
Jacob, Benjamin, 1778A, 1794D, 1829B
National Psalmody, 1819H
Jacob, Gordon, 1984B; *Elements of Orchestration*, 1962H; *How to Read a Score*, 1944H; *Orchestral Technique*, 1931H
Jacobi, Frederick, 1891A, 1952B
Jacobs, Arthur: *A Short History of Western Music*, 1973H
Jacobs, Max, String Quartet, 1912G
Jacobs, Paul, 1930A, 1951C, 1983B
Jacobson, Julian, 1974C
Jacobson, Robert: *Magnificence–Onstage at the Met*, 1985H
Jacobsthal, Gustav, 1845A, 1912B; *Mensuralnotenschrift des 12. und 13. Jahrhunderts*, 1871H
Jacoby, Josephine, 1875A, 1948B
Jacoby, Robert E., Symphony Hall, 1997G
Jacques, Reginald, 1894A, 1926D, 1931D, 1954E, 1969B
Jacques Orchestra (London), 1936G

F *Biographical*   G *Cultural Beginnings*   H *Musical Literature*
I *Musical Compositions*

Jacques-Dalcroze, Émile, 1865A, 1950B;
Rhythm, Music & Education, 1922H
Jadassohn, Otto, 1852F
Jadassohn, Salomon, 1831A, 1887E, 1902B ; *Die
Formen in den Werken der Tonkunst*, 1889H;
Harmonielehre, 1883H; *Kontrapunkt*, 1884H;
Die Kunst zu Modulieren und Präludieren,
1890H; *Lehrbuch der Instrumentation*, 1889H;
Methodik des Musiktheoretisches Unterrichts,
1898H; *Das Wesen der Melodie in der Tonkunst*,
1899H
Jadin, George, & Son, Organs, 1839G
Jadin, Hyacinthe, 1769A, 1802B
Jadin, Louis Emmanuel, 1768A, 1853B
Jadlowker, Hermann, 1877A, 1897C, 1953B
Jaëll, Alfred, 1832A, 1843C, 1882B
Jaëll, Marie Trautmann, 1846A, 1925B
Jaffe, Michael, 1938A
Jaffe, Stephen, 1954A, 1991E
Jagel, Frederick, 1897A, 1924C, 1982B
Jahn, Otto, 1813A, 1869B; *Gesammelte Aufsätze
über Musik*, 1866H
Jahns, Friedrich Wilhelm, 1809A, 1888B
Jahrbuch für Musikalische Wissenschaft, 1863G
Jakovlov, Jakov, 1958A
Jakubowski Publishing House, 1892G
Jalas, Jussi, 1908A, 1945D
James, Carolyne, 1945A
James, Jamie: *The Music of the Spheres*, 1993H
James, Philip, 1890A, 1930E, 1933DE, 1975B
James Harrison, Publisher, 1779G
Janáček, Leo, 1854A, 1872F, 1873D, 1881D,
1887F, 1928B
Janáček Academy of the Arts (Brno), 1947G
Janáček String Quartet (Brno), 1947G
Jander, Owen, 1930A
Janeček, Karel: *Basis of Modern Harmony*, 1965H
Janet et Cotelle, Publishers (Paris), 1810G
Janiewicz, Feliks, 1762A, 1787C, 1848B
Janiewicz's Music &...Instrument Warehouse,
1803G
Janigro, Antonio, 1918A, 1934C, 1954D, 1989B
Janis, Byron, 1928A, 1943C, 1965E, 1967F
Janitsch, Johann Gottlieb, 1763B
Janků, Hana, 1940A, 1959C, 1995B
Jannaconi, Giuseppe, 1811D, 1816B
Janotha, Natalia, 1856A, 1868C, 1932B
Janowitz, Gundula, 1937A, 1959C
Janowski, Marek, 1939A, 1969A, 1975D, 1983D,
1984D, 1986D
Jansen, Jacques, 1913A, 1941C
Janson, Jean-Baptiste Aimée, 1803B
Jansons, Arvad, 1952D
Jansons, Mariss, 1972E, 1979D, 1997D
Janssen, Herbert, 1892A, 1922C, 1965B
Janssen, Werner, 1899A, 1937D, 1946D, 1990B
Janssen Symphony Orchestra, 1940G
Janus Chorale of New York, 1969G
Japan (*see also* Osaka; Tokyo): New Directions,
1963G; New Symphony Orchestra, 1926G;

Shinko Sakkyokuka, 1930G; State
Philharmonic Orchestra, 1956G; Women's
Symphony Orchestra, 1963G, 1987G
Japanese Musicological Society (Tokyo), 1952G
Japanese Philharmonic Orchestra of Los
Angeles, 1961G
Japanese Society for Contemporary Music,
1937G
Jarboro, Caterina, 1968B
Jarecki, Henryk, 1877D
Jarmusiewicz, Jan, *A New System of Music*,
1843H
Järneffelt, Armas, 1898D, 1907D, 1923D, 1932D,
1942D, 1958B
Jaroff, Serge, 1896A, 1985B
Jaruwek, Józef, 1756A, 1792C, 1840B
Järvi, Neeme, 1937A, 1960D, 1963D, 1964D,
1971E, 1980F, 1982D, 1984D, 1990D, 1998F
Järvi, Paavo, 1962A
Jausions, Dom Paul, 1834A, 1870B
Jean, Kenneth, 1984E
Jean-Aubrey, Georges: *La musique française
d'aujourd'hui*, 1915H
Jeffrey, Francis, 1803D
Jehin-Prume, François, 1839A, 1899B
Jelinek, Hanns, 1901A, 1969B; *Anleitung zur
Zwölftonkomposition I*, 1952H; *Anleitung zur
Zwölfton kimposition II*, 1958H
Jellinek, George: *History Through the Opera
Glass*, 1994H
Jélyotte, Pierre de, 1797B
Jena Bürgerlicher Gesangverein, 1828G
Jenkins, Graeme, 1994D
Jenkins, Neil, 1945A, 1967C
Jenkins, Newell, 1915A, 1996B
Jenkins, Timothy, 1951A, 1974C, 1981E
Jenks, Stephen, 1772A, 1856B; *The Delight of
Harmony*, 1805H; *Laus Deo*, 1806H
Jensen, Niels Peter, 1802A, 1828D, 1846B
Jensen, Thomas, 1935D
Jenson, Dylana, 1961A, 1973C, 1978F
Jeppesen, Knud, 1892A, 1931D, 1974B;
Kontrapunkt, 1930H; *The Style of Palestrina &
the Dissonance*, 1922H
Jepson, Harry B., 1952B
Jepson, Helen, 1904A, 1928C, 1997B
Jeremiá, Otokar, 1892A, 1929D, 1962B
Jerger, Alfred, 1889A, 1917C, 1976B
Jeritza, Maria, 1887A, 1910C, 1982B
Jerrold's Magazine, 1845G
Jerse, T.: *Computer Music: Synthesis, Composition
& Performance*, 1985H
Jerusalem, Siegfried, 1940A, 1975C
Jerusalem, Israel: Academy & Conservatory II,
1947G; Archive of Oriental Music, 1935G;
Chamber Orchestra, 1964G; Institute of
Music, 1918G; Music Society, 1921G; String
Quartet, 1922G; Theater, 1971G
Jerusalem Trio, 1999E
Jeths, Willem, 1959A

❈

A   *Births*   B   *Deaths*   C   *Debuts*   D   *New Positions*
E   *Prizes/Honors*

La Jeune Belgique, 1881G
Jeunesses Musicales (Brussels), 1946G
Jeunesses Musicales World Orchestra, 1970G
Jewell, Kenneth, Chorale, 1962G
Jewell, Fred, Music Co., Publisher, 1920G
Jewish Liturgical Music Society of America, 1962G
Jewish Music Forum, 1939G
Jewish Music Research Center, 1964G
Ješek, Jaroslav, 1906A, 1942B
Jimenez, Bernal, 1910A, 1956B
Jiménez, Melchor López, 1784D
Jiménez-Mabarak, Carlos, 1916A, 1994B
Jindrak, Jindrich, 1931A, 1958C
Jirák, K. B., 1891A, 1930D, 1972B
Jirásek, Ivo, 1920A
Jirko, Ivan, 1926A, 1978B
Jo, Sumi, 1962A, 1986C
Joachim, Amalie, 1839A, 1854C, 1899B
Joachim, Irene, 1913A, 1938C
Joachim, Joseph, 1831A, 1835D, 1841F, 1843F, 1849F, 1866F, 1868D, 1877E, 1907B
Joachim String Quartet, 1869G
Jobin, Raoul, 1906A, 1930C
Jochum, Eugen, 1902A, 1926CD, 1934D, 1949D, 1954E, 1961D, 1969D, 1987B
Jochum, Georg Ludwig, 1940D
Joffman, Jan, Publishers, 1838G
Joffrey Ballet Co., 1956G
Johannesen, Grant, 1921A, 1944C, 1949E, 1959E, 1977D
Johannsson, Kristjan, 1950A, 1961C
Johanos, Donald, 1928A, 1962D, 1979D
Johanson, Gunnar, 1906A, 1918C, 1991B
Johns, Clayton, 1857A, 1932B; The Essentials of Pianoforte Playing, 1909H
Johns, Paul Emile, 1798A, 1860B
Johnson, Anthony, 1973C
Johnson, Camelia, 1960A, 1985C
Johnson, Charles L., Publisher, 1907G
Johnson, Edward, 1878A, 1912C, 1935D, 1959B
Johnson, Frank (Francis), 1792A, 1844B
Johnson, Graham, 1950A, 1972C, 1994E; A French Song Companion, 2000H; The Songmaker's Almanac, 1996H; The Spanish Song Companion, 1991H
Johnson, Hall, 1887A, 1970B; The Green Pastures Spirituals, 1930H
Johnson, H. Earle: Hallelujah, Amen! The Story of the Handel & Haydn Society of Boston, 1965H
Johnson, Hallvard, 1916A
Johnson, Hinrich Philipp, 1779B
Johnson, James: American Negro Spirituals, 1925H; The Scot's Musical Museum, 1787H
Johnson, James, Music Shop, 1790G
Johnson, Mary Jane, 1950A, 1981C
Johnson, Nancy, 1954A
Johnson, Patricia, 1934A, 1954C
Johnson, Scott, 1952A

Johnson, Thor, 1913A, 1940D, 1947D, 1958D, 1964D, 1967D, 1975B
Johnson, Thor, Living Tribute Fund, 1975G
Johnson, William A., Organ Builder, 1851G
Johnson, William Allen, 1816A, 1901B
Johnsson, Bengt, 1921A, 1944C
Johnston, Ben, 1926A
Johnston, Thomas, 1767B
Jokl, Fritzi, 1895A, 1917C
Jolas, Betsy, 1926A, 1953E, 1973E, 1983E
Jolivet, André, 1905A, 1943D, 1974B
Jommelli, Niccolò, 1769F, 1774B
Jonás, Alberto: Master School of Modern Pianist Playing & Virtuosity, 1922H
Jonas, Maryla, 1911A, 1926C, 1959B
Jonas, Oswald, 1897A, 1978B; Das Wesen des musikalischen Kunstwerk, 1934H
Jones, Alton, 1899A, 1924C, 1971B
Jones, Charles, 1910A, 1997B
Jones, Daniel, 1912A, 1993B; Music & Esthetic, 1954H
Jones, Della, 1946A, 1970C
Jones, Edward, 1752A, 1824B; The Bardic Museum, 1802H; Cambro-British Melodies, 1820H; Musical and Poetical Relicks of the Welsh Bards, 1784H
Jones, Geraint, 1917A, 1940C, 1998B
Jones, Gwyn Hughes, 1968A
Jones, Gwyneth, 1936A, 1962C, 1976E, 1986E, 1987E
Jones, Isola, 1949A, 1977C
Jones, Mason, 1919A; 20th Century Orchestral Studies, 1971H
Jones, Parry, 1891A, 1914C, 1963B
Jones, Philip, 2000B
Jones, Philip, Brass Ensemble, 1951G
Jones, Sissieretta, 1868A, 1888C, 1933B
Jones, William, 1783E, 1800B; The Nature and Excellence of Music, 1787H; Observations in a Journey to Paris, 1777H; Treatise on the Art of Music, 1784H
Jones Hall for the Performing Arts, 1966G
Jong, Marinus de, 1891A, 1984B
Jongen, Joseph, 1897E, 1920E, 1925D, 1953B
Jongen, Léon, 1884A, 1913E, 1939D, 1945E, 1969B
Joó, Árpád, 1948A, 1973D, 1977D, 1987D
Joplin, Scott, 1868A, 1917B, 1976E
Jordá, Enrique, 1911A, 1940D, 1948D, 1954D, 1970D, 1996B
Jordan, Armin, 1968D, 1973D, 1985D
Jordan, Arthur, Conservatory of Music, 1928G
Jordan, Irene, 1919A, 1946C
Jordania, Vakhtang, 1971E
Jörgen, Anton, 1926B
Jørgensen, Poul, 1934A, 1959C, 1961D
Jörn, Karl, 1873A, 1896C, 1947B
Joseffy, Rafael, 1852A, 1870C, 1915B
Joselson, Tedd, 1954A, 1974C
Josephs, Wilfred, 1927A, 1997B

F   *Biographical*   G   *Cultural Beginnings*   H   *Musical Literature*
I   *Musical Compositions*

Josephson, Jacob Axel, 1818A, 1880B
Josten, Werner, 1885A, 1963B
Journal d'Apollon pour le Forte-Piano, 1798G
Journal de Clavecin, 1762G
Journal de Guitare, 1788G
Journal de Musique, 1877G
Journal de Musique Française, Italienne (Echo), 1758G
Journal de Musique Française et Italienne, 1764G
Journal des Maîtrises, 1862G
Journal des Troubadours, 1806G
Journal of Band Research, 1964G
Journal of Music Theory, 1957G
The Journal of Musicology, 1982G
Journal of National Music, 1806G
Journal of Renaissance & Baroque Music, 1946G
Journal of the Acoustical Society of America, 1929G
Journal of the American Musicological Society, 1948G
Journal of the Arnold Schoenberg Institute, 1976G
Journal of the Conductor's Guild, 1980G
Journal of the Piano Technician's Guild, 1958G
Journal Musical Française, 1951G
Journet, Marcel, 1867A, 1891C, 1933B
Jousse Jean: *Lectures on Thoroughbass*, 1819H
Joy, Geneviève, 1919A
Jubiak, Teresa, 1965C
Juch, Emma, 1863A, 1881C, 1939B
Juch, Emma, Grand Opera Co., 1889G
Judd, Terence, 1976E
Judd, Terence, Piano Award, 1982G
Judd, William M., 1916A
Judd Concert Artist Bureau, 1969G
Jude, Marie-Josephe, 1968A
Judson, Arthur, 1881A, 1915D, 1961E, 1975B
Judson, Arthur, Concert Management, 1915G
Judson, O'Neill, Beall & Steinway, 1962G
Die Jugend, 1896G
Juhan, Alexander, 1765A, 1845B
Juilliard American Music Recording Institute, 1987G
Juilliard Musical Foundation, 1920G
Juilliard School of Music, 1946G
Juilliard String Quartet, 1946G
Jullien, Adolphe: *Musiciens d'Aujourd'hui I*, 1891H
Jullien, Louis, 1812A, 1838F, 1840D, 1856F, 1859F, 1860B
Jullien's Monster Concerts for the Masses, 1853G
June, Ava, 1934A, 1953C
Jung, Manfred, 1945A, 1974C
Jungwirth, Manfred, 1919A, 1942C
Júnior, Joaquim Casimiro, 1808A, 1860D, 1862B
Junker Carl L.: *Betrachtungen...mahlerey, ton' & bildhauer kunsts*, 1778H; *Einige der vornehmsten pflichten eines Kapellmeister oder Musikdirector*, 1782H; *Musikalischer Almanach*,

1783, 1783H; *Tonkunst*, 1777H; *Über den werth der Tonkunst*, 1786H
Juon, Paul, 1872A, 1940B
Jupiter Symphony, 1979G
Jurgensen, P. I., Publisher, 1861G
Jurinac, Sena, 1921A, 1942C
Jurjevskaya, Zinaida, 1922C, 1925C
Jurowski, Michail, 1945A, 1970F, 1992D
Just, Justin August, 1791B
Juyol, Suzanne, 1942C
JVC Classic Recordings, 1996G
Jyväskylä (Finland): Sinfonia, 1949G; Studio Choir, 1968G
Kaa, Franz Ignaz, 1777D
Kaart, Hans, 1956C
Kaasch, Donald, 1968A
Kabaivanska, Raina, 1934A, 1957C
Kabalevsky, Dmitri, 1904A, 1987B
Kabeláč, Miloslav, 1908A, 1932D, 1979B
Kabós, Ilona, 1893A, 1911C, 1915E, 1973B
Kaczkowski, Joachim, 1789A, 1810C
Kagel, Mauricio, 1931A, 1961F, 1969D
Kahane, Jeffrey, 1956A, 1978C, 1983E
Kahl, Willi, 1893A, 1962B
Kähler, Andreas Per, 1958A
Kahler, Lia, 1952A
Kahlert August: *Blätter aus der Brieftasches eines Musikers*, 1832H; *Tonleben*, 1838H
Kahn, Erich Itor, 1905A, 1948E, 1956B
Kahn, Otto Hermann, 1934B
Kaim Orchestra, 1893G
Kaipainen, Jouni, 1956A
Kajanus, Robert, 1882D, 1897D, 1933B
Kakhidze, Jansug, 1936A, 1973D
Kakova, Hans, 1985E
Kalbeck, Max, 1875D, 1883D, 1886D, 1890D; *Humoresken und Fantasien*, 1896H; *Opernabende I, II*, 1898H
Kalich, Gilbert, 1935A
Kalichstein, Joseph, 1946A, 1967C, 1969E
Kalichstein-Laredo-Robinson Trio, 1976G
Kalinnikov, Vasili, 1866A, 1901B
Kalisch, Paul, 1855A, 1879C, 1946B
Kalish, Gilbert, 1962C
Kalkbrenner, Christian, 1755A, 1806B; *Kurzer Abriss der Geschichte der Tonkunst*, 1792H; *Theorie der Tonkunst*, 1789H
Kalkbrenner, Frédéric, 1785A, 1801F, 1805C, 1818F, 1824F, 1828E, 1836E, 1849B; *Méthode pour apprendre le piano-forte à l'aide du guide-mains*, 1830H; *Traité d'harmonie du pianiste*, 1849H
Kallir, Lillian, 1931A, 1948C
Kalliwoda, Johann Wenzel, 1801A, 1821F, 1822D, 1866B
Kallstenius, Edvin, 1881A, 1967B
Kálmán, Oszkár, 1887A, 1913C, 1971B
Kalmus, Edwin F., 1893A
Kalmus, Edwin F., Publisher, 1926G

❄️

A *Births*   B *Deaths*   C *Debuts*   D *New Positions*
E *Prizes/Honors*

Kaludov, Kaludi, 1953A, 1978C
Kamienski, Matthias, 1821B
Kamiya, Michiko, 1997E
Kammel, Antonin, 1787B
Kammermusik der Staats-Kapelle Dresden, 1952G
Kammermusikkreis Ferdinand Conrac, 1956G
Kamu, Okko, 1946A, 1968C, 1969E, 1971D, 1975D, 1979D, 1988D, 1991D
Kandler, Franz S., 1820E
Kang, Dong-Suk, 1954A
Kang, Juliette, 1994E
Kangro, Raimo, 1949A
Kanita, Ernest, 1894A
Kanitz, Ernest, 1978B
Kanppertsbusch, Hans, 1922D, 1937D
Kansas City, Kansas: Gillis Opera House, 1902G
Kansas City, Missouri: Apollo Club, 1889G; Athenaeum, 1894G; Butler Standard Theater, 1900G; Coates Opera House, 1870G; Conservatory of Music, 1906G; Haydn Male Chorus, 1925G; Lyric Theater, 1958G; Musical Club, 1899G; Oratorio Society, 1897G; Philharmonic Orchestra, 1933G; Schubert Theater, 1906G; Symphony Orchestra, 1911G
The Kansas Folio, 1873G
Kantorow, Jean-Jacques, 1945A, 1964E, 1985D
Kapell, William, 1922A, 1941CE, 1953B
Kaplan, Abraham, 1956E
Kaplan, Mark, 1953A
Kapp, Julius, 1883A, 1962B
Kapp, Richard, 1936A
Kappa Kappa Psi Fraternity, 1919G
Kappel, Gertrude, 1884A, 1903C, 1971B
Kapyrin, Dmitri, 1960A
Karajan, Herbert von, 1908A, 1929CD, 1934D, 1948D, 1954D, 1955F, 1989B
Karajan Foundation, 1969G
Karamanov, Alemdar, 1934A
Karasik, Gita, 1952A, 1958C
Karasowski Moritz: *History of Polish Opera*, 1859H
Karayev, Kara, 1918A, 1982B
Karchin Louis, 1951A
Karel, Rudolf, 1880A, 1945B
Karg-Elert, Sigfrid, 1877A, 1931F, 1933B; *Vergleichende Orgel-Dispasitionen*, 1914H
Karis, Aleck, 1954A, 1981C
Karkoschka, Erhard, 1973D
Karl, Tom, 1846A, 1916B
Karlins, M. William, 1932A
Karlovitch, Jan: *Theory of Composition*, 1841H
Karlowicz, Mieczyslaw, 1876A, 1909B
Karlsbad, Germany: Labitzky Orchestra, 1825G
Karlsruhe, Germany: Grand Ducal Theater, 1810G

Karlsson, Erik, 1967A
Karneus, Katarina, 1965A
Kärntner Quintet, 1875G
Karpeles, Maud, 1885A, 1976B; *Folk Songs of Europe*, 1956H; *Introduction to English Folk Song*, 1973H
Karr, Gary, 1941A, 1962C
Kars, Jean-Rodolphe, 1947A, 1967C, 1968E
Karski, Dominik, 1972A
Kaschmann, Giuseppe, 1847A, 1869C, 1925B
Kasemets, Udo, 1919A
Kashin, Daniil Nikitich, 1769A, 1841B
Kashkashian, Kim, 1952A
Kashkin, Nikolai Dmitrievich, 1839A, 1920B; *Elementary Music Theory*, 1875H; *First 25 Years of the Moscow Conservatory*, 1891H
Kashperov, Vladimir, 1826A, 1894B
Kasrasvili, Makvala, 1942A
Kassel, Germany: Musikalische Gesellschaft, 1766G; State Theater, 1959G
Kassern, Tadeusz, 1904A, 1957B
Kastner, Jean-Georges, 1810A, 1867B; *Traité générale d'instrumentation*, 1837H
Kastner's Wiener Musikalische Zeitung, 1885G
Kastu, Matti, 1943A, 1973C
Katchen Julius, 1926A, 1937C, 1969B
Kates, Stephen, 1943A, 1963C, 1966F
Katim, Peter, 1930A
Katims, Milton, 1909A, 1954D, 1963E, 1972F, 1976D, 1985F, 1986E
Katin, Peter, 1948C
Katowice Radio Symphony Orchestra, 1945G
Katsaris, Cyprien, 1951A, 1970E
Katz, Israel, 1930A
Katz, Martin, 1945A
Katz, Mindru, 1925A, 1947C, 1978B
Katz, Paul, 1941A
Kauder, Hugo, 1888A, 1972B; *Counterpoint: An Introduction to Polyphonic Composition*, 1960H; *Entwurf einer neuen Melodie- und Harmonielehre*, 1932H
Kauer, Ferdinand, 1751A, 1831B; *Kurzgefasste generalbass-schule für Anfänger*, 1800H; *Singschule nach dem neuesten System, Tonkunst*, 1790H
Kaufmann, Julie, 1955A
Kaufman, Louis, 1927E, 1928E, 1999F
Kaufman, Walter, 1907A, 1984B
Kauntiz, Ernest: *A Counterpoint Manual*, 1948H
Kavafian, Ani, 1948A, 1969C, 1971E, 1976E
Kavafian, Ida, 1952A, 1978C
Kavakos, Leonidas, 1967A, 1984C, 1988E, 1989E
Kavrakos, Dimitri, 1946A, 1970C
Kawahito, Makiko, 1956A, 1985C
Kawai Piano Co. (Japan), 1925G
Kay, Hershy, 1917A, 1981B
Kay, Ulysses Simpson, 1917A, 1969E, 1979E, 1995B

❈

F *Biographical*   G *Cultural Beginnings*   H *Musical Literature*
I *Musical Compositions*

Kayser, Isfrid, 1771B
Kayser, Philipp Christoph, 1755A, 1823B
Kazaras, Peter, 1956A, 1981C
Kazarnovskaya, Ljuba, 1960A, 1982C
Kazyński, Wiktor, 1812A, 1867B; *History of Italian Opera*, 1851H
Kee, Piet, 1927A, 1941C
Keeble, John, 1786B; *The Theory of Harmonics*, 1784H
Keene, Christopher, 1946A, 1964F, 1965C, 1975D, 1979D, 1982D, 1989D 1995B
Keene, Constance, 1921A, 1943E
Kegel, Herbert, 1977D
Kehl, Johann Balthasar, 1778B
Keilberth, Joseph, 1908A, 1935D, 1940D, 1945D, 1949D, 1950D, 1959D, 1968B
Kelemen, Barnabas, 1978A
Kelemen, Zoltán, 1926A, 1959C, 1979B
Kell, Reginald, 1906A, 1981B
Keller, Hans, 1919A, 1985B; *Criticism*, 1987H
Keller, Hermann, 1885A, 1946D, 1967B; *Die Kunst des Orgelspiels*, 1941H; *Phrasierung und artikulation*, 1955H; *Schule der Choralimprovisation*, 1939H
Keller, Homer Todd, 1915A, 1996B
Keller, Matthias, 1813A, 1875B
Keller, Walter, 1873A, 1940B
Keller's Patent Steam Violin Manufactory, 1857G
Kelley, Edgar Stillman, 1857A, 1893D, 1902F, 1917E, 1944B; *Musical Instruments*, 1925H
Kellie, Lawrence, 1862A, 1886C, 1932B
Kellner, Johann Christoph, 1803B; *Grundriss des Generalbasses*, 1783H
Kellner, Johann Peter, 1772B
Kellogg, Clara Louise, 1842A, 1861C, 1916B
Kellogg, Paul, 1996D
Kelly, Bryan, 1934A
Kelly, Declan, 1998C
Kelly, Michael, 1762A, 1826B; *Reminiscences of M K, of the King's Theatre*, 1826H
Kelly, Michael, Publishers (London), 1801G
Kelly, Peter, 1965A
Kelly, Robert, 1916A
Kelm, Linda, 1944A, 1977C
Kelmperer, Otto, 1917D
Kemble, Adelaide, 1814A, 1835C, 1879B
Kementt, Waldemar, 1919A
Kemp, Barbara, 1881A, 1903C, 1959B
Kemp, Joseph, 1778A, 1824B; *A New System of Musical Education*, 1819H
Kempe, Rudolf, 1910A, 1935C, 1949D, 1952D, 1967D 1976B
Kemper, Paul van, 1934D
Kempers, Karel P. Bernet, 1974B; *Meesters der Muziek*, 1939H; *Muziekgeschiedenis*, 1932H
Kempf, Frederick, 1977A, 1985C
Kempff, Wilhelm, 1895A, 1918C, 1924D, 1991B
Kempster, David, 1970A

Kenins, Talivaldis, 1919A
Kennan, Kent, 1913A, 1936E; *Counterpoint Based on 18th* Century Practice, *1959H;* The Technique of Orchestration, *1952H*
Kennedy, Nigel, 1956A, 1977C
Kennedy, John F., Center for the Performing Arts, 1971G
Kenner, Kevin, 1963A, 1994E
Kennis, Guillaume, 1803D
Kenny, Sylia, 1922A, 1968B
Kenny, Yvonne D., 1950A, 1975C
Kent, James, 1776B
Kent Opera Co., 1969G
Kentner, Louis, 1905A, 1920C, 1987B
Kenton, Egon, 1987B
Kentucky (*see also* Louisville): Center for the Arts, 1983G; Opera Ass'n, 1952G
Kerker, Gustave, 1880D
Kerman, Joseph, 1924A, 1973E; *Contemplating Music: Challenges to Musicology*, 1990H; *A History of Art & Music*, 1968H; *Listen*, 1972H; *Opera as Drama*, 1956H
Kern, Adele, 1901A, 1924C, 1980B
Kern, Johannes, 1965A
Kern, Jerome, 1945B
Kernis, Aaron Jay, 1960A, 1985E
Kerns, Robert, 1960C
Kerr, Harrison, 1897A, 1929D, 1947D, 1978B
Kertész, István, 1929A, 1964D, 1965D, 1970F, 1973B
Kerwig, Käthe, 1891A
Kerzelli Music College, 1772G
Kes, Willem, 1888D, 1895D, 1901D, 1905D, 1934B
Ketèlby, Albert, 1875A, 1959B
Keuris, Tristan, 1946A, 1976E, 1996B
Key West Music Festival, 1997G (Florida)
Keyboard Classics, 1981G
Keyes, Christopher, 1963A
Keyes, John, 1964A
Keylin, Misha, 1970A, 1981C
Keynote, 1883G
Keystone Wind Ensemble, 1992G
Khachaturian, Aram, 1903A, 1948F, 1959E, 1978B
Khandoshkin, Ivan, 1804B
Khokhlov, Pavel, 1854A, 1879C, 1919B
Khrennikov, Tikhon, 1948D
Kiel, Friedrich, 1821A, 1865E, 1885B
Kiel, Germany: Opera, 1907G; Saint Nikolaichor, 1922G; Stadttheater, 1841G; Tivoli Theater, 1845G
Kienzel, Wilhelm, 1857A, 1883D, 1886D, 1890D
Kienzl, Wilhelm, 1941B; *Aus Kunst und Leben*, 1904H
Kiepura, Jan, 1902A, 1924C, 1966B
Kiesewetter, Raphael Georg, 1773A, 1850B; *Geschichte der europäisch-abendländischen, das*

❋

A *Births*   B *Deaths*   C *Debuts*   D *New Positions*
E *Prizes/Honors*

ist unserer heutigen Musik, 1834H; *Schicksale & beschaffenheit des...Gesanges*, 1841H; *Über die Octave des Pythagoras*, 1848H; *Die Verdienste der Niederlander um die Tonkunst*, 1826H
Kiesler, Kenneth, 1953A
Kiev, Russia: Opera Co., 1867G; Philharmonic Society, 1833G
Kilduff, Barbara (Jane), 1959A, 1986E, 1987C
Kilenyi, Edward, Jr., 1910A, 1929C
Kilenyi, Edward, Sr., 1884A, 1968B
Kilgen, Georg, & Son, Organ Builders, 1851G
Killebrew, Gwendolyn, 1939A, 1967C
Kilpinen, Yrjö, 1959A
Kim, Earl, 1920A, 1965E, 1971E, 1998B
Kim, Ettore, 1965A, 1990C
Kim, Hae-Jung, 1965A, 1985C
Kim, Lisa, 1995E
Kim, Michael (Injae), 1968A, 1983C
Kim, Young Uck, 1947A, 1963C
Kimball, W. W., Co, Publishers, 1857G
Kimball, W. W., Organ Co., 1880G
Kimball, Jacob, Jr, 1761A, 1826B; *The Essex Harmony*, 1800H; *The Rural Harmony*, 1793H
Kincaid, William, 1895A, 1967B
Kind, Johann Friedrich, 1768A, 1843B
Kinder, Ralph, 1876A
Kindler, Hans, 1892A, 1931D, 1949B
King, James, 1925A, 1961AC
King, Karl A., 1891A
King, Karl L., 1953E, 1871B
King, Matthew Peter, 1773A, 1823B; *A General Treatise on Music*, 1800H; *Introduction to Sight Singing*, 1806H
King Musical Instrument Co., 1893G
The King's Singers, 1970G
Kingston, Morgan, 1881A, 1909C, 1936B
Kinkel, Johanna, 1810A, 1858B
Kinkeldey, Otto, 1878A, 1915D, 1923D, 1966B
Kinsella, John, 1932A
Kipnis, Alexander, 1891A, 1915C, 1978B
Kirana Center for Indian Classical Music, 1971G
Kirby, F. E.: *Music in the Classic Period*, 1979H
Kirby, James, 1965A, 1991C
Kirchenburg Kirchenmusikschule, 1874G
Der Kirchenchor, 1947G
Kirchner, Leon, 1962E, 1977E
Kirchner, Theodor F., 1823A, 1873D, 1903B
Kirchschlager, Angela, 1965A
Kirckman, Jacob, 1792B
Kirckmann, Abraham, 1794B
Kirkbride, Simon Alexander, 1971A, 1996C
Kirkby, Emma, 1949A, 1974C
Kirkby-Lunn, Louise, 1873A, 1893C, 1930B
Kirkmann, Jan, 1799B
Kirkop, Oreste, 1998B
Kirkpatrick, John, 1905A, 1931C, 1949D, 1991B
Kirkpatrick, Ralph, 1911A, 1930C, 1984B

Kirnberger, Johann P., 1758D, 1783B; *Allzeit fertige Polonaisen- & Menuetten-componist*, 1757H; *Construction der gleichschwebenden Temperatur*, 1760H; *Gedanken über die verschiedenen Lehrarten in der Komposition*, 1782H; *Grundsätze des Generalbasses, als erste Linen zur Composition*, 1781H; *Die Kunst des reinen Satzes in der Musik I*, 1771H; *Die Kunst des reinen Satzes in der Musik II*, 1779H; *Wahren Grundsätze zum Gebrach der Harmonie*, 1773H
Kirshbaum, Ralph, 1946A, 1959C, 1970E
Kirsten, Dorothy, 1910A, 1940C, 1977E, 1992B
Kissin, Evgeny, 1971A, 1983C
Kist, Florentius C, 1841D; *Protestant Churchmusic in the Netherlands*, 1840H
Kistler Cyrill: *Harmonielehre*, 1879H; *Musikalische elementarlehre*, 1880H; *Über originalität in Tonkunst*, 1894H; *Volksschullehrer-Tonkünstlerlexicon*, 1887H
Kitajenki, Dimitri, 1990D
The Kitchen, 1971G
Kitchenor Centre in the Square, 1980G
Kite, Christopher, 1947A, 1972C
Kitson, Charles H., 1874A, 1913D, 1944B; *Applied Strict Counterpoint*, 1916H; *The Art of Counterpoint*, 1924H; *Evolution of Harmony*, 1914H; *Studies in Fugue*, 1909H
Kittel, Johann Christian, 1751D, 1762D, 1809B; *Der Angehende praktische Organist*, 1801H; *Neues Choralbuch*, 1803H
Kittl, Johann Friedrich, 1806A, 1843D, 1868B
Kitzler, Otto, 1868D
Kivy, Peter: *Music Alone*, 1990H; *Osmin's Rage*, 1988H; *Sound & Semblance*, 1991H
Kjerulf, Halfdan, 1815A, 1865E, 1868B
Kjos, Neil A., Music Co., 1936G
Klafsky, Katharina, 1855A, 1875C, 1896B
Klais, Johannes, Organ Co., 1882G
Klarwein, Franz, 1914A, 1937C
Klas, Eri, 1939A, 1975D, 1986C, 1991D
Klaus, Kenneth: *The Romantic Period in Music*, 1970H
Der Klavierlehrer, 1878G
Klavier Records, 1962G
Klebe, Giselher, 1925A
Klee, Bernhard, 1936A, 1992D
Kleiber, Carlos, 1930A, 1954D, 1964D, 1966D
Kleiber, Erich, 1890A, 1911C, 1912D, 1923D, 1936D, 1956B
Klein, Bernhard, 1793A, 1832B
Klein, Bruno Oscar, 1858A, 1911A
Klein, Henrik, 1756A, 1832B
Klein, Jacques, 1953E
Klein, Johann J., *Lehrbuchs der praktischen Musik*, 1801
Klein, Kenneth, 1939A, 1967D, 1980D, 1981D
Klein, Lothar, 1932A
Klein, Walter, 1928A

❋

F   *Biographical*   G   *Cultural Beginnings*   H   *Musical Literature*
I   *Musical Compositions*

Kleine Musikfeste (Lüdenscheid), 1938G
Kleines Festspielhaus (Salzburg), 1924G
Kleinknecht, Daniel, 1960A
Kleinknecht, Jakob F., 1761D, 1794B
Kleinknecht, Johann Wolfgang, 1786B
Kleinmichel, Richard, 1882D
Kleinsinger, George, 1914A, 1982B
Kleis, Johannes, Organ Builder, 1852G
Klementyev, Lev, 1868A, 1888C, 1910B
Klemm, Carl August, Publishing Co. (Leipzig), 1821G
Klemm and Brother, Instrument Dealers, 1819G
Klemperer, Otto, 1885A, 1910D, 1927D, 1933DF, 1939F, 1947D, 1955D, 1972F, 1973B; *Minor Recollections*, 1964H
Klengel, August Alexander, 1783A, 1852B
Kletzki, Paul, 1900A, 1923C, 1958D, 1964D, 1968D, 1973B
Klíč (Czechoslovakia), 1930G
Klimov, Valery A., 1931A, 1958E
Klindworth, Karl, 1830A, 1916B
Klingenberg, Friedrich, 1840D
Klöffler, Johann Friedrich, 1790B
Klosé, Hyacinthe-Eléonore, 1808A, 1864E, 1880B; *Grande Méthode pour la clarinette*, 1844H
Klose, Margarete, 1902A, 1927C, 1968B
Klughardt, August, 1847A, 1902B
Klusák, Jan, 1934A
Kmentt, Waldemar, 1929A, 1950C
Knabe, William, 1803A, 1833F, 1864B
Knabe & Gaehle, Piano Makers, 1837G
Knappertsbusch, Hans, 1888A, 1913D, 1918D, 1919D, 1936D, 1965B
Knecht, Justin H., 1752A, 1771D, 1817B; *Allgemeiner musikalischer Katechismus*, 1803H; *Erklärung einiger missverstandenen Grundsätze aus der Vogler'schen Theorie*, 1785H; *Gemeinnützliches elementarwerk der harmonie und des generalbasses I*, 1792H; *Kleines...Wörterbuch...der musikalischen Theorie*, 1795H
Kneisel, Franz, 1911E, 1915E
Kneisel String Quartet, 1886G
Knie, Roberta, 1938A, 1964C
Kniesel, Franz, 1865A, 1882C, 1926B
Knight, Gillian, 1968C
Knipper, Lev, 1898A
Knoch, Ernst, 1959B
Knopf, Alfred, 1984B
Knorr, Iwan, 1853A, 1916B; *Aufgaben für den Unterricht in der Harmonielehre*, 1903H; *Lehrbuch der Fugenkimposition*, 1911H
Knorr, Julius, 1807A, 1831C, 1861B; *Ausführliche klaviermethode: Schule der mechanik*, 1860H; *Ausführliche Klaviermethode*, 1859H; *Erklärendes Verzeichniss der hauptsächlichsten Musik-kunstwörter*, 1854H;

Methodischer leitfaden für Klavierlehrer, 1849H; *Neue pianoforteschule*, 1836H
Knosulov, Ivan, 1946A
Knote, Heinrich, 1870A, 1892C, 1953B
Knoxville, Tennessee: Civic Auditorium, 1961G; Opera Co., 1978G; Philharmonic Society, 1867G; Staub's Opera House, 1872G; Symphony Orchestra, 1935G
Knudsen Piano Factory, 1896G
Knüpfer, Paul, 1865A, 1885C, 1920B
Knussen, Oliver, 1952A
Knyvett, Charles, Jr., 1773A, 1859B
Knyvett, Charles, Sr., 1752A, 1796D, 1822B
Knyvett, William, 1779A, 1856B
Kobbé, Gustav, 1857A, 1918B; *Complete Opera Book*, 1919H ; *Famous American Songs*, 1906H; *How to Appreciate Music*, 1906H; *Opera Singers*, 1901H
Koblenz, Germany: Anschütz Vocal School, 1808G; Madrigal Choir, 1956G; Musikinstitut, 1808G; Verein der Musikfreunde, 1872G
Koc, Jozik, 1993C
Koch, Casper, 1872A, 1970B; *The Organ Student's Gradus ad Parnassum*, 1945H
Koch, Eduard Emil: *Geschichte desKirchenliedes und Kurchengesanges*, 1847H
Koch, Heinrich: *Handbuch bei dem Studium der Harmonie*, 1811H; *Musikalisches Lexikon*, 1802H; *Versuch einer anleitung zur Composition*, 1782H; *Versuch einer anleitung zur composition III*, 1793H
Koch, Sigurd von, 1919B
Koch International, 1975G
Koch International U.S.A., 1987G
Koch Music Academy, 1952G
Kochan, Günter, 1930A
Kochánski, Paul, 1887A, 1934B
Köchel, Ludwig, 1800A, 1877B; *Chronologisch-thematisches Verzeichnis sämtlicher Tonwerke Wolfgang Amade Mozarts*, 1862H
Kocher, Conrad, 1786A, 1827E, 1872B; *Die Tonkunst in der Kirche*, 1823H
Kocsis, Zoltán, 1952A, 1970C, 1973E, 1978E, 1983C
Kodalli, Yelda, 1968A, 1992C
Kodály, Zoltán, 1882A, 1905F, 1946F, 1967B; *Folk Music of Hungary*, 1960H
Kodoma, Momo, 2000C
Koechlin, Charles, 1867A, 1928F, 1936E, 1937EF, 1950B; *Théorie de la musique*, 1934H
Koeckert String Quartet, 1939G
Koehne, Graeme, 1956A
Koening, Joseph, Piano Builder, 1896G
Koessler, Hans, 1853A, 1926B
Kogan, Leonid, 1924A, 1941C, 1951E, 1965E, 1982B
Köhler, Ernst, 1779A, 1847B

❄️

A   *Births*   B   *Deaths*   C   *Debuts*   D   *New Positions*
E   *Prizes/Honors*

Kohler, Johannes, Instrument Maker, 1780G
Kohler, Linda, 1952A
Köhler, Louis, 1820A, 1886B; *Allgemeine Musiklehre*, 1883H; *Die Neue Richtung in der Musik*, 1864H; *Systematische lehrmethode für klavierspiel...I*, 1856H; *Systematische Lehrmethode für klavierspiel...II*, 1858H
Kohn, Otto Hermann, 1867A
Köhner, Basil, 1870D
Kohs, Ellis Bonoff, 1916A, 1946E, 2000B; *Musical Form*, 1976H; *Musical Composition: Projects in Ways & Means*, 1980H; *Music Theory, A Syllabus*, 1961H
Koivula, Hannu, 1993D
Kojian, Varujan, 1980D, 1981D, 1984D
Kokkonen, Joonas, 1921A, 1963E, 1968E, 1973E, 1996B; *Finnish Composers since the 1960s*, 1995H
Kokoma, Momo, 1972A
Kolb, Barbara, 1939A, 1969EF, 1973E
Kolb, Carlmann, 1765B
Kolbe, Oskar, 1836A, 1878B; *Handbuch der Harmonielehre*, 1873H
Kolisch, Rudolf, 1896A, 1978B
Kolisch String Quartet, 1922G
Kollmann, Augustus Frederic, 1756A, 1829B; *An Essay on Practical Harmony*, 1796H; *An Essay on Practical Musical Composition*, 1799H; *A New Theory of Musical Harmony*, 1806H; *A Practical Guide to Thoroughbass*, 1801H; *A Second Practical Guide to Thorough Bass*, 1807H
Kollmann, George A., 1789A, 1804C 1845B
Kollmann, Johanna Sophia, 17865A, 1806C, 1849B
Kollo, René, 1937A., 1965C
Kolly, Karl-Andreas, 1965A, 1982C
Kolodin, Irving, 1908A, 1932D, 1947D, 1988B; *The Composer as Listener*, 1958H; *The Continuity of Music*, 1969H; *The Critical Composer*, 1940H; *In Quest of Music*, 1980H; *The Opera Omnibus*, 1976H; *Orchestral Music*, 1955H
Koloman, D. Kern, 1947A; *Komponist und Musikerzieher*, 1971G
Kolozavár National Theater (Hungary), 1821G
Kolozavár Music Cons., 1837G
Kondo, Jo, 1947A
Kondrashin, Kyrill, 1914A, 1937D, 1943D, 1958F, 1960D, 1978F, 1979D, 1981B; *The Art of Conducting*, 1972H
Konetzni, Anny, 1902A, 1925C, 1968B
Konetzni, Hilde, 1905A, 1929C, 1980B
König, Johann Balthasar, 1758B
König & Bauer, Steam Press Manufacturers, 1817G
Königsberg, Germany: Leidertafel, 1824G; Philharmonic Society, 1838G; Singverein, 1818G

Königslow, Johann Wilhelm von, 1833B
Königslöw, Otto von, 1858D
Königsperger, Marianus, 1769B
Konjovic, Petar, 1883A, 1970B
Konsulov, Ivan, 1972C
Kontarsky, Bernhard, 1964E
Kontarsky Brothers Piano Duo, 1955G
Kontski, Antoine de, 1817A, 1825C, 1851F, 1899B
Kontski, Apollinaire de, 1861D
Konwitschny, Franz, 1901A, 1930D, 1938D, 1945D, 1949D, 1953D, 1955D, 1962B
Konya, Sándor, 1923A, 1951C
Konzerte fur Kenner und Liebhaber, 1787G
Kopylov, Alexander A., 1854A, 1911B
Korbay, Francis A., 1865C
Korbay, Francis Alexander, 1846A, 1913B
Kord, Kazimierz, 1977D, 1980DF
Korean Classical Music & Dance Co., 1973G
Korjus, Miliza, 1912A, 1933C
Korn, Artur, 1937A, 1963C
Korn, Clara Anna, 1866A, 1940B
Korn, Peter (Jona), 1998B
Korndorf, Nikolai, 1947A
Kornél, Ábrányi: *Harmony*, 1874H; *Music Aesthetic*, 1877H
Körner, Christian Gottfried, 1756A, 1831B; *Das Deutsche evangeliche Kirchenlied*, 1830H; *Gesangblätter aus den 16. Jahrhundort*, 1838H
Körner, Gotthilf, 1809A, 1865B
Körner, Gotthilf, Publishers, 1838G
Korngold, Erich Wolfgang, 1897A, 1957B
Korngold, Erich, Society, 1983G
Kornmüller, Otto, 1824A, 1907B; *Lexikon der Kirchlichen Tonkunst*, 1870H; *Die Musik beim liturgischen Hochamt*, 1871H
Korsakova, Natasha, 1973A
Korte, Karl, 1928A
Kortschak (Berkshire) String Quartet, 1913G
Kósa, György, 1897A, 1955E, 1984E
Koschat, Thomas, 1845A, 1914B
Koshetz, Nina, 1894A, 1913C, 1965B
Koshgarian, Richard: *American Orchestral Music: A Performance Catalogue*, 1992H
Koshkin, Nikita, 1956A
Koler, Zdeněk, 1958D, 1962D, 1963E, 1966D, 1971D, 1980D
Kosponth, Otto Carl, 1753A, 1817B
Kossmaly, Carl, 1812A, 1893A; *Über die anwendung des programm mes zur erklärung musikalischen compositionen*, 1858H
Kostelanetz, André, 1901A, 1930D, 1980B
Kostelanetz, Richard, 1940A, 1965E
Kostka, Stefan: *Materials & Techniques of Twentieth Century Music*, 1990H; *Tonal Harmony*, 1984H
Köstlin, Heinrich Adolf, 1846A, 1907B; *Geschichte der Musik um Umriss*, 1873H;

❋

F *Biographical*   G *Cultural Beginnings*   H *Musical Literature*
I *Musical Compositions*

Köstlin, Heinrich Adolf, (cont.)
  Tonkunst: Einführung in die Aesthetik der
  Musik, 1878H
Köstlin Karl R: Aesthetik I, 1863H
Kostova, Denitza, 1973A, 1992C
Kotek, Joseph, 1855A, 1885B
Kothe Bernhard: Abriss der Musikgeschichte für
  Lehrerseminare und Dilettanten, 1874H; Die
  Musik in der katholischen Kirche, 1862H
Kotkova, Hana, 1967A
Kotkova, Nina, 1977C
Kotoski, Dawn, 1967A
Kotzebue, August von, 1819F: Opera almanach,
  1815H
Kotzolt, Heinrich, 1814A, 1838C, 1881B
Kotzwara, Franz, 1791B
Kountz, Richard, 1896A, 1950B
Kousky, Petr Jiri, 1987E
Koussevitzky, Serge, 1874A, 1901C, 1907C,
  1917D, 1924D, 1926E, 1945E, 1947E, 1951B
Koussevitzky (Natalie) Music Foundation,
  1942G
Koussevitzky (Serge) Music Foundation,
  1949G
Koussevitzky Orchestra (Russia), 1909G
Kout, Jiri, 1937A, 1978D, 1985D, 1993D
Koutzen, Boris, 1901A, 1966B
Kouyoumdjian, Avedis, 1960A
Kovacevich, Stephen (Bishop), 1940A
Kovařovic, Karel, 1862A, 1900D, 1920B
Kowalski, Henri, 1841A, 1916B; A Travers
  l'Amérique 1872H
Kowalski, Jochen, 1954A, 1982C
Kox, Hans, 1930A
Košeluhová, Jitka, 1966A
Košená, Magdalena, 1973A, 1995E, 1996C
Kozeluch, Johann Antonin, 1784D
Kozeluch, Leopold, 1778F, 1792D, 1818B
Kozeluch Music Publishing Co., 1784G
Kozlovsky, Ivan, 1918C, 1993B
Kozlowski, Józef, 1757A, 1801D, 1831B
Kraayvanger, Heinz, 1904A, 1933C
Krafft, François-Joseph, 1769D, 1795B
Kraft, Anton, 1820B
Kraft, Leo, 1922A; Gradus: An Integrated
  Approach to Harmony, Counter-point &
  Analysis, 1976H; A New Approach to Keyboard
  Harmony, 1978H
Kraft, Nicolaus, 1778A, 1853A
Kraft, Norbert, 1985E
Kraft, William, 1872A, 1923A, 1984E, 1990E
Krainev, Vladimir, 1970E
Krainik, Ardis, 1981D, 1991D, 1997B
Krainis, Bernard, 2000B
Kraków, Poland: Bach Festival, Krakow-
  Katowice, 1985G; College of Music, 1945G;
  Conservatory of Music, 1881G;
  Krzyzanowski Concert Bureau, 1879G;
  Music Society, 1876G; Muza, 1866G; School

of Singing & Music, 1838G; Society of
  Friends of Music, 1817G
Kramer, A. Walter, 1890A, 1929D, 1936D, 1969B
Kramer, Christian, 1829E
Kramer, Jonathan, 1942A; Listen to the Music,
  1988H; The Time of Music, 1988H
Kramer, Toni, 1965C
Krämer and Bossler, Darmstadt Branch, 1785G
Kranich & Bach Piano Co., 1864G
Krantz, Eugen, 1890D; Lehrgang im
  Klavierunterricht, 1882H
Kranz, Johann Friedrich, 1752A, 1789D, 1810B
Krasnapolsky, Yuri, 1934A, 1974D
Krasner, Louis, 1903A, 1995B
Krasni String Quartet, 1998G
Krásová, Marta, 1901A, 1922C, 1970B
Kraus, Alfredo, 1927A, 1956CE, 1999B
Kraus, Ernst, 1863A, 1893C, 1941B
Kraus, Felix von, 1870A, 1896C, 1937B
Kraus, James Martin, String Quartet, 1993G
Kraus, Joseph Martin, 1756A, 1780E, 1788D,
  1792B; Etwas von und über Musik für Jahr
  1777, 1777H
Kraus, Lili, 1903A, 1942F, 1986B
Kraus, Michael, 1957A
Kraus, Otakar, 1909A, 1935C, 1980B
Krause, Christian Gottfired, 1770B; Von der
  musikalischen Poesie, 1752H
Krause, Emil, 1840A, 1916B; Ergänzungen:
  Aufgabenbuch für...Harmonielehre, 1869H
Krause, Karl C.F., 1781A, 1832B; Anfangsgründe
  der allge'meinen Theorie...Musik, 1838H;
  Darstellung aus der geschichte der Musik,
  1827H
Krause, Tom, 1934A, 1057C
Kraushaar, Otto, 1812A, 1866B; Accordliche
  Gegensatz & der Begründung der Scala, 1852H
Kraushaar Auditorium (Baltimore), 1962G
Krauss, Clemens, 1893A, 1924D, 1929D, 1934D,
  1937D, 1954B
Krauss, Gabrielle, 1842A, 1858C, 1906B
Kravis Center for the Performing Arts, 1992G
Krček, Jaroslav, 1939A
Krebs, Carl August, 1804A, 1827D, 1850D,
  1880B
Krebs, Johann Gottfried, 1814B
Krebs, Johann Tobias, 1762B
Krebs, Johann Ludwig, 1756D, 1780B
Kreek, Cyrillus, 1962B
Kreger, James, 1947A
Krehbiel, Henry, 1854A, 1874D, 1880D, 1923B;
  A Book of Operas, 1909H; How to Listen to
  Music, 1896H; The Pianoforte and Its Music,
  1911H
Krehl, Stephan: Kontrapunkt, 1908H; Theorie der
  Tonkunst und Kimpositonslehre, 1922H
Kreibé, Charles Frédéric, 1816D
Krein, Alexander, 1883A, 1951B
Kreisler, Fritz, 1875A, 1882F, 1904E, 1962B

❈

A Births   B Deaths   C Debuts   D New Positions
E Prizes/Honors

Krejci, Josef, 1865D, 1865D
Kremenliev, Boris, 1911A, 1988B
Kremer, Gidon, 1947A, 1968E, 1970E, 1974F, 1977C
Krenek, Ernst, 1900A, 1960E, 1963E, 1969E, 1991B; *Exploring Music*, 1966H; *Hamline Studies in Musicology*, 1945H; *Komponist und Hören*, 1964H; *Modal Counterpoint in the Style of the 16th Century*, 1959H; *Studies in Counterpoint Based on the Twelve-Tone Technique*, 1940H; *Tonal Counterpoint in the Style of the 18th Century*, 1958H; *Über neue Musik*, 1937H
Krenn Franz; *Musik- und Harmonielehre*, 1890H
Krennikov, Tikhon, 1913A
Kreppel, Walter, 1923A, 1945C
Kress, Georg Philipp, 1779B
Kretschmer, Edmund, 1830A, 1863D, 1908B
Kretzschmar, Hermann (August),1848A, 1877D, 1924B; *Führer durch den Konzert-Saal*, 1887H; *Geschichte der Oper*, 1919H
Kreubé, Charles Frédéric, 1777A, 1846B
Kreutzbach, Urban, Organ Builder, 1830G
Kreutzer, Conradin, 1780A, 1798F, 1800F, 1804F, 1812D, 1818D, 1822D, 1829D, 1883D, 1840D, 1849B
Kreutzer, Jean Nicolas, 1778A, 1832B
Kreutzer, Léon Charles, 1817A, 1868B; *Essai sur l'art lyrique au théâtre*, 1845H
Kreutzer, Rodolphe, 1766A, 1780C, 1785F, 1796F, 1798F, 1810F, 1824E, 1826F, 1831B; *Méthode de violon*, 1803H
Kreutzer String Quartet, 1988G
Kriegk, Johann Jacob, 1814B
Krikorian, Mari, 1946A, 1976C
Krilovici, Marina, 1942A, 1966C
Kringelborn, Solveig, 1963A, 1990C
Krips, Josef, 1902A, 1921C, 1926D, 1933D, 1947B, 1950D, 1954D, 1963D,
Kriscak, Manuela, 1965A, 1990C
Kritische Briefe uber die Tonkunst, 1759G
Kroeger, Ernest R., 1862A, 1915E, 1934B
Kroeger, Karl, 1932A
Kroeger School of Music, 1904G
Krohn, Ernst C., 1888A, 1953D, 1975B
Kroll, William, 1901A, 1915C, 1980B
Kroll String Quartet, 1944G
Krommer, Franz, 1759A, 1818D, 1831B
Kronold, Selma, 1861A, 1878C, 1920B
Kronos String Quartet, 1973G
Kroó, György, 1926A, 1963E
Kroyer, Theodor, 1873A, 1945B
Krückl, Franz, 1841A, 1868C, 1899B
Krueger, Karl, 1894A, 1926D, 1933D, 1943D, 1979B; *The Musical Heritage of the United States*, 1973H; *The Way of the Conductor*, 1958H
Krüger, Eduard: *Beiträge für leben und wissenschaft der Tonkunst*, 1847H; *Grundriss*

der Metrik, 1839H; *System der Tonkunst*, 1866H
Krüger, Felix: *Über das Bewusstein de Konsonanz*, 1901H
Kruis, M. H. van't, 1861A, 1919B
Krummel, D. W.: *Resources of American Music History*, 1981H
Krumpholtz, Anne-Marie, 1779C
Krumpholtz, Johann Baptist, 1790B
Krumpholz, Wenzel, 1817B
Krushelnitskaya, Salomea, 1872A, 1892C
Krzyzanowski, Stanislaw, Publisher, 1870G
Krzyzanowski Concert Bureau (Kraków), 1879G
Kubelík, Jan, 1880A, 1898C, 1940B
Kubelik, Rafael, 1914A, 1934C, 1937F, 1939D, 1948F, 1950D, 1961D, 1973D, 1996B
Kubera, Joseph, 1949A
Kubiak, Teresa, 1937A
Kubik, Gail, 1914A, 1950E, 1984B
Kubin String Quartet, 1972G
Kubo, Yoko, 1956A, 1979C
Kuchar, Theodore, 1992D, 1994D, 1996D
Kucharz, Johann B., 1751A, 1791D, 1829B
Küchler, Johann, 1790B
Kuchta, Gladys, 1923A, 1951C, 1998B
Kücken, Friedrich W., 1851D
Kuczinski, Paul, 1846A, 1897B
Kudelski, Karl Matthias, 1841D; *Kurzgefasste Harmonielehre*, 1865H
Kuebler, David, 1947A, 1972C
Kuen, Paul, 1910A, 1933C, 1966B
Kuerti, Anton, 1938A, 1948C, 1957E
Kufferath, Antonia, 1878C
Kufferath, Hubert F., 1818A, 1896B
Kufferath, Johann H., 1797A, 1823D, 1830D, 1864B
Kufferath, Louis, 1836D
Kuhlau, Friedrich, 1786A, 1813D, 1832B
Kuhlmann, Kathleen, 1950A, 1979C
Kuhmo, Finland: Arts Center, 1993G; Chamber Music Festival, 1970G
Kuhn, Gustav, 1947A, 1969C, 1970D, 1978D, 1979D, 1987D
Kuhn, Laura, 1953A
Kuhn, Pamela, 1960A, 1984C
Kühnau, Johann Christoph, 1788D, 1805B
Kui Dong, 1967A
Kuivila, Ron, 1955A
Kulinsky, Bohumil, 1959A
Kullak, Adolf, 1823A, 1862B; *Des Musikalisch-schöne*, 1858H
Kullak Franz: *Vortrag in der musik am Ende des 19 Jahrhunderts*, 1898H
Kullak, Theodor, 1818A, 1882B
Kullman, Charles, 1903A, 1924C, 1931C, 1983B
Kummer, Friedrich August, 1797A, 1879B
Kun Hu, 1963A
Kunc, Jan, 1923D

❂

F *Biographical*   G *Cultural Beginnings*   H *Musical Literature*
I *Musical Compositions*

Kunde, Gregory, 1954A, 1979C
Kunkel, Charles, 1840A, 1923B
Kunkel, Franz Joseph, 1808A, 1880B; *Kleine Musiklehre*, 1855H; *Die Neue Harmonielehr*, 1863H
Kunkel Brothers, Publishers, 1868G
Kunkel's Music Review, 1878G
Künneke, Eduard, 1885A, 1953B
Kunst und Industrie Comptoir (Pest), 1805G
Kunst und Industrie Comptoir (Vienna), 1801G
Kunstfest Weimar, 1990G
Kunsthumaniora, 1972G
Kunwald, Ernst, 1895D, 1897D, 1898D, 1902D, 1907D, 1912D
Kunz, Erich, 1909A, 1933C, 1995B
Kunzel, Erich, 1935A, 1957C, 1960D, 1965F, 1966F, 1974D, 1977D
Kunzen, Adolph Carl, 1752D, 1757D, 1781B
Kunzen, Friedrich Ludwig, 1761A, 1794D, 1797D, 1817B
Kunzen, Johann Paul, 1757B
Kupferberg, Herbert, 1918A
Kupferman, Meyer, 1926A, 1981E; *Atonal Jazz*, 1993H
Kupper, Anneliese, 1987B
Küpper, Leo, 1935A
Kurenko, Maria, 1890A, 1914C, 1980B
Kurka, Robert, 1921A, 1952E, 1957B
Kurll, Marguerita, 1997E
Kurpinski, Karol, 1785A, 1819D, 1842D, 1857B
Kürsteiner, Jean Paul, 1864A, 1943B
Kurt, Melanie, 1880A, 1902C, 1941B
Kurth, Ernst, 1886A, 1946B; *Grundlagen des Linearen Kontrapunkt*, 1917H; *Musikpsychologie*, 1931H; *Romantische Harmonik und ihre Krise in Wagners Tristan*, 1920H
Kurtz, Efrem, 1900A, 1921C, 1924D, 1943D, 1948D, 1995B
Kurz, Selma, 1874A, 1895C, 1933B
Kusche, Benno, 1916A, 1938C
Küster, Hermann, 1817A, 1857D, 1878B; *Über die Formen in der Musik*, 1872H
Kutcher String Quartet, 1924G
Kuula, Toiva, 1883A, 1918B
Kuusisto, Pekka, 1976B, 1995E
Küzdö, Victor, 1859A, 1882C, 1966B
Kuzumi, Karina, 1973A, 1986C, 1973B
Kvandal, Johan, 1919A, 1999B
Kwalwasser, Helen, 1947C
Kwalwasser, Jacob, 1894A, 1977B; *Exploring the Musical Mind*, 1955H; *Problems in Public School Music*, 1932H; *Tests & Measurements in Music*, 1927H
Kwella, Patrizia, 1953A, 1979C
Kyllonen, Timo-Juhani, 1955A
La Barbara, Joan, 1947A
Labarre, Théodore, 1805A, 1862E, 1870B
Labatt, Leonard, 1838A, 1866C, 1897B

Labbette, Dora, 1917C
Labèque, Katia, 1950A, 1961C, 1982F
Labèque, Marielle, 1952A, 1961C, 1982G
Labia, Maria, 1880A, 1905C, 1953B
Labitzky, Joseph, 1802A, 1881B
Lablache, Luigi, 1794A, 1812C, 1858B
Labo, Flaviano, 1927A, 1954C, 1991B
La Borde, Jean-Benjamin de, 1794B; *Essai sur la musique ancienne et moderne*, 1780H
LaBrecque, Rebecca, 1996B
Labunski, Wiktor, 1895A, 1941D, 1974B
Lacépède, Bernard Germain, 1756A, 1825B; *Poétique de la musique*, 1785H
Lach, Robert, 1874A, 1958B
Lachmann, Robert, 1892A, 1939B
Lachmund, Carl, 1857A, 1928B
Lachmund Conservatory, 1905G
Lachner, Franz, 1803A, 1827D, 1834D, 1836D, 1890B
Lachner, Ignaz, 1807A, 1831D, 1858D, 1895B
Lachner, Vincenz, 1811A, 1848D, 1893B
Lachnith, Ludwig Wenzel, 1820B
Lacombe Louis: *Philosophie et musique*, 1895H
Lacoste, Louis de, 1754B
Lacroix, Antoine, 1756A, 1806B
La Croix, François de, 1759B
Ladegast, Friedrich, 1905B
Ladergast, Friedrich, Organ Builder, 1818A, 1846G
Laderman, Ezra, 1924A, 1963E, 1973D, 1978D, 1986D, 1989D, 1991E
Ladmirault, Paul, 1877A, 1944B
Ladurner, Ignaz Antoine, 1766A, 1839B
Ladurner, Josef Alois, 1769A, 1851B
The Lady's Musical Magazine, 1788G
La Fage, Adrien (Juste) de, 1801A, 1829D, 1862; *Cours complet de plain-chant*, 1855H; *Histoire générale de la musique*, 1844H
Lafayette String Quartet, 1984G, 1988E
Lafont, Charles-Philippe, 1781A, 1839B
Lafont, Jean-Philippe, 1951A, 1974C
La Forge, Frank, 1879A, 1953B
La Garde, Pierre de, 1756E, 1792B
Lagoya, Alexander, 1999B
La Grande Écurie et la Chambre du Roy, 1966G
La Grange, Anne Caroline de, 1905B
LaGuardia High School of Music & the Arts, 1984G
Laguerre, Marie-Joséphine, 1755A, 1776C, 1783B
La Grange, Anne Carolin de, 1842C
La Hache, Theodore von, 1822A, 1869B
Lahee, Henry C., 1953B; *Annals of Music in America*, 1922H; *Famous Pianists of Today & Yesterday*, 1901H; *Grand Opera in America*, 1902H; *The Grand Opera Singers of Today*, 1912H; *The Organ & Its Masters*, 1903H; *The Orchestra*, 1925H

❀

A *Births*   B *Deaths*   C *Debuts*   D *New Positions*
E *Prizes/Honors*

La Houssaye, Pierre, 1777D, 1781D, 1790D, 1818B
Lahti, Finland: Performing Arts Center, 1983G; Sibelius Hall, 2000G; Symphony Orchestra, 1949G
Laidlaw, Anna Robena, 1819A, 1837C, 1901B
Lajante, Théodore de, 1873D
Lajtha, Lázló, 1951E
Lake, Mayhew, 1913D, 1955B
Lake George Opera Festival, 1962G
Lake Tahoe Summer Music Festival, 1983G
Lakes, Gary, 1950A, 1981CE
Laki, Krisztina, 1944A, 1976C
Lalande, Henriette C., 1798A, 1814C, 1867B
La Laurencie, Lionel de, 1861A, 1933B
Lalo, Édouard, 1823A, 1888E, 1892B
Lalo Pierre: *La musique*, 1899H
Lamb, James, 1887A
Lambda Phi Delta Music Sorority, 1916G
Lambert, Alexander, 1862A, 1929B
Lambert, Constant, 1905A, 1940D, 1951B
Lambert, George Jackson, 1794A, 1880B
Lambert, Johann, 1777B; *Observations sur les sons des flutes*, 1775H; *Remarques sur le tempérament*, 1774H; *Sur la vitesse du son*, 1768H; *Sur quelques instruments acoustiques*, 1763H
Lambert, Lucien, 1885E
Lamberti, Giorgio, 1938A, 1964C
Lambertini Piano Co., 1838G
Lambertini, Luigi, 1790A, 1864B
Lambertini, Luigi, Piano Maker, 1836G
Lambillotte, Louis, 1796A, 1855B; *Clef des mélodies grégoriennes*, 1851H; *Musée des organistes I*, 1842H
Lambord, Benjamin, 1879A, 1915B
Lambord Choral (Modern Music) Society, 1912G
Lamond, Frederic, 1868A, 1885C, 1948B
Lamoninary, Jacques-Philippe, 1802B
Lamont, Forrest, 1881A, 1914C, 1937B
La Montaine, John, 1920A, 1962E
Lamote de Grignon, Juan, 1872A, 1910D, 1949B; *Musique et musiciens français à Barcelona*, 1935H
Lamoureux, Charles, 1834A, 1872F, 1877D, 1878E, 1899B
Lampe, John F, 1751B
Lamperti, Francesco, 1811A, 1892B; *Treatise on the Art of Singing*, 1877H
Lanagevin, Claude, 1928A
Lancelot, James, 1952A, 1975C
Land, Jan Pieter, 1834A, 1897B
Landau, Siegfried, 1955D
Landon, H. C. Robbins: *Essays on the Viennese Classical Style*, 1970H; *Five Centuries of Music in Venice*, 1991H
Landouzy, Lise, 1861A, 1889C, 1942B

Landowska, Wanda, 1879A, 1919F, 1959B; *Musique ancienne*, 1909H
Landré, Guillaume, 1905A, 1947D, 1968B
Landré, Willem, 1874A, 1948B
Lane, Eastwood, 1879A, 1951B
Lane, Louis, 1923A, 1947F, 1956D, 1971E, 1972E
Lane, Jennifer, 1954A, 1968C
Lang, Benjamin, 1837A, 1858C, 1874D, 1895D, 1909B
Lang, David, 1957A, 1990E
Lang, Hans, 1902C
Lang, Johann Georg, 1798B
Lang, Josephine, 1815A, 1880B
Lang, Klaus, 1971B
Lang, Margaret Ruthven, 1867A, 1972B
Lang, Paul Henry, 1901A, 1945D, 1954D, 1955D, 1991B; *Contemporary Music in Europe*, 1965H; *Critic at the Opera*, 1971H; *Music in Western Civilization*, 1941H; *Problems of Modern Music*, 1960H
Langan, Kevin, 1955A, 1979C
Langbecker, Emanuel, 1792A, 1843B; *Das Deutsch-Evangelische Kirchenlied*, 1830H
Langdon, H. C. Robbins, 1926A
Langdon, Richard, 1753D, 1778D, 1782D, 1803B; *Divine Harmony*, 1774H
Langdon, Sophia, 1958A, 1981C
Lange, Francisco C., 1903A, 1997B
Lange, Hans, 1884A
Lange, Samuel de, Jr., 1885D, 1900D
Lange, Samuel de, Sr., 1811A, 1884B, 1911B
Lange-Müller, Peter Erasmus, 1850A, 1926B
Langendorff, Frieda, 1868A, 1901C, 1947B
Langenus, Gustave, 1883A, 1957B; *Complete Method for the Boehm Clarinet*, 1916H; *Modern Clarinet Playing*, 1913H
Langer, Hermann, 1857D
Langer, Milan, 1955A
Langert, Johann August, 1873D
Langgaard, Rued, 1893A, 1905C, 1952B
Langhans Friedrich: *Die Geschichte der musik des 17., 18., & 19. Jahrhunderts I*, 1882H; *Musikgeschichte in zwölf Vorträgen*, 1878H
Langhans, Wilhelm, 1832A, 1892B; *Das Musicalische Urteil und seine Ausbildung durch des Erziehung*, 1872H
Langlais, Jean, 1907A, 1945D, 1991B
Langlé, Honoré, 1807B; *Nouvelle méthode pour chiffrer les accords*, 1801H; *Traité d'harmonie et de modulation*, 1793H; *Traité de la basse sous le chant*, 1798H; *Traité de la fugue*, 1805H
Langridge, Philip, 1964C
Lanier, Sidney, 1842A, 1873F, 1881B
Lanner, Joseph, 1801A, 1843B
Lannoy, Edward, 1787A, 1853B
Lanowski, Paul M., 1900E
Lansky, Paul, 1977E
Lanza, Mario, 1921A, 1959B

※

F *Biographical*   G *Cultural Beginnings*   H *Musical Literature*
I *Musical Compositions*

Laparra, Raoul, 1903E
La Paz, Bolivia: Bolivian National Orchestra, 1940G; National Conservatory of Music, 1908G
La Pierre, Louis-Maurice de, 1753B
Laporte, André, 1931A, 1989D
Laporte, Joseph de, 1779B; *Anecdotes dramatiques*, 1775H; *Dictionnaire dramatique*, 1776H
La Pouplinière, Alexandre Jean de, 1762B
Larchet, John F., 1884A, 1967B
Laredo, Jaime, 1941A, 1959E
Laredo, Ruth, 1937A, 1962C
Larin, Sergei, 1989C
Lark String Quartet, 1985G
Larmore, Jennifer, 1958A, 1986C, 1994E
La Roux, François, 1955A
Larrivée, Henri, 1755C, 1802B
Larrocha, Alicia de, 1923A, 1935C, 1959D, 1961E, 1978E
Larsen, Jens Peter, 1902A, 1988B
Larsen, Libby, 1950A
Larsen, Knud, Musikforlag, Publisher, 1906G
Larsen-Todsen, Nanny, 1884A, 1906C, 1982B
Larsson, Lars-Erik, 1908A, 1929E, 1937D, 1986B
La Rue, Steven: *International Dictionary of Opera*, 1994H
Laruette, Jean-Louis, 1752C, 1792B
Laruette, Marie-Therese, 1758C
Laryngoscope, 1855G
La Salette, Joubert de, 1833B; *Considérations sur les divers systèmes de la musique ancienne et moderne*, 1810H; *De la fixité et de l'invariabilité des sons musicaux*, 1824H; *De la notation musicale en général, et en particulier de celle du système grec*, 1817H; *Sténographie musicale*, 1805H
Laschi, Luisa, 1784C
La Scola, Vincenzo, 1958A, 1983C
Laserna, Blas de, 1751A, 1816B
Lassalle, Jean-Louis, 1847A, 1868C, 1909B
La Salle String Quartet, 1949G
Lassen, Eduard, 1830A, 1851E, 1858D, 1904B
Lassen, Morten Ernst, 1969A
Las Vegas Symphony Orchestra, 1980G
László, Alexander, 1895A, 1970B; *Die Farblichtmusik*, 1925H
Laszló, Magda, 1919A, 1943C
Lateiner, Jacob, 1928A, 1944C
Latham, Alison: *The Cambridge Music Guide*, 1985H
Latham, William, 1917A
Latille, Gaetano, 1788B
Latin American Center for Advanced Musical Studies, 1962G
Latin American Music Center, 1961G
Latrobe, Christian Ignatius, 1758A, 1836B

Latrobe, John Antes, 1799A, 1878B; *The Music of the Church in its Various Branches, Congregational and Choral*, 1831H
Laub, Ferdinand, 1832A, 1875B
Laubach, Mark Edward, 1961A
Laube, Anton, 1771D, 1784B
Laube, Heinrich, 1849D, 1869D
Laubenthal, Horst, 1939A, 1967C
Laubenthal, Rudolf, 19131C, 1971B
Lauder, Harry, 1870A
Laudibus, 1995G
Laurel Festival of the Arts, 1990G
Laurencin, Ferdinand, 1819A, 1890B; *Zur Geschichte der Kirchenmusik bei den italienern un deutschen*, 1856H; *Die Harmonik der Neuzeit*, 1861H
Lauri-Volpi, Giacomo, 1892A, 1919C, 1979B
Lausanne, Switzerland: Beau-Rivage Orchestra, 1872G; Chamber Orchestra, 1940G; International Festival, 1955G
Lauska, Franz, 1764A, 1825B
Laussot, Jennie, 1850F
Lauterbach, Johann, 1832A
Lautten Compagney, 1984G
Lavenu, Lewis, Publisher (London), 1796G
Lavigna, Vincenzo, 1776A, 1836B
Lavignac, Albert, 1846A, 1916B; *Cours complet théorique de dictée musicale*, 1882H; *Cours d'harmonie...*, 1907H; *La musique et les musiciens*, 1895H
Lavigne, Jacques Émile, 1782A, 1809C, 1855B
La Violette, Wesley, 1894A, 1978B
Lavoix, Henri-Marie, 1865D; *Histoire de l'instrumentation*, 1878H; *La musique dans la nature*, 1877H; *La musique dans l'imagerie du moyen-âge*, 1875H
Lavotta, János, 1764A, 1820B
Lavrovskaya, Elizaveta A., 1845A, 1867C, 1919B
Law, Andrew, 1786E, 1821BE; *The Art of Playing the Organ & Pianoforte*, 1809H; *The Art of Singing*, 1794H; *Collection of Hymns for Social Worship*, 1782H; *Essays on Music*, 1814H; *Harmonie Companion & Guide to Social Worship*, 1807H; *Musical Primer*, 1803H; *The Rudiments of Music*, 1783H; *Select Harmony*, 1779H
Lawrence, Dorothea Dix, 1899A, 1929C, 1979B; *Folklore Songs of the United States*, 1959H
Lawrence, Marjorie, 1907A, 1932C, 1943F, 1979B; *Interrupted Melody*, 1949H
Lawrence, Robert, 1939D; *A Rage for Opera*, 1971H
Lawrence, Vera Brodsky, 1909A, 1996B; *Music for Patriots, Politicians & Presidents*, 1975H
Lawrence College Cons. Of Music, 1894G
Laycock, Mark, 1957A, 1979CE
Lays, François, 1758A, 1779C, 1831B
Layton, Billy Jim, 1924A, 1954E

A   *Births*   B   *Deaths*   C   *Debuts*   D   *New Positions*
E   *Prizes/Honors*

Lazarev, Alexander, 1945A, 1972E, 1973CD, 1988D
Lazaro, Hippolito, 1887A, 1911C, 1974B
Lazarof, Henri, 1932A
Lazarus, Henry, 1815A, 1838C, 1895B
Lazzari, Ferdinando Antonio, 1754B
Lazzari, Sylvio, 1857A, 1944B
Lazzari, Virgilio, 1887A, 1908C, 1953B
Leach, James, 1762A, 1798B
Leach, Joel: *Scoring for Percussion*, 1969H
League of Composers (N.Y.), 1923G
The League of Composers' Review, 1924G
League of Filipino Composers, 1955G
Leaper, Adrian, 1953A, 1982D, 1986F, 1994D
Leal, Eleutério, 1780D
Lear, Evelyn, 1926A, 1955C, 1985F
Le Beau, Luise Adolpha, 1850A, 1927B
Lebeuf, Abbé Jean, 1760B
LeBlanc, G., Corporation, 1946G
Leborne, Aimée Ambroise, 1797A, 1820E, 1853E, 1866B
Lebrecht, Norman: *The Companion to Twentieth-Century Music*, 1996H
Lebrun, Paul Henri, 1920B
Lebrun, Franziska D., 1772C, 1791B
Lebrun, Jean, 1759A, 1781C, 1792F, 1809B
Lebrun, Louis-Sébastien, 1764A, 1787C, 1829B
Lebrun, Ludwig August, 1752A, 1790B
Lebrun, Paul Henri, 1863A, 1891E
Lechner, Frederick, 1910A
Lecian, Krystof Filip, 1974A, 1994C
Leclair, Jean-Marie, *l'aîné*, 1764BF
Leclair, Jean-Marie, *le cadet*, 1777B
LeClerc, Charles-Nicolas, 1774B
Lecocq, Charles, 1832A, 1856E, 1918B
Lecuona, Ernesto, 1896A, 1963B
Lederer, Joseph, 1796B
Ledesma, Mariano Rodríques de, 1779A, 1807D
Leduc, Alphonse, Publishing Co., 1841G
Leduc, Pierre, 1755A, 1770C, 1816B
Leduc, Simon, 1763C, 1777B
Leduc, Simon et Pierre, Publishers (Paris), 1775G
Lee, Dai-Keong, 1915A
Lee, Everett, 1962D
Lee, Samuel, Music Store, 1752G
Lee, Sebastian, 1805A, 1831C, 1887B
Lee & Walker Publishing Co., 1848G
Leech, Richard, 1956A, 1980E, 1984C, 1988E
Leeds, England: Amateur Society, 1827G; Madrigal & Motet Society, 1850G; Music Hall II, 1794G; Philharmonic Society; Piano Competition, 1963G; String Quartet, 1909G
Leedy, Douglas, 1938A
Leedy Manufacturing Co., 1900G
Lees, Benjamin, 1924A
Leeuw, Ton de, 1926A, 1956E, 1982E, 1996B; *Music of the Twentieth Century*, 1964H

Lefébure-Wély, Louis, 1817A, 1847D, 1858D, 1869B; *Nouveau solfège*, 1780H
Lefebvre, Charles Édouard, 1843A, 1870E, 1917B
Lefèbvre, Joseph, 1761A
Lefebvre, Louis Antoine, 1763B
Lefèvre, Jean-Baptiste, 1784B
Lefevre, Jean Xavier, 1763A, 1783C, 1828B
Lefèbvre, Pierre, 1959A
Leffler-Burckard, Martha, 1865A, 1888A, 1954B
Lefkowitz, Mischa, 1954A, 1984C
Leger, Jean-François, 1956A, 1994F
Legge, Harry, 2000B
Leginska, Ethel, 1886A, 1907C, 1970B
Legnani, Luigi, 1790A, 1877B, 1819C
Legrand, Jean-Pierre, 1758D, 1809B
Legrand, Louis-Alexandre, 1773B
Legros, Joseph, 1764C, 1777D, 1793B
Lehár, Franz, 1870A, 1948B
Le Havre, France: École Saint Simeon, 1856G
Lehman String Quartet, 1892G
Lehmann, Friedrich: *Harmonic Analysis*, 1910H
Lehmann, Lilli, 1848A, 1865C, 1929B
Lehmann, Liza, 1862A, 1885C, 1918B
Lehmann, Lotte, 1888A, 1910C, 1976B; *Mein Weg*, 1913H
Lehmann, Marie, 1851A, 1865C, 1931B
Lehmann, Wilfred, 1952C
Leibl, Karl, 1784A, 1870B
Leibl, William, 1892E
Leibowitz, René, 1913A, 1972B; *The Evolution of Music*, 1952H; *Introduction to 12-tone Music*, 1949H; *Schoenberg & His School*, 1947H
Leibrock, Joseph: *Musikalische Akkordenlehre*, 1875H
Leichtentritt, Hugo, 1874A, 1951B; *Geschichte der musik*, 1905H; *Serge Koussevitzky, The Boston Symphony Orchestra & New American Music*, 1946H; *Musical Form*, 1951H; *Musikalische Formenlehre*, 1911H
Leider, Frida, 1888A, 1915C, 1975B
Leiferkus, Sergei, 1946A, 1972CE, 1977C
Leifs, Jón, 1899A, 1968B
Leighton, Kenneth, 1988B
Leinsdorf, Erich, 1912A, 1933C, 1938D. 1943D, 1947D, 1962D, 1963E, 1978D, 1993B; The Composer's Advocate, 1982H
Leipzig, Germany: Bach-Verein, 1847G; Concerts Spirituels, 1776G; Conservatory of Music, 1843G; Gewandhaus, 1780G; Gewandhaus Orchestra, 1781G; Hiller Singing School, 1771G; Männerchor, 1891G; Musikübende Gesellschaft, 1775G; Riedel Verein, 1854G; Schauspielhaus, 1766G; Singakademie, 1802G; Stadttheater, 1766G; State Opera Co., 1945G; Subscription (Liebhaber) Concerts, 1763G; Winderstein Orchestra, 1896G; Zöllner-Verein, 1833G; Zschocher'sches Musik-Institut, 1846G

❀

F *Biographical*   G *Cultural Beginnings*   H *Musical Literature*
I *Musical Compositions*

Leisner, David, 1953A
Leite, Antonio da Silva, 1759A, 1833B; *Estudo de Guitarra*, 1796H
Leitert, Johann G., 1852A, 1865C, 1901B
Leitner, Ferdinand, 1912A, 1945D, 1969D, 1976D, 1996B
Lekeu, Guillaume, 1870A, 1894B
Lemaire, Jean-Eugène, 1854A, 1928B
Leman, Juan, 1999B
Lemare, Edwin, 1865A, 1917D, 1934B
Lemeshev, Sergei, 1902A, 1926C, 1977B
Lemieux, Marie-Nicole, 2000E
Lemmens Institute of Church Music, 1879G
Lemmens-Sherrington, Helen, 1834A, 1856C, 1906B
Lemnitz, Tiana Luise, 1920C, 1994B
Lemoine, Antoine-Marcel, 1753A, 1816B
Lemoine, Henri, 1786A, 1854B
Lemoine Music Publishers, 1772G
Lemoyne, Jean-Baptiste, 1751A, 1796B
Lenard, Ondrej, 1942A
Lendvay, Kamilló, 1928A, 1989E, 1998E
Lenepveu, Charles, 1865E, 1887E, 1896E
Léner String Quartet, 1918G
Lengnick Music Publishers, 1893G
Lennon, John Anthony, 1950A, 1980E
Lenox, Massachusetts: Berkshire (Tanglewood) Music Center, 1940G; String Quartet, 1922G
Lentz, Heinrich Gerhard, 1764A, 1839B
Lenya, Lotte, 1981B
Lenz, Friedrich, 1953C
Lenz, Wilhelm von, 1809A, 1883B
Léon, Tania, 1943A
Leonard, Charles: *Foundations & Principles of Music Education*, 1959H
Leonard, Hal, Music, Inc., 1946G
Léonard, Hubert, 1819A, 1832C, 1890B
Leoncavallo, Ruggiero, 1857A, 1906F, 1919B
Leonhard, Julius Emil, 1810A, 1883B
Leonhardt, Gustav, 1928A, 1950C
Leoni, Franco, 1864A, 1949B
Leonova, Darya, 1829A, 1852C, 1896B
LePage, Jane: *Women Composers, Conductors & Musicians of the Twentieth Century*, 1980H
Le Passe-Temps (Canada), 1895G
Lepore, Paolo, 1985D
Leppard, Raymond, 1927A, 1952C, 1973D, 1983F, 1987D
Leppart, R.: *Music & Society*, 1988H
Leps, Wassili, 1932D
Lerdahl, Fred, 1943A, 1971E; *A Generative Theory of Tonal Music*, 1983H
Lermnitz, Tiana Luise, 1897A
Lerner, Mimi, 1954A, 1979C
Lerner, Bennett, 1944A, 1966C
Le Roux, François, 1980C
LeRoux, Maurice, 1923A
Leroux, Xavier, 1863A, 1885E, 1919B
Lert, Richard, 1980B

Le Rue, Jan, 1918A
Les Ballets de L'École, 1954G
Leschetizky, Theodor, 1830A, 1915B
Lescovar, Monika, 1980A, 1995C
Lesovichenko, Andrei, 19960A
Lessard, John, 1920A
Lessel, Franz, 1780A, 1838B
Lessing, Kolja, 1961A, 1981C
Lester, Joel: *Analytic Approaches to Twentieth-Century Music*, 1988H
Lesueur, Jean-François, 1760A, 1781D, 1784D, 1786D, 1788F, 1804D, 1837B; *Exposé d'une musique unie, imitative et particulière à chaque solemnité*, 1787H
Letorey, Omer, 1895E
Lettvin, Theodore, 1926A, 1940E, 1952C
Leuckart, Ernst Christoph, 1817B
Leuckart, F. Ernst, Publishing Co., 1782G
Leuckart Publishing House, 1856G
Leutgeb, Joseph Ignaz, 1811B
Lev, Ray, 1912A, 1931C, 1968B
Levadé, Charles, 1899E
Levant, Oscar, 1906A, 1972B; *A Smattering of Ignorance*, 1940H
Levarie, Siegmund: *Fundamentals of Harmony*, 1954H; *Tone: A Study in Musical Acoustics*, 1968H
Levasseur, Jean Henri, 1764A, 1826B
Levasseur, Nicolas, 1791A, 183C, 1869E, 1871B
Levasseur, Rosalie, 1766C, 1826B
Leventritt Foundation International Competition, 1940G
Leveridge, Richard, 1758B
Levering, Arthur, 1953A
Levi, Hermann, 1839A, 1859D, 1861D, 1864D, 1872D, 1900B
Levi, Yoel, 1950A, 1978F, 1980F, 1988D
Levine, Gilbert, 1948A, 1973C, 1987D, 1993F
Levine, James, 1943A, 1953C, 1964F, 1973D, 1984E, 1994F, 1997E, 2000E
Levinsky, Ilya, 1965A, 1987C
Levinson, Max, 1997E
Levitzki, Mischa, 1898A, 1941B
Levy, Alan H.: *Musical Nationalism*, 1983H
Levy, Daniel, 1947A
Lévy, Ernst: *Tone: A Study in Musical Acoustics*, 1968H
Lévy, Heniot, 1879A, 1899C, 1946B
Levy, Marvin David, 1932A, 1962E
Lewandowski, Lynne, 1953A
Lewenthal, Raymond, 1926A, 1988B
Lewin, David, 1933A; *Generalized Musical Intervals & Transformations*, 1987H
Lewin, Michael, 1956A
Lewis, Daniel, 1925A
Lewis, Henry, 1932A, 1968D, 1972F, 1989D, 1996B
Lewis, Mary, 1900A, 1941A, 1923C,
Lewis, Richard, 1914A, 1939C, 1963E, 1990B

❀

A   *Births*   B   *Deaths*   C   *Debuts*   D   *New Positions*
E   *Prizes/Honors*

Lewis, Robert Hall, 1926A, 1976E
Lewis, William, 1935A, 1953C
Lewis, William, & Son, Publisher, 1874G
Lewisohn Stadium (N.Y.), 1914G; concerts at,
   1918G
Lewkovitch, Bernard, 1927A, 1963E
Leybach, Ignace, 1844D
Leypoldt and Holt, Publishers, 1866G
Lhévinne, Josef, 1874A, 1895E, 1944B; *Basic*
   Principles in Pianoforte Playing, 1924H
Lhevinne, Rosina, 1976B
Lhoyer, Antoine de, 1768A, 1852A
Liadov, Anatoli, 1855A, 1876F, 1914B
Liadov, Constantin, 1850D
Liberati, Alessandro, 1927B
Libetto, Francesco, 1968A
Libon, Philippe, 1775A, 1838B
Licad, Cecile, 1961A, 1979C, 1981E
Liceo Musicale Giuseppe Tartini, 1903G
Licette, Miriam, 1892A, 1911C
Lichnowsky, Prince Carl, 1761A, 1814B
Lichtegg, Max, 1910A, 1936C
Lichtenstein, Karl August von, 1767A, 1825D,
   1845B
Lichtenstein, Romella, 1988C
Lichtenthal, Peter, 1780A, 1853B; *Dizionario e*
   bibliografia della musica, 1826H; *Estetica*,
   1831H; *Harmony Treatise*, 1816H; *Der*
   Musikalische Arzt, 1807H
Lickl, Johann Georg, 1769A, 1843B
Lidón, José, 1787D
Lie, Harald, 1902A, 1942B
Lieban, Julius, 1878C
Lieberman, Maurice: *Creative Counterpoint*,
   1966H
Liebermann, Lowell, 1961A
Liebermann, Rolf, 1910A, 1959D, 1973D, 1999B
Lieberson, Peter, 1946A
Liebig, Carl, 1808A, 1872B
Liebling, Emil, 1851A, 1914B
Liebling, Estelle, 1880A, 1898C, 1970B
Liebling, Georg, 1865A, 1946B
Liebling, Leonard, 1874A, 1911D, 1923D, 1945B
Liège, Belgium: Orchestre Philharmonique,
   1960G ; String Quartet, 1925G
Lienau, Emil Robert, 1838A, 1920B
Lierhammer, Theodor, 1866A, 1894C, 1937B
Lieurance, Thurlow, 1878A, 1940D, 1963B
Lifshitz, Constantin, 1977A
Ligabue, Ilva, 1998B
Ligendza, Catarina, 1937A, 1965C
Ligeti, György, 1923A, 1986E
Liljeblad, Ingeborg, 1887A, 1911C, 1942B
Lill, John, 1944A, 1963C, 1970D, 1978E
Lille Opera House, 1787G
Lillenas Music Publishing Co., 1924G
Lima, Arthur, 1950C
Lima, Jeronymo Francisco de, 1798D
Lima, Luis, 1948A, 1972E, 1973E, 1974C

Lima, Peru: Academy of Music, 1930G; Teatro
   Principal, 1889G
Lincke, Joseph, 1783A, 1837B
Lincke Georg F.: *Die Sitze der musikalischen*
   Haupt-Satze in einer harten un weichen Tonart,
   1766H
Lind, Eva, 1965A, 1983C
Lind, Jenny, 1820A, 1830F, 1838C, 1840E, 1849F,
   1850F, 1852F, 1887B
Lindberg, Magnus, 1958A
Lindberg, Oskar, 1887A, 1955B
Lindblad, Adolf Fredrik, 1801A, 1831E, 1878B
Lindblad, Adolf, Music School, 1827G
Lindholm, Berit, 1934A, 1963C, 1984E
Lindley, Robert, 1776A, 1855B
Lindpaintner, Peter J. von, 1791A, 1812D,
   1819D, 1856B
Lindroth, Scott, 1958A
Linley, Charles, 1774B
Linley, Elizabeth Ann, 1754A, 1767C, 1792B
Linley, Francis, 1770A, 1800B
Linley, Thomas, Jr., 1756A, 1763C, 1777E,
   1778B
Linley, Thomas, Sr., 1795B
Linley, William, 1771A, 1835B
Linn, Robert, 1925A
Linz, Austria: Bruckner Conservatorium,
   1822G; Liedertafel "Froshsinn," 1845G;
   Männergesangverein, 1845G; Music
   Academy, 1822G
Lipatti, Dinu, 1917A, 1950B
Lipinsky, Carl, 1790A, 1861B
Lipkin, Malcolm, 1932A, 1951C
Lipkin, Seymour, 1927A, 1938C, 1948E
Lipkovska, Lydia, 1882A, 1907C, 1955B
Lipman, Michael, 1954A, 1985C
Lipman, Samuel, 1934A, 1943C, 1977E, 1994B;
   The House of Music, 1982H; *Music after*
   Modernism, 1979H
Lipovek, Marjana, 1979C
Lipowsky, Felix Joseph, 1764A, 1842B;
   Baierisches Musiklexicon, 1811H
Lipowsky, Thaddäis Ferdinan, 1767B
Lipp, Wilma, 1943C
Lippert, Marian, 1939A, 1956C
Lippincott, J. B. & Co., Publishers, 1836G
Lippman, Edward A., 1920A; *Musical*
   Aesthetics, 1986H
Lipsett, Steven, 1996E
Lipsius, Marie (La Mara), 1837A, 1927B
Lipton, Martha, 1913A, 1944C
Lirico Arena Opera Co., 1913G
Lirou, Jean François, 1806B; *Explication du*
   système de l'harmonie, 1785H
Lisbon, Portugal: Choral Society, 1941G;
   Conservatório Nacional, 1835G; Orquestra
   da Real Academia, 1884G; Philharmonic
   Orchestra, 1937G; Sociedade Philarmonica,
   1822G; Symphony Orchestra, 1913G; Teatro

❖

F   *Biographical*   G   *Cultural Beginnings*   H   *Musical Literature*
       I   *Musical Compositions*

Lisbon, Portugal: (*cont.*)
  des Pacos de Ribeira, 1755G; Teatro do
  Salitre, 1785G; Teatro S. Carlos, 1793G
Lisinski, Vatroslav, Concert Auditorium, 1973G
Lissner, Gerda Foundation, 1994G
List, Eugene, 1918A, 1930C, 1985B
List, Emanuel, 1888A, 1922C, 1967B
Listemann, Bernhard, 1841A, 1917B
Listemann, Franz, 1873A, 1930B
Listemann, Fritz, 1839A, 1909B
Listemann Concert Co., 1885G
Liszt, Cosima, 1853F, 1857F
Liszt, Franz, 1811A, 1820CF, 1825F, 1834F,
  1836F, 1839F, 1840F, 1842F, 1848D, 1865F,
  1875E, 1879F, 1886B; *Des bohémiens et de leur*
  musique en Hongrie, 1859H
Liszt, Franz, Memorial Hall, 1925G
Liszt Piano Competition, 1961G
Litchfield County Choral Union, 1899G
Lithuania: Conservatory of Music, 1933G;
  Opera & Ballet Theater, 1948G; Opera
  Theater, 1920G; Radio Symphony Orchestra,
  1926G; State Philharmonic, 1940G;
Litolff, Henry C., 1832C
Litta, Marie, 1856A, 1876C, 1883B
Little, Tasmine, 1965A
Little, Vera, 1928A, 1950C
Little Rock, Arkansas: Chamber Music Society,
  1954G; Forest Park Theater, 1904G; Grand
  Opera House, 1873G; State Symphony,
  1940G; Symphony Orchestra, 1933G
Little, Brown & Co., Publishers, 1837G, 1847G
Littlejohn, David: *The Ultimate Art*, 1992H
Littolff, Henry Charles, 1818A, 1891B
Litton, Andrew, 1959A, 1979E, 1988D, 1994DF
Litvinne Félia, 1860A, 1882C, 1936B
Lively, David, 1953A, 1968C
Liverati, Giovanni, 1772A, 1799D, 1846B
Liverpool, England: Apollo Glee Club, 1796G;
  Concert Hall, 1786G; Goosens Male-Voice
  Choir, 1894G; Lieder Circle, 1968G;
  Philharmonic Hall, 1849G, 1939G;
  Philharmonic Society, 1840G; Rodewald
  Concert Society, 1911G; Saint George's Hall
  Concert Room, 1854G; Sinfonia, 1970G;
  Symphony Orchestra, 1943G
Livorno, Italy: Istituto Musicale Livornese,
  1875G; Società degli Esercizi Musicale,
  1809G; Teatro degli Armeni, 1782G; Teatro
  Goldoni, 1847G
Ljubljana, Slovenia: Philharmonische
  Gesellschaft, 1794G; Slovene Philharmonia,
  1901G; Slovene Regional Theater, 1892G;
  Theater of the Estates, 1765G
Ljungberg, Göta, 1893A, 1918C, 1955B
Llewellyn, Grant, 1960A, 1986E, 1990F
Llobet, Miguel, 1878A, 1938B
Lloveras, Juan, 1966C, 1998B
Lloyd, Charles H., 1849A, 1919B

Lloyd, David, 1920A, 1950C
Lloyd, Edward, 1845A, 1871C, 1927B
Lloyd, George, 1998B
Lloyd, Robert, 1940A, 1969C, 1991E
Lobe, Johann C., 1797A, 1846D, 1853D, 1881B;
  Aus dem leben eines musikers, 1859H;
  Compositionslehre, 1844H; *Consonanzen und*
  Dissonanzen, 1869H; *Katechismus der*
  Compositionslehre, 1872H; *Katechismus der*
  musik, 1851H; *Die Lehr von der thematischen*
  Arbeit, 1846H; *Lehrbuch der musikalischen*
  Composition, 1850H; *Musikalische Briefe eines*
  Wohlbekannten, 1852H; *Vereinfachte*
  harmonielehre, 1861H
Lobkowitz, Ferdinand P., 1784B
Lobkowitz, Joseph Franz, 1772A, 1816B
Locatelli, Pietro, 1759F, 1764B
Locatelli Trio, 1989G
Lockenhaus Music Festival, 1981G
Lockhart, James, 1981D
Lockhart, John, 1825D
Lockhart, Keith, 1992D, 1995D, 1998D
Locklair, Dan, 1949A, 1981E, 1989E
Lockwood, Lewis, 19895D
Lockwood, Normand, 1906A, 1929E
Locrian Chamber Players, 1994G
Loder, John D.: *General & Comprehensive*
  Instruction Book for Violin, 1814H; *The Whole*
  Modern Art of Bowing, 1842H
Loeffler, Charles Martin, 1861A, 1903F, 1908E,
  1919E, 1926E, 1931E, 1935B
Loesser, Arthur, 1894A, 1913C, 1969B, 1969B;
  Men, Women & Pianos, 1954H
Loewe, Carl, 1796A, 1819F. 1821D, 1866F,
  1869B; *Gesanglehre für Gymnasien, Seminarien*
  und, 1826H; *Musikalischer Gottesdienst*, 1851H
Loewe, Johann Carl, 1837E
Loewe, Sophie, 1815A, 1832C, 1866B
Loewenguth String Quartet, 1929G
Loft Recordings, 1995G
Logan, James, Library, 1751G
Logier, Johann Bernhard, 1777A, 1846B;
  Chiroplast Méthode de Piano, 1818H; *System*
  der Musikwissenschaft und der musikalischen
  Komposition, 1827H
Logroscino, Nicola Bonifacio, 1765B
Loh, Lisa, 1967A, 1993C
Lohfing, Max, 1870A, 1894C
Löhlein, Georg Simon, 1781B; *Clavier-Schule I*,
  1765H; *Clavier-Schule II*, 1781H; *Violinschule*,
  1774H
Lohmann, Lodger, 1954B
Lokot, Anna Kaskas, 1907A
Lolli, Antonio, 1758F, 1773F, 1779F, 1780DF,
  1783F, 1785F, 1802B; *École du violon en*
  quatuor, 1776H
Lomax, Alan, 1915A; *American Folk Song & Folk*
  Lore, 1942H; *Folk Songs Style & Culture*,
  1968H

❄

A   *Births*   B   *Deaths*   C   *Debuts*   D   *New Positions*
E   *Prizes/Honors*

Lomax, John Avery, 1867A
Lomax, John W., Jr.: *Plantation Songs of the Negro*, 1916H
Lombard, Alain, 1940A, 1972D, 1974D, 1988D
Lombardo, Bernard, 1960A
London, Edwin, 1929A
London, George, 1919A, 1941C, 1960F, 1971D, 1975D, 1985B
London, England: Abbey Glee Club, 1841G; Academy of Ancient Music, 1973G; Adelphi Glee Club, 1832G; Adelphi Theater, 1806G; Aeolian Hall, 1904G; Alexandra Choir, 1940G; Anacreontic Society, 1766G; Argyll Rooms, 1812G; Associated Board, Royal Schools, 1889G; Astley's Royal Amphitheatre, 1798G; Athenaeum Club, 1824G; Bach Cantata Club, 1926G; Bach Choir, 1875G; Bach Society, 1946G; Bach-Abel Subscription Concerts, 1765G; Barnby's Choir, 1864G; Baroque, 1978G; Baroque Ensemble, 1941G; Bath Festival, 1948G; Bechstein (Wigmore) Hall, 1901G; Beecham Orchestra, 1909G; Bibliographical Society, 1892G; Blagroves's Quartet Concerts, 1843G; Caecilian Society, 1785G; Cambridge Theatre, 1930G; Centre for Microtonal Music, 1990G; Chamber Orchestra, 1921G; Choral Society, 1903G; City Glee Club, 1853G; College of Music, 1887G; College of Organists, 1869G; Concertorres Sodales, 1798G; Concerti da Camera, 1853G; Concerts of Ancient Music, 1776G; Consort of Musicke, 1969G; Consort of Winds, 1948G; Contemporary Chamber Orchestra, 1982G; Covent Garden Theater II, 1809G; Covent Garden Theater III, 1858G; Crosby Hall, 1842G; Crystal Palace, 1851G; Delius Music Festival, 1929G; Deller Consort, 1950G; Donizetti Society, 1973G; Early Music Consort, 1967G; Elizabethan Singers, 1953G; Exeter Hall, 1831G; Forest Gate College of Music, 1885G; Galpin Society of London, 1946G; Ganz Orchestral Concerts, 1879G; Glee Club, 1787G; Gounod's Choir, 1870G; Guildhall School of Music, 1880G; Handel Festival, 1857G; Handel Opera Society, 1955G; Handel Society, 1882G; Hanover Square Concert Hall, 1775G; Harp Ensemble, 1925G; Haydn Orchestra, 1949G; Haymarket Theatre II, 1880G; Her Majesty's Theatre II, 1791G; Hullah's Singing School, 1841G; Independent Theatre Society, 1891G; Intimate Opera Co., 1930G; Irish Orchestra, 1911G; Jacques Orchestra, 1936G; Junior Orchestra, 1929G; Lyceum Theater, 1772G; Matthay Piano School, 1900G; Melos Ensemble, 1950G; Melophonic Society, 1837G; Mermaid Theater, 1951G; Metropolitan College of Music, 1889G;

Monteverdi Choir of London, 1964G; Motett Society, 1841; Musical Antiquarian Society, 1840G; Musical Society, 1858G; Musical Union, 1845G; Music Group of London, 1966G; National Opera Studio, 1978G; National Training School for Music, 1873G; New Philharmonic Society, 1852G; New Symphony Orchestra, 1905G; Noblemen & Gentlemen's Catch Club, 1761G; Noblemen's Subscription Concerts, 1791G; Opera Centre, 1963G; Opera House, 1911G; Organ School, 1865G; Palace Theatre, 1891G; Palm Court Orchestra, 1986G; People's Concert Society, 1878G; Philharmonic Choir, 1919G; Philharmonic Orchestra, 1932G, 1945G; Philharmonic Society, 1813G; Pine-Harrison English Opera Co., 1857G; Plainsong & Medieval Music Society, 1888G; Popular Concerts of Chamber Music, 1858G; Promenade Concerts, 1838G; Purcell Club, 1836G; Purcell Society, 1836G; Queen's Hall, 1893G; Queen's Hall Promenade Concerts, 1895G; Roxburghe Club, 1812G; Royal Academy of Music, 1822G, 1861G; Royal Albert Hall, 1871G; Royal Amateur Orchestral Society, 1872G; Royal Choral Society, 1871G; Royal College of Organists, 1864G; Royal Harmonic Institution, 1818G; Royal Italian Opera, 1847G; Royal Society of Female Musicians, 1839G; Sacred Harmony Society, 1832G; Sadler's Wells Music House II, 1765G; Saint George's Hall, 1867G; Saint James Hall, 1858G; Saint Martin's Hall, 1850G; Sainton-Dolby Vocal School, 1872G; Salomon Concert Series, 1786G; Sans Souci Theatre, 1792G; Savoy Theatre, 1881G; Sinfonia 21, 1989G; Società Armonica, 1827G; Society of British Musicians, 1834G; Society of Musical Graduates, 1790G; South Place Sunday Concerts, 1887G; Sterling Club, 1838G; Stock Exchange Choral Society, 1883G; Stock Exchange Orchestral Society, 1883G; Symphonic Players, 1946G; Symphony Chorus, 1966G; Symphony Orchestra, 1886G, 1904G; Sinfonietta, 1968G; Terre Nova, 1986G; Tonal Art Club, 1900G; Tonic Sol-Fa Association, 1853G; Trinity College of Music, 1872G; Union Support...Widows & Orphans, 1803G; Wagner Society, 1872G; Wind Players, 1942G; Working Men's Society, 1867G
London Magazine, 1819G
Long, Kathleen, 1896A, 1915C, 1968B
Long, Marguerite, 1874A, 1883C
Long, Zhou, 1953A
Longhi, Pietro, 1756E
Longines Symphonette, 1941G
Long Island Philharmonic Orchestra, 1979G
Longman and Broderip, Publishers, 1767G

�֎

F *Biographical*   G *Cultural Beginnings*   H *Musical Literature*
I *Musical Compositions*

Long Play Record, 1948G
Longo, Achille, 1900A, 1954I
Longo, Alessandro, 1864A, 1945B
Longyear, Rey, 1930A, 1995B; *Nineteenth Century Romanticism in Music*, 1969H
Loomis, Clarence, 1889A, 1965B
Loomis, Harvey Worthington, 1865A, 1930B
Loop, François, 1940A
Lopardo, Frank, 1957A, 1984C
Lopatnikoff, Nikolai, 1903A, 1953E, 1963E, 1976B
Lopaz, Vincent, 1894A
Lopes-Graça, Fernando, 1906A, 1994B
Lopez-Cobos, Jesús, 1940A, 1969CE, 1970D, 1984D, 1986D, 1990D
Lo Presti, Ronald, 1933A, 1985B
Lord Mornington's Musical Academy, 1757G
Lorée, François, Woodwind Maker, 1881G
Lorengar, Pilar, 1928A, 1952C, 1996B
Lorenz, Alfred, 1868A, 1939B
Lorenz, Max, 1901A, 1927C, 1975B
Lorenz Publishing Co., 1890G
Lorenzini, Raimondo, 1786D
Lornell, Kip: *Music of Multicultural America*, 1997H
Lortie, Louis, 1959A, 1984E
Lortzing, Albert, 1801A, 1844DF, 1846F, 1851B
Los Angeles, Victoria de, 1923A, 1944C
Los Angeles, California: Ambassador Auditorium, 1974G; Chamber Orchestra, 1969G; Child's Grand Opera House, 1884G; Conservatory of Music, 1883G; Ellie Clubs, 1888G; Festival Negro Chorus, 1941G; Grand Opera Association, 1924G; Japanese Philharmonic Orchestra, 1961G; Lyric Club, 1889G; Master Chorale, 1965G; Master Sinfonia, 1965G; Merced Theater, 1870G; Music Center Opera, 1986G; Music Festival, 1947G; Negro Chorus, 1936G; New Orchestra, 1948G; Opera Repertory Theater, 1980G; Oratorio Society, 1912G; (Philharmonic) Auditorium, 1906G; Philharmonic Institute, 1982G; Philharmonic Orchestra, 1919G; Philharmonic Society, 1878G; Piano Quartet, 1977G; Shrine Auditorium, 1927G; Symphony Orchestra, 1898G; Treble Clef, 1889G; Turnverein Hall, 1872G; USC School of Performing Arts, 1883G; Youth Orchestra, 1964G
Lose, C., & Co., Publishers (Copenhagen), 1802G
Lott, Felicity, 1947A, 1975C
Lotze, Rudolf: *Geschichte der Aesthetik in Deutschland*, 1868H
Loudová, Ivana, 1941A
Louel, Jean, 1943E
Loughran, James, 1931A, 1943E, 1961C, 1962D, 1965D, 1971D, 1979D, 1987D, 1993F
Louiré, Arthur Vincent, 1892A

Louis, Rudolf: *Harmonieléhre*, 1907H
Louisiana (*see also* New Orleans): Bohemian Composers Groups, 1957G; Philharmonic Orchestra, 1992G
Louisville, Kentucky: Academy of Music, 1954G; Chamber Music Society, 1938G; Conservatory of Music, 1915G; Greater Louisville Foundation for the Arts, 1949G; Macauley's Theater, 1873G; Orchestra Commissioning Project, 1948G; Philharmonic Society, 1866G; Records, 1953G; Symphony Orchestra, 1937G
Louten, Elodie, 1950A
Love, Shirley, 1940A, 1962C
Løveberg, Aase, 1923A, 1948C, 1978D
Löwe, Ferdinand, 1865A, 1898D, 1900D, 1925B
Lowe, Halifax, 1784C, 1790B
Löwe, Johanna Sophie, 1816A, 1866B
Lowe, Thomas, 1783B
Lowens, Irving, 1916A, 1953D, 1978D, 1983B; *Lectures on the History & Art of Music at the Library of Congress, 1946-63*, 1968H; *Music & Musicians in Early America*, 1964H; *Source Readings in American Music History*, 1966H
Lowenthal, Jerome, 1863C, 1932A, 1945C, 1957E, 1960E
Lozano, Fernando, 1964C, 1978D
Lu Siging, 1969A
Lübeck, Ernst, 1829A, 1841C, 1876B
Lübeck, Heinrich, 1799A, 1865B
Lübeck, Johann, 1827D, 1829D
Lübeck, Germany: Gesangverein (Singakademie), 1833G; North German Music Festival, 1839G; Opera House, 1799G
Lubimov, Alexei, 1944A, 1980E
Lubin, Germaine, 1890A, 1912C, 1979B
Lubin, Steven, 1942A, 1977C
Luboff, Norman, 1917A, 1987B
Luboff, Norman, Choir, 1963G
Luboshutz, Léa, 1885A, 1965B
Luboshutz, Pierre, 1891A, 1912C, 1937C, 1971B
Luc de Persuis, Louis, 1810D
Luca, Giuseppe de, 1950B
Luca, Libero de, 1942C
Luca, Sergiu, 1943A, 1952C
Lucas L.: *L'acoustique nouvelle*, 1854H
Lucas, Leighton, 1903A, 1982B
Lucca, Pauline, 1841A, 18759C, 1908B
Lucca Music Publishing House, 1825G
Lucca, Italy: Istituto Musicale, 1839G; Scuola Pubblica di Musica, 1839G
Lucchesi, Andrea, 1774D, 1801B, 1965A, 1983E
Lucchesi, Joseph, 1844D
Luccioni, José, 1903A, 1932C, 1978B
Lucerne, Switzerland: Festival, 1938; Festival Strings, 1956G; Kultur-und Kongresshaus, 1998G; Schweizerische Musikgesellschaft, 1808G
Luchetti, Veriano, 1939A, 1965C

❈

A   *Births*   B   *Deaths*   C   *Debuts*   D   *New Positions*
E   *Prizes/Honors*

Lucia, Fernando De, 1860A
Lucier, Alvin, 1931A
Lüdenscheider Musikvereiningung, 1935G
Luders, Gustav, 1913B
Ludgin, Chester, 1925A, 1956C
Ludikar, Pavel, 1882A, 1904C, 1970B
Ludwig, Carl F. W., 1983B
Ludwig, Christa, 1924A, 1946C, 1994E
Ludwig, Franz, 1889A, 1955B
Ludwig, Friedrich, 1872A, 1930B
Ludwig, Ilse, 1954C
Ludwig Johann A.: *Den unverschamten Entehrern der Orgeln*, 1764H; *Gedanken über die grossen Orgeln*, 1762H; *Versuch von den Eigenschaften einer...Orgelbauers*, 1759H
Ludwig, Leopold, 1908A, 1951D, 1979B
Luening, Otto, 1900A, 1934D, 1944D, 1946E, 1970F, 1981E, 1996B; *Electronic Tape Music*, 1952H
Lugo, Giuseppe, 1890A, 1930C
Luigini, Alexandre, 1850A, 1897D, 1906B
Luise Radecke, 1847A
Luke, Ray, 1926A
Lüller, August Liberhard, 1794D
Lumbye, Hans Christian, 1810A, 1874B
Lummis, Charles F., 1859A, 1928B
Lumsdaine, David, 1931A
Lundgren, Eva, 1953A
Lundquist, A., Publisher, 1856G
Lüneburg Musikverein, 1823G
Les Lunes, 1785G
Lunn, Charles, 1838A, 1906B; *Philosophy of Voice*, 1874H
Lunssens, Martin, 1895E
Luperi, Mario, 1954A, 1979C
Lupo, Benedetto, 1963A, 1976C
Lupot, Nicolas, 1758A, 1824B
Lupot, Nicolas, Violin Maker (Paris), 1798G
Lupu, Radu, 1945A, 1957C, 1966E, 1967E, 1969E
Luria, Juan, 1862A, 1885C, 1942B
Lussan, Zélie de, 1862A, 1878C, 1949B
Lussy, Mathis, 1828A, 1910B; *L'anacrouse dans la musique moderne*, 1903H; *Histoire de la notation musicale*, 1882H; *Traité de l'expression musicale*, 1873H
Lutkin, Peter Christian, 1858A, 1895D, 1931B
Lutoslawski, Witold, 1913A, 1985E, 1995B
Lutyens, Elisabeth, 1906A, 1969E, 1983B
Lux, Friedrich Orlando, 1820A, 1895B
Luxembourg Philharmonic Society, 1824G
Luzon, Benjamin, 1937A, 1965C
Luzzi, Luigi, 1828A, 1876B
Lvov, Alexei F., 1798A, 1833F, 1837D, 1870B; *On Free or Non-Symmetrical Rhythm*, 1858H
Lvov, Feodor, 1766A, 1766D, 1825D
Lvov: Cäcilien-Verein, 1826G; Mikuli School of Music, 1888G; Ossolineum, 1833G; Polish Opera Co., 1776G; Ukrainian Theater, 1864G

Lyatoshinsky, Boris, 1971E
Lybbert, Donald, 1923A, 1981B
Lyford, Ralph, 1882A, 1927B
Lympany, Moura, 1916A, 1928C
Lyndon-Gee, Christopher, 1954A
Lyne, Felice, 1887A, 1911C, 1935B
Lynes, Frank, 1858A, 1913B
Lynn, George, 1964D
Lyon & Healy Harp Co., 1899G
Lyons, James, 1759F, 1794B, 1925A, 1953D, 1957D, 1973B; *Modern Music*, 1957H; *Urania*, 1761H
Lyons Concert Hall, 1969G
Lyon, France: Berlioz Festival, 1979G; Concerts Symphonique du Grand Theatre, 1884G; Concerts Symphoniques Populaires, 1873G; Grand Theater, 1831G; Opéra de Lyon, 1969G; Société des Grands Concerts, 1905G; Société Symphonique Lyonnaise, 1898G
Lyras, Panayis, 1979E
Lyric Art Quartet-Quintet, 1953G
Lys, Edith de, 1961B
Ma, Yo Yo, 1955A, 1978E, 2000E
Maag, Peter, 1919A, 1949C, 1952D, 1955D, 1964D, 1969E, 1972D, 1973E, 1984D
Ma'alot Quintet, 1986G
Maas, Joseph, 1847A, 1871C, 1886B
Maas, Louis, 1852A, 1889B
Maatschaplpijmoor Tonkunst (Leiden), 1834G
Maazel, Lorin, 1930A, 1938C, 1942F, 1960F, 1965D, 1970F, 1972D, 1977D, 1982D, 1984F, 1986D, 1987F, 1992D, 1993D
Mabellini, Teodulo, 1817A, 1897B
Macal, Zdeněk, 1936A, 1963D, 1965E, 1966E, 1968D, 1970D, 1986C, 1988D
McAfee, Rhonda Jackson, 1956A, 1984C
MacArdle, Donald Wales, 1897A, 1964B
McArthur, Edwin, 1907A, 1938C, 1941F, 1945D, 1967D, 1987B
Macbeth, Florence, 1891A, 1913C, 1966B
McBeth, W. Francis, 1933A
McBride, Robert, 1911A, 1942E
McCalla, James, 1946A; *Chamber Music of Our Time*, 1991H
McCabe, John, 1939A
McCabe, Robin, 1949A
McCauley, Barry, 1950A, 1977C, 1980E
McCauley, John J., 1937A, 1975C
McCawley, Leon, 1973A, 1990C
McClary, Susan, 1946A; *Feminine Endings: Music, Gender & Sexuality*, 1991H; *Music & Society*, 1988H; *Power & Desire in Seventeenth-Century Music*, 1991H
McClellan, John J., 1900D
MacClintock, Carol: *Readings in the History of Music Performance*, 1979H
MacColl, Hugh, 1953B
McCollin, Frances, 1960B
MacCombie, Bruce, 1993D

❉

F *Biographical* G *Cultural Beginnings* H *Musical Literature*
I *Musical Compositions*

McConathy, O.: *Music in the Secondary School*, 1917H
McCormack, Elizabeth, 1964A, 1986C, 1987E
McCormack, John, 1884A, 1903F, 1906C, 1945B
McCoy, Seth, 1928A, 1997B
McCoy, William J., 1921E
McCracken, James, 1926A, 1952C, 1988B
McCracken Memorial Fund for Young Tenors, 1988G
McCreesh, Paul D., 1960A
MacCunn, Hamish, 1868A, 1916B
McCutchan, Robert: *Hymn Tune Names*, 1957H
McDaniel, Barry, 1930A, 1953C
McDonald, Harl, 1899A, 1939D, 1955B
MacDonald, Jeanette, 1903A, 1965B
McDonald, Robert, 1983E
McDonnell, Tom, 1940A, 1965C
MacDougall, Jamie, 1966A
MacDowell, Edward, 1860A, 1879F, 1882F, 1884F, 1888F, 1896DE, 1904EF, 1908B, 1960E
MacDowell, Edward, Medal, 1960G
MacDowell Chorus (Schola Cantorum–N.Y.), 1909G
MacDowell Colony (N.H.), 1907G
MacDowell Festival, 1910G
Macedonian Conservatory of Music, 1926G
McElhaney, Samantha Yvonne, 1995E
McEwen, John, 1868A, 1926E, 1931E, 1948B
McEwen, Terence A., 1929A, 1982D, 1998B
Macfarren, George, 1813A, 1883E, 1887B; *The Rudiments of Harmony*, 1860H; *Six Lectures on Harmony*, 1867H
McFerrin, Bobby, 1950A
McFerrin, Robert, 1921A, 1949C, 1955F
McGibbon, William, 1756B
McGill, Josephine: *Folk Songs of the Kentucky Mountains*, 1917H
McGill Conservatory of Music, 1904G
McGlaughlin, William, 1943A
MacGregor, Johanna, 1959A
McGurty, Mark, 1955A
Mach, Elyse: *Great Pianists Speak for Themselves*, 1980H
Mach, Ernst, 1838A, 1916B; *Beitrag zur geschichte der Musik*, 1892H; *Einlietung in die Helmholtz'sche musiktheorie*, 1866H; *Über musikalische Akustik*, 1865H; *Zur Theorie des Gehörorgans*, 1872H
Machabey, Armand, 1886A, 1966B; *La musique de danse*, 1966H; *La musicologie*, 1962H; *La musique et la médecine*, 1952H; *Précis-manual d'histoire de la musique*, 1942H; *Problèmes de notation musicale*, 1958H; *Sommaire de la méthode en musicologie*, 1930H; *Le théâtre musical en France*, 1933H
Machlis, Joseph, 1906A, 1998B; *American Composers of Our Time*, 1963H; *The Enjoyment of Music*, 1955H; *Introduction to Contemporary Music*, 1961H

McHose, Allen Irvine, 1902A, 1986B; *Basic Principles of the Technique of 18th Century Counterpoint*, 1951H; *Contrapuntal Harmonic Technique of the 18th Century*, 1947H; *Musical Style 1950-1920*, 1950H
Machover, Tod, 1953A, 1984E, 1987D; *The Extended Orchestra*, 1985H; *Some Thoughts on Computer Music*, 1984H
McInnes, Donald, 1939A
McIntire, Dennis, 1944A
McIntyre, Donald, 1934A, 1959C
Macintyre, Margaret, 1865A, 1888C, 1943B
MacKay, Ann, 1956A
McKay, George Frederick, 1899A, 1970B; *Creative Orchestration*, 1963H
Mackay, Penelope, 1943A, 1970C
Mackay, Robert, 1973A
Mackenzie, Alexander, 1847A, 1888D, 1890E, 1892D, 1895E, 1903E, 1922E, 1935B; *A Musician's Narrative*, 1927H
Mackenzie, Alexander C., 1890E, 1895E
Mackerras, Charles, 1925A, 1948C, 1954D, 1966D, 1970D, 1978E, 1979E, 1982D, 1987D, 1998D
Mackey, Stephen, 1956A
Mackie, David, 1986F
Mackinac Island Music Festival, 1986G
McKinley, Carl, 1895A, 1966B
McKinley, William Thomas, 1938A
McKinnan, James: *Ancient & Medieval Music*, 1990H; *The Temple, the Church Fathers & Early Western Chant*, 1998H
McLachlan, Murray, 1965A, 1983C
McLaughlin, Marie, 1954A, 1978C
McLean, Barton, 1938A
McLean, Priscilla, 1942A
Maclennan, Francis, 1879A, 1902C, 1935B
MacMillan, Ernest, 1893A, 1926D, 1931D, 1935E, 1973B; *Music in Canada*, 1955H
Macmillen, Francis, 1885A, 1903C, 1973B
MacMillan, James, 1959A
Macmillan and Co., Publisher, 1844G
McNair, Sylvia, 1956A, 1980C, 1990E
MacNaughton Concerts, 1931G
MacNaughton String Quartet, 1932G
MacNeil, Cornell, 1922A, 1950C
McPhee, Colin, 1900A, 1901A, 1931F, 1954E, 1964B
MacPherson, Stewart, 1865A; *Evolution of Musical Design*, 1908H; *Melody & Harmony*, 1920H; *Music & Its Appreciation*, 1910H; *Practical Counterpoint*, 1900H; *Practical Harmony*, 1894H; *Simple Introduction to the Principles of Tonality*, 1929H
Macura, Stanislav, 1946A
Macurdy, John, 1929A, 1952C
McWherter, Rod, 1936A
Maddison, Dorothy, 1956A, 1986C
Maddy, Joseph, 1891A, 1966B

❈

A *Births*   B *Deaths*   C *Debuts*   D *New Positions*
E *Prizes/Honors*

Madeira, Francis, 1917A, 1945D
Madeira, Jean, 1918A, 1943C, 1972B
Maderna, Bruno, 1920A, 1973B
Maderna Ensemble (Venice), 1975G
Madrid, Spain: Asociatión Artistico-Musical,
   1860G; Concerts Spirituales, 1859G; Grupo
   Nueva Musica, 1957G, 1958G; National
   Radio Orchestra of Madrid, 1953G; Royal
   Conservatory of Music, 1830G; Sociedad de
   Autores, Compositores, 1893G; Sociedad de
   Conciertos, 1866G; Teatro de la Zarzuela,
   1856G; Teatro Real, 1850G, 1997G; Unión
   Artistico-Musical, 1878G
Madrigalist Romani, 1926G
Madsen, Trygve, 1943A
Madzar, Alexander, 1968A, 1989E, 1996E
Mae, Vanessa, 1978A, 1990C
Maelzel, Johannes Nepomuk, 1772A, 1792F,
   1816F, 1838B
Magaloff, Nikita, 1912A, 1992B
Maganini, Quinto, 1897A, 1930D, 1939D,
   1974B
Maganini Chamber Symphony, 1932G
Le magasin de musique, (Paris), 1802G
Magasin Pittoresque, 1833G
Magazin der Musik, 1783G
Magdeburg Gelehrte Clubb, 1760G
Magee, Emily, 1994C
Magee, Gary, 1995C
Maggini String Quartet, 1988G
Maggio, Robert, 1964A
Maggio Musicale, 1933G
Magini-Coletti, Antonio, 1855A, 1880C, 1912B
Magnard, Albéric, 1865A, 1914B
Magnusson, Elizabeth, 1968A
Magnusson, Lars, 1955A, 1982C
Mahillon, Victor-Charles, 1924B; *Éléments
   d'acoustique musicale et instrumentale*, 1874H;
   Les instruments à vent, 1841A, 1907H
Mahillon Wind Instrument Co., 1836G
Mahler, Fritz, 1901A, 1947D, 1953D, 1973B
Mahler, Gustav, 1860A, 1881D, 1882D, 1886F,
   1888D, 1891D, 1897D, 1907DF, 1909D,
   1911B
Mahler, Gustav, Jugend-orchester, 1986G
Mahon, Elizabeth, 1778C
Mahon, John, 1772C, 1834B
Mahon, William, 1761A, 1774C, 1816B
Maier, Guy, 1891A, 1914C, 1956B
Maier, Julius: *Auswahl englischer Madrigale*,
   1863H; *Klassische kirchenwerke alter Meister*,
   1845H
Maillart, Aimé (Louis), 1817A, 1841E, 1871
Mailman, Martin, 1932A
Mainous, F.: *Programmed Rudiments of Music*,
   1979H; *Rudiments of Music*, 1970H
Mainwaring, John, 1760F, 1897B
Mainz, Germany: Civic Orchestra, 1876G;
   Liedertafel, 1831G; Nationaltheater, 1788G;

Philharmonische Verein, 1847G; Schumacher
   Conservatory, 1881C; Stadttheater, 1833G
Mainzer, Joseph, 1801A, 1851B; *Abécédaire de
   chant*, 1837H; *Esquisses musicales*, 1839H;
   Méthode de chant pour voix d'hommes, 1836H;
   Music and Education, 1848H; *The Musical
   Athenaeum*, 1842H; *Singschule*, 1831H
Mainzer's Musical Times and Singing Circular,
   1844G
Maisch, Ludwig, Publisher, 1810G
Maisky, Mischa, 1948A, 1965C
Maison, René, 1895A, 1920C, 1962B
Maison Pleyel, 1795G
Maissa, Nella, 1914A
Maitland, J. A. Fuller, 1856A, 1882D, 1884D,
   1936B
La Maîtresse, 1857G
Majer, Joseph Friedrich, 1768B
Majeske, Daniel, 1932A, 1993B
Majo, Gian Francesco, 1770B
Majo, Giuseppe de, 1771B
Makaymiuk, Jerzy, 1936A, 1964E, 1984D
Malachovsky, Martin, 1991C
Malagnini, Mario, 1959A
Malanotte, Adelaide, 1785A, 1806C, 1832B
Malas, Spiro, 1933A, 1959C
Malas-Godlewska, Ewa, 1955A, 1978C
Malaspina, Rita Orlandi, 1963C
Malát, Jiří, 1981D, 1988D, 1990D
Malats, Joaquín, 1872A, 1912B
Malaysian PO, 1998I
Malcuzynski, Witold, 1914A, 1940C, 1977B
Maldere, Pierre van, 1758D, 1762D, 1768B
Malfitano, Catherine, 1948A, 1972C
Malherbe, Charles, 1853A, 1911B; *Précis
   d'histoire de l'Opéra-Comique*, 1887H
Malibran, Maria, 1808A, 1825C, 1836BF
Malipiero, Francesco, 1824A, 1887B
Malipiero, Gian Francesco, 1882A, 1939D, 1973B
Maliponte, Adriana, 1938A, 1958C, 1960E
Malis, David, 1961A
Malko, Nikolai, 1883A, 1926D, 1956D, 1961B;
   The Conductor & His Baton, 1950H
Mallard's, Mother, Portable Masterpiece Co.,
   1969G
Mallet & Graupner Musical Academy, 1801G
Malling, Otto, 1848A, 1874D, 1899D, 1915B
Mallinger, Mathilde, 1847A, 1866C, 1920B
Malm, William P.: *Music Cultures of the Pacific,
   the Near East & Asia*, 1996H
Malmö Concert Hall, 1985G
Malmsjö Piano Co., 1843G
Malone, Carol, 1943A, 1966C
Malotte, Albert Hay, 1895A, 1964B
Malten, Therese, 1855A, 1873C, 1930B
Mamlok, Ursula, 1928A, 1981E
Mana-Zucca, 1890A, 1981B
Manahan, George, 1996D
Manalt, Francisco, 1759B

F *Biographical*   G *Cultural Beginnings*   H *Musical Literature*
            I *Musical Compositions*

Manawarda, Josef von, 1942B
Manchester, England: Camerata, 1972G; Free
  Trade Hall, 1856G; Hallé Orchestra, 1858G;
  Incorporated Society of Musicians, 1882G;
  International Cello Festival, 1988G;
  Manchester Festivals, 1777G; Opera Group,
  1964G; Royal College of Music, 1893G;
  Sinfonietta, 1986G; Vocal Union, 1867G
Mancinelli, Aldo, 1954E
Mancinelli, Luigi, 1848A, 1874CD, 1888D,
  1921B
Mancini, Giambattista, 1800B; Pensieri e
  riflessioni pratiche sopra il canto figurato,
  1774H
Mandac, Evelyn, 1945A, 1968C
Mandel, Alan, 1935A, 1948C
Mandel, Nancy, 1943A
Mandelbaum, Joel, 1932A
Mander, N. P., Ltd., Organ Builders (London),
  1936G
Mandini, Maria, 1783C
Mandini, Paolo, 1777C
Mandyczewski, Eusebius, 1929B
Mandyezewski, Eusebius, 1857A
Manén, Juan, 1883A, 1971B
Manfredini, Francesco Onofrio, 1762B
Manfredini, Vincenzo, 1758F, 1766F, 1798F,
  1799B; Difesa della musica moderna, 1788H;
  Regolo armoniche, 1775H
Mangold, Carl, 1813A, 1848D, 1889B
Mangold, Wilhelm, 1825D
Mangore, Augustin Barrios, 1885A, 1944B
Mann, Alfred: The Study of the Fugue, 1958H;
  The Theory of Fugue, 1955H
Mann, Robert, 1920A, 1941CE
Mann Music Center (Pennsylvania), 1930G
Manners, Charles, 1857A, 1882C, 1935B
Mannes, Clara Damrosch, 1869A, 1948B
Mannes, David, 1866A, 1959B
Mannes, David, School of Music, 1916G
Mannes, Leopold, 1899A, 1922C, 1950D, 1964B
Mannes Trio (New York), 1948G
Mannheim, Germany: Akademie-Konzerte,
  1778G; Conservatory of Music, 1806G;
  Harmonischer Verein, 1810G; Liederkranz,
  1842G; Liedertafel, 1840G; Musikverein,
  1829G; National Opera Co., 1779G; National
  Theater, 1779G, 1957G; Rheinischer
  Musikverein, 1816G
Manning, Jane, 1938A, 1964C
Manning, Peter, 1956A, 1987C
Mannion, Rosa, 1984C
Manowarda, Josef von, 1890A, 1911C
Manship, Paul, 1909E
Manski, Dorothée, 1891A, 1911C, 1967B
Mansouri, Lofti, 1977D, 1988D
Mansur, Cem, 1981D
Mantelli, Eugenia, 1860A, 1883C, 1926B
Mantinucci, Nicola, 1941A

Mantius, Eduard, 1806A, 1830C, 1874B
Mantua, Italy: Teatro Accademico, 1769G
Mantuani, Josef, 1860A, 1933B; Geschichte der
  Musik in Wien I, 1904H; Über den Beginn des
  Notendrucks, 1901H
Manuel da Silva, Francisco, 1834D
Manuguerra, Matteo, 1924A, 1962C, 1998D
Manurita, Giovanni, 1984B
Manz, Wolfgang, 1960A, 1981E, 1984C
Manzino, Leonardo, 1962A, 1983C
Mapleson, James H., 1862D, 1868D
Mara, Gertrud, 1767C, 1771F, 1833B
Mara, Yoshikazu, 1971A
Marachesi, Blanche, 1863A
Marachisio, Barbara, 1833A
Mařák, Otokar, 1872A, 1899C, 1939B
Marc, Alessandra, 1957A, 1987C
Marcel, Lucille, 1885A, 1908C, 1921B
Marcellus, Robert, 1996B
Marchal, André, 1894A
Marchant, Stanley, 1943E
Marchesi, Blanche, 1895C, 1940B
Marchesi, Filippo, 1886D
Marchesi, Luigi, 1754A, 1773C, 1829B
Marchesi de Castrone, Mathilde 1821A, 1844C,
  1913B
Marchesi de Castrone, Salvatore 1822A, 1908B
Marchetti, Fillippo, 1831A, 1902B
Marchisio Barbara, 1856C, 1919B
Marchisio, Carlotta, 1835A, 1856C, 1872B
Marco, Tomás, 1942A
Marcori, Adamo, 1799D
Marcoulescou, Yolanda, 1928A, 1948C
Marcoux, Vanni, 1877A, 1894C, 1948D, 1962B
Marcovici, Silvia, 1952A, 1967C, 1969E, 1970E
Marcussen, Jürgen, Organ Builders, 1806G
Mardiello, Catherine, 1958A
Maréchal, Adolphe, 1867A, 1891C, 1935B
Maréchal, Henri, 1842A, 1924B
Maréchal, Henri-Charles, 1870E
Marek, Czeslaw, 1891A, 1909C, 1985B; Lehre des
  Klavierspiels, 1972H
Marescalchi, Luigi, Publishers, 1770G
Maresch, Johann Anton, 1794B
Margison, Richard Charles, 1953A, 1991C
Margita, Stefan, 1956A
Margola, Franco, 1908A, 1974C, 1992B; Guida
  pratica per lo studio della composizione, 1954H
Margolina, Yelena, 1964A, 1974C
Marguillier, Cécile, 1938B
Margulies, Adele, 1863A, 1879C, 1949B
Margun Music, 1975G
Marguste, Anti, 1931A
Marherr, Elfriede, 1885A, 1916C
Maria, Dominique Della, 1800B
Marie, Gabriel, 1928B
Mariani, Angelo, 1821A, 1847D, 1852D, 1860D,
  1873B
Mariani, Mathilde, 1821A

A *Births*   B *Deaths*   C *Debuts*   D *New Positions*

E *Prizes/Honors*

Marie, Gabriel, 1852A, 1887D
Marin, Ion, 1960A
Marinelli, Gaetano, 1754A
Marini, Ignacio, 1811A, 1833C, 1873B
Marino, Amerigo, 1925A, 1988B
Marinuzzi, Gino, 1882A, 1928D
Mario, (Giovanni M.), 1810A, 1838C, 1883B
Mario, Queena, 1896A, 1918C, 1951B
Mark Educational Recordings, Inc., 1967G
Markevitch, Igor, 1912A, 1933C, 1983B, 1957D, 1965D, 1967D
Markiz, Lev, 1978E
Markov, Alexander, 1982E
Markova, Juliana, 1945A, 1973C
Marks, Alan, 1949A, 1966C, 1995B
Marks, Edward B., 1865A, 1945B
Marks, Edward B., Co., 1894G
Marlboro Music Festival & School (Vermont), 1950G
Marlboro Music School (Massachusetts), 1950G
Marlowe, Sylvia, 1908A, 1981B
Marmontel, Antoine-François, 1816A, 1898B; Éléments d'aesthétique musicale, 1884H; Histoire du piano et ses origines, 1885H; Les pianistes célèbres, 1878H
Marmontel Jean F.: Essai sur les révolutions de la musique en France, 1777H
Marpurg, Friedrich, 1864D, 1868D, 1873D
Marpurg, Friedrich Wilhelm, 1795B; Abhandlung von der Fuge I, 1753H; Abhandlung von der Fuge nach dem Grundsätzen den besten deutschen und ausländischen Meister, 1754H; Anfangsgründe der theoretischen musik, 1757H; Anleitung zum Clavierspielen der Schönen Ausübung der heutigen Zeit gemäss, 1755H; Anleitung zur Musik überhaupt und zur Singkunst besonders mit Übungsexampeln erläutert, 1763H; Anleitung zur Singecomposition, 1758H; Handbuch bey dem Generalbasse und der Composition, 1755H; Historisch-kritische beyträge IV, 1759H; Kritische Briefe über die Tonkunst...von einer musikalisch Gesellschat in Berlin, 1764H; Kritische einleitung in die Geschichte und Lehrsätze der alten und neuen Musik, 1759H; Die Kunst das Clavier zu spielen II, 1761H; Neue Methode, allerley Arten von Temperaturen dem Claviere aufs bequemste mitzutheilen, 1790H; Principes de clavecin, 1756H; Systematische Einleitung in die musikalische Setzkunst, nach den Lehrsätzen des Hernn Rameau, 1757H; Versuch über die musikalische Temperature..., 1776H
Marriner, Neville, 1924A, 1969D, 1978D, 1981D, 1985E
Marrocco, W. Thomas, 1909A, 1999B
Marrucino Theatre, 1997G
Marsalis, Wynton, 1961A, 1996E

Marschner, Heinrich, 1795A, 1813F, 1823F, 1827D, 1834E, 1861B
Marsee, Susanne, 1944A
Marseilles, France: Concerts Classiques, 1886G; École Communale de Musique, 1852G; Free School of Music, 1821G; Opéra de Marseilles, 1787G; Société Populaires...de Musique Classique, 1880G; Thubaneau Concert Society, 1806G; Trotebau Male Choir, 1832G
Marsh, Jane, 1945A
Marsh, Calvin, 1954C
Marsh, Jane, 1965C, 1966E
Marshall, Robert L., 1939A
Marshall, Margaret, 1949A, 1974E, 1975C
Marshall-Dean, Deirdre Pauline, 1965A
Marsick, Martin, 1848A, 1873C, 1924B
Marteau, Henri, 1874A, 1884C, 1934B
Martenot, Maurice, 1898A, 1980B
Martin, C. J., & Co., Guitar Makers, 1833G
Martin, François, 1757B
Martin, Frank, 1890A, 1974B
Martin, George C., 1897E
Martin, Janis, 1939A, 1960C
Martin, Jean-Blaise, 1768A, 1789C, 1837B
Martin, Laurent, 1959A
Martin, Marvis, 1981E
Martin, Mihaela, 1982E
Martin, Philip James, 1947A
Martin, Riccardo, 1874A, 1904C, 1952B
Martín y Soler, Vicente, 1754A, 1788D, 1795F, 1796F, 1806B
Martinelli, Giovanni, 1908C, 1969B
Martinez, Miguel Gomez, 1992D
Martini, G. B. "Padre," 1758E, 1776E, 1784B; Compendio della teoria de'numeri per uso del musico, 1769H; Esemplare ossia Saggio fondamentale pratico de contrap-punto I, 1774H; Regole agli organiste per accompagnare il canto fermo, 1756H; Saggio fondamentale pratico di contrapunto II, 1775H; Storia della musica I, 1757H; Storia della Musica II, 1770H; Storia della Musica III, 1781H
Martini, Jean Paul, 1798D, 1816B; Mélopée moderne, 1792H
Martini, Nino, 1905A, 1931C, 1976B
Martino, Donald, 1931A, 1967E, 1981E, 1987E
Martino, Tirimo, 1942A
Martinon, Jean, 1910A, 1948D, 1950D, 1958D, 1960D, 1963D, 1968D, 1974D, 1976B
Martins, João Carlos, 1966F
Martinsson, Håkon, 1982D
Martinů, Bohuslav, 1890A, 1932E, 1940F, 1946F, 1956F, 1959B
Martucci, Giuseppe, 1856A, 1886D
Martinucci, Nicola, 1966C
Martirano, Salvatore, 1927A, 1960E, 1995B
Marton, Eva, 1943A, 1968C
Martucci, Giuseppe, 1902D, 1909B

F *Biographical*   G *Cultural Beginnings*   H *Musical Literature*
I *Musical Compositions*

Martucci, Paolo, 1881A, 1902C, 1980B
Martzy, Johanna, 1924A, 1943C, 1979B
Maruzin, Yuri, 1947A
Marvin, Frederick, 1923A, 1948C
Marx, Adolf B., 1795A, 1824D, 1832D, 1850F,
  1866B; *Allgemeine Musiklehre*, 1839H; *Alte
  Musiklehre im streit mit unserer Zeit*, 1841H;
  Erinnerungen: aus Meinem Leben, 1865H; *Das
  Ideal und die Gegenwart*, 1867H; *Die Lehre von
  der musikalischen Komposition I, II*, 1837H; *Die
  Musik des 19. Jahrhundert und ihre Pflege*,
  1855H; *Über Malerei in der Tonkunst*, 1828H;
  *Über die Geltung Händelscher Sologesänge für
  unsere Zeit*, 1829H
Maryland: Handel Festival, 1981G; Music
  Critics Association, 1957G; Res Musica,
  1980G; Villa Pace, 1982G
Maryon, Edward, 1867A, 1954B
Märzendorfer, Ernst, 1921A
Mascagni, Pietro, 1863A, 1884F, 1890E, 1895D,
  1902F, 1945B
Mascherini, Enzo, 1916A, 1938C
Mascheroni, Edoardo, 1852A, 1941B
Masciti, Michele, 1760B
Maek, Vincenz, 1755A, 1831B
Mashek, Michal, 1980A
Ma Sicong, 1987B
Masini, Angelo, 1844A, 1867C
Masini, Galliano, 1896A, 1902A, 1923C,
  1986B
Mason, Anne, 1993F
Mason, Daniel Gregory, 1873A, 1913F, 1953B;
  The Art of Music, 1915H; *Artistic Ideals*,
  1925H; *Contemporary Composers*, 1918H; *The
  Dilemma of American Music*, 1928H; *From
  Grieg to Brahms*, 1902H; *Great Modern
  Composers*, 1916H; *A Guide to Music*, 1909H;
  Music as a Humanity, 1920H; *Orchestral
  Instruments*, 1908H; *The Romantic Composers*,
  1906H
Tune In, America!, 1931H
Mason, Edith, 1911C, 1973B
Mason, Lowell, 1792A, 1812F, 1818F, 1827F,
  1820D, 1827D, 1835E, 1837D, 1872B; *Address
  on Church Music*, 1826H; *The Boston Glee
  Book*, 1838H; *Boston Academy Collection of
  Church Music*, 1835H; *Cantica Laudis*, 1850H;
  Carmina Sacra, 1841H; *The Glee Hive*, 1851H;
  *Handel and Haydn Society's Collection of
  Church Music*, 1822H; *The Juvenile Lyre*,
  1831H; *The Juvenile Psalmist*, 1829H; *Lyra
  Sacra*, 1832H; *Manual of Instruction
  (Pestalozzian)*, 1834H; *The Modern Psalmist*,
  1839H; *Musical Notation in a Nutshell*, 1854H;
  Musical Letters from Abroad, 1853H; *New
  Carmina Sacra*, 1852H; *The Odeon: A Collection
  of Secular Melodies*, 1837H; *The Psaltery*,
  1845H; *The Sabbath School Harp*, 1837H;
  Sabbath School Songs, 1836H; *Spiritual Songs

for Worship*, 1831H; *The Vocalist*, 1844H;
  Young Men's Singing Book, 1855H
Mason, Luther Whiting, 1828A, 1896B
Mason, Marilyn, 1925A
Mason, William, 1829A, 1846C, 1849F, 1855F,
  1872E, 1908B, 1996D; *A Method for the Piano*,
  1867H; *Pianoforte Technics*, 1878H
Mason, William (poet), 1797B
Mason & Hamlin Organ Co., 1854G
Mason & Hamlin Piano Co., 1882G
Mason Brothers, Publishers, 1855G
Mason-Thomas Quintet, 1855G
Masrasvili, Makvala, 1968C
Massachusetts (*see also* Boston; Lenox; Salem;
  Springfield; Worcester): Berkshire Music
  Festival, 1934G; Dedham Chorus, 1954G;
  Folk Festival, 1944G; Marlboro Music
  School, 1950G; Musical Society, 1802G
Massart, Lambert, 1811A, 1822C, 1892B
Massé, Victor, 1822A, 1844E, 1856E, 1872E,
  1884B
Masselos, William, 1920A, 1939C, 1992B
Massenet, Jules, 1842A, 1863E, 1876E, 1878E,
  1912B
Massine, Leonide, 1915D, 1932D
Massine Ballet School, 1925G
Massini, Angelo, 1926B
Massol, Eugène Étienne, 1802A, 1825C, 1887B
Másson, Áskell, 1953A
Masson, Diego, 1935A
Masson, Paul-Marie, 1882A, 1954B
Masson, Elizabeth, 1806A, 1831C, 1865B;
  Original Jacobite Songs, 1839H
Massonneau, Louis, 1766A, 1848B
Masterson, Valerie, 1937A, 1963C, 1988E
Mastilović, Danica, 1859C, 1933A, 1959C
Mastini, Giovanni Battista, 1771B
Masur, Kurt, 1927A, 1955D, 1967D, 1970D,
  1990D, 1993E, 1997E, 2000D
Mata, Eduardo, 1942A, 1965D, 1966D, 1970D,
  1977D, 1988F, 1995B
Matačić, Lovro von, 1899A, 1938D, 1961D,
  1970D
Materna, Amalie, 1844A, 1865C, 1918B
Mates, Julian: *The American Musical State before
  1800*, 1962H
Matheopoulos, Helena: *Divo: Great Tenors,
  Baritones & Basses Discuss their Roles*, 1986H;
  Maestro: Encounters with Conductors, 1983H
Mather, Bruce, 1939A
Mathes, Rachel Clarke, 1941A, 1965C
Mathews, W. S. B., 1837A, 1878D, 1912A;
  Dictionary of Music Terms, 1896H; *How to
  Understand Music I*, 1880H; *A Hundred Years
  of Music in America*, 1889H; *Outlines of Music
  Form*, 1867H; *Primer of Musical Forms*, 1890H
Mathias, William (James), 1968E, 1992B
Mathieson, Muir, 1911A, 1932C, 1934D, 1975B
Mathieu, Julien-Amable, 1765D, 1811B

❄

A *Births*   B *Deaths*   C *Debuts*   D *New Positions*
E *Prizes/Honors*

Mathieu, Michel, 1768B
Mathis, Edith, 1938A, 1956C
Mathushek Piano Co., 1863G
Matiegka, Wenzel Thomas, 1773A, 1830B
Matsudaira, Yoriaki, 1931A
Matsudaira, Yoritsune, 1907A, 1935E, 1962E
Matsumura, Teizo, 1929A
Mattei, Peter, 1965A, 1990C
Mattei, Stanislao, 1770D, 1789D, 1799E, 1824E
Matthay, Tobias, 1858A, 1945B
Mattheson, Johann, 1764B; *George Frederick Handel*, 1761H; *Sieben Gespräche der Weisheit und Musik samt zwo Beylagen; als die dritte, Dosis der Panacea*, 1751H
Matthews, Andrea, 1956A, 1984C
Matthews, Dennis, 1919A, 1939C, 1988B
Mattila, Karita, 1960A, 1982C, 1983E
Matton, Roger, 1929A
Matzenauer, Margarete, 1881A, 1901C, 1963B
Matzka, George, 1876D
Matzmacher, Inge, 1985C
Mauceri, John, 1945A, 1980D, 1987D, 1990D
Maultsby, Nancy, 1993E
Maurel, Victor, 1848A, 1867C, 1923B; *L'art du chant*, 1897H
Maurer, Ludwig, 1789A, 1802C, 1878B
Mauricio, José, 1752A, 1791D, 1815B; *Metodo do musica*, 1806H
Mauro, Ermanno, 1939A, 1962C
Mautner, Michael, 1959A
Maw, Nicholas, 1935A
Max, Robert, 1968A
Maxakova, Mariya, 1902A, 1923C, 1974B
Maxfield, Richard, 1927A, 1969B
Maxwell John: *An Essay upon Tune*, 1781H
Maxwell, Peter, 1934A
Mayer, Charles, 1799A, 1862B
Mayer, Robert, 1939E
Mayer, Steven, 1992E
Mayer, William, 1925A
Mayer Auditorium & Madison Civic Center, 1980G
Maylath, Heinrich, 1827A, 1883B
Maynor, Dorothy, 1910A, 1939C, 1996B
Mayr, Richard, 1877A, 1902C, 1935B
Mayr, Simon, 1763A, 1781F, 1802D, 1845B; *Breve notizii istroiche della vite e delle opere de G. Haydn*, 1809H
Mayseder, Joseph, 1789A, 1800C, 1862E, 1863B
Mayuzumi, Toshiro, 1929A, 1997B
Mazas, Jacques-Féréol, 1782A, 1849B
Mazowsze State Song & Dance Ensemble, 1949G
Mazura, Franz, 1924A, 1949C
Mazurkovich, Yuri, 1941A, 1963C
Mazzaria, Lucia, 1964A, 1987C
Mazzinghi, Joseph, 1765A, 1785D, 1844B
Mazzoni, Antonio, 1751D, 1785B
Mazzucato, Alberto 1872D

Mc–. Names beginning with this prefix are alphabetized as if they were spelled Mac.
Meacham, Horace, 1789A, 1861B
Meacham, John, Jr., 1785A, 1844B
Mead String Quartet, 1902G
Meader, George, 1911C, 1963B, 1888A
Meadow Brook Festival, 1964G
Meadowmount School for String Players, 1944G
Meale, Richard, 1932A
Mechanical Orguinette Co., 1878G
Mechanical Organette & Music Co., 1888G
Mechem, Kirke, 1925A
Meck, Joseph, 1758B
Meck, Mme. Von, 1876F, 1877F, 1890F
Mediņ, Jāzeps, 1877A, 1916D, 1922D
Medtner, Nicolai, 1880A, 1900C, 1951B
Meerens, Charles, 1831A, 1909B; *Acoustique musicale*, 1892H; *L'avenir de la science musicale*, 1894H; *Le diapason et la notation musicale simplifiée*, 1873H; *La gamme musicale majeure et mineure*, 1890H; *Instruction élémentaire de calcul musical*, 1864H; *Phénomènes musico-physiologiques*, 1868H
Mees, Joseph-Henri, 1777A, 1858B
Mees Music Academy (Antwerp), 1824G
Meet the Composer Program, 1974G
Meet the Composer Residency Program, 1982G
Meeting of the Worlds Festival, 1990G
Mega-Hertz, 1969G
Mehlig, Anna, 1843A, 1866C, 1928B
Mehta, Zaren, 2000D
Mehta, Zubin, 1936A, 1961D, 1962D, 1974E, 1978D, 1980E
Méhul, Étienne, 1763A, 1772F, 1794F, 1795E, 1804E, 1817B; *Cours de composition*, 1809H
Mei, Eva, 1967A
Mei, Orazio, 1763D, 1788B
Mei-Figner, Medea, 1858A, 1874C, 1952B
Meier, Johanna, 1938A, 1969C, 1981F
Meier, Waltraud, 1956A, 1976C
Meigs, Melinda, 1953A, 1975C
Meininger Hoftheater, 1831G
Meisle, Kathryn, 1970B
Meissonier, Jean Louis, 1889E
Meissonier & Heugel Publishers, 1839G
Meisterarchiv, Austrian National Library, 1927G
Meiszner, Louise, 1945E
Melba, Nellie, 1861A, 1884C, 1918E, 1931B
Melbourne, Australia: Academy of Music, 1885G; Memorial Conservatorium, 1895G; Music Society of Victoria, 1861G; Philharmonic Society, 1852G; University Chair of Music, 1891G
Melbye, Mikael, 1955A, 1976C
Melchers, Hendrik Melcher, 1882A, 1961B
Melchert, Helmut, 1910A, 1939C

F *Biographical*   G *Cultural Beginnings*   H *Musical Literature*
I *Musical Compositions*

Melchior, Lauritz, 1890A, 1913C, 1918C, 1950F, 1973B
Melchior Heldentenor Foundation, 1968G
Melchissédec, Pierre L., 1843A, 1866C, 1925B
Melgunov, Julius N., 1846A, 1864C, 1893B
Melikov, Arif, 1933A
Meliponte Adriana, 1942A
Melis, Carmen, 1885A, 1905C, 1967B
Melis, György, 1923A, 1949C
Mellon, Alfred, 1865D
Melloni, Romeo, 1963A
Mellor, Alwyn, 1968A
Melnikov, Alexander, 1973A
Melnikov, Ivan, 1832A, 1867C, 1906B
Melodika, 1772G
Melodina, 1855G
Melodion, 1805G
La Mélomanie Revue Musicale, 1841G
Melos String Quartet, 1965G
Melrose, Leigh, 1972A
Melton, James, 1904A, 1932C, 1961B
Memphis, Tennessee: Greenlaw Opera House, 1866G; Opera Theater, 1956G; Symphony Orchestra I, 1909G; Symphony Orchestra II, 1947G
Mendel, Arthur, 1905A, 1952D, 1979B; Studies in the History of Musical Pitch, 1969H
Mendel, Hermann, 1870D
Mendelssohn, Felix, 1809A, 1816F, 1817F, 1818C, 1819F, 1825F, 1829F, 1830F, 1832F, 1833D, 1835DF, 1837EF, 1838F, 1842F, 1845F, 1846F, 1847BF,
Mendelssohn Choir of Indianapolis, 1916G
Mendelssohn Choir of Pittsburgh, 1909G
Mendelssohn Scholarship, 1856G
Mendius, Louise, 1988E
Mendocino Music Festival, 1987G
Meneely & Co., Bell Foundry, 1826G
Meneses, Antonio, 1957A, 1977E, 1982E
Le Ménestrel, 1833G
Mengal, Martin-Joseph, 1781A, 1835D, 1851B
Mengelberg, Willem, 1871A, 1891D, 1895D, 1922D, 1928E, 1951B
Menges, Isolde, 1893A, 1913C, 1976B
Menges String Quartet, 1931G
Mennin, Peter, 1923A, 1946E, 1958D, 1962D, 1970E, 1983B
Mennini, Louis, 1920A, 1949E
Menotti, Gian Carlo, 1911A, 1927F, 1945E, 1984E, 1991E
Menotti, Tatiana, 1911A, 1931C
Menter, Joseph, 1808A, 1856B
Menter, Sophie, 1846A, 1867C, 1918B
Mentzer, Susanne, 1957A, 1981C
Menuhin, Hephzibah, 1920A, 1928C, 1981B
Menuhin, Jeremy, 1951A, 1984C
Menuhin, Yehudi, 1916A, 1966E, 1976E, 1972D, 1985E, 1986E, 1999B; Theme & Variations, 1972H

Menuhin, Yehudi, School of Music, 1963G
Menzel, Wolfgang, 1798A
Meo, Cléotine de, 1904A, 1927C, 1930B
Mercadante, (Giuseppe) Saverio, 1795A, 1808F, 1833D, 1840D, 1870B
Mercadier, Jean Baptiste, 1815B; Nouveau système de musique..., 1776H
Der Mercur, 1909G
Mercure de France, 1890G
Mercure Musicale, 1905G
Mercurio, Steven, 1956A, 1991D
Mercury, 1919G
Méreaux, Nicolas-Jean Le Froid de, 1797B
Meredith, Morley, 2000B
Mériel, Paul, 1818A, 1897B
Merighi, Giorgio, 1939A, 1962C
Merikanto, Oskar, 1911D
Merk, Joseph, 1795A, 1852B
Merklin, Joseph, Organ Builders, 1843G
Merklin, Schütze et Cie., Organ Builders, 1853G
Merlet, Dominique, 1957E
Merli, Francesco, 1887A, 1916C, 1976B
Merö-Irion, Yolanda, 1887A, 1902C, 1963B
Merola, Gaetano, 1881A, 1923D, 1953B
Merola Opera Program, 1957G
Merquillier, Cécile, 1861A
Merrick, Frank, 1886A, 1895C, 1981B
Merrill, Robert, 1917A, 1944C; Between Acts, 1977H; Once More, From the Beginning, 1965H
Merrimack Lyric Opera, 1985G
Merriman, Margaret: A New Look at 16th Century Counterpoint, 1982H
Merriman, Nan, 1920A, 1942C
Merritt, Chris, 1952A, 1978C
Merryman, Majorie, 1991E
Merseburger, Carl, Publishing Co., 1849G
Mersmann, Hans, 1891A, 1947D, 1971B; Angewandte Musikästhetik, 1926H; Eine deutsche Musikgeschichte, 1934H; Die Kirchenmusik im XX. Jahrhundert, 1958H; Kulturgeschichte der Musik in Einzeldarstellungen, 1921H; Musikhören, 1937H; Neue Musik in den Strömungen unserer Zeit, 1949H; Volkslied und Gegenwart, 1936H
Mertens, Joseph, 1878D
Mertons, W.: American Minimal Music, 1991H
Mertz, Joseph Kasper, 1806A, 1856B
Mesplé, Mady, 1931A, 1953C
Messager, André, 1853A, 1874D, 1898D, 1929B
Messiaen, Olivier, 1908A, 1940F, 1966D, 1967E, 1992B; Technique of My Musical Language, 1944H
Messina, Italy: Accademia Fil-Armonica, 1833G; Accademia Peloritana, 1833G; Arena Peloro, 1882G; Melopea Accademia Filarmonica-Drammatica, 1867G; Società del Quartetto, 1880G; Società Orchestrale l'Avenire, 1886G

❄

A   Births   B   Deaths   C   Debuts   D   New Positions
E   Prizes/Honors

Mester, Jorge, 1935A, 1955C, 1967D, 1968E, 1971D, 1990D
Mestrino, Nicola, 1786C, 1789B
Metalov, Vasili, 1862A, 1926B
Metamorphosen Chamber Orchestra, 1994G
Metastasio, Pietro, 1782B
Metcalf, Frank J., 1865A, 1945B; *American Psalmody*, 1917H; *American Writers & Compilers of Sacred Music*, 1925H; *Stories of Hymn Tunes*, 1928H
Metcalf, William, 1929A, 1958C, 1997B
The Metronome, 1885G
Metternich, Josef, 1915A, 1945C
Mettraux, Laurent, 1970A
Metz Conservatory of Music, 1835G
Metzler, Valentine, Music Shop, 1788G
Metzler und Söhne, Organ Builders, 1890G
Metzmacher, Ingo, 1957A, 1995F, 1997D
Meulemans, Arthur, 1884A, 1966B
Meulen, Henk van der, 1955A
Mexican Academy of the Arts, 1966G
Mexican Symphony Orchestra, 1928G
Mexico City, Mexico: Eliazaga Conservatory of Music, 1825G; Palacio Nacional de Bella Artes, 1933G; Philharmonic Orchestra, 1978G; Sociedad Filharmónica, 1824G
Meyer, Conrad, Piano Maker, 1829G
Meyer, Edgar, 1960A, 2000E
Meyer, Friedrich, Publisher, 1781G
Meyer, Kerstin, 1928A, 1952C
Meyer, Krzysztof, 1943A
Meyer, Leonard B., 1918A; *Emotion & Meaning in Music*, 1956H; *Explaining Music, Essays & Explorations*, 1973H; *Music, the Arts, and Ideas*, 1967H; *The Rhythmic Structure of Music*, 1960H; *Style & Music*, 1989H
Meyer, Paul, 1965B, 1978C
Meyerbeer, Giacomo, 1791A, 1812F, 1815F, 1816F, 1823F, 1832E, 1834E, 1842DE, 1846B
Meyerhoff, Joseph, 1985E
Meyerhoff, Joseph, Symphony Hall, 1982G
Meyers, Anne Akiko, 1970A
Meyerson, Janice, 1950A
M'Guckin, Barton, 1852A, 1878C, 1917B
Miaskovsky, Nicolai, 1881A, 1899F
Miami, Florida: Center for the Fine Arts, 1984G; City Ballet, 1986G; Classic Opera, 1975G; Greater Miami Opera Association, 1941G; Greater Miami Symphony Orchestra, 1965G; Opera Guild, 1974G; Philharmonic Orchestra, 1965G; String Quartet, 1988G
Miami Beach Symphony Orchestra, 1953G
Miaskovsky, Nicolai, 1950B
Michaeau, Janine, 1914A
Michael, David Moritz, 1751A, 1827B
Michael, Najda, 1969A, 1993C
Michaelis, Ruth, 1909A, 1933C
Michaels, Timothy C., 1951A
Michailow, Zwetan, 1990C

Michalak, Thomas, 1965B
Michalowski, Alexander, 1851A, 1869C, 1938B
Michalski, Raymond, 1933A, 1978B
Micheau, Janine, 1933C, 1976B
Micheelsen, Hans Friedrich, 1902A, 1973B
Michelangeli, Arturo, 1920A
Michelangeli, Arturo Benedetti, 1920A, 1939E, 1995B
Micheli, Benedetto, 1784B
Micheli, Lorenzo, 1975A, 1994C
Michigan Opera Theater, 1971G
Midland-Odessa Symphony Orchestra, 1962G
Midori, 1971A, 1982C, 1994E
Midwest National Band & Orchestra Clinic, 1947G
Mielke, Antonia, 1852A, 1907B
Migenes, Julia, 1945A
Migenes (-Johnson), Julia, 1965C
Mignone, Francisco, 1897A, 1986B
Migot, Georges, 1891A, 1976B
Mikhailova, Maria, 1866A, 1892C, 1943B
Miki, Minoru, 1930A
Miklosa, Erika, 1993E
Mikuli, Carl, 1819A, 1858D, 1897B
Milan, Italy: Accademia Filarmonica, 1758G; Ars Antiqua, 1963G; Conservatory of Music, 1807G; La Scala Opera House, 1778G; Opera da Camera di Milano, 1957G; Pio Istituto Filarmonico, 1783G; Società dei Conceri Sinfonici Popolari, 1877G; Società del Quartetto, 1864G; Società del Quartetto Corale, 1875G; Studio di Fonologia Musicale, 1955; Teatro Carcano, 1803G; Teatro della Cannonbiana, 1779G; Teatro Fiando, 1815G; Teatro Lentasio, 1801G; Teatro Nuovo, 1938G; Teatro Re, 1813G
Milanollo, Teresa, 1827A, 1836C
Milanov, Michail, 19949A
Milanov, Zinka, 1906A, 1927C, 1966F, 1989B
Milburn, Ellsworth, 1938A
Milcheva-Nonova, Alexandrina, 1936A, 1961C
Milde, Hans Feodor von, 1821A, 1899B
Mildenberg, Albert, 1878A, 1918B
Mildenburg, Anna, 1872A, 1895C
Milder-Hauptmann, Anna, 1785A, 1803C, 1838B
Milenkovic, Stefan, 1977A
Miles, Alastair, 1961A
Milhaud, Darius, 1892A, 1920F, 1922F, 1940F, 1971F, 1974B; *Notes sans musique*, 1949H
Milhaud, Darius, Archive, 1985G
Milinkovič, Georgina von, 1913A, 1937C
Millard, Harrison, 1829A, 1895B
Miller, Arthur, 1984E
Miller, David Alan, 1992D
Miller, Dayton: *Anecdotal History of the Science of Sound*, 1935H; *Science of Musical Sounds*, 1916H

Miller, Edward, 1807B; *Elements of Thorough Bass and Composition*, 1787H; *Institutes of Music*, 1783H
Miller, Henry F., & Sons Piano Co., 1863G
Miller, Johann A., 1804B
Miller, Lajos, 1940A, 1968C
Miller, Marilyn, 1898A
Miller, Mildred, 1924A, 1949C
Miller, Ruth, 1892A, 1983B
Miller & Beecham, Publishers, 1853G
Millico, Giuseppe, 1802B
Millo, Mary, 1985C
Millo, Aprile, 1958A, 1977CE, 1978E, 1985E
Millöcker, Carl, 1864D, 1869D
Mills, Charles, 1914A, 1939D, 1982B
Mills, Erie, 1953A, 1979C
Mills, John, 1947A, 1971C
Mills, Jack, Inc. (Mills Music), 1919G
Mills, Sebastian Bach, 1838A, 1858C, 1898B
Mills Music, Inc., Publisher, 1928G
Milne, Lisa, 1994C
Milnes, Sherrill, 1935A, 1984E
Milstein, Nathan, 1903A, 1919C, 1925F, 1967E, 1983E, 1987E, 1992B
Milwaukee, Wisconsin: Academy of Music, 1864G; Bach Orchestra, 1855G; Civic Orchestra, 1921G; College of Music, 1874G; Conservatory of Music, 1878G; Grand Opera House, 1871G; Liederkranz, 1878G; Liedertafel, 1858G; Music Hall, 1864G; Musikverein, 1851G; Performing Arts Center, 1969G; School of Music, 1884G; Symphony Orchestra, 1958G
Mimaroglu, Ilhan, 1926A
Mims, Marilyn, 1962A
Minchev, Georgi, 1939A
Mineva, Stefka, 1949A, 1972C
Mingardo, Sara, 1970A
Minghini-Cattaneo, Irene, 1918C
Mingotti, Pietro, 1759B
Mingotti, Regina, 1808B
Minguet String Quartet, 1988G
Miniature Scores, 1802G
Minkowski, Marc, 1962A, 1997D
Minkus, Léon, 1826A, 1917B
Minneapolis, Minnesota: Academy of Music, 1871G; Auditorium, 1905G; Northwestern Cons. of Music, 1885G; Orchestra Hall, 1974G; Pence Opera House, 1867G; School of Fine Arts, 1886G; Symphony, 1903G
Minnesota: Composers Forum, 1973G; Opera Co., 1962G; Viennese Sommerfest, 1980G
Minoja, Ambrogio, 1752A, 1825B; *Lettere sopra il canto*, 1812H
Minot Opera Association, 1975G
Minton, Yvonne, 1938A, 1961, 1964C
Mintz, Shlomo, 1957A, 1966C
Mirecki, Franz, 1844D
Mirecourt Trio, 1973G

Miricioiu, Nelly, 1952A, 1974C
Mirigi, Angelo, 1801B
Mirtova, Nelly, 1962A
Mirzoyan, Edvard, 1921A
Miscellanea musicologica, 1956G
Mischakoff, Mischa, 1895A, 1912C, 1981B
Misón, Luis, 1756D, 1766B
Mississippi: Opera Association, 1945G; River Festival, 1969G
MIT Experimental Music Studio, 1971G
Mitchell, Donald: *The Language of Modern Music*, 1963H
Mitchell, Howard, 1911A, 1949D, 1969F, 1988B
Mitchell, Leona, 1948A, 1967C
Mitchell, Madelein Louise, 1957A, 1984C
Mitchell, William J., 1906A, 1971B; *Elementary Harmony*, 1939H
Mitropoulos, Dimitri, 1896A, 1936D, 1950D, 1960B
Mitsukuri, Shukichi, 1895A, 1971B; *Mitteilungsblatt der Internationalen Bruckner-Gesellschaft*, 1971G
Mitterwurzer, Anton, 1818A, 1876B
Miyoshi, Akira, 1933A
Mizler, Lorenz Christoph, 1778B
Mlynarski, Emil, 1870A, 1897D, 1898E, 1935B
Mochizuki, Misato, 1969A
Mocquereau, André, 1849A, 1930B
Mocquet, Jules, 1896E
Modarelli, Antonio, 1926D
Modena, Italy: Accademia Filarmonica, 1771G; Corale Rossini, 1887G; Scuola Communale di Musica, 1864G; Società Artistico-Filarmonica, 1881G; Teatro Comunale Nuovo, 1841G
Modern Liturgy, 1973G
Modern Music Masters Society, 1952G
Moderne Music, 1923G
Mödl, Martha, 1912A, 1942C
Moeck, Hermann, Publishing Co., 1930G
Moeller Organ Co., 1872G
Moeran, E. J., 1894A, 1950B
Moiseiwitsch, Benno, 1890A, 1899E
Moeschi, Alessandro, 1922B
Moevs, Robert, 1920A, 1952E, 1956E, 1974D
Moffat, Julie, 1966A, 1987C
Moffo, Anna, 1932A, 1955C
Mogilevsky, Evgeny, 1964E
Moiseiwitsch, Benno, 1908C, 1963B
Mokranjac (Serbian) Music School, 1899G
Mol, Pierre de, 1855E
Moldenhauer, Hans, 1906A, 1970E, 1987B; *Duo-Pianism*, 1950H
Moldoveanu, Nicolae, 1962A
Moldoveanu, Vasile, 1935A, 1966C
Molinari, Bernardino, 1880A, 1952B
Molique, Bernhard, 1802A, 1869B
Molique, Wilhelm B., 1817C
Moll, Kurt, 1938A, 1958C

�֍

A *Births*   B *Deaths*   C *Debuts*   D *New Positions*
E *Prizes/Honors*

Mollenhauer, Andreas, Woodwind Maker, 1822G
Mollenhauer, Eduard, 1827A, 1914B
Mollenhauer, Emil, 1855A, 1927B
Mollenhauer, Gustav, Woodwind Maker, 1837A, 1864G
Moller, John Christopher, 1755A, 1796D, 1803B
Möller, Johann Patroklus, 1772B
Möller, M. P., Organ Builder, 1875G
Möller, Niels, 1977D
Moller & Capron, Publishers, 1793G
Mollo, T., & Co., Publishers (Vienna), 1798G
Molnár, Antal, 1890A, 1983B; *Introduction to Contemporary Music*, 1929H; *Music Today*, 1936H; *The New Hungarian Music*, 1926H; *New Music*, 1925H; *Popular Musical Aesthetics*, 1940H; *Practical Music Aesthetics*, 1971H; *The Spirit of New Music*, 1948H; *The Spirit of the History of Music*, 1914H; *The World of the Composer*, 1969H
Molter, Johann Melchior, 1765B
Momigny, Jérôme-Joseph de, 1762A, 1842B; *A l'académie des Beaux-Arts*, 1831H; *Cours complet d'harmonie et de composition*, 1806H; *Cours général de musique*, 1834H; *Le nouveau solfège*, 1808H; *Première année de leçons de pianoforte*, 1803H; *La seule vraie théorie de la musique*, 1821H
Momigny Publishing House (Paris), 1800G
Mompou, Frederico, 1893A, 1987B
Mompou, Hippolyte, 1804A, 1819D, 1841B
Monasterio, Jesús de, 1836A, 1845C, 1903B
Monatschrift für Gottesdienst & Kirchliche Kunst, 1896G
Monatschrifte für Musikgeschichte, 1869G
Moncrieff, Gladys, 1892A, 1906C, 1976B
Le monde musical, 1889G
Mondonville, Jean Joseph de, 1755D, 1772B
Mongini, Pietro, 1830A, 1853C, 1874B
Moniuszko, Stanislaw, 1819A, 1840F, 1872B; *Textbook on Harmony*, 1871H
Monk, Edwin George, 1819A, 1859D, 1900B
Monk, Meredith, 1942A, 1995E
Monk, Meredith, Vocal Ensemble, 1978G
Monk, William Henry, 1823A, 1889B
Monmart, Bertha, 1951C
Monn, Johann Christoph, 1782B
Monsigny, Pierre A., 1754F, 1798F, 1800D, 1804E, 1817B
Montague, Diana, 1953A, 1977C
Monte Carlo, Monaco: Ballet Russe, 1932G; Concert Hall, 1872G; Opéra de Monte Carlo, 1879G; Opera Orchestra, 1863G; Playhouse, 1878G
Montefusco, Licinio, 1961C
Montero, Gabriel, 1970A
Montesanto, Luigi, 1887A, 1909C, 1954B
Monteux, Pierre, 1875A, 1911D, 1916F, 1917D, 1919D, 1924D, 1929D, 1936D, 1961D, 1964B

Montevideo, Uruguay: Beethoven Society, 1897G; Casa de Comedias, 1793G; La Lira Conservatory, 1873G; Municipal Orchestra, 1959G; Philharmonic Society, 1868G; Piano Competition, 1968G; Symphony Orchestra, 1931G; Teatro San Felipe, 1879G; Teatro Solis, 1856G; Verdi Institute, 1890G
Montgomery, Kathryn, 1952A, 1972C
Monthly Musical Record, 1871G
Monti, Marianna, 1814B
Monti, Nicola, 1920A, 1940C, 1993B
Monticelli, Angelo Maria, 1764B
Montreal, Canada: Concours International de Montreal, 1965G; Dominion College of Music, 1894G; Les Festivals de Montreal, 1936G; I Musici de Montreal, 1983G; Ladies' Morning Musical Club, 1882G; Mendelssohn Choir, 1864G; Opéra de Montreal, 1980G; Opera Guild of Canada, 1940G; Philharmonic Society I, 1848G; Philharmonic Society II, 1877G; Place des Arts, 1967G; Société des Concerts Symphoniques, 1935G; Société des Vents de Montréal, 1988G; Symphony Orchestra, 1934G; Théâtre de Société, 1789G; Tudor Singers, 1962G
Montsalvatge, Bassols Xavier, 1912A
Monza, Carlo, 1768DE, 1771E, 1775D, 1801B
Monzani, Theobald, 1762A
Monzani, Theobald, Flute Co., 1790G
Moody, Fanny, 1866A, 1885C, 1945B
Moody-Manners Opera Co., 1897G
Moog, R. A., Co., 1954G
Moog, Robert, 1934A
Moon, Chloe, 1952A
Moore, Douglas, 1893A, 1940D, 1951E, 1967E, 1969B; *From Madrigal to Modern Music*, 1942H; *Listening to Music*, 1932H
Moore, Gerald, 1899A, 1919C, 1987B; *The Unashamed Accompanist*, 1943H
Moore, Grace, 1898A, 1928C, 1947B
Moore, John W., 1807A, 1889B; *Sacred Minstrel*, 1842H; *The Sentimental Songbook*, 1878H; *Complete Encyclopedia of Music Elementary, Technical, Historical, Biographical, Vocal and Instrumental*, 1852H
Moore, Mary Carr, 1873A, 1911E, 1957B
Moore, Thomas, 1779A, 1852B; *Irish Melodies I*, 1808H
Moorehead, John, 1760A, 1804B
Moores School of Music Building (U. of Houston), 1997G
Moos, Paul: *Moderne Musikästhetik in Deutschland*, 1902H
Mooser, Aloys, 1770A, 1839B
Mora, Fernando de la, 1963A
Morales, Melesio, 1838A, 1908B
Moran, John, 1965A
Moran, Robert, 1937A
Moran-Olden, Fanny, 1855A, 1877C, 1905B

❀

F *Biographical*   G *Cultural Beginnings*   H *Musical Literature*
I *Musical Compositions*

Morata, Juan José, 1786D
Moravec, Ivan, 1930A, 1946C
Moravec, Vincent (Paul), 1957A, 1984E
Moravian Music Foundation, 1956G
Moravian Philharmonic Orchestra, 1945G
Moravian String Quartet, 1923G
Mordden, Ethan: *Demented: The World of the Opera Diva*, 1985H; *Opera in the Twentieth Century*, 1978H
Moréas, Jean, 1910B
Moreau, Henri, 1803B; *L'harmonie mise en pratique*, 1783H
Moreau, Léon, 1899E
Moreau, Jacobus Franciscus, 1751B
Moreira, António, 1758A, 1787D, 1790D, 1793D, 1819B
Morel, Auguste-François, 1809A, 1881B
Morel, Jean, 1903A, 1936D, 1956D, 1975B
Morell, Barry, 1927A, 1955C
Morellati, Paolo, 1763E, 1768D, 1807B
Morelli, Adriana, 1978C
Morelli, Carlo, 1897A, 1922C, 1970B
Morelli, Giacomo, 1819B
Morelot, Stéphan, 1820A, 1899B; *Manuel de Psalmodie*, 1855H; *De la musique au XV siècle*, 1856H
Morena, Berta, 1878A, 1898C, 1952B
Morère, Jean, 1836A, 1861C, 1887B
Moreschi, Alessandro, 1858A
Moret, Norbert, 1921A
Morgan, Beverly, 1952A, 1978C
Morgan, Helen, 1900A
Morgan, Michael, 1957A, 1982C, 1990D
Morgan Cons. of Music, 1877G
Mori, Nicolas, 1796A, 1804C, 1839B
Mori, Tadashi, 1967D
Moriani, Napoleone, 1806A, 1833C, 1878B
Morigi, Angelo, 1752A, 1788B
Morini, Erica, 1904A, 1916C, 1965B
Morison, Elsie, 1924A, 1948C
Morlacchi, Francesco, 1784A, 1810D, 1816E, 1841B
Mornington, Garret Wesley, 1781B
Moroi, Saburo, 1903I, 1967D, 1977B
Moross, Jerome, 1913A, 1983B
Morris, Harold, 1890A, 1964B
Morris, James, 1947A, 1967C
Morris, Joan, 1943A, 1973C
Morris, R. O.: *Contrapuntal Technique in the XVIth Century*, 1922H; *Introduction to Counterpoint*, 1944H; *The Structure of Music*, 1935H
Morris, Robert, 1943A; *Class Notes for Atonal Theory*, 1990H; *Composition with Pitch-Classes*, 1987H
Morris, Thomas, 1790B
Morris, Wyn, 1929A, 1957E, 1968E
Morris & Co., 1861G
Morrison, Alan, 1968A

Morrison, Angus, 1902A, 1923C
Morrison, Ray, 1946A
Morse, Charles Henry, 1853A, 1927B
Morse, Theodore, Publisher, 1898G
Morse & Haviland, Publishers (N.Y.), 1905G
Morse Music Co., 1897G
Mortelmans, Lodewijk, 1893E, 1925D, 1952B
Mortimer, Peter; *Choralgesang zur Zeit der Reformation*, 1821H
Mosca, Giuseppe, 1772A, 1817D, 1827D, 1839B
Mosca, Luigi, 1775A, 1824B
Mosca, Silvia, 1958A
Moscheles, Ignaz, 1794A, 1808C, 1821F, 1870B
Moscona, Nicola, 1907A, 1929C, 1975B
Moscow, Russia: Art Theater, 1898G; Association of Contemporary Music, 1923G; Bolshoi Kamenniy Theater, 1757G; Bolshoi Opera Co., 1776G; Bolshoi Opera Theater II, 1856G; Chamber Orchestra, 1955G; Choral Society, 1878G; Conservatory of Music, 1866G; Conservatory String Quartet, 1923G; Contemporary Music Ensemble, 1990G; Galitzin Boys Choir, 1842G; Historic Concerts, 1907G; Imperial Theater, 1806G; Opera House, 1759G; Petrovsky Theater, 1780G; Philharmonic Orchestra, 1864G, 1920G; Philharmonic Quartet, 1946G; Philharmonic Society, 1883G; Radio Symphony Orchestra, 1930G; Russian Music Circle, 1860G; Society for Jewish Music, 1923G; Soloists, 1984G; State Symphonic Kapelle of Moscow, 1982G; Symphonic Chapel, 1901G; Symphony Orchestra, 1989G; University Theater, 1757G; USSR State Choir, 1942G; Virtuosi, 1979G
Mosel, Ignaz Franz von, 1772A, 1844B; *Tonkunst in Wien während der letsten fünf Dezennien*, 1818H; *Über die Originalpartitur des Requiems von W.A. Mozart*, 1839H; *Versuch einer Aesthetik des dramatischen Tonsatzes*, 1813H
Moseley, Carlos, Music Pavilion, 1990G
Moser, Edda, 1938A, 1962C
Moser, Hans Joachim, 1927D, 1950D 1967B; *Geschichte der deutschen Musik I*, 1920H; *Geschichte der deutschen Musik II*, 1922H; *Geschichte der deutschen Musik III*, 1924H; *Lehrbuch der musikgeschichte*, 1936H; *Musik in Zeit und Raum*, 1960H; *Musikästhetik*, 1953H; *Musiklexikon*, 1935H; *Technik der deutschen Gesangskunst*, 1911H
Moser, Rudolf, 1892A, 1960B
Moser, Hans Joachim, 1889A
Möser, Karl, 1774A, 1851B
Moser, Thomas, 1945A, 1975C
Möser String Quartet (Berlin), 1811G
Mosewius, Johann T., 1788A, 1831D, 1832D, 1858B
Moskowski, Moritz, 1925B

❈

A *Births*   B *Deaths*   C *Debuts*   D *New Positions*
E *Prizes/Honors*

Mosolov, Alexander, 1973B
Mosonyi, Mihály, 1815A, 1870B
Moss, Lawrence, 1927A
Mossolov, Alexander, 1900A
Mostad, Jon, 1942A
Mostly Mozart Festival, 1966G
Moszkowski, Moritz, 1854A, 1873C
Motta & Ball, Piano Makers (London), 1794G
Motet Choir of the Hallgrim's Church, 1982G
Mott, Louise, 1972A
Mottl, Felix, 1856A, 1876F, 1893D, 1903D, 1911B
Mount-Edgcumbe, Richard, 1764A, 1839B; *Musical Reminiscences*, 1824H
Mountain, Henry, 1794B
Mourja, Graf, 1973A
Moxon, Edward, Publisher, 1830G
Mozart, Leopold, 1787B; *Fundamentals of Violin Playing*, 1756H
Mozart, Leopold, Conservatorium, 1925G
Mozart, Maria Anna, 1751A, 1829B
Mozart, Wolfgang A., 1756A, 1760F, 1762F, 1763F, 1764F, 1765F, 1766F, 1767F, 1768F, 1769F, 1770EF, 1772F, 1773F, 1774F, 1776F, 1777F, 1778F, 1779F, 1780F, 1781F, 1782F, 1784F, 1787F, 1789F, 1790F, 1791BF
Mozart Gesellschaft (Germany), 1951G
Mozart in Monterey, 1987G
Mozartean Players, The, 1978G
Mravina, Evgenia, 1864A, 1914B
Mravinsky, Evgeni, 1903A, 1932D, 1938D, 1988B
Mu Alpha Sinfonia Fraternity, 1898G
Mu Phi Epsilon Music Sorority, 1903G
Muck, Karl, 1859A, 1880C, 1886D, 1892D, 1906D, 1912D, 1919F, 1922D, 1940B
Muczynski, Robert, 1929A
Mudge, Richard, 1763B
Mudie's Lending Library, 1842G
Muff, Alfred, 1949A, 1974C
Muffat, Gottlieb, 1763F, 1770B
Muldowney, Dominic, 1952A, 1976D
Müller, Adolf, Jr., 1839A, 1901B
Müller, Adolf, Sr., 1801A, 1828D, 1886B
Müller, August E., 1767A, 1804D, 1810D, 1817B; *Kleines Elementarbuch für Klavierspielen*, 1807H; *Anweisung zum genauen Vortrage*, 1796H; *Elementarbuch für Flötenspieler*, 1815H; *Klavier- und Fortepiano-Schule*, 1804H
Muller, Barbel, 1991C
Müller, Christian, 1763B
Müller, Friedrich, 1786A, 1831D, 1871B
Müller, Georg Godfrey, 1762A, 1821B
Müller, Iwan, 1786A, 1854B
Müller, Maria, 1898A, 1919C, 1958B
Müller, Paul, 1898A
Müller, Rufus, 1958A
Müller, Wenzel, 1767A, 1786D, 1808D, 1835B

Müller String Quartet I, 1830G
Müller String Quartet II, 1855G
Müller-Blattau, Joseph, 1895A, 1952D, 1976B; *Das Deutsche Volkslied*, 1932H; *Einführung in die Musikgeschichte*, 1932H; *Gestaltung-Umgestaltung*, 1950H
Müller-Brühl, Helmut, 1964D
Müller-Zürich, Paul, 1993B
Mullings, Frank, 1881A, 1907C, 1953B
Mullova, Viktoria, 1959A, 1962C, 1981E, 1982E
Mumma, Gordon, 1935A
Munch, Charles, 1891A, 1932C, 1935D, 1938D, 1945E, 1949D, 1952F, 1968B; *Je suis chef d'orchestre*, 1954H
Münch, Hans, 1935D
Münchinger, Karl, 1915A, 1941D, 1990B
Muni, Nicholas, 1996D
Munich, Germany: Akademie der Tonkunst, 1874G; Akademischer Gesangverein, 1861G; ARTS, 1993G; Association for Contemporary Music, 1929G; Bavarian Academy of Arts & Sciences, 1801G; Bavarian State Opera, 1818G; Bürgersängerzunft, 1840G; Conservatory of Music, 1846G; Cuvilliestheater, 1753G; Genossenshaft Deutscher Tonsetzen, 1896G; Hoffman, Hans, School of Fine Arts, 1915G; Kaim Orchestra, 1893G; Kerzelli Music College, 1772G; Lehrergesangverein, 1878G; Liederkranz, 1826G; Liedertafel, 1841G; Musikalische Akademie, 1811G; National Theater, 1818G; Neuer Orchesterverein, 1879G; Opera Festival, 1875G; Oratorio Society, 1854G; Philharmonic Orchestra, 1893G, 1924G; Residenztheater, 1753G; Staatstheater am Gärtnerplatz, 1865G; Städtische Singschule, 1830G; Theater am Isartor, 1812G
Munsel, Patrice, 1925A, 1943C
Münster, Germany: Stierlin Music School, 1897G
Munteanu, Peter, 1940C
Munz, Mieczyslaw, 1900A, 1920C, 1976B
Muratore, Lucien, 1876A, 1902C, 1954B
Murdoch, John Spencer, Piano Maker, 1884G
Murgu, Corneliu, 1948A, 1978C
Murphy, John F., 1887E
Murphy, Suzanne, 1941A, 1976C
Murray, Ann, 1949A, 1974C
Murray, Michael, 1943A, 1968C
Murray, Thomas, 1943A
Murray, William, 1935A, 1956C
Mursell, James L.: *Human Values in Music Education*, 1934H; *Music & the Classroom Teacher*, 1951H; *Music Education: Principles & Programs*, 1956H; *Principles of Music Education*, 1927H; *The Psychology of Music*, 1937H; *The Psychology of School Music Teaching*, 1931H

F *Biographical*   G *Cultural Beginnings*   H *Musical Literature*
I *Musical Compositions*

Murska, Ilma de, 1836A, 1862C, 1889B
Musard, Philippe, 1792A, 1859B
Muse Française, 1823G
Museum of Musical Instruments, 1963G
Musgrave, Thea, 1928A
Music, 1891G
Music Academy of the West Summer Festival
  (Santa Barbara), 1947G
Music & Arts Programs of America, Inc.,
  1985G
Music & Drama, 1882G
Music & Letters, 1920G
Music & Musician, 1952G
Music & Musicians, 1915G
Music Appreciation Hour (W. Damrosch),
  1928G
Music Associates of America, 1980G
Music at La Gesse Foundation, 1981G
Music at the Gainey Center, 1990G
Music Board, Australian Council for the Arts,
  1973G
Music Cataloguing Bulletin, 1970G
Music Club of Richmond, Virginia, 1915G
Music Educator's National Conference, 1907G
Music for All Seasons, 1992G
Music Forum, 1967G
The Music Index, 1949G
Music Library Association, 1931G; Publication
  Prizes, 1977G
The Music Magazine, 1792G
Music of the Baroque, 1971G
Music of the West, 1945G
Music of Today, 1963G
Music Publisher's Ass'n of the U.S., 1895G
Music Review, 1940G
Music Review Weekly, 1888G
Music Society of Victoria, 1861G
Music Supervisor's National Conference,
  1907G
Music Teacher's National Association
  (MTNA), 1876G
Music Teacher's Training School, 1945G
Music Trade Journal, 1879G
Music Trades, 1890G, 1893G
The Music Trades Review, 1875G
Musica, 1947G
Musica Aeterna Chorus, 1961G
Musica Aeterna Orchestra, 1961G
Musica Camerit, 1983G
Musica Choir (University of Jyraskyla), 1977G
Musica Electronica Viva, 1966G
Musica Florea, 1992G
Musica Judaica, 1975G
Musica Nova, 1962G
Musica Romana, 1888G
Musica Sacra, 1866G
Musica Sacra: Revue du Chant Liturgique...,
  1874G
Musica Sacra Society, 1920G

Música Sacro-Hispana, 1907G
Musical Alliance of America, 1917G
Musical America, 1898G
Musical and Dramatic Times, 1875G
Musical Antiquary, 1909G
Musical Box, 1796G
Musical Canada, 1895G
Musical Contemporary, 1915G
The Musical Courier, 1880G
Musical Critic & Trade Review, 1878G
Musical Digest, 1920G
Musical Examiner, 1842G
Musical Harp, 1880G
Musical Herald, 1880G, 1897G
Musical Heritage Society, 1962G
The Musical Independent, 1868G
Musical Journal for the Piano Forte, 1800G
The Musical Leader & Concertgoer, 1895G
Musical Leaflet, 1872G
Musical Life, 1901G
Musical Magazine, 1835G, 1839G
Musical Messenger, 1891G, 1904G
Musical Million & Fireside Friend, 1870G
The Musical Observer, 1907G
Musical Opinion, 1877G
Musical Poetica, 1980G
The Musical Quarterly, 1915G
Musical Review, 1903G
Musical Review for the Blind, 1930G
Musical Standard, 1862G
Musical Viva (Australia), 1945G
Musical World, 1836G
Musical World & New York Musical Times, 1850G
The Musician, 1896G
Musicians Guild of America, 1956G
Musician's International Mutual Aid Fund,
  1974G
Musicians of the Old Post Road, 1989G
Musician's Memorial Chapel, 1955G
Musicians' National Protective Association,
  1871G
Le musicien, 1842G
Les musiciens du Louvre, 1984G
Musicologica Austriaca, 1977G
Musicwriter, 1954G
Die Musik, 1901G
Musik Hug (Zürich Publishing House), 1807G
Musik und Altar, 1947G
Musik-Pädagogische, 1911G
Musikalisch-Kritisches Repertorium, 1843G
Musikalisch-litterarischer Monatsbericht, 1829G
*Musikalisches Jugendblatt für Gesang, Clavier und
  Flöte*, 1830G
Musikalisches Kunstmagazin, 1782G
Musikalisches Magazin auf der Höhe, 1791G
Musikalische Realzeitung, 1788G
Musikalisches Wochenblatt, 1791G
Musikalische Zeitung, 1793G
Musikforlag, Norsk, Publisher, 1909G

❋

A *Births*   B *Deaths*   C *Debuts*   D *New Positions*
E *Prizes/Honors*

Die Musikforschun, 1948G
Musik-Pädagogische, 1911G
Die Musikpädagogische Bibliothek, 1928G
Musikinstrumenten-Zeitung, 1890G
Musil, Frantiek, 1908B
Musin, Ilya Alexandrovich, 1999B
Musin, Ovide, 1854A, 1929B
Musin Violin School (N.Y.), 1908G
Musique de Notre Temps, 1958G
Musique d'Aujourd'hui, 1958G
Mussolini Cesare: A New and Complete Treatise
   on the Theory and Practice of Music, 1795H
Mussorgsky, Modest, 1839A, 1856F, 1857F,
   1858F, 1863F, 1867F, 1869F, 1880F, 1881B
Mustafà, Domenico, 1829A, 1912B
Mustonen, Olli, 1967A
Müthel, Johann Gottfried, 1755D, 1788B
Muti, Riccardo, 1941A, 1967CE, 1969D, 1970D,
   1973D, 1975F, 1977F, 1979D, 1980D, 1986D
Mutter, Anne-Sophie, 1963A, 1976C, 1977F
Muza (Kraków), 1866G
Muzika (Moscow), 1910G
Muzika (Poland), 1924G
Muzio, Claudia, 1910C, 1936B
Muzio, Emanuele, 1821A, 1890B
Muzio, Claudia, 1889A
Muzyka Centrum Artistic Society, 1977G
Myers, Michael, 1955A, 1977C
Myers, Pamela, 1952A, 1977C
Myers, Rollo: Modern French Music, 1971H;
   Modern Music, 1923H
Myerscough, Nadia, 1967A
Mysliveček, Josef, 1761F, 1771E, 1781B
Nabokov, Nicolas, 1903A, 1970E, 1978B;
   Bagázh: Memoirs of a Russian Cosmopolitan,
   1975H; Old Friends & New Music, 1951H
Nacchini, Pietro, 1765B
Nachbaur, Franz, 1830A, 1857C, 1902B
Naderman, Jean-Henri, 1799B
Nadermann, François-Joseph, 1781A, 1835B
Nadien, David, 1946E
Nagamo, Kent, 1951A, 1978D, 1989D, 1991D,
   1994D, 1995F, 2000D
Nagel, Willibald, 1863A, 1929B; History of
   Music in England II, 1897H
Nägeli, Hans Georg, 1773A, 1833E, 1836B;
   Musikalisches Tabellwerk für Volks-schulen...,
   1828H; Verlesungen über Musik, 1825H
Nägeli, Hans, Publisher, 1792G
Nägeli Johann: Gesangsbildungslehre nach
   Pestalozzischen Grundsätzen, 1810H
Nagler, Georg K., 1835F
Nagy, János B., 1943A, 1971C
Nagy, Robert, 1929A
Nahan, Franko, 1861A
Nakamatsu, Jon, 1995E, 1997E
Nakamichi Baroque Music Festival, 1986G
Naldi, Giuseppe, 1770A, 1789C, 1820B
Namara, Marguerite, 1974B

Nancarrow, Conlon, 1912A, 1997B
Nancy, France: Conservatory of Music, 1870G;
   Municipal Theater, Place Stanislas, 1755G
Nantes, France; Graslin Theater, 1852G;
   Philharmonic Society, 1826G; Bressler's
   Conservatory, 1844G
Nantier-Didiée, Constance, 1831A, 1850C,
   1867B
Napier, Marita, 1939A, 1969C
Napier, William, Publisher, 177
Naples, Italy: Circolo Scarlatti, 1892G;
   Conservatory of Music, 1808G; San Carlo
   Theater II, 1816G; Società del Quartetto,
   1880G; Società Orchestrale, 1880G; Teatro del
   Fondo, 1779G
Nápravnik, Eduard, 1839A, 1869D, 1916B
Nardini, Pietro, 1762F, 1770D, 1793B
Nares, James, 1783B; A Concise and East Treatise
   on Singing with a Set of English Duets for
   Beginners, 1786H; A Regular Introduction to
   Playing on the Harpsichord or Organ, 1760H;
   Treatise on Singing, 1780H
Narmour, Eugene, 1939A; The Analysis &
   Cognition of Melodic Complexity, 1991H
Narvarro, Garcia, 1941A
Nash, Heddle, 1896A
Nash, Pamela, 1959A
Nash Ensemble, 1964G
Nash, Heddle, 1924C, 1961B
Nashville, Tennessee: Symphony Orchestra I,
   1904G; Symphony Orchestra II, 1920G;
   Symphony Orchestra III, 1946G
Nast, Minnie, 1874A, 1897C, 1956B
Nathan, Hans, 1910A, 1989B; William Billings,
   1975H
Nathan, Isaac, 1790A, 1864B; The Essay on the
   History and Theory of Music, and on the
   Qualities, Capabilities and Management of the
   Human Voice, 1823H
National Academy of the Recording Arts &
   Sciences, 1957G
National Arts Centre Festival Opera, 1971G
National Arts Centre Orchestra, 1969G
National Arts Foundation, 1947G
National Association for American Composers
   & Conductors, 1933G
National Association for Music Therapy, 1950G
National Association of Choir Directors, 1938G
National Association of College Wind &
   Percussion Instructors, 1951G
National Association of Composers, U.S.A.,
   1975
National Association of Harpists, 1919G
National Association of Jazz Educators, 1968G
National Association of Music Merchants,
   1919G
National Association of Negro Musicians,
   1919G
National Association of Organ Teachers, 1963G

❊

F   Biographical   G   Cultural Beginnings   H   Musical Literature
         I   Musical Compositions

National Association of Organists, 1908G
National Association of Performing Artists, 1935G
National Association of Schools of Music (NASM), 1924G
National Association of Teachers of Singing (NATS), 1944G
National Band Association (NBA), 1960G
National Bandmasters Fraternity, 1937G
National Bureau for the Advancement of Music, 1916G
National Catholic Bandmasters' Association, 1953G
National Catholic Music Educator's Association, 1942G
National Congress on Women in Music, 1981G
National Federation of Music Clubs, 1893G 98???
National Federation of Music Societies, 1935G
National Folk Festival Association, 1933G
National Foundation for Advancement in the Arts, 1981G
National Gazette & Literary Register, 1820G
National Guild of Piano Teachers, 1929G
National Hungarian Ass'n of Choral Societies, 1867G
National Institute of Arts and Letters, 1898G
National League of Composers, 1886G
National Museum of Dance, 1986G
National Museum of Women in the Arts, 1987G
National Music Camp (Interlochen, Mich.), 1928G
National Music Publishers' Association, 1917G
National Negro Opera Co., 1941G
National Opera Association, 1955G
National Opera Institute, 1969G
National Philharmonic of India, 2000G
National Piano Manufacturer's Ass'n, 1897G
National Sacred Harp Singing Convention, 1980G
National School Band Association, 1926G
National Symphony Orchestra of Colombia, 1936G
National Wa-Wan Society of America, 1907G
National Youth Orchestra of Great Britain, 1947G
Natorp, Bernhard; *Anleitung zur Unterweisung im Singen für Lehrer in Volksschulen*, 1813H; *Choralbuch für evangelische Kirchen*, 1829H; *Melodienbuch*, 1822H; *Über den Gesang in den Kirchen der Protestanten*, 1817H
Nau, Maria Dolores, 1818A, 1836C, 1891B
Naudin, Emilio, 1823A, 1843C, 1890B
Naudot, Jacques-Christophe, 1762B
Naumann, Emil, 1827A, 1888B; *Das Alter des Psalmengesänge*, 1867H; *Deutsche Tondichter*, 1871H; *Illustrierte Musikgeschichte I*, 1880H; *Der Moderne musikalishe Zopf*, 1880H: *Musikdrama oder Oper?*, 1876H; *Die Tonkunst*

in der Culturgeschichte, 1870H; *Über Einführung des Psalmengesanges in die evangelische Kirche*, 1856H; *Zukunftsmusik und die Musik der Zukunft*, 1877H
Naumann, Ernst, 1860D
Naumann, Johann G., 1757F, 1763F, 1765F, 1776D, 1777F, 1785F, 1801B
Naumann, Siegfried, 1950C
Naumburg, Walter, 1867A, 1959A
Naumburg Chamber Music Award, 1965G
Naumburg Music Foundation (N.Y.), 1926G
Naumburg Recording Award, 1949G
Nauss, Johann Xaver, 1764B
Grundlicher Unterriecht der General-Bass recht zu erlernen, 1751H
Navál, Franz, 1865A, 1888C, 1939B
Navarini, Francesco, 1853A, 1876C, 1923B
Navarra, André, 1931C, 1888B
Navarro, García, 1967E, 1970D, 1976D, 1980D, 1987D
Navarro, Luis Antonio, 1997D
Navoigille, Guillaume, *l'aîné*, 1811B
Naxos Classical Records, 1987G
Nàsadál, Maria, 1924C
Nazareth, Daniel, 1982D
NBC Symphony Orchestra, 1937G
NBC Television Opera Co., 1949G
Neal, James, 1990C
Neate, Charles, 1784A, 1800C, 1877B
Neate, Kenneth, 1997B
Nebe, Carl, 1858A, 1878C, 1908B
Nebelsin, Eloan, 1974A
Neblett, Carol, 1946A, 1969C
Nebra, Jose, 1751D, 1768B
Nedarejshvili, Zurab, 1957A
Nedbal, Oskar, 1896D
Netherlands: Nederlands Ballet Orchestra, 1965G; Nederlands Congresgebouw, 1969G; Nederlands Danstheater, 1959G
Neefe, Christian G., 1769F, 1779D, 1782D, 1796D, 1798B
Neel, Boyd, 1905A, 1981B
Neel, Boyd, Orchestra, 1932G
Negri, Giovanni B. de., 1856A, 1878C
Negri, Maria Rosa, 1760B
Negro Chorus of Los Angeles, 1936G
Negro Opera Co. (H. L. Freeman), 1920G
Neidlinger, Gustav, 1910A, 1931C, 1991B
Neikrug, Marc, 1946A, 1997D
Neimann, Albert, 1917A
Neithardts, August, 1793A, 1861B
Nel, Anton, 1961A, 1986C, 1987E
Nelepp, Georgi, 1904A, 1930C, 1957B
Nelhybel, Vaclav, 1919A, 1996B
Nelli, Herva, 1994B
Nelson, Robert: *Techniques & Materials of Tonal Music*, 1975H
Nelson, Jane, 1974E
Nelson, John, 1941A, 1967C, 1976D, 1985D, 1987G, 1999D

❈

A *Births*   B *Deaths*   C *Debuts*   D *New Positions*
E *Prizes/Honors*

Nelson, Judith, 1939A, 1979C
Nelson, Ron, 1929A
Nelsova, Zara, 1918A, 1931C
Nemenoff, Genia, 1905A, 1937C, 1989B
Németh, Mária, 1897A, 1923C, 1967B
Nèmethy, Ella, 1895A, 1919C, 1961B
Nentwig, Franz Ferdinand, 1929A, 1962C
Neri, Giulio, 1909A, 1935C, 1958B
Nerude, Wilma, 1838A, 1846C, 1911B
Nessi, Giuseppe, 1887A, 1910C, 1961B
Nessler, Victor E., 1841A, 1890B
Nesterenko, Evgeni, 1938A, 1963C, 1970E,
    1981E, 1982E, 1986E
Netherlands: Chamber Orchestra, 1955G; Lyric
    Theater, 1890G; Opera Co., 1964G; Opera
    Foundation, 1965G; Society for
    Contemporary Music, 1930G; Society for the
    History of Netherlands' Music, 1868G; Wind
    Ensemble, 1960G
Netrebko, Anna, 1994C
Nettl, Bruno, 1930A; *Contemporary Music &*
    Music Cultures, 1975H; *Introduction to Folk*
    Music in the United States, 1960H; *Music in*
    Primitive Cultures, 1956H; *The Western Impact*
    on World Music, 1985H
Nettl, Paul, 1889A, 1972B; *The Dance in*
    Classical Music, 1963H; *Forgotten Musicians*,
    1951H; *Musik-Barock in Böhmen und Mähren*,
    1927H; *The Story of Dance Music*, 1947H; *Vom*
    Ursprung der Musik, 1918H
Neubauer, Franz Christoph, 1795B; *Eine*
    Erleichterung zu der musikalische composition,
    1783H
Neuchatel Conservatory of Music, 1918G
Neue Berliner Musikzeitung, 1847G
Neue Mozart Ausgabe (Bärenreiter), 1955G
Neue Musikgesellschaft, 1918G
Neue Musikzeitung (Stuttgart), 1880G
Die Neue Schau, 1948G
Neue Schütz Gesellschaft, 1930G
Neue Wiener Musick- Zeitung, 1852G
Neue Zeitschrift für Musik, 1834G
Neuendorff, Adolph, 1843A, 1897B
Neuhaus, Heinrich, 1888A, 1964B
Neuhaus, Rudolf, 1914A, 1934C, 1990B
Neukomm, Sigismund von, 1778A, 1815E,
    1816DF, 1821F, 1858B
Neuls-Bates, Carol: *Women in American Music*,
    1979H
Neumann, Angelo, 1838A, 1859C, 1876D,
    1882D, 1910B
Neumann, Vácalv, 1920A, 1946D, 1948C,
    1956D, 1968D, 1969D, 1995B,
Neumann, Wolfgang, 1945A, 1973C
Neuner, Carl B., 1778A, 1830B
Neupert, Edmund, 1842A, 1888B
Neupert, Johann C., Piano & Harpsichord
    Maker, 1868G
Nevada, Emma, 1859A, 1880C, 1940B
Nevada, Mignon, 1886A, 1907C, 1971B

Neveu, Ginette, 1919A, 1927C, 1935E, 1949B
Nevin, Arthur, 1871A, 1943B
Nevin, Ethelbert, 1862A, 1901B
Nevins, Marian, 1884F
Nevskaya, Marina, 1965A, 1986C
Newark, New Jersey: Amateur Glee Club,
    1837G; Boys Chorus, 1966G; Chamber
    Orchestra, 1956G; College of Music, 1885G;
    Germania Men's Chorus, 1865G; Griffith
    Music Foundation, 1938G; Handel & Haydn
    Society, 1831G; Harmonic Society, 1860G;
    Krueger Auditorium, 1884G; Little
    Symphony, 1966G; Music Festival, 1915G;
    Oratorio Society, 1878G; Orpheus Club,
    1889G; Symphony Hall, 1925G; Symphony
    Orchestra, 1893G, 1914G
New & Unusual Music Festival, 1980G
Neway, Patricia, 1919A, 1946C
Newbolt, Henry, 1900D
Newcastle, England: Chamber Music Society,
    1880G; Newcastle & Gateshead Choral
    Union, 1888G
Newcomb, Ethel, 1875A, 1903C, 1959B
New Directions (Japan), 1963G
Newel Chamber Music Festival, 1972G
New England: Bach Festival, 1969G;
    Contemporary Music Ensemble, 1970G;
    Fiddling Contest, 1974G; Opera Theater,
    1946G; Music Conservatory, 1867G
New England Conservatory: Opera
    Workshop, 1942G; Piatigorsky Artist Award,
    1992G
New-Eröffnete Orchestra, 1988G
New Friends of Music, Inc., 1936G
New Haven, Connecticut: Musical Society,
    1832G; Oratorio Society, 1903G; Parker,
    Horatio, Choir, 1920G; Symphony Orchestra,
    1894G
New Hungarian Music Society, 1911G
New Ipswich Military Band, 1804G
New Irish Chamber Orchestra, 1970G
New Hampshire: Groton Academy, 1793G;
    Music Festival, 1986G; Music Festival of
    Center Harbor, 1953G
New Jersey: Garden State Arts Center, 1968G;
    Performing Arts Center, 1997G; Symphony
    Chorus, 1967G
Newlin, Dika, 1923A
New London, Connecticut: Chamber Choir,
    1981G; Orchestra, 1941G
Newman, Anthony, 1941A, 1967C
Newman, Edward, 1980E
Newman, Ernest, 1868A, 1920D, 1959B; *From*
    the World of Music, 1956H; *A Music Critic's*
    Holiday, 1925H; *The Testament of Music*,
    1962H
Newman, William, 1912A; *The Sonata in the*
    Baroque Era, 1959H; *The Sonata in the Classic*
    Era, 1963H; *The Sonata since Beethoven*,
    1969H

F *Biographical*   G *Cultural Beginnings*   H *Musical Literature*
I *Musical Compositions*

New Monthly Maagazine & Literary Journal, 1820G
New Music, 1926G
New Music America, 1980G
New Music American Festival, 1979G
New Music Distribution Service, 1972G
New Music for Young Ensembles, 1974G
New Music Quartet, 1947G
The New Musical and Universal Magazine, 1774G
The New Musical Magazine, 1783G
New Orleans, Louisiana: Camp Street Theater, 1824G; Classical Music Society, 1855G; Conservatory of Music, 1919G; French Opera Co. I, 1813G; French Opera Co. II, 1859G; French Opera House, 1859G; Opera Association, 1943G; Orpheum Theater, 1982G; Philharmonic Orchestra, 1936G; Philharmonic Society, 1824G, 1906G; Philharmonic Society, Friends of Art, 1853G; Saint Phillippe Theater, 1808G; Spectacle de la Rue St. Pierre, 1792G; Théâtre de St. Pierre, 1791G; Theater of the Performing Arts, 1973G
New Pittsburgh Chamber Orchestra, 1978G
Newport, Rhode Island: Classic Recordings, 1985G; Folk Festival, 1959G; Music Festival, 1969G; St. Cecilia Society, 1793G
New Prague Trio, 1971G
New Quarterly Musical Review, 1893G
New South Wales, Australia: Conservatory, 1916G; State Orchestra, 1916G
New World Festival of the Arts, 1982G
New World Records, 1975G
New World School of the Arts, 1988G
New World Symphony Orchestra, 1986G
New York City: Amato Opera Theater, 1948G; American Ballet Center, 1953G; American Ballet Theater, 1939G; American Music Center of New York, 1939G; Astor Place Opera House, 1847G; Bach Aria Group, 1946G; Bowery Theater, 1827G; Carnegie Hall, 1891G; Chamber Music Society of Lincoln Center, 1969G; Chamber Music Society of New York, 1914G; Chamber Opera Theater of New York, 1980G; Chamber Orchestra, 1930G; City Concerts, 1793G; Dance Theater of Harlem, 1969G; Franco-American Musical Society, 1920G; Goldman Band , 1911G; Grand (Pike's) Opera House, 1868G; Harlem Opera House, 1888G; Harmonic Choir of New York, 1975G; Hoffman School of the Fine Arts, 1934G; League of Composers, 1923G; Lewisohn Stadium, 1914G; Lewisohn Stadium Concerts, 1918G; Light Opera of Manhattan, 1969G; Lincoln Center Chamber Music Society, 1968G; Lincoln Center for the Performing Arts, 1962G; Lincoln Center Music Theater, 1964G; Lincoln Center

Summer Festival, 1967G; Little Orchestra Society of New York, 1947G; Little Symphony of New York, 1915G; Manhattan Chamber Orchestra, 1984G; Manhattan Opera Co. & House, 1906G; Manhattan Opera House I, 1898G; Manhattan School of Music, 1917G; Manhattan String Quartet, 1970G; Manhattan Symphony Orchestra, 1929G; Metropolitan Conservatory, 1886G; Metropolitan Opera Association, 1883G; Metropolitan Opera Broadcasts, 1931G; Metropolitan Opera Guild, 1935G; Metropolitan Opera House, 1966G; Metropolitan Opera Studio, 1960G; Metropolitan School of Music, 1895G; Musin Violin School, 1908G; New York City Center of Music & Drama, 1943G; New York City Opera, 1943G; New York City Symphony Orchestra, 1944G; Ninety Second Street Y Chamber Orchestra, 1977G; Opera Orchestra of New York, 1968G; Palace Theater, 1913G; Philharmonic Broadcasts, 1930G; Philharmonic Hall, 1962G; Philharmonic in the Parks, 1965G; Philharmonic Orchestra, 1842G; Philharmonic Society, 1890G; Phoenix Theater, 1934G; Russian Symphony Orchestra of New York, 1903G; Steinway Hall, 1866G; Symphony Orchestra, 1903G; Teacher's Institute of Lincoln Center, 1975G; Town Hall, 1921G; Tully, Alice, Hall, 1969G
New York State (*see also* New York City, Rochester): Academy of Music, 1854G; American Institute of Applied Music, 1886G; American Music Association, 1856G; Artist-Artisan Institute, 1888G; Brass Ensemble, 1948G; Camerata Singers, 1960G; Cantata Singers, 1934G; Caramoor Festival (Katonah), 1946G; Castle Gordon, 1845G;Chamber Soloists, 1957G; Church Choral Society, 1889G; Church Choral Union, 1881G; Church Music Association, 1868G; Clarion Concerts, 1956G; Clarion Music Society of New York, 1958G; College of Music, 1878G; Collegiate Chorale of New York, 1941G; Columbian Anacreontic Society, 1795G; Consortium for New Music, 1966G; Damrosch Opera Co., 1894G; Deutsche Liederkranz, 1847G; Dodsworth Hall Matinee Concerts, 1855G; Empire Theater, 1893G; Euterpe Choral Society, 1865G; Euterpean Society, 1800G; Festival of Contemporary Music, 1976G; Festival of the Arts, 1989G; Finger Lakes Performing Arts Center, 1983G; Foundation for Musical Performance, 1987G; Garcia Italian Opera Co., 1825G; Germania Theater, 1872G; Guildmant Organ School, 1899G; Handelian Academy, 1814G; Harmonic Society, 1773G; Harmonical Society, 1796G; Irving Hall

---
❄

A *Births*   B *Deaths*   C *Debuts*   D *New Positions*
E *Prizes/Honors*

Symphonic Soirées, 1864G; Italian Opera House, 1833G; Jullien's Monster Concerts, 1853G; Lyric Opera Co., 1972G; Kellogg Opera Co., 1873G; Männergesangverein Arion, 1854G; Manuscript Society, 1889G; Mendelssohn Glee Club, 1866G; Mollenhauer Studio of Music, 1865G; Music Critics' Circle Award, 1941G; Musical Art Society, 1894G; Musical Fund Society, 1828G; Musical Mutual Protective Union, 1863G; Musical Society, 1788G; Musicians Club of New York, 1911G; Musicological Society, 1930G; National Conservatory of Music, 1885G; National Orchestra of New York, 1930G; National Opera Co., 1885; New Music Ensemble, 1975G; Niblo's Gardens, 1827G; Normal Music Institute, 1853G; Olympia Music Hall, 1899G; Oratorio Society, 1873G; Orchestrette, 1933G; Orfeon Free School, 1861G; Palmo's Opera House, 1844G; Park Theater, 1798G; People's Choral Union, 1892G; People's Symphony Concerts, 1900G; Promenade Concerts, 1895G; Pro Musica, 1952G; Rosenfeld Musical Press Bureau, 1898G; Sacred Music Society, 1823G; Saint Cecilia Society, 1791G; Scandinavian Symphony of New York, 1913G; Scharwenka Conservatory, 1891G; Seventh Regiment Band, 1860G; Summer Terrace Garden Concerts, 1866G; Symphony Orchestra, 1878G; Theatrical Syndicate, 1896G; Uranian Society, 1793G; Virtuosi, 1982G; Vocal Arts Ensemble, 1971G; Westchester Philharmonic Orchestra, 1983G; Women's String Orchestra, 1896G; Woodwind Quartet, 1946G; Young People's Concerts, 1898G
New York Musical Review & Choral Advocate, 1850G
New York Philharmonic Journal, 1868G
Next Wave Festival, 1983G
Ney, Elly, 1882A, 1905C, 1968B
Nešadál, Maria, 1897A
Nezhdanova, Antonina, 1873A, 1902C, 1950B
NHK Electronic Music Studio, 1955G
NHK Symphony Orchestra, 1951G
Ni, Hai-Ye, 1990E
Nicander, Karl, 1827F
Niccolini, Giuseppe, 1819D
Nice Opera, 1885G
Nichelmann, Christoph, 1762B; *Die Melodie nach ihren Wesen*, 1755H
Nicholl, Horace, 1848A, 1922B
Nicholls, Agnes, 1877A, 1895C, 1959B
Nicholls, David: *American Experimental Music, 1890-1940*, 1990H
Nicholson, Charles, 1795A, 1837B
Nicholson, Stuart: *Reminiscing in Tempo: A Portrait of Duke Ellington*, 1999H
Nicodé, Jean-Louis, 1853A, 1919B

Nicolai, Elena, 1905A, 1938C, 1993B
Nicolai, David Traugott, 1764D, 1799B
Nicolai, Otto, 1810A, 1833C, 1837D, 1841E, 1848I, 1849BE
Nicolescu, Mariana, 1948A, 1972C
Nicolini, (Ernest-Nicolas), 1834A, 1857C, 1898B
Nicolini, Giuseppe, 1762A, 1842B
Nicolosi, Francesco, 1954A
Niecks, Friedrich, 1845A, 1857C, 1898E; *Concise Dictionary of Musical Terms*, 1884H
Niedermeyer, Louis, 1802A, 1861B; *Traité théorique et pratique de l'accompagnement du plain-chant*, 1857H; *Niederrheinische Musikzeitung*, 1853G
Niedzielski, Stanislaw, 1842A, 1866C, 1895B
Nielsen, Alice, 1868A, 1903C, 1943B
Nielsen, Carl, 1865A, 1901E, 1908D, 1931BD
Nielsen, Ludvig, 1935D
Nielsen, Svend, 1937A
Nielsen, Svend Hvidfelt, 1958A
Niemann, Albert, 1831A, 1917B
Niemann, Walter, 1876A, 1953B; *Meister des Klaviers*, 1919H
Niessen-Stone, Matja von, 1870A, 1890C, 1948B
Nietzsche, Friedrich, 1868F; *Der Fall Wagner*, 1888H; *Die Geburt der Tragödie aus dem Geiste der Musik*, 1872H
Nijinsky, Vaclav, 1890A
Nikisch, Arthur, 1855A, 1878D, 1889D, 1893D, 1895D, 1912F, 1922B
Nikkanen, Kurt, 1965A, 1978C
Nikolaidi, Elena, 1909A, 1936C
Nikolsky, André, 1959A, 1977C
Niles, John Jacob, 1892A, 1920C, 1980B; *Anglo-American Ballad Book*, 1945H; *Anglo-American Carol Study Book*, 1948H; *More Songs of the Hill People*, 1936H; *Songs of the Hill People*, 1934H
Nilsson, Birgit, 1918A, 1946C, 1968E, 1979F
Nilsson, Christine, 1843A, 1864C, 1921B
Nimsgern, Siegmund, 1940A, 1965C
Ning, Liang, 1957A, 1983C
Nini, Alessandro, 1843D
Nisard, Théodore, 1812A, 1888B; *Dictionnaire litugique, historique et pratique de plain-chant*, 1854H; *La science et la pratique de plain-chant*, 1847H; *Les vrais principes de l'accompagnement du plain-chant*, 1860H
Nishimura, Akira, 1953A, 1975E, 1977E, 1988E
Nissen, Hans Hermann, 1893A, 1920C, 1980B
Nissen, Henriette, 1819A, 1843C, 1879B
Nissman, Barbara, 1944A, 1971C
Nissim Composer Competition, 1982G
Nixon, Marni, 1930A
Nixon, Roger, 1921A
Noack, Fritz, Organ Co., 1960G
Nobel, T. Tertius, 1953B
Nobile Accademia di Musica, 1777G
Noble, Dennis, 1899A, 1924C

❊

F   *Biographical*   G   *Cultural Beginnings*   H   *Musical Literature*
I   *Musical Compositions*

Noble, Tertius, 1867A
Noble, Timothy, 1945A, 1981C
Noda, Ken, 1962A, 1977C
Nohr, Christian Friedrich, 1800A, 1875B
Nolfo, Ian de, 1997E
Noll, William, 1976D
Nonesuch Commission Award, 1982G
Noni, Alda, 1916A, 1937C
Nono, Luigi, 1924A, 1990B
Nopre, Gilles, 1965A
Norbert, Karl, 1893A, 1914C, 1938B
Norberg-Schulz, Elisabeth, 1959A
Norby, Eric, 1936A
Norden, Betsy, 1945A
Nordgren, Pehr Henrik, 1944A
Nordheim, Arne, 1931A, 1975E, 1980E
Nordheimer, A. & S., Publishers, 1842G
Nordica, Lillian, 1857A, 1876C, 1885F, 1914B
Nordiska Musikförlaget (Stockholm), 1915
Nordoff, Paul, 1909A, 1977B; *Music Therapy in
    Special Education*, 1971H
Nordqvist, Gustaf, 1949B
Nordraak, Rikard, 1842A, 1866B
Nordstrøm, H. H., 1947A
Norena, Eidé, 1884A, 1907C, 1968B
Norfolk: Chamber Music Festival, 1899G;
    Choral Festival, 1886G
Norfolk & Norwich Music Club, 1950G
Norfolk & Norwich Triennial Music Festival,
    1824G
Nørgård, Per, 1932A
Nørholm, Ib, 1956D, 1964D, 1971E, 1981E
Norlin Foundation, 1974G
Norlind, Tobias, 1879A, 1947B; *Allmän
    musikhistoria*, 1922H; *Allmänt musiklexicon*
    (completion), 1916H; *Bok on
    Musikinstrument, En*, 1928H; *Svensk
    musikhistoria*, 1901H; *Systematik der
    Saiteninstrumente II: Geschichte des klaviers*,
    1939H
Norman, Jerold, 1990B
Norman, Jessye, 1945A, 1968E, 1969C, 1982E,
    1987E
Norman, Ludvig, 1831A, 1861D, 1885B;
    Musikaliska uppsatser och Kritiker, 1888H
Norrington, Roger, 1934A, 1966D, 1978D,
    1990D, 1998D
Norris, David Owen, 1991E
Norris, Thomas, 1759C, 1776D
Norrköping Symphony Orchestra, 1912G
Norrland Opera (Sweden), 1947G
North American New Music Festival, 1983G
North American Phonograph Co., 1887G
North American Review, 1815G
North Beach Grand Opera, 1984G
North Carolina (*see also* Raleigh): Brevard
    Music Center (North Carolina), 1936G;
    School of the Arts, 1965G
North Country Chamber Players Summer
    Festival, 1978G

Northeastern Records, 1979G
Northern Greece Symphony Orchestra, 1959G
Northern Sinfonia (Newcastle-upon-Tyne),
    1958G
North-South Consonance Ensemble, 1980G
North/South Recordings, 1992G
North Tonawanda Barrel Organ Works, 1893G
Northwest Grand Opera Association, 1951G
Northwest Chamber Orchestra, 1973G
Northwest Grand Opera Association, 1951G
Northwest Regional Folklife Festival, 1972G
Northwest Symphony Orchestra, 1987G
Norton, Charles Eliot, 1827A
Norup, Bent, 1936A, 1970C
Norwegian Cultural Council Prize, 1970G
Norwegian Soloists Choir, 1950G
Norwegian Academy of Music, 1867G
Norwegian Choral Festival, 1849G
Norwich, England: Anacreontic Society, 1795G;
    Choral Society, 1824G; Madrigal Society,
    1838G; Norwich Festival, 1770G; Pantheon,
    1777G; Philharmonic Society, 1838G; Theater
    Royal, 1757G
Nosag Record Label, 1989G
Nosyrev, Mikhail, 1981B
Notas Musicales y Literarias, 1882G
Noté, Jean, 1859A, 1883C, 1922B
Note d'Archivo, 1924G
Notes (Music Library Association), 1943G
Nott, Jonathon, 1963A, 1991D, 1997D, 2000D
Nottebohm, Gustav, 1817A, 1882B
Nottingham, England: Festival, 1970G; Music
    & Drama Festival, 1970G; Royal Concert
    Hall, 1982G; Sacred Harmonic Society,
    1856G; Vocal Music Club, 1846G
Nourrit, Adolphe, 1802A, 1821C, 1839B
Nourrit, Louis, 1780A, 1805C, 1831B
Nouveaux Concerts Symphoniques, 1888G
Nouvelle Gazette Musicale, 1838G
La Nouvelle Revue, 1879G
Nouvelliste, 1840G
Nováček, Ottokar, 1866A, 1900B
Novachord, 1939G
Novães, Guiomar, 1895A, 1911C, 1979B
Novák, Vitěslav, 1870A, 1889F, 1949B
Noval, Tara, 1969A
Novarra, André, 1911A
Nova Stravaganza, 1988G
Novello, Alfred, 1810A, 1896B
Novello, Clara, 1818A, 1850F, 1832C, 1860F,
    1908B
Novello, Vincent, 1781A, 1861B
Novello and Co., Ltd., 1811G
Novitskaya, Ekaterina, 1978F
Novotná, Jarmila, 1907A, 1925C, 1994B
Nowak, Grzegorz, 1984E
Nowak, Lionel, 1911A, 1995B
Nowak, Maria Malgorzata, 1977A, 1995C
Nowowiejski, Feliks, 1877A, 1903E, 1909D,
    1946B

❄

A *Births*   B *Deaths*   C *Debuts*   D *New Positions*
                    E *Prizes/Honors*

Nozzari, Andrea, 1775A, 1794C, 1832B
Nucci, Leo, 1942A, 1967C, 1973E
Nuestra Música, 1946G
Nuevo Teatro Critico, 1891G
Nuitter Charles: *Origines de l'opéra français*,
    1886H
Nunns, R. & W., Piano Makers, 1823G
Nunns & Clark, Piano Makers, 1823G
Nuova Consonanza (Rome), 1960G
Nuremberg, Germany; Music Theater & Opera
    Co., 1905G; Ramann-Volkmann Music
    School, 1865G
Nureyev, Rudolph, 1961F
Nurmela, Kari, 1961C, 1984B
Nutida Musik (Sweden), 1954G
Nyack Symphonic Society, 1877G
Nyiregyházi, Ervin, 1903A, 1915C, 1973F,
    1977F, 1987B
Nykryn, Jan, 1995C
Nyman, Michael: *Experimental Music*, 1974H
Nystedt, Knut, 1915A, 1946D
Nystroem, Gösta, 1890A, 1966B
Nyvang, Michael, 1962A
Nyyd (Estonian festival), 1991G
Oakland, California: Morgan Conservatory of
    Music, 1877G; Orpheus Club, 1892G;
    Symphony Chorus, 1960G; Symphony
    Orchestra, 1933G
Oakley, Herbert, 1876E
Oberhoffer, Emil, 1867A, 1901D, 1903D, 1933B
Obin, Louis-Henri, 1820A, 1844C, 1895B
Oberlin, Russell, 1928A
Oberlin College Conservatory of Music, 1865G
Oberlin Trio, 1982G
Obermayer, J., Harp Maker, 1928G
Obermayr, Christine, 1959A, 1983C
Obetz, John, 1933A
Oborin, Lev, 1924C, 1927E
Obouhov, Nicolas: *Traité d'harmonie tonale,
    atonale et totale*, 1946H
Oboussier, Robert, 1942D, 1957B
Obradors, Fernando, 1897A, 1945B
Obradović, Alexander, 1977D
Obraztsova, Elena, 1937A, 1963C, 1970E, 1976E
O'Brien, Eugene, 1945A
Obukhov, Nicolai, 1892A
Obukhova, Nadezhda, 1886A, 1916C, 1961B
Očadlík, Mirko, 1904A, 1959D, 1964B
Ocean Records, 1997G
Očená, Andrej, 1911A
Ochmann, Wieslaw, 1937A, 1959C
Ochs, Siegfried, 1858A, 1929B
O'Connell, Charles, 1900A, 1962B
O'Connor, Mark, 1962A
O'Connor, Padraig, 1942A
O'Conor, John, 1947A, 1968C, 1973E
Odak, Krsto, 1965B
Odel, J. H./C. S., Organ Builders, 1859G
Odessa Philharmonic Orchestra, 1936G
Odnoposoff, Adolfo, 1917A, 1992B

Odnoposoff, Ricardo, 1914A, 1932E, 1937E
Oe, Hikari, 1963A
Oehl, Kurt, 1923A; *Musikliteratur im Überlick*,
    1988H
Oelze, Christiane, 1963A
Oestvig, Karl, 1889B, 1914C, 1968B
Oettingen Arthur von: *Harmoniesystem in
    dualer Entwickelung*, 1866H
Offenbach, Jacques, 1819A, 1839C, 1849D,
    1861EF, 1880B
Ogawa, Noriko, 1962A, 1982C, 1988E
Ogden, Will, 1921A, 1966D
Ogdon, John, 1937A, 1958C, 1961E, 1962E,
    1989B
Ogihara, Toshitsugu, 1910A, 1992B
Ogiński, Prince Michal Cleofas, 1765A, 1833B
Ogura, Roh, 1916A, 1990B
Ohana, Maurice, 1982E, 1985E
O'Hara, Geoffrey, 1882A, 1967B
O'Hara, Kane, 1782B
Ohlsson, Garrick, 1966E, 1968E, 1970CEF,
    1994E
Ohms, Elisabeth, 1888A, 1921C, 1974B
Oisley, Maurice d', 1882A, 1949B
Oistrakh, David, 1908A, 1927C, 1937E, 1964F,
    1974B
Oistrakh, Igor, 1931A, 1948C, 1952E
OK Mozart Festival, 1985G
Okada, Hiromi, 1985C
Okada, Yoshiko, 1961A, 1991C
Oke, Alan, 1954A
Okeh Records, 1918G
Oki, Masao, 1901A, 1971B
Oklahoma Sinphonia, 1979G
Olah, Tiberiu, 1928A
Olaño, Nemesio, 1880A
Olczewska, Maria, 1892A, 1915C, 1969B
Old American Co., 1767G
Oldberg, Arne, 1874A, 1962B
Oldham, Kevin, 1993B
Oldmixon, Georgina, 1767A, 1783C, 1835B
Oldroyd, George, 1886A, 1951B; *Polyphonic
    Writing for Voices in 6 & 8 Parts*, 1953H; *The
    Technique & Spirit of Fugue*, 1948H
Old time Fiddler's Contest, 1953G
Olefsky, Paul, 1948E
Oleg, Raphael, 1959A, 1986E
Olenin, Alexander, 1944B
Olénine d'Alheim, Marie, 1896C, 1970B
Olevsky, Estela, 1943A
Olevsky, Julian, 1926A, 1936C, 1985B
Oliphant, Thomas, 1799A, 1873B; *Brief Account
    of the Madrigal Society*, 1853H; *La musa
    madrigalesca*, 1837H; *A Short Account of
    Madrigals*, 1836H
Olitzka, Rosa, 1873A, 1891C, 1949B
Olitzka, Walter, 1903A, 1949B
Oliveira, Elmar, 1950A, 1964C, 1974E, 1978E,
    1983E
Oliveira, Jocy de, 1936A

❄

F *Biographical*   G *Cultural Beginnings*   H *Musical Literature*
          I *Musical Compositions*

Oliveiras, Pauline, 1932A
Oliver, Henry Kemble, 1800A, 1883E, 1885B;
   Oliver's Collection of Hymn and Psalm Tunes,
   1860H
Oliver, John, 1939A
Oliver, John, Chorale, 1977G
Oliver, Stephen, 1950A, 1992B
Olivera, Mercedes, 1919A, 1932C
Olivero, Magda, 1912A, 1933C
Olivet Cons. of Music, 1874G
Ollendorff, Fritz, 1912A, 1937C, 1977B
Ollila, Tuomas, 1965A, 1994D
Ollmann, Kurt, 1957A, 1979C
Ollone, Max d', 1897E, 1959B
Olmi, Paoli, 1991D
Olsen, Frode, 1982C
Olsen, Keith, 1957A, 1982C
Olsen, Poul Rovsing, 1922A, 1965E, 1982B
Olsen, Sparre, 1903A, 1936E, 1984B
Olsen, Stanford, 1959A, 1986E,
Olsson, Otto, 1879A, 1908D, 1915E, 1964B
Olsvai, Imre, 1931A
Olt, Harry: *Estonian Music*, 1980H
Oltrabella, Augusta, 1898A, 1901A, 1917C
Omaha: Festival of Contemporary Music,
   1986G; Opera Co., 1957G; Regional Ballet
   Co., 1965G
O'Mara, Joseph, 1861A, 1891C, 1927B
O'Mara Grand Opera Co., 1912G
Omilian, Jolanta, 1956A, 1979C
Oncina, Juan, 1925A, 1946C
Ondes Martinot (patent), 1922G
Ondříček, Emanuel, 1882A, 1958B
Onégin, Sigrid, 1889A, 1911C, 1943B
O'Neill, Dennis, 1948A, 1975C
O'Neill, Norman, 1908D, 1934B
Onslow, Georges, 1784A, 1842E, 1853B
Opalach, Jan, 1950A, 1980E
Opera America, 1970G
Opera Association of New Mexico, 1956G
Opera Ebony, 1976G
Opera Factory, 1982G
Opera for Youth (Sarasota), 1977G
Opéra Francais de New York, L', 1990G
Opera Go Round, 1978G
Opera in English, 1974G
Opera in the Ozarks (Eureka Springs), 1950G
The Opera Journal, 1968G
Opera Midwest, 1979G
Opera/Music Theater Institute, 1987G
Opera News, 1936G
Opera North Co., 1978G
Opera Northern Ireland, 1986G
The Opera Quarterly, 1983G
Opera Rara, 1970G
Opera St. Paul, 1981G
Ophecleide, 1821G
Opieński, Henryk, 1870A, 1908D, 1919D,
   1942B; *La musique polonaise*, 1918H

Oppens, Ursula, 1944A, 1969CE, 1976E
Oppitz, Gerhard, 1953A, 1977E
Opus, 1984G
Opus III Records, 1990G
Opus 7 Vocal Ensemble, 1992G
Oramo, Sakari, 1993D, 1998D
Orange County Performing Arts Center, 1986G
Orbán, György, 1947A
Orbelian, Constantine, 1991DF
Orbón, Julián, 1924A, 1946D, 1991B
Orchard, William, 1867A, 1923D, 1961B; *Music
   in Australia*, 1952H
Orchardson, William, 1907E
Orchesterschule der Sachsischen Staatskapelle,
   1923G
Orchestra of St. Luke's, 1974G
Orchestra of St. John's Smith Square, 1967G
Orchestra of the Scuola Veneziana, 1948G
Orchestra of the Twentieth Century, 1979G
Orchestra Van Wassenaer, 1990G
Orchestral Space Festival, 1966G
Orchestre Classique de Tunis, 1963G
Orchestrion, 1791G
Orchinnikov, Viacheslav, 1936A
Orchinikov, Vladimir, 1959A
Ord, Boris, 1929D, 1958E
Order of the Legion of Honor, 1802G
Ordoñez, Antonio, 1948A, 1982C
Ordonez, Carlos d', 1786B
Ordway Music Theater, 1985G
Ore, Cecile, 1954A
Oregon: Bach Festival, 1970G; Conservatory of
   Music II, 1945G; Repertory Singers, 1974G
Orejon y Aparicio, José, 1760D
Orel, Alfred, 1889A, 1918D, 1967B; *Aufsätze und
   Vorträge*, 1939H; *Kirchenmusikalische Liturgik*,
   1936H; *Musikstadt Wien*, 1953H
Orel, Dobroslav, 1870A, 1909D; *St. Wenceslas
   Elements in Music*, 137H; *A Theoretical and
   Practical Manuel of Roman Plainsong*, 1899H
Orense Conservatory of Music, 1957G
Orfeó Català, 1891G
Orfeo Baroque Orchestra, 1996G
Orff, Carl, 1895A, 1982B; *Musik, Werk, Bild*,
   1960H; *Orff-Schulwerk I*, 1930H
Orford String Quartet, 1965G
The Organ, 1921G
Organ & Piano Teacher's Association, 1966G
Organ Historical Society, 1956G
The Organist and Choirmaster, 1894G
Organist's Quarterly Journal, 1869G
L'Organo, 1960G
Orgel-Archiv, 1844G
Orgeni, Aglaja, 1841A, 1865C, 1926B
Orgitano, Vincenzo, 1787D
Orgonasova, Luba, 1961A
L'orgue et les organistes, 1923G
Original Creole Orchestra, 1912G
O'Riley, Christopher, 1956A, 1981C

❄

A   *Births*   B   *Deaths*   C   *Debuts*   D   *New Positions*
E   *Prizes/Honors*

Orion String Quartet, 1987G
Orkestr (Moscow), 1910G
Orlandini, Giuseppe Maria, 1760B
Orlandi-Malaspina, Rita, 1937A
Orlando di Lasso Choir, 1953G
Orleans, France: Institut Musical, 1834G;
Municipal Music School, 1868G; Société des
Concerts Populaires, 1884G
Orlov, Alexander, 1930D
Orlov, Nikolai, 1892A, 1964B
Ormandy, Eugene, 1899A, 1921F, 1924C,
1931D, 1934F, 1936D, 1944F, 1952E, 1970E,
1973F, 1975E, 1976E, 1979E, 1980F, 1982E,
1984F, 1985B
Ornstein, Leo, 1892A, 1911C, 1975E
Orozco, Rafael, 1946A, 1966E, 1996B
Orphei Dränger (Sweden), 1853G
L'orphéon, 1855G
Orpheonist & Philharmonic Journal, 1864G
Orpheus, 1972G
Orquesta Radio Naciónal (Argentina), 1951G
Orquesta Sinfonica del Estado del Mexico,
1971G
Orr, Buxton, 1997B
Orr, Robin, 1972E, 1977D
Orrego-Salas, Juan, 1919A, 1949D
Orsi, Romeo, 1843A, 1918B
Orstein School of Music, 1940G
Orth, John, 1850A, 1932B
Orth, Peter, 1979E
Orthel, Léon, 1905A, 1985B
Ortigue, Joseph d', 1802A, 1863D, 1866B;
Abécédaire du plain-chant, 1844H; *Le balcon de
l'opéra*, 1833H; *De l'école musicale italienne*,
1839H; *De la guerre des diletanti*, 1829H;
Musique à l'église, 1861H; *Traité théorique et
pratique de l'accompagnement du plain-chant*,
1857H
Ortiz, Cristina, 1950A, 1969E, 1971C
Ortmann, Otto R.: *Psychological Mechanics of
Piano Techniques*, 1929H
Osaka, Japan: International Festival, 1958G;
Music School, 1915G; Philharmonic
Orchestra, 1947G
Osborn-Hannah, Jane, 1873A, 1904C, 1943B
Osborne, Adrienne, 1873A, 1893C, 1951B
Osborne, John, Piano Maker, 1792A, 1815G,
1835B
Osborne, Nigel, 1948A
Osgood, Emma Aline, 1849A, 1911B
Osgood, George Laurie, 1844A, 1922B
Oskarsson, Gudjon, 1965A
Oslo (Christiania), Norway: Artisans' Glee
Society, 1845G; Cecilia Society, 1879G;
Commercial Choral Society, 187G;
Dramatiske Selskab, 178G; Johaniterne,
1875G; Musical Society, 1871G; Musikalske
Lyceum, 1810G; Musikforening, 1871G;
Norwegian Opera Co. (Oslo), 1950G; Opera

Club, 1926G; Organ School, 1883G; National
Theater, 1827G; Philharmonic Orchestra,
1871G. 1919G; Philharmonic Society, 1846G;
String Quartet, 1991G
Osten, Eva von der, 1881A, 1902C, 1936B
Osterc, Slavko, 1941B
Osthoff, Helmuth, 1896A, 1983B
Osthoff, Wolfgang, 1927A
Ostman, Arnold, 1939A, 1980D
Ostrava (Janácek) Philharmonic Orchestra,
1954G
Ostrčil, Otakar, 1879A, 1920D, 1935B
O'Sullivan, Denis, 1868A, 1895C, 1908B
Oswald, James, 1761E, 1769B
Otaka, Hisatada, 1911A, 1942D, 1951B
Otaka, Tadaaki, 1947A, 1974D, 1981D, 1987D,
1991F, 1992D
Otaño, Nemesio, 1907D, 1939D, 1956B; *El canto
popular montañes*, 1915H; *La música religiosa y
la legislación eclesiástica*, 1912H
Otescu, Ion Nonna, 1913E, 1918D, 1927D,
1940B
Otrabella, Augusta, 1981B
Ott, David, 1947A
Ottani, Bernardo, 1765E, 1769D
Ottawa, Canada; Choral Union, 1875G;
National Arts Centre, 1968G
Otte, Hans, 1926A
Otter, Anne Sofie von, 1955A, 1982C
Otterloo, Willem van, 1907A, 1937D, 1949D,
1967D, 1973D, 1974D 1978B
Ottman, Robert, 1914A; *Advanced Harmony,
Theory & Practice*, 1961H; *Basic Ear Training
Skills*, 1991H; *Elementary Harmony, Theory &
Practice*, 1961H; *Programmed Rudiments of
Music*, 1979H; *Rudiments of Music*, 1970H
Otto, Julius, 1804A, 1830D, 1893B
Otto, Lisa, 1919A, 1941C
Otto, Melitta, 1842A, 1860C, 1893B
Ötvos, Gabor, 1934A, 1958D, 1961D, 1967D,
1972D, 1981D
Oudin, Eugène, 1858A, 1886C, 1894B
Oudrid, Cristóbal, 1825A, 1877B
Oue, Eiji, 1956A, 1980E, 1981E, 1991D, 1995D
Oulibicheff, Alexander Dmitrievich, 1794A,
1858B
Oundjian, Peter, 1997D
Oury, Anna Caroline, 1808A, 1880B
Oury, Antonio James, 1800A, 1828C, 1883B
Ouseley, Frederick Gore, 1815A, 1889B; *A
Treatise on Counterpoint, Canon and Fugue,
Based on Cherubini*, 1869H; *A Treatise on
Musical Form and General Composition*, 1875H;
Treatise on Harmony, 1868H
Ousset, Cécile, 1936A
*Ovation: The Magazine for Classical Music
Listeners*, 1980G
Ovchinikov, Vladimir, 1987C
Overlook Lyric Theatre, 1992G

F   *Biographical*   G   *Cultural Beginnings*   H   *Musical Literature*
I   *Musical Compositions*

Overton, Hall, 1920A, 1964E, 1972B
Ovorin, Lev, 1907A
Owen, Barbara: *The Organ in New England*,
  1979H
Owen, Harold: *Modal & Tonal Counterpoint:*
  From Josquin to Stravinsky, 1992H
Owen, Morfydd, Llywn, 1891B
Owen, Richard, 1922A
Owings, John, 1943A, 1968E
Oxford University: Bach Choir, 1896G; Choral
  Society, 1819G; Holywell Hall, 1848G;
  Musical Club, 1872G; Musical Union, 1884G;
  Philharmonia Society, 1865G
Oxford Orchestra Society, 1902G
Oxford Schola Cantorum, 1960G
Oxinaga, Joaquin de, 1789B
Ozark Folk Festival, 1947G
Ozawa, Seiji, 1935A, 1959E, 1960E, 1961F,
  1965D, 1970D, 1971E, 1973D, 1979F, 1998E
Ozawa, Seiji, Hall (Tanglewood), 1994G
Ozi, Étienne, 1754A, 1813B; *Nouvelle méthode de*
  basson, 1803H
Ozim, Igor, 1931A, 1950E, 1953E
Paap, Wouter, 1908A, 1981B
Pablo, Luís de, 1930A
Pabst, Louis, 1846A, 1862C, 1903B
Pabst, Michael, 1955A, 1978C
Paccagnini, Angelo, 1930A, 1968D
Pacchiarotti, Gasparo, 1821B
Pace Jubilee Singers, 1925G
Pace-Handy Co., Publishers, 1908G
Pacetti, Iva, 1898A, 1920C, 1981B
Pachelbel, Wilhelm Kieronymus, 1764B
Pachler-Koschak, Marie Leopoldine, 1792A,
  1855B
Pachmann, Vladimir de, 1848A, 1869C, 1885E,
  1933B
Pacific Chamber Orchestra, 1985G
Pacific Coast Musician, 1911G
Pacific Contemporary Music Center, 1987G
Pacific Music Festival, 1990G
Pacific Northwest Wagner Festival, 1975G
Pacific World Artists, 1968G
Pacifica Quartet, 1998E
Pacini, Antonio Francesco, 1778A
Pacini, Antonio, Publisher (Paris), 1806G
Pacini, Giovanni, 1796A, 1867B; *Cenni storici*
  sulla musical e trattado di contrappunto, 1864H;
  Corso teorico-pratico de lezioni di armonia,
  1844H; *Memoria sul migliore indirizzo degli*
  studii musicali, 1863H
Pacini, Regina, 1871A, 1888C, 1965B
Paciorek, Grazyna, 1967A
Paciorkiewicz, Tadeusz, 1916A
Pacius, Fredrik, 1809A, 1891B
Packard Piano & Organ Co., 1871G
Pade, Steen, 1989D
Paderewski, Ignace Jan, 1860A, 1878D, 1881F,
  1888C, 1909D, 1912E, 1917E, 1922EF, 1941B,
  1992F

Paderewski, Ignace Jan, Foundation, 1896G
Padilla, Anna Maria, 1978A
Padilla, José, 1889A
Padilla, Lola Artôt de, 1876A, 1904C
Padlewski, Roman, 1915A, 1944B
Padua, Italy: I Solisti Veneti, 1959G; Istituto
  Mujsicale, 1878G; Teatro Nuovo, 1751G
Paër, Ferdinando, 1771A, 1801F, 1802D, 1805F,
  1807D, 1809F, 1812D, 1827F, 1828EF, 1831EF,
  1832DF, 1833F, 1834F, 1838F, 1839B
Paganelli, Giuiseppe, 1763B
Paganini, Niccolò, 1782A, 1794C, 1805D,
  1827E, 1840B
Paganini String Quartet, 1946G
Page, Charlotte, 1972A
Page, Christopher: *Voices & Instruments of the*
  Middle Ages, 1987H
Page, John, 1760A, 1812B; *Festive Harmony*,
  1804H; *Harmonia Sacra*, 1800H
Page, Robert, 1927A, 1975D
Page, Robert, Singers, 1982G
Page, Tim, 1997E; *Music from the Road: Views &*
  Reviews 1978-1992, 1992H
Pagliughi, Lina, 1907A, 1927C, 1980B
Pahissa, Jaime, 1880A, 1969B; *Espiritu cuerpo de*
  la música, 1945H; *Los grandes problemas de la*
  música, 1945H; *Sendas y cumbres de la música*
  española, 1955H
Paige, Norman, 1935A
Paik, Byung-Dong, 1936A
Paik, Kun-Woo, 1946A, 1954C, 1969E, 1971E
Paik, Nam June, 1932A
Paillard, Jean-François, 1928A; *La musique*
  française classique, 1960H
Paillard Chamber Orchestra, 1953G
Paine, John Knowles, 1839A, 1858F, 1862D,
  1869E, 1873F, 1875D, 1890E, 1906B
Paine, Thomas D., 1813A, 1895B
Paisible, Louis-Henri, 1782B
Paisiello, Giovanni, 1754F, 1759F, 1776F, 1784D,
  1802D, 1806E, 1816B
Paita, Carlos, 1932A
Pakhumutova, Alexandra, 1929A
Palace Theater (N.Y.), 1913G
Paladilhe, Emile, 1844A, 1860E, 1892E, 1897E,
  1926B
Palange, Louis, 1917A, 1979B
Palau Boix, Manuel, 1967B
Palazzesi, Matilde, 1824C
Palella, Antonio, 1761B
Páleníček, Josef, 1914A, 1991B
Paléographic Musicale, 1890G
Palermo, Sicily: Palermo Opera, 1897G; Teatro
  Massimo, 1897G
Palester, Roman, 1907A, 1989B
Palestine Conservatory of Music & Dramatic
  Art, 1933G
Palestrina Society, 1879G
Paley, Alexander, 1956A, 1969C
Paling, Willem, Piano Co., 1855G

※

A   *Births*   B   *Deaths*   C   *Debuts*   D   *New Positions*
E   *Prizes/Honors*

Palisca, Claude, 1921A, 1972D, 1986E; *Baroque Music*, 1968H; *Humanism in Italian Renaissance Musical Thought*, 1985H; *Music in Our Schools: A Search for Improvement*, 1964H; *Studies in the History of Italian Music & Music Theory*, 1994H
Palishvili, Zakhary Petrovich, 1871A
Palkovsk, Oldřich, 1907A
Palkovsk, Pavel, 1939A
Pallandios, Menelaos, 1914A, 1962D, 1969E
Pallemaerts, Korbay Edmundo, 1894D
Pallo, Imre, 1941A
Palm, Siegfried, 1927A
Palm Beach, Florida: Chamber Music Festival, 1992G
Palma, Athos, 1891A, 1951B; *Tratado completo de armonia*, 1941H
Palma, Sandro de, 1957A, 1976E
Palma, Silvestre (De), 1754A, 1834B
Palmer, Bessie, 1831A, 1854C, 1910B
Palmer, Felicity, 19441, 1970CE
Palmer, Horatio R, 1834A, 1888D, 1907B
Palmer, Larry, 1938A; *Harpsichord in America: A Twentieth Century Revival*, 1989H
Palmer, Michel, 1988D
Palmer, Robert, 1915A, 1946E
Palmer, Rudolph, 1952A
Palmer, Thomas, 1994B
Palmerini, Luigi, 1817D, 1838D
Palmgren, Selim, 1878A, 1950E, 1951B
Palombi, Antonello, 1990C
Palombo, Paul, 1937A
Palotta, Matteo, 1758B
Palschau, Johann Gottfried, 1813B
Pampani, Antonio Gaetano, 1767D
Pampanini, Rosetta, 1896A, 1920C, 1973B
Pan American Association of Composers, 1928G
Pan-American Union, Music Division, 1941G
Panagulias, Ann, 1989C
Pandolfini, Angelica, 1871A, 1894C, 1959B
Pandolfini, Francesco, 1836A, 1859C, 1916B
Panenka, Jan, 1944C, 1951E
Panerai, Rolando, 1924A, 1947C
Panhofer, Wolfgang, 1965A
Panizza, Ettore, 1875A, 1967B
Pann, Carter, 1972A
Pannain, Guido, 1891A, 1977B: *L'opera e le opere ed altri scritti di letteratura musicale*, 1958H; *Le origini della scuola musicale napoletano*, 1914H; *Ottocento musicale italiano: Saggi e note*, 1952H; *La vita del linguaggio musicale*, 1947H
Panni, Marcello, 1940A
Panofka, Heinrich, 1807A, 1827C, 1887B; *L'art de chanter*, 1854H
Panseron, Auguste-Mathieu, 1813E; *Traité de l'harmonie*, 1855H
Pantaleoni, Romilda, 1847A, 1868C, 1917B
Pantin Conservatory, 1972G
Pantinga, Leon: *Romantic Music*, 1983H

Panufnik, Andrzej, 1914A, 1944F, 1947E, 1957D, 1977F, 1991BE
Panufnik, Roxanne, 1968A
Panula, Jorma, 1930A, 1963D, 1965D, 1972D, 1986D
Panzarella, Anna Maria, 1970A
Panzéra, Charles, 1896A,1919C, 1976B; *L'art de chanter*, 1945H; *L'art vocal*, 1959H; *Votre voix: Directives générales*, 1967H
Paoli, Antonio, 1870A, 1946B
Paolis, Alessio de, 1898A, 1919C, 1964B
Paolucci, Giuseppe, 1756D, 1770D, 1776B; *Arte pratica de contrappunto*, 1772H
Pap, Janos, 1957A; *Fundamentals of Musical Acoustics*, 1992H
Papadakos, Dorothy, 1990D
Papadopoulos, Marios, 1973C
Papaioannou, Yannis, 1911A, 1989B
Papandopulo, Boris, 1906A, 1953D, 1959D, 1991B
Papavoine, 1793B
Pape, Gerard (Joseph), 1955A
Pape, Jean H., Piano Maker, 1815G
Pape, René, 1964A
Papenheim, Eugenie, 1924B
Papi, Gennaro, 1886A, 1916D, 1925D, 1941B
Papineau-Couture, Jean, 1916A, 1968D, 2000B
Papini, Guido, 1847A, 1860C, 1912B
Pappano, Antonio, 1992D
Pappenheim, Eugenie, 1849A, 1866C
Paradies, Domencio, 1791B
Paradis, Marie Theresia von, 1759A, 1775C, 1824B
Paranov, Moshe, 1895A, 1920C, 1938D, 1947D, 1994B
Paratore, Anthony, 1944A, 1973C
Paratore, Joseph, 1973C
Paray, Paul, 1886A, 1911E, 1920C, 1923D, 1928D, 1932D, 1944D, 1952D, 1979B
Parent String Quartet, 1892G
Parepa-Rosa, Euphrosyne, 1836A, 1855C, 1874B
Parepa-Rosa English Opera Co., 1869G
Pareto, Graziella, 1906C, 1973B
Paribeni, Giulio: *Storia e teoria della antica musica greco*, 1911H
Parik, Ivan, 1936A, 1992D
Parikian, Manoug, 1920A, 1947C
Pâris, Alain, 1947A, 1983D; *Les livrets d'opéra*, 1991H
Paris, France: Académie de Chant, 1842G; Association Artistique des...Châtelet, 1874G; Bureau de Musique, 1966G; Capet String Quartet II, 1903G; Capet String Quartet III, 1910G; Colonne Concerts, 1873G; Concerts de la Loge Olympique, 1769G; Concerts des Amateurs, 1769G; Concerts Ignace Pleyel, 1919G; Concerts Lamoureux, 1881G; Concerts Populaire de Musique Classique, 1861G; Concerts Valentino, 1837G; Confrère

---

❄

Paris, France: (cont.)
Liturgique, 1912G; Conservatoire Populaire
Mimi Pinson, 1902G; Conservatoire
Secondaire, 1810G; Conservatory of Music,
1795G; Duprez Vocal School, 1850G; École
l'Arcuiel, 1923G; École Monteux, 1932G;
École Normale de Musique, 1919G; École
Royale du Chant, 1784G; École Spéciale de
Chant, 1853G; Ensemble à Vent, 1980G;
Ensemble Baroque de Paris, 1953G;
Ensemble Moderne de Paris, 1963G; Festival
Estival de Paris, 1965G; Festival of 20th
Century Music, 1952G; French Conservatory
of Music, 1789g, 1887G; Institut Grégorien,
1924G; Institut National de Musique, 1793G;
Institution royale de musique classique,
1817G; Opera House, 1875G; L'Oiseau-Lyre,
1932G; Orchestre de Chambre Hewitt,
1939G; Orchestre de Paris, 1966G; Orphéon,
1833G; Palais Garnier, 1875G; Pastou Singing
School, 1819G; Philharmonic Orchestra,
1988G; Prix Chartier, 1861G; Schola
Cantorum, 1894G; Société Alard-
Franchomme, 1848G; Société Bourgault-
Ducoudray, 1868G; Société des
Compositeurs, 1863G; Société de l'Harmonie
Sacrée, 1873G; Société de Musique de
Chambre, 1835G; Société de Musique de
Chambre de la Société des Concerts du
Conservatoire de Paris, 1943G; Société de
Musique, Vocale, 1843G; Société des
Concerts de Chant Classique, 1860G; Société
des Concerts du Conservatoire, 1828G;
Société des Jeunes Artistes du Conservatoire,
1851G; Société des Oratorios, 1868G; Société
des Quintettes, Instruments à Vent, 1879G;
Société moderne d'instruments à vent,
1895G; Société musicale indépendante,
1090G; Société Nationale de Musique,
1870G; Société Ste. Cécile, 1849G; Symphony
Orchestra, 1929G, 1935G; Théâtre Antoine,
1897G; Théâtre des Champs-Elysées, 1913G;
Théâtre Libre, 1887G; Théâtre Français de la
Rue Richelieu, 1791G; Théâtre de la Porte-
St.-Martin, 1807G; Théâtre de Monsieur,
1789G; Théâtre des Arts, 1890G; Théâtre des
Jeunes-Artistes, 1798G; Théâtre-Lyrique,
1851G; Le Triton, 1932G
Park, Maria Hester, 1775A, 1822B
Parke, William Thomas, 1762A, 1847B
Parkening, Christopher, 1947A, 1959C, 1975F;
Guitar Method, 1973H
Parker, Henry Taylor, 1867A, 1934B; Eighth-
Notes, 1922H
Parker, Horatio, 1862A, 1881F, 1888D, 1893F,
1894D, 1902E, 1903D, 1904D, 1905E, 1911E,
1919B
Parker, Horatio, Choir (New Haven), 1920G
Parker, Jamie, 1963A, 1981C

Parker, J. C. D., 1828A, 1864D, 1916B; Manual of
Harmony, 1855H; Theoretical and Practical
Harmony, 1870H
Parker, Jon Kimura, 1959A, 1984CE
Parker, Louise, 1986B
Parker, Moises, 1976C
Parker, Roger, 1951A
Parker, William, 1943A, 1993B
Parker, William Frye, 1855A, 1871C, 1919B
Parkhurst, Howard E.: The Church Organist,
1913H
Parkman, Francis, 1915E
Parlow, Kathleen, 1890A, 1905C, 1963B
Parlow String Quartet, 1941G
Parma, Italy: Institute of Verdi Studies, 1959G;
Regia Scuola de Canto, 1769G; Scuola Canto
Corale, 1815G
Parmeggiani, Ettore, 1922C, 1960B
Parnas, Leslie, 1931A, 1957E
Parratt, Walter, 1841A, 1892E, 1893E, 1894E,
1908D, 1910E, 1912E, 1924B
Parratt, Willaim, 1872D, 1882D
Parrenin String Quartet, 1942G
Parris, Robert, 1924A
Parrish, Carl, 1904A, 1965B; Masterpieces of
Music before 1750, 1951H; The Notation of
Medieval Music, 1958H; A Treasury of Early
Music, 1958H
Parrish, Cheryl, 1954A, 1983C
Parrish, Lillian: Slave Songs of the Georgia Slave
Islands, 1942H
Parrott, Andrew, 1947A, 1989D
Parrott, Ian, 1916A; A Guide to Musical Thought,
1955H; Method in Orchestration, 1957H;
Pathways to Modern Music, 1947H
Parry, Charles Hubert, 1848A, 1874F, 1883E,
1884E, 1891EF, 1898E, 1894D,1903E, 1918B;
The Art of Music, 1893H; The Music of the
Seventeenth Century, 1902H; Studies of the
Great Composers, 1886H; Style in Musical Art,
1911H; Summary of the History & Development
of Mediaeval & Modern European Music,
1893H
Parry, John (I), 1782B; Cambrian Harmony: A
Collection of Ancient Welsh Airs, 1781H;
Collection of Welsh, English & Scotch Airs,
1761H
Parry, John (II), 1776A, 1851B
Parsadanian, Boris, 1925A
Parsch, Arnot, 1936A
Parsons, William, 1786E
Partch, Harry, 1901A, 1974B; Genesis of a New
Music, 1949H
Partos, Ödön, 1907A, 1951D, 1977B
Partridge, Ian, 1938A, 1958C, 1991E
Pas, Juan Carlos, 1972B
Pasatieri, Thomas, 1945A
Pascal Boyle Publishing Co, 1785G
Pasch, Oskar, 1874E

❋

A   Births   B   Deaths   C   Debuts   D   New Positions

E   Prizes/Honors

Pasdeloup, Jules-Étienne, 1819A, 1868D, 1887B
Pasero, Tancredi, 1893A, 1917C, 1983B
Pashchenko, Andrei, 1972B
Pashkevich, Vasily, 1797B
Pasini, Camille, 1935B
Pasini, Lina, 1872A, 1893C, 1959B
Pasini, Laura, 1894A, 1912C
Pasino, Gisella, 1987C
Paskalis, Kostas, 1929A, 1951C
Pasquali, Niccolò, 1757B; *The Art of Fingering
    the Harpsichord*, 1758H; *Thorough-Bass Made
    Easy*, 1757H
Pasqué, Ernst, 1821A, 1844C, 1892B
Pasquet, Nicolas, 1958A, 1987E, 1993D
Pasta, Giuditta, 1797A, 1815C, 1865B
Pasterwitz, Georg von, 1803B
Pastillie, William, 1954A
Pastou, Etienne: *École de la lyre harmonique*,
    1822H
Pásztory, Ditta, 1903A, 1981B
Patachich, Iván, 1922A
Pataky, Kálmán, 1896A, 1922C, 1964B
Patané, Giuseppe, 1932A, 1961D, 1962D,
    1987D, 1988D, 1989B
Paterno, Anton, Publisher, 1813G
Paterson and Sons, Publishers, 1819G
Paterson String Quartet, 1979G
Patey, Janet, 1842A, 1860C, 1894B
Patey, John, 1835A, 1858C, 1901B
Paton, Mary Ann, 1802A, 1822C, 1864B
Patorzhinsky, Ivan, 1896A, 1960B
Patriarco, Earle, 1994E
Patterson, Franklin Peale, 1871A, 1966B
Patterson, Paul, 1947A
Patterson, Russell, 1982E
Patterson, Susan, 1987E
Patterson's Church Music, 1813G
Patti, Adelina, 1843A, 1859C, 1919B
Patti, Carlotta, 1835A, 1861C, 1889B
Pattiera, Tino, 1890A, 1915C, 1966B
Pattison, John Nelson, 1845A, 1905B
Pattison, Lee, 1890A, 1913C, 1965B
Pattison-Maier, Two-Piano Team, 1916G
Patzak, Julius, 1898A, 1923C, 1974B
Pauer, Ernst, 1826A, 1851CF; *The Art of
    Pianoforte Playing*, 1877H; *The Birthday Book
    of Musicians and Composers*, 1881H; *A
    Dictionary of Pianists and Composers for the
    Pianoforte*, 1895H; *Elements of the Beautiful in
    Music*, 1877H; *Musical Forms*, 1878H
Pauer, Jiří, 1919A, 1958D, 1961E
Pauer, Ernst, 1905B
Pauer, Max von, 1866A, 1908D, 1924D, 1933D,
    1945B
Pauk, György, 1936A
Paul, Oscar, 1836A, 1898B; *Geschichte des
    Klaviers*, 1868H; *Handlexicon der Tonkunst*,
    1873H; *Musikalische Instrumente*, 1874H
Paul, Thomas, 1934A, 1961C

Paulin, Frédéric-Hubert, 1761B
Paull, Barberi, 1946A
Paulli, Holger Simon, 1810A, 1863D, 1891B
Paulson, Gustaf, 1966B
Paulus, Stephen, 1949A
Pauly, Reinhard: *Music in the Classical Period*,
    1965H
Pauly, Rosa, 1894A, 1918C, 1975B
Paumgartner, Bernhard, 1887A, 1917D, 1971B
Paur, Emil, 1855A, 1880D, 1893D, 1898D,
    1899D, 1904D, 1932B
Pauwels, Jean-Englebert, 1768A, 1804B
Pavarotti, Luciano, 1935A, 1961C, 1989F
Pavarotti International Voice Competition,
    1980G
Pavasi, Stefano, 1779A, 1818D, 1850B
Pavlovski, Anton, 1999B
Payer, Hieronymus, 1787A, 1845B
Payne, Anthony, 1965D, 1987D
Payne, Patricia, 1942A, 1974C
Paynter, John, 1996B; *Sound & Structure*, 1992H
Pazovsky, Ariy, 1953B
PBS Choral Society (Palestine), 1938G
Peabody, George, 1795A, 1869B
Peace, Albert, 1879D
Peacock, Lucy, 1947A, 1959C
Pearce, Alison, 1953A
Pearlman, Martin, 1945A
Pears, Peter, 1910A, 1942C, 1957E, 1978E,
    1986B
Pearsall, Robert Lucas, 1795A, 1856B
Pearson Electronic Sound Studio, 1969G
Pease, Alfred H., 1838A, 1864C, 1882B
Pease, James, 1916A, 1941C, 1967B
Pechaczek, Franz X., Jr., 1802C
Pechner, Gerhard, 1903A, 1927C, 1969B
Peckova, Dagmar, 1961A, 1987C
Pécs Symphony Orchestra, 1984G
Pederson, Monte, 1986C
Pederzini, Gianna, 1903A, 1923C, 1988B
Pedreira Music Academy, 1931G
Pedrell, Carlos, 1941B
Pedrell, Felipe, 1841A, 1894E, 1922B; *Diccinario
    téchnico de la música...espagñoles, portugueses y
    hispano-americanos antiquos y modernas*,
    1897H; *Documents pour servir â histoire de
    thêâtre musical*, 1906H; *Emporio cientifico e
    histórico de organograpia musicale española
    antigua*, 1901H; *Gramática musical...de la
    Teoria del solfee, en forma de dialogo*, 1872H;
    Jornadas de arte, 1911H; *Musicalerias*, 1906H;
    Músicos contemporáneos ye de otros tiempos,
    1910H; *Por nuestra música*, 1891H; *Práeticas
    preparatorias de instrumentación*, 1902H
Pedrollo, Arrigo, 1920D, 1942D
Pedrotti, Carlo, 1817A, 1841D, 1868D, 1882D,
    1893B
Peel, Ruth, 1966A
Peer-Southern Music Publishers, 1928G

❄

F *Biographical*   G *Cultural Beginnings*   H *Musical Literature*
I *Musical Compositions*

Peerce, Jan, 1904A, 1938C, 1971F, 1984B
Peeters, Flor, 1903A, 1952D, 1986B; *Ars Organi I*, 1953H
Peiko, Nicolai Ivanovich, 1916A
Peinbaur, Joseph, Sr., 1923B
Peineman, Edith, 1937A, 1956C
Peixe, César Guerra, 1914A, 1993B
Peixinho, Jorge, 1940A
Pekinel, Süher, 1951A
Pelemans, Willem, 1901A, 1991B
Pelinka, Werner, 1952A
Pélissier, Olympe, 1837F, 1846F
Pelissier Victor: *Columbian Melodies*, 1811H
Pellegrin, Claude Mathieu, 1763B
Pellegrini, Ferdinando, 1766B
Pellegrino, Ron: *The Electronic Arts of Sound & Light*, 1983H
Pelletier, Wilfrid, 1896A, 1934D, 1937E, 1942D, 1951D, 1982B
Pembaur, Joseph, Sr., 1874D
Pendachanska, Alexandrina, 1970A, 1987C
Penderecki, Krzysztof, 1933A, 1951F, 1953F, 1968E, 1972DE, 1983E, 1998E
Penenka, Jan, 1922A
Penherski, Zbigniew, 1935A
Peninsula Music Festival (Wisconsin), 1953G
Pennarini, Aloys, 1870A, 1893C, 1927B
Pennario, Leonard, 1924A, 1936C
Penson, Robertson & Co., (Scotland), 1807G
Pennsylvania Grand Opera Co., 1927G
Penny, Andrew, 1952A, 1979D, 1982D
Pensacola Chamber Music Festival, 1985G
Pentaton (Hungary), 1990G
Pente, Emilio, 1860A, 1895C, 1929B
Pentemuan Musik Surabaya (Indonesia), 1957G
Pentland, Barbara, 1912A
People to People Music Committee, 1968G
People's Chorus of New York, 1916G
Peoria Civic Center Theater (Ill.), 1982G
Pépin, Clermont, 1926A, 1949E, 1967C
Pepper, J. W., Publisher, 1876G
Pepper's Musical Times & Band Journal, J. W.'s, 1877G
Pepping, Ernst, 1956E
Pepusch, John Christopher, 1752B
Perabo, Ernst, 1845A, 1865C, 1920B
Peragallo, Mario, 1910A
Perahia, Murray, 1947A, 1968C, 1972E, 1973E
Peralta, Angela, 1845A, 1860C, 1883B
Peralta, Frances, 1933B
Percussive Arts Society, 1960G
Pereira-Salas, Eugenio, 1979B; *Art & Music in Contemporary Latin America*, 1968H
Perera, Ronald, 1941A; *Development & Practice of Electronic Music*, 1975H
Peress, Maurice, 1930A, 1970D, 1974D
Perez, David, 1752D, 1778B
Pérez-Casas, Bartolomeo, 1915D, 1956B

Performing Rights Society of Great Britain, 1914G
Pergament, Moses, 1893A, 1977B
Pergolesi Musical Institute (Ancona), 1920G
Peri, Achille, 1812A, 1880B
Perick, Christof, 1946A, 1977D, 1991D, 1992D
Périer, Jean Alexis, 1869A, 1892C, 1954B
Perikian, Manoug, 1987B
Perkins, John MacIver, 1935A, 1970D
Perkins, Walton, 1847A, 1907D, 1929B
Perkowski, Piotr, 1901A, 1990B
Perl, Alfredo, 1965A
Perle, George, 1915A, 1978E, 1985E, 1986E; *The Listening Composer*, 1990H; *Serial Composition & Atonality*, 1962H; *Twelve-Tone Tonality*, 1977H
Perlea, Jonel, 1900A, 1919C, 1929D, 1934D, 1936D, 1955D, 1970B
Perlman, Itzhak, 1945A, 1964E, 1986E
Perlongo, Daniel, 1942A, 1970E
Perne, François Louis, 1772A, 1819D, 1832B; *Cours d'harmonie et d'accompagnement*, 1822H
Pernerstorfer, Alois, 1912A, 1936C, 1978B
Pernet, André, 1894A, 1921C, 1941E, 1966B
Perosi, Don Lorenzo, 1894D, 1898D
Perotti, Giovanni Agostino, 1769A, 1817D, 1855B
Perotti, Giovanni Domenico, 1761A, 1825B
Perpetuum Mobile, 1983G
Perrachio, Luigi, 1883A
Perras, Margherita, 1908A, 1927C, 1984B
Pérrier, Jean, 1954A
Perrin, Jean, 1920A, 1989B
Perron, Karl, 1858A, 1884C, 1928B
Perry, Edward Baxter, 1855A, 1924B
Perry, Elisabeth, 1955A, 1978C
Perry, Eugene, 1955A, 1986C
Perry, George Frederick, 1793A, 1822D, 1862B
Perry, Janet, 1944A, 1969C
Perry, John, 1834D
Perry, Julia, 1924A, 1979B
Perry's Musical Magazine, 1881G
Persiani, Fanny, 1812A, 1832C, 1867B
Persiani, Giuseppe, 1799A, 1869B
Persichetti, Vincent, 1915A, 1948E, 1963D, 1965E, 1975E, 1987B; *Twentieth Century Harmony: Creative Aspects & Practice*, 1961H; *Twentieth Century Orchestral Music*, 1970H
Persinger, Louis, 1887A, 1897C, 1916D, 1965B
Perspectives of New Music, 1962G
Persuis, Louis Loiseau de, 1769A, 1819B
Perth, Australia: Fremantle Orchestra Society, 1887G
Perti, Giacomo Antonio, 1756B
Perticaroli, Sergio, 1952E
Pertile, Aureliano, 1885A, 1911C, 1952B
Pertusi, Michele, 1965A, 1984C

❄

A   *Births*   B   *Deaths*   C   *Debuts*   D   *New Positions*
E   *Prizes/Honors*

Perugia, Italy: Musical Institute, 1790G; Nuovo Teatro Civico del Verzaro, 1781G; Teatro della Nobile Academia del Casino, 1773G

Pesaro, Italy: Centre de Studi Rossiniani, 1940G; Liceo Musicale, 1882G; Teatro Nuovo, 1818G

Pescetti, Giovanni Battista, 1762D, 1766B

Peschka-Leutner, Minna, 1839A, 1856C, 1890B

Peek, Libor, 1987D, 1996E

Pessard, Emile-Louis, 1843A, 1866E, 1917B

Pest Philharmonic Society, 1853G, 1867G

Peter, Johann Friedrich, 1789F, 1813B

Peter, Simon, 1819B

Peter's Sax-Horn Journal, 1859G

Peter's Music Library, 1894G

Peters & Co. (Peters, Field & Co.), 1846G

Peters, Carl Friedrich, 1779A, 1827B

Peters, C. F., Publisher (Leipzig), 1814G

Peters, C. F., Corporation (New York), 1948G

Peters, John L., & Brother, Publishers, 1851G

Peters, Roberta, 1930A, 1950C, 1993E, 1998G

Peters, W. C., & Sons, Publishers, 1851G

Petersen, Dennis, 1954A

Petersen, Peter Nikolaus, 1761A, 1830B

Peterson, Claudette, 1953A, 1975C

Peterson, John Murray, 1957A

Peterson, Wayne, 1927A

Peterson-Berger, Wilhelm, 1867A, 1942B; *Svensk musikkultur*, 1911H

Petracchi, Francesco, 1937A

Petrassi, Goffredo, 1904A; *Taccuino di musica*, 1944H

Petrella, Clara, 1918A, 1939C, 1987B

Petrella, Errico, 1813A, 1877B

Petri, Egon, 1881A, 1902C, 1962B

Petri, Johann S.: *Anleitung zur praktischen Music*, 1767H

Petri, Michala, 1958A, 1969C

Petrić, Ivo, 1931A, 1977E, 1979D

Petridis, Petros, 1892A, 1959E, 1978B

Petrini, Francesco: *Nouveau Système de l'harmonie en 66 accords*, 1793H

Petronas Hall (Kuala Lumpur), 1998G

Petrov, Ivan, 1920A

Petrov, Nikolai, 1943A

Petrov, Osip, 1807A, 1826C, 1878B

Petrov, Petar, 1961A

Petrucci, Brizio, 1784D, 1828B

Petrutshenko, Natalia, 1963A

Pettersson, Allan, 1911A, 1980B

Petukhov, Mikhail, 1954A

Petyrek, Felix, 1951B

Pexinho, Jorge, 1995B

Peyser, Ethel: *How Opera Grew*, 1956H; *How to Enjoy Music*, 1933H; *Music Through the Ages*, 1932H

Peyser, Joan, 1931A, 1977D; *Music of My Time*, 1995H; *The New Music*, 1971H; *The Orchestra: Origins & Transformations*, 1986H

Pfeffinger, Philippe Jacques, 1790D

Pfeiffer, Theodore, 1853A, 1929B

Pfister, Hugo, 1914A, 1969B

Pfitzner, Hans, 1869A, 1907D, 1910D, 1949B

Pflüger, Hans Georg, 1999B

Pfordten Hermann von der: *Musikalische Essays I*, 1897H

Pflughaupt, Robert, 1833A, 1871B

Phaleron Conservatory of Music, 1934G

Phelps, Ellsworth C., 1827A, 1913B

Phi Beta Mu, 1912G, 1937G

Phi Mu Gamma Sorority, 1898G

Philadelphia, Pennsylvania: Academy of Vocal Arts, 1935G; Adgate Free School, 1785G; American Academy of Music, 1857G; American Conservatorio, 1822G; Bach Choir- 1934G; Bremner School of Music, 1763G; Chamber Music Association, 1917G; Chamber String Sinfonietta, 1925G; Chestnut Street Theater, 1794G; Chamber Symphony, 1966G; Chestnut Street Opera House, 1885G; Choral Arts Society, 1982G; Choral Society, 1897G; Civic Opera Co., 1924G; Combs Conservatory, 1885G; Composers Concerts, 1769G; Concert Soloists, 1965G; Conservatory of Music, 1877G; Eurydice Chorus, 1886G; Folk Festival, 1962G; Germania Orchestra, 1856G; Grand Opera House, 1888G; Harmonie, 1855G; Hinrichs Opera Co., 1888G; Little Symphony, 1909G; Logan, James, Library, 1751G; Männerchor, 1835G; Manuscript Music Society, 1892G; Mendelssohn Glee Club, 1874G; Musical Academy, 1870G; Musical Association, 1863G; Musical Fund Society, 1820G; Opera House, 1908G; Orchestra, 1999F; Palestrina Choir, 1915G; Pennsylvania Academy of Fine Arts, 1805G; Pennsylvania Opera Co., 1976G; Philadelphia Orchestra, 1900G; Philharmonic Society, 1837G; Presser Foundation, 1916G; Public Concerts, 1757G; Singers, 1971G; Singing City, 1947G; Southwark Theater, 1766G; Sternberg School of Music, 1890G; String Quartet, 1959G; Subscription Concerts, 1764G; Symphony Club, 1909G; Theater Opera House, 1793G; Treble Clef Club, 1884G; Uranian Society, 1784G; Virtuosi, 1991G; Woodwind Quintet, 1950G

Philharmonia Baroque Orchestra of the West, 1982G

Philharmonia Chorale, 1970G

Philharmonia Hungarica, 1957G

Philharmonia String Quartet, 1941G

Philidor, François-André, 1795B

Philipp, Isidore, 1863A, 1958B

Philippi, Maria, 1875A, 1901C, 1944B

Philippines: Conservatory of Music, 1916G; Cultural Center, 1969G; Music Promotion

F *Biographical*   G *Cultural Beginnings*   H *Musical Literature*

I *Musical Compositions*

Philippines: (cont.)
Foundation, 1956G; Opera Company of the Philippines, 1982G
Philips, Nathaniel, Publishers, 1839G
Phillipps, Adelaide, 1833A, 1853C, 1882B
Phillips, Burrill, 1907A, 1944E, 1988B
Phillips, Harvey, 1929A
Phillips, Henry, 1801A, 1824C, 1876B; Hints on Declamation, 1848H; Musical and Personal Recollections during Half a Century, 1864H
Phillips, Henry Gene, 1829A, 1876B
Phillips, John, 1960A
Phillips, Liz, 1951A
Phillips, Philip, Publishers, 1863G
Phillips, Xavier, 1971A, 1991E
Philogene, Ruby, 1993E
Phöbus, (Dresden), 1808G
Phoenix, Arizona: Arizona Opera Co., 1971G; Bach & Madrigal Society, 1958G; Boys Choir, 1949G; Lyric Opera Theater, 1963G; Opera Co., 1965G; Orpheus Male Choir, 1929G; Symphony Hall, 1972G; Symphony Orchestra, 1947G
Phonograph Monthly Review (American Record Guide), 1926G
Piacenza, Italy: Scuola Musicale, 1839G; Teatro Municipale, 1804G; Università de' Filarmonici, 1781G
Piano Repetitive Action, 1809G
Pianists Foundation of America, 1977G
Piano Technicians' Guild, 1958G
Il pianoforte, 1920G
The Pianoforte Magazine (London), 1797G
Piastro, Mishel, 1891A, 1941D, 1970B
Piatigorsky, Gregor, 1903A, 1928F, 1976B
Piatti, Alfredo, 1822A, 1837C, 1901B
Piau, Sandrine, 1969A
Piazzolla, Astor, 1992B
Piccaluga, Nino, 1893A, 1918C
Piccaver, Alfred, 1884A, 1907C, 1958B
Piccinni, Louis Alexandre, 1779A, 1850B
Piccinni, Luigi, 1764A, 1827B
Piccinni, Niccolò, 1776F, 1794F, 1798F, 1800B
Piccola Opera Co. (Detroit), 1961G
Piccola Accademi a Musicale, 1952G
Piccolomini, Marietta (Maria), 1834A, 1852C, 1899B
Pichl, Václav (Wenzel), 1805B
Picht-Axenfeld, Edith, 1935C
Pickard, John, 1963A
Picker, Tobias, 1954A, 1977E
Pierné, Gabriel, 1863A, 1882E, 1890D, 1910D, 1925E, 1937B
Pierrot Players (Fires of London), 1967G
Pijper, Willem, 1894A, 1947B
Pi Kappa Lambda Society, 1918G
Pikes Peak Center, 1982G
Piland, Jeanne, 1945A, 1972C
Pilarczyk, Helga, 1925A, 1951C

Pilcher, Henry, & Sons, Organ Builders, 1833G
Piles, Alphonse Fortia de: A Bas les Masques, 1813H; Quelques réflexions d'un homme du monde, 1812H
Pilotti, Giuseppe, 1784A, 1838B
Pilou, Jeannette, 1931A, 1958C
Pilsen Radio Symphony Orchestra, 1946G
Piltti, Lea, 1904A, 1926C
Pimsleur, Solomon, 1900A, 1962B
Pincherle, Marc, 1888A, 1974B; Feuillets d'histoire du violon, 1927H; Le monde des virtuoses, 1961H; Musical Creation, 1961H; Les violinistes compositeurs et virtuoses, 1922H
Pingoud, Ernest, 1887A, 1942B
Pini-Corsi, Antonio, 1858A, 1878C, 1918B
Pinkham, Daniel, 1923A
Pinnock, Trevor, 1946A, 1968C, 1973D, 1989D, 1992E
Pinschof, Thomas, 1965C
Pinto, Amelia, 1878A, 1899C, 1946A
Pinto, Thomas, 1783B
Pinza, Ezio, 1892A, 1914C, 1950F, 1957B
Pinzauti, Alessandro, 1989C
The Pioneer, 1854G
Pipkov, Lubomir, 1904A, 1974B
Pipp, Wilma, 1925A
Pique, François-Louis, 1758A
Pirani, Eugenio, 1852A, 1939B
Pirazzini, Miriam, 1944C
Pirenesi, Giovanni, Publishing House, 1761G
Pirogov, Alexander, 1899A, 1924C, 1964B
Pirro, André, 1869A, 1943B
Pirrotta, Nino, 1908A, 1998B
Pisa, Italy: Accademia dei Constanti, 1798G; Accademie de Revvivati, 1823G; Benvenuti Music School, 1824G; Giuseppe Verdi Choir, 1961G; Regio Teatro Nuovo, 1867G; Scuola Communale de Music, 1906G; Scuola Corale 1855G; Società Amici della Musica, 1920G; Società Filarmonica Pisana, 1765G; Teatro dei Nobili Fratelli Prini, 1772G; Teatro Diurno, 1807G
Pisari, Pasquale, 1778B
Pisaroni, Benedetta Rosmunda, 1793A, 1811C, 1813F, 1872B
Piek, Jan Křtitel, 1814A, 1835C, 1873B
Pisendel, Johann Georg, 1755B
Pisk, Paul, 1893A, 1921D, 1948D, 1990B; A History of Music & Musical Style, 1963H
Piston Valve, 1815G
Piston, Walter, 1894A, 1916F, 1924F, 1935E, 1938E, 1940E, 1955E, 1963E, 1974E, 1976B; Counterpoint, 1947H; Harmony, 1941H; Orchestration, 1955H; Principles of Harmonic Analysis, 1933H
Pitsch, Karel Frant, 1786A, 1858B
Pittel, Harvey, 1943A, 1970E, 1971C
Pittman, Richard, 1997D

�֍

A Births   B Deaths   C Debuts   D New Positions
E Prizes/Honors

Pittsburgh, Pennsylvania: American Wind Symphony, 1960G; Apollonian Society, 1807G; Bach Choir, 1934G; Benedum Center, 1988G; Cardwell School of Music, 1927G; Carnegie Hall, 1895G; Chamber Opera Theater, 1978G; Civic Light Opera Ass'n, 1945G; Germania Orchestra, 1873G; Madrigal Singers, 1963G; Mendelssohn Choir, 1909G; Mozart Club, 1879G; Music Festival, 1879G; New Music Ensemble, 1975G; Opera Co., 1939G; Oratorio Society, 1960G; Orchestra Association, 1910G; Orchestral Society, 1854G; Symphony Orchestra, 1895G, 1926G; Teutonia Männerchor, 1854G; Youth Symphony Orchestra, 1945G

Pixis, Francilla Göhringer, 1816A, 1834C

Pixis, Friedrich Wilhelm, Jr., 1810D

Pixis, Johann Peter, 1788A, 1874B

Pizarro Artur, 1968B, 1987E, 1990E

Pizzetti, Ildebrando, 1880A, 1917D, 1924D, 1947D, 1968B; *Intermezzi critici*, 1921H; *La musica dei greci*, 1914H; *Musica e dramma*, 1945H; *La musica Italiana del'800*, 1947H; *Musicisti contemporanei*, 1914H

Placidi, Tommaso, 1964A, 1992E

Plagge, Wolfgang, 1960A, 1972C

Plaichinger, Thila, 1868A, 1893C, 1939B

Le plain-chant, 1859G

Planchet, Dominique, 1946B

Plançon, Pol-Henri, 1851A, 1877C, 1914B

Planer, Minna, 1834F, 1836F

Planquette, Jean-Robert, 1848A, 1903B

Plantade, Charles-Henri, 1764A, 1814E, 1816D, 1839B

Plantanida, Giovanni, 1758E

Plantinga, Leon, 1935A, 1979D; *Romantic Music*, 1985H

Plaschke, Friedrich, 1875A, 1900C, 1951B

Plasson, Michel, 1933A, 1962E, 1968D, 1994D

Platania, Pietro, 1828A, 1907B

Platel, Nicolas-Joseph, 1776A, 1835B

Platt, Peter, 1994D, 2000B; *A Form of Infinity: Music & the Human Spirit*, 1995H

Platti, Giovanni Benedetto, 1763B

Player Piano, 1863G

Pleasants, Henry, 1910A, 1930D, 1945D, 1967D, 2000B; *The Agony of Modern Music*, 1955H; *Opera in Crisis: Tradition, Present, Future*, 1989H

Pleeth, William, 1916A, 1932C, 1999B

Pleskow, Raoul, 1931A, 1974E

Plessis, Hubert du, 1922A

Pletnev, Mikhail, 1957A, 1978E, 1990D

Pleyel, Camille, 1788A, 1855B

Pleyel, Ignace Joseph, 1757A, 1783D, 1791F, 1831B

Pleyel Piano Factory, 1807G

Plfüger, Hans George, 1944A

Plishka, Paul, 1941A, 1961C

Plotkin, Fred: *Opera 101*, 1994H

Plowright, Jonathan, 1959A, 1984C

Plowright, Rosalind, 1949A, 1968C, 1979E

Plumeri, Johnterryl, 1944A

Pocci, Franz, 1807A, 1876B

Pocono Boy Singers, 1970G

Podles, Ewa, 1952A, 1975C

Poell, Alfred, 1929C

Pogorelich, Ivo, 1958A, 1980EF, 1981C

Pogorelich Piano Competition, 1993G

Pohl, Carl Ferdinand, 1819A, 1887B; *Die Gesellschaft der Musikfreunde und ihr Conservatorium in Wien*, 1871H

Pohl, Richard, 1826A, 1896B; *Akustische Briefe...*, 1853H

Pohlenz, Christian August, 1790A, 1827D, 1843B

Pohlig, Karl, 1858A, 1907D, 1928B

Poise, Ferdinand, 1828A, 1892B

Poisot Charles: *History of Music in France*, 1860H

Poissl, Johann Nepomuk, 1783A, 1865B

Pokorn, Franz Xaver, 1794B

Polacco, Giorgio, 1873A, 1912D, 1922D, 1960B

Polansky, Larry, 1954A; *New Instrumentation & Orchestration*, 1986H

Polaski, Deborah, 1949A

Pole, William: *Philosophy of Music*, 1879H

Poleri, Daivd, 1921A, 1945C, 1967B

Poli, Afro, 1907A, 1926C

Poli-Randaccio, Tina, 1877A, 1901C, 1956B

Poland (*see also* Breslau, Gdansk, Karków): Association of Polish Composers, 1930G; Association of Young Polish Composers, 1905G; Group 49, 1949G: National Radio Symphony Orchestra, 1934G, 1935G; Polish Composers Union, 1926G; Polish Radio Choir, 1947G; Polish Radio Symphony Orchestra, 1945G; Polish Society of Music Writers and Critics, 1924G; Young Polish Composers Publishing Co., 1905G

Polisi, Joseph W., 1984D

Polivnick, Paul, 1947A, 1985D

Polko, Elise: *Musikalische Märchen*, 1852H

Poll, Afro, 1988B

Pollak, Anna, 1912A, 1945C, 1996B

Pollard, Mark, 1957A

Pollard Opera Co. of New Zealand, 1904G

Polledro, Giovanni Battista, 1781A, 1797C, 1824D, 1853B

Pollet, Françoise, 1949A, 1983C

Pollini, Bernhard, 1838A, 1857C, 1897B

Pollini, Francesco, 1762A, 1846B; *Metodo per Clavicembalo*, 1811H

Pollini, Maurizio, 1942A, 1960E

Polosov, Vyachesav, 1950A, 1977C

Polyansky, Valeri, 1992D

Polyphonie, 1947G

F   *Biographical*   G   *Cultural Beginnings*   H   *Musical Literature*
I   *Musical Compositions*

Polyplectron, 1828G
Polytonal Clavichord, 1769G
Ponce, Manuel, 1882A, 1948B
Poncet, Tony, 1955C
Ponchielli, Amilcare, 1834A, 1886B
Pond, Sylvanus Billings, 1792A, 1871B; *The United States Psalmody*, 1841H
Ponder, Michael, 1948A, 1973C
Poné, Gundaris, 1981E, 1982E, 1984E, 1988E
Poniatowski, Józef, 1816A, 1873B; *Le progrès de la musique dramatique*, 1859H
Ponnelle, Jean-Pierre, 1932A, 1988B
Ponochevny, Andrey, 1998E
Pons, Lily, 1898A, 1927C, 1976B
Pons, José, 1768A, 1791D, 1793D, 1818B
Pons, Juan, 1946A
Ponselle, Carmela, 1892A, 1923C, 1977B
Ponselle, Rosa, 1897A, 1918C, 1981B
Ponte, Lorenzo da, 1791F, 1838B
Ponti, Michael, 1937A, 1964E
Pöntinen, Roland, 1983C
Pontoglio, Cipriano, 1831A, 1892B
Poole, Elizabeth, 1820A, 1834C, 1906B
Poole, Geoffrey, 1949A, 1977E, 1990E
Poole, Valter, 1984B
Poot, Marcel, 1901A, 1949D, 1988B
Pope, René, 1987C
Popov, Gavriil, 1904A, 1972B
Popov, Valery, 1965A
Popov, Vladimir, 1947A, 1977C
Popp, Lucia, 1939A, 1963C, 1993B
Popper, David, 1843A, 1913B
Populaire et Classique, 1845G
Porpora, Nicola A., 1752F, 1768B
Porro, Pierre-Jean, 1831B
Porro, Pierre-Jean, Publisher, 1786G
Porta, Bernardo, 1758A, 1829B
Porta, Giovanni Battista, 1755B
Portable Grand (Upright) Piano, 1800G
Porter, Quincy, 1897A, 1938D, 1942D, 1943E, 1944E, 1946E, 1966B
Porter, Samuel, 1757D, 1810B
Portland, Maine: Beethoven Musical Society, 1819G; Chamber Music Society, 1982G; Chandler's Band, 1867G; Choral Arts Society, 1972G; Civic Band, 1827G; Handel & Haydn Society, 1828G; Handel Society of Maine, 1814G; Lyric Theater, 1953G; Maine Music Festival, 1897G; Opera Repertory Co., 1995G; Sacred Music Society, 1836G; String Quartet, 1969G; Symphony Orchestra, 1923G
Portland, Oregon: Apollo Club, 1883G; Civic Auditorium, 1917G; Ellison-White Conservatory, 1918G; Marquam Grand Theater, 1890G; Mechanic's Band, 1864G; Opera Association, 1950G; Opera Co., 1917G; Philharmonic Music Society, 1866G; Symphonic Choir, 1946G; Symphony Orchestra, 1896G

Portugal, Marcos António, 1762A, 1771F, 1783E 1800D, 1811D, 1830B
Posen: Agthe Music Academy, 1826G
Posselt, Ruth, 1914A, 1935F
Posseur, Henri, 1929A
Post, Merriweather, Pavilion of Music, 1967G
Pothier, Joseph, 1835A, 1923B
Pötinen, Roland, 1963A
Potsdam Musikschule, 1875G
Pott, August Friedrich, 1806A, 1824C, 1883B
Pott, Francis John, 1957A
Potter, Archibald, 1918B, 1980B
Potter, (Philip) Cipriani, 1792A, 1816C, 1871B
Potter, John: *Observations on the Present State of Music & Musicians*, 1762H
Potter, Richard, 1806B
Pougin, Arthur, 1834A, 1921B
Poulenard, Isabelle, 1961A
Poulenc, Francis, 1899A, 1920F, 1963B
Poulet, Michel, 1960A
Poulet, Gerard, 1956E
Powell, Claire, 1954A, 1979C
Powell, John, 1882A, 1924E, 1963B
Powell, Maud, 1868A, 1904F, 1920B
Powell, Maud, String Quartet, 1894G
Powell, Maud, Trio, 1908G
Powell, Mel, 1933A, 1963E, 1969D, 1998B
Powell, Samuel, 1775B
Powell Verne Q., 1879A, 1968B
Powell, Vernon Q., Flutes, Inc., 1926G
Powell Hall (St. Louis), 1968G
Power, James, 1766A, 1836B
Power, James, Publisher, 1807G
Power Center for the Performing Arts, 1971G
Powers, Marie, 1974B
Powers, William, 1941A
Powley, John, 1816D
Pownall, Mary Ann, 1751A, 1770C, 1797B
Poznan Chamber Orchestra, 1963G
Poznanski, Barrett Isaac, 1840A, 1896B
Prades Music Festival, 1950G
Pradher, Louis Barthélemy, 1781A, 1843B
Praeger, Heinrich Aloys, 1783A, 1854B
Prague, Czechoslovakia: Academy of the Arts, 1947G; Brass Ensemble, 1979C; Bustelli Opera Co., 1764G; Conservatory of Music, 1811G; Deutsche Akademie für Musik, 1920G; German Philharmonic Orchestra, 1939G; German Opera, 1807G; German Theater, 1888G; Hlahol Choral Society, 1861G; Italian Opera House, 1784G; Kammermusikverein, 1876G; Mozart Society, 1837G; National Theater, 1881G; National Opera House I, 1862G; National Opera House II, 1883G; Proksch Music School, 1830G; Saint Cecilia Society, 1840G; Saxophone Quartet, 1980G; Smetana Museum, 1928G; Smetana Theater, 1885G; Society for Modern Music, 1920G; Soc.,

---

A Births   B Deaths   C Debuts   D New Positions
E Prizes/Honors

Promotion of Church Music, 1826G; Spring Festival, 1946G; Ständetheater, 1781G; String Quartet, 1920G; Symphony Orchestra, 1934G; Theater of the States, 1807G; Tonkünstler-Societät, 1803G; Tyl Theater, 1783G; Zofin Academy of Music, 1840G

Prandelli, Giacinto, 1914A, 1942C

Prang Educational Co. (Boston), 1882G

Prati, Alessio, 1775F, 1788B

Pratico, Bruno, 1962A

Pratt, Awagadin, 1966A, 1992EF, 1993C

Pratt, Carroll: *The Meaning of Music*, 1931H; *Music as the Language of Emotion*, 1952H

Pratt, John, 1772A, 1855B

Pratt, Silas Gamaliel, 1846A, 1871D, 1875F, 1916B

Pratt, Waldo Selden, 1857A, 1939B; *Music of the Pilgrims*, 1921H; *Musical Ministries in the Church*, 1901H; *The New Encyclopedia of Music & Musicians*, 1924H; *The Problem of Music in the Church*, 1930H

Pratt Institute of Music & Art, 1906G

Prausnitz, Frederik, 1920A, 1961D, 1971D, 1974E; *Score & Podium*, 1983H

Predieri, Luca Antonio, 1767B

Pregardien, Christoph, 1956A

Preger, Kurt, 1970A, 1933C, 1960B

Preger, Richard von, 1899D

Preindl, Joseph, 1756A, 1787D, 1793D, 1809D, 1823B; *Wiener Tonschule (posthumous publication)*, 1827H

Preisler, Frantisek, Jr., 1973A, 1993C, 1997D

Preobrazhensky, Anton, 1870A, 1929B; *Dictionary of Russian Church Chant*, 1896H; *On Church Chant*, 1897H; *Sacred Music in Russia*, 1914H

Pressenda, Franciscus, 1777A, 1854B

Presser, Theodore, 1848A, 1925B

Presser, Theodore, Publisher, 1883G

Presser Foundation (Philadelphia), 1916G

Presser Home for Retired Music Teachers, 1906G

Preston, John, and Son, Violin Maker, 1774G

Preston, Katherine, 1950A

Preston, Robert, 1942A

Preston, Simon, 1938A, 1962C, 1970D, 1981D

Preston, Stephen, 1968C

Prêtre, Georges, 1924A, 1946C

Prevedi, Bruno, 1959C, 1988B

Previn, André, 1929A, 1967D, 1968D, 1976D, 1985D, 1999E

Previtali, Fernando, 1907A, 1928D, 1936D, 1953D, 1984B

Prévost, André, 1934A

Prévost, Eugène-Prosper, 1809A, 1831E, 1838D, 1872B

Prey, Hermann, 1929A, 1952C, 1998B

Preyer, Carl Adolph, 1863A, 1947B

Preyer, Gottfried von, 1844D

Prianishnikov, Ippolit Petrovich, 1847A, 1876C, 1921B

Pribyl, Lubos, 1975A, 1989D, 1992C

Price, Florence B., 1888A, 1953B

Price, Leontyne, 1927A, 1961E, 1965E, 1980E, 1981E, 1985E

Price, Margaret, 1941A, 1962C, 1982E, 1992E

Priestman, Brian, 1927A, 1964D, 1970D, 1978D, 1980D

Primavera, Carmen, Violin Maker, 1888G

Primavera String Quartet, 1975G

Primrose, William, 1903A, 1937F, 1963F, 1982B; *Technique Is Memory*, 1963H

Primrose String Quartet, 1939G

Pring, Katherine, 1940A, 1966C

PRISM, 1983G

Pritchard, John, 1921A, 1957D, 1962DE, 1978D, 1982D, 1983E, 1986D, 1989B

Prix Chartier, 1861G

Prix Clara Haskil, 1965G

Prix de Rome in Music (French), 1803G

Pro-Arte String Quartet, 1912G

Probst Music Publishing Co., 1823G

Pro Cantione Antiqua, 1968G

Proch, Heinrich, 1837D, 1840D

Prochazkova, Jarmila, 1961A

Proconart Ensemble for Contemporary Music, 1989G

Proctor, Norma, 1928A, 1948C

Prohaska, Carl, 1869A, 1927B

Prohaska, Felix, 1912A, 1945D, 1956D, 1961D, 1965D, 1987B

Prohaska, Jaro, 1891A, 1922C, 1965B

Prokofiev, Serge, 1891A, 1945F, 1948F, 1949F, 1953B

Proksch, Josef, 1794A, 1864B; *Allgemeine Musiklehre*, 1857H

Pro Musica Antiqua (Belgium), 1933G

Pro Musicis Foundation, 1965G

Prony, Gaspard-Clair, 1755A, 1839B; *Instruction élémentaire sur les moyens de calculer les intervalles musicaux*, 1832H; *Rapport sur la nouvelle harpe à double mouvement*, 1815H

Proske, Carl, 1794A, 1861B

Prota, Gabriele, 1806D

Protokoll der Schweizerischen Musikgesellschaft, 1808G

Prout, Ebenezer, 1835A, 1854F, 1859F, 1871D, 1895E, 1909B; *Applied Forms*, 1895H; *Counterpoint, Strict and Free*, 1890H; *Double Counterpoint, Canon and Fugue*, 1891H; *Harmony, Its Theory and Practice*, 1889H; *Instrumentation*, 1876H; *Musical Form*, 1893H; *The Orchestra I*, 1898H

Provedi Francesco: *Paragone della musica antica e della moderna*, 1752H

Providence, Rhode Island: Opera House, 1871G, 1897G ; Opera Theater, 1978G; Musical Institute, 1864G; Symphony

❀

F *Biographical*   G *Cultural Beginnings*   H *Musical Literature*
I *Musical Compositions*

Providence, Rhode Island: (*cont.*)
  Orchestra, 1932G; Tourjée Music Institute, 1859G
Prowse, Keith, and Co., 1775G
Pruckner, Caroline, 1832A, 1850C, 1908B; *Theorie und Praxis der Gesangskunst,* 1872H
Prudent, Emile, 1817A, 1863B
Pruett, James W., 1987D
Prüfer, Arthur, 1860A, 1944B
Prumier, Ange-Conrad, 1820A, 1884B
Prumier, Antoine, 1794A, 1868B
Prunell-Friend, Augustin, 1996C
Prunières, Henry, 1886A, 1942B; *Le ballet de Cour en France avant Benserade et Lully,* 1914H; *La musique de chambre et de l'écurie,* 1912H; *Nouvelle histoire de la musique I,* 1934H; *Nouvelle histoire de la musique II,* 1936H
Pruslin, Stephen, 1940A, 1970C
Pryor, Arthur, 1870A, 1942B
Pryor, Arthur, Band, 1903G
Pryor, Gwenneth, 1965C
Psalterium, 1907G
Puccini, Giacomo (I), 1781B
Puccini, Giacomo (II), 1858A, 1907F, 1924B
Puchat, Max, 1884E
Puente, Giuseppe del, 1841A, 1900B
Puerto Rico: Biennial of 20th Century Music, 1978G; Casals Festival, 1957G; Conservatory of Music, 1960G; Symphony Orchestra, 1958G
Puget, Paul-Charles, 1873E
Puget Music Publications, 1970G
Pugliese, Michael, 1956A
Pugnani, Gaetano, 1754F, 1767D, 1770F, 1776D, 1780F, 1798B
Pugni, Cesare, 1802A, 1851F, 1870B
Pugno, Raoul, 1852A, 1858C, 1914B
Pulitzer Prize for Music, 1943G
Pulitzer Prize Music Scholarship, 1917G
Purcell, Kevin John, 1959A
Purcell Consort of Voices, 1963G
Purcell Room & Queen Elizabeth Hall, 1967G
Purcell String Quartet, 1969G
Purday & Button, Publishers (London), 1805G
Purdie, Robert, Publisher, 1809G
Pustet, Friedrich, Publisher, 1826JG
Putnam, Ashley, 1952A, 1976C
Putnam, G. P., & Son, 1866G
Puzzi, Giovanni, 1792A, 1817C, 1876B
Pyne, Louisa, 1832A, 1904B
Qiuntón, José, 1925A
Quadrivium, 1956G
Quaile, Elizabeth, 1874A, 1951B
Quallenberg, Johann Michael, 1786B
Quanta, 1970G (Mexico)
Quantz, Johann Joachim, 1773B; *New Church Melodies,* 1760H; *Versuch einer Anweisung, die Flöte traversiere zu spielen,* 1752H

Quarterly Music Register, 1812G
Quarterly Musical Magazine & Review, 1818G
Quarterly Review, 1809G
Quarter-Tone Clarinet, 1922G
Quarter-Tone Piano, 1928G
Quartet of the Americas, 1976G
Quartet Renaixement, 1912G
Quartet Veronique, 1989G
Quartetto, David, 1995G
Quartetto Aria, 1993G
Quartetto Italiano, 1945G
Quartetto Fiorentino, 1865G
Quebec, Canada: Academie de musique, 1868G; Harmonic Society, 1820G; Opéra de Quebec, 1970G; Société Sainte Cécile, 1869G; Société Symphonique de Québec, 1903G
Queen Elisabeth Music Competition, 1952G
Queler, Eve, 1936A, 1968D
Quilico, Gino, 1955A, 1977C
Quilico, Louis, 1925A, 1954C, 2000B
Quinault, Marie-Anne-Catherine, 1791B
Quinet, Fernand, 1924D, 1938D, 1948D
Quink, 1978G
Quinke, W. A., & Co., 1906G
Quintanar, Héctor, 1936A
Quintetto Briccialdi, 1992G
Quintetto dell Regina, 1881G
Quito, Ecuador: Conservatorio Nacional, 1870G; Philharmonic Society, 1952G
Quittmeyer, Susan, 1955A
Quivar, Florence, 1944A
Quog Music Theater, 1970G
Raabe, Peter, 1872A, 1899D, 1945B
Raaff, Anton, 1797B
Rääts, Jaan, 1932A
Rabaud, Henri, 1873A, 1894E, 1908D, 1914D, 1918DE, 1920D, 1949B
Rabin, Michael, 1936A, 1949E, 1950C, 1972B
Rabin, Shira, 1970A, 1979C
Rabinof, Benno, 1908A, 1927C, 1975B
Racette, Patricia, 1965A, 1990C, 1994E, 1998E
Rachmaninoff, Sergei, 1873A, 1882F, 1895F, 1899C, 1909F, 1918F, 1943B
Rachmaninoff String Quartet, 1974G
Rackham Symphony Choir, 1949G
Radecke, Luise, 1867C
Radecke, Robert, 1863D
Radev, Mariana, 1911A, 1937C
Radicati, Felice Alessandro, 1775A, 1815D, 1820B
Radio Eireann (RTE) Symphony Orchestra, 1948G
Radio City Music Hall, 1932G
Radoux, Jean-Théodore, 1859E, 1872D
Radziwill, Prince Anton Heinrich, 1775A, 1833B
Raekalllio, Matti (Juhani), 1954A, 1971C
Raff, Joseph Joachim, 1822A, 1843F, 1877D, 1882B

A *Births*   B *Deaths*   C *Debuts*   D *New Positions*
E *Prizes/Honors*

Raffanti, Dano, 1948A, 1976C
Raffell, Anthony, 1940A, 1966C
Raftery, J. Patrick, 1951A, 1980C, 1981E
Ragin, Derek Lee, 1958A, 1983C, 1986E
Ragnarsson, Hjalmar, 1952A
Rahbari, Alexander, 1988D
Rahn, John, 1944A; *Basic Atonal Theory*, 1980H;
    A Theory for All Music, 1983H
Raida, Karl Alexander, 1878D
Railton, Ruth, 1915B, 1936C
Raim, Cynthia, 1979E
Raimondi, Gianni, 1923A, 1947C
Raimondi, Ignazio, 1813D
Raimondi, Pietro, 1786A, 1824d, 1852D,1853B
Raimondi, Ruggero, 1941A, 1964C
Rainer (family), 1839F
Rainforth, Elizabeth, 1814A, 1836C, 1877B
Rainger, Ralph, 1942B
Rains, Leon, 1954B
Raisa, Rosa, 1893A, 1913C, 1963B
Raisa-Rimini Singing School, 1937G
Raitzin, Misha, 1990B
Raivez, José, 1916C
Rajski, Wojciech, 1948A, 1971D, 1978D
Rakhmadiev, Erkegali, 1932A
Rakov, Nikolai, 1908A, 1990B
Rakowski, David, 1958A, 1995E
Raleigh, N.C.: Grass Roots Opera Co., 1948G;
    National Opera Co., 1955G; North Carolina
    Symphony, 1932G
Ralf, Oscar, 1881A, 1905C, 1964B
Rameau, Jean-Philippe, 1764B; *Code de musique
    pratique*, 1760H; *Nouvelles réflexions sur le
    principe sonore*, 1759H; *Observations sur notre
    instinct pour la musique*, 1754H
Ramey, Samuel, 1942A, 1968C
Ramiro, Yordi, 1948A, 1977C
Rampal, Jean-Pierre, 1922A, 2000B
Rampini, Domenico, 1801D
Rampini, Giacomo, 1779D, 1799D, 1811B
Rampini, Giovanni Giacomo, 1760B
Ran, Shulamit, 1949A
Randall, John, 1777D
Randegger, Alberto, Jr., 1880A, 1918B
Randel, Don M.: *New Harvard Dictionary of
    Music*, 1986H
Randle, Thomas, 1958A
Randolph, Harold, 1898D
Randová, Eva, 1936A, 1968C
Rands, Bernard, 1934A, 1983E, 1987E
Rangström, Ture, 1884A, 1922D, 1947B
Ranjbaran, Behzad, 1996C
Ránki, Dezsó, 1951A, 1969E
Rankin, Nell, 1926A, 1949C
Rapchak, Lawrence, 1951A
Rapee, Erno, 1891A, 1912D, 1931D, 1945B
Raphael, Günter, 1960B
Le rappel, 1869G
Rappoldi, Laura, 1853A, 1868C, 1925B

Rasbach, Oscar, 1975B
Rascher, Sigurd, 1907A
Rascher Saxophone Quartet, 1969G
Rasilainen, Ari, 1959A, 1994D
Raskin, Judith, 1928A, 1956C, 1984B
Rasmussen, Karl Aage, 1947A
Rasmussen, Paula, 1965A
Rasponi, Lanfranco: *The Last Prima Donnas*,
    1983H
Rasse, François, 1899E, 1925D
La Rassegna Musicale, 1928G
Rastall, Richard: *The Notation of Western Music*,
    1982H
Rastrelli, Joseph, 1799A, 1828E, 1830D,
    1842B
Ratez, Emile-Pierre, 1851A, 1934B
Rathaus, Karol, 1895A, 1954B
Ratisbon. See Regensburg, Germany
Ratner, Leonard Gilbert, 1916A; *Harmony:
    Structure & Style*, 1962H
Ratti, Cencetti and Co. Publishers (Rome),
    1821G
Rattle, Simon, 1955A, 1980D, 1981F, 1988F,
    1994E
Rattray, David: *Masterpieces of Italian Violin
    Making*, 2000H
Rauch, Frantiek, 1932C
Rauch, Johann Baptist, 1779D
Rauchs, Béatrice, 1962A
Raumklang, 1993G
Raupach, Hermann Friedrich, 1758D
Rautawaara, Aulikki, 1906A, 1932C, 1990B
Rautio, Nina, 1957A, 1981C
Rauzzini, Venanzio, 1765C, 1810B
Ravel, Maurice, 1875A, 1895F, 1897F, 1920E,
    1928EF, 1922F, 1937B
Ravinia Festival (Chicago), 1936G
Ravinia Opera (Chicago), 1911G
Ravinia Park Concerts, 1906G
Rawlins, Emily, 1950A, 1973C
Rawsthorne, Alan, 1905A, 1971B
Raylor, Raynor, 1792F
Rayner, Sydney, 1927C, 1981B
Razumovsky, Count Andreas, 1752A, 1836B
Razumovsky String Quartet, 1808G
RCA Victor Co., 1929G
Read, Daniel, 1757A, 1836B; *The American
    Singing Book*, 1785H; *American Singing Book
    Supplement*, 1787H; *Columbian Harmonist I*,
    1793H; *Columbian Harmonist II*, 1794H
Read, Gardner, 1913A, 1943E, 1945D;
    *Compendium of Modern Instrumental
    Techniques*, 1993H; *Contemporary Instrumental
    Techniques*, 1976H; *Modern Rhythmic Notation*,
    1978H; *Music Notation*, 1964H; *Pictographic
    Score Notation*, 1998H; *Source Book of Proposed
    Music Notation Reforms*, 1987H; *Style &
    Orchestration*, 1979H; *Thesaurus of Orchestral
    Devices*, 1953H; *Twentieth Century Notation*,

F   *Biographical*   G   *Cultural Beginnings*   H   *Musical Literature*
        I   *Musical Compositions*

Read, Gardner, (cont.)
  1967H; *Twentieth-Century Microtonal Notation*, 1990H
Reading, John, 1764B
Real Orquestra Sinfónica de Sevilla, 1991G
Reardon, John, 1930A, 1954C, 1988B
Rebel, François, 1751D, 1757D, 1760E, 1775B
Reber, Napoléon-Henri, 1807A, 1855E, 1880B; *Traité d'harmonie*, 1862H
Rebikov, Vladimir, 1866A, 1920B
Rebling, Gustav, 1902B
Recio, Marie, 1841F
Reconnaissance des Musiques Modernes, 1967G
Recording Industries Association of America, 1952G
Red Army Song & Dance Ensemble, 1928G
Redlands Bowl Summer Music Festival, 1924G
Redlich, Hans F., 1903A, 1968B
Redwoods Summer Music Festival, 1982G
Reed, Alfred, 1921A
Reed, George, Music Store (Boston) 1839G
Reed, G. P. & Co., Boston, 1839G
Reed, H. Owen, 1910A; *Basic Contrapuntal Techniques*, 1964H; *Basic Music*, 1954H; *Materials of Music Composition*, 1980H; *Scoring for Percussion*, 1969H
Reese, Gustave, 1899A, 1940D, 1944D, 1950D, 1977B; *Fourscore Classics of Music Literature*, 1957H; *Music in the Middle Ages*, 1940H; *Music in the Renaissance*, 1954H
Reeve, William, 1757A, 1815B
Reeves, Sims, 1818A, 1838C, 1900B
Regensburg, Germany: Liederkranz, 1837G; Musikverein, 1846G; Ratisbon School of Church Music, 1874G; Saint Cecilia Society, 1767G
Reger, Max, 1873A, 1911D, 1916B; *Beiträge zur Mondulationslehre*, 1903H
Reggiani, Hilde, 1912A, 1933C, 1996B
Regnault, Alexandre, 1866E
Regnault, Jean-Baptiste, 1783E
Régolo, Hungary, 1833G
Rehfuss, Heinz, 1917A, 1938C, 1988B
Rehkemper, Heinrich, 1894A, 1919C, 1949B
Reich, Steve, 1936A, 1994E, 2000E; *Writings about Music*, 1974H
Reich, Willi, 1898A, 1932D, 1980B
Reicha, Anton, 1770A, 1799F, 1801F, 1808F, 1829F, 1831E, 1835E, 1836B, 1906B; *L'art du compositeur dramatique*, 1833H; *Cours de composition musicale*, 1818H; *Traité de haute composition musicale I*, 1824H
Reicha, Josef, 1752A, 1795B
Reichardt, Alexander, 1825A, 1843C, 1885B
Reichardt, Johann Friedrich, 1752A, 1775D, 1785F, 1790F, 1814B; *Briefe auf einer Reise nach Wien*, 1810H; *Briefe über Frankreich*, 1793H; *Schreiben über die berlinische musik*, 1775H;

Studien für Tonkünstlerund Musikfreunde, 1792H; *Über des Pflichten des Ripienviolinistens*, 1776H; *Über die deutsche komische oper*, 1774H; *Vertraute Briefe aus Paris*, 1804H
Reichardt, Luise, 1779A, 1794C, 1826B
Reicher-Kinderman, Hedwig, 1853A, 1871C, 1883B
Reichmann, Theodor, 1849A, 1869C, 1903B
Reigny, Louis-Abel Belfroy de, 1757A, 1811B
Die Reihe (Vienna), 1958G
Reimann, Aribert, 1936A
Reimann, Heinrich, 1850A, 1893D, 1906B
Reimer, Bennett: *A Philosophy of Music Education*, 1970H
Reimers, Paul, 1878A, 1902C, 1942B
Reims, France: Académie de Musique, 1752G; Société Philharmonique, 1833G
Reina, Domenico, 1797A, 1829C, 1843B
Reinach, Théodore, 1860A, 1928B
Reinagle, Alexander, 1756A, 1786F, 1793F, 1809B
Reinecke, Carl, 1824A, 1843F, 1854D, 1859D, 1860D, 1875E, 1897D, 1910B; *Aus dem Reich der Töne*, 1907H; *Meister der Tonkunst*, 1903H; *Rathschläge und Winke für Clavierschüler*, 1890H
Reiner, Fritz, 1888A, 1909C, 1911D, 1914D, 1922D, 1938D, 1948D, 1953D, 1963B
Reinhardt, Delia, 1892A, 1913C, 1974B
Reinhardt, Heinrich, 1865A, 1922B
Reinhold, Frederick Charles, 1815B, 1755C
Reinhold, Henry Theodore, 1751B
Reinhold, Theodor Christlieb, 1755B
Reining, Maria, 1903A, 1931C, 1991B
Reinmar, Hans, 1895A, 1919C, 1961B
Reinthaler, Carl, 1822A, 11858D, 882E, 1896B
Reisenauer, Alfred, 1863A, 1881C, 1907B
Reisenberg, Nadia, 1904A, 1922C, 1983B
Reiss, Albert, 1870A, 1897C, 1940B
Reissiger, Carl Gottlob, 1798A, 1826D, 1828D, 1856D, 1859B
Reissiger, Friedrich August, 1809A, 1840D,. 1883B
Reissmann, August, 1825A, 1903B; *Aesthetik der Tonkunst, Zur*, 1879H; *Deutsche Lied in seiner historischen Entwicklung*, 1861H; *Grundriss der Musikgeschichte*, 1865H
Relache, 1977G
Relfe, John, 1763A, 1837B; *Guida Armonica*, 1798H; *Lucidus Ordo*, 1821H; *Remarks, the Present State of Musical Instruction*, 1819H
Rellstab, Johann Carl, 1759A, 1813B
Rellstab, Ludwig, 1799A, 1860B
Rellstab Music Lending Library, 1783G
Remedios, Albert, 1935A
Reményi, Ede, 1828A, 1846C, 1848F, 1853F, 1898B
Reményi, Eduard, 1848F, 1853F

❄

A *Births*   B *Deaths*   C *Debuts*   D *New Positions*
E *Prizes/Honors*

Remick, Jerome H., 1868B
Remmert, Birgit, 1966A
Remoortel, Edouard van, 1926A, 1951D, 1958D, 1977B
Renaissance City Chamber Players, 1984G
Renard, Marie, 1863A, 1882C, 1939B
Renaud, Maurice, 1861A, 1883C, 1933B
Rendall, David, 1948A, 1975C
Rendano, Alfonso, 1853A
Renié, Henriette, 1875A, 1956B
Rennert, Wolfgang, 1980D
Rensburg, Jacques, 1846A, 1872C, 1910B
Renzetti, Donato, 1950A
Répertoire international des sources musicales, 1952G
Répertoire international d'iconographie musicale, 1971G
Répertoire international de littérature musicale, 1966G
A Repertoire of Music, 1873G
Répertoire des clavecinistes (Zurich), 1803G
Repin, Vadim, 1971A, 1984C
Resnik, Regina, 1922A, 1942C, 1993D
Respighi, Ottorino, 1879A, 1902F, 1913F, 1924D, 1925F, 1926F, 1932E, 1936B
Reszke, Edouard De, 1853A
Reszke, Jean De, 1850A
Reszke, Josephine De, 1855A
Rethberg, Elizabeth, 1894A, 1915C, 1976B
Réthy, Ester, 1935C
Réti, Rudolf, 1885A, 1957B; *The Thematic Process in Music*, 1951H; *Tonality, Atonality & Pantonality*, 1958H; *Tonality in Modern Music*, 1962H
Reubke, Adolf, 1805A, 1875B
Reubke, Julius, 1834A, 1858B
Reuchsel, Amédée, 1931B
Reuss-Belce, Luise, 1860A, 1881C, 1945B
Reuter Organ Co., 1917G
Reuter, Rudolph Ernst, 1888A
Reutter, Georg von, 1772B
Revelli, William D., 1902A, 1935D, 1941D, 1994B
Review of New music Publicaations, 1784G
Revista Brasileira de Musica, 1934G
Revista de Studi Crociani, 1964G
Revista di Cultura Organaria e Organistica, 1960G
Revista Musical Chilena, 1945G
Revista Musical Mexicana, 1942G
Revista Musicale Italiana, 1894G
Revue belge de musicologie, 1946G
Revue de la musique religieuse, 1845G
Revue de Paris, 1829G, 1851G
Revue d'histoire et de critique musicale, 1901G
Revue fantaisiste, 1859G
Revue félibré-anne, 1885G
Revue indépendante, 1841G
Revue internationale de musique, 1938G

La revue musicale, 1827G, 1920G
La revue musicale belge, 1925G
Revue musicale de la Suisse romande, 1948G
Revue musicale de Lyon, 1903G
Revue musicale Suisse, 1861G
Revue rétrospective, 1832G
Revueltas, Silvestre, 1899A, 1940B
Révy, Aurelie, 1879A, 1897C, 1957B
Rey, Isabel, 1966A, 1987C
Rey, Jean-Baptiste, 1776E, 1781D, 1810B
Rey, Louis-Charles, 1811B
Reyer, Ernest, 1823A, 1909B
Reyer, Louis-Etienne, 1862E, 1876E
Reykjavik, Iceland: Chamber Ensemble, 1974G; College of Music, 1930G
Reynolds, Anna, 1931A, 1960C
Reynolds, Roger, 1934A, 1971E, 1989E; *Mind Models*, 1975H; *A Searcher's Path*, 1987H
Reyzen, Mark, 1895A, 1921C
Rezende, Marisa, 1944A
Rezniček, Emil von, 1860A, 1896D, 1945B
Rezucha, Bystrik, 1968D
Rhein-Mosel-Halle, 1962G
Rheinberger, Joseph, 1839A, 1860D, 1864D, 1877D, 1887E, 1901B
Rheinische Musik-Zeitung für Kunstfreunde und..., 1850G
Rheinische Philharmonic (Rhenish) Orchestra, 1945G
Rheinsberg Chamber Orchestra, 1991G
Rhineland Chamber Orchestra, 1957G
Rhode Island (*see also* Providence): Civic Chorale, 1956G; Philharmonic Orchstra, 1945G; Verdi Festival, 1967G
Rhodes, Jane, 1929A, 1953C
Rhodes, Philip, 1940A
Rhys-Davies, Jennifer, 1953I
Riaño, Juan Facundo, 1828A, 1901B; *Critical and Bibliographical Notes on Early Spanish Music*, 1887H
Riavez, José, 1890A, 1958B
Ribla, Gertrude, 1918A
Ricci, Federico, 1809A, 1877B
Ricci, Luigi, 1805A, 1836D, 1859B
Ricci, Ruggiero, 1918A, 1928C
Ricciarelli, Katia, 1946A, 1969C, 1970E, 1971E
Riccius, Karl August, 1830A, 1893B
Rice, Fenlon B., 1871D
Rich, Alan, 1924A, 1963D; *Music: Mirror of the Arts*, 1969H
Richards, (Henry) Brinley, 1817A, 1885B
Richards, Leslie, 1950A
Richardson, Alfred Madeley, 1868A, 1949B
Richardson, Mark, 1966A
Richardson, Stephen, 1965A
Richault, Charles-Simon, 1780A, 1866B
Richault, Charles S., Publishing Co. (Paris), 1805G
Richings, Mary Caroline, 1827A, 1852C, 1882B

F *Biographical*   G *Cultural Beginnings*   H *Musical Literature*
I *Musical Compositions*

Richings Grand Opera Co., 1859G
Richmond Symphony Orchestra, 1957G
Richter, Caspar, 1944A, 1972C
Richter, Ernst Friedrich, 1808A, 1879B;
Lehrbuch der fuge, 1859H; *Lehrbuch der
harmonie*, 1853H
*Lehrbuch des einfachen und doppelten
Kontrapunkts*, 1872H
Richter, Franz Xaver, 1769D, 1789B; *Traité
d'harmonie et de composition*, 1804H
Richter, Hans, 1843A, 1871D, 1875D, 1897D,
1916B
Richter, Karl, 1926A, 1947D, 1981B
Richter, Marga, 1926A
Richter, Sviatoslav, 1915A, 1934C, 1949E, 1997B
Richter-Haaser, Hans, 1912A, 1928C
Rickenbacher, Karl-Anton, 1976D, 1978D
Ricordi, Giovanni, 1785A, 1853B
Ricordi, Tito, 1811A, 1888B
Ricordi, New York Branch, 1911G
Ricordi & Co., Publishers (Milan), 1808G
Ridderbusch, Karl, 1932A, 1961C, 1997B
Riddle, Nelson, 1921A
Rider-Kelsey, Corinne, 1877A, 1897C, 1947B
Ridinger, Johann, 1759D
Riedel, Carl, 1827A, 1868D, 1888B
Riedel, Deborah, 1958A, 1986C
Riegel, Kenneth, 1938A, 1965C
Riedt, Friedrich Wilhelm, 1784B; *Versuch uber
die musikalischen Intervalle*, 1753H
Riegel, Henri Joseph, 1799B
Rieger, Franz, Organ Builder, 1845G
Riegger, Wallingford, 1885A, 1914F, 1917F,
1922E, 1924E, 1925E, 1961BE
Riem, Friedrich Wilhelm, 1779A, 1807D,
1857B
Riemann, Hugo, 1849A, 1919B; *Elementar-
Schulbuch der Harmonielehre*, 1906H; *Die
Entwickelung unserer Notenschrift*, 1881H;
Folkloristische Tonalitätsstudien, 1916H;
*Geschichte der Musik seit Beethoven (1800-
1900)*, 1901H; *Geschichte der Musiktheorie*,
1898H; *Geschichte der Notenschrift*, 1878H;
Grosse Kompositionslehre I, 1902H; *Grosse
Kompositionslehre III*, 1913H; *Grundriss der
Musikwissenschaft*, 1908H; *Handbuch der
Musikgeschichte I*, 1903H; *Katechismus der
Orchestrierung*, 1902H; *Lehrbuch des...
Kontrapunkts*, 1888H; *Musikalische Rückblick*,
1900H; *Musiklexikon*, 1882H; *Opern-
Handbuch*, 1887H; *Skizze einer neuen Methode
der Harmonielehre*, 1880H; *System der
musikalischen Rhythmik un Metrik*, 1903H;
*Verloren gegangene selbstverständlichkeiten in
der musik des 15.-16. Jahrhunderts*, 1907H
Riemenschneider, Albert, 1878A, 1950B
Riepel, Joseph, 1782B; *Anfangsgrunde zur
musikalischen Setzkunst*, 1752H
Rieppe, Karl Joseph, 1775B

Ries, Ferdinand, 1784A, 1801F, 1804C, 1813F,
1834D, 1836D
Ries, Franz, 1755A, 1846B, 1932B
Ries, Hubert, 1835D, 1886B
Rieter, Jakob Biedermann, Publishers, 1849G
Rieti, Vittorio, 1898A, 1994B
Rietsch, Heinrich, 1860A, 1927B
Rietz, Eduard, 1802A, 1818C, 1826D, 1832B
Rietz, Julius, 1812A, 1848D, 1877B
Rifkin, Joshua, 1944A
Riga, Latvia: City Theater, 1782G; Latvian
Conservatory of Music, 1919G; Opera
Festival, 1998G; Musikalische Gesellschaft,
1760G; Symphony Orchestra, 1761G
Rigal, Joel, 1979C
Rigby, Jean, 1954A, 1982C
Rigel, Henri-Jean, 1772A, 1852B
Righetti-Giorgi, Geltrude, 1793A, 1814C, 1862B
Righini, Vincenzo, 1756A, 1775C, 1787D,
1793D, 1812B
Rignold, Hugo, 1905A, 1948D, 1957D, 1960D,
1976B
Riisager, Knudåge, 1897A, 1974B
Rijksmusiekacademie, 1970G
Riley, Edward, Music Publisher, 1811G
Riley, Terry, 1935A
Rilling, Helmuth, 1933A, 1954D, 1965D
Rimbault, Edward, 1816A, 1842E, 1876B; *The
Organ, Its History and Construction*, 1857H;
*Pianoforte: Its Origin, Progress and
Construction*, 1860H
Rimmer, F.: *A History of Scottish Music*, 1973H
Rimsky-Korsakov, Nicolai, 1844A, 1856F,
1862F, 1865F, 1873F, 1874F, 1892F, 1908B;
Autobiography, 1876H; *My Musical Life*,
1906H; *Principles of Orchestration*, 1896H;
Textbook on Harmony, 1884H
Rinaldi, Alberto, 1939A, 1963C
Rinaldi, Margherita, 1935A, 1958C
Rinck, Johann Christian, 1770A, 1790D, 1813D,
1846B
Ringborg, Patrik Erland, 1965A, 1989C
Ringer, Alexander: *The Early Romantic Era
Between Revolutions*, 1990H
Ringholz, Teresa, 1958A, 1982C
Ringborg, Tobias, 1973A, 1994C
Rinkevicius, Gintaras, 1960A
Rintzler, Marius, 1932A, 1964C
Rio, Anita, 1873A, 1901C, 1971B
Rio de Janeiro, Brazil: Clube Mozart, 1867G;
Conservatorio Imperial de Música, 1847G;
Imperial Academy of Music, 1857G;
National Conservatory of Music, 1942G;
National Opera, 1857G; Opera Nova, 1776G;
Opera Velha, 1767G; Real Teatro de Sao Joao,
1823G; Sociedad de Concertos Clássicos,
1883G; Sociedad de Concertos Populares,
1896G; Sociedade de Concertos Sinfonicos,
1912G; Sociedade Beneficencia Musical,

A *Births*   B *Deaths*   C *Debuts*   D *New Positions*
E *Prizes/Honors*

1833G; Symphony Orchestra, 1949G; Teatro Ginásio Dramático, 1855G

Riotte, Philipp Jakob, 1776A, 1856B

Ripa, Antonio, 1768D

Rippon, Michael, 1938A, 1969C

Risler, Edouard, 1873A, 1894C, 1929B

Risler, Paul, 1951B

Risley, Patricia, 1968A, 1985C

Ristenpart, Karl, 1900A, 1932D, 1946D, 1953D, 1967B

Ristori, Giovanni Alberto, 17153B

Ritchie, Anthony, 1960A

Ritchie, John, 1921A

Ritschel, Johannes, 1766B

Ritter, Alexander, 1833A, 1856D, 1896B

Ritter, August G., 1811A, 1844D, 1885B

Ritter, Frédéric Louis, 1826A, 1891B; *History of Music I*, 1870H; *Music in America*, 1883H; *Music in Its Relation to Intellectual Life*, 1891H

Ritter, Johann C., 1767B

Ritter, Johann N., 1782B

Ritter, Peter, 1763A, 1803D, 1846B

Ritter, Rudolf, 1878A, 1910C

Ritter String Quartet, 1905G

Ritter-Ciampi, Gabriella, 1886A, 1917C

Riva, Ambroglio, 1975C

Riva, Douglas, 1951A, 1982C

Rivé-King, Julie, 1854A, 1875C, 1937B

Riverbend Music Center, 1984G

Rivinius, Gustav, 1990E

Rivoli, Ludwika, 1814A, 1830C, 1878B

Rivoli, Paulina, 1823A, 1837C, 1881B

Rizdale, Robert, 1920A

Rizzi, Carlo, 1960A, 1982C

Roads, Curtis: *Composers & the Computer*, 1985H

Roark-Strummer, Diana, 1977C

Roark-Strummer, Linda, 1952A

Robb, John Donald, 1892A, 1941D, 1990B

Robbins Music Corporation, 1927G

Robert, Jean-Louis, 1979B

Roberti, Margherita, 1957C

Roberton, Hugh, 1931E

Roberts, Brenda, 1945A, 1968C

Roberts, Kathleen, 1967C

Roberts, Megan, 1952A

Roberts, Stefanovich, 1966A

Roberts, Susan, 1960A

Robertson, Christopher, 1964A

Robertson, David, 1958A, 1985D, 1992D, 1999D

Robertson, Leroy, 1896A, 1925D, 1948D, 1971B

Robeson, Lila, 1960B

Robeson, Paul, 1898A, 1936F, 1976B, 1989D

Robinette, Robert, 1929A

Robinson, Anatasia, 1755B

Robinson, Forbes, 1926A, 1954C, 1987B

Robinson, Ray: *Choral Music*, 1978H

Robinson, Sharon, 1949A, 1974C

Robinson, Stephen, 1953A

Robinson, Faye, 1943A, 1972C

Robison, Paula, 1941A, 1961C, 1964E, 1966E

Robles, Daniel Alomias, 1871A, 1942B

Robles, Marisa, 1937A, 1954C

Robson, Christopher, 1976C

Robson, Paul, 1925C

Robyn, Alfred George, 1860A, 1935B

Roca, Matheo Tollis de la, 1757D

Rocca, Giuseppe, 1807A, 1865B

Rocca, Lodovico, 1940D

Rochat, Michel, 19985D

Rochberg, George, 1918A, 1950E, 1951D, 1960D, 1985E, 1986E, 1893F; *Aesthetics of Survival*, 1984H; *The Hexachord & its Relation to the Twelve-tone Row*, 1955H

Rochester, N.Y.: American Opera Co., 1885G, 1922G, Chamber Orchestra, 1964G; Eastman School of Music, 1921G; Eastman Theater, 1921G; Eastman Theater Orchestra (Rochester Philharmonic), 1921G; Institute of Musical Art, 1905G, 1913G; Music Publishers, 1965G; Opera Theater of Rochester, 1962G; Oratorio Society, 1945G; Symphony Orchestra, 1922G

Rochlitz, Johann F, 1798D, 1805D; *Für Freunde der Tonkunst I*, 1824H

Rockefeller, Martha Baird, Fund for Music, 1962G

Röckel, August, 1783A, 1876B

Röckel, Joseph A., 1806C

Rockport Chamber Music Festival, 1982G

Rockstro, William, 1823A, 1895B; *General History of Music*, 1886H; *A History of Music*, 1879H; *Practical Harmony*, 1881H; *Rules of Counterpoint*, 1882H

Rockwell, John: *All American Music*, 1983H

Rocky Ridge Music Center, 1942G

Rode, Halfdán, 1871A, 1894C, 1945B

Rode, Jacques-Pierre, 1774A, 1790C, 1803F, 1830B

Rode, Wilhelm, 1887A, 1909C, 1959B

Rodeheaver, Homer, 1880A

Röder, Carl Gottlieb, 1812A, 1883B

Röder, Carl G., Engraver, 1846G

Rodescu, Julian, 1980C

Rodgers, Joan, 1956A, 1982C

Rodgers, Richard, 1955E, 1978E, 1979B

Rodgers Organ Co., 1958G

Rodó, Gabriel, 1904A, 1951D, 1963B

Rodolphe, Jean Joseph, 1812B

Rodrigo, Joaquín, 1901A, 1999B

Rodrigues de Ledesma, Mariano, 1779A, 1848B

Rodriguez, Robert Xavier, 1946A

Rodriguez, Santiago, 1952A, 1961C, 1975E

Rodriguez, Vicente, 1760B

Rodriguez de Hita, Antonio: *Diapason instructivo*, 1757H

Rodzinski, Artur, 1892A, 1920C, 1926F, 1929D, 1932D, 1933D, 1947D, 1958B

F *Biographical*   G *Cultural Beginnings*   H *Musical Literature*
I *Musical Compositions*

Roe, Betty, 1930A
Roeckel, August, 1838D, 1843D
Roeckel, Edward, 1816A, 1836C, 1899B
Roelstraete, Herman, 1925A
Roeseler, Marcella, 1890A, 1910C, 1957B
Rogé, Pascal, 1951A, 1962C, 1973E
Rogel, José, 1829A, 1901B
Roger, Gustave-Hippolyte, 1815A, 1838C,
  1879B
Roger, Miguel, 1954A
Roger-Ducasse, Jean, 1873A, 1954B
Rogers, Bernard, 1893A, 1913D, 1920E, 1947E,
  1968B; *The Art of Orchestration,* 1951H
Rogers, Clara Kathleen, 1931B
Rogers, Clara Kellogg, 1844A, 1863C
Rogers, Francis, 1870A, 1898C, 1951B
Rogers, George, & Sons, Piano Makers, 1843G
Rogers, Leslie-Jane, 1962A
Rogister, Jean, 1879A, 1964B
Rogliano, Marco, 1967A, 1989C
Rögner, Heinz, 1973D
Rohan, Jindrich, 1919A
Rohr, Otto von, 1916A, 1938C
Rojas, Rafael, 1962A
Rokitansky, Hans von, 1835A, 1856C, 1909B
Roland de Lattre Choral Society, 1841G
Rolandi, Gianna, 1952A, 1975C
Rolfe, William, & Co., Piano Maker, 1785G
Roll, Michael, 1946A, 1958C, 1963E
Rolla, Alessandro, 1757A, 1803D, 1841B
Rolland, Romain, 1866A, 1944B; *Goethe et
  Beethoven,* 1930H; *The Life of Beethoven,*
  1903H; *Musiciens d'aujourd'hui,* 1908H;
  Musiciens d'autrefois, 1908H
Rolland, Sophie, 1963A, 1982C
Rolle, Johann Heinrich, 1785B
Röllig, Carl Leopold, 1804B
Rollinson, Thomas H., 1844A, 1928B
Rolnick, Neil B., 1947A, 1994D
Roloff, Roger, 1975C, 1984E
Rolton, Julian, 1965A
Roman, Johan Helmich, 1758B
Roman, Stella, 1904A, 1932C, 1992B
Romani, Carlo, 1824A, 1875B
Romani, Felice, 1788A, 1865B
Romania (*see also* Bucharest): Liti Muzica,
  1916G; Opera Co., 1877G; Opera House,
  1953G; Orchestral Society, 1874G; State
  Philharmonic Orchestra of Romania, 1955G
Romantic Music Festival, 1968G
Romberg, Andreas J., 1767A, 1774C, 1815D,
  1821B
Romberg, Bernhard Heinrich, 1767A, 1841B
Romberg, Sigmund, 1887A, 1951A
Rome, Italy: Accademie Filarmonica Romana,
  1821G; American School of Classical Studies,
  1895G; Contemporary Music Festival,
  1954G; Liceo Musicale, 1877G; Opera Co.,
  1946G; Piano Quartet, 1956G; Quintetto dell
  Regina, 1881G; Scuola Gregoriana, 1880G;

Scuola Nazionale de Musica, 1905G; Società
  Romana del Quartetto, 1867G; Societana
  Filarmonicǎ Românǎ I, 1868G; Societana
  Filarmonicǎ Românǎ II, 1894G; Teatro
  Costanzi, 1888G
Romer, Emma, 1814A, 1830C, 1868B
Romero, Patricia, 1953A, 1976C
Romero family, 1958F
Romero de Avila Manuel: *Arte de canto, llano y
  organo,* 1761H
Römhild, Theodor, 1756B
Ronald, Landon, 1873A, 1910D, 1922E, 1938B
Ronconi, Domenico, 1772A, 17797C, 1839B
Ronconi, Giorgio, 1810A, 1831C, 1890B
Ronconi, Sebastiano, 1814A, 1836C, 1900B
Ronger, Florimond (Hervé), 1825A, 1892B
Röntgen, Julius, 1914D
Ronzi de Begnis, Giuseppina, 1816C
Roocroft, Amanda, 1966A, 1988E, 1990C
Roos, Lars Anders, 1945A
Roosenschoon, Hans, 1952A
Root, Frederick, 1846A, 1871F, 1916B
Root, George Frederick, 1820A, 1839F, 1895B;
  The Young Ladies Choir, 1846H; *Young Men's
  Singing Book,* 1855H
Root and Cady, Publishers, 1858G
Root & Sons Music Co., 1875G
Rootering, Jan Hendrik, 1950A, 1980C
Rootham, Cyril, 1938A
Ropartz, Joseph Guy, 1864A, 1886F, 1894D,
  1919D, 1955B
Rorem, Ned, 1923A, 1968E, 1979E; *Critical
  Affairs: a Composer's Journal,* 1970H; *The Final
  Diary, 1961-1972,* 1974H; *Knowing When to
  Stop,* 1994H; *Music & People,* 1968H; *Music
  from Inside Out,* 1967H; *Setting Tone,* 1983H;
  Settling the Score, 1988H
Rosa, Carl, 1842A, 1889B
Rosa, Carl, Opera Co., 1875G
Rosa, Carlantonio de, 1762A, 1847B
Rosa, Evelyn de la, 1954A
Rosa, Franz de Paula, 1779A
Rosamonde String Quartet, 1981G
Rosand, Aaron, 1927A
Rosbaud, Hans, 1895A, 1921D, 1928D, 1945D,
  1947D, 1948D, 1962B
Rosé, Arnold, 1863A, 1879C, 1946B
Rose, Bernard, 1916A
Rose, Jerome, 1938A, 1953C, 1961E
Rose, Leonard, 1918A, 1944C, 1951F, 1984B
Rose, Peter, 1961A, 1986C
Rose-Stern-Istomin Trio, 1961G
Roseingrave, Thomas, 1766B
Rösel, Peter, 1945A
Rosell, Lars-Erik, 1944A
Rosellen, Henri, 1811A, 1876B
Rosen, Charles, 1927A, 1951C, 1992E; *The
  Frontiers of Meaning,* 1994H; *The Romantic
  Generation,* 1995H; *Sonata Forms,* 1980H
Rosen, Jerome, 1921A

❀

A *Births*   B *Deaths*   C *Debuts*   D *New Positions*
              E *Prizes/Honors*

Rosen, Max, 1900A, 1915C, 1956B
Rosen, Nathaniel, 1948A, 1969C, 1970E, 1977E, 1978E
Rosenberg, Hilding, 1892A, 1985B
Rosenbloom, David, 1947A, 1984D, 1990D; *Extended Musical Interface with the Human Nervous System*, 1990H
Rosenblum, Mathew, 1954A
Rosenfeld, Paul, 1890A, 1946B; *Discoveries of a Music Critic*, 1936H; *An Hour with American Music*, 1929H; *Modern Tendencies in Music*, 1927H; *Musical Portraits: Interpretations of Twenty Modern Composers*, 1920H
Rosenhain, Jacob, 1813A, 1894B
Rosenshein, Neil, 1947A, 1972C
Rosenstiel, Leonie: *The Schirmer History of Music*, 1982H
Rosenstock, Joseph, 1895A, 1920D, 1927D, 1948D, 1958D, 1960D
Rosenthal, Harold: *Sopranos of Today*, 1956H
Rosenthal, Manuel, 1904A, 1944D, 1949D, 1964D
Rosenthal, Moriz, 1862A, 1876C, 1946B; *Schule des höheren Klavierspiel*, 1892H
Rosetti, Antonio, 1785D, 1789D, 1792B
Rosing, Vladimir, 1890A, 1912C, 1923D, 1963B
Rosing-Schow, Niels, 1954A
Roslavets, Nicolai, 1881A, 1944B
Rösler, Endre, 1904A, 1927C, 1963B
Rösler, Johann Joseph, 1771A, 1813B
Rosner, Arnold, 1945A
Ross, Elinor, 1958C
Ross, Glynn, 1963D
Ross, Hugh, 1898A, 1922D, 1927D, 1990B
Ross, John J., 1783D
Ross, Susanna, 1950A, 1973C
Ross, William P., Harpsichord Shop, 1964G
Rosseau, Marcel Samuel, 1905E
Rosseau, Samuel-Alexandre, 1879E
Rossi, Giovanni, 1828A, 1864D, 1873D, 1886B
Rossi, Giulio, 1865A, 1887C, 1931B
Rossi Giuseppe, 1809F; *Alli intendenti di Contrappunto*, 1809H
Rossi, Lauro, 1810A, 1831D, 1835D, 1850D, 1870D, 1885B
Rossi, Mario, 1902A, 1946E, 1992B
Rossi-Lemeni, Nicola, 1920A, 1946C, 1991B
Rossini, Gioacchino, 1792A, 1802F, 1805F, 1806F, 1810F, 1815F, 1822F, 1823F, 1824D, 1826EF,1829E, 1830F, 1836F, 1837F, 1846F, 1855F, 1868B
Rössl-Majdan, Hildegard, 1921A, 950C
Rost, Andrea, 1965A, 1989C
Rostand, Aaron, 1948C
Rostand, Claude, 1912A, 1970B; *Dictionnaire de la musique contemporaine*, 1970H
Rostock, Germany: Konzertverein, 1877G; Singakademie, 1819G; Stadt- und Theaterorchester, 1897G

Rostropovich, Mstislav, 1927A, 1935C, 1950E, 1955F, 1963E, 1974F, 1977D, 1985E, 1987E, 1989F, 1990F, 1992E, 1993E
Rostropovich Cello Competition, 1981G
Rosvaenge, Helge, 1897A, 1921C, 1972B
Rota, Nino, 1911A, 1979B
Rotary Valve, 1827G
Roth, Daniel, 1942A, 1972D, 1985D
Roth, Feri, 1969B
Roth, Wilhelm August, 1757D, 1765B
Rothauser, Therese, 1865A, 1887C, 1943B
Rothenberg, Ned, 1956A
Rothenberger, Annaliese, 1924A, 1943C
Rother, Artur, 1938D, 1946D, 1972B
Rothier, Léon, 1874A, 1899C, 1951B
Rothmüller, Marko, 1908A, 1932C, 1993B
Rothwell, Walter Henry, 1872A, 1904D, 1919D, 1927B
Rotterdam, Holland: Association for the Promotion...of Music, 1829G; Concert Hall, 1966G; Duitse Opera, 1860G; Eruditio Musica, 1826G; Symphony Orchestra, 1918G
Röttger, Heinz, 1909A, 1954D
Rouart-Lerolle et Cie. (Paris), 1905G
Rouen, France: Municipal Conservatory of Music, 1945G; Théâtre de Rouen, 1776G; Théâtre des Arts, 1962G
Rouget de Lisle, Claude-Joseph, 1760A, 1836B
Rouleau, Joseph, 1929A, 1955C
Round Top Festival-Institute (Texas), 1970G, 1971G
Rouse, Christopher, 1949A
Roussakis, Nicolas, 1934A, 1969E, 1994B
Rousseau, Jean-Jacques, 1754F, 1756F, 1762F, 1770F; *Dictionnaire de musique*, 1767H; *Lettre sur la musique française*, 1753H
Rousseau, Marcel, 1955B
Rousseau, Samuel-Alexandre, 1892E
Roussel, Albert, 1869A, 1887F, 1894F, 1898F, 1937B
Rousselière, Charles, 1950B
Rousset, Christophe, 1961A, 1983E
Roussier, Abbé Pierre-Joseph, 1792B; *L'harmonie pratique*, 1775H; *Mémoire sur la musique des anciens*, 1770H; *Mémoire sur la nouvelle Harpe de M. Cousineau*, 1782H; *Observations sur differents points d'harmonie*, 1755H; *Traité des accords, et de leur succession*, 1764H
Routh, Francis: *Contemporary British Music*, 1972H; *Contemporary Music: An Introduction*, 19668H; *The Organ*, 1958H
Routley, Erik: *The Church & Music*, 1950H; *The Music of the Christian Hymns*, 1981H; *Twentieth Century Church Music*, 1964H; *Words, Music & the Church*, 1968H
Rouvier, Jacques, 1967E
Roux, Michel, 1924A, 1948C, 1998B
Rovere, Agostino, 1804A, 1826C, 1865B

F *Biographical*   G *Cultural Beginnings*   H *Musical Literature*
I *Musical Compositions*

Rowicki, Witold, 1914A, 1945D, 1950D, 1958D, 1982D, 1989B
Roy, Klaus George, 1924A
Royal Bohemian Academy of Sciences, 1784G
Royal Festival Hall, 1951G
Royal Flemish Opera Co., 1893G
Royal Military School of Music, 1856G
Royal Northern College of Music, 1972G
Royal Opera House Renovation, 1999G
Royal Philharmonic Orchestra, 1946G
Royal Scottish Academy of Music, 1890G
Royal Welsh Ladies' Choir, 1881G
Royer, Joseph-Nicolas, 1755B
Rózavölgyi & Fárza, Publishers, 1850G
Rôze, Marie-Hippolyte, 1846A, 1865C, 1926B
Rozhdestvensky, Gennadi, 1931A, 1961D, 1965D, 1982D, 1991D
Rozkon, Josef Richard, 1833A, 1913B
Rózsa, Miklós, 1995B
Rozsnyai, Károly, Publisher, 1889G
Rozsnyai, Zoltán, 1927A, 1990B
Różycki, Ludomir, 1908D, 1920D, 1953B
RTF Chamber Orchestra, 1952G
RTF Singers, 1953G
RTF Symphony, 1947G
Ruan, Joshua, 1964A
Ruano, Cándido José, 1760A, 1782D, 1792D, 1803B
Rubbra, Edmund, 1901A, 1986B; Counterpoint, 1960H
Ruben, Cristina, 1985C
Rubens, Sibylla, 1970A
Rubenson, Albert, 1826A, 1901B
Rubin, Joel Edward, 1955A
Rubin, Marcel, 1905A, 1995B
Rubinelli, Giovanni B., 1753A, 1771C, 1829B
Rubini, Giovanni Battista, 1794A, 1854B
Rubinstein, Anton, 1829A, 1858D, 1859D, 1862D, 1887D, 1894B
Rubinstein, Artur, 1887A, 1900C, 1976EF, 1978E, 1982B
Rubinstein, Beryl, 1898A, 1916C, 1932D, 1952B; An Outline of Piano Pedagogy, 1929H
Rubinstein, Joseph, 1847A, 1884B
Rubinstein, Nicolai, 1835A, 1855F, 1866D, 1881B
Rubinstein Piano Master Competition, 1974G
Rubio, Samuel, 1912A, 1986B
Rubsamen, Walter, 1911A, 1965D, 1973B; Chanson & Madrigal 1480, 1530, 1964H; Literary Sources of Secular Music in Italy c. 1500, 1943H
Ruch Muzyczny, 1857G
Rückauf, Anton, 1855A, 1903B
Rudakova, Larissa, 1964A
Rudel, Julius, 1921A, 1957D, 1979D, 1985E
Rudel, Julius, Award, 1969G
Ruders, Poul, 1949A
Rudersdorff, Hermine, 1822A, 1840C, 1882B

Rudhyar, Dane, 1895A, 1985B
Rudolf, Max, 1902A, 1923C, 1945D, 1958D, 1973D, 1988E, 1995B; The Grammar of Conducting, 1950H
Rudy, Mikhail, 1953A, 1977C
Ruebush, Kieffer & Co., Publishers, 1872G
Ruetz, Caspar; Widerlegte vorurtheile von der Beshaffenheit der heutigen Kirchenmusik und von der Lebens-Art einiger Musicorum, 1752H
Rufer, Josef, 1893A, 1985B; Die Komposition mit zwölf Tönen, 1952H; Musiker über Musik, 1955H
Ruffo, Titta, 1877A, 1898C, 1953B
Ruggi, Francesco, 1767A, 1845B
Ruggles, Carl, 1876A, 1907F, 1954E, 1960E, 1971B
Ruiter, Wim de, 1943A
Rumford, Robert Kennerley, 1870A
Rummel, Christian, 1787A, 1815D, 1849B
Rummel, Franz, 1853A, 1872C, 1901B
Rummel, Walter, 1953B
Rummel, Walter Morse, 1887A
Runciman, John F., 1894D
Rung, Henrik, 1807A, 1871B
Runge, Paul, 1848A, 1911B
Rungenhagen, Carl F., 1778A, 1833D, 1851B
Rünger, Gertrude, 1899A, 1924C, 1965B
Runnicles, Donald, 1954A, 1984D, 1992D
Ruoff, Axel D., 1957A
Ruohonen, Seppo, 1946A, 1973C
Rupp, Franz, 1901A, 1992B
Ruppe, Christian Friedrich, 1753A, 1790D, 1826B
Ruppe, Friedrich Christian, 1771A, 1834B
Rusconi, Gerardo, 1922A, 1974B
Rush, Loren, 1935A, 1969E
Rushton, Julian, 1941A
Russ Cerri, Giannina, 1903C
Russell, Alexander, 1880A, 1953B
Russell, Charles E.: The American Orchestra & Theodore Thomas, 1927H
Russell, Ella, 1864A
Russell, George, 1908C; The Lydian Chromatic Concept of Tonal Organization, 1953H
Russell, Henry, 1812A, 1900B
Russell, Lillian, 1922B
Russell, William, 1777A, 1813B, 1905A, 1992B
Russell & Tolman, Publishers, 1858G
Russia: Archangelsky Chorus, 1880G; Baroque Chamber Ensemble, 1968G; Koussevitzky Orchestra, 1909G
Russian Arts Foundation, 1992G
Russian Cinematographic Symphony Orchestra, 1924G
Russian Musical Gazette, 1893G
Russian Musical Review, 1885G
Russian Musical Society, 1860G
Russian National Orchestra, 1990G
Russian Orchestra of the Americas, 1976G

❄

A   Births   B   Deaths   C   Debuts   D   New Positions
E   Prizes/Honors

Russian Protective Collective of Composers, 1925G
Russian Royal Court Theater, 1756G
Russian State Symphonic Capella, 1971G
Russian Symphony Orchestra of New York, 1903G
Russo, William, 1928A
Russolo, Luigi: *L'arte dei rumori*, 1916H
Rust, Friedrich W., 1775D, 1796B
Rust, Giacomo, 1777D, 1783D
Rust, Wilhelm, 1822A, 1861D, 1892B
Rutini, Giovanni Marco, 1762E, 1769D, 1797B
Rutkowski, Bronislaw, 1898A, 1955D, 1964B
Rutkowski, Frank, 1932A
Rutkowski & Robinette, Harpsichord Makers, 1957G
Rutman, Neil, 1953A, 1985C
Rutter, Claire, 1972A
Rutter, John, 1945A, 1975D
Ruud, Ole Kristian, 1958A, 1987D, 1992E, 1996D
Ruyneman, Daniel, 1886A, 1963B
Ruzicka, Peter, 1948A, 1979D, 1988D, 1997D
Růžička, Rudolf, 1941A
Ryabchikov, Victor, 1954A
Ryabov, Vladimir, 1950A
Ryan, Thomas, 1827A, 1903B
Ryba, Jakub Jan, 1765A, 1815B
Rybner, Cornelius, 1855A, 1904D, 1929B
Rychlik, Jan, 1916A, 1964B
Rychlik, József, 1946A
Ryder, Arthur Hilton, 1875A
Ryder, Thomas Philander, 1836A, 1887B
Ryelandt, Joseph, 1870A, 1924D, 1965B
Ryker, Robert, 2000D
Rysanek, Leonie, 1926A, 1949C, 1998B
Rytel, Piotr, 1884A, 1970B
Rzewski, Frederic, 1938A
Saar, Louis Victor, 1868A, 1937B
Saar, Mart, 1882A, 1963B
Saar Radio Chamber Orchestra, 1968G
Saarbrücken Radio Symphony Orchestra, 1936G
Saariaho, Kaija, 1952A
Saarinen, Gloria, 1934A
Sabata, Victor de, 1892A, 1967B
Sabatino, Nicolo, 1796B
Sabbatini, Giuseppe, 1957A, 1987C
Sabbatini, Luigi Antonio, 1767D, 1809B; *Elementi teorici della musica colla pratica dei medesimi, in duetti e terzetti a canone accompagnate dal basso*, 1789H; *Trattato sopra le fughe*, 1802H; *La vera idea delle musicale numeriche signature*, 1799H
Sabin, Wallace Arthur, 1860A, 1937B
Saccani, Rico, 1984E, 1997D, 1998D
Sacchi, Don Giovenale, 1789B; *Della divisione del tempo nella musica nel ballo e nella poesia*, 1770H; *Delle quinte successive nel contrappunto e delle regolo degli accompagnamenti*, 1780H

Sacchini, Antonio, 1768D, 1786B
Saccoman, Lorenzo, 1964C
Sacconi, Fernando, 1895A, 1973B
Sacher, Paul, 1906A, 1999B
Sacher, Paul, Foundation, 1986G
Sachs, Curt, 1881A, 1933F, 1959B; *The Commonwealth of Art*, 1946H; *The Evolution of Piano Music*, 1944H; *Geist und Werden der musikinstrumente*, 1929H; *Handbuch der Musikinstrumentenkunde*, 1920H; *The History of Musical Instruments*, 1940H; *Das Klavier*, 1923H; *Die moderne Musikinstrumente*, 1923H; *Musikgeschichte der Stadt Berlin bis zum Jahre 1800*- 1908H; *Our Musical Heritage*, 1948H; *Reallexikon der musikinstrumente*, 1913H; *Rhythm & Tempo, A Study in Music History*, 1953H; *The Rise of Music in the Ancient World*, 1943H; *Vergleichende Musikwissenschaft in ihren Grundzügen*, 1930H; *World History of Dance*, 1937H
Sachs, Joel, 1939A
Sack, Erna, 1898A, 1925C, 1972B
The Sackbut, 1920G
Sacred Music Society of America, 1976G
Sadie, Stanley, 1967D; *The Cambridge Music Guide*, 1985H; *The Norton/Grove Concise Encyclopedia of Music*, 1988H; *The Norton/Grove Dictionary of Women Composers*, 1995H; *The New Grove Dictionary of Music & Musicians*, 1980H; *The New Grove Dictionary of Musical Instruments*, 1984H; *The New Grove Dictionary of Opera*, 1992H
Sado, Yutaka, 1961A, 1989E, 1995E
Saenger, Gustav, 1904D
Saeverud, Harald, 1992B
Safonov, Vasili, 1852A, 1880C, 1889D, 1906D, 1918B
Safranek, Vincent F., 1867A, 1955B
Sahl, Michael: *Making Changes: A Practical Guide to Vernacular Harmony*, 1977H
Sainsbury John H.: *A Dictionary of Musicians*, 1824H
Sainsbury, Lionel, 1958A
Saint-Aubin, Jeanne Charlotte, 1764A, 1786C, 1850B
Saint Cecilia Society of America, 1873G
Saint Cecilia Orchestra of New York, 1987G
Saint-Georges, Joseph Boulogne de, 1739A, 1763F, 1772C, 1773D, 1792F, 1797F, 1799B
Saint Gervais, France: Semaines Saintes, 1892G
Saint-Huberty, Antoinette C., 1777C
Saint-Huberty, Cécile, 1756A, 1812B
Saint Lawrence String Quartet, 1989G
Saint-Léon, Arthur, 1821A, 1834C, 1870B
Saint Louis, Missouri: Amateur Orchestra, 1893G; Apollo Club, 1894G; Bach Society, 1942G; Balmer & Weber Music House, 1848G; Beethoven Conservatory, 1871G; Brass Quintet, 1964; Choral Society, 1880G;

F *Biographical*   G *Cultural Beginnings*   H *Musical Literature*
I *Musical Compositions*

Saint Louis, Missouri: (*cont.*)
Choral Symphony Society, 1880G; College of
Music, 1880G; Conservatory of Music,
1872G; Institute of Music, 1924G; Kunkel's
Popular Concerts, 1884G; Municipal Opera
Ass'n & Theater, 1919G; Musical Fund
Society, 1838G; Musical Union, 1881G;
Musicians' Mutual Benefit Ass'n, 1885G;
Opera Theater, 1976G, 1977G; Philharmonic
Orchestra, 1838G; Philharmonic Quintet
Club, 1878G; Philharmonic Society II, 1860G;
Philharmonic Society III, 1893G; Powell
Symphony Hall, 1868G; Sacred Music
Society, 1840G; Symphony Chorus, 1976G;
Symphony Orchestra, 1880G, 1907G; Youth
Symphony Orchestra, 1970G
Saint Magnus Festival, 1977G
Saint Michael's Sinfonia, 1981G
Saint Olaf Choir, 1911G
Saint Olaf Lutheran Choir, 1955G
Saint Pancras (Camden) Festival, 1954G
Saint Paul, Minnesota: Chamber Orchestra,
1959G; Opera Association, 1933G; Opera
House, 1866G; Schubert Club, 1882G
Saint Petersburg, Russia: Andreyev Balalaika
Orchestra, 1886G; Free School of Music,
1870G; Hermitage Theater, 1783G; Imperial
Russian Music Society, 1859G; Kühner Music
School, 1892G; Large Stone Theater, 1757G;
Male Chorus, 1993G; Marjinsky (Kirov)
Theater, 1860G; Maresch Hunting Horn
Ensemble, 1751G; Music Club, 1772G; Music
Lover's Society, 1828G; Philharmonic
Society, 1802G; Popular Concerts, 1893G;
Russian Imperial Chapel Choir, 1779G;
Russian Public Symphony Concerts, 1885G;
Small Opera Theater, 1833G; Society for
Quartet (Chamber) Music, 1872G; State
Symphony Orchestra, 1969G; String Quartet,
1985G; Symphony Orchestra, 1963G
Saint-Marcoux, Micheline Coulombe, 1938A,
1985B
Saint-Saëns, Camille, 1835A, 1846C, 1852E.
1857D, 1861D, 1868E, 1875F, 1881E, 1892E,
1906F, 1915F, 1921B; *Harmonie et mélodie*,
1885H; *Portraits et souvenirs*, 1899H;
Problèmes et mystères, 1894H
Saint-Sevin, Joseph Barnabé, 1802B; *Les
principes du violon*, 1761H
Sainton, Prosper, 1813A, 1846D, 1890B
Sainton-Dolby, Charlotte, 1821A, 1842C, 1885B
Saitenharmonika, 1789G
Sakamoto, Ryuichi, 1952A
Sakari, Petri, 1958A, 1988D
Sala, Nicola, 1801B; *Regole del contrappunto
prattico*, 1794H
Salaman, Charles, 1814A, 1901B
Salamunovich, Paul, 1991D
Salas y Castro, Esteban, 1764D, 1803B

Salazar, Adolfo, 1911A, 1958B; *Momentos
decisivos en la música*, 1957H
Salazar, Felix, 1948D
Salazar, Manuel, 1887A, 1913C, 1950B
Saldoni, Baltasar, 1807A, 1889B
Salem, Massachusetts: Mozart Association,
1826G; Whittlesey's Music School, 1835G
Salerno-Sonnenberg, Nadja, 1961A, 1981E,
1982C, 1999E
Sales, Pietro Pompeo (de Sala), 1797B
Saléza, Albert, 1867A, 1888C, 1916B
Salieri, Antonio, 1774D, 1788D, 1825B
Salignac, Thomas, 1867A, 1893C, 1945B
Sallinen, Aulis, 1935A, 1976D, 1979E
Salmagundi, 1807G
Salmanov, Vadim Nikolayevich, 1912A, 1978B
Salmenhaara, Erkki, 1941A
Salminen, Matti, 1945A, 1969C
Salmon, Eliza, 1787A, 1803C, 1849B
Salomon String Quartet, 1981G
Salmond, Felix, 1888A, 1909C, 1952B
Salomon, Johann Peter, 1780F, 1786F, 1815B
Salonen, Esa-Pekka, 1958A, 1979C, 1984D,
1992DF
Salonika State Conservatory of Music, 1915G
Salter, Mary Elizabeth, 1856A, 1938B
Salter, Stephen, 1996E
Salterio Sacro-hispano, 1882G
Salt Lake City, Utah: Theater, 1862G;
Symphonic Choir, 1949G; Symphony Hall,
1979G; Utah Chorale, 1950G; Utah
Symphony Orchestra I, 1892G
Saltzmann-Stevens, Minnie, 1874A, 1909C,
1950B
Salvarezza, Antonio, 1935C
Salvatore, Ramon, 1977C
Salvayre, Gaston, 1872E
Salvi, Lorenzo, 1810A, 1830C, 1879B
Salvini-Donatelli, Fanny, 1815A, 1839C, 1891B
Salzburg, Austria: Festival, 1877G; Grosses
Festspielhaus, 1960G; Internationale Mozart-
Stiftung, 1870G; Internationale Stifung
Mozarteum, 1841G; Liedertafel, 1847G;
Music Festival, 1917G; Salzburgischer
Sängerbund, 1865G; Singakademie, 1847G;
Mozarteum, 1870G
Salzédo, Carlos, 1885A, 1921D, 1961B; *The Art
of Modulating*, 1950H; *Method for the Harp*,
1929H; *Modern Study of the Harp*, 1921H
Salzedo, Leonard, 2000B
Salzedo Harp Colony, 1931G
Salzer, Felix, 1904A, 1986B; *Counterpoint in
Composition*, 1969H; *Structural Hearing*,
1952H
Salzman, Eric, 1933A, 1958D, 1963D, 1984D;
*Making Changes: A Practical Guide to
Vernacular Harmony*, 1977H; *The New Music
Theater*, 1998H; *Twentieth-Century Music*,
1967H

❈

A　*Births*　　B　*Deaths*　　C　*Debuts*　　D　*New Positions*
E　*Prizes/Honors*

Samaroff, Olga, 1882A, 1905C, 1911F, 1948B; *The Layman's Music Book*, 1935H; *The Magic World of Music*, 1936H

Samenspraaken over Musikaale Beginselen, 1756G

Saminsky, Lazare, 1882A, 1959B; *Living Music of the Americas*, 1949H; *Music of Our Day*, 1932H

Physics & Metaphysics of Music & Essays on the Philosophy of Mathematics, 1957H

Sammarco, Mario, 1868A, 1888C, 1930B

Sammartini, Giovanni Battista, 1775B

Sammut, Thomas, 1970A

Samoshka, Vitaly, 1973A, 1998E

Samuel, Adolphe, 1845E, 1871D

Samuel, Gerhard, 1994E

San Antonio, Texas: Beethoven Concert Hall, 1895G; Chamber Music Society, 1942G; Festival, 1982G; Fiesta San Jacinto, 1891G; Grand Opera House, 1886G; Opera Co., 1945G; Symphony Orchestra, 1939G; Theater for the Performing Arts, 1968G

San Carlo Opera Co. (NY), 1913G

Sanchez, Ana Maria, 1966A, 1994C

Sanchez-Gutierrez, 1964A

Sand, Annemarie, 1958A

Sand, George, 1837F, 1838F, 1847F

Sandberger, Adolf, 1864A, 1943B

Sanderling, Kurt, 1912A, 1941D, 1960D

Sanderling, Michael, 1967A

Sanderling, Thomas, 1942A, 1962C, 1966D, 1984D, 1992D

Sanders, Robert, 1906A, 1938D, 1974B

Sanders, Samuel, 1937A, 1949C, 1999B

Sanderson, Sibyl, 1865A, 1888C, 1903B

San Diego, California: Civic Grand Opera Association, 1919G; Harmonie Cornet Band, 1875G; Louis Opera House, 1887G; Morning Choral House, 1924G; Opera Institute, 1981G; Opera Co., 1964G; Philharmonic Chorus, 1919G; Polyphonia, 1933G; Symphony Hall, 1985G; Symphony Orchestra, 1902G

Sándor, György, 1912A, 1930C; *On Piano Playing: Motion, Sound & Expression*, 1981H

Sandpoint Music Festival, 1982G

Sandström, Jan, 1954A

Sandunova, Elizaveta Semyonova, 1777A, 1790C, 1826B

San Francisco, California: Bendix Music Conservatory, 1895G; Biscacciante Opera Co., 1861G; Boy's Chorus, 1951G; Chamber Music Society, 1960G; Chamber Symphony, 1983G; Conservatory Artists Ensemble, 1966G; Conservatory of Music, 1915G; Contemporary Music Players, 1974G; Fisher Opera House, 1892G; German Theater, 1869G; Horton Hall, 1870G; Opera Auditions, 1954G; Opera Co., 1923G; Oratorio Society, 1860G; Philharmonic Society, 1852G; Pocket Opera, 1968G;

Sinfonia San Francisco, 1981G; Symphony Orchestra, 1895G, 1911G; Tivoli Theater I, 1877G; Tivoli Theater II, 1879G; Tivoli Theater III, 1879G, 1890G; Wade's Opera House, 1876G; Young Memorial Museum, 1895G; Youth Orchestra, 1981G

Sangiovanni, Antonio, 1831A, 1892B

San Jose Community Opera Theater, 1980G

San Juan, Puerto Rico: Municipal Theater, 1832G

Sankey, Ira D., 1840A, 1908B; *My Life*, 1905H; *Story of the Gospel Hymns*, 1906H

Sanromá, Jesús María, 1902A, 1984B

San Salvatore, El Salvador: Schola Cantorum, 1869G

Santa Barbara, California.: Music Academy of the West (Santa Barbara), 1947G; Symphony Orchestra, 1953G

Santa Fe, New Mexico: Chamber Music Festival, 1973G; Concert Association, 1937G; Desert Chorale, 1983G; Opera Co., 1957G; Opera Festival, 1957G; Opera House, 1968G; Symphony Orchestra I, 1953G; Symphony Orchestra II, 1984G

Santelmann, William F., 1940D

Santi, Anna de, 1786C

Santi, Nello, 1931A, 1951C, 1958D, 1986D

Santiago, Theresa, 1994E

Santiago, Chile: National Ballet, 1942G; Escuela Moderna de Musica, 1940G; Municipal Philharmonic Orchestra, 1955G; Municipal Theater, 1857G; National Conservatory of Music, 1849G; Sociedad de Música Clásica, 1879G; Sociedad del Cuarteto, 1886G; Symphony Orchestra, 1827G; Symphony Orchestra of Chile, 1941G; Teatro de la Victoria, 1844G

Santini, Fortunato, 1778A, 1861B

Santley, Charles, 1834A, 1857C, 1887E, 1907E, 1922B

Santo Domingo: Music Festival, 1997G; National Symphony Orchestra, 1941G; National Theater, 1976G

Santoro, Claudio, 1919A, 1948E, 1989B

Santos, João Paulo, 1959A

Santos, Joly Braga, 1924A, 1988B

Santucci, Marco, 1762A, 1797D, 1843B

Sanzogno, Nino, 1911A, 1937D, 1983B

São Paulo, Brazil: Clube Haydn, 1883G

Sapelnikov, Vasili, 1867A, 1888C, 1941B

Saperton, David, 1889A, 1900C, 1970B

Sapio, Romualdo, 1858A, 1883C, 1943B

Sapp, Allen Dwight, 1922A, 1999B

Sarajevo, Bosnia and Herzegovina: National Theater, 1921G; Philharmonic Society, 1923G

Sarasate, Pablo de, 1844A, 1856F, 1859F, 1866F, 1908B

Saraste, Jukka-Pekka, 1956A, 1980C, 1987D, 1994D

F *Biographical*   G *Cultural Beginnings*   H *Musical Literature*
I *Musical Compositions*

Saratoga, New York: Festival of the Performing Arts, 1966G; Performing Arts Center, 1966G; Springs Festival, 1937G
Saratoga-Potsdam Choral Institute, 1970G
Sarfaty, Regina, 1932A, 1954C, 1957E
Sargeant, Winthrop, 1934D, 1947D; *Divas*, 1973H; *Geniuses, Goddesses & People*, 1949H; *Listening to Music*, 1958H
Sargent, Malcolm, 1895A, 1921C, 1939D, 1942D, 1947E, 1950D, 1967B
Sargent, Winthrop, 1903A, 1986B
Sari, Ada, 1886A, 1912C, 1968B
Sarrette, Bernard, 1765A, 1797D, 1858B
Sarti, Giuseppe, 1752D, 1753D, 1765F, 1768F, 1770D, 1775D, 1779D, 1784DF, 1787F, 1793F, 1802B; *Trattato del basso generale*, 1791H
Scalabrini, Paolo, 1775D
Sasetti & Co., Publishers, 1848G
Sass, Sylvia, 1951A, 1971C
Sasson, Deborah, 1955A, 1979C
Satanowski, Robert, 1951D, 1954D, 1960D, 1962D, 1963D, 1969D, 1975D, 1977D, 1981D
Satie, Erik, 1866A, 1882F, 1925B
Sato, Sumiko, 1967A
Satoh, Sômei, 1947A
Sattler, Joachim, 1899A, 1926C
Satukangas, Arto, 1962A
Sauer, Emil von, 1942B
Sauguet, Henri, 1901A, 1976E, 1989B
Saunders, Arlene, 1935A, 1958C, 1961E
Saunders, Christopher, 1971A
Sauret, Emile, 1852A, 1866C, 1920B
Sauzay, Eugène, 1809A, 1901B
Savage, Henry W., 1859A, 1927B
Savage, Robert, 1993B
Savage, Stephen (Leon), 1942A, 1966C
Savard, Augustin, 1814A, 1881B; *Cours complet d'harmonie théorique et pratique*, 1853H; *Principes de la musique*, 1861H
Savard, Marie-Emmanuel, 1886E
Savart, Félix, 1791A, 1821E, 1841B; *Sur la communication des mouvements vibratoires entre les corps solides*, 1820H; *Sur la communication des mouvements vibratoires par les liquides*, 1826H; *Mémoire sur la construction des instruments à cordes et archet*, 1819H; *Sur la voix humaine*, 1825H
Savary, Jean, Bassoon Maker, 1823G
Saville, Frances, 1863A, 1892C, 1935B
Savonlinna Opera Festival, 1967G
Savova, Galina, 1945A
Sawallisch, Wolfgang, 1923A, 1953D, 1960D, 1961D, 1970D, 1971D, 1993D
Sax, Adolphe, 1814A, 1894B
Sax, Charles-Joseph, Instrument Maker, 1815G
Saxby, Joseph, 1997B
Saxophone, 1840G
Saxton, Robert, 1953A

Sayao, Bidú, 1902A, 1925C, 1987E, 1999B
Saygun, Ahmed Adnan, 1907A, 1991B
Saylor, Bruce, 1946A
Sbriglia, Jean-Baptiste, 1853C, 1916B
Sbriglia, Giovanni Battista, 1829A
Scaccia, Angelo Maria, 1761B
Scacciati, Bianca, 1894A, 1917C, 1948B
Scalchi, Sofia, 1850A, 1866C, 1922B
Scaltri, Roberto, 1969A, 1986C
Scandiuzzi, Roberto, 1982C
Scaria, Emil, 1838A, 1860C, 1886B
Scarlatti, Domenico, 1757B
Scarlatti, Giuseppe, 1777B
Scarlatti, Tommaso, 1760B
Scarmolin, Anthony Louis, 1890A
Scarmolin, Louis, 1969B
Schaab, Robert, 1817A, 1887B
Schachner, Rudolf Joseph, 1821A, 1896B
Schacht, Theodor, 1823B
Schachter, Carl: *Counterpoint in Composition*, 1969H
Schack, Benedikt, 1758A, 1786C, 1826B
Schad, Joseph, 1812A, 1879B
Schade, Michael, 1965A, 1990C
Schaefer, Karl L., 1931B
Schaefer, Peter, 1956A
Schaeffer, Boguslaw, 1929A; *History of Music, Styles & Authors*, 19797H; *Introduction to Contemporary Composition*, 1975H
Schaeffer, Ferdinand, 1930D
Schaeffer, Pierre, 1910A, 1948F, 1959D, 1995B; *Machines à communiquer*, 1972H; *A la recherche d'une musique concrète*, 1952H; *Traité des objets musicaux*, 1966H
Schaeffner, André, 1895A, 1980B; *Origines des instruments de musique*, 1936H
Schaeuble, Hans, 1906A, 1988B
Schäfer, Michael, 1956A
Schafer, R. Murray, 1933A
Schäffer, August, 1814A, 1879B
Schaffrath, Christoph, 1763B
Schagidullin, Albert, 1991C
Schale, Christian Friedrich, 1763D
Schalk, Franz, 1863A, 1886C, 1931B
Schard, Joseph, 1812A
Scharwenka, Franz Xaver, 1850A, 1924B; *Meisterschule des klavierspiels*, 1907H
Scharwenka, Philipp, 1847A, 1917B
Scharwenka Cons. of Music, 1881G
Schat, Peter, 1935A
Schauensee, Max de, 1942D
Schaum, John W., 1905A, 1988B
Schebest, Agnes, 1813A, 1869B
Schech, Marianne, 1914A, 1937C
Schechner-Waagen, Nanette, 1806A, 1860B
Scheel, Fritz, 1852A, 1895D, 1900D, 1907B
Scheff, Fritzi, 1879A, 1896C, 1954B
Scheibe, Johann Adolf, 1776B; *Abhandlung über das recitativ*, 1765H; *Abhandlung vom*

A *Births*   B *Deaths*   C *Debuts*   D *New Positions*
E *Prizes/Honors*

Ursprung und Alter der Musik, 1754H; *Über die musikalische composition I*, 1773H
Scheibler, Johann Heinrich, 1777A, 1837B; *Der Physikalische und musikalische Tonmerrer*, 1834H
Scheidemantel, Karl, 1859A, 1923B
Scheider, Urs, 1982D
Scheidl, Theodor, 1880A, 1910C, 1959B
Scheidt, Selma von, 1874A, 1891C, 1959B
Schein, Ann, 1939A, 1958C
Schein String Quartet, 1984G
Schelble, Johann Nepomuk, 1789A, 1808C, 1837B
Schelle, Michael, 1950A
Schellenberg, Arno, 1908A, 1929C
Schellendorf, Hans B. von, 1888D
Scheller, Jacob, 1759A, 1803B
Schelling, Ernest, 1876A, 1939A, 1913E, 1936D
Schenig, Francis, 1835D
Schenk, Andrew, 1941A, 1992B
Schenk, Erich, 1902A, 1974B
Schenk, Johann Baptist, 1753A, 1836B
Schenker, Heinrich, 1868A, 1935B; *Harmonielehre*, 1906H; *Kontrapunki I*, 1910H; *Kontrapunkt II*, 1922H; *Der Tonwille*, 1924H
Schenly, Paul, 1948A
Scheppen, Hilde, 19334C
Scherchen, Hermann, 1891A, 1914F, 1922D, 1928D, 1939D, 1944D, 1966B; *Lehrbuch des Dirigierens*, 1929H
Schering, Arnold, 1877A, 1941B; *Geschichte der Music in Beispielen*, 1931H
Scherman, Thomas, 1917A, 1960E, 1979B
Schermerhorn, Kenneth, 1929A, 1957D, 1963D, 1968D, 1982D, 1983D, 1984D, 1986F
Schertzinger, Victor, 1941B
Scherzer, Otto, 1860D
Schetky, George, 1776A, 1831B
Schetky, George, Publishers (Philadelphia), 1802G
Schetky, Johann G. C., 1824B
Schexnayder, Brian, 1953A, 1980C
Schiassi, Gaetano Maria, 1754B
Schicht, Johann Gottfried, 1753A, 1785d, 1810D, 1823B; *Grundregeln der Harmonie nach dem Verwechslungssystem*, 1812H
Schick, George, 1958D, 1969D
Schick, Margarete Luise, 1773A, 1791C, 1809B
Schickele, Peter, 1935A
Schickhardt, Johann Christian, 1762B
Schiedermair, Ludwig, 1957B; *Deutsche Musik im Europäischen Raum*, 1954H; *Die deutsche Oper*, 1930H; *Einführung in das Studium der musikgeschichte*, 1918H; *Musikalische Begegnungen: Erlebnis und erinnerung*, 1948H
Schiedmayer, J. & P., Piano Makers, 1853G
Schiedmayer und Söhne, Piano Makers, 1809G
Schiedermair, Ludwig, 1876A

Schiedermayer, Johann Baptist, 1779A, 1840B; *Theoretisch-praktische Chorallehre zum Gebranch beim katholischen Kirchenritus*, 1828H
Schierbeck, Poul, 1888A, 1947E, 1949B
Schiff, András, 1953A, 1963C, 1991E
Schiff, Heinrich, 1951A, 1988C, 1990D
Schikaneder, Emanuel, 1751A, 1812B
Schilke, Renold, 1910A, 1982B
Schilke Music Products, 1956G
Schiller, Allan, 1943A, 1954C
Schiller, Madeline, 1845A, 1862C, 1911B
Schilling, Gustav, 1803A, 1880B; *Enzyklopädie der gesamten musikalischen Wissenschaften I*, 1835H; *Lehrbuch der allgemeinen Musikwissenschaft*, 1840H; *Musikalische dynamik*, 1843H; *Die musikalische Europa*, 1842H; *Musikalisches Handwörterbuch*, 1830H; *Versuch einer Philosophie des Schönen in...Musik*, 1838H
Schillinger, Joseph, 1895A, 1943B; *Kaleidophone*, 1940H; *The Schillinger Method of Musical Composition*, 1946H
Schillings, Max von, 1867A, 1919D, 1933B
Schiml, Marga, 1945A, 1967C
Schimmel Piano Factory, 1885G
Schimon-Regan, Anna, 1841A, 1864C, 1902B
Schindelmeisser, Ludwig, 1811A, 1847D, 1853D, 1864B
Schindler, Anton, 1795A, 1814F, 1822F, 1824F, 1826F, 1831D, 1864B; *Aesthetik der tonkunst*, 1846H
Schindler, Anton Felix, 1864B
Schindler, Kurt, 1907D
Schiøtz, Aksel, 1906A, 1938C, 1975B
Schipa, Tito, 1888A, 1910C, 1965B
Schipper, Emil, 1882A, 1904C, 1957B
Schippers, Thomas, 1930A, 1951D, 1959F, 1970D, 1977BF
Schirmer, Ernest C., 1865A, 1958B
Schirmer, E.C., Co. (Boston), 1921G
Schirmer, Gustav (I), 1829A, 1893B
Schirmer, Gustav (II), 1864A, 1907B
Schirmer, Gustav (III), 1890A, 1965B
Schirmer, G., Publishing Co., 1866G
Schirmer, Ulf, 1959A, 1995D
Schirp, Wilhelm, 1906A, 1928C
Schirz, Francesco, 1809A, 1883B
Schläger, Hans, 1820A, 1885B
Schlaefer, Jean-Claude, 1961A
Schleifer, M. F.: *Women Composers: Music Through the Ages, Vol. I*, 1996H
Schlesinger, Adolph Martin, 1769A, 1838B
Schlesinger, Daniel, 1799A
Schlesinger, Maurice, Publishers (Paris), 1821G
Schlesinger'sche...Musikalienhandlung (Berlin), 1795G
Schlesingersche Buch- und Musikalienhandlung, 1810G

Schleswig-Holstein Festival, 1986G
Schlicker, Herman, 1974B
Schlicker Organ Co., 1932G
Schlimbach, Johann C., Organ & Piano Builder,
 1806G
Schlösser, Adolph, 1830A, 1847C, 1913B
Schlösser, Louis, 1800A, 1886B
Schlosskirchenchor, 1855G
Schlusnus, Heinrich, 1888A, 1914C, 1952B
Schlüter, Erna, 1904A, 1922C
Schmedes, Erik, 1868A, 1891C, 1898C, 1931B
Schmid, Benjamin, 1986C
Schmid, Erich, 1907A, 1904A, 1960B
Schmid, Johann Michael, 1756D, 1792B
Schmid-Lindner, August, 1870A, 1889E,
 1959B
Schmidl, Carlo, Publisher, 1889G
Schmidt, Andreas, 1960A, 1984C
Schmidt, Annerose, 1956E
Schmidt, Arthur P., 1846A, 1866F, 1921B
Schmidt, Arthur P., Co., Publisher, 1876G
Schmidt, Franz, 1874A, 1927D, 1939B
Schmidt, Franz, Gesellschaft (Vienna), 1951G
Schmidt, Gustav, 1816A, 1876D, 1882B
Schmidt, Heinrich: *Die Orgel in unserer Zeit*,
 1904H
Schmidt Johann M.: *Musico-Theologia*, 1754H
Schmidt, Johann Philipp, 1779A, 1853B
Schmidt, Joseph, 1904A, 1928C, 1942B
Schmidt, Ole, 1928A, 1959D, 1969D, 1971D,
 1979D, 1990F
Schmidt, Trudeliese, 1941A, 1965C
Schmidt, Wolfgang, 1955A
Schmidt-Isserstedt, Hans, 1900A, 1935D,
 1943D, 1945D, 1955D, 1973B
Schmiege, Marilyn, 1955A, 1978C
Schmitt, Aloys, 1788A, 1866B
Schmitt, Florent, 1870A, 1900E, 1922D, 1929D,
 1936E, 1958B
Schmitt, Georg Aloys, 1857D
Schmitt, Georges: *Nouveau manuel complet de
 l'organiste I*, 1855H
Schmitt-Walter, Karl, 1900A, 1921C, 1985B
Schmittbaur, Joseph Aloys, 1809B
Schmitz, Elie Robert, 1889A, 1949B; *The Capture
 of Inspiration*, 1935H
Schmitz, Eugen, 1882A, 1939D, 1959B
Schnabel, Artur, 1882A, 1890C, 1951B; *Music &
 the Line of Most Resistance*, 1942H
Schnabel, Joseph I., 1804D
Schnabel, Michael, Piano Co., 1814G
Schnaut, Gabriele, 1951A, 1976C
Schneeberger, Hans, 1926A, 1946C
Schnéevoigt, Georg, 1927D
Schneider, Alexander, 1908A, 1945E, 1988E,
 1993B
Schneider, David E., 1963A
Schneider, Edward Faber, 1872A, 1950B
Schneider, Conrad Michael, 1752B

Schneider, Friedrich, 1786A, 1821D, 1853B;
 Elementarbuch der Harmonie und Tonsetzkunst,
 1820H; *Handbuch des Organisten*, 1830H;
 Vorschule der Musik, 1827H
Schneider, Georg Abraham, 1770A, 1820D,
 1825D, 1839B
Schneider, Heidi, 1946E
Schneider, Hortense, 1838A, 1853C, 1920B
Schneider, Johann, 1789A, 1825D, 1864B
Schneider, Johann Christian Friedrich, 1812D
Schneider, Julius, 1805A, 1885B
Schneider, Mischa, 1985B
Schneider, Peter, 1939A, 1960C
Schneider, Urs, 1991D, 1962D
Schneider String Quartet, 1952G
Schneiderhan String Quartet, 1937G
Schnittke, Alfred, 1934A, 1998B
Schnitzer, Arlene, Concert Hall, 1984G
Schnoor, Hans, 1893A, 1976B
Schnoor von Carolsfeld, Ludwig 1836A,
 1854C, 1865B
Schnorr von Carolsfeld, Malvina, 1825A,
 1841C, 1904B
Schoberlechner, Charles Franz, 1797A, 1809C,
 1843B
Schobert, Johann, 1767F, 1767B
Schock, Rudolf, 1915A, 1937C, 1986B
Schoeck, Othmar, 1886A, 1945D, 1957B
Schoen-René, Anna, 1864A, 1887C, 1942B;
 America's Musical Heritage, 1941H
Schoenberg, Arnold, 1874A, 1951B; *Composing
 with Twelve Tones*, 1922H; *Fundamentals of
 Musical Composition*, 1948H; *Harmonielehre*,
 1911H; *Manual of Counterpoint*, 1912H;
 Models for Beginners in Composition, 1942H;
 Structural Functions of Harmony, 1948H; *Style
 & Idea*, 1950H; *Theory of Composition*, 1940H
Schoenberg Institute, 1974G
Schoenberg String Quartet, 1977G
Schoenefeld, Henry, 1857A, 1936B
Schöffler, Paul, 1897A, 1925C, 1977B
Schola de Montpelier, 1905G
Schola Cantorum Basiliensis, 1933G
Schola Cantorum of Copenhagen, 1953G
Schola Cantorum of Iceland, 1996G
Schola Cantorum of Mexico, 1939G
Schola Cantorum of Norway, 1964G
Scholes, Percy, 1877A, 1958B; *Puritans & Music
 in England & New England*, 1934H
Scholl, Andreas, 1967A, 1992C
Scholl, Klaus, 1757A, 1844B
Scholz, Bernhard E, 1871D
Schonberg, Harold C., 1915A, 1948D, 1950D,
 1939D, 1971D; *Chamber & Solo Instrument
 Music*, 1955H; *Facing the Music*, 1981H;
 *Glorious Ones: Classical Music's Legendary
 Performers*, 1985H; *The Great Conductors*,
 1967H; *The Great Pianists*, 1963H; *Loves of the
 Great Composers*, 1970H

A *Births*   B *Deaths*   C *Debuts*   D *New Positions*
          E *Prizes/Honors*

Schönberger, Benno, 1863A, 1878C, 1930B
Schöne, Lotte, 1891A, 1912C, 1977B
Schønwandt, Michael, 1953A, 1977C, 1979D, 1987D, 1988D, 1989F, 1990D, 1992D
School for...New Serial Techniques, 1965G
School Music Monthly, 1908G
The School Musician, 1929G
School Music Review, 1892G
School of Dalcroze Eurythmics, 1913G
School of English Church Music, 1927G
Schorr, Friedrich, 1888A, 1912C, 1953B
Schott, Anton, 1846A, 1871C, 1913B
Schotts, B., Söhne, Publishers, 1770G
Schrade, Leo, 1903A, 1964B; *Tragedy in the Art of Music*, 1964H
Schrader, Barry, 1945A; *Introduction to Electro-Acoustical Music*, 1982H
Schradieck, Henry, 1846A, 1918B
Schramm, Hermann, 1871A, 1895C, 1951B
Schramm, Johann Jacob, 1808B
Schreiber Cornet Co., 1867G
Schreier, Peter, 1935A
Schreiner, Alexander, 1901A, 1939D
Schreiner Music Store & Publishing Co., 1861G
Schreker, Franz, 1878A, 1934B
Schreyer, Gregor, 1768B
Schrider, Christopher, 1751B
Schrøder, Jens, 1943D
Schröder, Karl, (I), 1816A, 1890B
Schröder, Karl, (II), 1848A, 1872D, 1886D, 1890D, 1935B
Schröder-Devrient, Wilhelmine, 1804A, 1821C, 1823F, 1860B, 1921C
Schröder-Feinen, Ursula, 1936A, 1961C
Schroeder & Gunther, Publishers, 1879G
Schroeder String Quartet, 1871G
Schröter Christoph G.: *Deutliche answeisung zum generalbass*, 1772H; *Letzte beschäftigung mit musikalischen dingen*, 1782H
Schröter, Corona E., 1751A, 1764C, 1802B
Schröter, Gottlieb, 1782B
Schrott, Thomas, 1966A
Schub, André-Michel, 1952A, 1974CE, 1977E, 1981E
Schuback, Thomas, 1982D
Schubart, Christian Friedrich Daniel, 1768D, 1777F, 1791B; *Ideen zu einer aesthetik der Tonkunst*, 1784H; *Leben und gesinnungen*, 1791H; *Musikalisches Rhapsodien*, 1786H
Schubaur, Johann Lukas, 1815B
Schubert, Richard, 1885A
Schubert, Franz, 1797A, 1808F, 1811F, 1814F, 1816F, 1817F, 1818F, 1819F, 1822F, 1828B
Schubert, Franz Anton, 1768A, 1827B
Schubert, Georgine, 1840A, 1839C, 1878B
Schubert, Joseph, 1757A, 1837B
Schubert, Maschinka (Schneider), 1815A, 1832C, 1882B
Schubert, Richard, 1909C, 1959B

Schubert Alley (New York), 1913G
Schubert String Quartet, 1877G
Schuberth, E., Publisher, 1872G
Schuberth, Julius, 1804A, 1875B
Schuberth, J, & Co., 1826G; Leipzig Branch, 1832G
Schuch, Ernst von, 1845A, 1872D, 1914B
Schuch-Proska, Clementine, 1850A, 1873C, 1932B
Schulhoff, Julius, 1825A, 1842C, 1898B
Schuller, Gunther, 1925A, 1959F, 1960E, 1967DE, 1970E, 1980E, 1981E, 1982E, 1984D. 1989E, 1991E, 1994E, 1997E; *Horn Technique*, 1962H; *Musings: The Musical Worlds of Gunther Schuller*, 1986H
Schultz, Andrew, 1196A
Schultz, Jan, 1987E
Schultz, Robert, 1981D
Schulz, Johann Abraham, 1780D, 1787D, 1800B; *Gedanken über den Einfluss der Musik auf die Bildung eines Volks*, 1790H
Schulz, Johann Philipp, 1773A, 1810D, 1827B
Schulz, Leo, 1865A, 1876C, 1944B
Schulz, Walther, 1979C
Schulze, J. F., & Sons, Organ Builders, 1825G
Schuman, Patricia, 1954A
Schuman, William, 1910A, 1930F, 1939F, 1943E, 1945D, 1946E, 1957E, 1962D, 1964E, 1965E, 1968F, 1971E, 1973E, 1985E, 1987E, 1981E, 1982E, 1989E, 1992B
Schuman, William, Award, 1981G
Schumann, Clara (Wieck), 1819A, 1828C, 1837F, 1840F, 1844F, 1896B
Schumann, Elisabeth, 1888A, 1909C, 1952B
Schumann, Robert, 1810A, 1828F, 1829F, 1830F, 1831F, 1832F, 1833F, 1837F, 1840F, 1842F, 1843F, 1844F, 1853F, 1854F, 1856B
Schumann, Robert, Piano Competition, 1956G
Schumann-Heink, Ernestine, 1861A, 1876C, 1936B
Schunk, Robert, 1948A, 1973C
Schuppanzigh, Ignaz, 1776A, 1798D, 1828D, 1830B
Schuppanzigh String Quartet, 1808G
Schuré Edouard: *Le drame musical*, 1875H; *Histoire du Lied*, 1868H
Schürer, Georg, 1786B
Schurig, Wolfram, 1967A
Schürmann, Georg Caspar, 1751B
Schuster, Ignaz, 1801C
Schuster, Joseph, 1812B
Schütz, Siiri, 1974A, 1991C
Schütz, Heinrich, Chorale, 1962G
Schütz, Heinrich, Tage, 1955G
Schützendorf, Alfons, 1882A, 1904C, 1946B
Schützendorf, Gustav, 1883A, 1905C, 1937B
Schützendorf, Leo, 1886A, 1908C, 1931B
Schwäbischer Sängerbund, 1849G
Schwager, Myron, 1974D

❀

F   *Biographical*   G   *Cultural Beginnings*   H   *Musical Literature*
I   *Musical Compositions*

Schwanenberg, Johann Gottfried, 1762D
Schwanenberger, Johann, 1804B
Schwann, William, 1913A, 1998B
Schwann Record Catalog, 1949G
Schwann-2: Record and Tape Guide, 1964G
Schwantner, Joseph, 1943A
Schwartz, Elliott, 1936A, 1975D, 1984D;
   Contemporary Composers on Contemporary
   Music, 1967H; *Electronic Music: A Listener's*
   Guide, 1973H; *Music Since 1945*, 1993H;
   Music: Ways of Listening, 1982H
Schwartz, Sergiu, 1957A, 1980C
Schwartzer Zither Factory, 1866G
Schwarz, Boris, 1906A, 1920C, 1948D, 1983B;
   Great Masters of the Violin, 1983H; *Music &*
   Musical Life in Soviet Russia, 1972H
Schwarz, Gerard, 1947A, 1975F, 1976D, 1978D,
   1983D, 1987E, 1989E
Schwarz, Hanna, 1943A, 1970C
Schwarz, Joseph, 1880A, 1900C, 1926B
Schwarz, K. Robert: *Minimalists*, 1996H
Schwarz, Vera, 1912C
Schwarzenberg, Elisabeth, 1956C
Schwarzer Zither Factory, 1872G
Schwarzkopf, Elisabeth, 1915A, 1938C, 1975F
Schweitzer, Albert, 1875A, 1952E, 1965B
Schweitzer, Anton, 1766D, 1778D, 1787B
Schweitzerische Musikpädagogische Blätter,
   1949G
Schweizerische Musikzeitung, 1861G
Schweizerisches Jahrbuch für Musikwissenschaft,
   1924G
Schweizerische Musikpädagogische Verband,
   1893G
Schwencke, Christian Friedrich, 1767A, 1822B
Schwencke, Friedrich Gottlieb, 1823A, 1852D,
   1896B
Schwencke, Johann Friedrich, 1792A, 1852B
Schwerin Landestheater, 1882G
Schwets, Stanislav, 1974A, 1996CE
SchwetzingenRococo Theater, 1752G
Schwieger, Hans, 1906A, 1948D
Schwindl, Friedrich, 1786B
Schymberg, Hjordis, 1934C
Sciutti, Graziella, 1927A, 1951C
Scogna, Flavio, 1956A
Scott, Cyril, 1879A, 1970B
Scott, Francis George, 1880A, 1958B
Scott, James, 1885A
Scott, Stephen, 1944A
Scott, Vanessa, 1955A, 1982C
Scottsdale Center for the Arts, 1976G
Scotti, Antonio, 1866A, 1889C, 1936B
Scottish Baroque Ensemble, 1968G
Scottish Chamber Orchestra, 1974G
The Scottish Minstrel, 1820G
Scottish Music Archive, 1969G
Scottish Opera Co., 1962G
Scottish Rite Symphony Orchestra, 1952G

Scotto, Renata, 1933A, 1952C
Scovotti, Jeanette, 1936A, 1960C
Scratch Orchestra, 1969G
Scriabin, Alexander, 1872A, 1896F, 1906F,
   1908F, 1915B
Scribner, Norman, 1936A
Scribner, Norman, Choir, 1971G
Scribner's Magazine, 1887G
Scribner's Monthly, 1870G
Scuderi, Vincenzo, 1961A
Scudo, Pierre, 1806A, 1864B; *Critique et*
   littérature musicale I, 1850H
Sculthorpe, Peter, 1929A
Scuola Superiore de Musica Sacra, 1910G
Seagle, Oscar, 1877A, 1896C, 1945B
Seal Bay Festival, 1995G
Search, Frederick Preston, 1889A, 1959B
Searle, Humphrey, 1915A, 1982B; *Twentieth*
   Century Counterpoint, 1954H
Seashore, Carl Emil, 1866A, 1949B; *In Search of*
   Beauty in Music, 1947H; *Measures of Musical*
   Talent, 1919H; *The Psychology of Musical*
   Talent, 1919H
Seattle, Washington: Center Opera House,
   1962G; Chamber Music Festival, 1982G;
   Frye's Opera House, 1884G; Moore Theater,
   1907G; Norwegian Male Chorus, 1889G;
   Opera Association, 1963G 64???????; Squire's
   Opera House, 1879G; Symphony Orchestra
   I, 1903G; Symphony Orchestra II, 1908G
Seaver/NEA Conductors Award, 1985G
Seay, Albert: *Music in the Medieval World*,
   1965H
Sebastian, Bruno, 1947A, 1969C
Sebastian, John, 1944A
Sebastiani, Sylvia, 1942A, 1969C
Sechter, Simon, 1788A, 1867B; *Die Grundsätze*
   der musikalischen Komposition, 1853H;
   Praktische Generalbass-Schule, 1835H
Seckendorff, Karl Siegmund, 1785B
Il secolo, 1866G
Second, Sarah Mahon, 1785C
Secunde, Nadine, 1953A
Sedares, James, 1986D, 1979F
Sedie, Enrico Delle, 1907B
Sedivka, Jan, 1961D
Sedona Chamber Music Festival, 1985G
Seefehlner, Egon, 1976D
Seefried, Irmgard, 1919A, 1940C, 1988B
Seeger, Charles, 1886A, 1979B; *Music as*
   Recreation, 1940H; *Studies in Musicology 1935-*
   75, 1977H
Seesaw Music Corp., 1963
Segal, Uriel, 1981D
Seger, Josef Ferdinand, 1782B
Segerstam, Leif, 1944A, 1965D, 1968D, 1975D,
   1977D, 1983D, 1989D, 1995D
Segovia, Andrés, 1893A, 1909C, 1987B
Segreva, Caroline, 1905A, 1934C, 1998B

❄

A   *Births*   B   *Deaths*   C   *Debuts*   D   *New Positions*
E   *Prizes/Honors*

Seguin, Arthur P., 1809A, 1829C, 1852B
Segurola, Andrés de, 1874A, 1953B
Seiber, Mátyás, 1905A, 1960B
Seidel, Friedrich Ludwig, 1765A, 1792D, 1808D, 1822D, 1831B
Seidel, Johann Julius, 1810A, 1856B; *Die Orgel un ihr Bau*, 1843H
Seidel, Toscha, 1899A, 1918C, 1962B
Seideman, Wladyslaw, 1849A, 1874C
Seidl, Anton, 1850A, 1879D, 1883D, 1885D, 1891D, 1898B
Seidl, Arthur, 1863A, 1928B
Seidl-Kraus, Auguste, 1853A, 1939B
Seifert, Ernst Hubertus, Organ Builder, 1885G
Seiffert, Max, 1868A, 1948B; *Geschichte der Klaviermusik*, 1899H, 1901H
Seiffert, Peter, 1954A
Seifriz, Max, 1854D
Seinemeyer, Meta, 1895A, 1918C, 1929B
Seipenbusch, Edgar, 1936A
Seiss, Isodor, 1870D
Seitz, Roland Forrest, 1867A, 1946B
Séjan, Nicolas, 1773D, 1783D, 1790D, 1807D, 1814D, 1819B
Selby, Kathryn, 1962A, 1981C
Selby, William, 1760D, 1771F, 1776D, 1778D, 1798B
Seligmann, Hippolyte-Prosper, 1817A, 1882B
Selika, Marie, 1937B
Selivochin, Vladimir, 1968E
Sellars, Peter, 1957A, 1983E
Sellick, Phyllis, 1933C
Sellner, Joseph, 1787A, 1843B
Selmer, Henri, et Cie., 1885G
Selmexzi, Györgi, 1952A
Semanas de Música Religiosa, 1962G
Sembrich, Marcella, 1858A, 1877C, 1935B
Semet, Théophile, 1824A, 1888B
Semkow, Jerzy, 1928A, 1959D, 1966D, 1976D, 1985D
Sempere, José, 1986C
Sendrey, Aladár (Alfred Szendrei), 1884A
Senefelder, A, Gleissner, Fr, & Co., (Munich), 1796G
Senesino, Francisco, 1759B
Senff, Bartholf, 1815A, 1900B
Senff, Gartolf, Publisher, 1847G
Senn, Marta, 1958A
Senofsky, Berl, 1925A, 1947E, 1955E
Sequin, Arthur, 1828C
Sequoia String Quartet, 1972G
Serafin, Tullio, 1878A. 1898C, 1909D, 1924D, 1934D, 1956D, 1968B
Serassi, Andrea L., 1799B
Serassi, Giuseppe, Jr., 1817B; *Sugli Organi*, 1816H
Serassi, Giuseppe, Sr., 1760B
Serebrier, José, 1938A, 1949C, 1962F, 1968F, 1976E, 1984D

Sereni, Mario, 1928A, 1953C
Serge Modular Music Systems, 1974G
Serkin, Peter, 1947A, 1903A, 1991B
Serkin, Rudolf, 1915C, 1963E, 1968D, 1979E, 1981E, 1988E
Serly, Tibor, 1900A, 1901A, 1978B; *Modus Lascivus: The Road to Enharmonicism*, 1976H; *The Rhetoric of Melody*, 1978H; *A, Second Look at Harmony*, 1965H
Serocki, Kazimierz, 1922A, 1981B
Serov, Alexander, 1820A, 1849F, 1851F, 1871B
Serpette, Gaston, 1871E
Serra, Luciana, 1946A, 1966C
Servadei, Annette, 1945A, 1972C
Servais, Adrien-François, 1807A, 1866B
Servais, François M., 1873E
Servais, Joseph, 1850A, 1867C, 1885B
Sessions, Roger, 1896A, 1928E, 1938E, 1953DE, 1958E, 1961E, 1966D, 1968EF, 1974E, 1985B; *Harmonic Practice*, 1951H; *The Musical Experience of Composer, Performer, Listener*, 1950H; *Questions about Music*, 1970H; *Reflections on the Music Life in the United States*, 1956H; *Roger Sessions on Music, The Collected Essays*, 1979H
Settlement Music School, 1908G
Ševčik, Otakar, 1852A, 1873C, 1934B; *Violine-Schule für Anfänger*, 1904H; *Schule der Violine-Technik*, 1881H
Sevenars Summer Music Festival, 1968G
Seventh Army Symphony Orchestra, 1952G
Sévérac, Déodat de, 1872A, 1921B
Severn, Edmund, 1862A, 1942B
Sevitzky, Fabien, 1893A, 1923F, 1937D, 1959D, 1965D, 1967B
Sewanee Summer Music Center, 1957G
Seward, Theodore, 1868D, 1881D
Seydel, Karl, 1879A, 1901C, 1947B
Seydelmann, Franz, 1787D, 1806B
Seyfarth Music, Publishers, 1868G
Seyfried, Ignaz Xaver, 1776A, 1801D, 1841B
Seyfried Johann: *Wiener Tonschule*, 1832H
Sgambati, Giovanni, 1841A, 1914B
Sgouros, Dimitris, 1969A, 1982C
Shacklock, Constance, 1913A, 1945C
Shade, Ellen, 1948A, 1972C
Shade, Nancy, 1949A, 1968C
Shäfer, Markus, 1961A
Shafir, Shuylamith, 1934C
Shaham, Gil, 1971A, 1981C
Shaham, Hagai, 1990E
Shaham, Rinat, 1998C
Shallon, David, 2000B
Shane, Rita Frances, 1940A
Shanet, Howard, 1918A, 1972D
Shanghai, China: String Quartet, 1983G; Symphony Orchestra, 1879G
Shanks, Donald, 1940A
Shao, En, 1954A

F *Biographical*   G *Cultural Beginnings*   H *Musical Literature*
I *Musical Compositions*

Shapero, Harold, 1920A, 1941E
Shapey, Ralph, 1921A, 1966E, 1982E, 1989E, 1991E
Shapiro, Gerald, 1942A
Shapiro, Bernstein & Co., 1895G
Shapirra, Elyakum, 1969D
Shapleigh, Bertram, 1871A, 1940B
Shaporin, Yuri, 1887A, 1966B
Sharp, Cecil, 1859A, 1923E, 1924B; *English Folksongs from the Southern Appalachians,* 1917H; *Folksongs of England,* 1912H
Sharp, Geoffrey, 1914A
Sharpe, Ethel, 1872A, 1891C, 1947B
Shasby, Anne, 1945A, 1971C
Shattinger, Adam & Oliver, Publishers, 1876G
Shaw, Arnold: *The Schillinger System of Musical Composition,* 1941H
Shaw, George Bernard: *How to Become a Music Critic,* 1960H; *Music in London, Three Volumes,* 1932H; *The Perfect Wagnerite,* 1898H
Shaw, Harold, 1923A
Shaw, Mary, 1834C, 1844F, 1876B
Shaw, Joseph P., Publishing Co., 1854G
Shaw, Oliver, 1779A, 1848B; *Melodia Sacra,* 1819H
Shaw, Robert, 1916A, 1967D, 1988EF, 1991E, 1992E, 1999B
Shaw, Robert, Chorale, 1948G
Shaw Attractions, Inc., 1978G
Shaw Concerts, Inc., 1969G
Shawn, Allen, 1948A
Shawnee Press (Words & Music), 1947G
Shchedrin, Rodion, 1932A
Shchetinsky, Alexander, 1961A
Shea's Buffalo Theater, 1926G
Shebalin, Meredith, 1902A
Shebalin, Vissarion, 1942D, 1963B
Sheehan, Joseph, 1869A, 1895C, 1936B
Sheffield, England: Amateur Musical Society, 1864G; Bach Society, 1950G; Music Festival, 1895G; Tonic Sol-Fa Ass'n, 1876G
Shelley, Harry Rowe, 1858A, 1947B
Shelley, Howard, 1950A, 1971C
Shelobinsky, Valeri, 1913A
Shelton, Lucy, 1944A, 1980E
Sheng, Bright, 1955A
Shepherd, Arthur, 1880A, 1920F, 1928D, 1938E, 1958B
Shepherd, John, Music Press, 1964G
Sheridan, Margaret, 1889A, 1918C, 1958B
Sherman, Russell, 1930A, 1945C
Sherman, Clay & Co., 1871G
Sherman & Hyde, Publishers, 1871G
Sherwood, William Hall, 1854A, 1911B
Shicoff, Neil, 1949A, 1975C
Shield, William, 1817E, 1829B; *An Introducton to Harmony,* 1799H; *Rudiments of Thorough Bass,* 1815H
Shields, Ren, 1913B

Shifrin, Seymour, 1926A, 1979B
Shifrin, David, 2000E
Shilkret, Nathaniel, 1895A, 1916D, 1989B
Shimell, William, 1953A, 1980C
Shimizu, Kazune, 1960A
Shinko Sakkyokuka (Japan), 1930G
Shinn F. W.: *Musical Memory and its Cultivations,* 1898
Shinner, Emily, 1862A, 1881C, 1901B
Shinner String Quartet, 1887G
Shinozaki, Yasuo, 1968A, 1993C
Shira, Francesco, 1833D, 1844D, 1848D
Shirley, George, 1934A, 1959C
Shirley-Quirk, John, 1931A, 1961C
Shirreff, Jane, 1811A, 1831C, 1883B
Shkolnik, Sheldon, 1990B
Shoemaker, Carolie J., 1963
Shoo, David Ik-Sung, 1988C
Shore, Bernard, 1896A, 1925C
Shore, Clare, 1954A
Shore, John, 1752B
Shostakovich, Dmitri, 1906A, 1948F, 1966F, 1973E, 1975B
Shostakovich, Maxim, 1938A, 1963F, 1965C, 1968F, 1981E, 1986D,
Shrubsole, William, 1760A, 1782D, 1806B
Shuard, Amy, 1924A ,1949C, 1975B
Shudi, Joshua, Harpsichord Maker, 1767G
Shui, Lan, 1985CD, 1997D
Shuk, Isaac, 1973B
Shulamit Conservatory of Music, 1920G
Shulman, Alan, 1915A
Shumsky, Oscar, 1917A, 1925C, 2000B
Shumway, Nehemiah: *American Harmony,* 1801H
Shure, Leonard, 1910A, 1927C, 1995B
Sibelius, Jan, 1865A, 1885F, 1897E, 1899F, 1904F, 1906E, 1908F, 1912F, 1914E, 1957B
Sibelius Violin Competition, 1965G
Siboni, Guiseppe Vincenze, 1780A, 1797C, 1819D, 1839B
Sicilian Symphony Orchestra, 1958G
Sidlin, Murry, 1940A
Sidnell, Robert: *Materials of Music Composition,* 1980H
Siebenkäs, Johann, 1764D, 1775D, 1781B
Sieber, Ferdinand, 1822A, 1895B; *Vollständiges lehrbuch der gesangkunst für Lehrer und Schüler,* 1854H
Sieber, Jean Georges, Publisher, 1770G
Sieber, Georges-Julien, Publisher (Paris), 1799G
Siebert, Dorothea, 1945C
Siegel, Carl F. W., Publishing Co., 1846G
Siegel, Jeffrey, 1942A, 1958C
Sieglitz, George, 1854A, 1880C, 1917B
Siegmeister, Elie, 1909A, 1978E, 1990E, 1991B; *Harmony & Melody,* 1965H; *Invitation to Music,* 1961H; *The Music Lover's Handbook,* 1943H

A *Births* B *Deaths* C *Debuts* D *New Positions*
E *Prizes/Honors*

Siegmund-Schultze, Walther, 1916A, 1993B
Siehr, Gustav, 1837A, 1896B
Siehr, Gustav, 1863C
Siemonn, George, 1930D
Siems, Margarethe, 1879A, 1902C, 1952B
Siepi, Cesare, 1923A, 1941C
Sierra, Roberto, 1953A
Sieveking, Martinus, 1867A, 1950B
Sigismondi, Giuseppe, 1808D
Sigma Alpha Iota Music Sorority, 1903G
Signale für die Musikalische Welt, 1843G
Signorini, Francisco, 1860A, 1882C, 1927B
Signum Record Label, 1997G
Sigurbjörnsson, Thorkell, 1938A
Siki, Béla, 1923A, 1943E, 1945C
Silas, Edouard, 1827A, 1909B
Silbermann, Gottfried, 1753B
Silbermann, Johann Andreas, 1783B
Silberstein, Lilya, 1965A
Silcher, Friedrich, 1789A, 1817D, 1825E, 1860B;
   Harmonie- und kompositionslehre, 1851H
Silesian Music Festival, 1876G
Silesian Philharmonic Choir, 1974G
Silja, Anja, 1935A, 1956C
Sills, Beverly, 1929A, 1947C, 1955F, 1970E,
   1979D, 1980E, 1985E, 1994D
Siloti, Alexander, 1863A, 1880C, 1945B
Silva, Francisco Manuel da, 1795A, 1865B
Silva, Luigi, 1903A, 1961B
Silver Burdett Co, Publisher, 1885G
Silver, Charles, 1891E
Silver, Sheil, 1948A
Silveri, Paolo, 1913A, 1939C
Silverstein, Joseph, 1932A, 1959E, 1960E,
   1983D, 1986F, 1987D, 1995F
Silvestre, Pierre, Violin Maker, 1829G
Silvestri, Constantin, 1913A, 1923C, 1935D,
   1947D, 1961D, 1969B
Simándy, József, 1916A, 1938C, 1997B
Simionato, Giulietta, 1910A, 1935C
Simmonds, William H., 1823A, 1876B
Simmons, Calvin, 1950A, 1978D, 1979E,
   1982B
Simmons, William B., Organ Builder, 1845G
Simon, Abbey, 1922A, 1940CE
Simon, Geoffrey, 1969D, 1987D
Simon, Joanna, 1940A, 1962E
Simon, Pierre, Bowmaker, 1846G
Simon, Prosper-Charles, 1788A, 1866B;
   Nouveau manuel complet de l'organiste II,
   1863H
Simon, Stephen, 1937A
Simon & Schuster, 1924G
Simon-Girard, Juliette, 1859A, 1877C, 1959B
Simoneau, Léopold, 1916A, 1941C
Simonetti, Riccardo, 1970A
Simonis, Jean-Marie, 1931A
Simonov Yuri, 1941A, 1970D, 1994D
Simons, Marijn, 1982A

Simonsen, Rudolph, 1889A, 1911C, 1931D,
   1947B
Simpson, Joy, 1987B
Simpson, Methven, Publisher, 1851G
Simpson, Robert, 1921A, 1997B
Simrock, Friedrich August, 1901B
Simrock, Nikolaus, 1751A, 1832B
Simrock, Peter Joseph, 1792A, 1868B
Simrock Music Publishers, 1793G
Sims, Ezra, 1928A, 1985E
Sinaisky, Vassily, 1973E, 1991D
Sinclair, John, 1791A, 1810C, 1811C, 1857B
Sinding, Christian, 1856A, 1890E, 1921F,
   1941B
Sinfonia of Westminster, 1996G
Sinfonia Varsovia, 1984G
Sinfonian, 1901G
Singapore Symphony Orchestra, 1979G
Singer, Peter: *Metaphysische blicke in die Tonwelt*,
   1847H
Singer Pur, 1991G
Singers Development Foundation, 1991G
Singher, Martial, 1904A, 1930C, 1959E, 1962D,
   1990B
Singleton, Alvin, 1940A
Die Singphoniker, 1980G
Sinigaglia, Leone, 1868A, 1944B
Sinopoli, Giuseppe, 1946A, 1971F, 1982D,
   1983D, 1984D, 1986F
Siona, 1875G
Siow, Lee-Chin, 1994E
Sisman, Elaine, 1952A
Sitka Summer Music Festival, 1972G
Sitkovetsky, Dmitri, 1954A, 1979E
Sitsky, Larry, 1934A; *Music of the Repressed
   Russian Avant-Garde*, 1994H
Siukola, Heikki, 1943A
Sivori, Ernesto Camillo, 1815A, 1827C, 1886E,
   1894B
Sixt, Johann Abraham, 1757A, 1797B
Sjöberg, Gilla-Maria, 1987C
Sjögren, Emil, 1853A, 1918B
Skalkottas, Nikos, 1904A, 1949B
Škampa Quartet, 1989G
Skaraborg Vocal Ensemble, 1989G
Skilton, Charles Sanford, 1868A, 1903D, 1941B
Skinner, Ernest M., 1866A, 1960B; *The
   Composition of the Organ*, 1947H; *The Modern
   Organ*, 1915H
Skinner Organ Co., 1901G
Skovhus, Bo, 1962A, 1988C
Skripka, Sergei, 1977D
Škroup, František Jan, 1801A, 1837D, 1862B
Skrowaczewski, Stanislaw, 1923A, 1954D,
   1956D, 1960D, 1984D
Slack, Karen, 1994E
Slater, Moses, Brass Instruments, 1865G
Slatinaru, Maria, 1938A, 1969C
Slatkin, Felix, 1915A, 1963B

❈

Slatkin, Leonard, 1944A, 1968F, 1974F, 1979D, 1985D, 1986F, 1989D, 1992E, 1995F, 1996D
Slava Osterc Ensemble, 1962G
Slavák, Ladislav, 1919A
Slavenski, Josip, 1896A, 1955B
Slavík, Josef, 1806A, 1821C, 1833B
Slawson, Wayne, 1932A
Sleeper, Henry Dike, 1865A, 1902D, 1948B
Slenczynska, Ruth, 1925A, 1936C
Slezak, Leo, 1873A, 1896C, 1946B
Sli-sadih, Franghiz, 1947A
Slingerland Banjo & Drum Co., 1921G
Slivinski, Joseph von, 1865A, 1890C, 1930B
Sloane, A. Baldwin, 1925B
Sloane, Steven, 1998D
Sloboda, John: *The Musical Mind*, 1985H; *Musical Perceptions*, 1993H
Slobodskaya, Oda, 1888A, 1918C, 1970B
Slonimsky, Nicholas, 1923F, 1991E, 1995B; *Lexicon of musical Invective*, 1952H; *Music of Latin-America*, 1945H; *Music Since 1900*, 1937H; *Supplement to Music Since 1900*, 1986H; *Thesaurus of Scales & Melodic Patterns*, 1947H
Sloper, Lindsay, 1826A, 1846C, 1887B
Slovak Chamber Orchestra, 1960G
Slovak Philharmonic Society, 1949G
Slovák, Ladislav, 1961D, 1972D, 1999B
Smallens, Alexander, 1889A, 1919D, 1972B
Smart, Georg, Publisher, 1770G
Smart, George Thomas, 1776A, 1791D, 1811E, 1822D, 1867B
Smart, Henry, Piano Maker, 1821G
Smart, Henry Thomas, 1813A, 1879B
Smetáček, Václav, 1906A, 1934D, 1942D, 1986B
Smetana, Bedřich, 1824A, 1843F, 1848F, 1861F, 1866D, 1874F, 1884BF
Smetana, Bedřich, Museum (Prague), 1928G
Smetana (Czech) String Quartet, 1934G
Smetana String Quartet, 1945G
Smirnov, Dmitri, 1882A, 1903C, 1944B
Smirnova, Tamara, 1958A, 1975C
Smit, Leo (American), 1921A, 1999B
Smit, Leo (Dutch), 1900A, 1939C, 1943B
Smith, Bessie, 1894A
Smith, Carlton Sprague, 1905A, 1931D, 1994B
Smith, Cecil, 1936D, 1948D, 1956B; *Worlds of Music*, 1952H
Smith, Craig, 1960A
Smith, David Stanley, 1910E, 1920D, 1949B
Smith, Gayle, 1943A
Smith, Geoff: *New Voices: American Composers Talk about Their Music*, 1995H
Smith, Gregg, 1931A
Smith, Gregg, Singers, 1955G
Smith, Hale, 1925A
Smith, John Christopher, 1754D, 1795B; *Collection of English Songs, c. 1500*, 1779H

Smith, John Stafford, 1836B; *Musical Antiqua I, II*, 1812H
Smith, Julian, 1973C
Smith, Lawrence Leighton, 1936A, 1964E, 1973D, 1983D
Smith, Leland, 1925A; *Handbook of Harmonic Analysis*, 1963H
Smith, Moses, 1901A, 1924D, 1934D, 1964B
Smith, Patrick J., 1932A, 1970D
Smith, William O., 1926A, 1957E
Smith Publications, 1974G
Smith String Quartet, 1990G
Smith, White & Perry, Publishers, 1867G
Smith-Brindle, Reginald: *The New Music*, 1975H
Smither, Howard, 1925A; *A History of the Oratorio*, 1977H
Smithson, Henriette, 1833F
Smitkova, Jane, 1967C
Smits, Stefanie, 1966A, 1996C
Smolenskaya, Eugenia, 1945C
Smolensky, Stepan, 1848A, 1909B
Smoshka, Vitaly, 1999E
SMU Conservatory Summer Music Festival, 1976G
Smulders, Charles, 1889E
Smyth, Ethel, 1858A, 1922E, 1944B
Snetzler, Johann, 1785B
Snetzler, John, Organ Builder, 1775G
Sobinov, Leonid, 1897C, 1934B
Sobolewski, Edward, 1804A, 1872B; *Das Geheimnis der neuester Schule der Musik*, 1859H
Sobolov, Leonid, 1872A
Sociedad de Autores, Compositores y Editores..., 1893G
Sociedade Beneficencia Musical, 1833G
Società Corale G. B. Martini, 1902G
Società Italiana de Musicologia, 1964G
Società Italiana de Musique Moderna, 1917G
Societá Polifonica Romana, 1919G
Societas Universalis Sanctae Caeciliae, 1947G
Société Anonyme des Editions Maurice Senart, 1908G
Société de Musique Contemporaine du Québec, 1965G
Société de Musique d'Autrefois, 1925G
Société de Musique de Chambre Amingaud, 1855G
Société de Musique de Chambre de Versailles, 1944G
Société de Musique Helvétique, 1808G
Société des Concerts Cortot, 1903G
Société des Concerts d'Autrefois, 1906G
Société des Concerts Populaires, 1914G
Société des Derniers Quators de Beethoven, 1834G
Société des Instruments Anciens Casadesus, 1901G

A *Births*   B *Deaths*   C *Debuts*   D *New Positions*
E *Prizes/Honors*

Société d'Études Musicales, Publisher, 1903G
Société Française de Musicologie, 1917G
Society for the Publication of Danish Music, 1871G
Society for Asian Music (N.Y.), 1960G
Society for Contemporary Music, 1927G
Society for Electro-Acoustic Music in the United States, 1984G
Society for Ethnomusicology, 1955G
Society for Forgotten Music, 1948G
Society for New Music, 1971G
Society for Research in Asiatic Music, 1936G
Society for the Improvement of Musical Art in Bohemia, 1810G
Society for the Preservation & Encouragement of Barber Shop Quartet Singing, 1938G
Society for the Preservation of the American Musical Heritage, 1958G
Society for the Publication of American Music, 1919G
Society of Advertising Music Producers, Arrangers & Composers, 1976G
Society of American Musicians & Composers, 1889G
Society of Black Composers, 1968G
Society of British Composers, 1905G
Society of Composers, Inc, 1966G
Society of European State Authors & Composers, 1931G
Society of Friends of Music (N.Y.), 1913G
Society of Norwegian Composers, 1917G
Society of Private Music Performance, 1918G
Society of Romanian Composers, 1920G
Society of St. Gregory of America, 1914G
Society of Swedish Composers, 1918G
Society of the Classic Guitar, 1936G
Society of Women Musicians, 1911G
Söderblom, Ulf, 1977E
Söderlind, Ragnar, 1945A
Söderström, Elisabeth, 1927A, 1947C
Sofia, Bulgaria: Festival Sinfonietta, 1977G; National Opera, 1908G; State Music Academy, 1904G; State Philharmonic Orchestra, 1946G
Sofronitzky, Vladimir, 1901A, 1961B
Sohier, Charles-Joseph 1759B
Sohmer & Co., Piano Makers, 1872G
Sojer, Hans, 1967C
Sokoloff, Nicolai, 1886A, 1914D, 1918D, 1938D, 1965B
Sokoloff, Nikolai Alexandrovich, 1859A, 1922B
Sokoloff, Vladimir, 1936A, 1955C, 1997B
Sokolov, Grigory, 1964E
Solano, Francisco Ignacio, 1800B; *Dissertação sobre o caracter do musica*, 1780H; *Exame instructive sobre a Musica multiforme, metrica e rythmica*, 1790H; *Llave de la modulación y antigüedades de la música en que se trate del fundamento necessario para saber modular*,

1762H; *Nova instrucção musical, ou Theorica pratica*, 1764H; *Nova tratado de musica metrica e rythmica*, 1779H
Solari, Christy, 1894A, 1916C
Solberg, Leif, 1914A
Soldat, Marie, 1864A, 1882E, 1955B
Soldat, Marie, String Quartet I (Vienna), 1887G
Soldat, Marie, String Quartet II, 1889G
Soler, Antonio, 1752F, 1757D, 1783B
Solère, Pedro Etienne, 1753A, 1817B
Soli Deo Gloria, 193G
Solisti New York, 1980G
Sollberger, Harvey, 1938A, 1965E
Solomon, 1902A, 1911C, 1956F, 1988B
Solomon, Izler, 1910A, 1932C, 1936D, 1941D, 1956D, 1987B
Solovox, 1940G
Soltesz, Stefan, 1949A, 1983CD, 1985D
Solti, George, 1912A, 1936C, 1944E, 1947D, 1952D, 1961D, 1969D, 1971F, 1972E, 1974F, 1988E, 1993E, 1997B
Solyom, Janos, 1959C, 1986E
Somer, Hilde, 1922A, 1979B
Somers, Harry, 1925A, 1999B
Somervell, Arthur, 1929E
Something Else Press, 1964G
Somigli, Franca, 1901A, 1927C, 1974B
Somis, Giovanni Battista, 1763B
Somis, Lorenzo Giovanni, 1775B
Sommer, Hans, 1837A, 1922B; *Genossenschaft Deutscher Komponisten*, 1898H
Song Messenger of the North-West, 1863G
Somogi, Judith, 1937A, 1977D, 1982D, 1984F 1988B
Son, Dan Thai, 1958A, 1976B
Sonatori di Praga, 1963G
Songwriters Hall of Fame, 1977G
Songwriters' Protective Association, 1931G
Sonneck, Oscar G. T., 1873A, 1902D, 1915D, 1917D, 1928B; *Bibliography of Early Secular American Music*, 1905H; *Early Concert Life in America*, 1907H; *Early Opera in America*, 1915H; *Miscellaneous Studies in the History of Music*, 1921H; *Suum cuique: Essays on Music*, 1916H
Sonneck Society, 1975G
Sonnichsen, Soren, Publisher, 1783G
Sonntag, Ulrike, 1983C
Sons of Orpheus, The (Sweden), 1853G
Sontag, Henriette, 1806A, 1821C, 1854B, 1921C
Soot, Fritz, 1878A, 1908C, 1965B
Sooter, Edward, 1934A, 1966C
Sopkin, Henry, 1903A, 1944D, 1988B
Sor, Fernando, 1778A, 1819F, 1813F, 1823F, 1839B; *Méthode pour la guitare*, 1830H
Sorabji, K. S., 1892A, 1988B
Sorel, Claudette, 1999B
Sørensen, Bent, 1958A

❈

F *Biographical*   G *Cultural Beginnings*   H *Musical Literature*
I *Musical Compositions*

Sorge, Georg Andreas, 1778B; *Anleitung zur Fantasie*, 1767H; *Kurze erklarung des Canonis Harmonici*, 1763H
Sorkočević, Luka, 1789B
Sotin, Hans, 1939A, 1962C
Soubre, Etienne-Joseph, 1841E, 1844D, 1862D
Souez, Ina, 1903A, 1928C, 1992B
Soulacroix, Gabriel, 1853A, 1878C, 1905B
Souliotis, Elena, 1943A, 1964C
Sound Celebration, 1987G
Sound-Space Centre, 1995G
Soundings, 1972G
Sounds Positive, 1987G
Souris, André, 1899A, 1927E, 1937D
Sousa, John Philip, 1854A, 1875F, 1892F, 1880D, 1900F, 1910F, 1920E, 1923E, 1924F, 1929E, 1932B, 1973E; *Marching Along: Recollections of Men, Women & Music*, 1928H; *National, Patriotic & Typical Airs of all Countries*, 1890H
Sousa, John Philip, Band, 1892G
Soustrot, Marc, 1976D
Southard, Lucien H., 1827A, 1868D, 1881B; *A Course in Harmony*, 1855H; *Union Glee Book*, 1852H
South Australian Orchestra, 1921G
South Africa (*see also* Capetown): African Music Society, 1947G; College of Music, 1920G; National Symphony Orchestra of the South African Broadcasting Corporation, 1954G
Southeastern Composers' League, 1952G
Southeastern Music Center Summer Festival, 1983G
Southern, Eileen, 1920A, 1973D; *Biographical Dictionary of Afro-American & African Musicians*, 1982H; *The Music of Black Americans*, 1971H; *Readings in Black American Music*, 1971H
Southern, Hugh, 1989D
Southern Music Co., Publisher (San Antonio), 1935G, 1957G
Southern Musical Advocate & Singers' Friend, 1859G
Southern Symphony Orchestra, 1938G
Southwell, William, Piano Maker, 1782G
Southwest German Radio Symphony Orchestra, 1946G
Souzay Gérard, 1918A, 1945C
Soviero, Diana, 1952A, 1974C, 1979E
Soviet Emigré Music Festival, 1979G
Soviet Emigré Orchestra, 1979G
Sowerby, Leo, 1895A, 1921E, 1927D, 1935E, 1968B; *Ideals in Church Music*, 1956H
Sowerby, Leo, Society, 1971G
Sowinski, Wojciech A., 1803A, 1828C, 1880B; *Musiciens polonais et slaves, anciens et modernes*, 1857H
Soyer, Roger, 1939A, 1962C
Spaeth, Sigmund, 1885A, 1965B; *The Art of Enjoying Music*, 1933H; *At Home with Music*,

1945H; *The Common Sense of Music*, 1924H; *Fifty Years with Music*, 1959H; *Fun with Music*, 1941H; *Great Program Music*, 1940H; *Great Symphonies*, 1936H; *A Guide to Great Orchestra Music*, 1943H; *The Importance of Music*, 1963H; *Music for Everybody*, 1934H; *Music for Fun*, 1939H; *Stories Behind the World's Greatest Music*, 1937H; *They Still Sing of Love*, 1929H; *Words & Music*, 1926H
Spalding, Albert, 1888A, 1905C, 1926E, 1937E
Spalding, W. R.: *Modern Harmony in Its Theory & Practice*, 1905H
Spangler, Johann Georg, 1752A, 1802B
Spani, Hina, 1896A, 1915C, 1969B
Spanish Radio & Television Symphony Orchestra, 1965G
Spano, Robert, 1995D, 1996D
Spanuth, August, 1857A, 1874C, 1920B; *Meisterschule des klavierspiels: Methodik des Klavierspiels*, 1907H
Spark, William, 1861E; *A Lecture on Church Music*, 1851H
Spasov, Ivan, 1934A, 1996B
Spaulding, Albert, 1953B
Speaks, Oley, 1874A, 1948B
Specht, Richard: *Kritisches Skizzenbuch*, 1900H
Speculum Musicae, 1971G
Speiser, Elizabeth, 1940A
Spelman, Timothy Mather, 1891A, 1970B
Spemann, Alexander, 1967A, 1989C
Spence, Patricia, 1961A
Sperry, Paul, 1934A, 1969C, 1989D
Sperski, Krzysztof, 1964C
Speyer, Wilhelm, 1790A, 1878B
Der Spiegel, 1918G
Spiegelmann, Joel, 1933A
Spiers, Colin, 1957A
Spies, Claudio, 1969E
Spies, Herminie, 1857A, 1882C, 1883C, 1893B
Spiess, Ludovic, 1938A, 1962C, 1964E
Spiess, Meinrad, 1761B
Spinnler, Burkhard, 1954A, 1978C
Spitalny, Phil, 1889A, 1970B
Spitalny, Phil, & His All-Girl Orchestra, 1934G
Spitta, Julius Philipp, 1841A, 1894B
Spivacke, Harold, 1904A, 1937D, 1977B
Spivakov, Vladimir, 1944A, 1969E, 1970F
Spivakovsky, Tossy, 1907A, 1917C, 1998B
Spletter, Carla, 1932C
Spohr, Louis, 1784A, 1799F, 1802F, 1804F, 1817D, 1819F, 1820F, 1821F, 1822D, 1859B; *Violin School*, 1831H
Spokane Conservatory of Music, 1942G
Spontini, Gaspare Luigi, 1774A, 1795F, 1803F, 1810D, 1814F, 1818E, 1820D, 1839D, 1841F, 1851B
Spoorenberg, Erna, 1926A, 1947C
Spotorno, Marianangela, 1992C
Spratling, Huw, 1949A

✵

A   *Births*   B   *Deaths*   C   *Debuts*   D   *New Positions*

E   *Prizes/Honors*

Spring Opera Theater, 1962G
Springfield, Massachusetts: Orchestral Club,
  1875G; Orpheus Society, 1873G; Symphony
  Chorus, 1944; Symphony Hall, 1913G; Tonic
  Sol-Fa Association, 1883G
Staatliche Hochschule für Musik und
  Darstellende Kunst, 1973G
Stabell, Carsten, 1960A, 1984C
Stabile, Mariano, 1888A, 1909C, 1968B
Stade, Friedrich: *Vom Musikalisch-Schönon*,
  1870H
Stader, Maria, 1939E, 1999B
Stadler, Anton, 1753A, 1812B
Stadtfeldt, Alexandre, 1849E
Staffless Music Notation, 1802G
Stahl, David, 1976D
Stahlman, Sylvia, 1998B
Stainer, John, 1840A, 1872D, 1888E, 1888F,
  1901B; *Music in Relation to the Intellect and
  Emotions*, 1892H; *Music of the Bible*, 1879H;
  The Theory of Harmony, 1871H
Stainer & Bell, Publishers, 1907G
Stair, Patty, 1869A, 1926B
Stalingrad Philharmonic Orchestra, 1935G
Stamenova, Galina, 1958A, 1984C
Stamitz, Carl Philipp, 1801B
Stamitz, Johann, 1757B
Stamm, Harald, 1938A, 1968C
Standard Grand Opera Co. of Seattle, 1914G
Stanford, Charles Villiers, 1852A, 1873D,
  1901DE, 1924B; *Musical Composition*, 1911H
Stanford Center for Computer Research in
  Music & Acoustics, 1975G
Stanhope, David, 1986D
Stanhope, Paul Thomas, 1969A
Stanick, Toni Elisabeth, 1996C
Stanislavsky Opera Theater, 1928G
Stankovich, Yevhen, 1942A
Stankovsky, Róbert, 1964A, 1987D, 1988F
Stanley, John, 1779E, 1786B
Stapp, Gregory Lee, 1954A, 1968C
Stapp, Olivia, 1940A, 1960C
Starer, Robert, 1924A, 1994E, 1995E; *Rhythmic
  Training*, 1969H
Stark, John, & Son, Pianos, 1882G
Starker, János, 1924A, 1935C, 1958F
Starobin, David, 1915A, 1978C
Starr, Susan, 1942A
Starzer, Joseph, 1787B
Stasov, Vladimir, 1824A, 1867F, 1870F, 1906B
Staudigl, Joseph, Jr., 1850A, 1875C, 1916B
Staudigl, Joseph, Sr., 1807A, 1861B
Stavenhagen, Bernhard, 1890E
Steane, John B.: *Voices: Singers & Critics*, 1992H
Stebbins, George C., 1846A, 1945B
Stebbins, George W., 1869A, 1930B
Steber, Eleanor, 1914A, 1940C, 1990B
Steber, Eleanor, Music Foundation, 1975G
Steber, Eleanor, Vocal Competition, 1979G

Steck, George, & Co., Piano Makers, 1857G
Steele, John, 1876E
Stefan, Paul, 1879A, 1943B
Stefanescu, Ana Camelia, 1974A
Stefani, Jan, 1779D, 1829B
Stefani, Józef, 1800A, 1867B
Stefano, Giuseppe di, 1921A
Steffan, Joseph Anton, 1797B
Stefiuk, Maria, 1982C
Steger, Ingrid, 1927A, 1951C
Stegmann, Carl David, 1751A, 1772C, 1798D,
  1826B
Stegmayer, Matthäus, 1771A, 1820B
Stegmayer, Ferdinand, 1803A, 1863B
Stegnani, Ebe, 1904A
Stehle, J. Gustav, 1874D
Stehle, Sophie, 1838A, 1860C, 1921B
Steibelt, Daniel, 1765A, 1784F, 1796F, 1790F,
  1799F, 1800F, 1808D, 1823B; *Méthode de
  pianoforte*, 1805H
Steidry, Fritz, 1883A
Steiert, Catherine, 1979E
Steiger, Rand, 1957A
Steiger, Anna, 1960A, 1983C
Stein, Erwin, 1958B
Stein, Fritz, 1879A, 1933D, 1961B
Stein, Horst, 1928A, 1951D, 1955D, 1963D,
  1972D, 1973D, 1980D, 1985D, 1987D
Stein, Irwin, 1885A
Stein, Johann A., Organ Builder, 1751G
Stein, Leon, 1910A; *Structure & Style*, 1962H
Stein, Leonard, 1916A
Stein Organ Works, 1893G
Steinbach, Fritz, 1855A, 1886D, 1903D, 1916B
Steinberg, Michael: *The Symphony–A Listener's
  Guide*, 1995H
Steinberg, Pinchas, 1989D
Steinberg, William, 1899A, 1938F, 1945D,
  1952D, 1969D, 1978B
Steiner, Elisabeth, 1935A, 1961C
Steiner, Emma, 1850A, 1928B
Steiner, Johann Ludwig, 1761B
Steiner, Moritz, 1900F
Steingardt, Arnold, 1958E
Steingräber, Theodor, 1830A, 1904B
Steingräber, Theodor, Publishing House,
  1878G
Steingruber, Ilona, 1912A, 1942C, 1962B
Steinhardt, Milton, 1909A
Steinke, Greg, 1988D
Steinmetz, Werner, 1959A
Steinmeyer Organ Co., 1847G
Steinway & Sons, 1853G
Steinweg, Heinrich E., 1797A, 1871B
Stella, Antonietta, 1950C
Stenborg, Carl, 1752A, 1773C, 1813B
Stendhal Quartet, 1981G
Stenhammar, Wilhelm, 1871A, 1890F, 1902C,
  1906D, 1927B

❋

F   *Biographical*   G   *Cultural Beginnings*   H   *Musical Literature*
I   *Musical Compositions*

Stenz, Marcus, 1965A, 1998D
Stephănescu, George, 1843A, 1925B
Stephen, Pamela, 1990C
Stephens, Catherine, 1794A, 1813C, 1882B
Steptoe, Roger (Guy), 1953A
Stereo Review, 1958G
Sterkel, (Abbée) Johann Franz, 1793D, 1817B
Sterling, Antoinette, 1850A, 1873C, 1904B
Sterling Club, 1838G
Sterling, Elizabeth, 1895B
Sterling, Winthrop Smith, 1859A, 1943B
Stern, Isaac, 1920A, 1936C, 1956F, 1960F, 1971F, 1979F, 1984E, 1986E, 1987E, 1988E
Stern, Leo, 1862A, 1904B
Stern, Joseph, & Co., 1894G
Stern, Michael, 1996D
Stern Grove Midsummer Music Festival, 1938G
Sternberg, Constantin, 1852A, 1924B; *Tempo Rubato & Other Essays*, 1920H
Sternberg, Jonathan, 1919A
Steuerman, Jean Louis, 1963C
Steuermann, Edward, 1892A, 1952E, 1964B
Stevens, Denis: *Tudor Church Music*, 1955H
Stevens, George, 1803A, 1894B
Stevens, Halsey, 1908A, 1961E, 1989B
Stevens, John: *Words & Music in the Middle Ages*, 1988H
Stevens, Risë, 1913A, 1936C, 1975D, 1981D, 1990E
Stevenson, John Andrew 1802E
Stevenson, Robert, 1916A; *Foundations of New World Opera*, 1973H; *Patterns of Protestant Church Music*, 1953H; *Protestant Church Music in America*, 1966H
Stevenson, Ronald, 1928A
Steward & Chickering, Piano Makers, 1823G
Stewart, Humphrey, 1932B
Stewart, Reginald, 1900A, 1933D, 1941D, 1942D, 1984B
Stewart, Robert, 1852D, 1872E
Stewart, Thomas, 1928A, 1954C
Stich, Jan Václav, 1803B; *Hornschule*, 1798H
Stich-Randall, Teresa, 1927A, 1947C
Stiedry, Fritz, 1916D, 1923D, 1929D, 1933F, 1946D, 1968B
Stieff Piano Co., 1852G
Stigelli, Giorgio, 1815A, 1868B
Stignani, Ebe, 1925C, 1974B
Still, William Grant, 1895A, 1911F, 1947E, 1949F, 1978B
Stilwell, Richard, 1942A, 1962C
Die Stimme: Centralblatt für Stimmung Tonbildung, 1906G
Stirling, Elizabeth, 1819A, 1895B
Stock, Frederick, 1872A, 1895F, 1899F, 1905D, 1912E, 1942B
Stockhausen, Julius, 1826A, 1906B; *Gesangsmethode I*, 1886H

Stockhausen, Karlheinz, 1928A, 1951F, 1958F, 1963F
Stockhoff, Walter William, 1876A, 1968B
Stockholm, Sweden: Bellmanska Söllskapet, 1891G; Concert Hall (Konserthus), 1926G; Drottningholm Palace Theater I, 1754G; Drottningholm Palace Theater II, 1812G; Filharmoniska Sällskapet, 1900G; Konsertförening, 1902G; New Music Society, 1800G; New Swedish Theater, 1784G; Nya Harmonska Sällskapet, 1869G; Opera Co., 1898G; Opera House, 1782G; Royal Opera House, 1898G; Sinfonietta, 1980G; Swedish National Opera, 1773G; Swedish Nationl theater, 1773G; Swedish Royal Academy of Music, 1771G; Symphony Orchestra, 1914G
Stockley's Concerts, 1873G
Stodart, Robert, Piano Co., 1775G
Stoeckel, Carl, 1858A, 1925B
Stoeckel, Gustave, 1819A, 1907B
Stoepel, Helene, 1850F
Stoessel, Albert, 1894A, 1914C, 1923D, 1931E, 1943B; *The Technic of the Baton*, 1920H
Stoessel, George, 1927D
Stojowski, Sigismund, 1869A, 1946B
Stokes, Eric, 1930A, 1999B
Stokes, Fredrick A., Co., 1890G
Stokowski, Leopold, 1882A, 1909D, 1911F, 1912D, 1922E, 1940F, 1945F, 1955D, 1968E, 1977B; *Music for Us All*, 1943H
Stokowski Conducting Prize, 1979G
Stoltz, Rosine, 1815A, 1832C, 1903B
Stolz, Catherine, 1987E
Stolz, Robert, 1880A, 1905D, 1975B
Stolz, Teresa, 1834A, 1857C, 1902B
Stolze, Gerhard, 1926A, 1949C, 1979B
Stolzenberg, Hertha, 1889A, 1910C, 1960B
Stolzman, Richard, 1942A, 1976C, 1977E, 1986E
Stone, Carl, 1953A, 1992D
Stone, Kurt, 1911A, 1989B; *Notation in the Twentieth Century*, 1980H
Stone, Marcus, 1887E
Stone, William, 1975C
Stöpel Franz: *Grundzuge der Geschichte der modernen Musik*, 1821H
Stör, Karl, 1857D
Storace, Nancy, 1765A, 1780C, 1817B
Storace, Stephen, 1762A, 1796B
Storchio, Rosina, 1876A, 1892C, 1945B
Storrs, Caryl B., 1902D
Stott, Kathryn, 1958A, 1978C
Stoughton Musical Society, 1786G
Stour Music Festival, 1963G
Stout, Alan, 1932A
Stovanov, Boyko Stoykov, 1953A, 1983D, 1984D
Stracciari, Riccardo, 1875A, 1898C, 1955B
Straeten, Edmund Van der, 1826A, 1895B
Straka, Peter, 1950A, 1978C

A *Births*   B *Deaths*   C *Debuts*   D *New Positions*
E *Prizes/Honors*

Strakosch, Maurice, 1857D
Strang, Gerald, 1908A, 1965D, 1983B
Strange, Allen: *Electronic Music: Systems, Techniques & Controls*, 1972H
Stransky, Josef, 1872A, 1898D, 1911D, 1936B
Strasbourg, France: Académie de Chant, 1827G; Conservatory of Music, 1854G; International Music Festival, 1932G; Union Alsacienne de Musique, 1830G
Strasfogel, Ignace, 1994B
Stratas, Teresa, 1938A, 1958C
Stratton, John F., Brass Instrument Factory, 1857G
Stratton String Quartet, 1925G
Straube, Karl, 1873A, 1902D, 1950B
Straus, Oscar, 1870A, 1954B
Strauss, Axel, 1998E
Strauss, Eduard, 1835A, 1862C, 1900F, 1916B
Strauss, Franz, 1822A, 1905B
Strauss, Johann, Jr., 1825A, 1863F, 1867F, 1872F 1899B
Strauss, Johann, Sr., 1804A, 1833F, 1849B
Strauss, Josef, 1827A, 1853C, 1870B
Strauss, Richard, 1864A, 1885F, 1884CF, 1886F, 1889F, 1894D, 1989D, 1902E, 1904F, 1914E, 1919D, 1947F, 1949B
Strauss, Richard, Institute, 1964G
Stravinsky, Feodor, 1843A, 1873C, 1902B
Stravinsky, Igor, 1882A, 1902F, 1908F, 1910F, 1914F, 1925F, 1935F, 1939F, 1949E, 1951E, 1956E, 1962E, 1971B; *Chroniques de ma vie*, 1935H; *Poetics of Music*, 1946H
Streich, Rita, 1920A, 1943C, 1987B
Streicher, Nannette, Piano Co. (Vienna), 1802G
Streit, Kurt, 1959A, 1987C
Strepponi, Giuseppina, 1815A, 1834C, 1859F, 1897B
Strickland, Lily, 1887A, 1958B
Strickland, William, 1914A, 1946D, 1991B
Stringer, Mark, 1961A, 1989D
Stringfield, Lamar, 1897A, 1959B; *America & Her Music*, 1931H
Stringham, Edwin John, 1890A, 1932D, 1938D, 1974B
Strohm, Reinhard: *The Rise of European Music, 1380-1500*, 1993H
Strolling Players Amateur Orchestral Society, 1882G
Strong, George Templeton, 1856A, 1948B
Strong, Susan, 1870A, 1793C, 1946B
Strozzi, Violetta de, 1891A
Strube, Gustav, 1900D, 1916D; *The Theory & Use of Chords*, 1928H
Struckmann, Falk, 1958A, 1985C
Strummer, Peter, 1948A, 1972C
Strumpf, Carl, 1936B
Strunk, Oliver, 1901A, 1934D, 1980B; *Essays on Music in the Byzantine World*, 1977H; *Essays on Music in the Western World*, 1974H; *Source*

Readings in Music History, 1950H; *State & Resources of Musicology in the United States*, 1932H
Stuck, Jean-Baptiste, 1755B
Stucken, Frank Van der, 1895D
Stuckenschmidt, H. H., 1901A, 1929D, 1957D, 1974E, 1988B; *Glanz und elend der Musikkritik*, 1957H; *Music from 1925 to 1975*, 1976H; *Twentieth Century Music*, 1968H
Stückgold, Grete, 1895A, 1917C, 1977B
Stucky, Steven, 1949A, 1982E, 1991D
Studebaker, Thomas, 1970A, 1995C
Studer, Cheryl, 1955A
Studio de Musique Contemporaine, 1959G
Studio de Musique Electronique, 1958G
Studio di Fonologia, Milan, 1954G
Studio ESPACES, 1976G
Studio Musicologia, 1961G
Stulberg, Neal, 1954A
Stumm, Johann Heinrich, 1788B
Stumm, Johann Philipp, 1776B
Stumpf, Carl, 1848A; *Tonpsychologie I*, 1883H
Stumpf, Peter Daniel, 1963A, 1979C
Stuntz, Joseph Hartmann, 1793A, 1859B
Stupel, Ilya, 1949A, 1990D
Stuttgart, Germany: Bach Collegium, 1965G; Chamber Orchestra, 1845G, 1945G; Faiszt Organ School, 1847G; Künstler- und Dilettantenschule für Klavier, 1874G; Liederkranz, 1824G; Musikschule, 1857G; Orchestral Association, 1911G; Oratorienchor, 1847G; Schola Cantorum, 1960G
Subotnick, Morton, 1933A, 1979E
Suburban Opera Society (PA), 1963G
Sucher, Josef, 1843A, 1888D, 1908B
Sucher, Rosa, 1849A, 1871C
Suchoff, Benjamin, 1918A; *A Musician's Guide to Desktop Computing*, 1993H
Sudds, William, 1843A, 1920B
Suderberg, Robert, 1936A, 1971E, 1974D
Sugár, Rezső, 1919A, 1988B
Suggia, Guilhermina, 1888A, 1950B
Suhonen, Antti, 1956A, 1986C
Suhonen String Quartet, 1964G
Suitner, Othmar, 1922A, 1945D, 1960D, 1964D
Suk, Josef, I, 1874A, 1898F, 1935B
Suk, Josef, II, 1929A, 1940C, 1964E
Suk, Váa, 1933B
Sukerlan, Ananda, 1968A
Šulek, Stjepan, 1986B
Sullivan, Arthur, 1842A, 1856E, 1861D, 1867F, 1871F,1878E, 1879E, 1883E, 1900B
Sullivan, Cornelius, 1983E
Sullivan, Daniel, 1764B
Sullivan, George J., Arena, 1982G
Sullivan, Jack: *New World Symphonies*, 1999H
Sultanov, Aleksei, 1989E

❈

F   *Biographical*   G   *Cultural Beginnings*   H   *Musical Literature*
I   *Musical Compositions*

Sulzer, Johann Georg, 1779B; *Allgemeine theorie der schönen kunste*, 1775H; *Pensées sur l'origine des sciences et...Beaux-Arts*, 1757H
Sulzer, Salomon: *Schir Zion*, 1838H
Sume, Razvan Gabriel, 1977A, 1988C
Sumera, Lepo, 1950A, 2000B
Summers, Jonathan, 1975C
Summers, Patrick, 1960A, 1998D
Summit Brass, 1984G
Summy, Clayton F., Co., Publishers, 1888G
Summy-Birchard Co., Publisher, 1957G
Sun, Leland, 1964A
Sun Valley Music Festival, 1982G
Sundelius, Marie, 1884A, 1916C, 1958B
Sunderland, Susan, 1819A, 1905B
Sundine, Stephanie, 1954A, 1981C
Suñol, Gregoria Maria, 1930D
Suolahti, Heikki, 1920A, 1936B
Supervia, Conchita, 1895A, 1910C, 1936B
Supičić, Ivo, 1928A
Suppan, Wolfgang, 1933A
Suppé, Franz von, 1819A, 1845D, 1865D, 1895B
Supraphon Records, 1946G
Supries, Joseph, 1787D
Surdin, Morris, 1979B
Surinach, Carlos, 1915A, 1966E, 1997B
Surette, Thomas W.: *Course of Study on the Development of Symphonic Music*, 1915H; *Music & Life*, 1917H
Susa, Conrad, 1935A
Susskind, Walter, 1913A, 1934C, 1943D, 1946D, 1953D, 1956D, 1962D, 1968D, 1980B
Süssmayr, Franz Xaver, 1766A, 1792D, 1784F, 1788F, 1794F, 1803B
Sustaining Pedal for Piano, 1874G
Sustikova, Vera: *History of Czech Musical Culture*, 1986H
Sutej, Vjekoslav, 1993D
Suter, Herman, 1921D
Suter, Robert, 1919A
Sutermeister, Heinrich, 1910A, 1995B
Suthaus, Ludwig, 1906A, 1928C, 1971B
Sutherland, Joan, 1926A, 1947C, 1979E, 1992E
Sutherland, Margaret, 1897A, 1970E, 1984B
Sutro, Ottilie, 1872A, 1894C, 1970B
Sutro, Rose Laura, 1870A, 1894C, 1957B
Suvini Zerboni, Publisher, 1930G
Suwardi, Aloysius, 1951A
Suzuki, Masaaki, 1954A
Suzuki, Shin'ichi, 1898A, 1998B
Suzuki, Yuki Kazu, 1954A
Suzuki String Quartet, 1928G
Svanholm, Set, 1904A, 1930C, 1956D, 1964B
Svéd, Alexander, 1928C
Svéd, Sándor, 1904A, 1930C, 1979B
Svenden, Brigitta, 1952A, 1981C
Svendsen, Johan, 1840A, 1883D, 1911B
Svetlanov, Evgeny, 1928A, 1965D, 1992D
Svetlev, Michail, 1943A, 1971C

Sviridov, Georgi, 1915A, 1998B
Sewanee Summer Music Center, 1957G
Swan, Timothy, 1758A, 1842B; *New England Harmony*, 1801H; *The Songster's Assistant*, 1800H; *The Songster's Museum*, 1803H
Swan, Alfred, 1890A
Swann, Frederick, 1931A, 1983D
Swann, Jeffrey, 1975E
Swanson, Howard, 1907A, 1978B
Swarowsky, Hans, 1899A, 1946D, 1947D, 1957D, 1975B
Swarthout, Gladys, 1900A, 1924C, 1969B
Swayne, Giles, 1946A
Swedish Archives of the History of Music, 1965G
Swedish Arts Council, 1974G
Swedish Brass Quartet, 1997G
Swedish Composer's Society, 1924G
Swedish Folksoper, 1993F
Swedish Institute for National Concerts, 1963G
Swedish Performing Rights Society, 1923G
Sweet, Sharon, 1951A, 1985C
Swenson, Ruth Ann, 1959A, 1983C, 1993E
Swieten, Baron Gottfried von, 1803B
Switzerland (*see also* Basel, Berne, Geneva, Lausanne, Lucerne, Zürich): Center for Computer Music, 1985G; Gstaad Festival, 1956G; Musicological Society, 1899G; Orchestre de la Suisse Romande, 1918G; Orchestre della Svizzera italiana, 1991G; Woodwind Quintet, 1985G;
Swoboda, Henry, 1897A, 1990B
Swolfs, Laurent, 1867A, 1901C, 1954B
Syberg, Franz, 1904A, 1955B
Sydeman, William, 1928A, 1962E
Sydney, Australia: International Piano Competition, 1977G; Opera House, 1973G; Symphony Orchestra, 1946G
Sydsvenska Filharmoniska Forening, 1902G
Sykes, James, 1908A, 1938C, 1985B
Sylvester, Michael, 1951A, 1987C
Symonette, Randolph, 1910A, 1998B
Symphonia (Netherlands), 1923G
Symphony Magazine, 1948G
Symphony Orchestra of Russia, 1991G
Synowiec, Ewa, 1942A
Syracuse, New York: Civic Center, 1976G; Opera Theater of Syracuse, 1974G; Philharmonic Orchestra, 1941G; Symphony Orchestra, 1921G; Syracuse University Oratorio Society, 1975G; Symphony Orchestra, 1892G
Szabó, Ferenc, 1902A, 1951E, 1958D, 1969B
Szabo, Peter, 1965A, 1981C
Szabolcsi, Bence: *A Concise History of Hungarian Music*, 1964H; *A History of Melody*, 1950H
Szalowski, Antoni, 1907A
Szantho, Enid, 1907A, 1928C
Szász, Tibor, 1948A

❋

A *Births*　　B *Deaths*　　C *Debuts*　　D *New Positions*

E *Prizes/Honors*

Székely, Endre, 1912A, 1989B
Székely, Mihály, 1901A, 1923C, 1963B
Szekelyhidy, Ferenc, 1885A, 1954B
Szelényi, István, 1972B; *The Harmonic Realm of Romantic Music*, 1959H; *The History of Hungarian Music*, 1965H; *The Interrelations of the History of Music & That of Philosophy*, 1944H; *Methodical Theory of Modulation*, 1927H
Szeligowski, Tadeusz, 1963B
Szell, George, 1897A, 1924D, 1942D, 1946D, 1970B
Szeluto, Apolinary, 1966B
Szendrei, Aladár, 1976B; *Dirigierkunde*, 1932H; *Music in the Social & Religious Life of Antiquity*, 1974H; *Rundfunk und Musikpflege*, 1931H
Szendrenze, Katalin, 1989C
Szenkar, Eugen, 1924D, 1944D, 1952D
Szervánszky, Endre, 1911A, 1951E, 1955E, 1977B
Szeryng, Henryk, 1918A, 1933C, 1988B
Szigeti, Joseph, 1892A, 1905C, 1973B
Szikaly, Erika, 1960C
Szoboda, Tomás, 1939A
Szokolay, Sándor, 1931A, 1966E, 1987E
Szőllősy, András, 1921A, 1971E, 1985E
Sztompka, Henryk, 1901A, 1932C, 1964
Szulc, Józef Zygmunt, 1875A, 1956B
Szumowska, Antoinette, 1868A, 1938B
Szweykowski, Zigmunt, 1929A
Szymanowska, Maria Agate, 1789A, 1810C, 1828F, 1831B
Szymanowski, Karol, 1882A, 1917F, 1927D, 1937B; *The Educational Role of Musical Culture in Society*, 1931H
Tabachnik, Michel, 1942A, 1975D
Tabakov, Emil, 1977E, 1985D
Table Book, 1845G
Taccani, Giuseppe, 1885A, 1905C, 1959
Tacchinardi, Nicola, 1772A, 1859B
Tacchino, Gabriel, 1934A, 1953CE, 1956E
Tacet Record Label, 1989G
Tachezi, Herbert, 1930A
Taddei, Giuseppe, 1916A, 1936C
Tadeo, Giorgio, 1929A, 1953C
Tadolini, Eugenia, 1809A, 1828C
Tadolini, Giovanni, 1811D, 1825E, 1829D
Tag, Christian Gotthilf, 1811B
Tagliabue, Carlo, 1898A, 1978B
Tagliaferro, Magda, 1893A, 1908C, 1986B
Tagliafico, Joseph, 1821A, 1844C, 1900B
Tagliapietra, Gino, 1887A, 1954B
Tagliavini, Ferruccio, 1913A, 1938C, 1995B
Tagliavini, Franco, 1934A, 1961C
Tagliavini, Luigi F., 1929A
Taglioni, Ferdinando, 1849D
Tagore, Surindro, 1840A, 1914B
Tailleferre, Germaine, 1892A, 1920F, 1983B

Taillon, Jocelyn, 1941A, 1968C
Taipei International Chamber Music Festival, 1997G
Tajo, Italo, 1915A, 1935C, 1993B
Takács, Jenő, 1902A, 1942D, 1962E, 1999B
Takács String Quartet, 1975G
Takahashi, Aki, 1944A, 1970C
Takahaski, Yuji, 1938A
Takata, Sabura, 1913A
Takeda, Yoshimi, 1933A
Takemitsu, Toru, 1930A, 1996B
Takezawa, Kyoko, 1986E
Taktakashvili, Shalva, 1952D, 1965B
Taktakishvili, Otar, 1924A, 1989B
Tal, Josef, 1910A, 1948D
Talbot, Michael, 1943A
Talich, Václav, 1883A, 1908D, 1912D, 1919D, 1928E, 1935D, 1937F, 1949D, 1961B
Talich String Quartet, 1962G
Tallahassee Symphony Orchestra, 1981G
Talley, Marion, 1906A, 1926C, 1983B
Tallis Scholars, 1973G
Talma, Louise, 1906A, 1927E, 1928E, 1960E, 1974E, 1996B; *Functional Harmony*, 1970H; *Harmony for the College Student*, 1966H
Talmi, Yoav, 1943A, 1974D, 1984D, 1990D
Talon, Pierre, 1785B
Talons Lyriques, 1991G
Taltabull, Cristòpher, 1964B
Talvela, Martti, 1935A, 1961C, 1989B
Tamagno, Francesco, 1850A, 1869C, 1905B
Tamberg, Eino, 1930A
Tamberlik, Enrico, 1820A, 1841C, 1889B
Tamburini, Antonio, 1800A, 1818C, 1876B
Tamburini Organ Co., 1893G
Tampa Performing Arts Complex, 1987G
Tampere, Finland: Philharmonic Hall, 1990G; Philharmonic Orchestra, 1930G
Tams, Arthur W., 1848A, 1864C
Tan, Margaret Leng, 1945A
Tan, Melvyn, 1956B
Tanabe, Hisao, 1883A, 1984B; *Acoustics of Music*, 1951H; *History of Oriental Music*, 1930H; *Lectures on Japanese Music*, 1919H
Tanaka, Karen, 1961A, 1987E
Tanaka, Toshimitsu, 1930A
Tandler, Adolph, 1913D
Tanev, Alexander, 1928A
Taneyev, Alexander, 1885D, 1918B
Taneyev, Sergei, 1875C, 1915B
Taneyev String Quartet, 1946G
Tangeman, Nell, 1917A, 1945C, 1965B
Tanglewood Festival, 1937G
Tanglewood Music Shed, 1938G
Tango, Egisto, 1873A, 1893C, 1951B
Taniev, Alexander, 1850A
Taniev, Sergei, 1856A
Tannenbaum, Elias, 1924A

❋

F *Biographical*   G *Cultural Beginnings*   H *Musical Literature*
I *Musical Compositions*

Tannenberg, David, 1757F, 1765F, 1804B
Tanski, Claudius, 1959A
Tansman, Alexandre, 1897A, 1941E, 1986B
Tans'ur, William, 1783B; *The Elements of Music Displayed*, 1772H; *Melodia Sacra*, 1771H; *The Psalmsinger's Jewel*, 1760H; *The Royal Melody Compleat*, 1755H
Tänzler, Hans, 1897A, 1903C, 1953B
Taos Chamber Music Festival, 1963G
Taphouse, Charles, & Son, Ltd. (Oxford), 1857G
Tapia, Lynette, 1996E
Tapper, Bertha Feiring, 1859A
Tapper, Thomas, 1864A, 1901D, 1958B; *The Education of the Music Teacher*, 1914H; *Essentials of Music History*, 1913H; *The Music Life*, 1891H
Tappert, Wilhelm, 1830A, 1866D, 1907B; *Musik und musikalische Erziehung*, 1866H; *Musikalische Studien*, 1868H
Tappolet, Willy, 1890A, 1907B, 1981B
Tappy, Eric, 1931A, 1959C
Tapray, Jean-François, 1763D, 1776D, 1819B
Tarack, Gerald, 1929A, 1952C
Tarack Chamber Players, 1974G
Tarade, Théodore, 1788B; *Nouveaux principes de musique et de violon*, 1774H
Taranov, Gleb, 1904A, 1989B
Tăranu, Carnel, 1934A
Tarchi, Angelo, 1755A, 1816B
Tardos, Béla, 1966B
Tariol-Baugé, Anne, 1944B
Tarp, Svend Erik, 1908A, 1994B
Tarr, Edward H., 1936A; *Die Trompete*, 1977H
Tarr, Edward, Brass Ensemble, 1967G
Tárrega, Francisco, 1852A, 1909B
Tartini, Giuseppe, 1768F, 1770B; *De' principi dell'armonia musicale contenuta nel diatonico genere*, 1767H; *Trattato de musica secondo la vera sienza dell'armonia*, 1754H
Tartu Music Academy (Estonia), 1920G
Taruskin, Richard, 1945A; *Opera & Drama in Russia*, 1981H; *Test & Act: Essays on Music & Performance*, 1995H
Tas, Rudi, 1957A
Tashi, 1973G
Taskin, Emil-Alexandre, 1853A, 1875C, 1897B
Taskin, Pascal, 1793B
Tassinari, Pia, 1903A, 1929C, 1995B
Tata Theater (National Center, Bombay), 1980G
Tate, Jeffrey, 1943A, 1978C, 1984D, 1986D, 1990E, 1991D
Tate, Phyllis, 1911A, 1987B
Tattermuschová, Helena, 1933A, 1955C
Tattersal William: *Improved Psalmody*, 1794H
Tatum, Nancy, 1934A, 1962C
Tau Beta Sigma Music Sorority, 1939G
Taub, Bruce J., 1948A
Taub, Robert (David), 1955A, 1981C

Taube, Michael, 1924D, 1972B
Tauber, Richard, 1891A, 1913C, 1948B
Tauberová, Marie, 1911A, 1934C
Taubert, Wilhelm, 1811A, 1845D 1891B
Taubman, Horst, 1912A, 1935C, 1991B
Taubman, Howard, 1907A, 1935D, 1955D, 1996B; *Music as a Profession*, 1939H; *Music on My Beat*, 1943H; *The New York Times Guide to Listening Pleasure*, 1968H; *The Pleasure of Their Company: A Reminiscence*, 1994H
Taucher, Curt, 1908C, 1954B
Tauchnitz Publishing House, 1837G
Taudou, Antoine, 1869E
Tauriello, Antonio, 1931A
Taurizian, Mikhail, 1938D
Tausch, Franz, 1762A, 1817B
Tausch, Julius, 1827A, 1855D, 1895B
Tausig, Carl, 1841A, 1858C, 1871B
Tausinger, Jan, 1921A, 1980B
Tauwitz, Eduard, 1846D
Tavener, John, 1944A
Taverner Choir, 1973G
Tavrizian, Mikhail, 1907A, 1957B
Tawa, Nicholas E.: *The Coming of Age of American Art Music*, 1991H; *Mainstream Music of Early Twentieth Century America*, 1992H
Taws, Joseph C., 1803A
Taylor, Clifford, 1923A, 1987B
Taylor, Daniel, 1969A
Taylor, Deems, 1885A, 1921D, 1924E, 1927DE, 1931D, 1933D, 1935E, 1942D, 1966B; *Of Men & Music*, 1937H; *Music to My Ears*, 1949H; *The Well Tempered Listener*, 1940H
Taylor, Deems, Awards, 1967G
Taylor, Edward, 1784A, 1863B; *Vocal Schools of Italy in the 16th Century*, 1839H
Taylor, James, 1966A, 1990C
Taylor, Janis, 1946A, 1971C
Taylor, Raynor, 1765D, 1795D, 1825B
Tchaikovsky, André, 1935A, 1955C, 1982B
Tchaikovsky, Boris, 1925A, 1996B
Tchaikovsky, Peter Ilyich, 1840A, 1859F, 1863F, 1866D, 1876F, 1877F, 1887F, 1890F, 1891F, 1893B, 1915B; *Practical Study of Harmony*, 1871H
Tchaikovsky Competition, 1958G
Tchakarov, Emil, 1948A, 1974D, 1991B
Tcherepnin, Alexander, 1899A, 1922C, 1967F, 1974E, 1977B
Tcherepnin, Alexander, Society, 1983G
Tcherepnin, Ivan, 1943A, 1998B
Tcherepnin, Nicolai, 1873A, 1918D, 1925D, 1938D, 1945B
Tcherepnin, Serge, 1941A
Tchesnokov, Pavel, 1944B
Tear, Robert, 1939A, 1963C, 1984E
Teatro Grattacielo, 1994G
Teatro Nacional (Guatamala), 1977G

Tebaldi, Renata, 1922A, 1944C
Tebaldini, Giovanni, 1897D, 1952B; *Metodo teorica pratico per organo*, 1897H; *La musica sacra in Italia*, 1894H
Tebenikhin, Amir, 1999E
Tedeschi, Alfio, 1882A, 1903C, 1967B
Tedesco, Fortunata, 1826A, 1844C
Teichmüller, Robert, 1863A, 1939B; *Internationale moderne Klaviermusik*, 1927H
Te Kanawa, Kiri, 1944A, 1969C, 1982E
Tel Aviv, Israel: Leviyim, Beit, Music School, 1914G; National Opera, 1948G; String Quartet, 1962G
Telemann Georg Michael: *Unterricht in Generalbass-Spielen*, 1773H
Telemann, George Philipp, 1767B; *Sammlung alter und neuer Kirchenmelodien*, 1812H; *Über die wahl der melodie eines Kirchenliedes*, 1821H
Telemann Chamber Orchestra, 1952G
Telford and Telford, Organ Builders, 1830G
Tellefsen, Thomas, 1823A, 1841C, 1874B
Tellefson, Arvo, 1973E
Telmányi, Emil, 1892A, 1911C, 1919C, 1988B
Telva, Marian, 1897A, 1920C, 1962B
Temianka, Henri, 1906A, 1932C, 1961D, 1992B; *Facing the Music*, 1973H
Temirkanov, Yuri, 1938A, 1965C, 1968D, 1977D, 1979F, 1988D, 1992D, 1999D
Temperley, Nicholas, 1932A; *Music of the English Parish Church*, 1979H
Templeton, Alec, 1909A, 1963B
Templeton, John, 1802A, 1831C, 1886B
Ten Centuries Concerts, 1961G
Tenducci, Giusto Ferdinando, 1758F, 1790B
Tengstrand, Per, 1995E, 1997E
Tenney, James, 1934A, 1982E; *A History of Consonance & Dissonance*, 1988H
Tennstedt, Klaus, 1926A, 1952C, 1958D, 1962D, 1971F, 1972D, 1978D, 1983D, 1998B
Tenschert, Roland, 1970B; *Musikerbrevier*, 1894A, 1940H; *Salzburg und seine Festspiele*, 1947H
Tension-Resonator, 1902G
Teodor Burada (Romanian Academy), 1878G
Teodorini, Elena, 1857A, 1880C, 1926B
Teramoto, Mariko, 1948A
Terasova, Natalya, 1986E
Terényi, Ede, 1934A
Terfel, Bryn, 1965A, 1990C
Terhune, Anice, 1873A, 1964B
Ternina, Milka, 1863A, 1882C, 1941B
Terradellas, Domingo, 1751B
Terry, Charles Sanford, 1864A, 1936B; *The Revised English Hymnal*, 1933H
Terry, R. R., 1865A, 1901D, 1922E, 1938B; *Catholic Church Music*, 1907H; *The Westminster Hymnal*, 1912H
Terterian, Avet, 1929A, 1994B
Tertis, Lionel, 1876A, 1950E, 1975B

Tervani, Irma, 1908C, 1936B
Terzakis, Dimitri, 1938A
Terziani, Eugenio, 1847D, 1867D
Terziani, Pietro, 1865A, 1784E, 1816D
Teschemacher, Margarete, 1903A, 1924C, 1959B
Tesi-Tramontini-Vittoria, 1775B
Tesoro Musical, 1917G
Tess, Giulia, 1889A, 1904C, 1976B
Tessarini, Carlo, 1766B; *Grammatica de musica* (English translation), 1765H
Tessier, André, 1886A, 1931B
Testori, Carlo Giovanni, 1782B; *La Musica raggionata*, 1767H
Tetrazzini, Eva, 1862A, 1882C, 1938B
Tetrazzini, Luisa, 1871A, 1890C, 1940B; *How to Sing*, 1923H
Tetzlaff, Christian, 1966A, 1980C
Teubner, B. G., Publishing House, 1811G
Der Teutsche Merkur, 1773G
Texas: Chamber Orchestra, 1979G; Composers Forum, 1985G; Girls' Choir, 1962G
Teyber, Anton, 1754A, 1822B
Teyber, Franz, 1756A, 1810BD
Teyber, Therese, 1760A, 1778C, 1830B
Teyte, Maggie, 1888A, 1907C, 1958E, 1976B
Thalben-Ball, George, 1967E, 1982E,1978B
Thalberg, Sigismond, 1812A, 1827C,1836F, 1855F, 1857F, 1871B
Thalberg, Zaré, 1858A, 1875C, 1915B
Thayer, Alexander W., 1817A, 1897B; *Chronologisches Verzeichnis der Werke Ludwig von Beethoven*, 1865H
Thayer, Whitney Eugene, 1838A, 1889B
Thea Dispeker Art Management, 1947G
Théâtre de Jorat (Mézières), 1908G
Theatrical Censor and Musical Review, 1828G
Thebom, Blanche, 1918A, 1941C
Thedéan, Torleif, 1962A
Theodorakis, Mikis, 1925A, 1993D
Theodorini, Helena, 1862A, 1879C
Theremin, Leon, 1896A, 1993B
Therrien, Jeanne, 1944E
Theyard, Harry, 1939A
Thibaud, Jacques, 1880A, 1898C, 1953B
Thibaudet, Jean-Yves, 1961A
Thibaut, Charles, 1792A, 1818C
Thibault, Geneviève, 1902A, 1975B
Thibaut Anton: *Über Reinheit der Tonkunst*, 1825H
Thiel, Carl, 1894E
Thielemann, Christian, 1959A, 1985D, 1988D, 1997D
Thiemé Frédéric: *Éléments de musique pratique*, 1784H; *Nouvelle théorie sur les differens mouvemens des airs*, 1801H
Thienen, Marcel van, 1922A
Thill, Georges, 1897A, 1924C, 1984B
Thillon, Sophie Anne, 1819A, 1838C, 1903B

❀

F *Biographical*   G *Cultural Beginnings*   H *Musical Literature*
I *Musical Compositions*

Thilman, Johannes Paul, 1906A, 1973B; *Musikalische formenlehre*, 1952H; *Neue musik*, 1950H; *Probleme der neuen Polyphonie*, 1949H

Thomán, István, 1862A, 1940B

Thomán, Mária, 1899A, 1948A

Thomán, Valerie, 1878A, 1948A

Thomas, Ambroise, 1811A,1832E, 1845E, 1851E, 1871D, 1896B

Thomas, Augusta Read, 1964A

Thomas, Caryl, 1958A, 1981C

Thomas, Christian G.: *Praktische beiträge zur geschichte der Musik*, 1778H

Thomas, David, 1943A

Thomas, Jess, 1927A, 1957C, 1993B

Thomas, John Charles, 1891A, 1913F, 1924C, 1960B

Thomas, John Rogers, 1829B, 1896B

Thomas, Isaiah, 1792F

Thomas, Mary, 1935A, 1997B

Thomas, Michael Tilson, 1944A, 1968E, 1969F, 1971DE, 1988D, 1993E, 1995D

Thomas, Rudolf, 1939D

Thomas, Theodore, 1835A, 1853F, 1859F, 1862D,1866F, 1869F, 1875F, 1877D, 1880D, 1891D, 1899F, 1905B

Thomas, Theodore, Orchestra, 1862G

Thomé, Francis, 1850A, 1909B

Thommessen, Olav Anton, 1946A

Thompson, John, 1805A, 1841B

Thompson, John M.: *The Oxford History of New Zealand Music*, 1991H

Thompson, John S., 1889A, 1963B

Thompson, John Winter, 1867A, 1951B

Thompson, Lesleigh, 1966A

Thompson, Oscar, 1887A, 1928D, 1936D, 1937D, 1945B; *How to Understand Music*, 1935H; *International Cyclopedia of Music & Musicians*, 1939H; *Practical Music Criticism*, 1934H; *Tabulated Biographical History of Music*, 1936H

Thompson, Peter, Publishing House, 1751G

Thompson, Randall, 1899A, 1938E, 1939D, 1941D, 1984B; *College Music*, 1935H

Thompson, Roy, Hall, 1982G

Thompson, Will, Publisher, 1875G

Thomson, Bryden, 1928A, 1968D, 1977D, 1979D, 1984D, 1988D, 1991B

Thomson, César, 1857A, 1931B

Thomson, George, 1757A, 1851B; *Original Scottish Airs I*, 1793H; *Select Collection of Original Irish Airs*, 1816H; *Select Collection of Original Welsh Airs*, 1809H

Thomson, Heather, 1962C

Thomson, Neil, 1966A

Thomson, Virgil, 1896A, 1921F, 1925F, 1940D, 1948E, 1959E, 1966E, 1968E, 1977E, 1983E, 1988E, 1989B; *American Music Since 1910*, 1871H; *The Art of Judging Music*, 1948H; *Music Reviewed*, 1967H; *Music, Right & Left*,

1951H; *Music with Words: A Composer's View*, 1989H; *The Musical Scene*, 1945H; *The State of Music*, 1939H

Thórarinsson, Leifur, 1934A, 1998B

Thorborg, Kerstin, 1896A, 1924C, 1970B

Thorburn, Melissa, 1956A

Thoresen, Lasse, 1949A

Thorn, Penelope, 1957A

Thorne, Francis, 1922A, 1988E

Thorne Music Fund, 1965G

Thorpe Davie, Cedric, 1983B

Thorvaldsson, Tórame, 1975C

Thouvenel String Quartet, 1975G

Thrane, Waldemar, 1790A, 1828B

Thuille, Ludwig, 1861A, 1907B

Thurber, Jeannette, 1946B

Thuringian Academic Singing-Circle, 1969G

Thursby, Emma, 1845A, 1931B

Thurston, Frederick, 1901A, 1952E, 1953B; *The Clarinet*, 1939H; *Clarinet Technique*, 1956H

Thybo, Leif, 1922A

Tibbett, Lawrence, 1896A, 1923C, 1960B

Tibbits, George, 1933A

Tiby, Ottavio, 1955B; *Acustica musicale e organologia degli strumenti musicali*, 1933H

Tichatschek, Joseph, 1807A, 1837C, 1886B

Tichchenko, Boris, 1978E

Tichel, Framl, 1958A

Ticknor & Fields Publishing House (Boston), 1832G

Tiensuu, Jukka, 1948A

Tiersot, Julien, 1857A, 1936B; *La musique aux temps romantiques*, 1930H

Tiessen, Heinz, 1887A, 1971B

Tietjens, Therese, 1831A, 1877B

Tiffany, Young & Ellis (Tiffany & Co.), 1837G

Tigranian, Armen, 1939E, 1950B

Tijarković, Ivo, 1976B

Tikka, Kari, 1946A, 1968C, 1970D, 1972D, 1975D, 1979D, 1986D

Tikotsky, Evgeni, 1944E, 197B

Till, Johann Christian, 1762A, 1844B

Tilli, Johan, 1967A

Tillyard, H. J. W., 1881A, 1968B; *Byzantine Music & Hymnography*, 1923H

Tilmant, Théophile (Alexandre), 1799A, 1834D, 1860D, 1878B

Timbrell, Charles: *French Pianism: A Historical Perspective (2nd edition)*, 1999H

Timm, Henry Christian, 1811A, 1835C, 1892B

Timmermans, Ferdinand, 1891A, 1967B

Timofeeva, Lubov, 1951A, 1969E

Tinel, Edgar, 1877E

Tinsley, Pauline, 1928A, 1951C

Tintner, George, 1917A, 1973D, 1977D, 1987D, 1999B

Tiomkin, Dimitri, 1979B

Tipo, Maria, 1931A, 1949E

A *Births*   B *Deaths*   C *Debuts*   D *New Positions*

E *Prizes/Honors*

Tippett, Michael, 1905A, 1940D, 1943F, 1959E, 1965F, 1966E, 1998B
Tiraboschi, Girolamo, 1784B; *Biblioteca Modenese I*, 1781H; *Storia della letteratura italiana*, 1772H
Tischer und Jagenberg (Cologne), 1909G
Tischhauser, Franz, 1921A, 1971D
Tischler, Hans, 1915A; *The Perceptive Music Listener*, 1955H; *Practical Harmony*, 1964H
Tisné, Antoine, 1932A
Titl, Anton Emil, 1809A, 1882B
Titov, Alexei Nikolaivich, 1769A, 1827B
Titov, Nikolai Alexievich, 1800A, 1875B
Titus, Alan, 1945A, 1969C
Titus, Graham, 1949A, 1974C
Titus, Hiram, 1947A
Titz, Heinrich, 1759B
Tivoli Gardens Concert Hall, 1956G
Tjeknavorian, Loris, 1937A, 1989D
Tobias, Johann, 1758B
Tobin, Tim, 1991E
Toch, Ernst, 1887A, 1909E, 1910E, 1956E, 1964B; *The Shaping Forces in Music*, 1948H
Toch, Ernst, Archive, 1974G
Tocchi, Gian Luca, 1901A
Tocco, James, 1943A, 1973E
Toczyska, Stefania, 1943A, 1973C
Toda, Kunio, 1915A
Todi, Luiza Rosa, 1753A, 1770C, 1787F, 1833B
Todisco, Nunzio, 1942A
Toduiţă, Sigismund, 1908A, 1991B
Toebosch, Louis, 1916A, 1946D, 1965D
Toeschi, Alessandro, 1758B
Toeschi, Carl Joseph, 1788B
Toeschi, Johann Baptist, 1793D
Toeschi, Johann Christoph, 1800B
Tofts, Catherine, 1756B
Togni, Camillo, 1993B
Tokatyan, Armand, 1896A, 1921C, 1960B
Tokody, Ilona, 1953A, 1973C
Tokyo, Japan: Kosei Wind Orchestra (Tokyo), 1984G; Metropolitan Symphony Orchestra, 1965G; Music School, 1887G; New Composer's Association, 1949G; Opera (Niki Kai), 1952G; Philharmonic Orchestra, 1940G; String Quartet, 1969G; Symphony Orchestra, 1937G; University of Arts, 1949G;
Toldrá, Eduardo, 1895A, 1912C, 1944D
Tollefsen, Carl H., 1882A, 1963B
Tollefsen Trio, 1909G
Tolonen, Jouko, 1912A, 1956D, 1986B
Tomáek, Jaroslav, 1970B
Tomáek, Václav Jan, 1774A, 1790F, 1794F, 1797F, 1824F, 1850B
Tomasi, Henri, 1901A, 1971B
Tomasini, Alois Luigi, 1808B
Tómasson, Haukur, 1960A
Tómasson, Jónas, 1946A

Tomeoni, Florido: *Théorie de la musique vocale*, 1799H
Tomilin, Victor, 1908A, 1941B
Tomkison, Thomas, Piano Maker (London), 1798G
Tomlinson, John, 1946A, 1970C
Tommasini, Vincenzo, 1878A, 1950B
Tomotani, Kāji, 1947A
Tomowa-Sintow, Anna, 1941A, 1965C
Tone, Yasunao, 1935A
Tonelli, Antonio, 1765B; *Trattado di Musica*, 1755H
Tonger, P. J., Music Publisher, 1822G
Toni, Alceo, 1969B
Tonic Sol-Fa Advocate, 1881G
Tonic Sol-Fa College, 1867G, 1869G
Tonic Sol-Fa Reporter, 1853G
Töpfer, Johann Gottlob, 1791A, 1830D, 1870B; *Abhandlung über den saitenbezug der Pianoforte*, 1842H; *Anleitung zur erhalung und stimmung der Orgel*, 1840H; *Die Orgel, Zweck und beschaffenheit Teile*, 1843H; *Scheibler'sche stimm-methode*, 1842H; *Theoretisch-praktische Orgelschule*, 1845H
Topilow, Carl, 1947A
Töpper, Hertha, 1924A, 1945C
Torachi, Luigi, 1858A, 1894D
Toradze, Alexander, 1952A, 1961C, 1983F
Toradze, David, 1922A
Torchi, Luigi, 1920B
Torgerson, Torleif, 1967A
Torjussen, Trygve, 1977B
Torkanowsky, Werner, 1926A, 1961E, 1963D, 1992B
Torke, Michael, 1961A, 1986E
Törne, Bengt von, 1967B
Toronto, Canada: C.B.C. Opera Co., 1948G; College of Music, 1888G; Esprit Orchestra, 1983G; Grand Opera House, 1874G; Massey Hall, 1894G; Mendelssohn Choir, 1894G; Metropolitan Choral Society, 1858G; Musical Society, 1836G; New Symphony Orchestra of Toronto, 1923G; Philharmonic Society, 1845G; Repertory Orchestra, 1964G; Royal Conservatory of Music, 1886G; Saint Lawrence Hall, 1851G; Symphony Orchestra I, 1906G; Symphony Orchestra II, 1934G
Torrefranca, Fausto, 1883A, 1907D, 1955B; *Le origine italiane del romanticismo musicale: I primitivi della sonata moderne*, 1930H; *La vita musicale dello spirito: La musica, le arti, il dramma*, 1910H
Torres, Jesús, 1965A
Torres, Victor, 1991C
Torres-Santos, Raymond, 1958A
Torricella, Christoph, 1798B
Tortelier, Paul, 1914A, 1931C, 1990B
Tortelier, Yan Pascal, 1947A, 1962C, 1989D, 1992D

❖

F *Biographical*   G *Cultural Beginnings*   H *Musical Literature*
I *Musical Compositions*

Torzewski, Marek, 1984C
Toscanini, Arturo, 1867A, 1895D, 1886C, 1898D, 1906D, 1908D, 1915F, 1928D, 1929F, 1930F, 1937D, 1940F, 1950F, 1954F, 1957B, 1987G
Toselli, Enrico, 1883A, 1926B
Tosti, (Francesco) Paolo, 1846A, 1908E, 1916B
Totenberg, Roman, 1911A, 1923C, 1932E, 1978D
Tóth, Aladár, 1898A, 1946D, 1952E
Tottmann Albert: *Abriss der Musikgeschichte*, 1883H
Toulouse, France: Chamber Orchestra, 1853G; Conservatory of Music, 1820G; National Chamber Orchestra, 1953G
Tourangeau, Huguette, 1940A, 1962C
Tourel, Jennie, 1900A, 1906A, 1931C, 1973B, 1992F
Tourjée, Eben, 1834A, 1867D, 1869E, 1876D, 1891B
Tournemire, Charles, 1870A, 1898D, 1939B; *Petite méthode d'orgue*, 1949H; *Précis d'exécution de registration et d'improvisation à l'orgue*, 1936H
Tours, Jacques, 1759A, 1811B
Tourte, François, 1835B
Touyère, Raymond, 1941A, 1993B
Tovey, Donald, 1875A, 1898F, 1935E, 1940B; *Companion to Bach's Art of the Fugue*, 1931H; *Essays & Lectures on Music*, 1949H; *Essays in Musical Analysis I*, 1935H; *Essays in Musical Analysis: Chamber Music*, 1944H; *The Mainstream of Music*, 1949H; *A Musician Talks*, 1941H
Tower, Joan, 1938A, 1983E, 1990E, 1998E
Toyama, Yuzo, 1931A
Toye, Francis, 1883A, 1964B; *Italian Opera*, 1952H; *The Well-Tempered Musician*, 1925H
Toye, Geoffrey, 1942B
Tozzi, Antonio, 1761E, 1774D
Tozzi, Giorgio, 1923A, 1948C
Tracey, Minnie, 1870A, 1891C, 1929B
Tracy, Hugh, 1903A, 1977B
Traetta, Filippo, 1777A, 1799F, 1822F, 1854B; *Introduction to the Art and Science of Music*, 1829H; *Rudiments of Singing I*, 1841H
Traetta, Tommaso, 1758D, 1765D, 1775F, 1799B
Trago, José, 1856A, 1880C, 1934B
Trakas, Christopher, 1985E
Trambitsky, Victor, 1970B
Trampler, Walter, 1915A, 1933C
Trần, Van Khê, 1921A, 1964D
Trapp, Maria von, 1987B
Trapp, Max, 1971B
Trattner, Johann Thomas, 1798B
Traubel, Helen, 1899A, 1923C, 1953F, 1972B
Traubmann, Sophie, 1867A, 1885C, 1951B
Trautonium, 1930G
Trautwein Music Publishers, 1820G

Travenol, Louis: *Histoire du théâtre de l'opéra en France*, 1753H; *Mémoire sur le sieur Travenol, ex-musicien du roi de Pologne*, 1758H
Travers, John, 1758B
Travis, Roy, 1922A
Traxel, Josef, 1916A, 1942C, 1975B
Trebelli, Zélia, 1838A, 1859C, 1892B
Tredici, David Del, 1937A
Tree, Ann Maria, 1801A, 1819C, 1862B
Tree, Michael, 1954C
Treger, Charles, 1935A, 1946C, 1962E, 1984D
Treigle, Norman, 1927A, 1947C, 1975B
Treitler, Leo, 1931A; *Music & the Historical Imagination*, 1989H
Tremaine, Henry B., 1866A, 1832
Tremaine Brothers (Tremaine Piano Co.), 1876G
Tremblay, Edith, 1972E
Tremblay, George, 1911A, 1982B; *The Definitive Cycle of the Twelve-Tone Row & its Application in all Fields of Composition*, 1974H
Tremblay, Gilles, 1932A
Tremont String Quartet, 1977G
Trento, Vittorio, 1761A, 1806D, 1833B
Treptow, Günther, 1907A, 1936C, 1981B
Tretyakov, Viktor, 1966E
Tréville, Yvonne de, 1881A, 1898C, 1954B
Trial, Antoine, 1764C, 1795B
Trial, Armand-Emmanuel, 1771A, 1803B
Trial, Jean-Claude, 1767D, 1771B
Trial, Marie-Jeanne, 1766C, 1818B
Triay, Raphael R., 1836D
Tribolet, Marianne de, 1768A, 1795C, 1813B
Tricht, Käte van, 1909A
Triebensee, Josef, 1772A, 1846B
Triebert, Guillaume, Woodwind Maker, 1810G
Trieste, Italy: Academy of Music, 1822G; Liceo Musicale, 1887G; Opera Co., 1801G; Sinico Singing School, 1843G; Società Filarmonico-drammatica, 1829G; Teatro Grande, 1801G; Teatro Nuovo, 1801G
Trifunović, Vitomir, 1916A
Trimarchi, Domenico, 1940A, 1964C
Trimble, Lester, 1923A, 1952D, 1957D, 1961E, 1963D, 1967F, 1968D, 1986B
Trinitatis Kantori, 1993G
Trio, 1790G, 1994G
Trio de Lutèce (Carlos Salzedo), 1913G
Trio Mezzena-Bonucci, 1992G
Trio Wanderer, 1987G
Tritto, Giacomo, 1799D, 1824B; *Scuola di contrappunto*, 1823H
Trochléon, 1812G
Trognitz, R. E., 1902D
Trojahn, Manfred, 1949A, 1975E
Trojan, Václav, 1907A, 1983B
Tromlitz, Johann Georg, 1805B; *Ausführlicher und gründlicher unterricht die Flöte zu spielen,*

A *Births*   B *Deaths*   C *Debuts*   D *New Positions*
E *Prizes/Honors*

1791H; *Kurze abhandlung vom flötenspiel*,
1786H
Trondheim, Norway: Practical Musical Society,
1815G; Symphony Orchestra, 1909G
Trost, Tobias Heinrich, 1759B
Trostiansky, Alexander, 1972A
Tröstler Bernhard: *Traité général et raisonné de
Musique*, 1825H
Troszel, Wilhelm, 1823A, 1843C, 1887B
Trotter, Thomas, 1957A, 1980C
Trotyako, Viktor, 1946A
Troupenas, Eugéne, Publishers, 1825G
Trowell, Brian, 1931A
Trow–Piccolo, Lynne, 1975C
Troxell, Barbara, 1916A, 1984B
Troyanos, Tatiana, 1938A, 1963C, 1993B
Troyat, Henri, 1959E
Truax, Barry, 1947A; *Acoustic Communication*,
1085H; *Handbook for Acoustic Ecology*, 1978H
Trúbner & Co., 1851G
Truhn, Friedrich Hieronymus, 1811A, 1886B
Trunk, Richard, 1925D, 1934D
Trussel, Jacques, 1943A, 1970C
Trutovsky Vasili: *Russian Folksongs II*, 1778H
Trydell John: *Analogy of Harmony*, 1769H; *Two
Essays on the Theory and Practice of Music*,
1766H
Tryon, Valerie, 1934A, 1953C
Trythall, Gil, 1930A; *Eighteenth Century
Counterpoint*, 1993H; *Principles & Practice of
Electronic Music*, 1974H; *Sixteenth Century
Counterpoint*, 1994H
Trythall, Richard A., 1939A, 1964E
Tschudi, Burkhard, 1773B
Tseytlin, Lev, 1881A, 1952B
Tsintsadze, Sulkhan, 1925A, 1991B
Tsitsaros, Christos, 1961B
Tsontakis, George, 1951A, 1990E
Tsoupaki, Calliope, 1963A
Tsují, Shōichi, 1895A, 1987B
Tsutsumi, Tsuyoshi, 1942A, 1955C, 1963E
Tsvetanov, Tsvetan, 1931A, 1982B
Tua, Teresina, 1867A, 1895F, 1955B
Tubb, Carrie, 1876A, 1976B
Tubists Universal Brotherhood Association,
1972G
Tucci, Gabriella, 1929A, 1951CE
Tucker, Richard, 1913A, 1943C, 1975B
Tucker, Richard, Music Foundation., 1975G
Tucker, Sophie, 1884A
Tuckerman, Samuel Parkman, 1819A, 1864D,
1890B; *A Collection of Cathedral Chants*,
1858H; *Episcopal Harp*, 1844H; *Trinity
Collection of Church Music*, 1864H
Tuckey, William, 1770F
Tuckwell, Barry, 1931A
Tucson, Arizona: Arizona Chamber Orchestra,
1967G; Boys' Choir, 1939G; Desert Singing
Guild, 1948G; Festival in the Sun, 1990G;

Music Hall, Tucson Community Center,
1971G; Opera Co., 1972G; Symphony
Orchestra, 1929G; Winter Chamber Music
Festival, 1994G; Youth Symphony Orchestra,
1960G
Tudor, David, 1926A, 1996B, 1992E
Tudoran, Ionel, 1913A, 1936C
Tuesday Morning Music Club (Springfield),
1902G
Tufts, John Wheeter, 1825A, 1908B
Tully, Alice, 1902A, 1927C, 1969D, 1985E,
1993B
Tully, Alice, Hall, 1969G
Tulou, Jean-Louis, 1786A, 1865B; *Flute Method*,
1836H
Tulou-Nonon Flute Co., 1831G
Tulsa, Oklahoma: Commercial Club Band,
1902G; Grand Opera House, 1906G; Little
Symphony, 1979G; Opera Club, 1902G;
Performing Arts Center, 1977G;
Philharmonic Orchestra, 1947G; Youth
Symphony Orchestra, 1963G
Tůma, Frantiek Ignác, 1774B
Tůma, Jaroslav, 1956A
Tumagian, Eduard, 1944A, 1968C
Tumanyan, Barseg, 1958A, 1980C, 1983E
Tunley, David, 1930A
Tuomela, Tapio, 1958A
Tupkov, Dimiter, 1929A
Turban, Charles Paul, 1845A, 1905B
Turban, Ingolf, 1964A, 1986C
Turchaninov, Peter Ivanovich, 1779A, 1856B
Turchi, Guido, 1967D
Tureck, Rosalyn, 1914A, 1935C, 1958F, 1977E
Tureck Bach Ensemble & Institute, 1981G
Turetzky, Bertram, 1933A, 1964C; *The
Contemporary Contrabass*, 1974H
Turgeon, Edward/Anne, 1998E
Turin, Italy: Accademia Filarmonica, 1814G;
Concerti Popolari, 1872G; Liceo Musicale,
1866G; Scuola Gratuita de Canto, 1872G;
Società Corale, 1875G; Società del Quartetto,
1862G; Teatro Regio II, 1973G
Turina, Joaquin, 1882A, 1949B; *Enciclopedia
abreviada de música*, 1917H; *Tratado de
composición*, 1946H
Turini, Ronald, 1934A
Türk, Daniel Gottlob, 1774D, 1779D, 1787D,
1813B; *Anleitung zu Temperaturberechnungen*,
1808H; *Clavierschule*, 1789 H; *Kurze
Anweisung zum Klavierspielen*, 1792H; *Kurze
anweisung zum generalbassspielen*, 1791H; *Von
den wichtigsten Pflichten eines Organisten: ein
Beytrag zur verbesserung der musikalischen
Liturgie*, 1787H
Turkish National School for Opera & Drama,
1936G
Turnage, Mark-Anthony, 1960A
Turner, Eva, 1892A, 1916C, 1962E, 1990B

❋

F   *Biographical*   G   *Cultural Beginnings*   H   *Musical Literature*
I   *Musical Compositions*

Turner, Robert, 1920A
Turner, W. J.: *English Music*, 1941H; *Facing the Music: Reflections of a Music Critic*, 1933H; *Music: A Short History*, 1932H; *Music: An Introduction to Its Nature & Appreciation*, 1936H; *Music & Life*, 1922H; *Musical Meanderings*, 1928H; *Orpheus, or The Music of the Future*, 1926H; W. J., *Variations on a Theme of Music*, 1924H
Turner & Steere Organ Co., 1867G
Turnovsky, Martin, 1928A, 1952C, 1958E, 1959D, 1960D, 1963D, 1966D, 1975D, 1979D, 1992D
Turok, Paul, 1929A, 1964D, 1980D
Turovsky, Yuri, 1939A
Turp, André, 1950C
Turpin, Tom, 1873A, 1922B
Türrschmidt, Carl, 1753A, 1791B
Turski, Zbigniew, 1908A, 1979B
Tusler, Robert L., 1920A; *Music: Catalyst for Healing*, 1991H
Tuthill, Burnet C., 1888A, 1924D, 1935D, 1937D, 1938D, 1982B
Tuukkanen, Kalervo, 1909A, 1979B
Tüür, Erkki-Sven, 1959A
Tuvas, Linda, 1972A
Tuxen, Erik, 1902A, 1927D, 1936D, 1945D, 1957B
Tveitt, Geirr, 1908A, 1981B
Tworkov, Jack, 1981E
Tyl, Noel, 1936A
Tyndall John: *Sound*, 1867H; *On the Transmission of Sound by the Atmosphere*, 1874H
Tynes, Margaret, 1929A, 1952C
Tyrrell, Lisa Jane, 1967A
Tyson, Alan, 1926A, 1989E, 2000B
Tzarth, Georg, 1778B
Ubani, Edurne, 1990C
Uber, Christian F., 1781A, 1808D, 1814D, 1822B
Uberti, Antonio, 1783B
Uchida, Mitsuko, 1948A, 1963C, 1968E, 1970F
Ude, Armin, 1959C
Ugalde, Delphine, 1829B, 1848C, 1910B
Ughi, Uto, 1944A, 1951C
Ugolinus, Blasius, 1771B
Uhde, Hermann, 1914A, 1936C, 1965B
Uhl, Fritz, 1928A, 1952C
Uhlik, Tomâslav, 1956A
Ukrainian State Symphony Orchestra, 1937G
Ulbrich, Andrea Edina, 1964A
Ulehla, Ludmila: *Contemporary Harmony*, 1966H
Ulfung, Ragnar, 1927A, 1952C, 1977D
Ullman & Strakosch Opera Co., 1857G
Ulivieri, Nicola, 1993C
Uliyanich, Victor, 1956A
Ulms Conservatory of Music, 1921G

Ulrich, Homer, 1906A, 1953D, 1987B; *Chamber Music*, 1948H; *The Education of a Concertgoer*, 1949H; *Famous Women Singers*, 1953H; *A History of Music & Musical Style*, 1963H; *Symphonic Music*, 1952H; *A Survey of Choral Music*, 1973H
Ulrich, Hugo, 1827A, 1872B
Ulster Symphony Orchestra, 1966G
Ultan, Lloyd: *Music Theory: Problems & Practice in the Middle Ages & Renaissance*, 1977H
Ultima Festival, 1991G
Umbreit, Karl Gottlieb, 1763A, 1829B
Umeå Symphony Orchestra, 1991G
Umlauf, Ignaz, 1778D
Umlauf, Michael, 1781A, 1842B
Umstatt, Joseph, 1752D, 1762B
Ung, Chinary, 1942A, 1964F, 1989E
Unger, Caroline, 1803A, 1824C, 1877B
Unger, Georg, 1837A, 1867C, 1887B
Unger, Heinz, 1895A, 1965B
Unger, Max, 1883A, 1959B
Union of Musical Artists for...Widows & Orphans, 1803G
Union Musical de Québec, 1866G
Unión musical Española, Publishing Co., 1900G
United Artists Records, 1958G
United States Army Music School, 1911G
United States Marine Band, 1802G
United States Marine Fife & Drum Corps, 1798G
Universal Edition (Vienna), 1901G
University of Chicago Press, 1964G
University of Michigan School of Music, 1879G
University of Nebraska School of Music, 1880G
Unpartheiische Kritik, 1798G
Unpublished Editions, 1972G
Unwin, Nicholas, 1962A
Uppman, Theodor, 1920A, 1941C
Upshaw, Dawn, 1960A, 1985CE
Upton, George P., 1834A, 1863D, 1919B; *Musical Memories: My Recollections of Celebrities of the Half-Century, 1850-1900*, 1908H; *Musical Pastels–The Standard Light Operas*, 1902H; *The Song*, 1915H
Upton, William Treat, 1870A, 1961B; *The Art-Song in America*, 1930H
Urbánek, Franz A., Publisher, 1872G
Urbani, Edurne, 1979A, 1992C
Urbani, Peter, Publisher (Edinburgh), 1795G
Urbany String Quartet, 1813G
Urhan, Chrétien, 1790A, 1845B
Urlus, Jacques, 1867A, 1894C, 1935B
Urso, Camilla, 1842A, 1852C, 1902B
Urspruch, Anton, 1850A, 1907B
Ursprung, Otto, 1879A, 1960B; *Die Katholische kirchenmusik*, 1931H
Ursuleae, Viorica, 1894A, 1922C, 1985B
Usandizaga, José María, 1887A, 1915A

❉

A   *Births*   B   *Deaths*   C   *Debuts*   D   *New Positions*
E   *Prizes/Honors*

USC School of the Performing Arts, 1883
Ussachevsky, Vladimir, 1911A, 1963E, 1973E
USSR International Music Festival, 1981G
USSR State Choir (Moscow), 1942G
USSR State Symphony Orchestra, 1936G
Utah (*see also* Salt Lake City): Opera Co.,
    1976G; Oratorio Society, 1914G; State
    Symphony Orchestra, 1940G; Symphony
    Orchestra, 1946G
Uttini, Francesco A., 1755F, 1767DE, 1788F,
    1795B
Vaccai, Nicola, 1790A, 1821F, 1838D, 1848B
Vachon, Pierre, 1756C, 1803B
Vačkář, Václav, 1881A
Vadé, Jean-Joseph, 1757B
Vaghi, Giacomo, 1901A, 1978B
Vähi, Peeter, 1955A
Valasek, Erno, 1941E
Valda, Giulia, 1855A, 1879C, 1925B
Valdengo, Giuseppe, 1914A, 1936C
Valdes, Maximiano, 1989D
Valdrighi, Luigi Francesco, 1827A, 1899B
Valek, Vladimir, 1977D, 1985D, 1995D
Valen, Fartein, 1887A, 1927D, 1935E, 1952B
Valencia Municipal Orchestra, 1943G
Valente, Benita, 1934A, 1960C
Valenti, Fernando, 1926A, 1950C, 1990B
Valentin, Erich, 1906A, 1993B
Valentin de Carvalho, Publisher, 1914G
Valentini-Terrani, Lucia, 1948A, 1969C, 1998B
Valentino, Frank, 1907A, 1991B
Valentino, Henri J., 1785A, 1820D, 1831D,
    1865B
Valeri, Gaetano, 1760A, 1785D, 1805D, 1822B
Valero, Fernando, 1878C
Valesi, Giovanni, 1816B
Valleria, Alwina, 1848A, 1871C, 1883F, 1925B
Valletti, Cesare, 1922A, 1947C, 2000B
Vallotti, Francesco Antonio, 1780B
Valverde, Joaquín, 1846A, 1910B
Van Allen, Richard, 1935A, 1966C
Vanaud, Marcel, 1952A
Vanaud, Marcel, 1975C
Vanbrugh String Quartet, 1985G
Vancouver, Canada: Opera Co., 1959G;
    Chamber Choir, 1971G; International
    Festival, 1958G; Opera Association, 1961G;
    Symphony Orchestra, 1931G
Van Dam, José, 1940A, 1960C, 1964E
Van den Borren, Charles, 1874A, 1909D, 1919D,
    1966B; *La musique en Belgique du moyen-âge à
    nos jours*, 1950H; *Origine et développement de
    l'art polyphonique vocal du XVIe siècle*, 1920H;
    Sources of Keyboard Music in England, 1912H
Van den Hoek, Martijn, 1955A
VanderCook, Hale A., 1864A, 1949B; *A Course
    in Band & Orchestra Directing*, 1916H;
    Teaching the High School Band, 1926H
VanderCook's College of Music, 1909G

Van der Straeten, Edmond, 1875C
Van der Stucken, Frank, 1858A, 1906A, 1929E
Van de Vate, Nancy, 19930A
Van Dresser, Marcia, 1877A, 1903C, 1937B
Van Dyck, Ernest, 1861A, 1883C, 1923B
Vaness, Carol, 1952A, 1979C
Vanguard Recording Society, 1949G
Vanguard Records, 1950
Van Hagen, Peter, Sr., 1803B
Vanhall Johann Baptist, 1813B
Van Hoose, Ellison, 1868A, 1897C, 1936B
Van Hove, Luc, 1957A
Vanhulst, Henri, 1943A
Van Kampen, Christopher, 1967C
Vankatova, Dagmar, 1963A, 1995C
Van Keulen, Isabelle, 1966A
Van Nes, Jard, 1948A, 1983C
Vannuccini, Luigi, 1828A, 1911B
Van Rooy, Anton, 1870A, 1897C, 1932B
Vänskä, Osmo, 1953A, 1982E, 1988D, 1993D,
    1996D
Van Slyck, Nicholas, 1962D
Van Vechten, Carl, 1964B, 1994B; *Interpreters &
    Interpretations*, 1917H; *Music after the Great
    War*, 1915H; *Red: Papers on Musical Subjects*,
    1925H
Van Vulpen Brothers, Organ Builders, 1940G
Van Zandt, Jennie, 1840A, 1864C
Van Zandt, Marie, 1858A, 1879C, 1919B
Van Zanten, Cornelia, 1946B
Vanzo, Alain, 1928A, 1954C
Varady, Julia, 1962C
Varèse, Edgard, 1883A, 1915F, 1955E, 1957EF,
    1962E, 1965BE
Varesi, Felice, 1813A, 1834C, 1889B
Varga, Tibor, 1921A, 1931C
Varga, Gilbert, 1985D, 1998D
Vargas, Ramon, 1960A, 1988C
Varlamov, Alexander, 1801A, 1832D, 1848B
Varney, Astrid, 1918A, 1941C
Varney, Pierre Joseph, 1811A, 1840D, 1879B
Varsova, Valeria, 1919C
Varviso, Silvio, 1924A, 1944C, 1965D, 1972D
Vasarely, Victor, Foundation, 1977G
Vasary, Tamas, 1989D
Vashegyi, György, 1970A
Vasilenko, Sergei, 1872A, 1956B
Vasks, Peteris, 1946A
Vassiliev, Alexander, 1970A, 1994C
Vaucorbeil, Auguste-Emmanuel, 1821A,
    1884B
Vaughan, Denis Edward, 1926A
Vaughan, Elizabeth, 1937A, 1959E, 1960C
Vaughan-Williams, Ralph, 1872A, 1894F, 1897F,
    1908F, 1919E, 1922F, 1932F, 1954F, 1958B; *The
    English Hymnal*, 1906H
Veasey, Josephine, 1930A, 1955C
Vechten, Carl Van, 1880A
Vedernikov, Alexander, 1991D

Vega, Aurelio de la: *The New Romanticism*, 1951H
Vegh String Quartet, 1940G
Végh, Sándor, 1912A, 1997B
Veinus, Abraham, 1916A, 1938D; *The Concerto*, 1944H; *Pocket Book of Great Operas*, 1944H; *Understanding Music: Style, Structure & History*, 1958H
Velcovici, Oana, 1973C
Velis, Andrea, 1932A, 1954C, 1994B
Vellinger String Quartet, 1990G
Velluti, Giovanni B., 1781A, 1801C, 1861B
Veltman, Michael, 1960A
Veltri, Michelangelo, 1940A, 1964C, 1966D, 1984D, 1997B
Venezuela Symphony Orchestra, 1930G
Vengerov, Maxim, 1974A, 1985C, 1990E
Vengerova, Isabelle, 1877A
Vengerova, Isabelle, 1950E, 1956B
Venice, Italy: Festival of Contemporary Music, 1930G; Maderna Ensemble, 1975G
Venta, Matthias, 1776B
Ventre, Carlo, 1965A
Veracini, Francesco Maria, 1768B
Vera-Rivera, Santiago Oscar, 1950A
Verbier Festival & Academy, 1994G
Verbitskaya, Eugenia, 1904A, 1926C
Verbrugghen, Henri, 1873A, 1915D, 1923D, 1934B
Vercoe, Barry: *Man–Computer Interaction in Creative Applications*, 1975H
Verdehr, Walter, 1941A
Verdery, Benjamin, 1955A
Verdi, Giuseppe, 1813A, 1832F, 1835D, 1840F, 1848F, 1857F, 1859F, 1860F, 1865F, 1874F, 1901B
Verdière, René, 1927C
Vered, Ilana, 1939A
Verein zur Erforschung alter Choralhandschriften, 1872G
Vergara, Victoria, 1948A, 1977C
Vergnes, Paul-Henri, 1905A, 1929C
Vergnet, Edmund A., 1850A, 1874C, 1904B
Verhulst, Johannes, 1816A, 1860D, 1891B
Verin, Nicolas, 1958A
Verkrnova, Denisa, 1993C
Vermeer String Quartet, 1969G
Vermeulen, Matthijs, 1888A, 1967B
Vernerová-Nováková, Ludmila, 1962A, 1987C
Vernon, Joseph, 1751C
Vernon, Richard, 1950A, 1972C
Véron, Louis, 1830D
Verrall, John, 1908A; *Basic Theory of Scales, Modes & Intervals*, 1969H; *The Elements of Harmony*, 1937H; *Fugue & Invention in Theory & Practice*, 1966H
Verrett, Shirley, 1931A, 1955E, 1957C, 1958E
Verroust, Denis, 1958A
Verschraegen, Herman, 1974D

Vertavo String Quartet, 1984G
Verteljahrsschrift für Musikwissenschaft, 1884G
Vertovsky, Alexei, 1799A, 1825D, 1842D, 1862B
Veskrnova, Denisa, 1973A
Vesque von Püttlinger, Johann, 1803A, 1883B; *Das musikaliche Autorecht*, 1865H
Vestris, Lucia E., 1797A, 1815C, 1856B
Vetö, Iámás, 1987D
Veyron-Lacroix, Robert, 1922A, 1949C, 1991B
Vezzani, César, 1886A, 1911C, 1951B
Viala, Jean-Luc, 1957A, 1983C
Vianesi, Auguste C., 1837A, 1870D, 1887D, 1908B
Viardo, Vladimit, 1973E
Viardot-Garcia, Pauline, 1821A, 1837C, 1910B
Vibert, Nicolas, 1752B
Vicar, Jan, 1949A
Vickers, Jon, 1926A, 1952C
Victor Talking Machine Co., 1901G
Victory, Gerard, 1921A, 1995B
Vidal, Paul, 1883E
Vienna, Austria: Bella Musica, 1977G; Capella Academica, 1965G; Concentus Musicus, 1953G; Octet, 1948G; Rosé String Quartet, 1882G;
Viennese Summerfest (Atlanta), 1989G
Viennese Sommerfest (Minnesota), 1980G
Viens, Michael C., 1953A
Vierk, Lois V., 1951A
Vierling, Georg, 1826A, 1901B
Vierling, Johann G., 1773B, 1813B
Vierne, Louis, 1870A, 1900D, 1937B
Vierteljahrsschrift für Musikwissenschaft, 1844G
Vieru, Anatol, 1947D, 1998B
Vieuxtemps, Henri, 1820A, 1833F, 1846F, 1857F, 1870F, 1881B
Viglione-Borghese, Domenico, 1877A, 1899C, 1957B
Vignas, Francisco, 1863A, 1888C, 1933B
Vignoles, Roger, 1945A, 1967C
Vigny, Alfred Victor, 1845E
Vilanova, Ramón, 1801A, 1830D, 1870B
Vilback, Renaud, 1844E
Viljakainen, Raili, 1954A, 1978C
Villa-Lobos, Heitor, 1887A, 1932F, 1944F, 1959B
Villani, Luisa, 1885A, 1907C
Villaroel, Veronica, 1965A, 1986C
Villette, Pierre, 1926A, 1998B
Villoteau, Guillaume A., 1759A, 1839B
Vilnius, Lithuania: Lithuanian Opera & Ballet Theater, 1948G; Lithuanian State Philharmonic, 1940G;
Vinay, Ramón, 1912A, 1931C, 1943C, 1996B
Vincent, Alexandre J., 1797A, 1868B
Vincent, Heinrich J., 1819A,
Vincent, John, 1901A, 1977B; *The Diatonic Modes in Modern Music*, 1951H
Vine, Carl, 1954A
Viner, William Letton, 1790A, 1867B

A *Births*   B *Deaths*   C *Debuts*   D *New Positions*

E *Prizes/Honors*

Vinogradsky, Alexander, 1912B
Vinohrady Theater (Prague), 1907G
Vinton, John: *Dictionary of Contemporary Music*, 1974H
Vinzing, Ute, 1936A, 1967C
The Violinist, 1900G
Viotta, Henri, 1848A, 1896D, 1903D, 1933B
Viotti, Giovanni Battista, 1755A, 1766F, 1770F, 1780F, 1782C, 1783F, 1818F, 1819D, 1824B
Virgil Practice Clavier Co., 1890G
Virginia: Opera Association, 1975G; Opera (Norfolk), 1974G; School of the Arts, 1983G
Virtuosi della Rosa, 1985G
Virtuosi per Musica di Pianoforte, 1968G
Virtuosi Woodwind Quintet, 1983G
Virués, José, 1770A, 1840B
Visconti, Piero, 1975C
Visek, Tomás, 1957A
Vishnevskaya, Galina, 1926A, 1944C, 1955F, 1974F
Vitásek, Jan August, 1770A, 1814D, 1826D, 1839B
Vito-Delvaux, Berthe de, 1915A
Vitzthumb, Ignaz, 1769D, 1786D
Vivier, Eugène, 1817A, 1900B
Vix, Geneviève, 1879A, 1906C, 1939B
Vixell, Ingmar, 1955C
Vlach String Quartet, 1951G
Vladigerov, Pantcho, 1899A
Vocal Normal School, 1912G
Vodenicharov, Boyan, 1960A
Vogel, Adolf, 1897A, 1923C, 1969B
Vogel, Emil, 1859A, 1908B
Vogel, Jaroslav, 1949D, 1970B
Vogel, Johann Christoph, 1756A, 1788B
Vogel, Wilhelm Moritz, 1846A, 1922B
Vogelstrom, Fritz, 1882A, 1903C, 1963B
Voggenhuber, Vilma von, 1862C
Voggenhuber, Vilma von, 1845A, 1862C, 1888B
Vogl, Heinrich, 1845A, 1865C, 1900B
Vogl, Johann Michael, 1768A, 1795C, 1840B
Vogler, Georg "Abbe," 1763F, 1773F, 1774E, 1775F, 1781F, 1783F, 1784D, 1786DF, 1792F, 1793F, 1807D
Vogler, Jan, 1964A
Vogler, Johann Caspar, 1763B
Vogrich, Max, 1852A, 1916B
Vogt, Gustave, 1781A, 1829E, 1870B
Vogt, Johann, 1823A, 1888B
Vogt, Lars, 1970A
Vogt'sche Konservatorium, 1899G
Voigt, Deborah, 1960A, 1990E, 1991CE, 1993E
Voigt, Johann Georg, 1769A, 1811B
Voketaitis, Arnold, 1958C
Volckmar, Wilhelm, 1812A, 1887B
Völker, Franz, 1899A, 1926C, 1965B
Volkert, (Johann) Franz, 1767A, 1814D, 1845B
Volkland, Alfred, 1841A, 1905B
Volkmann, Robert, 1815A, 1883B

Volkov, Feodor, 1761D
Volmer, Arvo, 1993D
Volodos, Árcadi, 1972A
Volpe, Arnold, 1869A, 1904D, 1922D, 1940B
Volpe, Armond, 1869A
Volpe Symphony of New York, 1904G
Von Huene, Friedrich, Recorder/Flute Maker, 1960G
Vonk, Hans, 1942A, 1966D, 1973D, 1976D, 1980D, 1985D, 1991D, 1995F, 1996D
Von Magnus, Elisabeth, 1965A
Von Stade, Frederica, 1945A, 1970C, 1986E
Voorhees, Donald, 1903A, 1989B
Voříek, Jan Václav, 1791A, 1818D, 1825B
Votalpek, Ralph, 1939A, 1959CE, 1962E
La Voz de la Musica, 1907G
Vronsky, Vitya, 1909A, 1992B
Vronsky, Peter, 1946A, 1971C, 1983D
Vroons, Frans, 1911A, 1937C, 1983B
Vuillaume, Jean, Violin Maker, 1798A, 1828G, 1875B
Vuillermoz, Emile, 1878A, 1960B; *Histoire de la musique*, 1949H; *Musique d'aujour'hui*, 1923H
Waart, Edo de, 1941A, 1964CE, 1966D, 1973D, 1977D, 1986D, 1988D, 1993D
Wachovia Little Symphony, 1978G
Wachs, Paul Étienne, 1851A, 1914B
Wachtel, Theodor, 1823A, 1893B
Wächter, Eberhard, 1929A, 1953C, 1992B
Wackernagel, Philipp, 1800A, 1877B; *Das deutsche Kirchenlied von der ältesten Zeit*, 1841H
Wade, Joseph Augustine, 1796A, 1845B
Waelput, Hendrik, 1869D, 1867E, 1884D
Wagenaar, Bernard, 1894A, 1925E, 1971B
Wagenaar, Johan, 1862A, 1887D, 1941B
Wagenseil, Georg Christoph, 1777B; *Geig-Fundamenta, oder Rudimenta Pandurietae*, 1751H
Wagner, Georg Gottfried, 1756B
Wagner, Johann G, 1789B
Wagner, Johanna, 1826A, 1844C, 1894B
Wagner, Joseph Frederick, 1900A, 1925D, 1974B; *Orchestration*, 1958H; *Scoring for Band*, 1960H
Wagner, Karl Jakob, 1772A, 1808D, 1822B
Wagner, Melinda, 1999E
Wagner, Minna, 1858F, 1859F, 1862F
Wagner, Peter, 1865A, 1931B
Wagner, Richard, 1813A, 1814F, 1822F, 1824F, 1826F, 1830F, 1831F, 1834DF, 1836F, 1837D, 1839F, 1840F, 1842F, 1843D, 1846F, 1848F, 1850, 1853F, 1854F, 1855F, 1857F, 1858F, 1859F, 1860F, 1862F, 1864F, 1865F, 1868F, 1870F, 1872F, 1874F, 1883B; *Art and Revolution*, 1849H; *Kunst un Klima*, 1850H; *Das Kunstwerke der Zukunft*, 1850H; *Oper und Drama*, 1851H; *Über des Dirigieren*, 1869H
Wagner, Roger, 1914A, 1951D, 1992B

❖

Wagner, Roger, Chorale, 1946G
Wagner, Siegfried, 1869A, 1930B
Wagner, Wieland, 1917A, 1966B
Wagner Museum (Tribschen), 1933G
Wagner Tubas, 1870G
Wailly, Paul de, 1854A, 1933B
Wainwright, John, 1768B
Wainwright, Richard, 1757A, 1775D, 1782D, 1825B
Wainwright, Robert, 1768D, 1775D, 1782B
Wakasugi, Hiroshi, 1977D, 1981D, 1987D, 1995D
Walcker, Eberhard F., 1794A, 1872
Walcker, Eberhard, Organ Builder, 1820G
Wald, Max, 1889A, 1954B
Waldbauer-Kerpoly String Quartet, 1909G
Walden, Valerie: *One Hundred Years of Violoncello*, 1998H
Walden String Quartet, 1934G
Waldhans, Jiří, 1923A, 1962D
Waldman, Frederic, 1903A, 1995B
Waldmann, Maria, 1865C
Waldrop, Gideon W., 1986D
Waldstein, Ferdinand, 1762A, 1823B
Waldteufel, Emil, 1837A, 1915B
Walker, Alan: *An Anatomy of Musical Criticism*, 1966H
Walker, Diana, 1958A, 1983C
Walker, Edyth, 1867A, 1894C,
Walker, George, 1922A, 1945C, 1982E, 1999E
Walker, Jayne, 1958A, 1984C
Walker, Joseph: *Historical Account & Critical Essay on the Opera*, 1805H; *Historical Memoirs of the Irish Bards*, 1786H
Walker, Penelope, 1956A, 1976C
Walker, Sandra, 1948A, 1972C
Walker, Sarah, 1943A, 1969C
Walker, William: *The Christian Harmony*, 1866H; *Southern Harmony*, 1835H
Wallace, William V, 1812A, 1835F, 1838F, 1841F, 1844F, 1845F, 1850F, 1865B
Wallaschek, Richard, 1860A, 1917B; *Ästhetik der Tonkunst*, 1886H; *On the Origin of Music*, 1891H; *Primitive Music*, 1893H
Wallenstein, Alfred, 1898A, 1912C, 1935D, 1943D, 1983B
Wallenstein Sinfonietta, 1933G
Wallfisch, Elizabeth, 1952A, 1969C
Wallfisch, Rafael, 1953A
Wallin, Rolf, 1957A
Wallnöfer, Adolf, 1854A, 1878C, 1946B
La Wallonie, 1886G
Walmisley, Thomas Forbes, 1814D
Walsh, Luise, 1966A
Walt, Deon van der, 1958A
Walter, Alfred, 1966D, 1984D
Walter, Anton, 1790E
Walter, Bruno, 1876A, 1889F, 1893F, 1894F, 1901F, 1913D, 1933F, 1936D, 1947D,

1962B; *Of Music & Music-Making*, 1961H
Walter, Gustav, 1834A, 1855C, 1910B
Walter, William E., 1924D
Walther, Geraldine, 1979E
Walthrop, Gideon, 2000B
Walton, William, 1902A, 1983B, 1942E, 1951E, 1967E
Waltz, Gustavus, 1759B
Wambach, Emile, 1854A, 1913D, 1924B
Wanami, Takoyoshi, 1963C
Wand, Günter, 1912A, 1939D, 1947D, 1982D
Ward, David, 1922A, 1953C, 1983B
Ward, Frank Edwin, 1872A, 1953B
Ward, Genevieve, 1833A, 1861C, 1922B
Ward, John M., 1917A
Ward, Joseph, 1962C
Ward, Robert, 1917A, 1946E, 1956D, 1967D, 1972E, 1994B
Ward, Thomas, 1884F
Ward-Steinman, David, 1936A; *Toward a Comparative Structural Theory of the Arts*, 1989H
Ware, Harriet, 1877A, 1962B
Ware, Henry, (Cardiff) Symphony Orchestra, 1918G
Warfield, Gerald, 1940B
Warfield, Sandra, 1929A, 1953C
Warfield, William, 1920A, 1950C
Waring, Fred, 1900A, 1984B
Waring, Fred, Glee Club, 1938G
Waring, Fred, Music Workshop, 1947G
Waring's, Fred, Pennsylvanians, 1916G
Warlock, Peter, 1894A, 1930B
War Memorial Opera House, 1932G
Warmuth, Carl, Publisher, 1843G
Warner, Wendy, 1991E
Warner Brothers Music, 1929G
Warner Brothers Records, 1958G
Warnier, Vincent, 1996D
Warnots, Elly Elisabeth, 1862A, 1878C
Warnots, Henri, 1832A, 1856C, 1893B
Warnot's Music School, 1870G
Waroblewski, Patrick, 1984E
Warren, Elinor Remick, 1900A, 1991B
Warren, George William, 1828A, 1902B
Warren, Kenneth, & Son School of Violinmaking, 1975G
Warren, Leonard, 1911A, 1939C, 1960B
Warren, Richard Henry, 1859A, 1933B
Warren, Samuel Prowse, 1841A, 1915B
Warren, Samuel R., Organ Builder, 1836G
Warriner, Solomon: *Musica Sacra*, 1816H; *Springfield Collection of Sacred Music*, 1813H
Warsaw, Poland: Amateur Music Society, 1817G; Autumn Festival of Contemporary Music (Warsaw), 1956G; Chopin, Frederick, Institute, 1934G; Chopin Piano Competition, 1949G; Grand Opera, 1833G; Grand Theater,

A *Births*   B *Deaths*   C *Debuts*   D *New Positions*
E *Prizes/Honors*

1825G; Katski (Kontski) Music Conservatory, 1861G; Music Society, 1870G; National Philharmonic Hall, 1955G; Philharmonic Orchestra I, 1901G; Philharmonic Orchestra II, 1950G; Society, Religious & National Music, 1814G

Wartel, Pierre-François, 1806A, 1831C, 1882B

Warton, Joseph, 1800B

Washburn, Robert, 1928A, 1982D

Washington Auditorium, 1924G

Washington Community Opera Ass'n, 1918G

Washington Guitar Quintet, 1986G

Washington Opera, 1980G

Washington Performing Arts Society, 1966G

Washington Symphony Orchestra, 1966G

Washington, D.C.: American Music Festival, 1942G; Cathedral Choral Society, 1942G; Choral Society, 1869G; College of Church Musicians, 1962G; Dodsworth Band, 1860G; Inter-American Music Festival, 1958G; Library of Congress, 1800G; Library of Congress, Music Div., 1897G; National Gallery Orchestra, 1943G; National Institute for Music Theater, 1969G; National Society of Arts and Letters, 1944G; National Symphony Orchestra, 1931G; Opera Society of Washington, 1956G; Permanent Chorus, 1899G; Philharmonic Society, 1850G; Sängerbund, 1851G; Terrace Theater, 1979G; Twentieth Century Consort, 1975G; Violins of Lafayette, 1995G

Wasielewski, Wilhelm von: *Geschichte der Instrumental-Musik in SVI. Jahrhundert.*, 1878H

Wass, Robert, 1764B

Wasserman, Ellen, 1972E

Watanabe, Akeo, 1919A, 1945C, 1948D, 1956D, 1972D, 1988D, 1990B

Watanabe, Yoko, 1956A, 1978C

Waterloo Music Festival, 1968G (NJ)

Wathey, Andrew, 1958A

Watkins, Glenn: *Soundings: Music in the Twentieth Century*, 1988H

Watson, Chester, 1979B

Watson, Claire, 1924A, 1951C, 1976F, 1986B

Watson, Janice, 1964A

Watt, Henry: *The Foundations of Music*, 1919H; *The Psychology of Sound*, 1917H

Watson, Henry C., 1863D

Watts, André, 1946A, 1955C, 1988E

Watts, Helen, 1927A, 1953C

Watts, Isaac: *The Psalms of David*, 1818H

Watts, John, 1930A, 1982B; *Psalms of David Imitated*, 1773H

Watts, Wintter, 1884A, 1923E, 1962B

Watzke, Rudolf, 1892A, 1923C

Wa-Wan Press (Boston), 1901G

Waxman, Donald, 1925A

Waxman, Franz, 1906A, 1967B

Wayditch, Gabriel von, 1969B

Waylett, Harriett, 1800A, 1816C, 1851B

Weathers, Felicia, 1937A, 1961C

Weaver, Powell, 1890A, 1951B

Webb, Daniel: *Observations on the Correspondance between Poetry and Music*, 1769H

Webb, Frank Rush, 1851A, 1934B

Webb, George James, 1803A, 1830D, 1887B; *The Odeon: A Collection of Secular Melodies*, 1837H

Webbe, Samuel, Jr., 1770A, 1843B

Webbe, Samuel, Sr., 1816B

Webber, Andrew Lloyd, 1997E

Webber, Julian Lloyd, 1951A, 1972C, 1986F

Weber, Aloysia, 1760A, 1779C, 1839B

Weber, Ben, 1916A, 1950E, 1965E, 1971E, 1979B

Weber, Bernhard Anselm, 1764A, 1792D, 1821B

Weber, Bernard Christian, 1758B

Weber, Carl Maria von, 1786A, 1796F, 1797F, 1798F, 1800F, 1801F, 1803F, 1804D, 1806F, 1807D, 1808F, 1810F, 1812F, 1813D, 1817D, 1820F, 1821F, 1823F, 1826BF,

Weber, Christian L., Publisher, 1773G

Weber, Friedrich Dionys, 1766A, 1811D, 1842B; *Allgemeine theoretisch-praktische Vorschule der Musik*, 1828H; *Theoretisch-prakisches Lehrbuch der Harmonie I*, 1830H

Weber, Gottfried, 1779A, 1824D, 1839B; *Allgemeine Musiklehre zum Selbstunterrichte*, 1822H; *Generalbasslehre zum selbstunterrichte*, 1833H; *Versuch einer geordneten Theorie der Tonsetzkunst I*, 1817H

Weber, Joseph Miroslav, 1854A, 1906B

Weber, Josepha, 1759A, 1819B

Weber, Louis, Publisher, 1904G

Weber, Ludwig, 1899A, 1920C, 1974B

Weber, Peter, 1955A, 1976C

Weber Piano Co., 1852G

Webern, Anton, 1883A, 1904F, 1945B

Webster, Beveridge, 1908A, 1999B

Wechsler, Bert, 1997A

Weckerlin, Jean Baptiste, 1821A, 1876D, 1910B

Wedekind, Erika, 1868A, 1894C, 1944B

Wedge, George, 1964B; *Advanced Ear Training*, 1922H; *Keyboard Harmony*, 1924H

Wedge, George Anson, 1890A

Weede, Robert, 1903A, 1927C, 1972B

Weekblad voor Musiek, 1894G

Wegelius, Martin, 1846A, 1882D, 1906B; *Treatise on General Musical Seience and Analysis I*, 1888H; *Foundations of General Music Science*, 1887H; *Homophonic Writing*, 1897H

Wegelius Chamber Orchestre, 1986G

Wegner, Walburga, 1908A, 1940C, 1993B

Wehr, David Allen, 1987E

Wehrmann, Henry, Jr., 1956B

Weichsel, Elizabeth, 1783F

Weichsell, Frederica, 1764C, 1786B

Weidemann, Friedrich, 1871A, 1796C, 1919B

F   *Biographical*   G   *Cultural Beginnings*   H   *Musical Literature*
I   *Musical Compositions*

Weidig, Adolf, 1867A, 1931B; *Harmonic Material & Its Uses*, 1923H
Weidinger, Christine, 1946A, 1972C
Weidt, Lucie, 1876A, 1940B
Weigall, Hugo, 1975E
Weigel Hall (Ohio State U.), 1980G
Weigl, Karl, 1949B
Weigl, Johann Baptist, 1783A, 1852B
Weigl, Joseph, Jr., 1766A, 1782F, 1790F, 1846B
Weigl, Joseph, Sr., 1820B
Weigl, Karl, 1881A
Weigl, Thaddäus, 1776A, 1844B
Weigl, Thaddäus, Publisher (Vienna), 1803G
Weigle, Jörg-Peter, 1953A, 1986D, 1995D
Weikert, Ralf, 1940A, 1981D, 1984D
Weikl, Bernd, 1942A, 1968C
Weil, Hermann, 1876A, 1901C, 1949B
Weill, Kurt, 1900A, 1933F, 1950B
Weill, Kurt, Foundation for Music, 1962G
Weill, Kurt, Prize, 1995G
Weimar, Germany: Ducal Orchestral School, 1872G; Institute for Folk Music, 1950G; Kunstfest, 1990G; Liszt Hochschule, 1872G; National Theater, 1825G; Neu-Weimar-Verein, 1854G
Weinberg, Henry, 1968E
Weinberg, Jacob, 1879A, 1956B
Weinberger, Jaromir, 1896A, 1967B
Weinberger, Josef, Publisher, 1885G
Weiner Konzerthausgesellschaft, 1900G
Weiner, Lazar, 1897A, 1982B
Weiner, Léo, 1922E
Weingartner, Felix, 1863A, 1881F, 1883F, 1884C, 1887D, 1891D, 1908D, 1912D, 1919D, 1927D, 1942B
Weinlig, Christian Ehregott, 1767D, 1785D; *Vorlesungen über Grundbasse und Composition überhaupt*, 1811H
Weinlig, (Christian) Theodor, 1780A, 1814D, 1823D, 1842B; *Theoretisch-praktische Anleitung zur Fuge, für den Selstunterricht*, 1845H
Weinmann, Karl, 1873A, 1929B
Weinrich, Carl, 1904A, 1991B
Weinstock, Herbert, 1905A, 1971B; *Men of Music*, 1939H; *Music As an Art*, 1953H; *The Opera: A History of Its Creation & Performance*, 1941H
Weintraub Music Co. (NY), 1950G
Weir, Judith, 1954A
Weisbach, Hans, 1961B
Weisberg, Arthur, 1931A; *The Art of Wind Playing*, 1973H; *Performing Twentieth-Century Music*, 1993H
Weiser, Bernhard, 1998B
Weisgall, Hugo, 1912A, 1949D, 1954E, 1963D, 1990D, 1994E, 1995E, 1997B
Weismann, Julius, 1879A, 1950B
Weiss, Adolph, 1891A, 1926F, 1955E, 1971B
Weiss, Willoughby Hunter, 1820A, 1842C, 1867B

Weissenberg, Alexis, 1929A, 1945C, 1947E, 1966F
Weitzmann, Carl F., 1808A, 1880B; *Geschichte der harmonie*, 1849H; *Geschichte des Clavierspiele*, 1863H; *Harmonie system*, 1860H; *Der Letzte der Virtuosen*, 1868H; *Die neue Harmonielehre im Streit mit der Alten*, 1861H; *Der Übermässige Dreiklang*, 1853H
Welcher, Dan, 1948A
Welcker Music Publishers, 1762G
Weldon, George, 1906A, 1943D, 1963B
Weldon, Georgina 1837A, 1870C, 1914B
Welin, Karl-Erik, 1934A, 1992B
Welitsch, Ljuba, 1913A, 1936C, 1996B
Welker, Hartmut, 1941A, 1974C
Weller, Dieter, 1937A, 1963C
Weller, Walter, 1939A, 1969D, 1977D, 1980D, 1991D, 1994D
Weller String Quartet, 1958G
Wellesley College School of Music, 1878G
Wellesley, Garret, 1760E
Wellesz, Egon, 1885A, 1957E, 1961E, 1974B; *Byzantinische Musik*, 1927H; *Byzantinische Musik, Das Musikwerk*, 1959H; *Essays on Opera*, 1950H; *Origin of Schoenberg's 12-tone System*, 1958H
Wellington Orchestra Society, 1892G
Welser-Moest, Franz, 1960A, 1985D, 1990D, 1995D
Welsh Folk Song Society, 1906G
Welsh Music Festival, 1859G
Welsh National Opera Co., 1946G
Welsh Philharmonia, 1970G
Welte, Emil, 1841A, 1923B
Welte, Michael, 1807A, 1880B
Welting, Patricia, 1949A, 1986BF
Welting, Ruth, 1970C, 1999B
Wendling, Dorothea, 1767A, 1784C, 1811B
Wendling, Elisabeth Augusta, 1752A, 1794B
Wendling, Franz, 1786B
Wendling, Johann Baptist, 1797B
Wenkel, Ortrun, 1964C
Wennberg, Siv, 1944A, 1972C
Werckmeister, Andreas: *Die musicalische Temperatur*, 1996H
Werlein, P. F., Publisher, 1853G
Werner, Eric, 1901A, 1988B; *From Generation to Generation: Studies on Jewish Musical Tradition*, 1962H; *Sacred Bridge: Literary Parallels in Synagogue & Early Church*, 1959H; *Sacred Bridge II: Liturgical Parallels in Synagogue & Early Church*, 1984H
Werner, Gregor Joseph, 1766B
Werner, Johann Gottlob, 1777A, 1822B; *Harmonielehre I*, 1818H; *Orgelschule*, 1805H; *Orgelschule II*, 1823H
Wernick, Richard, 1934A, 1976E, 1987E
Werrenrath, Reinald, 1883A, 1919C, 1953B
Wertheim Performing Arts Center, 1996G
Wescott, Mark, 1971E

❀

A *Births*   B *Deaths*   C *Debuts*   D *New Positions*
E *Prizes/Honors*

Wesendonck, Mathilde, 1854F
Wesley, Charles (I), 1788B
Wesley, Charles (II), 1757A, 1834B
Wesley, John, 1791B; *The Power of Music*, 1779H; *Sacred Melody*, 1765H; *Select Hymns with Tunes Annext*, 1761H
Wesley, Samuel, 1766A, 1787F, 1837B; *Eight Lessons for Harpsichordists*, 1777H
Wesley, Samuel Sebastian, 1810A, 1826D, 1829D, 1832D, 1835D, 1842D, 1847F, 1849D, 1850D, 1865D, 1874E, 1876B; *A Few Words on Cathedral Music*, 1849H; *The Psalter*, 1843H
Wesolowska, Anna, 1967C
Wessel, Marc, 1894A, 1973B
Wessel & Stodart, 1823G
Wessely, Carl B., 1788D, 1796D
Wessely, Hans, 1862A, 1926B
Wessely, Othmar, 1922A, 1998B
West, Benjamin: *Sacra Concerto; or the Voice of Melody*, 1760H
West, Ewan: *The Oxford Dictionary of Opera*, 1992H
West Australian Symphony Orchestra, 1950G
West Bay Opera (San Francisco), 1956G
West Coast Festival of Sound Poetry, 1977G
Westenburg, Richard, 1932A
Westenholz, Barbara Lucietta, 1776B
Westenholz, Carl, 1789B
Westenholz, Sophia Maria, 1759A, 1838B
Westerberg, Stig, 1918A, 1949D, 1957D, 1978D
Westergaard, Peter, 1931A; *An Introduction to Tonal Theory*, 1975H
Western Arts Music Festival, 1972G
Western Journal of Music, 1856G
Western Opera Theater, 1966G
Western (Brainard's) Musical World, 1864G
Western Slope Summer Music Festival, 1997G
Western Wind, 1969G
Westminster Choir (New York), 1921G
Westminster Choir School, 1926G
Westminster Presbyterian Church Choir, 1920G
Westminster Recordings, 1949G
Westminster Review, 1824G
Westphal, Rudolf, 1826A, 1892B
Westphalian Music Festival, 1852G
Westrup, Jack Allen, 1959D, 1961E; *Musical Interpretation*, 1971H
West Virginia Opera Theater, 1972G
Wettergren, Gertrud, 1897A, 1922C
Wetz, Richard, 1935B
Wetzler, Hermann, 1870A, 1943B
Wetzler Symphony Concerts (N.Y.), 1903G
Weyditch, Gabriel von, 1888A
Weyse, Christoph Ernst, 1774A, 1805D, 1842B
Wharton Center for the Performing Arts, 1982G
Whear, Paul William, 1925A
Wheeler, Anthony, 1958A
Whelpley, Benjamin Lincoln, 1886C, 1864A, 1946B

White, Carolina, 1886A
White, Clarence C., 1880A, 1960B
White, David H., 1981D
White, Emily, 1962A, 1988C
White, Harry, *Music and the Church*, 1993H; *Music & Irish Cultural History*, 1995H; *Musicology in Ireland*, 1991H
White, John, 1855A, 1902B
White, John (Reeves), 1924A, 1984B
White, Michael, 1931A
White, Paul, 1895B, 1973B
White, Richard G., 1851D
White, Robert, 1936A
White, Ruth, 1925A
White, Wendy, 1989C
White, Willard, 1948A, 1974C
White, William C., 1881A, 1964B; *A History of Military Music in America*, 1943H
Whitehill, Clarence, 1871A, 1898C, 1932B
Whitewater Opera Co., 1972G
Whithorne, Emerson, 1884A, 1958B
Whiting, Arthur Battelle, 1861A, 1905E, 1936B
Whiting, George E., 1840A, 1923B
Whitley, William, Instrument Shop, 1810G
Whitlock, Percy, 1903A, 1946B
Whitmer, Carl, 1873A
Whitmer, T. Carl, 1959B; *The Art of Improvisation*, 1934H
Whitney, Myron, 1836A, 1858C, 1910B
Whitney, Samuel B., 1842A, 1914B
Whitney, Robert, 1904A, 1937D, 1956D, 1986B
Whittal, Arnold: *Music Analysis in Theory & Practice*, 1987H
Whittall, Gertrude C., 1867A, 1965B
Whittall Foundation (Library of Congress), 1936F
Whittall Pavilion (Library of Congress), 1938G
Whittenberg, Charles, 1927A, 1984B
Wichita Symphony Orchestra, 1944G
Wichmann, Hermann, 1824A, 1905B
Wick, Tilman, 1959A, 1976C
Wickham, Florence, 1880A, 1902C, 1962B
Widdop, Walter, 1892A, 1923C, 1949B
Widén, Anna Kristina, 1972A
Widhalm, Leopold, 1776B
Widmann, Jörg, 1973A, 1996E
Widor, Charles-Marie, 1844A, 1860D, 1870D, 1910E, 1937B; *L'orgue moderne*, 1928H; *Technique de l'orchestre moderne*, 1904H
Wieck, Clara, 1836E
Wieck, Friedrich, 1785A, 1828F, 1873B; *Clavier und gesang*, 1853H
Wieck, Marie, 1832A, 1843C, 1916B
Wiecks, Frederick, 1924B
Wiedebein, Gottlob, 1779A, 1854B
Wiedemann, Ernst Johann, 1797A, 1873B
Wiedemann, Hermann, 1879A, 1905C, 1944B
Wiegand, Heinrich, 1842A, 1870C, 1899B
Wiehmayer, Theodor, 1870A, 1890C, 1947B
Wieland, Christoph M., 1773D

❉

F *Biographical*   G *Cultural Beginnings*   H *Musical Literature*
I *Musical Compositions*

Wielhorsky, Count Mikhail, 1788A, 1856B
Wiemann, Ernst, 1919A, 1938C, 1980B
Wiener, Otto, 2000B
Wiener Festwochen, 1951G
Die Wiener Solisten, 1959G
Wiener Theatre-Zeitung, 1806G
Wiener Urtext Editions, 1972G
Wieniawski, Henryk, 1835A, 1848C, 1849F,
 1851F, 1880B
Wieniawski, Jozef, 1837A, 1912B
Wieprecht, Friedrich Wilhelm, 1802A, 1872B
Wiesbaden, Germany: Spangenberg Music
 Cons., 1890G
Wigglesworth, Frank, 1918A, 1945E, 1961E,
 1996B
Wigglesworth, Mark, 1964A, 1991D, 1996D
Wihan String Quartet, 1985G
Wikmanson, Johan, 1753A, 1800B
Wilcox, Carol Ann, 1945A
Wilcox & White, Organ Makers, 1876G
Wild, Earl, 1915A, 1934C
Wildbrunn, Helene, 1882A, 1906C, 1972B
Wilder, Alec, 1907A, 1980B
Wildmann, Maria, 1920B
Wildner, Johannes, 1956A
Wilford & Associates, Artist Management,
 1953G
Wilhelm, Alexander, 1908A
Wilhelm, August, 1845A, 1854C, 1908B
Wilhelm, Guillaume-Louis, 1781A, 1842B
Wilke, Christian F, 1769A, 1848B; *Beiträge zur
 geschichte der neuen Orgelbaukunst*, 1846H
Wilkins, Christopher, 1991D
Willan, Healey, 1880A, 1933D, 1968B
Willcocks, David, 1960D, 1977E
Willcox, J. H., Co., Organ Builders, 1869G
Willen, Niklas Olov, 1988C
Willent-Bordogni, Jean-Baptiste, 1809A, 1852B;
 The Psalmody, 1770H; *The Universal Psalmist*,
 1763H
Williams, Adrien, 1956A
Williams, Alberto, 1862A, 1919E, 1952B
Williams, Alberto, Cons. of Music, 1893G
Williams, Bradley, 1991C
Williams, Camilla, 1922A, 1946C
Williams, Clifton, 1923A, 1976B
Williams, George E., 1814D
Williams, Grace, 1906A, 1977B
Williams, Harry Evan, 1867A, 1918B
Williams, Huw, 1971A
Williams, Janet, 1970C
Williams, John (Towner), 1932A, 1980D
Williams, John (Christopher), 1941A, 1952F,
 1955C, 1962F
Williams, John M., 1884A, 1974B
Williams Music Publishers (London), 1808G
Williams, R. S., & Sons, 1854G
Williamson, John Finley, 1887A, 1932F, 1964B
Williamson, Malcolm, 1931A, 1975E

Willig, George, Publisher (Philadelphia),
 1794G
Willis, Henry, 1901B
Willis, Henry, Organ Builder, 1821A, 1845G
Willis, Helen, 1959A, 1983C
Willis, Richard S., 1819A, 1852D, 1900B; *Church
 Chorals & Choir Studies*, 1850H
Willis Music Co., 1899G
Willmers, Heinrich R., 1821A, 1844C, 1878B
Willson, Meredith, 1902A, 1984B
Wilms, Jan Willems, 1772A, 1847B
Wilms, Johann Wilhelm, 1772A, 1847B
Wilson, Grenville D., 1833A, 1897B
Wilson, John, 1996D
Wilson, Mary Ann, 1802A, 1821C, 1867B
Wilson, Neal, 1956A
Wilson, Neil, 2000B
Wilson, Olly, 1937A, 1995E
Wilson, Ransom, 1951A
Wilson, Richard, 1941A, 1979D, 1985D
Wilson, Steuart, 1948E
Wilt, Marie, 1865C
Winbergh, Gösta, 1943A, 1971C
Wincenc, Carol, 1949A, 1978E
Winchester, England: Hamshire Music
 Festival, 1760G
Winckelmann, Hermann, 1849A
Windgassen, Fritz, 1909C
Windgassen, Wolfgang, 1914A, 1941C, 1974B
Windham Chamber Music Festival, 1997G
Winding, August, 1835A, 1891D, 1899B
Windingstad, Ole, 1913D, 1940D, 1945D, 1959B
Winds Quarterly, 1980G
Windsor Symphony Orchestra, 1981G
Winkelmann, Hermann, 1875C, 1912B
Winn, James: *Unsuspected Eloquence*, 1981H
Winn, William, 1828A, 1855C, 1868B
Winner, Septimus, 1827A, 1902B
Winnipeg, Canada: Philharmonic Choir,
 1922G; Symphony Orchestra, 1948G
Winograd, Arthur, 1920A
Winslow, Walter, 1998B
Winson, Phil: *Computer-Assisted Music
 Composition*, 1987H
Winston, Jeannie, 1845A, 1929B
Winter, Louise, 1959A
Winter, Peter (von), 1754A, 1798D, 1814E,
 1825B; *Vollständige singschule*, 1825H
Winter Garden (New York), 1911G
Winterfeld, Carl von, 1784A, 1852B; *Der
 Evangelische Kirchengesant I*, 1843H; *Johannes
 Gabrieli und sein zeitalter*, 1834H; *Martin
 Luthers deutsche geistliche Lieder*, 1840H;
 *Musiktreilben und Musikempfindungen im 16.
 Und 17. Jahrhundert*, 1851H; *Zur geschichte
 heiliger Tonkunst I*, 1850H
Winterhalter, Hugo, 1950D
Winternitz, Emanuel, 1898A, 1983B
Winternitz-Dorda, Martha, 1885A, 1906C

A *Births*   B *Deaths*   C *Debuts*   D *New Positions*
E *Prizes/Honors*

Winter Park Bach Festival, 1935G
Winterthur Stadtorchesster, 1875G
Wiorda, Walter, 1997B; *Das Musikalische Kunstwerk*, 1983H
Wippern, Louise, 1837A, 1857C, 1878B
Wirén, Dag, 1905A, 1946E, 1986B
Wirl, Eric, 1885A, 1906C, 1954B
Wirth, Emanuel, 1842A, 1923B
Wise, Patricia, 1944A, 1966C
Wissmer, Pierre, 1915A, 1992B
Wit, Antoni, 1970D, 1974D, 1977D, 1983D, 1987D
Witherspoon, Herbert, 1873A, 1898C, 1925D, 1931D, 1935B; *Singing: a Treatise for Teachers & Singers*, 1925H
Witmark, M., Publisher, 1885G
Witt, Friedrich, 1770A, 1802D, 1836B
Witt, Marie, 1833A, 1891B
Wittassek, Johann Nepomuk, 1770A, 1839B
Witte, Erich, 1932C
Wittgenstein, Paul, 1887A, 1912C, 1914F, 1958E, 1961B; *School for the Left Hand*, 1957H
Wittich, Marie, 1868A, 1882C, 1931B
Wittinger, Robert, 1945A
Wixell, Ingvar, 1931A, 1952C
Wochentliche Nachrichten und Anmerkungen, 1766G
Wodzinska, Marie, 1837F
Woffington, Robert, Organ/Piano Maker (Dublin), 1785G
Wohlfahrt, Heinrich, 1797A
Woldemar, Michel, 1815B; *Méthode pour le violon*, 1798H
Wöldike, Mogens, 1895A, 1988B
Wolf, Ernst W., 1763D, 1772D, 1792B; *Kleine musikalische Reise*, 1782H; *Musikalischer unterricht fur Liebhaber und diejenigen, welche die Music treiben und lehren wollen*, 1788H; *Vorbericht als eine Anleitung zum guten Vortrag beim Klavier-Spielen*, 1785H
Wolf, Georg F., 1761A, 1785D, 1801D, 1814D; *Kurzegefasstes musikalisches Lexikon*, 1787H; *Kurzer aber deutlicher Unterricht in Klavierspielen*, 1781H
Wolf, Hugo, 1860A, 1884D, 1897F, 1898F, 1903B
Wolf, Hugo, String Quartet, 1993G
Wolf, Johannes, 1869A, 1947B; *Handbuch der Notationskunde I*, 1913H; *Handbuch der Notationskunde II*, 1919H
Wolfe, Jacques, 1896A
Wolf, Marcus, 1962A, 1976C
Wolf Trap Farm, Performing Arts, 1971G
Wolf-Ferrari, Ermanno, 1876A, 1892F, 1903D, 1948B
Wolfahrt, Karl, Musikskola (Stockholm), 1913G
Wolfe, Jacques, 1973B
Wolfe, Duain, 1994D
Wolff, Albert, 1884A, 1911C, 1919D, 1925D, 1928D, 1970B

Wolff, Beverly, 1928A, 1952C
Wolff, Christian, 1934A, 1975E, 1996E
Wolff, Fritz, 1894A, 1925C, 1957B
Wolff, Hermann, Concert Management, 1881G
Wolff, Hugh, 1953A, 1985D, 1995D
Wolfl, Joseph, 1773A, 1790F, 1794F, 1795F, 1805F, 1812B
Wolfram, Joseph Maria, 1789A
Wolfrum, Philipp, 1854A, 1919B
Wollanck, Friedrich, 1781A, 1831B
Wollenhaupt, Hermann Adolf, 1827A, 1863B
Wollfisch, Peter, 1948E
Wolpe, Stefan, 1902A, 1949E, 1966E, 1972B
Wolzogen, Hans, 1848A, 1938B; *Grossmeister deutscher Musik*, 1897H
Women's Philharmonic, 1980G
Women's Symphony Orchestra of Chicago, 1925G
Wong, Albert, 1989A
Wong, Samuel, 1996D
Wood, B. F., Publisher, 1893G
Wood, Charles, 1866A, 1926B
Wood, David Duffle, 1838A, 1910B
Wood, Haydn, 1882A, 1959B
Wood, Henry J., 1869A, 1911E, 1926E, 1944B; *About Conducting*, 1945H
Wood, James Peter, 1953A
Wood, Mary Knight, 1857A, 1944B
Woodbury, Arthur, 1967D
Woodbury, Isaac B., 1819A, 1850D, 1858B
Woodman, Huntington, 1861A, 1943B
Woodridge, H. E., 1845A
Woods, Elaine, 1979C
Woodward, Richard, 1765D, 1771E, 1777B
Woodward, Roger, 1942A, 1968E, 1970C
Wooldridge, H. E., 1917B
Woolf, Benjamin E., 1836A, 1901B
Woolf, Randall, 1959A
Woolhouse Wesley: *A Catechism of Music*, 1843H; *Essay on Musical Intervals*, 1835H
Woolrich, John, 1954A
Worcester, England: Concert Club, 1951G; Music Festival, 1858G; Musical Society, 1870G
Worcester, Massachusetts: Glee Club, 1810C
Worcestershire Philharmonic Society, 1898G
Words & Music, Publisher, 1939G
Wordsworth, William, 1908A, 1988B
Worgan, James, 1753B, 1790B
Worgen, John, 1751D, 1760D
Work, Frederick J., 1942B
Work, Henry Clay, 1832A, 1863D, 1884B
Work, John W., 1925B, 1967B; *Folk Song of the American Negro*, 1915H
Workman, William, 1940A, 1965C
World Cello Congress, 1988G
World Center for Jewish Music, 1938G
World Music Bank for...Contemporary Music, 1957G

※

F   *Biographical*   G   *Cultural Beginnings*   H   *Musical Literature*
I   *Musical Compositions*

World Peace Jubilee & Int'l Musical Festival, 1872G

World Saxophone Quartet, 1976G

Worms, Germany: Casino- und Musikgesellschaft, 1783G; Musikgesellschaft und Liedertafel, 1812G

Wormser, André, 1851A, 1875E, 1926B

Wörner, Karl H., 1910A, 1969B; *Geschichte der Musik*, 1954H; *Musik der Gegenwart*, 1949H; *Musiker-Wörte*, 1949H; *Neue Musik in der Entscheidung*, 1954H; *Das Zeitalter der thematischen Prozesse in der Geschichte der Musik*, 1969H

Wortham, Gus S., Theater Center, 1987G

Wranitzky, Anton, 1761A, 1797D, 1814D, 1820B; *Violin Fondament*, 1804H

Wranitzky, Paul, 1756A, 1790F, 1808B

Wray, Margaret Jane, 1989E

Wright, Thomas, 1763A, 1829B

Wu, Mary Mei-Loc, 1964A, 1979C

Wüerst, Richard, 1824A, 1881B

Wüllmer, Franz, 1832A, 1871D, 1877D, 1882D, 1884D, 1902B

Wüllner, Ludwig, 1858A, 1938B

Wunderlich, Fritz, 1930A, 1955C, 1966B

Wuorinen, Charles, 1938A, 1967E, 1985E, 1986E; *Simple Composition*, 1979H

Wüppertal, Germany: City Orchestra, 1849G; Elberfelder Gesangverein, 1811G; Konzertgesellschaft, 1861G; Städischer Singverein Barmen, 1817G; Theater am Brausenwerth, 1888g

Würfel, Wenzel Wilhelm, 1790A

Wurlitzer, Franz, 1853F

Wurlitzer, Howard E., 1871A, 1928B

Wurlitzer, Rudolph, 1831A, 1914B

Wurlitzer, Rudolph H., 1873A, 1948B

Wurlitzer Electronic Organ, 1947G

Wutlizer Organ Co., 1856G

Wurlitzer Hope-Jones Unit Orchestra, 1910G

Wurm, Marie, 1938B

Württemberg, Germany: Evangelical Kirchengesangverein, 1877G; Evangelical Fesstival, 1877G; State Opera, 1912G

Würzburg, Germany: Institute of Music, 1804G; Mozart Festival, 1923G; Royal Music School, 1804G; Stadttheater, 1966G

Wylde, Henry, 1822A, 1890B

Wylie, Phillip, 1971B

Wyman Music School, 1869G

Wyn-Davies, Catrin, 1969A

Wyner, Yehudi, 1929A

Wyner, Susan Davenny, 1943A, 1972C, 1973E

Wyner, Yehudi, 1961E, 1999E

Wynne, Sarah Edith, 1842A, 1862C, 1897B

Xenakis, Iannis, 1922A; *Musiques formelles*, 1963H

Xerox Pianists Program, 1982G

Yablonsky, Dmitri, 1962A

Yaddo Artist's Colony, 1924G

Yaddo Music Festival, 1932G

Yahr, Carol, 1959A, 1987C

Yakupova, Natalia, 1977A

Yale University: Electronic Music Studio, 1960G; Fine Arts Department, 1864G; Glee Club, 1861G, 1921G; Music Classes, 1855G; School of Music, 1894

Yamada, Kōsaku, 1886A, 1915D, 1965B

Yamaha Co., 1887G

Yamaha Foundation, 1966G

Yang, Sungsie, 1966A, 1977C

Yannay, Yehuda, 1937A

The Yard, 1983G

Yardumian, Richard, 1917A, 1985

Yasser, Joseph: *A Theory of Evolving Tonality*, 1932H

Yates, Peter, 1976B; *Twentieth Century Music*, 1967H

Yeend, Frances, 1918A, 1948C

Yepes, Narciso, 1927A, 1947C, 1997B

Yestadt, James, 1960D

Yevtushenko, Evgeny, 1933A

Yggdrasil String Quartet, 1990G

Yi, Chen, 1953A, 1994E

Yi, Suk Won: *Modern Music*, 1997H; *Psychology of Music*, 1994H; *A Theory of Melodic Contour*, 1990H

Yinen, Israel, 1956A

Ying String Quartet, 1992G

Yip, Wing-Sie, 1960A, 1985E, 1986D

Yns, Jean, 1960A

Yoes, Janice, 1943A, 1973C

Yomiuri Nippon Symphony Orchestra, 1962G

Yon, Pietro Alessandro, 1886A, 1926D, 1943B

Yoo, Yung Wook, 1998E

York, John, 1974C

York, England: Choral Society, 1833G; Symphony Orchestra, 1898G

Yoshimatsu, Takashi, 1953A

Young, Alexander, 1920A, 1950C

Young, Cecilia, 1789B

Young, Elizabeth, 1756C

Young, Isabella, 1751C, 1791B

Young, Josephine, 1988C

Young, La Monte, 1935A

Young, Polly, 1762C, 1799B

Young, Simone, 1961A, 1985C, 1993D

Young Artists Development Program, 1980G

Young Concert Artists, 1961G

Young Men's Symphony Orchestra of New York, 1902G

Young People's Philharmonic, 1977G

Young Polish Composers Publishing Co., 1905G

Youngstown Opera Co., 1975G

Youth Symphony of Seattle, 1942G

Youth Symphony of the U.S., 1979G

Ysaÿe, Eugène, 1858A, 1918D, 1931B

❄

A　*Births*　　B　*Deaths*　　C　*Debuts*　　D　*New Positions*

E　*Prizes/Honors*

Yugoslav Academy of Arts & Sciences, Music, 1953G
Yun, Isang, 1917A, 1995B
Yurisich, Gregory, 1978C
Zabaleta, Nicanor, 1907A, 1926C, 1993B
Zaccaria, Nicola, 1923A, 1949C
Zach, Jan, 1773B
Zach, Max, 1905D, 1907D, 1921B
Zach, Miriam Susan, 1954A
Zachariassen, Mathias, 1968A, 1994C
Zack, Arthur, 1936D
Zador, Eugene, 1894A, 1977B
Zadora, Michael, 1882A, 1946B
Zagreb, Yugoslavia: Festival of Contemporary Music, 1961G; I Solisti di Zagreb, 1950G; Musikverein, 1827G; Opera Co., 1870G; Opera House, 1895G; Philharmonic Orchestra, 1920G
Zagrosek, Lothar, 1982D
Zaimont, Judith Lang, 1945A; *Twentieth Century Music*, 1980H
Zajick, Dolora, 1952A, 1986CE
Zamboni, Luigi, 1767A, 1791C, 1837B
Zamboni, Maria, 1898A, 1921C
Zampieri, Giuseppe, 1945C, 1981B
Zampieri, Maria, 1951A, 1972C
Zandonai, Riccardo, 1883A, 1939D, 1944B
Zanelli, Renato, 1892A, 1916C, 1924C, 1935B
Zanetti, Francesco, 1760D, 1788B
Zani, Andrea, 1757B
Zanotti, Giovanni, 1774D, 1817B
Zarębski, Julius, 1854A, 1885B
Zareska, Eugenia, 1941C
Zaslaw, Neal, 1939A; *The Classical Era*, 1990H
Zavateri, Lorenzo Gaetano, 1764B
Zawisza, Philip, 1992E
Zazofsky, Peter, 1955A, 1977F, 1979E
Zech, Frederick, Jr., 1926B
Zech, Jacob, Piano Maker, 1856G
Zech, Max, 1864A
Zecchi, Carlo, 1903A, 1920C, 1984B
Zechwer, Camille, 1875A, 1917D, 1924B
Zeckwer, Richard, 1876D
Zehetmair, Thomas, 1961A, 1978E
Zehetmair String Quartet, 1997G
Zeisler, Fannie B., 1863A, 1875C
Zeitlin, Zvi, 1923A, 1940C
Zeitschrift für Instrumentenbau, 1879G
Zeitschrift für Katholische Kirchenmusik, 1868G
Zeitschrift für Musiktheorie, 1967G
Zeitschrift für Musikwissenschaft, 918G
Zeitschrift für Spielmusik, 1948G
Zelter, Carl F., 1758A, 1800D, 1809D, 1815D, 1822D, 1832B
Zeltzer, Sandra, 1995C
Zemlinsky, Alexander, 1871A, 1900D, 1904D, 1927D, 1933F, 1942B
Zenatello, Giovanni, 1876A, 1898C, 1949B
Zenck, Hermann, 1950B

Zender, Hans, 1972D
Zenészeti Lapok, 1860G
Zerr, Anna, 1822A, 1839C, 1881B
Zerrahn, Carl, 1866D, 1909B
Zeuner, Charles, 1795A, 1857B; *The American Harp*, 1832H; *Church Music*, 1831H
Zhelobinsky, Valeri, 1946B
Zhou, Qiam, 1987E
Zhuk, Isaak, 1902A, 1917C
Zich, Otakar, 1934B
řídek, Ivo, 1926A, 1945C
Ziegler, Delores, 1951A, 1978C
Ziehn, Bernhard, 1845A, 1912B; *Canonical Studies*, 1912H
Ziesler, Fanny Bloomfield, 1927B
Zilberstein, Lilya, 1987E
Zilcher, Hermann, 1920D
Ziliani, Alessandro, 1906A, 1929C, 1977B
Zillig, Winfried, 1905A, 1959C, 1963B; *Variationen über neue Musik*, 1959H
Zimbalist, Efrem, 1889A, 1907C, 1911F, 1985B
Zimerman, Krystian, 1956A, 1975E
Zimmer, Ján, 1926A, 1993B
Zimmer, Richard, 1985D
Zimmerman, Franklin B., 1923A
Zimmerman, Pierre-Joseph, 1785A, 1853B
Zimmermann, Agnes, 1845A, 1863C, 1925B
Zimmermann, Anne, 1852F
Zimmermann, Anton, 1781B
Zimmermann, Bernd, 1918A, 1970B; *Intervall und Zeit*, 1974H
Zimmermann, Erich, 1892A, 1918C, 1968B
Zimmermann, Frank Peter, 1965A, 1975C
Zimmermann, Heinz, 1930A
Zimmermann, Udo, 1943A, 1986D, 1993D
Zimmermann Publishing Co., 1876G
Zinck, Hardenack: *Kompositionen für den Gesang & das Clavier I*, 1791H; *Kompositionen für den Gesang & das Clavier II, III*, 1792H
Zingarelli, Nicola A., 1752A, 1772F, 1793D, 1794D, 1811F, 1813D, 1816D, 1822E, 1837B,
Zinman, David, 1965A, 1974D, 1979D, 1985D, 1995D, 1998D
Zinman, David, 1936A, 1982F, 1983F, 1998E
Zinn, M.: *Basics of Music*, 1987H
Zitek, Otakar: *On New Opera*, 1920H
Zítek, Vilém, 1890A, 1917C, 1956B
Znaider, Nikolaj, 1975A
Zoellner Conservatory of Music, 1922G
Zoghby, Linda, 1949A, 1973C
Zollman, Ronald, 1950A, 1989D
Zöllner, Carl Friedrich, 1800A, 1860B
Zolotarev, Vasili, 1955E, 1964B
Zoltán, Aladár, 1965D
Zoras, Leonidas, 1948D, 1958D, 1968D, 1987B
Zorn, John, 1953A
Zouhar, Vit, 1966A
Zschau, Marilyn, 1944A, 1967C
Zsolt, Nándor, 1936A

F   *Biographical*   G   *Cultural Beginnings*   H   *Musical Literature*
I   *Musical Compositions*

Zuckerkandl, Victor: *The Sense of Music*, 1959H;
 Sound & Symbol: Music & the External World,
 1956H
Zuckermann, Gizella Augusta, 1890A
Zuckert, Leon, 1904A, 1992B
Zuk, Zbigniew, 1955A
Zukerkman, Eugenia, 1944A, 1971C,
Zukerman, Pinchas, 1948A, 1967E, 1980D,
 1998D
Zukofsky, Paul, 1943A, 1952C
Zumpe, Johannes, Piano Maker, 1761G
Zumsteeg, Johann Rudolf, 1760A, 1791D,
 1802B
Zupko, Ramon, 1932A, 1982E
Zürich, Switzerland: Allgemeine
 Musikgesellschaft, 1812G; Conservatory of

Music, 1876G; Hausermann Privatchor,
 1897G; Hegar Music School, 1878G;
 Lehrergesangverein, 1891G; Male Chorus,
 1862G; Opera Co., 1891G; Opera House,
 1891G; Sängerverein, 1826G; Schweizerische
 Musikpädagogische Verband, 1893G;
 Tonhall-Gesellschaft, 1868G; Zürcherische
 Singinstitut, 1805G
Zweers, Bernard, 1924B
Zweig, Fritz, 1927D, 1934D, 1984B
Zwickau Theater, 1823G
Zwilich, Ellen Taaffe, 1974E, 1975F, 1983F,
 1984E, 1992E
Zylis-Gara, Teresa, 1935A, 1954E, 1956C,
 1960E
Zysset, Martin, 1992C

❄

A *Births* B *Deaths* C *Debuts* D *New Positions*
E *Prizes/Honors*